gage

Canadian

THESAURUS

gagelearning

© **1998 Gage Learning Corporation**
164 Commander Blvd., Toronto, ON M1S 3C7

Gage acknowledges the use of the Chambers Paperback Thesaurus. © 1995, in the making of this work.

We acknowledge the financial support of the Government of Canada through the Book Publishing Industry Development Program for our publishing activities.

We acknowledge the government of Ontario through the Ontario Media Development Corporation's Ontario Book Initiative.

National Library of Canada Cataloguing in Publication Data

Main entry under title:

Gage Canadian thesaurus
ISBN 0-7715-1985-0
1. English language – Synonyms and antonyms.
PE1591.G332 1997 423'.1 C97-930980-8

ISBN 0-7715-**1985-0**

12 13 14 KRO 05 04 03

Printed and Bound in Canada

GAGE CANADIAN THESAURUS

Lexicographer   Debbie Sawczak

Editorial Team   Joe Banel
Kim Blakey
Caroline Cobham
Susan Cox
George Davidson
Ruth Dyck
Darleen Rotozinski
Catherine Schwarz
Anne Seaton
John Simpson
Carol Waldock

General Series   T.K. Pratt
Editor   Professor Emeritus of English
University of Prince Edward Island

Gage would like to thank the following educators for reviewing the thesaurus:

Mike Bruce
York Region School Board
Ontario

Michael Budd
Languages Program Consultant
Essex County Board of Education
Ontario

Anna Carino
Metro Separate School Board
Ontario

John Cassano
Integrated Programs Consultant
York Region Board of Education
Ontario

Robert Dawe
Program Co-ordinator
Avalon Consolidated School Board
Newfoundland

Wanda Gibbons
Westwind Regional School Division
Alberta

Barbara Harris
Linguistics Professor
University of Victoria

Pauline McCabe
Former Language Arts Co-ordinator
London and Middlesex County
R.C. School Board, Ontario

Teresa Paoli
Metro Separate School Board
Ontario

Mary Ellen Perley-Waugh
Edmonton Public School Board
Alberta

Wendy Phillips
Richmond School District
British Columbia

Ian Scott
York Region Board of Education
Ontario

THE GAGE CANADIAN REFERENCE SERIES

General Series Editor: T. K. Pratt

Gage Canadian Dictionary
Gage Canadian Thesaurus
Gage Canadian Concise Dictionary
Gage Canadian Intermediate Dictionary
Gage Canadian Junior Dictionary
Gage Canadian School Dictionary
Gage Canadian School Thesaurus

-osis *(cont.)*
avitaminosis
biocenosis
brucellosis
byssinosis
carcinomatosis
chlorosis
cirrhosis
coccidiosis
cyanosis
cyclosis
dermatosis
diagnosis
diarthrosis
diverticulosis
ecchymosis
enarthrosis
endocytosis
endometriosis
endosmosis
endostosis
enosis
exosmosis
exostosis
fibrinosis
fibrosis
fluorosis
furunculosis
gliomatosis
gnotobiosis
gomphosis
gummosis
haematosis
halitosis
hallucinosis
heterosis
hidrosis
homozygosis
hydronephrosis
hyperkeratosis
hyperostosis
hypervitaminosis
hypnosis
ichthyosis
kenosis
keratosis
ketosis
kurtosis
kyphosis
leptospirosis
leucocytosis
lordosis
meiosis
melanosis
metamorphosis
metempsychosis
miosis
mitosis
molybdosis
mononucleosis
morphosis
mycosis
mycotoxicosis
myxomatosis
narcosis

necrobiosis
necrosis
nephrosis
neurosis
ornithosis
osmosis
osteoporosis
osteosis
otosclerosis
parabiosis
parasitosis
pediculosis
phagocytosis
phimosis
pneumoconiosis
pollenosis
polyposis
prognosis
proptosis
psittacosis
psychoneurosis
psychosis
ptosis
pyrosis
salmonellosis
sarcoidosis
sarcomatosis
sclerosis
scoliosis
self-hypnosis
siderosis
silicosis
sorosis
spirillosis
spirochetosis
spondylosis
steatosis
stenosis
strongylosis
sycosis
symbiosis
synarthrosis
syndesmosis
syssarcosis
theriomorphosis
thrombosis
thyrotoxicosis
torulosis
toxicosis
toxoplasmosis
trichinosis
trichosis
trophoneurosis
tuberculosis
virosis
xerosis
zoonosis
zygosis
zymosis

-pathy
allopathy
anthropopathy
antipathy

apathy
cardiomyopathy
dyspathy
empathy
enantiopathy
homeopathy
homoeopathy
hydropathy
idiopathy
kinesipathy
myocardiopathy
naturopathy
neuropathy
nostopathy
osteopathy
protopathy
psychopathy
sociopathy
sympathy
telepathy
theopathy
zoopathy

-phagous
anthropophagous
bacteriophagous
carpophagous
coprophagous
endophagous
entomophagous
geophagous
hippophagous
hylophagous
ichthyophagous
lithophagous
meliphagous
monophagous
mycophagous
myrmecophagous
necrophagous
omophagous
pantophagous
phyllophagous
phytophagous
polyphagous
rhizophagous
saprophagous
sarcophagous
scatophagous
xylophagous
zoophagous

-phobia
acrophobia
aerophobia
agoraphobia
ailurophobia
algophobia
androphobia
anemophobia
anthropophobia
arachnophobia
archaeophobia

arithmophobia
astraphobia
bathophobia
bibliophobia
carcinophobia
claustrophobia
cynophobia
ergophobia
gerontophobia
graphophobia
gynophobia
hierophobia
hippophobia
homophobia
hydrophobia
hypsophobia
monophobia
mysophobia
narcophobia
necrophobia
neophobia
nosophobia
nyctophobia
ochlophobia
pantophobia
pathophobia
phagophobia
photophobia
scopophobia
symmetrophobia
taphophobia
technophobia
thanatophobia
theophobia
toxicophobia
triskaidekaphobia
xenophobia
zoophobia

-phone
aerophone
allophone
Anglophone
audiophone
chordophone
detectophone
diaphone
Dictaphone
earphone
Francophone
geophone
gramophone
headphone
heckelphone
homophone
hydrophone
idiophone
interphone
megaphone
metallophone
microphone
optophone
phone
photophone

-phone *(cont.)*

polyphone
radiophone
radiotelephone
sarrusophone
saxophone
sousaphone
speakerphone
sphygmophone
telephone
vibraphone
videophone
xylophone

-phonic

allophonic
antiphonic
aphonic
cacophonic
chordophonic
dodecaphonic
dysphonic
euphonic
homophonic
microphonic
monophonic
polyphonic
quadraphonic
radiotelephonic
stentorophonic
stereophonic
symphonic
tautophonic
telephonic
xylophonic

-phyte

aerophyte
bryophyte
dermatophyte
endophyte
epiphyte
gametophyte
geophyte
halophyte
heliophyte
holophyte
hydrophyte
lithophyte
mesophyte
microphyte
neophyte
oophyte
osteophyte
phanerophyte
phreatophyte
protophyte
psammophyte
pteridophyte
saprophyte
schizophyte
spermatophyte
sporophyte

thallophyte
tracheophyte
tropophyte
xerophyte
zoophyte
zygophyte

-saurus

Albertosaurus
allosaurus
ankylosaurus
Apatosaurus
Argentinosaurus
brachiosaurus
brontosaurus
Centrosaurus
hadrosaurus
Ichthyosaurus
Lambeosaurus
megalosaurus
Pachyrhinosaurus
Panoplosaurus
Plateosaurus
Plesiosaurus
Stegosaurus
Styracosaurus
Teleosaurus
Titanosaurus
tyrannosaurus
Ultrasaurus

-scope

auriscope
baroscope
bioscope
bronchoscope
chronoscope
Cinemascope
colposcope
cryoscope
cystoscope
dichroscope
electroscope
endoscope
epidiascope
fetoscope
fluoroscope
galvanoscope
gastroscope
gyroscope
hagioscope
helioscope
hodoscope
horoscope
hydroscope
hygroscope
iconoscope
kaleidoscope
kinescope
lactoscope
laparoscope
laryngoscope
lychnoscope

megascope
microscope
nephoscope
ophthalmoscope
oscilloscope
otoscope
periscope
pharyngoscope
polariscope
proctoscope
pseudoscope
radarscope
radioscope
retinoscope
rhinoscope
roentgenoscope
scintilloscope
scope
seismoscope
sigmoidoscope
skiascope
spectrohelioscope
spectroscope
spinthariscope
statoscope
stereoscope
stethoscope
stroboscope
tachistoscope
telescope
thermoscope
ultramicroscope
vitascope

-sophy

anthroposophy
gymnosophy
pansophy
philosophy
sciosophy
theosophy

-stat

aerostat
antistat
appestat
bacteriostat
barostat
chemostat
coelostat
cryostat
gyrostat
heliostat
hemostat
humidistat
hydrostat
hygrostat
pyrostat
rheostat
siderostat
thermostat

-therapy

actinotherapy
aromatherapy
art therapy
autotherapy
balneotherapy
chemotherapy
cryotherapy
electrotherapy
heliotherapy
hydrotherapy
hypnotherapy
immunotherapy
kinesitherapy
musicotherapy
narcotherapy
occupational therapy
organotherapy
pet therapy
phototherapy
physiotherapy
psychotherapy
pyretotherapy
radiotherapy
roentgenotherapy
serotherapy
thermotherapy

-tomy

adenoidectomy
anatomy
appendectomy
arteriotomy
autotomy
cholecystectomy
cholecystotomy
choledochostomy
choledochotomy
colostomy
colotomy
cordotomy
craniotomy
cystectomy
cystotomy
dichotomy
duodenectomy
embryectomy
encephalotomy
enterostomy
gastrectomy
gastrotomy
glossectomy
hepatectomy
herniotomy
hysterectomy
hysterotomy
iridectomy
keratectomy
keratotomy
laparotomy
laryngectomy
laryngotomy
leucotomy
lipectomy

-tomy *(cont.)*
lithotomy
lobectomy
lobotomy
lumpectomy
mastectomy
meniscectomy
microtomy
necrotomy
nephrectomy
nephrotomy
neurectomy
neuroanatomy
neurotomy
oophorectomy
orchidotomy
orchiectomy
osteotomy
ovariectomy
ovariotomy
pharyngectomy
phlebotomy

pleurotomy
pneumectomy
pogonotomy
prostatectomy
rhytidectomy
salpingectomy
sclerotomy
splenectomy
stapedectomy
stereotomy
strabotomy
sympathectomy
tenotomy
tetrachotomy
thymectomy
tonsillectomy
tonsillotomy
topectomy
tracheotomy
trichotomy
tubectomy
ultramicrotomy

varicotomy
vasectomy
zootomy

-urgy

chemurgy
dramaturgy
electrometallurgy
hierurgy
hydrometallurgy
liturgy
metallurgy
pyrometallurgy
thaumaturgy
theurgy
zymurgy

-vorous

apivorous
baccivorous

carnivorous
frugivorous
graminivorous
granivorous
herbivorous
insectivorous
lignivorous
mellivorous
nucivorous
omnivorous
piscivorous
sanguinivorous
sanguivorous
vermivorous

-tomy (cont.)
lithotomy
lobectomy
lobotomy
lumpectomy
mastectomy
meniscectomy
microtomy
necrotomy
nephrectomy
nephrotomy
neurectomy
neurotomy
oophorectomy
orchidotomy
orchiectomy
osteotomy
ovariectomy
ovariotomy
pharyngectomy
phlebotomy

pleurotomy
pneumectomy
popotomy
prostatectomy
thyroidectomy
salpingectomy
sclerotomy
splenectomy
stapedectomy
stereotomy
strabotomy
sympathectomy
tenotomy
tetrachotomy
thymectomy
tonsillectomy
tonsillotomy
topectomy
tracheotomy
trichotomy
tubectomy
ultramicrotomy

vagotomy
vasectomy
zootomy

-urgy
chemurgy
dramaturgy
electrometallurgy
liturgy
hydrometallurgy
metallurgy
pyrometallurgy
thaumaturgy
theurgy
zymurgy

-vorous
apivorous
baccivorous

carnivorous
frugivorous
graminivorous
granivorous
herbivorous
insectivorous
lignivorous
mellivorous
nucivorous
omnivorous
piscivorous
sanguinivorous
sanguivorous
vermivorous

CONTENTS

Thesaurus

Appendixes

What is a thesaurus?

A thesaurus has much in common with a dictionary; but whereas a dictionary explains the meaning of a word, a thesaurus supplies alternatives for it. The *Gage Canadian Thesaurus* is an essential tool for anyone who wants to create something satisfying with words—a quick, convenient source of synonyms and related terms that help express ideas in a more precise and interesting manner.

It is over 130 years since Peter Mark Roget published his *Thesaurus*. His purpose was to provide the reader with a wide choice of expressions for a general concept. His method was to classify these within a framework of ideas based on seventeenth-century philosophical and scientific principles. This meant that a very full alphabetical index was needed to allow readers to locate the general concept they wanted to express. It was probably the complications of this concept-based system that ensured the continued popularity of the more "user-friendly" type of word-finding book already in production in Roget's time: a simple alphabetical list of words, each with its own group of synonyms.

The *Gage Canadian Thesaurus* belongs to this last type—it contains almost 18 000 of the commonest, most synonym-rich words and expressions, listed alphabetically, each with a wide variety of substitutable words, phrases, and idioms covering its full range of meanings. Where appropriate, antonyms are also listed, and attention is drawn to any word which is easily confused with the one being looked up.

The *Gage Canadian Thesaurus* has all the recognized usefulness of any thesaurus—but its special advantage is that it is designed for Canadians. It incorporates vocabulary unique to Canada, uses Canadian spellings, and omits usage and vocabulary that are strictly British or American. It follows the basic conventions of the *Gage Canadian Dictionary*, while occasionally expanding its range to include a lesser-known but particularly apt or colourful synonym.

Why use a thesaurus?

The more regularly you use a thesaurus, the more obvious its usefulness becomes. A thesaurus jogs your memory—it comes to your rescue as you struggle to encapsulate an idea in a forgotten *mot juste* that hovers tantalizingly at the tip of your tongue. It lets you gear your writing to a certain audience by choosing simpler or more advanced vocabulary. It may help you find the politically more sensitive equivalent for a given term.

A thesaurus is indispensable to the journalist, writer, and reporter seeking precision with variety and freshness. It is also the perfect tool for the player of word games and the crossword enthusiast.

Besides, a thesaurus is just plain fun to use. It is fun to notice all the different meanings of a word, the different nuances within a meaning, all the possible overtones and connections, and the different social contexts suggested by everything from slang to oratory. What you find, in fact, is a delicious list of possible alternatives that have more or less of a particular ingredient, are more or less formal, are more or less euphonious—that, in short, have more or less of the precise flavour sought by the user. English has its international origins to thank for its richness and subtle variety, and in Canadian English this breadth is complemented by the specific contribution of our own cultural history.

With this fun comes the opportunity to enhance your personal command of words and increase your general knowledge; words that may be less familiar to you will trigger investigations in your dictionary and lead to exploratory forays into the remote corners of the language.

Added features of this thesaurus

As a catalogue of synonyms, a thesaurus has a natural bias toward abstract terms. (There are more different names for an idea or an action or a quality than for a concrete object.) But in the *Gage Canadian Thesaurus*, this natural bias of the main text has been balanced by the addition of a section that is a relative newcomer to this type of thesaurus: an appendix of concrete and technical terms arranged in categories such as architecture, astronomy, furniture, fabrics, musical instruments, vehicles, and so on. There are also lists of collective nouns (*a charm of goldfinches, a leap of leopards...*), names for collectors and enthusiasts (do you know what a chronic punster is called?), the First Nations of Canada, Canadian public offices, colour terms (how many different kinds of yellow can you name?), and other useful and interesting categories. A full list of the categories appears on the page just preceding the appendixes.

A second appendix contains words arranged by suffix. Here are those *-ologies, -phobias, -isms,* and *-graphies* you keep forgetting and losing track of, along with unfamiliar ones to pique your curiosity, thoroughly inventoried for you in dozens of lists. This is another innovative and intriguing addition to the standard thesaurus. These two appendixes will be invaluable extras not only for the crossword solver but for all types of thesaurus user.

Finally, the inclusion of many idiomatic phrases in the main text widens its scope, while the "confusable word" warnings will keep writers on their toes and help them say what they really mean.

How to use this thesaurus

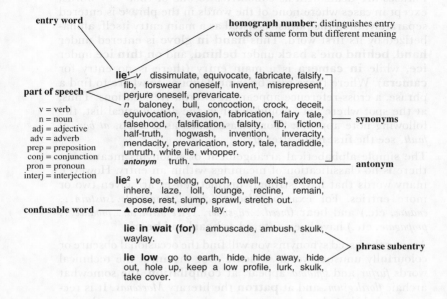

entry word

homograph number; distinguishes entry words of same form but different meaning

part of speech

v = verb
n = noun
adj = adjective
adv = adverb
prep = preposition
conj = conjunction
pron = pronoun
interj = interjection

lie¹ *v* dissimulate, equivocate, fabricate, falsify, fib, forswear oneself, invent, misrepresent, perjure oneself, prevaricate.
n baloney, bull, concoction, crock, deceit, equivocation, evasion, fabrication, fairy tale, falsehood, falsification, falsity, fib, fiction, half-truth, hogwash, invention, inveracity, mendacity, prevarication, story, tale, taradiddle, untruth, white lie, whopper.
antonym truth.

synonyms

antonym

lie² *v* be, belong, couch, dwell, exist, extend, inhere, laze, loll, lounge, recline, remain, repose, rest, slump, sprawl, stretch out.
▲ *confusable word* lay.

confusable word

lie in wait (for) ambuscade, ambush, skulk, waylay.

lie low go to earth, hide, hide away, hide out, hole up, keep a low profile, lurk, skulk, take cover.

phrase subentry

Given the deliberately simple arrangement of the thesaurus, little explanation is needed. But to take the entry **happy** as an example: the part of speech, *adj*, is given, and then a list of synonymous words and phrases in alphabetical order—*advantageous, appropriate, apt, auspicious, blessed, blissful, convenient, delighted, ecstatic, elated. . . .* If none of the synonyms will do, most if not all have entries of their own, providing further alternatives. Likewise with the antonyms: at **help** the word *hinder* is supplied as an antonym; the entry **hinder** will turn up further opposites to *help*.

Separate parts of speech have separate lists of synonyms; thus at **flash**, two distinct lists are provided for the word as noun and as verb. The list for each new part of speech begins on a new line.

Phrases are dealt with as subentries to one of their key words, except in cases where none of the words in the phrase is entered separately; then the phrase is listed as a main entry itself, alphabetized by its first word. Thus **hand in glove** is entered under **hand**, **behind one's back** under **behind**, and **on thin ice** under **ice**, while **in camera** is a main entry (there is no entry for **camera**). Where there may be some doubt as to where to find a phrase, a cross-reference appears at alternative locations. Thus, at the spot where "at" would occur in the alphabetical list, the following note appears: "For phrases such as *at a loss, at bay, at fault,* see the first noun after *at*."

The simple alphabetical arrangement of synonyms means that there is no classification of meanings within an entry. However, many words that have strongly distinct senses are given two or more entries. For example, **bear** (*carry...transport...sustain... endure*, etc.) and **bear** (*breed...engender...give birth to...produce... propagate*, etc.) have been entered as **bear**[1] and **bear**[2].

Among the listed synonyms you will find the occasional obscure or colourfully unusual word. At **scale**[2], for instance, the technical words *furfur* and *squama* appear; at **compilation**, the somewhat archaic *florilegium*, and at **patron** the literary *Maecenas*. It is recommended that the thesaurus be used in conjunction with your dictionary. As a general policy, truly arcane terms are excluded from the synonym lists. The appendixes, however, are another matter—there the adventurous user will find more latitude.

Happy exploring!

A

abandon v abdicate, back-pedal (from), cede, chuck, desert, desist, discontinue, ditch, drop, evacuate, forgo, forsake, give up, jilt, leave, leave behind, leave in the lurch, quit, relinquish, renounce, repudiate, resign, scrap, sink, surrender, vacate, waive, withdraw from, yield.

antonyms continue, persist, support.

n dash, recklessness, wantonness, wildness.

antonym restraint.

abandoned[1] *adj* cast aside, cast away, cast out, derelict, deserted, desolate, discarded, dropped, forlorn, forsaken, jilted, left, neglected, outcast, rejected, relinquished, scorned, unoccupied, vacant.

antonyms cherished, occupied, retained.

abandoned[2] *adj* corrupt, debauched, depraved, dissipated, dissolute, profligate, reprobate, sinful, wanton, wicked.

antonyms restrained, sober.

abandonment n apostasy, cession, decampment, dereliction, desertion, desistance, discontinuance, discontinuation, dropping, evacuation, forsaking, giving up, jilting, leaving, neglect, relinquishment, renunciation, resignation, sacrifice, scrapping, surrender, waiver.

abase v belittle, cast down, debase, degrade, demean, discredit, disgrace, dishonour, downgrade, humble, humiliate, lower, malign, mortify, reduce, vitiate.

antonyms elevate, honour.

abasement n belittlement, debasement, degradation, demotion, depravation, deterioration, disgrace, dishonour, downgrading, humbling, humiliation, lowering, mortification, reduction, shame, vitiation.

antonyms elevation, promotion.

abashed *adj* affronted, ashamed, astounded, bewildered, chagrined, confounded, confused, cowed, discomfited, discomposed, disconcerted, discountenanced, discouraged, dismayed, dumfounded, embarrassed, floored, humbled, humiliated, mortified, nonplussed, perturbed, shamefaced, taken aback.

antonyms at ease, audacious, composed.

abate v alleviate, appease, attenuate, decline, decrease, deduct, diminish, discount, dull, dwindle, ease, ebb, fade, fall off, lessen, let up, mitigate, moderate, mollify, pacify, quell, rebate, reduce, relieve, remit, sink, slacken, slake, slow, subside, subtract, taper off, wane, weaken.

antonyms increase, strengthen.

abatement n alleviation, allowance, assuagement, attenuation, cessation, decline, decrease, deduction, diminution, discount, dulling, dwindling, easing, ebb, extenuation, fading, falloff, lessening, letup, mitigation, moderation, mollification, palliation, quelling, rebatement, reduction, relief, remission, slackening, slowing, softening, subsidence, subtraction, tapering off, tempering, waning, weakening.

antonyms crescendo, increase.

abbey n abbacy, cloister, convent, friary, monastery, nunnery, priory, seminary.

abbot or **abbess** n abbé, archimandrite, general, head monk (or nun), mother superior, prior, superior.

abbreviate v abridge, abstract, clip, compress, condense, contract, curtail, cut, digest, epitomize, lessen, précis, reduce, shorten, shrink, summarize, trim, truncate.

antonyms amplify, extend.

abbreviation n abridgment, abstract, abstraction, clipping, compendium, compression, condensation, conspectus, contraction, curtailment, digest, epitome, précis, reduction, résumé, shortening, summarization, summary, summation, synopsis, trimming, truncation.

antonyms expansion, extension.

abdicate v abandon, abjure, abnegate, cede, forgo, give up, quit, relinquish, renounce, repudiate, resign, retire, step down, surrender, vacate, yield.

abdication n abandonment, abjuration, abnegation, cession, giving up, quitting, relinquishment, renunciation, resignation, retirement, surrender.

abdomen n belly, breadbasket, corporation, guts, midriff, paunch, pot, stomach, tummy.

abdominal *adj* coeliac, gastric, intestinal, stomachic, ventral, ventricular, visceral.

abduct v abduce, appropriate, carry off, kidnap, lay hold of, make off with, rape, run away with, run off with, seduce, seize, snatch, spirit away.

abduction n appropriation, kidnapping, rape, seduction, seizure, theft.

aberrant *adj* abnormal, anomalous, atypical, corrupt, corrupted, defective, degenerate, depraved, deviant, different, divergent, eccentric, egregious, erroneous, incongruous, irregular, odd, peculiar, perverse, perverted, queer, quirky, rambling, roving, straying, untypical, wandering, wrong.

antonyms normal, straight, typical.

aberration *n* aberrancy, abnormality, anomaly, defect, delusion, deviation, divergence, eccentricity, freak, hallucination, irregularity, lapse, nonconformity, oddity, peculiarity, quirk, rambling, rogue, straying, vagary, wandering.

antonyms conformity, normalcy.

abet *v* aid, assist, back, condone, connive (with or at), egg on, encourage, goad, help, incite, promote, prompt, sanction, second, spur, succour, support, sustain, uphold, urge.

antonym discourage.

abettor *n* accessory, accomplice, assistant, associate, backer, confederate, conniver, co-operator, encourager, fomenter, goad, helper, henchman, inciter, instigator, prompter, second, supporter.

abeyance *n* adjournment, deferral, discontinuation, inactivity, intermission, lull, postponement, recess, remission, reservation, suspension, waiting.

antonyms activity, continuation.

in abeyance dormant, hanging, inactive, on ice, pending, shelved, suspended.

abhor *v* abominate, despise, detest, execrate, hate, loathe, recoil from, shrink from, shudder at, spurn.

antonyms adore, approve, love.

abhorrence *n* abomination, animosity, aversion, detestation, disgust, distaste, enmity, execration, hate, hatred, horror, loathing, odium, repugnance, revulsion.

antonyms adoration, approval, love.

abhorrent *adj* abominable, anathema, detestable, disgusting, distasteful, execrable, hated, hateful, heinous, horrible, horrid, loathsome, nauseating, obnoxious, odious, offensive, repellent, repugnant, repulsive, revolting.

antonym attractive.

abide *v* accept, bear, brook, continue, endure, last, outlive, persist, put up with, remain, stand, stay, stomach, submit to, suffer, survive, tarry, tolerate.

antonyms dispute, quit.

abide by acknowledge, acquiesce in, adhere to, agree to, carry out, comply with, conform to, discharge, follow, fulfil, go along with, hold to, keep to, obey, observe, stand by, submit to.

abiding *adj* constant, continual, continuing, continuous, durable, enduring, eternal, everlasting, fast, firm, immortal, immutable, indissoluble, lasting, permanent, persistent, persisting, stable, steadfast, surviving, sustained, tenacious, unchangeable, unchanging, unending.

antonyms ephemeral, transient.

ability *n* adeptness, adroitness, aptitude, capability, capacity, competence, competency, deftness, dexterity, endowment, energy, expertise, expertness, facility, faculty, flair, forte, genius, gift, knack, know-how, long suit, potentiality, power, proficiency, qualification, savoir-faire, savvy, skill, strength, talent, touch.

antonyms inability, incompetence.

abject *adj* base, contemptible, cringing, debased, degenerate, degraded, deplorable, despicable, dishonourable, execrable, fawning, forlorn, grovelling, hopeless, humiliating, ignoble, ignominious, low, mean, miserable, outcast, pathetic, pitiable, servile, slavish, sordid, submissive, vile, wretched.

antonym exalted.

abjuration *n* abnegation, abstention, avoidance, denial, disavowal, disclaiming, eschewal, forswearing, recantation, refusal, rejection, relinquishment, renunciation, repudiation, retraction, sacrifice.

antonyms assent, insistence, retention, support.

abjure *v* abandon, abnegate, abstain from, avoid, deny, disavow, discard, disclaim, disown, eschew, forsake, forswear, give up, recant, refrain from, reject, relinquish, renege on, renounce, repudiate, retract, sacrifice, swear off.

antonyms assent to, insist on, retain, support.

▲ *confusable word* adjure.

ablaze *adj* afire, aflame, aglow, alight, angry, aroused, blazing, brilliant, burning, enraged, enthusiastic, excited, exhilarated, fervent, fiery, flaming, flashing, frenzied, fuming, furious, glaring, gleaming, glowing, ignited, illuminated, impassioned, incandescent, incensed, lighted, lit, luminous, on fire, passionate, radiant, raging, sparkling, stimulated.

able *adj* accomplished, adept, adequate, adroit, agile, capable, clever, competent, deft, dexterous, effective, efficient, experienced, expert, fit, fitted, gifted, ingenious, masterful, masterly, nimble, powerful, practised, proficient, qualified, skilful, skilled, strong, talented.

antonyms incapable, incompetent.

able-bodied *adj* firm, fit, hale, hardy, healthy, hearty, lusty, powerful, robust, sound, stalwart, staunch, stout, strapping, strong, sturdy, tough, vigorous.

antonyms delicate, infirm.

ablution *n* bath, bathing, cleansing, purgation, purging, purification, shower, wash, washing.

abnegate *v* abandon, abdicate, abjure, abstain from, cede, concede, decline, deny, disallow, eschew, forbear, forgo, forsake, give up, pass up, refrain from, reject, relinquish, renounce, sacrifice, submit, surrender, yield.

abnegation *n* abandonment, abjuration, abstinence, cession, concession, continence, disallowance, eschewal, forbearance, giving up, refusal, rejection, relinquishment, renunciation, sacrifice, submission, surrender.

antonyms demand, indulgence, insistence.

abnormal *adj* aberrant, anomalous, atypical, bizarre, curious, deformed, deviant, diseased, divergent, eccentric, erratic, exceptional, extraordinary, irregular, monstrous, morbid, odd, paranormal, peculiar, perverted, queer, singular, strange, uncanny, uncommon, unexpected, unhealthy, unnatural, untypical, unusual, wayward, weird.

antonyms normal, regular, typical.

abnormality *n* aberration, anomaly, atypicalness, bizarreness, deformity, deviation, disease, divergence, dysfunction, eccentricity, exception, flaw, irregularity, monstrosity, morbidity, oddity, peculiarity, queerness, singularity, strangeness, uncommonness, unexpectedness, unnaturalness, untypicalness, unusualness, weirdness.

antonym normality.

abode *n* domicile, dwelling, dwelling-place, habitat, habitation, home, house, lodging, pad, place, quarters, residence.

abolish *v* abrogate, annihilate, annul, blot out, cancel, destroy, do away with, eliminate, end, eradicate, expunge, exterminate, extinguish, extirpate, get rid of, invalidate, nix, nullify, obliterate, overthrow, overturn, put an end to, put the kibosh on, quash, repeal, repudiate, rescind, revoke, scrap, sink, stamp out, suppress, terminate, vitiate, void, wipe out.

antonyms continue, retain.

abolition *n* abolishment, abrogation, annihilation, annulment, cancellation, destruction, dissolution, elimination, end, ending, eradication, expunction, extermination, extinction, extirpation, invalidation, nullification, obliteration, overthrow, overturning, quashing, repeal, repudiation, rescission, revocation, suppression, termination, vitiation, voiding, withdrawal.

antonyms continuance, retention.

abominable *adj* abhorrent, accursed, appalling, atrocious, base, beastly, contemptible, damnable, despicable, detestable, disgusting, execrable, foul, hateful, heinous, hellish, horrible, horrid, loathsome, monstrous, nauseating, nauseous, obnoxious, odious, repellent, reprehensible, repugnant, repulsive, revolting, terrible, vile, villainous, wretched.

antonyms delightful, desirable.

abominate *v* abhor, condemn, despise, detest, execrate, hate, loathe.

antonyms adore, esteem, love.

abomination *n* abhorrence, anathema, animosity, animus, antipathy, aversion, bête noire, bugbear, curse, detestation, disgrace, disgust, distaste, evil, execration, hate, hatred, horror, hostility, loathing, odium, offence, plague, repugnance, revulsion, torment.

antonyms adoration, delight.

aboriginal *adj* ancient, autochthonous, domestic, earliest, endemic, first, indigenous, native, original, primal, primary, primeval, primordial, pristine.

abort *v* arrest, call off, check, cut off, end, fail, frustrate, halt, miscarry, nullify, stop, terminate, thwart.

antonym continue.

abortion *n* disappointment, failure, fiasco, feticide, frustration, misadventure, misbirth, miscarriage, premature end, termination, thwarting.

antonyms continuation, fruition, realization, success.

abortive *adj* barren, bootless, failed, failing, fruitless, futile, ineffective, ineffectual, miscarried, sterile, unavailing, unproductive, unsuccessful, useless, vain.

antonym successful.

abound *v* be plentiful, brim over, crowd, exuberate, flourish, increase, luxuriate, multiply, overflow, proliferate, run riot, superabound, swarm, swell, teem, thrive.

antonym be in short supply.

abounding *adj* abundant, bountiful, copious, filled, flourishing, flowing, flush, full, lavish, luxuriant, overflowing, plenteous, plentiful, prodigal, profuse, prolific, rank, replete, rich, superabundant, teeming, unstinting.

antonym lacking.

about *prep* adjacent to, all over, anent, around, as regards, beside, busy with, circa, close to, concerned with, concerning, connected with, encircling, encompassing, engaged in, in regard to, in the matter of, near, nearby, of, on, over, re, referring to, regarding, relating to, relative to, respecting, round, surrounding, through, throughout, touching, with reference to, with regard to, with respect to.

adv active, almost, approaching, approximately, around, astir, close to, from place to place, here and there, hither and thither, in motion, in the region of, more or less, nearing, nearly, present, roughly, stirring, to and fro.

about to all but, intending to, on the point of, on the verge of, preparing to, ready to.

about-turn *n* about-face, apostasy, backtracking, flip-flop, reversal, right about-face, turnabout, turnaround, U-turn, volte face.

above *prep* atop, before, beyond, exceeding, higher than, in excess of, on top of, over, prior to, superior to, surpassing, upon.

antonyms below, beneath, under.

adv aloft, earlier, heavenwards, in heaven, on high, overhead, supra.

antonym below.

adj above-mentioned, above-stated, aforementioned, aforesaid, earlier, foregoing, preceding, previous, prior.

above suspicion above reproach, blameless, guiltless, honourable, innocent, irreproachable, pure, sinless, unimpeachable, virtuous.

aboveboard *adj* candid, fair, fair and square, forthright, frank, guileless, honest, honourable, legitimate, licit, on the level, on the up and up, open, overt, reputable, square, straight, straightforward, true, trustworthy, truthful, upright, veracious.

antonyms shady, underhand.

abrade *v* chafe, erase, erode, file, grind, rub off, scour, scrape, triturate, wear away, wear down, wear off.

abrasion *n* abrading, attrition, chafe, chafing, erosion, friction, grating, graze, grinding, rubbing, scouring, scrape, scraping, scratch, scratching, scuff, scuffing, trituration, wearing away, wearing down.

abrasive[1] *adj* abradant, attritional, biting, caustic, chafing, erosive, frictional, grating, harsh, rough, scraping, scratching, scratchy, scuffing, sharp.

antonyms gentle, lubricating, smooth.

abrasive[2] *adj* annoying, biting, caustic, galling, grating, harsh, hurtful, irritating, nasty, rough, sharp, unpleasant.

antonyms inoffensive, pleasant, smooth, sweet.

abreast (of) *adj* acquainted, au courant, au fait, aware, conversant, familiar, in touch, informed, knowledgeable, on the ball, up (on), up to date.

antonyms out of touch, unaware.

abridge *v* abbreviate, abstract, circumscribe, clip, compress, concentrate, condense, contract, curtail, cut, cut down, decrease, digest, diminish, dock, epitomize, lessen, lop, précis, prune, reduce, shorten, summarize, synopsize, trim, truncate.

antonyms amplify, expand, extend, pad.

abridgment *n* abbreviation, abstract, compendium, compression, concentration, condensation, conspectus, contraction, curtailment, cutting, decrease, digest, diminishing, diminution, epitome, lessening, limitation, outline, précis, pruning, reduction, restriction, résumé, shortening, summary, synopsis, truncation.

antonyms expansion, padding.

abroad *adv* about, around, at large, away, circulating, current, elsewhere, extensively, far, far and wide, forth, in circulation, in foreign parts, out, out of the country, outdoors, outside, overseas, publicly, widely.

abrogate *v* abolish, annul, cancel, countermand, discontinue, dissolve, end, invalidate, nullify, override, overrule, quash, recall, repeal, repudiate, rescind, retract, reverse, revoke, scrap, set aside, terminate, void, withdraw.

antonyms establish, institute.

▲ *confusable word* arrogate.

abrogation *n* abolition, annulling, annulment, cancellation, countermanding, discontinuation, ending, invalidation, nullification, overriding, overruling, quashing, repeal, repudiation, rescission, retraction, reversal, revocation, scrapping, setting aside, termination, voiding, withdrawal.

antonyms continuation, retention.

abrupt *adj* blunt, brief, brisk, broken, brusque, curt, direct, disconnected, discontinuous, discourteous, gruff, hasty, headlong, hurried, impolite, irregular, jerky, precipitate, precipitous, quick, rapid, rough, rude, sharp, sheer, short, snappy, steep, sudden, surprising, swift, terse, unannounced, unceremonious, uncivil, unexpected, unforeseen, ungracious.

antonyms ceremonious, expansive, gradual, leisurely, smooth, well-planned.

abscond *v* beat it, bolt, clear out (or off), decamp, disappear, escape, flee, flit, fly, hightail it, make off (or away), quit, run off, scram, skedaddle, take French leave, take off, vamoose.

absence *n* absenteeism, absent-mindedness, abstraction, dearth, default, defect, deficiency, distraction, inattention, lack, need, non-appearance, non-attendance, non-existence, omission, paucity, preoccupation, privation, reverie, scarcity, truancy, unavailability, vacancy, vacuity, want.

antonyms alertness, attention, existence, presence.

absent *adj* absent-minded, absorbed, abstracted, away, bemused, blank, daydreaming, dead to the world, distracted, distrait, dreamy, elsewhere, empty, faraway, gone, heedless, inattentive, lacking, missing, musing, non-existent, not present, oblivious, out, preoccupied, spaced-out, spacy, truant, unavailable, unaware, unconscious, unheeding, unthinking, vacant, vague, wanting, withdrawn, wool-gathering.

antonyms aware, present.

absent-minded *adj* absent, absorbed, abstracted, bemused, distracted, distrait, dreaming, dreamy, engrossed, faraway, forgetful, heedless, impractical, inattentive, musing, oblivious, otherworldly, pensive, preoccupied, scatterbrained, spaced-out, spacy, unaware, unconscious, unheeding, unthinking, withdrawn, wool-gathering.

antonyms attentive, matter-of-fact, practical.

absent-mindedness *n* absence, absorption, abstraction, distraction, dreaminess, forgetfulness, heedlessness, inattention, muse, pensiveness, preoccupation, unawareness, vacancy, vagueness.

antonyms alertness, attentiveness, presence of mind.

absolute *adj* absolutist, actual, almighty, arbitrary, autarchical, autocratic, autonomous, categorical, certain, complete, conclusive, consummate, decided, decisive, definite, definitive, despotic, diametric, dictatorial, downright, entire, exact, exhaustive, final, full, genuine, independent, indubitable, infallible, non-relative, omnipotent, out-and-out, outright, peremptory, perfect, positive, precise, pure, sheer, sovereign, supreme, sure, terminative, thorough, total, totalitarian, tyrannical, unadulterated, unalloyed, unambiguous, unbounded, unconditional, uncontrolled, undivided, unequivocal, unlimited, unmitigated, unmixed, unqualified, unquestionable, unrestrained, unrestricted, utter.

antonyms conditional, partial, relative.

absolutely *adv* actually, arbitrarily, autocratically, autonomously, bang (on), categorically, certainly, completely, conclusively, consummately, dead, decidedly, decisively, definitely, despotically, diametrically, dictatorially, entirely, exactly, exhaustively, finally, fully, genuinely, indubitably, infallibly, peremptorily, perfectly, positively, precisely, purely, sovereignly, supremely, surely, thoroughly, totally, truly, tyrannically, unambiguously, unconditionally, unequivocally, unmitigatedly, unquestionably, unrestrainedly, utterly, wholly.

absolution *n* acquittal, amnesty, deliverance, discharge, dispensation, emancipation, exculpation, exemption, exoneration, forgiveness, forgiving, freeing, indulgence, justification, liberation, mercy, pardon, purgation, redemption, release, remission, shriving, vindication.

antonym condemnation.

absolve *v* acquit, clear, deliver, discharge, emancipate, exculpate, excuse, exempt, exonerate, forgive, free, justify, let off, liberate, loose, pardon, ransom, redeem, release, remit, set free, shrive, vindicate.

antonyms charge, condemn.

absorb *v* adsorb, apprehend, assimilate, captivate, comprehend, consume, co-opt, devour, digest, drink in, engage, engross, engulf, enthrall, enwrap, exhaust, fascinate, fill (up), fix, grip, hold, imbibe, immerse, incorporate, ingest, involve, monopolize, occupy, preoccupy, receive, retain, rivet, soak up, sorb, submerge, suck up, take in, understand, utilize.

antonyms bore, dissipate, exude, put off.

absorbed *adj* captivated, concentrating, consumed, engaged, engrossed, enthralled, enwrapped, fascinated, fixed, gripped, held, immersed, intent, involved, lost, obsessed, occupied, preoccupied, rapt, riveted, wrapped up.

antonyms bored, distracted.

absorbent *adj* absorptive, assimilative, blotting, penetrable, permeable, pervious, porous, receptive, retentive, spongy.

antonym impermeable.

absorbing *adj* amusing, arresting, captivating, compulsive, consuming, diverting, engaging, engrossing, entertaining, enthralling, fascinating, gripping, interesting, intriguing, involving, preoccupying, riveting, spellbinding, unputdownable.

antonyms boring, off-putting.

absorption *n* adsorption, assimilation, attentiveness, captivation, concentration, consumption, digestion, engagement, exhaustion, fascination, holding, imbibition, immersion, incorporation, ingestion, intentness, involvement, occupation, osmosis, preoccupation, raptness, soaking up, sucking up.

abstain (from) *v* avoid, cease, decline, deny, desist, eschew, forbear, forgo, give up, keep from, pass up, refrain, refuse, reject, renounce, resist, shun, stop, swear off, withold.

antonym indulge.

abstemious *adj* abstinent, ascetic, austere, continent, disciplined, frugal, moderate, restrained, self-denying, self-disciplined, sober, sparing, temperate.

antonyms gluttonous, immoderate, intemperate, luxurious, wanton.

abstinence *n* abstemiousness, asceticism, avoidance, continence, forbearance, frugality, moderation, non-indulgence, refraining, self-denial, self-discipline, self-restraint, soberness, sobriety, teetotalism, temperance.

antonym self-indulgence.

abstinent *adj* abstaining, abstemious, continent, disciplined, forbearing, frugal, moderate, self-controlled, self-denying, self-disciplined, self-restrained, sober, temperate.

antonyms immoderate, self-indulgent, voluptuous, wanton.

abstract *adj* abstruse, academic, arcane, complex, conceptual, deep, discrete, general, generalized, hypothetical, indefinite, intellectual, metaphysical, non-concrete, occult, philosophical, profound, recondite, separate, subtle, theoretical, unpractical, unrealistic.

antonym concrete.

n abbreviation, abridgment, abstractive, compendium, compression, condensation, conspectus, digest, epitome, essence, outline, précis, recapitulation, résumé, summary, synopsis.

v abbreviate, abridge, compress, condense, detach, digest, dissociate, epitomize, extract, isolate, outline, précis, purloin, remove, separate, shorten, steal, summarize, withdraw.

antonyms expand, insert.

abstracted *adj* absent, absent-minded, bemused, distrait, dreamy, faraway, inattentive, pensive, preoccupied, remote, spaced-out, unfocussed, withdrawn, wool-gathering.

antonyms alert, on the ball.

abstraction *n* absence, absent-mindedness, absorption, bemusedness, concept, conception, dissociation, distraction, dream, dreaminess, formula, generalization, generality, hypothesis, idea, inattention, notion, pensiveness, preoccupation, remoteness, separation, theorem, theory, thought, withdrawal, wool-gathering.

abstruse *adj* abstract, arcane, complex, cryptic, dark, deep, devious, difficult, enigmatic, esoteric, hermetic, hidden, incomprehensible, mysterious, mystical, obscure, occult, perplexing, profound, puzzling, recondite, subtle, tortuous, unfathomable, vague.

antonyms concrete, obvious.

▲ *confusable word* obtuse.

absurd *adj* anomalous, comical, crazy, daft, derisory, fantastic, farcical, foolish, funny, humorous, idiotic, illogical, implausible, incongruous, irrational, laughable, ludicrous, meaningless, nonsensical, paradoxical, preposterous, ridiculous, risible, senseless, silly, stupid, unreasonable, untenable.
antonyms logical, rational, sensible.

absurdity *n* comicality, craziness, daftness, farce, farcicality, fatuity, fatuousness, folly, foolery, foolishness, idiocy, illogicality, incongruity, irrationality, joke, ludicrousness, meaninglessness, nonsense, nonsensicality, preposterousness, ridiculousness, senselessness, silliness, stupidity, unreasonableness.

abundance *n* affluence, ampleness, amplitude, bonanza, bounty, copiousness, exuberance, fortune, fullness, glut, heap, lavishness, luxuriance, milk and honey, munificence, oodles, opulence, plenitude, plenteousness, plenty, plethora, prodigality, profusion, riches, richness, scads, wealth.
antonyms dearth, scarcity.

abundant *adj* ample, bounteous, bountiful, copious, exuberant, filled, full, generous, in plenty, lavish, luxuriant, overflowing, plenteous, plentiful, prodigal, profuse, rank, rich, superabundant, teeming, unstinted, well-provided, well-supplied.
antonyms scarce, sparse.

abuse *v* batter, bully, bullyrag, calumniate, castigate, curse, damage, deceive, defame, degrade, denigrate, disparage, exploit, harass, harm, hurt, ill-treat, impose on, injure, insult, inveigh against, libel, malign, maltreat, manhandle, mar, misapply, miscall, misemploy, mistreat, misuse, molest, objurgate, oppress, rape, revile, scold, slander, slate, smear, spoil, swear at, take advantage of, traduce, upbraid, vilify, violate, vituperate, wrong.
antonyms care for, cherish, compliment, praise.
n affront, blame, calumniation, calumny, castigation, censure, contumely, curses, cursing, damage, defamation, denigration, derision, diatribe, disparagement, execration, exploitation, harassment, harm, hurt, ill-treatment, imposition, injury, insults, invective, libel, malediction, maltreatment, manhandling, misapplication, misconduct, misdeed, mistreatment, misuse, obloquy, offence, oppression, opprobrium, rape, reproach, revilement, scolding, sin, slander, spoiling, swearing, tirade, traducement, upbraiding, vilification, violation, vitriol, vituperation, wrong, wrongdoing.
antonyms attention, care, praise.

abusive *adj* blistering, brutal, calumniating, calumnious, castigating, censorious, contumelious, cruel, defamatory, degrading, denigrating, derisive, derogatory, destructive, disparaging, harmful, hurtful, injurious, insulting, invective, libellous, maligning, objurgatory, offensive, opprobrious, pejorative, reproachful, reviling, rough, rude, scathing, scolding, slanderous, traducing, upbraiding, vilifying, vituperative.
antonyms complimentary, courteous, kind.

abut *v* adjoin, be adjacent (to), be contiguous (with), border, conjoin, connect, impinge, join, meet, touch, verge.

abysmal[1] *adj* abyssal, bottomless, boundless, complete, deep, endless, extreme, immeasurable, incalculable, infinite, profound, thorough, unending, unfathomable, vast, yawning.

abysmal[2] *adj* abominable, appalling, atrocious, awful, bad, miserable, pathetic, rotten, terrible, unbearable, wretched.

abyss *n* abysm, Avernus, canyon, chasm, crater, crevasse, depth, fissure, gorge, gulf, pit, profound, swallow, void.

academic *adj* abstract, bookish, collegiate, conjectural, donnish, educational, erudite, highbrow, hypothetical, impractical, instructional, learned, lettered, literary, notional, pedagogical, scholarly, scholastic, speculative, studious, theoretical, well-read.
n academician, don, fellow, lecturer, man of letters, master, pedant, professor, pundit, savant, scholar, scholastic, schoolman, student, tutor.

accede *v* accept, acquiesce, admit, agree, assent, assume, attain, capitulate, cave in, comply, concede, concur, consent, defer, endorse, go along (with), grant, inherit, submit, succeed (to), yield.
antonyms demur, object, veto.

accelerate *v* advance, dispatch, expedite, facilitate, forward, further, hasten, hurry, open the throttle, pick up speed, precipitate, promote, quicken, speed, speed up, spur, step on the gas, step up, stimulate.
antonyms delay, slow down.

accent *n* accentuation, articulation, beat, cadence, emphasis, enunciation, force, ictus, inflection, intensity, intonation, modulation, pitch, pronunciation, pulsation, pulse, rhythm, stress, thesis, timbre, tonality, tone.
v accentuate, emphasize, stress, underline, underscore.

accentuate *v* accent, deepen, emphasize, highlight, intensify, italicize, spotlight, strengthen, stress, underline, underscore.
antonyms play down, weaken.

accept *v* abide (by), accede, accommodate, acknowledge, acquiesce, admit, adopt, affirm, agree to (or with), approve, assent (to), assume, avow, bear, believe, bow to, brook, concur with, consent to, contain, co-operate with, defer to, go along with, handle, jump at, put up with, receive, recognize, stand, stomach, submit to, suffer, swallow, take, take in, take on, tolerate, undertake, welcome, yield to.
antonyms demur, reject.
▲ *confusable word* except.

acceptable *adj* adequate, admissible, agreeable, all right, average, conventional, correct, desirable, done, gratifying, moderate,

passable, pleasant, pleasing, proper, reasonable, respectable, satisfactory, standard, suitable, tolerable, unexceptionable, unexceptional, unobjectionable, welcome.
antonyms unsatisfactory, unwelcome.

acceptance *n* accedence, accepting, accession, acknowledgment, acquiescence, admission, adoption, affirmation, agreement, approbation, approval, assent, belief, compliance, concession, concurrence, consent, co-operation, credence, OK, permission, ratification, recognition, seal of approval, stamp of approval, submission, tolerance, toleration, undertaking.
antonyms dissent, refusal.

accepted *adj* acceptable, acknowledged, admitted, agreed, agreed upon, approved, authorized, common, confirmed, consuetudinary, conventional, correct, customary, established, normal, orthodox, proper, ratified, received, recognized, regular, sanctioned, standard, time-honoured, traditional, universal, unwritten, usual.
antonym unorthodox.

access¹ *n* attack, burst, fit, flood, surge, upsurge, upsurgence, wave.

access² *n* adit, admission, admittance, approach, attack, avenue, door, entering, entrance, entree, entry, fit, flood, gateway, increase, ingress, key, onset, passage, passageway, path, retrieval, road, surge, upsurge, upsurgence, wave, way in.
antonyms egress, outlet.
v enter, find, gain admittance to, get at, locate, open, reach, retrieve.

accessible *adj* achievable, affable, approachable, at hand, attainable, available, come-at-able, comprehensible, conversable, cordial, exposed, friendly, get-at-able, handy, liable, near, nearby, obtainable, on hand, open, procurable, reachable, ready, sociable, subject, susceptible, understandable, user-friendly, vulnerable, wide open.
antonym inaccessible.

accession *n* accedence, acceptance, acquiescence, acquisition, addition, agreement, assumption, attaining, attainment, augmentation, concurrence, consent, enlargement, entering upon, extension, increase, installation, purchase, submission, succession, taking over, yielding.

accessory¹ *n* abettor, accomplice, assistant, associate, colleague, confederate, conniver, help, helper, partner.
adj abetting, aiding, ancillary, assisting, auxiliary, contributory, incidental, secondary, subordinate, subsidiary.

accessory² *n* accent, accompaniment, accoutrement, addition, adjunct, adornment, aid, appendage, attachment, component, convenience, decoration, embellishment, extension, extra, frill, helper, ornament, side item, supplement, trimming.
adj additional, adventitious, ancillary, extra, incidental, secondary, subsidiary, supplemental, supplementary.

accident *n* blow, calamity, casualty, chance, collision, contingency, contretemps, crash, disaster, fate, fluke, fortuity, fortune, happenstance, hazard, luck, misadventure, miscarriage, mischance, misfortune, mishap, pile-up, serendipity.

accidental *adj* adventitious, adventive, casual, chance, contingent, extrinsic, flukey, fortuitous, haphazard, inadvertent, incidental, random, serendipitous, unanticipated, uncalculated, uncertain, unexpected, unforeseen, unintended, unintentional, unlooked-for, unplanned, unpremeditated, unwitting.
antonyms intentional, intrinsic, premeditated.

accidentally *adv* adventitiously, bechance, by accident, by chance, by mistake, casually, extrinsically, fortuitously, haphazardly, inadvertently, incidentally, involuntarily, randomly, serendipitously, unconsciously, undesignedly, unexpectedly, unintentionally, unwittingly.
antonyms intentionally, intrinsically.

acclaim *v* announce, applaud, approve, celebrate, cheer, clap, commend, crown, declare, endorse, eulogize, exalt, extol, hail, honour, laud, praise, rave about, salute, welcome.
antonyms boo, criticize, demean, pan, slam.
n acclamation, applause, approbation, approval, celebration, cheering, clapping, commendation, eulogizing, eulogy, exaltation, fanfare, honour, laudation, ovation, plaudits, praise, rave reviews, two thumbs up, welcome.
antonyms brickbats, criticism, vituperation.

acclamation *n* acclaim, adulation, applause, approbation, bravos, cheer, cheering, cheers, commendation, declaration, éclat, endorsement, enthusiasm, extolling, homage, laudation, ovation, paean, panegyric, plaudit, praise, salutation, shouting, tribute.
antonym disapproval.

acclimatize *v* accommodate, acculturate, accustom, adapt, adjust, attune, conform, familiarize, find one's legs, get used to, habituate, inure, naturalize, settle in.

acclivity *n* ascent, gradient, hill, incline, rise, rising ground, slope.

accolade *n* award, bravo, honour, kudos, laurels, praise, recognition.

accommodate¹ *v* acclimatize, accustom, adapt, adjust, afford, aid, assist, attune, cater to, comply, conform, entertain, fit, furnish, harmonize, help, make room for, modify, oblige, provide, reconcile, serve, suit, supply.

accommodate² *v* billet, board, cater for, domicile, entertain, fit, harbour, house, lodge, make room for, put up, quarter, serve, settle, shelter.

accommodating *adj* complaisant, considerate, co-operative, friendly, helpful, hospitable, indulgent, kind, obliging, polite, sympathetic, unselfish, willing.
antonyms contrary, disobliging, inconsiderate, selfish.

accommodation¹ *n* adaptation, adjustment, assistance, compliance, compromise, conformity, fitting, harmonization, harmony, help, modification, reconciliation, settlement.

accommodation² *n* bed and breakfast, billet, board, digs, domicile, dwelling, harbouring, house, housing, lodgings, place, quartering, quarters, residence, room(s), shelter, sheltering.

accompaniment *n* accessory, attendance, background, backup, complement, concomitant, obbligato, supplement, support, vamp.

accompany *v* attend, belong to (or with), chaperone, co-exist, coincide, complement, conduct, consort, convoy, escort, follow, go with, occur with, squire, supplement, usher.

accompanying *adj* accessory, added, additional, appended, associate, associated, attached, attendant, background, complementary, concomitant, concurrent, connected, fellow, joint, related, subsidiary, supplemental, supplementary.

accomplice *n* abettor, accessory, ally, assistant, associate, coadjutor, collaborator, colleague, confederate, conspirator, helper, helpmate, henchman, mate, participator, partner, shill.

accomplish *v* achieve, attain, bring about (or off), carry out (or off or through), compass, complete, conclude, consummate, discharge, do, effect, effectuate, engineer, execute, finish, fulfil, manage, obtain, perform, produce, pull off, realize, swing.

accomplished *adj* able, adept, adroit, consummate, cultivated, expert, facile, gifted, masterly, polished, practised, professional, proficient, skilful, skilled, talented.
antonym inexpert.

accomplishment *n* ability, achievement, act, aptitude, art, attainment, capability, carrying out, completion, conclusion, consummation, coup, deed, discharge, doing, effecting, execution, exploit, faculty, feat, finishing, forte, fruition, fulfilment, gift, management, perfection, performance, production, proficiency, realization, skill, stroke, talent, triumph.

accord¹ *v* allow, bestow, concede, confer, endow, give, grant, present, render, tender, vouchsafe.
antonyms refuse, withhold.

accord² *v* agree, assent, concur, conform, correspond, fit, harmonize, jibe, jive, line up, match, square, suit, tally.
antonym disagree.
n accordance, agreement, assent, concert, concurrence, conformity, congruence, congruity, correspondence, harmony, rapport, symmetry, sympathy, unanimity, unity.
antonym discord.

accordance *n* accord, agreement, assent, concert, concurrence, conformity, congruence, consistency, consonance, correspondence, harmony, rapport, sympathy, unanimity.

accordingly *adv* appropriately, as a result, as requested, consequently, correspondingly, duly, ergo, fitly, hence, in accord therewith, in accordance, in consequence, properly, so, suitably, therefore, thus.

according to after, after the manner of, agreeably to, as determined by, as prescribed by, commensurate with, consistent with, in accordance with, in compliance with, in conformity with, in keeping with, in line with, in obedience to, in proportion to, in relation with, in the light of, in the manner of, obedient to, on the basis of, proportionate(ly) to, with reference to.

accost *v* address, approach, buttonhole, confront, detain, greet, hail, halt, importune, salute, solicit, stop, waylay.

account¹ *n* advantage, basis, benefit, cause, chronicle, communiqué, concern, consequence, consideration, description, detail, distinction, esteem, estimation, explanation, ground, grounds, history, honour, import, importance, interest, memoir, merit, motive, narration, narrative, note, portrayal, presentation, profit, rank, reason, recital, record, regard, relation, report, reputation, repute, sake, score, significance, sketch, standing, statement, story, tale, use, value, version, worth, write-up.
v adjudge, appraise, assess, believe, consider, count, deem, esteem, estimate, gauge, hold, judge, rate, reckon, regard, think, value, weigh.

account for answer for, clarify, clear up, destroy, elucidate, explain, illuminate, justify, kill, rationalize, vindicate.

account² *n* balance, bill, book, books, charge, check, computation, inventory, invoice, ledger, reckoning, register, score, statement, tab, tally.

accountable *adj* amenable, answerable, blamable, bound, chargeable, charged with, culpable, liable, obligated, obliged, reporting, responsible.

accoutrements *n* accessories, adornments, apparel, appurtenances, array, attire, caparison, clothes, clothing, decorations, dress, equipage, equipment, fittings, fixtures, furnishings, garb, gear, habiliments, kit, ornamentation, outfit, paraphernalia, tackle, trappings, traps, trimmings.

accredited *adj* appointed, approved, attested, authorized, certified, credentialed, endorsed, guaranteed, licensed, official, qualified, recognized, sanctioned, vouched for.
antonyms unauthorized, unrecognized.

accretion *n* accession, accrual, accumulation, addition, agglomeration, amassment, amplification, augmentation, coherence, cohesion, enlargement, fusion, growth, increase, increment, supplement.
antonyms decrease, deduction.

accrue *v* accumulate, amass, arise, be added, build up, collect, compound, earn, emanate, enlarge, ensue, fall due, flow, follow, gain, gather, grow, increase, issue, proceed, redound, result, spring (up).

accumulate v accrue, agglomerate, aggregate, amass, assemble, build up, collect, cumulate, gather, grow, hoard, increase, multiply, pile up, stash, stockpile, store.
antonyms diffuse, disseminate.

accumulation n accretion, agglomeration, aggregation, amassment, assemblage, augmentation, backlog, buildup, collection, conglomeration, gathering, growth, heap, hoard, increase, mass, pile, reserve, stack, stock, stockpile, store.

accuracy n authenticity, carefulness, closeness, correctness, exactitude, exactness, faithfulness, faultlessness, fidelity, meticulousness, minuteness, niceness, nicety, precision, rigorousness, scrupulosity, scrupulousness, strictness, truth, truthfulness, veracity, veridicality, verity.
antonym inaccuracy.

accurate adj authentic, bang on, careful, close, correct, dead on, exact, factual, faithful, faultless, just, letter-perfect, mathematical, meticulous, minute, nice, on the mark, perfect, precise, proper, regular, right, right on, rigorous, scrupulous, sound, strict, true, truthful, unerring, veracious, veridical, well-aimed, well-directed, well-judged, word-perfect.
antonyms inaccurate, wrong.

accursed adj abominable, anathematized, bedevilled, bewitched, blighted, condemned, confounded, cursed, damned, despicable, detestable, doomed, execrable, foredoomed, hateful, hellish, hopeless, horrible, ill-fated, ill-omened, jinxed, luckless, maledict, miserable, ruined, star-crossed, undone, unfortunate, unholy, unlucky, wretched.
antonym blessed.

accusation n allegation, arraignment, attribution, charge, citation, complaint, crimination, denunciation, gravamen, impeachment, imputation, incrimination, indictment, plaint, recrimination.

accuse v arraign, attaint, blame, censure, charge, cite, criminate, denounce, impeach, impugn, incriminate, indict, inform against, recriminate, tax.

accustom v acclimatize, acculturate, acquaint, adapt, adjust, familiarize, habituate, harden, inure, season, train.

accustomed adj acclimatized, acquainted, adapted, common, confirmed, consuetudinary, conventional, customary, established, everyday, expected, familiar, familiarized, fixed, general, given (to), habitual, habituated, in the habit of, inured, normal, ordinary, prevailing, regular, routine, seasoned, set, traditional, trained, used (to), usual, wonted.
antonym unaccustomed.

ace n adept, champ, champion, dab (hand), expert, genius, maestro, master, nonpareil, pro, star, talent, virtuoso, whiz, winner, wizard.
antonyms colt, novice.
adj brilliant, champion, crack, excellent, expert, fine, first-class, gifted, great, hell of a,

masterly, matchless, nonpareil, outstanding, star, superb, superlative, tiptop, virtuoso.

acerbic adj abrasive, acid, acidulous, acrid, acrimonious, astringent, biting, bitter, brusque, caustic, churlish, corrosive, curt, cutting, harsh, incisive, mordacious, mordant, nasty, rancorous, rude, sarcastic, severe, sharp, snarky, sour, stern, stinging, tart, trenchant, unfriendly, unkind, verjuiced.
antonym mild.

ache v agonize, covet, crave, desire, grieve, hanker, hunger, hurt, itch, long, mourn, need, pain, pine, pound, smart, sorrow, suffer, throb, twinge, yearn.
n anguish, craving, desire, grief, hankering, hunger, hurt, itch, longing, misery, mourning, need, pain, pang, pining, pounding, smart, smarting, soreness, sorrow, suffering, throb, throbbing, yearning.

achieve v accomplish, acquire, attain, bring about, carry out, compass, complete, consummate, do, earn, effect, effectuate, execute, finish, fulfil, gain, get, manage, obtain, perform, produce, pull off, reach, realize, score, strike, succeed, swing, win.
antonyms fail, miss.

achievement n accomplishment, acquirement, act, attainment, completion, deed, effort, execution, exploit, feat, fruition, fulfilment, magnum opus, performance, production, qualification, realization, stroke, success.

achiever n doer, go-getter, performer, succeeder.

acid adj acerbic, acidulous, acrid, astringent, biting, bitter, blistering, caustic, corrosive, cutting, harsh, hurtful, ill-natured, incisive, mordant, nasty, pungent, sarcastic, searing, sharp, snarky, sour, stinging, tart, trenchant, venomous, verjuiced, vinegarish, vinegary, vitriolic.
antonyms saccharine, sugary, sweet.

acid test proof of the pudding, where the rubber hits the road.

acknowledge v accede, accept, accredit, acquiesce, address, admit, affirm, allow, answer, attest, avouch, concede, confess, confirm, declare, endorse, give the time of day to, grant, greet, hail, notice, own, pay tribute to, profess, react to, recognize, reply to, respond to, return, salute, tip one's hat to, vouch for, witness, yield.

acknowledged adj accepted, accredited, admitted, affirmed, answered, approved, attested, avowed, conceded, confessed, declared, endorsed, professed, recognized, returned.

acknowledgment n acceptance, accession, accreditation, acquiescence, addressing, admission, affirmation, allowing, answer, appreciation, avowal, confession, credit, declaration, endorsement, gratitude, greeting, hail, hailing, honour, notice, profession, reaction, realization, recognition, recompense, reply, response, return, salutation, salute, thanks, tribute, yielding.

acme *n* apex, apogee, climax, crest, crown, culmination, height, high point, maximum, optimum, peak, pinnacle, sublimation, sublimity, summit, top, vertex, zenith.
antonym nadir.

acolyte *n* adherent, admirer, altar boy, assistant, attendant, follower, helper, lackey, slave.

acquaint *v* accustom, advise, apprise, brief, bring up to date, clue in, enlighten, familiarize, fill in, give (someone) the lowdown, inform, notify, tell.

acquaintance *n* associate, association, awareness, chum, cognizance, colleague, companionship, confrère, contact, conversance, conversancy, experience, familiarity, fellowship, friendship, intimacy, knowledge, relationship, understanding.

acquainted *adj* abreast, au courant, au fait, aware, cognizant, conversant, familiar, in the know, informed, knowledgeable.

acquiesce *v* accede, accept, agree, allow, approve, assent, comply, concur, conform, consent, defer, fall into line, give in, go along (with), submit, yield.
antonyms disagree, object.

acquiescence *n* acceptance, accession, agreement, approval, assent, compliance, concurrence, conformity, consent, deference, giving in, obedience, sanction, submission, yielding.
antonyms disagreement, rebelliousness.

acquiescent *adj* acceding, accepting, agreeable, amenable, approving, assenting, biddable, complaisant, compliant, concurrent, conforming, consenting, docile, obedient, submissive, yielding.

acquire *v* achieve, amass, appropriate, attain, buy, collect, cop, develop, earn, gain, gather, get, learn, net, obtain, pick up, procure, purchase, realize, receive, secure, snag, win.
antonyms forfeit, forgo, pass up, relinquish.

acquirements *n* accomplishments, achievements, acquisitions, attainments, attributes, culture, erudition, knowledge, learning, mastery, qualifications, skills.

acquisition *n* accession, achievement, acquirement, appropriation, attainment, buy, gain, gaining, learning, obtainment, possession, prize, procurement, property, purchase, pursuit, securing, takeover.

acquisitive *adj* avaricious, avid, covetous, grabbing, grasping, greedy, insatiable, mercenary, possessive, predatory, rapacious, voracious.
antonym generous.

acquisitiveness *n* avarice, avidity, covetousness, graspingness, greed, predatoriness, rapacity, voracity.

acquit *v* absolve, bear, behave, clear, comport, conduct, deliver, discharge, dismiss, exculpate, excuse, exonerate, free, fulfil, liberate, pay, pay off, perform, release, relieve, repay, reprieve, satisfy, settle, vindicate.
antonym convict.

acquittal *n* absolution, clearance, deliverance, discharge, dismissal, dispensation, exculpation, excusing, exoneration, freeing, liberation, release, relief, reprieve, vindication.
antonym conviction.

acquittance *n* discharge, dispensation, payment, quittance, release, satisfaction, settlement.

acrid *adj* acerbic, acid, acrimonious, astringent, biting, bitter, burning, caustic, cutting, harsh, incisive, irritating, malicious, mordant, nasty, pungent, sarcastic, sardonic, searing, sharp, stinging, trenchant, venomous, virulent, vitriolic.

acrimonious *adj* abusive, acerbic, astringent, atrabilious, biting, bitter, caustic, censorious, churlish, crabbed, cutting, hostile, ill-tempered, irascible, mordant, nasty, peevish, petulant, pungent, rancorous, sarcastic, severe, sharp, spiteful, splenetic, tart, testy, trenchant, virulent, waspish.
antonyms irenic, kindly, peaceable.

acrimony *n* acerbity, asperity, astringency, bitterness, churlishness, gall, harshness, hostility, ill temper, ill will, irascibility, mordancy, nastiness, peevishness, petulance, rancour, resentment, sarcasm, spleen, tartness, trenchancy, virulence, waspishness.

acrobat *n* aerialist, balancer, contortionist, equilibrist, funambulist, gymnast, somersaulter, stuntman, stuntwoman, tightrope walker, trapeze artist, tumbler.

act[1] *n* affectation, attitude, bit, counterfeit, dissimulation, fake, feigning, feint, front, gig, make-believe, performance, piece, pose, posture, pretence, put-on, routine, sham, show, sketch, skit, spiel, stance.
v act out, affect, assume, characterize, counterfeit, dissimulate, fake (it), feign, imitate, impersonate, mime, mimic, perform, personate, personify, play, portray, pose, posture, pretend, put on, represent, sham, simulate.

act[2] *n* bill, decree, edict, law, ordinance, resolution, statute.

act[3] *n* accomplishment, achievement, action, blow, deed, doing, enactment, enterprise, execution, exertion, exploit, feat, gest, manoeuvre, measure, move, operation, proceeding, step, stroke, transaction, turn, undertaking.
v acquit oneself, bear oneself, behave, carry oneself, comport oneself, conduct oneself, do, enact, execute, exert an influence, function, move, operate, perform, react, seem, serve, strike, take effect, take steps (or measures), work.

act up carry on, cause trouble, fool around, give trouble, horse around, make trouble, make waves, malfunction, mess around, misbehave, rock the boat.

act on[1] affect, alter, change, have an effect on, influence, manipulate, modify, operate on, sway, transform.

act on[2] carry out, comply with, conform to,

execute, follow, fulfil, heed, implement, obey, put into practice.

acting *adj* deputy, interim, pro tem, provisional, reserve, standby, stopgap, substitute, supply, surrogate, temporary.

n affectation, airs, bluff, characterization, counterfeiting, dissimulation, dramatics, enactment, game-playing, histrionics, imitation, impersonation, imposture, melodrama, performance, performing, play-acting, portrayal, posing, posturing, pretence, pretending, put-on, role-playing, shamming, stagecraft, theatre, theatrics.

action *n* accomplishment, achievement, act, activity, affray, agency, battle, case, cause, combat, conflict, contest, deed, effect, effort, encounter, endeavour, energy, engagement, enterprise, exercise, exertion, exploit, feat, fight, fighting, force, fray, function(ing), influence, lawsuit, litigation, liveliness, mechanism, motion, move, movement, operation, performance, power, proceeding, process, prosecution, skirmish, sortie, spirit, stroke, suit, undertaking, vigour, vim, vitality, warfare, work, working, works.

actions *n* bearing, behaviour, comportment, conduct, demeanour, deportment, manners, ways.

activate *v* actuate, animate, arouse, bestir, drive, energize, excite, fire, galvanize, impel, initiate, mobilize, motivate, move, prompt, propel, rouse, set in motion, set off, start, stimulate, stir, switch on, trigger, turn on.

antonyms arrest, deactivate, stop.

active *adj* acting, activist, agile, alert, alive, ambitious, animated, assertive, assiduous, astir, bustling, busy, committed, devoted, diligent, doing, effectual, energetic, engaged, enterprising, enthusiastic, forceful, full, functioning, hardworking, in force, in operation, industrious, involved, light-footed, live, lively, moving, nimble, occupied, on the go, on the move, operating, operative, quick, running, sedulous, spirited, sprightly, spry, stirring, strenuous, thoroughgoing, vibrant, vigorous, vital, vivacious, working, zealous.

antonyms dormant, inactive, inert, passive.

activity *n* act, action, activeness, animation, avocation, bustle, commotion, deed, endeavour, enterprise, exercise, exertion, hobby, hustle, industry, interest, job, labour, life, liveliness, motion, movement, occupation, pastime, project, pursuit, scheme, stir, task, undertaking, venture, work.

actor *n* actress, agent, artist, comedian, doer, executor, factor, ham, impersonator, masquerader, mime, mummer, operative, operator, participant, participator, performer, perpetrator, personator, play-actor, player, practitioner, Thespian, tragedian, trouper, worker.

actual *adj* authentic, bona fide, categorical, concrete, confirmed, corporeal, current, de facto, definite, existent, existing, extant, factual, genuine, historical, legitimate, live, living, material, physical, positive, present, present-day, prevailing, real, realistic, substantial, tangible, true, truthful, verified, veritable.

antonyms apparent, imaginary, theoretical.

actuality *n* concreteness, corporeality, fact, factuality, historicity, materiality, reality, realness, substance, substantiality, truth, verity.

actually *adv* as a matter of fact, concretely, currently, de facto, effectively, essentially, in effect, in fact, in reality, in truth, indeed, literally, palpably, physically, really, tangibly, truly, verily, veritably.

actuate *v* activate, animate, arouse, cause, dispose, drive, excite, impel, influence, inspire, mobilize, motivate, move, prod, prompt, propel, quicken, rouse, spur, stimulate, stir, urge.

acumen *n* acuteness, astuteness, cleverness, discernment, discrimination, gumption, ingenuity, insight, intelligence, intuition, judgment, judiciousness, keenness, penetration, perception, perceptiveness, percipience, perspicacity, perspicuity, quickness, sagacity, sapience, sharpness, shrewdness, smartness, wisdom, wit.

antonym obtuseness.

acute¹ *adj* astute, canny, clever, critical, crucial, cutting, dangerous, discerning, discriminating, distressing, excruciating, exquisite, extreme, fierce, grave, incisive, ingenious, insightful, intense, intuitive, judicious, keen, observant, overpowering, overwhelming, penetrating, perceptive, percipient, perspicacious, piercing, poignant, pointed, powerful, racking, sagacious, sapient, sensitive, serious, severe, sharp, shooting, shrewd, shrill, smart, stabbing, subtle, sudden, urgent, violent.

antonyms chronic, mild, obtuse.

acute² *adj* abrupt, aciculate, apiculate, cuspidal, cuspidate, needle-shaped, peaked, pointed, sharp, sharpened.

antonym obtuse.

acuteness *n* acuity, astuteness, canniness, cleverness, criticality, danger, dangerousness, discernment, discrimination, fierceness, gravity, ingenuity, insight, intensity, intuitiveness, keenness, perception, perceptiveness, percipience, perspicacity, poignancy, powerfulness, sagacity, sapience, sensitivity, seriousness, severity, sharpness, shrewdness, shrillness, smartness, subtlety, suddenness, urgency, violence, wit.

adage *n* aphorism, apothegm, axiom, byword, dictum, epigram, gnome, maxim, motto, precept, proverb, saw, saying, sentence.

adamant *adj* adamantine, determined, firm, fixed, flinty, hard, immovable, impenetrable, indestructible, inexorable, inflexible, infrangible, insistent, intransigent, obdurate, resolute, rigid, rocklike, rocky, set, steely, stiff, stony, stubborn, tough, unbending, unbreakable, uncompromising, unrelenting, unshakable, unyielding.

antonyms flexible, pliant, yielding.

adapt *v* acclimatize, accommodate, adjust, alter, apply, become accustomed, become habituated, become used, change, comply, conform, convert, customize, fashion, fit, harmonize, match, metamorphose, modify, prepare, proportion, qualify, refashion, remodel, shape, suit, tailor, translate.

▲ *confusable word* adopt.

adaptable *adj* accommodating, adjustable, alterable, amenable, changeable, compliant, conformable, convertible, easy-going, flexible, malleable, modifiable, plastic, pliable, pliant, resilient, tractable, translatable, variable, versatile.

antonyms inflexible, refractory.

adaptation *n* acclimatization, accommodation, adjustment, alteration, change, conversion, habituation, modification, naturalization, refashioning, refitting, remodelling, reshaping, reworking, shift, transformation, translation, variation, version.

add *v* adjoin, affix, annex, append, attach, calculate, combine, compute, count, factor in, include, join, juxtapose, reckon, subjoin, superimpose, tack on, total.

antonym subtract.

add to aggravate, amplify, augment, broaden, compound, enhance, enlarge, exacerbate, extend, further, heighten, increase, intensify, magnify, multiply, prolong, raise, supplement.

add up add, amount (to), be consistent, be logical, be plausible, be reasonable, calculate, come (to), compute, count, count up, hang together, hold water, imply, indicate, make sense, mean, reckon, ring true, signify, stand to reason, sum up, tally, total.

added *adj* additional, adjunct, extra, fresh, further, increased, new, supplementary.

addendum *n* addition, adjunct, affix, appendage, appendix, attachment, augmentation, codicil, epilogue, extension, extra, postscript, supplement.

addict *n* acid head, adherent, buff, devotee, dope fiend, enthusiast, fan, fiend, follower, freak, head, hophead, junkie, mainliner, nut, pillhead, pillpopper, pothead, tripper, user.

addicted *adj* absorbed, accustomed, dedicated, dependent, devoted, enslaved, habituated, hooked, obsessed.

addiction *n* craving, dependency, enslavement, habit, monkey (on one's back), obsession.

addition *n* accession, accessory, accretion, addend, addendum, adding, additive, adjoining, adjunct, adjunction, affix, affixing, amplification, annex, annexation, appendage, appendix, appurtenance, attachment, augmentation, calculation, computation, counting, enlargement, extension, extra, gain, inclusion, increase, increment, inpouring, reckoning, summation, supplement, totalling.

additional *adj* added, additive, adscititious, adventitious, adventive, affixed, appended, excrescent, extra, fresh, further, increased, more, new, other, repeat, reserve, second (third, etc.), spare, supplementary.

addled *adj* bad, bamboozled, befuddled, bewildered, confused, dazed, flustered, foolish, gone bad, mixed up, muddled, off, perplexed, putrid, rancid, rotten, silly, spoiled, turned, unbalanced.

antonyms clear, fresh.

address¹ *n* abode, department, direction, domicile, dwelling, home, house, inscription, location, lodging, place, residence, situation, superscription, whereabouts.

address² *n* declamation, discourse, disquisition, dissertation, harangue, lecture, oration, sermon, speech, talk.

v accost, address (oneself) to, apostrophize, apply (oneself) to, approach, attend to, bespeak, buttonhole, concentrate on, devote (oneself) to, discourse (on or to), discuss, engage in, focus on, greet, hail, handle, harangue, invoke, lecture, orate, salute, sermonize, speak, speak to, take care of, take on, talk, talk to, treat, turn to, undertake.

address³ *n* adroitness, application, art, bearing, deftness, dexterity, discretion, dispatch, expedition, expertise, expertness, facility, ingenuity, manner, skilfulness, skill, tact.

addresses *n* advances, approaches, attentions, courting, courtship, lovemaking, overtures, proposals, suit, wooing.

adept *adj* able, accomplished, ace, adroit, agile, deft, dexterous, experienced, expert, facile, masterful, masterly, nimble, polished, practised, proficient, skilful, skilled, versed.

antonyms bungling, incompetent, inept.

n ace, dab (hand), expert, genius, maestro, master, old hand, past master, pro, virtuoso, wizard.

antonyms bungler, incompetent, klutz.

adequacy *n* acceptability, adequateness, capability, commensurateness, competence, efficacy, fairness, fitness, passability, presentability, requisiteness, satisfactoriness, serviceability, sufficiency, suitability, tolerability.

antonyms inadequacy, insufficiency.

adequate *adj* able, acceptable, capable, commensurate, competent, condign, efficacious, enough, equal, fair, fit, passable, presentable, requisite, respectable, satisfactory, serviceable, sufficient, suitable, tolerable.

antonyms inadequate, insufficient.

adhere *v* abide (by), accrete, agree, attach (itself or oneself), belong, bond, cleave, cling, coalesce, cohere, comply with, fasten (itself or oneself), follow, fulfil, heed, hold, hold fast, join, keep, link, maintain, mind, obey, observe, respect, stand by, stick, stick fast, support, unite.

adherence *n* allegiance, attachment, constancy, devotion, faithfulness, fidelity, fulfilment, heed, holding fast, loyalty, obedience, observance, respect, support.

adherent *n* admirer, advocate, aficionado, devotee, disciple, enthusiast, fan, follower, hanger-on, henchman, partisan, proponent, satellite, sectary, supporter, upholder, votary.

adhesion *n* adhesiveness, attachment, bond, coherence, cohesion, grip, sticking, union.

adhesive *adj* adherent, attaching, bonding, clinging, cohesive, gluey, glutinous, gummy, mucilaginous, sticky, tacky, tenacious.
n cement, glue, gum, mountant, mucilage, paste, tape.

adieu *n* bon voyage, cheerio, congé, departure, farewell, goodbye, leave-taking, parting, valediction, valedictory.

adjacent *adj* abutting, adjoining, alongside, beside, bordering, close, contiguous, coterminous, juxtaposed, near, neighbouring, next, proximate, touching, vicinal.

adjoin *v* abut, add, affix, annex, append, approximate, attach, border, communicate with, connect, couple, interconnect, join, juxtapose, link, meet, touch, unite, verge.

adjoining *adj* abutting, adjacent, bordering, connecting, contiguous, interconnecting, joined, juxtaposed, near, neighbouring, next, next door, proximate, touching, verging, vicinal.

adjourn *v* break up, close, defer, delay, discontinue, dismiss, end, interrupt, knock off, let out, pause, postpone, prorogue, put off, quit, recess, stay, stop, suspend, terminate, wrap up.
antonym convene.

adjournment *n* break, close, deferment, deferral, delay, discontinuation, dismissal, dissolution, end, interruption, pause, postponement, prorogation, putting off, recess, stay, suspension, termination, wrap-up.

adjudicate *v* adjudge, arbitrate, decide, determine, judge, pronounce, rate, ref, referee, settle, umpire.

adjudication *n* adjudgment, arbitration, conclusion, decision, determination, finding, judgment, pronouncement, rating, refereeing, ruling, settlement, verdict.

adjunct *n* accessory, addendum, addition, add-on, annex, appanage, appendage, appendix, appurtenance, attachment, auxiliary, complement, extension, supplement.

adjure *v* appeal to, ask, beg, beseech, charge, command, conjure, direct, enjoin, entreat, implore, importune, invoke, order, plead with, pray, request, supplicate.
▲ *confusable word* abjure.

adjust *v* acclimatize, accommodate, accustom, adapt, align, alter, arrange, balance, change, compose, conform, convert, customize, dispose, fine-tune, fit, fix, harmonize, jiggle, measure, modify, move, order, proportion, realign, reconcile, rectify, redress, refashion, regulate, remodel, reposition, reshape, set, settle, settle in, shape, square, suit, temper, tune.
antonyms derange, disarrange, upset.

adjustable *adj* adaptable, alterable, customizable, flexible, malleable, modifiable, mouldable, movable, tractable.
antonyms fixed, inflexible.

adjustment *n* acclimatization, accommodation, adaptation, alignment, alteration, arrangement, arranging, conforming, conversion, customization, fitting, fixing, harmonization, modification, naturalization, ordering, position(ing), realignment, reconciliation, rectification, redress, refashioning, regulation, remodelling, reorientation, repositioning, setting, settlement, settling in, shaping, tuning.

ad-lib *v* extemporize, improvise, invent, make up (as one goes along), play by ear, wing it.
adj extemporaneous, extempore, extemporized, impromptu, improvised, made up, off-the-cuff, spontaneous, unpremeditated, unprepared, unrehearsed.
antonym prepared.

ad lib *adv* extemporaneously, extempore, impromptu, impulsively, off the cuff, off the top of one's head, on the spur of the moment, spontaneously, without preparation.

administer *v* apply, assign, conduct, contribute, control, direct, disburse, dispense, dispose, distribute, dole out, execute, give, govern, head, impose, lead, manage, measure out, mete out, officiate, organize, oversee, perform, preside over, provide, regulate, rule, run, superintend, supervise, supply.

administration *n* administering, application, conduct, control, direction, directorship, disbursement, dispensation, disposal, distribution, execution, executive, governing, governing body, government, leadership, management, ministry, organization, overseeing, performance, provision, regime, regulation, rule, ruling, running, settlement, superintendence, supervision, supply, term of office.

administrative *adj* authoritative, directorial, executive, governmental, gubernatorial, legislative, management, managerial, organizational, regulatory, supervisory.

administrator *n* boss, controller, curator, custodian, director, distributor, governor, guardian, leader, manager, organizer, overseer, ruler, superintendent, supervisor, trustee.

admirable *adj* commendable, creditable, deserving, desirable, enviable, estimable, excellent, fine, honourable, laudable, meritorious, noble, praiseworthy, respectable, respected, superior, valuable, wonderful, worthy.
antonyms contemptible, despicable.

admiration *n* adoration, affection, amazement, appreciation, approbation, approval, astonishment, awe, delight, esteem, idolization, praise, regard, respect, reverence, surprise, veneration, wonder, wonderment, worship.
antonym contempt.

admire *v* adore, applaud, appreciate, approve, esteem, iconize, idolize, laud, look up to, praise, prize, respect, revere, value, venerate, wonder at, worship.

antonym despise.

admirer *n* adherent, aficionado, beau, boyfriend, devotee, disciple, enthusiast, fan, follower, gallant, idolator, idolizer, lover, partisan, suitor, supporter, sweetheart, votary, wooer, worshipper.

antonyms critic, opponent.

admissible *adj* acceptable, allowable, allowed, equitable, justifiable, lawful, legitimate, licit, passable, permissible, permitted, tolerable, tolerated.

antonyms illegitimate, inadmissible.

admission *n* acceptance, access, acknowledgment, admittance, admitting, affirmation, allowance, avowal, concession, confession, declaration, disclosure, divulgence, entrance, entrée, entry, entry fee, exposé, granting, inclusion, ingress, initiation, introduction, owning, profession, revelation.

antonyms denial, exclusion.

admit *v* accept, acknowledge, affirm, agree, allow, allow to enter, avow, be amenable (to), concede, confess, declare, disclose, divulge, give access, grant, initiate, introduce, let, let in, permit, profess, receive, recognize, reveal, take in.

antonyms deny, exclude, gainsay.

admittance *n* acceptance, access, admitting, allowing, entrance, entry, ingress, letting in, passage, reception.

admixture *n* addition, amalgamation, blend, combination, commixture, fusion, intermixture, mingling, tincture, trace.

admonish *v* advise, berate, caution, censure, check, chide, counsel, enjoin, exhort, forewarn, rebuke, reprehend, reprimand, reproach, reprove, scold, upbraid, urge, warn.

admonition *n* advice, berating, caution, censure, counsel, exhortation, injunction, rebuke, reprehension, reprimand, reproach, reproof, scolding, urging, warning.

admonitory *adj* admonishing, advisory, cautionary, censorious, exhortative, exhortatory, hortatory, injunctive, rebuking, reprimanding, reproachful, reproving, scolding, warning.

ado *n* agitation, bother, business, bustle, ceremony, commotion, confusion, deal, delay, disturbance, excitement, ferment, flurry, furor, fuss, hassle, hue and cry, hullabaloo, hurly-burly, hype, kafuffle, pother, rigmarole, stir, to-do, trouble, tumult, turmoil, uproar.

antonyms calm, tranquillity.

adolescence *n* boyhood, boyishness, childishness, development, girlhood, girlishness, immaturity, juvenescence, juvenility, minority, puberty, pubescence, puerility, teens, transition, youth, youthfulness.

antonym senescence.

adolescent *adj* boyish, childish, girlish, growing, half-grown, immature, juvenescent, juvenile, maturing, pre-adult, pubescent, puerile, teenage, young, youthful.

n bobbysoxer, juvenile, minor, pre-adult, teenager, young adult, youngster, youth.

Adonis *n* charmer, dish, dream, dreamboat, Ganymede, god, golden boy, good-looker, he-man, hunk, idol, knockout, matinée idol, pin-up.

adopt *v* accept, affect, appropriate, approve, assume, back, choose, embrace, endorse, espouse, follow, foster, maintain, ratify, sanction, select, support, take in, take on, take up.

antonyms disown, repudiate.

▲ *confusable word* adapt.

adoption *n* acceptance, affectation, appropriation, approval, assumption, choice, embrace(ment), embracing, endorsement, espousal, following, fostering, maintenance, ratification, sanction, selection, support.

adorable *adj* appealing, attractive, bewitching, captivating, charming, cute, darling, dear, delightful, enchanting, fetching, lovable, pleasing, precious, sweet, winning, winsome.

antonym hateful, ugly.

adoration *n* admiration, cult, esteem, estimation, exaltation, glorification, honour, idolatry, idolization, love, magnification, reverence, veneration, worship.

antonyms abhorrence, detestation.

adore *v* admire, cherish, dote on, esteem, exalt, glorify, honour, idolatrize, idolize, love, magnify, revere, reverence, venerate, worship.

antonyms abhor, hate.

adorn *v* apparel, array, beautify, bedeck, bedizen, bejewel, crown, deck, decorate, doll up, embellish, emblazon, enhance, enrich, furbish, garnish, gild, grace, impearl, ornament, tart up, trick out, trim.

adornment *n* accessory, beautification, bedizenment, decorating, decoration, embellishment, fallal, flounce, frill, frippery, furbelow, garnish, gilding, ornament, ornamentation, ornateness, trappings, trimming.

adrift *adj* aimless, amiss, anchorless, astray, at sea, directionless, goalless, insecure, lost, off course, purposeless, rootless, rudderless, unsettled, wandering, wrong.

antonyms anchored, stable.

adroit *adj* able, adept, apt, artful, clever, cunning, deft, dexterous, expert, ingenious, masterful, neat, nimble, proficient, quick, resourceful, skilful, skilled, slick.

antonyms clumsy, inept, maladroit.

adroitness *n* ability, ableness, address, adeptness, aptness, artfulness, cleverness, cunning, deftness, dexterity, expertise, facility, finesse, ingeniousness, ingenuity, legerdemain, masterfulness, mastery, neatness, nimbleness, proficiency, quickness, resourcefulness, skilfulness, skill.

antonyms clumsiness, ineptitude.

adulation *n* blandishment, bootlicking, fawning, flattery, idolatry, idolization, personality cult, sycophancy, worship.

antonym abuse.

adulatory *adj* blandishing, bootlicking, fawning, flattering, fulsome, grovelling, idolatrous, obsequious, praising, servile, slavish, sycophantic, unctuous, worshipful.
antonym unflattering.

adult *adj* developed, full-grown, (fully) grown, grown-up, mature, of age, ripe, ripened.
antonym immature.

adulterate *v* attenuate, bastardize, contaminate, corrupt, dash, debase, defile, depreciate, devalue, dilute, doctor, infect, load, mix, pollute, taint, thin, vitiate, water down, weaken.
antonym purify, refine.

adumbrate *v* augur, bedim, chart, conceal, darken, delineate, draft, eclipse, forecast, foreshadow, foretell, hint at, indicate, obfuscate, obscure, outline, overshadow, portend, predict, prefigure, presage, prognosticate, prophesy, silhouette, sketch, suggest, trace, veil.

advance *v* accelerate, adduce, advocate, aid, allege, ameliorate, assist, benefit, bring forward, cite, elevate, expedite, facilitate, foster, furnish, further, get worse, go ahead, go forward, grow, hasten, improve, increase, lend, make, make progress, make strides, move on, multiply, offer, pay beforehand, posit, present, press on, proceed, proffer, profit, progress, promote, propound, prosper, provide, put, put forward, raise, send forward, speed, submit, suggest, supply, thrive, upgrade.
antonyms demote, hinder, impede, retard, retreat.
n advancement, amelioration, betterment, breakthrough, credit, deposit, development, down payment, furtherance, gain, growth, headway, improvement, increase, loan, preferment, prepayment, profit, progress, promotion, raise, retainer, rise, step.
antonym recession.
adj beforehand, early, foremost, forward, in front, leading, preliminary, preparatory, prior.

in advance ahead, ahead of time, beforehand, before the fact, down, earlier, early, in front, in the forefront, in the lead, in the van, in the vanguard, previously, sooner, up front.

advanced *adj* ahead, avant-garde, developed, extreme, foremost, forward, forward-looking, higher, high-level, imaginative, late, leading, original, precocious, progressive, sophisticated.
antonyms backward, retarded.

advancement *n* advance, advocacy, amelioration, betterment, development, expedition, facilitation, forward movement, fostering, furthering, gain, growth, headway, improvement, maturation, onward movement, preferment, progress, promotion, raising, rise, suggestion.
antonyms demotion, retardation.

advances *n* addresses, approach, approaches, attentions, headway, moves, overtures, progress, proposals, proposition, strides.

advantage *n* account, aid, ascendancy, asset, assistance, avail, benefit, blessing, boon, boot, convenience, dominance, edge, expediency, fruit, gain, good, help, hold, interest, lead, leverage, precedence, pre-eminence, profit, purchase, service, start, superiority, sway, upper hand, use, usefulness, utility, welfare.
antonyms disadvantage, hindrance.

advantageous *adj* auspicious, beneficial, convenient, favourable, gainful, helpful, opportune, profitable, propitious, remunerative, rewarding, superior, useful, valuable, worthwhile.
antonym disadvantageous.

advent *n* accession, appearance, approach, arrival, coming, dawn, entrance, inception, introduction, occurrence, onset, visitation.

adventitious *adj* accidental, added, additional, casual, chance, contingent, extra, extraneous, extrinsic, foreign, fortuitous, incidental, non-essential, serendipitous, supervenient, unexpected.
antonyms inherent, intrinsic.

adventure *n* challenge, chance, contingency, danger, enterprise, event, excitement, experience, exploit, gest, happening, hazard, incident, occurrence, peril, risk, speculation, thrills, undertaking, venture.

adventurer *n* cowboy, daredevil, derring-doer, filibuster, fortune hunter, freebooter, freelancer, gambler, hero, heroine, knight-errant, madcap, mercenary, opportunist, rogue, soldier of fortune, speculator, swashbuckler, thrill-seeker, traveller, venturer, voyager, wanderer.

adventurous *adj* adventuresome, audacious, bold, dangerous, daredevil, daring, dauntless, doughty, enterprising, foolhardy, game, hazardous, headstrong, impetuous, intrepid, perilous, plucky, rash, reckless, risky, spunky, swashbuckling, temerarious, venturesome.
antonyms cautious, chary, prudent.

adversary *n* antagonist, assailant, attacker, competitor, contestant, enemy, foe, foeman, opponent, opposer, rival.
antonyms ally, supporter.

adverse *adj* antagonistic, bad, conflicting, contrary, counter, counter-productive, deleterious, detrimental, disadvantageous, harmful, hostile, hurtful, inauspicious, inexpedient, inimical, injurious, inopportune, negative, noxious, opposing, opposite, repugnant, uncongenial, unfavourable, unfortunate, unfriendly, unlucky, unpropitious, untoward.
antonyms advantageous, propitious.
▲ *confusable word* averse.

adversity *n* affliction, bad fortune, bad luck, calamity, catastrophe, contretemps, difficulty, disaster, distress, hard knocks, hard luck, hard times, hardship, ill fortune, ill luck, mischance, misery, misfortune, mishap, poor luck, reverse, setback, sorrow, suffering, trial, tribulation, trouble, woe, wretchedness.
antonym prosperity.

advertise *v* announce, blazon, broadcast, bruit, declare, display, flaunt, herald, hype (up), make known, plug, praise, proclaim, promote, promulgate, publicize, publish, puff, push, shout from the rooftops, spread abroad, tout, trumpet.

advertisement *n* ad, announcement, bill, billboard, blurb, broadcast, brochure, circular, classified(s), commercial, display, flyer, handbill, handout, hype, leaflet, (newspaper) insert, notice, placard, plug, poster, promotion, propaganda, propagation, publicity, puff, puffery, sign, trumpet-blowing, word from our sponsor.

advice *n* admonition, caution, communication, counsel, direction, do's and don'ts, exhortation, guidance, help, hint(s), information, injunction, instruction, intelligence, memorandum, notice, notification, opinion, recommendation, rede, suggestion, tip(s), view, warning, wisdom, word.

advisable *adj* advantageous, appropriate, apt, beneficial, correct, desirable, expedient, fit, fitting, judicious, meet, politic, profitable, proper, prudent, recommended, seemly, sensible, sound, suggested, suitable, wise.
antonyms inadvisable, injudicious.

advise *v* acquaint, apprise, caution, counsel, enjoin, forewarn, guide, inform, instruct, make aware, notify, recommend, report to, suggest, teach, tell, tutor, urge, warn.

adviser *n* aide, authority, coach, confidant(e), consultant, counsel, counsellor, éminence grise, guide, helper, instructor, lawyer, mentor, monitor, preceptor, righthand man, solicitor, supervisor, teacher, therapist, tutor, vizier.

advisory *adj* advising, consultative, consulting, counselling, helping, hortatory, recommending.

advocacy *n* activism, adoption, advancement, approval, backing, campaigning, championing, championship, defence, encouragement, espousal, justification, lobby(ing), patronage, pleading, promotion, promulgation, propagation, proposal, recommendation, spokesmanship, support, upholding, urging.

advocate *v* adopt, advise, approve, argue for, campaign for, champion, countenance, defend, encourage, endorse, espouse, favour, justify, lobby for, patronize, plead for, press for, promote, propose, recommend, speak (out or up) for, subscribe to, support, uphold, urge.
antonyms deprecate, disparage, impugn.
n activist, apologist, apostle, attorney, backer, barrister, campaigner, champion, counsel, counsellor, defender, interceder, intercessor, lawyer, lobbyist, mediator, patron, pleader, promoter, proponent, proposer, solicitor, speaker, spokesman, supporter, upholder, vindicator.
antonyms critic, opponent.

aegis *n* advocacy, auspices, backing, championship, favour, guardianship, patronage, protection, shelter, sponsorship, support, wing.

aerial *adj* aeolian, airy, atmospheric, elevated, ethereal, high-flown, incorporeal, insubstantial, lofty, unreal.

affability *n* accessibility, amiability, amicability, approachability, benevolence, benignity, civility, congeniality, conversableness, cordiality, courtesy, easiness, friendliness, geniality, good humour, good nature, graciousness, kindliness, mildness, obligingness, openness, pleasantness, sociability, suavity, urbanity, warmth.
antonyms brusqueness, coolness, reserve, reticence, unfriendliness.

affable *adj* agreeable, amiable, amicable, approachable, benevolent, benign, civil, congenial, cordial, courteous, expansive, free, friendly, genial, good-humoured, good-natured, gracious, kindly, mild, obliging, open, pleasant, sociable, suave, urbane, warm.
antonyms brusque, cool, reserved, reticent, unfriendly.

affair *n* activity, adventure, amour, business, ceremony, circumstance, concern, connection, do, episode, event, happening, incident, interest, intrigue, liaison, matter, occurrence, operation, organization, outfit, party, proceeding, project, question, reception, relationship, responsibility, romance, schmozzle, subject, topic, transaction, undertaking.

affect[1] *v* act on, agitate, alter, apply to, attack, bear upon, change, concern, determine, disturb, faze, grieve, grip, have an effect on, impinge upon, impress, influence, interest, involve, melt, modify, move, overcome, penetrate, pertain to, perturb, prevail over, regard, relate to, seize, soften, stir, strike, sway, touch, transform, trouble, tug at the emotions (or heartstrings) of, upset.

affect[2] *v* act, adopt, aspire to, assume, contrive, counterfeit, fake, feign, imitate, pretend, profess, put on, sham, simulate, stage.

▲ *confusable word* effect.

affectation *n* act, affectedness, appearance, artificiality, euphuism, façade, fakery, false display, imitation, insincerity, ladyism, mannerism, phoniness, pose, posturing, pretence, pretension, pretentiousness, semblance, sham, show, simulation, staginess, theatricalism, theatricality, unnaturalness.
antonyms artlessness, ingenuousness.

affected[1] *adj* afflicted, agitated, altered, changed, concerned, damaged, distressed, gripped, hurt, impaired, impressed, influenced, injured, melted, moved, perturbed, smitten, stirred, swayed, touched, troubled, upset.

affected[2] *adj* artificial, assumed, bogus, camp, chi-chi, conceited, contrived, counterfeit, cutesy, euphuistic, exaggerated, fake, feigned, fussy, insincere, lah-di-dah, mannered, mincing, namby-pamby, phony, pompous, posing, posturing, precious, pretended, pretentious, put-on, self-conscious, sham, simulated, spurious, staged, stagy, stiff, studied, unnatural.
antonyms genuine, natural.

affecting *adj* emotional, heart-wrenching, impressive, moving, pathetic, piteous, pitiable, pitiful, poignant, sad, saddening, stirring, touching, troubling.

affection *n* affinity, amity, attachment, care, desire, devotion, favour, feeling, fondness, friendliness, good will, inclination, kindness, liking, love, passion, predisposition, regard, sympathy, tenderness, warmth.

antonyms antipathy, dislike.

affectionate *adj* amiable, amorous, attached, caring, demonstrative, devoted, doting, fond, friendly, kind, loving, passionate, responsive, solicitous, tender, touchy-feely, warm, warm-hearted.

antonyms cold, undemonstrative.

affiliate *v* ally, amalgamate, annex, associate, band together, combine, confederate, conjoin, connect, federate, incorporate, join, merge, relate, syndicate, unite.

affiliation *n* alliance, amalgamation, association, coalition, combination, confederation, connection, federation, incorporation, joining, league, merger, merging, relationship, syndication, union.

affinity *n* alliance, analogy, attraction, closeness, compatibility, connection, correspondence, fondness, homogeneity, inclination, kinship, leaning, likeness, liking, partiality, predisposition, proclivity, propensity, rapport, relation, relationship, resemblance, similarity, similitude, sympathy.

antonyms aversion, dissimilarity.

affirm *v* assert, asseverate, attest, aver, avouch, avow, build up, certify, confirm, corroborate, declare, depose, encourage, endorse, maintain, pronounce, ratify, state, support, swear, testify, uphold, witness to.

affirmation *n* affirmance, assertion, asseveration, attestation, averment, avouchment, avowal, certification, confirmation, corroboration, declaration, deposition, encouragement, endorsement, oath, pronouncement, ratification, statement, support, testimony, witness.

affirmative *adj* agreeing, approving, assenting, assertory, asseverative, concurring, confirming, consenting, corroborative, emphatic, encouraging, positive, supportive, upbuilding.

antonyms dissenting, negative.

affix *v* add, adjoin, annex, append, assign, attach, attribute, bind, connect, fasten, glue, join, nail, paste, pin, rivet, screw, stick, subjoin, tack, tag.

antonym detach.

afflict *v* beset, burden, distress, grieve, harass, harm, harrow, hurt, oppress, pain, plague, rack, smite, strike, torment, torture, trouble, try, visit, wound, wring.

antonyms comfort, solace.

affliction *n* adversity, calamity, cross, curse, depression, disaster, disease, distress, grief, hardship, hurt, illness, misery, misfortune, ordeal, pain, plague, scourge, sickness, sorrow, suffering, torment, trial, tribulation, trouble, visitation, woe, wretchedness.

antonyms comfort, consolation, solace.

affluence *n* abundance, money, opulence, plenty, profusion, property, prosperity, riches, substance, wealth, wealthiness.

antonym poverty.

affluent *adj* comfortable, flourishing, flush, high-income, loaded, moneyed, opulent, pecunious, prosperous, rich, rolling (in dough, etc.), successful, wealthy, well-fixed, well-heeled, well-off, well-to-do.

antonyms impecunious, impoverished, poor.

afford *v* absorb, bear, bestow, cope with, engender, furnish, generate, give, grant, handle, impart, manage, offer, produce, provide, render, spare, stand, supply, sustain, yield.

affray *n* brawl, brush, contest, disturbance, dogfight, Donnybrook, encounter, feud, fight, fisticuffs, fracas, fray, free-for-all, melee, quarrel, riot, row, scrap, scrimmage, scuffle, set-to, skirmish, squabble, tussle, wrangle.

affront *v* abuse, anger, annoy, bend out of shape, displease, gall, incense, insult, irritate, nettle, offend, outrage, pique, provoke, slight, snub, vex.

antonyms appease, compliment.

n abuse, discourtesy, disrespect, facer, indignity, injury, insult, offence, outrage, provocation, rudeness, slap in the face, slur, snub, vexation, wrong.

antonym compliment.

afoot *adv* about, abroad, afloat, around, astir, brewing, circulating, current, going around, going on, in preparation, in progress, in the air, in the offing, in the pipeline, in the wind, up.

afraid *adj* alarmed, anxious, apprehensive, cowardly, diffident, distrustful, faint-hearted, fearful, frightened, intimidated, jittery, jumpy, mistrustful, nervous, regretful, reluctant, scared, sorry, spooked, suspicious, timid, timorous, tremulous, unhappy, worried.

antonyms confident, unafraid.

afresh *adv* again, anew, da capo, de novo, newly, once again, once more, over, over again.

after *adv, prep* afterwards, as a result of, behind, below, following, in consequence of, later, post, since, subsequent to, subsequently, succeeding, thereafter, upon.

antonym before.

aftermath *n* after-effects, backwash, by-products, consequences, effects, end, fall-out, outcome, repercussion, results, upshot, wake.

again *adv* afresh, also, anew, another time, besides, bis, da capo, de novo, ditto, encore, furthermore, in addition, moreover, on the other hand, once more.

against *prep* abutting, across (from), adjacent to, athwart, at variance with, close up to, con, confronting, contra, counter to, facing, fronting, hostile to, in contact with, in contradiction to, in contrast to, in defiance of, in exchange for, in opposition to, in the face of, next to, on, opposed to, opposing, opposite to, resisting, touching, versus.

antonyms for, pro.

age *n* agedness, caducity, date, datedness, day, days, decline, decrepitude, dotage, duration, eld, elderliness, eon, epoch, era, generation, lifetime, majority, maturity, obsolescence, old age, period, senescence, senility, seniority, span, superannuation, the sere and yellow, time, years.

antonyms salad days, youth.

v cure, decline, degenerate, deteriorate, grow old, mature, mellow, obsolesce, ripen, season.

aged *adj* advanced, age-old, ancient, antiquated, antique, decrepit, elderly, geriatric, grey, hoary, obsolescent, obsolete, old, patriarchal, senescent, sere, superannuated, timeworn, venerable, worn out.

antonyms young, youthful.

agency *n* action, activity, broker, brokerage, bureau, business, department, effect, effectuation, efficiency, finger, force, hand, influence, instrumentality, intercession, intervention, means, mechanism, mediation, medium, office, offices, operation, organization, power, vehicle, work, workings.

agenda *n* axe to grind, calendar, diary, goal, list, menu, objective, plan, program, schedule, timetable, (ulterior) motive.

agent *n* actor, agency, attorney, author, broker, cause, channel, delegate, deputy, doer, emissary, envoy, executor, factor, force, functionary, go-between, instrument, intermediary, legate, manager, means, middleman, mover, negotiator, operative, operator, organ, performer, rep, representative, substitute, surrogate, vehicle, vicar, worker.

ages *n* a dog's age, centuries, decades, donkey's years, eons, years.

aggrandize *v* advance, amplify, augment, dignify, elevate, enhance, enlarge, ennoble, enrich, exaggerate, exalt, glamorize, glorify, increase, inflate, magnify, promote, upgrade, widen.

antonyms belittle, debase.

aggravate *v* annoy, compound, exacerbate, exaggerate, exasperate, frustrate, harass, hassle, heighten, incense, increase, inflame, intensify, irk, irritate, magnify, needle, nettle, peeve, pester, provoke, tease, vex, worsen.

antonyms alleviate, appease, mollify.

aggravation *n* annoyance, bore, drag, exacerbation, exaggeration, exasperation, frustration, hassle, heightening, increase, inflammation, intensification, irksomeness, irritant, irritation, magnification, pain (in the neck), peeve, provocation, teasing, thorn in the flesh (or side), vexation, worsening.

aggregate *n* accumulation, agglomeration, aggregation, amount, assemblage, body, bulk, cluster, collection, combination, conglomeration, entirety, generality, heap, herd, lump, mass, mixture, pile, sum, throng, total, totality, whole.

adj accumulated, added, assembled, clustered, collected, collective, combined, complete, composite, conglomerate, corporate, cumulative, mixed, total, united.

antonyms individual, particular.

v accumulate, add up, agglomerate, amass, amount to, assemble, cluster, collect, combine, conglomerate, heap, mix, pile, total.

aggregation *n* accumulation, agglomeration, amassment, assemblage, cluster, collection, combination, congeries, conglomeration, heap, mass, pile, stack.

aggression *n* act of war, aggressiveness, antagonism, assault, attack, bellicosity, belligerence, combativeness, destructiveness, encroachment, hostility, impingement, incursion, injury, intrusion, invasion, jingoism, militancy, offence, offensive, onslaught, provocation, pugnacity, raid, violence.

aggressive *adj* abrasive, argumentative, assertive, bareknuckle, bellicose, belligerent, bold, butch, chauvinistic, chippy, combative, competitive, contentious, destructive, disputatious, dominating, domineering, dynamic, energetic, enterprising, forceful, go-ahead, hostile, intrusive, invasive, jingoistic, militant, obnoxious, offensive, overassertive, proactive, provocative, pugnacious, pushing, pushy, quarrelsome, scrappy, triumphalist, vigorous, violent, zealous.

antonyms passive, peaceable, submissive.

aggressor *n* assailant, assaulter, attacker, intruder, invader, offender, provoker.

antonym victim.

aggrieved *adj* afflicted, affronted, bent out of shape, distressed, disturbed, harmed, hurt, ill-used, injured, insulted, maltreated, mistreated, miffed, offended, pained, peeved, put out, saddened, unhappy, wronged.

antonym pleased.

aghast *adj* amazed, appalled, astonished, astounded, awestruck, confounded, dismayed, distressed, horrified, horror-struck, shocked, startled, stunned, stupefied, thunderstruck.

agile *adj* active, acute, adroit, alert, brisk, clever, fleet, flexible, limber, lissome, lithe, lively, mobile, nimble, quick, quick-witted, sharp, sprightly, spry, supple, swift.

antonyms clumsy, stiff, torpid.

agility *n* activity, acuteness, adroitness, alertness, briskness, cleverness, flexibility, lissomeness, litheness, liveliness, mobility, nimbleness, quickness, quick-wittedness, sharpness, sprightliness, spryness, suppleness, swiftness.

antonyms sluggishness, stiffness, torpidity.

aging *adj* elderly, geriatric, obsolescent, senescent.

agitate[1] *v* alarm, arouse, beat, churn, confuse, convulse, discompose, disconcert, disquiet, distract, disturb, excite, ferment, flurry, fluster, incite, inflame, perturb, rattle, rile, rock, roil, rouse, ruffle, shake, stimulate, stir, toss, trouble, unnerve, unsettle, upset, work up, worry.

antonyms calm, tranquillize.

aim

agitate² *v* campaign, issue demands, lobby, press, push.

agitated *adj* anxious, churning, discomposed, distracted, dithery, excited, feverish, flappable, flurried, flustered, in a dither, in a flap, in a lather, in a tizzy, insecure, jumpy, nervous, perturbed, rattled, restive, restless, riled, ruffled, tumultuous, twitchy, uneasy, unnerved, unsettled, upset, worked up.

antonyms calm, composed.

agitation *n* agitprop, alarm, anxiety, arousal, campaigning, churning, clamour, commotion, confusion, controversy, convulsion, discomposure, disquiet, distraction, disturbance, dither, ebullition, excitement, ferment, fever, flap, flurry, fluster, fomentation, fuss, hassle, lather, incitement, lobbying, moil, outcry, rocking, shake, shaking, solicitude, stimulation, stir, stirring, tail-spin, tizzy, tossing, trouble, tumult, turbulence, turmoil, uneasiness, unrest, upset, welter, worry.

antonyms calm, tranquillity.

agitator *n* agent provocateur, bellwether, demagogue, firebrand, fomenter, inciter, instigator, mob orator, rabble-rouser, revolutionary, soapbox orator, stirrer, troublemaker, tub-thumper.

agog *adj* avid, breathless, curious, desirous, eager, enthralled, enthusiastic, excited, expectant, impatient, in suspense, keen, on tenterhooks.

antonyms incurious, laid-back.

agonize *v* afflict, bleed, distress, excruciate, feel anguish, harrow, labour, pain, rack, strain, strive, struggle, suffer, toil, torment, torture, trouble, worry, wrestle, writhe.

agony *n* affliction, anguish, distress, misery, pain, pangs, paroxysm, spasm, suffering, throes, torment, torture, tribulation, woe, wretchedness.

agrarian *adj* agricultural, agronomic, farming, geoponic, georgic, rural.

agree *v* accede, accord, acquiesce, adhere, admit, assent, chime, coincide, commit, comply, concede, concur, confess, conform, consent, consort, contract, correspond, cotton, covenant, engage, fit, get along, grant, harmonize, jibe, jive, match, pledge, preconcert, promise, see eye to eye, settle, side (with), square, suit, tally, yield.

antonyms conflict, disagree.

agree upon arrange, establish, fix, set, settle.

agreeable *adj* acceptable, acquiescent, amenable, amicable, appropriate, approving, attractive, befitting, compatible, complying, concurring, conformable, congenial, consenting, consistent, enjoyable, fitting, gemütlich, gratifying, in accord, likable, palatable, pleasant, pleasing, pleasurable, proper, suitable, sympathetic, well-disposed, willing.

antonyms disagreeable, distasteful, incompatible, nasty.

agreement¹ *n* acceptance, accord, accordance, adherence, affinity, analogy, closing, compatibility, complaisance, compliance, concert, concord, concurrence, conformity, congruence, congruity, consensus, consentience, consistency, consonance, consort, convention, correspondence, harmony, modus vivendi, resemblance, similarity, suitableness, sympathy, unanimity, union, unison, unity.

antonym disagreement.

agreement² *n* arrangement, bargain, compact, concordat, contract, covenant, convention, deal, entente, pact, resolution, settlement, treaty, understanding.

agricultural *adj* agrarian, agronomic, farming, geoponic, georgic, rural.

agriculture *n* agribusiness, agronomy, cultivation, culture, farming, geoponics, husbandry, tillage.

aground *adv, adj* ashore, beached, foundered, grounded, high and dry, marooned, on the rocks, stranded, stuck, wrecked.

antonym afloat.

ague *n* fever, fit, malaria, quaking, shivering, trembling, tremors.

ahead *adv, adj* advanced, along, at an advantage, at the head, before, earlier on, forward, in advance, in front, in the forefront, in the lead, in the vanguard, leading, onward, superior, to the fore, winning.

aid *v* abet, accommodate, assist, befriend, boost, conduce to, ease, encourage, expedite, facilitate, favour, help, minister to, oblige, promote, prop up, rally around, relieve, second, serve, subsidize, succour, support, sustain.

antonyms impede, obstruct.

n a leg up, assistance, assistant, benefit, contribution, donation, encouragement, favour, good offices, help, helper, kindness, ministration, patronage, prop, relief, service, sponsorship, subsidy, subvention, succour, support, supporter, sustenance.

antonyms impediment, obstruction.

aide *n* adjutant, adviser, advocate, aide-de-camp, assistant, attaché, attendant, confidant(e), disciple, follower, helper, henchman, right-hand man, servant, supporter.

ail *v* afflict, be ill, be indisposed, be sick, bother, decline, distress, droop, fail, languish, pain, pine, sicken, suffer, trouble, upset, weaken, worry.

antonyms comfort, flourish.

ailing *adj* debilitated, diseased, feeble, frail, ill, indisposed, infirm, invalid, languishing, off-colour, out of sorts, peaked, poorly, sick, sickly, suffering, under the weather, unsound, unwell, weak, weakly.

antonyms flourishing, healthy.

ailment *n* affliction, complaint, condition, disability, disease, disorder, illness, indisposition, infection, infirmity, malady, sickness, weakness.

aim *v* address, aspire, attempt, beam, design, direct, draw a bead (on), endeavour, essay, head, hope, intend, level, mean, plan, point, propose, purpose, resolve, seek, set one's sights (on), sight, strive, take aim, target, train, try, want, wish, zero in (on).

n ambition, aspiration, course, desideratum, design, desire, direction, dream, end, goal, hope, intent, intention, mark, motive, object, objective, plan, purpose, target, wish.

aimless *adj* casual, chance, desultory, directionless, erratic, feckless, frivolous, goalless, haphazard, irresolute, pointless, purposeless, rambling, random, stray, undirected, unguided, unmotivated, unpredictable, vagrant, wayward.

antonyms determined, positive, purposeful.

air *n* ambience, appearance, aria, atmosphere, aura, bearing, blast, breath, breeze, carriage, character, demeanour, diapason, draft, effect, ether, feeling, flavour, heavens, lay, look, manner, melody, mien, mood, oxygen, port, quality, sky, song, strain, style, theme, tone, touch, tune, waft, welkin, whiff, wind, zephyr.

v aerate, broadcast, circulate, communicate, declare, disclose, display, disseminate, divulge, expose, express, freshen, give vent to, make known, make public, proclaim, publicize, publish, reveal, tell, utter, vent, ventilate, voice.

airily *adv* affectedly, animatedly, blithely, breezily, brightly, buoyantly, cheerfully, daintily, delicately, ethereally, flippantly, gaily, gracefully, happily, haughtily, high-spiritedly, insouciantly, jauntily, light-heartedly, lightly, nonchalantly, superciliously, unconcernedly.

antonyms concernedly, thoughtfully.

airless *adj* breathless, close, frowzy, fusty, heavy, muggy, musty, oppressive, stale, stifling, stuffy, suffocating, sultry, unventilated.

antonyms airy, fresh.

airman or **airwoman** *n* ace, aviator, flyer, pilot.

airs *n* affectation, affectedness, arrogance, artificiality, haughtiness, hauteur, pomposity, posing, pretensions, pretentiousness, staginess, superciliousness, swank.

airtight *adj* closed, hermetic, impenetrable, impermeable, sealed, tight, tight-fitting, windproof.

airy *adj* aerial, blithe, blowy, bodiless, breezy, buoyant, cheerful, cheery, debonair, delicate, disembodied, drafty, ethereal, fanciful, flimsy, fresh, frolicsome, gay, graceful, gusty, happy, haughty, high-spirited, illusory, imaginary, immaterial, incorporeal, insouciant, insubstantial, jaunty, light, light-hearted, lively, lofty, merry, nimble, nonchalant, offhand, open, roomy, spacious, spectral, sportive, sprightly, supercilious, trifling, uncluttered, unreal, unsubstantial, vaporous, visionary, weightless, well-ventilated, windy.

antonyms close, heavy, oppressive, stuffy.

aisle *n* alleyway, ambulatory, cloister, corridor, division, gangway, lane, passage, passageway, path, walkway.

akin *adj* affiliated, alike, allied, analogous, cognate, comparable, congenial, connected, consanguineous, consonant, corresponding, kin, kindred, like, parallel, related, similar.

antonym alien.

alacrity *n* alertness, avidity, briskness, celerity, cheerfulness, dispatch, eagerness, enthusiasm, gaiety, gusto, liveliness, promptitude, promptness, quickness, readiness, relish, speed, sprightliness, swiftness, willingness, zeal.

antonyms dilatoriness, slowness.

alarm *v* affright, agitate, daunt, dismay, distress, frighten, give (someone) a turn, panic, put the wind up (someone), scare, startle, terrify, terrorize, unnerve.

antonyms calm, reassure, soothe.

n alarm bell, alert, anxiety, apprehension, beeper, bell, buzzer, consternation, danger signal, detector, dismay, distress, distress signal, fear, fright, horror, panic, scare, security system, signal, siren, terror, tocsin, trepidation, unease, uneasiness, warning.

antonym composure.

alarming *adj* daunting, dire, direful, dismaying, distressing, disturbing, dreadful, frightening, ominous, scary, shocking, startling, terrifying, threatening, unnerving.

antonym reassuring.

alarmist *n* Cassandra, doom and gloom merchant, doomsayer, fearmonger, Jeremiah, jitterbug, pessimist, prophet of doom, scaremonger.

antonym optimist.

alas *interj* alack, alackaday, good lack, oy veh, welladay, wellaway, woe, woe is me.

albeit *conj* although, even if, even though, howbeit, notwithstanding that, though.

alchemy *n* hermetics, magic, sorcery, witchcraft, wizardry.

alcohol *n* booze, drink, firewater, hard stuff, hooch, John Barleycorn, (jungle) juice, liquor, medicine, moonshine, mountain dew, rotgut, spirits, the bottle.

alcoholic *adj* ardent, brewed, distilled, fermented, hard, inebriant, inebriating, intoxicating, spirituous, strong, vinous.

n bibber, dipsomaniac, drunk, drunkard, hard drinker, inebriate, lush, rubby, soak, sot, sponge, tippler, toper, wino.

alcoholism *n* alcohol abuse, alcohol addiction, crapulence, dipsomania, drunkenness, vinosity.

alcove *n* bay, booth, bower, carrel, compartment, corner, cubbyhole, cubicle, niche, nook, recess.

alert *adj* active, alive, attentive, awake, aware, brisk, careful, circumspect, heedful, lively, nimble, observant, on the ball, on the beam, on the lookout, on the qui vive, on the stick, perceptive, perky, prepared, quick, ready, sharp, sharp-eared, sharp-eyed, sharp-witted, spirited, sprightly, streetwise, vigilant, wakeful, wary, watchful, wide awake.

antonyms drowsy, inattentive, listless, slow.

n alarm, signal, siren, tocsin, warning.

v forewarn, inform, notify, signal, tip off, warn.

alertness n activeness, attention, attentiveness, briskness, carefulness, circumspection, heedfulness, liveliness, nimbleness, perceptiveness, perkiness, preparedness, presence of mind, promptitude, quickness, readiness, spiritedness, sprightliness, vigilance, wakefulness, wariness, watchfulness.
antonyms drowsiness, inattention, listlessness, slowness.

alias n allonym, anonym, assumed name, false name, nickname, nom de guerre, nom de plume, pen name, pseudonym, screen name, sobriquet, stage name.
adv a.k.a., alias dictus, also, also called, also known as, formerly, otherwise, otherwise called, otherwise known as.

alibi n cover-up, defence, excuse, explanation, justification, plea, pretext, reason, story.

alien adj adverse, antagonistic, conflicting, contrary, estranged, exotic, extraneous, extraterrestrial, foreign, inappropriate, incompatible, incongruous, inimical, opposed, outlandish, remote, repugnant, separated, strange, unfamiliar, unknown.
antonym akin.
n creature from outer space, emigrant, extraterrestrial, foreigner, freak, immigrant, newcomer, outlander, outsider, spacedweller, spaceman, stranger, weirdo.
antonym native.

alienate v antagonize, disaffect, disenchant, divert, divorce, drive away, drive a wedge between, estrange, separate, set against, turn away, turn off, withdraw.
antonyms attract, disarm, set at ease, unite.

alienation n antagonization, apathy, disaffection, disjunction, disunion, diversion, divorce, estrangement, indifference, remoteness, rupture, separation, severance, turnoff, withdrawal.
antonym endearment.

alight[1] v come down, come to rest, debark, descend, detrain, disembark, dismount, get down, get off, land, light, perch, settle, touch down.
antonyms ascend, board, rise, take off.

alight[2] adj ablaze, afire, aflame, aglow, blazing, bright, brilliant, burning, fiery, flaming, flaring, glowing, ignited, illuminated, illumined, lighted, lit, lit up, on fire, radiant, shining.
antonyms dark, extinguished, out.

align v adjust, affiliate, ally, arrange in line, associate, bring into line, bring into sync, co-ordinate, even, even up, join, level, line up, make even, make flush, make parallel, order, range, regularize, regulate, square, straighten.

alignment n adjustment, affiliation, alliance, arrangement, association, conformity, co-operation, co-ordination, evening, evening up, line, lining up, order, ranging, regularization, regulating, regulation, sequence, step, straightening, sympathy, sync, union.

alike adj akin, analogous, cognate, comparable, corresponding, duplicate, equal, equivalent, even, homologous, identical, parallel, similar, the same, uniform.
antonyms different, unlike.
adv analogously, correspondingly, equally, evenly, identically, in common, similarly, the same, uniformly.

alive adj active, alert, animate, animated, awake, breathing, brisk, cheerful, eager, energetic, existent, existing, extant, functioning, having life, in effect, in existence, in force, in operation, lifelike, live, lively, living, operative, quick, real, responsive, sensitive, spirited, sprightly, spry, subsisting, vibrant, vigorous, vital, vivacious, zestful.
antonyms dead, lifeless.

alive with abounding in, bristling with, bustling with, buzzing with, crawling with, crowded with, infested with, lousy with, overflowing with, overrun by, swarming with, teeming with, thronged with.

all adj complete, each, each and every, entire, every, every bit of, every one of, every single, full, greatest, perfect, the sum of, the total of, the totality of, the utmost, the whole of, total, utter.
antonyms no, not a bit, not any, not a single, partial, part of.
n aggregate, entirety, everything, heart and soul, sum, sum total, total, total amount, totality, universe, utmost, whole, whole amount, whole heart, whole-hearted effort.
adv altogether, completely, entirely, fully, holus-bolus, outright, totally, utterly, wholesale, wholly.

all being well Deo volente, DV, God willing, if I'm spared.

all in beat, dog-tired, done in, exhausted, finished, spent, tired (out), weary, whacked out, worn out.

all right acceptable, adequate, allowable, average, fair, hale, healthy, OK, passable, permissible, right as rain, safe, satisfactory, secure, sound, standard, unharmed, unhurt, unimpaired, uninjured, unobjectionable, well, whole.
antonyms injured, unacceptable.
adv acceptably, adequately, appropriately, certainly, for sure, OK, passably, reasonably, satisfactorily, suitably, unobjectionably, well, well enough, you bet.
antonyms unacceptably, unsatisfactorily.

all the time always, at all times, constantly, continually, continuously, ever, everlastingly, perpetually, the whole time, unceasingly.

all thumbs butterfingered, clumsy, ham-fisted, inept, maladroit, unhandy.

allay v alleviate, appease, assuage, blunt, calm, check, diminish, dull, ease, lessen, lull, mitigate, moderate, mollify, pacify, quell, quiet, reduce, relieve, slake, smooth over, soften, soothe, subdue, tranquillize.
antonyms exacerbate, intensify.

allegation n accusation, affirmation, assertion, asseveration, attestation, averment, charge, claim, declaration, deposition, plea, profession, statement, testimony.

allege v affirm, assert, asseverate, attest, aver, charge, claim, contend, declare, depose, hold, insist, maintain, plead, posit, profess, put forward, state.

alleged adj accused, affirmed, asserted, averred, claimed, declared, described, designated, doubtful, dubious, inferred, ostensible, professed, purported, reputed, so-called, stated, supposed, suspected.

allegiance n adherence, constancy, devotion, duty, faithfulness, fealty, fidelity, friendship, homage, loyalty, obedience, obligation, support.

antonyms disloyalty, enmity.

allegorical adj emblematic, figurative, parabolic, representative, significative, symbolic.

allegory n analogy, apologue, comparison, emblem, fable, metaphor, myth, parable, story, symbol, symbolism, tale, type.

allergic adj affected, antipathetic, averse, disinclined, hostile, hypersensitive, opposed, sensitized, sensitive.

antonym tolerant.

allergy n antipathy, aversion, disinclination, dislike, hostility, hypersensitivity, intolerance, opposition, sensitivity.

antonyms affinity, tolerance.

alleviate v abate, allay, assuage, blunt, check, cushion, deaden, diminish, dull, ease, lessen, lighten, lull, mitigate, moderate, mollify, palliate, quell, quench, quiet, reduce, relieve, slacken, slake, smooth over, soften, soothe, subdue, temper.

antonym aggravate.

alleviation n abatement, assuagement, diminution, dulling, easing, lessening, lightening, lulling, mitigation, moderation, mollification, palliation, quelling, quenching, reduction, relief, slackening, slaking.

antonym aggravation.

alley n alleyway, back street, entry, gate, lane, passage, passageway, pathway, walk.

alliance n affiliation, affinity, agreement, association, bloc, bond, cartel, coalition, combination, compact, concordat, confederacy, confederation, conglomerate, connection, consortium, faction, federation, guild, league, link, marriage, pact, partnership, syndicate, treaty, union, yoke.

antonyms divorce, enmity, estrangement, hostility.

allied adj affiliated, amalgamated, associate(d), bound, combined, confederate(d), connected, correlate(d), hand in glove, in cahoots, in league, joined, joint, kindred, leagued, linked, married, related, tied, unified, united, wed.

antonym estranged.

allocate v allot, allow, apportion, appropriate, assign, budget, designate, dispense, distribute, earmark, grant, mete, parcel out, ration, set aside, share out.

allocation n allotment, allowance, apportionment, appropriation, budget, grant, lot, measure, portion, quota, ration, share, stint.

allot v allocate, allow, apportion, appropriate, assign, budget, designate, dispense, distribute, divvy up, earmark, grant, measure out, mete, parcel out, ration, set aside, share out.

▲ *confusable word* a lot.

allotment n allocation, allowance, apportionment, appropriation, division, grant, lot, measure, partition, percentage, portion, quota, ration, share, stint.

all-out adj complete, determined, energetic, exhaustive, full, full-scale, intensive, maximum, no-holds-barred, outright, powerful, resolute, supreme, thorough, thoroughgoing, total, undivided, unlimited, unremitting, unrestrained, unstinted, utmost, vigorous, whole-hearted, wholesale.

antonyms half-hearted, perfunctory.

allow v accord, acknowledge, acquiesce, admit, allocate, allot, apportion, approve, assign, authorize, bear, brook, concede, confess, deduct, endure, give, give leave, grant, let, own, permit, provide, put up with, sanction, spare, stand, suffer, tolerate.

antonyms deny, forbid.

allow for arrange for, bear in mind, consider, count on, expect, foresee, include, keep in mind, keep in view, make allowances for, make concessions for, make provision for, plan for, provide for, reckon on (or with), take into account.

antonym discount.

allowable adj acceptable, admissible, all right, appropriate, approved, apt, legal, legitimate, licit, permissible, sanctionable, sufferable, suitable, supportable, tolerable.

antonym unacceptable.

allowance n admission, allocation, allotment, amount, annuity, apportionment, concession, deduction, discount, grant, lot, measure, pension, pin money, pocket money, portion, provision, quota, ration, reduction, remittance, sanction, share, stint, stipend, subsidy, sufferance, tolerance, weighting.

alloy n admixture, amalgam, blend, coalescence, combination, composite, compound, fusion, hybrid, mix, mixture.

v admix, adulterate, amalgamate, blend, combine, compound, debase, fuse, impair, mix, qualify, temper.

allude (to) v adumbrate, advert, cite, hint (at), imply, insinuate, intimate, mention, refer (to), remark (on), speak (of), suggest, touch (upon).

▲ *confusable word* elude.

allure v attract, beckon, beguile, captivate, charm, coax, decoy, enchant, enrapture, entice, entrance, fascinate, interest, inveigle, lead on, lure, seduce, tempt, win over.

antonym repel.

n appeal, attraction, captivation, charm,

enchantment, enticement, fascination, glamour, lure, magnetism, seductiveness, temptation.

alluring *adj* arousing, attractive, beguiling, bewitching, captivating, come-hither, enchanting, engaging, enticing, fascinating, fetching, intriguing, seductive, sensuous, sexy, tempting, voluptuous, winning.

antonyms repellent, unattractive.

allusion *n* citation, hint, implication, innuendo, insinuation, intimation, mention, observation, quotation, reference, remark, suggestion.

▲ *confusable word* illusion.

ally *n* abettor, accessory, accomplice, associate, coadjutor, collaborator, colleague, confederate, confrère, consort, co-worker, friend, helper, helpmate, partner, sidekick, supporter.

antonyms antagonist, enemy.

v affiliate, amalgamate, associate, band together, collaborate, combine, confederate, conjoin, connect, fraternize, join, join forces, league, marry, team up, unite, wed.

antonym estrange.

almanac *n* annual, calendar, ephemeris, register, yearbook.

almighty *adj* absolute, all-powerful, awful, deafening, enormous, excessive, great, intense, invincible, omnipotent, overpowering, overwhelming, plenipotent, sovereign, supreme, terrible, thunderous, unlimited.

antonyms impotent, insignificant, weak.

almost *adv* about, all but, approaching, approximately, around, as good as, close to, just about, just short of, little short of, nearing, nearly, not far from, not quite, practically, toward, virtually, well-nigh.

alms *n* benefaction, beneficence, bounty, charity, donation, gift, largesse(e), offerings, relief.

alone *adv, adj* abandoned, all by one's lonesome, apart, by itself, by oneself, deserted, desolate, detached, discrete, forlorn, forsaken, hors concours, incomparable, isolated, just, lonely, lonesome, matchless, mere, nonpareil, on one's own, only, peerless, separate, simply, single, single-handed, singular, sole, solitary, unaccompanied, unaided, unassisted, unattended, uncombined, unconnected, unequalled, unescorted, unique, unparalleled, unsurpassed.

aloof *adj* chilly, cold, cool, detached, distant, forbidding, formal, haughty, inaccessible, indifferent, offish, remote, reserved, reticent, snobbish, stand-offish, supercilious, unapproachable, uncompanionable, unforthcoming, unfriendly, uninterested, uninvolved, unresponsive, unsociable, unsympathetic.

antonyms involved, sociable, warm.

aloofness *n* coolness, distance, indifference, offishness, remoteness, reserve, stand-offishness, uncompanionability.

antonyms sociability, warmth.

aloud *adv* audibly, clamorously, clangorously, clearly, distinctly, intelligibly, loudly, noisily, orally, out loud, plainly, resoundingly, sonorously, vocally, vociferously.

antonym silently.

already *adv* at present, before now, beforehand, by now, by that time, by then, by this time, even now, heretofore, hitherto, just now, previously.

▲ *confusable word* all ready.

also *adv* additionally, along with that, and, as well, besides, ditto, eke, further, furthermore, in addition, including, moreover, plus, therewithal, to boot, too.

alter *v* adapt, adjust, amend, change, convert, cook (the books), customize, doctor, edit, emend, metamorphose, modify, qualify, recast, reform, remodel, reshape, revise, shift, take liberties with, transfigure, transform, transmute, transpose, turn, vary.

antonym fix.

alteration *n* adaptation, adjustment, amendment, change, conversion, difference, diversification, doctoring, edit(ing), emendation, metamorphosis, modification, reformation, remodelling, reshaping, revision, shift, transfiguration, transformation, transmutation, transposition, variance, variation, vicissitude.

antonyms fixity, sameness.

altercation *n* argument, bickering, clash, conflict, confrontation, contention, controversy, debate, disagreement, discord, dispute, dissension, fight, fracas, quarrel, row, sparring, spat, squabble, tiff, wrangle.

alternate *v* change, fluctuate, follow one another, interchange, intersperse, oscillate, reciprocate, rotate, substitute, take turns, transpose, vary, vascillate.

adj alternating, alternative, another, different, every other, every second, interchanging, other, reciprocal, reciprocating, reciprocatory, rotating, second, substitute.

alternative *n* backup, choice, fallback, option, other course, recourse, substitute.

adj alternate, another, backup, different, fringe, other, second, substitute, unconventional, unorthodox.

although *conj* admitting that, albeit, conceding that, despite the fact that, even if, even though, granted that, howbeit, if, notwithstanding that, though, while.

altitude *n* elevation, height, loftiness, stature, tallness.

antonym depth.

altogether *adv* absolutely, all in all, all told, as a whole, collectively, completely, entirely, fully, generally, holus-bolus, in all, in general, in sum, in toto, on the whole, perfectly, quite, thoroughly, totally, utterly, wholesale, wholly.

▲ *confusable word* all together.

altruism *n* charity, compassion, considerateness, disinterestedness, generosity, humanity, neighbourliness, philanthropy, public-spiritedness, self-abnegation, self-denial, selflessness, self-sacrifice, social conscience, unselfishness.

antonym selfishness.

altruistic *adj* benevolent, charitable, compassionate, considerate, disinterested, generous, giving, humane, humanitarian, philanthropic, public-spirited, self-abnegating, self-denying, selfless, self-sacrificing, unselfish.

always *adv* all the time, aye, consistently, constantly, continually, continuously, endlessly, eternally, ever, everlastingly, evermore, every time, for aye, forever, in perpetuum, invariably, perpetually, regularly, repeatedly, sempiternally, unceasingly, unfailingly, without exception.

antonym never.

amalgam *n* admixture, aggregate, alloy, amalgamation, blend, coalescence, combination, commixture, composite, compound, dental filling, fusion, mixture, union.

amalgamate *v* alloy, ally, blend, coalesce, combine, commingle, compound, fuse, incorporate, integrate, intermix, join, merge, mingle, synthesize, unite.

antonym separate.

amalgamation *n* admixture, alliance, alloy, amalgam, amalgamating, blend, coalescence, coalition, combination, commingling, composite, compound, fusion, incorporation, integration, joining, merger, mingling, mixing, mixture, synthesis, unification, union.

amass *v* accumulate, agglomerate, agglutinate, aggregate, assemble, collect, compile, forgather, garner, gather, heap up, hoard, pile up, rake in (or up), scrape together.

amateur *n* aficionado, buff, dabbler, dilettante, do-it-yourselfer, fancier, ham, layman, non-professional.

antonym professional.

amateurish *adj* amateur, clumsy, crude, dilettantish, incompetent, inept, inexpert, unaccomplished, unprofessional, unskilful, untrained.

antonyms professional, skilled.

amatory *adj* amorous, aphrodisiac, erogenous, erotic, erotogenic, lascivious, libidinous, love, lovemaking, passionate, romantic, sensual, sexual, sexy.

amaze *v* alarm, astonish, astound, awe, baffle, bewilder, blow away, confound, daze, dazzle, dumfound, electrify, flabbergast, floor, shock, stagger, startle, stun, stupefy, surprise, wow.

amazement *n* admiration, astonishment, awe, bafflement, bewilderment, confusion, disbelief, incomprehension, incredulity, incredulousness, marvel, shock, stupefaction, surprise, wonder, wonderment.

ambassador *n* agent, apostle, commissioner, consul, deputy, diplomat, emissary, envoi (extraordinaire), envoy, legate, minister, nuncio, plenipotentiary, representative.

ambience *n* air, atmosphere, aura, character, climate, décor, environment, feel, feeling, flavour, impression, milieu, mood, quality, setting, spirit, surroundings, tenor, tone, vibes, vibrations.

ambiguity *n* ambivalence, confusion, double meaning, doubt, doubtfulness, dubiety, dubiousness, enigma, equivocacy, equivocality, equivocation, fuzziness, imprecision, inconclusiveness, indefiniteness, indeterminateness, obscurity, puzzle, tergiversation, uncertainty, unclearness, vagueness, weasel word(s), woolliness.

antonym clarity.

ambiguous *adj* ambivalent, amphibological, confused, confusing, cryptic, Delphic, double-barrelled, double-meaning, doubtful, dubious, enigmatic, equivocal, fuzzy, imprecise, inconclusive, indefinite, indeterminate, obscure, oracular, puzzling, uncertain, unclear, vague, woolly.

antonym clear.

ambit *n* circuit, compass, confines, domain, environs, extent, limits, precincts, range, scope, sphere.

ambition *n* aim, aspiration, avidity, craving, design, desire, dream, drive, eagerness, end, enterprise, goal, hankering, hope, hunger, ideal, industry, initiative, intent, longing, object, objective, purpose, push, striving, target, wish, yearning, zeal.

antonyms aimlessness, apathy, indifference, lethargy.

ambitious *adj* arduous, aspiring, assertive, avid, bold, challenging, demanding, desirous, difficult, driven, eager, elaborate, energetic, enterprising, enthusiastic, exacting, formidable, go-ahead, grandiose, hard, hopeful, impressive, industrious, intent, keen, purposeful, pushy, strenuous, striving, zealous.

antonyms aimless, apathetic, easy, indifferent, lethargic, unambitious.

ambivalence *n* ambiguity, clash, conflict, confusion, contradiction, doubt, emotional tug-of-war, equivocation, fluctuation, hesitancy, inconclusiveness, inconsistency, indecision, instability, irresolution, mixed feelings, opposition, struggle, uncertainty, vacillation, wavering.

antonyms certainty, resolve, single-mindedness.

ambivalent *adj* ambiguous, clashing, conflicting, confused, contradictory, doubtful, equivocal, fluctuating, hesitant, inconclusive, inconsistent, irresolute, mixed, opposed, uncertain, undecided, unresolved, unsettled, unsure, vacillating, warring, wavering.

antonym unequivocal.

amble *v* dawdle, drift, meander, mosey, perambulate, promenade, ramble, saunter, stroll, toddle, walk, wander.

antonyms march, stride.

ambush *n* ambuscade, attack, concealment, cover, hiding, hiding place, retreat, shelter, snare, surprise attack, trap, waylaying.

v ambuscade, bushwhack, ensnare, entrap, lie in wait for, pounce on, surprise, trap, waylay.

ameliorate *v* advance, alleviate, amend, assuage, benefit, better, ease, elevate, emend, enhance, improve, meliorate, mend, mitigate, raise, redress, reform, relieve, revise.

antonyms exacerbate, worsen.

amenable *adj* accountable, acquiescent, agreeable, answerable, biddable, chargeable, complaisant, conformable, docile, flexible, liable, open, persuadable, responsible, responsive, submissive, susceptible, tractable.

antonym intractable.

amend *v* adjust, alter, ameliorate, better, change, clarify, correct, emend, emendate, enhance, fix, improve, mend, modify, qualify, rectify, redress, reform, remedy, repair, revise.

antonyms impair, worsen.

amendment *n* addendum, addition, adjunct, adjustment, alteration, amelioration, betterment, change, clarification, correction, corrigendum, emendation, enhancement, improvement, mending, modification, qualification, rectification, redress, reform, remedy, repair, revision.

antonyms deterioration, impairment.

amends *n* atonement, compensation, expiation, indemnification, indemnity, mitigation, quittance, recompense, redress, reparation, requital, restitution, restoration, satisfaction.

amenity *n* advantage, attraction, charm, comfort, convenience, facility, pleasantness, refinement, service.

antonyms inconvenience, unpleasantness.

amiable *adj* accessible, affable, agreeable, amicable, approachable, attractive, benign, biddable, charming, cheerful, companionable, complaisant, congenial, conversable, delightful, engaging, friendly, gemütlich, genial, good-humoured, good-natured, good-tempered, kind, kindly, likable, lovable, obliging, pleasant, pleasing, sociable, sweet, sweet-tempered, warm, winning, winsome.

antonyms hostile, unfriendly.

amicable *adj* amiable, brotherly, civil, civilized, conciliatory, cordial, courteous, easy, frank, fraternal, friendly, good-natured, harmonious, kind, kindly, neighbourly, open, peaceable, peaceful, polite, sisterly, sociable.

antonym hostile.

amid *prep* among, in the middle of, in the midst of, in the thick of, 'midst, surrounded by.

amiss *adj* awry, defective, erroneous, fallacious, false, faulty, imperfect, imprecise, improper, inaccurate, inappropriate, incorrect, out of kilter, out of order, unsuitable, untoward, wonky, wrong.

adv ill, otherwise than intended, the wrong way, wrongly.

antonyms right, well.

take amiss misconstrue, misinterpret, misunderstand, take offence at, take the wrong way.

amity *n* accord, agreement, amicability, brotherhood, brotherliness, comity, comradeship, concord, co-operation, cordiality, entente, fellowship, fraternity, friendliness, friendship, good will, harmony, kindliness, kindness, peace, peaceability, peacefulness, sisterhood, sympathy, understanding.

antonyms discord, hostility.

amnesty *n* absolution, dispensation, forgiveness, immunity, indulgence, lenience, mercy, pardon, remission, reprieve.

among *prep* amid, between, in the middle of, in the midst of, in the thick of, surrounded by, together with, with.

amoral *adj* abandoned, free-living, intemperate, lax, loose, non-moral, uninhibited, unmoral, unrestrained.

antonym moral.

▲ *confusable word* immoral.

amorous *adj* affectionate, amatory, ardent, attached, doting, enamoured, erotic, fond, impassioned, in love, lovesick, loving, passionate, tender.

antonyms cold, indifferent.

amorphous *adj* chaotic, characterless, featureless, formless, inchoate, indeterminate, indistinct, irregular, nebulous, nondescript, shapeless, undefined, unformed, unshaped, unshapen, unstructured, vague.

antonyms definite, distinctive, shapely.

amount *n* expanse, extent, figure, lot, magnitude, mass, measure, number, quantity, quantum, quota, sum, sum total, supply, total, volume.

amount to add up to, aggregate to, approximate to, become, be equivalent to, be in effect, be little short of, be tantamount to, be virtually, come (out) to, equal, grow to (be), mean, purport, run to, total, turn out to be, work out to.

amour *n* affair, affaire de coeur, conquest, entanglement, intimacy, intrigue, involvement, liaison, love affair, relationship, romance.

ample *adj* abundant, big, bountiful, broad, capacious, commodious, complete, considerable, copious, enough, expansive, extensive, full, generous, goodly, great, handsome, large, lavish, liberal, more than enough, munificent, plenteous, plentiful, plenty, profuse, rich, roomy, spacious, substantial, sufficient, thorough, unrestricted, unstinting, voluminous, wide.

antonyms insufficient, meagre.

amplify *v* add to, augment, boost, broaden, bulk out, deepen, develop, dilate, elaborate, enhance, enlarge, expand, expatiate, extend, fill out, heighten, increase, intensify, lengthen, magnify, raise, strengthen, supplement, widen.

antonym reduce.

amplitude *n* abundance, ampleness, bigness, breadth, bulk, capaciousness, capacity, compass, completeness, copiousness, dimension, expanse, extent, fullness, greatness, hugeness, largeness, magnitude, mass, plenitude, plentifulness, plethora, profusion, range, reach, richness, scope, size, spaciousness, sweep, vastness, volume, width.

antonym inadequately.

amputate *v* curtail, cut off, dissever, dock, excise, lop off, remove, separate, sever, truncate.

amuck *adv* berserk, crazy, in a frenzy, in a fury, insane, like a madman, mad, out of control, wild.

amulet *n* charm, fetish, juju, lucky charm, pentacle, phylactery, talisman.

amuse *v* absorb, beguile, busy, charm, cheer, cheer up, delight, disport, divert, engross, enjoy (oneself), enliven, entertain, interest, occupy, please, recreate, regale, relax, slay, tickle.

antonyms anger, bore, sadden.

amusement[1] *n* beguilement, delight, disportment, distraction, diversion, enjoyment, entertainment, fun, hilarity, laughter, merriment, mirth, pleasure, recreation, regalement, sport.

antonyms boredom, disgust.

amusement[2] *n* attraction, entertainment, game, hobby, interest, joke, lark, pastime, pleasure, prank, recreation, ride, sideshow.

amusing *adj* charming, cheerful, cheering, comical, delightful, diverting, droll, enjoyable, entertaining, facetious, fun, funny, hilarious, humorous, interesting, jocular, jolly, killing, laughable, ludicrous, merry, pleasant, pleasing, rib-tickling, risible, sportive, witty.

antonyms boring, gloomy, sad, serious, unentertaining.

anachronism *n* antique, archaism, atavism, back number, dinosaur, fogey, fossil, throwback.

analogous *adj* akin, alike, comparable, correlative, corresponding, equivalent, homologous, like, matching, parallel, reciprocal, related, similar.

antonym disparate.

analogy *n* agreement, comparison, correlation, correspondence, equivalence, homologue, homology, likeness, parallel, parallelism, relation, resemblance, semblance, similarity, similitude.

analyse *v* anatomize, appraise, assay, assess, break down, categorize, classify, consider, criticize, diagnose, dissect, divide, estimate, evaluate, examine, explain, inquire into, interpret, investigate, judge, parse, reduce, resolve, review, scrutinize, separate, sift, size up, study, test.

analysis *n* account, anatomization, anatomy, appraisal, assay, assessment, breakdown, criticism, diagnosis, dissection, division, estimation, evaluation, examination, exegesis, explanation, explication, exposition, inquiry, interpretation, investigation, judgment, opinion, parsing, reasoning, reduction, resolution, review, scrutiny, separation, sifting, study, test, understanding, view.

analytical *adj* anatomical, critical, detailed, diagnostic, discrete, dissecting, explanatory, expository, inquiring, inquisitive, interpretative, interpretive, investigative, left-brain, linear,

logical, methodical, questioning, rational, searching, studious, systematic.

anarchic *adj* anarchistic, anti-government, chaotic, confused, disordered, disorderly, disorganized, iconoclastic, lawless, libertarian, nihilistic, rebellious, revolutionary, riotous, ungoverned, unruly.

antonyms orderly, submissive.

anarchist *n* anarch, iconoclast, insurgent, libertarian, nihilist, rebel, revolutionary, terrorist.

anarchy *n* anarchism, a zoo, bedlam, chaos, confusion, disorder, disorganization, iconoclasm, insurrection, lawlessness, libertarianism, mayhem, misgovernment, misrule, mutiny, nihilism, pandemonium, rebellion, revolution, riot, unrule.

antonyms control, order, rule.

anathema *n* abhorrence, abomination, ban, bane, bête noire, bugbear, condemnation, curse, damnation, denunciation, excommunication, execration, imprecation, malediction, object of loathing, pariah, proscription, taboo.

anatomize *v* analyse, break down, dissect, divide, examine, pull apart, resolve, scrutinize, separate, study, vivisect.

anatomy *n* analysis, build, composition, constitution, construction, dissection, frame, framework, make-up, structure, vivisection.

ancestor *n* antecedent, antecessor, forebear, forefather, foremother, forerunner, precursor, predecessor, primogenitor, progenitor.

antonym descendant.

ancestral *adj* atavistic, familial, genealogical, genetic, hereditary, lineal, original, parental.

ancestry *n* ancestors, antecedents, antecessors, background, blood, derivation, descent, extraction, family, forebears, forefathers, genealogy, heredity, heritage, house, line, lineage, origin, parentage, pedigree, progenitors, roots, stirps, stock.

anchor *n* grapnel, kedge, killick, mainstay, pillar of strength, prop, security, stability, staff, stay, support.

v affix, attach, fasten, fix, ground, make fast, moor, root, secure.

anchorage *n* harbour, harbourage, haven, mooring, port, protection, refuge, sanctuary, shelter.

anchorite *n* anchoret, ascetic, eremite, hermit, holy man or woman, marabout, recluse, solitary, stylite.

ancient *adj* aged, age-old, antediluvian, antiquated, antique, archaic, bygone, démodé, early, fossilized, hoary, immemorial, obsolete, old, olden, old-fashioned, original, outmoded, out-of-date, prehistoric, primeval, primordial, pristine, superannuated, timeworn, venerable.

antonyms modern, new, young.

ancillary *adj* accessory, additional, auxiliary, contributory, dependent, extra, secondary, subordinate, subsidiary, supplementary.

androgynous *adj* bisexual, epicene, gynandrous, hermaphrodite, hermaphroditic.

anecdote *n* exemplum, fable, illustration, parable, reminiscence, sketch, story, tale, yarn.

anemic *adj* ashen, bloodless, blue, chalky, characterless, colourless, dull, enervated, exsanguine, feeble, frail, ineffectual, infirm, insipid, pale, pallid, pasty, sallow, sickly, spiritless, wan, weak, whey-faced, white.
antonyms full-blooded, ruddy, sanguine.

anesthetic *n* analgesic, anodyne, narcotic, opiate, painkiller, palliative, sedative, soporific, stupefacient, stupefactive.

anesthetize *v* benumb, chloroform, deaden, desensitize, dope, drug, dull, etherize, lull, make oblivious, numb, put to sleep, put under, sedate, stupefy.

angel *n* archangel, backer, benefactor, celestial being, cherub, darling, divine messenger, fairy godmother, guardian spirit, heavenly being, ideal, malaika, paragon, patron, principality, saint, seraph, sponsor, supporter, treasure.
antonyms devil, fiend.

angelic *adj* adorable, beatific, beautiful, celestial, cherubic, divine, ethereal, exemplary, heavenly, holy, innocent, lovely, pious, pure, radiant, saintly, seraphic, unworldly, virtuous.
antonyms devilish, fiendish.

anger *n* annoyance, antagonism, bad blood, bile, bitterness, choler, dander, displeasure, dudgeon, exasperation, fury, indignation, ire, irritability, irritation, outrage, passion, pique, rage, rancour, resentment, spleen, temper, vexation, wrath.
antonyms forbearance, good pleasure.
v affront, aggravate, annoy, antagonize, bend out of shape, bother, bug, cheese off, disgruntle, displease, enrage, exasperate, fret, frustrate, gall, incense, infuriate, irk, irritate, madden, miff, needle, nettle, offend, outrage, pique, provoke, put out, raise the hackles of, rankle, rile, ruffle, tee off, tick off, upset, vex.
antonyms appease, calm, please.

angle *n* approach, aspect, bend, bias, corner, crook, crotch, cusp, diagonal, direction, elbow, facet, flexure, outlook, perspective, point, point of view, position, side, slant, slope, standpoint, turn, vertex, viewpoint.

angle for aim for, be after, be out for, contrive to get, fish for, have one's eye on, hunt, invite, scheme, seek, solicit.

angry *adj* aggravated, annoyed, antagonized, bent out of shape, bitter, burned up, cheesed off, choked, choleric, cross, disgruntled, displeased, enraged, exasperated, fed up, frustrated, furious, heated, hopping mad, hot (under the collar), in a fury, in a rage, incensed, indignant, inflamed, infuriated, irascible, irate, ireful, irked, irritable, irritated, mad, miffed, needled, nettled, on the rampage, on the warpath, outraged, painful, passionate, piqued, provoked, put out, raging, rancorous, ratty, raw, resentful, riled, sore, splenetic, teed off, ticked off, tumultuous, upset, uptight, wrathful, wroth.
antonyms calm, content.

angst *n* anxiety, apprehension, depression, dread, foreboding, future shock, mal du siècle, malaise, midlife crisis, Weltschmerz, worry.

anguish *n* agony, desolation, distress, dole, dolour, grief, heartache, heartbreak, misery, pain, pangs, rack, sorrow, suffering, torment, torture, wretchedness.
antonyms happiness, solace.

anguished *adj* afflicted, agonized, angst-ridden, distressed, dolorous, harrowed, miserable, racked, stricken, suffering, tormented, tortured, wretched.

angular *adj* bony, gangling, gangly, gauche, gaunt, gawky, geometrical, lank, lanky, lean, pointed, pointy, rangy, rawboned, rectangular, scrawny, skinny, spare, square, thin, ungainly.

anima *n* feminine side (or nature or principle), impetus, intention, life, motive, purpose, soul, spirit, will, yin.

animal *n* barbarian, beast, brute, creature, critter, cur, mammal, monster, non-human, pet, pig, savage, swine.
adj bestial, bodily, brutish, carnal, faunal, feral, fleshly, gross, gut, inhuman, instinctive, non-human, physical, piggish, savage, sensual, visceral, wild.

animate *v* activate, arouse, embolden, encourage, energize, enliven, excite, fire, galvanize, goad, hearten, impel, incite, inspire, inspirit, invigorate, irradiate, kindle, move, quicken, reactivate, revive, revivify, rouse, spark, spur, stimulate, stir, suffuse, urge, vitalize, vivify.
antonyms dampen, deaden, inhibit.
adj alive, breathing, live, living, sentient.
antonyms inanimate, lifeless.

animated *adj* active, airy, alive, ardent, bouncy, brisk, bubbly, buoyant, eager, ebullient, elated, energetic, enthusiastic, excited, exhilarated, extrovert(ed), fervent, full of life, gay, glowing, high-spirited, impassioned, lively, outgoing, passionate, peppy, quick, radiant, sparkling, spirited, sprightly, vehement, vibrant, vigorous, vital, vivacious, vivid, zestful, zesty.
antonyms dull, inert, lifeless, sluggish, spiritless.

animation *n* action, activity, ardour, bounce, briskness, buoyancy, ebullience, elation, energy, enthusiasm, excitement, exhilaration, fervour, gaiety, high spirits, life, liveliness, passion, pep, radiance, sparkle, spirit, sprightliness, verve, vibrancy, vigour, vitality, vivacity, zeal, zest, zing.
antonyms dullness, inertia.

animosity *n* acrimony, animus, antagonism, antipathy, bad blood, bitterness, enmity, feud, feuding, hate, hatred, hostility, ill will, loathing, malevolence, malice, malignity, odium, rancour, resentment, spite.
antonym good will.

animus[1] *n* acrimony, animosity, antagonism, antipathy, bad blood, bitterness, enmity, hate, hatred, hostility, ill feeling, ill will, loathing, malevolence, malice, malignity, odium, rancour, resentment.

antonym sympathy.

animus² *n* impetus, intention, life, masculine side (or nature or principle), motive, purpose, soul, spirit, will, yang.

annals *n* accounts, archives, chronicles, history, journals, memoirs, memorials, records, registers, reports.

annex *v* acquire, add, adjoin, affix, append, appropriate, arrogate, attach, connect, conquer, expropriate, fasten, filch, grab, incorporate, join, occupy, purloin, scoff, seize, steal, subjoin, swipe, tack, take (over), unite, usurp.

n addendum, addition, adjunct, appendix, attachment, backhouse, ell, expansion, extension, outbuilding, outhouse, supplement, wing.

annexation *n* addition, amalgamation, annexing, appropriation, arrogation, attachment, augmentation, combination, conquest, expropriation, occupation, seizure, takeover, theft, usurpation.

annihilate *v* abolish, assassinate, destroy, eliminate, eradicate, erase, exterminate, extinguish, extirpate, liquidate, murder, nullify, obliterate, raze, rub out, stamp out, terminate, thrash, trounce, wipe out.

annihilation *n* abolition, assassination, defeat, destruction, elimination, eradication, erasure, extermination, extinction, extirpation, liquidation, nullification, obliteration, termination.

annotate *v* comment, commentate, elucidate, explain, footnote, gloss, interpret, note.

annotation *n* comment, commentary, elucidation, endnote, exegesis, explanation, explication, footnote, gloss, interpretation, marginalia, note, scholia, scholium.

announce *v* advertise, air, blazon, broadcast, call (out), declare, disclose, divulge, intimate, leak, make known, proclaim, promulgate, propound, publicize, publish, report, reveal, signal, state.

antonym suppress.

announcement *n* advertisement, airing, broadcast, bulletin, commercial, communiqué, declaration, disclosure, dispatch, divulgence, intimation, message, notification, proclamation, promulgation, publication, report, revelation, statement.

announcer *n* anchor, broadcaster, commentator, crier, harbinger, herald, messenger, news anchor, newscaster, news reader, reporter.

annoy *v* aggravate, anger, badger, bait, bore, bother, bug, displease, disturb, exasperate, gall, get, get on (someone's) nerves, get (someone's) goat, get under (someone's) skin, harass, harm, harry, hassle, incommode, irk, irritate, madden, miff, molest, needle, nettle, peeve, pester, pique, plague, provoke, put out, rile, ruffle, tease, tee off, tick off, trouble, vex.

antonyms gratify, leave in peace, please.

annoyance *n* aggravation, anger, bind, bore, bother, displeasure, disturbance, exasperation, harassment, headache, inconvenience, irritant, irritation, nuisance, pain, pest, pique, plague, provocation, tease, thorn in the flesh (or side), trouble, vexation.

antonym pleasure.

annoyed *adj* bored, bugged, displeased, exasperated, fed up, galled, harassed, irked, irritated, miffed, nettled, peeved, piqued, provoked, put out, riled, teed off, ticked off, vexed.

antonym pleased.

annoying *adj* aggravating, boring, bothersome, displeasing, disturbing, exasperating, galling, harassing, irksome, irritating, maddening, offensive, off-putting, peeving, pesky, pestersome, pestiferous, pestilent, pestilential, plaguesome, plaguey, provoking, teasing, tiresome, troublesome, vexatious.

antonyms pleasing, welcome.

annual *n* almanac, annal, ephemeris, yearbook.

annul *v* abolish, abrogate, cancel, countermand, invalidate, negate, nullify, quash, recall, repeal, rescind, retract, reverse, revoke, suspend, void, withdraw.

antonyms enact, restore.

annulment *n* abolition, abrogation, cancellation, cassation, countermanding, invalidation, negation, nullification, quashing, recall, repeal, rescindment, rescission, retraction, reversal, revocation, suspension, voiding, withdrawal.

antonyms enactment, restoration.

anodyne *adj* alleviative, analgesic, bland, blunting, calmative, deadening, desensitizing, dulling, febrifugal, harmless, inoffensive, mild, narcotic, numbing, painkilling, pain-relieving, palliative, sedative, tranquillizing.

antonym irritant.

n alleviative, analgesic, febrifuge, narcotic, painkiller, pain-reliever, palliative, sedative, tranquillizer.

antonym irritant.

anoint *v* appoint, bless, consecrate, daub, dedicate, embrocate, grease, hallow, lard, lubricate, oil, ordain, rub, sanctify, smear.

anointing *n* appointing, blessing, consecration, dedication, embrocation, hallowing, ordination, sanctification, unction.

anomalous *adj* aberrant, abnormal, atypical, bizarre, deviant, eccentric, exceptional, extraordinary, freakish, incongruous, inconsistent, irregular, odd, peculiar, quirky, rare, singular, strange, untypical, unusual, weird.

antonyms normal, regular.

anomaly *n* aberration, abnormality, departure, deviance, deviant, deviation, divergence, eccentricity, exception, freak, incongruity, inconsistency, irregularity, misfit, oddball, oddity, peculiarity, rarity.

anonymous *adj* characterless, faceless, impersonal, incognito, innominate, nameless,

nondescript, unacknowledged, unattributed, uncredited, unidentified, unknown, unnamed, unnoticed, unsigned, unspecified.
antonyms distinctive, identifiable, named.

anorak *n* all-weather coat (or jacket), bush jacket, car coat, golf jacket, jacket, lumber jacket, mackinaw, parka, stadium coat, windbreaker.

answer *n* acknowledgment, apology, backtalk, comeback, counterargument, countercharge, counterclaim, defence, explanation, plea, reaction, rebuttal, reciprocation, refutation, rejoinder, reply, report, resolution, response, retaliation, retort, return, riposte, solution.
v acknowledge, agree, balance, conform, correlate, correspond, counter, do, echo, explain, fill, fit, fulfil, match, meet, pass, qualify, react, rebut, reciprocate, refute, rejoin, reply, resolve, respond, retaliate, retort, return, riposte, satisfy, serve, solve, suffice, suit, work.
answer back argue, be cheeky, be lippy, be mouthy, contradict, retort, sass, sauce, talk back.
antonym acquiesce.

answerable *adj* accountable, amenable, blamable, chargeable, liable, responsible, to blame.

ant *n* emmet, hymenopteran, pismire, termite.

antagonize *v* alienate, anger, annoy, disaffect, drive away, embitter, estrange, insult, irritate, offend, provoke, repel.
antonym disarm.

antagonism *n* animosity, animus, antipathy, bad blood, competition, conflict, dislike, enmity, friction, hate, hatred, hostility, ill feeling, ill will, opposition, rivalry.
antonyms rapport, sympathy.

antagonist *n* adversary, competitor, contender, contestant, disputant, enemy, foe, opponent, opposer, rival.
antonyms ally, supporter.

antagonistic *adj* adversarial, adverse, antipathetic, at variance, averse, bellicose, belligerent, conflicting, contentious, contrary, hostile, ill-disposed, incompatible, inimical, opposed, pugnacious, unfriendly, unsympathetic.
antonyms friendly, sympathetic.

antecedents *n* ancestors, ancestry, antecessors, background, blood, descent, dossier, extraction, family, forebears, forefathers, forerunners, genealogy, history, line, lineage, past, pedigree, precursors, prodromes, progenitors, record, stock.

antedate *v* antecede, anticipate, come before, forego, forerun, go before, precede, predate.
antonym follow.

antediluvian *adj* anachronistic, ancient, antiquated, antique, archaic, bygone, démodé, fossilized, obsolete, old-fashioned, out of the ark, out-of-date, passé, prehistoric, primal, primeval, primitive, primordial, superannuated.
antonyms modern, up-to-date, with it.

anterior *adj* antecedent, earlier, foregoing, former, preceding, previous, prior, prodromal, prodromic.
antonym subsequent.

anthem *n* canticle, chant, chorale, hymn, introit, paean, psalm, song.

anthology *n* analects, choice, collection, compendium, compilation, digest, garland, miscellany, selection, treasury.

anticipate *v* antedate, apprehend, await, bank on, beat to it, count upon, expect, forecast, foresee, forestall, foretaste, foretell, hope for, intercept, look for, look forward to, precede, predate, predict, pre-empt, prevent.

anticipation *n* apprehension, expectancy, expectation, foresight, foretaste, forethought, forewarning, hope, preconception, premonition, prescience, presentiment, waiting.

anticipatory *adj* anticipative, expectant, hopeful, intuitive, preparatory, prodromal, prodromic.

anticlimax *n* bathos, comedown, damp squib, disappointment, fiasco, letdown.

anticlockwise *adj* dextrorse, levorotatory.

antics *n* buffoonery, capers, clownery, clowning, didoes, doings, escapades, foolery, foolishness, frolics, larks, mischief, monkeyshines, playfulness, pranks, silliness, skylarking, stunts, tomfoolery, tricks, zaniness, zanyism.

antidote *n* antitoxin, antivenin, corrective, counteragent, countermeasure, cure, detoxicant, neutralizer, preventive, remedy, specific, treacle.

antipathetic *adj* abhorrent, allergic, anathema, antagonistic, averse, disgusting, distasteful, hateful, horrible, hostile, incompatible, inimical, loathsome, obnoxious, odious, offensive, repellent, repugnant, repulsive, revolting.
antonyms agreeable, harmonious, sympathetic.

antipathy *n* abhorrence, allergy, animosity, animus, antagonism, aversion, bad blood, contrariety, disgust, dislike, distaste, enmity, hate, hatred, hostility, ill will, incompatibility, loathing, odium, opposition, rancour, repugnance, repulsion, resentment.
antonyms rapport, sympathy.

antiquary *n* antiquarian, archaeologist, archaist, bibliophile, collector, paleologist.

antiquated *adj* anachronistic, ancient, antediluvian, antique, archaic, dated, démodé, elderly, fogeyish, fossilized, obsolete, old, old-fashioned, old-fogeyish, outdated, outmoded, out-of-date, outworn, passé, quaint, superannuated.
antonyms forward-looking, modern, new.

antique *adj* aged, ancient, antiquarian, archaic, elderly, obsolete, old, old-fashioned, outdated, quaint, superannuated, vintage.
n antiquity, bibelot, curio, curiosity, heirloom, knick-knack, museum piece, object of virtu, period piece, rarity, relic.

antiquity *n* age, agedness, ancient times, ancientness, antique, distant past, eld, elderliness, hoariness, old age, olden days, oldness, time immemorial, venerableness.

antonyms modernity, novelty.

antiseptic *adj* aseptic, bactericidal, clean, disinfectant, germ-free, germicidal, hygienic, medicated, pure, sanitary, sanitized, sterile, uncontaminated, unpolluted.

n bactericide, cleanser, decontaminant, disinfectant, germicide, purifier.

antisocial *adj* alienated, anarchic, antagonistic, asocial, belligerent, disorderly, disruptive, hostile, misanthropic, rebellious, reserved, retiring, unacceptable, unapproachable, uncommunicative, unfriendly, unsociable, withdrawn.

antonyms acceptable, sociable.

antithesis *n* antipode, contradiction, contradistinction, contraposition, contrariety, contrary, contrast, converse, inverse, inversion, opposite, opposite extreme, opposition, polarity, reversal, reverse.

antithetical *adj* antipodal, antipodean, antithetic, contradictory, contrary, contrasted, contrasting, converse, counter, inverse, opposed, opposite, polarized, poles apart, reverse.

anxiety *n* angst, anxiousness, apprehension, care, concern, disquiet, disquietude, distress, dread, eagerness, foreboding, fretfulness, impatience, keenness, misgiving, nervousness, presentiment, restlessness, solicitude, suspense, tension, unease, uneasiness, worriment, worry.

antonym composure.

anxious[1] *adj* afraid, angst-ridden, apprehensive, biting one's nails, careful, concerned, disquieted, distressed, disturbed, fearful, fretful, in suspense, jittery, nervous, on tenterhooks, overwrought, restless, solicitous, suspenseful, taut, tense, troubled, uneasy, unquiet, watchful, worried.

antonym composed.

anxious[2] (**to** or **for**) *adj* avid, desirous (of), eager, expectant, hungry, impatient, intent (on), itching, keen (to or on), longing, looking forward (to), lustful (for), thirsty, yearning.

antonyms reluctant (to), uninterested (in), unwilling (to).

apace *adv* at full speed, at top speed, double-quick, expeditiously, fast, hastily, posthaste, quickly, rapidly, speedily, swiftly, without delay.

apart *adv* afar, alone, aloof, aside, asunder, away, by oneself, cut off, distant, distinct, divorced, excluded, independent, independently, individually, into parts, isolated, on one's own, privately, separate, separated, separately, singly, to bits, to one side, to pieces.

apartment *n* accommodation, chambers, compartment, condominium, flat, living quarters, lodgings, maisonette, pad, penthouse, quarters, rental unit, room, rooms, suite, tenement.

apathetic *adj* cold, cool, emotionless, impassive, incurious, indifferent, insensible, insentient, lackadaisical, lethargic, listless, numb, passionless, passive, phlegmatic, sluggish, torpid, unambitious, unconcerned, unemotional, unfeeling, uninterested, uninvolved, unmotivated, unmoved, unresponsive.

antonyms concerned, responsive.

apathy *n* accidie, coldness, coolness, emotionlessness, impassibility, impassivity, incuriousness, indifference, inertia, insensibility, lack of ambition or motivation, lack of interest or involvement, lethargy, listlessness, passiveness, passivity, phlegm, sluggishness, torpor, unconcern, unfeelingness, uninterestedness, unresponsiveness.

antonyms ambition, concern, interest, involvement, motivation, warmth.

ape *v* affect, be (or do) a takeoff of (or on), caricature, copy, counterfeit, echo, emulate, imitate, mimic, mirror, mock, parody, parrot, take off (on).

n baboon, barbarian, boor, brute, chimpanzee, fool, gibbon, gorilla, idiot, ignoramus, klutz, know-nothing, monkey, oaf, orangutan, philistine, savage.

aperture *n* breach, cavity, chink, cleft, crack, eye, eyelet, fissure, foramen, gap, hole, interstice, mouth, opening, orifice, passage, perforation, rent, rift, slit, slot, space, vent, window.

apex *n* acme, apogee, climax, consummation, crest, crown, crowning point, culmination, height, high point, peak, pinnacle, point, summit, tip, top, vertex, zenith.

antonym nadir.

aphorism *n* adage, apothegm, axiom, dictum, epigram, gnome, maxim, mot, motto, precept, proverb, saw, saying, sentence.

aplomb *n* assurance, audacity, balance, calmness, composure, confidence, coolness, equanimity, poise, sang-froid, savoir faire, self-assurance, self-confidence, self-possession.

antonym discomposure.

apocalyptic *adj* fatidic, ominous, oracular, portentous, prophetic, revelational, revelatory, signal, threatening, vatic, warning.

apocryphal *adj* concocted, doubtful, dubious, equivocal, fabricated, fictitious, imaginary, legendary, mythical, phony, questionable, spurious, unauthenticated, uncanonical, unsubstantiated, unsupported, unverified.

antonym true.

apogee *n* acme, apex, climax, consummation, crest, crown, culmination, height, high point, meridian, peak, pinnacle, summit, tip, top, vertex, zenith.

antonyms nadir, perigee.

apologetic *adj* compunctious, conscience-stricken, contrite, defensive, excusatory, penitent, regretful, remorseful, repentant, rueful, sorry.

antonym defiant.

n apologia, argument, defence, justification, rationale.

apologist *n* advocate, champion, defender, endorser, justifier, pleader, seconder, spokesperson, supporter, upholder, vindicator.

antonym critic.

apology *n* acknowledgment, apologia, confession, defence, excuse, explanation, expression of regret (or remorse), extenuation, justification, palliation, plea, semblance, substitute, travesty, vindication.

antonym defiance.

apostasy *n* defection, desertion, disloyalty, faithlessness, falseness, heresy, perfidy, rattery, ratting, recidivism, recreancy, renunciation, treachery, unfaithfulness.

antonyms loyalty, orthodoxy.

apostate *n* defector, deserter, heretic, recidivist, recreant, renegade, tergiversator, traitor, turncoat.

antonyms adherent, believer, convert, loyalist.

adj backslidden, disloyal, faithless, fallen away, false, heretical, lapsed, perfidious, recreant, renegade, traitorous, treacherous, unfaithful, unorthodox, untrue.

antonyms faithful, true.

apostatize *v* backslide, defect, desert, lapse, recant, reject the faith, renege, tergiversate, turn back, withdraw.

apostle *n* advocate, champion, crusader, evangelist, exponent, herald, messenger, missionary, pioneer, preacher, promoter, propagandist, propagator, proponent, proselytizer.

apothegm *n* adage, aphorism, axiom, dictum, epigram, gnome, maxim, mot, motto, precept, proverb, saw, saying, sentence.

apotheosis *n* adoration, deification, elevation, exaltation, glorification, idealization, idolization, immortalization, worship.

apotheosize *v* adore, deify, elevate, exalt, glorify, idealize, idolize, immortalize, worship.

appal *v* alarm, astound, daunt, disconcert, disgust, dishearten, dismay, frighten, harrow, horrify, intimidate, outrage, petrify, scare, shock, terrify, unnerve.

antonyms encourage, reassure.

appalling *adj* alarming, astounding, atrocious, awful, daunting, dire, disheartening, dismaying, dreadful, fearful, frightening, frightful, ghastly, grim, harrowing, hideous, horrible, horrid, horrific, horrifying, intimidating, loathsome, petrifying, scary, shocking, startling, terrible, terrifying, unnerving, wretched.

antonym reassuring.

apparatus *n* accoutrements, appliance, bureaucracy, business, contraption, device, equipment, framework, gadget, gear, gizmo, hierarchy, implements, machine, machinery, materials, means, mechanism, network, organization, outfit, rig, setup, structure, stuff, system, tackle, tools, utensils.

apparel *n* accoutrements, array, attire, clothes, clothing, costume, dress, duds, equipment, fashions, garb, garments, gear, guise,

habiliments, habit, outfit, raiment, robes, suit, togs, trappings, vestments, wardrobe, wear, weeds.

apparent¹ *adj* clear, conspicuous, declared, discernible, distinct, evident, indubitable, manifest, marked, noticeable, obvious, open, outward, overt, patent, perceptible, plain, unmistakable, visible.

antonyms hidden, imperceptible, obscure.

apparent² *adj* on paper, ostensible, outward, seeming, specious, spurious, superficial.

antonyms actual, real.

apparition *n* chimera, eidolon, ghost, manifestation, materialization, phantasm, phantom, presence, revenant, shade, shadow, spectre, spirit, spook, umbra, vision, visitant, visitation, wraith.

appeal¹ *n* adjuration, application, entreaty, invocation, orison, petition, plea, prayer, request, solicitation, suit, supplication.

v address, adjure, apply, ask, beg, beseech, call, call upon, entreat, implore, invoke, petition, plead, pray, refer, request, resort to, solicit, sue, supplicate.

appeal² *n* allure, attraction, attractiveness, beauty, charisma, charm, enchantment, fascination, interest, magnetism, winsomeness.

v allure, attract, charm, draw, engage, entice, fascinate, interest, invite, lure, please, tempt.

appear *v* act, arise, arrive, attend, become manifest, be outwardly, be published, bob up, come into sight, come into view, come forth, come on the scene, come out, come to light, come up, crop up, develop, emerge, enter, issue, leak out, look, loom, make the scene, materialize, occur, perform, play, rise, seem, show, show up, surface, take part, transpire, turn out, turn up.

antonym disappear.

appearance¹ *n* advent, appearing, arrival, coming, début, emergence, introduction, presence.

antonym disappearance.

appearance² *n* air, aspect, bearing, cast, demeanour, dress, expression, externals, face, facies, figure, form, front, grooming, image, impression, look, looks, manner, mien, physiognomy, presence, the cut of one's jib.

antonym character.

appearance(s)³ *n* air, façade, front, guise, illusion, pretence, seeming, semblance, show.

antonym reality.

appease *v* accede to, accommodate, allay, assuage, blunt, calm, compose, conciliate, diminish, ease, give a sop to, humour, lessen, lull, mitigate, mollify, pacify, placate, propitiate, quell, quench, quiet, reconcile, satisfy, soften, soothe, subdue, tranquillize.

antonym aggravate.

appeasement *n* acceding, accommodation, assuagement, compromise, concession, conciliation, humouring, lessening, mitigation, mollification, pacification, placation, propitiation, quelling, quenching, quieting,

reconciliation, satisfaction, softening, sop, subduing.
antonyms aggravation, resistance.

appellation *n* address, denomination, description, designation, epithet, handle, label, moniker, name, nickname, sobriquet, style, term, title.

append *v* add, adjoin, affix, annex, attach, conjoin, fasten, join, stick on, subjoin, tack on.

appendage *n* accessory, addendum, addition, add-on, adjunct, affix, ancillary, annex, appendix, appurtenance, attachment, auxiliary, excrescence, extra, extremity, limb, member, projection, prosthesis, protuberance, supplement, tab, tag.

appendix *n* addendum, addition, adjunct, appendage, codicil, epilogue, excursus, postscript, rider, supplement.

appertaining (to) *adj* applicable, applying, belonging, characteristic, connected, germane, having to do (with), pertinent, related, relating, relevant, to do (with).

appetite *n* appetence, craving, demand, desire, eagerness, hankering, hunger, inclination, keenness, liking, longing, passion, predilection, proclivity, propensity, relish, stomach, taste, thirst, willingness, yearning, zeal, zest.
antonym distaste.

appetizer *n* antipasto, apéritif, canapé, cocktail, foretaste, hors d'oeuvre, preview, sample, taste, taster, tidbit, whet.

appetizing *adj* appealing, delicious, inviting, lip-smacking, moreish, mouthwatering, palatable, piquant, savoury, scrumptious, succulent, tasty, tempting, toothsome, yummy.
antonym disgusting.

applaud *v* acclaim, approve, cheer, clap, commend, compliment, congratulate, encourage, endorse, eulogize, extol, hail, laud, praise, salute, welcome.
antonyms censure, disparage.

applauding *adj* acclamatory, adulatory, approving, commendary, complimentary, congratulatory, laudatory, plauditory.
antonym abusive.

applause *n* acclaim, acclamation, accolade, approbation, approval, cheering, cheers, commendation, congratulation, encomium, eulogies, eulogizing, hand, laudation, ovation, plaudits, praise.
antonyms censure, disparagement.

appliance *n* apparatus, contraption, contrivance, device, gadget, gizmo, implement, instrument, machine, mechanism, tool.

applicable *adj* apposite, appropriate, apropos, apt, befitting, fit, fitting, germane, legitimate, pertinent, proper, related, relevant, suitable, suited, timely, to the purpose, useful, valid.
antonym inapplicable.

applicant *n* aspirant, candidate, claimant, competitor, contestant, inquirer, interviewee, petitioner, postulant, suitor.

application[1] *n* appositeness, apposition, exercise, extension, function, germaneness, lesson, moral, pertinence, practice, purpose, reference, relevance, use, value.

application[2] *n* assiduity, attention, attentiveness, commitment, dedication, diligence, effort, exercise, industry, keenness, perseverance, practice, sedulity, sedulousness.

application[3] *n* appeal, claim, claim form, form, inquiry, petition, reference, request, request form, requisition, solicitation, suit.

application[4] *n* balm, cream, dressing, emollient, liniment, lotion, medication, ointment, poultice, preparation, salve, unguent.

apply[1] *v* administer, appose, assign, bring into play, bring to bear, direct, employ, engage, execute, exercise, implement, ply, practise, resort to, set, use, utilize, wield.

apply[2] *v* appertain, be applicable or relevant, be apt or suitable, fit, have force, pertain, refer, relate, suit.

apply[3] **(oneself, one's energies, etc.)** *v* address, bend, buckle down, commit, concentrate, dedicate, devote, direct, focus, get serious, give, knuckle down, persevere, settle down, study, throw.

apply[4] *v* appeal, ask for, claim, indent for, inquire, petition, put in, request, requisition, solicit, sue.

apply[5] *v* cover with, dab, lay (on), paint, place, plaster, put on, rub, smear, spread on, use.

appoint *v* allot, arrange, assign, call, charge, choose, command, commission, constitute, co-opt, decide, decree, delegate, designate, destine, detail, determine, devote, direct, elect, engage, establish, fix, install, name, nominate, ordain, provide, select, set, settle.
antonyms dismiss, reject.

appointed[1] *adj* allotted, arranged, assigned, called, chosen, commanded, commissioned, co-opted, decided, decreed, delegated, designated, determined, directed, elected, established, fixed, installed, invested, named, nominated, ordained, preordained, provided, selected, set, settled.

appointed[2] *adj* equipped, fitted out, furnished, supplied.

appointment *n* allotment, arrangement, assignation, assignment, call, choice, choosing, commissioning, consultation, date, decision, decree, delegation, designation, determination, election, engagement, installation, interview, investiture, job, meeting, naming, nomination, office, ordaining, ordination, place, position, post, provision, rendezvous, selection, session, situation, station, tryst, visit.

appointments *n* accoutrements, appurtenances, equipage, equipment, fittings, fixtures, furnishings, furniture, gear, outfit, paraphernalia, trappings.

apportion *v* accord, allocate, allot, assign, award, deal, dispense, distribute, divide, divvy up, dole out, grant, measure out, mete, parcel out, portion out, ration, share.

apportionment *n* allocation, allotment, assignment, dealing, dispensation, dispensing, distribution, division, divvying up, doling, measuring, meting, parcelling out, partitioning, sharing.

apposite *adj* applicable, appropriate, apropos, apt, befitting, condign, felicitous, germane, pertinent, proper, relevant, suitable, suited, to the point, to the purpose.
antonym inapposite.

appraisal *n* appreciation, assay, assaying, assessment, estimate, estimation, evaluation, examination, inspection, judgment, once-over, opinion, pricing, rating, reckoning, review, sizing-up, survey, valuation.

appraise *v* assay, assess, estimate, evaluate, examine, gauge, inspect, judge, price, rate, review, size up, survey, valuate, value.

appreciable *adj* apparent, ascertainable, clear, considerable, definite, detectable, discernible, distinguishable, evident, marked, material, measurable, noticeable, obvious, perceivable, perceptible, pronounced, recognizable, significant, substantial, undeniable, visible.
antonyms imperceptible, negligible.

appreciate[1] *v* acknowledge, admire, be grateful or thankful for, be sensible of, be sensitive to, cherish, comprehend, dig, do justice to, enjoy, esteem, estimate, know, like, perceive, prize, realize, recognize, regard, relish, respect, savour, sympathize with, take kindly to, treasure, understand, value.
antonyms despise, overlook.

appreciate[2] *v* enhance, gain, grow, improve, increase, inflate, mount, rise, strengthen.
antonym depreciate.

appreciation[1] *n* acclaim, acclamation, acknowledgment, admiration, appraisal, assessment, awareness, cognizance, comprehension, criticism, enjoyment, esteem, estimation, gratefulness, gratitude, indebtedness, judgment, knowledge, liking, notice, obligation, perception, praise, realization, recognition, regard, relish, respect, responsiveness, review, sensitivity, sympathy, thankfulness, thanks, tribute, understanding, valuation, view.
antonyms ignorance, ingratitude, insensitivity, neglect.

appreciation[2] *n* climb, enhancement, gain, growth, improvement, increase, inflation, rise.
antonym depreciation.

appreciative *adj* admiring, aware, beholden, cognizant, conscious, encouraging, enthusiastic, grateful, indebted, knowledgeable, mindful, obliged, perceptive, pleased, regardful, respectful, responsive, sensible, sensitive, supportive, sympathetic, thankful, understanding.
antonym ungrateful.

apprehend[1] *v* arrest, bust, capture, catch, collar, detain, get, grab, haul in, nab, pinch, reel in, run in, seize, take.

apprehend[2] *v* appreciate, assimilate, believe, comprehend, conceive, consider, cotton on (to), discern, grasp, imagine, know, perceive, realize, recognize, register, see, twig (to), understand.

apprehension[1] *n* arrest, capture, catching, detention, seizure, taking.

apprehension[2] *n* alarm, anxiety, apprehensiveness, concern, disquiet, doubt, dread, fear, foreboding, misgiving, mistrust, nervousness, premonition, presentiment, qualm, suspicion, unease, uneasiness, worry.

apprehension[3] *n* assimilation, awareness, belief, comprehension, concept, conception, discernment, grasp, idea, impression, intellect, intellection, intelligence, ken, knowledge, notion, opinion, perception, registration, thought, understanding, uptake, view.

apprehensive *adj* afraid, alarmed, anxious, concerned, disquieted, distrustful, disturbed, doubtful, fearful, mistrustful, nervous, solicitous, suspicious, uneasy, worried.
antonym confident.

apprentice *n* beginner, cheechako, cub, greenhorn, learner, neophyte, newcomer, novice, probationer, pupil, recruit, starter, student, tenderfoot, trainee, tyro.
antonym expert.

apprise *v* acquaint, advise, brief, bring up to date, clue in, enlighten, fill in, give (someone) the lowdown, inform, make aware, notify, tell, tip off, warn.

approach *v* address, advance, appeal to, apply to, approximate, ask, attack, be like, begin, broach, catch up (to), come close (to), come near (to), commence, compare with, draw near (to), embark on, gain on, introduce, make advances to, make overtures to, meet, near, raise, reach, resemble, set about, sound out, start on, undertake, verge on.
n access, advance, advent, appeal, application, approximation, arrival, attitude, avenue, course, doorway, entrance, invitation, landfall, likeness, manner, means, method, mode, modus operandi, nearing, offer, overture, passage, procedure, proposal, proposition, resemblance, road, semblance, style, system, technique, way.

approachable *adj* accessible, affable, agreeable, attainable, congenial, conversable, cordial, easy, friendly, informal, open, reachable, sociable, warm.
antonym unapproachable.

approbation *n* acceptance, acclaim, acclamation, applause, approval, assent, authorization, commendation, congratulation, encouragement, endorsement, esteem, favour, kudos, laudation, praise, ratification, recognition, regard, sanction, support, validation.
antonym disapprobation.

appropriate *adj* applicable, apposite, appurtenant, apropos, apt, bang on, becoming, befitting, belonging, condign, congruous, correct, felicitous, fit, fitting, germane, meet, merited, opportune, pertinent, proper, relevant, right, seasonable, seemly, suitable, timely, to the point, well-chosen, well-suited, well-timed.

antonym inappropriate.

v allocate, allot, annex, apportion, arrogate, assign, assume, claim, commandeer, confiscate, devote, earmark, embezzle, expropriate, filch, impound, impropriate, misappropriate, pilfer, pocket, possess oneself of, pre-empt, purloin, seize, set apart, steal, take, usurp.

appropriateness *n* applicability, appositeness, aptness, becomingness, condignness, congruity, congruousness, correctness, felicitousness, felicity, fitness, germaneness, justice, justness, opportuneness, pertinence, properness, propriety, relevance, rightness, seemliness, suitability, timeliness.

appropriation *n* allocation, allotment, annexation, apportionment, assignment, assumption, commandeering, confiscation, dispensation, earmarking, expropriation, impoundment, misappropriation, pre-emption, seizure, setting apart, usurpation.

approval *n* acclaim, acclamation, acquiescence, admiration, adoption, agreement, applause, appreciation, approbation, assent, authorization, blessing, certification, commendation, concurrence, confirmation, consent, countenance, endorsement, esteem, favour, go-ahead, good opinion, green light, imprimatur, leave, licence, liking, OK, permission, plaudits, praise, ratification, recommendation, regard, respect, sanction, support, thumbs up, validation.

antonym disapproval.

approve *v* accede to, accept, acclaim, admire, adopt, advocate, agree to, allow, applaud, appreciate, assent to, authorize, back, bless, commend, concur, confirm, consent to, countenance, endorse, esteem, favour, like, OK, pass, permit, praise, ratify, recommend, respect, rubber-stamp, sanction, second, support, take kindly to, uphold, validate, welcome.

antonyms disapprove, look askance at, take a dim view of.

approved *adj* acceptable, accepted, authorized, comme il faut, conventional, correct, favoured, official, orthodox, permissible, permitted, preferred, proper, recognized, recommended, sanctioned.

antonym unorthodox.

approximate *adj* ballpark, close, comparable, conjectural, estimated, extrapolated, guessed, inexact, like, loose, near, relative, rough, similar, verging on.

antonym exact.

v approach, be like, be on the order of, be tantamount to, border on, resemble, verge on.

approximately *adv* about, almost, around, circa, close to, coming up to, give or take, in round numbers, in the region of, in the vicinity of, just about, loosely, more or less, nearly, not far off, pushing, roughly, -odd, some, somewhere around, upwards of, well-nigh.

antonym exactly.

approximation *n* approach, ballpark figure, conjecture, correspondence, estimate, estimation, extrapolation, guess, guesstimate, likeness, match, proximity, resemblance, rough calculation, rough idea, semblance, similarity.

antonyms exactitude, precision.

appurtenance *n* accessory, accompaniment, addition, adjunct, appanage, appendage, attachment, auxiliary, concomitant, incidental, subordinate, subsidiary, supplement.

appurtenances *n* accessories, accompaniments, accoutrements, apparatus, appendages, equipment, gear, impedimenta, kit, paraphernalia, trappings, traps.

apropos *adj* applicable, apposite, appropriate, apt, befitting, belonging, condign, correct, fit, fitting, germane, meet, opportune, pertinent, proper, related, relevant, right, suitable, timely, to the point.

antonym inappropriate.

adv appositely, appropriately, aptly, by the bye, by the way, en passant, in passing, incidentally, opportunely, pertinently, properly, relevantly, suitably, to the point.

antonym inappropriately.

apropos of about, as regards, in connection with, in relation to, in respect of, on the subject of, re, regarding, respecting, speaking of, with reference to, with regard to, with respect to.

apt *adj* accurate, adept, applicable, apposite, appropriate, apropos, astute, bang on, befitting, bright, clever, condign, correct, disposed, expert, fair, fit, fitting, germane, gifted, given, inclined, ingenious, intelligent, just, liable, likely, meet, pertinent, prone, proper, quick, ready, relevant, seasonable, sharp, skilful, smart, suitable, talented, teachable, tending, timely.

antonyms inapt, inept, poor, unfortunate, unsuitable.

aptitude *n* ability, aptness, bent, capability, capacity, cleverness, disposition, facility, faculty, flair, gift, inclination, intelligence, knack, leaning, penchant, predilection, proclivity, proficiency, propensity, quickness, talent, tendency.

antonym inaptitude.

aptness *n* accuracy, applicability, appositeness, appropriateness, becomingness, bent, capacity, cleverness, condignness, congruity, congruousness, correctness, disposition, felicitousness, felicity, fitness, fittingness, germaneness, inclination, leaning, liability, likelihood, likeliness, opportuneness, pertinence, predilection, proclivity, proficiency, proneness, propensity, properness, quickness, readiness, relevance, rightness, suitability, tendency, timeliness.

arbiter *n* adjudicator, arbitrator, authority, controller, dictator, expert, go-between, intermediary, judge, master, mediator, negotiator, pundit, referee, ruler, umpire.

arbitrary *adj* absolute, autocratic, capricious, chance, despotic, dictatorial, domineering, erratic, fanciful, high-handed, imperious, inconsistent, irrational, magisterial, overbearing, peremptory, personal, random, subjective, summary, tyrannical, tyrannous, unreasonable, unreasoned, unsupported, whimsical, wilful.

antonyms circumspect, consistent, rational, reasoned.

arbitrate *v* adjudge, adjudicate, decide, determine, facilitate, intervene in, judge, mediate, pass judgment, referee, settle, umpire.

arbitration *n* adjudication, arbitrament, decision, determination, intervention, judgment, mediation, negotiation, settlement.

arbitrator *n* adjudicator, arbiter, facilitator, go-between, intermediary, judge, mediator, moderator, negotiator, referee, umpire.

arcade *n* cloister, colonnade, covered way, gallery, loggia, mall, peristyle, portico, precinct, stoa.

arcane *adj* abstruse, cabalistic, cryptic, enigmatic, esoteric, hidden, mysterious, mystical, obscure, occult, profound, recondite, secret.

antonym commonplace.

arch[1] *n* arc, archway, bend, bow, concave, concavity, cupola, curvature, curve, dome, flexure, semicircle, span, vault.

v arc, bend, bow, camber, curve, embow, extend, vault.

arch[2] *adj* accomplished, chief, consummate, coy, egregious, expert, finished, first, first-class, foremost, frolicsome, greatest, highest, knowing, leading, main, major, master, mischievous, pert, playful, pre-eminent, primary, principal, provocative, roguish, saucy, sly, top, waggish, wily.

archaic *adj* ancient, antediluvian, antiquated, antique, démodé, fossilized, obsolete, old, old-fashioned, outdated, outmoded, out-of-date, passé, primitive, quaint, superannuated.

antonym modern.

archetype *n* classic, conception, exemplar, form, idea, ideal, model, original, paradigm, pattern, precursor, prime example, prototype, standard, type.

architect *n* artist, author, constructor, contriver, creator, designer, deviser, engineer, fabricator, fashioner, founder, instigator, inventor, maker, master builder, originator, planner, prime mover, shaper.

architecture *n* architectonics, arrangement, building, composition, construction, design, framework, layout, make-up, plan, planning, structure, style.

archive *n* library, muniment room, museum, record office, registry, repository.

archives *n* annals, chronicles, deeds, documents, ledgers, memorabilia, memorials, muniments, papers, records, registers, roll(s).

ardent *adj* amorous, avid, devoted, eager, earnest, enthusiastic, fervent, fervid, fierce, fiery, heated, hot, hot-blooded, impassioned, intense, keen, lusty, passionate, perfervid,

spirited, vehement, warm, whole-hearted, zealous.

antonyms cool, indifferent, lukewarm, unenthusiastic.

ardour *n* animation, avidity, devotion, eagerness, earnestness, empressement, enthusiasm, feeling, fervour, fire, heat, heatedness, intensity, keenness, lust, passion, spirit, vehemence, warmth, zeal, zest.

antonyms coolness, indifference.

arduous *adj* backbreaking, burdensome, daunting, difficult, exacting, exhausting, fatiguing, formidable, gruelling, hard, harsh, herculean, laborious, onerous, punishing, rigorous, severe, strenuous, taxing, tiring, toilsome, tough, troublesome, trying, uphill, wearisome.

antonym easy.

area *n* arena, bailiwick, ballpark, breadth, compass, department, district, domain, environs, expanse, extent, field, locality, neck of the woods, neighbourhood, part, patch, portion, province, range, realm, region, scope, section, sector, size, sphere, stretch, terrain, territory, tract, width, zone.

arena *n* amphitheatre, area, battlefield, battleground, bowl, coliseum, field, ground, hockey rink, lists, park, ring, rink, scene, skating rink, sphere, stadium, stage.

argot *n* cant, dialect, idiom, jargon, lingo, parlance, patois, slang, terminology, usage, vernacular, vocabulary.

argue[1] **(for** or **that)** *v* assert, bear out, claim, contend, demonstrate, denote, evidence, hold, imply, indicate, maintain, manifest, plead, prove, reason, show, suggest.

argue[2] **(with)** *v* altercate, argufy, bicker, convince, debate, disagree, discuss, dispute, expostulate, fall out, fence, feud, fight, haggle, have it out, join issue, moot, persuade, plead, prevail upon, quarrel, question, reason, remonstrate, squabble, take issue, talk (into), wrangle.

argument[1] *n* abstract, argumentation, assertion, case, claim, contention, defence, demonstration, dialectic, exposition, gist, ground, logic, outline, plea, pleading, plot, polemic, position, proposition, reason, reasoning, story, story line, summary, synopsis, thesis.

argument[2] *n* altercation, beef, bickering, bone to pick, clash, contention, controversy, debate, difference, disagreement, discussion, dispute, expostulation, feud, fight, pleading, polemic, quarrel, questioning, reasoning, remonstrance, remonstration, row, set-to, shouting match, squabble, wrangle.

argumentative *adj* belligerent, captious, chippy, combative, confrontational, contentious, contrary, disputatious, disputative, dissentious, litigious, opinionated, perverse, polemic, quarrelsome.

antonym complaisant.

arid *adj* baked, barren, boring, colourless, desert, desiccated, dreary, droughty, dry, dull, empty, flat, infertile, jejune, lifeless, moistureless, monotonous, parched, sere, spiritless, sterile, tedious, thirsty, torrefied, torrid, uninspired, uninteresting, unproductive, vapid, waste, waterless.

antonyms fertile, lively, moist.

aright *adv* accurately, aptly, comme il faut, correctly, de règle, duly, en règle, exactly, fitly, justly, properly, righteously, rightly, suitably, truly, uprightly, well.

arise *v* appear, ascend, begin, be resurrected, climb, come to light, commence, crop up, derive, emanate, emerge, ensue, flow, follow, get up, gird oneself, go up, grow, happen, issue, lift, occur, originate, proceed, result, rise, set in, soar, spring, stand up, start, stem, tower, wake up.

aristocracy *n* blue bloods, élite, gentility, gentry, haut monde, nobility, noblemen, noblesse, patricians, peerage, quality, ruling class, titled class, top drawer, upper class, upper crust.

antonyms canaille, the plebs.

aristocrat *n* blue blood, eupatrid, grand seigneur, grande dame, gentleman, gentlewoman, grandee, lady, lord, lordling, nob, noble, nobleman, noblewoman, patrician, peer, peeress.

antonym commoner.

aristocratic *adj* blue-blooded, courtly, dignified, elegant, élite, fine, gentle, gentlemanly, haughty, highborn, lordly, noble, patricianly, polished, refined, supercilious, thoroughbred, titled, upper-class, upper-crust, well-born, well-bred.

antonyms plebeian, vulgar.

arithmetic *n* algorism, algorithm, calculation, ciphering, computation, count, counting, mathematics, numbers, numeration, reckoning.

arm[1] *n* appendage, authority, bough, brachium, branch, channel, control, department, detachment, division, estuary, extension, firth, force, influence, inlet, limb, might, offshoot, power, projection, section, sector, sound, strait, sway, tributary, upper limb.

arm[2] *v* accoutre, ammunition, array, brace, equip, forearm, fortify, furnish, gird, issue (with), munition, outfit, prepare, prime, protect, provide, reinforce, steel, strengthen, supply.

armaments *n* ammunition, arms, artillery, cannon, defences, fortifications, guns, matériel, munitions, ordnance, weaponry, weapons.

armed *adj* accoutred, armoured, arrayed, braced, briefed, equipped, fitted out, forearmed, fortified, furnished, girded, guarded, panoplied, prepared, primed, protected, provided, steeled, strengthened.

antonyms unarmed, unprepared.

armour *n* armature, carapace, chain mail, iron cladding, mail, panoply, shell, steel plating.

armoured *adj* armour-plated, bombproof, bulletproof, ironclad, mail-clad, mailed, panoplied, protected, steel-plated.

armoury *n* ammunition dump, arsenal, depot, magazine, ordnance depot, panoply, repertoire, repository, reserve, stock, stock-in-trade, stockpile.

arms[1] *n* armaments, defences, firearms, guns, instruments of war, ordnance, weaponry, weapons.

arms[2] *n* armorial bearings, blazonry, crest, escutcheon, hatchment, heraldry, insignia, scutcheon, shield.

army *n* armed force, array, cohorts, corps, force(s), gang, horde, host, land forces, legions, military, militia, mob, multitude, pack, soldiers, soldiery, swarm, the service, throng, troops.

aroma *n* bouquet, fragrance, odour, perfume, redolence, savour, scent, smell.

aromatic *adj* balmy, fragrant, odoriferous, perfumed, pungent, redolent, savoury, spicy, sweet-smelling.

antonym acrid.

around *prep* about, across, approximately, circa, circling, encircling, enclosing, encompassing, environing, more or less, on all sides of, on every side of, roughly, surrounding, through(out).

adv about, abroad, all over, at hand, close, close by, everywhere, here and there, in all directions, in the air, in various places, near, nearby, nigh, on all sides, to and fro.

arouse *v* agitate, animate, awaken, bestir, call forth, enliven, evoke, excite, foment, foster, galvanize, goad, incite, inflame, instigate, kindle, move, prompt, provoke, quicken, raise, rouse, sharpen, spark, spur, startle, stimulate, stir up, summon up, wake up, waken, warm, whet, whip up.

antonyms calm, lull, quieten.

arraign *v* accuse, attack, blame, call to account, charge, denounce, find fault with, haul up, impeach, impugn, incriminate, indict, prosecute.

arrange[1] *v* adjust, align, array, categorize, class, classify, collocate, concert, construct, contrive, co-ordinate, decorate, design, determine, devise, dispose, distribute, file, fix, form, format, group, lay out, line up, marshal, methodize, order, organize, plan, position, preconcert, prepare, project, range, rank, schedule, set up, settle, sift, sort, sort out, stage-manage, style, systematize, tidy, trim.

arrange[2] *v* adapt, harmonize, instrument, orchestrate, score, set.

arrangement[1] *n* adjustment, agreement, alignment, array, battery, classification, compact, compromise, construction, contrivance, deal, design, display, disposition, form, grouping, layout, line-up, marshalling, method, modus vivendi, order, ordering, organization, plan, planning, preparation, provision, ranging, ranking, schedule, scheduling, scheme, settlement, setup,

---

spacing, structure, system, tabulation, taxis, terms.

arrangement² *n* adaptation, harmonization, instrumentation, interpretation, orchestration, score, setting, version.

arrant *adj* absolute, atrocious, barefaced, blatant, brazen, complete, downright, egregious, extreme, flagrant, gross, incorrigible, infamous, monstrous, notorious, out-and-out, outright, rank, thorough, thoroughgoing, undisguised, unmitigated, unregenerate, utter, vile.

array *n* apparel, arrangement, assemblage, attire, battery, clothes, collection, display, dress, equipage, exhibition, exposition, finery, formation, garb, garments, habiliments, line-up, marshalling, muster, order, panoply, parade, raiment, regalia, robes, show, supply. *v* accoutre, adorn, align, apparel, arrange, assemble, attire, bedeck, bedizen, caparison, clothe, deck out, decorate, display, dispose, doll up, draw up, dress, equip, exhibit, garb, group, line up, marshal, muster, order, outfit, parade, range, robe, show, suit up, supply, trick out, wrap.

arrest *v* absorb, apprehend, block, bust, capture, catch, check, collar, cop, delay, detain, divert, end, engage, engross, fascinate, grip, halt, hinder, hold, impede, inhibit, interrupt, intrigue, lay hands on, nab, nip in the bud, obstruct, pinch, prevent, restrain, retard, run in, seize, slow, staunch, stay, stem, stop, suppress. *n* apprehension, blockage, bust, capture, cessation, check, cop, delay, detention, end, halt, hindrance, inhibition, interruption, nabbing, obstruction, prevention, restraint, seizure, stay, stoppage, suppression, suspension.

arresting *adj* amazing, attention-getting, attractive, captivating, conspicuous, engaging, extraordinary, fascinating, impressive, notable, noteworthy, noticeable, outstanding, remarkable, striking, stunning, surprising. *antonyms* inconspicuous, unremarkable.

arrival *n* accession, advent, appearance, approach, caller, comer, coming, débutant(e), entrance, entrant, entry, incomer, landfall, newcomer, visitant, visitor. *antonym* departure.

arrive *v* alight, appear, attain, come, enter, get it all together, get there, get to the top, land, make it, make one's appearance or entrance, materialize, reach, show, show up, succeed, turn up. *antonym* depart.

arrogance *n* airs, brass, conceit, conceitedness, condescension, contempt, contemptuousness, contumely, disdain, disdainfulness, haughtiness, hauteur, high-handedness, hubris, imperiousness, insolence, loftiness, lordliness, presumption, presumptuousness, pretension, pretentiousness, pride, scorn, scornfulness, superciliousness, superiority, uppishness. *antonym* humility.

arrogant *adj* assuming, brassy, conceited, condescending, contemptuous, contumelious, disdainful, haughty, high and mighty, high-handed, hubristic, imperious, insolent, lordly, on one's high horse, overbearing, overweening, presumptuous, proud, scornful, supercilious, superior. *antonym* humble.

arrogate *v* appropriate, ascribe, assume, attribute, commandeer, confiscate, demand, expropriate, grab, impute, misappropriate, possess oneself of, presume, seize, usurp.

▲ *confusable word* abrogate.

arrow *n* barb, bolt, dart, flight, indicator, pointer, shaft.

arsenal *n* ammunition dump, armoury, collection, depot, magazine, ordnance depot, repertoire, repository, reserve, stock, stockpile, store, storehouse, supply, warehouse.

arson *n* fire-setting, incendiarism, pyromania.

arsonist *n* firebug, fire-setter, incendiary, pyromaniac.

art¹ *n* address, adroitness, aesthetics, aptitude, artistry, artwork, craftsmanship, creativity, dexterity, draftsmanship, drawing, expertise, facility, finesse, graphics, illustrations, knack, mastery, method, métier, painting, profession, science, sculpture, skill, strategy, trade, virtu, virtuosity, visuals.

art² *n* artfulness, artifice, cleverness, contrivance, craft, craftiness, cunning, deceit, deviousness, foxiness, guile, ingenuity, slyness, strategy, subtlety, trick, trickery, wile(s), wiliness.

artful *adj* adept, adroit, canny, clever, crafty, cunning, deceitful, designing, devious, dexterous, dodgy, foxy, ingenious, masterly, politic, resourceful, rusé, scheming, sharp, shrewd, skilful, sly, smart, subtle, tricksy, tricky, vulpine, wily. *antonyms* artless, ingenuous, naïve.

article *n* account, bit, clause, commodity, composition, constituent, detail, dissertation, division, element, entity, entry, essay, feature, head, heading, item, matter, object, paper, paragraph, part, particular, piece, point, report, review, section, story, thing, unit.

articulate¹ *adj* clear, coherent, comprehensible, distinct, eloquent, expressive, facile, fluent, intelligible, lucid, meaningful, understandable, verbal, vocal, well-spoken. *v* communicate, enounce, enunciate, express, phrase, pronounce, put, put into words, say, speak, state, talk, utter, verbalize, vocalize, voice, word.

articulate² *v* attach, connect, couple, fasten, fit together, hinge, interlock, join, joint, link.

articulation¹ *n* delivery, diction, enunciation, expression, phrasing, pronunciation, saying, speaking, statement, talking, utterance, verbalization, vocalization, voicing, wording.

articulation² *n* conjunction, connection, coupling, hinge, interlinking, interlock, joint, jointing, juncture, link.

artifice *n* adroitness, artfulness, chicanery, cleverness, contrivance, cozenage, craft, craftiness, cunning, deception, deftness, device, dodge, duplicity, expedient, facility, finesse, fraud, guile, hoax, invention, machination, manipulation, manoeuvre, ruse, scheme, shift, skill, slyness, stratagem, strategy, subterfuge, subtlety, tactic, trick, trickery, wile.

artificer *n* architect, artisan, builder, constructer, contriver, craftsman, creator, designer, deviser, fabricator, fashioner, framer, inventor, maker, mechanic, originator.

artificial *adj* affected, assumed, bogus, contrived, counterfeit, ersatz, factitious, fake, false, feigned, forced, imitation, insincere, made-up, man-made, mannered, manufactured, meretricious, mock, non-natural, phony, plastic, pretended, pseudo, sham, simulated, specious, spurious, stagy, synthetic, unnatural.

antonyms genuine, natural.

artillery *n* battery, cannon, cannonry, field guns, fieldpieces, gunnery, guns, heavy metal, ordnance.

artisan *n* artificer, craftsman, craftswoman, expert, handcrafter, handicraftsman, handicraftswoman, journeyman, technician, worker.

artist *n* aesthete, colourist, craftsman, craftswoman, draftsman, draftswoman, entertainer, expert, filmmaker, maestro, master, muralist, musician, painter, performer, portraitist, portrait painter, professional, sculptor, singer, songwriter, water-colourist.

artistic *adj* aesthetic, arty, beautiful, bohemian, creative, cultivated, cultured, decorative, elegant, exquisite, graceful, harmonious, imaginative, ornamental, refined, sensitive, skilled, stylish, talented, tasteful.

antonym inelegant.

artistry *n* accomplishment, art, brilliance, craft, craftsmanship, creativity, deftness, expertise, finesse, flair, genius, imagination, mastery, proficiency, sensibility, sensitivity, skill, style, talent, taste, touch, virtuosity, workmanship.

antonym ineptitude.

artless *adj* candid, childlike, direct, frank, genuine, guileless, honest, humble, ingenuous, innocent, naïf, naïve, naked, natural, open, plain, pure, simple, sincere, straightforward, true, trustful, trusting, unadorned, unaffected, uncontrived, undesigning, unpretentious, unsophisticated, unwary, unworldly.

antonym artful.

artlessness *n* candour, directness, frankness, genuineness, honesty, humbleness, humility, ingenuousness, innocence, naïveté, naïvety, naturalness, openness, purity, simplicity, sincerity, straightforwardness, trustfulness, unpretentiousness, unwariness, unworldliness.

antonym cunning.

as *conj, prep* because, being, considering that, for example, for instance, given that, in that, in the capacity of, in the character of, in the guise of, in the manner of, in the part of, in the role of, inasmuch as, in view of the fact that, like, seeing that, since, such as, that, to wit, when, while.

as for as regards, in connection with, in reference to, on the subject of, with reference to, with regard to, with relation to, with respect to.

as it were as it might be, in a manner of speaking, in a way, in some way, so to say, so to speak.

ascend *v* clamber up, climb, float up, fly up, gain altitude, go up, lift, lift off, mount, move up, rise, scale, slope upwards, soar, take off, tower.

antonym descend.

ascendancy *n* authority, command, control, dominance, domination, dominion, edge, hegemony, influence, leadership, lordship, mastery, overlordship, power, predominance, pre-eminence, prestige, prevalence, reign, rule, sovereignty, superiority, supremacy, sway, upper hand.

antonyms decline, subordination.

ascendant *adj* ascending, authoritative, climbing, commanding, controlling, dominant, influential, levitating, lifting, mounting, powerful, predominant, pre-eminent, prevailing, rising, ruling, sovereign, superior, supreme, uphill, uppermost.

antonyms descending, subordinate.

ascension *n* arising, ascent, climb, levitation, lifting, mounting, rise, rising.

antonym descent.

ascent *n* acclivity, advancement, ascending, ascension, brae, clamber, clambering, climb, climbing, elevation, escalation, gradient, hill, incline, mounting, rise, rising, scaling, slope.

antonym descent.

ascertain *v* confirm, detect, determine, discover, establish, find out, fix, identify, learn, locate, make certain, settle, verify.

ascetic *n* abstainer, anchorite, celibate, flagellant, hermit, monk, nun, puritan, recluse, solitary, Spartan, stylite.

antonyms epicure, voluptuary.

adj abstemious, abstinent, austere, celibate, continent, frugal, harsh, plain, puritanical, rigorous, self-controlled, self-denying, self-disciplined, severe, simple, Spartan, stern, strict, temperate.

antonyms epicurean, sensual, voluptuous.

asceticism *n* abstemiousness, abstinence, austerity, celibacy, continence, frugality, harshness, moderation, monasticism, plainness, puritanism, rigorousness, rigour, self-abnegation, self-control, self-denial, self-discipline, simplicity, temperance.

antonyms sensuality, voluptuousness.

ascribe *v* accredit, arrogate, assign, attribute, chalk up, charge, credit, impute, put down.

ashamed *adj* abashed, apologetic, bashful, blushing, chagrined, confused, conscience-stricken, crestfallen, discomfited, discomposed, distressed, embarrassed, guilty, humbled, humiliated, mortified, prudish, red in the face, redfaced, remorseful, self-conscious, shamefaced, sheepish, shy, sorry.

antonyms defiant, shameless.

ashen *adj* anemic, ashy, blanched, bleached, colourless, ghastly, grey, leaden, livid, pale, pallid, pasty, wan, white.

antonym ruddy.

aside *adv* alone, apart, away, in isolation, in reserve, on one side, out of the way, privately, secretly, separately.

n departure, digression, excursion, excursus, interpolation, interposition, parenthesis, soliloquy, stage whisper, whisper.

asinine *adj* absurd, boneheaded, brainless, cretinous, daft, doltish, dopey, dumb, dunderheaded, fatuous, feebleminded, foolish, goofy, gormless, half-witted, idiotic, ignorant, imbecile, imbecilic, inane, moronic, senseless, silly, stupid, witless.

antonyms intelligent, sensible.

ask *v* appeal, apply, beg, beseech, bid, claim, clamour, crave, demand, enquire, entreat, implore, importune, indent, interrogate, invite, order, petition, plead, pray, press, query, question, quiz, request, require, seek, solicit, sue, summon, supplicate.

askance *adv* contemptuously, disapprovingly, disdainfully, distrustfully, doubtfully, dubiously, indirectly, mistrustfully, obliquely, sceptically, scornfully, sideways, suspiciously.

askew *adv, adj* agley, aslant, asquint, asymmetrical(ly), awry, cock-eyed, crooked(ly), lopsided(ly), oblique(ly), off-centre, out of line, skew(ed).

asleep *adj* benumbed, catching z's, comatose, dead, dead to the world, dormant, dozing, fast asleep, inactive, in dreamland, inert, in never-never land, napping, numb, out, out for the count, out like a light, reposing, sleeping, slumbering, snoozing, snoring, sound asleep, unconscious.

aspect *n* air, angle, appearance, attitude, bearing, condition, countenance, demeanour, direction, elevation, exposure, expression, face, facet, feature, look, manner, mien, outlook, physiognomy, point of view, perspective, position, prospect, scene, side, standpoint, view, viewpoint, visage.

asperity *n* acerbity, acidity, acrimony, astringency, bitterness, causticity, churlishness, crabbedness, crossness, curtness, harshness, irascibility, irritability, peevishness, roughness, severity, sharpness, sourness, tartness.

antonym mildness.

aspersion *n* abuse, animadversion, bad press, bad rap, calumny, censure, criticism, defamation, denigration, detraction, disparagement, insult, mudslinging, negative hype, obloquy, reproach, slander, slur, smear, traducement, vilification, vituperation.

antonyms commendation, compliment.

asphyxiate *v* burke, choke, garrote, smother, stifle, strangle, strangulate, suffocate, throttle.

aspirant *n* applicant, aspirer, candidate, competitor, contestant, hopeful, postulant, seeker, striver, suitor.

aspiration *n* aim, ambition, desire, dream, eagerness, endeavour, goal, hankering, hope, ideal, intent, longing, object, objective, purpose, wish, yearning.

aspire *v* aim, desire, dream, hanker, hope, intend, long, purpose, pursue, seek, wish, yearn.

aspiring *adj* ambitious, aspirant, eager, endeavouring, enterprising, hopeful, keen, longing, optimistic, striving, wishful, would-be.

asquint *adj, adv* askew, aslant, awry, cockeyed, crooked(ly), indirect(ly), oblique(ly), off-centre, skew(ed).

antonym straight.

ass¹ *n* blockhead, bonehead, cretin, dipstick, dolt, dope, dunce, fool, half-wit, idiot, moron, nincompoop, ninny, nitwit, numskull, schmuck, simpleton, twerp, twit, witless wonder.

ass² *n* burro, donkey, hinny, jackass, jenny, mule.

assail *v* abuse, assault, attack, belabour, berate, beset, bombard, charge, criticize, encounter, fall upon, impugn, invade, lay into, malign, pelt, revile, set about, set upon, strike, vilify.

assailant *n* abuser, adversary, aggressor, assailer, assaulter, attacker, invader, opponent, reviler.

assassin *n* bravo, cutthroat, eliminator, executioner, hatchet man, hired gun, hit man, homicide, killer, liquidator, murderer, ninja, slayer, terminator, thug.

assassinate *v* dispatch, do in, eliminate, hit, kill, knock off, liquidate, murder, rub out, slay, terminate.

assault *n* aggression, attack, blitz, charge, incursion, invasion, offensive, onset, onslaught, raid, storm, storming, strike.

v assail, attack, beset, charge, fall on, hit, invade, lay hands on, set upon, storm, strike.

assay *v* analyse, appraise, assess, estimate, evaluate, examine, inspect, investigate, prove, test, try, weigh.

n analysis, assaying, attempt, endeavour, essay, evaluation, examination, inspection, investigation, test, trial, try, valuation, venture.

assemblage *n* accumulation, aggregation, array, assembly, body, collection, company, congeries, conglomeration, constellation, crowd, flock, galaxy, gathering, group, mass, multitude, rally, throng.

assemble *v* accumulate, amass, build, collect, compose, congregate, construct, convene, convocate, convoke, erect, fabricate, flock, forgather, gather, group, join up, levy, make, manufacture, marshal, meet, mobilize, muster, muster (up), piece together, put together, rally, round up, set up, summon.

antonyms disassemble, disperse, take apart.

assembly *n* agora, assemblage, body, building, collection, company, conclave, conference, congregation, congress, consistory, construction, convention, convocation, council, crowd, diet, divan, ecclesia, erection, fabrication, fitting, flock, folkmoot, gathering, group, indaba, joining, levy, manufacture, mass, meeting, moot, multitude, rally, setting up, synod, throng.

assent *v* accede, accept, acquiesce, agree, allow, approve, concede, concur, consent, grant, permit, sanction, submit, subscribe, yield.

antonym disagree.

n acceptance, accession, accord, acquiescence, agreement, approval, concession, concurrence, consent, permission, sanction, submission.

assert *v* advance, affirm, allege, asseverate, attest, aver, avouch, avow, claim, contend, declare, defend, dogmatize, hold, insist, lay down, maintain, predicate, press, profess, promote, pronounce, protest, say, state, swear, testify to, thrust forward, uphold.

antonym deny.

assertion *n* affirmance, affirmation, allegation, asseveration, attestation, averment, avowal, claim, contention, declaration, dictum, ipse dixit, predication, profession, pronouncement, say-so, statement, word.

antonym denial.

assertive *adj* aggressive, bold, bumptious, confident, decided, dogmatic, emphatic, firm, forceful, forward, insistent, opinionated, self-assured, strong-willed.

antonym diffident.

assertiveness *n* aggressiveness, boldness, bumptiousness, decisiveness, dogmatism, forcefulness, forwardness, insistence, positiveness, self-assurance, self-confidence.

assess *v* appraise, compute, consider, determine, estimate, evaluate, fix, gauge, impose, investigate, judge, levy, rate, review, size up, tax, value, weigh.

assessment *n* appraisal, calculation, consideration, determination, estimate, estimation, evaluation, gauging, judgment, opinion, rating, review, taxation, valuation.

asset *n* advantage, aid, benefit, blessing, bonus, boon, good point, help, plus, resource, service, strength, virtue.

antonym liability.

assets *n* capital, estate, finances, funds, goods, holdings, means, money, possessions, property, reserves, resources, securities, wealth, wherewithal.

asseverate *v* affirm, assert, attest, aver, avouch, avow, certify, declare, maintain, profess, pronounce, protest, state, swear, testify.

asseveration *n* affirmation, assertion, assurance, attestation, averment, avowal, declaration, deposition, predication, profession, pronouncement, protestation, statement, vow.

assiduity *n* application, assiduousness, attentiveness, care, carefulness, conscientiousness, constancy, dedication, devotion, diligence, indefatigability, industriousness, industry, labour, perseverance, persistence, sedulity, sedulousness, steadiness, tirelessness.

antonym negligence.

assiduous *adj* attentive, conscientious, constant, dedicated, devoted, diligent, hardworking, indefatigable, industrious, persevering, persistent, religious, sedulous, steady, studious, unflagging, untiring.

antonym negligent.

assign *v* accredit, allocate, allot, appoint, apportion, arrogate, ascribe, attribute, chalk up, choose, consign, credit, delegate, designate, determine, dispense, distribute, fix, give, grant, impose, name, nominate, put down, select, set, specify.

assignation[1] *n* allocation, allotment, apportionment, lot, portion, share.

assignation[2] *n* appointment, arrangement, date, engagement, meeting, rendezvous, tryst.

assignment *n* allocation, allotment, appointment, apportionment, ascription, attribution, charge, commission, consignment, delegation, designation, determination, dispensation, distribution, duty, errand, giving, grant, imposition, job, mission, nomination, position, post, responsibility, selection, specification, task.

assimilate *v* absorb, accept, acclimatize, accommodate, acculturate, accustom, adapt, adjust, blend, comprehend, conform, digest, fit, homogenize, imbibe, incorporate, ingest, intermix, internalize, learn, merge, mingle, register, take in.

antonym reject.

assimilation *n* absorption, acceptance, acclimatization, accommodation, acculturation, adaptation, adjustment, comprehension, conformity, homogenization, incorporation, ingestion, internalization, learning, registration.

antonym rejection.

assist *v* abet, accommodate, aid, back, benefit, boost, collaborate, co-operate, enable, expedite, facilitate, further, give a hand, give a leg up, help, lend a hand, rally around, reinforce, relieve, second, serve, succour, support, sustain.

antonyms hinder, thwart.

assistance *n* a hand, a leg up, abetment, accommodation, adjutancy, aid, backing, benefit, boost, collaboration, comfort, co-operation, furtherance, help, reinforcement, relief, succour, support, sustainment.

antonyms hindrance, opposition.

assistant *n* abettor, accessory, accomplice, adjutant, aide, ally, ancillary, associate, auxiliary, backer, coadjutor, collaborator, colleague, confederate, co-operator, girl Friday, helper, helpmate, henchman, man Friday, partner, person Friday, right-hand man, second, subordinate, subsidiary, supporter.

associate *v* accompany, affiliate, ally, amalgamate, combine, confederate, conjoin, connect, consort, correlate, couple, deal, fraternize, give the time of day (to), hang around, have anything to do (with), hobnob, identify, join, keep company, league, link, mingle, mix, pair, pass the time of day, relate, socialize, unite, yoke.

n affiliate, ally, assistant, bedfellow, coadjutor, collaborator, colleague, companion, compeer, comrade, confederate, confrère, co-worker, fellow, follower, friend, mate, partner, peer, sidekick.

association *n* affiliation, alliance, analogy, band, bloc, bond, cartel, clique, club, coalition, combination, combine, companionship, company, compound, comradeship, concomitance, confederacy, confederation, connection, consortium, conspiracy, co-operative, corporation, correlation, familiarity, federation, fellowship, fraternization, fraternity, friendship, Gesellschaft, group, intimacy, joining, juxtaposition, league, linkage, organization, pairing, partnership, relation, relations, relationship, resemblance, society, syndicate, syndication, tie, trust, union, Verein.

assorted *adj* different, differing, divergent, divers, diverse, diversified, heterogeneous, manifold, miscellaneous, mixed, motley, multifarious, multiform, several, sundry, varied, variegated, various.

assortment *n* arrangement, array, assemblage, categorization, choice, classification, collection, disposition, distribution, diversity, farrago, grading, grouping, hodgepodge, jumble, medley, mélange, miscellany, mishmash, mixture, pot-pourri, range, ranging, salad, salmagundi, selection, sifting, sorting, variety.

assuage *v* allay, alleviate, appease, calm, dull, ease, lessen, lighten, lower, lull, mitigate, moderate, mollify, pacify, palliate, quench, quiet(en), reduce, relieve, satisfy, slake, soften, soothe, still, tranquillize.
antonym exacerbate.

assume[1] *v* accept, believe, deduce, expect, fancy, guess, hypothesize, imagine, infer, postulate, premise, presume, presuppose, suppose, surmise, suspect, take, take for granted, think, understand.

assume[2] *v* accept, acquire, adopt, affect, appropriate, arrogate, bear, commandeer, counterfeit, don, embrace, expropriate, fake, feign, pre-empt, pretend (to), put on, seize, sham, shoulder, simulate, strike, take, take on, take over, take up, undertake, usurp.

assumed *adj* affected, bogus, counterfeit, fake, false, feigned, fictitious, hypothetical, made-up, phony, pretended, pseudonymous, sham, simulated, specious, spurious.

assuming *adj* arrogant, audacious, bold, brassy, brazen, bumptious, cocksure, conceited, forward, impertinent, impudent, overassertive, overconfident, presumptuous, pretentious, pushy, self-assertive, self-assured, self-important.
antonym unassuming.

assumption[1] *n* belief, conjecture, expectation, fancy, guess, guesswork, hypothesis, inference, postulate, postulation, premise, presupposition, supposition, surmise, suspicion, theory, understanding.

assumption[2] *n* acceptance, acquisition, adoption, appropriation, arrogation, expropriation, pre-emption, seizure, usurpation.

assumption[3] *n* arrogance, audacity, brass, bumptiousness, conceit, gall, imposition, impudence, nerve, presumption, presumptuousness, pride, self-assuredness, self-importance.

assurance *n* affirmation, aplomb, assertion, asseveration, assuredness, audacity, boldness, certainty, certitude, chutzpah, confidence, conviction, coolness, courage, declaration, firmness, gall, guarantee, nerve, oath, pledge, poise, positiveness, profession, promise, protestation, security, self-assurance, self-confidence, self-reliance, sureness, vow, word.
antonym uncertainty.

assure *v* affirm, attest, boost, certify, clinch, comfort, confirm, convince, embolden, encourage, ensure, guarantee, hearten, persuade, pledge, promise, reassure, seal, secure, soothe, strengthen, swear, tell, vow.

assured *adj* assertive, audacious, bold, brassy, certain, clinched, cocksure, confident, confirmed, definite, ensured, fixed, guaranteed, indisputable, indubitable, in the bag, irrefutable, overconfident, pert, poised, positive, sealed, secure, self-assured, self-confident, self-possessed, settled, sure, unquestionable.
antonym uncertain.

assuredly *adv* certainly, definitely, indisputably, indubitably, irrefutably, surely, truly, undoubtedly, unquestionably, without doubt.

astir *adv, adj* active, afoot, around, awake, busy, circulating, in motion, in the air, roused, up, up and about.

astonish *v* amaze, astound, awe, baffle, bewilder, blow away, confound, daze, dazzle, dumfound, electrify, flabbergast, floor, knock the socks off, nonplus, shock, stagger, startle, stun, stupefy, surprise, take (someone's) breath away, wow.

astonished *adj* aghast, amazed, astounded, awed, baffled, bewildered, blown away, bug-eyed, confounded, dazed, dazzled, dumfounded, electrified, flabbergasted, floored, gaping, incredulous, nonplussed, shocked, staggered, startled, stunned, surprised, thunderstruck.

astonishing *adj* amazing, astounding, awesome, baffling, bewildering, breathtaking, dazzling, electrifying, extraordinary, impressive, incredible, prodigious, shocking, staggering, startling, striking, stunning, stupefying, stupendous, surprising, unbelievable, wondrous.

astonishment *n* amazement, awe, bafflement, bewilderment, confusion, consternation, dismay, shock, stupefaction, surprise, wonder, wonderment.

astound v amaze, astonish, awe, baffle, bewilder, blow away, boggle, confound, daze, dazzle, dumfound, electrify, flabbergast, floor, knock the socks off, overwhelm, shake, shock, stagger, stun, stupefy, surprise, wow.

astounded adj amazed, awed, baffled, bewildered, blown away, boggled, bug-eyed, confounded, dazed, dazzled, dumfounded, electrified, flabbergasted, floored, incredulous, overwhelmed, shaken, shocked, staggered, stunned, stupefied, thunderstruck, wonderstruck, wowed.

astounding adj amazing, astonishing, baffling, bewildering, boggling, breathtaking, dazzling, electrifying, impressive, incredible, mind-boggling, overwhelming, prodigious, shocking, staggering, striking, stunning, stupefying, stupendous, surprising, unbelievable.

astray adv adrift, amiss, awry, lost, off course, off the mark, off the rails, off (the) track, to the bad, wide, wrong.

astringent adj acerb, acerbic, acid, austere, biting, caustic, contractile, contractive, exacting, grim, hard, harsh, puckery, rigorous, scathing, severe, stern, strict, stringent, styptic, trenchant.
antonym bland.

astronomical adj astrophysical, celestial, cosmological, enormous, high, huge, Uranian.

astronomy n astrodynamics, astrography, astrophysics, cosmography, cosmology, star-gazing, uranography, uranology.

astute adj acute, adroit, artful, calculating, canny, clever, crafty, cunning, discerning, foxy, intelligent, keen, knowing, penetrating, perceptive, percipient, perspicacious, politic, prudent, sagacious, sharp, shrewd, sly, smart, subtle, wily, wise.
antonym stupid.

astuteness n acumen, acuteness, adroitness, artfulness, canniness, cleverness, craftiness, cunning, discernment, insight, intelligence, keenness, penetration, perceptiveness, percipience, perspicacity, prudence, sagacity, sharpness, shrewdness, slyness, smartness, subtlety, wiliness.
antonym stupidity.

asunder adv apart, in half, in pieces, in twain, in two, into pieces, to bits, to pieces.

asylum n cover, harbour, haven, hospital, institution, mental hospital, refuge, retreat, safety, sanctuary, shelter.

asymmetrical adj awry, crooked, disproportionate, dissymmetric, gibbous, irregular, lopsided, skew(ed), unbalanced, unequal, uneven, unmatched, unsymmetrical.
antonym symmetrical.

asymmetry n disproportion, dissymmetry, imbalance, inequality, irregularity, lopsidedness, skewness, unevenness.
antonym symmetry.

at
For phrases such as at a loss, at bay, at fault, see the first noun after at.

atheism n disbelief, godlessness, impiety, infidelity, irreligion, non-belief, rationalism, scepticism, unbelief.

atheist n disbeliever, irreligionist, naturalist, non-believer, rationalist, sceptic, unbeliever.

atheistic adj disbelieving, godless, impious, irreligious, irreverent, rationalistic, sceptical, unbelieving, unreligious.
antonym religious.

athlete n agonist, competitor, contender, contestant, gymnast, jock, runner, sportif, sportsman, sportswoman.

athletic adj active, brawny, energetic, fit, husky, muscular, powerful, robust, sinewy, sportif, strapping, strong, sturdy, thewy, vigorous, well-knit, well-proportioned, wiry.
antonym bookish, inactive, puny, weak.

athletics n agonistics, callisthenics, contests, events, exercises, games, gymnastics, races, sports, track events.

atmosphere n aerospace, aerosphere, air, ambience, aura, character, climate, environment, feel, feeling, flavour, heavens, milieu, mood, quality, sky, spirit, surroundings, tenor, tone, vibrations.

atmospheric adj aerial, climatic, meteorological.

atom n bit, crumb, grain, hint, iota, jot, mite, molecule, morsel, particle, scintilla, scrap, shred, smidgen, speck, spot, tittle, trace, whit.

atone v compensate, expiate, make amends, make right, make satisfaction for, make up for, offset, pay for, propitiate, put right, recompense, reconcile, redeem, redress, remedy.

atonement n amends, compensation, expiation, indemnity, payment, penance, propitiation, recompense, redress, reparation, repayment, restitution, restoration, satisfaction.

atrocious adj abominable, appalling, awful, barbaric, brutal, criminal, cruel, diabolical, evil, execrable, fell, fiendish, flagitious, ghastly, grievous, heinous, hideous, horrific, horrible, horrifying, infamous, infernal, inhuman, monstrous, ruthless, savage, shocking, terrible, unspeakable, vicious, vile, villainous, wicked.

atrocity n abomination, atrociousness, barbarity, barbarousness, brutality, crime, cruelty, enormity, evil, flagitiousness, ghastliness, heinousness, hideousness, horror, infamy, inhumanity, monstrosity, monstrousness, outrage, ruthlessness, savagery, viciousness, vileness, villainy, wickedness.

atrophy n decay, decline, degeneration, deterioration, diminution, emaciation, marasmus, shrivelling, tabes, tabescence, wasting, withering.
v decay, decline, degenerate, deteriorate, diminish, dwindle, emaciate, fade, shrink, shrivel, waste, wither.

attach *v* add, adhere, affix, annex, append, ascribe, assign, associate, attract, attribute, belong, bind, captivate, connect, couple, fasten, fix, impute, join, link, place, put, secure, stick, tie, unite, weld.

antonyms detach, unfasten.

attached *adj* affectionate, affiliated, associated, close, connected, fond, involved, loving.

attachment *n* accessory, accoutrement, adapter, addition, adhesion, adjunct, affection, affinity, allegiance, annexation, appendage, appurtenance, attraction, bond, closeness, codicil, confiscation, connection, connector, coupling, devotion, esteem, extension, extra, fastener, fastening, fidelity, fitting, fixture, fondness, friendship, involvement, joint, junction, juncture, liking, link, love, loyalty, partiality, predilection, regard, seizure, supplement, tenderness, tie.

attack *n* abuse, access, aggression, assailment, assault, attempt, bash, battery, blitz, bombardment, bout, broadside, censure, charge, convulsion, criticism, fit, foray, impugnment, incursion, inroad, invasion, invective, kamikaze, offensive, onset, onslaught, paroxysm, raid, rush, seizure, spasm, spell, strike, stroke.

v abuse, assail, assault, bash, belabour, berate, blame, blast, censure, charge, chastise, criticize, crucify, denounce, dig into, dive into, dump on, fall on, flay, go after, have at, have one's knife in, impugn, invade, inveigh against, jump on, lash, lay into, light into, make at, malign, mob, plunge into, raid, rate, revile, rush, set about, set on, snipe at, stick it to, storm, strafe, strike, tuck into, vilify, visit, wade into.

attacker *n* abuser, aggressor, assailant, assaulter, critic, invader, mugger, persecutor, raider, reviler, traducer.

antonyms defender, protector, supporter.

attain *v* accomplish, achieve, acquire, arrive at, bag, compass, complete, earn, effect, fulfil, gain, get, grasp, net, obtain, procure, reach, realize, secure, touch, win.

attainable *adj* accessible, achievable, available, doable, feasible, fulfillable, graspable, manageable, obtainable, possible, potential, practicable, probable, procurable, reachable, realistic, within reach.

antonyms out of reach, unattainable.

attainment *n* ability, accomplishment, achievement, acquirement, acquisition, art, competence, completion, consummation, feat, fulfilment, mastery, procurement, reaching, realization, skill, success.

attempt *n* assault, assay, attack, bash, bid, coup d'essai, crack, effort, endeavour, essay, experiment, move, push, shot, stab, struggle, trial, try, undertaking, venture.

v aspire, endeavour, essay, experiment, have a bash, have a crack, have a shot, seek, strive, tackle, take a stab at, try, try one's hand at, try one's luck at, undertake, venture.

attend *v* accompany, appear, arise from, assist, be all ears, be in attendance (at), be present, care for, chaperone, companion, concentrate, conduct, convoy, escort, follow, frequent, give ear, go (along) with, guard, hear, hearken, heed, help, lend a hand to, lend an ear, listen, look after, mark, mind, minister to, note, notice, nurse, observe, pay attention, pay heed, regard, result from, see (to), serve, show up (at), squire, study at, succour, take care of, tend, turn out (for or to), usher, visit, wait on, watch, worship at.

attend to concentrate on, control, cope with, deal with, direct, handle, look after, manage, oversee, see to, supervise, take care of, take on.

attendance *n* accompaniment, appearance, assistance, attending, audience, crowd, escort, gate, house, ministration, presence, service, showing, turnout, waiting.

attendant *n* acolyte, aide, assistant, auxiliary, batman, butler, chaperone, clerk, companion, custodian, equerry, escort, famulus, flunkey, follower, gentleman's gentleman, guard, guide, helper, lackey, lady-in-waiting, lady's-maid, livery servant, marshal, menial, page, retainer, servant, steward, underling, usher, valet, waiter.

adj accessory, accompanying, associated, attached, concomitant, consequent, ensuing, incidental, related, resultant, subsequent.

attention *n* alertness, attentiveness, awareness, care, civility, concentration, concern, consciousness, consideration, courtesy, deference, ear, gallantry, heed, heedfulness, intentness, mindfulness, ministration, notice, observation, politeness, recognition, regard, respect, service, thought, thoughtfulness, treatment, vigilance.

antonyms disregard, inattention.

attentive *adj* accommodating, alert, awake, careful, civil, concentrating, concerned, conscientious, considerate, courteous, deferential, devoted, gallant, gracious, heedful, helpful, intent, kind, mindful, obliging, observant, polite, regardant, solicitous, studious, thoughtful, vigilant, watchful.

antonyms heedless, inattentive, inconsiderate.

attenuate *v* adulterate, debase, decrease, devaluate, dilute, diminish, draw out, elongate, enervate, enfeeble, extend, lengthen, rarefy, reduce, refine, sap, spin out, stretch out, taper, thin, thin out, water down, weaken.

antonyms concentrate, intensify, strengthen, thicken.

attest (to) *v* adjure, affirm, assert, asseverate, authenticate, aver, back up, bear out, bespeak, certify, confirm, corroborate, declare, demonstrate, depose, endorse, evidence, manifest, prove, ratify, seal, show, substantiate, swear, testify, verify, vouch, warrant, witness.

attestation *n* affirmation, asseveration, assurance, averment, avowal, certification, confirmation, corroboration, declaration, deposition, endorsement, evidence, testification, testimony, vouch, witness.

attire *n* accoutrements, apparel, array, caparison, clothes, clothing, costume, dress, duds, finery, garb, garments, gear, get-up, habiliments, habit, outfit, raiment, robes, togs, uniform, vestment, wear, weeds.
v accoutre, adorn, apparel, array, caparison, clothe, costume, deck out, dress, equip, fit out, garb, outfit, prepare, robe, turn out, uniform.

attitude *n* affectation, air, approach, aspect, bearing, carriage, condition, demeanour, disposition, feeling, manner, mien, mindset, mood, opinion, outlook, perspective, point of view, pose, position, posture, stance, view, Weltanschauung.

attract *v* allure, appeal to, bewitch, captivate, charm, decoy, draw, enchant, engage, entice, fascinate, incline, induce, interest, inveigle, invite, lure, pull, seduce, tempt.
antonym repel.

attraction *n* allure, amenity, appeal, attractiveness, bait, captivation, charisma, charm, crowd-puller, draw, enchantment, entertainment, enticement, event, fascination, inducement, interest, invitation, lure, magnetism, pull, seduction, show, sight, temptation.
antonym repulsion.

attractive *adj* agreeable, alluring, appealing, beautiful, captivating, catchy, charismatic, charming, comely, cute, enchanting, engaging, enticing, fair, fascinating, fetching, glamorous, good-looking, gorgeous, handsome, interesting, inviting, lovely, magnetic, nubile, personable, pleasant, pleasing, prepossessing, pretty, seductive, stunning, tempting, toothsome, voluptuous, winning, winsome.
antonyms plug-ugly, repellent, unattractive.

attribute *v* accredit, apply, arrogate, ascribe, assign, blame, charge, credit, impute, put down, refer.
n affection, aspect, character, characteristic, facet, feature, idiosyncrasy, mark, peculiarity, point, property, quality, quirk, sign, symbol, trait, virtue.

attribution *n* accreditation, application, ascription, assignment, charge, crediting, imputation.

attrition *n* abrasion, attenuation, chafing, debilitation, detrition, erosion, fretting, friction, gradual loss, grinding, harassment, harrying, rubbing, scraping, weakening, wear, wearing away, wearing down.

attune *v* acclimatize, accustom, adapt, adjust, assimilate, co-ordinate, familiarize, harmonize, modulate, reconcile, regulate, set, tune.

atypical *adj* aberrant, abnormal, anomalous, deviant, different, divergent, eccentric, exceptional, extraordinary, freakish, irregular, unexpected, untypical, unusual.
antonym typical.

auburn *adj* chestnut, copper, henna, nutbrown, red, russet, rust, tawny, titian.

audacious *adj* adventuresome, adventurous, assuming, assured, bold, brassy, brave, brazen, cheeky, courageous, dare-devil, daring, dauntless, death-defying, disrespectful, fearless, forward, impertinent, impudent, insolent, intrepid, nervy, pert, plucky, presumptuous, rash, reckless, risky, rude, saucy, shameless, unabashed, valiant, venturesome.
antonyms cautious, reserved, timid.

audacity *n* adventuresomeness, adventurousness, assurance, audaciousness, boldness, brass, bravery, brazenness, cheek, chutzpah, courage, daring, dauntlessness, defiance, derring-do, effrontery, fearlessness, foolhardiness, forwardness, gall, guts, impertinence, impudence, insolence, intrepidity, nerve, pertness, presumption, rashness, recklessness, rudeness, sauce, shamelessness, valour, venturesomeness.
antonyms caution, reserve, timidity.

audible *adj* appreciable, clear, detectable, discernible, distinct, hearable, perceptible, recognizable.
antonym inaudible.

audience *n* assemblage, assembly, auditorium, congregation, crowd, devotees, fans, following, gallery, gathering, hearers, hearing, house, interview, listeners, market, meeting, onlookers, public, readers, reception, spectators, turnout, viewers.

audit *n* analysis, balancing, check, checking, cross-check, examination, inspection, investigation, review, scrutiny, statement, verification.
v analyse, attend, balance, check, cross-check, examine, inspect, investigate, review, scrutinize, sit in on, verify.

auditor *n* accountant, actuary, analyst, examiner, inspector, scrutinizer.

au fait abreast of, acquainted, au courant, clued in, conversant, hip, in the know, in the swim, in touch, knowledgeable, on the ball, posted, up-to-date, well up, well-informed.

augment *v* add to, amplify, boost, dilate, eke out, enhance, enlarge, expand, extend, grow, heighten, increase, inflate, intensify, magnify, multiply, raise, reinforce, strengthen, supplement, swell.
antonym decrease.

augur *n* auspex, divinator, diviner, oracle, prognosticator, prophet, seer, soothsayer.
v bespeak, betoken, bode, forebode, foreshadow, foretoken, harbinger, herald, import, portend, predict, prefigure, presage, promise, prophesy, signify.

augury *n* auspice, divination, foreboding, forerunner, forewarning, fortunetelling, harbinger, haruspication, herald, interpretation, omen, portent, precursor, prediction, presage, prodrome, prognostication, promise, prophecy, reading, sign, soothsaying, token, warning.

august *adj* awful, dignified, exalted, glorious, grand, imposing, impressive, lofty, magnificent, majestic, monumental, noble, regal, revered, solemn, splendid, stately, venerable.

aura *n* air, ambience, aroma, atmosphere, effluvium, emanation, feel, feeling, hint, mood, nimbus, odour, quality, scent, suggestion, vibes, vibrations.

auspices *n* aegis, authority, backing, care, championship, charge, control, guidance, influence, oversight, patronage, protection, responsibility, sponsorship, superintendence, supervision, support, tutelage, umbrella.

auspicious *adj* bright, encouraging, favourable, felicitous, fortunate, happy, hopeful, lucky, opportune, optimistic, promising, propitious, rosy.

antonyms inauspicious, ominous.

austere *adj* abstemious, abstinent, ascetic, astringent, bleak, chaste, cold, conservative, continent, Dantean, Dantesque, economical, exacting, forbidding, formal, frugal, grave, grim, hard, harsh, inflexible, plain, puritanical, restrained, rigid, rigorous, self-denying, self-disciplined, serious, severe, simple, sober, solemn, spare, Spartan, stark, stern, strict, stringent, unadorned, unembellished, unornamented.

antonyms elaborate, extravagant, genial.

austerity *n* abstemiousness, abstinence, asceticism, chasteness, chastity, coldness, continence, economy, formality, frugality, gravity, grimness, hardness, harshness, inflexibility, plainness, puritanism, reserve, restraint, rigidity, rigour, self-control, self-denial, self-discipline, seriousness, severity, simplicity, sobriety, solemnity, spareness, Spartanism, starkness, sternness, strictness, stringency.

antonyms elaborateness, extravagant, geniality.

authentic *adj* accurate, actual, authoritative, bona fide, certain, credible, dependable, factual, faithful, genuine, honest, kosher, legitimate, original, pure, real, reliable, simon-pure, true, true-to-life, trustworthy, valid, veracious, veritable.

antonyms counterfeit, inauthentic, spurious.

authenticate *v* accredit, attest, authorize, avouch, certify, confirm, corroborate, endorse, guarantee, validate, verify, vouch for, warrant.

authentication *n* accreditation, attestation, authorization, certification, confirmation, corroboration, endorsement, guarantee, validation, verification, voucher, warrant.

authenticity *n* accuracy, actuality, authoritativeness, certainty, correctness, credibility, dependability, factualness, faithfulness, fidelity, genuineness, honesty, legitimacy, purity, reality, realness, reliability, trustworthiness, truth, truthfulness, validity, veracity, veritableness, verity.

antonyms invalidity, spuriousness.

author *n* architect, begetter, composer, creator, designer, dramatist, fabricator, fashioner, father, forger, founder, framer, initiator, inventor, maker, mover, novelist, originator, parent, pen, penman, penwoman, planner, playwright, poet, prime mover, producer, writer.

authoritarian *n* absolutist, autocrat, despot, dictator, disciplinarian, fascist, tyrant.

adj absolute, autocratic, despotic, dictatorial, disciplinarian, doctrinaire, dogmatic, domineering, harsh, heavy, imperious, inflexible, oppressive, repressive, right-wing, rigid, severe, strict, tyrannical, unyielding.

antonym liberal.

▲ *confusable word* authoritative.

authoritarianism *n* absolutism, autocracy, despotism, dictatorship, fascism, totalitarianism, tyranny.

antonyms laissez faire, liberalism.

authoritative *adj* accepted, accurate, approved, assured, authentic, authorized, cathedral, commanding, confident, convincing, decisive, definitive, dependable, factual, faithful, learned, legitimate, magisterial, masterly, official, reliable, sanctioned, scholarly, sound, sovereign, true, trustworthy, truthful, valid, veritable.

antonym unreliable.

▲ *confusable word* authoritarian.

authoritatively *adv* accurately, commandingly, conclusively, confidently, convincingly, decisively, ex cathedra, legitimately, magisterially, officially, reliably, soundly.

authority[1] *n* administration, ascendancy, attestation, authorization, charge, command, control, domination, dominion, evidence, force, government, imperium, influence, jurisdiction, justification, licence, management, might, officialdom, permission, permit, power, pre-eminence, prerogative, responsibility, right, rule, sanction, say-so, sovereignty, statement, strength, supremacy, sway, testimony, textbook, warrant, weight, word.

authority[2] *n* arbiter, bible, connoisseur, expert, judge, leader, master, professional, pundit, sage, scholar, specialist.

authorization *n* accreditation, approval, certification, commission, confirmation, go-ahead, green light, leave, licence, mandate, permission, permit, ratification, sanction, warrant.

authorize *v* accredit, allow, approve, commission, confirm, consent to, countenance, empower, enable, entitle, legalize, license, mandate, permit, ratify, sanction, validate, warrant.

autocracy *n* absolutism, autarchy, authoritarianism, despotism, dictatorship, fascism, Hitlerism, totalitarianism, tyranny.

antonym democracy.

autocrat *n* absolutist, autarch, authoritarian, Caesar, despot, dictator, fascist, Hitler, khan, panjandrum, totalitarian, tyrant.

autocratic *adj* absolute, all-powerful, autarchic, authoritarian, despotic, dictatorial, domineering, imperious, overbearing, totalitarian, tyrannical, tyrannous.

antonyms democratic, liberal.

automatic *adj* automated, certain, habitual, inescapable, inevitable, instinctive, involuntary, knee-jerk, mechanical, mechanized, natural, necessary, perfunctory, push-button, reflex, robot, robotlike, routine, self-acting, self-activating, self-moving, self-propelling, self-regulating, spontaneous, unavoidable, unbidden, unconscious, unthinking, unwilled, vegetative.

automaton *n* machine, mechanical man, robot.

autonomous *adj* autarkic, free, independent, self-determining, self-governing, self-ruling, sovereign, voluntary.

antonym subject.

autonomy *n* autarky, free will, freedom, home rule, independence, self-determination, self-government, self-rule, sovereignty.

antonyms compulsion, subjection.

auxiliary *adj* accessory, aiding, ancillary, assistant, assisting, backup, emergency, for reinforcement, helping, reinforcing, reserve, secondary, spare, subsidiary, substitute, supplementary, supporting, supportive.

n accessory, accomplice, ally, ancillary, assistant, associate, backup, companion, confederate, helper, partner, reinforcement, reserve, second, subordinate, substitute, supporter.

avail *v* advance, aid, assist, benefit, boot, help, profit, serve, work.

n advantage, aid, assistance, benefit, boot, good, help, profit, purpose, service, use, value.

avail oneself of capitalize on, exploit, make the most of, make use of, profit by, profit from, take advantage of, turn to account, use, utilize.

available *adj* accessible, at hand, convenient, disengaged, free, handy, obtainable, on hand, on tap, procurable, ready, to hand, unbooked, unoccupied, unreserved, vacant, within reach.

antonyms spoken for, unavailable.

avalanche *n* barrage, cascade, cataclysm, deluge, flood, inundation, landslide, rockslide, snowslide, torrent.

avant-garde *adj* advanced, adventurous, enterprising, experimental, far out, forward-looking, innovative, inventive, pioneering, progressive, unconventional, way out.

antonyms conservative, dyed-in-the-wool.

avarice *n* acquisitiveness, cheeseparing, covetousness, cupidity, greed, greediness, meanness, miserliness, money-grubbing, niggardliness, parsimoniousness, parsimony, penny-pinching, penuriousness, predatoriness, rapacity, stinginess, tight-fistedness.

antonym generosity.

avaricious *adj* acquisitive, cheeseparing, covetous, grasping, greedy, mean, miserable, miserly, money-grubbing, niggardly, parsimonious, penny-pinching, penurious, predatory, rapacious, Scroogelike, stingy, tight, tight-fisted.

antonym generous.

avenge *v* exact justice for, punish, repay, requite, take revenge for, take vengeance for, vindicate.

avengement *n* punishment, repayment, reprisal, requital, retaliation, retribution, revenge, vengeance.

avenger *n* punisher, requiter, retributor, vindicator.

avenging *adj* retaliatory, retributive, talionic, vengeful, vindictive.

avenue *n* access, alley, approach, boulevard, channel, course, drive, driveway, entrance, entrée, entry, means, pass, passage, path, pathway, road, route, street, thoroughfare, vista, walk, way.

aver *v* affirm, allege, assert, asseverate, attest, avouch, avow, declare, insist, maintain, profess, protest, say, state, swear, testify, witness.

average *n* commonplace, mean, mediocrity, medium, midpoint, norm, par, rule, run-of-the-mill, standard.

antonyms exception, extreme.

adj common, commonplace, everyday, fair, garden-variety, general, indifferent, intermediate, mean, medial, median, mediocre, medium, middle, middling, moderate, normal, ordinary, passable, regular, run-of-the-mill, satisfactory, so-so, standard, tolerable, typical, undistinguished, unexceptional, unremarkable, usual.

antonyms exceptional, extreme.

averse *adj* antagonistic, antipathetic, disinclined, hostile, ill-disposed, inimical, loath, opposed, reluctant, unsympathetic, unwilling.

antonyms sympathetic, willing.

▲ *confusable word* adverse.

aversion *n* abhorrence, abomination, anathema, animosity, antagonism, antipathy, detestation, disapproval, disgust, disinclination, dislike, distaste, hate, hatred, horror, hostility, loathing, odium, opposition, phobia, repugnance, repulsion, revulsion, unwillingness.

antonyms liking, sympathy.

avert *v* avoid, deflect, evade, fend off, foil, forestall, frustrate, obviate, parry, preclude, prevent, stave off, turn, turn aside, turn away, ward off.

aviation *n* aeronautics, flight, flying.

aviator *n* ace, aeronaut, airman, airwoman, bush pilot, flier, pilot.

avid *adj* acquisitive, ardent, avaricious, covetous, dedicated, devoted, eager, enthusiastic, fanatical, fervent, grasping, greedy, hungry, insatiable, intense, keen, passionate, rapacious, ravenous, thirsty, voracious, zealous.

antonym indifferent.

avidity *n* acquisitiveness, ardour, avarice, covetousness, craving, cupidity, desire, devotion, eagerness, enthusiasm, fanaticism, fervour, greed, greediness, hankering, hunger, insatiability, intensity, keenness, longing, passion, rapacity, ravenousness, thirst, voracity, zeal.

antonym indifference.

avocation *n* business, calling, distraction, diversion, employment, hobby, interest, job, occupation, pastime, profession, pursuit, recreation, relaxation, sideline, trade, vocation, work.

avoid *v* abstain from, avert, balk at, bypass, circumvent, dodge, duck, elude, escape, eschew, evade, get out of, give a wide berth to, keep from, obviate, prevent, refrain from, shirk, shun, sidestep, steer clear of.

avoidable *adj* avertible, eludible, escapable, evadable, evitable, preventable, unnecessary.
antonym inevitable.

avoidance *n* abstention, abstinence, circumvention, dodge, dodging, eluding, elusion, escape, eschewal, evasion, prevention, refraining, shirking, shunning.

avow *v* acknowledge, admit, affirm, assert, asseverate, attest, aver, confess, declare, maintain, own, proclaim, profess, recognize, state, swear, testify.

avowal *n* acknowledgment, admission, affirmation, assertion, asseveration, attestation, averment, confession, declaration, oath, owning, proclamation, profession, recognition, statement, swearing, testimony.

avowed *adj* acknowledged, admitted, card-carrying, confessed, declared, open, overt, professed, self-confessed, self-proclaimed, sworn.

avowedly *adv* admittedly, candidly, confessedly, frankly, openly, overtly, professedly.
antonym secretly.

await *v* anticipate, be in store for, expect, hope for, lie in wait for, look for, look forward to, wait for.

awake *v* arouse, awaken, rouse, wake, wake up.
adj alert, alive, aroused, astir, attentive, awakened, aware, conscious, heedful, observant, on the ball, on the stick, responsive, sensitive, vigilant, wakeful, waking, watchful, wide awake.

awaken *v* activate, alert, animate, arouse, awake, call forth, enliven, evoke, excite, fan, inspire, kindle, prompt, provoke, revive, rouse, stimulate, stir up, unearth, vivify, wake, waken.
antonyms lull, quell, quench.

awakening *n* activation, animation, arousal, awaking, birth, enlivening, evocation, inspiration, kindling, prompting, provocation, revival, rousing, stimulation, vivification, wakening, waking.

award *v* accord, adjudge, allot, allow, apportion, assign, bestow, confer, distribute, endow, gift, give, grant, present.
n adjudication, allotment, allowance, bestowal, conferment, conferral, decision, decoration, dispensation, endowment, gift, grant, judgment, order, presentation, prize, trophy.

aware *adj* acquainted, alive to, appreciative, apprised, attentive, au courant, cognizant, conscious, conversant, enlightened, familiar, heedful, hip, informed, knowing, knowledgeable, mindful, observant, on the ball, on the qui vive, sensible, sensitive, sentient, sharp, shrewd.
antonyms insensitive, unaware.

awareness *n* acquaintance, appreciation, attention, cognizance, consciousness, enlightenment, familiarity, knowledge, observation, perception, realization, recognition, sensibility, sensitivity, sentience, understanding.
antonyms insensitivity, unawareness.

awe *n* admiration, amazement, apprehension, astonishment, dread, fear, respect, reverence, veneration, wonder, wonderment.
antonym contempt.
v amaze, astonish, cow, daunt, frighten, impress, intimidate, overwhelm, stun, terrify.

awe-inspiring *adj* amazing, astonishing, awesome, awful, breathtaking, daunting, fearsome, formidable, impressive, intimidating, magnificent, overwhelming, terrible, wonderful, wondrous.
antonyms contemptible, tame.

awesome *adj* alarming, amazing, astonishing, august, awe-inspiring, awful, breathtaking, daunting, dread, dreadful, fearful, fearsome, formidable, frightening, imposing, impressive, intimidating, magnificent, majestic, moving, overwhelming, redoubtable, solemn, stunning, stupefying, stupendous, terrible, terrifying, wonderful, wondrous.

awe-struck *adj* afraid, amazed, astonished, awed, breathless, cowed, daunted, dumfounded, fearful, frightened, impressed, intimidated, overwhelmed, speechless, struck dumb, stunned, terrified, wonder-struck.

awful *adj* abysmal, alarming, amazing, appalling, atrocious, august, awe-inspiring, awesome, dire, disgusting, dread, dreadful, fearful, fearsome, frightful, ghastly, gruesome, harrowing, hideous, horrendous, horrible, horrific, horrifying, majestic, nasty, shocking, solemn, terrible, ugly, unbearable, unpleasant, woeful, wretched.

awfully *adv* abysmally, appallingly, atrociously, badly, disgracefully, disgustingly, disputably, dreadfully, exceedingly, exceptionally, excessively, extremely, greatly, immensely, inadequately, quite, reprehensibly, shockingly, shoddily, terribly, unforgivably, unpleasantly, very, wickedly, woefully, wretchedly.

awkward *adj* all thumbs, annoying, blundering, bungling, butter-fingered, clownish, clumsy, compromising, cubbish, cumbersome, delicate, difficult, disobliging, embarrassed, embarrassing, exasperating, farouche, fiddly, gauche, gawky, graceless, ham-fisted, ill at ease, inconvenient, inelegant, inept, inexpedient, inexpert, inopportune, intractable, klutzy, maladroit, painful, perplexing, perverse, prickly, risky, sticky, thorny, ticklish, touchy, troublesome, uncomfortable, unco-operative, unco-ordinated, uncouth, underfoot, ungainly, ungraceful, unhandy, unhelpful, unmanageable, unpleasant, unrefined, unskilful, untimely, untoward, unwieldy, vexatious, vexing.

antonyms amenable, convenient, elegant, graceful, straightforward.

awkwardness *n* clumsiness, coarseness, cumbersomeness, delicacy, difficulty, discomfort, embarrassment, fiddliness, gaucheness, gaucherie, gawkiness, gracelessness, inconvenience, inelegance, ineptitude, intractability, klutziness, maladroitness, painfulness, perversity, prickliness, risk, riskiness, stiffness, touchiness, troublesomeness, unco-operativeness, uneasiness, ungainliness, unhandiness, unhelpfulness, unmanageability, unpleasantness, untimeliness, unwieldiness, vexatiousness.
antonyms amenability, convenience, elegance, grace, straightforwardness.

awning *n* baldachin, canopy, covering, sunshade, tarpaulin, windbreak.

awry *adv, adj* agley, amiss, askew, asymmetrical, cock-eyed, crooked, misaligned, oblique, off-centre, out of kilter, skew(ed), twisted, uneven, unevenly, wonky, wrong.
antonyms straight, symmetrical.

axe *v* cancel, chop, cleave, cut, cut back (or off or down), discharge, discontinue, dismiss, eliminate, fell, fire, get rid of, hew, remove, sack, split, terminate, throw out, withdraw.

axiom *n* adage, aphorism, apothegm, byword, dictum, epigram, fundamental, gnome, maxim, postulate, precept, principle, proverb, truism, truth.

axiomatic *adj* absolute, accepted, aphoristic, apodictic, apothegmatic, assumed, certain, epigrammatic, fundamental, given, gnomic, indubitable, manifest, presupposed, proverbial, self-evident, taken for granted, understood, unquestioned.

axis *n* alliance, arbor, axle, bloc, centre line, coalition, compact, entente, league, longitude, pact, pivot, plumb line, shaft, spindle, vertical.

axle *n* arbor, axis, hinge, mandrel, pin, pivot, shaft, spindle.

B

babble *v* blab, burble, chatter, gabble, gibber, gurgle, jabber, mumble, murmur, prate, prattle, purl, twaddle.

n babel, burble, chatter, clamour, drivel, gabble, gibberish, gurgle, murmur, prattle, purl, purling, twaddle.

babbling *adj* burbling, chattering, drivelling, drooling, gabbling, gibbering, gurgling, incoherent, jabbering, long-tongued, murmuring, prattling, rambling, unintelligible.

babe *n* baby, bairn, child, infant, newborn, nursling, papoose, suckling, wean, weanling, youngling.

babel *n* babble, bedlam, chaos, clamour, commotion, confusion, din, disorder, hubbub, hullabaloo, pandemonium, tumult, turmoil, uproar.

antonyms calm, order.

baby *n* babe, bairn, child, infant, newborn, nursling, papoose, suckling, toddler, weanling, youngling.

adj babyish, childish, diminutive, dwarf, immature, Lilliputian, little, midget, mini, miniature, minute, new, newborn, pygmy, small, small-scale, tiny, toy, young, wee.

v coddle, cosset, humour, indulge, mollycoddle, overindulge, pamper, pander to, pet, spoil, spoon-feed.

babyish *adj* baby, childish, foolish, immature, infantile, jejune, juvenile, naïve, namby-pamby, puerile, regressive, silly, sissy, soft, spoiled.

antonyms mature, precocious.

bacchanalian *adj* bacchic, debauched, Dionysian, dissolute, drunken, frenzied, intemperate, licentious, maenadic, orgiastic, riotous, saturnalian, wanton, wild.

back¹ *v* advocate, aid, assist, bankroll, boost, buttress, champion, countersign, encourage, endorse, favour, finance, fund, promote, sanction, second, side with, sponsor, subsidize, support, sustain, underwrite.

antonyms discourage, oppose.

back down accede, back-pedal, capitulate, cave (in), concede, give in, retreat, submit, surrender, withdraw, yield.

back out (of) abandon, apostatize, back-pedal, cancel, chicken out, cop out, default (on), flip-flop, give up, go back on, recant, renege, resign, revoke, wimp out, withdraw.

back up¹ affirm, aid, assist, bolster,

champion, confirm, corroborate, endorse, reinforce, second, substantiate, support, uphold, vouch for.

antonym let down, undermine.

back up² back-pedal, backtrack, do an about-face, flip-flop, recede, recoil, regress, retire, retrace one's steps, retreat, retrogress, reverse, turn back, withdraw.

back² *n* backside, end, hind part, hindquarters, posterior, rear, reverse, stern, tail, tail end, verso.

adj end, hind, hindmost, posterior, rear, reverse, tail.

back³ *adj* accumulated, backlogged, delayed, earlier, elapsed, former, outdated, overdue, past, previous, prior, superseded.

backbite *v* abuse, attack, bad-mouth, bash, calumniate, criticize, defame, denigrate, disparage, libel, malign, revile, slander, talk down, traduce, vilify, vituperate.

antonym praise.

backbiting *n* abuse, aspersion, bad-mouthing, calumniation, calumny, cattiness, criticism, defamation, denigration, detraction, disparagement, gossip, malice, revilement, rumourmongering, scandalmongering, slander, spite, spitefulness, vilification, vituperation.

antonym praise.

backbone *n* basis, character, core, courage, determination, firmness, foundation, grit, hardihood, mainstay, mettle, nerve, pluck, power, resolution, resolve, spine, stamina, staunchness, steadfastness, strength, support, tenacity, toughness, vertebral column, will.

antonyms spinelessness, weakness.

backbreaking *adj* arduous, crushing, exhausting, gruelling, hard, heavy, killing, laborious, punishing, strenuous, tiring, toilsome, wearing, wearisome.

antonym easy.

backer *n* advocate, benefactor, champion, funder, patron, promoter, second, seconder, sponsor, subscriber, subsidizer, supporter, underwriter, well-wisher.

backfire *v* boomerang, come home to roost, fail, flop, miscarry, rebound, recoil, ricochet.

background *n* breeding, briefing, circumstances, credentials, culture, dossier, education, environment, experience, fond, grounding, history, information, milieu, preparation, record, setting, situation, surroundings, tradition, upbringing.

backhanded *adj* ambiguous, double-edged, doubtful, dubious, equivocal, indirect, ironic, oblique, sarcastic, sardonic, two-edged.

antonyms direct, sincere, wholehearted.

backing *n* accompaniment, advocacy, aid, assistance, championing, championship, encouragement, endorsement, favour, financing, funding, funds, grant, helpers, moral support, patronage, reinforcement, sanction, seconding, sponsorship, subsidization, subsidy, support.

backlash *n* backfire, boomerang, counterblast, kickback, reaction, recoil, repercussion, reprisal, resentment, response, retaliation.

backlog *n* accumulation, excess, hoard, mountain, overstock, oversupply, reserve, surplus.

backslide *v* apostatize, default, defect, fall from grace, lapse, regress, relapse, renege, retrogress, revert, sin, slip, stray, weaken.

antonym persevere.

backslider *n* apostate, defaulter, defector, deserter, recidivist, recreant, renegade, reneger, turncoat.

backsliding *n* apostasy, defaulting, defection, desertion, lapse, perfidy, recidivism, recreancy, relapse.

backward *adj* backwater, bashful, behind, behindhand, diffident, dull, en arrière, hesitant, hesitating, immature, late, old-fashioned, primitive, rearward, retarded, retrograde, reverse, shy, slow, tardy, uncultured, underdeveloped, unsophisticated.

antonyms forward, precocious.

backwoods *n* back of beyond, badlands, boondocks, boonies, bush, outback, sticks, wilderness.

adj backward, boorish, crude, rough, rugged, rustic, uncivilized, uncultured, unrefined, unsophisticated.

bacteria *n* bacilli, bugs, cocci, germs, microbes, micro-organisms, pathogens, spirilla.

bad *adj* abysmal, acute, adverse, ailing, appalling, atrocious, base, blameworthy, conscience-stricken, corrupt, criminal, damaging, dangerous, decayed, defective, deficient, deleterious, delinquent, despondent, detrimental, difficult, disastrous, discouraged, discouraging, diseased, disobedient, distressed, distressing, evil, fallacious, faulty, frustrating, gloomy, grave, grim, guilty, harmful, ill, immoral, imperfect, inadequate, incorrect, inferior, injurious, low, malicious, mean, melancholy, mischievous, mouldy, naughty, nauseous, negative, no-good, noxious, obnoxious, off, offensive, painful, poor, problem, putrid, rainy, rancid, regretful, remorseful, rotten, rough, rueful, ruinous, sad, serious, severe, shabby, shocking, shoddy, sick, sinful, sorry, sour, spoilt, stormy, substandard, terrible, tough, troubled, unco-operative, unethical, unfair, unfavourable, unfortunate, unhealthy, unpleasant, unruly,

unsatisfactory, unsuccessful, unwell, upset, vile, wicked, wretched, wrong.

bad blood acrimony, anger, animosity, animus, antagonism, bad feeling, bitterness, dislike, distrust, enmity, feud, grudge, hard feelings, hatred, hostility, ill feeling, ill will, malevolence, malice, nastiness, odium, rancour, resentment, vendetta.

bad form bad manners, bad style, barbarism, faux pas, gaucherie, impropriety, indecorum, inelegance, infelicity, mauvais ton, no-no, solecism.

bad luck adversity, blow, hard luck, hard times, hoodoo, ill luck, misadventure, mischance, misfortune, reverse, setback, worse luck.

antonym luck.

bad manners boorishness, coarseness, crudeness, discourtesy, disrespect, gaucherie, impoliteness, incivility, inconsideration, indecorum, indelicacy, rudeness, unmannerliness.

antonym politeness.

bad taste coarseness, crudeness, disgustingness, grossness, indecency, indelicacy, obscenity, offensiveness, poor taste, smuttiness, tactlessness, tastelessness, vulgarity.

antonyms delicacy, tastefulness.

bad time difficulty, going-over, grilling, mauvais quart d'heure, pain, third degree, torture, trouble.

badge *n* brand, device, emblem, identification, insignia, logo, mark, sign, stamp, token, trademark.

badger *v* bait, bug, bully, bullyrag, chivvy, goad, harass, harry, hassle, hound, importune, nag, persecute, pester, plague, torment.

badinage *n* banter, chaff, drollery, give and take, humour, jocularity, joking, joshing, kibbitzing, mockery, persiflage, raillery, repartee, ribbing, teasing, waggery, word-play.

badly *adv* acutely, critically, crucially, deeply, desperately, gravely, greatly, intensely, painfully, seriously, severely.

antonyms mildly, slightly.

bad-tempered *adj* bitchy, cantankerous, captious, choleric, crabby, cranky, cross, crotchety, dyspeptic, fractious, grouchy, grumpy, ill-humoured, ill-tempered, impatient, irascible, irritable, moody, peevish, petulant, querulous, snappish, splenetic, sulky, sullen, testy, touchy, vixenish.

antonyms equable, genial.

baffle *v* amaze, astound, balk, bamboozle, bemuse, bewilder, check, confound, confuse, daze, defeat, disconcert, dumfound, flabbergast, floor, flummox, foil, frustrate, hinder, mystify, nonplus, perplex, puzzle, stump, stun, stymie, throw (off), throw for a loop, thwart.

antonyms enlighten, help.

baffling *adj* amazing, astounding, bemusing, bewildering, confusing, extraordinary, frustrating, mysterious, mystifying, perplexing, puzzling, stupefying, surprising, unfathomable.

antonyms enlightening, explanatory.

bag *v* acquire, appropriate, capture, catch, commandeer, corner, gain, get, grab, kill, land, nab, obtain, pick up, reserve, secure, seize, shoot, snag, take, trap.
n backpack, carrier, carry-all, carry-on, container, duffel bag, grab bag, grip, gunny sack, gym bag, handbag, hand luggage, haversack, knapsack, overnighter, pack, poke, pouch, purse, reticule, rucksack, sachet, sack, satchel, scrip, shopping bag, shoulder bag, suitcase, tote (bag), valise.

baggage *n* accoutrements, bags, belongings, equipment, gear, impedimenta, luggage, paraphernalia, stuff, suitcases, supplies, things, traps, viatica.

baggy *adj* billowing, bulging, droopy, flaccid, floppy, ill-fitting, loose, oversize, pouchy, roomy, sagging, slack.
antonyms firm, tight.

bail *n* bond, guarantee, guaranty, pledge, security, surety, warranty.
bail out¹ aid, assist, cover for, finance, go bail for, help out, pick up the pieces for, relieve, rescue, save.
bail out² back out, cop out, escape, quit, retreat, wimp out, withdraw.

bailiff *n* agent, constable, deputy, factor, magistrate, office, sheriff.

bait *n* allurement, attraction, bribe, carrot, decoy, enticement, incentive, inducement, lure, sweetener, temptation.
antonyms disincentive, poison pill.
v annoy, bully, bullyrag, gall, goad, harass, hound, irk, irritate, needle, persecute, provoke, tease, torment.

balance *v* adjust, calculate, compare, compute, consider, counteract, counterbalance, counterpoise, deliberate, equalize, equate, equilibrate, equipoise, equiponderate, estimate, evaluate, level, match, neutralize, offset, parallel, poise, settle, square, stabilize, steady, tally, total, weigh.
antonyms overbalance, unbalance.
n composure, correspondence, difference, equality, equanimity, equilibrium, equipoise, equity, equivalence, evenness, parallelism, parity, poise, remainder, residue, rest, self-possession, stability, stasis, steadiness, surplus, symmetry.
antonyms imbalance, instability.

balanced *adj* calm, equanimous, equitable, even-handed, fair, impartial, just, level-headed, self-possessed, sensible, stable, steady, together, unbiased, unprejudiced, well-adjusted, well-rounded.
antonyms prejudiced, unbalanced.

balcony *n* gallery, gods, terrace, upper circle, veranda.

bald *adj* bald-headed, baldpated, bare, barren, bleak, depilated, direct, downright, exposed, forthright, glabrous, hairless, naked, outright, peeled, plain, severe, simple, stark, straight, straightforward, treeless, unadorned,

uncompromising, uncovered, undisguised, unvarnished.
antonyms adorned, embellished, euphemistic, hirsute, softened.

balderdash *n* a crock, baloney, bull, bunk, cardboard, claptrap, crap, drivel, eyewash, falderal, gibberish, guff, hogwash, humbug, malarkey, moonshine, nonsense, old wives' tales, poppycock, rot, rubbish, stuff and nonsense, tommyrot, trash, tripe, twaddle.

baldness *n* alopecia, bald-headedness, bareness, barrenness, bleakness, directness, forthrightness, glabrousness, hairlessness, nakedness, plainness, starkness.
antonyms hirsuteness, lushness.

bale *n* bundle, fardel, pack, package, parcel, truss.

baleful *adj* baneful, deadly, destructive, evil, fell, glowering, harmful, hurtful, ill-meaning, injurious, lowering, malevolent, malignant, menacing, noxious, ominous, pernicious, ruinous, sinister, threatening, venomous, woeful.
antonyms auspicious, favourable.

balk *v* baffle, bar, boggle, check, counteract, defeat, demur, disconcert, dodge, draw back, evade, falter, feel (or have) qualms, flinch, foil, forestall, frustrate, hang back, hesitate, hinder, jib, make difficulties, obstruct, prevent, quail, recoil, refuse, resist, scruple, shirk, shrink, shy (away), stall, thwart.

ball¹ *n* bauble, bobble, bullet, clew, clump, conglomeration, drop, globe, globule, orb, pellet, pill, shot, slug, sphere, spheroid, wad.
on the ball alert, attentive, aware, informed, in touch, on one's toes, on the beam, quick, ready, wide-awake.

ball² *n* assembly, carnival, dance, dinner-dance, do, fandango, hop, masquerade, party, ridotto, rout, soirée.

ballad *n* carol, composition, ditty, epic, folk song, lay, lyric, ode, poem, shanty, song.

balloon *v* bag, belly, billow, blow up, bulge, dilate, distend, enlarge, expand, inflate, puff out, swell.

ballot *n* election, plebiscite, poll, polling, referendum, vote, voting.

ballyhoo *n* ado, advertising, agitation, buildup, clamour, commotion, disturbance, excitement, fanfare, fuss, hubbub, hue and cry, hullabaloo, hype, noise, promotion, propaganda, publicity, racket, tumult, uproar.

balm *n* anodyne, balsam, bromide, calmative, comfort, consolation, cream, curative, embrocation, emollient, lenitive, liniment, lotion, ointment, palliative, restorative, salve, sedative, solace, unguent.
antonyms irritant, vexation.

balmy¹ *adj* clement, gentle, mild, pleasant, soft, summery, temperate, warm.
antonym inclement.

balmy² *adj* barmy, bats, batty, bonkers, cracked, crackers, crazy, daffy, daft, dippy, dotty, foolish, idiotic, insane, loony, mad, nuts,

nutty, odd, off one's nut, off one's rocker, out of one's mind, round the bend, silly, stupid.
antonyms rational, sane, sensible.

bamboozle *v* baffle, befool, befuddle, bemuse, cheat, con, confound, confuse, cozen, deceive, defraud, delude, dupe, fool, hoax, hoodwink, mystify, perplex, puzzle, snow, stump, swindle, trick.

ban *v* anathematize, banish, bar, blackball, blacklist, censor, debar, disallow, exclude, excommunicate, forbid, interdict, ostracize, outlaw, prohibit, proscribe, restrict, squelch, suppress.
antonyms legalize, permit.
n anathematization, boycott, censorship, condemnation, curse, denunciation, embargo, excommunication, interdiction, outlawing, prohibition, proscription, restriction, stoppage, suppression, taboo.
antonyms dispensation, legalization, permission.

banal *adj* boring, bromidic, clichéd, cliché-ridden, commonplace, corny, dull, empty, everyday, hackneyed, humdrum, jejune, ordinary, pedestrian, platitudinous, prosaic, stale, stereotyped, stock, threadbare, tired, trite, unimaginative, unoriginal, vapid.
antonym original.

banality *n* bromide, cliché, commonplace, dullness, platitude, prosaicism, triteness, triviality, truism, vapidity.
antonym originality.

band[1] *n* bandage, bandeau, bandolier, belt, binding, bond, chain, cord, fascia, fasciole, fetter, fillet, ligature, line, manacle, ribbon, sash, shackle, strap, strip, stripe, swath, tape, tie, vitta, zone.

band[2] *n* association, body, brigade, bunch, clique, club, combo, company, contingent, corps, coterie, crew, ensemble, flock, gang, group, herd, horde, orchestra, party, posse, society, troop, troupe, waits.
v affiliate, ally, amalgamate, collaborate, consolidate, federate, gang up, gather, group, join, league, merge, unite.
antonyms disband, disperse.

bandage *n* compress, dressing, gauze, ligature, plaster, swaddle, swathe, tourniquet.
v bind, cover, dress, swaddle, swathe.

bandit *n* brigand, buccaneer, cowboy, dacoit, desperado, footpad, freebooter, gangster, gunman, highwayman, hijacker, marauder, mugger, outlaw, pirate, privateer, racketeer, road agent, robber, ruffian, thief, thug.

banditry *n* brigandage, dacoity, freebooting, heist, highway robbery, hijacking, holdup, piracy, privateering, robbery, stick-up, theft.

bandy[1] *v* barter, exchange, interchange, pass, reciprocate, swap, throw, toss, trade.

bandy[2] *adj* bandy-legged, bent, bowed, bowlegged, crooked, curved, valgus.

bane *n* adversity, affliction, annoyance, bête noire, blight, burden, calamity, curse, despair, destruction, disaster, distress, downfall, evil, irritation, misery, misfortune, nuisance, ordeal, pest, pestilence, plague, ruin, scourge, sorrow, thorn in the flesh (or in one's side), torment, trial, trouble, vexation, woe.
antonym blessing.

baneful *adj* deadly, deleterious, destructive, disastrous, fell, harmful, hurtful, injurious, malevolent, noxious, pernicious, pestilential, ruinous, sinister, venomous.
antonym beneficent.

bang *n* blow, boom, box, bump, clang, clap, clash, collision, crash, cuff, detonation, explosion, hit, knock, noise, peal, pop, punch, report, shot, slam, smack, stroke, thud, thump, wallop, whack, whap.
v bash, beat, boom, bump, clang, clatter, crash, detonate, drum, echo, explode, hammer, hit, kick, knock, peal, pound, pummel, punch, rap, slam, strike, thump.
adv directly, hard, headlong, noisily, plumb, precisely, right, slap, smack, square, squarely, straight, suddenly.

banish *v* ban, bar, blacklist, debar, deport, discard, dislodge, dismiss, dispel, eject, eliminate, eradicate, evict, exclude, excommunicate, exile, expatriate, expel, get rid of, ostracize, oust, outlaw, remove, send away, shut out, turn out.
antonyms recall, welcome.

banishment *n* deportation, eviction, exile, expatriation, expulsion, ostracism, ostracization, outlawry, proscription.
antonyms recall, return, welcome.

bank[1] *n* accumulation, cache, depository, fund, hoard, pool, repository, reserve, reservoir, savings, stock, stockpile, store, storehouse, treasury.
v accumulate, deposit, hoard, keep, save, stockpile, store up.
antonym spend.

bank[2] *n* acclivity, banking, bar, brink, camber, dike, earthwork, edge, embankment, esker, heap, margin, mass, moraine, mound, pile, rampart, ridge, shallow, shelf, shoal, shore, side, slope, tilt.
v aggrade, camber, cant, drift, heap, incline, mass, mound, pile up, pitch, slant, slope, tilt, tip.

bank[3] *n* array, bench, echelon, file, group, line, rank, row, series, tier.

bank note *n* bill, greenback, note, paper money, treasury note.

bankrupt *adj* beggared, broke, depleted, destitute, devoid, empty, exhausted, failed, impecunious, impoverished, insolvent, lacking, penurious, ruined, spent, used up.
antonyms solvent, wealthy.
n debtor, insolvent, pauper.

bankruptcy *n* beggary, destitution, economic disaster, exhaustion, failure, indebtedness, insolvency, lack, liquidation, penury, poverty, receivership, ruin, ruination.
antonyms solvency, wealth.

banner *n* banderole, burgee, colours, ensign, flag, gonfalon, labarum, oriflamme, pennant, pennon, standard, streamer, vexillum, wall hanging.

banquet *n* binge, dinner, feast, meal, reception, regale, repast, revel, supper, treat.

banter *n* badinage, chaff, chaffing, cross-talk, derision, jesting, joking, kibbitzing, kidding, mockery, persiflage, pleasantry, raillery, repartee, ribbing, ridicule, waggery, word play.

baptism *n* beginning, chrism, christening, debut, dedication, dunking, immersion, initiation, introduction, launch, launching, plunging, purification, sprinkling, washing.

baptize *v* admit, call, christen, cleanse, dedicate, dunk, enrol, immerse, initiate, introduce, launch, name, plunge, purify, recruit, sprinkle, style, term, title, wash.

bar[1] *n* barricade, barrier, batten, check, crosspiece, determent, deterrent, hindrance, impediment, obstacle, obstruction, paling, pole, preventive, rail, railing, rod, shaft, stake, stanchion, stick, stop.

v ban, barricade, blackball, bolt, debar, deny entry to, exclude, fasten, forbid, hinder, interdict, latch, lock, obstruct, preclude, prevent, prohibit, secure.

bar[2] *n* beer parlour, bierkeller, brasserie, canteen, counter, estaminet, gin mill, gin palace, gin shop, honky-tonk, inn, joint, lounge, pub, saloon, tavern, watering hole.

bar[3] *n* advocates, attorneys, barristers, bench, counsel, court, courtroom, dock, law court, lawyers, tribunal.

bar[4] *n* block, cake, chunk, ingot, lump, nugget, slab, stick, wedge.

barb *n* affront, arrow, barbule, bristle, cut, dart, dig, fluke, gibe, insult, jab, point, prickle, prong, quill, rebuff, sarcasm, shot, sneer, snipe, spicule, spike, spur, stab, thorn, thrust.

barbarian *n* animal, ape, beast, boor, brute, clod, hooligan, hun, ignoramus, illiterate, lowbrow, oaf, philistine, pig, ruffian, savage, swine, vandal, vulgarian, yahoo.

adj boorish, brutish, coarse, crude, lowbrow, philistine, rough, savage, uncivilized, uncouth, uncultivated, uncultured, unsophisticated, vulgar.

barbaric *adj* barbarous, boorish, brutal, brutish, coarse, crude, cruel, ferocious, fierce, inhuman, primitive, rude, savage, uncivilized, uncouth, vulgar, wild.

antonyms civilized, humane.

barbarism *n* abuse, atrocity, barbarity, brutishness, coarseness, corruption, crudity, cruelty, enormity, misuse, outrage, savagery, solecism, vulgarism.

barbarity *n* barbarousness, boorishness, brutality, brutishness, cruelty, ferocity, inhumanity, rudeness, ruthlessness, savagery, viciousness, wildness.

antonyms civilization, civility, humanity.

barbarous *adj* barbarian, barbaric, brutal, brutish, coarse, crude, cruel, ferocious, heartless, heathenish, ignorant, inhuman, monstrous, philistine, primitive, rough, rude, ruthless, savage, uncivilized, uncouth,

uncultured, unlettered, unrefined, vicious, vulgar, wild.

antonyms civilized, cultured, educated.

barbed *adj* acerbic, acid, catty, caustic, critical, cutting, hooked, hostile, hurtful, jagged, nasty, piercing, pointed, prickly, pronged, sharp, snide, spiked, spiny, thorny, toothed, trenchant, unkind.

bare *adj* austere, bald, barren, basic, blank, bleak, defoliated, denuded, direct, empty, essential, explicit, exposed, hard, lacking, literal, mean, naked, napless, nude, open, peeled, plain, poor, scanty, scarce, severe, sheer, shorn, simple, spare, stark, sterile, straight, straightforward, stripped, unadorned, unarmed, unclad, unclothed, uncovered, undisguised, undressed, unembellished, unforested, unfurnished, unprovided, unsheathed, untimbered, unvarnished, unwooded, vacant, void, wanting, woodless, worn.

barefaced *adj* arrant, audacious, bald, blatant, bold, brash, brazen, flagrant, glaring, impudent, insolent, manifest, naked, obvious, open, overt, palpable, patent, shameless, transparent, unabashed, unconcealed, undisguised.

barefoot *adj* shoeless, unshod.
antonym shod.

barely[1] *adv* almost, by the skin of one's teeth, hardly, just, scarcely.

barely[2] *adv* austerely, explicitly, nakedly, openly, plainly, scantily, severely, simply, sparely, starkly.

bargain *n* agreement, arrangement, buy, compact, contract, covenant, deal, discount, exchange, find, giveaway, negotiation, pact, pledge, promise, reduction, sale, settlement, snip, steal, stipulation, trade, transaction, treaty, understanding, value.

v agree, barter, broker, buy, contract, covenant, deal, dicker, exchange, haggle, higgle, negotiate, promise, sell, trade, traffic, transact.

bargain for anticipate, consider, contemplate, count on, envisage, envision, expect, foresee, imagine, look for, plan for, reckon on/with.

bargaining *n* barter, bartering, dealing, dickering, exchanging, haggling, higgling, horse-dealing, horse-trading, negotiation, sale, selling, trading, trafficking, wheeling and dealing.

barge[1] *v* butt (in), cannon, elbow, encroach, gatecrash, hit, impinge, impose, interfere, interrupt, intrude, muscle in, push, push in, thrust oneself.

barge[2] *n* canal boat, flatboat, houseboat, lighter, riverboat, transport.

bark *n* bawl, bay, cough, growl, shout, snap, snarl, woof, yap, yell, yelp.

v advertise, bawl, bay, bluster, cough, growl, shout, snap, snarl, woof, yap, yell, yelp.

barmy *adj* balmy, batty, cracked, crackers, crazy, daft, dippy, dotty, foolish, idiotic, insane, loony, mad, nuts, nutty, odd, off one's nut, off one's rocker, one brick short of a load, out of one's mind, silly, stupid.

antonyms rational, sane, sensible.

baroque *adj* bizarre, byzantine, convoluted, elaborate, exaggerated, extravagant, exuberant, fanciful, fantastic, flamboyant, florid, grotesque, labyrinthine, ornate, overdecorated, overdone, overwrought, rococo, whimsical.

antonym plain.

barracks *n* accommodation, billet, camp, cantonment, casern, encampment, garrison, guardhouse, lodging, quarters.

barrage *n* assault, attack, battery, bombardment, broadside, burst, cannonade, deluge, flood, fusillade, gunfire, hail, inundation, mass, onset, onslaught, plethora, profusion, rain, salvo, shelling, shower, storm, stream, torrent, volley.

barred *adj* banned, blackballed, disallowed, excluded, forbidden, interdicted, outlawed, prohibited, proscribed, taboo.

antonym permissible.

barrel *n* butt, cask, drum, hogshead, keg, puncheon, tierce, tun, wood.

barren *adj* arid, boring, childless, desert, desolate, dry, dull, empty, flat, fruitless, infecund, infertile, jejune, lacklustre, pointless, profitless, stale, sterile, treeless, unbearing, uncultivable, unfruitful, uninformative, uninspiring, uninstructive, uninteresting, unproductive, unprolific, unrewarding, useless, vapid, waste.

antonyms fertile, productive, useful.

barricade *n* barrier, blockade, bulwark, fence, obstruction, palisade, protection, rampart, screen, stockade.

v bar, block, blockade, defend, fence (in or off), fortify, obstruct, palisade, protect, screen.

barrier *n* bail, bar, barricade, blockade, boom, boundary, bulkhead, check, difficulty, ditch, drawback, fence, fortification, handicap, hindrance, hurdle, impediment, limitation, obstacle, obstruction, railing, rampart, restriction, stop, stumbling-block, transverse, wall.

barrow *n* handbarrow, handcart, pushcart, wheelbarrow.

bartender *n* barkeeper, barmaid, barman, publican, tapster.

barter *v* bargain, exchange, sell, swap, trade, traffic, truck.

base¹ *n* basis, beachhead, bed, bottom, camp, centre, core, crux, essence, essential, foot, foundation, fundamental, groundwork, headquarters, heart, holder, home, key, keystone, origin, pedestal, plinth, post, principal, rest, root, seat, settlement, socket, socle, source, stand, standard, starting-point, station, substrate, substructure, support, underlay, underpinning, understructure.

v build, centre, construct, establish, found, ground, locate, rest, root, seat, station, support.

be based be according (to), depend, derive,

go (by), hinge, originate, proceed (from), rest.

base² *adj* abject, common, contemptible, corrupt, cowardly, debased, degraded, degrading, depraved, despicable, disgraceful, disreputable, evil, good-for-nothing, grovelling, humble, ignoble, ignominious, immoral, infamous, inferior, knavish, low, lowbrow, lowly, low-minded, mean, menial, miserable, paltry, pitiful, poor, scandalous, servile, shameful, slavish, sordid, sorry, ungenerous, unworthy, valueless, vile, villainous, vulgar, wicked, worthless, wretched.

base³ *adj* adulterated, alloyed, artificial, bastard, counterfeit, debased, degraded, fake, forged, fraudulent, impure, inferior, pinchbeck, spurious.

baseborn *adj* bastard, common, humble, illegitimate, inferior, lowborn, low-bred, lower-class, lowly, plebeian, proletarian, vulgar.

antonyms highborn, noble.

baseless *adj* gratuitous, groundless, indefensible, unattested, unauthenticated, uncalled-for, unconfirmed, uncorroborated, unfounded, ungrounded, unjustifiable, unjustified, unsubstantiated, unsupported.

antonym justifiable.

baseness *n* contemptibility, cowardliness, degradation, depravation, depravity, despicability, disgracefulness, ignominy, infamy, inferiority, knavery, lowliness, meanness, misery, poverty, servility, shame, shamefulness, slavishness, sordidness, sorriness, subservience, turpitude, unworthiness, vileness, villainy, vulgarity, wickedness, worthlessness, wretchedness.

bash *v* bang, batter, beat, belt, biff, break, club, crash, crush, dent, hammer, hit, pound, punch, slam, slug, smack, smash, sock, stave, strike, swipe, wallop, whap.

n attempt, crack, shot, stab, try, turn, whirl.

bashful *adj* abashed, backward, blushing, confused, coy, diffident, embarrassed, hesitant, inhibited, modest, nervous, reserved, reticent, retiring, self-conscious, self-effacing, shamefaced, sheepish, shrinking, shy, timid, timorous, unforthcoming.

antonym confident.

bashfulness *n* backwardness, coyness, diffidence, embarrassment, hesitancy, inhibition, modesty, reserve, self-consciousness, self-effacement, shamefacedness, sheepishness, shyness, timidity, timorousness.

antonym confidence.

basic *adj* central, core, crucial, elementary, essential, fundamental, important, inalienable, indispensable, inherent, intrinsic, key, main, necessary, primary, radical, root, rudimentary, simple, underlying, vital.

antonyms inessential, peripheral.

basically *adv* at bottom, at heart, au fond, essentially, fundamentally, in brief, inherently, in short, intrinsically, primarily, principally, radically, underlyingly, vitally.

basics *n* bedrock, brass tacks, core, elements, essentials, facts, first thing(s), fundamentals, grass roots, necessaries, nitty-gritty, nuts and bolts, practicalities, principles, rock bottom, rudiments, underpinnings.

basin *n* bowl, cavity, crater, depression, dip, dish, hollow, lavabo, laver, porringer, sink, stoup, washbasin.

basis *n* base, bottom, core, essential, fond, footing, foundation, fundamental, ground, groundwork, heart, keynote, pedestal, premise, principle, support, thrust, underpinnings.

on the basis of according to, (as) determined by, (as) indicated by, based on, by virtue of, commensurate with, depending on, going by, in view of, with reference to.

bask *v* bathe, delight (in), enjoy, gloat, laze, lie, lounge, luxuriate, relax, relish, revel, savour, sunbathe, take pleasure, wallow, warm oneself.

basket *n* bassinet, creel, frail, hamper, junket, pannier, punnet.

bass *adj* baritone, deep, deep-toned, grave, low, low-pitched, low-toned, resonant, sepulchral, sonorous.

bastard *n* by-blow, illegitimate child, love child, misfortune, natural child, whoreson.
adj abnormal, adulterated, anomalous, artificial, base, baseborn, counterfeit, false, illegitimate, imperfect, impure, inferior, irregular, misbegotten, sham, spurious, synthetic.
antonyms genuine, legitimate.

bastardize *v* adulterate, cheapen, corrupt, debase, defile, degrade, demean, depreciate, devalue, distort, lower, pervert, profane, vitiate.

bastion *n* bulwark, buttress, citadel, defence, fastness, fortification, fortress, mainstay, pillar, prop, redoubt, rock, stronghold, support, tower of strength.

batch *n* amount, assemblage, assortment, bunch, collection, consignment, contingent, group, lot, pack, parcel, quantity, set.

bath *n* ablution, cleansing, douche, douse, scrubbing, shower, soak, spa, tub, wash, whirlpool.
v bathe, clean, douse, lave, shower, soak, tub, wash.

bathe *v* baptize, cleanse, cover, dunk, flood, immerse, moisten, rinse, soak, steep, suffuse, swim, wash, wet.

bathetic *adj* anticlimactic, sublime to ridiculous.

bathos *n* anticlimax, comedown, letdown.

bathroom *n* can, facilities, john, ladies' room, lavatory, men's room, outhouse, powder room, restroom, toilet, washroom, w.c.

battalion *n* army, brigade, company, contingent, corps, division, force, herd, horde, host, legion, mass, multitude, phalanx, platoon, regiment, squadron, throng.

batten *v* bar, barricade, board up, clamp down, fasten, fix, nail down, secure, tighten.

batter *v* abuse, assault, bash, beat, belabour, bruise, buffet, crush, dash, deface, demolish, destroy, disfigure, distress, hurt, injure, knock around, lash, maltreat, mangle, manhandle, mar, maul, mistreat, pelt, pound, pummel, rough up, ruin, shatter, slap around, smash, thrash, wallop.

battered *adj* abused, beaten, bruised, crumbling, crushed, damaged, dented, dilapidated, ill-treated, injured, ramshackle, scuffed, tumbledown, weather-beaten, worn.

battery *n* arsenal, artillery, assault, attack, barrage, beating, cannon, cannonry, cell, emplacements, guns, mayhem, onslaught, progression, range, row, sequence, series, set, thrashing, violence.

battle *n* action, campaign, clash, combat, conflict, contest, controversy, crusade, debate, disagreement, dispute, encounter, engagement, fight, fray, hostilities, row, skirmish, strife, struggle, war, warfare.
v agitate, argue, campaign, clamour, combat, contend, contest, crusade, dispute, feud, fight, strive, struggle, war.

battle-axe *n* disciplinarian, harridan, martinet, Tartar, termagant, virago.

battle cry *n* catchword, motto, slogan, war cry, war whoop, war song, watchword.

batty *adj* balmy, barmy, bats, bonkers, cracked, crackers, crazy, daffy, daft, demented, dippy, dotty, eccentric, idiotic, insane, loony, lunatic, mad, nuts, nutty, odd, off one's rocker, peculiar, queer, screwy, touched.
antonym sane.

bauble *n* bagatelle, doodad, falderal, gewgaw, gimcrack, kickshaw, knick-knack, plaything, tinsel, toy, trifle, trinket.

bawd *n* brothel keeper, hooker, madam, panderess, pimp, procuress, prostitute, streetwalker, whore.

bawdy *adj* blue, coarse, dirty, erotic, gross, improper, indecent, indecorous, indelicate, lascivious, lecherous, lewd, libidinous, licentious, lustful, obscene, pornographic, prurient, ribald, risqué, rude, salacious, smutty, suggestive, vulgar.
antonyms chaste, clean.

bawl *v* bellow, blubber, call, caterwaul, clamour, cry, halloo, holler, howl, roar, shout, sob, squall, vociferate, wail, weep, yell, yowl.

bay[1] *n* arm, bight, cove, embayment, gulf, inlet.

bay[2] *n* alcove, booth, carrel, compartment, cubicle, embrasure, niche, nook, opening, recess, stall.

bay[3] *n* bark, bawl, bell, bellow, cry, halloo, holler, howl, roar, yell, yowl.

at bay caught, cornered, trapped, up against it (or the wall), with one's back to the wall.

bayonet *v* impale, knife, pierce, skewer, spear, stab, stick, thrust through.

bazaar *n* agora, exchange, fair, flea market, market, marketplace, mart, rummage sale, sale, souk.

be *v* abide, arise, befall, breathe, come about, come to pass, consist, continue, develop, dwell, endure, exist, happen, inhabit, inhere, last, live, obtain, occur, persist, prevail, remain, reside, stand, stay, survive, take place.

beach *n* coast, foreshore, littoral, margin, plage, sand, sands, seaboard, seashore, seaside, shingle, shore, strand, water's edge.

beachcomber *n* forager, loafer, loiterer, scavenger, scrounger, wayfarer.

beacon *n* beam, bonfire, flare, guiding light, light, lighthouse, pharos, rocket, searchlight, sign, signal, watch fire.

bead *n* ball, blob, bubble, dot, drop, droplet, foam, froth, glob, globule, head, moulding, pearl, pellet, pill, spherule.

beak *n* bill, bow, mandibles, nib, nose, nozzle, proboscis, projection, prow, ram, rostrum, snout, stem.

beaked *adj* curved, hooked, pointed, rostral, rostrate, sharp.

beam *n* arbor, bar, boom, girder, gleam, glimmer, glint, glow, joist, plank, radiation, rafter, ray, shaft, spar, stanchion, stream, support, timber, transom.
v broadcast, emit, glimmer, glow, grin, laugh, radiate, send forth, shine, smile, transmit.

beaming *adj* beautiful, bright, brilliant, cheerful, effulgent, flashing, gleaming, glimmering, glowing, grinning, happy, joyful, lambent, radiant, refulgent, shining, smiling, sparkling, sunny.
antonyms lowering, sullen.

bear¹ *v* abide, accept, admit, allow, assume, beget, bring, bring forth, bring oneself (to), brook, carry, cherish, convey, endure, entertain, give, hack, harbour, have, head, hold, lend, lie, live with, maintain, move, permit, possess, put up with, shoulder, stomach, suffer, support, sustain, sweep, take, tolerate, tote, transport, undergo, uphold, weather, weigh (upon).

bear down (on) advance on, approach, attack, burden, close in, compress, converge on, encumber, near, oppress, press down, push, push down, strain, weigh down.

bear in mind be cognizant of, be mindful of, beware, consider, heed, include, watch out for, note, reckon with, remember, take into consideration.

bear on affect, appertain to, be relevant to, concern, connect with, have a bearing on, have to do with, influence, involve, pertain to, refer to, relate to, touch on.

bear oneself acquit oneself, act, behave, carry oneself, comport oneself, conduct oneself, deport oneself, perform.

bear out attest, bear witness, confirm, corroborate, demonstrate, endorse, illustrate, justify, prove, substantiate, support, testify, uphold, vindicate.

bear up carry on, cope, endure, hang in, hold up, keep one's chin up, persevere, soldier on, suffer, withstand.

bear with be patient with, endure, forbear, make allowances for, put up with, suffer, tolerate.

bear witness attest, confirm, corroborate, demonstrate, depone, depose, evidence, evince, give evidence, prove, show, testify, testify to, vouch for.

bear² *v* breed, bring forth, develop, drop, engender, generate, give birth to, produce, propagate, yield.

bearable *adj* acceptable, endurable, livable(-with), manageable, sufferable, supportable, sustainable, tolerable.

beard *v* brave, challenge, confront, dare, defy, face, oppose.
n bristles, brush, face fungus, facial hair, goatee, imperial, moustache, mutton chops, sideburns, stubble, tuft, vandyke, whiskers.

bearded *adj* awned, bewhiskered, bristly, bushy, hairy, hirsute, shaggy, stubbly, tufted, unshaven, whiskered.
antonyms beardless, clean-shaven, smooth.

bearer *n* beneficiary, carrier, consignee, conveyor, courier, holder, messenger, payee, porter, possessor, post, runner, servant.

bearing *n* air, application, aspect, attitude, behaviour, carriage, charge, coat of arms, comportment, connection, course, demeanour, deportment, device, direction, import, manner, mien, pertinence, posture, presence, reference, relation, relevance, significance.

bearings *n* course, direction, inclination, location, orientation, position, situation, tack, track, way, whereabouts.

beast *n* animal, ape, barbarian, brute, creature, devil, fiend, monster, pig, sadist, savage, swine.

beastly *adj* abominable, awful, barbarous, bestial, brutal, brutish, coarse, cruel, depraved, disagreeable, feral, fierce, foul, ghastly, horrible, inhuman, mean, monstrous, nasty, repulsive, rotten, sadistic, savage, sensual, swinish, terrible, unpleasant, vile, wild.

beat¹ *v* bang, bash, baste, bastinado, batter, belabour, belt, bludgeon, bruise, buffet, cane, clobber, club, contuse, cream, crush, cudgel, curry, drub, flog, forge, fustigate, hammer, hit, horsewhip, impinge, knock, knout, lash, lay into, make mincemeat out of, maul, mill, mix, model, pelt, pound, punch, shape, slug, smack, smash, sock, stamp, stave, stir, strap, strike, swipe, tan, thrash, thump, thwack, trounce, welt, whale, wham, whip, work.
adj all in, dead tired, dog-tired, drained, exhausted, fatigued, pooped, tired, wearied, whacked, worn out, zonked.

beat it buzz off, get lost, go away, hop it, leave, scarper, scat, scoot, scram, shoo, shove off, skedaddle, take off, vamoose.

beat up assault, attack, batter, hammer, knock around, rough up, thrash.

beat² *v* best, blow out of the water, clobber, conquer, cream, defeat, euchre, excel over, hammer, horsewhip, make mincemeat out of, outdo, outrun, outstrip, overcome, overwhelm, pound, rout, slaughter, subdue, surpass, thump, trounce, vanquish, whip.

beat³ *v* flutter, hammer, palpitate, patter, pound, pulsate, pulse, quake, quiver, race, shake, throb, thump, tremble, vibrate.

n accent, cadence, flutter, measure, metre, palpitation, pulsation, pulse, rhyme, rhythm, stress, throb, time.

beat⁴ *n* circuit, course, journey, path, round, rounds, route, territory, walk, way.

beaten¹ *adj* baffled, bested, broken, cowed, crushed, defeated, disappointed, disheartened, frustrated, hangdog, overcome, ruined, subdued, surpassed, thwarted, vanquished, worsted.

beaten² *adj* fashioned, forged, formed, hammered, malleated, shaped, stamped, worked, wrought.

beaten³ *adj* blended, foamy, frothy, mixed, pounded, stirred, tenderized, whipped, whisked.

beatific *adj* angelic, blessed, blissful, celestial, cherubic, divine, ecstatic, exalted, glorious, heavenly, joyful, rapturous, seraphic, serene, sublime.

beatify *v* bless, exalt, glorify, sanctify.

beatitude *n* beatification, blessedness, bliss, ecstasy, exaltation, felicity, happiness, holiness, joy, saintliness, sanctity.

beau *n* admirer, Adonis, boyfriend, cavalier, coxcomb, dandy, escort, fiancé, fop, gallant, ladies' man, lover, popinjay, suitor, swain, sweetheart, swell.

beautician *n* beauty specialist, cosmetician, friseur, hairdresser, stylist.

beautiful *adj* alluring, appealing, attractive, beauteous, becoming, charming, comely, dazzling, delightful, elegant, exquisite, fair, fine, glorious, good-looking, gorgeous, graceful, handsome, lovely, pleasing, pretty, pulchritudinous, radiant, ravishing, stunning, well-proportioned.

antonyms plain, ugly.

beautify *v* adorn, array, bedeck, bedizen, deck, decorate, doll up, embellish, enhance, garnish, gild, glamorize, grace, improve, ornament, tart up, titivate.

antonyms disfigure, spoil.

beauty¹ *n* allure, attractiveness, bloom, charm, comeliness, elegance, excellence, exquisiteness, fairness, glamour, glory, grace, handsomeness, loveliness, pleasure, pulchritude, seemliness, symmetry.

antonym ugliness.

beauty² *n* belle, charmer, corker, dazzler, fair maiden, femme fatale, fine specimen, gem, goddess, good-looker, jewel, knockout, lovely, siren, stunner, Venus.

antonym frump.

becalmed *adj* at a standstill, idle, motionless, still, stranded, stuck.

because (of) *conj, prep* as, by reason of, by virtue of, due to, for, forasmuch as, for the sake of, inasmuch as, in that, in view of the fact that, on account of, on the grounds that, out of, owing to, seeing that, since, thanks to.

beckon *v* allure, attract, bid, call, coax, decoy, draw, entice, gesticulate, gesture, invite, lead on, lure, motion, nod, pull, signal, summon, tempt, wave.

become¹ *v* befit, behoove, embellish, enhance, fit, flatter, grace, harmonize with, ornament, set off, suit.

become² *v* change into, develop into, evolve into, get, grow (into), grow to be, turn (into).

becoming *adj* appropriate, attractive, befitting, charming, comely, comme il faut, compatible, complimentary, congruous, decent, decorous, enhancing, fit, fitting, flattering, graceful, maidenly, meet, neat, pretty, proper, seemly, suitable, tasteful, worthy.

antonym unbecoming.

bed¹ *n* bedroll, bedstead, berth, bunk, cot, cote, couch, cradle, crib, divan, futon, hammock, kip, mattress, pallet, palliasse, rollaway, the sack.

bed² *n* base, bottom, channel, foundation, garden, groundwork, layer, matrix, patch, plot, row, stratus, strip, substratum, underlay, wadi, watercourse.

v base, embed, establish, fix, found, ground, implant, insert, plant, settle.

bedaub *v* befoul, begrime, bemire, besmear, besmirch, bespatter, blotch, cake, daub, foul, plaster, smear, smirch, soil, spatter, splash, splatter, stain, sully.

bedclothes *n* bedding, bed linen, bedspread, blankets, comforter, counterpane, coverlet, covers, duvet, duvet cover, eiderdown, pillowcases, pillow shams, pillowslips, quilts, sheets, spread.

bedeck *v* adorn, array, beautify, bedight, bedizen, deck (out), decorate, embellish, festoon, garnish, ornament, trick out, trim.

antonym strip.

bedevil *v* afflict, annoy, befuddle, beset, besiege, bewitch, bug, confound, confuse, distress, fret, frustrate, harass, irk, irritate, muddle, pester, plague, tease, torment, torture, trouble, vex, worry.

bedew *v* dampen, drench, imbue, moisten, shower, soak, spray, sprinkle, water, wet.

bedim *v* becloud, befog, cloak, cloud, darken, dim, fog, obscure, overcast, shade, shadow, veil.

bedlam *n* anarchy, a zoo, babel, chaos, clamour, commotion, confusion, furor, hubbub, hullabaloo, madhouse, mayhem, noise, pandemonium, tumult, turmoil, uproar.

antonym calm.

bedraggled *adj* bespattered, blowsy, dirty, dishevelled, disordered, messy, muddied, muddy, scruffy, slovenly, sodden, soiled, stained, sullied, unkempt, untidy.

antonym tidy.

beef *n* axe to grind, bitch, bone to pick, complaint, criticism, dispute, dissatisfaction, grievance, gripe, grouse, grumble, objection, protest.

v bellyache, bitch, bleat, complain, criticize, find fault, fuss, gripe, grouse, grumble, moan, natter, object, squawk, whine, yammer.
antonym approve.

beefy *adj* brawny, bulky, burly, chubby, chunky, corpulent, fat, fleshy, heavy, hefty, hulking, muscular, plump, portly, pudgy, rotund, solid, stalwart, stocky, strapping, sturdy.
antonym slight.

beetle *v* dash, hurry, nip, run, rush, scamper, scoot, scurry, tear, zip, zoom.

beetling *adj* beetle, jutting, overhanging, pendent, poking, projecting, prominent, protruding, thrusting.

befall *v* arrive, bechance, betide, chance, fall, happen, occur, supervene, take place.

befitting *adj* appropriate, becoming, comme il faut, correct, decent, fit, fitting, meet, proper, right, seemly, suitable, tasteful.
antonym unbecoming.

before *adv* ahead, earlier, formerly, heretofore, hitherto, in advance, in front, previously, sooner.
prep above, ahead of, earlier than, in advance of, in anticipation of, in front of, in preparation for, previous to, prior to, rather than, sooner than.
conj lest, rather than, until.

beforehand *adv* ahead, already, before, earlier, in advance, preliminarily, previously, sooner.

befoul *v* bedung, begrime, bemire, besmirch, bespatter, defile, dirty, foul, muddy, pollute, smear, smirch, soil, stain, sully, tarnish.

befriend *v* accept, aid, assist, back, benefit, comfort, encourage, favour, help, patronize, receive, stand by, succour, support, sustain, take a liking to, take in, take under one's wing, uphold, welcome.
antonym neglect.

befuddle *v* baffle, bamboozle, befog, bewilder, confuse, daze, disorient, hocus, muddle, puzzle, stupefy, throw (off), throw for a loop.

befuddled *adj* baffled, bewildered, blank, confused, dazed, fuddled, groggy, hazy, inebriated, intoxicated, muddled, woozy.
antonym lucid.

beg *v* adjure, beseech, bum, cadge, crave, desire, entreat, implore, importune, mooch, pester, petition, plead, pray, request, scrounge, solicit, sponge, supplicate, touch.
beg (the question) avoid, dodge, duck, equivocate, evade, hedge, shirk, shun, sidestep, take for granted.

beget *v* breed, bring, cause, create, effect, engender, father, generate, get, give birth to, give rise to, give way to, lead to, occasion, procreate, produce, propagate, result in, sire, spawn, yield.

beggar¹ *n* bankrupt, bum, cadger, down-and-outer, Lazarus, mendicant, moocher, pauper, rubby, scrounger, sponger, starveling, supplicant, tramp, vagrant.

beggar² *v* baffle, challenge, defy, exceed, surpass, transcend.

beggarly *adj* abject, contemptible, despicable, destitute, impoverished, inadequate, indigent, low, meagre, mean, miserly, needy, niggardly, paltry, pathetic, penurious, pitiful, poor, poverty-stricken, stingy, vile, wretched.
antonyms affluent, generous.

beggary *n* bankruptcy, destitution, indigence, mendicancy, need, neediness, pauperism, penury, poverty, vagrancy, want, wretchedness.
antonyms affluence, plenty.

begging *adj* beseeching, entreating, imploring, longing, pleading, wistful.
n bumming, cadging, entreaty, mendicancy, mendicity, mooching, pestering, petitioning, prayers, scrounging, soliciting, sponging, supplication.

begin *v* activate, actuate, appear, arise, commence, crop up, dawn, emerge, happen, inaugurate, initiate, instigate, institute, introduce, open, originate, prepare, set about, set in, set in motion, set off, set out (on), spring, start, trigger.
antonyms end, finish.

beginner *n* abecedarian, amateur, apprentice, cheechako, cub, dude, fledgling, freshman, greenhorn, initiate, Johnny-come-lately, learner, neophyte, novice, recruit, rookie, starter, student, tenderfoot, tyro, trainee.
antonyms expert, old hand, veteran.

beginning *n* birth, commencement, embryo, establishment, fountainhead, germ, inauguration, inception, inchoation, initiation, introduction, onset, opening, origin, outset, preface, prelude, prime, rise, root, rudiments, seed, source, start, starting point.
antonyms end, finish.
adj early, elementary, first, inaugural, inceptive, inchoative, incipient, initial, introductory, nascent, primal, primary, primeval.

begrudge *v* covet, envy, grudge, mind, resent, stint.
antonym allow.

beguile *v* amuse, bamboozle, charm, cheat, cheer, cozen, deceive, delight, delude, distract, divert, dupe, engross, entertain, fool, hoodwink, mislead, occupy, pass, snow, trick, wile.

beguiling *adj* alluring, appealing, attractive, bewitching, captivating, charming, disarming, diverting, enchanting, entertaining, enticing, interesting, intriguing, tempting, winsome.
antonyms offensive, repulsive.

behalf *n* account, advantage, authority, benefit, defence, good, interest, name, part, profit, sake, side, support.

behave *v* acquit, act, bear, comport, conduct, deal, deport, function, operate, perform, react, respond, run, work.

behaviour *n* action, actions, bearing, carriage, comportment, conduct, dealings, demeanour, deportment, doings, functioning, habits, lifestyle, manner, manners, operation, performance, practice, reaction, response, ways.

behead v decapitate, execute, guillotine.

behest n authority, bidding, charge, command, commandment, decree, dictate(s), direction, fiat, injunction, insistence, instruction, mandate, order, ordinance, precept, requirement, wish.

behind prep after, at the bottom of, backing, causing, following, for, in back of, initiating, instigating, in the wake of, later than, responsible for, supporting, to the rear of.

adv after, afterwards, backlogged, behindhand, en arrière, following, in arrears, in debt, next, overdue, subsequently.

n backside, bottom, buns, butt, buttocks, cheeks, derrière, duff, posterior, rear, rear end, rump, seat, tail.

behind one's back covertly, deceitfully, secretly, sneakily, sub rosa, surreptitiously, treacherously.

behind the times antiquated, dated, démodé, living in the past, obsolete, old hat, old-fashioned, out of date, outdated, outmoded, passé, square.

behold v consider, contemplate, descry, discern, espy, eye, look at, note, notice, observe, perceive, regard, scan, see, survey, view, watch, witness.

interj ecce, lo, look, mark, note, notice, observe, presto, see, ta-da, voilà, watch.

beholden adj bound, grateful, indebted, obligated, obliged, owing, thankful.

behoove v advance, be to (one's) advantage, become, be expedient for, befit, be fitting for, be necessary for, benefit, beseem, be suitable for, profit.

beige adj biscuit, buff, café au lait, camel, cream, ecru, fawn, khaki, light brown, mushroom, natural, neutral, oatmeal, off-white, sand, tan.

being[1] n actuality, animation, entity, essence, existence, life, living, nature, reality, self, soul, spirit, substance.

being[2] n animal, beast, body, creature, entity, human being, individual, mortal, sentient, thing.

belabour v abuse, attack, bash, batter, beat, belt, berate, castigate, censure, chastise, criticize, exaggerate, flay, flog, harp on, lambaste, lay into, overdo, overemphasize, thrash, whip.

belated adj behindhand, delayed, late, overdue, retarded, tardy, unpunctual.

antonyms punctual, timely.

belch v burp, discharge, disgorge, emit, eruct, eructate, erupt, gush, hiccup, spew, vent, vomit.

n burp, eructation, eruption, hiccup.

beleaguered adj assailed, badgered, bedevilled, beset, besieged, bothered, harassed, harried, hedged about, hedged in, persecuted, plagued, surrounded, tormented, vexed, worried.

belie v conceal, confute, contradict, deny, disappoint, disguise, disprove, falsify, gainsay, give the lie to, misrepresent, negate, refute, repudiate, run counter to, understate.

antonym attest.

belief n acceptance, assumption, assurance, confidence, conviction, credence, credit, credo, creed, doctrine, dogma, expectation, faith, feeling, ideology, impression, intuition, ism, judgment, notion, opinion, persuasion, premise, presumption, presupposition, principle, principles, reliance, sureness, tenet, theory, trust, understanding, view.

antonyms disbelief, doubt, known fact, unbelief.

believable adj acceptable, authentic, authoritative, conceivable, convincing, credible, creditable, imaginable, likely, plausible, possible, probable, realistic, reliable, thinkable, true to life, trustworthy.

antonyms inconceivable, unconvincing.

believe v accept, assume, be under the impression, conjecture, consider, count on, credit, deem, depend on, feel, gather, guess, hold, imagine, judge, maintain, postulate, presume, reckon, rely on, speculate, suppose, swallow, swear by, think, trust, understand.

antonyms disbelieve, doubt.

believer n adherent, advocate, catechumen, convert, devotee, disciple, follower, (one of) the faithful, proponent, proselyte, supporter, upholder, votary, zealot.

antonyms apostate, sceptic, unbeliever.

belittle v denigrate, deprecate, depreciate, deride, derogate, detract, diminish, dismiss, disparage, downgrade, humiliate, lessen, minimize, put down, ridicule, run down, scorn, underestimate, underrate, undervalue.

antonyms build up, exaggerate, exalt, maximize.

bellicose adj aggressive, antagonistic, argumentative, bareknuckle, belligerent, combative, contentious, defiant, hawkish, hostile, jingoistic, militant, militaristic, provocative, pugnacious, quarrelsome, sabre-rattling, warlike, war-loving, warmongering.

antonym peaceable.

belligerence n aggression, aggressiveness, animosity, antagonism, argumentativeness, bellicosity, combativeness, contentiousness, pugnacity, quarrelsomeness, unfriendliness, violence.

antonym complaisance.

belligerent adj aggressive, antagonistic, argumentative, bellicose, bullying, chippy, combative, confrontational, contentious, forceful, militant, pugnacious, quarrelsome, violent, warlike, warring.

antonym peaceable.

bellow v, n bay, bell, call, clamour, cry, halloo, holler, howl, roar, scream, shout, yell.

belly n abdomen, bowels, breadbasket, corporation, gut, guts, insides, middle, paunch, pot, stomach, tummy, uterus, vitals, womb.

v bag, balloon, billow, blow up, bulge, dilate, distend, expand, fill out, inflate, swell.

antonyms deflate, shrink.

belong *v* appertain, attach, be affiliated, be a member, be associated, be attached, be connected, be intrinsic, be linked, be part (of), be relevant, be tied, come under the heading/rubric (of), fit (with), go (with), have its proper place, have membership, inhere, link up (with), pertain, relate, tie up (with).

belonging *n* acceptance, affinity, association, attachment, closeness, compatibility, fellow feeling, fellowship, home, inclusion, kinship, link, linkage, loyalty, membership, rapport, relationship.

antonym antipathy.

belonging to affiliated to, associated with, essential to, held by, included in, inherent in, intrinsic to, native to, owned by.

antonym alien to.

belongings *n* accoutrements, chattels, effects, gear, goods, impedimenta, kit, paraphernalia, possessions, stuff, things, traps.

beloved *adj* admired, adored, cherished, darling, dear, dearest, favourite, loved, pet, precious, prized, revered, sweet, treasured.

n adored, darling, dear, dearest, favourite, inamorata, inamorato, lover, pet, precious, sweet, sweetheart.

below *adv* beneath, down, infra, lower, lower down, under, underneath.

prep beneath, inferior to, lesser than, 'neath, subject to, subordinate to, under, underneath, unworthy of.

below par below average, imperfect, inadequate, inferior, lacking, not oneself, off, off-colour, poor, poorly, second-rate, substandard, under the weather, unfit, unhealthy, wanting.

below the belt cowardly, dirty, dishonest, foul, low, mean, unfair, unjust, unscrupulous, unsporting, unsportsmanlike.

belt *n* area, band, cincture, cingulum, cummerbund, district, girdle, girth, layer, region, sash, strait, stretch, strip, swathe, tract, waistband, zone.

v circle, encircle, gird, girdle, ring, surround.

bemoan *v* bewail, deplore, grieve for (or over), lament, mourn, regret, rue, sigh for, sorrow over, weep for (or over).

antonyms gloat over, rejoice over.

bemuse *v* amaze, bewilder, confuse, daze, distract, muddle, overwhelm, perplex, puzzle, stun, stupefy.

antonyms enlighten, illuminate.

bemused *adj* absent-minded, absorbed, befuddled, bewildered, blank, confused, dazed, distracted, engrossed, fuddled, half-drunk, lost, muddled, perplexed, stunned, stupefied, tipsy.

antonyms clear, clear-headed, lucid.

bench[1] *n* bleachers, board, counter, form, ledge, pew, seat, settle, stall, table, terrace, tier, workbench, worktable.

bench[2] *n* court, courtroom, judge, judges, judgeship, judicature, judiciary, magistracy, magistrate, magistrates, tribunal.

benchmark *n* criterion, example, level, model, norm, point of reference, reference, reference point, standard, touchstone, yardstick.

bend *v* aim, apply, arc, bow, buckle, compel, constrain, contort, crimp, crouch, curve, deflect, direct, dispose, diverge, divert, dogleg, double (back or over), embow, flex, fold, head, incline, incurvate, incurve, influence, lean, loop, mould, nerve, persuade, pervert, shape, stoop, subdue, submit, sway, swerve, turn, twist, veer, warp, yield.

n angle, arc, bight, bow, corner, crook, curvature, curve, dogleg, elbow, flexure, hook, incurvation, incurvature, incurve, inflexure, loop, turn, twist, zigzag.

beneath *adv* below, down, lower (down), under, underneath.

prep below, ill befitting, inferior to, infra dig(nitatem), lower than, 'neath, subject to, subordinate to, unbecoming to, under, underneath, unworthy of.

benediction *n* beatitude, Benedictus, benison, blessing, closing prayer, consecration, dismissal, favour, grace, invocation, orison, prayer, thanksgiving.

antonyms anathema, curse, execration.

benefaction *n* aid, almsgiving, backing, beneficence, benevolence, bequest, bestowal, boon, bounty, charity, contribution, donation, endowment, generosity, gift, grant, gratuity, help, legacy, liberality, munificence, offering, patronage, philanthropy, present, sponsorship, subsidy.

benefactor *n* angel, backer, contributor, donor, endower, friend, helper, patron, philanthropist, provider, sponsor, subscriber, subsidizer, supporter, well-wisher.

antonyms opponent, persecutor.

beneficence *n* aid, altruism, benefaction, benevolence, bestowal, big-heartedness, bounty, charity, compassion, donation, generosity, gift, goodness, helpfulness, kindness, largesse, liberality, love, munificence, open-handedness, open-heartedness, present, relief, succour, unselfishness, virtue.

antonym meanness.

beneficent *adj* altruistic, benevolent, benign, big-hearted, bounteous, bountiful, charitable, compassionate, generous, giving, helpful, kind, liberal, munificent, open-handed, open-hearted, unselfish.

antonym mean.

beneficial *adj* advantageous, benign, benignant, edifying, favourable, gainful, healthful, helpful, improving, nourishing, nutritious, profitable, restorative, rewarding, salubrious, salutary, serviceable, upbuilding, useful, valuable, wholesome.

antonym harmful.

beneficiary *n* assignee, devisee, donee, heir, heiress, heritor, inheritor, legatee, payee, receiver, recipient, successor.

benefit *n* advantage, aid, asset, assistance, avail, betterment, blessing, boon, edification, favour, gain, good, help, improvement, plus, profit, return, reward, sake, service, use, weal, welfare.
antonym harm.
v advance, aid, ameliorate, assist, avail, better, enhance, further, help, improve, profit, promote, serve, support.
antonyms harm, hinder, undermine.

benefits *n* advantages, bonuses, extras, freebies, perks, perquisites, pluses.
antonym disadvantages.

benevolence *n* altruism, beneficence, benignity, big-heartedness, bounty, charity, compassion, fellow feeling, generosity, good-heartedness, goodness, good will, graciousness, humanity, kind-heartedness, kindliness, kindness, loving-kindness, mercy, munificence, sympathy.
antonym meanness.

benevolent *adj* altruistic, beneficent, benign, bounteous, bountiful, caring, charitable, compassionate, considerate, generous, good-hearted, good-will, gracious, humane, humanitarian, kind, kind-hearted, kindly, liberal, loving, merciful, philanthropic, solicitous, well-disposed.
antonyms cruel, malevolent, mean.

benign *adj* amiable, anodyne, auspicious, balmy, beneficent, benevolent, complaisant, curable, curative, favourable, friendly, generous, genial, gentle, good, gracious, harmless, healthful, kind, kindly, liberal, lucky, mild, obliging, propitious, refreshing, restorative, salubrious, salutary, sympathetic, temperate, warm, wholesome.
antonyms harmful, hostile, malign, malignant.

bent *adj* angled, arched, bowed, criminal, crooked, curved, dishonest, distorted, doubled, falcate, folded, hunched, inflexed, perverted, retroverted, shady, sinister, stooped, twisted, untrustworthy, warped.
antonym straight.
n ability, aptitude, capacity, facility, faculty, flair, forte, gift, inclination, knack, leaning, penchant, predilection, predisposition, preference, proclivity, propensity, talent, tendency.

bent for bound for, headed for, heading for, hellbent for.

bent on bound and determined, determined, fixed, hellbent on, insistent, resolved, set on.

benumbed *adj* anesthetized, dazed, deadened, desensitized, dull, frozen, immobilized, insensible, insensitive, inured, numb, numbed, paralysed, stunned, stupefied, unconscious, unfeeling, unresponsive, unthinking.

bequeath *v* assign, bestow, commit, demise, devise, endow with, entrust, gift, give, grant, hand down, impart, pass on, settle, transmit, will.

bequest *n* bequeathal, bequeathment, bestowal, demise, devisal, devise, donation, dower, endowment, estate, gift, heritage, inheritance, legacy, patrimony, settlement, trust.

berate *v* castigate, censure, chastise, chew out, chide, criticize, dress down, get on (someone's) case, give a piece of one's mind, give heck, give (someone) what for, jump down the throat of, jump on, light into, rail at, rake over the coals, rate, read the riot act to, rebuke, reprimand, reproach, reprove, revile, sail into, scold, tell off, upbraid, vituperate.
antonym praise.

bereave *v* afflict, deprive, despoil, dispossess, divest, orphan, rob, strip, widow.

bereavement *n* death, deprivation, despoliation, dispossession, loss.

bereft *adj* denuded, deprived, despoiled, destitute, devoid, empty, lacking, minus, robbed, shorn, stripped, void, wanting.

berserk *adj* amuck, beside oneself, crazy, demented, deranged, enraged, frantic, frenzied, furious, insane, mad, maniacal, manic, out of one's mind, rabid, raging, raving, uncontrollable, violent, wild.
antonyms calm, sane.

berth *n* anchorage, bed, billet, bunk, cot, dock, employment, hammock, harbour, harbourage, haven, job, landfall, pier, place, port, position, post, quay, sea room, shelter, sinecure, slip, space, standing, timber limit, wharf.

give a wide berth to avoid, beware (of), fight shy of, keep away from, keep one's distance from, shun, skirt, steer clear of.
v anchor, dock, drop anchor, land, moor, park, position, tie up.
antonym weigh anchor.

beseech *v* adjure, ask, beg, call on, conjure, crave, desire, entreat, implore, importune, petition, plead, pray, solicit, sue, supplicate.

beset *v* assail, attack, badger, bedevil, besiege, encircle, enclose, encompass, entangle, environ, harass, hassle, hem in, perplex, pester, plague, surround.

besetting *adj* constant, habitual, harassing, irresistible, nagging, persistent, plaguing, recurring, troublesome, unconquerable.

beside *prep* abreast of, abutting on, adjacent, alongside, at the side of, bordering on, by, close to, hand in hand with, near, neighbouring, next door to, next to, overlooking, with.
▲ *confusable word* besides.

beside oneself berserk, crazed, delirious, demented, deranged, distracted, distraught, frantic, frenzied, furious, insane, mad, out of one's mind, unbalanced, unhinged, wild.

beside the point extraneous, immaterial, inapplicable, incidental, inconsequential, irrelevant, neither here nor there, pointless, secondary, unimportant, unrelated.
antonym relevant.

besides *adv* additionally, also, as well, extra, further, furthermore, in addition, into the bargain, moreover, to boot, too, withal.
prep apart from, as well as, in addition to, other than, over and above.

▲ *confusable word* beside.

besiege *v* assail, badger, beleaguer, beset, blockade, bother, confine, encircle, encompass, environ, harass, harry, hound, importune, nag, pester, plague, surround, trouble.

besmirch *v* bedaub, begrime, bemire, bespatter, daub, defame, defile, dirty, dishonour, drag through the mud, muddy, slander, smear, soil, spatter, stain, sully, tarnish.
antonym enhance.

besotted *adj* befuddled, bewitched, confused, doting, drunk, foolish, hypnotized, inebriated, infatuated, intoxicated, muddled, obsessed, smitten, stupefied, witless.
antonyms disenchanted, indifferent, sober.

bespeak *v* attest, bear out, betoken, betray, demonstrate, denote, display, evidence, forebode, foretell, imply, indicate, manifest, predict, proclaim, reveal, show, signify, suggest, testify to.

best *adj* choicest, correct, excellent, fanciest, finest, first, first-class, first-rate, foremost, greatest, highest, ideal, incomparable, largest, leading, matchless, most advantageous, most apt, nonpareil, optimal, optimum, outstanding, perfect, pre-eminent, preferable, preferred, principal, right, superlative, supreme, transcendent, unequalled, unsurpassed.
adv exceptionally, most excellently, superlatively, surpassingly.
n choicest, cream, crème de la crème, élite, favourite, finest, first, first choice, flower, hardest, pick, prime, the tops, top, utmost.
v beat, conquer, defeat, get the better of, lick, outclass, outdo, outperform, outrun, outstrip, outwit, surpass, thrash, trounce, vanquish, worst.

bestial *adj* animal, barbaric, barbarous, beastly, brutal, brutish, carnal, degraded, depraved, feral, filthy, gross, inhuman, savage, sensual, sordid, subhuman, swinish, vile.
antonyms civilized, humane.

bestir *v* activate, actuate, animate, arouse, awaken, energize, exert, galvanize, incite, motivate, move, rouse, stimulate, stir (up), wake.
antonyms calm, lull, quell.

bestow *v* accord, apportion, award, bequeath, confer, donate, endow with, entrust, give, grant, impart, lavish, lend, present, transmit.
antonym deprive.

bestowal *n* benefaction, bequeathal, bequeathment, bequest, conferral, conferring, donation, gift, giving, granting, imparting, presentation, transmission.

bet *n* ante, bid, gamble, hazard, pledge, risk, speculation, stake, venture, wager.
v ante, bid, chance, gamble, hazard, lay, pledge, risk, speculate, stake, venture, wager.

bête noire abomination, anathema, aversion, bane, bogey, bugbear, curse, pet hate.
antonym favourite.

betide *v* bechance, befall, hap, happen to, occur, overtake, supervene.

betimes *adv* early, expeditiously, in (good) time, promptly, punctually, seasonably, soon, speedily.
antonym late.

betoken *v* augur, bespeak, bode, declare, denote, evidence, forebode, foreshow, import, indicate, manifest, mark, mean, portend, presage, prognosticate, promise, represent, signify, suggest, symbolize.

betray *v* abandon, beguile, bespeak, deceive, delude, desert, disappoint, disclose, divulge, double-cross, dupe, ensnare, entrap, evince, expose, fail, forsake, give away, inform on, jilt, lead down the garden path, leave in the lurch, let down, manifest, mislead, rat on, reveal, seduce, sell, sell down the river, sell out, show, stab in the back, tattle on, tell on, turn in, turn over, turn Queen's (or King's) evidence, uncover.
antonyms defend, fulfil, protect.

betrayal *n* abandonment, apostasy, backstabbing, deception, desertion, disappointment, disclosure, disloyalty, divulgence, double cross, double-dealing, duplicity, exposure, faithlessness, falseness, giveaway, Judas kiss, perfidy, rattery, ratting, revelation, seduction, sell-out, treachery, treason, trickery, unfaithfulness.
antonyms loyalty, protection.

betrayer *n* apostate, backstabber, conspirator, deceiver, deserter, double-crosser, informer, renegade, snake in the grass, tattler, traitor.
antonyms protector, supporter.

betroth *v* affiance, contract, engage, espouse, give the hand of, pledge, plight, plight one's troth, promise.

betrothal *n* engagement, espousal, pledging, plight, promise, troth, vow.

better *adj* bigger, cured, finer, fitter, grander, greater, healthier, higher, higher-quality, improved, larger, longer, more apt, more worthwhile, on the mend, nobler, preferable, progressing, recovered, recovering, restored, stronger, superior, surpassing, well, worthier.
antonyms ill, inferior, worse.
v advance, ameliorate, amend, beat, best, cap, correct, edify, enhance, exceed, excel over, further, go one further than, improve, improve on, increase, meliorate, mend, outdo, outperform, outstrip, overtake, overtop, overtrump, raise, rectify, redress, reform, strengthen, surpass, top, trump.
antonyms deteriorate, worsen.

betterment *n* advancement, amelioration, edification, enhancement, furtherance, improvement, melioration, strengthening.
antonyms deterioration, impairment.

between *prep* amid, among, betwixt, inter-, 'mid.

between ourselves confidentially, entre nous, in confidence, in secret, privately, sub rosa, within these four walls.

bevel *n* angle, bezel, bias, cant, chamfer, diagonal, mitre, oblique, slant, slope.
v bias, cant, chamfer, mitre, slant.

beverage *n* draft, drink, libation, liquid, liquor, potable, potation, potion.

bevy *n* band, bunch, collection, company, flock, gaggle, gang, gathering, group, harem, herd, knot, pack, phalanx, troupe.

bewail *v* bemoan, cry over, deplore, grieve for (or over), keen, lament, moan, mourn, regret, repent, rue, sigh over, sorrow over.
antonyms gloat over, glory in, rejoice over, vaunt.

beware *v* avoid, give a wide berth to, guard against, heed, look out, mind, shun, steer clear of, take heed, watch out (for), ware.
antonyms court, trifle with.

bewilder *v* baffle, bamboozle, befuddle, bemuse, buffalo, confound, confuse, daze, dazzle, discombobulate, disconcert, disorient, flummox, fuddle, maze, muddle, mystify, perplex, puzzle, stump, stun, stupefy, throw for a loop, tie in knots.

bewildered *adj* at a loss, awed, baffled, bamboozled, bemused, blank, confused, dazed, dazzled, discombobulated, disconcerted, disoriented, dizzy, flummoxed, lost, muddled, mystified, nonplussed, perplexed, puzzled, stunned, stupefied, surprised, taken aback.
antonyms collected, unperturbed.

bewitch *v* allure, attract, beguile, captivate, charm, enchant, enrapture, ensorcel, enthrall, entrance, fascinate, hex, hoodoo, hypnotize, jinx, mesmerize, obsess, possess, spellbind, transfix, voodoo, witch.

bewitching *adj* alluring, beguiling, charming, enchanting, entrancing, fascinating, glamorous, hypnotic, intriguing, mesmerizing, seductive, tantalizing, witching.
antonym repellent.

beyond *prep* above, across, before, beggaring, behind, further than, on the far (or other) side of, out of range of, out of reach of, over, past, remote from, superior to, transcending, yonder side of.

beyond price inestimable, invaluable, irreplaceable, precious, priceless, without price.

beyond words indescribable, ineffable, inexpressible, unimaginable, unspeakable, unutterable.

bias *n* angle, bent, bigotry, distortion, editorialization, favouritism, imbalance, inclination, intolerance, leaning, lopsidedness, one-sidedness, parti pris, partiality, predisposition, prejudice, slant, tendency, tendentiousness, turn, unfairness, warp.
antonyms fairness, impartiality.
v angle, distort, editorialize, influence, jaundice, load, predispose, prejudice, slant, sway, twist, warp, weight.

biassed *adj* angled, bigoted, blinkered, distorted, embittered, jaundiced, loaded, lopsided, one-sided, partial, predisposed, prejudiced, slanted, swayed, tendentious, twisted, unbalanced, unfair, warped, weighted.
antonyms fair, impartial.

bibulous *adj* alcoholic, crapulous, dipsomaniac, drunken, inebriate, intemperate, thirsty, tipsy.
antonyms sober, temperate.

bicker *v* altercate, argue, clash, disagree, dispute, feud, fight, haggle, have it out, quarrel, row, scrap, spar, squabble, wrangle.
antonym agree.

bicycle *n* bike, cycle, penny-farthing, racer, tandem, two-wheeler, velocipede.

bid *v* ask, call, charge, command, desire, direct, enjoin, instruct, invite, offer, proclaim, propose, request, require, say, suggest, summon, tell, wish.
n amount, ante, attempt, crack, effort, endeavour, offer, price, proposal, proposition, stab, submission, sum, tender, try, venture.

biddable *adj* acquiescent, agreeable, amenable, complaisant, co-operative, docile, obedient, responsive, teachable, tractable.
antonym recalcitrant.

bidding *n* behest, call, charge, command, demand, dictate, direction, injunction, instruction, invitation, order, request, requirement, summons.

big¹ *adj* adult, baggy, beefy, boastful, bombastic, Brobdingnagian, bulky, burly, buxom, colossal, considerable, corpulent, elder, elephantine, eminent, enormous, extensive, gargantuan, gigantic, great, grown, grown-up, heavy, huge, hulking, immense, important, influential, large, leading, loose, main, mammoth, massive, mature, momentous, ponderous, powerful, prime, principal, prodigious, prominent, roomy, serious, significant, sizable, spacious, stout, strapping, substantial, tall, titanic, vast, voluminous, weighty, whopping.
antonyms little, small.

big shot big cheese, big gun, big name, big noise, big wheel, bigwig, celebrity, dignitary, heavyweight, mogul, nob, notability, notable, panjandrum, personage, somebody, VIP, visiting fireman.
antonym nonentity.

big² *adj* altruistic, benevolent, big-hearted, charitable, decent, generous, good, gracious, heroic, kind, lofty, magnanimous, noble, tolerant, unselfish.

bigamy *n* diandry.

bigot *n* chauvinist, dogmatist, fanatic, jingoist, racist, religionist, sectarian, sexist, zealot.
antonyms humanitarian, liberal.

bigoted *adj* biassed, blinkered, chauvinist, closed, dogmatic, fanatical, illiberal, intolerant, jingoistic, narrow, narrow-minded, obstinate, opinionated, prejudiced, racist, sectarian.
antonyms broad-minded, liberal, tolerant.

bigotry *n* bias, chauvinism, discrimination, dogmatism, fanaticism, ignorance, illiberality, injustice, intolerance, jingoism, mindlessness, narrow-mindedness, prejudice, racism, religionism, sectarianism, unfairness.

bigwig *n* big cheese, big gun, big name, big noise, big shot, big wheel, celebrity, dignitary, heavyweight, mogul, nabob, nob, notability, notable, panjandrum, personage, somebody, VIP.

antonyms nobody, nonentity.

bile *n* anger, bad temper, bitterness, choler, gall, ill humour, irascibility, irritability, peevishness, poison, rancour, sourness, spleen, testiness.

bilingual *adj* diglot.

bilious *adj* bad-tempered, choleric, crabby, cross, crotchety, grouchy, grumpy, ill-humoured, irritable, liverish, nauseated, nauseating, nauseous, out of sorts, peevish, poisonous, queasy, sick, sickly, sour, testy.

bilk *v* bamboozle, cheat, con, cozen, deceive, defraud, do (out of), fleece, foil, rook, soak, sting, swindle, thwart, trick.

bill[1] *n* account, act (of parliament), advertisement, bank note, broadsheet, broadside, bulletin, card, catalogue, charges, check, chit, circular, flyer, greenback, handbill, handout, inventory, invoice, leaflet, legislation, list, listing, note, notice, placard, playbill, poster, program, reckoning, roster, schedule, score card, score sheet, statement, syllabus, tab, tally.

v advertise, announce, charge, debit, invoice, list, post, reckon, record.

bill[2] *n* beak, mandible, nib, rostrum.

billet *n* accommodation, barracks, berth, housing, lodgment, lodging, quarterage, quarters.

v accommodate, berth, board, house, lodge, put up, quarter, station.

billow *v* balloon, belly, bulge, expand, fill out, heave, puff out, roll, seethe, spread, surge, swell, undulate, wave.

billowy *adj* billowing, heaving, rippling, rolling, surging, swelling, swirling, tossing, undulating, waving.

bind *v* attach, bandage, border, chafe, cinch, clamp, colligate, commit, compel, confine, constipate, constrain, cover, detain, dress, edge, encase, engage, fasten, finish, force, glue, hamper, harden, hinder, hitch, hobble, hogtie, indenture, lash, obligate, oblige, pledge, require, restrain, restrict, rub, seal, secure, stick, stiffen, strap, swaddle, swathe, thicken, tie, trim, truss, wrap.

n catch-22, difficulty, dilemma, hole, impasse, nuisance, predicament, quandary, tight spot.

binding *adj* compulsory, conclusive, imperative, indissoluble, irrevocable, mandatory, obligatory, permanent, strict, unalterable, unbreakable.

n bandage, border, covering, deligation, edging, stricture, syndesis, tape, trimming, wrapping.

binge *n* banquet, bender, blind, bout, feast, fling, guzzle, jag, orgy, spree.

antonym fast.

v overeat, overindulge, pig out, scarf.

biography *n* account, adventures, autobiography, biopic, curriculum vitae, exposé, fortunes, hagiography, history, life, life story, memoir, memoirs, recollections, record.

birdlike *adj* aquiline, avian, hawklike, ornithoid.

birth *n* ancestry, background, beginning, blood, breeding, childbirth, delivery, derivation, descent, emergence, extraction, family, genealogy, genesis, line, lineage, nativity, nobility, origin, parentage, parturition, pedigree, race, rise, source, stirps, stock.

give birth to bear, beget, bring forth, engender, father, generate, give rise to, produce, spark.

birthmark *n* angioma, beauty spot, blotch, mole, naevus, port wine stain, strawberry mark.

birthplace *n* fount, incunabula, native country, native town, origin, place of origin, provenance, roots, source.

biscuit *n* cake, cookie, cracker, hardtack, rusk, scone, wafer.

bisect *v* bifurcate, cross, divide, halve, intersect, separate, split.

bisexual *adj* androgynous, epicene, gynandromorphic, gynandromorphous, gynandrous, hermaphrodite, hermaphroditic.

antonyms heterosexual, homosexual.

bishop *n* archbishop, diocesan, exarch, metropolitan, patriarch, prelate, primate, suffragan.

bit *n* act, atom, chip, crumb, drop, flake, fragment, grain, instant, iota, jiffy, jot, minute, mite, moment, morsel, part, particle, period, piece, routine, scrap, second, segment, shard, share, shred, sip, sippet, slice, snippet, speck, spell, time, tittle, while, whit.

bit by bit gradually, in dribs and drabs, insidiously, in stages, little by little, piecemeal, seriatim, slowly (but surely), step by step.

antonym all at once, wholesale.

bitch *v* beef, bellyache, carp, complain, fuss, gripe, groan, grouse, grumble, kvetch, moan, nag, natter, whine, yammer.

bitchy *adj* backbiting, catty, cruel, ill-tempered, malicious, mean, nasty, poisonous, savage, snarky, snide, spiteful, venomous, vicious, vindictive, vixenish, waspish.

antonym kind.

bite *v* burn, chomp, clamp, corrode, crunch, crush, cut, gnaw, hurt, nibble, nip, pierce, pinch, rend, seize, smart, snap, sting, tear, tingle, wound.

n edge, food, grip, kick, morsel, mouthful, nibble, nip, piece, pinch, piquancy, prick, punch, pungency, refreshment, smarting, snack, spice, sting, taste, tingle, wound.

bite the dust collapse, crumple, die, drop, drop dead, expire, fall, give up the ghost, go down, perish.

biting *adj* astringent, bitter, blighting, blistering, caustic, cold, crushing, cutting, cynical, freezing, harsh, hurtful, incisive, ironic, mordant, nipping, penetrating, piercing, raw, sarcastic, savage, scathing, severe, sharp, smarting, stinging, tart, trenchant, withering, wounding.

antonyms bland, mild.

bitter *adj* acerb, acerbic, acid, acrid, acrimonious, astringent, begrudging, biting, blistering, calamitous, caustic, crabbed, cruel, crushing, cynical, dire, disillusioned, disillusioning, distressing, embittered, fierce, freezing, galling, grievous, harsh, hateful, heartbreaking, hostile, intense, ironic, jaundiced, merciless, painful, poignant, poisoned, rancorous, raw, resentful, ruthless, sarcastic, savage, severe, sharp, sore, sour, stinging, sullen, tart, unsweetened, vexatious, vinegary, waspish.

antonyms contented, genial, sweet.

bitterness *n* acerbity, acidity, acrimony, animosity, asperity, astringency, causticity, cynicism, disillusionment, grudge, heartbreak, hostility, irony, mordancy, pain, painfulness, pique, rancour, resentment, sarcasm, sharpness, sourness, sting, tartness, venom, virulence, wormwood.

antonyms contentment, geniality, sweetness.

bizarre *adj* abnormal, comical, curious, deviant, eccentric, extraordinary, extravagant, fantastic, freakish, grotesque, ludicrous, odd, offbeat, off the wall, outlandish, outré, peculiar, quaint, queer, ridiculous, strange, unusual, way out, weird, wild, wild and woolly.

antonym normal.

bizarreness *n* bizarrerie, curiousness, eccentricity, freakishness, grotesqueness, grotesquerie, oddity, oddness, outlandishness, queerness, singularity, strangeness, weirdness.

antonym normality.

blab *v* blabber, blurt, disclose, divulge, gossip, leak, let slip, let the cat out of the bag, reveal, spill the beans, squeal, tattle, tell.

antonyms hide, hush up, keep mum, keep quiet, keep under wraps.

blabber *v* blab, blather, chatter, gab, gabble, gibber, jabber, natter, prattle, run off at the mouth, wag one's tongue, yak, yap.

black *adj* baleful, begrimed, charred, coal-black, dark, darksome, depressing, dingy, dirty, dismal, doleful, dusky, ebony, filthy, funereal, gloomy, grim, grimy, grubby, hopeless, horrible, inky, jet, jet-black, jetty, menacing, moonless, murky, ominous, overcast, pitch-black, pitch-dark, pitchy, raven, sable, sad, soiled, sombre, sooty, stained, starless, Stygian, sullen, swarthy, threatening, thunderous.

black out censor, collapse, conceal, cover up, darken, eclipse, extinguish, faint, flake out, keel over, lose consciousness, obliterate, pass out, shade, suppress, swoon, withhold.

black sheep disgrace, drop-out, ne'er-do-well, outcast, pariah, prodigal, reject, renegade, reprobate, wastrel.

antonym pride.

blackball *v* ban, bar, blacklist, boycott, debar, exclude, ostracize, oust, reject, repudiate, snub, veto.

blacken *v* befoul, begrime, besmirch, calumniate, cloud, darken, defame, defile, denigrate, detract from, dishonour, malign, revile, slander, smear, smirch, smudge, soil, stain, sully, taint, tarnish, traduce, vilify.

antonyms enhance, praise.

blackguard *n* bastard, blighter, cad, churl, clod, creep, cur, devil, knave, miscreant, rascal, reprobate, rogue, rotter, scoundrel, stinker, swine, villain, wretch.

blacklist *v* ban, bar, blackball, boycott, debar, disallow, exclude, expel, ostracize, proscribe, reject, repudiate, snub, taboo, veto.

antonyms accept, allow.

blackmail *n* bloodsucking, coercion, exaction, extortion, hush money, intimidation, milking, payoff, protection, ransom, threat.

v bleed, bribe, coerce, compel, force, hold to ransom, lean on, milk, squeeze, threaten.

blackmailer *n* bloodsucker, extortioner, extortionist, vampire.

blackout *n* ban, censorship, coma, concealment, cover-up, faint, power cut, secrecy, suppression, swoon, syncope, unconsciousness.

bladder *n* bag, bursa, caecum, capsule, cell, cyst, pocket, pouch, receptacle, sac, theca, utricle, vesica, vesicle.

blade *n* beau, cavalier, cutlass, dagger, dirk, edge, falchion, gallant, knife, rapier, sabre, scalpel, scimitar, skate, snickersnee, sword, swordsman, vane.

blamable *adj* accountable, answerable, at fault, blameworthy, censurable, culpable, guilty, liable, reprehensible, reproachable, reprovable, responsible, wrong.

blame *n* accountability, accusation, animadversion, castigation, censure, charge(s), condemnation, criticism, culpability, fault, guilt, incrimination, liability, obloquy, onus, rap, recrimination, reprimand, reproach, reproof, responsibility, stricture.

v accuse, attribute to, censure, charge, chide, condemn, criticize, disapprove, find fault with, get on (someone's) case, hold accountable, hold responsible, lay to (someone's) account, make liable, rebuke, reprehend, reprimand, reproach, reprove, tax, stick (someone) with, upbraid.

antonym exonerate.

blameless *adj* above reproach, clean, clear, faultless, guiltless, holy, immaculate, impeccable, inculpable, innocent, irreprehensible, irreproachable, irreprovable, perfect, pure, righteous, sinless, spotless, stainless, sterling, unblamable, unblemished, unimpeachable, unspotted, unsullied, untarnished, upright, virtuous.

antonym guilty.

blameworthy *adj* censurable, culpable, discreditable, disreputable, flagitious, guilty, indefensible, inexcusable, reprehensible, reproachable, shameful, unworthy.

antonym blameless.

blanch *v* bleach, blench, drain, etiolate, fade, pale, whiten.

antonyms blush, colour, redden.

bland *adv* affable, amiable, anodyne, balmy, boring, calm, characterless, congenial, courteous, demulcent, dull, fair-spoken, flat, friendly, gentle, gracious, harmless, humdrum, hypo-allergenic, impassive, inscrutable, insipid, mild, monotonous, nondescript, non-irritant, safe, smooth, soft, soothing, suave, tasteless, tedious, temperate, unexciting, uninspiring, uninteresting, urbane, vapid, weak.

antonyms piquant, sharp.

blandishments *n* blarney, cajolery, coaxing, compliments, enticements, fawning, flattery, inducements, ingratiation, inveiglement, lipsalve, persuasiveness, smooth talk, soft soap, sweet talk, sycophancy, wheedling.

blank *adj* apathetic, bald, bare, bewildered, clean, clear, confounded, confused, deadpan, dull, dumfounded, empty, expressionless, featureless, flat, glazed, hollow, impassive, indifferent, inscrutable, lifeless, nonplussed, plain, poker-faced, sheer, spotless, staring, stark, uncomprehending, unfilled, unmarked, unrhymed, utter, vacant, vacuous, vague, void, white.

n break, emptiness, gap, nothingness, oblivion, space, tabula rasa, vacancy, vacuity, vacuum, void.

blanket *n* carpet, cloak, coat, coating, cover, covering, coverlet, envelope, film, housing, layer, mackinaw, manta, mantle, rug, sheet, wrapper, wrapping.

adj across-the-board, all-embracing, all-inclusive, comprehensive, inclusive, overall, sweeping, wide-ranging.

v cloak, cloud, coat, conceal, cover, deaden, eclipse, hide, mask, muffle, obscure, surround.

blankness *n* abstraction, bareness, dullness, emptiness, expressionlessness, featurelessness, flatness, hollowness, impassivity, incomprehension, indifference, inscrutability, obliviousness, plainness, starkness, vacancy, vacuity, void.

blare *v* blast, boom, clamour, clang, honk, hoot, resound, roar, scream, shriek, toot, trumpet.

blarney *n* blandishment, cajolery, coaxing, eloquence, flattery, persuasiveness, smooth talk, soft soap, spiel, sweet talk, wheedling.

blasé *adj* apathetic, bored, dulled, glutted, indifferent, jaded, nonchalant, offhand, sated, satiated, surfeited, unconcerned, unexcited, unfazed, unimpressed, unimpressible, uninspired, uninterested, unmoved, weary, world-weary.

antonyms enthusiastic, excited.

blaspheme *v* abuse, curse, damn, defile, desecrate, execrate, imprecate, profane, revile, swear.

blasphemous *adj* execratory, godless, hubristic, impious, imprecatory, irreligious, irreverent, profane, sacrilegious, ungodly.

blasphemy *n* curse, cursing, defilement, desecration, execration, expletive, hubris, impiety, impiousness, imprecation, irreverence, outrage, profanation, profaneness, profanity, sacrilege, swearing, violation.

blast[1] *v, n* blare, blow, boom, honk, hoot, roar, scream, shriek, sound, wail.

blast[2] *n* bang, bluster, burst, clap, crack, crash, detonation, discharge, draft, eruption, explosion, gale, gust, outburst, salvo, squall, storm, tempest, volley, wind.

v assail, attack, blight, blow up, burst, castigate, crucify, demolish, destroy, devastate, explode, flay, kill, lash, lay waste, ruin, shatter, shrivel, storm at, wither.

blasted *adj* blighted, desolated, destroyed, devastated, ravaged, ruined, scorched, shattered, wasted, withered.

blatant *adj* arrant, bald, barefaced, brazen, clamorous, conspicuous, egregious, flagrant, flaunted, flaunting, glaring, loud, naked, noisy, obtrusive, obvious, ostentatious, outright, overt, prominent, pronounced, sheer, unmitigated, utter.

blaze *n* blast, bonfire, brilliance, burst, conflagration, eruption, explosion, fire, flame(s), flare, flare-up, flash, fury, glare, glow, light, outbreak, outburst, radiance, rush, storm.

v beam, burn, burst, erupt, explode, fire, flame (up), flare (up), flash, fume, glare, gleam, glow, seethe, shine, storm.

blazon *v* announce, broadcast, bruit, celebrate, display, flaunt, flourish, inscribe, make known, noise abroad, paint, proclaim, publicize, publish, trumpet, vaunt.

antonyms hush up, keep quiet, keep under wraps.

bleach *v* blanch, decolorize, etiolate, fade, lighten, pale, peroxide, whiten.

n chlorine, decolorizer, Javel water, peroxide, whitener.

bleak *adj* bare, barren, bitter, blasted, cheerless, chilly, cold, colourless, comfortless, delightless, depressing, desolate, discouraging, disheartening, dismal, dreary, empty, exposed, forbidding, gaunt, gloomy, grey, grim, harsh, hopeless, joyless, leaden, loveless, naked, raw, sombre, stark, weather-beaten, windswept, windy.

antonyms cheerful, congenial, cosy.

bleary *adj* blurred, blurry, cloudy, dim, fogged, foggy, fuzzy, hazy, indistinct, misty, muddy, murky, obscured, rheumy, watery.

bleat *v* baa, beef, bellyache, bitch, blat, complain, growl, grumble, moan, whine, yammer.

bleed *v* blackmail, deplete, drain, empty, exhaust, exploit, extort, extract, extravasate, exude, fleece, flow, gush, hemorrhage, leech, menstruate, milk, ooze, run, sap, seep, soak, spread, spurt, squeeze, suck dry, suffer, trickle, weep.

bleed for ache for, break for, feel

compassion for, go out to, hurt for, pity.

blemish *n* birthmark, blot, blotch, blur, defect, deformity, disfigurement, disgrace, dishonour, fault, flaw, imperfection, mackle, macula, mark, naevus, pimple, pock, smudge, speck, spot, stain, taint, zit.

v besmirch, blot, blotch, blur, damage, deface, disfigure, flaw, impair, injure, maculate, mar, mark, smirch, smudge, spoil, spot, stain, sully, taint, tarnish.

blench *v* balk, blanch, boggle, cower, draw back, falter, flinch, hesitate, jib, pale, quail, quake, quiver, recoil, shrink, shudder, shy, start, wince.

blend *v* alloy, amalgamate, coalesce, combine, complement, compound, fit, fuse, harmonize, intermix, match, meld, merge, mingle, mix, shade, synthesize, temper, unite.

antonyms clash, separate.

n alloy, amalgam, amalgamation, combination, composite, compound, concoction, fusion, harmonization, harmony, interunion, meld, mix, mixture, synthesis, union.

bless *v* anoint, approve, consecrate, dedicate, endorse, endow, exalt, extol, favour, gift, glorify, grace, hallow, lay hands on, magnify, ordain, praise, pray over, prosper, protect, provide, sanction, sanctify, shine upon, speed, thank.

antonyms condemn, curse.

blessed *adj* adored, anointed, beatified, blissful, consecrated, contented, divine, endowed, exalted, favoured, fortunate, glad, glorified, hallowed, happy, holy, joyful, joyous, lucky, magnified, prosperous, revered, sacred, sanctified.

antonym cursed.

blessedness *n* beatitude, bliss, blissfulness, contentment, felicity, happiness, holiness, joy, sanctity.

blessing *n* advantage, anointing, approbation, approval, authorization, backing, benedicite, benediction, benefit, benison, boon, bounty, commendation, concurrence, consecration, consent, darshan, dedication, favour, gain, gift, godsend, grace, help, invocation, kiddush, kindness, leave, permission, prayer, sanction, service, support, thanksgiving, windfall.

antonyms bane, blight, condemnation, curse.

blather *n* blather, chatter, chit-chat, claptrap, drivel, gabble, gibberish, gobbledegook, jabbering, loquacity, moonshine, nonsense, prattle, twaddle.

v blabber, blather, chatter, gab, gabble, go on, jabber, natter, prattle, twaddle.

blight *n* affliction, bane, blight, cancer, canker, check, contamination, corruption, curse, decay, depression, disease, evil, fungus, infestation, mildew, pest, pestilence, plague, pollution, rot, scourge, setback, woe.

antonyms blessing, boon.

v annihilate, blast, crush, dash, destroy, disappoint, euchre, frustrate, injure, mar, ruin, shatter, shrivel, spoil, undermine, wither, wreck.

antonym bless.

blind *adj* amaurotic, bat-blind, beetle-eyed, blinkered, blotto, careless, closed, concealed, darkened, dazzled, dim, drunk, drunken, eyeless, floundering, frantic, hasty, headlong, heedless, hidden, ice-blind, ignorant, impetuous, inattentive, inconsiderate, indifferent, indiscriminate, injudicious, insensate, insensitive, intoxicated, irrational, mad, mindless, neglectful, oblivious, prejudiced, purblind, random, rash, reckless, sand-blind, senseless, sightless, sloshed, snow-blind, sozzled, stone-blind, stumbling, thick, thoughtless, unaware, uncontrollable, uncritical, undiscerning, unobservant, unobserving, unquestioning, unreasoned, unreasoning, unseeing, unsighted, unthinking, violent, visionless, wild.

antonyms aware, circumspect, clear, judicious, sighted.

n camouflage, cloak, cover, cover-up, distraction, façade, feint, front, hiding place, mask, masquerade, screen, shade, smoke screen.

blindfold *v* bamboozle, beguile, blind, deceive, delude, dupe, fool, hoodwink, mislead, pull the wool over (someone's) eyes.

antonym enlighten.

blindly *adv* aimlessly, carelessly, confusedly, frantically, headlong, heedlessly, hook line and sinker, impetuously, impulsively, incautiously, inconsiderately, indiscriminately, injudiciously, irrationally, madly, mindlessly, passionately, precipitately, purposelessly, randomly, recklessly, senselessly, stumblingly, thoughtlessly, uncritically, unquestioningly, unthinkingly, wildly, wilfully.

antonyms cautiously, circumspectly.

blindness *n* heedlessness, ignorance, indifference, insensitivity, narrow-mindedness, neglect, prejudice, sightlessness, thoughtlessness, unawareness.

antonyms awareness, sight, sightedness.

blink *v* bat, condone, connive at, disregard, flash, flicker, flutter, glimmer, glint, glitter, ignore, nictitate, overlook, scintillate, shine, sparkle, squint, twinkle, wink.

blink at close (or shut) one's eyes to, condone, connive at, disregard, ignore, overlook, turn a blind eye to, wink at.

bliss *n* beatitude, blessedness, blissfulness, darshan, ecstasy, elation, euphoria, felicity, gladness, happiness, heaven, joy, nirvana, paradise, rapture.

antonyms damnation, misery.

blissful *adj* beatific, blessed, contented, ecstatic, elated, enraptured, euphoric, happy, heavenly, joyful, joyous, peaceful, rapturous.

antonym wretched.

blister *n* abscess, blain, bleb, boil, bubble, bulla, canker, carbuncle, cyst, furuncle, papilla, papilloma, pimple, pock, pustule, sore, swelling, ulcer, vesicle, welt, wen.

blistering *adj* burning, cruel, cutting, excoriating, hot, intense, killing, sarcastic, savage, scathing, scorching, stifling, sweltering, vesicant, vesicatory, vicious, virulent, withering.

antonyms mild, refreshing, soothing.

blithe *adj* airy, animated, buoyant, carefree, careless, casual, cheerful, cheery, debonair, gay, gladsome, happy, heedless, jaunty, light-hearted, lightsome, lively, merry, mirthful, nonchalant, playful, sprightly, sunny, thoughtless, unconcerned, untroubled, vivacious.

antonym morose.

blizzard *n* flurry, snow squall, snowstorm, squall, storm, tempest, whiteout.

bloated *adj* blown up, bombastic, dilated, distended, dropsical, enlarged, expanded, glutted, inflated, edematous, puffy, sated, swollen, tumescent, tumid, turgid.

antonyms shrivelled, shrunken, thin.

blob *n* ball, bead, bubble, dab, dewdrop, drop, droplet, glob, globule, gob, lump, mass.

bloc *n* alliance, axis, cabal, cartel, clique, coalition, combine, entente, faction, federation, group, league, megacorporation, monopoly, party, ring, section.

block *n* bar, barrier, blockage, brick, cake, chunk, complex, cube, delay, group, hang-up, hindrance, hunk, impediment, ingot, jam, let, lump, mass, neighbourhood, obstacle, obstruction, piece, resistance, section, set, sheet, slab, square, stoppage, street, stretch, unit.

v arrest, bar, blockade, check, choke, clog, close, dam up, foil, halt, hinder, impede, obstruct, obturate, occlude, oppilate, plug, resist, stonewall, stop, stop up, thwart, veto.

blockade *n* barricade, barrier, beleaguerment, closure, encirclement, obstruction, siege, stoppage.

blockage *n* block, blocking, clot, embolism, hindrance, impediment, jam, log-jam, obstruction, occlusion, stoppage.

blockhead *n* bonehead, chump, clown, dipstick, dolt, dope, dork, doze, dullard, dummy, dunce, dunderhead, fathead, fool, goof, idiot, ignoramus, ninny, nitwit, noodle, numskull, pinhead, twit.

antonyms brain, genius.

bloke *n* blighter, bod, body, bugger, chap, character, customer, fellow, guy, individual, personage.

blond or **blonde** *adj* bleached, fair, fair-haired, fair-skinned, flaxen, flaxen-haired, golden, golden-haired, light-coloured, light-haired, straw-coloured, tow-headed.

blood[1] *n* ancestry, birth, consanguinity, dander, descent, extraction, family, kindred, kinship, lineage, relations, relationship, royalty, stock, temper, temperament.

blood[2] *n* bloodshed, carnage, gore, killing, murder, slaughter, violence.

bloodcurdling *adj* chilling, dreadful, ear-piercing, eldritch, fearful, frightening, frightful, hair-raising, horrible, horrifying, scary, spine-chilling, terrifying, weird.

bloodless *adj* anemic, ashen, chalky, cold, cold-hearted, colourless, cruel, drained, feeble, inhuman, insipid, languid, lifeless, listless, non-violent, pale, pallid, passionless, pasty, peaceable, sallow, sickly, spiritless, torpid, unemotional, unfeeling, wan.

antonyms bloody, ruddy, vigorous.

bloodshed *n* bloodletting, butchery, carnage, gore, killing, massacre, murder, slaughter, slaying.

bloodsucker *n* blackmailer, extortioner, extortionist, leech, parasite, sponger, vampire.

bloodthirsty *adj* barbaric, barbarous, brutal, cruel, ferocious, inhuman, murderous, ruthless, sanguinary, savage, slaughterous, vicious, warlike.

bloody *adj* bleeding, bloodstained, blooming, brutal, cruel, ferocious, fierce, gaping, murderous, raw, sanguinary, sanguineous, savage.

bloom *n* beauty, blossom, blossoming, blow, blush, bud, efflorescence, florescence, flourishing, flower, flush, freshness, glow, health, heyday, lustre, perfection, prime, radiance, rosiness, spring, summer, vigour.

v blossom, blow, bud, burgeon, develop, flourish, grow, open, prosper, sprout, succeed, thrive, wax.

antonym wither.

blooming *adj* blossoming, bonny, burgeoning, florescent, flourishing, flowering, glowing, healthful, healthy, rosy, ruddy, thriving.

antonym ailing.

blooper *n* bêtise, blunder, botch, clanger, clunker, error, fault, faux pas, fluff, gaffe, gaucherie, howler, inaccuracy, indiscretion, mistake, oversight, pratfall, slip, slip-up, solecism.

blossom *n* bloom, bud, floret, flower, flowers.

v bloom, blow, burgeon, develop, effloresce, flourish, flower, grow, mature, progress, prosper, thrive.

antonym wither.

blot *n* blemish, blotch, defect, disgrace, fault, flaw, mackle, macula, mark, patch, smear, smudge, speck, splotch, spot, stain, taint.

v besmirch, bespatter, blur, disfigure, disgrace, maculate, mar, mark, smirch, smudge, soil, spoil, spot, stain, sully, taint, tarnish.

blot out cancel, darken, delete, destroy, eclipse, efface, erase, expunge, obliterate, obscure, shadow, wipe out.

blotch *n* blemish, blot, mark, patch, smudge, splash, splotch, spot, stain.

blotchy *adj* blemished, patchy, reddened, smeary, smudgy, spotted, spotty, stained, uneven.

blow[1] *v* bear, blare, blast, breathe, buffet, carry, drift, drive, exhale, fan, fling, flow, flutter, mouth, pant, pipe, play, puff, rush, sound, stream, sweep, toot, trumpet, waft, whirl, whisk, wind.

n blast, draft, flurry, gale, gust, puff, squall, tempest, wind.

blow over cease, die down, disappear,

blurt

dissipate, end, finish, fizzle out, pass, peter out, subside, vanish.

blow up balloon, belly out, bloat, dilate, distend, enlarge, exaggerate, expand, fill, fill out, hype, inflate, magnify, overblow, overhype, overstate, puff up, pump up, swell.

blow² *n* affliction, bang, bash, bat, belt, biff, bombshell, bop, box, buffet, calamity, catastrophe, clap, clip, clout, clump, comedown, concussion, disappointment, disaster, haymaker, jolt, knock, knuckle sandwich, misfortune, punch, rabbit-punch, rap, reverse, setback, shock, slap, slug, smack, sock, stroke, swash, swat, swipe, thump, uppercut, upset, wallop, welt, whack, whap.

blow up blast, blow a fuse, blow one's top, bomb, burst, detonate, dynamite, erupt, explode, go off, go off the deep end, have a bird, have a fit, hit the roof, lose one's cool, lose it, lose one's temper, rage, rupture, shatter.

blown *adj* breathless, effete, jaded, shot, spent, stale, tired, used up, worthless.

blowout *n* bash, celebration, binge, blast, burst, carousal, detonation, eruption, explosion, feast, party, puncture, rupture, spree.

blowy *adj* blustery, breezy, drafty, fresh, gusty, squally, stormy, windy.

blowsy *adj* bedraggled, dishevelled, draggle-tailed, florid, flushed, frowzy, messy, red-faced, ruddy, slatternly, slipshod, sloppy, slovenly, sluttish, tousled, ungroomed, unkempt, untidy.

antonyms neat, smart.

bludgeon *n* baton, billy, club, cudgel, knobkerrie, nightstick, shillelagh, stick, truncheon.

v badger, batter, beat, browbeat, bulldoze, bully, clobber, club, coerce, cudgel, force, harass, hector, intimidate, steamroller, strike, terrorize, threaten, torment.

blue¹ *adj* aquamarine, azure, cerulean, cobalt, cyan, indigo, navy, sapphire, turquoise, ultramarine.

blue² *adj* black, bleak, dejected, depressed, despondent, dismal, dispirited, doleful, downcast, downhearted, down in the dumps, gloomy, glum, heavy-hearted, low, melancholy, miserable, morose, sad, unhappy.

antonym cheerful.

blue³ *adv* bawdy, coarse, dirty, improper, indecent, lewd, naughty, obscene, offensive, pornographic, risqué, smutty, vulgar.

antonym decent.

blue-pencil *v* bowdlerize, censor, clean up, correct, edit, expurgate, purge.

blueprint *n* archetype, design, draft, guide, guidelines, instructions, model, outline, pattern, pilot, plan, project, prototype, sketch.

blues *n* blue devils, dejection, depression, despondency, doldrums, dumps, gloom, gloominess, glumness, melancholy, miseries, moodiness.

antonym euphoria.

bluff¹ *n* bank, cape, cliff, crag, escarpment, foreland, headland, height, knoll, peak, precipice, promontory, ridge, scarp, slope.

adj affable, blunt, candid, direct, downright, frank, genial, good-natured, hearty, open, outspoken, plain-spoken, straightforward.

antonyms diplomatic, refined.

bluff² *v* bamboozle, deceive, fake, feign, fib, hoodwink, lead on, lie, mislead, pretend, psych out, pull (someone's) leg, sham.

n bluster, boast, braggadocio, bravado, deceit, deception, fake, fanfaronade, feint, fib, humbug, idle boast (or threat), lie, pretence, sham, show, subterfuge, trick.

blunder *n* bêtise, blooper, boner, booboo, clanger, clinker, clunker, error, fault, faux pas, fluff, gaffe, gaucherie, goof, howler, impropriety, inaccuracy, indiscretion, misstep, mistake, oversight, pratfall, slip, slip-up, solecism.

v blow it, botch, bumble, bungle, err, fall on one's face, flounder, flub, fluff, fumble, goof, mess up, miscalculate, misjudge, mismanage, muff (it), put one's foot in it, slip a cog, slip up, stumble, trip.

blunderer *n* botcher, bungler, duffer, fool, goof, incompetent, oaf.

blunt *adj* abrupt, bluff, brusque, candid, curt, direct, discourteous, downright, dull, dulled, edgeless, explicit, forthright, frank, honest, impolite, insensitive, obtuse, outspoken, plain-spoken, pointless, retuse, rounded, rude, straightforward, stubby, stumpy, tactless, thick, trenchant, unceremonious, uncivil, unpolished, unsharpened.

antonyms sharp, tactful.

v allay, alleviate, anesthetize, buffer, dampen, deaden, dull, hebetate, numb, obtund, palliate, soften, stupefy, take the edge off, weaken.

antonyms intensify, sharpen.

bluntness *n* abruptness, brusqueness, candidness, candour, dullness, forthrightness, frankness, hebetude, insensitivity, lack of ceremony, obtuseness, obtusity, tactlessness.

antonyms sharpness, tact.

blur *v* becloud, befog, blear, blemish, blot, blotch, cloud, darken, dim, fog, mask, obfuscate, obscure, scumble, smear, smudge, soften, spot, stain.

n blear, blot, blotch, cloudiness, confusion, dimness, fog, fuzziness, haze, indistinctness, muddle, obscurity, smear, smudge, spot, stain.

blurb *n* advertisement, commendation, copy, hype, puff, spiel.

blurred *adj* beclouded, bleary, blurry, clouded, confused, dim, faint, foggy, fuzzy, hazy, ill-defined, indistinct, misty, nebulous, unclear, vague.

antonym distinct.

blurt *v* babble, blab, cry, disclose, divulge, ejaculate, exclaim, gush, leak, let slip, reveal, spill, spout, utter.

antonyms clam up, guard one's lips, hush up, keep quiet.

blush *v* be ashamed, colour, crimson, flush, glow, mantle, redden.
antonym blanch.
n colour, flush, glow, pink, red, reddening, redness, rosiness, ruddiness, suffusion.

blushing *adj* abashed, ashamed, confused, discomfited, embarrassed, flushed, glowing, pink, red, red-faced, rosy, sheepish, suffused.
antonyms composed, pale.

bluster *v* be all bark and no bite, be all talk, boast, brag, browbeat, bully, domineer, hector, rant, roar, rodomontade, roister, storm, strut, swagger, swell, talk big, vaunt.
n (big) show, bluff, boasting, bombast, bounce, braggadocio, bragging, bravado, crowing, fanfaronade, parade, racket, rodomontade, swagger, swaggering, vapour, vauntery.

blusterer *n* bigmouth, big talker, boaster, braggart, roisterer, show-off, swaggerer, swank, swashbuckler, swasher, windbag.

blustery *adj* big-mouthed, boasting, boisterous, gusty, loud, loud-mouthed, noisy, squally, stormy, tempestuous, tumultuous, violent, wild, windy.
antonym calm.

board¹ *n* beam, billboard, blackboard, bulletin board, chalkboard, clapboard, deal, lath, notice board, panel, plank, rafter, sheet, shelf, sign, signboard, slab, slat, stud, table, timber, two-by-four, whiteboard.

board² *n* commons, food, grub, meals, provisions, rations, repasts, table, victuals.
v accommodate, bed, billet, feed, house, lodge, put up, quarter, room, table.

board³ *n* advisers, chamber, commission, committee, conclave, consistory, council, directorate, directors, elders, jury, leadership, panel, trustees.

board⁴ *v* catch, embark, embus, emplane, enter, mount.

boast *v* be all talk, blazon, blow, bluster, brag, claim, crow, exaggerate, exhibit, gasconade, possess, puff oneself up, rodomontade, show off, sport, strut, swagger, talk big, trumpet, vaunt.
antonyms deprecate oneself, put oneself down.
n avowal, brag, claim, fanfaronade, gasconade, joy, pride, rodomontade, vaunt.

boaster *n* bigmouth, big talker, blowhard, braggart, gascon, show-off, swaggerer, swelled head, vaunter.

boastful *adj* braggart, bragging, cocky, conceited, crowing, egotistical, proud, puffed-up, self-important, swaggering, swanky, too big for one's boots (or britches), vain, vainglorious, vaunting, windy.
antonym modest.

boasting *n* big talk, bluster, bragging, conceit, exaggeration, fanfaronade, gasconade, jactation, jactitation, ostentation, rodomontade, showing off, strutting, swagger, swank, vaingloriousness, vainglory, vauntery, vaunting, windiness.

antonym modesty.

boat *n* barge, bark, barque, bateau, canoe, cockboat, cockleboat, coracle, craft, dinghy, dugout, ferry, gondola, houseboat, junk, kayak, ketch, longliner, motorboat, punt, riverboat, rowboat, sailboat, speedboat, umiak, vessel, water-craft, yacht.

bob *v* bounce, duck, hop, jerk, jolt, jounce, jump, leap, nod, oscillate, quiver, shake, skip, spring, twitch, waggle, weave, wobble.

bode *v* adumbrate, augur, betoken, forebode, foreshadow, foreshow, foretell, forewarn (of), import, indicate, intimate, omen, portend, predict, presage, prophesy, signify, threaten, warn (of).

bodily *adj* actual, carnal, concrete, corporal, corporeal, earthly, fleshly, incarnate, material, physical, real, somatic, substantial, tangible.
antonym spiritual.
adv actually, altogether, as a whole, bag and baggage, collectively, completely, concretely, corporeally, en masse, entirely, fully, in toto, physically, totally, wholly.
antonyms in spirit, piecemeal.

body¹ *n* being, bod, build, bulk, cadaver, carcass, consistency, corpse, creature, density, figure, firmness, form, frame, human, individual, mass, material, matter, mortal, opacity, person, physique, relics, remains, richness, shape, solidity, stiff, substance, substantiality, tabernacle, thickness, torso, trunk, volume.

body² *n* association, band, bevy, bloc, cartel, collection, company, confederation, congress, corporation, corpus, crowd, group, horde, league, majority, mass, mob, multitude, organization, society, syndicate, throng, unit.

body snatcher *n* desecrator, resurrectionist.

bog *n* fen, marsh, marshland, mire, morass, moss, muskeg, quagmire, quicksand, slough, swamp, swampland, wetland.

bog down delay, flounder, get mired, get stuck, halt, hinder, impede, mire, overwhelm, retard, sink, slow down, slow up, stall, stick.

boggle *v* balk, be overwhelmed, blench, dither, doubt, equivocate, falter, fight shy, flinch, hang back, hesitate, jib, jump, overwhelm, pause, recoil, reel, shilly-shally, shrink, shy (away), stagger, start, startle, vacillate, waver.

boggy *adj* fennish, fenny, marshy, miry, morassy, mucky, muddy, oozy, quaggy, soft, spongy, swampy, waterlogged, wet.
antonym arid.

bogus *adj* artificial, counterfeit, dummy, ersatz, fake, false, forged, fraudulent, imitation, phony, pinchbeck, pseudo, sham, spoof, spurious, unauthentic.
antonym genuine.

bogey *n* bête noire, bogeyman, bugaboo, bugbear, goblin, hobgoblin, imp, incubus, nightmare, spectre, spook.

bohemian *adj* alternative, artistic, art(s)y, bizarre, carefree, eccentric, exotic, irregular, nonconformist, offbeat, outré, unconventional, unorthodox, way out.

booby

antonyms bourgeois, conventional.

n beatnik, drop-out, gypsy, hippie, iconoclast, nonconformist.

antonyms bourgeois, conformist.

boil¹ *v* agitate, brew, bubble, churn, decoct, effervesce, erupt, explode, fizz, foam, froth, fulminate, fume, gurgle, parboil, rage, rave, seethe, simmer, sizzle, spume, steam, stew, storm, wallop.

boil down abridge, abstract, concentrate, condense, decrease, digest, distil, epitomize, reduce, summarize, synopsize.

boil² *n* abscess, anthrax, blain, bleb, blister, carbuncle, furuncle, gathering, gumboil, inflammation, pimple, pock, pustule, sty, tumour, ulcer, whelk.

boiling *adj* angry, baking, blistering, bubbling, enraged, flaming, frying, fuming, furious, gurgling, hot, incensed, indignant, infuriated, roasting, scorching, seething, sweltering, torrid, turbulent.

boisterous *adj* blustery, bouncy, clamorous, disorderly, exuberant, gusty, impetuous, loud, noisy, obstreperous, rackety, raging, rambunctious, riotous, roistering, rollicking, rough, rowdy, squally, tempestuous, termagant, tumultuous, turbulent, unrestrained, unruly, uproarious, vociferous, wild.

antonyms calm, quiet, restrained.

bold *adj* adventurous, audacious, brash, brave, brazen, bright, cheeky, colourful, confident, conspicuous, courageous, daring, dauntless, enterprising, extrovert, eye-catching, fearless, flamboyant, flashy, forceful, forward, fresh, gallant, heroic, impudent, insolent, intrepid, jazzy, lively, loud, malapert, outgoing, pert, plucky, prominent, pronounced, saucy, shameless, showy, spirited, striking, strong, temerarious, unabashed, unashamed, unbashful, valiant, valorous, venturesome, vivid.

antonyms diffident, restrained.

bolster *v* aid, assist, augment, boost, brace, buoy up, buttress, firm up, help, maintain, prop, reinforce, shore up, stay, stiffen, strengthen, supplement, support.

antonym undermine.

bolt *n* arrow, bar, bound, catch, dart, dash, elopement, escape, fastener, flight, flit, latch, lock, missile, peg, pin, projectile, rivet, rod, rush, shaft, sprint, thunderbolt.

v abscond, bar, bound, cram, dart, dash, devour, elope, escape, fasten, fetter, flee, fly, gobble, gorge, gulp, guzzle, jump, latch, leap, lock, run, rush, secure, spring, sprint, stuff, wolf.

bomb *n* A-bomb, bombshell, charge, egg, explosive, flop, grenade, mine, missile, Molotov cocktail, mortar bomb, projectile, rocket, shell, torpedo, washout.

v attack, blow up, bombard, come a cropper, come to grief, destroy, fail, fall flat, flop, misfire, shell, strafe, tear, torpedo.

bombard *v* assail, assault, attack, barrage, batter, beset, besiege, blast, blitz, bomb, cannonade, deluge, harass, hound, importune, inundate, pelt, pester, pound, shell, strafe.

bombardment *n* air raid, assault, attack, barrage, blitz, bombing, cannonade, fire, flak, fusillade, salvo, shelling, strafe.

bombast *n* bluster, brag, braggadocio, euphuism, fustian, gasconade, grandiloquence, grandiosity, heroics, histrionics, magniloquence, pomposity, pretentiousness, rant, rodomontade, verbosity, wordiness.

antonyms reserve, restraint.

bombastic *adj* bloated, convoluted, declamatory, elaborate, euphuistic, fustian, grandiloquent, grandiose, high-flown, histrionic, inflated, magniloquent, pompous, turgid, verbose, windy, wordy.

bona fide actual, authentic, genuine, honest, kosher, lawful, legal, legitimate, real, true, valid.

antonym bogus.

bond *n* adhesion, affiliation, affinity, agreement, attachment, band, binding, chain, compact, connection, contract, copula, cord, covenant, fastening, fetter, ligament, ligature, link, manacle, nexus, obligation, pledge, promise, relation, shackle, tie, union, vinculum, word.

v adhere, attach, bind, connect, fasten, fuse, glue, gum, paste, seal, unite.

bondage *n* captivity, confinement, durance, duress, enslavement, enthrallment, imprisonment, incarceration, restraint, serfdom, servitude, slavery, subjection, subjugation, subservience, thrall, thralldom, vassalage, yoke.

antonyms freedom, independence.

bonfire *n* beacon, conflagration, feu de joie, pyre.

bonny *adj* attractive, beautiful, blithe, blooming, bouncing, buxom, cheerful, cheery, comely, fair, fine, gay, goodly, handsome, joyful, lovely, merry, pretty, shapely, sunny, sweet, wholesome, winsome.

antonym ill-favoured.

bonus *n* advantage, asset, baksheesh, benefit, bounty, bribe, commission, dividend, extra, freebie, gift, gratuity, handout, honorarium, merit pay, perk, perquisite, plus, pourboire, premium, prize, profit, reward, tip.

antonyms disadvantage, disincentive, liability.

bon vivant epicure, epicurean, gastronome, gourmet, hedonist, luxurist, pleasure-seeker, voluptuary.

bony *adj* angular, drawn, emaciated, gangling, gaunt, gawky, knobby, lanky, lean, osseous, rawboned, sclerous, scrawny, sharp, skinny, thin.

antonym plump.

booboo *n* ball-up, bêtise, blooper, blunder, botch, clanger, clunker, error, fault, faux pas, fluff, gaffe, gaucherie, howler, inaccuracy, indiscretion, mistake, oversight, pratfall, slip, slip-up, solecism.

booby *n* blockhead, chump, clod, clown, dimwit, dope, duffer, dunce, dunderhead, fool, goof, halfwit, idiot, nincompoop, ninny, nitwit, palooka, schmuck, simpleton.

antonym genius.

booby prize consolation prize, wooden spoon.

book *n* album, anthology, booklet, catalogue, codex, companion, diary, hornbook, incunabulum, jotter, lectionary, manual, manuscript, notebook, pad, paperback, publication, roll, scroll, text, textbook, tome, tract, volume, work.

v arrange, arrest, bag, charter, engage, enter, insert, list, log, note, organize, pencil in, post, procure, program, record, register, reserve, schedule.

antonym cancel.

bookish *adj* academic, cultured, donnish, erudite, highbrow, intellectual, learned, lettered, literary, pedantic, scholarly, scholastic, studious, well-read.

antonyms lowbrow, unlettered.

boom[1] *v* bang, blare, blast, crash, explode, resound, reverberate, roar, roll, rumble, sound, thunder.

n bang, blast, burst, clap, crash, explosion, reverberation, roar, rumble, thunder.

boom[2] *v* advance, develop, escalate, expand, explode, flourish, gain, go from strength to strength, grow (by leaps and bounds or like a house on fire), increase, intensify, prosper, spurt, strengthen, succeed, swell, thrive.

antonyms collapse, fail.

n advance, boost, development, escalation, expansion, explosion, gain, growth, improvement, increase, jump, spurt, upsurge, upturn.

antonyms collapse, failure.

boon *n* advantage, benefaction, benefit, blessing, donation, favour, gift, godsend, good, grant, gratification, gratuity, kindness, present, windfall.

antonyms blight, disadvantage.

boor *n* barbarian, brute, bumpkin, churl, clodhopper, Goth, hog, kern, lummox, oaf, peasant, philistine, rustic, vulgarian.

antonyms aesthete, charmer.

boorish *adj* awkward, barbaric, churlish, clodhopping, clownish, coarse, crude, gross, gruff, ill-bred, loutish, lubberly, oafish, piggish, rough, rude, rustic, swinish, uncivilized, uncouth, uneducated, unmannerly, unrefined, vulgar.

antonyms cultured, polite, refined.

boorishness *n* awkwardness, barbarity, bluntness, coarseness, crudeness, gaucherie, grossness, ignorance, impoliteness, loutishness, lubberliness, philistinism, piggishness, roughness, rudeness, rudery, rusticity, swinishness, uncouthness, vulgarity.

antonyms politeness, refinement.

boost *n* addition, advancement, assistance, ego trip, encouragement, enhancement, expansion, fillip, hand, heave, help, hoist, hype, improvement, increase, increment, jump,

leg up, lift, praise, promotion, push, rise, supplement, thrust.

antonyms blow, setback.

v advance, advertise, aid, amplify, assist, augment, bolster, develop, elevate, encourage, enhance, enlarge, expand, foster, further, heave, heighten, hoist, hype, improve, increase, inspire, jack up, lift, plug, praise, promote, push, raise, supplement, support, sustain, thrust.

antonyms hinder, undermine.

boot[1] *n* bootee, galosh, gumboot, hiker, kamik, larrigan, mukluk, overshoe, riding-boot, rubber, topboot, wader, wellie, wellington.

v bounce, dismiss, eject, expel, fire, give the bum's rush, give the heave, kick, kick out, knock, oust, punt, sack, shove.

boot[2] *v* aid, avail, benefit, help, profit, serve.

booth *n* bay, box office, carrel, compartment, concession, cubicle, hut, kiosk, stall, stand, ticket office, wicket.

bootless *adj* barren, fruitless, futile, ineffective, pointless, profitless, sterile, unavailing, unproductive, unsuccessful, useless, vain, worthless.

antonyms profitable, useful.

bootlicking *n* backscratching, crawling, cringing, deference, fawning, flattery, grovelling, ingratiation, lackeying, obsequiousness, servility, sycophancy, toadying.

booty *n* boodle, gains, goods, haul, loot, pickings, pillage, plunder, spoil, spoils, swag, takings, winnings.

border *n* borderline, bound, boundary, bounds, brim, brink, circumference, confine, confines, demarcation, edge, fringe, frontier, guilloche, hem, limit, limits, line, lip, list, march, margin, mat, perimeter, periphery, rim, screed, selvage, skirt, surround, trim(ming), valance, verge.

border on abut, adjoin, appear like, approach, approximate, be adjacent to, be akin to, be contiguous with, communicate with, connect, contact, impinge, join, neighbour, resemble, tend toward, touch, verge on.

bordered *adj* bounded, circumscribed, edged, framed, fringed, hemmed, limbate, marginate(d), margined, rimmed, skirted, surrounded, trimmed.

borderline *adj* ambivalent, doubtful, grey, iffy, in-between, indecisive, indefinite, indeterminate, marginal, neither fish nor fowl, problematic, uncertain.

antonyms certain, definite.

bore[1] *v* burrow, countermine, dig, drill, gouge, mine, penetrate, perforate, pierce, sap, sink, tunnel, undermine.

bore[2] *v* fatigue, jade, pester, tire, turn off, weary.

antonyms charm, engage, interest, thrill.

n annoyance, bind, bother, drag, dullard, headache, nuisance, pain, pain in the neck, pest, schmo, trial, turn-off, vexation, vieux jeu, yawn.

antonym pleasure.

boredom *n* accidie, apathy, doldrums, dullness, ennui, flatness, irksomeness, listlessness, monotony, sameness, tediousness, tedium, vapours, weariness, wearisomeness, world-weariness.

antonym interest.

boring *adj* commonplace, dead, draggy, dreary, dry, dull, flat, ho-hum, humdrum, insipid, irksome, monotonous, repetitious, routine, soporific, stale, stupid, tedious, tiresome, tiring, trite, unamusing, unedifying, uneventful, unexciting, unfunny, unimaginative, uninspired, uninteresting, unvarying, vapid, wearisome.

antonyms entertaining, interesting, original.

borrow *v* adopt, appropriate, bum, cadge, copy, derive, draw, filch, mooch, obtain, pilfer, pirate, plagiarize, scrounge, sponge, steal, take, use, usurp.

borrowing *n* adoption, appropriation, cadging, calque, copy, copying, crib, imitation, loan, loan-translation, loanword, plagiarism, plagiarization, scrounging, sponging.

bosom *n* breast, bust, centre, chest, circle, core, heart, midst, protection, sanctuary, shelter.

adj boon, cherished, close, confidential, dear, favourite, inseparable, intimate.

boss¹ *n* administrator, baron, captain, chief, director, employer, executive, foreman, gaffer, governor, head, head honcho, leader, manager, master, overseer, owner, superintendent, supervisor, top banana, top dog.

v administrate, command, control, direct, employ, manage, oversee, run, superintend, supervise.

boss around browbeat, bulldoze, bully, dominate, domineer, dragoon, hector, oppress, order around, overbear, push around, tyrannize.

boss² *n* knob, nub, omphalos, point, protuberance, stud, tip.

bossy *adj* arrogant, authoritarian, autocratic, demanding, despotic, dictatorial, domineering, exacting, hectoring, high-handed, imperious, insistent, lordly, oppressive, overbearing, pushy, tyrannical.

antonym unassertive.

botch *v* ball up, blunder (through), bugger up, bungle, butcher, flub, foul up, fudge, fumble, goof, louse up, mar, mess up, mismanage, muff, ruin, screw up, spoil, wreck.

antonyms accomplish, succeed.

n blunder, bungle, failure, farce, fiasco, flop, hash, mess, miscarriage, muddle, shambles.

antonym success.

bother *v* alarm, annoy, bore, bug, chivvy, concern, dismay, distress, disturb, dog, harass, harry, hassle, inconvenience, irk, irritate, molest, nag, pester, plague, pother, trouble, upset, vex, worry.

n aggravation, annoyance, consternation, difficulty, drag, flurry, fuss, hassle, headache, inconvenience, irritation, kafuffle, nuisance, pain, palaver, perplexity, pest, pother, problem, schmozzle, strain, trouble, vexation, worry.

bothersome *adj* aggravating, annoying, boring, burdensome, cumbersome, distressing, exasperating, inconvenient, infuriating, irksome, irritating, laborious, tedious, tiresome, troublesome, vexatious, vexing, wearisome.

bottle *n* carafe, carboy, cruse, decanter, demijohn, flacon, flagon, flask, jar, jug, phial, vial.

bottle up check, conceal, contain, curb, hide, hold in (or back), inhibit, keep pent up, quell, rein in, restrain, restrict, suppress.

antonyms unbosom, unburden, vent.

bottleneck *n* block, blockage, clogging, congestion, hindrance, holdup, jam, logjam, obstacle, obstruction, snarl-up, traffic jam.

bottom¹ *n* base, basis, bed, core, depths, essence, floor, foot, foundation, fundus, ground, groundwork, heart, nadir, origin, pedestal, plinth, principle, root, seat, socle, sole, source, substance, substratum, substructure, support, underneath, underside, understratum.

bottom line effect, essence, gist, main point, minimum, real issue, straight goods, upshot.

bottom² *n* backside, behind, bum, buns, butt, buttocks, derrière, duff, posterior, rear, rear end, rump, seat, tail.

bottomless *adj* abysmal, abyssal, boundless, deep, endless, fathomless, immeasurable, inexhaustible, infinite, limitless, measureless, profound, unbounded, unending, unfathomable, unfathomed, unlimited, unplumbed.

antonym shallow.

bottomless pit abode of the damned, abysm, abyss, chasm, crevasse, fire and brimstone, Gehenna, gulf, Hades, Hell, hellfire, infernal regions, inferno, maw, Sheol.

boulevard *n* avenue, drive, parade, promenade, prospect, row, street, terrace, thoroughfare.

bounce *v* bob, bound, bump, dismiss, eject, jounce, jump, kick out, leap, oust, rebound, recoil, ricochet, spring, throw out.

n animation, bound, buoyancy, cheeriness, dynamism, ebullience, elasticity, energy, exuberance, gaiety, give, go, life, liveliness, pep, perkiness, rebound, recoil, resilience, spirit, spring, springiness, vigour, vitality, vivacity, zip.

bouncing *adj* blooming, bonny, healthy, lively, robust, strong, thriving, vigorous.

bouncy *adj* animated, bubbly, buoyant, cheery, ebullient, elastic, energetic, exuberant, gay, jaunty, light-hearted, lively, peppy, perky, resilient, spirited, springy, vigorous, vivacious.

bound¹ *adj* bandaged, beholden, cased, certain, chained, committed, compelled, constrained, destined, doomed, duty-bound, fastened, fated, fixed, forced, held, liable, manacled, obligated, obliged, pinioned, pledged, required, restricted, secured, sure, tied, tied up, wound, wrapped.

bound² v bob, bounce, caper, frisk, galumph, gambol, hurdle, jump, leap, lope, lunge, pounce, prance, scamper, skip, spring, vault.

n bob, bounce, caper, dance, frisk, gambol, jump, leap, lope, lunge, pounce, prance, scamper, skip, spring, vault.

boundary n abuttal, barrier, border, borderline, bounds, bourn, brink, confines, demarcation, edge, extremity, fringe, frontier, junction, limit(s), line, march, margin, mete, perimeter, termination, verge.

bounded adj bordered, circumscribed, confined, controlled, defined, delimited, demarcated, edged, encircled, enclosed, encompassed, hemmed in, limited, restrained, restricted, surrounded, terminated.

boundless adj countless, endless, illimitable, immeasurable, immense, incalculable, indefatigable, inexhaustible, infinite, interminable, interminate, limitless, measureless, prodigious, unbounded, unconfined, unending, unflagging, unlimited, untold, vast.

antonym limited.

bounds n borders, boundary, circumference, confines, edges, extremities, fringes, frontiers, limits, marches, margins, periphery, rim.

bountiful adj abundant, ample, bounteous, copious, exuberant, generous, lavish, liberal, luxuriant, magnanimous, munificent, open-handed, overflowing, plenteous, plentiful, princely, profuse, prolific, ungrudging, unstinting.

antonyms meagre, mean, sparse.

bounty¹ n beneficence, benevolence, charity, generosity, gift, grace, grant, kindness, largesse, liberality, philanthropy.

bounty² n bonus, gratuity, premium, recompense, reward.

bouquet n aroma, arrangement, boutonnière, bunch, buttonhole, corsage, fragrance, garland, nosegay, odour, perfume, posy, redolence, savour, scent, smell, spray, wreath.

bourgeois adj Biedermeier, circumscribed, commonplace, conformist, conservative, conventional, dull, hidebound, humdrum, kitschy, materialistic, middle-class, narrow, pedestrian, pretentious, smug, staid, suburban, suburb(i)an, tawdry, traditional, trite, trivial, unadventurous, unimaginative, uninspired, unoriginal, vulgar.

antonyms bohemian, original, unconventional.

n conformist, petit bourgeois, philistine, plebeian, stick-in-the-mud.

antonyms bohemian, nonconformist.

bout n battle, competition, confrontation, contest, course, encounter, engagement, fight, fit, heat, match, patch, period, round, run, run-in, session, set-to, skirmish, spell, spree, stint, stretch, struggle, term, time, turn.

bovine adj beefy, dense, dull, dumb, heavy, hulking, obtuse, slow, slow-witted, sluggish, stolid, stupid, thick.

antonym quick.

bow¹ v accept, acquiesce, bend, bob, capitulate, cave (in), comply, concede, consent, curtsey, defer, depress, droop, fall into line, genuflect, give in, incline, knuckle under, kowtow, nod, stoop, submit, surrender, truckle, yield.

n acknowledgment, bending, bob, curtsey, genuflexion, inclination, kowtow, nod, obeisance, salaam, salutation.

bow out abandon, back out, chicken out, defect, desert, drop out, give up, opt out, pull out, quit, resign, retire, stand down, step down, weasel out, wimp out, withdraw.

bow² n beak, head, prow, rostrum, stem.

bowdlerize v blue-pencil, censor, clean up, cut, edit, emasculate, excise, expunge, expurgate, launder, modify, mutilate, purge, purify, scrub (up), soften, tame.

bowels n belly, centre, core, depths, entrails, guts, heart, hold, innards, inside, insides, interior, intestines, middle, viscera, vitals.

bower n alcove, arbour, belvedere, boudoir, dwelling, gazebo, grot, grotto, hideaway, pleasance, recess, retreat, sanctuary, shelter, summerhouse.

bowl¹ n amphitheatre, basin, cup, dish, pan, porringer, receptacle, sink, stadium, tureen, vessel.

bowl² v fling, hurl, pitch, revolve, roll, rotate, spin, throw, trundle, whirl.

bowl over amaze, astonish, astound, blow away, dumfound, fell, flabbergast, floor, knock down, overwhelm, shock, stagger, startle, surprise, topple, unbalance.

bowlegs n bandiness, bandy legs, valgus.

box¹ n booth, cage, canister, carton, case, casket, chest, coffer, coffin, compartment, container, coop, crate, cubbyhole, cubicle, pack, package, pigeonhole, portmanteau, present, pyx, pyxis, receptacle, rectangle, square, trunk.

v case, encase, pack, package, wrap.

box in cage, circumscribe, confine, contain, coop up, cordon off, corner, double-park, enclose, fence in, hem in, imprison, restrict, surround, trap, wall in.

box² v bop, buffet, clout, cuff, fight, hit, punch, rap, slap, sock, spar, strike, thwack, wallop, whack, wham, whap.

n blow, bop, buffet, clout, cuff, punch, rap, slap, stroke, thump, wallop, wham, whap.

boxing n fisticuffs, prizefighting, pugilism, sparring, the noble art.

adj fistic, fistical, pugilistic.

boy n chap, cub, duffer, fellow, gamin, gossoon, imp, junior, kid, lad, man-child, nipper, puppy, schoolboy, servant, stripling, tyke, urchin, whippersnapper, youngling, youngster, young'un, youth.

boycott v ban, bar, black, blackball, blacklist, cold-shoulder, disallow, embargo, exclude, ignore, ostracize, proscribe, refuse, reject, spurn.

antonyms encourage, support.

boyfriend *n* admirer, beau, date, lover, man, steady, suitor, swain, sweetheart, young man.

boyish *adj* adolescent, childish, gamine, immature, innocent, juvenile, playful, puerile, tomboyish, unfeminine, unmaidenly, young, youthful.

brace[1] *n* bracer, bracket, buttress, clamp, cleat, corset, prop, reinforcement, shoring, stanchion, stay, strap, strut, support, truss, vise.

v bolster, buttress, clamp, fasten, fortify, jam, prop, reinforce, shore (up), steady, strap, strengthen, support, tie, tighten, wedge.

brace[2] *n* couple, duo, pair, twosome.

braces *n* galluses, suspenders.

bracing *adj* brisk, crisp, energizing, enlivening, exhilarating, fortifying, fresh, invigorating, refreshing, restorative, reviving, rousing, stimulating, strengthening, tonic.

antonym debilitating.

brackish *adj* bitter, briny, saline, salt, saltish, salty.

antonym fresh.

brag *v* bluster, boast, claim, crow, exaggerate, rodomontade, swagger, talk big, trumpet, vaunt.

antonym deprecate.

braggart *n* bigmouth, big talker, bluffer, blusterer, boaster, gascon, show-off, swaggerer, swashbuckler.

bragging *n* big talk, bluster, boastfulness, boasting, braggadocio, bravado, exaggeration, fanfaronade, gasconade, jactation, jactitation, rodomontade, showing off, strutting, swagger, swank, talk, vauntery.

antonyms modesty, unobtrusiveness.

braid *v* entwine, interlace, intertwine, interweave, lace, plait, ravel, twine, twist, weave, wind.

antonyms undo, untwist.

brain[1] *n* boffin, designer, egghead, engineer, expert, genius, highbrow, intellect, intellectual, inventor, mastermind, master planner, prodigy, pundit, sage, savant, scholar, scientist, thinker, wizard.

antonym simpleton.

brain[2] *n* cerebrum, grey matter, intellect, mind, sensorium.

v bludgeon, clobber, club, cudgel, knock out, poleaxe.

brainless *adj* asinine, crazy, daft, dunderheaded, foolish, half-witted, idiotic, incompetent, inept, mindless, moronic, senseless, stupid, thoughtless, unintelligent, witless.

antonyms sensible, shrewd, wise.

brains *n* capacity, common sense, grey matter, head, intellect, intelligence, mind, reason, sagacity, savvy, sense, shrewdness, smarts, understanding, wit.

brain-teaser *n* conundrum, mind-bender, poser, problem, puzzle, riddle.

brainwash *v* condition, drill, grill, indoctrinate, persuade, pressure, program, propagandize, re-educate, reprogram.

brainwashing *n* conditioning, doublethink, drill(ing), grilling, indoctrination, menticide, mind-bending, persuasion, pressure, programming, propagandizing, re-education, reprogramming, thought control, unlearning.

brainy *adj* bright, brilliant, clever, intellectual, intelligent, quick, sapient, smart.

antonym dull.

brake *n* check, constraint, control, curb, drag, inhibitor, red light, rein, restraint, restriction, retardant.

v check, curb, decelerate, drag, halt, moderate, pull up, put the brakes on, rein in, retard, slacken, slow, stop.

antonym accelerate.

branch *n* arm, bough, chapter, department, division, limb, local, lodge, office, offshoot, outlet, part, prong, ramification, ramus, section, shoot, sprig, subdivision, subsection, switch, wing.

branch (out) bifurcate, broaden (out), develop, diversify, divide, enlarge, expand, extend, fork, move on, multiply, proliferate, ramify, vary.

brand *n* brand name, class, emblem, grade, hallmark, kind, label, line, logo, make, mark, marker, marque, sign, sort, species, stamp, stigma, symbol, trademark, type, variety.

v burn, call, censure, denounce, discredit, disgrace, label, mark, scar, stain, stamp, stigmatize, taint, type.

brandish *v* display, exhibit, flash, flaunt, flourish, parade, raise, shake, swing, wave, wield.

brash *adj* assuming, assured, audacious, bold, brassy, brazen, bumptious, cocky, foolhardy, forward, hasty, heedless, impertinent, impetuous, impudent, impulsive, incautious, indiscreet, insolent, malapert, precipitate, rash, reckless, rude, temerarious.

antonyms cautious, reserved, unobtrusive.

brass *n* assurance, audacity, brazenness, cheek, chutzpah, cockiness, effrontery, gall, impertinence, impudence, insolence, nerve, presumption, rudeness, self-assurance, temerity.

antonyms circumspection, timidity.

brassy *adj* blaring, blatant, bold, brash, brazen, dissonant, flamboyant, flashy, forward, garish, gaudy, grating, hard, harsh, jangling, jarring, jazzy, loud, loud-mouthed, noisy, obtrusive, pert, piercing, raucous, saucy, showy, shrill, strident.

brat *n* ankle-biter, cub, gamin, guttersnipe, jackanapes, kid, nipper, puppy, rascal, ruffian, rugrat, urchin, varmint, whippersnapper, youngster.

bravado *n* big talk, bluffing, bluster, boastfulness, boasting, bombast, braggadocio, bragging, fanfaronade, parade, pretence, rodomontade, show, showing off, swagger, swaggering, swank, swashbuckling, talk, vauntery, vaunting.

antonyms modesty, restraint.

brave *adj* audacious, bold, courageous, daring, dauntless, doughty, fearless, fine, gallant, game, glorious, gutsy, hardy, heroic, indomitable, intrepid, manly, plucky, resolute, resplendent, splendid, spunky, stalwart, stoical, stout-hearted, unafraid, undaunted, unflinching, valiant, valorous, womanly.

antonyms cowardly, craven, timid.

v accost, bear, beard, challenge, confront, dare, defy, encounter, endure, face, face up to, meet, stand up to, suffer, venture (into or upon), withstand.

antonyms evade, flinch at, shy away from.

bravery *n* audacity, boldness, courage, daring, dauntlessness, doughtiness, fearlessness, fortitude, gallantry, grit, guts, hardihood, hardiness, heroism, indomitability, intrepidity, mettle, nerve, pluck, pluckiness, resoluteness, resolution, spirit, spunk, stalwartness, stoicism, stomach, stout-heartedness, valiance, valour.

antonyms cowardice, timidity.

bravura *n* animation, audacity, boldness, brilliance, brio, daring, dash, display, élan, energy, exhibitionism, extravagance, flair, flamboyance, liveliness, ostentation, panache, pizzazz, punch, spirit, verve, vigour, virtuosity.

antonym restraint.

brawl *n* affray, altercation, argument, battle, broil, bust-up, clash, dispute, dogfight, Donnybrook, dustup, fight, fracas, fray, free-for-all, melee, punch-up, quarrel, row, ruckus, rumpus, scrap, scuffle, squabble, tumult, tussle, uproar, wrangle.

v altercate, argue, battle, dispute, fight, quarrel, row, scrap, scuffle, squabble, tussle, wrangle, wrestle.

brawn *n* beef, beefiness, bulk, bulkiness, flesh, heft, mass, meat, might, muscle, muscles, muscularity, power, robustness, sinew(s), strength, thews.

brawny *adj* athletic, beefy, bovine, bulky, burly, fleshy, hardy, hefty, herculean, hulking, husky, lusty, massive, muscular, powerful, robust, sinewy, solid, stalwart, strapping, strong, sturdy, thewy, vigorous, well-built, well-knit.

antonyms frail, slight.

bray *v* bawl, bellow, blare, bleat, heehaw, hoot, roar, trumpet.

n bawl, bellow, blare, blast, cry, heehaw(ing), hoot, roar, shout.

brazen *adj* assured, audacious, barefaced, blatant, bold, brash, brassy, cocksure, defiant, flagrant, forward, immodest, impudent, insolent, malapert, pert, saucy, shameless, unabashed, unashamed.

antonym shamefaced.

breach *n* alienation, aperture, break, break-up, chasm, cleft, contravention, crack, crevice, difference, disaffection, disagreement, discontinuity, disobedience, disruption, dissension, dissociation, division, estrangement, failure, fissure, gap, gulf, hole,

infraction, infringement, lapse, neglect, offence, omission, opening, parting, quarrel, rent, rift, rupture, schism, scission, separation, severance, split, transgression, trespass, variance, violation.

bread *n* aliment, cash, chapati, dough, fare, finance, food, funds, money, moolah, necessities, nourishment, nutriment, pita, provisions, roti, staff of life, subsistence, sustenance, tortilla, viands, victuals, wherewithal.

breadth *n* amplitude, area, beam, broadness, bulk, compass, comprehensiveness, dimension, expanse, extensiveness, extent, inclusiveness, latitude, magnitude, measure, range, reach, scale, scope, size, span, spread, sweep, thickness, vastness, wideness, width.

break *v* absorb, announce, appear, bankrupt, batter, beat, better, breach, bud, burst, bust, check, cleave, contravene, cow, crack, crash, cripple, crush, cushion, cut, damage, dash, dawn, decipher, defeat, degrade, demolish, demoralize, destroy, dig, diminish, disclose, discontinue, disintegrate, disobey, dispirit, disregard, divide, divulge, domesticate, emerge, enervate, enfeeble, erupt, escape, exceed, excel, explode, flee, flout, fly, fracture, fragment, free, give way, go kaput (or phut), happen, humiliate, impair, impart, incapacitate, inform, infract, infringe, interrupt, lessen, master, moderate, modify, occur, open, oppress, outdo, outstrip, part, pause, pierce, plough, proclaim, reduce, rend, rest, reveal, rive, ruin, separate, sever, shatter, shiver, smash, snap, soften, solve, splinter, split, stave, stop, subdue, surpass, suspend, tame, tear, tell, train, transgress, undermine, undo, violate, weaken, worst, yield.

n abruption, advantage, alienation, breach, breather, chance, cleft, crack, crevice, disaffection, discontinuity, disruption, divergence, division, escape, estrangement, fissure, flight, fracture, gap, gash, halt, hiatus, hole, interlude, intermission, interruption, interval, lapse, letup, lull, opening, opportunity, parting, pause, quarrel, recess, reduction, rent, respite, rest, rift, rupture, schism, separation, split, suspension, tear, time-out.

break away abscond, apostatize, bolt, depart, detach (oneself), escape, flee, fly, leave, part company, quit, revolt, run away, secede, separate, split.

break down[1] collapse, conk out, crack up, crush, demolish, fail, give way, go kaput (or phut), grind down, seize up, stop.

break down[2] analyse, anatomize, atomize, biodegrade, categorize, classify, compartmentalize, decay, decompose, disintegrate, dissect, divide.

break in burgle, burst in, encroach (on), impinge (on), interfere, interject, interpose, interrupt, intervene, intrude, invade, irrupt.

break off cease, desist, detach, disconnect, discontinue, dissever, end, finish, halt, interrupt, part, pause, separate, sever, snap off, splinter, split off, stop, suspend, terminate.

break out arise, begin, burst (out),

commence, emerge, erupt, escape, flare up, flee, happen, occur, start.

break the ice begin, lead the way, oil the works, put (someone) at ease, relax, start (or get) the ball rolling, unbend.

break through achieve, advance, emerge, gain ground, leap forward, make headway, pass, penetrate, progress, succeed.

break up adjourn, analyse, anatomize, crack up, decompose, demolish, destroy, disband, disintegrate, dismantle, dismiss, disperse, disrupt, dissolve, divide, divorce, part, scatter, separate, sever, split, stop, suspend, terminate.

break with abandon, dissociate oneself (from), ditch, drop, finish with, jilt, part with, reject, renounce, repudiate, separate (from).

breakable *adj* brittle, crumbly, delicate, flimsy, fragile, frail, frangible, friable, insubstantial.

antonyms durable, sturdy.

breakaway *adj* apostate, dissenting, heretical, maverick, rebel, renegade, schismatic, seceding, secessionist.

breakdown[1] *n* cataclasm, collapse, decay, decomposition, disintegration, disruption, failure, interruption, mishap, stoppage.

breakdown[2] *n* analysis, categorization, classification, dissection, itemization.

break-in *n* burglary, home invasion, housebreaking, intrusion, larceny, robbery, theft.

breakthrough *n* advance, development, discovery, find, finding, gain, headway, improvement, invention, leap, progress, step.

break-up *n* adjournment, breakdown, crumbling, decay, disintegration, dismissal, dispersal, dissolution, divorce, finish, parting, recess, rift, separation, split, splitting, spring, termination, thaw.

breakwater *n* dike, dock, jetty, mole, pier, quay, wharf.

breast *n* bosom, bust, chest, front, heart, mammary gland, teat, thorax.

breath *n* air, animation, aroma, being, breathing, breeze, exhalation, existence, flatus, flutter, fragrance, gasp, gulp, gust, hint, inhalation, life, murmur, odour, pant, pneuma, puff, respiration, scent, sigh, smell, sniff, spirit, suggestion, suspicion, vapour, vitality, waft, wheeze, whiff, whisper, wind.

under one's breath in a low voice, in an aside, in an undertone, inaudibly, in a whisper, in whispers, quietly, sotto voce, voicelessly.

breathe *v* blow, exhale, expire, express, exude, imbue, impart, infuse, inhale, inject, inspire, instil, live, murmur, ooze, pant, puff, respire, say, sigh, snore, suspire, transfuse, utter, voice, wheeze, whisper.

breather *n* break, breathing-space, constitutional, halt, pause, recess, relaxation, respite, rest, walk.

breathless *adj* agog, anxious, avid, choking, dyspneal, eager, excited, exhausted, expectant, gasping, gulping, hushed, impatient, panting, puffing, rapt, short-winded,

spent, tense, wheezing, wheezy, wide-eyed, winded.

breathtaking *adj* affecting, amazing, astonishing, awe-inspiring, awesome, dazzling, dizzying, exciting, impressive, magnificent, moving, overwhelming, stirring, stunning, thrilling.

breeches *n* galligaskins, jodhpurs, knee-breeches, knickerbockers, knickers, leggings, moleskins, pantaloons, pants, plus fours, trousers.

breed *v* arouse, bear, beget, bring forth, bring up, cause, create, cross, cultivate, develop, discipline, educate, engender, foster, generate, hatch, induce, instruct, make, mate, multiply, nourish, nurture, occasion, originate, procreate, produce, propagate, raise, rear, reproduce, spawn, train.

n blood, family, ilk, kind, line, lineage, order, pedigree, progeny, race, sort, species, stock, strain, type, variety.

breeding *n* ancestry, background, civility, courtesy, cultivation, culture, development, education, gentility, lineage, manners, nurture, polish, politeness, raising, rearing, refinement, reproduction, training, upbringing, urbanity.

antonyms coarseness, ill-manneredness, vulgarity.

breeding-ground *n* hotbed, nest, nursery, school, source, training ground.

breeze *n* air, breath, cat's-paw, draft, flurry, gale, gust, puff, waft, whiff, wind, zephyr.

v blow, drift, flit, float, glide, hurry, sail, sally, sweep, trip, wander.

breezy *adj* airy, animated, blithe, blowing, blowy, blustery, bright, bubbly, buoyant, carefree, careless, casual, cheerful, cheery, debonair, easy-going, exhilarating, fresh, gusty, informal, insouciant, jaunty, light, light-hearted, lively, nonchalant, sprightly, squally, sunny, untroubled, vivacious, windy.

antonyms calm, staid, tense.

brevity *n* abruptness, briefness, brusqueness, conciseness, concision, crispness, curtness, economy, ephemerality, epigrammatism, evanescence, impermanence, incisiveness, laconicism, laconism, pithiness, shortness, succinctness, summariness, terseness, transience, transitoriness.

antonyms longevity, permanence, verbosity.

brew *v* boil, build up, concoct, contrive, cook, decoct, develop, devise, excite, ferment, foment, gather, hatch, infuse, mix, plan, plot, prepare, project, scheme, seethe, soak, steep, stew, threaten.

n beverage, blend, bouillon, brewage, broth, concoction, distillation, drink, fermentation, gruel, infusion, liquor, mixture, potion, preparation, stew.

bribable *adj* bent, buyable, corrupt, corruptible, purchasable, venal.

antonym incorruptible.

bribe *n* allurement, baksheesh, boodle, enticement, graft, grease, hush money, incentive, inducement, kickback, payoff, payola, protection money, slush fund, sweetener.

v buy off, buy over, corrupt, grease the palm of, reward, square, suborn.

bribery *n* corruption, graft, greasing, inducement, lubrication, palm-greasing, payola, protection, subornation.

bric-à-brac *n* antiques, baubles, bibelots, collectibles, curios, curiosities, gauds, gewgaws, gimcracks, kickshaws, knick-knacks, ornaments, trinkets, virtu.

brick *n* adobe, block, bomb, breeze block, brickbat, chunk, firebrick, header, hunk, quoin, slab, stretcher.

bridal *adj* conjugal, connubial, hymeneal, marital, marriage, matrimonial, nuptial, spousal, wedding.

bridge *n* arch, band, bond, causeway, connection, flyover, link, overpass, pontoon bridge, span, tie, tombolo, viaduct, yoke.

v attach, bind, connect, couple, cross, fill, join, link, span, traverse, unite, yoke.

bridle[1] *v* check, contain, control, curb, draw oneself up, govern, master, moderate, rein in, repress, restrain, subdue.

bridle[2] *v* be indignant, bristle, draw oneself up, take offence, take umbrage.

brief *adj* abrupt, aphoristic, blunt, brusque, capsular, clipped, compendious, compressed, concise, crisp, cursory, curt, ephemeral, epigrammatic, fast, fleeting, fugitive, hasty, laconic, limited, momentary, passing, pithy, quick, sharp, short, short-lived, sketchy, succinct, summary, surly, swift, telegraphic, temporary, terse, thumbnail, transient, transitory.

antonyms long, long-lived, verbose.

n advice, argument, briefing, case, data, defence, demonstration, directions, directive, dossier, file, information, instructions, mandate, orders, outline, précis, presentation, statement, submission, summary.

v acquaint, advise, direct, explain, familiarize, fill in, gen up, give a rundown, give the lowdown, guide, inform, instruct, prepare, prime.

briefing *n* advice, conference, directions, filling-in, gen, guidance, information, instruction, instructions, lowdown, meeting, notification, orders, preamble, preparation, priming, rundown.

briefly *adv* abruptly, brusquely, concisely, cursorily, curtly, fleetingly, hastily, hurriedly, in brief, in outline, in short, in sum, laconically, momentarily, precisely, quickly, shortly, sketchily, succinctly, summarily, temporarily, tersely.

antonyms at length, fully, permanently.

brigade *n* band, body, company, contingent, corps, crew, force, group, guard, outfit, party, squad, team, troop, unit.

brigand *n* bandit, dacoit, desperado, footpad, freebooter, gangster, heister, highwayman, holdup artist, marauder, outlaw, pirate, plunderer, robber, ruffian.

bright *adj* ablaze, acute, astute, auspicious, beaming, blazing, brainy, breezy, brilliant, burnished, cheerful, clear, clear-headed, clever, cloudless, dazzling, effulgent, encouraging, excellent, favourable, flashing, fulgent, gay, genial, glad, glaring, gleaming, glistening, glittering, glorious, glowing, golden, happy, hopeful, illuminated, illustrious, ingenious, intelligent, intense, inventive, jolly, joyful, joyous, keen, lambent, light-hearted, limpid, lively, lucent, lucid, luminous, lustrous, merry, observant, optimistic, pellucid, perceptive, percipient, perspicacious, polished, promising, propitious, prosperous, quick, quick-witted, radiant, resplendent, rosy, scintillating, sharp, sheeny, shimmering, shining, shiny, smart, sparkling, splendid, sunny, translucent, transparent, twinkling, unclouded, undulled, untarnished, vivacious, vivid, wide-awake.

antonyms depressing, dim, dreary, dull, pale, stupid.

brighten *v* burnish, cheer up, clear up, encourage, enliven, gladden, hearten, illuminate, light up, lighten, perk up, polish, rub up, sharpen, shine.

antonyms darken, dull, tarnish.

brightness *n* acuteness, aptitude, astuteness, blaze, braininess, brains, breeziness, brilliance, brilliancy, cheer, cheerfulness, clearness, cleverness, effulgence, fulgency, fulgor, gaiety, gladness, glare, gleam, glitter, glory, glow, hopefulness, illumination, intelligence, joy, liveliness, lucency, luminosity, lustre, optimism, perceptiveness, promise, propitiousness, quickness, quick-wittedness, radiance, refulgence, resplendence, sharpness, sheen, shine, smartness, sparkle, splendour, vivacity, vividness.

antonyms cheerlessness, darkness, dullness.

brilliance *n* animation, blaze, braininess, bravura, brightness, brilliancy, cleverness, coruscation, distinction, éclat, effulgence, excellence, flair, fulgency, genius, giftedness, glare, glory, grandeur, greatness, illustriousness, intellect, intelligence, intensity, inventiveness, lambency, lucency, luminosity, lustre, pizzazz, radiance, refulgence, resplendence, scintillation, sheen, shine, sparkle, splendour, talent, virtuosity, vivacity, vividness, wit.

brilliant *adj* ablaze, accomplished, adroit, animated, astute, blazing, brainy, bright, celebrated, clever, coruscating, dazzling, distinguished, effulgent, eminent, exceptional, expert, famous, gemmy, gifted, glaring, glittering, glorious, illustrious, ingenious, intellectual, intelligent, intense, inventive, lambent, luminous, masterly, outstanding, refulgent, scintillating, shining, showy, skilful, sparkling, splendid, star, starlike, superb, talented, virtuoso, vivacious, vivid, witty.

antonyms dull, restrained, stupid, undistinguished.

brim *n* brink, edge, lip, rim, top, verge.

bring *v* accompany, add, attract, bear, beget, carry, cause, compel, conduct, convey, convince, create, deliver, draw, earn, effect, engender, escort, fetch, force, gather, generate, get, give, gross, guide, impel, induce, inflict, influence, introduce, lead, make, motivate, move, net, occasion, persuade, present, produce, prompt, return, submit, take, transfer, transport, usher, wreak, yield.

bring about accomplish, achieve, cause, compass, create, effect, effectuate, engender, engineer, fulfil, generate, lead to, manage, manipulate, manoeuvre, occasion, produce, realize, result in.

bring around argue around, convince, persuade, prevail upon (or with), restore, revive, wake up, win over.

bring down abase, break, debase, defeat, degrade, destroy, fell, floor, humble, lay low, level, lower, overthrow, overturn, reduce, ruin, shoot, topple, undermine.

bring forth afford, bear, beget, cause, create, engender, furnish, generate, lead to, produce, provide, result in, supply, yield.

bring home (to) clinch, convince, drive home, emphasize, impress upon, persuade, prove.

bring in accrue, earn, fetch, gross, introduce, net, produce, profit, realize, return, yield.

bring off accomplish, achieve, bring about, compass, discharge, execute, fulfil, make fly, manage, perform, pull off, succeed in, swing.

bring on accelerate, advance, cause, expedite, generate, give rise to, induce, inspire, lead to, occasion, precipitate, prompt, provoke.

antonyms inhibit, prevent, suppress.

bring out draw out, elicit, emphasize, enhance, highlight, introduce, issue, print, publish, underline, underscore, utter.

bring to light dig up, disclose, discover, disinter, exhume, expose, reveal, show, uncover, unearth, unveil.

bring to nothing defeat, destroy, knock the bottom out of, mar, negate, nullify, ruin, scupper, spoil, undermine, undo, vitiate.

bring up advance, broach, disgorge, educate, evoke, form, foster, introduce, mention, nurture, propose, puke, raise, rear, regurgitate, suggest, teach, throw up, touch on, train, vomit.

brink *n* bank, brim, edge, extremity, fringe, limit, lip, margin, point, rim, threshold, verge, waterside.

brisk *adj* active, agile, alert, allegro, bracing, bright, businesslike, bustling, busy, cheery, crisp, effervescing, efficient, energetic, exhilarating, expeditious, fresh, invigorating, keen, lively, nimble, nippy, no-nonsense, prompt, quick, rapid, ready, refreshing, sharp, smart, snappy, speedy, spirited, sprightly, spry, stimulating, vigorous.

antonym sluggish.

bristle *n* barb, hair, prickle, spine, stubble, thorn, vibrissa, whisker.

v be indignant, bridle, draw oneself up, horripilate, prickle, react, rise, seethe.

bristling *adj* abounding, crawling, horripilant, incensed, indignant, seething, swarming, teeming.

bristly *adj* bearded, bewhiskered, bristling, hairy, hirsute, hispid, horripilant, prickly, rough, scratchy, spiny, stubbly, thorny, unshaven, whiskered.

antonyms clean-shaven, smooth.

brittle *adj* anxious, breakable, crackly, crisp, crumbling, crumbly, delicate, edgy, fragile, frail, frangible, friable, irritable, nervous, nervy, shattery, shivery, short, tense.

antonyms durable, resilient, sturdy.

broach *v* break open, bring up, crack open, introduce, launch into, mention, open, pierce, propose, puncture, raise, start, suggest, tap, uncork, utter.

broad *adj* all-embracing, ample, blue, capacious, catholic, coarse, comprehensive, eclectic, encyclopedic, enlightened, expansive, extensive, far-reaching, general, generous, gross, improper, inclusive, indecent, indelicate, large, latitudinous, liberal, obvious, roomy, spacious, square, strong, sweeping, tolerant, universal, unlimited, unrefined, vast, voluminous, vulgar, well-rounded, wide, wide-ranging, widespread.

antonym narrow.

broadcast *v* advertise, air, announce, beam, cable, circulate, disseminate, proclaim, promulgate, publicize, publish, radio, relay, report, show, spread, televise, transmit.

n airing, program, relay, show, telecast, transmission.

broaden *v* augment, branch out, develop, diversify, enlarge, enlighten, expand, extend, increase, open up, spread, stretch, supplement, swell, thicken, widen.

broad-minded *adj* catholic, cosmopolitan, dispassionate, enlightened, flexible, free-thinking, indulgent, liberal, loose, open-minded, permissive, progressive, receptive, tolerant, unbiassed, unprejudiced.

broadside *n* assault, attack, barrage, battering, blast, bombardment, brickbat, broadsheet, cannonade, counterblast, denunciation, diatribe, fulmination, harangue, invective, pamphlet, philippic.

brochure *n* advertisement, booklet, broadsheet, broadside, circular, flyer, folder, handbill, handout, leaflet, pamphlet.

broil *n* affray, altercation, argument, brawl, brouhaha, dispute, disturbance, fracas, fray, imbroglio, quarrel, scrimmage, scrum, strife, tumult, wrangle.

v bake, barbecue, fry, grill, roast, toast.

broke *adj* bankrupt, bust, destitute, impecunious, impoverished, insolvent, penniless, penurious, ruined, stone-broke, strapped.

antonyms affluent, solvent.

broken *adj* bankrupt, beaten, betrayed, browbeaten, burst, contravened, contrite, crippled, crushed, defeated, defective, demolished, demoralized, destroyed, disconnected, discontinuous, dishonoured, disjointed, dismantled, disobeyed, dispersed, disregarded, disturbed, domesticated, down, dud, erratic, faulty, feeble, fractured, fragmentary, fragmented, halting, hesitating, humbled, imperfect, incoherent, incomplete, infirm, infringed, intermittent, interrupted, isolated, kaput, on the blink (or fritz), oppressed, out of order (or service), overcome, overpowered, rent, retracted, ruined, run-down, ruptured, separated, severed, shattered, shivered, spasmodic, spent, splintered, stammering, subdued, tamed, traduced, transgressed, unkempt, vanquished, variegated, violated, wasted, weak.

broken-down *adj* collapsed, decayed, dilapidated, disintegrated, dismantled, inoperative, kaput, out of order, ruined, run-down, shabby, tumbledown.

broken-hearted *adj* crestfallen, dejected, desolate, despairing, despondent, devastated, disappointed, disconsolate, grief-stricken, hard-hit, heartbroken, heartsick, heartsore, inconsolable, miserable, mournful, prostrated, sorrowful, unhappy, wretched.

broker *n* agent, dealer, distributor, factor, handler, intermediary, manager, middleman, negotiator, stockbroker.

bromide *n* anodyne, banality, cliché, commonplace, platitude, stereotype, truism.

bronze *adj* auburn, brazen, brown, chestnut, copper, copper-coloured, golden, nut-brown, reddish-brown, rust, tan, titian.

brooch *n* badge, breastpin, clasp, clip, pin.

brood *v* agonize, cover, dwell (on), fret, hatch, incubate, meditate, mope, mull (over), muse, ponder, rehearse, repine, ruminate, sulk.
n birth, chicks, children, clutch, family, hatch, issue, litter, offspring, progeny, tribe, young.

brook¹ *n* beck, burn, channel, creek, freshet, inlet, mill, rill, rivulet, runnel, stream, streamlet, watercourse.

brook² *v* abide, accept, allow, bear, countenance, endure, permit, put up with, stand, stomach, submit to, suffer, support, swallow, take, tolerate.

broom *n* besom, brush, sweeper, wisp.

brothel *n* bagnio, bawdy-house, bordello, cathouse, house of ill fame, house of ill repute, whorehouse.

brother *n* associate, blood brother, brer, chum, colleague, companion, compeer, comrade, confrère, cousin, fellow, fellow believer, fellow creature, friar, friend, kin, kinsman, mate, monk, pal, partner, relation, relative, religious, sibling.

brotherhood *n* affiliation, affinity, alliance, association, belonging, bond, bondedness, camaraderie, clan, clique, communion, community, comradeship, confederacy, confederation, confraternity, coterie, fellowship, fraternity, guild, league, order, relationship, society, union.

brotherly *adj* affectionate, amicable, caring, comradely, concerned, cordial, fraternal, friendly, kind, loving, neighbourly, platonic, sympathetic.
antonyms callous, unbrotherly.

brow *n* appearance, aspect, bearing, brink, cliff, countenance, crest, crown, edge, expression, eyebrow, face, forehead, front, mien, peak, rim, summit, tip, top, verge, visage.

browbeat *v* batter, bludgeon, bulldoze, bully, coerce, cow, domineer, dragoon, hector, hound, intimidate, oppress, overbear, threaten, tyrannize.
antonym coax.

brown *adj* auburn, bay, bronze, bronzed, browned, brunette, chestnut, chocolate, cinnamon, coffee, dark, dun, dusky, fuscous, ginger, hazel, mahogany, russet, rust, rusty, sunburnt, tan, tanned, tawny, titian, toasted, umber, vandyke brown, walnut.

brown study absence, absent-mindedness, absorption, abstraction, contemplation, meditation, musing, pensiveness, preoccupation, reflection, reverie, rumination.

browned off angry, annoyed, cheesed off, discontented, disgruntled, displeased, fed up, mad, put out, teed off, ticked off, upset.

brownie *n* elf, fairy, goblin, hob, kobold, leprechaun, nix, nixie, pixie, Puck, Robin Goodfellow, sprite.

browse *v* crop, dip into, eat, feed, flick through, graze, leaf through, munch, nibble, page (through), pasture, peruse, scan, scroll (through), skim, surf (the Net), survey, window-shop.

bruise *v* blacken, blemish, contuse, crush, discolour, grieve, hurt, injure, insult, mar, mark, offend, pound, pulverize, wound.
n black eye, blemish, bump, contusion, discoloration, injury, mark, rainbow, shiner, swelling.

brunt *n* burden, force, impact, impetus, pressure, shock, strain, stress, thrust, violence, weight.

brush¹ *n* besom, broom, currycomb, sweeper.
v buff, burnish, caress, clean, contact, curry, flick, glance, graze, kiss, paint, polish, rub, scrape, shine, stroke, sweep (across), touch.

brush aside belittle, dismiss, disregard, flout, ignore, minimize, override, pooh-pooh.

brush off cast off (or aside), cold-shoulder, discourage, disdain, dismiss, disown, disregard, ignore, rebuff, refuse, reject, repudiate, repulse, scorn, slight, snub, spurn.
antonyms cultivate, encourage.

brush up bone up, cram, dust off, freshen up, improve, read up, refresh one's memory, relearn, study.

brush² *n* brushwood, bushes, ground cover, scrub, shrubs, thicket, underbrush, undergrowth, underwood.

brush³ *n* clash, conflict, confrontation, dustup, encounter, fight, fracas, incident, run-in, scrap, set-to, skirmish, tussle.

buffoon

brushoff *n* cold shoulder, discouragement, dismissal, go-by, rebuff, refusal, rejection, repudiation, repulse, slight, snub.
antonym encouragement.

brusque *adj* abrupt, blunt, curt, discourteous, gruff, hasty, impolite, rude, sharp, short, surly, tactless, tart, terse, uncivil, undiplomatic.
antonyms courteous, tactful.

brutal *adj* animal, barbarous, beastly, bestial, bloodthirsty, boarish, brute, brutish, callous, carnal, coarse, crude, cruel, ferocious, harsh, heartless, hurtful, inhuman, inhumane, insensitive, merciless, pitiless, remorseless, rough, rude, ruthless, sadistic, savage, severe, uncivil, uncivilized, unfeeling, unmannerly, unsympathetic, vicious.
antonyms humane, kindly.

brutality *n* atrocity, barbarism, barbarity, bloodthirstiness, brutishness, callosity, callousness, coarseness, cruelty, ferocity, heartlessness, inhumanity, mercilessness, pitilessness, roughness, ruthlessness, sadism, savageness, savagery, severity, viciousness.
antonyms gentleness, kindness.

brutalize[1] *v* decivilize, dehumanize, desensitize, harden, inure.
antonym civilize.

brutalize[2] *v* attack, maul, mistreat, savage, torture.
antonyms gentle, succour.

brute *n* animal, barbarian, beast, boor, creature, devil, fiend, monster, ogre, sadist, savage, swine.
antonym gentleman.
adj bestial, bodily, carnal, coarse, depraved, fleshly, gross, instinctive, mindless, physical, senseless, sensual, unthinking.
antonym refined.

brutish *adj* barbarian, barbaric, barbarous, boorish, coarse, crass, crude, feral, gross, insensitive, loutish, rude, savage, stupid, subhuman, swinish, uncivilized, uncouth, unfeeling, unmannerly, vulgar.
antonym refined.

bubble[1] *n* ball, bead, bladder, blister, blob, drop, droplet, globule, vesicle.
v babble, boil, burble, effervesce, fizz, foam, froth, gurgle, murmur, percolate, purl, ripple, roil, seethe, sparkle, trill.

bubble[2] *n* bagatelle, daydream, delusion, fantasy, fraud, illusion, toy, trifle, vanity.

bubbles *n* barm, effervescence, fizz, foam, froth, head, lather, mousse, spume, suds.

bubbly *adj* animated, bouncy, buoyant, carbonated, cheery, ebullient, effervescent, elated, excited, fizzy, foamy, happy, light-hearted, lively, merry, sparkling, spirited, sudsy.
antonym flat.

buccaneer *n* corsair, filibuster, freebooter, pirate, privateer, sea robber, sea rover, sea wolf.

buck[1] *n* beau, blade, blood, coxcomb, dandy, fop, gallant, playboy, popinjay, spark, swell.

buck[2] *v* bound, dislodge, jerk, jump, leap, prance, spring, start, throw, unseat, vault.

buck up brighten, cheer, cheer up, encourage, gladden, hearten, improve, inspirit, perk up, rally, stimulate, take heart.
antonyms dishearten, lose heart.

buck[3] *v* challenge, defy, fight, resist.

buckle[1] *n* bend, bulge, contortion, distortion, kink, twist, warp, wrinkle.
v bend, bulge, cave in, collapse, contort, crumple, distort, fold, skew, twist, warp, wrinkle.

buckle[2] *n* catch, clasp, clip, closure, fastener, hasp.
v attach, clasp, close, connect, fasten, hitch, hook, make fast, secure.

bucolic *adj* agrarian, agricultural, countrified, country, pastoral, rural, rustic.
antonyms industrial, urban.

bud *n* embryo, germ, shoot, sprig, sprout.
v burgeon, develop, grow, pullulate, shoot, sprout.
antonyms waste away, wither.

budding *adj* aspiring, beginning, burgeoning, developing, embryonic, emerging, fledgling, flowering, germinal, growing, hopeful, incipient, intending, nascent, potential, promising.
antonym experienced.

buddy *n* alter ego, chum, companion, comrade, crony, friend, mate, pal, partner, playmate, sidekick, soul mate.

buddy-buddy *adj* backslapping, condescending, effusive, familiar, on first-name basis, palsy-walsy, smarmy, superfriendly, thick.

budge *v* bend, change, convince, dislodge, give an inch, give (way), influence, move, persuade, propel, push, remove, roll, shift, slide, stir, sway, yield.

budget *n* allocation, allotment, allowance, cost, estimate, finances, funds, means, resources.
v allocate, allot, apportion, cost, estimate, plan, ration.

buff[1] *adj* dun, fawn, fulvous, khaki, sandy, straw, tan, yellowish, yellowish-brown.
v brush, burnish, polish, polish up, rub, shine, smooth.

buff[2] *n* addict, admirer, aficionado, bug, cognoscente, connoisseur, devotee, enthusiast, expert, fan, fiend, freak, lover.

buffer *n* bulwark, bumper, cushion, fender, intermediary, pad, pillow, safeguard, screen, shield, shock absorber.

buffet *v* bang, batter, beat, box, bump, clobber, clout, cuff, flail, hit, jar, knock, pound, pummel, push, rap, shove, slap, strike, thump, wallop.
n bang, blow, box, bump, clout, cuff, jar, jolt, knock, push, rap, shove, slap, smack, thump, wallop.

buffoon *n* clown, comedian, comic, droll, fool, harlequin, jester, joker, merry-andrew, mountebank, scaramouch, tomfool, wag, zany.

buffoonery *n* clowning, drollery, farce, foolery, harlequinade, jesting, nonsense, pantomime, silliness, tomfoolery, waggishness, zaniness, zanyism.

bug[1] *n* catch, defect, error, failing, fault, flaw, gremlin, imperfection, kink, knot, problem, snag.

bug[2] *n* bacterium, craze, disease, fad, germ, infection, insect, mania, micro-organism, obsession, rage, virus.

v annoy, badger, bother, brown off, disturb, get, harass, irk, irritate, needle, nettle, pester, plague, tease, tick off, vex, worry.

bug[3] *n* addict, admirer, buff, devotee, enthusiast, fan, fiend, freak, lover, maniac.

bugbear *n* anathema, bane, besetting fear, bête noire, bogey, bugaboo, devil, dread, fiend, horror, mumbo jumbo, nightmare, pet hate, pet peeve.

build *v* assemble, augment, base, begin, constitute, construct, crescendo, cultivate, deepen, develop, edify, enlarge, erect, escalate, establish, expand, extend, fabricate, form, formulate, found, grow, improve, increase, initiate, institute, intensify, knock together, make, originate, raise, rise, slap together, strengthen.

antonyms destroy, knock down, lessen, weaken.

n body, figure, form, frame, physique, shape, size, structure.

build up accumulate, advertise, amass, amplify, assemble, boost, develop, edify, encourage, enhance, expand, extend, fortify, gather, grow, heighten, hype, improve, increase, intensify, nurture, pile up, plug, promote, publicize, puff, reinforce, strengthen.

antonyms lessen, weaken.

building *n* architecture, construction, domicile, dwelling, edifice, erection, establishment, high-rise, house, megastructure, plant, structure, tower.

antonym destruction.

buildup[1] *n* accretion, accumulation, backlog, deposit, development, enlargement, escalation, expansion, growth, increase, mass, stockpile, store.

antonyms decrease, reduction.

buildup[2] *n* advertising, ballyhoo, hype, plug, promotion, publicity, puff.

built-in *adj* automatic, essential, fundamental, implicit, included, incorporated, inherent, inseparable, integral, intrinsic, necessary.

bulbous *adj* balloonlike, bellied, bellying, bloated, bulging, convex, distended, globular, rounded, swelling, swollen.

bulge *n* belly, boost, bump, distension, hump, increase, intensification, lump, projection, protrusion, protuberance, rise, surge, swelling, upsurge.

v bag, belly, bulb, dilate, distend, enlarge, expand, hump, increase, project, protrude, sag, swell.

bulging *adj* bellied, bulbous, bunchy, convex, rounded, swelling, swollen.

bulk *n* amplitude, bigness, body, dimensions, extensity, extent, generality, immensity, largeness, magnitude, majority, mass, most, plurality, preponderance, size, substance, thickness, volume, weight.

bulky *adj* big, cumbersome, enormous, heavy, hefty, huge, hulking, immense, large, massive, massy, ponderous, substantial, unmanageable, unwieldy, voluminous, weighty.

antonyms compact, handy, insubstantial, small.

bulldoze *v* browbeat, buffalo, bully, clear, coerce, cow, demolish, drive, flatten, force, hector, intimidate, knock down, level, propel, push, push through, railroad, raze, shove, thrust.

bullet *n* ball, missile, pellet, plumb, projectile, shot, sinker, slug, weight.

bulletin *n* announcement, communication, communiqué, dispatch, dope, memo, message, news brief, newsflash, newsletter, notification, report, statement, update.

bull's-eye *n* bull, centre, gold, jackpot.

antonym miss.

bully *n* bouncer, browbeater, bully boy, coercionist, intimidator, oppressor, persecutor, ruffian, termagant, tormentor, tough, tyrant.

v abuse, bluster, browbeat, bulldoze, bullyrag, coerce, cow, domineer, hassle, hector, intimidate, oppress, overbear, persecute, pick on, push around, swagger, terrorize, threaten, torment, tyrannize.

bulwark *n* bastion, buffer, buttress, defence, embankment, fortification, guard, mainstay, outwork, rampart, redoubt, safeguard, security, support.

bum *n* cad, clod, good-for-nothing, heel, idler, jerk, lazybones, loafer, loser, lowlife, meanie, rat, rotter, tramp.

bumbling *adj* awkward, blundering, botching, bungling, clumsy, foozling, incompetent, inefficient, inept, lumbering, maladroit, muddled, stumbling.

antonyms competent, efficient.

bump *v* bang, bounce, butt, collide (with), crash, displace, hit, jar, jerk, jolt, jostle, jounce, knock, lay off, move, rattle, remove, shake, shift, slam, strike.

n bang, blow, bulge, collision, contusion, crash, hit, hump, impact, jar, jolt, knob, knock, knot, lump, node, nodule, protuberance, rap, shock, smash, swelling, thud, thump.

bump off assassinate, dispatch, do in, eliminate, kill, liquidate, murder, put out of the way, remove, rub out, terminate.

bumper *adj* abundant, bountiful, enormous, excellent, exceptional, generous, great, huge, jumbo, large, massive, prodigal, spanking, teeming, unusual, whacking, whopping.

antonyms miserly, small.

bumpkin *n* boor, clodhopper, clown, cornball, hayseed, hick, hillbilly, lummox, oaf, peasant, provincial, rube, rustic, yokel.

antonym man of the world.

bumptious *adj* arrogant, boastful, brash, brassy, brazen, cocky, conceited, egotistic, forward, full of oneself, impudent, overbearing, overconfident, pompous, presumptuous, pushy, self-assertive, self-important, showy, swaggering, vainglorious, vaunting.
antonyms humble, modest.

bumpy *adj* bouncy, choppy, irregular, jarring, jerky, jolting, jolty, knobby, lumpy, rough, rutted, uneven.
antonym smooth.

bunch *n* assortment, band, batch, bouquet, bundle, clump, cluster, collection, crew, crowd, fascicle, fascicule, flock, gang, gathering, group, handful, heap, knot, lot, mass, mob, multitude, number, parcel, party, pile, quantity, sheaf, spray, stack, swarm, team, troop, tuft.
v assemble, bundle, cluster, collect, congregate, crowd, flock, group, herd, huddle, mass, pack.
antonyms scatter, spread out.

bunched *adj* clumped, clustered, concentrated, crowded together, fascicular, fasciculate, gathered, grouped, massed.
antonyms scattered, spread out.

bundle *n* accumulation, assortment, bag, bale, batch, bunch, carton, collection, consignment, fascicle, fascicule, group, heap, mass, pack, package, packet, pallet, parcel, pile, quantity, roll, shock, shook, stack, stook, swag.
v bale, bind, bunch, fasten, group, lump, pack, palletize, tie, truss, wrap.

bung *n* cork, stopper.

bungle *v* blunder, botch, bugger up, bumble, flub, foozle, foul up, fudge up, fumble, goof, louse up, mar, mess up, miscalculate, mishandle, mismanage, muff, ruin, screw up, spoil.
n blunder, booboo, botched job, fiasco, flop, foul-up, mess, screw-up.

bungler *n* blunderer, botcher, butterfingers, fool, foozler, fumbler, goof, incompetent, muddler, oaf.

bungling *adj* awkward, blundering, botching, clumsy, foozling, fumbling, ham-fisted, incompetent, inept, inexpert, maladroit, unskilful.

bunk *n* a crock, balderdash, baloney, bilge, bosh, bull, bunkum, claptrap, crap, eyewash, garbage, guff, hogwash, hooey, horsefeathers, malarkey, moonshine, nonsense, piffle, poppycock, rot, rubbish, stuff and nonsense, taradiddle, tomfoolery, tommyrot, trash, tripe, twaddle.
antonym sense.

buoy *n* beacon, bellbuoy, float, marker, signal.
buoy up boost, cheer, comfort, encourage, hearten, lift, raise, support, sustain.
antonym depress.

buoyant *adj* afloat, animated, blithe, bobbing, bouncy, breezy, bright, bubbly, bullish, carefree, cheerful, cheery, debonair, floatable, floating, happy, jaunty, joyful, light, light-hearted, lively, optimistic, peppy, resilient, rising, sanguine, sprightly, sunny, weightless.

antonym depressed.

burble *n* babble, gurgle, lapping, murmur, purl, purling.
v babble, gurgle, lap, murmur, purl.

burden *n* affliction, anxiety, bear, bother, bulk, care, cargo, clog, dead weight, drift, encumbrance, gist, grievance, inconvenience, load, main point, millstone, obligation, obstruction, onus, oppression, oppressiveness, pain, responsibility, sorrow, strain, stress, trial, trouble, weight, worry.
v bother, encumber, handicap, inconvenience, lade, lie hard on, lie heavy on, load, oppress, overload, overwhelm, strain, tax, worry.
antonyms disburden, lighten, relieve.

burdensome *adj* crushing, difficult, distressing, exacting, heavy, irksome, onerous, oppressive, taxing, troublesome, trying, wearisome, weighty.
antonyms easy, light.

bureau *n* agency, branch, counter, department, desk, division, office, service.

bureaucracy *n* administration, city hall, civil service, directorate, government, ministry, officialdom, officialese, officials, paper mill, red tape, regulations, the authorities, the powers that be, the system.

bureaucrat *n* administrator, apparatchik, bureaucratist, civil servant, functionary, mandarin, minister, office holder, officer, official, paper pusher, pencil pusher, rubber stamp, suit.

burglar *n* cat burglar, cracksman, housebreaker, intruder, picklock, pilferer, robber, safecracker, thief, yegg.

burglary *n* break-in, cat burglary, home invasion, housebreaking, larceny, pilferage, robbery, stealing, theft, thieving.

burial *n* burying, entombment, exequies, funeral, inhumation, interment, obsequies, sepulture.

burlesque *n* caricature, lampoon, mock, mockery, parody, ridicule, satire, sendup, spoof, takeoff, travesty.
adj caricaturic, comic, derisive, droll, farcical, mocking, parodying, satirical.
antonym serious.
v ape, caricature, exaggerate, imitate, lampoon, mock, parody, ridicule, satirize, send up, spoof, take off, travesty.

burly *adj* athletic, beefy, big, brawny, bulky, heavy, hefty, hulking, husky, muscular, powerful, stocky, stout, strapping, strong, sturdy, thickset, well-built.
antonyms puny, slim, small, thin.

burn *v* bite, blaze, brand, calcine, cauterize, char, combust, conflagrate, consume, corrode, deflagrate, expend, flame, flare, flash, flicker, fume, glow, hurt, ignite, incinerate, kindle, light, long, oxidize, pain, parch, rip off, roast, scorch, sear, seethe, shrivel, simmer, singe, smart, smoke, smoulder, spend, sting, take advantage of, tingle, toast, use, waste, wither, yearn.

burning *adj* ablaze, acrid, acute, aflame, alight, ardent, biting, blazing, caustic, compelling, consuming, corrosive, critical, crucial, eager, earnest, essential, excessive, fervent, fiery, flaming, flashing, frantic, frenzied, gleaming, glowing, hot, ignited, illuminated, impassioned, important, intense, irritating, painful, parching, passionate, piercing, pressing, prickling, roasting, scorching, searing, significant, smarting, smouldering, stinging, tingling, urgent, vehement, vital, zealous.
antonyms apathetic, cold, mild, unimportant.

burnish *v* brighten, buff, furbish, polish, polish up, rub, shine.
antonym tarnish.
n gloss, lustre, patina, polish, sheen, shine.

burrow *n* den, earth, hole, lair, retreat, shelter, tunnel, warren.
v delve, dig, earth, excavate, mine, rummage, tunnel, undermine.

burst *v* barge, blow up, break, crack, dehisce, disintegrate, erupt, explode, fragment, gush, irrupt, pierce, prick, puncture, rend, rip, rupture, rush, shatter, shiver, split, spout, spring, spurt, tear.
n bang, blast, blasting, blowout, blowup, breach, break, crack, discharge, eruption, explosion, fit, gallop, gush, gust, outbreak, outburst, outpouring, rupture, rush, spate, split, spurt, surge, torrent, volley.

bury *v* absorb, conceal, cover, embed, enclose, engage, engross, engulf, enshroud, entomb, hide, immerse, implant, inhume, inter, interest, lay to rest, lose, occupy, secrete, sepulchre, shroud, sink, submerge.
antonyms disinter, uncover.

bus *n* charabanc, coach, jeepney, jitney, minibus, omnibus, van.

bush *n* backwoods, boscage, brush, deep woods, forest, hedge, plant, scrub, scrubland, shrub, shrubbery, thicket, wilderness, wilds, wooded area, woodland, woods.

bush-league *adj* amateur, backward, minor, one-horse, second-rate, small, small-time, small-town, third-rate, unprofessional.

bushy *adj* bosky, bristling, bristly, coarse, fluffy, fuzzy, luxuriant, rough, shaggy, spreading, stiff, thick, unruly, wiry.
antonyms neat, tidy, trim, well-kept.

busily *adv* actively, assiduously, briskly, diligently, earnestly, energetically, hard, industriously, intently, purposefully, strenuously.

business *n* affair, assignment, bargaining, call, calling, career, ceremony, commerce, company, concern, corporation, craft, dealings, duty, enterprise, errand, establishment, firm, function, fuss, industry, issue, job, line, line of work, manufacturing, marketing, matter, merchandising, métier, mission, occupation, organization, palaver, problem, profession, pursuit, question, responsibility, right, sale, sales, selling, stuff, subject, task, to-do, topic, trade, trading, transaction(s), venture, vocation, work.

businesslike *adj* brisk, cold, correct, efficient, emotionless, formal, impersonal, matter-of-fact, methodical, no-nonsense, orderly, organized, practical, precise, professional, regular, routine, systematic, thorough, unemotional, well-ordered.
antonyms disorganized, inefficient, unprofessional.

businessman or **businesswoman** *n* capitalist, employer, entrepreneur, executive, financier, homme (or femme) d'affaires, industrialist, merchant, trader, tradesperson, tycoon.

buskers *n* mariachi, street band, street entertainers, street musicians, travelling minstrels, travelling musicians.

bust *n* bosom, breast, carving, chest, head, sculpture, statue, statuette, torso.

bustle *v* buzz, dash, flit, flutter, fuss, hasten, hurry, rush, scamper, scramble, scurry, scuttle, stir, tear.
n activity, ado, agitation, bother, commotion, excitement, flurry, fuss, haste, hurly-burly, hurry, palaver, pother, stir, to-do, toing and froing, tumult.

bustling *adj* active, astir, busy, buzzing, crowded, energetic, eventful, full, humming, lively, restless, rushing, stirring, swarming, teeming, thronged.
antonym quiet.

bust-up *n* brawl, disruption, disturbance, Donnybrook, fight, quarrel, separation.

busy *adj* active, assiduous, brisk, cluttered, crowded, diligent, employed, energetic, engaged, engrossed, full, fussy, hectic, industrious, inquisitive, interfering, in use, lively, meddlesome, meddling, nosey, occupied, officious, prying, restless, slaving, stirring, strenuous, tied up, tireless, tiring, troublesome, unleisured, working.
antonyms free, idle, lethargic, quiet.
v absorb, bother, concern, employ, engage, engross, immerse, interest, occupy.

busybody *n* eavesdropper, gossip, intriguer, intruder, meddler, Nosey Parker, pry, scandalmonger, snoop, snooper, troublemaker.

butcher *n* destroyer, killer, murderer, slaughterer, slayer.
v assassinate, botch, carve, clean, cut up, destroy, dress, exterminate, joint, kill, liquidate, mangle, massacre, murder, mutilate, prepare, ruin, slaughter, slay, spoil, wreck.

butchery *n* bloodletting, bloodshed, carnage, killing, mass destruction, massacre, murder, slaughter.

butler *n* manservant, sommelier, wine steward, wine waiter.

butt[1] *n* base, end, foot, haft, handle, hilt, shaft, shank, stock, stub, tail, tip.

butt[2] *n* dupe, laughing-stock, mark, object, point, subject, target, victim.

butt[3] *v, n* bump, jab, knock, poke, prod, push, ram, shove, thrust.

butt in   cut in, interfere, interpose, interrupt, intrude, meddle.

butter up   blarney, cajole, coax, flatter, soft-soap, wheedle.

buttocks   *n*   backside, beam end, behind, bottom, bum, buns, butt, cheeks, derrière, duff, fanny, haunches, hind end, hindquarters, nates, posterior, rear (end), rump, seat.

button   *n*   bud, catch, clasp, fastening, frog, knob, pimple.

buttonhole   *v*   accost, bore, catch, corral, detain, grab, importune, nab, pin, rope in, waylay.

buttress   *n*   abutment, brace, mainstay, pier, prop, reinforcement, shore, stanchion, stay, strut, support.
v   bolster up, brace, hold up, prop up, reinforce, shore up, strengthen, support, sustain, uphold.
antonym   weaken.

buxom   *adj*   ample, bosomy, busty, chesty, comely, curvy, hearty, jocund, jolly, lively, lusty, merry, plump, robust, Rubenesque, voluptuous, well-rounded, winsome.
antonyms   petite, slim, small.

buy   *v*   acquire, bribe, corrupt, fix, get, obtain, procure, purchase, square, suborn.
antonym   sell.
n   acquisition, bargain, deal, purchase.

buyer   *n*   emptor, purchaser, shopper, vendee.
antonyms   seller, vendor.

buzz   *n*   activity, bombination, brushcut, bustle, buzzing, call, drone, euphoria, excitement, gossip, hearsay, high, hiss, hum, murmur, news, purr, report, ring, ringing, rumour, rush, scandal, shave, stir, susurration, susurrus, whir, whisper, whiz.
v   bombinate, call, drone, hum, murmur, reverberate, ring, shave, summon, susurrate, whir, whisper, whiz.

by   *prep*   along, alongside, beside, by means of, near, next to, over, past, through, using, via, with.
adv   aside, at hand, away, close, handy, near(by), past.

by all means   absolutely, certainly, doubtlessly, of course, positively, surely, you bet.

by any means   anyhow.

by chance   mayhap, perchance.

by degrees   bit by bit, gently, gradually, imperceptibly, inch by inch, in stages, little by little, slowly, step by step.
antonyms   all at once, quickly, suddenly.

by far   by a long chalk, by a long shot, easily, far and away, immeasurably, incomparably, much.

by fits and starts   erratically, fitfully, in dribs and drabs, intermittently, irregularly, now and again, on and off, spasmodically, sporadically, unsystematically.
antonyms   constantly, continuously.

by halves   imperfectly, incompletely, scrappily, skimpily, sloppily.
antonyms   completely, thoroughly, totally.

by heart   by rote, down pat, from memory, parrot-fashion, pat, word for word.

by mistake   accidentally, inadvertently, in error, mistakenly, unintentionally.

by no means   in no way, not at all, not in the least, not the least bit, on no account.

by repute   putatively, reportedly, reputedly, supposedly.

by the way   apropos, by the bye, en passant, in passing, speaking of which.

bygone   *adj*   ancient, antiquated, departed, erstwhile, forgotten, former, lost, of yore, olden, past, previous.
antonyms   modern, recent.

bypass   *v*   avoid, circumvent, detour around, go over (someone's) head, ignore, neglect, outflank, set aside, skip, skirt, slight.

by-product   *n*   after-effect, aftermath, consequence, epiphenomenon, fall-out, repercussion, result, side effect, waste product.

bystander   *n*   eyewitness, looker-on, observer, onlooker, passer-by, spectator, watcher, witness.

byword   *n*   adage, aphorism, apothegm, catchword, dictum, epithet, gnome, household word, maxim, motto, precept, proverb, saw, saying, slogan, watchword.

C

cab *n* hackney carriage, limo, minicab, taxi, taxicab.

cabal *n* caucus, clique, coalition, conclave, confederacy, conspiracy, coterie, faction, intrigue, junta, junto, league, machination, party, plot, plotters, scheme, set.

cabin *n* berth, chalet, compartment, cot, cottage, crib, deckhouse, hovel, hut, lodge, quarters, room, shack, shanty, shed.

cabinet *n* almirah, case, chiffonier, closet, commode, credenza, cupboard, dresser, locker, wall unit.

cable *n* chain, cord, hawser, line, mooring, rope.

cache *n* accumulation, fund, garner, hoard, repository, reserve, stash, stockpile, store, storehouse, supply, treasure store.
v bury, conceal, hide, secrete, stash, store, stow.

cackle *v, n* babble, chatter, chuckle, crow, gabble, gibber, giggle, jabber, laugh, prattle, snicker, snigger, titter.

cacophonous *adj* discordant, dissonant, grating, harsh, inharmonious, jarring, raucous, strident.
antonyms harmonious, pleasant.

cacophony *n* caterwauling, discord, disharmony, dissonance, stridency.
antonym harmony.

cad *n* blackguard, caitiff, churl, clod, creep, cur, dastard, heel, jerk, knave, poltroon, rat, rotter, scum, skunk, swine, worm.
antonym gentleman.

cadence *n* accent, beat, close, inflection, intonation, lilt, measure, metre, modulation, pattern, pulse, rate, resolution, rhythm, stress, swing, tempo, throb.

cadge *v* beg, bum, freeload, hitch, mooch, scrounge, sponge.

cadre *n* basis, core, framework, hierarchy, infrastructure, nucleus, official.

café *n* bistro, cafeteria, coffee bar, coffee shop, estaminet, greasy spoon, restaurant, snack bar, tea room.

cage *v* confine, coop up, encage, fence in, immure, impound, imprison, incarcerate, lock up, mew, restrain, shut up.
antonyms free, let out.
n aviary, coop, corral, enclosure, pen, pound.

cagey *adj* careful, cautious, chary, circumspect, discreet, guarded, non-committal, secretive, shrewd, wary, wily.
antonyms frank, indiscreet, open.

cajole *v* beguile, blandish, blarney, coax, decoy, dupe, entice, entrap, flatter, induce, inveigle, lure, manoeuvre, mislead, seduce, soft-soap, soothe, sweet-talk, tempt, wheedle, wile.
antonyms bully, force.

cake *v* bake, cement, coagulate, coat, condense, congeal, consolidate, cover, dry, encrust, harden, inspissate, solidify, thicken.
n bar, block, chunk, loaf, lump, mass, slab.

calamitous *adj* cataclysmic, catastrophic, deadly, devastating, dire, disastrous, dreadful, fatal, ghastly, grievous, ruinous, tragic, woeful.
antonyms fortunate, happy.

calamity *n* adversity, affliction, cataclysm, catastrophe, desolation, disaster, distress, downfall, misadventure, mischance, misfortune, mishap, reverse, ruin, scourge, tragedy, trial, tribulation, woe.
antonyms blessing, godsend.

calculate *v* aim, assess, cipher, compute, consider, count, determine, enumerate, estimate, figure, find, gauge, intend, judge, plan, rate, reckon, value, weigh, work out.

calculated *adj* considered, deliberate, intended, intentional, planned, premeditated, purposed, purposeful, purposive, willful.
antonyms unintended, unplanned.

calculating *adj* canny, cautious, contriving, crafty, cunning, designing, devious, Machiavellian, manipulative, politic, scheming, sharp, shrewd, sly.
antonyms artless, naïve, open.

calculation *n* answer, caution, ciphering, circumspection, computation, deliberation, estimate, estimation, figurework, figuring, forecast, foresight, forethought, judgment, manipulation, number crunching, planning, precaution, reckoning, result, scheming.

calibre *n* ability, bore, capacity, character, diameter, distinction, gauge, league, measure, merit, quality, scope, size, stature, strength, worth.

call *v* announce, appoint, arouse, assemble, awaken, bid, bill, christen, command, consider, contact, convene, convoke, cry, declare, decree, denominate, designate, elect, entitle, estimate, gather, hail, halloo, invite, judge, label, muster, name, nickname, ordain, phone, proclaim, rally, regard, rouse, shout, style, summon, telephone, term, think, title, waken, yell.

n announcement, appeal, claim, command, cry, demand, excuse, grounds, invitation, justification, need, occasion, order, plea, reason, request, right, ring, scream, shout, signal, summons, urge, visit, whoop, yell.

call for[1] appeal for, demand, entail, involve, necessitate, need, occasion, order, recommend, request, require, solicit, suggest, urge.

call for[2] collect, fetch, pick up.

call it a day finish, knock off, leave off, pack it in, pack up, quit, shut up shop, stop, throw in the towel.

call off abandon, abort, break off, can, cancel, discontinue, drop, skip, withdraw.

call on appeal, appeal to, ask, bid, drop in on, entreat, go and see, invite, invoke, request, summon, supplicate, visit.

call the shots call the tune, command, dictate, give the orders, govern, lead, rule, rule the roost.

calling *n* business, career, employment, field, job, line, métier, mission, occupation, profession, trade, vocation, work.

callous *adj* casehardened, cold, hard-bitten, hard-boiled, hardened, hard-hearted, heartless, indifferent, indurated, insensate, insensible, insensitive, inured, obdurate, soulless, thick-skinned, uncaring, unfeeling, unresponsive, unsouled, unsympathetic.

antonyms kind, sensitive, sympathetic.

callow *adj* fledgling, green, guileless, immature, inexperienced, jejune, juvenile, naïve, puerile, raw, unfledged, uninitiated, unsophisticated, untried, young, youthful.

antonym experienced.

calm *adj* balmy, collected, composed, cool, dispassionate, equable, equanimous, even-keeled, even-tempered, halcyon, impassive, imperturbable, laid-back, mild, pacific, passionless, peaceful, phlegmatic, placid, quiet, relaxed, restful, sedate, self-collected, self-composed, self-possessed, serene, smooth, still, stilly, stoical, tranquil, unapprehensive, unclouded, undisturbed, unemotional, uneventful, unexcitable, unexcited, unflappable, unflustered, unmoved, unperturbed, unruffled, untroubled, windless.

antonyms excitable, panicky, rough, stormy, wild, worried.

v compose, hush, mollify, pacify, placate, quieten, relax, soothe.

antonyms excite, irritate, worry.

n calmness, dispassion, hush, order, peace, peacefulness, quiet, repose, serenity, stillness.

antonyms restlessness, storminess.

calmness *n* ataraxia, ataraxy, calm, composure, cool, coolness, dispassion, equability, equanimity, hush, impassiveness, impassivity, imperturbability, motionlessness, peace, peacefulness, phlegm, placidity, poise,

quiet, repose, restfulness, sang-froid, self-possession, serenity, smoothness, stillness, stoicism, tranquillity, unexcitableness, unflappableness.

antonyms excitability, restlessness, storminess.

calumniate *v* asperse, backbite, badmouth, blacken, defame, denigrate, detract, disparage, libel, malign, misrepresent, revile, slander, stigmatize, traduce, vilify.

calumny *n* abuse, aspersion, backbiting, calumniation, defamation, denigration, derogation, detraction, disparagement, insult, libel, lying, misrepresentation, obloquy, revilement, slander, smear, stigma, vilification, vituperation.

camaraderie *n* brotherhood, brotherliness, companionship, comradeship, esprit de corps, fellowship, fraternization, friendly spirit, friendship, intimacy, loyalty, sisterhood, sisterliness, togetherness.

camouflage *n* blind, cloak, concealment, cover, covering, deception, disguise, front, guise, mask, masquerade, screen, subterfuge.

v cloak, conceal, cover, disguise, hide, mask, obfuscate, obscure, screen, veil.

antonyms reveal, uncover.

camp[1] *adj* affected, artificial, campy, effeminate, exaggerated, homosexual, mannered, ostentatious, overdone, over the top, posing, posturing, theatrical, tongue-in-cheek.

camp[2] *n* caucus, clique, crowd, faction, group, party, school, section, set, side.

campaign *n* attack, crusade, drive, expedition, jihad, mission, movement, offensive, operation, promotion, push, tour.

v advocate, agitate, attack, canvass, champion, crusade, electioneer, fight, gladhand, lobby, mainstreet, promote, push.

camp follower *n* hanger-on, henchman, lackey, minion, toady.

can *n* canister, cannikin, container, jar, jerrycan, pail, receptacle, tin.

canal *n* waterway.

cancel *v* abandon, abolish, abort, abrogate, annul, call off, can, countermand, delete, drop, efface, eliminate, erase, expunge, mothball, neutralize, nullify, obliterate, quash, redeem, repeal, rescind, revoke, scrap, scrub, strike off (or out).

cancel out balance out, compensate for, counterbalance, neutralize, offset.

cancellation *n* abandoning, abandonment, abolition, abrogation, annulment, deletion, elimination, neutralization, nullification, obliteration, quashing, recision, redemption, repeal, revocation.

cancer *n* blight, canker, carcinoma, corruption, evil, growth, malignancy, melanoma, pestilence, plague, rot, sickness, tumour.

candelabrum *n* candlestick, menorah.

candid *adj* artless, blunt, clear, direct, fair, forthright, frank, free, guileless, ingenuous, just, open, outspoken, plain, sincere, straight, straightforward, truthful, unbiassed, uncontrived, unequivocal, unposed, unprejudiced, upfront.

antonyms cagey, devious, evasive.

candidate *n* applicant, aspirant, competitor, contender, contestant, entrant, examinee, nominee, possibility, pretender, prospect, runner, suitor.

candour *n* artlessness, bluntness, directness, fairness, forthrightness, frankness, guilelessness, honesty, ingenuousness, naïvety, openness, outspokenness, plain speech, simplicity, sincerity, straightforwardness, truthfulness, unequivocalness.

antonyms cageyness, deviousness, evasiveness.

cane *n* ferule, Malacca cane, stick, walking-stick.

canker *n* blight, boil, cancer, corrosion, corruption, infection, lesion, rot, sore, ulcer.

canny *adj* acute, artful, astute, careful, cautious, circumspect, clever, judicious, knowing, lucky, perspicacious, prudent, sagacious, sharp, shrewd, skilful, sly, subtle, wise, worldly-wise.

antonyms foolish, imprudent.

canon *n* catalogue, criterion, dictate, formula, law, list, precept, principle, regulation, roll, rule, standard, statute, yardstick.

canonical *adj* accepted, approved, authoritative, authorized, orthodox, recognized, regular, sanctioned.

antonym uncanonical.

canopy *n* awning, baldachin, cope, covering, marquee, shade, sunshade, tabernacle, tester, umbrella.

cant¹ *n* argot, bull, harangue, humbug, hypocrisy, insincerity, jargon, lingo, platitude(s), pretentiousness, rhetoric, sanctimoniousness, slang, spiel, thieves' Latin, vernacular.

cant² *n* angle, bevel, incline, jerk, rise, slant, slope, tilt, toss.

cantankerous *adj* bad-tempered, captious, choleric, contrary, crabby, cranky, crotchety, crusty, difficult, disagreeable, grouchy, grumpy, ill-humoured, ill-natured, irascible, irritable, peevish, perverse, piggish, quarrelsome, testy.

antonyms good-natured, pleasant.

canter *n* amble, dogtrot, jog, jog-trot, lope.

v amble, jog, lope, run, trot.

canvass *v* agitate, analyse, ask for, campaign, debate, discuss, dispute, electioneer, examine, inspect, investigate, poll, scan, scrutinize, seek, sift, solicit, study.

n examination, investigation, poll, scrutiny, survey, tally.

canyon *n* barranca, box-canyon, cañon, chasm, coulee, flume, gorge, gulch, gully, ravine, rift, valley.

cap *v* beat, better, complete, cover, crown, eclipse, exceed, excel, finish, outdo, outstrip, surpass, top, transcend.

n balmoral, beanie, beret, biretta, bonnet, fez, glengarry, hat, lid, shako, skullcap, tam, Tam o' Shanter, top, yarmulke.

capability *n* ability, capacity, competence, facility, faculty, feature, function, means, possibility, potential, potentiality, power, proficiency, qualification, skill, talent.

capable *adj* able, accomplished, adept, adequate, amenable, apt, clever, competent, efficient, experienced, gifted, intelligent, masterly, proficient, qualified, skilful, skilled, susceptible, talented.

antonyms incapable, incompetent, useless.

capacious *adj* ample, big, broad, comfortable, commodious, comprehensive, expansive, extensive, generous, huge, large, roomy, sizable, spacious, vast, voluminous, wide.

antonyms cramped, small.

capacity *n* ability, amplitude, appointment, aptitude, aptness, brains, calibre, capability, cleverness, compass, competence, competency, dimensions, extent, facility, faculty, forte, function, genius, gift, intelligence, magnitude, measure, office, position, post, power, range, relation, role, room, scope, size, space, strength, talent, volume.

cape¹ *n* head, headland, ness, peninsula, point, promontory, tongue.

cape² *n* cloak, coat, cope, mantle, pelisse, poncho, robe, shawl, wrap.

caper *v* bounce, bound, capriole, cavort, dance, frisk, frolic, gambol, hop, jump, lark, leap, revel, romp, skip, sport, spring.

n affair, antic, business, capriole, dido, escapade, gambol, high jinks, hop, jape, jest, jump, lark, leap, mischief, prank, revel, stunt.

capital¹ *adj* cardinal, central, chief, controlling, essential, first, foremost, great, important, leading, main, major, overruling, paramount, pre-eminent, primary, prime, principal, upper-case.

antonyms minor, unimportant.

capital² *n* assets, cash, finance, finances, financing, funds, investment(s), means, money, principal, property, resources, seed money, stock, wealth, wherewithal.

capitulate *v* accede, cave in, collapse, defer, fall, give in, relent, resist, submit, succumb, surrender, throw in the towel (or sponge), yield.

antonym fight on.

caprice *n* arbitrariness, changeableness, fad, fancy, fantasia, fantasy, fickleness, fitfulness, freak, humoresque, humour, impulse, inconstancy, notion, quirk, vagary, vapour, whim, whimsy.

capricious *adj* arbitrary, changeable, crotchety, erratic, fanciful, fickle, fitful, freakish, humorous, impulsive, inconstant, mercurial, odd, queer, quirky, uncertain, unpredictable, variable, wayward, whimsical.

antonyms sensible, steady.

capsize *v* invert, keel over, overturn, tip (over), turn over, turn turtle, upset.

capsule *n* bolus, cartridge, case, lozenge, module, pellet, pericarp, pill, pod, receptacle, sheath, shell, spaceship, tablet, troche, vessel.

captain *n* boss, chief, chieftain, commander, head, leader, master, officer, patron, pilot, skip, skipper.

captious *adj* acrimonious, argumentative, cantankerous, carping, cavilling, censorious, crabbed, crabby, critical, cross, disparaging, faultfinding, fussy, hypercritical, irritable, nagging, nit-picking, peevish, picky, quibbling, testy, touchy.
antonyms amiable, good-natured, pleasant.

captivate *v* allure, attract, beguile, besot, bewitch, charm, dazzle, enamour, enchain, enchant, enrapture, enslave, ensnare, enthrall, entrance, fascinate, hypnotize, infatuate, lure, mesmerize, seduce, win.
antonyms bore, appal, repel.

captive *n* abductee, convict, detainee, hostage, internee, prisoner, slave.
adj caged, confined, enchained, enslaved, ensnared, held fast, imprisoned, incarcerated, restricted, subjugated.
antonym free.

captivity *n* bondage, confinement, custody, detention, durance, duress, enchainment, enthralment, imprisonment, incarceration, internment, restraint, servitude, slavery, thralldom, vassalage.
antonym freedom.

capture *v* apprehend, arrest, bag, catch, collar, cop, corral, lay hold of, lift, nab, secure, seize, snaffle, snare, take, trap.
n apprehension, arrest, catch, imprisonment, seizure, taking, trapping.

car *n* auto, automobile, buggy, crate, cruiser, dragster, gas guzzler, horseless carriage, hot rod, jalopy, machine, motor, motor car, roadster, sedan, vehicle, wagon, (set of) wheels.

carafe *n* bottle, decanter, flagon, flask, jug, pitcher.

carbuncle *n* anthrax, boil, furuncle, inflammation, lesion, pimple, pustule, sore, sty.

carcass *n* body, cadaver, corpse, framework, hulk, relics, remains, shell, skeleton, stiff.

card *n* eccentric, joker, life of the party, wag, wit.

cardinal *adj* capital, central, chief, essential, first, foremost, fundamental, greatest, highest, important, key, leading, main, paramount, pre-eminent, primary, prime, principal.

care *n* affliction, anxiety, attention, burden, carefulness, caution, charge, circumspection, concern, consideration, control, custody, direction, disquiet, forethought, guardianship, hardship, heed, interest, keeping, management, meticulousness, ministration, nursing, nurture, pains, pressure, protection, prudence, regard, responsibility, solicitude, stress, supervision, surveillance, tribulation, trouble, vexation, vigilance, ward, wardship, watchfulness, woe, worry.
antonyms carelessness, inattention, thoughtlessness.

care for attend, delight in, desire, enjoy, foster, like, look after, look out for, love, mind, minister to, nurse, nurture, prize, protect, take pleasure in, tend, want, watch over.

career *n* calling, course, employment, job, lifework, livelihood, occupation, passage, path, progress, pursuit, race, vocation.
v bolt, dash, gallop, hurtle, race, run, rush, shoot, speed, tear.

carefree *adj* airy, blithe, breezy, buoyant, careless, casual, cheerful, cheery, easygoing, gay, happy, happy-go-lucky, insouciant, jaunty, laid-back, leisurely, light-hearted, lightsome, playful, relaxed, sunny, untroubled, unworried.
antonyms anxious, worried.

careful *adj* accurate, alert, attentive, cautious, chary, circumspect, concerned, conscientious, considerate, discreet, fastidious, guarded, heedful, judicious, meticulous, mindful, on one's guard, painstaking, particular, precise, protective, prudent, punctilious, scrupulous, solicitous, thoughtful, thrifty, vigilant, wary, watchful.
antonyms careless, inattentive, thoughtless.

caregiver *n* babysitter, day-care worker, guardian, nanny, nurse.

careless *adj* absent-minded, casual, cavalier, cursory, derelict, forgetful, haphazard, heedless, hit-or-miss, inaccurate, inattentive, incautious, inconsiderate, indiscreet, irresponsible, lackadaisical, messy, neglectful, negligent, nonchalant, offhand, perfunctory, reckless, regardless, remiss, shoddy, slack, slapdash, slipshod, sloppy, thoughtless, uncaring, unconcerned, unguarded, unmindful, unstudied, unthinking.
antonyms accurate, careful, meticulous, thoughtful.

caress *v* canoodle, cuddle, embrace, fondle, hug, kiss, neck, nuzzle, paw, pet, rub, stroke, touch.
n cuddle, embrace, hug, kiss, pat, stroke, touch.

caretaker *n* cleaner, concierge, curator, custodian, janitor, keeper, maintenance worker, porter, sanitation engineer, superintendent, warden, watchman.

careworn *adj* exhausted, fatigued, gaunt, haggard, lined, tired, weary, worn, worn-out.
antonyms lively, sprightly.

cargo *n* baggage, consignment, contents, freight, goods, haul, lading, load, merchandise, payload, shipment, tonnage, wares.

caricature *n* burlesque, cartoon, distortion, exaggeration, farce, lampoon, mimicry, parody, pasquinade, representation, satire, sendup, stereotype, takeoff, travesty.
v burlesque, distort, exaggerate, lampoon, mimic, mock, parody, pasquinade, ridicule, satirize, send up, take off (or on).

carnage *n* bloodbath, bloodshed, butchery, destruction, havoc, holocaust, immolation, massacre, murder, shambles, slaughter.

carnal *adj* animal, bestial, bodily, brutish, corporeal, earthly, erotic, fleshly, human, impure, lascivious, lecherous, lewd, libidinous, licentious, lustful, mundane, natural, physical, profane, prurient, salacious, secular, sensual, sensuous, sexual, sublunary, temporal, unchaste, unregenerate, unspiritual, voluptuous, wanton, worldly.
antonyms chaste, pure, spiritual.

carnival *n* celebration, fair, festival, fête, fiesta, gala, holiday, jamboree, jubilee, Mardi Gras, merrymaking, revelry, wassail.

carol *n* canticle, canzonet, chorus, ditty, hymn, lay, motet, noel, song, strain, wassail.

carouse *v* booze, drink, imbibe, live it up, party, quaff, revel, roister, wassail.
n drinking-bout, party, revel, wassail.

carousing *n* bacchanalia, boozing, celebrating, debauchery, drinking, merrymaking, orgy, party, partying, revelry, wassailing.

carp *v* bitch, cavil, censure, complain, criticize, cut up, find fault, grumble, hypercriticize, knock, nag, natter, nit-pick, quibble, reproach.
antonym praise.

carpet *n* Axminster, broadloom, dhurrie, kilim, mat, rug, runner, tapis, Wilton.

carping *adj* argumentative, captious, cavilling, critical, faultfinding, grouchy, hypercritical, nagging, nit-picking, picky, quibbling, reproachful, sour.
n bitching, captiousness, cavilling, censure, complaints, criticism, disparagement, faultfinding, hypercriticism, knocking, nagging, negativism, nit-picking, reproofs.
antonyms compliments, praise.

carriage *n* air, bearing, behaviour, cab, carrying, coach, comportment, conduct, conveyance, conveying, delivery, demeanour, deportment, freight, gait, manner, mien, posture, presence, trap, transport, transportation, vehicle, wagon, wagonette.

carrier *n* bearer, conveyor, delivery-person, messenger, porter, runner, transmitter, transporter, vector.

carry *v* bear, blow, bring, broadcast, cart, communicate, comport, conduct, convey, convince, display, disseminate, drive, extend, fetch, gain, give, haul, hump, impel, influence, keep up, lift, lug, maintain, motivate, move, offer, print, project, publish, reach, relay, schlep, send, shoulder, spur, stand, stock, support, sustain, take, tolerate, tote, transfer, transmit, transport, truck, underpin, uphold, win.

carry off accomplish, bring off, capture, pull off, seize, succeed with (or at), swing, win.

carry on administer, conduct, continue, endure, flirt, fuss, last, maintain, make a fuss, make a hullabaloo, make a scene, manage, misbehave, operate, perpetuate, persevere, persist, proceed, run.

carry out accomplish, achieve, bring off, discharge, do, effect, execute, fulfil, implement, perform, realize.

cart *n* barrow, buggy, bundlebuggy, caddie, chaise, curricle, dogcart, float, gig, gurney, handcart, shay, trap, tray, trolley, truck, tumbrel, wagon, wain, wheelbarrow.
v bear, carry, convey, haul, hump, lug, move, schlep, tote, transport, truck.

carton *n* box, case, container, crate, pack, package, packet, parcel.

cartoon *n* animation, caricature, comic strip, drawing, lampoon, parody, representation, sketch, takeoff.

cartridge *n* canister, capsule, case, cassette, charge, container, cylinder, magazine, refill, round, shell.

carve *v* chip, chisel, cut, engrave, etch, fashion, form, grave, hack, hew, incise, indent, inscribe, make, sculp(t), sculpture, slash, slice, tool, whittle.

carving *n* bust, engraving, etching, gravure, incision, lithoglyph, petroglyph, sculpture, statue, statuette.

cascade *n* avalanche, cataract, deluge, falls, flood, fountain, outpouring, rush, series, shower, torrent, waterfall.
antonym trickle.
v descend, flood, gush, overflow, pitch, plunge, pour, rush, shower, spill, surge, tumble.

case¹ *n* box, cabinet, caddy, canister, capsule, carton, cartridge, casing, casket, chest, compact, container, cover, covering, crate, envelope, etui, folder, holder, housing, integument, jacket, receptacle, sheath, shell, showcase, suitcase, tray, trunk, wrapper, wrapping.
v encase, enclose, skin.

case² *n* action, affair, argument, cause, circumstances, client, condition, context, contingency, dispute, event, example, illustration, instance, lawsuit, matter, occasion, occurrence, patient, point, position, proceedings, process, situation, specimen, state, state of affairs, suit, thesis, trial.
v investigate, reconnoitre.

cash *n* banknotes, bills, bread, bullion, change, coin, coinage, currency, dough, funds, hard currency, hard money, money, notes, payment, ready, ready money, resources, specie, wherewithal.
v encash, liquidate, realize, redeem.

cashier¹ *n* accountant, attendant, banker, bursar, checkout, clerk, purser, teller, treasurer.

cashier² *v* defrock, discard, discharge, dismiss, drum out, expel, fire, sack, unfrock.

cask *n* barrel, butt, firkin, hogshead, puncheon, tub, tun, vat, wood.

casket *n* box, caddy, case, chest, coffer, coffin, jewel box, pyxis.

cast¹ *v* add, allot, appoint, arrange, assign, bestow, calculate, categorize, choose, chuck, compute, deposit, diffuse, direct, distribute, drive, drop, figure, fling, forecast, form, found, hurl, impel, launch, lob, model, mould, pick, pitch, project, radiate, reckon, roll, scatter, select, set, shape, shed, shy, sling, spread, throw, toss, total.

n air, appearance, aspect, complexion, demeanour, fling, form, kind, lob, look, manner, mien, mould, quality, roll, semblance, shade, sort, stamp, style, throw, tinge, tint, tone, toss, turn, type.

cast down crush, deject, depress, desolate, discourage, dishearten, dispirit, sadden.

antonyms encourage, lift up.

cast off (or **away** or **aside**) abandon, chuck, discard, dispense with, ditch, drop, dump, get rid of, jettison, leave behind, reject, scrap, shed, throw out, toss out, unload.

cast² *n* actors, artistes, characters, company, dramatis personae, entertainers, performers, players, troupe.

caste *n* class, degree, estate, grade, lineage, order, position, race, rank, station, status, stratum.

castigate *v* beat, berate, cane, censure, chasten, chastise, chew out, chide, correct, criticize, discipline, flail, flay, flog, lash, punish, rake over the coals, rebuke, reprimand, scold, scourge, whip.

castle *n* casbah, château, citadel, donjon, fastness, fortress, keep, mansion, palace, peel, schloss, stronghold, tower.

castrate *v* emasculate, fix, geld, neuter, sterilize, unman, unsex.

casual *adj* accidental, apathetic, blasé, carefree, careless, cavalier, chance, contingent, cursory, easygoing, fortuitous, incidental, indifferent, informal, insouciant, irregular, lackadaisical, laid-back, nonchalant, occasional, offhand, perfunctory, random, relaxed, serendipitous, stray, unceremonious, unconcerned, unexpected, unforeseen, unintentional, unpremeditated.

antonyms deliberate, painstaking, planned.

casualty *n* death, injured, injury, loss, sufferer, victim, wounded.

casuistry *n* chicanery, equivocation, sophism, sophistry, speciousness.

cat *n* feline, gib, grimalkin, mouser, puss, pussy, tabby, tom, tomcat.

cataclysm *n* blow, calamity, catastrophe, collapse, convulsion, debacle, devastation, disaster, upheaval.

catacomb *n* burial vault, cave, crypt, ossuary, tomb, vault.

catalogue *n* calendar, directory, gazetteer, index, inventory, list, litany, record, register, roll, roster, schedule, syllabus, table.

v accession, alphabetize, classify, codify, file, index, inventory, list, record, register.

catapult *v* heave, hurl, hurtle, launch, pitch, plunge, precipitate, propel, shoot, throw, toss.

cataract *n* cascade, deluge, downpour, falls, rapids, torrent, waterfall.

catastrophe *n* adversity, affliction, blow, calamity, cataclysm, conclusion, culmination, debacle, denouement, devastation, disaster, end, failure, fiasco, finale, ill, mischance, misfortune, mishap, outcome, reverse, ruin, termination, tragedy, trial, trouble, upheaval, upshot.

catcall *n* boo, gibe, hiss, jeer, raspberry, whistle.

v boo, deride, gibe, give (someone) the bird, heckle, hiss, jeer, razz, whistle.

catch *v* apprehend, arrest, bewitch, captivate, capture, charm, clutch, contract, cop, delight, detect, develop, discern, discover, distinguish, enchant, enrapture, ensnare, entangle, entrap, expose, fascinate, grab, grasp, grip, hear, nab, nail, net, notice, perceive, recognize, see, seize, sense, snag, snare, snatch, surprise, take, take in, twig, understand, unmask.

antonyms drop, free, miss.

n bolt, clasp, clip, detent, disadvantage, drawback, fastener, hasp, hitch, hook, latch, obstacle, pawl, ratchet, snag, trap, trick.

catch sight of espy, glimpse, notice, recognize, spot, spy, view.

catch up close the gap, draw level (with), gain on, make up for lost time, overtake.

catching *adj* attractive, captivating, charming, communicable, contagious, enchanting, fascinating, fetching, infectious, infective, taking, transferable, transmissible, transmittable, winning, winsome.

antonyms boring, non-communicable, ugly, unattractive.

catchword *n* buzzword, byword, catch phrase, motto, parrot-cry, password, refrain, slogan, watchword.

catchy *adj* attractive, captivating, confusing, deceptive, haunting, memorable, popular, punchy, singable, tricky.

antonyms boring, dull.

catechize *v* cross-examine, disciple, drill, examine, grill, instruct, interrogate, question, test.

catechumen *v* convert, disciple, initiate, learner, neophyte, novice, proselyte, pupil, tyro.

categorical *adj* absolute, clear, direct, downright, emphatic, explicit, express, positive, total, unambiguous, unconditional, unequivocal, unqualified, unquestionable, unreserved.

antonyms qualified, tentative, vague.

categorize *v* class, classify, grade, group, list, order, pigeonhole, rank, sort.

category *n* class, classification, department, division, grade, grouping, head, heading, list, order, rank, rubric, section, sort, type.

cater (to) *v* furnish, humour, indulge, outfit, pander, provide, provision, purvey, serve, supply, victual.

caterwaul *v* bawl, cry, howl, meow, scream, screech, shriek, squall, wail, yowl.

catharsis *n* abreaction, abstersion, cleansing, lustration, purgation, purging, purification, purifying, release.

cathedral *n* dome, minster, shrine.

catholic *adj* all-embracing, all-inclusive, broad, broad-minded, charitable, comprehensive, eclectic, ecumenical, general, global, inclusive, liberal, tolerant, universal, whole, wide, wide-ranging, worldwide.

antonyms exclusive, narrow, narrow-minded.

cattle *n* beasts, cows, kine, livestock, neat, steers, stock.

catty *adj* backbiting, bitchy, ill-natured, malevolent, malicious, mean, rancorous, snarky, sniping, spiteful, venomous, vicious, vixenish, waspish.

antonyms kind, pleasant.

caucus *n* assembly, clique, conclave, convention, council, gathering, get-together, meeting, parley, session, set.

cause *n* agency, agent, basis, beginning, causation, creator, end, enterprise, genesis, goal, grounds, interest, mainspring, maker, motivation, motive, movement, object, origin, originator, producer, purpose, reason, root, source, spring, stimulus, trigger, undertaking.

antonyms effect, result.

v begin, bring about, bring on, compel, create, effect, engender, force, generate, give rise to, impel, incite, induce, motivate, move, occasion, originate, precipitate, produce, provoke, result in, stimulate, trigger.

caustic *adj* acerbic, acid, acidic, acidulous, acrid, acrimonious, astringent, biting, bitter, blistering, burning, corroding, corrosive, cutting, escharotic, harsh, keen, mordant, pungent, sarcastic, scathing, searing, severe, stinging, trenchant, virulent, waspish, withering.

antonyms mild, soothing.

caution *n* admonition, advice, alertness, caginess, care, carefulness, cautiousness, caveat, chariness, circumspection, counsel, deliberation, discretion, forethought, guardedness, heed, heedfulness, injunction, judiciousness, prudence, vigilance, wariness, warning, watchfulness.

antonyms foolhardiness, heedlessness, recklessness.

verb admonish, advise, enjoin, urge, warn.

cautious *adj* alert, cagey, careful, chary, circumspect, discreet, Fabian, guarded, heedful, judicious, prudent, scrupulous, tentative, unadventurous, vigilant, wary, watchful.

antonyms foolhardy, heedless, imprudent, incautious.

cavalcade *n* array, march-past, parade, procession, retinue, series, spectacle, train, troop.

cavalier *n* attendant, beau, blade, chevalier, equestrian, escort, gallant, gentleman, horseman, knight, partner, royalist.

adj arrogant, careless, casual, cavalierish, condescending, curt, disdainful, flippant, free-and-easy, gay, haughty, insolent, lofty, loose, lordly, offhand, scornful, supercilious, swaggering.

cave *n* cavern, cavity, cellar, crypt, den, grotto, hole, hollow, vault.

cave in accede, capitulate, collapse, fall, fall in, give in, give way, yield.

caveat *n* admonition, alarm, caution, notice, warning.

cavern *n* cave, cavity, crypt, den, grotto, hole, hollow, vault.

cavernous *adj* deep, deep-set, echoing, gaping, hollow, resonant, reverberant, sepulchral, sunken, yawning.

cavil *v* carp, censure, complain, hypercriticize, find fault, nit-pick, object, quibble.

n complaint, criticism, objection, quibble.

cavilling *adj* captious, carping, censorious, critical, faultfinding, hypercritical, nit-picking, quibbling.

cavity *n* antrum, belly, caries, cell, chamber, crater, dent, gap, hole, hollow, passage, pit, pothole, sinus, space, vacuole, ventricle, well, womb.

cavort *v* caper, caracole, dance, frisk, frolic, gambol, hop, leap, play, prance, romp, skip, sport.

cease *v* call a halt, call it a day, come to an end, conclude, desist, die, discontinue, end, fail, finish, halt, knock off, pack in, quit, refrain (from), stay, stop, terminate.

antonyms begin, start.

ceaseless *adj* constant, continual, continuous, endless, eternal, everlasting, incessant, indefatigable, inexhaustible, interminable, never-ending, non-stop, ongoing, perennial, perpetual, persistent, unending, unremitting, untiring.

antonyms irregular, occasional.

cede *v* abandon, abdicate, allow, concede, convey, give up, grant, hand over, relinquish, renounce, resign, sign over, surrender, transfer, turn over, yield.

celebrate *v* acclaim, bless, commemorate, commend, emblazon, eulogize, exalt, extol, glorify, hail, have a bash, honour, hype (up), keep, laud, lionize, live it up, make merry, observe, officiate at, party, perform, praise, proclaim, publicize, rejoice, remember, revel, reverence, solemnize, toast, tout, wassail, whoop it up.

celebrated *adj* acclaimed, big, distingué, distinguished, eminent, exalted, famed, famous, glorious, illustrious, lionized, notable, popular, pre-eminent, prominent, renowned, revered, well-known.

antonyms obscure, unknown.

celebration *n* acclamation, anniversary, carousal, commemoration, commendation, emblazonment, exaltation, feast, festival, festivity, gala, glorification, honouring, jollification, jubilee, junketing, keeping, laudation, merrymaking, observance, orgy, party, performance, praise, proclamation, publicization, rejoicing, remembrance, revel, revelry, shindig, solemnization.

celebrity *n* big name, big shot, big wheel, bigwig, celeb, dignitary, distinction, éclat, eminence, fame, glory, honour, luminary, name, notability, notable, personage, personality, popularity, pre-eminence, prestige, prominence, renown, reputation, repute, star, stardom, superstar, VIP, visiting fireman.
antonyms nobody, obscurity.

celerity *n* dispatch, expedition, fleetness, haste, promptness, quickness, rapidity, speed, swiftness, velocity.
antonyms sloth, slowness.

celestial *adj* angelic, astral, divine, elysian, empyrean, eternal, ethereal, godlike, heavenly, immortal, paradisaical, seraphic, spiritual, starry, sublime, supernatural, transcendental.
antonyms earthly, mundane.

celibacy *n* abstinence, bachelorhood, chastity, continence, singleness, spinsterhood, virginity.

cell *n* category, caucus, cavity, chamber, compartment, cubicle, dungeon, nucleus, pigeonhole, room, stall, subgroup(ing), unit.

cellar *n* basement, crypt, storeroom, vault, wine collection.

cement *v* attach, bind, bond, combine, fix, glue, gum, join, seal, stick, unite, weld.
n adhesive, bond, binder, concrete, glue, gum, mortar, mucilage, paste, plaster, sealant.

cemetery *n* boneyard, burial ground, churchyard, God's acre, graveyard, necropolis.

censor *v* amend, beep, black out, blue-pencil, bowdlerize, cut, edit, expurgate, screen, suppress.
▲ *confusable word* censure.

censorious *adj* captious, carping, cavilling, condemnatory, critical, disapproving, disparaging, faultfinding, judgmental, hypercritical, severe.
antonyms approving, complimentary, laudatory.

censure *n* accusation, blame, castigation, charge, condemnation, criticism, denunciation, disapproval, obloquy, rebuke, remonstrance, reprehension, reprimand, reproach, reprobation, reproof, stricture, telling-off, vituperation.
antonyms approval, compliments, praise.
v accuse, animadvert (on), berate, blame, blast, castigate, charge, chide, condemn, criticize, decry, denounce, get on someone's case, inveigh against, jump on, rebuke, reprehend, reprimand, reproach, reprobate, reprove, scold, slam, tell off, upbraid.
antonyms approve, comment, compliment, praise.
▲ *confusable word* censor.

central *adj* chief, core, crucial, essential, focal, fundamental, important, inner, interior, key, main, major, mean, median, mid, middle, pivotal, primary, principal, vital.
antonyms marginal, minor, peripheral.

centralize *v* amalgamate, compact, concentrate, consolidate, converge, focus, gather together, incorporate, rationalize, streamline, unify.
antonym decentralize.

centre *n* bull's-eye, core, crux, eye, focus, heart, hub, Mecca, mid, middle, midpoint, nave, navel, nucleus, omphalos, pivot.
antonyms edge, margin, outskirts, periphery.
v balance, cluster, concentrate, converge, focus, gravitate, hinge, pivot, revolve.

centrepiece *n* cynosure, epergne, flagship, focus, highlight, jewel, main attraction (or event or feature), ornament, pearl.

centrifugal *adj* diffusive, divergent, diverging, efferent, radial, radiating, scattering, spreading.
antonym centripetal.

centripetal *adj* afferent, clustering, concentrating, convergent, converging.
antonym centrifugal.

ceremonial *adj* dress, formal, liturgical, official, ritual, ritualistic, solemn, stately.
antonym informal.
n ceremony, formality, protocol, rite, ritual, solemnity.

ceremonious *adj* courtly, deferential, dignified, formal, grand, officious, polite, pompous, precise, proper, punctilious, ritual, solemn, starchy, stately, stiff.
antonyms informal, relaxed, unceremonious.

ceremony *n* ado, big deal, bother, business, celebration, ceremonial, circumstance, commemoration, decorum, etiquette, event, form, formality, function, fuss, niceties, observance, pageantry, parade, pomp, propriety, protocol, rite, ritual, service, show, solemnities, to-do.

certain *adj* ascertained, assured, bound, conclusive, confident, constant, convinced, convincing, decided, definite, dependable, destined, determinate, established, express, fated, fixed, given, incontrovertible, individual, indubitable, ineluctable, inescapable, inevitable, inexorable, irrefutable, known, one, particular, plain, positive, reliable, resolute, resolved, satisfied, settled, some, special, specific, stable, steady, sure, true, trustworthy, undeniable, undoubted, unequivocal, unfailing, unmistakable, unquestionable.
antonyms doubtful, hesitant, uncertain, unsure.

certainly *adv* absolutely, conclusively, decidedly, definitely, doubtlessly, gladly, incontrovertibly, naturally, of course, positively, surely, undeniably, undoubtedly, unmistakably, unquestionably, without question.

certainty *n* assurance, authoritativeness, certitude, conclusiveness, confidence, conviction, definiteness, determinacy, fact, faith, incontrovertibility, indubitableness, inevitability, positiveness, reality, reliability, sureness, sure thing, surety, trust, trustworthiness, truth.
antonyms doubt, hesitation, uncertainty.

certificate *n* attestation, authentication, authorization, award, coupon, credentials, diploma, document, endorsement, guarantee, licence, papers, pass, permit, qualification, testimonial, validation, voucher, warrant.

certify *v* accredit, ascertain, assure, attest, authenticate, authorize, avow, confirm, corroborate, declare, endorse, evidence, guarantee, license, notarize, show, testify, validate, verify, vouch, witness.

cessation *n* abeyance, arrest, break, desistance, discontinuance, discontinuation, end, ending, halt, halting, hiatus, intermission, interruption, interval, letup, pause, recess, remission, respite, rest, standstill, stay, stoppage, stopping, suspension, termination. *antonyms* commencement, continuation, resumption.

chafe *v* abrade, anger, annoy, exasperate, fret, fume, gall, get, grate, heat, incense, inflame, irk, irritate, offend, peeve, provoke, rankle, rasp, rub, scrape, scratch, vex, wear, worry.

chaff *n* badinage, banter, jesting, jokes, joking, joshing, persiflage, raillery, ribbing, taunting, teasing. *v* banter, bug, deride, jeer (at), josh, laugh at, mock, pull (someone's) leg, rib, ridicule, scoff, taunt, tease.

chagrin *n* annoyance, discomfiture, discomposure, displeasure, disquiet, dissatisfaction, embarrassment, exasperation, fretfulness, humiliation, indignation, irritation, mortification, peevishness, spleen, vexation. *antonyms* delight, pleasure. *v* annoy, disconcert, displease, disquiet, dissatisfy, embarrass, exasperate, humiliate, irk, irritate, mortify, peeve, vex.

chain *n* bond, catena, concatenation, coupling, fetter, fob, gyve, link, manacle, progression, restraint, sequence, series, set, shackle, string, succession, suite, train, vinculum. *v* bind, confine, enslave, fasten, fetter, gyve, handcuff, manacle, restrain, secure, shackle, tether, trammel. *antonyms* free, release.

chairperson *n* chair, chairman, chairwoman, convenor, director, facilitator, master of ceremonies, MC, president, presider, speaker, spokesperson, toastmaster, toastmistress.

chalk up accumulate, achieve, ascribe, attribute, charge, credit, enter, gain, log, mark, record, register, score, tally, win.

chalky *adj* ashen, calcareous, cretaceous, pale, pallid, powdery, wan, white.

challenge *v* accost, beard, brave, call, confront, dare, defy, demand, dispute, draw a line in the sand, impugn, invite, object, provoke, put to the test, query, question, stimulate, tax, test, threaten, throw down the gauntlet. *n* call, confrontation, dare, defiance, gauntlet, hurdle, interrogation, invitation, line in the sand, objection, obstacle, poser, provocation, question, test, threat, trial, ultimatum.

chamber *n* apartment, assembly, bedchamber, bedroom, boudoir, camera, cavity, compartment, council, cubicle, enclosure, hall, legislature, office, parliament, room, suite, vault, ventricle.

champion *n* backer, challenger, conqueror, defender, guardian, hero, nonpareil, paladin, patron, protector, Roland, titleholder, titleist, upholder, victor, vindicator, warrior, winner. *v* advocate, back, defend, espouse, maintain, promote, stand up for, support, uphold.

chance *n* accident, act of God, coincidence, contingency, destiny, fate, fortuity, fortune, gamble, happenstance, hazard, likelihood, luck, misfortune, occasion, odds, opening, opportunity, peril, possibility, probability, prospect, providence, risk, scope, shot, try, turn, uncertainty. *antonyms* certainty, law, necessity. *v* gamble, happen, hazard, risk, stake, try, turn out, venture, wager. *adj* accidental, casual, coincidental, contingent, fortuitous, inadvertent, incidental, random, serendipitous, unforeseeable, unforeseen, unintended, unintentional, unlooked-for. *antonyms* certain, deliberate, intentional.

chancy *adj* dangerous, dicey, hazardous, problematic, risky, speculative, tricky, uncertain. *antonyms* safe, secure .

change *v* alter, alternate, amend, barter, convert, correct, denature, diversify, edit, exchange, fluctuate, interchange, metamorphose, moderate, modify, mutate, permute, rearrange, reform, remodel, reorganize, replace, restyle, shift, substitute, swap, switch, take liberties with, trade, transfigure, transform, transmute, transpose, turn, turn around, turn upside down, vacillate, vary, veer. *n* alteration, alternation, amendment, break, chop, conversion, correction, difference, diversion, edit, exchange, fluctuation, innovation, interchange, metamorphosis, metanoia, metastasis, metathesis, modification, mutation, novelty, permutation, rearrangement, reform, reorganization, revolution, sea change, shift, substitution, switch, switchover, trade, transformation, transition, transmutation, transposition, turning, upheaval, variation, variety, vicissitude.

changeable *adj* capricious, chameleon(ic), changeful, erratic, fickle, fitful, fluid, inconstant, irregular, kaleidoscopic, labile, mercurial, mobile, mutable, protean, shifting, uncertain, unpredictable, unreliable, unsettled, unstable, unsteady, vacillating, variable, vicissitudinous, volatile, wavering. *antonyms* constant, reliable, unchangeable.

channel *n* artery, avenue, band, bed, canal, chamber, chamfer, communication, conduit, course, creekbed, direction, duct, euripus, fairway, flume, fluting, frequency, furrow, gat, groove, gulley, gut, gutter, instrument, main, means, medium, millrace, passage, path, race, riverbed, route, sound, station, strait, streambed, trough, watercourse, waterway, way.

v conduct, convey, direct, flute, furrow, groove, guide, send, transmit.

chant n carol, chorus, drone, intonation, mantra, melody, monotone, psalm, recitation, recitative, refrain, shanty, singsong, slogan, song, war cry.

v cantillate, carol, chorus, croon, descant, drone, intone, recite, sing.

chaos n anarchy, bedlam, confusion, disorder, disorganization, entropy, lawlessness, mayhem, mess, pandemonium, shambles, snafu, tumult, unreason, uproar.

antonym order.

chaotic adj anarchic, confused, deranged, disordered, disorganized, lawless, purposeless, rampageous, riotous, snafu, topsy-turvy, tumultuous, uncontrolled.

antonyms organized, purposive.

chap n bloke, character, codger, customer, duffer, fellow, gentleman, guy, individual, person, shaver, sort, type.

chapel n bethel, church, group devotions, meeting house, prayers, shrine.

chaperone n bodyguard, companion, duenna, escort, gooseberry, governess, supervisor.

v accompany, attend, escort, guard, matronize, protect, safeguard, shepherd, supervise, watch over.

chapter n assembly, branch, chapel, clause, division, episode, local, part, period, phase, section, stage, topic.

char v blacken, brown, burn, carbonize, cauterize, scorch, sear, singe.

character[1] n attributes, backbone, bent, calibre, cast, characteristic, complexion, constitution, disposition, feature, honour, individuality, integrity, kidney, make-up, nature, peculiarity, personality, physiognomy, principle, quality, rank, rectitude, reputation, sort, spine, stamp, strength, temper, temperament, trait, type, uprightness.

character[2] n card, cove, customer, eccentric, fellow, guy, individual, oddball, oddity, original, part, person, persona, role, sort, type, weirdo.

character[3] n cipher, device, emblem, figure, hieroglyph, ideogram, ideograph, letter, logo, mark, rune, sign, symbol, type.

characteristic adj classic, discriminative, distinctive, distinguishing, idiosyncratic, individual, peculiar, representative, singular, special, specific, symbolic, symptomatic, typical, vintage.

antonyms uncharacteristic, untypical.

n attribute, faculty, feature, hallmark, idiosyncrasy, lineament, mannerism, mark, peculiarity, property, quality, symptom, thing, trait.

characterize v brand, describe, distinguish, identify, indicate, inform, mark, portray, represent, stamp, typify.

charade n fake, farce, mockery, pantomime, parody, pasquinade, pretence, travesty.

charge v accuse, adjure, afflict, arraign, ascribe, ask, assail, assault, attack, attribute, bid, blame, burden, command, debit, demand, enjoin, entrust, exact, exhort, fill, impeach, impute, indict, instruct, lade, load, order, require, rush, set on, storm, suffuse, tax.

n accusation, adjuration, allegation, amount, assault, attack, behest, burden, care, command, cost, custody, damage, debit, demand, dictate, direction, duty, exhortation, expenditure, expense, fee, imputation, indictment, injunction, instruction, mandate, office, onset, onslaught, order, outlay, payment, price, rate, responsibility, rush, safekeeping, sortie, trust, toll, ward.

charisma n allure, appeal, attraction, charm, duende, dynamism, fascination, magnetism, power.

charismatic adj alluring, appealing, attractive, charming, dynamic, fascinating, inspiring, magnetic, pentecostal, powerful, winning.

charitable adj accommodating, beneficent, benevolent, benign, benignant, bountiful, broad-minded, clement, compassionate, considerate, eleemosynary, favourable, forgiving, generous, gracious, humane, indulgent, kind, kindly, lavish, lenient, liberal, magnanimous, mild, philanthropic, sympathetic, tolerant, understanding.

antonyms uncharitable, unforgiving.

charity n affection, agape, almsgiving, altruism, assistance, benefaction, beneficence, benevolence, benignity, benignness, bountifulness, bounty, clemency, compassion, dole, endowment, fund, generosity, gift, goodness, handout, humanity, indulgence, love, philanthropy, relief, tender-heartedness.

charlatan n cheat, con man, fake, fraud, impostor, mountebank, phony, pretender, quack, quacksalver, sham, swindler, trickster.

charm v allure, attract, beguile, bewitch, cajole, captivate, delight, enamour, enchant, engage, enrapture, enthrall, entrance, fascinate, mesmerize, please, win.

n abraxas, allure, allurement, amulet, appeal, attraction, attractiveness, charisma, desirability, duende, enchantment, fascination, fetish, idol, incantation, juju, magic, magnetism, mascot, phylactery, sorcery, spell, talisman, trinket.

charming adj appealing, attractive, bewitching, captivating, cute, delectable, delightful, engaging, eye-catching, fetching, gallant, honeyed, irresistible, lovely, pleasant, pleasing, quaint, seductive, sweet, winning, winsome.

antonyms ugly, unattractive.

chart n blueprint, diagram, figure, flowchart, graph, map, nomogram, pie chart, plan, table, tabulation.

v delineate, draft, draw, graph, map out, mark, outline, place, plan, plot, sketch.

charter n accreditation, authorization, bill, bond, concession, constitution, contract, deed, document, engagement, franchise, hiring, indenture, licence, list, permit, prerogative, privilege, right, statement.

v authorize, commission, employ, engage, hire, lease, rent, sanction.

chary *adj* careful, cautious, circumspect, guarded, heedful, leery, prudent, reluctant, slow, sparing, suspicious, uneasy, unwilling, wary.

antonyms heedless, unwary.

chase *v* course, drive, expel, follow, hunt, hurry, pursue, run (after), rush, track.

n coursing, hunt, hunting, pursuit, race, run, rush, venery.

chasm *n* abysm, abyss, breach, canyon, cavity, cleft, crater, crevasse, fissure, gap, gorge, gulf, hiatus, hollow, opening, ravine, rent, rift, split, void.

chassis *n* anatomy, bodywork, bones, frame, framework, fuselage, skeleton, structure, substructure, undercarriage.

chaste *adj* austere, decent, decorous, elegant, immaculate, incorrupt, innocent, maidenly, modest, moral, neat, pure, refined, restrained, simple, unaffected, undefiled, unsullied, unvulgar, vestal, virginal, virginly, virtuous, wholesome.

antonyms indecorous, lewd.

chasten *v* admonish, chastise, correct, cow, curb, discipline, humble, reprove, sober, soften, subdue, tame.

chastise *v* beat, berate, castigate, censure, correct, discipline, flog, give (someone) what for, lash, punish, reprove, scold, scourge, smack, spank, upbraid, whip.

chastity *n* abstinence, celibacy, continence, decorum, innocence, maidenhood, modesty, purity, restraint, self-restraint, simplicity, temperateness, virginity, virtue.

antonym lechery.

chat *n* chatter, chinwag, confab, gab, gossip, heart-to-heart, natter, parley, rap, session, talk, tête-à-tête, visit.

v chatter, chew the fat, gossip, jaw, natter, rap, shoot the breeze, talk, visit, yackety-yak.

chatter *n* babble, blather, blether, chat, chinwag, gab, gossip, jabber, natter, prate, prating, prattle, prattlement, tonguewagging, twaddle.

v babble, blab, blabber, blather, blether, chat, clack, clatter, gab, gossip, go on, jabber, natter, prate, prattle, prittle-prattle, quack, talk a blue streak, twaddle, yackety-yak.

chatterer *n* bigmouth, blabbermouth, blatherskite, chatterbox, gabber, gossip, loudmouth, magpie, prattlebox, windbag.

chattering *adj* blathering, clacking, gabby, long-tongued, nattering, prattling, talkative.

chatty *adj* colloquial, conversative, familiar, friendly, gabby, gossipy, informal, long-tongued, newsy, prattling, talkative.

antonym quiet.

chauvinist *adj* flag-flapping, jingoish, jingoistic, nationalistic, parochial, racist, sexist, supremicist, triumphalist.

cheap *adj* à bon marché, bargain, base, budget, cockamamie, common, contemptible, crappy, cut-price, despicable, dirt-cheap, economical, economy, flimsy, inexpensive, inferior, knock-down, low, low-budget, low-cost, low-priced, mean, paltry, poor, reasonable, reduced, sale, schlocky, scurvy, second-rate, shoddy, sordid, tatty, tawdry, uncostly, vulgar, worthless.

antonyms costly, excellent, noble, superior.

cheapen *v* belittle, debase, degrade, demean, denigrate, depreciate, derogate, devalue, discredit, disparage, downgrade, lower, prostitute.

antonym enhance.

cheat *v* baffle, bamboozle, beguile, bilk, burn, check, chicane, chisel, con, cozen, deceive, defeat, defraud, deprive, diddle, do, double-cross, dupe, finagle, fleece, fob, foil, fool, frustrate, fudge, grift, gudgeon, gull, gyp, hand (someone) a lemon, hoax, hocus, hoodwink, mislead, prevent, rip off, scam, screw, sell (someone) a bill of goods, short-change, short-shrift, scam, skin, swindle, take (in), thwart, touch, trick, trim, victimize.

n artifice, bilker, charlatan, cheater, con artist, con man, cozener, deceiver, deception, dodger, double-crosser, extortioner, fraud, grifter, hoax, impostor, imposture, knave, picaroon, rip-off, rogue, scam, shark, sharp, sharper, short-changer, swindle, swindler, trick, trickery, trickster, welsher.

check¹ *v* audit, compare, confirm, examine, give the once-over, inspect, investigate, monitor, note, probe, research, scrutinize, study, test, track, verify.

n audit, examination, inspection, investigation, research, scrutiny, tab, test.

check out examine, investigate, test.

check² *v* arrest, bar, bridle, control, curb, damp(en), delay, halt, hinder, hold back, impede, inhibit, keep back, limit, obstruct, repress, restrain, retard, stop, thwart.

n blow, constraint, control, curb, damper, disappointment, frustration, hindrance, impediment, inhibition, limitation, obstruction, restraint, reverse, setback, stoppage.

cheek¹ *n* audacity, backchat, backtalk, boldness, brass, brazenness, chutzpah, disrespect, effrontery, gall, hardihood, impertinence, impudence, insolence, lip, nerve, sauce, temerity.

cheek² *n* bum, buttock, chap, face, jowl.

cheeky *adj* audacious, bold, brassy, brazen, disrespectful, forward, impertinent, impudent, insolent, insulting, irreverent, lippy, malapert, pert, saucy, shameless.

antonyms polite, respectful.

cheer *v* acclaim, animate, applaud, brighten, chant, chat up, clap, comfort, console, elate, elevate, encourage, enliven, exhilarate, gladden, hail, hearten, hurrah, inspirit, solace, uplift, warm.

antonyms boo, dishearten, jeer.

n acclamation, animation, applause, bravo, buoyancy, cheerfulness, comfort, encouragement, gaiety, gladness, glee, hoorah, hopefulness, hurrah, joy, liveliness, merriment, merrymaking, mirth, optimism, ovation, plaudit, solace.

cheerful *adj* animated, blithe, bouncy, bright, bubbly, buoyant, cheery, chipper, chirpy, chirrupy, contented, enlivening, eupeptic, gay, gaysome, genial, glad, gladsome, happy, hearty, hopeful, jaunty, jolly, jovial, joyful, joyous, light-hearted, lightsome, light-spirited, merry, optimistic, perky, pleasant, sparkling, sprightly, sunny, upbeat, winsome.
antonyms sad, grim.

cheering *adj* auspicious, bright, comforting, encouraging, enlivening, gladdening, heartening, hopeful, inspiring, optimistic, promising, propitious, reassuring, stirring.
antonyms depressing, disheartening.

cheerless *adj* austere, barren, bleak, cold, comfortless, dank, dark, dejected, depressed, desolate, despondent, dingy, disconsolate, dismal, dolorous, drab, dreary, dull, forlorn, gloomy, grim, joyless, lonely, melancholy, miserable, mournful, sad, sombre, sorrowful, spiritless, sullen, sunless, unhappy, uninviting, winterly, woebegone, woeful.
antonyms bright, cheerful.

cheers *interj* bottoms up, (here's) mud in your eye, l'chaim, prosit, skoal, skol, slàinte, your health.

chemical *n* additive, compound, drug, element, insecticide, pesticide, preservative, substance, synthetic.

cherish *v* cling to, entertain, foster, harbour, hold dear, love, make much of, nourish, nurse, nurture, prize, shelter, support, sustain, tender, treasure, uphold, value.

cherubic *adj* adorable, angelic, appealing, cute, heavenly, innocent, lovable, lovely, seraphic, shining, sweet.

chest *n* ark, box, case, casket, coffer, commode, crate, dresser, strongbox, trunk.

chestnut *n* cliché, oldie, vieux jeu, warhorse.

chew *v* bite, champ, chomp, crunch, gnaw, grind, masticate, munch.

chic *adj* à la mode, chi-chi, elegant, fashionable, modish, smart, stylish, trendy.
antonyms démodé, outmoded, unfashionable.

chicanery *n* artifice, cheating, chicane, deception, deviousness, dodge, double-dealing, duplicity, intrigue, jiggery-pokery, sharp practice, skulduggery, sophistry, stratagems, subterfuge, trickery, underhandedness, wiles, wire pulling.

chicken feed *n* coppers, paltry sum, peanuts, pennies, pin money, pittance.

chide *v* admonish, bawl out, berate, blame, censure, chew out, criticize, dress down, give (someone) what for, lecture, objurgate, rate, rebuke, reprehend, reprimand, reproach, reprove, scold, tell off, upbraid.
antonym praise.

chief *adj* capital, cardinal, central, dominant, especial, essential, first, foremost, grand, greatest, highest, key, leading, main, major, outstanding, paramount, predominant, pre-eminent, premier, primary, prime, principal,

senior, superior, supreme, top, uppermost, vital.
antonyms junior, minor, unimportant.

n boss, captain, chieftain, cock of the walk, commander, coryphaeus, director, duke, governor, head, leader, lord, manager, master, paramount, paramount chief, principal, ringleader, ruler, superintendent, superior, supremo, suzerain.

chiefly *adv* especially, essentially, for the most part, generally, mainly, mostly, predominantly, primarily, principally, usually.

child *n* anklebiter, babe, baby, bairn, bambino, brat, chit, colt, cub, descendant, duffer, elf, face (or mouth) to feed, infant, issue, juvenile, kid, kiddy, little one, minor, niño, nipper, nursling, offspring, papoose, pickaninny, product, progeny, pup, rugrat, shaver, small fry, spawn, sprout, suckling, tadpole, toddler, tot, tyke, weanling, youngling, youngster.

child prodigy whiz kid, wunderkind.

childbirth *n* accouchement, childbearing, childbed, confinement, delivery, labour, lying-in, parturition, travail.

childhood *n* adolescence, babyhood, boyhood, early years, girlhood, immaturity, infancy, innocence, minority, schooldays, youth.

childish *adj* babyish, boyish, foolish, frivolous, girlish, immature, infantile, irresponsible, juvenile, puerile, silly, simple, trifling, weak, young.
antonyms adult, sensible.

childlike *adj* artless, credulous, guileless, ingenuous, innocent, naïve, natural, pure, simple, trustful, trusting.

children *n* daughters, descendants, line, offspring, progeny, seed, sons, spawn.

chill *adj* aloof, biting, bleak, chilly, cold, cool, cutting, depressing, distant, freezing, frigid, hostile, icy, penetrating, raw, sharp, stony, unfriendly, unresponsive, unsympathetic, unwelcoming, wintry.
antonyms friendly, warm.

v alarm, cool, dampen, depress, discourage, dishearten, dismay, freeze, frighten, refrigerate, terrify.

n bite, cold, coldness, coolness, coolth, crispness, frigidity, nip, rawness, sharpness.

chilly *adj* aloof, blowy, blustery, breezy, brisk, cold, cool, crisp, drafty, fresh, frigid, hostile, nippy, penetrating, sharp, stony, unenthusiastic, unfriendly, unresponsive, unsympathetic, unwelcoming.
antonyms friendly, warm.

chimera *n* bogey, delusion, dream, fancy, fantasy, figment of the imagination, hallucination, idle fancy, ignis fatuus, illusion, mirage, monster, monstrosity, spectre, will-o'-the-wisp.

chimeric *adj* absurd, delusive, fabulous, fanciful, fantastic, hallucinatory, illusive, illusory, imaginary, impossible, quixotic, unfounded, unreal, vain, visionary, whimsical, wild.

antonym real.

china *n* bone china, ceramics, dinnerware, earthenware, faience, porcelain, pottery, tableware, tea set, terracotta.

chink[1] *n* aperture, cleft, crack, crevice, cut, fissure, flaw, gap, opening, rift, slot, space.

chink[2] *n* clink, jangle, jingle, ping, ring, ting, tinkle.

chip *n* dent, flake, flaw, fragment, nick, notch, paring, piece, scrap, scratch, shard, shaving, sliver, spall, wafer.

v chisel, damage, nick, notch, spall, whittle.

chip in contribute, donate, do one's part, give one's share, interpose, interrupt, participate, pay, share the load (or cost), subscribe.

chippy *adj* aggressive, argumentative, belligerent, contentious, irascible, pugnacious, quarrelsome, scrappy, short-tempered, touchy.

chirp *v, n* cheep, chirrup, peep, pipe, tweet, twitter, warble, whistle.

chirpy *adj* blithe, bright, cheerful, cheery, chipper, chirrupy, gay, happy, jaunty, merry, perky, sprightly, sunny.

antonyms downcast, sad.

chivalrous *adj* bold, brave, chivalric, courageous, courteous, courtly, gallant, generous, gentlemanly, helpful, heroic, honourable, knightly, polite, true, valiant.

antonyms cowardly, ungallant.

chivalry *n* boldness, bravery, courage, courtesy, courtliness, gallantry, generosity, gentlemanliness, helpfulness, honour, knight-errantry, knighthood, politeness.

choice *n* alternative, choosing, decision, dilemma, election, espousal, opting, option, pick, preference, say, selection, variety.

adj best, dainty, elect, elite, excellent, exclusive, exquisite, fancy, fine, hand-picked, nice, plum, precious, prime, prize, rare, select, special, superior, uncommon, unusual, valuable.

antonyms commonplace, inferior.

choke *v* asphyxiate, bar, block, clog, congest, constrict, dam, gag, obstruct, occlude, overpower, reach, retch, smother, stifle, stop, strangle, suffocate, suppress, throttle.

choleric *adj* angry, bad-tempered, cantankerous, crabbed, crabby, crotchety, fiery, grouchy, grumpy, hasty, hot, hot-tempered, ill-tempered, irascible, irritable, petulant, quick-tempered, testy, touchy.

antonyms calm, placid.

choose *v* adopt, appoint, cull, decide, designate, desire, elect, espouse, favour, fix on, opt for, pick, please, plump for, predestine, prefer, see fit, select, settle on, single out, take, vote for, wish.

choosy *adj* discriminating, exacting, fastidious, finicky, fussy, hard to please, particular, picky, selective.

antonym undemanding.

chop *v* amputate, cleave, cut, cut back, divide, fell, hack, hew, lop, reduce, sever, shear, slash, slice, truncate.

chop up cube, cut up, dice, divide, fragment, mince, slice (up).

choppy *adj* blustery, broken, rough, ruffled, squally, stormy, tempestuous, wavy, whitecapped.

antonym calm.

chore *n* bother, burden, drag, drudgery, duty, errand, job, stint, task.

chortle *v* cackle, chuckle, crow, giggle, guffaw, laugh, snigger, snort.

chorus *n* burden, call, choir, chorale, choristers, ensemble, hymn, refrain, response, shout, singers, song, strain, unison, vocalists.

chosen *adj* destined, elect, elite, favoured, peculiar, predilect, preferred, selected.

christen *v* baptize, besprinkle, call, designate, inaugurate, name, sprinkle, style, term, title.

Christmas *n* Advent, Epiphany, Nativity, Noel (Nowell), Xmas, Yule, Yuletide.

chronic *adj* confirmed, continual, deep-rooted, deep-seated, habitual, incessant, incurable, ineradicable, ingrained, inveterate, ongoing, perpetual, persistent, recurring.

antonym temporary.

chronicle *n* account, annals, chanson de geste, diary, epic, gest, history, journal, memoir, narrative, record, register, saga, story.

v enter, list, narrate, record, recount, register, relate, report, tell, write down.

chronicler *n* annalist, diarist, historian, historiographer, narrator, recorder, reporter, scribe.

chronological *adj* consecutive, historical, linear, ordered, progressive, sequential.

chubby *adj* buxom, fat, flabby, fleshy, heavy, overweight, paunchy, plump, portly, rotund, round, stout, tubby.

antonyms skinny, slim.

chuck *v* cast, discard, fling, get rid of, heave, hurl, jettison, pitch, reject, scrap, shy, sling, throw, toss.

chuckle *v* chortle, crow, exult, giggle, laugh, snigger, snort, titter.

chum *n* buddy, companion, comrade, crony, friend, mate, pal.

antonym enemy.

chummy *adj* affectionate, buddy-buddy, close, familiar, friendly, intimate, matey, pally, palsy-walsy, sociable, thick.

chunk *n* bar, block, dollop, hunk, lump, mass, piece, portion, slab, wad, wedge.

chunky *adj* beefy, brawny, fat, heavy, solid, square, stocky, stubby, thick, thickset.

antonym slim.

church *n* basilica, bethel, cathedral, house of God, house of prayer, kirk, minster, preaching-house, steeple-house.

adj canon, clerical, ecclesiastic, ecclesiastical, ecclesiological, parish, parochial, religious.

churl *n* boor, cad, clod, jerk, oaf.

churlish *adj* boorish, brusque, harsh, ill-tempered, impolite, loutish, morose, oafish, rude, sullen, surly, uncivil, unmannerly, unneighbourly, unsociable, vulgar.
antonyms polite, urbane.

churn *v* agitate, beat, boil, convulse, foam, froth, heave, knot, seethe, swirl, toss, turn, writhe.

chute *n* channel, flume, funnel, gutter, hopper, incline, ramp, runway, shaft, slide, slope, trough.

cigarette *n* cancer stick, cig, coffin nail, fag, gasper, joint, smoke, snout, whiff.

cinch *n* duck soup, piece of cake, snap, sure thing, walk-over.

cinema *n* big screen, filmhouse, film theatre, flicks, movies, movie theatre.

cipher *n* character, code, cryptograph, device, digit, figure, logo, mark, monogram, nil, nobody, nonentity, nothing, nought, number, numeral, symbol, zero.

circle *n* ambit, area, assembly, band, bounds, circuit, circumference, class, clique, club, coil, company, compass, cordon, coterie, crowd, cycle, disc, domain, enclosure, fellowship, field, fraternity, globe, group, gyre, lap, loop, orb, orbit, perimeter, province, radius, range, realm, revolution, ring, round, roundabout, roundel, scene, school, set, society, sphere, turn.
v belt, circumambulate, circumnavigate, circumscribe, coil, compass, curl, curve, eddy, encircle, enclose, encompass, envelop, gird, girdle, hem in, loop, pivot, revolve, ring, rotate, spiral, surround, tour, turn, wheel, whirl.

circuit *n* ambit, area, boundary, bounds, circumference, compass, course, district, journey, lap, limit, orbit, perambulation, range, region, revolution, round, route, tour, track, tract.

circuitous *adj* cagey, circumlocutory, convoluted, devious, indirect, labyrinthine, meandering, oblique, periphrastic, rambling, roundabout, tortuous, winding.
antonyms direct, straight.

circular *adj* annular, discoid(al), disc-shaped, hoop-shaped, ring-shaped, round.
n ad, advertisement, announcement, flyer, handbill, leaflet, letter, memo, notice, pamphlet.

circulate *v* broadcast, cycle, diffuse, disseminate, distribute, flow, give currency to, go around, issue, make the rounds, promulgate, propagate, publicize, publish, revolve, rotate, send around, spread, spread abroad, swirl, whirl.

circumference *n* border, boundary, bounds, circuit, edge, extremity, fringe, limits, margin, outline, perimeter, periphery, rim, verge.

circumlocution *n* euphemism, indirectness, periphrasis, prolixity, redundancy, roundaboutness, wordiness.

circumscribe *v* bound, confine, curtail, define, delimit, delineate, demarcate, encircle,

enclose, encompass, environ, hem in, limit, pen in, restrain, restrict, surround, trim.

circumspect *adj* attentive, canny, careful, cautious, deliberate, discreet, discriminating, guarded, heedful, judicious, observant, politic, prudent, sagacious, sage, vigilant, wary, watchful.
antonyms unguarded, unwary.

circumstance *n* accident, ceremony, chance, coincidence, condition, contingency, detail, display, element, event, fact, factor, fortuity, fuss, happening, happenstance, incident, item, luck, occurrence, particular, pomp, position, respect, situation.

circumstances *n* background, conditions, context, means, position, resources, situation, state, state of affairs, station, status, times.

circumstantial *adj* conjectural, contingent, detailed, evidential, exact, hearsay, incidental, indirect, inessential, inferential, irrelevant, minor, minute, particular, presumptive, provisional, specific, unimportant.
antonyms hard, inexact, vague.

circumvent *v* bypass, dodge, elude, evade, foil, frustrate, get out of, get past, hoodwink, mislead, outflank, outgeneral, outwit, overreach, sidestep, steer clear of, thwart, trick.

cistern *n* basin, pool, reservoir, sink, tank, vat.

citadel *n* acropolis, bastion, castle, château, fortification, fortress, keep, refuge, stronghold, tower.

citation *n* award, clip, clipping, commendation, excerpt, mention, passage, quotation, quote, reference, source, subpoena, summons.

cite *v* adduce, advance, appeal to, call on, enumerate, excerpt, extract, mention, name, quote, refer to, specify, subpoena, summon.

citizen *n* burgess, burgher, city-dweller, civilian, denizen, dweller, freeman, inhabitant, national, native, oppidan, passport-holder, ratepayer, resident, subject, townsman, urbanite.

city *n* city hall, cityscape, conurbation, downtown, inner city, megalopolis, metropolis, municipal government, municipality, town, urban centre, urban core.

civic *adj* borough, city, communal, community, local, municipal, oppidan, public, urban.

civil *adj* accommodating, affable, amicable, civilized, citizen's, complaisant, courteous, domestic, home, interior, internal, mannerly, municipal, non-criminal, obliging, polite, political, private, respectful, secular, temporal.
antonym uncivil.

civil servant bureaucrat, government employee, government official, paper pusher, pencil pusher.

civilization *n* advancement, amenities, conveniences, cultivation, culture, development, education, enlightenment, kultur, (modern) amenities, progress, refinement, sophistication, urbanity.
antonyms barbarity, primitiveness, wilderness.

civilize v ameliorate, cultivate, educate, enlighten, humanize, improve, meliorate, perfect, polish, refine, sophisticate, tame.

civilized adj advanced, couth, cultivated, cultured, educated, enlightened, humane, polite, refined, sophisticated, tolerant, urbane.
antonyms barbarous, primitive, uncouth.

civility n affability, amenity, amiability, amicability, comity, complaisance, cordiality, courteousness, courtesy, couth, good breeding, manners, politeness, politesse, tact.
antonyms rudeness, uncouthness.

claim v affirm, allege, arrogate, ask for, assert, aver, collect, demand, exact, hold, insist, maintain, need, pick up, profess, request, require, state, take, uphold.
n affirmation, allegation, application, assertion, call, demand, insistence, petition, pretension, privilege, protestation, request, requirement, right, title.

claimant n applicant, petitioner, pretendant, pretender, suppliant, supplicant.

clairvoyant adj extrasensory, fey, oracular, prescient, prophetic, psychic, second-sighted, sibylline, telepathic, vatic, visionary.
n augur, diviner, fortuneteller, oracle, prophet, prophetess, seer, sibyl, soothsayer, telepath, telepathist, visionary.

clamber v ascend, claw, climb, crawl, descend, scale, scrabble, scramble, shin, shinny.

clammy adj close, damp, dank, heavy, moist, muggy, pasty, slimy, sticky, sweating, sweaty, viscid.

clamorous adj blaring, deafening, insistent, loud, noisy, riotous, tumultuous, uproarious, vehement, vociferant, vociferous, yammering.
antonym silent.

clamour n agitation, babel, blare, brouhaha, commotion, complaint, din, hubbub, hue and cry, hullabaloo, jammering, noise, outcry, racket, shouting, uproar, vociferation.
antonym silence.

clamp n brace, bracket, fastener, grip, press, vice.
v brace, clap, clinch, fasten, fix, impose, press, secure.

clamp down on crack down on, get tough on, lower the boom on, put paid to, put the kibosh on, take stern (or stiff) measures against, toughen up on.

clan n band, brotherhood, clique, confraternity, coterie, extended family, faction, family, fraternity, gens, group, house, kingroup, phratry, race, sect, sept, set, society, sodality, tribe.

clandestine adj backroom, behind-door, cloak-and-dagger, closet, concealed, covert, furtive, hidden, private, secret, sly, sneaky, stealthy, surreptitious, underground, underhand, under-the-counter.
antonym open.

clang v bong, chime, clank, clash, jangle, peal, resound, reverberate, ring, toll.

n bong, clank, clash, clatter, jangle, peal, reverberation .

clannish adj cliquey, cliquish, close, closed, exclusive, insular, inward-looking, narrow, parochial, sectarian, select, tight-knit, unfriendly.
antonyms friendly, open.

clap v acclaim, applaud, bang, cheer, impose, pat, slap, smack, thrust, thwack, wallop, whack.

claptrap n balderdash, baloney, blarney, bombast, bull, bunk, bunkum, codswallop, drivel, eyewash, falderal, guff, hogwash, hokum, hot air, humbug, malarkey, nonsense, rot, rubbish, tommyrot, tripe, twaddle.

clarification n definition, elucidation, explanation, exposition, gloss, illumination, interpretation, simplification.
antonym obfuscation.

clarify v cleanse, define, elucidate, explain, gloss, illuminate, purify, refine, resolve, shed/throw light on, simplify.
antonym obscure.

clarity n clearness, comprehensibility, definition, distinctness, explicitness, intelligibility, limpidity, lucidity, lucidness, obviousness, precision, resolution, sharpness, simplicity, transparency, unambiguousness.
antonyms obscurity, vagueness.

clash v bang, clang, clank, clatter, conflict, crash, disagree, feud, fight, grapple, jangle, jar, quarrel, war, wrangle.
n brush, clank, clatter, collision, conflict, confrontation, disagreement, discord, disharmony, encounter, fight, jangle, jar, mismatch, noise, run-in, showdown.

clasp n agraffe, brooch, buckle, catch, clip, closure, embrace, fastener, fastening, grasp, grip, hasp, hold, hook, hug, pin, snap.
v attach, close, clutch, concatenate, connect, embrace, enclasp, enfold, fasten, grasp, grip, hold, hug, press, seize, squeeze.

class[1] n calibre, caste, category, classification, denomination, department, description, division, genre, genus, grade, group, grouping, ilk, kidney, kind, league, order, phylum, quality, rank, section, set, sort, species, status, style, taxon, type.
v assort, brand, categorize, classify, codify, designate, grade, group, rank, rate, sort.

class[2] n course, lecture, lesson, seminar, study group, teach-in, tutorial, workshop.

class[3] n dash, dignity, elegance, excellence, flair, refinement, style, subtlety, swank, taste.

classic adj abiding, ageless, archetypal, Augustan, best, characteristic, chaste, consummate, deathless, definitive, enduring, established, excellent, exemplary, finest, first-rate, high-calibre, high-quality, ideal, immortal, lasting, master, masterly, model, paradigmatic, par excellence, quality, quintessential, refined, standard, time-honoured, traditional, typical, undying, vintage.
antonym second-rate.

n chef d'oeuvre, exemplar, masterpiece, masterwork, model, paradigm, pièce de résistance, prototype, standard.

classical *adj* Attic, Augustan, chaste, elegant, established, excellent, graceful, grecian, Greek, harmonious, Hellenic, Latin, orthodox, pure, refined, regular, restrained, Roman, standard, symmetrical, traditional, well-proportioned.

classification *n* analysis, arrangement, cataloguing, categorization, codification, division, grading, pigeonholing, sorting, taxis, taxonomy.

classify *v* arrange, assort, catalogue, categorize, codify, dispose, distribute, divide, grade, pigeonhole, rank, sort, systematize, tabulate.

classy *adj* dignified, elegant, exclusive, exquisite, fine, grand, high-class, posh, refined, select, smart, stylish, superior, swanky, tasteful, tony, up-market.
antonyms dowdy, plain, unstylish.

clause *n* article, chapter, codicil, condition, heading, item, paragraph, part, passage, point, provision, proviso, rider, section, sentence, specification, stipulation, subpoint, subsection.

claw *n* clutch, griffe, grip, gripper, nail, nipper, paw, pincer, pounce, talon, tentacle, unguis.
v dig, graze, lacerate, mangle, maul, rip, scrabble, scrape, scratch, tear.

clean *adj* antiseptic, chaste, clarified, clear, complete, conclusive, decent, decisive, decontaminated, disinfected, drug-free, elegant, entire, exemplary, even, faultless, final, flawless, fresh, germ-free, good, graceful, guiltless, honest, honourable, hygienic, immaculate, innocent, laundered, moral, neat, perfect, polished, pure, purified, regular, sanitary, sanitized, scrubbed-up, sharp, simple, smooth, sober, spotless, squeaky-clean, sterile, sterilized, straight, thorough, tidy, total, trim, unadulterated, unblemished, uncluttered, uncontaminated, undefiled, unimpaired, unpolluted, unsoiled, unspotted, unstained, unsullied, upright, virtuous, washed, whole, wholesome.
antonyms dirty, indecent, polluted, squalid, unsterile.
v bath, cleanse, deodorize, deterge, disinfect, dust, freshen, launder, lave, mop, neaten, purge, purify, rinse, sanitize, scour, scrub, sponge, sterilize, swab, sweep, tidy (up), vacuum, wash, wipe.
antonyms defile, dirty, stain.

cleaner *n* caretaker, char, charlady, charwoman, janitor, sanitation engineer.

cleanse *v* absolve, absterge, clean, clear, deterge, detoxicate, detoxify, disinfect, lustrate, purge, purify, rinse, sanitize, scavenge, scour, scrub, sterilize, wash.
antonyms defile, dirty, pollute.

cleanser *n* abstergent, detergent, disinfectant, purifier, rinse, scourer, scouring-powder, soap, solvent.

clear *adj* apparent, audible, bright, categorical, certain, clean, cloudless, coherent, comprehensible, conspicuous, crystalline, decided, definite, diaphanous, direct, disengaged, distinct, eidetic, empty, evident, explicit, express, fair, fine, free, glassy, guiltless, halcyon, hyaline, immaculate, incontrovertible, innocent, intelligible, light, limpid, lucid, manifest, marked, noticeable, obvious, open, palpable, patent, pellucid, perceptible, perspicuous, plain, positive, precise, pronounced, pure, recognizable, see-through, sharp, sheer, shining, smooth, sunny, sure, translucent, transparent, unambiguous, unblemished, unclouded, uncompromising, undeniable, undimmed, undulled, unequivocal, unhampered, unhindered, unimpeded, unmistakable, unobstructed, unquestionable, untarnished, untroubled, well-defined.
antonyms blocked, cloudy, congested, fuzzy, vague.
v absolve, acquire, acquit, approve, authorize, brighten, bus, clarify, clean, cleanse, debug, decongest, disengage, disentangle, earn, empty, erase, excuse, exonerate, extricate, fix, free, gain, get past (or over), get through, jump, justify, leap, liberate, lighten, make, miss, open, pass, pass over, purify, reap, refine, remove, rid, settle, strip, submit for approval, tidy, unblock, unclog, uncloud, unload, vault, vindicate, wipe.
antonyms block, condemn, defile, dirty.

clear out beat it, clean out, clear off, decamp, depart, empty, leave, remove, throw out, unclog, vacate, withdraw.

clear up answer, brighten, clarify, deal with, elucidate, explain, fix, remove, resolve, settle, solve, sort out, tidy up, unravel.

clearance *n* allowance, authorization, consent, endorsement, gap, go-ahead, headroom, leave, margin, OK, permission, sale, sanction, settlement, space, the green light.

clear-cut *adj* categorical, clear, definite, distinct, explicit, plain, precise, specific, straightforward, unambiguous, unequivocal, well-defined.
antonyms ambiguous, vague.

clearing *n* dell, glade, hollow, opening, space.

cleave[1] *v* adhere, attach oneself, cling, cohere, hold, remain, stick, unite (oneself).

cleave[2] *v* break, chop, crack, dissever, disunite, divide, halve, hew, open, part, pierce, rend, rive, separate, sever, slice, split, sunder.
antonyms join, unite.

cleft *n* breach, break, chasm, chink, crack, cranny, crevice, fissure, fracture, gap, opening, rent, split.
adj cloven, divided, hewed, parted, rent, riven, ruptured, separated, severed, split, sundered, torn.
antonym solid.

clement *adj* balmy, benevolent, calm, compassionate, fair, fine, forbearing, forgiving, generous, gentle, humane, indulgent, kind, kind-hearted, lenient, magnanimous, merciful, mild, moderate, soft-hearted, temperate, tender-hearted.

antonyms harsh, ruthless.

clench *v* clasp, close, clutch, double, grasp, grip, grit, hold.

clergy *n* church leaders, churchmen, clergymen, clerics, ecclesiastics, ministers, ministry, pastors, presbyterate, priesthood, rabbis, spiritual authorities, the church, the cloth.

clergyman *n* bishop, chaplain, churchman, cleric, curate, deacon, dean, divine, dominie, father, Levite, man of God, minister, padre, parson, pastor, presbyter, priest, rabbi, rector, reverend, sky pilot, vicar.

clerical *adj* church, deaconal, ecclesiastical, ministerial, pastoral, priestly, sacerdotal.

clerk *n* account-keeper, assistant, bookkeeper, cashier, copyist, officer, official, paper shuffler, pencil pusher, receptionist, record-keeper, salesperson, scribe, shop assistant, writer.

clever *adj* able, adroit, apt, astute, brainy, bright, canny, capable, cunning, deep, dexterous, discerning, expert, facile, gifted, ingenious, intelligent, inventive, keen, knowing, knowledgeable, quick, quick-witted, resourceful, sagacious, shrewd, skilful, smart, smart-alecky, smart-ass, talented, witty.

antonyms foolish, naïve, senseless, slow.

clever dick smart aleck, smartass, smartypants, wiseacre, wise guy, witmonger.

cliché *n* banality, bromide, byword, chestnut, commonplace, platitude, stereotype, tag, truism.

click *v, n* beat, clack, snap, snick, snip, tick.

client *n* applicant, buyer, consumer, customer, dependant, habitué, john, patient, patron, protégé, shopper.

clientele *n* business, clients, customers, following, market, patronage, patrons, regulars, trade.

cliff *n* bluff, crag, escarpment, face, overhang, precipice, rock face, scar, scarp.

climactic *adj* critical, crucial, culminative, decisive, exciting, orgasmic, orgastic, paramount, peak.

antonyms bathetic, trivial.

climate *n* ambience, atmosphere, clime, country, disposition, feeling, milieu, mood, region, setting, sky, temper, temperature, tendency, trend, weather.

climax *n* acme, apogee, critical point, culmination, head, height, highlight, high point, moment of decision, orgasm, peak, summit, top, turning point, zenith.

antonyms bathos, low point, nadir.

climb *v* ascend, clamber, mount, rise, scale, shinny, shin up, soar, spiral increase, swarm (up), top.

climb down back down, backpedal, clamber down, descend, dismount, eat crow, eat one's words, retract, retreat.

clinch *v* assure, bolt, cap, clamp, conclude, confirm, cuddle, decide, determine, embrace,

fasten, fix, grasp, hug, nail, rivet, seal, secure, settle, squeeze, tack, verify.

cling (to) *v* adhere, attach oneself, clasp, cleave, clutch, embrace, fasten itself, grasp, grip, hang on, hold, hug, stick.

clinical *adj* analytical, antiseptic, businesslike, cold, detached, disinterested, dispassionate, emotionless, impersonal, objective, scientific, sterile, unemotional.

antonyms biassed, passionate, subjective.

clip[1] *v* crop, curtail, cut, dock, elide, pare, poll, pollard, prune, shear, shorten, snip, swallow, trim, truncate.

clip[2] *v* box, cheat, clobber, clout, cuff, fleece, gyp, hit, knock, overcharge, punch, rip off, short-change, slap, slug, smack, sock, thump, wallop, whack.

n blow, box, clout, cuff, hit, knock, punch, skelp, slap, smack, sock, thump, wallop, whack.

clip[3] *n* gallop, lick, rate, speed.

clip[4] *v* attach, fasten, fix, hold, pin, staple.

clipping *n* citation, cutting, excerpt, extract, piece.

clique *n* band, bunch, circle, clan, club, coterie, crew, crowd, faction, gang, group, grouplet, mates, mob, pack, set.

cloak *n* blind, cape, coat, cover, front, mantle, mask, pretext, robe, screen, shield, wrap.

v camouflage, conceal, cover, disguise, hide, mask, obscure, screen, veil, wrap.

clod *n* boor, cad, churl, creep, cur, dastard, jerk, nincompoop, scoundrel, twerp.

clodhopper *n* booby, boor, bumpkin, lummox, oaf, ox, stubble-jumper, yokel.

clog *v* ball up, block, burden, congest, dam up, fill, hamper, hinder, impede, jam, obstruct, occlude, shackle, stop up, stuff.

antonyms clear, unblock.

n ball and chain, burden, dead weight, drag, encumbrance, hindrance, impediment, obstruction, sabot, wood block, wooden sandal, wooden shoe.

cloistered *adj* cloistral, confined, enclosed, hermitic, insulated, protected, reclusive, restricted, secluded, sequestered, sheltered, shielded, withdrawn.

antonyms open, urbane.

close[1] *v* agree, bar, bear down (on), block, cease, catch up, choke, clinch, clog, come to terms, complete, conclude, confine, connect, converge (on), cork, culminate, discontinue, end, fill, finish, gain (on), grapple, heal, home (in), lock, make a deal, obstruct, plug, reach an agreement, seal, secure, settle, shut, stop, strike a bargain, surround, terminate, wind up.

n cadence, cessation, closing, closure, completion, conclusion, culmination, denouement, end, ending, finale, finish, stop, termination, wind-up.

close[2] *adj* accurate, adjacent, adjoining, affectionate, airless, alert, approaching, approximate, assiduous, at hand, attached, attentive, careful, close-fisted, close-knit, close-lipped, close-mantled, close-woven, compact, confidential, confined, congested, conscientious, cramped, crowded, dear, dense, detailed, devoted, dogged, exact, faithful, familiar, handy, hard by, heavy, hidden, humid, illiberal, imminent, impending, impenetrable, inseparable, intense, intent, intimate, jam-packed, keen, literal, loving, mean, minute, miserly, muggy, narrow, near, nearby, neighbouring, niggardly, nigh, oppressive, packed, painstaking, parsimonious, penurious, precise, private, reserved, reticent, rigorous, searching, secluded, secret, secretive, short, solid, stale, stifling, stingy, strict, stuffy, suffocating, sweltering, taciturn, thick, thorough, tight, tight-fisted, uncommunicative, unforthcoming, ungenerous, unventilated, vigilant.

antonyms broad, careless, cool, distant, unfriendly.

closed *adj* concluded, decided, ended, exclusive, fastened, finished, locked, narrow, over, resolved, restricted, sealed, settled, shut, terminated, wound up.

antonyms open, unfastened, unsettled.

closure *n* cap, cessation, closing, completion, cloture, conclusion, end, finish, healing, junction, juncture, lid, plug, resolution, seal, settlement, stoppage, stopper, termination, wind-up.

antonym opening.

clot[1] *n* coalesence, coagulation, curd, embolism, embolus, glob, gob, lump, mass, occlusion, thrombus.

v coagulate, coalesce, congeal, curdle, jell, thicken.

cloth *n* dishcloth, duster, fabric, facecloth, material, rag, stuff, textile, tissue, towel.

clothe *v* accoutre, apparel, array, attire, bedizen, caparison, cover, deck, drape, dress, enwrap, equip, garb, habit, invest, outfit, rig, robe, swathe, vest, wrap.

antonyms unclothe, undress.

clothes *n* apparel, attire, clothing, costume, dress, duds, garb, garments, gear, get-up, habiliments, habit, outfit, raiment, rig, suit, threads, toggery, togs, uniform, vestments, vesture, wardrobe, wear, weeds.

cloud(s) *n* billow, brume, crowd, darkness, darkspot, flock, fog, gloom, haze, horde, host, mass, mist, multitude, murk, mushroom, nebula, nebulosity, obscurity, shower, swarm, throng, thunderhead, vapour, woolpack.

v becloud, blur, cast suspicion on, confuse, darken, defame, dim, disgrace, disorient, distort, dull, eclipse, impair, mist (over or up), muddle, muddy, obfuscate, obscure, overcast, overshadow, shade, shadow, stain, veil.

antonym clear.

cloudy *adj* blurred, blurry, confused, dark, dim, dismal, dull, emulsified, fuzzy, gloomy, grey, hazy, indistinct, leaden, lightless, lowering, muddy, murky, nebulous, obfuscated, obscure, opaque, overcast, sombre, sullen, sunless, troubled, vague.

antonyms clear, sunny.

clout *v* bash, box, clip, clobber, cuff, hit, knock, punch, slap, slug, smack, sock, strike, thump, wallop, whack.

n authority, bash, clip, cuff, influence, knock, power, prestige, pull, punch, say, slap, slug, smack, sock, standing, thump, wallop, weight, whack, wham.

cloven *adj* bisected, cleft, divided, riven, split.

antonym solid.

clown *n* boor, buffoon, clodhopper, comedian, comic, dolt, fool, fruitcake, goof, harlequin, idiot, jester, joker, merry-andrew, mime, mountebank, oaf, Pantaloon, Pierrot, prankster, punchinello, scaramouch, silly, yahoo, yokel, zany.

clowning *n* antics, buffoonery, cutting up, harlequinade, foolishness, goofing around, jesting, joking, messing around, pantaloonery, pranks, silliness, skylarking.

clownish *adj* awkward, clumsy, comic, crude, foolish, galumphing, goofy, graceless, ill-bred, oafish, rough, rustic, silly, slapstick, ungainly, unsophisticated, zany.

antonyms graceful, sophisticated.

cloy *v* choke, disgust, glut, gorge, nauseate, sate, satiate, sicken, smother, surfeit, tire, weary.

antonyms please, whet.

cloying *adj* excessive, nauseating, oversweet, sickening, sickly, smothering.

club[1] *n* bat, billy, bludgeon, cudgel, mace, stick, truncheon.

v bash, baste, batter, beat, bludgeon, clobber, clout, hammer, hit, pummel, strike, wallop, whack.

club[2] *n* association, band, bunch, circle, clique, combination, company, coterie, fraternity, gang, group, guild, lodge, order, set, society, sodality, sorority, union.

clue *n* evidence, hint, idea, indication, inkling, intimation, lead, notion, pointer, sign, suggestion, suspicion, tip, tip-off, trace.

clump *n* bunch, bundle, cluster, mass, shock, thicket, tuffet, tuft.

v clomp, lumber, plod, stamp, stomp, stump, thud, thump, tramp, tread, trudge.

clumsy *adj* all thumbs, awkward, blundering, bumbling, bungling, butterfingered, crude, cumbersome, gauche, gawky, graceless, ham-fisted, heavy, hulking, ill-made, inelegant, inept, inexpert, klutzy, left-handed, lubberly, lumbering, maladroit, ponderous, rough, unco-ordinated, uncouth, ungainly, ungraceful, unhandy, unrefined, unskilful, unwieldy.

antonym graceful.

cluster *n* assemblage, batch, bunch, clump, collection, constellation, gaggle, gathering, glomeration, group, knot, mass.

v assemble, bunch, clump, collect, flock, gather, group.

clutch *v* catch, clasp, embrace, grab, grasp, grip, hang on to, seize.

clutches n claws, control, custody, dominion, embrace, grasp, grip, hands, keeping, mercy, paws, possession, power, sway, talons.

clutter n busyness, confusion, disarray, disorder, hodgepodge, jumble, litter, mess, muddle, untidiness.

v cover, crowd, encumber, fill, litter, scatter, strew.

coach¹ n drillmaster, guide, instructor, prompter, teacher, trainer, tutor.

v drill, guide, instruct, prepare, prime, prompt, teach, train, tutor.

coach² n bus, carriage, charabanc, landau, motorbus, motor coach, omnibus.

coagulate v clot, congeal, curdle, jell, solidify, thicken.

antonym melt.

coalesce v amalgamate, blend, cohere, combine, consolidate, fuse, incorporate, integrate, merge, unite.

coalition n affiliation, alliance, amalgam, amalgamation, association, bloc, combination, compact, confederacy, confederation, conjunction, federation, fusion, integration, league, merger, union.

coarse adj bawdy, blowzy, boorish, brutish, coarse-grained, crass, crude, earthy, foul-mouthed, gross, homespun, ill-mannered, immodest, impolite, improper, impure, indecent, indelicate, inelegant, loutish, offensive, profane, Rabelaisian, raw, ribald, rough, rude, smutty, uncivil, uncouth, uneven, unfinished, unmannerly, unpolished, unprocessed, unrefined, vulgar.

antonyms fine, polite, refined, sophisticated.

coarsen v anesthetize, blunt, deaden, degenerate, desensitize, deteriorate, dull, harden, indurate, roughen.

antonyms civilize, sensitize.

coast n coastline, littoral, seaboard, seaside, shore.

v cruise, drift, freewheel, glide, sail.

coat n anorak, Burberry, cloak, coating, covering, duffel (coat), fleece, fur, hair, hide, jacket, layer, mackinaw, mackintosh, mantle, melton, overcoat, overlay, parka, pelt, raincoat, ski jacket, topcoat, wash, windbreaker, wool.

v apply, cover, dip, dust, laminate, plaster, plate, smear, spread.

coating n coat, covering, dusting, film, finish, glaze, lamination, layer, membrane, patina, pellicle, sheet, skin, varnish, veneer, wash.

coax v beguile, cajole, convince, decoy, draw, elicit, entice, flatter, inveigle, persuade, soft-soap, sweet-talk, wheedle, wile.

antonym force.

cobble v mend, patch together, slap together.

cock n capon, chanticleer, rooster.

cock-eyed adj absurd, askew, asymmetrical, awry, crazy, crooked, cross-eyed, daft, lopsided, ludicrous, nonsensical, preposterous, skew(ed), squint, squint-eyed.

antonyms sensible, sober.

cocksure adj arrogant, brash, brassy, brazen, bumptious, cocky, hubristic, overconfident, presumptuous, self-assured, self-confident.

antonym modest.

cocky adj arrogant, brash, brassy, brazen, cocksure, conceited, egotistical, fresh, pert, self-assured, swaggering, too big for one's boots (or britches), vain.

cocoon v cover, encase, envelop, insulate, preserve, protect, sheathe, shelter, wrap.

coddle v baby, cosset, humour, indulge, mollycoddle, overprotect, pamper, pet, spoil.

code n canon, cipher, convention, cryptograph, custom, ethics, etiquette, instructions, language, manners, program, protocol, regulations, rules, signal, system.

v encipher, encode, program.

codify v catalogue, classify, code, digest, organize, summarize, systematize, tabulate, write down.

coerce v bludgeon, browbeat, bulldoze, bully, compel, constrain, drag, dragoon, drive, force, intimidate, press-gang, pressure, railroad, threaten.

antonyms coax, persuade.

co-existent adj coeval, co-existing, coincident, concomitant, contemporaneous, contemporary, simultaneous, synchronous.

coffer n ark, case, casket, chest, repository, strongbox, treasure chest, treasury.

cogency n conviction, force, persuasiveness, potency, power, strength, urgency, weight.

antonym weakness.

cogent adj compelling, conclusive, convincing, effective, forceful, forcible, influential, irresistible, persuasive, potent, powerful, strong, unanswerable, urgent, weighty.

antonyms ineffective, unsound.

cogitate v cerebrate, consider, contemplate, deliberate, meditate, mull, muse, ponder, reflect, ruminate, think.

cognate adj affiliated, akin, alike, allied, analogous, associated, connected, kindred, parallel, related, similar.

antonym unconnected.

cognition n apprehension, awareness, comprehension, intelligence, interpretation, learning, perception, reasoning, understanding.

cognizance n acknowledgment, apprehension, awareness, cognition, consciousness, knowledge, notice, perception, percipience, recognition, regard.

antonym unawareness.

cognizant adj acquainted, aware, conscious, familiar, informed, knowledgeable, witting.

antonym unaware.

cohere v accord, adhere, agree, bond, cling, coalesce, combine, consolidate, correspond, fuse, hang together, harmonize, hold, jibe, make sense, square, stick, unite.

antonym separate.

coherence n agreement, cohesion, comprehensibility, concordance, congruity, connectedness, consistency, consonance, correspondence, intelligibility, rationality, sense, unity.

antonym incoherence.

coherent *adj* articulate, comprehensible, consistent, intelligible, logical, lucid, meaningful, ordered, orderly, organized, rational, reasoned, sensible, systematic.

cohort *n* accomplice, assistant, associate, band, colleague, companion, company, comrade, contingent, corps, crony, division, follower, henchman, legion, mate, minion, myrmidon, partner, regiment, sidekick, squadron, supporter, toady, troop.

coil *v* convolute, curl, entwine, loop, snake, spiral, twine, twist, wind, wreathe, writhe.

n bight, convolution, curl, loop, spiral, twist.

coin *v* conceive, create, devise, forge, form, introduce, invent, make up, mint, originate, think up.

n bit, cash, change, copper, jitney, loose change, money, piece, silver, small change, specie.

coincide *v* accord, agree, co-exist, concur, correspond, harmonize, jibe, match, square, tally.

coincidence *n* accident, chance, coexistence, concomitance, concord, concurrence, conjunction, correlation, correspondence, eventuality, fluke, fortuity, luck, synchronicity, synchronism.

coincidental *adj* accidental, casual, chance, coincident, concomitant, concurrent, flukey, fortuitous, lucky, random, simultaneous, synchronous, unintentional, unplanned.

antonyms deliberate, planned.

coitus *n* congress, copulation, coupling, lovemaking, marriage bed, mating, sexual intercourse, union.

cold *adj* algid, aloof, apathetic, arctic, benumbed, biting, bitter, bleak, chill, chilled, chilly, cold-blooded, cool, dead, distant, emotionless, freezing, frigid, frosty, frozen, gelid, glacial, icy, inclement, indifferent, inhospitable, lukewarm, nippy, numb(ed), passionless, raw, shivery, spiritless, stand-offish, stark, stony, undemonstrative, unfeeling, unfriendly, unheated, unmoved, unresponsive, unsympathetic, wintry.

antonyms friendly, warm.

n catarrh, chill, chilliness, coldness, frigidity, frostiness, hypothermia, iciness, inclemency.

antonyms friendliness, warmth.

cold fish iceberg.

cold-blooded *adj* barbaric, barbarous, brutal, callous, cruel, dispassionate, emotionless, fell, flinty, heartless, inhuman, merciless, obdurate, pitiless, ruthless, savage, steely, stony-hearted, uncompassionate, unemotional, unfeeling, unmoved.

antonyms compassionate, merciful.

cold-hearted *adj* callous, cold, detached, flinty, frigid, frozen, heartless, indifferent, inhuman, insensitive, stony-hearted, uncaring, uncompassionate, unfeeling, unkind, unresponsive, unsympathetic.

antonym warm-hearted.

collaborate *v* cabal, co-author, collude, conspire, co-operate, co-produce, fraternize, participate, team up.

collaboration *n* alliance, association, concert, co-operation, partnership, tandem, teamwork.

collaborator *n* assistant, associate, caballer, co-author, collaborationist, colleague, confederate, co-worker, fellow-traveller, partner, quisling, teammate, traitor, turncoat.

collapse *v* break (down), capitulate, cave in, crash, crumple, disintegrate, fail, faint, fall, fold, founder, go to pieces, sink, subside, telescope.

n breakdown, capitulation, cave-in, crash, debacle, detumescence, disintegration, downfall, exhaustion, failure, fainting, flop.

collar *v* apprehend, appropriate, arrest, capture, catch, grab, lay hold of, nab, reel in, seize.

n dog collar, gorget, neck, neckband, ring, ruff.

collate *v* adduce, arrange, collect, compare, compile, compose, gather, order, sort.

collateral *n* assurance, deposit, funds, guarantee, pledge, security, surety.

adj additional, concurrent, confirmatory, corresponding, corroborative, indirect, parallel, related, supplementary, supporting.

colleague *n* aide, ally, assistant, associate, auxiliary, bedfellow, coadjutor, cohort, collaborator, companion, compeer, comrade, confederate, confrère, co-worker, fellow, helper, mate, partner, peer, schoolmate, teammate, workmate.

collect *v* accumulate, acquire, aggregate, amass, assemble, cluster, congregate, convene, forgather, gather, gather together, heap up, hoard, muster, obtain, pick up, pile up, raise, rally, save, stockpile.

collected *adj* assembled, calm, composed, confident, cool, efficient, gathered, imperturbable, poised, self-possessed, serene, together, unperturbed, unruffled.

antonyms discombobulated, disorganized, jittery.

collection *n* accumulation, anthology, assemblage, assembly, assortment, caboodle, cluster, company, compilation, congeries, conglomerate, conglomeration, congregation, convocation, crowd, festschrift, gathering, group, harvest(ing), heap, hoard, ingathering, job lot, mass, miscellany, pile, set, stockpile, store.

collective *adj* combined, common, concerted, co-operative, corporate, joint, shared, unified, united.

n commune, co-op, corporation, group, kibbutz.

collision *n* accident, bump, clash, clashing, conflict, confrontation, crash, encounter, fender bender, impact, opposition, pile-up, rencounter, skirmish, smash, smash-up.

colloquial *adj* conversational, demotic, everyday, familiar, idiomatic, informal, non-technical, vernacular.
antonym formal.

collude *v* abet, cabal, collaborate, complot, connive, conspire, contrive, intrigue, machinate, plot, scheme.

collusion *n* cahoots, collaboration, complicity, connivance, conspiracy, intrigue, league.

colonize *v* annex, conquer, develop, people, pioneer, populate, settle, subjugate.

colonist *n* colonial, colonizer, emigrant, frontiersman, homesteader, immigrant, pioneer, planter, settler.

colonnade *n* arcade, cloister(s), columniation, peristyle, portico.

colony *n* dependency, outpost, possession, province, settlement, territory.

colossal *adj* Brobdingnagian, elephantine, enormous, gargantuan, gigantic, herculean, heroic, huge, immense, leviathan, mammoth, massive, monstrous, monumental, mountainous, prodigious, titanic, vast.
antonym tiny.

colour *n* animation, appearance, bloom, blush, brilliance, chroma, colorant, coloration, complexion, disguise, dye, façade, flush, glow, guise, hue, liveliness, paint, pigment, pigmentation, plausibility, pretence, pretext, race, reason, rosiness, ruddiness, semblance, shade, timbre, tincture, tinge, tint, variety, vividness, wash, water-colour.
v blush, burn, colourwash, disguise, distort, dye, embroider, encolour, exaggerate, falsify, flush, misrepresent, paint, pervert, prejudice, redden, slant, stain, strain, taint, tinge, tint.

colourful *adj* bright, brilliant, checkered, descriptive, distinctive, expressive, evocative, graphic, intense, interesting, jazzy, kaleidoscopic, lively, motley, multicoloured, parti-coloured, picturesque, psychedelic, rich, stimulating, unusual, varied, variegated, vibrant, vivid.
antonyms colourless, drab, plain.

colourless *adj* achromatic, achromic, anemic, ashen, bleached, characterless, drab, dreary, dull, faded, flat, forgettable, insipid, lacklustre, livid, neutral, nondescript, one-dimensional, pale, sickly, tame, transparent, uninteresting, unmemorable, vacuous, vapid, wan, washed out.
antonym colourful.

colours *n* banner, colour, emblem, ensign, flag, standard, uniform.

column *n* anta, cavalcade, file, line, list, obelisk, pilaster, pillar, post, procession, queue, rank, row, shaft, string, support, train, upright.

columnist *n* correspondent, critic, editor, journalist, reporter, reviewer, writer.

coma *n* catalepsy, catatonia, insensibility, oblivion, sopor, stupor, torpor, trance, unconsciousness.

comatose *adj* asleep, cataleptic, insensible, stupefied, torpid, unconscious.

antonym conscious.

comb *v* brush, card, curry, hackle, hunt, rake, ransack, rummage through, scour, screen, search, sift, sweep.
n crest, hackle.

combat *n* action, armed conflict, battle, clash, contest, duel, encounter, engagement, fight, hostilities, skirmish, struggle, war, warfare.
v battle (against), contend (with), contest, defy, engage, fight, oppose, resist, strive (against), struggle (against), withstand.

combatant *n* adversary, antagonist, belligerent, contender, enemy, fighter, opponent, serviceman, soldier, warrior.
adj active, battling, belligerent, combating, contending, fighting, opposing, warring.

combative *adj* aggressive, antagonistic, argumentative, bellicose, belligerent, contentious, militant, pugnacious, quarrelsome, truculent, warlike.
antonyms pacific, peaceful.

combination *n* alliance, amalgam, amalgamation, association, blend, cabal, cartel, coalescence, coalition, combine, composite, composition, compound, confederacy, confederation, conjunction, consortium, conspiracy, federation, fusion, integration, marriage, meld, merger, mix, mixture, pooling, syndicate, unification, union.

combine *v* amalgamate, associate, bind, blend, bond, compound, conjoin, co-operate, fuse, incorporate, integrate, join, marry, meld, merge, mix, pool, synthesize, unify, unite, wed.
antonym separate.

combustible *adj* excitable, explosive, flammable, ignitable, incendiary, inflammable, volatile.
antonyms incombustible, non-flammable.

come *v* advance, amount, appear, approach, arrive, attain, become, derive, draw near, enter, extend, happen, materialize, move, near, occur, originate, pass, progress, reach.
antonyms depart, go, leave.

come about arise, befall, come to pass, develop, fall out, happen, occur, result, transpire.

come across appear, bump into, chance upon, come upon, discover, encounter, find, happen on, light on, meet, notice, seem, unearth.

come along accompany, arise, arrive, chug along, develop, happen, improve, mend, progress, rally, recover, recuperate, tag along.

come apart break, crumble, disintegrate, fall to pieces, separate, split, tear.

come around accede, acquiesce, awake, awaken, concede, drop by, give in, mellow, recover, relent, revive, visit, wake, waken, yield.

come between alienate, disunite, divide, embitter, estrange, interfere, intervene, meddle, mediate, part, separate, split up.

come by acquire, get, obtain, procure, secure.

come clean confess, fess up, own up, spill

the beans, tell the truth.

come down　contract, decline, degenerate, descend, deteriorate, fall, fall off, worsen.

come in　appear, arrive, enter, finish, show up.

come on　advance, appear, approach, begin, develop, enter, improve, make overtures, proceed, progress, take place, thrive.

come out　come to light, emerge, end up, make oneself known, result, show up, take a stand, turn out.

come out with　declare, disclose, divulge, offer, publish, record, release, say, state.

come through　bleed, deliver (the goods), endure, show through, succeed, survive, undergo, withstand.

come to grief　bomb, come to nothing, come unstuck, fail, flop, get hurt, go down, miscarry.

antonyms　succeed, triumph.

come to life　revive, rouse.

antonym　collapse, die.

come to light　appear, come out, emerge, transpire, turn out (or up).

come up with　advance, arrive at, concoct, cook up, create, devise, discover, fabricate, find, furnish, hit on, invent, make up, offer, present, produce, propose, provide, submit, suggest, think of, think out, think up, work out.

comeback　*n*　quip, rally, rebound, recovery, rejoinder, repartee, reply, response, resurgence, retaliation, retort, return, revival, riposte, triumph.

comedian　*n*　card, clown, comic, gagster, humorist, jester, joker, jokesmith, laugh, wag, wit.

comedown　*n*　anticlimax, blow, decline, deflation, degradation, demotion, descent, disappointment, humiliation, letdown, reverse, setback, slap in the face.

comedy　*n*　clowning, drollery, facetiousness, farce, fun, hilarity, humour, jesting, joking, light fare (or piece), sitcom, slapstick, wisecracking, witticisms.

comely　*adj*　attractive, beautiful, becoming, blooming, bonny, buxom, decent, decorous, fair, fit, fitting, good-looking, graceful, handsome, lovely, pleasing, pretty, proper, pulchritudinous, seemly, suitable, wholesome, winsome.

comeuppance　*n*　chastening, dues, (just) deserts, merit, punishment, rebuke, recompense, requital, retribution.

comfort　*v*　alleviate, assuage, calm, cheer, console, ease, encourage, gladden, hearten, inspirit, reassure, refresh, relieve, solace, soothe, strengthen, succour.
n　aid, alleviation, cheer, compensation, consolation, cosiness, ease, easy street, encouragement, help, luxury, opulence, palliative, reassurance, relief, satisfaction, snugness, solace, succour, support, warmth, well-being.

antonyms　distress, torment.

comfortable　*adj*　adequate, affluent, agreeable, ample, at ease, at home, commodious, contented, cosy, easy, gemütlich, happy, homey, loose, loose-fitting, pleasant, prosperous, relaxed, relaxing, restful, roomy, secure, snug, soothed, soothing, well-off, well-to-do.

antonyms　poor, uncomfortable.

comforting　*adj*　cheering, consolatory, consoling, encouraging, gratifying, heartwarming, inspiriting, reassuring, soothing, uplifting.

antonym　worrying.

comic　*adj*　amusing, comical, droll, facetious, farcical, funny, humorous, jocular, joking, light, waggish, witty.

antonyms　serious, tragic, unfunny.

n　buffoon, clown, comedian, droll, gagster, humorist, jester, joker, jokesmith, wag, wit.

comical　*adj*　absurd, amusing, comic, diverting, droll, entertaining, farcical, funny, hilarious, humorous, laughable, ludicrous, odd, priceless, queer, quirky, quizzical, rich, ridiculous, risible, sidesplitting, silly, strange, whimsical.

antonyms　sad, unamusing.

coming　*adj*　approaching, aspiring, due, forthcoming, future, imminent, impending, near, next, nigh, promising, rising, up-and-coming.

n　accession, advent, approach, arrival, entrance.

command　*v*　bid, charge, compel, control, decree, demand, direct, dominate, enjoin, govern, have at one's disposal, head, instruct, lead, manage, order, overlook, oversee, reign over, require, rule, supervise.

n　authority, behest, bidding, charge, commandment, control, decree, dictate, diktat, direction, directive, domination, dominion, edict, fiat, government, grasp, injunction, instruction, management, mandate, mastery, order, power, precept, requirement, rule, supervision, sway, ukase, ultimatum.

commandeer　*v*　appropriate, confiscate, expropriate, grab, hijack, requisition, seize, sequester, sequestrate, usurp.

commander　*n*　admiral, boss, captain, chief, commander-in-chief, commanding officer, director, general, head, imperator, leader, marshal, officer, ruler.

commanding　*adj*　advantageous, assertive, authoritative, autocratic, compelling, controlling, decisive, dominant, dominating, forceful, imposing, impressive, peremptory, powerful, superior.

commemorate　*v*　celebrate, honour, immortalize, keep, mark, memorialize, observe, pay tribute (to), re-enact, remember, salute, solemnize.

commemorative　*adj*　celebratory, dedicatory, in memoriam, memorial.

commence　*v*　begin, embark on, inaugurate, initiate, introduce, open, originate, start.

antonyms　cease, finish.

commend v acclaim, applaud, approve, cite, commit, compliment, confide, consign, credit, deliver, endorse, entrust, eulogize, extol, praise, recommend, yield.
antonym criticize.

commendable *adj* admirable, creditable, deserving, estimable, excellent, exemplary, laudable, meritorious, noble, praiseworthy, worthy.
antonyms blameworthy, poor.

commensurate *adj* appropriate, co-extensive, comparable, compatible, consistent, corresponding, due, equivalent, fitting, just, meet, proportionate.
antonym disproportionate.

comment (on) v animadvert, annotate, criticize, descant, elucidate, enlarge, expand, explain, gloss, interpose, interpret, mention, note, observe, opine, remark, say.
n animadversion, annotation, commentary, criticism, elucidation, explanation, exposition, footnote, illustration, marginalia, marginal note, note, observation, remark, scholium, statement.

commentary *n* analysis, criticism, critique, description, elucidation, exegesis, explanation, exposition, interpretation, narration, narrative, notes, review, treatise, voice-over.

commentator *n* annotator, critic, expositor, glosser, interpreter, reporter, scholiast, sportscaster.

commerce *n* business, communication, dealing(s), exchange, interchange, intercourse, merchandising, relations, trade, traffic.

commercial *adj* business, exploitative, exploited, marketable, materialistic, mercantile, mercenary, monetary, pecuniary, popular, profitable, profit-making, saleable, sales, sellable, trade, trading, venal.

commiseration *n* compassion, condolence, consolation, pity, sympathy.

commission *n* allowance, appointment, authority, board, brokerage, charge, committee, compensation, council, cut, delegation, deputation, duty, errand, fee, function, mandate, mission, order, percentage, rake-off, representatives, service, task force, trust.
v appoint, ask for, authorize, contract, delegate, depute, empower, engage, mandate, nominate, order, request, select, send.

commit v bind, commend, confide, confine, consecrate, consign, dedicate, deliver, deposit, devote, do, engage, entrust, give, imprison, incarcerate, involve, obligate, perpetrate, pledge.

commit oneself bind oneself, cross the Rubicon, decide, pass the point of no return, pledge, promise, take a stand, take the plunge, undertake.

commitment *n* adherence, assurance, dedication, devotion, duty, engagement, guarantee, involvement, liability, loyalty, obligation, pledge, promise, responsibility, tie, undertaking, vow, word, zeal.

committed *adj* active, ardent, card-carrying, dedicated, devoted, devout, diligent, engagé, fervent, obligated, passionate, pledged, red-hot, serious, whole-hearted, zealous.
antonyms apathetic, half-hearted, uncommitted.

committee *n* advisory group, board, cabinet, commission, council, jury, panel, table, task force, team think-tank, working party.

commodities *n* consumer items, goods, merchandise, output, produce, products, saleables, stock, things, wares.

common *adj* accepted, average, base, coarse, collective, commonplace, communal, conventional, customary, daily, everyday, familiar, frequent, general, habitual, hackneyed, inferior, joint, low, mundane, mutual, obscure, ordinary, pedestrian, plain, plebeian, popular, prevailing, prevalent, public, regular, routine, run-of-the-mill, shared, simple, standard, stock, undistinguished, unexceptional, universal, unrefined, untitled, vulgar, widespread, workaday.
antonyms noteworthy, uncommon.

common sense discretion, gumption, intuition, judgment, level head, level-headedness, mother wit, native intelligence, practicality, prudence, soundness, wits.

commonplace *adj* cliché(d), common, customary, everyday, humdrum, obvious, ordinary, pedestrian, quotidian, stale, threadbare, tired, trite, undistinguished, unexceptional, uninteresting, widespread, worn out.
antonyms exceptional, innovative, rare.
n banality, cliché, platitude, truism.

common-sense *adj* astute, common-sensical, down-to-earth, hard-headed, intuitive, judicious, level-headed, matter-of-fact, practical, pragmatic, realistic, reasonable, sane, sensible, sound.
antonyms counter-intuitive, foolish.

commotion *n* ado, agitation, ballyhoo, brouhaha, bustle, bust-up, disorder, disturbance, excitement, ferment, fracas, furor, fuss, hoo-ha, hoopla, hubbub, hue and cry, hullabaloo, hurly-burly, kafuffle, perturbation, pother, racket, riot, rumpus, stink, to do, tumult, uproar, upset.

communal *adj* collective, common, communistic, community, general, joint, public, shared.
antonyms personal, private.

commune *n* collective, colony, communion, community, co-operative, encampment, fellowship, kibbutz, settlement.
v communicate, confer, converse, discourse, have fellowship, hold converse, make contact.

communicable *adj* catching, contagious, conveyable, impartible, infectious, infective, spreadable, transferable, transmissible, transmittable.

communicate v announce, bestow, connect, contact, convey, correspond, declare, diffuse, disclose, disseminate, divulge, e-mail, express, fax, impart, intimate, pass along (or on), proclaim, promulgate, publish, report, reveal, signify, speak, spread, telegraph, telex, transmit, unfold, wire.

communication *n* announcement, bulletin, communiqué, connection, contact, conversation, converse, correspondence, declaration, diffusion, disclosure, dispatch, dissemination, divulgation, e-mail, expression, fax, information, intelligence, intercourse, intimation, message, news, proclamation, promulgation, report, revelation, statement, telex, transmission, word.

communicative *adj* candid, chatty, conversable, conversational, expansive, extrovert, forthcoming, frank, free, friendly, informative, loquacious, open, outgoing, sociable, talkative, unreserved, voluble.

antonym reticent.

communion *n* affinity, closeness, communing, community, concord, connection, converse, empathy, Eucharist, fellow feeling, fellowship, harmony, Holy Communion, intercourse, Lord's Supper, Mass, participation, rapport, relationship, Sacrament, sympathy, togetherness, unity.

communiqué *n* announcement, bulletin, communication, dispatch, message, report, statement.

community *n* affinity, association, body politic, brotherhood, coincidence, colony, commonness, commonwealth, commune, company, concurrence, confraternity, convent, district, fellowship, fraternity, identity, kibbutz, kindredness, likeness, locality, monastery, neighbourhood, people, populace, population, public, residents, sameness, similarity, sisterhood, society.

commute[1] *v* adjust, alter, change, curtail, decrease, exchange, lighten, mitigate, modify, reduce, remit, shorten, soften, substitute.

commute[2] *v* alternate, drive, journey, travel.

commuter *n* exurbanite, straphanger, suburbanite, traveller.

antonyms cocooner, local, urbanite.

compact[1] *adj* brief, close, compendious, compressed, concise, condensed, dense, firm, impenetrable, solid, succinct, well-knit.

antonyms diffuse, rambling, rangy.

v compress, condense, consolidate, cram, flatten, pack, ram, squeeze, tamp.

compact[2] *n* agreement, alliance, arrangement, bargain, bond, concordat, contract, covenant, deal, entente, pact, settlement, treaty, understanding.

companion *n* accomplice, aide, ally, assistant, associate, attendant, buddy, chaperone, cohabitant, cohort, colleague, compeer, complement, comrade, confederate, confidant(e), confrere, consort, counterpart, crony, duenna, escort, fellow, follower, friend, helper, intimate, mate, partner, satellite, sidekick, shadow, squire, twin.

companionable *adj* affable, amiable, approachable, congenial, conversable, convivial, extrovert, familiar, friendly, genial, gregarious, informal, neighbourly, outgoing, personable, sociable, sympathetic, warm.

antonym unfriendly.

companionship *n* camaraderie, companionhood, company, comradeship, confraternity, conviviality, esprit de corps, fellowship, fraternity, friendship, rapport, society, support, sympathy, togetherness.

company[1] *n* assemblage, assembly, association, band, body, business, circle, collection, community, concern, concourse, consortium, convention, corporation, coterie, crew, crowd, ensemble, establishment, firm, fraternity, gathering, group, guild, house, outfit, partnership, party, society, sorority, syndicate, throng, troop, troupe.

company[2] *n* attendance, callers, companionhood, companionship, fellowship, guests, party, presence, society, support, visitors.

comparable *adj* akin, alike, analogous, approaching, cognate, commensurate, correspondent, corresponding, equal, equivalent, in the same league, kindred, like, parallel, proportionate, related, similar, tantamount.

antonym unlike.

compare *v* approach, balance, collate, contrast, correlate, emulate, equal, equate, juxtapose, liken, match, parallel, resemble, rival, weigh.

comparison *n* analogy, collation, comparability, contrast, correlation, distinction, juxtaposition, likeness, parallel, parallelism, relation, resemblance, similarity, similitude.

compass *n* area, boundary, bounds, circle, circuit, circumference, diapason, enclosure, extent, field, gamut, girth, limit, range, reach, realm, round, scale, scope, space, sphere, stretch, zone.

v accomplish, achieve, beset, besiege, blockade, circumscribe, comprehend, contrive, devise, effect, encircle, enclose, encompass, environ, grasp, manage, realize, surround, understand.

compassion *n* charity, clemency, commiseration, concern, condolence, empathy, fellow feeling, heart, humanity, kindness, loving-kindness, mercy, pity, sorrow, sympathy, tenderness, understanding, yearning.

antonym indifference.

compassionate *adj* benevolent, caring, charitable, clement, empathetic, humane, humanitarian, kind-hearted, kindly, lenient, merciful, supportive, sympathetic, tender, tender-hearted, understanding, warm-hearted.

antonym indifferent.

compatible *adj* accordant, adaptable, agreeable, conformable, congenial, congruent, congruous, consistent, consonant, harmonious, in accord, kindred, like-minded, reconcilable, suitable, sympathetic.

antonyms antagonistic, antipathetic, incompatible.

compel *v* browbeat, bulldoze, bully, cause, coerce, constrain, dragoon, drive, enforce, exact, force, impel, make, obligate, oblige, press-gang, pressure, railroad, strong-arm, urge.

compelling *adj* binding, coercive, cogent, conclusive, convincing, enchanting, enthralling, fascinating, forceful, gripping, hypnotic, imperative, incontrovertible, irrefragable, irrefutable, irresistible, mesmeric, overriding, peremptory, persuasive, powerful, pressing, spellbinding, telling, unanswerable, unavoidable, unputdownable, urgent, weighty.

compendious *adj* abbreviated, abridged, brief, compact, comprehensive, concise, condensed, contracted, epitomized, short, shortened, succinct, summarized, summary, synoptic.

antonym enlarged.

compendium *n* abridgment, abstract, brief, companion, condensation, conspectus, digest, encapsulation, epitome, handbook, manual, précis, recapitulation, summary, synopsis, vade mecum.

compensate *v* atone, balance, cancel (out), counterbalance, countervail, expiate, guerdon, indemnify, make up, offset, recompense, recover, recuperate, redeem, redress, refund, reimburse, remunerate, (re)pay, requite, restore, reward, satisfy.

compensation *n* amends, atonement, consolation, damages, guerdon, honorarium, indemnification, indemnity, payment, quittance, recompense, redress, refund, reimbursement, remuneration, reparation, repayment, requital, restitution, restoration, return, reward, satisfaction.

compete *v* battle, challenge, contend, contest, duel, enter, fight, oppose, rival, strive, struggle, try, tussle, vie.

competent *adj* able, adept, adequate, appropriate, capable, clever, efficient, equal, expert, fit, legitimate, masterly, pertinent, proficient, qualified, satisfactory, skilful, skilled, strong, sufficient, suitable, trained, well-qualified.

antonym incompetent.

competition *n* battle, challenge, challenger(s), championship, combativeness, competitiveness, competitors, contention, contest, cup, event, field, match, opposition, quiz, race, rivalry, rival(s), series, strife, struggle, tournament, tourney, trial.

competitive *adj* aggressive, agonistic, ambitious, antagonistic, combative, contentious, cutthroat, emulous, keen, pugnacious, pushy, vying.

antonyms sluggish, unambitious.

competitor *n* adversary, agonist, antagonist, challenger, competition, contender, contestant, emulator, entrant, opponent, opposition, rival.

compilation *n* anthology, arrangement, assemblage, assortment, collation, collection, combination, florilegium, garnering, selection, thesaurus, treasury, unification.

compile *v* anthologize, arrange, assemble, collate, collect, combine, compose, cull, garner, gather, marshal, organize, unite.

complacent *adj* content(ed), gloating, gratified, pleased with oneself, proud, satisfied, self-assured, self-congratulatory, self-contented, self-righteous, self-satisfied, serene, smug, unconcerned.

antonyms diffident, discontented.

complain *v* beef, bellyache, bemoan, bewail, bitch, bleat, carp, deplore, find fault, fuss, grieve, gripe, groan, grouch, grouse, growl, grumble, kvetch, lament, moan, murmer, natter, nit-pick, protest, raise a stink, squawk, squeal, wail, whine, yammer.

complaining *adj* bleating, cantankerous, captious, carping, cranky, critical, dissatisfied, faultfinding, fussy, grumbling, hypercritical, moaning, nagging, nattering, nit-picking, peevish, petulant, protesting, querulous, whining, whiny, yammering.

antonym contented.

complaint[1] *n* accusation, annoyance, beef, bellyache, bitch, bleat, bone to pick, censure, charge, criticism, dissatisfaction, faultfinding, gravamen, grievance, gripe, grouse, grumble, lament, moan, peeve, plaint, problem, protest, remonstrance, squawk, stricture, wail, whine.

complaint[2] *n* affliction, ailment, disease, disorder, illness, indisposition, malady, malaise, problem, sickness, trouble, upset.

complaisant *adj* accommodating, acquiescent, agreeable, amenable, amiable, biddable, compliant, conformable, co-operative, deferential, docile, easy, obedient, obliging, tractable.

antonyms obstinate, perverse.

complement *n* addition, aggregate, capacity, companion, completion, consummation, counterpart, quota, sum, supplement.

▲ *confusable word* compliment.

complementary *adj* companion, correlative, corresponding, dovetail(ing), interdependent, interrelated, interrelating, interwoven, (well-)matched.

complete *adj* absolute, accomplished, achieved, all, all-inclusive, comprehensive, concluded, consummate, ended, entire, exhaustive, faultless, finished, full, intact, integral, out-and-out, perfect, plenary, radical, root-and-branch, self-contained, thorough, thoroughgoing, total, unabbreviated, unabridged, unbroken, uncut, undivided, unedited, unexpurgated, unimpaired, unqualified, utter, whole, whole-hog.

antonyms imperfect, incomplete, partial. *v* accomplish, achieve, cap, carry through, clinch, close, complement, conclude, consummate, cover, crown, discharge, do, end, fill in (or out or up), finalize, finish, follow through, fulfil, get through, perfect, terminate, top off, wind up.

▲ *confusable word* replete.

completely *adv* absolutely, altogether, diametrically, en bloc, en masse, entirely, every inch, from first to last, fully, heart and soul, hook line and sinker, in full, in toto, lock stock and barrel, perfectly, quite, radically, root and branch, solidly, thoroughly, totally, utterly, wholly.

completion *n* accomplishment, achievement, close, closure, complement, conclusion, consummation, crowning, culmination, discharge, end, finalization, finish, fruition, fulfilment, perfection, plenitude, realization, settlement, termination.

complex *adj* ambivalent, Byzantine, circuitous, complicated, composite, compound, convoluted, Daedalian, devious, diverse, elaborate, heterogeneous, interwoven, intricate, involved, knotty, labyrinthine, manifold, mingled, mixed, multifarious, multipartite, multiple, polymerous, ramified, tangled, tortuous.

antonym simple.

n aggregate, composite, compound, development, establishment, fixation, hang-up, idée fixe, installation web, maze, network, obsession, organization, phobia, preoccupation, scheme, structure, syndrome, synthesis, system, tangle.

complexion *n* appearance, aspect, cast, character, colour, colouring, composition, constitution, countenance, disposition, guise, hue, kind, look, make-up, nature, pigmentation, skin, stamp, temperament, type.

complexity or **complexities** *n* circuitousness, circuity, complication, convolution, deviousness, diversity, elaboration, entanglement, ins and outs, intricacy, involution, involvement, knot(s), multifariousness, multiplicity, ramification, repercussion, tangle(s), tortuousness, twists and turns.

antonym simplicity.

compliance *n* acquiescence, agreement, assent, complaisance, concession, concurrence, conformability, conformity, consent, co-operation, deference, obedience, observance, passivity, submission, submissiveness, yielding.

antonyms defiance, disobedience.

compliant *adj* accommodating, acquiescent, agreeable, amenable, biddable, complaisant, conformable, co-operative, deferential, docile, obedient, obliging, passive, submissive, tractable, yielding.

antonyms disobedient, intractable.

complicate *v* compound, confuse, elaborate, embroil, entangle, foul up, involve, mix up, muddle, tangle (up).

antonym simplify.

complicated *adj* baroque, Byzantine, circuitous, complex, convoluted, devious, difficult, elaborate, entangled, fancy, intricate, involved, knotty, labyrinthine, messy, ornate, perplexing, problematic, puzzling, Rube Goldberg, tangled, tortuous, troublesome.

antonyms easy, simple, straightforward.

complication *n* complexity, complicatedness, confusion, difficulty, drawback, elaboration, entanglement, factor, fancy, intricacy, mixture, obstacle, problem, ramification, repercussion, rigmarole, snag, twist.

complicity *n* abetment, agreement, approval, collaboration, collusion, concurrence, connivance, co-operation, implication, involvement, knowledge, participation.

antonyms ignorance, innocence.

compliment *n* accolade, admiration, approval, bouquet, commendation, congratulations, courtesy, encomium, eulogy, favour, felicitation, flattery, honour, plaudit, praise, tribute.

antonyms criticism, insult.

v admire, applaud, commend, congratulate, eulogize, extol, felicitate, flatter, laud, praise, salute.

antonyms bad-mouth, condemn, insult.

▲ *confusable word* complement.

complimentary *adj* admiring, appreciative, approving, commendatory, congratulatory, courtesy, eulogistic, favourable, flattering, free, gratis, honorary, laudatory, panegyrical.

antonyms critical, insulting, unflattering.

compliments *n* best wishes, congratulations, devoirs, greetings, regards, remembrances, respects, salutation.

comply *v* accede, accommodate, accord, acquiesce, agree, assent, conform, consent, co-operate, defer, fall in, follow, fulfil, obey, observe, perform, respect, satisfy, submit, yield.

antonyms disobey, resist.

component *n* bit, constituent, element, factor, ingredient, item, part, piece, spare part, unit.

compose *v* adjust, arrange, build (up), calm, collect, compound, constitute, construct, contrive, control, create, devise, draw up, fashion, form, frame, indite, invent, make, meditate the muse, prepare, produce, quell, quiet, recollect, reconcile, redact, regulate, resolve, settle, still, tranquillize, write.

▲ *confusable word* comprise.

composed *adj* assured, calm, collected, confident, cool, imperturbable, level-headed, placid, poised, relaxed, self-assured, self-possessed, serene, together, tranquil, unfazed, unflappable, unruffled, unworried.

antonym agitated.

composer *n* arranger, author, bard, creator, maker, minstrel, originator, poet, songsmith, songwriter, troubadour, tunesmith, writer.

composite *adj* agglutinate, blended, combined, complex, compound, conglomerate, fused, mixed, patchwork, synthesized.

antonyms homogeneous, uniform.

n agglutination, alloy, amalgam, blend, combination, compound, conglomerate, fusion, mixture, pastiche, patchwork, synthesis.

composition *n* air, alloy, arrangement, balance, blend, combination, compromise, concord, configuration, constitution, creation, creative writing, design, essay, exercise, fantasia, form, formulation, ingredients, invention, layout, make-up, making, mixture, opus, organization, piece, placement, production, proportion, settlement, song, structure, study, theme, work, writing.

composure *n* aplomb, assurance, calm, calmness, confidence, cool, coolness, dignity, dispassion, ease, equanimity, impassivity, imperturbability, placidity, poise, sang-froid, savoir-faire, sedateness, self-assurance, self-possession, serenity, tranquillity, unflappability.
antonym discomposure.

compound *v* aggravate, alloy, amalgamate, augment, blend, coalesce, combine, complicate, compose, concoct, exacerbate, fuse, heighten, increase, intensify, magnify, mingle, mix, multiply, synthesize, unite, worsen.
n alloy, amalgam, amalgamation, blend, combination, composite, composition, conglomerate, conglomeration, fusion, medley, mixture, synthesis.
adj complex, complicated, composite, conglomerate, intricate, mixed, multiple.

comprehend *v* appreciate, apprehend, assimilate, compass, comprise, conceive, conceptualize, contain, cover, discern, embrace, encompass, fathom, get, get one's mind around, grasp, include, know, penetrate, perceive, realize, see, see daylight, sense, tumble to, twig, understand.
antonym misunderstand.

comprehensible *adj* clear, coherent, conceivable, explicit, fathomable, graspable, intelligible, knowable, lucid, plain, rational, simple, straightforward, understandable.
antonym incomprehensible.

▲ *confusable word* comprehensive.

comprehensive *adj* across-the-board, all-embracing, all-inclusive, blanket, broad, catholic, compendious, complete, encyclopedic, exhaustive, extensive, full, general, inclusive, omnibus, sweeping, thorough, wide.
antonyms incomplete, selective.

▲ *confusable word* comprehensible.

compress *v* abbreviate, abridge, compact, concentrate, condense, constrict, contract, cram, crowd, crush, flatten, impact, jam, press, reduce, shorten, squash, squeeze, squish, stuff, summarize, synopsize, wad, wedge.
antonyms diffuse, expand, separate.

compression *n* abbreviation, abridgment, concentration, condensation, consolidation, constriction, crushing, digest, impaction, pressure, reduction, squashing, squeezing, squishing.
antonyms enlargement, expansion.

comprise *v* comprehend, consist of, contain, cover, embody, embrace, encompass, include, incorporate, involve, subsume, take in.

▲ *confusable word* compose.

compromise¹ *v* accommodate (oneself), adapt, adjust, arbitrate, bargain, concede,

make concessions, meet halfway, negotiate, reach an agreement, settle.
antonyms follow the hard line, not budge, stand pat.
n accommodation, accord, adjustment, agreement, bargain, concession, co-operation, happy medium, settlement, trade-off, via media.
antonyms hard line, intransigence.

compromise² *v* bargain away, discredit, dishonour, embarass, endanger, expose, give up, hazard, imperil, jeopardize, lose, prejudice, put at risk, sacrifice, undermine, weaken.

compulsion *n* coercion, constraint, drive, duress, exigency, force, impulse, necessity, need, obligation, obsession, preoccupation, pressure, urge, urgency.
antonyms freedom, liberty.

compulsive *adj* besetting, compelling, driving, hardened, hopeless, incorrigible, incurable, irredeemable, irrepressible, irresistible, obsessive, overmastering, overpowering, overwhelming, uncontrollable, urgent.

compulsory *adj* binding, de rigueur, enforced, forced, imperative, mandatory, obligatory, required, requisite, stipulated, stipulatory.
antonyms optional, voluntary.

compunction *n* contrition, hesitancy, hesitation, misgiving, penitence, qualm, regret, reluctance, remorse, repentance, scruple, sorrow, unease, uneasiness.
antonyms callousness, defiance.

compute *v* add up, assess, calculate, count, enumerate, estimate, evaluate, figure (out), measure, reckon, register, tally, total, work out.

comrade *n* Achates, ally, associate, brother, buddy, chum, cohort, colleague, companion, compatriot, compeer, confederate, co-worker, crony, fellow, friend, mate, pal, partner, sidekick, sister.

con *v* bamboozle, beguile, bilk, bluff, bunco, cheat, cozen, deceive, defraud, diddle, do, double-cross, dupe, fiddle, fool, goldbrick, gull, hoax, hoodwink, humbug, inveigle, mislead, put one over on, racket, rip off, rook, suck in, swindle, take in, trick.
n bluff, confidence game, deception, fraud, grift, hoax, racket, rip-off, scam, swindle, trick.

concatenation *n* chain, connection, course, interlinking, interlocking, linking, nexus, procession, progression, sequence, series, string, succession, trail, train.

concave *adj* bowl-shaped, cupped, depressed, emaciated, excavated, hollow, hollowed, incurvate, incurved, indented, scooped-out, sunken.
antonym convex.

conceal *v* bury, cache, camouflage, cloak, cover, disguise, dissemble, hide, keep dark, mask, obscure, screen, secrete, shelter, stash, suppress, veil.
antonym reveal.

concealed *adj* camouflaged, clandestine, covered, covert, disguised, hidden, inconspicuous, masked, screened, secret, secreted, ulterior, unseen, veiled.

antonyms clear, plain.

concede *v* accept, acknowledge, admit, allow, cede, confess, forfeit, give up, grant, own, recognize, relinquish, sacrifice, surrender, yield.

antonyms deny, dispute.

conceit *n* arrogance, assumption, cockiness, complacency, conceitedness, egotism, narcissism, pride, self-absorption, self-conceit, self-importance, self-love, self-pride, self-satisfaction, swagger, vainglory, vanity.

antonyms diffidence, modesty.

conceited *adj* arrogant, assuming, bigheaded, cocky, complacent, egotistical, hoity-toity, immodest, narcissistic, overweening, preening, self-absorbed, self-aggrandizing, self-important, self-satisfied, stuck-up, swell-headed, uppity, vain, vainglorious, windy.

antonyms diffident, modest.

conceivable *adj* believable, comprehensible, credible, fathomable, imaginable, likely, plausible, possible, probable, supposable, tenable, thinkable.

antonym inconceivable.

conceive (of) *v* appreciate, apprehend, believe, comprehend, contrive, create, design, develop, devise, dream (up), envisage, envision, fancy, form, formulate, grasp, ideate, imagine, invent, originate, plan, produce, project, realize, suppose, think (up), understand, visualize.

concentrate *v* accumulate, attend, attract, boil down, centre, cluster, collect, condense, congregate, converge, crowd, draw, fix, focus, gather, intensify, pay attention, strengthen, thicken.

antonyms disperse, separate, thin, weaken.

n decoction, distillate, distillation, elixir, essence, extract.

concentrated *adj* all-out, concerted, condensed, deep, dense, evaporated, focussed, intense, intensified, intensive, reduced, rich, single-minded, strengthened, thickened.

antonyms desultory, diffuse, diluted.

concept *n* abstraction, clue, conception, conceptualization, construct, design, idea, image, impression, inkling, invention, notion, picture, theory, understanding, view, vision, visualization.

conception *n* appreciation, apprehension, beginning, birth, clue, comprehension, concept, design, envisagement, envisioning, fertilization, formation, germination, idea, image, imagination, impregnation, impression, inception, inkling, insemination, invention, knowledge, launch, notion, origin, outset, perception, picture, plan, understanding, vision, visualization.

concern *v* affect, bear on, bother, disquiet, distress, disturb, interest, involve, pertain to, perturb, regard, relate to, touch, trouble, upset, worry.

n affair, anxiety, apprehension, attention, burden, business, care, charge, company, consideration, corporation, department, disquiet, disquietude, distress, enterprise, establishment, firm, heed, house, importance, interest, involvement, issue, job, matter, mission, organization, outfit, perturbation, reference, regard, relation, relevance, responsibility, solicitude, task, unease, uneasiness, worry.

antonym unconcern.

concerned *adj* active, anxious, apprehensive, attentive, at issue, at stake, bothered, caring, connected, disquieted, distressed, disturbed, exercised, implicated, in question, interested, involved, perturbed, solicitous, troubled, uneasy, unhappy, upset, worried.

antonym unconcerned.

concerning *prep* about, anent, apropos of, as regards, bearing on, germane to, in regard to, in the matter of, on the subject of, pertaining to, re, regarding, relating to, relevant to, respecting, to do with, touching, with reference to, with regard to, with respect to.

concert¹ *n* accord, agreement, concord, concordance, consonance, co-operation, diapason, hand in hand, harmony, in unison, jointly, unanimity, union, unison.

antonym disunity.

in concert co-operatively, hand in hand, in unison, jointly, together.

concert² *n* appearance, engagement, gig, musical, performance, presentation, production, recital, show, symphony.

concerted *adj* collaborative, collective, combined, concentrated, co-operative, co-ordinated, focussed, joint, organized, planned, prearranged, shared, united.

antonyms disorganized, separate, unco-ordinated.

concession *n* acknowledgment, adjustment, admission, allowance, assent, boon, cession, compromise, exception, favour, grant, indulgence, nod, permit, privilege, sacrifice, surrender, yielding.

conciliate *v* appease, bring around, disarm, disembitter, make amends to, make peace with, mollify, pacify, placate, propitiate, satisfy, soften, soothe, win over.

antonym antagonize.

conciliator *n* dove, intercessor, intermediary, mediator, negotiator, peacemaker, reconciler.

antonym troublemaker.

conciliatory *adj* disarming, forgiving, irenic, mollifying, pacific, pacificatory, peaceable, placatory, propitiative, propitiatory, reconciliatory.

antonym antagonistic.

concise *adj* abbreviated, abridged, aphoristic, brief, clean, compact, compendious, compressed, condensed, encapsulated, epigrammatic, gnomic, laconic, pithy, punchy, short, succinct, summary, synoptic, terse, thumbnail, tight, to the point, uncluttered.

antonyms diffuse, expansive, rambling.

conclave n assembly, cabal, cabinet, confab, confabulation, conference, conspiracy, conventicle, convention, council, meeting, parley, powwow, session.

conclude v assume, cease, clinch, close, complete, culminate, decide, deduce, determine, effect, end, establish, figure out, finish, gather, infer, judge, reason, reckon, resolve, settle, suppose, surmise, terminate, wind up.

conclusion n answer, assumption, clincher, close, closure, completion, consequence, conviction, culmination, decision, deduction, end, finale, finis, finish, illation, inference, issue, judgment, outcome, resolution, result, settlement, solution, termination, upshot, verdict, wind-up.

conclusive adj clear, clinching, convincing, decisive, definite, definitive, final, incontrovertible, irrefragable, irrefutable, ultimate, unanswerable, unappealable, unarguable, undeniable.

antonym inconclusive.

concoct v brew, come up with, contrive, construct, cook up, decoct, design, develop, devise, fabricate, form, formulate, hatch, invent, make up, plan, plot, prepare, weave.

concoction n blend, brew, combination, compound, contrivance, creation, decoction, dish, fable, fabrication, mixture, myth, potion, preparation, story.

concomitant adj accompanying, associated, attendant, co-existent, coincidental, collateral, concurrent, contemporaneous, contributing, incidental, linked, secondary, side, simultaneous, synchronous, syndromic.

antonyms accidental, unrelated.

n accompaniment, by-product, epiphenomenon, incidental, secondary, side effect, symptom.

concord n accord, agreement, amicability, amity, brotherliness, compact, concert, concordat, consensus, consonance, convention, diapason, entente, friendship, harmony, peace, protocol, rapport, treaty, unanimity, unison.

antonym discord.

concrete adj actual, calcified, definite, explicit, factual, firm, hard, material, perceptible, petrified, physical, ponderable, real, seeable, sensible, solid, solidified, specific, substantial, tactile, tangible, touchable, visible.

antonym abstract.

concupiscence n appetite, desire, horniness, lasciviousness, lechery, lewdness, libidinousness, libido, lubricity, lust, lustfulness, randiness, ruttishness.

concur v accede, accord, acquiesce, agree, approve, assent, coincide, combine, consent, conspire, co-operate, harmonize, join, meet, unite.

antonym disagree.

concurrent adj co-existent, coincident, concerted, concomitant, confluent, consistent, contemporaneous, convergent, co-operative, co-ordinate, harmonious, juxtaposed, simultaneous, synchronous, unanimous, united.

concussion n agitation, blow, impact, rocking, shaking, shock.

condemn v ban, blame, castigate, censure, come down hard on, consign, convict, damn, decry, denounce, deprecate, disapprove, doom, excommunicate, pan, proscribe, reprehend, reprobate, sentence, slam, slate, write off.

antonyms approve, praise.

condemnatory adj accusatory, accusing, censorious, critical, damnatory, damning, denunciatory, deprecatory, disapproving, incriminating, judgmental, negative, proscriptive.

antonyms approving, complimentary, indulgent, laudatory.

condense v abbreviate, abridge, abstract, boil down, capsulize, compact, compress, concentrate, crystallize, decoct, distil, encapsulate, epitomize, evaporate, inspissate, liquefy, precipitate, précis, reduce, shorten, solidify, strengthen, summarize, synopsize, thicken.

antonyms dilute, expand.

condescend v bend, deign, lower oneself, patronize, see fit, stoop, submit, unbend, vouchsafe.

condescending adj de haut en bas, disdainful, gracious, haughty, imperious, lofty, lordly, patronizing, pitying, pretentious, snooty, stooping, supercilious, superior, unbending.

antonyms humble.

condign adj adequate, apposite, appropriate, deserved, due, earned, fitting, just, meet, merited, proper, suitable, well-earned, well-merited.

antonym unjust.

condiment n accompaniment, garnish, relish, sauce, seasoning, spice, trimming.

condition n ailment, article, caste, circumstance, class, complaint, defect, demand, disease, disorder, estate, fettle, fitness, form, health, infirmity, kilter, level, limitation, malady, obligation, order, plight, position, prerequisite, problem, provision, proviso, qualification, rank, requirement, requisite, restriction, shape, situation, state, status, stipulation, terms, trim, understanding, weakness.

v accustom, adapt, adjust, attune, determine, educate, groom, habituate, hone, inure, prepare, prime, ready, repair, season, train, tune.

conditional adj contingent, dependent, limited, provisional, qualified, relative, restricted, tied.

antonym unconditional.

conditioned adj acclimatized, accustomed, adapted, adjusted, attuned, determined, familiar, familiarized, groomed, habituated, honed, inured, learned, prepared, primed, seasoned, trained, tuned, used.

conditioning *n* acculturation, adjustment, education, familiarization, grooming, hardening, honing, inurement, preparation, priming, reorientation, seasoning, training, tune-up, tuning.

conditions *n* atmosphere, background, circumstances, context, environment, habitat, medium, milieu, setting, situation, surroundings.

condolence *n* commiseration, condolences, consolation, pity, support, sympathy.
antonym congratulation.

condone *v* accept, allow, brook, disregard, excuse, forgive, ignore, indulge, overlook, pardon, tolerate.
antonyms censure, denounce, forbid.

conducive *adj* advantageous, beneficial, contributive, contributory, encouraging, favourable, helpful, leading, productive, promotive, stimulative, tending.
antonyms adverse, inimical, unfavourable.

conduct *n* actions, administration, attitude, bearing, behaviour, comportment, control, demeanour, deportment, direction, discharge, escort, handling, management, manners, mien, orchestration, organization, performance, running, supervision, ways.
v accompany, administer, attend to, bear, carry, carry out, chair, control, convey, direct, do, escort, govern, guide, handle, hold, lead, manage, orchestrate, organize, pilot, run, steer, supervise, transact, usher.

conduct oneself acquit oneself, act, behave, comport oneself, demean oneself, deport oneself.

conduit *n* aqueduct, canal, channel, chute, culvert, ditch, drain, duct, flume, gutter, main, passage, pipe, tube, watercourse, waterway.

confederacy *n* alliance, Bund, cabal, coalition, compact, confederation, conspiracy, federation, junta, league, partnership, union.

confederate *adj* allied, associated, combined, federal, federated, united.
n abettor, accessory, accomplice, ally, assistant, associate, collaborator, colleague, companion, conspirator, crony, friend, henchman, partner, supporter.
v ally, amalgamate, associate, bind, combine, federate, join, league (together), merge, unite.

confer¹ *v* consult, converse, deliberate, discourse, discuss, lay heads together, parley, powwow, talk,

confer² *v* accord, award, bestow, give, grant, impart, lend, present, vouchsafe.

conference *n* assembly, colloquium, confab(ulation), congress, consultation, convention, convocation, debate, diet, discussion, forum, indaba, league, meeting, moot, powwow, seminar, symposium, synod, teach-in.

confess *v* acknowledge, admit, affirm, allow, assert, avow, bare one's soul, betray, blurt (out), come clean, concede, confide, declare, disclose, divulge, fess up, grant, let out, make a clean breast of (it), own, own up, profess, recognize, reveal, testify to (or about), unbosom oneself, unburden oneself.
antonyms conceal, deny.

confidant(e) *n* bosom friend, companion, crony, duenna, familiar, friend, inseparable, intimate, repository.

confide *v* admit, breathe, confess, disclose, divulge, entrust, impart, reveal, share, trust, unburden, whisper.
antonyms hide, suppress.

confidence¹ *n* aplomb, assurance, belief, boldness, calmness, composure, coolness, courage, credence, dependence, faith, firmness, morale, nerve, reliance, savoir-faire, self-assurance, self-confidence, self-possession, self-reliance, trust.
antonyms diffidence, distrust.

confidence² *n* communication, confession, disclosure, divulgence, secret revelation, unburdening

in confidence in private, privately, secretly, sub rosa, under the rose.

confident *adj* assertive, assured, bold, certain, composed, convinced, cool, dauntless, fearless, persuaded, positive, sanguine, satisfied, secure, self-assured, self-confident, self-possessed, self-reliant, sure, unabashed, unbashful, unselfconscious.
antonyms diffident, sceptical.

confidential *adj* classified, close, closed, familiar, hush-hush, in camera, intimate, private, privy, restricted, secret, tête-à-tête, trusted, trusty.
antonyms common, public.

confidentially *adv* behind closed doors, between you me and the bedpost (lamppost, gatepost), in camera, in confidence, in privacy, in private, in secret, on the quiet, personally, privately, sub rosa, under the rose, within these four walls.
antonym openly.

configuration *n* arrangement, cast, composition, conformation, contour, deployment, disposition, figure, form, Gestalt, outline, setup, shape, structure.

confine *v* bind, bound, cage, chamber, circumscribe, constrain, cramp, crib, detain, enclose, immure, imprison, incarcerate, inhibit, intern, keep, keep prisoner, limit, mew, restrain, restrict, shackle, shut up, trammel.
antonym free.

confined *adj* circumscribed, claustrophobic, cramped, housebound, limited, narrow, pokey, restricted, small.
antonyms free, unrestricted.

confinement¹ *n* constraint, custody, detention, house-arrest, imprisonment, incarceration, internment, time.
antonym freedom.

confinement² *n* accouchement, birth, childbed, childbirth, delivery, labour, lying-in, parturition, time, travail.

confines n border(s), boundary, bounds, circumference, edge, frontier, limits, parameters, perimeter, precincts.

confirm v approve, ascertain, assure, attest, authenticate, back, buttress, check, clinch, corroborate, double-check, endorse, establish, evidence, finalize, firm up, fix, fortify, prove, ratify, reinforce, settle, strengthen, substantiate, support, validate, verify, witness to.
antonym deny.

confirmation n acceptance, agreement, approval, assent, attestation, authentication, backing, clincher, corroboration, endorsement, establishment, evidence, proof, ratification, reinforcement, substantiation, support, testimony, validation, verification, witness.
antonym denial.

confirmed adj authenticated, card-carrying, certain, chronic, committed, congenital, decided, deep-rooted, deep-seated, definite, down to the ground, dyed-in-the-wool, engagé, entrenched, established, habitual, hardened, incorrigible, incurable, ingrained, inured, inveterate, irredeemable, known, long-established, long-standing, proved, proven, rooted, seasoned, staunch, substantiated.
antonyms uncommitted, unconfirmed.

confiscate v appropriate, commandeer, distrain, escheat, expropriate, impound, remove, seize, sequester, sequestrate.
antonym restore.

conflagration n blaze, deflagration, fire, hellfire, holocaust, inferno, wildfire.

conflict n ambivalence, antagonism, antipathy, argument, Armageddon, battle, brawl, clash, collision, combat, confrontation, contention, contradiction, difference, disagreement, discord, disharmony, dissension, dissonance, encounter, engagement, feud, fight, fracas, friction, hostility, incompatibility, inconsistency, interference, opposition, quarrel, set-to, skirmish, strife, struggle, turmoil, unrest, variance, war, warfare.
antonyms agreement, concord.
v battle, clash, collide, combat, contend, contradict, differ, disagree, fight, interfere, oppose, war.
antonym agree.

in conflict at daggers drawn, at loggerheads, at odds, at swords' points, at variance, at war, disagreeing, disunited, in disagreement, opposed.
antonyms at peace, in agreement.

conflicting adj ambivalent, antagonistic, clashing, contradictory, contrary, discordant, incompatible, inconsistent, irreconcilable, opposed, opposing, opposite, paradoxical, warring.
antonym compatible.

confluence n assemblage, assembly, concourse, concurrence, conflux, conjunction, convergence, crowd, gathering, host, junction, meeting, multitude, throng, union.

conform v accommodate, accord, adapt, adjust, agree, align, assimilate, bend, be (or fall) in line, comply, copy, correspond, fit, follow, harmonize, match, obey, quadrate, square, suit, tailor, tally, yield.
antonym differ.

conformation n anatomy, arrangement, build, composition, configuration, form, framework, Gestalt, outline, shape, structure.

conformist n bourgeois, conventionalist, follower, rubber-stamp, stick-in-the-mud, traditionalist, yes-man.
antonyms bohemian, maverick, nonconformist.

conformity n accordance, affinity, agreement, allegiance, compliance, congruity, consonance, correspondence, harmony, likeness, obedience, observance, orthodoxy, resemblance, sameness, similarity.
antonyms difference, nonconformity.

confound v abash, amaze, astonish, astound, baffle, bamboozle, bewilder, boggle, confuse, cut the ground from under someone's feet, damn, demolish, demoralize, destroy, discombobulate, discomfit, dismay, dumfound, flabbergast, floor, frustrate, mistake, mix up, mystify, nonplus, overthrow, overwhelm, perplex, pull the rug out from under someone, ruin, shake, startle, stupefy, stymie, surprise, throw, throw for a loop, thwart, unshape, upset.

confounded adj abominable, arrant, blasted, bloody, consummate, cursed, damned, darned, detestable, egregious, godawful, hateful, insufferable, rank.

confront v accost, address, beard, brave, call to account, challenge, defy, encounter, eyeball, face, front, oppose, stand up to.
antonym evade.

confrontation n battle, collision, combat, conflict, contest, crisis, disagreement, encounter, engagement, face-off, fight, meeting, quarrel, set-to, showdown.

confuse v abash, addle, baffle, ball up, befuddle, bemuse, bewilder, buffalo, confound, darken, disarrange, discombobulate, discomfit, discompose, disconcert, discountenance, disorder, disorient, distract, embarrass, embrangle, flummox, fluster, involve, jumble, mistake, mix up, mortify, muddle (up), mystify, nonplus, obscure, perplex, psych out, puzzle, rattle, shame, shuffle, tangle, tie in knots, upset.
antonyms clarify, enlighten, reassure.

confusing adj ambiguous, baffling, bewildering, complicated, contradictory, convoluted, cryptic, dazzling, difficult, inconclusive, inconsistent, involved, labyrinthine, mazelike, misleading, muddling, overwhelming, perplexing, puzzling, tangled, tortuous, unclear, unintelligible, unpredictable.
antonyms clear, definite.

confusion n abashment, Babel, ball-up, befuddlement, bemusement, bewilderment, blur, bustle, chagrin, chaos, clutter, cock-up, combustion, commotion, crossed signals, disarrangement, discomfiture, disorder, disorganization, disorientation, distraction, embarrassment, embroilment, fluster, fog, hodgepodge, hugger-mugger, imbroglio, jumble, maze, mess, mishmash, misinformation, misunderstanding, mix-up, muddle, mystification, overthrow, palaver, perplexity, perturbation, puzzlement, rush, shambles, shame, shuffle, tangle, tizzy, turmoil, uncertainty, untidiness, upheaval, welter.

antonyms clarity, composure, order.

confute *v* confound, controvert, disprove, give the lie to, impugn, invalidate, knock down, negate, nullify, oppugn, overthrow, overturn, rebut, refute, knock (or punch or shoot) holes in, vitiate.

antonyms confirm, prove.

congeal *v* clot, coagulate, coalesce, concrete, curdle, freeze, fuse, gel, gelatinize, harden, jell, jelly, set, solidify, stiffen, thicken.

antonyms dissolve, melt, separate.

congenial *adj* affable, agreeable, companionable, compatible, complaisant, cosy, favourable, friendly, gemütlich, genial, homey, kindly, kindred, like-minded, pleasant, pleasing, personable, relaxing, sociable, suitable, sympathetic, warm, well-suited.

antonym disagreeable.

congenital *adj* complete, connate, constitutional, deep-rooted, deep-seated, hereditary, inborn, inbred, ingenerate, inherent, inherited, innate, inveterate, natural, thorough, utter.

congested *adj* blocked, clogged, crammed, crowded, engorged, full, jammed, overcharged, overcrowded, overfilled, overflowing, overfull, packed, stuffed, swarming, swollen, teeming, thronged.

antonym clear.

congestion *n* bottleneck, clogging, crowdedness, crowding, engorgement, fullness, gridlock, jam, log-jam, overcrowding, overfullness, snarl-up, surfeit, traffic jam.

conglomerate *adj* agglutinated, aggregate, amassed, clustered, coherent, composite, heterogeneous, massed.

v accumulate, agglomerate, agglutinate, aggregate, amass, assemble, clump, cluster, cohere, collect, congregate, foregather, gather, mass.

antonym separate.

n agglomerate, aggregate, composite, congeries, mass, megacorporation, multinational.

conglomeration *n* accumulation, agglomeration, agglutination, aggregation, assemblage, bundle, cluster, combination, composite, congeries, hodgepodge, jumble, mass, medley, mixture.

congratulations *n* compliments, felicitations, good wishes, greetings, pat on the back.

antonyms commiserations, condolences.

congregate *v* accumulate, assemble, bunch, clump, cluster, collect, concentrate,

conglomerate, convene, converge, crowd, flock, foregather, gather, mass, meet, muster, rally, rendezvous, throng.

antonyms dismiss, disperse.

congregation *n* assemblage, assembly, brethren, church, cluster, concourse, crowd, fellowship, flock, gathering, host, laity, multitude, muster, parish, parishioners, pew-warmers, throng, worshippers.

congress *n* assembly, conclave, conference, convention, convocation, council, diet, forum, legislature, meeting, parliament, synod.

congruity *n* agreement, coincidence, compatibility, concurrence, conformity, congruence, congruousness, consistency, consonance, correspondence, felicitousness, fittingness, harmony, identity, match, parallelism, suitability.

antonym incongruity.

conjectural *adj* academic, assumed, hypothetical, posited, postulated, speculative, supposed, suppositional, surmised, tentative, theoretical.

antonyms factual, real.

conjecture *v* assume, estimate, extrapolate, fancy, guess, hypothesize, imagine, infer, opine, reckon, speculate, suppose, surmise, suspect, theorize.

n assumption, conclusion, estimate, extrapolation, fancy, guess, guesstimate, guesswork, hypothesis, inference, notion, opinion, presumption, projection, speculation, supposition, surmise, theorizing, theory.

conjugal *adv* bridal, connubial, epithalamic, hymeneal, marital, married, matrimonial, nuptial, spousal, wedded.

conjunction *n* association, coincidence, combination, concert, concomitance, concurrence, conjuncture, connection, junction, juxtaposition, syzygy, unification, union.

conjure *v* adjure, beseech, call on, compel, entreat, implore, invoke, pray, raise, rouse, summon, supplicate.

conjure up arouse, awaken, contrive, create, evoke, excite, produce, recall, recollect.

conjurer *n* illusionist, magician, miracle-worker, prestidigitator, sorcerer, thaumaturge, wizard.

conk out break down, collapse, die, fail, faint, fall asleep, go kaput.

con man *n* bluffer, crook, deceiver, fraud, grifter, imposter, pretender, rip-off artist, rook, shark, swindler, trickster.

connect *v* affiliate, affix, ally, associate, catenate, cohere, combine, communicate, concatenate, conjoin, couple, fasten, hitch, hook up, join, link, plug in, relate, tie, unite.

antonym disconnect.

connection[1] *n* affiliation, affinity, alliance, arthrosis, association, attachment, bond, catenation, circuit, coherence, commerce, communication, concatenation, conjunction, contact, context, correlation, correspondence, coupling, fastening, hookup, interrelation, intimacy, junction, link, marriage, point of

articulation, reference, regard, relationship, relevance, tie, tie-in, union.
antonym disconnection.

connection² *n* acquaintance, ally, associate, contact, friend, kin, kindred, kinsman, relation, relative, sponsor.

connivance *n* abetment, abetting, collusion, complicity, condoning, consent, jobbery.

connive *v* cabal, collude, conspire, intrigue, look the other way, plot, scheme.
    connive at abet, aid, blink at, condone, disregard, let go, overlook, shut one's eyes to, turn a blind eye to, wink at.

connoisseur *n* aficionado, appreciator, arbiter, authority, buff, cognoscente, devotee, expert, judge, savant, specialist, virtuoso.

connotation *n* association, colouring, hint, implication, load, nuance, overtone, significance, suggestion, undertone.

connote *v* betoken, hint at, imply, import, indicate, intimate, involve, purport, signify, suggest.

connubial *adj* bridal, conjugal, epithalamic, hymeneal, marital, married, matrimonial, nuptial, wedded.

conquer *v* acquire, annex, beat, best, checkmate, crush, defeat, discomfit, get the better of, humble, master, occupy, overcome, overpower, overrun, overthrow, prevail (over), quell, rout, seize, subdue, subjugate, succeed (at), surmount, take over, triumph (over), vanquish, win (over), woo, worst.
antonyms surrender, yield.

conquest *n* acquisition, annexation, appropriation, capture, coup, defeat, discomfiture, invasion, mastery, occupation, overthrow, rout, seduction, subjection, subjugation, suit, takeover, triumph, vanquishment, victory.

conscience *n* ethics, integrity, morals, principles, scruples, standards, superego.

conscience-stricken *adj* ashamed, compunctious, contrite, disturbed, guilt-ridden, guilty, penitent, regretful, remorseful, repentant, sorry, troubled, uneasy.
antonyms unashamed, unrepentant.

conscientious *adj* careful, diligent, faithful, hard-working, high-minded, honest, honourable, incorruptible, just, meticulous, moral, painstaking, particular, principled, punctilious, responsible, serious, scrupulous, solicitous, straightforward, strict, thorough, upright, well-intentioned.
antonyms careless, irresponsible.

conscious *adj* alert, alive, attentive, awake, aware, calculated, cognizant, deliberate, heedful, intentional, knowing, mindful, percipient, premeditated, rational, reasoning, reflective, regardful, responsible, self-conscious, sensible, sensitive, sentient, studied, willful, witting.
antonym unconscious.

consciousness *n* apprehension, awareness, intuition, knowledge, realization, recognition, sensibility, sentience.

antonym unconciousness.

consecrate *v* beatify, dedicate, devote, exalt, hallow, ordain, revere, sanctify, set aside, venerate.

consecutive *adj* chronological, continuous, following, linear, running, sequential, seriatim, succeeding, successive, unbroken, uninterrupted.
antonym discontinuous.

consensus *n* agreement, concord, concurrence, consent, consentience, harmony, like-mindedness, unanimity, unity.
antonym disagreement.

consent *v* accede, acquiesce, agree, allow, approve, assent, authorize, comply, concede, grant, permit, yield.
antonyms oppose, refuse.
    n acquiescence, agreement, approval, assent, authorization, blessing, compliance, concurrence, go-ahead, green light, permission, sanction.
antonyms opposition, refusal.

consequence *n* account, concern, distinction, effect, eminence, end, fall-out, import, importance, interest, moment, notability, note, outcome, rank, repercussion, result, side effect, significance, standing, status, upshot, weight.
antonym cause.

consequent *adj* ensuing, following, resultant, resulting, sequent, sequential, subsequent, succeeding.

consequential *adj* consequent, far-reaching, grave, important, impressive, indirect, momentous, noteworthy, resultant, serious, significant, weighty.
antonyms inconsequential, unimportant.

consequently *adv* accordingly, consequentially, ergo, hence, inferentially, necessarily, so, subsequently, therefore, thus.

conservation *n* care, custody, ecology, economy, guardianship, husbandry, keeping, maintenance, preservation, protection, safeguarding, safe-keeping, saving, upkeep.
antonyms destruction, neglect, waste.

conservative *adj* anti-change, bourgeois, cautious, conventional, die-hard, establishmentarian, guarded, hidebound, middle-of-the-road, moderate, old-fashioned, orthodox, predictable, quiet, reactionary, restrained, rightist, right-wing, safe, sober, staid, Tory, traditional, unexaggerated, unprogressive.
antonyms left-wing, radical.
    n diehard, fogey, moderate, mossback, reactionary, right-winger, stick-in-the-mud, Tory, traditionalist.
antonyms iconoclast, left-winger, radical.

conserve *v* guard, hoard, husband, keep, maintain, nurse, preserve, protect, save.
antonyms squander, use, waste.

consider *v* allow for, believe, bethink, cogitate, contemplate, count, deem, deliberate, discuss, entertain, esteem, examine, judge, meditate, mull over, muse, ponder, rate, reckon with, reflect, regard, remember, respect, revolve, ruminate, study, take into account, think, weigh.

antonym ignore.

considerable *adj* ample, appreciable, big, distinguished, goodly, great, important, influential, large, marked, much, noteworthy, noticeable, reasonable, remarkable, renowned, significant, sizable, substantial, tidy, venerable.

antonyms insignificant, slight.

considerate *adj* attentive, charitable, concerned, forbearing, gracious, heedful, kind, kindly, mindful, obliging, other-oriented, respectful, sensitive, solicitous, tactful, thoughtful, unselfish.

antonyms selfish, thoughtless.

consideration *n* acknowledgment, analysis, attention, attentiveness, cogitation, concern, considerateness, contemplation, deliberation, discussion, examination, factor, fee, issue, kindliness, kindness, meditation, payment, perquisite, point, recognition, recompense, reflection, regard, remuneration, respect, review, reward, rumination, scrutiny, solicitude, study, tact, thought, thoughtfulness, tip, unselfishness.

antonyms disdain, disregard.

consign *v* assign, commend, commit, convey, deliver, devote, entrust, hand over, relegate, ship, sign over, transfer, transmit.

consignment *n* assignment, batch, cargo, committal, delivery, dispatch, distribution, goods, load, relegation, sending, shipment, transmittal.

consist (in) *v* inhere, lie, reside.

consist of comprise, contain, embody, embrace, include, incorporate, involve, take in.

consistency *n* accordance, agreement, body, coherence, compatibility, concordance, congruity, constancy, correspondence, density, evenness, firmness, harmony, identity, regularity, sameness, steadfastness, steadiness, thickness, uniformity, viscosity.

antonym inconsistency.

consistent *adj* accordant, agreeing, coherent, compatible, congruous, consonant, constant, dependable, harmonious, in accordance, in harmony, logical, of a piece, persistent, predictable, regular, steady, strong, unchanging, undeviating, unfailing, uniform.

antonyms erratic, inconsistent, patchy.

consolation *n* aid, alleviation, assuagement, cheer, comfort, ease, easement, encouragement, help, relief, solace, succour, support.

antonym discouragement.

console *v* assuage, calm, cheer, comfort, encourage, hearten, solace, soothe, succour.

antonyms agitate, upset.

consolidate *v* ally, amalgamate, cement, combine, compact, compress, condense, confederate, conjoin, federate, fortify, fuse, harden, join, merge, reinforce, roll into one,

secure, solidify, stabilize, strengthen, thicken, unify, unite.

consonant *adj* according, compatible, concordant, conformable, congruous, consistent, correspondent, fitting, harmonious, in accord(ance), suitable.

antonym dissonant.

consort *n* associate, companion, escort, fellow, helpmate, helpmeet, husband, partner, spouse, wife.

v accord, agree, associate, correspond, fraternize, hang out, harmonize, have converse, jibe, keep company, mingle, mix, square, tally.

conspectus *n* abstract, compendium, digest, epitome, outline, précis, report, résumé, review, statement, summary, survey, syllabus, synopsis.

conspicuous *adj* apparent, blatant, clear, discernible, evident, flagrant, flashy, garish, glaring, hard to ignore, hard to miss, manifest, marked, noticeable, obvious, ostentatious, patent, perceptible, remarkable, showy, striking, unconcealable, visible.

antonym inconspicuous.

conspiracy *n* cabal, cahoots, collusion, confederacy, fix, frame-up, intrigue, league, machination, plot, ring, scheme.

conspire *v* cabal, collude, combine, concur, conduce, confederate, contribute, contrive, co-operate, intrigue, league together, machinate, manoeuvre, plot, scheme, tend.

constancy *n* consistency, dependability, determination, devotion, evenness, faithfulness, fidelity, firmness, fixedness, immutability, loyalty, permanence, perseverance, regularity, resolution, stability, staunchness, steadfastness, steadiness, tenacity, uniformity.

antonyms inconstancy, irregularity.

constant *adj* ceaseless, changeless, continual, continuous, dependable, determined, devoted, dogged, endless, eternal, even, everlasting, faithful, firm, fixed, habitual, immutable, incessant, interminable, invariable, loyal, never-ending, non-stop, permanent, perpetual, persevering, persistent, regular, relentless, resolute, stable, staunch, steadfast, steady, sustained, tried-and-true, true, trustworthy, trusty, unalterable, unaltered, unbroken, unceasing, unchangeable, unchanged, unchanging, unfailing, unflagging, uniform, uninterrupted, unrelenting, unremitting, unshakable, unshaken, unvarying, unwavering.

antonyms fickle, fitful, irregular, occasional, variable.

constantly *adv* always, ceaselessly, continually, continuously, endlessly, everlastingly, every time you turn around, forever, incessantly, interminably, invariably, non-stop, perpetually, relentlessly, steadfastly, uniformly.

antonym occasionally.

constellation *n* arrangement, clump, cluster, collection, galaxy, gathering, knot, set.

consternation *n* alarm, amazement, anxiety, awe, bewilderment, confusion, dismay, disquietude, distress, dread, fear, fright, horror, panic, perturbation, shock, terror, trepidation. *antonym* composure.

constituent *adj* basic, component, elemental, essential, inherent, integral, intrinsic.
n bit, component, element, essential, factor, ingredient, part, portion, section, unit. *antonym* whole.

constitute *v* amount to, appoint, authorize, be, be in fact, build, commission, compose, construct, create, delegate, depute, draw up, elect, empower, enact, equal, establish, fix, form, found, make, make up, name, nominate, ordain, represent.

constitution *n* appointment, build, character, commissioning, composition, configuration, construction, delegation, disposition, election, enactment, establishment, form, formation, founding, habit, health, make-up, nature, organization, physique, set-up, structure, temper, temperament.

constitutional *adj* chartered, congenital, immanent, inborn, inherent, innate, intrinsic, lawful, legal, organic, statutory, vested.
n airing, promenade, stroll, turn, walk.

constrain *v* bind, bulldoze, chain, check, coerce, compel, confine, constrict, cramp, curb, drive, force, hinder, impel, limit, necessitate, oblige, pressure, railroad, restrain, restrict, strong-arm, twist the arm of, urge.

constrained *adj* embarrassed, forced, guarded, inhibited, reserved, reticent, stiff, strained, subdued, uneasy, unnatural. *antonyms* free, relaxed.

constraint *n* awkwardness, check, coercion, compulsion, confinement, curb, damper, duress, force, hindrance, limitation, necessity, pressure, restraint, restriction, stiffness, stricture.

constrict *v* choke, compress, constrain, contract, cramp, inhibit, limit, narrow, pinch, reduce, restrict, shrink, squeeze, strangle, strangulate, tighten. *antonym* expand.

construct *n* fabrication, invention, model, paradigm, systemization. *v* assemble, build, compose, create, design, engineer, erect, establish, fabricate, fashion, form, formulate, found, frame, knock together, make, manufacture, organize, piece together, raise, shape. *antonyms* demolish, destroy.

construction *n* assembly, arrangement, building, composition, constitution, creation, edifice, erection, fabrication, figure, form, formation, interpretation, meaning, model, organization, shape, structure. *antonym* destruction.

constructive *adj* advantageous, affirmative, beneficial, edifying, helpful, positive, practical, productive, upbuilding, useful, valuable. *antonyms* destructive, negative, unhelpful.

construe *v* analyse, decipher, deduce, explain, expound, infer, interpret, parse, read, render, take, translate, understand.

consult *v* ask, call on, commune, confer, consider, debate, deliberate, discuss, interrogate, parley, powwow, question, refer to, regard, respect, see, seek advice, take into account, talk.

consultation *n* appointment, colloquy, conference, council, deliberation, dialogue, discussion, examination, hearing, interview, meeting, parley, powwow, session, talk.

consume *v* absorb, annihilate, deplete, destroy, devastate, devour, drain, drink, eat, engross, engulf, envelop, exhaust, expend, gobble, guzzle, monopolize, ravage, spend, squander, swallow, take (up), use (up), vanish, waste.

consumed *adj* absorbed, devoured, dominated, engrossed, filled, monopolized, obsessed, overwhelmed, preoccupied, taken up, wasted, wrapped up.

consumer *n* buyer, customer, end user, purchaser, shopper, user.

consuming *adj* absorbing, compelling, compulsive, devouring, dominating, engrossing, gripping, immoderate, monopolizing, obsessive, overpowering, overwhelming, tormenting.

consummate *v* accomplish, achieve, cap, compass, complete, conclude, crown, effectuate, finish, fulfil, perfect, perform, realize, seal.
adj absolute, accomplished, complete, distinguished, finished, matchless, peerless, perfect, polished, practised, skilled, superb, superior, supreme, total, transcendent, ultimate, unqualified, utter. *antonym* imperfect.

consummation *n* accomplishment, achievement, actualization, cap, completion, crown, crowning, culmination, end, fulfilment, perfection, realization.

consumption *n* consuming, depletion, devouring, diminution, dissipation, emaciation, exhaustion, expenditure, gobbling, guzzling, loss, phthisis, ravaging, tabes, tabescence, TB, tuberculosis, use, waste, wasting.

contact *n* acquaintance, approximation, association, communication, connection, contiguity, impact, junction, liaison, meeting, tangency, touch, union.
v approach, call, connect with, get hold of, notify, phone, reach, touch.

contagious *adj* catching, communicable, epidemic, infectious, pestiferous, spreading, transmissible, zymotic.

contain *v* accommodate, check, comprehend, comprise, control, curb, embody, embrace, enclose, hold, include, incorporate, keep in, limit, put a lid on, repress, restrain, stifle, stop, take in. *antonym* exclude.

contaminate *v* adulterate, befoul, besmirch, corrupt, debase, defile, dirty, foul, infect, pollute, soil, stain, sully, taint, tarnish, vitiate.

antonym purify.

contamination *n* adulteration, contagion, corruption, debasement, decay, defilement, dirt, dirtiness, filth, foulness, impurity, infection, poisoning, pollution, rottenness, stain, taint, vitiation.

antonym purification.

contemplate *v* behold, cogitate, consider, deliberate, envisage, expect, eye, gaze at, intend, mean, meditate, mull over, muse (on), observe, plan, ponder, propose, reflect on, regard, ruminate, study, survey, think (about), view.

contemplative *adj* devotional, introspective, meditative, musing, pensive, rapt, reflective, ruminative, thoughtful.

antonyms impulsive, thoughtless.

contemporary *adj* à la mode, coeval, co-existent, co-existing, concurrent, contemporaneous, coterminous, current, latest, modern, modern-day, newfangled, present, present-day, recent, synchronous, up-to-date, up-to-the-minute, with it.

antonyms preceding, succeeding.

contempt *n* condescension, contumely, derision, despite, detestation, disdain, disgrace, dishonour, disregard, disrespect, flouting, humiliation, loathing, mockery, neglect, scorn, shame, slight(ing).

antonyms admiration, regard.

contemptible *adj* abject, base, cheap, degenerate, despicable, detestable, disgraceful, dishonourable, ignominious, loathsome, low, low-down, mean, paltry, pitiful, scurvy, shabby, shameful, sleazy, slimy, vile, worthless, wretched.

antonyms admirable, honourable.

▲ *confusable word* contemptuous.

contemptuous *adj* arrogant, cavalier, condescending, contumacious, contumelious, cynical, derisive, disdainful, disrespectful, haughty, high and mighty, insolent, insulting, scornful, sneering, snobby, supercilious, withering.

antonyms humble, polite, respectful.

▲ *confusable word* contemptible.

contend *v* affirm, allege, argue, assert, aver, avow, battle, clash, compete, cope, debate, declare, dispute, grapple, hold, jostle, maintain, skirmish, strive, struggle, vie, wrestle.

content[1] *v* appease, gratify, humour, indulge, mollify, pacify, placate, please, reconcile, satisfy, suffice for.

antonym displease.

adj agreeable, at peace, comfortable, contented, fulfilled, glad, gratified, happy, pleased, satisfied, thankful, untroubled.

antonym dissatisfied.

content[2] *n* burden, capacity, essence, gist, ideas, load, matter, meaning, measure, proportion, significance, size, subject matter, substance, text, volume.

contented *adj* at peace, cheerful, comfortable, content, equanimous, gratified, happy, placid, pleased, relaxed, satisfied, serene.

antonym discontented.

contention *n* affirmation, allegation, argument, assertion, asseveration, claim, competition, contest, controversy, debate, declaration, discord, dispute, dissension, enmity, feuding, hostility, position, rivalry, stand, strife, struggle, thesis, wrangling.

contentious *adj* antagonistic, argumentative, bickering, captious, cavilling, chippy, combative, confrontational, controversial, debatable, disputatious, factious, hostile, litigious, peevish, perverse, polarizing, problematic, pugnacious, quarrelsome, querulous, wrangling.

antonyms co-operative, peaceable, uncontroversial.

contentment *n* comfort, content, contentedness, ease, equanimity, fulfilment, gratification, happiness, peace, peacefulness, placidity, pleasure, repletion, satisfaction, serenity.

antonym dissatisfaction.

contents *n* chapters, constituents, divisions, elements, ingredients, insides, items, load, parts, subjects, themes, topics.

contest *n* affray, altercation, argument, battle, combat, competition, conflict, controversy, debate, discord, dispute, encounter, fight, game, match, meet, olympiad, race, rivalry, set-to, struggle, sweepstakes, tournament, trial.

v argue against, challenge, compete, contend, debate, deny, dispute, doubt, fight, litigate, oppose, question, refute, strive (for), vie.

contestant *n* agonist, aspirant, candidate, competitor, contender, entrant, hopeful, participant, player.

context *n* background, circumstances, collocation, conditions, connection, environment, frame of reference, framework, milieu, setting, situation, surroundings, venue.

contiguous *adj* abutting, adjacent, adjoining, bordering, coterminous, in contact, juxtaposed, juxtapositional, near, neighbouring, next, tangential, touching.

antonyms distort, separate.

continent *adj* abstemious, abstinent, ascetic, austere, celibate, chaste, moderate, pure, restrained, self-controlled, self-restrained, sober, temperate, virginal.

antonym incontinent.

contingency *n* accident, arbitrariness, chance, emergency, event, eventuality, fortuity, happening, incident, juncture, possibility, randomness, uncertainty.

contingent *n* batch, body, bunch, company, complement, delegation, deputation, detachment, group, mission, quota, section, set.

adj accidental, conditional, dependent, hinging, possible, turning, uncertain, unexpected.

continual *adj* ceaseless, constant, continuous, endless, eternal, everlasting, frequent, incessant, interminable, non-stop, oft-repeated, ongoing, perpetual, persistent, recurrent, regular, repeated, repetitive, unbroken, unceasing, uninterrupted, unremitting.

antonyms occasional, temporary.

continually *adv* always, ceaselessly, constantly, endlessly, eternally, everlastingly, every time you turn around, forever, incessantly, interminably, non-stop, perpetually, persistently, repeatedly, unremittingly.

antonym occasionally.

continuance *n* adjournment, continuation, duration, endurance, period, permanence, postponement, prolongation, protraction, term, time.

continuation *n* addition, appendix, epilogue, extension, furtherance, maintenance, perpetuation, postscript, prolongation, resumption, sequel, supplement.

antonyms cessation, termination.

continue *v* abide, adjourn, carry on, endure, extend, go on, keep up, last, lengthen, maintain, postpone, persevere, persist, proceed, project, prolong, pursue, put off, reach, recommence, remain, rest, resume, stay, stick at, survive, sustain.

antonyms discontinue, stop.

continuing *adj* abiding, enduring, lasting, ongoing, progressive, sustained.

continuity *n* cohesion, connection, constancy, extension, flow, interrelationship, linkage, permanence, progression, sequence, stability, succession.

antonym discontinuity.

continuous *adj* ceaseless, connected, consecutive, constant, continued, endless, extended, non-stop, perpetual, progressive, prolonged, successive, sustained, unbroken, unceasing, undivided, uninterrupted, unremitting.

antonyms discontinuous, intermittent, separate, sporadic.

continuum *n* line, progression, range, spectrum, spiral, whole.

contort *v* convolute, deform, disfigure, distort, gnarl, knot, misshape, squirm, twist, warp, wrench, wriggle, writhe.

contour *n* aspect, curve, figure, form, lie, lines, outline, profile, relief, shape, silhouette.

contraband *adj* banned, black-market, bootleg, forbidden, hot, illegal, illicit, interdicted, prohibited, proscribed, smuggled, unlawful, verboten.

contract[1] *v* abbreviate, close, compress, condense, constrict, curl up, elide, epitomize, lessen, narrow, purse, reduce, shorten, shrink, tense, tighten, wrinkle.

antonyms dilate, enlarge, expand, lengthen.

contract[2] *v* agree, arrange, bargain, commit, covenant, engage, negotiate, pledge, promise, stipulate, subcontract.

n agreement, arrangement, bargain, bond, commission, commitment, compact, concordat, convention, covenant, deal, engagement, instrument, pact, pledge, settlement, stipulation, subcontract, transaction, treaty, understanding.

contract[3] *v* acquire, catch, come down with, develop, incur.

contraction *n* abbreviation, astringence, compression, constriction, cramp, diminution, elision, narrowing, pain, pursing, reduction, retrenchment, shortening, shrinkage, tensing, tightening.

antonyms dilation, expansion, growth.

contradict *v* belie, challenge, clash (with), conflict (with), contravene, controvert, counter, deny, disaffirm, dispute, gainsay, impugn, negate, oppose, sauce, talk back (to).

antonyms agree (with), confirm, corroborate.

contradiction *n* antithesis, conflict, confutation, contravention, converse, counterstatement, denial, disaffirmation, gainsaying, incongruity, inconsistency, inverse, negation, opposite, oxymoron, paradox, reverse.

antonyms agreement, confirmation, corroboration.

contradictory *adj* antithetical, clashing, conflicting, contrary, counter, discrepant, dissident, double-mouthed, incompatible, inconsistent, irreconcilable, opposed, opposite, oxymoronic, paradoxical.

antonym consistent.

contraption *n* apparatus, contrivance, device, gadget, gizmo, mechanism, rig, thingamabob, thingamajig, widget.

contrary *adj* adverse, antagonistic, awkward, balky, bloody-minded, cantankerous, clashing, contradictory, counter, cross-grained, cussed, difficult, discordant, disobliging, froward, hostile, inconsistent, inimical, intractable, obstinate, opposed, opposite, paradoxical, perverse, stubborn, unaccommodating, wayward, wilful.

antonyms like, obliging, similar.

n antithesis, converse, opposite, reverse.

contrast *n* comparison, contradistinction, contraposition, contrariety, counterpoint, difference, differentiation, disparity, dissimilarity, distinction, divergence, foil, opposition, resolution, set-off, sharpness.

antonym similarity.

v compare, countervail, differ, differentiate, discriminate, distinguish, oppose, set off.

contravene *v* break, contradict, counteract, counter, cross, disobey, fly in the face of, hinder, infract, infringe, interfere with, oppose, overstep, refute, run counter to, thwart, transgress against, trespass against (or on), violate.

antonym uphold.

contribute v add, afford, bestow, chip in, conduce, donate, furnish, give, help, kick in, lead, pitch in, provide, put up, sponsor, subscribe, supply, underwrite.
antonyms subtract, withhold.

contribution n addition, bestowal, donation, gift, grant, gratuity, handout, input, offering, subscription.

contributor n backer, benefactor, bestower, columnist, conferrer, correspondent, donor, freelance, freelancer, giver, journalist, patron, reporter, subscriber, supporter.

contrite adj broken-spirited, chastened, conscience-stricken, guilt-ridden, hat in hand, humble, penitent, penitential, regretful, remorseful, repentant, sorrowful, sorry.

contrition n broken spirit, compunction, humility, penitence, remorse, repentance, sackcloth and ashes, self-reproach, sorrow.

contrivance n apparatus, appliance, artifice, contraption, design, device, dodge, equipment, excogitation, expedient, fabrication, gadget, gear, implement, intrigue, invention, inventiveness, knack, machination, machine, manoeuvre, mechanism, plan, plot, ruse, scheme, stratagem, trick.

contrive v arrange, compass, concoct, construct, create, design, devise, effect, engineer, excogitate, fabricate, frame, improvise, invent, manage, manoeuvre, plan, plot, scheme, think up, wangle.

contrived adj artificial, elaborate, false, forced, laboured, mannered, overdone, planned, recherché, strained, unnatural.
antonym natural.

control v boss, bridle, check, command, conduct, confine, constrain, contain, curb, determine, direct, dominate, govern, lead, limit, manage, manipulate, master, monitor, monopolize, overpower, oversee, pilot, possess, regiment, regulate, restrain, rule, run, stage-manage, steer, subdue, superintend, supervise, suppress, verify.
n authority, brake, charge, check, clutches, command, curb, direction, discipline, dominion, governance, government, guidance, jurisdiction, leading-strings, leash, limitation, management, mastery, monopoly, oversight, possession, regulation, restriction, rule, subjection, superintendence, supervision, suppression, supremacy, the reins.

controversial adj contentious, controvertible, debatable, disputable, disputed, divisive, doubtful, polarizing, polemic, provocative, questionable, touchy.

controversy n altercation, argument, contention, debate, disagreement, discussion, dispute, dissension, polemic, quarrel, squabble, strife, war of words, wrangle, wrangling.
antonyms accord, agreement.

controvert v argue, challenge, contest, contradict, counter, debate, deny, disaffirm, discuss, dispute, gainsay, oppose, rebut, refute, wrangle.

contumacious adj disobedient, haughty, headstrong, insubordinate, intractable, intransigent, mulish, obdurate, obstinate, perverse, pig-headed, rebellious, recalcitrant, refractory, stiff-necked, stubborn, wilful.
antonym obedient.

contumely n abuse, affront, arrogance, contempt, derision, disdain, humiliation, incivility, indignity, insolence, insult, invective, obloquy, opprobrium, rudeness, scorn, superciliousness.

convene v assemble, call, collect, congregate, convoke, gather, meet, muster, rally, summon.

convenience n accessibility, accommodation, advantage, amenity, appliance, availability, comfort, ease, facility, handiness, help, leisure, opportuneness, opportunity, satisfaction, service, serviceability, suitability, use, usefulness, utility.

convenient adj accessible, advantageous, at hand, available, handy, helpful, labour-saving, nearby, opportune, seasonable, serviceable, suitable, suited, useful, utile, well-timed.
antonyms awkward, inconvenient.

convention n agreement, assembly, bargain, code, compact, conclave, concordat, conference, congress, contract, convocation, council, custom, delegates, etiquette, formality, matter of form, meeting, pact, practice, propriety, protocol, representatives, stipulation, synod, tradition, treaty, understanding, usage.

conventional adj accepted, agreed, arbitrary, bourgeois, common, commonplace, copybook, correct, customary, decorous, established, expected, formal, formalist, habitual, hackneyed, hidebound, iconic, nomic, normal, ordinary, orthodox, pedestrian, prevailing, prevalent, proper, prosaic, regular, ritual, routine, run-of-the-mill, safe, standard, stereotyped, straight, stylized, traditional, tried and true, typical, understood, unoriginal, uptight, usual, wonted.
antonyms exotic, unconventional, unusual.

converge v approach, coincide, combine, concentrate, concur, congregate, focus, gather, home in, intersect, join, meet, merge, mingle.
antonyms disperse, diverge.

convergence n approach, assimilation, blending, coincidence, concentration, concurrence, confluence, conflux, conjunction, intersection, junction, meeting, merging, mingling, union.
antonym divergence.

conversant with acquainted with, au fait with, experienced in, familiar with, informed about, knowledgeable about, practised in, proficient in, skilled in, versed in.
antonym ignorant of.

conversation n chat, chinwag, chit-chat, colloquy, communication, communion, confab, confabulation, conference, consultation, converse, dialogue, discourse, discussion, exchange, gab session, gossip, interchange, intercourse, powwow, rap (session), socializing, talk, tête-à-tête.

conversational *adj* affable, chatty, colloquial, communicative, confabulatory, informal, interlocutory, sociable, relaxed, talkative, talky.

converse[1] *v* chat, chew the fat, colloquize, commune, confabulate, confer, dialogue, discourse, gab, rap, shoot the breeze, socialize, talk.

converse[2] *n* antithesis, contrary, counterpart, inverse, obverse, opposite, reverse.
adj antipodal, antipodean, contrary, counter, inverse, opposite, reverse, reversed, transposed.

conversion *n* about-face, adaptation, alteration, appropriation, change, evangelism, metamorphosis, metanoia, modification, permutation, proselytization, rebirth, reconstruction, reformation, regeneration, remodelling, reorganization, switch, transfiguration, transformation, transmogrification, transmutation, turnaround.

convert *v* adapt, alter, appropriate, baptize, change, convince, evangelize, exchange, go over, metamorphose, modify, permute, proselytize, reform, regenerate, remodel, reorganize, restyle, revise, save, switch, transfigure, transform, transmogrify, transmute, transpose, turn, win (over).
n catechumen, disciple, neophyte, proselyte.

convex *adj* bulbous, bulging, curved, gibbous, humped, protuberant, rounded, swelling, tumid.
antonym concave.

convey *v* bear, bequeath, bring, carry, cede, communicate, conduct, deliver, demise, devolve, disclose, express, fetch, forward, grant, guide, impart, move, pass (on), relate, reveal, send, take, tell, transfer, transmit, transport, waft, will.

conveyance *n* carriage, communication, conduct, deed, delivery, forwarding, movement, shipment, transfer, transference, transferral, transmission, transport, transportation, transshipment, vehicle.

conviction *n* assurance, belief, certainty, certitude, confidence, creed, earnestness, faith, fervour, firmness, guilt, opinion, persuasion, principle, tenet, view.

convince *v* assure, confirm, persuade, reassure, satisfy, sway, win over.

convincing *adj* believable, cogent, conclusive, credible, impressive, incontrovertible, likely, persuasive, plausible, powerful, probable, realistic, telling, verisimiliar.
antonyms dubious, improbable.

convivial *adj* backslapping, cheerful, cordial, festal, festive, friendly, fun-loving, gay, genial, gregarious, hearty, hilarious, jolly, jovial, lively, merry, mirthful, party-going, sociable.
antonym taciturn.

convocation *n* assemblage, assembly, conclave, concourse, congregation, congress, convention, council, diet, forgathering, gathering, graduation, meeting, muster, summons, synod.

convoke *v* assemble, call, collect, convene, gather, muster, rally, round up, summon.

convoluted *adj* baroque, complex, complicated, gyrose, intricate, involved, labyrinthine, mazelike, meandering, spiral, tangled, tortuous, twisting, whorled, winding.
antonym straightforward.

convolution *n* coil, coiling, complexity, contortion, curlicue, gyrus, helix, intricacy, involution, loop, sinousness, sinuosity, spiral, tortuousness, twist, volution, whorl, winding.

convoy *n* attendance, attendant, escort, fleet, guard, protection, train.

convulsion *n* agitation, commotion, contortion, contraction, cramp, disturbance, eruption, explosion, fit, furore, outburst, paroxysm, seizure, shaking, spasm, throe, tremor, turbulence, turmoil, upheaval.

convulsive *adj* churning, contorting, fitful, involuntary, jerky, paroxysmal, spasmodic, spastic, sporadic, sudden, twitchy, uncontrollable, violent.

cook up *v* brew, concoct, contrive, devise, fabricate, improvise, invent, plan, plot, prepare.

cool[1] *adj* air-conditioned, aloof, analytical, apathetic, audacious, blasé, bold, brazen, calm, cheeky, chilled, chilling, chilly, coldish, collected, composed, crisp, dégagé, deliberate, detached, dispassionate, distant, downbeat, elegant, frigid, imperturbable, incurious, indifferent, laid-back, level-headed, lukewarm, nippy, nonchalant, objective, offhand, placid, quiet, refreshing, relaxed, reserved, reviving, self-controlled, self-possessed, serene, snobby, stand-offish, together, unapproachable, uncommunicative, unconcerned, unemotional, unenthusiastic, unexcited, unfazed, unfriendly, unheated, uninterested, unresponsive, unruffled, unwelcoming.
antonyms excited, friendly, hot, warm.
v abate, air-condition, allay, assuage, calm (down), chill, dampen, defuse, die down, fan, flag, freeze, lessen, moderate, quiet, refresh, refrigerate, temper, ventilate.
antonyms excite, heat, warm.
n calmness, collectedness, composure, control, nerve, poise, sangfroid, self-control, self-discipline, self-possession, temper.

cool[2] *adj* acceptable, cosmopolitan, fashionable, groovy, in, neat(o), snazzy, sophisticated, stylish, suave, trendy, urbane.

coop *n* box, cage, enclosure, hutch, jail, mew, pen, pound, prison.
v cage, confine, immure, impound, imprison, intern, lock up, pen, shut up.

co-operate *v* abet, aid, assist, collaborate, combine, comply, concur, conduce, conspire, fall in (line), give and take, help, join forces, join hands, participate, play along, play ball, team up, unite.
antonyms hinder, obstruct, oppose, resist.

co-operative *adj* accommodating, collective, combined, concerted, co-ordinated, helpful, joint, obliging, responsive, shared, supportive, synergetic, synergic, synergistic, unified, united.

co-ordinate *v* administrate, codify, convene, correlate, harmonize, integrate, manage, match, mesh, orchestrate, organize, relate, set up, synchronize, systematize, tabulate.

adj co-equal, correlative, correspondent, equal, equiponderant, equipollent, equivalent, independent, parallel.

copacetic *adj* all right, hunky-dory, manageable, peachy, satisfactory, under control.

cope *v* carry on, do all right, get by, handle it, hold one's own, hold up, make shift, make do, manage, survive.

cope with be up to, contend with, deal with, dispatch, encounter, grapple with, handle, manage, struggle with, tangle with, tussle with, weather, wrestle with.

copious *adj* abundant, ample, bounteous, bountiful, extensive, exuberant, full, generous, great, huge, inexhaustible, lavish, liberal, luxuriant, overflowing, plenteous, plentiful, profuse, rich, superabundant.

antonyms meagre, scarce.

cop out (of) abandon, abdicate, back out, desert, dodge, drop out, evade, give up, quit, renege, renounce, revoke, shirk, skip, turn back, weasel out, wimp out, withdraw.

cop-out *n* alibi, dodge, excuse, evasion, fraud, pretence, pretext.

copulation *n* carnal knowledge, coitus, congress, coupling, covering, joining, lovemaking, mating, mounting, serving, sex, sexual intercourse, treading, union.

copy *n* calque, caption, carbon copy, counterfeit, crib, double, duplicate, echo, ectype, emulation, engrossment, exemplar, facsimile, fake, fax, forgery, image, imitation, likeness, loan translation, model, pattern, photocopy, plagiarization, print, reconstruction, replica, replication, representation, reproduction, tenor, text, tracing, transcript, transcription, writing.

antonym archetype, original.

v ape, borrow, counterfeit, crib, duplicate, echo, emulate, engross, facsimile, follow, imitate, (im)personate, mimic, mirror, mock, parody, parrot, photocopy, plagiarize, reconstruct, repeat, replicate, reproduce, simulate, transcribe.

coquettish *adj* amorous, arch, come-hither, coy, dallying, flirtatious, flirty, inviting, teasing, vampish.

cord *n* band, bond, cable, connection, fibre, gimp, line, link, piping, rope, strand, string, tie, twine, wale, wire.

cordial *adj* affable, affectionate, agreeable, amiable, cheerful, earnest, friendly, genial, heartfelt, hearty, hospitable, invigorating, pleasant, sincere, sociable, stimulating, warm, warm-hearted, welcoming, whole-hearted.

antonyms aloof, cool, hostile.

cordon *n* barrier, braid, chain, fence, line, ribbon, ring, rope.

cordon off encircle, enclose, fence off, isolate, rope off, separate, surround.

core *n* bottom, centre, crux, depths, essence, germ, gist, heart, heartwood, kernel, nitty-gritty, nub, nucleus, pith.

antonyms exterior, perimeter, surface.

corner *n* angle, bend, cranny, crook, hideaway, hide-out, hidey-hole, hole, intersection, joint, monopoly, niche, nook, part, pickle, predicament, recess, retreat, spot, vertex.

corny *adj* banal, clichéd, commonplace, contrived, dull, feeble, hackneyed, hokey, maudlin, mawkish, old-fashioned, overdone, platitudinous, sappy, sentimental, stale, stereotyped, tacky, trite, unsophisticated.

antonyms clever, new, original, sophisticated, subtle.

corollary *n* conclusion, consequence, deduction, illation, induction, inference, result, upshot.

corporate *adj* allied, amalgamated, collaborative, collective, combined, communal, concerted, joint, merged, pooled, shared, united.

corporation *n* association, body, combine, company, conglomerate, council, legal entity, society, unit.

corporeal *adj* actual, bodily, concrete, fleshly, human, material, mortal, physical, real, substantial, tangible, visible.

antonym spiritual.

corps *n* band, body, brigade, cohort, company, contingent, crew, detachment, detail, division, force, phalanx, regiment, squad, squadron, team, troop, unit.

corpse *n* body, cadaver, carcass, remains, skeleton, stiff.

corpulence *n* adiposity, blubber, bulk(iness), burliness, chubbiness, embonpoint, fatness, fleshiness, obesity, plumpness, portliness, rotundity, stoutness, tubbiness.

antonym thinness.

corpulent *adj* adipose, beefy, big, bulky, burly, chubby, chunky, fat, fattish, fleshy, heavy, large, obese, overweight, plump, portly, potbellied, pudgy, roly-poly, rotund, stout, tubby, well-padded.

antonym thin.

corpus *n* aggregation, body, collection, compilation, entirety, oeuvre, whole.

corral *n* coop, enclosure, fold, kraal, pen, pound, sty.

v buttonhole, capture, collar, collect, hem in, reel in, surround.

correct *v* adjust, admonish, amend, blue-pencil, chasten, chastise, chide, counteract, counterbalance, cure, debug, discipline, emend, emendate, fix, grade, improve, mark, punish, rectify, redress, reform, regulate, remedy, reprimand, reprove, right, set right.

adj acceptable, accurate, appropriate, by the

book, comme il faut, conventional, diplomatic, done, equitable, established, exact, expected, faultless, fitting, flawless, in order, jake, just, kosher, legitimate, OK, orthodox, precise, prim, prissy, proper, regular, right, seemly, standard, strict, traditional, true, well-formed, word-perfect.

antonyms inaccurate, incorrect, out of line, wrong.

correction *n* adjustment, admonition, alteration, amendment, castigation, chastisement, discipline, emendation, improvement, modification, punishment, rectification, reformation, regulation, remedy, reprimand, reproof, righting.

corrective *adj* admonitory, ameliorative, curative, disciplinary, emendatory, medicinal, penal, punitive, reformatory, rehabilitative, remedial, restorative, therapeutic.

correctly *adv* accurately, appropriately, aright, by the book, comme il faut, faithfully, faultlessly, justly, legitimately, perfectly, precisely, properly, right, rightly.

antonyms incorrectly, wrongly.

correlate *v* associate, compare, connect, co-ordinate, correspond, equate, interact, link, parallel, relate, tie in.

correlation *n* alternation, association, connection, correspondence, equivalence, interaction, interchange, interdependence, interrelationship, link, reciprocity, relationship, tie-in.

correspond *v* accord, agree, answer, coincide, communicate, complement, concur, conform, correlate, dovetail, fit, harmonize, jibe, jive, match, parallel, square, tally, write.

correspondence *n* agreement, analogy, coincidence, communication, comparability, comparison, concurrence, conformity, congruity, consonance, correlation, equivalence, fitness, harmony, homology, letters, mail, match, parallelism, relation, resemblance, respondence, similarity, writing.

antonyms divergence, incongruity.

correspondent *n* contributor, journalist, penpal, reporter, writer.

corresponding *adj* accordant, analogous, answering, coincident, collateral, comparable, complementary, concurrent, congruent, consonant, correlative, correspondent, equivalent, homologous, identical, interrelated, like, matching, parallel, reciprocal, related, similar, synonymous.

corridor *n* aisle, ambulatory, cloister, foyer, hall, hallway, isthmus, landlink, lobby, passage, passageway, thoroughfare, walkway, vestibule.

corroborate *v* authenticate, back up, bear out, confirm, document, endorse, establish, prove, ratify, reinforce, substantiate, support, sustain, underpin, uphold, validate.

antonym contradict.

corrode *v* canker, consume, corrupt, crumble, deteriorate, disintegrate, eat away (at), erode, fret, impair, oxidize, rust, waste, wear away.

corrosive *adj* abrasive, acid, acrid, biting, caustic, consuming, corroding, cutting, incisive, mordant, sarcastic, trenchant, truculent, venomous, virulent, wasting, wearing.

corrupt *adj* adulterated, altered, bent, bribed, contaminated, crooked, debased, decayed, defiled, degenerate, demoralized, depraved, dishonest, dissolute, distorted, doctored, falsified, fraudulent, immoral, impure, infected, perverted, poisoned, polluted, profligate, putrescent, putrid, rotten, shady, substandard, tainted, twisted, unethical, unprincipled, unscrupulous, venal, vicious, warped.

antonyms honest, trustworthy, upright.

v adulterate, alter, barbarize, bend, bribe, canker, contaminate, debase, debauch, defile, demoralize, deprave, distort, doctor, empoison, falsify, fix, infect, pervert, pollute, putrefy, rot, seduce, spoil, suborn, subvert, taint, twist, vitiate, warp.

antonym purify.

corruption *n* adulteration, baseness, bribery, bribing, crookedness, debasement, decadence, decay, defilement, degeneration, degradation, demoralization, depravity, dishonesty, distortion, doctoring, evil, extortion, falsification, fiddling, foulness, fraud, fraudulence, graft, immorality, impurity, infection, iniquity, jobbery, leprosy, malversation, perversion, pollution, profiteering, profligacy, putrefaction, putrescence, rot, rottenness, shadiness, sinfulness, turpitude, twistedness, ulcer, unscrupulousness, venality, vice, viciousness, virus, warpedness, wickedness.

antonyms honesty, purification.

cosmetic *adj* non-essential, superficial, surface.

antonym essential.

cosmic *adj* boundless, grandiose, huge, illimitable, immense, infinite, limitless, measureless, universal, vast.

cosmopolitan *adj* broadminded, catholic, international, multicultural, multiethnic, sophisticated, universal, unprejudiced, urbane, well-travelled, worldly, worldly-wise.

antonyms insular, parochial, rustic.

cosmos *n* creation, galaxy, order, system, universe, world.

cosset *v* baby, cherish, coddle, cuddle, mollycoddle, overprotect, pamper, pet.

cost *n* amount, charge, damage, detriment, disbursement, expenditure, expense, figure, harm, hurt, injury, loss, outlay, payment, penalty, price, rate, sacrifice, sum, worth.

v demand, estimate, lose, require, set one back, take.

costly *adj* damaging, dear, deleterious, detrimental, disastrous, excessive, exorbitant, expensive, extortionate, harmful, highly-priced, injurious, lavish, loss-making, luxurious, opulent, precious, priceless, pricy, rich, ruinous, steep, sumptuous, valuable.

antonyms cheap, inexpensive.

costume *n* apparel, attire, clothing, disguise, dress, ensemble, garb, gear, get-up, livery, masquerade, outfit, raiment, robes, suit, uniform, vestment.

cosy *adj* buddy-buddy, comfortable, comfy, compact, friendly, homelike, homey, intimate, secure, sheltered, snug, warm.

antonyms cold, uncomfortable.

coterie *n* caucus, cenacle, circle, clique, gang, group, outfit, set.

coterminous *adj* abutting, adjacent, bordering, co-extensive, contiguous, neighbouring.

cottage *n* cabin, chalet, hut, lodge, shack, summer house, villa, woodland retreat.

couch *v* cradle, express, frame, lower, phrase, support, utter, word.

n bed, chaise longue, chesterfield, day bed, divan, lounge, ottoman, settee, sofa.

cough *n* ahem, bark, hack, tussis.

v bark, clear one's throat, hack, harrumph, hawk, hem.

cough up deliver, expectorate, fork out (or over), give, hand over, pay, pay out, shell out, spit up, surrender.

council *n* assembly, board, cabinet, chamber, commission, committee, conclave, conference, congress, consistory, consultation, convention, convocation, diet, directorate, divan, ministry, panchayat, panel, parley, parliament, soviet, syndicate, synod.

▲ *confusable word* counsel.

counsel *n* admonition, advice, advocate, attorney, barrister, caution, consideration, consultation, deliberation, direction, guidance, information, lawyer, plan, purpose, recommendation, solicitor, suggestion, warning.

v admonish, advise, advocate, caution, direct, exhort, guide, instruct, recommend, suggest, urge, warn.

▲ *confusable word* council.

hold (or **take**) **counsel** confer, consult, deliberate, parley, talk.

counsellor *n* adviser, attorney, cabin supervisor, councillor, lawyer, representative, social worker, therapist, vizier.

count *v* add, calculate, check, compute, consider, deem, enumerate, esteem, hold, include, judge, list, matter, number, rate, reckon, regard, score, signify, tally, tell, think, total, tot up, weigh.

n addition, calculation, computation, enumeration, figure, number, numbering, poll, reckoning, score, sum, tally, total.

count for nothing cut no ice, make no difference.

count on bank on, believe, depend on, expect, figure on, intend, plan on, reckon on, rely on, trust.

countenance *n* acquiescence, air, appearance, approval, aspect, backing, demeanour, endorsement, expression, face, favour, features, look, mien, physiognomy, sanction, support, visage.

v acquiesce to, agree to, allow, approve,

back, brook, condone, encourage, endorse, endure, permit, sanction, support, tolerate.

counter¹ *adv* against, contrarily, contrariwise, conversely, in opposition.

adj adverse, against, antithetical, conflicting, contradictory, contrary, contrasting, obverse, opposed, opposing, opposite.

antonyms concurring, corroborating.

v answer, contradict, meet, offset, oppose, parry, resist, respond, retaliate, retort, return.

counter² *n* bean, chip, coin, disc, jeton, marker, piece, tiddlywink, token.

counter³ *n* bar, checkout, cupboard, desk.

counteract *v* act against, annul, cancel (out), check, compensate for, contravene, counterbalance, countervail, defeat, foil, frustrate, hinder, invalidate, negate, neutralize, nullify, offset, oppose, resist, thwart, undo.

antonyms assist, support.

counterbalance *v* balance, cancel (out), compensate for, counterpoise, countervail, equalize, make up for, neutralize, offset.

counterfeit *v* copy, fabricate, fake, feign, forge, imitate, impersonate, pretend, sham, simulate.

adj bogus, copied, ersatz, faked, false, feigned, forged, fraudulent, imitation, phony, pretend(ed), pseudo, sham, simulated, spurious, supposititious.

antonym genuine.

n copy, fake, forgery, fraud, imitation, phantasm, phony, pretence, reproduction, sham, simulacrum.

countermand *v* abrogate, annul, cancel, override, recall, repeal, rescind, reverse, revoke, withdraw.

counterpart *n* colleague, complement, copy, correlative, correspondent, duplicate, equal, equivalent, fellow, homologue, match, mate, opposite number, parallel, peer, twin.

countless *adj* endless, incalculable, infinite, innumerable, legion, limitless, measureless, multitudinous, myriad, numberless, uncounted, unnumbered, unsummed, untold.

antonym limited.

countrified *adj* Arcadian, bucolic, hick, homespun, idyllic, pastoral, provincial, rural, rustic, rusticated.

antonyms oppidan, urban.

country¹ *n* citizenry, citizens, clime, commonwealth, community, electorate, fatherland, homeland, kingdom, land, motherland, nation, people, populace, public, realm, society, (sovereign) state, voters.

country² *n* backwoods, boondocks, countryside, electorate, farmland, green belt, land, outback, outdoors, parts, provinces, region, sticks, terrain, territory.

adj agrarian, agricultural, Arcadian, bucolic, cracker-barrel, farming, georgic, homespun, landed, pastoral, provincial, rural, rustic, rusticated.

antonyms oppidan, urban.

county *n* canton, department, district, province, region, shire, township.

coup *n* accomplishment, action, blow, coup d'état, deed, exploit, feat, manoeuvre, master-stroke, overthrow, rebellion, revolt, revolution, stratagem, stroke, stunt, takeover, tour de force, triumph, uprising, victory.

coup de grâce clincher, come-uppance, death-blow, final stroke, kibosh, kill, quietus.

couple *n* brace, Darby and Joan, duet, duo, dyad, pair, span, team, twain, twosome, yoke.
v attach, buckle, clasp, combine, conjoin, connect, copulate, fornicate, hitch, join, link, marry, pair, unite, wed, yoke.

courage *n* boldness, bravery, daring, dauntlessness, fearlessness, firmness, fortitude, gallantry, grit, guts, hardihood, heroism, mettle, moxie, nerve, pluck, resolution, spirit, spunk, stomach, stout-heartedness, valour.
antonym cowardice.

courageous *adj* audacious, bold, brave, daring, dauntless, fearless, gallant, gutsy, hardy, heroic, high-hearted, indomitable, intrepid, lion-hearted, plucky, resolute, spunky, stout-hearted, valiant, valorous.
antonym cowardly.

courier *n* bearer, carrier, emissary, envoy, guide, herald, legate, messenger, nuncio, pursuivant, representative, runner.

course *n* advance, bed, channel, circuit, continuity, current, development, diadrom, direction, duration, flight-path, flow, hippodrome, lap, layer, line, march, movement, orbit, order, passage, passing, path, period, piste, plan, policy, procedure, program, progress, race, racecourse, racetrack, raceway, regimen, road, round, route, row, seminar, sequence, series, subject, succession, sweep, tack, term, time, track, trajectory, unfolding, vector, way.
v chase, dash, flow, fly, follow, gush, hunt, move, pour, pursue, race, run, scud, scurry, speed, stream, surge.

court *n* advances, attendants, bailey, bar, bench, cloister, cortege, courtyard, durbar, entourage, hall, law court, manor, overtures, palace, piazza, plaza, quad, quadrangle, retinue, square, suit, suite, train, tribunal, wooing, yard.
v attract, be seeing, butter up, chase, cultivate, dance attendance on, date, flatter, go out with, invite, lionize, make overtures to, pander to, prompt, provoke, pursue, seek, serenade, solicit, take out, woo.

courteous *adj* affable, attentive, ceremonious, civil, considerate, courtly, debonair, gallant, gracious, mannerly, obliging, polished, polite, refined, respectful, thoughtful, urbane, well-bred, well-mannered.
antonyms discourteous, rude.

courtesan *n* call girl, Delilah, demi-mondaine, harlot, hetaira, kept woman, lady of the night, mistress, paramour, prostitute, scarlet woman, whore, woman of easy virtue.

courtesy *n* affability, attention, breeding, civility, comity, consideration, courteousness, courtliness, favour, gallantness, gallantry, generosity, graciousness, greeting, kindness, manners, polish, politeness, thoughtfulness, urbanity.
antonyms discourtesy, rudeness.

courtier *n* attendant, bootlicker, chamberlain, flatterer, follower, henchman, lady, lord, major-domo, noble, nobleman, page, pursuivant, squire, steward, sycophant, toady, train-bearer.

courtly *adj* affable, aristocratic, ceremonious, chivalric, chivalrous, civil, decorous, dignified, elegant, flattering, formal, gallant, high-bred, ingratiating, lordly, obliging, obsequious, polished, polite, refined, stately, sycophantic, toadying.
antonyms inelegant, provincial, rough.

courtyard *n* area, atrium, enclosure, garden, patio, peristyle, playground, quad, quadrangle, yard.

cove *n* anchorage, bay, bight, creek, estuary, fiord, firth, frith, harbour, inlet, sound.

covenant *n* agreement, arrangement, bargain, bond, commitment, compact, concordat, contract, convention, engagement, oath, pact, pledge, promise, testament, treaty, trust, undertaking, vow.
v agree, bargain, contract, engage, pledge, promise, stipulate, swear, undertake, vow.

cover *v* aim at, answer (for), block, brood, camouflage, canopy, canvass, clad, cloak, clothe, coat, compensate, comprehend, comprise, conceal, consider, contain, copulate with, curtain, daub, deal with, defend, discuss, disguise, dress, eclipse, embrace, encase, encompass, encrust, enshroud, envelop, fill in, front, guard, hide, hood, house, include, incorporate, insure, invest, investigate, layer, mantle, mask, obscure, offset, overlay, overspread, pay (for), plaster, protect, reinforce, report on, screen, secrete, shade, sheathe, shelter, shield, shroud, stand in, substitute (for), suffice (for), suffuse, support, swathe, take in, travel, work, wrap, veil.
n bedspread, binding, blanket, blind, camouflage, canopy, cap, case, cloak, clothing, coating, compensation, concealment, covering, coverture, cover-up, defence, disguise, dress, envelope, façade, front, guard, indemnity, insurance, jacket, lid, mask, payment, pretence, pretext, protection, refuge, reimbursement, sanctuary, screen, sheath, shelter, shield, shutter, sleeve, smoke, spread, thicket, throw, top, underbrush, undergrowth, veil, wrapper.

cover up bury, conceal, cover, dissemble, dissimulate, hide, hush up, keep quiet, suppress, whitewash.
antonym uncover.

coverage *n* account, analysis, attention, description, handling, insurance, protection, reportage, reporting, treatment.

covering *n* blanket, blind, cap, carpet, casing, cloak, clothing, coating, cocoon, cope, cover, curtain, exoskeleton, housing, integument, layer, mask, masking, overlay, protection, shade, sheath, shelter, tegmen, top, wrap, wrapper, wrapping.

adj accompanying, descriptive, explanatory, introductory, masking, obscuring, protective.

covert *adj* clandestine, concealed, disguised, dissembled, furtive, hidden, masked, private, secret, sneaky, stealthy, surreptitious, ulterior, under the table, underhand, unsuspected, veiled.

antonym open.

cover-up *n* complicity, concealment, conspiracy, dissemblance, dissimulation, front, pretence, smoke screen, whitewash.

covet *v* crave, desire, envy, fancy, hanker for, long for, lust after, thirst for, want, yearn for, yen for.

antonym abjure.

covetous *adj* acquisitive, avaricious, close-fisted, envious, grasping, greedy, insatiable, jealous, rapacious, thirsting, yearning.

antonyms content, generous, satisfied, temperate.

covey *n* band, bevy, brood, clump, cluster, clutch, drove, flight, flock, gaggle, group, handful, knot, skein.

cow *v* awe, break, browbeat, bulldoze, bully, daunt, dishearten, dismay, dominate, domineer over, frighten, intimidate, overawe, scare, subdue, terrorize, unnerve.

antonyms embolden, encourage.

coward *n* caitiff, chicken, craven, dastard, faint-heart, lowlife, poltroon, recreant, renegade, scaredy-cat, skulker, sneak, wretch, yellow-belly.

antonym hero.

cowardice *n* chicken-heartedness, faint-heartedness, fear, gutlessness, pusillanimity, recreancy, spinelessness, timorousness.

antonyms courage, valour.

cowardly *adj* base, caitiff, chicken, chicken-hearted, chicken-livered, craven, dastardly, faint-hearted, fearful, gutless, lily-livered, low, low-down, mean, pusillanimous, recreant, scared, shrinking, soft, spineless, timorous, unheroic, weak, weak-kneed, white-livered, yellow, yellow-bellied.

antonyms courageous, plucky, stout-hearted.

cowboy *n* broncobuster, buckaroo, cattleman, cowgirl, cowhand, cowpoke, cowpuncher, drover, gaucho, herder, herdsman, rancher, ranchero, rodeo rider, roughrider, stockman, vaquero, wrangler.

cower *v* cringe, crouch, flinch, grovel, huddle, quail, quake in one's boots, recoil, shake, shiver, shrink, skulk, tremble.

coy *adj* arch, backward, bashful, coquettish, demure, diffident, evasive, flirtatious, kittenish, maidenly, modest, prudish, reserved, retiring, self-effacing, shrinking, shy, skittish, timid, virginal.

antonyms forward, impudent, sober.

cozen *v* bamboozle, beguile, bilk, cheat, circumvent, con, deceive, defraud, diddle, do, double-cross, dupe, finagle, gull, hoodwink, hornswoggle, inveigle, sweet-talk, swindle, trick.

crabby *adj* acid, acrid, acrimonious, bad-tempered, captious, churlish, crabbed, cranky, cross, cross-grained, crotchety, difficult, fretful, grouchy, harsh, ill-humoured, ill-tempered, irascible, irritable, misanthropic, morose, peevish, petulant, prickly, snappish, snappy, sour, splenetic, surly, tart, testy.

antonyms good-natured, sweet-tempered.

crack *v* break, break into, burst, chap, chip, chop, cleave, collapse, crackle, craze, decipher, detonate, explode, falter, fathom, fracture, give in, give way, jimmy, penetrate, pop, rive, rupture, snap, spring, spring a leak, solve, splinter, split, succumb, waver, yield.

n attempt, blow, breach, break, burst, chink, chip, clap, cleft, clip, cranny, crevasse, crevice, dig, expert, explosion, fissure, flaw, fracture, gag, gap, instant, interstice, jab, jibe, joke, line, moment, pop, quip, remark, report, retort, rift, slap, smack, snap, stab, try, whack, wisecrack, witticism.

adj ace, brilliant, choice, elite, excellent, expert, first-class, first-rate, hand-picked, masterly, outstanding, star, superior, top-notch.

crack down on act against, check, clamp down on, come down hard on, end, get tough on, lower the boom on, put a stop to, put the kibosh on, stop, take stiff (or stern) measures against, toughen up on.

crack up break down, collapse, fall apart, go crackers, go crazy, go nuts, go round the bend, go to pieces, lose it, snap.

crackdown *n* campaign, clampdown, crushing, end, get-tough, repression, stop, suppression.

cracked *adj* bats, batty, broken, chipped, crackbrained, crackers, crackpot, crazed, crazy, daft, damaged, defective, deranged, eccentric, faltering, faulty, fissured, flawed, fractured, grating, imperfect, insane, loony, nuts, nutty, off one's rocker, one brick short of a load, out of one's mind, rent, riven, ruptured, split, sprung, torn, uneven.

antonyms flawless, perfect, sane.

crackle *v* crepitate, decrepitate, pop, rustle, snap.

n crepitation, crepitus, decrepitation, rustle.

crackpot *n* crackbrain, crazy, eccentric, flake, fruitcake, idiot, loon, nut.

cradle *n* babyhood, bassinet, bed, beginning(s), berceau, birthplace, crib, frame, holder, incubator, incunabula, infancy, origin, rest, stand.

v bear, couch, hold, lay, lull, nestle, nurse, rock, shelter, support, tend.

craft¹ *n* aircraft, barque, boat, plane, spacecraft, spaceship, vessel.

craft² *n* ability, art, artfulness, artifice, artisanship, artistry, business, calling, cleverness, contrivance, craftiness, cunning, deceit, dexterity, duplicity, employment, expertise, expertness, guile, hand(i)craft, hand(i)work, ingenuity, line, occupation, pursuit, scheming, ship, shrewdness, skill, stratagem, subterfuge, subtlety, technique, trade, trickery, vocation, wiles, wiliness, vulpinism, work, workmanship.

antonyms artlessness, bungling, clumsiness.

craftsman *n* artificer, artisan, maker, master, smith, technician, wright.

craftsmanship *n* artisanship, artistry, expertise, facture, mastery, skill, technique, workmanship.

crafty *adj* artful, astute, calculating, canny, cunning, deceitful, designing, devious, duplicitous, foxy, fraudulent, guileful, insidious, knowing, Machiavellian, scheming, sharp, shrewd, sly, subtle, tricksy, tricky, vulpine, wily.

antonyms artless, innocent, straightforward.

crag *n* aiguille, bluff, cliff, peak, pinnacle, rock, tor.

craggy *adj* cragged, hard, jagged, rocky, rough, rugged, stony, uneven.

antonyms rolling, smooth.

cram *v* compact, compress, crowd, crush, feed one's face, fill, force, glut, gorge, gormandize, grind, hit the books, jam, overcrowd, overeat, overfeed, overfill, pack, press, ram, satiate, shove, squeeze, study, stuff.

cramp[1] *v* check, circumscribe, confine, constrain, frustrate, hamper, hamstring, handicap, hinder, impede, inhibit, limit, restrict, shackle, squeeze, stymie, thwart, tie.

cramp[2] *n* ache, charley horse, contraction, convulsion, crick, muscle fatigue, pain, pang, pins and needles, spasm, stiffness, stitch, twinge.

cramped *adj* awkward, circumscribed, claustrophobic, close, confined, confining, incapacious, narrow, restricted, small, squished, squeezed, tight, uncomfortable.

antonym roomy, spacious.

crank *n* eccentric, grouch, grump, loon, madman, nut, weirdo.

cranky *adj* bad-tempered, bizarre, capricious, crabby, cross, crotchety, eccentric, erratic, freakish, freaky, fretful, funny, fussy, grouchy, idiosyncratic, ill-humoured, ill-natured, irritable, odd, peculiar, peevish, petulant, prickly, queer, quirky, sour, splenetic, strange, surly, tart, unreliable, wacky.

antonyms cheerful, happy, normal, sensible.

cranny *n* chink, cleavage, cleft, crack, crevice, fissure, gap, hole, interstice, nook, opening.

crap *n* baloney, bull, bunk, bunkum, claptrap, crud, dirt, eyewash, falderal, garbage, grunge, hogwash, malarkey, nonsense, rot, rubbish, tommyrot, tripe, twaddle.

crash *n* accident, bang, bankruptcy, boom, breakdown, bump, clang, clash, clatter, clattering, collapse, collision, debacle, depression, din, downfall, failure, impact, jar, jolt, noise, pile-up, racket, slamming, smash, smashing, smash-up, wreck.

v bang, bomb, break, break down, bump,

burst, clang, clash, collapse, collide, dash, fail, fall, flop, fold (up), go bust, go under, hang, hurtle, intrude (on), lurch, miscarry, overbalance, pass out, pitch, plunge, run afoul, shatter, shiver, slam, sleep, smash, sprawl, surge, topple.

adj compressed, concentrated, emergency, fast-paced, immediate, intensive, round-the-clock, telescoped, urgent.

crass *adj* boorish, bovine, cheap, coarse, crude, gross, in bad taste, indelicate, inelegant, insensitive, lumpish, oafish, rude, sleazy, tacky, tactless, tawdry, unrefined, unsubtle, vulgar.

antonyms classy, refined, sensitive, tasteful.

crater *n* basin, cavity, chasm, cirque, depression, hole, hollow, pit, pothole.

crave *v* ask, be dying for, beg, beseech, cry out for, desire, fancy, hanker after, hunger after, long for, need, pine for, require, seek, solicit, thirst for, want, yearn for, yen for.

antonyms dislike, spurn.

craven *adj* base, caitiff, chicken-hearted, chicken-livered, cowardly, dastardly, faint-hearted, fearful, gutless, lily-livered, low, mean-spirited, pusillanimous, recreant, scared, spiritless, timorous, unheroic, weak, yellow, yellow-bellied.

antonym courageous.

n caitiff, coward, dastard, poltroon, recreant, skulker, yellow-belly.

antonym hero.

craving *n* appetence, appetite, desire, hankering, hunger, longing, lust, need, thirst, urge, yearning, yen.

antonyms dislike, distaste.

craw *n* crop, esophagus, gizzard, gullet, maw, throat.

crawl *v* creep, cringe, drag, eat crow, eat dirt, eat humble pie, fawn, go on all fours, go on hands and knees, grovel, inch, slither, swarm, teem, toady, truckle, wriggle, writhe.

craze *n* cult, dernier cri, enthusiasm, fad, fanaticism, fashion, frenzy, infatuation, mania, novelty, obsession, passion, preoccupation, rage, thing, trend, vogue.

v bewilder, confuse, dement, derange, distemper, distract, enrage, infatuate, inflame, madden, unbalance, unhinge.

crazed *adj* beside oneself, demented, distracted, hysterical, maddened, maenadic, possessed, wild.

antonym sane.

crazy *adj* absurd, bananas, barmy, bats, batty, berserk, beyond the pale, birdbrained, bizarre, bonkers, cockeyed, cracked, crazed, cuckoo, daffy, daft, delirious, demented, deranged, devoted, dippy, eager, eccentric, enamoured, enthusiastic, fanatical, fantastic, far out, foolhardy, foolish, half-baked, hysterical, ill-conceived, impracticable, imprudent, infatuated, insane, irrational, irresponsible, ludicrous, lunatic, loco, loony, mad, maniacal, nonsensical, nuts, nutty, odd, off one's rocker, outrageous, passionate, pixilated, potty, preposterous, quixotic, ridiculous, senseless, short-sighted, silly, smitten, strange, touched, unbalanced, unhinged, unreasonable, unwise, unworkable, up the wall, wacky, way out, weird, wild, zany, zealous.

antonyms sane, sensible.

go crazy crack up, go bananas, go batty, go beserk, go bonkers, go mad, go nuts, go off the deep end, go off the rails, go round the bend, go wild, lose it, lose one's head, lose one's marbles, lose one's mind, run amuck.

creaky *adj* creaking, croaky, grating, rasping, raspy, rusty, scratchy, squeaking, squeaky, unoiled.

cream *n* best, cosmetic, crème de la crème, elite, emulsion, flower, liniment, lotion, oil, ointment, paste, pick, salve, sauce, unguent.

creamy *adj* buttery, cream-coloured, creamed, lush, milky, off-white, oily, rich, smooth, soft, unctuous, velvety.

crease *v* corrugate, crimp, crinkle, crumple, fold, pucker, ridge, ruck, ruckle, rumple, wrinkle.

n corrugation, crumple, fold, goal, groove, line, overlap, pucker, ridge, ruck, ruckle, rumple, tuck, wrinkle.

create *v* appoint, author, beget, bring about, build, cause, coin, compose, concoct, constitute, construct, design, develop, devise, effect, engender, establish, fabricate, form, formulate, foster, found, generate, give rise to, hatch, initiate, install, institute, invent, invest as, make, occasion, originate, produce, set up, sire, spawn.

antonym destroy.

creation *n* achievement, appointment, brainchild, chef d'oeuvre, coining, composition, concoction, constitution, construction, cosmos, development, establishment, fabrication, fathering, formation, fostering, foundation, generation, genesis, handiwork, inception, institution, invention, magnum opus, making, nature, origination, pièce de résistance, procreation, production, siring, spawning, universe, world.

antonym destruction.

creative *adj* artistic, clever, fecund, fertile, gifted, imaginative, ingenious, inspired, inventive, original, productive, resourceful, stimulating, talented, unique, visionary.

antonym unimaginative.

creator *n* architect, auteur, author, begetter, builder, demiurge, designer, father, First Cause, framer, God, initiator, inventor, maker, originator, producer, Supreme Being.

creature *n* animal, beast, being, body, brute, bug, character, critter, dependant, fellow, hanger-on, henchman, hireling, individual, instrument, lackey, man, minion, mortal, person, puppet, soul, toady, tool, woman, wretch.

credence *n* belief, confidence, credit, dependence, endorsement, faith, recommendation, reliance, support, trust.

antonym distrust.

credentials *n* accreditation, attestation, authorization, background, card, certificate, deed, diploma, documents, endorsement, ID, identification, letters of credence, licence, passport, permit, qualifications, recommendation, references, testimonials, title, voucher, warrant.

credibility *n* believableness, clout, integrity, likeliness, plausibility, probability, realism, reliability, reputation, respectability, solid, tenability, trustworthiness.

antonym implausibility.

credible *adj* believable, conceivable, convincing, dependable, honest, imaginable, likely, persuasive, plausible, possible, probable, realistic, reasonable, reliable, respectable, rock-solid, sincere, supposable, tenable, thinkable, trustworthy, trusty.

antonyms implausible, unreliable.

▲ *confusable word* creditable.

credit *n* acclaim, acknowledgment, approval, belief, character, commendation, confidence, credence, distinction, esteem, faith, fame, glory, honour, kudos, loan, praise, recognition, reliance, reputation, repute, standing, status, thanks, tribute, trust.

antonyms dishonour, low reputation, shame.

v accept, acknowledge, add, ascribe, attribute, believe, buy, chalk up to, recognize, subscribe to, swallow, take seriously, take to heart, trust.

antonym disbelieve.

creditable *adj* admirable, commendable, estimable, excellent, exemplary, good, honourable, laudable, meritorious, praiseworthy, reputable, respectable, sterling, worthy.

antonyms blameworthy, shameful.

▲ *confusable word* credible.

credulity *n* credulousness, dupability, gullibility, naïveté, simplicity, stupidity, trustfulness.

antonym scepticism.

credulous *adj* dupable, gullible, naïve, trusting, uncritical, unsuspecting, unsuspicious, wide-eyed.

antonym sceptical.

creed *n* articles of faith, belief, belief system, canon, catechism, confession, credo, doctrine, dogma, faith, persuasion, principles, tenets, theological summation.

creek *n* bay, bight, brook, cove, fiord, firth, inlet, rivulet, stream, streamlet, tributary, watercourse.

creep *v* cower, crawl, dawdle, drag, edge, grovel, inch, insinuate oneself, kowtow, ride (up), shiver, shudder, skulk, slink, slip, slither, sneak, steal, tiptoe, worm, wriggle.

n jerk, lowlife, pervert, sleaze, slimeball, sneak, undesirable, weirdo.

creepy *adj* disgusting, disturbing, eerie, frightening, ghoulish, gruesome, hair-raising, horrible, macabre, menacing, nightmarish, ominous, repugnant, repulsive, scary, sinister, spooky, terrifying, threatening, unearthly, unpleasant, weird.

antonyms normal, pleasant.

crescent-shaped *adj* bow-shaped, falcate, falciform, lunate, sickle-shaped.

crest *n* aigrette, apex, badge, caruncle, coat of arms, cockscomb, comb, crown, device, emblem, head, height, insignia, mane, panache, peak, pinnacle, plume, ridge, summit, symbol, top, topknot, tuft.

crestfallen *adj* chagrined, chapfallen, dejected, depressed, despondent, disappointed, disconsolate, discouraged, disheartened, dispirited, downcast, downhearted, woebegone.

antonym elated.

cretin *n* dimwit, dunce, fool, half-wit, idiot, imbecile, moron, simpleton.

crevasse *n* abyss, bergschrund, chasm, cleavage, cleft, crack, fissure, gap, rent, rift.

crevice *n* chink, cleavage, cleft, crack, cranny, fissure, fold, fracture, gap, groove, hole, interstice, opening, rift, slit, split.

crew *n* assemblage, attendants, band, brigade, bunch, company, complement, contingent, corps, crowd, gang, hands, henchmen, herd, horde, lot, lower deck, mob, pack, party, posse, set, squad, staff, swarm, team, troop.

crib *n* bassinet, bed, bin, borrowing, box, bunker, cheat sheet, cradle, cribbing, framework, key, manger, plagiarism, rack, raft, scaffolding, stall, translation.

v borrow, cheat, copy, pinch, pirate, plagiarize, purloin, steal.

crick *n* cramp, pain, spasm, stiffness, subluxation, twinge.

v jar, sprain, twist, wrench.

crime *n* atrocity, corruption, delinquency, fault, felony, flagitiousness, guilt, illegality, iniquity, injustice, law-breaking, malefaction, malfeasance, misconduct, misdeed, misdemeanour, offence, outrage, scandal, sin, transgression, trespass, unrighteousness, vice, villainy, violation, wickedness, wrong, wrongdoing.

criminal *n* bad guy, con, convict, crook, culprit, delinquent, evildoer, felon, jail-bird, lawbreaker, malefactor, offender, sinner, thug, transgressor, villain.

adj bent, corrupt, crooked, culpable, deplorable, felonious, flagitious, illegal, immoral, indictable, iniquitous, lawless, malfeasant, nefarious, outrageous, peccant, preposterous, scandalous, unconscionable, unjust, unlawful, unrighteous, vicious, villainous, wicked, wrong.

antonyms honest, upright.

cringe *v* bend, blench, bootlick, bow, cower, crawl, creep, crouch, dodge, duck, fawn, flinch, grovel, kowtow, quail, quiver, recoil, shrink, shy, startback, stoop, toady, tremble, truckle, wince.

crinkle *n* curl, fold, pucker, ruffle, rumple, rustle, twist, wave, wrinkle.

v crackle, crease, crimp, crimple, crumple, curl, fold, pucker, ruffle, rumple, rustle, twist, wrinkle.

crinkly *adj* crackly, creased, curly, frizzy, gathered, kinky, puckered, ruffled, rumpled, wrinkled, wrinkly.

antonyms smooth, straight.

cripple *v* damage, debilitate, disable, enfeeble, hamstring, handicap, hinder, hobble, impair, incapacitate, lame, maim, paralyse, ruin, sabotage, spoil, vitiate, weaken.

crippled *adj* deformed, disabled, halt, handicapped, incapacitated, invalid, lame, maimed, paralysed, paraplegic.

crisis *n* calamity, catastrophe, climacteric, climax, confrontation, conjuncture, crossroads, crunch, crux, culmination, difficulty, dilemma, disaster, emergency, exigency, extremity, head, height, impasse, mess, moment of decision, pinch, plight, predicament, quandary, strait, trouble, turning point.

crisp *adj* bracing, brand-new, brief, brisk, brittle, brusque, clear, concise, cool, crispy, crunchy, decisive, firm, forthright, fresh, incisive, invigorating, lively, neat, newly pressed, nippy, pithy, refreshing, short, smart, snappy, succinct, tart, terse.

antonyms crumbly, flabby, limp, vague.

criterion *n* benchmark, canon, diagnostic, gauge, measure, norm, precedent, principle, proof, rule, shibboleth, standard, test, touchstone, yardstick.

critic *n* analyst, animadverter, appraiser, arbiter, attacker, authority, carper, caviller, censor, censurer, commentator, connoisseur, detractor, evaluator, expert, expositor, faultfinder, judge, Momus, nit-picker, pundit, reviewer, reviler, vilifier.

critical[1] *adj* analytical, appraising, captious, carping, cavilling, censorious, derogatory, diagnostic, disapproving, discerning, discriminating, disparaging, evaluative, fastidious, faultfinding, judgmental, judicious, nagging, negative, niggling, nit-picking, penetrating, perceptive, picky, pressing, serious, sharp-tongued, uncomplimentary, urgent, vital.

antonyms uncritical.

critical[2] *adj* all-important, climacteric, crucial, dangerous, deciding, decisive, determining, essential, grave, high-priority, imperative, key, momentous, perilous, pivotal, precarious, pressing, serious, urgent, vital.

criticize *v* analyse, animadvert, appraise, bad-mouth, blame, carp, cavil at, censure, condemn, crab, critique, decry, disapprove, disparage, evaluate, excoriate, find fault (with), give someone what for, judge, knock, nag, nit-pick, pan, put down, review, roast, scarify, slam, slash, slate, snipe, tear apart.

antonym praise.

criticism *n* analysis, animadversion, appraisal, appreciation, blame, brickbat, cavil(ling), censure, comment, commentary, condemnation, critique, disapproval, disparagement, dissection, evaluation, faultfinding, flak, jab, judgment, knocking, panning, rap, review, slating, static, stricture, thrust.

antonym praise.

critique *n* analysis, appraisal, assessment, commentary, essay, evaluation, examination, review.

croak *v* caw, die, expire, gasp, groan, grumble, grunt, kick the bucket, moan, pass away, perish, snuff it, squawk, wheeze.

crony *n* accomplice, ally, associate, buddy, chum, colleague, companion, comrade, confederate, follower, friend, henchman, mate, pal, sidekick.

crook *n* cheat, criminal, defrauder, fraud, knave, racketeer, robber, rogue, shark, shyster, swindler, thief, villain.

crooked[1] *adj* bent, corrupt, crafty, criminal, deceitful, discreditable, dishonest, dishonourable, dubious, fraudulent, illegal, knavish, questionable, shady, shifty, treacherous, underhand, unethical, unlawful, unprincipled, unscrupulous.

antonym honest.

crooked[2] *adj* angled, askew, asquint, asymmetrical, awry, bent, bowed, crippled, curved, deformed, disfigured, distorted, hooked, irregular, lopsided, meandering, misaligned, misshapen, off-centre, out of alignment, skew(ed), slanted, slanting, tilted, tortuous, twisted, twisting, uneven, warped, winding, zigzag.

antonym straight.

crop[1] *n* fruits, gathering, generation, growth, harvest, ingathering, produce, vintage, yield.

v browse, clip, curtail, cut, dock, graze, lop, mow, nibble, pick, prune, reduce, shear, shingle, shorten, snip, top, trim.

crop up appear, arise, arrive, emerge, happen, occur, pop up, show up, spring up, surface.

crop[2] *n* craw, esophagus, gizzard, gullet, maw, throat.

cross *adj* angry, annoyed, cantankerous, captious, contrary, crabby, cranky, crosswise, crotchety, crusty, decussate, disagreeable, displeased, fractious, fretful, grouchy, grumpy, hybrid, ill-humoured, ill-tempered, impatient, interchanged, intersecting, irascible, irritable, mad, opposing, opposite, out of sorts, peeved, peevish, perpendicular, petulant, querulous, reciprocal, short, snappish, splenetic, sulky, sullen, testy, transverse, unfavourable, vexed, waspish.

antonyms calm, cheerful, placid, pleasant.

v annoy, bestride, blend, block, bridge, cancel, crisscross, crossbreed, cross-fertilize, cross-pollinate, deny, foil, ford, frustrate, hinder, hybridize, interbreed, intercross, interfere with, intersect, intertwine, lace, meet, mix, mongrelize, obstruct, oppose, resist, span, strike, stroke, thwart, traverse.

n affliction, amalgam, ankh, blend, burden, Calvary, combination, crossbreed, crossing, crossroads, crucifix, grief, Holy Rood, hybrid, hybridization, intersection, load, misfortune, mixture, mongrel, rood, thorn (in the flesh or side), trial, tribulation, trouble, woe.

cross swords argue, bicker, dispute, feud,

fight, quarrel, spar, take issue, wrangle.

cross-examine *v* catechize, give (someone) the third degree, grill, interrogate, pump, question, quiz.

crosspatch *n* bear, crank, curmudgeon, grouch, grump, killjoy, scold, shrew, sorehead, sourpuss.

cross-question *v* cross-examine, debrief, examine, grill, quiz, test.

crosswise *adv* across, aslant, athwart, crisscross, crossways, diagonally, over, perpendicularly, sideways, transversely.

crotchety *adj* bad-tempered, cantankerous, contrary, crabby, cranky, cross, crusty, curmudgeonly, difficult, disagreeable, fractious, grouchy, grumpy, ill-humoured, ill-tempered, irascible, irritable, obstreperous, peevish, prickly, snappish, surly, testy.

antonyms calm, placid, pleasant.

crouch *v* bend, bow, cower, cringe, duck, hunch, kneel, squat, stoop.

crow *v* bluster, boast, brag, coo, exult, flourish, gloat, prate, rejoice, triumph, vaunt.

crowd *n* army, assembly, audience, bunch, caboodle, circle, clique, company, concourse, flock, full house, gate, group, herd, hoi polloi, horde, host, lot, many-headed beast (or monster), mass, masses, mob, multitude, pack, people, plebs, populace, press, proletariat, public, rabble, riffraff, ruck, set, spectators, swarm, the many, throng, troupe.

v bundle, clog, cluster, clutter, compress, congest, congregate, cram, cramp, elbow, fill, flock, forgather, gather, huddle, interfere with, jostle, mass, mob, overfill, overpopulate, pack, pile, press, push, shove, squeeze, stream, surge, swarm, throng.

crowded *adj* busy, clogged, cluttered, congested, crammed, cramped, filled, full, huddled, jammed, jam-packed, mobbed, overflowing, packed, populous, swarming, teeming, thronged, tight.

antonym empty.

crown *n* acme, apex, bays, blue ribbon, cap, chaplet, circlet, consummation, coronal, coronet, crest, diadem, forehead, garland, governor general, head, highest distinction, high point, honour(s), king, kudos, laurels, laurel wreath, monarch, monarchy, pate, perfection, pinnacle, prize, queen, reward, royalty, ruler, skull, sovereign, sovereignty, summit, throne, tiara, tip, top, trophy, ultimate, zenith.

v adorn, biff, box, cap, clout, complete, consummate, cuff, dignify, enthrone, finish, fulfil, honour, install, perfect, punch, reward, round off, surmount, top, top off, wreathe.

crowning *adj* climactic, consummate, culminating, final, finishing, paramount, sovereign, supreme, top, ultimate, unmatched, unsurpassed.

n coronation, enthronement, installation.

crucial *adj* central, critical, decisive, essential, important, key, momentous, pivotal, pressing, urgent, vital.

antonym unimportant.

crucify *v* attack, blame, burn at the stake, criticize, excoriate, execute, harrow, have for lunch, lampoon, mock, pan, persecute, punish, rack, ridicule, savage, scapegoat, slam, torment, torture, vilify.

crude *adj* amateurish, bawdy, blue, boorish, clumsy, coarse, crass, dirty, graceless, gross, immature, inartistic, indecent, lewd, makeshift, natural, obscene, outline, primitive, raw, rough, rough-hewn, rude, rudimentary, sketchy, smutty, tactless, tasteless, unanalysed, uncouth, undeveloped, undigested, unfinished, unformed, unpolished, unprepared, unprocessed, unrefined, unsubtle, vulgar.
antonyms finished, polite, refined, tasteful.

crudity *n* bawdiness, clumsiness, coarseness, crassness, crudeness, impropriety, indecency, indelicacy, lewdness, loudness, obscenity, offensiveness, primitiveness, roughness, rudeness, smuttiness, tactlessness, tastelessness, vulgarity.
antonyms polish, politeness, tastefulness.

cruel *adj* atrocious, barbarous, barberic, bitter, bloodthirsty, brutal, brutish, butcherly, callous, cold-blooded, compassionless, cutting, depraved, excruciating, fell, ferocious, fierce, flinty, grim, hard, hard-hearted, harsh, heartless, hellish, hurtful, implacable, inclement, inexorable, inhuman, inhumane, malevolent, marble-breasted, mean, merciless, monstrous, murderous, painful, pitiless, ravening, raw, relentless, remorseless, ruthless, sadistic, savage, severe, spiteful, stony-hearted, unfeeling, ungentle, unkind, unmerciful, unnatural, unrelenting, unsparing, vengeful, vicious.
antonyms compassionate, kind, merciful.

cruelty *n* atrocity, barbarity, bestiality, bloodthirstiness, brutalism, brutality, brutishness, callousness, compassionlessness, depravity, ferocity, fiendishness, hard-heartedness, harshness, heartlessness, hurtfulness, inhumanity, mercilessness, murderousness, pitilessness, ruthlessness, sadism, savagery, severity, spite, spitefulness, tyranny, ungentleness, unkindness, vengefulness, venom, viciousness.
antonyms compassion, kindness, mercy.

crumb *n* atom, bit, grain, hint, iota, jot, mite, morsel, particle, scrap, shred, sliver, snippet, soupçon, speck, suggestion.

crumble *v* break down, break up, collapse, comminute, crush, decay, decompose, degenerate, deteriorate, disintegrate, fall down (or apart), fragment, granulate, grind, moulder, perish, powder, pulverize, triturate.

crumbly *adj* decaying, friable, powdery, short, weak.

crummy *adj* cheap, contemptible, crappy, dirty, grotty, inferior, low-down, miserable, pathetic, poor, rotten, second-rate, shabby, shoddy, third-rate, trashy, useless, weak, worthless.
antonym excellent.

crumple *v* collapse, crease, crush, fall, pucker, rumple, scrunch, wrinkle.

crunch *v* chomp, grind, masticate, munch.
n crisis, emergency, pinch, shortage, squeeze, test.

crusade *n* battle, campaign, cause, drive, expedition, holy war, jihad, movement, offensive, push, revival, struggle, undertaking, war.
v battle, campaign, carry the torch, fight, lobby, preach, push, speak out.

crusader *n* activist, advocate, campaigner, champion, enthusiast, fighter, lobbyist, missionary, reformer, soldier, torchbearer, zealot.

crush *v* abash, break, bruise, chagrin, comminute, compress, conquer, contuse, crease, crumble, crumple, crunch, disappoint, embrace, enfold, extinguish, flatten, grind (down), hug, humiliate, hurt, mangle, mash, mortify, oppress, overcome, overpower, overwhelm, pound, press, pulverize, quash, quell, rumple, smash, squash, squeeze, squelch, steam-roller, stomp on, subdue, trample, triturate, vanquish, wound, wrinkle.
n check, crowd, huddle, infatuation, jam, press, pressure, puppy love, stampede, the hots.

crust *n* caking, coat, coating, concretion, covering, exterior, gall, heel, impertinence, incrustation, nerve, (outer) layer, outside, rind, scab, shell, surface.

crusty *adj* brittle, brusque, cantankerous, captious, choleric, crabbed, crabby, crisp, crispy, cross, curt, firm, friable, grouchy, gruff, hard, ill-humoured, irritable, peevish, short, short-tempered, snappish, splenetic, surly, testy, touchy.
antonyms calm, pleasant, soft, soggy.

crux *n* central point, core, essence, heart, main issue, nub, vexed question.

cry *v* advertise, announce, bark, bawl, beg, bellow, beseech, bewail, blubber, boohoo, broadcast, bruit, call, caterwaul, clamour, ejaculate, entreat, exclaim, halloo, hawk, holler, howl, implore, keen, lament, mewl, meow, noise, plead, pray, proclaim, roar, scream, screech, shout, shriek, snivel, sob, squall, squeal, trumpet, vociferate, wail, weep, whimper, whine, whoop, yell, yowl.
n announcement, appeal, battle cry, bawl, bellow, blubbering, call, caterwaul, ejaculation, entreaty, exclamation, holler, hoot, howl, keening, lament, lamentation, meow, outcry, petition, plaint, plea, prayer, proclamation, report, roar, rumour, scream, screech, shriek, slogan, snivelling, sobbing, squall, squawk, squeal, supplication, utterance, wail, watchword, weeping, whoop, yell, yelp, yoohoo.

crybaby *n* baby, fusspot, milquetoast, sissy, softy, suck, whiner, wimp.

cryptic *adj* abstruse, ambiguous, apocryphal, arcane, cabalistic, dark, Delphic, enigmatic, esoteric, hidden, mysterious, obscure, occult, oracular, perplexing, puzzling, recondite, secret, strange, veiled.
antonyms clear, obvious, straightforward.

crystallize *v* coalesce, emerge, form, harden, jell, materialize, resolve itself, solidify, take shape.

cub *n* babe, beginner, fledgling, greenhorn, kid, lad, learner, novice, offspring, pup, puppy, recruit, tenderfoot, trainee, whelp, whippersnapper, young, youngster, youth.
antonym adult.

cubbyhole *n* carrel, cell, compartment, cubicle, den, hideaway, hole, niche, pigeonhole, recess, slot.

cubicle *n* booth, box, carrel, cell, compartment, stall.

cuddle *v* canoodle, clasp, cosset, dandle, embrace, fondle, hug, nestle, pet, snuggle.

cuddly *adj* affectionate, cosy, cuddlesome, huggable, lovable, soft, warm.

cudgel *n* bastinado, baton, bludgeon, club, shillelagh, stick, truncheon.
v bang, bash, baste, bastinado, batter, beat, bludgeon, clobber, club, drub, maul, pound, pummel, thump, thwack, whack.

cue *n* catchword, feed line, hint, incentive, key, nod, prompt(ing), reminder, sign, signal, stimulus, suggestion.

cuff *v* bash, bat, beat, belt, box, clobber, clout, knock, pummel, punch, slap, smack, strike, swat, thump, whack.
n belt, blow, box, clout, knock, punch, rap, slap, smack, swat, thump, whack.

cull *v* choose, collect, decimate, downsize, gather, glean, pick, pick out, pluck, reduce, select, sift, thin, winnow.

culminate *v* climax, close, conclude, consummate, end (up), finish, peak, terminate.
antonyms begin, start.

culmination *n* acme, apex, apogee, climax, completion, conclusion, consummation, crown, finale, height, meridian, peak, perfection, pinnacle, summit, top, zenith.
antonyms beginning, start.

culpable *adj* answerable, at fault, blamable, blameworthy, censurable, chargeable, guilty, (in the) wrong, liable, offending, peccant, reprehensible, responsible, sinful, to blame.
antonyms blameless, innocent.

culprit *n* criminal, delinquent, evildoer, felon, guilty party, lawbreaker, malefactor, miscreant, offender, rascal, sinner, transgressor, wrongdoer.

cult *n* admiration, believers, craze, denomination, devotees, devotion, faith, following, group, idolization, religion, religious body, reverence, sect, veneration, worship.

cultivate *v* advance, ameliorate, better, broaden, civilize, court, culture, deepen, develop, dig (up), discipline, educate, elevate, encourage, enrich, farm, fertilize, forward, foster, further, grow, improve, patronize, plant, plough, polish, prepare, promote, pursue, raise, refine, school, support, tend, till, train, work (at).
antonym neglect.

cultivation *n* advancement, advocacy, agronomy, breeding, care, civility, civilization, culture, development, discrimination, education, encouragement, enhancement, enlightenment, farming, fostering, furtherance, gardening, gentility, husbandry, learning, letters, manners, nurture, patronage, planting, ploughing, polish, promotion, pursuit, refinement, schooling, support, taste, tillage, tilling, tilth, work(ing).

cultural *adj* aesthetic, artistic, art(s)y, broadening, customary, enriching, ethnic, human, learned, liberal, social, societal.

culture *n* accomplishment, aesthetics, agriculture, agronomy, arts, breeding, civilization, cultivation, customs, education, enlightenment, ethnic group, ethos, fine arts, gentility, heritage, husbandry, Kultur, lifestyle, mores, national character, polish, politeness, refinement, social norms, society, sophistication, taste, urbanity, value system.

cultured *adj* accomplished, advanced, aesthetic, art(s)y, civilized, educated, enlightened, genteel, highbrow, polished, refined, urbane, well-bred, well-read.
antonyms ignorant, uncultured.

culvert *n* channel, conduit, ditch, drain, drainpipe, gutter, sewer, watercourse.

cumbersome *adj* awkward, bulky, burdensome, clumsy, cumbrous, heavy, hefty, incommodious, inconvenient, inefficent, inelegant, onerous, oppressive, unhandy, unmanageable, unwieldy.
antonyms convenient, manageable.

cumulative *adj* accumulative, additive, aggregate, building, collective, combined, compound(ed), growing, increasing, linear, progressive.

cunning *adj* adroit, artful, astute, canny, clever, crafty, deep, deft, devious, dexterous, foxy, guileful, imaginative, ingenious, knowing, Machiavellian, rusé, sharp, shifty, shrewd, skilful, sly, sneaky, subtle, tricky, vulpine, wily.
antonyms gullible, naïve.
n ability, adroitness, art, artfulness, artifice, astuteness, cleverness, craft, craftiness, deceitfulness, deftness, deviousness, dexterity, finesse, foxiness, guile, ingenuity, shrewdness, skill, slyness, subtlety, trickery, vulpinism, wiliness.
antonyms openness, simplicity.

cup *n* beaker, cannikin, chalice, cupel, cupful, cupule, demitasse, dish, draft, drink, goblet, mug, potion, tankard, tazza, teacup, trophy.

cupboard *n* almirah, armoire, cabinet, closet, locker, pantry, press, tack box.

cupidity *n* acquisitiveness, avarice, avidity, covetousness, desire, eagerness, graspingness, greed, greediness, hankering, hunger, itch(ing), longing, rapaciousness, rapacity, voracity, yearning.

cur *n* blackguard, canine, coward, dastard, good-for-nothing, heel, hound, mongrel, mutt, rat, rotter, scoundrel, stray, swine, villain, wretch.

curative *adj* alleviative, corrective, febrifugal, healing, healthful, health-giving, medicinal, remedial, restorative, salutary, therapeutic, tonic, vulnerary.

curb *v* bit, bridle, check, contain, control, curtail, hinder, hold back, inhibit, lessen, moderate, muzzle, pull over, reduce, rein in, repress, restrain, restrict, retard, slow (down), subdue, suppress.
antonyms encourage, foster, goad.
n brake, bridle, check, control, deterrent, limitation, rein, restraint.

curdle *v* clot, coagulate, congeal, ferment, sour, thicken, turn.

cure¹ *v* alleviate, correct, ease, heal, help, mend, rehabilitate, relieve, remedy, restore.
n alleviation, antidote, corrective, detoxicant, healing, medicine, panacea, panpharmacon, recovery, relief, remedy, restorative, solution, specific, treatment, vulnerary.

cure² *v* age, brine, dry, kipper, mature, pickle, preserve, salt, smoke, treat.

curio *n* antique, bibelot, curiosity, knick-knack, object of virtu, relic, souvenir, trinket.

curiosity *n* celebrity, freak, inquisitiveness, interest, nosiness, novelty, oddity, phenomenon, prying, rarity, sight, snooping, spectacle, wonder.

curious *adj* bizarre, eccentric, enquiring, exotic, extraordinary, funny, inquisitive, interested, meddling, mysterious, nosy, novel, odd, peculiar, peeping, peering, prying, puzzled, puzzling, quaint, queer, questioning, rare, singular, snoopy, strange, unconventional, unexpected, unique, unusual.
antonyms incurious, indifferent, normal, ordinary, uninterested.

curl *v* bend, coil, convolute, corkscrew, crimp, crimple, crinkle, crisp, curve, entwine, frizz, loop, meander, ripple, scroll, spiral, turn, twine, twirl, twist, wind, wreathe, writhe.
antonyms flatten, straighten, uncurl.
n coil, curlicue, kink, ring, ringlet, spiral, swirl, tress, twist, whorl, wreath.

curly *adj* corkscrew, crimped, crimpy, crinkly, curled, curling, frizzy, kinky, spiralled, wavy, whorled, winding.
antonyms flat, poker-straight, straight.

currency *n* acceptance, bills, circulation, coinage, coins, commonness, contemporariness, exposure, legal tender, medium of exchange, money, notes, popularity, prevalence, publicity, reign, timeliness, transmission, up-to-dateness, usage, vogue.

current *adj* accepted, circulating, common, contemporary, extant, fashionable, general, in use, ongoing, popular, present, present-day, prevailing, prevalent, reigning, rife, trendy, up-to-date, up-to-the-minute, used, widespread.
antonyms antiquated, old-fashioned.
n course, draft, drift, electricity, flow, jet, juice, mainstream, power, progression, river, stream,

tendency, thermal, tide, trend, undercurrent, undertow, voltage, wind.

curse *n* affliction, anathema, ban, bane, blasphemy, blight, burden, calamity, cross, denunciation, disadvantage, disaster, evil, excommunication, execration, expletive, handicap, hindrance, imprecation, jinx, malediction, misfortune, oath, obscenity, plague, profanity, scourge, spell, swearing, swear-word, trouble, woe.
antonyms advantage, blessing.
v accurse, afflict, anathematize, ban, blaspheme, blight, blow, burden, confound, cuss, damn, denounce, destroy, doom, excommunicate, execrate, fulminate, handicap, imprecate, jinx, plague, scourge, swear, trouble, vex.
antonym bless.

cursed *adj* abominable, accursed, anathematized, bedevilled, bewitched, blasted, blessed, blighted, confounded, damnable, damned, detestable, devilish, doomed, excommunicate, execrable, fell, fey, fiendish, foredoomed, hateful, hexed, ill-fated, infamous, infernal, jinxed, loathsome, odious, pernicious, pestilential, star-crossed, unholy, unsanctified, vile, villainous.

cursory *adj* brief, careless, casual, desultory, fleeting, hasty, hurried, offhand, passing, perfunctory, quick, rapid, slapdash, slight, summary, superficial.
antonyms in-depth, painstaking, thorough.

curt *adj* abrupt, blunt, brief, brusque, gruff, laconic, offhand, rude, sharp, short, short-spoken, snappish, summary, surly, tart, terse, unceremonious, uncivil, ungracious.
antonyms chatty, courteous, voluble.

curtail *v* abbreviate, abridge, chop, circumscribe, curb, cut, cut back (or down or off), decrease, dock, lessen, lop, pare, prune, reduce, restrict, retrench, shorten, trim, truncate.
antonyms extend, lengthen, prolong.

curtain *v* close off, conceal, drape, hide, screen, shield, shroud, shutter, veil.
n arras, backdrop, drapery, hanging, portière, screen, shroud, tapestry, veil.

curtsy *n* bob, bow, genuflection, kowtow, salaam.

curvaceous *adj* bosomy, buxom, comely, curvy, Junoesque, shapely, voluptuous, well-proportioned, well-rounded, well-stacked.

curve *v* arc, arch, bend, bow, coil, decurve, flex, hook, incurvate, incurve, inflect, spiral, swerve, turn, twist, wind.
n arc, bend, camber, curvature, graph, half-moon, incurvation, incurvature, inflexure, loop, trajectory, turn.

curved *adj* arced, arched, arcuate, bent, bowed, crooked, falcate, flexed, humped, incurvate, incurved, inflected, rounded, serpentine, sinuous, spiral, sweeping, turning, twisted, twisting, winding.
antonym straight.

cushion n beanbag, bolster, buffer, fallback, hassock, headrest, pad, pillion, pillow, shock absorber, squab.

v allay, bolster, buttress, cradle, dampen, deaden, lessen, mitigate, muffle, pillow, protect, soften, stifle, support, suppress.

cushy adj comfortable, easy, luxurious, plum, soft, undemanding.

antonyms demanding, rough, Spartan, tough.

custodian n caretaker, castellan, chatelaine, conservator, curator, guardian, janitor, keeper, overseer, protector, sexton, steward, superintendent, warden, warder, watchdog, watchman.

custody n arrest, care, charge, confinement, custodianship, detention, durance, duress, guardianship, holding, imprisonment, incarceration, keeping, observation, possession, preservation, protection, retention, safekeeping, supervision, trusteeship, tutelage, ward, wardship, watch.

custom n business, clientele, consuetude, convention, customers, etiquette, fashion, form, formality, habit, habitude, manner, mode, observance, patronage, policy, practice, praxis, procedure, ritual, routine, rule, style, trade, tradition, usage, use, way, wont.

customary adj accepted, accustomed, acknowledged, common, confirmed, conventional, established, everyday, familiar, fashionable, favourite, general, habitual, normal, ordinary, popular, prevailing, regular, routine, traditional, usual, wonted.

antonyms occasional, rare, unusual.

customer n buyer, client, consumer, habitué, patron, prospect, purchaser, regular, shopper, vendee.

cut v abbreviate, abridge, abscind, avoid, bisect, carve, castrate, chip, chisel, chop, cleave, clip, cold-shoulder, condense, crop, cross, curtail, decrease, delete, dilute, dissect, dissolve, divide, dock, edit (out), engrave, excise, exclude, fell, gash, geld, graze, grieve, hack, harvest, hew, hurt, ignore, incise, indent, insult, interrupt, intersect, lacerate, lop, lower, mow, nick, notch, operate on, pain, pare, part, penetrate, pierce, prune, punch, reap, record, reduce, remove, saw, scissor, score, scrape, sculpt, sculpture, segment, sever, shape, share, shave, shorten, skin, skip, slash, slice, slight, slit, snip, snub, split, spurn, sting, stop, strike, style, sunder, trim, truncate, veer, whittle, wound.

n abscission, barb, blow, carving, chop, commission, cutback, decrease, decrement, diminution, division, economy, engraving, fall, fashion, form, gash, gravure, graze, groove, haircut, incision, indentation, jab, kerf, kickback, laceration, lowering, nick, notch, percentage, piece, portion, rakeoff, rebuff, reduction, saving, scrape, section, share, shortcut, slash, slice, slight, slit, snick, snip, snub, stroke, style, trim, wound.

cut and dried boring, carved in stone, decided, fixed, organized, passionless, planned out, prearranged, predetermined, routine, settled, sewn up. antonyms original, spontaneous, uncertain, up in the air

cut back check, crop, curb, decrease, economize, lessen, lop, lower, prune, reduce, retrench, slash, trim.

cut down abase, chop, decrease, diminish, dispatch, fell, hew, humiliate, kill, lessen, level, lop, lower, massacre, mow (down), raze, reduce, slaughter, slay.

cut in break in, butt in, interject, interpose, interrupt, intervene, intrude.

cut it bear inspection, come up to scratch, cut the cheese, do, make the grade, measure up, pass muster, wash.

cut off abscind, amputate, block (off), chop, disconnect, discontinue, disinherit, disown, end, excise, exscind, halt, intercept, interrupt, intersect, isolate, lop, obstruct, prune, remove, renounce, separate, sever, shut off, stop, suspend, terminate, turn off.

cut out abstain from, cease, debar, delete, depart, die, displace, eliminate, excise, exclude, exsect, extract, give up, oust, remove, shape, stall, stop, supersede, supplant, suppress, take French leave.

cut out (for) adapted, adequate, competent, designed, equipped, fitted, made, meant, qualified, right, suitable, suited.

cut short abbreviate, abort, arrest, check, crop, curtail, cut off, dock, end, halt, interrupt, shorten, stop, terminate, truncate.

antonym prolong.

cut up act up, butcher, carve, chop, clown around, criticize, crucify, dice, divide, hurt, lacerate, mince, pan, ridicule, show off, slash, slate, slice, split, tear apart, vilify, wound.

cutback n (budget) cut, curtailment, decrease, decrement, economy, lessening, reduction, retrenchment.

cute adj adorable, affected, appealing, artless, attractive, bonny, bright-eyed, charming, cherub-faced, clever, contrived, cutesy, dainty, darling, endearing, good-looking, handsome, hokey, huggable, ingenious, innocent, kissable, lovable, mannered, naïve, overdone, precious, pretty, quaint, rosy-cheeked, self-conscious, sweet, (un)self-conscious, winsome.

cutoff n deadline, end, exit, expiry date, limit, line, off-ramp, termination.

cut-rate adj bargain, cheap, cut-price, low-priced, reduced, sale.

cutthroat n assassin, bravo, butcher, executioner, hatchet man, hit man, homicide, killer, liquidator, murderer, slayer, thug.

adj barbarous, bloodthirsty, bloody, brutal, competitive, cruel, dog-eat-dog, extreme, ferocious, fierce, homicidal, merciless, murderous, relentless, ruthless, savage, stop-at-nothing, thuggish, unprincipled, vicious, violent.

cutting adj acid, acrimonious, barbed, biting, bitter, caustic, chill, hurtful, incisive, keen, malicious, mordant, numbing, penetrating, piercing, pointed, raw, sarcastic, sardonic, scathing, severe, sharp, stinging, trenchant, wounding.

n bit, clipping, piece, sample, scion, scrap, slice, slip, snippet, swatch.

cutting edge *n* advance force, effectiveness, force, forefront, front line(s), sharpness, vanguard.

cybernetics *n* artificial intelligence, communication science, computer science, electronic communications, information science, organic programming.

cycle *n* age, alternation, circle, circuit, eon, epoch, era, pattern, period, phase, revolution, rotation, round, sequence, series, set, vicious circle.

cyclic *adj* circular, periodic, regularly alternating, repeating.

cyclone *n* hurricane, monsoon, tempest, tornado, twister, typhoon, whirlwind, windstorm.

cylinder *n* barrel, bobbin, column, drum, map case, piston chamber, platen, reel, roll, roller, scroll case, spindle, spool, tube.

cynic *n* doubter, killjoy, misanthrope, misanthropist, pessimist, sceptic, scoffer, spoilsport.

cynical *adj* bitter, black, contemptuous, derisive, disillusioned, distrustful, doubting, ironic, jaded, mephistophelian, misanthropic, mistrustful, mocking, negative, pessimistic, sarcastic, sardonic, sceptical, scoffing, scornful, sharp-tongued, sneering, streetwise.

cynicism *n* bitterness, disbelief, disillusionment, distrust, doubt, jadedness, misanthropy, mistrust, negativity, pessimism, sarcasm, scepticism.

czar *n* autocrat, big wheel, boss, chief, decision-maker, dictator, emperor, king, mogul.

D

dab¹ v blot, daub, flick, pat, stipple, swab, tap, touch, wipe.

n bit, dollop, drop, fleck, flick, pat, smear, smidgen, smudge, speck, spot, stroke, tap, touch, trace.

dab² n ace, adept, dab hand, expert, past master, wizard.

dabble v dip into, fiddle, moisten, paddle, putter, spatter, splash, sprinkle, tinker, toy, trifle, wet

dabbler n amateur, dilettante, putterer, sciolist, tinkerer, trifler.

antonyms connoisseur, expert, professional.

daft adj absurd, asinine, berserk, besotted, crackers, crazy, daffy, delirious, demented, deranged, dopey, dotty, foolish, giddy, hysterical, idiotic, inane, infatuated, insane, lunatic, mad, nuts, nutty, potty, scatty, screwy, silly, simple, stupid, touched, unhinged, witless.

antonyms bright, sane, wise.

dagger n bayonet, dirk, kris, kukri, poniard, skean, stiletto, yataghan.

daily adj circadian, common, commonplace, customary, day-to-day, diurnal, everyday, normal, ordinary, quotidian, regular, routine.

dainty adj choice, choosy, delectable, delicate, delicious, exquisite, fastidious, fine, finicking, finicky, fussy, graceful, mignon, mincing, neat, nice, palatable, particular, petite, pretty, refined, savoury, tasty, tender, toothsome.

antonyms clumsy, gross.

n bonbon, delicacy, sweetmeat, tidbit, treat.

dale n clough, combe, dell, dingle, glen, vale, valley.

dally v dawdle, delay, dilly-dally, dither, drag one's feet, fiddle-faddle, flirt, fool around, frivol, linger, loiter, play, procrastinate, sport, take one's own sweet time, tarry, toy, trifle.

antonyms hasten, hurry.

dam n barrage, barrier, blockage, check, dike, embankment, hindrance, obstruction, reservoir, restraint, wall.

v barricade, block, check, choke, confine, contain, hold back, obstruct, restrain, restrict, staunch, stem.

damage n cost, destruction, detriment, devastation, harm, hurt, impairment, injury, loss, mischief, mutilation, scathe.

antonym repair.

v deface, harm, hurt, impair, incapacitate, injure, mar, mutilate, play havoc with, ruin, spoil, tamper with, weaken, wreak havoc on, wreck.

antonyms fix, repair.

damages n amercement, compensation, costs, fine, indemnity, reimbursement, reparation, satisfaction.

damaging adj deleterious, destructive, detrimental, devastating, disadvantageous, harmful, hurtful, injurious, pernicious, prejudicial, ruinous, unfavourable.

antonyms favourable, helpful.

dame n baroness, dowager, lady, matron, noblewoman, peeress.

damn v abuse, anathematize, blacklist, blaspheme, blast, castigate, censure, condemn, criticize, curse, denounce, doom, excoriate, execrate, imprecate, objurgate, pan, revile, sentence, slam, slate, swear.

antonyms bless, praise.

n brass farthing, darn, dash, hoot, iota, jot, tinker's damn, two hoots, whit.

damnable adj abominable, accursed, atrocious, culpable, cursed, despicable, detestable, execrable, hateful, horrible, iniquitous, offensive, rotten, sinful, wicked.

antonyms admirable, praiseworthy.

damnation n anathema, ban, condemnation, curse, denunciation, doom, excommunication, objurgation, perdition, proscription.

damned adj accursed, anathematized, blasted, bloody, condemned, confounded, cussed, cursed, darned, dashed, despicable, detestable, deuced, doggone, doomed, dratted, flipping, goddamned, hateful, infamous, infernal, jiggered, loathsome, lost, reprobate, revolting, rotten, wicked.

antonym blessed.

damning adj accusatory, condemnatory, damnatory, denunciatory, dooming, implicative, imprecatory, incriminating, inculpatory, unflattering.

damp n clamminess, dampness, dankness, dew, drizzle, fog, humidity, mist, moistness, moisture, vapour, wet.

antonym dryness.

adj clammy, dank, dewy, dripping, drizzly, humid, misty, moist, muggy, sodden, soggy, sopping, vaporous, vapourish, wet.

antonyms arid, bone-dry.

v allay, bedew, check, chill, cool, curb, dampen, dash, deaden, deject, depress, diminish, discourage, dispirit, dull, inhibit, moderate, moisten, restrain, smother, stifle, wet.
antonyms dry, encourage.

dampen *v* bedew, besprinkle, check, dash, deaden, decrease, depress, deter, diminish, dishearten, dismay, dull, lessen, moderate, moisten, muffle, reduce, restrain, smother, spray, stifle, throw cold water on, wet.
antonyms dry, encourage.

dance *v* boogie, caper, foot (it),frolic, gambol, hoof (it), hop, jig, jive, prance, rock, skip, spin, stomp, sway, swing, tango, tread a measure, trip the light fantastic, waltz, whirl.
n ball, ballet, barn dance, corroboree, hop, prom, shindig.

dancer *n* ballerina, ballet dancer, ballroom dancer, belly-dancer, coryphée, danseur, danseuse, hoofer, prima ballerina, tap-dancer.

dandy *n* Adonis, beau, blade, blood, buck, clotheshorse, Corinthian, coxcomb, dude, exquisite, fop, man about town, peacock, popinjay, swell.
adj capital, dapper, dashing, excellent, fine, first-rate, foppish, great, hunky-dory, jim-dandy, lovely, peachy, perfect, spiffy, splendid, swell.

danger *n* endangerment, hazard, insecurity, jeopardy, liability, menace, peril, precariousness, risk, threat, trouble, vulnerability.
antonyms safety, security.

dangerous *adj* alarming, breakneck, chancy, compromising, critical, daring, deadly, grave, hairy, harmful, hazardous, insecure, menacing, nasty, parlous, perilous, precarious, reckless, risky, serious, severe, threatening, ticklish, treacherous, ugly, unsafe, vulnerable.
antonyms harmless, safe, secure.

dangle *v* droop, flap, flaunt, hang, sway, swing, tantalize, trail, wave.

dangling *adj* disconnected, drooping, hanging, loose, pendulous, swaying, swinging, trailing.

dank *adj* clammy, damp, dewy, dripping, moist, rheumy, slimy, soggy.
antonym dry.

dapper *adj* active, brisk, chic, dandy, dashing, natty, neat, nimble, smart, spiffy, spruce, spry, stylish, trim, well-dressed, well-groomed.
antonyms dishevelled, dowdy, scruffy, shabby, sloppy.

dappled *adj* brindled, checkered, dotted, flecked, freckled, mottled, piebald, pied, speckled, spotted, stippled, variegated.

dare *v* adventure, beard, brave, challenge, defy, goad, have the gall, hazard, presume, risk, taunt, throw down the gauntlet, venture.
n challenge, gamble on, gauntlet, provocation, taunt.

daredevil *n* adventurer, desperado, exhibitionist, hotspur, madcap, stuntman.
antonym coward.
adj adventurous, audacious, bold, daring,

death-defying, fearless, foolhardy, madcap, rash, reckless, risky.
antonyms cautious, prudent, timid.

daring *adj* adventuresome, adventurous, audacious, bold, brave, brazen, daredevil, dauntless, fearless, foolhardy, game, impulsive, intrepid, plucky, rash, reckless, risky, valiant, venturesome.
antonyms afraid, safe, timid.
n audacity, boldness, bravery, bravura, courage, defiance, derring-do, fearlessness, foolhardiness, gall, grit, guts, hardihood, intrepidity, nerve, pluck, prowess, rashness, spirit, spunk, temerity.
antonyms cowardice, timidity.

dark *adj* abstruse, angry, aphotic, arcane, atrocious, baleful, benighted, black, bleak, brunette, cheerless, cloudy, coal-black, concealed, cryptic, damnable, darkling, dark-skinned, darksome, deep, depressed, depressing, dim, dingy, dismal, doleful, dour, drab, dusky, ebony, enigmatic, evil, forbidding, foul, frowning, gloomy, glowering, glum, grim, hellish, hidden, horrible, ignorant, infamous, infernal, jet-black, joyless, lightless, lowering, melanic, melanous, midnight, morbid, morose, mournful, murk, murky, mysterious, mystic, nasty, nefarious, obscure, occult, ominous, overcast, pitch-black, pitch-dark, pitchy, puzzling, recondite, sable, satanic, scowling, secret, shadowy, shady, sinful, sinister, sombre, sulky, sullen, sunless, swarthy, tenebrous, threatening, uncultivated, unenlightened, unilluminated, unlettered, unlit, vile, wicked.
antonyms bright, happy, light, lucid.
n concealment, darkness, dimness, dusk, evening, gloom, ignorance, murk, murkiness, night, nightfall, nighttime, obscurity, secrecy, twilight, yin.
antonyms brightness, light.

darken *v* becloud, bedim, blacken, cloud, cloud over, deepen, deject, depress, dim, dispirit, eclipse, embrown, obscure, overshadow, sadden, shade, shadow.
antonyms brighten, lighten.

darling *n* apple of one's eye, baby, beloved, blue-eyed boy, dear, dearest, fair-haired boy, favourite, honey, ladylove, love, pet, poppet, sweetheart, sweetie, treasure, true-love.
adj adored, beloved, cherished, dear, pet, precious, sweet, treasured, white-haired.

dart *v* bound, cast, dash, flash, fling, flit, fly, race, run, rush, scoot, scurry, send, shoot, spring, sprint, start, tear, throw, whiz.
n arrow, barb, bolt, dig, flight, gibe, jab, shaft, shot, snipe, stab.

dash[1] *v* blight, break, cast, chagrin, confound, crash, damp, dampen, depress, destroy, disappoint, discourage, fling, foil, frustrate, hurl, ruin, shatter, shiver, slam, sling, smash, spatter, splash, splatter, splinter, spoil, strike, throw, thwart.
n bit, blow, bravura, brio, check, daring, drop, élan, flair, flavour, flourish, hint, little, panache, pinch, pizzazz, smack, smash, soupçon, spirit,

splatter, sprinkling, stroke, style, suggestion, tinge, touch, verve, vigour, vivacity.

dash² *v* be off like a shot, bolt, bound, dart, fly, gallop, haste(n), hurry, race, run, rush, speed, spring, sprint, streak, tear.

antonym dawdle.

n bolt, break, dart, race, run, rush, sprint, spurt.

dashing *adj* bold, dapper, daring, dazzling, debonair, doggy, elegant, exuberant, flamboyant, gallant, impressive, jaunty, lively, plucky, showy, smart, spirited, sporty, stylish, swashbuckling.

antonyms drab, nerdy.

dastard *n* cad, caitiff, coward, craven, cur, heel, milksop, poltroon, recreant, sneak, worm, yellow-belly.

dastardly *adj* base, caitiff, contemptible, cowardly, craven, despicable, faint-hearted, ignoble, lily-livered, low, low-down, mean, poltroon, pusillanimous, recreant, sneaking, sneaky, spiritless, timorous, underhand(ed), vile, yellow.

antonyms brave, heroic, noble.

data *n* brief, bumf, details, documents, dope, facts, figures, file, info, information, input, lowdown, material, poop, statistics.

date¹ *n* age, epoch, era, juncture, period, point, point in time, stage, time.

date² *n* appointment, assignation, boyfriend, engagement, escort, girlfriend, meeting, outing, partner, rendezvous, steady, tryst.

dated *adj* antiquated, archaic, démodé, obsolescent, obsolete, old-fashioned, out, outdated, outmoded, out-of-date, passé, superseded, unfashionable.

antonyms fashionable, on the cutting edge, up-to-date, up-to-the-minute.

daub *v* bedaub, begrime, besmear, blot, blur, coat, cover, dab, deface, dirty, grime, paint, plaster, smear, smirch, smudge, soil, spatter, splatter, stain, sully.

n blob, blot, blotch, dab, mark, smear, spatter, splash, splatter, splotch, spot, stain.

daunt *v* alarm, appal, cow, demoralize, deter, discourage, dishearten, dismay, dispirit, frighten, give pause to, intimidate, overawe, overcome, put off, scare, shake, subdue, terrify, unnerve.

antonyms encourage, hearten.

dauntless *adj* bold, brave, courageous, daring, doughty, fearless, gallant, game, heroic, indomitable, intrepid, lion-hearted, plucky, resolute, stout-hearted, undaunted, unflinching, valiant, valorous.

antonyms discouraged, disheartened, wimpy.

dawdle *v* dally, delay, dilly-dally, fiddle, fritter, hang about, idle, lag, loaf, loiter, poke along, potter, putter, shilly-shally, trail, waste time.

antonym hurry.

dawdler *n* laggard, lingerer, loafer, loiterer, poke, shilly-shallier, slowcoach, slowpoke, snail, tortoise.

dawn *n* advent, aurora, beginning, birth, break of day, cockcrow, crack of dawn, dawning, daybreak, daylight, dayspring, emergence, first light, genesis, inception, morning, onset, origin, outset, peep of day, rise, start, sunrise, sunup.

antonyms decline, dusk, sundown, sunset, wane.

v appear, begin, break, brighten, develop, emerge, gleam, glimmer, grow light, lighten, occur, open, originate, rise, unfold.

dawn on become clear to, click (for), come (home) to, hit, occur to, register with, strike.

day *n* age, ascendancy, date, daylight, daytime, epoch, era, generation, period, time.

antonym night.

day after day always, continually, day in day out, endlessly, forever, monotonously, one day at a time, perpetually, persistently, regularly, relentlessly.

day by day daily, each day, every day, from day to day, gradually, one day at a time, progressively, slowly but surely, steadily.

daybreak *n* break of day, cockcrow, crack of dawn, dawn, daylight, dayspring, first light, morning, peep of day, sunrise, sunup.

antonyms sundown, sunset.

daydream *n* castle in Spain, castle in the air, dream, fantasy, figment of one's imagination, fond hope, have one's head in the clouds, imagining, musing, phantasm, pipe dream, reverie, stargazing, vision, wish, woolgathering.

v build castles in Spain, build castles in the air, dream, fancy, fantasize, hallucinate, imagine, muse, stargaze.

daydreamer *n* dreamer, fantasizer, stargazer, visionary, woolgatherer.

daze *v* amaze, astonish, astound, befog, benumb, bewilder, blind, confuse, dazzle, dumfound, flabbergast, numb, paralyse, perplex, razzle-dazle, shock, stagger, startle, stun, stupefy, surprise.

n bewilderment, confusion, distraction, narcosis, shock, stupor, trance.

dazed *adj* baffled, befuddled, bemused, bewildered, confused, disoriented, dizzy, dopy, dumbstruck, flabbergasted, fuddled, groggy, light-headed, mesmerize, muddled, nonplussed, numbed, perplexed, punch-drunk, shocked, staggered, stunned, stupefied, woozy.

dazzle *v* amaze, astonish, awe, bedazzle, blind, blur, confuse, daze, fascinate, hypnotize, impress, mesmerize, overawe, overcome, overpower, overwhelm, stupefy.

n brilliance, glitter, magnificence, razzle-dazzle, razzmatazz, scintillation, sparkle, splendour.

dazzling *adj* amazing, astounding, awe-inspiring, awesome, brilliant, fascinating, foudroyant, glaring, glittering, glorious, impressive, radiant, ravishing, remarkable, scintillating, sensational, shining, sparkling, splendid, stunning, sublime, superb, virtuoso.

dead¹ *adj* apathetic, barren, boring, callous, cold, comatose, deadbeat, deceased, defunct, departed, dog-tired, dull, exhausted, extinct, flat, frigid, glassy, glazed, gone, inactive, inanimate, indifferent, inert, inoperative, insensate, insensible, insipid, late, lifeless, lukewarm, no longer with us, numb, obsolete, passé, paralysed, perished, spent, spiritless, stagnant, stale, sterile, stiff, still, tasteless, tired, torpid, uninteresting, unmoved, unresponsive, useless, vapid, wooden, worn-out.

antonyms active, alive, animated.

dead² *adj* absolute, complete, downright, outright, perfect, total, unqualified, utter.

adv absolutely, completely, entirely, exactly, perfectly, precisely, quite, squarely, totally.

deaden *v* abate, allay, alleviate, anesthetize, benumb, blunt, cushion, damp, dampen, desensitize, diminish, dull, hush, impair, lessen, muffle, mute, numb, obtund, paralyse, quieten, reduce, smother, stifle, suppress, weaken.

antonym enliven.

deadlock *n* halt, impasse, stalemate, standstill.

deadly *adj* accurate, baleful, baneful, boring, cruel, dangerous, death-dealing, deathful, deathlike, deathly, destructive, devastating, dull, effective, exact, fatal, ghastly, ghostly, grim, implacable, lethal, malignant, monotonous, mortal, noxious, pernicious, pestilent, poisonous, precise, sure, tedious, true, unerring, unfailing, uninteresting, venomous, wearisome.

antonyms harmless, healthy.

deadpan *adj* blank, dispassionate, empty, expressionless, impassive, inexpressive, inscrutable, poker-faced, straight-faced, unexpressive.

deaf *adj* hard of hearing, heedless, indifferent, oblivious, stone-deaf, unconcerned, unhearing, unmindful, unmoved, unresponsive.

antonyms aware, conscious.

deafening *adj* booming, ear-piercing, earsplitting, fortissimo, piercing, resounding, ringing, roaring, stentorian, thunderous.

antonyms pianissimo, quiet.

deal *v* allot, apportion, assign, bargain, bestow, deliver, dispense, distribute, divide, do business, dole out, give, mete out, negotiate, sell, share, stock, trade, traffic, treat.

n agreement, amount, arrangement, bargain, buy, contract, degree, distribution, exchange, extent, hand, pact, portion, quantity, round, settlement, share, transaction, understanding.

deal with attend to, consider, cope with, cover, do business with, field, handle, manage, oversee, respond to, see to, take care of, treat.

dealer *n* chandler, chapman, distributor, horse trader, marketer, merchandiser, merchant, monger, peddler, retailer, trader, tradesman, wholesaler.

dealings *n* actions, behaviour, business, commerce, conduct, interchange, intercourse, relations, trade, traffic, transactions, truck.

dear *adj* beloved, cherished, close, costly, darling, esteemed, expensive, familiar, favourite, high-priced, intimate, loved, overpriced, precious, pricey, prized, respected, treasured, valued.

antonyms cheap, hated.

n angel, beloved, darling, dearie, dearie, honey, love, loved one, precious, sweetheart, sweetie, treasure.

for dear life desperately, energetically, for all one is worth, intensely, strenuously, urgently, vigorously, with might and main.

dearly *adv* affectionately, devotedly, extremely, fondly, greatly, lovingly, profoundly, tenderly.

dearth *n* absence, deficiency, exiguousness, famine, inadequacy, insufficiency, lack, need, paucity, poverty, scarcity, shortage, sparseness, sparsity, want.

antonyms abundance, excess.

death *n* bane, bereavement, cessation, curtains, decease, demise, departure, destroying angel, destruction, dissolution, downfall, dying, end, eradication, exit, expiration, extinction, fatality, finish, grave, Grim Reaper, loss, passing, quietus, release, ruin, ruination, undoing.

antonyms birth, life.

deathless *adj* ageless, enduring, eternal, everlasting, immortal, imperishable, incorruptible, memorable, never-ending, timeless, undying, unforgettable.

deathly *adj* ashen, beastly, cadaverous, deadly, deathlike, fatal, gaunt, ghastly, grim, haggard, intense, mortal, pale, pallid, terrible, wan.

debacle *n* cataclysm, catastrophe, collapse, defeat, devastation, disaster, downfall, fiasco, havoc, overthrow, rout, ruin, ruination, stampede.

debar *v* bar, blackball, deny, exclude, obstruct, preclude, prevent, prohibit, segregate, shut out, stop.

antonym admit.

debase *v* abase, adulterate, bastardize, cheapen, contaminate, corrupt, debauch, defile, degrade, demean, depreciate, devalue, diminish, disgrace, dishonour, humble, humiliate, impair, lower, pollute, reduce, shame, taint, vitiate.

antonyms elevate, exalt, upgrade.

debased *adj* adulterated, base, corrupt, debauched, degenerate, degraded, demeaned, depraved, depreciated, devalued, diminished, fallen, impure, low, lowered, mean, mixed, perverted, polluted, reduced, shameful, sordid, tainted, vile.

antonyms elevated, pure.

debatable *adj* arguable, borderline, contentious, contestable, controversial, controvertible, disputable, doubtful, dubious, moot, open to question, problematic, questionable, subject to interpretation, uncertain, undecided, unsettled.

antonyms certain, unquestionable.

debate *v* argue, consider, contend, contest, controvert, deliberate, discuss, dispute, meditate on, mull over, ponder, question, reflect, revolve, ruminate, weigh, wrangle.

antonym agree.

n altercation, argument, consideration, contention, controversy, deliberation, discussion, disputation, dispute, polemic, reflection.

antonym agreement.

debauch *v* corrupt, debase, deflower, demoralize, deprave, over-indulge, pervert, pollute, ravish, ruin, seduce, spoil, subvert, violate, vitiate.

antonyms cleanse, purge, purify.

n bacchanalia, bender, binge, bout, fling, orgy, saturnalia, spree.

debauched *adj* corrupt, corrupted, debased, degenerate, degraded, depraved, dissipated, dissolute, immoral, intemperate, lewd, licentious, perverted, profligate, wanton.

antonyms decent, pure, virtuous.

debauchee *n* bacchanalian, bacchant, libertine, Lothario, playboy, profligate, rake, rakehell, roué, sensualist, wanton.

debauchery *n* carousal, debauchment, depravity, dissipation, excess, immorality, incontinence, indulgence, intemperance, lewdness, licentiousness, lust, orgies, overindulgence, revelry, riot, wantonness.

debilitate *v* devitalize, drain, enervate, enfeeble, exhaust, fatigue, incapacitate, prostrate, sap, undermine, unman, weaken, wear out.

antonyms energize, invigorate, strengthen.

debility *n* asthenia, decrepitude, enervation, enfeeblement, exhaustion, faintness, feebleness, frailty, incapacity, infirmity, languor, malaise, prostration, sickliness, weakness.

antonyms strength, vigour.

debonair *adj* affable, breezy, buoyant, charming, cheerful, courteous, dashing, elegant, gallant, gay, jaunty, light-hearted, refined, sprightly, suave, urbane, well-bred.

debris *n* bits, brash, detritus, drift, dross, duff, eluvium, exuviae, fragments, litter, moraine, pieces, remains, rubbish, rubble, ruins, sweepings, trash, waste, wreck, wreckage.

debt *n* arrears, bill, claim, debit, due, duty, indebtedness, liability, obligation, score, sin.

antonyms asset, credit.

debtor *n* bankrupt, borrower, defaulter, insolvent, mortgager.

antonym creditor.

debunk *v* deflate, demythologize, disparage, explode, expose, lampoon, puncture, ridicule, show up.

debut *n* appearance, beginning, bow, entrance, inauguration, initiation, introduction, launching, première, presentation.

decadence *n* corruption, debasement, decay, decline, degeneracy, degeneration, deterioration, dissipation, dissolution, fall, perversion, retrogression.

antonyms flourishing, rise.

decadent[1] *adj* corrupt, debased, debauched, decaying, declining, degenerate, degraded, depraved, dissolute, effete, immoral, self-indulgent.

antonym moral.

decadent[2] *adj* lavish, luxurious, opulent, rich, self-indulgent, sumptuous.

antonyms ascetic, spartan.

decamp *v* abscond, bolt, desert, escape, flee, flit, fly, go AWOL, hightail (it), make off, run away, scarper, skedaddle.

decapitate *v* behead, execute, guillotine.

decay *v* atrophy, biodegrade, break down, canker, collapse, corrode, crumble, decline, decompose, degenerate, deteriorate, disintegrate, dissolve, dwindle, moulder, perish, putrefy, rot, shrivel, sink, spoil, wane, waste away, wear away, wither.

antonyms flourish, grow, ripen.

n atrophy, breakdown, caries, collapse, corrosion, crumbling, death, decadence, decline, decomposition, decrepitude, degeneracy, degeneration, deterioration, dissolution, disintegration, dwindling, erosion, fading, failure, fall, gangrene, putrefaction, putrescence, putridity, putridness, rot, rotting, wane, waning, wasting, weakening, withering.

decayed *adj* addled, bad, carious, carrion, corroded, decomposed, off, putrefied, putrid, rank, rotten, spoiled, wasted, withered.

decaying *adj* collapsing, crumbling, declining, decomposing, decrepit, degenerating, deteriorating, disintegrating, dying, foul, gangrenous, on the wane, perishing, putrescent, rotting, spoiling, wasting.

decease *n* death, demise, departure, dissolution, dying, expiration, expiry, passing, release.

v croak, die, expire, give up the ghost, go to meet one's maker, kick the bucket, leave the land of the living, pass away, pass on, pass over, perish, shuffle off this mortal coil.

deceased *adj* dead, defunct, departed, expired, extinct, finished, former, gone, late, lifeless, lost.

n dead, decedent, departed.

deceit *n* artifice, blind, cheat, cheating, chicanery, con, cozenage, craftiness, cunning, deceitfulness, deception, dissimulation, double-dealing, duplicity, fake, falsehood, feint, fraud, fraudulence, guile, hypocrisy, imposition, imposture, lying, lie, misrepresentation, pretence, prevarication, ruse, sham, shift, slyness, snow job, stratagem, subterfuge, swindle, treachery, trick, trickery, underhandedness, wile.

antonyms honesty, openness.

deceitful *adj* cheating, collusive, counterfeit, crafty, deceiving, deceptive, designing, dishonest, disingenuous, dissembling, double-dealing, duplicitous, fallacious, false, fraudulent, guileful, hypocritical, illusory, insincere, knavish, lying, prevaricating, Punic, rusé, scheming, sneaky, treacherous, tricky, two-faced, underhanded, untrustworthy, wily.

antonyms honest, open, trustworthy.

deceive *v* bamboozle, befool, beguile, betray, cheat, con, cozen, delude, diddle, disappoint, double-cross, dupe, ensnare, entrap, fool, gammon, gull, have, hoax, hoodwink, impose on, lead astray, lead down the garden path, lead on, mislead, outwit, pull one over on, pull the wool over (someone's) eyes, snow, swindle, take for a ride, take in, trick, two-time.

antonym enlighten.

deceiver *n* betrayer, charlatan, cheat, con man, cozener, crook, deluder, diddler, dissembler, dissimulator, double-dealer, fake, fraud, hypocrite, impostor, inveigler, liar, mountebank, phony, pretender, sharper, swindler, trickster.

decency *n* appropriateness, civility, correctness, courtesy, decorum, etiquette, fitness, good form, good manners, helpfulness, modesty, propriety, respectability, seemliness, thoughtfulness.

antonyms discourtesy, indecency.

decent *adj* acceptable, accommodating, adequate, ample, appropriate, average, becoming, befitting, chaste, clothed, comme il faut, competent, courteous, covered, decorous, dressed, fair, fit, fitting, friendly, generous, gracious, helpful, kind, modest, nice, obliging, passable, polite, presentable, proper, pure, reasonable, respectable, respectful, satisfactory, seemly, sufficient, suitable, thoughtful, tolerable.

antonyms disobliging, indecent, poor.

deception *n* artifice, blind, bluff, cheat, con, craftiness, cunning, deceitfulness, deceit, deceptiveness, decoy, defraudation, dissembling, dissimulation, double-dealing, duplicity, feint, flimflam, fraud, fraudulence, guile, hoax, hypocrisy, illusion, imposition, imposture, insincerity, legerdemain, lie, pretence, ruse, sell, sham, smoke and mirrors, snare, snow job, stratagem, subterfuge, treachery, trick, trickery, wile.

antonyms artlessness, openness.

deceptive *adj* ambiguous, catchy, delusive, delusory, dishonest, elusive, fake, fallacious, false, fraudulent, illusive, illusory, misleading, sham, specious, spurious, treacherous, tricky, unreliable.

antonyms artless, genuine, open.

decide *v* adjudge, adjudicate, choose, conclude, decree, determine, elect, end, fix, judge, opt, purpose, reach a decision, resolve, settle.

decided *adj* absolute, assertive, categorical, certain, clear-cut, decisive, definite, deliberate, determined, distinct, emphatic, express, firm, fixed, forthright, indisputable, marked, noticeable, positive, pronounced, resolved, resolute, settled, strong-willed, sure,

unambiguous, undeniable, undisputed, unequivocal, unfaltering, unhesitating, unmistakable, unquestionable.

antonyms indecisive, undecided.

decidedly *adv* absolutely, categorically, certainly, clearly, decisively, definitely, distinctly, downright, indisputably, markedly, noticeably, positively, quite, unequivocally, unmistakably, unquestionably, very.

decider *n* clincher, coup de grâce, determiner, floorer, tie breaker.

deciding *adj* chief, clinching, conclusive, critical, crucial, decisive, definitive, determining, final, influential, pivotal, prime, principal, significant, supreme.

antonym insignificant.

decipher *v* construe, crack, decode, decrypt, deduce, explain, figure out, interpret, make out, read, solve, transliterate, understand, unfold, unravel, unscramble.

antonym encode.

decision *n* arbitrament, arbitration, choice, conclusion, decisiveness, determination, finding, firmness, judgment, outcome, purpose, purposefulness, resoluteness, resolution, resolve, result, ruling, settlement, verdict.

moment of decision climax, crisis, crunch, critical juncture, point of no return, Rubicon, turning point, watershed.

decisive *adj* absolute, clinching, conclusive, critical, crucial, decided, definite, definitive, determinate, determined, fateful, final, firm, forceful, forthright, influential, momentous, pivotal, positive, resolute, significant, strong-minded, supreme.

antonyms indecisive, insignificant.

deck *v* adorn, apparel, array, attire, beautify, bedeck, bedizen, clothe, decorate, doll up, drape, dress, embellish, festoon, garland, grace, gussy up, ornament, prettify, pretty up, primp, prink, smarten, spiff up, titivate, tog out, tog up, trick out, trim.

declaim *v* harangue, hold forth, lecture, mouth, orate, perorate, pontificate, preach, preachify, proclaim, rant, recite, rhetorize, sermonize, soapbox, speak, speechify, spiel, spout, tub-thump, wax eloquent.

declamation *n* address, bombast, harangue, lecture, oration, peroration, pontification, rant, recitation, rhetoric, sermon, speil, speech, tirade, tub thumping.

declamatory *adj* bombastic, fustian, grandiloquent, grandiose, high-flown, inflated, magniloquent, oratorical, orotund, overblown, pompous, pontifical, ranting, rhetorical, stagy, soapbox, stilted, theatrical, tub-thumping, turgid.

declaration *n* acknowledgment, affirmation, announcement, assertion, asseveration, attestation, averment, avouchment, avowal, claim, confession, deposition, disclosure, edict, manifesto, notification, proclamation, profession, promulgation, pronouncement, pronunciamento, protestation, revelation, statement, testimony.

declare *v* acknowledge, affirm, announce, assert, attest, aver, avouch, avow, certify, claim, communicate, confess, confirm, convey, disclose, maintain, make known, manifest, proclaim, profess, pronounce, reveal, show, state, swear, testify (to), witness (to).

decline[1] *v* decay, decrease, degenerate, deny, deteriorate, diminish, droop, drop, dwindle, ebb, fade, fail, fall, fall off, flag, forgo, languish, lessen, pine, refuse, reject, shrink, sink, slacken (off), turn down, wane, weaken, worsen.

n abatement, decay, declension, decrease, decrepitude, degeneration, deterioration, deviation, diminution, downswing, downtrend, downturn, drop, dwindling, enfeeblement, failure, fall off, lessening, phthisis, recession, senility, slump, weakening, worsening.

decline[2] *v* descend, dip, fall off, sink, slant, slope.

n declination, declivity, descent, dip, downgrade, grade, hill, incline, obliqueness, obliquity, slope.

declivity *n* declination, decline, descent, incline, slant, slope.

antonym acclivity.

decode *v* decipher, decrypt, interpret, translate, transliterate, unscramble.

antonym encode.

decompose *v* analyse, atomize, biodegrade, break down, break up, crumble, decay, disintegrate, dissolve, distil, divide, fall apart, fractionate, putrefy, rot, separate, spoil.

antonyms combine, unite.

decomposition *n* analysis, atomization, biodegradation, breakdown, break-up, corruption, decay, disintegration, dissolution, distillation, division, electrolysis, fractionation, hydrolysis, putrefaction, putrescence, putridity, rot, separation.

antonyms combination, unification.

décor *n* colour scheme, decoration, embellishments, furnishings, ornamentation, scenery, theme.

decorate[1] *v* adorn, beautify, bedeck, colour, deck, do up, embellish, enrich, fancy up, festoon, furbish, garland, garnish, grace, gussy up, hang, impearl, ornament, paint, paper, prettify, renovate, stud, tart up, trick out, trim, wallpaper.

decorate[2] *v* belaurel, bemedal, cite, crown, honour.

decorated *adj* baroque, elaborate, embellished, figured, garnished, ornamented, ornate, rococo.

antonym plain.

decoration[1] *n* adornment, arabesque, bauble, beautification, curlicue, elaboration, embellishment, enrichment, flounce, flourish, frill, frou-frou, furbelow, garland, garnish, ornament, ornamentation, scroll, spangle, squiggle, trimming, trinket.

decoration[2] *n* award, badge, colours, crown, emblem, garter, laurel, laurel wreath, medal, order, ribbon, star.

decorative *adj* adorning, baroque, beautifying, embellishing, enhancing, fancy, non-functional, ornamental, ornate, pretty, rococo, superfluous.

antonyms plain, ugly.

decorous *adj* appropriate, becoming, befitting, comely, comme il faut, correct, courtly, decent, dignified, fit, maidenly, mannerly, modest, polite, proper, refined, restrained, sedate, seemly, staid, suitable, well-behaved.

antonym indecorous.

decorum *n* behaviour, breeding, courtliness, decency, deportment, dignity, etiquette, gentility, good manners, grace, gravity, modesty, politeness, propriety, protocol, punctilio, respectability, restraint, seemliness, self-control.

antonyms bad manners, indecorum.

decoy *n* attraction, bait, carrot front, deke, ensnarement, enticement, inducement, lure, pretence, shill, trap.

v allure, attract, bait, beguile, deceive, deke, draw, ensnare, entice, entrap, inveigle, lead, lure, seduce, set up, tempt.

decrease *v* abate, ablate, curtail, cut down, decline, diminish, drop, dwindle, ebb, ease, fall off, lessen, lower, peter out, reduce, shrink, slacken, slim, subside, taper off, wane.

antonym increase.

n abatement, ablation, cutback, decline, decrement, degression, diminution, downswing, downtread, downturn, dwindling, ebb, falling-off, fall off, lessening, loss, lowering, reduction, shrinkage, subsidence.

antonym increase.

decree *n* act, command, decretal, dictum, edict, enactment, law, mandate, order, ordinance, precept, proclamation, regulation, rescript, ruling, statute, ukase, writ.

v command, decide, declare, determine, dictate, enact, lay down, mandate, ordain, order, prescribe, proclaim, pronounce, rule.

decreed *adj* declared, enacted, mandated, ordained, prescribed, proclaimed, ruled, written.

decrepit *adj* aged, antiquated, battered, broken-down, crippled, crumbling, debilitated, deteriorated, dilapidated, doddering, feeble, frail, incapacitated, infirm, ramshackle, rickety, run-down, superannuated, tumble-down, wasted, weak, worn-out.

antonyms fit, maintained, well, youthful.

decrepitude *n* debility, decay, degeneration, deterioration, dilapidation, disability, dotage, feebleness, frailty, incapacity, infirmity, invalidity, old age, senescence, senility, wasting, weakness.

antonyms good repair, youth.

decry *v* belittle, blame, censure, condemn, criticize, cry down, declaim against, denounce, deplore, depreciate, derogate, detract (from), devalue, disapprove, discredit, disparage, inveigh against, rail against, run down, talk down, traduce.

antonyms praise, value.

dedicate v address, allocate, allot, assign, bless, commend, commit, consecrate, devote, earmark, give over to, hallow, inscribe, offer, pledge, present, sacrifice, sanctify, set apart, surrender, turn over.

dedicated adj committed, devoted, enthusiastic, faithful, given over (to), loyal, purposeful, single-hearted, single-minded, sworn, tireless, whole-hearted, zealous.
antonyms apathetic, uncommitted.

dedication[1] n adherence, allegiance, attachment, commitment, devotedness, devotion, faithfulness, loyalty, self-sacrifice, single-mindedness, tirelessness, whole-heartedness, zeal.
antonym apathy.

dedication[2] n address, blessing, commendation, consecration, donation, hallowing, inscription, presentation, sanctification.

deduce v conclude, derive, draw, gather, glean, infer, reason, surmise, understand.

deducible adj a fortiori, a posteriori, derivable, inferable, traceable.

deduct v decrease by, discount, knock off, rebate, reduce by, remove, subtract, take away, withdraw, withhold.
antonym add.

deduction[1] n assumption, conclusion, corollary, finding, inference, reasoning, result.

deduction[2] n abatement, allowance, decrease, diminution, discount, rebate, reduction, subduction, subtraction, withholding.
antonyms addition, increase.

deed[1] n achievement, act, action, exploit, fact, feat, gest(e), performance, reality, truth.

deed[2] n contract, document, indenture, instrument, record, title.

deem v account, adjudge, believe, conceive, consider, esteem, estimate, hold, imagine, judge, reckon, regard, suppose, think.

deep adj absorbed, abstract, abstruse, abyssal, acute, arcane, astute, bass, booming, bottomless, broad, close, consuming, cryptic, dark, discerning, engrossed, esoteric, extreme, far, fathomless, full-toned, grave, great, hidden, in-depth, immersed, inmost, inner, innermost, intense, learned, lost, low, low-pitched, mysterious, obscure, penetrating, powerful, preoccupied, profound, rapt, recondite, resonant, rich, sage, sagacious, secret, sonorous, sound, strong, unfathomable, unfathomed, unplumbed, unsoundable, unsounded, vivid, weighty, well-guarded, wide, wise, yawning.
antonyms open, shallow, superficial.
n high seas, main, ocean, sea.

deepen v darken, dredge, excavate, grow, hollow, increase, intensify, lower, magnify, reinforce, scoop out, strengthen.
antonyms fill in, lessen.

deeply adv acutely, completely, gravely, greatly, intensely, passionately, profoundly, seriously, severely, sorely, strongly, thoroughly, tenderly, to the quick, unfathomably, very much.
antonyms slightly, superficially.

deep-seated adj confirmed, deep, deep-rooted, entrenched, fixed, ineradicable, ingrained, inveterate, rooted, settled, subconscious, unconscious.
antonyms eradicable, temporary.

deer n buck, caribou, doe, elk, fawn, hart, hind, reindeer, roe, stag.

deface v blemish, blot, damage, deform, destroy, disfigure, impair, injure, mar, mutilate, obliterate, spoil, sully, tarnish, vandalize.
antonym repair.

de facto adv actually, in effect, in reality, really. adj actual, existing, real.

defamation n aspersion, calumny, denigration, derogation, disparagement, innuendo, libel, mudslinging, obloquy, opprobrium, scandal, slander, slur, smear, traducement, vilification.
antonym praise.

defamatory adj abusive, calumnious, contumelious, denigrating, derogatory, disparaging, injurious, insulting, libellous, pejorative, slanderous, vilifying, vituperative.
antonym complimentary.

defame v asperse, belie, besmirch, blacken, calumniate, cast aspersions on, cloud, denigrate, discredit, disgrace, dishonour, disparage, libel, malign, slander, smear, speak evil of, stigmatize, traduce, vilify, vituperate.
antonyms compliment, praise.

default n absence, automatic value, defect, deficiency, dereliction, duck, failure, fault, lack, lapse, neglect, non-payment, present value, want.
v backslide, dodge, evade, fail, neglect, renege, revert, welsh.

defeat v baffle, balk, beat, best, blow out of the water, checkmate, clobber, confound, conquer, counteract, cream, crush, disappoint, discomfit, down, euchre, foil, frustrate, get the better of, lick, overcome, overpower, overthrow, overwhelm, quell, repulse, rout, ruin, subdue, subjugate, thrash, thump, thwart, triumph over, trounce, vanquish, vote down, whip.
n beating, conquest, debacle, disappointment, discomfiture, downfall, failure, frustration, licking, overthrow, rebuff, repulse, reverse, rout, ruin, setback, thrashing, thwarting, trouncing, Waterloo.

defeatist n fatalist, futilitarian, negative, pessimist, prophet of doom, quitter.
antonym optimist.
adj cynical, despairing, despondent, fatalistic, gloomy, helpless, hopeless, pessimistic, resigned, resourceless.
antonym optimistic.

defecate v do a big job, egest, empty one's bowels, evacuate, excrete, have a bowel movement, move one's bowels, poo, relieve oneself, void (excrement).

defecation n egestion, elimination, evacuation, excrement, excretion, movement, voiding.

defect *n* blemish, bug, deficiency, demerit, error, failing, fault, flaw, frailty, imperfection, inadequacy, lack, mistake, shortcoming, spot, taint, want, weakness.

v abandon, apostatize, backslide, break faith, desert, forsake, rebel, renege, revolt, tergiversate, turn away.

defection *n* abandonment, apostasy, backsliding, dereliction, desertion, rebellion, recreancy, renegation, revolt, tergiversation.

defective *adj* abnormal, broken, deficient, dysfunctional, faulty, flawed, imperfect, inadequate, incomplete, insufficient, kaput, out of order, subnormal.

antonyms normal, operative.

defector *n* apostate, deserter, Judas, quisling, rat, recreant, renegade, runaway, tergiversator, turncoat.

defence[1] *n* armament, barricade, bastion, buckler, bulwark, buttress, cover, deterrence, fastness, fortification, guard, immunity, muniment, munition, protection, rampart, resistance, safeguard, security, shelter, shield.

antonym attack.

defence[2] *n* alibi, apologia, apology, argument, case, denial, excuse, exoneration, explanation, extenuation, justification, palliation, plea, pleading, rebuttal, vindication.

defenceless *adj* endangered, exposed, helpless, imperilled, naked, powerless, unarmed, undefended, unguarded, unprotected, unshielded, vulnerable, wide open.

antonym protected.

defend *v* argue for, assert, bulwark, champion, cover, endorse, espouse, fortify, guard, justify, maintain, plead, preserve, protect, safeguard, screen, secure, shelter, shield, speak up for, stand by, stand up for, support, sustain, uphold, vindicate, watch over.

antonym attack.

defendant *n* accused, appellant, offender, prisoner, respondent.

defender *n* advocate, bodyguard, champion, counsel, endorser, escort, guard, patron, protector, upholder, shield, sponsor, supporter, upholder, vindicator.

antonym attacker.

defensible *adj* arguable, holdable, impregnable, justifiable, pardonable, permissible, plausible, safe, secure, tenable, unassailable, valid, vindicable.

antonyms indefensible, insecure.

defensive *adj* adversarial, apologetic, aposematic, cautious, confrontational, defending, opposing, protective, safeguarding, self-justifying, self-vindicating, touchy, wary, watchful.

antonym bold.

defer[1] *v* abeyance, adjourn, delay, hold in, hold over, postpone, procrastinate, prorogue, put off, put on ice, shelve, stay, suspend, waive.

defer[2] *v* accede, aquiesce, bow, capitulate, comply, give way, go along, give precedence, kowtow, respect, submit, yield.

deference *n* acquiescence, attention, capitulation, civility, complaisance, compliance, consideration, courtesy, esteem, homage, honour, obedience, obeisance, obsequiousness, politeness, regard, respect, reverence, submission, submissiveness, thoughtfulness, veneration, yielding.

deferential *adj* complaisant, compliant, considerate, courteous, dutiful, ingratiating, obedient, obeisant, obsequious, polite, regardful, respectful, reverential, submissive.

antonyms arrogant.

deferment *n* adjournment, deferral, delay, moratorium, postponement, procrastination, putting off, stay, suspension.

defiance *n* antiauthoritarianism, brazenness, challenge, confrontation, contempt, contumacy, disobedience, disregard, insolence, insubordination, obstinacy, opposition, provocation, rebellion, rebelliousness, recalcitrance, resistance, spite.

antonyms acquiescence, submissiveness.

defiant *adj* aggressive, antiauthoritarian, audacious, bold, brazen, challenging, contumacious, daring, disobedient, incorrigible, insolent, insubordinate, intransigent, mutinous, obstinate, provocative, rebellious, recalcitrant, refractory, resistant, truculent, unco-operative, unrepentant.

antonyms acquiescent, submissive.

deficiency *n* absence, dearth, defect, deficit, demerit, failing, fault, flaw, frailty, imperfection, inadequacy, insufficiency, lack, paucity, scantiness, scarcity, shortage, shortcoming, want, weakness.

antonym superfluity.

deficient *adj* defective, exiguous, faulty, flawed, impaired, imperfect, inadequate, incomplete, inferior, insufficient, lacking, scanty, scarce, short, skimpy, unsatisfactory, wanting, weak.

antonyms excessive, superfluous.

deficit *n* arrears, default, deficiency, lack, loss, negative balance, shortage, shortfall.

antonym excess.

defile[1] *v* abuse, befoul, besmirch, contaminate, corrupt, debase, deflower, degrade, desecrate, dirty, disgrace, dishonour, foul, make impure, mar, pollute, profane, rape, ravish, seduce, smear, soil, spoil, stain, sully, taint, tarnish, violate, vitiate.

antonyms cleanse, purify.

defile[2] *n* canyon, gorge, gulch, gully, pass, ravine.

defiled *adj* befouled, besmirched, corrupted, debased, degraded, desecrated, dirtied, dirty, dishonoured, impure, maculate, polluted, profaned, ravished, spoilt, stained, sullied, tainted, unclean.

antonyms clean, cleansed, pure.

definable *adj* ascertainable, definite, describable, determinable, determinate, distinct, explicable, expressible, identifiable, limitable, specific.

antonyms indefinable, vague.

define *v* articulate, bound, characterize, circumscribe, delimit, delineate, demarcate, describe, designate, detail, determine, elucidate, explain, expound, express, fix, identify, interpret, limit, make clear, mark out, outline, pin down, put into words, put one's finger on, specify, spell out.

definite *adj* assured, categotical, certain, clear, clear-cut, decided, determined, distinct, established, exact, explicit, express, final, fixed, guaranteed, marked, obvious, particular, positive, precise, settled, specific, substantive, sure, unequivocal, undeniable, undoubted, unmistakable.

antonyms indefinite, vague.

definitely *adv* absolutely, beyond doubt, categorically, certainly, clearly, decidedly, doubtless, doubtlessly, easily, finally, indeed, indubitably, obviously, plainly, positively, surely, undeniably, unequivocally, unmistakably, unquestionably, without doubt, without fail.

definition[1] *n* articulation, clarification, delimitation, delineation, demarcation, description, determination, elucidation, establishment, explanation, exposition, interpretation, meaning, outline.

definition[2] *n* clarity, clearness, contrast, distinctness, focus, precision, resolution, sharpness.

definitive *adj* absolute, authoritative, characteristic, complete, conclusive, correct, decisive, defining, distinguishing, exact, exhaustive, final, identifying, perfect, reliable, standard, ultimate.

antonyms incidental, interim, provisional, tentative.

deflate[1] *v* abash, bring down a notch, chasten, collapse, contract, dash, debunk, disconcert, dispirit, empty, exhaust, flatten, humble, humiliate, knock down, mortify, puncture, put down, put in his (or her) place, shrink, take the wind out of (someone's) sails.

antonyms inflate, puff up.

deflate[2] *v* decrease, depreciate, depress, devalue, diminish, lessen, lower, reduce.

antonym increase.

deflect *v* avert, bend, change course, deviate, diverge, divert, glance (off), ricochet, shy, sidetrack, slew, stave off, swerve, turn, turn aside, twist, veer, ward off, wind.

deflection *n* aberration, averting, bend, bending, declination, deviation, divergence, diversion, drift, refraction, sidetrack, swerve, turn, turning, veer.

deflower *v* assault, corrupt, defile, desecrate, despoil, dishonour, force, harm, mar, molest, rape, ravish, ruin, seduce, spoil, violate.

deflowering *n* corruption, defilement, defloration, desecration, dishonour(ing), rape, ravishment, violation.

deform *v* disfigure, distort, malform, mangle, mar, pervert, ruin, spoil, twist, warp.

deformed *adj* bent, blemished, buckled, contorted, crippled, crooked, defaced, defective, depraved, disfigured, distorted, gnarled, maimed, malformed, mangled, marred, misbegotten, misshapen, mutilated, perverted, ruined, spoilt, twisted, warped.

deformity *n* abnormality, defect, depravity, disfigurement, distortion, irregularity, malformation, misshapenness, ugliness.

defraud *v* beguile, bilk, cheat, con, cozen, deceive, delude, diddle, do (out of), dupe, embezzle, fleece, gull, gyp, rip off, rob, soak, swindle, trick.

defray *v* clear, cover, discharge, foot, meet, pay, repay, settle.

antonym incur.

defrayal *n* clearance, defrayment, discharge, payment, settlement.

antonym incurrence.

deft *adj* able, adept, adroit, agile, clever, dexterous, expert, handy, nimble, proficient, skilful, smooth.

antonym clumsy.

defunct *adj* dead, deceased, departed, expired, extinct, gone, inoperative, invalid, kaput, non-existent, obsolete, outdated, passé.

antonyms alive, live, operative.

defy *v* baffle, beard, beat, brave, challenge, confront, contemn, dare, defeat, despise, disregard, elude, face, flout, foil, frustrate, provoke, rebel (against), repel, repulse, resist, scorn, slight, spurn, thwart, withstand.

antonyms comply with, flinch, quail, yield.

degeneracy *n* corruption, debasement, decadence, decay, decline, decrease, degradation, depravation, depravity, deterioration, dissolution, dissoluteness, effeteness, falling-off, immorality, inferiority, lapsing, poorness, reprobation, turpitude.

antonyms morality, uprightness.

degenerate *adj* base, corrupt, debased, debauched, decadent, degraded, depraved, deteriorated, dissipated, dissolute, effete, fallen, immoral, lapsed, perverted, reprobate.

antonyms regenerate, upright, virtuous.

v age, decay, decline, decrease, descend, deteriorate, fall off, lapse, regress, retrogress, rot, sink, slip, worsen.

antonyms improve, progress, regenerate, rise.

degeneration *n* corruption, debasement, decay, decline, degeneracy, degradation, descent, deterioration, dissipation, dissolution, falling-off, lapse, regression, retrogression.

antonyms improvement, progress, regeneration.

degradation *n* abasement, debasement, decadence, decline, degeneracy, degeneration, demotion, derogation, deterioration, discredit, disgrace, dishonour, downgrading, humiliation, ignominy, indignity, lowering, mortification, perversion, shame.

antonyms enhancement, ennoblement, exaltation, dignity, virtue.

degrade v abase, adulterate, break, brutalize, cheapen, corrupt, debase, demean, demote, depose, deteriorate, discredit, disennoble, disgrace, dishonour, downgrade, humble, humiliate, impair, injure, lower, pervert, shame, unfrock, vitiate, weaken.

antonyms enhance, ennoble, improve.

degraded adj abased, base, corrupt, debased, debauched, decadent, déclassé, depraved, disgraced, dissolute, low, mean, profligate, reprobate, sordid, vicious, vile.

antonyms moral, upright.

degrading adj base, cheapening, contemptible, debasing, demeaning, disgraceful, dishonourable, humiliating, ignoble, infra dig, lowering, shameful, undignified, unworthy.

antonym enhancing.

degree n amount, calibre, class, division, doctorate, extent, gradation, grade, intensity, interval, level, limit, mark, measure, notch, order, point, position, proportion, quality, quantity, range, rank, rate, ratio, scale, scope, severity, stage, standard, standing, station, status, step, unit.

dehydrate v desiccate, drain, dry out, dry up, effloresce, evaporate, exsiccate, parch.

deification n adoration, apotheosis, elevation, exaltation, glorification, idolization, worship.

deify v adore, apotheosize, elevate, enthrone, exalt, extol, glorify, idealize, idolize, immortalize, venerate, worship.

deign v condescend, consent, demean oneself, lower oneself, stoop, vouchsafe.

deity n Allah, demigod, demigoddess, deva, divinity, god, goddess, godhead, godhood, idol, immortal, Jehovah, kami, power, spirit.

deject v cast down, crush, dampen, daunt, demoralize, depress, discourage, dishearten, dismay, dispirit, sadden.

dejected adj blue, cast down, crestfallen, demoralized, depressed, despairing, despondent, disconsolate, discouraged, disheartened, dismal, dispirited, doleful, down, downcast, downhearted, forlorn, gloomy, glum, low, low-spirited, melancholy, miserable, morose, sad, spiritless, woebegone, wretched.

antonyms bright, happy, high-spirited.

dejection n blues, depression, despair, despondency, disconsolateness, discouragement, downheartedness, dumps, gloom, gloominess, low spirits, melancholy, sadness, sorrow, unhappiness.

antonyms happiness, high spirits.

de jure according to law, by law, by right(s), legally, rightfully.

delay v arrest, bog down, check, dawdle, defer, detain, dilly-dally, drag, filibuster, halt, hinder, hold back, hold over, hold up, impede, lag, linger, loiter, mire, obstruct, play for time, postpone, procrastinate, prolong, protract, put on hold, put off, retard, set back, shelve, stall, stave off, stop, suspend, tarry, temporize.

antonyms accelerate, expedite, hurry.

n check, dawdling, deferment, detention, dilly-dallying, halt, hindrance, holdup, impediment, interruption, interval, lag, lingering, loitering, obstruction, postponement, procrastination, stalling, setback, stay, stoppage, suspension, tarrying, wait.

antonyms hastening, hurry.

without delay at once, here and now, immediately, pronto, right away, straightaway, straightway, there and then.

delectable adj adorable, agreeable, ambrosial, appetizing, charming, dainty, delicious, delightful, enjoyable, enticing, finger-licking, flavourful, gratifying, inviting, lip-smacking, luscious, lush, mouthwatering, palatable, pleasant, pleasurable, satisfying, savoury, scrumptious, sweet, tasty, toothsome, yummy.

antonyms horrid, unpleasant.

delectation n amusement, delight, diversion, enjoyment, entertainment, gratification, happiness, pleasure, relish, satisfaction.

antonym distaste.

delegate n agent, ambassador, attendee, commissioner, conferee, deputy, envoy, legate, messenger, nuncio, representative.

v appoint, assign, authorize, charge, commission, consign, depute, deputize, designate, devolve, empower, entrust, give, hand over, mandate, name, nominate, pass on, transfer.

delegation n appointment, commission, contingent, deputation, deputization, embassy, legation, mission.

delete v blot out, blue-pencil, cancel, cross out, dele, edit, edit out, efface, erase, expunge, obliterate, remove, rub out, strike, strike out, take out, wipe out.

antonyms add in, enter, input.

deleterious adj bad, damaging, destructive, detrimental, harmful, hurtful, injurious, negative, noxious, pernicious, prejudicial, ruinous.

antonyms enhancing, helpful.

deliberate v cogitate, consider, consult, debate, discuss, meditate, mull over, ponder, reflect, ruminate, think, weigh.

adj advised, calculated, careful, cautious, circumspect, conscious, considered, designed, heedful, intentional, measured, methodical, planned, ponderous, prearranged, premeditated, prudent, purposeful, slow, studied, thoughtful, unhurried, volitive, willful, willed, witting.

antonyms chance, unintentional.

deliberately adv advisedly, by arrangement, by design, calculatingly, carefully, circumspectly, consciously, designedly, determinedly, emphatically, expressly, in cold blood, intentionally, knowingly, methodically, on purpose, pointedly, purposefully, purposely, resolutely, slowly, unhurriedly, wilfully, with malice aforethought, wittingly.

antonyms by chance, involuntarily, unintentionally.

deliberation n calculation, canniness, care, carefulness, caution, circumspection, cogitation, conference, consideration, consultation, coolness, debate, discussion, forethought, meditation, prudence, purpose, reflection, rumination, speculation, study, thought.

delicacy n accuracy, daintiness, dainty, diplomacy, discretion, discrimination, elegance, exquisiteness, fastidiousness, fineness, finesse, lightness, luxury, niceness, nicety, precision, refinement, relish, savoury, sensibility, sensitiveness, sensitivity, subtlety, sweetmeat, tact, thorniness, tidbit, treat.

antonyms indelicacy, tactlessness.

delicate adj accurate, ailing, careful, choice, complicated, considerate, critical, dainty, debilitated, deft, diaphanous, difficult, diplomatic, discreet, discriminating, eggshell, elegant, elfin, exquisite, faint, fastidious, fine, finicky, flimsy, fragile, frail, fussy, gauzy, gentle, graceful, hazardous, kid-glove, light, minute, muted, pale, pastel, precarious, precise, prudish, pure, refined, risky, savoury, scrupulous, sensible, sensitive, sickly, skilled, slender, slight, soft, squeamish, sticky, subdued, subtle, tactful, tender, ticklish, touchy, weak.

antonyms coarse, gross, harsh, imprecise, strong, thorny.

delicious adj agreeable, ambrosial, appetizing, charming, choice, dainty, delectable, delightful, enjoyable, entertaining, exquisite, finger-licking, flavourful, lip-smacking, luscious, mouthwatering, nectarous, palatable, pleasant, pleasing, savoury, scrumptious, tasty, toothsome, yummy.

antonym unpleasant.

delight n amusement, attraction, beauty, bliss, ecstasy, enchantment, enjoyment, felicity, gladness, gratification, happiness, heaven, joy, jubilation, pleasure, rapture, satisfaction, thrill, treat.

antonyms bane, dismay, displeasure.

v amuse, charm, cheer, divert, enchant, gladden, gratify, please, ravish, rejoice, satisfy, thrill, tickle.

antonyms dismay, displease.

delight in appreciate, enjoy, get a kick out of, get one's jollies out of, get a thrill out of, gloat over, glory in, indulge in, joy in, like, love, relish, rejoice in, revel in, savour, take pleasure in, take pride in.

delighted adj captivated, charmed, ecstatic, elated, enchanted, glad, gratified, happy, joyous, jubilant, overjoyed, over the moon, pleased, pleased as Punch, thrilled, tickled pink.

antonyms dismayed, displeased.

delightful adj agreeable, amusing, attractive, captivating, charming, congenial, delectable, enchanting, engaging, enjoyable, entertaining, fascinating, fetching, gratifying, heavenly, lovely, pleasant, pleasing, pleasurable, rapturous, ravishing, sweet, thrilling.

antonyms horrible, loathsome, off-putting.

delimit v bound, define, demarcate, determine, establish, fix, mark (out or off).

delineate v characterize, chart, depict, describe, design, draw, figure, limn, outline, paint, picture, portray, render, represent, set out, sketch, trace.

delineation n account, characterization, chart, depiction, description, design, diagram, drawing, outline, picture, portrait, portrayal, representation, sketch, tracing.

delinquency n crime, criminality, failure, fault, guilt, law-breaking, misbehaviour, misconduct, misdeed, misdemeanour, neglect, offence, wrongdoing.

delinquent n behind, criminal, culprit, defaulter, evildoer, hooligan, law-breaker, malefactor, miscreant, outstanding, offender, overdue, rough, tough, wrongdoer, young offender.

adj careless, culpable, guilty, neglectful, negligent, remiss.

antonyms blameless, careful.

delirious adj beside oneself, crazy, demented, deranged, ecstatic, euphoric, excited, frantic, frenzied, hallucinating, hysterical, incoherent, insane, light-headed, mad, maenadic, out of one's mind, raving, unglued, unhinged, wild.

antonyms calm, sane.

delirium n derangement, ecstasy, fever, frenzy, fury, hallucination, hysteria, insanity, jimjams, lunacy, madness, passion, rage, raving.

deliver v acquit, administer, aim, announce, bear, birth, bring, bring forth, bring into the world, carry, cart, cede, commit, convey, cough up, deal, declare, direct, discharge, dispense, distribute, emancipate, extricate, fork over, free, give, give birth, give forth, give up, grant, hand over, inflict, launch, let go, liberate, loose, make over, pass, present, proclaim, pronounce, publish, ransom, read, redeem, release, relinquish, rescue, resign, save, set free, strike, supply, surrender, throw, transfer, transport, turn over, utter, yield.

deliverance n emancipation, escape, extrication, judgment, liberation, opinion, redemption, release, rescue, salvation, utterance.

delivery[1] n cession, commital, consignment, conveyance, dispatch, dispensing, distribution, passage, shipment, supply, surrender, transfer, transmission, transmittal, transport, yield.

delivery[2] n articulation, elocution, enunciation, intonation, manner, presentation, speech, utterance.

delivery[3] n accouchement, birthing, childbirth, confinement, labour, parturition, travail.

dell n dingle, glen, hollow, vale, valley.

delude v bamboozle, beguile, cheat, con, cozen, deceive, dupe, flatter (oneself), fool, gull, hoax, hoodwink, impose on, lead astray, misguide, misinform, mislead, snow, take in, trick.

deluge n avalanche, barrage, cataclysm, downpour, flood, hail, inundation, overflow, overload, rush, spate, torrent.

v bury, douse, drench, drown, engulf, flood,

inundate, overload, overrun, overwhelm, soak, submerge, swamp.

delusion *n* deception, error, fallacy, fancy, fantasy, fata Morgana, hallucination, illusion, mirage, misapprehension, misbelief, misconception, phantasm.

deluxe all dressed, choice, costly, elegant, exclusive, expensive, grand, luxurious, opulent, palatial, plush, posh, rich, select, special, splendid, sumptuous, superior, with all the extras (or trimmings), top-of-the-line.

antonyms bare-bones, economy, lower-end.

delve (into) *v* burrow, dig, examine, explore, investigate, poke, probe, research, root, rummage (in), search, study.

demagogue *n* agitator, firebrand, haranguer, orator, populist, rabble-rouser, tub-thumper.

demand *v* ask, call for, challenge, claim, exact, expect, inquire, insist on, involve, necessitate, need, order, request, require, take, want.

antonyms cede, supply.

n behest, bidding, call, challenge, charge, claim, desire, expectation, inquiry, insistence, interrogation, market, necessity, need, order, question, request, requirement, requisition, want.

antonym supply.

demanding *adj* back-breaking, challenging, clamorous, difficult, exacting, exhausting, exigent, fatiguing, hard, imperious, importunate, insistent, nagging, persistent, pressing, taxing, tough, trying, urgent, wearing.

antonyms easy, easy-going, generous, undemanding, unselfish.

demarcate *v* define, delimit, delineate, determine, differentiate, distinguish, establish, fix the boundary of, mark, mark off (or out), separate.

demarcation *n* boundary, bourn, confine, delimitation, differentiation, distinction, division, enclosure, limit, line, margin, pale, separation.

demean[1] *v* abase, behave, condescend, conduct, debase, degrade, deign, descend, humble, lower, stoop.

antonym enhance.

demean[2] *v* acquit, bear, carry, depart.

demeanour *n* air, bearing, behaviour, carriage, comportment, conduct, deportment, manner, mien, port.

demented *adj* crazed, crazy, deranged, distracted, distraught, dotty, feeble-minded, frenzied, insane, irrational, lunatic, mad, maenadic, maniacal, manic, non compos mentis, nutty, out of one's mind, unbalanced, unglued, unhinged.

antonym sane.

demigod *n* daemon, demigoddess, idol, kami, minor deity, power, spirit.

demise *n* collapse, conveyance, death, decease, departure, dissolution, downfall, end, expiration, failure, fall, passing, ruin, termination, transfer.

v bequeath, convey, grant, hand down (or over), grant, lease, leave, pass, transfer, will.

democracy *n* autonomy, commonwealth, egalitarianism, free-market economy, liberty, majority rule, populism, republic, self-government.

democratic *adj* autonomous, egalitarian, free, popular, populist, representative, republican, self-governing.

antonyms autocratic, totalitarian.

demolish *v* annihilate, blow apart (or up), bulldoze, consume, crash, defeat, dilapidate, destroy, devour, dismantle, down, eat up, flatten, knock down, level, overthrow, overturn, pull down, pulverize, raze, ruin, shatter, shred, smash, tear down, unbuild, undo, waste, wreck.

antonym build up.

demon[1] *n* afreet, daemon, devil, evil spirit, fallen angel, fiend, genie, genius, goblin, guardian spirit, incubus, jinni, monster, numen, spirit, succubus, villain, warlock.

demon[2] *n* ace, addict, dab (hand), fanatic, fiend, master, past master, whirlwind, wizard.

demoniac *adj* crazed, demonic, demoniacal, devilish, diabolical, fiendish, frantic, frenetic, frenzied, furious, hectic, hellish, infernal, mad, maniacal, manic, possessed, raging, satanic.

demonstrable *adj* apparent, arguable, attestable, axiomatic, certain, clear, evident, evincible, incontrovertible, indubitable, irrefutable, obvious, palpable, patent, positive, provable, self-evident, substantiable, undeniable, unmistakable, verifiable.

antonyms untestable, unverifiable.

demonstrate[1] *v* act out, attest (to), bear out, display, establish, evidence, evince, exhibit, explain, expound, express, illustrate, indicate, manifest, model, prove, show, substantiate, teach, testify to.

demonstrate[2] *v* march, parade, picket, protest, rally.

demonstration[1] *n* affirmation, attestation, confirmation, demo, display, evidence, example, exhibition, explanation, exposition, expression, illustration, indication, manifestation, modelling, presentation, proof, substantiation, test, testimony, trial, validation.

demonstration[2] *v* demo, march, parade, picket, protest, rally, sit-in, walk.

demonstrative *adj* affectionate, conclusive, convincing, effusive, emotional, evincive, expansive, explanatory, expository, expressive, free, illustrative, incontrovertable, indicative, irrefutable, loving, open, symptomatic, touchy-feely, unreserved, unrestrained.

antonyms cold, inconclusive, unconvincing, undemonstrative, weak.

demoralization *n* corruption, crushing, debasement, dejection, depravation, depression, despondency, devitalization, discomfiture, discouragement, disheartenment, enervation, lowering, panic, perturbation, perversion, trepidation, unmanning, vitiation, weakening.

antonym encouragement.

demoralize *v* corrupt, cripple, crush, daunt, debase, debauch, deject, deprave, depress, devitalize, disconcert, discourage, dishearten, dispirit, enfeeble, grind down, lower, panic, pervert, rattle, sap, shake, undermine, unman, unnerve, vitiate, weaken, wear down.

antonym encourage.

demoralized *adj* bad, base, broken, corrupt, corrupted, crippled, crushed, degenerate, dejected, depraved, depressed, despondent, devitalized, discouraged, disheartened, dispirited, dissolute, downcast, immoral, low, reprobate, sinful, subdued, unmanned, unnerved, weakened, wicked.

antonyms encouraged, heartened.

demote *v* declass, degrade, downgrade, move down, reduce, relegate.

antonyms promote, upgrade.

demotic *adj* common, everyday, ordinary, plebian, popular, vernacular, vulgar.

demur *v* balk, cavil, disagree, dispute, dissent, doubt, hesitate, object, pause, protest, refuse, take exception, waver.

demurral *n* compunction, demurral, demurrer, dissent, hesitation, misgiving, objection, protest, qualm, reservation, scruple.

demure *adj* coy, decorous, diffident, grave, maidenly, modest, priggish, prim, prissy, prudish, reserved, reticent, retiring, sedate, shy, sober, staid, strait-laced.

antonym forward.

den *n* cave, cavern, cloister, cubbyhole, earth, haunt, hideaway, hide-out, hidey-hole, hole, lair, retreat, sanctuary, sanctum, shelter, study.

denial *n* abjuration, abnegation, contradiction, denegation, deprivation, disaffirmation, disavowal, disclaimer, dismissal, dissent, gainsaying, negation, prohibition, rebuff, refusal, rejection, renunciation, repudiation, repulse, retraction, revocation, self-denial, veto, withholding.

denigrate *v* abuse, assail, bash, belittle, besmirch, blacken, calumniate, criticize, decry, defame, denounce, disparage, impugn, put down, malign, revile, run down, slander, smear, vilify.

antonym praise.

denigration *n* aspersion, backbiting, bashing, decrial, defamation, denunciation, derogation, detraction, disparagement, mudslinging, obloquy, put-down, scurrility, slander, smear(ing), vilification.

antonym praise.

denizen *n* citizen, dweller, frequenter, habitant, habitué, immigrant, inhabitant, occupant, resident.

denominate *v* baptize, call, christen, designate, entitle, label, name, style, term, title.

denomination *n* appellation, body, category, church, class, classification, communion, creed, designation, grade, group, kind, label, name, persuasion, religion, school, sect, size, sort, style, taxon, term, title, unit, value.

denote *v* betoken, express, imply, import, indicate, mark, mean, show, signify, stand for, symbolize, typify.

dénouement *n* climax, close, conclusion, culmination, ending, finale, finish, outcome, payoff, resolution, solution, termination, unravelling, upshot.

denounce *v* accuse, anathematize, arraign, assail, attack, brand, castigate, censure, condemn, criticize, declaim against, decry, denigrate, disown, fulminate against, impugn, inveigh against, proscribe, revile, stigmatize, vilify.

antonym praise.

dense *adj* blockish, close, close-textured, compact, compressed, condensed, crowded, dull, heavy, impenetrable, intense, jam-packed, obtuse, opaque, packed, profound, slow, slow-witted, solid, stolid, stupid, thick, thick-headed.

antonyms clever, sparse.

denseness *n* dullness, obtuseness, slowness, stolidity, stupidity, thickheadedness.

antonym acuteness.

density *n* body, bulk, close-texturedness, compactness, denseness, heaviness, impenetrability, mass, solidity, solidness, substance, thickness.

antonym sparseness.

dent *n* chip, concavity, crater, depression, dimple, dint, hollow, impression, indentation, pit.

v dint, gouge, indent, push in, stave in.

make a dent in eat into, make an impression on, make inroads into, take a chunk out of.

denude *v* bare, defoliate, deforest, divest, expose, strip, uncover.

antonym cover.

denunciation *n* accusation, assailment, attack, castigation, censure, condemnation, criticism, decrial, decrying, denouncement, disowning, fulmination, incrimination, invective, obloquy, proscription, stigmatization.

antonyms compliment, praise.

denunciatory *adj* accusatory, accusing, attack, censorious, comminatory, condemnatory, condemning, decrying, execratory, fulminatory, incriminatory, recriminatory, reproachful.

antonym complimentary.

deny *v* abjure, contradict, decline, disaffirm, disagree with, disallow, disavow, disbelieve, discard, disclaim, discredit, disown, disprove, forbid, gainsay, ignore, negate, oppose, rebuff, recant, refuse, refute, reject, renounce, repudiate, repulse, revoke, trample on, traverse, turn down, veto, withhold.

antonyms admit, allow.

deodorant *n* air-freshener, antiperspirant, deodorizer, room freshener.

deodorize *v* aerate, freshen, purify, refresh, sweeten, ventilate.

depart *v* absent oneself, be off, break away, decamp, deviate, die, differ, digress, disappear, diverge, escape, exit, go, go (away), leave, make off, migrate, quit, remove, retire, retreat, set forth, skedaddle, stray, swerve, take off, take one's leave, vanish, vary, veer, withdraw.
antonyms arrive, keep to.

departed *adj* dead, deceased, defunct, expired, late.

department *n* area, branch, bureau, district, division, domain, faculty, field, function, line, ministry, office, province, realm, region, responsibility, section, sector, sphere, station, subdivision, unit.

departure *n* abandonment, break, branching, branching out, change, death, deviation, difference, digression, disappearance, divergence, exit, exodus, going, innovation, leave-taking, leaving, parting, removal, retirement, shift, variation, veering, withdrawal.
antonym arrival.

depend on anticipate, bank on, be based on, be conditional on, be contingent on, be determined by, be a function of, calculate on, count on, expect, hang on, hinge on, lean on, reckon on, rely on, rest on, revolve around, trust in, turn on, turn to.

dependable *adj* certain, conscientious, faithful, gilt-edged, honest, reliable, responsible, steady, sterling, sure, trustworthy, trusty, unfailing.
antonyms undependable, unreliable.

dependant *n* child, client, hanger-on, henchman, minion, minor, protégé, relative, retainer, subordinate, vassal.

dependence *n* addiction, attachment, belief, confidence, contingency, craving, dependency, expectation, faith, helplessness, hope, insecurity, need, reliance, subordination, subservience, trust, vassalage, vulnerability, weakness.
antonyms independence, self-sufficiency.

dependent *adj* addicted, conditional, contingent, controlled (by), defenceless, depending, determined (by), feudal, hanging down, helpless, immature, influenced (by), insecure, needy, related (to), reliant, relying, resulting (from), subject, subject (to), subordinate, tied (to), tributary, vulnerable, weak.
antonyms independent, self-sufficient.

depict *v* caricature, characterize, delineate, describe, detail, draw, illustrate, limn, narrate, outline, paint, picture, portray, render, reproduce, represent, sculpt, show, sketch, trace.

depiction *n* caricature, delineation, description, drawing, illustration, image, likeness, outline, picture, portrayal, representation, sketch.

deplete *v* attenuate, bankrupt, consume, decimate, decrease, diminish, drain, empty, exhaust, expend, impoverish, lessen, make a dent in, make an impression in, reduce, use up.

antonyms augment, increase, replenish, spare.

depleted *adj* attenuated, consumed, decimated, decreased, diminished, drained, dwindling, emptied, exhausted, lessened, reduced, spent, used up, weakened, worn out.
antonyms augmented, increased, replenished.

depletion *n* attenuation, consumption, decimation, decrease, deficiency, diminution, draining, dwindling, emptying, exhaustion, expenditure, lessening, lowering, reduction, shrinkage.
antonyms increase, replenishment, supply.

deplorable *adj* blameworthy, calamitous, dire, disastrous, disgraceful, dishonourable, disreputable, distressing, execrable, grievous, heartbreaking, lamentable, miserable, opprobrious, pitiable, pitiful, regrettable, reprehensible, sad, scandalous, shameful, unfortunate, wretched.
antonyms excellent, praiseworthy.

deplore *v* abhor, bemoan, bewail, censure, condemn, denounce, deprecate, disapprove, execrate, grieve over, lament, mourn, regret.
antonym praise.

deploy *v* arrange, dispose, distribute, embattle, extend, position, spread out, station, use, utilize.

depopulate *v* dispeople, empty, evacuate, unpeople.

deport[1] *v* banish, evict, exile, expatriate, expel, extradite, oust, remove, resettle.

deport[2] *v* acquit, act, bear, behave, carry, comport, conduct, demean, hold, manage.

deportation *n* banishment, eviction, exile, expatriation, expulsion, extradition, removal, resettlement, transportation.

deportment *n* actions, air, appearance, aspect, bearing, behaviour, carriage, cast, comportment, conduct, demeanour, etiquette, manner, mien, pose, posture, stance.

depose *v* cashier, declare, degrade, demote, depone, dethrone, discrown, disestablish, dismiss, displace, downgrade, oust, remove, testify, topple.

deposit[1] *v* drop, dump, insert, lay (down), leave, pay, park, place, plunk (down), precipitate, put (down), seat, set, settle, sit, unload.
n accumulation, alluvium, deposition, dregs, hypostasis, lees, precipitate, sediment, silt.

deposit[2] *v* bank, consign, entrust, file, invest, lodge, reposit, rest, save, store.
n bail, down payment, instalment, money, part(ial), part payment, pledge, retainer, security, stake.

deposition[1] *n* demotion, dethronement, discoronation, dismissal, displacement, ousting, removal, toppling.

deposition[2] *n* affidavit, declaration, denunciation, evidence, information, statement, testimony.

depository n bond, depository, depot, dump, repository, store, storehouse, trustee, warehouse.

depot n arsenal, bond, depository, distribution centre, dump, garage, receiving-house, repository, station, storehouse, storeroom, terminal, terminus, warehouse.

deprave v brutalize, corrupt, debase, debauch, degrade, demoralize, pervert, seduce, subvert, vitiate.

antonym improve.

depraved adj abandoned, base, brutalized, corrupt, debased, debauched, degenerate, degraded, demoralized, dissolute, evil, twisted, immoral, perverted, profligate, reprobate, shameless, sinful, vicious, vile, warped, wicked.

antonym upright.

▲ *confusable word* deprived.

depravity n baseness, bestiality, corruption, criminality, debasement, debauchery, degeneracy, degradation, demoralization, depravation, dissoluteness, evil, immorality, iniquity, perversion, profligacy, reprobacy, sinfulness, turpitude, twistedness, vice, viciousness, vileness, wickedness.

antonym uprightness.

deprecate v belittle, condemn, denounce, deplore, disapprove of, disparage, object to, plead against, protest against, put down, reject.

antonyms approve, commend, take a stand against.

▲ *confusable word* depreciate.

deprecation n belittling, condemnation, denunciation, disapproval, dismissal, disparagement, objection, opposition, protestation, put-down, rejection.

antonyms commendation, encouragement.

deprecatory adj apologetic, belittling, censorious, condemnatory, derogatory, disapproving, dismissive, disparaging, perjorative, protesting, regretful, reproachful.

antonyms commendatory, encouraging.

depreciate v belittle, cheapen, decrease, decry, deflate, denigrate, deride, derogate, detract, devaluate, devalue, disparage, downgrade, drop, fall, lessen, lower, minimize, misprise, reduce, ridicule, scorn, slight, slump, traduce, trivialize, underestimate, underrate, undervalue.

antonyms appreciate, overrate, praise.

▲ *confusable word* deprecate.

depreciation n belittlement, cheapening, deflation, depression, derogation, detraction, devaluation, disparagement, downgrading, drop, fall, misprizing, pejoration, slump.

antonyms appreciation, exaggeration, praise.

depredation n denudation, desolation, despoiling, despoliation, destruction, devastation, harrying, laying waste, looting, marauding, pillage, pillaging, plunder, plundering, raiding, ransacking, rape, rapine, ravaging, raven, robbery, spoliation, stripping, theft.

depress v burden, chill, damp, daunt, debilitate, decrease, deject, devaluate, devalue, devitalize, diminish, discourage, dishearten, dispirit, downgrade, drain, enervate, engloom, exhaust, flatten, impair, inhibit, lessen, lower, oppress, overburden, press, reduce, sadden, sap, squash, slow, tire, undermine, upset, weaken, weary.

antonyms cheer, energize, gladden, revitalize, stimulate.

depressant n calmative, downer, relaxant, sedative, tranquilliser.

antonym stimulant.

depressed[1] adj blue, cast down, cheerless, crestfallen, debilitated, dejected, demoralized, despairing, deprived, despondent, desponding, destitute, devitalized, disadvantaged, discouraged, disheartened, dispirited, distressed, down, downbeat, downcast, downhearted, enervated, exanimate, glum, hopeless, lethargic, limp, low, low-spirited, melancholy, miserable, moody, morose, needy, pessimistic, poor, sad, spiritless, unhappy.

antonym cheerful.

depressed[2] adj concave, dented, dinted, dished, hollow, indented, recessed, sunken.

antonyms convex, prominent, protuberant, swelling.

depressing adj black, bleak, burdensome, cheerless, daunting, dejecting, demoralizing, devitalizing, discouraging, disheartening, dismal, dispiriting, distressing, dreary, enervating, gloomy, grey, heartbreaking, hopeless, lugubrious, melancholy, oppresive, sad, saddening, sombre.

antonym encouraging.

depression[1] n blues, cabin fever, decline, dejection, despair, despondency, dispiritedness, doldrums, dolefulness, downheartedness, dullness, dumps, ennui, exanimation, gloom, gloominess, glumness, hard times, heart-heaviness, hopelessness, inactivity, low spirits, lowness, malaise, mal du siècle, megrims, melancholia, melancholy, moroseness, panophobia, recession, sadness, slump, spiritlessness, stagnation, unhappiness, vapours, weltschmerz, worldweariness.

antonyms cheerfulness, prosperity.

depression[2] n basin, bowl, cavity, concavity, dent, dimple, dint, dip, dish, excavation, fossa, fovea, hollow, hollowness, impression, indentation, navel, pit, sag, sink, umbilicus, valley.

antonyms convexity, prominence, protuberance, swelling.

deprivation n denial, denudation, deprival, despoliation, destitution, disadvantage, dispossession, distress, divestment, expropriation, hardship, loss, need, poverty, privation, removal, want, withdrawal, withholding.

antonym bestowal.

deprive v bereave, defraud, denude, deny, despoil, dispossess, divest, expropriate, mulct, rob, starve, strip.

antonym bestow.

deprived *adj* bereft, denuded, depressed, destitute, disadvantaged, forlorn, impoverished, in want, lacking, necessitous, needy, poor, underdeveloped, undernourished.

antonyms fortunate, prosperous.

▲ *confusable word* depraved.

depth *n* abstruseness, abysm, abyss, centre, complexity, deepness, discernment, drop, exhaustiveness, extent, gulf, heart, insight, intensity, intensiveness, interior, lowness, measure, middle, obscurity, penetration, perspective, pit, profoundness, profundity, reconditeness, richness, sagacity, shrewdness, strength, thoroughness, three-dimensionality, wisdom.

in depth comprehensively, exhaustively, extensively, in detail, intensively, thoroughly.

antonyms broadly, superficially.

deputation *n* appointment, assignment, commission, delegates, delegation, deputies, deputing, designation, embassy, legation, mission, nomination, representatives.

depute *v* appoint, authorize, charge, commission, delegate, empower, entrust, mandate, nominate.

deputize *v* commission, delegate, depute, double, replace, represent, stand in for, substitute for, understudy.

deputy *n* agent, alternate, ambassador, assistant, coadjutor, commissary, commissioner, delegate, henchman, legate, lieutenant, nuncio, proxy, representative, second-in-command, substitute, suffragan, surrogate, vicar, vicegerent.

adj assistant, subordinate, substitute, suffragan, surrogate, vice.

derange *v* confound, confuse, craze, dement, disarrange, disarray, discompose, disconcert, disorder, displace, disturb, drive crazy, madden, make insane, ruffle, unbalance, unhinge, unsettle, upset.

deranged *adj* aberrant, batty, berserk, brainsick, confused, crazed, crazy, delirious, delusional, demented, disarranged, disordered, distracted, distraught, disturbed, frantic, frenzied, hallucinating, insane, irrational, loony, lunatic, mad, maddened, mentally ill, nutty, of unsound mind, unbalanced, unhinged.

antonyms calm, sane.

derangement *n* aberration, agitation, alienation, brainsickness, confusion, craziness, delirium, dementia, disarrangement, disarray, disorder, distraction, disturbance, frenzy, hallucinations, illness, insanity, irregularity, jumble, lunacy, madness, mania, mental disorder (or illness), muddle.

antonyms order, sanity.

derelict *adj* abandoned, deserted, desolate, dilapidated, discarded, forlorn, forsaken, neglected, negligent, remiss, ruined.

n down-and-out, drifter, hobo, outcast, rubby, street person, tramp, vagrant, wastrel.

dereliction *n* abandonment, abdication, apostasy, betrayal, default, delinquency, desertion, evasion, failure, faithlessness, fault, forsaking, neglect, negligence, remissness, renegation.

antonyms devotion, faithfulness, fulfilment.

deride *v* belittle, contemn, detract, disdain, disparage, flout, gibe, insult, jeer at, knock, laugh at, lampoon, make fun of, mock, parody, pillory, pooh-pooh, rail at, ridicule, satirize, scoff at, scorn, sneer, taunt.

antonyms praise, respect.

de rigueur comme il faut, compulsory, conventional, correct, decent, decorous, done, fitting, necessary, obligatory, proper, required, right, the done thing.

derision *n* contempt, contumely, disdain, disparagement, disrespect, insult, lampooning, laughter, mockery, parodying, raillery, ridicule, satire, scoffing, scorn, sneering.

antonyms praise, reverence.

derisive *adj* contemptuous, derisory, disdainful, disparaging, disrespectful, insulting, irreverent, jeering, mocking, parodying, ridiculing, satiristic, scornful, taunting.

antonyms appreciative, flattering.

derisory *adj* absurd, contemptible, derisive, insulting, laughable, ludicrous, mockable, outrageous, preposterous, ridiculous, risible.

derivation *n* ancestry, basis, beginning, deduction, descent, etymology, extraction, foundation, genealogy, inference, origin, root, source.

derivative *adj* borrowed, conventional, copied, copycat, daughter, derived, hackneyed, imitative, inferred, regurgitated, rehashed, secondary, second-hand, transmitted, trite, unadventurous, unimaginative, uninventive, unoriginal.

n branch, by-product, derivation, descendant, development, offshoot, outgrowth, product, refinement, spinoff.

derive *v* arise, borrow, collect, deduce, descend, develop, draw, emanate from, extract, flow, follow, gain, gather, get, glean, grow, infer, issue, lift, obtain, originate, proceed, receive, spring, stem, trace.

derogate *v* become worse, belittle, decry, defame, degenerate, denigrate, depreciate, deteriorate, detract, devalue, deviate, diminish, disparage, insult, lessen, misprise, put down, rundown, slight, take away (from), talk down, trivialize, undermine.

antonyms add to, appreciate, praise.

derogatory *adj* aspersory, belittling, critical, damaging, defamatory, depreciatory, destructive, detractive, disparaging, injurious, insulting, offensive, pejorative, slighting, snide, (term) of contempt, uncomplimentary, unfavourable, unflattering.

antonyms appreciative, favourable, flattering.

descend *v* alight, arrive, assail, assault, attack, condescend, degenerate, deign, derive, deteriorate, develop, dip, dismount, drop, fall, gravitate, incline, invade, issue, leap, originate, plummet, plunge, pounce, proceed, raid, sink, slant, slope, spring, stem, stoop, subside, swoop.

descendants n children, family, house, issue, line, lineage, offspring, posterity, progeny, race, scions, seed, sons and daughters, successors.

descent n ancestry, assault, attack, comedown, debasement, decadence, declination, decline, declivity, degradation, deriviation, deterioration, dip, drop, extraction, fall, family tree, foray, genealogy, heredity, incline, incursion, inheritance, invasion, line, lineage, origin, parentage, plunge, pounce, raid, slant, slope, stoop, swoop.

antonyms ascent, improvement.

describe v characterize, define, delineate, depict, detail, draw, enlarge on, explain, express, illustrate, mark out, narrate, outline, portray, present, recount, relate, report, represent, sketch, specify, tell, trace.

description n account, brand, breed, category, characterization, class, delineation, depiction, detailling, explanation, exposition, genre, ilk, image, kidney, kind, narration, narrative, order, outline, portrayal, presentation, report, representation, sketch, sort, species, specification, type, variety, wordpainting, wordpicture.

descriptive adj blow-by-blow, circumstantial, colourful, depictive, detailed, explanatory, expressive, full, graphic, illustrative, immediate, pictorial, picturesque, specific, vivid.

antonyms cursory, laconic.

descry v catch sight of, detect, discern, discover, distinguish, espy, glimpse, make out, mark, notice, observe, perceive, recognize, see, sight, spot, spy.

desecrate v abuse, blaspheme, contaminate, debase, defile, despoil, dishonour, insult, invade, pervert, pollute, profane, vandalize, violate.

desecration n blasphemy, contamination, debasement, defilement, dishonouring, impiety, insult, invasion, perversion, pollution, profanation, sacrilege, vandalism, violation.

desert[1] n badlands, solitude, vacuum, void, waste, wasteland, wilderness, wild, wilds.
adj arid, bare, barren, desolate, droughty, dry, infertile, lonely, solitary, sterile, uncultivated, uninhabitable, uninhabited, unpeopled, unproductive, untilled, waste, waterless, wild.

desert[2] v abandon, abscond, apostatize, backslide, be unfaithful to, betray, break faith with, decamp, deceive, defect, fail, forsake, give up (on), go AWOL, jilt, leave, leave holding the baby/bag, leave in the lurch, maroon, quit, rat on, relinquish, renege, renounce, resign, strand, tergiversate, vacate.

desert[3] n comeuppance, demerit, deserts, due, guerdon, meed, merit, payment, recompense, remuneration, requital, retribution, return, reward, right, virtue, worth.

deserted adj abandoned, alone, bereft, betrayed, derelict, desolate, empty, forlorn, forsaken, friendless, godforsaken, isolated, left holding the baby (or bag), left in the lurch, lonely, marooned, neglected, solitary, stranded, underpopulated, unfriended, unoccupied, unpopulous, vacant, vacated.

antonym populous.

deserter n absconder, apostate, backslider, betrayer, defector, delinquent, escapee, fugitive, rat, renegade, runaway, traitor, truant.

desertion n abandonment, absconding, apostasy, betrayal, defection, delinquency, departure, dereliction, escape, evasion, flight, forsaking, jilting, relinquishment, renunciation, tergiversation, truancy.

deserve v ask for, be worthy (of), earn, gain, incur, justify, merit, rate, warrant.

deserved adj apposite, appropriate, apt, condign, due, earned, fair, fitting, in order, just, justifiable, justified, legitimate, meet, merited, proper, right, rightful, suitable, warranted, well-earned.

antonyms gratuitous, undeserved.

deserving adj admirable, commendable, creditable, estimable, exemplary, laudable, meritorious, praiseworthy, righteous, virtuous, worthy.

antonyms undeserving, unworthy.

desiccated adj arid, dead, dehydrated, drained, dried, dry, dry as dust, exsiccated, lifeless, moistureless, parched, passionless, sere, spiritless, sterile.

desiccation n aridity, dehydration, dryness, exsiccation, parching, sterility.

desideratum n aim, aspiration, dream, essential, gap, goal, heart's desire, hope, ideal, lack, lacuna, need, object, objective, sine qua non, want, wish.

design[1] n agenda, architecture, arrangement, blueprint, composition, configuration, conformation, construction, contrivance, delineation, draft, drawing, figure, form, logo, model, motif, organization, outline, pattern, prototype, purpose, schema, shape, sketch, structure, style.
v conceive, construct, contrive, create, delineate, describe, destine, develop, devise, draft, draw, draw up, fabricate, fashion, form, invent, make, model, originate, outline, plan, shape, sketch, structure, tailor, trace.

design[2] n aim, conspiracy end, goal, intent, intention, intrigue, machination, manoeuvre, meaning, object, objective, plan, plot, project, purpose, scheme.

designate v allot, appoint, assign, bill, call, characterize, choose, christen, code-name, deem, define, delegate, denominate, denote, depute, describe, docket, earmark, entitle, indicate, label, mark out, name, nickname, nominate, point out, select, set aside, show, slate, specify, stipulate, style, term, ticket, title.

designation n appointment, category, characterization, classification, code-name, definition, delegation, denomination, deputjation, description, docket, epithet, indication, label, mark, name, nickname, nomination, selection, specification, title.

designedly *adv* calculatedly, consciously, deliberately, intentionally, knowingly, on purpose, premeditatedly, purposely, studiously, willfully, willingly, with malice aforethought, wittingly.
antonyms innocently, unwittingly.

designer *n* architect, artificer, author, contriver, couturier, creator, deviser, fashioner, framer, inventor, maker, mastermind, originator, planner, stylist.

designing *adj* artful, calculating, conniving, conspiring, contriving, crafty, cunning, deceitful, devious, disingenuous, guileful, insidious, intriguing, Machiavellian, manipulative, manoeuvering, plotting, scheming, sharp, shrewd, sly, treacherous, tricky, underhanded, unscrupulous, wily.
antonym artless.

desirability *n* advantage, advisability, allure, attraction, attractiveness, beauty, benefit, merit, profit, seductiveness, usefulness, value, worth.
antonyms disadvantage, inadvisability, undesirability.

desirable *adj* adorable, advantageous, advisable, agreeable, alluring, appetizing, appropriate, attractive, beneficial, captivating, covetable, coveted, eligible, enviable, excellent, expedient, fascinating, fetching, good, nubile, pleasing, plummy, preferable, profitable, seductive, sensible, sexy, suitable, tempting, worthwhile.
antonym undesirable.

desire *v* ask (for), aspire (to), beg, covet, crave, entreat, fancy, hanker after, hunger for, importune, itch, long (for), look for, need, petition, request, require, seek, solicit, thirst (after or for), want, wish (for), yearn (for).
n appeal, appetence, appetite, ardour, aspiration, concupiscence, covetousness, craving, cupidity, entreaty, greed, hankering, itch, lasciviousness, lechery, libido, longing, lust, lustfulness, need, passion, petition, request, solicitation, supplication, want, wish, yearning, yen.

desired *adj* appropriate, correct, coveted, expected, express, fitting, longed-for, looked-for, necessary, needed, particular, proper, requested, required, right, sought-after, wanted, wished-for.
antonyms undesired, unintentional.

desirous *adj* ambitious, anxious, aspiring, avid, burning, craving, eager, enthusiastic, greedy, hopeful, hoping, itching, keen, longing, ready, willing, wishing, yearning.
antonyms reluctant, unenthusiastic.

desist *v* abstain, break off, cease, come to a halt, cut out, discontinue, end, forbear, give in, give over, give up, halt, leave off, pause, peter out, refrain, remit, stop, suspend.
antonyms continue, resume.

desolate *adj* abandoned, alone, arid, bare, barren, bereft, bleak, cheerless, comfortless, companionless, dejected, depopulated, depressed, depressing, derelict, deserted, desolated, despondent, devastated, disconsolate, disheartened, dismal, dismayed, distressed, downcast, dreary, empty, forlorn, forsaken, gloomy, godforsaken, inconsolable, isolated, joyless, laid waste, lonely, melancholy, miserable, ravaged, ruined, solitary, unfrequented, unhappy, uninhabited, unpopulated, waste, wild, wretched.
antonym cheerful.
v cast down, denude, depopulate, depress, desert, despoil, destroy, devastate, dishearten, distress, lay waste, pillage, plunder, ravage, ruin, spoil, waste, wreck.

desolation *n* abandonment, anguish, barrenness, bereavement, bleakness, comfortlessness, dejection, depopulation, desolateness, despair, desperation, despondency, devastation, disconsolateness, dismay, distress, dreariness, emptiness, forlornness, gloom, gloominess, grief, havoc, isolation, loneliness, melancholy, misery, ravages, ruin, ruination, sadness, solitariness, solitude, sorrow, unhappiness, wildness, woe, wretchedness.

despair *v* capitulate, collapse, crumple, despond, give in, give up (hope), lose heart, lose hope, quit, surrender.
antonym hope.
n anguish, defeatism, dejection, depression, desperation, despondency, disconsolateness, emptiness, forlornness, gloom, hopelessness, inconsolableness, melancholy, misery, pain, resignation, resourcelessness, sorrow, wretchedness.
antonyms cheerfulness, resilience.

despairing *adj* anxious, broken-hearted, crushed, dejected, depressed, desolate, desperate, despondent, disconsolate, disheartened, dispirited, distracted, distraught, downcast, forlorn, frantic, grief-stricken, heartbroken, hopeless, inconsolable, melancholy, miserable, sorrowful, suicidal, woebegone, wretched.
antonyms cheerful, resilient.

desperado *n* bandit, brigand, criminal, cutthroat, dacoit, gangster, gunman, heavy, highway robber, hood, hoodlum, law-breaker, mugger, outlaw, ruffian, thug.

desperate *adj* acute, audacious, critical, dangerous, daring, despairing, despondent, determined, dire, do-or-die, drastic, extreme, foolhardy, forlorn, frantic, frenzied, grave, great, hasty, hazardous, headlong, hopeless, inconsolable, incurable, irremediable, irretrievable, madcap, miserable, precipitate, rash, reckless, risky, serious, severe, temerarious, urgent, violent, wild, wretched.

desperately *adv* agonizingly, appallingly, badly, critically, dangerously, distractedly, excrutiatingly, fearfully, frantically, frenziedly, frightfully, gravely, hopelessly, miserably, perilously, seriously, severely, shockingly, terribly, urgently, violently, wildly.

desperation *n* agony, anguish, anxiety, despair, despondency, disconsolateness, distraction, distress, foolhardiness, frenzy, hastiness, heedlessness, hoplessness, madness, misery, pain, rashness, recklessness, sorrow, trouble, unhappiness, worry.

despicable *adj* abhorrent, abject, base, cheap, contemptible, degraded, detestable, disgraceful, disgusting, disreputable, hateful, ignoble, ignominious, infamous, low, low-down, mean, miserable, nasty, reprehensible, reprobate, rotten, scurvy, shameful, sordid, unprincipled, vile, worthless, wretched.
antonyms laudable, noble.

despise *v* abhor, condemn, contemn, deplore, deride, detest, disdain, dislike, disregard, have contempt for, hate, ignore, loathe, look down on, misprize, revile, scorn, slight, spurn, undervalue.
antonyms appreciate, prize.

despite *prep* against, defying, heedless of, in spite of, in the face of, in the teeth of, notwithstanding, regardless of, undaunted by, undeterred by.

despoil *v* bereave, denude, deprive, destroy, devastate, dispossess, divest, loot, maraud, pillage, plunder, rape, ransack, ravage, rifle, rob, spoliate, strip, vandalize, wreck.
antonyms adorn, enrich.

despoliation *n* denudation, depredation, despoilment, destruction, devastation, havoc, looting, marauding, pillage, plunder, rape, rapine, ravaging, raven, ruin, spoliation, vandalism, wreckage.
antonyms adornment, enrichment.

despond *v* capitulate, despair, lose courage, lose heart, lose hope, quit, surrender.
antonym hope.

despondency *n* broken-heartedness, dejection, depression, despair, desperation, disconsolateness, discouragement, dispiritedness, downheartedness, forlornness, gloom, glumness, hopelessness, inconsolability, melancholia, melancholy, misery, sadness, sorrow, unhappiness, wretchedness.
antonyms cheerfulness, hopefulness.

despondent *adj* blue, broken-hearted, dejected, depressed, despairing, disconsolate, discouraged, disheartened, dispirited, doleful, down, downcast, downhearted, forlorn, gloomy, glum, hopeless, inconsolable, low, low-spirited, melancholy, miserable, morose, mournful, overwhelmed, sad, sorrowful, woebegone, wretched.
antonyms cheerful, hopeful.

despot *n* absolutist, autocrat, boss, dictator, Hitler, monocrat, oppressor, overlord, tyrant.
antonyms democrat, egalitarian, liberal.

despotic *adj* absolute, absolutist, arbitrary, arrogant, autachie, authoritarian, autocratic, bossy, dictatorial, domineering, imperious, monocratic, oppressive, overbearing, peremptory, totalitarian, tyrannical.
antonyms democratic, egalitarian, liberal, tolerant.

despotism *n* absolutism, autarchy, authoritarianism, autocracy, dictatorship,

monarchism, monocracy, oppression, repression, totalitarianism, tyranny.
antonyms democracy, egalitarianism, liberalism, tolerance.

destination *n* aim, ambition, aspiration, end, goal, harbour, haven, journey's end, object, objective, port of call, station, stop, target, terminus.

destine *v* allot, appoint, assign, consecrate, decree, design, designate, devote, doom, earmark, fate, foredoom, foreordain, intend, mark out, mean, ordain, predestinate, predestine, predetermine, preordain, purpose, reserve.

destined *adj* assigned, booked, bound, certain, designed, directed, doomed, en route, fated, foreordained, headed, heading, ineluctable, inescapable, inevitable, intended, in the cards, meant, ordained, predestined, predetermined, preordained, routed, unavoidable.

destiny *n* cup, doom, fate, fortune, karma, kismet, lot, portion, predestiny.

destitute *adj* bankrupt, beggared, bereft, deprived, devoid (of), dispossessed, distressed, down- and-out, impecunious, impoverished, indigent, insolvent, in want (of), lacking, necessitous, needy, penniless, penurious, poor, poverty-stricken, strapped, wanting.
antonyms prosperous, wealthy.

destitution *n* bankruptcy, beggary, distress, impecuniousness, indigence, lack, need, neediness, pauperism, pennilessness, penury, poverty, privation, starvation, straits, want.
antonyms prosperity, wealth.

destroy *v* annihilate, break, crush, demolish, devastate, dismantle, dispatch, eliminate, eradicate, euchre, exterminate, extinguish, extirpate, gut, kill, lay waste, level, nullify, overthrow, ravage, raze, ruin, sabotage, scuttle, shatter, slay, smash, stamp out, thwart, torpedo, undermine, undo, vandalize, vaporize, waste, wipe out, wreck, zap.
antonym create.

destroyer *n* angel of death, annihilator, demolisher, desolater, despoiler, destroying angel, devestator, Grim Reaper, iconoclast, juggernaut, kiss of death, liquidator, ransacker, ravager, slayer, smasher, undoer, vandal, wrecker.
antonym creator.

destruction *n* annihilation, bane, crushing, defeat, demolition, desolation, devastation, downfall, elimination, end, eradication, extermination, extinction, extirpation, havoc, killing, liquidation, massacre, nullification, overthrow, ravagement, ruin, ruination, shattering, slaughter, slaying, smashing, undoing, vandalism, wastage, wrack, wreckage.
antonym creation.

destructive *adj* adverse, antagonistic, baleful, baneful, calamitous, cataclysmic, catastrophic, contrary, damaging, deadly, deathful, deleterious, derogatory, detrimental, devastating, disastrous, disparaging, disruptive, fatal, harmful, hostile, hurtful, injurious, invalidating, lethal, malignant, negative, noxious, nullifying, pernicious, pestiferous, pestilent, pestilential, ruinous, slaughterous, subversive, undermining, vexatious, vicious.

antonyms creative, positive, productive.

desultory *adj* accidental, aimless, capricious, cursory, digressional, disconnected, discursive, disorderly, disorganized, erratic, fitful, haphazard, inconsistent, inconstant, irregular, irrelevant, loose, maundering, meandering, peripatetic, rambling, random, unconnected, unco-ordinated, undirected, unmethodical, unsystematic, wandering.

antonyms concerted, methodical, systematic.

detach *v* abstract, alienate, cut off, disconnect, disengage, disentangle, disjoin, dissociate, distance, disunite, divide, estrange, free, isolate, loosen, make aloof, make uninvolved, remove, set apart, segregate, separate, sever, take off, uncouple, undo, unfasten, unfix, unhitch, unhook, unlink.

antonym attach.

detached *adj* absent, abstract(ed), aloof, cool, disconnected, discrete, disinterested, disjoined, dispassionate, dissociated, distant, divided, free, free-standing, impartial, impassive, impersonal, independent, loosened, neutral, objective, removed, reserved, separate, severed, unattached, unbiassed, uncommitted, unconcerned, unconnected, unimpassioned, uninvolved, unprejudiced.

antonyms concerned, connected, involved.

detachment¹ *n* aloofness, coolness, disconnection, disengagement, disinterest, disinterestedness, disjoining, dissociation, distance, fairness, impartiality, impassivity, indifference, isolation, laissez-faire, neutrality, non-partisanship, objectivity, remoteness, removal, separation, severance, severing, unconcern, uncoupling, unfastening, uninvolvement.

antonyms attachment, concern, involvement.

detachment² *n* assignment, body, brigade, corps, detail, force, party, patrol, squad, task force, unit.

detail¹ *n* aspect, attribute, complexity, complication, component, elaborateness, elaboration, element, fact, factor, feature, incidental, ingredient, intricacy, item, meticulousness, minuteness, nicety, particular, particularity, point, refinement, respect, specific, specificity, technicality, thoroughness, triviality.

v catalogue, delineate, depict, describe, dilate upon, elaborate on, enumerate, individualize, itemize, list, narrate, particularize, portray, recite, recount, rehearse, relate, specify.

in detail at length, comprehensively, exhaustively, fully, in depth, in particular, inside out, item by item, particularly, point by point, thoroughly.

antonyms broadly, superficially.

detail² *n* assignment, duty, force, group, job, party, squad, task, task force.

v allocate, appoint, assign, commission, delegate, depute, send.

detailed *adj* amplified, blow-by-blow, circumstantial, complex, complicated, comprehensive, descriptive, elaborate, exact, exhaustive, extensive, fine, full, intricate, itemized, meticulous, minute, particular, particularized, specific, thorough, unabridged, unsparing.

antonyms brief, cursory, summary.

details *n* complexities, complications, ins and outs, intricacies, minutiae, niceties, particularities, particulars, specifics, trivia, trivialities.

detain *v* arrest, buttonhole, check, confine, delay, detain in custody, hinder, hold, hold back, hold up, impede, incarcerate, intern, keep, prevent, restrain, retain in custody, retard, slow, stay, stop, waylay.

antonym release.

detect *v* ascertain, catch (out), descry, discern, discover, distinguish, espy, expose, find, identify, nose out, note, notice, observe, perceive, recognize, reveal, scent, sight, smell out, sniff at, snoop out, spot, spy, track down, unearth, uncover, unmask.

detection *n* discernment, discovery, exposé, exposure, identification, nosing out, observation, perception, recognition, revelation, sighting, smelling out, sniffing out, snooping out, tracking down, uncovering, unearthing, unmasking.

detective *n* agent, busy, constable, cop, copper, dick, gumshoe, investigator, private eye, private investigator, shamus, sleuth, sleuth-hound.

detention *n* arrest, confinement, constraint, custody, delay, detainment, hindrance, holding back (or up), imprisonment, incarceration, internment, quarantine, restraint.

antonym release.

deter *v* cause to think twice, caution, check, damp, daunt, discourage, dissuade, frighten (off), give pause to, hinder, inhibit, intimidate, prevent, prohibit, put off, repel, restrain, stop, turn off, warn (off).

antonym encourage.

deteriorate *v* atrophy, backslide, corrode, crumble, decay, decline, decompose, degenerate, depreciate, disintegrate, ebb, fade, fail, fall off, go downhill, lapse, relapse, slide, slip, tabesce, weaken, worsen.

antonym improve.

deterioration *n* atrophy, corrosion, debasement, decline, degeneration, degradation, depreciation, descent, dilapidation, disintegration, downturn, drop, failing, fall, falling-off, lapse, pejoration, retrogression, slump, tabes, tabescence, vitiation, wastage, worsening.

antonym improvement.

determinate *adj* certain, clear-cut, conclusive, decided, defined, definite, definitive, delimited, determined, distinct, established, explicit, express, fixed, limited, positive, precise, quantified, settled, specific, specified.

antonym indeterminate.

determination *n* assessment, arbitration, backbone, calculation, conclusion, constancy, conviction, decision, dedication, definition, doggedness, drive, establishment, finding, firmness, fortitude, indomitability, insistence, intention, judgment, obstinacy, perseverance, persistence, pertinacity, purpose, resoluteness, resolution, resolve, settlement, single-mindedness, solution, specification, spire, steadfastness, strength of character, stubbornness, tenacity, verdict, will, willpower.

antonym irresolution.

determine *v* affect, arbitrate, ascertain, assess, calculate, certify, check, choose, conclude, control, decide, define, detect, dictate, direct, discover, elect, end, establish, figure (out), find (out), finish, fix, govern, guide, identify, impel, influence, inform, intend, lead, learn, limit, modify, ordain, purpose, regulate, resolve, rule, settle, shape, terminate, verify.

determined *adj* bent, constant, convinced, decided, dogged, firm, fixed, indivertible, insistent, intent, obstinate, persevering, persistent, pertinacious, purposeful, resolute, resolved, set, single-minded, steadfast, strong-minded, strong-willed, stubborn, tenacious, tough-minded, undissuadable, unflinching, unhesitating, unwavering.

antonyms irresolute, wishy-washy.

deterrent *n* bar, barrier, check, curb, difficulty, discouragement, disincentive, hindrance, impediment, obstacle, obstruction, repellent, restraint, turnoff, warning.

antonym incentive.

detest *v* abhor, abominate, deplore, despise, dislike, execrate, hate, have an aversion to, loathe, recoil from.

antonym adore.

detestable *adj* abhorred, abhorrent, abominable, accursed, despicable, disgusting, execrable, foul, hated, hateful, heinous, loathsome, nauseating, noisome, obnoxious, odious, offensive, pestiferous, pestilent, pestilential, repellent, repugnant, repulsive, revolting, rotten, shocking, sordid, swinish, vile, villainous.

antonyms admirable, adorable, pleasant.

detestation *n* abhorrence, abomination, anathema, animosity, animus, antipathy, aversion, disgust, dislike, enmity, execration, hate, hatred, hostility, loathing, odium, repugnance, revulsion.

antonyms adoration, approval, love.

dethrone *v* depose, oust, topple, uncrown, unseat.

antonyms crown, enthrone.

detonate *v* blast, blow up, discharge, explode, fulminate, ignite, kindle, set off, spark, trigger.

detonation *n* bang, blast, blowup, boom, burst, discharge, explosion, fulmination, igniting, ignition, kindling, report, triggering.

detour *n* bypass, by-path, byroad, byway, deviation, digression, diversion, excursus.

detract from *v* bash, belittle, criticize, denigrate, depreciate, derogate, devaluate, dilute, diminish, lessen, lower, mar, negate, nullify, put down, reduce, spoil, talk down, take away, trivialize, vitiate, weaken.

antonyms add to, enhance, praise.

▲ *confusable word* distract.

detraction *n* abuse, aspersion, bashing, belittling, belittlement, belittling, calumniation, calumny, criticism, defamation, denigration, depreciation, derogation, devaluation, disparagement, innuendo, insinuation, misrepresentation, muckraking, negation, put-down, reduction, revilement, scandalmongering, scurrility, slander, traducement, weakening, vituperation.

antonyms appreciation, enhancement, praise.

detractor *n* backbiter, basher, belittler, critic, defamer, denigrator, disparager, enemy, muckraker, opponent, reviler, scandalmonger, slanderer, traducer, vilifier.

antonyms flatterer, supporter.

detriment *n* damage, disadvantage, disservice, evil, harm, hurt, ill, impairment, injury, loss, menace, mischief, prejudice, threat.

antonym advantage.

detrimental *adj* adverse, baleful, damaging, dangerous, deleterious, destructive, disadvantageous, harmful, hurtful, inimical, injurious, noxious, pernicious, prejudicial, unfavourable, untoward.

antonym advantageous.

detritus *n* debris, fragments, garbage, junk, litter, remains, rubbish, scum, waste, wreckage.

de trop needless, redundant, supererogatory, superfluous, supernumerary, surplus, unnecessary, unneeded, unwanted, unwelcome.

devaluation *n* belittle, decrease, deflation, depreciation, denigration, disparagement, lowering, put-down, reduction, trivialization.

devalue *v* decrease, deflate, denigrate, devaluate, disparage, lower, reduce, trivialize.

devastate *v* annihilate, break the heart (or spirit) of, confound, crush, demolish, desolate, despoil, destroy, humiliate, lay low, lay waste, level, maraud, overwhelm, pillage, plunder, ransack, ravage, raze, ruin, sack, shatter, spoil, spoliate, undo, waste, wreck.

devastation *n* annihilation, broken-heartedness, brokenness, crushing, demolition, denudation, depredation, desolation, despoliation, destruction, havoc, humiliation, pillage, plunder, ravage(s), ruin, ruination, sack, spoliation, wasting, wrack, wreckage.

devastator *n* annihilator, crusher, demolisher, desolater, despoiler, destroyer, devourer,

devote

humiliator, plunderer, ravager, spoliator, undoer, vandal, wrecker.

develop v acquire, advance, amplify, augment, begin, bloom, blossom, branch out, breed, broaden, burgeon, build up, change, civilize, come up with, commence, contract, create, cultivate, elaborate (on), engender, enlarge, ensue, establish, evolve, expand, flourish, flower, follow, form, foster, generate, grow, happen, improve (on), industrialize, invent, make headway, mature, move on, originate, perfect, pick up, produce, progress, promote, prosper, refine, result, ripen, sprout, start, thrive, transpire, unfold.

development n advance, advancement, amplification, blooming, blossoming, building, burgeoning, change, circumstance, construction, creation, cultivation, elaboration, enlargement, establishment, event, evolution, expansion, extension, flowering, formation, furtherance, growth, happening, improvement, incident, increase, invention, issue, maturation, maturity, occurrence, outcome, phenomenon, phylogenesis, phylogeny, production, progress, progression, promotion, refinement, result, ripening, situation, spread, unfolding, unravelling, upbuilding, upshot.

deviant adj aberrant, abnormal, anomalous, antinormative, bent, bizarre, deviate, devious, disordered, divergent, freakish, freaky, heretical, heterodox, heteromorphic, irregular, kinky, non-conforming, perverse, perverted, queer, quirky, screwy, twisted, unnatural, unorthodox, wayward.

antonym normal.

n anomoly, deviate, eccentric, freak, kook, misfit, oddball, pervert, queer, screwball.

antonym straight.

deviate v depart, differ, digress, divagate, diverge, drift, err, go astray, part, stray, swerve, turn, turn aside, vary, veer, wander, yaw.

deviation n aberrance, aberrancy, aberration, abnormality, alteration, anomaly, antinormativity, change, deflection, departure, detour, digression, discrepancy, disparity, divagation, divergence, driftage, eccentricity, fluctuation, freak, freakishness, heteromorphism, heteromorphy, inconsistency, irregularity, kinkiness, quirk, quirkiness, shift, variance, variation, wandering.

antonym conformity.

device n apparatus, appliance, artifice, badge, blazon, colophon, contraption, contrivance, crest, design, dodge, emblem, expedient, figure, gadget, gambit, gimmick, gizmo, implement, improvisation, insignia, instrument, invention, logo, machination, mechanism, manoeuvre, motif, motto, plan, plot, ploy, ruse, scheme, shield, shift, stratagem, strategy, stunt, symbol, tactic, token, tool, trick, utensil, wile.

devil n adversary, Apollyon, archfiend, bastard, beast, Beelzebub, Belial, blighter, bogey, bogeyman, brute, cad, creature, demon, Evil One, fiend, hell, imp, incubus, Lucifer, Mephistopheles, monkey, monster, ogre, Old Nick, Prince of Darkness, rascal, rogue, rotter, Satan, savage, scamp, scoundrel, Shaitan, Slanderer, succubus, swine, the Enemy, terror, unfortunate, villain, wretch.

devilish adj accursed, black-hearted, damnable, dark, demonic, demonical, diabolical, evil, execrable, fiendish, hellish, impious, infernal, iniquitous, mischievous, monstrous, nefarious, satanic, villainous, wicked.

devil-may-care adj careless, casual, cavalier, easygoing, flippant, frivolous, happy-go-lucky, heedless, insouciant, jaunty, lackadaisical, laid-back, nonchalant, reckless, swaggering, swashbuckling, unconcerned, unworried.

devilment n devilry, deviltry, knavery, mischief, mischievousness, naughtiness, rascality, roguery, roguishness, sport, teasing.

deviltry n black magic, chicanery, cruelty, dark deeds, devilment, devilry, diablerie, diabolism, evil, hanky-panky, high jinks, jiggery-pokery, knavery, malevolence, malice, mischief, mischievousness, monkey business, naughtiness, prankishness, pranks, rascality, roguery, roguishness, sorcery, sport, trickiness, tricks, vice, viciousness, villainy, wickedness.

devious adj calculating, circuitous, confusing, convoluted, crafty, crooked, cunning, deceitful, deviating, dishonest, disingenuous, double-dealing, erratic, evasive, excursive, indirect, insidious, insincere, labyrinthine, manipulative, misleading, rambling, roundabout, scheming, slippery, sly, subtle, surreptitious, tortuous, treacherous, tricky, underhand(ed), wandering, wily, winding.

antonyms artless, candid, straightforward, up-front.

deviousness n circuitousness, craftiness, crookedness, cunning, deceit, dishonesty, disingenuity, evasion, evasiveness, indirectness, insincerity, slipperiness, slyness, subtlety, trickiness, underhandedness .

antonyms artlessness, openness.

devise v arrange, come up with, compass, compose, conceive, concoct, construct, contrive, craft, create, design, excogitate, forge, form, formulate, frame, imagine, invent, plan, plot, prepare, project, scheme, shape, think up, work out.

devoid of adj barren of, bereft of, deficient in, denuded of, destitute, empty of, free of, innocent of, lacking, sans, void of, wanting in, without.

antonyms blessed, endowed.

devolution n decentralization, degeneration, delegation, dispersal, distribution, passage, retrogression, transference.

antonym centralization.

devolve v be handed down, commission, consign, convey, delegate, deliver, depute, entrust, fall (to), hand down, pass, rest (with), transfer.

devote v allocate, allot, apply, appropriate, assign, commit, concentrate, consecrate, dedicate, direct, focus, give (oneself), pledge, reserve, sacrifice, set apart, set aside.

devoted *adj* adoring, ardent, assiduous, attentive, caring, committed, concerned, constant, dedicated, devout, faithful, fond, loving, loyal, single-minded, staunch, steadfast, tireless, true, unremitting, unswerving, wholehearted, zealous.

antonyms inconstant, indifferent, negligent.

devotee *n* addict, adherent, admirer, aficionado, buff, devil, disciple, enthusiast, fan, fanatic, fiend, follower, hound, supporter, votary, zealot.

antonyms adversary, sceptic.

devotion *n* adherence, adoration, affection, allegiance, ardour, assiduity, attachment, commitment, consecration, constancy, dedication, devoutness, earnestness, faith, faithfulness, fervour, fidelity, fondness, godliness, holiness, indefatigability, love, loyalty, passion, piety, prayer, regard, religiousness, reverence, sanctity, sedulousness, single-mindedness, spirituality, steadfastness, support, tirelessness, whole-heartedness, worship, zeal.

antonyms inconstancy, negligence.

devotional *adj* inspirational, contemplative, meditative, religious, reverential, sacred, solemn, spiritual, worshipful.

devour *v* absorb, annihilate, bolt, consume, cram (in), destroy, dispatch, down, eat (up), engulf, feast on, feast one's eyes on, gobble (up), gorge (oneself), gulp, guzzle, polish off, ravage, raven, relish, revel in, spend, stuff, swallow (up), waste, wolf (down).

devourer *n* consumer, destroyer, glutton, gobbler, gormandizer, gourmand, guzzler, waster.

devout *adj* ardent, constant, deep, devoted, earnest, faithful, fervent, genuine, godly, heartfelt, holy, intense, orthodox, passionate, pious, practising, prayerful, profound, pure, religious, reverent, saintly, serious, sincere, staunch, steadfast, unswerving, wholehearted, zealous.

antonyms insincere, uncommitted.

dewy *adj* blooming, doe-eyed, fresh, innocent, moist, refreshing, sparkling, starry-eyed, wet, youthful.

dexterity *n* ability, address, adroitness, agility, aptitude, art, artistry, cleverness, cunning, deftness, effortlessness, expertise, expertness, facility, finesse, handiness, ingenuity, legerdemain, mastery, neatness, nimbleness, proficiency, readiness, skilfulness, skill, smoothness, tact, touch.

antonyms clumsiness, ineptitude.

dexterous *adj* able, active, acute, adept, adroit, agile, apt, clever, cunning, deft, expert, facile, handy, ingenious, light-handed, masterly, neat, nimble, nimble-fingered, proficient, skilful, skilled.

antonyms clumsy, inept.

diabolical *adj* abominable, black, cruel, damnable, dark, demoniacal, devilish, dreadful, fiendish, heinous, hellish, infernal, knavish, monstrous, nasty, outrageous, shocking, tricky, vicious, vile, villainous, wicked.

diadem *n* circlet, coronet, crown, mitre, tiara.

diagnose *v* analyse, assess, determine, distinguish, examine, explain, figure out, identify, interpret, pinpoint, pronounce upon, recognize.

diagnosis *n* analysis, answer, assessment, conclusion, examination, explanation, identification, interpretation, opinion, pronouncement, scrutiny, verdict.

diagnostic *adj* analytical, demonstrative, distinctive, distinguishing, indicative, interpret(at)ive, recognizable, symptomatic.

diagonal *adj* angled, cater-corner, cater-corner(ed), cornerwise, crooked, cross, crossways, crosswise, kitty-corner(ed), oblique, slanting, slanted, slantways, slantwise, sloping.

diagonally *adv* aslant, at an angle, cornerwise, crosswise, obliquely, on the bias, on the slant, slantwise.

diagram *n* chart, cross section, drawing, exploded view, figure, flow chart, graph, illustration, layout, nomogram, outline, picture, plan, representation, schema, sketch.

diagrammatic *adj* graphic, illustrative, representational, schematic, sketchy.

antonyms imaginative, impressionistic.

dialect *n* accent, diction, idiom, jargon, language, lingo, localism, patois, pronunciation, provincialism, regionalism, speech, tongue, vernacular.

dialectic *adj* analytical, argumentative, deductive, inductive, logical, polemic, ratiocinative, rational, rationalistic.

n analysis, argument, argumentation, casuistry, contention, debate, deduction, dialectics, discourse, discussion, disputation, induction, logic, polemic(s,) ratiocination, rationale, reasoning, sophistry.

dialogue *n* causerie, colloquy, communication, confabulation, conference, conversation, converse, debate, discourse, discussion, exchange, interchange, lines, script, table talk, talk.

diametrical *adj* antipodal, antithetic(al), contrary, contrasting, counter, diametrical, opposed, opposite.

diaphanous *adj* cobwebby, delicate, filmy, fine, gauzy, gossamer, light, pellucid, see-through, sheer, thin, translucent, transparent.

antonyms heavy, opaque, thick.

diarrhea *n* dysentery, looseness, loose stools, Montezuma's revenge, the runs, the trots.

antonym constipation.

diary *n* appointment book, chronicle, commonplace book, day book, engagement book, journal, journal intime, logbook.

diatribe *n* abuse, attack, blast, castigation, criticism, denunciation, harangue, insult, invective, lecture, onslaught, philippic, reviling, stricture, tirade, upbraiding, vituperation.

antonyms bouquet, encomium, praise.

dicey *adj* chancy, close, dangerous, difficult, dubious, hairy, iffy, nip and tuck, precarious, problematic, risky, ticklish, touch and go, tricky, uncertain.

antonyms certain, easy.

dictate *v* command, decree, direct, enjoin, hand down, impose, instruct, lay down, ordain, order, prescribe, pronounce, rule, transmit.

n behest, bidding, command, decree, determine, dictum, direction, edict, fiat, injunction, instruction, law, mandate, order, ordinance, precept, prescription, principle, requirement, rule, ruling, statute, word.

dictator *n* absolute ruler, autarch, autocrat, Big Brother, boss, despot, Hitler, tyrant.

dictatorial *adj* absolutist, almighty, arbitrary, autarchic, authoritarian, autocratic, bossy, despotic, dogmatic, domineering, imperious, magisterial, oppressive, overbearing, peremptory, repressive, totalitarian, tyrannical.

antonyms democratic, egalitarian, liberal, tolerant.

dictatorship *n* absolute rule, absolutism, autarchy, authoritarianism, autocracy, despotism, fascism, Hitlerism, totalitarianism, tyranny.

antonyms democracy, egalitarianism.

diction *n* articulation, delivery, elocution, enunciation, expression, fluency, idiom, inflection, intonation, language, parlance, phraseology, phrasing, pronunciation, register, speech, style, terminology, usage, vocabulary, wording, word choice.

dictionary *n* concordance, encyclopedia, glossary, lexicon, onomasticon, thesaurus, vocabulary, wordbook.

dictum *n* adage, aphorism, axiom, command, decree, dictate, edict, fiat, gnome, maxim, order, precept, principle, pronouncement, proverb, ruling, saw, saying, utterance.

didactic *adj* educational, educative, homiletic, instructive, moral, moralizing, pedagogical, pedantic, preceptive, prescriptive, teacherlike.

die *v* be no more, bite the dust, breathe one's last, cash in one's chips, croak, cross over, decay, decease, decline, depart, disappear, dwindle, ebb, end, expire, fade, finish, fizzle out, give up the ghost, go to a better place, go to glory, go to meet one's maker, kick, kick the bucket, languish, lapse, lose one's life, pass away (or on), pass over, perish, peter out, pop off, run down, shuffle off this mortal coil, sink, starve, stop, subside, succumb, suffer, vanish, wane, wilt, wither.

be dying for desire, hunger for, languish for, long for, pine for, want, wish for, yearn for.

die-hard *n* Blimp, fanatic, hard-liner, intransigent, reactionary, rightist, stick-in-the-mud, ultra conservative, zealot.

adj blimpish, confirmed, dyed-in-the-wool, entrenched, fanatical, hard-core, hard-line, immovable, incorrigible, incurable, inflexible, intransigent, irreconcilable, obstinate, reactionary, resolute, rigid, stubborn, ultra conservative, uncompromising, unyielding.

antonyms flexible, progressive, wishy-washy.

diet[1] *n* aliment, comestibles, commons, cuisine, dietary, eating, edibles, fare, fast, food, foodstuffs, menu, nourishment, nutriment, nutrition, provisions, rations, regime, regimen, sustenance, viands, victuals.

v abstain, count one's calories, fast, lose weight, reduce, slim, weight-watch.

a steady diet of prolonged exposure to, overindulgence in, exclusive consumption (or use) of.

diet[2] *n* assembly, chamber, congress, convention, convocation, council, court, divan, legislature, meeting, parliament, session, sitting, synod.

differ *v* argue, be at odds, be opposed, clash, conflict, contradict, contrast, debate, demur, depart, deviate, disagree, dispute, dissent, diverge, fall out, oppose, part company with, quarrel, take issue, vary.

antonyms agree, conform, see eye to eye.

difference *n* alteration, argument, balance, change, clash, conflict, contention, contrariety, contrast, controversy, debate, deviation, differentia, differentiation, disagreement, discordance, discrepancy, discreteness, disparateness, disparity, dispute, dissimilarity, distinction, distinctness, divergence, diversity, exception, falling out, idiosyncrasy, misunderstanding, nuance, peculiarity, quarrel, remainder, rest, set-to, singularity, spat, tiff, unlikeness, variation, variety, wrangle.

antonyms agreement, conformity, uniformity.

different *adj* altered, anomalous, assorted, at odds, at variance, atypical, bizarre, changed, clashing, conflicting, contrary, contrasting, deviating, discrepant, discrete, disparate, dissimilar, distinct, distinctive, divergent, divers, diverse, eccentric, extraordinary, inconsistent, individual, manifold, many, miscellaneous, multifarious, numerous, one of a kind, opposed, original, other, peculiar, rare, separate, several, singular, special, strange, sundry, unalike, uncommon, unconventional, unique, unlike, unusual, varied, various.

antonyms conventional, normal, same, similar, uniform.

differentiate *v* alter, change, contrast, demarcate, discern, discriminate, distinguish, diverge, identify, individualize, mark off, modify, particularize, separate, specialize, tell apart, transform.

antonyms assimilate, associate, confuse, link.

differentiation *n* alteration, change, contrast, demarcation, differentia, discrimination, distinction, distinguishing, divergence, individualization, modification, particularization, separation, specialization.

antonyms assimilation, association, confusion, connection.

difficult *adj* abstract, abstruse, arduous, argumentative, Augean, awkward, baffling, burdensome, captious, challenging, complex, complicated, contrary, dark, delicate, demanding, disruptive, enigmatic, fastidious, formidable, fractious, fussy, Gordian, grim, hard, hard to please, herculean, iffy, intractable, intricate, involved, knotty, laborious, obscure, obstinate, obstreperous, onerous, painful, perplexing, perverse, problematic, puzzling, recalcitrant, refractory, steep, sticky, stiff, straitened, strenuous, stubborn, taxing, thorny, ticklish, tiresome, toilsome, tough, troublesome, trying, unamenable, unco-operative, unmanageable, uphill, wearisome.

antonyms easy, straightforward.

difficulty *n* abstruseness, arduousness, awkwardness, bad patch, block, challenge, complexity, complication, delicacy, dilemma, distress, fix, hang-up, hardship, hiccup, hindrance, hole, hurdle, impediment, intractability, intricacy, jam, laboriousness, mess, objection, obstacle, opposition, pain, painfulness, perplexity, pickle, pinch, pitfall, plight, predicament, problem, quandary, scruple, spot, strain, straits, steepness, strenuousness, stickiness, stumbling-block, thorniness, ticklishness, tiresomeness, trial, tribulation, trouble, troublesomeness, unco-operativeness, vexed question, weariness.

antonyms advantage, ease.

in difficulties in a hole, in dire straits, in trouble, up the creek, up the pole.

diffidence *n* abashment, backwardness, bashfulness, doubt, fear, hesitancy, hesitation, humility, inhibition, insecurity, meekness, modesty, reluctance, reserve, self-consciousness, self-distrust, self-doubt, self-effacement, shamefacedness, sheepishness, shyness, tentativeness, timidity, timidness, timorousness, unassertiveness.

antonym confidence.

diffident *adj* abashed, backward, bashful, distrustful, doubtful, hesitant, inhibited, insecure, meek, modest, reluctant, reserved, self-conscious, self-effacing, shamefaced, sheepish, shrinking, shy, suspicious, tentative, timid, timorous, unadventurous, unassertive, unassuming, unobtrusive, unsure, withdrawn.

antonym confident.

diffuse *adj* circuitous, circumlocutory, copious, diffused, digressive, disconnected, discursive, dispersed, long-winded, loose, maundering, meandering, prolix, rambling, round about, scattered, spread-out, unconcentrated, unco-ordinated, unfocussed, vague, verbose, waffling, wordy.

antonyms concentrated, succinct.

v circulate, dispense, disperse, disseminate, dissipate, distribute, propagate, scatter, spread, winnow.

antonyms concentrate, suppress.

dig¹ *v* burrow, delve, drive, excavate, go (into), gouge, grub, hoe, investigate, jab, mine, penetrate, pierce, poke, probe, prod, punch, quarry, research, rummage, scoop, search, thrust, till, tunnel.

n aspersion, barb, crack, cut, gibe, insinuation, insult, jab, jeer, poke, prod, punch, quip, slur, sneer, stab, taunt, thrust, wisecrack.

antonym compliment.

dig up discover, disinter, dredge, excavate,

exhume, expose, find, rake up, retrieve, root out (or up), tear up, track down, uncover, unearth, uproot.

antonyms bury, obscure.

dig² *v* adore, appreciate, be crazy about, be into, catch on to, enjoy, fancy, follow, get a kick out of, get off on, get one's jollies out of, go for, go overboard about, groove, like, love, relish, understand, warm to.

antonym hate.

digest *v* abridge, absorb, arrange, assimilate, bear, classify, codify, compress, condense, consider, contemplate, dispose, dissolve, endure, grasp, incorporate, ingest, internalize, macerate, master, meditate (on), methodize, ponder, process, reduce, shorten, stand, stomach, study, summarize, systematize, tabulate, take in, tolerate, understand.

n abbreviation, abridgment, abstract, compendium, compression, condensation, epitome, précis, reduction, résumé, summary, synopsis.

digestion *n* abridgment, absorption, assimilation, dyspepsia, eupepsia, ingestion, internalization, processing, transformation.

dignified *adj* august, decorous, distinguished, exalted, formal, grave, honourable, imposing, impressive, lofty, lordly, majestic, noble, orotund, reserved, solemn, stately.

antonym undignified.

dignify *v* adorn, advance, aggrandize, apotheosize, distinguish, elevate, ennoble, exalt, glorify, honour, promote, raise.

antonyms degrade, demean.

dignitary *n* big name, big shot, bigwig, celebrity, heavy, notability, notable, personage, pillar, VIP, visiting fireman, worthy.

dignity *n* amour-propre, courtliness, decorum, elevation, eminence, excellence, glory, grandeur, gravity, greatness, honour, importance, loftiness, majesty, nobility, nobleness, pride, propriety, rank, respectability, self-esteem, self-possession, self-regard, self-respect, solemnity, standing, stateliness, station, status.

digress *v* branch off depart, deviate, divagate, diverge, drift, expatiate, go off on a tangent, ramble, stray, wander.

digression *n* aside, departure, detour, deviation, divagation, divergence, diversion, excursion, footnote, obiter dictum, parenthesis, sidetrack, side trip, straying, wandering.

dilapidated *adj* battered, broken-down, collapsing, crumbling, decayed, decaying, decrepit, deteriorated, mouldering, neglected, ramshackle, rickety, ruined, ruinous, run-down, shabby, shaky, tumbledown, uncared-for, worn-out.

dilapidation *n* collapse, decay, decrepitude, demolition, destruction, deterioration, disintegration, disrepair, dissolution, downfall, ruin, ruination, waste.

dilate *v* amplify, broaden, descant, detail, develop, distend, dwell (on), elaborate, enlarge, expand, expatiate, expound, extend, increase, open, puff out (or up), spin out, spread (out), stretch, swell, wax eloquent, widen.

antonyms abbreviate, constrict, curtail.

dilated *adj* bloated, distended, enlarged, expanded, extended, inflated, outspread, stretched, swollen, tumescent, varicose, wide open.

antonyms contracted, shortened.

dilation *n* broadening, dilatation, distension, enlargement, expansion, extension, increase, spread, stretching, swelling, widening.

antonyms constriction, contraction.

dilatory *adj* backward, behindhand, dallying, dawdling, delaying, dilly-dallying, indolent, lackadaisical, laggard, lingering, loitering, procrastinating, slack, slothful, slow, sluggish, tardy, tarrying.

antonyms diligent, prompt.

dilemma *n* bind, catch-22, corner, difficulty, embarrassment, fix, jam, mess, perplexity, pickle, pinch, plight, predicament, problem, puzzle, quandary, spot, strait, tough call.

dilettante *n* aesthete, amateur, dabbler, sciolist, trifler.

diligence *n* activity, application, assiduity, assiduousness, attention, attentiveness, care, careful effort, conscientiousness, constancy, doggedness, earnestness, heedfulness, industry, intentness, laboriousness, perseverance, pertinacity, sedulousness, tirelessness.

antonym laziness.

diligent *adj* active, assiduous, attentive, busy, careful, conscientious, constant, dogged, earnest, hardworking, indefatigable, industrious, laborious, painstaking, persevering, persistent, pertinacious, sedulous, studious, tireless.

antonyms dilatory, lazy.

dilly-dally *v* back and fill, dally, dawdle, delay, dither, drag one's feet, falter, hem and haw, hesitate, hover, linger, loiter, poke along, potter, procrastinate, putter, shilly-shally, tarry, trifle, vacillate, waste time, waver.

dilute *v* adulterate, allay, attenuate, cut, dash, decrease, diffuse, diminish, emasculate, lessen, mitigate, neutralize, reduce, soften, take the edge off, temper, thin (out), water down, weaken.

antonym concentrate.

adj adulterated, attenuate(d), cut, diluted, emasculated, thin, watered down, waterish, weak.

antonym concentrated.

dim *adj* bleary, blurred, cloudy, confused, dark, darkish, dense, depressing, dingy, discouraging, dull, dumb, dusky, faint, feeble, foggy, fuzzy, gloomy, grey, hazy, ill-defined, imperfect, indistinct, intangible, lack-lustre, misty, muted, obscure, obscured, obtuse, opaque, overcast, pale, remote, shadowy, slim, slow, sombre, stupid, tenebrous, thick, unclear, unfavourable, unilluminated, unpromising, vague, weak.

antonyms bright, clear, distinct.

v becloud, bedim, blear, blur, cloud, darken, dull, fade, lower, obfuscate, obscure, tarnish.

antonyms brighten, illuminate.

dimension(s) *n* amplitude, bulk, capacity, extent, greatness, importance, largeness, magnitude, measure, range, scale, scope, size.

diminish *v* abate, belittle, cheapen, contract, curtail, cut (down), decline, decrease, de-emphasize, demean, depreciate, devalue, dwindle, ebb, fade, fall off, fizzle out, lessen, lower, minify, minimize, peter out, recede, reduce, shrink, shrivel, sink, slacken, subside, taper off, wane, weaken.

antonyms enhance, enlarge, increase.

diminishing *adj* abating, contracting, declining, decreasing, decrescent, dwindling, ebbing, fading, lessening, lowering, receding, shrinking, shrivelling, subsiding, waning.

antonyms growing, increasing.

diminution *n* abatement, contraction, curtailment, cut, cutback, decay, decline, decrease, diminishing, ebb, fading, lessening, reduction, retrenchment, shortening, shrinkage, subsidence, wane, weakening.

antonyms enlargement, increase.

diminutive *adj* baby, bantam, dinky, doll-sized, Lilliputian, little, midget, mini, miniature, minute, petite, pocket(-sized), pygmy, small, tiny, toy, wee.

antonyms big, great, huge, large.

n hypocorism, pet-name.

dimple *n* concavity, dent, depression, dint, dip, fovea, hollow, umbilicus.

dimwit *n* blockhead, bonehead, booby, dope, dullard, dummy, dunce, dunderhead, idiot, ignoramus, nitwit, numskull, twit, witless wonder.

din *n* babble, clamour, clangour, clash, clatter, commotion, crash, hubbub, hullabaloo, noise, outcry, pandemonium, racket, row, shout, uproar.

antonyms calm, quiet.

dine *v* banquet, break bread, eat, feast, feed on, lunch, regale oneself, sup.

dingy *adj* cheerless, colourless, dark, dim, dirty, discoloured, drab, dreary, dull, dusky, faded, fuscous, gloomy, grey, grimy, grungy, murky, run-down, seedy, shabby, soiled, sombre.

antonyms bright, clean.

dinner *n* banquet, blowout, collation, feast, lunch, meal, refection, repast, spread, supper.

dint *n* concavity, dent, depression, dimple, dip, hollow, impression, indentation, pit, stroke.

by dint of by (sheer) force of, by means of, by the expedient of.

dip *v* bathe, coat, decline, decrease, descend, disappear, douse, droop, drop, duck, dunk, fade, fall, immerse, infuse, ladle, lower, plunge, rinse, sag, scoop, set, sink, slope (downward), slump, souse, spoon, submerge, subside, tilt.

n concavity, decline, depression, dilution, dive, drenching, ducking, fall, hole, hollow, immersion, incline, infusion, lowering, plunge, sag, slip, slope, slump, soaking, suspension, swim.

dip into browse, dabble, draw on, make withdrawals on, peruse, sample, skim, start using, tap, touch, try.

diplomacy *n* delicacy, discretion, finesse, manoeuvring, politeness, savoir-faire, skill, statecraft, statesmanship, subtlety, tact, tactfulness, sensitivity.

diplomat *n* ambassador, conciliator, consul, expatriate, go-between, high commissioner, mediator, moderator, negotiator, peacemaker, politician, tactician.

diplomatic *adj* discreet, judicious, polite, politic, prudent, sagacious, sensitive, subtle, tactful.

antonyms rude, tactless, thoughtless.

dire *adj* alarming, appalling, awful, calamitous, cataclysmic, catastrophic, critical, crucial, cruel, crying, desperate, disastrous, dismal, distressing, drastic, dreadful, exigent, extreme, fearful, gloomy, grave, grim, horrible, horrid, ominous, portentous, pressing, ruinous, serious, terrible, urgent, woeful.

direct *v* address, administer, advise, aim, bid, charge, command, conduct, control, dictate, dispose, enjoin, fix, focus, forward, govern, guide, handle, instruct, intend, label, lead, level, mail, manage, mastermind, mean, order, oversee, point, project, regulate, route, rule, run, send, show, stage-manage, superintend, superscribe, supervise, tell, train, turn.

adj absolute, blunt, candid, categorical, diametric, downright, exact, explicit, express, face-to-face, first-hand, forthright, frank, head-on, honest, immediate, man-to-man, matter-of-fact, no- nonsense, non-stop, open, outright, outspoken, personal, plain, plain-spoken, point-blank, pointed, prompt, shortest, sincere, straight, straightforward, through, truthful, unambiguous, unbroken, undeviating, unequivocal, uninterrupted.

antonyms crooked, devious, indirect, underhand.

direction *n* address, administration, aim, angle, approach, bearing, bent, bias, charge, command, control, course, current, drift, end, government, guidance, instruction, label, leadership, line of action, management, mark, order, orientation, path, proclivity, purpose, road, route, superintendence, superscription, supervision, tack, tendency, tenor, track, trend, way.

directions *n* briefing, guidance, guidelines, indication, instructions, orders, plan, recipe, recommendations, regulations.

directive *n* charge, command, decree, dictate, diktat, edict, fiat, imperative, injunction, instruction, mandate, notice, order, ordinance, regulation, ruling.

directly *adv* absolutely, at once, bluntly, candidly, dead, due, exactly, explicitly, face-to-face, forthwith, frankly, honestly,

immediately, instantaneously, instantly, matter-of-factly, openly, personally, plainly, point-blank, pointedly, precisely, promptly, pronto, quickly, right away, speedily, straight, straightaway, straightforwardly, truthfully, unequivocally, unerringly, unswervingly.

antonym indirectly.

directness *n* bluffness, bluntness, candour, forthrightness, frankness, honesty, outspokenness, plain speaking, sincerity, straightforwardness.

director *n* administrator, auteur, boss, chair, chairman, chairperson, chairwoman, chief, conductor, controller, executive, governor, head, leader, manager, monitor, organizer, principal, producer, supervisor.

dirge *n* dead march, elegy, funeral march, lament, monody, requiem, threnody.

dirt *n* clay, corruption, crud, dope, dust, earth, excrement, filth, gossip, grime, ground, grunginess, guck, gunk, impurity, indecency, loam, lowdown, mire, muck, mud, obscenity, ordure, poop, pornography, scoop, slime, smudge, smut, soil, stain, tarnish.

antonyms cleanliness, cleanness.

dirty *adj* angry, base, begrimed, black, blue, cheap, clouded, contemptible, corrupt, cowardly, crooked, cruddy, dark, despicable, dishonest, dull, filthy, foul, fraudulent, grimy, grubby, grungy, gunky, ignominious, illegal, indecent, low, low-down, maculate, mean, messy, miry, mucky, muddy, nasty, obscene, off-colour, piggish, polluted, pornographic, risqué, salacious, scruffy, scurvy, shabby, smutty, soiled, sordid, squalid, sullied, treacherous, unclean, unethical, unfair, unhygenic, unkempt, unsanitary, unscrupulous, unsporting, unsportsmanlike, unsterile, unswept, untidy, vile, vulgar, yucky.

antonyms clean, spotless.

v bedaub, begrime, besmear, besmirch, bespatter, blacken, blot, contaminate, corrupt, defile, foul, mess up, muddy, pollute, smear, smirch, smudge, soil, spoil, stain, sully.

antonyms clean, cleanse, immaculate, purify, squeaky-clean.

disability *n* disadvantage, disorder, disqualification, handicap, hindrance, limitation, weakness.

antonyms asset, strength.

disable *v* cripple, damage, deactivate, debilitate, disarm, disqualify, enfeeble, hamstring, handicap, immobilize, impair, incapacitate, inoperative, invalidate, lame, paralyse, prostrate, unfit, unman, weaken.

disabled[1] *adj* crippled, handicapped, immobilized, incapacitated, maimed, mangled, mutilated, paralysed, weak, weakened, wrecked.

antonyms able, strong.

disabled[2] *adj* challenged, differently abled, hemiplegic, paraplegic, quadriplegic.

antonym able-bodied.

disadvantage *n* burden, damage, debit, detriment, disability, disservice, downside, drawback, flaw, fly in the ointment, handicap, hardship, harm, hindrance, hurt, impediment, inconvenience, injury, liability, loss, minus, nuisance, prejudice, privation, snag, trouble, unfavourableness, weakness.

antonyms advantage, asset, benefit.

v hamper, handicap, hinder, hold-back, inconvenience.

antonyms aid, help.

disadvantaged *adj* deprived, handicapped, hindered, impeded, impoverished, struggling, underprivileged.

antonym privileged.

disadvantageous *adj* adverse, burdensome, damaging, deleterious, detrimental, harmful, hurtful, ill-timed, inauspicious, inconvenient, inexpedient, injurious, inopportune, prejudicial, unfavourable.

antonym advantageous.

disaffected *adj* alienated, antagonistic, antipathetic(al), discontented, disenchanted, disgruntled, disloyal, dissatisfied, estranged, hostile, mutinous, rebellious, seditious, unfriendly.

antonym contented.

disaffection *n* alienation, animosity, antagonism, antipathy, aversion, coolness, desertion, disagreement, discontent(ment), discord, disenchantment, disgruntlement, disharmony, dislike, disloyalty, dissatisfaction, estrangement, hostility, ill will, repugnance, resentment, unfriendliness.

antonym contentment.

disagree *v* altercate, argue, be at cross purposes, be at loggerheads, be at odds, be at variance, bicker, bother, clash, conflict, contend, contest, contradict, counter, cross words, depart, deviate, differ, disaccord, dispute, dissent, diverge, fall out, nauseate, object, oppose, quarrel, run counter to, sicken, spar, spat, squabble, take issue, tiff, vary, wrangle.

antonym agree.

disagreeable *adj* bad-tempered, churlish, contrary, cross, difficult, disgusting, disobliging, displeasing, distasteful, ill-natured, ill-tempered, irritable, nasty, objectionable, obnoxious, offensive, peevish, repellent, repugnant, repulsive, rude, surly, unamiable, unappetizing, unfriendly, ungracious, uninviting, unpalatable, unpleasant, unsavoury.

antonyms agreeable, friendly, pleasant.

disagreement *n* altercation, argument, clash, conflict, contradiction, contrariety, controversy, debate, difference, disaccord, discord, discrepancy, disparity, dispute, dissent, dissimilarity, dissimilitude, divergence, division, falling-out, incompatibility, incongruity, inconsistency, misunderstanding, opposition, quarrel, spat, squabble, strife, tiff, unlikeness, variance, wrangle.

antonym agreement.

disallow *v* abjure, annul, ban, cancel, debar, deny, disaffirm, disavow, disclaim, dismiss, embargo, exclude, forbid, interdict, nullify, prohibit, proscribe, refuse, reject, repudiate, veto.

antonyms allow, permit.

disallowed *adj* annulled, banned, cancelled, debarred, denied, excluded, forbidden, impermissible, interdicted, prohibited, proscribed, rejected, vetoed.

antonyms allowed, permissible.

disappear *v* be lost from sight, cease, decamp, dematerialize, depart, dissolve, ebb, end, escape, evanesce, evaporate, fade, flee, fly, go, leave the scene, melt away, pass (out of sight), perish, recede, retire, scarper, take off, vamoose, vanish, wane, withdraw.

antonym appear.

disappearance *n* dematerialization, departure, desertion, disappearing, dispersal, dispersion, dissipation, evanescence, evaporation, fading, flight, going, loss, melting, passing, vanishing, wane, withdrawal.

antonym appearance.

disappoint *v* chagrin, dash, deceive, defeat, delude, disenchant, disgruntle, dishearten, disillusion, dismay, displease, dissatisfy, fail, foil, frustrate, hamper, hinder, hurt, let down, sadden, stand up, thwart, vex.

antonyms delight, please, satisfy.

disappointed *adj* chagrined, depressed, despondent, discontented, discouraged, disenchanted, disgruntled, disillusioned, dissatisfied, displeased, distressed, downhearted, frustrated, hurt, let down, saddened, thwarted.

antonyms delighted, pleased, satisfied.

disappointing *adj* anticlimactic, depressing, disagreeable, discouraging, inadequate, inferior, insufficient, pathetic, poor, sad, sorry, unhappy, unsatisfactory, unworthy.

antonyms encouraging, pleasant, satisfactory.

disappointment[1] *n* bafflement, chagrin, discontent, discouragement, disenchantment, disgruntlement, disillusionment, dismay, displeasure, dissatisfaction, distress, frustration, regret.

antonyms delight, pleasure, satisfaction.

disappointment[2] *n* blow, bomb, calamity, comedown, disaster, failure, fiasco, flop, frost, lemon, letdown, misfortune, setback.

antonyms boost, success.

disapproval *n* blame, censure, condemnation, criticism, denunciation, deprecation, disapprobation, disfavour, dislike, disparagement, displeasure, dissatisfaction, objection, opposition, refusal, rejection, reproach, reproof, thumbs down.

antonyms approbation, approval, thumbs up.

disapprove (of) *v* blame, censure, condemn, denounce, deplore, deprecate, disallow, discountenance, dislike, disparage, look askance at, look down one's nose at, object to, raise one's eyebrows at, reject, spurn, take a dim view of, take exception to.

antonym approve of.

disapproving *adj* censorious, condemnatory, critical, deprecatory, disparaging, negative, reproachful, unfavourable.

disarm[1] *v* deactivate, declaw, demilitarize, demobilize, disable, disband, make harmless, take the teeth out of, unarm.

antonym arm.

disarm[2] *v* appease, calm, charm, conciliate, mollify, persuade, placate, win over.

disarming *adj* charming, conciliatory, irresistible, likable, mollifying, persuasive, winning.

disarrange *v* confuse, derange, disarray, discompose, dislocate, disorder, disorganize, disturb, jumble, mess up, muss (up), scatter, scramble, shuffle, throw out of kilter, unsettle, upset.

antonym arrange.

disarray *n* chaos, clutter, confusion, discomposure, disharmony, dishevelment, dislocation, dismay, disorder, disorderliness, disorganization, disunity, indiscipline, jumble, mess, muddle, muss, shambles, tangle, unruliness, untidiness, upset.

antonyms array, order.

disaster *n* accident, act of God, blow, calamity, cataclysm, catastrophe, debacle, failure, flop, misadventure, mischance, misfortune, mishap, reverse, ruin, ruination, stroke of misfortune, tragedy, trouble.

antonyms success, triumph.

disastrous *adj* adverse, calamitous, cataclysmic, catastrophic, destructive, detrimental, devastating, dire, dreadful, fatal, grievous, hapless, harmful, ill-fated, ill-starred, miserable, ruinous, terrible, tragic, unfortunate, unlucky.

antonyms fortunate, successful, triumphant.

disband *v* break up, demobilize, dismiss, disperse, dissolve, part company, retire, scatter, separate.

antonyms assemble, band, combine.

disbelief *n* amazement, distrust, doubt, dubiety, incredulity, mistrust, rejection, scepticism, suspicion, unbelief, wonder.

antonym belief.

disbelieve *v* discount, discredit, doubt, mistrust, reject, repudiate, suspect.

antonyms believe, trust.

disbeliever *n* agnostic, atheist, doubter, doubting Thomas, questioner, sceptic, scoffer, unbeliever.

antonym believer.

disbursement *n* disbursal, disposal, expenditure, outlay, payment, spending.

disc *n* circle, disk, diskette, face, plate, record, ring, roundel.

discard *v* abandon, cast aside, chuck, dispense with, dispose of, ditch, drop, dump, get rid of, give up, jettison, leave behind, reject, relinquish, remove, repudiate, scrap, shed, throw aside, throw away (or out), toss out.

antonyms adopt, embrace, espouse.

discern *v* ascertain, behold, descry, detect, determine, differentiate, discover, discriminate, distinguish, espy, judge, make out, notice, observe, perceive, recognize, see, sense, tell.

discernible *adj* apparent, appreciable, clear, detectable, discoverable, distinct, distinguishable, manifest, noticeable, observable, perceptible, perceivable, recognizable, sensible, undiscernable, visible.

antonym invisible.

discerning *adj* acute, astute, clear-sighted, critical, discriminating, eagle-eyed, insightful, intelligent, judicious, knowing, penetrating, perceptive, percipient, perspicacious, piercing, sagacious, sensitive, sharp, shrewd, subtle, wise.

antonym obtuse.

discernment *n* acumen, acuteness, ascertainment, astuteness, awareness, clear-sightedness, differentiation, discovery, discrimination, insight, intelligence, judgment, keenness, observation, penetration, perception, perceptiveness, percipience, perspicacity, recognition, sagacity, sharpness, shrewdness, understanding, wisdom.

discharge *v* absolve, accomplish, acquit oneself of, cancel, carry out, cashier, clear, detonate, disburden, dismiss, dispense with, drum out, egest, eject, emit, empty, excrete, execute, exempt, exonerate, expel, explode, exude, fire, free, fulfil, give off, give the boot to, gush, honour, leak, let go, let off, let out, liberate, meet, offload, ooze, oust, pardon, pay, perform, pour forth, release, relieve, remove, run, sack, satisfy, send away (or out), set off, settle, shoot, spread, unburden, unload, vent, void, volley.

antonyms charge, employ, engage, hire.

n accomplishment, acquittal, blast, burst, clearance, congé, demobilization, detonation, disburdening, discharging, dismissal, effluent, ejecta, ejection, emission, emptying, excretion, execution, exhaust, exoneration, explosion, exudation, expulsion, firing, flow, flux, fluxion, fulfilment, fusillade, liberation, observance, ooze, pardon, payment, performance, pus, quietus, quittance, release, remittance, report, salvo, secretion, seepage, settlement, shot, suppuration, the boot, the sack, unburdening, unloading, vent, voidance, voiding, volley.

disciple *n* acolyte, adherent, apostle, believer, catechumen, convert, devotee, follower, learner, partisan, proselyte, pupil, student, supporter, votary.

disciplinarian *n* authoritarian, autocrat, control freak, despot, martinet, stickler, taskmaster, tyrant.

discipline *n* area of study, castigation, chastening, chastisement, control, correction, course, curriculum, drill, exercise, field, method, obedience, orderliness, practice, punishment, regimen, regulation, restraint, science, self-control, specialty, strictness, subject, training.

antonyms carelessness, negligence.

v break in, castigate, chasten, chastise, check, control, correct, drill, educate, exercise,

discontinuous

form, govern, habituate, instruct, inure, penalize, prepare, punish, rap the knuckles of, regulate, reprimand, reprove, restrain, slap the wrist of, teach, toughen, train.

disciplined *adj* controlled, orderly, restrained, self-controlled, well-behaved.

disclaim *v* abandon, abjure, abnegate, decline, deny, disacknowledge, disaffirm, disallow, disavow, disown, forswear, reject, renounce, repudiate.

antonyms accept, acknowledge, claim.

disclaimer *n* abjuration, abnegation, contradiction, denial, disacknowledgment, disavowal, disownment, rejection, renunciation, repudiation, retraction.

disclose *v* broadcast, communicate, confess, discover, divulge, exhibit, expose, impart, lay bare, leak, let slip, make known, publish, relate, reveal, show, tell, bare, unbosom, unburden, uncover, unfold, unveil, utter.

antonyms conceal, hide.

disclosure *n* acknowledgment, admission, announcement, apocalypse, baring, broadcast, communication, confession, declaration, discovery, divulgence, exposé, exposure, leak, publication, revelation, uncovering.

discoloration *n* blemish, blot, blotch, bruise, ecchymosis, mark, patch, splotch, spot, stain.

discolour *v* blemish, disfigure, fade, mar, mark, rust, soil, spot, stain, streak, tarnish, tinge, weather, yellow.

discomfit *v* abash, baffle, balk, beat, checkmate, confound, confuse, defeat, demoralize, discombobulate, discompose, disconcert, embarrass, faze, flurry, fluster, foil, frustrate, humble, humiliate, outwit, overcome, overthrow, perplex, perturb, rattle, rout, ruffle, thwart, trump, unsettle, vanquish, worry, worst.

discomfiture *n* abashment, chagrin, confusion, defeat, demoralization, disappointment, discombobulation, discomposure, embarrassment, failure, frustration, humiliation, overthrow, rout, ruin, shame, undoing, unease, vanquishment.

discomfort *n* ache, annoyance, discomposure, disquiet, distress, embarrassment, hardship, hurt, inquietude, irritant, irritation, malaise, trouble, uneasiness, unpleasantness, unpleasantry, vexation.

antonyms comfort, ease.

discompose *v* agitate, annoy, bewilder, confuse, disarrange, discomfit, disconcert, dishevel, disorder, displease, disquiet, disturb, embarrass, faze, flurry, fluster, fret, irritate, make uneasy, mix up, perturb, put out of countenance, rattle, ruffle, rumple, throw off, tousle, unsettle, upset, vex, worry.

antonym compose.

discomposure *n* agitation, anxiety, confusion, discomfiture, discomfort, disconcertedness, dislocation, disorder, disquiet, disquietude, distraction, disturbance, embarrassment, fluster, inquietude, malaise, nervousness, perturbation, uneasiness.

antonym composure.

disconcert *v* abash, agitate, alarm, annoy, baffle, balk, bewilder, confuse, discombobulate, discomfit, discompose, disorder, disturb, embarrass, flurry, fluster, frustrate, hinder, mix up, nonplus, perplex, perturb, put out of countenance, rattle, ruffle, throw off, throw someone for a loop, thwart, trouble, unbalance, undo, unsettle, upset, worry.

disconcerted *adj* abashed, agitated, alarmed, annoyed, bewildered, confused, discombobulated, discomfited, distracted, disturbed, embarrassed, fazed, flurried, flustered, mixed up, nonplussed, out of countenance, perturbed, rattled, ruffled, taken aback, thrown for a loop, thrown off, troubled, unsettled, upset.

disconcerting *adj* alarming, awkward, baffling, bewildering, bothersome, confusing, discombobulating, dismaying, distracting, distressing, disturbing, embarrassing, off-putting, perplexing, troublesome, troubling, upsetting.

disconnect *v* break, cut off, detach, disengage, part, separate, sever, uncouple, unfasten, unhitch, unhook, unlink, unplug, unyoke.

antonyms attach, connect, engage.

disconnected *adj* broken, confused, disjointed, free, garbled, illogical, incoherent, irrational, jumbled, loose, rambling, separate, telegraphic, unconnected, unco-ordinated, unfasten, unintelligible, wandering.

antonyms attached, coherent, connected, fluent.

disconsolate *adj* brokenhearted, cheerless, crushed, dejected, depressed, desolate, despairing, dispirited, forlorn, gloomy, grief-stricken, heartbroken, heavy-hearted, hopeless, inconsolable, melancholy, miserable, sad, unhappy, woeful, wretched.

antonyms cheerful, cheery.

discontent *n* displeasure, disquiet, dissatisfaction, envy, fretfulness, impatience, regret, restlessness, uneasiness, unhappiness, unrest, vexation.

antonym content.

discontented *adj* bad-tempered, complaining, disaffected, disgruntled, displeased, dissatisfied, fretful, grumbling, impatient, miserable, restless, unhappy, vexed.

antonyms contented, happy, satisfied.

discontinue *v* abandon, break off, cancel, cease, drop, end, finish, halt, interrupt, pause, quit, stop, suspend, terminate.

antonym continue.

discontinuity *n* breach, break, change, disconnectedness, disconnection, disjointedness, disruption, gap, incoherence, inconsistency, interruption, irregularity, lacuna, rupture.

antonym continuity.

discontinuous *adj* broken, disconnected, discrete, disjointed, disjunct, erratic, fitful, inconsistent, intermittent, interrupted, irregular, periodic, spasmodic.

antonym continuous.

discord *n* cacophony, clash(ing), conflict, contention, difference, din, disagreement, discordance, disharmony, dispute, dissension, dissonance, disunity, division, fighting, friction, incompatibility, jangle, jar(ring), opposition, quarrelling, racket, strife, variance, wrangling.

antonyms agreement, concord, harmony.

discordant *adj* at odds, cacophonous, clashing, conflicting, contradictory, contrary, different, disagreeing, disharmonic, disharmonious, dissonant, grating, harsh, incompatible, incongruous, inconsistent, inharmonious, jangling, jarring, opposite, shrill, strident, unmelodious, untuneful.

antonyms concordant, harmonious.

discount¹ *v* disbelieve, discredit, dismiss, disregard, forget about, gloss over, ignore, mark down, overlook, rebate, reject.

discount² *n* abatement, allowance, concession, cut, deduction, markdown, rebate, reduction.

discountenance *v* abash, chagrin, confuse, disapprove (of), discompose, disconcert, discourage, embarrass, frown on, humble, humiliate, put out of countenance, shame.

antonyms countenance, support.

discourage *v* check, chill, cow, curb, damp, dampen, dash, daunt, deject, demoralize, deprecate, depress, deter, discountenance, disfavour, dishearten, dismay, dispirit, dissuade, frighten away (or off), hinder, inhibit, intimidate, overawe, prevent, put off, restrain, scare away (or off), unman, unnerve.

antonyms encourage, favour, hearten, inspire.

discouraged *adj* chapfallen, crestfallen, dashed, daunted, dejected, demoralized, depressed, despondent, deterred, disappointed, disheartened, dismayed, dispirited, downcast, downhearted, glum, pessimistic.

antonyms encouraged, heartened.

discouragement *n* constraint, curb, damp, damper, dejection, demoralization, depression, despair, despondency, deterrent, disappointment, discomfiture, disincentive, dismay, downheartedness, hindrance, hopelessness, impediment, negative reinforcement, obstacle, opposition, pessimism, rebuff, restraint, setback, stumbling-block.

antonyms encouragement, incentive.

discouraging *adj* dampening, daunting, depressing, disappointing, disheartening, dispiriting, dissuasive, inauspicious, off-putting, unfavourable, unpropitious.

antonyms encouraging, heartening.

discourse *n* address, chat, communication, conversation, converse, descant, dialogue, discussion, disquisition, dissertation, essay, homily, lecture, lucubration, oration, rhetoric, sermon, speech, talk, treatise, writing.

v confer, converse, debate, declaim, descant, expound, dialogue, discuss, expatiate, go on, jaw, lecture, lucubrate, speechify, talk, write.

discourteous *adj* abrupt, bad-mannered, boorish, brusque, curt, disrespectful, ill-bred, ill-mannered, impolite, insolent, offhand, rude, slighting, unceremonious, uncivil, uncourteous, ungracious, unmannerly.

antonyms courteous, polite, respectful.

discourtesy *n* abruptness, affront, bad manners, boorishness, brusquerie, curtness, disrespect(fulness), ill breeding, impertinence, impoliteness, incivility, indecorousness, indecorum, insolence, insult, rudeness, slight, snub, ungraciousness, unmannerliness.

antonyms courtesy, politeness.

discover *v* ascertain, come across (or upon), conceive, contrive, descry, detect, determine, devise, dig up, discern, disclose, espy, exposé, find, find out, invent, learn, light on, locate, notice, originate, perceive, pioneer, realize, recognize, reveal, see, spot, uncover, unearth.

antonyms conceal, hide.

discoverer *n* author, explorer, finder, founder, initiator, inventor, originator, pioneer.

discovery *n* ascertainment, breakthrough, coup, detection, disclosure, espial, exploration, find, finding, innovation, introduction, invention, locating, location, origination, revelation, uncovering.

antonym concealment.

discredit *v* bring into disrepute, cast aspersions on, cast suspicion on, challenge, debunk, defame, denigrate, deny, disbelieve, discount, disgrace, dishonour, dismiss, disparage, disprove, dispute, distrust, doubt, explode, expose, invalidate, mistrust, question, refute, suspect, slander, slur, smear, undermine, vilify.

antonyms believe, credit.

n aspersion, blame, disgrace, dishonour, disrepute, distrust, doubt, ignominy, ill repute, imputation, mistrust, odium, opprobium, question, refute, reproach, scandal, scepticism, shame, slur, smear, stigma, suspicion.

antonym credit.

discreditable *adj* blameworthy, degrading, disgraceful, dishonourable, humiliating, ignoble, ignominious, improper, infamous, reprehensible, scandalous, shameful, unbecoming, unprincipled, unworthy.

antonyms creditable, worthy.

discredited *adj* debunked, discarded, disgraced, dishonoured, disproved, exploded, exposed, outworn, refuted, rejected.

discreet *adj* careful, cautious, circumspect, considerate, delicate, diplomatic, discerning, guarded, judicious, modest, polite, politic, prudent, reserved, restrained, sagacious, sensible, tactful, wary.

antonyms careless, indiscreet, ostentatious, tactless.

▲ *confusable word* discrete.

discrepancy *n* conflict, contrariety, difference, disagreement, discordance, disparity, dissimilarity, dissonance, divergence, imparity, incongruity, inconsistency, inequality, variance, variation.

antonym consistency

discrete *adj* detached, disconnected, discontinuous, disjoined, disjunct, distinct, individual, separate, unattached.

▲ *confusable word* discreet.

discretion *n* care, carefulness, caution, choice, circumspection, consideration, diplomacy, discernment, good sense, heedfulness, inclination, judgment, judiciousness, liking, maturity, mind, option, pleasure, preference, prudence, responsibility, sagacity, sense, tact, volition, wariness, will, wisdom, wish.

antonym indiscretion.

discriminate *v* differentiate, discern, distinguish, make a distinction, separate, sift, tell apart.

antonyms confound, confuse.

discriminate against be biassed against, be prejudiced against, disfavour, treat unfairly, victimize.

discriminating *adj* acute, analytical, astute, critical, cultivated, differentiating, discerning, fastidious, informed, insightful, particular, penetrating, perceptive, percipient, percipacious, refined, selective, sensitive, subtle, tasteful.

discrimination¹ *n* bias, bigotry, favouritism, inequity, intolerance, Jim Crow, prejudice, unfairness.

discrimination² *n* acumen, acuteness, critical appreciation, discernment, insight, judgment, keenness, penetration, perception, percipience, refinement, sagacity, subtlety, taste.

discriminatory *adj* biassed, favouring, inequitable, loaded, one-sided, partial, partisan, preferential, prejudiced, prejudicial, unfair, unjust, weighted.

antonyms fair, impartial, unbiassed.

discursive *adj* circuitous, desultory, diffuse, digressive, discursory, erratic, long-winded, loose, meandering, peripatetic, prolix, rambling, wide-ranging.

antonyms brief, short.

discuss *v* argue, confer, consider, consult, converse, debate, deliberate, dialogue, examine, explain, expound, lay heads together, rap, talk about, talk over.

discussion *n* analysis, argument, colloquium, colloquy, confab, confabulation, conference, conferencing, consideration, consultation, conversation, debate, deliberation, dialogue, discourse, examination, exchange, gabfest, interchange, rap, review, scrutiny, seminar, symposium, talk, talkfest, teleconferencing.

disdain *v* belittle, contemn, deride, despise, disregard, look down on, look down one's nose at, misprize, pooh-pooh, rebuff, reject, scorn, slight, sneer at, spurn, undervalue.

antonyms admire, respect.

n arrogance, contempt, contumely, deprecation, derision, dislike, haughtiness,

hauteur, imperiousness, indifference, scorn, sneering, snobbishness, superciliousness.

antonyms admiration, respect.

disdainful *adj* arrogant, contemptuous, derisive, haughty, hoity-toity, imperious, insolent, proud, scornful, sneering, snobby, snooty, snotty, supercilious, superior, uppity.

antonyms admiring, respectful.

disease *n* affliction, ailment, blight, cancer, canker, complaint, condition, contagion, contamination, disorder, distemper, epidemic, idiopathy, ill health, illness, indisposition, infection, infirmity, malady, malaise, murrain, pestilence, plague, sickness.

antonym health.

diseased *adj* ailing, cancerous, contaminated, corrupt, disordered, infected, poisoned, rotten, sick, sickly, tainted, unhealthy, unsound, unwell, unwholesome.

antonym healthy.

disembark *v* alight, arrive, debark, deplane, detrain, get off, go ashore, land, pile out, unload.

antonym embark.

disembodied *adj* bodiless, ghostly, immaterial, incorporeal, intangible, phantom, spectral, spiritual, unbodied.

disembowel *v* draw, eviscerate, exenterate, gut.

disenchanted *adj* blasé, cynical, disappointed, disillusioned, fed up, indifferent, jaded, jaundiced, soured, undeceived.

disenchantment *n* cynicism, disappointment, disillusion, disillusionment, revulsion.

disengage *v* detach, disconnect, disentangle, disentwine, disjoin, disunite, divide, ease out, extricate, free, liberate, loosen, release, separate, set free, undo, unloose, untie, untwine, withdraw.

antonyms attach, connect, engage.

disengaged *adj* detatched, disconnected, disentangled, extricated, fancy-free, freed, heart-whole, inactive, liberated, loose, released, separate(d), unattached, unconnected, unhitched, unoccupied, untied.

antonyms connected, joined, united.

disentangle *v* clarify, detach, disconnect, disembarrass, disengage, disentwine, extricate, free, loose, resolve, separate, sever, simplify, unfold, unravel, unsnarl, untangle, untwine, untwist.

antonym entangle.

disfavour *n* black books, disapprobation, disapproval, discredit, disesteem, disgrace, disgust, dislike, disservice, displeasure, disrepute, injury, injustice, unpopularity, the doghouse, wrong.

antonym favour.

disfigure *v* blemish, damage, deface, deform, distort, injure, maim, mar, mutilate, scar, spoil, uglify.

antonym adorn.

disfigurement *n* blemish, damage, defacement, defect, deformity, disgrace, distortion, impairment, injury, mutilation, scar, sore, spot, stain, uglification.

antonym adornment.

disgorge *v* belch, cast forth (or up), discharge, effuse, eject, empty, expel, pour forth (or out), regurgitate, release, relinquish, renounce, spew, spill, spit up, spout, surrender, throw up, vomit.

disgrace *n* aspersion, attaint, blemish, blot, defamation, degradation, discredit, disesteem, disfavour, dishonour, disrepute, ignominy, infamy, obloquy, odium, opprobium, reproach, scandal, shame, slur, stain, stigma, the doghouse.

antonyms esteem, honour, respect.

v abase, defame, degrade, discredit, disfavour, dishonour, humiliate, reproach, shame, slur, stain, stigmatize, sully, taint.

antonyms honour, respect.

disgraceful *adj* appalling, blameworthy, contemptible, degrading, detestable, discreditable, dishonourable, disreputable, dreadful, ignominious, infamous, low, mean, opprobrious, scandalous, shameful, shocking, unworthy.

antonyms honourable, respectable.

disgruntled *adj* annoyed, browned off, cheesed off, degraded, discontented, displeased, dissatisfied, grumpy, irritated, malcontent, out of humour, peeved, peevish, petulant, put out, sulky, sullen, testy, teed off, ticked off, vexed.

antonyms pleased, satisfied.

disguise *v* camouflage, cloak, conceal, cover(up), dissemble, dissimulate, dress up, explain away, fake, falsify, fudge, hide, mask, misrepresent, screen, secrete, shroud, veil.

antonyms expose, reveal, uncover.

n camouflage, cloak, concealment, costume, cover, coverture, deception, dissimulation, façade, front, get-up, guise, mask, masquerade, pretence, screen, semblance, travesty, trickery, veil, veneer.

disguised *adj* camouflaged, cloaked, covert, dressed up, incognito, made up, masked, undercover, unrecognizable.

disgust *v* appal, displease, gross out, nauseate, offend, outrage, put off, repel, revolt, scandalize, sicken, turn off.

antonyms delight, gratify, tempt.

n abhorrence, abomination, antipathy, aversion, detestation, dislike, disrelish, distaste, hatefulness, hatred, loathing, nausea, odium, repugnance, repulsion, revulsion.

antonyms admiration, liking.

disgusting *adj* abominable, detestable, distasteful, foul, grisly, gross, hateful, loathsome, nasty, nauseating, nauseous, noisome, noxious, objectionable, obnoxious, obscene, odious, offensive, repellent, repugnant, repulsive, revolting, shameless, sickening, ugly, unappetizing, vile, vulgar, yucky.

antonyms attractive, delightful, pleasant.

dish[1] *n* bowl, container, entree, fare, food, menu item, (fruit) nappie, plate, platter, porringer, ramekin, recipe, salver, trencher.

dish out allocate, deal out, dispense, distribute, dole out, give out, hand out, inflict, ladle out, mete out.

dish up dispense, ladle, offer, prepare, present, produce, scoop, serve, spoon.

dish[2] *v* defeat, euchre, finish, ruin, spoil, torpedo, wreck.

disharmony *n* clash, conflict, disaccord, disagreement, discord, discordance, dissension, dissonance, disunity, friction, incompatibility, incongruity, strife.

antonym harmony.

dishearten *v* cast down, crush, damp(en), dash, daunt, deject, demoralize, depress, deter, disappoint, discourage, dismay, dispirit, weary.

antonyms encourage, hearten.

disheartened *adj* crestfallen, crushed, daunted, dejected, depressed, disappointed, discouraged, dismayed, dispirited, downcast, downhearted, weary.

antonyms encouraged, heartened.

dishevelled *adj* bedraggled, blowsy, disarranged, disordered, frowzy, messy, mussy, ruffled, rumpled, slovenly, tousled, uncombed, unkempt, untidy.

antonyms neat, spruce, tidy.

dishonest *adj* bent, cheating, corrupt, crafty, crooked, deceitful, deceiving, deceptive, designing, disingenuous, disreputable, double-dealing, false, fraudulent, guileful, immoral, insincere, knavish, lying, mendacious, perfidious, shady, sharp, sneaky, swindling, treacherous, tricky, underhand, unethical, unfair, unprincipled, unscrupulous, untrustworthy, untruthful, weaselly, wrongful.

antonyms fair, honest, scrupulous, trustworthy.

dishonesty *n* cheating, chicanery, corruption, craft, criminality, crookedness, deceit, double-dealing, duplicity, falsehood, falsity, fraud, fraudulence, graft, guile, immorality, improbity, insincerity, lies, lying, mendacity, perfidy, stealing, treachery, trickery, unscrupulousness, untrustworthiness, wiliness.

antonyms honesty, truthfulness.

dishonour *v* abase, blacken, break, corrupt, debase, debauch, defame, defile, deflower, degrade, demean, discredit, disgrace, disobey, disparage, drag in the dirt (or mud), flout, insult, pollute, profane, rape, ravish, seduce, shame, sully, violate.

antonym honour.

n abasement, abuse, affront, aspersion, degradation, discourtesy, discredit, disfavour, disgrace, disrepute, ignominy, indignity, infamy, insult, lower, obloquy, odium, offence, opprobrium, outrage, reproach, scandal, shame, slight, slur.

antonym honour.

dishonourable *adj* base, blackguardly, contemptible, corrupt, cowardly, dastardly, degraded, degrading, despicable, discreditable, disgraceful, disreputable, ignoble, ignominious, infamous, low, mean, reprehensible, scandalous, shameful, shameless, treacherous, unethical, unprincipled, unscrupulous, untrustworthy, unworthy.

antonym honourable.

disillusioned *adj* cynical, disabused, disappointed, disenchanted, enlightened, indifferent, undeceived, unenthusiastic.

disincentive *n* barrier, damper, deterrent, discouragement, dissuasion, hindrance, impediment, obstacle, repellent, restriction, restraint, turn-off.

antonyms encouragement, incentive.

disinclination *n* averseness, aversion, demur, dislike, loathness, objection, reluctance, resistance, unwillingness.

antonym inclination.

disinclined *adj* antipathetic, averse, hesitant, indisposed, loath, reluctant, resistant, undisposed, unenthusiastic, unwilling.

antonyms inclined, willing.

disinfect *v* clean, cleanse, decontaminate, deodorise, fumigate, purge, purify, sanitize, sterilize.

antonyms contaminate, infect.

disinfectant *n* antiseptic, cleanser, germicide, sanitizer, sterilizer.

disinfection *n* antisepsis, cleansing, decontamination, fumigation, purification, sanitization, sterilization.

disingenuous *adj* artful, cunning, deceitful, designing, devious, dishonest, duplicitous, guileful, insidious, insincere, shifty, two-faced, uncandid, wily.

antonyms artless, frank, ingenuous, naïve.

disintegrate *v* break up, crumble, decompose, dissolve, disunite, fall apart, moulder, rot, separate, shatter, splinter.

antonyms combine, merge, unite.

disinterest *n* apathy, detachment, disinterestedness, dispassion, impartiality, indifference, neutrality, unconcern, uninvolvement.

antonym interest.

disinterested *adj* detached, dispassionate, impartial, impersonal, neutral, unbiassed, uninvolved, unprejudiced, unselfish.

antonyms biassed, concerned, interested, prejudiced.

▲ *confusable word* uninterested.

disjoin *v* detach, disconnect, disengage, dismember, dissociate, disunite, divide, divorce, isolate, partition, segregate, separate, sever, split, uncouple.

antonyms connect, join.

disjoint *v* anatomize, break up, come apart, disarrange, disarticulate, discompose, disconnect, dislocate, dismember, disorder, displace, dissect, luxate, put out of joint, take apart, unjoint.

disjointed *adj* aimless, broken (up), cobbled together, confused, disarticulated, disconnected, discontinuous, dislocated, disordered, displaced, disunited, divided, fitful, incoherent, loose, out of joint, rambling, separated, spasmodic, split, unconnected, unjointed.

antonym coherent.

dislike *n* animosity, animus, antagonism, antipathy, aversion, detestation, disapprobation, disapproval, disgust, disinclination, displeasure, disrelish, distaste, enmity, hatred, hostility, loathing, repugnance.

antonyms attachment, liking, predilection.

v abhor, abominate, despise, detest, disapprove, disfavour, disrelish, hate, loathe, scorn, shun.

antonyms favour, like, prefer.

dislocate *v* derange, disarrange, disarray, disarticulate, disengage, disjoint, disorder, displace, disrupt, disturb, luxate, mess up, misplace, shift, unhinge, upset.

dislocation *n* derangement, disarrangement, disarray, disarticulation, disengagement, disorder, disorganization, disruption, disturbance, luxation, misplacement, unhinging.

antonym order.

dislodge *v* displace, disturb, eject, extricate, force out, loosen free, move, oust, pry off (or out), remove, shift, unstick, uproot.

disloyal *adj* apostate, disaffected, double-dealing, faithless, false, inconstant, perfidious, seditious, subversive, traitorous, treacherous, treasonable, treasonous, two-faced, unfaithful, unpatriotic, untrustworthy.

antonym loyal.

disloyalty *n* apostasy, betrayal, defection, desertion, double-dealing, falseness, falsity, inconstancy, infidelity, lese-majesty, perfidiousness, perfidy, sedition, treachery, treason, unfaithfulness.

antonym loyalty.

dismal *adj* black, bleak, cheerless, dark, defection, depressing, disheartening, discouraging, doleful, dolorous, dreary, forlorn, funereal, gloomy, grey, grim, hopeless, incompetent, inept, joyless, lachrymose, lonesome, long-faced, long-visaged, lowering, low-spirited, lugubrious, melancholy, miserable, poor, sad, sepulchral, sombre, sorrowful.

antonyms bright, cheerful.

dismantle *v* demolish, demount, disassemble, dismember, dismount, knock down, raze, strike, strip, take apart, unbuild.

antonym assemble.

dismay *v* affright, alarm, appal, consternate, daunt, depress, disappoint, disconcert, discourage, dishearten, disillusion, dispirit, distress, frighten, horrify, paralyse, put off, scare, terrify, trouble, unnerve, unsettle.

antonyms encourage, hearten.

n agitation, alarm, anxiety, apprehension, consternation, disappointment, distress, dread, fear, fright, funk, panic, terror, trepidation, upset.

antonyms boldness, courage, heart confidence.

dismember *v* amputate, anatomize, disassemble, disjoint, dislimb, dislocate, dismantle, dissect, divide, mutilate, rend, sever.

antonyms assemble, join.

dismemberment *n* amputation, anatomization, disassembly, dislocation, dismantling, dissection, division, mutilation.

antonyms assembly, joining, unifying.

dismiss *v* adjourn, axe, banish, bounce, cashier, disband, discharge, discount, disregard, dissolve, drop, fire, give a pink slip to, give the boot, lay off, let go, oust, pooh-pooh, reject, release, relegate, remove, repudiate, sack, send packing, set aside, shelve, spurn, write off.

antonyms accept, appoint.

dismissal *n* adjournment, congé, dear John letter, discharge, dismission, dissolution, end, expulsion, firing, golden handshake, marching orders, notice, ouster, release, rejection, removal, repudiation, the boot, the bum's rush, the sack, walking orders, walking papers, walking-ticket.

antonym appointment.

dismissive *adj* contemptuous, disdainful, off-hand, scornful, sneering.

antonyms concerned, interested.

dismount *v* alight, descend, disassemble, dismantle, get down, light, take apart, unhorse, unmount.

antonym mount.

disobedience *n* contrariness, contravention, contumacy, defiance, indiscipline, infraction, insubordination, intractability, mutiny, non-compliance, non-obedience, non-observance, obstreperousness, rebellion, recalcitrance, refractoriness, revolt, transgression, unruliness, violation, waywardness, willfulness.

antonym obedience.

disobedient *adj* contrary, contumacious, defiant, disorderly, froward, insubordinate, intractable, mischievous, naughty, non-compliant, obstreperous, rebellious, refractory, undisciplined, unruly, wayward, wild, willful.

antonym obedient.

disobey *v* contravene, defy, disregard, flout, ignore, infringe, overstep, rebel against, resist, transgress, violate.

antonym obey.

disoblige *v* deny, give offence to, inconvenience, refuse.

antonym oblige.

disobliging *adj* awkward, bloody-minded, contrary, cussed, disagreeable, discourteous, inaccommodating, rude, unaccommodating, uncivil, unco-operative, unhelpful.

antonyms complaisant, obliging.

disorder[1] *n* anarchy, chaos, clutter, commotion, confusion, derangement, disarray, disorderliness, disorganization, disruption, disturbance, failure, hubbub, hullabaloo, irregularity, jumble, mess, misrule, muddle, muss, mussiness, riot, rumpus, shambles, tumult, turmoil, untidiness, uproar.

antonym order.

v clutter, confound, confuse, derange, disarrange, discompose, dislocate, disorganize, disrupt, disturb, jumble, mess up, mix up, muddle, scatter, scramble, shuffle, unsettle, upset.

antonyms arrange, organize.

disorder[2] *n* affliction, ailment, complaint, condition, disease, illness, indisposition, malady, neurosis, psychosis, sickness, syndrome.

disordered[1] *adj* confused, deranged, disarranged, dislocated, disorganized, displaced, disturbed, higgledy-piggledy, jumbled, messed up, messy, misplaced, muddle, mussy, out of kilter, scrambled, topsy-turvy, turbid, untidy.

antonyms ordered, tidy.

disordered[2] *adj* deranged, diseased, morbid, sickened, unbalanced, unhealthy, unsound.

disorderly *adj* badly-behaved, chaotic, confused, disorganized, disruptive, higgledy-piggledy, indiscriminate, irregular, jumbled, lawless, messy, obstreperous, rambunctious, rebellious, refractory, riotous, rowdy, stormy, systemless, tumultuous, turbulent, undisciplined, ungovernable, unlawful, unmanageable, unruly, unsystematic, untidy, upside-down.

antonyms tidy, well-behaved.

disorganization *n* chaos, confusion, derangement, disarray, disjointedness, dislocation, disorder, disorderliness, disruption, incoherence, messiness, systemlessness, unconnectedness.

antonyms order, tidiness.

disorganize *v* break up, confound, confuse, derange, destroy, desystematize, disarrange, discompose, disorder, disrupt, disturb, jumble, mess up, muddle, play havoc with, unsettle, upset.

antonym organize.

disorganized *adj* chaotic, confused, disordered, disorderly, haphazard, jumbled, messy, misplaced, muddled, scrambled, shuffled, structureless, systemless, topsy-turvy, unmethodical, unorganized, unregulated, unsifted, unsorted, unstructured, unsystematic, unsystematized, untidy .

antonyms organized, tidy.

disorient *v* bewilder, confuse, disconcert, dislocate, faze, mislead, mix up, muddle, perplex, puzzle, unsettle, upset.

disoriented *adj* adrift, astray, at sea, bewildered, confused, disconcerted, displaced, lost, mixed up, muddled, perplexed, puzzled, unbalanced, unsettled, upset.

disown v abandon, abnegate, cast off, cut off, deny, disallow, disavow, disclaim, disinherit, reject, renounce, repudiate, wash one's hands of.

antonym accept.

disparage v belittle, criticize, decry, defame, degrade, denigrate, deprecate, depreciate, deride, derogate, detract from, devalue, discredit, disdain, dishonour, dismiss, downgrade, malign, minimize, put down, ridicule, run down, scorn, slander, talk down, traduce, underestimate, underrate, undervalue, vilify.

antonym praise.

disparagement n aspersion, belittlement, contempt, contumely, criticism, debasement, decrial, decrying, denunciation, deprecation, depreciation, derision, derogation, detraction, discredit, disdain, minimization, putdown, ridicule, scorn, slander, underestimation, vilification.

antonym praise.

disparaging adj belittling, contemptuous, denigrating, deprecatory, depreciatory, derisive, derogation, disdainful, insulting, pejorative, scornful.

disparate adj contrary, contrasting, different, discordant, discrepant, dissimilar, distinct, diverse, unequal, unlike.

antonyms equal, similar.

disparity n contrast, difference, discrepancy, disproportion, dissimilarity, dissimilitude, distinction, gap, imbalance, imparity, incongruity, inequality, unevenness, unlikeness.

antonyms equality, similarity.

dispassionate adj calm, collected, composed, cool, detached, disinterested, fair, impartial, impersonal, imperturbable, indifferent, moderate, neutral, objective, quiet, serene, sober, temperate, unbiassed, unemotional, unexcitable, unexcited, uninvolved, unmoved, unprejudiced, unruffled.

antonyms biassed, emotional.

dispatch¹ v accomplish, conclude, discharge, dismiss, dispose of, eat up, expedite, finish, perform, settle, take care of.

antonym impede.

n alacrity, celerity, efficiency, expedition, haste, promptude, promptness, quickness, rapidity, speed, swiftness.

antonyms delay, dilatoriness, slowness.

dispatch² v consign, convey, express, fire off, forward, mail, remit, send away (or off), transmit.

n account, bulletin, communication, communiqué, document, instruction, item, letter, message, missive, news, piece, release, report, story.

dispatch³ v assassinate, bump off, dissolve, do away with, do in, execute, get rid of, kill, murder, put out of the way, rub out, slaughter, slay, waste.

dispel v allay, banish, dismiss, disperse, dissipate, dissolve, drive away (or off), eliminate, expel, get rid of, melt away, resolve, rout, scatter.

antonym give rise to.

dispensable adj disposable, expendable, extra, inessential, needless, non-essential, replaceable, superfluous, unimportant, unnecessary, unneeded.

antonym indispensable.

dispensation n administration, allotment, appointment, apportionment, arrangement, award, bestowal, conferment, disbursement, distribution, dole, economy, endowment, exception, exemption, immunity, indulgence, licence, management, order, part, permission, plan, portion, privilege, quota, regime, regulation, relaxation, relief, remission, reprieve, scheme, setup, share, stewardship, supplying rule, system.

dispense v administer, allocate, allot, apply, apportion, assign, carry out, deal out, disburse, discharge, distribute, dole out, enforce, excuse (from), execute, exempt, give out, implement, let off, measure, mete out, mix, prepare, release, relieve, supply.

▲ *confusable word* disperse.

dispense with abolish, cancel, dispose of, disregard, do away with, do without, drop, forgo, forget (about), get rid of, ignore, obviate, omit, pass over, scrap, skip, waive.

antonyms accept, use.

disperse v broadcast, circulate, diffuse, disappear, disband, dismiss, dispel, disseminate, dissipate, dissolve, distribute, drive off, evanesce, melt away, rout, scatter, separate, spread, strew, vanish.

antonym gather.

▲ *confusable word* dispense.

dispersion n broadcast, circulation, diaspora, diffusion, dispersal, dissemination, dissipation, dissolution, distribution, scattering, spread.

dispirit v damp(en), dash, deject, depress, discourage, dishearten, put a damper on, sadden.

antonym encourage.

dispirited adj cast down, crestfallen, dejected, depressed, despondent, discouraged, disheartened, down, downcast, gloomy, glum, low, morose, sad.

antonym encouraged.

displace v crowd out, denote, depose, derange, disarrange, discharge, dislocate, dislodge, dismiss, dispossess, disturb, eject, evict, fire, luxate, misplace, move, oust, remove, replace, sack, shift, succeed, supersede, supplant, transpose, unsettle.

display v blazon, demonstrate, disclose, evidence, evince, exhibit, expose, flash, flaunt, flourish, manifest, model, parade, present, reveal, show, show off, showcase, splash, sport, spotlight, spread out, unfold, unfurl, unveil.

antonym hide.

n array, demonstration, exhibit booth, exhibition, exposition, exposure, manifestation, ostentation, pageant(ry), parade, pomp, presentation, revelation, scene, show, spectacle, splash.

displease *v* aggravate, anger, annoy, bother, bug, disgust, dissatisfy, exasperate, gall, get, huff, incense, infuriate, irk, irritate, miff, nettle, offend, peeve, pique, provoke, put out, rile, tee off, tick off, turn off, upset, vex.

antonyms calm, please.

displeased *n* aggravated, angry, annoyed, botched, disgusted, exasperated, furious, in a huff, irritated, miffed, nettled, offended, peeved, piqued, put out, teed off, ticked off, upset.

antonym pleased.

displeasure *n* anger, annoyance, disapprobation, disapproval, discontent, disfavour, disgruntlement, dudgeon, indignation, irritation, offence, pique, resentment, vexation, wrath.

antonyms gratification, pleasure.

disport *v* amuse, beguile, caper, cavort, divert, entertain, frisk, frolic, gambol, play, revel, romp, sport.

disposal *n* arrangement, array, assignment, bequest, bestowal, clearance, consignment, control, discarding, dispensation, disposition, distribution, dumping, jettisoning, management, ordering, positioning, regulation, removal, riddance, sale, scrapping, selling, settlement, transfer.

antonym provision.

dispose *v* adjust, align, arrange, array, bias, condition, determine, group, incline, induce, influence, lay, lead, marshal, motivate, move, order, place, position, predispose, prompt, put, range, rank, regulate, set, settle, situate, subject.

dispose of arrange, consume, deal with, decide, destroy, discard, dispatch, dispense with, dump, eat up, end, finish (up), get rid of, give away, jettison, scrap, sell, settle, throw away, transfer, unload.

antonym provide.

disposed *adj* apt, given, inclined, liable, likely, minded, moved, predisposed, prone, ready, subject, willing.

antonym disinclined.

disposition *n* adjustment, arrangement, bent, bias, character, classification, constitution, control, direction, disposal, distribution, grain, grouping, habit, inclination, kidney, leaning, make-up, management, nature, ordering, organization, placement, predisposition, proclivity, proneness, propensity, readiness, regulation, removal, settlement, spirit, temper, temperament, tendency, transfer.

dispossess *v* deprive, dislodge, divest, eject, evict, expel, expropriate, oust, rob, strip, unhouse.

antonyms give, provide.

dispossession *n* dethronement, dethroning, divestiture, divestment, ejection, eviction, expropriation, expulsion, ouster, ousting.

antonym possession.

disproportion *n* asymmetry, discrepancy, disparity, imbalance, imparity, inequality, lopsidedness, unevenness.

antonyms balance, equality.

disproportionate *adj* asymmetrical, disproportional, excessive, inappropriate, incommensurate, inordinate, lopsided, unbalanced, unequal, uneven, unreasonable.

antonyms appropriate, balanced.

disprove *v* confute, contradict, controvert, discredit, explode, expose, invalidate, negate, refute.

antonym prove.

disputable *adj* arguable, contentious, controversial, debatable, doubtful, dubious, inconclusive, litigious, moot, questionable, uncertain.

antonym indisputable.

disputation *n* argumentation, controversy, debate, dispute, dissension, polemics.

disputatious *adj* argumentative, cantankerous, captious, cavilling, contentious, litigious, polemic, pugnacious, quarrelsome.

dispute *v* altercate, argue, brawl, call into question, challenge, clash, contend (for), contest, contradict, controvert, debate, deny, disagree with, discuss, doubt, fight (against), fight (for), gainsay, impugn, litigate, moot, oppose, oppugn, quarrel with, question, resist, spar, squabble, traverse, wrangle.

antonym agree.

n altercation, argument, brawl, conflict, contention, controversy, debate, disagreement, discord, discussion, dissension, disturbance, feud, friction, quarrel, spar, squabble, strife, wrangle.

antonym agreement.

disputant *n* adversary, antagonist, arguer, contender, contestant, debater, litigant, opponent.

disqualified *adj* debarred, disabled, eliminated, excluded, ineligible, invalid, invalidated, unfit.

antonyms accepted, eligible, qualified.

disqualify *v* debar, disable, disentitle, eliminate, exclude, incapacitate, invalidate, preclude, prohibit, rule out, unfit.

antonyms accept, allow.

disquiet(ude) *n* alarm, angst, anxiety, concern, distress, disturbance, fear, foreboding, fretfulness, nervousness, perturbation, restlessness, trouble, uneasiness, unrest, worry.

antonym calmness.

v agitate, alarm, annoy, bother, concern, discompose, disconcert, distress, disturb, fret, perturb, pester, plague, shake, trouble, unsettle, upset, vex, worry.

antonym calm.

disquieting *adj* alarming, annoying, bothersome, disconcerting, distressing, disturbing, irritating, perturbing, troubling, unnerving, unsettling, upsetting, vexing, worrying.

antonym calming.

disquisition *n* descant, discourse, dissertation, essay, exposition, lecture, monograph, paper, sermon, thesis, treatise.

disregard *v* brush aside, brush away, brush off, cold-shoulder, contemn, despise, discount, disdain, dismiss, disobey, forget (about), ignore, laugh off, make light of, neglect, never mind (imperatively), overlook, pass over, pooh-pooh, slight, snub, turn a blind eye to, write off.

antonyms note, pay attention to.

n brushoff, contempt, disdain, disesteem, dismissal, disrespect, heedlessness, ignoring, inattention, inconsiderateness, indifference, neglect, negligence, oversight, slight, snubbing, thoughtlessness.

antonym attention.

disrepair *n* collapse, decay, deterioration, dilapidation, ruin, ruination, shabbiness.

antonyms good repair, restoration.

disreputable *adj* base, contemptible, derogatory, discreditable, disgraceful, dishonourable, ignominious, infamous, low, mean, notorious, opprobrious, scandalous, seedy, shady, shameful, shocking, unprincipled.

antonyms decent, honourable.

disrepute *n* discredit, disesteem, disfavour, disgrace, dishonour, ignominy, infamy, obloquy, shame.

antonyms esteem, honour.

disrespect *n* cheek, contempt, discourtesy, dishonour, disregard, flippancy, impertinence, impoliteness, impudence, incivility, insolence, insult, irreverence, mouthiness, rudeness, sauce, unmannerliness.

antonym respect.

disrespectful *adj* cheeky, contemptuous, discourteous, flippant, impertinent, impolite, impudent, insolent, insulting, irreverent, mouthy, rude, saucy, smart-alecky, uncivil, unmannerly.

antonym respectful.

disrobe *v* bare, denude, divest of, strip, unclothe, uncover, undress.

antonyms cover, dress.

disrupt *v* agitate, break into, break up, confuse, derange, dislocate, disorder, disorganize, disturb, interrupt, interfere with, intrude in (or upon), obstruct, shatter, split, spoil, unsettle, upset.

disruption *n* cataclysm, confusion, derangement, disarray, disorder, disorderliness, dissolution, disturbance, interference, interruption, obstruction, stoppage, upheaval, upset.

disruptive *adj* boisterous, disorderly, distracting, disturbing, obstreperous, troublesome, turbulent, undisciplined, unruly, unsettling, upsetting.

antonym well-behaved.

dissatisfaction *n* annoyance, chagrin, disappointment, discomfort, discontent, dislike, displeasure, distress, exasperation, frustration,

irritation, regret, resentment, restlessness, unfulfilment, unhappiness, unrest.

antonyms fulfilment, satisfaction.

dissatisfied *adj* disappointed, discontented, disgruntled, displeased, frustrated, restless, unfulfilled, unhappy, unsatisfied.

antonyms fulfilled, satisfied.

dissatisfy *v* annoy, disappoint, discontent, disgruntle, displease, exasperate, fall short, frustrate, irritate, leave something to be desired, put out.

dissect *v* analyse, anatomize, break down, cut up, dismember, examine, inspect, investigate, pore over, scrutinize, study.

dissection *n* analysis, anatomization, anatomy, autopsy, breakdown, dismemberment, examination, inspection, investigation, necropsy, scrutiny, study.

dissemble *v* affect, camouflage, cloak, conceal, counterfeit, cover up, disguise, dissimulate, fake, falsify, feign, hide, mask, pretend, put on, sham, simulate.

antonyms admit, unmask.

dissembler *n* charlatan, con, confidence man, con man, deceiver, dissimulator, fake, feigner, fraud, hypocrite, impostor, phony, pretender, trickster, whited sepulchre.

disseminate *v* broadcast, circulate, diffuse, disperse, dissipate, distribute, proclaim, promulgate, propagate, publicize, publish, scatter, sow, spread.

dissemination *n* broadcast(ing), circulation, diffusion, dispersion, dissipation, distribution, promulgation, propagation, publication, publicization, publishing, scattering, sowing, spread.

dissension *n* conflict, contention, difference, disagreement, discord(ance), dispute, dissent, division, friction, quarrel(ing), schism, strife, variance.

antonyms agreement, peace.

dissent *v* decline, differ, disagree, object, oppose, protest, quibble, refuse.

antonyms agree, consent.

n difference, disagreement, discord, dissension, dissidence, heterodoxy, non-conformance, nonconformity, objection, opposition, quibble, recusancy, refusal, resistance.

antonyms agreement, conformity.

dissenter *n* disputant, dissident, heretic, nonconformist, objector, protestant, protester, recusant, schismatic, sectary.

antonym conformist.

dissentient *adj* conflicting, differing, disagreeing, dissenting, dissident, non-conformist, heretical, heterodox, objecting, opposing, protesting, recusant.

antonyms agreeing, conforming, conformist.

dissertation *n* critique, discourse, discussion, disquisition, essay, exposition, monograph, paper, prolegomena, thesis, treatise.

disservice *n* bad turn, disfavour, harm, injury, injustice, unkindness, wrong.

antonym favour.

dissever *v* break apart, cleave, disunite, divide, divorce, part, rend, rift, rive, separate, sever, split, sunder.

dissidence *n* difference, disagreement, discordance, dispute, dissent, feud, heterodoxy, non-conformity, opposition, protest, recusancy, rupture, schism, variance.
antonyms agreement, peace.

dissident *adj* differing, disagreeing, discordant, dissentient, dissenting, heretical, heterodox, nonconformist, recusant, schismatic.
antonyms acquiescent, agreeing.
n agitator, dissenter, heretic, protester, rebel, recusant, schismatic.
antonym assenter.

dissimilar *adj* contrasting, different, disparate, divergent, diverse, heterogeneous, incompatible, incongruous, mismatched, unlike, unrelated, various.
antonyms compatible, similar.

dissimilarity *n* contrast, difference, discrepancy, disparity, dissimilitude, distinction, divergence, diversity, heterogeneity, incomparability, incompatibility, incongruity, mismatch, unlikeness, unrelatedness.
antonyms compatibility, similarity.

dissimulate *v* camouflage, cloak, conceal, disguise, dissemble, hide, mask, pretend.

dissimulation *n* act, affectation, concealment, deceit, deception, dissembling, double-dealing, duplicity, feigning, hypocrisy, play-acting, pretence, sham, wile.
antonym openness.

dissipate *v* burn up, consume, deplete, disappear, disintegrate, dispel, disperse, dissolve, evaporate, expend, fritter away, indulge, lavish, scatter, spend, squander, vanish, wanton, waste away.
antonyms accumulate, conserve.

dissipated *adj* abandoned, consumed, debauched, dissolute, exhausted, intemperate, profligate, rakish, scattered, spent, squandered, wanton, wasted, wild.
antonyms conserved, virtuous.

dissipation *n* abandonment, amusement, debauchery, disappearance, disintegration, dispersion, dissemination, dissoluteness, dissolution, diversion, excess, extravagance, fast life, intemperance, prodigality, profligacy, rakishness, scattering, squandering, vanishing, wantonness, waste.
antonyms conservation, virtue.

dissociate *v* break off, break up, decompose, detach, disband, disconnect, disrupt, distance, disunite, divorce, isolate, leave, quit, segregate, separate, sever, split (off).
antonyms attach, share.

dissociation *n* break, detachment, disconnection, disengagement, dissevering, distancing, disunion, division, divorce, isolation, segregation, separation, severance, severing, split.
antonyms association, union.

dissolute *adj* abandoned, corrupt, debauched, degenerate, depraved, dissipated, immoral, lax, lewd, libertine, licentious, loose, profligate, rakish, unrestrained, vicious, wanton, wild.
antonym virtuous.

dissoluteness *n* abandon, corruption, debauchery, degeneracy, depravity, dissipation, immorality, laxness, lewdness, licence, licentiousness, looseness, profligacy, rakishness, vice, wantonness, wildness.
antonym virtue.

dissolution *n* abolition, adjournment, breakdown, break-up, collapse, conclusion, death, decay, decomposition, demise, destruction, disappearance, disassembly, disbandment, discontinuation, disintegration, dismissal, dispersal, disruption, divorce, end, ending, evaporation, extinction, fall, finish, liquefaction, liquidity, melting, overthrow, parting, resolution, ruin, separation, solution, suspension, termination.
antonym unification.

dissolve *v* adjourn, break up, clear up, conclude, crumble, decompose, deliquesce, destroy, diffuse, disappear, discontinue, disintegrate, dismiss, disperse, dissipate, disunite, divorce, dwindle, end, evanesce, evaporate, explain, fade (away), flux, fuse, liquefy, loose, melt, overthrow, perish, recess, ruin, separate, sever, soften, solve, suspend, terminate, vanish, wind up.

dissonance *n* cacophony, clash, conflict, difference, disagreement, discord, discord(ance), discrepancy, disharmony, disparity, dissension, harshness, incompatability, incongruity, inconsistency, jangle, jarring, variance.
antonyms consonance, harmony.

dissonant *adj* anomalous, cacophonous, different, differing, disagreeing, discordant, discrepant, disharmonious, dissentient, grating, harsh, incompatible, incongruous, inconsistent, inharmonious, irreconcilable, irregular, jangling, jarring, raucous, tuneless, unmelodious.
antonyms compatible, harmonious.

dissuade *v* caution (against), deter, discourage, disincline, divert, expostulate with, put off, remonstrate with, talk (out), warn (against).
antonym persuade.

dissuasion *n* caution, determent, deterrence, deterring, discouragement, expostulation, remonstration.
antonym persuasion.

distance *n* absence, aloofness, coldness, coolness, difference, dissociation, extent, frigidity, gap, interval, isolation, length, range, reach, remoteness, remove, reserve, restraint, separation, space, span, stand-offishness, stiffness, stretch, width.
v detach, disassociate, disengage, divorce, isolate, remove, separate, withdraw.

distant *adj* absent, aloof, apart, away, cold, cool, dreamy, faint, far, faraway, far away, far-flung, far-off, formal, haughty, indirect, indistinct, isolated, obscure, outlying,

distaste *n* abhorrence, antipathy, aversion, detestation, discontent(ment), disfavour, disgust, disinclination, dislike, displeasure, disrelish, dissatisfaction, horror, loathing, repugnance, revulsion.

antonym inclination.

distasteful *adj* abhorrent, aversive, disagreeable, displeasing, loathsome, nasty, nauseous, objectionable, obnoxious, offensive, repugnant, repulsive, unattractive, unappetizing, undesirable, uninviting, unpalatable, unpleasant, unsavoury.

antonym pleasing.

distend *v* balloon, bloat, bulge, dilate, enlarge, expand, fill out, increase, inflate, intumesce, puff out, stretch (out), swell, widen.

antonym deflate.

distended *adj* ballooning, bloated, bulging, dilated, emphysematic, enlarged, expanded, inflated, puffed out, puffy, stretched out, swollen, tumescent, varicose.

antonym deflated.

distension *n* ballooning, bloat, bulge, bulging, dilatation, dilation, emphysema, enlargement, expansion, extension, inflation, intumescence, puffiness, spread, swelling, tumescence.

distil *v* capture the essence of, condense, drip, encapsulate, evaporate, extract, flow, purify, rarefy, refine, sublimate, trickle, vaporize.

distinct *adj* apparent, clear, clear-cut, decided, definite, detached, different, discrete, dissimilar, evident, individual, lucid, manifest, marked, noticeable, obvious, palpable, patent, plain, recognizable, separate, several, sharp, unambiguous, unconnected, unmistakable, well-defined.

antonyms fuzzy, hazy, indistinct.

distinction[1] *n* contradistinction, contrast, definitive, dichotomy, difference, differential, differentiation, discernment, discrimination, dissimilarity, distinctiveness, division, distinguishing feature, individuality, mark, nuance, particularity, peculiarity, quality, separation.

distinction[2] *n* account, celebrity, consequence, credit, dignity, eminence, excellence, fame, glory, greatness, honour, importance, merit, note, prestige, prominence, quality, rank, renown, reputation, repute, significance, superiority, worth.

antonym insignificance.

distinctive *adj* characteristic, contrastive, definitive, different, dignity, discriminative, distinguishing, extraordinary, idiosyncratic, individual, inimitable, original, peculiar, singular, special, typical, uncommon, unique.

antonym common.

distinctness *n* clarity, clearness, definition, definiteness, difference, discreteness, disparateness, dissimilarity, dissociation, distinctiveness, individuality, lucidity, obviousness, palpability, plainness, resolution, sharpness, unmistakeableness, vividness.

antonyms fuzziness, haziness, indistinctness.

distinguish *v* ascertain, categorize, celebrate, characterize, classify, contrastive, desury, determine, differentiate, dignify, discern, discriminate, honour, immortalize, individualize, judge, know, make out, mark, perceive, pick out, recognize, see, separate, signalize, single out, tell, tell apart.

distinguishable *adj* appreciable, clear, different, discernible, distinct, evident, manifest, noticeable, observable, obvious, perceptible, plain, recognizable, unidentical.

antonyms identical, indistinct, indistinguishable.

distinguished *adj* acclaimed, celebrated, distingué, eminent, excellent, extraordinary, famed, famous, great, illustrious, marked, notable, noted, noteworthy, outstanding, renowned, signal, striking, well-known.

antonyms insignificant, ordinary.

distinguishing *adj* characteristic, contrastive, differentiating, discriminative, distinctive, individual, marked, peculiar, salient, signal, typical, unique.

distort *v* bend, bias, buckle, colour, contort, deform, disfigure, falsify, garble, misrepresent, misshape, pervert, skew, slant, stretch, twist, warp, weight, wrench.

distorted *adj* askew, awry, bent, biassed, contorted, deformed, false, garbled, lopsided, misleading, misrepresented, misshapen, skewed, slanted, twisted, warped, weighted, wry.

antonym straight.

distortion *n* bend, bias, buckle, colouring, contortion, crookedness, deformity, falsification, malformation, misrepresentation, obliquity, perversion, skewness, slantedness, twistedness, warpedness.

distract *v* agitate, amuse, awry, beguile, bewilder, confound, confuse, derange, discompose, disconcert, disturb, divert, engross, entertain, faze, frazzle, madden, occupy, perplex, preoccupy, sidetrack, torment, trouble.

▲ *confusable word* detract.

distracted *adj* agitated, bemused, bewildered, confounded, confused, crazy, deranged, distraught, flustered, frantic, frazzled, frenzied, grief-stricken, insane, mad, maddened, occupied, overwrought, perplexed, preoccupied, puzzled, raving, troubled, wild, worked-up, wrought-up.

antonyms calm, untroubled.

distracting *adj* annoying, bewildering, confusing, disconcerting, disturbing, irritating, off-putting, perturbing.

distraction *n* abstraction, a frazzle, agitation, amusement, annoyance, beguilement, bewilderment, confusion, delirium, derangement, desperation, disturbance, diversion, divertissement, entertainment, escape, frenzy, incoherence, interference, interruption, irritation, pastime, preoccupation, recreation, relief.

distraught adj agitated, anguished, anxious, beside oneself, confused, crazed, crazy, delirious, distracted, distressed, frantic, grief-stricken, hysterical, mad, out of one's mind, overwrought, raving, upset, wild, worked-up, wrought-up.

antonyms calm, untroubled.

distress n adversity, affliction, agony, anguish, anxiety, calamity, deprivation, desolation, destitution, difficulty, discomfort, grief, hardship, heartache, indigence, misery, misfortune, need, pain, pauperism, peril, poverty, privation, sadness, sorrow, strait(s), suffering, torment, torture, trial, trouble, woe, worry, wretchedness.

antonyms comfort, ease, security.

v afflict, aggrieve, agitate, bother, disturb, grieve, harass, harrow, pain, perplex, sadden, torment, trouble, upset, worry, wound.

antonyms assist, comfort.

distressed adj afflicted, aggrieved, agitated, agonizing, anxious, broken up, damaged, destitute, distracted, distraught, grieved, indigent, needy, poor, poverty-stricken, saddened, shaken, straitened, tormented, troubled, upset, worried, wretched.

antonyms calm, untroubled.

distressing adj afflictive, disquieting, distressful, disturbing, grievous, harrowing, heartbreaking, hurtful, lamentable, nerve-wracking, painful, perturbing, sad, trying, unnerving, upsetting, worrisome, worrying.

antonyms assuaging, pleasant.

distribute v administer, allocate, allot, apportion, arrange, assign, assort, bestow, carve up, categorize, circulate, class, classify, deal out, deliver, diffuse, dish out, dispense, disperse, dispose, divide, divvy up, dole out, give out, group, hand out, market, measure out, mete out, parcel out, pass out, retail, scatter, sell, share, spread, strew, wholesale.

antonyms collect, gather in.

distribution n allocation, allotment, apportionment, arrangement, assortment, bestowal, bestowing, circulation, classification, dealing, delivery, diffusion, dispensation, dispersal, dispersion, disposition, division, dole, handling, mailing, marketing, partition, propagation, retailing, scattering, sharing, spread, spreading, trading.

antonyms collection, gathering.

district n area, canton, community, division, locale, locality, municipality, neck of the woods, neighbourhood, parish, precinct, quarter, region, sector, township, vicinity, ward.

distrust v disbelieve, discredit, doubt, mistrust, question, suspect.

antonym trust.

n disbelief, doubt, leeriness, misgiving,

mistrust, paranoia, qualm, question, scepticism, suspicion, uneasiness, wariness.

antonym trust.

distrustful adj chary, cynical, disbelieving, distrusting, doubtful, doubting, dubious, leery, mistrustful, paranoid, sceptical, suspicious, uneasy, untrusting, wary.

antonyms trustful, unsuspecting.

disturb v agitate, alarm, annoy, bother, bug, concuss, confound, confuse, derange, disarrange, discompose, disconcert, disorder, disorganize, disquiet, disrupt, distract, distress, excite, faze, fluster, get on someone's nerves, harass, inconvenience, interfere with, interrupt, make uneasy, mess with, molest, muddle (up), perturb, pester, rouse, ruffle, shake, startle, tamper with, trouble, unsettle, unblance, upset, worry.

antonyms calm, quiet, reassure.

disturbance n affray, agitation, annoyance, bother, brawl, bust-up, commotion, confusion, derangement, discomposure, disorder, distraction, fracas, fray, hubbub, interruption, intrusion, misarrangement, molestation, perturbation, riot, ruckus, shake-up, trouble, tumult, turmoil, uneasiness, unrest, upheaval, uproar, upset.

antonyms peace, quiet.

disturbed adj agitated, alarmed, anxious, apprehensive, bothered, concerned, confused, deranged, disarranged, discomposed, disconcerted, disordered, disquieted, disrupted, distracted, distressed, flustered, maladjusted, neurotic, perturbed, restless, shaken, troubled, unbalanced, uneasy, upset, worried.

antonyms calm, sane.

disturbing adj agitating, alarming, disconcerting, discouraging, dismaying, disquieting, distressful, distressing, frightening, perturbing, threatening, troubling, unsettling, upsetting, worrying.

antonym reassuring.

disunion n alienation, breach, detachment, disagreement, disconnection, discord, disharmony, disjunction, dissension, dissevance, dissidence, disunity, division, estrangement, feud, partition, rift, rupture, schism, separation, severance, split.

antonym unification.

disunite v alienate, detach, disband, disconnect, disengage, disjoin, disrupt, divide, estrange, part, segregate, separate, sever, split, sunder.

antonym unify.

disunity n alienation, breach, conflict, disagreement, discord, discordance, disharmony, dissension, dissent, dissidence, disunion, estrangement, rupture, schism, split, strife, variance.

antonyms unity, cohesion.

disuse n abandonment, decay, desuetude, discontinuance, idleness, neglect.

antonym use.

ditch *n* channel, drain, dike, furrow, gully, gutter, jilt, moat, trench, watercourse.

v abandon, chuck, discard, dispose of, drop, dump, get rid of, jettison, scrap, throw out.

dither *v* back and fill, dilly-dally, faff around, falter, hesitate, hem and haw, hover,oscillate, shilly-shally, stall, teeter, vacillate, waffle (back and forth), waver.

antonym decide.

n bother, flap, fluster, flutter, indecision, panic, pother, stew, tizzy, twitter.

antonym decision.

divan *n* chaise longue, chesterfield, couch, council (chamber), lounge, ottoman, settee, smoking room, sofa.

dive¹ *v* descend, dip, drop, duck, fall, jump, leap, nose-dive, pitch, plummet, plunge, sound, submerge, swoop.

n drop, fall, jump, leap, lunge, nose-dive, plunge, swoop.

dive² *n* den, doss house, dump, fleapit, hellhole, hole, honky-tonk, joint.

diverge *v* bifurcate, branch (off), conflict, depart, deviate, differ, digress, disagree, dissent, divagate, divide, drift apart, fork, part ways, radiate, separate, split, spread, stray, turn away, vary, wander.

antonyms agree, come together, join.

divergence *n* branching-out, conflict, deflection, departure, deviation, difference, digression, disagreement, disparity, divagation, division, fork, parting of the ways, radiating, ramification, separation, split, spread(ing), straying, variation, wandering.

antonym convergence.

divergent *adj* conflicting, deviating, different, differing, disagreeing, dissenting, dissimilar, diverging, diverse, divided, radiating, separate, split, spreading, straying, variant, varying, wandering.

antonyms convergent, parallel, uniform.

diverse *adj* assorted, different, differing, discrete, disparate, dissimilar, distinct, divergent, divers, diversified, heterogeneous, manifold, many, miscellaneous, multifarious, multiform, numerous, separate, several, some, sundry, unlike, varied, various, varying.

antonyms identical, uniform.

diversify *v* assort, branch out, change, distribute, expand, mix, spread out, variegate, vary.

diversion¹ *n* deflection, detour, deviation, digression, distraction, feint, redirection, sidetrack.

diversion² *n* amusement, beguilement, delight, divertissement, enjoyment, entertainment, game, pastime, play, pleasure, recreation, relaxation, sport.

diversity *n* assortment, difference, dissimilarity, distinctiveness, divergence, diverseness, diversification, heterogeneity, medley, multifariousness, multiplicity, range, unlikeness, variance, variegation, variety.

antonyms sameness, similarity, uniformity.

divert¹ *v* avert, deflect, delight, detract, distract, entertain, redirect, sidetrack, switch, turn aside.

divert² *v* amuse, beguile, delight, entertain, regale.

diverting *adj* amusing, beguiling, enjoyable, entertaining, fun, funny, humorous, pleasant.

antonyms boring, irritating.

divest *v* denude, deprive, dispossess, free, rid, rob, shear, strip, take away.

antonyms endow, invest.

divide *v* alienate, allocate, allot, apportion, arrange, bisect, break apart, break (up), categorize, classify, cleave, cut(up), deal (out), compartmentalize, dispense, distribute, disunite, divvy up, drive apart, estrange, graduate, group, parcel out, part, partition, portion, segment, segregate, separate, sever, share, sort, split, subdivide, sunder.

antonyms bring together, collect, gather, join.

dividend *n* benefit, bonus, cut, divvy, extra, gain, gratuity, interest, plus, portion, return, share, surplus.

divination *n* augury, clairvoyance, divining, foretelling, fortunetelling, -mancy, prediction, presaging, prognostication, prophecy, second sight, soothsaying.

divine *adj* angelic, beatific, beautiful, blissful, celestial, consecrated, delightful, exalted, excellent, glorious, godlike, heavenly, holy, marvellous, mystical, perfect, rapturous, religious, sacred, sanctified, spiritual, splendid, superhuman, superlative, supernatural, supreme, transcendent, wonderful.

n churchman, clergyman, cleric, ecclesiastic, minister, parson, pastor, prelate, priest, reverend, theologian.

v apprehend, conjecture, deduce, foretell, guess, infer, intuit, perceive, prognosticate, suppose, surmise, suspect, understand.

diviner *n* astrologer, augur, clairvoyant, divinator, dowser, fortuneteller, haruspex, oracle, prophet, psychic, seer, sibyl, soothsayer.

divinity *n* daemon, deity, deva, genius, god, goddess, godhead, godhood, holiness, kami, sanctity, spirit, theology.

division *n* allotment, apportionment, arrangement, bisection, borderline, boundary, branch, breach, breakup, categorization, category, chapter, class, classification, compartment, cutting, demarcation, department, detachment, dichotomy, disagreement, discord, dissension, distribution, disunion, divide, divider, dividing, estrangement, feud, grouping, part, partition, portion, rupture, schism, scission, section, sector, segment, segmentation, separation, sept, severance, sharing, side, split, splitting, stream, subdivision, sundering, ward, watershed, wing.

antonyms agreement, multiplication, unification.

divorce n annulment, breach, break, break-up, decree nisi, diffarreation, dissolution, disunion, rupture, separation, severance, split-up.
v dissever, dissociate, disunite, divide, get, part, separate, sever, split up, sunder.
antonyms marry, unify.

divulge v betray, broadcast, communicate, confess, declare, disclose, expose, impart, leak, let slip, proclaim, promulgate, publish, reveal, spill, tell, uncover.

divvy n cut, dividend, percentage, portion, quota, share, whack.
divvy up apportion, carve up, deal out, distribute, divide up, dole out, measure out, parcel out, share, share out, split.

dizzy adj befuddled, bemused, bewildered, confused, dazed, dazzled, faint, fickle, flighty, foolish, frivolous, giddy, light-headed, lofty, muddled, reeling, scatter-brained, shaky, staggering, steep, swimming, vertiginous, wobbly, woozy.

do v accomplish, achieve, act, arrange, be enough, behave, bring about, carry out, cause, cheat, complete, conclude, cover, create, deal with, defraud, discharge, effect, end, execute, explore, fare, finish, fix, give, happen, implement, make, manage, organize, pass muster, perform, prepare, present, proceed at, produce, put on, render, satisfy, serve, solve, suffice, suit, tour, transact, travel, undertake, use, visit, work (around, at, through), work out.
n affair, celebration, event, function, gathering, get-together, occasion, party.
do away with abolish, bump off, destroy, discard, discontinue, do in, eliminate, exterminate, get rid of, kill, liquidate, murder, remove, slay.
do for[1] defeat, destroy, finish (off), kill, ruin, shatter, slay.
do for[2] fend for, look after.
do in butcher, dispatch, eliminate, execute, exhaust, fag, fatigue, kill, liquidate, murder, rub out, slaughter, slay, tire out, waste, wear out, weary.
do (out of) bilk, cheat, con, cozen, deceive, defraud, deprive, diddle, dupe, fleece, rook, swindle, trick.
do's and don'ts code, customs, etiquette, instructions, niceties, p's and q's, protocol, punctilios, regulations, rules, standards.
do up buckle up, button up, clean, close, fasten, iron, lace up, prepare, press, ready, style, tie, wrap up, zip up.
do without abstain from, dispense with, forgo, give up, relinquish, renounce, skip, spare, waive.

docile adj amenable, biddable, complaisant, compliant, ductile, manageable, meek, obedient, obliging, pliable, pliant, submissive, teachable, tractable, unprotesting, unquestioning, yielding.
antonyms truculent, unco-operative.

docility n amenability, biddableness, complaisance, compliance, ductility, manageability, meekness, obedience, pliability, pliancy, submissiveness, teachability, tractability.
antonyms truculence, unco-operativeness.

dock[1] n dry-dock, harbour, landing, marina, pier, platform, quay, shipyard, waterfront, wharf.
v anchor, berth, drop anchor, join, land, link up, moor, put in, rendezvous, tie up, unite.

dock[2] v clip, crop, curtail, cut, decrease, deduct, diminish, enter, lessen, list, reduce, schedule, shorten, subtract, truncate, withhold.

docket n bill of goods, bill of lading, certificate, chit, counterfoil, label, list, schedule, tab, tag, tally, ticket, worksheet.
v catalogue, enter, file, index, label, list, mark, register, schedule, tag, ticket.

doctor n clinician, general practitioner, GP, hakim, intern, internist, leech, medic, medico, physician, resident, surgeon.
v adulterate, alter, change, cook, coroner, cut, dilute, falsify, fix, fudge, hocus, medicate, mend, misrepresent, patch, practise, repair, spike, tamper with, tend, treat.

doctrinaire adj dogmatic, fanatical, hypothetical, ideological, impractical, inflexible, insistent, legalistic, opinionated, pedantic, rigid, speculative, theoretical, unrealistic.
antonym flexible.

doctrine n article of faith, belief, canon, concept, conviction, credo, creed, dogma, ism, precept, principle, teaching, tenet.

document n certificate, deed, form, instrument, paper, parchment, record, report.
v authenticate, back, certify, cite, corroborate, demonstrate, detail, enumerate, illustrate, instance, list, particularize, prove, reference, show, substantiate, support, validate, verify.

dodder adj aged, decrepit, faltering, feeble, infirm, shaky, shambling, tottery, trembly, unsteady, weak.
antonyms hale, youthful.

dodge v avoid, dart, deceive, duck, elude, equivocate, evade, fend off, fudge, hedge, parry, shift, shirk, shuffle, sidestep, swerve.
n chicane, contrivance, device, fakery, feint, manoeuvre, ploy, ruse, scheme, shift, shuffle, stratagem, subterfuge, trick, wile.

dodger n evader, shirk(er), slacker, slyboots, trickster.

doer n accomplisher, achiever, activist, bustler, busy bee, dynamo, go-getter, going concern, live wire, organizer, powerhouse, worker, workhorse.

doff v discard, lift, get rid of, raise, remove, shed, take off, throw aside, tip, touch.
antonym don.

dog n beast, bitch, blackguard, canine, cur, Fido, heel, hound, knave, mongrel, mutt, pooch, pup, puppy, scoundrel, tyke, villain.
v beset, harry, harass, haunt, hound, plague, pursue, shadow, tail, track, trail, trouble, worry.

dogged adj determined, firm, indefatigable, indomitable, obstinate, persevering, persistent, pertinacious, relentless, resolute, single-minded, staunch, steadfast, steady, stubborn, tenacious, unflagging, unshakable, unyielding.

antonym irresolute.

doggedness n determination, endurance, indomitablity, obstinacy, perseverance, persistence, pertinacity, relentlessness, resolution, single-mindedness, staunchiness, steadfastness, steadiness, stubbornness, tenaciousness, tenacity.

dogma n article, article of faith, belief, conviction, credo, creed, doctrine, precept, principle, teaching, tenet.

dogmatic adj arbitrary, authoritative, canonical, categorical, close-minded, dictatorial, didactic, doctrinaire, emphatic, ex cathedra, fanatical, imperious, inflexible, magisterial, narrow, narrow-minded, opinionated, oracular, overbearing, peremptory, pontifical, positive, rigid.

dogmatism n arbitrariness, bigotry, fanaticism, imperiousness, inflexibility, legalism, narow-mindedness, opinionatedness, peremptoriness, positiveness, presumption, rigidity.

do-gooder n activist, bleeding heart, goody-goody, hero, martyr, Quixote, reformer, saint, torchbearer.

dog-tired adj asleep on one's feet, beat, dead, dead tired, done in, drained, exhausted, fagged, washed out, weary, whacked (out), wiped, worn out, zonked.

doings n actions, activities, acts, adventures, affairs, behaviour, business, comings and goings, concerns, conduct, dealings, deeds, events, exploits, goings-on, handiwork, happenings, movements, proceedings, transactions.

doldrums n accidie, accidia, apathy, blahs, blues, boredom, depression, dullness, dumps, ennui, gloom, inertia, lassitude, listlessness, low-spiritedness, malaise, stagnation, tedium, torpor.

dole n allocation, allotment, allowance, alms, apportionment, benefit(s), charity, division, donation, gift, grant, gratuity, handout, modicum, pittance, portion, quota, ration, relief, share, social assistance, social security, welfare.

dole (out) administer, allocate, allot, apportion, assign, deal, dispense, distribute, divide, give, hand out, issue, mete, ration, share.

doleful adj blue, cheerless, depressing, dismal, distressing, dolorous, down in the dumps, dreary, forlorn, funereal, gloomy, lugubrious, melancholy, mournful, painful, pathetic, pitiful, rueful, sad, sombre, sorrowful, woebegone, woeful, wretched.

antonym cheerful.

doll n china doll, dolly, figurine, kewpie doll, marionette, moppet, plaything, poppet, puppet, toy.

doll up deck out, dress up, gussy up, preen, primp, prink, spiff up, tart up, titivate, trick out (or up).

dollar n buck, greenback, loonie, money, smacker.

dollop n ball, blob, dose, glob, gob, gobbet, lump.

dolorous adj anguished, distressful, distressed, distressing, doleful, forlorn, grievous, harrowing, heartbreaking, heartbroken, heart-rending, lugubrious, melancholy, miserable, mournful, painful, rueful, sad, sombre, sorrowful, woebegone, woeful, wretched.

antonym happy.

dolour n anguish, distress, grief, heartache, heartbreak, lamentation, misery, mourning, sadness, sorrow, suffering.

antonyms celebration, joy.

dolt n ass, beetlebrain, beetlehead, birdbrain, blockhead, bonehead, booby, calf, chump, clunk, dimwit, dope, dullard, dunce, dunderhead, fool, galoot, goof, half-wit, idiot, ignoramus, loggerhead, lout, lubber, lunkhead, lurdan(e), mutt, muttonhead, ninny, nitwit, numskull, palooka, simpleton.

doltish adj boneheaded, brainless, dense, dimwitted, dopey, dozey, dull, dumb, foolish, half-witted, idiotic, mindless, muttonheaded, obtuse, silly, slow, stupid, thick.

antonyms brainy, clever.

domain n area, authority, bailiwick, demesne, department, discipline, dominion, empire, estate, field, jurisdiction, kingdom, lands, orbit, province, purview, realm, region, scope, specialty, sphere, territory.

domestic adj autochthonous, cultivated, domesticated, domiciliary, familial, family, home, home-bred, home-loving, homemade, house, housebroken, household, house-trained, indigenous, internal, native, pet, private, stay-at-home, tame, trained.

n au pair, char, charwoman, daily help, help, housekeeper, maid, scullery maid, servant.

domesticate v acclimatize, accustom, adopt, break (in), cultivate, familiarize, habituate, house-train, naturalize, tame, train, transfer.

domesticated adj broken (in), domestic, home-loving, housebroken, house-proud, house-trained, housewifely, naturalized, tame, tamed.

antonyms feral, wild.

domesticity n domestication, familism, homecraft, homemaking, housekeeping, housewifery.

domicile n abode, dwelling, habitation, home, house, lodging(s), quarters, residence.

dominance n ascendancy, authority, command, control, domination, government, hegemony, leadership, mastery, power, precedence, predominance, pre-eminence, prevalence, primacy, prominance, rule, superiority, supremacy, sway.

dominant *adj* ascendant, authoritative, besetting, chief, commanding, controlling, governing, influential, leading, main, outstanding, paramount, predominant, pre-eminent, presiding, prevailing, prevalent, primary, prime, principal, prominent, ruling, superior, supreme.

antonym subordinate.

dominate *v* bestride, control, direct, domineer over, dwarf, eclipse, govern, have the whip hand over, keep under one's thumb, lead, master, monopolize, oppress, outshine, overbear, overlook, overrule, overshadow, predominate, prevail over, rule over, suppress, tower over, tyrannize.

domination *n* ascendancy, authority, command, control, despotism, dictatorship, hegemony, influence, leadership, mastery, oppression, overlordship, power, repression, rule, subjection, subordination, superiority, suppression, supremacy, sway, tyranny.

domineer over *v* boss, browbeat, bully, command, hector, intimidate, lord it (over), menace, overbear, ride roughshod over, rule, threaten, throw one's weight around, tyrannize.

domineering *adj* arrogant, authoritarian, autocratic, bossy, coercive, despotic, dictatorial, harsh, high-handed, imperious, intimidating, ironfisted, iron-handed, magisterial, masterful, oppressive, overbearing, pushy, severe, tyrannical.

antonyms meek, obsequious, servile.

dominion *n* ascendancy, authority, command, control, country, domain, domination, empire, government, hegemony, jurisdiction, kingdom, lordship, mastery, power, realm, rule, sovereignty, supremacy, sway, territory.

don *v* affect, assume, clothe oneself in, dress in, get into, put on.

antonym doff.

donate *v* bequeath, bestow, chip in, confer, contribute, cough up, fork out, give, impart, make a gift of, present, proffer, subscribe, throw in.

donation(s) *n* alms, benefaction, boon, conferment, contribution, generosity, gift, grant, gratuity, largesse(e), offering, present, presentation, subscription, support.

done *adj* acceptable, accomplished, advised, agreed, completed, concluded, consummated, conventional, cooked, cooked to a turn, correct, de rigueur, ended, executed, finished, OK, over, past, perfected, proper, ready, realized, settled, spent, taken care of, terminated, through.

done for beaten, broken, dashed, defeated, destroyed, doomed, finished, foiled, lost, ruined, undone, vanquished, wrecked.

done in all in, beat, bushed, dead, dead beat, dead tired, dog-tired, drained, exhausted, fagged, frazzled, pooped out, tired out, washed out, whacked (out), wiped, worn out, worn to a frazzle, zonked.

Don Juan *n* amoroso, Casanova, gigolo, ladies' man, lady-killer, libertine, lover, philanderer, romancer, romeo, seducer, womanizer.

donkey *n* ass, burro, hinny, jackass, jennet, jenny, mule.

donnish *adj* academic, bookish, erudite, formal, formalistic, learned, pedagogic, pedantic, precise, scholarly, scholastic.

donor *n* benefactor, contributor, donator, fairy godmother, giver, granter, philanthropist, provider, sponsor, subscriber, supporter, underwriter.

antonym beneficiary.

doom *n* Armageddon, catastrophe, condemnation, death, deathknell, decision, decree, destiny, destruction, doomsday, downfall, fate, fortune, judgment, Judgment Day, karma, kismet, Last Judgment, lot, portion, ruin, sentence, verdict.

v condemn, consign, damn, destine, foredoom, foreordain, judge, predestine, preordain, sentence.

doomed *adj* accursed, bedevilled, bewitched, bound (to), condemned, cursed, fated, hopeless, ill-fated, ill-omened, ill-starred, luckless, star-crossed.

door *n* doorstep, doorway, egress, entrance, entry, exit, gate, gateway, ingress, opening, portal, threshold, vomitorium, vomitory.

doorkeeper *n* commissionaire, concierge, doorman, gatekeeper, janitor, porter.

dope¹ *n* details, drugs, facts, forecast, gen, grease, hallucinogen, heroin, info, information, lowdown, narcotic, news, poop, prediction, oil, opiate, scoop, tip, varnish.

v anesthetize, doctor, drug, inject, load, medicate, sedate, stupefy.

dope² *n* birdbrain, blockhead, bonehead, dimwit, dolt, dullard, dunce, fool, half-wit, idiot, ignoramus, imbecile, ninny, simpleton, witless wonder.

dopey *adj* brainless, dazed, dense, dimwitted, doltish, dozy, drowsy, drugged, dumb, foolish, groggy, hazy, idiotic, senseless, silly, simple, slow, stupefied, stupid, thick, witless, woozy.

antonyms alert, bright.

dormant *adj* asleep, comatose, fallow, hibernating, inactive, inert, inoperative, latent, quiescent, sleeping, sluggish, slumbering, suspended, torpid, undeveloped, unrealized.

antonym active.

dose *n* dosage, draught, drench, hit, measure, portion, potion, prescription, quantity, shot, slug.

v administer, dispense, drench, medicate, treat.

dot *n* atom, circle, dab, decimal point, dit, ellipsis point, fleck, full stop, iota, jot, mark, mite, mote, period, pinpoint, point, speck, spot, title.

v bespeckle, dab, dabble, fleck, punctuate, spot, sprinkle, stipple, stud.

on the dot exactly, on time, precisely, promptly, punctually, to the minute.

dotage *n* anility, decrepitude, feebleness, old age, second childhood, senility, weakness.
antonym youth.

dote on admire, adore, be crazy about, idolize, indulge, love, pamper, prize, spoil, treasure.

doting *adj* adoring, devoted, fond, foolish, indulgent, lovesick, loving, soft.

dotty *adj* batty, crazy, eccentric, enthusiastic, feeble, feeble-minded, loopy, peculiar, shaky, touched, unbalanced, unsteady, weird.
antonym sensible.

double *adj* binate, coupled, diploid, doubled, dual, duple, duplex, duplicate, geminate, paired, twin, twofold.
v bend, duplicate, enlarge, fold, geminate, grow, increase, magnify, multiply, repeat, stoop, turn sharply.
n bend, clone, copy, counterpart, dead ringer, doppelgänger, duplicate, image, impersonator, look-alike, match, mate, replica, ringer, spit, spitting image, substitute, twin, understudy.

double back backtrack, circle, dodge, evade, loop, retrace one's steps, return, reverse.

double entendre ambiguity, double meaning, innuendo, play on words, pun, suggestiveness, wordplay.

on the double at full speed, at once, briskly, immediately, in double-quick time, lickety-split, like lightning, posthaste, promptly, pronto, quickly, tout de suite, without delay.

double-cross *v* betray, cheat, con, cozen, defraud, hoodwink, mislead, swindle, trick, two-time.

double-dealer *n* betrayer, cheat, con man, cozener, deceiver, dissembler, double-crosser, fraud, hypocrite, Machiavellian, rogue, swindler, traitor, two-timer.

double-dealing *n* bad faith, betrayal, cheating, deceit, deception, dishonesty, duplicity, foul play, hypocrisy, Machiavellianism, mendacity, perfidy, treachery, trickery, two-timing.
adj cheating, crooked, deceitful, dishonest, duplicitous, fraudulent, hypocritical, lying, Machiavellian, perfidious, scheming, shifty, sneaky, swindling, treacherous, tricky, two-faced, two-timing, underhanded, unscrupulous, untrustworthy, wily.

doubly *adv* again, bis, twice, twofold.

doubt *v* be dubious, be uncertain, debate, demur, discredit, distrust, fear, fluctuate, have misgivings, hesitate, mistrust, query, question, suspect, vacillate, waver.
antonyms believe, trust.
n ambiguity, apprehension, confusion, difficulty, dilemma, disquiet, distrust, dubiety, fear, hesitancy, hesitation, incredulity, indecision, irresolution, misgiving, mistrust, perplexity, problem, qualm, quandary, question, reservation, scepticism, scruple, suspense, suspicion, uncertainty, vacillation.
antonyms belief, certainty, confidence, trust.

without doubt certainly, doubtless, no doubt, unquestionably.

doubter *n* agnostic, cynic, disbeliever, doubting Thomas, questioner, sceptic, scoffer, unbeliever.
antonym believer.

doubtful *adj* ambiguous, borderline, debatable, disreputable, distrustful, dubious, dubitable, equivocal, grey, hazardous, hesitant, hesitating, iffy, inconclusive, indefinite, indeterminate, in doubt, irresolute, litigious, noncommittal, obscure, perplexed, precarious, problematic, problematical, questionable, sceptical, shady, suspect, suspicious, tentative, uncertain, unclear, unconfirmed, unconvinced, undecided, unresolved, unsettled, unsure, vacillating, vague, wavering.
antonyms certain, definite.

doubtless *adv* assuredly, certainly, clearly, indisputably, most likely, obviously, of course, without question, presumably, probably, surely, truly, undoubtedly, unquestionably, without a doubt.

doughty *adj* able, bold, brave, courageous, daring, dauntless, fearless, gallant, game, hardy, heroic, intrepid, plucky, redoubtable, resolute, stout-hearted, strong, valiant, valorous.
antonyms cowardly, weak.

dour *adj* austere, dismal, dreary, forbidding, gloomy, grim, hard, humourless, inflexible, morose, obstinate, rigid, rigorous, severe, sour, Spartan, stern, stiff, strict, stubborn, sullen, uncompromising, unfriendly, unyielding.
antonyms bright, cheery, easy-going.

douse *v* blow out, dip, drench, duck, dunk, extinguish, immerge, immerse, plunge, put out, saturate, smother, snuff (out), soak, souse, steep, submerge.

dovetail (with) *v* accord, agree, coincide, complement, conform, correspond, fit, harmonize, interlock, join, link, match, mortise, splice, tailor, tally, tenon, unite.

dowdy *adj* dingy, drab, frowzy, frumpish, frumpy, old-fashioned, scrubby, shabby, slovenly, tacky, tatty, unfashionable, unmodish.
antonyms dressy, smart, spruce.

down¹ *n* bloom, defeat, eiderdown, floccus, floss, fluff, fuzz, nap, pile, shag, thistledown, wool.

down² *v* deck, get down, drink, fell, floor, gulp, gobble, guzzle, lay down, lay out, knock back, knock down, put down, quaff, swallow, throw, topple, toss off.

down and out derelict, destitute, homeless, impoverished, on one's uppers, on skid row, penniless, ruined.

down at the heel dowdy, impoverished, out at the elbows, run-down, seedy, shabby, slipshod, slovenly, worn.

down in the mouth blue, cast down, chapfallen, crestfallen, dejected, depressed, discouraged, disheartened, dispirited, down, down the dumps, downcast, downhearted, gloomy, glum, in low spirits, in the doldrums, melancholy, sad, unhappy.

down the drain blown, down the tubes,

lost, out the window, ruined, shot, up the spout, wasted.

down with abolish, away with, end, exterminate, get rid of, remove.

down-and-outer *n* bag lady, beggar, bum, derelict, loser, outcast, pauper, rubby, street person, tramp, vagabond, vagrant.

downcast *adj* cheerless, chapfallen, crestfallen, daunted, dejected, depressed, despondent, disappointed, disconsolate, discouraged, disheartened, dismayed, dispirited, down, downhearted, glum, miserable, sad, unhappy.

antonyms cheerful, elated, happy.

downfall *n* breakdown, cloudburst, collapse, comedown, debacle, deluge, descent, destruction, disgrace, downpour, failure, fall, humiliation, overthrow, rainstorm, ruin, undoing, Waterloo.

downgrade *v* belittle, decry, degrade, demote, denigrate, detract from, devalue, disparage, drop, humble, lower, minimize, put down, reduce in rank, run down.

antonyms improve, upgrade.

downhearted *adj* blue, chapfallen, crestfallen, dejected, depressed, despondent, discouraged, disheartened, dismayed, dispirited, downcast, gloomy, glum, jaw-fallen, low-spirited, sad, sorrowful, unhappy.

antonyms cheerful, enthusiastic, happy.

downpour *n* cloudburst, deluge, downfall, flood, inundation, rainstorm, torrent.

downright *adj* absolute, blatant, blunt, candid, categorical, clear, complete, direct, explicit, forthright, frank, honest, open, out-and-out, outright, outspoken, plain, positive, pure (and simple), sheer, simple, sincere, straightforward, thoroughgoing, total, undisguised, unequivocal, unmitigated, unqualified, utter, wholesale.

down-to-earth *adj* common-sense, common-sensical, hard-headed, matter-of-fact, mundane, no-nonsense, plain-spoken, practical, realistic, sane, sensible, simple, unsentimental.

antonyms fantastic, impractical, visionary.

downtrodden *adj* abused, afflicted, distressed, exploited, helpless, ill-treated, oppressed, subjugated, subservient, trampled on, trampled underfoot, tyrannized, victimized.

downward *adj* declining, descending, downhill, falling, sliding, slippery, slipping.

antonym upward.

downy *adj* feathery, fleecy, floccose, fluffy, plumose, silky, soft, velvety, woolly.

dowry *n* dot, dower, endowment, faculty, gift, inheritance, legacy, portion, provision, share, talent.

doze *v* catnap, drop off, drowse, kip, nap, nod, nod off, sleep, slumber, snooze.

n catnap, forty winks, kip, nap, shut-eye, siesta, sleep, snooze.

drab *adj* blah, bleak, boring, cheerless, colourless, dingy, dismal, dreary, dull, dun-coloured, flat, gloomy, grey, humdrum,

insipid, lacklustre, monotonous, mousy, nondescript, shabby, sombre, unattractive, uninspired, vapid, washed out.

antonym bright.

draft[1] *v* call up, compose, delineate, design, draw, draw up, formulate, make up, outline, prepare, plan, redact, sketch.

n abstract, delineation, outline, plan, protocol, rough, sketch, version.

draft[2] *n* bill, cheque, order, postal order.

draft[3] *n* ale, beer, breath, cup, current, damper, demand, depth, dose, dragging, drain, drawing, drench, drink, flow, haulage, influx, lager, load, lungful, movement, portion, potation, puff, pulling, quantity, tap, tax, traction.

draft[4] *v* call up, conscript, enlist, select.

drag *v* cart, crawl, creep, dawdle, draggle, draw, hale, haul, inch, lag, linger, loiter, lug, pull, schlep, shamble, shuffle, straggle, sweep, tow, trail, traipse, trudge, tug.

n annoyance, bore, bother, brake, bummer, burden, downer, drug, hindrance, hook, impediment, inconvenience, influence, net, nuisance, pain, pest, pill, puff.

drag on, drag out clout, draw out, extend, hang on, lengthen, persist, prolong, protract, pull, spin out, stoneboat, street, thoroughfare, weight.

drag one's feet be a stick in the mud, be slow, dally, dawdle, delay, hang back, lag, obstruct, procrastinate, stall, take one's sweet time, waste time.

dragoon *v* browbeat, bully, coerce, compel, constrain, drive, force, impel, intimidate, oppress, persecute, strong-arm.

drain (off) *v* bleed, consume, deplete, deprive, devitalize, discharge, dissipate, down, draw off, drink up, dry, ebb, empty, ennervate, evacuate, exhaust, finish, flow (off or out), leach, leak, milk, ooze, quaff, remove, sap, seep, strain, swallow, tap, tax, trickle, use up, wear out, weary, withdraw.

antonym fill.

n channel, conduit, culvert, demand, depletion, ditch, draft, drag, duct, exhaustion, exodus, outlet, pipe, reduction, sap, sewer, sink, strain, tax, tap, trench, watercourse, withdrawal.

drainage *n* bilge, leaching, seepage, sewage, sewerage, waste.

dram *n* drop, glass, measure, shot, slug, snifter, snort, tot.

drama *n* acting, crisis, dramatics, dramatization, dramaturgy, emotion, excitement, histrionics, intensity, kabuki, melodrama, pathos, play, scene, show, spectacle, stage-craft, story, suspense, tension, theatre, theatre arts, theatricals, Thespian art.

dramatic *adj* affecting, breathtaking, climactic, dramaturgic, effective, electrifying, emotional, exaggerated, exciting, expressive, graphic, histrionic, impressive, meaningful, melodramatic, moving, powerful, sensational, stagy, startling, striking, sudden, suspenseful, tense, theatrical, Thespian, thrilling, vivid.

antonyms normal, ordinary.

dramatize *v* act, exaggerate, overdo, overstate, play-act, put on, stage.

dramatist *n* comedian, dramaturge, playwright, scriptwriter, tragedian.

drape *v* adorn, array, cloak, cover, dangle, droop, drop, enwrap, festoon, fold, hang, suspend, swathe, vest, wrap.

drapery *n* arras, backdrop, blind(s), covering(s), curtain(s), hanging(s), portière, tapestry, valance.

drastic *adj* desperate, dire, draconian, extreme, far-reaching, forceful, harsh, heroic, radical, severe, strong.

antonym mild.

draw[1] *v* allure, attract, borrow, breathe (in), bring, bring forth, cause, choose, close, deduce, delineate, depict, derive, design, drag, drain, elicit, empty, engage, entice, eviscerate, evoke, extort, extract, get, haul, induce, infer, influence, inhale, inspire, interest, invite, make, map out, mark out, outline, paint, pencil, persuade, pick, portray, puff, pull, receive, respire, select, sketch, steep, stretch, suck, take, tow, trace, tug, unsheathe, withdraw.

antonyms drive away, repel.

n appeal, attraction, bait, enticement, interest, lure, pull.

draw back cringe, flinch, recoil, retract, retreat, shrink, start back, withdraw.

draw on apply, employ, exploit, extract, make use of, put to use, rely on, take from, use, tap.

draw out drag out, elongate, extend, lengthen, prolong(ate), protract, spin out, stretch, string out.

antonyms compact, curtail, shrink.

draw the line distinguish, lay down the law, make a distinction, object, put one's foot down, restrict, say no, set a limit.

draw up arrange, compose, draft, formulate, frame, halt, prepare, pull up, redact, stop, stop short, write out.

draw[2] *n* dead heat, deadlock, impasse, stalemate, tie.

drawback *n* block, defect, deficiency, detriment, difficulty, disability, disadvantage, downside, fault, flaw, fly in the ointment, handicap, hindrance, hitch, impediment, imperfection, nuisance, obstacle, snag, stumbling block, trouble.

antonym advantage.

drawing *n* cartoon, delineation, depiction, graphic, illustration, outline, picture, portrait, portrayal, representation, sketch, study.

drawn *adj* anxious, fatigued, haggard, pinched, strained, stressed, taut, tense, tired, worn.

dread *v* cringe at, fear, flinch from, quail at, shrink from, shudder at, shy away from, tremble at.

n alarm, apprehension, aversion, awe, dismay, disquiet, fear, fright, horror, misgiving, terror, trepidation, worry.

antonyms confidence, security.

adj alarming, awe-inspiring, awful, dire, dreaded, dreadful, formidable, fearsome, frightening, frightful, ghastly, grisly, gruesome, horrible, terrible, terrifying.

dreadful *adj* alarming, appalling, awe-inspiring, awful, dire, distressing, fearful, formidable, frightful, ghastly, grievous, grisly, gruesome, harrowing, hideous, horrendous, horrible, monstrous, shocking, terrible, tragic.

antonym comforting.

dream *n* ambition, aspiration, beauty, castle in Spain, castle in the air, charm, daydream, delight, delusion, design, dreamboat, heart's desire, fantasy, goal, hallucination, hope, illusion, imagination, marvel, notion, phantasm, pie in the sky, pipe-dream, reverie, speculation, trance, vagary, vision, wish.

v build castles in the air, conjure, daydream, envisage, envision, fancy, fantasize, hallucinate, have one's head in the clouds, imagine, muse, speculate, stargaze, think, visualize.

dream up conceive, concoct, contrive, cook up, create, devise, hatch, imagine, invent, think up.

dreamer *n* daydreamer, Don Quixote, fantasizer, fantasist, idealist, romancer, stargazer, theorizer, utopian, visionary, woolgatherer.

antonyms pragmatist, realist.

dreaminess *n* absent-mindedness, abstraction, dimness, ethereality, fancifulness, insubstantiality, preoccupation, unreality, vagueness.

dreamlike *adj* chimerical, fanciful, fantastic, hallucinatory, illusory, imaginary, insubstantial, intangible, phantasmagorical, phantasmal, phantom, surreal, trancelike, unreal, unsubstantial, visionary.

dreamy absent, abstracted, daydreaming, dim, distant, dreamlike, faraway, gentle, impractical, lulling, many, misty, moony, musing, pensive, preoccupied, quixotic, romantic, shadowy, soft, soothing, speculative, starry-eyed, unrealistic, vague, visionary, wistful, wonderful.

antonyms down-to-earth, realistic.

dreary *adj* bleak, boring, cheerless, colourless, comfortless, commonplace, dark, depressing, dismal, doleful, downcast, drab, drear, dull, gloomy, glum, humdrum, joyless, leaden, lifeless, lonely, lonesome, melancholy, monotonous, mournful, overcast, routine, sad, solitary, sombre, sorrowful, tedious, trite, uneventful, uninteresting, wearisome, wretched.

antonyms bright, interesting.

dredge up *v* dig (up), discover, drag (up), draw (up), expose, fish up, raise, rake (up), scoop (up), scrape, uncover, unearth.

dregs *n* bitter end, canaille, deposit, dross, grounds, leavings, lees, leftovers, outcasts, rabble, residue, residuum, riffraff, scourings, scum, sediment, tailings, trash, waste.

drench v douse, drown, duck, flood, imbrue, imbue, immerse, inundate, saturate, soak, sop, souse, steep, wet.

dress n accoutrements, apparel, array, attire, caparison, clothes, clothing, costume, duds, ensemble, frock, garb, garment, garments, gear, get-up, gown, guise, habiliments, habit, outfit, raiment, robe(s), suit, togs, vestment(s).
v accoutre, adorn, align, apparel, arrange, array, attire, bandage, bedeck, bedizen, bind up, caparison, change, clothe, clothes, deck out, decorate, drape, embellish, finish, furbish, garb, garnish, groom, habit, ornament, plaster, prepare, put on, rig, robe, set, smooth, straighten, tend, treat, trim.
antonyms disrobe, strip, undress.

dress down bawl out, berate, call down, call on the carpet, castigate, chew out, chide, give (someone) what for, haul up, rake over the coals, rap the knuckles of, rebuke, reprimand, reprove, scold, take to task, tear into, tear a strip off, tell off, upbraid.

dress up adorn, beautify, deck (out), disguise, doll up, embellish, gild, glorify, gussy up, improve, refurbish, rig out (or up), spiff up, tart up, titivate, trick out.

dressing n bandage, compress, medicine ligature, medicine, pad, plaster, poultice, sauce, spica, stuffing, tourniquet.

dressing gown bathrobe, housecoat, kimono, negligee, peignoir, robe.

dressmaker n couturier, coutouriere, modiste, seamstress, tailor.

dressy adj classy, elaborate, elegant, fancy, formal, natty, ornate, ritzy, showy, smart, stylish, swanky.
antonyms casual, dowdy, scruffy.

dribble v drip, drivel, drizzle, drool, drop, leak, ooze, run, slaver, slobber, spit up, trickle.
n drip, drool, droplet, leak, saliva, seepage, slobber, spit, spittle, spit-up, sprinkling, trickle.

dried adj arid, baked, caked, chapped, dehydrated, desiccated, drained, exsiccated, mummified, parched, sere, shrivelled, wilted, withered, wizened.

drift v accumulate, amass, coast, drive, float, freewheel, gather, heap up, meander, mosey, pile up, rove, shift, stray, waft, wander.
n accumulation, bank, course, current, direction, dune, flow, gist, heap, implication, import, intention, mass, meaning, moraine, mound, movement, pile, punch, purport, ridge, shift, significance, sweep, tendency, tenor, thrust, trend.

drifter n beachcomber, hobo, itinerant, rolling stone, rover, swagman, tramp, vagabond, vagrant, wanderer.

drill[1] v coach, drum, exercise, hammer, instruct, pound, practise, rehearse, teach, train, tutor.
n coaching, exercise, instruction, practice, preparation, rehearsal, repetition, training.

drill[2] **(into, through)** v bore, penetrate, perforate, pierce, puncture, transpierce.
n awl, bit, borer, gimlet.

drink v absorb, booze, carouse, down, drain, gulp (down), guzzle, hit the bottle, imbibe, indulge, knock back, lush, partake of, quaff, revel, sip, suck (up), sup, swallow, swig, swill, swizzle, tank up, tipple, tope, toss off, wassail, water.
n alcohol, ambrosia, aperitif, beverage, booze, cold one, dose, dram, draft, glass, gulp, hooch, liquid, liquor, noggin, peg, plonk, potion, refreshment, sip, slug, snifter, snort, spirits, suck, swallow, swig, swizzle, tall one, tankard, taste, the bottle, tipple, toss, tot.

drink in absorb, assimilate, attend to, be absorbed by, hang on, ingest, inhale, lap up, soak up, take in.

drink to pledge (the health of), salute, toast.

drinker n alcoholic, bibber, carouser, dipsomaniac, drunk, drunkard, guzzler, inebriate, lush, rummy, soak, sot, souse, sponge, tippler, toper, wino.
antonyms abstainer, teetotaller.

drip v dribble, drizzle, drop, exude, filter, plop, splash, sprinkle, trickle, weep.
n dribble, dripping, drop, IV, leak, milk-sop, ninny, softy, trickle, weakling, wet.

drive v actuate, aim, bear, blow, carry, coerce, compel, constrain, dash, dig, direct, drill, force, goad, guide, hammer, handle, herd, hit, impel, manage, motivate, motor, move, obtain, operate, overburden, overwork, plunge, power, prod, propel, push, ram, ride, roll, rush, send, sink, spur, steer, strike, task, tax, thrust, transport, travel, urge.
n action, ambition, appeal, avidity, campaign, crusade, determination, driveway, dynamism, eagerness, effort, energy, enterprise, excursion, get-up-and-go, herding, hit, impulse, initiative, jaunt, journey, lane, motivation, outing, pressure, push, ride, road, run, spin, stroke, transport, trip, vigour, vim, zip.

drive at aim at (or for), allude to, get at, hint at, imply, insinuate, intend, intimate, mean, refer to, signify, suggest.

drive up the wall annoy, derange, drive bonkers, drive round the bend, exasperate, infuriate, irritate, madden, make (someone) climb the walls, make (someone) scream, make (someone) tear his (or her) hair out.

drivel n baloney, blather, bunkum, claptrap, crap, eyewash, foolishness, gibberish, gobbledygook, guff, gush, inanities, mumbo jumbo, nonsense, prattle, slush, waffle.

driver n busman, cabdriver, charioteer, chauffeur, coachman, engineer, jehu, motorist, trucker, vetturino, waggoner.

driving adj compelling, dynamic, energetic, forceful, galvanic, heavy, impelling, motivating, rhythmic, sweeping, urgent, vigorous, violent.

drizzle n mist, mizzle, Scotch mist, shower, spray.
v dribble, mizzle, rain, shower, spit, spray, sprinkle.

droll *adj* amusing, clownish, comic, comical, curious, diverting, eccentric, entertaining, farcical, funny, humorous, jocular, laughable, ludicrous, odd, quaint, queer, ridiculous, risible, waggish, whimsical, witty.

drollery *n* absurdity, archness, banter, buffoonery, comicalness, farce, fun, funniness, humour, jesting, jocularity, quaintness, oddity, pleasantry, waggery, waggishness, whimsicality, wit.

drone *v* bombinate, buzz, chant, drawl, hum, intone, purr, thrum, vibrate, whine, whir.

n buzz, chant, hum, murmur, purr, thrum, vibration, whine, whir.

drool *v* dribble, drivel, lick one's lips (or chops), salivate, slaver, slobber, water at the mouth.

drool over be gaga over, dote on, enthuse about, fondle, gloat at (or over), gush about, lust for (or after), rave about, swoon over.

droop *v* bend (down), dangle, decline, despond, diminish, drop, fade, feel faint, fall down, falter, flag, go slack, hang (down), sag, languish, lose heart, sink, slouch, slump, wane, weaken, wilt, wither.

antonyms perk up, revive, straighten.

drooping *adj* blue, dejected, discouraged, disheartened, dispirited, doleful, downcast, droopy, floppy, languid, languorous, lethargic, limp, listless, low, pendulous, sagging, wilting.

antonyms firm, fresh, gay, perky, taut.

drop *n* abyss, bead, bubble, chasm, cliff, dab, dash, decline, declivity, decrease, descent, deterioration, downturn, driblet, drip, droplet, drop-off, fall, fall off, glob, globule, gutta, iota, lowering, mouthful, nip, ounce, pearl, pinch, plunge, precipice, reduction, shot, sip, slope, slump, spot, taste, tear, tot, trace, trickle.

v abandon, bite the dust, chuck, close, collapse, decline, decrease, delete, depreciate, depress, descend, desert, die, diminish, discontinue, discard, dismiss, disown, dispense with, ditch, dive, dribble, drip, droop, dump, end, fall, forget, forsake, get rid of, give (something) a rest, give up, jilt, jettison, kill, lapse, layout, leave, leave out (or off), lessen, lose, lower, omit, plummet, plunge, quit, reject, relinquish, scrap, shed, sink, skip, spend, stop, terminate, throw over, toss out, trickle, tumble, unload.

antonyms mount, rise.

drop off catnap, decline, decrease, deliver, depreciate, diminish, doze off, drowse, dwindle, fall off, take forty winks, leave, left off (or out), lessen, nod off, slacken, snooze.

antonyms awake, increase.

drop out (of) abandon, back out, cry off, give up, leave, quit, stop, throw in the towel, withdraw.

drop-out *n* beatnik, bohemian, deviant, dissenter, dissentient, hippie, loner, malcontent, non-conformist, quitter, rebel, renegade.

droppings *n* do, dung, egesta, excrement, excreta, feces, guano, manure, ordure, plops, poop, scat, stools, turds.

dross *n* crust, debris, dregs, impurities, lees, refuse, remains, rubbish, scoria, scum, slag, trash, waste.

drought *n* aridity, dearth, deficiency, dehydration, desiccation, drouth, dryness, dry spell, famine, insufficiency, lack, need, scarcity, shortage, want.

drove *n* crowd, drift, flock, herd, horde, mob, multitude, press, swarm, throng.

in droves in crowds, in flocks, in force, in herds, in hordes, in large numbers, in strength, in troops.

antonyms a few at a time, one by one.

drown *v* deaden, deluge, drench, engulf, extinguish, flood, go under, immerse, inundate, muffle, obliterate, overcome, overpower, overwhelm, quench, silence, sink, stifle, submerge, suppress, swallow up, swamp, wash away, wipe out.

drowsiness *n* cobwebs, doziness, fog, grogginess, lethargy, mist, narcosis, oscitancy, sleepiness, sluggishness, somnolence, torpor.

drowsy *adj* comatose, dazed, dopey, dozy, dreamy, drugged, heavy, inactive, lethargic, lulling, nodding, restful, sleepy, sluggish, somnolent, soothing, soporific, tired, torpid.

antonyms alert, awake.

drubbing *n* beating, clobbering, defeat, flogging, hammering, hiding, licking, pounding, pummelling, shutout, thrashing, trouncing, walloping, whipping, whitewash.

drudge *n* devil, dogsbody, factotum, fag, galleyslave, grind, hack, jackal, lackey, maidservant, maid of all work, manservant, man of all work, menial, scullion, servant, slave, toiler, worker.

v break one's back, fag, grind, labour, moil, plod, plug away, slave, slog, sweat, toil, work, work one's fingers to the bone.

antonyms idle, laze.

drudgery *n* backbreaking work, chore, donkey-work, faggery, grind, hackwork, (hard) labour, moil, slave labour, slavery, slogging, sweat, toil.

drug *n* anesthetic, chloroform, depressant, dope, downer, kef, medicament, medication, medicine, mickey, Mickey Finn, narcotic, opiate, physic, pill, poison, potion, remedy, sedative, stimulant.

v anesthetize, chloroform, deaden, dope, dose, drench, hype, knock out, medicate, numb, poison, put under, sedate, spike, stupefy, upper.

drug addict *n* acid head, acid freak, dope fiend, druggie, head, hophead, hype, junkie, tripper.

drugged *adj* chloroformed, comatose, doped, dopey, high, knocked out, medicated, sedated, spaced out, spiked, stoned, stupefied, tripping, turned on, zonked.

drum *v* beat, pitter-patter, pulsate, rap, reverberate, tap, tattoo, throb, thrum.

drum into din into, drill into, drive home to, hammer into, harp at, instil in, pound into, reiterate to.

drum up attract, call together, canvass for, collect, gather, muster, obtain, petition for, raise, round up, solicit, summon.

drunk *adj* besotted, blind, blotto, boozy, corked, drunken, excited, hammered, impaired, inebriate(d), in liquor, in one's cups, intoxicated, liquored, lit up, loaded, maudlin, merry, pickled, pie-eyed, plastered, rubby, sloshed, smashed, soaked, sottish, soused, sozzled, stewed, stoned, tanked, three sheets to the wind, tight, tipsy, under the influence, well-oiled, wet.
antonym sober.
n alcoholic, boozer, drunkard, inebriate, lush, rubby, rummy, soak, sot, souse, toper, wino.
antonym teetotaller

drunkard *n* alcoholic, bacchanal, bacchanalian, bacchant, carouser, dipsomaniac, drinker, drunk, lush, soak, sot, souse, sponge, tippler, wino.

drunken *adj* bacchanalian, bacchic, bibulous, boozing, boozy, crapulent, crapulous, debauched, Dionysiac, Dionysian, dissipated, drunk, inebriate(d), intoxicated, orgiastic, riotous, Saturnalian, sodden, sottish, spongy, under the influence.
antonym sober.

drunkenness *n* alcoholism, bibulousness, dipsomania, inebriation, inebriety, insobriety, intemperance, intoxication, sottishness, tipsiness.
antonyms sobriety, teetotalism.

dry *adj* arid, bald, barren, blah, boring, brittle, deadpan, dehydrated, desiccated, dreary, dried up (or out), droll, droughty, drouthy, dull, ironic, juiceless, low-key, moistureless, monotonous, non-perishable, parched, plain, pro-prohibition, sapless, sarcastic, sec, sere, sharp, shrivelled, sober, stale, tearless, tedious, thirsty, tiresome, torrid, unadorned, unbuttoned, uninteresting, waterless, withered, witty, xeric.
antonyms interesting, moist, sweet, wet.
v dehumidify, dehydrate, desiccate, detoxicate, detoxify, drain, evaporate, exsiccate, harden, mummify, parch, sear, shrivel, welt, wilt, wither, wizen.
antonyms irrigate, soak, wet.

drying *n* dehumidification, dehydration, desiccation, evaporation, exsiccation.

dryness *n* aridity, aridness, barrenness, dehydration, drought, drouth, dullness, moisturelessness, sarcasm, tedium, thirst, thirstiness, tiresomeness, torridity, waterlessness, xerosis.
antonym wetness.

dual *adj* binary, combined, coupled, diploid, double, duplex, duplicate, geminate, matched, paired, twin, twofold.

dub *v* call, christen, denominate, designatedness, entitle, knight, label, name, nickname, rub, scrape, smooth, style, tag, term, title.

dubiety *n* doubt, doubtfulness, dubiousness, incertitude, indecision, misgiving, mistrust, qualms, scepticism, suspicion, uncertainty.
antonym certainty.

dubious *adj* debatable, doubtful, fishy, hesitant, iffy, indefinite, indeterminate, obscure, problematic, questionable, sceptical, shady, speculative, suspect, suspicious, uncertain, unconvinced, undecided, undependable, unreliable, unsettled, unsure, untrustworthy, wavering.
antonyms certain, reliable, trustworthy.

duck[1] *v* abdicate, avoid, bend, bob, bow, cop out of, crouch, dodge, drop, escape, evade, get out of, lower, shirk, shun, sidestep, squat, stoop, wangle (one's way) out of.

duck[2] *v* dip, dive, douse, dunk, immerse, plunge, souse, submerge, wet.

duct *n* artery, canal, channel, conduit, fistula, funnel, passage, pipe, shaft, tube, vas, vein, vent, vessel.

ductile *adj* amenable, biddable, compliant, docile, extensible, flexible, malleable, manageable, manipul(at)able, plastic, pliable, pliant, tractable, yielding.
antonyms intractable, refractory.

dud *n* bomb, bum steer, failure, fizzle, flop, lemon, misfit, washout.
adj broken, dead, failed, ineffective, inoperative, kaput, nugatory, unsatisfactory, valueless, worthless.

due *adj* adequate, ample, appropriate, becoming, bound, deserved, enough, expected, fit, fitting, in arrears, just, justified, mature, merited, necessary, needed, obligatory, outstanding, owed, owing, payable, plenty of, proper, required, requisite, returnable, right, rightful, scheduled, slated, sufficient, suitable, unpaid, well-earned.
n birthright, comeuppance, just deserts, merits, prerogative, privilege, reward, right(s), wages.
adv dead, direct, directly, exactly, precisely, straight.

duel *n* affair of honour, clash, competition, contest, duello, encounter, engagement, fight, match, rivalry, single combat, struggle.
v battle, clash, compete, contend, contest, cross swords, fight, rival, struggle, vie.

dues *n* charge(s), contribution, fee, levy, subscription, tax.

duffer *n* blunderbuss, blunderer, Boeotian, bonehead, booby, bungler, codger, dolt, galoot, geezer, klutz, lummox, oaf, tyke.

dull *adj* apathetic, blockish, blunt(ed), Boeotian, boring, bovine, callous, cloudy, commonplace, dead, dense, depressed, dim, dimwitted, dismal, doltish, drab, dreary, dry, dulled, dullish, edgeless, empty, faded, featureless, flat, gloomy, grey, heavy, humdrum, indifferent, indistinct, insensible, insensitive, insipid, lacklustre, leaden, lifeless, listless, monotonous, mopey, muffled, muted, overcast, passionless, pedestrian, plain, prosaic, run-of-the-mill, slack, sleepy, slow, sluggish, sombre, staid, stodgy, stolid, stultifying, stupid, subdued, subfusc, sunless, tame, tedious, thick, tiresome, toneless, torpid, turbid, uneventful, unexciting, unfunny, unimaginative, unintelligent, uninteresting, unlively, unresponsive, unsharpened, unsunny, vacuous, vapid.

antonyms alert, bright, clear, exciting, sharp.

v allay, alleviate, assuage, blunt, cloud, damp(en), darken, deaden, deject, depress, dim, discourage, dishearten, dispirit, fade, hebetate, lessen, mitigate, moderate, muffle, mute, numb, obscure, obtund, palliate, paralyse, relieve, soften, stultify, stupefy, subdue, tarnish.

antonyms brighten, sharpen, stimulate.

dullard *n* blockhead, bonehead, chump, cretin, dimwit, dolt, dope, dummy, dunce, dunderhead, idiot, ignoramus, imbecile, loggerhead, moron, nitwit, noodle, numskull, oaf, simpleton.

antonym brain.

duly *adv* accordingly, appropriately, befittingly, condignly, correctly, decorously, deservedly, enough, fitly, fittingly, properly, punctually, rightfully, suitably, sure enough as expected (or required).

dumb *adj* aphonic, dense, dimwitted, dull, foolish, inarticulate, mum, mute, silenced, silent, soundless, speechless, stupid, thick, tongue-tied, unexpressed, unintelligent, voiceless, wordless.

antonyms articulate, intelligent.

dumfounded *adj* amazed, astonished, astounded, bewildered, bowled over, breathless, confounded, confused, dumb, flabbergasted, floored, knocked (over) sideways, nonplussed, overcome, overwhelmed, paralysed, speechless, staggered, startled, stunned, taken aback, thrown, thunderstruck.

dummy *n* blockhead, bonehead, copy, counterfeit, dimwit, dolt, dope, dullard, dunce, duplicate, figure, fool, form, goose, ignoramus, imitation, lay figure, know-nothing, layout, manikin, mannequin, mock-up, model, ninny, nitwit, numskull, pacifier, sample, sham, simpleton, soother, space cadet, substitute, teat, volume.

adj artificial, bogus, counterfeit, fake, false, imitation, make-believe, mock, phony, practice, sham, simulated, substitute, trial.

dump *v* abandon, cast off (or away), chuck, copy, deposit, discard, discharge, dispose of, ditch, drop, empty out, get rid of, jettison, let fall, offload, park, print out, reject, scrap, throw away, throw down, tip, toss out, trash, unload.

n dive, garbage pit, hellhole, hole, hovel, joint, junkyard, landsite, mess, midden, pigsty, refuse heap, rubbishheap, shack, shanty, slum, transfer station, trash pile.

dump on disapproval of, disparage, express contempt for, make a scapegoat of, take one's feelings out on, vent feelings on.

dumpy *adj* chubby, chunky, fat, homely, plump, pudgy, roly-poly, short, squab, squat, stout, stubby, tubby.

antonyms rangy, tall, thin.

dun *v* beset, harass, harry, importune, pester, plague, press, urge.

dunce *n* ass, blockhead, bonehead, cretin, dimwit, dolt, duffer, dullard, dummy, dunderhead, goose, half-wit, idiot, ignoramus, know-nothing, moron, nincompoop, ninny, nitwit, numskull, simpleton, space cadet.

antonyms brain, intellectual.

dung *n* droppings, excrement, feces, filth, guano, manure, ordure, scat, turd(s).

dungeon *n* cage, cell, donjon, jail, keep, lockup, oubliette, pit, prison, slammer, vault.

dupe *n* cat's-paw, easy mark, fall guy, gudgeon, gull, instrument, pawn, pigeon, puppet, push-over, sap, simpleton, sitting duck, stooge, sucker, tool, victim.

v bamboozle, beguile, cheat, con, cozen, deceive, defraud, delude, fool,gammon, grift, gull, hoax, hoodwink, humbug, outwit, overreach, pull the wool over (someone's) eyes, rip off, suck in, swindle, take in, trick.

duplicate *adj* corresponding, geminate, identical, matched, matching, second, twin, twofold.

n carbon copy, clone, copy, counterpart, double, facsimile, match, photocopy, replica, reproduction.

v clone, copy, (dead) ringer, ditto, double, echo, geminate, mimeograph, photocopy, repeat, replicate, reproduce.

duplication *n* clone, cloning, copying, gemination, photocopying, repetition, replication, reproduction, xerography.

duplicity *n* betrayal, deceit, deception, dishonesty, dissimulation, double cross, double-dealing, falsehood, fraud, guile, hypocrisy, mendacity, perfidy, treachery.

durability *n* dependability, endurance, imperishability, longevity, permanence, persistence, reliability, stability, strength, sturdiness, toughness.

antonyms fragility, impermanence, weakness.

durable *adj* abiding, constant, dependable, enduring, fast, firm, fixed, hard-wearing, imperishable, lasting, long-lasting, permanent, persistent, reliable, resistant, robust, sound, stable, strong, sturdy, substantial, tough, unfading.

antonyms fragile, flimsy, impermanent, perishable, weak.

duration *n* continuance, continuation, extent, fullness, length, long haul, period, perpetuation, prolongation, span, spell, stretch, term, time period.

duress *n* blackmail, bullying, captivity, coercion, compulsion, confinement, constraint, detention, force, hardship, imprisonment, incarceration, pressure, restraint, threat.

dusk *n* crepuscule, dark, darkness, day's end, evening, eventide, gloaming, gloom, murk,

nightfall, obscurity, shade, shadow(s), sundown, sunset, twilight.
antonyms brightness, dawn.

duskiness *n* darkness, dimness, gloom, gloominess, murkiness, obscurity, shadiness, shadowiness, swarthiness.
antonyms brightness, lightness, whiteness.

dusky *adj* cloudy, crepuscular, dark, dark-hued, darkish, dim, gloomy, murky, obscure, overcast, sable, shadowy, shady, sooty, subfusc, swarthy, tenebrous, twilight, twilit, veiled.
antonyms bright, light, white.

dust *n* dirt, earth, grime, grit, ground, particles, pollen, powder, soil.
v burnish, clean, coat, dredge, polish, powder, scatter, sift, spray, spread, sprinkle, wipe.

raise a dust cause a disturbance, create confusion, create turmoil, make a fuss, make a hullabaloo, make a to-do, raise a stink, raise Cain.

dust storm *n* dust devil, duster, sandstorm.

dustup *n* argument, brawl, brush, commotion, conflict, confrontation, disagreement, dispute, disturbance, encounter, fight, fistcuffs, fracas, punch-up, quarrel, scrap, scuffle, set-to, skirmish, tussle.

dusty *adj* chalky, crumbly, dirty, dry, dust-coated, dust-covered, filthy, friable, granular, greyish, gritty, grubby, powdery, sandy, sooty, unswept.
antonyms clean, polished, solid.

dutiful *adj* acquiescent, complaisant, compliant, conscientious, deferential, devoted, docile, duteous, filial, obedient, punctilious, regardful, respectful, reverential, submissive.

duty *n* assignment, business, calling, charge, chore, customs, deference, detail, devoirs, engagement, excise, function, impost, job, levy, loyalty, mission, obedience, obligation, office, patrol, province, respect, responsibility, reverence, service, tariff, task, tax, toll, work.

on duty at work, busy, engaged, working.

dwarf *n* elf, gnome, goblin, homunculus, hop-o'-my-thumb, Lilliputian, manikin, midget, pygmy, Tom Thumb.
adj baby, bonsai, diminutive, dwarfed, dwarfish, Lilliputian, mini, miniature, petite, pint-size(d), pocket, pocket-size(d), pygmy, small, stunted, tiny, toy, undersized.
antonym large.
v check, dim, diminish, dominate, lower, minimize, overshadow, retard, stunt.

dwell (in) *v* abide, bide, hang out, inhabit, live, lodge, people, populate, quarter, remain, reside, rest, settle, sojourn, stay, stop, tenant.

dwell on belabour, elaborate on, emphasize, expatiate on, flog, go on about, harp on about, linger over, meditate on, mull over, muse on, press.
antonym pass over.

dweller *n* denizen, inhabitant, occupant, occupier, resident.

dwelling *n* abode, domicile, dwelling place, establishment, habitation, home, house, hut, igloo, lodge, lodging, longhouse, quarters, residence, tent, tepee, wigwam.

dwindle *v* abate, decay, decline, decrease, die, die out, diminish, disappear, ebb, fade, fall (off), lessen, peter out, shrink, shrivel, sink, subside, tail off, taper off, vanish, wane, waste away, weaken, wither.
antonym increase.

dye *n* colorant, colour, colouring, colouring agent, hue, pigment, stain, tinge, tint.
v colour, pigment, stain, tincture, tinge, tint.

dyed-in-the-wool *adj* card-carrying, complete, confirmed, deep-rooted, die-hard, entrenched, established, firm, fixed, hard-core, hardened, inflexible, inveterate, long-standing, settled, staunch, thoroughgoing, true, trueblue, unchangeable, unchanging, uncompromising, unshakable, unwavering.
antonym superficial.

dying *adj* at death's door, declining, disappearing, ebbing, expiring, fading, failing, final, going, in extremis, moribund, not long for this world, obsolescent, passing, perishing, sinking, vanishing.
antonyms coming, reviving.

dynamic *adj* active, animated, charismatic, driving, electric, energetic, forceful, high-powered, inspiring, lively, powerful, self-starting, spirited, vigorous, vital, zippy.
antonyms apathetic, inactive, slow.

dynamism *n* animation, charisma, drive, energy, enterprise, forcefulness, get-up-and-go, go, initiative, liveliness, pep, vigour, vim, vitality, spiritedness, zap, zip.
antonyms apathy, inactivity, slowness.

dynasty *n* ascendancy, authority, dominion, empire, family, government, house, line, regime, reign, rule, sovereignty, succession, sway.

dyspeptic *adj* bad-tempered, crabby, crotchety, gloomy, grouchy, peevish, pessimistic, short-tempered, snappish, testy, touchy.

E

each *adv* apiece, individually, one by one, per capita, per head, per person, respectively, separately, severally, singly.

eager *adj* agog, all ready, anxious, ardent, athirst, avid, champing at the bit, desirous, enthusiastic, expectant, fervent, fervid, greedy, gung-ho, hot, hungry, impatient, interested, keen, longing, (more than) willing, perfervid, raring, thirsty, yearning, zealous.
antonyms apathetic, unenthusiastic.

eagerly *adv* ardently, avidly, enthusiastically, fain, fervently, greedily, hungrily, keenly, thirstily, willingly, zealously.
antonyms apathetically, listlessly.

eagerness *n* alacrity, ardour, avidity, breathless anticipation, enthusiasm, fervency, fervidness, fervour, greediness, heartiness, hunger, impatience, impetuosity, keenness, longing, readiness, thirst, willingness, yearning, zeal.
antonyms apathy, disinterest.

ear *n* ability, appreciation, attention, audience, consideration, discrimination, hearing, heed, notice, perception, regard, sensitivity, skill, taste.
give ear attend, hark(en), hear, incline one's ear, lend one's ear(s), list(en), pay (or take) heed.

early *adj* advanced, former, forward, matutinal, of long ago, of yore, prehistoric, premature, primeval, primitive, primordial, prior, undeveloped, untimely, young.
adv ahead of time, beforehand, betimes, in advance, in good time, prematurely, too soon.
antonym late.

earmark *v* allocate, designate, hold, keep back, label, put aside, reserve, set aside, tag.

earn *v* acquire, attain, bring in, collect for one's services, deserve, draw (wages), gain, get, gross, make, merit, net, obtain, procure, pull down, rate, realize, reap, receive, warrant, win, work for.
antonyms lose, spend.

earnest *adj* ardent, attentive, determined, devoted, enthusiastic, fervent, firm, fixed, grave, heartfelt, impassioned, passionate, purposeful, resolute, resolved, serious, sincere, solemn, steady, thoughtful, urgent, vehement, warm, whole-hearted, zealous.
antonyms apathetic, flippant, unenthusiastic.
n assurance, deposit, down payment,

foretaste, guarantee, indemnity, insurance, pledge, promise, security, token.

earnestly *adv* ex animo, fervently, firmly, gravely, passionately, purposefully, resolutely, seriously, sincerely, solemnly, surely, thoughtfully, warmly, whole-heartedly, zealously.
antonyms flippantly, listlessly, tongue in cheek.

earnestness *n* ardour, determination, devotion, enthusiasm, fervency, fervour, gravity, passion, purposefulness, resolution, seriousness, sincerity, urgency, vehemence, warmth, whole-heartedness, zeal.
antonyms apathy, flippancy.

earnings *n* emoluments, gain, income, pay, proceeds, profits, receipts, remuneration, return, revenue, reward, salary, stipend, takings, wages.
antonyms expenses, outgoings.

Earth *n* blue planet, Gaeia, geosphere, globe, middle-earth, middle-world, Midgard, orb, planet, sphere, world.

earth *n* clay, clods, dirt, dry land, ground, humus, land, loam, mould, sod, soil, topsoil.

earthenware *n* ceramics, crockery, crocks, pots, pottery, terra cotta.
adj ceramic, clay, fictile, terra cotta.

earthly *adj* base, carnal, conceivable, corporeal, earthbound, earthen, fleshly, human, imaginable, material, materialistic, mortal, mundane, non-spiritual, physical, possible, practical, secular, slightest, sublunary, tellurian, telluric, temporal, terrestrial, worldly.
antonyms eternal, heavenly, spiritual.

earthquake *n* earth tremor, quake, seism, tremor, upheaval.

earthy *adj* bawdy, blue, coarse, crude, down-to-earth, for real, hearty, honest, indecorous, lusty, natural, plain, raunchy, ribald, robust, rough, rustic, simple, uninhibited, unrefined, unsophisticated, vulgar.
antonyms cultured, refined.

ease *n* affluence, aid, aplomb, calmness, comfort, composure, content, contentment, convenience, deftness, dexterity, easement, easiness, easing, effortlessness, facileness, facility, flexibility, freedom, informality, insouciance, leisure, liberty, luxury, naturalness, nonchalance, peace, peace of mind, poise, prosperity, quiet, quietude, readiness, relaxation, repose, rest, restfulness, serenity, simplicity, solace, tranquillity, unconstraint, unreservedness.

antonyms difficulty, discomfort, hardship, inconvenience.

v abate, aid, allay, alleviate, appease, assist, assuage, calm, comfort, disburden, edge, expedite, extenuate, facilitate, forward, further, guide, inch, lessen, lighten, loosen, manoeuvre, mitigate, moderate, mollify, pacify, palliate, quiet, reduce, relax, relieve, simplify, slide, slip, smooth, soften, solace, soothe, steer, still, take the edge off, tranquillize.

antonyms hinder, retard, torment.

at ease calm, comfortable, easy, insouciant, natural, relaxed, unconstrained, untroubled.

antonyms anxious, ill at ease, out of place, strained, tense, uncomfortable, uneasy.

ease off abate, decline, decrease, die away, die down, ease up, lessen, let up, lighten, loosen, moderate, relent, slacken, slow down, subside, wane.

antonym increase.

easily¹ *adv* comfortably, conveniently, effortlessly, facilely, freely, quickly, readily, simply, smoothly, standing on one's head, with one arm tied behind one's back, with one's eyes closed.

antonym laboriously.

easily² *adv* absolutely, beyond question, by far, certainly, clearly, definitely, doubtless, far and away, hands down, indisputably, indubitably, plainly, probably, simply, surely, undeniably, undoubtedly, unequivocally, unquestionably, very likely, well, without a doubt.

easy *adj* accommodating, a cinch, affable, amenable, at ease, biddable, calm, carefree, casual, child's play, comfortable, compliant, contented, cushy, docile, easeful, easy as falling off a log, easy as pie, easygoing, effortless, facile, flexible, friendly, gentle, good-natured, graceful, gracious, gullible, idiotproof, indulgent, informal, lax, leisurely, lenient, liberal, light, like taking candy from a baby,loose, luxurious, manageable, mild, moderate, natural, nonchalant, no sweat, painless, peaceful, permissive, pleasant, pliant, problem-free, quiet, relaxed, serene, simple, slow, smooth, soft, straightforward, submissive, suggestible, susceptible, temperate, tolerant, tractable, tranquil, trusting, unburdensome, uncomplicated, unconstrained, undemanding, undisturbed, unexacting, unforced, unhurried, unlaboured, unoppressive, untroubled, unworried, user-friendly, yielding.

antonyms demanding, difficult, impossible, oppressive, unaccommodating.

easygoing *adj* accommodating, adaptable, amenable, calm, carefree, casual, complacent, downbeat, easy, equanimous, even-tempered, flexible, happy-go-lucky, indulgent, insouciant, laid-back, lax, lenient, liberal, mild, moderate, nonchalant, permissive, phlegmatic, placid, relaxed, serene, tolerant, unconcerned, uncritical, undemanding, unhurried, unworried.

antonyms fussy, intolerant.

eat *v* banquet, break bread, chew, chomp, consume, corrode, destroy, devour, dine, dissolve, eat up, erode, feed, grub, ingest, knock back, munch, nibble, nosh, pig (out), rot, scarf, swallow, wear away.

eat one's words abjure, back-pedal, eat crow, recant, rescind, retract, take back, unsay, withdraw (statement).

eatable *adj* comestible, digestible, edible, esculent, good, harmless, palatable, wholesome.

antonym unpalatable.

eatables *n* chow, chuck, comestibles, dainties, eats, food, grub, refreshments, snacks, tuck, victuals.

eavesdrop *v* bug, intercept, listen in, monitor, overhear, snoop, spy, tap, wiretap.

eavesdropper *n* listener-in, little pitcher with big ears, monitor, overhearer, snoop, spy.

ebb *v* abate, decay, decline, decrease, degenerate, deteriorate, die down, diminish, drift away, drop, dwindle, fade away, fall, fall away, fall back, flag, flow back, go out, lessen, peter out, quiet, recede, retire, retreat, retrocede, run down or out, shrink, sink, slacken, subside, taper off, wane, weaken, withdraw.

antonyms increase, rise.

n decay, decline, decrease, degeneration, deterioration, diminution, drop, dwindling, ebb tide, flagging, lessening, low tide, low water, refluence, reflux, regression, retreat, retrocession, shrinking, sinking, slackening, subsidence, wane, waning, weakening, withdrawal.

antonyms flow, increase, rising.

ebony *adj* black, coal-black, dark, inky, jet, jet-black, obsidian, pitch-black, pitchy, sable, sooty.

ebullience *n* animation, boiling, breeziness, brightness, bubbliness, bubbling, buoyancy, chirpiness, ebullition, effervescence, effusiveness, enthusiasm, excitement, exuberance, ferment, fermentation, foaminess, frothiness, high spirits, liveliness, seething, vivacity, zest.

antonyms apathy, dullness, lifelessness.

ebullient *adj* animated, boiling, breezy, bright, bubbling, bubbly, buoyant, chirpy, effervescent, effusive, enthusiastic, excited, exuberant, foaming, foamy, frothing, frothy, high-spirited, irrepressible, lively, seething, vivacious, zestful.

antonyms apathetic, dull, lifeless.

eccentric *adj* aberrant, bizarre, capricious, dotty, erratic, far-out, flaky, fruity, funny, idiosyncratic, irregular, nuts, nutty, odd, offbeat, off-centre, off the wall, outlandish, peculiar, queer, quirky, screwball, screwy, singular, strange, uncommon, unconventional, wacky, way-out, weird, whimsical.

antonyms conventional, normal.

n character, crackpot, crank, flake, fruitcake, nonconformist, nut, oddball, oddity, queer fish, screwball, strange duck, weirdo.

eccentricity *n* aberration, bizarreness, caprice, capriciousness, foible, idiosyncrasy, irregularity, nonconformity, oddity, outlandishness, peculiarity, queerness, quirk, singularity, strangeness, unconventionality, weirdness, whim, whimsicality.
antonyms normalcy, normality, ordinariness.

ecclesiastic *n* abbé, bishop, churchman, clergyman, cleric, curate, divine, man (or woman) of the cloth, member of the clergy, minister, parson, pastor, priest, rector, vicar.

ecclesiastical *adj* church, churchly, churchy, clerical, divine, holy, ministerial, pastoral, priestly, religious, spiritual, templar.

echelon *n* degree, grade, level, place, position, rank, rung, status, step, tier.

echo *v* ape, be reminiscent of, copy, give back, imitate, mimic, mirror, parallel, parrot, rebound, recall, re-echo, re-evoke, reflect, reiterate, repeat, reproduce, resemble, resonate, resound, reverberate, ring, second.
n answer, copy, evocation, hint, image, imitation, intimation, memory, mirror image, parallel, recurrence, reflection, reiteration, reminder, repeat, repetition, reproduction, resonance, resounding, response, reverberation, suggestion, sympathy, trace, vestige.

echoic *adj* answering, echoing, imitative, onomatopoeic, onomatopoetic, repetitious, reverberating.

éclat *n* acclaim, acclamation, applause, approval, brilliance, celebrity, display, distinction, fame, glory, lustre, ostentation, plaudits, pomp, renown, repute, show, showmanship, splendour, success.
antonyms disapproval, dullness.

eclectic *adj* all-embracing, broad, catholic, comprehensive, diverse, diversified, general, heterogeneous, liberal, many-styled, multifarious, run on, selective, varied, wide-ranging.
antonyms narrow, one-sided.

eclipse *v* block, blot out, cloud, conceal, cover, darken, dim, dwarf, efface, exceed, excel, extinguish, obscure, outdo, outshine, overshadow, shroud, surpass, throw into the shade, transcend, veil.
n blocking, covering, darkening, decline, diminution, dimming, extinction, obscuration, occultation, overshadowing, shading.

economic *adj* budgetary, business, commercial, financial, fiscal, industrial, mercantile, monetary, money-making, pecuniary, profit-making, trade, viable.
antonyms expensive, uneconomic.

economical *adj* careful, cheap, cost-effective, economizing, economy-size, efficient, fair, frugal, inexpensive, labour-saving, low, low-priced, modest, profitable, prudent, reasonable, saving, scrimping, sparing, thrifty, time-saving.

antonyms expensive, uneconomical.

economize *v* cut back, cut corners, husband (one's resources), retrench, save, scrape, scrimp, skimp, tighten one's belt.
antonym squander.

economy *n* frugality, husbandry, parsimony, prudence, restraint, retrenchment, saving, scrimping, skimping, sparingness, thrift, thriftiness.
antonyms improvidence, prodigality.

ecstasy *n* bliss, cloud nine, delight, delirium, elation, euphoria, exaltation, frenzy, heaven, joy, rapture, ravishment, rhapsody, seventh heaven, sublimation, trance, transport(s).
antonym torment.

ecstatic *adj* beside oneself, blissful, delirious, elated, enraptured, entranced, euphoric, exultant, frenzied, in raptures, in (the seventh) heaven, joyful, joyous, jubilant, on cloud nine, overjoyed, over the moon, rapturous, rhapsodic, transported.
antonyms disappointed, downcast.

eddy *n* backwash, backwater, countercurrent, counterflow, swirl, vortex, whirlpool, whirlwind.
v circle, spiral, swirl, whirl.

edge *n* acerbity, acridity, acuteness, advantage, arris, ascendancy, bezel, bite, bitterness, blade, border, bound, boundary, brim, brink, card up one's sleeve, contour, cutting edge, effectiveness, force, forefront, fringe, hardness, harshness, incisiveness, inside track, keenness, lead, limit, line, lip, margin, outline, perimeter, periphery, pungency, rim, sharpness, side, sting, threshold, trenchancy, upper hand, urgency, verge.
v border, bound, creep, ease, fringe, hem, hone, inch, rim, shape, sharpen, side, sidle, skirt, steal, strop, trim, verge, whet, worm.

on edge a bundle of nerves, anxious, apprehensive, edgy, excited, fidgety, ill at ease, impatient, irritable, keyed up, nervous, on tenterhooks, restive, restless, tense, touchy, uptight, wired.

edgy *adj* all nerves, anxious, ill at ease, impatient, irascible, irritable, keyed up, nervous, on edge, prickly, restive, sharp, tense, testy, touchy.
antonyms calm, relaxed.

edible *adj* comestible, digestible, eatable, esculent, good, harmless, palatable, safe, tasty, wholesome.
antonym inedible.

edict *n* act, command, decree, dictate, dictum, diktat, enactment, fiat, injunction, law, mandate, manifesto, order, ordinance, proclamation, pronouncement, pronunciamento, regulation, rescript, ruling, statute, ukase.

edification *n* benefit, enlightenment, guidance, improvement, instruction, nurture, upbuilding.

edifice *n* building, construction, erection, establishment, structure.

edify v benefit, build up, educate, elevate, enlighten, guide, improve, inform, instruct, nurture, school, teach, train, tutor.

edit v adapt, amend, annotate, assemble, blue-pencil, bowdlerize, censor, check, condense, correct, emend, format, polish, rearrange, redact, reorder, rephrase, revise, rework, rewrite, select.

edition n copy, exemplar, impression, issue, number, printing, run, version, volume.

educate v better (oneself), catechize, civilize, coach, cultivate, develop, discipline, drill, edify, enlighten, exercise, ground, improve, improve the mind (of), indoctrinate, inform, instruct, school, teach, train, tutor.

educated adj civilized, cultivated, cultured, enlightened, erudite, informed, instructed, knowledgeable, learned, lettered, literate, literary, nurtured, polished, refined, schooled, sophisticated, taught, trained, tutored, well-bred, well-read, well-versed.

antonyms uncultured, uneducated.

education n academic background, breeding, civilization, coaching, cultivation, culture, development, discipline, drilling, edification, enlightenment, erudition, guidance, improvement, indoctrination, instruction, knowledge, learning, literacy, nurture, scholarship, schooling, teaching, training, tuition, tutelage.

educational adj academic, cultural, didactic, edifying, educative, enlightening, improving, informative, instructive, scholastic.

antonym uninformative.

educator n academic, coach, consultant, edifier, educationalist, instructor, lecturer, pedagogue, preceptor, professor, schoolmaster, schoolmistress, schoolteacher, teacher, trainer, tutor.

eerie adj chilling, creepy, eldritch, fearsome, frightening, ghastly, ghostly, hair-raising, mysterious, scary, spectral, spine-chilling, spooky, strange, uncanny, unearthly, unnatural, weird.

antonyms natural, ordinary.

efface v annihilate, blank out, blot out, blue-pencil, cancel, cross out, delete, destroy, dim, do away with, eclipse, eliminate, eradicate, erase, excise, expunge, extirpate, obliterate, raze, remove, rub out, wipe off the map, wipe out.

effect n aftermath, avail, clout, conclusion, consequence, drift, éclat, effectiveness, efficacy, efficiency, end, end result, enforcement, essence, force, fruit, impact, import, impression, influence, issue, meaning, outcome, power, product, purport, result, sense, sequel, significance, strength, tenor, upshot, use, validity, weight.

v accomplish, achieve, actuate, bring about, cause, complete, consummate, contrive, create, do, effectuate, execute, fulfil, implement, initiate, make, perform, produce, wreak.

▲ *confusable word* affect.

in effect active, actually, effective, effectively, essentially, for practical purposes, in actuality, in fact, in force, in operation, in reality, in the end, in truth, operative, really, to all intents and purposes, valid, virtually, when all is said and done.

effective adj able, active, actual, adequate, capable, cogent, compelling, competent, convincing, effectual, efficacious, efficient, eloquent, forceful, forcible, implemental, impressive, in operation, moving, operative, persuasive, potent, powerful, productive, real, serviceable, striking, telling, useful, virtual.

antonyms ineffective, useless.

effectiveness n ability, capability, clout, cogency, effect, efficacy, efficiency, force, potency, power, strength, success, usefulness, utility, validity, vigour, virtue, weight.

antonyms ineffectiveness, uselessness.

effects n belongings, chattels, gear, goods, movables, paraphernalia, possessions, property, stuff, things, trappings.

effectual adj authoritative, binding, capable, effective, efficacious, efficient, forcible, operative, potent, powerful, productive, sound, successful, telling, useful, valid.

antonyms ineffective, useless.

effeminate adj delicate, epicene, feminine, pansy, sissy, soft, tender, unmanly, weak, womanish.

antonym manly.

effervesce v boil, bubble (over), ferment, fizz, foam, froth, sparkle.

effervescence n animation, bubbles, bubbliness, buoyancy, ebullience, enthusiasm, excitedness, excitement, exhilaration, exuberance, ferment, fermentation, fizz, foam, foaming, froth, frothiness, gaiety, high spirits, liveliness, sparkle, vim, vitality, vivacity, zing, zip.

effervescent adj animated, bubbling, bubbly, buoyant, carbonated, ebullient, enthusiastic, excited, exhilarated, exuberant, fermenting, fizzing, fizzy, foaming, frothing, frothy, gay, irrepressible, lively, merry, sparkling, vital, vivacious, zingy.

antonyms apathetic, dull, flat.

effete adj barren, characterless, corrupt, debased, debilitated, decadent, decayed, decrepit, degenerate, dissipated, drained, emasculated, enervated, enfeebled, exhausted, feeble, fruitless, incapable, ineffective, ineffectual, infecund, infertile, insipid, overrefined, played out, spent, spoiled, sterile, tired out, unfruitful, unproductive, unprolific, used up, wasted, weak, worn out, vapid.

antonym vigorous.

efficacious adj active, adequate, capable, competent, effective, effectual, efficient, operative, potent, powerful, productive, strong, successful, sufficient, useful, valid.

antonyms ineffective, useless.

efficacy n ability, adequacy, capability, competence, effect, effectiveness, efficiency,

force, influence, potency, power, strength, success, sufficiency, usefulness, utility, virtue.
antonyms ineffectiveness, uselessness.

efficiency *n* ability, adeptness, capability, competence, economy, effectiveness, efficacy, mastery, performance, power, practicality, productivity, proficiency, readiness, skilfulness, skill.
antonyms inefficiency, waste.

efficient *adj* able, adept, businesslike, capable, competent, economical, effective, effectual, orderly, organized, practical, powerful, productive, ready, skilful, streamlined, well-conducted, well-oiled, well-ordered, well-organized, well-regulated.
antonyms inefficient, wasteful.

effigy *n* carving, dummy, figure, icon, idol, image, likeness, picture, portrait, representation, statue.

effluent *n* discharge, effluence, effluvium, efflux, emanation, emission, exhalation, industrial waste, outflow, pollutant, pollution, sewage, waste.

effort *n* accomplishment, achievement, act, application, attempt, bother, creation, deed, elbow grease, endeavour, energy, essay, exertion, feat, force, job, labour, muscle, nisus, opus, pains, power, shot, stab, strain, stretch, striving, struggle, toil, travail, trouble, try, undertaking, work.

effortless *adj* deft, easy, easy as falling off a log, facile, like taking candy from a baby, painless, simple, smooth, uncomplicated, undemanding, unlaboured.
antonym difficult.

effrontery *n* arrogance, audacity, boldness, brashness, brass, brazenness, cheek, cheekiness, disrespect, face, front, gall, impertinence, impudence, insolence, nerve, presumption, presumptuousness, rudeness, shamelessness, temerity.

effusion *n* discharge, effluence, efflux, expression, flood, gush, gushing, outflow, outpouring, seepage, stream, unburdening, voidance, word salad, writing.

effusive *adj* demonstrative, ebullient, emotional, enthusiastic, expansive, extravagant, exuberant, fulsome, gushing, gushy, lavish, outgoing, overemotional, overflowing, profuse, talkative, unreserved, unrestrained, voluble, wordy.
antonyms quiet, restrained.

egghead *n* brain, Einstein, genius, highbrow, intellect, intellectual, literati (pl.), member of the intelligentsia, scholar.

egg on cheer on, drive, encourage, exhort, goad, incite, prick, prod, prompt, push, spur, stimulate, urge.
antonym discourage.

egoism *n* amour-propre, egocentricity, narcissism, self-absorption, self-centredness, self-importance, self-interest, selfishness, self-love, self-regard, self-seeking.
antonym altruism.

egoist *n* egocentric, narcissist, self-seeker.

egoistic *adj* egocentric, narcissistic, self-absorbed, self-centred, self-important, self-involved, selfish, self-pleasing, self-seeking.
antonym altruistic.

egotism *n* big-headedness, boastfulness, conceit, egocentricity, egomania, narcissism, self-admiration, self-aggrandizement, self-centredness, self-conceit, self-congratulation, self-importance, self-interest, self-love, self-praise, self-pride, superiority, swelled head, vainglory, vanity.
antonym humility.

egotist *n* big-head, boaster, braggadocio, braggart, egomaniac, know-it-all, narcissist, swaggerer.

egotistic *adj* big-headed, boastful, boasting, bragging, conceited, egocentric, egoistic, egomaniacal, full of oneself, narcissistic, on an ego trip, opinionated, proud, self-centred, self-important, superior, vain, vainglorious.
antonym humble.

egregious *adj* bad, extraordinary, flagrant, glaring, grievous, gross, heinous, infamous, insufferable, intolerable, monstrous, notorious, outrageous, rank, remarkable, scandalous, shocking, unconscionable.
antonym slight.

egress *n* emergence, escape, exit, exodus, issue, out, outlet, vent, way out.

ejaculate¹ *v* discharge, eject, emit, expel, spew, spurt.

ejaculate² *v* blurt (out), burst out, cry, exclaim, shout, yell.

ejaculation¹ *n* discharge, ejection, emission, expulsion, spurt.

ejaculation² *n* blurt(ing), cry, exclamation, expletive, outburst, shout, yell.

eject *v* banish, belch, boot out, bounce, deport, discharge, disgorge, dislodge, dismiss, dispossess, drive out, emit, evacuate, evict, expel, fire, force out, get rid of, kick out, oust, remove, sack, spew, spout, throw out, turn out, unhouse, vomit.

ejection *n* banishment, defenestration, deportation, discharge, disgorgement, dislodgement, dismissal, dispossession, evacuation, eviction, expulsion, firing, ouster, ousting, removal, sacking, spouting.

eke out add to, augment, economize (on or with), husband, increase, make (something) stretch, round out, stretch (out), supplement, top off.

elaborate *adj* careful, complex, complicated, convoluted, daedal, Daedalian, decorated, detailed, exact, extravagant, fancy, fussy, intricate, involute(d), involved, laboured, minute, ornamental, ornate, ostentatious, painstaking, perfected, precise, Rube Goldberg, showy, skilful, studied, thorough.
antonyms plain, simple.

elaborate (on) *v* amplify, complicate, decorate, detail, develop, devise, embellish, enhance, enlarge, expand, expatiate, explain, flesh out, garnish, improve, ornament, polish, refine.

antonyms précis, simplify.

élan *n* animation, brio, dash, eagerness, enthusiasm, esprit, flair, flourish, heart, liveliness, oomph, panache, pizzazz, soul, spirit, style, verve, vigour, vivacity, zest.

antonyms apathy, lifelessness.

elapse *v* expire, glide by, go by, lapse, pass (by), run its course, run out, slip away.

elastic *adj* accommodating, adaptable, adjustable, bendable, bouncy, buoyant, distensible, ductile, extendible, extensible, extensile, flexible, irrepressible, plastic, pliable, pliant, resilient, rubbery, springy, stretch, stretchable, stretchy, supple, tolerant, variable, yielding.

antonym rigid.

elasticity *n* adaptability, adjustability, bounce, buoyancy, ductility, flexibility, give, irrepressibility, plasticity, pliability, pliancy, resilience, rubberiness, spring, springiness, stretch, stretchability, stretchiness, suppleness, tolerance, variability.

antonym rigidity.

elated *adj* blissed out, delighted, ecstatic, euphoric, exalted, excited, exhilarated, exultant, glad, gleeful, happy, in high spirits, joyful, joyous, jubilant, on cloud nine, overjoyed, over the moon, pleased (as punch), proud, rejoicing.

antonym downcast.

elation *n* bliss, delight, ecstasy, euphoria, exaltation, exhilaration, exultation, gladness, glee, happiness, high spirits, joy, joyfulness, joyousness, jubilation, rapture, rejoicing, transports (of delight).

antonym depression.

elbow *v* bulldoze, bump, crowd, hustle, jostle, knock, nudge, plough, push, shoulder, shove, thrust.

elbowroom *n* freedom, latitude, Lebensraum, leeway, play, room, scope, space.

elder *adj* ancient, earlier, first-born, former, of yore, olden, older, prior, senior.

antonym younger.

n ancestor, ancient, antique, chieftain, councillor, deacon, dean, doyen(ne), forebear, forefather, presbyter, senior, wise one.

elderly *adj* aged, aging, hoary, old, senior, well on in years.

antonyms young, youthful.

eldest *adj* first, first-begotten, first-born, oldest.

antonym youngest.

elect *v* appoint, choose, designate, determine, in support, opt (for or to), pick, place in office, predestine, prefer, select, vote.

adj choice, chosen, designate, designated, elite, hand-picked, picked, predestined, preferred, presumptive, prospective, select, selected, to be.

election *n* appointment, ballot, choice, choosing, decision, determination, judgment,

option, predestination, preference, selection, vote, voting in.

elector *n* chosen, constituent, (registered) voter, selector.

electric *adj* brilliant, charged, dazzling, dynamic, electrifying, exciting, galvanic, galvanizing, jolting, rousing, startling, stimulating, stirring, supercharged, thrilling.

antonyms tedious, unexciting.

electrify *v* amaze, animate, astonish, astound, energize, excite, fire (up), galvanize, invigorate, jolt, rouse, shock, stagger, startle, stimulate, stir, stun, thrill.

antonym bore.

elegance *n* beauty, chic, courtliness, dignity, distinction, exquisiteness, gentility, good breeding, good taste, grace, gracefulness, grandeur, handsomeness, luxury, polish, propriety, refinement, richness, style, sumptuousness, taste.

antonym inelegance.

elegant *adj* à la mode, apt, artistic, beautiful, chic, choice, comely, courtly, cultivated, debonair, delicate, excellent, exquisite, fashionable, fine, genteel, graceful, grandiose, handsome, in good taste, luxurious, modish, neat, nice, polished, refined, simple, smart, smooth, stylish, sumptuous, superior, tasteful, well-bred.

antonyms clumsy, inelegant.

elegiac *adj* dirgelike, doleful, epicedial, funereal, keening, lamenting, melancholy, mournful, nostalgic, plaintive, sad, threnodic, valedictory.

antonym happy.

elegy *n* coronach, dirge, epicedium, funeral song, keen, lament, plaint, requiem, threnody.

element *n* bit, component, constituent, factor, feature, field, fragment, habitat, hint, ingredient, medium, member, milieu, modicum, natural environment, note, part, piece, streak, tinge, trace, unit.

elementary *adj* basic, beginning, clear, easy, elemental, facile, fundamental, initial, introductory, original, plain, primary, principial, rudimentary, simple, straightforward, uncomplicated.

antonyms advanced, complex.

elements *n* basics, components, constituents, essentials, foundations, fundamentals, ingredients, introduction, principia, principles, rudiments, weather.

elevate *v* advance, aggrandize, augment, boost, brighten, buoy up, cheer (up), elate, escalate, exalt, excite, exhilarate, gladden, glorify, hearten, heighten, hoist (up), increase, intensify, lift up, magnify, prefer, promote, raise, sublimate, swell, upgrade, uplift, upraise.

antonyms lessen, lower.

elevated *adj* buoyed up, cheerful, cheery, dignified, elated, exalted, excited, exhilarated, flowery, glorified, glorious, grand, grandiloquent, heartened, heightened, high, high-flown, high-minded, inflated, in high spirits, joyful, lofty, majestic, noble, overjoyed, proud, raised, sublime, uplifted, uplifting.

antonyms base, informal, lowly.

elevation *n* acclivity, advancement, aggrandizement, altitude, eminence, exaltation, exaltedness, glorification, grandeur, grandiloquence, height, hill, hillock, increase, loftiness, mountain, nobility, preferment, promotion, raising, rise, sublimation, sublimity, upgrading, upliftment.

antonyms baseness, informality.

elfin *adj* arch, charming, delicate, elfish, elflike, frolicsome, impish, mischievous, petite, playful, puckish, small, sprightly, tiny.

elicit *v* cause, draw forth (or out), educe, evoke, exact, extort, extract, fish for, get, induce, obtain, prompt, wrest, wring.

eligible *adj* acceptable, appropriate, available, desirable, fit, marriageable, proper, qualified, suitable, suited, worthy.

antonym ineligible.

eliminate *v* annihilate, bump off, cut out, delete, dispense with, dispose of, disqualify, disregard, do away with, drop, eject, eradicate, exclude, excrete, expel, exterminate, extinguish, get rid of, ignore, kill, knock off, knock out, liquidate, murder, omit, reject, remove, rub out, slay, stamp out, take out, terminate, waste.

antonym accept.

elite *n* aristocracy, best, cream, cream of the crop, crème de la crème, elect, establishment, flower, gentry, high society, inner circle, intelligentsia, leaders, meritocracy, nobility, pick, upper class.

adj aristocratic, best, choice, chosen, exclusive, first-class, hand-picked, high-class, noble, selected, superior, top, top-class, upper-class.

antonyms ordinary, run-of-the-mill.

elixir *n* concentrate, cure-all, essence, extract, medicine, mixture, nostrum, panacea, potion, principle, quintessence, remedy, solution, syrup, tincture, treacle.

elliptical[1] *adj* egg-shaped, oval, oviform, ovoid.

elliptical[2] *adj* abstruse, ambiguous, concentrated, concise, condensed, cryptic, econmical, incomprehensible, laconic, obscure, recondite, telegraphic, terse, unfathomable.

antonym clear.

elocution *n* articulation, declamation, delivery, diction, enunciation, oratory, pronunciation, public speaking, rhetoric, speech, speechmaking, utterance.

elongated *adj* extended, lengthened, long, prolonged, protracted, stretched.

elope *v* abscond, bolt, cut and run, decamp, disappear, escape, leave, run away, run off, slip away, steal away.

eloquence *n* articulateness, expression, expressiveness, fluency, forcefulness, oratory, persuasiveness, rhetoric.

antonym inarticulateness.

eloquent *adj* articulate, Demosthenic, expressive, fluent, forceful, graceful, honeyed, meaningful, moving, persuasive, pregnant, revealing, silver-tongued, speaking, stirring, suggestive, telling, vivid, vocal, voluble, well-expressed, well-spoken, well-turned.

antonyms inarticulate, tongue-tied.

elucidate *v* annotate, clarify, explain, explicate, expound, gloss, illuminate, illustrate, interpret, spell out, unfold.

antonyms confuse, obscure.

elucidation *n* annotation, clarification, comment, commentary, explanation, explication, exposition, footnote, gloss, illumination, illustration, interpretation, marginalia, note.

elude *v* avoid, baffle, beat, circumvent, confound, dodge, duck, escape, evade, flee, foil, frustrate, give (someone) the slip, outrun, outwit, shirk, shun, stump, thwart.

▲ *confusable word* allude.

elusive *adj* baffling, cagey, elusory, evasive, fleeting, fugitive, illusory, indefinable, intangible, puzzling, shifty, slippery, subtle, transient, transitory, tricky, unanalysable.

emaciated *adj* anorexic, atrophied, attenuated, bony, cadaverous, gaunt, haggard, hollow-cheeked, lean, meagre, peaked, pinched, scrawny, skeletal, skinny, tabescent, thin, wan, wasted.

antonyms plump, well-fed.

emaciation *n* atrophy, attenuation, gauntness, haggardness, leanness, meagreness, scrawniness, tabes, tabescence, thinness, wanness, wasting away.

antonym plumpness.

emanate *v* arise, come (forth), derive, diffuse, discharge, emerge, emit, exhale, exude, flow, give off, give out, issue (forth), originate, proceed, radiate, send out, spread, spring, stem, vent.

emanation *n* arising, derivation, diffusion, discharge, ectoplasm, effluence, effluent, effluvium, efflux, effusion, emergence, emission, exhalation, flow, mephitis, origination, proceeding, radiation, spreading, venting.

emancipate *v* deliver, disencumber, disenthrall, enfranchise, free, liberate, loose, manumit, release, set free, unbind, unchain, unfetter, unshackle.

antonym enslave.

emancipation *n* deliverance, enfranchisement, freedom, liberation, liberty, loosing, manumission, release, unbinding, unchaining, unfettering, unshackling.

antonym enslavement.

emasculate *v* castrate, cripple, debilitate, enervate, impoverish, neuter, soften, take the teeth out of, unman, water down, weaken.

antonyms boost, vitalize.

embalm *v* cherish, consecrate, enshrine, immortalize, mummify, preserve, store, treasure.

embankment *n* bank, barrier, buttress, causeway, defences, earthwork, levee, rampart, ridge.

embargo *n* ban, bar, barrier, blockage, boycott, check, hindrance, impediment, injunction, interdict, interdiction, prohibition, proscription, restraint, restriction, seizure, stoppage, trade sanction.
v ban, bar, block, boycott, check, impede, interdict, outlaw, prohibit, proscribe, restrict, seize, stop.
antonym allow.

embark *v* board, emplane, go aboard, take ship.
antonym disembark.

embark on begin, broach, commence, engage in, enter into or upon, initiate, launch, start, set out on, undertake.
antonym finish.

embarrass *v* abash, chagrin, confuse, crush, discomfit, discomfort, discompose, disconcert, discountenance, fluster, humiliate, mortify, shame, show up, throw into confusion.

embarrassed *adj* abashed, awkward, blushing, chagrined, discomfited, discomposed, disconcerted, discountenanced, flustered, humiliated, mortified, red-faced, self-conscious, shamed, shamefaced, sheepish, uncomfortable, with egg on one's face.
antonym unembarrassed.

embarrassing *adj* awkward, compromising, crushing, discomfiting, disconcerting, distressing, humbling, humiliating, mortifying, sensitive, shameful, shaming, sticky, touchy, uncomfortable.

embarrassment *n* abashment, awkwardness, bind, chagrin, confusion, constraint, difficulty, discomfiture, discomfort, discomposure, disconcertedness, distress, excess, humiliation, mess, mortification, overabundance, pickle, predicament, scrape, self-consciousness, shame, shamefacedness, sheepishness, superabundance, superfluity, surfeit, surplus.

embassy *n* consulate, delegation, deputation, embassade, legation, mission.

embed *v* bury, fix, implant, impress, insert, plant, root, set, sink.

embellish *v* add bells and whistles, adorn, beautify, bedeck, deck, decorate, dress up, elaborate, embroider, enhance, enrich, exaggerate, fancy up, festoon, garnish, gild, grace, improve (upon), ornament, stretch, trim, varnish.
antonyms denude, simplify.

embellishment *n* adornment, curlicue, decoration, elaboration, embroidery, enhancement, enrichment, exaggeration, flourish, frill, garnish, garniture, gilding, improvement, ornament, ornamentation, squiggle, trill, trimming, vignette.

embers *n* ashes, cinders, coals, remains.

embezzle *v* abstract, appropriate, defalcate, divert, feather one's nest with, filch, have one's hand in the till, misapply, misappropriate, misuse, peculate, pilfer, pinch, purloin, steal.

embezzlement *n* abstraction, appropriation, defalcation, diversion of funds, filching, fraud, larceny, misapplication, misappropriation, misuse, peculation, pilferage, pilfering, purloining, stealing, theft, thievery, thieving.

embezzler *n* cheat, defalcator, fraud, peculator, pilferer, thief, white-collar thief.

embitter *v* acerbate, aggravate, alienate, anger, antagonize, disaffect, disillusion, empoison, envenom, exacerbate, poison, sour, worsen.
antonym pacify.

emblazon *v* adorn, blazon, colour, decorate, depict, embellish, extol, flaunt, glorify, honour, illuminate, laud, ornament, paint, praise, proclaim, publicize, publish, trumpet.

emblem *n* badge, crest, device, figure, image, insignia, mark, representation, sign, symbol, token, totem, type.

emblematic *adj* evocative, figurative, representative, representing, symbolic, typical.

embodiment *n* codification, collection, combination, consolidation, example, exemplar, exemplification, expression, incarnation, inclusion, incorporation, integration, manifestation, materialization, paragon, personification, realization, reification, representation, symbol, type.

embody *v* body forth, codify, collect, combine, comprehend, comprise, concretize, consolidate, contain, corporealize, embrace, encarnalize, encompass, exemplify, express, incarnate, include, incorporate, integrate, manifest, materialize, personify, realize, reify, represent, stand for, symbolize, typify.

embolden *v* animate, cheer on, encourage, fire (up), hearten, inflame, inspire, inspirit, invigorate, nerve, rouse, stimulate, stir (up), strengthen, vitalize.
antonym dishearten.

embrace *v* accept, adopt, canoodle, clasp, comprehend, comprise, contain, cover, cuddle, embody, embosom, encircle, enclose, encompass, enfold, enwrap, envelop, espouse, grab, grasp, hold, hug, include, incorporate, neck, receive, seize, squeeze, subsume, surround, take up, welcome.
n clasp, clinch, cuddle, grasp, hug, squeeze.

embrocation *n* cream, lotion, liniment, ointment, salve.

embroider *v* embellish, enhance, exaggerate, fancy up, ornament, stretch.

embroidery *n* fancywork, needlepoint, needlework, ornamentation, tapestry, tatting.

embroil *v* confound, confuse, distract, encumber, enmesh, ensnare, entangle, implicate, incriminate, involve, mire, mix up, muddle, perplex, throw into confusion.

embryo *n* beginning, germ, nucleus, root, rudiment, seed, zygote.

embryonic *adj* beginning, early, emerging, germinal, inchoate, incipient, incomplete, primary, rudimentary, seminal, undeveloped.
antonyms advanced, developed.

emend *v* alter, amend, correct, edit, improve, rectify, redact, revise, rewrite.

emendation *n* alteration, amendment, correction, corrigendum, edit(ing), improvement, rectification, redaction, revision.

emerge *v* appear, arise, come forth, come into view, come out, crop up, debouch, develop, emanate, issue, materialize, proceed, rise, surface, transpire.
antonyms disappear, fade.

emergence *n* advent, apparition, appearance, arrival, coming, dawn, development, disclosure, eclosion, emanation, emersion, issue, materialization, rise.
antonyms decline, disappearance.

emergency *n* crisis, crunch, danger, difficulty, exigency, extremity, necessity, pass, pinch, plight, predicament, quandary, scrape, strait, urgency.
adj alternative, backup, extra, fallback, reserve, safety, spare, substitute.

emergent *adj* budding, coming, dawning, developing, emerging, forthcoming, new, rising, surfacing.
antonyms declining, disappearing.

emigration *n* departure, exodus, expatriation, journey, migration, removal.

eminence[1] *n* celebrity, dignity, distinction, esteem, fame, greatness, high standing, illustriousness, importance, influence, notability, note, pre-eminence, prestige, prominence, rank, renown, reputation, repute, superiority.

eminence[2] *n* elevation, height, hill, hillock, knob, knoll, peak, prominence, ridge, rise, summit.

eminent *adj* august, celebrated, conspicuous, distinguished, elevated, esteemed, exalted, famous, grand, great, high, high-ranking, illustrious, important, lofty, notable, noted, noteworthy, outstanding, paramount, par excellence, pre-eminent, prestigious, prominent, renowned, reputable, respected, revered, signal, superior, superlative, well-known.
antonyms unimportant, unknown.
▲ *confusable word* imminent.

eminently *adv* conspicuously, exceedingly, exceptionally, extremely, greatly, highly, notably, outstandingly, remarkably, signally, strikingly, superlatively, surpassingly.

emissary *n* agent, ambassador, courier, delegate, deputy, diplomat, envoy, herald, legate, messenger, nuncio, plenipotentiary, representative, scout, spy.

emission *n* diffusion, discharge, ejaculation, ejection, emanation, exhalation, exhaust, exudation, issuance, issue, mephitis, radiation, release, transmission, utterance, vent, venting.

emit *v* diffuse, discharge, eject, emanate, exhale, express, exude, give off, give out, issue, radiate, send out, shed, utter, vent.
antonym absorb.

emollient *adj* assuaging, balsamic, demulcent, lenitive, mitigative, mollifying, softening, soothing.
n balm, cream, lenitive, liniment, lotion, moisturizer, oil, ointment, poultice, salve, unguent.

emolument *n* allowance, benefit, compensation, earnings, fee, gain, hire, honorarium, pay, payment, profits, recompense, remuneration, return, reward, salary, stipend, wages.

emotion *n* affect, agitation, ardour, enthusiasm, excitement, feeling, fervour, fire, heat, passion, pathos, perturbation, reaction, sensation, sentiment, soul, tenderness, vehemence, warmth.

emotional *adj* affected, affecting, ardent, demonstrative, emotive, enthusiastic, excitable, exciting, expressive, feeling, fervent, fervid, fiery, heartwarming, heated, hot-blooded, impassioned, moved, moving, passionate, pathetic, poignant, responsive, roused, sensitive, sentimental, soulful, stirred, stirring, supercharged, susceptible, tearjerking, temperamental, tempestuous, tender, thrilling, touching, visceral, volcanic, warm, zealous.
antonyms calm, cold, detached, emotionless, unemotional.

emotionless *adj* blank, cold, cold-blooded, cool, detached, distant, expressionless, frigid, glacial, impassive, imperturbable, indifferent, passionless, phlegmatic, remote, stoic, stony, toneless, unaffected, unaroused, undemonstrative, unemotional, unexcitable, unfeeling, unmoved.
antonym emotional.

emperor *n* czar, dynast, imperator, kaiser, king, mikado, overlord, ruler, shogun, sovereign.

emphasis *n* accent, accentuation, attention, concentration, concern, focus, force, import, importance, insistence, intensity, interest, positiveness, pre-eminence, priority, prominence, significance, stress, underscoring, urgency, weight.

emphasize *v* accent, accentuate, belabour, dwell on, enhance, feature, highlight, insist on, intensify, magnify, play up, point up, press home, punctuate, (put in the) foreground, spotlight, stress, underline, underscore, weight.
antonyms depreciate, play down, understate.

emphatic *adj* absolute, categorical, certain, decided, definite, direct, distinct, earnest, energetic, forceful, forcible, graphic, important, impressive, insistent, marked, momentous, noticeable, positive, powerful, pronounced, punctuated, resounding, significant, striking, strong, telling, unequivocal, unmistakable, vigorous.
antonyms quiet, understated, unemphatic.

empire *n* authority, bailiwick, command, commonwealth, control, domain, dominion, government, imperium, jurisdiction, kingdom, power, realm, rule, sovereignty, supremacy, sway, territory.

empirical *adj* concrete, experiential, experimental, observable, observed, practical, pragmatic, trial-and-error.

antonyms conjectural, speculative, theoretical.

employ *v* apply, apprentice, bring to bear, commission, engage, enlist, exercise, exert, hire, indenture, occupy, ply, practise, retain, spend, take on, take up, use, utilize.

n employment, hire, pay, service.

employed *adj* active, busy, earning, engaged, hired, occupied, salaried, working.

antonym unemployed.

employee *n* hired hand, hireling, jobholder, retainer, staffer, staff member, wage earner, worker, working person, workman.

employer *n* boss, business, company, establishment, firm, manager, master, organization, outfit, owner, patron, proprietor, taskmaster.

employment *n* application, appointment, avocation, business, calling, employ, engagement, enlistment, exercise, hiring, job, line, métier, occupation, profession, pursuit, retainment, service, trade, use, utilization, vocation, work.

antonym unemployment.

emporium *n* bazaar, establishment, market, marketplace, mart, shop, store, superstore, warehouse.

empower *v* accredit, allow, authorize, commission, delegate, enable, enfranchise, entitle, license, permit, qualify, sanction, warrant.

emptiness *n* absentness, aimlessness, banality, bareness, barrenness, blankness, cheapness, desertedness, desolation, destitution, discontent, dissatisfaction, ennui, expressionlessness, frivolity, futility, hollowness, hunger, idleness, inanity, ineffectiveness, insincerity, insubstantiality, longing, meaninglessness, purposelessness, restlessness, senselessness, silliness, triviality, trivialness, unfulfilment, unreality, vacancy, vacuity, vacuousness, vacuum, valuelessness, vanity, vapidity, void, waste, worthlessness.

antonym fullness.

empty *adj* absent, aimless, banal, bare, barren, blank, bootless, cheap, clear, deserted, desolate, destitute, dissatisfied, drained, effete, exhausted, expressionless, famished, foolish, frivolous, fruitless, futile, hollow, hungry, idle, inane, ineffective, insincere, insubstantial, meaningless, powerless, purposeless, ravenous, restless, senseless, silly, starving, superficial, trivial, unfed, unfilled, unfrequented, unfulfilled, unfurnished, uninhabited, unintelligent, unoccupied, unreal, untenanted, vacant, vacuous, vain, valueless, vapid, void, wasted, worthless.

antonyms filled, full, replete.

v clear, consume, debouch, deplete, discharge, drain, dump, eject, evacuate, exhaust, flow out, gut, pour out, unburden, unload, vacate, void.

antonym fill.

empty-headed *adj* brainless, dizzy, fatuous, flighty, frivolous, giddy, harebrained, inane, scatterbrained, silly, stupid, thoughtless, vacuous.

emulate *v* challenge, compete with, contend with, copy, echo, follow, follow in the footsteps of, imitate, match, mimic, rival, strive to equal, take off on, vie with.

enable *v* accredit, allow, authorize, capacitate, commission, empower, endue, enfranchise, equip, facilitate, fit, license, make possible, permit, prepare, qualify, sanction, warrant.

antonyms inhibit, prevent.

enact *v* act (out), command, decree, depict, dramatize, establish, impersonate, legalize, legislate, ordain, order, pass, perform, personate, play, portray, proclaim, put on, ratify, represent, stage.

antonym repeal.

enactment *n* acting, authorization, command, commandment, decree, depiction, dictate, dramatization, edict, impersonation, law, legislation, order, ordinance, performance, personation, playing, portrayal, proclamation, ratification, regulation, representation, staging, statute.

antonym repeal.

enamoured *adj* besotted, bewitched, captivated, charmed, enchanted, enraptured, entranced, fascinated, fond, impressed, infatuated, in love, smitten, starry-eyed (about), stuck (on), taken.

encampment *n* base, bivouac, camp, campsite, cantonment, quarters, tents.

encapsulate *v* abridge, capture, compress, condense, digest, embody, epitomize, exemplify, put in a nutshell, précis, represent, sum up, summarize, typify.

encase *v* cake, cover, enclose, encrust, house, lay, overlay, plate, sheathe.

enchant *v* beguile, bewitch, captivate, cast a spell (on), charm, delight, enamour, enrapture, ensorcel, enthrall, entrance, fascinate, hypnotize, mesmerize, spellbind, transport, witch.

antonyms bore, disenchant.

enchanter *n* conjurer, hypnotist, magician, magus, mesmerist, necromancer, sorcerer, sorceress, spellbinder, warlock, witch, wizard.

enchanting *adj* alluring, appealing, attractive, bewitching, captivating, charming, delightful, endearing, engaging, enthralling, entrancing, fascinating, lovely, mesmerizing, pleasant, ravishing, spellbinding, winsome, witching, wonderful.

antonyms boring, repellent.

enchantment *n* allure, allurement, beguilement, bewitchment, captivation, charm, conjuration, delight, entrancement, fascination, glamour, hypnotism, incantation, magic,

mesmerism, necromancy, rapture, ravishment, sorcery, spell, transport, witchcraft, wizardry.
antonym disenchantment.

enchantress *n* charmer, Circe, conjurer, femme fatale, hypnotist, lamia, magician, necromancer, seductress, siren, sorceress, spellbinder, temptress, vamp, witch.

encircle *v* begird, besiege, circle, circumscribe, close in on, compass, enclose, encompass, enfold, engird, enlace, envelop, environ, gird, girdle, go around, hem in, loop, ring, surround.

enclose *v* bound, circumscribe, close in, compass, comprehend, confine, contain, coop up, corral, cover, embosom, embrace, encage, encase, encircle, enclasp, encompass, environ, fence in, hedge, hem in, hold, include, incorporate, immure, insert, pen, send (or forward) herewith, shut in, wall in, surround, wrap.

enclosed *adj* bound, caged, cocooned, confined, contained, cooped up, corralled, encased, encircled, encompassed, fenced in, immured, imprisoned, included, shut in, surrounded.
antonyms open, unenclosed.

enclosure *n* arena, circumscription, compound, corral, court, encasement, enceinte, fold, fortification, kraal, paddock, pen, pinfold, pound, ring, seraglio, stockade, sty, the enclosed.

encompass *v* besiege, circle, circumscribe, combine, comprise, contain, cover, embody, embrace, encircle, enclose, envelop, environ, extend around, girdle, hem in, hold, include, incorporate, involve, ring, subsume, surround, take in.

encounter *v* be faced with, chance upon, clash with, collide with, combat, come upon, confront, contend with, cross swords with, engage in battle, experience, face, fight, grapple with, happen on, meet, meet (up) with, ran up against, run across, run into, struggle with.
n action, battle, brush, clash, collision, combat, conflict, confrontation, contest, dispute, engagement, fight, meeting, run-in, set-to, skirmish.

encourage *v* abet, advance, advise, advocate, affirm, aid, animate, boost, buoy up, cheer (on), comfort, console, conduce (or be conducive) to, confirm, egg on, embolden, entice, exhort, favour, forward, foster, further, hearten, help, incite, inspire, inspirit, motivate, persuade, promote, rally, reassure, recommend, rouse, spirit, spur (on), stimulate, strengthen, succour, support, sustain, urge (on).
antonyms depress, discourage, dissuade.

encouragement *n* a boost, advocacy, aid, cheer, come-on, comfort, consolation, emboldenment, exhortation, favour, help, incentive, incitement, inspiration, pat on the back, promotion, reassurance, stimulation, stimulus, succour, support, urging.
antonyms disapproval, discouragement.

encouraging *adj* affirmative, affirming, auspicious, bright, cheerful, cheering, come-hither, comforting, heartening, hopeful, hortative, hortatory, incentive, inspiring, inviting, positive, promising, reassuring, rosy, stimulating, supportive, upbuilding, uplifting.
antonym discouraging.

encroach (on) *v* appropriate, arrogate, impinge, impose, infringe, intrude, invade, make inroads (into), muscle in, obtrude, overstep, take liberties (with), trench, trespass, usurp, violate.

encroachment *n* appropriation, arrogation, impingement, incursion, infringement, inroad, intrusion, invasion, obtrusion, trespass, usurpation, violation.

encumber *v* burden, clog, cramp, embarrass, hamper, handicap, hinder, hold back, impede, incommode, inconvenience, obstruct, oppress, overload, retard, saddle, slow down, trammel, weigh down.

encumbrance *n* annoyance, burden, clog, cumbrance, difficulty, drag, embarrassment, excess baggage, handicap, hindrance, impediment, inconvenience, liability, load, millstone, obstacle, obstruction, onus.
antonym aid.

encyclopedic *adj* all-embracing, all-encompassing, all-inclusive, broad, compendious, complete, comprehensive, exhaustive, extensive, thorough, universal, varied, vast, wide-ranging.
antonyms incomplete, narrow.

end *n* aim, annihilation, aspiration, attainment, bit, bound, boundary, butt, cessation, close, closure, completion, conclusion, consequence, consummation, culmination, curtains, death, demise, denouement, destiny, destruction, dissolution, doom, downfall, edge, ending, expiration, expiry, extermination, extinction, extreme, extremity, fall of the curtain, fate, final curtain, finale, fine, finis, finish, fragment, goal, halt, intent, intention, issue, last part, limit, object, objective, outcome, part, payoff, piece, point, purpose, reason, remainder, remnant, resolution, result, rest, ruin, ruination, scrap, side, solution, stop, stoppage, stub, tail end, termination, terminus, tip, upshot, wind-up.
antonyms beginning, opening, start.
v abate, abolish, abort, adjourn, annihilate, break up, cease, close, complete, conclude, culminate, cut off, destroy, dissolve, expire, exterminate, extinguish, finish (off or up), kill, resolve, ruin, silence, stop, surpass, terminate, wind up, wrap up.
antonyms begin, start.

endanger *v* compromise, expose, hazard, imperil, jeopardize, risk, threaten.
antonyms protect, shelter, shield.

endearing *adj* adorable, attractive, charming, delightful, enchanting, engaging, lovable, prepossessing, sweet, winning, winsome.

endearment *n* affection, attachment, blandishment, caress, diminutive, fondness, honeyed word, hypocorism, kindness, love, pet name, sweet nothing.

endeavour *n* aim, attempt, crack, effort, enterprise, essay, go, nisus, project, shot, stab, trial, try, undertaking, venture.

v aim, aspire, attempt, essay, exert oneself, labour, make an effort, strive, struggle, take pains, try, undertake, venture.

ending *n* break-up, cessation, climax, close, completion, conclusion, consummation, culmination, denouement, end, epilogue, finale, finish, halting, last part, resolution, termination, wind-up.

antonyms beginning, start.

endless *adj* boundless, ceaseless, constant, continual, continuous, eternal, everlasting, immortal, incessant, infinite, interminable, interminate, limitless, measureless, monotonous, never-ending, non-stop, overlong, perpetual, Sisyphean, timeless, unbounded, unbroken, undivided, undying, unending, uninterrupted, unlimited, unremitting.

endorse *v* adopt, advocate, affirm, approve, authorize, back, champion, confirm, consent to, countenance, countersign, favour, OK, ratify, recommend, rubber-stamp, sanction, sign, subscribe to, superscribe, support, undersign, vouch for, warrant.

antonyms denounce, disapprove.

endorsement *n* advocacy, affirmation, approbation, approval, authorization, backing, championship, commendation, confirmation, consent, corroboration, countersignature, favour, fiat, OK, ratification, recommendation, sanction, seal of approval, signature, stamp of approval, superscription, support, testimonial, thumbs up, warrant.

antonyms denouncement, disapproval.

endow (with) *v* award, bequeath, bless, dower, empower, endue, enrich, favour, finance, fund, furnish, gift, give, grant, invest, leave, present, provide, supply, will.

antonym divest.

endowment *n* ability, aptitude, award, benefaction, bequest, bestowal, donation, dowry, empowerment, faculty, flair, fund, genius, gift, grant, income, largesse, legacy, power, presentation, property, provision, revenue, talent.

endurable *adj* bearable, sufferable, supportable, sustainable, tolerable.

antonyms intolerable, unbearable.

endurance *n* constancy, continuation, continuity, doggedness, durability, fortitude, immutability, lastingness, longevity, patience, permanence, perseverance, persistence, pertinacity, resignation, resolution, stability, stamina, staying power, stick-to-itiveness, strength, submission, sufferance, sustaining power, tenacity, tolerance, toleration.

endure *v* abide, allow, bear, brave, brook, continue, cope with, countenance, digest, experience, go through, hang in (there), hold, hold up, last, live, live through, live to fight another day, persevere, persist, prevail, put up with, remain, see (it) through, stand, stay (the course), stick, stomach, submit to, suffer, survive, sustain, swallow, tolerate, tough it out, undergo, weather, withstand.

antonyms cease, end.

enduring *adj* abiding, constant, continuing, durable, eternal, firm, immortal, imperishable, lasting, living, long-lasting, long-standing, perennial, permanent, persistent, persisting, prevailing, remaining, steadfast, steady, surviving, timeless, tough, unfaltering, unwavering.

antonyms changeable, fleeting, unending, unfailing.

enemy *n* adversary, antagonist, competitor, foe, opponent, rival, sworn enemy, the opposition.

antonyms ally, friend.

energetic *adj* active, animated, brisk, dynamic, forceful, forcible, full of life, high-powered, indefatigable, lively, peppy, pithy, potent, powerful, spirited, sprightly, spry, strenuous, strong, thoroughgoing, tireless, vigorous, zippy.

antonyms idle, inactive, lazy, sluggish.

energize *v* activate, animate, electrify, enliven, fire (up), galvanize, inspirit, invigorate, liven, motivate, move to action, pep up, quicken, refresh, stimulate, vitalize, vivify.

antonym drain.

energy *n* activity, animation, ardour, brio, drive, effort, élan, enthusiasm, exertion, fire, force, forcefulness, fuel, get-up-and-go, intensity, juice, life, liveliness, pep, peppiness, power, spirit, sprightliness, stamina, steam, strength, tirelessness, verve, vigour, vim, vitality, vivacity, vroom, zeal, zest, zip.

antonyms inertia, lethargy, weakness.

enervate *v* burn out, debilitate, deplete, devitalize, do in, drain, enfeeble, exhaust, fatigue, incapacitate, paralyse, poop (out), prostrate, run down, sap the strength of, take it out of, tire, weaken, wear out.

antonyms activate, energize.

enervated *adj* burned out, debilitated, depleted, devitalized, done in, drained, effete, enfeebled, exhausted, fatigued, feeble, incapacitated, languid, limp, paralysed, pooped (out), prostrate, prostrated, run-down, sapped, spent, tired, undermined, washed out, weak, weakened, worn out.

antonyms active, energetic.

enervation *n* burnout, debilitation, debility, depletion, effeteness, enfeeblement, exhaustion, fatigue, feebleness, impotence, incapacity, infirmity, languor, lassitude, paralysis, powerlessness, prostration, tiredness, weakening, weakness, weariness.

enfeeble *v* debilitate, deplete, devitalize, disable, emasculate, enervate, exhaust, fatigue, impoverish, sap, undermine, unhinge, unnerve, weaken, wear out.

antonym strengthen.

enfold *v* clasp, embrace, encircle, enclose, encompass, envelop, enwrap, fold, hold, hug, shroud, surround, swathe, wrap (up).

enforce v administer, apply, carry out, compel, exact, execute, force, implement, impose, insist on, make mandatory, prosecute, put into effect, reinforce, require.

enforced adj binding, compelled, compulsory, dictated, imposed, involuntary, mandatory, necessary, obligatory, ordained, prescribed, required, unavoidable.

enforcement n administration, application, carrying out, coercion, compulsion, constraint, execution, force, implementation, imposition, insistence, obligation, pressure, prosecution, requirement.

enfranchise v emancipate, empower, entitle, free, liberate, manumit, release, set free.
antonym disenfranchise.

enfranchisement n emancipation, empowerment, entitlement, freedom, freeing, liberation, manumission, release, setting free, suffrage.
antonym disenfranchisement.

engage v absorb, activate, affiance, agree, allure, apply, appoint, arrest, assail, attack, attract, bespeak, betroth, bind, book, busy oneself, captivate, catch, charm, charter, combat, commission, commit (oneself) to, contract, covenant, draw, draw (in or out), employ, engross, enlist, enrol, fascinate, fight with, fit into, fix, grab, grip, guarantee, hire, interact with, interconnect, interlock, involve, join, keep busy, lease, meet, mesh, obligate, oblige, occupy, operate, partake, participate, pledge, practise, prearrange, preoccupy, promise, rent, retain, secure, take on, take part, tie up, undertake, vouch, vow.
antonyms discharge, disengage, dismiss.

engaged adj absorbed, activated, affianced, betrothed, booked, busy, committed, contacted, employed, engrossed, immersed, involved, occupied, pledged, preoccupied, promised, reserved, spoken for, tied up, unavailable, wrapped up.

engagement n activation, affiance, agreement, appointment, arrangement, battle, betrothal, booking, combat, commission, commitment, compact, conflict, confrontation, contract, date, employment, encounter, fight, gig, hire, interaction, job, meeting, mesh(ing), oath, obligation, pact, pledge, position, post, promise, situation, stint, troth, undertaking, vow, word, work.
antonym disengagement.

engaging adj agreeable, alluring, appealing, attractive, beguiling, captivating, charming, enchanting, fascinating, likable, lovable, pleasant, pleasing, prepossessing, winning, winsome.
antonyms boring, loathsome, repellent.

engender v arouse, beget, breed, bring about (or forth), cause, create, encourage, excite, father, generate, give rise to, hatch, incite, induce, lead to, make, occasion, precipitate, procreate, produce, propagate, provoke, sire, spawn.

engine n agency, agent, apparatus, appliance, contraption, contrivance, device, dynamo,

implement, instrument, machine, means, mechanism, motor, tool, turbine, weapon.

engineer n architect, brains, contriver, designer, deviser, driver, inventor, mastermind, operator, originator, planner.
v concoct, contrive, control, create, devise, direct, drive, effect, finagle, lead, machinate, manage, manipulate, manoeuvre, mastermind, originate, oversee, plan, plot, wangle.

engrave v blaze, carve, chase, chisel, cut (in), embed, enchase, etch, fix, grave, impress, imprint, infix, ingrain, inscribe, lodge, mark, photoengrave, print.

engraving n blaze, block, carving, chasing, chiselling, cutting, drypoint, enchasing, etching, gravure, impression, inscription, mark, photoengraving, photogravure, plate, print, woodcut.

engross v absorb, arrest, captivate, engage, fixate, hold, immerse, involve, monopolize, occupy, preoccupy, rivet, wrap up.

engrossed adj absorbed, captivated, caught up, engaged, enthralled, fascinated, fixated, immersed, intent, in the grip (of), intrigued, lost, preoccupied, rapt, riveted, spellbound, taken (up), wrapped up.
antonyms bored, disinterested.

engrossing adj absorbing, captivating, compelling, enthralling, fascinating, gripping, interesting, intriguing, riveting, spellbinding, suspenseful, taking, unputdownable.
antonym boring.

engulf v absorb, bury, consume, deluge, drown, encompass, engross, envelop, flood, immerse, inundate, overrun, overwhelm, plunge, submerge, swallow up, swamp.

enhance v add to, amplify, augment, boost, complement, elevate, embellish, escalate, exalt, heighten, improve, increase, intensify, lift, magnify, maximize, optimize, raise, reinforce, strengthen.
antonyms decrease, minimize.

enigma n brain teaser, conundrum, mystery, perplexity, poser, problem, puzzle, puzzler, riddle.

enigmatic adj ambiguous, baffling, cryptic, Delphic, doubtful, equivocal, impenetrable, incomprehensible, indecipherable, inexplicable, inscrutable, mysterious, obscure, perplexing, puzzling, recondite, strange, uncertain, unfathomable, unintelligible.
antonyms simple, straightforward.

enjoin v advise, ban, bar, bid, call upon, charge, command, counsel, demand, direct, disallow, exhort, forbid, impose, instruct, interdict, issue an injunction to, order, preclude, prescribe, prohibit, proscribe, require, restrain, urge, warn.

enjoy v appreciate, bask in, be amused by, be blessed with, be fond of, be turned on by, delight in, dig, experience, find stimulating, have, have a weakness for, indulge in, like, love, possess, rejoice in, relish, revel in, savour, take pleasure in, use.
antonyms abhor, detest.

enjoy oneself have a ball, have a good time, have fun, make merry, party.

enjoyable adj agreeable, amusing, delectable, delicious, delightful, entertaining, fun, fun-and-games, fun-filled, good, gratifying, pleasant, pleasing, pleasurable, satisfying, to one's liking or task.
antonyms disagreeable, unpleasant.

enjoyment n amusement, benefit, comfort, delectation, delight, diversion, entertainment, exercise, fun, fun and games, gaiety, gladness, gratification, gusto, happiness, indulgence, jollity, joy, kicks, pleasure, possession, recreation, relish, satisfaction, use, zest.
antonyms displeasure, dissatisfaction.

enlarge (on) v add to, amplify, augment, balloon, bloat, blow up, broaden, descant, develop, dilate, distend, elaborate, elongate, expand, expatiate, extend, greaten, grow, increase, inflate, intumesce, lengthen, magnify, stretch, swell (up), wax, widen.
antonyms decrease, diminish, shrink.

enlargement n addition, amplification, aneurysm, augmentation, blowup, broadening, dilation, distension, edema, elaboration, emphysema, expansion, extension, growth, increase, increment, intumescence, magnification, protuberance, supplementation, swelling (up).
antonyms contraction, decrease, shrinkage.

enlighten v advise, broaden the mind of, civilize, counsel, edify, educate, illuminate, illumine, indoctrinate, inform, instruct, teach, undeceive.
antonyms confuse, puzzle.

enlightened adj aware, broad-minded, civilized, cultivated, educated, illuminated, informed, knowledgeable, liberal, literate, open-minded, reasonable, refined, sophisticated, wise.
antonyms blind, blinkered, confused, ignorant.

enlightenment n awareness, broad-mindedness, civilization, comprehension, cultivation, edification, education, illumination, information, insight, instruction, knowledge, learning, literacy, open-mindedness, refinement, sapience, sophistication, teaching, understanding, wisdom.
antonyms confusion, ignorance.

enlist v call (on or up), conscript, draft, employ, engage, enrol, enter, gather, interest in, join (up), muster, obtain, procure, recruit, register, secure, sign up (or on), volunteer.

enliven v animate, brighten, buoy up, cheer (up), energize, excite, exhilarate, fire (up), galvanize, gladden, hearten, inspire, inspirit, invigorate, juice up, kindle, liven (up), pep up, perk up, quicken, rouse, spark, stimulate, vitalize, vivify, wake up.
antonyms dampen, subdue.

en masse all at once, all together, as a group, as a whole, as one, collectively, en bloc, in a body, in large numbers, together, wholesale.

enmity n acrimony, animosity, animus, antagonism, antipathy, aversion, bad blood, bitterness, contention, feud, hate, hatred, hostility, ill will, malevolence, malice, malignity, rancour, spite, unfriendliness, venom.
antonyms amity, friendship.

ennoble v aggrandize, dignify, elevate, enhance, exalt (to the skies), glorify, honour, lift up, lionize, magnify, purify, raise, refine, uplift.

ennui n accidie, boredom, dissatisfaction, languor, lassitude, listlessness, restlessness, tedium, the doldrums, weariness, Weltschmerz, world-weariness.

enormity n abomination, atrociousness, atrocity, baseness, crime, depravity, evil, evilness, flagitiousness, heinousness, horror, hugeness, iniquity, magnitude, monstrosity, monstrousness, nefariousness, outrage, outrageousness, turpitude, viciousness, vileness, villainy, wickedness.
antonyms triviality, unimportance.

enormous adj abominable, astronomical, atrocious, Brobdingnagian, colossal, cyclopean, daunting, depraved, disgraceful, evil, excessive, gargantuan, gigantic, gross, heinous, herculean, horrific, huge, hulking, immense, jumbo, large, leviathan, mammoth, massive, monstrous, mountainous, nefarious, odious, outrageous, prodigious, titanic, tremendous, vast, vicious, vile, villainous, wicked.
antonyms small, tiny.

enough adj abundant, adequate, ample, lots (of), plenty (of), sufficient.
n abundance, adequacy, plenitude, plenty, repletion, sufficiency.
adv abundantly, adequately, amply, aplenty, fairly, fully, moderately, passably, quite, reasonably, satisfactorily, sufficiently, tolerably.

enquire see **inquire**

enquiry see **inquiry**

enrage v acerbate, aggravate, anger, drive mad, exasperate, incense, inflame, infuriate, irritate, madden, make (someone's) blood boil, raise the hackles of, provoke.
antonyms calm, placate, soothe.

enraged adj aggravated, angered, angry, exasperated, fighting mad, fit to be tied, foaming at the mouth, fuming, furious, hopping mad, hot (under the collar), incensed, inflamed, infuriated, irate, irritated, livid, mad (as a hornet), rabid, raging, ranting, raving, seething, smouldering, storming, wild.
antonym calm.

enrapture v beguile, bewitch, captivate, charm, delight, enchant, enravish, enthral, entrance, fascinate, ravish, spellbind, thrill, transport.

enrich v adorn, aggrandize, ameliorate, augment, cultivate, decorate, deepen, develop, embellish, endow, enhance, fertilize, fortify, grace, improve, ornament, prosper, refine, supplement.

antonym impoverish.

enrol *v* accept, admit, chronicle, engage, enlist, enregister, impanel, inscribe, join up, list, matriculate, note, record, recruit, register, sign on, sign up, take on.

antonyms leave, reject.

enrolment *n* acceptance, admission, engagement, enlistment, impanelment, matriculation, recruitment, register, registration.

ensconce *v* conceal, entrench, establish, hide, install, locate, lodge, nestle, park, place, put, settle, shelter.

ensemble *n* acting company, aggregate, assemblage, band, (chamber) orchestra, chorale, chorus, collection, combo, company, corps de ballet, costume, entirety, get-up, group, kit, outfit, rig, set, suit, totality, troupe, whole.

enshrine *v* apotheosize, cherish, consecrate, dedicate, embalm, exalt, glorify, hallow, idolize, keep sacred, preserve, revere, sanctify, treasure.

enshroud *v* cloak, clothe, cloud, conceal, cover, enclose, enfold, envelop, enwrap, enwreathe, hide, obscure, shroud, veil, wrap.

ensign *n* badge, banner, colours, flag, gonfalon, insignia, oriflamme, pennant, pennon, standard, streamer.

enslave *v* bind, conquer, dominate, enchain, enthral, hold captive, make a chattel of, overcome, shackle, subject, subjugate, take captive.

antonyms emancipate, free.

enslavement *n* bondage, captivity, domination, enthralment, oppression, repression, serfdom, servitude, slavery, subjection, subjugation, thralldom, vassalage.

antonym emancipation.

ensnare *v* catch, embroil, enmesh, entangle, entrap, lure, net, snare, snarl, suck in, trap.

ensue *v* arise, come next, eventuate, fall out (from), flow (from), follow, happen (next), issue, proceed, result, succeed, supervene, turn out.

antonym precede.

ensuing *adj* consequent, eventual, following, resulting, subsequent, succeeding, supervenient.

ensure *v* assure, clinch, confirm, guarantee, guard, insure, make sure or certain, protect, safeguard, secure, warrant.

entail *v* call for, demand, impose, involve, mean, necessitate, occasion, require, take.

entangle *v* ball up, catch, complicate, confuse, draw in, embroil, enlace, enmesh, ensnare, entrap, foul, hook, implicate, involve, jumble (up), knot, mat, mix up, muddle, ravel, snag, snare, snarl, tangle, trammel, trap, twist (up).

antonym disentangle.

entanglement *n* complexity, complication, confusion, difficulty, embarrassment, ensnarement, entrapment, imbroglio, intrigue,

involvement, love affair, jumble, knot, liaison, mess, mix-up, muddle, predicament, snare, snarl, tangle, tie, toils, trap.

antonym disentanglement.

entente *n* agreement, arrangement, bargain, compact, deal, entente cordiale, pact, treaty, understanding.

enter *v* appear, arrive (at), board, come in/into, embark (upon), enlist, enrol, go in (or into), hand in, input, inscribe, insert, join, list, log, participate (in), penetrate, pierce, present, record, register, set down, sign up, submit, take part, tender, write (down).

antonyms delete, issue, leave.

enter (up)on begin, commence, embark (up)on, set (up)on, start, take up, undertake.

enterprise[1] *n* activity, adventuresomeness, alertness, audacity, boldness, daring, drive, dynamism, eagerness, effort, energy, enthusiasm, get-up-and-go, gumption, imagination, initiative, push, readiness, resourcefulness, self-motivation, spirit, spunk, vigour, what it takes, zeal.

antonyms apathy, inertia.

enterprise[2] *n* adventure, business, company, concern, effort, endeavour, establishment, firm, operation, plan, program, project, undertaking, venture.

enterprising *adj* active, adventuresome, adventurous, alert, ambitious, aspiring, audacious, bold, brave, courageous, daring, dynamic, eager, energetic, enthusiastic, hustling, imaginative, intrepid, keen, ready, resourceful, self-motivated, self-reliant, spirited, up-and-coming, venturesome, vigorous, zealous.

antonyms lethargic, unadventurous.

entertain *v* accommodate, amuse, beguile, charm, cheer, cherish, conceive, consider, contemplate, countenance, delight, divert, fete, foster, harbour, hold in the mind, host, imagine, lodge, maintain, occupy, please, put up, receive, recreate, regale, support, treat.

antonyms bore, reject.

entertainer *n* artist, artiste, comedian, diseur, diseuse, performer, stand-up comic, troubadour, trouper.

entertaining *adj* amusing, beguiling, charming, cheering, delightful, diverting, droll, enjoyable, fun, funny, humorous, interesting, more fun than a barrel of monkeys, pleasant, pleasing, pleasurable, witty.

antonym boring.

entertainment *n* amusement, cheer, distraction, diversion, enjoyment, extravaganza, fun, hospitality, kicks, pastime, play, pleasure, recreation, show, spectacle, sport, treat.

enthral *v* beguile, captivate, cast a spell over, charm, enchant, enrapture, enravish, enslave, entrance, fascinate, grip, hypnotize, intrigue, mesmerize, rivet, spellbind, thrill.

antonyms bore, weary.

enthralling *adj* beguiling, captivating, charming, compelling, enchanting, entrancing, fascinating, gripping, hypnotic, hypnotizing, intriguing, mesmeric, mesmerizing, riveting, spellbinding, thrilling, unputdownable.

antonym boring.

enthuse *v* be ecstatic, carry on, drool, emote, excite, go on (about), gush, impassion, inflame, rave, rhapsodize, wax lyrical.

enthusiasm *n* animation, ardour, avidity, craze, devotion, eagerness, ebullience, excitement, exuberance, fad, fervour, frenzy, heart and soul, hobby, hobbyhorse, infatuation, interest, keenness, liveliness, mania, oomph, passion, relish, spirit, vehemence, warmth, whole-heartedness, willingness, zeal, zest.

antonym apathy.

enthusiast *n* addict, admirer, aficionado, buff, bug, devotee, eager beaver, fan, fanatic, fiend, follower, freak, hound, lover, nut, supporter, zealot.

antonym detractor.

enthusiastic *adj* ardent, avid, devoted, eager, ebullient, enthused, excited, exuberant, fervent, fervid, forceful, glowing, gung-ho, hearty, keen, keen as mustard, lively, passionate, spirited, unstinting, vehement, vigorous, warm, whole-hearted, willing, zealous.

antonyms apathetic, reluctant, unenthusiastic.

entice *v* allure, attract, beguile, blandish, cajole, coax, decoy, draw, induce, inveigle, lead on, lure, persuade, prevail on, seduce, suck in, sweet talk, tantalize, tempt, wheedle.

enticement *n* allurement, attraction, bait, beguilement, blandishments, cajolery, coaxing, come-on, decoy, inducement, inveiglement, lure, persuasion, seduction, sweet talk, temptation.

entire *adj* absolute, complete, full, in one piece, intact, integrated, perfect, sound, thorough, total, unabridged, unbroken, uncut, undamaged, undiminished, undivided, unified, unmarked, unmarred, unmitigated, unqualified, unreserved, unrestricted, whole.

antonyms impaired, incomplete, partial.

entirely *adv* absolutely, altogether, completely, every inch, exclusively, fully, hook line and sinker, in toto, lock stock and barrel, only, perfectly, solely, thoroughly, totally, unreservedly, utterly, wholly, without a qualification, without exception, without reservation.

antonym partially.

entirety *n* absoluteness, aggregate, completeness, ensemble, fullness, sum total, totality, unity, universality, whole, wholeness.

antonyms element, incompleteness, part.

entitle *v* accredit, allow, authorize, call, christen, denominate, designate, empower, enable, enfranchise, label, license, name, permit, tag, term, title.

entity *n* being, body, creature, essence, existence, individual, object, organism, presence, substance, thing.

entombment *n* burial, inhumation, interment, sepulture.

entourage *n* associates, attendants, claque, companions, company, cortege, coterie, court, escort, followers, following, retainers, retinue, satellites, staff, suite, train.

entrails *n* bowels, entera, guts, haslet, innards, insides, intestines, offal, viscera.

entrance¹ *n* access, admission, admittance, appearance, arrival, avenue, beginning, commencement, debut, door, doorway, entranceway, entree, entry, foyer, gate, ingress, inlet, introduction, lobby, narthex, opening, passage, passageway, portal, start, vestibule.

antonyms departure, exit.

entrance² *v* bewitch, captivate, cast a spell on, charm, delight, enchant, enrapture, enthral, fascinate, hypnotize, magnetize, mesmerize, ravish, spellbind, transport.

antonyms bore, repel.

entrant *n* beginner, candidate, competitor, contender, contestant, convert, entry, initiate, neophyte, newcomer, novice, participant, player, probationer, tyro.

entrap *v* allure, beguile, capture, catch, decoy, embroil, enmesh, ensnare, entangle, entice, implicate, inveigle, involve, lure, net, seduce, snare, trap, trick.

entreat *v* adjure, appeal to, ask, beg, beseech, call on, conjure, cry to, enjoin, exhort, go cap in hand to, go on bended knee to, implore, importune, invoke, petition, plead with, pray, request, sue, supplicate.

entreaty *n* adjuration, appeal, cry, exhortation, importunity, invocation, petition, plea, prayer, request, solicitation, suit, supplication.

entrench *v* anchor, dig in, embed, encroach, ensconce, establish, fix, fortify, impinge, infix, infringe, ingrain, install, interlope, intrude, lodge, plant, root, seat, set, settle, trespass.

antonym dislodge.

entrenched *adj* deep-rooted, deep-seated, established, firm, fixed, implanted, inbred, indelible, ineradicable, ingrained, rooted, set, unshakable, well-established.

entrepreneur *n* businessman, businesswoman, contractor, financier, impresario, industrialist, magnate, tycoon.

entrust *v* assign, authorize, charge, commend, commit, confide, consign, delegate, deliver, give, hand over, invest, trust, turn over.

entry¹ *n* access, admission, admittance, appearance, avenue, door, doorway, entrance, entranceway, entree, entryway, foyer, gate, ingress, narthex, opening, passage, passageway, portal, threshold, vestibule.

antonym exit.

entry² *n* article, candidate, competitor, contestant, entrant, heading, headword, item, jotting, listing, memo, memorandum, minute, notation, note, participant, player, record, registration, statement, submission.

entwine *v* braid, embrace, encircle, enlace, entwist, enwreathe, interlace, interlink, intertwine, interweave, knit, plait, surround, twine, twist, weave, wind.

antonym unravel.

enumerate *v* call the roll of, cite, count, detail, itemize, list, mention, name, number, quote, recapitulate, recite, recount, rehearse, relate, specify, spell out, tally.

enunciate *v* announce, articulate, broadcast, declare, enounce, proclaim, promulgate, pronounce, propound, publish, say, sound, speak, state, utter, verbalize, vocalize, voice.

envelop *v* blanket, cloak, conceal, cover, embrace, encase, encircle, enclose, encompass, enfold, engulf, enshroud, enwrap, enwreathe, hide, obscure, sheathe, shroud, surround, swaddle, swathe, veil, wrap.

envelope *n* case, casing, coating, cover, covering, integument, jacket, sheath, shell, skin, theca, wrapper, wrapping.

enviable *adj* advantageous, blessed, covetable, desirable, excellent, favoured, fine, fortunate, good, lucky, much to be desired, privileged, worth having.

antonym unenviable.

envious *adj* begrudging, covetous, discontented, dissatisfied, green, green-eyed, green with envy, grudging, jaundiced, jealous, malcontent, resentful, spiteful.

environment *n* ambience, atmosphere, background, conditions, context, domain, element, entourage, habitat, locale, medium, milieu, scene, setting, situation, surroundings, territory.

environmentalist *n* conservationist, earth activist, ecologist, nature lover.

environs *n* district, locality, neighbourhood, outskirts, precincts, purlieus, suburbs, surroundings, vicinage, vicinity.

envisage *v* anticipate, conceive of, conceptualize, contemplate, envision, expect, fancy, foresee, have in mind, ideate, imagine, picture, preconceive, predict, see, visualize.

envoy *n* agent, ambassador, courier, delegate, deputy, diplomat, emissary, intermediary, legate, messenger, minister, nuncio, plenipotentiary, representative.

envy *n* covetousness, cupidity, dissatisfaction, enviousness, green-eyed monster, grudge, ill will, jaundiced eye, jealousy, malice, malignity, resentment, spite.

v begrudge, covet, crave, grudge, resent, view with a jaundiced eye.

enwrap *v* encase, enclose, enfold, enshroud, envelop, enwind, enwreathe, parcel, sheathe, shroud, swaddle, swathe, wimple, wind, wrap.

ephemeral *adj* brief, evanescent, fleeting, flitting, fly-by-night, fugitive, impermanent, momentary, passing, short, short-lived, temporary, transient, transitory.

antonyms enduring, lasting, perpetual.

epic *adj* colossal, grand, grandiloquent, great, heroic, Homeric, huge, imposing, impressive, larger than life, lofty, majestic, monumental, stirring, titanic, vast.

antonym ordinary.

epicure *n* arbiter of taste, bon vivant, connoisseur, epicurean, gastronome, glutton, gourmand, gourmet, hedonist, pleasure seeker, sensualist, sybarite, voluptuary.

epicurean *adj* gluttonous, gourmandising, hedonistic, libertine, luxury-loving, pleasure-seeking, self-indulgent, sensual, sybaritic, unrestrained, voluptuous.

epidemic *adj* epizootic, pandemic, prevailing, prevalent, rampant, rife, sweeping, wide-ranging, widespread.

n growth, outbreak, pandemic, pestilence, plague, rash, scourge, spread, upsurge, wave.

epigram *n* aphorism, apothegm, bon mot, gnome, maxim, proverb, quip, witticism.

epigrammatic *adj* aphoristic, apothegmatic, concise, gnomic, laconic, piquant, pithy, pointed, sharp, short, succinct, terse, witty.

epilogue *n* afterword, coda, conclusion, postscript.

antonyms foreword, preface, prologue.

episode *n* adventure, affair, chapter, circumstance, digression, event, experience, happening, incident, instalment, interlude, occasion, occurrence, parenthesis, part, passage, scene, section.

episodic *adj* anecdotal, digressive, disconnected, disjointed, incidental, intermittent, linear, occasional, parenthetic, picaresque, sporadic.

epistle *n* communication, dispatch, encyclical, letter, line, message, missive, note.

epithet *n* appellation, curse, denomination, description, designation, dirty name, dirty word, expletive, four-letter word, label, name, nickname, sobriquet, swearword, tag, title, ugly name.

epitome *n* abbreviation, abridgment, abstract, archetype, classic example, compendium, compression, condensation, conspectus, contraction, digest, embodiment, essence, exemplar, ideal, image, model, personification, précis, quintessence, recapitulation, reduction, representation, résumé, shortening, summary, summation, syllabus, synopsis, type.

epitomize *v* abbreviate, abridge, abstract, compress, condense, contract, curtail, cut, embody, encapsulate, exemplify, illustrate, incarnate, personify, précis, recap, reduce, represent, shorten, summarize, sum up, symbolize, typify.

antonyms elaborate, expand.

epoch *n* age, eon, era, period, time.

equable *adj* agreeable, calm, composed, consistent, constant, easygoing, equanimous, equitable, even, even-tempered, imperturbable, level-headed, moderate, phlegmatic, placid, serene, stable, steady, temperate, tranquil, unchanging, unexcitable, unflappable, uniform, unruffled, unvarying.

antonyms excitable, variable.

equal (to) *adj* able (to do), adequate (for), alike, balanced, capable (of), commensurate (with), competent, corresponding, egalitarian, equable, equalized, equivalent, even,

even-handed, evenly-balanced, evenly-matched, evenly-proportioned, fair, fifty-fifty, fit (for), identical, impartial, interchangeable, like, matched, on a par (with), proportionate, ready (for), regular, split down the middle, sufficient (for), suitable (for), symmetrical, tantamount, the same, uniform, unvarying, up (to).

antonyms different, inequitable, unequal.

n brother, co-equal, colleague, compeer, counterpart, equivalent, fellow, match, mate, opposite number, parallel, peer, rival, twin.

v balance, compare with, correspond to, equalize, match, parallel, rival, square with, tally with.

equality *n* balance, co-equality, correspondence, egalitarianism, equitability, equivalence, evenness, fairness, identity, imbalance, likeness, par, parity, proportion, sameness, similarity, symmetry, uniformity.

antonym inequality.

equalize *v* balance, draw level, equate, even up, level, match, regularize, smooth, square, standardize.

equanimity *n* aplomb, calm, calmness, composure, coolness, equability, equableness, even-temperedness, imperturbability, level-headedness, peace, phlegm, placidity, poise, presence of mind, sang-froid, self-possession, serenity, steadiness, tranquillity.

antonyms alarm, anxiety, discomposure.

equanimous *adj* calm, composed, cool, equable, even-tempered, imperturbable, level-headed, peaceful, phlegmatic, placid, self-controlled, self-possessed, serene, steady, tranquil.

antonyms anxious, excitable, volatile.

equate *v* balance, bracket (with), compare, equalize, level, liken, match, pair, parallel, put on a par, square.

equation *n* calculation, formula, reckoning.

equestrian *n* cavalier, dressagist, horseback rider, horseman, knight, postilion, rider.

equilibrium *n* balance, calm, calmness, collectedness, composure, cool, coolness, counterbalance, counterpoise, equality, equanimity, equipoise, equiponderance, evenness, poise, rest, self-possession, serenity, stability, steadiness, symmetry.

antonym imbalance.

equip *v* accoutre, arm, array, attire, bedight, deck out, dress, endow, endue, fit out, furnish, kit out, outfit, prepare, provide, ready, supply.

equipage *n* accoutrements, apparatus, baggage, carriage, coach, equipment, gear, impedimenta, material, munitions, outfit, retinue, rig, stores, suite, train, trappings, turnout.

equipment *n* accessories, accoutrements, apparatus, appurtenances, baggage, equipage, furnishings, furniture, gear, impedimenta, implements, kit, material, matériel, muniments, outfit, paraphernalia,

stuff, supplies, tackle, things, tools, wherewithal.

equipoise *n* balance, ballast, counterbalance, counterpoise, counterweight, equibalance, equilibrium, equiponderance, evenness, poise, stability, steadiness, symmetry.

antonym imbalance.

equitable *adj* disinterested, dispassionate, ethical, even-handed, fair, fair-minded, fair-and-square, honest, impartial, just, legitimate, proper, proportionate, reasonable, right, rightful, square, unbiassed, unprejudiced.

antonyms inequitable, unfair.

equity *n* disinterestedness, equality, even-handedness, fair-mindedness, fairness, fair play, honesty, impartiality, integrity, justice, reasonableness, rectitude, righteousness, rightness, uprightness.

antonym inequity.

equivalence *n* agreement, alikeness, analogy, comparability, conformity, correspondence, equality, evenness, homology, identity, interchangeability, interchangeableness, likeness, match, parallel, parity, sameness, similarity, substitutability, synonymy.

antonyms dissimilarity, inequality, unlikeness.

equivalent *adj* alike, analagous, commensurate, comparable, convertible, correspondent, corresponding, equal, equipollent, equipotent, even, homologous, identical, interchangeable, similar, substitutable, synonymous, tantamount, the same, twin.

antonyms dissimilar, unlike.

n correspondent, counterpart, equal, homologue, match, opposite number, parallel, peer, substitute, twin.

equivocal *adj* ambiguous, ambivalent, casuistic, confusing, Delphic, doubtful, dubious, evasive, indefinite, indeterminate, misleading, mixed, oblique, obscure, oracular, questionable, self-contradictory, suspicious, uncertain, undecided, vague.

antonyms clear, unequivocal.

equivocate *v* dodge, evade, fence, fudge, hedge, mislead, palter, parry, prevaricate, pussyfoot, quibble, shift, shuffle, sidestep, sit on the fence, tergiversate, waffle, weasel.

equivocation *n* ambiguity, casuistry, confusion, double talk, doubtfulness, evasion, fencing, fudging, hedging, prevarication, quibbling, shifting, shuffling, sophistry, tergiversation, waffle, weasel words.

antonyms directness, forthrightness.

era *n* age, century, cycle, day, days, eon, epoch, generation, period, stage, time.

eradicate *v* abolish, annihilate, blot out, demolish, deracinate, destroy, do away with, efface, eliminate, erase, excise, expunge, exterminate, extinguish, extirpate, get rid of, obliterate, pull up by the roots, raze, remove all trace of, root out, rub out, stamp out, suppress, unroot, uproot, weed out, wipe out.

eradication *n* abolition, annihilation, deracination, destruction, effacement, elimination, erasure, expunction, extermination, extinction, extirpation, obliteration, removal, riddance, suppression.

erasable *adj* effaceable, eradicable, removable, washable.
antonyms ineradicable, permanent.

erase *v* blot out, cancel, cleanse, delete, efface, eliminate, eradicate, expunge, get rid of, kill, obliterate, remove, rub out, wipe out.

erasure *n* cancellation, cleansing, deletion, effacement, elimination, eradication, erasement, expunction, obliteration, removal.

erect *adj* engorged, firm, hard, perpendicular, proud, raised, rigid, standing, stiff, straight, tall, taut, tense, tumescent, upright, upstanding, vertical.
antonyms limp, relaxed.
v assemble, build, construct, create, establish, fabricate, form, found, initiate, institute, mount, organize, pitch, put up, raise, rear, set up.

ergo *adv* accordingly, because of this (or that), consequently, for this reason, given this (or that), hence, in consequence, in view of this, on account of this, propter hoc, so, then, therefore, this being the case, thus.

erode *v* abrade, break down, consume, corrade, corrode, decay, destroy, deteriorate, disintegrate, eat away, grind down, spoil, undermine, wear away, wear down.

eroded *adj* abraded, corraded, corroded, destroyed, disintegrated, eaten away, fragmented, ground down, undermined, weatherworn, worn away.

erosion *n* abrasion, attrition, corrasion, corrosion, depletion, destruction, deterioration, diminution, disintegration, fragmentation, undermining, wear and tear.

erosive *adj* caustic, corrosive, destructive, gnawing, nibbling, undermining, wearing.

erotic *adj* amatory, amorous, aphrodisiac, carnal, concupiscent, erogenous, erotogenic, fleshly, libidinous, lustful, rousing, seductive, sensual, sexual, sexy, stimulating, suggestive, titillating, venereal, voluptuous.

err *v* be (in the) wrong, blunder, deviate, fail, go astray, go off the straight and narrow, go wrong, lapse, misapprehend, misbehave, miscalculate, misjudge, mistake, misunderstand, offend, sin, slip up, stray, stumble, transgress, trespass, trip up, wander.

errand *n* assignment, charge, commission, duty, job, message, mission, task.

errant *adj* aberrant, deviant, deviating, drifting, erring, itinerant, journeying, loose, lost, nomadic, offending, peccant, peripatetic, rambling, roaming, roving, sinful, sinning, stray, straying, vagrant, wandering, wayward, wrong.

erratic *adj* aberrant, abnormal, capricious, changeable, desultory, deviant, directionless, disordered, eccentric, fitful, fluctuating, inconsistent, inconstant, irregular, meandering, shifting, temperamental, uncertain, uneven, unpredictable, unreliable, unstable, unsteady, unusual, variable, wandering, wayward.
antonyms consistent, reliable, stable, straight.

erring *adj* aberrant, backsliding, delinquent, deviant, disobedient, errant, faithless, guilty, lapsed, peccant, sinful, sinning, straying, wandering, wayward.

erroneous *adj* amiss, contrary to fact, fallacious, false, faulty, flawed, illogical, imperfect, inaccurate, incorrect, in error, inexact, invalid, mistaken, specious, spurious, unfounded, unsound, untrue, wrong.
antonym correct.

error *n* barbarism, bêtise, blooper, blunder, boner, bungle, corrigendum, delinquency, delusion, deviation, erratum, erroneousness, fallacy, fault, faux pas, flaw, gaucherie, howler, ignorance, ignoratio elenchi, illusion, inaccuracy, incorrectness, inexactitude, iniquity, lapse, lapsus linguae, malapropism, misapprehension, miscalculation, misconception, misdeed, misjudgment, misprint, mistake, misunderstanding, offence, omission, oversight, sin, slip, slip-up, solecism, transgression, trespass, wrong, wrongdoing.

erstwhile *adj* bygone, ex, former, late, old, once, one-time, past, previous, quondam, sometime, that once was, whilom.

erudite *adj* academic, cultivated, cultured, educated, highbrow, knowledgeable, learned, lettered, literate, profound, scholarly, well-educated, well-read, wise.
antonym unlettered.

erudition *n* booklearning, education, knowledge, knowledgeableness, learnedness, learning, letters, profoundness, profundity, scholarliness, scholarship, wisdom.

erupt *v* belch, break (forth or out), burst (forth or out), eject, eruct, eructate, explode, flare, gush, issue forth, rift, spew, spout, vent, vomit.

eruption *n* discharge, ejection, eructation, explosion, flare-up, inflammation, outbreak, outburst, rash, venting.

escalate *v* accelerate, ascend, climb, expand, extend, grow, increase, intensify, mount, rise, spiral, step up.
antonym diminish.

escapade *n* adventure, antic, caper, deed, doings, exploit, fling, gest, lark, prank, romp, scrape, spree, stunt, tear, trick.

escape *v* abscond, avoid, baffle, bolt, break free, break loose, break out, bust out, circumvent, decamp, defect, disappear, do a disappearing act, dodge, duck out (of), elude, emanate, evade, flee, flit, flow, fly, fly the coop, foil, free oneself (from), get away (from), get free (of), get out (of), give the slip, go on the lam, gush, issue, leak, ooze, pour forth, scarper, seep, shake off, skedaddle, skip out, skip town, slip away, slip out of (someone's) grasp, sneak out, take it on the run, take to one's heels, throw off, trickle, vamoose.
n absconding, avoidance, bolt, break, breakout, circumvention, (close) call, (close) shave, decampment, deliverance, distraction, diversion, elusion, escape mechanism,

escapism, evasion, flight, flight of fancy, getaway, jailbreak, out, outlet, pastime, prisonbreak, recreation, release, relaxation, relief, safety valve.

escape route   bolthole, egress, escape road, exit, loophole, out, outlet, secret passage, way out.

escapee *n* absconder, defector, deserter, escape artist, fugitive, jailbreaker, runaway.

escapist *n* daydreamer, dreamer, fantasizer, non-realist, ostrich, wishful thinker.

antonym realist.

eschew *v* abjure, abstain from, avoid, disdain, forgo, forswear, give up, have nothing to do with, keep clear of, never touch, pass up, refrain from, renounce, repudiate, shun, spurn, swear off.

antonym embrace.

escort *n* aide, attendant, beau, bodyguard, chaperone, companion, company, convoy, cortege, entourage, gigolo, guard, guardian, guide, partner, pilot, procession, protection, protector, retinue, safe-conduct, safeguard, squire, suite, train.

v accompany, chaperone, conduct, convoy, go with, guard, guide, lead, partner, protect, shepherd, squire, usher.

esoteric *adj* abstruse, arcane, cabalistic, confidential, cryptic, hermetic, hidden, inner, inscrutable, inside, mysterious, mystic, mystical, obscure, occult, private, recondite, secret.

antonyms exoteric, familiar, popular.

especial *adj* chief, definite, eminent, exceptional, exclusive, express, extraordinary, individual, marked, notable, noteworthy, outstanding, particular, peculiar, pre-eminent, principal, private, remarkable, signal, singular, special, specific, striking, uncommon, unique, unusual.

especially *adv* chiefly, conspicuously, eminently, exceedingly, exceptionally, expressly, extraordinarily, in chief, in the main, mainly, markedly, mostly, notably, noticeably, outstandingly, particularly, passing, peculiarly, predominantly, pre-eminently, principally, remarkably, signally, singularly, specially, specifically, strikingly, supremely, uncommonly, uniquely, unusually, very.

espionage *n* cloak-and-dagger work, counter-intelligence, infiltration, intelligence, reconnaissance, secret investigation, spying, surveillance, undercover operations.

espousal *n* adoption, advocacy, affiance, alliance, backing, betrothal, betrothing, bridal, championing, championship, defence, embrace, engagement, marriage, nuptials, spousal(s), support, troth-plighting, wedding.

espouse *v* adopt, advocate, affiance, back, befriend, betroth, champion, choose, convert to, defend, embrace, marry, opt for, patronize, support, take to wife, take up, wed.

espy *v* behold, catch sight of, descry, detect, discern, discover, distinguish, glimpse, make out, notice, observe, perceive, see, sight, spot, spy.

essay[1] *n* article, assignment, commentary, composition, critique, discourse, disquisition, dissertation, leader, paper, piece, review, squib, term paper, thesis, tract, treatise.

essay[2] *n* attempt, bash, bid, crack, effort, endeavour, experiment, go, shot, stab, test, trial, try, undertaking, venture, whack, whirl.

v attempt, endeavour, give (something) a go (or a whirl), have a bash (or crack or go or stab) at, make an effort, strain, strive, tackle, take on, test, try, undertake.

essence *n* attar, attributes, being, centre, character, characteristics, concentrate, core, crux, decoction, distillate, drift, elixir, ens, entity, extract, fragrance, gist, heart, kernel, life, lifeblood, marrow, meaning, meat, nature, perfume, pith, principle, properties, qualities, quality, quintessence, scent, solution, soul, spirit, spirits, substance, tincture, virtuality.

essential *adj* absolute, a must, basic, cardinal, characteristic, constituent, crucial, definitive, elemental, elementary, formal, fundamental, important, indispensable, indivisible, inherent, innate, intrinsic, key, main, material, necessary, needed, principal, quintessential, required, requisite, substantive, vital.

antonym inessential.

n basic, constituent, definitive, feature, first principle, fundamental, must, necessity, quintessence, requirement, requisite, rudiment, sine qua non.

antonym inessential.

essentially *adv* basically, effectually, for all practical purposes, for the most part, fundamentally, in essence, in substance, in the main, materially, on the whole, per se, primarily, substantially, to all intents and purposes.

establish *v* affirm, ascertain, attest to, authenticate, authorize, base, certify, confirm, constitute, corroborate, create, decree, demonstrate, enact, ensconce, entrench, fix, form, found, ground, implant, inaugurate, ingrain, install, institute, introduce, invent, lodge, nail down, ordain, organize, originate, plant, prove, ratify, root, seat, secure, settle, set up, show, start, station, substantiate, validate, verify.

established *adj* accepted, attested, certified, confirmed, conventional, customary, ensconced, entrenched, experienced, firm, fixed, ingrained, known, ordained, proved, proven, recognized, respected, secure, settled, stated, steadfast, traditional, understood, well-known.

antonyms impermanent, unreliable.

establishment *n* abode, building, business, company, concern, confirmation, construction, corporation, creation, demonstration, determination, domicile, dwelling, edifice, enactment, enterprise, erection, factory, firm, formation, foundation, founding, home, house, household, implantation, inauguration, inception, installation, institute, institution, introduction, invention, ordination, organization, outfit, plant, proof, residence, ruling class, setup, structure, system, the powers that be, the system, validation, verification.

estate *n* assets, barony, belongings, caste, class, condition, demesne, domain, effects, estancia, fortune, goods, grade, hacienda, holdings, house and grounds, lands, lot, manor, order, period, place, position, possessions, property, ranch, rank, situation, stage, standing, state, station, status, wealth.

esteem *v* account, adjudge, admire, approve of, believe, cherish, consider, count, deem, have a high opinion of, hold, honour, judge, like, love, prize, rate, reckon, regard, regard highly, respect, revere, reverence, think, treasure, value, venerate, view.
n admiration, consideration, good opinion, high regard, honour, love, regard, respect, reverence, veneration.

esteemed *adj* admirable, admired, beloved, distinguished, excellent, highly-regarded, honourable, honoured, notable, prized, reputable, respectable, respected, revered, treasured, valued, venerable, venerated, well-respected, well-thought-of, worthy.

estimable *adj* admirable, calculable, commendable, considerable, countable, distinguished, esteemed, excellent, good, honourable, laudable, measurable, meritorious, notable, noteworthy, praiseworthy, reputable, respectable, respected, valuable, valued, worthy.
antonyms contemptible, despicable, insignificant.

estimate *v* appraise, assess, calculate, compute, conjecture, consider, count, evaluate, gauge, guess, judge, number, rank, rate, reckon, surmise, value.
n appraisal, approximation, assessment, calculation, computation, conjecture, estimation, evaluation, guess, guesstimate, judgment, reckoning, surmise, valuation.

estimation *n* account, admiration, appraisal, appreciation, assessment, belief, calculation, computation, conception, consideration, credit, esteem, estimate, evaluation, good opinion, honour, judgment, opinion, rating, reckoning, regard, respect, reverence, veneration, view.

estrange *v* alienate, antagonize, come between, disaffect, disassociate, disunite, divide, drive a wedge between, drive apart, part, put a barrier between, separate, set at odds, set at variance, sever, sunder.
antonyms ally, attract, bind, unite.

estrangement *n* alienation, antagonism, antagonization, antipathy, breach, break-up, disaffection, disharmony, dissociation, disunity, division, hostility, parting, parting of the ways, separation, severance, split, sundering, unfriendliness.

estuary *n* arm, bay, creek, fiord, firth, inlet, mouth, wash.

et cetera and all, and all that, and God knows what else, and more of the same, and others, and so forth, and so on, and stuff like that, and suchlike, and that sort of thing, and the like, and the rest, and whatnot, et al, et alia, et alii, cum multis abiis, etc.

etch *v* burn, carve, cut, engrave, fix, furrow, grave, hatch, impress, imprint, incise, ingrain, inscribe, stamp.

etching *n* carving, cut, design, engraving, impression, imprint, print, sketch.

eternal *adj* abiding, ageless, boundless, ceaseless, changeless, constant, deathless, durable, endless, enduring, eonian, everlasting, illimitable, immortal, immutable, imperishable, incessant, indestructible, infinite, interminable, lasting, limitless, never-ending, perennial, permanent, perpetual, sempiternal, timeless, unceasing, unchanging, undying, unending, unextinguishable, unremitting, without end.
antonyms changeable, ephemeral, temporal.

eternally *adv* ceaselessly, constantly, endlessly, ever and always, everlastingly, forever, immutably, incessantly, indestructibly, in perpetuity, interminably, lastingly, never-endingly, perennially, permanently, perpetually, to the end of time, unceasingly, unendingly, world without end.
antonyms briefly, temporarily.

eternity *n* afterlife, age, ages, ceaselessness, changelessness, endlessness, eon, everlasting, everlastingness, Ewigkeit, forever, heaven, hereafter, illimitability, immortality, immutability, imperishability, incorruptibility, incorruption, infinitude, infinity, long time, next world, paradise, perpetuity, sempiternity, timelessness, world to come.

ethereal *adj* aerial, airy, celestial, delicate, diaphanous, empyreal, exquisite, fairy, fine, ghostly, gossamer, heavenly, immaterial, impalpable, incorporeal, insubstantial, intangible, light, otherworldly, rarefied, refined, spiritual, subtle, tenuous, unearthly, unworldly, vaporous.
antonyms earthly, solid.

ethical *adj* conscientious, correct, decent, fair, fitting, full of integrity, good, high-minded, honest, honourable, just, moral, noble, principled, proper, right, righteous, seemly, unimpeachable, upright, virtuous.
antonym unethical.

ethics *n* code, code of ethics, conscience, deontology, integrity, moral code, morality, moral philosophy, moral values, principles, probity, propriety, rules, standards, values.

ethos *n* attitudes, beliefs, character, code, culture, ethics, ideology, manners, morality, mores, outlook, principle(s), rationale, spirit, standards, tenor, value system, Zeitgeist.

etiquette *n* ceremony, civility, code, convention, conventionalities, correct deportment, correctness, courtesy, customs, decorum, formalities, manners, politeness, propriety, protocol, rules (of conduct), seemliness, social code, social convention, usage, use.

etymology *n* derivation, descent, folk etymology, lexicology, origin, pedigree, philology, semantics, source, word history, word lore.

eulogistic *adj* acclamatory, adulatory, approbatory, celebratory, commendatory, complimentary, congratulatory, encomiastic, favourable, flattering, laudatory, panegyrical.
antonym unfavourable.

eulogize *v* acclaim, adulate, applaud, approve, celebrate, commend, compliment, congratulate, exalt, extol, flatter, glorify, honour, laud, magnify, make much of, pay tribute to, praise, praise to the skies.
antonym condemn.

eulogy *n* acclaim, acclamation, accolade, adulation, applause, bouquet, commendation, compliment, encomium, exaltation, glorification, homage, laud, laudation, paean, panegyric, plaudits, praise, tribute.
antonym condemnation.

euphemism *n* evasion, fig leaf, genteelism, hypocorism, overniceness, polite term, politically correct term, politeness, substitution, understatement.

euphonious *adj* clear, consonant, dulcet, euphonic, harmonious, honeyed, lyrical, mellifluous, mellow, melodic, melodious, musical, pleasant, pleasing (to the ear), silvery, soft, sugared, sweet, sweet-sounding, sweet-toned, symphonious, tuneful.
antonym cacophonous.

euphony *n* consonance, euphoniousness, harmoniousness, harmony, mellifluousness, mellowness, melodiousness, melody, music, musicality, sweet sound, tunefulness.
antonym cacophony.

euphoria *n* bliss, buzz, cloud nine, ecstasy, ecstatics, elation, enthusiasm, exaltation, exhilaration, exuberance, exultation, glee, high, high spirits, intoxication, joy, joyfulness, joyousness, jubilation, rapture, (seventh) heaven, transport.
antonym depression.

euphoric *adj* blissful, ecstatic, elated, enraptured, enthusiastic, exalted, exhilarated, exultant, gleeful, happy, high, in (seventh) heaven, intoxicated, joyful, joyous, jubilant, on cloud nine, overjoyed, rapturous, thrilled (to death).
antonym depressed.

euthanasia *n* assisted suicide, mercy killing, quietus.

evacuate *v* abandon, clear, clear out, decamp, depart, desert, empty, forsake, leave, quit, remove, retire from, vacate, withdraw from.

evacuation[1] *n* abandonment, clearance, clearing (out), clearout, departure, desertion, exodus, leaving, quitting, removal, retreat, vacation, withdrawal.

evacuation[2] *n* catharsis, defecation, discharge, ejection, elimination, emptying, excretion, expulsion, purgation, purging, voidance.

evade *v* avoid, baffle, balk at, chicken out of, circumvent, cop out of, dodge, duck, elude, equivocate, escape, fence, fend off, fudge, get

around, get away from, give the runaround, give the slip, hedge, outwit, parry, prevaricate, put off, quibble, shake, shirk, sidestep, temporize.
antonym face.

evaluate *v* analyse, appraise, assay, assess, calculate, compute, estimate, gauge, judge, measure, price, rank, rate, reckon, size up, value, weigh.

evaluation *n* analysis, appraisal, assessment, calculation, computation, estimate, estimation, judgment, opinion, rating, reckoning, valuation.

evanescence *n* brevity, briefness, disappearance, ephemerality, ephemeralness, evaporation, fleetingness, fugitiveness, impermanence, inconstancy, instability, momentariness, temporariness, transience, transitoriness.
antonym permanence.

evanescent *adj* brief, changing, ephemeral, fading (away), fleeting, fugitive, impermanent, insubstantial, momentary, passing, perishable, short-lived, temporary, tenuous, transient, transitory, unstable, vanishing.
antonym permanent.

evangelical *adj* Bible-believing, born-again, campaigning, crusading, evangelistic, fundamentalist, gospel, missionary, propagandizing, propagandistic, proselytizing, zealous.

evangelize *v* baptize, campaign, convert, crusade, missionize, preach, propagandize, proselytize, spread the gospel.

evaporate *v* condense, dematerialize, disappear, dispel, disperse, dissipate, dissolve, distil, dry (up), evanesce, exhale, fade (away), go up in smoke, melt (away), vanish, vanish into thin air, vaporize.

evaporation *n* condensation, dematerialization, disappearance, dispelling, dispersal, dissipation, dissolution, distillation, drying, evanescence, fading, melting (away), vanishing, vaporization.

evasion *n* artifice, avoidance, casuistry, circumvention, cop-out, cunning, dodge, elusion, equivocation, escape, euphemism, evasiveness, excuse, fencing, fudging, hedging, obfuscation, obliqueness, parrying, pretext, prevarication, put-off, ruse, shiftiness, shirking, shuffling, sophism, sophistry, subterfuge, trickery, weasel words.
antonyms directness, frankness.

evasive *adj* ambiguous, cagey, casuistic, deceptive, elusive, elusory, equivocating, fencing, hedging, indirect, mealy-mouthed, misleading, oblique, parrying, prevaricating, secretive, shifty, shuffling, slippery, sophistic, tricky, uncommunicative, unforthcoming, vague, weaselly.
antonyms direct, forthright, frank.

eve *n* brink, edge, evening, moment, point, threshold, verge.

even *adj* abreast, alike, alongside, balanced, calm, co-equal, commensurate, comparable, constant, cool, drawn, equable, equal, equalized, equanimous, equitable, even-handed, even-tempered, exact, fair, fair and square, fifty-fifty, flat, flush, horizontal, identical, impartial, impassive, imperturbable, interchangeable, just, level, like, matching, metrical, moderate, monotonous, neck and neck, on a level, on a par, peaceful, placid, planar, plumb, proportionate, quits, regular, rhythmic, serene, side by side, similar, smooth, square, stable, steady, straight, symmetrical, tied, tranquil, true, unbroken, undisturbed, unexcitable, unexcited, uniform, unruffled, unvarying, unwavering, well-balanced.

antonyms unequal, uneven.

adv all the (more), as well, directly, exactly, indeed, just, so much as, still, yet.

v align, balance, equal, equalize, flatten, flush, level, match, regularize, regulate, smooth, square, stabilize, steady, straighten.

even so all the same, despite that, however, however that may be, in any case, in spite of that, nevertheless, nonetheless, notwithstanding (that), still, yet.

even-handed *adj* balanced, disinterested, dispassionate, equitable, fair, fair and square, impartial, just, neutral, non-discriminatory, objective, square, unbiassed, unprejudiced, without fear or favour.

antonym inequitable.

evening *n* close of day, crepuscule, day's end, dusk, eve, even, eventide, gloaming, Hesperus, night, nightfall, sundown, sunset, twilight, vesper.

adj crepuscular, twilight, vespertine.

evenness *n* alikeness, balance, calmness, commensurateness, comparability, constancy, coolness, equability, equableness, equality, equanimity, flatness, impassivity, imperturbability, levelness, monotony, peaceableness, placidity, proportion, regularity, rhythm, rhythmicality, serenity, similarity, smoothness, stability, steadiness, straightness, symmetry, tranquillity, trueness, uniformity.

antonyms inequality, unevenness.

event *n* adventure, affair, case, circumstance, competition, contest, entertainment, episode, eventuality, experience, fact, game, happening, incident, instance, match, milestone, occasion, occurrence, outcome, possibility, result, tournament, turn of events, upshot.

even-tempered *adj* calm, composed, cool, cool-headed, equable, equanimous, impassive, imperturbable, level-headed, peaceable, peaceful, phlegmatic, placid, serene, stable, steady, tranquil, unexcitable, unflappable.

antonym excitable.

eventful *adj* active, busy, consequential, critical, crucial, decisive, epochal, exciting, fateful, full of incident, historic, important, interesting, memorable, momentous, notable, noteworthy, portentous, remarkable, significant, unforgettable.

antonyms dull, ordinary, uneventful.

eventual *adj* coming, concluding, consequent, ensuing, final, future, impending, later, planned, projected, prospective, resulting, subsequent, ultimate.

eventuality *n* case, chance, circumstance, contingency, event, happening, happenstance, likelihood, off chance, outcome, outside chance, possibility, probability.

eventually *adv* after all, all in good time, at last, at length, by and by, finally, in due course (of time), in one's own good time, in the end, in the long run, sooner or later, subsequently, ultimately.

ever *adv* always, at all, at all times, at any time, by any chance, ceaselessly, constantly, continually, endlessly, eternally, everlastingly, evermore, forever, in any case, in any circumstances, incessantly, on any account, perpetually, unceasingly, unendingly.

everlasting *adj* abiding, boring, ceaseless, changeless, constant, continual, continuous, deathless, durable, endless, enduring, eternal, immortal, imperishable, incessant, indestructible, infinite, interminable, lasting, monotonous, never-ending, permanent, perpetual, relentless, sempiternal, tedious, timeless, tiresome, unceasing, unchanging, undying, unfading, uninterrupted, unremitting, without end.

antonyms temporary, transient.

evermore *adv* always, eternally, ever, ever after, for all time, for aye, forever, for ever and a day, for ever and ever, for good, for keeps, henceforth, hereafter, in perpetuum, in saecula saeculorum, till doomsday, to the end of time, unceasingly.

everted *adj* evaginated, extrorse, inside out, outside in, reversed, turned inside out, wrong side out.

everybody *n* all and sundry, each and every one, each one, everybody and his brother (or dog), everyone, every Tom Dick and Harry, one and all, the (whole) world, tout le monde.

everyday *adj* accustomed, banal, boring, circadian, common, common-or-garden, commonplace, conventional, customary, daily, diurnal, dull, familiar, frequent, habitual, informal, monotonous, mundane, normal, ordinary, plain, prosaic, quotidian, regular, routine, run-of-the-mill, simple, stock, unexceptional, unimaginative, usual, wonted, workaday.

antonyms exceptional, special.

everyone *n* all and sundry, each one, everybody, every man Jack, every mother's son, one and all, the whole human race, the whole world, tout le monde.

everything *n* all, every last thing, lock stock and barrel, the aggregate, the entirety, the lot, the sum, the total, the whole ball of wax, the whole bunch, the whole (kit and) caboodle, the whole lot, the whole shebang, the whole shooting match, the (whole) works.

everywhere *adv* all along the line, all around, all over, around (or throughout) the world, far and near, far and wide, from Dan to

Beersheba, high and low, in every corner of the world, in every direction, left right and centre, omnipresent, passim, ubiquitous, universally.

evict v boot out, cast out, chuck out, defenestrate, dislodge, dispossess, eject, expel, expropriate, force out, give the bum's rush, kick out, oust, put out, remove, show the door, turf out, turn out.

eviction n defenestration, dislodgment, dispossession, ejection, expropriation, expulsion, ouster, removal, the bum's rush.

evidence n affirmation, attestation, clues, confirmation, corroboration, data, declaration, demonstration, deposition, documentation, facts, grounds, hint, indication, manifestation, mark, pledge, proof, sign, substantiation, suggestion, symptom, testimony, token, voucher, witness.

v affirm, attest to, betray, confirm, demonstrate, denote, display, establish, evince, exhibit, illustrate, indicate, manifest, point to, prove, reveal, show, signify, testify to, witness.

evident adj apparent, clear, clear-cut, conspicuous, detectable, discernible, distinct, incontestable, incontrovertible, indisputable, irrefutable, manifest, noticeable, obvious, ostensible, palpable, patent, perceptible, plain, tangible, undeniable, unmistakable, visible.

antonym uncertain.

evidently adv apparently, clearly, distinctly, manifestly, obviously, ostensibly, outwardly, patently, plainly, seemingly, undoubtedly, unmistakably, unquestionably.

evil adj adverse, bad, baleful, baneful, base, blackguardly, black-hearted, calamitous, catastrophic, corrupt, criminal, cruel, damnable, deadly, deleterious, depraved, destructive, detrimental, devilish, dire, disastrous, flagitious, foul, ghastly, ghoulish, grievous, grim, harmful, heinous, hurtful, immoral, inauspicious, infamous, inimical, iniquitous, injurious, knavish, malefic, maleficent, malevolent, malicious, malignant, mephitic, mischievous, miscreant, nefarious, noisome, noxious, offensive, peccant, perfidious, pernicious, pestiferous, pestilential, poisonous, putrid, rank, reprobate, ruinous, sinful, sinister, ugly, unfortunate, unlucky, unpleasant, unspeakable, vicious, vile, villainous, wicked, woeful, wrong.

n abomination, adversity, affliction, atrocity, badness, bane, baseness, calamity, catastrophe, corruption, curse, damage, demonry, depravity, disaster, distress, flagitiousness, foulness, harm, havoc, heinousness, hydra, ill, immorality, impiety, improbity, iniquity, injury, knavery, maleficence, malignity, mischief, misdeed, misery, misfortune, monstrosity, peccancy, perfidy, reprobacy, ruin, sin, sinfulness, turpitude, ulcer, unrighteousness, vice, viciousness, villainy, wickedness, woe, wrong, wrongdoing.

evil eye baleful glare, blight, charm, curse, hex, hoodoo, jinx, malevolent gaze, spell, voodoo.

evil spirit bogey, demon, devil, evil genius, fiend, ghost, ghoul, goblin, gremlin, hobgoblin, imp, incubus, kelpie, kobold, nightmare, nix, nixie, succubus, troll.

evildoer n bad guy, blackguard, criminal, delinquent, knave, malefactor, malfeasant, miscreant, offender, reprobate, rogue, scamp, scapegrace, scoundrel, sinner, villain, wrongdoer.

evince v attest, bespeak, betoken, betray, declare, demonstrate, display, evidence, exhibit, express, indicate, make clear, manifest, reveal, show, signify.

antonyms conceal, suppress.

eviscerate v devitalize, disembowel, draw, exenterate, gut, weaken.

evocation n activation, actuation, arousal, conjuration, echo, elicitation, excitation, kindling, recall, stimulation, stirring, suggestion, summoning up.

evocative adj impressionistic, powerful, speaking, stirring, striking, suggestive, vivid.

evoke v activate, actuate, arouse, awaken, bring forth, call forth, call up, conjure up, dredge up, educe, elicit, excite, induce, kindle, produce, prompt, provoke, raise, recall, stimulate, stir, summon (up).

antonyms quell, suppress.

▲ **confusable word** invoke.

evolution n adaptation, advance, advancement, ascent, change, Darwinism, descent, development, emergence, growth, improvement, maturation, progress, progression, refinement, ripening, specialization, speciation, unfolding.

evolve v derive, descend, develop, elaborate, emerge, grow, improve, mature, originate, progress, unfold.

exacerbate v add to, aggravate, amplify, deepen, embitter, exaggerate, further provoke, heighten, increase, inflame, intensify, magnify, sharpen, worsen.

antonym soothe.

exact adj absolute, accurate, bang on, blow-by-blow, careful, close, correct, dead on, definite, detailed, explicit, express, factual, faithful, fastidious, finicky, flawless, identical, just, letter-perfect, literal, methodical, meticulous, minute, nice, orderly, painstaking, particular, perfectionistic, precise, punctilious, religious, right, rigorous, scrupulous, severe, specific, strict, true, unambiguous, unequivocal, unerring, veracious, very, word-perfect.

antonym inexact.

v bleed, call for, charge, claim, command, compel, demand, extort, extract, force, impose, insist on, levy, require, requisition, squeeze, take, wrest, wring.

exacting adj arduous, demanding, difficult, exigent, fastidious, fussy, hard, hard to please, harsh, imperious, laborious, oppressive, painstaking, particular, rigid, rigorous, severe, stern, strict, stringent, taxing, toilsome, tough, trying, tyrannical, unsparing.

antonyms easy, tolerant.

exaction n blackmail, bleeding, charge, compulsion, demand, extortion, fee, imposition, milking, rapacity, requirement, requisition, toll.

exactitude n accuracy, attention to, care, carefulness, clarity, correctness, detail, exactness, faithfulness, flawlessness, fidelity, meticulousness, nicety, orderliness, painstakingness, perfectionism, precision, punctilio, punctuality, rigorousness, rigour, scrupulosity, scrupulousness, strictness, thoroughness, truth, veracity.

antonyms carelessness, inaccuracy.

exactly adv absolutely, accurately, bang (on), carefully, correctly, dead (on), definitely, explicitly, expressly, faithfully, flawlessly, just, literally, literatim, methodically, on the dot, particularly, plumb, precisely, punctiliously, quite, religiously, right, rigorously, scrupulously, sharp, specifically, squarely, straight, strictly, to a T, to the letter, to the minute, truly, truthfully, unambiguously, unequivocally, unerringly, veraciously, verbatim, with deadly accuracy, word for word.

interj absolutely, indeed, just so, of course, precisely, quite right, true.

exaggerate v amplify, blow up, caricature, distort, embellish, embroider, hyperbolize, increase, inflate, intensify, lay it on (thick), magnify, misrepresent, overdo, overdraw, overemphasize, overestimate, overrate, oversell, overstate, pile it on, stretch, stretch the truth, talk big.

antonyms belittle, understate.

exaggerated adj amplified, bombastic, blown out of (all) proportion, burlesqued, caricatured, disproportionate, distorted, embellished, euphuistic, excessive, extravagant, hyperbolic, inflated, on the high side, overblown, overdone, overestimated, overrated, overstated, pretentious, tall, turgid.

antonym understated.

exaggeration n amplification, burlesque, caricature, distortion, embellishment, excess, extravagance, hyperbole, inflation, magnification, overemphasis, overestimation, overkill, overrating, overstatement, parody, pretension, pretentiousness, stretching it, tall story, tall tale.

antonyms meiosis, understatement.

exalt v acclaim, adore, aggrandize, apotheosize, applaud, bless, deify, dignify, elate, elevate, ennoble, enthrone, excite, exhilarate, extol, fire (up), glorify, heighten, honour, idolize, laud, lift (up or high), lionize, magnify, praise, praise to the skies, promote, put on a pedestal, raise, revere, reverence, transport, uplift, venerate, worship.

antonym debase.

exaltation[1] n acclaim, acclamation, adoration, adulation, aggrandizement, apotheosis, blessing, deification, dignifying, elevation, eminence, ennoblement, enthronement, extolment, glorification, grandeur, honouring, idealization, idolization, laudation, lionization, loftiness, magnification, panegyric, plaudits,

praise, promotion, raising, reverence, tribute, uplifting, veneration, worship.

antonym debasement.

exaltation[2] n bliss, ecstasy, elation, elevation, euphoria, excitement, exhilaration, joy, joyfulness, joyousness, jubilation, rapture.

exalted[1] adj august, awe-inspiring, awesome, deified, dignified, elevated, eminent, ennobled, glorified, glorious, grand, high, high-minded, high-ranking, honoured, idealized, inflated, lifted high, lionized, lofty, lordly, noble, prestigious, princely, raised, stately, sublime, superior, transcendent, uplifted.

antonym debased.

exalted[2] adj blissful, ecstatic, elated, elevated, excited, exhilarated, exultant, euphoric, happy, in high spirits, in seventh heaven, joyful, joyous, jubilant, rapturous, transported.

examination n analysis, assay, audit, catechism, check, checkup, contemplation, critique, cross-examination, cross-questioning, exam, exploration, hearing, inquest, inquiry, inquisition, inspection, interrogation, investigation, observation, once-over, oral defence, perusal, probe, questioning, quiz, research, review, scan, scrutiny, search, sifting, study, survey, test, trial.

examine v analyse, assay, assess, audit, case, catechize, check (out), consider, contemplate, cross-examine, cross-question, explore, eye, eyeball, grill, inquire into, inspect, interrogate, investigate, observe, peruse, ponder, pore over, probe, question, quiz, research, review, scan, scrutinize, sift through, study, survey, take a (close) look at, test, try, vet, weigh.

examiner n adjudicator, assessor, auditor, censor, critic, cross-examiner, evaluator, inspector, investigator, judge, marker, observer, proctor, questioner, reader, reviewer, scrutineer.

example n archetype, case, case in point, citation, exemplar, exemplification, exemplum, ideal, illustration, instance, lesson, model, object lesson, occurrence, paradigm, paragon, pattern, precedent, prototype, representative, sample, specimen, standard, taste, type, warning.

for example e.g., exempli gratia, par exemple, zum Beispiel.

exasperate v aggravate, anger, annoy, bug, enrage, gall, get, get in (someone's) hair, get on (someone's) nerves, get (someone's) goat, get to, get under (someone's) skin, goad, incense, inflame, infuriate, irk, irritate, madden, nettle, peeve, pique, plague, provoke, rankle, rile, rouse, rub the wrong way, ruffle (someone's) feathers, try the patience of, vex.

antonyms calm, soothe.

exasperated adj aggravated, angered, angry, annoyed, at the end of one's rope or tether, bored, bugged, fed up, galled, incensed, indignant, infuriated, irked, irritated, maddened, nettled, peeved, piqued, provoked, riled, vexed.

exasperating *adj* aggravating, annoying, a pain (in the neck), bothersome, disagreeable, galling, infuriating, irksome, irritating, maddening, pesky, pestiferous, pestilential, provoking, troublesome, vexatious, vexing.

exasperation *n* aggravation, anger, annoyance, displeasure, dissatisfaction, fury, gall, indignation, inflammation, ire, irritation, passion, pique, provocation, rage, resentment, vexation, wrath.
antonym calmness.

excavate *v* burrow, cut, delve, dig, dig out, dig up, disinter, exhume, gouge (out), hollow (out), mine, quarry, sap, scoop (out), stope, trench, tunnel, uncover, undermine, unearth.

excavation *n* burrow, cavity, cut, cutting, dig, digging, diggings, ditch, dugout, hole, hollow, mine, mining, pit, quarry, sapping, shaft, stope, trench, trough, undermining.

exceed *v* beat, better, cap, eclipse, excel, go beyond (or over), outdistance, outdo, outreach, outrival, outrun, outshine, outstrip, overstep, overtake, pass, surpass, top, transcend.

exceeding *adj* amazing, astonishing, exceptional, excessive, extraordinary, extreme, great, outstanding, pre-eminent, superlative, surpassing, transcendent, unequalled, unprecedented, unusual.

exceedingly *adv* amazingly, astonishingly, awfully, enormously, especially, exceptionally, excessively, extraordinarily, extremely, greatly, highly, hugely, inordinately, intensely, only too, overly, passing, superlatively, surpassingly, unprecedentedly, unusually, vastly, very.

excel *v* beat, better, cap, eclipse, exceed, outclass, outdo, outperform, outrank, outrival, outshine, outstrip, overshadow, pass, predominate over, shine, stand out, surpass, top, trump.

excellence *n* class, distinction, eminence, fineness, goodness, greatness, high calibre, merit, nobility, perfection, pre-eminence, purity, quality, skilfulness, superiority, supremacy, transcendence, virtue, water, worth.
antonym inferiority.

excellent *adj* a beaut, a cut above, admirable, A-one, bang-up, boss, brave, bully, capital, champion, choice, commendable, corking, crack, distinguished, estimable, exemplary, exquisite, fine, first-class, first-rate, good, great, high-calibre, high-quality, highly skilled, hot, hot stuff, in a class by itself, laudable, marvellous, meritorious, nonpareil, notable, noted, noteworthy, of the first water, outstanding, peerless, prime, remarkable, ripping, select, splendid, sterling, stunning, superb, supereminent, superior, superlative, surpassing, tiptop, top-flight, top-notch, topping, unequalled, unexampled, unexceptionable, up to scratch or snuff, wonderful, worthy.
antonym inferior.

except *prep* apart from, bar, barring, besides, but, except for, excepting, excluding, exclusive of, leaving out, less, minus, not counting, omitting, other than, outside of, save, saving.
v eliminate, exclude, exempt, leave out, omit, pass over, rule out.
▲ *confusable word* accept.

exception *n* abnormality, anomaly, curiosity, departure, deviation, exclusion, exemption, freak, inconsistency, irregularity, issue, objection, oddity, omission, rare instance, special case.

exceptional *adj* aberrant, abnormal, anomalous, atypical, curious, deviant, excellent, extraordinary, freakish, irregular, marvellous, notable, noteworthy, odd, out of the ordinary, outstanding, peculiar, phenomenal, quirky, rare, remarkable, singular, special, strange, striking, superior, superlative, uncommon, unconventional, unequalled, unexpected, unusual.
antonyms mediocre, unexceptional.

exceptionally *adv* abnormally, amazingly, especially, excellently, extraordinarily, marvellously, notably, outstandingly, peculiarly, phenomenally, remarkably, singularly, splendidly, strikingly, superlatively, uncommonly, unusually, wonderfully.

excerpt *n* citation, extract, extraction, fragment, part, passage, portion, quotation, quote, scrap, section, selection.
v borrow, cite, crib, cull, extract, lift, quote, select.

excess *n* balance, debauchery, diarrhea, dissipation, dissoluteness, excessiveness, exorbitance, extravagance, extreme(s), glut, gluttony, immoderation, intemperance, leftover, libertinism, licentiousness, nimiety, overabundance, overage, overdose, overflow, overindulgence, overkill, overload, plethora, prodigality, remainder, superabundance, superfluity, surfeit, surplus, unrestraint.
antonyms dearth, insufficiency.
adj additional, extra, leftover, redundant, remaining, residual, spare, superfluous, supernumerary, surplus, unneeded, unwanted.
antonym insufficient.

excessive *adj* disproportionate, exaggerated, exorbitant, extravagant, extreme, fanatical, high, immoderate, inordinate, intemperate, needless, nimious, outrageous, overdone, overmuch, over the top, prodigal, profligate, steep, stiff, supererogatory, superfluous, unasked-for, uncalled-for, unconscionable, undue, unnecessary, unneeded, unreasonable, unrestrained.
antonym insufficient.

excessively *adv* disproportionately, exaggeratedly, exorbitantly, extravagantly, extremely, fanatically, immoderately, inordinately, intemperately, needlessly, outrageously, overly, overmuch, prodigally, superfluously, to a fault, to extremes, too, too much, unconscionably, unduly, unnecessarily, unreasonably.
antonym insufficiently.

exchange *v* bandy, barter, change, commute, convert, interchange, reciprocate, replace, substitute, swap, switch, toss back and forth, trade.

n banter, bargain, barter, bourse, chat, commerce, communication, conversation, converse, conversion, deal, dealing(s), dialogue, interchange, intercourse, market, quid pro quo, reciprocation, reciprocity, replacement, substitution, swap, switch, tit for tat, trade, traffic, truck.

excise[1] *n* customs, duty, impost, levy, surcharge, tariff, tax, toll, value-added tax, VAT.

excise[2] *v* bowdlerize, censor, cut (away), cut out, delete, eradicate, erase, expunge, expurgate, extirpate, extract, remove.

excision *n* bowdlerization, deletion, eradication, expunction, expurgation, extirpation, extraction, removal.

excitable *adj* edgy, emotional, explosive, feisty, fiery, hasty, high-strung, hot-headed, hot-tempered, inflammable, irascible, mercurial, nervous, nervy, passionate, prickly, quick-tempered, restive, restless, sensitive, susceptible, temperamental, unstable, violent, volatile, volcanic.

antonyms calm, impassive.

excite *v* activate, actuate, affect, agitate, animate, arouse, awaken, discompose, disturb, elate, electrify, fire (up), foment, fluster, galvanize, ignite, impassion, impress, incite, induce, inflame, inspire, instigate, interest, kindle, motivate, move, provoke, quicken, raise to a fever pitch, rattle, rouse, stimulate, stir to action, stir (up), sway, thrill, titillate, touch, turn on, upset, waken, whet, work into a lather, work up.

antonyms bore, quell.

excited *adj* aflame, agitated, agog, animated, aroused, awakened, breathless, Corybantic, discomposed, disturbed, eager, elated, emotional, enthused, enthusiastic, feverish, flurried, flustered, high, impassioned, keyed up, lathered up, moved, nervous, overwrought, restive, restless, roused, ruffled, stimulated, stirred (up), thrilled, titillated, turned on, upset, whipped up, wild, worked up, wrought up.

antonyms apathetic, bored.

excitement *n* action, activity, ado, adventure, agitation, animation, anticipation, arousal, brouhaha, clamour, commotion, discomposure, eagerness, elation, emotion, enthusiasm, excitation, exhilaration, ferment, fervour, fever, flurry, flutter, fomentation, furor, fuss, heat, hubbub, hue and cry, hurly-burly, incitement, kafuffle, kicks, passion, perturbation, restlessness, stimulation, stimulus, stirring up, thrill(s), titillation, unrest.

antonyms apathy, calm.

exciting *adj* action-packed, adventurous, arousing, breathtaking, cliff-hanging, electrifying, encouraging, enthralling, exhilarating, impressive, inspiring, intoxicating, moving, piquant, promising, provocative, rousing, sensational, stimulating, stirring, suspenseful, swashbuckling, tantalizing, thrilling, titillating.

antonyms boring, unexciting.

exclaim *v* blurt (out), call (out), cry (out), declare, ejaculate, interject, shout (out), vociferate.

exclamation *n* call, cry, ejaculation, expletive, interjection, outburst, outcry, shout, vociferation.

exclamatory *adj* blurted, dramatic, ejaculatory, interjectional, melodramatic, sensationalist, theatrical.

exclude *v* anathematize, ban, bar, blackball, blacklist, boycott, cut off, debar, disallow, eliminate, embargo, except, excommunicate, expel, forbid, freeze out, ignore, interdict, keep out, leave out, lock out, omit, ostracize, preclude, prohibit, proscribe, reject, remove, repudiate, rule out, send to Coventry, shut out, slight, veto.

antonyms admit, allow, include.

exclusion *n* ban, bar, barring, boycott, debarment, elimination, embargo, exception, excommunication, expulsion, forbidding, interdict, non-admission, omission, ostracization, preclusion, prohibition, proscription, rejection, removal, repudiation, veto.

antonyms admittance, allowance, inclusion.

exclusive *adj* absolute, choice, clannish, classy, cliquey, cliquish, closed, complete, confined, definitive, discriminative, esoteric, excluding, full, high-end, insular, limited, luxurious, monopolistic, narrow, one of a kind, only, peculiar, posh, pricey, private, restricted, restrictive, select, selective, snobbish, sole, total, undivided, unique, unshared, upscale, whole.

exclusive of barring, debarring, except, except for, excepting, excluding, leaving out, not counting, not including, omitting, ruling out.

antonym inclusive of.

excommunicate *v* anathematize, ban, banish, bar, blacklist, condemn, curse, cut off, debar, denounce, eject, exclude, execrate, exile, expel, outlaw, proscribe, remove, repudiate, unchurch.

excrescence *n* appendage, bump, growth, intumescence, knob, lump, misgrowth, outgrowth, process, projection, prominence, protrusion, protuberance, swelling, tumour, wart.

excrete *v* defecate, discharge, egest, eject, eliminate, evacuate, expel, exude, give off, pass, relieve oneself, secrete, urinate, void.

excretion *n* defecation, discharge, droppings, dung, egesta, ejection, elimination, evacuation, excrement, excreta, exudate, expulsion, exudation, feces, ordure, perspiration, pus, scat, secretion, stool, sweat, urination, urine, voidance, waste (matter).

excretory *adj* defecatory, egestive, emunctory, excremental, excretive, exudative, fecal, perspiratory, sudatory, sudorific, urinary.

excruciating *adj* acute, agonizing, bitter, burning, exquisite, extreme, harrowing, insufferable, intense, intolerable, painful, piercing, racking, savage, searing, severe, sharp, stabbing, tormenting, torturing, torturous, unbearable, unendurable.

exculpate *v* absolve, acquit, clear, deliver, discharge, excuse, exonerate, forgive, free from blame, justify, let off, pardon, prove innocent, release, vindicate.

antonyms blame, condemn.

exculpation *n* absolution, acquittal, clearing, discharge, excuse, exoneration, freedom, justification, pardon, release, vindication.

antonym condemnation.

excursion *n* airing, breather, day trip, detour, deviation, digression, divagation, drive, episode, excursus, expedition, jaunt, journey, junket, outing, pleasure trip, ramble, ride, sashay, tour, trip, walk, wandering.

excusable *adj* allowable, defensible, explainable, explicable, forgivable, ignorable, justifiable, minor, pardonable, permissible, slight, tolerable, understandable, venial, vindicable, warrantable.

antonym blameworthy.

excuse *v* absolve, acquit, apologize for, clear of blame, condone, defend, discharge, exculpate, exempt, exonerate, explain, extenuate, forgive, free, ignore, indulge, justify, let off, liberate, mitigate, overlook, palliate, pardon, release, relieve, spare, tolerate, vindicate, warrant, wink at.

n alibi, apology, cop-out, defence, evasion, exculpation, exemption, exoneration, expedient, explanation, extenuation, grounds, justification, makeshift, mitigation, out, palliation, plea, pretence, pretext, put-off, rationale, rationalization, reason, regrets, semblance, substitute, travesty, vindication.

execrable *adj* abhorrent, abominable, accursed, appalling, atrocious, awful, base, cursed, damnable, deplorable, despicable, detestable, disgusting, foul, frightful, hateful, heinous, horrible, loathsome, nauseous, obnoxious, odious, offensive, repulsive, revolting, shocking, sickening, terrible, vile.

antonyms admirable, estimable.

execrate *v* abhor, abominate, anathematize, berate, blast, condemn, curse, damn, denounce, deplore, despise, detest, excoriate, fulminate against, hate, inveigh against, loathe, revile, vilify, vituperate.

antonyms commend, praise.

execration *n* abhorrence, abomination, anathema, condemnation, contempt, curse, damnation, detestation, excoriation, fulmination, hate, hatred, imprecation, invective, loathing, malediction, odium, revilement, vilification, vituperation.

antonyms commendation, praise.

execute[1] *v* behead, burn at the stake, capitally punish, crucify, decapitate, electrocute, garrote, guillotine, hang, kill, liquidate, lynch, put to death, shoot.

execute[2] *v* accomplish, administer, carry out, complete, consummate, deliver, discharge, dispatch, do, effect, effectuate, enact, enforce, expedite, finish, fulfil, implement, perform,

prosecute, put into effect, realize, render, run, seal, serve, sign, transact, validate.

execution[1] *n* auto-da-fé, beheading, burning, capital punishment, crucifixion, death, death penalty, decapitation, dispatch, electrocution, firing squad, garrote, guillotining, hanging, killing, lynching, lynch law, shooting, the (electric) chair.

execution[2] *n* accomplishment, administration, completion, consummation, delivery, discharge, dispatch, effectuation, enactment, enforcement, implementation, manner, mode, operation, performance, prosecution, realization, rendering, rendition, style, technique, transaction, warrant, writ.

executioner *n* assassin, exterminator, garrotter, hangman, headsman, hired gun, hit man, killer, liquidator, lyncher, murderer, slayer.

executive *n* administration, administrator, (board of) directors, board of governors, controller, director, directorate, executive officer(s), government, hierarchy, leadership, management, manager, official, organizer.

adj administrative, controlling, decision-making, directing, directorial, governing, gubernatorial, guiding, leading, managerial, organizational, organizing, regulating, supervisory.

exemplar *n* archetype, copy, embodiment, epitome, example, exemplification, ideal, illustration, instance, model, paradigm, paragon, pattern, prototype, representative, specimen, standard, type, yardstick.

exemplary *adj* admirable, admonitory, cautionary, commendable, correct, deterrent, estimable, excellent, faultless, flawless, good, honourable, ideal, laudable, meritorious, model, monitory, praiseworthy, punctilious, sterling, unexceptionable, warning, worthy.

antonyms imperfect, unworthy.

exemplify *v* demonstrate, depict, display, embody, epitomize, evidence, exhibit, illustrate, instance, instanciate, manifest, represent, show, typify.

exempt *v* absolve, acquit, discharge, dismiss, except, excuse, exonerate, free, let off, liberate, make an exception for, release, relieve, spare.

adj absolved, acquitted, clear, discharged, excepted, excluded, excused, free, immune, liberated, released, spared.

antonym liable.

exemption *n* absolution, discharge, dispensation, exception, exclusion, exoneration, freedom, immunity, indulgence, pardon, privilege, release.

antonym liability.

exercise *v* agitate, annoy, apply, bring to bear, burden, carry out, discharge, discipline, distress, disturb, drill, employ, engross, exert, fulfil, keep fit, make use of, occupy, perform, perturb, ply, practise, preoccupy, put into use, train, trouble, try, upset, use, utilize, vex, warm up, wield, work, work out, worry.

n action, activity, aerobics, application,

assignment, athletics, constitutional, daily dozen, discharge, discipline, drill, drilling, effort, employment, enjoyment, exertion, fitness routine, fulfilment, implementation, labour, lesson, participation, practice, problem, task, training, use, utilization, war game, working, workout, working out.

exert v apply, bring to bear, employ, exercise, expend, put forth, use, utilize, wield.

exert oneself apply oneself, concentrate, do one's best, endeavour, labour, spare no effort, strain, strive, struggle, sweat, take pains, toil, try hard, work.

exertion n action, application, assiduity, attempt, diligence, effort, employment, endeavour, exercise, industry, labour, pains, perseverance, sedulousness, strain, stretch, struggle, toil, travail, use, utilization, work.

antonyms idleness, rest.

exhalation n air, breath, breathing (out), discharge, effluvium, efflux, emanation, emission, exhaust, expiration, fume(s), miasma, mist, outflow, respiration, smoke, steam, vapour(s).

antonym inhalation.

exhale v breathe (out), discharge, emanate, emit, expel, expire, exude, give off, issue, pass off, respire.

antonym inhale.

exhaust v bankrupt, beggar, burn out, consume, cripple, debilitate, deplete, disable, dissipate, do in, drain, dry up, empty, enervate, enfeeble, expend, fatigue, finish, impoverish, overtax, overtire, overwork, prostrate, run through, sap, spend, squander, strain, tax, tire (out), tucker out, use up, waste, weaken, wear out, weary.

antonym refresh.

n discharge, effluvium, emanation, emission, exhalation, fumes, miasma.

exhausted adj all gone, all in, bare, barren, beat, burned out, bushed, consumed, crippled, dead, dead beat, dead on one's feet, dead tired, debilitated, depleted, disabled, dissipated, dog-tired, done for, done in, drained, dry, effete, empty, enervated, enfeebled, expended, fagged (out), fatigued, finished, gone, jaded, pooped, prostrated, ready to drop, run ragged, sapped, spent, squandered, tired out, tuckered out, used up, washed-out, washed-up, wasted, weak, weary, whacked (out), worn out, worn to a frazzle, zonked.

antonyms conserved, fresh, vigorous.

exhausting adj arduous, backbreaking, crippling, debilitating, difficult, draining, enervating, fatiguing, formidable, gruelling, hard, killing, laborious, punishing, sapping, severe, strenuous, taxing, testing, tiring, vigorous.

antonyms effortless, refreshing.

exhaustion n burnout, consumption, debilitation, depletion, effeteness, emptying, enervation, fatigue, feebleness, impoverishment, inanition, jet lag, lassitude, prostration, tiredness, weariness.

antonym freshness.

exhaustive adj all-embracing, all-inclusive, complete, comprehensive, definitive, detailed, encyclopedic, extensive, far-reaching, full, full-scale, in-depth, intensive, sweeping, thorough, thoroughgoing, total.

antonym incomplete.

exhibit v demonstrate, disclose, display, evidence, evince, expose, flaunt, indicate, manifest, parade, present, put on display, reveal, show, showcase, sport.

antonym hide.

n booth, collection, display, evidence, exhibition, illustration, model, show, showcase.

exhibition n array, demonstration, display, exhibit, expo, exposition, fair, flaunting, manifestation, performance, presentation, show, showcase, showing, spectacle.

exhibitionist n attention-seeker, extrovert, flasher, pervert, self-advertiser, show-off.

exhilarate v animate, cheer, delight, elate, energize, enliven, exalt, excite, gladden, hearten, inspirit, invigorate, lift, refresh, stimulate, thrill, vitalize.

antonyms bore, discourage.

exhilarating adj cheering, energizing, enlivening, euphoriant, exalting, exciting, exhilarant, gladdening, inspiring, invigorating, refreshing, stimulating, thrilling, vitalizing.

antonyms boring, discouraging.

exhilaration n animation, ardour, cheer, delight, elation, euphoria, exaltation, excitement, gaiety, gladness, glee, gleefulness, gusto, high spirits, hilarity, joy, joyfulness, liveliness, merriment, mirth, sprightliness, stimulation, thrill, zeal.

antonyms boredom, discouragement.

exhort v admonish, advise, beseech, bid, call upon, caution, counsel, encourage, enjoin, entreat, implore, inspire, persuade, plead with, preach (to), press, remind, spur, stir up, urge, warn.

exhortation n admonition, advice, beseeching, bidding, caution, counsel, encouragement, enjoinder, entreaty, homily, lecture, persuasion, plea, preaching, reminder, sermon, urging, warning.

exhortatory adj admonitory, begging, beseeching, cautionary, encouraging, imploring, persuasive, preachy.

exhume v bring to light, bring to the surface, dig up, disentomb, disinhume, disinter, excavate, unbury, unearth.

antonym bury.

exigency n acuteness, bind, constraint, crisis, criticalness, crunch, demand, difficulty, distress, emergency, extremity, fix, hardship, imperativeness, jam, juncture, necessity, need, needfulness, pass, pickle, pinch, plight, predicament, pressure, quandary, requirement, scrape, strait, stress, urgency.

exigent adj acute, arduous, compelling, constraining, critical, crucial, demanding, difficult, exacting, exhausting, hard, harsh, high-priority, imperative, importunate, insistent,

life-and-death, necessary, needful, pressing, rigorous, severe, stiff, strict, stringent, taxing, tough, urgent.
antonym mild.

exile *n* banishment, deportation, deportee, émigré, expatriate, expatriation, expulsion, ostracism, outcast, proscription, refugee, separation.
v banish, deport, drive out, expatriate, expel, ostracize, oust, proscribe.

exist *v* abide, be, be available, be extant, be found, be on the books, be real, breathe, continue, endure, happen, have one's being, last, live, obtain, occur, prevail, remain, reside, stand, subsist, survive.

existence *n* actuality, being, breath, continuance, continuation, duration, endurance, esse, history, inbeing, life, lifestyle, occurrence, presence, reality, subsistence, survival, way of life.
antonym non-existence.

existent *adj* actual, around, current, enduring, existing, extant, living, obtaining, on the books, present, prevailing, real, remaining, standing, surviving.
antonym non-existent.

exit *n* adieu, aperture, congé, death, departure, door, doorway, egress, evacuation, exodus, farewell, gate, going, leave-taking, outlet, retirement, retreat, vent, way out, withdrawal.
antonym entrance.
v depart, die, find vent, go offstage, go out (or away), issue, leave, retire, retreat, take one's leave, withdraw.

exodus *n* departure, emigration, evacuation, exit, flight, hegira, leaving, long march, migration, retirement, retreat, withdrawal.

exonerate *v* absolve, acquit, clear, declare innocent, deliver, discharge, dismiss, exculpate, excuse, exempt, free, justify, let off, liberate, prove innocent, release, relieve, vindicate.
antonym incriminate.

exoneration *n* absolution, acquittal, clearing, deliverance, discharge, dismissal, exception, exculpation, exemption, freeing, immunity, justification, liberation, release, relief, vindication.
antonym incrimination.

exorbitance *n* excess, excessiveness, extravagance, immoderateness, inordinateness, monstrousness, outrageousness, preposterousness, unfairness, unreasonableness.
antonyms fairness, reasonableness.

exorbitant *adj* enormous, exaggerated, excessive, extortionate, extravagant, extreme, immoderate, inflated, inordinate, monstrous, outrageous, over the top, preposterous, tall, unconscionable, undue, unreasonable, unwarranted.
antonyms fair, reasonable.

exorcise *v* adjure, banish, cast out, deliver, drive out, expel, get rid of, lay (ghosts), purify.

exotic *adj* alien, bizarre, colourful, curious, different, extraordinary, fascinating, foreign, foreign-looking, glamorous, imported, introduced, mysterious, outlandish, out-of-the-way, outré, peculiar, rare, recherché, strange, striking, unfamiliar, unusual.
antonyms familiar, ordinary, run-of-the-mill.

expand *v* amplify, augment, bloat, blow up (or out), branch out, broaden, develop, dilate, distend, diversify, elaborate, embellish, enlarge (on), expatiate, expound, extend, fatten, fill out, flesh out, grow, increase, inflate, lengthen, magnify, multiply, open (out), outspread, prolong, protract, puff out, snowball, spread (out), spread outward, stretch (out), swell (out), unfold, unfurl, unravel, unroll, wax, widen.
antonyms contract, précis.

expanse *n* area, body, breadth, extent, field, plain, range, sheet, space, spread, surface, stretch, sweep, tract, vastness, wideness.

expansible *adj* distensible, distensile, expandable, expansile, extensible, extensile, inflatable, stretchy.

expansion *n* amplification, augmentation, branching out, development, dilatation, dilation, distension, diversification, enlargement, extension, growth, increase, inflation, magnification, multiplication, spread(ing), swelling, unfolding, unfurling.
antonym contraction.

expansive *adj* affable, all-embracing, broad, communicative, comprehensive, dilating, distensible, easy, effusive, elastic, expanding, expatiating, extendable, extensive, extrovert(ed), far-reaching, free, friendly, garrulous, genial, inclusive, loquacious, open, outgoing, sociable, spacious, stretchy, swelling, talkative, thorough, unreserved, voluminous, warm, wide, wide-ranging, widespread.
antonyms cold, reserved.

expatiate (on) *v* amplify, descant (on), develop, dilate on, dwell on, elaborate on, embellish, enlarge on, expand (on), expound on.

expatriate *n* deportee, displaced person, DP, emigrant, émigré, exile, foreigner, refugee.
v banish, deport, eject, exile, expel, ostracize, oust, proscribe.
adj banished, emigrant, émigré, exiled.

expect *v* anticipate, assume, await, bank on, bargain for, believe, calculate on, conjecture, contemplate, count on, demand, envisage, forecast, foresee, guess, have in mind, hope for, imagine, insist on, look for, look forward to, predict, presume, project, reckon (on), suppose, surmise, take for granted, think, trust, wait for, want.

expectancy *n* alertness, anticipation, curiosity, eagerness, expectation, hope, optimism, readiness, suspense, waiting.

expectant *adj* agog, alert, anticipating, anxious, awaiting, curious, eager, enceinte, expecting, full of anticipation, gravid, hopeful, in expectation, in suspense, on tenterhooks, optimistic, pregnant, ready, waiting, watchful.

expectantly *adv* eagerly, expectingly, hopefully, in anticipation, optimistically, with bated breath, with breathless anticipation.

expectation *n* anticipation, apprehension, assumption, assurance, belief, calculation, chance, confidence, demand, eagerness, expectancy, fear, forecast, hope, insistence, likelihood, optimism, outlook, possibility, prediction, presumption, probability, projection, promise, prospect, requirement, supposition, surmise, suspense, trust, understanding, want, wish.

expected *adj* anticipated, assumed, awaited, due, eagerly awaited, hoped-for, imminent, long-awaited, longed-for, long-overdue, predicted, promised, taken for granted, understood.

antonym unexpected.

expecting *adj* carrying a child, enceinte, expectant, gravid, in the family way, pregnant, with child.

expediency *n* advantage, advantageousness, advisability, appropriateness, aptness, benefit, convenience, desirability, effectiveness, fitness, gainfulness, helpfulness, judiciousness, meetness, opportunism, practicality, pragmatism, profitability, profitableness, propriety, prudence, self-interest, suitability, timeliness, usefulness, utilitarianism, utility, wisdom.

expedient *adj* advantageous, advisable, appropriate, beneficial, convenient, desirable, effective, fitting, helpful, judicious, meet, opportune, opportunistic, politic, practical, pragmatic, profitable, proper, prudent, serviceable, suitable, timely, useful, utilitarian, wise, worthwhile.

antonym inexpedient.

n artifice, contrivance, device, dodge, makeshift, manoeuvre, means, measure, method, resort, resource, ruse, scheme, shift, stopgap, stratagem, substitute.

▲ *confusable word* expeditious.

expedite *v* accelerate, advance, aid, assist, dispatch, facilitate, forward, further, hasten, hurry, precipitate, promote, quicken, rush, speed up.

antonym delay.

expedition[1] *n* campaign, company, crusade, enterprise, excursion, exploration, explorers, hike, journey, mission, outing, party, pilgrimage, quest, raid, ramble, safari, sail, team, tour, travellers, trek, trip, undertaking, voyage, voyagers.

expedition[2] *n* alacrity, briskness, celerity, dispatch, expeditiousness, facilitation, furtherance, haste, hurry, immediacy, promptness, quickness, rapidity, readiness, speed, swiftness.

antonym delay.

expeditious *adj* active, alert, brisk, diligent, efficient, fast, hasty, immediate, instant, prompt, quick, rapid, ready, speedy, swift.

antonym slow.

▲ *confusable word* expedient.

expel *v* ban, banish, bar, belch, blackball, boot out, breathe out, cast out, disbar, discharge, dislodge, dismiss, drive out, drum out, egest, eject, evict, exclude, exile, expatriate, extrude, force out, give the boot, oust, proscribe, remove, send packing, spew, suspend, throw out, turf out.

antonym admit.

expend *v* consume, disburse, dissipate, employ, exhaust, fork out, lay out, pay (out), shell out, spend, use, use up, waste.

antonym save.

expendable *adj* consumable, dispensable, disposable, inessential, non-essential, replaceable, unimportant, unnecessary.

antonyms indispensable, necessary.

expenditure *n* application, charge, consumption, cost, debit, disbursement, expense, outgo, outgoings, outlay, output, payment, spending.

antonyms profit, revenue, savings.

expense *n* charge, cost, damage, disbursement, expenditure, loss, outlay, output, payment, price, sacrifice, spending, toll, use.

expenses *n* costs, charges, damages, debits, expenditures, incidentals, outlay, overhead.

expensive *adj* beyond one's means, capital-intensive, costly, dear, excessive, exorbitant, extortionate, extravagant, high-priced, inordinate, lavish, overpriced, rich, steep, stiff.

antonyms cheap, inexpensive.

experience *n* adventure, affair, contact, doing, encounter, episode, event, exposure, familiarity, first-hand knowledge, happening, incident, involvement, know-how, knowledge, observation, occurrence, ordeal, practical knowledge, practice, proof, taste, test, the school of hard knocks, training, trial, understanding.

antonym inexperience.

v apprehend, behold, empathize, encounter, endure, face, feel, have, know, live through, meet (with), observe, perceive, sample, sense, suffer, survive, sustain, take part in, taste, try, undergo.

experienced *adj* accomplished, adept, broken-in, capable, competent, expert, familiar, habitual, hardened, knowing, knowledgeable, master, mature, practised, professional, qualified, schooled, seasoned, skilful, sophisticated, streetwise, tested, trained, travelled, tried, veteran, well-versed, wise, worldly, worldly-wise.

antonym inexperienced.

experiment *n* assay, attempt, ballon d'essai, experimentation, foray, investigation, pilot project, procedure, proof, research, sally, test, trial, trial and error, trial run, venture.

v assay, dabble, explore, investigate, research, sample, test, try, verify.

experimental *adj* avant-garde, empirical, exploratory, heuristic, hit-or-miss, pilot, preliminary, probationary, provisional, speculative, tentative, test, trial, trial-and-error.

expert *n* ace, adept, authority, boffin, connoisseur, dab (hand), maestro, master, maven, past master, pro, professional, specialist, virtuoso, wizard.

adj able, adept, adroit, apt, authoritative, brilliant, crack, deft, dexterous, experienced, facile, finished, handy, knowledgeable, master, masterly, polished, practised, professional, proficient, qualified, shark, skilful, skilled, trained, virtuoso, well-versed.

antonym novice.

expertise *n* ability, adeptness, adroitness, command, competence, deftness, dexterity, expertness, facility, finesse, judgment, knack, know-how, knowledge, masterliness, mastery, proficiency, savoir-faire, skilfulness, skill, virtuosity, wizardry.

antonym inexpertness.

expiate *v* atone for, do penance for, make amends for, make up for, propitiate, purge, wipe out.

expiation *n* amends, atonement, compensation, penance, propitiation, purging, ransom, recompense, redemption, redress, reparation, shrift.

expiatory *adj* atoning, expiating, propitiatory, purgative, redemptive.

expiration *n* cessation, close, conclusion, death, decease, demise, departure, dissolution, end, exhalation, expiry, finis, finish, lapse, termination.

antonyms beginning, continuation.

expire *v* become invalid, become void, breathe out, cease, close, conclude, decease, depart, die, discontinue, end, exhale, finish, lapse, pass, pass away, perish, run out, stop, terminate.

antonyms begin, continue.

explain *v* account for, annotate, articulate, clarify, clear up, construe, decipher, decode, define, demonstrate, describe, elucidate, excuse, explicate, expound, gloss, illustrate, interpret, justify, lay out, make clear, rationalize, resolve, set out (or forth), shed light on, simplify, solve, spell out, teach, translate, unfold, unravel, untangle.

antonyms obfuscate, obscure.

explanation *n* account, annotation, answer, apology, articulation, cause, clarification, comment, construction, defense, definition, demonstration, description, éclaircissement, elucidation, excuse, exegesis, explication, exposition, footnote, gloss, illustration, interpretation, justification, key, legend, meaning, motive, rationale, rationalization, reason, resolution, significance, solution, theory, translation, whys and wherefores.

explanatory *adj* annotative, apologetic, clarifying, demonstrative, descriptive, elucidative, exegetical, explicative, expository, illuminative, illustrational, illustrative, interpretive, justifying, rationalizing.

explicable *adj* accountable, definable, describable, determinable, explainable, intelligible, interpretable, justifiable, resolvable, solvable, understandable.

explicate *v* analyse, clarify, construct, develop, elucidate, evolve, explain, expound, formulate, interpret, lay out, set forth, unfold, unravel, untangle, work out.

antonyms confuse, obscure.

explicit *adj* blow-by-blow, candid, categorical, clear, declared, definite, detailed, direct, distinct, express, flat (-out), forthright, frank, graphic, implicit, open, outspoken, patent, plain, positive, precise, specific, stated, straight, straightforward, straight-out, unambiguous, understood, unequivocal, unmincing, umistakable, unqualified, unreserved.

antonyms inexplicit, vague.

▲ *confusable word* implicit.

explode *v* belie, blast, blow to bits, blow sky-high, blow up, boom, burst, debunk, detonate, discharge, discredit, disprove, erupt, fly apart, fulminate, give the lie to, go off, go up in smoke, invalidate, knock the bottom out of, poke full of holes, rebut, refute, repudiate, set off, shatter, skyrocket.

antonym prove.

exploit *n* accomplishment, achievement, adventure, attainment, deed, feat, gest, stunt, tour de force.

v abuse, bleed, capitalize on, cash in on, fleece, impose on, make capital of, manipulate, milk, misuse, oppress, profit by, rape, rip off, skin, soak, take advantage of, turn to account, use, utilize.

exploitation *n* abuse, imposition, manipulation, misuse, rape, rip-off, sexploitation.

exploration *n* analysis, close look, examination, expedition, inquiry, inquisition, investigation, probe, reconnaissance, research, safari, search, study, survey, touring, travel, voyage.

exploratory *adj* analytical, examining, experimental, fact-finding, investigative, pilot, probing, searching, tentative, trial.

explore *v* analyse, case, examine, inquire into, investigate, look into, probe, prospect, reconnoitre, research, scout, search through, sift through, survey, tour, travel, traverse.

explosion *n* bang, blast, blowup, bomb, boom, burst, clap, crack, debunking, detonation, discharge, discrediting, eruption, fit, flare-up, fulmination, outbreak, outburst, paroxysm, refutation, report, shattering.

explosive *adj* charged, dangerous, excitable, fiery, hazardous, perilous, stormy, tense, touchy, ugly, unstable, violent, volatile, volcanic.

antonym calm.

n cordite, dynamite, gelignite, gunpowder, lyddite, melinite, nitroglycerine, powder, TNT.

exponent *n* advocate, apologist, backer, believer, champion, commentator, defender, demonstration, elucidator, example, exegete, exemplar, expositor, expounder, illustration, interpreter, model, promoter, propagandist, proponent, representative, sample, specimen, spokesman, spokesperson, spokeswoman, supporter, symbol, type, upholder.

expose v air, bare, betray, blow the whistle on, bring into the open, bring to light, debunk, denounce, detect, disclose, display, divulge, exhibit, lay bare, lay open (to view), make known, manifest, present, reveal, show (up), uncover, unearth, unmask, unveil.

antonyms cover, shelter.

expose to acquaint with, bring in contact with, familiarize with, introduce to, lay open to, make liable to, make vulnerable to, open up to, put at risk of, subject to.

antonym protect from.

exposé n account, article, documentary, disclosure, divulgence, exposure, revelation, uncovering, unmasking.

exposed adj bare, exhibited, in (plain) view, laid bare, liable, naked, on display, on show, open, prey (to), revealed, showing, susceptible, unconcealed, uncovered, unprotected, unsheltered, unveiled, visible, vulnerable.

antonyms covered, sheltered.

exposition n account, commentary, critique, demonstration, description, discourse, display, elucidation, exegesis, exhibition, explanation, explication, expo, fair, illustration, interpretation, lecture, monograph, paper, piece, presentation, show, study, thesis, treatise.

expository adj descriptive, elucidative, exegetical, explanatory, explicative, hermeneutic, illustrative, interpretive.

expostulate v argue, dissuade, object, plead, protest, reason, remonstrate, warn against.

exposure n acquaintance, airing, aspect, baring, betrayal, cold, contact, conversance, denunciation, detection, disclosure, discovery, display, divulgence, exhibition, experience, exposé, familiarity, frontage, introduction, knowledge, liability, manifestation, openness, orientation, outlook, presentation, publicity, revelation, risk, showing, susceptibility, uncovering, unearthing, unmasking, unveiling, view, vulnerability.

expound v describe, elucidate, explain, explicate, hold forth (on), illustrate, interpet, lecture (on), preach, sermonize about, set forth, spell out, unfold.

express v affirm, articulate, assert, asseverate, bespeak, communicate, conceive, convey, couch, declare, denote, depict, designate, disclose, divulge, embody, enunciate, evince, extract, force out, formulate, indicate, intimate, make known, manifest, phrase, press out, pronounce, put, put across, put into words, represent, reveal, say, share, show, signify, speak, squeeze out, stand for, state, symbolize, tell, utter, verbalize, voice, word.

adj categorical, clear, clear-cut, definite, direct, distinct, emphatic, especial, exact,

explicit, fast, high-speed, intentional, manifest, non-stop, outright, particular, plain, pointed, positive, precise, quick, rapid, singular, special, specific, speedy, stated, swift, unambiguous, unqualified.

antonym vague.

expression n affirmation, air, appearance, aspect, assertion, asseveration, communication, conveyance, countenance, declaration, delivery, demonstration, diction, disclosure, embodiment, enunciation, extraction, face, feeling, figure of speech, idiom, indication, intonation, language, locution, look, manifestation, maxim, mien, phrase, phraseology, phrasing, pronouncement, reflection, reflex, representation, saying, set (or stock) phrase, show, sign, soul, speaking, speech, statement, style, symbol, term, token, turn of phrase, utterance, verbalization, verbalism, voicing, word, wording.

expressionless adj blank, deadpan, dull, empty, flat, glassy, impassive, inscrutable, lifeless, mechanical, monotone, poker-faced, straight-faced, vacuous, wooden.

antonym expressive.

expressive adj allusive, articulate, demonstrative, descriptive, eloquent, emphatic, evocative, forcible, indicative, lively, meaningful, mobile, moving, poignant, pointed, pregnant, representative, revealing, significant, speaking, striking, strong, suggestive, telling, vivid.

antonyms expressionless, poker-faced.

expressly adv absolutely, categorically, clearly, decidedly, definitely, distinctly, especially, exactly, explicitly, flat out, in so many words, intentionally, manifestly, on purpose, outright, particularly, plainly, pointedly, positively, precisely, purposely, specially, specifically, straight out, unambiguously, unequivocally.

expropriate v annex, appropriate, arrogate, assume, commandeer, confiscate, dispossess, foreclose (on), impound, requisition, seize, sequester, take, unhouse.

expulsion n banishment, debarment, disbarment, discharge, dislodgment, dismissal, egestion, ejection, eviction, exclusion, excommunication, exile, expatriation, extrusion, proscription, removal, suspension.

expunge v annul, blot out, cancel, delete, efface, erase, expurgate, extinguish, obliterate, remove, scratch (out), wipe out.

expurgate v blue-pencil, bowdlerize, censor, clean up, cut (out), emend, excise, get rid of, purge, purify, sanitize.

exquisite adj acute, admirable, beautiful, charming, choice, consummate, cultivated, dainty, delicate, delicious, discerning, discriminating, elegant, excellent, excruciating, fine, flawless, impeccable, incomparable, intense, keen, lovely, matchless, nonpareil, of the first water, outstanding, peerless, perfect, piercing, poignant, polished, precious, rare, refined, select, selective, sensitive, sharp, splendid, stabbing, striking, superb, superlative, unparalleled, unsurpassed.

antonyms coarse, flawed, imperfect, poor, ugly.

extant *adj* alive, around, existent, existing, in existence, living, on the books, remaining, subsistent, subsisting, surviving.

antonyms dead, extinct, non-existent.

extemporaneous *adj* ad lib, extemporary, extempore, free, impromptu, improvised, made-up, makeshift, offhand, off-the-cuff, on-the-spot, spontaneous, spur-of-the-moment, unplanned, unpremeditated, unprepared, unrehearsed.

antonym planned.

extemporize *v* ad lib, compose offhand, do offhand, improvise, make up, play by ear, talk off the top of one's head, wing it.

extend *v* add onto, advance, attain, augment, bestow (on), broaden, confer (on), continue, dilate, drag out, draw out, elongate, enlarge, expand, give, grant, grow, hold out, impart, increase, lengthen, offer, present, proffer, prolong, protract, pull out, reach, spin out, spread, stretch (out), supplement, uncoil, unfold, unfurl, unroll, widen.

antonym shorten.

extension *n* accretion, addendum, addition, adjunct, annex, appendage, arm, augmentation, branch, broadening, continuance, continuation, deferment, delay, development, dilatation, distension, el, elongation, enhancement, enlargement, expansion, grace, increase, lengthening, postponement, prolongation, protraction, spread, stretching, supplement, widening, wing.

extensive *adj* all-inclusive, ample, broad, comprehensive, expanded, expansive, extended, far-flung, far-reaching, general, great, huge, large, large-scale, lengthy, long, pervasive, prevalent, protracted, sprawling, spread out, stretched out, sweeping, thorough, thoroughgoing, universal, unrestricted, vast, voluminous, wholesale, wide, widespread.

antonyms narrow, restricted.

extent *n* amount, amplitude, area, bounds, breadth, compass, degree, dimension(s), distance, duration, expanse, extensiveness, length, magnitude, measure, proportions, quantity, range, reach, scope, size, spread, stretch, sweep, term, time, volume, width.

extenuate *v* decrease, diminish, excuse, lessen, minimize, mitigate, moderate, modify, palliate, qualify, reduce, soften, temper, weaken.

antonyms clinch, increase, strengthen.

extenuating *adj* excusatory, justifying, lenitive, mitigating, moderating, palliative, qualifying, softening.

antonyms clinching, strengthening.

exterior *n* appearance, aspect, coating, covering, externals, façade, face, finish, outside, shell, skin, superficies, surface.

antonym interior.

adj external, extraneous, extrinsic, outer, outermost, outside, outward, superficial, surface.

antonym interior.

exterminate *v* abolish, annihilate, deracinate, destroy, eliminate, eradicate, extinguish, extirpate, get rid of, kill (off), massacre, purge (of), wipe out.

extermination *n* annihilation, deracination, destruction, elimination, eradication, extinction, extirpation, genocide, killing (off), massacre, purge, riddance.

external *adj* alien, apparent, exoteric, exotic, exterior, extramural, extraneous, extrinsic, foreign, independent, outer, outermost, outside, outward, superficial, surface, visible.

antonym internal.

extinct *adj* abolished, a thing of the past, dead, defunct, doused, ended, exterminated, extinguished, gone (forever), gone the way of the dinosaurs, inactive, lost, no more, obsolete, out, quenched, terminated, vanished, wiped out.

antonyms extant, living.

extinction *n* abolition, annihilation, death, destruction, dousing, eradication, extermination, extinguishment, extirpation, obliteration, oblivion, quietus, wiping out.

extinguish *v* abolish, annihilate, destroy, douse, eliminate, end, eradicate, erase, expunge, exterminate, extirpate, kill, out, put out, quench, remove, slake, smother, snuff out, stifle, suppress.

extirpate *v* abolish, annihilate, cut out, deracinate, destroy, eliminate, eradicate, erase, excise, expunge, exterminate, extinguish, remove, root out, tear up by the roots, uproot, wipe out.

extol *v* acclaim, applaud, celebrate, commend, cry up, eulogize, exalt, glorify, laud, lift up, magnify, panegyrize, praise, puff.

antonyms blame, denigrate.

extort *v* blackmail, bleed, bully, by force, coerce, demand, exact, extract, gouge, milk, squeeze, wrest, wring.

extortion *n* blackmail, coercion, demand, exaction, exorbitance, expensiveness, force, gouging, highway robbery, oppression, overcharging, rapacity.

extortionate *adj* bloodsucking, exacting, excessive, exorbitant, extravagant, grasping, hard, harsh, immoderate, inflated, inordinate, oppressive, outrageous, preposterous, rapacious, rigorous, severe, sky-high, unreasonable, usurious.

antonym reasonable.

extra *adj* accessory, added, additional, ancillary, a plethora of, auxiliary, excess, for good measure, fresh, further, inessential, leftover, more, more than enough, more than usual, needless, other, over and above, redundant, reserve, spare, supererogatory, superfluous, supernumerary, supplemental, supplementary, surplus, unnecessary, unneeded, unused.

antonym integral.

n accessory, addition, adjunct, appendage, appurtenance, attachment, bells and whistles, bonus, complement, excess, extension, frill(s), leftovers, non-essential, overabundance, plus, spare, superfluity, supernumerary, supplement, surplus.

adv especially, exceedingly, exceptionally, extraordinarily, extremely, particularly, remarkably, uncommonly, unusually, ultra-, very.

extract *v* abstract, choose, cite, cull, decoct, deduce, derive, develop, distil, draw (off or out), educe, elicit, evoke, evolve, exact, excerpt, express, extirpate, extort, get, glean, harvest, obtain, pull (out), quote, reap, remove, select, take out, uproot, withdraw, wrest, wring.

antonym insert.

n abstract, citation, clip, clipping, concentrate, cutting, decoction, distillate, distillation, essence, excerpt, extraction, flavouring, juice, passage, preparation, quotation, selection.

extraction *n* ancestry, birth, blood, derivation, descent, distillation, drawing off (or out), extirpation, extract, family, lineage, origin, parentage, pedigree, pulling (out), removal, separation, stock, withdrawal.

antonym insertion.

extraneous *adj* accidental, additional, adventitious, alien, external, extrinsic, foreign, immaterial, impertinent, inapplicable, inapposite, inappropriate, inapt, incidental, inessential, irrelevant, needless, non-essential, peripheral, redundant, strange, superfluous, supplementary, tangential, unconnected, unessential, unnecessary, unneeded, unrelated.

antonym integral.

extraordinary *adj* amazing, bizarre, curious, exceptional, extraordinaire, fantastic, marvellous, notable, noteworthy, odd, out of the ordinary, outstanding, particular, peculiar, phenomenal, rare, remarkable, singular, special, strange, striking, surprising, uncommon, uncontemplated, unfamiliar, unheard-of, unimagined, unique, unprecedented, unusual, unwonted, weird, wonderful.

antonyms commonplace, ordinary, run-of-the-mill.

extrapolate *v* derive, infer, predict, project.

extravagance *n* absurdity, dissipation, exaggeration, excess, exorbitance, folly, hyperbole, immoderation, improvidence, intemperance, lavishness, outrageousness, overspending, preposterousness, prodigality, profligacy, profusion, recklessness, squandering, thriftlessness, unreasonableness, unrestraint, unthriftiness, waste, wastefulness, wildness.

antonyms moderation, thrift.

extravagant *adj* absurd, boastful, costly, exaggerated, excessive, exorbitant, expensive, extortionate, extreme, fanciful, fancy, fantastic, flamboyant, flashy, foolish, grandiose, hyperbolic, immoderate, improvident, imprudent, inordinate, intemperate, lavish, ornate, ostentatious, outrageous, outré, overpriced, preposterous, prodigal, profligate, reckless, showy, spendthrift, steep, tall, thriftless, unrealistic, unreasonable, unrestrained, unthrifty, wasteful, wild.

antonyms moderate, thrifty.

extravaganza *n* display, gala, pageant, show, spectacle, spectacular.

extreme *adj* acute, beyond the pale, die-hard, dire, Draconian, drastic, dyed-in-the-wool, egregious, exaggerated, exceptional, excessive, exquisite, extraordinary, extravagant, fanatical, far out, farthest, final, great, greatest, harsh, high, highest, immoderate, infinite, inordinate, intemperate, intense, last, maximal, maximum, out-and-out, outermost, outrageous, over the top, radical, rank, red-hot, remotest, rigid, severe, stern, strict, strong, supreme, terminal, ultimate, ultra, unbending, uncommon, uncompromising, unreasonable, unusual, utmost, utter, uttermost, violent, worst, zealous.

antonyms mild, moderate.

n acme, apex, apogee, boundary, climax, depth, edge, end, excess, extremity, height, limit, maximum, minimum, nadir, peak, pinnacle, pole, terminus, top, ultimate, utmost, zenith.

extremely *adv* acutely, awfully, exceedingly, exceptionally, excessively, extraordinarily, greatly, highly, incredibly, inordinately, intensely, in the extreme, markedly, mortally, overly, quite, radically, severely, terminally, terribly, too, ultra-, uncommonly, unusually, utterly, very.

extremism *n* excess, fanaticism, militance, radicalism, terrorism, ultraism, zealotry.

antonyms moderation, restraint.

extremist *n* die-hard, fanatic, militant, radical, terrorist, ultra, ultraconservative, zealot.

antonym moderate.

extremity *n* acme, acuteness, apex, apogee, border, bound, boundary, brim, brink, climax, consummation, crisis, crunch, danger, depth, desperate measure, desperation, edge, emergency, end, excess, extreme, farthest point, foot, frontier, full extent, hand, hardship, height, limit, margin, maximum, minimum, nadir, need, pass, peak, peril, pinnacle, plight, pole, rim, suffering, terminal, terminus, tip, top, trouble, ultimate, utmost, verge, zenith.

extricate *v* clear, deliver, disembarrass, disembroil, disengage, disentangle, extract, free, liberate, release, remove, rescue, withdraw.

antonym involve.

extrinsic *adj* accidental, alien, external, extraneous, foreign, imported, inessential, non-essential, outside, superficial.

antonyms essential, intrinsic.

extroversion *n* amiability, amicability, exuberance, friendliness, heartiness, sociability.

extrovert(ed) *adj* amiable, amicable, exuberant, friendly, hail-fellow-well-met, hearty, other-oriented, outgoing, people-oriented, sociable, social, talkative, vocal.
antonym introvert(ed).
n joiner, life (and soul) of the party, mixer, people-person, socializer.
antonyms introvert, loner.

exuberance *n* abundance, animation, buoyancy, cheerfulness, copiousness, eagerness, ebullience, effervescence, effusiveness, energy, enthusiasm, excitement, exhilaration, fulsomeness, gaiety, high spirits, lavishness, life, liveliness, lushness, luxuriance, plenitude, prodigality, productivity, profusion, proliferousness, rambunctiousness, richness, spirit, sprightliness, superabundance, superfluity, vigour, vitality, vivacity, zest.
antonyms apathy, lifelessness, scantiness.

exuberant *adj* abundant, animated, buoyant, cheerful, copious, eager, ebullient, effervescent, effusive, elaborate, elated, energetic, enthusiastic, excessive, excited, exhilarated, fulsome, gay, high-spirited, lavish, lively, lush, luxuriant, overflowing, plenteous, plentiful, prodigal, productive, profuse, proliferous, prolific, rambunctious, rich, sparkling, spirited, sprightly, superabundant, superfluous, teeming, unrestrained, vigorous, vivacious, zestful.
antonyms apathetic, lifeless, scant.

exude *v* bleed, discharge, display, emanate, emit, excrete, exhibit, flow out, glow (with), issue, leak, manifest, ooze, perspire, radiate, secrete, seep, show, sweat, trickle, weep, well (up).

exult *v* celebrate, crow, delight, gloat, glory, jubilate, rejoice, relish, revel, triumph.

exultant *adj* crowing, delighted, elated, exulting, flushed, gleeful, in high feather, joyful, joyous, jubilant, over the moon, overjoyed, rejoicing, revelling, transported, triumphant.
antonym depressed.

exultation *n* celebration, crowing, delight, elation, glee, gloating, glorying, joy, jubilation, rejoicing, revelling, transport, triumph.
antonym depression.

eye *n* appreciation, attention, belief, discernment, discrimination, eyeball, gaze, glance, judgment, look, mind, opinion, optic, orb, peeper, perception, protection, recognition, regard, supervision, surveillance, taste, view, watch.
v contemplate, examine, gaze at, give the eye, glance at, inspect, leer at, look at, make eyes at, observe, ogle, peruse, regard, scan, scrutinize, stare at, study, survey, view, watch.

an eye for an eye justice, reciprocation, repayment, reprisal, requital, retaliation, retribution, revenge, talion, talionic code, tit for tat, vengeance.

eye-catching *adj* appealing, arresting, attractive, beautiful, captivating, conspicuous, gorgeous, showy, spectacular, striking, stunning.
antonyms plain, unattractive.

eyeful *n* a good looker, beauty, dazzler, knockout, look, show, sight, sight for sore eyes, spectacle, stunner, view, vision.

eyeglasses *n* glasses, lorgnette, pince-nez, specs, spectacles.

eyesight *n* observation, perception, range (or field) of vision, seeing distance, sight, view, vision.

eyesore *n* blemish, blight, blot, disfigurement, disgrace, horror, mess, monstrosity, sight, ugliness.

eyewitness *n* beholder, bystander, looker-on, observer, onlooker, passer-by, spectator, viewer, watcher, witness.

F

fable *n* allegory, apologue, fabliau, fabrication, fairy story, fairy tale, falsehood, fantasy, fib, fiction, figment, invention, legend, lie, make-believe, myth, narrative, old wives' tale, parable, romance, saga, story, tale, tall tale, untruth, yarn.

fabled *adj* celebrated in story and song, fabulous, fairy-tale, famed, famous, fantastic, feigned, fictional, fictitious, invented, legendary, made up, mythical, renowned, storied.

antonym unknown.

fabric *n* cloth, constitution, construction, foundations, framework, infrastructure, make-up, material, organization, structure, stuff, textile, texture, warp and woof, weave, web.

fabricate *v* assemble, build, coin, concoct, construct, cook up, create, devise, erect, fake, falsify, fashion, feign, forge, form, frame, invent, make, make up, manufacture, trump up.

fabrication *n* assemblage, assembly, building, cock-and-bull story, concoction, construction, erection, fable, fairy story, fairy tale, fake, falsehood, fiction, figment (of someone's imagination), fish story, forgery, frame-up, imagination, invention, lie, make-believe, manufacture, myth, production, story, tall tale, untruth.

antonym truth.

fabulous *adj* amazing, apocryphal, astounding, breathtaking, exaggerated, exciting, fabled, false, fantastic, feigned, fictitious, imaginary, immense, inconceivable, incredible, invented, legendary, marvellous, mythical, phenomenal, renowned, spectacular, superb, unbelievable, unreal, wonderful.

antonyms moderate, real, small.

façade *n* appearance, cloak, cover, disguise, exterior, face, front, frontage, guise, mask, pretence, semblance, show, veil, veneer.

face *n* air, appearance, aspect, audacity, authority, boldness, brass, cheek, confidence, countenance, cover, dial, dignity, disguise, effrontery, expression, exterior, façade, facet, favour, features, front, frown, gall, grimace, hardihood, honour, image, impudence, insolence, kisser, lineaments, look, mask, metope, moue, mug, nerve, outside, physiognomy, pout, presence, prestige, presumption, pride, reputation, sauce, scowl,

self-respect, side, smirk, snoot, standing, status, surface, typeface, veneer, visage, wall.

v accept, admit, beard, clad, coat, confront, cope with, cover, deal with, defy, dress, encounter, experience, finish, front in, front on, give on to, handle, level, line, look out on, meet, oppose, overlay, overlook, present, sheathe, surface, tackle, turn toward, veneer.

face down abash, confuse, disconcert, embarass, get the better of, humiliate, stare down, outface.

faceless anonymous, characterless, featureless, generic, impersonal, nameless, nondescript.

face to face with across from, à deux, confronting, eye to eye, eyeball to eyeball, in a close encounter, in confrontation, in person, nose to nose, opposite, personally, tête-à-tête, vis-à-vis, with one's own eyes.

face up to accept, acknowledge, come to terms with, confront, cope with, deal with, meet head-on, recognize, square up to, stand up to.

facelift *n* beautification, change, cosmetic surgery, plastic surgery, overhaul, redecoration, rejuvenation, renovation, restoration, revamping, rhytidectomy.

facet *n* angle, aspect, characteristic, face, feature, part, phase, plane, point, side, slant, surface, view.

facetious *adj* amusing, comical, droll, flippant, frivolous, funny, humorous, jesting, jocose, jocular, merry, playful, pleasant, tongue-in-cheek, unserious, waggish, witty.

antonym serious.

facile *adj* adept, adroit, agreeable, amenable, complaisant, cursory, dexterous, easy, effortless, expert, fluent, glib, hasty, insincere, light, mild, pat, plausible, proficient, quick, ready, shallow, simple, simplistic, skilful, slick, smooth, superficial, uncomplicated, yielding.

antonyms clumsy, implausible, profound.

facilitate *v* assist, ease, expedite, forward, further, grease, help, lead, make easy, promote, speed up.

facilities *n* accommodations, amenities, appliances, conveniences, equipment, furnishings, lavatory, means, resources, restroom, toilet, washroom.

facility *n* ability, adeptness, adroitness, bent, building, dexterity, ease, efficiency, effortlessness, expertness, fluency, gift, knack, proficiency, quickness, readiness, skilfulness, skill, smoothness, talent.

facing n cladding, coating, façade, false front, lining, overlay, plating, reinforcement, revetment, sheathing, surface, trim(ming), veneer.

facsimile n carbon, carbon copy, close, copy, duplicate, image, imitation, likeness, fax, mimeograph, photocopy, photostat, print, replica, reproduction, transcript.

fact(s) n act, actuality, certainty, circumstance, datum, deed, detail, event, fait accompli, gospel, happening, incident, item, occurrence, particular, point, reality, specific, truth.

in fact actually, as a matter of fact, indeed, in effect, in point of fact, in reality, in truth, really, to tell the truth, truly.

faction[1] n band, bloc, cabal, cadre, camp, caucus, clique, coalition, combination, confederacy, contingent, coterie, crowd, division, gang, Ginger Group, group, grouplet, junta, lobby, minority, party, pressure group, ring, section, sector, set, side, splinter group, splinter party, subgroup, troop.

faction[2] n conflict, contention, disagreement, discord, disharmony, dissension, disunity, division, divisiveness, fighting, friction, infighting, mutiny, quarrelling, rebellion, sedition, strife.

antonyms agreement, peace.

factious adj argumentative, contentious, disputatious, dissident, divisive, factional, insurrectionary, litigious, malcontent, mutinous, partisan, quarrelsome, rebellious, refractory, rival, sectarian, seditious, troublemaking.

antonyms calm, co-operative.

factitious adj affected, artificial, assumed, contrived, counterfeit, engineered, fabricated, fake, false, feigned, imitation, insincere, made-up, manufactured, mock, phony, pinchbeck, put-on, sham, simulated, spurious, supposititious, synthetic, unnatural, unreal.

antonyms genuine, natural, spontaneous.

▲ _confusable word_ fictitious.

factor n agent, aspect, building block, cause, circumstance, component, condition, consideration, deputy, determinant, element, force, influence, ingredient, item, manager, middleman, multiplicand, multiplicational, multiplier, parameter, part, particular, point, representative, steward, thing, unknown quantity, variable.

factory n assembly plant, drudge, manufacturing plant, manufactory, mill, plant, shop, works.

factotum n candystriper, do-all, famulus, gopher, handyman, jack of all trades, man of all work, odd-jobber, person Friday.

facts n data, details, evidence, gen, info, information, lowdown, poop, scoop, score, story.

factual adj accurate, authentic, certain, circumstantial, close, correct, credible, detailed, evidential, exact, faithful, genuine, historical, literal, objective, precise, real, straight, sure, true, unadorned, unbiassed, veritable.

antonym false.

faculties n capabilities, functions, intelligence, powers, reason, senses, wits.

faculty[1] n academics, department, discipline, lecturers, profession, professors, school, staff, teachers.

faculty[2] n ability, adroitness, aptitude, bent, capability, capacity, cleverness, dexterity, facility, gift, knack, power, propensity, readiness, skill, talent.

fad n affectation, craze, cult, fancy, fashion, mania, mode, rage, trend, vogue.

fade v age, bet, blanch, bleach, blench, decline, decolour, decolorize, deteriorate, die away, dim, diminish, disappear, discolour, disperse, dissolve, droop, dull, dwindle, ebb, etiolate, evanesce, fail, fall, flag, languish, pale, perish, recede, shrivel, vanish, wane, weaken, wilt, wither, yellow.

faded adj bleached, dim, discoloured, dull, etiolated, indistinct, lustreless, pale, passé, past it, washed-out, weatherworn.

antonym bright.

fail v abandon, bomb, cease, collapse, come to grief, come to nothing, conk out, crack up, crash, cut out, decline, desert, die, disappoint, droop, dwindle, fade, fall, fall short, flop, flub, flunk, fold, forget, forsake, founder, give out, give up, go bankrupt, go bust, go phut, go under, gutter, languish, let down, malfunction, miscarry, misfire, miss, neglect, omit, peter out, run out, sink, underachieve, underperform, wane, weaken.

antonyms gain, improve, prosper, succeed.

without fail conscientiously, constantly, dependably, faithfully, like clockwork, predictably, punctually, regularly, reliably, religiously, unfailingly, without exception.

antonyms unpredictably, unreliably.

failing n blemish, blind spot, defect, deficiency, drawback, error, failure, fault, flaw, foible, frailty, imperfection, inadequacy, lapse, peccadillo, shortcoming, weakness.

antonyms advantage, strength.

adj collapsing, decaying, declining, deteriorating, drooping, dwindling, dying, fading, flagging, languishing, moribund, unhealthy, unsuccessful, waning, weak, weakening.

antonyms thriving, vigorous.

prep in default of, in the absence of, lacking, wanting, without.

failure n abortion, also-ran, bankruptcy, bomb, breakdown, bummer, collapse, crash, damp squib, death, decay, decline, default, defeat, deficiency, dereliction, deterioration, disappointment, downfall, dud, failing, fiasco, flop, frost, frustration, good-for-nothing, inadequacy, incompetence, incompetent, ineffectiveness, insolvency, loser, loss, malfunction, miscarriage, neglect, negligence, non-performance, non-success, omission, remissness, ruin, shortcoming, slip-up, stoppage, turkey, washout, wreck, write-off. *antonym* success.

faint *adj* bleached, blurred, cowardly, delicate, dim, distant, dizzy, drooping, dull, enervated, exhausted, faded, faltering, faraway, fatigued, feeble, giddy, half-hearted, hazy, hushed, ill-defined, indistinct, irresolute, languid, lethargic, light, light-headed, low, muffled, muted, remote, slight, soft, subdued, thin, unenthusiastic, vague, vertiginous, weak, whispered, woozy. *antonyms* clear, strong.
v black out, collapse, droop, drop, flag, flake out, keel over, pass out, swoon.
n blackout, collapse, dead faint, swoon, syncope, unconsciousness.

faint-hearted *adj* chicken, cowardly, diffident, fearful, half-hearted, irresolute, lily-livered, spiritless, timid, timorous, weak, weak-kneed, yellow. *antonym* courageous.

fair¹ *adj* adequate, all right, appropriate, average, beauteous, beautiful, bonny, bright, clean, clear, clement, cloudless, comely, considerable, decent, disinterested, dispassionate, equal, equitable, even-handed, favourable, fine, good, handsome, honest, honourable, impartial, just, lawful, legitimate, likely, lovely, mediocre, middling, moderate, not bad, objective, OK, on the level, passable, pleasant, pretty, pretty good, promising, proper, rainless, reasonable, respectable, satisfactory, so-so, sporting, sportsmanlike, square, sunny, sunshiny, tolerable, trustworthy, unbiassed, unclouded, unprejudiced, upright, well-favoured. *antonyms* biassed, cloudy, foul, inclement, poor, unfair.

fair² *adj* blond(e), fair-haired, fair-headed, flaxen, golden, light, pale yellow, straw-coloured, towheaded. *antonyms* dark, raven-haired, swarthy.

fair³ *n* amusement park, bazaar, carnival, expo, exposition, festival, fête, gala, kermis, market, show.

fairly *adv* absolutely, actually, adequately, deservedly, et bono, equitably, fully, honestly, impartially, justly, moderately, objectively, plainly, positively, pretty, properly, quite, rather, really, reasonably, somewhat, tolerably, unbiassedly, veritably. *antonym* unfairly.

fairness *n* decency, disinterestedness, equitableness, equity, even-handedness, good sportsmanship, impartiality, justice, legitimacy, rightfulness, rightness, unbiassedness, uprightness. *antonyms* bias, unfairness.

fairy *n* brownie, elf, fay, hob, hobgoblin, gnome, imp, leprechaun, Mab, peri, pixie, puck, Robin Goodfellow, sprite.

fairy tale cock-and-bull story, dream, fable, fabrication, fairy story, fantasy, fiction, folk tale, invention, lie, make-believe (story), myth, romance, tall tale, untruth.

fairyland *n* Eden, faerie, land of make-believe, lotus land, magic kingdom, never-never-land, paradise, toyland, utopia.

faith *n* allegiance, assurance, belief, church, communion, confidence, constancy, conviction, credence, credit, creed, denomination, dependence, dogma, faithfulness, fealty, fidelity, honesty, honour, loyalty, persuasion, piety, pledge, promise, reliance, religion, sincerity, trust, truth, truthfulness, vow, word, word of honour. *antonyms* mistrust, treachery, unbelief, unfaithfulness.

faithful *adj* accurate, card-carrying, close, constant, dependable, devoted, devout, exact, just, loyal, obedient, pious, precise, reliable, soothfast, staunch, steadfast, strict, true, true-blue, true-hearted, trusty, truthful, unchanging, unswerving, unwavering, zealous. *antonyms* disloyal, inaccurate, treacherous.
n adherents, believers, brethren, communicants, congregation, fans, followers, supporters.

faithfulness *n* accuracy, adherence, closeness, constancy, dependability, devotion, exactness, fealty, fidelity, justice, loyalty, staunchness, steadfastness, trustworthiness, truth. *antonyms* disloyalty, inaccuracy, treachery.

faithless *adj* adulterous, apostate, delusive, disloyal, doubting, false, false-hearted, fickle, inconstant, perfidious, Punic, recreant, traitorous, treacherous, unbelieving, unfaithful, unreliable, untrue, untrustworthy, untruthful. *antonyms* believing, faithful.

faithlessness *n* adultery, apostasy, betrayal, disloyalty, falseness, fickleness, inconstancy, infidelity, perfidy, traitorousness, treachery, unfaithfulness, untrustworthiness. *antonyms* belief, faithfulness.

fake *v* affect, assume, bluff, copy, counterfeit, fabricate, falsify, feign, forge, imitate, improvise, pretend, put on, sham, simulate.
n charlatan, copy, counterfeit, falsification, forgery, fraud, hoax, imitation, impersonator, impostor, mountebank, reproduction, sham, simulation, substitute.
adj affected, artificial, assumed, bogus, counterfeit, ersatz, false, forged, hyped-up, imitation, mock, pinchbeck, pretended, pseudo, sham, simulated, spurious, synthetic. *antonym* genuine.

fall *v* abate, arrive, backslide, become, be defeated, be overthrown, capitulate, cascade, cave in, chance, collapse, come, come about, come a cropper, come down, come to pass, crash, decline, decrease, depreciate, descend, devolve, die, diminish, dive, droop, drop, drop dead, drop down, dwindle, ebb, err, fall away, fall off, fall out, falter, flag, give in, give up, give way, go astray, go down, hang down, happen, incline, keel over, lag, lapse, lessen, lose position or power, measure one's length, meet one's end, nose-dive, occur, offend, perish, pitch, plummet, plunge, settle, sin, sink, slip (downward), slope, slump, stumble, subside, succumb, surrender, take a spill, topple, transgress, trespass, trip, tumble, yield, yield to temptation.

antonym rise.

n abatement, autumn, backsliding, capitulation, capture, collapse, death, decline, declivity, decrease, defeat, degradation, descent, destruction, diminution, dip, dive, downfall, downgrade, drop, failure, incline, lapse, lessening, nose-dive, overthrow, plunge, reduction, ruin, sin, slant, slip, slope, slump, spill, surrender, transgression, tumble.

antonym rise.

fall apart break, break down (or up), crack up, crumble, decay, decompose, disband, disintegrate, disperse, dissolve, rot, shatter.

fall asleep doze off, drop off, nod off.

fall back on go back to, have recourse to, look to, resort to, turn to, use.

fall for accept, be deceived by, be taken in by, fall in love with, swallow.

fall guy dupe, patsy, scapegoat, victim.

fall in cave in, collapse, come down, conform, crumble, fail, give way, join, line up, sink.

fall in with accept, acquiesce, agree with, assent to, come across, comply, concur with, conform, converge, co-operate with, go along with, join with, meet, support.

fall off decelerate, decline, decrease, deteriorate, drop, falter, lessen, slacken, slow, slump, subside, wane, worsen.

fall on assail, assault, attack, be incumbent on, descend on, devolve to, jump (on), lay into, pounce on, snatch.

fall out[1] altercate, argue, bicker, clash, differ, disagree, fight, quarrel, squabble.

antonym agree.

fall out[2] chance, happen, occur, result, take place, transpire, turn out.

fall through collapse, come to nothing, fail, fizzle out, founder, miscarry.

antonym succeed.

fall to apply oneself (to), begin, commence, dig in, eat, set about, start.

fallacious *adj* casuistic, deceptive, delusive, delusory, erroneous, false, ill-founded, illogical, ill-reasoned, illusory, incorrect, misleading, mistaken, sophistic, spurious, unsound, untrue, wrong.

antonyms correct, true.

fallacy *n* casuistry, deceit, deception, deceptiveness, delusion, error, falsehood, falseness, falsity, faultiness, flaw, illusion, inconsistency, misapprehension, misconception, mistake, myth, sophism, sophistry, unsoundness, untruth.

antonym truth.

fallible *adj* errant, erring, frail, human, imperfect, mortal, uncertain, weak.

antonym infallible.

fallow *adj* dormant, idle, inactive, inert, resting, uncultivated, undeveloped, unplanted, unproductive, unseeded, unsown, unstimulated, untilled, unused.

false *adj* artificial, bastard, bogus, cockamamie, concocted, counterfeit, deceitful, deceiving, deceptive, delusive, dishonest, dishonourable, disloyal, double-dealing, double-faced, duplicitous, erroneous, ersatz, faithless, fake, fallacious, false-hearted, faulty, feigned, fictitious, forged, fraudulent, groundless, hypocritical, ill-founded, illusive, imitation, improper, inaccurate, inauthentic, incorrect, inexact, invalid, lying, mendacious, misleading, mistaken, mock, off-pitch, perfidious, pretended, pseudo, sham, simulated, spurious, synthetic, treacherous, treasonable, trumped-up, truthless, two-faced, unauthentic, unfaithful, unfounded, unreal, unreliable, unsound, untrue, untrustworthy, untruthful, wrong.

antonyms genuine, honest, reliable, true.

falsehood *n* cock-and-bull story, deceit, deception, dishonesty, dissimulation, fable, fabrication, falsity, fib, fiction, fish story, inaccuracy, inexactitude, inveracity, lie, (little) white lie, mendacity, misstatement, perjury, prevarication, story, tall tale, unfact, untruth, untruthfulness, whopper.

antonyms truth, truthfulness.

falsification *n* adulteration, alteration, change, counterfeit, deceit, dissimulation, distortion, fake, forgery, misrepresentation, misstatement, perversion, tampering.

falsify *v* adulterate, alter, belie, cook, counterfeit, disprove, distort, doctor, fake, forge, garble, lie about, misrepresent, misstate, pervert, sophisticate, take liberties with, tamper with.

falter *v* balk, break, draw back, fail, fall (off), flag, flinch, halt, hem and haw, hesitate, lose one's nerve or resolve, shake, shy, stammer, stumble, stutter, totter, tremble, vacillate, waver, weaken.

faltering *adj* broken, failing, flagging, hesitant, irresolute, shaky, stammering, stumbling, tentative, timid, trembling, uncertain, unsteady, wavering, weak.

antonyms firm, strong.

fame *n* celebrity, credit, eminence, esteem, glory, honour, illustriousness, kudos, name, notoriety, prominence, renown, reputation, repute, stardom.

famed *adj* acclaimed, celebrated, eminent, famous, noted, notorious, prominent, recognized, renowned, well-known, widely-known.

antonym unknown.

familiar *adj* accustomed, acquainted, amicable, bold, buddy-buddy, chummy, close, common, common-or-garden, confidential, conventional, cordial, customary, disrespectful, domestic, easy, everyday, forward, free, free and easy, frequent, friendly, habitual, household, impudent, informal, intimate, intrusive, mundane, near, open, ordinary, overfree, palsy-walsy, personal, presuming, presumptuous, private, recognizable, relaxed, repeated, routine, stock, unceremonious, unconstrained, unreserved, usual, well-known.

antonyms formal, reserved, unfamiliar.

familiar with abreast of, accustomed to, acquainted with, aware of, conscious of, conversant with, experienced with, habituated to, intimate with, knowledgeable about, used to, versed in, well-informed about.

antonyms ignorant of, unacquainted with, unused to.

familiarity *n* acquaintance, acquaintanceship, awareness, background, boldness, cheek, closeness, conversance, disrespect, ease, experience, forwardness, freedom, friendliness, grasp, impertinence, impudence, informality, intimacy, liberties, liberty, naturalness, openness, presumption, sociability, unceremoniousness, understanding.

antonyms formality, reserve, unfamiliarity.

familiarize *v* acclimatize, accustom, acquaint, brief, coach, habituate, inform, inure, popularize, prime, school, season, train.

family *n* ancestors, ancestry, background, birth, blood, brood, category, children, clan, class, classification, community, descendants, descent, dynasty, extraction, folks, forebears, forefathers, genealogy, genre, group, house, household, issue, kin, kind, kindred, kinsmen, kith and kin, line, lineage, ménage, offspring, parentage, pedigree, people, progeny, race, relations, relatives, roots, sept, stem, stirps, stock, strain, subdivision, tribe, upbringing.

family tree ancestry, extraction, genealogy, line, lineage, pedigree, roots, stirps.

famine *n* dearth, destitution, hunger, scarcity, shortage, starvation, want.

antonym plenty.

famished *adj* famishing, hungry, ravening, ravenous, starved, starving, voracious.

antonym sated.

famous *adj* acclaimed, celebrated, conspicuous, distinguished, eminent, excellent, glorious, great, honoured, illustrious, legendary, lionized, notable, noted, notorious, prominent, remarkable, renowned, reputable, signal, well-known.

antonym unknown.

fan¹ *v* aggravate, agitate, air-condition, air-cool, arouse, blow, cool, kindle, excite, impassion, increase, provoke, refresh, revive, rouse, stimulate, stir up, ventilate, whip up, winnow, work up.

n air-conditioner, blower, extractor fan, propeller, punkah, vane, ventilator.

fan² *n* adherent, admirer, aficionado, believer, buff, devotee, endorser, enthusiast, fiend, follower, freak, groupie, lover, nut, rooter, supporter, zealot.

fanatic *n* activist, addict, bigot, energumen, extremist, freak, militant, nut, visionary, zealot.

fanatical *adj* bigoted, burning, compulsive, demoniacal, extreme, fervid, fiery, frenzied, immoderate, mad, obsessive, overenthusiastic, overzealous, passionate, rabid, unreasonable, visionary, wild-eyed.

antonyms moderate, unenthusiastic.

fanaticism *n* bigotry, compulsiveness, extremism, fervidness, immoderacy, immoderateness, immoderation, infatuation, madness, monomania, narrow-mindedness, obsessiveness, overenthusiasm, zealotism, zealotry.

antonym moderation.

fanciful *adj* airy-fairy, chimeric, curious, dream, extravagant, fabulous, fairy-tale, fantastic, ideal, imaginary, imaginative, make-believe, metaphysical, mythical, poetic, quaint, romantic, unreal, vaporous, visionary, whimsical, wild.

antonym ordinary.

fancy *v* be attracted to, believe, conceive, conjecture, crave, desire, dream of, favour, go for, guess, hanker for, have an eye for, imagine, infer, like, long for, lust after, picture, prefer, reckon, relish, suppose, surmise, take a liking to, take to, think, think likely, wish for, yearn for, yen for.

antonym dislike.

n caprice, chimera, conception, daydream, delusion, desire, dream, fantasy, fondness, hankering, idea, image, imagination, impulse, inclination, liking, notion, partiality, penchant, phantasm, predilection, preference, thought, urge, vision, whim.

antonyms dislike, fact, reality.

adj baroque, choice, decorated, decorative, elaborate, elegant, embellished, extravagant, fanciful, fantastic, formal, frilly, fussy, intricate, ornamented, ornate, rococo, showy, skilful, souped-up, Sunday, top-grade, whimsical, with all the bells and whistles.

antonym plain.

fanfare *n* ceremony, fanfaronade, flourish, fuss, pomp and circumstance, show, trump, trumpet call.

fang *n* canine, prong, tang, tooth, tusk.

fantasize *v* build castles in the air, daydream, dream, hallucinate, imagine, invent, live in a dream, romance, romanticize.

fantastic *adj* absurd, ambitious, bizarre, chimeric, enormous, excellent, exotic, extravagant, extreme, fabricated, fabulous, fanciful, far-fetched, first-rate, freakish, grandiose, great, grotesque, illusory, imaginative, implausible, incredible, irrational, ludicrous, mad, magical, make-believe, marvellous, mind-boggling, mythical, out of this world, outlandish, overwhelming, peculiar, phantasmagoric, preposterous, quaint, queer, ridiculous, rococo, sensational, severe, strange, superb, tall, tremendous, unbelievable, unlikely, unreal, unrealistic, visionary, weird, whimsical, wild, wonderful.

antonyms ordinary, plain, poor.

fantasy *n* apparition, caprice, creativity, daydream, delusion, dream, fancy, fantasia, fantasizing, flight of fancy, hallucination, illusion, imagination, invention, myth, mirage, nightmare, pipe dream, reverie, romance, self-deception, unreality, vision, whim, whimsy.

antonym reality.

far *adv* a good way (off), a long way (off), afar, considerably, decidedly, deep, greatly, incomparably, miles, unquestionably, very much, way.

antonym near.

adj a long way away, distal, distant, faraway, far-flung, far-off, far-removed, further, godforsaken, isolated, long, opposite, other, outlying, out-of-the-way, remote, removed.

antonyms close, nearby.

far and wide all around, around the world, broadly, everywhere, extensively, far and near, (from or to) the four corners of the earth, hither and thither, widely, worldwide.

so far hitherto, thus far, till now, to date, up to now.

faraway *adj* absent, absent-minded, abstracted, distant, dreamy, far, far-flung, far-off, lost, outlying, remote.

antonyms alert, attentive, focussed, nearby, neighbouring.

farce *n* absurdity, broad humour, buffoonery, burlesque, comedy, commedia dell'arte, joke, low comedy, mockery, nonsense, parody, ridiculousness, satire, sham, slapstick, travesty.

farcical *adj* absurd, amusing, burlesque, Chaplinesque, comic, derisory, droll, facetious, funny, improbable, laughable, ludicrous, nonsensical, preposterous, pretence, ridiculous, risible, silly, slapstick, stupid.

antonyms deep, sensible, serious, solemn.

fare¹ *n* admission, charge, cost, fee, passage, passenger, price, rider, ticket, traveller.

fare² *n* board, commons, diet, eatables, food, meals, menu, provisions, rations, sustenance, table, victuals.

fare³ *v* be, do, eat, get along, get on, go, go on, happen, make out, manage, proceed, prosper, turn out.

farewell *n* adieu, departure, Godspeed, goodbye, leave-taking, parting, send-off, valediction.

antonym hello.

adj final, last, parting, swan(song), valedictory.

interj aloha, bon voyage, bye-bye, cheers, ciao, Godspeed, goodbye, good luck, so long.

far-fetched *adj* contrived, crazy, doubtful, dubious, fantastic, forced, hard to swallow, implausible, improbable, incredible, preposterous, recherché, strained, unbelievable, unconvincing, unlikely, unnatural, unrealistic.

antonym plausible.

farm *n* acreage, acres, croft, farmland, farmplace, farmstead, grange, holding, homestead, land, market garden, plantation, quarter section, ranch, station.

v cultivate, plant, raise crops, till, work the land.

farmer *n* agriculturist, agronomist, cattleman, crofter, husbander, husbandman, kulak, market gardener, rancher, rustic, sodbuster, stubble-jumper.

farming *n* agriculture, agronomy, crofting, husbandry, ranching.

farrago *n* gallimaufery, hash, hodgepodge, jumble, medley, mélange, miscellany, mishmash, mixture, potpourri, salmagundi.

far-reaching *adj* broad, consequential, extensive, important, momentous, pervasive, significant, sweeping, widespread.

antonym insignificant.

far-sighted *adj* acute, astute, canny, cautious, circumspect, discerning, far-seeing, foresighted, forward-looking, long-sighted, judicious, politic, presbyopic, prescient, provident, prudent, sagacious, sage, shrewd, wise.

antonyms imprudent, short-sighted, unwise.

fascinate *v* absorb, allure, attract, beguile, bewitch, captivate, charm, delight, enamour, enchant, engross, enrapture, enthrall, entrance, hypnotize, infatuate, interest, intrigue, mesmerize, rivet, spellbind, transfix.

antonyms bore, turn off.

fascinated *adj* absorbed, beguiled, bewitched, captivated, charmed, enamoured, enchanted, engrossed, enthralled, entranced, glued (to), hooked, hypnotized, infatuated, interested, intrigued, mesmerized, smitten, spellbound.

antonyms bored, turned off, uninterested.

fascinating *adj* absorbing, alluring, bewitching, captivating, charming, compelling, delightful, enchanting, engaging, engrossing, enthralling, enticing, gripping, interesting, intriguing, irresistible, mesmerizing, ravishing, riveting, seductive, unputdownable, witching.

antonyms boring, uninteresting.

fascination *n* absorption, allure, attraction, bewitchment, charm, enchantment, enthusiasm, glamour, idée fixe, infatuation, interest, lure, magic, magnetism, obsession, pull, sorcery, spell, witchery.

antonym boredom.

fascism *n* absolutism, authoritarianism, autocracy, despotism, dictatorship, Hitlerism, right-wing extremism, totalitarianism.

fascist *n* absolutist, authoritarian, autocrat, Blackshirt, Hitlerist, Hitlerite, right-wing extremist, totalitarian.

adj absolutist, authoritarian, autocratic, fascistic, Hitlerist, Hitlerite, totalitarian.

fashion *n* beau monde, convention, craze, cult, custom, cut, dernier cri, fad, haut ton, haute couture, high society, jet set, latest, line, look, manner, method, mode, rage, style, trend, usage, vogue, way.

v accommodate, adapt, adjust, alter, carve, construct, contrive, craft, create, design, devise, fit, forge, form, improvise, make, manufacture, model, modify, mould, sculpt, shape, suit, tailor, work.

fashionable *adj* à la mode, all the rage, chic, chi-chi, contemporary, cool, cult, current, customary, genteel, high-toned, hot, in, in style, in vogue, latest, modern, modish, popular, prestigious, prevailing, smart, snazzy, stylish, swagger, swanky, tony, trendsetting, trendy, up-to-date, up-to-the-minute, with it.

antonym unfashionable.

fast[1] *adj* accelerated, brisk, fleet, flying, hasty, hurried, mercurial, quick, rapid, speedy, swift, time-saving, winged.

antonym slow.

adv apace, at high speed, hastily, hell for leather, hurriedly, instantaneously, like a flash, like a shot, on the double, posthaste, presto, quickly, rapidly, speedily, swiftly.

antonym slowly.

fast[2] *adj* close, colourfast, confirmed, constant, fastened, firm, fixed, fortified, immovable, impregnable, lasting, locked, loyal, permanent, secure, sound, staunch, steadfast, tight, unflinching, unwavering.

antonyms impermanent, loose.

adv close, completely, deeply, firmly, fixedly, hard, near, permanently, rigidly, securely, sound(ly), thoroughly, tightly, unflinchingly.

antonym loosely.

fast[3] *adj* dissipated, dissolute, extravagant, free, immoral, intemperate, licentious, loose, profligate, promiscuous, rakish, reckless, self-indulgent, unchaste, unrestrained, wanton, whorish, wild.

antonyms chaste, moral.

fast[4] *v* abstain, diet, go hungry, starve.

n abstinence, diet, fasting, starvation diet.

antonyms gluttony, gorge oneself, self-indulgence.

fasten *v* affix, aim, anchor, attach, belay, bind, bolt, bond, buckle, button, chain, clamp, clip, close, concentrate, connect, direct, fix, focus, glue, grip, impose, impute, join, knot, lace, latch, link, lock, moor, nail, pin, rivet, seal, secure, shut, spar, staple, stick, tack, tie, zip up.

antonyms unfasten, untie.

fastening *n* bolt, bond, catch, clasp, clip, closing, copula, dome, fastener, hand eye, hasp, holder, hook, latch, latchet, link, lock, nexus, snap, tie, vinculum.

fastidious *adj* choosy, critical, dainty, difficult, discriminating, finical, finicky, fussy, hypercritical, meticulous, overnice, particular, pernickety, picky, precise, punctilious, squeamish.

antonym easy-going.

fasting *n* abstinence, dieting, self-denial, starvation.

antonyms gluttony, self-indulgence.

fat *adj* abdominous, adipose, affluent, beefy, blubbery, broad, corpulent, elephantine, fattened, fattish, fatty, fertile, flabby, fleshed, fleshy, flourishing, flowing with milk and honey, fruitful, greasy, gross, heavy, lucrative, lush, obese, oily, oleaginous, overweight, paunchy, pinguid, plentiful, plump, portly, potbellied, productive, profitable, prosperous, pudgy, remunerative, rich, roly-poly, rotund, round, small, solid, squab, squat, stout, stupid, suety, thick, thriving, tubby, wealthy, well-upholstered, well-fed.

antonyms thin, unproductive.

n adipose tissue, blubber, brown fat, cellulite, corpulence, embonpoint, excess, fatness, flab, lard, luxury, obesity, overweight, paunch, pinguidity, plumpness, pot (belly), speck, shortening, superfluity, surplus, wealth.

fatal *adj* baleful, baneful, calamitous, catastrophic, deadly, decisive, destructive, disastrous, fateful, final, incurable, killing, lethal, malignant, mortal, pernicious, ruinous, terminal, vital.

antonym harmless.

fatality *n* casualty, deadliness, death, disaster, fate, lethalness, loss (of life), mortality, unavoidability.

fate *n* chance, cup, death, destiny, destruction, divine will, doom, downfall, end, fortune, future, handwriting on the wall, horoscope, inevitability, issue, karma, kismet, lot, nemesis, outcome, portion, predestination, predestiny, providence, ruin, stars.

fated *adj* destined, doomed, fateful, foreordained, ineluctable, inescapable, inevitable, in the cards, predestined, pre-elected, preordained, sure, unavoidable, unfortunate, written, written in the stars.

antonym avoidable.

fateful *adj* calamitous, critical, crucial, deadly, decisive, destructive, disastrous, fatal, fated, important, lethal, momentous, ominous, pivotal, portentous, prophetic, ruinous, significant.

antonym unimportant.

fathead *n* ass, booby, dimwit, dolt, dope, dumbo, dunce, dunderhead, fool, goose, idiot, imbecile, jackass, nincompoop, nitwit, numskull, twit.

father *n* abbé, abbot, ancestor, architect, author, begetter, confessor, creator, curé, dad, daddy, elder, forebear, forefather, founder, governor, inventor, leader, maker, old man, originator, pa, padre, papa, pappy, parent, pastor, pater, paterfamilias, patriarch, patron, pop, pops, predecessor, priest, prime mover, procreator, progenitor, senator, sire.

v beget, conceive, create, dream up, engender, establish, foist, found, get, institute, invent, nurture, originate, procreate, produce, raise, rear, sire.

fatherland *n* birthplace, home, homeland, mother country, motherland, native land, native soil, old country.

fatherly *adj* affectionate, avuncular, benevolent, benign, fatherlike, forbearing, gentle, indulgent, kind, kindly, nurturing, paternal, patriarchal, protective, supportive, tender, warm.

antonyms cold, harsh, unkind.

fathom *v* comprehend, estimate, gauge, get to the bottom of, grasp, interpret, measure, penetrate, plumb, plummet, probe, see, sound, understand, work out.

fatigue *v* do in, drain, exhaust, fag (out), flag, flake out, jade, overtire, poop (out), shatter,

fatigued 236

antonym refresh.

n debility, decay, degeneration, ennui, exhaustion, heaviness, languor, lassitude, lethargy, listlessness, overtiredness, overwork, strain, tiredness, weariness.

antonyms energy, freshness.

fatigued *adj* all in, beat, bushed, dead-beat, dead-tired, dog-tired, exhausted, fagged, flagging, flaked out, frazzled, jaded, overtired, pooped (out), run-down, tired, tired out, tuckered (out), wasted, weary, whacked, worn-out, worn to a frazzle, zonked.

antonym refreshed.

fatness *n* bulk, bulkiness, chubbiness, corpulence, embonpoint, flab, flesh, fleshiness, girth, grossness, heaviness, healthiness, obesity, plumpness, pudginess, portliness, roundness, rotundity, size, stoutness, tubbiness, weight.

fatten *v* bloat, broaden, build up, coarsen, cram, distend, enrich, expand, feed, feed up, fertilize, make better, nourish, overfeed, spread, stuff, swell, thicken, thrive.

fatty *adj* adipose, fat, greasy, lardy, oily, oleaginous, pinguid, suety.

n blimp, fatso, heavyweight, lump, podge, pudding, pudge, roly-poly, tub (of lard).

fatuity *n* absurdity, asininity, brainlessness, daftness, fatuousness, folly, foolishness, idiocy, imbecility, inanity, ludicrousness, mindlessness, senselessness, stupidity, thoughtlessness.

antonym sense.

fatuous *adj* absurd, asinine, brainless, daft, dense, empty-headed, foolish, idiotic, imbecile, inane, ludicrous, mindless, moronic, puerile, silly, stupid, thoughtless, vacuous, weak-minded, witless.

antonym sensible.

fault *n* blemish, blunder, boner, booboo, breach, break, crack, culpability, defect, deficiency, delinquency, demerit, error, failing, flaw, frailty, goof, imperfection, inaccuracy, indiscretion, infirmity, lack, lapse, liability, misconduct, misdeed, mistake, negligence, offence, omission, oversight, peccadillo, responsibility, shortcoming, sin, slip, slip-up, snag, solecism, transgression, trespass, vice, weakness, wrong.

antonyms advantage, strength.

v blame, call to account, censure, criticize, find fault with, impugn, object to, pick apart, pick at, pick holes in, point the finger at.

antonym praise.

at fault accountable, answerable, blamable, blameworthy, culpable, guilty, in the wrong, responsible, to blame, wrong.

to a fault excessively, immoderately, in the extreme, needlessly, out of all proportion, over the top, overly, overmuch, preposterously, ridiculously, to extremes, unduly.

faultfinder *n* carper, caviller, fussbudget, griper, grumbler, hairsplitter, hypercritic,

kvetch(er), nag, nagger, niggler, nit-picker, pettifogger.

faultfinding *adj* captious, carping, cavilling, censorious, critical, finger-pointing, fussy, grumbling, hairsplitting, hypercritical, nagging, niggling, nit-picking, pettifogging, petulant, picky, querulous.

antonym complimentary.

faultless *adj* accurate, blameless, correct, exemplary, flawless, guiltless, immaculate, impeccable, innocent, irreproachable, model, paragonic, perfect, picture perfect, pure, sinless, spotless, stainless, unblemished, unerring, unspotted, unsullied, untainted, word perfect.

antonym imperfect.

faulty *adj* bad, blemished, broken, casuistic, damaged, defective, erroneous, fallacious, false, flawed, illogical, impaired, imperfect, imprecise, inaccurate, incorrect, inoperative, invalid, malfunctioning, out of order, specious, unsound, weak, wrong.

faux pas blunder, boner, booboo, breach, clanger, error, gaffe, gaucherie, goof, impropriety, indiscretion, misstep, slip, social sin, solecism.

favour *n* acceptance, approbation, approval, backing, badge, benefit, bias, boon, countenance, courtesy, decoration, esteem, favouritism, friendliness, gift, good opinion, good turn, good will, grace, indulgence, keepsake, kindness, liking, memento, partiality, patronage, present, regard, rosette, service, smile, souvenir, support, token.

antonym disfavour.

v abet, accommodate, advance, advocate, aid, approve, assist, back, befriend, be on the side of, be partial to, bestow (something) on, champion, choose, commend, conduce to, countenance, encourage, esteem, facilitate, fancy, go for, have in one's good books, help, indulge, like, look like, oblige, opt for, pamper, patronize, prefer, promote, recommend, resemble, reward, smile on, spare, spoil, succour, support, take after, take kindly to, value, vote for.

antonyms disapprove of, hinder, inhibit, thwart.

in favour of all for, approving, backing, for, on the side of, pro, supporting, to the advantage of.

favourable *adj* advantageous, affirmative, agreeable, amicable, approving, auspicious, beneficial, benign, commendatory, complimentary, consenting, convenient, encouraging, enthusiastic, fair, favonian, friendly, good, helpful, hopeful, kind, opportune, optimistic, positive, profitable, promising, propitious, reassuring, roseate, suitable, supportive, sympathetic, welcoming, well-disposed, well-minded.

antonyms disapproving, negative, unfavourable.

favourably *adv* advantageously, affirmatively, agreeably, approvingly, auspiciously, benignly, conveniently, encouragingly, enthusiastically, fortunately, graciously, opportunely, optimistically, positively, profitably, propitiously, supportively, sympathetically, well.

antonyms negatively, unfavourably.

favoured *adj* advantaged, approved, blessed, chosen, elite, favourite, fortunate, highly esteemed, lucky, pet, preferred, privileged, recommended, selected, well thought of.

favourite *adj* best-liked, best-loved, choice, dearest, most esteemed, favoured, pet, popular, preferred, top.

antonyms hated, unfavourite, unpopular.

n apple of one's eye, beloved, blue-eyed boy, choice, chosen one, darling, dear, first choice, idol, pet, pick, predicted winner, preference, teacher's pet, top of the list, top pick, white-haired boy.

antonyms black sheep, pet hate.

favouritism *n* bias, discrimination, inequality, injustice, nepotism, old-boy network, one-sidedness, partiality, partisanship, preference, preferential treatment, unfairness.

antonym impartiality.

fawn[1] **(on)** *v* bootlick, bow and scrape, court, crawl, creep, cringe, curry favour, dance attendance, flatter, grovel, ingratiate oneself, kneel, kowtow (to), pay court, suck up, toady, truckle.

fawn[2] *adj* beige, buff, dun, grey-brown, khaki, sand-coloured, sandy.

fawning *adj* abject, apple-polishing, bootlicking, crawling, cringing, deferential, flattering, grovelling, ingratiating, obsequious, servile, slavish, smarmy, sycophantic, toad-eating, toadying, unctuous.

antonyms cold, proud.

fear *n* agitation, alarm, anxiety, apprehension, apprehensiveness, awe, bogey, bugbear, butterflies in one's stomach, cold sweat, concern, consternation, cravenness, danger, dismay, disquietude, distress, doubt, dread, foreboding(s), fright, funk, horror, likelihood, misgiving(s), mistrust, nervousness, nightmare, panic, phobia, qualms, reverence, risk, solicitude, spectre, suspicion, terror, (the) jitters, timidity, trembling, tremors, trepidation, unease, uneasiness, veneration, wonder, worry.

antonyms courage, fortitude.

v anticipate, apprehend, cower before, dread, expect, foresee, quake (at), respect, reverence, shudder at, shrink from, suspect, take fright at, tremble at, venerate, worry about.

fear for tremble for, worry about.

fearful[1] *adj* afraid, alarmed, anxious, apprehensive, cowering, diffident, faint-hearted, frightened, hesitant, intimidated, jittery, jumpy, nervous, nervy, panicky, pusillanimous, scared, shrinking, spooked, tense, timid, timorous, trembling, uneasy.

antonym courageous.

fearful[2] *adj* appalling, atrocious, awful, dire, distressing, dreadful, egregious, fearsome, frightening, frightful, ghastly, grievous, grim,

gruesome, hair-raising, heinous, hideous, horrendous, horrible, horrific, monstrous, severe, shocking, terrible, unspeakable.

antonym delightful.

fearless *adj* bold, brave, confident, courageous, daring, dauntless, doughty, gallant, game, gutsy, heroic, imperturbable, indomitable, intrepid, lion-hearted, plucky, resolute, strong, unabashed, unafraid, unalarmed, unapprehensive, unblenching, unblinking, undaunted, unflinching, unshrinking, valiant, valorous.

antonyms afraid, timid.

fearlessness *n* boldness, bravery, confidence, courage, dauntlessness, daring, guts, indomitability, intrepidity, intrepidness, lion-heartedness, nerve, pluck, pluckiness, prowess, valour.

antonyms fear, timidness.

fearsome *adj* alarming, appalling, awe-inspiring, awesome, awful, daunting, dismaying, fearful, formidable, frightening, frightful, hair-raising, horrendous, horrible, horrific, horrifying, intimidating, menacing, scary, terrible, terrifying, unnerving.

antonym delightful.

feasible *adj* achievable, attainable, convenient, doable, expedient, likely, possible, practicable, practical, realistic, realizable, reasonable, viable, workable.

antonym impossible.

feast *n* banquet, barbecue, binge, blowout, carousal, carouse, celebration, dinner, enjoyment, entertainment, feed, festival, fête, gala, holiday, holy day, jollification, junket, meal, potlatch, repast, revel(s), saint's day, spread, table, treat.

v delight, eat one's fill, entertain, feed, gorge, gormandize, gratify, indulge, make merry, overindulge, pig out, regale, rejoice, stuff, stuff oneself (or one's face), thrill, treat, wine and dine.

feat *n* accomplishment, achievement, act, attainment, deed, exploit, performance, trick.

feather *n* aigrette, egret, pinion, plume, plumule, quill.

feathery *adj* downy, feathered, featherlike, fluffy, light, pennate, plumate, plumed, plumose, plumy, soft, wispy.

feature *n* article, aspect, attraction, attribute, character, characteristic, column, documentary, drawing card, facet, hallmark, highlight, innovation, item, lineament, main attraction, mark, movie, peculiarity, piece, point, property, quality, report, show, special, speciality, story, trait, write-up.

v accentuate, emphasize, headline, highlight, play up, present, promote, push, recommend, show, showcase, spotlight, star.

features *n* appearance, countenance, face, lineaments, looks, mug, physiognomy.

febrile *adj* burning, delirious, fevered, feverish, fiery, flushed, hot, inflamed, pyretic.

feces *n* body waste, dregs, droppings, dung, excrement, excreta, manure, ordure, scat, sediment, solid waste, stools.

feckless *adj* aimless, careless, feeble, futile, gormless, hopeless, incompetent, ineffective, ineffectual, irresponsible, shiftless, useless, vain, weak, worthless.

antonyms efficient, sensible.

fecund *adj* fertile, fructiferous, fruitful, productive, prolific, teeming.

antonym infertile.

fecundity *n* fertility, fructiferousness, fruitfulness, prolificacy, productiveness.

antonym infertility.

federate *v* affiliate, ally, amalgamate, associate, combine, confederate, integrate, join together, league, syndicate, unify, unite.

antonyms disunite, separate.

federation *n* affiliation, alliance, amalgamation, association, Bund, coalition, combination, confederacy, confederation, co-partnership, entente, federacy, league, society, syndicate, union.

fed up annoyed, bored, browned off, cheesed off, discontented, dissatisfied, exasperated, peeved, sick and tired, teed off, ticked off, tired, tired to death, wearied, weary.

antonym contented.

fee *n* account, bill, charge, compensation, cost(s), emolument, hire, honorarium, pay, payment, price, recompense, remuneration, retainer, reward, terms, toll.

feeble *adj* debilitated, delicate, doddering, effete, enervated, enfeebled, etoliated, exhausted, failing, faint, faltering, flat, flimsy, forceless, frail, inadequate, incompetent, indecisive, indistinct, ineffective, ineffectual, inefficient, infirm, insignificant, insufficient, lame, languid, paltry, poor, powerless, puny, shaky, sickly, silly, slight, tame, thin, unconvincing, unhealthy, weak, weakened, weakly.

antonyms dynamic, strong, vigorous, worthy.

feeble-minded *adj* addle-brained, addle-pated, cretinous, dimwitted, dull, dumb, half-witted, idiotic, imbecilic, lacking, mentally deficient, moronic, retarded, simple, simple-minded, slow, slow on the uptake, slow-witted, soft in the head, stupid, two bricks short of a load, unintelligent, vacant, weak-minded.

antonyms bright, intelligent.

feebleness *n* debility, delicacy, effeteness, enervation, etiolation, exhaustion, faintness, flimsiness, forcelessness, frailness, frailty, inadequacy, incapacity, incompetence, indecisiveness, ineffectiveness, ineffectualness, infirmity, insufficiency, lameness, languor, lassitude, sickliness, weakness.

antonyms power, strength, vitality.

feed *v* augment, bolster, cater to (or for), dine, eat, encourage, fare, foster, fuel, gratify, graze, grub, nourish, nurture, pass, pasture, provide for, provision, satisfy, strengthen, subsist, supply, support, sustain, victual.

n banquet, cue, feast, fodder, food, forage, line, meal, nosh, pasturage, pasture, provender, repast, silage, spread, tuck-in, victuals.

feed in inject, input, key in, load, supply.

feed on consume, devour, eat, exist on, live on, partake of, prey on.

feel *v* be, believe, consider, deem, empathize, endure, enjoy, experience, explore, find, finger, fondle, fumble, go through, grope, handle, have, have a hunch, hold, intuit, judge, maul, notice, observe, paw, perceive, reckon, resemble, rummage, search, seem, sense, stroke, suffer, sympathize, test, think, touch, try, undergo.

n ambience, appreciation, atmosphere, bent, feeling, finish, gift, impression, instinct, intuition, knack, quality, sense, surface, texture, touch, vibes.

feel for be sorry for, bleed for, commiserate (with), condole (with), crave, empathize with, have compassion for, pity, sympathize with.

feel like desire, fancy, feel up to, have a yen for, seem like, want.

feel out assess, explore, get (or form) an impression of, look into, probe, sound out, try out, look into.

feeler *n* advance, antenna, approach, ballon d'essai, hanking, hint, overture, probe, suggestion, tentacle, trawl, trial balloon.

feeling *n* affect, affection, air, ambience, appreciation, apprehension, ardour, atmosphere, aura, belief, compassion, concern, consciousness, emotion, empathy, esthesia, feel, fervour, fondness, heart, heat, hunch, idea, impression, inclination, inkling, instinct, intuition, mood, notion, opinion, passion, perception, pity, point of view, presentiment, quality, sensation, sense, sensibility, sensitivity, sentience, sentiment, sentimentality, soul, suspicion, sympathy, touch, understanding, vibes, vibrations, view, warmth.

feelings *n* affections, ego, emotions, heart, passions, self-esteem, sensitivities, sentiments, soul, susceptibilities.

feign *v* act, affect, assume, counterfeit, dissemble, dissimulate, fabricate, fake, forge, go through the motions of, imitate, invent, make a pretense of, make a show of, pretend, put on, sham, simulate.

feigned *adj* affected, artificial, assumed, counterfeit, fabricated, fake, false, falsified, imaginary, imitation, inauthentic, insincere, invented, personated, pretend, pretended, pseudo, put-on, sham, simulated, spurious, unauthentic.

antonyms genuine, sincere.

feint *n* artifice, blind, bluff, deception, distraction, dodge, expedient, gambit, manoeuvre, mock assault, play, pose, pretence, pretext, pulled punch, ruse, stratagem, subterfuge, thrust, wile.

felicitous *adj* apposite, appropriate, apropos, apt, delightful, effective, expedient, fitting, fortunate, happy, inspired, loquent, lucky, neat, opportune, pleasant, propitious, prosperous, suitable, timely, well-chosen, well-timed, well-turned.

antonyms inappropriate, inept.

felicity *n* applicability, appositeness, appropriateness, aptness, blessedness, blessing, bliss, blissfulness, delectation, delight, ecstasy, effectiveness, eloquence, good fortune, grace, happiness, joy, propitiousness, propriety, suitability, suitableness.

antonyms inappropriateness, ineptitude, sadness.

feline *adj* catlike, graceful, leonine, seductive, sensual, sinuous, sleek, slinky, smooth, stealthy.

fell *adj* baneful, barbarous, bloody, cruel, deadly, destructive, fatal, ferocious, fierce, grim, implacable, inhuman, maleficent, malevolent, malicious, malign, malignant, merciless, mortal, nefarious, noxious, pernicious, pestilential, pitiless, relentless, ruinous, ruthless, sanguinary, savage, terrible, vicious.

antonyms benign, gentle, kind

v chop down, cut down, demolish, drop, flatten, floor, hew down, knock down, lay low, lay out, level, prostrate, raze, strike down.

fellow[1] *n* beau, bloke, boy, bugger, bud, buddy, cat, chap, character, codger, cuss, customer, fella, feller, guy, individual, joker, kipper, lad, man, person.

fellow[2] *n* associate, brother, colleague, companion, compeer, comrade, counterpart, co-worker, crony, equal, fellow member, friend, match, mate, member, neighbour, partner, peer, teammate, twin.

adj associate, associated, co-, like, related, similar.

fellow feeling *n* commiseration, compassion, empathy, sympathy, understanding.

fellowship *n* accord, amity, affiliation, association, award, brotherhood, camaraderie, club, commonality, communion, companionableness, companionship, company, community, endowment, familiarity, fraternization, fraternity, friendship, guild, intercourse, intimacy, kindliness, league, order, partnership, sharing, sisterhood, sociability, society, sodality, togetherness.

femme fatale charmer, coquette, enchantress, Jezebel, lamia, seductress, siren, tease, temptress, vamp.

fen *n* bog, marsh, morass, muskeg, quagmire, slough, swamp.

fence[1] *n* barricade, barrier, boundary, defence, guard, hedge, paling, palisade, rail, rampart, stockade, wall, windbreak.

v bound, circumscribe, confine, coop, defend, encircle, enclose, fortify, guard, hedge, pen, protect, restrict, secure, separate, surround.

on the fence between two stools, dithering, irresolute, shilly-shallying, uncertain, uncommitted, undecided, unsure, vacillating.

fence[2] *v* beat around the bush, be evasive, cavil, dodge, equivocate, evade, hedge, parry, prevaricate, pussyfoot, quibble, shift, stonewall, tergiversate, use weasel words.

fend for do for, look after, maintain, provide for, shift for, support, sustain.

fend off avert, beat off, defend, deflect, hold at bay, keep off, parry, repel, repulse, resist, shut out, stave off, ward off.

feral *adj* bestial, brutal, brutish, fell, ferocious, fierce, savage, unbroken, uncultivated, undomesticated, untamed, vicious, wild.

antonym tame.

ferment *v* agitate, boil, brew, bubble, concoct, effervesce, excite, fester, foam, foment, froth, heat, incite, inflame, leaven, provoke, rise, rouse, seethe, sour, stir up, work, work up.

n agitation, brouhaha, commotion, disruption, excitement, fermentation, fever, frenzy, furor, glow, heat, hubbub, imbroglio, leavening, stew, stir, tumult, turbulence, turmoil, unrest, uproar, volatility, yeast, zymosis.

antonym calm.

ferocious *adj* barbaric, barbarous, bloodthirsty, bloody, brutal, brutish, cruel, fearsome, feral, fiendish, fierce, homicidal, inhuman, intense, merciless, murderous, pitiless, predatory, rapacious, ravening, relentless, ruthless, sadistic, sanguinary, savage, truculent, vicious, violent, warlike, wild.

antonyms gentle, mild.

ferocity *n* barbarity, bloodthirstiness, brutality, cruelty, ferity, ferociousness, fiendishness, fierceness, inhumanity, murderousness, pitilessness, rapacity, relentlessness, ruthlessness, sadism, savageness, savagery, truculence, viciousness, violence, wildness.

antonyms gentleness, mildness.

ferret out dig up, disclose, discover, disinter, drive out, elicit, extract, find, hunt down, nose out, root out, run to earth, search out, seek out, smell out, sniff out, trace, track down, unearth, worm out.

ferry *v* carry, chauffeur, convey, drive, move, run, shift, ship, shuttle, taxi, transport.

fertile *adj* abundant, fat, fecund, flowering, fructiferous, fruit-bearing, fruitful, generative, lively, lush, luxuriant, plenteous, plentiful, potent, productive, prolific, rich, teeming, verdant, yielding.

antonyms arid, barren.

fertility *n* abundance, fatness, fecundity, fruitfulness, liveliness, lushness, luxuriance, plenteousness, potency, productiveness, prolificacy, prolificness, richness.

antonyms aridity, barrenness.

fertilization *n* dressing, dunging, enrichment, fecundation, implantation, impregnation, insemination, manuring, mulching, pollination, top dressing.

fertilize *v* compost, dress, dung, enrich, fecundate, feed, fructify, impregnate, inseminate, manure, mulch, pollinate, top-dress.

fertilizer *n* compost, dressing, dung, guano, manure, marl, muck, plant food.

fervent *adj* animated, ardent, devout, eager, earnest, eloquent, emotional, energetic, enthusiastic, excited, fervid, fiery, full-blooded, glowing, heartfelt, hearty, hot, impassioned, intense, passionate, perfervid, soniful, spirited, vehement, vigorous, warm, whole-hearted, zealous.

fervour *n* animation, ardour, eagerness, earnestness, eloquence, emotion, empressement, energy, enthusiasm, excitement, fervency, fervidity, fervidness, fire, heat, intensity, passion, soulfulness, spirit, spiritedness, unction, unctuousness, vehemence, vigour, warmth, whole-heartedness, zeal.

antonym apathy.

fester *v* chafe, decay, gall, gather, irk, maturate, putrefy, rankle, rot, smoulder, suppurate, ulcerate.

antonyms dissipate, heal.

festering *adj* discharging, galling, gathering, infected, inflamed, maturating, poisonous, purulent, pussy, putrescent, rankling, septic, smouldering, suppurating, ulcerated, venomous, virulent.

festival *n* anniversary, blowout, carnival, celebration, commemoration, entertainment, fair, feast, fest, festivities, fete, field day, fiesta, gala, holiday, holy day, jubilee, junket, merrymaking, potlatch, saint's day, treat.

festive *adj* carnival, celebratory, cheery, Christmassy, convivial, cordial, en fête, festal, gala, gay, gleeful, happy, hearty, holiday, jolly, jovial, joyful, joyous, jubilant, merry, mirthful, rollicking, sportive, uproarious.

antonyms gloomy, sober, sombre.

festivities *n* bacchanalia, banqueting, carousal, celebration, entertainment, feasting, festival, fun and games, glorification, jollification, jollities, junketings, party, partying, rejoicings, revelries, revels.

festivity *n* amusement, conviviality, do, enjoyment, feasting, festal, fun, gaiety, garden party, jollification, jollity, joviality, joyfulness, junketing, merriment, merrymaking, mirth, party, pleasure, revelry, sport, wassail.

festoon *n* chaplet, decoration, garland, lei, ornament, swag, wreathe.

v adorn, array, bedeck, bedizen, beribbon, deck, decorate, drape, garland, garnish, hang, ornament, swathe, wreath.

fetch *v* attract, be sold for, bring (in or forth), carry, conduct, convey, deliver, draw, earn, elicit, escort, evoke, get, go for, lead, make, obtain, produce, provoke, realize, retrieve, sell for, summon, transport, uplift, utter, yield.

fetch up arrive, come, come to a halt, end up, finish, finish up, halt, land, reach, stop, turn up.

fetching *adj* alluring, attractive, beguiling, captivating, charming, cute, disarming, enchanting, enticing, fascinating, pretty, sweet, taking, winning, winsome.

antonym repellent.

fete *n* bazaar, carnival, celebration, entertainment, fair, festival, gala, garden party, sale of work.

v banquet, bring out the red carpet for, entertain, honour, lionize, make much of, regale, treat, welcome, wine and dine.

fetid *adj* bad, corrupt, disgusting, filthy, foul, malodorous, mephitic, nauseating, noisome, noxious, odorous, offensive, rancid, rank, reeking, sickly, smelly, stinking.

antonym fragrant.

fetish *n* amulet, charm, cult object, fixation, idée fixe, idol, image, ju-ju, mania, obsession, phylactery, rabbit's-foot, talisman, thing, totem.

fetter *v* bind, chain, confine, curb, encumber, gyve, hamper, hamstring, hobble, manacle, pinion, restrain, restrict, shackle, tie (up), trammel, truss.

antonym free.

fetters *n* bilboes, bondage, bonds, bracelets, captivity, chains, check, constraint, curb, gyves, hampers, handcuffs, hindrances, hobbles, inhibitions, irons, manacles, obstructions, restraints, shackles, trammels.

feud *n* animosity, antagonism, argument, bad blood, bickering, bitterness, clash, conflict, contention, disagreement, discord, dispute, dissension, enmity, estrangement, faction, feuding, grudge, hostility, ill will, quarrel, rivalry, row, squabble, strife, variance, vendetta, war.

antonyms agreement, peace.

v altercate, argue, be at odds, bicker, brawl, clash, contend, dispute, duel, fight, quarrel, row, squabble, war, wrangle.

antonym agree.

fever *n* agitation, calenture, craze, delirium, ecstasy, excitement, fad, ferment, fervour, feverishness, flush, frenzy, heat, illness, intensity, passion, pyrexia, rage, restlessness, sickness, temperature, turmoil, unrest.

fevered *adj* burning, febrile, feverish, feverous, fever-ridden, fiery, flushed, hectic, hot, pyretic, pyrexial, pyrexic.

antonym cool.

feverish *adj* agitated, anxious, burning, distracted, eager, excited, fanatical, febrile, fevered, feverous, flurried, flushed, flustered, frantic, frenetic, frenzied, hasty, hectic, hot, hurried, impatient, inflamed, nervous, obsessive, overwrought, pyretic, restless.

antonyms calm, cool.

feverishness *n* agitation, bustle, commotion, distraction, excitement, ferment, fever, flurry, flush, franticness, frenzy, fuss, haste, hurry, kafuffle, pother, pyrexia, restlessness, stir, turmoil.

antonyms calmness, coolness.

few *adj* few and far between, hard to come by, in short supply, inadequate, inconsiderable, infrequent, insufficient, meagre, negligible, rare, scant, scanty, scarce, scattered, sparse, sporadic, thin, uncommon.

pron a couple, a handful, not many, oddments, one or two, scarcely any, a scattering, small number, a small quantity, some, a sprinkling.

fewness n dearth, inadequacy, infrequency, insufficiency, lack, negligibility, paucity, rareness, rarity, scantiness, scarceness, scarcity, sparseness, thinness, uncommonness, want.
antonyms abundance, glut.

fiancé(e) n betrothed, bridegroom-to-be, bride-to-be, husband-to-be, intended, wife-to-be.

fiasco n bummer, catastrophe, debacle, disappointment, disaster, failure, flop, letdown, mess, non-success, washout.
antonym success.

fiat n authorization, command, decree, dictate, dictum, diktat, directive, edict, go-ahead, injunction, mandate, OK, order, ordinance, permission, prescript, proclamation, sanction, ukase, warrant.

fib n concoction, evasion, fabrication, falsehood, falsity, fantasy, fiction, invention, lie, (little) white lie, misrepresentation, prevarication, story, tale, untruth, whopper, yarn.
v dissemble, evade, fabricate, falsify, fantasize, invent, lie, prevaricate, sidestep, tell a whopper.

fibre n backbone, bast, calibre, character, courage, determination, essence, fibril, filament, grit, guts, nature, nerve, pile, pluck, resolution, roughage, sinew, spirit, stamina, staple, strand, strength, string, substance, tenacity, tendon, tendril, texture, thread, toughness, villus.

fibrous adj fibrillar, fibrillate, fibrillose, fibrillous, fibroid, filamentary, filar, filiform, filose, sinewy, stringy, tendinous, threadlike, wiry.

fickle adj capricious, chameleon, chameleonlike, changeable, changing with the wind, disloyal, erratic, faithless, fitful, flighty, fluctuating, inconstant, irresolute, mercurial, mutable, quick-changing, quicksilver, treacherous, unfaithful, unpredictable, unreliable, unstable, unsteady, vacillating, variable, volatile.
antonym constant.

fickleness n capriciousness, changeability, changeableness, disloyalty, faithlessness, fitfulness, flightiness, inconstancy, mutability, treachery, unfaithfulness, unpredictability, unreliability, unsteadiness, variability, volatility.
antonym constancy.

fiction n canard, cock-and-bull story, concoction, convenience, fable, fabrication, fairy tale, falsehood, fancy, fantasy, feigning, fib, figment of the imagination, fish story, improvisation, invention, legend, lie, make-believe, myth, novel, parable, romance, story, storytelling, tale, tall tale, untruth, whopper, yarn.
antonym truth.

fictional adj fabricated, fabulous, fictitious, fictive, imaginary, invented, legendary, made-up, mythical, non-existent, unreal.

antonyms real, true.

fictitious adj aprocryphal, artificial, assumed, bogus, counterfeit, fabricated, false, falsified, fanciful, feigned, fictive, fraudulent, hypothetical, imaginary, imagined, improvised, invented, made-up, make-believe, mythical, non-existent, spurious, supposed, suppositional, supposititious, unreal, untrue.
antonyms genuine, real.
▲ *confusable word* factitious.

fiddle[1] v bugger (around), fidget, finger, fool (around), idle, mess (around), play, putter, tamper, tinker, toy, trifle, waste (around).

fiddle[2] v cheat, cook, cook the books, diddle, finagle, fix, gerrymander, graft (around), interfere, juggle, manoeuvre, racketeer, swindle, tamper, wangle.
n chicanery, con, fix, fraud, graft, monkey business, racket, rip-off, sharp practice, swindle, trickery, wangle.

fiddle[3] n viol, viola, viola da braccio, viola da spalla, viola d'amore, violin.

fiddling adj insignificant, negligible, paltry, pettifogging, petty, trifling, trivial.
antonyms important, significant.

fidelity n accuracy, adherence, allegiance, authenticity, closeness, constancy, correspondence, dedication, dependability, devotedness, devotion, dutifulness, exactitude, exactness, faith, faithfulness, fealty, incorruptibility, integrity, loyalty, precision, reliability, sense of duty, staunchness, steadfastness, true-heartedness, trustworthiness.
antonyms inaccuracy, inconstancy, treachery.

fidget v be on tenterhooks, be uneasy, bustle, chafe, fiddle, fret, jerk, jiggle, jitter, jump, mess around, play around, squirm, toy, twitch, worry, wriggle.

fidgets n agitation, anxiety, creeps, discomposure, edginess, excitement, fidgetiness, heebie-jeebies, jimjams, jitteriness, jitters, jumpiness, nerves, nerviness, nervousness, restlessness, shakes, twitchiness, unease, uneasiness, willies.

fidgety adj active, agitated, excited, impatient, jerky, jittery, jumpy, nervous, nervy, on edge, on tenterhooks, restive, restless, skittish, squirmy, twitchy, uneasy.
antonym still.

field[1] n arena, background, ballpark, battlefield, battleground, expanse, glebe, grassland, green, greensward, lawn, lea, mead, meadow, paddock, pasture, pitch, playing field, stadium, surface, theatre, turf.

field[2] n applicants, candidates, competition, competitors, contenders, contestants, entrants, opponents, opposition, possibilities, runners.

field[3] n area, bailiwick, ballpark, bounds, confines, department, discipline, domain, environment, forte, limits, line, métier, profession, province, purview, range, scope, sphere, territory, trade.

field[4] v answer, catch, cope with, deal with, defend, deflect, handle, parry, pick up, protect, put into the field, receive, retrieve, return, run, stop.

fiend *n* addict, aficionado, barbarian, beast, brute, demon, devil, devotee, enthusiast, evil spirit, fanatic, freak, ghoul, goblin, hellhound, hobgoblin, incubus, lamia, maniac, mephistopheles, monster, nut, ogre, Satan, savage, succubus.

fiendish *adj* accursed, baleful, black-hearted, cruel, damnable, demoniacal, devilish, diabolical, evil, hellish, impious, implacable, infernal, inhuman, alefic, maleficent, malevolent, malicious, malign, malignant, Mephistophelian, mischievous, monstrous, nefarious, satanic, savage, terrible, ungodly, unspeakable, vicious, vile, wicked.

fierce *adj* active, ardent, baleful, barbarous, bitter, blustery, boisterous, brutal, cruel, cutthroat, dangerous, eager, extreme, fanatic(al), fearsome, fell, feral, ferocious, fervid, fiery, frightening, furious, grim, howling, implacable, intense, keen, menacing, merciless, murderous, passionate, powerful, raging, relentless, savage, stern, stormy, strong, tempestuous, threatening, tigerlike, truculent, tumultuous, uncontrollable, unrelenting, untamable, untamed, vicious, violent, warlike, wild, zealous.

antonyms calm, gentle, kind.

fierceness *n* ardour, avidity, bitterness, bluster, destructiveness, fanaticism, fearsomeness, ferity, ferocity, fervidness, fervour, fieriness, intensity, keenness, mercilessness, passion, relentlessness, ruthlessness, savageness, sternness, storminess, strength, tempestuousness, viciousness, violence, wildness, zeal.

antonyms gentleness, kindness.

fiery *adj* ablaze, afire, aflame, aglow, ardent, blazing, burning, choleric, easily aroused, eloquent, excitable, febrile, feisty, fervent, fervid, fevered, feverish, fierce, flaming, glowing, heated, hot, hot-headed, hot-tempered, impatient, impetuous, impulsive, inflamed, irascible, irritable, passionate, peppery, perfervid, red-hot, spirited, sultry, torrid, truculent, violent, volcanic, zealous.

antonyms cold, impassive.

fight *v* altercate, argue, assault, battle, bear arms (against), bicker, box, brawl, carry on, clash, close, combat, compete, conduct, conflict, contend, contest, cross swords, defy, dispute, do battle (with), engage, exchange blows, fence, feud, go to war, grapple, joust, lock horns, mix it up, oppose, prosecute, quarrel, resist, scrap, scuffle, skirmish, spar, squabble, stand up to (or against), strive, struggle (against), take the field, tilt, tussle, wage, wage war, war (against), work, work against, wrangle, wrestle.

n action, affray, altercation, argument, battle, belligerence, bicker, bout, boxing match, brawl, brush, clash, conflict, contest, courage, dispute, dogfight, duel, encounter, engagement, feistiness, fisticuffs, fracas, fray, free-for-all, hostilities, joust, melee, mettle,

militancy, passage of arms, pluck, quarrel, resilience, resistance, riot, row, rumble, scrap, scuffle, set-to, shootout, skirmish, spat, spirit, spunk, squabble, strength, struggle, tenacity, tiff, tug-of-war, tussle, war, wrangle.

fight back[1] defend oneself, give as good as one gets, put up a fight, reply, resist, retaliate, retort, show fight.

fight back[2] bite back, bottle up, contain, control, curb, fight down, hold back, hold in check, repress, resist, restrain, swallow, suppress.

fight off beat off, hold off, keep at bay, overcome, put to flight, rebuff, repel, repress, repulse, resist, rout, stave off, turn back, ward off.

fight shy of avoid, balk at, disdain, eschew, give a wide berth to, keep at arm's length, keep or stay away from, shun, spurn, steer clear of.

fighter *n* adventurer, antagonist, battler, belligerent, boxer, brave, bruiser, champion, combatant, contender, contestant, disputant, fighting man, filibuster, free lance, gladiator, man-at-arms, mercenary, militant, prizefighter, pugilist, soldier, soldier of fortune, swordsman, trooper, warrior, wrestler.

fighting *n* action, arguing, battle, bickering, bloodshed, boxing, brawling, clash, combat, conflict, contention, dissension, encounter, engagement, feuding, fisticuffs, fray, hostilities, infighting, melee, pugilism, quarrelling, scuffle, scuffling, squabbling, strife, struggle, war, warfare, warring, wrangling, wrestling.

figment *n* concoction, creation, deception, delusion, fable, fabrication, fairy tale, falsehood, fancy, fiction, illusion, improvisation, invention, mare's nest, product, production, work.

figurative *adj* allegorical, descriptive, emblematic, evocative, extended, fanciful, imagistic, metaphorical, non-literal, parabolic, pictorial, picturesque, poetic, representational, representative, symbolic, tropical, typical.

antonym literal.

figure *n* amount, apparition, body, build, celebrity, character, cipher, configuration, conformation, cost, depiction, design, device, diagram, digit, dignitary, drawing, embellishment, emblem, form, frame, human form, illustration, image, motif, notable, number, numeral, outline, pattern, person, personage, personality, physique, picture, price, proportions, representation, shadow, shape, silhouette, sketch, sum, symbol, torso, total, trope, value.

v add, appear, assume, be conspicuous, be logical, believe, calculate, compute, consider, count, do arithmetic, estimate, feature, guess, judge, make sense, opine, presume, reckon, stand to reason, surmise, tally, think, tot up, work out.

figure of speech conceit, expression, figurative, figure, image, imagery, metaphor, rhetorical device, simile, trope, turn of phrase.

figure out calculate, come up with, comprehend, compute, decipher, excogitate, fathom, make head or tail of, make out, puzzle out, reason out, reckon, resolve, see, solve, think out (or up), understand, work out.

figured *adj* adorned, decorated, embellished, formed, marked, ornamented, patterned, printed, shaped, sprigged, variegated.

antonym plain.

figurehead *n* bust, carving, cipher, dummy, front, front man, image, man of straw, mouthpiece, name, nominal head, nonentity, nonperson, puppet, rubber stamp, statue, straw man, titular head, token.

filament *n* cilium, fibre, fibril, hair, staple, strand, string, thread, whisker, wire.

filch *v* abstract, appropriate, borrow, crib, embezzle, fake, finger, lift, make off with, misappropriate, palm, peculate, pilfer, pinch, plagiarize, poach, purloin, rip off, scoff, snaffle, snitch, steal, swipe, take, thieve.

file¹ *v* abrade, grate, grind, hone, pare, plane, rasp, rub (down), sand, scour, scrape, shape, sharpen, shave, smooth, trim, whet.

file² *n* binder, cabinet, case, catalogue, documents, dossier, folder, index, information, list, portfolio, record, registry .

v apply, catalogue, document, enter, index, make application, memorize, pigeonhole, process, record, register, send in, store, submit.

file³ *n* column, cortege, line, parade, procession, queue, row, stream, string, trail, train.

v defile, march, parade, stream, trail, troop.

filial *adj* affectionate, daughterlike, daughterly, devoted, dutiful, fond, loving, loyal, respectful, sonlike, sonly.

antonyms disloyal, unfilial.

filibuster¹ *n* delay, hindrance, impediment, obstruction, peroration, postponement, procrastination, speechifying.

v delay, hinder, impede, obstruct, perorate, prevent, procrastinate, put off, speechify.

antonym expedite.

filibuster² *n* adventurer, buccaneer, corsair, free lance, freebooter, pirate, rover, sea robber, sea rover, soldier of fortune.

filigree *n* fret work, interlace, lace, lacework, lattice, lattice work, openwork, pattern, scrollwork, tracery, wirework.

fill *v* assign, block, bung, charge, clog, close, congest, cork, cram, crowd, discharge, drench, engage, engorge, execute, fulfil, furnish, glut, gorge, hold, imbue, impregnate, inflate, load, meet, occupy, officiate, overspread, pack, perform, permeate, pervade, plug, replenish, sate, satiate, satisfy, saturate, seal, soak, stock, stop (up), stuff, suffuse, supply, surfeit, swell, take up.

antonyms clear, empty.

one's fill abundance, ample, enough, full measure, plenty, sufficiency, sufficient.

fill in acquaint with, act for, advise, answer, apprise, brief, bring up to date, complete, deputize, fill out, inform, put wise, replace,

represent, stand in, sub, substitute, understudy.

filling *n* contents, filler, grouting, innards, inside, insides, padding, rubble, stuffing, wadding.

adj ample, big, generous, heavy, large, nutritious, satisfying, solid, square, substantial, sustaining.

antonym insubstantial.

fillip *n* boost, flick, goad, impetus, incentive, prod, push, shove, spur, stimulant, stimulus, tap, zest.

antonym damper.

film¹ *n* bloom, blur, cloud, coat, coating, covering, dusting, fog, gauze, glaze, haze, haziness, integument, layer, membrane, mist, opacity, pellicle, screen, scum, sheet, skin, tissue, veil, web.

v blear, blur, cloud, dull, glaze, haze, mist, screen, veil.

film² *n* documentary, epic, feature film, flick, horse opera, motion picture, movie, oldie, picture, short, video, western.

v photograph, shoot, take, video, videotape.

filmy *adj* cobwebby, delicate, diaphanous, fine, flimsy, floaty, fragile, gauzy, gossamer, indistinct, insubstantial, light, see-through, sheer, shimmering, thin, translucent, transparent.

antonym opaque.

filter *v* clarify, dribble, escape, exude, filtrate, flow, leach, leak, ooze, pass, penetrate, percolate, purify, refine, screen, seep, sieve, sift, strain, transpire, transude, trickle, well.

n colander, gauze, membrane, mesh, riddle, sieve, sifter, strainer.

filth *n* bilge, carrion, coarseness, contamination, corruption, crud, defilement, dirt, dirty-mindedness, dung, excrement, excreta, feces, filthiness, foulness, garbage, grime, grossness, grunge, impurity, indecency, muck, nastiness, obscenity, ordure, pollution, pornography, putrefaction, putrescence, refuse, scatology, sewage, slime, sludge, smut, smuttiness, soil, sordidness, squalor, uncleanness, vileness, vulgarity.

antonyms cleanliness, decency, purity.

filthy *adj* base, bawdy, begrimed, black, blackened, blue, coarse, contemptible, corrupt, depraved, despicable, dirty, dirty-minded, fecal, feculent, foul, foul-mouthed, grimy, gross, grubby, grungy, impure, indecent, lewd, licentious, low, mean, miry, mucky, muddy, nasty, nasty-minded, obscene, offensive, polluted, pornographic, putrid, scatological, scurrilous, slimy, smoky, smutty, sooty, sordid, squalid, swinish, unclean, unwashed, vicious, vile, vulgar.

antonyms clean, decent, inoffensive, pure.

final *adj* absolute, clinching, closing, concluding, conclusive, decided, deciding, decisive, definite, definitive, departing, determinate, dying, eleventh-hour, end, eventual, farewell, finished, incontrovertible, irrefragable, irrefutable, irrevocable, last, last-minute, latest, parting, settled, terminal, terminating, ultimate, unanswerable, undeniable.

finale *n* climax, close, conclusion, crescendo, crowning glory, culmination, curtain, denouement, end, epilogue, final curtain, finis, last act, supreme moment.

finality *n* certitude, conclusiveness, conviction, decidedness, decisiveness, definiteness, firmness, inevitability, inevitableness, irreversibility, irrevocability, resolution, ultimacy, unanswerability, unavoidability.

finalize *v* agree, clinch, complete, conclude, decide, dispose of, end, finish, get signed and sealed, resolve, round off, seal, settle, sew up, tie up, work out, wrap up.

finally *adv* absolutely, at last, at length, completely, conclusively, convincingly, decisively, definitely, eventually, forever, for good, for good and all, in conclusion, in the end, inescapably, inexorably, irreversibly, irrevocably, last, last but not least, lastly, once and for all, permanently, ultimately, when all is said and done.

finance *n* accounting, accounts, banking, business, commerce, economics, investment, money, money management, money matters, stock market, trade.

v back, bail out, bankroll, capitalize, float, fund, guarantee, pay for, set up, subsidize, support, underwrite.

finances *n* affairs, assets, bank account, bread, budget, capital, cash, coffers, funds, income, liquidity, money, moolah, money matters, purse, resources, revenues, wealth, wherewithal.

financial *adj* budgetary, commercial, economic, fiscal, monetary, money, pecuniary.

financier *n* banker, broker, financialist, gnome, investor, moneylender, money-maker, speculator, stockbroker.

find *v* achieve, acquire, arrive at, ascertain, attain, bring, catch, chance on, come across, come upon, conclude, consider, contribute, declare, descry, detect, discover, earn, encounter, espy, experience, expose, feel, ferret out, furnish, gain, get, happen on, hit on, hunt down, judge, learn, light on, locate, meet, note, notice, observe, obtain, perceive, procure, provide, reach, realize, receive, recognize, recover, rediscover, regain, remark, repossess, retrieve, rule, see, spot, stumble on, supply, think, track down, turn up, uncover, unearth, win.

n acquisition, asset, bargain, catch, discovery, finding, good buy.

find fault (with) bitch, carp, cavil, censure, complain, criticize, depreciate, disparage, gripe, hypercriticise, kvetch, nag, niggle, nit-pick, pettifog, pick holes, point the finger, pull to pieces, quarrel with, quibble, reprove, take to task.

antonym praise.

find out ascertain, catch, detect, dig up, disclose, discover, establish, expiscate, expose, figure out, learn, note, observe,

perceive, realize, reveal, rumble, show up, sus out, tumble to, uncover, unmask.

finding *n* award, breakthrough, conclusion, decision, decree, discovery, evidence, find, judgment, pronouncement, recommendation, verdict.

fine[1] *adj* A-O.K., A-one, abstruse, acceptable, acute, admirable, agreeable, all right, attractive, balmy, beau, beaut, beautiful, bonny, brave, bright, brilliant, choice, clear, clement, cloudless, convenient, copacetic, critical, cutting, dainty, dandy, delicate, diaphanous, discriminating, dry, elegant, elusive, exact, excellent, exceptional, expensive, expert, exquisite, fair, fastidious, fine-drawn, first-class, first-rate, flimsy, fragile, gauzy, good, good-looking, goodly, gorgeous, gossamer, great, hair-splitting, handsome, honed, hunky, hunky-dory, impressive, in apple pie order, in good health, intelligent, jake, keen, light, lovely, magnificent, masterful, masterly, meticulous, minute, nice, of high quality, OK, ornate, outstanding, peachy (keen), pleasant, polished, powdery, precise, pure, quick, rainless, rare, refined, robust, satisfactory, select, sensitive, sharp, sheer, showy, skilful, skilled, slender, slight, small, smart, solid, splendid, sterling, strong, sturdy, stylish, sublime, subtle, suitable, sunny, superior, supreme, tasteful, tenuous, thin, tickety-boo, tiny, unalloyed, virtuoso, well, well-favoured, wiredrawn.

fine[2] *v* mulct, penalize, punish, sting.

n amercement, damages, forfeit, forfeiture, mulct, penalty, punishment.

finery *n* bedizenment, decorations, frills and furbelows, frippery, gaud, gaudery, gauds, gear, gewgaws, glad rags, jewellery, ornamentation, ornaments, showiness, splendour, Sunday best, trappings.

finesse *n* address, adeptness, adroitness, artfulness, artifice, cleverness, craft, deftness, delicacy, diplomacy, discretion, elegance, expertise, gracefulness, know-how, neatness, polish, quickness, refinement, savoir-faire, skill, sophistication, strategem, subtlety, tact.

v bluff, evade, manipulate, manoeuvre, trick.

finger[1] *v* caress, feel, fiddle with, fondle, handle, manipulate, maul, meddle with, palpate, paw, play around with, pinky, stroke, touch, toy with.

n claw, digit, digital, index, talon.

finger[2] *v* accuse, betray, condemn, filch, inform on, pilfer, point out, rat on, steal.

finicky *adj* choosy, critical, dainty, delicate, difficult, fastidious, finical, fussy, hypercritical, meticulous, nice, nit-picking, overnice, particular, pernickety, precise, scrupulous, squeamish, tricky.

antonyms easy, easygoing.

finish (off, up, or **with)** *v* accomplish, achieve, annihilate, best, bring (or come) to an end, buff, burnish, cease, close, coat, complete, conclude, consume, consummate, culminate, deal with, defeat, destroy, devour, discharge, dispatch, dispose of, do, drain, drink, eat, elaborate, empty, encompass, end, euchre, execute, exhaust, expend, exterminate, face, finalize, fulfil, get rid of, gild, hone, kill, lacquer, overcome, overpower, overthrow, perfect, polish, put an end to, put the last hand to, refine, resolve, round off, rout, ruin, settle, smooth, smooth off, sophisticate, spend, stain, stop, terminate, texture, use (up), veneer, wax, wind up, worst, zap.

n annihilation, appearance, bankruptcy, burnish, cessation, close, closing, closure, completion, conclusion, coup de grâce, culmination, cultivation, culture, curtain, curtains, death, defeat, demise, denouement, downfall, elaboration, end, end of the road, ending, finale, gloss, grain, liquidation, lustre, patina, perfection, polish, refinement, ruin, shine, smoothness, sophistication, surface, termination, texture, wind-up.

finished *adj* accomplished, bankrupt, beaten, classic, closed, consummate, cultivated, dead ended, defeated, dog-tired, done, done for, done in, doomed, drained, elegant, empty, exhausted, expert, faultless, flawless, gone, impeccable, lost, masterly, over, perfected, played out, polished, professional, proficient, refined, ruined, skilled, smooth, sophisticated, spent, through, undone, urbane, used up, virtuoso, washed-up, wrecked, zonked.

antonyms coarse, crude, unfinished.

finite *adj* bounded, calculable, circumscribed, compassable, definable, delimited, demarcated, fixed, limited, measurable, restricted, terminable.

antonym infinite.

fire *n* animation, ardour, balefire, barrage, blaze, bombardment, bonfire, brio, broadside, burning, cannonade, combustion, conflagration, dash, eagerness, earnestness, élan, eloquence, enthusiasm, excitement, feeling, fervency, fervidness, fervour, feu de joie, fever, fierceness, fireworks, flak, flames, force, fusillade, gunfire, hail, heat, impetuosity, inferno, inflammation, intensity, life, light, liveliness, lustre, pain, passion, radiance, salvo, scintillation, shelling, signal fire, sniping, sparkle, spirit, splendour, trial, trouble, verve, vigour, virtuosity, vivacity, volley, warmth, zeal.

v activate, animate, arouse, boot out, cashier, depose, detonate, discharge, dismiss, eject, electrify, enkindle, enliven, excite, explode, fire away, galvanize, get rid of, give a pink slip to, give marching orders, give the boot to, give the bum's rush to, hurl, ignite, impassion, incite, inflame, inspire, inspirit, kindle, launch, let go, let off, light, loose, put a match to, quicken, rouse, sack, send off, set alight, set fire to, set off, set on fire, shell, shoot, show the door, stimulate, stir, throw, touch off, trigger off, whet.

on fire ablaze, aflame, alight, ardent, blazing, burning, eager, enthusiastic, excited, fiery, fired up, flaming, ignited, in flames, inspired, kindled, passionate.

firearm *n* automatic, gun, handgun, musket, muzzle-loader, pistol, repeater, revolver, rifle, shooter, shooting iron, shotgun, weapon.

fireworks *n* crackers, explosions, feux d'artifice, fire, firecrackers, gunfire, hysterics, illuminations, pyrotechnics, rage, rockets, Roman candles, rows, six-shooter, sparklers, sparks, storm, tantrum, temper, torpedoes, trouble, uproar.

firm¹ *adj* abiding, adamant, anchored, balanced, braced, cast-iron, cemented, changeless, committed, compact, compressed, concentrated, congealed, constant, convinced, crisp, definite, dense, dependable, determined, dogged, durable, embedded, enduring, established, faithful, fast, fastened, fixed, grounded, hard, hardened, immovable, impregnable, indurate, inelastic, inflexible, iron-fisted, iron-handed, iron-hearted, jelled, motionless, obdurate, permanent, positive, reliable, resolute, resolved, rigid, robust, secure, secured, set, settled, solid, solidified, stable, stationary, staunch, steadfast, steady, stiff, strict, strong, sturdy, substantial, sure, taut, tight, true, unalterable, unassailable, unbending, unchanging, undeviating, unfailing, unfaltering, unflinching, unmoved, unmoving, unshakable, unshakeable, unshaken, unshifting, unswerving, unwavering, unyielding, well-knit.

antonyms infirm, soft, unsound.

firm² *n* association, business, company, concern, conglomerate, corporation, enterprise, establishment, house, institution, organization, outfit, partnership, set-up, syndicate.

firmness *n* an iron fist, an iron hand, changelessness, compactness, constancy, conviction, density, dependability, determination, doggedness, durability, fixedness, fixity, hardness, immovability, impregnability, indomitability, inelasticity, inflexibility, obduracy, reliability, resistance, resolution, resolve, rigidity, solidity, soundness, stability, staunchness, steadfastness, steadiness, stiffness, strength, strength of will, strictness, sureness, tautness, tension, tightness, unshakability, will, willpower.

antonyms infirmity, uncertainty, unsoundness.

first *adj* basic, cardinal, chief, earliest, eldest, elementary, embryonic, foremost, front, fundamental, head, highest, initial, introductory, key, leading, lowest, maiden, main, most, oldest, opening, original, paramount, preceding, predominant, pre-eminent, premier, primal, primary, prime, primeval, primitive, primordial, principal, prior, pristine, rudimentary, ruling, senior, sovereign, uppermost.

adv at the outset, before all else, beforehand, early on, firstly, for the first time, in front, in preference, in the beginning, initially, originally, preferably, primarily, rather, sooner, to begin with, to start with.

first name baptismal name, Christian name, font name, forename, given name.

first-hand *adj* direct, eyewitness, immediate, personal, straight from the horse's mouth.

antonyms hearsay, indirect.

first-rate *adj* A-one, admirable, crack, elite, excellent, exceptional, exclusive, fine, first-class, leading, matchless, nonpareil, outstanding, peerless, prime, second-to-none, splendid, superb, superior, superlative, tiptop, top, top-flight, top-notch, top-quality, tops, world-class.

antonym inferior.

fiscal *adj* budgetary, capital, economic, financial, monetary, money, pecuniary, treasury.

fish *v* angle, cast, fly-fish, harvest, trawl, troll.
n aquatic, chap, drip, dupe, fellow.

fish for angle for, delve for, elicit, hunt for, invite, look for, search for, seek, solicit.

fish out come up with, dredge up, extract, extricate, find, haul up, produce, rescue, withdraw.

fish out of water freak, maverick, misfit, nonconformist, rogue, square peg in a round hole.

antonym conformist.

fisher *n* angler, fisherman, fly-fisher, handliner, rod-fisher, rodman, rodsman.

fishy *adj* deceptive, dishonest, doubtful, dubious, fishlike, funny, glassy, implausible, improbable, inexpressive, irregular, odd, piscatorial, piscatory, piscine, queer, questionable, shady, suspect, suspicious, unlikely, vacant.

antonyms honest, legitimate.

fissile *adj* brittle, cleavable, divisible, easily split, fissionable, flaky, scissile, separable, severable.

fission *n* breaking, cleavage, disintegration, division, parting, rending, rupture, schism, scission, separation, severance, splitting.

fissure *n* breach, break, chasm, chink, cleavage, cleft, crack, cranny, crevasse, crevice, discontinuity, fault, foramen, fracture, gap, gash, hole, interstice, opening, rent, rift, rupture, slit, split, sulcus, vein.

fist *n* duke, grasp, hand, handwriting, mitt, paw.

fit¹ *adj* able, able-bodied, adapted, adequate, apposite, appropriate, apt, becoming, capable, commensurate, competent, condign, convenient, correct, deserving, due, eligible, equipped, expedient, fit as a fiddle, fitted, fitting, hale, hearty, healthy, in fine fettle, in good form, in good health, in good shape, in good trim, in the pink, meet, prepared, proper, qualified, ready, right, robust, satisfactory, seemly, sound, strapping, strong, sturdy, sufficient, suitable, suited, trained, trim, well, well-chosen, well-suited, worthy.

antonym unfit.

v accommodate, accord, adapt, adjust, agree (with), alter, arrange, assimilate, belong, change, concur, conform, correspond, customize, dispose, dovetail, equip, fashion, figure, follow, go, harmonize, interlock, jibe,

jive, join, match, measure, meet, modify, outfit, place, position, prepare, reconcile, shape, square, stack up, suit, supply, tailor, tally.

fit out accommodate, accoutre, arm, caparison, equip, kit out, outfit, prepare, provide, rig out, supply.

fit² *n* access, attack, bird, bout, burst, bustle, caprice, convulsion, eruption, explosion, fancy, frenzy, hissy-fit, humour, hysterics, kittens, mood, outbreak, outburst, paroxysm, seizure, spasm, spell, storm, surge, tantrum, whim.

fitful *adj* broken, desultory, discontinuous, disturbed, erratic, fluctuating, haphazard, inconstant, intermittent, irregular, jerky, occasional, spasmodic, sporadic, uneven, unstable, unsteady, variable.

antonyms regular, steady.

fitfully *adv* brokenly, desultorily, discontinuously, erratically, haphazardly, in fits and starts, in snatches, intermittently, interruptedly, irregularly, off and on, shakily, spasmodically, sporadically, unevenly, unsteadily.

antonyms regularly, steadily.

fitness *n* adaptation, adequacy, applicability, appropriateness, aptness, competence, condition, eligibility, haleness, health, healthiness, pertinence, preparedness, propriety, qualifications, readiness, robustness, seemliness, strength, suitability, vigour.

antonym unfitness.

fitted *adj* accoutred, adapted, appointed, armed, booted and spurred, built-in, caparisoned, equipped, fit, furnished, kitted, outfitted, permanent, prepared, provided, qualified, rigged out, right, suitable, supplied, tailor-made.

antonym unfitted.

fitting *adj* apposite, appropriate, apt, becoming, comme il faut, condign, correct, decent, decorous, deserved, desirable, expedient, harmonious, meet, merited, proper, right, seasonable, seemly, suitable, timely, well-chosen.

antonym unsuitable.

n accessory, attachment, component, connection, fitment, fixture, part, piece, unit.

fittings *n* accessories, accoutrements, appointments, appurtenances, conveniences, equipment, extras, fixtures, furnishings, furniture, trimmings.

fivefold *adj* pentaploid, quintuple, quintuplicate.

fix¹ *v* adjust, agree on, anchor, appoint, arrange, arrive at, attach, bind, bribe, cement, conclude, confirm, congeal, connect, consolidate, correct, couple, decide, define, determine, direct, embed, establish, fasten, fiddle, finalize, firm, focus, freeze, get even with, get revenge on, glue, harden, hold steady, implant, inculcate, influence, install, irradicate, limit, link, locate, make, make firm, manipulate, manoeuvre, memorize, mend, nail, name, ordain, pin, place, plant, point, position, prearrange, preordain, produce, punish, regulate, repair, resolve, restore, rig, rigidify, rivet, root, seal, seat, secure, see to, set, settle, set up, show, solidify, sort, sort out, specify, stabilize, stack (the deck), stick, stiffen, straighten, swing, teach a lesson to, thicken, tidy, tie.

n awkward position, corner, difficulty, dilemma, embarrassment, hole, jam, mess, muddle, pickle, plight, predicament, put-up job, quagmire, quandary, scrape, set-up, spot.

fix up accommodate, agree on, arrange (for), bring about, decorate, equip, fix, furnish, mend, organize, plan, produce, provide with, put in order, refurbish, renovate, repair, set up, settle, sort out, supply.

fix² *n* dose, hit, injection, jag, pop, score, shot, slug.

fixation *n* attachment, complex, compulsion, fetish, hang-up, idée fixe, infatuation, mania, monomania, obsession, preoccupation, thing.

fixed *adj* agreed, anchored, arranged, attached, bribed, castrated, decided, definite, determinate, determined, entrenched, established, fast, fiddled, fiducial, firm, framed, immovable, inflexible, ingrained, intent, invariable, lasting, level, manipulated, packed, permanent, planned, prearranged, put-up, resolute, resolved, rigged, rigid, rooted, secure, set, settled, spayed, standing, stacked, stated, steadfast, steady, sterilized, stiff, sure, unalterable, unbending, unblinking, unchangeable, unchanging, undeviating, unflinching, unvarying, unwavering, unyielding.

antonyms alterable, variable.

fixity *n* determination, doggedness, firmness, fixedness, intentness, permanence, perseverance, persistence, resoluteness, resolve, stability, steadiness, strength, tenacity.

fizz *v* bubble, effervesce, fizzle, froth, fume, hiss, sizzle, sparkle, spit, sputter.

fizzle out abort, burn out, collapse, come to nothing, die away, die down, disappear, dissipate, evaporate, fail, fall through, fold, peter out, run out of steam, stop, subside, taper off, wind down.

fizzy *adj* aerated, bubbling, bubbly, carbonated, effervescent, frothy, gassy, sparkling.

flabbergasted *adj* amazed, astonished, astounded, bowled over, confounded, dazed, disconcerted, dumfounded, nonplussed, overcome, overwhelmed, speechless, staggered, stunned, stupefied.

flabbiness *n* bloat, bloatedness, embonpoint, fat, flab, flaccidity, flesh, fleshiness, heaviness, laxness, limpness, looseness, overweight, pendulousness, plumpness, slackness.

antonyms firmness, leanness, strength.

flabby *adj* baggy, drooping, effete, enervated, fat, feckless, feeble, flaccid, fleshy, floppy, hanging, impotent, ineffective, ineffectual, inert, lax, limp, loose, nerveless, pendulous, plump, sagging, slack, sloppy, soft, spineless, toneless, unfit, untoned, weak, yielding.

antonyms firm, lean, strong.

flaccid *adj* clammy, drooping, flabby, floppy, hypotonic, inert, lax, limp, loose, nerveless, relaxed, sagging, slack, soft, toneless, weak.

antonym firm.

flaccidity *n* clamminess, droopiness, flabbiness, floppiness, limpness, looseness, nervelessness, slackness, softness, tonelessness.

antonym firmness.

flag¹ *v* abate, decline, degenerate, deteriorate, die, diminish, droop, dwindle, ebb, fade, fail, faint, fall (off), falter, flop, languish, lessen, peter out, sag, sink, slow, slump, subside, succumb, taper off, tire, wane, weaken, weary, wilt.

antonym revive.

flag² *n* banderole, banner, burgee, colours, ensign, gonfalon, jack, Jolly Roger, labarum, oriflamme, pennant, pennon, standard, streamer.

v docket, hail, indicate, label, mark, motion, note, salute, signal, tab, tag, warn, wave.

flagellation *n* beating, castigation, chastisement, flaying, flogging, hiding, lashing, scourging, tanning, thrashing, whaling, whipping.

flagrant *adj* arrant, atrocious, audacious, barefaced, blatant, bold, brazen, conspicuous, crying, egregious, enormous, flagitious, flaunted, glaring, heinous, immodest, infamous, notorious, open, ostentatious, outrageous, outright, overt, rank, scandalous, shameless, unashamed, undisguised.

antonyms covert, secret.

flail *v* beat, thrash, thresh, whip.

flair *n* ability, accomplishment, acumen, aptitude, artistry, chic, creativity, dash, discernment, discrimination, elegance, facility, faculty, feel, genius, gift, knack, mastery, nose, panache, perception, skill, style, stylishness, talent, taste, verve.

antonym ineptitude.

flak *n* abuse, animadversions, artillery, aspersions, bad press, censure, complaints, condemnation, criticism, disapprobation, disapproval, disparagement, faultfinding, gunfire, hostility, invective, opposition, strictures.

flake *n* bit, chip, disc, eccentric, floccule, floccus, fruitcake, lamella, lamina, layer, nut, oddball, paring, particle, peeling, scale, shaving, sliver, squama, wafer, weirdo.

v blister, chip, delaminate, exfoliate, peel, scale, split.

flaky *adj* bizarre, dry, eccentric, exfoliative, furfuraceous, laminar, layered, nutty, oddball, powdery, scabrous, scaly, scurfy, weird.

flamboyance *n* brightness, brilliance, colour, dash, élan, extravagance, glamour, ornateness, ostentation, panache, pizzazz, rococo, showiness, style, theatricality.

antonyms diffidence, restraint.

flamboyant *adj* baroque, brilliant, colourful, dashing, dazzling, elaborate, exciting, extravagant, flaming, flashy, florid, gaudy, glamorous, high-spirited, jaunty, lively, ornate, ostentatious, rich, rococo, showy, striking, stylish, swashbuckling, theatrical.

antonyms modest, restrained.

flame *v* beam, blaze, burn, burst forth (or out), flare, flash, flush, glare, glow, radiate, redden, shine.

n affection, ardour, beau, blaze, brightness, enthusiasm, fervency, fervour, fire, heart-throb, intensity, keenness, light, lover, passion, radiance, sweetheart, tongue, warmth, zeal.

flaming *adj* ablaze, afire, alight, angry, ardent, aroused, blazing, bright, brilliant, burning, fervid, fiery, flashing, flaring, flushed, frenzied, glowing, hot, impassioned, intense, raging, red, red-hot, scintillating, smouldering, vehement, vivid.

flammable *adj* burnable, combustible, combustive, deflagrable, fiery, ignitable, inflammable.

antonyms fire-resistant, flameproof, incombustible, non-flammable, non-inflammable.

flange *n* flare, knob, lip, rim, skirt, splay.

flank *n* edge, flitch, fringe, ham, haunch, hip, loin, quarter, side, thigh, wing.

v accompany, border, bound, confine, edge, fringe, go around, guard, line, protect, screen, skirt, wall.

flap¹ *v* agitate, beat, dither, flail, flutter, fuss, panic, shake, swing, swish, thrash, thresh, vibrate, wag, wave.

n agitation, bustle, commotion, dither, fluster, flutter, fuss, kafuffle, pother, state, stew, sweat, tizzy, twitter.

flap² *n* aileron, apron, cover, fly, fold, lapel, lappet, lug, overlap, skirt, tab, tag, tail.

flare (up) *v* blaze, burn (up), burst, dazzle, erupt, explode, flame (up), flash, flicker, flutter, glare, signal, waver.

n bell-bottom, blaze, broadening, burst, flame, flange, flash, flicker, glare, gore, outburst, splay, spread, torch, widening.

flare out broaden, splay, spread out, widen.

flare up become angry, blaze (forth), blow one's top, erupt, explode, fly off the handle, lose one's cool.

flash *v* appear, blaze, bolt, brandish, coruscate, dart, dash, display, exhibit, expose, flare, flaunt, flicker, flourish, fly, fulminate, glare, gleam, glint, glisten, glitter, light, race, scintillate, shimmer, shine, shoot, show, signal, sparkle, speed, sprint, streak, sweep, twinkle, whistle.

n blaze, bulletin, burst, coruscation, dazzle, demonstration, display, flare, flicker, gleam, hint, instant, item, jiff, jiffy, manifestation, moment, outburst, ray, scintillation, second, shaft, shake, shimmer, show, sign, spark, sparkle, split second, streak, touch, trice, twinkle, twinkling.

flashing *adj* coruscant, coruscating, dancing, flaring, flickering, fulgent, glinting, glittering, lambent, scintillating, shiny, sparkling, twinkling.

antonym steady.

flashy *adj* bold, brassy, cheap, chintzy, flamboyant, flash, garish, gaudy, glamorous, glittery, glitzy, jazzy, loud, meretricious, obtrusive, ostentatious, raffish, rakish, ritzy, shiny, showy, slick, snazzy, tacky, tasteless, tawdry, tinselly, vulgar.

antonyms plain, simple, tasteful.

flask *n* canteen, carafe, flacon, hipflask, phial, pocket flask, vial.

flat¹ *adj* at full length, even, horizontal, lamellar, lamellate, lamelliform, level, levelled, low, outstretched, pancakelike, planar, plane, prone, prostrate, reclining, recumbent, smooth, spread-eagled, supine, unbroken, uniform.

n lowland, marsh, morass, moss, mud flat, plain, shallow, shoal, strand, swamp.

flat out all out, at full speed, at full tilt, at top speed, bluntly, double-quick, flatly, for all one is worth, full speed ahead, hell for leather, point-blank, posthaste, straight out.

flat² *adj* boring, burst, cardboard, collapsed, colourless, deflated, depressed, dull, emotionless, empty, expressionless, flavourless, insipid, jejune, lacklustre, lifeless, mechanical, monotonous, one-dimensional, pointless, prosaic, punctured, spiritless, stale, tedious, unidimensional, uninteresting, unpalatable, vapid, watery, weak, wooden.

flat³ *adj* absolute, blunt, categorical, direct, downright, explicit, final, fixed, flat-out, out-and-out, peremptory, point-blank, positive, straight, total, uncompromising, unconditional, unequivocal, unqualified.

antonym equivocal.

adv absolutely, categorically, completely, entirely, exactly, flatly, flat out, point-blank, precisely, totally, utterly.

flat⁴ *n* apartment, bachelor(ette), bed-sitting room, maisonette, pad, penthouse, pied-à-terre, rooms, place, suite, tenement.

flatly *adv* absolutely, categorically, completely, peremptorily, point-blank, positively, uncompromisingly, unconditionally, unhesitatingly.

flatten *v* compress, crush, deck, demolish, even out, fell, floor, iron out, knock down, lay out, level, overwhelm, plane, planish, plaster, press (out), prostrate, raze, roll, slight, smooth, squash, straighten, subdue, trample.

flatter *v* adulate, become, blandish, blarney, bootlick, butter up, cajole, claw, compliment, court, enhance, eulogize, fawn on, humour, inveigle, laud, oil, play up to, praise, set off, show to advantage, soap, soft-soap, soothe, suit, sweet-talk, sycophantize, wheedle.

antonym criticize.

flatterer *n* adulator, backscratcher, bootlicker, cajoler, encomiast, eulogist, eulogizer, fawner, flunkey, groveller, lackey, sycophant, toady, wheedler.

antonyms critic, opponent.

flattering *adj* adulatory, backscratching, becoming, blandishing, cajoling, complimentary, effective, effusive, enhancing, favourable, fawning, fulsome, gratifying, honeyed, honey-tongued, ingratiating, kind, laudatory, obsequious, servile, smooth-spoken, smooth-tongued, sugared, sugary, sycophantic, unctuous, wheedling.

antonyms candid, uncompromising, unflattering.

flattery *n* adulation, backscratching, blandishment, blarney, bootlicking, butter, cajolement, cajolery, eulogy, fawning, fulsomeness, ingratiation, obsequiousness, servility, soap, soft sawder, soft soap, sugar, sweet talk, sycophancy, sycophantism, toadyism, unctuousness, wheedling.

antonym criticism.

flatulence *n* belching, bloat, borborygmus, eructation, flatulency, flatus, gas, gassiness, pomposity, prolixity, turgidity, wind, windiness.

flatulent *v* bloated, distended, empty, gaseous, gassy, pompous, prolix, swollen, turgid, vain, windy.

flaunt *v* air, boast, brandish, dangle, display, exhibit, flash, flourish, parade, show off, sport, vaunt, wave, wield.

▲ *confusable word* flout.

flavour *n* aroma, aspect, characteristic, essence, extract, feel, feeling, flavouring, hint, odour, piquancy, property, quality, relish, sapidity, savour, savouriness, seasoning, smack, soupçon, spice, stamp, style, suggestion, tang, taste, tastiness, tinge, tone, touch, zest, zing.

v contaminate, ginger up, imbue, infuse, lace, leaven, season, spice, taint.

antonym tastelessness.

flavourful *adj* delicious, flavoursome, palatable, sapid, savoury, spicy, tasty, toothsome.

antonyms insipid, tasteless.

flavouring *n* essence, extract, seasoning, spice, spirit, tincture, zest.

flaw *n* blemish, breach, break, cleft, crack, crevice, defect, disfigurement, error, failing, fallacy, fault, fissure, fracture, imperfection, lapse, macula, mark, mistake, rent, rift, shortcoming, slip, speck, split, spot, tear, vice, weakness.

antonyms perfection, virtue.

flawed *adj* blemished, broken, chipped, cracked, damaged, defective, disfigured, erroneous, fallacious, faulty, illogical, imperfect, marked, marred, spoiled, spoilt, unsound, vicious, vitiated.

antonyms flawless, perfect.

flawless *adj* accurate, faultless, immaculate, impeccable, intact, irreproachable, perfect, sound, spotless, stainless, unblemished, unbroken, undamaged, unexceptionable, unsullied, whole.

antonyms flawed, imperfect.

flay *v* castigate, cheat, excoriate, execrate, flense, flog, lambaste, lash, pull to pieces, revile, rob, scold, scourge, skin, skin alive, tear into, tear a strip off, upbraid, whip.

flea-bitten *adj* crawling, dingy, flea-ridden, flyblown, frowzy, grotty, grubby, grungy, infested, insalubrious, lousy, mangy, mean, moth-eaten, mucky, pedicular, ratty, run-down, scabby, scruffy, scurfy, seedy, sleazy, sordid, squalid, tatty, unhealthy, unhygienic.

antonym salubrious.

fleck *v* bespeckle, besprinkle, dapple, dot, dust, flake, floccule, mark, mottle, speck, speckle, spot, sprinkle, stipple, streak, variegate.

n dot, flake, macula, mark, particle, patch, point, spatter, speck, speckle, spot, streak.

fledgling *n* apprentice, beginner, chick, greenhorn, learner, neophyte, nestling, newcomer, novice, novitiate, recruit, rookie, spring chicken, tenderfoot, trainee, tyro, youngster.

flee *v* abscond, avoid, beat a hasty retreat, bolt, cut and run, decamp, depart, disappear, escape, fly, get away, leave, make off, make oneself scarce, run off, scarper, scram, shun, skedaddle, split, take flight, take it on the lam, take off, take to one's heels, vamoose, vanish, withdraw.

antonyms stand, stay.

fleece *v* bilk, bleed, cheat, clip, con, defraud, diddle, mulct, overcharge, plunder, rifle, rip off, rob, rook, shear, skin, soak, squeeze, steal, sting, swindle.

fleecy *adj* downy, flocculent, fluffy, hairy, lanuginose, napped, pilose, shaggy, soft, velvety, white, woolly.

antonyms bald, smooth.

fleet[1] *n* argosy, armada, escadrille, flotilla, group, navy, squadron, task force.

fleet[2] *adj* expeditious, fast, flying, light-footed, mercurial, meteoric, nimble, quick, rapid, speedy, swift, winged.

antonyms slow, sluggish.

fleeting *adj* brief, disappearing, ephemeral, evanescent, flitting, flying, fugitive, gone with the wind, impermanent, momentary, passing, short, short-lived, temporary, transient, transitory, vanishing.

antonyms enduring, lasting.

fleetness *n* celerity, dispatch, expedition, expeditiousness, light-footedness, nimbleness, quickness, rapidity, speed, speediness, swiftness, velocity.

antonym sluggishness.

flesh *n* animality, beef, blood, body, brawn, carnal nature, corporeality, family, fat, fatness, flesh and blood, food, humankind, human nature, human race, kin, kindred, kinsfolk, kith and kin, matter, meat, physicality, pulp, relations, relatives, sensuality, substance, tissue.

flesh and blood *adj* corporeal, human, incarnate, mortal, physical, real, real-life.

fleshiness *n* adiposity, chubbiness, corpulence, embonpoint, flabbiness, heaviness, obesity, plumpness, portliness, stoutness, tubbiness.

fleshly *adj* animal, bestial, bodily, brutish, carnal, corporal, corporeal, earthly, earthy, erotic, human, lustful, material, mortal, mundane, physical, secular, sensual, terrestrial, worldly.

antonym spiritual.

fleshy *adj* ample, beefy, brawny, chubby, chunky, corpulent, fat, flabby, hefty, meaty, obese, overweight, paunchy, plump, portly, pudgy, rotund, stout, tubby, well-padded.
antonym thin.

flex *v* angle, bend, bow, contract, crook, curve, double up, ply, tighten, try.
antonyms extend, straighten.

flexibility *n* adaptability, adjustability, agreeability, amenability, bendability, complaisance, elasticity, flexion, give, limberness, pliability, pliancy, resilience, spring, springiness, suppleness, tensility, versatility.
antonym inflexibility.

flexible *adj* accommodating, adaptable, adapting, adjustable, agreeable, amenable, bending, bendable, biddable, complaisant, compliant, discretionary, docile, double-jointed, ductile, elastic, flexile, gentle, limber, lissome, lithe, loose-jointed, loose-limbed, manageable, mobile, mouldable, open, plastic, pliable, pliant, responsive, springy, stretchy, supple, tensile, tractable, variable, versatile, willowy, yielding.
antonym inflexible.

flibbertigibbet *n* airhead, birdbrain, bubblebrain, butterfly, chatterbox, featherbrain, flapper, madcap, rattlebrain, scatterbrain, will-o'-the-wisp.

flick *v* bat, blow, click, crack, dab, fillip, flip, flutter, hit, jerk, rap, snap, snick, strike, tap, touch, wave, whip.
n click, crack, fillip, flick, flip, flutter, movie, rap, snap, snick, tap, touch.

flicker *v* coruscate, flare, flash, flutter, glimmer, gutter, quiver, scintillate, shimmer, sparkle, twinkle, vibrate, waver.
n atom, breath, coruscation, drop, flare, flash, gleam, glimmer, glint, indication, inkling, iota, scintillation, spark, trace, vestige.

flickering *n* burning, coruscant, coruscating, glimmering, guttering, lambent, sparkling, twinkling, unsteady.

flight¹ *n* aeronautics, air transport, air travel, aviation, cloud, echelon, escadrille, flock, flying, formation, journey, mounting, soaring, squadron, swarm, trip, unit, voyage, wing, winging.

flight² *n* breakaway, departure, escape, exit, exodus, fleeing, getaway, hegira, retreat, running away.

flightiness *n* capriciousness, changeability, dizziness, empty-headedness, fickleness, flippancy, foolishness, frivolity, giddiness, inconstancy, irresponsibility, levity, light-headedness, lightness, mercurialness, silliness, volatility, wildness.
antonym steadiness.

flighty *adj* birdbrained, birdwitted, bubblebrained, bubbleheaded, capricious, changeable, dizzy, empty-headed, fickle, foolish, frivolous, giddy, hare-brained, impetuous, impulsive, inconstant, irresponsible, light-headed, mercurial,

scatterbrained, silly, skittish, superficial, thoughtless, unbalanced, unstable, unsteady, volatile, wild.
antonym steady.

flimsy *adj* cardboard, chiffon, cobwebby, delicate, diaphanous, ethereal, feeble, fragile, frail, frivolous, gauzy, gimcrack, gossamer, implausible, inadequate, insubstantial, jerrybuilt, light, makeshift, meagre, poor, rickety, shaky, shallow, sheer, slapped-together, slight, superficial, thin, transparent, trivial, unconvincing, unsatisfactory, unsubstantial, vaporous, weak.
antonym sturdy.

flinch *v* balk, blench, cower, cringe, draw back, duck, flee, quail, quake, recoil, retreat, shake, shirk, shiver, shrink, shudder, shy, shy away, start, swerve, tremble, wince, withdraw.

fling *v* bung, cant, cast, catapult, chuck, heave, hurl, jerk, let fly, lob, pitch, precipitate, propel, send, shoot, shy, sling, slug, throw, toss.
n attempt, bash, binge, cast, crack, gamble, go, heave, indulgence, lob, pitch, shot, spree, stab, throw, toss, trial, try, turn, venture, whirl.

flip *v* about-face, cast, fillip, flap, flick, flip-flop, jerk, pitch, snap, spin, throw, toss, turn (over), twirl, twist.
n about-face, bob, fillip, flap, flick, flip-flop, jerk, toss, turn, twirl, twist.

flip (through) flick, glance, page, riffle, scan, skim, skip, thumb.

flippancy *n* casualness, cavalierness, cheek, cheekiness, disrespect, frivolity, glibness, impertinence, impudence, irreverence, levity, persiflage, pertness, sauciness, superficiality.
antonym earnestness.

flippant *adj* brash, careless, casual, cavalier, cheeky, cocky, disrespectful, flip, frivolous, glib, impertinent, impudent, irreverent, malapert, nonchalant, offhand, pert, rude, saucy, smartass, superficial, unserious.
antonym earnest.

flirt *v* coquet, dally, flutter, jerk, ogle, philander, tease, toss.
n coquette, heartbreaker, hussy, philanderer, tease, trifler, wanton.

flirt with chat up, come on to, consider, dabble in, entertain, make advances to, make eyes at, make up to, play with, toy with, trifle with, try.

flirtation *n* affair, amorousness, amour, chatting up, come-on, coquetry, dalliance, dallying, intrigue, philandering, sport, teasing, toying, trifling.

flirtatious *adj* amorous, arch, come-hither, coquettish, coy, enticing, flirty, loose, promiscuous, provocative, sportive, teasing, wanton.

flit *v* bob, dance, dart, elapse, flash, fleet, flitter, flutter, fly, pass, skim, slip, speed, whisk, wing.

flitting *adj* bobbing, dancing, darting, ephemeral, fleet, fleeting, flittering, fluttering, skimming.

float *v* bob, drift, glide, hang, hover, initiate, launch, poise, promote, ride, sail, set up, slide, swim, waft.

antonym sink.

floating *adj* afloat, bobbing, buoyant, buoyed up, changing, fluctuating, free, migratory, movable, sailing, swimming, unattached, uncommitted, unfixed, unsinkable, unsubmerged, variable, wandering, water-borne.

flock *v* bunch, cluster, collect, congregate, converge, crowd, gather, gravitate, group, herd, huddle, mass, swarm, throng, troop.

n assembly, bevy, collection, colony, company, congregation, convoy, crowd, drove, flight, gaggle, gathering, group, herd, horde, host, mass, multitude, pack, shoal, skein, swarm, throng.

flog *v* beat, belabour, birch, cane, chastise, drive, drub, flagellate, flay, hide, horsewhip, knout, larrup, lash, overexert, overtax, overwork, peddle, punish, push, scourge, sell, switch, tax, thrash, trounce, welt, whack, whale, whip.

flogging *n* beating, caning, drubbing, flagellation, flaying, hiding, horsewhipping, lashing, scourging, thrashing, trouncing, whaling, whipping.

flood *v* bog down, brim, choke, cover, deluge, drench, drown, engulf, fill, flow, glut, gush, immerse, inundate, overcome, overflow, oversupply, overwhelm, pour, rush, saturate, soak, submerge, surge, swamp, swarm, sweep.

n abundance, alluvion, bore, cataclysm, debacle, deluge, diluvium, downpour, eagre, flash flood, flow, freshet, glut, inundation, outpouring, overflow, plethora, profusion, rush, spate, stream, superfluity, tidal wave, tide, torrent.

antonyms dearth, drought, trickle.

floor *n* base, basis, deck, étage, landing, level, platform, right to speak, stage, storey, tier.

v baffle, beat, bewilder, confound, conquer, defeat, discomfit, disconcert, down, dumfound, flummox, frustrate, knockdown, nonplus, overcome, overthrow, overwhelm, perplex, prostrate, puzzle, stump, stun, throw, throw for a loop, trounce, worst.

flop *v* bomb, close, collapse, crash, droop, drop, fail, fall, flap flat, flap, fold, founder, hang, misfire, plop, plump, rest, sack out, sag, sleep, slump, topple, tumble.

n debacle, disaster, failure, fiasco, loser, no go, non-starter, turkey, washout.

floppy *adj* baggy, dangling, droopy, flabby, flaccid, flapping, flappy, flopping, hanging, limp, loose, pendulous, sagging, soft.

antonym firm.

flora *n* botany, herbage, plant life, plants, vegetable kingdom, vegetation.

florid *adj* baroque, blowsy, bombastic, busy, coloratura, elaborate, embellished, euphuistic, figurative, flamboyant, flourishy, flowery, flushed, fussy, grandiloquent, high-coloured, high-falutin, high-flown, ornamental, ornate,

overelaborate, purple, raddled, red, reddish, rococo, rubicund, ruddy, showy.

antonyms pale, plain.

flotsam *n* debris, detritus, jetsam, junk, oddments, scum, sweepings, wreckage.

flounce *v* bob, bounce, fling, jerk, spring, stamp, stomp, storm, throw, toss, turn, twist.

n frill, fringe, furbelow, ruffle, trimming, valance.

flounder *v* blunder, bungle, falter, flail, fumble, grope, muddle, plunge, stagger, struggle, stumble, thrash, toss, tumble, wallop, wallow, welter.

▲ *confusable word* founder.

flourish¹ *v* advance, bloom, blossom, boom, burgeon, develop, do well, flower, get on, grow, increase, mushroom, progress, prosper, succeed, thrive, wax.

antonyms fail, languish.

flourish² *v* brandish, display, flaunt, flutter, parade, shake, sweep, swing, swish, twirl, vaunt, wag, wave, wield.

n arabesque, brandishing, ceremony, curlicue, dash, decoration, display, élan, embellishment, fanfare, flair, ornament, ornamentation, panache, parade, pizzazz, plume, shaking, show, squiggle, sweep, twirling, wave.

flourishing *adj* blooming, booming, burgeoning, developing, going strong, growing, in the pink, lush, luxuriant, mushrooming, progressing, prospering, rampant, rank, riotous, successful, thriving.

antonyms failing, languishing.

flout *v* affront, contemn, defy, deride, disregard, insult, jeer at, mock, outrage, reject, ridicule, scoff at, scorn, scout, spurn, taunt.

antonym respect.

▲ *confusable word* flaunt.

flow *v* arise, bubble, cascade, circulate, course, deluge, derive, distil, drift, emanate, emerge, flood, glide, gush, inundate, issue, move, originate, overflow, pour, proceed, purl, result, ripple, rise, roll, run, rush, slide, slip, spew, spill, spring, spurt, squirt, stream, surge, sweep, swirl, teem, well, whirl.

n abundance, cascade, course, current, deluge, drift, effluence, efflux, effusion, emanation, flood, flowage, flux, fluxion, gush, influx, outflow, outpouring, plenty, plethora, spate, spurt, stream, succession, tide, train, wash.

flower *n* acme, best, best part or time, bloom, blossom, choice, cream, crème de la crème, efflorescence, elite, floret, floweret, freshness, height, high point, pick, prime, vigour, zenith.

v blossom, blow, burgeon, dehisce, effloresce, flourish, mature, open, peak, thrive, unfold.

flowering *adj* blooming, bloomy, blossoming, efflorescent, florescent, in bloom, in flower.

n anthesis, blooming, blossoming, burgeoning, development, florescence, flourishing, flowerage, maturing.

flowery *adj* affected, baroque, elaborate, embellished, euphuistic, fancy, figurative, floral, floriated, florid, fulsome, high-flown, ornate, overelaborate, overwrought, rhetorical.
antonym plain.

flowing *adj* abounding, brimming, cantabile, cascading, continuous, cursive, easy, eloquent, facile, falling, flooded, fluent, fluid, full, gushing, overrun, prolific, rich, rolling, running, rushing, smooth, streaming, surging, sweeping, teeming, unbroken, uninterrupted, voluble.
antonyms hesitant, interrupted.

fluctuate *v* alter, alternate, change, ebb and flow, float, hesitate, oscillate, rise and fall, seesaw, shift, shuffle, sway, swing, undulate, vacillate, vary, veer, waver.

fluctuating *adj* capricious, changeable, fickle, inconstant, irregular, irresolute, mutable, oscillating, oscillatory, rising and falling, swaying, swinging, unstable, unsteady, vacillant, vacillating, vacillatory, variable, wavering.
antonym stable.

fluctuation *n* alternation, ambivalence, capriciousness, change, ficklessness, inconstancy, instability, irresolution, oscillation, rise and fall, shift, swing, unsteadiness, ups and downs, vacillation, variability, variableness, variation, wavering.

fluency *n* articulateness, assurance, command, control, ease, eloquence, facility, glibness, mastery, readiness, slickness, smoothness, volubility.
antonym incoherence.

fluent *adj* articulate, easy, effortless, eloquent, facile, flowing, fluid, glib, mellifluous, natural, ready, smooth, smooth-spoken, tongued, voluble, well-versed.
antonym tongue-tied.

fluff *n* down, dust, dustball, error, floccus, floss, frivolity, froth, fuzz, lightness, lint, mistake, nap, particle, pile, softness, superficiality.
v ball up, botch, bungle, err, fumble, mess up, muddle, muff, screw up, spoil.
antonym bring off.

fluffy *adj* downy, feathery, fleecy, flocculent, flossy, fuzzy, gossamer, hairy, light, nappy, shaggy, soft, superficial, velvety, woolly.
antonym smooth.

fluid *adj* adaptable, adjustable, aqueous, changeable, convertible, easy, elegant, feline, flexible, floating, flowing, fluctuating, fluent, fluidic, graceful, indefinite, liquefied, liquid, melted, mercurial, mobile, molten, mutable, protean, running, runny, shifting, sinuous, smooth, unstable, vaporous, watery.
antonyms solid, stable.
n gas, humour, juice, liquid, liquor, sap, solution.

fluke *n* accident, blessing, break, chance, coincidence, fortuity, freak, happenstance, lucky break, lucky chance, of good luck (or fortune), quirk, serendipity, stroke, twist of fate, windfall.

flukey *adj* accidental, chance, chancy, coincidental, fortuitous, fortunate, freakish, iffy, incalculable, lucky, quirky, random, serendipitous, uncertain, unexpected.

flummox *v* baffle, bamboozle, befuddle, bewilder, confound, confuse, defeat, euchre, floor, fox, mystify, nonplus, perplex, puzzle, stump, stymie, thwart.

flummoxed *adj* at a loss, at sea, baffled, befuddled, bewildered, confounded, confused, floored, foxed, mystified, nonplussed, perplexed, puzzled, stumped, stymied, thwarted.

flunkey *n* assistant, bootlicker, creature, cringer, drudge, errand boy, footman, hanger-on, lackey, manservant, menial, minion, slave, toady, tool, underling, valet, yes man.

flurry *n* ado, agitation, burst, bustle, commotion, confusion, disturbance, excitement, ferment, flap, flaw, fluctuation, fluster, flutter, furor, fuss, gust, hubbub, hurry, kafuffle, outbreak, pother, rush, spell, spurt, squall, stir, to-do, tumult, upset, whirl.
v abash, agitate, bewilder, bother, bustle, confuse, disconcert, discountenance, disturb, fluster, flutter, fuss, hassle, hurry, hustle, perturb, rattle, ruffle, unsettle, upset.

flush[1] *v* blush, burn, colour, crimson, excite, flame, glow, mantle, redden, rouge, suffuse, turn red, warm.
antonym pale.
n bloom, blush, colour, freshness, glow, radiance, reddening, redness, rosiness, ruddiness, rush, vigour, warmth.

flush[2] *v* cleanse, douche, drench, eject, empty (out), evacuate, expel, hose, rinse, swab, syringe, wash.
adj abundant, affluent, full, generous, in funds, in the money, lavish, liberal, moneyed, overflowing, plentiful, prodigal, prosperous, rich, rolling, wealthy, well-heeled, well-off, well-supplied, well-to-do.

flush[3] *adj* aligned, even, flat, level, plane, smooth, square, true.

flush[4] *v* dig out, disturb, drive out, fly up, force out, rouse, rout, run to earth, start (up), uncover.

flushed *adj* ablaze, aflame, aglow, animated, aroused, blowsy, blushing, burning, crimson, elated, embarrassed, enthused, excited, exhilarated, exultant, febrile, feverish, glowing, hectic, high, hot, inspired, intoxicated, red, rosy, rubicund, ruddy, sanguine, scarlet, thrilled.
antonym pale.

fluster *v* abash, agitate, bother, bustle, confound, confuse, discombobulate, discompose, disconcert, discountenance, disturb, embarrass, excite, faze, flurry, hassle, heat, hurry, perturb, pother, rattle, ruffle, shake (up), unnerve, unsettle, upset.
antonym calm.

n agitation, bustle, commotion, discomposure, distraction, disturbance, dither, embarrassment, faze, flap, flurry, flutter, furor, kafuffle, perturbation, pucker, ruffle, state, tizzy, turmoil, twitter.
antonym calm.

fluted *adj* chamfered, channelled, corrugated, furrowed, gouged, grooved, ribbed, ridged, rutted.

flutter *v* agitate, bat, beat, bustle, confuse, dance, discompose, excite, flap, flicker, flit, flitter, fluctuate, hover, palpitate, quiver, ripple, ruffle, shiver, toss, tremble, vibrate, wave, waver.
n agitation, bustle, commotion, confusion, discomposure, dither, excitement, flicker, flurry, fluster, nervousness, palpitation, perturbation, quiver, quivering, shiver, shudder, state, tremble, tremor, tumult, twitching, upset, vibration.

fluttering *adj* beating, dancing, flapping, flickering, flitting, hovering, palpitating, quivering, tossing, trembling, wavering, waving.

flux *n* alteration, change, chaos, development, discharge, flow, fluctuation, fluidity, instability, modification, motion, movement, mutability, mutation, rate of flow, stir, transition, unrest.
antonym stability.

fly *v* abscond,avoid, bolt, career, carry, charge, clear out, dart, dash, decamp, disappear, display, elapse, escape, flap, flee (from), flit, float, flutter, get away, glide, hare, hasten, hasten away, hedge-hop, hightail it, hoist, hover, hurry, light out, mount, operate, pass, pilot, race, raise, retreat, roll by, run, run away, run for it, run full tilt, run off, rush, sail, scamper, scarper, scoot, shoot, show, shun, skim, soar, speed, sprint, take flight, take off, take to one's heels, take wing, tear, travel, vamoose, wave, whisk, whiz, wing, zoom.

fly at assail, assault, attack, charge (at), fall upon, go for, have at, light into, pitch into, rush at.

fly in the face of affront, contradict, counteract, defy, disobey, flout, insult, oppose.

fly-by-night *adj* brief, cowboy, discreditable, disreputable, dubious, ephemeral, here today gone tomorrow, impermanent, irresponsible, questionable, shady, short-lived, undependable, unreliable, untrustworthy.
antonym reliable.

flying *adj* airborne, brief, express, fast, flapping, fleet, fleeting, floating, fluttering, fugitive, flyaway, gliding, hasty, hovering, hurried, mercurial, mobile, quick (or short), rapid, rushed, short-lived, soaring, speedy, streaming, taken on the fly, transitory, vanishing, volant, waving, wind-borne, winged, winging.

foam *n* barm, bubbles, effervescence, foaminess, froth, frothiness, head, lather, scum, spume, spumescence, suds, surf.
v boil, bubble, effervesce, fizz, froth, lather, spume.

foamy *adj* barmy, bubbly, foam-flecked, foaming, foamlike, frothy, lathery, light, spumescent, spumy, sudsy.

fob off appease, cheat, deceive, dump, foist, get rid of, give a sop to, impose, inflict, palm off, pass off, placate, put off, stall, trick, unload.

focus *n* axis, centre, centre of attraction, core, crux, cynosure, focal point, heart, hinge, hub, kernel, linchpin, nucleus, pivot, target.
v aim, centre, converge, direct, fix, focalize, home in, join, meet, rivet, spotlight, zero in, zoom in.

fodder *n* browsing, feed, food, foodstuff, forage, fuel, nourishment, provender, rations, raw material, silage.

foe *n* adversary, antagonist, enemy, foeman, ill-wisher, opponent, rival.
antonym friend.

fog *n* bewilderment, blanket, blindness, blur, brume, confusion, daze, gloom, haze, miasma, mist, muddle, murk, murkiness, obscurity, peasouper, perplexity, puzzle, puzzlement, smog, stupor, trance, vagueness.
v becloud, bedim, befuddle, bewilder, blanket, blind, blur, cloud, confuse, darken, daze, dim, dull, mist, muddle, obfuscate, obscure, perplex, shroud, steam up, stupefy.

fogey *n* anachronism, antique, archaism, dodo, eccentric, fossil, fuddy-duddy, geezer, moss-back, oddity, period piece, relic, square, stick-in-the-mud.

foggy *adj* beclouded, befogged, befuddled, bewildered, blurred, blurry, brumous, clouded, cloudy, confused, dark, dazed, dim, grey, hazy, indistinct, misty, muddled, murky, muzzy, nebulous, obscure, puzzled, shadowy, smoggy, stupefied, stupid, unclear, vague, vaporous.
antonym clear.

foible *n* crotchet, defect, eccentricity, failing, fault, habit, idiosyncrasy, imperfection, infirmity, oddity, oddness, peculiarity, quirk, shortcoming, strangeness, weakness.

foil[1] *v* baffle, balk, bring to nothing, check, checkmate, circumvent, counter, defeat, disappoint, elude, euchre, frustrate, hinder, nullify, obstruct, outsmart, outwit, prevent, spike (someone's) guns, spoil, stop, stump, thwart.
antonym abet.

foil[2] *n* antithesis, background, balance, complement, contrast, opposite, relief, setting.

foist *v* fob off, force, get rid of, impose, insert, insinuate, interpolate, introduce, palm off, pass off, thrust, unload, wish on.

fold *v* bend, break down, clasp, close, collapse, crash, crease, crimp, crumple, dog-ear, double, embrace, enclose, end, enfold, entwine, envelop, fail, gather, go bust, go under, hug, intertwine, overlap, pleat, shut down, terminate, tuck, wrap, wrap up.
n bend, corrugation, crease, crimp, furrow, layer, overlap, pleat, plicature, turn, wimple, wrinkle.

folder *n* binder, brochure, envelope, file, folio, holder, pamphlet, portfolio.

foliage *n* foliation, foliature, greenery, leafage, verdure, vernation.

folk *n* clan, family, kin, kindred, kinsfolk, kinsmen, nation, people, race, society, tribe.

adj ancestral, ethnic, indigenous, national, native, traditional, tribal.

folklore *n* beliefs, fables, folk tales, legends, lore, mythology, myths, superstitions, tales, tradition.

follow *v* accompany, accept, accord, act according to, attend, catch, catch on (to), chase, come after, come next, comply, comprehend, conform, cultivate, dangle, develop, dog, emanate, ensue, escort, fathom, get, get the picture, get the drift (of), grasp, haunt, heed, hound, hunt, imitate, keep abreast of, keep up with, live up to, mind, note, obey, observe, pursue, realize, regard, result (from), see, shadow, stalk, succeed, supersede, supervene, supplant, support, tag along, tail, track, trail, twig (to), understand, use, watch.

antonyms desert, precede.

follow through carry out, carry through, complete, conclude, consummate, continue, finish, fulfil, implement, pursue, see through.

follow up check out, consolidate, continue, follow, investigate, pursue, reinforce, substantiate.

follower *n* acolyte, adherent, admirer, aficionado, apostle, backer, believer, buff, cohort, companion, convert, devotee, disciple, emulator, fan, fancier, freak, habitué, hanger-on, heeler, helper, henchman, imitator, lackey, minion, partisan, pupil, representative, retainer, seeker, sidekick, successor, supporter, votary, worshipper, yes man.

antonyms leader, opponent.

following *adj* attendant, coming, consecutive, consequent, consequential, ensuing, later, next, resulting, sequent, subsequent, succeeding, successive.

n attendance, audience, backing, circle, claque, clientele, coterie, entourage, fans, followers, patronage, public, retinue, suite, support, supporters, train.

folly *n* absurdity, craziness, daftness, fatuity, foolishness, idiocy, illogicality, imbecility, imprudence, indiscretion, insanity, irrationality, irresponsibility, lack of sense, lunacy, madness, nonsense, preposterousness, rashness, recklessness, senselessness, silliness, stupidity, unreason, unwisdom.

antonyms prudence, rationality, wisdom.

foment *v* activate, agitate, arouse, brew, encourage, excite, foster, goad, heat (up), incite, instigate, kindle, promote, prompt, provoke, quicken, raise, rouse, spur, stimulate, stir up, whip up, work up.

antonym quell.

fomenter *n* abettor, agitator, demagogue, firebrand, hatemonger, incendiary, inciter, instigator, mob-orator, rabble-rouser, troublemaker, tubthumper, warmonger.

antonym peacemaker

fond *adj* absurd, adoring, affectionate, amorous, caring, credulous, deluded, devoted, doting, empty, foolish, indulgent, loving, naïve, over-optimistic, sanguine, tender, uxorious, vain, warm.

antonyms hostile, realistic.

fond of addicted to, attached to, crazy about, enamoured of, hooked on, keen on, mad about, partial to, predisposed toward, stuck on, sweet on, taken with, wild about.

fondle *v* caress, coddle, cuddle, dandle, pat, pet, snuggle, stroke, touch.

fondly *adv* absurdly, adoringly, affectionately, credulously, dearly, foolishly, indulgently, lovingly, naïvely, overoptimistically, sanguinely, stupidly, tenderly, vainly.

fondness *n* affection, attachment, devotion, enthusiasm, fancy, inclination, infatuation, kindness, leaning, liking, love, partiality, penchant, predilection, preference, soft spot, susceptibility, taste, tenderness, weakness.

antonym aversion.

food *n* aliment, ambrosia, board, bread, cheer, chow, comestibles, commons, cooking, cuisine, diet, eatables, eats, edibles, fare, fast food, feed, fodder, foodstuff, forage, grub, junk food, larder, meal, meat, menu, nosh, nourishment, nutriment, nutrition, pap, provender, provisions, rations, refreshment(s), scoff, stores, subsistence, sustenance, table, tack, tuck, tuck-in, viands, victuals.

fool *n* addle-pate, ass, birdbrain, blockhead, bonehead, buffoon, chucklehead, chump, clod, clot, clown, cluck, comedian, comic, coxcomb, cuckoo, dimwit, dolt, dope, droll, dumb-bell, dumb cluck, dumbo, dummy, dunce, dunderhead, dupe, easy mark, fall guy, fathead, featherbrain, goon, goose, greenhorn, gudgeon, gull, halfwit, harlequin, idiot, ignoramus, illiterate, imbecile, jackass, jerk, jester, knucklehead, laughingstock, loggerhead, loon, lowbrow, lunatic, merry-andrew, mooncalf, moron, muttonhead, nerd, nincompoop, ninny, nit, nitwit, noodle, numskull, patsy, peabrain, pigeon, Pierrot, puddinghead, punchinello, pushover, sap, saphead, schlep, schmo, schmuck, silly, silly-billy, simpleton, sitting duck, softhead, softy, stooge, stupe, stupid, sucker, thickhead, tomfool, twerp, twit, want-wit, wooden-head, zany, zombie.

v act the fool, act up, bamboozle, be silly, beguile, bluff, cavort, cheat, clown, con, cozen, cut capers, cut up didos, daff, deceive, delude, diddle, dupe, feign, frolic, gull, have on, hoax, hoodwink, horse around, jest, joke, kid, lark, meddle, mess, mess around, mislead, monkey (around), play, play the fool, play up, pretend, put one over on, string, string along, swindle, take in, tamper, tease, toy, trick, trifle.

fool around dawdle, idle, kill time, lark, lark about, mess around, play around, trifle.

foolery *n* antics, buffoonery, capers, carryings-on, childishness, clownery, clowning around, dido, drollery, farce, folly, fooling around, high jinks, horseplay, larks, mischief, monkey around, monkey business, nonsense, practical jokes, pranks, shenanigans, silliness, tomfoolery, waggery, zaniness.

foolhardy *adj* adventurous, adventuresome, bold, daredevil, harebrained, hot-headed, ill-advised, ill-considered, impetuous, imprudent, incautious, irresponsible, madcap, precipitate, rash, reckless, temerarious, unheeding, unwary, venturesome, venturous.

antonym cautious.

fooling *n* banter, bluffing, buffoonery, clownishness, deception, drollery, farce, jesting, joking, kidding, mockery, mocking, nonsense, pretence, shamming, skylarking, teasing, tricks, trifling, waggery, zaniness.

foolish *adj* absurd, all wet, birdbrained, brainless, cock-eyed, crazy, daft, dilly, doltish, dotty, dunderheaded, empty-headed, fatuous, featherbrained, flighty, half-baked, half-witted, harebrained, idiotic, ill-advised, ill-considered, ill-judged, imbecile, imbecilic, imprudent, incautious, indiscreet, inept, injudicious, lean-witted, loony, ludicrous, mad, moronic, nonsensical, potty, ridiculous, sappy, senseless, short-sighted, silly, simple, simple-minded, soft-headed, stupid, thoughtless, tomfool, trivial, unintelligent, unreasonable, unwise, weak, wet, witless.

antonym wise.

foolishly *adv* absurdly, doltishly, fatuously, fondly, idiotically, ill-advisedly, imprudently, incautiously, indiscreetly, ineptly, injudiciously, mistakenly, ridiculously, senselessly, short-sightedly, stupidly, unwisely.

antonym wisely.

foolishness *n* absurdity, bunk, bunkum, claptrap, flightiness, folly, foolery, idiocy, imprudence, inanity, incaution, incautiousness, indiscretion, ineptitude, insipience, irresponsibility, luncay, malarkey, nonsense, rubbish, silliness, stupidity, thoughtlessness, triviality, unreason, unwisdom, weakness.

antonyms prudence, wisdom.

foolproof *adj* certain, fail-safe, guaranteed, idiot-proof, infallible, never-failing, reliable, safe, sure-fire, trouble-free, unassailable, unbreakable.

antonym unreliable.

footing *n* base, basis, establishment, foothold, footwork, foundation, ground, groundwork, niche, position, purchase, rank, relations, relationship, settlement, standing, state, status, support, surface, terms, total.

footnote(s) *n* annotation, apparatus, commentary, comment, explanation, marginalia, note, reference, scholia.

footprint *n* footmark, imprint, paw mark, paw print, spoor, trace, track, trail, vestige.

footstep *n* footfall, plod, step, tramp, tread, trudge.

fop *n* beau, clotheshorse, coxcomb, dandy, dude, exquisite, macaroni, pansy, peacock, popinjay, swell.

foppish *adj* affected, coxcomical, dainty, dandified, dandyish, dapper, dressy, finical,

la-di-da, natty, overdressed, preening, prinking, spruce, vain.

antonym unkempt.

for
For phrases such as *for dear life*, *for example*, *for the time being*, see the first noun after *for*.

forage *n* feed, fodder, food, foodstuff, pasturage, provender.

v cast around, explore, hunt, plunder, raid, ransack, rummage, scavenge, scour, scrounge, search, seek.

foray *n* depredation, descent, excursion, incursion, inroad, invasion, irruption, offensive, raid, reconnaissance, sally, sortie, swoop.

forbear *v* abstain, avoid, cease, decline, desist, eschew, hesitate, hold, hold back, keep from, omit, pause, refrain, restrain oneself, stay, stop, withhold.

forbearance *n* abstinence, avoidance, clemency, endurance, indulgence, leniency, lenity, long-suffering, mildness, moderation, patience, refraining, resignation, restraint, self-control, sufferance, temperance, tolerance, toleration.

antonym intolerance.

forbearing *adj* clement, easy, forgiving, gentle, indulgent, lenient, long-suffering, merciful, mild, moderate, patient, restrained, self-controlled, temperate, tolerant.

antonyms intolerant, merciless.

forbid *v* ban, block, contra-indicate, debar, deny, disallow, exclude (from), hinder, inhibit, interdict, outlaw, preclude, prevent, prohibit, proscribe, refuse, rule out, veto.

antonym allow.

forbidden *adj* against the rules, banned, barred, debarred, disallowed, interdit, not allowed, out of bounds, outlawed, prohibited, proscribed, taboo, verboten, vetoed.

forbidding *adj* abhorrent, awesome, daunting, formidable, frightening, gaunt, grim, hostile, inhospitable, menacing, off-putting, ominous, repellent, repulsive, sinister, stern, threatening, unapproachable, unfriendly.

antonyms approachable, congenial.

force¹ *n* aggression, arm-twisting, beef, big stick, binding power, bite, clout, coercion, cogency, compulsion, constraint, drive, duress, dynamism, effect, effectiveness, efficacy, emphasis, energy, enforcement, fierceness, forcefulness, impact, impetus, import, impulse, incentive, influence, intensity, life, mailed fist, meaning, might, momentum, motivation, muscle, persistence, persuasiveness, potency, power, pressure, punch, shock, steam, stimulus, strength, stress, teeth, validity, vehemence, vigour, violence, vis, vitality, weight.

v break (open or through), bulldoze, coerce, compel, constrain, drag, drive, exact, extort, impel, impose, lean on, make, necessitate, obligate, oblige, overpower, press, press-gang, pressure, pressurize, prise, propel, push, railroad, steamroller, strong-arm, thrust, twist (someone's) arm, urge, wrench, wrest, wring.

force² *n* armed forces, army, battalion, body, corps, detachment, detail, division, effective, enomoty, host, legion, patrol, phalanx, regiment, squad, squadron, team, troop, unit, Wehrmacht.

in force¹ current, effective, in effect, in operation, in use, on the books, operative, valid, working.

antonym inoperative.

in force² in crowds, in droves, in flocks, in hordes, in large numbers, in strength.

forced *adj* affected, artificial, coerced, compelled, compulsory, contrived, enforced, false, feigned, insincere, involuntary, laboured, mandatory, obligatory, stiff, stilted, strained, synthetic, unnatural, unspontaneous, wooden.

antonyms spontaneous, voluntary.

forceful *adj* cogent, compelling, convincing, domineering, drastic, dynamic, effective, emphatic, energetic, persuasive, pithy, potent, powerful, strong, telling, urgent, vigorous, weighty.

antonym feeble.

forcible *adj* active, aggressive, coercive, cogent, compelling, compulsory, convincing, drastic, effective, efficient, energetic, forceful, impressive, mighty, pithy, potent, powerful, strong, telling, urgent, vehement, violent, weighty.

antonym feeble.

forcibly *adv* against one's will, by main force, compulsorily, obligatorily, under compulsion, under duress, violently, willy-nilly.

ford *n* causeway, crossing, drift, passage, shoal.

forebear *n* ancestor, antecedent, antecessor, father, forefather, forerunner, predecessor, primogenitor, progenitor.

antonym descendant.

forebode *v* augur, betoken, foreshadow, foreshow, foretell, foretoken, forewarn, import, indicate, omen, portend, predict, presage, prognosticate, promise, signify, warn.

foreboding *n* anticipation, anxiety, apprehension, apprehensiveness, augury, boding, chill, dread, fear, foreshadowing, foretoken, hoodoo, intuition, misgiving, omen, portent, prediction, prefigurement, premonition, presage, presentiment, prodrome, prognostication, sign, token, warning, worry.

forecast *v* augur, bode, calculate, conjecture, divine, estimate, expect, foresee, foretell, plan, predict, prognosticate, prophesy.

n augury, conjecture, foresight, forethought, guess, guesstimate, outlook, planning, prediction, prognosis, prognostication, projection, prophecy.

forefather *n* ancestor, antecedent, antecessor, father, forebear, forerunner, predecessor, primogenitor, procreator, progenitor.

antonym descendant.

forefront *n* avant-garde, centre, cutting edge, firing line, fore, foreground, front, front line, lead, limelight, prominence, spearhead, spotlight, van, vanguard.

antonym rear.

foregoing *adj* above, aforementioned, antecedent, anterior, earlier, former, preceding, previous, prior, prodromal, prodromic.

foregone *adj* anticipated, cut-and-dried, foreseen, inevitable, open and shut, predetermined, predictable.

antonym unpredictable.

foreground *n* centre, fore, forefront, front, limelight, prominence.

antonym background.

forehead *n* brow, front, temples.

foreign *adj* adventitious, adventive, alien, borrowed, distant, exotic, external, extraneous, extrinsic, imported, incongruous, irrelevant, non-native, outlandish, outside, overseas, remote, strange, unassimilable, uncharacteristic, unfamiliar, unknown, unnative, unrelated.

antonym native.

foreigner *n* alien, Ausländer, barbarian, boat person, displaced person, DP, outlander, outsider, refugee, stranger, tourist, uitlander, visitor.

antonym native.

foreknowledge *n* clairvoyance, foresight, forewarning, precognition, predetermination, premonition, prescience, prevision, prognostication, second sight.

foreman *n* chair, chief, floor manager, gaffer, ganger, inspector, overseer, steward, straw boss, super, superintendent, supervisor.

foremost *adj* cardinal, central, chief, first, front, headmost, highest, inaugural, initial, leading, main, most salient, paramount, pre-eminent, primary, prime, principal, supreme, uppermost.

foreordain *v* appoint, destine, doom, fate, foredoom, ordain, prearrange, predestine, predetermine, preordain.

foreordained *adj* appointed, foredoomed, prearranged, predestined, predetermined, preordained.

forerunner *n* ancestor, announcer, antecedent, antecessor, envoy, forebear, foregoer, foretoken, harbinger, herald, indication, messenger, omen, portent, precursor, predecessor, premonition, preparer, prodrome, progenitor, prognostic, prototype, sign, token.

antonyms aftermath, result.

foresee *v* anticipate, augur, divine, envisage, expect, forebode, forecast, foreknow, foretell, predict, prognosticate, prophesy, vaticinate.

foreshadow *v* adumbrate, anticipate, augur, betoken, bode, forebode, foreshow, foretoken, imply, import, indicate, omen, portend, predict, prefigure, presage, promise, prophesy, signal.

foresight *n* anticipation, care, caution, circumspection, clairvoyance, far-sightedness, forethought, perspicacity, precaution, preparedness, prescience, prevision, providence, provision, prudence, readiness, sagacity, sense, vision.

antonym improvidence.

forest *n* greenwood, plantation, trees, wood, woods, woodland.

forestall *v* anticipate, avert, balk, circumvent, deal with · in advance, frustrate, head off, hinder, intercept, obstruct, obviate, parry, preclude, pre-empt, prevent, steal (someone's) thunder, thwart, ward off.
antonyms encourage, facilitate.

forester *n* backwoodsman, dendrologist, forest ranger, gamekeeper, naturalist, woodsman.

forestry *n* arboriculture, dendrology, silviculture, woodcraft, woodsmanship.

foretaste *n* appetizer, example, foreknowledge, foretoken, forewarning, indication, prelude, preview, sample, specimen, token, warning, whet, whiff.

foretell *v* adumbrate, augur, bode, forebode, forecast, foreshadow, foreshow, forespeak, forewarn, portend, predict, presage, prognosticate, project, prophesy, signify, soothsay, vaticinate.

forethought *n* anticipation, carefulness, circumspection, far-sightedness, foresight, planning, precaution, premeditation, preparation, providence, provision, prudence.
antonym improvidence.

foretold *adj* forecast, foreseen, foreshadowed, foreshown, forespoken, predicted, presaged, prophesied, written.
antonym unforeseen.

forever *adv* always, ceaselessly, constantly, continually, endlessly, eternally, everlastingly, evermore, for all time, for always, forever and a day, for good and all, for keeps, in perpetuity, in saecula saeculorum, incessantly, interminably, permanently, perpetually, persistently, till the cows come home, till the end of time, unremittingly, world without end.

forewarn (of) *v* admonish, advise, alert, apprise, caution, dissuade, forebode, portend, precaution, tip off, warn.

foreword *n* exordium, introduction, preamble, preface, preliminary, proem, prolegomenon, prologue.
antonyms epilogue, postscript.

forfeit *n* amercement, damages, escheat, fine, forfeiture, loss, mulct, penalization, penalty, surrender.
v abandon, forgo, give up, lose, relinquish, renounce, sacrifice, surrender.

forfeiture *n* attainder, confiscation, escheat, forgoing, giving up, loss, relinquishment, sacrifice, sequestration, surrender.

forge *v* beat out, cast, coin, construct, contrive, copy, counterfeit, create, devise, fabricate, fake, falsify, fashion, feign, form, frame, hammer out, imitate, invent, make, mould, shape, simulate, work.

forge ahead *v* advance, boldly go, gain ground, improve, make great strides, make headway, make one's way, pioneer, press on, proceed, progress, push back the frontier(s), push on.

forgery *n* coining, copy, counterfeit, counterfeiting, dud, fabrication, fake,

falsification, fraud, fraudulence, imitation, look-alike, phony, sham.
antonym original.

forget *v* consign to oblivion, discount, dismiss, disregard, disremember, fail, ignore, lose sight of, neglect, omit, overlook, put aside, think no more of, unlearn.
antonym remember.

forgetful *adj* absent-minded, abstracted, amnesiac, amnesic, careless, dreamy, heedless, inattentive, lax, neglectful, negligent, oblivious, unmindful, unretentive, woolgathering.
antonyms attentive, heedful.

forgetfulness *n* absent-mindedness, abstraction, amnesia, carelessness, dreaminess, heedlessness, inattention, lapse, laxness, Lethe, oblivion, obliviousness, wool-gathering.
antonyms attentiveness, heedfulness.

forgivable *adj* excusable, innocent, minor, pardonable, petty, slight, trifling, venial.
antonym unforgivable.

forgive *v* absolve, acquit, condone, exculpate, excuse, exonerate, forget, forgive and forget, let off, overlook, pardon, reconcile with, remit, shrive.
antonym censure.

forgiveness *n* absolution, acquittal, amnesty, clemency, condonation, exculpation, exoneration, mercy, pardon, reconciliation, remission, shrift, shriving.
antonyms blame, censure.

forgiving *adj* clement, compassionate, forbearing, humane, indulgent, lenient, magnanimous, merciful, mild, remissive, soft-hearted, sparing, tolerant.
antonym censorious.

forgo *v* abandon, abjure, abstain from, avoid, do without, eschew, forfeit, give up, pass up, refrain from, relinquish, renounce, resign, sacrifice, surrender, waive.
antonyms claim, indulge in, insist on.

forgotten *adj* blotted out, buried, bygone, disregarded, ignored, irrecoverable, irretrievable, lost, neglected, obliterated, omitted, out of mind, overlooked, past, past recall, past recollection, unrecalled, unremembered, unretrieved.
antonym remembered.

fork *v* bifurcate, branch, branch off, diverge, divide, furcate, part, ramify, separate, split.
n bifurcation, branch(ing), divergence, division, furcation, intersection, junction, prong, ramification, separation, split.

forked *adj* bifurcate, branched, branching, cloven, divergent, diverging, divided, forking, furcate, pronged, ramified, split, tined, zigzag.
fork out or over cough up, deliver, give up, hand over, lay out, pay out (or up), relinquish, spend, surrender.
have a forked tongue be a deceiver, be untrustworthy, equivocate, have lying lips, lie, mislead, prevaricate, speak out of both sides of one's mouth, talk fast.

forlorn *adj* abandoned, abject, bereft, cheerless, comfortless, deserted, desolate, desperate, destitute, disconsolate, forgotten, forsaken, friendless, helpless, homeless, hopeless, lonely, lost, miserable, neglected, pathetic, piteous, pitiable, pitiful, unhappy, woebegone, woeful, wretched.
antonym hopeful.

form *v* accumulate, acquire, appear, arrange, assemble, be born, become, build, combine, compose, comprise, conceive, concoct, constitute, construct, contract, contrive, create, crystallize, cultivate, design, develop, devise, discipline, dispose, draw up, educate, establish, evolve, fabricate, fashion, forge, formulate, found, frame, give shape to, group, grow, hatch, instruct, invent, make, make up, manufacture, materialize, model, mould, order, organize, pattern, plan, produce, put together, rear, rise, school, serve as, settle, shape, take order, take shape, teach, train, turn (into).
n anatomy, appearance, application, arrangement, aspect, behaviour, being, body, build, cast, ceremony, character, class, condition, conduct, configuration, construction, convention, custom, cut, description, design, document, etiquette, fashion, fettle, figure, fitness, formality, format, formation, formula, frame, framework, genre, Gestalt, grade, guise, harmony, health, kind, manifestation, manner, manners, matrix, method, mode, model, motif, mould, nature, order, orderliness, organization, outline, paper, pattern, person, physique, plan, practice, procedure, proportion, protocol, questionnaire, rank, ritual, rule, schedule, semblance, shape, sheet, silhouette, sort, species, spirits, stamp, structure, style, symmetry, system, trim, type, variety, way.

formal *adj* academic, aloof, approved, ceremonial, ceremonious, conventional, correct, exact, explicit, express, fixed, full-dress, impersonal, lawful, legal, methodical, nominal, official, perfunctory, precise, prescribed, prim, proper, punctilious, recognized, regular, reserved, rigid, ritualistic, set, solemn, starch, starched, starchy, stiff, stiff-necked, stilted, strict, unbending.
antonym informal.

formality *n* ceremoniousness, ceremony, convenance, convention, conventionality, correctness, custom, decorum, etiquette, form, formalism, gesture, matter of form, politeness, pomp, procedure, propriety, protocol, punctilio, red tape, rite, ritual, stiffness.
antonym informality.

format *n* appearance, arrangement, configuration, construction, dimensions, form, layout, look, make-up, pattern, plan, shape, structure, style, type.

formation *n* accumulation, appearance, array, arrangement, compilation, composition, configuration, constitution, construction, creation, crystallization, design, development, disposition, emergence, establishment, evolution, fabrication, figure, format, forming, generation, genesis, grouping, manufacture, order, organization, pattern, production, rank, shaping, structure.

formative *adj* controlling, determinative, determining, developmental, dominant, guiding, impressionable, influential, malleable, mouldable, moulding, pliant, sensitive, shaping, susceptible.
antonym destructive.

former *adj* above, aforementioned, aforesaid, ancient, antecedent, anterior, bygone, departed, earlier, erstwhile, ex-, first mentioned, foregoing, late, long ago, of yore, old, old-time, one-time, past, preceding, pre-existent, previous, prior, pristine, quondam, sometime, then, whilom.
antonyms current, future, later, present, prospective, subsequent.

formerly *adv* already, at one time, before, days of yore, earlier, erstwhile, heretofore, historically, hitherto, in the (good) old days, lately, long ago, once, once upon a time, previously, whilom.
antonyms currently, hereafter, later, now, nowadays, presently, subsequently, thereafter, these days, today.

formidable *adj* alarming, appalling, arduous, awesome, challenging, colossal, dangerous, daunting, difficult, dismaying, dreadful, enormous, fearful, frightening, frightful, great, horrible, huge, impressive, indomitable, intimidating, leviathan, mammoth, menacing, mighty, onerous, overwhelming, powerful, puissant, redoubtable, shocking, staggering, terrible, terrific, terrifying, threatening, toilsome, tremendous, weighty.
antonyms easy, genial.

formless *adj* amorphous, chaotic, confused, disorganized, inchoate, incoherent, indefinite, indeterminate, nebulous, shapeless, unformed, unshaped, vague.
antonyms definite, orderly.

formula *n* algorithm, axiom, blueprint, code, form, formulary, method, modus operandi, password, precept, prescription, principle, procedure, recipe, rite, ritual, rubric, rule, rule of thumb, schema, way, wording.

formulate *v* block in, block out, codify, couch, create, define, detail, develop, devise, draw up, evolve, express, form, frame, invent, originate, particularize, phrase, plan, specify, systematize, word, work out, write up.

forsake *v* abandon, abdicate, cast off, desert, discard, disown, forgo, forswear, give up, jettison, jilt, leave, leave in the lurch, quit, reject, relinquish, renounce, repudiate, surrender, throw over, turn one's back on, vacate, yield.
antonyms abide by, cherish, resume, revert to.

forsaken *adj* abandoned, cast off, deserted, desolate, destitute, discarded, disowned, forlorn, friendless, ignored, isolated, jilted, left in the lurch, lonely, lorn, lovelorn, marooned, outcast, rejected, shunned, solitary, unloved.
antonyms cared for, cherished, loved.

forswear v abandon, abjure, deny, disavow, disclaim, disown, drop, forgo, forsake, give up, lie, perjure oneself, recant, reject, renege, renounce, repudiate, retract, swear off.
antonym revert to.

fort n acropolis, bastion, blockhouse, bridgehead, camp, castle, citadel, fastness, fortification, fortress, garrison, Martello (tower), post, redoubt, station, stronghold, tower.

forte n aptitude, bent, gift, long suit, métier, skill, specialty, strength, strong point, talent.
antonyms inadequacy, weak point.

forthcoming[1] adj accessible, approaching, at hand, available, coming, emerging, expected, future, imminent, impending, in preparation, in the offing, in the pipeline, in the works, obtainable, projected, prospective, ready, soon to appear.
antonyms past, unavailable.

forthcoming[2] adj accommodating, chatty, communicative, conversational, expansive, frank, free, informative, loquacious, obliging, open, sociable, talkative, unreserved.
antonyms awkward, secretive, taciturn, unaccommodating, uncommunicative.

forthright adj aboveboard, blunt, bold, candid, direct, foursquare, frank, open, outspoken, plain-speaking, plain-spoken, straightforward, straight-from-the-shoulder, trenchant, unequivocal.
antonyms devious, mealy-mouthed, tactful.

forthwith adv at once, directly, immediately, instanter, instantly, posthaste, promptly, pronto, quickly, right away, straightaway, tout de suite, without delay.

fortification n abatis, barricade, bastion, bulwark, buttressing, castle, citadel, defence, earthwork, embattlement, entrenchment, fastness, fort, fortress, keep, Martello (tower), muniment, outwork, protection, rampart, redoubt, reinforcement, stockade, strengthening, stronghold.

fortify v add to, boost, brace, bulwark, buttress, cheer, confirm, defend, embattle, embolden, encourage, entrench, garrison, hearten, invigorate, lace, load, mix, protect, reassure, reinforce, secure, shore up, spike, steel, stiffen, strengthen, support, sustain, wall.
antonyms dilute, weaken.

fortitude n backbone, braveness, bravery, courage, dauntlessness, determination, endurance, fearlessness, firmness, grit, guts, hardiness, indomitability, intrepidity, long-suffering, patience, perseverance, pluck, resoluteness, resolution, staying power, stout-heartedness, strength, strength of mind, valour, virtue, willpower.
antonyms cowardice, weakness.

fortress n alcazar, bastion, burg, casbah, castle, citadel, fastness, fort, fortification, stronghold.

fortuitous adj accidental, adventitious, arbitrary, casual, chance, coincidental, contingent, felicitous, flukey, fortunate, happy, incidental, lucky, providential, quirky, random, serendipitous, unexpected, unforeseen, unintentional, unplanned.
antonyms intentional, planned.

fortunate adj advantageous, auspicious, blessed, bright, convenient, encouraging, favourable, favoured, felicitous, fortuitous, golden, happy, helpful, lucky, opportune, profitable, promising, propitious, prosperous, providential, rosy, serendipitous, successful, timely, well-off, well-timed.
antonym unfortunate.

fortunately adv happily, luckily, providentially.
antonym unfortunately.

fortune[1] n affluence, an arm and a leg, assets, bundle, estate, income, king's ransom, means, mint, opulence, packet, pile, possessions, property, prosperity, riches, small fortune, success, treasure, wad, wealth.

fortune[2] n accident, chance, circumstances, contingency, cup, destiny, doom, expectation, experience, fate, fortuity, hap, happenstance, kismet, life, lot, luck, portion, providence, star.

fortune-telling n augury, card reading, chiromancy, crystal gazing, divination, palmistry, prediction, prognostication, prophecy, second sight.

forward[1] adj advanced, eager, early, enterprising, fore, foremost, forward-looking, front, onward, precocious, premature, progressive, ready, well-advanced, well-developed.
antonyms retrograde, slow.
adv ahead, en avant, forth, forward, into consideration, into view, on, onward, out, outward, to light, to the fore, to the surface, up.
antonym backward.
v accelerate, advance, aid, assist, back, courier, deliver, dispatch, encourage, expedite, facilitate, favour, fax, foster, freight, further, hasten, help, hurry, mail, promote, push, readdress, redirect, route, send, send on, ship, speed, support, transmit.
antonyms impede, obstruct.

forward[2] adj aggressive, assertive, assuming, audacious, brassy, bold, brash, brazen, brazenfaced, cheeky, confident, familiar, fresh, impertinent, impudent, malapert, officious, overweening, pert, presuming, presumptuous, pushy.
antonym diffident.

forward-looking adj avant-garde, dynamic, enlightened, enterprising, far-sighted, go-getting, innovative, liberal, modern, progressive, reformative, visionary.
antonyms conservative, retrograde.

forwardness n aggressiveness, assurance, audacity, boldness, brashness, brazenness, cheek, cheekiness, eagerness, impertinence, impudence, malapertness, overconfidence, pertness, pushiness, presumption, presumptuousness.
antonyms reserve, retiring.

fossilized adj aged, anachronistic, antediluvian, antiquated, archaic, archaistic, dead, démodé, extinct, hardened, inflexible, obsolete, old-fashioned, old-fogeyish, ossified, outdated, outmoded, out-of-date, passé, petrified, prehistoric, stone-age, superannuated.
antonym up-to-date.

foster v accommodate, advance, aid, bring up, care for, cherish, cultivate, encourage, entertain, feed, foment, harbour, make much of, nourish, nurse, nurture, promote, raise, rear, stimulate, support, sustain, take care of.
antonyms discourage, neglect.

foul adj abhorrent, abominable, abusive, bad, base, blasphemous, blue, blustery, choked, clogged, coarse, contaminated, crooked, decaying, despicable, detestable, dirty, disagreeable, disfigured, disgraceful, disgusting, dishonest, dishonourable, entangled, evil, fetid, filthy, foggy, foul-mouthed, fraudulent, gross, hateful, heinous, impure, indecent, inequitable, infamous, iniquitous, lewd, loathsome, low, malodorous, mephitic, murky, nasty, nauseating, nefarious, noisome, notorious, noxious, objectionable, obscene, offensive, polluted, profane, putrid, rainy, rank, reeking, repulsive, revolting, rotten, rough, rude, scandalous, scatological, scurrilous, shady, shameful, smelly, smutty, snarky, squalid, stagnant, stinking, stormy, sullied, tainted, unclean, underhand, unfair, unfavourable, unjust, unpleasant, unsportsmanlike, untidy, venomous, vicious, vile, vituperative, vulgar, wet, wicked, wild.
antonyms clean, fair, pure, worthy.
v befoul, begrime, besmear, besmirch, block, catch, choke, clog (up), collide, contaminate, defile, dirty, disgrace, dishonour, ensnare, entangle, jam, pollute, smear, snarl, soil, stain, sully, taint, twist.
antonyms clean, clear, disentangle.

foul play chicanery, corruption, crime, deception, dirty work, double-dealing, duplicity, fraud, funny business, jiggery-pokery, perfidy, roguery, sharp practice, skulduggery, treachery, villainy, violence.
antonyms fair play, justice.

foul up ball up, bangle, botch, muck up, mess up, screw up.

foul-mouthed adj abusive, blasphemous, coarse, foul-spoken, foul-tongued, mouthy, obscene, offensive, profane, rude, vulgar.

found v base, begin, build, constitute, construct, create, endow, erect, establish, fix, ground, inaugurate, initiate, institute, organize, originate, plant, raise, rest, root, set up, start, sustain.

foundation n base, basis, bedrock, beginning, bottom, endowment, establishment, fond, footing, ground, groundwork, inauguration, institution, organization, premise, preparation, setting up, substance, substratum, substructure, underpinning.

founder[1] n architect, author, beginner, benefactor, builder, constructor, designer, endower, establisher, father, framer, generator, initiator, institutor, inventor, maker, matriarch, mother, organizer, originator, patriarch.

founder[2] v abort, break down, bog down, capsize, collapse, come to grief, come to nothing, fail, fall, fall through, get mired, go lame, lurch, miscarry, misfire, sink, sprawl, stagger, stick, stumble, submerge, subside, trip.
▲ confusable word flounder.

foundling n enfant trouvé, orphan, outcast, stray, urchin, waif.

fountain n fons et origo, font, fount, fountainhead, inspiration, jet, origin, reservoir, source, spout, spray, spring, waterworks, well, wellhead, wellspring.

fourfold adj four times as much or as many, quadruple, quadruplex, quadruplicate, tetraploid.

foursquare adv firmly, frankly, honestly, resolutely, squarely, unyieldingly.
adj direct, firm, forthright, frank, honest, immovable, outspoken, resolute, solid, steady, straightforward, strong, unyielding.
antonyms uncertain, wavering.

fox n crafty devil, cunning devil, dodger, horse trader, reynard, slick customer, sly one, slyboots, trickster.

foxy adj artful, astute, canny, clever, crafty, cunning, devious, guileful, knowing, seductive, sharp, shrewd, sly, tricky, vulpine, wily.
antonyms naïve, open.

foyer n antechamber, anteroom, entrance hall, hall(way), lobby, narthex, reception (room), vestibule.

fracas n affray, brawl, commotion, disturbance, Donnybrook, fight, fray, free-for-all, melee, quarrel, riot, row, ruckus, rumpus, scrimmage, scuffle, shindy, trouble, uproar.

fractious adj awkward, bad-tempered, captious, choleric, crabby, cross, crotchety, fretful, froward, grouchy, irascible, irritable, peevish, petulant, quarrelsome, querulous, recalcitrant, refractory, testy, touchy, ungovernable, unruly.
antonyms complaisant, placid.

fracture n breach, break, cleft, crack, fissure, gap, opening, rent, rift, rupture, schism, scission, split.
v break, crack, rupture, splinter, split.
antonym join.

fragile adj breakable, brittle, dainty, delicate, feeble, fine, flimsy, frail, frangible, infirm, insubstantial, slight, transient, weak.
antonyms durable, robust, tough.

fragility n breakability, brittleness, delicacy, feebleness, frailty, frangibility, infirmity, weakness.
antonyms durability, robustness, strength.

fragment n bit, chip, crumb, excerpt, flake, flinder, fraction, frazzle, fritter, morsel, part, particle, piece, portion, remnant, scrap, shard, shatter, shiver, shred, sliver, smithereen.
v break, break up, come apart, come to

pieces, crumble, disintegrate, disunite, divide, flake, fractionalize, frazzle, fritter, shatter, shiver, shred, splinter, split, split up, tear into bits.

antonyms hold together, join.

fragmentary *adj* broken, disconnected, discrete, disjointed, fractional, fractionary, incoherent, incomplete, partial, piecemeal, scattered, scrappy, separate, sketchy, unsystematic.

antonym complete.

fragrance *n* aroma, balm, balminess, bouquet, essence, odour, perfume, redolence, scent, smell.

fragrant *adj* aromatic, balmy, balsamy, odoriferous, odorous, perfumed, redolent, scented, sweet, sweet-scented, sweet-smelling.

antonyms smelly, unscented.

frail *adj* breakable, brittle, decrepit, delicate, feeble, flimsy, fragile, frangible, infirm, insubstantial, irresolute, puny, slight, tender, thin, transient, unhealthy, unsound, vulnerable, weak.

antonyms firm, robust, strong, tough.

frailty *n* blemish, defect, deficiency, failing, fallibility, fault, feebleness, flaw, foible, frailness, imperfection, infirmity, peccadillo, puniness, shortcoming, sickliness, susceptibility, vice, weakness.

antonyms firmness, robustness, strength, toughness.

frame *v* assemble, block (in or out), build, case, compose, conceive, concoct, constitute, construct, contrive, cook up, create, devise, draft, draw up, enclose, enframe, fabricate, fashion, forge, form, formulate, hatch, institute, invent, make, manufacture, map out, model, mould, mount, plan, put together, redact, set up, shape, sketch, surround, trap, victimize.

n anatomy, body, build, carcass, casing, chassis, construction, fabric, flake, form, framework, housing, morphology, mount, mounting, physique, plan, scaffolding, scheme, setting, shape, shell, skeleton, structure, system.

frame of mind attitude, disposition, fettle, humour, mood, morale, outlook, spirit, state, temper, vein.

frame-up *n* fabrication, fix, put-up job, scheme, set-up, trap, trumped-up charge.

framework *n* bare bones, context, core, fabric, foundation, frame, gantry, groundwork, outline, paradigm, plan, schema, setting, shell, skeleton, structure, system.

franchise *n* authorization, chain, charter, concession, exemption, freedom, immunity, liberty, prerogative, privilege, right, suffrage, voice, vote.

frank *adj* artless, blunt, candid, communicative, direct, downright, forthright, four-square, free, honest, ingenuous, open, outright, outspoken, plain, plain-spoken, simple-hearted, sincere, straight, straightforward, transparent, truthful, unaffected, unconcealed, undisguised, unreserved, unrestricted.

antonyms evasive, insincere.

frankly *adv* bluntly, candidly, directly, flat out, forthrightly, freely, honestly, in all honesty, in plain words, in truth, openly, plainly, sincerely, straight, straight from the shoulder, to be frank, to be (perfectly) honest, unreservedly, without reservation.

antonyms evasively, insincerely.

frankness *n* bluntness, candour, forthrightness, glasnost, ingenuousness, openness, outspokenness, plain speaking, truthfulness, unreserve.

frantic *adj* anxious, berserk, beside oneself, desperate, distracted, distraught, fraught, frenetic, frenzied, furious, hectic, mad, overwrought, raging, raving, wild.

antonym calm.

fraternity *n* affiliation, association, brotherhood, camaraderie, circle, clan, club, companionship, company, comradeship, confrèrie, confraternity, fellowship, guild, kinship, league, lodge, order, set, society, sodality, sorority, union.

fraternize *v* affiliate, associate, be friendly, consort, co-operate, forgather, hobnob, mingle, mix, socialize, sympathize, unite.

antonyms ignore, shun.

fraud¹ *n* artifice, cheat, chicane, chicanery, counterfeit, craft, deceit, deception, dishonesty, double-dealing, duplicity, fake, fakery, forgery, fraudulence, guile, hoax, humbug, imposture, sham, sharp practice, spuriousness, swindle, swindling, take-in, theft, treachery, trick, trickery.

fraud² *n* bluffer, charlatan, cheat, counterfeit, deceiver, double-dealer, hoaxer, impostor, malingerer, mountebank, phony, pretender, quack, swindler, trickster.

fraudulent *adj* bogus, counterfeit, crafty, criminal, crooked, deceitful, deceptive, dishonest, double-dealing, duplicitous, false, knavish, phony, sham, specious, spurious, swindling, treacherous.

antonyms genuine, honest.

fraught *adj* abounding, accompanied, agitated, attended, bristling, burdened, charged, filled, full, heavy, laden, loaded, replete, stuffed, weighted (down).

antonyms calm, untroublesome.

fray *n* affray, battle, brawl, broil, clash, combat, conflict, disturbance, Donnybrook, dustup, fight, free-for-all, melee, quarrel, riot, row, ruckus, rumble, rumpus, scuffle, set-to, shindy.

frayed *adj* edgy, frazzled, on edge, ragged, ravelled, raw, strained, tattered, threadbare, unravelled, worn.

antonyms calm, tidy.

freak¹ *n* aberration, abnormality, anomaly, caprice, crotchet, eccentric, fad, fancy, folly, grotesque, irregularity, malformation, misfit, misgrowth, monster, monstrosity, mutant, oddity, queer fish, quirk, rara avis, teratism, twist, vagary, weirdo, whim, whimsy.

adj aberrant, abnormal, atypical, bizarre, capricious, erratic, exceptional, flukey, fortuitous, odd, queer, strange, surprise, unaccountable, unexpected, unforeseen, unparalleled, unpredictable, unpredicted, unusual.

antonyms common, expected.

freak² *n* addict, aficionado, buff, devotee, enthusiast, fan, fanatic, fiend, lover, monomaniac, nut, votary.

freakish *adj* aberrant, abnormal, arbitrary, bizarre, capricious, changeable, eccentric, erratic, fanciful, fantastic, fitful, freaky, grotesque, malformed, monstrous, odd, outlandish, outré, preternatural, strange, teratoid, unconventional, unpredictable, unusual, vagarious, way out, wayward, weird, whimsical.

antonym ordinary.

free *adj* able, allowed, at large, at leisure, at liberty, autarkic, autonomous, available, bounteous, bountiful, broad, buckshee, candid, careless, casual, charitable, clear, complimentary, cost-free, dégagé, democratic, disengaged, easy, emancipated, empty, extra, familiar, footloose, forward, frank, free and easy, free of charge, generous, gratis, hospitable, idle, impertinent, independent, informal, irresponsible, laid-back, lavish, lax, leisured, liberal, liberated, libertine, licentious, loose, munificent, natural, off the hook, on the house, on the loose, open, open-handed, permitted, prodigal, relaxed, released, self-governing, self-ruling, sovereign, spare, spontaneous, unattached, unbidden, unceremonious, unchaste, uncommitted, unconstrained, unemployed, unencumbered, unengaged, unfastened, unfettered, unforced, unhampered, unhindered, unimpeded, uninhabited, uninhibited, unobstructed, unoccupied, unpaid, unpreoccupied, unregimented, unregulated, unrestrained, unrestricted, unsparing, unstinting, untrammelled, unused, vacant, voluntary, welcome, wild, willing, without charge.

antonyms attached, confined, costly, formal, mean, niggardly, restricted, tied.

adv as a gift, compliments of (someone), for free, for love, for nothing, gratis, with compliments, without charge.

v absolve, acquit, clear, declassify, decolonize, decontrol, deliver, detach, disburden, discharge, disembarrass, disengage, disentangle, emancipate, enfranchise, exempt, extricate, let go, let loose, liberate, loose, manumit, ransom, release, relieve, rescue, rid, set free, turn loose, unbind, unburden, uncage, unchain, undo, unfetter, unhand, unleash, unlock, unloose, unmanacle, unpeg, unshackle, unstick, untether, untie, unyoke.

antonyms confine, enslave, imprison.

free hand authority, carte blanche, discretion, freedom, full authority, full permission, latitude, liberty, permission, power, scope.

free from or of devoid of, exempt from, immune to, innocent of, lacking, not liable to,

safe from, sans, unaffected by, unencumbered by, unhampered by, untouched by, without.

freebooter *n* bandit, brigand, buccaneer, filibuster, highwayman, looter, marauder, pillager, pirate, plunderer, raider, robber, rover.

freedom *n* abandon, ability, autonomy, boldness, brazenness, candour, carte-blanche, deliverance, directness, discretion, disrespect, ease, elbow-room, emancipation, enfranchisement, exemption, facility, familiarity, flexibility, forwardness, frankness, free rein, home rule, immunity, impertinence, impunity, independence, informality, ingenuousness, lack of restraint or reserve, latitude, laxity, leeway, leisure, liberty, licence, manumission, openness, opportunity, overfamiliarity, play, power, presumption, privilege, range, release, right, room, scope, self-government, space, unconstraint.

antonyms confinement, reserve, restriction.

freely *adv* abundantly, amply, bountifully, candidly, cleanly, copiously, easily, extravagantly, fluently, frankly, generously, lavishly, liberally, loosely, of one's own accord, of one's own free will, open-handedly, openly, plainly, readily, smoothly, spontaneously, unchallenged, unreservedly, unstintingly, volubly, voluntarily, willingly, without restraint.

antonyms evasively, meanly, roughly, under duress.

free will *n* autarky, autonomy, election, freedom of decision, independence, liberty, self-determination, self-sufficiency, spontaneity, volition.

freeze *v* anesthetize, benumb, chill, congeal, cut off, discontinue, fix, form ice, glaciate, halt, harden, hold, ice, ice over, inhibit, numb, peg, prohibit use of, rigidify, shelve, solidify, stiffen, stop, suspend.

n abeyance, cold snap, discontinuation, embargo, freeze-up, frost, halt, interruption, moratorium, postponement, shutdown, standstill, stay, stoppage, suspension.

freezing *adj* arctic, below-zero, biting, bitter, brumous, chill, chilled, chilly, cold, cutting, frigid, frosty, gelid, glacial, icy, numbing, penetrating, polar, raw, Siberian, wintry.

antonyms hot, warm.

freight *n* bulk, burden, cargo, carriage, charge, consignment, contents, conveyance, duty, fee, goods, haul, lading, load, merchandise, payload, shipment, tonnage, transportation.

frenetic *adj* breathless, demented, distraught, excited, fanatical, frantic, frenzied, hyperactive, insane, mad, maniacal, obsessive, phrenetic, rushed, unbalanced, wild.

antonyms calm, placid.

frenzied *adj* agitated, convulsive, distracted, distraught, excited, feverish, frantic, frenetic, furious, hysterical, mad, maniacal, overactive, overzealous, panicked, rabid, uncontrolled, violent, wild.

antonyms calm, placid.

frenzy *n* agitation, bout, burst, convulsion, delirium, derangement, distraction, excitement, fit, fury, hysteria, insanity, lunacy, madness,

mania, outburst, panic, paroxysm, passion, rage, seizure, spasm, transport, turmoil, violence.
antonyms calm, placidness.

frequency *n* constancy, frequentness, oftenness, periodicity, prevalence, recurrence, repetition.
antonym infrequency.

frequent[1] *adj* common, commonplace, constant, continual, customary, everyday, familiar, habitual, incessant, numerous, persistent, recurrent, recurring, regular, reiterated, repeated, usual.
antonym infrequent.

frequent[2] *v* attend, crowd, hang around, hang out at, haunt, patronize, resort to, visit.

frequenter *n* attender, client, customer, denizen, guest, habitué, haunter, patron, regular.

frequently *adv* commonly, continually, customarily, habitually, many a time, many times, much, oft, often, oftentimes, over and over, persistently, repeatedly.
antonyms infrequently, seldom.

fresh[1] *adj* added, additional, alert, artless, auxiliary, blooming, bold, bouncing, bracing, brand-new, bright, brisk, callow, chipper, clean, clear, cool, creative, crisp, dewy, different, energetic, extra, fair, further, glowing, green, healthy, imaginative, inexperienced, innovative, inventive, invigorated, invigorating, keen, lively, modern, modernistic, more, natural, new, new-fangled, nippy, novel, original, outdoorsy, presumptuous, pure, raw, recent, refreshed, refreshing, renewed, rested, restored, revived, rosy, ruddy, spanking, sparkling, spick-and-span, sprightly, spry, stiff, strong, supplementary, sweet, unconventional, uncultivated, undimmed, unhackneyed, unjaded, unjaundiced, unpolluted, unsoured, unspoiled, untrained, untried, unusual, unwarped, unwearied, up-to-date, verdant, vernal, vigorous, virescent, vital, vivid, warm, wholesome, young, youthful.
antonyms experienced, faded, old hat, stale, tired.

fresh[2] *adj* bold, brazen, cheeky, disrespectful, familiar, flip, forward, impudent, insolent, lippy, malapert, mouthy, pest, saucy.

freshen *v* air, clean (up), deodorize, do up, enliven, invigorate, liven, purify, refresh, reinvigorate, restore, resuscitate, revitalize, spruce up, tart up, titivate, touch up, ventilate, vitalize, wash up.
antonym tire.

freshman *n* beginner, first-year, freshy, frosh, (grade) niner, novice.

freshness *n* bloom, brightness, cleanness, clearness, dewiness, glow, newness, novelty, originality, shine, sparkle, vigour, virescence, wholesomeness.
antonyms staleness, tiredness.

fret *v* abrade, agitate, agonize, annoy, bother, brood, chafe, chagrin, corrode, distress, disturb, eat into, erode, fray, gall, goad, grieve,

harass, irk, irritate, nag, nettle, peeve, pique, provoke, rankle, repine, rile, ripple, rub, ruffle, torment, trouble, vex, wear, wear away, worry.
antonym calm.

fretful *adj* agitated, bad-tempered, cantankerous, captious, complaining, cross, crotchety, edgy, fractious, irritable, peevish, petulant, querulous, short-tempered, snappish, snappy, splenetic, testy, touchy, uneasy, unhappy.
antonym calm.

friable *adj* brittle, crisp, crumbly, powdery, pulverizable.
antonyms clayey, solid.

friar *n* brother, mendicant, monastic, monk, religieux, religious.

friction *n* abrasion, animosity, antagonism, attrition, bad blood, bad feeling, bickering, chafing, conflict, contention, disagreement, discord, disharmony, dispute, dissension, erosion, fretting, grating, hostility, ill feeling, incompatibility, irritation, opposition, quarrelling, rasping, resentment, resistance, rivalry, rubbing, scraping, wearing away, wrangling.

friend *n* Achates, adherent, advocate, ally, alter ego, associate, backer, benefactor, boon companion, bosom friend, buddy, chum, companion, comrade, confidant(e), crony, familiar, intimate, kindred spirit, mate, nitchie, pal, partisan, partner, patron, playmate, sidekick, soul mate, supporter, well-wisher.
antonym enemy.

friendless *adj* abandoned, alienated, alone, deserted, desolate, estranged, forlorn, forsaken, helpless, isolated, lonely, lonesome, ostracized, shunned, solitary, unattached, unbefriended, uncared-for, unfriended, unloved.

friendliness *n* affability, amiability, approachability, companionability, congeniality, conviviality, friendship, Gemütlichkeit, geniality, kindliness, neighbourliness, sociability, warmth.
antonyms coldness, unsociableness.

friendly *adj* affable, affectionate, amiable, amicable, approachable, attached, attentive, auspicious, beneficial, benevolent, benign, buddy-buddy, chummy, close, congenial, comfortable, companionable, comradely, conciliatory, confiding, convivial, cordial, familiar, favonian, favourable, fond, fraternal, friendlike, gemütlich, genial, good, helpful, homelike, hospitable, informal, intimate, kind, kindly, neighbourly, on good terms, outgoing, palsy-walsy, peaceable, propitious, receptive, sociable, sympathetic, thick, warm, welcoming, well-disposed.
antonyms cold, hostile, unsociable.

friendship *n* affection, affinity, alliance, amity, attachment, benevolence, closeness, companionship, concord, familiarity, fellowship, fondness, friendliness, good will, harmony, intimacy, love, neighbourliness, rapport, regard.
antonym enmity.

fright *n* alarm, apprehension, consternation, dismay, dread, eyesore, fear, funk, horror, mess, monstrosity, panic, quaking, scare, scarecrow, shock, sight, spectacle, sweat, terror, the shivers, trepidation.

frighten v affright, alarm, appal, cow, daunt, dismay, give one a turn, intimidate, paralyse, petrify, scare, scare stiff, scare the daylights out of, scare the pants off, scare out of one's wits, scare to death, shake, shock, spook, startle, terrify, terrorize, unman, unnerve.

antonyms calm, reassure.

frightened adj affrighted, afraid, alarmed, cowed, dismayed, fearful, frozen, in a fright, panicky, petrified, scared, scared out of one's wits, scared to death, scared stiff or silly, startled, terrified, terrorized, terror-stricken, unnerved.

antonyms calm, courageous.

frightening adj alarming, appalling, bad, bloodcurdling, creepy, daunting, dismaying, dreadful, fearful, fearsome, hair-raising, horrifying, intimidating, menacing, scary, shocking, spine-chilling, spooky, terrifying, traumatic, unnerving.

antonym reassuring.

frightful adj alarming, appalling, atrocious, awful, bad, dire, disagreeable, dread, dreadful, fearful, fearsome, frightening, ghastly, great, grim, grisly, gruesome, harrowing, hideous, horrendous, horrible, horrid, horrifying, insufferable, macabre, petrifying, severe, shocking, terrible, terrific, terrifying, traumatic, ugly, unnerving, unpleasant, unspeakable.

antonyms agreeable, pleasant.

frigid adj aloof, arctic, austere, chill, chilly, cold, cold-hearted, cool, forbidding, formal, frost-bound, frosty, frozen, gelid, glacial, icy, lifeless, passionless, passive, repellent, rigid, stand-offish, stiff, unanimated, unapproachable, unbending, unfeeling, unfriendly, unloving, unresponsive, wintry.

antonyms responsive, warm.

frigidity n aloofness, austerity, chill, chilliness, cold-heartedness, coldness, frostiness, iciness, impassivity, lifelessness, passivity, stiffness, unapproachability, unresponsiveness, wintriness.

antonyms responsiveness, warmth.

frill n edging, extra, flounce, furbelow, gathering, lace, orphrey, purfle, ruche, ruching, ruff, ruffle, superfluity, trimming, tuck, valance.

frills n accessories, additions, affectation, bells and whistles, decoration, embellishment, extras, fanciness, fandangles, finery, flounces, frilliness, frippery, froth, frou-frous, gewgaws, icing (on the cake), luxuries, mannerisms, nonsense, ornamentation, ostentation, smocking, superfluities, trimmings.

frilly adj fancy, flouncy, frothy, lacy, ornate, overornate, ruched, ruffled.

antonyms plain, unadorned.

fringe n border, borderline, edge, edging, fimbriation, limits, marches, margin, outskirts, perimeter, periphery, trimming.

adj alternative, borderline, marginal, unconventional, unofficial, unorthodox.

v border, edge, enclose, fimbriate, skirt, surround, trim.

fringed adj bordered, edged, fimbriated, fringy, skirted, tasselled, trimmed.

frippery n adornments, baubles, decorations, fanciness, fandangles, finery, flashiness, foppery, frilliness, frills, froth, fussiness, gaudiness, gewgaws, glad rags, knick-knacks, meretriciousness, nonsense, ornamentation, ornaments, ostentation, pretentiousness, showiness, superfluity, tawdriness, trifles, trinkets, trivia, triviality.

antonym plainness.

frisk[1] v bounce, caper, cavort, curvet, dance, frolic, gambol, hop, jump, leap, pirouette, play, prance, rollick, romp, skip, sport, trip.

frisk[2] v check, inspect, search, shake down.

frisky adj bouncy, coltish, frolicsome, gamesome, gay, high-spirited, in high spirits, kittenish, lively, playful, raring to go, rollicking, romping, skittish, spirited, sportive.

antonym quiet.

fritter away v blow, dissipate, go through, idle away, misspend, run through, spend foolishly, squander, wanton, waste.

frivolity n childishness, flightiness, flippancy, flummery, folly, foolishness, frivolousness, froth, fun, gaiety, giddiness, jest, levity, light-heartedness, lightness, nonsense, puerility, shallowness, silliness, superficiality, trifling, triviality.

antonym seriousness.

frivolous adj bubble-brained, bubble-headed, childish, dizzy, empty-headed, extravagant, facetious, flighty, flip, flippant, foolish, giddy, idle, ill-considered, impractical, jocular, juvenile, light, light-minded, petty, pointless, puerile, shallow, silly, superficial, trifling, trivial, unimportant, unserious, vacuous, vain.

antonym serious.

frizzy adj crimped, crisp, curled, curly, flyaway, frizzed, kinky, wiry.

antonym straight.

frolic v caper, cavort, cut capers, frisk, gambol, lark, make merry, play, rollick, romp, skylark, sport, wanton.

n amusement, antic, drollery, escapade, fun, fun and games, gaiety, gambol, game, high jinks, hoot, lark, merriment, prank, revel, rig, romp, skylarking, sport, spree.

frolicsome adj coltish, frisky, full of fun, gamesome, gay, kittenish, lively, merry, playful, rollicking, sportive, sprightly, wanton.

antonym quiet.

from
For phrases such as from hand to mouth, from time to time, see the first noun after from.

front n affection, air, anterior, appearance, aspect, battlefield, bearing, beginning, blind, countenance, cover, cover-up, decoy, demeanour, disguise, expression, exterior, façade, face, facing, fakery, figurehead, fore, forefront, foreground, forehead, forepart, front line, frontage, gall, hardihood, head,

fuddled

impertinence, lead, manner, mask, mien, nerve, obverse, pretence, pretext, screen, show, top, van, vanguard.
antonym back.
adj anterior, first, fore, foremost, frontal, head, lead, leading.
antonyms back, last, least, posterior.
v confront, cover, defy, face, look over, meet, oppose, overlook.
in front ahead, before, first, in advance, in the van, in the vanguard, leading, leading the way, preceding, to the fore.
antonym behind.

frontier *n* border, borderland, borderline, bound, boundary, bourn, confines, defy, edge(s), hinterland, limit, march, marches, perimeter, verge, wild west.
adj backwoods, outlying, pioneering.

frost *n* coldness, disappointment, failure, freeze, freeze-up, frigidity, hoarfrost, Jack Frost, rime.

frosty *adj* chilly, cold, discouraging, frigid, frozen, hoary, hostile, ice-capped, icicled, icy, off-putting, rimy, stand-offish, stiff, unfriendly, unwelcoming, white, wintry.
antonym warm.

froth *n* bubbles, effervescence, fluff, foam, frivolity, head, lather, scum, shallowness, spume, spumescence, suds, superficiality, triviality, trumpery.
v bubble, effervesce, ferment, fizz, foam, lather.

frothy *adj* barmy, bubbling, bubbly, empty, foaming, foamy, frilly, frivolous, insubstantial, light, slight, spumescent, spumy, sudsy, superficial, trifling, trivial, trumpery, vain.
antonym flat.

frown *v* glare, glower, grimace, lower, scow, show disapproval.
n dirty look, glare, glower, grimace, moue, scowl.

frown on deprecate, disapprove of, discountenance, discourage, dislike, look askance at, look down on, object to, take a dim view of.
antonym approve of.

frowzy *adj* blowsy, dirty, dishevelled, draggle-tailed, frumpish, frumpy, messy, slatternly, sloppy, slovenly, sluttish, ungroomed, unkempt, untidy, unwashed.
antonym well-groomed.

frozen *adj* arctic, chilled, fixed, frigid, frosted, icebound, ice-cold, ice-covered, icy, in abeyance, numb, pegged, petrified, rigid, rooted, shelved, solidified, stiff, stock-still, stopped, suspended, turned to stone.
antonym warm.

frugal *adj* abstemious, careful, cheap, cheeseparing, economical, meagre, niggardly, parsimonious, penny-pinching, penny-wise, provident, prudent, saving, sparing, Spartan, thrifty, ungenerous.
antonym wasteful.

frugality *n* carefulness, conservation, economizing, economy, frugalness, good management, husbandry, parsimony, penny-pinching, providence, prudence, scrimping, thrift, thriftiness.
antonym wastefulness.

fruit *n* advantage, benefit, consequence, crop, effect, fruitage, harvest, outcome, produce, product, profit, result, return, reward, yield.

fruitful *adj* abundant, advantageous, beneficial, bountiful, copious, effective, fecund, fertile, flush, fructiferous, gainful, plenteous, plentiful, productive, profitable, profuse, prolific, rewarding, rich, spawning, successful, teeming, thriving, useful, well-spent, worthwhile.
antonyms barren, fruitless.

fruitfulness *n* fecundity, feracity, fertility, productiveness, profitability, usefulness.
antonym fruitlessness.

fruition *n* accomplishment, actualization, attainment, completion, consummation, enjoyment, fulfilment, materialization, maturation, maturity, perfection, realization, ripeness, success.
antonym failure.

fruitless *adj* abortive, barren, futile, hopeless, idle, ineffective, ineffectual, pointless, profitless, unavailing, unfruitful, unproductive, unprofitable, unsuccessful, useless, vain.
antonyms fruitful, successful.

fruity *adj* bawdy, blue, flavourful, fruitlike, full, indecent, indelicate, juicy, mellow, racy, resonant, rich, ripe, risqué, salacious, saucy, sexy, smutty, spicy, suggestive, titillating, vulgar.
antonyms decent, light.

frump *n* dowd, dowdy, draggle-tail, fright, mopsy, scarecrow, slattern, slob, sloven.

frumpish *adj* badly-dressed, blowsy, dated, dingy, dowdy, drab, dreary, frowzy, frumpy, ill-dressed, out of date, unfashionable.
antonyms chic, well-groomed.

frustrate *v* baffle, balk, block, check, circumvent, confront, counter, countermine, crab, defeat, depress, disappoint, discourage, dishearten, euchre, foil, forestall, inhibit, neutralize, nullify, outwit, spike, spoil, stymie, thwart.
antonyms fulfil, further, promote.

frustrated *adj* defeated, disappointed, discontented, discouraged, disheartened, embittered, foiled, irked, resentful, scunnered, thwarted.
antonym fulfilled.

frustration *n* annoyance, balking, circumvention, contravention, curbing, defeat, disappointment, discontent, dissatisfaction, failure, foiling, irritation, neutralization, non-fulfilment, non-success, obstruction, resentment, thwarting, vexation.
antonyms fulfilment, furthering, promoting.

fuddled *adj* bemused, confused, dazed, drunk, groggy, hazy, inebriated, intoxicated, muddled, muzzy, sozzled, stupefied, tipsy, woozy.

antonyms clear, sober.

fuddy-duddy *n* back number, conservative, dodo, fogey, fossil, museum piece, old fogey, square, stick-in-the-mud, stuffed shirt.

adj carping, censorious, fusty, old-fashioned, old-fogeyish, prim, stick-in-the-mud, stuffy.

antonym up-to-date.

fudge *v* avoid, cheat, cook, dodge, equivocate, evade, fake, falsify, fiddle, fix, hedge, misrepresent, shuffle, stall, waffle, walsh.

fuel *n* ammunition, encouragement, fodder, food, impetus, incitement, material, means, nourishment, provocation.

v encourage, fan, feed, fill up, fire, incite, inflame, nourish, stoke up, sustain.

antonyms damp down, discourage.

fugitive *n* criminal, deserter, escapee, refugee, renegade, runaway.

adj brief, elusive, ephemeral, escaped, evanescent, fleeing, fleeting, flitting, flying, intangible, momentary, passing, runaway, short, short-lived, temporary, transient, transitory, unstable, wandering.

antonym permanent.

fulfil *v* accomplish, achieve, act on, answer, carry out, complete, comply with, conclude, conform to, consummate, discharge, effect, effectuate, execute, fill, finish, gratify, implement, indulge, keep, meet, obey, observe, perfect, perform, realize, satisfy.

antonyms break, defect, fail, frustrate.

fulfilment *n* accomplishment, achievement, attainment, bringing about, carrying out, completion, consummation, contentment, crowning, discharge, effectuation, end, execution, gratification, implementation, indulgence, observance, perfection, performance, realization, satisfaction, success.

antonyms failure, frustration.

full *adj* abundant, adequate, all-inclusive, ample, baggy, brimful, brimming, broad, buxom, chock-a-block, chock-full, clear, complete, comprehensive, copious, crammed, crowded, curvaceous, deep, detailed, distinct, entire, exhaustive, extensive, filled, generous, gorged, intact, jammed, large, loaded, loud, maximum, orotund, packed, plenary, plenteous, plentiful, plump, replete, resonant, rich, rounded, sated, satiated, satisfied, saturated, sonorous, stocked, sufficient, thorough, unabbreviated, unabridged, uncut, unedited, unexpurgated, unrestricted, voluminous, voluptuous.

antonyms empty, incomplete.

in full completely, entirely, fully, in its entirety, in total, in toto, totally, unabridged, uncut, wholly.

antonyms partially, partly.

full of absorbed by (or in), engrossed in, ocupied with, taken up with.

to the full completely, entirely, fully, thoroughly, to the utmost, utterly.

full-blooded *adj* bona fide, genuine, gutsy, hearty, lusty, mettlesome, real, red-blooded, thoroughbred, vigorous, virile, whole-hearted.

fullfledged *adj* complete, experienced, full-blown, graduate, mature, professional, proficient, qualified, senior, trained.

full-grown *adj* adult, developed, full-blown, full-size, grown, grown-up, marriageable, mature, nubile, of age, ripe.

antonyms undeveloped, young.

fullness *n* abundance, adequateness, ampleness, breadth, broadness, clearness, completeness, comprehensiveness, copiousness, curvaceousness, dilation, distension, enlargement, entirety, extensiveness, glut, loudness, orotundity, plenitude, plenty, profusion, repletion, resonance, richness, roundness, satiety, saturation, strength, sufficiency, swelling, totality, tumescence, vastness, voluptuousness, wealth, wholeness.

antonyms emptiness, incompleteness.

full-scale *adj* all-encompassing, all-out, complete, comprehensive, exhaustive, extensive, full-dress, full-size, in-depth, intensive, major, proper, sweeping, thorough, thoroughgoing, wide-ranging.

antonyms half-hearted, partial.

fully *adv* absolutely, abundantly, adequately, altogether, amply, at least, completely, comprehensively, enough, entirely, every inch, from first to last, heartily, heart and soul, in all respects, intimately, lock stock and barrel, perfectly, plentifully, positively, quite, satisfactorily, sufficiently, thoroughly, totally, unreservedly, utterly, wholly.

antonym half-heartedly, partly, with reservation.

fulminate *v* detonate, discharge, explode, go off, thunder.

antonym praise.

fulminate against animadvert on, blast, censure, criticize, curse, denounce, fume at, inveigh against, rage at, rail at, rant against, revile, vituperate.

fulmination *n* blast, censure, condemnation, criticism, denunciation, detonation, diatribe, explosion, invective, obloquy, philippic, ranting, reprobation, thundering, tirade.

antonym praise.

fulsome *adj* abundant, adulatory, cloying, effusive, excessive, extravagant, fawning, gross, immoderate, ingratiating, inordinate, insincere, nauseating, nauseous, offensive, overdone, profuse, rank, saccharine, sickening, smarmy, sycophantic, unctuous.

antonym sincere.

fumble *v* blunder, botch, bumble, bungle, feel around, flail, flounder, flub, fluff, grope, mishandle, mismanage, muff, mumble, paw, scrabble, spoil.

fume *v* boil, chafe, get steamed up, give off, rage, rant, reek, seethe, smoke, smoulder, storm.

fumes *n* effluvium, exhalation, exhaust, gas, haze, mephitis, miasma, pollution, reek, smog, smoke, stench, vapour.

fumigate v cleanse, deodorize, disinfect, purify, sanitize, sterilize.

fuming adj angry, boiling, enraged, fizzing, incensed, infuriated, irate, raging, roused, seething, spitting, steamed up.

antonym calm.

fun n amusement, buffoonery, cheer, clowning, distraction, diversion, enjoyment, entertainment, foolery, fooling around, frolic, gaiety, game, high, high jinks, horseplay, jest, jesting, jocularity, joking, jollity, joy, junketing, merriment, merrymaking, mirth, play, playfulness, pleasure, recreation, ridicule, romp, skylarking, sport, teasing, treat, waggery, whoopee.

for fun all in good fun, facetiously, for kicks, for laughs, for thrills, in fun, in jest, jokingly, light-heartedly, mischievously, playfully, roguishly, sportively, teasingly, tongue in cheek.

function[1] n activity, business, capacity, charge, concern, duty, employment, exercise, faculty, job, mission, occupation, office, operation, part, post, province, purpose, raison d'être, responsibility, role, situation, task, utility.

v act, be in running order, be used, behave, do duty, go, officiate, operate, perform, run, serve, work.

function[2] n affair, dinner, do, gathering, junket, luncheon, party, reception, shindig, social event.

functional adj acting, hard-wearing, long-wearing, operating, operational, operative, plain, practical, serviceable, useful, utilitarian, working.

antonyms effective, inoperative, ornate, useless.

functionary n agent, bureaucrat, dignitary, employee, office-bearer, officeholder, officer, official, operator.

functionless adj aimless, decorative, futile, hollow, idle, inactive, inert, irrelevant, needless, otiose, pointless, redundant, superfluous, useless.

antonym useful.

fund n cache, capital, collection, endowment, foundation, hoard, kitty, mine, pool, repository, reserve, reservoir, source, stack, stock, store, storehouse, supply, treasury, vein, well.

v back, capitalize, endow, finance, float, promote, stake, subsidize, support, underwrite.

fundamental adj axiomatic, basal, basic, basilar, cardinal, central, constitutional, crucial, elementary, essential, first, important, indispensable, integral, intrinsic, key, keynote, main, necessary, organic, primal, primary, prime, principal, radical, rudimentary, simple, underlying, vital.

antonym advanced.

n axiom, basic, cornerstone, essential, first principle, foundation, keystone, law, principle, rudiment, rule, sine qua non.

fundamentally adv at bottom, at heart, au fond, basically, essentially, in essence, intrinsically, primarily, principally, radically.

fundamentals n basics, brass tacks, business, essentials, nitty-gritty, practicalities.

funds n assets, backing, bread, capital, cash, dough, finances, hard cash, means, money, moola, pelf, ready money, resources, savings, the ready, the wherewithal.

funeral n burial, exequies, inhumation, interment, memorial service, obsequies.

funereal adj black, dark, deathlike, depressing, dirgelike, dismal, dreary, exequial, feral, gloomy, grave, lamenting, lugubrious, mournful, sad, sepulchral, solemn, sombre, woeful.

antonyms happy, lively.

funk v balk at, blench, chicken out of, cop out, dodge, duck out of, flinch from, recoil from, shirk from, shrink.

funnel v channel, conduct, convey, direct, feed, filter, move, pass, pipe, pour, siphon, transfer.

funny adj a card, a caution, a hoot, a scream, absurd, amusing, comic, comical, curious, diverting, droll, dubious, eccentric, entertaining, facetious, farcical, fishy, funny ha-ha, funny peculiar, hilarious, humorous, jocose, jocular, jolly, killing, laughable, ludicrous, mirth-provoking, mysterious, odd, peculiar, perplexing, puzzling, queer, remarkable, rib-tickling, rich, ridiculous, riotous, risible, side-splitting, silly, slapstick, strange, suspicious, tricky, unusual, waggish, weird, witty.

antonyms sad, solemn, unamusing, unfunny.

fur n coat, down, fell, fleece, hide, pelage, pelt, skin, wool.

furious adj agitated, angry, boiling, boisterous, enraged, fierce, frantic, frenzied, fuming, incensed, infuriated, intense, irate, livid, mad, maddened, maenadic, raging, savage, stormy, tempestuous, tumultuous, turbulent, unrestrained, up in arms, vehement, violent, wild, wrathful, wroth.

antonyms calm, pleased.

furnish v afford, appoint, bestow, decorate, endow, equip, fit out, fix up, give, grant, offer, outfit, present, provide, provision, reveal, rig, stake, stock, store, suit, supply.

antonym divest.

furniture n appliances, appointments, appurtenances, chattels, effects, equipment, fittings, furnishing, goods, household goods, movables, possessions, things.

furor n commotion, craze, disturbance, enthusiasm, excitement, flap, frenzy, fury, fuss, hue and cry, hullabaloo, mania, outburst, outcry, rage, stir, to-do, tumult, uproar.

antonym calm.

furrow n chamfer, channel, corrugation, crack, crease, crow's-foot, flute, fluting, groove, hollow, line, rut, seam, trench, valley, wrinkle.

v corrugate, crease, draw together, flute, knit, plough, seam, wrinkle.

furrowed adj channelled, corrugated, creased, fluted, gouged, grooved, knit, ribbed, ridged, rutted, seamed, wrinkled.

further *adj* additional, extra, farther, fresh, more distant, new, opposite, other, renewed, supplementary.

v accelerate, advance, aid, assist, champion, contribute to, ease, encourage, expedite, facilitate, forward, foster, hasten, help, patronize, promote, push, speed, succour.

antonyms frustrate, stop.

furtherance *n* advancement, advocacy, aid, backing, boosting, carrying-out, championship, facilitation, progression, promotion, prosecution, pursuit.

furthermore *adv* additionally, also, as well, besides, further, in addition, into the bargain, likewise, moreover, not to mention, to boot, too, what's more.

furthest *adj* extreme, farthest, furthermost, most distant, most extreme, outermost, outmost, remotest, ultimate, uttermost.

antonym nearest.

furtive *adj* backdoor, backstairs, clandestine, cloaked, conspiratorial, covert, hidden, secret, secretive, skulking, slinking, sly, sneaking, sneaky, stealthy, surreptitious, underhand(ed).

antonym open.

fury *n* anger, desperation, ferocity, fierceness, force, frenzy, impetuosity, intensity, ire, madness, passion, power, rage, savagery, severity, tempestuousness, turbulence, vehemence, violence, wrath.

antonym calm.

fuse *v* agglutinate, amalgamate, ankylose, blend, coalesce, combine, come together, commingle, commix, federate, integrate, intermingle, intermix, join, meld, melt, merge, smelt, solder, unite, weld.

fusillade *n* barrage, broadside, burst, discharge, fire, gunfire, hail, outburst, salvo, volley.

fusion *n* alloy, amalgam, amalgamation, blend, blending, coalescence, commingling, commixture, federation, integration, melting, merger, merging, mixture, smelting, synthesis, union, uniting, welding.

fuss *n* ado, agitation, a to-do, bother, brouhaha, bustle, commotion, confusion, ceremony, difficulty, display, dispute, excitement, fidget, flap, flurry, fluster, flutter, furor, hassle, hue and cry, hurry, kafuffle, objection, outcry, palaver, pother, quarrel, row, squabble, stew, stir, trouble, unrest, uproar, upset, worry.

antonym calm.

v bustle, chafe, complain, feel anxious, fidget, flap, fret, fume, make an issue, nag, niggle, nit-pick, stew, take pains, worry.

fussiness *n* busyness, choosiness, daintiness, elaborateness, fastidiousness, finickness, frilliness, meticulousness, niceness, niggling, ornatness, particularity, perfectionism, pernicketiness, pickiness.

antonym unfastidiousness.

fuss-budget *n* faultfinder, fidget, fuss-pot, hypercritic, nit-picker, old woman, perfectionist, worrier.

fussy *adj* bustling, busy, choosy, cluttered, dainty, detailed, difficult, discriminating, exacting, fancy, fastidious, faultfinding, finicking, finicky, frilly, hard to please, meticulous, niggling, nit-picking, old womanish, ornate, overdecorated, overelaborate, overparticular, particular, pernickety, picky, restless, squeamish.

antonyms easy-going, laid-back, plain, uncritical, undemanding.

fustiness *n* airlessness, closeness, dampness, mouldiness, mustiness, staleness, stuffiness.

antonym airiness.

fusty *adj* airless, antediluvian, antiquated, archaic, close, damp, dank, ill-smelling, malodorous, mildewed, mildewy, mouldering, mouldy, musty, old-fashioned, old-fogeyish, outdated, out-of-date, passé, rank, stale, stuffy, trite, unventilated.

antonyms airy, up-to-date.

futile *adj* abortive, aimless, barren, bootless, empty, forlorn, fruitless, hollow, hopeless, idle, ineffective, ineffectual, meaningless, nugatory, otiose, pointless, profitless, Sisyphean, sterile, trifling, trivial, unavailing, unimportant, unproductive, unprofitable, unsuccessful, useless, vain, valueless, worthless.

antonyms fruitful, profitable.

future *n* by-and-by, expectation, fate, fortune, futurity, hereafter, outlook, prospects, time to come.

antonym past.

adj approaching, coming, designate, destined, eventual, expected, fated, forthcoming, imminent, impending, in the offing, later, projected, prospective, rising, subsequent, to be, to come, ultimate, unborn.

antonym past.

fuzz *n* down, fibre, flock, floss, fluff, hair, lint, nap, pile.

fuzzy *adj* bleary, blurred, blurry, distant, distorted, downy, faint, fluffy, formless, frizzy, hairy, hazy, ill-defined, indistinct, linty, muffled, napped, obscure, shadowy, unclear, unfocussed, vague, woolly.

antonyms base, distinct.

G

gab v babble, blabber, blather, buzz, chat, chatter, converse, drivel, gossip, jabber, jaw, prattle, rap, rattle on, socialize, talk, wag one's tongue, yak, yap.

n blab, blarney, blathering, chat, chatter, chinwag, chitchat, conversation, drivel, gossip, palaver, prattle, prattling, rap, small talk, tête-à-tête, tongue-wagging, yak, yakety-yak, yapping.

gabble v babble, blab, blabber, blather, cackle, chatter, gaggle, gibber, gush, jabber, prattle, rattle on, splutter, spout, sputter.

n babble, blabbering, blathering, cackling, chatter, drivel, gibberish, nonsense, prattle, twaddle.

gabby adj chattery, chatty, effusive, garrulous, gossipy, long-winded, loquacious, prolix, talkative, voluble, verbose.

antonyms quiet, reticent, taciturn.

gad about gallivant, ramble, range, roam, rove, run around, stray, traipse, wander.

gadabout n gallivanter, pleasure-seeker, rambler, rover, runabout, social butterfly, wanderer.

gadget n appliance, contraption, contrivance, convenience, device, doodad, doohickey, gimmick, gizmo, invention, novelty, thing, thingamabob, thingamajig, tool, widget.

gaffe n blooper, blunder, boner, booboo, breach of etiquette, clanger, faux pas, gaucherie, goof, howler, indiscretion, mistake, slip-up, solecism.

gaffer n boss, foreman, ganger, manager, overseer, superintendent, supervisor.

gag[1] v choke, choke up, gasp, heave, muffle, muzzle, quiet, retch, silence, stifle, still, stop up, suppress, throttle.

gag[2] n comic routine, funny, hoax, jest, joke, one-liner, pun, quip, wisecrack, witticism.

gaiety n animation, blitheness, blithesomeness, brightness, brilliance, celebration, cheerfulness, colour, colourfulness, conviviality, effervescence, elation, exhilaration, festivity, flamboyance, fun, glee, good cheer, good humour, high spirits, hilarity, joie de vivre, jollification, jollity, joviality, joyousness, light-heartedness, liveliness, merriment, merrymaking, mirth, revelry, revels, sparkle, sprightliness, vivacity.

antonyms drabness, dreariness, sadness.

gaily adv blithely, brightly, brilliantly, cheerfully, cheerily, colourfully, fancily, flamboyantly, gleefully, happily, joyfully, joyously, light-heartedly, merrily.

antonyms drearily, sadly.

gain v achieve, acquire, advance, arrive at, attain (to), avail, bag, be up (by), bring in, capture, clear, collect, come to, earn, enlist, gather, get, get to, glean, grow by (or in), harvest, increase by (or in), make, net, obtain, pick up, procure, profit, progress, put on, reach, realize, reap, secure, win, win over.

antonym lose.

n accretion, achievement, acquisition, advance, advancement, advantage, attainment, benefit, dividend, earnings, emolument, gravy, growth, headway, improvement, income, increase, increment, lucre, proceeds, profit, progress, pudding, return, revenue, rise, strides, velvet, winnings, yield.

antonyms loss, losses.

gain on approach, catch up, catch up with, close with, come up with, encroach on, leave behind, level with, make inroads into, narrow the gap, outdistance, overtake.

gain time delay, dilly-dally, drag one's feet, hedge, hem and haw, play for time, procrastinate, stall, stonewall, temporize.

gainful adj advantageous, beneficial, fruitful, lucrative, moneymaking, paid, paying, productive, profitable, remunerative, rewarding, useful, worthwhile.

antonym useless.

gains n booty, earnings, fruits, pickings, prize, proceeds, profits, revenue, takings, velvet, winnings.

antonym losses.

gainsay v contradict, contravene, controvert, deny, disaffirm, disagree with, dispute, nay-say.

antonyms confirm, echo.

gait n bearing, carriage, manner, pace, step, stride, tread, walk.

gala n bash, carnival, celebration, festival, festivity, fête, jamboree, jubilee, Mardi Gras, pageant, party, procession.

gale n blast, burst, cyclone, eruption, explosion, fit, howl, hurricane, outbreak, outburst, peal, ripsnorter, shout, squall, storm, tempest, tornado, typhoon, windstorm.

gall¹ *n* acrimony, animosity, animus, antipathy, bad blood, bile, bitterness, brass, brazenness, cheek, chutzpah, effrontery, enmity, hostility, impertinence, impudence, insolence, malevolence, malice, malignity, nerve, presumption, presumptuousness, rancour, sauciness, sourness, spite, spleen, venom.
antonyms friendliness, modesty, reserve.

gall² *v* abrade, aggravate, annoy, bother, bug, chafe, exasperate, excoriate, fret, get (to), get under (one's) skin, irk, irritate, nettle, peeve, pester, plague, provoke, rankle, rile, rub raw, rub the wrong way, ruffle, vex.

gallant *adj* attentive, august, bold, brave, chivalrous, courageous, courteous, courtly, daring, dashing, dauntless, dignified, doughty, elegant, fearless, game, gentlemanly, glorious, gracious, grand, heroic, high-spirited, honourable, imposing, indomitable, intrepid, lion-hearted, lofty, magnanimous, magnificent, manful, manly, mettlesome, noble, plucky, polite, splendid, stately, valiant, valorous.
antonyms cowardly, craven, ungentlemanly.
n admirer, adventurer, beau, blade, boyfriend, buck, cavalier, champion, dandy, daredevil, escort, fop, hero, knight, ladies' man, lady-killer, lover, paramour, suitor, wooer.

gallantry *n* attention, attentiveness, boldness, bravery, chivalry, courage, courageousness, courteousness, courtesy, courtliness, daring, dash, dauntlessness, derring-do, elegance, fearlessness, gentlemanliness, graciousness, heroism, intrepidity, manliness, mettle, nerve, nobility, pluck, politeness, prowess, spirit, valiance, valour.
antonyms cowardice, ungentlemanliness.

gallery *n* arcade, art gallery, balcony, circle, collection, gods, grandstand, loggia, museum, passage, spectators, walk.

galley *n* bireme, longboat, quadrireme, quinquereme, trireme.

galling *adj* aggravating, annoying, bitter, bothersome, exasperating, infuriating, irksome, irritating, nettling, plaguing, provoking, rankling, vexatious, vexing.
antonym pleasing.

gallivant *v* gad about, ramble, range, roam, rove, run around, stray, traipse, travel, wander.

gallop *v* bolt, career, dart, dash, fly, galumph, hasten, hie, hurry, lope, race, run, rush, scud, shoot, speed, sprint, tear, thunder, zoom.

gallows *n* gibbet, hanging, scaffold, the rope.

galore *adv* aplenty, everywhere, heaps of, in abundance, in profusion, lots of, millions of, on every hand, scads of, stacks of, to spare, tons of.

galvanize *v* animate, arouse, awaken, electrify, excite, fire, inspire, invigorate, jolt, move, prod, provoke, quicken, rouse, shock, spur, startle, stimulate, stir, thrill, vitalize, wake.
antonym retard.

gambit *n* artifice, device, manoeuvre, move, ploy, stratagem, tactic, trick, wile.

gamble *v* back, bet, chance, game, hazard, lay on the line, play, risk, speculate, stake, stick one's neck out, take a chance, try one's luck, venture, wager.
n bet, chance, game of chance, leap in the dark, lottery, risk, speculation, uncertainty, venture, wager.

gambol *v* bounce, bound, caper, cavort, curvet, cut capers, frisk, frolic, hop, jump, prance, rollick, romp, skip.
n antic, bound, caper, frisk, frolic, hop, jump, prance, skip, spring.

game¹ (or **games**) *n* adventure, amusement, business, competition, contest, dance, design, device, distraction, diversion, enterprise, entertainment, event, frolic, fun, jest, joke, lark, line, match, meet, merriment, merrymaking, occupation, pastime, plan, play, plot, ploy, proceeding, recreation, romp, round, routine, scheme, sport, stratagem, strategy, tactic, tournament, trick, undertaking, venture.

game² *n* animals, bag, flesh, game birds, meat, prey, quarry, spoils.

game³ *adj* bold, brave, courageous, dauntless, desirous, disposed, dogged, eager, fearless, gallant, gamy, heroic, inclined, interested, intrepid, persevering, persistent, plucky, prepared, ready, resolute, spirited, spunky, unflinching, valiant, valorous, willing.
antonyms cowardly, unwilling.

game⁴ *adj* bad, crippled, deformed, disabled, gammy, gouty, hobbling, incapacitated, injured, lame, maimed.

gamin(e) *n* gutter child, guttersnipe, imp, orphan, ragamuffin, street child, tatterdemalion, urchin, waif.

gamut *n* catalogue, compass, diapason, field, inventory, range, scale, scope, series, spectrum, sweep.

gang *n* band, circle, clique, club, company, coterie, crew, crowd, group, herd, horde, lot, mob, pack, party, ring, set, shift, squad, team, troupe.

gangling *adj* all arms and legs, angular, awkward, bony, gangly, gauche, gawky, lanky, long-limbed, loose-jointed, rangy, raw-boned, skinny, spindly, tall, ungainly.

gangster *n* bandit, brigand, criminal, crook, desperado, heavy, hood, hoodlum, mafioso, mobster, racketeer, robber, rough, ruffian, thug, tough.

gap *n* blank, breach, break, chink, cleft, crack, cranny, crevice, difference, disagreement, discontinuity, disparateness, disparity, divergence, divide, hiatus, hole, inconsistency, interlude, intermission, interruption, interspace, interstice, interval, lacuna, lull, omission, opening, pause, recess, rent, rift, space, vacuity, void.

gape *v* crack, dehisce, gawk, goggle, open, stare, wonder, yawn.

gaping *adj* broad, cavernous, chasmlike, dehiscent, great, huge, open, vast, wide, yawning.

garage *n* auto shop, auto mechanics, carport, engine shop, hangar, repair shop, service station.

garb *n* accoutrements, apparel, appearance, array, aspect, attire, clothes, clothing, costume, covering, dress, fashion, garments, gear, guise, habiliment, habit, mode, outfit, raiment, robes, suit, uniform, vestments, wear. *v* apparel, array, attire, clad, clothe, cover, dress, robe.

garbage *n* bits and pieces, debris, detritus, dross, filth, flotsam, jetsam, junk, litter, muck, odds and ends, offal, refuse, rubbish, schlock, scourings, scraps, slops, sweepings, swill, trash, waste.

garble *v* confuse, corrupt, distort, doctor, edit, falsify, jumble, misinterpret, misquote, misreport, misrepresent, misstate, mistranslate, mix up, muddle, mutilate, pervert, scramble, slant, tamper with, twist.
antonym decipher.

garden *n* backyard, orchard, park, patch, plot, yard.

gargantuan *adj* big, Brobdingnagian, colossal, elephantine, enormous, giant, gigantic, huge, immense, large, leviathan, mammoth, massive, monstrous, monumental, mountainous, outsize, prodigious, titanic, towering, tremendous, vast.
antonym small.

gargoyle *n* carving, freak, grotesque, ornament, spout.

garish *adj* cheap, chintzy, electric, flashy, flaunting, fluorescent, gaudy, glaring, glittering, glitzy, loud, meretricious, overdone, raffish, showy, splashy, tacky, tasteless, tawdry, vulgar.
antonyms modest, plain, quiet.

garland *n* bays, chaplet, coronal, crown, daisy chain, festoon, honours, laurels, lei, swag, wreath.
v adorn, crown, deck, engarland, festoon, wreathe.

garments *n* apparel, array, attire, clothes, clothing, costume, dress, duds, garb, gear, get-up, habiliment, habit, outfit, raiment, robes, togs, uniform, vestments, wear.

garner *v* accumulate, amass, assemble, collect, cull, deposit, earn, gain, gather, harvest, hoard, lay up, put by, reserve, save, stockpile, store, stow away, win.
antonym dissipate.

garnish *v* adorn, beautify, bedeck, deck, decorate, embellish, enhance, furnish, grace, ornament, set off, trim.
antonym divest.
n adornment, decoration, embellishment, enhancement, garnishment, garniture, ornament, ornamentation, relish, trim, trimming.

garrison *n* armed force, barracks, base, camp, casern, command, detachment, encampment, force, fort, fortification, fortress, guard, post, station, stronghold, troops, unit.

v assign, defend, furnish, guard, man, mount, occupy, place, position, post, protect, station.

garrulity *n* babble, babbling, chatter, chattering, chattiness, diffuseness, effusiveness, gabbiness, garrulousness, gassing, gift of the gab, glibness, long-windedness, loquaciousness, loquacity, prating, prattle, prolixity, prosiness, talkativeness, verbosity, volubility, windiness, wordiness.
antonyms taciturnity, terseness.

garrulous *adj* babbling, chattering, chatty, diffuse, effusive, gabby, gassy, glib, gossiping, gushing, long-winded, loquacious, mouthy, prating, prattling, prolix, prosy, talkative, verbose, voluble, windy, wordy.
antonyms taciturn, terse.

gash *v* cleave, cut, gouge, incise, lacerate, nick, notch, rend, score, slash, slit, split, tear, wound.
n cleft, cut, gouge, incision, laceration, nick, notch, rent, score, slash, slit, split, tear, wound.

gasp *v* blow, breathe, choke, ejaculate, gulp, pant, puff, utter, wheeze.
n blow, breath, ejaculation, exclamation, gulp, pant, puff, wheeze.

gate *n* barrier, door, doorway, entrance, exit, gateway, opening, passage, port, portal, portcullis, valve, wicket.

gather *v* accumulate, amass, assemble, assume, build, clasp, collect, compile, compose, conclude, congregate, convene, cull, deduce, deepen, draw, embrace, enfold, figure (out), flock, fold, forgather, form a head, garner, glean, group, grow, harvest, heap, hear, heighten, hoard, hold, hug, increase, infer, intensify, learn, make out, marshal, mass, muster, pick, pile up, pleat, pluck, pucker, rake up, rally, reap, rise, round up, ruche, ruffle, select, shirr, smock, stockpile, surmise, swell, thicken, tuck, understand.
antonyms dissipate, scatter.

gathering *n* accumulation, acquisition, aggregate, assemblage, assembly, collection, company, concentration, conclave, concourse, congregation, congress, convention, convocation, crowd, flock, get-together, group, heap, hoard, jamboree, knot, mass, meeting, moot, muster, party, pile, procurement, rally, roundup, rout, stockpiling, throng, turnout.
antonym scattering.

gauche *adj* awkward, clumsy, farouche, gawky, graceless, ignorant, ill-bred, ill-mannered, indiscreet, inelegant, inept, insensitive, maladroit, tactless, uncouth, uncultured, ungainly, ungraceful, unpolished, unsophisticated.
antonym graceful.

gaucherie *n* awkwardness, bad taste, blooper, blunder, boner, booboo, clanger, clumsiness, faux pas, gaffe, gaucheness, goof, gracelessness, ignorance, ill-breeding, indiscretion, inelegance, ineptness, insensitivity, maladroitness, mistake, slip, solecism, tactlessness.

antonym elegance.

gaudy *adj* bright, chintzy, flashy, florid, garish, glaring, glitzy, loud, meretricious, ostentatious, raffish, showy, splashy, tacky, tasteless, tawdry, tinselly, vulgar.
antonyms drab, plain, quiet.

gauge[1] *v* adjudge, appraise, ascertain, assess, calculate, check, compute, count, determine, estimate, evaluate, figure, guess, judge, measure, rate, reckon, value, weigh.
n basis, criterion, example, exemplar, guide, guideline, indicator, measure, meter, micrometer, model, pattern, rule, sample, standard, test, touchstone, yardstick.

gauge[2] *n* bore, calibre, capacity, degree, depth, extent, height, magnitude, measure, scope, size, span, thickness, width.

gaunt *adj* angular, attenuated, bare, bleak, bony, cadaverous, desolate, dismal, dreary, emaciated, forbidding, forlorn, grim, haggard, harsh, hollow-eyed, lank, lean, meagre, pinched, rawboned, scraggy, scrawny, shrunken, skeletal, skinny, spare, thin, wasted.
antonyms hale, plump.

gauzy *adj* delicate, diaphanous, filmy, flimsy, gossamer, insubstantial, light, see-through, sheer, thin, transparent.
antonyms heavy, thick.

gawk *v* gape, gaze, goggle, look, ogle, stare.

gawky *adj* awkward, clownish, clumsy, gangling, gauche, loutish, lumbering, lumpish, maladroit, oafish, uncouth, ungainly, ungraceful.
antonym graceful.

gay[1] *adj* animated, blithe, boon, bright, brilliant, carefree, cavalier, cheerful, cheery, colourful, convivial, debonair, festive, flamboyant, flashy, fresh, frolicsome, fun-loving, gamesome, glad, gleeful, happy, hilarious, insouciant, jolly, jovial, joyful, joyous, light-hearted, lightsome, lively, merry, playful, pleasure-seeking, rakish, rollicking, showy, sparkling, sportive, sunny, vivacious, vivid, waggish.
antonyms gloomy, sad.

gay[2] *adj* homosexual, lesbian, queer.
antonyms heterosexual, straight.
n homosexual, lesbian, queer, sapphist.
antonym heterosexual.

gaze *v* contemplate, gape, gawk, look, ogle, regard, stare, view, watch.
n attention, eye, look, regard, stare.

gazebo *n* belvedere, hut, pavilion, shelter, summerhouse.

gazette *n* dispatch, journal, magazine, newsletter, newspaper, notice, organ, paper, periodical, record, tabloid.

gear[1] *n* accessories, accoutrements, apparatus, apparel, armour, array, attire, baggage, belongings, business, clothes, clothing, costume, doings, dress, effects, equipment, garb, garments, get-up, habit, harness, instruments, kit, luggage, machinery, outfit, paraphernalia, possessions, rig, stuff,

supplies, tackle, things, togs, tools, trappings, traps, wear, works.
v adapt, adjust, aim, equip, fit, harness, rig, subordinate, suit, tailor, target.

gear[2] (or **gears**) *n* cam, cam-wheel, cog, cogwheel, gearing, gearshift, gearwheel, mechanism, pinion, rack, stickshift, transmission, workings, works, worm gear.

gelatinous *adj* congealed, gluey, glutinous, gooey, gummy, jellied, jellified, jelly, jellylike, mucilaginous, rubbery, sticky, viscid, viscous.

gem *n* angel, bijou, brick, flower, honey, jewel, masterpiece, pearl, pièce de résistance, precious stone, prize, stone, sweetheart, treasure.

gen *n* background, data, details, dirt, facts, info, information, lowdown, poop, scoop, story.

genealogy *n* ancestry, background, bloodline, derivation, descent, extraction, family, family history, family tree, line, lineage, pedigree, progeniture, roots, stirps, stock, strain.

general *adj* accepted, accustomed, across-the-board, all-inclusive, approximate, blanket, broad, catholic, characteristic, collective, common, comprehensive, conventional, customary, ecumenical, encyclopedic, everyday, extensive, generic, habitual, ill-defined, imprecise, inaccurate, indefinite, indiscriminate, inexact, loose, miscellaneous, normal, ordinary, panoramic, popular, prevailing, prevalent, public, regular, sweeping, total, typical, universal, unspecific, usual, vague, widespread.
antonyms limited, particular, uncommon.
n chief, C. in C., commander, commander-in-chief, (field) marshal, generalissimo, hetman, leader, officer.

generality *n* approximateness, breadth, catholicity, commonness, comprehensiveness, ecumenicity, extensiveness, generalization, imprecision, indefiniteness, inexactitude, looseness, miscellaneity, popularity, prevalence, sweeping statement, universality, vagueness.
antonyms detail, exactitude, particular, rarity.

generally *adv* approximately, as a rule, broadly, by and large, characteristically, chiefly, commonly, conventionally, customarily, extensively, for the most part, habitually, in the main, largely, mainly, mostly, normally, on average, on the whole, ordinarily, popularly, predominantly, principally, publicly, regularly, typically, universally, usually, widely.
antonyms narrowly, rarely.

generate *v* arouse, beget, breed, bring about, cause, create, effect, engender, excite, father, form, gender, give rise to, initiate, make, originate, procreate, produce, propagate, spawn, whip up.
antonyms prevent, quash.

generation *n* age, age group, begetting, breeding, brood, cohort, creation, crop, day(s), engendering, engenderment, epoch, era, formation, genesis, origination, period, procreation, production, progeniture, propagation, reproduction, time(s).

generic *adj* all-inclusive, blanket, collective, common, comprehensive, general, inclusive, non-proprietary, non-specific, sweeping, typical, universal, wide.

antonyms particular, proprietary.

generosity *n* altruism, beneficence, benevolence, big-heartedness, bounty, charity, goodness, high-mindedness, hospitality, kindness, large-heartedness, largesse, liberality, magnanimity, munificence, nobleness, open-handedness, philanthropy, soft-heartedness, unselfishness, unsparingness.

antonyms meanness, selfishness.

generous *adj* abundant, altruistic, ample, beneficent, benevolent, big-hearted, bounteous, bountiful, charitable, copious, free, full, giving, good, high-minded, hospitable, kind, large-hearted, lavish, liberal, lofty, magnanimous, munificent, noble, open-handed, overflowing, philanthropic, plentiful, princely, rich, soft-hearted, ungrudging, unreproachful, unresentful, unselfish, unsparing, unstinting.

antonyms mean, selfish.

genesis *n* beginning, birth, commencement, creation, dawn, engenderment, formation, foundation, founding, generation, germ, inception, initiation, origin, outset, propagation, rise, root, source, spark, start.

antonym end.

genial *adj* affable, agreeable, amiable, cheerful, cheery, comforting, congenial, convivial, cordial, easy-going, expansive, friendly, good-natured, hearty, jolly, jovial, kind, kindly, merry, open, pleasant, sunny, sunshiny, warm, warm-hearted, winsome.

antonym cold.

geniality *n* affability, agreeableness, amiability, cheerfulness, cheeriness, congeniality, conviviality, cordiality, friendliness, good nature, heartiness, jollity, joviality, kindliness, kindness, mirth, openness, pleasantness, sunniness, warm-heartedness, warmth, winsomeness.

antonym coldness.

genie *n* demon, fairy, jinni, spirit.

genitals *n* genitalia, private parts, privates, pudenda, pudendum.

genius[1] *n* adept, brain, expert, intellect, maestro, master, master hand, mastermind, mind, past master, prodigy, virtuoso, whiz, wizard, wunderkind.

genius[2] *n* ability, aptitude, bent, brightness, brilliance, capacity, endowment, faculty, flair, gift, inclination, intellect, knack, power(s), propensity, talent.

genius[3] *n* character, daemon, defining quality, double, embodiment, epitome, essence, genie, incarnation, ka, personification, spirit.

genocide *n* annihilation, ethnic purge, ethnocide, extermination, massacre, slaughter.

genre *n* brand, category, character, class, form, genus, group, kind, race, school, sort, species, strain, style, type, variety.

genteel *adj* aristocratic, civil, courteous, courtly, cultivated, cultured, elegant, fashionable, formal, gentlemanly, graceful, ladylike, mannerly, polished, polite, refined, respectable, stylish, urbane, well-bred, well-mannered.

antonyms crude, rough, unpolished.

gentility *n* aristocracy, blue blood, breeding, civility, courtesy, courtliness, cultivation, culture, decorum, elegance, elite, etiquette, formality, gentle birth, gentry, good family, high birth, mannerliness, manners, nobility, polish, politeness, propriety, rank, refinement, respectability, upper class, urbanity.

antonyms crudeness, discourteousness, roughness.

gentle *adj* amiable, aristocratic, balmy, benign, bland, broken, calm, clement, compassionate, courteous, cultured, docile, easy, elegant, genteel, gentlemanly, gradual, highborn, humane, imperceptible, kind, kindly, ladylike, lamblike, lenient, light, low, maidenly, manageable, meek, merciful, mild, moderate, muted, noble, pacific, peaceful, placid, polished, polite, quiet, refined, serene, slight, slow, smooth, soft, soothing, sweet, sweet-tempered, tame, temperate, tender, tractable, tranquil, untroubled, upper-class, well-born, well-bred.

antonyms crude, fierce, rough, unpolished.

gentleman *n* don, escort, gent, gentilhomme, grandee, hidalgo, landowner, sahib, Señor, Signor(e), sir, squire.

gentlemanly *adj* chivalrous, civil, civilized, courteous, cultivated, gallant, genteel, gentlemanlike, gentlewomanly, honourable, mannerly, noble, obliging, polished, polite, refined, reputable, suave, urbane, well-bred, well-mannered.

antonyms impolite, rough.

gentlewoman *n* donna, lady, landowner, madame, mademoiselle, memsahib, Señora, Señorita, Signora, Signorina.

gentry *n* aristocracy, elite, gentility, gentlefolk, landed class, nobility, nobles, quality, squirearchy, titled class, upper class.

genuine *adj* actual, artless, authentic, bona fide, candid, earnest, frank, heartfelt, honest, kosher, legitimate, natural, original, pukka, pure, real, simon-pure, sincere, sound, sterling, sure-enough, true, unadulterated, unaffected, unalloyed, unfeigned, veritable.

antonyms artificial, counterfeit, feigned, insincere.

genus *n* breed, category, class, division, genre, group, kind, order, race, set, sort, species, taxon, type.

geography *n* layout, lie of the land, physical features, topography.

germ *n* bacterium, beginning, bud, bug, cause, egg, embryo, genesis, microbe, micro-organism, nucleus, origin, ovule, ovum, root, rudiment, seed, source, spark, spore, sprout, virus, zyme.

germane *adj* akin, allied, applicable, apposite, appropriate, apropos, apt, cognate, connected, fitting, kin, kindred, material, pertinent, proper, related, relevant, suitable, to the point.
antonyms irrelevant, tangential.

germinal *adj* beginning, developing, embryonic, incipient, preliminary, rudimentary, seminal, sprouting, undeveloped.

germinate *v* bud, develop, generate, grow, originate, pullulate, root, shoot, sprout, swell, vegetate.

Gestalt *n* configuration, construct, form, pattern, structure, system.

gestation *n* conception, development, drafting, evolution, formation, growth, incubation, maturation, planning, pregnancy, ripening.

gesticulate *v* gesture, indicate, motion, point, sign, signal, wave.

gesture *n* act, action, charade, expression, gesticulation, indication, motion, pose, posturing, pretence, sign, signal, token, wave.
v gesticulate, indicate, motion, point, sign, signal, wave.

get *v* achieve, acquire, annoy, arouse, arrange, arrest, arrive (at), attain, baffle, bag, become, bother, bring, bug, capture, catch, catch on, coax, coerce, collar, come, come by, come down with, communicate with, comprehend, confound, contact, contract, contrive, convince, cotton on, earn, enlist, excite, fathom, fell, fetch, fix, follow, force, gain, glean, grab, grow, hear, hit, impress, incite, induce, influence, inherit, irk, irritate, kill, make, manage, manipulate, motivate, move, mystify, nab, net, nonplus, notice, obtain, perceive, perplex, persuade, pick up, pique, prevail upon, procure, puzzle, reach, realize, reap, receive, secure, see, seize, snag, spur, stimulate, stir, strike, stump, sway, touch, trap, turn, twig to, understand, upset, vex, wangle, wax, wheedle, win.
antonyms lose, misunderstand, pacify.

get across bring home to, communicate, convey, cross, ford, impart, negotiate, put over, transmit, traverse.

get ahead advance, do well, flourish, get there, go places, make good, make it, make strides, progress, prosper, succeed, thrive.
antonyms fail, fall behind.

get along agree, co-exist, cope, fare, get by, get on, hit it off, make shift, make out, manage, progress, shift, survive.
antonym argue.

get a move on get cracking, get going, go to it, hurry (up), jump to it, make haste, make it snappy, move it, shake a leg, speed up, step on it.
antonym slow down.

get around avoid, bypass, cajole, circumvent, coax, evade, outmanoeuvre, outsmart, outwit, overcome, persuade, prevail upon, skirt, talk over, talk around, trick, wheedle, win over.

get at access, annoy, attack, attain, bribe, buy off, carp at, corrupt, criticize, find fault with, hint (at), imply, influence, irritate, mean,

nag, pervert, pick on, reach, suborn, suggest, tamper with.
antonym praise.

get away break free, decamp, depart, disappear, escape, flee, get out, leave, run away, set out, start out.

get back get even, get one's own back (on), recoup, recover, regain, repossess, retaliate, retrieve, return, revenge oneself (on), revert, revisit.

get by cope, exist, fare, get along, make both ends meet, make it, manage, pass muster, shift, squeak by, subsist, survive.

get down alight, climb down, depress, descend, disembark, dishearten, dismount, dispirit, lower, sadden.
antonyms board, encourage.

get even even the score, get one's own back, pay back, reciprocate, repay, requite, revenge oneself, settle the score.

get off alight, disembark, dispatch, escape, get away, get one's jollies or kicks (out of), send, take off.

get on advance, agree, ascend, board, climb on, cope, embark, fare, get along, hit it off, make out, manage, mount, proceed, progress, prosper, succeed.
antonyms alight, argue.

get out break out, clear out, decamp, deliver, escape, evacuate, exit, extract, extricate (oneself), flee, flit, free oneself, leave, produce, publish, quit, scarper, scram, vacate, wash out, withdraw.
antonym board.

get out of avoid, dodge, escape, evade, shirk, wangle one's way out of, weasel out of.

get over adjust to, cross, ford, forget, get past, master, outgrow, overcome, put behind one, recover from, shake off, surmount, survive, traverse.

get ready arrange, fix up, get set, gird one's loins, make ready, prepare, psych oneself up, ready, rehearse, set out, set up.

get rid of chuck, delete, dispense with, dispose of, do away with, dump, eject, eliminate, expel, exterminate, jettison, jilt, kill, remove, rid oneself of, scrap, shake off, shed, throw out (or away or off), unload.
antonyms accumulate, acquire.

get the better of beat, best, defeat, do in, outdo, outfox, outsmart, outwit, surpass, worst.

get the message catch on, comprehend, get it, get the point, see, take the hint, twig, understand.
antonym misunderstand.

get there advance, arrive, go places, make good, make it, progress, prosper, succeed.

get to annoy, bother, bug, get one's goat, get on one's nerves, get under one's skin, hurt, irk, irritate, tick off.

get together accumulate, agree, arrange, assemble, collaborate, collect, congregate, convene, co-ordinate, gather, join, meet, muster, organize, put heads together, rally, reconcile, scrape together, unite.

get under one's skin annoy, get, get to,

infuriate, irk, irritate, needle, nettle, press one's buttons.

antonym pacify.

get up arise, ascend, climb, mount, organize, prepare, rise, scale, stand.

getaway *n* breakaway, breakout, decampment, departure, escape, exit, flight, start.

get-together *n* do, function, gabfest, gathering, party, reception, reunion, social, soirée.

gewgaw *n* bagatelle, bauble, bijou, doodad, gaud, gimcrack, kickshaw, knick-knack, novelty, ornament, plaything, toy, trifle, trinket.

ghastly *adj* appalling, ashen, awful, cadaverous, deathlike, deathly, dreadful, frightful, ghostly, grim, grisly, gruesome, hideous, horrendous, horrible, horrid, livid, loathsome, lurid, pale, pallid, repellent, shocking, spectral, terrible, terrifying, wan.

antonym delightful.

ghost *n* apparition, astral body, eidolon, fetch, glimmer, hint, larva, manes, phantasm, phantom, possibility, revenant, semblance, shade, shadow, simulacrum, soul, spectre, spirit, spook, suggestion, trace, umbra, visitant, wraith.

ghostly *adj* chthonian, eerie, eldritch, faint, ghostlike, illusory, insubstantial, pale, phantasmal, phantom, spectral, spooky, supernatural, uncanny, unearthly, weird, white, wraithlike.

ghoulish *adj* grisly, gruesome, horrible, macabre, morbid, revolting, sick, unhealthy, unwholesome.

giant *n* behemoth, colossus, Goliath, Hercules, Jotun, leviathan, monster, titan.

adj Atlantean, Brobdingnagian, colossal, cyclopean, elephantine, enormous, gargantuan, gigantesque, gigantic, herculean, huge, immense, jumbo, king-size, large, leviathan, mammoth, monstrous, outsize, prodigious, titanic, vast.

gibber *v* babble, blab, blabber, blather, cackle, chatter, gabble, jabber, prattle, rave.

gibberish *n* abracadabra, babble, balderdash, blather, claptrap, drivel, gabbling, gobbledegook, jabbering, jargon, mumbo-jumbo, nonsense, prattle, raving, twaddle.

antonym sense.

gibe (at) *v* deride, flout, jeer at, make fun of, mock, poke fun at, rail at, rib, ridicule, scoff at, scorn, sneer at, taunt, tease, twit.

n barb, crack, cut, derision, dig, jab, jeer, mockery, poke, put-down, raillery, ridicule, sarcasm, scoff, snipe, taunt, thrust.

giddiness *n* dizziness, faintness, light-headedness, nausea, vertigo, wobbliness, wooziness.

giddy *adj* capricious, careless, changeable, dizzy, dizzying, erratic, faint, fickle, flighty, frivolous, heedless, impulsive, inconstant, irresolute, irresponsible, light-headed, reckless, reeling, scatterbrained, silly, thoughtless,

unbalanced, unstable, unsteady, vacillating, vertiginous, volatile, wild.

antonyms sensible, sober.

gift *n* ability, aptitude, benefaction, beneficence, bequest, bonus, boon, bounty, capacity, contribution, donation, earnest, endowment, faculty, flair, freebie, genius, grant, gratuity, knack, largesse, legacy, love token, manna, offering, potlatch, power, present, sop, talent.

gifted *adj* able, accomplished, ace, adroit, bright, brilliant, capable, expert, intelligent, masterly, skilful, skilled, talented.

antonym dull.

gigantic *adj* Atlantean, Brobdingnagian, colossal, cyclopean, elephantine, enormous, gargantuan, giant, herculean, huge, immense, king-size, leviathan, mammoth, monstrous, outsize, prodigious, stupendous, titanic, tremendous, vast.

antonym tiny.

giggle *v, n* chortle, chuckle, guffaw, laugh, shriek, snicker, snigger, tee-hee, titter.

gild *v* adorn, array, beautify, bedeck, brighten, coat, deck, dress up, embellish, embroider, enhance, enrich, festoon, garnish, grace, ornament, paint, trim.

gilded *adj* gilt, gold, golden, inaurate.

gimcrack *adj* cheap, chintzy, shoddy, showy, tawdry, tinselly, trashy, trumpery, useless, worthless.

antonyms solid, well-made.

gimmick *n* angle, attraction, contrivance, device, dodge, gadget, gambit, gizmo, hook, incentive, lure, manoeuvre, ploy, scheme, stratagem, stunt, trick.

gingerly *adv* carefully, cautiously, charily, circumspectly, daintily, delicately, fastidiously, gently, hesitantly, reluctantly, squeamishly, suspiciously, timidly, warily.

antonyms carelessly, roughly.

gird *v* arm, belt, bind, blockade, brace, encircle, enclose, encompass, enfold, engird, environ, equip, fortify, girdle, hem in, pen, prepare, ready, ring, steel, surround.

girdle *n* band, belt, cestus, cincture, cingulum, corset, cummerbund, fillet, foundation (garment), sash, support, waistband, zone.

v bind, bound, encircle, enclose, encompass, engird, environ, gird (around), go around, hem, ring, surround.

girl *n* chit, colleen, damsel, daughter, demoiselle, filly, flapper, flibbertigibbet, fräulein, gal, girlfriend, lass, lassie, maid, maiden, miss, moppet, peach, poppet, princess, sheila, sweetheart, wench.

girth *n* band, bellyband, bulk, cinch, circumference, measure, saddle band, size, strap, waist.

gist *n* core, direction, drift, effect, essence, force, idea, import, marrow, matter, meaning, nub, pith, point, purport, quintessence, sense, significance, substance.

give _v_ accord, administer, allot, allow, announce, apportion, assign, award, bend, bestow, cause, cede, commit, communicate, concede, confer, consign, contribute, deal, deliver, devote, do, donate, emit, engender, entrust, furnish, grant, hand (over), host, impart, issue, lead, lend, make, make over, offer, open (out), pass, pay, perform, permit, present, produce, proffer, pronounce, provide, put forward, relinquish, render, set forth, show, state, stretch, supply, surrender, transmit, utter, vouchsafe, yield.

antonyms keep, take, withstand.

give away betray, disclose, divulge, expose, inform on, leak, let out, let slip, rat on, reveal, uncover.

give in admit defeat, back down, break down, capitulate, cave in, collapse, come around, comply, concede, crack, give way, quit, submit, surrender, yield.

antonyms hang tough, hold out, stand pat.

give off discharge, emit, excrete, exhale, exude, ooze, pour out, produce, put out, release, send out, throw out, vent.

give on to lead to, open on to, overlook.

give out announce, broadcast, communicate, deal out, discharge, disseminate, distribute, dole out, emit, exhale, exude, give off, hand out, impart, mete out, outpour, pass out, pour out, produce, publicize, publish, release, send out, transmit, utter, vent.

give rise to breed, bring about, bring on, cause, effect, engender, generate, lead to, occasion, precipitate, produce, provoke, result in, trigger.

give up abandon, abjure, capitulate, cease, cede, cut out, desist, despair, do without, drop, forswear, hand over, hang up one's skates, leave off, lose hope, pack it in, quit, release, relinquish, renounce, resign, stop, surrender, throw in the towel, waive.

antonyms cling to, hang in, persevere.

give way accede, acquiesce, back down, bend, break (down), cave in, cede, collapse, concede, crack, crumple, fall, give ground, give place, sink, submit, subside, withdraw, yield.

antonyms hold out, resist, withstand.

give-and-take _n_ adaptability, commonality, compromise, co-operation, exchange, flexibility, good will, interchange, mutual aid, reciprocity, sharing, teamwork, turntaking, willingness.

given _adj_ addicted, agreed, apt, assumed, axiomatic, disposed, granted, inclined, known, liable, likely, prone, specified, taken for granted, understood.

glacial _adj_ antagonistic, arctic, biting, bitter, chill, chilly, cold, freezing, frigid, frosty, frozen, gelid, hostile, icy, inimical, piercing, polar, raw, Siberian, stiff, unfriendly, wintry.

antonym warm.

glad _adj_ blithe, blithesome, bright, cheerful, cheering, cheery, comforting, content, delighted, delightful, encouraged, encouraging,

felicitous, gay, gleeful, gratified, gratifying, happy, heartening, jocund, jovial, joyful, joyous, merry, over the moon, overjoyed, pleasant, pleased, pleasing, rejoicing, uplifting, willing.

antonym sad.

gladden _v_ brighten, cheer, comfort, delight, elate, encourage, exhilarate, gratify, hearten, please, rejoice.

antonym sadden.

gladly _adv_ blithely, blithesomely, cheerfully, fain, freely, gaily, gleefully, happily, jovially, joyfully, joyously, merrily, readily, willingly, with good grace, with pleasure.

antonyms sadly, unwillingly.

gladness _n_ blitheness, blithesomeness, brightness, cheerfulness, delight, felicity, gaiety, glee, happiness, high spirits, hilarity, jollity, joy, joyousness, mirth, pleasure, rejoicing.

antonym sadness.

glamorous _adj_ alluring, attractive, beautiful, bewitching, captivating, charming, classy, dazzling, elegant, enchanting, entrancing, exciting, exotic, fascinating, glittering, glossy, gorgeous, lovely, prestigious, romantic, smart.

antonyms boring, drab, plain.

glamour _n_ allure, appeal, attraction, beauty, bewitchment, cachet, charm, enchantment, fascination, magic, magnetism, prestige, ravishment, romance, witchery.

glance[1] _v_ allude to, browse, dip, flip, glimpse, leaf, look, mention, peek, peep, riffle, scan, skim, thumb, touch on, view.

_n_ allusion, browse, coup d'oeil, gander, glimpse, look, mention, once-over, peek, peep, reference, squint, view.

glance[2] _v_ bounce, brush, cannon, carom, coruscate, flash, gleam, glimmer, glint, glisten, glister, glitter, graze, rebound, reflect, ricochet, shimmer, shine, skim, twinkle.

glare _v_ blaze, coruscate, dazzle, flame, flare, frown, glower, look daggers, lower, scowl, shine, stare (down).

_n_ black look, blaze, brightness, brilliance, dirty look, flame, flare, flashiness, frown, garishness, gaudiness, glitz, glow, glower, light, look, loudness, lower, scowl, showiness, stare, tawdriness.

glaring _adj_ blatant, blazing, bright, brilliant, conspicuous, dazzling, dreadful, egregious, flagrant, flashy, garish, gross, horrendous, loud, manifest, obvious, open, outrageous, outstanding, overt, patent, rank, terrible, unconcealed, visible.

antonyms dull, hidden, minor.

glass _n_ beaker, crystal, goblet, lens, looking glass, magnifying glass, mirror, pane, pocket lens, schooner, tumbler, vitrics, window.

glass case display (or curio) cabinet, showcase, vitrine.

glassy _adj_ blank, clear, cold, dazed, dull, empty, expressionless, fishy, fixed, glasslike, glazed, glossy, hyaline, icy, lifeless, shiny, slick, slippery, smooth, transparent, vacant, vitreous, vitriform.

glaze v burnish, coat, crystallize, enamel, frost, furbish, gloss, ice, lacquer, polish, varnish.

n coating, enamel, finish, frosting, gloss, icing, lacquer, lustre, patina, polish, shine, varnish.

gleam n beam, brightness, brilliance, coruscation, flash, flicker, glimmer, glint, gloss, glow, hint, inkling, lustre, ray, sheen, shimmer, shine, sparkle, suggestion, trace.

v coruscate, flare, flash, glimmer, glint, glisten, glister, glitter, glow, scintillate, shimmer, shine, sparkle.

gleaming adj ablaze, bright, brilliant, burnished, glistening, glossy, glowing, lustrous, polished, shimmering, shining, sparkling.

antonym dull.

glean v accumulate, amass, collect, cull, find out, garner, gather, harvest, learn, pick (up), reap, select.

glee n cheeriness, delight, elation, exhilaration, exuberance, exultation, fun, gaiety, gladness, gratification, high spirits, hilarity, jocularity, jollity, joviality, joy, joyfulness, joyousness, liveliness, merriment, mirth, pleasure, sprightliness, triumph, verve.

gleeful adj cheery, cock-a-hoop, crowing, delighted, elated, exuberant, exultant, gay, gleesome, gloating, gratified, happy, jovial, joyful, joyous, jubilant, merry, mirthful, over the moon, overjoyed, pleased, triumphant.

antonym sad.

glib adj artful, easy, facile, fast-talking, fluent, garrulous, insincere, pat, platitudinous, plausible, quick, ready, simplistic, slick, slippery, smooth, smooth-spoken, smooth-tongued, suave, superficial, talkative, voluble.

antonyms implausible, tongue-tied.

glibness n fast talk, insincerity, pat answers, patter, platitude(s), plausibility, slickness, smoothness, smooth talk, suaveness, suavity, superficiality.

glide v coast, cruise, drift, float, flow, fly, glissade, roll, run, sail, skate, skim, slide, slip, soar, volplane.

glimmer v blink, flicker, gleam, glint, glisten, glitter, glow, shimmer, shine, sparkle, twinkle.

n blink, flicker, gleam, glimpse, glint, glow, grain, hint, inkling, ray, shimmer, spark, sparkle, suggestion, trace, twinkle.

glimpse n flash, glance, look, peek, peep, sight, sighting, squint.

v catch sight of, descry, espy, sight, spot, spy, view.

glint v flash, gleam, glimmer, glitter, reflect, shine, sparkle, twinkle.

n flash, gleam, glimmer, glitter, reflection, shine, sparkle, twinkle, twinkling.

glisten v coruscate, flash, glance, gleam, glimmer, glint, glister, glitter, scintillate, shimmer, shine, sparkle, twinkle.

glitter v coruscate, flash, glare, gleam, glimmer, glint, glisten, scintillate, shimmer, shine, sparkle, twinkle.

n beam, brightness, brilliance, display, fanciness, flash, flashiness, gaudiness, glamour, glare, gleam, glitz, lustre, pageantry, radiance, scintillation, sheen, shimmer, shine, show, showiness, spangles, sparkle, splendour, tinsel.

gloat v crow, exult, eye, glory, ogle, rejoice, relish, revel in, rub it in, triumph, vaunt.

global adj across-the-board, all-encompassing, all-inclusive, all-out, comprehensive, encyclopedic, exhaustive, general, international, pandemic, planetary, spherical, thorough, total, unbounded, universal, unlimited, world, worldwide.

antonyms limited, parochial.

globe n ball, earth, orb, planet, round, roundure, sphere, world.

globular adj ball-shaped, globate, globoid, globose, orbicular, round, spherical, spheroid.

globule n ball, bead, bubble, drop, droplet, particle, pearl, pellet, vesicle.

gloom, gloominess n blackness, blues, cheerlessness, cloud, cloudiness, dark, darkness, dejection, depression, desolation, despair, despondency, dimness, downheartedness, dreariness, dullness, dusk, duskiness, gloominess, glumness, low spirits, melancholy, misery, moroseness, murk, murkiness, obscurity, pessimism, sadness, shade, shadow, sorrow, twilight, unhappiness, woe.

antonym brightness.

gloomy adj bad, black, bleak, blue, chapfallen, cheerless, comfortless, crepuscular, crestfallen, dark, darksome, dejected, delightless, depressed, depressing, despairing, despondent, dim, disheartened, disheartening, dismal, dispirited, dispiriting, down (in the dumps or mouth), downbeat, downcast, downhearted, dreary, dull, dusky, glum, joyless, long-faced, long-visaged, low-spirited, melancholy, miserable, moody, morose, murky, obscure, overcast, pessimistic, sad, saddening, saturnine, sepulchral, shadowy, sombre, Stygian, sullen, tenebrous.

antonym bright.

glorification n adoration, aggrandizement, beatification, canonization, celebration, deification, doxology, elevation, ennoblement, exaltation, glamorization, idolization, magnification, panegyric, praise, praising, romanticization, veneration, worship.

antonyms abasement, blame, vilification.

glorify v adore, adorn, aggrandize, apotheosize, beatify, bless, canonize, celebrate, deify, dignify, elevate, enhance, ennoble, enshrine, eulogize, exalt, extol, honour, hymn, idolize, illuminate, immortalize, laud, lift up, magnify, panegyrize, praise, put on a pedestal, raise, revere, sanctify, venerate, worship.

antonyms abase, denounce, vilify.

glorious *adj* beautiful, bright, brilliant, celebrated, dazzling, delightful, distinguished, divine, effulgent, elevated, eminent, enjoyable, excellent, famed, famous, fine, gorgeous, grand, great, heavenly, honoured, illustrious, magnificent, majestic, marvellous, noble, noted, pleasurable, radiant, renowned, resplendent, shining, splendid, sublime, superb, triumphant, wonderful.
antonyms dreadful, inglorious, plain, unknown.

glory *n* accolades, adoration, beauty, benediction, blessing, bliss, brightness, brilliance, celebrity, credit, dignity, distinction, effulgence, eminence, exaltation, fame, gloria, gorgeousness, grandeur, greatness, heaven, homage, honour, illustriousness, immortality, kudos, laudation, lustre, magnificence, majesty, nobility, pageantry, pomp, praise, prestige, radiance, recognition, renown, resplendence, richness, splendour, sublimity, thanksgiving, triumph, veneration, worship.
antonyms blame, shame.
v boast, crow, delight, exult, gloat, pride oneself, rejoice, relish, revel, triumph, vaunt.

gloss¹ *n* appearance, brightness, brilliance, burnish, façade, front, gleam, lustre, mask, polish, semblance, sheen, shine, show, surface, varnish, veneer, window-dressing.
gloss over camouflage, conceal, disguise, double-glaze, downplay, explain away, gild, glaze over, hide, mask, smooth over, sweep under the rug, veil, whitewash.

gloss² *n* annotation, comment, commentary, definition, elucidation, explanation, footnote, interpretation, note, scholium, translation.
v annotate, comment, construe, define, elucidate, explain, interpret, translate.

glossary *n* dictionary, lexicon, phrasebook, vocabulary, wordbook, word list.

glossy *adj* bright, brilliant, burnished, enamelled, glassy, glazed, lustrous, polished, sheeny, shining, shiny, silken, silky, sleek, smooth.
antonyms dull, mat.

glow *n* ardour, bloom, blush, brightness, brilliance, burning, effulgence, enthusiasm, excitement, fervour, flush, gleam, glimmer, incandescence, intensity, lambency, light, luminosity, passion, phosphorescence, radiance, reddening, redness, rosiness, splendour, vehemence, vividness, warmth.
v blush, brighten, burn, colour, flush, gleam, glimmer, radiate, redden, shine, smoulder, thrill, tingle.

glower *v* frown, give someone the evil eye, glare, look daggers, lower, scowl.
n black look, dirty look, frown, glare, look, lower, scowl, stare.

glowing *adj* adulatory, aglow, beaming, bright, complimentary, ecstatic, enthusiastic, eulogistic, flaming, florid, flushed, lambent, laudatory, luminous, panegyric, positive, rave, red, rhapsodic, rich, ruddy, suffused, vibrant, vivid, warm.
antonyms dull, restrained.

glue *n* adhesive, cement, epoxy, gum, isinglass, mucilage, paste, size, superglue.
v affix, attach, cement, fix, gum, paste, seal, stick.

gluey *adj* adhesive, glutinous, gummy, sticky, tacky, viscid, viscous.

glum *adj* chapfallen, crestfallen, dejected, doleful, down, gloomy, gruff, grumpy, ill-humoured, low, moody, morose, pessimistic, saturnine, sour, sulky, sullen, surly.
antonyms ecstatic, happy.

glut *n* excess, overabundance, oversupply, plethora, saturation, superabundance, superfluity, surfeit, surplus.
antonyms lack, scarcity.
v choke, clog, cram, deluge, fill, flood, gorge, inundate, overfeed, overload, oversupply, sate, satiate, saturate, stuff, surfeit.

glutinous *adj* adhesive, cohesive, gluey, gummy, mucilaginous, ropy, sticky, syrupy, tacky, viscid, viscous.

glutton *n* cormorant, gannet, gobbler, gorger, gormandizer, gourmand, greedyguts, guzzler, hog, omnivore, pig, trencherman, vulture, whale.
antonym ascetic.

gluttonous *adj* edacious, esurient, gluttonish, gormandizing, greedy, hoggish, insatiable, omnivorous, piggish, rapacious, ravenous, voracious.
antonyms abstemious, ascetic.

gluttony *n* edacity, esurience, gormandizing, gourmandise, gourmandism, greed, greediness, insatiability, omnivorousness, piggishness, rapaciousness, rapacity, voraciousness, voracity.
antonyms abstinence, asceticism.

gnarled *adj* contorted, distorted, gnarly, knarred, knobby, knotted, knotty, knurled, knurly, leathery, rough, rugged, twisted, weather-beaten, wrinkled.

gnaw (at) *v* bite, chew, consume, corrode, devour, distress, eat (away), erode, fret, harry, haunt, munch, nag, nibble, niggle, plague, prey, torment, trouble, wear, worry.

go (to, with) *v* accord, advance, agree, appeal, attend, beat it, become, belong, bet, blend, connect, continue, correspond (to), decamp, decease, defecate, depart, deteriorate, develop, die, disappear, drive, elapse, endure, extend, fare, fit, flow, fly, frequent, function, harmonize, head (for), jibe, jive, journey, lapse, last, lead, leave, make (for), match, mosey, move, nip, operate, pass, pass away, proceed, progress, reach, refer, relieve oneself, repair, resort, retreat, roll, run, sail, sally, scram, serve, shift, shove off, slip, sound, span, spread, stretch, suit, take one's leave, tend, travel, trot, turn out, urinate, vanish, wag, walk, wend one's way, withdraw, work.
n animation, bid, crack, drive, dynamism, energy, force, get-up-and-go, life, move, oomph, pep, shot, spirit, stab, try, verve, vigour, vim, vitality, vivacity, whack, zest.

interj giddy-up, move it, mush, shoot, start.

go about address, approach, begin, set about, start, tackle, undertake.

go ahead advance, begin, continue, march on, move, proceed, progress, shoot.

go along (with) accept, accompany, acquiesce, agree, attend, be associated or connected, chaperone, comply, concur, conduct, escort, hold (with), tag along.

go at attack, blame, criticize, impugn, jump on, lunge at, rush, sail into, set about, set upon.

go away bugger off, decamp, depart, disappear, exit, get lost, leave, recede, retreat, scat, scram, vanish, withdraw.

go back (on) backslide, break, forsake, renege, repudiate, retract, retreat, return, revert.

go by adopt, believe, elapse, flow, follow, heed, observe, pass, proceed, trust.

go down collapse, decline, decrease, degenerate, descend, deteriorate, drop, fail, fall, founder, go under, happen, lose, set, sink, subside, succumb.

go far advance, blaze a trail, do well, progress, prosper, succeed.

go for admire, assail, assault, attack, be fond of, be into, choose, dig, enjoy, fall on, favour, fetch, hold with, like, lunge at, obtain, pick, prefer, reach for, seek.

go in for adopt, be fond of, embrace, engage in, enjoy, enter (for), espouse, follow, like, participate in, practise, pursue, sign up, take part in, take up, undertake.

go into analyse, begin, check out, consider, delve into, develop, discuss, dissect, enquire into, enter, examine, investigate, make a study of, probe, pursue, review, scrutinize, study, take up, undertake.

go mad go bonkers, go crazy, go nuts, go round the bend, lose one's mind (or marbles or reason), take leave of one's senses.

go missing be nowhere to be found, disappear, get lost, scarper, vamoose, vanish.

go off abscond, blow up, cut out, decamp, depart, deteriorate, detonate, explode, fire, happen, leave, part, proceed, quit, rot, sour, spoil, take place, turn, vamoose, vanish.

go on advance, blather, chatter, continue, endure, fuss, hang in, happen, hold out, last, persist, prattle, proceed, progress, ramble on, rattle on.

go out become passé, date, depart, die out, exit, expire, fade out, leave, lose currency (or favour), obsolesce, sally forth, see (each other).

go over be accepted, be a hit, detail, enumerate, examine, fly, inspect, list, peruse, read, recall, recapitulate, rehearse, reiterate, review, scan, skim, study, succeed.

go through be approved (by), bear, brave, check, consume, detail, endure, enumerate, examine, exhaust, experience, explore, face, finish, get passed, hunt through, inspect, inventory, investigate, list, look through, read (through), rehearse, rummage through, search,

sift through, sort (through), squander, suffer, tolerate, undergo, use (up), wear out.

go to bed bed down, go to sleep, hit the hay, hit the sack, kip, kip down, retire, turn in.

go together accord, agree, blend, chime, fit, go halves, harmonize, jibe, jive, match.

go to pieces break down, capitulate, collapse, crack up, crumble, crumple, disintegrate, fall apart, have a nervous breakdown, lose control, lose one's head (or nerve), snap.

go to seed decay, decline, degenerate, deteriorate, go downhill, go down the drain (or tubes), go to pot, go to rack and ruin, go to the dogs, go to waste, lie fallow.

go under close down, collapse, default, die, drown, fail, fold, founder, go bankrupt, go down, sink, succumb.

go with accompany, choose, complement, conduct, court, date, decide on, escort, fit, go steady with, match, settle on, suit, take.

go wrong break down, come to grief, come to nothing, come ungummed, come unstuck, conk out, err, fail, fall through, flop, get lost, go astray, go off the rails, go on the blink, go phut, lapse, malfunction, miscarry, misfire, sin, slip up.

goad *n* fillip, impetus, incentive, incitement, irritation, jab, motivation, nudge, poke, pressure, prod, prompt, push, spur, stimulation, stimulus, thrust, urge.

v annoy, arouse, badger, bullyrag, chivvy, drive, egg on, exasperate, excite, exhort, harass, hassle, hector, hound, impel, incite, infuriate, irritate, lash, madden, nag, needle, nudge, persecute, prick, prod, prompt, propel, push, spur, stimulate, sting, urge, vex, worry.

go-ahead *n* agreement, assent, authorization, clearance, consent, cue, fiat, green light, leave, OK, permission, sanction, sign, signal.

antonyms ban, embargo, moratorium, veto.

goal *n* aim, ambition, aspiration, bourn, design, destination, end, grail, intention, mark, object, objective, point, purpose, target.

gob[1] *n* drool, saliva, slobber, spit, spittle, sputum.

v dribble, drool, expectorate, slaver, slobber, spit.

gob[2] *n* blob, dollop, glob, gobbet, lump, mass.

gobble (down) *v* bolt, consume, cram (in), devour, gorge oneself on, gulp, guzzle, pig out on, put away, shovel (in), stuff (in), swallow, wolf (down).

go-between *n* agent, arbitrator, broker, contact, dealer, factor, intercessor, intermediary, internuncio, liaison, mediator, medium, messenger, middleman, negotiator, ombudsman, pander, pimp, procurer.

goblet *n* chalice, cup, grail, wine glass.

goblin *n* bogey, brownie, bugbear, demon, fiend, gremlin, hobgoblin, imp, kelpie, kobold, fiend, nix, nixie, spirit, sprite, troll.

godforsaken *adj* abandoned, backward, benighted, bleak, deserted, desolate, dismal, dreary, empty, forlorn, gloomy, isolated, lonely, miserable, neglected, remote, unfrequented, wild, wretched.

antonym congenial.

godless *adj* atheistic, depraved, evil, impious, irreligious, irreverent, profane, sacrilegious, secular, ungodly, unholy, unprincipled, unrighteous, wicked, worldly.

antonyms godly, pious.

godlike *adj* celestial, deiform, divine, exalted, glorious, heavenly, holy, sublime, superhuman, theomorphic, transcendent.

godly *adj* blameless, devout, god-fearing, good, holy, innocent, pious, pure, religious, righteous, saintly, virtuous.

antonyms godless, impious.

godsend *n* blessing, boon, fluke, lucky break, manna, miracle, stroke of luck, windfall.

antonyms affliction, blow, bolt from the blue, bombshell, setback, thorn in the side.

goggle *v* bulge, gape, gawk, go round (as saucers), ogle, pop (out), stare.

going-over *n* analysis, beating, castigation, chastisement, check, checkup, chiding, critique, doing, dressing-down, drubbing, examination, hiding, inspection, investigation, lecture, perusal, probe, rebuke, reprimand, review, scolding, scouring, scrutiny, study, survey, thrashing, thumping, tongue-lashing, trouncing, whipping.

golden *adj* advantageous, aureate, auric, auspicious, best, blissful, blond(e), bright, brilliant, delightful, excellent, fair, favourable, favoured, flaxen, flourishing, full, gilt, glorious, halcyon, happy, inaurate, invaluable, joyful, lustrous, mellow, opportune, precious, priceless, promising, propitious, prosperous, resplendent, rich, rosy, shimmering, shining, successful, timely, valuable, xanthous, yellow.

gold mine *n* dripping roast, fountain, Golconda, gold dust, golden goose, repository, storehouse, treasury, widow's cruse.

gone *adj* absent, away, broken, bygone, consumed, dead, deceased, defunct, departed, disappeared, dizzy, done, ecstatic, elapsed, ended, enraptured, extinct, faded, faint, finished, giddy, inspired, kaput, lost, missed, missing, over, over and done with, past, pregnant, spent, transported, used (up), vanished.

goo *n* crud, glop, grease, grime, grunge, guck, gunk, matter, mire, muck, mud, mush, ooze, scum, slime, slop, sludge, slush, stickiness.

good *adj* able, acceptable, accomplished, adept, adequate, admirable, adroit, advantageous, agreeable, altruistic, amiable, ample, appropriate, approved, approving, at ease, auspicious, authentic, balmy, beneficent, beneficial, benevolent, benign, blameless, bona fide, bright, brotherly, buoyant, calm, capable, charitable, cheerful, choice, clean, clear, clement, clever, cloudless, comfortable, commendable, competent, complete, congenial, considerate, convenient, correct, darb, decorous, delicious, dependable, deserving, desirable, dexterous, drinkable, dutiful, easy, eatable, edible, efficient, enjoyable, entire, estimable, ethical, excellent, exemplary, expert, fair, favourable, fine, first-class, first-rate, fit, fitting, friendly, full, genuine, gracious, gratifying, great, happy, healthful, healthy, helpful, holy, honest, honourable, humane, innocent, kind, kindly, large, legitimate, long, loyal, mannerly, merciful, meritorious, mild, moral, nice, noble, nourishing, nutritious, obedient, obliging, opportune, orderly, pious, pleasant, pleasing, pleasurable, polite, positive, potable, practicable, praiseworthy, precious, presentable, professional, proficient, profitable, proper, propitious, pure, real, reasonable, reliable, right, righteous, safe, salubrious, salutary, satisfactory, satisfying, seemly, serviceable, sizable, skilful, skilled, solid, sound, splendid, substantial, successful, sufficient, suitable, sunny, super, superior, supportive, sustaining, talented, tested, thorough, true, trustworthy, uncorrupted, untainted, upright, usable, useful, valid, valuable, virtuous, well-behaved, well-mannered, whole, wholesome, workable, worthwhile, worthy.

n advantage, avail, behalf, behoof, benefit, boon, convenience, excellence, gain, goodness, interest, merit, morality, probity, profit, rectitude, right, righteousness, service, uprightness, use, usefulness, virtue, weal, welfare, well-being, worth, worthiness.

for good finally, forever, irreparably, irreversibly, irrevocably, once and for all, permanently.

good-bye *n, interj* adieu, adiós, arrivederci, au revoir, auf Wiedersehen, bon voyage, ciao, farewell, Godspeed, leave-taking, parting, valediction, valedictory.

good-for-nothing *n* black sheep, bum, drone, idler, layabout, lazybones, loafer, loser, lowlife, ne'er-do-well, no-account, profligate, rapscallion, rascal, reprobate, scapegrace, waster, wastrel.

antonyms achiever, success, winner.

adj do-nothing, feckless, idle, indolent, irresponsible, no-good, profligate, reprobate, slothful, useless, worthless.

antonyms conscientious, successful.

good health *interj* à votre santé, cheers, Gesundheit, l'chaim, prosit, salud, salute, skoal, your health.

n haleness, hardiness, health, healthiness, heartiness, lustiness, robustness, soundness, strength, vigour, vitality.

antonyms ill health, invalidism.

good-humoured *adj* affable, amiable, approachable, blithe, cheerful, congenial, expansive, genial, good-tempered, happy, jocund, jovial, pleasant.

antonym ill-humoured.

good-looking *adj* attractive, beautiful, bonny, comely, easy on the eye, fair, handsome, personable, presentable, pretty, well-favoured, well-looking, well-proportioned.

antonyms ill-favoured, plain, ugly.

good-luck charm amulet, fetish, phylactery, porte-bonheur, rabbit's foot, talisman.

antonyms curse, evil eye, jinx.

goodly *adj* ample, considerable, generous, good, large, significant, sizable, substantial, sufficient, tidy.

antonym inadequate.

good-natured *adj* agreeable, amenable, approachable, benevolent, cheerful, easy-going, friendly, generous, gentle, good-hearted, happy, helpful, kind, kind-hearted, kindly, neighbourly, obliging, open-minded, positive, sweet, sweet-tempered, sympathetic, tolerant, upbeat, warm, warm-hearted.

antonyms difficult, grouchy, ill-natured.

goodness *n* altruism, beneficence, benefit, benevolence, condescension, excellence, fairness, friendliness, generosity, good will, graciousness, holiness, honesty, honour, humaneness, humanity, integrity, justice, kindliness, kindness, mercy, merit, morality, nourishment, nutrition, piety, probity, purity, quality, rectitude, richness, righteousness, salubriousness, saintliness, superiority, unselfishness, uprightness, value, virtue, wholesomeness, worth.

antonyms badness, inferiority, wickedness.

goods *n* appurtenances, articles, bags and baggage, belongings, chattels, commodities, effects, furnishings, furniture, gear, iktas, merchandise, movables, paraphernalia, possessions, property, stock, stuff, traps, vendibles, wares.

good will *n* altruism, amity, benevolence, compassion, co-operation, favour, friendliness, friendship, generosity, heartiness, kindliness, loving-kindness, sympathy, willingness, zeal.

antonyms hostility, ill will.

goody-goody *adj* bleeding-heart, holier-than-thou, pious, priggish, sanctimonious, self-righteous, smug, ultra-virtuous, unctuous.

gooey *adj* gluey, glutinous, gummy, grungy, maudlin, mawkish, mucilaginous, mushy, sentimental, sloppy, slushy, soft, sticky, syrupy, tacky, thick, viscid, viscous.

goose flesh *n* creeps, goose bumps, goose pimples, heebie-jeebies, horripilation, horrors, jimjams, shivers, shudders.

gore[1] *n* blood, bloodiness, bloodshed, butchery, carnage, slaughter.

gore[2] *v* impale, penetrate, pierce, rend, spear, spit, stab, stick, transfix, wound.

n flare, gusset.

gorge[1] *n* abyss, barranca, canyon, chasm, cleft, clough, defile, fissure, gap, gulch, gully, pass, ravine.

gorge[2] (oneself) (on) *v* bolt, cram, devour, feed, fill, fill one's face, glut, gobble, gormandize, gulp, guzzle, hog, make a pig of oneself, overeat, ravin, sate, satiate, stuff, surfeit, wolf.

antonym abstain (from).

gorgeous *adj* attractive, beautiful, bright, brilliant, dazzling, delightful, elegant, enjoyable, exquisite, fine, flamboyant, glamorous, glittering, glorious, good, good-looking, grand, lovely, luxuriant, luxurious, magnificent, opulent, pleasing, ravishing, resplendent, rich, showy, splendid, splendiferous, stunning, sumptuous, superb.

antonyms dull, plain, seedy.

gory *adj* blood-soaked, bloodstained, bloodthirsty, bloody, brutal, ensanguined, murderous, sanguinary, sanguineous, savage.

gospel *n* certainty, credo, creed, doctrine, evangel, fact, good news, message, news, revelation, teaching, testament, tidings, truth, verity.

gossamer *adj* airy, cobwebby, delicate, diaphanous, fine, flimsy, gauzy, insubstantial, light, sheer, shimmering, silky, thin, translucent, transparent.

antonyms heavy, opaque, thick.

gossip[1] *n* blather, bush telegraph, causerie, chinwag, chitchat, hearsay, idle talk, jaw, newsmongering, prattle, report, rumour, scandal, schmooze, small talk, the grapevine, tittle-tattle, yakety-yak.

gossip[2] *n* babbler, blatherer, blatherskite, busybody, chatterbox, chatterer, gossipmonger, newsmonger, Nosey Parker, prattler, quidnunc, rumourer, scandalmonger, talebearer, tattler, telltale, whisperer.

v blather, bruit, chat, gabble, jaw, prattle, rumour, tattle, tell tales, whisper.

gouge *v* chisel, claw, cut, dig, extort, extract, force, gash, grave, groove, hack, hollow, incise, overcharge, scoop, score, scratch, slash, swindle.

n cut, furrow, gash, groove, hack, hollow, incision, notch, scoop, score, scratch, slash, trench.

gourmand *n* cormorant, free-liver, gannet, glutton, gorger, gormandizer, guzzler, hog, omnivore, overeater, pig, trencherman, whale.

antonym ascetic.

gourmet *n* bon vivant, connoisseur, dainty eater, epicure, epicurean, gastronome.

antonym omnivore.

govern *v* administer, allay, bridle, check, command, conduct, contain, control, curb, decide, determine, direct, discipline, guide, influence, inhibit, lead, manage, master, order, oversee, pilot, preside over, quell, regulate, reign over, restrain, rule, steer, subdue, superintend, supervise, tame, underlie.

governess *n* companion, duenna, guide, mentor, teacher, tutor.

governing *adj* commanding, dominant, dominative, guiding, leading, legislative, overriding, predominant, prevailing, reigning, ruling, supreme, transcendent, uppermost.

government *n* administration, authority, charge, command, control, direction, domination, dominion, Establishment, executive, governance, guidance, kingcraft, law, management, ministry, polity, powers-that-be, raj, régime, regulation, restraint, rule, state, statecraft, superintendence, supervision, surveillance, sway.

governor *n* administrator, alderman, board member, boss, chief, commander, commissioner, comptroller, controller, corrector, director, executive, gubernator, hakim, head, leader, manager, overseer, ruler, superintendent, supervisor.

gown *n* costume, dress, dressing-gown, frock, garb, garment, habit, kimono, kirtle, negligee, nightie, robe.

grab *v* annex, appropriate, bag, capture, catch, catch hold of, cling to, clutch, collar, commandeer, grasp, grip, impress, latch on to, nab, pluck, seize, snap up, snatch, strike, suit, usurp.

grace[1] *n* attractiveness, beauty, breeding, charm, comeliness, courtesy, cultivation, decency, decorum, deftness, ease, elegance, eloquence, etiquette, finesse, fluency, gracefulness, loveliness, mannerliness, manners, merit, pleasantness, poise, polish, propriety, refinement, shapeliness, tact, tastefulness, unction, virtue.

v adorn, beautify, bedeck, deck, decorate, dignify, distinguish, dress, elevate, embellish, enhance, enrich, favour, garnish, glorify, honour, ornament, prettify, set off, trim.

antonyms deface, detract from, spoil.

grace[2] *n* benefaction, beneficence, benevolence, benignity, benison, charity, clemency, compassion, consideration, favour, forgiveness, generosity, goodness, good will, graciousness, indulgence, kindliness, kindness, leniency, lenity, love, loving-kindness, mercy, pardon, quarter, reprieve.

grace[3] *n* benediction, benedictus, blessing, consecration, prayer, thanks, thanksgiving.

graceful *adj* agile, balletic, beautiful, becoming, charming, comely, deft, easy, elegant, facile, feat, feline, fine, flowing, fluid, gracile, lightsome, natural, pleasing, pliant, slender, smooth, suave, supple, tasteful, willowy.

antonyms awkward, graceless.

graceless *adj* awkward, barbarous, boorish, brazen, clumsy, coarse, crude, forced, gauche, gawky, ill-mannered, improper, incorrigible, indecorous, inelegant, inept, loutish, oafish, reprobate, rough, rude, shameless, uncouth, ungainly, ungraceful, unmannerly, unsophisticated, untutored, vulgar.

antonym graceful.

gracious *adj* accommodating, affable, amenable, amiable, beneficent, benevolent, benign, benignant, charitable, chivalrous, civil, compassionate, complaisant, condescending, considerate, cordial, courteous, courtly, elegant, friendly, grand, hospitable, indulgent, kind, kindly, lenient, loving, luxurious, merciful, mild, obliging, pleasant, pleasing, polite, refined, sweet, well-mannered.

antonym ungracious.

gradation *n* ablaut, change, classification, continuum, degree, grade, grading, grouping, increment, level, mark, measurement, notch, nuance, ordering, place, point, position, progress, progression, rank, shade, shading, sorting, stage, step, succession.

grade *n* acclivity, bank, category, class, declivity, degree, downgrade, echelon, gradation, gradient, group, hill, incline, level, mark, notch, place, position, quality, rank, rating, rise, rung, size, slope, upgrade.

v arrange, blend, categorize, class, classify, evaluate, group, label, level, mark, order, pigeonhole, range, rank, rate, shade, size, sort.

gradient *n* acclivity, bank, decline, declivity, downgrade, grade, hill, incline, rise, slope, upgrade.

gradual *adj* cautious, continuous, deliberate, even, gentle, graduated, incremental, leisurely, measured, moderate, piecemeal, progressive, regular, slow, steady, step-by-step, successive, unhurried.

antonyms precipitate, sudden.

gradually *adv* bit by bit, by degrees, cautiously, drop by drop, evenly, gently, gingerly, imperceptibly, inch by inch, inchmeal, incrementally, little by little, moderately, piecemeal, progressively, slowly, steadily, step by step, unhurriedly.

graduate[1] **(from)** *v* arrange, calibrate, classify, complete, finish, grade, index, make the grade, mark off, measure off, pass, proportion, pro-rate, regulate.

graduate[2] *n* alumna, alumnus, bachelor, doctor, fellow, graduand, licentiate, master.

graft *n* bud, engraftment, heteroplasty, implant, implantation, insert, scion, shoot, splice, sprout, transplant.

v engraft, implant, insert, join, splice, transplant.

grain *n* atom, bit, cereals, crumb, doit, fibre, fragment, granule, grist, grits, iota, jot, kernel, marking, mite, molecule, morsel, mote, nap, ounce, particle, pattern, piece, scintilla, scrap, scruple, seed, smidgen, spark, speck, suspicion, texture, trace, weave, whit.

grammarian *n* linguist, pedant, philologist, style guru.

grand *adj* A-one, admirable, ambitious, august, chief, condescending, dignified, elevated, eminent, exalted, excellent, fine, first-class, first-rate, glorious, gracious, grandiose, great, haughty, head, highest, illustrious, imperious, imposing, impressive, large, lofty, lordly, luxurious, magnificent, main, majestic, marvellous, monumental, noble, opulent, ostentatious, palatial, patronizing, pompous, pre-eminent, pretentious, princely, principal, regal, senior, splendid, stately, striking, sublime, sumptuous, superb, supreme, wonderful.

grandeur *n* augustness, dignity, graciousness, greatness, hauteur, imperiousness, importance, loftiness, magnificence, majesty, nobility, pomp, splendour, state, stateliness, sublimity.

antonyms humbleness, lowliness, simplicity.

grandfather *n* gaffer, grampa, gramps, grandad, granddaddy, grandpa, grandpapa, grandpappy, grandsire, opa.

grandiloquence *n* affectation, bombast, euphuism, floweriness, fustian, magniloquence, orotundity, pomposity, pretentiousness, purple prose, rhetoric, turgidity.

antonyms plainness, restraint, simplicity.

grandiloquent *adj* bombastic, euphuistic, florid, flowery, fustian, high-flown, high-sounding, inflated, magniloquent, orotund, pompous, pretentious, purple, rhetorical, swollen, turgid.

antonyms plain, restrained, simple.

grandiose *adj* affected, ambitious, bombastic, euphuistic, extravagant, flamboyant, grand, high-flown, imposing, impressive, lofty, magnificent, majestic, monumental, noble, ostentatious, overambitious, pompous, ponderous, pretentious, showy, stately, weighty.

antonym unpretentious.

grandmother *n* gammer, gramma, gran, grandma, grandmama, granny, oma.

grant *v* accede to, accord, acknowledge, admit, agree to, allocate, allot, allow, apportion, assign, award, bestow (on), cede, concede, confer (on), consent to, dispense, donate, give, impart, permit, present, provide, transfer, transmit, vouchsafe.

antonyms deny, refuse.

n allocation, allotment, allowance, annuity, award, benefaction, bequest, boon, bounty, bursary, concession, donation, endowment, gift, honorarium, present, scholarship, subsidy, subvention, transfer payment.

granular *adj* crumbly, grainy, granulated, granulose, gravelly, gritty, rough, sandy.

granule *n* atom, bead, crumb, fragment, grain, iota, jot, molecule, particle, pellet, scrap, seed, speck.

graph *n* chart, curve, diagram, figure, grid, table.

graphic *adj* blow-by-blow, clear, cogent, delineated, delineative, descriptive, detailed, diagrammatic, drawn, evocative, explicit, expressive, forcible, illustrative, image-laden, lifelike, lively, lucid, pictorial, picturesque, representational, specific, striking, telling, visual, vivid.

antonyms abstract, vague.

grapple (with) *v* attack, battle, catch, clash (with), clasp, clinch, close (with), clutch, combat, come to grips (with), confront, contend (with), cope (with), deal (with), do battle (with), encounter, engage, face, fight (with), grab, grasp, grip, hug, lay hold (of), make fast, pin down, seize, snatch, struggle (with), tackle, tussle (with), wrestle (with).

antonyms avoid, evade.

grasp *v* apprehend, catch, catch on to, clasp, clinch, clutch, comprehend, fathom, follow, get, grab, grapple, grip, hold, lay hold of, master, perceive, realize, see, seize, snatch, twig to, understand.

n acquaintance, apprehension, awareness, capacity, clasp, clutches, compass, competence, comprehension, control, embrace, expertise, extent, familiarity, grip, hold, intimacy, ken, knowledge, mastery, perception, possession, power, range, reach, realization, scope, sway, sweep, tenure, understanding.

grasping *adj* acquisitive, avaricious, close-fisted, covetous, greedy, mean, mercenary, miserly, niggardly, parsimonious, penny-pinching, rapacious, selfish, stingy, tight-fisted, usurious.

antonym generous.

grass *n* fog, grama, grassland, green, greensward, hay, herbage, lawn, pasturage, pasture, sod, sward, turf, verdure.

grasshopper *n* cicada, cricket, katydid, locust.

grassland *n* downs, lea, llano, meadow, meadowland, pampas, pasture, plain, prairie, savanna, steppe, sward, veld.

grate[1] *v* comminute, creak, granulate, gride, grind, mince, pulverize, rasp, rub, scrape, scratch, set one's teeth on edge, shred, triturate.

grate[2] **(on)** *v* aggravate, annoy, chafe, exasperate, fret, gall, get on one's nerves, irk, irritate, jar, nettle, peeve, rankle, rub the wrong way, set one's teeth on edge, vex.

grateful *adj* appreciative, beholden, indebted, mindful, obliged, sensible, thankful.

antonym ungrateful.

gratification *n* contentment, delight, elation, enjoyment, fruition, fulfilment, glee, indulgence, joy, jubilation, kicks, pleasure, recompense, relish, reward, satisfaction, thrill, triumph.

antonym disappointment, frustration.

gratify *v* appease, cater to, content, delight, fulfil, give in to, gladden, humour, indulge, pander to, please, pleasure, recompense, requite, reward, satisfy, thrill.

antonyms disappoint, frustrate, thwart.

gratifying *v* comfortable, comforting, delightful, fulfilling, heartening, heartwarming, pleasant, pleasing, pleasurable, rewarding, satisfying, thrilling, welcome.

antonyms disappointing, frustrating.

grating[1] *adj* aggravating, annoying, cacophonous, disagreeable, discordant, displeasing, exasperating, galling, grinding, harsh, irksome, irritating, jarring, rasping, raucous, scraping, squeaky, strident, unharmonious, unmelodious, unpleasant, vexatious.

antonyms harmonious, pleasing.

grating[2] *n* grid, grill, grille, grillwork, hack, lattice, latticework, trellis, trelliswork, wicket.

gratitude *n* acknowledgment, appreciation, gratefulness, indebtedness, mindfulness, obligation, recognition, thankfulness, thanks, thanksgiving.

antonym   ingratitude.

gratuitous¹ *adj* buckshee, complimentary, free, gratis, unasked-for, undeserved, unearned, unmerited, unpaid, unrewarded, voluntary.

antonyms   due, earned, owing, paid, required.

gratuitous² *adj* baseless, causeless, groundless, irrelevant, needless, purposeless, reasonless, redundant, superfluous, unasked-for, uncalled-for, unfounded, unjustified, unnecessary, unprovoked, unsolicited, unwarranted, wanton.

antonyms   justified, necessary, reasonable.

gratuity *n* baksheesh, bonus, gift, largesse, perquisite, pourboire, present, recompense, reward, tip, Trinkgeld.

grave¹ *n* barrow, burial place, cairn, cemetery plot, crypt, mausoleum, pit, sepulchre, tomb, vault.

grave² *adj* acute, critical, crucial, dangerous, dignified, disquieting, dour, earnest, exigent, gloomy, grievous, grim, grim-faced, hazardous, heavy, important, leaden, long-faced, momentous, muted, pensive, perilous, ponderous, preoccupied, pressing, quiet, reserved, restrained, sad, sage, saturnine, sedate, serious, severe, significant, sober, solemn, sombre, staid, subdued, thoughtful, threatening, unsmiling, urgent, vital, weighty.

antonyms   flippant, gay, light, slight, trivial.

gravelly *adj* grainy, granular, grating, gritty, gruff, guttural, harsh, hoarse, pebbly, rasping, rough, shingly, throaty.

antonyms   clear, fine, powdery, smooth.

gravestone *n* cross, headstone, marker, monument, stele, tombstone.

graveyard *n* boneyard, burial ground, burial place, cemetery, churchyard, God's acre, Golgotha, necropolis.

gravitate *v* be drawn, descend, drop, fall, head (for), incline, lean, move, precipitate, settle, sink, tend.

gravity *n* acuteness, consequence, demureness, dignity, earnestness, exigency, gloom, gloominess, grievousness, grimness, hazardousness, importance, magnitude, moment, momentousness, pensiveness, perilousness, ponderousness, reserve, restraint, sedateness, seriousness, severity, significance, sobriety, solemnity, sombreness, thoughtfulness, urgency, weightiness.

antonyms   flippancy, gaiety, levity, slightness, triviality.

graze¹ *v* batten, browse, crop, feed, fodder, pasture.

graze² *v* abrade, bark, brush, chafe, gride, rub, score, scrape, scratch, shave, skim, skin, touch.

n abrasion, score, scrape, scratch.

grease *n* dope, dripping(s), fat, grime, grunge, lard, liniment, lubricant, oil, ointment, petrolatum, petroleum jelly, sebum, suet, tallow, unction, unguent, wax.

greasy *adj* fatty, fawning, glib, grimy, grovelling, grungy, ingratiating, lardy, oily, oleaginous, sebaceous, slick, slimy, slippery, smarmy, smeary, smooth, suety, sycophantic, tallowy, toadying, unctuous, waxy.

great *adj* able, ace, active, adept, admirable, adroit, august, big, blatant, bulky, celebrated, chief, colossal, consequential, considerable, crack, critical, crucial, devoted, dignified, distinguished, egregious, eminent, enormous, enthusiastic, exalted, excellent, excessive, expert, extended, extensive, extravagant, extreme, fabulous, famed, famous, fantastic, favourite, fine, first-rate, flagrant, generous, gigantic, glorious, good, glaring, grand, grave, great-hearted, grievous, heavy, heroic, high, high-minded, huge, idealistic, illustrious, immense, important, impressive, inordinate, invaluable, keen, large, leading, lengthy, lofty, long, magnanimous, main, major, mammoth, manifold, marked, marvellous, massive, masterly, momentous, multitudinous, munificent, noble, nonpareil, notable, noteworthy, noticeable, outstanding, paramount, ponderous, precious, pre-eminent, priceless, primary, princely, principal, prodigious, proficient, prominent, pronounced, remarkable, renowned, senior, serious, significant, skilful, skilled, strong, stupendous, sublime, superb, superior, superlative, talented, terrific, tremendous, valuable, vast, virtuoso, voluminous, weighty, wonderful, world-class, zealous.

antonyms   insignificant, lowly, small, unimportant, unimpressive.

greatly *adv* abundantly, considerably, deeply, enormously, exceedingly, extensively, extremely, highly, hugely, immensely, impressively, markedly, mightily, much, notably, noticeably, powerfully, remarkably, significantly, substantially, superlatively, tremendously, vastly.

greatness *n* celebrity, depth, dignity, distinction, egregiousness, eminence, excellence, extent, fame, flagrancy, force, generosity, genius, glory, grandeur, gravity, great-heartedness, heroism, high-mindedness, hugeness, illustriousness, immensity, import, importance, intensity, loftiness, magnanimity, magnitude, majesty, mass, moment, momentousness, nobility, note, potency, power, prodigiousness, renown, seriousness, significance, size, stateliness, strength, sublimity, superbness, urgency, vastness, weight, weightiness.

antonyms   insignificance, pettiness, smallness.

greed *n* acquisitiveness, avidity, covetousness, craving, cupidity, desire, eagerness, edacity, esurience, gluttony, gormandizing, gormandism, gourmandise, greediness, hunger, insatiability, insatiableness, itchy palm, longing, rapacity, ravenousness, selfishness, voraciousness, voracity.

antonyms   abstemiousness, contentment.

greedy *adj* acquisitive, anxious, avaricious, avid, covetous, craving, curious, desirous, eager, edacious, esurient, gluttonish, gluttonous, gormandizing, grasping, hoggish, hungry, impatient, insatiable, itchy-palmed, money-grubbing, piggish, rapacious, ravenous, selfish, voracious, wolfish.

antonyms abstemious, content.

green *adj* blooming, budding, burgeoning, callow, covetous, emerald, envious, fertile, flourishing, fresh, glaucous, grassy, growing, grudging, ignorant, ill, immature, inexperienced, inexpert, jealous, leafy, living, naïve, nauseous, new, pale, pliable, raw, recent, resentful, sick, starry-eyed, supple, tender, thriving, unpractised, unripe, unseasoned, unsophisticated, untrained, untried, unversed, verdant, verdurous, virescent, virid, viridescent, wan, wet behind the ears, young.

n common, golf course, golf links, greensward, lawn, sward, turf.

greenery *n* foliage, greenness, vegetation, verdancy, verdure, virescence, viridescence, viridity.

greenhorn *n* apprentice, beginner, catechumen, cheechako, fledgling, ignoramus, ingénue, initiate, learner, naïf, neophyte, newcomer, novice, novitiate, recruit, rookie, tenderfoot, tyro.

antonyms old hand, veteran.

greenhouse *n* conservatory, glasshouse, hothouse, nursery, pavilion, vinery.

greet *v* accost, acknowledge, address, give the time of day to, hail, halloo, meet, pass the time of day, receive, salute, wave to, welcome.

antonym ignore.

greeting *n* accost, acknowledgment, address, aloha, hail, kiss of peace, reception, salaam, salutation, salute, salve, the time of day, welcome.

greetings *n, interj* best wishes, civilities, compliments, devoirs, formalities, good wishes, hail, hello, love, regards, respects, salutations, welcome.

gregarious *adj* affable, chummy, companionable, convivial, cordial, extrovert, friendly, outgoing, pally, sociable, social, warm.

antonyms solitary, unsociable, withdrawn.

grey *adj* aged, ambiguous, ancient, anonymous, ashen, bloodless, characterless, cheerless, cloudy, colourless, dark, depressing, dim, dismal, drab, dreary, dull, elderly, fuzzy, glaucous, gloomy, griseous, grizzle, grizzled, hoar, hoary, indeterminate, indistinct, leaden, livid, mature, murky, neutral, old, overcast, pale, pallid, sombre, sunless, uncertain, unclear, unidentifiable, venerable, wan.

grid *n* array, chart, grating, gridiron, grill, grille, lattice, matrix, network, table.

grief *n* ache, affliction, agony, anguish, bereavement, blow, burden, dejection, desolation, distress, dole, dolour, heartache, heartbreak, lamentation, misery, mourning, pain, regret, remorse, sadness, sorrow, suffering, tragedy, trial, tribulation, trouble, woe.

antonym happiness.

grief-stricken *adj* aching, afflicted, agonized, broken, broken-hearted, crushed, desolate, despairing, devastated, disconsolate, distracted, distressed, grieving, heartbroken, inconsolable, mourning, overcome, overwhelmed, sad, sorrowful, sorrowing, stricken, unhappy, woebegone, wretched.

antonym overjoyed.

grievance *n* beef, bitch, bone to pick, charge, complaint, gravamen, gripe, grouse, grudge, hardship, injury, injustice, moan, objection, peeve, resentment, wrong.

grieve¹ *v* afflict, break one's heart, crush, cut to the quick, disappoint, displease, distress, disturb, harrow, hurt, injure, offend, pain, sadden, trouble, upset, wound.

grieve² (over, for) *v* ache, agonize, bemoan, bewail, complain, deplore, eat one's heart out, hurt, lament, mourn, regret, rue, sorrow, suffer, wail, weep.

grievous *adj* appalling, atrocious, burdensome, calamitous, damaging, deplorable, devastating, distressing, dreadful, egregious, flagrant, glaring, grave, harmful, heartbreaking, heart-rending, heavy, heinous, hurtful, injurious, intolerable, lamentable, monstrous, offensive, oppressive, outrageous, overwhelming, painful, pitiful, serious, severe, shameful, shocking, sorrowful, tragic, unbearable, unconscionable, unforgivable, unpardonable.

grim *adj* adamant, bleak, cruel, doom-laden, dour, fearsome, ferocious, fierce, forbidding, formidable, frightening, frightful, ghastly, grave, grisly, gruesome, harsh, horrible, implacable, macabre, merciless, morose, relentless, repellent, resolute, ruthless, severe, sinister, stern, sullen, terrible, unpleasant, unrelenting, unwelcome, unyielding.

antonyms benign, congenial, pleasant.

grimace *n* face, frown, moue, pout, scowl, smirk, sneer, wry face.

v frown, make (or pull) a face, mop (and mow), mug, pout, scowl, smirk, sneer.

grime *n* dirt, filth, grease, grunge, guck, gunk, muck, smut, soot, squalor.

grimy *adj* begrimed, besmeared, besmirched, contaminated, dirty, filthy, foul, grubby, smudgy, smutty, soiled, sooty, squalid.

antonyms clean, pure.

grind¹ *v* abrade, bray, comminute, crush, file, gnash, granulate, grate, grit, kibble, mill, polish, pound, powder, pulverize, sand, scrape, sharpen, smooth, triturate, whet.

n coarseness, fineness, texture.

grind² *v* beaver, drudge, labour, lucubrate, slave, slog, sweat, toil, work one's fingers to the bone.

n chore, drudgery, exertion, labour, round, routine, slavery, sweat, task, toil.

grind down afflict, burden, crush, harass, harry, hound, oppress, persecute, plague, trouble, tyrannize.

grip *n* acquaintance, clasp, clutches, comprehension, control, domination, embrace, grasp, handclasp, handle, hold, influence, keeping, mastery, perception, possession, power, purchase, sway, understanding.

v absorb, catch, clasp, clutch, engross, enthrall, entrance, fascinate, grasp, hold, involve, latch on to, mesmerize, rivet, seize, spellbind.

gripe *v* beef, bellyache, bitch, carp, complain, groan, grouch, grouse, grumble, kvetch, moan, nag, whine.

n beef, bitch, complaint, grievance, griping, groan, grouse, grumble, moan, objection.

gripping *adj* absorbing, compelling, engrossing, enthralling, entrancing, exciting, fascinating, riveting, spellbinding, suspenseful, thrilling, unputdownable.

grisly *adj* abominable, appalling, awful, dreadful, frightful, ghastly, grim, gruesome, hair-raising, hideous, horrible, horrific, macabre, revolting, shocking, sickening, terrible, terrifying.
antonym delightful.

grit¹ *n* dust, gravel, particles, pebbles, sand, shingle.
v clench, gnash, grate, grind, lock.

grit² *n* backbone, bravery, courage, determination, doggedness, endurance, fortitude, gameness, guts, hardihood, mettle, nerve, perseverance, pluck, resolution, spine, spirit, spunk, stamina, staying power, steadfastness, stick-to-it-iveness, tenacity, toughness.

gritty¹ *adj* abrasive, dusty, grainy, granular, gravelly, pebbly, rough, sandy, shingly.
antonyms fine, smooth.

gritty² *adj* brave, courageous, determined, dogged, game, gutsy, hardy, mettlesome, persevering, plucky, resolute, spirited, spunky, steadfast, tenacious, tough.
antonyms cowardly, spineless, wishy-washy.

grizzled *adj* canescent, grey, grey-haired, grey-headed, greying, griseous, grizzly, hoar, hoary, pepper-and-salt.

groan *n* complaint, cry, lament, moan, objection, outcry, protest, sigh, wail.
antonym cheer.

v complain, cry (out), lament, moan, object, protest, sigh, wail.
antonym cheer.

groceries *n* food, foodstuffs, pantry stock, provisions, shopping, victuals.

groggy *adj* befuddled, confused, dazed, dizzy, dopey, faint, fuddled, half-asleep, half-awake, light-headed, punch-drunk, reeling, sedated, shaky, stunned, stupid, unsteady, weak, wobbly, woozy.
antonym lucid.

groom *v* brush, clean, coach, curry, dress, drill, educate, neaten, nurture, preen, prepare, prime, primp, prink, ready, school, smarten, spruce up, tart up, tend, tidy, titivate, train, turn out, tutor.

groove *n* canal, chamfer, channel, chase, cut, cutting, flute, furrow, gutter, hollow, indentation, kerf, rabbet, rut, score, sulcus, trench.
antonym ridge.

grooved *adj* chamfered, channelled, fluted, furrowed, rabbeted, rutted, scored, sulcate.
antonym ridged.

groovy *adj* cool, exciting, far out, fashionable, hip, in, sixties.
antonym square.

grope *v* cast about (or around), feel, feel around, feel up, finger, fish, flounder, fumble, goose, grabble, probe, scrabble, search.

gross¹ *adj* apparent, arrant, bawdy, bestial, big, blatant, blue, boorish, broad, brutish, callous, coarse, colossal, corpulent, crass, crude, dense, disgusting, egregious, extreme, fat, filthy, flagrant, foul, general, glaring, great, grievous, heinous, horrid, imprecise, improper, impure, indecent, indelicate, indiscriminate, insensitive, large, lewd, low, lumpish, manifest, massive, nauseating, obese, obscene, obvious, offensive, off-putting, outrageous, outright, plain, rank, repellent, repulsive, revolting, ribald, rough, rude, sensual, serious, shameful, shameless, sheer, shocking, sickening, smutty, tasteless, uncivil, uncouth, uncultured, undiscriminating, undisguised, unmitigated, unrefined, unseemly, unsophisticated, unwieldy, utter, vulgar.
antonyms delicate, fine, seemly, slight.

gross out disgust, horrify, nauseate, offend, put off, repel, revolt, sicken.

in the gross as a whole, en bloc, en masse, in aggregate, in bulk, in toto, wholesale.

gross² *n* aggregate, bulk, entirety, sum, total, totality, whole.
adj aggregate, all-inclusive, before deductions, complete, entire, inclusive, total, whole.
v bring (in), earn, make, rake in, take (in), total.

grossness *n* bawdiness, bestiality, blatancy, broadness, brutishness, coarseness, corpulence, crassness, crudity, egregiousness, fatness, filthiness, flagrancy, foulness, generality, greatness, grievousness, heinousness, hugeness, imprecision, impurity, incivility, indecency, indelicacy, insensitivity, lewdness, licentiousness, lumpishness, obesity, obscenity, obviousness, offensiveness, outrageousness, rankness, repulsiveness, ribaldry, rudeness, sensuality, seriousness, shamefulness, shamelessness, smut, smuttiness, tastelessness, uncouthness, unseemliness, unwieldiness, vulgarity.
antonyms delicacy, fineness, seemliness, slightness.

grotesque *adj* absurd, antic, bizarre, deformed, distorted, extravagant, fanciful, fantastic, freakish, gruesome, hideous, incongruous, laughable, ludicrous, macabre, malformed, misshapen, monstrous, odd, outlandish, preposterous, ridiculous, rococo, strange, ugly, unnatural, unsightly, weird.

n bizarrerie, extravaganza, fantastic figure, gargoyle, grotesquerie, manikin.

grotto *n* catacomb, cave, cavern, chamber, grot, souterrain, subterranean (chamber), underground chamber.

grouch *v* beef, bellyache, bitch, carp, complain, find fault, gripe, grouse, grumble, moan, snap, sulk, whine.

antonym acquiesce.

n beef, bellyacher, churl, complainer, complaint, crab, crank, crosspatch, crotcheteer, curmudgeon, faultfinder, grievance, gripe, griper, grouse, grouser, grumble, grumbler, malcontent, moan, moaner, murmur, murmurer, mutterer, objection, whiner.

grouchy *adj* bad-tempered, cantankerous, captious, churlish, complaining, crabby, cranky, cross, crotchety, discontented, dissatisfied, grumbling, grumpy, ill-tempered, irascible, irritable, peevish, petulant, querulous, snappish, sulky, surly, testy, truculent.

antonym contented.

ground *n* arena, background, ballpark, bottom, clay, clod, deck, dirt, dry land, dust, earth, field, foundation, land, loam, mould, park, pitch, sod, soil, stadium, surface, terra firma, terrain, turf.

v acquaint (with), anchor, base, build up, coach, drill, establish, familiarize (with), fix, found, initiate, instruct, introduce (to), prepare, root, set, settle, teach, train, tutor.

groundless *adj* absurd, baseless, empty, false, foundationless, gratuitous, idle, illusory, imaginary, irrational, unauthorized, uncalled-for, unfounded, unjustified, unproven, unprovoked, unreasonable, unsubstantiated, unsupported, unwarranted.

antonyms justified, reasonable.

ground rule *n* guideline, principle, rule of thumb.

grounds¹ *n* area, estate, gardens, holding, land, lawns, park, premises, property, yard.

grounds² *n* argument, base, basis, call, cause, excuse, foundation, justification, motive, occasion, premise, pretext, principle, rationale, reason, score.

grounds³ *n* deposit, dregs, lees, precipitate, precipitation, sediment, settlings.

groundwork *n* base, basis, cornerstone, essentials, footing, foundation, fundamentals, homework, preliminaries, preparation, research, spadework, underpinnings.

group *n* aggregate, assemblage, association, band, batch, bevy, bracket, branch, bunch, category, caucus, cell, circle, class, classification, classis, clique, clump, cluster, clutch, cohort, collection, collective, colony, combination, company, conclave, conglomeration, congregation, constellation, corps, coterie, covey, crowd, department, detachment, division, ensemble, faction, family, flock, gaggle, gang, gathering, genus, grouping, herd, knot, lobby, lot, nexus, organization, pack, party, pride, radical, sample, set, species, squad, squadron, team, troop, unit.

v arrange, assemble, associate, assort, band, bracket, categorize, class, classify, cluster, collect, combine, congregate, crowd, deploy, dispose, fraternize, gather, link, marshal, mass, order, organize, put together, range, sort, team (up).

grouse *v* beef, bellyache, bitch, carp, complain, find fault, fret, fuss, gripe, grouch, grumble, moan, murmur, mutter, repine, whine.

antonym acquiesce.

n bellyache, complaint, grievance, gripe, grouch, grumble, grumbling, moan, murmur, muttering, objection, peeve, whine.

grove *n* arbour, avenue, bosk, brake, clump, coppice, copse, covert, orchard, plantation, patch, spinney, stand, thicket, woods.

grovel *v* abase oneself, backscratch, bootlick, cower, crawl, creep, cringe, crouch, demean oneself, fawn, flatter, ingratiate oneself, kowtow, sneak, sycophantize, toady.

grovelling *adj* backscratching, bootlicking, cowering, cringing, fawning, flattering, ingratiating, obsequious, servile, sycophantic, toadying, wormy.

antonyms independent, outspoken, proud, straightforward.

grow *v* advance, arise, become, branch out, breed, broaden, burgeon, cultivate, deepen, develop, diversify, enlarge, escalate, evolve, expand, extend, farm, flourish, flower, germinate, get, heighten, improve, increase, intensify, issue, learn, mature, mount, multiply, nurture, originate, produce, progress, proliferate, propagate, prosper, raise, ripen, rise, shoot, spread, spring, sprout, stem, stretch, swell, thicken, thrive, turn, vegetate, wax, widen.

antonyms decrease, fail, halt, shrivel, wane.

growl *v* complain, grumble, rumble, snarl.

grown-up *adj* adult, big, full-grown, fully-fledged, mature, of age.

antonyms childish, immature.

n adult, big person, man, woman.

antonym child.

growth *n* accretion, advance, advancement, aggrandizement, augmentation, broadening, change, crop, cultivation, deepening, development, diversification, enlargement, escalation, evolution, excrescence, expansion, extension, flowering, gall, germination, heightening, improvement, increase, intensification, intumescence, learning, lump, maturation, multiplication, outgrowth, produce, production, progress, proliferation, prosperity, protuberance, ripening, rise, shooting, spread, sprouting, stretching, success, swelling, thickening, transformation, tumour, vegetation, waxing, widening.

antonyms decrease, failure, stagnation, stoppage.

grub¹ *v* burrow, delve, dig, explore, ferret, forage, hunt, investigate, nose, probe, pull up, root, rootle, rummage, scour, uproot.

n caterpillar, chrysalis, larva, maggot, nymph, pupa, worm.

grub² *n* chow, commons, eats, edibles, fodder, food, meal(s), nosh, provisions, rations, scoff, snack(s), sustenance, victuals.

grubby *adj* crummy, dirty, filthy, fly-blown, frowzy, grimy, grungy, messy, mucky, scruffy, seedy, shabby, slovenly, smudgy, smutty, soiled, sordid, squalid, unkempt, untidy, unwashed.
antonyms clean, smart.

grudge *n* animosity, animus, antagonism, antipathy, aversion, bitterness, chip on one's shoulder, dislike, enmity, envy, grievance, hard feelings, hate, ill will, jealousy, malevolence, malice, pique, rancour, resentment, spite.
antonyms favour, regard.
v begrudge, envy, mind, regret, resent, stint, take exception to.
antonyms applaud, approve.

grudging *adj* cautious, forced, guarded, half-hearted, hesitant, niggardly, reluctant, resentful, uncharitable, unenthusiastic, ungenerous, unwilling.

gruelling *adj* arduous, backbreaking, brutal, crushing, demanding, difficult, exhausting, fatiguing, fierce, grinding, hard, harsh, laborious, punishing, severe, stiff, strenuous, taxing, tiring, tough, trying, uphill, wearing, wearying.
antonym easy.

gruesome *adj* abominable, awful, chilling, creepy, fearful, fearsome, ghastly, grim, grisly, hideous, horrible, horrid, horrific, horrifying, loathsome, macabre, monstrous, repellent, repugnant, repulsive, shocking, sick, spine-chilling, terrible.
antonyms charming, congenial.

gruff *adj* abrupt, bad-tempered, blunt, brusque, churlish, crabby, croaking, crusty, curt, discourteous, gravelly, grouchy, grumpy, guttural, harsh, hoarse, husky, ill-humoured, ill-natured, impolite, low, rasping, rough, rude, sour, sullen, surly, throaty, uncivil, ungracious, unmannerly.
antonyms clear, courteous, sweet.

grumble *v* beef, bellyache, bitch, bleat, carp, complain, croak, find fault, fuss, gripe, grouch, grouse, growl, gurgle, moan, murmur, mutter, repine, roar, rumble, whine.
antonym acquiesce.
n beef, bitch, bleat, complaint, grievance, gripe, grouch, grouse, growl, gurgle, moan, murmur, muttering, objection, roar, rumble, whine.

grumpy *adj* bad-tempered, cantankerous, churlish, crabby, cranky, cross, crotchety, discontented, grouchy, grumbling, ill-tempered, irritable, peevish, petulant, quarrelsome, querulous, snappish, sulky, sullen, surly, testy, truculent.
antonyms cheerful, contented.

guarantee *n* assurance, attestation, bond, certainty, collateral, covenant, earnest, endorsement, guaranty, insurance, oath, pledge, promise, security, surety, testimonial,
undertaking, voucher, warranty, word, word of honour.
v answer for, assure, avouch, back up, certify, ensure, insure, maintain, make certain, make sure of, pledge, promise, protect, secure, stand behind, swear, underwrite, vouch for, warrant.

guarantor *n* angel, backer, bailsman, bondsman, covenanter, insurer, sponsor, supporter, underwriter, voucher, warrantor.

guard *v* be on the qui vive, be on the watch, beware, conserve, cover, defend, escort, husband, keep, look out, mind, oversee, patrol, police, preserve, protect, safeguard, save, screen, secure, sentinel, shelter, shield, supervise, tend, ward, watch.
n attention, backstop, barrier, buffer, bulwark, bumper, care, convoy, custodian, defence, defender, escort, guarantee, hedge, lookout, minder, pad, patrol, picket, precaution, protection, protector, rampart, safeguard, screen, security, sentinel, sentry, shield, surveillance, vigilance, wall, warden, warder, wariness, watch, watchfulness, watchman.
on guard alert, cautious, chary, circumspect, on the alert, on the lookout, on the qui vive, prepared, ready, vigilant, wary, watchful, wide-awake.

guarded *adj* cagey, careful, cautious, circumspect, discreet, disingenuous, non-committal, prudent, reserved, restrained, reticent, secretive, suspicious, uncommunicative, unforthcoming, wary, watchful.
antonyms frank, open, whole-hearted.

guardian *n* attendant, baby-sitter, caregiver, champion, conservator, curator, custodian, defender, depositary, depository, escort, fiduciary, foster parent, guard, houseparent, keeper, minder, nanny, preserver, protector, trustee, warden, warder.

guardianship *n* aegis, attendance, care, companionship, curatorship, custodianship, custody, defence, escort, guard, guidance, hands, keeping, patronage, protection, safekeeping, trust, trusteeship, wardship.

guerrilla *n* bushwhacker, franc-tireur, freedom-fighter, guerrillero, irregular, maquis, partisan, rebel, resistance fighter, sniper.

guess *v* assume, believe, conjecture, daresay, divine, estimate, fancy, fathom, feel, figure, figure out, guesstimate, hazard, hypothesize, imagine, intuit, judge, opine, predict, reckon, solve, speculate, suppose, surmise, suspect, theorize, think, work out.
n assumption, belief, conjecture, estimate, fancy, feeling, guesstimate, hypothesis, intuition, judgment, notion, opinion, prediction, reckoning, shot (in the dark), speculation, supposition, surmise, suspicion, theory.

guesswork *n* assumption, conjecture, estimation, hypothesizing, inference, intuition, presumption, presupposition, reckoning, speculation, supposition, surmise, suspicion, theory.

guest *n* boarder, caller, company, freeloader, habitué, invitee, lodger, parasite, regular, roomer, visitant, visitor.

guesthouse *n* boarding house, hospice, hostel, hostelry, hotel, inn, pension, rooming house.

guidance *n* advice, aegis, auspices, clues, conduct, control, counsel, counselling, direction, government, guidelines, help, illumination, indications, instruction, leadership, management, pointers, recommendation, steering, teaching.

guide *v* accompany, advise, attend, command, con, conduct, convoy, counsel, direct, educate, escort, govern, handle, head, influence, instruct, lead, manage, manoeuvre, oversee, pilot, point, rule, shape, shepherd, steer, superintend, supervise, teach, train, usher, vector.

n ABC, adviser, attendant, beacon, chaperone, cicerone, clue, companion, conductor, consultant, counsellor, courier, criterion, director, directory, dragoman, escort, example, exemplar, guidebook, guideline, guru, handbook, ideal, index, indication, informant, inspiration, instructions, interpreter, key, landmark, leader, legend, lodestar, manual, mark, marker, master, mentor, model, pattern, pilot, pointer, reference (point), sign, signpost, standard, steersman, teacher, template, tracker, usher, vade mecum.

guiding *adj* advisory, consultative, consulting, counselling, directorial, formative, governing, influential, instructional, instructive, managing, piloting, shepherding, steering, supervisory, tutorial.

guild *n* association, brotherhood, chapel, club, company, corporation, fellowship, fraternity, league, lodge, order, organization, society, (trade) union.

guile *n* art, artfulness, artifice, cleverness, craft, craftiness, cunning, deceit, deception, deviousness, disingenuity, duplicity, gamesmanship, knavery, ruse, slyness, treachery, trickery, trickiness, wiliness.

antonyms artlessness, guilelessness.

guileful *adj* artful, clever, crafty, cunning, deceitful, devious, disingenuous, duplicitous, foxy, sly, sneaky, treacherous, tricky, underhand, wily.

antonyms artless, guileless.

guileless *adj* artless, candid, direct, frank, genuine, honest, ingenuous, innocent, naïve, natural, open, simple, sincere, straightforward, transparent, trusting, truthful, unreserved, unsophisticated, unworldly.

antonyms artful, guileful.

guilt *n* blamability, blame, blameworthiness, compunction, conscience, criminality, culpability, delinquency, disgrace, dishonour, guiltiness, infamy, iniquity, regret, remissness, remorse, responsibility, self-condemnation, self-reproach, self-reproof, shame, sinfulness, stain, stigma, troubled conscience, wickedness, wrong.

antonyms innocence, shamelessness.

guiltless *adj* blameless, clean, clear, immaculate, impeccable, inculpable, innocent, irreproachable, pure, sinless, spotless, unimpeachable, unspotted, unstained, unsullied, untainted, untarnished.

antonyms guilty, tainted.

guilty *adj* ashamed, blamable, blameworthy, compunctious, conscience-stricken, convicted, criminal, culpable, delinquent, errant, erring, evil, felonious, guilt-ridden, hangdog, illicit, iniquitous, nefarious, nocent, offending, regretful, remorseful, reprehensible, responsible, rueful, shamefaced, sheepish, sinful, wicked, wrong.

antonyms guiltless, innocent.

guise *n* air, appearance, disguise, dress, façade, fashion, form, front, likeness, manner, mask, mode, pretence, semblance, shape, show.

gulch *n* arroyo, canyon, coulee, defile, gorge, gully, ravine, streambed, valley, wadi.

gulf *n* abyss, basin, bay, bight, breach, chasm, cleft, gap, gorge, rent, rift, separation, split, void, whirlpool.

gull[1] *n* mew, sea bird, seagull, tern.

gull[2] *n* cheat, con, deceive, dupe, hoax, pull the wool over one's eyes, put one over on, swindle, take (in), trick.

gullet *n* craw, crop, maw, esophagus, throat, weasand.

gullibility *n* credulity, foolishness, innocence, naïvety, simplicity, trustfulness.

antonym astuteness.

gullible *adj* born yesterday, credulous, foolish, green, innocent, naïve, trusting, unsuspecting.

antonyms astute, nobody's fool.

gully *n* channel, coulee, ditch, gulch, gutter, ravine, watercourse.

gulp *v* bolt, choke, devour, gasp, gobble, gormandize, guzzle, knock back, quaff, stifle, stuff, swallow, swig, swill, toss off, wolf.

antonyms nibble, sip.

n draft, lungful, mouthful, slug, swallow, swig.

gum *n* adhesive, cement, glue, goo, mucilage, paste, resin, sap.

v affix, cement, clog, fix, glue, paste, seal, stick.

gumboil *n* abscess, infection, swelling.

gummy *adj* adhesive, gluey, gooey, sticky, tacky, viscid, viscous.

gumption *n* astuteness, cleverness, common sense, discernment, enterprise, horse sense, initiative, mother wit, native intelligence, resourcefulness, sagacity, savvy, shrewdness, spirit, wit(s).

antonym foolishness.

gun *n* cannon, equalizer, fieldpiece, firearm, mortar, musket, peacemaker, persuader, piece, pistol, rifle, shooter, shooting iron, shotgun, tool.

gunman *n* assassin, bandit, bravo, desperado, gangster, gunslinger, hatchet man, hit man, killer, marksman, mobster, murderer, sniper, terrorist, thug.

gurgle v babble, bubble, burble, coo, crow, lap, murmur, plash, purl, ripple, splash.
n babble, burbling, murmur, purl, ripple.

guru n authority, expert, guide, instructor, leader, luminary, maharishi, master, mentor, pundit, sage, savant, Svengali, swami, teacher, tutor.

gush v babble, blather, burst, cascade, chatter, drivel, effuse, enthuse, flood, flow, jabber, jet, pour, rave, run, rush, spout, spurt, stream.
n babble, burst, cascade, chatter, drivel, ebullition, effusion, eruption, exuberance, flood, flow, jet, outburst, outflow, rush, slop, spout, spurt, stream, tide, torrent.

gushing adj cloying, effusive, emotional, excessive, fulsome, gushy, mawkish, overdone, overenthusiastic, saccharine, sentimental.
antonyms restrained, sincere.

gust n blast, breeze, burst, flaw, flurry, gale, puff, rush, squall, williwaw.
v blast, blow, bluster, breeze, puff, squall.

gusto n appetite, appreciation, brio, delight, élan, enjoyment, enthusiasm, exhilaration, exuberance, fervour, liking, pleasure, relish, verve, zeal, zest.
antonyms apathy, distaste.

gusty adj blowy, blustering, blustery, breezy, squally, stormy, tempestuous, windy.
antonym calm.

gut v clean, clean out, despoil, disembowel, draw, dress, empty, eviscerate, exenterate, gill, pillage, plunder, ransack, ravage, rifle, sack, strip.
adj basic, deep-seated, emotional, heartfelt, innate, instinctive, intuitive, involuntary, natural, spontaneous, strong, unthinking, visceral.

gutless adj abject, chicken, chicken-hearted, chicken-livered, cowardly, craven, emasculated, faint-hearted, feeble, irresolute, lily-livered, spineless, submissive, timid, weak, weak-kneed, weak-willed, wimpy, wishy-washy.
antonym courageous.

guts n audacity, backbone, belly, boldness, bowels, chutzpah, courage, daring, endurance, entrails, forcefulness, fortitude, grit, hardihood, innards, insides, intestines, inwards, mettle, nerve, pluck, spirit, spunk, stamina, staying power, stomach, tenacity, toughness, viscera.
antonym spinelessness.

gutsy adj bold, brave, courageous, daring, determined, forceful, gallant, game, indomitable, mettlesome, passionate, plucky, resolute, spirited, spunky, staunch, tough.
antonyms quiet, spineless, timid.

gutter n channel, conduit, ditch, drain, duct, pipe, sluice, trench, trough, tube.

guttersnipe n gamin, ragamuffin, street child, tatterdemalion, urchin, waif.

guttural adj deep, grating, gravelly, gruff, harsh, hoarse, husky, low, rasping, rough, thick, throaty.
antonym dulcet.

guy n bloke, cat, chap, codger, customer, duffer, fellow, geezer, individual, lad, man, person, tyke, youth.

guzzle v gulp, knock back, quaff, swig, swill, toss off.

Gypsy, gypsy n Bohemian, nomad, rambler, roamer, Romany, rover, traveller, tzigane, vagabond, vagrant, wanderer.

gyrate v bump and grind, circle, pirouette, revolve, rotate, spin, spiral, twirl, whirl.

gyrating adj gyral, revolving, rotating, spinning, twirling, whirling.

gyration n convolution, gyre, pirouette, revolution, rotation, spin, spinning, spiral, twirl, whirl, whirling.

H

habit¹ *n* accustomedness, addiction, bent, constitution, convention, custom, dependence, disposition, fixation, force of habit, habitude, inclination, manner, mannerism, mode, nature, obsession, practice, proclivity, propensity, quirk, routine, rut, second nature, tendency, trick, usage, vice, way, weakness, wont.

habit² *n* apparel, attire, clothes, clothing, dress, garb, garment, habiliment, outfit.

habitat *n* abode, domain, element, environment, home, locality, surroundings, terrain, territory.

habitation *n* abode, cottage, domicile, dwelling, dwelling place, home, house, hut, inhabitance, living quarters, lodging, mansion, occupancy, occupation, quarters, residence, tenancy.

habitual *adj* accustomed, chronic, common, confirmed, constant, customary, established, familiar, fixed, frequent, hardened, ingrained, inveterate, natural, normal, ordinary, persistent, recurrent, regular, routine, standard, traditional, usual, wonted.

antonym occasional.

habituate *v* acclimatize, accustom, adapt, break in, condition, discipline, familiarize, harden, inure, school, season, tame, train.

habitué *n* denizen, fan, frequenter, patron, regular, regular customer.

hack¹ *v* bark, chop, cope with, cough, cut, gash, haggle, handle, hew, kick, lacerate, mangle, mutilate, notch, rasp, sever, slash, tolerate.

n bark, chop, cough, cut, gash, notch, rasp, slash.

hack² *n* crock, drudge, hack writer, horse, jade, journalist, mercenary, nag, scribbler, slave, workhorse.

hackneyed *adj* banal, clichéd, common, commonplace, corny, dull, familiar, hand-me-down, overused, overworked, pedestrian, played-out, stale, stereotyped, stock, threadbare, timeworn, tired, trite, unoriginal, well-known, worn-out.

antonyms arresting, new.

hag *n* battle-axe, beldam, crone, fury, harpy, harridan, ogress, shrew, termagant, virago, vixen, witch.

haggard *adj* cadaverous, careworn, drawn, emaciated, gaunt, ghastly, hollow-eyed, peaked, pinched, shrunken, thin, wan, wasted, workworn, worn, wrinkled.

antonym hale.

haggle (with) *v* argue, bargain, beat down, bicker, chaffer, dicker, dispute, drive a (hard) bargain, higgle, niggle, palter, quarrel, squabble, work out a deal, wrangle.

hail¹ *v* assail, barrage, batter, bombard, pelt, rain, shower, storm, volley.

n barrage, bombardment, rain, shower, storm, torrent, volley.

hail² *v* acclaim, accost, acknowledge, address, applaud, call, cheer, exalt, flag down, glorify, greet, halloo, honour, salute, shout, signal (to), wave (to or at), welcome.

n call, cry, halloo, shout.

hair *n* locks, mane, mop, shock, tresses, vibrissa, villus.

hairdo *n* coiffure, cut, haircut, hairstyle, perm, permanent wave, set, style.

hairdresser *n* barber, beautician, coiffeur, coiffeuse, friseur, hairstylist, stylist.

hairless *adj* bald, baldheaded, baldpated, beardless, clean-shaven, depilated, glabrous, naked, shorn, smooth, smooth-faced, tonsured.

antonym hairy.

hairpiece *n* fall, switch, toupee, wig.

hair-raising *adj* alarming, bloodcurdling, breathtaking, creepy, eerie, exciting, frightening, ghastly, ghostly, horrifying, paralyzing, petrifying, scary, shocking, spine-chilling, startling, terrifying, thrilling.

antonym calming.

hair's-breadth *n* fraction, hair, inch, jot, whisker.

antonym mile.

hair-splitting *adj* captious, carping, cavilling, faultfinding, fine, finicky, fussy, nice, niggling, nit-picking, overnice, over-refined, pettifogging, picky, quibbling, subtle, word-splitting.

antonym unfussy.

hairy¹ *adj* bearded, bewhiskered, bushy, crinite, fleecy, furry, fuzzy, hirsute, hispid, pilose, risky, scary, shaggy, stubbly, unshaven, unshorn, villous, woolly.

antonyms bald, clean-shaven.

hairy² *adj* bad, dangerous, dicey, difficult, harrowing, hazardous, perilous, risky, rough, scary, tricky.

halcyon *adj* balmy, calm, carefree, flourishing, gentle, golden, happy, mild, pacific, peaceful, placid, pleasant, prosperous, quiet, serene, still, tranquil, undisturbed.
antonyms chaotic, disastrous, stormy.

hale *adj* able-bodied, athletic, blooming, fit, flourishing, full of beans, healthy, hearty, in fine fettle, in the pink, robust, sound, spry, strong, vigorous, well, youthful.
antonym ill.

half *n* bisection, division, fifty percent, fraction, half-share, hemisphere, portion, section, segment, semester.
adj divided, fractional, halved, incomplete, limited, moderate, part, partial, semi-.
antonym whole.
adv barely, imperfectly, in part, inadequately, incompletely, partially, partly, slightly.
antonym completely.

half-baked *adj* brainless, crazy, foolish, harebrained, ill-conceived, ill-judged, impractical, senseless, short-sighted, silly, stupid, unplanned.
antonym sensible.

half-caste *n* mestiza, mestizo, Métis, Métisse, mulatta, mulatto, quadroon, quarter-blood.

half-hearted *adj* apathetic, cool, indifferent, lackadaisical, lacklustre, listless, lukewarm, neutral, passive, perfunctory, unenthusiastic, uninterested, weak.
antonym enthusiastic.

halfway *adv* barely, imperfectly, in the middle, incompletely, midway, moderately, nearly, partially, partly, rather, slightly.
antonym completely.
adj central, equidistant, incomplete, intermediate, mid, middle, midway, partial, part-way.
antonym complete.

half-wit *n* cretin, dimwit, dolt, dullard, dunce, dunderhead, fool, idiot, imbecile, moron, nitwit, nut, simpleton.
antonym brain.

half-witted *adj* addle-brained, backward, barmy, batty, crazy, cretinous, dull, dull-witted, feeble-minded, foolish, idiotic, moronic, nuts, nutty, silly, simple, simple-minded, stupid, two bricks short of a load.
antonym clever.

hall *n* assembly-room, auditorium, basilica, building, chamber, concert hall, concourse, corridor, entrance, entry, foyer, hallway, lobby, passageway, salon, saloon, vestibule.

hallmark *n* authentication, badge, brand name, device, emblem, endorsement, indication, label, mark, seal, sign, stamp, symbol, trademark.

hallowed *adj* age-old, beatified, blessed, consecrated, dedicated, established, holy, honoured, inviolable, revered, sacred, sacrosanct, sainted, sanctified.

hallucinate *v* daydream, fantasize, freak out, imagine, see things, trip out.

hallucination *n* aberration, apparition, delusion, dream, fantasy, figment (of the imagination), illusion, mirage, phantasmagoria, pink elephants, trip, vision.

halo *n* aura, aureole, circle, corona, gloria, gloriole, glory, halation, nimbus, radiance.

halt *v* arrest, block, break off, call it a day, cease, check, curb, desist, discontinue, draw up, end, impede, obstruct, pack it in, quit, rest, stem, stop, terminate, wait.
antonyms assist, continue, start.
n arrest, break, close, delay, end, impasse, interruption, pause, stand, standstill, stop, stoppage, termination, way station.
antonyms continuation, start.

halting *adj* awkward, broken, faltering, hesitant, imperfect, laboured, slow, stammering, stumbling, stuttering, uncertain.
antonym fluent.

halve *v* bisect, cut, divide, go Dutch, in half, lessen, reduce, share, split.

hammer *v* bang, beat, clobber, defeat, din, drive, drive home, drub, drum, grind, hit, impress (upon), knock, make, nag, pound, shape, slate, thrash, thump, trounce, worst.
n ball-peen, beetle, gavel, mall, mallet, maul.

hammer out complete, contrive, excogitate, fashion, finish, forge, form, negotiate, produce, settle, shape, sort out, thrash out, work out.

hamper *v* bind, burden, cramp, cumber, curb, curtail, distort, embarrass, encumber, entangle, fetter, frustrate, hamstring, handicap, hinder, hobble, hold up, impede, interfere with, obstruct, prevent, restrain, restrict, shackle, slow down, thwart, trammel.
antonyms aid, expedite.

hamstrung *adj* balked, crippled, disabled, foiled, frustrated, helpless, hors de combat, incapacitated, paralysed, stymied.

hand¹ *n* ability, agency, aid, applause, art, artistry, assistance, calligraphy, chirography, clap, control, direction, fist, flipper, governance, handwriting, help, influence, mitt, ovation, palm, part, participation, paw, penmanship, script, share, skill, support.
v aid, assist, conduct, convey, deliver, give, guide, help, lead, offer, pass, present, provide, transmit, yield.

at hand approaching, at one's elbow, at one's fingertips, available, close, handy, immediate, imminent, impending, in the offing, near, nearby, nigh, on tap, ready.

from hand to mouth dangerously, from day to day, improvidently, in poverty, insecurely, necessitously, on the breadline, precariously, uncertainly.

hand down announce, bequeath, give, grant, pass on, transfer, will.

hand in glove allied, in cahoots, thick, in collusion, in league, intimate.

hand out deal out, deliver, disburse, dish out, dispense, disseminate, distribute, dole out, give (out), mete (out).

hand over deliver, donate, fork out, give up,

present, release, relinquish, surrender, transfer, turn over, yield up.

antonym retain.

hand² *n* artificer, artisan, craftsman, employee, farm hand, hired man, hireling, labourer, operative, operation, worker, workman.

handbook *n* Baedeker, companion, guide, guidebook, instruction book, manual, resource book, rule book, vade mecum.

handcuff *v* fasten, fetter, manacle, restrain, secure, shackle, tie.

handcuffs *n* bracelets, cuffs, fetters, manacles, mittens, shackles, wristlets.

handful *n* few, scattering, smattering, sprinkling.

antonym lot.

handicap *n* barrier, block, burden, defect, disability, disadvantage, drawback, encumbrance, hindrance, impairment, impediment, impost, limitation, millstone, obstacle, odds, penalty, restriction, shortcoming, stumbling-block.

antonyms assistance, benefit.

v burden, disadvantage, encumber, hamper, hamstring, hinder, impede, limit, restrict.

antonyms assist, further.

handicraft *n* art, artisanship, craft, craftsmanship, handiwork, skill, workmanship.

handiness *n* accessibility, adroitness, aptitude, availability, cleverness, closeness, convenience, deftness, dexterity, efficiency, expertise, knack, practicality, proficiency, proximity, skill, usefulness, workability.

antonym clumsiness.

handiwork *n* achievement, artifact, craft, creation, design, doing, handicraft, handwork, invention, product, result, work.

handle *n* ear, grasp, grip, haft, handgrip, helve, hilt, knob, lug, name, stock, title.

v administer, carry, conduct, control, cope with, deal in, deal with, direct, discourse upon, discuss, feel, finger, fondle, grasp, have (or take) charge of, hold, manage, manipulate, manoeuvre, market, maul, operate, paw, pick up, see to, sell, steer, stock, supervise, take care of, touch, trade in, traffic in, treat, use, wield.

handling *n* administration, approach, conduct, direction, discussion, management, manipulation, operation, running, transaction, treatment.

handout¹ *n* alms, charity, dole, donation, freebie, issue, largesse(e).

handout² *n* bulletin, circular, free sample, leaflet, literature, notes, pamphlet, press release, statement.

hand-picked *adj* choice, chosen, elect, elite, picked, recherché, screened, select, selected.

hands *n* authority, care, charge, clutches, command, control, custody, disposal, grasp, grip, governance, guardianship, guidance, jurisdiction, keeping, possession, power, supervision, tutelage.

hands down easily, effortlessly, in a walk,

no sweat, with both hands tied behind one's back, with ease.

antonym with difficulty.

handsome *adj* abundant, admirable, ample, attractive, beau, beautiful, becoming, bountiful, comely, considerable, elegant, fine, generous, good-looking, graceful, gracious, large, liberal, magnanimous, majestic, personable, plentiful, seemly, sizable, stately, well-favoured, well-mannered, well-proportioned.

antonyms mean, ugly.

handsomely *adv* abundantly, amply, beautifully, bountifully, generously, lavishly, liberally, magnanimously, munificently, plentifully, richly, unsparingly, unstintingly.

antonym stingily.

handwriting *n* cacography, calligraphy, chirography, fist, graphology, hand, longhand, penmanship, scrawl, script.

handy *adj* accessible, adept, adroit, at hand, available, clever, close, convenient, deft, dexterous, expert, helpful, manageable, near, nearby, neat, nimble, practical, proficient, ready, serviceable, skilful, skilled, useful.

antonyms clumsy, inconvenient, unwieldy.

handyman *n* do-it-yourselfer, factotum, famulus, Jack of all trades, man of the world, Mr. Fix-it, odd-jobber.

hang *v* attach, bow, cling, cover, dangle, deck, decorate, depend, drape, droop, drop, execute, fasten, fix, float, furnish, gibbet, hesitate, hinge, hold, hover, incline, lean, loll, lower, remain, rest, sag, stick, string up, suspend, swing, trail, turn, waver, weep.

hang around associate with, consort, dally, frequent, hang out, haunt, linger, loiter, resort to, tarry, waste time.

hang back balk, demur, drag one's feet, hesitate, hold back, pull back, recoil, shy away.

hang fire delay, hang back (or on), hold back, hold on, postpone, procrastinate, stall, stick, stop, vacillate, wait.

antonym press on.

hang on carry on, cling, clutch, continue, endure, grasp, grip, hang fire, hang in there, hold fast, hold on, hold out, hold the line, persevere, persist, remain, rest, stick it out, stop, wait.

antonym give up.

hang over impend, loom, menace, threaten.

hangdog *adj* abject, browbeaten, cowed, cringing, defeated, downcast, furtive, guilty, miserable, shamefaced, sneaking, wretched.

antonym bold.

hanger-on *n* adherent, camp follower, dependant, follower, freeloader, lackey, leech, minion, parasite, sponger, sycophant, toadeater, toady.

hanging¹ *adj* dangling, drooping, flapping, flopping, floppy, loose, pendent, pendulous, pensile, suspended, swinging, unattached, undecided, unresolved, unsettled, unsupported.

hanging² *n* cover, dossal, drape, drapery, drop, pendant.

hangout *n* den, dive, gathering place, haunt, home, joint, pad, rendezvous, resort, stamping ground, watering hole.

hangover *n* after-effects, crapulence, morning after.

hang-up *n* block, delay, difficulty, idée fixe, inhibition, mental block, obsession, obstacle, preoccupation, problem, thing (about).

hank *n* coil, length, loop, piece, roll, skein.

hanker for (or **after**) covet, crave, desire, hunger for, itch for, long for, lust after, pant for, pine for, thirst for, want, wish, yearn for, yen for.

antonym dislike.

hankering *n* craving, desire, hunger, itch, longing, pining, thirst, urge, wish, yearning, yen.

antonym dislike.

hanky-panky *n* cheating, chicanery, deception, devilry, dishonesty, funny business, jiggery-pokery, knavery, machinations, mischief, monkey business, nonsense, shenanigans, subterfuge, trickery, tricks.

antonym openness.

haphazard *adj* accidental, aimless, arbitrary, careless, casual, chance, disorderly, disorganized, flukey, hit-or-miss, indiscriminate, promiscuous, random, slapdash, slipshod, unmethodical, unordered, unsystematic.

antonyms deliberate, planned.

hapless *adj* cursed, down on one's luck, ill-fated, ill-starred, jinxed, luckless, miserable, out of luck, star-crossed, unfortunate, unhappy, unlucky, wretched.

antonym lucky.

happen *v* appear, arise, befall, chance, come about, crop up, develop, ensue, eventuate, fall out, follow, materialize, occur, result, supervene, take place, transpire, turn out.

happen on chance on, come on, discover, find, hit on, light on, stumble on.

happening *n* accident, adventure, affair, case, chance, circumstance, episode, event, experience, incident, occasion, occurrence, phenomenon, proceeding, scene.

happily *adv* agreeably, appropriately, aptly, auspiciously, blithely, by chance, cheerfully, contentedly, delightedly, enthusiastically, favourably, felicitously, fittingly, fortunately, freely, gaily, gladly, gleefully, gracefully, heartily, joyfully, joyously, luckily, merrily, opportunely, propitiously, providentially, seasonably, successfully, willingly, with pleasure.

antonym unhappily.

happiness *n* beatitude, blessedness, bliss, cheer, cheerfulness, cheeriness, chirpiness, contentment, delight, ecstasy, elation, enjoyment, euphoria, exuberance, felicity, gaiety, gladness, high spirits, joy, joyfulness, jubilation, light-heartedness, merriment, pleasure, satisfaction, well-being.

antonym unhappiness.

happy *adj* advantageous, appropriate, apt, auspicious, blessed, blissful, blithe, cheerful, content, contented, convenient, delighted, ecstatic, elated, enviable, euphoric, expedient, exuberant, favourable, felicitous, fit, fitting, fortunate, glad, gratified, happy as a lark, idyllic, in raptures, in (seventh) heaven, jolly, joyful, joyous, jubilant, lucky, merry, on cloud nine, opportune, over the moon, overjoyed, pleased (as punch), promising, propitious, radiant, satisfactory, Saturnian, seasonable, starry-eyed, successful, sunny, thrilled, tickled pink, timely, well-chosen, well-timed.

antonym unhappy.

happy medium golden mean, juste milieu, middle course, middle ground, via media.

antonym excess.

happy-go-lucky *adj* blithe, carefree, casual, cheerful, devil-may-care, easygoing, heedless, improvident, insouciant, irresponsible, laid back, light-hearted, nonchalant, reckless, unconcerned, untroubled, unworried.

antonyms anxious, wary.

harangue *n* address, declamation, diatribe, discourse, exhortation, homily, lecture, oration, peroration, philippic, sermon, speech, spiel, tirade.

v address, declaim, descant, exhort, hold forth, lecture, orate, perorate, preach, preachify, rant, sermonize, speechify, spout.

harass *v* annoy, badger, bait, beleaguer, besiege, bother, chivvy, distress, disturb, exasperate, exhaust, fatigue, harry, hassle, hound, molest, perplex, persecute, pester, plague, tease, tire, torment, trouble, vex, wear out, weary, worry.

antonym assist.

harassed *adj* beleaguered, careworn, distraught, distressed, harried, hassled, hounded, pestered, plagued, pressured, strained, stressed, tormented, troubled, vexed, worried.

antonym carefree.

harbinger *n* avant-coureur, forerunner, foretoken, herald, indication, messenger, omen, portent, precursor, presage, sign, warning.

harbour *n* anchorage, asylum, cove, covert, destination, haven, marina, outport, port, refuge, roadstead, sanctuary, sanctum, security, shelter.

v believe, cherish, cling to, conceal, entertain, foster, hide, hold, house, imagine, lodge, maintain, nurse, nurture, protect, retain, secrete, shelter, shield.

hard *adj* acrimonious, actual, addictive, adverse, alcoholic, angry, antagonistic, arduous, backbreaking, baffling, bare, bitter, burdensome, calamitous, callous, cast-iron, cold, compact, complex, complicated, concrete, cruel, crusty, dark, definite, demanding, dense, difficult, disagreeable, disastrous, distressing, draining, driving, exacting, exhausting, fatiguing, fierce, firm, flinty, forceful, formidable, glutinous, grievous, grim, habit-forming, hard-hearted, harsh, heartless, heavy, herculean, hostile, impenetrable, implacable, indisputable, industrious, inflexible, intolerable, intricate, involved, irony, knotty, laborious, marblelike, obdurate, painful, perplexing, persistent, pitiless, plain, powerful, puzzling, rancorous, real, resentful, rigid, rigorous, ruthless, severe, shrewd, solid, stable, stark, stern, stiff, stony, strenuous, strict, stringent, strong, stubborn, tangled, thorny, tight, tiring, toilsome, tough, unbending, undeniable, unfathomable, unfeeling, ungentle, unjust, unkind, unpleasant, unrelenting, unsparing, unsympathetic, unvarnished, unyielding, uphill, verified, vigorous, violent, wearisome, wearying.

antonyms harmless, kind, mild, non-alcoholic, pleasant, pleasing, soft, yielding.

adv agonizingly, assiduously, badly, bitterly, close, completely, determinedly, diligently, distressingly, doggedly, earnestly, energetically, fiercely, forcefully, forcibly, fully, hardly, harshly, heavily, industriously, intensely, intently, keenly, laboriously, near, painfully, persistently, powerfully, rancorously, reluctantly, resentfully, rigorously, roughly, severely, sharply, slowly, solidly, sorely, steadily, strenuously, strictly, stringently, strongly, untiringly, vigorously, violently, with might and main, with a will.

antonyms gently, mildly, moderately, unenthusiastically.

hard and fast binding, carved in stone, fixed, immutable, incontrovertible, inflexible, invariable, rigid, set, strict, stringent, unalterable, unchangeable, unchanging.

antonym flexible.

hard up bankrupt, broke, bust, cleaned out, desperate, destitute, feeling the pinch, impecunious, impoverished, in the red, penniless, penurious, poor, short, strapped for cash.

antonym rich.

hard-bitten *adj* callous, case-hardened, cynical, down-to-earth, hard-boiled, hard-headed, hard-nosed, matter-of-fact, practical, realistic, ruthless, shrewd, tough, unsentimental, unyielding.

antonym callow.

hard-core *adj* blatant, card-carrying, dedicated, die-hard, dyed-in-the-wool, explicit, extreme, fanatical, intransigent, obstinate, rigid, staunch, steadfast.

antonym moderate.

harden *v* accustom, anneal, bake, brace, brutalize, buttress, cake, case-harden, clot, concrete, congeal, fortify, freeze, gird, habituate, indurate, inure, nerve, reinforce, season, set, solidify, steel, stiffen, strengthen, temper, toughen, train, vulcanize.

antonym soften.

hardened *adj* accustomed, callous, chronic, fixed, habitual, habituated, heartless, incorrigible, inured, inveterate, irredeemable, obdurate, reprobate, seasoned, set, shameless, solidified, toughened, unfeeling.

antonyms callow, soft.

hard-headed *adj* astute, clear-thinking, cool, hard-boiled, level-headed, practical, pragmatic, realistic, sensible, shrewd, tough, unsentimental.

antonyms sentimental, unrealistic.

hard-hearted *adj* callous, cold, cold-hearted, cruel, hard, heartless, indifferent, inhuman, inhumane, insensitive, intolerant, merciless, pitiless, stony, stony-hearted, uncaring, uncompassionate, unfeeling, unkind, unmerciful, unsympathetic.

antonyms kind, merciful.

hard-hitting *adj* condemnatory, critical, forceful, no-holds-barred, strongly-worded, tough, unsparing, vigorous.

antonym mild.

hardihood *n* assurance, audacity, backbone, boldness, brass, bravery, brazenness, cheek, courage, crust, daring, determination, effrontery, firmness, foolhardiness, fortitude, gall, grit, guts, hardiness, impertinence, impetuousness, impudence, intrepidity, mettle, nerve, pluck, prowess, rashness, recklessness, resolution, spirit, spunk, strength, temerity.

antonyms sense, timidity.

hardiness *n* boldness, courage, endurance, fortitude, hardihood, intrepidity, resilience, resolution, robustness, ruggedness, strength, sturdiness, toughness, valour.

antonyms fragility, frailty, timidity.

hard-line *adj* aggressive, definite, extreme, immoderate, inflexible, intransigent, militant, stern, tough, uncompromising, undeviating, unyielding.

antonym moderate.

hardly *adv* barely, by no means, faintly, harshly, infrequently, just, no way, not at all, not quite, only, only just, probably not, rarely, roughly, scarcely, severely, strictly, with difficulty.

antonyms easily, very.

hardness *n* callousness, coldness, difficulty, firmness, harshness, heartlessness, inhumanity, insensitivity, laboriousness, obduracy, pitilessness, rigidity, rigour, severity, solidity, steel, sternness, strictness, toughness.

antonyms ease, mildness, softness.

hard pressed *adj* hard put, harried, under pressure, up against it, with one's back to the wall.

antonyms relaxed, untroubled.

hardship *n* adversity, affliction, austerity, burden, calamity, destitution, difficulty, fatigue, grievance, labour, misery, misfortune, need, oppression, persecution, poverty, privation, straits, suffering, toil, torment, trial, tribulation, trouble, want.

antonym ease.

hard-wearing *adj* durable, long-lasting, resilient, resistant, rugged, stout, strong, sturdy, tough.

antonym delicate.

hardworking *adj* assiduous, busy, conscientious, diligent, energetic, indefatigable, industrious, sedulous, workaholic, zealous.

antonym lazy.

hardy *adj* audacious, bold, brave, brazen, courageous, daring, enduring, firm, fit, foolhardy, hale, headstrong, healthy, hearty, heroic, impudent, intrepid, lusty, manly, plucky, rash, reckless, resolute, robust, rugged, sound, spartan, stalwart, stout, stout-hearted, strong, sturdy, tough, valiant, valorous, vigorous.

antonyms unhealthy, weak.

harebrained *adj* asinine, careless, daft, empty-headed, flighty, foolhardy, foolish, giddy, half-baked, harum-scarum, headlong, heedless, imprudent, inane, mindless, rash, reckless, scatterbrained, unstable, unsteady, wild.

antonym sensible.

harem *n* purdah, seraglio, women's quarters, zenana.

hark *v* attend, give ear, hear, hearken, listen, mark, note, notice, pay attention, pay heed.

hark back go back, recall, recollect, regress, remember, reminisce (about), revert.

harlot *n* call girl, hooker, hussy, hustler, loose woman, prostitute, slut, streetwalker, strumpet, tart, tramp, whore.

harm *n* abuse, damage, detriment, disservice, evil, hurt, ill, immorality, impairment, iniquity, injury, loss, mischief, misfortune, scathe, sin, sinfulness, vice, wickedness, wrong.

antonyms benefit, service.

v abuse, blemish, damage, hurt, ill-treat, ill-use, impair, injure, maltreat, mar, molest, ruin, scathe, spoil, wound.

antonyms benefit, improve.

harmful *adj* adverse, baleful, baneful, damaging, deleterious, destructive, detrimental, disadvantageous, evil, hurtful, injurious, malicious, noxious, pernicious, pestiferous, pestilent, pestilential, unhealthy, unwholesome.

antonym harmless.

harmless *adj* gentle, innocent, innocuous, innoxious, inoffensive, meek and mild, non-harzardous, non-toxic, safe, unharmed, uninjured, unobjectionable, unscathed.

antonym harmful.

harmonious *adj* agreeable, amicable, balanced, compatible, concordant, congenial, congruous, consonant, co-ordinated, cordial, correspondent, dulcet, euphonic, euphonious, eurhythmic, friendly, harmonic, harmonizing, in accord, in harmony, like-minded, matching, mellifluous, melodious, musical, ordered, sweet-sounding, sympathetic, symphonious, tuneful.

antonym inharmonious.

harmonize *v* accommodate, accord, adapt, agree, align, arrange, attune, blend, chime, cohere, compose, conform, co-ordinate, correspond, dovetail, jibe, match, order, reconcile, square, suit, tally, tone.

antonym clash.

harmony *n* accord, agreement, amicability, amity, balance, compatibility, concord, conformity, congruity, consensus, consistency, consonance, co-operation, co-ordination, correspondence, counterpoint, diapason, euphony, eurhythmy, fitness, friendship, good will, harmonics, like-mindedness, melodiousness, melody, order, parallelism, peace, rapport, suitability, symmetry, sympathy, tune, tunefulness, unanimity, understanding, unity.

antonym discord.

harness *n* equipment, gear, reins, straps, tack, tackle, trappings.

v apply, channel, control, couple, employ, exploit, make use of, mobilize, saddle, turn to account, use, utilize, yoke.

harp on belabour, dwell on, emphasize, flog (to death), labour, nag about, press, reiterate, repeat, stress.

harpoon *n* arrow, barb, dart, spear, trident.

harpy *n* gold digger, harridan, man-eater, vamp, vampire.

harridan *n* battle-axe, dragon, fury, gorgon, harpy, hellcat, nag, scold, shrew, Tartar, termagant, virago, vixen, witch, Xanthippe.

harried *adj* agitated, anxious, beleaguered, beset, bothered, distressed, hagridden, harassed, hard-pressed, hassled, plagued, pressured, ravaged, tormented, troubled, worried.

antonym untroubled.

harrow *v* distress, harass, lacerate, rend, tear, torment, torture, vex, wound, wrack, wring.

antonyms assuage, hearten.

harrowing *adj* agonizing, alarming, chilling, distressing, disturbing, excruciating, frightening, heart-rending, lacerating, nerve-wracking, terrifying, tormenting, traumatic, wracking.

antonyms calming, heartening.

harry *v* annoy, attack, badger, bedevil, besiege, chivvy, despoil, devastate, disturb, fret, harass, hassle, maraud, molest, persecute, pester, pillage, plague, plunder, raid, ravage, rob, sack, tease, torment, trouble, vex, worry.

antonyms aid, calm.

harsh *adj* abrasive, abusive, acerbic, acrimonious, austere, bitter, bleak, brutal, coarse, comfortless, croaking, crude, cruel, discordant, dissonant, dour, draconian, forbidding, glaring, grating, grim, guttural, hard, jarring, pitiless, punitive, rasping, raucous, relentless, rough, ruthless, scabrous, severe, sharp, Spartan, stark, stern, strict, strident, stringent, unfeeling, ungentle, unkind, unmelodious, unpleasant, unrelenting.

antonyms mild, smooth, soft.

harum-scarum *adj* careless, erratic, flighty, giddy, haphazard, harebrained, hasty, ill-considered, impetuous, imprudent, irresponsible, precipitate, rash, reckless, scatterbrained, wild.

antonym sensible.

harvest n collection, consequence, crop, effect, fruition, gathering, harvesting, harvest time, ingathering, produce, product, reaping, result, return, yield.
v collect, garner, gather, glean, mow, pick, pluck, reap (in), win.

hash[1] n botch, confusion, hodgepodge, jumble, mess, mishmash, mixture, mix-up, muddle, shambles.

hash[2] n fricassee, goulash, hot pot, lobscouse, mulligan, ragout, scouse, stew.

hashish n bhang, cannabis, dope, grass, hash, hemp, joint, marijuana, MaryJane, pot, reefer, weed.

hassle n altercation, annoyance, argument, bickering, bother, commotion, difficulty, disagreement, dispute, fight, inconvenience, nuisance, pain, problem, quarrel, squabble, struggle, trial, trouble, tussle, upset, wrangle.
antonyms agreement, peace.
v annoy, argue (with), badger, be on (someone's) case, bother, bug, chivvy, harass, harry, hound, nag, pester, quarrel (with).
antonyms assist, calm.

haste n alacrity, briskness, bustle, celerity, dispatch, expedition, fleetness, hastiness, hurry, hurrying, hustle, impetuosity, nimbleness, precipitance, precipitation, promptness, quickness, rapidity, rashness, recklessness, rush, rushing, speed, swiftness, urgency, velocity.
antonyms care, deliberation, slowness.

hasten v accelerate, advance, be quick, bolt, dash, dispatch, expedite, facilitate, fly, gallop, goad, hightail it, hurry, make haste, move along, move it, precipitate, press, push, quicken, race, run, rush, scurry, scuttle, speed, speed up, sprint, step on it, step up, tear, trot, urge.
antonym dawdle.

hastily adv apace, double-quick, fast, heedlessly, hurriedly, impetuously, impulsively, on the double, posthaste, precipitately, prematurely, promptly, quickly, rapidly, rashly, recklessly, speedily, straightaway.
antonyms carefully, deliberately, slowly.

hasty adj brief, brisk, brusque, cursory, eager, excited, expeditious, fast, fiery, fleet, fleeting, foolhardy, headlong, heedless, hot-headed, hot-tempered, hurried, impatient, impetuous, impulsive, indiscreet, irascible, irritable, passing, passionate, perfunctory, precipitate, premature, prompt, quick, quick-tempered, rapid, rash, reckless, rushed, short, snappish, snappy, speedy, superficial, swift, thoughtless, urgent.
antonyms careful, deliberate, placid, slow.

hat n balaclava, beret, biretta, boater, bonnet, bowler, cap, lid, nightcap, panama, poke bonnet, skullcap, sombrero, southwester, top hat, trilby, tuque, turban, yarmulke.

hatch v be born, breed, brood, conceive, concoct, contrive, cook up, design, develop, devise, dream up, incubate, originate, plan, plot, project, scheme, think up.

hate v abhor, abominate, bear ill will to, be unwilling, despise, detest, dislike, execrate, hesitate, loathe.
antonym like.

hateful adj abhorrent, abominable, damnable, despicable, detestable, disgusting, execrable, forbidding, foul, heinous, horrible, loathsome, malicious, nasty, obnoxious, odious, offensive, repellent, repugnant, repulsive, revolting, vile.
antonym pleasing.

hatred n abhorrence, abomination, animosity, animus, antagonism, antipathy, aversion, despite, detestation, dislike, enmity, execration, hate, hostility, ill will, loathing, misandry, misanthropy, odium, repugnance, revulsion.
antonym like.

haughtiness n airs, aloofness, arrogance, conceit, contempt, contemptuousness, disdain, hauteur, insolence, loftiness, pomposity, pride, snobbishness, snootiness, superciliousness.
antonyms friendliness, humility.

haughty adj arrogant, assuming, cavalier, conceited, contemptuous, disdainful, high, high and mighty, hoity-toity, imperious, lofty, on one's high horse, overweening, proud, puffed up, scornful, snobbish, snooty, snotty, stuck-up, supercilious, superior.
antonyms friendly, humble.

haul v bouse, carry, cart, convey, drag, draw, hale, heave, hump, lug, move, pull, tow, trail, transport, trice, tug.
n booty, catch, drag, find, gain, harvest, heave, loot, pull, spoils, swag, take, takings, tug, yield.

haunches n bottom, buttocks, derrière, hips, hunkers, nates, rear end, rump, thighs.

haunt v beset, dog, frequent, hound, obsess, plague, possess, prey on, torment, trouble, visit, walk in, worry.
n den, gathering place, hangout, meeting place, rendezvous, resort, stamping ground, watering hole.

haunted adj cursed, eerie, ghostly, hagridden, jinxed, obsessed, plagued, possessed, preoccupied, spooky, tormented, troubled, worried.

haunting adj disturbing, eerie, evocative, indelible, memorable, nostalgic, persistent, poignant, recurrent, recurring, unforgettable.
antonym unmemorable.

have v accept, acquire, allow, bear, beget, cheat, comprehend, comprise, consider, contain, deceive, deliver, dupe, embody, endure, enjoy, entertain, experience, feel, fool, gain, get, give birth to, harbour, hold, include, keep, know, obtain, occupy, outwit, own, permit, possess, procure, produce, put up with, receive, retain, secure, suffer, sustain, swindle, take, tolerate, trick, undergo, understand.

have done with be through with, cease, desist, finish with, give up, stop, throw over, wash one's hands of.

have to be compelled to, be forced to, be

obliged to, be required to, have got to, must, ought to, should.

haven *n* anchorage, asylum, destination, harbour, port, refuge, retreat, roadstead, sanctuary, sanctum, shelter.

havoc *n* carnage, chaos, confusion, damage, depopulation, desolation, despoliation, destruction, devastation, disorder, disruption, mayhem, rack and ruin, ravages, ruin, shambles, slaughter, waste, wreck.

hawk[1] *v* bark, cry, market, offer, peddle, sell, tout, vend.

hawk[2] *n* buzzard, falcon, goshawk, haggard, tercel, warmonger.

hawker *n* cheapjack, colporteur, coster, costermonger, crier, huckster, pedlar, vendor.

haywire *adj* amiss, balled up, chaotic, confused, crazy, disarranged, disordered, disorganized, erratic, in disarray, kaput, mad, tangled, topsy-turvy, wild.

antonyms correct, in order.

hazard *n* accident, chance, coincidence, danger, deathtrap, endangerment, gamble, imperilment, jeopardy, luck, mischance, misfortune, mishap, obstacle, peril, risk, threat.

antonym safety.

v advance, attempt, chance, conjecture, dare, endanger, expose, gamble, imperil, jeopardize, offer, presume, proffer, put forward, risk, speculate, stake, submit, suggest, suppose, threaten, venture, volunteer.

hazardous *adj* chancy, dangerous, dicey, difficult, fraught with danger, hairy, haphazard, insecure, perilous, precarious, risky, thorny, ticklish, uncertain, unpredictable, unsafe.

antonyms safe, secure.

haze *n* cloud, confusion, daze, dimness, film, fog, mist, nebulosity, nebulousness, obscurity, smog, smokiness, steam, unclearness, vagueness, vapour.

hazy *adj* blurry, clouded, cloudy, confused, dim, dull, faint, foggy, fuzzy, ill-defined, in a daze, indefinite, indistinct, loose, milky, misty, muddled, muzzy, nebulous, obscure, overcast, smoky, uncertain, unclear, vague, veiled.

antonyms clear, definite.

head *n* apex, aptitude, bean, beginning, boss, brain, brains, capacity, cape, captain, caption, caput, chief, chieftain, chump, climax, commander, commencement, cock, conclusion, conk, cranium, crest, crisis, crown, culmination, director, end, faculty, flair, foam, fore, forefront, foreland, front, froth, godfather, head teacher, heading, headland, headmaster, headmistress, height, intellect, intelligence, leader, likeness, manager, master, mastermind, mental ability, mentality, mind, nob, noddle, noggin, noodle, nut, origin, pate, peak, pinnacle, pitch, point, portrait, promontory, rest room, rise, sconce, skull, source, start, subject, summit, superintendent, supervisor, talent, tip, toilet, top, topic, topknot, turning point, understanding, upperworks, van, vanguard, vertex, zenith.

antonyms foot, subordinate, tail.

adj arch, chief, commanding, directing, dominant, first, foremost, front, governing, highest, leading, main, pre-eminent, premier, prime, principal, supreme, top, topmost.

v cap, come to a head, command, control, crown, direct, front, govern, guide, lead, manage, oversee, point, precede, rule, run, steer, superintend, supervise, top.

head for aim for, be bound for, direct toward, gravitate toward, make a beeline for, make for, point to, steer for, turn for, zero in on.

head off avert, deflect, distract, divert, fend off, forestall, intercept, interpose, intervene, parry, prevent, stop, turn aside, ward off.

head over heels completely, headfirst, headlong, intensely, recklessly, thoroughly, uncontrollably, utterly, whole-heartedly, wildly.

headache *n* annoyance, bane, bother, hassle, inconvenience, migraine, neuralgia, nuisance, problem, trouble, vexation, worry.

head honcho *n* big cheese, captain, CEO, chief, leader, ruler, sachem, top banana, top dog.

heading *n* caption, descriptor, direction, division, headline, name, rubric, section, superscription, title, top part.

headland *n* bill, bluff, cape, cliff, foreland, head, peninsula, point, promontory.

headlong *adj* breakneck, dangerous, hasty, headfirst, headforemost, head-on, hell-for-leather, helter-skelter, impetuous, impulsive, inconsiderate, precipitate, reckless, thoughtless.

adv at breakneck speed, hastily, headfirst, headforemost, head-on, heedlessly, hellbent, hell for leather, helter-skelter, hurriedly, lickety-split, pell-mell, precipitately, rashly, thoughtlessly, wildly.

headquarters *n* base camp, centre, head office, high command, HQ, nerve centre, praetorium.

headstrong *adj* bullheaded, contrary, foolhardy, fractious, froward, heedless, imprudent, impulsive, intractable, mulish, obstinate, perverse, pig-headed, rash, reckless, self-willed, stubborn, ungovernable, unruly, wilful.

antonyms biddable, docile, obedient.

headway *n* advance(s), advancement, improvement(s), inroad(s), progress, progression.

heady *adj* exciting, exhilarating, hasty, impetuous, impulsive, inconsiderate, inebriant, intoxicating, overpowering, potent, precipitate, rash, reckless, stimulating, strong, thoughtless, thrilling.

heal *v* alleviate, ameliorate, assuage, compose, conciliate, cure, harmonize, mend, patch up, physic, reconcile, regenerate, remedy, restore, salve, settle, soothe, treat.

healing *adj* analeptic, assuaging, comforting, curative, emollient, gentle, healthful, healthy, lenitive, medicinal, mild, mitigative, palliative, remedial, restorative, restoring, sanative, soothing, styptic, therapeutic, vulnerary.

health n condition, constitution, fettle, fitness, form, good condition, haleness, healthiness, robustness, salubrity, shape, soundness, state, strength, tone, vigour, vitality, weal, welfare, well-being, wholesomeness.

antonyms disease, infirmity.

healthy *adj* active, alive and kicking, beneficial, blooming, bracing, fine, fit, fit as a fiddle, flourishing, good, hale (and hearty), hardy, healthful, health-giving, hearty, hygienic, in fine feather, in fine fettle, in fine form, in good condition, in good shape, in the pink, invigorating, large, nourishing, nutritious, physically fit, robust, salubrious, salutary, sound, strong, sturdy, vigorous, well, wholesome.

antonyms diseased, ill, infirm, sick, unhealthy.

heap n abundance, accumulation, aggregation, collection, cumulus, hoard, lot, mass, mound, mountain, pile, ruck, stack, stockpile, store, ton.

v accumulate, amass, assign, augment, bank, bestow, build, burden, collect, confer, gather, give generously, hoard, increase, lavish, load, mound, pile, shower, stack, stockpile, store.

heaps n a lot, abundance, great deal, lashings, load(s), lots, mass, millions, mint, ocean(s), oodles, plenty, pot(s), quantities, scores, stack(s), tons.

hear v acknowledge, ascertain, attend, be told, catch, discover, eavesdrop, examine, find, gather, hark, hearken, heed, judge, learn, listen (to), overhear, perceive, pick up, try, understand.

hearing n audience, audition, auditory range, ear, earshot, inquest, inquiry, inquisition, interview, investigation, perception, range, reach, review, sound, trial.

hearsay n bruit, buzz, gossip, grapevine, report, rumour, scuttlebutt, talk, talk of the town, tittle-tattle, unconfirmed report, word of mouth.

antonym hard evidence.

heart n affection, benevolence, boldness, bravado, bravery, centre, character, compassion, concern, core, courage, crux, disposition, emotion, essence, feeling, fervour, fortitude, guts, hub, humanity, inclination, kernel, love, marrow, mettle, middle, mind, nature, nerve, nerve centre, nub, nucleus, pith, pity, pluck, purpose, quintessence, resolution, root, sentiment, soul, spirit, spunk, sympathy, temperament, tenderness, ticker, understanding, will.

heart and soul absolutely, completely, devotedly, eagerly, entirely, gladly, heartily, unreservedly, whole-heartedly.

heartache n affliction, agony, anguish, bitterness, dejection, despair, despondency, distress, grief, heartbreak, heartsickness, pain, remorse, sadness, sorrow, suffering, torment, torture.

heartbreak n agony, anguish, dejection, desolation, despair, grief, misery, pain, sadness, sorrow, suffering.

antonyms elation, joy, relief.

heartbreaking *adj* agonizing, bitter, desolating, disappointing, distressing, grievous, harrowing, heart-rending, pitiful, poignant, sad, sorrowful, tragic.

antonyms heartening, heartwarming, joyful.

heartbroken *adj* broken-hearted, crestfallen, crushed, dejected, desolate, despondent, disappointed, disconsolate, disheartened, dispirited, down, downcast, grieved, heartsick, miserable, woebegone.

antonyms delighted, elated.

hearten v animate, assure, buck up, buoy up, cheer (up), comfort, console, embolden, encourage, gladden, incite, inspire, inspirit, pep up, reassure, revivify, rouse, stimulate.

antonym dishearten.

heartfelt *adj* ardent, cordial, deep, devoted, devout, earnest, fervent, genuine, hearty, honest, impassioned, profound, sincere, unfeigned, warm, whole-hearted.

antonyms false, insincere.

heartily *adv* absolutely, completely, cordially, deeply, eagerly, earnestly, enthusiastically, feelingly, fervently, genuinely, gladly, profoundly, resolutely, sincerely, strongly, thoroughly, totally, unfeignedly, very, very much, vigorously, warmly, with a will, zealously.

antonym reluctantly.

heartless *adj* brutal, callous, cold, cold-blooded, cold-hearted, cruel, hard, hard-hearted, harsh, inhuman, merciless, pitiless, severe, stern, uncaring, unfeeling, unkind.

antonyms considerate, kind, merciful, sympathetic.

heart-rending *adj* affecting, agonizing, distressing, harrowing, heartbreaking, moving, pathetic, piteous, pitiful, poignant, sad, tear-jerking, tragic.

heart-throb n dreamboat, matinée idol, pin-up, star.

heartwarming *adj* affecting, cheering, encouraging, gladsome, gratifying, heartening, moving, pleasant, pleasing, rewarding, satisfying, touching, warming.

antonym heartbreaking.

hearty *adj* active, affable, ample, ardent, cordial, doughty, eager, earnest, ebullient, effusive, energetic, enthusiastic, exuberant, fervent, filling, friendly, generous, genial, genuine, hale, hardy, healthy, heartfelt, honest, jovial, nourishing, real, robust, sincere, sizable, solid, sound, square, stalwart, strong, substantial, true, unfeigned, unreserved, vigorous, warm, well, whole-hearted.

antonyms cold, emotionless.

heat n agitation, anger, ardour, earnestness, excitement, fervour, fever, fieriness, fury, hotness, impetuosity, incandescence, intensity, passion, pressure, sizzle, sultriness, swelter, temperature, torridity, torture, trial, vehemence, violence, warmness, warmth, zeal.

antonyms cold(ness), coolness.

v animate, boil, chafe, excite, flush, glow, impassion, incite, inflame, inspirit, reheat, rouse, stimulate, stir, toast, warm up.

antonyms chill, cool.

heated *adj* acrimonious, angry, bitter, excited, fierce, fiery, frenzied, furious, hot, impassioned, intense, passionate, perfervid, raging, stormy, tempestuous, vehement, violent, warmed, zealous.

antonym dispassionate.

heathen *n* animist, barbarian, gentile, idolator, idolatress, infidel, pagan, pantheist, philistine, polytheist, savage, unbeliever.

antonym believer.

adj barbaric, gentile, godless, heathenish, idolatrous, infidel, irreligious, pagan, philistine, savage, unbelieving, uncivilized, unenlightened.

antonyms Christian, godly.

heave *v* billow, breathe, bulge, cast, chuck, dilate, drag, elevate, exhale, expand, fling, gag, groan, haul, heft, hitch, hoist, hurl, let fly, lever, lift, palpitate, pant, pitch, puff, pull, raise, retch, rise, send, sigh, sling, sob, spew, surge, suspire, swell, throb, throw, throw up, toss, tug, vomit.

heaven *n* an exalted state, bliss, ecstasy, Elysian fields, Elysium, empyrean, enchantment, ether, felicity, fiddler's green, firmament, happiness, happy hunting ground, hereafter, next world, nirvana, paradise, rapture, sky, transport, utopia, Valhalla, welkin, Zion.

antonym hell.

heavenly *adj* alluring, ambrosial, angelic, beatific, beautiful, blessed, blissful, celestial, delightful, divine, Elysian, empyrean, entrancing, excellent, exquisite, extra-terrestrial, glorious, godlike, holy, immortal, lovely, paradisiacal, rapturous, ravishing, seraphic, sublime, superb, superhuman, supernal, supernatural, wonderful.

antonym hellish.

heavens *n* ether, firmament, sky, the blue, the wild blue yonder, welkin.

heavily *adv* awkwardly, closely, clumsily, compactly, completely, considerably, copiously, decisively, deep, deeply, dejectedly, densely, dully, excessively, fast, frequently, gloomily, hard, heftily, laboriously, painfully, ponderously, profoundly, roundly, sluggishly, solidly, sound, soundly, thick, thickly, thoroughly, to excess, utterly, weightily, woodenly.

antonym lightly.

heaviness *n* arduousness, burdensomeness, deadness, dejection, depression, despondency, drowsiness, dullness, gloom, gloominess, glumness, gravity, grievousness, heftiness, languor, lassitude, melancholy, numbness, onerousness, oppression, oppressiveness, ponderousness, sadness, seriousness, severity, sleepiness,

sluggishness, somnolence, torpor, weight, weightiness.

antonyms lightness, liveliness.

heavy *adj* abundant, apathetic, boisterous, brooding, bulky, burdened, burdensome, clumpy, coarse, complex, considerable, copious, deep, dense, difficult, drowsy, dull, encumbered, excessive, gloomy, grave, grieving, grievous, hard, harsh, hefty, inactive, indolent, inert, intolerable, laborious, laden, large, leaden, listless, loaded, loud, lumpish, massive, melancholy, onerous, oppressed, oppressive, ponderous, portly, profound, profuse, rough, sad, serious, severe, slow, sluggish, sober, solemn, sombre, sorrowful, squab, squat, stodgy, stormy, stupid, tedious, tempestuous, thick, torpid, turbulent, vexatious, violent, wearisome, weighted (down), weighty, wild, wooden.

antonyms airy, insignificant, light.

heavy-handed *adj* autocratic, awkward, bungling, clumsy, cruel, domineering, graceless, harsh, inconsiderate, inept, inexpert, insensitive, maladroit, oppressive, overbearing, tactless, thoughtless, unsubtle.

heavy-hearted *adj* crushed, depressed, despondent, discouraged, disheartened, downcast, downhearted, forlorn, gloomy, glum, heartsick, heartsore, melancholy, miserable, morose, mournful, sad, sorrowful.

antonym light-hearted.

heckle *v* annoy, bait, barrack, catcall, disrupt, gibe, harass, interrupt, jeer, pester, shout down, taunt.

hectic *adj* animated, boisterous, chaotic, excited, fast, fevered, feverish, flurrying, flustering, frantic, frenetic, frenzied, furious, heated, rapid, riotous, tumultuous, turbulent, wild.

antonym leisurely.

hector *v* badger, bluster, browbeat, bully, bullyrag, chivvy, harass, huff, intimidate, menace, nag, provoke, threaten, worry.

hedge *n* barrier, boundary, compensation, counterbalance, dike, guard, hedgerow, insurance, protection, quickset, screen, windbreak.

v block, circumscribe, confine, cover, dodge, duck, equivocate, fortify, guard, hem in, hinder, insure, obstruct, protect, quibble, restrict, safeguard, shield, sidestep, stall, take precautions, temporize, waffle.

hedonism *n* dolce vita, epicureanism, epicurism, gratification, luxuriousness, pleasure-seeking, self-indulgence, sensualism, sensuality, sybaritism, voluptuousness.

antonym asceticism.

hedonist *n* bon vivant, epicure, epicurean, pleasure-seeker, sensualist, swinger, sybarite, voluptuary.

antonym ascetic.

heed *n* attention, care, caution, consideration, ear, heedfulness, mind, note, notice, reck, regard, respect, thought, watchfulness.

antonyms inattention, indifference, unconcern.

v attend, consider, follow, listen, mark, mind, note, obey, observe, pay attention, regard, take notice of.

antonyms disregard, ignore.

heedful *adj* attentive, careful, cautious, chary, circumspect, mindful, observant, prudent, regardful, vigilant, wary, watchful.

antonym heedless.

heedless *adj* careless, foolhardy, imprudent, inattentive, incautious, inconsiderate, incurious, inobservant, neglectful, negligent, oblivious, precipitate, rash, reckless, thoughtless, uncaring, unconcerned, unheedful, unheeding, unmindful, unobservant, unthinking.

antonym heedful.

heel[1] *n* crust, end, hallux, hock, remainder, spur, stub, stump.

heel[2] *n* blackguard, bounder, cad, hallux, rotter, scoundrel, stern, swine.

hefty *adj* ample, beefy, big, brawny, bulky, burly, colossal, considerable, cumbersome, forceful, heavy, hulking, husky, large, massive, muscular, ponderous, powerful, robust, solid, strapping, strong, substantial, thumping, tremendous, unwieldy, vigorous, weighty.

antonyms light, slight, small.

height *n* acme, altitude, apex, apogee, ceiling, climax, crest, crown, culmination, degree, dignity, elevation, eminence, exaltation, extremity, grandeur, highness, hill, limit, loftiness, maximum, mountain, ne plus ultra, peak, pinnacle, prominence, size, stature, summit, tallness, top, ultimate, utmost, vertex, zenith.

antonym depth.

heighten *v* add to, aggrandize, aggravate, amplify, augment, elevate, enhance, ennoble, exalt, greaten, improve, increase, intensify, magnify, raise, sharpen, strengthen, uplift.

antonyms decrease, diminish.

heinous *adj* abhorrent, abominable, atrocious, awful, bad, base, evil, execrable, flagrant, grave, hateful, hideous, immitigable, infamous, iniquitous, monstrous, nefarious, odious, outrageous, revolting, shocking, unspeakable, vicious, villainous, wicked.

heir *n* beneficiary, co-heir, co-heiress, heir apparent, heir-at-law, heiress, heritor, inheritor, scion, successor.

hell *n* abyss, Acheron, affliction, agony, anguish, bottomless pit, depths, Erebus, Gehenna, Hades, hellfire, infernal regions, inferno, lower regions, martyrdom, misery, nether world, Niflheim, nightmare, ordeal, suffering, Tartarus, Tophet, torment, trial, underworld, wretchedness.

antonym heaven.

hellbent *adj* bent, dead set, determined, fixed, intent, resolved, set, settled.

hellish *adj* abominable, accursed, atrocious, barbarous, cruel, damnable, damned, demoniacal, detestable, devilish, diabolical, execrable, fiendish, infernal, inhuman,

monstrous, nefarious, Stygian, sulphurous, vicious, violent, wicked.

antonym heavenly.

helm *n* command, control, driver's seat, position of leadership, reins, rudder, saddle, tiller, wheel.

hello *interj* bonjour, ciao, chimo, greetings, hail, hey, hi, hiya, how do you do, howdy, salutations, salve.

antonym goodbye.

help *v* abet, abstain from, aid, alleviate, ameliorate, assist, avoid, back, befriend, control, co-operate with, cure, ease, eschew, facilitate, forbear, further, heal, improve, keep from, lend a hand, mitigate, prevent, promote, refrain from, relieve, remedy, resist, restore, save, second, serve, shun, stand by, stop, subsidize, succour, support, withstand.

antonym hinder.

n advice, aid, aide, assistance, assistant, avail, benefit, co-operation, daily, employee, guidance, hand, helper, helping hand, leg up, remedy, servant, service, support, use, utility, worker.

antonym hindrance.

helper *n* abettor, adjutant, aide, ally, assistant, attendant, auxiliary, benefactor, coadjutor, collaborator, colleague, deputy, girl Friday, helpmate, man Friday, mate, P.A., partner, personal assistant, person Friday, right-hand man, Samaritan, second, subordinate, subsidiary, supporter.

helpful *adj* accommodating, advantageous, beneficent, beneficial, benevolent, caring, considerate, constructive, co-operative, favourable, fortunate, friendly, instrumental, kind, neighbourly, practical, productive, profitable, serviceable, supportive, sympathetic, timely, useful.

antonyms futile, useless, worthless.

helping *n* amount, dollop, piece, plateful, portion, ration, serving, share.

helpless *adj* abandoned, debilitated, defenceless, dependent, destitute, disabled, exposed, feeble, forlorn, friendless, impotent, incapable, incompetent, infirm, paralysed, powerless, unfit, unprotected, vulnerable, weak.

antonyms competent, enterprising, independent, resourceful, strong.

helpmate *n* assistant, associate, better half, companion, consort, helper, helpmeet, husband, other half, partner, spouse, support, wife.

helter-skelter *adv* carelessly, confusedly, hastily, headlong, hurriedly, impulsively, in disorder, pell-mell, rashly, recklessly, wildly.

adj anyhow, confused, disordered, disorderly, disorganized, haphazard, higgledy-piggledy, hit-or-miss, hurried, jumbled, muddled, random, topsy-turvy, unsystematic.

hem *n* border, edge, edging, fringe, margin, skirt, trimming.

v beset, border, circumscribe, confine, edge,

encircle, enclose, engird, environ, fimbriate, gird, hedge, restrain, restrict, skirt, surround.

hence *adv* accordingly, ergo, therefore, thus.

henceforth *adv* from now on, hence, henceforward, hereafter, hereinafter, in future.

henchman *n* aide, associate, attendant, bodyguard, cohort, crony, follower, hanger-on, heavy, heeler, jackal, lackey, minder, minion, myrmidon, right-hand man, running dog, satellite, sidekick, subordinate, supporter.

henpeck *v* badger, browbeat, bully, carp at, cavil, chide, chivvy, criticize, domineer, find fault with, harass, hector, intimidate, nag, niggle at, pester, scold, torment.

henpecked *adj* browbeaten, bullied, cringing, dominated, intimidated, meek, obedient, subject, subjugated, timid.
antonym dominant.

herald *n* courier, crier, delegate, forerunner, harbinger, indication, messenger, omen, precursor, sign, signal, token.
v advertise, announce, broadcast, forebode, foretoken, harbinger, indicate, pave the way, portend, precede, presage, proclaim, prognosticate, promise, publicize, publish, show, trumpet, usher in.

heraldry *n* arms, badge, blazonry, ceremony, crest, emblazonry, emblem, ensign, escutcheon, hatchment, insignia, pageantry, pomp, regalia.

herculean *adj* arduous, athletic, brawny, colossal, daunting, demanding, difficult, enormous, exacting, exhausting, formidable, gigantic, great, gruelling, hard, heavy, huge, husky, laborious, large, mammoth, massive, mighty, muscular, onerous, powerful, prodigious, rugged, sinewy, stalwart, strapping, strenuous, strong, sturdy, titanic, toilsome, tough, tremendous.

herd *n* assemblage, canaille, collection, cowherd, crowd, crush, drove, flock, goatherd, herdboy, herdsman, horde, mass, mob, multitude, populace, press, rabble, riffraff, shepherd, swarm, the hoi polloi, the masses, the plebs, throng.
v assemble, associate, collect, congregate, drive, flock, force, gather, goad, guard, guide, huddle, lead, muster, protect, rally, shepherd, spur, watch.

herder *n* cowboy, cowgirl, cowherd, cowman, cowpoke, cowpuncher, drover, gaucho, goatherd, grazier, herdsman, stockman, vaquero, wrangler.

hereafter *adv* after this, eventually, hence, henceforth, henceforward, in (the) future, later.
n afterlife, afterworld, Elysian fields, happy hunting ground, heaven, life after death, next world.

here and there from pillar to post, hither and thither, passim, sparsely, sporadically, to and fro.

hereditary *adj* ancestral, bequeathed, congenital, family, genetic, handed down, inborn, inbred, inheritable, inherited, innate,

patrimonial, traditional, transmissible, transmittable, transmitted, willed.

heresy *n* apostasy, dissidence, error, free thinking, free thought, heterodoxy, iconoclasm, impiety, revisionism, schism, unorthodoxy.
antonym orthodoxy.

heretic *n* apostate, dissenter, dissident, free thinker, iconoclast, nonconformist, renegade, revisionist, schismatic.
antonym conformist.

heretical *adj* free-thinking, heterodox, iconoclastic, idolatrous, impious, infidel, irreverent, rationalistic, revisionist, schismatic, unorthodox.
antonyms conformist, conventional, orthodox.

heritage *n* bequest, birthright, deserts, due, endowment, estate, history, inheritance, legacy, lot, past, patrimony, portion, record, share, tradition.

hermetic *adj* airtight, obscure, resistant, sealed, secret, shut, watertight.

hermit *n* anchorite, ascetic, eremite, loner, monk, recluse, solitary.

hero(ine) *n* celebrity, champion, conqueror, exemplar, god, goddess, good guy, heart-throb, ideal, idol, male (or female) lead, paragon, protagonist, star, superstar, victor.

heroic *adj* bold, brave, classic, classical, courageous, daring, dauntless, doughty, elevated, epic, extravagant, fearless, gallant, game, grand, grandiose, gritty, Homeric, intrepid, legendary, lion-hearted, mythological, noble, spunky, stout-hearted, undaunted, valiant, valorous.
antonyms cowardly, pusillanimous, timid.

heroism *n* boldness, bravery, courage, courageousness, daring, derring-do, fearlessness, fortitude, gallantry, gameness, grit, intrepidity, prowess, spirit, valour.
antonyms cowardice, pusillanimity, timidity.

hero-worship *n* admiration, adoration, adulation, deification, idealization, idolization, veneration.

hesitancy *n* demur, disinclination, doubt, doubtfulness, dubiety, dubiousness, hesitation, indecision, irresolution, misgiving, qualm, reluctance, reservation, uncertainty, unwillingness, wavering.
antonyms certainty, willingness.

hesitant *adj* cautious, diffident, dilatory, doubtful, half-hearted, halting, hesitating, irresolute, reluctant, sceptical, shy, timid, uncertain, undecided, unsure, unwilling, vacillating, wavering.
antonyms resolute, staunch.

hesitate *v* balk, be reluctant, be uncertain, be unwilling, boggle, delay, demur, dither, doubt, falter, fumble, halt, pause, scruple, shilly-shally, shrink, shy away, stammer, stumble, stutter, think twice, vacillate, wait, waver.

hesitation *n* caution, delay, demurral, doubt, dubiety, faltering, fumbling, hesitancy, indecision, irresolution, misdoubt, misgiving(s), pause, qualm(s), reluctance, scruple(s), second thought(s), stammering, stumbling, stuttering, uncertainty, unwillingness, vacillation.

antonyms alacrity, assurance, eagerness.

heterodox *adj* dissident, free-thinking, heretical, iconoclastic, non-conformist, revisionist, schismatic, unorthodox, unsound.

antonym orthodox.

heterogeneous *adj* assorted, catholic, contrary, contrasted, different, discrepant, disparate, dissimilar, divergent, diverse, diversified, incongruous, miscellaneous, mixed, motley, multiform, opposed, polymorphic, unlike, unrelated, varied.

antonym homogeneous.

hew *v* axe, carve, chop, conform, cut, fashion, fell, form, hack, lop, make, model, sculpt, sculpture, sever, shape, smooth, split.

heyday *n* bloom, boom time, florescence, flower, flowering, golden age, pink, prime, salad days, vigour.

hiatus *n* aperture, blank, breach, break, chasm, discontinuance, discontinuity, gap, interruption, interval, lacuna, lapse, opening, rift, space, void.

hidden *adj* abstruse, cabalistic, clandestine, close, concealed, covered, covered up, covert, cryptic, dark, hermetic, latent, mysterious, mystic, mystical, obscure, occult, recondite, secluded, secret, shrouded, ulterior, unapparent, unseen, veiled.

antonyms open, showing.

hide[1] *v* abscond, bury, cache, camouflage, cloak, conceal, cover, disguise, earth, eclipse, ensconce, go to ground, go underground, hole up, keep dark, keep secret, lie low, mask, obscure, screen, secrete, shadow, shelter, shroud, stash, suppress, take cover, veil, withhold.

antonyms display, reveal, show.

hide[2] *n* fell, pelt, skin.

hideaway *n* cachette, cloister, haven, hide-out, hiding place, nest, refuge, retreat, sanctuary.

hidebound *adj* conventional, entrenched, narrow, narrow-minded, rigid, set, set in one's ways, strait-laced, stubborn, ultraconservative, unprogressive.

antonyms liberal, unconventional.

hideous *adj* abominable, appalling, atrocious, awful, beastly, detestable, disgusting, dreadful, frightful, ghastly, grim, grisly, gross, grotesque, gruesome, horrendous, horrible, horrid, loathsome, macabre, monstrous, odious, repulsive, revolting, shocking, sickening, terrible, terrifying, ugly, unsightly, unspeakable.

antonym beautiful.

hide-out *n* den, hangout, hideaway, hiding place, hole, lair, retreat.

hiding[1] *n* beating, caning, drubbing, flogging, hammering, larruping, lathering, leathering, licking, spanking, tanning, thrashing, walloping, whaling, whipping.

hiding[2] *n* camouflage, concealment, disguise, screening, secretion, veiling.

in hiding concealed, hidden, under cover.

hiding place *n* cachette, concealment, cover, den, haven, hideaway, hide-out, hole, lair, mew, recess, refuge, retreat, sanctuary, secret place, stash.

hierarchy *n* echelons, grading, layers, levels, pecking order, ranking, scale, strata.

higgledy-piggledy *adv* anyhow, any old how, any which way, confusedly, every which way, haphazardly, helter-skelter, indiscriminately, pell-mell, randomly, topsy-turvy.

adj confused, disorderly, disorganized, haphazard, indiscriminate, jumbled, muddled, random, topsy-turvy.

high *adj* acute, alto, arrogant, boisterous, bouncy, capital, cheerful, chief, consequential, costly, dear, delirious, despotic, distinguished, domineering, elated, elevated, eminent, euphoric, exalted, excessive, excited, exhilarated, exorbitant, expensive, extraordinary, extravagant, extreme, exuberant, freaked out, gamy, grand, grave, great, haughty, high-pitched, honourable, important, inebriated, influential, intense, intensified, intoxicated, joyful, lavish, leading, light-hearted, lofty, lordly, luxurious, main, merry, mountain(s)-high, noble, ostentatious, overbearing, overjoyed, penetrating, piercing, piping, powerful, prominent, proud, pungent, rich, ruling, serious, sharp, shrill, significant, smelly, soaring, soprano, spaced-out, steep, stiff, stoned, strident, strong, superior, tainted, tall, towering, treble, tripping, tumultuous, turbulent, tyrannical, vainglorious.

antonyms deep, low, lowly, short.

n apex, apogee, delirium, ecstasy, euphoria, height, intoxication, level, peak, record, summit, top, trip, zenith.

antonyms low, nadir.

high and dry abandoned, bereft, destitute, helpless, in difficulty, marooned, stranded, stuck, up the creek.

high and mighty arrogant, cavalier, conceited, disdainful, haughty, imperious, overbearing, overweening, self-important, snobbish, stuck-up, superior.

high society aristocracy, beau monde, beautiful people, crème de la crème, elite, gentry, grand monde, haut monde, jet set, nobility, smart set, top drawer, upper classes, upper crust, VIPs.

antonym hoi polloi.

high spirits boisterousness, bounce, buoyancy, exhilaration, exuberance, good humour, hilarity, joie de vivre, liveliness, sparkle, vivacity.

highborn *adj* aristocratic, blue-blooded, gentle, noble, patrician, pedigreed, thoroughbred, wellborn, well-connected.

highbrow *n* aesthete, Brahmin, brain, egghead, intellectual, longhair, mastermind, savant, scholar, snob.

adj bookish, brainy, cultivated, cultured, deep, intellectual, learned, long-haired, serious, sophisticated.

antonym lowbrow.

high-class *adj* A-one, choice, classy, deluxe, elite, exclusive, first-rate, high-quality, posh, quality, select, superb, superior, the tops, tiptop, top-flight, upper-class.
antonyms mediocre, ordinary.

highest *adj* apical, apogean, peak, record, top, topmost, upmost, uppermost, zenithal.
antonyms bottom(most), lowest.

highfalutin *adj* affected, big, bombastic, florid, grandiose, high-flown, high-sounding, la-di-da, lofty, magniloquent, pompous, pretentious, supercilious, swanky.

high-flown *adj* elaborate, elevated, exaggerated, extravagant, florid, grandiose, highfalutin, inflated, la-di-da, lofty, magniloquent, overblown, overdone, pretentious, turgid.

high-handed *adj* arbitrary, autocratic, bossy, despotic, dictatorial, discourteous, disdainful, domineering, imperious, inconsiderate, oppressive, overbearing, peremptory, self-willed, tyrannical, willful.

highlight *n* best, climax, cream, feature, focal point, focus, high point, high spot, peak, zenith.
v accent, accentuate, emphasize, feature, focus on, illuminate, play up, point up, set off, show up, spotlight, stress, underline.

highly *adv* appreciatively, approvingly, considerably, decidedly, eminently, enthusiastically, exceptionally, extraordinarily, extremely, favourably, greatly, immensely, supremely, tremendously, vastly, very, very much, warmly, well, with approval.

high-minded *adj* elevated, ethical, fair, good, honest, honourable, idealistic, lofty, magnanimous, moral, noble, principled, pure, righteous, scrupulous, upright, virtuous, worthy.
antonyms immoral, unscrupulous.

high-powered *adj* aggressive, driving, dynamic, effective, energetic, enterprising, forceful, go-ahead, go-getting, industrious, vigorous.

high-priced *adj* costly, dear, excessive, exorbitant, expensive, extortionate, high, pricey, steep, stiff, unreasonable.
antonym cheap.

high-quality *adj* blue-chip, choice, classy, deluxe, first-rate, gilt-edged, high-class, quality, select, superior, tiptop.

high-sounding *adj* affected, artificial, bombastic, extravagant, flamboyant, florid, grandiloquent, grandiose, highfalutin, high-flown, magniloquent, orotund, ostentatious, overblown, pompous, ponderous, pretentious.

high-spirited *adj* animated, boisterous, bold, bouncy, daring, dashing, ebullient, effervescent, energetic, exuberant, frolicsome, happy, lively, mettlesome, peppy, sparkling, spirited, spunky, vibrant, vital, vivacious.
antonyms downcast, glum.

high-strung *adj* edgy, excitable, irascible, irritable, jittery, nervous, nervy, neurotic, restless, sensitive, skittish, stressed, taut, temperamental, tense.
antonyms calm, relaxed.

hijack *v* commandeer, expropriate, kidnap, seize, skyjack, snatch, steal.

hike¹ *v* back-pack, foot (it), footslog, hoof it, leg it, plod, ramble, ride shank's mare, tramp, trek, trudge, walk.
n march, plod, ramble, tramp, trek, trudge, walk.

hike² *v* increase, jack up, raise.
n increase, rise.

hilarious *adj* amusing, comical, convivial, entertaining, funny, gay, happy, humorous, hysterical, jolly, jovial, joyful, joyous, killing, merry, mirthful, noisy, rollicking, sidesplitting, uproarious.
antonyms grave, serious.

hilarity *n* amusement, boisterousness, cheerfulness, conviviality, entertainment, exhilaration, exuberance, frivolity, gaiety, glee, high spirits, jollification, jollity, joviality, joyousness, laughter, levity, merriment, mirth, uproariousness.
antonyms gravity, seriousness.

hill *n* acclivity, berg, brae, butte, climb, elevation, eminence, fell, gradient, heap, height, hillock, hilltop, hummock, incline, knoll, kop, kopje, mesa, moraine, mound, mount, mountain, pile, prominence, rise, slope, stack, tor.

hillock *n* anthill, barrow, dune, hummock, knap, knoll, kopje, molehill, mound, pingo, protuberance, ridge, swell.

hilt *n* grip, haft, handgrip, handle, helve.
to the hilt absolutely, completely, entirely, fully, totally, wholly.

hind *adj* after, back, caudal, hinder, posterior, rear, tail.
antonym fore.

hinder *v* arrest, block, check, counteract, debar, delay, deter, encumber, frustrate, hamper, hamstring, handicap, hold back, hold up, impede, interrupt, obstruct, oppose, prevent, restrain, retard, slow down, stop, stymie, thwart, trammel.
antonyms aid, assist, help.

hindmost *adj* concluding, endmost, final, furthest, lag, last, rearmost, remotest, tail, terminal, trailing, ultimate.
antonym foremost.

hindrance *n* bar, barrier, check, delay, demurral, deterrent, difficulty, drag, drawback, encumbrance, handicap, hitch, impediment, interruption, limitation, obstacle, obstruction, restraint, restriction, snag, stoppage, stumbling-block, trammel.
antonyms aid, assistance, help.

hinge *v* be contingent, centre, depend, hang, pivot, rest, revolve (around), turn.
n articulation, axis, condition, factor, foundation, joint, premise, principle.

hint *n* advice, allusion, breath, clue, dash, help, implication, indication, inkling, innuendo, insinuation, intimation, mention, pointer, reminder, scintilla, sign, signal, smidgen, soupçon, spark, speck, suggestion, suspicion, taste, tinge, tip, tip-off, touch, trace, undertone, whiff, whisper, wrinkle.

v allude, imply, indicate, insinuate, intimate, mention, prompt, suggest, tip off.

hinterland *n* back country, backwater, backwoods, boondocks, boonies, bush, interior, outback, sticks, wilds.

hip *n* buttocks, croup, haunch, hindquarters, loin, pelvis, posterior, rump.

hippie *n* beatnik, bohemian, drop-out, flower child.

hire *v* appoint, book, charter, commission, employ, engage, lease, let, rent, reserve, retain, sign up, take on.

antonyms dismiss, fire.

n charge, cost, fare, fee, hiring, payment, price, rent, rental, toll.

hirsute *adj* bearded, bewhiskered, bristly, crinite, fuzzy, hairy, hispid, shaggy, unshaven, whiskered, whiskery.

antonyms bald, hairless.

hiss *n* boo, Bronx cheer, buzz, catcall, contempt, derision, hissing, hoot, jeer, mockery, raspberry, sibilance, sibilation, whistle, whiz.

v boo, catcall, condemn, damn, decry, deride, give the Bronx cheer, give the raspberry, hoot, jeer, mock, revile, ridicule, shrill, sibilate, wheeze, whir, whistle, whiz.

historic *adj* celebrated, consequential, epoch-making, extraordinary, famed, famous, important, momentous, notable, outstanding, red-letter, remarkable, renowned, significant.

historical *adj* actual, archival, attested, authentic, documented, factual, real, traditional, true, verifiable.

history *n* account, annals, antecedents, antiquity, autobiography, biography, chronicle, chronology, days of old, days of yore, genealogy, memoirs, narration, narrative, olden days, recapitulation, recital, record, relation, saga, story, tale, the past.

histrionic *adj* affected, artificial, bogus, dramatic, forced, ham, insincere, melodramatic, ranting, sensational, theatrical, unnatural.

histrionics *n* dramatics, overacting, performance, ranting and raving, scene, staginess, tantrums, temperament, theatricality.

hit *v* accomplish, achieve, affect, arrive at, attack, attain, bang, bash, batter, bean, beat, belt, bump, chop, clip, clobber, clock, clout, collide with, crown, cuff, damage, dawn on, devastate, flog, floor, fustigate, gain, get to, impinge on, influence, knock, lob, move, occur to, overwhelm, punch, reach, secure, shoot, slap, slog, slug, smack, smash, smite, sock, strike, swat, swipe, take a swipe at, thump, touch, volley, wallop, whack, wham, whop.

n blow, bump, chop, clash, clout, collision, cuff, impact, knock, rap, sell-out, sensation, shot, slap, slog, slug, smack, smash, sock, stroke, success, swipe, triumph, wallop, winner.

hit back get even, reciprocate, retaliate, strike back.

hit on arrive at, chance on, contrive, discover, guess, invent, light on, realize, stumble on.

hit out at assail, attack, castigate, condemn, criticize, denounce, inveigh against, lash out at, rail.

hitch *v* attach, catch, connect, couple, fasten, harness, heave, hike (up), hitchhike, hoist, jerk, join, pull, tether, thumb a lift, tie, tug, unite, yank, yoke.

antonyms unfasten, unhitch.

n bug, catch, check, delay, difficulty, drawback, fastening, hindrance, holdup, impediment, mishap, obstacle, problem, snag, stick, stoppage, trouble.

hitherto *adv* beforehand, heretofore, previously, so far, thus far, till now, until now, up to now.

hit-or-miss *adj* aimless, apathetic, careless, casual, cursory, disorganized, haphazard, indiscriminate, lackadaisical, perfunctory, random, slipshod, sloppy.

hoard *n* accumulation, cache, fund, heap, mass, pile, profusion, repository, reserve, reservoir, stockpile, store, supply, treasure-trove.

v accumulate, amass, cache, coffer, collect, deposit, garner, gather, hive, husband, lay up, put by, reposit, save, stash away, stockpile, store, treasure.

antonyms spend, squander, use.

hoarder *n* collector, gatherer, miser, niggard, pack rat, squirrel.

hoarse *adj* croaky, discordant, grating, gravelly, growling, growly, gruff, guttural, harsh, husky, rasping, raspy, raucous, rough, throaty.

antonyms clear, smooth.

hoary *adj* aged, ancient, antiquated, antique, canescent, frosty, grey, grey-haired, grey-headed, grizzled, old, senescent, silvery, venerable, white, white-haired.

hoax *n* cheat, con, deception, fast one, flimflam, fraud, grift, hocus-pocus, humbug, imposture, joke, leg-pull, practical joke, prank, put-on, rip-off, ruse, sham, snow job, spoof, stratagem, string, swindle, trick.

v bamboozle, befool, beguile, bluff, con, deceive, delude, dupe, flimflam, fool, gammon, gull, have on, hoodwink, hornswoggle, humbug, lead on, pull someone's leg, put something over on one, snow, spoof, string along, stuff, swindle, take for a ride, take in, trick.

hobble *v* clog, cripple, dodder, falter, fasten, fetter, halt, hamshackle, hamstring, limp, restrict, shackle, shamble, shuffle, stagger, stumble, tie, totter.

hobby *n* avocation, diversion, pastime, pursuit, recreation, relaxation, sideline.

hobgoblin *n* apparition, bogey, bugaboo, bugbear, elf, goblin, hob, imp, spectre, spirit, sprite.

hobnob *v* associate, consort, fraternize, hang around or about, hang out, keep company, mingle, mix, pal around, socialize.

hocus-pocus *n* abracadabra, artifice, cant, cheat, chicanery, conjuring, deceit, deception, delusion, finesse, gibberish, gobbledegook, hoax, humbug, imposture, jargon, jugglery, legerdemain, magic, mumbo-jumbo, nonsense, prestidigitation, rigmarole, sleight of hand, swindle, trickery, trompe-l'oeil.

hodgepodge *n* assortment, collage, collection, confusion, congeries, conglomeration, farrago, gallimaufery, hash, jumble, medley, mélange, mess, miscellany, mishmash, mix, mixed bag, mixture, omnium gatherum, pastiche, potpourri.

hogwash *n* balderdash, bilge, bunk, bunkum, claptrap, drivel, eyewash, hooey, humbug, nonsense, piffle, rot, rubbish, swill, taradiddle, trash, tripe, twaddle.

hoi polloi *n* canaille, citizenry, commonalty, riffraff, the common people, the great unnumbered, the great unwashed, the herd, the masses, the plebs, the populace, the proletariat, the rabble, the third estate.
antonyms aristocracy, elite, nobility.

hoist *v* elevate, erect, heave, jack up, lift, raise, rear, uplift, upraise.
n crane, davit, elevator, jack, lift, tackle, winch.

hoity-toity *adj* arrogant, conceited, disdainful, flighty, haughty, high and mighty, lofty, overweening, pompous, proud, scornful, silly, snobbish, snooty, stuck-up, supercilious, uppity.

hold *v* accommodate, account, adhere, arrest, assume, be in force, be the case, be true, bear, believe, bond, brace, call, carry, carry on, celebrate, check, clasp, cleave, clinch, cling, clip, clutch, conduct, confine, consider, contain, continue, convene, cradle, curb, deem, defend, delay, detain, embrace, endure, enfold, entertain, esteem, exist, grasp, grip, harbour, have, hold good, imprison, judge, keep, keep back, keep on, last, leave out, maintain, occupy, omit, operate, own, persevere, persist, possess, preside over, presume, prop, reckon, regard, remain, remain true, remain valid, reserve, resist, restrain, retain, run, seat, shoulder, solemnize, stand up, stay, stick, stop, summon, support, suspend, sustain, take, think, view, wear.
n anchorage, authority, clasp, clout, clutch, control, delay, dominance, dominion, foothold, footing, grasp, grip, halt, influence, leverage, mastery, possession, prop, pull, purchase, stay, support, sway, vantage.

hold back check, control, curb, desist, forbear, inhibit, refuse, repress, restrain, retain, stifle, suppress, withhold.
antonym release.

hold forth declaim, descant, discourse, go on, harangue, lecture, orate, preach, sermonize, speak, speechify, spiel, spout.

hold off avoid, defer, delay, fend off, keep off, postpone, put off, rebuff, refrain, repel, repulse, stave off, wait.

hold on abide, carry on, continue, endure, hang in (there), hang on, hold one's course, hold steady, keep going, persevere, stay on, wait.

hold out continue, endure, extend, give, hang on, keep back, last, offer, persevere, persist, present, proffer, stand fast.

hold over adjourn, defer, delay, postpone, put off, shelve, suspend.

hold up brace, delay, detain, display, endure, exhibit, hinder, impede, last, lift, present, raise, retard, show, slow, stop, support, survive, sustain, waylay, wear.

hold water bear scrutiny, hold true, make sense, pass the test, ring true, stand up to scrutiny, wash, work.

hold with accept, agree to, approve of, countenance, go along with, subscribe to, support.

holder *n* bearer, case, container, cover, cradle, custodian, housing, incumbent, keeper, occupant, owner, possessor, proprietor, purchaser, receptacle, rest, sheath, stand.

holdings *n* assets, bonds, estate, investments, land, possessions, property, real estate, resources, securities, shares, stocks.

holdup[1] *n* bottleneck, delay, difficulty, gridlock, hitch, obstruction, setback, snag, stoppage, (traffic) jam, trouble, wait.

holdup[2] *n* heist, mugging, robbery, stick-up.

hole *n* aglu, aperture, breach, break, burrow, cave, cavern, cavity, chamber, covert, crack, defect, den, depression, dilemma, dimple, discrepancy, dive, dump, earth, error, excavation, eyelet, fallacy, fault, fissure, fix, flaw, foramen, fovea, gap, hollow, hovel, imbroglio, inconsistency, indentation, jam, joint, lair, loophole, mess, nest, opening, orifice, outlet, perforation, pit, pocket, pool, pore, pothole, predicament, puncture, quandary, rent, retreat, scoop, scrape, shaft, shelter, slum, split, spot, tangle, tear, tight spot, vent, ventage.

hole-and-corner *adj* backdoor, backstairs, clandestine, covert, furtive, hush-hush, secret, secretive, shady, sneaky, stealthy, surreptitious, underhand, under-the-counter.
antonyms open, public.

holiday *n* anniversary, break, celebration, day off, feast, festival, festivity, fete, furlough, gala, holy day, leave, recess, respite, rest, sabbatical, saint's day, time off, vacation.

holier-than-thou *adj* complacent, goody-goody, pietistic, pious, priggish, religiose, sanctimonious, self-approving, self-righteous, self-satisfied, smug, unctuous.
antonyms humble, meek.

holiness *n* blessedness, devoutness, divinity, godliness, goodness, piety, purity, religiousness, righteousness, sacredness, saintliness, sanctity, sinlessness, spirituality, unworldliness, virtuousness.

antonyms impiety, wickedness.

holler *n, v* bawl, bellow, call, cheer, clamour, cry, hail, halloo, howl, hurrah, huzzah, roar, shout, shriek, whoop, yell, yelp, yowl.

hollow *adj* artificial, cavernous, concave, coreless, cynical, deaf, deceitful, deceptive, deep, deep-set, depressed, dished, dull, empty, expressionless, faithless, false, famished, flat, fleeting, flimsy, fruitless, futile, gaunt, hungry, hypocritical, indented, insincere, lantern-jawed, low, meaningless, muffled, muted, pointless, Pyrrhic, ravenous, reverberant, rumbling, sepulchral, specious, starved, sunken, toneless, unavailing, unfilled, unreal, unreliable, unsound, useless, vacant, vain, void, weak, worthless.

n aperture, basin, bottom, bowl, cave, cavern, cavity, channel, concave, concavity, combe, crater, cup, dale, dell, den, dent, depression, dimple, dingle, dint, dish, excavation, fossa, fovea, gap, geode, glen, groove, hole, indentation, invagination, navel, opening, pit, trough, umbilicus, vacuity, valley, well, womb.

v burrow, channel, dent, dig, dint, dish, excavate, furrow, gouge, groove, indent, pit, scoop.

holocaust *n* annihilation, carnage, conflagration, destruction, devastation, extermination, extinction, genocide, hecatomb, immolation, inferno, killing, mass murder, massacre, pogrom, sacrifice, slaughter.

holy *adj* blessed, consecrated, dedicated, devout, divine, evangelical, evangelistic, faithful, god-fearing, godlike, godly, good, hallowed, perfect, pious, pure, pure in heart, religious, righteous, sacred, sacrosanct, saintly, sanctified, sinless, spiritual, sublime, unworldly, venerable, venerated, virtuous.

antonyms impious, unsanctified, wicked.

homage *n* acknowledgment, admiration, adoration, adulation, allegiance, awe, deference, devotion, duty, esteem, faithfulness, fealty, fidelity, honour, loyalty, obeisance, praise, recognition, regard, respect, reverence, service, tribute, veneration, worship.

home *n* abode, almshouse, asylum, birthplace, domicile, dwelling, dwelling place, element, environment, family, fireside, habitat, habitation, halfway house, haunt, hearth, home ground, home town, homestead, hospice, hospital, house, household, institution, native heath, nest, nursing home, pad, pied-à-terre, residence, retirement residence, roof, roof over one's head, sanatorium, stamping ground, territory.

adj domestic, domiciliary, familiar, family, homegrown, homemade, household, in-house, inland, internal, intimate, local, national, native, plain, residential.

at home at ease, comfortable, contented, conversant, experienced, familiar, in one's element, knowledgeable, proficient, relaxed, skilled, well-versed.

antonyms ill at ease, like a fish out of water, unfamiliar.

homeland *n* country of birth, fatherland, mother country, motherland, native country, native heath, native land, native soil.

homeless *adj* abandoned, destitute, disinherited, displaced, dispossessed, down-and-out, exiled, forlorn, forsaken, houseless, itinerant, outcast, unsettled, vagabond, wandering.

n derelicts, down-and-outs, nomads, squatters, street people, tramps, travellers, vagrants.

homely *adj* horse-faced, plain, ugly, unalluring, unattractive, unglamorous, unlovely, unprepossessing.

antonyms beautiful, gorgeous.

Homeric *adj* epic, grand, heroic, imposing, impressive, poetic, Virgilian.

homesickness *n* Heimweh, loneliness, longing, nostalgia, yearning.

antonym wanderlust.

homespun *adj* amateurish, artless, coarse, crude, folksy, homely, homemade, inelegant, plain, rough, rude, rustic, unpolished, unrefined, unsophisticated.

antonym sophisticated.

homey *adj* comfortable, comfy, congenial, cosy, domestic, easy, everyday, familiar, folksy, friendly, gemütlich, homelike, homespun, informal, intimate, modest, natural, ordinary, plain, relaxed, simple, snug, unaffected, unassuming, unpretentious, unsophisticated, welcoming.

antonyms formal, unfamiliar.

homicidal *adj* bloodthirsty, deadly, death-dealing, killing, lethal, maniacal, mortal, murderous, sanguinary, violent.

homicide *n* assassin, assassination, bloodshed, cutthroat, killer, killing, liquidator, manslaughter, murder, murderer, slayer, slaying.

homily *n* address, discourse, harangue, heart-to-heart, lecture, preachment, sermon, spiel, talk.

homogeneity *n* agreement, akinness, analogousness, comparability, consistency, consonance, correspondence, identicalness, likeness, oneness, resemblance, sameness, similarity, similitude, uniformity.

antonyms difference, disagreement.

homogeneous *adj* akin, alike, analogous, cognate, comparable, consistent, consonant, harmonious, identical, indiscrete, kindred, of a piece, similar, uniform, unvarying.

antonym different.

homologous *adj* analogous, comparable, correspondent, corresponding, equivalent, like, matching, parallel, related, similar.

antonyms different, dissimilar.

homosexual *n* gay, homophile, lesbian, queen, queer, Sapphist.

antonyms heterosexual, straight.

adj gay, homoerotic, lesbian, pederastic, queer, Sapphic.

antonyms heterosexual, straight.

homosexuality *n* gayness, homoeroticism, homoerotism, Sapphism.

antonym heterosexuality.

hone *v* edge, file, grind, point, polish, rasp, sharpen, strop, whet.

honest *adj* aboveboard, authentic, bona fide, candid, chaste, conscientious, decent, direct, equitable, ethical, fair, fair and square, forthright, foursquare, frank, genuine, high-minded, honourable, humble, impartial, ingenuous, just, law-abiding, legitimate, modest, objective, on the level, open, outright, outspoken, plain, plain-spoken, proper, pure, real, reliable, reputable, respectable, scrupulous, seemly, simple, sincere, soothfast, square, straight, straightforward, true, trustworthy, trusty, truthful, unaffected, undisguised, unequivocal, unfeigned, unreserved, upright, veracious, virtuous.

antonyms covert, devious, dishonest, dishonourable.

honestly *adv* by fair means, candidly, cleanly, conscientiously, directly, dispassionately, equitably, ethically, fairly, frankly, honourably, in all sincerity, in good faith, justly, lawfully, legally, legitimately, objectively, on the level, openly, outright, plainly, really, scrupulously, sincerely, straight, straight out, truly, truthfully, undisguisedly, unreservedly, uprightly, verily.

antonyms dishonestly, dishonourably.

honesty *n* artlessness, bluntness, candour, equity, even-handedness, explicitness, fairness, faithfulness, fidelity, frankness, genuineness, honour, incorruptibility, integrity, justice, justness, morality, objectivity, openness, outspokenness, plainness, plain speaking, probity, rectitude, reputability, scrupulousness, sincerity, sooth, squareness, straightforwardness, straightness, trustworthiness, truthfulness, unreserve, uprightness, veracity, verity, virtue.

antonyms deviousness, dishonesty.

honorary *adj* complimentary, ex officio, formal, honorific, honoris causa, in name only, nominal, titular, unofficial, unpaid, virtute officii.

antonyms gainful, paid, salaried, waged.

honour *n* acclaim, accolade, acknowledgment, admiration, adoration, chastity, commendation, compliment, credit, decency, deference, dignity, distinction, duty, elevation, esteem, fairness, fame, favour, glory, good name, goodness, homage, honesty, honourableness, innocence, integrity, kudos, laudation, laurels, loyalty, modesty, morality, pleasure, praise, principles, privilege, probity, purity, rank, recognition, rectitude, regard, renown, reputation, repute, respect, reverence, righteousness, self-respect, tribute, trust, trustworthiness, uprightness, veneration, virginity, virtue, worship.

antonyms disgrace, dishonour, obloquy.

v accept, acclaim, acknowledge, admire, adore, applaud, appreciate, carry out, cash, celebrate, clear, commemorate, commend, compliment, credit, crown, decorate, dignify, discharge, esteem, exalt, execute, fete, fulfil, give kudos to, glorify, hallow, keep, laud, lionize, observe, pass, pay, pay homage, perform, praise, prize, remember, respect, revere, reverence, take, value, venerate, worship.

antonyms betray, debase, disgrace, dishonour.

honourable *adj* creditable, distinguished, eminent, equitable, estimable, ethical, fair, great, high-minded, honest, illustrious, irreproachable, just, meritorious, moral, noble, prestigious, principled, proper, renowned, reputable, respectable, respected, right, righteous, sincere, straight, true, trustworthy, trusty, unexceptionable, upright, upstanding, venerable, virtuous, worthy.

antonyms dishonest, dishonourable, unworthy.

honours *n* awards, bouquets, crowns, decorations, dignities, distinctions, kudos, laurels, prizes, rewards, titles, trophies.

antonyms aspersions, indignities.

hood[1] *n* amaut, capuche, cover, cowl, crest, domino.

hood[2] *n* bully, criminal, delinquent, gangster, hoodlum, hooligan, rowdy, ruffian, tough.

hoodwink *v* bamboozle, befool, cheat, con, cozen, deceive, delude, dupe, flimflam, fool, gammon, gull, gyp, have on, hoax, impose on, mislead, play one for a sucker, rook, sell a bill of goods, swindle, take in, trick.

hoof *n* cloven hoof, foot, trotter, ungula.

hoofed *adj* bovine, cloven-footed, cloven-hoofed, equine, ungulate.

hook *n* agraffe, anchor, barb, blow, catch, clasp, claw, fastener, fluke, hamulus, hanger, hasp, holder, link, lock, lure, peg, sickle, snag, snare, springe, trap.

v angle, attract, bag, catch, clasp, collar, curve, enmesh, ensnare, entangle, entrap, fasten, fix, grab, hitch, lure, nab, secure, snare, suck in, trap.

hooked[1] *adj* aquiline, barbed, beaked, beaky, bent, curled, curved, falcate, hamate, sickle-shaped, unciform, uncinate.

hooked[2] *adj* addicted, dependent, devoted, enamoured, obsessed, sucked in.

hooligan *n* apache, delinquent, hellion, holy terror, hood, hoodlum, mischief-maker, mugger, rough, roughneck, rowdy, ruffian, terror, thug, tough, toughie, vandal.

hoop *n* annulus, bail, band, belt, circlet, girdle, loop, ring, round, wheel.

hoot *n* beep, bit, boo, call, card, catcall, caution, cry, hiss, howl, jeer, laugh, raspberry, scream, shout, shriek, toot, whistle, whoop, yell.

v beep, boo, catcall, condemn, cry, decry, deride, explode, hiss, howl, howl down, jeer, ridicule, scream, shout, shriek, toot, ululate, whistle, whoop, yell, yell at.

hop *v* bound, caper, dance, fly, frisk, hitch, hobble, jump, jump over, leap, limp, nip, prance, skip, spring, trip, vault.

n ball, barn dance, bounce, bound, crossing, dance, flight, jump, leap, skip, social, spring, step, trip, vault.

hope *n* ambition, anticipation, aspiration, assumption, assurance, belief, confidence, conviction, desire, dream, expectancy, expectation, faith, hopefulness, longing, optimism, possiblity, promise, prospect, refuge, wish.

antonyms apathy, despair, pessimism.

v anticipate, aspire, assume, await, believe, contemplate, desire, expect, foresee, long, reckon on, rely on, trust, wish, wish for.

antonym despair.

hopeful *adj* assured, auspicious, bright, bullish, buoyant, cheerful, confident, encouraging, expectant, favourable, heartening, optimistic, probable, promising, propitious, reassuring, rosy, sanguine.

antonyms despairing, discouraging, pessimistic.

n contender, great white hope, optimist, white hope, wunderkind.

hopefully *adv* all being well, cheerfully, conceivably, confidently, deo volente, eagerly, expectantly, expectedly, feasibly, God willing, optimistically, probably, sanguinely, with a bit of luck.

hopeless *adj* beyond hope, defeatist, dejected, demoralized, despairing, desperate, despondent, disconsolate, downhearted, foolish, forlorn, futile, helpless, impossible, impracticable, inadequate, incompetent, incorrigible, incurable, ineffectual, irredeemable, irremediable, irreparable, irreversible, lost, madcap, no-win, past cure, pessimistic, pointless, poor, reckless, unachievable, unattainable, useless, vain, woebegone, worthless, wretched.

antonyms curable, hopeful, optimistic.

horde *n* band, bevy, crew, crowd, drove, flock, gang, group, herd, host, mob, multitude, pack, press, swarm, throng, troop.

horizon *n* ken, perspective, prospect, purview, range, realm, scope, skyline, sphere, stretch, verge, vista.

horny[1] *adj* callous, calloused, ceratoid, corneous, hard, horned.

antonyms hornless, soft.

horny[2] *adj* ardent, concupiscent, hot, lascivious, lecherous, libidinous, lustful, priapic, prurient, randy, ruttish.

antonyms cold, frigid.

horrible *adj* abhorrent, abominable, annoying, appalling, atrocious, awful, beastly, bloodcurdling, cruel, disagreeable, dreadful, fearful, fearsome, frightful, ghastly, grim, grisly, gruesome, heinous, hideous, horrid, horrific, loathsome, macabre, nasty, repulsive, revolting, shameful, shocking, terrible, terrifying, unkind, unpleasant, weird.

antonyms agreeable, pleasant.

horrid *adj* abominable, alarming, appalling, awful, beastly, bloodcurdling, cruel, despicable, disagreeable, disgusting, dreadful, formidable, frightening, frightful, hair-raising, harrowing, hateful, hideous, horrible, horrific, mean, nasty, odious, offensive, repulsive, revolting, shocking, terrible, terrifying, unkind, unpleasant.

antonyms agreeable, lovely, pleasant.

horrific *adj* appalling, awful, dreadful, frightening, frightful, ghastly, grim, grisly, hair-raising, harrowing, horrendous, horrifying, scaring, scary, shocking, spine-chilling, terrifying.

horrify *v* abash, affright, alarm, appal, disgust, dismay, frighten, harrow, intimidate, outrage, petrify, scandalize, scare, shock, sicken, startle, terrify, unnerve.

antonyms delight, gratify, please.

horror *n* abhorrence, abomination, alarm, antipathy, apprehension, aversion, awe, awfulness, consternation, detestation, disgust, dismay, dread, fear, fright, frightfulness, ghastliness, grimness, hatred, hideousness, horripilation, loathing, outrage, panic, repugnance, revulsion, shock, terror.

antonyms delight, pleasure.

the horrors cold shivers, goose bumps, goose flesh, goose pimples, the chills, the creeps, the heebie jeebies, the jimjams.

horror-struck *adj* aghast, appalled, frightened, horrified, petrified, shocked, stunned.

antonyms delighted, pleased.

horse *n* bayard, bronco, cayuse, charger, cob, colt, crock, dobbin, equine, filly, foal, gelding, hack, hackney, horseflesh, hoss, jade, jennet, mare, mount, mustang, nag, pacer, palfrey, plug, pony, quarter horse, racehorse, stallion, steed, trotter, warhorse, workhorse.

horse sense brains, common sense, gumption, head, judgment, mother wit, native intelligence, nous, practicality, practical wisdom, sense.

antonym stupidity.

horseman or **horsewoman** *n* broncobuster, buckaroo, cavalier, cavalryman, cowboy, dragoon, equestrian, equestrienne, gaucho, horse-soldier, hussar, jockey, mountie, RCMP officer, rider, roughrider.

horsemanship *n* dressage, equestrianism, equitation, haute école, manège.

horseplay *n* buffoonery, capers, clowning, clowning around, fooling, fooling around, fun and games, high jinks, pranks, romping, rough-and-tumble, roughhousing, rough stuff, rumpus, skylarking.

hortatory *adj* advisory, didactic, edifying, encouraging, exhortatory, exhorting, heartening, homiletic, hortative, inspiriting, instructive, pep, practical, stimulating.

horticulture *n* arboriculture, cultivation, floriculture, gardening, silviculture.

hospitable *adj* accessible, amenable, amicable, approachable, bountiful, congenial, convivial, cordial, friendly, gemütlich, generous, genial, gracious, kind, liberal, livable, open-handed, open-hearted, receptive, responsive, sociable, tolerant, welcoming.

antonyms hostile, inhospitable.

hospital *n* asylum, clinic, infirmary, lazaretto, nursing home, sanatorium, sick bay.

hospitality *n* cheer, congeniality, conviviality, cordiality, friendliness, generosity, graciousness, open-handedness, open-heartedness, sociability, warmth, welcome.

antonyms hostility, inhospitality.

host¹ *n* anchor, announcer, compère, emcee, entertainer, innkeeper, landlord, master of ceremonies, M.C., presenter, proprietor.

v compère, introduce, present.

host² *n* army, array, band, company, drove, horde, legion, multitude, myriad, pack, swarm, throng.

hostel *n* boarding house, dormitory, doss house, flophouse, Gasthaus, guest house, hospice, hostelry, hotel, inn, pension, residence, youth hostel.

hostile *adj* adverse, alien, antagonistic, anti, antipathetic, bellicose, belligerent, contrary, ill-disposed, inhospitable, inimical, malevolent, opposed, opposite, oppugnant, rancorous, unfriendly, ungenial, unkind, unpropitious, unsympathetic, unwelcoming, warlike, warring.

antonyms friendly, sympathetic.

hostilities *n* battle, bloodshed, conflict, encounter, fighting, state of war, strife, war, warfare.

hostility *n* abhorrence, animosity, animus, antagonism, antipathy, aversion, breach, detestation, disaffection, dislike, enmity, estrangement, hate, hatred, ill will, malevolence, malice, opposition, resentment, unfriendliness.

antonyms friendliness, sympathy.

hot *adj* acrid, angry, animated, approved, ardent, biting, blistering, boiling, burning, charged, clever, close, dangerous, eager, excellent, excited, exciting, favoured, febrile, fervent, fervid, fevered, feverish, fierce, fiery, flaming, fresh, glowing, heated, hotheaded, impetuous, impulsive, in demand, in fashion, in vogue, incandescent, inflamed, intense, irascible, latest, lustful, near, new, passionate, peppery, perfervid, piping, piquant, popular, pungent, quick, raging, recent, risky, roasting, scalding, scorching, searing, sensual, sharp, sizzling, skilful, sought-after, spicy, steaming, stolen, stormy, strong, sultry, sweltering, torrid, touchy, tropical, vehement, violent, voluptuous, warm, zealous.

antonyms calm, cold, mild, moderate.

hot air balderdash, blather, bluster, bombast, bosh, bull, bunk, bunkum, cant, claptrap, emptiness, eyewash, flatulence, foam, froth, fustion, gas, gobbledygook, guff, malarkey, nonsense, rant, vapour, verbiage, wind, words.

antonym wisdom.

hotbed *n* breeding ground, cradle, den, hive, nest, nidus, nursery, school, seedbed.

hotblooded *adj* ardent, bold, eager, excitable, fervent, fiery, heated, high-spirited, impetuous, impulsive, lustful, lusty, passionate, perfervid, precipitate, rash, reckless, sensual, spirited, temperamental, warm-blooded, wild.

antonyms cool, dispassionate.

hotel *n* auberge, beer parlour, boarding house, doss house, flophouse, Gasthaus, guest house, hostelry, inn, motel, pension, pub, public house, tavern.

hotfoot *adv* at top speed, hastily, helter-skelter, hurriedly, in haste, pell-mell, posthaste, promptly, quickly, rapidly, speedily, with dispatch, without delay.

antonyms dilatorily, slowly.

hothead *n* daredevil, desperado, fire-eater, hotspur, madcap, madman, terror.

hot-headed *adj* daredevil, fiery, foolhardy, hasty, headstrong, hot-tempered, impetuous, impulsive, intemperate, madcap, over-eager, precipitate, quick-tempered, rash, reckless, unruly, volatile.

antonyms calm, cool.

hothouse *n* conservatory, glasshouse, greenhouse, nursery, plant house, vinery.

hot-tempered *adj* choleric, explosive, fiery, hasty, irascible, irritable, petulant, quick-tempered, short-tempered, testy, violent, volcanic, wrathful.

antonyms calm, cool, imperturbable.

hound *v* annoy, badger, chase, chivvy, drive, dun, follow, goad, harass, harry, hunt (down), impel, importune, persecute, pester, prod, provoke, pursue.

house *n* abode, ancestry, audience, blood, building, business, church, clan, company, concern, domicile, dwelling, dynasty, edifice, establishment, family, family tree, firm, gens, habitation, home, homestead, hostelry, hotel, household, inn, kindred, line, lineage, lodgings, maisonette, ménage, organization, outfit, parliament, partnership, pied-à-terre, public house, race, residence, roof, stem, tavern, temple, theatre, tribe.

v accommodate, bed, billet, board, contain, cover, domicile, harbour, hold, keep, lodge, place, protect, put up, quarter, sheathe, shelter, store, take in.

housebroken *adj* domesticated, house-trained, tame, tamed, well-mannered.

antonym unsocial.

household *n* establishment, family, family circle, home, house, ménage, set-up.

adj common, domestic, domiciliary, established, everyday, familiar, family, home, ordinary, plain, well-known.

householder *n* franklin, freeholder, head of the household, home-owner, landlord, occupant, occupier, owner, property owner, proprietor, resident, tenant.

housekeeper *n* chatelaine, concierge, help, home economist, househusband, housewife, manager.

housewife or **househusband** *n* consort, hausfrau, home economist, homemaker, housekeeper, manager, mate.

housing *n* accommodation, case, casing, container, cover, covering, dwellings, enclosure, habitation, holder, homes, houses, living quarters, matrix, protection, roof, sheath, shelter.

hovel *n* cabin, cot, den, dive, dump, hole, hut, hutch, shack, shanty, shed, slum.

hover *v* dally, dither, falter, flap, float, flutter, fly, hang, hang about, hang back, hesitate, impend, linger, loom, menace, pause, poise, threaten, wait, waver.

however *conj* anyhow, anyway, but, even so, howbeit, in spite of that, nevertheless, nonetheless, notwithstanding, regardless, still, though, yet.

howl *n* bay, bellow, clamour, cry, groan, holler, hoot, outcry, roar, scream, shout, shriek, ululation, wail, yell, yelp, yowl.

v bellow, cry, holler, hoot, lament, roar, scream, shout, shriek, ululate, wail, weep, yell, yelp, yowl.

howler *n* bêtise, blooper, blunder, boner, bull, clanger, error, gaffe, good one, goof, joke, malapropism, mistake, screamer, solecism.

hub *n* axis, centre, core, focal point, focus, heart, linchpin, middle, nave, nerve centre, pivot.

hubbub *n* ado, agitation, babel, bedlam, brouhaha, chaos, clamour, coil, confusion, din, disorder, disturbance, fuss, hue and cry, hullabaloo, hurly-burly, kafuffle, noise, palaver, pandemonium, racket, riot, row, ruckus, ruction, rumpus, tumult, turbulence, uproar, upset.

antonym calm.

huckster *n* barker, chapman, dealer, haggler, hawker, packman, pedlar, pitcher, seller, tinker, trader, vendor.

huddle *n* clump, clutch, conclave, confab, conference, confusion, crowd, discussion, disorder, group, heap, jumble, knot, mass, meeting, mess, muddle.

v cluster, conglomerate, congregate, converge, crouch, crowd, cuddle, curl up, flock, gather, gravitate, group, hunch up, nestle, press, snuggle, throng.

antonym disperse.

hue *n* aspect, cast, character, colour, complexion, dye, light, nuance, shade, tincture, tinge, tint, tone, type.

hue and cry ado, brouhaha, chase, clamour, furor, howls, hullabaloo, outcry, pursuit, ruction, ruckus, rumpus, to-do, uproar.

huff *n* anger, bad mood, mood, passion, pet, pique, snit, the sulks, tiff.

huffy *adj* angry, crabby, cross, crotchety, crusty, disgruntled, grumpy, irritable, miffed, moody, morose, offended, peevish, pettish, petulant, querulous, resentful, short, snappy, sulky, surly, testy, touchy, waspish.

antonyms cheery, happy.

hug *v* cherish, clasp, cling to, cuddle, embrace, enclose, enfold, grip, hold, nurse, retain, skirt, squeeze.

n clasp, clinch, cuddle, embrace, hold, squeeze.

huge *adj* astronomical, Brobdingnagian, bulky, colossal, Cyclopean, elephantine, enormous, extensive, gargantuan, giant, gigantesque, gigantic, great, gross, immense, jumbo, large, larger than life, leviathan, mammoth, massive, monumental, mountainous, outsize, oversize, prodigious, stupendous, thundering, titanic, tremendous, towering, unwieldy, vast, walloping, whacking.

antonyms dainty, tiny.

hugeness *n* bulk, bulkiness, enormity, extensiveness, gigantism, greatness, grossness, immensity, largeness, massiveness, over-development, overgrowth, prodigiousness, size, stupendousness, tremendousness, unwieldiness, vastness.

antonyms daintiness, smallness.

hulk *n* clod, derelict, frame, hull, lout, lubber, lump, oaf, ox, shell, shipwreck, wreck.

hulking *adj* awkward, bulky, cloddish, clumsy, cumbersome, galumphing, gross, huge, loutish, lubberly, lumbering, lumpish, massive, oafish, overgrown, ponderous, ungainly, unwieldy.

antonyms delicate, small.

hull[1] *n* body, casing, covering, frame, framework, hulk, skeleton, structure.

hull[2] *n* capsule, case, epicarp, husk, legume, peel, pod, rind, shell, shuck, skin, theca.

v husk, pare, peel, shell, shuck, skin, strip, trim.

hullabaloo *n* agitation, babel, bedlam, brouhaha, chaos, clamour, commotion, confusion, din, disturbance, furor, fuss, hubbub, hue and cry, hurly-burly, kafuffle, noise, outcry, pandemonium, panic, racket, ruckus, ruction, rumpus, to-do, tumult, turmoil, uproar.

hum *v* bombinate, bustle, buzz, croon, drone, lilt, move, mumble, murmur, pulsate, pulse, purr, sing, stir, throb, thrum, vibrate, whir, whiz, zoom.

n bombination, bustle, busyness, buzz, crown, drone, mumble, murmur, noise, pulsation, pulse, purr, purring, singing, stir, susurration, throb, thrum, vibration, whir, whiz.

human *adj* anthropoid, approachable, compassionate, considerate, fallible, fleshly, forgivable, hominoid, humane, kind, kindly, mortal, natural, open, reasonable, responsive, susceptible, understandable, understanding, vulnerable, warm.

antonym inhuman.

n being, body, child, creature, hominid, Homo sapiens, human being, individual, living soul, man, mortal, person, soul, woman.

humane *adj* beneficent, benevolent, benign, charitable, civilizing, clement, compassionate, forbearing, forgiving, gentle, good, good-natured, human, humanizing, kind,

kind-hearted, kindly, lenient, loving, magnanimous, merciful, mild, sympathetic, tender, understanding.

antonym inhumane.

humanitarian *adj* altruistic, beneficent, benevolent, charitable, compassionate, humane, philanthropic, public-spirited.

n altruist, benefactor, do-gooder, Good Samaritan, philanthropist.

antonyms egoist, self-seeker.

humanitarianism *n* altruism, beneficence, benevolence, charitableness, charity, compassion, generosity, good will, humanism, loving-kindness, philanthropy.

antonyms egoism, self-seeking.

humanity *n* altruism, benevolence, benignity, brotherly love, charity, compassion, empathy, Everyman, fellow feeling, flesh, generosity, gentleness, good will, Homo sapiens, human nature, human race, humankind, humaneness, kind-heartedness, kindness, loving-kindness, mankind, mercy, mortality, people, philanthropy, pity, sympathy, tenderness, tolerance, understanding.

antonym inhumanity.

humanize *v* break, civilize, cultivate, domesticate, edify, educate, enlighten, improve, mellow, polish, reclaim, refine, soften, tame, temper.

antonym brutalize.

humble *adj* abject, common, commonplace, courteous, deferential, docile, homespun, humdrum, inferior, insignificant, low, lowborn, lowly, mean, meek, modest, obedient, obliging, obscure, ordinary, penitent, plebeian, polite, poor, respectful, self-effacing, simple, submissive, subservient, supplicatory, unassertive, unassuming, undistinguished, unimportant, unostentatious, unpretending, unpretentious.

antonyms assertive, important, pretentious, proud.

v abase, abash, break, bring down, bring low, chagrin, chasten, confound, conquer, crush, debase, deflate, degrade, demean, demote, discomfit, discredit, disgrace, humiliate, lower, mortify, put in one's place, reduce, shame, sink, subdue, take down a peg.

antonyms exalt, raise.

humbly *adv* abjectly, deferentially, diffidently, docilely, hat in hand, meekly, modestly, on bended knee, penitently, respectfully, simply, submissively, subserviently, unassumingly, unpretentiously.

antonyms boastfully, confidently, defiantly.

humbug *n* baloney, bull, bunk, bunkum, cant, charlatan, charlatanism, cheat, claptrap, con, con man, deceit, deception, dodge, eyewash, fake, faker, fakery, feint, foolishness, fraud, fudge, gaff, gammon, hoax, hollowness, hype, hypocrisy, imposition, impostor, imposture, mountebank, nonsense, phony, pretence, quack, quackery, rubbish, ruse, sham, shenanigans, snow job, swindle, swindler, trick, trickery, trickster, wile.

v bamboozle, befool, beguile, cheat, cozen,

deceive, delude, dupe, fool, gammon, gull, hoax, hoodwink, impose, mislead, pull a fast one on, snow, swindle, trick.

humdrum *adj* boring, commonplace, dreary, droning, dull, everyday, humble, monotonous, mundane, nine-to-five, ordinary, prosy, repetitious, routine, tedious, tiresome, uneventful, uninteresting, unvaried, wearisome.

antonyms exceptional, unusual.

humid *adj* clammy, damp, dank, moist, muggy, soggy, steamy, sticky, sultry, vaporous, watery, wet.

antonym dry.

humidity *n* clamminess, damp, dampness, dankness, dew, humidness, moistness, moisture, mugginess, sogginess, steaminess, sultriness, vaporousness, wetness.

antonym dryness.

humiliate *v* abase, abash, belittle, bring down, bring low, chagrin, chasten, confound, crush, debase, deflate, degrade, discomfit, discredit, disgrace, embarrass, humble, mortify, put down, put in one's place, shame, subdue, undignify.

antonyms boost, dignify, exalt, vindicate.

humiliating *adj* chastening, crushing, debasing, deflating, degrading, demeaning, discomfiting, disgraceful, disgracing, embarrassing, humbling, ignominious, inglorious, insulting, mortifying, shameful, shaming, snubbing.

antonyms gratifying, triumphant.

humiliation *n* abasement, affront, chagrin, condescension, deflation, degradation, discomfiture, discrediting, disgrace, dishonour, embarrassment, humbling, ignominy, indignity, mortification, put-down, rebuff, resignation, shame, snub.

antonyms gratification, triumph.

humility *n* abjectness, courtesy, deference, diffidence, docility, humbleness, insignificance, lowliness, meekness, modesty, obedience, obscurity, resignation, respectfulness, self-abasement, servility, simplicity, submissiveness, subservience, unassertiveness, unimportance, unpretentiousness.

antonym pride.

hummock *n* barrow, elevation, hillock, hump, knoll, morraine, mound, prominence.

humorist *n* buffoon, clown, comedian, comedienne, comic, droll, eccentric, entertainer, funny man, jester, joker, parodist, satirist, wag, wisecracker, wit, zany.

humorous *adj* absurd, amusing, comic, comical, entertaining, facetious, farcical, funny, hilarious, humoristic, jocose, jocular, laughable, ludicrous, merry, playful, pleasant, Rabelaisian, satirical, sidesplitting, waggish, whimsical, wisecracking, witty, zany.

antonym humourless.

humour *n* amusement, badinage, banter, bent, bias, caprice, choler, comedy, conceit, disposition, drollery, facetiousness, fancy, farce, frame of mind, fun, funniness, gags, jesting, jests, jocoseness, jocosity, jocularity, jokes, joking, ludicrousness, melancholy, mood, nature, phlegm, pleasantries, propensity, quirk, raillery, repartee, spirits, temper, temperament, vagary, vein, whim, wisecracks, wit, witticisms, wittiness.

v accommodate, appease, coax, comply with, cosset, favour, flatter, go along with, gratify, indulge, mollify, pamper, spoil.
antonym thwart.

humourless *adj* austere, boring, cheerless, crass, dour, dry, dull, glum, grim, heavy-going, inflated, mirthless, morose, obtuse, self-important, tedious, thick, thick-skinned, thick-witted, unamused, unamusing, unfunny, unwitty.
antonyms humorous, witty.

hump *n* bulge, bump, excrescence, hill, hunch, knob, lump, mound, projection, prominence, protrusion, protuberance, swelling.
v arch, curve, heave, hoist, hunch, hurry, hustle, lift, lug, move, rush, shoulder.

humped *adj* arched, bent, bowed, crooked, curved, gibbous, humpbacked, hunchbacked, hunched.
antonyms flat, straight.

hunch *n* bulge, feeling, guess, guesswork, hump, idea, impression, inkling, intuition, premonition, presentiment, suspicion.
v arch, bend, crouch, curl up, curve, draw in, huddle, hump, jerk, shrug, squat, stoop, tense.

hunchback *n* gibbosity, humpback, kyphosis, Quasimodo.

hunch-backed *adj* bowed, crooked, deformed, gibbous, humped, humpbacked, hunched, kyphotic, misshapen, stooped.
antonyms straight, upright.

hunger *n* aching void, appetence, appetite, craving, desire, emptiness, esurience, famine, greed(iness), hungriness, itch, longing, lust, rapacity, ravenousness, starvation, taste, thirst, voracity, yearning, yen.
antonyms appeasement, satisfaction.
v be famished, be ravenous, be starved, feel hunger, starve.
antonyms be full, be satisfied.

hunger for ache for, crave, desire, hanker after, hanker for, itch to, long for, lust for, pine for, starve for, thirst for, want, wish, yearn for.

hungry *adj* aching, athirst, avid, covetous, craving, desirous, eager, empty, esurient, famished, famishing, greedy, hollow, hungering, hungry as a bear, hungry as a horse, keen, lean, longing, peckish, ravenous, starved, starving, underfed, undernourished, voracious, yearning.
antonyms replete, satisfied.

hunk *n* Adonis, block, chunk, clod, dollop, dreamboat, gobbet, lump, mass, piece, slab, slice, wedge.

hunt *v* cast a net for, chase, chevy, course, dog, drive out, ferret, forage, gun for, harry, hound, investigate, look for, persecute, pursue, quest for, rummage, scour, search, seek, stalk, track, trail.
n battue, chase, chevy, dragnet, hue and cry, hunting, investigation, pursuit, quest, search.

hunted *adj* angst ridden, anxious, careworn, desperate, distraught, gaunt, haggard, hagridden, harassed, harried, haunted, persecuted, stricken, terror-stricken, tormented, worn, worried.
antonym serene.

hunter *n* chaser, chasseur, huntsman, investigator, pursuer, searcher, seeker, woodsman.

hunting *adj* chasing, pursuing, questing, searching, seeking.

hurdle *n* barricade, barrier, complication, difficulty, fence, handicap, hedge, hindrance, impediment, jump, obstacle, obstruction, problem, snag, stumbling-block, wall.

hurl *v* cast, catapult, chuck, dash, fire, fling, heave, launch, let fly, pitch, project, propel, send, shy, sling, throw, toss.

hurly-burly *n* agitation, bedlam, brouhaha, bustle, chaos, commotion, confusion, disorder, distraction, excitement, frenzy, furor, hassle, hubbub, hustle, noise, storm and stress, Sturm und Drang, tumult, turbulence, turmoil, upheaval.

hurricane *n* cyclone, gale, squall, storm, tempest, tornado, twister, typhoon, whirlwind.

hurried *adj* breakneck, brief, careless, cursory, hasty, headlong, hectic, passing, perfunctory, precipitate, quick, reckless, rushed, shallow, short, slam-bang, slapdash, speedy, superficial, swift, unthorough.
antonym leisurely.

hurry *v* accelerate, bustle, dash, dispatch, expedite, floor it, fly, get a move on, get moving, goad, hasten, hightail it, hump, hustle, jump to it, look lively, make a dash for it, make haste, move, quicken, rush, scoot, scramble, scurry, scuttle, shake a leg, speed up, spur, step on it, step on the gas, urge on.
antonyms dally, delay.
n bustle, celerity, commotion, dispatch, expedition, flurry, haste, hustle, precipitance, precipitation, quickness, rush, scurry, speed, sweat, urgency.
antonyms calm, leisureliness.

hurt *v* abuse, ache, afflict, aggrieve, annoy, bruise, burn, cut to the quick, damage, disable, distress, grieve, harm, impair, injure, maim, maltreat, mar, offend, pain, sadden, smart, spoil, sting, suffer, throb, tingle, torture, upset, wound.
antonyms assuage, heal.
n abuse, ache, bruise, damage, detriment, disadvantage, discomfort, distress, harm, impairment, injury, lesion, loss, mischief, pain, pang, scathe, sore, soreness, suffering, wound, wrong.
adj aggrieved, bruised, crushed, cut, damaged, distressed, grazed, harmed, hurting, injured, maimed, miffed, offended, pained,

piqued, rueful, sad, saddened, scarred, scraped, scratched, wounded.
antonyms unhurt, unscathed.

hurtful *adj* catty, cruel, cutting, damaging, deleterious, derogatory, destructive, detrimental, disadvantageous, distressing, harmful, humiliating, injurious, malefic, maleficent, malicious, malignant, mean, mischievous, nasty, pernicious, pestiferous, pestilential, pointed, prejudicial, scathing, spiteful, unkind, upsetting, vicious, wounding.
antonyms helpful, kind.

hurtle *v* bowl, charge, chase, crash, dash, fly, plunge, race, rattle, rush, scoot, scramble, shoot, speed, spin, spurt, tear.

husband[1] *v* budget, conserve, economize, eke out, hoard, ration, reserve, save, save up, store, use sparingly.
antonyms squander, waste.

husband[2] *n* benedict, consort, hubby, man, married man, mate, old man, spouse.

husbandry *n* agriculture, agronomy, conservation, cultivation, economy, farming, frugality, good housekeeping, land management, management, thrift, thriftiness, tillage.
antonym wastefulness.

hush *v* calm, compose, mollify, mute, muzzle, quieten, settle, shush, silence, soothe, still.
antonyms disturb, rouse.
n calm, calmness, peace, peacefulness, quiet, quietness, repose, serenity, silence, soundlessness, stillness, tranquillity.
antonyms clamour, uproar.
interj be quiet, button your lip, hold your tongue, leave it out, not another word, pipe down, put a lid on it, quiet, say no more, sh, shush, shut up, silence, stow it, whisht.
antonyms say something, speak up.

hush up conceal, cover up, gag, keep dark, keep under wraps, muzzle, smother, soft-pedal, squash, stifle, suppress.
antonyms publicize, reveal.

hush-hush *adj* classified, confidential, restricted, secret, top-secret, under wraps, undisclosed, unpublished.
antonyms open, public.

husk *n* bark, bract, bran, case, chaff, covering, glume, hull, pod, rind, shell, shuck, tegmen.

huskiness *n* croakiness, dryness, gruffness, gutturalness, harshness, hoarseness, roughness, throatiness.
antonym clarity.

husky[1] *adj* croaking, croaky, gruff, guttural, harsh, hoarse, low, rasping, raucous, rough, throaty.

husky[2] *adj* beefy, brawny, burly, hefty, muscular, powerful, rugged, stocky, strapping, strong, sturdy, thickset, tough.

hussy *n* baggage, broad, floozy, jade, minx, piece, slut, strumpet, tart, temptress, tramp, trollop, vamp, wanton, wench.

hustle *v* bustle, crowd, elbow, force, haste, hasten, hurry, impel, jog, jostle, pressure, push, rush, sell, shove, solicit, thrust.

hut *n* booth, cabin, caboose, crib, den, hogan, house, hovel, hutch, kiosk, lean-to, shack, shanty, shebang, shed, shelter, stall, tilt.

hybrid *n* amalgam, combination, composite, compound, conglomerate, cross, crossbreed, half-blood, half-breed, mixture, mongrel, mule, pastiche.
adj bastard, combined, composite, compound, crossbred, crossed, heterogeneous, hyphenated, interbred, mixed, mongrel, mule, patchwork.
antonyms pure, purebred.

hybridization *n* bastardization, compositeness, crossbreeding, crossing, heterogeneity, interbreeding.
antonym purity.

hygiene *n* asepsis, cleanliness, disinfection, healthfulness, purity, salubriousness, salubrity, sanitariness, sanitation, sterility, wholesomeness.
antonyms filth, insanitariness.

hygienic *adj* aseptic, clean, cleanly, disinfected, germ-free, healthy, pure, salubrious, salutary, sanitary, sterile, wholesome.
antonym unhygienic.

hymn *n* anthem, cantata, canticle, carol, chant, chorale, dithyramb, doxology, introit, mantra, Mass, motet, offertory, om, paean, psalm, recessional, Requiem, song of praise.

hype *n* advertisement, advertising, ballyhoo, blurb, buildup, fuss, plugging, promo, promotion, publicity, puffery, razzmatazz, trumpet-blowing.

hyperbole *n* enlargement, exaggeration, excess, extravagance, magnification, overkill, overplay, overstatement.
antonyms meiosis, understatement.

hypercritical *adj* captious, carping, cavilling, censorious, faultfinding, finicky, fussy, hairsplitting, nagging, niggling, nit-picking, overcritical, overparticular, pedantic, pernickety, quibbling, strict.
antonyms tolerant, uncritical.
▲ *confusable word* hypocritical.

hypnotic *adj* compelling, dazzling, fascinating, irresistible, magnetic, mesmeric, mesmerizing, narcotic, opiate, sleep-inducing, somniferous, soothing, soporific, spellbinding.

hypnotism *n* animal magnetism, hypnosis, hypnotherapy, mesmerism, suggestion.

hypnotize *v* bewitch, captivate, dazzle, entrance, fascinate, magnetize, mesmerize, spellbind, stupefy.

hypochondria *n* low spirits, melancholia, neurosis, psychosomatic illness, valetudinarianism.

hypochondriac *n* psychosomatic, neurotic, valetudinarian.
adj neurotic, psychosomatic, valetudinarian.

hypocrisy   *n*   affectation, cant, deceit, deceitfulness, deception, dissembling, double talk, duplicity, falsity, imposture, insincerity, lip-service, pharisaism, phoniness, pietism, pretence, quackery, sanctimony, sanctimoniousness, self-righteousness, speciousness, two-facedness.
    antonyms   humility, sincerity.

hypocrite   *n*   canter, charlatan, deceiver, dissembler, fraud, impostor, mountebank, Pharisee, phony, pietist, pretender, pseud, whited sepulchre.

hypocritical   *adj*   assumed, canting, deceitful, deceptive, dissembling, double-faced, duplicitous, false, fraudulent, hollow, insincere, pharisaic, phony, pietistic, sanctimonious, self-righteous, specious, spurious, two-faced.
    antonyms   genuine, humble, sincere.
    ▲ *confusable word*   hypercritical.

hypothesis   *n*   assumption, conjecture, guess, postulate, postulatum, premise, presumption, proposition, starting point, supposition, theory, thesis.

hypothetical   *adj*   academic, assumed, conditional, conjectural, imaginary, postulated, presumed, proposed, putative, speculative, supposed, suppositional, theoretical.
    antonyms   actual, real.

hysteria   *n*   agitation, frenzy, hysterics, instability, madness, mania, neurosis, panic, psychoneurosis, unreason.
    antonyms   calm, composure, reason.

hysterical   *adj*   berserk, comical, crazed, distracted, distraught, emotional, excited, farcical, frantic, frenzied, hilarious, mad, neurotic, overwrought, overzealous, priceless, psychoneurotic, psychosomatic, raving, sidesplitting, uncontrollable, uproarious.
    antonyms   calm, composed.

hysterics   *n*   drama, dramatics, emotionalism, emotionality, histrionics, melodrama, theatrics.

ice *n* chill, chilliness, coldness, distance, formality, frazil, frigidity, frost, frostiness, hoarfrost, ice cream, iciness, icing, reserve, rime, sorbet, stiffness, verglas.

v freeze, frost, glaciate, glaze.

on thin ice at risk, in jeopardy, insecure, open to attack, precarious, unsafe, vulnerable.

ice-cold *adj* algid, arctic, biting, bitter, chilled to the bone, freezing, frigid, frostbitten, frosty, frozen, frozen to the marrow, gelid, glacial, icy, icy cold, raw, refrigerated.

iced *adj* frappé, frosted, glazed.

icon *n* figure, idol, image, picture, portrait, portrayal, representation, symbol.

iconoclasm *n* criticism, demythologization, denunciation, disabusing, dissent, dissidence, heresy, irreverence, opposition, questioning, radicalism, scepticism, subversion, unbelief, undeceiving.

antonyms credulity, trustfulness.

iconoclast *n* critic, denouncer, denunciator, destroyer, dissenter, dissident, heretic, image breaker, opponent, questioner, radical, rebel, sceptic, subversive, unbeliever.

antonyms believer, devotee.

iconoclastic *adj* critical, denunciatory, dissentient, dissident, heretical, impious, innovative, irreligious, irreverent, questioning, radical, rebellious, sceptical, subversive.

antonyms trustful, uncritical, unquestioning.

icy *adj* algid, aloof, arctic, biting, bitter, chill, chilling, chilly, cold, distant, forbidding, formal, freezing, frigid, frost-bound, frosty, frozen, frozen over, gelid, glacial, glassy, hoary, hostile, ice-cold, indifferent, raw, reserved, reticent, rimy, slippery, steely, stiff, stony, unfriendly.

idea *n* abstraction, aim, approximation, archetype, belief, clue, conceit, concept, conception, conceptualization, conclusion, conjecture, construct, conviction, design, doctrine, end, essence, estimate, fancy, form, guess, guesstimate, hint, hypothesis, idée fixe, image, import, impression, inkling, intention, interpretation, intimation, judgment, meaning, notion, object, opinion, pattern, perception, plan, point, purpose, reason, recommendation, scheme, sense, significance, solution, suggestion, surmise, suspicion, teaching, theme, theory, thought, type, understanding, view, viewpoint, vision.

ideal *n* archetype, criterion, dream, dreamboat, epitome, example, exemplar, image, last word, model, ne plus ultra, nonpareil, paradigm, paragon, pattern, perfection, pink of perfection, principle, prototype, standard, type.

adj abstract, archetypal, best, classic, complete, conceptual, consummate, dream, fanciful, highest, hypothetical, imaginary, impractical, model, optimal, optimum, perfect, quintessential, supreme, theoretical, transcendent, transcendental, unattainable, unreal, utopian, visionary.

idealist *n* dreamer, escapist, immaterialist, perfectionist, romantic, romanticist, utopian, visionary.

antonyms pragmatist, realist.

idealistic *adj* impracticable, impractical, optimistic, perfectionist, quixotic, romantic, starry-eyed, unrealistic, utopian, visionary.

antonyms pragmatic, realistic.

idealization *n* apotheosis, deification, ennoblement, exaltation, glorification, romanticization, romanticizing, worship.

idealize *v* apotheosize, deify, ennoble, exalt, glorify, put on a pedestal, romanticize, utopianize, worship.

antonyms caricature, travesty.

idée fixe complex, fixation, fixed idea, hang-up, leitmotiv, mania, monomania, obsession, one-track mind, preoccupation, ruling passion.

identical *adj* alike, cloned, coincident, congruent, corresponding, duplicate, equal, equivalent, indistinguishable, interchangeable, like, matching, monozygotic, same, selfsame, synonymous, twin.

antonym different.

identifiable *adj* ascertainable, clear, detectable, discernible, distinguishable, known, namable, noticeable, observable, obvious, perceptible, recognizable, unmistakable.

antonyms indefinable, unfamiliar, unidentifiable, unknown.

identification *n* association, cataloguing, classifying, connection, credentials, detection, diagnosis, documents, empathy, fellow feeling, ID, involvement, labelling, naming, papers, pinpointing, rapport, recognition, relating, relationship, sympathy.

identify *v* catalogue, classify, detect, diagnose, distinguish, finger, give a name to, know, label, make out, name, pick out, pinpoint, place, recognize, single out, specify, spot, tag.

identify with agree with, ally with, associate with, connect with, empathize with, equate with, feel for, link with, relate to, respond to.

identity *n* accord, coincidence, congruence, correspondence, empathy, existence, individuality, likeness, oneness, particularity, personality, rapport, sameness, self, selfhood, singularity, unanimity, uniqueness, unity.

ideologist *n* ideologue, theorist, thinker, visionary.

ideology *n* belief(s), concept(s), convictions, creed, doctrine(s), dogma, ethics, faith, ideas, metaphysics, philosophy, principles, speculation, tenets, Weltanschauung, world view.

idiocy *n* amentia, asininity, cretinism, fatuity, fatuousness, folly, foolishness, imbecility, inanity, insanity, irrationality, lunacy, senselessness, silliness, stupidity, tomfoolery.

antonyms sanity, wisdom.

idiom *n* colloquialism, dialect, expression, idiolect, jargon, language, locution, parlance, phrase, regionalism, set phrase, style, talk, turn of phrase, usage, vernacular.

idiomatic *adj* characteristic, colloquial, correct, dialectal, grammatical, idiolectal, local, native, vernacular.

idiosyncrasy *n* characteristic, eccentricity, feature, freak, habit, kink, mannerism, oddity, oddness, peculiarity, quirk, singularity, trait.

idiosyncratic *adj* characteristic, distinctive, eccentric, individual, individualistic, inimitable, odd, peculiar, quirky, typical.

antonyms common, general.

idiot *n* ament, ass, birdbrain, blockhead, boob, booby, clod, crazy, cretin, cuckoo, dimwit, dolt, dullard, dumb-bell, dummy, dunderhead, fathead, featherbrain, fool, half-wit, imbecile, klutz, knucklehead, lamebrain, mental defective, mooncalf, moron, natural, nincompoop, ninny, nitwit, saphead, schlep, schmo, schmuck, simpleton, thickhead.

idiotic *adj* asinine, birdbrained, brainless, clueless, crazy, cretinous, daft, dimwitted, dumb, fatheaded, fatuous, foolhardy, foolish, half-witted, harebrained, imbecile, imbecilic, inane, insane, knuckleheaded, loony, lunatic, moronic, nutty, sappy, screwy, senseless, simple, stupid, thick, thick-headed, tomfool, unintelligent.

antonyms sane, sensible.

idle *adj* abortive, bootless, dead, dormant, dronish, empty, foolish, frivolous, fruitless, futile, good-for-nothing, groundless, inactive, indolent, ineffective, ineffectual, inoperative, jobless, lackadaisical, lazy, leisure, mothballed, motionless, nugatory, of no avail, otiose, pointless, purposeless, redundant, shiftless, slothful, slow, sluggish, stationary, superficial, torpid, trivial, unavailing, unbusy, unemployed, unproductive, unsuccessful, unused, useless, vain, workshy, worthless.

antonyms active, effective, purposeful.

v coast, dally, dawdle, drift, fool, fritter, goof

off, kill (time), laze, lie around, loaf, loiter, lounge, putter, rest on one's laurels, shirk, slack, take it easy, tick over, vegetate, waste (time), while.

antonyms act, work.

idleness *n* dolce far niente, ease, flânerie, inaction, inactivity, indolence, inertia, inoccupation, laziness, lazing, leisure, loafing, shiftlessness, sloth, slothfulness, sluggishness, torpor, unemployment, vegetating.

antonyms activity, employment.

idler *n* clock watcher, dawdler, do-nothing, drone, fainéant, flâneur, good-for-nothing, goof-off, laggard, layabout, lazybones, loafer, lotus-eater, lounger, malingerer, ne'er-do-well, shirker, slacker, sloth, slouch, sluggard, waster, wastrel.

idling *adj* dawdling, drifting, hanging around, loafing, puttering, resting, resting on one's oars, shirking, taking it easy, ticking over.

idol *n* Baal, beloved, darling, deity, favourite, fetish, god, golden calf, graven image, hero, icon, image, joss, juju, mumbo jumbo, pet, pin-up, superstar.

idolatrous *adj* adoring, adulatory, idolizing, idol-worshipping, reverential, uncritical, worshipful.

idolatry *n* admiration, adoration, adulation, deification, devotion, exaltation, glorification, hero-worship, iconolatry, idolism, idolizing, idol worship, respect.

antonym vilification.

idolize *v* admire, adore, apotheosize, cherish, deify, dote on, exalt, glorify, hero-worship, iconize, lionize, love, respect, revere, reverence, venerate, worship.

antonym vilify.

idyllic *adj* arcadian, charming, delightful, halcyon, happy, heavenly, idealized, innocent, pastoral, peaceful, picturesque, rustic, simple, unspoiled.

antonym disagreeable.

ignite *v* burn, catch fire, combust, conflagrate, fire, flare up, inflame, kindle, light, set alight, set fire to, set on fire, spark off, touch off.

antonym quench.

ignoble *adj* abject, base, baseborn, caddish, common, contemptible, cowardly, craven, dastardly, degenerate, degraded, despicable, disgraceful, dishonourable, heinous, humble, infamous, low, lowborn, lowly, mean, petty, plebeian, shabby, shameless, unworthy, vile, vulgar, worthless, wretched.

antonyms honourable, noble.

ignominious *adj* abject, contemptible, crushing, degrading, despicable, discreditable, disgraceful, dishonourable, disreputable, humiliating, indecorous, inglorious, mortifying, scandalous, shameful, sorry, undignified.

antonyms honourable, triumphant.

ignominy *n* contempt, contemptible, degradation, discredit, disgrace, dishonour, disrepute, humiliation, indignity, infamy, mortification, obloquy, odium, opprobrium, reproach, scandal, shame, stigma.

antonyms credit, honour.

ignoramus *n* ass, blockhead, bonehead, booby, cheechako, dolt, donkey, duffer, dullard, dunce, fool, greenhorn, illiterate, know-nothing, lowbrow, numskull, simpleton.
antonyms highbrow, intellectual, scholar.

ignorance *n* benightedness, blindness, crassness, denseness, greenness, illiteracy, illiterateness, inexperience, innocence, naïvety, nescience, oblivion, stupidity, unawareness, unconsciousness, unfamiliarity.
antonyms knowledge, wisdom.

ignorant *adj* as thick as two short planks, benighted, blind, bookless, clueless, crass, dense, green, gross, half-baked, idealess, ill-informed, illiterate, ill-versed, inexperienced, innocent, innumerate, insensitive, know-nothing, naïve, nescient, oblivious, stupid, thick, unaccustomed, unacquainted, unaware, unconscious, uncultivated, uneducated, unenlightened, uninformed, uninitiated, uninstructed, unintelligent, unknowing, unlearned, unlettered, unread, unscholarly, unschooled, untaught, untrained, untutored, unwitting.
antonyms knowledgeable, learned, wise.

ignore *v* blink, cold-shoulder, cut, disregard, neglect, omit, overlook, pass over, pay no attention to, pigeonhole, reject, send to Coventry, set aside, shun, shut one's eyes to, slight, take no notice of, turn a blind eye to, turn a deaf ear to, turn one's back on.
antonyms note, notice.

ilk *n* brand, breed, cast, character, class, description, kidney, kind, make, nature, sort, stamp, style, type, variety.

ill[1] *adj* ailing, bedridden, diseased, faint, frail, green about the gills, in a bad way, indisposed, infirm, in poor health, invalid, laid low, laid up, nauseous, not up to snuff, off-colour, on the sick list, out of sorts, poorly, queasy, seedy, sick, sick as a dog, sick to one's stomach, under the weather, unhealthy, unwell, valetudinarian, weak.
antonym well.
n affliction, ailment, complaint, disease, disorder, illness, indisposition, infection, infirmity, malady, malaise, sickness, weakness.

ill[2] *adj* acrimonious, adverse, antagonistic, bad, cantankerous, cross, cruel, damaging, deleterious, detrimental, difficult, disturbing, evil, foul, harmful, harsh, hateful, hostile, hurtful, inauspicious, incorrect, inimical, iniquitous, injurious, malevolent, malicious, mean, ominous, reprehensible, ruinous, sinister, sullen, surly, threatening, unfavourable, unfortunate, unfriendly, unhealthy, unkind, unlucky, unpromising, unpropitious, unwholesome, vile, wicked, wrong.
antonyms beneficial, fortunate, good, kind.
n abuse, affliction, badness, cruelty, damage, depravity, destruction, evil, harm, hurt, ill-usage, injury, malice, meanness, mischief, misery, misfortune, pain, sorrow, suffering,

trial, tribulation, trouble, unkindness, unpleasantness, wickedness, woe.
adv amiss, badly, by no means, cruelly, hard, hardly, harmfully, harshly, inauspiciously, insufficiently, poorly, scantily, scarcely, unfavourably, unfortunately, unluckily, wrongfully.
antonym well.

ill at ease anxious, awkward, disquieted, disturbed, edgy, embarrassed, fidgety, hesitant, like a cat on hot bricks, nervous, on edge, on tenterhooks, restless, self-conscious, strange, tense, uncomfortable, uneasy, unrelaxed, unsettled, unsure, worried.
antonym at ease.

ill-advised *adj* daft, foolhardy, foolish, hasty, hazardous, ill-considered, ill-judged, impolitic, imprudent, inappropriate, incautious, indiscreet, injudicious, misguided, overhasty, rash, reckless, short-sighted, thoughtless, unseemly, unwise, wrong-headed.
antonym sensible.

ill-assorted *adj* discordant, incompatible, incongruous, inharmonious, misallied, mismatched, uncongenial, unsuited.
antonym harmonious.

ill-bred *adj* bad-mannered, boorish, churlish, coarse, crass, crude, discourteous, ill-mannered, impolite, indelicate, rude, uncivil, uncivilized, uncouth, ungallant, ungentlemanly, ungracious, unladylike, unmannerly, unrefined, vulgar.
antonyms refined, urbane.

ill-considered *adj* careless, foolish, hasty, heedless, ill-advised, ill-judged, improvident, imprudent, injudicious, overhasty, poorly timed, precipitate, rash, unwise.
antonym sensible.

ill-defined *adj* blurred, blurry, dim, fuzzy, hazy, imprecise, indefinite, indistinct, nebulous, shadowy, unclear, vague, woolly.
antonym clear.

ill-disposed (to) *adj* against, antagonistic, anti, antipathetic, averse, hostile, inimical, opposed, unfavourable, unfriendly, unsympathetic, unwelcoming.
antonym well-disposed.

illegal *adj* actionable, banned, black-market, contraband, criminal, felonious, forbidden, illicit, outlawed, pirate, prohibited, proscribed, unauthorized, unconstitutional, under-the-counter, unlawful, unlicensed, unsanctioned, verboten, wrongful.
antonym legal.

illegality *n* crime, criminality, felony, illegitimacy, illicitness, lawlessness, unconstitutionality, unlawfulness, wrong, wrongfulness, wrongness.
antonym legality.

illegible *adj* crabbed, faint, hieroglyphic, indecipherable, indistinct, obscure, scrawled, scribbled, undecipherable, unreadable.
antonym legible.

illegitimacy *n* bar sinister, bastardism, bastardy, baton sinister, illegality, illicitness, irregularity, unconstitutionality, unlawfulness.
antonym legitimacy.

illegitimate *adj* bastard, born out of wedlock, illegal, illicit, illogical, improper, incorrect, invalid, misbegotten, natural, spurious, unauthorized, unconstitutional, unjustifiable, unjustified, unlawful, unsanctioned, unsound, unwarrantable, unwarranted.
antonym legitimate.

ill-fated *adj* blighted, doomed, forlorn, hapless, ill-omened, ill-starred, inauspicious, luckless, star-crossed, unfortunate, unhappy, unlucky.
antonym lucky.

ill-favoured *adj* hideous, homely, offensive, plain, repulsive, ugly, unattractive, unlovely, unpleasant, unprepossessing, unsightly.
antonym beautiful.

ill feeling *n* animosity, animus, antagonism, bad blood, bitterness, disgruntlement, dislike, dissatisfaction, dudgeon, enmity, frustration, grudge, hard feelings, hostility, ill will, odium, offence, rancour, resentment, sourness, spite.
antonyms friendship, goodwill.

ill humour *n* acrimony, choler, crabbiness, disagreeableness, discontent, distemper, grumpiness, irascibility, moroseness, petulance, spleen, sulkiness, the dumps.
antonym amiability.

ill-humoured *adj* acrimonious, bad-tempered, cantankerous, crabbed, crabby, cross, cross-grained, disagreeable, grumpy, huffy, impatient, irascible, irritable, moody, morose, peevish, petulant, sharp, snappish, snappy, sulky, sullen, tart, testy, waspish.
antonym amiable.

illiberal *adj* bigoted, close-fisted, hidebound, intolerant, mean, miserly, narrow-minded, niggardly, parsimonious, petty, prejudiced, reactionary, small-minded, sordid, stingy, tight, tightfisted, uncharitable, ungenerous.
antonym liberal.

illiberality *n* bigotry, intolerance, meanness, miserliness, narrow-mindedness, narrowness, niggardliness, parsimony, pettiness, prejudice, small-mindedness, stinginess.
antonym liberality.

illicit *adj* black-market, bootleg, clandestine, contraband, criminal, felonious, forbidden, furtive, guilty, illegal, illegitimate, ill-gotten, immoral, improper, inadmissible, prohibited, unauthorized, unlawful, unlicensed, unsanctioned, verboten, wrong.
antonyms legal, licit.

illiterate *adj* analphabetic, benighted, ignorant, uncultured, uneducated, unlettered, untaught, untutored.
antonym literate.

ill-judged *adj* daft, foolhardy, foolish, hasty, ill-advised, ill-considered, impolitic, imprudent, incautious, indiscreet, injudicious, misguided, overhasty, rash, reckless, short-sighted, stupid, unwise, wrong-headed.
antonym sensible.

ill-mannered *adj* badly-behaved, bad-mannered, boorish, churlish, coarse, crude, discourteous, ill-behaved, ill-bred, impolite, insensitive, insolent, loutish, rude, uncivil, uncouth, ungallant, unmannerly.
antonym polite.

ill-natured *adj* bad-tempered, churlish, crabbed, crabby, cross, cross-grained, disagreeable, disobliging, malevolent, malicious, malignant, mean, nasty, perverse, petulant, spiteful, sulky, sullen, surly, unfriendly, unkind, unpleasant, vicious, vindictive.
antonym good-natured.

illness *n* affliction, ailment, attack, complaint, disability, disease, disorder, distemper, dyscrasia, idiopathy, ill-being, ill-health, indisposition, infirmity, malady, malaise, sickness.
antonym health.

illogical *adj* absurd, erroneous, fallacious, faulty, foolish, illegitimate, inconclusive, inconsistent, incorrect, invalid, irrational, meaningless, senseless, sophistic, specious, spurious, unreasonable, unscientific, unsound.
antonym logical.

ill-omened *adj* doomed, ill-fated, inauspicious, star-crossed, unfortunate, unhappy, unlucky.
antonym fortunate.

ill-tempered *adj* bad-tempered, choleric, crabby, cross, curt, grumpy, ill-humoured, ill-natured, impatient, irascible, irritable, sharp, spiteful, testy, tetchy, touchy, vicious, vixenish.
antonym good-tempered.

ill-timed *adj* awkward, inappropriate, inconvenient, inept, inexpedient, inopportune, mistimed, tactless, unseasonable, untimely, unwelcome.
antonym well-timed.

ill-treat *v* abuse, damage, harass, harm, harry, ill-use, injure, maltreat, manhandle, mishandle, mistreat, misuse, neglect, oppress, wrong.
antonym care for.

illuminate *v* adorn, beacon, brighten, clarify, clear up, decorate, edify, elucidate, enlighten, explain, illumine, illustrate, inform, instruct, irradiate, light, light up, limn, ornament.
antonyms darken, divest.

illuminating *adj* edifying, enlightening, explanatory, helpful, informative, instructive, revealing, revelatory.
antonym unhelpful.

illumination *n* adornment, awareness, beam, brightening, brightness, clarification, decoration, edification, enlightenment, explanation, insight, inspiration, instruction, light, lighting, lights, limning, ornamentation, perception, radiance, ray, revelation, splendour, understanding.
antonym darkness.

illusion *n* apparition, chimera, daydream, deception, delusion, error, fallacy, fancy, fantasy, figment, hallucination, ignis fatuus, legerdemain, maya, mirage, misapprehension, misconception, phantasm, semblance, sleight of hand, smoke and mirrors, will-o'-the-wisp.

antonym reality.

▲ *confusable word* allusion.

illusory *adj* apparent, barmecidal, beguiling, chimeric, deceitful, deceptive, deluding, delusive, fallacious, false, hallucinatory, illusive, misleading, mistaken, seeming, sham, unreal, unsubstantial, untrue, vain.

antonym real.

illustrate *v* adorn, clarify, decorate, demonstrate, depict, draw, elucidate, emphasize, exemplify, exhibit, explain, illuminate, instance, interpret, ornament, picture, represent, show, sketch.

illustrated *adj* decorated, embellished, illuminated, pictorial.

illustration *n* adornment, analogy, case, case in point, clarification, decoration, delineation, demonstration, diagram, drawing, elucidation, example, exemplification, explanation, figure, graphic, half-tone, instance, interpretation, map, painting, photograph, picture, plate, representation, sketch, specimen.

illustrative *adj* delineative, descriptive, diagrammatic, explanatory, explicatory, expository, graphic, illustrational, illustrating, interpretive, pictorial, representational, representative, sample, specimen, typical.

illustrious *adj* bright, brilliant, celebrated, distinguished, eminent, exalted, excellent, famed, famous, glorious, great, magnificent, noble, notable, noted, outstanding, prominent, remarkable, renowned, resplendent, signal, splendid.

antonyms inglorious, shameful.

ill will *n* acrimony, animosity, animus, antagonism, antipathy, aversion, bad blood, dislike, enmity, envy, grudge, hard feelings, hatred, hostility, malevolence, malice, odium, rancour, resentment, spite, unfriendliness, venom.

antonyms friendship, good will.

image *n* appearance, conceit, concept, conception, counterpart, dead ringer, Doppelgänger, double, effigy, eidolon, facsimile, figure, figure of speech, icon, idea, idol, impression, likeness, perception, persona, picture, portrait, reflection, replica, representation, semblance, similitude, simulacrum, spit, spitting image, statue, symbol, trope, type, visualization.

imaginable *adj* believable, comprehensible, conceivable, credible, likely, plausible, possible, predictable, supposable, thinkable, visualizable.

antonym unimaginable.

imaginary *adj* assumed, barmecidal, chimeric, dreamlike, fake, fancied, fanciful, feigned, fictional, fictitious, hallucinatory, hypothetical, ideal, illusive, illusory, imagined, insubstantial, invented, invisible, legendary, made-up, mythological, non-existent, phantasmal, pretended, shadowy, supposed, unreal, unsubstantial, visionary.

antonym real.

imagination *n* chimera, conception, creativity, enterprise, fancy, flights of fancy, idea, ideality, illusion, image, imaginativeness, ingenuity, innovativeness, insight, inspiration, invention, inventiveness, notion, resourcefulness, supposition, the mind's eye, unreality, vision, wit(s).

antonyms reality, unimaginativeness.

imaginative *adj* clever, creative, dreamy, enterprising, fanciful, fantastic, fertile, ingenious, innovative, inspired, inventive, original, poetic, resourceful, visionary, vivid.

antonym unimaginative.

imagine *v* apprehend, assume, believe, conceive, conceptualize, conjecture, conjure up, create, deduce, deem, devise, dream up, envisage, envision, fancy, fantasize, frame, gather, guess, ideate, infer, invent, judge, picture, plan, project, realize, scheme, suppose, surmise, suspect, take it, think, think of, think up, visualize.

imbalance *n* bias, disparity, disproportion, distortion, imparity, inequality, lopsidedness, partiality, top-heaviness, unequalness, unevenness, unfairness.

antonym parity.

imbecile *n* ament, blockhead, bungler, clown, cretin, dolt, dotard, fool, half-wit, idiot, moron, simpleton, thickhead.

adj anile, asinine, doltish, fatuous, feeble-minded, foolish, idiotic, imbecilic, inane, ludicrous, moronic, senile, simple, stupid, thick, witless.

antonyms intelligent, sensible.

imbibe *v* absorb, acquire, assimilate, consume, drink, drink in, gain, gather, gulp, ingest, knock back, lap up, learn, quaff, receive, sip, soak up, swallow, swig, take in, tipple.

imbroglio *n* confusion, difficulty, dilemma, disagreement, embroilment, entanglement, involvement, mess, misunderstanding, muddle, predicament, quandary, scrape, tangle.

imbue *v* bathe, colour, dye, fill, impregnate, inculcate, indoctrinate, infuse, ingrain, inspire, instil, moisten, permeate, pervade, saturate, stain, steep, suffuse, tinge, tint.

imitate *v* affect, ape, borrow, burlesque, caricature, clone, copy, counterfeit, do, duplicate, echo, emulate, follow, follow suit, forge, impersonate, mimic, mirror, mock, monkey, parody, parrot, personate, repeat, reproduce, ridicule, send up, simulate, spoof, take off.

imitation *n* aping, borrowing, copy, counterfeit, counterfeiting, duplication, echoing, facsimile, fake, forgery, impersonation, impression, likeness, mimesis, mimicry, mockery, onomatopoeia, parody, reflection, repetition, replica, reproduction, resemblance, sham, simulation, substitute, substitution, takeoff, travesty.

adj artificial, dummy, ersatz, mock, phony, pinchbeck, pseudo, reproduced, sham, simulated, substitute, synthetic.

antonym genuine.

imitative adj apish, copied, copycat, copying, derivative, echoic, mimetic, mimicking, mock, onomatopoeic, parodistic, parrotlike, plagiarized, pseudo, put-on, repetitious, second-hand, simulated, unoriginal.

imitator n ape, aper, copier, copycat, copyist, duplicator, echo, epigone, follower, forger, impersonator, impostor, impressionist, mimic, parodist, parrot, plagiarist, simulator.

immaculate adj blameless, clean, faultless, flawless, guiltless, impeccable, incorrupt, innocent, neat, perfect, pure, scrupulous, sinless, spick-and-span, spotless, spruce, stainless, trim, unblemished, uncontaminated, undefiled, unexceptionable, unpolluted, unsullied, untainted, untarnished, virtuous.
antonyms contaminated, spoiled.

immaterial adj airy, disembodied, ethereal, extraneous, ghostly, impertinent, inapposite, inconsequential, inconsiderable, incorporeal, inessential, insignificant, insubstantial, irrelevant, metaphysical, minor, spiritual, trifling, trivial, unimportant, unnecessary, unsubstantial.
antonyms important, material, physical, solid.

immature adj adolescent, babyish, callow, childish, crude, embryonic, green, immatured, imperfect, inexperienced, infantile, jejune, juvenile, premature, puerile, raw, under-age, undeveloped, unfinished, unfledged, unformed, unprepared, unready, unripe, unseasonable, untimely, young.
antonym mature.

immeasurable adj bottomless, boundless, endless, illimitable, immense, immensurable, incalculable, inestimable, inexhaustible, infinite, limitless, measureless, unbounded, unfathomable, unlimited, unmeasurable, vast.
antonym limited.

immediacy n directness, imminence, instancy, instantaneity, promptness, simultaneity, spontaneity, swiftness, urgency.
antonyms remoteness, unimportance.

immediate adj actual, adjacent, at hand, close, contiguous, current, direct, existing, extant, imminent, instant, instantaneous, near, nearest, neighbouring, next, on hand, present, pressing, primary, prompt, proximate, recent, unhesitating, up-to-date, urgent.
antonym distant.

immediately adv at once, at the drop of a hat, closely, directly, forthwith, hastily, in less than no time, instantly, lickety-split, like a shot, nearly, now, off the top of one's head, on the instant, posthaste, promptly, pronto, right away, straightaway, straight off, tout de suite, unhesitatingly, without delay, yesterday.
antonyms eventually, never.

immemorial adj age-old, ancestral, ancient, archaic, fixed, hoary, long-standing, time-honoured, traditional.
antonym recent.

immense adj astronomical, boundless, Brobdingnagian, colossal, cosmic, cyclopean, elephantine, enormous, extensive, giant, gigantic, great, herculean, huge, illimitable, immeasurable, infinite, jumbo, large, limitless, mammoth, massive, monstrous, monumental, prodigious, stupendous, titanic, towering, tremendous, vast.
antonym minute.

immensity n bulk, enormousness, expanse, extent, greatness, hugeness, infinity, magnitude, massiveness, scope, size, sweep, vastness.
antonym minuteness.

immerse v absorb, bathe, dip, douse, duck, dunk, engross, plunge, sink, submerge, submerse.

immersed adj absorbed, buried, busy, consumed, deep, engrossed, involved, occupied, preoccupied, rapt, submerged, sunk, taken up, wrapped up.

immersion n absorption, baptism, bath, concentration, dip, dipping, dousing, ducking, dunking, engrossment, involvement, plunging, preoccupation, submergence.

immigrant n incomer, migrant, newcomer, settler, wetback.
antonym emigrant.

immigrate v come in, migrate, move in, remove, resettle, settle.
antonym emigrate.

imminence n approach, immediacy, impendence, instancy, menace, propinquity, threat.
antonym remoteness.

imminent adj afoot, approaching, at hand, brewing, close, coming, expected, forthcoming, gathering, impending, in the air, in the offing, looming, menacing, near, nigh, overhanging, threatening.
antonym far-off.
▲ *confusable word* eminent.

immobile adj at a standstill, at rest, cataplectic, catatonic, expressionless, fixed, frozen, immobilized, immotile, immovable, motionless, rigid, riveted, rooted, solid, stable, static, stationary, stiff, still, stock-still, stolid, unexpressive, unmoving.
antonyms mobile, moving.

immobility n catatonia, disability, firmness, fixedness, fixity, immovability, inertness, motionlessness, stability, steadiness, stillness.
antonym mobility.

immobilize v cripple, disable, fix, freeze, halt, paralyse, stop, transfix.
antonym mobilize.

immoderate adj egregious, enormous, exaggerated, excessive, exorbitant, extravagant, extreme, hubristic, inordinate, intemperate, over the top, profligate, steep, unbridled, uncalled-for, unconscionable, uncontrolled, undue, unjustified, unreasonable, unrestrained, unwarranted, wanton.
antonym moderate.

immoderately adv exaggeratedly, excessively, exorbitantly, extravagantly, extremely, inordinately, too much, unduly, unjustifiably, unreasonably, unrestrainedly, wantonly, without measure.

antonym moderately.

immoderation *n* excess, exorbitance, extravagance, gluttony, immoderateness, intemperance, overindulgence, prodigality, unreason, unrestraint.

antonym moderation.

immodest *adj* bawdy, bold, brazen, coarse, conceited, depraved, forward, fresh, gross, immoral, improper, impudent, impure, indecent, indecorous, indelicate, lewd, obscene, pushy, revealing, risqué, rude, shameless, titillating, unblushing, unchaste, unmaidenly.

antonym modest.

immodesty *n* audacity, bawdiness, boldness, brass, coarseness, conceit, forwardness, gall, impropriety, impudence, impurity, indecorousness, indecorum, indelicacy, lewdness, obscenity, shamelessness, temerity.

antonym modesty.

immoral *adj* abandoned, bad, corrupt, debauched, degenerate, depraved, dishonest, dissolute, evil, foul, impure, indecent, iniquitous, lecherous, lewd, licentious, nefarious, obscene, pornographic, profligate, reprobate, sinful, unchaste, unethical, unprincipled, unrighteous, unscrupulous, vicious, vile, wanton, wicked, wrong.

antonym moral.

▲ *confusable word* amoral.

immorality *n* badness, corruption, debauchery, depravity, dissoluteness, evil, iniquity, libertinism, licence, licentiousness, profligacy, sin, turpitude, vice, wickedness, wrong.

antonym morality.

immortal *adj* abiding, ambrosial, constant, deathless, endless, enduring, eternal, everlasting, godlike, imperishable, incorruptible, indestructible, lasting, perennial, perpetual, sempiternal, timeless, undying, unfading, unforgettable.

antonym mortal.

n deity, divinity, genius, god, goddess, great, hero, Olympian.

immortality *n* celebrity, deathlessness, deification, endlessness, eternal life, eternity, everlasting life, fame, glorification, gloriousness, glory, greatness, incorruptibility, indestructibility, perpetuity, renown, timelessness.

antonym mortality.

immortalize *v* apotheosize, celebrate, commemorate, deify, enshrine, eternalize, eternize, exalt, glorify, hallow, memorialize, perpetuate, solemnize.

immovable *adj* adamant, constant, determined, entrenched, fast, firm, fixed, immutable, impassive, inflexible, jammed, not to be budged, obdurate, obstinate, resolute, rigid, rooted, secure, set, stable, stationary, steadfast, steely, stony, stuck, unchangeable, unimpressionable, unmovable, unshakeable, unshaken, unwavering, unyielding.

antonym movable.

immune *adj* clear, exempt, free, insusceptible, insusceptive, invulnerable, proof, protected, resistant, safe, unaffected, unsusceptible.

antonym susceptible.

immunity *n* amnesty, charter, exemption, exoneration, franchise, freedom, immunization, indemnity, insusceptibility, invulnerability, liberty, licence, pardon, prerogative, privilege, protection, release, resistance, right, safety.

antonym susceptibility.

immunization *n* injection, inoculation, jab, needle, protection, shot, vaccination.

immunize *v* inject, inoculate, protect, safeguard, vaccinate.

immure *v* cage, cloister, confine, enclose, fence in, imprison, incarcerate, jail, lock up, shut up, wall in.

antonym free.

▲ *confusable word* inure.

immutable *adj* abiding, changeless, constant, durable, enduring, fixed, inflexible, invariable, lasting, permanent, perpetual, sacrosanct, solid, stable, steadfast, unalterable, unchangeable.

antonym mutable.

imp *n* brat, demon, devil, flibbertigibbet, gamin, minx, prankster, rascal, rogue, scamp, sprite, trickster, urchin.

impact *n* aftermath, bang, blow, brunt, bump, burden, collision, concussion, consequences, contact, crash, effect, force, impression, influence, jolt, knock, meaning, power, repercussions, shock, significance, smash, stroke, thrust, thump, weight.

v affect, alter, clash, collide, crash, crush, determine, fix, force into, hit, influence, pack in, press in, strike, wedge.

impair *v* blunt, craze, damage, debilitate, decrease, deteriorate, devalue, diminish, enervate, enfeeble, harm, hinder, injure, lessen, mar, reduce, spoil, undermine, vitiate, weaken, worsen.

antonym enhance.

impaired *adj* damaged, defective, drunk, faulty, flawed, imperfect, poor, under the influence, unsound, vicious, vitiated.

antonym enhanced.

impairment *n* damage, deterioration, disablement, disadvantage, dysfunction, fault, flaw, harm, hurt, imperfection, incapacity, injury, reduction, ruin, vitiation.

antonym enhancement.

impale *v* lance, perforate, pierce, puncture, run through, skewer, spear, spike, spit, stab, stick, thrust through, transfix.

impalpable *adj* airy, delicate, disembodied, elusive, fine, immaterial, imperceptible, inapprehensible, incorporeal, insensible, insubstantial, intangible, shadowy, slight, tenuous, thin, unsubstantial.

antonym palpable.

imparity n bias, disparity, disproportion, imbalance, inequality, inequity, partiality, unequalness, unevenness, unfairness.
antonym parity.

impart v afford, bestow, communicate, confer, contribute, convey, disclose, discover, divulge, give, grant, hand over, lend, make known, offer, pass on, relate, reveal, tell, transfer, yield.

impartial adj detached, disinterested, dispassionate, equal, equitable, even-handed, fair, impersonal, just, neutral, non-discriminating, non-partisan, objective, open-minded, unbiassed, unprejudiced.
antonym biassed.

impartiality n detachment, disinterest, disinterestedness, dispassion, equality, equity, even-handedness, fairness, justice, neutrality, non-partisanship, objectivity, open-mindedness, unbiassedness.
antonym bias.

impassable adj blocked, closed, impenetrable, obstructed, pathless, trackless, unnavigable, unpassable.
antonym passable.

impasse n blind alley, corner, cul-de-sac, dead end, deadlock, end of one's rope, halt, hole, nonplus, stalemate, stand-off, standstill.

impassioned adj animated, ardent, blazing, enthusiastic, excited, fervent, fervid, fiery, furious, glowing, heated, inflamed, inspired, intense, passionate, rousing, spirited, stirring, vehement, vigorous, violent, vivid, warm.
antonyms apathetic, mild.

impassive adj aloof, apathetic, callous, calm, composed, cool, dispassionate, emotionless, expressionless, immobile, impassible, imperturbable, indifferent, inscrutable, insensible, insusceptible, laid-back, phlegmatic, placid, poker-faced, reserved, serene, stoical, stolid, stone-faced, unconcerned, unemotional, unexcitable, unfeeling, unimpressible, unmoved, unruffled.
antonyms moved, responsive, warm.

impassivity n aloofness, calmness, composure, coolness, dispassion, impassibility, impassiveness, imperturbability, indifference, inscrutability, insensibility, phlegm, sang-froid, stoicism, stolidity.
antonyms compassion, responsiveness, warmth.

impatience n agitation, anxiety, avidity, brusqueness, eagerness, edginess, haste, hastiness, heat, impetuosity, impulsiveness, intolerance, irritability, nervousness, rashness, restiveness, restlessness, shortness, snappishness, testiness, uneasiness, vehemence.
antonym patience.

impatient adj abrupt, brusque, chafing, champing at the bit, curt, demanding, eager, edgy, fretful, hasty, headlong, hot-tempered, impetuous, impulsive, intolerant, irritable, precipitate, quick-tempered, restless, snappy, testy, vehement, violent.

antonym patient.

impeach v accuse, arraign, blame, cast doubt on, censure, challenge, charge, denounce, disparage, impugn, indict, peach on, question, tax, tell on.

impeachment n accusation, arraignment, charge, deposal, disparagement, indictment.

impeccable adj blameless, exact, exquisite, flawless, immaculate, incorrupt, innocent, irreproachable, perfect, precise, pure, scrupulous, sinless, squeaky-clean, stainless, unblemished, unerring, unimpeachable.
antonym flawed.

impecunious adj broke, cleaned out, destitute, feeling the pinch, hard up, impoverished, indigent, insolvent, penniless, penurious, poor, poverty-stricken, stone-broke.
antonym rich.

impede v bar, block, check, clog, curb, delay, disrupt, hamper, hinder, hobble, hold up, let, obstruct, prevent, restrain, retard, slow, stop, thwart, trammel.
antonym aid.

impediment n bar, barrier, block, burden, check, clog, curb, defect, difficulty, drag, encumbrance, hindrance, let, log, obstacle, obstruction, snag, stammer, stumbling-block, stutter.
antonym aid.

impel v actuate, cause, compel, constrain, drive, drive forward, empower, excite, force, goad, incite, induce, influence, inspire, instigate, motivate, move, oblige, poke, power, prod, prompt, propel, push, spur, stimulate, urge.
antonym dissuade.

impending adj approaching, brewing, close, coming, forthcoming, gathering, hovering, imminent, in store, looming, menacing, near, nearing, overhanging, threatening.
antonym remote.

impenetrable adj arcane, baffling, cabalistic, cryptic, dark, dense, enigmatic, fathomless, hermetic, hidden, impassable, impermeable, impervious, impregnable, inaccessible, incomprehensible, indiscernible, inexplicable, inscrutable, inviolable, mysterious, obscure, solid, thick, unfathomable, unintelligible, unpierceable.
antonyms intelligible, penetrable.

impenitence n defiance, hard-heartedness, incorrigibility, obduracy, recidivism, remorselessness, stubbornness.
antonym penitence.

impenitent adj defiant, hardened, incorrigible, obdurate, recidivisitic, remorseless, unabashed, unashamed, uncontrite, unreformed, unregenerate, unremorseful, unrepentant.
antonyms contrite, penitent.

imperative adj authoritative, commanding, compulsory, crucial, essential, indispensable, mandatory, necessary, obligatory, pressing, urgent, vital.
antonyms humble, optional.

imperceptible *adj* faint, fine, gradual, impalpable, inappreciable, inaudible, inconsequential, indiscernible, indistinguishable, infinitesimal, insensible, invisible, microscopic, minute, shadowy, slight, small, subtle, tiny, undetectable, unnoticeable.
antonym perceptible.

imperceptibly *adv* gradually, inappreciably, indiscernibly, insensibly, invisibly, little by little, minutely, slowly, subtly, unnoticeably, unobtrusively, unseen.
antonym perceptibly.

imperceptive *adj* crass, dim, dull, insensitive, obtuse, superficial, unappreciative, unaware, undiscerning, unobservant, unperceptive, unseeing.
antonym perceptive.

imperfect *adj* abortive, broken, damaged, defective, deficient, faulty, flawed, impaired, incomplete, inexact, inferior, limited, partial, patchy, rudimentary, unfinished, unideal.
antonym perfect.

imperfection *n* blemish, blot, blotch, crack, defect, defectiveness, deficiency, dent, failing, fallibility, fault, flaw, foible, frailty, glitch, inadequacy, incompleteness, inferiority, insufficiency, peccadillo, shortcoming, stain, taint, weakness.
antonyms asset, perfection.

imperial *adj* august, exalted, grand, great, imperatorial, imperious, kingly, lofty, magnificent, majestic, noble, princely, queenly, regal, royal, sovereign, superior, supreme.

imperialism *n* acquisitiveness, colonialism, empire-building, expansionism, sovereignty.

imperil *v* compromise, endanger, expose, gamble with, hazard, jeopardize, put in danger, risk, threaten.

imperious *adj* arrogant, authoritarian, autocratic, bossy, commanding, compelling, demanding, despotic, dictatorial, domineering, exacting, haughty, high-and-mighty, high-handed, imperative, lordly, magisterial, necessary, obligatory, overbearing, overweening, peremptory, tyrannical, urgent.
antonym humble.

imperishable *adj* abiding, deathless, enduring, eternal, everlasting, immortal, incorruptible, indestructible, inextinguishable, perennial, permanent, perpetual, undying, unfading, unforgettable.
antonym perishable.

impermanent *adj* brief, changeable, elusive, ephemeral, evanescent, fleeting, fly-by-night, flying, fugitive, inconstant, momentary, mortal, passing, perishable, short-lived, temporary, transient, transitory, unfixed, unsettled, unstable.
antonym permanent.

impermeable *adj* damp-proof, dense, hermetic, impassable, impenetrable, impervious, non-porous, proof, resistant, waterproof, water-repellent, water-resistant.
antonym permeable.

impersonal *adj* aloof, bureaucratic, businesslike, cold, detached, dispassionate, faceless, formal, frosty, glassy, impartial, inhuman, neutral, official, remote, reticent, unfriendly, unprejudiced, unsympathetic.
antonym friendly.

impersonate *v* act, ape, caricature, do, do a take off on, imitate, masquerade as, mimic, mock, parody, personate, pose as, represent.

impersonation *n* aping, burlesque, caricature, imitation, impression, mimicry, parody, sendup, spoof, takeoff.

impertinence *n* audacity, backchat, back talk, boldness, brass, brazenness, cheek, chutzpah, discourtesy, disrespect, effrontery, forwardness, impoliteness, impudence, incivility, insolence, irrelevance, malapertness, nerve, pertness, presumption, rudeness, sauce, sauciness.
antonyms politeness, relevance.

impertinent *adj* bold, brattish, brazen, bumptious, cheeky, discourteous, disrespectful, forward, fresh, ill-mannered, impolite, impudent, insolent, irrelevant, malapert, not to the point, out of place, pert, presumptuous, rude, saucy, uncivil, unmannerly.
antonyms polite, relevant.

imperturbable *adj* calm, collected, complacent, composed, cool, equanimous, impassive, optimistic, sanguine, sedate, self-possessed, stoical, tranquil, unexcitable, unflappable.
antonyms jittery, touchy.

impervious *adj* blind, closed, damp-proof, hermetic, immune, impassable, impenetrable, impermeable, inaccessible, invulnerable, resistant, sealed, unaffected, unmoved, unreceptive, unswayable, untouched.
antonyms pervious, responsive.

impetuosity *n* ardour, dash, élan, haste, hastiness, impetuousness, impulsiveness, precipitance, precipitateness, rashness, vehemence, violence.
antonym circumspection.

impetuous *adj* ardent, eager, furious, hasty, headlong, impassioned, impulsive, overhasty, passionate, precipitate, precipitous, rash, spontaneous, sudden, unplanned, unpremeditated, unreflected, unrestrained, unthinking.
antonym circumspect.

impetuously *adv* impulsively, passionately, precipitately, precipitously, rashly, recklessly, spontaneously, suddenly, unthinkingly, vehemently.
antonym circumspectly.

impetus *n* drive, energy, force, goad, impulse, impulsion, incentive, momentum, motivation, motive, power, push, spur, stimulus.

impiety *n* blasphemy, godlessness, iniquity, irreligion, irreverence, profaneness, profanity, sacrilege, sacrilegiousness, sinfulness, ungodliness, unholiness, unrighteousness, wickedness.
antonym piety.

impinge *v* affect, clash, collide, come into contact (with), dash, encroach, enter, hit, influence, infringe, intrude, invade, obtrude, strike, touch, touch on, trespass, violate.

impious *adj* blasphemous, godless, iniquitous, irreligious, irreverent, profane, sacrilegious, sinful, ungodly, unholy, unrighteous, wicked.
antonym pious.

impish *adj* arch, devilish, elfin, frolicsome, gamin, mischievous, naughty, prankish, puckish, rascally, roguish, sportive, tricksy, waggish, wanton, wicked.
antonym demure.

implacability *n* implacableness, inexorability, inflexibility, intractability, intransigence, irreconcilability, mercilessness, pitilessness, rancour, relentlessness, remorselessness, ruthlessness, unforgivingness, vengefulness.
antonym placability.

implacable *adj* cruel, immovable, inappeasable, inexorable, inflexible, intractable, intransigent, irreconcilable, merciless, pitiless, rancorous, relentless, remorseless, revengeful, ruthless, unappeasable, unbending, uncompromising, unforgiving, unrelenting, unyielding.
antonym placable.

implant *v* embed, fix, graft, inculcate, indoctrinate, infix, infuse, ingraft, inoculate, inseminate, insert, inset, instil, place, plant, root, sow.

implausible *adj* dubious, far-fetched, flimsy, improbable, incredible, suspect, thin, transparent, unbelievable, unconvincing, unlikely, unreasonable, weak.
antonym plausible.

implement *n* agent, apparatus, appliance, device, gadget, gimmick, gizmo, instrument, tool, utensil.
v accomplish, bring about, carry out, complete, discharge, do, effect, enforce, execute, fulfil, perfect, perform, put into effect, realize.

implementation *n* accomplishment, carrying out, completion, discharge, effecting, enforcement, execution, fulfilling, fulfilment, performance, performing, realization.

implicate *v* associate, compromise, connect, embroil, entail, entangle, imply, incriminate, inculpate, involve, point a finger at, suggest, throw suspicion on.
antonyms absolve, exonerate.

implicated *adj* accused, associated, compromised, embroiled, entangled, entailed, fingered, implied, incriminated, inculpated, involved, suspected.
antonym exonerated.

implication *n* accusation, association, assumption, conclusion, connection, entailment, entanglement, hint, incrimination, inference, innuendo, insinuation, involvement, meaning, overtone, presupposition, ramification, repercussion, significance, signification, suggestion, undertone.

implicit *adj* absolute, contained, firm, fixed, full, implied, inherent, intrinsic, latent, presupposed, steadfast, tacit, total, undeclared, underlying, understood, unhesitating, unqualified, unquestioning, unreserved, unshakable, unshaken, unspoken, wholehearted.
antonym explicit.
▲ *confusable word* explicit.

implicitly *adv* absolutely, by implication, completely, firmly, unconditionally, unhesitatingly, unquestioningly, unreservedly, utterly, without question.
antonyms explicitly, with reservation.

implied *adj* assumed, hinted, implicated, implicit, indirect, inherent, insinuated, suggested, tacit, undeclared, underlying, understood, unexpressed, unspoken, unstated.
antonym stated.

implore *v* ask, beg, beseech, crave, entreat, importune, plead, pray, solicit, supplicate, wheedle.

imply *v* betoken, connote, denote, entail, evidence, hint, import, indicate, insinuate, intimate, involve, mean, point to, presuppose, promise, require, signify, suggest.
antonym state.
▲ *confusable word* infer.

impolite *adj* abrupt, bad-mannered, boorish, churlish, coarse, cross, discourteous, disrespectful, gauche, ill-bred, ill-mannered, indecorous, indelicate, insolent, loutish, rough, rude, tactless, uncivil, uncourteous, undiplomatic, ungallant, ungentlemanly, ungracious, unladylike, unmannerly, unrefined.
antonym polite.

impoliteness *n* abruptness, bad manners, boorishness, churlishness, coarseness, crassness, discourtesy, disrespect, gaucherie, ill breeding, incivility, indelicacy, insolence, lack of diplomacy, rudeness, tactlessness, ungraciousness, unmannerliness.
antonym politeness.

impolitic *adj* daft, foolish, ill-advised, ill-considered, ill-judged, imprudent, indiscreet, inexpedient, injudicious, misguided, rash, undiplomatic, unwise.
antonym politic.

import *n* bearing, concernment, consequence, drift, essence, gist, implication, importance, importation, intention, magnitude, meaning, moment, nub, purport, sense, significance, substance, thrust, weight.
v betoken, bring in, imply, indicate, introduce, mean, purport, signify.

importance *n* authority, concern, concernment, consequence, consideration, distinction, eminence, esteem, gravity, import, influence, interest, mark, moment, momentousness, pre-eminence, prestige, prominence, repute, significance, standing, status, substance, value, weight, worth.
antonym unimportance.

important *adj* authoritative, basic, earth-shaking, earth-shattering, eminent,

essential, far-reaching, foremost, grave, heavy, high-level, high-ranking, influential, key, keynote, large, leading, material, meaningful, momentous, notable, noteworthy, on the map, outstanding, powerful, pre-eminent, primary, prominent, relevant, salient, seminal, serious, signal, significant, substantial, urgent, valuable, valued, weighty.
antonym unimportant.

importunate *adj* annoying, demanding, imploring, insistent, persistent, pertinacious, pestering, pressing, tenacious, urgent, wheedling.

importune *v* badger, beset, besiege, cajole, dun, entreat, harass, hound, insist (on), pester, plague, plead with, press, pressure, solicit, urge.

importunity *n* cajolery, entreaty, harassment, insistence, persistence, pertinacity, solicitation, urging.

impose[1] *v* burden, charge, decree, demand, dictate, encumber, enforce, enjoin, establish, exact, fix, inflict, institute, introduce, lay, levy, make mandatory, ordain, place, prescribe, promulgate, put, saddle, set.

impose[2] *v* butt in, encroach, foist, force, gate-crash, horn in, interpose, intrude, obtrude, presume, take liberties, trespass.

impose on abuse, cheat on, deceive, exploit, fool, hoodwink, inconvenience, mislead, play on, take advantage of, trick, use.

imposing *adj* august, commanding, dignified, distinguished, effective, grand, grandiose, impressive, majestic, orotund, pompous, stately, striking, weighty.
antonyms modest, unimposing.

imposition[1] *n* application, decree, demand, exaction, infliction, introduction, levying, promulgation.

imposition[2] *n* burden, charge, constraint, deception, duty, encroachment, fraud, intrusion, levy, liberty, presumption, punishment, task, tax, trick.

impossibility *n* hopelessness, impracticability, inability, inconceivability, unattainability, untenability, unviability.
antonym possibility.

impossible *adj* absurd, hopeless, impracticable, inadmissible, inconceivable, insoluble, intolerable, ludicrous, outrageous, preposterous, unacceptable, unachievable, unattainable, ungovernable, unobtainable, unreasonable, untenable, unthinkable, unviable, unworkable.
antonym possible.

impostor *n* charlatan, cheat, con man, deceiver, fake, fraud, grifter, hypocrite, impersonator, mountebank, phony, pretender, quack, rogue, sham, swindler, trickster.

imposture *n* artifice, cheat, con, counterfeit, deception, fraud, grift, hoax, impersonation, quackery, swindle, trick.

impotence *n* disability, enervation, feebleness, frailty, futility, helplessness, impuissance, inability, inadequacy, incapacity, incompetence,

ineffectiveness, inefficacy, inefficiency, infirmity, paralysis, powerlessness, resourcelessness, sterility, uselessness, weakness.
antonym strength.

impotent *adj* disabled, enervated, feeble, frail, helpless, impuissant, inadequate, incapable, incapacitated, incompetent, ineffective, infirm, paralysed, powerless, resourceless, sterile, unable, unmanned, useless, weak.
antonyms potent, strong.

impoverish *v* bankrupt, beggar, break, consume, denude, deplete, despoil, diminish, drain, exhaust, pauperize, reduce, ruin, weaken.
antonym enrich.

impoverished *adj* arid, bankrupt, barren, decayed, denuded, depleted, destitute, distressed, drained, empty, exhausted, impecunious, in reduced circumstances, indigent, jejune, meagre, necessitous, needy, on the rocks, penurious, poor, poorly off, reduced, spent, straitened, used up.
antonym rich.

impracticability *n* futility, hopelessness, impossibility, impracticality, infeasibility, unsuitableness, unviability, unworkability, uselessness.
antonym practicability.

impracticable *adj* awkward, doctrinaire, impossible, impractical, inapplicable, infeasible, unachievable, unattainable, unfeasible, unpractical, unserviceable, unsuitable, unworkable, useless, visionary.
antonym practicable.

impractical *adj* academic, idealistic, impossible, impracticable, inoperable, ivory-tower, non-viable, romantic, starry-eyed, theoretical, unbusinesslike, unfeasible, unrealistic, unserviceable, unusable, unwieldy, unworkable, visionary, wild.
antonym practical.

imprecation *n* abuse, anathema, blasphemy, curse, denunciation, execration, malediction, profanity, swearing, vilification, vituperation.

imprecise *adj* ambiguous, careless, equivocal, estimated, fluctuating, hazy, ill-defined, inaccurate, indefinite, indeterminate, inexact, inexplicit, loose, rough, sloppy, unprecise, unscholarly, unscientific, vague, woolly.
antonym precise.

impregnable *adj* fast, fortified, immovable, impenetrable, indestructible, invincible, invulnerable, secure, solid, strong, unassailable, unbeatable, unconquerable.
antonym vulnerable.

impregnate *v* fecundate, fertilize, fill (with), fructify, imbrue, imbue, infuse, inseminate, inspire, knock up, percolate, permeate, pervade, saturate, soak, steep, suffuse.

impregnation *n* fecundation, fertilization, fertilizing, fructification, fructifying, imbruement, imbuement, insemination, saturation, soaking.

impress *v* affect, emboss, engrave, excite, fix, grab, imprint, inculcate, incuse, indent, influence, inspire, instil, make one's mark on, mark, move, name-drop, print, stamp, stand out, stir, strike, sway, touch, wow.

impressed adj affected, engraved, excited, fixed, grabbed, imprinted, indented, infixed, influenced, marked, moved, stamped, stirred, struck, taken, touched, turned on.

antonym unimpressed.

impression[1] n awareness, belief, concept, consciousness, conviction, effect, fancy, feeling, hunch, idea, impact, influence, memory, notion, opinion, reaction, recollection, sense, suspicion, sway.

impression[2] n copy, dent, edition, engram, hollow, impress, imprint, imprinting, incuse, indentation, issue, mark, niello, outline, pressure, printing, stamp, stamping.

impression[3] n aping, burlesque, imitation, impersonation, mimicry, parody, sendup, takeoff.

impressionability n greenness, ingenuousness, naïvety, pliancy, receptiveness, receptivity, sensitivity, suggestibility, susceptibility, teachability, vulnerability.

impressionable adj educable, gullible, ingenuous, naïve, open, receptive, responsive, sensitive, suggestible, susceptible, vulnerable.

impressive adj convincing, effective, eloquent, exciting, forcible, foudroyant, imposing, moving, powerful, stirring, striking, touching.

antonym unimpressive.

imprint n brand mark, effect, impression, indentation, logo, mark, print, sign, stamp.

v brand, engrave, etch, fix, impress, mark, press, print, stamp.

imprison v cage, confine, constrain, coop up, detain, encage, enchain, fence in, immure, incarcerate, intern, jail, lock up, put away, send down.

antonym free.

imprisoned adj behind bars, caged, captive, confined, cooped up, doing time, immured, in captivity, incarcerated, in prison, jailed, locked up, put away, sent down.

antonym free.

imprisonment n captivity, confinement, custody, detention, durance, duress, enchainment, immurement, incarceration, internment, time.

antonym freedom.

improbable adj doubtful, dubious, fanciful, far-fetched, implausible, preposterous, questionable, tall, unbelievable, uncertain, unconvincing, unexpected, unlikely, weak.

antonym probable.

impromptu adj ad lib, extemporaneous, extempore, extemporized, improvised, offhand, off-the-cuff, spontaneous, unpremeditated, unprepared, unrehearsed, unscripted, unstudied.

antonyms planned, rehearsed.

adv ad lib, extemporaneously, extempore, off the cuff, off the top of one's head, on the spur of the moment, spontaneously.

n ad lib, extemporization, improvisation, playing by ear, voluntary.

improper adj bad, erroneous, false, illegitimate, ill-timed, impolite, inaccurate, inadmissible, inapplicable, inapposite, inappropriate, inapt, incongruous, incorrect, indecent, indecorous, indelicate, inexpedient, infelicitous, inopportune, irregular, malapropos, off-colour, out-of-place, risqué, smutty, suggestive, unbecoming, uncalled-for, unfit, unfitting, unjustifiable, unmaidenly, unparliamentary, unprintable, unquotable, unrepeatable, unseasonable, unseemly, unsuitable, untimely, untoward, unwarranted, vulgar, wrong.

antonym proper.

impropriety n bad taste, blunder, faux pas, gaffe, gaucherie, immodesty, incongruity, indecency, indecorousness, indecorum, injustice, lapse, mistake, slip, solecism, unseemliness, unsuitability, untimeliness, vulgarity.

antonym propriety.

improve v advance, ameliorate, amend, augment, better, correct, cultivate, culture, deodorize, develop, enhance, further, gentrify, get better, help, increase, look up, make better, meliorate, mend, mend one's ways, perk up, pick up, polish, progress, rally, recover, rectify, recuperate, refine, reform, restore, rise, touch up, turn over a new leaf, turn the corner, up, upgrade.

antonyms decline, diminish.

improvement n advance, advancement, amelioration, amendment, augmentation, bettering, betterment, correction, development, enhancement, furtherance, gain, gentrification, increase, melioration, progress, rally, recovery, rectification, reformation, restoration, rise, upswing.

antonyms decline, retrogression.

improvident adj careless, extravagant, feckless, heedless, imprudent, negligent, prodigal, profligate, rash, rashness, reckless, shiftless, short-sighted, spendthrift, thoughtless, thriftless, uneconomical, unprepared, unthrifty, wasteful.

antonym thrifty.

improving adj convalescing, edifying, educational, instructive, meliorative, on the mend, recuperating, uplifting.

antonyms harmful, unedifying.

improvisation n ad hockery, ad lib, ad libbing, expedient, extemporization, extemporizing, impromptu, invention, makeshift, spontaneity, vamp.

improvise v ad lib, coin, concoct, contrive, devise, extemporize, fake it, invent, make do with, make it up, play it by ear, throw together, vamp, wing it.

improvised adj ad hoc, ad lib, extemporaneous, extempore, extemporized, improvisational, improvisatorial, makeshift, off-the-cuff, spontaneous, stopgap, unprepared, unrehearsed.

antonym rehearsed.

imprudent *adj* careless, foolhardy, foolish, hasty, heedless, ill-advised, ill-considered, ill-judged, impolitic, improvident, incautious, inconsiderate, indiscreet, injudicious, irresponsible, overhasty, rash, reckless, short-sighted, temerarious, unthinking, unwise.
antonym prudent.

impudence *n* assurance, audacity, backchat, back talk, boldness, brass, brazenness, cheek, chutzpah, disrespect, effrontery, face, gall, impertinence, impudicity, insolence, lip, malapertness, nerve, pertness, presumption, presumptuousness, rudeness, sauciness, shamelessness.
antonyms demureness, modesty, politeness.

impudent *adj* audacious, bold, boldfaced, brazen, brazenfaced, cheeky, cocky, disrespectful, forward, fresh, immodest, impertinent, insolent, malapert, pert, presumptuous, rude, saucy, shameless.
antonyms demure, modest, polite.

impugn *v* assail, attack, call in question, censure, challenge, controvert, criticize, deny, dispute, oppose, question, renounce, resist, take issue with, vituperate.
antonym praise.

impulse *n* caprice, catalyst, desire, drive, feeling, force, impetus, incitement, inclination, influence, instinct, momentum, motive, movement, notion, passion, pressure, push, resolve, stimulus, surge, thrust, urge, whim, wish.

impulsive *adj* hasty, headlong, impetuous, instinctive, intuitive, passionate, precipitate, quick, rash, reckless, spontaneous, sudden, unconsidered, unpredictable, unpremeditated.
antonyms cautious, well thought out.

impulsiveness *n* haste, hastiness, impetuosity, impetuousness, precipitateness, precipitation, rashness, recklessness.
antonym caution.

impunity *n* amnesty, dispensation, exemption, freedom, immunity, liberty, licence, non prosequitur, permission, security.
antonym liability.

impure *adj* admixed, adulterated, alloyed, bad, carnal, coarse, contaminated, corrupt, debased, defiled, dirty, feculent, filthy, foul, gross, immodest, immoral, indecent, indelicate, infected, lascivious, lewd, licentious, lustful, mixed, obscene, polluted, prurient, salacious, smutty, spoiled, sullied, tainted, turbid, unchaste, unclean, unrefined, unwholesome, vicious, vitiated.
antonyms chaste, pure.

impurity *n* admixture, adulteration, befoulment, carnality, coarseness, contaminant, contamination, corruption, defilement, dirt, dirtiness, dross, feculence, filth, foreign body, foreign matter, foulness, grime, grossness, immodesty, immorality, indecency, infection, lasciviousness, lewdness, licentiousness, mark, mixture, obscenity, pollutant, pollution, prurience, salaciousness, scum, smuttiness, spot, stain, taint, turbidity, turbidness, unchastity, uncleanness, vulgarity.

antonyms chasteness, purity.

imputable *adj* ascribable, attributable, blameworthy, chargeable, referable, traceable.

imputation *n* accusation, arrogation, ascription, aspersion, attribution, blame, censure, charge, insinuation, libel, reproach, slander, slur, suggestion.

impute *v* accredit, accuse, ascribe, assign, attribute, blame, charge, credit, put down to, refer.

in
For phrases such as *in a state*, *in addition*, *in the making*, see the first noun after *in*.

inability *n* disability, disqualification, handicap, impotence, inadequacy, incapability, incapacity, incompetence, ineptitude, ineptness, powerlessness, weakness.
antonym ability.

inaccessible *adj* hard to get at, impassible, isolated, out-of-the-way, remote, solitary, unapproachable, unattainable, unfrequented, unreachable.
antonym accessible.

inaccuracy *n* carelessness, corrigendum, defect, discrepancy, erratum, erroneousness, error, fault, faultiness, imprecision, incorrectness, inexactness, looseness, miscalculation, misrepresentation, mistake, slip, unfaithfulness, unreliability.
antonym accuracy.

inaccurate *adj* careless, defective, discrepant, erroneous, faulty, imprecise, incorrect, in error, inexact, loose, mistaken, out, unfaithful, unreliable, unrepresentative, unsound, wide of the mark, wild, wrong.
antonym accurate.

inaccurately *adv* carelessly, erroneously, imperfectly, imprecisely, incorrectly, in error, inexactly, loosely, mistakenly, unfaithfully, unreliably.
antonym accurately.

inaction *n* dormancy, idleness, immobility, inactivity, inertia, motionlessness, passiveness, rest, stagnation, stasis, torpidity, torpor.
antonyms action, activeness.

inactivate *v* cripple, disable, immobilize, incapacitate, knock the bottom out of, mothball, paralyse, put out of commission, scupper, stop.
antonym activate.

inactive *adj* dormant, dull, hibernating, idle, immobile, in abeyance, incapacitated, indolent, inert, inoperative, jobless, kicking one's heels, latent, lazy, lethargic, low-key, mothballed, out of service, out of work, passive, quiet, sedentary, sleepy, slothful, slow, sluggish, somnolent, stagnant, stagnating, torpid, unemployed, unoccupied, unused.
antonym active.

inactivity *n* abeyance, dilatoriness, dolce far niente, dormancy, dullness, heaviness, hibernation, idleness, immobility, inaction, inactiveness, indolence, inertia, inertness, languor, lassitude, laziness, lethargy, motionlessness, passivity, quiescence, rest, sloth, sluggishness, stagnation, stasis, torpidity, torpor, unemployment, vegetation. *antonym* activeness.

inadequacy *n* dearth, defect, defectiveness, deficiency, failing, fault, faultiness, imperfection, inability, inadequateness, inaptness, incapacity, incompetence, incompleteness, ineffectiveness, ineffectuality, ineffectualness, inefficacy, inefficiency, inferiority, insufficiency, lack, meagreness, paucity, poverty, scantiness, shortage, shortcoming, skimpiness, unfitness, unsatisfactoriness, unsuitableness, want, weakness. *antonym* adequacy.

inadequate *adj* defective, deficient, faulty, imperfect, inapt, incapable, incommensurate, incompetent, incomplete, ineffective, ineffectual, inefficacious, inefficient, inept, inferior, insubstantial, insufficient, leaving a little (or a lot or much) to be desired, meagre, niggardly, poor, scanty, short, sketchy, skimpy, sparse, unequal, unfitted, unqualified, unsatisfactory, wanting. *antonym* adequate.

inadmissible *adj* disallowed, immaterial, improper, inappropriate, irrelevant, prohibited, unacceptable, unallowable. *antonym* admissible.

inadvertence *n* accident, blunder, booboo, carelessness, clanger, error, goof, heedlessness, inadvertence, inattention, inconsideration, inobservance, mistake, neglect, negligence, oversight, remissness, thoughtlessness. *antonym* care.

inadvertent *adj* accidental, careless, chance, heedless, inattentive, negligent, thoughtless, unguarded, unheeding, unintended, unintentional, unplanned, unpremeditated, unthinking, unwitting. *antonym* deliberate.

inadvertently *adv* accidentally, by accident, by mistake, carelessly, heedlessly, involuntarily, mistakenly, negligently, remissly, thoughtlessly, unguardedly, unintentionally, unpremeditatedly, unthinkingly, unwittingly. *antonym* deliberately.

inadvisable *adj* daft, foolish, ill-advised, ill-judged, impolitic, imprudent, incautious, indiscreet, inexpedient, injudicious, misguided, unwise. *antonym* advisable.

inalienable *adj* absolute, entailed, imprescriptible, indefeasible, infrangible, inherent, inviolable, non-negotiable, non-transferable, permanent, sacrosanct, unassailable, unremovable, untransferable. *antonym* impermanent.

inane *adj* asinine, daft, drippy, empty, fatuous, foolish, frivolous, futile, idiotic, imbecilic, meaningless, mindless, nutty, puerile, senseless, silly, soppy, stupid, trifling, trivial, unintelligent, vacuous, vain, vapid, worthless. *antonym* sensible.

inanimate *adj* abiotic, dead, defunct, dormant, dull, exanimate, extinct, heavy, inactive, inert, inorganic, insensate, insentient, languid, leaden, lifeless, listless, slow, spiritless, stagnant, torpid. *antonyms* alive, animate, lively, living.

inanity *n* asininity, bêtise, daftness, drippiness, emptiness, fatuity, folly, foolishness, frivolity, futility, imbecility, puerility, senselessness, silliness, stupidity, triviality, vacuity, vapidity, waffle. *antonym* sense.

inapplicable *adj* inapposite, inappropriate, inapt, inconsequent, irrelevant, unrelated, unsuitable, unsuited. *antonym* applicable.

inappropriate *adj* disproportionate, ill-fitted, ill-suited, ill-timed, improper, inapt, in bad taste, incongruous, infelicitous, malapropos, out-of-place, tactless, tasteless, unbecoming, unbefitting, unfit, unfitting, unseemly, unsuitable, untimely. *antonym* appropriate.

inappropriately *adv* inaptly, malapropos, tactlessly, tastelessly, unsuitably. *antonym* appropriately.

inapt *adj* awkward, clumsy, crass, dull, gauche, ill-fitted, ill-suited, ill-timed, inapposite, inappropriate, incompetent, inept, inexpert, infelicitous, inopportune, maladroit, slow, stupid, tactless, unapt, unfortunate, unhappy, unskilful, unsuitable, unsuited. *antonyms* apt, suitable.

inaptitude *n* awkwardness, clumsiness, crassness, inaptness, incompetence, inopportuneness, lack of skill, maladroitness, tactlessness, unfitness, unreadiness, unskilfulness, unsuitableness. *antonym* aptitude.

inarticulate *adj* blurred, dumb, dysarthric, dysphasic, dyspraxic, faltering, halting, hesitant, incoherent, incomprehensible, indistinct, muffled, mumbled, mute, silent, speechless, tongue-tied, unclear, unintelligible, unspoken, unuttered, unvoiced, voiceless, wordless. *antonym* articulate.

inattention *n* absence of mind, absent-mindedness, carelessness, daydreaming, disregard, distraction, forgetfulness, heedlessness, inadvertence, inattentiveness, neglect, negligence, preoccupation, woolgathering. *antonym* attentiveness.

inattentive *adj* absent-minded, careless, distracted, distrait, dreaming, dreamy, heedless, inadvertent, neglectful, negligent, preoccupied, regardless, remiss, unheeding, unmindful, unobservant, vague, woolgathering. *antonym* attentive.

inaudible *adj* faint, imperceptible, indistinct, low, muffled, mumbled, mumbling, muted, noiseless, out of earshot, silent. *antonym* audible.

inaugural *adj* consecratory, dedicatory, exordial, first, initial, introductory, launching, maiden, opening, preliminary.

inaugurate *v* begin, commence, commission, consecrate, dedicate, enthrone, handsel, induct, initiate, innovate, install, instate, institute, introduce, invest, kick off, launch, open, ordain, originate, set up, start, start off, usher in.

inauguration *n* beginning, consecration, enthronement, handsel, inception, induction, initiation, installation, installing, institution, investiture, launch, launching, opening, setting up.

inauspicious *adj* bad, discouraging, doomed, ill-boding, ill-fated, ill-omened, ominous, threatening, unfavourable, unfortunate, unlucky, unpromising, unpropitious, untimely, untoward.
antonym auspicious.

inborn *adj* congenital, connate, hereditary, inbred, ingenerate, ingrained, inherent, inherited, innate, instinctive, intuitive, native, natural.
antonym learned.

inbred *adj* bred in the bone, connate, constitutional, genetic, hereditary, inborn, ingenerate, ingrained, inherent, innate, native, natural.
antonym learned.

incalculable *adj* boundless, countless, enormous, immeasurable, immense, incomputable, inestimable, infinite, innumerable, limitless, measureless, numberless, uncountable, unforeseeable, unknown, unlimited, unmeasurable, unpredictable, untold, vast.
antonym limited.

in camera behind closed doors, in closed session, in judge's chambers, in private, in secret, privately, secretly, sub rosa, under the rose.
antonym openly.

incantation *n* abracadabra, chant, charm, conjuration, formula, hex, invocation, mantra, om, rune, spell.

incapable *adj* feeble, helpless, impotent, inadequate, incompetent, ineffective, ineffectual, inept, insufficient, not cut out, not equal, powerless, unable, unequipped, unfit, unfitted, unqualified, weak.
antonyms capable, sober.

incapacitate *v* cripple, disable, disqualify, hamstring, immobilize, lay up, paralyse, prostrate, put out of action, scupper, unfit.
antonyms facilitate, set up.

incapacitated *adj* crippled, disabled, disqualified, drunk, hamstring, immobilized, indisposed, laid up, out of action, prostrate, scuppered, tipsy, unfit, unwell, weakened.
antonym operative.

incapacity *n* disability, disqualification, feebleness, impotence, inability, inadequacy, incapability, incompetency, ineffectiveness, powerlessness, unfitness, unskilfulness, weakness.
antonym capability.

incarcerate *v* cage, commit, confine, coop up, detain, encage, enclose, immure, impound, imprison, intern, jail, lock up, put away, restrain, restrict, send down, shut in, wall in.
antonym free.

incarceration *n* bondage, captivity, confinement, custody, detention, imprisonment, internment, jail, restraint, restriction.
antonym freedom.

incarnate *adj* embodied, made flesh, personified, typified.

incarnation *n* appearance, avatar, embodiment, exemplification, impersonation, manifestation, materialization, personification, type.

incautious *adj* careless, hasty, heedless, ill-advised, ill-judged, improvident, imprudent, impulsive, inattentive, inconsiderate, indiscreet, injudicious, negligent, overhasty, precipitate, rash, reckless, thoughtless, unguarded, unthinking, unwary.
antonym cautious.

incendiary[1] *n* arsonist, firebomber, firebug, incendiaire, pyromaniac.

incendiary[2] *n* agitator, demagogue, firebrand, inciter, instigator, insurgent, rabble-rouser, revolutionary.
adj dissentious, inciting, inflammatory, provocative, rabble-rousing, seditious, subversive.
antonym calming.

incense[1] *n* adulation, aroma, balm, bouquet, flattery, fragrance, homage, joss stick, oblation, perfume, scent, worship.

incense[2] *v* anger, enrage, exasperate, excite, inflame, infuriate, irritate, madden, make one see red, make one's blood boil, make one's hackles rise, provoke, raise one's hackles, rile.
antonym calm.

incensed *adj* angry, enraged, exasperated, fuming, furious, in a state, indignant, infuriated, in high dudgeon, irate, ireful, livid, mad, maddened, steamed up, ticked off, up in arms, worked up, wrathful.
antonym calm.

incentive *n* bait, carrot, cause, consideration, encouragement, enticement, impetus, impulse, inducement, lure, motivation, motive, reason, reward, spur, stimulant, stimulus.
antonym disincentive.

inception *n* beginning, birth, commencement, dawn, inauguration, initiation, installation, kickoff, origin, outset, rise, start.
antonym end.

incessant *adj* ceaseless, constant, continual, continuous, endless, eternal, everlasting, interminable, never-ending, non-stop, perpetual, persistent, relentless, unbroken, unceasing, unending, unrelenting, unremitting, weariless.
antonym intermittent.

income

incidence n amount, commonness, degree, extent, frequency, occurrence, prevalence, range, rate.

incident n adventure, affair, brush, circumstance, clash, commotion, confrontation, contretemps, disturbance, episode, event, fight, happening, mishap, occasion, occurrence, scene, skirmish.

incidental adj accidental, accompanying, ancillary, attendant, casual, chance, concomitant, contingent, contributory, fortuitous, incident, inconsequential, inessential, irrelevant, minor, non-essential, occasional, odd, random, related, secondary, subordinate, subsidiary.
antonym essential.

incidentally adv accidentally, by chance, by the by, by the way, casually, digressively, en passant, fortuitously, in passing, parenthetically.

incidentals n contingencies, epiphenomena, extras, non-essentials, odds and ends.
antonym essentials.

incinerate v burn, char, cremate, destroy, reduce to ashes.

incipient adj beginning, commencing, developing, embryonic, inceptive, inchoate, nascent, originating, rudimentary, starting.
antonym developed.

incise v carve, chisel, cut, cut into, engrave, etch, gash, groove, notch.

incised adj carved, cut, engraved, grooved, notched.

incision n cut, engraving, gash, groove, notch, opening, slash, slit.

incisive adj acid, acute, astute, biting, caustic, cutting, discerning, keen, mordant, penetrating, perceptive, perspicacious, piercing, sagacious, sarcastic, sardonic, satirical, severe, sharp, tart, trenchant.
antonym woolly.

incite v abet, animate, drive, egg on, encourage, excite, foment, goad, impel, inflame, instigate, prompt, provoke, put up to, rabble-rouse, rouse, set on, solicit, spur, stimulate, stir up, urge on, whip up.
antonym restrain.

incitement n abetment, agitation, encouragement, excitation, exhortation, goad, impetus, impulse, incentive, inducement, instigation, motivation, motive, prompting, provocation, rabble-rousing, spur, stimulus.
antonyms check, discouragement.

inciting adj agitative, exciting, incendiary, incitive, inflammatory, instigative, provocative, rabble-rousing.
antonym calming.

incivility n bad manners, boorishness, coarseness, discourteousness, discourtesy, disrespect, ill-breeding, impoliteness, inurbanity, lack of courtesy, roughness, rudeness, unmannerliness, vulgarity.
antonym civility.

inclement adj bitter, boisterous, callous, cold, cruel, draconian, foul, harsh, intemperate, merciless, pitiless, rigorous, rough, severe, stormy, tempestuous, tyrannical, unfeeling, ungenial, unkind, unmerciful.
antonym clement.

inclination[1] n affection, aptitude, bent, bias, desire, disposition, fancy, fondness, leaning, liking, partiality, penchant, predilection, predisposition, preference, prejudice, proclivity, proneness, propensity, stomach, taste, tendency, turn, turn of mind, wish.
antonym disinclination.

inclination[2] n angle, bend, bending, bow, bowing, deviation, gradient, incline, leaning, nod, pitch, slant, slope, tilt.

incline[1] v affect, be willing, bias, dispose, influence, nod, persuade, predispose, prefer, prejudice, sway, tend.

incline[2] v bend, bevel, bow, cant, deviate, diverge, lean, slant, slope, tend, tilt, tip, veer.
n acclivity, ascent, declivity, descent, dip, grade, gradient, hill, ramp, rise, slope.

inclined[1] adj apt, disposed, given, liable, likely, minded, of a mind, predisposed, prone, tending, willing.
antonym disinclined.

inclined[2] adj bent, inclining, leaning, oblique, slanting, sloping, tilted.
antonyms flat, level.

include v add, allow for, comprehend, comprise, connote, contain, cover, embody, embrace, enclose, encompass, incorporate, involve, number among, rope in, subsume, take in, take into account.
antonyms exclude, ignore.

inclusion n addition, incorporation, insertion, involvement.
antonym exclusion.

inclusive adj across-the-board, all-embracing, blanket, catch-all, compendious, comprehensive, full, general, overall, sweeping, umbrella.
antonyms exclusive, narrow.

incognito adj anonymous, disguised, in disguise, masked, masquerading, unknown, unrecognizable, unrecognized, veiled.
antonyms openly, undisguised.

incoherent adj confused, disconnected, discontinuous, disjointed, dislocated, disordered, illogical, inarticulate, inconsequent, inconsistent, jumbled, loose, muddled, rambling, stammering, stuttering, uncohesive, unconnected, unco-ordinated, unintelligible, vague, wandering.
antonym coherent.

incombustible adj fireproof, fire-resistant, flameproof, flame-resistant, nonflammable, non-inflammable, unburnable, uninflammable.
antonym combustible.

income n earnings, gain(s), interest, means, pay, proceeds, profits, receipts, remuneration, returns, revenue, salary, takings, wages, yield.
antonym expenses.

incoming *adj* accruing, approaching, arriving, coming, ensuing, entering, landing, new, next, returning, succeeding.

antonym outgoing.

incommensurate *adj* disproportionate, dissimilar, inadequate, incommensurable, inconsistent, inequitable, insufficient, out of proportion, unequal.

antonym appropriate.

incommunicable *adj* indescribable, ineffable, inexpressible, unimpartable, unspeakable, unutterable.

antonym expressible.

incomparable *adj* brilliant, dissimilar, incommensurable, inimitable, matchless, paramount, peerless, superb, superlative, supreme, transcendent, unequalled, unmatched, unparalleled, unrelated, unrivalled, without equal.

antonyms poor, run-of-the-mill.

incomparably *adv* brilliantly, by far, eminently, far and away, immeasurably, peerlessly, superbly, superlatively.

antonyms poorly, slightly.

incompatibility *n* antagonism, clash, conflict, difference, discord, discrepancy, disparateness, disparity, enmity, incongruity, inconsistency, irreconcilability, lack of harmony, mismatch, uncongeniality.

antonym compatibility.

incompatible *adj* antagonistic, antipathetic, clashing, conflicting, contradictory, different, disagreeing, discordant, discrepant, disparate, ill-assorted, incongruous, inconsistent, inconsonant, inharmonious, irreconcilable, mismatched, uncongenial, unsuitable, unsuited.

antonym compatible.

incompetence *n* bungling, inability, inadequacy, incapability, incapacity, ineffectiveness, ineffectuality, ineffectualness, inefficiency, ineptitude, ineptness, inferiority, insufficiency, lack of skill, stupidity, unfitness, uselessness.

antonym competence.

incompetent *adj* bungling, floundering, incapable, incapacitated, ineffective, ineffectual, inept, inexpert, inferior, insufficient, stupid, unable, unfit, unfitted, unskilful, useless.

antonym competent.

incomplete *adj* broken, defective, deficient, fragmentary, imperfect, inexhaustive, insufficient, lacking, part, partial, short, unaccomplished, undeveloped, undone, unexecuted, unfinished, wanting.

antonym complete.

incomprehensible *adj* above one's head, arcane, baffling, beyond belief, beyond one's comprehension, beyond one's grasp, enigmatic, impenetrable, inapprehensible, inconceivable, inscrutable, mysterious, obscure, opaque, perplexing, puzzling, unbelievable, unfathomable, unimaginable, unintelligible, unthinkable.

antonym comprehensible.

inconceivable *adj* implausible, impossible, incredible, mind-boggling, out of the question, staggering, unbelievable, unheard-of, unimaginable, unknowable, unthinkable.

antonym conceivable.

inconclusive *adj* ambiguous, indecisive, indeterminate, open, uncertain, unconvincing, undecided, unproved, unsatisfying, unsettled, vague.

antonym conclusive.

incongruity *n* conflict, difference, discrepancy, disharmony, disparity, inappropriateness, inaptness, incompatibility, inconsistency, inequality, inharmoniousness, nonconformity, unsuitability.

antonyms consistency, harmoniousness.

incongruous *adj* absurd, clashing, conflicting, contradictory, contrary, different, disconsonant, discordant, extraneous, improper, inappropriate, inapt, incoherent, incompatible, inconsistent, out of keeping, out of place, unbecoming, unsuitable, unsuited.

antonyms consistent, harmonious.

inconsequential *adj* illogical, immaterial, inconsequent, inconsiderable, insignificant, minor, negligible, paltry, petty, trifling, trivial, unimportant.

antonym important.

inconsiderable *adj* exiguous, inconsequential, insignificant, light, minor, negligible, petty, piddling, piffling, slight, small, small-time, trifling, trivial, unimportant, unnoticeable.

antonym considerable.

inconsiderate *adj* careless, discourteous, heedless, imprudent, indelicate, insensitive, intolerant, rash, rude, self-centred, selfish, tactless, thoughtless, unconcerned, ungracious, unkind, unthinking, unwise.

antonym considerate.

inconsistency *n* changeableness, contrariety, difference, disagreement, discrepancy, disparity, divergence, fickleness, illogic, incompatibility, incongruity, inconsonance, inconstancy, instability, paradox, unpredictability, unreliability, unsteadiness, variance.

antonym consistency.

inconsistent *adj* at odds, at variance, capricious, changeable, conflicting, contradictory, contrary, different, discordant, discrepant, erratic, fickle, illogical, incoherent, incompatible, incongruous, inconstant, irreconcilable, irregular, paradoxical, unpredictable, unstable, unsteady, variable, varying.

antonym constant.

inconsistently *adv* contradictorily, differently, eccentrically, erratically, illogically, inequably, paradoxically, randomly, unequally, unfairly, unpredictably, variably.

antonym consistently.

inconsolable *adj* broken-hearted, desolate, desolated, despairing, devastated, disconsolate, heartbroken, wretched.

antonym consolable.

inconspicuous *adj* camouflaged, hidden, insignificant, low-key, modest, muted, ordinary, plain, quiet, retiring, unassuming, unnoticeable, unobtrusive, unostentatious.
antonym conspicuous.

inconstant *adj* capricious, chameleonlike, changeable, changeful, erratic, fickle, fluctuating, inconsistent, irregular, irresolute, mercurial, mutable, uncertain, undependable, unfaithful, unreliable, unsettled, unstable, unsteady, vacillating, variable, varying, volatile, wavering, wayward.
antonym constant.

incontestable *adj* certain, clear, evident, incontrovertible, indisputable, indubitable, irrefutable, obvious, self-evident, sure, undeniable, unquestionable.
antonym uncertain.

incontinent *adj* debauched, dissipated, dissolute, enuretic, excessive, intemperate, lascivious, lecherous, lewd, licentious, loose, lustful, profligate, promiscuous, unbridled, unchaste, unchecked, uncontrollable, uncontrolled, ungovernable, ungoverned, unrestrained, wanton.
antonym continent.

incontrovertible *adj* certain, clear, established, evident, incontestable, indisputable, indubitable, irrefutable, positive, self-evident, sure, undeniable, unquestionable, unshakable.
antonym uncertain.

inconvenience *n* annoyance, awkwardness, bother, cumbersomeness, difficulty, disadvantage, disruption, disturbance, drawback, fuss, hindrance, impediment, imposition, nuisance, trouble, uneasiness, unhandiness, unsuitableness, untimeliness, unwieldiness, upset, vexation.
antonym convenience.
v bother, discommode, disrupt, disturb, irk, put out, put to trouble, take liberties, trouble, upset.
antonym convenience.

inconvenient *adj* annoying, awkward, bothersome, cumbersome, difficult, disadvantageous, disturbing, embarrassing, inopportune, tiresome, troublesome, unhandy, unmanageable, unseasonable, unsocial, unsuitable, untimely, untoward, unwieldy, vexatious.
antonym convenient.

incorporate *v* absorb, amalgamate, assimilate, blend, coalesce, combine, consolidate, embody, fuse, incarnate, include, integrate, merge, mix, subsume, unite.
antonyms separate, split off.

incorporation *n* absorption, affiliation, amalgamation, assimilation, association, blend, coalescence, combination, company, embodiment, federation, fusion, inclusion, integration, merger, society, unification, unifying.
antonyms separation, splitting off.

incorporeal *adj* bodiless, ethereal, ghostly, illusory, immaterial, intangible, phantasmal, spectral, spiritual, unreal, unsubstantial.
antonym real.

incorrect *adj* erroneous, false, faulty, flawed, illegitimate, imprecise, improper, inaccurate, inappropriate, in error, inexact, mistaken, out, specious, ungrammatical, unidiomatic, unsuitable, untrue, wrong.
antonym correct.

incorrectness *n* erroneousness, error, fallacy, falseness, faultiness, illegitimacy, impreciseness, imprecision, impropriety, inaccuracy, inexactness, speciousness, ungrammaticality, unsoundness, unsuitability, wrongness.
antonym correctness.

incorrigible *adj* confirmed, hardened, hopeless, impenitent, incurable, indocile, intractable, inveterate, irreclaimable, irredeemable, ungovernable, unreformable, unreformed, unteachable.
antonym reformable.

incorruptibility *n* honesty, honour, indestructibility, integrity, justness, nobility, probity, uprightness, virtue.
antonym corruptibility.

incorruptible *adj* everlasting, honest, honourable, immortal, imperishable, incorrupt, indestructible, just, straight, trustworthy, unbribable, undecaying, upright.
antonym corruptible.

increase *v* add to, advance, aggrandize, aggravate, amplify, augment, boost, broaden, build up, develop, dilate, eke out, enhance, enlarge, escalate, expand, extend, greaten, grow, heighten, hike (up), increment, inflate, intensify, lengthen, magnify, maximize, mount, multiply, proliferate, prolong, propagate, pullulate, raise, snowball, soar, spread, step up, strengthen, swell, wax.
antonym decrease.
n addition, amplification, augmentation, boost, development, enlargement, escalation, expansion, extension, gain, growth, increment, intensification, offspring, propagation, proliferation, rise, spread, step-up, surge, upsurge, upsurgence, upturn.
antonym decrease.

on the increase accelerating, ballooning, escalating, expanding, growing, increasing, multiplying, on the rise, proliferating, rising, spreading, waxing.
antonym on the wane.

increasing *adj* advancing, broadening, crescent, developing, expanding, growing, intensifying, mounting, rising, rocketing, snowballing, spreading, sprouting, swelling, waxing, widening.
antonym decreasing.

incredible *adj* absurd, amazing, astonishing, astounding, extraordinary, fabulous, fantastic, far-fetched, great, implausible, impossible, improbable, inconceivable, inspired, marvellous, preposterous, prodigious,

remarkable, superb, superhuman, unbelievable, unimaginable, unthinkable, wonderful.
antonyms believable, run-of-the-mill.

incredulity *n* disbelief, distrust, doubt, doubting, incredulousness, scepticism, unbelief.
antonym credulity.

incredulous *adj* disbelieving, distrustful, doubtful, doubting, dubious, mistrustful, sceptical, suspicious, unbelieving, uncertain, unconvinced.
antonym credulous.

increment *n* accretion, accrual, accruement, addition, advancement, augmentation, enlargement, expansion, extension, gain, growth, increase, step up, supplement.
antonym decrease.

incriminate *v* accuse, arraign, blame, charge, criminate, impeach, implicate, inculpate, indict, involve, point the finger at, recriminate, stigmatize.
antonym exonerate.

incubator *n* breeding place, brooder, hatchery, hotbed, nest, nidus.

incubus *n* affliction, angst, burden, cross, demon, devil, dread, evil spirit, fear, fiend, load, nightmare, oppression, pressure, sorrow, spirit, stress, succubus, trial, worry.

inculcate *v* drill into, drum into, engrain, hammer into, implant, impress, indoctrinate, infuse, instil, teach.

inculpate *v* accuse, blame, censure, charge, connect, criminate, drag into, impeach, implicate, incriminate, involve, recriminate.
antonym exonerate.

incumbent *adj* binding, compulsory, mandatory, necessary, obligatory, overhanging, prescribed, resting (on), up to.

incur *v* arouse, bring down, bring upon, contract, draw, earn, expose oneself to, gain, induce, meet with, provoke, run into, run up, suffer.

incurable *adj* dyed-in-the-wool, fatal, hopeless, immedicable, incorrigible, inoperable, inveterate, irrecoverable, irremediable, recidivistic, remediless, terminal, unmedicable, untreatable.
antonym curable.

incurious *adj* apathetic, careless, inattentive, indifferent, unconcerned, uncurious, uninquiring, uninquisitive, uninterested, uninteresting, unobservant, unreflective.
antonym curious.

incursion *n* attack, foray, infiltration, inroad(s), intrusion, invasion, irruption, penetration, raid.

indebted *adj* beholden, grateful, in debt, obligated, obliged, thankful.

indecent *adj* bawdy, blue, coarse, crude, dirty, filthy, foul, gross, immodest, improper, impure, indecorous, indelicate, lewd, licentious, near the bone, obscene, offensive, outrageous, pornographic, Rabelaisian, racy, risqué, salacious, scatological, smutty, tasteless,

unbecoming, unchaste, uncomely, unseemly, vile, vulgar.
antonyms decent, modest.

indecipherable *adj* crabbed, cramped, illegible, indistinct, indistinguishable, tiny, unclear, unintelligible, unreadable.
antonym readable.

indecision *n* ambivalence, doubt, hesitancy, hesitation, indecisiveness, irresoluteness, irresolution, shilly-shallying, uncertainty, vacillation, wavering.
antonym decisiveness.

indecisive *adj* doubtful, faltering, hesitating, hung, inconclusive, indefinite, indeterminate, in two minds, irresolute, pussyfooting around, tentative, uncertain, unclear, undecided, undetermined, unproved, unsure, vacillating, vague, wavering.
antonym decisive.

indecorous *adj* boorish, churlish, coarse, crude, ill-bred, immodest, impolite, improper, indecent, rough, rude, tasteless, uncivil, uncouth, undignified, unmannerly, unseemly, untoward, vulgar.
antonym decorous.

indeed *adv* actually, certainly, doubtlessly, forsooth, positively, really, strictly, to be sure, truly, undeniably, undoubtedly, verily, veritably.

indefatigable *adj* assiduous, diligent, dogged, industrious, inexhaustible, patient, persevering, pertinacious, relentless, sedulous, tireless, undying, unfailing, unflagging, unremitting, unresting, untiring, unwearied, unwearying.
antonyms flagging, slothful.

indefensible *adj* faulty, inexcusable, insupportable, unacceptable, unforgivable, unjustifiable, unjustified, unpardonable, untenable, unwarrantable, wrong.
antonym defensible.

indefinable *adj* dim, hazy, impalpable, indescribable, indistinct, inexplicable, inexpressible, nameless, obscure, subtle, unclear, unrealized, vague.
antonym definable.

indefinite *adj* ambiguous, confused, doubtful, equivocal, evasive, formless, general, ill-defined, imprecise, indeterminate, indistinct, inexact, loose, obscure, uncertain, unclear, undecided, undefined, undetermined, unfixed, unfocussed, unformed, unformulated, unknown, unlimited, unresolved, unsettled, vague.
antonyms clear, limited.

indefinitely *adv* ad infinitum, continually, endlessly, eternally, for ever, for life, sine die, time without end, vaguely, world without end.

indelible *adj* deeply felt, enduring, indestructible, ineffaceable, ineradicable, inerasable, inexpungible, inextirpable, ingrained, lasting, permanent, unerasable.
antonyms erasable, impermanent.

indelicate *adj* blue, coarse, crude, embarrassing, gross, immodest, improper, in bad taste, indecent, indecorous, low, obscene, off-colour, offensive, risqué, rude, suggestive, tasteless, unbecoming, unmaidenly, unseemly, untoward, vulgar, warm.

antonym delicate.

indemnify *v* compensate, endorse, exempt, free, guarantee, insure, make restitution to, pay, protect, recompense, reimburse, remunerate, repair, repay, requite, satisfy, secure, underwrite.

indemnity *n* amnesty, atonement, compensation, excusal, exemption, guarantee, immunity, impunity, insurance, pardon, privilege, protection, recompense, redress, reimbursement, remuneration, reparation, requital, restitution, satisfaction, security.

indent¹ *v* cut, dent, dint, mark, nick, notch, pink, press in, scallop, serrate, stamp.

indent² *v* ask for, demand, order, request, requisition.

indentation *n* bash, cut, dent, depression, dimple, dint, dip, hollow, indention, jag, nick, notch, pit.

indented *adj* dented, impressed, notched, zigzag.

independence *n* autarky, autonomy, decolonization, enfranchisement, freedom, home rule, individualism, liberty, manumission, neutrality, self-determination, self-government, self-reliance, self-rule, self-sufficiency, separation, sovereignty, uhuru, unconventionality.

antonyms conventionality, dependence.

independent *adj* absolute, autarkic, autocephalous, autogenous, autonomous, decontrolled, disinterested, distinct, free, freelance, individualistic, liberated, maverick, nonaligned, non-partisan, neutral, objective, one's own man, on one's feet, self-contained, self-determining, self-employed, self-governing, self-reliant, self-sufficient, self-supporting, separate, separated, sovereign, unaided, unbiassed, unconnected, unconstrained, uncontrolled, unconventional, uninfluenced, unrelated.

antonyms conventional, dependent, timid.

independently *adv* alone, autonomously, by oneself, freelance, individually, on one's own, on one's own (two) feet, separately, solo, unaided.

antonym together.

indescribable *adj* beyond words, extraordinary, incommunicable, indefinable, ineffable, inexpressible, unspeakable, unutterable.

antonym describable.

indestructible *adj* abiding, durable, enduring, eternal, everlasting, immortal, imperishable, incorruptible, indissoluble, infrangible, lasting, permanent, perpetual, unbreakable, undestroyable, unfading.

antonyms breakable, mortal.

indeterminacy *n* impreciseness, inconclusiveness, indefiniteness, inexactness, open-endedness, uncertainty, vagueness.

antonym definiteness.

indeterminate *adj* imprecise, inconclusive, indefinite, inexact, open-ended, uncertain, undecided, undefined, undetermined, unfixed, unspecified, unstated, unstipulated, vague.

antonyms exact, limited.

index *n* clue, guide, hint, indication, indicator, map, mark, needle, pointer, sign, symptom, table, token.

indicate *v* add up to, bespeak, betoken, denote, designate, display, evince, express, hint at, imply, make known, manifest, mark, mean, point out, point to, read, record, register, reveal, show, signify, specify, suggest, telegraph, tip off.

indicated *adj* advisable, called-for, desirable, implied, necessary, needed, recommended, required, shown, suggested.

indication *n* clue, evidence, explanation, forewarning, hint, index, inkling, intimation, manifestation, mark, note, omen, portent, prognostic, sign, signal, signpost, suggestion, symptom, warning.

indicative *adj* denotative, exhibitive, pointing out, showing, significant, suggestive, symptomatic.

indicator *n* bellwether, blinker, display, gauge, gnomon, guide, index, mark, marker, meter, pointer, sign, signal, signpost, symbol.

indict *v* accuse, arraign, censure, charge, criminate, impeach, incriminate, prosecute, recriminate, summon, summons, tax.

antonym exonerate.

indictment *n* accusation, allegation, arraignment, charge, crimination, impeachment, incrimination, prosecution, recrimination, summons.

antonym exoneration.

indifferent *adj* aloof, apathetic, average, callous, careless, cold, cool, detached, disinterested, dispassionate, distant, equitable, fair, heedless, immaterial, impartial, impervious, inattentive, incurious, insignificant, insipid, mediocre, middling, moderate, neutral, nonchalant, not bad, objective, ordinary, passable, perfunctory, regardless, reluctant, so-so, stoical, unbiassed, uncaring, unconcerned, undistinguished, unenquiring, unenthusiastic, unexcited, unimportant, unimpressed, uninspired, uninterested, uninvolved, unmoved, unprejudiced, unresponsive, unsympathetic.

antonyms biassed, interested.

indigence *n* deprivation, destitution, distress, necessity, need, neediness, pennilessness, penury, poverty, privation, want.

antonym affluence.

indigenous *adj* aboriginal, autochthonous, home-grown, inherent, innate, intrinsic, local, native, original.

antonym foreign.

indigent *adj* destitute, down-and-out, impecunious, impoverished, in forma pauperis, in need, in want, necessitous, needy, penniless, penurious, poor, poverty-stricken, straitened.

antonym affluent.

indignant *adj* angered, angry, annoyed, beside oneself, disgruntled, exasperated, fuming, furious, heated, huffy, in a huff, in a snit, incensed, irate, livid, mad, marked, miffed, peeved, provoked, resentful, riled (up), scornful, sore, ticked off, wrathful, wroth.
antonym pleased.

indignation *n* anger, disapproval, exasperation, fury, ire, pique, rage, resentment, scorn, umbrage, wrath.
antonym pleasure.

indignity *n* abuse, affront, aspersion, contempt, contumely, disgrace, dishonour, disrespect, humiliation, incivility, injury, insult, obloquy, opprobrium, outrage, put-down, reproach, slight, snub.
antonym honour.

indirect *adj* ancillary, backhanded, circuitous, circumlocutory, collateral, crooked, devious, incidental, meandering, mediate, oblique, periphrastic, rambling, roundabout, secondary, slanted, subsidiary, subtle, tactful, tortuous, unintended, wandering, winding, zigzag.
antonym direct.

indirectly *adv* by agent, circuitously, circumlocutorily, deviously, in a roundabout way, not in so many words, obliquely, periphrastically, second-hand, subtly, tactfully.
antonym directly.

indiscernible *adj* hidden, impalpable, imperceptible, indistinct, indistinguishable, infinitesimal, invisible, minuscule, minute, tiny, unapparent, undiscernible.
antonym clear.

indiscreet *adj* careless, foolish, hasty, heedless, ill-advised, ill-considered, ill-judged, impolitic, imprudent, incautious, injudicious, naïve, rash, reckless, tactless, temerarious, undiplomatic, unthinking, unwise.
antonym discreet.

indiscretion *n* error, error of judgment, faux pas, folly, foolishness, gaffe, imprudence, misdeed, mistake, rashness, recklessness, slip, slip of the tongue, tactlessness, temerity.
antonym discretion.

indiscriminate *adj* aimless, careless, chaotic, confused, desultory, extensive, general, haphazard, higgledy-piggledy, hit or miss, indiscriminating, indiscriminative, jumbled, mingled, miscellaneous, mixed, mongrel, motley, promiscuous, random, sweeping, uncritical, undifferentiated, undiscriminating, undistinguishable, unmethodical, unparticular, unselective, unsystematic, wholesale.
antonyms deliberate, selective.

indiscriminately *adv* carelessly, extensively, haphazardly, in the mass, randomly, unsystematically, wholesale, without fear or favour.
antonyms deliberately, selectively.

indispensable *adj* basic, crucial, essential, imperative, key, necessary, needed, needful, required, requisite, vital.
antonym unnecessary.

indisposed[1] *adj* ailing, ill, laid up, poorly, sick, sickly, under the weather, unwell.
antonym well.

indisposed[2] *adj* averse, disinclined, loath, not of a mind (to), not willing, reluctant, unwilling.
antonym inclined.

indisposition[1] *n* ailment, bug, illness, sickness.
antonym health.

indisposition[2] *n* aversion, disinclination, dislike, distaste, hesitancy, reluctance, unwillingness.
antonym inclination.

indisputable *adj* absolute, certain, evident, incontestable, incontrovertible, indubitable, irrebuttable, irrefragable, irrefutable, positive, sure, true, unanswerable, unassailable, undeniable, unqualified, unquestionable.
antonym doubtful.

indissoluble *adj* abiding, binding, enduring, eternal, firm, fixed, imperishable, incorruptible, indestructible, inseparable, inviolable, lasting, permanent, sempiternal, solid, unbreakable.
antonym impermanent.

indistinct *adj* ambiguous, bleary, blurred, confused, dim, distant, doubtful, faint, fuzzy, hazy, ill-defined, indefinite, indeterminate, indiscernible, indistinguishable, misty, muffled, mumbled, obscure, shadowy, slurred, unclear, undefined, unintelligible, vague.
antonym distinct.

indistinguishable *adj* alike, identical, interchangeable, same, tantamount, twin.
antonyms distinguishable, unalike.

individual *n* being, body, character, creature, living being, mortal, party, person, personage, soul.
adj characteristic, discrete, distinct, distinctive, exclusive, identical, idiosyncratic, one, own, particular, peculiar, personal, personalized, proper, respective, separate, several, single, singular, special, specific, unique.

individualism *n* anarchism, egocentricity, egoism, free thinking, free thought, independence, individuality, libertarianism, originality, self-direction, self-interest, selfishness, self-reliance.
antonym conventionality.

individualist *n* anarchist, egoist, free thinker, independent, libertarian, lone wolf, loner, maverick, misfit, nonconformist, original.
antonym conventionalist.

individualistic *adj* anarchistic, characteristic, distinctive, egocentric, egoistic, iconoclastic, idiosyncratic, independent, individual, libertarian, non-conforming, non-conformist, original, particular, selfish, self-reliant, special, typical, unconventional, unique.
antonym conventionalistic.

individuality *n* character, discreteness, distinction, distinctiveness, originality, particularity, peculiarity, personality, separateness, singularity, uniqueness.

antonym sameness.

individually *adv* independently, particularly, personally, separately, seriatim, severally, singly.
antonym together.

indivisible *adj* all of a piece, cohesive, impartible, inseparable, non-divisible, simple, unbreakable, unitary.
antonym divisible.

indoctrinate *v* brainwash, catechize, drill, ground, imbue, initiate, instruct, school, teach, train.

indolence *n* fainéance, heaviness, idleness, inaction, inactivity, inertia, inertness, languidness, languor, laziness, lethargy, shirking, slacking, sloth, slowness, sluggishness, torpidity, torpor.
antonyms activeness, enthusiasm, industriousness.

indolent *adj* fainéant, idle, inactive, inert, lackadaisical, languid, lazy, lethargic, listless, lumpish, slack, slothful, slow, sluggard, sluggish, torpid.
antonyms active, enthusiastic, industrious.

indomitable *adj* bold, intrepid, invincible, irrepressible, resolute, staunch, steadfast, unbeatable, unconquerable, undaunted, unflinching, ungovernable, untameable, unyielding.
antonyms compliant, timid.

indubitable *adj* certain, evident, incontestable, incontrovertible, indisputable, irrebuttable, irrefragable, irrefutable, obvious, sure, unanswerable, unarguable, undeniable, undoubtable, undoubted, unquestionable, veritable.
antonym arguable.

induce *v* actuate, bring about, cause, convince, draw, effect, encourage, engender, generate, get, give rise to, impel, incite, influence, instigate, lead on, lead to, move, occasion, persuade, press, prevail upon, produce, prompt, talk into.

inducement *n* allure, attraction, bait, carrot, cause, come-on, consideration, encouragement, impulse, incentive, incitement, influence, lure, motive, persuasion, reason, reward, spur, stimulus.
antonym disincentive.

induct *v* bring in, consecrate, enthrone, inaugurate, initiate, install, introduce, invest, ordain, swear in.

induction¹ *n* conclusion, deduction, generalization, inference.

induction² *n* consecration, enthronement, inauguration, initiation, installation, institution, introduction, investiture, ordination.

indulge *v* baby, be intemperate, coddle, cosset, favour, foster, give in to, go along with, gratify, humour, mollycoddle, pamper, pander to, pet, satiate, satisfy, spoil, treat (oneself), yield to.

indulge in enjoy, give free rein to, give oneself up to, give way to, luxuriate in, revel in, wallow in.

indulgence *n* appeasement, consideration, courtesy, excess, extravagance, favour, forbearance, good will, gratification, immoderateness, immoderation, intemperance, intemperateness, kindness, leniency, luxury, pampering, partiality, patience, permissiveness, privilege, prodigality, profligacy, profligateness, satiation, satisfaction, self-gratification, self-indulgence, spoiling, tolerance, treat, understanding.
antonyms moderation, strictness.

indulgent *adj* complaisant, compliant, considerate, easy-going, favourable, fond, forbearing, gentle, gratifying, intemperate, kind, kindly, lenient, liberal, mild, patient, permissive, prodigal, self-indulgent, tender, tolerant, understanding.
antonyms moderate, strict.

industrialist *n* baron, boss, businessperson, capitalist, captain of industry, financier, magnate, manufacturer, producer, tycoon.

industrious *adj* active, assiduous, busy, conscientious, diligent, energetic, hardworking, painstaking, persevering, persistent, productive, purposeful, sedulous, steady, tireless, zealous.
antonym indolent.

industry *n* activity, application, assiduity, business, commerce, determination, diligence, effort, industriousness, labour, manufacturing, perseverance, production, tirelessness, toil, trade, vigour, work, zeal.
antonym indolence.

inebriate *v* addle, befuddle, besot, carry away, exhilarate, go to one's head, intoxicate, make drunk, make one see double, stupefy.
antonyms dampen, sober up.

inebriated *adj* befuddled, blind drunk, blotto, corked, drunk, feeling no pain, half-cut, half-drunk, high, incapable, inebriate, in one's cups, in the sauce, intoxicated, merry, pie-eyed, plastered, sloshed, smashed, sottish, sozzled, stoned, three sheets to the wind, tight, tipsy, under the influence, under the table.
antonym sober.

inedible *adj* deadly, harmful, injurious, noxious, poisonous, uneatable, unfit for human consumption.
antonym edible.

ineducable *adj* doltish, incorrigible, indocile, slow, stupid, thick, unteachable.
antonym educable.

ineffable *adj* incommunicable, indescribable, inexpressible, unspeakable, unutterable.
antonym describable.

ineffective *adj* bootless, emasculate, feeble, fruitless, futile, idle, incompetent, ineffectual, inefficacious, inefficient, inept, lame, powerless, unavailing, unproductive, unsuccessful, useless, vain, weak, worthless.
antonym effective.

ineffectual *adj* abortive, barren, emasculate(d), fruitless, impotent, inadequate,

incompetent, ineffective, inefficacious, sterile, unsuccesful, useless.

antonym effectual.

inefficacy *n* futility, inadequacy, ineffectiveness, ineffectuality, inefficiency, unproductiveness, uselessness.

antonym efficacy.

inefficiency *n* carelessness, disorganization, incompetence, muddle, negligence, slackness, sloppiness, waste, wastefulness.

antonym efficiency.

inefficient *adj* haywire, incapable, incompetent, inept, inexpert, money-wasting, negligent, slipshod, sloppy, time-wasting, unskilful, wasteful.

antonym efficient.

inelegant *adj* awkward, barbarous, clumsy, coarse, crass, crude, gauche, graceless, indelicate, laboured, rough, uncourtly, uncouth, uncultivated, ungainly, ungraceful, unpolished, unrefined, unsophisticated.

antonym elegant.

ineligible *adj* disqualified,* inappropriate, incompetent, unacceptable, undesirable, unequipped, unfit, unfitted, unqualified, unsuitable, unworthy.

antonym eligible.

inept *adj* absurd, awkward, bungling, clumsy, fatuous, foolish, gauche, inappropriate, inapt, incompetent, inexpedient, inexpert, infelicitous, irrelevant, maladroit, malapropos, meaningless, ridiculous, unable, unfit, unhandy, unskilful, unsuitable, unworkmanlike.

antonyms adroit, apt.

ineptitude *n* absurdity, awkwardness, clumsiness, crassness, fatuity, foolishness, gaucheness, gaucherie, inability, inappropriateness, incapacity, incompetence, ineptness, inexpediency, inexpertness, irrelevance, pointlessness, stupidity, unfitness, unhandiness, uselessness.

antonyms aptitude, skill.

inequality *n* bias, difference, disparity, disproportion, dissimilarity, diversity, imparity, inadequacy, irregularity, non-uniformity, preferentiality, prejudice, unequalness, unevenness.

antonym equality.

inequitable *adj* biassed, discriminatory, one-sided, partial, partisan, preferential, prejudiced, unequal, unfair, unjust, wrongful.

antonym equitable.

inequity *n* abuse, bias, discrimination, injustice, maltreatment, mistreatment, one-sidedness, partiality, prejudice, unfairness.

antonym equity.

inert *adj* apathetic, dead, dormant, dull, idle, immobile, inactive, inanimate, indolent, insensible, languid, lazy, leaden, lifeless, motionless, nerveless, numb, passive, quiescent, senseless, slack, sleepy, slothful, slow, sluggish, somnolent, static, still, torpid, unmoving, unreacting, unresponsive.

antonyms alive, animated.

inertia *n* accidie, apathy, deadness, drowsiness, dullness, idleness, immobility, inactivity, indolence, insensibility, languor, lassitude, laziness, lethargy, listlessness, nervelessness, numbness, passivity, sleepiness, sloth, sluggishness, somnolence, stillness, stupor, torpor, unresponsiveness.

antonyms activity, liveliness.

inescapable *adj* certain, destined, fated, ineluctable, inevitable, inexorable, irrevocable, necessary, sure, unalterable, unavoidable, unpreventable.

antonym escapable.

inessential *adj* accidental, dispensable, expendable, extraneous, extrinsic, irrelevant, needless, non-essential, optional, redundant, secondary, spare, superfluous, surplus, unessential, unimportant, unnecessary.

antonym essential.

n accessory, appendage, expendable, extra, extravagance, frill, luxury, non-essential, superfluity, trimming.

antonym essential.

inestimable *adj* beyond price, immeasurable, immense, incalculable, incomputable, infinite, invaluable, measureless, precious, priceless, prodigious, uncountable, unfathomable, unlimited, untold, vast.

antonym insignificant.

inevitable *adj* assured, automatic, certain, compulsory, decreed, destined, fated, fixed, ineluctable, inescapable, inexorable, irrevocable, mandatory, necessary, obligatory, ordained, settled, sure (as death and taxes), unalterable, unavertable, unavoidable, unpreventable.

antonyms alterable, avoidable, uncertain.

inevitably *adv* as a matter of course, automatically, certainly, incontestably, ineluctably, inescapably, necessarily, of necessity, perforce, predictably, surely, unavoidably.

inexact *adj* erroneous, fuzzy, imprecise, inaccurate, incorrect, indefinite, indeterminate, indistinct, lax, loose, muddled, vague, woolly.

antonym exact.

inexactitude *n* blunder, error, fuzziness, imprecision, inaccuracy, incorrectness, indefiniteness, laxness, looseness, miscalculation, mistake, vagueness, woolliness.

antonym exactitude.

inexcusable *adj* blameworthy, indefensible, inexpiable, intolerable, outrageous, reprehensible, shameful, unacceptable, unconscionable, unforgivable, unjustifiable, unpardonable, unwarrantable.

antonyms excusable, venial.

inexhaustible *adj* abundant, bottomless, boundless, endless, fathomless, illimitable, indefatigable, infinite, limitless, measureless, never-ending, never-failing, tireless, unbounded, unfailing, unflagging, unlimited, untiring, unwearied, unwearying.

antonym limited.

inexorable adj cruel, hard, harsh, immovable, implacable, ineluctable, inescapable, inevitable, inflexible, intransigent, irreconcilable, irrevocable, merciless, obdurate, pitiless, relentless, remorseless, severe, strict, unalterable, unappeasable, unavertable, unbending, uncompromising, unrelenting, unyielding.
antonyms flexible, lenient, yielding.

inexpedient adj detrimental, disadvantageous, foolish, ill-advised, ill-chosen, ill-judged, impolitic, impractical, imprudent, inadvisable, inappropriate, indiscreet, injudicious, misguided, senseless, silly, unadvisable, undesirable, undiplomatic, unfavourable, unsuitable, unwise, wrong.
antonym expedient.

inexpensive adj affordable, bargain, budget, cheap, economical, low-cost, low-priced, modest, reasonable, uncostly.
antonym expensive.

inexperience n callowness, greenness, ignorance, immaturity, inexpertness, innocence, naïvety, nescience, newness, rawness, strangeness, unexpertness, unfamiliarity, unsophistication, verdancy.
antonym experience.

inexperienced adj amateur, callow, fresh, green, ignorant, immature, inexpert, innocent, nescient, new, raw, unaccustomed, unacquainted, unbearded, unfamiliar, unpractical, unpractised, unschooled, unseasoned, unskilled, unsophisticated, untrained, untravelled, untried, unused, unversed, verdant.
antonym experienced.

inexpert adj amateurish, awkward, blundering, bungling, clumsy, incompetent, inept, maladroit, unhandy, unpractised, unprofessional, unproficient, unskilful, unskilled, untaught, untrained, untutored, unworkmanlike.
antonym expert.

inexplicable adj baffling, enigmatic, impenetrable, incomprehensible, incredible, inexplainable, inscrutable, insoluble, miraculous, mysterious, mystifying, puzzling, strange, unaccountable, unexplainable, unfathomable, unintelligible, unsolvable.
antonym explicable.

inexplicably adv bafflingly, incomprehensibly, incredibly, miraculously, mysteriously, mystifyingly, puzzlingly, strangely, unaccountably, unexplainably.
antonym explicably.

inexpressible adj beyond words, incommunicable, indefinable, indescribable, ineffable, nameless, undescribable, unsayable, unspeakable, untellable, unutterable.

inexpressive adj bland, blank, deadpan, emotionless, empty, expressionless, immobile, impassive, inanimate, inscrutable, lifeless, poker-faced, stolid, stony, unexpressive, vacant.
antonym expressive.

inextinguishable adj deathless, enduring, eternal, everlasting, immortal, imperishable, indestructible, irrepressible, lasting, unconquerable, undying, unquellable, unquenchable, unstoppable, unsuppressible.
antonyms impermanent, perishable.

inextricably adv indissolubly, inseparably, intricately, irresolubly, irretrievably, irreversibly.

infallibility n accuracy, dependability, faultlessness, impeccability, inerrancy, inevitability, irrefutability, irreproachability, omniscience, perfection, reliability, safety, supremacy, sureness, trustworthiness, unerringness.
antonym fallibility.

infallible adj accurate, certain, dependable, fail-safe, faultless, foolproof, impeccable, inerrant, irreproachable, omniscient, perfect, reliable, sound, sure, sure-fire, trustworthy, unbeatable, unerring, unfailing, unfaltering, unfaulty, unimpeachable.
antonym fallible.

infamous adj abhorrent, abominable, atrocious, bad, base, dastardly, despicable, detestable, discreditable, disgraceful, dishonourable, disreputable, egregious, evil, execrable, flagitious, hateful, heinous, ignoble, ignominious, ill-famed, iniquitous, knavish, loathsome, monstrous, nefarious, notorious, odious, opprobrious, outrageous, scandalous, scurvy, shameful, shocking, vile, villainous, wicked.
antonym glorious.

infamy n atrocity, baseness, crime, dastardliness, depravity, discredit, disgrace, dishonour, disrepute, enormity, ignominy, improbity, notoriety, obloquy, odium, opprobrium, outrageousness, scandal, shame, stain, stigma, turpitude, villainy, wickedness, wrong.
antonym glory.

infancy n babyhood, beginnings, birth, childhood, commencement, cradle, dawn, early days, embryonic stage, emergence, genesis, inception, origins, outset, start, youth.
antonym adulthood.

infant n babe, babe in arms, baby, beginner, child, innocent, neonate, newborn, nursling, suckling, weanling, youngling.
antonym adult.
adj baby, babyish, childhood, childish, dawning, developing, early, emergent, fledgling, growing, immature, inchoate, incipient, initial, juvenile, nascent, newborn, rudimentary, unfledged, unformed, weanling, young, youthful.
antonym adult.

infantile adj adolescent, babyish, childish, immature, juvenile, puerile, tender, undeveloped, young, youthful.
antonyms adult, mature.

infatuated adj befooled, beguiled, besotted, bewitched, captivated, crazy, crazy in love, deluded, dotty, enamoured, enraptured, fascinated, fixated, gaga, hypnotized,

intoxicated, mad, mesmerized, obsessed, possessed, ravished, smitten, spellbound.
antonyms disenchanted, indifferent.

infatuation *n* besottedness, case, crush, dotage, fascination, fixation, folly, fondness, intoxication, madness, mania, obsession, passion.
antonyms disenchantment, indifference.

infect *v* affect, blight, canker, contaminate, corrupt, defile, enthuse, influence, inject, inspire, pervert, poison, pollute, taint, touch, vitiate.

infection *n* contagion, contamination, corruption, defilement, disease, epidemic, illness, inflammation, influence, miasma, pestilence, poison, pollution, sepsis, taint, virus.

infectious *adj* catching, communicable, contagious, contaminating, corrupting, deadly, defiling, epidemic, infective, miasmal, miasmic, pestilential, poisoning, poisonous, polluting, spreading, transmissible, transmittable, venemous, virulent, vitiating, zymotic.

infelicitous *adj* gauche, ill-timed, inappropriate, inopportune, maladroit, tactless, unapt, unfortunate, unhappy, unsuitable, untimely.
antonym felicitous.

infelicity *n* despair, gaucheness, inappositeness, inappropriateness, inaptness, incongruity, inopportuneness, misery, misfortune, sadness, sorrow, tactlessness, unfitness, unfortunateness, unhappiness, unsuitability, untimeliness, woe, wretchedness, wrongness.
antonyms aptness, felicity, happiness.

infer *v* assume, conclude, conjecture, construe, deduce, derive, extract, extrapolate, gather, presume, reason, surmise, understand.
▲ *confusable word* imply.

inference *n* assumption, conclusion, conjecture, consequence, construction, corollary, deduction, extrapolation, illation, interpretation, presumption, reading, surmise.

inferior *adj* bad, crummy, grotty, humble, imperfect, inadequate, indifferent, junior, lesser, low, lower, low-grade, mean, mediocre, menial, minor, one-horse, poor, poorer, schlocky, secondary, second-class, second-rate, shoddy, slipshod, slovenly, subordinate, subsidiary, substandard, under, underneath, undistinguished, unimportant, unsatisfactory, unworthy, worse.
antonym superior.
n junior, menial, minion, servant, subordinate, underling, vassal.
antonym superior.

inferiority *n* badness, baseness, deficiency, humbleness, imperfection, inadequacy, insignificance, lowliness, meanness, mediocrity, shoddiness, slovenliness, subordination, subservience, unimportance, unworthiness, worthlessness.
antonym superiority.

infernal *adj* abominable, accursed, Acherontic, chthonian, damnable, damned, demonic, devilish, diabolical, fiendish, Hadean, hellish, malevolent, malicious, Mephistophelian, Plutonian, satanic, Stygian, Tartarean, terrible, underworld.
antonym heavenly.

infertile *adj* arid, barren, dried-up, effete, infecund, infructuous, non-productive, parched, sterile, unbearing, unfruitful, unimaginative, unproductive.
antonym fertile.

infest *v* beset, flood, infiltrate, invade, overrun, overspread, penetrate, permeate, pervade, plague, ravage, swarm, throng.

infested *adj* alive, beset, bristling, crawling, infiltrated, lousy, overrun, overspread, permeated, pervaded, plagued, ravaged, ridden, swarming, teeming, verminous.

infidel *n* atheist, disbeliever, freethinker, giaour, heathen, heretic, iconoclast, irreligionist, pagan, sceptic, unbeliever.
antonym believer.

infidelity *n* adultery, apostasy, bad faith, betrayal, cheating, disbelief, disloyalty, duplicity, faithlessness, false-heartedness, falseness, iconoclasm, irreligion, perfidy, recreancy, scepticism, traitorhood, traitorousness, treachery, unbelief, unfaithfulness.
antonym fidelity.

infiltrate *v* creep into, filter (through or into), infuse oneself, insinuate, interpenetrate, invade, penetrate, percolate, permeate, pervade, soak into (or through).

infiltration *n* infusion, insinuation, interpenetration, invasion, penetration, percolation, permeation, pervasion.

infiltrator *n* insinuator, intruder, penetrator, seditionary, spy, subversive, subverter.

infinite *adj* absolute, bottomless, boundless, countless, enormous, eternal, everlasting, extensive, fathomless, huge, illimitable, immeasurable, immense, incomputable, inestimable, inexhaustible, interminable, limitless, measureless, never-ending, numberless, perpetual, stupendous, total, unbounded, uncountable, uncounted, unfathomable, untold, vast, wide.
antonym finite.

infinitesimal *adj* atomic, exiguous, imperceptible, inappreciable, inconsiderable, insignificant, microscopic, minuscule, minute, negligible, paltry, teeny, tiny, unnoticeable, wee.
antonyms significant, substantial.

infinity *n* boundlessness, countlessness, endlessness, eternity, everlasting, everlastingness, for ever, illimitibleness, immeasurableness, immensity, inexhaustibility, infinitude, interminableness, limitlessness, perpetuity, vastness.
antonyms finiteness, limitation.

infirm *adj* ailing, crippled, debilitated, decrepit, doddering, enfeebled, failing, faltering, feeble, fickle, frail, hesitant, inconstant, indecisive, insecure, irresolute, lame, poorly, sickly, unhealthy, unreliable, unstable, wavering, weak, wobbly.

antonyms healthy, strong.

infirmity *n* ailment, complaint, debility, decrepitude, defect, deficiency, disease, disorder, failing, fault, feebleness, foible, frailty, ill health, illness, imperfection, instability, malady, sickliness, sickness, unhealthiness, vulnerability, weakness.

antonyms health, strength.

inflame *v* aggravate, agitate, anger, arouse, embitter, enkindle, enrage, exacerbate, exasperate, excite, fan, fire, foment, fuel, galvanize, heat, ignite, impassion, incense, incite, increase, infatuate, infuriate, intensify, intoxicate, kindle, madden, provoke, rile, rouse, stimulate, worsen.

antonyms cool, quench.

inflamed *adj* angry, burning, chafing, enraged, erythematous, excited, festering, fevered, feverish, fiery, heated, hot, impassioned, incensed, infected, poisoned, red, septic, sore, swollen.

inflammable *adj* burnable, choleric, combustible, deflagrable, excitable, flammable, incendiary, irascible, short-tempered, volatile.

antonyms flameproof, incombustible, nonflammable, non-inflammable.

inflammation *n* abscess, burning, empyema, erythema, heat, incitement, infection, painfulness, rash, redness, sepsis, sore, soreness, tenderness.

inflammatory *adj* anarchic, demagogic, explosive, fiery, incendiary, incitative, inflaming, instigative, insurgent, intemperate, provocative, rabble-rousing, rabid, riotous, seditious.

antonyms calming, pacific.

inflate *v* aerate, aggrandize, amplify, balloon, bloat, blow up, bombast, boost, dilate, distend, enlarge, escalate, exaggerate, expand, increase, puff out, puff up, pump up, swell, tumefy.

antonym deflate.

inflated *adj* ballooned, bloated, blown up, bombastic, dilated, distended, euphuistic, exaggerated, flatulent, grandiloquent, increased, magniloquent, ostentatious, overblown, pompous, puffed out, puffed up, swollen, tumefied, tumid, turgid.

antonym deflated.

inflation *n* aggrandizement, ballooning, bloating, dilation, distension, enhancement, enlargement, escalation, exaggeration, expansion, extension, hyperinflation, increase, intensification, rise, spread, swelling, tumefaction, tumescence, turgidity.

antonym deflation.

inflexible *adj* adamant, diehard, dyed-in-the-wool, entrenched, fast, firm, fixed, hard, hardened, immovable, immutable, implacable, inelastic, inexorable, intractable, intransigent, iron, non-flexible, obdurate,

obstinate, relentless, resolute, rigid, rigorous, set, steadfast, steely, stiff, strict, stringent, stubborn, taut, unaccommodating, unadaptable, unalterable, unbending, unchangeable, uncompromising, unpliable, unpliant, unsupple, unyielding.

antonym flexible.

inflict *v* administer, afflict, apply, burden, deal, deliver, enforce, exact, force, impose, lay, levy, mete, perpetrate, visit, wreak.

infliction *n* administration, affliction, bane, burden, castigation, chastisement, exaction, imposition, nemesis, pain, penalty, perpetration, punishment, retribution, suffering, trouble, visitation, worry, wreaking.

influence *n* agency, ascendancy, authority, bias, charisma, clout, connections, control, credit, direction, domination, drag, effect, éminence grise, good offices, guidance, hold, importance, leverage, magnetism, mastery, power, pressure, prestige, pull, reach, rule, scope, spell, standing, strength, string-pulling, sway, teaching, training, weight.

v affect, alter, arouse, bend, bias, cause, change, control, direct, dispose, dominate, guide, head, impel, incite, incline, induce, instigate, manipulate, manoeuvre, modify, motivate, move, persuade, point, predispose, prejudice, prompt, pull, pull strings, rouse, sway, teach, train, weigh with.

influential *adj* ascendant, authoritative, charismatic, cogent, compelling, controlling, dominant, dominating, effective, efficacious, forcible, guiding, important, instrumental, leading, momentous, moving, persuasive, potent, powerful, significant, strong, telling, weighty, well-placed.

antonym ineffectual.

influx *n* accession, arrival, convergence, flood, flow, incursion, inflow, inrush, instreaming, inundation, invasion, rush.

inform¹ *v* acquaint, advise, apprise, brief, clue in, clue up, divulge, enlighten, fill in, illuminate, instruct, keep posted, notify, sing, talk, teach, tell, tip off, turn state's evidence, wise up.

inform on accuse, betray, blab on, blow the whistle on, denounce, incriminate, inculpate, peach on, rat on, snitch on, squeak, squeal on, tattle on, tell on, tell tales, turn in.

inform² *v* animate, characterize, endue, fill, illuminate, imbue, infuse, inspire, invest, irradiate, light up, permeate, suffuse, typify.

informal *adj* approachable, casual, colloquial, congenial, cosy, easy, everyday, familiar, free, free and easy, homey, irregular, natural, offhand, relaxed, relaxing, simple, unbuttoned, unceremonious, unconstrained, unofficial, unorthodox, unpretentious, unsolemn, vernacular.

antonym formal.

informality *n* approachability, casualness, congeniality, cosiness, ease, familiarity, freedom, homeliness, irregularity, naturalness, offhandedness, relaxation, simplicity, unceremoniousness, unpretentiousness.

antonym formality.

informally *adj* casually, colloquially, confidentially, cosily, easily, en famille, familiarly, freely, offhandedly, simply, unceremoniously, unofficially.

antonym formally.

information *n* advices, blurb, briefing, bulletin, clue(s), communication, communiqué, complaint, consciousness-raising, data, databank, database, dope, dossier, enlightenment, facts, gen, illumination, info, input, instruction, intelligence, knowledge, lowdown, message, news, notice, report, tidings, word.

informative *adj* advisory, chatty, communicative, constructive, edifying, educational, educative, enlightening, gossipy, illuminating, informational, instructive, newsy, revealing, revelatory, useful, valuable.

antonym uninformative.

informed *adj* abreast, acquainted, apprised, au courant, au fait, authoritative, aware, briefed, clued in, clued up, conversant, enlightened, erudite, expert, familiar, filled in, genned up, hip, in the know, knowledgeable, learned, on top (of), posted, prepared, primed, scholarly, trained, up (on), up-to-date, versed, well-informed, well-read, well-researched.

antonyms ignorant, unaware.

informer *n* accuser, betrayer, canary, denouncer, denunciator, fink, Judas, peacher, singer, sneak, snitch, squeaker, squealer, stool pigeon, tattletale, tattler, telltale, traitor, whistle-blower, witness.

infrequent *adj* exceptional, intermittent, occasional, rare, scarce, sparse, spasmodic, sporadic, uncommon, unusual.

antonym frequent.

infringe *v* break, contravene, defy, disobey, encroach, flout, ignore, impinge, infract, intrude, invade, overstep, transgress, trespass, violate.

infringement *n* breach, contravention, defiance, encroachment, evasion, impingement, infraction, intrusion, invasion, non-compliance, non-observance, transgression, trespass, violation.

infuriate *v* anger, antagonize, bug, enrage, exasperate, incense, irritate, madden, provoke, put someone's back up, rile, rouse, vex.

antonyms calm, mollify.

infuriated *adj* agitated, angry, beside oneself, enraged, exasperated, fit to be tied, flaming, fuming, furious, heated, in a rage, incensed, irate, irritated, maddened, provoked, roused, vexed, violent, wild.

antonyms calm, gratified, pleased.

infuriating *adj* aggravating, annoying, exasperating, frustrating, galling, intolerable, irritating, maddening, mortifying, pesky, pestiferous, pestilential, provoking, thwarting, unbearable, vexatious.

antonyms agreeable, pleasing.

infuse *v* breathe into, brew, draw, fill, imbue, impart to, implant, inculcate, inject, inspire,

instil, introduce, macerate, saturate, soak, steep.

infusion *n* brew, imbuement, implantation, inculcation, infusing, inspiration, instillation, maceration, soaking, steeping.

ingenious *adj* adept, adroit, apt, artistic, bright, brilliant, clever, crafty, creative, cunning, daedal, Daedalian, daedalic, deft, dexterous, fertile, Gordian, imaginative, innovative, intricate, inventive, masterful, masterly, original, pretty, ready, resourceful, Rube Goldberg, shrewd, skilful, sly, subtle.

antonyms clumsy, unimaginative.

▲ *confusable word* ingenuous.

ingenuity *n* adroitness, cleverness, cunning, deftness, faculty, flair, genius, gift, ingeniousness, innovativeness, invention, inventiveness, knack, originality, resourcefulness, sharpness, shrewdness, skill, slyness, turn.

antonyms clumsiness, dullness.

ingenuous *adj* artless, candid, childlike, frank, guileless, honest, innocent, naïf, naïve, natural, open, plain, simple, sincere, trustful, trusting, unreserved, unsophisticated, unstudied.

antonyms artful, sly.

▲ *confusable word* ingenious.

inglorious *adj* discreditable, disgraceful, dishonourable, disreputable, humiliating, ignoble, ignominious, infamous, mortifying, obscure, shameful, unheroic, unhonoured, unknown, unrenowned, unsuccessful, unsung.

antonym glorious.

ingrain *v* dye, embed, engrain, entrench, fix, imbue, implant, impress, imprint, infix, instil, root.

ingrained *adj* deep-rooted, deep-seated, entrenched, fixed, fundamental, hereditary, immovable, inborn, inbred, inbuilt, indelible, ineradicable, infixed, inherent, intrinsic, inveterate, permanent, rooted.

antonym superficial.

ingratiate oneself (with) *v* blandish, bootlick, butter up, cosy up (to), crawl, curry favour, fawn (on), flatter, get in (with), grovel (before), insinuate oneself, suck up (to), toady (to).

ingratiating *adj* agreeable, bland, bootlicking, charming, crawling, fawning, flattering, obsequious, pleasing, servile, smooth-tongued, suave, sycophantic, timeserving, toadying, unctuous.

ingratitude *n* non-recognition, thanklessness, unappreciativeness, ungraciousness, ungratefulness.

antonym gratitude.

ingredient *n* component, constituent, element, factor, part.

inhabit *v* abide in, bide in, colonize, dwell in, exist in, live in, lodge in, make one's home in, occupy, people, populate, possess, reside at, settle, settle in, stay, take up one's abode at, tenant.

inhabitant *n* aborigine, autochthon, burgher, citizen, denizen, dweller, habitant, indigen, indweller, inmate, landed immigrant, lodger, native, occupant, occupier, resident, residentiary, resider, settler, tenant.

inhabited *adj* colonized, developed, held, lived-in, occupied, overrun, peopled, populated, possessed, settled, tenanted.
antonym uninhabited.

inhalation *n* breath, breathing, inhaling, inspiration, respiration, spiration, suction, taking in.

inhale *v* breathe in, draw, draw in, inbreathe, inspire, respire, suck in, take in, whiff.

inharmonious *adj* antipathetic, atonal, cacophonous, clashing, colliding, conflicting, discordant, dissonant, grating, harsh,, incompatible, inconsonant, jangling, jarring, raucous, strident, tuneless, unharmonious, unmelodious, unmusical, untuneful.
antonym harmonious.

inherent *adj* basic, characteristic, congenital, connate, essential, fundamental, hereditary, immanent, inborn, inbred, inbuilt, ingrained, inherited, innate, instinctive, intrinsic, inwrought, native, natural.

inherit *v* accede to, assume, be bequeathed, be left, come in for, come into, fall heir to, receive, succeed to.

inheritance *n* accession, bequest, birthright, descent, heredity, heritage, legacy, patrimony, reversion, succession.

inheritor *n* beneficiary, co-heir, co-heiress, devisee, heir, heir apparent, heiress, heritor, joint heir, legatee, next in line, recipient, reversionary, successor.

inhibit *v* arrest, bar, bridle, check, constrain, cramp, curb, debar, discourage, forbid, frustrate, hinder, hold back, impede, interfere with, obstruct, prevent, prohibit, repress, restrain, staunch, stem, stop, suppress, thwart.

inhibited *adj* bashful, bridled, constrained, curbed, diffident, frustrated, guarded, repressed, reserved, restrained, reticent, self-conscious, shamefaced, shy, strained, subdued, tense, uptight, withdrawn.
antonym uninhibited.

inhibition *n* bar, check, constraint, embargo, hang-up, hindrance, impediment, interdict, interference, obstacle, obstruction, prohibition, repression, reservation, restraint, restriction, retention, reticence, self-consciousness, shyness, suppression.
antonym freedom.

inhospitable *adj* antisocial, bare, barren, bleak, cold, cool, desolate, forbidding, hostile, inimical, intolerant, sterile, unaccommodating, uncivil, uncongenial, unfavourable, unfriendly, ungenerous, uninhabitable, unkind, unneighbourly, unreceptive, unsociable, unwelcoming, xenophobic.
antonyms favourable, hospitable.

inhospitality *n* coldness, coolness, hostility, incivility, inimicality, intolerance, uncongeniality, unfriendliness, unkindness, unneighbourliness, unreceptiveness, unsociability, xenophobia.
antonym hospitality.

inhuman *adj* animal, barbaric, barbarous, bestial, brutal, brutish, callous, cold-blooded, cruel, diabolical, fiendish, heartless, inhumane, insensate, merciless, pitiless, remorseless, ruthless, sadistic, savage, unfeeling, vicious.
antonym human.

inhumane *adj* brutal, callous, cold-hearted, cruel, heartless, indurate, inhuman, insensitive, pitiless, uncaring, uncompassionate, unfeeling, unkind, unsympathetic.
antonym humane.

inhumanity *n* atrocity, barbarism, barbarity, brutality, brutishness, callousness, cold-bloodedness, cold-heartedness, cruelty, hard-heartedness, heartlessness, pitilessness, ruthlessness, sadism, unkindness, viciousness, violence.
antonym humanity.

inimical *adj* adverse, antagonistic, antipathetic, contrary, destructive, disaffected, harmful, hostile, hurtful, ill-disposed, inhospitable, injurious, intolerant, noxious, opposed, oppugnant, pernicious, repugnant, unfavourable, unfriendly, unwelcoming.
antonyms favourable, friendly, sympathetic.

inimitable *adj* consummate, distinctive, exceptional, incomparable, matchless, nonpareil, peerless, second to none, sublime, superlative, supreme, unequalled, unexampled, unique, unmatched, unparalleled, unrivalled, unsurpassable, unsurpassed, without equal.

iniquitous *adj* abominable, accursed, atrocious, awful, base, criminal, dreadful, evil, flagitious, heinous, immoral, infamous, malicious, nefarious, reprehensible, reprobate, sinful, unjust, unrighteous, vicious, wicked.
antonym virtuous.

iniquity *n* abomination, baseness, crime, enormity, evil, evildoing, heinousness, impiety, infamy, injustice, misdeed, offence, sin, sinfulness, ungodliness, unrighteousness, vice, viciousness, wickedness, wrong, wrongdoing.
antonym virtue.

initial *adj* beginning, commencing, early, embryonic, first, formative, inaugural, inceptive, inchoate, incipient, infant, introductory, opening, original, prefatory, primary.
antonym final.

initially *adv* at first, at the beginning, at the outset, at the start, first, firstly, first of all, in the beginning, in the first place, introductorily, originally, prefatorily, to begin with, to start with.
antonym finally.

initiate *v* activate, actuate, begin, cause, coach, commence, inaugurate, indoctrinate, induce, induct, install, instate, institute, instruct, introduce, invest, launch, open, originate, prompt, start, stimulate, teach, train.
n beginner, catechumen, cheechako, convert, entrant, fledgling, greenhorn, learner, member, neophyte, newcomer, novice, novitiate, probationer, proselyte, recruit, tenderfoot, tyro.

initiation *n* admission, beginning, commencement, debut, enrolment, entrance, entry, inauguration, inception, induction, installation, instatement, instruction, introduction, investiture, reception, rite of passage.

initiative *n* advantage, ambition, drive, dynamism, energy, enterprise, first move, first step, forcefulness, get-up-and-go, go, innovativeness, inventiveness, lead, opening gambit, opening move, originality, push, recommendation, resource, resourcefulness.

inject *v* add, bring, fix, hit, infuse, inoculate, insert, instil, interject, interpolate, introduce, jab, mainline, pop, shoot, shoot up, throw in, vaccinate.

injection *n* dose, fix, hit, infusion, inoculation, insertion, interjection, interpolation, introduction, jab, mainlining, popping, shot, vaccination, vaccine.

injudicious *adj* foolish, hasty, ill-advised, ill-judged, ill-timed, impolitic, imprudent, inadvisable, incautious, inconsiderate, indiscreet, inexpedient, misguided, rash, stupid, unthinking, unwise, wrong-headed.
antonym judicious.

injunction *n* admonition, behest, command, dictate, direction, directive, enjoinment, exhortation, instruction, interdict, mandate, order, precept, prohibition, ruling.

injure *v* abuse, aggrieve, blemish, blight, break, cripple, crush, cut, damage, deface, disable, disfigure, harm, hurt, ill-treat, impair, maim, maltreat, mar, ruin, scathe, spoil, tarnish, undermine, vandalize, vitiate, weaken, wound, wrong.

injured *adj* abused, aggrieved, blemished, broken, cut to the quick, defamed, disabled, disgruntled, displeased, grieved, hurt, ill-treated, insulted, lamed, long-suffering, maligned, maltreated, misused, offended, pained, put out, stung, tarnished, undermined, unhappy, upset, vilified, weakened, wounded, wronged.

injurious *adj* adverse, bad, baneful, calumnious, corrupting, damaging, deleterious, destructive, detrimental, disadvantageous, harmful, hurtful, iniquitous, insulting, libellous, mischievous, noxious, pernicious, prejudicial, ruinous, slanderous, unconducive, unhealthy, unjust, wrongful.
antonyms beneficial, favourable.

injury *n* abuse, annoyance, damage, detriment, disablement, disservice, evil, grievance, harm, hurt, ill, impairment, indignity, injustice, insult, lesion, loss, mischief, prejudice, ruin, scathe, trauma, vexation, wound, wrong.

injustice *n* bad turn, bias, discrimination, disparity, favouritism, imposition, inequality, inequitableness, inequity, iniquity, misdeed, one-sidedness, oppression, partiality, partisanship, prejudice, unevenness, unfairness, unjustness, unlawfulness, unreason, wrong.
antonym justice.

inkling *n* allusion, clue, conception, glimmering, hint, idea, indication, intimation, notion, pointer, sign, suggestion, suspicion, the faintest, the foggiest, vague idea, whisper.

inlaid *adj* damascened, enchased, set, studded, tessellated.

inland *adj* central, domestic, inner, interior, internal, upcountry.

inlay *n* damascene, insert, inset, tessellation.

inlet *n* bay, bight, cove, creek, entrance, fiord, gulf, ingress, opening, passage, passageway.

inmost *adj* basic, buried, central, closest, dearest, deep, deepest, esoteric, essential, hidden, innermost, interior, intimate, personal, private, secret.

inn *n* alehouse, auberge, caravansary, hospice, hostelry, hotel, khan, local, motel, motor inn, pub, public house, roadhouse, saloon, tavern.

innards *n* entrails, guts, inner mechanism, insides, interior, intestines, inwards, mechanism, organs, viscera, vitals, workings, works.

innate *adj* basic, congenital, connate, constitutional, essential, fundamental, hereditary, immanent, inborn, inbred, ingenerate, ingrained, inherent, inherited, instinctive, intrinsic, intuitive, native, natural.

inner *adj* central, concealed, emotional, esoteric, essential, hidden, innermost, inside, interior, internal, intimate, inward, mental, middle, personal, private, psychic, psychological, secret, spiritual.
antonyms outer, patent.

innkeeper *n* aubergiste, boniface, host, hostess, hotelier, hotel-keeper, innholder, landlady, landlord, mine host, publican, restaurateur.

innocence *n* artlessness, blamelessness, chastity, credulousness, freshness, greenness, guilelessness, guiltlessness, gullibility, harmlessness, honesty, ignorance, immaturity, incorruptibility, incorruption, inexperience, ingenuousness, innocuity, innocuousness, inoffensiveness, irreproachability, naïvety, naturalness, nescience, probity, purity, righteousness, simplicity, sinlessness, stainlessness, trustfulness, unawareness, unfamiliarity, unimpeachability, unsophistication, unworldliness, virginity, virtue.
antonyms experience, guilt, knowledge.

innocent *adj* Arcadian, artless, benign, blameless, chaste, childlike, clear, credulous, dewy-eyed, faultless, frank, free, fresh, green, guileless, guiltless, gullible, harmless, honest, immaculate, immature, impeccable, incorrupt, ingenuous, innocuous, inoffensive, intact, irreproachable, naïve, natural, nescient, not guilty, open, pristine, pure, righteous, simple, sinless, spotless, stainless, trustful, trusting, unblemished, uncontaminated, unimpeachable, unobjectionable, unoffending, unsophisticated, unsullied, unsuspicious, untainted, untouched, unworldly, verdant, virginal, well-intentioned, well-meaning, well-meant.
antonyms experienced, guilty, knowing.

n babe, babe in arms, babe in the woods, child, infant, ingénue.

antonyms connoisseur, expert.

innocently *adv* artlessly, blamelessly, credulously, guilelessly, harmlessly, ingenuously, innocuously, inoffensively, like a lamb to the slaughter, simply, trustfully, trustingly, unoffendingly, unsuspiciously.

innocuous *adj* bland, harmless, hypo-allergenic, innocent, innoxious, inoffensive, non-irritant, safe, unimpeachable, unobjectionable, unprovocative.

antonym harmful.

innovation *n* alteration, change, departure, introduction, modernization, modernism, neologism, neoterism, newness, novelty, originality, progress, reform, variation.

innovative *adj* adventurous, bold, creative, daring, enterprising, fresh, go-ahead, groundbreaking, imaginative, inventive, modernizing, new, on the move, original, progressive, reforming, resourceful, revolutionary.

antonyms conservative, unimaginative.

innuendo *n* aspersion, hint, implication, imputation, insinuation, intimation, overtone, slant, slur, suggestion, whisper.

innumerable *adj* countless, incalculable, incomputable, infinite, many, multitudinous, myriad, numberless, numerous, uncountable, uncounted, unnumbered, untold.

inoculate *v* immunize, inject, protect, safeguard, vaccinate.

inoculation *n* immunization, injection, protection, shot, vaccination.

inoffensive *adj* gentle, harmless, humble, innocent, innocuous, innoxious, mild, mousy, non-provocative, peaceable, quiet, retiring, unassertive, unobjectionable, unobtrusive, unoffending.

antonyms malicious, offensive.

inoperable *adj* impracticable, impractical, intractable, irremovable, non-viable, unrealistic, unusable, unworkable.

antonyms operable, practicable.

inoperative *adj* broken, broken-down, defective, hors de combat, idle, in disrepair, ineffective, ineffectual, inefficacious, invalid, non-active, non-functioning, nugatory, out of action, out of commission, out of order, out of service, unserviceable, unusable, unused, unworkable, useless.

antonym operative.

inopportune *adj* badly timed, clumsy, ill-chosen, ill-timed, inappropriate, inauspicious, inconvenient, inexpedient, infelicitous, malapropos, mistimed, tactless, unfortunate, unpropitious, unseasonable, unsuitable, untimely.

antonym opportune.

inordinate *adj* disproportionate, exaggerated, excessive, exorbitant, extravagant, hubristic, immoderate, intemperate, over the top, overweening, preposterous, prohibitive, unconscionable, undue, unreasonable, unrestrained, unwarranted.

antonyms moderate, reasonable.

input *v* capture, code, enter, feed in, insert, key in, process, store, type in.

inquietude *n* agitation, anxiety, apprehension, discomposure, disquiet, disquietude, jumpiness, nervousness, perturbation, restlessness, solicitude, trepidation, unease, uneasiness, worry.

antonym composure.

inquire *v* ask, delve, examine, explore, inspect, interrogate, investigate, look into, probe, query, quest, question, reconnoitre, scout, scrutinize, search, want to know.

inquirer *n* examiner, explorer, inquisitor, interrogator, interviewer, investigator, quester, questioner, researcher, searcher, seeker, student.

inquiring *adj* analytical, curious, doubtful, eager, examining, inquisitive, interested, interrogatory, investigating, investigative, nosey, outward-looking, probing, prying, querying, questing, questioning, sceptical, searching, wondering.

antonym incurious.

inquiry *n* examination, exploration, inquest, interrogation, investigation, post-mortem, probe, query, question, research, scrutiny, search, study, survey, witch hunt.

inquisition *n* catechism, cross-examination, cross-questioning, examination, grilling, inquest, inquiry, interrogation, investigation, questioning, quizzing, third degree, tribunal, witch hunt.

inquisitive *adj* curious, eager, inquiring, intrusive, investigative, meddlesome, nosey, peeping, peering, probing, prying, questing, questioning, snooping, snoopy.

antonym incurious.

inroad *n* advance, attack, encroachment, foray, impingement, incursion, intrusion, invasion, irruption, onslaught, raid, sally, sortie, trespass.

insane *adj* barmy, batty, bizarre, bonkers, brainsick, cracked, crackers, crazed, cuckoo, daft, delirious, demented, deranged, distracted, disturbed, fatuous, foolish, idiotic, impractical, irrational, irresponsible, loony, lunatic, mad, manic, mental, mentally ill, mentally unsound, non compos mentis, nuts, nutty, preposterous, psychotic, queer, schizoid, schizophrenic, screwy, senseless, stupid, touched, unbalanced, unhinged.

antonym sane.

insanitary *adj* contaminated, dirty, disease-ridden, feculent, filthy, foul, impure, infected, infested, insalubrious, noisome, noxious, polluted, unclean, unhealthful, unhealthy, unhygienic, unsalutary, unsanitary.

antonym sanitary.

insanity *n* aberration, alienation, amentia, brainsickness, brainstorm, craziness, delirium, dementia, derangement, folly, frenzy, infatuation, irresponsibility, lunacy, madness, mania, mental disorder, mental illness, neurosis, preposterousness, psychoneurosis, psychosis, senselessness, stupidity.

antonym sanity.

insatiable *adj* bottomless, esurient, gluttonous, greedy, immoderate, incontrollable, inordinate, insatiate, intemperate, persistent, quenchless, rapacious, ravenous, unappeasable, uncurbable, unquenchable, unsatisfiable, voracious.

antonym moderate.

inscribe¹ *v* carve, cut, engrave, etch, fix, grave, impress, imprint, incise, stamp.

inscribe² *v* address, autograph, dedicate, enlist, enrol, enter, record, register, sign, write, write on.

inscription *n* autograph, caption, dedication, engraving, epigraph, epitaph, label, legend, lettering, motto, saying, signature, words.

inscrutable *adj* baffling, blank, cryptic, deadpan, deep, enigmatic, esoteric, expressionless, hidden, impassive, impenetrable, incomprehensible, inexplicable, mysterious, poker-faced, sphinxlike, undiscoverable, unexplainable, unfathomable, unintelligible, unknowable, unsearchable.

antonyms clear, comprehensible, expressive.

insecure *adj* afraid, anxious, apprehensive, assailable, dangerous, defenceless, diffident, endangered, exposed, fearful, flimsy, insubstantial, jerry-built, loose, nervous, perilous, precarious, pregnable, rickety, rocky, shaky, uncertain, unconfident, uneasy, unguarded, unprotected, unreliable, unsafe, unshielded, unsound, unstable, unsteady, unsure, vulnerable, weak, wobbly, worried.

antonyms confident, safe, secure.

insecurity *n* anxiety, apprehension, assailability, danger, defencelessness, diffidence, dubiety, fear, flimsiness, frailness, instability, nervousness, peril, precariousness, ricketiness, risk, shakiness, uncertainty, uneasiness, unreliability, unsafeness, unsafety, unsteadiness, unsureness, vulnerability, weakness, worry.

antonyms confidence, safety, security.

insensibility *n* apathy, callousness, coma, incognizance, indifference, inertness, insensitivity, lethargy, nervelessness, numbness, oblivion, obliviousness, thoughtlessness, torpor, unawareness, unconsciousness, unperceptiveness.

antonyms consciousness, sensibilty.

insensible¹ *adj* anesthetized, apathetic, callous, cataleptic, cold, hard-hearted, impassive, impervious, incognizant, indifferent, inert, insensate, nerveless, numb, numbed, oblivious, senseless, stupid, torpid, unaffected, unaware, unconscious, unfeeling, unmindful, unmoved, unnoticing, unobservant, unperceptive, unresponsive, unsusceptible, untouched.

antonyms conscious, sensible.

insensible² *adj* imperceptible, inappreciable, minuscule, minute, negligible, tiny, unnoticeable.

antonym appreciable.

insensitive *adj* anesthetized, blunted, callous, crass, dead, hardened, immune, impenetrable, imperceptive, impervious, indifferent, insensible, insusceptible, inured, obtuse, pachydermal, proof against, tactless, thick-skinned, unaffected, uncaring, unconcerned, unfeeling, unimpressionable, unmoved, unreactive, unresponsive, unsensitive, unsusceptible.

antonym sensitive.

inseparable *adj* bosom, bound up in (or with), close, conjoined, devoted, impartible, inalienable, indissoluble, individuate, indivisible, inextricable, inseverable, intimate, joined, thick as thieves, undividable.

antonym separable.

insert *v* ease in, embed, engraft, enter, fit into (or between), implant, infix, inject, inset, intercalate, interject, interlaminate, interlard, interleave, interline, interpolate, interpose, introduce, place, pop in (or between), put (in), set (into), squeeze in, stick in, thrust (in).

n ad, advertisement, empiecement, enclosure, engraftment, godet, graft, gusset, implant, insertion, inset, interjection, notice.

insertion *n* addition, entry, implant, inclusion, insert, inset, intercalation, interpolation, introduction, intrusion, supplement.

inside *n* content, contents, inner part, interior. *adv* indoors, inly, internally, inwardly, privately, secretly, within. *adj* classified, confidential, esoteric, exclusive, hush-hush, inner, innermost, interior, internal, intramural, inward, private, restricted, secret.

insides *n* belly, bowels, entera, entrails, gut, guts, innards, organs, stomach, viscera, vitals.

insidious *adj* artful, crafty, crooked, cunning, deceitful, deceptive, designing, devious, disingenuous, duplicitous, furtive, guileful, intriguing, Machiavellian, slick, sly, smooth, sneaking, stealthy, subtle, surreptitious, treacherous, tricky, wily.

insight *n* acumen, acuteness, apprehension, awareness, comprehension, discernment, grasp, ingenuity, intuition, intuitiveness, judgment, observation, penetration, perception, percipience, perspicacity, sagacity, sensitivity, shrewdness, understanding, vision, wisdom.

insightful *adj* acute, astute, aware, comprehending, discerning, intelligent, observant, penetrating, perceptive, percipient, perspicacious, sagacious, sage, shrewd, understanding, wise.

antonym superficial.

insignia *n* badge, brand, crest, decoration, emblem, ensign, hallmark, mark, regalia, sign, symbol, trademark.

insignificance *n* immateriality, inconsequence, inconsequentiality, insubstantiality, irrelevance, meaninglessness, meanness, negligibility, nugatoriness, paltriness, pettiness, tininess, triviality, unimportance, worthlessness.

antonym significance.

insignificant *adj* humble, immaterial, inappreciable, inconsequential, inconsiderable, insubstantial, meagre, meaningless, minor, negligible, no big deal, nondescript, nonessential, nugatory, paltry, petty, piddling, scanty, scrub, small, tiny, trifling, trivial, unimportant, unsubstantial.
antonym significant.

insincere *adj* affected, artificial, canting, deceitful, deceptive, devious, dishonest, disingenuous, dissembling, dissimulating, double-dealing, duplicitous, evasive, faithless, false, hollow, hypocritical, lip-deep, lying, mendacious, perfidious, phony, pretended, pretentious, specious, two-faced, unfaithful, ungenuine, untrue, untruthful.
antonym sincere.

insincerity *n* affectation, artificiality, cant, deceitfulness, deviousness, dishonesty, disingenuousness, dissembling, dissimulation, duplicity, evasiveness, faithlessness, falseness, falsity, hollowness, hypocrisy, lip service, mendacity, perfidy, phoniness, pretence, untruthfulness.
antonym sincerity.

insinuate *v* allude, get at, hint, imply, indicate, intimate, introduce, suggest.

insinuate oneself curry favour, get in (with), ingratiate oneself, work oneself (into), worm oneself (into), wriggle one's way (into).

insinuation *n* allusion, aspersion, hint, implication, infiltration, ingratiating, innuendo, intimation, introduction, slant, slur, suggestion.

insipid *adj* anemic, banal, bland, boring, characterless, colourless, commonplace, dead, diluted, drab, dry, dull, flat, flavourless, humdrum, jejune, lifeless, limp, mediocre, monotonous, prosaic, prosy, savourless, spiritless, stale, tame, tasteless, trite, unappetizing, unimaginative, uninteresting, unsavoury, vapid, watery, weak, wishy-washy.
antonyms appetizing, piquant, stimulating, tasty.

insist (on) *v* assert, asseverate, aver, claim, contend, demand, emphasize, harp, hold, maintain, persist, protest, reiterate, repeat, request, stand firm, stress, submit, swear (up and down), vow.

insistence *n* assertion, averment, certainty, contention, demand, determination, doggedness, emphasis, encouragement, entreaty, exhortation, firmness, importunity, persistence, persuasion, pressing, reiteration, relentlessness, solicitation, stress, tenacity, urgency, urging.

insistent *adj* demanding, dogged, emphatic, exigent, forceful, importunate, incessant, peremptory, persevering, persistent, pressing, relentless, tenacious, unrelenting, unremitting, urgent.

insobriety *n* drunkenness, inebriation, inebriety, intemperance, intemperateness, intoxication, tipsiness.
antonym sobriety.

insolence *n* arrogance, audacity, backchat, back talk, boldness, brazenness, cheek,

cheekiness, chutzpah, contemptuousness, contumely, defiance, disrespect, effrontery, forwardness, gall, hubris, impertinence, impudence, incivility, insubordination, insults, lip, malapertness, offensiveness, pertness, presumption, presumptuousness, rudeness, sauce, sauciness.
antonyms politeness, respect.

insolent *adj* arrogant, audacious, bold, brazen, cheeky, contemptuous, contumelious, defiant, disrespectful, forward, fresh, hubristic, impertinent, impudent, insubordinate, insulting, malapert, pert, presumptuous, rude, saucy, uncivil.
antonyms polite, respectful.

insoluble *adj* baffling, impenetrable, indecipherable, inexplicable, inextricable, intractable, mysterious, mystifying, obscure, perplexing, unaccountable, unexplainable, unfathomable, unsolvable.
antonym explicable.

insolvency *n* bankruptcy, default, failure, liquidation, receivership, ruin.
antonym solvency.

insolvent *adj* bankrupt, broke, bust, defaulting, destitute, failed, flat broke, in receivership, on the rocks, ruined.
antonym solvent.

insomnia *n* insomnolence, restlessness, sleeplessness, tossing and turning, wakefulness.
antonym sleep.

insouciance *n* breeziness, carefreeness, carelessness, casualness, cavalierness, ease, flippancy, heedlessness, indifference, jauntiness, light-heartedness, nonchalance, unconcern.
antonyms anxiety, care.

insouciant *adj* airy, breezy, buoyant, carefree, casual, cavalier, easygoing, flippant, gay, happy-go-lucky, heedless, incurious, indifferent, jaunty, light-hearted, nonchalant, sunny, unconcerned, untroubled, unworried.
antonyms anxious, careworn.

inspect *v* audit, check (out), examine, give the once-over, go over, investigate, look over, peruse, scan, scrutinize, search, study, survey, take a close look at, vet, view.

inspection *n* audit, autopsy, check, checkup, conning, examination, investigation, once-over, perusal, post-mortem, quality control, reconnaissance, review, scan, scrutiny, search, surveillance, survey, vetting.

inspector *n* auditor, censor, checker, conner, critic, examiner, investigator, reviewer, scrutineer, scrutinizer, surveyor, tester, viewer.

inspiration *n* afflatus, arousal, awakening, brainstorm, brain wave, creativity, encouragement, enthusiasm, exaltation, genius, Hippocrene, illumination, influence, insight, Muse, revelation, soul, spur, stimulation, stimulus, Svengali, trigger.

inspire *v* activate, affect, animate, arouse, encourage, enkindle, enliven, enthuse, excite, fill, fire up, galvanize, hearten, imbue, impel, influence, infuse, inspirit, instil, motivate, move, quicken, spark, spur, stimulate, stir, suggest, trigger.

inspired *adj* afflated, aroused, brilliant, dazzling, elated, enthralling, enthused, enthusiastic, exalted, exciting, exhilarated, fired, fired-up, galvanized, imaginative, impressive, invigorated, memorable, outstanding, reanimated, stimulated, superb, thrilled, thrilling, uplifted, well-chosen, well-expressed, wonderful.

antonyms dull, uninspired.

inspiring *adj* affecting, emboldening, encouraging, exciting, exhilarating, heartening, inspirational, inspiriting, invigorating, motivating, moving, rousing, stimulating, stirring, uplifting.

antonyms dull, uninspiring.

inspirit *v* animate, breathe life into, cheer, embolden, encourage, enliven, exhilarate, fire, galvanize, hearten, incite, inspire, invigorate, move, nerve, quicken, refresh, rouse, stimulate, vitalize, vivify.

instability *n* capriciousness, changeability, fickleness, fitfulness, flimsiness, fluctuation, fluidity, frailty, imbalance, impermanence, inconstancy, insecurity, insolidity, insubstantiality, irresoluteness, irresolution, lability, mutability, oscillation, precariousness, shakiness, shiftiness, transience, uncertainty, undependability, unpredictability, unreliability, unsafeness, unsoundness, unsteadiness, vacillation, variability, volatility, wavering, weakness.

antonym stability.

install *v* build in, consecrate, crown, ensconce, establish, fix, inaugurate, induct, initiate, instate, institute, introduce, lay, locate, lodge, ordain, place, place in office, plant, position, put, put in, set, settle, set up, site, situate, station.

installation *n* base, consecration, equipment, establishment, fitting, inauguration, induction, instalment, instatement, investiture, location, machinery, ordination, placing, plant, positioning, post, siting, station, system.

instalment *n* chapter, delivery, division, episode, fascicle, part, payment, portion, remittance, section, segment.

instance *n* case, case in point, citation, example, illustration, occasion, occurrence, precedent, sample, situation, time.

v adduce, cite, exemplify, mention, name, point to, quote, refer to, specify.

instant *n* flash, jiffy, juncture, less than no time, minute, mo, moment, no time, occasion, point, second, shake, split second, the wink of an eye, tick, trice, twinkling, two shakes.

adj fast, immediate, instantaneous, on-the-spot, precooked, pressing, prompt, quick, rapid, ready-mixed, speedy, split-second, swift, unhesitating, urgent.

instantaneous *adj* direct, immediate, instant, on-the-spot, prompt, rapid, unhesitating.

antonym eventual.

instantaneously *adv* at once, directly, forthwith, immediately, instantly, on the spot, promptly, rapidly, straight away, there and then, unhesitatingly.

antonym eventually.

instantly *adv* at once, directly, forthwith, immediately, in a flash, in a jiffy, in no time, in short order, instantaneously, like a shot, now, on the spot, pronto, right away, straight away, there and then, tout de suite, without delay.

antonym eventually.

instead *adv* alternatively, as an alternative, preferably, rather.

instead of as an alternative to, as proxy for, as a substitute for, in default of, in lieu of, in place of, in preference to, on behalf of, rather than.

instigate *v* actuate, cause, encourage, foment, generate, impel, incite, influence, initiate, inspire, kindle, move, persuade, prompt, provoke, put others up to, rouse, set in motion, set on, spur, stimulate, stir up, urge, whip up, work up.

instigation *n* behest, bidding, encouragement, incentive, incitement, initiative, insistence, persuasion, prompting, urging.

instigator *n* agent provocateur, agitator, firebrand, fomenter, goad, incendiary, inciter, leader, mischief-maker, motivator, prime mover, provoker, rabble-rouser, ringleader, spur, troublemaker.

instil *v* drill into, engender, engraft, imbue, impart, implant, impress, inculcate, indoctrinate, infix, infuse, inject, insinuate, introduce.

instinct *n* ability, aptitude, faculty, feel, feeling, flair, gift, gut feeling, gut reaction, id, impulse, intuition, knack, nose, predisposition, proclivity, sixth sense, talent, tendency, urge.

instinctive *adj* animal, automatic, gut, immediate, impulsive, inborn, inherent, innate, intuitive, involuntary, knee-jerk, mechanical, native, natural, reflex, spontaneous, subliminal, unconscious, unlearned, unpremeditated, unthinking, visceral.

antonyms conscious, deliberate, voluntary.

institute[1] *v* appoint, begin, commence, create, enact, establish, fix, found, inaugurate, induct, initiate, install, introduce, invest, launch, open, ordain, organize, originate, pioneer, settle, set up, start.

antonyms abolish, cancel, discontinue.

institute[2] *n* custom, decree, doctrine, dogma, edict, law, maxim, precedent, precept, principle, regulation, rescript, rule, tenet, ukase.

institute[3] *n* academy, association, college, collegiate, conservatory, educational institution, foundation, guild, institution, organization, school, seminary, society, university.

institution[1] *n* beginning, consecration, creation, enactment, establishment, formation, foundation, founding, inception, initiation, installation, introduction, investiture, organization, setting up.

insuppressible

institution² *n* convention, custom, fixture, law, practice, rite, ritual, rule, tradition, usage.

institution³ *n* academy, college, collegiate, concern, corporation, establishment, foundation, hospital, institute, organization, school, seminary, society, university.

institutional *adj* accepted, bureaucratic, cheerless, clinical, cold, conventional, customary, drab, dreary, dull, established, forbidding, formal, impersonal, institutionary, monotonous, orthodox, regimented, ritualistic, routine, set, societal, uniform, unwelcoming.
antonyms individualistic, unconventional.

instruct *v* acquaint, advise, apprise, bid, brief, catechize, charge, coach, command, counsel, direct, discipline, drill, educate, enjoin, enlighten, ground, guide, inform, mandate, notify, order, school, teach, tell, train, tutor.

instruction *n* apprenticeship, briefing, catechesis, catechizing, coaching, command, direction, directive, discipline, drilling, education, enlightenment, grounding, guidance, information, injunction, lesson(s), mandate, order, preparation, ruling, schooling, teaching, training, tuition, tutelage, tutoring.

instructions *n* advice, book of words, commands, directions, guidance, handbook, information, key, legend, manual, orders, recommendations, rules.

instructive *adj* advisory, didactic, edificatory, edifying, educational, educative, enlightening, helpful, illuminating, improving, inculcative, informative, instructing, instructional, prescriptive, revealing, useful.
antonym unenlightening.

instructor *n* adviser, catechist, catechizer, coach, demonstrator, edifier, Egeria, exponent, guide, guru, maharishi, master, mentor, mistress, pedagogue, preceptor, professor, schoolmaster, schoolmistress, teacher, trainer, tutor.

instrument *n* agent, apparatus, appliance, cat's-paw, channel, contraption, contrivance, device, doodad, dupe, factor, force, gadget, implement, means, mechanism, medium, minion, organ, pawn, puppet, tool, utensil, vehicle, way, widget.

instrumental *adj* active, assisting, auxiliary, conducive, contributive, contributory, facilitative, helpful, helping, implemental, influential, involved, subsidiary, useful.
antonyms obstructive, unhelpful.

insubordinate *adj* contumacious, defiant, disobedient, disorderly, fractious, impertinent, impudent, insurgent, mutinous, rebel, rebellious, recalcitrant, refractory, riotous, rude, seditious, turbulent, undisciplined, ungovernable, unruly.
antonyms docile, obedient.

insubstantial *adj* chimeric, ephemeral, false, fanciful, feeble, flimsy, frail, idle, illusory, imaginary, immaterial, impalpable, incorporeal, poor, slight, tenuous, thin, unreal, unreliable, unsubstantial, vaporous, weak, yeasty.
antonyms real, strong.

insufferable *adj* dreadful, impossible, insupportable, intolerable, obnoxious, odious, outrageous, past bearing, too much, unbearable, unendurable, unlivable, unspeakable.
antonyms pleasant, tolerable.

insufficiency *n* dearth, deficiency, inadequacy, inadequateness, lack, meagreness, need, paucity, poverty, scantiness, scarcity, shortage, sparsity, want.
antonyms excess, sufficiency.

insufficient *adj* a shortage of, deficient, inadequate, incommensurate, in short supply, lacking, not enough, poor, scanty, scarce, short, sparse, wanting.
antonyms excessive, sufficient.

insular *adj* blinkered, circumscribed, closed (off), contracted, cut off, detached, ethnocentric, illiberal, inward-looking, isolated, limited, narrow, narrow-minded, parochial, petty, prejudiced, provincial, secluded, separate, xenophobic.
antonym cosmopolitan.

insularity *n* ethnocentrism, isolation, narrow-mindedness, parochialism, prejudice, xenophobia.
antonyms open-mindedness, openness.

insulate *v* cocoon, cushion, cut off, isolate, protect, quarantine, separate (from others), sequester, set apart, shield, wrap.

insulation *n* air space, buffer, cushioning, deadening, isolation, padding, protection, sound barrier, stuffing, wrapping.

insult *v* abuse, affront, call names, degrade, disparage, fling/throw mud at, give offence to, humiliate, injure, libel, miscall, offend, outrage, revile, slander, slight, snub, vilify, vilipend.
antonyms compliment, honour.
n abuse, affront, aspersion, contumely, degradation, humiliation, indignity, insolence, libel, offence, outrage, rudeness, slander, slap in the face, slight, snub.
antonyms compliment, honour.

insulting *adj* abusive, affronting, contemptuous, contumelious, degrading, disparaging, humiliating, insolent, libellous, offensive, rude, scurrilous, slanderous, slighting.
antonyms complimentary, respectful.

insuperable *adj* formidable, impassable, impregnable, insurmountable, invincible, overwhelming, unconquerable.
antonym surmountable.

insupportable *adj* dreadful, indefensible, insufferable, intolerable, obnoxious, too much, unbearable, unendurable, unjustifiable, untenable.
antonym bearable.

insuppressible *adj* energetic, go-getting, incorrigible, irrepressible, lively, obstreperous, uncontrollable, ungovernable, unruly, unstoppable, unsubduable.
antonym suppressible.

insurance n assurance, cover, coverage, guarantee, indemnification, indemnity, policy, premium, protection, provision, safeguard, security, warranty.

insure v assure, cover, guarantee, indemnify, protect, underwrite, warrant.

insurer n assurer, guarantor, insurance agent, underwriter.

insurgent n guerrilla, insurrectionist, mutineer, partisan, rebel, resister, revolter, revolutionist, revolutionary, rioter.

adj disobedient, guerrilla, insubordinate, insurrectionary, mutinous, partisan, rebel, rebellious, revolting, revolutionary, riotous, seditious.

insurmountable adj beyond one's power, hopeless, impassable, impossible, insuperable, invincible, overwhelming, unclimbable, unconquerable, unscalable, unsurmountable.

antonym surmountable.

insurrection n civil disorder, coup, coup d'état, insurgence, mutiny, putsch, rebellion, revolt, revolution, riot, rising (up), sedition, uprising.

intact adj all in one piece, complete, entire, flawless, inviolate, perfect, scatheless, sound, together, unbroken, undamaged, undefiled, undivided, unharmed, unhurt, unimpaired, uninjured, unscathed, unspoiled, untouched, unviolated, virgin, whole.

antonyms broken, damaged, harmed.

intangible adj dim, elusive, ethereal, evanescent, immaterial, impalpable, imperceptible, imponderable, incorporeal, indefinite, insubstantial, invisible, shadowy, unreal, unsubstantial, vague.

antonyms real, tangible.

integral adj basic, complete, component, constituent, elemental, entire, essential, full, fundamental, indispensable, intact, intrinsic, necessary, requisite, undivided, unitary, whole.

antonyms accessory, partial.

integrate v amalgamate, assimilate, blend, bring together, coalesce, combine, commingle, desegregate, fuse, harmonize, incorporate, intermix, join, knit, merge, mesh, mix, unify, unite.

antonym separate.

integrated adj cohesive, combined, concordant, connected, desegregated, harmonious, interrelated, joined, part and parcel, unified, unsegregated, unseparated.

antonym unintegrated.

integration n amalgamation, assimilation, blending, combination, combining, commingling, desegregation, fusing, harmony, incorporation, mixing, mixture, unification, unity.

antonym separation.

integrity n candour, coherence, cohesion, completeness, goodness, honesty, honour, incorruptibility, principle(s), probity, purity, rectitude, righteousness, sincerity, soundness, unity, uprightness, virtue, virtuousness, wholeness.

antonyms dishonesty, incompleteness, unreliability.

intellect n brain, brain power, brains, egghead, genius, headpiece, highbrow, intellectual, intellectualist, intelligence, mental ability, mind, nous, reason, sense, thinker, understanding.

antonym dunce.

intellectual adj bookish, cerebral, discursive, highbrow, intelligent, mental, noetic, rational, scholarly, studious, thoughtful.

antonym lowbrow.

n academic, egghead, highbrow, intellectualist, mastermind, thinker.

antonym lowbrow.

intelligence[1] n acuity, acumen, aptitude, brain power, brains, brightness, capacity, cleverness, comprehension, discernment, disclosure, grey matter, intellect, intellectuality, mental ability, mind, nous, penetration, perception, quickness, reason, savvy, smarts, understanding.

antonym foolishness.

intelligence[2] n data, facts, findings, gen, information, knowledge, lowdown, news, notice, notification, report, rumour, tidings, tip-off, word.

intelligent adj acute, alert, apt, brainy, brilliant, bright, clever, discerning, educable, enlightened, instructed, knowing, penetrating, perceptive, perspicacious, quick, quick-witted, rational, razor-sharp, sharp, smart, thinking, well-informed.

antonyms foolish, unintelligent.

intelligentsia n academics, brains, eggheads, highbrows, illuminati, intellectual elite, intellectuals, literati.

intelligibility n articulateness, clarity, clearness, comprehensibility, comprehensibleness, distinctness, explicitness, lucidity, lucidness, plainness, simplicity, understandability.

antonym unintelligibility.

intelligible adj articulate, clear, comprehensible, decipherable, distinct, fathomable, lucid, open, penetrable, plain, understandable.

antonym unintelligible.

intemperate adj drunk, drunken, excessive, extravagant, extreme, gluttonous, immoderate, incontinent, inordinate, intoxicated, irrestrainable, licentious, overindulgent, passionate, prodigal, profligate, self-indulgent, severe, tempestuous, unbridled, uncontrollable, ungovernable, unrestrained, violent, wild.

antonym temperate.

intend v aim, consign, contemplate, design, destine, determine, earmark, have a mind, have in mind, mark out, mean, plan, project, propose, purpose, set apart.

intended adj affianced, betrothed, calculated, conscious, deliberate, designate, designated, designed, destined, future, intentional, meant, planned, proposed, prospective.

antonym accidental.

n betrothed, fiancé, fiancée, husband-to-be, prospective husband or wife, wife-to-be.

intense *adj* acute, agonizing, ardent, burning, concentrated, consuming, driven, eager, earnest, energetic, extreme, fanatical, fervent, fervid, fierce, forceful, forcible, great, harsh, heightened, impassioned, intensive, keen, passionate, powerful, profound, severe, strenuous, strong, vehement.
antonyms apathetic, mild.

intensely *adv* acutely, ardently, deeply, extremely, fervently, fiercely, greatly, passionately, profoundly, strongly, very.
antonym mildly.

intensification *n* acceleration, building-up, buildup, deepening, escalation, exacerbation, heightening, increase, worsening.
antonym lessening.

intensify *v* add to, aggravate, amplify, boost, build up, deepen, emphasize, enhance, escalate, exacerbate, fire, fuel, gain strength, heat up, heighten, increase, magnify, quicken, redouble, reinforce, sharpen, step up, strengthen, whet, worsen.
antonyms damp down, die down.

intensity *n* ardour, concentration, depth, drive, earnestness, emotion, energy, extremity, fanaticism, fervency, fervour, fierceness, fire, force, heatedness, intenseness, keenness, magnitude, passion, potency, power, severity, strength, vehemence, vigour, vividness, voltage, zeal.

intensive *adj* all-encompassing, all-out, comprehensive, concentrated, crash, detailed, exhaustive, in detail, in-depth, thorough, thoroughgoing.
antonym superficial.

intent *adj* absorbed, attentive, concentrated, earnest, engrossed, fixed, industrious, intense, piercing, rapt, resolute, single-minded, steady, watchful.
antonyms absent-minded, distracted.
n aim, design, end, goal, intention, meaning, object, objective, plan, purpose.

intent on absorbed in, bent on, committed to, concentrating on, determined to, engrossed in, occupied with, preoccupied by (or with), resolved to, set on, wrapped up in.

to all intents and purposes as good as, practically, pretty much, pretty well, virtually.

intention *n* aim, design, end, end in view, goal, idea, intent, meaning, motive, object, objective, plan, point, purpose, target, view.

intentional *adj* calculated, conscious, deliberate, designed, done on purpose, intended, meant, planned, prearranged, preconcerted, premeditated, purposed, studied, willful.
antonym accidental.

intentionally *adv* by design, consciously, deliberately, designedly, in cold blood, meaningly, on purpose, purposely, willfully, with malice aforethought.
antonyms accidentally, inadvertently.

intently *adv* attentively, carefully, closely, fixedly, hard, keenly, searchingly, staringly, steadily, watchfully, zealously.
antonym absent-mindedly.

inter *v* bury, entomb, inhume, inurn, lay in the grave, lay to rest, put six feet under.
antonym exhume.

interbreed *v* cross, crossbreed, hybridize, miscegenate, mongrelize.

intercede *v* advocate, arbitrate, interpose, intervene, mediate, plead, speak.

intercept *v* arrest, block, catch, check, cut off, deflect, delay, frustrate, head off, impede, interrupt, obstruct, retard, seize, stop, take, thwart.

intercession *n* advocacy, agency, beseeching, entreaty, good offices, intervention, mediation, petition, plea, pleading, prayer, solicitation, supplication.

interchange *n* alternation, crossfire, exchange, interplay, intersection, junction, reciprocation, trading.

interchangeable *adj* alike, commutable, equivalent, exchangeable, identical, indistinguishable, reciprocal, similar, standard, synonymous, the same, transposable.
antonym different.

intercourse[1] *n* association, commerce, communication, communion, congress, connection, contact, conversation, converse, correspondence, dealings, interaction, intercommunication, traffic, truck.

intercourse[2] *n* act of love, carnal knowledge, coitus, copulation, intimacy, lovemaking, making it, sex, sex act, sexual intercourse, sexual relations, sleeping together, venery.

interdict *v* ban, bar, debar, disallow, forbid, outlaw, preclude, prevent, prohibit, proscribe, rule out, veto.
antonym allow.
n ban, disallowance, injunction, interdiction, prohibition, proscription, taboo, veto.
antonym permission.

interest *n* activity, advantage, advocacy, affair, a piece of the action, attention, attentiveness, attraction, backing, behalf, benefit, claim, commitment, concern, consequence, curiosity, diversion, dividend, fascination, favour, finger, gain, hobby, importance, investment, involvement, matter, moment, note, notice, part, participation, pastime, patronage, portion, preoccupation, profit, pursuit, regard, relevance, right, share, significance, stake, stock, weight.
antonyms boredom, irrelevance.
v amuse, appeal to, attract, concern, divert, engage, engross, entice, fascinate, intrigue, involve, move, touch, warm.
antonym bore.

in the interest of for the sake of, on behalf of, on the part of, to the advantage of, to the benefit of.

interested *adj* attentive, attracted, biassed, concerned, curious, drawn, engrossed, fascinated, implicated, intent, involved, keen, partial, partisan, predisposed, prejudiced, responsive, simulated.

antonyms apathetic, indifferent, unaffected.

interesting *adj* absorbing, alluring, amusing, appealing, attractive, compelling, curious, engaging, engrossing, entertaining, gripping, intriguing, provocative, stimulating, thought-provoking, unusual, viewable, visitable.

antonym boring.

interfere *v* butt in, interlope, intermeddle, interpose, intervene, intrude, meddle, poke one's nose in, prevent, stick one's oar in.

antonyms assist, forbear.

interfere with arrest, block, conflict with, frustrate, hamper, handicap, hinder, impede, inhibit, intrude on, meddle with, tamper with, trammel.

interference *n* butting in, blocking, do-goodism, hampering, hindering, hindrance, impedance, intervention, intrusion, meddlesomeness, meddling, obstruction, opposition, paternalism, prying, static, white noise.

antonyms assistance, forbearance.

interim *adj* acting, improvised, intervening, makeshift, pro tem, provisional, provisory, stand-in, stopgap, temporary.

n interregnum, interval, meantime, meanwhile.

interior *adj* central, domestic, hidden, home, inland, inly, inner, inside, internal, intimate, inward, mental, middle, personal, private, remote, secret, spiritual, upcountry.

antonyms exterior, external.

n bowels, centre, core, heart, heartland, hinterland, inland area, inside, insides, middle, upcountry.

interject *v* inject, insert, insinuate, intercalate, interpolate, interpose, intersperse, interrupt, introduce, throw in.

interjection *n* injection, insertion, insinuation, interpolation, interposition, introduction.

interlace *v* braid, crochet, cross, enlace, entwine, interlock, intermix, intersperse, intertwine, interweave, interwreathe, knit, plait, reticulate, twine, twist together, weave.

interlink *v* clasp together, interconnect, interlock, interrelate, intertwine, interweave, knit, link, link together, lock together, mesh.

antonym separate.

interlock *v* interdigitate, intertwine, lock together.

interloper *n* buttinsky, gate-crasher, intruder, trespasser, uninvited guest.

interlude *n* break, breather, breathing space, breathing spell, breathing time, hiatus, interim, intermission, interval, letup, lull, pause, recess, respite, rest, spell, time-out.

intermediary *n* agent, broker, go-between, intercessor, internuncio, intervener, mediator, middleman, ombudsman, ombudswoman.

intermediate *adj* halfway, in-between, intermediary, interposed, intervening, mean,

medial, median, medium, mid, middle, midway, transitional.

antonym extreme.

interment *n* burial, burying, entombment, funeral, inhumation, obsequies, sepulture.

antonym exhumation.

interminable *adj* ceaseless, dragging, endless, everlasting, lengthy, long, long-drawn-out, long-winded, never-ending, overlong, perpetual, prolix, prolonged, protracted, tedious, tiring, wearisome.

antonym limited.

intermingle *v* amalgamate, blend, combine, commingle, commix, fuse, interlace, intermix, interweave, merge, mingle, mix, mix together, mix up.

antonym separate.

intermission *n* break, breather, breathing space, cessation, discontinuity, entr'acte, interlude, interruption, interval, letup, lull, pause, recess, remission, respite, rest, stoppage, suspension.

intermittent *adj* broken, discontinuous, fitful, irregular, occasional, periodic, punctuated, recurrent, recurring, remittent, spasmodic, sporadic, stop-go.

antonym continuous.

intern *v* confine, detain, hold, immure, imprison, incarcerate, jail, lock up, throw in prison.

antonym free.

internal *adj* domestic, in-house, inner, inside, interior, intimate, inward, private, subjective.

antonym external.

international *adj* cosmopolitan, general, global, intercontinental, interterritorial, universal, worldwide.

antonym parochial.

internecine *adj* bloody, civil, deadly, destructive, disastrous, exterminating, fatal, fratricidal, internal, mortal, murderous, ruinous.

interplay *n* communication, exchange, give-and-take, interaction, interchange, meshing, reciprocation, reciprocity.

interpolate *v* add, insert, intercalate, interject, interpose, introduce.

interpose *v* come between, insert, intercede, interfere, interject, interrupt, intervene, introduce, intrude, mediate, place between, step in, thrust in.

antonym forbear.

interpret *v* analyse, clarify, construe, decipher, decode, diagnose, elucidate, explain, explicate, expound, paraphrase, put a construction on, read (into), render, solve, take, throw light on, translate, understand, unfold.

interpretation *n* anagoge, analysis, clarification, construal, construction, decipherment, diagnosis, elucidation, exegesis, explanation, explication, exposition, meaning, performance, portrayal, reading, rendering, rendition, sense, signification, take, translation, understanding, version.

interpreter *n* analyst, annotator, commentator, critic, dragoman, elucidator, exegete, explainer, explicator, exponent, expositor, hermeneutist, scholiast, translator, ulema.

interpretive *adj* clarifiying, exegetical, explanatory, explicatory, expository, hermeneutic.

interrogate *v* ask (of), catechize, cross-examine, cross-question, debrief, examine, give (someone) the third degree, grill, inquire (of), pump, question, quiz.

interrogation *n* catachesis, cross-examination, cross-questioning, examination, grilling, inquiry, inquisition, probing, question, questioning, third degree.

interrupt *v* barge in, break, break in (upon), break off, butt in, check, cut, cut off, cut short, delay, disconnect, discontinue, disjoin, disturb, disunite, divide, heckle, hinder, hold up, interfere, interject, intrude, obstruct, punctuate, separate, sever, stay, stop, suspend.

antonym forbear.

interrupted *adj* broken (off), cut off, disconnected, discontinuous, disjunctive, disturbed, incomplete, intermittent, suspended, uneven, unfinished.

antonyms complete, continuous.

interruption *n* breach, break, cessation, disconnection, discontinuance, disruption, dissolution, disturbance, disuniting, division, halt, hiatus, hindrance, hitch, impediment, intermission, interval, intrusion, letup, obstacle, obstruction, pause, separation, severance, stop, stoppage, suspension.

intersect *v* bisect, crisscross, cross, cut, cut across, decussate, divide, divide up, meet.

intersection *n* bisection, crossing, crossroads, decussation, division, interchange, junction.

intersperse *v* dot, interlard, intermix, interweave, pepper, scatter, sprinkle.

intertwine *v* braid, convolute, cross, entwine, interlace, intertangle, intertwist, interweave, interwreathe, inweave, link, reticulate, twist together.

interval *n* break, delay, distance, entr'acte, gap, hiatus, in-between, interim, interlude, intermission, interspace, interstice, meantime, meanwhile, opening, pause, period, playtime, rest, season, space between, spell, term, time between, wait.

intervene *v* arbitrate, befall, come (between), ensue, happen, intercede, interfere, interpose oneself, interrupt, intrude, involve oneself, mediate, occur, step in, succeed, supervene, take a hand.

intervening *adj* in-between, interjacent, interposing, intervenient, mediating.

intervention *n* agency, intercession, interference, interposition, intervening, intrusion, mediation.

interview *n* appointment, audience, conference, consultation, dialogue, evaluation, inquiry, inquisition, meeting, oral, oral examination, press conference, talk.

v examine, interrogate, question.

interviewer *n* cross-examiner, examiner, inquisitor, interlocutor, interrogator, investigator, questioner, reporter.

interweave *v* blend, braid, crisscross, cross, interlace, intertangle, intertwine, intertwist, interwork, interwreathe, reticulate, splice.

interwoven *adj* blended, connected, entwined, inmixed, interconnected, interlaced, interlocked, intermingled, intertangled, intertwisted, interworked, interwreathed, interwrought, knit.

intestinal *adj* abdominal, celiac, duodenal, ileac, internal, stomachic, visceral.

intestines *n* bowels, chitterlings, entrails, guts, innards, insides, offal, viscera, vitals.

intimacy *n* affinity, brotherliness, chumminess, closeness, coitus, confidence, copulating, copulation, familiarity, fornication, fraternization, friendship, inseparability, intercourse, lovemaking, sexual intercourse, sisterliness, understanding.

intimate[1] *v* allude, hint, imply, indicate, insinuate, suggest, to drop a hint.

intimate[2] *adj* as thick as thieves, bosom, buddy-buddy, cherished, close, confidential, cosy, dear, deep, deep-seated, devoted, familiar, friendly, informal, inmost, innermost, inseparable, internal, near, on intimate terms, palsy-walsy, penetrating, personal, private, privy, profound, secret, warm, well-known.

antonyms cold, distant, unfriendly.

n Achates, alter ego, associate, best friend, bosom buddy, buddy, chum, companion, comrade, confidant(e), crony, familiar, friend, lover, mate, pal, repository.

antonym stranger.

intimately *adv* affectionately, arm in arm, closely, confidentially, confidingly, deeply, familiarly, inside out, personally, profoundly, tenderly, thoroughly, warmly.

antonyms coldly, distantly.

intimation *n* allusion, clue, cue, hint, implication, indication, inkling, innuendo, insinuation, suggestion.

intimidate *v* alarm, appal, browbeat, bulldoze, bully, coerce, cow, daunt, dishearten, dismay, dispirit, frighten, lean on, overawe, psych out, put pressure on, scare, strong-arm, subdue, terrify, terrorize, threaten.

antonym persuade.

intimidation *n* arm-twisting, browbeating, bullying, coercion, fear, menaces, pressure, strong-arm tactics, terror, terrorization, terrorizing, threats.

antonym persuasion.

intolerable *adj* abhorrent, abominable, beyond the pale, excruciating, impossible, insufferable, insupportable, painful, unacceptable, unbearable, unconscionable, unendurable, unforgivable, unpardonable.

antonym tolerable.

intolerant *adj* bigoted, chauvinistic, discriminatory, dogmatic, fanatical, illiberal, impatient, narrow, narrow-minded, opinionated, opinionative, opinioned, persecuting,

prejudiced, racist, small-minded, uncharitable, unforbearing, unindulgent, untolerating, xenophobic.
antonym tolerant.

intonation *n* accentuation, cadence, chant, incantation, inflection, mantra, melody, modulation, tone.

intone *v* chant, croon, declaim, intonate, pronounce, recite, sing, utter.

intoxicate *v* addle, befuddle, besot, elate, excite, exhilarate, fuddle, go to one's head, inebriate, inflame, stimulate, stupefy, thrill.
antonym sober up.

intoxicated *adj* addled, befuddled, besotted, blind drunk, blotto, bombed, canned, cut, delirious, dizzy, drunk, drunk as a lord, drunken, ecstatic, elated, enraptured, euphoric, excited, exhilarated, feeling no pain, fuddled, high, incapable, inebriate, inebriated, infatuated, in liquor, in one's cups, lit up, mellow, pickled, pie-eyed, pixilated, plastered, reeling, roaring drunk, seeing double, sloshed, smashed, sottish, sozzled, stewed, stiff, stimulated, stoned, the worse for liquor, three sheets to the wind, tiddly, tight, tipsy, under the influence, zonked.
antonym sober.

intoxicating *adj* alcoholic, exciting, exhilarating, heady, inebriant, intoxicant, spirituous, stimulating, strong, thrilling.
antonym sobering.

intoxication *n* a high, besottedness, delirium, drunkenness, elation, euphoria, exaltation, excitement, exhilaration, inebriation, inebriety, infatuation, insobriety, tipsiness.
antonym sobriety.

intractability *n* cantankerousness, contrariness, incorrigibility, indiscipline, indocility, mulishness, obduracy, obstinacy, perverseness, perversity, pig-headedness, self-will, stubbornness, unamenability, unco-operativeness, ungovernability, waywardness.
antonym amenability.

intractable *adj* bull-headed, cantankerous, contrary, difficult, fractious, headstrong, incurable, indomitable, insoluble, intransigent, obdurate, obstinate, perverse, pig-headed, recalcitrant, refractory, self-willed, stubborn, unamenable, unbending, unco-operative, undisciplined, ungovernable, unmanageable, unruly, unyielding, wayward, wild, willful.
antonym amenable.

intransigent *adj* hard-line, immovable, implacable, inflexible, intractable, irreconcilable, obdurate, obstinate, stubborn, tenacious, tough, unamenable, unbending, uncompromising, unpersuadable, unyielding.
antonym amenable.

intrepid *adj* audacious, bold, brave, courageous, daring, dashing, dauntless, doughty, fearless, gallant, game, gutsy, heroic, lion-hearted, nervy, plucky, resolute, stalwart, stout-hearted, unafraid, undaunted, unflinching, valiant, valorous.

antonyms cowardly, timid.

intricacy *n* complexity, complexness, complication, convolution, difficulty, elaborateness, entanglement, intricateness, involution, involvement, knottiness, labyrinth, obscurity, perplexity.
antonym simplicity.

intricate *adj* bewildering, Byzantine, complex, complicated, convoluted, daedal, Daedalian, detailed, difficult, elaborate, entangled, fancy, Gordian, involved, involute, knotty, labyrinthine, many-faceted, mazelike, perplexing, rococo, sophisticated, subtle, tangled, tortuous.
antonym simple.

intrigue[1] *v* attract, charm, fascinate, interest, puzzle, rivet, tantalize, tickle one's fancy, titillate.
antonym bore.
n affair, amour, entanglement, flirtation, intimacy, liaison, romance.

intrigue[2] *n* cabal, chicanery, collusion, conspiracy, double-dealing, influence, knavery, machination(s), manipulation, manoeuvre, plot, ruse, scheme, sharp practice, stratagem, string pulling, trickery, wheeling and dealing, wile, wire pulling.
v connive, conspire, machinate, manipulate, manoeuvre, plot, scheme.

intriguer *n* conniver, conspirator, intrigant(e), Machiavellian, machinator, operator, plotter, schemer, string puller, wangler, wheeler-dealer.

intriguing *adj* alluring, beguiling, bewitching, captivating, compelling, diverting, exciting, fascinating, interesting, puzzling, tantalizing, titillating.
antonyms boring, uninteresting.

intrinsic *adj* basic, built-in, central, congenital, constitutional, elemental, essential, fundamental, genuine, implicit, inborn, inbred, inherent, innate, integral, interior, internal, inward, native, natural, underlying.
antonym extrinsic.

introduce *v* acquaint, add, advance, air, announce, begin, bring in, bring up, broach, commence, conduct, establish, familiarize, found, inaugurate, initiate, inject, insert, institute, interpolate, interpose, launch, lead in, lead into, make known, market, moot, open, organize, pioneer, preface, present, propose, put forward, put in, recommend, ring in, set forth, start, submit, suggest, throw in, usher in, ventilate.
antonym take away.

introduction *n* addition, baptism, commencement, debut, entrance, establishment, exordium, foreword, inauguration, induction, initiation, injection, innovation, insertion, institution, interjection, interpolation, intro, launch, lead-in, opening, overture, pioneering, preamble, preface, preliminaries, prelude, presentation, prodrome, proem, prolegomena, prolegomenon, prologue, unveiling.
antonym withdrawal.

introductory *adj* beginner, beginning, early, elementary, exordial, first, inaugural, initial, initiatory, opening, precursory, prefatory, preliminary, preparatory, proemial, prolegomenous, starting.

introspection *n* heart-searching, introversion, navel-gazing, self-analysis, self-examination, self-observation, soul-searching.

introspective *adj* contemplative, introverted, inward-looking, meditative, navel-gazing, pensive, ruminative, subjective, thoughtful.
antonym outward-looking.

introverted *adj* indrawn, inner-directed, introspective, introversive, inward-looking, reserved, self-centred, self-contained, withdrawn.
antonym extroverted.

intrude *v* barge in, butt in, disturb, encroach, infringe, interfere, interlope, interrupt, meddle, obtrude, sneak in, trespass, violate.
antonyms stand back, withdraw.

intruder *n* burglar, buttinsky, gate-crasher, infiltrator, interloper, invader, poacher, prowler, raider, snooper, trespasser, unwelcome guest.

intrusion *n* aggression, encroachment, incursion, infringement, ingression, interference, interloping, interruption, invasion, meddling, obtrusion, trespass, violation.
antonym withdrawal.

intrusive *adj* disturbing, forward, importunate, interfering, interruptive, invasive, meddlesome, nosey, obtrusive, presumptuous, prying, pushy, uncalled-for, unwanted, unwelcome.
antonyms unintrusive, welcome.

intuition *n* discernment, feeling, feeling in one's bones, gut feeling, hunch, insight, instinct, perception, presentiment, reflex, sixth sense.
antonym reasoning.

intuitive *adj* automatic, innate, instinctive, intuitional, involuntary, natural, reflex, spontaneous, unreflecting, untaught.
antonym reasoned.

inundate *v* bury, deluge, drown, engulf, fill, flood, glut, overflow, overrun, overwhelm, spill over, submerge, swamp.

inundation *n* deluge, deluvion, deluvium, flood, glut, overflow, spillover, submergence, tidal wave, torrent.
antonym trickle.

inure *v* accustom, break in, condition, desensitize, familiarize, habituate, harden, numb, steel, strengthen, temper, toughen.
▲ *confusable word* immure.

invade *v* assail, assault, attack, break in on, burst in on, descend upon, encroach (on), enter, fall upon, infest, infringe (on), interfere with, intrude upon, irrupt, occupy, overrun, overspread, penetrate, pervade, raid, rush into, seize, swarm (over), violate.
antonym withdraw.

invader *n* aggressor, assailant, attacker, encroacher, infiltrator, intruder, raider, trespasser.

invalid[1] *adj* ailing, bedridden, disabled, failing, feeble, frail, ill, infirm, poorly, run-down, sick, sickly, valetudinarian, weak.
antonym healthy.
n convalescent, patient, shut-in, sufferer, valetudinarian.

invalid[2] *adj* baseless, fallacious, false, ill-founded, illogical, incorrect, inoperative, nugatory, null, null and void, unfounded, unscientific, unsound, untrue, void, worthless.
antonym valid.

invalidate *v* abrogate, annul, cancel, disprove, give the lie to, make worthless, negate, nullify, overrule, overthrow, quash, rescind, rule out, undermine, undo, vitiate, void, weaken.
antonym validate.

invalidity *n* fallaciousness, fallacy, falsity, illogicality, inconsistency, incorrectness, invalidness, speciousness, unsoundness, voidness, worthlessness.

invaluable *adj* beyond price, costly, indispensable, inestimable, precious, priceless, valuable.
antonym worthless.

invariable *adj* changeless, consistent, constant, fixed, immutable, inflexible, permanent, regular, rigid, set, static, unalterable, unchangeable, unchanging, unfailing, uniform, unvarying, unwavering.
antonym variable.

invariably *adv* always, consistently, customarily, habitually, inevitably, perpetually, regularly, unfailingly, universally, without exception, without fail.
antonym variably.

invasion *n* aggression, assault, attack, breach, encroachment, foray, incursion, infiltration, infraction, infringement, inroad, interference, intrusion, irruption, offensive, onslaught, overrunning, raid, seizure, usurpation, violation.
antonym withdrawal.

invective *n* abuse, berating, billingsgate, castigation, censure, contumely, curse, denunciation, diatribe, obloquy, opprobrium, philippic, reproach, revilement, sarcasm, scolding, tirade, tongue-lashing, vilification, vituperation.
antonym praise.

inveigh against *v* berate, blame, castigate, censure, condemn, damn, decry, denounce, expostulate, fulminate with, lambaste, rail against, recriminate, reproach, scold, sound off against, tongue-lash, upbraid, vituperate.
antonym praise.

inveigle *v* allure, bamboozle, beguile, cajole, charm, coax, con, decoy, ensnare, entice, entrap, lead on, lure, manipulate, manoeuvre, persuade, seduce, sweet-talk, wheedle, wile.

invent *v* coin, conceive, concoct, contrive, cook up, create, design, develop, devise, discover, dream up, fabricate, formulate, frame, imagine, improvise, innovate, make up, originate, think up, trump up.

invention *n* brainchild, coinage, concoction, contraption, contrivance, creation, creativeness, creativity, deceit, design, development, device, discovery, excogitation, fabrication, fake, falsehood, fantasy, fib, fiction, figment of the imagination, forgery, gadget, genius, imagination, ingenuity, innovation, inspiration, inventiveness, inveracity, lie, originality, origination, prevarication, resourcefulness, sham, story, tall tale, untruth, yarn.
antonym truth.

inventive *adj* creative, daedal, Daedalian, excogitative, fertile, imaginative, ingenious, innovative, inspired, original, resourceful.
antonym uninventive.

inventor *n* architect, author, builder, coiner, creator, designer, deviser, discoverer, innovator, maker, originator.

inventory *n* account, catalogue, equipment, file, list, listing, record, register, roll, roster, schedule, stock, store.

inverse *adj* contrary, converse, inverted, opposite, reverse, reversed, transposed, upside down.

inversion *n* antipode, antithesis, contraposition, contrariety, contrary, hysteron proteron, opposite, reversal, transposal, transposition.

invert *v* capsize, introvert, inverse, overturn, reverse, transpose, turn turtle, turn upside down, upset, upturn.
antonym right.

invest[1] *v* contribute, devote, expend, lay out, provide, put in, sink, spend, supply.

invest[2] *v* authorize, charge, consecrate, crown, empower, endow, endue, enthrone, establish, inaugurate, induct, install, license, ordain, sanction, vest.
antonym divest.

investigate *v* analyse, enquire into, examine, explore, gather evidence, go into, inspect, look into, probe, research, scrutinize, search, see how the land lies, sift through, study.

investigation *n* analysis, examination, exploration, fact-finding, hearing, inquest, inquiry, inspection, mission, probe, research, review, scrutiny, search, study, survey, witch hunt.

investigative *adj* exploratory, fact-finding, heuristic, inspecting, investigating, research, researching.

investigator *n* detective, dick, enquirer, examiner, gumshoe, inquisitor, PI, private detective, private eye, private investigator, researcher, shamus, sleuth, sleuthhound.

investment *n* ante, asset, contribution, investing, speculation, stake, transaction, venture.

inveterate *adj* chronic, confirmed, deep-dyed, deep-rooted, deep-seated, diehard, dyed-in-the-wool, entrenched, established, habitual, hard-core, hardened, incorrigible, incurable, ineradicable, ingrained, irreversible, long-standing, obstinate, recidivistic, set in one's ways.

invidious *adj* discriminating, discriminatory, harmful, hateful, injurious, malicious, objectionable, odious, offensive, repugnant, slighting, undesirable.
antonym desirable.

invigorate *v* animate, brace, buck up, energize, enliven, exhilarate, fortify, freshen, galvanize, give new life to, hearten, inspirit, liven up, nerve, pep up, perk up, quicken, refresh, rejuvenate, revitalize, revive, stimulate, strengthen, vitalize, vivify.
antonyms dishearten, weary.

invigorating *adj* bracing, energizing, enlivening, exhilarating, fresh, healthful, inspiriting, quickening, refreshing, rejuvenating, restorative, rousing, salubrious, stimulating, strengthening, tonic, uplifting, vitalizing, vivifying.
antonyms disheartening, wearying.

invincible *adj* impenetrable, impregnable, indestructible, indomitable, inexpugnable, insuperable, invulnerable, unassailable, unbeatable, unconquerable, unsurmountable, unyielding.
antonym beatable.

inviolable *adj* hallowed, holy, impregnable, inalienable, incorruptible, invulnerable, sacred, sacrosanct, unalterable, untouchable.
antonym violable.

inviolate *adj* intact, pristine, pure, sacred, stainless, unaltered, unbroken, undamaged, undefiled, undisturbed, unhurt, uninjured, unpolluted, unprofaned, unscathed, unspoiled, unstained, unsullied, untouched, virgin, whole.
antonym sullied.

invisible *adj* behind the scenes, concealed, disguised, hidden, imperceptible, inappreciable, inconspicuous, indiscernible, infinitesimal, microscopic, out of sight, unapparent, undetectable, undetected, unperceivable, unseen.
antonym visible.

invitation *n* allurement, asking, begging, bidding, call, challenge, come-on, coquetry, enticement, exhortation, incitement, inducement, invite, overture, provocation, request, solicitation, summons, supplication, tantalization, temptation.

invite *v* allure, ask, ask for, attract, beckon, beg, bid, bring on, call, court, draw, encourage, entice, extend an invitation to, lead, provoke, request, seek, solicit, summon, tempt, welcome.
antonyms force, order.

inviting *adj* alluring, appealing, appetizing, attractive, beguiling, captivating, delightful, engaging, enticing, fascinating, intriguing, magnetic, mouthwatering, pleasing, provocative, seductive, tantalizing, tempting, warm, welcoming, winning.
antonym uninviting.

invocation n adjuration, appeal, beseeching, conjuration, entreaty, imploring, incantation, petition, prayer, supplication.

invoke v adjure, appeal to, apply, base on, beg, beg for, beseech, call forth (or up), call upon, conjure, conjure up, entreat, evoke, implore, petition, pray, resort to, solicit, summon, supplicate, use.
▲ *confusable word* evoke.

involuntary adj automatic, blind, compulsory, conditioned, forced, instinctive, instinctual, obligatory, reflex, reluctant, spontaneous, unconscious, uncontrolled, unintentional, unpremeditated, unthinking, unwilled, unwilling, vegetative.
antonym voluntary.

involve v absorb, affect, associate, call for, comprise, concern, connect, contain, cover, draw in, embrace, engage, engross, enmesh, entail, entangle, hold one's attention, immerse, implicate, imply, include, incorporate, incriminate, inculpate, make a party to, mean, mix up, necessitate, occupy, preoccupy, presuppose, require, rivet, take in, touch.

involved adj caught up (or in), complex, complicated, confusing, convoluted, difficult, elaborate, intricate, knotty, labyrinthine, sophisticated, tangled, tortuous.
antonyms simple, uninvolved.

involved in (or with) a part of, caught up in (or with), concerned in (or with), engrossed in, implicated in, in on, mixed up in (or with), occupied in (or with), participating in, tangled up in (or with).

involvement n absorption, association, commitment, complexity, complication, concern, connection, convolution, dedication, difficulty, engrossment, enmeshment, entanglement, imbroglio, implication, interest, intricacy, involution, participation, problem.

invulnerable adj impenetrable, impregnable, indestructible, insusceptible, invincible, inviolable, proof against attack, protected, safe, secure, unassailable, unwoundable.
antonym vulnerable.

inward adj entering, essential, hidden, inbound, incoming, inflowing, ingoing, inherent, inly, inmost, inner, innermost, inpouring, inside, interior, internal, intimate, intrinsic, penetrating, personal, private, privy, secret.
antonyms external, outward.

inwardly adv at heart, deep down, inly, in one's heart of hearts, inside, internally, privately, secretly, to oneself, under the surface, within.
antonyms externally, outwardly.

iota n atom, bit, drop, grain, hint, jot, mite, particle, scintilla, scrap, smidgen, soupçon, spark, speck, tittle, trace, whit.

irascibility n asperity, bad temper, cantankerousness, choler, crabbiness, crankiness, crossness, edginess, fieriness, ill temper, impatience, irritability, irritation, petulance, shortness, snappishness, snarkiness, testiness, touchiness.
antonym placidness.

irascible adj bad-tempered, cantankerous, chippy, choleric, crabbed, crabby, cranky, cross, edgy, fiery, fractious, hasty, hot-tempered, huffy, ill-natured, ill-tempered, irritable, peppery, petulant, prickly, quick-tempered, short-tempered, snappish, snarky, testy, touchy, volcanic.
antonym placid.

irate adj angered, angry, annoyed, cross, enraged, exasperated, fuming, furious, hot under the collar, in a huff, in a rage, incensed, indignant, infuriated, in high dudgeon, ireful, irritated, livid, mad, piqued, provoked, riled, teed off, ticked off, up in arms, worked up, wrathful, wroth.
antonym calm.

ire n anger, annoyance, choler, displeasure, exasperation, fury, indignation, infuriation, passion, rage, wrath.
antonym calmness.

iridescent adj glittering, moiré, nacreous, opalescent, opaline, pearl-like, pearly, polychromatic, prismatic, rainbow, rainbow-coloured, rainbowlike, rainbowy, shimmering, shot.

irk v aggravate, annoy, bore, bother, bug, disgust, distress, exasperate, gall, get, get to, get under one's skin, irritate, nettle, peeve, plague, provoke, put out, rile, rub the wrong way, ruffle, try one's patience, vex, weary.
antonym please.

irksome adj aggravating, annoying, boring, bothersome, burdensome, disagreeable, exasperating, galling, infuriating, irritating, tedious, tiresome, troublesome, trying, vexatious, vexing, wearisome.
antonym pleasing.

iron adj adamant, cruel, fast-binding, firm, fixed, hard, harsh, heavy, immovable, implacable, indomitable, inflexible, insensitive, obdurate, rigid, robust, steel, steely, stone, strict, strong, tough, unbending, uncompromising, unyielding.
antonyms pliable, weak.
v flatten, press, smooth, uncrease.

iron out clear up, deal with, eliminate, eradicate, erase, fix, get rid of, put right, reconcile, resolve, settle, smooth over, solve, sort out, square away, straighten out.

ironic adj caustic, contemptuous, contrary to expectation, cynical, derisive, incongruous, mocking, paradoxical, sarcastic, sardonic, satirical, scoffing, scornful, sneering, wry.

irons n bilboes, bonds, chains, fetters, gyves, handcuffs, manacles, shackles, trammels.

irony n burlesque, contrariety, contrariness, cynicism, incongruity, mockery, paradox, sarcasm, satire.

irradiate v brighten (up), enlighten, give out, illume, illuminate, illumine, lighten, light (up), make bright, radiate, shed light on, shine on, throw light on.

irrational adj aberrant, absurd, baseless, brainless, crazy, demented, faulty, flawed, foolish, illogical, injudicious, insane, mindless, muddle-headed, nonsensical, preposterous, reasonless, scatterbrained, senseless, silly, unfounded, unreasonable, unreasoning, unsound, unstable, unthinking, unwise, wild, without rhyme or reason.

antonym rational.

irreconcilable *adj* clashing, conflicting, hard-line, implacable, incompatible, incongruous, inconsistent, inexorable, inflexible, intransigent, opposed, poles apart, unappeasable, uncompromising, unconformable, unreconcilable.

antonym reconcilable.

irrecoverable *adj* beyond recall, irreclaimable, irredeemable, irremediable, irreparable, irretrievable, lost, past saving, unrecoverable, unsalvageable, unsavable.

antonym recoverable.

irrefutable *adj* absolute, apodictic, axiomatic, certain, demonstrable, impregnable, incontestable, incontrovertible, indisputable, indubitable, invincible, irrebuttable, irrefragable, irresistible, self-evident, sure, unanswerable, unassailable, undeniable, ungainsayable, unquestionable.

antonym refutable.

irregular *adj* aberrant, abnormal, anomalistic, anomalous, asymmetrical, broken, bumpy, craggy, crooked, deformed, disconnected, discontinuous, disorderly, eccentric, erratic, exceptional, extraordinary, fitful, fluctuating, freak, haphazard, heterodox, hit or miss, holey, illegal, improper, inappropriate, inconsistent, inordinate, intermittent, jagged, lopsided, lumpy, malformed, non-uniform, occasional, odd, patchy, peculiar, pitted, queer, quirky, ragged, random, rough, serrated, shifting, snatchy, spasmodic, sporadic, uncertain, unconnected, unconventional, unequal, uneven, unorthodox, unprocedural, unpunctual, unsteady, unsymmetrical, unsystematic, unusual, variable, wavering.

antonyms conventional, regular, smooth.

irregularity *n* aberration, abnormality, anomaly, asymmetry, breach, bumpiness, confusion, crookedness, deformity, desultoriness, deviation, discontinuity, disorderliness, disorganization, eccentricity, freak, haphazardness, heterodoxy, inconsistency, inequality, jaggedness, lopsidedness, lumpiness, malformation, malfunction, malpractice, non-uniformity, oddity, patchiness, peculiarity, raggedness, randomness, roughness, singularity, uncertainty, unconnectedness, unconventionality, unevenness, unorthodoxy, unpunctuality, unsteadiness.

antonyms conventionality, regularity, smoothness.

irregularly *adv* anyhow, by fits and starts, disconnectedly, eccentrically, erratically, every which way, fitfully, haphazardly, inconsistently, intermittently, jerkily, non-uniformly, now and again, occasionally, off and on, spasmodically, sporadically, unevenly, unmethodically, unsystematically.

antonym regularly.

irrelevance *n* immateriality, inapplicability, inappositeness, inappropriateness, inaptness, inconsequence, unconnectedness, unimportance, unrelatedness.

antonym relevance.

irrelevant *adj* beside the point, extraneous, immaterial, impertinent, inadmissible, inapplicable, inapposite, inappropriate, inapt, inconsequent, inessential, nothing to do with the case, off the subject, peripheral, tangential, unconnected, unrelated.

antonym relevant.

irreligious *adj* agnostic, atheistic, blasphemous, free-thinking, godless, heathen, heathenish, iconoclastic, impious, irreverent, pagan, profane, rationalistic, sacrilegious, sceptical, sinful, unbelieving, undevout, ungodly, unholy, unreligious, unrighteous, wicked.

antonyms pious, religious.

irremediable *adj* beyond redemption, beyond remedy, deadly, fatal, hopeless, immedicable, incorrigible, incurable, inoperable, irreclaimable, irrecoverable, irredeemable, irreparable, irreversible, mortal, remediless, terminal.

antonym remediable.

irremovable *adj* durable, fast, fixed, frozen, immovable, indestructible, ineradicable, ingrained, inoperable, obdurate, obstinate, permanent, persistent, rooted, set, stuck.

antonym removable.

irreparable *adj* beyond remedy, incurable, irreclaimable, irrecoverable, irremediable, irretrievable, irreversible, past hope, unrepairable.

antonyms recoverable, remediable.

irreplaceable *adj* essential, indispensable, inimitable, invaluable, matchless, peerless, priceless, unique, unmatched, vital.

antonym replaceable.

irrepressible *adj* boisterous, bubbling over, buoyant, ebullient, effervescent, indomitable, inextinguishable, insuppressible, resilient, uncontainable, uncontrollable, ungovernable, uninhibited, unmanageable, unquenchable, unrestrained, unstoppable.

antonyms depressed, depressive, despondent, resistible.

irreproachable *adj* blameless, faultless, guiltless, immaculate, impeccable, inculpable, innocent, irreprehensible, irreprovable, perfect, pure, reproachless, stainless, unblemished, unimpeachable, unsullied, untainted, virtuous.

antonyms blameworthy, culpable.

irresistible *adj* alluring, beguiling, charming, compelling, enchanting, fascinating, great, imperative, ineluctable, inescapable, inevitable, inexorable, overpowering, overwhelming, potent, powerful, pressing, ravishing, resistless, seductive, strong, tempting, unavoidable, uncontrollable, urgent.

antonyms avoidable, resistible.

irresolute *adj* dithering, doubtful, faint-hearted, fickle, fluctuating, half-hearted, hesitant, hesitating, inconstant, indecisive, infirm, in two minds, on the fence, shifting, shilly-shallying, tentative, undecided, undetermined, unresolved, unsettled, unstable, unsteady, vacillating, variable, wavering, weak.

antonym resolute.

irresponsible *adj* birdbrained, carefree, careless, featherbrained, feckless, flibbertigibbity, flighty, fly-by-night, footloose, giddy, harebrained, harum-scarum, heedless, ill-considered, immature, light-hearted, madcap, negligent, rash, reckless, scatterbrained, shiftless, thoughtless, undependable, unreliable, untrustworthy, wild.

antonym responsible.

irretrievable *adj* beyond recall, hopeless, irreclaimable, irrecoverable, irredeemable, irremediable, irreparable, irreversible, irrevocable, lost, unrecallable, unrecoverable, unsalvageable.

antonyms recoverable, reversible.

irreverence *n* blasphemy, cheek, cheekiness, derision, discourtesy, disrespect, flippancy, godlessness, iconoclasm, impertinence, impiety, impudence, irreligion, levity, mockery, profanity, sacrilege, sauce.

antonym reverence.

irreverent *adj* blasphemous, cheeky, contemptuous, derisive, discourteous, disparaging, disrespectful, flip, flippant, godless, iconoclastic, impertinent, impious, impudent, irreligious, mocking, profanatory, profane, rude, sacrilegious, saucy, tongue-in-cheek.

antonym reverent.

irreversible *adj* final, hopeless, immedicable, immutable, incurable, inoperable, irremediable, irreparable, irretrievable, irrevocable, lasting, lost, permanent, remediless, unalterable, unchangeable.

antonyms curable, remediable, reversible.

irrevocable *adj* carved in stone, certain, changeless, fated, fixed, hopeless, immutable, inexorable, invariable, irremediable, irrepealable, irretrievable, irreversible, predestined, predetermined, settled, sure, unalterable, unchangeable.

antonyms alterable, flexible, mutable, reversible.

irrigate *v* dampen, flood, flush (out), inundate, moisten, sluice, wash (out), water, wet.

irritability *n* crankiness, edge, edginess, erethism, excitability, fractiousness, fretfulness, hypersensitivity, ill humour, ill temper, impatience, irascibility, peevishness, petulance, prickliness, snappishness, testiness, tetchiness, touchiness.

antonyms bonhomie, cheerfulness, complacence, good humour.

irritable *adj* bad-tempered, cantankerous, captious, choleric, crabby, cranky, cross, crotchety, crusty, edgy, excitable, feisty, fractious, fretful, hypersensitive, ill-humoured, ill-tempered, impatient, in a huff, irascible, nettlesome, on edge, peevish, petulant, prickly, querulous, short, short-tempered,

snappish, snappy, snarky, snarling, testy, tetchy, thin-skinned, touchy.

antonyms cheerful, complacent.

irritant *n* annoyance, bother, goad, irritation, menace, nuisance, pain, pest, pinprick, plague, provocation, salt in the wound, tease, thorn in the flesh (or side), trouble, vexation.

antonyms pleasure, sop, sweetness.

irritate *v* acerbate, aggravate, anger, annoy, bedevil, bother, bug, chafe, enrage, exacerbate, exasperate, faze, fret, gall, get one's back up, get on one's nerves, get to, harass, incense, inflame, infuriate, intensify, irk, needle, nettle, offend, pain, peeve, pester, pique, provoke, put out, rankle, rile, rouse, rub salt in (the wound), rub the wrong way, ruffle, ruffle one's feathers, set on edge, stick in one's craw, vex.

antonyms gratify, mollify, placate, please.

irritated *adj* angry, annoyed, bothered, cross, displeased, edgy, exasperated, harassed, huffy, impatient, intensified, irked, irritable, nettled, peeved, piqued, provoked, put out, ratty, riled, roused, ruffled, ticked off, uptight, vexed.

antonyms composed, gratified, pleased.

irritating *adj* abrasive, aggravating, annoying, bothersome, displeasing, disturbing, exasperating, galling, infuriating, irksome, maddening, nagging, pesky, pestiferous, pestilent, pestilential, plaguy, provoking, thorny, troublesome, trying, upsetting, vexatious, vexing, worrisome.

antonyms pleasant, pleasing.

irritation *n* aggravation, anger, annoyance, bore, crossness, displeasure, dissatisfaction, exasperation, fretfulness, fury, goad, impatience, indignation, irritability, irritant, itch, nuisance, pain, pain in the neck, pest, pinprick, provocation, shortness, snappiness, tease, testiness, vexation, wrath.

antonyms pleasure, satisfaction.

island *n* atoll, cay, holm, isle, islet, key, reef, sandbar.

isolate *v* abstract, alienate, cut off, detach, disconnect, dissociate, distance, divorce, exclude, factor out, identify, insulate, keep apart, ostracize, pinpoint, quarantine, remove, seclude, segregate, separate, sequester, set apart, shut off, withdraw.

antonyms assimilate, incorporate.

isolated *adj* abnormal, alienated, alone, anomalous, atypical, backwoods, deserted, detached, dissociated, eremitic, exceptional, excluded, freak, godforsaken, incommunicado, insular, lonely, monastic, outlying, out-of-the-way, random, reclusive, remote, retired, secluded, separated, sequestered, shut off, single, solitary, sporadic, unfrequented, unique, unrelated, untrodden, untypical, unusual, unvisited, withdrawn.

antonyms populous, typical.

isolation *n* alienation, aloofness, detachment, disconnection, dissociation, exile, insularity, insulation, lazaretto, loneliness, quarantine, reclusion, remoteness, removal, retirement, seclusion, segregation, self-sufficiency, separation, solitariness, solitude, withdrawal.

issue¹ *n* bone of contention, bottom line, business at hand, concern, controversy, crux of the matter, debate, matter for debate, matter in hand, point at issue, problem, question, subject, topic.

issue² *n* copy, delivery, discharge, dissemination, distribution, edition, emanation, emergence, flow, focus of attention (or interest), granting, impression, instalment, issuance, issuing, printing, promulgation, propagation, publication, release, supply, supplying.

v announce, bring out, broadcast, circulate, deal out, deliver, discharge, distribute, emit, give out, mint, produce, promulgate, publicize, publish, put out, release, send out, supply.

issue³ *n* conclusion, consequence, culmination, debouchement, denouement, effect, end product, outcome, payoff, result, upshot.

v arise, burst forth, debouch, emanate, emerge, flow, leak, originate, proceed, rise, spring, stem.

issue⁴ *n* brood, children, descendants, heirs, offspring, posterity, progeny, scions, seed, young.

itch *v* crawl, prickle, tickle, tingle.

n craving, desire, eagerness, hankering, hunger, irritation, itchiness, keenness, longing, lust, passion, prickling, scabies, tingling, urge, yearning, yen.

itch (for or **to)** ache, be burning (to), be dying, be eager, be impatient, be raring (to), be spoiling (for), crave, desire, hanker (for or after), have a hankering, have a yen, long, lust (after or for), pine, yearn.

item *n* article, aspect, bulletin, component, consideration, detail, element, entry, factor, feature, ingredient, matter, minute, note, notice, object, paragraph, part, particular, piece, point, report, thing.

itemize *v* catalogue, count (up), detail, document, enumerate, give full particulars, go into detail, index, instance, inventory, list, mention, name, number, particularize, record, specify, spell out, tabulate.

itinerancy *n* drifting, globetrotting, hoboism, nomadism, peregrination, roaming, rootlessness, roving, travelling, vagabondism, vagrancy, wandering, wanderlust, wayfaring.

itinerant *adj* ambulatory, drifting, journeying, migratory, nomadic, peregrine, peripatetic, rambling, roaming, rootless, roving, travelling, vagabond, vagrant, wandering, wayfaring.

antonyms settled, stationary.

n drifter, globetrotter, gypsy, hobo, nomad, perigrinator, peripatetic, pilgrim, roamer, rolling stone, Romany, rover, tinker, tramp, traveller, vagabond, vagrant, wanderer, wayfarer.

itinerary *n* circuit, course, directory, guidebook, line, path, plan, program, route, schedule, tour.

J

jab v clap, clip, dig, elbow, hit, jog, jostle, lunge, nudge, pierce, poke, prod, punch, stab, tap, thrust, thump.

jabber v babble, blather, chatter, drivel, gab, gabble, jaw, mumble, natter, prate, prattle, ramble, run off at the mouth, talk nonsense, tattle, yap.

jacket n blazer, blouson, case, casing, coat, cover, covering, envelope, folder, jerkin, mackinaw, sheath, shell, skin, sleeve, tabard, windbreaker, wrap, wrapper, wrapping.

jackpot n award, big one, big time(s), bonanza, kitty, pool, pot, prize, reward, stakes, winnings.

jaded adj blasé, blunted, bored, cloyed, dispirited, dulled, effete, exhausted, fagged, fatigued, fed-up, played-out, satiated, sick and tired, spent, surfeited, tired, tired out, weary, world-weary, worn out.

antonyms fresh, refreshed.

jag¹ n arête, barb, denticle, nick, notch, point, projection, protrusion, snag, spur, tooth.

jag² n bout, fit, spell, spree, tear.

jagged adj barbed, broken, craggy, denticulate, hackly, indented, irregular, nicked, non-uniform, notched, pointed, pointy, ragged, ridged, rough, saw-edged, serrated, snagged, spiky, toothed, uneven.

antonym smooth.

jail n bridewell, brig, cage, calaboose, can, cell(s), clink, cooler, coop, custody, dungeon, guardhouse, hole, hoosegow, house of correction, inside, jailhouse, jug, lockup, pen, penitentiary, pokey, prison, reform school, reformatory, slammer, solitary confinement, stockade.

v cage, confine, coop up, detain, encage, immure, impound, imprison, incarcerate, intern, keep in custody, keep under lock and key, lock up, send down, shut up.

jailer n captor, guard, keeper, screw, turnkey, warden, warder.

jam¹ v block (up), clog, compact, confine, congest, cram, crowd, crush, fill up, force, obstruct, overload, pack, press, push, ram, sandwich, shove, squash, squeeze, stall, stick, stuff, throng, thrust, wedge.

n bottleneck, concourse, crowd, crush, gridlock, herd, horde, mass, mob, multitude, pack, press, swarm, throng, traffic jam.

jam² n bind, corner, difficulty, dilemma, fix, hole, hot water, imbroglio, impasse, pickle, pinch, plight, predicament, quandary, scrape, sorry plight, spot, straits, tangle, tight corner, tight spot, trouble.

jam³ n confiture, conserve, jelly, marmalade, preserve, spread.

jamboree n blowout, carnival, carousal, carouse, celebration, convention, festival, festivity, fete, field day, frolic, gala, gathering, get-together, jubilee, junket, party, potlatch, rally, shindig, spree.

jangle v chime, clank, clash, clatter, jar, jingle, rattle, ring, upset, vibrate.

n cacophony, clang, clangour, clash, din, dissonance, harshness, jar, noise, racket, rattle, reverberation, ringing.

antonyms euphony, harmony.

janitor n caretaker, cleaner, concierge, custodian, doorkeeper, doorman, porter.

jar¹ n amphora, bottle, can, carafe, container, crock, cruet, cruse, ewer, flagon, jug, pitcher, pot, receptacle, stamnos, stoup, urn, vase, vessel.

jar² v agitate, annoy, clash, conflict (with), discompose, disturb, grate (on), grind, hit a sour note, interfere (with), irritate, jangle, jolt, rasp, rattle, rock, shake, shock, startle, upset, vibrate.

n clash, clamour, discord, dissonance, grating, harshness, irritation, jangle, jolt, rasping, rattle, shake, shock, start.

jargon n argot, balderdash, bunkum, cant, claptrap, computerese, criminalese, dialect, diplomatese, drivel, gabble, gibberish, gobbledygook, idiom, jive, lingo, mumbo jumbo, nonsense, palaver, parlance, patois, rigmarole, rubbish, slang, tongue, twaddle, unintelligibility, vernacular.

jarring adj cacophonous, clashing, discordant, dissonant, disturbing, grating, irritating, jangling, jolting, nerve-wracking, rasping, strident, upsetting.

jaundiced adj biassed, bitter, cynical, disbelieving, distorted, distrustful, envious, hostile, jaded, jealous, misanthropic, partial, pessimistic, preconceived, prejudiced, resentful, sceptical, sour, suspicious.

antonyms fresh, naïve, optimistic.

jaunty adj breezy, buoyant, carefree, cheeky, chic, chipper, dapper, debonair, gay, high-spirited, insouciant, light-hearted, lively, perky, self-confident, showy, smart, sprightly, spruce, stylish, trim.

antonyms anxious, depressed, dowdy, seedy.

jaw¹ *n* chops, flews, jaws, mandible, masticator, maw, maxilla, mouth, muzzle, trap.

jaw² *v* babble, berate, blather, chat, chatter, criticize, gab, gabble, gas, gossip, jabber, lecture, natter, prate, revile, scold, talk, yak.

n chat, chatter, chinwag, gab, gossip, guff, natter, prattle, talk.

jazz *n* bebop, blues, boogie, boogie-woogie, crap, Dixieland, guff, hard rock, heavy metal, lies, New Wave, ragtime, rhythm, rock, spiel, swing, talk.

jazzy *adj* animated, avant-garde, bold, fancy, flashy, gaudy, lively, showy, smart, snazzy, spirited, stylish, swinging, vivacious, wild, zestful.

antonyms conservative, prosaic, square.

jealous *adj* begrudging, careful, covetous, desirous, envious, green, green-eyed, green with envy, grudging, guarded, heedful, jaundiced, mistrustful, possessive, proprietorial, protective, resentful, solicitous, suspicious, vigilant, wary, watchful, zealous.

jealousy *n* covetousness, distrust, enviousness, envy, green-eyed monster, grudge, heart burning, ill will, mistrust, possessiveness, resentment, spite, suspicion, vigilance, watchfulness.

jeer *n* abuse, aspersion, boo, catcall, chaff, crack, derision, dig, gibe, hiss, hoot, mockery, put-down, ragging, raillery, raspberry, ridicule, scoff, sneer, taunt, thrust.

jeer at banter, barrack, boo, chaff, deride, flout, gibe, heckle, hector, knock, make a laughingstock of, mock, put down, rag, rail at, razz, ride, ridicule, scoff at, sneer at, take a crack (at), taunt, twit.

jejune *adj* arid, banal, barren, callow, childish, colourless, dry, dull, empty, foolish, immature, impoverished, inane, insipid, juvenile, meagre, naïve, prosaic, puerile, senseless, shallow, silly, simple, spiritless, trite, uninteresting, unoriginal, unsophisticated, vapid, wishy-washy.

antonyms mature, meaningful.

jell *v* clot, coagulate, congeal, crystallize, form, gel, gelatinize, harden, jellify, jelly, set, solidify, take form, take shape, thicken.

antonym disintegrate.

jeopardize *v* compromise, endanger, expose, gamble with (or away), hazard, imperil, menace, put at risk, put in danger, risk, stake, threaten, venture.

antonyms protect, safeguard.

jeopardy *n* danger, endangerment, exposure, hazard, imperilment, insecurity, peril, plight, precariousness, risk, venture, vulnerability.

antonyms safety, security.

jerk¹ *n* bounce, bump, jig, jog, jolt, lurch, pluck, pull, shrug, throw, toss, tug, tweak, twist, twitch, wrench, yank.

v bounce, bump, flirt, jog, jolt, jounce, lurch, pluck, pull, shrug, start, start suddenly, throw, thrust, toss, tug, tweak, twist, twitch, wrench, yank.

jerk² *n* bum, cad, clod, clot, clown, creep, dimwit, dolt, dope, fool, halfwit, heel, idiot, klutz, louse, ninny, schlep, schmo, schmuck, twit.

jerky *adj* bouncy, bumpy, convulsive, disconnected, discontinuous, fitful, incoherent, in fits and starts, irregular, jolting, jumpy, paroxysmal, rough, shaky, spasmodic, tremulous, twitchy, uncontrolled, unco-ordinated.

antonym smooth.

jerry-built *adj* cheap, cheapjack, defective, faulty, flimsy, insubstantial, ramshackle, rickety, shoddy, slapped together, slipshod, unsubstantial.

antonyms firm, stable, substantial.

jersey *n* guernsey, jumper, pullover, sweater, sweat shirt, woolly.

jest *n* banter, bon mot, clowning, crack, fooling, fun, gag, hoax, jape, jeu d'esprit, joke, josh, kidding, pleasantry, prank, quip, ribbing, sally, sport, teasing, trick, waggery, wisecrack, witticism.

v banter, chaff, clown, fool, gibe, jeer (at), joke, josh, kid, mock, quip, rag, rib, scoff, tease, trifle, twit.

jester *n* buffoon, card, clown, comedian, comic, cutup, droll, fool, gagster, harlequin, humorist, joker, life of the party, merry-andrew, merryman, mummer, pantaloon, prankster, quipster, wag, wit, zany.

jet¹ *n* atomizer, ejection, flow, fountain, gush, issue, nozzle, rush, spout, spray, sprayer, spring, sprinkler, spurt, squirt, stream, surge.

jet² *adj* black, charcoal, coal-black, ebon, ebony, inky, jetty, pitch-black, pitchy, raven, sable, sloe, sooty.

jetsam *n* lagan, junk, refuse, rubbish, trash, wreckage.

jettison *v* abandon, chuck (out), discard, ditch, dump, eject, expel, heave out, offload, scrap, throw out, toss overboard, unload.

antonyms load, take on.

jetty *n* barrier, breakwater, dock, mole, pier, quay, seawall, wharf.

jewel *n* bijou, brilliant, diamond, find, gaud, gem, gemstone, humdinger, locket, masterpiece, ornament, paragon, pearl, precious stone, pride and joy, prize, rarity, rock, sparkler, stone, treasure, trinket, wonder.

jewellery *n* bijouterie, bijoux, finery, gauds, gems, jewels, ornaments, regalia, treasure, trinkets.

Jezebel *n* Delilah, femme fatale, harlot, hussy, man-eater, scarlet woman, seductress, she-devil, temptress, vamp, wanton, whore, witch.

jib *v* back off, balk, pull back, recoil, refuse, retreat, shrink, stall, stop short.

jibe *see* **gibe**

jiffy *n* flash, instant, less than no time, minute, moment, no time, sec, second, split second, tick, trice, twinkling, two shakes, two ticks.
antonym age.

jig *v* bob, bobble, bounce, caper, dance, hop, jerk, jiggle, jounce, jump, prance, shake, skip, twitch, wiggle, wobble.

jiggery-pokery *n* bunk, chicanery, deceit, deception, dishonesty, fraud, funny business, hanky-panky, humbug, monkey business, subterfuge, trickery.

jiggle *v* agitate, bounce, fidget, jerk, jig, jog, joggle, shake, shimmy, twitch, waggle, wiggle, wobble.

jilt *v* abandon, betray, brush off, chuck, desert, discard, ditch, drop, forsake, leave at the alter, leave in the lurch, reject, repudiate, spurn, throw over.
antonym cleave to.

jingle¹ *v* chime, chink, clatter, clink, jangle, peal, rattle, ring, sound, tinkle, tintinnabulate.
n clang, clangour, clink, jangle, pealing, rattle, reverberation, ringing, tinkle, tintinnabulation.

jingle² *n* chant, chime, chorus, couplet, ditty, doggerel, limerick, melody, poem, rhyme, song, tune, verse.

jingoism *n* chauvinism, flagwaving, imperialism, insularity, nationalism, parochialism, patriotism, xenophobia.

jinx *n* bad luck, charm, curse, evil eye, gremlin, hex, hoodoo, Jonah, magic, plague, spell, voodoo.
v bedevil, bewitch, bring bad luck to, curse, doom, hex, hoodoo, plague, put a spell on.

jitters *n* agitation, anxiety, edginess, fidgets, heebie-jeebies, jimjams, nerves, nervousness, tenseness, the creeps, the screaming meemies, the shakes, the shivers, the willies.

jittery *adj* agitated, anxious, edgy, fidgety, flustered, jumpy, nervous, on edge, panicky, perturbed, quaking, quivering, shaky, shivery, trembling, uneasy.
antonyms calm, composed, confident.

job *n* activity, affair, assignment, batch, burglary, business, calling, capacity, caper, career, charge, chore, commission, concern, consignment, contract, contribution, course of action, craft, duty, employment, enterprise, errand, function, heist, line of work, livelihood, lot, matter, métier, mission, occupation, office, opening, output, part, placement, position, post, proceeding, profession, project, province, pursuit, responsibility, robbery, role, situation, stint, task, theft, trade, undertaking, vacancy, venture, vocation, work.

jobless *adj* idle, inactive, laid off, on the dole, out of work, unemployed, unoccupied, unused, workless.
antonym employed.

jockey *v* angle, challenge, compete, edge, engineer, finagle, jostle, manipulate, manoeuvre, negotiate, pull strings, vie.

jocose *adj* blithe, comical, droll, facetious, funny, humorous, jesting, jocular, jocund, joking, jovial, merry, mirthful, mischievous, playful, sportive, teasing, waggish, witty.
antonym morose.

jocular *adj* amusing, arch, blithe, comical, droll, entertaining, facetious, frolicsome, funny, humorous, jesting, jocose, jocund, joking, jolly, jovial, merry, playful, roguish, sportive, teasing, waggish, whimsical, witty.
antonym serious.

jocularity *n* absurdity, comicality, drollery, facetiousness, fooling, gaiety, hilarity, humour, jesting, jocoseness, jocosity, jolliness, joviality, laughter, merriment, playfulness, pleasantry, roguishness, sport, sportiveness, teasing, waggery, waggishness, whimsicality, whimsy, wit, wittiness.

jog¹ *v* activate, arouse, bounce, bump, jar, jerk, jiggle, joggle, jolt, jostle, jounce, nudge, poke, prod, prompt, push, remind, rock, shake, shove, stimulate, stir, yank.
n jerk, jiggle, jolt, nudge, poke, prod, push, reminder, shake, shove, yank.

jog² *v, n* canter, dogtrot, jogtrot, lope, lumber, pace, pad, run, trot.

joie de vivre blitheness, bounce, buoyancy, cheerfulness, ebullience, enjoyment, enthusiasm, gaiety, get-up-and-go, gusto, joy, joyfulness, life, liveliness, merriment, mirth, pleasure, relish, spirit, zest.
antonym depression.

join *v* abut, accompany, accrete, add (to), adjoin, affiliate (with), amalgamate, annex, append, assemble, associate (with), attach (to), border, border on, bring together, butt, cement, cohere, combine, conglomerate, conjoin, conjugate, connect, couple, dock, enlist, enrol, enter, fasten, juxtapose, knit, knit together, link, march with, marry, meet, merge with, reach, sign up (for), splice, take part in, team up with, tie, touch, unite (with), verge on, yoke.
antonyms leave, separate.

join in chip in, contribute, co-operate (in), help (with), lend a hand (with), partake (in), participate (in), pitch in, take part (in).

join up enlist, enrol, enter, sign up.

joint¹ *n* articulation, commissure, connection, geniculation, hinge, intersection, junction, juncture, knot, nexus, node, seam, union.
adj adjunct, amalgamated, collective, combined, communal, concerted, consolidated, co-operative, co-ordinated, joined, mutual, shared, united.
v articulate, carve, connect, couple, cut up, dismember, dissect, divide, fasten, fit, geniculate, join, segment, sever, sunder, unite.

joint² *n* dance hall, den, dive, hangout, haunt, hole, honky-tonk, nightclub, nightspot, place, pub.

joke *n* buffoon, butt, byword, clown, conceit, farce, figure of fun, frolic, fun, funny, gag, good one, hoot, howler, jape, jest, jeu d'esprit, knee slapper, lark, laughingstock, play, pun, quip, rib tickler, sally, scream, sport, whimsy, wisecrack, witticism, yarn.

v banter, chaff, clown, crack a funny, deride, fool, frolic, gambol, jest, kid, laugh (at), make fun of, mock, pull someone's leg, quip, rally, rib, ridicule, spoof, taunt, tease, twit, wisecrack.

joker *n* buffoon, card, character, clown, comedian, comic, cutup, droll, gagster, humorist, jester, jokesmith, jokester, kidder, prankster, sport, trickster, wag, wit.

jollification *n* celebration, conviviality, festivity, frolic, gaiety, jollity, junket, merriment, merrymaking, party, revelry, shindig, spree.

antonym lamentation.

jolly *adj* blithe, blithesome, carefree, cheerful, cheery, convivial, exuberant, festive, frisky, frolicsome, fun-filled, fun-loving, funny, gay, gladsome, happy, hearty, hilarious, jaunty, jocular, jocund, jovial, joyful, joyous, jubilant, merry, mirthful, playful, sportive, sprightly, sunny.

antonym sad.

jolt *v* astonish, astound, bounce, bump, discompose, disconcert, disturb, jar, jerk, jog, joggle, jostle, jounce, knock, knock one's socks off, nonplus, perturb, pull one up short, push, shake (up), shock, shove, stagger, startle, stun, surprise, upset.

n blow, bolt from the blue, bombshell, bump, hit, impact, jar, jerk, jog, jump, lurch, shake, shock, start, surprise, thunderbolt, turn.

jostle *v* bump, butt, compete, crowd, elbow, force, hustle, jockey, jog, joggle, jolt, press, push (against), rough up, scramble, shake, shoulder, shove, squeeze, thrust.

jot *n* atom, bit, detail, drop, fraction, gleam, glimmer, grain, hint, iota, mite, morsel, particle, scintilla, scrap, smidgen, speck, spot, tittle, trace, trifle, whit.

jot down enter, list, note, record, register, scribble down, take down, write down.

journal *n* annals, book, chronicle, daily, datebook, daybook, diary, ephemeris, gazette, log, magazine, monthly, newspaper, organ, paper, periodical, publication, record, record book, register, review, tabloid, weekly.

journalism *n* copy writing, correspondence, feature writing, Fleet Street, fourth estate, gossip writing, Grub Street, newswriting, press, reportage, reporting, writing.

journalist *n* broadcaster, chronicler, columnist, commentator, contributor, correspondent, diarist, editor, editorialist, feature writer, hack, hatchet man, leg man, newshound, newsman, newspaperman, newswriter, periodicalist, pressman, reporter, scribe, stringer.

journey *n* course, excursion, expedition, grand tour, haj, jaunt, junket, odyssey, outing, passage, peregrination, pilgrimage, progress, ramble, route, safari, sally, tour, travel(s), trek, trip, voyage, wanderings.

v fly, gallivant, go, hit the road/trail, jaunt, peregrinate, ramble, range, roam, rove, safari, take a trip, tour, tramp, travel, traverse, trek, voyage, wander, wend one's way.

journeyer *n* explorer, globe-trotter, haji, peregrinator, pilgrim, rambler, tourist, traveller, trekker, tripper, voyager, voyageur, wanderer, wayfarer.

joust *n* combat, contest, encounter, engagement, pas d'armes, skirmish, tilt, tournament, tourney, trial.

jovial *adj* affable, animated, blithe, buoyant, cheerful, cheery, convivial, cordial, ebullient, expansive, Falstaffian, fun-loving, gay, glad, good-humoured, happy, hilarious, jaunty, jocose, jocular, jocund, jolly, jubilant, light-hearted, merry, mirthful.

antonyms morose, sad, saturnine.

joy *n* bliss, delight, ecstasy, elation, euphoria, exaltation, exhilaration, exultation, felicity, gaiety, gem, gladness, gladsomeness, glee, gratification, happiness, jewel, joyfulness, joyousness, pleasure, prize, rapture, ravishment, rejoicing, satisfaction, transport, treasure, treat, triumph, wonder.

antonyms mourning, sorrow.

joyful *adj* blissful, blithe, blithesome, delighted, ecstatic, elated, enraptured, glad, gladsome, gleeful, gratified, happy, in seventh heaven, jocund, jolly, jovial, joyous, jubilant, light-hearted, merry, on cloud nine, pleased, rapturous, satisfied, transported, triumphant.

antonyms mournful, sorrowful.

joyless *adj* bleak, cheerless, dejected, depressed, despondent, discouraged, discouraging, dismal, dispirited, doleful, dour, downcast, dreary, forlorn, gloomy, glum, grim, miserable, pleasureless, sad, sombre, sunless, unhappy.

antonym joyful.

joyous *adj* blessed, blissful, cheerful, ecstatic, festal, festive, glad, gladsome, happy, joyful, jubilant, merry, rapturous.

antonym sad.

jubilant *adj* celebratory, crowing, delighted, elated, enraptured, euphoric, excited, exuberant, exultant, flushed with success, glad, gratified, joyous, over the moon, overjoyed, rejoicing, thrilled, triumphal, triumphant.

antonyms defeated, depressed.

jubilation *n* celebration, ecstasy, elation, euphoria, excitement, exultation, festivity, jamboree, jollification, joy, jubilee, rejoicing, triumph.

antonyms depression, lamentation.

jubilee *n* anniversary, carnival, celebration, commemoration, festival, festivity, fete, gala, joy, potlatch, rejoicing.

Judas *n* betrayer, deceiver, quisling, renegade, tergiversator, traitor, turncoat.

judge *n* adjudicator, arbiter, arbiter elegantiae, arbitrator, assessor, authority, connoisseur, critic, Daniel, evaluator, expert, hakim, jurist, justice, justice of the piece, justiciary, magistrate, mediator, moderator, pundit, referee, umpire, virtuoso.

v adjudge, adjudicate, appraise, arbitrate, ascertain, assess, conclude, condemn, consider, criticize, decide, decree, deem, determine, discern, distinguish, esteem, estimate, evaluate, examine, find, gauge, hear, hold, mediate, opine, pass judgment on, rate, reckon, referee, regard, review, rule, sentence, sit, sit in judgment, suppose, think, try, umpire, weigh.

judgment n acumen, adjudication, appraisal, arbitration, assessment, assize, award, belief, circumspection, common sense, conclusion, condemnation, consideration, conviction, criticism, damnation, decision, decree, deduction, determination, diagnosis, discernment, discretion, discrimination, doom, estimate, expertise, finding, intelligence, judiciousness, just deserts, mediation, opinion, order, perceptiveness, percipience, perspicacity, prudence, punishment, result, retribution, ruling, sagacity, sense, sentence, shrewdness, taste, understanding, valuation, verdict, view, virtuosity, wisdom.

judicial adj critical, decretory, discriminating, fair, forensic, impartial, judiciary, judicious, juridical, legal, magisterial, official.

judicious adj acute, astute, canny, careful, circumspect, considered, diplomatic, discerning, discreet, discriminating, expedient, informed, percipient, perspicacious, politic, prescient, prudent, rational, reasonable, sagacious, sage, sapient, sensible, shrewd, skilful, sober, sound, thoughtful, wary, well-advised, well-judged, wise.

antonym injudicious.

jug n amphora, blackjack, carafe, churn, container, crock, ewer, flagon, jar, pitcher, stoup, urn, vessel.

juggle v alter, change, cook, doctor, fake, falsify, fix, manipulate, manoeuvre, misrepresent, modify, rig, stack, tamper with.

juice n ambrosia, beverage, current, electricity, essence, extract, fluid, gas, gasoline, latex, liquid, liquor, milk, nectar, power, sap, secretion, serum.

juicy adj ambrosial, colourful, interesting, lactiferous, lively, luscious, lush, moist, naughty, provocative, racy, randy, risqué, sappy, sensational, serous, spicy, succulent, suggestive, titillating, vivid, watery.

antonym dry.

jumble v confuse, disarrange, disarray, disorder, disorganize, mix, mix up, muddle, scramble, shuffle, tangle, tumble.

antonym order.

n agglomeration, chaos, clutter, confusion, congeries, conglomeration, disarrangement, disarray, disorder, farrago, gallimaufry, hodgepodge, litter, medley, mess, miscellany, mishmash, mixed bag, mixture, mix-up, muddle, pastiche, potpourri, rat's nest.

jumbled adj chaotic, confused, disarrayed, disordered, disorganized, helter-skelter, higgledy-piggledy, mixed, mixed-up, motley, muddled, scrambled, shuffled, tangled, tumbled, unsorted, untidy.

antonym orderly.

jump¹ v bounce, bound, caper, capriole, clear, curvet, dance, frisk, frolic, gambol, hop, hurdle, jig, leap (over), pounce, prance, skip, spring, vault.

n bounce, bound, caper, capriole, curvet, dance, frisk, frolic, hop, jeté, leap, pounce (on), prance, skip, spring, vault.

jump² v avoid, bypass, digress, disregard, escape, evade, flee, ignore, leave out, miss, omit, overshoot, pass over, run away from, shy away from, skip, switch.

n breach, break, flight, gap, hiatus, interruption, interval, lacuna, lapse, omission, switch.

jump³ v advance, appreciate, ascend, boost, escalate, gain, hike, increase, mount, rise, spiral, surge.

n advance, ascent, augmentation, boost, escalation, increase, increment, interval, mounting, rise, upsurge, upturn.

jump⁴ v be startled, flinch, jerk, jump out of one's skin, lurch, recoil, start, twitch.

n jar, jerk, jolt, lurch, spasm, start, twitch.

jump⁵ n fence, gate, hedge, hurdle, obstacle, rail.

jump at accept, agree to, be eager for, fall for, grab, pounce on, seize, snatch, swoop down on.

antonym recoil.

jump on attack, berate, blame, castigate, censure, chide, criticize, dress down, fly at, jump all over, jump down one's throat, light into, rake over the coals, rate, rebuke, reprimand, reproach, reprove, revile, rip into, scold, upbraid.

jumpy adj agitated, anxious, apprehensive, discomposed, edgy, fearful, fidgety, jittery, nervous, nervy, on edge, restive, restless, shaky, tense, uneasy.

antonyms calm, composed.

junction n abutment, combination, concurrence, confluence, conjunction, connection, coupling, intersection, interstice, join, joining, joint, juncture, juxtaposition, linking, meeting (point), nexus, seam, union.

juncture n bond, conjunction, connection, convergence, crisis, crux, intersection, join, joining, joint, junction, link, minute, moment, nexus, occasion, period, point, predicament, seam, stage, time, turn, union, weld.

junior adj cadet, inferior, lesser, lower, minor, secondary, subordinate, subsidiary, younger.

antonym senior.

junk n clutter, debris, detritus, dregs, garbage, litter, oddments, odds and ends, refuse, rejectamenta, rubbish, rummage, schlock, scrap, trash, truck, waste, wreckage.

junta n cabal, camarilla, cartel, clique, conclave, confederacy, coterie, council, faction, gang, group, league, oligarchy, party, ring, set.

jurisdiction n area, authority, bailiwick, bounds, charge, cognizance, command, commission, control, domination, dominion, field, governance, judicature, power, prerogative, protectorship, province, range, reach, responsibility, rule, scope, sovereignty, sphere, sway, territory, zone.

jury *n* jurors, panel, tales, talesmen, veniremen.

just *adj* accurate, apposite, appropriate, apt, beyond reproach, blameless, condign, conscientious, correct, decent, deserved, disinterested, due, equitable, even-handed, exact, fair, fair and square, fair-minded, faithful, fitting, good, honest, honourable, impartial, impeccable, irreproachable, justified, lawful, legal, legitimate, meet, merited, precise, proper, pure, reasonable, right, righteous, rightful, sound, suitable, true, unbiased, unimpeachable, unprejudiced, upright, virtuous, well-chosen, well-deserved, well-founded.

antonym unjust.

justice[1] *n* amends, appositeness, appropriateness, compensation, correction, dharma, equality, equitableness, equity, fairness, fair shake, fitness, honesty, impartiality, integrity, justifiability, justness, law, lawfulness, legality, legitimacy, nemesis, propriety, reasonableness, recompense, rectitude, redress, reparation, requital, right, rightfulness, rightness, satisfaction, square deal.

antonym injustice.

justice[2] *n* J.P., judge, judiciary, justice of the peace, justiciary, magistrate.

justifiable *adj* allowable, defensible, excusable, explainable, explicable, fit, forgivable, justified, lawful, legitimate, licit, logical, maintainable, pardonable, proper,

reasonable, right, sound, tenable, understandable, valid, vindicable, warrantable, warranted, well-founded.

antonyms culpable, illicit, unjustifiable.

justification *n* absolution, apology, approval, authorization, basis, defence, exculpation, excuse, exoneration, explanation, extenuation, foundation, grounds, justice, mitigation, palliation, plea, rationalization, reason, substance, vindication, warrant.

justify *v* absolve, acquit, condone, confirm, defend, exculpate, excuse, exonerate, explain, forgive, legalize, legitimize, maintain, pardon, substantiate, support, sustain, uphold, validate, vindicate, warrant.

justly *adv* accurately, condignly, conscientiously, correctly, deservedly, duly, equally, equitably, even-handedly, fairly, honestly, impartially, lawfully, legitimately, objectively, properly, rightfully, rightly, uprightly, without fear or favour.

antonym unjustly.

jut out *v* beetle, bulge, extend, impend, overhang, poke out, project, protrude, stick out.

antonym recede.

juvenile *n* adolescent, boy, child, girl, halfling, infant, kid, minor, young person, youngster, youth.

antonym adult.

adj adolescent, babyish, boyish, callow, childish, girlish, immature, impressionable, inexperienced, infantile, jejune, puerile, tender, undeveloped, unsophisticated, young, youthful.

antonym mature.

juxtaposition *n* adjacency, apposition, closeness, contact, contiguity, immediacy, nearness, propinquity, proximity, vicinity.

antonyms dissociation, separation.

K

kaleidoscopic *adj* changeable, ever-changing, fluctuating, fluid, manifold, many-coloured, many-splendoured, mobile, motley, multicoloured, multifarious, polychromatic, polychrome, variegated.

antonyms dull, monochrome, monotonous.

kaput *adj* broken, conked out, dead, defunct, destroyed, done for, extinct, fini, finished, no more, on the blink (or fritz), ruined, smashed, undone, useless, wrecked.

karma *n* destiny, doom, fate, judgment, kismet, lot.

keel over black out, capsize, collapse, crumple, drop, faint, fall, founder, go out like a light, overturn, pass out, swoon, topple over, upset.

keen *adj* acid, acrid, acrimonious, acerbic, acute, ardent, assiduous, astute, avid, biting, brilliant, canny, caustic, clever, cutting, deep-felt, diligent, discerning, discriminating, eager, earnest, ebullient, edged, enthusiastic, fervid, fierce, forthright, impassioned, incisive, industrious, intense, mordant, penetrating, perceptive, perfervid, perspicacious, piercing, pointed, pungent, quick, razorlike, rigorous, sardonic, satirical, scathing, sedulous, sensitive, severe, sharp, shrewd, shrill, stinging, strong, tart, trenchant, vigorous, witty, zealous.

antonyms apathetic, blunt, dull.

keen on fond of, into, taken with, wild about.

keenness *n* acerbity, acidity, acrimony, acuity, ardour, assiduity, astuteness, avidity, avidness, bitterness, canniness, causticity, cleverness, diligence, discernment, eagerness, earnestness, ebullience, edge, enthusiasm, fervour, forthrightness, harshness, impatience, incisiveness, industriousness, industry, insight, intelligence, intensity, intentness, mordancy, passion, penetration, perfervidity, pungency, quickness, rigour, sedulity, sensitivity, severity, sharpness, shrewdness, sternness, trenchancy, virulence, wittiness, zeal, zest.

antonyms apathy, bluntness, dullness.

keep¹ *v* accumulate, amass, carry, collect, conserve, control, deal in, deposit, garner, hang on to, have, heap, hold, hold on to, maintain, pile, place, possess, preserve, retain, stack, stock, store.

keep an eye on guard, keep tabs on, keep track of, keep under surveillance, look after,

look to, monitor, observe, regard, scrutinize, stand guard over, supervise, survey, watch.

keep at be steadfast, beaver away at, carry on with, complete, continue with, drudge away at, endure, finish, grind away at, keep one's nose to the grindstone, labour at, last, maintain, persevere (in), persist in, plug away at, remain, slave away at, slog at, stay at (or with), stick at (or with), toil at.

antonyms abandon, neglect.

keep on carry on, continue, endure, hold on, keep at, keep going, last, maintain, persevere, persist, prolong, remain, retain, soldier on, stay, stay the course.

keep on at badger, carp at, chivvy, dun, go on at, harass, harry, importune, nag, pester, plague, pursue.

keep one's distance (from) avoid, be aloof, give a wide berth (to), keep at arm's length, keep (oneself) to oneself, shun, withdraw (from).

keep secret conceal, dissemble, hide, keep back, keep dark, keep mum, keep quiet, keep (something) to oneself, keep under one's hat, keep under wraps, suppress, wash one's dirty linen at home.

antonym reveal.

keep track of follow, grasp, keep up with, monitor, oversee, plot, record, trace, track, understand, watch.

keep up (with) be equal (to), be on a par (with), compete (with), contend (with), continue, emulate, equal, keep informed, keep pace, maintain, match, pace, persevere (in), preserve, rival, support, sustain, vie (with).

keep² *v* be responsible for, board, care for, control, defend, feed, foster, guard, harbour, have, have charge of, have custody of, keep from harm, look after, maintain, manage, mind, nourish, nurture, operate, protect, provide for, provision, safeguard, secure, shelter, shield, subsidize, support, sustain, take care of, tend, victual, watch, watch over.

n board, custody, food, livelihood, living, maintenance, means, nourishment, nurture, subsistence, support, upkeep.

keep³ (from) *v* block, check, constrain, curb, delay, deter, hamper, hamstring, hinder, hold back, hold up, impede, inhibit, interfere (with), keep at bay, keep back, limit, obstruct, prevent, restrain.

keep back check, conceal, constrain,

control, curb, delay, hide, hinder, hold back, hush up, impede, keep in, keep secret, keep to oneself, limit, prohibit, quell, ration, reserve, restrain, restrict, retain, retard, slow, stifle, stop, suppress, withhold.

keep in bottle up, conceal, confine, control, detain, hide, inhibit, keep back, quell, restrain, retain, stifle, stop up, suppress.

antonyms declare, release.

keep⁴ *v* adhere to, celebrate, commemorate, comply with, fulfil, hold, honour, keep faith with, keep in mind, keep up (with), maintain, mark, obey, observe, perform, perpetuate, remember, respect, ritualize, solemnize.

keep⁵ *n* bastion, castle, citadel, donjon, dungeon, fastness, fort, fortress, Martello, peel tower, stronghold, tower.

keeper *n* attendant, caretaker, conservator, curator, custodian, defender, governor, guard, guardian, herder, inspector, jailer, mahout, overseer, possessor, preserver, protector, shepherd, steward, superintendent, supervisor, warden, warder.

keeping *n* accord, accordance, aegis, agreement, balance, care, celebration, charge, compliance, conformity, congruity, consistency, correspondence, cure, custody, guardianship, harmony, keep, maintenance, obedience, observance, patronage, possession, preservation, proportion, protection, protectorship, safekeeping, supervision, surveillance, trust, tutelage, ward.

in keeping with appropriate to, befitting, fitting with, in agreement with, in harmony with, of a piece with, suitable to.

keepsake *n* favour, memento, pledge, relic, remembrance, reminder, souvenir, token, token of esteem, trophy.

keg *n* barrel, butt, cask, drum, firkin, hogshead, puncheon, tierce, tun, vat.

ken *n* awareness, cognizance, compass, comprehension, experience, field, field of vision, grasp, knowledge, perception, range, range of knowledge, reach, scope, sight, understanding, view, vision, visual field.

kerchief *n* babushka, bandana, chador, cravat, fichu, headcloth, headscarf, headsquare, madras, neckcloth, neckerchief, scarf, shawl, square.

kernel *n* centre, core, essence, germ, gist, grain, heart, marrow, middle, nitty-gritty, nub, nut, pith, seed, substance.

key *n* answer, clue, code, crib, cue, digital, explanation, glossary, guide, index, indicator, interpretation, lead, means, pointer, secret, solution, table, translation.

adj basic, cardinal, central, chief, core, crucial, decisive, essential, fundamental, important, influential, leading, main, major, pivotal, principal, salient.

key in enter, input, load, process, type.

keynote *n* accent, centre, core, emphasis, essence, gist, guiding principle, heart, kernel, leitmotiv, main idea, marrow, meat, motif, pith, substance, theme.

keystone *n* base, basis, core, cornerstone, crux, foundation, fundamental, ground, linchpin, mainspring, motive, pivot, principle, quoin, root, source, spring.

kick *v* abandon, boot, break, desist from, discontinue, drop, foot, give up, leave off, overcome, punt, quit, rid oneself of, shake off, spurn, stop, toe.

n bang, bite, buzz, charge, dash, élan, enjoyment, excitement, feeling, force, gratification, gusto, intensity, jolt, panache, pep, pizzazz, pleasure, power, punch, pungency, rush, satisfaction, snap, sparkle, stimulation, strength, tang, thrill, verve, vitality, zest, zing, zip.

kick off begin, break the ice, commence, die, get under way, inaugurate, initiate, introduce, kick the bucket, open, open the proceedings, set the ball rolling, start.

kick out chuck out, defenestrate, discharge, dismiss, eject, evict, expel, fire, force out, get rid of, give a pink slip to, give the bum's rush, oust, put out, reject, remove, sack, throw out, toss out, turn out.

kickoff *n* beginning, blastoff, commencement, face-off, inception, introduction, onset, opening, outset, start, word go.

kid¹ *n* babe, babe in arms, baby, bairn, bambino, boy, child, girl, halfling, infant, juvenile, kiddie, kiddo, lad, lass, nipper, shaver, spring chicken, stripling, teenager, tot, weanling, whippersnapper, youngster, youth.

kid² *v* bamboozle, beguile, con, cozen, delude, dupe, fool, gull, hoax, hoodwink, humbug, jest, joke, josh, mock, pretend, pull someone's leg, put on, put one over on, rag, razz, ridicule, tease, trick.

kidnap *v* abduct, capture, carry off, hijack, remove, seize, skyjack, snatch, steal.

kill *v* abolish, annihilate, assassinate, bump off, butcher, cancel, cease, cut down, deaden, defeat, delete, destroy, dispatch, dispose of, do away with, do in, do to death, eliminate, end, eradicate, execute, exterminate, extinguish, extirpate, finish off, get rid of, give the deathblow to, gun down, halt, hush up, knock off, knock on the head, liquidate, mar, martyr, massacre, mop up, murder, neutralize, nip in the bud, nullify, obliterate, purge, put an end to, put a stop to, put down, put out of one's misery, put the kibosh on, put to death, quash, quell, rub out, ruin, scotch, shoot (to death), slaughter, slay, smite, smother, spoil, stifle, still, stop, suppress, top, turn off, use up, veto, vitiate, waste, while away, zap.

antonym bring to life.

n climax, conclusion, coup de grâce, death, deathblow, dénouement, end, finish, mop-up, quarry, shootout, slaughter.

killer *n* assassin, butcher, button man, cutthroat, destroyer, executioner, exterminator, fratricide, gun, gunman, hatchet man, hired gun, hit man, homicide, infanticide, liquidator, matricide, murderer, parricide, patricide, regicide, shooter, slaughterer, slayer, sororicide, thug, trigger man, uxoricide.

killing¹ n assassination, bloodshed, carnage, elimination, ethnocide, execution, extermination, fatality, fratricide, genocide, homicide, infanticide, liquidation, manslaughter, massacre, matricide, murder, parricide, patricide, pogrom, regicide, slaughter, slaying, sororicide, thuggee, uxoricide.

adj deadly, death-dealing, deathly, debilitating, enervating, exhausting, fatal, fatiguing, final, hard, laborious, lethal, mortal, murderous, prostrating, punishing, tiring, vital.

killing² n big hit, big win, bonanza, bundle, clean-up, coup, fortune, gain, hit, lucky break, profit, success, wad, windfall, winner.

killing³ adj absurd, amusing, comical, funny, hilarious, hysterical, ludicrous, sidesplitting, uproarious.

kill-joy n complainer, crepehanger, cynic, dampener, damper, grouch, meanie, misery, moaner, party pooper, pessimist, prophet of doom, sceptic, spoilsport, wet blanket, whiner.

antonyms enthusiast, optimist, sport.

kin n affines, affinity, blood, clan, connection, connections, consanguinity, cousins, extended family, extraction, family, flesh and blood, kindred, kinsfolk, kinship, kinsmen, kinswomen, kith, lineage, people, relations, relationship, relatives, stock, tribe.

adj affinal, akin, allied, close, cognate, connected, consanguineous, interconnected, kindred, linked, near, related, similar, twin.

kind¹ n brand, breed, category, character, class, description, family, genus, habit, ilk, kidney, like manner, manner, mould, natural group, nature, persuasion, race, set, sort, species, stamp, style, temperament, type, variety.

in kind in like manner, in the same manner, similarly, tit for tat.

kind² adj accommodating, affectionate, altruistic, amiable, amicable, avuncular, beneficent, benevolent, benign, benignant, bonhomous, boon, bounteous, bountiful, brotherly, charitable, clement, compassionate, congenial, considerate, cordial, courteous, diplomatic, fatherly, favourable, forgiving, friendly, generous, gentle, giving, good, gracious, helpful, hospitable, humane, indulgent, kind-hearted, kindly, lenient, loving, merciful, mild, motherly, neighbourly, obliging, philanthropic, propitious, sisterly, soft-hearted, solicitous, sweet, sympathetic, tactful, tender, tender-hearted, thoughtful, understanding, warm, warm-hearted.

antonyms cruel, inconsiderate, unhelpful, unkind.

kindle v activate, agitate, animate, arouse, awaken, brighten, catch fire, enkindle, excite, fan, fire, foment, ignite, incite, induce, inflame, initiate, inspire, inspirit, light, light up, provoke, rouse, set alight (or ablaze), set on fire, sharpen, stimulate, stir (up).

kindliness n amiability, beneficence, benevolence, benignity, charity, compassion, friendliness, generosity, humanity, kindness, loving-kindness, solicitousness, sympathy, warmth.

antonyms cruelty, meanness, unkindness.

kindly adj agreeable, beneficent, beneficial, benevolent, benign, benignant, big-hearted, charitable, comforting, compassionate, cordial, favourable, generous, genial, gentle, giving, good-hearted, good-natured, hearty, helpful, indulgent, kind, mild, patient, pleasant, polite, sympathetic, tender, warm.

antonyms cruel, inconsiderate, uncharitable, unpleasant.

adv agreeably, charitably, comfortingly, considerately, cordially, generously, gently, graciously, indulgently, in good part, kind-heartedly, patiently, politely, tenderly, thoughtfully, warmly, with good will.

antonyms cruelly, ungraciously, unkindly.

kindness n affection, aid, altruism, amiability, assistance, benefaction, beneficence, benevolence, benignity, bonhomie, bounty, charity, chivalry, clemency, compassion, cordiality, courtesy, favour, forbearance, friendliness, gallantry, generosity, gentleness, good will, goodness, grace, help, hospitality, humaneness, humanity, indulgence, kindliness, liberality, loving-kindness, magnanimity, mildness, munificence, obligingness, patience, philanthropy, service, tactfulness, tenderness, tolerance, understanding, warmth.

antonyms cruelty, illiberality, inhumanity, unkindness.

kindred n affines, affinity, clan, connections, consanguinity, extended family, family, flesh, folk, kin, kinsfolk, kinship, kinsmen, kinswomen, lineage, people, relations, relationship, relatives.

adj affiliated, affinal, akin, allied, cognate, common, congenial, connected, corresponding, kin, like, matching, related, similar.

king n boss, chief, chieftain, doyen, emir, emperor, khan, kingpin, leader, leading light, lord, luminary, majesty, monarch, overlord, paramount, patriarch, potentate, prince, rajah, ruler, shah, sovereign, sultan, superstar, suzerain, top dog.

kingdom n area, commonwealth, country, division, domain, dominion, dynasty, empire, field, land, monarchy, nation, palatinate, principality, province, realm, reign, sovereign state, sovereignty, sphere, state, sultanate, territory, tract of land.

kingly adj august, dignified, glorious, grand, grandiose, imperial, imperious, imposing, lordly, majestic, monarchical, noble, regal, royal, sovereign, splendid, stately, sublime, supreme.

kink¹ n bend, bug, coil, complication, corkscrew, crick, crimp, curl, defect, deformity, dent, difficulty, distortion, entanglement, flaw, hindrance, hitch, imperfection, inadequac, indentation, knot, loop, snag, tangle, tv, unsoundness, warp, weak point, wrinkle.

v bend, coil, crimp, curl, tangle, twist.

kink² *n* caprice, conceit, crotchet, eccentricity, fetish, foible, freak, idiosyncrasy, oddity, quirk, singularity, vagary, whim.

kinky¹ *adj* coiled, crimped, crumpled, curled, curly, frizzy, tangled, twisted, wrinkled.

kinky² *adj* bizarre, capricious, cranky, crotchety, degenerate, depraved, deviant, eccentric, freakish, idiosyncratic, licentious, odd, offbeat, outlandish, peculiar, perverted, queer, quirky, strange, unconventional, unnatural, warped, weird, whimsical.

kinsfolk *n* affines, clan, connections, cousins, family, kin, kindred, relations, relatives.

kinship *n* accord, affinity, alliance, association, bearing, blood ties, common ancestry, community, conformity, connection, consanguinity, correspondence, family tie, kin, relation, relationship, similarity.

kiosk *n* bookstall, booth, box, concession, counter, hut, newsstand, stall, stand.

kismet *n* cup, destiny, doom, fate, fortune, handwriting on the wall, joss, karma, lot, portion, predestiny, providence.

kiss¹ *v* buss, canoodle, neck, osculate, peck, salute, smack, smooch.
n buss, osculate, osculation, peck, salute, smack, smacker.

kiss² *v* brush, caress, fan, glance, graze, lick, pet, scrape, sweep, touch.

kit *n* accoutrements, apparatus, appurtenances, baggage, effects, equipage, equipment, gear, impedimenta, implements, instruments, luggage, matériel, muniments, outfit, paraphernalia, provisions, rig, rig-out, set, supplies, tackle, tools, trappings, utensils.
kit out accoutre, arm, deck out, dress, equip, fit, fit out, fix up, furnish, habilitate, outfit, prepare, rig out, supply.

kittenish *adj* arch, coquettish, coy, cute, flirtatious, frisky, frolicsome, playful, sportive.
antonym staid.

knack *n* ability, adroitness, aptitude, art, bent, capacity, dexterity, expertise, expertness, eye (for), facility, faculty, flair, forte, genius, gift, handiness, hang, ingenuity, propensity, quickness, skilfulness, skill, talent, trick, trick of the trade, turn.

knapsack *n* backpack, bag, duffel bag, haversack, musette (bag), pack, rucksack, satchel.

knave *n* bastard, blackguard, blighter, bounder, cheat, dastard, devil, mischief-maker, rapscallion, rascal, reprobate, rogue, rotter, scallywag, scamp, scapegrace, scoundrel, stinker, swindler, swine, varlet, varmint, villain.
antonym paragon.

knavery *n* chicanery, corruption, deceit, deception, devilry, dishonesty, double-dealing, duplicity, fraud, hanky-panky, imposture, knavishness, mischief, mischief-making, monkey business, rascality, reprobacy, roguery, trick, trickery, villainy.

knavish *adj* contemptible, corrupt, damnable, dastardly, deceitful, deceptive, devilish, dishonest, dishonourable, fiendish, fraudulent, low, lying, mischievous, rascally, recreant, reprobate, roguish, scoundrelly, tricky, unprincipled, unscrupulous, vile, villainous, wicked.
antonyms honest, honourable, scrupulous.

knead *v* form, knuckle, make pliant, manipulate, massage, mould, ply, press, rub, shape, squeeze, work.

kneel *v* bend the knee, bow down, fall at someone's feet, fall to one's knees, genuflect, get down on one's knees, humble oneself, make obeisance.

knell *n* chime, peal, ringing, sound, tintinnabulation, toll.

knickers *n* bloomers, boxers, breeks, briefs, drawers, knickerbockers, panties, shorts, underpants, underwear.

knick-knack *n* bagatelle, bauble, bibelot, bijou, bric-a-brac, curio, guad, gewgaw, gimrack, gizmo, kickshaw, ornament, plaything, pretty, toy, trifle, trinket.

knife *n* barong, blade, bolo, carver, cutter, dagger, flick-knife, jack-knife, kukri, machete, parang, penknife, pocketknife, shiv, skean, switchblade, ulu, weapon, whittle.
v cut, impale, lacerate, pierce, play one false, rip, run through, stab in the back, stick, slash, stab, wound.

knight *n* caballero, cavalier, champion, chevalier, freelance, gallant, hero, horseman, knight-at-arms, knight errant, Lancelot, man-at-arms, preux chevalier, Ritter, (Sir) Galahad, soldier, warrior.

knightly *adj* bold, brave, chivalrous, courageous, courtly, dauntless, gallant, gracious, heroic, honourable, intrepid, noble, soldierly, valiant, valorous.
antonyms cowardly, ignoble, ungallant.

knit *v* ally, bind, connect, crease, crotchet, fasten, furrow, heal, interlace, intertwine, join, knot, link, loop, mend, secure, tie, unite, weave, wrinkle.

knob *n* ball, boll, boss, bulge, bump, caput, door-handle, hill, hummock, knot, knurl, lump, mound, nub, projection, protrusion, protuberance, stud, swelling, tuber, tumour.

knock¹ *v* box, buffet, clap, cuff, hammer, hit, pound, punch, rap, slap, smack, smite, strike, tap, thump, thwack.
n blow, box, chop, clip, clout, cuff, hammering, hit, pounding, rap, slap, smack, thump.
knock around¹ associate, gad bout, drift, go around, loaf (around), ramble, range, roam, rove, saunter (through or around), traipse (all over), travel, wander.
knock around² abuse, bash, batter, beat up, biff, bruise, buffet, damage, hit, hurt, knock senseless, maltreat, manhandle, maul, mistreat.
knock down batter, bowl over, clout, collide with, cut down, deck, demolish, destroy, down, fell, floor, lay out, level, pound, raze, smash, strike down, take down, tear down, wallop, wreck.
knock off¹ cease, clock out, complete,

conclude, finish, pack (it) in, stop, stop work, take a break, terminate.

knock off[2] assassinate, bump off, do away with, do in, kill, liquidate, murder, rub out, slay, waste.

knock[2] *v* abuse, belittle, carp at, cavil, censure, condemn, criticize, deprecate, disapprove of, disparage, find fault with, grumble at, lambaste, pan, reject, run down, slam, vilify, vilipend.

n blame, censure, condemnation, criticism, defeat, disapproval, rebuff, rejection, reversal, setback, stricture.

antonyms boost, praise.

knockout *n* beauty, bestseller, coup de grâce, dazzler, grand slam, hit, KO, sensation, smash, smash hit, stunner, success, triumph, winner.

antonyms flop, loser.

knoll *n* barrow, hill, hillock, hummock, knob, kopje, mound, pingo, rise.

knot *v* bind, entangle, entwine, knit, loop, secure, tangle, tether, tie, weave.

n aggregation, bond, bow, braid, bunch, burl, clump, cluster, collection, connection, difficulty, dilemma, gnarl, group, heap, hitch, joint, knag, knar, ligature, loop, lump, mass, node, nodule, pile, problem, puzzle, rosette, tangle, tie, tuft.

knotty *adj* baffling, bumpy, Byzantine, complex, complicated, difficult, gnarled, hard, intricate, knobby, knotted, mystifying, nodose, nodular, nubby, perplexing, problematic, puzzling, rough, rugged, thorny, tricky, troublesome.

know *v* apprehend, be acquainted with, be certain (of), be expert in, be familiar with, be up on, comprehend, discern, distinguish, experience, fathom, have down pat, identify, intuit, ken, learn, make out, notice, perceive, realize, recognize, see, tell, undergo, understand, wist.

know-how *n* ability, adroitness, aptitude, capability, dexterity, experience, expertise, faculty, flair, gumption, ingenuity, knack, knowledge, proficiency, savoir-faire, savvy, skill, talent.

knowing *adj* acute, astute, aware, calculated, canny, clever, competent, conscious, cunning, deliberate, discerning, eloquent, experienced, expert, expressive, gnostic, hip, intelligent, intentional, knowledgeable, meaningful, perceptive, sagacious, shrewd, significant, skilful, well-informed, wise, worldly-wise.

antonyms ignorant, obtuse.

knowingly *adv* calculatedly, consciously, deliberately, designedly, intentionally, on purpose, pointedly, purposely, studiedly, willfully, with (full) intent, with one's eyes open, wittingly.

knowledge *n* ability, acquaintance, acquaintanceship, apprehension, booklearning, cognizance, cognition, comprehension, consciousness, discernment, education, enlightenment, erudition, familiarity, gnosis, grasp, information, instruction, intelligence, intimacy, judgment, know-how, learning, notice, pansophism, recognition, savvy, scholarship, schooling, science, the know, tuition, understanding, wisdom.

antonym ignorance.

knowledgeable *adj* acquainted, au courant, au fait, aware, book-learned, bright, cognizant, conscious, conversant, educated, erudite, experienced, familiar, in the know, intelligent, knowing, learned, lettered, scholarly, well-informed.

antonym ignorant.

known *adj* acknowledged, admitted, ascertained, avowed, celebrated, commonplace, confessed, decided, definite, familiar, famous, manifest, noted, obvious, patent, perceived, plain, public (or common) knowledge, published, recognized, understood, well-known.

knuckle under accede, acquiesce, assent, capitulate, comply, defer, fall in line, give in, give up, give way, resign oneself, submit, succumb, surrender, truckle, yield.

kowtow *v* bend, bow, bow and scrape, court, cringe, defer, fawn, flatter, genuflect, grovel, kneel, pander, prostrate oneself, suck up, toady, truckle.

kudos *n* acclaim, applause, bouquets, credit, distinction, esteem, fame, glory, honour, laudation, laurels, plaudits, praise, prestige, regard, renown, repute, strokes.

L

label *n* badge, brand, categorization, characterization, classification, company, description, docket, epithet, mark, marker, sticker, tag, tally, ticket, trademark.

v brand, call, categorize, characterize, class, classify, define, describe, designate, docket, identify, mark, name, stamp, tag.

laborious *adj* arduous, assiduous, backbreaking, burdensome, difficult, diligent, fatiguing, forced, hard, hardworking, heavy, herculean, indefatigable, industrious, laboured, onerous, painstaking, persevering, ponderous, sedulous, strained, strenuous, tireless, tiresome, toilsome, tough, unflagging, uphill, wearing, wearisome.

antonyms easy, effortless, relaxing, simple.

labour¹ *n* chore, donkey-work, drudgery, effort, employees, exertion, grind, hands, industry, job, labourers, moil, pains, slog, sweat, task, toil, undertaking, work, workers, workforce.

v drudge, endeavour, grind, heave, moil, pitch, plod, roll, slave, strain, strive, struggle, suffer, sweat, toil, toss, travail, work.

antonyms idle, laze, loaf, lounge.

labour² *n* birth, childbirth, contractions, delivery, labour pains, pains, parturition, throes, travail.

laboured *adj* affected, awkward, complicated, contrived, difficult, forced, heavy, overdone, overwrought, ponderous, stiff, stilted, strained, studied, unnatural.

antonyms easy, natural.

labourer *n* carrier, drudge, farm hand, hand, hireling, hobo, hod, husbandman, manual worker, navvy, worker, working man, working woman, workman.

labyrinth *n* circumvolution, coil, complexity, complication, convolution, entanglement, Gordian knot, intricacy, jungle, maze, perplexity, puzzle, riddle, tangle, windings.

labyrinthine *adj* Byzantine, complex, confused, convoluted, Daedalian, faveolate, Gordian, intricate, involved, knotty, mazy, perplexing, puzzling, tangled, tortuous, winding.

antonyms simple, straightforward.

lace¹ *n* crochet, filigree, netting, openwork, tatting.

lace² *n* bootlace, cord, lanyard, shoelace, string, thong, tie.

v attach, bind, close, do up, fasten,

intertwine, interweave, interwork, string, thread, tie.

lace³ *v* add to, fortify, intermix, mix in, spike.

lacerate *v* afflict, claw, cut, distress, gash, harrow, jag, lancinate, maim, mangle, rend, rip, shred, slash, tear, torment, torture, wound.

laceration *n* cut, gash, injury, lancination, maim, mutilation, rent, rip, slash, tear, wound.

lachrymose *adj* crying, dolorous, lugubrious, mournful, sad, sobbing, tearful, teary, weeping, weepy, woeful.

antonyms happy, laughing.

lack *n* absence, dearth, deficiency, deprivation, destitution, emptiness, insufficiency, need, privation, scantiness, scarcity, shortage, shortcoming, shortness, vacancy, void, want.

antonyms abundance, profusion.

v miss, need, require, want.

lackadaisical *adj* abstracted, apathetic, dreamy, dull, enervated, fainéant, half-hearted, idle, indifferent, indolent, inert, languid, languorous, lazy, lethargic, limp, listless, slack, spiritless, supine.

antonyms active, dynamic, energetic, vigorous.

lackey *n* attendant, creature, fawner, flatterer, flunky, footman, gofer, hanger-on, instrument, manservant, menial, minion, parasite, pawn, servitor, sycophant, toady, tool, valet, yes-man.

lacking *adj* defective, deficient, flawed, impaired, inadequate, minus, missing, needing, sans, short of, wanting, without.

lacklustre *adj* boring, dim, drab, dry, dull, flat, leaden, lifeless, lustreless, mundane, muted, prosaic, sombre, spiritless, unimaginative, uninspired, vapid.

antonyms brilliant, polished.

laconic *adj* brief, close-mouthed, compact, concise, crisp, curt, pithy, sententious, short, succinct, taciturn, terse.

antonyms garrulous, verbose, wordy.

lacuna *n* blank, break, cavity, gap, hiatus, omission, space, void.

lad *n* boy, bucko, chap, fellow, guy, juvenile, kid, laddie, nipper, schoolboy, shaver, stripling, youngster, youth.

laden *adj* burdened, charged, chock-a-block, chock-full, encumbered, fraught, full, hampered, heavy, jammed, loaded, oppressed, packed, stuffed, taxed, weighed down, weighted.

antonym empty.

la-di-da *adj* affected, conceited, foppish, highfalutin, hoity-toity, mannered, mincing, overrefined, posh, precious, pretentious, snobbish, snooty, stuck-up.

ladies' man Casanova, Don Juan, gigolo, heart-breaker, libertine, Lothario, philanderer, rake, roué, stud, wolf, womanizer.

ladle *v* bail, dip, dish, lade, scoop, shovel, spoon.

ladle out disburse, dish out, distribute, dole out, hand out, serve out.

lady *n* begum, dame, damsel, don(n)a, female, Frau, gentlewoman, hidalga, madam(e), matron, memsahib, milady, mistress, noblewoman, senora, signora, woman.

ladylike *adj* courtly, cultured, decorous, elegant, genteel, matronly, modest, polite, proper, queenly, refined, respectable, well-bred.

lag *v* dawdle, delay, hang back, idle, linger, loiter, mosey, saunter, shuffle, stay behind, straggle, tarry, trail.

antonym lead.

laggard *n* dawdler, idler, layabout, lingerer, loafer, loiterer, lounger, saunterer, slowcoach, slowpoke, slugabed, sluggard, snail, straggler.

antonyms dynamo, go-getter, live wire.

lagoon *n* bayou, bog, fen, lake, marsh, pond, pool, shallows, shoal, slough, swamp.

laid-back *adj* at ease, calm, casual, cool, easy-going, free and easy, low-key, passionless, relaxed, unflappable, unhurried, untroubled, unworried.

antonyms tense, uptight.

laid up bedridden, disabled, hors de combat, housebound, ill, immobilized, incapacitated, injured, on the sick list, out of action, sick.

lair *n* burrow, den, earth, form, hideout, hole, nest, refuge, retreat, roost, sanctuary, stronghold.

lake *n* lagoon, mere, reservoir, slough, tarn.

lambaste *v* batter, beat, berate, blast, bludgeon, castigate, censure, chew out, cudgel, drub, flay, flog, hammer, leather, rebuke, reprimand, reprove, roast, scold, strike, thrash, upbraid, whip.

lambent *adj* brilliant, dancing, flickering, fluttering, gleaming, glistening, glowing, incandescent, licking, light, luminous, lustrous, radiant, refulgent, shimmering, sparkling, touching, twinkling.

lame *adj* crippled, defective, disabled, disappointing, feeble, flimsy, game, half-baked, halt, handicapped, hobbling, inadequate, insufficient, limping, poor, thin, unconvincing, unsatisfactory, weak.

v cripple, damage, disable, hamstring, hobble, hurt, incapacitate, injure, maim, wing.

lament *v* bemoan, bewail, complain, deplore, grieve, keen, mourn, regret, sorrow, ululate, wail, weep, yammer.

antonyms celebrate, rejoice.

n complaint, coronach, dirge, elegy, jeremiad, keening, lamentation, moan, moaning, monody, plaint, requiem, threnody, ululation, wail, wailing.

lamentable *adj* deplorable, disappointing, distressing, grievous, inadequate, insufficient, low, meagre, mean, miserable, mournful, pitiful, poor, regrettable, sorrowful, tragic, unfortunate, unsatisfactory, woeful, wretched.

lamentation *n* deploration, dirge, grief, grieving, jeremiad, keen, keening, lament, moan, mourning, plaint, sobbing, sorrow, ululation, wailing, weeping.

antonyms celebration, rejoicing.

laminate *v* coat, cover, exfoliate, face, flake, foliate, layer, plate, separate, split, stratify, veneer.

lamp *n* beacon, flare, floodlight, lantern, light, limelight, searchlight, spotlight, torch.

lampoon *n* burlesque, caricature, parody, pasquinade, satire, sendup, skit, spoof, squib, takeoff.

v burlesque, caricature, make fun of, mock, parody, pasquinade, ridicule, satirize, send up, spoof, squib, take off (on).

lampooner *n* caricaturist, parodist, pasquinader, satirist.

land[1] *n* country, countryside, dirt, district, earth, estate, farmland, fatherland, ground, grounds, loam, motherland, nation, property, province, real estate, realty, region, shore, soil, solid ground, terra firma, territory, tract.

v alight, arrive, berth, bring, come to rest, debark, deposit, disembark, dock, drop, end up, plant, touch down, turn up, wind up.

land[2] *v* achieve, acquire, capture, gain, get, net, obtain, secure, win.

landlord *n* freeholder, host, hotelier, innkeeper, lessor, owner, proprietor.

antonym tenant.

landmark *n* beacon, boundary, cairn, feature, milestone, monument, signpost, turning point, watershed.

landscape *n* aspect, countryside, outlook, panorama, prospect, scene, scenery, view, vista.

landslide *adj* decisive, emphatic, overwhelming, runaway.

lane *n* alley(way), avenue, by-path, byroad, byway, channel, driveway, footpath, gut, passage(way), path(way), towpath, way.

language *n* argot, cant, conversation, dialect, diction, discourse, expression, idiolect, idiom, interchange, jargon, langue, lingo, lingua franca, parlance, parole, patois, phraseology, phrasing, speech, style, talk, terminology, tongue, utterance, vernacular, vocabulary, wording.

languid *adj* debilitated, drained, drooping, dull, enervated, faint, feeble, heavy, inactive, indifferent, inert, lackadaisical, languorous, lazy, lethargic, limp, listless, pining, sickly, slow, sluggish, spiritless, torpid, unenthusiastic, uninterested, weak, weary.

antonyms alert, lively, vivacious.

languish *v* brood, decline, desire, despond, droop, fade, fail, faint, flag, grieve, hanker, hunger, long, mope, pine, repine, rot, sicken, sigh, sink, sorrow, suffer, sulk, want, waste, waste away, weaken, wilt, wither, yearn.

antonym flourish.

languishing *adj* brooding, declining, deteriorating, dreamy, drooping, droopy, fading, failing, flagging, longing, lovelorn, lovesick, melancholic, moping, nostalgic, pensive, pining, sickening, sinking, soulful, sulking, tender, wasting away, weak, weakening, wilting, wistful, withering, woebegone, yearning.

antonyms flourishing, thriving.

languor *n* apathy, asthenia, calm, debility, dreaminess, drowsiness, enervation, ennui, faintness, fatigue, feebleness, frailty, heaviness, hush, indolence, inertia, lassitude, laziness, lethargy, listlessness, lull, oppressiveness, relaxation, silence, sleepiness, sloth, stillness, torpor, weakness, weariness.

antonyms alacrity, gusto.

lank *adj* attenuated, drooping, dull, emaciated, flabby, flaccid, gaunt, lanky, lean, lifeless, limp, long, lustreless, rawboned, scraggy, scrawny, skinny, slender, slim, spare, straggling, thin.

antonyms bulky, burly.

lanky *adj* angular, bony, gangling, gangly, gaunt, loose-jointed, rangy, rawboned, scraggy, scrawny, spare, tall, thin, twiggy, weedy.

antonyms short, squat.

lap[1] *v* drink, lick, sip, sup, tongue.

lap[2] *v* gurgle, plash, purl, ripple, slap, slosh, splash, swish, wash.

lap[3] *n* ambit, circle, circuit, course, distance, loop, orbit, round, tour.

v cover, encase, enfold, envelop, fold, surround, swaddle, swathe, turn, twist, wrap.

lapse *n* aberration, backsliding, break, caducity, decline, descent, deterioration, drop, error, failing, fall, fault, gap, indiscretion, intermission, interruption, interval, lull, mistake, negligence, omission, oversight, passage, pause, relapse, slip.

v backslide, decline, degenerate, deteriorate, drop, end, expire, fail, fall, run out, sink, slide, slip, stop, terminate, worsen.

lapsed *adj* discontinued, ended, expired, finished, invalid, obsolete, out of date, outdated, outworn, run out, unrenewed.

larceny *n* burglary, expropriation, heist, misappropriation, pilfering, piracy, purloining, robbery, stealing, theft.

large *adj* abundant, ample, big, broad, bulky, capacious, colossal, comprehensive, considerable, copious, enormous, extensive, full, generous, giant, gigantic, goodly, grand, grandiose, great, herculean, huge, immense, jumbo, king-size, liberal, mammoth, man-size, massive, monumental, outsize, Patagonian, plentiful, plonking, queen-size, roomy, sizable,

spacious, spanking, substantial, sweeping, tidy, vast, wide.

antonyms diminutive, little, slight, small, tiny.

at large at liberty, evading capture, footloose, free, independent, liberated, loose, on the loose, on the run, out there, roaming, unapprehended, uncaptured, unconfined, unconstrained.

largely *adv* abundantly, by and large, chiefly, considerably, extensively, for the most part, generally, greatly, highly, mainly, mostly, predominantly, primarily, principally, widely.

largeness *n* bigness, breadth, broadness, bulk, bulkiness, dimension, enormity, enormousness, expanse, extent, greatness, heaviness, heftiness, height, immensity, magnitude, mass, massiveness, measure, mightiness, obesity, prodigiousness, size, vastness, wideness, width.

antonym smallness.

large-scale *adj* broad, country-wide, epic, expansive, extensive, far-reaching, global, nationwide, sweeping, vast, wholesale, wide, wide-ranging.

antonym minor.

largesse *n* aid, allowance, alms, benefaction, bequest, bounty, charity, donation, endowment, generosity, gift, grant, handout, liberality, munificence, open-handedness, philanthropy, present.

antonym meanness.

lark *n* antic, caper, escapade, fling, frolic, fun, gambol, game, jape, mischief, prank, revel, romp, spree.

v caper, cavort, frolic, gambol, play, rollick, romp, skylark, sport.

lascivious *adj* bawdy, blue, coarse, crude, dirty, horny, indecent, lecherous, lewd, libidinous, licentious, lustful, obscene, offensive, pornographic, prurient, randy, ribald, salacious, scurrilous, sensual, smutty, suggestive, unchaste, voluptuous, vulgar, wanton.

lash[1] *n* blow, cat, cat-o'-nine-tails, hit, quirt, stripe, stroke, swipe, whip.

v attack, beat, belabour, berate, birch, buffet, castigate, censure, chastise, criticize, dash, drum, flagellate, flay, flog, hammer, hit, horsewhip, knock, lambaste, lampoon, larrup, pound, ridicule, satirize, scold, scourge, smack, strike, tear into, thrash, upbraid, welt, whip.

lash[2] *v* affix, bind, fasten, join, make fast, rope, secure, strap, tether, tie.

lass *n* damsel, girl, lassie, maid, maiden, miss.

lassitude *n* apathy, drowsiness, dullness, enervation, ennui, exhaustion, fatigue, heaviness, languor, lethargy, listlessness, oscitancy, prostration, sluggishness, tiredness, torpor, weariness.

antonyms energy, vigour.

last[1] *adj* aftermost, closing, concluding, conclusive, definitive, endmost, extreme, farthest, final, furthest, hindmost, latest, rearmost, remotest, terminal, ultimate, utmost.

antonyms first, initial.
adv after, at the end, behind, finally, ultimately.

antonyms first, firstly.

n close, completion, conclusion, curtain, end, ending, finale, finish, termination.

antonyms beginning, start.

at last at length, at long last, eventually, finally, in conclusion, in due course, in the end, in the final analysis, in time, ultimately.

last word¹ final decision, final say, ultimatum.

last word² best, cream, crème de la crème, dernier cri, latest, ne plus ultra, newest, perfection, pick, quintessence, rage, the in thing, ultimate, vogue.

last² v abide, carry on, continue, endure, hold on, hold out, keep (on), perdure, persist, remain, stand up, stay, survive, wear.

last-ditch adj all-out, desperate, eleventh-hour, final, frantic, heroic, last-chance, last-gasp, straining, struggling.

lasting adj abiding, continuing, deep-rooted, durable, enduring, hard-wearing, immutable, indelible, indestructible, lifelong, long-standing, long-term, perennial, permanent, perpetual, sempiternal, unceasing, unchanging, undying, unending.

antonyms ephemeral, fleeting, short-lived.

lastly adv finally, in conclusion, in the end, to sum up, ultimately.

antonym firstly.

latch n bar, bolt, catch, fastening, hasp, hook, lock.

latch on to apprehend, attach oneself to, comprehend, get, grasp, pick up on, seize, twig, understand.

late¹ adj behind, behindhand, belated, delayed, dilatory, last-minute, overdue, slow, tardy, unpunctual.

antonyms early, punctual.

adv behindhand, belatedly, dilatorily, formerly, recently, slowly, tardily, unpunctually.

antonyms early, punctually.

late² adj dead, deceased, defunct, departed, ex-, former, old, past, preceding, previous.

lately adv formerly, heretofore, latterly, recently.

lateness n belatedness, delay, dilatoriness, retardation, tardiness, unpunctuality.

antonym earliness.

latent adj concealed, dormant, hidden, inherent, invisible, lurking, potential, quiescent, secret, underlying, undeveloped, unexpressed, unrealized, unseen, veiled.

antonyms active, live, patent.

later adv after, afterwards, next, sequentially, subsequently, successively, thereafter.

antonym earlier.

lateral adj askance, edgeways, flanking, indirect, marginal, oblique, side, side-to-side, sideward, sideways.

antonym central.

latest adj current, fashionable, in, modern, most recent, newest, ultimate, up-to-date, up-to-the-minute, with it.

antonym earliest.

lather¹ n bubbles, foam, froth, soapsuds, suds.
v foam, froth, shampoo, soap, whip up.

lather² n agitation, dither, fever, flap, fluster, flutter, fret, fuss, pother, state, stew, sweat, tizzy, twitter.

latitude n breadth, clearance, compass, elbowroom, extent, field, freedom, indulgence, laxity, leeway, liberty, licence, play, range, reach, room, scope, space, span, spread, sweep, width.

latrine n can, outhouse, privy, toilet, washroom.

latter adj closing, concluding, ensuing, last, last-mentioned, later, latest, modern, recent, second, succeeding, successive.

antonym former.

latterly adv hitherto, lately, of late, recently.

antonym formerly.

lattice n espalier, fretwork, grate, grating, grid, grille, latticework, mesh, network, openwork, reticulation, tracery, trellis, web.

laud v acclaim, applaud, approve, celebrate, extol, glorify, hail, honour, magnify, praise.

antonyms blame, condemn, curse, damn.

laudable adj admirable, commendable, creditable, estimable, excellent, exemplary, meritorious, of note, praiseworthy, sterling, worthy.

antonyms damnable, execrable.

laudation n acclaim, acclamation, accolade, adulation, blessing, celebrity, commendation, devotion, encomium, eulogy, extolment, glorification, glory, homage, kudos, paean, panegyric, praise, reverence, tribute, veneration.

antonyms condemnation, criticism.

laudatory adj acclamatory, adulatory, approbatory, approving, celebratory, commendatory, complimentary, encomiastic, eulogistic, glorifying, panegyrical.

antonym damning.

laugh v break up, cachinnate, chortle, chuckle, giggle, guffaw, roar, roll on the floor, shriek, snicker, snigger, split one's sides, titter, yuk.

antonym cry.

n belly laugh, chortle, chuckle, giggle, guffaw, fit of laughter, hoot, horse laugh, joke, lark, scream, snicker, snigger, titter, yuk.

laugh at belittle, deride, jeer at, lampoon, make fun of, mock, ridicule, scoff at, scorn, take the mickey out of, taunt.

laugh off belittle, brush aside, dismiss, disregard, ignore, make little of, minimize, pooh-pooh, shrug off.

laughable adj absurd, amusing, comical, derisory, diverting, droll, farcical, funny, hilarious, humorous, ludicrous, mirthful, mockable, nonsensical, preposterous, ridiculous, risible.

antonyms impressive, serious, solemn.

laughing *adj* cackling, cheerful, cheery, chortling, chuckling, giggling, gleeful, guffawing, happy, hooting, jocund, jolly, jovial, merry, mirthful, shrieking, snickering, sniggering, tittering.

laughingstock *n* ass, butt, chump, fair game, figure of fun, fool, joke, stooge, target, victim.

laughter *n* amusement, cachinnation, chortling, chuckling, convulsions, giggling, glee, guffawing, hilarity, joviality, laughing, merriment, mirth, tittering.

launch *v* begin, cast, commence, discharge, dispatch, embark on, establish, fire, float, found, inaugurate, initiate, instigate, introduce, open, project, propel, send off, set afloat, set in motion, start, throw.

lavatory *n* bathroom, can, cloakroom, comfort station, convenience, head, john, ladies' room, latrine, loo, men's room, powder room, privy, public convenience, rest toom, toilet, urinal, washroom, water closet, W.C.

lavish *adj* abundant, bountiful, copious, effusive, exaggerated, excessive, extravagant, exuberant, free, generous, gorgeous, immoderate, improvident, intemperate, liberal, lush, luxuriant, munificent, open-handed, opulent, plentiful, princely, prodigal, profuse, prolific, sumptuous, thriftless, unlimited, unreasonable, unrestrained, unstinting, wasteful, wild.

antonyms economical, frugal, parsimonious, scanty, sparing, thrifty.

v bestow, deluge, dissipate, expend, heap, pour, shower, spend, squander, waste.

law *n* act, axiom, canon, charter, code, command, commandment, constitution, consuetude, covenant, criterion, decree, dharma, edict, enactment, formula, institute, jurisprudence, order, ordinance, precept, principle, regulation, rule, standard, statute.

law-abiding *adj* compliant, decent, dutiful, good, honest, honourable, lawful, obedient, orderly, peaceable, peaceful, principled, upright, upstanding.

antonym lawless.

lawbreaker *n* convict, criminal, crook, culprit, delinquent, felon, infractor, miscreant, offender, outlaw, pirate, racketeer, scofflaw, sinner, transgressor, trespasser, wrongdoer.

lawful *adj* allowable, authorized, constitutional, hal(l)al, kosher, legal, legalized, legitimate, licit, permissible, proper, rightful, valid, warranted.

antonyms illegal, illicit, lawless, unlawful.

lawless *adj* anarchic(al), chaotic, disorderly, felonious, insubordinate, insurgent, mutinous, rebellious, reckless, riotous, ruleless, seditious, unbridled, ungoverned, unrestrained, unruly, wild.

antonym lawful.

lawsuit *n* action, argument, case, cause, charge, contest, dispute, indictment, litigation, proceedings, process, prosecution, suit, trial.

lawyer *n* advocate, attorney, barrister, counsel, counsellor, legist, solicitor.

lax *adj* broad, careless, casual, derelict, easygoing, flabby, flaccid, general, imprecise, inaccurate, indefinite, inexact, lenient, loose, neglectful, negligent, overindulgent, remiss, shapeless, slack, slipshod, soft, vague, wide, wide-open, yielding.

antonyms rigid, strict, stringent.

laxative *n* aperient, cathartic, purgative, purge, salts, stool softener.

adj aperient, cathartic, lenitive, purgative.

laxness *n* carelessness, freedom, heedlessness, imprecision, indifference, indulgence, laissez-faire, latitude, latitudinarianism, laxity, leniency, looseness, neglect, negligence, nonchalance, permissiveness, slackness, sloppiness, slovenliness, softness, tolerance.

antonyms severity, strictness.

lay¹ *v* advance, allocate, allot, appease, apply, arrange, ascribe, assess, assign, attribute, bet, charge, concoct, contrive, deposit, devise, dispose, establish, gamble, hazard, impose, impute, leave, locate, lodge, organize, place, plan, plant, plot, posit, position, prepare, present, put, quiet, register, risk, set, set down, set out, spread, stake, submit, tax, wager.

▲ *confusable word* lie.

lay aside abandon, cast aside, discard, dismiss, ignore, pigeonhole, postpone, put (or set) aside, put off, reject, shelve, store.

lay bare disclose, divulge, exhibit, exhume, explain, expose, reveal, show, uncover, unveil.

lay down affirm, assert, assume, couch, discard, drop, establish, formulate, give, give up, ordain, postulate, prescribe, quit, relinquish, sacrifice, state, stipulate, submit, surrender, yield.

lay down the law crack down, dictate, dogmatize, pontificate, put one's foot down, read the riot act, rule the roost.

lay hands on acquire, assault, attack, beat up, bless, clasp, clutch, confirm, consecrate, discover, find, get, get hold of, grab, grasp, grip, lay hold of, lay into, ordain, seize, set on, unearth.

lay in accumulate, amass, build up, collect, gather, glean, hoard, stock up, stockpile, store (up).

lay into assail, attack, belabour, berate, chastise, chew out, lambaste, let fly at, pitch into, set about, slam, tear into, turn on.

lay it on butter up, exaggerate, flatter, overdo it, overpraise, soft soap, sweet talk.

lay off axe, cease, desist, discharge, dismiss, drop, give it a rest, give over, give up, leave alone, leave off, let go, let up, make redundant, oust, pay off, quit, stop, withhold.

lay on burden with, charge with, encumber with, inflict on, saddle with.

lay out arrange, demolish, design, disburse, display, exhibit, expend, fell, flatten, fork out, give, invest, knock out, pay, plan, set out, shell out, spend, spread out.

lay to rest allay, alleviate, assuage, calm, relieve, settle, soothe, still, suppress.

lay up   accumulate, amass, garner, hive, hoard, hospitalize, incapacitate, keep, preserve, put away, salt away, save, squirrel away, store up, treasure.

lay waste   depredate, desolate, despoil, destroy, devastate, pillage, rape, ravage, raze, ruin, sack, spoil, vandalize.

lay² *adj*   amateur, inexpert, laic, non-professional, non-specialist, secular.

lay³ *n*   ballad, canzonet, lyric, madrigal, ode, poem, roundelay, song.

layabout *n*   beachcomber, good-for-nothing, idler, laggard, loafer, lounger, ne'er-do-well, shirker, slugabed, waster.

layer *n*   bed, blanket, coat, coating, cover, covering, film, folium, lame, lamella, lamina, mantle, plate, ply, row, seam, sheet, stratum, table, thickness, tier.

layman *n*   amateur, layperson, outsider, parishioner.

layoff *n*   discharge, dismissal, redundancy, unemployment.

layout *n*   arrangement, blueprint, design, draft, formation, geography, map, outline, plan, sketch.

laze *v*   dawdle, idle, lie around, loaf, loll, lounge, sit around.

laziness *n*   idleness, inactivity, indolence, otiosity, slackness, sloth, slothfulness, slowness, sluggishness.

antonym industriousness.

lazy *adj*   dormant, drowsy, idle, inactive, indolent, inert, languid, languorous, lethargic, otiose, remiss, shiftless, slack, sleepy, slothful, slow, slow-moving, sluggish, somnolent, torpid, workshy.

antonyms active, diligent, energetic, industrious.

lazybones *n*   dawdler, goldbricker, goof-off, idler, laggard, loafer, lounger, shirker, sleepyhead, slouch, slugabed, sluggard.

leach *v*   drain, extract, filter, filtrate, percolate, seep, strain.

lead *v*   antecede, cause, command, conduct, direct, dispose, draw, escort, exceed, excel, experience, govern, guide, have, head, incline, induce, influence, live, manage, outdo, outstrip, pass, persuade, pilot, precede, preside over, prevail, prompt, spend, steer, supervise, surpass, transcend, undergo, usher.

antonym follow.

n advance, advantage, clue, direction, edge, example, first place, guidance, guide, hint, indication, leadership, margin, model, precedence, primacy, principal, priority, protagonist, starring role, start, suggestion, supremacy, tip, title role, trace, van, vanguard.

adj chief, first, foremost, head, leading, main, premier, primary, prime, principal, star.

lead off   begin, commence, get going, inaugurate, initiate, kick off, open, start, start off, start out, start the ball rolling.

lead on   beguile, deceive, draw on, entice, hoax, inveigle, lure, persuade, seduce, string along, tempt, trick.

lead to   bring about, bring on, cause, conduce, contribute to, produce, result in, tend toward.

lead up to   approach, intimate, introduce, make advances, make overtures, overture, pave the way, prepare (the way) for.

leaden *adj*   ashen, bleak, burdensome, crushing, cumbersome, dark, dingy, dismal, dreary, dull, gloomy, grey, greyish, heavy, humdrum, inert, laboured, lacklustre, languid, lead, lifeless, listless, lowering, lustreless, onerous, oppressive, overcast, plodding, prosaic, sluggish, sombre, spiritless, stiff, stilted, wooden.

leader *n*   bellwether, big cheese, boss, captain, chief, chieftain, commander, conductor, coryphaeus, counsellor, director, doyen(ne), figurehead, flagship, groundbreaker, guide, head, head honcho, kingpin, lead, mahatma, mover, pacesetter, pilot, pioneer, point, principal, ringleader, ruler, skipper, superior.

antonym follower.

leadership *n*   administration, authority, command, control, direction, directorship, domination, guidance, hegemony, influence, initiative, management, pre-eminence, premiership, running, superintendency, supremacy, sway.

leading *adj*   cardinal, chief, dominant, first, foremost, governing, greatest, highest, main, number one, outstanding, pacesetting, paramount, pre-eminent, primary, prime, principal, ruling, superior, supreme.

antonym subordinate.

leaf *n*   blade, bract, calyx, cotyledon, flag, folio, frond, needle, pad, page, sepal, sheet.

v browse, flip, glance, riffle, skim, thumb.

leaflet *n*   advertisement, booklet, brochure, circular, flyer, handbill, handout, pamphlet.

leafy *adj*   bosky, foliate, green, shaded, shady, verdant, wooded, woody.

league *n*   alliance, association, band, Bund, cartel, category, class, coalition, combination, combine, compact, confederacy, confederation, consortium, federation, fellowship, fraternity, group, guild, level, partnership, sorority, syndicate, union.

v ally, amalgamate, associate, band, collaborate, combine, confederate, consort, join forces, unite.

in league   allied, collaborating, conniving, conspiring, hand in glove, in cahoots, in collusion.

antonym at odds.

leak *n*   aperture, break, chink, crack, crevice, disclosure, divulgence, drip, fissure, flaw, hole, leakage, leaking, oozing, opening, percolation, perforation, puncture, seepage.

v break (the news), discharge, disclose, divulge, drain, dribble, drip, escape, exude, give away, let slip, let the cat out of the bag, make known, make public, ooze, pass, pass on, percolate, reveal, seep, spill, spill the beans, tell, trickle, weep.

leaky *adj* cracked, holey, leaking, perforated, permeable, porous, punctured, split.

lean[1] *v* bend, confide, count on, depend, favour, incline, list, prefer, prop, recline, rely, repose, rest, slant, slope, tend, tilt, tip, trust.

lean[2] *adj* angular, bare, barren, bony, emaciated, gaunt, inadequate, infertile, lank, meagre, pitiful, poor, rangy, scanty, scraggy, scrawny, skinny, slender, slim, spare, sparse, svelte, thin, unfruitful, unproductive, wiry.

antonyms fat, fleshy.

lean on force, persuade, pressure, put pressure on.

leaning *n* aptitude, bent, bias, disposition, inclination, liking, partiality, penchant, predilection, proclivity, proneness, propensity, susceptibility, taste, tendency.

leap *v* advance, bounce, bound, caper, capriole, cavort, clear, curvet, escalate, frisk, gambol, hasten, hop, hurry, increase, jump, jump (over), reach, rocket, rush, skip, soar, spring, surge, vault.

antonyms drop, fall, sink.

learn *v* acquire, ascertain, assimilate, attain, catch on to, con, detect, determine, discern, discover, find out, gather, get down pat, grasp, hear, imbibe, internalize, learn by heart, master, memorize, pick up, see, study (up on), take in, understand.

learned *adj* academic, accomplished, adept, bookish, cultured, erudite, experienced, expert, highbrow, intellectual, knowledgeable, lettered, literate, proficient, sage, scholarly, skilled, versed, well-informed, well-read, wise.

antonyms ignorant, illiterate, uneducated.

learner *n* abecedarian, apprentice, beginner, catechumen, cheechako, disciple, greenhorn, neophyte, novice, pupil, rookie, scholar, student, tenderfoot, trainee, tyro.

learning *n* acquirements, attainments, culture, edification, education, enlightenment, erudition, information, knowledge, letters, literature, lore, research, scholarship, schooling, study, tuition, wisdom.

lease *v* charter, farm out, hire, hire out, let, loan, rent, sublet.

leash *n* check, control, curb, discipline, harness, hold, lead, rein, restraint, tether.

least *adj* fewest, last, lowest, meanest, merest, minimum, minutest, poorest, slightest, smallest, tiniest.

antonym most.

leathery *adj* chewy, coriaceous, durable, hard, hardened, leathern, rough, rugged, tough, wrinkled.

leave[1] *v* abandon, bequeath, cause, cease, commit, consign, decamp, depart, deposit, desert, disappear, drop, entrust, exit, flit, forget, forsake, give over, give up, go, go away, hand down, hold in abeyance, ignore, let stand, move (away from), pull out, quit, refer, relinquish, renounce, retire, set aside, set out, surrender, take off, transmit, will, withdraw.

antonym arrive.

leave off abstain, break off, cease, desist,

discontinue, end, give over, halt, knock off, lay off, quit, refrain, stop, terminate.

leave out bar, cast aside, count out, cut (out), disregard, eliminate, except, exclude, ignore, neglect, omit, overlook, pass over, reject.

leave[2] *n* allowance, authorization, concession, consent, dispensation, freedom, furlough, holiday, indulgence, liberty, licence, permission, R&R, sabbatical, sanction, time off, vacation.

antonyms active service, refusal, rejection.

leaven *v* elevate, expand, ferment, imbue, inspire, lighten, permeate, pervade, quicken, raise, stimulate, suffuse, work.

leavings *n* bits, debris, detritus, dregs, droppings, dross, fragments, garbage, leftovers, litter, oddments, pieces, refuse, remains, remnants, residue, scraps, spoil, sweepings, trash, waste.

lecher *n* adulterer, Casanova, debaucher, Don Juan, fornicator, goat, libertine, philanderer, profligate, rake, roué, satyr, seducer, sensualist, wanton, wolf, womanizer.

lecherous *adj* carnal, concupiscent, lascivious, lewd, libidinous, licentious, lubricous, lustful, prurient, randy, raunchy, salacious, unchaste, wanton, womanizing.

lecture *n* address, castigation, censure, chiding, diatribe, discourse, disquisition, dressing down, going over, harangue, instruction, lesson, rebuke, reprimand, reproof, scolding, sermon, speech, talk, talking to, telling off, tirade.

v address, admonish, berate, call on the carpet, castigate, censure, chew out, chide, discourse, expound, harangue, hold forth, preach, rate, reprimand, reprove, scold, sermonize, speak, talk (to), teach, tell off.

ledge *n* berm, mantel(piece), projection, ridge, shelf, sill, step.

leech *n* bloodsucker, freeloader, hanger-on, parasite, sponger, sycophant, usurer.

leer *v* eye, gloat, goggle, grin, ogle, smirk, squint, stare, wink.

leery *adj* careful, cautious, chary, distrustful, doubting, dubious, guarded, hesitant, on one's guard, sceptical, shy, suspicious, uncertain, unsure, wary.

lees *n* deposit, dregs, grounds, precipitate, refuse, residue, sediment, settlings.

leeway *n* elbowroom, latitude, margin, play, room, scope, slack, space.

left *adj* communist, left-hand, leftist, left-wing, liberal, port, progressive, radical, red, sinistral, socialist.

antonym right.

leftovers *n* debris, dregs, garbage, leavings, litter, oddments, odds and ends, refuse, remainder, remains, remnants, residue, scraps, surplus, sweepings, trash.

leg *n* brace, gam, lap, limb, member, part, pin, portion, prop, section, segment, shank, stage, stretch, stump, support, upright.

on one's last legs at death's door, dying,

exhausted, fading fast, failing, moribund, with one foot in the grave, worn-out.

legacy *n* bequest, birthright, devise, endowment, estate, gift, heirloom, heritage, inheritance, patrimony.

legal *adj* aboveboard, allowable, allowed, authorized, constitutional, forensic, judicial, juridical, lawful, legalized, legit, legitimate, licit, permissible, proper, rightful, sanctioned, valid, warrantable.

antonym illegal.

legality *n* admissibleness, constitutionality, lawfulness, legitimacy, permissibility, rightfulness, validity.

antonym illegality.

legalize *v* allow, approve, authorize, codify, decriminalize, legitimate, legitimize, license, permit, sanction, validate, warrant.

legate *n* ambassador, delegate, deputy, emissary, envoy, messenger, nuncio.

legatee *n* beneficiary, co-heir(ess), devisee, heir(ess), inheritor, recipient.

legation *n* commission, consulate, delegation, deputation, embassy, ministry, mission, representation.

legend[1] *n* celebrity, fable, fiction, folk tale, household name, luminary, marvel, myth, narrative, phenomenon, prodigy, saga, spectacle, story, tale, tradition, wonder.

legend[2] *n* caption, cipher, code, device, imprint, inscription, key, motto.

legendary *adj* apocryphal, celebrated, fabled, fabulous, famed, famous, fanciful, fictional, fictitious, illustrious, immortal, mythical, renowned, romantic, storied, storybook, traditional, unhistoric(al), well-known.

legerdemain *n* artfulness, artifice, chicanery, contrivance, craftiness, cunning, deception, feint, flimflam, fraud, hocus-pocus, manipulation, manoeuvring, monkey business, prestidigitation, sleight of hand, smoke and mirrors, subterfuge, trickery, wiles.

legible *adj* clear, decipherable, discernible, distinct, intelligible, neat, readable.

antonym illegible.

legion *n* army, battalion, brigade, cohort, company, division, drove, force, horde, host, mass, multitude, myriad, number, regiment, swarm, throng, troop.

adj countless, illimitable, innumerable, multitudinous, myriad, numberless, numerous.

legislate *v* authorize, codify, constitute, constitutionalize, enact, enforce, establish, formalize, ordain, prescribe.

legislation *n* act, authorization, bill, charter, codification, constitutionalization, enactment, law, lawmaking, measure, prescription, regulation, ruling, statute.

legislative *adj* congressional, judicial, juridical, jurisdictional, lawgiving, lawmaking, ordaining, parliamentary, senatorial, synodical.

legislature *n* assembly, chamber, congress, council, diet, governing body, house, parliament, senate.

legitimate *adj* acknowledged, admissible, authentic, authorized, correct, genuine, just, justifiable, kosher, lawful, legal, legit, licit, logical, proper, real, reasonable, rightful, sanctioned, sensible, statutory, true, true-born, valid, warranted, well-founded.

antonym illegitimate.

legitimize *v* authorize, charter, entitle, legalize, legitimate, license, permit, sanction.

leisure *n* breather, ease, freedom, holiday, letup, liberty, opportunity, pause, quiet, recreation, relaxation, respite, rest, retirement, spare time, time off, vacation.

antonyms toil, work.

at leisure at ease, at liberty, disengaged, free, idle, off the hook, unbusy, unengaged, unoccupied.

antonyms booked up, busy, tied down, tied up.

leisurely *adj* carefree, comfortable, deliberate, easy, easygoing, gentle, indolent, laid-back, lazy, lingering, loose, peaceful, relaxed, restful, slow, tranquil, unhurried.

antonyms hectic, hurried, rushed.

lend *v* add, advance, afford, bestow, confer, contribute, furnish, give, grant, impart, lease, loan, present, provide, supply.

antonym borrow.

lend a hand aid, assist, do one's bit, give a helping hand, give a leg up, help, help out, pitch in.

lend an ear give ear, hearken, heed, listen, pay attention, take notice.

length *n* distance, duration, elongation, extensiveness, extent, lengthiness, longitude, measure, period, piece, portion, prolixity, protractedness, reach, section, segment, space, span, stretch, tediousness, term.

at length at last, at long last, completely, comprehensively, eventually, exhaustively, extensively, finally, for ages, for hours, fully, in depth, in detail, interminably, in the end, in time, thoroughly, to the full, ultimately.

lengthen *v* continue, draw out, eke, eke out, elongate, expand, extend, increase, pad out, prolong, protract, spin out, stretch.

antonym shorten.

lengthwise *adv* endways, endwise, horizontally, lengthways, longitudinally, vertically.

lengthy *adj* diffuse, drawn-out, extended, interminable, lengthened, long, long-drawn, long-winded, loquacious, marathon, overlong, prolix, prolonged, protracted, rambling, tedious, verbose, voluble.

antonym short.

leniency *n* clemency, compassion, forbearance, gentleness, indulgence, lenience, lenity, mercy, mildness, moderation, permissiveness, pity, soft-heartedness, softness, tenderness, tolerance.

antonym severity.

lenient *adj* clement, compassionate, easy-going, forbearing, forgiving, gentle,

indulgent, kind, merciful, mild, permissive, soft, soft-hearted, sparing, tender, tolerant.
antonym severe.

lenitive *adj* alleviating, alleviative, assuaging, calmative, calming, easing, laxative, mitigating, mitigative, mollifying, palliative, relieving, soothing.
antonym irritant.

lens *n* eye, eyeglass, eyepiece, glass, loupe, magnifying glass, monocle, ocular.

leper *n* lazar, outcast, pariah, undesirable, untouchable.

lesbian *n* gay, homophile, homosexual, sapphist.

lesion *n* abrasion, bruise, contusion, cut, gash, hurt, impairment, injury, scrape, scratch, sore, trauma, wound.

lessen *v* abate, abridge, bate, contract, curtail, deaden, decrease, de-escalate, degrade, die down, diminish, downplay, dwindle, ease, erode, fail, flag, impair, let up, lighten, lower, minimize, mitigate, moderate, narrow, reduce, shrink, slack, slow down, tail off, weaken.
antonym increase.

lessening *n* abatement, bating, contraction, curtailment, deadening, decline, decrease, de-escalation, diminution, dwindling, ebbing, erosion, failure, flagging, letup, minimization, moderation, petering out, reduction, shrinkage, slackening, waning, weakening.
antonym increase.

lesser *adj* inferior, lower, minor, secondary, slighter, smaller, subordinate.
antonym greater.

lesson¹ *n* assignment, class, coaching, drill, example, exemplar, exercise, homework, instruction, lection, lecture, period, practice, reading, recitation, schooling, task, teaching, tutorial, tutoring.

lesson² *n* admonition, censure, chiding, deterrent, example, message, model, moral, precept, punishment, rebuke, reprimand, reproof, scolding, warning.

let¹ *v* allow, authorize, cause, empower, enable, entitle, give leave, give permission, give the go ahead, give the green light, hire, lease, make, permit, rent.
antonym forbid.

let down abandon, betray, desert, disappoint, disenchant, disillusion, dissatisfy, fail, fall short, jilt, sell out.
antonyms come through for, satisfy.

let go¹ dismiss, free, liberate, manumit, release, set free, spare, unhand.
antonyms catch, imprison.

let go² drop, excuse, forget (about), ignore, let fall by the wayside, let slide, neglect, overlook.

let in accept, admit, embrace, include, incorporate, induct, receive, take in, welcome.
antonym bar.

let off absolve, acquit, clear, detonate, discharge, dispense, emit, excuse, exempt,

exonerate, explode, exude, fire, forgive, give off, ignore, pardon, release, reprieve, spare.
antonym punish.

let on admit, disclose, divulge, give away, leak, let out, make believe, make known, make out, pretend, profess, reveal, say, tell.
antonym keep mum.

let out betray, discharge, disclose, emit, free, give, give vent to, leak, let fall, let go, let slip, liberate, make known, produce, release, reveal, tell, utter.
antonym keep in.

let up abate, cease, decrease, diminish, ease, ease up, end, halt, moderate, slacken, stop, subside.
antonym continue.

let slip blab, blurt out, come out with, disclose, divulge, give away, leak, let out, let the cat out of the bag, reveal, tell.
antonym keep mum.

let² *n* check, constraint, hindrance, impediment, interference, obstacle, obstruction, prohibition, restraint, restriction.
antonym assistance.

letdown *n* anticlimax, betrayal, blow, desertion, disappointment, disillusionment, fiasco, flop, frustration, setback, washout.
antonyms satisfaction, success.

lethal *adj* baleful, dangerous, deadly, deathful, deathly, destructive, devastating, fatal, killing, mortal, murderous, noxious, pernicious, poisonous, virulent.
antonym harmless.

lethargic *adj* apathetic, comatose, debilitated, drowsy, dull, enervated, heavy, hebetudinous, inactive, indifferent, inert, languid, lazy, listless, sleepy, slothful, slow, sluggish, somnolent, stupefied, torpid.
antonym lively.

lethargy *n* apathy, drowsiness, dullness, hebetude, inaction, indifference, inertia, languor, lassitude, listlessness, sleepiness, sloth, slowness, sluggishness, stupor, torpidity, torpor.
antonym liveliness.

letter¹ *n* acknowledgment, answer, billet, card, chit, communication, dispatch, encyclical, epistle, line, message, missive, note, reply.

letter² *n* character, grapheme, initial, logogram, logograph, monogram, sign, symbol.

to the letter accurately, exactly, literally, literatim, precisely, strictly, word for word.

lettered *adj* accomplished, bookish, cultivated, cultured, educated, erudite, highbrow, informed, knowledgeable, learned, literary, literate, scholarly, studied, versed, well-educated, well-read.
antonym ignorant.

letters *n* academia, belles-lettres, books, culture, erudition, humanities, learning, literature, scholarship, writing.

letup *n* abatement, break, breather, cessation, interval, lessening, lull, pause, recess, remission, respite, slackening.

level¹ *adj* abreast, aligned, balanced, calm, champaign, commensurate, comparable, consistent, equable, equal, equivalent, even, even-tempered, flat, flush, horizontal, neck and neck, on a par, on equal terms, plane, proportionate, smooth, stable, steady, uniform, unruffled.

antonyms behind, uneven, unstable.

v aim, beam, bulldoze, couch, demolish, destroy, devastate, direct, equalize, even out, even up, flatten, flush, focus, knock down, lay low, plane, point, pull down, raze, smooth, tear down, train, wreck.

n altitude, bed, class, degree, echelon, elevation, floor, grade, height, horizontal, layer, plain, plane, position, rank, stage, standard, standing, status, storey, stratum, zone.

level² *v* be up front, come clean, confess, fess up, make a clean breast of it, open up, spill the beans, tell the truth.

antonym prevaricate.

on the level aboveboard, candid, fair, frank, genuine, honest, open, sincere, square, straight, straightforward, up front.

level-headed *adj* balanced, calm, collected, commonsensical, composed, cool, dependable, even-kneeled, even-tempered, phlegmatic, reasonable, sane, self-possessed, sensible, steady, together, unflappable.

lever *n* bar, crowbar, handle, jimmy.

v dislodge, force, heave, jimmy, move, pry, purchase, raise, shift.

leverage *n* advantage, ascendancy, authority, clout, force, influence, pull, purchase, rank, strength, weight.

leviathan *n* behemoth, colossus, giant, hulk, mammoth, monster, titan, whale.

levity *n* facetiousness, fickleness, flightiness, flippancy, frivolity, giddiness, irreverence, light-heartedness, silliness, skittishness, triviality, whifflery.

antonyms seriousness, sobriety.

levy *v* assemble, call, call up, charge, collect, conscript, demand, exact, gather, impose, mobilize, muster, press, raise, summon, tax.

n assessment, collection, contribution, duty, exaction, excise, fee, gathering, imposition, impost, subscription, tariff, tax, toll.

lewd *adj* bawdy, blue, carnal, crude, dirty, impure, indecent, lascivious, libidinous, licentious, loose, lubricous, lustful, obscene, pornographic, profligate, salacious, smutty, unchaste, vile, vulgar, wanton, wicked.

antonyms chaste, polite.

lewdness *n* bawdiness, carnality, crudity, debauchery, depravity, impurity, indecency, lasciviousness, lechery, licentiousness, lubricity, lustfulness, obscenity, pornography, priapism, profligacy, randiness, salaciousness, smut, smuttiness, unchastity, vulgarity, wantonness.

antonyms chasteness, politeness.

lexicographer *n* dictionary-writer, glossarist, lexiconist, vocabulist.

lexicon *n* dictionary, encyclopedia, glossary, phrasebook, vocabulary, wordbook, wordlist.

liability *n* accountability, albatross, answerability, arrears, burden, culpability, debit, debt, disadvantage, drag, drawback, duty, encumbrance, handicap, hindrance, impediment, inconvenience, indebtedness, likeliness, millstone, minus, nuisance, obligation, onus, responsibility.

antonyms asset(s), unaccountability.

liable *adj* accountable, amenable, answerable, apt, bound, chargeable, disposed, exposed, inclined, likely, obligated, open, predisposed, prone, responsible, subject, susceptible, tending, vulnerable.

antonyms unaccountable, unlikely.

liaison *n* affair, amour, communication, conjunction, connection, contact, entanglement, interchange, intermediary, intrigue, link, love affair, romance, union.

liar *n* Ananias, deceiver, dissembler, fabricator, falsifier, fibber, fraud, perjurer, Pinocchio, prevaricator, storyteller.

libel *n* aspersion, calumny, defamation, denigration, obloquy, slander, slur, smear, vilification, vituperation.

antonym praise.

v asperse, blacken, calumniate, defame, derogate, malign, revile, slander, slur, smear, traduce, vilify, vituperate.

antonym praise.

libellous *adj* calumnious, defamatory, defaming, derogatory, false, injurious, malicious, maligning, scurrilous, slanderous, traducing, untrue, vilifying, vituperative.

antonyms laudative, praising.

liberal *adj* abundant, advanced, altruistic, ample, beneficent, bounteous, bountiful, broad, broad-minded, catholic, charitable, copious, enlightened, flexible, free, freehanded, general, generous, Grit, handsome, high-minded, humanistic, humanitarian, indulgent, inexact, kind, large-hearted, latitudinarian, lavish, lenient, libertarian, loose, magnanimous, munificent, open-handed, open-hearted, permissive, plentiful, profuse, progressive, radical, reformist, rich, tolerant, unbiassed, unbigoted, unprejudiced, unstinting, Whig.

antonyms conservative, illiberal, mean, narrow-minded.

liberality *n* altruism, beneficence, benevolence, bounty, breadth, broad-mindedness, candour, catholicity, charity, freehandedness, generosity, impartiality, kindness, large-heartedness, largesse, latitude, liberalism, libertarianism, magnanimity, munificence, open-handedness, open-mindedness, permissiveness, philanthropy, progressivism, tolerance, toleration.

antonyms illiberality, meanness.

liberate *v* deliver, discharge, disenthral, emancipate, enfranchise, free, let go, let loose, let out, manumit, ransom, redeem, release, rescue, set free, uncage, unchain, unfetter, unpen, unshackle.

antonyms enslave, imprison, restrict.

liberation *n* deliverance, emancipation, enfranchisement, freedom, freeing, liberating, liberty, manumission, ransoming, redemption, release, uncaging, unchaining, unfettering, unpenning, unshackling.

antonyms enslavement, imprisonment, restriction.

liberator *n* deliverer, emancipator, freer, manumitter, ransomer, redeemer, rescuer, saviour.

antonyms enslaver, jailer.

libertarian *n* anarchist, free-thinker, libertine.

adj anarchistic.

liberties *n* audacity, disrespect, familiarity, forwardness, impertinence, impropriety, impudence, insolence, misuse, overfamiliarity, presumption, presumptuousness.

antonyms politeness, respect.

libertine *n* debaucher, lecher, loose liver, playboy, profligate, rake, reprobate, roué, seducer, sensualist, swinger, voluptuary, wanton, womanizer.

liberty *n* authorization, autonomy, carte blanche, dispensation, disrespect, emancipation, exemption, familiarity, franchise, free rein, freedom, immunity, impertinence, independence, latitude, leave, liberation, licence, permission, prerogative, presumption, privilege, release, right, sanction, self-determination, sovereignty.

antonyms imprisonment, restriction, slavery.

at liberty at large, at leisure, disengaged, footloose, free, idle, loose, on the loose, unconfined, unconstrained, unrestricted, welcome (to).

libidinous *adj* carnal, concupiscent, debauched, impure, incontinent, lascivious, lecherous, lewd, loose, lustful, prurient, randy, ruttish, salacious, sensual, unchaste, wanton, wicked.

antonyms modest, temperate.

library *n* Athenaeum, bibliotheca, den, reading room, reference room, stack, study.

libretto *n* book, lines, lyrics, script, text, words.

licence¹ *n* authorization, authority, carte blanche, certificate, charter, dispensation, entitlement, exemption, freedom, immunity, imprimatur, independence, latitude, leave, liberty, permission, permit, privilege, right, self-determination, warrant.

antonym restriction.

licence² *n* abandon, amorality, anarchy, debauchery, disorder, dissipation, dissoluteness, excess, immoderation, impropriety, indulgence, intemperance, irresponsibility, lawlessness, laxity, profligacy, unruliness.

antonyms decorum, temperance.

license *v* accredit, allow, approve, authorize, certificate, certify, commission, empower, entitle, permit, sanction, warrant.

antonym ban.

licentious *adj* abandoned, debauched, disorderly, dissolute, immoral, impure, lascivious, lax, lewd, libertine, libidinous, lubricous, lustful, profligate, promiscuous, sensual, uncontrollable, uncontrolled, uncurbed, unruly, wanton.

antonyms modest, temperate.

lick¹ *v* brush, dart, flick, lap, play over, smear, taste, tongue, touch, wash.

n bit, brush, dab, hint, little, sample, smack, smidgen, speck, spot, stroke, taste, touch.

lick one's lips anticipate, drool over, enjoy, relish, savour.

lick² *v* beat, best, defeat, flog, outdo, outstrip, overcome, rout, slap, smack, spank, strike, surpass, thrash, top, trounce, vanquish, wallop.

lick³ *n* clip, gallop, pace, rate, speed.

licking *n* beating, defeat, drubbing, flogging, hiding, skelping, smacking, spanking, tanning, thrashing, trouncing, whipping.

lie¹ *v* dissimulate, equivocate, fabricate, falsify, fib, forswear oneself, invent, misrepresent, perjure oneself, prevaricate.

n baloney, bull, concoction, crock, deceit, equivocation, evasion, fabrication, fairy tale, falsehood, falsification, falsity, fib, fiction, half-truth, hogwash, invention, inveracity, mendacity, prevarication, story, tale, taradiddle, untruth, white lie, whopper.

antonym truth.

lie² *v* be, belong, couch, dwell, exist, extend, inhere, laze, loll, lounge, recline, remain, repose, rest, slump, sprawl, stretch out.

▲ *confusable word* lay.

lie in wait (for) ambuscade, ambush, skulk, waylay.

lie low go to earth, hide, hide away, hide out, hole up, keep a low profile, lurk, skulk, take cover.

life¹ *n* activity, behaviour, being, breath, conduct, continuance, course, creatures, duration, entity, essence, existence, fauna, flora and fauna, growth, history, lifeblood, lifestyle, lifetime, livelihood, organisms, sentience, soul, span, the world, this mortal coil, time, viability, vital flame, vital spark, way of life, wildlife.

life² *n* autobiography, biography, career, conduct, confessions, history, life history, memoirs, story.

life³ *n* animation, brio, energy, go, heart, high spirits, liveliness, oomph, sparkle, spirit, verve, vigour, vitality, vivacity, zest.

lifeless *adj* abiotic, apathetic, bare, barren, cold, colourless, comatose, dead, deceased, defunct, desert, dull, empty, extinct, flat, heavy, hollow, inanimate, inert, insensate, insensible, insipid, lacklustre, lethargic, listless, nerveless, out cold, out for the count, passive, pointless, slow, sluggish, spent, spiritless, static, sterile, stiff, torpid, unconscious, uninhabited, unproductive, waste, wooden.

antonyms alive, lively.

lifelike *adj* authentic, exact, expressive, faithful, graphic, natural, photographic, pictorial, picturesque, real, realistic, true, true-to-life, undistorted, vivid.

antonyms inexact, unnatural.

lifelong *adj* abiding, constant, deep-rooted, deep-seated, enduring, entrenched, inveterate, lasting, lifetime, long-lasting, long-standing, perennial, permanent, persistent.

antonyms impermanent, temporary.

lifetime *n* career, course, day(s), existence, life, life span, period, span, time.

lift[1] *v* advance, ameliorate, annul, arrest, ascend, boost, buoy up, cancel, climb, collar, copy, countermand, dignify, disappear, disperse, dissipate, draw up, elevate, end, enhance, exalt, heft, hoist, improve, mount, pick up, promote, raise, rear, relax, remove, rescind, revoke, rise, stop, terminate, up, upgrade, uplift, upraise, vanish.

antonyms drop, fall, impose, lower.

n boost, encouragement, fillip, pick-me-up, reassurance, shot in the arm, spur, uplift.

antonym discouragement.

lift[2] *v* appropriate, crib, pilfer, pinch, pirate, plagiarize, pocket, purloin, steal, take, thieve.

lift[3] *n* drive, hitch, ride, run, transport.

ligature *n* band, bandage, binding, bond, connection, cord, ligament, link, rope, strap, string, thong, tie, tourniquet.

light[1] *n* beacon, blaze, brightness, brilliance, bulb, candle, cockcrow, dawn, day, daybreak, daylight, daytime, effulgence, flame, flare, flash, glare, gleam, glim, glint, glow, illumination, incandescence, lambency, lamp, lantern, lighter, lighthouse, luminescence, luminosity, lustre, match, morn, morning, phosphorescence, radiance, ray, refulgence, scintillation, shine, sparkle, star, sunrise, sunshine, taper, torch, window, yang.

antonym darkness.

v animate, beacon, brighten, cheer, fire, floodlight, ignite, illuminate, illumine, inflame, irradiate, kindle, light up, lighten, put on, set alight, set fire to, switch on, turn on.

antonyms darken, extinguish.

adj bleached, blond, bright, brilliant, faded, faint, fair, glowing, illuminated, lightsome, lucent, luminous, lustrous, pale, pastel, shining, sunny, well-lit.

antonym dark.

light[2] *n* angle, approach, aspect, attitude, awareness, clue, comprehension, context, elucidation, enlightenment, example, exemplar, explanation, hint, illustration, information, insight, interpretation, knowledge, model, paragon, point of view, slant, understanding, viewpoint.

in (the) light of bearing (or keeping) in mind, because of, considering, in view of, taking into account.

light[3] *adj* airy, buoyant, crumbly, delicate, digestible, diverting, easy, effortless, facile, faint, flimsy, friable, frugal, idle, imponderous, inconsequential, inconsiderable, indistinct, insignificant, insubstantial, lightweight, manageable, mild, moderate, modest, porous, portable, restricted, sandy, scanty, simple, slight, small, soft, spongy, superficial, thin, tiny, trifling, trivial, underweight, unsubstantial, untaxing, volatile, weak, worthless.

antonyms harsh, heavy, important, severe, solid, stiff.

light[4] *adj* agile, amusing, animated, blithe, buoyant, carefree, cheerful, cheery, diverting, easy, facile, funny, gay, gentle, graceful, humorous, light-footed, light-headed, light-hearted, lithe, lively, loose, merry, nimble, slight, sprightly, sunny, superficial, undemanding, unexacting, unheeding.

antonyms clumsy, sad, sober.

lighten[1] *v* beacon, brighten, illume, illuminate, illumine, light up, shine.

antonym darken.

lighten[2] *v* alleviate, ameliorate, assuage, brighten, buoy up, cheer, disburden, disencumber, ease, elate, encourage, facilitate, gladden, hearten, inspire, inspirit, lessen, lift, mitigate, perk up, reduce, relieve, revive, unload, uplift.

antonyms burden, depress, oppress.

light-fingered *adj* crafty, crooked, dishonest, furtive, pilfering, shifty, sly, thieving, thievish.

antonym honest.

light-footed *adj* active, agile, buoyant, fleet, graceful, lightsome, lithe, nimble, sprightly, spry, swift, tripping, winged.

antonyms clumsy, slow.

light-headed *adj* birdbrained, delirious, dizzy, faint, featherbrained, fickle, flighty, flippant, foolish, frivolous, giddy, hazy, inane, light-minded, shallow, silly, superficial, thoughtless, trifling, unsteady, vacuous, vertiginous, woozy.

antonym sober.

light-hearted *adj* blithe, blithesome, bright, carefree, cheerful, effervescent, elated, frolicsome, gay, glad, gleeful, happy-go-lucky, insouciant, jocund, jolly, jovial, joyful, joyous, light-spirited, merry, perky, playful, sunny, untroubled, upbeat.

antonym sad.

lightly *adv* a bit, airily, breezily, carelessly, delicately, easily, effortlessly, facilely, faintly, flippantly, frivolously, gaily, gently, gingerly, heedlessly, indifferently, moderately, readily, simply, slightingly, slightly, softly, sparingly, sparsely, thinly, thoughtlessly, timidly, wantonly.

antonyms heavily, soberly.

lightness *n* agility, airiness, animation, blitheness, buoyancy, cheerfulness, cheeriness, crumbliness, delicacy, delicateness, facileness, faintness, fickleness, flimsiness, frivolity, gaiety, grace, idleness, inconsequentiality, indistinctness, insignificance, levity, light-heartedness, litheness, liveliness, mildness, minuteness, moderation, nimbleness, porosity, porousness, sandiness, scantiness, slightness, triviality, wantonness.

antonyms clumsiness, harshness, heaviness,

importance, sadness, severity, sobriety, solidness, stiffness.

light on chance on, come across, discover, encounter, find, happen upon, hit on, spot, stumble on.

lightweight *adj* inconsequential, inferior, insignificant, lesser, negligible, nugatory, paltry, petty, slight, trifling, trivial, unimportant, valueless, worthless.

antonyms important, major.

likable *adj* agreeable, amiable, appealing, attractive, charming, congenial, engaging, friendly, genial, lovable, nice, pleasant, pleasing, sympathetic, winning, winsome.

antonym disagreeable.

like¹ *adj* akin, alike, allied, analogous, approximating, cognate, corresponding, equivalent, homologous, identical, matching, parallel, related, relating, resembling, same, similar.

antonym unlike.

n counterpart, equal, fellow, match, opposite number, parallel, peer, twin.

prep in the same manner as, along the lines of, similar to.

like² *v* admire, adore, appreciate, approve, be fond of, be partial to, care to, cherish, choose, choose to, cotton to, delight in, desire, dig, enjoy, esteem, fancy, feel inclined, go for, hold dear, love, prefer, prize, relish, revel in, select, take a shine to, take kindly to, take pleasure in, take to, want, wish.

antonym dislike.

n choice, cup of tea, favourite, liking, love, partiality, penchant, predilection, preference.

antonym dislike.

likelihood *n* chance, liability, likeliness, possibility, probability, prospect, reasonableness, verisimilitude.

antonym unlikeliness.

likely *adj* acceptable, agreeable, anticipated, appropriate, apt, befitting, believable, bright, credible, disposed, expected, fair, favourite, feasible, fit, foreseeable, hopeful, inclined, liable, odds-on, on the cards, plausible, pleasing, possible, predictable, probable, promising, prone, proper, qualified, reasonable, suitable, tending, up-and-coming, verisimilar.

antonyms unlikely, unsuitable.

adv doubtless, in all probability, like as not, like enough, no doubt, odds on, presumably, probably.

like-minded *adj* agreeing, as one, compatible, harmonious, in accord, in agreement, in harmony, in rapport, of one mind, of the same mind, unanimous.

antonym disagreeing.

liken *v* associate, compare, equate, juxtapose, link, match, parallel, relate, set beside.

likeness *n* affinity, appearance, copy, correspondence, counterpart, delineation, depiction, effigies, effigy, facsimile, form, guise, image, model, photograph, picture, portrait, replica, representation, reproduction,

resemblance, semblance, similarity, similitude, simulacrum, study.

antonym unlikeness.

likewise *adv* also, besides, by the same token, eke, further, furthermore, in addition, moreover, similarly, too.

antonym contrariwise.

liking *n* affection, affinity, appreciation, attraction, bent, bias, desire, favour, fondness, inclination, love, partiality, penchant, predilection, preference, proneness, propensity, satisfaction, soft spot, stomach, taste, tendency, weakness.

antonym dislike.

lilt *n* air, beat, cadence, measure, rhythm, song, sway, swing.

lily-white *adj* chaste, incorrupt, innocent, irreproachable, milk-white, pure, spotless, uncorrupt, uncorrupted, unsullied, untainted, untarnished, virgin, virtuous.

antonym corrupt.

limb *n* appendage, arm, bough, branch, extension, extremity, fork, leg, member, offshoot, part, projection, ramus, spur, wing.

limber *adj* agile, elastic, flexible, flexile, graceful, lissome, lithe, loose-jointed, loose-limbed, plastic, pliable, pliant, supple.

antonym stiff.

limber up exercise, loosen up, prepare, warm up, work out.

antonym stiffen up.

limelight *n* attention, big time, celebrity, fame, prominence, public notice, publicity, recognition, renown, stardom, the public eye, the spotlight.

limit *n* bitter end, border, bound, boundary, bourn, brim, brink, ceiling, check, compass, confines, curb, cutoff point, deadline, edge, end, extent, frontier, limitation, maximum, mete, obstruction, perimeter, periphery, precinct, restraint, restriction, rim, saturation point, termination, terminus, threshold, ultimate, utmost, verge.

v bound, check, circumscribe, condition, confine, constrain, curb, delimit, demarcate, fix, hem in, hinder, ration, restrain, restrict, specify.

antonyms extend, free.

limitation *n* block, check, condition, constraint, control, curb, definitude, delimitation, demarcation, disadvantage, drawback, impediment, liability, obstruction, qualification, reservation, restraint, restriction, snag.

antonyms asset, extension, furtherance.

limited *adj* bounded, checked, circumscribed, confined, constrained, controlled, cramped, curbed, defined, determinate, diminished, finite, fixed, hampered, hemmed in, inadequate, insufficient, minimal, narrow, reduced, restricted, short, unsatisfactory.

antonym limitless.

limitless *adj* boundless, countless, endless, illimitable, immeasurable, immense, immensurable, incalculable, inexhaustible, infinite, measureless, never-ending, numberless, unbounded, undefined, unending, unlimited, untold, vast.

antonym limited.

limp[1] *v* falter, halt, hitch, hobble, hop, shamble, shuffle, stumble.

n claudication, hitch, hobble, lameness.

limp[2] *adj* debilitated, drooping, enervated, exhausted, flabby, flaccid, flexible, flexile, floppy, lax, lethargic, limber, loose, pliable, pooped, relaxed, slack, soft, spent, tired, toneless, weak, worn out.

antonym strong.

limpid *adj* bright, clear, comprehensible, crystal-clear, crystalline, glassy, hyaline, intelligible, lucid, pellucid, pure, still, translucent, transparent, unruffled, untroubled.

antonyms muddy, ripply, turbid, unintelligible.

line[1] *n* band, bar, border, borderline, boundary, cable, chain, channel, column, configuration, contour, cord, crease, crow's foot, dash, demarcation, disposition, edge, figure, filament, file, firing line, formation, front, front line, frontier, furrow, groove, limit, mark, outline, position, procession, profile, queue, rank, rope, row, rule, score, scratch, sequence, series, silhouette, stipe, strand, streak, string, stripe, stroke, tail, thread, trail, trenches, underline, wire, wrinkle.

v border, bound, crease, cut, draw, edge, fringe, furrow, hatch, inscribe, mark, rank, rim, rule, score, skirt, verge.

line up align, arrange, array, assemble, dispose, book, engage, fall in, form ranks, hire, lay on, marshal, obtain, order, organize, prepare, procure, produce, queue up, range, regiment, schedule, secure, sign up, straighten.

line[2] *n* activity, approach, area, avenue, axis, belief, business, calling, course, course of action, department, direction, employment, field, forte, ideology, interest, line of country, job, method, occupation, path, policy, position, practice, procedure, profession, province, pursuit, route, scheme, specialization, specialism, specialty, system, track, trade, trajectory, vocation.

line[3] *n* ancestry, breed, family, lineage, pedigree, race, stirps, stock, strain, succession.

line[4] *n* card, clue, hint, indication, information, lead, letter, memo, memorandum, message, note, postcard, report, word.

line[5] *v* ceil, cover, encase, face, fill, reinforce, strengthen, stuff.

lineage *n* ancestors, ancestry, birth, blood, breed, descendants, descent, extraction, family, forebears, forefathers, genealogy, heredity, house, line, offspring, origin, pedigree, progeny, race, stirps, stock, succession.

lineaments *n* appearance, aspect, configuration, countenance, face, features, lines, outline(s), physiognomy, traits, visage.

lined *adj* furrowed, lineate, ruled, wizened, worn, wrinkled.

antonyms smooth, unlined.

linen *n* bed linen, napery, sheets, table linen.

lines[1] *n* appearance, configuration, contour, convention, cut, example, model, outline, pattern, plan, principle, procedure, shape, style.

lines[2] *n* book, libretto, part, script, text, words.

line-up *n* arrangement, array, bill, cast, queue, row, selection, team.

linger *v* abide, continue, dally, dawdle, delay, dilly-dally, endure, hang around, hang on, hold out, idle, lag, last out, loiter, persist, procrastinate, remain, stay, stop, survive, tarry, wait.

antonyms leave, rush.

lingering *adj* dragging, long-drawn-out, persistent, prolonged, protracted, remaining, slow.

antonym quick.

lingo *n* argot, cant, dialect, -ese, idiom, jargon, language, parlance, patois, patter, speech, talk, terminology, tongue, vernacular, vocabulary.

liniment *n* balm, balsam, cream, embrocation, emollient, lotion, ointment, salve, unguent, wash.

lining *n* backing, encasement, inlay, interfacing, interlining, padding, stiffening.

link *n* association, attachment, bond, communication, component, connection, constituent, division, element, joint, knot, liaison, member, part, piece, relationship, tie, tie-up, union.

v associate, attach, bind, bracket, catenate, concatenate, connect, couple, fasten, identify, join, relate, tie, unite, yoke.

antonyms separate, unfasten.

link up ally, amalgamate, connect, dock, hook up, join, join forces, merge, team up, unify.

antonym separate.

lion-hearted *adj* bold, brave, courageous, daring, dauntless, fearless, gallant, heroic, intrepid, resolute, stalwart, stout-hearted, valiant, valorous.

antonym cowardly.

lionize *v* acclaim, adulate, aggrandize, celebrate, eulogize, exalt, fete, glorify, hero-worship, honour, idolize, magnify, praise, sing the praises of.

antonym vilify.

lip[1] *n* border, brim, brink, edge, margin, rim, verge.

lip[2] *n* backtalk, cheek, effrontery, impertinence, impudence, insolence, rudeness, sauce, sauciness.

antonym politeness.

liquefaction *n* deliquescence, dissolution, dissolving, fusion, liquefying, melting, thawing.

antonym solidification.

liquefy *v* condense, deliquesce, dissolve, fluidize, flux, fuse, liquesce, macerate, melt, run, smelt, thaw.

antonym solidify.

liquid n beverage, drink, fluid, juice, liquor, lotion, potation, sap, solution.

adj aqueous, clear, convertible, dulcet, flowing, fluid, limpid, liquefied, liquescent, mellifluous, melted, molten, negotiable, running, runny, serous, shining, smooth, soft, sweet, thawed, translucent, transparent, watery, wet.

antonyms harsh, solid.

liquidate v abolish, annihilate, annul, assassinate, bump off, cancel, cash, clear, destroy, discharge, dispatch, dissolve, do away with, do in, eliminate, exterminate, finish off, honour, kill, massacre, murder, obliterate, pay, pay off, realize, redeem, remove, rub out, sell off, sell up, settle, silence, square, terminate, wipe out.

liquor[1] n alcohol, booze, drink, grog, hard stuff, hootch, intoxicant, juice, moonshine, potation, rotgut, sauce, spirits, strong drink.

liquor[2] n broth, distillate, essence, extract, gravy, infusion, juice, liquid, stock.

lissome adj agile, flexible, graceful, light, limber, lithe, lithesome, loose-jointed, loose-limbed, nimble, pliable, pliant, supple, willowy.

antonym stiff.

list[1] n catalogue, directory, enumeration, file, index, inventory, invoice, listing, litany, muster, program, record, register, roll, schedule, series, syllabus, table, tabulation, tally.

v alphabetize, bill, book, catalogue, chronicle, classify, enrol, enter, enumerate, file, index, itemize, note, record, register, schedule, set down, tabulate, write down.

list[2] v cant, careen, heel, heel over, incline, lean, slope, tilt, tip.

n cant, leaning, slant, slope, tilt.

listen v attend, be all ears, get a load of, give ear, hang on (someone's) words, hang on (someone's) lips, hark, hear, hearken, heed, keep one's ears open, lend an ear, listen up, mind, obey, observe, pay attention, prick up one's ears, take in, take notice.

listless adj apathetic, bored, depressed, enervated, heavy, impassive, inattentive, indifferent, indolent, inert, languid, languishing, lethargic, lifeless, limp, lymphatic, mopish, sluggish, spiritless, supine, torpid, uninterested, vacant.

antonym lively.

listlessness n accidie, apathy, enervation, ennui, inattention, indifference, indolence, languidness, languor, lassitude, lethargy, lifelessness, sloth, sluggishness, spiritlessness, supineness, the blahs, torpidity, torpor, weariness.

antonym liveliness.

litany n account, catalogue, enumeration, invocation, list, narration, narrative, petition, prayer, recital, recitation, refrain, repetition, supplication, tale.

literal adj accurate, actual, boring, close, colourless, direct, down-to-earth, dull, exact, factual, faithful, genuine, matter-of-fact,

pedantic, plain, precise, prosaic, prosy, real, simple, strict, true, unexaggerated, unimaginative, uninspired, unvarnished, verbatim, word-for-word.

antonym loose.

literally adv actually, closely, exactly, faithfully, literatim, plainly, precisely, really, simply, strictly, to the letter, truly, verbatim, word-for-word.

antonyms figuratively, loosely.

literary adj academic, bookish, cultivated, cultured, erudite, formal, highbrow, learned, lettered, literate, poetic, refined, scholarly, well-read.

literate adj able, articulate, cultivated, cultured, educated, erudite, informed, intelligent, knowledgeable, learned, lettered, proficient, scholarly, well-read, well-versed.

antonym illiterate.

literature n belles-lettres, blurb, brochure(s), bumf, circular(s), handout(s), information, leaflet(s), letters, lore, pamphlet(s), paper(s), writings.

lithe adj double-jointed, flexible, flexile, limber, lissome, lithesome, loose-jointed, loose-limbed, pliable, pliant, supple.

antonym stiff.

litigant n claimant, complainant, contender, contestant, disputant, litigator, party, petitioner, plaintiff.

litigation n case, contention, lawsuit, (legal) action, process, prosecution, suit.

litigious adj argumentative, belligerent, contentious, disputatious, quarrelsome.

antonym easygoing.

litter[1] n clutter, confusion, debris, detritus, disarray, disorder, fragments, jumble, mess, muck, refuse, rubbish, scatter, scoria, shreds, untidiness, wastage.

v clutter, scatter, strew.

antonym tidy.

litter[2] n brood, family, issue, offspring, progeny, young.

litter[3] n bier, couch, palanquin, pallet, sedan chair, stretcher.

little adj babyish, bantam, base, brief, cheap, diminutive, dinky, dwarf, elfin, fleeting, hasty, immature, inconsiderable, infant, infinitesimal, insignificant, insufficient, junior, lightweight, Lilliputian, meagre, mean, microscopic, midget, mini, miniature, minor, minute, negligible, nugatory, paltry, passing, peewee, petite, petty, piddling, pint-sized, pygmy, scant, short, short-lived, skimpy, slender, small, sparse, tiny, transient, transitory, trifling, trivial, undersized, undeveloped, unimportant, wee, young.

antonyms important, large, long.

adv barely, hardly, infrequently, rarely, scarcely, seldom.

antonyms frequently, greatly.

n bit, dab, dash, dribble, driblet, fragment, hint, modicum, particle, pinch, smack, smear, smidgen, snippet, speck, splash, spot, sprinkling, taste, touch, trace, trifle.

antonym lot.

little by little bit by bit, by degrees, gradually, imperceptibly, piecemeal, progressively, slowly, step by step.

antonyms all at one go, quickly.

liturgical *adj* ceremonial, eucharistic, formal, hieratic, ritual, sacerdotal, sacramental, solemn.

antonym secular.

liturgy *n* celebration, ceremony, form, formula, office, rite, ritual, sacrament, service, usage, worship.

live¹ *v* abide, be, breathe, continue, draw breath, dwell, earn a living, endure, exist, fare, feed, get along, hang out, inhabit, last, lead, lodge, make ends meet, pass, persist, prevail, remain, reside, settle, stay, subsist, survive.

antonyms cease, die.

live it up celebrate, go on a spree, have a ball, live high, make merry, make whoopee, paint the town red, revel.

live² *adj* active, alert, alight, alive, animate, blazing, breathing, bright, brisk, burning, connected, controversial, current, dynamic, earnest, energetic, existent, glowing, hot, ignited, lively, living, pertinent, pressing, prevalent, relevant, sentient, smouldering, topical, unsettled, viable, vigorous, vital, vivid, wide awake.

antonyms apathetic, dead, out.

liveable *adj* acceptable, adequate, bearable, comfortable, endurable, habitable, inhabitable, possible, satisfactory, sufferable, supportable, tolerable, worthwhile.

antonyms unbearable, uninhabitable.

livelihood *n* employment, income, job, living, maintenance, means, occupation, subsistence, support, sustenance, work.

liveliness *n* activity, animation, boisterousness, brio, briskness, dynamism, energy, gaiety, quickness, smartness, spirit, sprightliness, vitality, vivacity.

antonyms apathy, inactivity.

livelong complete, enduring, entire, full, long, protracted, whole.

antonym partial.

lively *adj* active, agile, alert, animated, astir, blithe, blithesome, breezy, bright, brisk, bustling, busy, buzzing, cheerful, chipper, chirpy, colourful, crowded, energetic, eventful, exciting, forceful, frisky, frolicsome, gay, heated, invigorating, keen, lightsome, merry, mettlesome, moving, nimble, peppy, perky, quick, racy, refreshing, skittish, snappy, sparkling, spirited, sprightly, spry, stimulating, stirring, swinging, vigorous, vivacious, vivid, zippy.

antonyms apathetic, inactive, moribund.

liven up animate, brighten, buck up, energize, enliven, heat up, invigorate, pep up, perk up, put life into, rouse, spark, stir, stir up, vitalize, vivify.

antonyms deaden, dishearten.

livery *n* apparel, attire, clothes, clothing, costume, dress, garb, gear, get up, habit, raiment, regalia, suit, uniform, vestments.

live wire ball of fire, dynamo, eager beaver, go-getter, hustler, life and soul of the party, self-starter, workaholic.

antonym wet blanket.

livid¹ *adj* angry, beside oneself, boiling, enraged, exasperated, fuming, furious, incensed, indignant, infuriated, irate, ireful, mad, outraged, ticked off, waxy.

antonym calm.

▲ *confusable word* lurid.

livid² *adj* angry, ashen, black-and-blue, blanched, bloodless, bruised, contused, discoloured, doughy, greyish, leaden, pale, pallid, pasty, purple, wan, waxen, waxy.

antonyms healthy, rosy.

living *adj* active, alive, animated, breathing, existing, live, lively, strong, vigorous, vital.

antonyms dead, sluggish.

n being, benefice, existence, income, job, life, livelihood, maintenance, occupation, profession, property, subsistence, support, sustenance, way of life, work.

load *n* affliction, albatross, bale, burden, cargo, consignment, encumbrance, freight, goods, lading, millstone, onus, oppression, pressure, shipment, trouble, weight, worry.

v burden, charge, cram, encumber, fill, fortify, freight, hamper, heap, lade, oppress, overburden, pack, pile, prime, saddle with, stack, stuff, trouble, weigh down, weight, worry.

loaded *adj* affluent, artful, biassed, burdened, charged, drunk, fixed, flush, freighted, full, high, inebriated, insidious, intoxicated, laden, manipulative, moneyed, prejudicial, primed, rich, rolling, tight, tipsy, tricky, under the influence, wealthy, weighted, well-heeled, well-off, well-to-do.

antonyms poor, sober, straightforward, unloaded.

loads *n* a million, dozens, heaps, hordes, hundreds, lots, millions, scores, thousands, tons.

loaf¹ *n* block, cake, cube, lump, mass, slab.

loaf² *v* gold brick, goof off, idle, laze, lie around, loiter, loll, lounge around, malinger, moon, stand around, take it easy.

antonym toil.

loafer *n* beachcomber, bum, deadbeat, drone, goldbricker, good-for-nothing, goof-off, idler, layabout, lazybones, lounger, malingerer, ne'er-do-well, shirker, slouch, sluggard, wastrel.

antonym worker.

loan *n* accommodation, advance, allowance, calque, credit, lend-lease, mortgage.

v accommodate, advance, allow, credit, lend, let out, oblige.

antonym borrow.

loath *adj* against, averse, backward, counter, disinclined, grudging, hesitant, indisposed, opposed, reluctant, resisting, unwilling.

antonym willing.

loathe v abhor, abominate, despise, detest, dislike, execrate, hate.
antonym like.

loathing n abhorrence, abomination, antipathy, aversion, detestation, disgust, dislike, execration, hatred, horror, nausea, odium, repugnance, repulsion, revulsion.
antonym liking.

loathsome adj abhorrent, abominable, detestable, disgusting, execrable, hateful, horrible, loathful, nasty, nauseating, obnoxious, odious, offensive, repellent, repugnant, repulsive, revolting, vile.
antonym likeable.

lob v chuck, fling, heave, hurl, launch, lift, loft, pitch, shy, throw, toss.

lobby[1] v call for, campaign for, demand, influence, persuade, press for, pressure, promote, pull strings, push for, solicit, urge.
n ginger group, pressure group.

lobby[2] n anteroom, corridor, entrance hall, entryway, foyer, hall, hallway, narthex, passage, passageway, porch, vestibule, waiting room.

local adj community, confined, district, limited, narrow, neighbourhood, parish, parochial, provincial, regional, restricted, small-town, vernacular, vicinal.
antonym distant.
n denizen, inhabitant, native, resident, yokel.
antonyms newcomer, outsider.

locale n area, locality, location, locus, place, position, scene, setting, site, spot, venue, zone.

locality n area, district, environs, locale, location, neck of the woods, neighbourhood, place, point, position, region, scene, setting, site, spot, vicinity, zone.

localize v ascribe, assign, circumscribe, concentrate, confine, contain, delimit, limit, narrow down, pinpoint, restrain, restrict, specify, zero in on.

locate v detect, discover, establish, find, fix, identify, lay one's hands on, pinpoint, place, put, run to earth, seat, set, settle, situate, track down, unearth.

location n bearings, locale, locus, place, point, position, site, situation, spot, ubiety, venue, whereabouts.

lock[1] n bolt, clasp, fastening, latch, padlock.
v bolt, clasp, clench, close, clutch, disengage, embrace, encircle, enclose, engage, entangle, entwine, fasten, grapple, grasp, hug, join, latch, link, mesh, press, seal, secure, shut, unite, unlock.

lock out ban, bar, debar, exclude, keep out, ostracize, refuse admittance to, shut out.

lock up cage, close up, confine, detain, immure, imprison, incarcerate, jail, pen, secure, shut, shut in, shut up.
antonym release.

lock[2] n braid, curl, plait, ringlet, shock, strand, tress, tuft.

lockup n brig, can, cell, clink, cooler, hoosegow, jail, jailhouse, jug, pen, penitentiary, prison, slammer.

locomotion n action, ambulation, headway, motion, movement, moving, progress, progression, travel, travelling.

locution n accent, articulation, cliché, collocation, diction, expression, idiom, inflection, intonation, phrase, phrasing, saying, style, term, turn of speech, wording.

lodge[1] n abode, cabin, chalet, cot, cottage, den, gatehouse, haunt, house, hut, lair, retreat, shelter.
v accommodate, billet, board, deposit, dig, embed, entertain, file, get stuck, harbour, implant, lay, place, put, put on record, put up, quarter, register, room, set, shelter, sojourn, stay, stick, stop, submit.

lodge[2] n assemblage, association, branch, chapter, club, group, society.

lodger n boarder, guest, inmate, paying guest, renter, resident, roomer, tenant.

lodgings n abode, accommodation, apartments, billet, boarding, digs, dwelling, habitation, pad, quarters, residence, rooms, shelter.

lofty adj arrogant, condescending, dignified, disdainful, distinguished, elevated, esteemed, exalted, grand, haughty, high, high and mighty, illustrious, imperial, imposing, lordly, majestic, noble, patronizing, proud, raised, renowned, sky-high, snooty, soaring, stately, sublime, supercilious, superior, tall, towering.
antonyms humble, low(ly), modest.

log[1] n billet, block, bole, chunk, stump, timber, trunk.

log[2] n account, chart, daybook, diary, journal, listing, logbook, record, tally.
v book, chart, note, record, register, report, tally, write down, write in, write up.

logic n argument, argumentation, cogency, consistency, deduction, dialectic(s), ratiocination, rationale, rationality, reason, reasoning, sense, soundness.

logical adj clear, cogent, coherent, consistent, deducible, elenctic, judicious, necessary, obvious, pertinent, plausible, rational, reasonable, relevant, sensible, sound, valid, well-founded, well-grounded, well-organized, wise.
antonyms illogical, irrational.

logistics n co-ordination, engineering, management, masterminding, orchestration, organization, planning, plans, practicalities.

loins n genitalia, groin, manliness, potency, power, strength, virility.

loiter v dally, dawdle, delay, dilly-dally, hang around, idle, lag, linger, loaf, loll, lollygag, mooch, saunter, skulk, stroll.

loll v dangle, depend, droop, drop, flap, flop, hang, lean, loaf, lounge, recline, relax, sag, slouch, slump, sprawl.

lone adj deserted, individual, isolated, lonesome, one, only, separate, separated, single, sole, solitary, unaccompanied, unattached, unattended.

antonym accompanied.

loneliness *n* aloneness, desolation, forlornness, friendlessness, isolation, lonesomeness, seclusion, solitariness, solitude.

lonely *adj* abandoned, alone, apart, companionless, destitute, estranged, forlorn, forsaken, friendless, isolated, lonesome, outcast, out-of-the-way, remote, secluded, sequestered, solitary, unfrequented, uninhabited, untrodden.

loner *n* hermit, individualist, lone wolf, maverick, outsider, pariah, recluse, solitary, solitudinarian.

lonesome *adj* cheerless, companionless, deserted, desolate, dreary, forlorn, friendless, gloomy, isolated, lone, lonely, solitary.

long[1] *adj* dragging, elongated, expanded, expansive, extended, extensive, far-reaching, interminable, late, lengthy, lingering, long-drawn, marathon, prolonged, protracted, slow, spread out, stretched, sustained, tardy.

antonyms abbreviated, brief, fleeting, short.

as long as assuming, on condition that, only if, only while, provided (that), so long as, supposing, with the provision or proviso that, with (or on) the understanding that.

long[2] **(for** or **to)** *v* covet, crave, desire, dream of, hanker for, have a yen for, hunger after, itch for, lust after, pine for, thirst for, want, wish (for), yearn for.

long-drawn *adj* interminable, lengthy, long-winded, marathon, overextended, overlong, prolix, prolonged, protracted, spun out, tedious.

antonyms brief, curtailed.

longing *n* ambition, appetence, aspiration, coveting, craving, desire, hankering, hungering, itch, thirst, urge, wish, yearning, yen.

adj anxious, ardent, avid, craving, desirous, eager, hungry, languishing, pining, wishful, wistful, yearning.

long-lasting *adj* durable, enduring, long-lived, long-standing.

antonyms ephemeral, short-lived, transient.

long-lived *adj* abiding, continuing, durable, enduring, entrenched, established, evergreen, imperishable, lasting, lifelong, long-lasting, long-standing, prolonged, protracted.

antonyms brief, ephemeral, short-lived.

long-standing *adj* abiding, deep-rooted, enduring, established, fixed, hallowed, long-lived, time-honoured, traditional.

long-suffering *adj* easygoing, forbearing, forgiving, patient, placid, resigned, stoical, tolerant, uncomplaining.

long-winded *adj* circumlocutory, diffuse, discursive, garrulous, lengthy, long-drawn, overlong, prolix, prolonged, rambling, repetitious, tedious, verbose, voluble, wordy.

antonyms brief, compact, curt, terse.

look *v* appear, behold, cast a glance, check out, consider, contemplate, display, evidence, examine, exhibit, eye, gape, gawk, gawp, gaze, get a load of, glance, goggle, inspect, observe, ogle, peep, regard, rubberneck, scan, scrutinize, see, seem, seem to be, show, stare, steal a glance, study, survey, take a gander, take in, view, watch.

n air, appearance, aspect, bearing, complexion, countenance, demeanour, effect, examination, expression, eyeful, face, fashion, gander, gaze, glance, glimpse, guise, inspection, look-see, manner, mien, observation, once-over, peek, review, semblance, sight, survey, view.

look after attend to, care for, chaperone, guard, keep an eye on, mind, nurse, protect, serve, supervise, take care of, take charge of, tend, watch.

antonym neglect.

look back (on) hark back (to), mull over, muse, recall, recollect, reflect, reminisce, review, ruminate.

look down on contemn, despise, disdain, hold in contempt, look down one's nose at, misprize, pooh-pooh, scorn, sneer at, spurn, turn one's nose up at.

antonyms approve, esteem.

look for forage for, hunt, hunt for, hunt out, pursue, quest, search for, seek.

look forward to anticipate, await, count on, envisage, envision, expect, hope for, long for, look for, wait for.

look into check out, delve into, enquire about, examine, explore, fathom, follow up, go into, inspect, investigate, look over, plumb, probe, research, scrutinize, study.

look like resemble, take after.

look out be careful, be on the qui vive, beware, keep an eye out, keep one's eyes peeled (or skinned), pay attention, watch out.

look out on face, front, front on, give on (to), overlook.

look over cast an eye over, check, examine, flick through, give a once-over, inspect, look through, monitor, peruse, scan, view.

look to anticipate, await, count on, expect, have recourse to, hope for, reckon on, rely on.

look up[1] call on, drop by, drop in on, find, hunt for, look in on, pay a visit to, research, search for, seek out, stop by, track down, visit.

look up[2] ameliorate, come on, get better, improve, meliorate, perk up, pick up, progress, shape up.

look up to admire, esteem, have a high opinion of, honour, respect, revere.

look-alike *n* clone, dead ringer, doppelgänger, double, living image, replica, ringer, spit, spit and image, spitting image, twin.

look out *n* affair, beacon, business, citadel, concern, guard, post, problem, readiness, sentinel, sentry, tower, vedette, vigil, watch, watchman, watch tower, weather eye, worry.

loom *v* appear, bulk, dominate, emerge, hang over, hover, impend, materialize, menace, mount, overhang, overshadow, overtop, rise, soar, take shape, threaten, tower.

loop n arc, bend, circle, coil, convolution, curl, curve, eyelet, hoop, kink, loophole, noose, ring, spiral, turn, twirl, twist, whorl.

v bend, braid, circle, coil, connect, curl, curve round, fold, gird, join, knot, roll, spiral, turn, twist.

loophole n aperture, avoidance, escape, evasion, excuse, get-out, opening, plea, pretence, pretext, slot, subterfuge.

loose¹ adj baggy, crank, diffuse, disconnected, disordered, easy, floating, free, hanging, ill-defined, imprecise, inaccurate, indefinite, indistinct, inexact, insecure, loosened, movable, rambling, random, relaxed, released, shaky, slack, slackened, sloppy, unattached, unbound, unconfined, unfastened, unfettered, unrestricted, unsecured, untied, vague, wobbly.

antonyms close, compact, precise, strict, taut, tense, tight.

v absolve, detach, disconnect, disengage, ease, free, let go, liberate, loosen, release, set free, slacken, unbind, unbrace, unclasp, uncouple, undo, unfasten, unhand, unleash, unlock, unloose, unmoor, unpen, untie.

antonyms bind, fasten, fix, secure.

loose² adj abandoned, careless, debauched, disreputable, dissipated, dissolute, fast, heedless, immoral, imprudent, lax, lewd, libertine, licentious, negligent, profligate, promiscuous, rash, thoughtless, unchaste, unmindful, wanton.

antonyms strict, stringent, tight.

▲ confusable word lose.

loosen v deliver, detach, free, let go, let out, liberate, release, separate, set free, slacken, unbind, undo, unfasten, unloose, unloosen, unstick, untie.

antonym tighten.

loosen up ease up, go easy, lessen, let up, mitigate, moderate, relax, soften, unbend, weaken.

loot n boodle, booty, cache, goods, haul, plunder, prize, riches, spoils, swag.

v burglarize, despoil, maraud, pillage, plunder, raid, ransack, ravage, rifle, rob, sack.

lop v abscind, chop, clip, crop, curtail, cut, detach, dock, hack, prune, sever, shorten, trim, truncate.

lope v bound, canter, gallop, run, spring, stride.

lopsided adj askew, asquint, asymmetrical, awry, cockeyed, crooked, disproportionate, ill-balanced, off balance, one-sided, out of true, tilting, unbalanced, unequal, uneven, warped.

antonyms balanced, straight, symmetrical.

loquacious adj babbling, blathering, chattering, chatty, gabby, garrulous, gassy, gossipy, multiloquent, talkative, voluble, wordy.

antonyms succinct, taciturn, terse.

lord n baron, commander, count, daimio, duke, earl, governor, Herr, king, leader, liege, liege

lord, master, monarch, noble, nobleman, overlord, peer, potentate, prince, ruler, seigneur, seignior, sovereign, superior, suzerain, viscount.

lord it (over) act big, boss around, domineer, oppress, order around, pull rank (with), put on airs (with), repress, swagger, tyrannize.

lordly adj aristocratic, arrogant, authoritarian, condescending, despotic, dictatorial, dignified, disdainful, domineering, exalted, gracious, grand, haughty, high and mighty, high-handed, hoity-toity, imperial, imperious, lofty, majestic, masterful, noble, overbearing, patronizing, princely, proud, regal, stately, stuck-up, supercilious, swanky, tyrannical.

antonyms humble, low(ly), mean.

lore n beliefs, doctrine, erudition, experience, know-how, knowledge, learning, letters, mythos, saws, sayings, scholarship, schooling, teaching, traditions, wisdom.

lose v capitulate, come to grief, concede, default, dissipate, dodge, drop, elude, escape, evade, expend, fail, fall short, forfeit, forget, get the worst of, give (someone) the slip, leave behind, lose out on, misfile, mislay, misplace, miss, misspend, outdistance, outrun, outstrip, overtake, pass, pass up, shake off, slip away from, squander, stray from, suffer defeat, take a licking, throw off, wander from, waste, yield.

antonyms gain, make, win.

▲ confusable word loose.

loss n bereavement, cost, damage, death, debit, debt, decrease, defeat, deficiency, deficit, depletion, deprivation, destruction, detriment, disadvantage, disappearance, failure, forfeiture, harm, hurt, impairment, injury, losing, misfortune, privation, reduction, ruin, shortfall, shrinkage, squandering, waste, write-off.

antonyms benefit, gain.

at a loss at one's wits' end, baffled, bewildered, confounded, confused, disconcerted, floored, flummoxed, helpless, lost, nonplussed, perplexed, puzzled, resourceless, speechless, stuck, stumped, taken aback, thrown for a loop, thrown off.

losses n casualties, costs, damage, dead, death toll, disprofit, fatalities, missing, wounded.

lost adj abandoned, abolished, absent, absorbed, abstracted, adrift, annihilated, astray, baffled, bewildered, confused, consumed, damned, demolished, depraved, destroyed, devastated, disappeared, disoriented, dissipated, distracted, dreamy, engrossed, entranced, errant, exterminated, fallen, forfeited, frittered away, irreclaimable, misapplied, misdirected, mislaid, misplaced, missed, missing, misspent, misused, mystified, obliterated, off-course, off-track, perished, perplexed, preoccupied, puzzled, rapt, ruined, spellbound, squandered, stray(ed), unrecallable, unrecapturable, unrecoverable, untraceable, vanished, wandering, wasted, wayward, wiped out, wrecked.

antonym found.

lot[1] *n* assortment, batch, collection, consignment, crowd, group, quantity, set.

lot[2] *n* allowance, cut, dole, parcel, part, percentage, piece, portion, quota, ration, share.

lot[3] *n* accident, chance, destiny, doom, fate, fortune, hazard, luck, plight.

loth *see* **loath**

lotion *n* balm, cream, embrocation, fomentation, liniment, salve, solution.

lots *n* abundance, a great deal, heaps, oodles, plenty, scads, tons.

lottery *n* chance, draw, gamble, hazard, raffle, risk, sweepstake, tombola, toss-up, uncertainty, venture.

loud *adj* blaring, blatant, boisterous, booming, brash, brassy, brazen, clamorous, coarse, crass, crude, deafening, ear-piercing, earsplitting, flamboyant, flashy, garish, gaudy, glaring, loudmouthed, lurid, mouthy, noisy, obstreperous, offensive, ostentatious, piercing, raucous, resounding, rowdy, showy, sonorous, stentorian, strident, strong, tasteless, thundering, tumultuous, turbulent, uproarious, vehement, vocal, vociferous, vulgar.

antonyms low, quiet, soft.

loudly *adv* clamorously, deafeningly, fortissimo, lustily, noisily, resoundingly, shrilly, stridently, strongly, uproariously, vehemently, vigorously, vocally, vociferously.

antonyms quietly, softly.

loudmouth *n* bigmouth, blusterer, boaster, brag, braggadocio, braggart, swaggerer, windbag.

lounge *v* dawdle, idle, kill time, laze, lie around, lie back, loaf, loiter, loll, potter, recline, relax, slump, sprawl, take it easy, waste time.

lousy *adj* awful, bad, base, contemptible, crappy, despicable, dirty, hateful, inferior, lice-infested, lice-ridden, low, mean, measly, miserable, no good, pedicular, poor, rotten, second-rate, shoddy, slovenly, terrible, trashy, vicious, vile.

antonyms excellent, superb.

lout *n* bear, booby, boor, bumpkin, chucklehead, churl, clod, clown, dolt, gawk, hick, hobbledehoy, klutz, lubber, lummox, oaf, ox, yahoo.

loutish *adj* bearish, boorish, bungling, churlish, clodhopping, coarse, doltish, gawky, gross, ill-bred, ill-mannered, lubberly, lumpish, oafish, rough, stolid, swinish, thick, uncouth, unmannerly.

lovable *adj* adorable, amiable, attractive, captivating, charming, cuddly, delightful, enchanting, endearing, engaging, fetching, likeable, lovely, pleasing, sweet, taking, winning, winsome.

antonym hateful.

love *v* adore, adulate, appreciate, cherish, delight in, desire, dote on, enjoy, fancy, hold dear, idolize, like, prize, relish, savour, take

pleasure in, think the world of, treasure, want, worship.

antonyms detest, hate, loathe.

n adoration, adulation, affection, agape, amity, amorousness, appreciation, ardour, attachment, delight, devotion, enjoyment, enthusiasm, fondness, friendship, inclination, infatuation, keenness, liking, partiality, passion, rapture, regard, relish, soft spot, taste, tenderness, warmth, weakness, zeal.

antonyms detestation, hate, loathing.

for love as a favour, for free, for nothing, for pleasure, free, free of charge, gratis, voluntarily.

in love with besotted with, charmed with, crazy about, doting on, enamoured of, enraptured by, gaga over, hooked on, infatuated by, nuts about, smitten with, stuck on.

not for love or money by no means, never, not for anything, not for the world, on no condition, under no circumstances.

love affair *n* affair, amour, appreciation, enthusiasm, infatuation, intrigue, liaison, love, mania, passion, relationship, romance.

loveless *adj* cold, cold-hearted, disliked, forsaken, friendless, frigid, hard, heartless, icy, insensitive, lovelorn, passionless, unappreciated, uncherished, unfeeling, unfriendly, unloved, unloving, unresponsive, unvalued.

antonyms beloved, passionate.

lovely *adj* admirable, adorable, agreeable, amiable, attractive, beautiful, captivating, charming, comely, delightful, enchanting, engaging, enjoyable, exquisite, graceful, gratifying, handsome, idyllic, nice, pleasant, pleasing, pretty, sweet, taking, winning.

antonyms hideous, ugly, unlovely.

lovemaking *n* carnal knowledge, coitus, congress, copulation, courtship, dalliance, foreplay, gallantry, intercourse, intimacy, making out, mating, necking, petting, sexual intercourse, sexual relations, sexual union, venery, wooing.

lover[1] *n* admirer, amoroso, beau, beloved, boyfriend, Casanova, Don Juan, fiancé(e), flame, gigolo, girlfriend, inamorata, inamorato, Lothario, mistress, paramour, philanderer, stud, suitor, swain, sweetheart.

lover[2] *n* aficionado, buff, bug, devotee, enthusiast, fan, hound, nut.

lovesick *adj* desiring, infatuated, languishing, longing, lovelorn, pining, yearning.

loving *adj* affectionate, amative, amatory, amorous, ardent, cordial, dear, demonstrative, devoted, doting, fond, friendly, kind, passionate, solicitous, tender, warm, warm-hearted.

low *adj* abject, base, baseborn, below the belt, blue, browned off, cheap, coarse, common, contemptible, crude, dastardly, debilitated, deep, deficient, degraded, dejected, depleted, depraved, depressed, despicable, despondent, dirty, disgraceful, disheartened, dishonourable, disreputable, down, down in the dumps, downcast, dying, economical, exhausted, fed up, feeble, forlorn, frail, gloomy, glum, gross, humble, hushed, ignoble, ill, ill-bred, inadequate, inexpensive, inferior, insignificant, little, lowborn, low-grade, lowly, low-lying, meagre, mean, mediocre, meek, menial, miserable, moderate, modest, morose, muffled, muted, nasty, obscure, paltry, plain, plebeian, poor, prostrate, puny, quiet, reasonable, reduced, rough, rude, sad, scant, scurvy, second-rate, servile, shallow, shoddy, short, simple, sinking, small, soft, sordid, sparse, squat, stricken, stunted, subdued, substandard, sunken, trifling, unbecoming, undignified, unfair, unhappy, unpretentious, unrefined, unworthy, vile, vulgar, weak, whispered, worthless.

antonyms elevated, fair, high, lofty, noble.

low point all-time low, low-watermark, nadir, perigee.

lowborn *adj* base, common, humble, mean, plebeian, unexalted.

lowbrow *adj* crude, ignorant, rude, uncultivated, uncultured, uneducated, unlearned, unlettered, unrefined, unscholarly.

antonym highbrow.

lowdown *n* dope, gen, info, information, inside story, intelligence, news.

lower *adj* inferior, insignificant, junior, lesser, low-level, lowly, minor, secondary, second-class, smaller, subordinate, subservient, under, unimportant.

v abase, abate, belittle, condescend, couch, curtail, cut, debase, decrease, degrade, deign, demean, demolish, depress, devalue, diminish, discredit, disgrace, downgrade, drop, fall, humble, humiliate, lessen, let down, minimize, moderate, prune, raze, reduce, sink, slash, soften, stoop, submerge, take down, tone down.

antonyms elevate, increase, raise, rise.

lowering *adj* black, brooding, clouded, cloudy, dark, darkening, forbidding, foreboding, gloomy, glowering, grey, grim, heavy, impending, menacing, minatory, ominous, overcast, scowling, sullen, surly, threatening.

low-grade *adj* bad, cheapjack, inferior, poor, second-class, second-rate, substandard, third-rate.

antonyms good, quality.

low-key *adj* downbeat, laid-back, low-pitched, modulated, muffled, muted, quiet, restrained, slight, soft, softened, soft-sell, subdued, toned-down, understated.

lowly *adj* average, common, docile, dutiful, homespun, humble, ignoble, inferior, lowborn, mean, meek, mild, modest, obscure, ordinary, plain, plebeian, poor, proletarian, simple, submissive, subordinate, unassuming, unexalted, unpretentious.

antonyms lofty, noble.

low-minded *adj* coarse, crude, depraved, dirty, disgusting, filthy, foul, gross, immoral, indecent, obscene, rude, smutty, uncouth, vulgar.

antonym high-minded.

low-spirited *adj* apathetic, blue, browned off, dejected, depressed, despondent, discouraged, dispirited, down, down in the dumps, downhearted, fed up, gloomy, glum, heavy-hearted, low, miserable, moody, sad, unhappy.

antonyms cheerful, high-spirited.

loyal *adj* attached, constant, dependable, devoted, dutiful, faithful, honest, patriotic, sincere, staunch, steadfast, true, true-blue, true-hearted, trustworthy, trusty, unswerving, unwavering.

antonyms disloyal, traitorous.

loyalty *n* allegiance, constancy, dependability, devotion, faithfulness, fealty, fidelity, honesty, patriotism, reliability, sincerity, staunchness, steadfastness, true-heartedness, trueness, trustiness, trustworthiness.

antonyms disloyalty, treachery.

lubberly *adj* awkward, blundering, bungling, churlish, clodhopping, clownish, clumsy, coarse, crude, dense, doltish, gawky, heavy-handed, inept, klutzy, loutish, lumbering, lumpish, oafish, obtuse, thick, uncouth, ungainly.

lubricate *v* butter, dress, grease, lard, oil, smear, smooth, wax.

lucid *adj* beaming, bright, brilliant, clear, clear-cut, clear-headed, compos mentis, comprehensible, crystalline, diaphanous, distinct, effulgent, evident, explicit, glassy, gleaming, intelligible, limpid, luminous, obvious, pellucid, perspicuous, plain, pure, radiant, rational, reasonable, resplendent, sane, sensible, shining, sober, sound, translucent, transparent, vitreous.

antonyms dark, murky, unclear.

luck *n* accident, blessing, break, chance, destiny, fate, fluke, fortuity, fortune, godsend, good fortune, hap, happenstance, hazard, prosperity, serendipity, stroke, success, windfall.

antonym misfortune.

luckily *adv* felicitously, fortuitously, fortunately, haply, happily, opportunely, propitiously, providentially.

antonym unfortunately.

luckless *adj* calamitous, catastrophic, cursed, disastrous, doomed, fey, hapless, hopeless, ill-fated, ill-starred, inauspicious, jinxed, star-crossed, unfortunate, unhappy, unlucky, unpropitious, unsuccessful.

antonym lucky.

lucky *adj* advantageous, adventitious, auspicious, blessed, charmed, favoured, flukey, fortuitous, fortunate, opportune, propitious, prosperous, providential, serendipitous, successful, timely.

antonyms luckless, unlucky.

lucrative *adj* advantageous, fat, fecund, fertile, fruitful, gainful, money-making, paying, productive, profitable, remunerative, well-paid.

antonym unprofitable.

lucre *n* bread, dough, gain(s), mammon, money, moolah, pelf, profit, riches, spoils, velvet, wealth.

ludicrous *adj* absurd, amusing, burlesque, comic, comical, crazy, droll, farcical, funny, incongruous, laughable, nonsensical, odd, outlandish, preposterous, ridiculous, risible, silly, zany.

lug *v* carry, drag, haul, heave, hump, pull, schlep, tote, tow, yank.

luggage *n* baggage, bags, cases, gear, impedimenta, kit, paraphernalia, suitcases, things, trunks.

lugubrious *adj* dismal, doleful, dreary, funereal, gloomy, glum, melancholy, morose, mournful, sad, sepulchral, serious, sombre, sorrowful, woebegone, woeful.

antonyms cheerful, jovial, merry.

lukewarm *adj* apathetic, cool, half-hearted, indifferent, Laodicean, phlegmatic, tepid, unconcerned, unenthusiastic, uninterested, unresponsive.

lull *v* abate, allay, assuage, calm, cease, compose, decrease, diminish, dope, dwindle, ease off, hush, let up, lullaby, moderate, pacify, put to sleep, quell, quiet, quieten down, sedate, slacken, soothe, still, subdue, subside, tranquillize, wane.

antonym agitate.

n calm, calmness, hush, letup, pause, peace, quiet, respite, silence, stillness, tranquillity.

antonym agitation.

lumber¹ *n* beams, boards, lathing, logs, timbers, planks, posts, siding, wood.

lumber² *v* clump, galumph, plod, shamble, shuffle, stomp, stump, trudge, trundle, waddle.

lumbering *adj* awkward, blundering, bovine, bumbling, clumsy, elephantine, heavy, heavy-footed, hulking, lubberly, lumpish, massive, ponderous, ungainly, unwieldy.

antonyms agile, nimble.

luminary *n* big gun, big name, celebrity, dignitary, leader, leading light, lion, notable, personage, star, superstar, VIP, visiting fireman, worthy.

luminescent *adj* bright, effulgent, fluorescent, glowing, luminous, phosphorescent, radiant, shining.

luminous *adj* bright, brilliant, glowing, illuminated, lighted, lit, lucent, luminescent, luminiferous, lustrous, radiant, resplendent, shining, vivid.

lump¹ *n* ball, bulge, bump, bunch, cake, chump, chunk, clod, clot, cluster, cyst, dab, gob, gobbet, goose egg, group, growth, hunch, hunk, knob, mass, nodule, nub, nubbin, nugget, piece, protrusion, protuberance, spot, swelling, tuber, tumescence, tumour, wedge, wen.

v coalesce, collect, combine, consolidate, group, mass, unite.

lump² *v* bear (with), brook, endure, put up with, stand, stomach, suffer, swallow, take, tolerate.

lumpish *adj* awkward, boorish, bovine, bungling, clumsy, doltish, dull-witted, elephantine, gawky, heavy, lethargic, lumbering, oafish, obtuse, stolid, stupid, ungainly.

lumpy *adj* bumpy, bunched, clotted, curdled, grainy, granular, knotty, nodose, nodular, nodulose, uneven.

antonyms even, smooth.

lunacy *n* aberration, absurdity, craziness, dementia, derangement, folly, foolhardiness, foolishness, idiocy, imbecility, insanity, madness, mania, psychosis, senselessness, stupidity, tomfoolery.

antonym sanity.

lunatic *n* crackpot, kook, loony, madman, maniac, nut, nutcase, psychopath.

adj barmy, bonkers, bughouse, crackpot, crazy, cuckoo, daft, demented, deranged, harebrained, insane, irrational, loco, loony, mad, maniacal, meshuga, moonstruck, non-compos mentis, nuts, nutty, psychotic, squirrelly, touched, unhinged, wacko.

antonyms sane, sensible.

lunge *v* bound, charge, cut, dash, dive, fall (upon), grab, hit, jab, leap, pitch into, plunge, poke, pounce, set upon, stab, strike, thrust.

n charge, cut, jab, pass, pounce, spring, stab, swing, swipe, thrust.

lurch *v* heave, lean, list, pitch, reel, rock, roll, stagger, stumble, sway, tilt, totter, wallow, weave, welter.

lure *v* allure, attract, beckon, decoy, draw, ensnare, entice, inveigle, invite, lead on, seduce, tempt.

n allurement, attraction, bait, carrot, come-on, decoy, drawing card, enticement, hook, inducement, magnet, siren, song, temptation, train.

lurid *adj* ashen, bloody, disgusting, exaggerated, fiery, flaming, ghastly, glaring, glowering, gory, graphic, grim, grisly, gruesome, intense, livid, loud, macabre, melodramatic, pale, pallid, revolting, sallow, sanguine, savage, sensational, shocking, startling, unrestrained, violent, vivid, wan.

▲ *confusable word* livid.

lurk *v* crouch, hide, hide out, lie in wait, lie low, prowl, skulk, slink, sneak, snoop.

luscious *adj* appetizing, delectable, delicious, honeyed, juicy, luxuriant, luxurious, mouth-watering, palatable, rich, savoury, scrumptious, succulent, sweet, tasty, toothsome, yummy.

antonyms austere, dry.

lush *adj* abundant, dense, elaborate, extravagant, flourishing, grand, green, juicy, lavish, luxuriant, luxurious, opulent, ornate, overgrown, palatial, plush, prolific, rank, ripe, ritzy, succulent, sumptuous, superabundant, teeming, tender, verdant.

lust *n* appetence, appetite, avidity, carnality, concupiscence, covetousness, craving, cupidity, desire, greed, lasciviousness, lechery, lewdness, libido, licentiousness, longing, passion, prurience, salaciousness, sensuality, thirst, wantonness.

lust after crave, be greedy for, desire, have the hots for, hunger for, need, slaver over, thirst for, want, yearn for, yen for.

lustful *adj* carnal, concupiscent, craving, goatish, hankering, horny, lascivious, lecherous, lewd, libidinous, licentious, passionate, prurient, randy, raunchy, ruttish, sensual, unchaste, wanton.

lustily *adv* forcefully, hard, loudly, powerfully, robustly, stoutly, strongly, vigorously, with all one's might, with might and main.

antonym weakly.

lustiness *n* energy, haleness, hardihood, hardiness, health, healthiness, power, robustness, stoutness, strength, sturdiness, toughness, vigour, virility.

lustre *n* brightness, brilliance, burnish, dazzle, distinction, effulgence, fame, gleam, glint, glitter, glory, gloss, glow, honour, illustriousness, lambency, luminousness, prestige, radiance, renown, resplendence, sheen, shimmer, shine, sparkle.

lustrous *adj* bright, burnished, dazzling, gleaming, glistening, glittering, glossy, glowing, lambent, luminous, radiant, shimmering, shining, shiny, sparkling.

antonyms dull, lacklustre, matt.

lusty *adj* blooming, brawny, energetic, enthusiastic, gutsy, hale, healthy, hearty, in fine fettle, muscular, powerful, red-blooded, robust, rugged, stalwart, stout, strapping, strong, sturdy, vigorous, virile.

antonyms effete, weak.

luxuriance *n* abundance, copiousness, denseness, excess, exuberance, fecundity, fertility, lavishness, lushness, profusion, rankness, richness, sumptuousness.

luxuriant *adj* abundant, ample, baroque, copious, dense, elaborate, excessive,

extravagant, exuberant, fancy, fecund, fertile, festooned, flamboyant, florid, flowery, lavish, lush, opulent, ornate, overflowing, plenteous, plentiful, prodigal, productive, profuse, prolific, rank, rich, riotous, rococo, sumptuous, superabundant, teeming, thriving.

antonyms barren, infertile.

luxuriate *v* abound, bask, bloom, burgeon, delight, enjoy, flourish, grow, have a ball, indulge, live high off the hog, live the life of Riley, prosper, relish, revel, savour, thrive, wallow.

luxurious *adj* comfortable, costly, decadent, deluxe, epicurean, expensive, hedonistic, lavish, magnificent, opulent, pampered, plush, rich, ritzy, self-indulgent, sensual, splendid, sumptuous, sybaritic, voluptuous, well-appointed.

antonyms ascetic, austere, economical, frugal, scant(y), spartan.

luxury *n* affluence, bliss, comfort, decadence, delight, dolce vita, enjoyment, extra, extravagance, fleshpots, frill, gratification, hedonism, indulgence, milk and honey, non-essential, opulence, pleasure, richness, satisfactiion, splendour, sumptuousness, treat, voluptuousness, well-being.

antonym essential.

lying *adj* deceitful, dishonest, dissembling, double-dealing, duplicitous, false, guileful, mendacious, perfidious, treacherous, two-faced, untruthful.

antonyms honest, truthful.

n deceit, dishonesty, dissimulation, double-dealing, duplicity, fabrication, falsity, fibbing, guile, mendacity, perjury, prevarication, untruthfulness.

antonyms honesty, truthfulness.

lyrical *adj* carried away, ecstatic, effusive, emotional, enthusiastic, expressive, impassioned, inspired, musical, passionate, poetic, rapturous, rhapsodic.

lyrics *n* book, libretto, text, words.

M

macabre *adj* cadaverous, deathlike, deathly, dreadful, eerie, frightening, frightful, ghastly, ghostly, ghoulish, grim, grisly, gruesome, hideous, horrible, horrid, morbid, spooky, uncanny, weird.

macerate¹ *v* chew (up), liquefy, mash, pulp, soak, soften, steep.

macerate² *v* attenuate, consume, emaciate, thin, waste (away).

Machiavellian *adj* amoral, artful, astute, calculating, crafty, cunning, deceitful, designing, double-dealing, foxy, guileful, intriguing, opportunist, perfidious, scheming, shrewd, sly, underhand, unscrupulous, wily.

machinate *v* conspire, contrive, design, devise, engineer, finagle, hatch, intrigue, manoeuvre, plan, plot, rig, scheme, wangle.

machination *n* artifice, cabal, conspiracy, design, device, dodge, finagling, intrigue, manoeuvre, plot, ploy, ruse, scheme, shenanigans, stratagem, trick, trickery.

machine *n* agency, agent, apparatus, appliance, automaton, automobile, contraption, contrivance, device, engine, gadget, instrument, machinery, mechanism, motor, organization, robot, set-up, structure, system, tool.

machine gun *n* Bren gun, gatling gun, mitrailleur, mitrailleuse, pompom, submachine gun, Tommy gun.

machinery *n* agency, apparatus, channels, enginery, engines, equipment, gear, instruments, machines, mechanism, organization, procedure, structure, system, tools, works.

mad *adj* abandoned, aberrant, angry, avid, bananas, barmy, batty, berserk, boisterous, bonkers, cracked, crackers, crackpot, crazed, crazy, cuckoo, daft, delirious, demented, deranged, distracted, dotty, energetic, enraged, exasperated, excited, fanatical, foolhardy, foolish, frantic, frenetic, frenzied, fuming, furious, harebrained, impassioned, imprudent, in a huff, incensed, inflamed, infuriated, insane, irate, ireful, irrational, irritated, keen, livid, loony, ludicrous, lunatic, madcap, mental, moonstruck, non compos mentis, nonsensical, not all there, nuts, nutty, off one's head, off one's nut, off one's rocker, off one's trolley, out of one's mind, overzealous, possessed, preposterous, psychotic, rabid, raging, raving, reckless, resentful, riotous, round the bend, screwball, screwy, senseless, touched, unbalanced, uncontrolled, unhinged, unreasonable, unrestrainable, unrestrained, unsound, unstable, unwise, wacky, wild, wrathful.

antonyms lucid, rational, sane.

mad about crazy about, devoted to, enamoured of, enthusiastic about, fond of, gaga over, gone on, hooked on, infatuated with, keen on, nuts about, wild about.

madcap *adj* birdbrained, crazy, daredevil, flighty, foolhardy, foolish, harebrained, heedless, hot-headed, ill-advised, impetuous, imprudent, impulsive, lively, rash, reckless, silly, stupid, thoughtless, wild.

madden *v* annoy, craze, dement, derange, enrage, exasperate, incense, inflame, infuriate, irritate, provoke, unhinge, upset, vex.

antonyms calm, pacify, please.

made-up *adj* artificial, fabricated, fairy-tale, false, fictional, imaginary, invented, make-believe, mythical, specious, trumped-up, unreal, untrue.

madhouse *n* asylum, Babel, bedlam, chaos, disarray, disorder, funny farm, loony bin, nuthouse, pandemonium, snake pit, turmoil, uproar.

madly *adv* absurdly, crazily, deliriously, dementedly, desperately, devotedly, distractedly, energetically, exceedingly, excessively, excitedly, extremely, fanatically, foolishly, frantically, frenziedly, furiously, hastily, hurriedly, hysterically, insanely, intensely, irrationally, like mad, ludicrously, nonsensically, passionately, quickly, rabidly, rapidly, recklessly, senselessly, speedily, to distraction, unreasonably, violently, wildly.

madman *n* bedlamite, crackpot, fanatic, kook, loony, lunatic, maniac, mental case, nut, nutcase, psycho, psychopath, psychotic, screwball.

madness *n* abandon, aberration, absurdity, anger, ardour, craze, craziness, daftness, delusion, dementia, demoniacism, derangement, distraction, enthusiasm, exasperation, excitement, fanaticism, folly, fondness, foolhardiness, foolishness, frenzy, furor, fury, infatuation, insanity, intoxication, ire, keenness, lunacy, lycanthropy, mania, monomania, moon-madness, nonsense, nuttiness, passion, preposterousness, psychopathy, psychosis, rage, raving, riot, unrestraint, uproar, wackiness, wildness, wrath, zeal.

antonym sanity.

maelstrom *n* agitation, bedlam, chaos, Charybdis, confusion, disorder, mess, pandemonium, swirl, tumult, turmoil, uproar, vortex, whirlpool.

maestro *n* expert, genius, master, prodigy, teacher, virtuoso, wizard.

magazine¹ *n* fanzine, gazette, journal, monthly, paper, periodical, quarterly, rag, review, weekly.

magazine² *n* ammunition dump, arsenal, depot, ordnance, store, storehouse.

magic *n* allurement, black art, charm, charms, conjuring, conjury, diablerie, enchantment, entrancement, fascination, glamour, hocus-pocus, hoodoo, illusion, jugglery, legerdemain, magnetism, marvel, medicine, miracle, necromancy, occultism, sleight of hand, sorcery, sortilege, spell, spells, trickery, voodoo, witchcraft, witchery, wizardry, wonder work.

adj alluring, bewitching, charismatic, charming, enchanting, entrancing, fascinating, hermetic, magical, magnetic, marvellous, miraculous, sorcerous, spellbinding, spellful.

magician *n* adept, conjurer, enchanter, enchantress, expert, genius, illusionist, maestro, mage, magus, marvel, master, miracle worker, necromancer, prestidigitator, prodigy, sorcerer, spellbinder, thaumaturge, theurgist, trickster, virtuoso, warlock, whiz, witch, witch doctor, wizard, wonder worker.

magisterial *adj* arrogant, assertive, authoritarian, authoritative, bossy, commanding, despotic, dictatorial, domineering, high-handed, imperious, lordly, masterful, overbearing, peremptory.

magistrate *n* aedile, arbitrator, bailiff, bailie, J.P., judge, jurat, justice, justice of the peace, stipendiary, tribune.

magnanimity *n* altruism, beneficence, big-heartedness, bountifulness, charitableness, charity, generosity, high-mindedness, largesse, liberality, munificence, nobility, open-handedness, philanthropy, selflessness, unselfishness.

antonym meanness.

magnanimous *adj* altruistic, beneficent, big, big-hearted, bountiful, charitable, forgiving, free, generous, great-hearted, handsome, high-minded, kind, kindly, large-hearted, large-minded, liberal, munificent, noble, open-handed, philanthropic, selfless, tolerant, ungrudging, unselfish, unstinting.

antonyms mean, paltry, petty.

magnate *n* aristocrat, baron, bashaw, big cheese, big noise, big shot, big wheel, bigwig, captain of industry, chief, fat cat, grandee, leader, magnifico, merchant, mogul, nabob, noble, notable, personage, plutocrat, prince, tycoon, VIP.

magnet *n* attraction, attractor, bait, draw, enticement, lodestone, lure, pull, solenoid.

antonym repellent.

magnetic *adj* absorbing, alluring, attractive, captivating, charismatic, charming, enchanting, engrossing, entrancing, fascinating, gripping, hypnotic, irresistible, mesmerizing, seductive.

antonyms repellent, repugnant, repulsive.

magnetism *n* allure, appeal, attraction, attractiveness, charisma, charm, draw, drawing power, enchantment, fascination, grip, hypnotism, lure, magic, mesmerism, power, pull, seductiveness, spell.

magnification *n* aggrandizement, amplification, augmentation, blowup, boost, buildup, deepening, dilation, enhancement, enlargement, exaggeration, expansion, extolment, heightening, increase, inflation, intensification, lionization.

antonyms diminution, reduction.

magnificence *n* brilliance, glory, gorgeousness, grandeur, grandiosity, impressiveness, luxuriousness, luxury, majesty, nobility, opulence, pomp, resplendence, splendour, stateliness, sublimity, sumptuousness.

antonyms modesty, plainness, simplicity.

magnificent *adj* august, brilliant, elegant, elevated, exalted, excellent, fine, glorious, gorgeous, grand, grandiose, imposing, impressive, lavish, luxurious, majestic, noble, opulent, outstanding, plush, posh, princely, regal, resplendent, rich, ritzy, splendid, splendiferous, stately, sublime, sumptuous, superb, superior, swanky, transcendent.

antonyms humble, modest, plain, simple.

magnify *v* aggrandize, aggravate, amplify, augment, blow up, boost, build up, deepen, dilate, dramatize, enhance, enlarge, exaggerate, expand, glorify, greaten, heighten, increase, inflate, intensify, lionize, overdo, overemphasize, overestimate, overplay, overrate, overstate, play up, praise.

antonyms belittle, play down.

magniloquence *n* bombast, euphuism, fustian, grandiloquence, loftiness, orotundity, pomposity, pretentiousness, rhetoric, turgidity.

antonyms simplicity, straightforwardness.

magniloquent *adj* bombastic, declamatory, elevated, euphuistic, exalted, fustian, grandiloquent, grandiose, high-falutin, high-flown, high-sounding, lofty, orotund, overblown, pompous, pretentious, rhetorical, sonorous, stilted, turgid.

antonyms simple, straightforward.

magnitude *n* amount, amplitude, bigness, brightness, bulk, capacity, consequence, dimensions, eminence, enormousness, expanse, extent, grandeur, greatness, hugeness, immensity, importance, intensity, largeness, mark, mass, measure, moment, note, proportions, quantity, significance, size, space, strength, vastness, volume, weight.

magnum opus chef d'oeuvre, masterpiece, master work, pièce de résistance.

maid *n* abigail, bonne, damsel, dresser, femme de chambre, fille de chambre, gentlewoman, girl, handmaid, housemaid, lady's maid, lass, maiden, maid of all work, maid servant, miss, nymph, servant, serving maid, soubrette, tirewoman, virgin, waitress, wench.

maiden *n* damosel, damsel, demoiselle, girl, lass, mademoiselle, maid, miss, nymph, spinster, virgin, wench.

adj chaste, female, first, fresh, inaugural, initial, initiatory, intact, introductory, new, pure, spinster, unbroached, uncaptured, undefiled, unmarried, unpolluted, untapped, untried, unused, unwed, virgin, virginal.

antonyms defiled, deflowered, unchaste.

maidenly *adj* becoming, chaste, decent, decorous, demure, gentle, girlish, modest, proper, pure, reserved, seemly, undefiled, vestal, virginal, virtuous.

antonym immodest.

mail *n* correspondence, delivery, letters, packages, parcels, post.

v airmail, courier, dispatch, forward, post, send (off), ship.

maim *v* cripple, disable, hack, haggle, hamstring, hurt, impair, incapacitate, injure, lame, mangle, mar, mutilate, savage, wound.

antonyms heal, repair.

main¹ *adj* basic, capital, cardinal, central, chief, critical, crowning, crucial, dominant, essential, extensive, first, foremost, general, great, greatest, head, key, leading, necessary, outstanding, paramount, particular, predominant, pre-eminent, premier, primary, prime, principal, ruling, staple, supreme, vital.

antonyms minor, unimportant.

main² *n* force, might, potency, power, puissance, strength, vigour.

antonym weakness.

main³ *n* aqueduct, cable, channel, conduit, duct, line, pipe, pipeline.

mainly *adv* above all, as a rule, chiefly, especially, for the most part, generally, in general, in the main, largely, mostly, on the whole, overall, predominantly, primarily, principally, substantially, usually.

mainspring *n* cause, driving force, fountainhead, generator, incentive, inspiration, motivation, motive, origin, prime mover, source, wellspring.

mainstay *n* anchor, backbone, bulwark, buttress, linchpin, pillar, prop, reinforcement, support.

mainstream *adj* accepted, average, conventional, established, general, normal, orthodox, received, regular, standard.

antonyms heterodox, peripheral.

maintain *v* advocate, affirm, allege, argue, assert, asseverate, aver, avouch, avow, back, believe, care for, carry on, champion, claim, conserve, contend, continue, declare, defend, feed and clothe, fight for, finance, hold, insist, keep, keep up, look after, make good, nurture, observe, perpetuate, practise, preserve, profess, prolong, provide for, retain, run, stand by, state, supply, support, sustain, take care of, uphold, vindicate.

antonyms deny, neglect, oppose.

maintenance *n* aliment, alimony, allowance, backing, care, conservation, continuance, continuation, defence, keep, keeping, livelihood, living, nurture, perpetuation, preservation, prolongation, protection, provision, repairs, retainment, subsistence, supply, support, sustainment, sustenance, upkeep.

antonym neglect.

majestic *adj* august, awe-inspiring, awesome, dignified, distinguished, elevated, exalted, grand, grandiose, imperial, imperious, imposing, impressive, kingly, lofty, magisterial, magnificent, monumental, noble, pompous, princely, queenly, regal, resplendent, royal, splendid, stately, sublime, superb.

antonyms unimportant, unimpressive.

majesty *n* augustness, awe-inspiring, awesomeness, dignity, exaltedness, glory, grandeur, grandiosity, impressiveness, kingliness, loftiness, magnificence, nobility, pomp, queenliness, regalness, resplendence, resplendent, royalty, splendour, state, stateliness, sublimity.

antonyms unimportance, unimpressiveness.

major *adj* better, bigger, chief, critical, crucial, elder, grave, great, greater, higher, important, key, keynote, larger, leading, main, notable, older, outstanding, pre-eminent, principal, radical, senior, serious, significant, superior, supreme, vital, weighty.

antonym minor.

majority *n* adulthood, better part, bulk, lion's share, manhood, mass, maturity, most, plurality, preponderance, seniority, superiority, the many, womanhood, years of discretion.

antonyms childhood, minority.

make¹ *v* coerce, compel, constrain, dragon (into), drive, force, impel, induce, oblige, press, pressure (into), prevail upon, require.

make² *v* accomplish, acquire, act, add up to, amount to, appoint, arrange, arrive at, assemble, assign, attain, be, become, beget, blaze, bring about, build, calculate, carry out, carve (out), catch, cause (to), clear, complete, compose, conclude, constitute, construct, contract, contribute, convert, craft, create, crochet, design, designate, do, draw (up), earn, effect, elect, embody, enact, engage in, engender, enter upon, erect, establish, estimate, execute, fabricate, fashion, fix, force, forge, form, frame, gain, gauge, generate, get, give rise to, inaugurate, install, invest, judge, knit, lead to, manufacture, meet, mould, net, nominate, occasion, ordain, originate, pass, perform, prepare, produce, put into effect, put together, raise, reach, reckon, render, result in, sew, shape, submit, suppose, synthesize, take in, think of as, tie, total, trace, turn, weave, win, write out (or up).

antonyms dismantle, lose.

n brand, build, character, composition, constitution, construction, cut, designation, disposition, form, humour, kind, make-up, manner, manufacture, mark, model, nature, shape, sort, stamp, structure, style, temper, temperament, texture, type, variety.

make believe act as if, dream, enact, fantasize, feign, imagine, make like, play, play-act, pretend, role-play, sham.

make do cope, get along, get by, improvise, make out, make shift, make the best (of) things, manage, muddle through, scrape by, survive.

make eyes at come on to, flirt with, give (someone) the come-on, leer at, make sheep's eyes at, ogle.

make for aim for, be conducive to, contribute to, facilitate, favour, forward, further, head for, promote, result in.

make fun of deride, lampoon, laugh at, laugh to scorn, make a laughingstock of, make sport of, mock, parody, poke fun at, rag, razz, rib, ride, ridicule, roast, satirize, scoff at, send up, sneer at, take off, taunt.

antonym praise.

make inroads into consume, deplete, eat away at, eat into, eat up, encroach upon, get on with, lessen, make a dent in, make progress with.

antonym add to.

make it arrive, come through, get on, get there, make good, pass, prosper, pull through, reach one's goal, succeed, survive.

antonym fail.

make love bill and coo, canoodle, copulate, cuddle, embrace, enjoy, go to bed, make out, neck, pet, romance, sleep together, smooch.

make merry carouse, celebrate, feast, frolic, junket, kick up one's heels, paint the town red, revel, whoop it up.

antonym mourn.

make no difference be all the same, be six of one and half a dozen of the other, be immaterial, count for nothing, cut no ice, have no effect.

antonym matter.

make off abscond, beat a hasty retreat, bolt, clear off, clear out, cut and run, decamp, depart, flee, fly, leave, run away, run for it, run off, take to one's heels.

make off with abduct, appropriate, carry off, filch, kidnap, make away with, pilfer, pinch, purloin, run away with, run off with, steal, swipe, walk off with.

antonym bring.

make one's mark be a hit, get on, go over big, make good, make it, make it big, make the big time, prosper, succeed.

antonym fail.

make out¹ assert, claim, convey the impression, crack up, fob off (as), imply, let on, make as if, pass off (as), pretend, represent, show.

antonym fail.

make out² comprehend, decipher, descry, detect, discern, distinguish, espy, fathom, figure out, follow, grasp, make head or tail of, make sense of, perceive, recognize, see, understand, work out.

make out³ cope, fare, get along, manage, prosper, succeed, survive, thrive.

make out⁴ complete, draw up, fill out (or in), inscribe, write (out).

make sense of apprehend, comprehend, fathom, figure out, grasp, make head or tail of, make anything of, make out, understand.

make tracks beat it, dash, dash off, depart, disappear, get a move on, get going, go, hit the road, hurry, leave, make off, scram, set out, split, take off.

antonym stay put.

make up¹ arrange, assemble, coin, collect, complement, complete, compose, comprise, concoct, constitute, construct, cook up, create, devise, dream up, fabricate, feign, fill out, form, formulate, frame, hatch, invent, meet, originate, parcel, prepare, put together, repair, supplement, supply, trump up, write.

make up² bury the hatchet, call it quits, come round, come to terms, forgive and forget, let bygones be bygones, make peace, mend one's fences, reconcile, patch things up, settle differences, shake hands, smooth things over.

make up for atone for, balance, compensate for, expiate, make amends for, make restitution for, offset, recompense, redeem, redress.

make up one's mind choose, decide, determine, resolve, settle.

antonym waver.

make up to befriend, butter up, chat up, cosy up to, court, curry favour with, fawn on, flatter, flirt with, ingratiate oneself with, make overtures to, toady to, woo.

make-believe *n* charade, dream, fantasy, imagination, play-acting, pretence, role-playing, unreality.

antonym reality.

adj dream, fairy-tale, fake, fantasized, fantasy, feigned, fictional, imaginary, imagined, made-up, mock, pretend, pretended, sham, simulated, unreal.

antonym real.

maker *n* architect, artist, author, builder, constructor, contriver, creator, director, fabricator, framer, manufacturer, originator, producer.

antonym destroyer.

makeshift *adj* expedient, extemporaneous, haywire, improvised, jerry-built, make-do, provisional, rough and ready, stopgap, substitute, temporary.

antonyms finished, permanent.

n band-aid, expedient, improvisation, shift, stopgap, substitute.

make-up¹ *n* cosmetics, greasepaint, maquillage, paint, powder, war paint.

make-up² *n* arrangement, assembly, build, cast, character, complexion, composition, configuration, constitution, construction, disposition, figure, form, format, formation, make, nature, organization, stamp, structure, style, temper, temperament.

making n assemblage, assembly, building, composition, construction, creation, fabrication, forging, manufacture, modelling, moulding, production.
antonym dismantling.

in the making budding, coming, developing, embryonic, emergent, growing, nascent, potential, up and coming.

makings n beginnings, capability, capacity, earnings, gains, income, ingredients, materials, possibilities, potential, potentiality, proceeds, profits, promise, qualities, returns, revenue, takings.

maladjusted adj alienated, confused, disturbed, estranged, hung-up, muddled, neurotic, unbalanced, unstable.
antonym well-adjusted.

maladministration n blundering, bungling, corruption, dishonesty, incompetence, inefficiency, malfeasance, malpractice, malversation, misconduct, misfeasance, misgovernment, mismanagement, misrule.

maladroit adj all thumbs, awkward, bungling, butterfingered, clumsy, gauche, gawky, graceless, inelegant, inept, inexpert, ungainly, unhandy, unskilful, untoward.
antonyms adroit, tactful.

malady n affliction, ailment, breakdown, complaint, disease, disorder, distemper, illness, indisposition, infirmity, malaise, sickness.
antonym health.

malaise n agitation, angst, anxiety, culture shock, depression, discomfort, disquiet, distemper, doldrums, enervation, future shock, illness, indisposition, lassitude, melancholy, sadness, sickness, unease, uneasiness, weakness, weltschnerg.
antonyms happiness, well-being.

malapropos adj ill-timed, inapposite, inappropriate, inapt, inexpedient, inopportune, misapplied, tactless, uncalled-for, unseemly, unsuitable, untimely.
antonyms appropriate, tactful.
adv inapposdely, inappropriately, inaptly, inopportunely, tactlessly, unseasonably, unsuitably.
antonyms appropriately, tactfully.

malcontent adj bellyaching, complaining, disaffected, discontented, disgruntled, dissatisfied, dissentient, factious, grouchy, grousing, grumbling, ill-disposed, morose, negative, rebellious, resentful, restive, unhappy, unsatisfied.
antonym contented.
n agitator, bellyacher, complainer, grouch, grouser, grumbler, mischief-maker, moaner, rebel, troublemaker.

male adj bull, cock, manlike, manly, masculine, virile.
antonym female.
n boy, back, bull, cock, daddy, dog, father, hombre, homme, man.
antonym female.

malediction n anathema, anathematization, curse, damnation, damning, denunciation, execration, imprecation, malison.
antonyms blessing, praise.

malefactor n convict, criminal, crook, culprit, delinquent, evildoer, felon, lawbreaker, miscreant, offender, outlaw, public enemy, sinner, transgressor, villain, wrongdoer.

maleficent adj baleful, baneful, deleterious, destructive, detrimental, evil, harmful, hurtful, injurious, malefactory, malefic, malign, malignant, noxious, pernicious, threatening.
antonyms beneficent, harmless.

malevolence n bitterness, hate, hatred, hostility, ill will, malice, maliciousness, malignancy, malignity, rancour, spite, spitefulness, vengefulness, venom, viciousness, vindictiveness.
antonym benevolence.

malevolent adj baleful, bitter, despiteful, evil-minded, hostile, ill-natured, malicious, malign, malignant, pernicious, rancorous, spiteful, vengeful, venomous, vicious, vindictive, vitriolic.
antonym benevolent.

malformation n abnormality, crookedness, deformity, distortion, irregularity, misshapenness, warp, warpedness, warping.

malformed adj abnormal, bent, contorted, crooked, deformed, distorted, imperfect, irregular, misshapen, twisted, warped.
antonym perfect.

malfunction n breakdown, defect, failure, fault, flaw, glitch, impairment.
v break down, fail, go wrong, misbehave.

malice n animosity, animus, bad blood, bitterness, enmity, hate, hatred, ill will, malevolence, maliciousness, malignity, rancour, spite, spitefulness, spleen, vengefulness, venom, viciousness, vindictiveness.
antonym kindness.

malicious adj baleful, bitchy, bitter, catty, evil-minded, hateful, ill-natured, injurious, malevolent, malignant, mean, mischievous, pernicious, rancorous, resentful, spiteful, vengeful, venomous, vicious.
antonyms kind, thoughtful.

malign adj bad, baleful, baneful, deleterious, destructive, evil, harmful, hostile, hurtful, injurious, malevolent, malicious, malignant, noxious, pernicious, poisonous, venomous, vicious, wicked.
antonym benign.
v abuse, bad-mouth, blacken the name of, calumniate, cast aspersion on, cast a slur on, defame, denigrate, derogate, disparage, harm, injure, libel, revile, run down, slander, smear, traduce, vilify, vilipend.
antonym praise.

malignant adj baleful, cancerous, cankered, dangerous, deadly, destructive, devilish, evil, fatal, harmful, hostile, hurtful, inimical, injurious, irremediable, malevolent, malicious, malign, pernicious, spiteful, uncontrollable, venomous, vicious, viperous, virulent.

antonyms harmless, kind.

malignity *n* animosity, animus, bad blood, balefulness, banefulness, deadliness, destructiveness, harmfulness, hate, hatred, hostility, hurtfulness, ill will, malevolence, malice, maliciousness, perniciousness, rancour, spite, spitefulness, vengefulness, venom, viciousness, vindictiveness, virulence, wickedness.

antonyms harmlessness, kindness.

malinger *v* dodge, goof off, goldbrick, lie down on the job, loaf, shirk, slack.

antonym toil.

malingerer *n* dodger, goldbricker, goof-off, lead-swinger, loafer, shirker, slacker, truant.

antonym toiler.

malleable *adj* adaptable, biddable, compliant, conformable, ductile, governable, impressionable, manageable, plastic, pliable, pliant, soft, tractable, tractile, workable, yielding.

antonyms intractable, unworkable.

malnutrition *n* anorexia (nervosa), cachexia, hunger, inanition, starvation, undernourishment.

antonym nourishment.

malodorous *adj* evil-smelling, fetid, foul-smelling, mephitic, miasmal, miasmatic, miasmic, nauseating, noisome, noxious, offensive, putrid, rank, reeking, smelly, stinking.

antonym sweet-smelling.

malpractice *n* abuse, dereliction, malfeasance, malversation, misbehaviour, misconduct, misfeasance, mismanagement, misuse, negligence.

maltreat *v* abuse, bully, damage, harm, hurt, ill-treat, ill-use, injure, mistreat, misuse, molest.

antonym care for.

mammoth *adj* astronomical, Brobdingnagian, colossal, elephantine, enormous, formidable, gargantuan, giant, gigantic, herculean, huge, immense, jumbo, leviathan, massive, mighty, monumental, mountainous, prodigious, stupendous, titanic, vast.

antonym small.

man[1] *n* adult, beau, bloke, body, boyfriend, cat, chap, dude, fellow, gentleman, guy, human, human being, husband, individual, lover, male, partner, person, spouse.

v crew, fill, garrison, occupy, operate, people, staff, take charge of.

man in the street average person, common man, Everyman, John Doe, John Q. Public, little guy, ordinary Joe, Tom Dick or Harry.

man of fashion buck, dandy, dude, homme du monde, man about town, swell, toff.

to a man bar one, every one, nem. con., none, one and all, unanimously, without exception.

man[2] *n* attendant, employee, follower, hand, henchman, hireling, manservant, retainer, servant, soldier, subject, subordinate, valet, vassal, worker, workman.

man[3] *n* Homo sapiens, humanity, humankind, human race, humans, mankind, mortals, people.

manacle *v* bind, chain, check, clap in irons, confine, constrain, curb, fetter, gyve, hamper, hamstring, handcuff, hogtie, inhibit, put in chains (or irons), restrain, shackle, trammel.

antonym unshackle.

manacles *n* bonds, bracelets, chains, fetters, gyves, handcuffs, irons, shackles.

manage *v* accomplish, administer, arrange, bring about, bring off, carry on, come through, command, concert, conduct, contrive, control, cope, cope with, deal with, direct, dominate, effect, engineer, fare, get along, get by, get on, govern, guide, hack, handle, influence, make do, make out, make shift, manipulate, muddle through, operate, oversee, pilot, ply, preside over, regulate, rule, run, solicit, stage-manage, steer, steward, succeed, superintend, supervise, survive, train, use, wield.

antonym fail.

manageable *adj* amenable, biddable, compliant, controllable, convenient, doable, docile, governable, handy, pliant, practicable, submissive, tameable, tractable, wieldable, wieldy, workable, yielding.

antonym unmanageable.

management *n* administration, board, bosses, care, charge, command, conduct, control, direction, directorate, directors, employers, executive, executives, governance, government, governors, guidance, handling, managers, manipulation, operation, responsibility, rule, running, stewardship, superintendence, supervision, supervisors.

manager *n* administrator, big boss, boss, captain, conductor, controller, director, executive, factor, gaffer, governor, head, impresario, master, organizer, overseer, proprietor, steward, straw boss, superintendent, supervisor.

mandate *n* authorization, authority, charge, command, commission, decree, directive, edict, fiat, full power, injunction, instruction(s), licence, order, precept, rescript, right, sanction, ukase, warrant.

mandatory *adj* a must, binding, compulsory, de rigueur, imperative, necessary, obligatory, prescriptive, required, requisite.

antonym optional.

manful *adj* bold, brave, courageous, daring, determined, gallant, hardy, heroic, indomitable, intrepid, lion-hearted, manly, noble, noble-minded, plucky, powerful, resolute, stalwart, steadfast, stout, stout-hearted, strong, unflinching, valiant, vigorous.

antonyms half-hearted, timid.

mangle *v* butcher, crush, cut, deform, destroy, disfigure, distort, hack, haggle, lacerate, maim, mar, maul, mutilate, rend, ruin, spoil, tear, twist, wreck.

mangy *adj* dirty, grotty, mean, moth-eaten, ratty, scabby, scruffy, seedy, shabby, shoddy, squalid, tatty.

antonyms clean, neat, spruce.

manhandle *v* carry, haul, heave, knock around, lift, maltreat, manoeuvre, maul, mishandle, mistreat, misuse, paw, push around, rough up, shove.

manhood *n* adulthood, bravery, courage, determination, firmness, fortitude, hardihood, machismo, manfulness, manliness, masculinity, maturity, mettle, resolution, spirit, strength, valour, virility.

antonym timidness.

mania *n* aberration, compulsion, craving, craze, craziness, delirium, dementia, derangement, enthusiasm, fad, fanaticism, fetish, fixation, frenzy, infatuation, insanity, itch, lunacy, madness, obsession, overzealousness, passion, preoccupation, rage, thing (about).

maniac *n* détraquéa(e), enthusiast, fan, fanatic, fiend, freak, loony, lunatic, madman, madwoman, mental case, nutcase, psycho, psychopath, psychotic.

maniacal *adj* berserk, crazed, crazy, demented, deranged, frenzied, hysterical, insane, lunatic, mad, maniacal, psychotic, raving, screwy, unbalanced, unhinged, wild.

antonym sane.

manifest *adj* apparent, clear, conspicuous, distinct, evident, glaring, noticeable, obvious, open, palpable, patent, plain, unconcealed, undeniable, unmistakable, visible.

antonym unclear.

v appear, demonstrate, display, establish, evidence, evince, exhibit, expose, illustrate, indicate, prove, reveal, set forth, show.

antonym hide.

manifestation *n* appearance, demonstration, disclosure, display, exhibition, exposure, expression, evidence, indication, instance, mark, materialization, reflection, reflex, revelation, show, sign, symptom, token.

manifesto *n* declaration, platform, policies, policy, position paper, pronunciamento.

manifold *adj* abundant, assorted, copious, diverse, diversified, kaleidoscopic, many, multifarious, multifold, multiple, multiplex, multiplied, multitudinous, numerous, varied, various.

antonym simple.

manipulate *v* change, control, cook, doctor, engineer, exploit, gerrymander, guide, handle, influence, juggle with, manage, manoeuvre, negotiate, operate, ply, rig, shuffle, steer, tamper with, use, wield, work.

mankind *n* Homo sapiens, human race, humanity, humankind, mortals, people.

manliness *n* boldness, bravery, courage, fearlessness, firmness, hardihood, heroism, independence, intrepidity, manfulness, manhood, masculinity, mettle, resolution, stalwartness, stout-heartedness, valour, vigour, virility.

antonym timidity.

manly *adj* bold, brave, courageous, daring, dauntless, fearless, gallant, hardy, heroic, male, masculine, muscular, noble, powerful, resolute, robust, stalwart, stout-hearted, strapping, strong, sturdy, valiant, valorous, vigorous, virile.

antonyms timid, unmanly.

man-made *adj* artificial, ersatz, fake, imitation, manufactured, plastic, simulated, synthetic.

antonym natural.

manner *n* address, air, appearance, approach, aspect, bearing, behaviour, brand, breed, category, character, comportment, conduct, custom, demeanour, deportment, description, fashion, form, genre, habit, kind(s), line, look, means, method, mien, mode, nature, practice, presence, procedure, process, routine, sort, style, tack, tenor, tone, type, usage, variety, way, wise, wont.

mannered *adj* affected, artificial, campy, euphuistic, posed, precious, pretentious, pseudo, put-on, stilted, unnatural.

antonym natural.

mannerism *n* characteristic, eccentricity, foible, habit, idiosyncrasy, peculiarity, quirk, trait, trick.

mannerly *adj* civil, civilized, courteous, decorous, deferential, formal, genteel, gentlemanly, gracious, ladylike, polished, polite, refined, respectful, well-behaved, well-bred, well-mannered.

antonym unmannerly.

manners *n* bearing, behaviour, breeding, comportment, conduct, courtesy, decorum, demeanour, deportment, etiquette, formalities, good form, mores, polish, politeness, proprieties, protocol, p's and q's, refinement, social conduct, social graces.

antonyms impoliteness, indecorousness.

mannish *adj* butch, hoydenish, manlike, masculine, tomboyish, unfeminine, unladylike, unwomanly, viragoish.

antonym womanish.

manoeuvre *n* action, artifice, device, dodge, exercise, gambit, intrigue, machination, move, movement, operation, plan, plot, ploy, ruse, scheme, stratagem, subterfuge, tactic, trick.

v angle, contrive, deploy, devise, direct, drive, engineer, exercise, finagle, guide, handle, intrigue, jockey, machinate, manage, manipulate, move, navigate, negotiate, pilot, plan, plot, pull strings, scheme, steer, wangle.

manor *n* barony, big house, château, hall, Hof, Schloss, seat, villa.

manse *n* glebe-house, parsonage, rectory, vicarage.

manservant *n* butler, gentleman's gentleman, retainer, valet, valet de chambre.

mansion *n* abode, big house, castle, château, dwelling, habitation, hall, home, house, manor, manor house, palace, residence, Schloss, seat, villa.

mantle *n* blanket, canopy, cape, cloak, cloud, cover, covering, curtain, hood, mantlet, pall, pelisse, robe, screen, shawl, shroud, veil, wrap.

manual¹ *n* bible, book of words, companion, guide, guidebook, handbook, instructions, primer, textbook, vade mecum.

manual² *adj* hand, hand-operated, human, physical.

antonym automatic.

manufacture *v* assemble, build, churn out, compose, concoct, construct, cook up, create, devise, fabricate, forge, form, hatch, invent, make, make up, mass-produce, mould, process, produce, shape, think up, trump up, turn out.

n assembly, construction, creation, fabrication, facture, formation, making, mass production, production.

manufacturer *n* builder, constructor, creator, fabricator, factory owner, industrialist, maker, producer.

manure *n* compost, droppings, dung, fertilizer, guano, muck, ordure.

manuscript *n* autograph, deed, document, handwriting, holograph, palimpsest, parchment, scroll, text, vellum.

many *adj* abundant, copious, countless, divers, frequent, innumerable, manifold, multifarious, multifold, multitudinous, myriad, numerous, profuse, sundry, umpteen, untold, varied, various, zillions of.

antonym few.

map *n* atlas, chart, graph, plan, plot, representation, street plan.

mar *v* blemish, blight, blot, botch, damage, deface, detract from, disfigure, flaw, foul up, harm, hurt, impair, injure, maim, mangle, mutilate, pollute, ruin, scar, spoil, stain, sully, taint, tarnish, vitiate, wreck.

antonym enhance.

maraud *v* despoil, forage, foray, freeboot, harry, loot, pillage, plunder, raid, ransack, ravage, sack, spoliate.

marauder *n* bandit, brigand, buccaneer, corsair, freebooter, looter, outlaw, pillager, pirate, plunderer, raider, ravager, robber, spoliater.

march *v* countermarch, file, flounce, goose-step, pace, parade, slog, stalk, step, stride, strut, stump, tramp, tread, trudge, walk, waltz.

n advance, career, demonstration, development, evolution, footslog, goose step, hike, pace, parade, passage, procession, progress, progression, quickstep, step, stride, tramp, trek, walk.

margin *n* allowance, border, bound, boundary, brim, brink, compass, confines, edge, latitude, leeway, limit, perimeter, periphery, play, rim, room, scope, side, skirt, space, surplus, verge.

antonyms centre, core.

marginal *adj* bordering, borderline, doubtful, infinitesimal, insignificant, limited, low, minimal, minor, negligible, peripheral, slight, small.

antonyms central, core.

marina *n* dock, harbour, mooring, port, yacht station.

marine *adj* deep-sea, maritime, nautical, naval, ocean-going, oceanic, oceanographic, pelagic, saltwater, sea, seafaring, seagoing, thalassic.

n bluejacket, fleet, leatherneck, sailor, seascape.

mariner *n* bluejacket, deckhand, hand, Jack Tar, matelot, navigator, sailor, salt, seafarer, seaman, tar.

marital *adj* bridal, conjugal, connubial, hymeneal, married, matrimonial, nuptial, spousal, wedded.

maritime *adj* coastal, littoral, marine, nautical, naval, oceanic, pelagic, sea, seafaring, seaside, thalassic.

mark¹ *n* blaze, blemish, blot, blotch, bruise, dent, fingermark, fingerprint, footprint, impression, incision, line, lineament, nick, pock, pockmark, print, scar, scratch, smudge, splotch, stain, stamp, streak, trace, track, trail, vestige.

v blemish, blot, blotch, bruise, dent, nick, scar, scratch, smudge, splotch, stain, streak, traumatize, colour-code, impress.

mark² *n* aim, criterion, earmark, end, goal, object, objective, purpose, sign, standard, target, yardstick.

mark³ *n* badge, brand, characteristic, device, diacritic, distinction, emblem, feature, hallmark, indicator, index, label, marque, measure, seal, signature, symbol, symptom, token.

v attend, betoken, brand, characterize, denote, distinguish, exemplify, hearken, heed, identify, imprint, label, list(en), mind, note, notice, observe, print, regard, remark, stamp, take to heart, watch.

of mark eminent, distinguished, famous, important, influential, notable, noteworthy, prestigious, of consequence, of distinction, of high standing, of note, of quality, of renown, of status.

mark⁴ *n* grade, rating, result, score, standing.

v appraise, assess, correct, evaluate, grade, judge, rate, score.

marked *adj* apparent, clear, considerable, conspicuous, decided, destined, distinct, doomed, emphatic, evident, glaring, indicated, manifest, notable, noted, noticeable, obvious, outstanding, patent, prominent, pronounced, recognizable, remarkable, salient, signal, singled out, striking, strong, suspected, watched.

antonyms slight, unnoticeable.

market *n* bazaar, clientele, demand, fair, marketplace, mart, need, outlet, shop, souk, store, trade.

v deal in, flog, hawk, merchandise, peddle, retail, sell, vend.

antonym buy.

marketable *adj* in demand, merchantable, saleable, sought after, vendible, wanted.

marksman or **markswoman** *n* crack shot, deadeye, dead shot, good shot, sharpshooter, sniper.

maroon *v* abandon, cast away, desert, isolate, leave, put ashore, strand.
antonym rescue.

marriage *n* alliance, amalgamation, association, confederation, coupling, espousal, joining, link, match, (holy) matrimony, merger, nuptials, spousal(s), union, wedding, wedlock.
antonym divorce.

married *adj* conjugal, connubial, coupled, hitched, husbandly, joined, marital, mates, matrimonial, nuptial, one, spliced, spousal, united, wed, wedded, wifely, yoked.
antonyms divorced, single.

marrow *n* centre, core, cream, essence, gist, heart, kernel, nub, pith, quick, quintessence, soul, spirit, stuff, substance.

marry *v* ally, bond, espouse, get hitched, get married, get spliced, head to the altar, join (together), knit, link, match, merge, splice, take to husband (or wife), tie, tie the knot, unify, unite, wed, yoke.
antonyms divorce, separate.

marsh *n* bayou, bog, fen, maremma, marshland, mire, morass, moss, muskeg, quagmire, soak, swale, swamp, swampland, wetland.

marshal *v* align, arrange, array, assemble, collect, conduct, convoy, deploy, dispose, distribute, draw up, escort, gather, group, guide, lead, line up, muster, order, organize, prepare, rank, shepherd, take, usher.

marshy *adj* boggy, fenny, miry, mucky, quaggy, spongy, swampy, waterlogged, wet.
antonym solid.

martial *adj* bellicose, belligerent, brave, combative, heroic, militant, military, scrappy, soldierlike, soldierly, warlike.
antonym pacific.

martinet *n* disciplinarian, formalist, Simon Legree, slave-driver, stickler, taskmaster, tyrant.

martyrdom *n* agony, anguish, death, excruciation, ordeal, persecution, self-immolation, self-sacrifice, suffering, torment, torture.

marvel *n* genius, miracle, nonesuch, paragon, phenom, phenomenon, prodigy, rarity, sensation, spectacle, whiz, wonder.
v gape, gaze, goggle, wonder.

marvellous *adj* amazing, astonishing, astounding, awesome, beyond belief, breathtaking, excellent, exquisite, extraordinary, fabulous, fantastic, fine, glorious, gorgeous, great, hell of a, implausible, improbable, incredible, magnificent, miraculous, phenomenal, prodigious, remarkable, sensational, singular, smashing, spectacular, splendid, stupendous, super, superb, surprising, terrific, the best, unbelievable, unlikely, unsurpassed, wonderful, wondrous.
antonyms ordinary, plausible, run-of-the-mill.

masculine *adj* butch, gallant, macho, male, manlike, manly, mannish, muscular, red-blooded, tomboyish, tough, virile.

antonym feminine.

masculinity *n* animus, hoydenism, maleness, manhood, manliness, mannishness, masculineness, potency, tomboyishness, unladylikeness, unwomanliness, virilism, virility, yang.
antonym femininity.

mash *v* beat, comminute, crush, grind, pound, powder, pulp, pulverize, pummel, smash, squash, triturate.

mask *n* blind, camouflage, cloak, concealment, cover, cover-up, disguise, domino, façade, false face, false front, front, guise, pretence, pretext, screen, semblance, show, smoke screen, veil, veneer, visor.
v camouflage, cloak, conceal, cover (up), disguise, hide, obscure, screen, shield, shroud, suppress, veil.
antonym uncover.

masked *adj* camouflaged, cloaked, concealed, covered, disguised, incognito, screened, shielded, shrouded, veiled, visored.
antonyms uncovered, unshielded.

masquerade *n* act, cloak, costume, costume ball, cover, cover-up, deception, disguise, dissimulation, domino, fakery, fancy-dress party, front, guise, imposture, mask, masked ball, masque, mummery, pose, pretence, put-on, screen, sham, subterfuge.
v act the part, be disguised, disguise oneself, dissemble, dissimulate, impersonate, mask, misrepresent oneself, pass oneself off, play, pose, pretend, profess.

mass *n* accumulation, aggregate, aggregation, assemblage, band, batch, block, body, bulk, bunch, chunk, cluster, collection, combination, concretion, congeries, conglomeration, crowd, dimension, entirety, extent, gob, group, heap, horde, host, hunk, lion's share, load, lot, lump, magnitude, majority, mob, multitude, piece, pile, plurality, preponderance, quantity, size, solid, stack, sum, sum total, throng, totality, troop, welter, whole.
adj across-the-board, blanket, comprehensive, extensive, general, indiscriminate, large-scale, massive, pandemic, popular, sweeping, wholesale, widespread.
antonym limited.
v assemble, cluster, collect, congregate, crowd, forgather, gather, muster, rally.
antonym separate.

massacre *n* annihilation, blood bath, butchery, carnage, decimation, extermination, genocide, holocaust, killing, murder, slaughter.
v annihilate, butcher, decimate, exterminate, kill, mow down, murder, slaughter, slay, wipe out.

massage *n* back rub, effleurage, kneading, manipulation, rubbing, rubdown, shiatsu, stimulation.
v knead, manipulate, rub, rub down.

massive *adj* big, broad, bulky, colossal, cyclopean, enormous, extensive, gargantuan, gigantic, great, heavy, hefty, huge, hulking, immense, imposing, impressive, jumbo, large,

large-scale, mammoth, monster, monstrous, monumental, ponderous, rounceval, solid, substantial, titanic, vast, weighty, whacking, whopping, widespread.

antonyms slight, small.

master *n* ace, adept, artisan, authority, baas, boss, bwana, captain, champion, chief, commander, controller, dab (hand), director, doyen, educator, employer, expert, genius, governor, guide, guru, head, Herr, instructor, leader, lord, maestro, manager, overlord, overseer, owner, past master, pedagogue, preceptor, principal, pro, ruler, sahib, schoolmaster, skipper, superintendent, superior, swami, teacher, tutor, victor, virtuoso, wizard.

antonyms amateur, learner, pupil, servant, slave.

adj ace, adept, chief, consummate, controlling, crack, expert, foremost, governing, grand, great, leading, main, masterful, masterly, predominant, prime, principal, proficient, skilful, skilled, virtuoso.

antonyms copy, subordinate, unskilled.

v acquire, bridle, check, command, conquer, control, curb, defeat, direct, dominate, get the better of, get the hang of, govern, grasp, learn, manage, overcome, quash, quell, regulate, rule, subdue, subjugate, suppress, tame, triumph over, vanquish.

masterful *adj* adept, adroit, arrogant, authoritative, autocratic, bossy, clever, consummate, crack, deft, despotic, dexterous, dictatorial, domineering, excellent, expert, exquisite, fine, finished, first-rate, high-handed, imperious, magisterial, masterly, overbearing, overweening, peremptory, powerful, professional, proficient, self-willed, skilful, skilled, superior, superlative, supreme, tyrannical, virtuoso.

antonyms clumsy, humble, unskilful.

masterly *adj* adept, adroit, clever, consummate, crack, dexterous, excellent, expert, exquisite, fine, finished, first-rate, masterful, polished, skilful, skilled, superb, superior, superlative, supreme.

antonyms clumsy, poor, unskilled.

mastermind *v* conceive, contrive, design, devise, direct, dream up, forge, frame, hatch, manage, organize, originate, plan.

n architect, authority, brain(s), creator, director, engineer, expert, genius, intellect, manager, organizer, originator, planner, prime mover, virtuoso.

masterpiece *n* chef d'oeuvre, classic, gem, jewel, magnum opus, master work, museum piece, pièce de résistance, tour de force, work of art.

mastery *n* ability, acquirement, advantage, ascendancy, attainment, authority, cleverness, command, comprehension, conquest, control, deftness, dexterity, domination, dominion, expertise, familiarity, finesse, grasp, know-how, knowledge, mastership, pre-eminence, proficiency, prowess, rule, skill, superiority, supremacy, sway, triumph, understanding, upper hand, victory, virtuosity, whip hand.

antonyms clumsiness, unfamiliarity.

masticate *v* chomp, chew, crunch, eat, knead, munch, ruminate.

masturbation *n* auto-eroticism, onanism, playing with oneself, self-stimulation.

mat *n* carpet, covering, doormat, drugget, felt, rug, underlay, welcome mat.

match[1] *n* bout, competition, contest, game, test, trial, venue.

v oppose, pit (against).

match[2] *n* affiliation, alliance, combination, companion, complement, copy, counterpart, couple, dead ringer, double, duet, duplicate, equal, equivalent, image, like, look-alike, marriage, mate, pair, pairing, parallel, partnership, peer, replica, ringer, rival, spit, spitting image, tally, twin, union.

v accord, adapt, agree, ally, be comparable, be compatible, be in harmony, be in sync, blend, coincide, combine, compare, complement, co-ordinate, correspond (to), couple, emulate, equal, fit together, give in kind, go together, go with, harmonize, join, link, make (or be) parallel, marry, mate, measure up to, pair, resemble, rival, suit, synchronize, tally, team, unite, yoke.

antonyms clash, separate.

match[3] *n* friction match, fuse, fusee, igniter, light, lucifer, matchstick, safety match, spill, taper, vesta, vesuvian.

matching *adj* alike, analogous, companion, comparable, co-ordinated, co-ordinating, corresponding, cut from the same cloth, duplicate, equal, equivalent, harmonious, identical, like, of a kind, parallel, pared, similar, the same, twin.

antonyms clashing, different.

matchless *adj* consummate, excellent, exquisite, incomparable, inimitable, nonpareil, peerless, perfect, superlative, supreme, unequalled, unique, unmatched, unparalleled, unrivalled, unsurpassed.

antonyms commonplace, poor.

mate *n* assistant, associate, buddy, chum, colleague, companion, compeer, comrade, confidant(e), counterpart, co-worker, crony, double, equivalent, fellow, fellow worker, friend, helper, helpmate, helpmeet, husband, match, one's better half, pal, parallel, partner, peer, sidekick, spouse, twin, wife.

v become partners, breed, come together, copulate, couple, get married, join, marry, match, pair (up), wed, yoke.

material *n* body, bumf, cloth, constituents, data, documents, elements, evidence, fabric, facts, fodder, grist for the mill, information, literature, matter, notes, stuff, substance, textile, work.

adj applicable, apposite, apropos, bodily, central, concrete, consequential, corporeal, essential, fleshly, germane, grave, gross, important, indispensable, key, meaningful, momentous, non-spiritual, palpable, pertinent, physical, relevant, serious, significant, substantial, tangible, temporal, vital, weighty, worldly.

meagre

antonyms ethereal, immaterial.

materialistic *adj* banausic, Mammonistic, mercenary, moneygrubbing, pothunting.

antonym spiritual.

materialize *v* appear, arise, be realized, happen, occur, take shape, turn up.

antonym disappear.

materially *adv* considerably, gravely, greatly, much, noticeably, palpably, physically, seriously, significantly, substantially, tangibly, visibly.

antonym insignificantly.

maternal *adj* loving, motherlike, motherly, protective.

antonym paternal.

mating *n* breeding, copulating, copulation, coupling, fusing, joining, jointing, making it, matching, sex act, sexual intercourse, sexual relations, twinning, uniting.

matrimonial *adj* conjugal, connubial, marital, marriage, married, nuptial, spousal, wedded, wedding.

matrimony *n* espousals, marriage, marriage sacrament, nuptials, spousal, wedded state, wedlock.

matron *n* dame, dowager, housemother, housewife, matriarch.

matted *adj* disheveled, knotted, massed, shaggy, snarled, tangled, tousled, uncombed.

antonyms tidy, untangled.

matter[1] *n* affair, basis, body, business, cause, concern, consequence, content, context, difficulty, episode, essence, event, gist, grounds, import, importance, incident, interest, issue, item, material, meat, moment, note, occurrence, problem, proceeding, purport, question, sense, significance, situation, stuff, subject, substance, sum, sum and substance, text, thesis, thing, topic, transaction, trouble, upset, weight, worry.

antonym insignificance.

v be of consequence, carry weight, count, cut ice, make a difference, mean much, mean something, signify.

no matter (what) at all costs, at any cost, come hell or high water, come what may, in any case, never mind, notwithstanding, regardless (of), unconditionally, whatever (happens), willy-nilly, without fail.

matter[2] *n* discharge, purulence, pus, secretion, suppuration.

v discharge, fester, run, secrete, suppurate, weep.

matter-of-fact *adj* businesslike, deadpan, direct, down-to-earth, dry, dull, emotionless, flat, forthright, lifeless, literal, mundane, plain, practical, prosaic, simple, sober, unembellished, unimaginative, unsentimental, unvarnished.

antonyms emotional, imaginative.

mature *adj* adult, aged, complete, developed, due, experienced, finished, fit, full-blown, full-grown, fully developed, fullfledged, grown, grown-up, matured, mellow, nubile, of age,

payable, perfect, perfected, prepared, ready, ripe, ripened, seasoned, well-thought-out.

antonym immature.

v accrue, age, bloom, come of age, develop, evolve, fall due, grow (up), maturate, mellow, perfect, ripen, season.

maturity *n* adulthood, completion, experience, fullness, majority, manhood, maturation, matureness, nubility, perfection, readiness, ripeness, wisdom, womanhood.

antonym immaturity.

maudlin *adj* beery, corny, drunk, emotional, fuddled, gushy, half-drunk, lachrymose, mawkish, melodramatic, mushy, nostalgic, schmaltzy, sentimental, slushy, soppy, tearful, theatrical, tipsy, weepy.

antonym matter-of-fact.

maul *v* abuse, batter, beat, beat up, bruise, claw, ill-treat, injure, knock around, lacerate, maltreat, mangle, manhandle, molest, paw, pound, pummel, rough up, thrash.

maunder *v* babble, blather,chatter, drivel, gabble, grumble, mutter, prattle, ramble, rattle on, wander.

maw *n* abyss, black hole, chasm, craw, crop, gulf, gullet, jaws, mouth, stomach, throat.

mawkish *adj* disgusting, emotional, foul, gushy, insipid, jejune, loathsome, maudlin, mushy, nauseating, offensive, schmaltzy, sentimental, sickening, sloppy, slushy, soppy.

antonyms matter-of-fact, pleasant.

maxim *n* adage, aphorism, apothegm, axiom, byword, dictum, epigram, gnome, mot, motto, precept, proverb, rule, saw, saying, truism.

maximize *v* accentuate, bring out, concentrate, emphasize, enhance, exaggerate, heighten, increase, intensify, magnify, play up, stress.

maximum *adj* biggest, greatest, highest, largest, maximal, most, paramount, supreme, topmost, utmost.

antonym minimum.

n apex, apogee, ceiling, crest, extremity, height, highest point, most, ne plus ultra, peak, pinnacle, summit, tip, top, upper limit, utmost, zenith.

antonym mimimum.

maybe *adv* by chance, conceivably, feasibly, mayhap, peradventure, perchance, perhaps, possibly.

antonym definitely.

▲ *confusable word* may be.

maze *n* bewilderment, confusion, convolutions, imbroglio, intricacy, labyrinth, meshes, muddle, perplexity, puzzle, snarl, tangle, web.

meadow *n* common, field, grassland, green, holm, lea, mead, pasture, veld.

meagre *adj* barren, bony, deficient, emaciated, exiguous, gaunt, hungry, inadequate, infertile, insubstantial, lank, lean, little, negligible, paltry, penurious, poor, puny, scanty, scraggy, scrawny, scrimpy, short, skimpy, skinny, slender, slight, small, spare, sparse, starved, thin, underfed, unfruitful, unproductive, weak.

antonyms fertile, substantial.

meal¹ *n* banquet, barbecue, blowout, breakfast, brunch, collation, dinner, feast, feed, lunch, luncheon, mess, nosh, picnic, refreshments, repast, scoff, snack, spread, supper, tea, tiffin, tuck-in.

meal² *n* cornmeal, farina, flour, grits, oatmeal, powder.

mealy-mouthed *adj* equivocal, euphemistic, fawning, flattering, glib, hesitant, indirect, insincere, mincing, obsequious, overdelicate, over-squeamish, prim, reticent, smooth-tongued, weaselly.

mean¹ *adj* bad-tempered, callous, cheeseparing, churlish, close-fisted, cruel, cutting, disagreeable, discourteous, grudging, hard-hearted, harsh, heartless, hostile, hurtful, illiberal, inconsiderate, insensitive, low, malicious, malignant, mean-spirited, miserly, nasty, niggardly, ornery, parsimonious, penny-pinching, petty, rude, ruthless, selfish, small-minded, snippy, sour, spiteful, stingy, thoughtless, tight, tight-fisted, unfeeling, unfriendly, ungenerous, ungiving, unhandsome, unkind, unpleasant, vicious, vindictive.
antonyms generous, kind.

mean² *adj* ace, accomplished, crack, crackerjack, excellent, expert, good, great, ruthless, skilled, top-notch.

mean³ *adj* abject, base, baseborn, beggarly, common, contemptible, degraded, despicable, disgraceful, dishonourable, down-at-heel, humble, ignoble, inconsiderable, inferior, insignificant, low, lowborn, lowly, meagre, menial, mercenary, miserable, obscure, one-horse, ordinary, paltry, penurious, plebeian, poor, proletarian, run-down, scurvy, seedy, shabby, shameful, sordid, shoddy, squalid, tawdry, undistinguished, vile, vulgar, wretched, skimpy, small, unimportant.
antonyms noble, superior.

mean⁴ *v* adumbrate, aim, aspire, augur, be indicative of, bespeak, betoken, cause, communicate, connote, contemplate, convey, denote, design, desire, destine, drive at, engender, entail, express, fate, foreshadow, foretell, get at, give rise to, have a mind (to), have every intention, have in mind, herald, hint (at), imply, import, indicate, insinuate, intend, involve, lead to, make, match, necessitate, omen, plan, portend, predestine, preordain, presage, produce, promise, propose, purport, purpose, refer to, represent, result in, say, set out, signify, spell, stand for, suggest, symbolize, want, wish.

mean⁵ *adj* average, halfway, intermediate, medial, median, medium, middle, middling, moderate, normal, standard.
antonym extreme.
n average, balance, compromise, golden mean, halfway point, happy medium, median, middle, middle course, middle ground, middle way, mid-point, norm, via media.
antonym extreme.

meander *v* amble, curve, ramble, snake, stray, stroll, turn, twist, twist and turn, wander, wind, zigzag.

meandering *adj* circuitous, convoluted, curving, indirect, roundabout, serpentine, sinuous, snaking, snaky, tortuous, twisting, wandering, winding.
antonym straight.

meaning *n* aim, connotation, construction, denotation, design, drift, end, explanation, force, gist, goal, idea, implication, import, intention, interpretation, matter, message, object, plan, point, purport, purpose, sense, significance, signification, substance, thrust, upshot, validity, value, worth.

meaningful *adj* communicative, dense, eloquent, expressive, important, material, meaning, pointed, pregnant, purposeful, relevant, sententious, serious, significant, speaking, suggestive, telling, useful, valid, worthwhile.
antonym meaningless.

meaningless *adj* absurd, aimless, empty, expressionless, futile, hollow, inane, inconsequential, insignificant, insubstantial, nonsense, nonsensical, nugatory, pointless, purposeless, senseless, trifling, trivial, unenforceable, useless, vain, valueless, without rhyme or reason, worthless.
antonym meaningful.

meanness *n* abjectness, baseness, beggarliness, churlishness, close-fistedness, contemptibleness, degradation, despicableness, disagreeableness, disgracefulness, dishonourableness, humbleness, humility, illiberality, inferiority, insignificance, lowliness, malice, maliciousness, malignity, meagerness, mean-spiritedness, mediocrity, miserliness, nastiness, niggardliness, obscurity, paltriness, parsimony, penuriousness, penurity, pettiness, poorness, poverty, rudeness, scurviness, seediness, selfishness, shabbiness, shamefulness, shoddiness, skimpiness, smallness, sordidness, sourness, squalor, stinginess, tawdriness, tight-fistedness, unfriendliness, unkindness, unpleasantness, viciousness, vileness, wretchedness.
antonyms generosity, kindness, nobility, superiority.

means *n* ability, affluence, agency, assets, avenue, capacity, capital, channel, course, estate, expedient, fortune, funds, income, instrument, machinery, manner, measure, medium, method(s), mode, money, process, property, resources, riches, substance, tool, way, wealth, wherewithal.

meanwhile *adv* at the same time, between now and then, concurrently, for now, for the moment, for the time being, in the interim, in the interval, in the meantime, in the meanwhile, meantime, simultaneously, until then.

measly *adj* beggarly, contemptible, meagre, mean, miserable, miserly, niggardly, paltry, pathetic, petty, piddling, pitiful, poor, puny,

scanty, skimpy, small, stingy, trivial, ungenerous, unsatisfactory.
antonym generous.

measurable *adj* appreciable, assessable, calculable, computable, determinable, fathomable, gaugeable, material, mensurable, perceptible, quantifiable, quantitative, significant.
antonyms measureless, unmeasurable.

measure *n* allotment, allowance, amount, amplitude, beat, bounds, cadence, capacity, control, course, criterion, degree, demarche, enactment, estimate, example, expedient, extent, foot, gauge, index, indicator, jigger, law, limit, magnitude, manoeuvre, mark, means, measuring stick, method, metre, model, modicum, norm, portion, preventive measure, procedure, proceeding, proportion, quantity, quota, range, ration, reach, resolution, restraint, rhythm, rule, scale, scope, share, sign, size, standard, statute, step, system, test, touchstone, yardstick.

v appraise, assess, calculate, calibrate, compare, compute, determine, estimate, evaluate, fathom, gauge, judge, mark off (or out), measure off (or out), plumb, quantify, rate, size (up), sound, step, survey, value, weigh.

for good measure as a bonus, as an extra, besides, gratis, in addition, into the bargain, to boot.

measure off circumscribe, delimit, demarcate, determine, fix, limit, mark off (or out), measure (out), pace out.

measure out allot, apportion, assign, deal out, dispense, distribute, divide, dole out, hand out, issue, measure (off), mete out, parcel out, pour out, proportion, share out.

measure up be comparable, do, fill the bill, make the grade, pass muster, shape up, suffice.

measure up to come up to, compare with, equal, hold a candle to, match, meet, rival, stack up with, touch.

measured *adj* calculated, considered, deliberate, even, exact, gauged, leisurely, metrical, metronomic, modulated, periodic, planned, precise, predetermined, premeditated, quantified, reasoned, regular, regulated, restrained, rhythmical, sedate, slow, sober, standard, steady, studied, unhurried, uniform, verified, weighed, well-thought-out.

measureless *adj* bottomless, boundless, endless, immeasurable, immense, incalculable, inestimable, infinite, innumerable, limitless, unbounded, unlimited, vast.
antonym measurable.

measurement *n* amount, amplitude, appraisal, appreciation, area, assessment, calculation, calibration, capacity, computation, depth, dimension, estimation, evaluation, extent, gauging, height, judgment, length, magnitude, mass, measure, mensuration, size, survey, valuation, volume, weight, width.

meat[1] *n* aliment, cheer, chow, comestibles, (daily) bread, eats, fare, flesh, food, grub,

nourishment, nutriment, provender, provisions, rations, subsistence, sustenance, viands, victuals.

meat[2] *n* content, core, crux, essence, fundamentals, gist, heart, kernel, marrow, nub, nucleus, pith, point, substance.

meaty *adj* beefy, brawny, burly, corpulent, deep, fleshy, hearty, heavy, husky, interesting, meaningful, muscular, pithy, profound, rich, sententious, significant, solid, strapping, sturdy, substantial.

mechanic *n* engineer, fitter, fixer, machinist, mechanician, mender, operative, operator, repairer, servicer, technician.

mechanical *adj* automated, automatic, cold, cursory, dead, dull, emotionless, expressionless, habitual, impersonal, instinctive, involuntary, lacklustre, lifeless, machine-driven, machinelike, matter-of-fact, mechanistic, mindless, perfunctory, robotic, routine, spiritless, unanimated, unconscious, unfeeling, unthinking, wooden.

mechanism *n* agency, apparatus, appliance, components, contrivance, device, execution, functioning, gadgetry, gears, innards, instrument, lever, machine, machinery, means, medium, method, motor, moving parts, operation, performance, procedure, process, structure, system, tool, workings, works.

medal *n* award, decoration, honour, medallion, order, prize, reward, trophy.

meddle *v* interfere, interlope, interpose, intervene, intrude, monkey, pry, put one's oar in, snoop, stick one's nose in, tamper.

meddlesome *adj* busybody, interfering, intruding, intrusive, meddling, mischievous, officious, prying, snoopy.

mediate *v* arbitrate, conciliate, intercede, interpose, intervene, moderate, negotiate, reconcile, referee, resolve, settle, step in, umpire.

mediation *n* arbitration, conciliation, good offices, intercession, interposition, intervention, negotiation, parley, reconciliation.

mediator *n* advocate, arbiter, arbitrator, broker, counsellor, facilitator, go-between, intercessor, intermediary, judge, liaison, middleman, moderator, negotiator, ombudsman, ombudswoman, peacemaker, referee, third party, umpire.

medical *adj* Hippocratic, iatric, medicinal.

medical practitioner allopath, consultant, doc, doctor, general practitioner, G.P.,healer, homeopath, intern, medic, medical officer, medico, M.O., physician, sawbones, surgeon.

medicinal *adj* analeptic, curative, healing, homeopathic, medical, medicative, remedial, restorative, sanative, therapeutic.

medicine *n* cure, drug, electuary, elixir, febrifuge, Galenical, herbs, materia, medicament, medication, mixture, nostrum, panacea, physic, remedy, specific, syrup, tincture, vermifuge.

medicine-man *n* angakog, folk healer, shaman, witch doctor.

medieval *adj* antediluvian, antiquated, antique, archaic, Gothic, old-fashioned, old-world, outmoded, primitive, unenlightened.

mediocre *adj* amateurish, average, commonplace, fair to middling, indifferent, inexpert, inferior, insignificant, lacklustre, mean, medium, middling, nothing to brag (or write home) about, ordinary, passable, pedestrian, run-of-the-mill, second-rate, so-so, undistinguished, unexceptional, uninspired, unskilful.

antonyms excellent, exceptional, extraordinary.

mediocrity *n* amateurishness, cipher, indifference, inferiority, insignificance, lightweight, nobody, nonentity, ordinariness, pedestrianism, poorness, second-rater, unimportance.

meditate *v* be in a brown study, cerebrate, cogitate, consider, contemplate, deliberate, devise, excogitate, intend, mull over, muse, plan, ponder, purpose, reflect, ruminate, scheme, speculate, study, think, think over.

meditation *n* brown study, cerebration, cogitation, concentration, contemplation, devotions, excogitation, musing, pondering, quiet time, reflection, reverie, ruminating, rumination, speculation, study, thought.

meditative *adj* cogitative, contemplative, deliberative, musing, pensive, quiet, reflective, ruminant, ruminative, studious, thoughtful.

medium[1] *adj* average, fair, intermediate, mean, medial, median, mediocre, medium-sized, middle, middling, midway, moderate, standard.

n aurea mediocratis, average, centre, compromise, golden mean, happy medium, mean, middle, middle ground, midpoint, via media, way.

medium[2] *n* agency, agent, avenue, base, channel, excipient, form, instrument, instrumentality, means, mode, organ, substance, vehicle, way.

medium[3] *n* chancellor, clairvoyant, go-between, intermediary, necromancer, psychic, spiritualist.

medium[4] *n* ambience, atmosphere, circumstances, climate, conditions, element, environment, habitat, influences, milieu, setting, surroundings.

medley *n* all sorts, assemblage, assortment, collection, confusion, conglomeration, farrago, gallimaufery, hash, hodgepodge, jumble, macédoine, mélange, miscellany, mishmash, mixed bag, mixture, odds and ends, omnium-gatherum, pastiche, patchwork, potpourri, salmagundi, variety.

meek *adj* accommodating, acquiescent, compliant, deferential, docile, forbearing, gentle, humble, lamblike, long-suffering, lowly, mild, modest, obedient, pacific, patient, peaceful, resigned, self-effacing, soft, subdued, submissive, tame, timid, unambitious, unassuming, unimposing, unobtrusive, unpretentious, unresisting, yielding.

antonyms arrogant, rebellious.

meet (with) *v* abut, adjoin, answer, assemble, bear, be introduced to, be united, bump into, chance on, collect, collide (with), come across, come face to face (with), come together, comply (with), confront, congregate, connect (with), contact, convene, converge, cross, deal with, discharge, encounter, endure, equal, experience, face (up to), forgather, fulfil, gather, go through, gratify, handle, happen on, intersect, join up, link up, make contact (with), match, measure up to, muster, pay (off), rally, rencounter, rendezvous, respond to, run across, run into, satisfy, touch, undergo.

meeting *n* abutment, assembly, assignation, audience, collision, conclave, concourse, conference, confluence, confrontation, congregation, conjunction, consultation, conventicle, convention, convergence, convocation, council, crossing, encounter, engagement, forum, gathering, get-together, indaba, intersection, introduction, joining, junction, meet, moot, rally, rencounter, rendezvous, reunion, session, synod, tryst, union.

meeting point *n* confluence, convergence, crossroads, interface, intersection, junction.

megalomania *n* conceitedness, delusions of grandeur, egoism, folie de grandeur, overestimation, self-importance.

melancholy *adj* blue, dejected, depressed, depressing, despondent, disconsolate, dismal, dispirited, doleful, down, down in the dumps, down in the mouth, downcast, downhearted, dreary, gloomy, glum, heavy-hearted, in the doldrums, joyless, low, low-spirited, lugubrious, melancholic, miserable, moody, mournful, pensive, sad, sombre, sorrowful, unhappy, wistful, woebegone, woeful.

antonyms cheerful, gay, happy, joyful.

n blues, dejection, depression, despondency, doldrums, dole, dolour, dreariness, gloom, gloominess, glumness, low spirits, pensiveness, sadness, sorrow, unhappiness, wistfulness, woe.

antonym exhilaration.

mélange *n* all sorts, assortment, confusion, conglomeration, farrago, gallimaufrey, hash, hodgepodge, jumble, medley, miscellany, mishmash, mix, mixed bag, mixture, odds and ends, pastiche, potpourri, salmagundi.

melee *n* affray, battle royal, brawl, broil, dogfight, Donnybrook, fight, fracas, fray, free-for-all, riot, row, ruckus, rumble, rumpus, scrimmage, scrum, scuffle, set-to, tussle.

mellifluous *adj* dulcet, euphonious, flowing, honeyed, melodious, mellow, pleasant, silvery, smooth, soft, soothing, sweet, sweet-sounding, tuneful.

antonyms discordant, grating, harsh.

mellow *adj* cheerful, dulcet, expansive, full, full-flavoured, genial, happy, intoxicated, jolly, jovial, juicy, laid-back, mature, mellifluous, melodious, placid, pleasant, relaxed, resonant, rich, ripe, rounded, seasoned, serene, smooth, soft, sweet, tipsy, tranquil, warm.

mental¹

antonyms immature, unripe.

v evolve, improve, mature, perfect, relax, ripen, season, soften, sweeten, temper.

melodious *adj* arioso, concordant, dulcet, euphonious, harmonious, lyric, melodic, musical, silvery, sonorous, sweet-sounding, tuneful.

antonyms discordant, grating, harsh.

melodramatic *adj* blood-and-thunder, emotionalistic, exaggerated, hammy, histrionic, overdone, overdramatic, overemotional, overwrought, schmaltzy, sensational, stagy, theatrical.

melody *n* air, aria, arietta, euphony, harmony, melodiousness, music, musicality, refrain, song, strain, theme, tonality, tune, tunefulness.

melt *v* deliquesce, diffuse, disappear, disarm, dissolve, flux, fuse, liquefy, mollify, relax, soften, thaw, touch, uncongeal, unfreeze, warm.

antonyms freeze, harden, solidify.

melt away dematerialize, disappear, disperse, dissipate, dissolve, ebb away, evanesce, evaporate, fade, vanish.

member *n* adherent, affiliate, appendage, arm, component, constituent, element, extremity, initiate, leg, limb, organ, part, portion.

membership *n* affiliates, associates, body, constituency, enrolment, fellows, fellowship, members, participation, subscription, voting rights.

membrane *n* diaphragm, film, hymen, integument, pellicle, scum, skin, tissue, veil, velum.

memento *n* keepsake, memorial, record, relic, remembrance, reminder, souvenir, token, trophy.

memoir *n* account, biography, documentation, journal, life, monograph, record, report, study, treatise.

memoirs *n* annals, autobiography, chronicles, confessions, diary, experiences, history, journals, life, life story, memories, personalia, profile, recollections, records, reminiscences.

memorable *adj* catchy, celebrated, distinguished, extraordinary, famous, historic, illustrious, important, impressive, marvellous, momentous, notable, noteworthy, outstanding, remarkable, signal, significant, striking, unforgettable.

antonym forgettable.

memorial *n* cairn, cromlech, dolmen, gravestone, martyry, mausoleum, memento, menhir, monolith, monument, plaque, record, remembrance, souvenir, tombstone.

adj celebratory, commemorative, monumental.

memorize *v* commit to memory, con, get letter perfect, learn, learn by heart, learn by rote, learn verbatim, learn word for word.

antonym forget.

memory *n* commemoration, database, engram, memorial, memoriam, memory bank, name, observance, recall, recollection, remembrance, reminiscence, renown, reputation, repute, retention, storage.

antonym forgetfulness.

menace *v* alarm, be imminent, browbeat, bully, cow, frighten, impend, intimidate, loom, lower, terrorize, threaten.

n annoyance, commination, danger, hazard, intimidation, jeopardy, nuisance, peril, pest, plague, scare, sword of Damocles, terror, threat, troublemaker, warning.

menacing *adj* alarming, baleful, Damoclean, dangerous, foreboding, frightening, impending, intimidating, intimidatory, looming, lowering, minacious, minatory, ominous, portentous, sinister, threatening.

mend *v* ameliorate, amend, better, bushel, cobble, convalesce, correct, cure, darn, emend, fix, heal, improve, patch, recover, rectify, recuperate, refit, reform, remedy, renew, renovate, repair, restore, retouch, revise, solder.

antonyms break, destroy, deteriorate.

on the mend convalescent, convalescing, healing, improving, recovering, recuperating, reviving.

mendacious *adj* deceitful, deceptive, dishonest, duplicitous, fallacious, false, forsworn, fraudulent, insincere, inveracious, lying, perfidious, perjured, prevaricating, untrue, untruthful.

antonyms honest, truthful.

mendacity *n* deceit, deceitfulness, dishonesty, distortion, duplicity, falsehood, falsification, fraudulence, insincerity, inveracity, lie, lying, mendaciousness, misrepresentation, perfidy, perjury, prevarication, untruth, untruthfulness.

antonyms honesty, truthfulness.

mendicant *adj* begging, cadging, petitionary, scrounging, supplicant.

n almsman, beachcomber, beggar, bum, cadger, hobo, moocher, panhandler, pauper, scrounger, tramp, vagabond, vagrant.

menial *adj* abject, base, boring, degrading, demeaning, dull, fawning, grovelling, hack, humble, humdrum, ignoble, ignominious, low, lowly, mean, obsequious, routine, servile, slavish, subservient, sycophantic, unskilled.

n creature, dog's-body, domestic, drudge, flunkey, lackey, maid of all work, peon, roustabout, scullion, serf, servant, slave, underling.

menstruation *n* catamenia, courses, discharge, flow, friend, grandmother, menorrhoea, menses, menstrual flow, monthlies, period, that time (of month), the curse.

mensuration *n* appraisal, assessment, calculation, calibration, computation, estimation, evaluation, measurement, measuring, quantification, survey, surveying, valuation.

mental¹ *adj* abstract, cerebral, cognitive, conceptual, ideational, intellectual, noetic, rational, theoretical.

antonym physical.

mental² *adj* crazy, cuckoo, deranged, disturbed, insane, loony, lunatic, mad, psychiatric, psychotic, temperamental, unbalanced, unstable.
antonyms balanced, sane.

mentality *n* attitude, brains, character, comprehension, disposition, endowment, faculty, frame of mind, intellect, intelligence, IQ, make-up, mental age, mental capacity, mind, mindset, outlook, personality, psychology, rationality, stance, understanding, wits.

mentally *adv* emotionally, intellectually, inwardly, psychologically, rationally, subjectively, temperamentally.

mention *v* acknowledge, adduce, allude to, bring up, broach, call attention to, cite, communicate, declare, disclose, divulge, hint at, impart, intimate, make known, name, point out, refer to, remark upon, report, reveal, say, speak about (or of), specify, state, touch on.
n acknowledgment, allusion, announcement, citation, indication, notification, observation, recognition, reference, remark, tribute.

mentioned *adj* above-mentioned, aforementioned, aforesaid, cited, forementioned, forenamed, quoted, reported, stated.

mentor *n* adviser, coach, counsellor, guide, guru, instructor, pedagogue, swami, teacher, trainer, tutor.

menu *n* bill of fare, carte du jour, list, schedule.

mercantile *adj* business, commercial, industrial, merchant, trade, trading.

mercenary *adj* acquisitive, avaricious, bought, covetous, grasping, greedy, hack, hired, Mammonistic, materialistic, meretricious, moneygrubbing, paid, sordid, venal.

merchandise *n* commodities, goods, inventory, produce, products, saleables, staples, stock, stock in trade, vendibles, wares.
v carry, deal in, distribute, market, peddle, retail, sell, supply, trade, traffic in, vend, wholesale.

merchant *n* broker, dealer, distributor, jobber, marketer, merchandiser, retailer, salesman, seller, shopkeeper, trader, tradesman, trafficker, vendor, wholesaler.

merciful *adj* beneficent, benignant, clement, compassionate, condoling, forbearing, forgiving, generous, gracious, humane, humanitarian, kind, lenient, liberal, mild, pitying, soft-hearted, sparing, sympathetic, tender-hearted.
antonyms cruel, merciless.

merciless *adj* barbarous, callous, cruel, hard, hard-hearted, harsh, heartless, implacable, inexorable, inhuman, inhumane, pitiless, relentless, remorseless, ruthless, savage, severe, unappeasable, unforgiving, unmerciful, unpitying, unsparing.
antonym merciful.

mercurial *adj* active, capricious, chameleonlike, changeable, erratic, fickle, fleetfooted, flighty, impetuous, impulsive, inconstant, irrepressible, lively, mobile, nimble, quick, spirited, sprightly, swift, temperamental, unpredictable, unstable, variable, volatile.
antonyms saturnine, stable.

mercy *n* benevolence, blessing, boon, charity, clemency, compassion, favour, forbearance, forgiveness, generosity, godsend, grace, humanitarianism, humanity, kindness, leniency, pity, quarter, relief, tender-heartedness.
antonyms cruelty, revenge.

mere *adj* bare, common, paltry, petty, plain, pure, pure and simple, sheer, simple, stark, unadorned, unadulterated, unenhanced, unmitigated, unmixed, utter.

merge *v* amalgamate, blend, bring together, coalesce, combine, come together, commingle, confederate, consolidate, converge, fuse, incorporate, intermix, join, meet, meld, melt (into), mingle, mix, unite.

merger *n* amalgamation, coalescence, coalition, combination, confederation, consolidation, fusion, incorporation, joining, union.

merit *n* advantage, asset, class, credit, due, excellence, good, goodness, integrity, justification, quality, right, strength, strong point, talent, value, virtue, worth, worthiness.
antonyms demerit, fault.
v deserve, earn, incur, justify, rate, warrant.

merited *adj* appropriate, condign, deserved, due, earned, entitled, fitting, just, justified, rightful, warranted, worthy.
antonyms inappropriate, unjustified.

meritorious *adj* admirable, commendable, creditable, deserving, estimable, excellent, exemplary, good, honourable, laudable, praiseworthy, right, righteous, upright, virtuous, worthful, worthy.
antonym unworthy.

merriment *n* amusement, cheerfulness, conviviality, festivity, frolic, fun, gaiety, glee, hilarity, jocosity, jocularity, jocundity, jollity, joviality, laughter, levity, liveliness, merrymaking, mirth, revelry, sport, waggery.
antonyms gloom, gravity, sadness, seriousness.

merry *adj* amusing, blithe, blithesome, boon, carefree, cheerful, chirpy, comic, comical, convivial, facetious, festive, frolicsome, fun-loving, funny, gay, glad, gleeful, happy, hilarious, humorous, intoxicated, jocose, jocular, jocund, jolly, joyful, joyous, light-hearted, mirthful, playful, riotous, rollicking, saturnalian, sportful, sportive, squiffy, tipsy, vivacious.
antonyms gloomy, glum, grave, melancholy, serious, sober, sombre.

merry-go-round *n* carousel, mad round, roundabout, whirl, whirligig.

merrymaking *n* carousal, carouse, carousing, celebration, conviviality, festivity, fun, fun and games, gaiety, jollification, jollity, larking, merriment, party, partying, rejoicings, revels, revelry.

mesh *n* chicken wire, entanglement, interlacement, knit, lattice, meshwork, net, netting, network, plexus, reticulation, tangle, tracery, weave, web.
v catch, connect, co-ordinate, dovetail, engage, enmesh, entangle, fit, harmonize, interact, interlock, intermesh, interweave, knit, match, net, snare.

mesmerize *v* benumb, captivate, engross, enthrall, entrance, fascinate, grip, hypnotize, magnetize, spellbind, stupefy.

mess *n* botch, bungle, chaos, clutter, confusion, difficulty, dilemma, dirtiness, disarray, disorder, disorganization, fiasco, fix, hash, hot water, imbroglio, jam, jumble, litter, mishmash, mix-up, muddle, muss, perplexity, pickle, pigsty, plight, predicament, shambles, schmozzle, stew, turmoil, untidiness, uproar.
antonyms order, tidiness.

mess around amuse oneself, dabble, fiddle, interfere, meddle, muck around, play, play (around), putter, tamper, tinker, toy, trifle, waste time.
antonyms order, tidy.

mess up[1] befoul, besmirch, clutter, dirty, disarrange, disarray, dishevel, foul, litter, make a mess of, mix up, muss, pollute, put in, tousle.

mess up[2] blow (it), botch, bungle, disrupt, flub, goof, jumble, louse up, make a hash of, muck up, muddle, ruin, spoil, tangle, wreck.

mess with fiddle with, interfere with (or in), meddle with, play with, tamper with, tangle with, tinker with.

message *n* bulletin, cable, commission, communication, communiqué, dispatch, errand, fax, gist, idea, import, information, intimation, lesson, letter, meaning, memorandum, mission, missive, moral, news, note, notice, point, purport, task, telegram, telex, tidings, word.

messenger *n* agent, ambassador, carrier, courier, delegate, delivery boy, emissary, envoy, errand boy, go-between, harbinger, herald, internuncio, Mercury, nuncio, runner, send.

messy *adj* badly done, botched, chaotic, cluttered, complicated, confused, difficult, dirty, dishevelled, disordered, disorganized, grubby, grungy, (in) a shambles, littered, muddled, mussy, rumpled, slobby, sloppy, slovenly, unkempt, untidy, yucky.
antonyms neat, ordered, tidy.

metamorphosis *n* alteration, change, change-over, conversion, make-over, metamorphism, metanoia, modification, mutation, permutation, rebirth, remodelling, reshaping, transfiguration, transformation, translation, transmogrification, transmutation, transubstantiation.

metaphor *n* allegory, analogy, apologue, emblem, figure of speech, image, symbol, trope.

metaphorical *adj* allegorical, emblematic, figurative, Pickwickian, symbolic, tropological.

metaphysical *adj* abstract, abstruse, basic, deep, esoteric, essential, eternal, fundamental, general, high-flown, ideal, immaterial, impalpable, incorporeal, insubstantial, intangible, intellectual, occult, ontological, oversubtle, philosophical, profound, rarefied, recondite, speculative, spiritual, subjective, supernatural, theoretical, transcendental, universal, unreal, unsubstantial.

mete out administer, allot, apportion, assign, deal out, dispense, distribute, dole out, give out, hand out, measure out, parcel out, pass around, portion, ration out.

meteor *n* aerolite, bolide, comet, fireball, meteorite, meteoroid, shooting star.

meteoric *adj* brief, brilliant, dazzling, fast, fleeting, instantaneous, momentary, overnight, rapid, spectacular, speedy, sudden, swift, transitory.

meteorologist *n* aerologist, climatologist, weatherman, weather forecaster, weather prophet.

method *n* approach, consistency, course, design, discipline, fashion, form, manner, mode, modus operandi, order, orderliness, organization, pattern, plan, planning, practice, procedure, process, program, purpose, regularity, routine, rule, scheme, structure, style, system, technique, way.

methodical *adj* businesslike, consistent, deliberate, disciplined, efficient, meticulous, neat, ordered, orderly, organized, painstaking, planned, precise, punctilious, regular, routinized, scrupulous, structured, systematic, tidy.
antonyms confused, desultory, irregular.

meticulous *adj* accurate, careful, detailed, exact, fastidious, fussy, microscopic, painstaking, particular, perfectionistic, precise, punctilious, scrupulous, strict, thorough.
antonyms careless, slapdash.

métier *n* business, calling, craft, field, forte, line, occupation, profession, pursuit, specialty, sphere, talent, trade, vocation.

metropolis *n* capital, city, megacity, megalopolis, metropolitan area, urban centre.

mettle *n* ardour, backbone, boldness, bravery, calibre, character, courage, daring, disposition, fire, fortitude, gameness, ginger, grit, guts, hardihood, heart, indomitability, kidney, life, make-up, nature, nerve, pith, pluck, quality, resolve, spirit, spunk, temper, temperament, valour, vigour.

mew *v* caterwaul, cry, meow, mewl, pule, whine.

mewl *v* blubber, cry, pule, snivel, wail, whimper, whine.

miasma *n* effluvium, fetor, mephitis, odour, pollution, reek, smell, stench, stink.

miasmal *adj* fetid, foul, insalubrious, malodorous, mephitic, miasm(at)ic, noisome, noxious, offensive, pestilent, poisonous, polluted, putrid, reeking, smelly, stinking, toxic, unwholesome.

microbe *n* bacillus, bacterium, bug, germ, micro-organism, pathogen, virus.

microscopic *adj* imperceptible, inappreciable, indiscernible, infinitesimal, invisible, minuscule, minute, negligible, tiny.

antonyms huge, vast.

midday *n* lunchtime, noon, noonday, noontide, noontime, twelve noon.

middle *adj* central, halfway average, inner, inside, intermediate, intervening, mean, medial, median, mediate, medium, mid, middling, midmost.

n average, centre, focus, golden mean, halfway mark, halfway point, happy medium, heart, inside, mean, middle way, midpoint, midriff, midsection, midst, thick, via media, waist.

antonyms beginning, border, edge, end, extreme.

in the middle of among, busy with, during, engaged in, in the midst of, in the process of, occupied with, surrounded by, while.

middle-class *adj* bourgeois, conventional, preppy, suburban, white collar.

middleman *n* agent, broker, distributor, entrepreneur, fixer, go-between, intermediary, mediator, merchant, negotiator, retailer, trader.

middling *adj* adequate, average, fair, indifferent, mean, median, mediocre, medium, middle, moderate, modest, OK, ordinary, passable, run-of-the-mill, so-so, tolerable, unexceptional, unremarkable.

midget *n* dwarf, gnome, homunculus, Lilliputian, manikin, midge, peewee, pygmy, shrimp, Tom Thumb.

antonym giant.

adj dwarf, elfin, Lilliputian, little, miniature, pocket, pocket-size, pygmy, small, teeny, tiny, toy, undersized, wee.

antonym giant.

midst *n* bosom, centre, core, depths, epicentre, heart, hub, interior, middle, midpoint, thick.

in the midst of among, during, in the middle of, in the thick of, surrounded by.

midway *adv* betwixt and between, halfway, in the middle, in midcourse, partially, partway.

mien *n* air, appearance, aspect, aura, bearing, carriage, complexion, countenance, demeanour, deportment, look, manner, presence, semblance.

miffed *adj* aggrieved, annoyed, chagrined, disgruntled, displeased, huffy, hurt, in a huff, irked, irritated, nettled, offended, peevish, piqued, put out, resentful, sulking, ticked off, upset, vexed.

antonyms delighted, pleased.

might *n* authority, clout, efficacy, force, heftiness, muscularity, potency, power, powerfulness, prowess, puissance, strength, sway, valour, vigour.

mightily *adv* decidedly, energetically, exceedingly, extremely, forcefully, greatly, highly, hugely, intensely, lustily, manfully, much, potently, powerfully, strenuously, strongly, very, very much, vigorously, with might and main.

mighty *adj* bulky, colossal, considerable, doughty, enormous, forceful, gigantic, grand, great, hardy, hefty, huge, immense, indomitable, large, lusty, manful, massive, monumental, muscular, potent, powerful, prodigious, puissant, robust, stalwart, stout, strapping, strenuous, strong, stupendous, sturdy, titanic, towering, tremendous, vast, vigorous.

antonyms frail, weak.

migrant *n* drifter, emigrant, globetrotter, gypsy, hobo, immigrant, itinerant, nomad, rover, tinker, transient, traveller, trekker, vagrant, wanderer.

adj drifting, globetrotting, gypsy, immigrant, itinerant, migratory, nomadic, roving, shifting, transient, travelling, vagrant, wandering.

migrate *v* drift, emigrate, expatriate, immigrate, journey, move, roam, rove, shift, transmigrate, travel, trek, voyage, wander.

mild *adj* amiable, balmy, bland, calm, clement, compassionate, docile, easy, easygoing, equable, forbearing, forgiving, gentle, good-natured, indulgent, kind, lenient, light, meek, mellow, merciful, moderate, pacific, passive, peaceable, placid, pleasant, serene, smooth, soft, sweet-tempered, temperate, tender, tranquil, warm.

antonyms fierce, harsh, stormy, strong, violent.

mildewy *adj* damp, dank, fetid, fusty, mildewed, mouldy, musty, rotten.

mildness *n* blandness, calmness, clemency, docility, forbearance, gentleness, good nature, indulgence, kindness, leniency, lenity, meekness, mellowness, moderation, passivity, placidity, smoothness, softness, temperateness, tenderness, tractability, tranquillity, warmth.

antonyms ferocity, harshness, strength, violence.

milestone *n* accomplishment, breakthrough, critical development, event, key advance, landmark, turning point.

milieu *n* arena, atmosphere, background, element, environment, locale, location, medium, scene, setting, sphere, surroundings, venue.

militant *adj* active, aggressive, bellicose, belligerent, combative, contentious, embattled, extremist, fanatical, fighting, hawkish, overassertive, overzealous, pugnacious, pushy, trigger-happy, triumphalist, vigorous, warlike, warring.

n activist, aggressor, battler, combatant, extremist, fanatic, fighter, partisan, struggler, triumphalist, warrior, zealot.

military *adj* armed, martial, service, soldierlike, soldierly, warlike.

n (armed) forces, (armed) services, army, soldiers, soldiery.

militate (against) *v* act, argue, contend, count, counter, counteract, hinder, operate, oppose, prevent, tell, thwart, weigh, work.

▲ *confusable word* mitigate.

milk *v* bleed, drain (from), draw from, draw off, exploit, express, extract, impose on, pump, siphon, squeeze (out), take advantage of, tap, use, wring.

milksop *n* coward, chicken, gutless wonder, jellyfish, milquetoast, mollycoddle, namby-pamby, pansy, sissy, weakling, wimp.

milky *adj* alabaster, albescent, chalky, clouded, cloudy, milk-white, opaque, white, whitish.

mill[1] *n* coffee mill, crusher, grinder, millstone, pulverizer, quern.

v comminute, crush, granulate, grate, grind, pound, powder, press, pulverize, roll.

mill[2] *n* factory, foundry, plant, shop, works.

mill[3] *v* crowd, scurry, seethe, swarm, throng, wander.

millstone *n* affliction, albatross, burden, drag, encumbrance, grindstone, handicap, load, quernstone, weight.

mime *n* charade(s), dumb show, gesture, (hand) motions, mimicry, mummery, pantomime.

v act out, gesture, impersonate, mimic, represent, signal, simulate.

mimic *v* act like, ape, caricature, copy, echo, imitate, impersonate, look like, mime, mirror, mock, parody, parrot, personate, resemble, simulate, take off (on).

n ape, caricaturist, copy, copycat, copyist, imitator, impersonator, impressionist, parodist, parrot.

adj apish, echoic, fake, imitation, imitative, make-believe, mimetic, mock, pseudo, sham, simulated.

mimicry *n* apery, burlesque, caricature, copying, imitating, imitation, impersonation, impression, mimesis, mimicking, mockery, parody, parrotry, takeoff.

mince[1] *v* chop, crumble, crush, cut (up), dice, grind, hash.

mince[2] *v* diminish, euphemize, extenuate, hold back, moderate, palliate, play down, soften, spare, suppress, tone down, weaken.

mince[3] *v* attitudinize, pose, posture, simper.

mincing *adj* affected, comcombical, dainty, dandified, delicate, effeminate, foppish, la-di-da, niminy-piminy, precious, pretentious, prim, prissy, simpering.

mind[1] *n* attention, attitude, belief, bent, brains, concentration, desire, disposition, fancy, feeling, genius, grey matter, head, imagination, inclination, intellect, intellectual, intelligence, intention, judgment, leaning, marbles, memory, mentality, mindset, mood, notion, opinion, outlook, point of view, psyche, purpose, rationality, reason, recollection, remembrance, sanity, sense, senses, sensorium, sentiment, spirit, tendency, thinker, thinking, thought(s), understanding, urge, view, will, wish, wits.

in (or **of**) **two minds** dithering, hesitant, hesitating, shilly-shallying, uncertain, undecided, unsure, vacillating, wavering.

antonym certain.

mind's eye contemplation, head, imagination, memory, mind, recollection, remembrance.

mind[2] *v* be unwilling (to), care, demur, disapprove (of), dislike, object (to), resent, take amiss, take offence (at).

mind[3] *v* adhere to, attend (to), be careful (of), be on one's guard, care for, comply with, ensure, follow, guard, have charge of, heed, keep an eye on, listen to, look after, make certain, mark, note, notice, obey, observe, pay attention, pay heed to, regard, respect, see (to it), take care (of), take heed, tend, watch (out for).

mindful *adj* alert, alive (to), attentive, aware, careful, chary, cognizant, compliant, conscious, considerate, heedful, obedient, observant, regardful, remembering, remindful, respectful, sensible, thoughtful, wary, watchful.

antonyms heedless, inattentive, mindless.

mindless *adj* asinine, automatic, brainless, brutish, careless, foolish, forgetful, gratuitous, heedless, idiotic, illogical, imbecilic, inattentive, incurious, irrational, mechanical, moronic, neglectful, negligent, oblivious, obtuse, stupid, thoughtless, unaware, unintelligent, unmindful, unreasoning, unthinking, witless.

antonyms intelligent, mindful, thoughtful.

mine[1] *n* abundance, coal field, colliery, deposit, excavation, fund, hoard, lode, pit, reserve, sap, shaft, source, stock, store, supply, treasury, trench, tunnel, vein, wealth.

v delve (for), dig for, dig up, excavate, extract, hew, quarry, remove, sap, subvert, tunnel, undermine, unearth, weaken.

mine[2] *n* ashcan, bomb, booby trap, depth charge, egg, explosive, land mine.

mingle *v* alloy, associate, blend, circulate, coalesce, combine, commingle, compound, consort, fraternize, hobnob, intermingle, intermix, interweave, join, keep company, merge, mix, rub shoulders, socialize.

miniature *adj* baby, diminutive, dwarf, Lilliputian, little, midget, mini, minuscule, minute, peewee, pint-sized, pocket, pocket-size, pygmy, reduced, scaled-down, small, teensy, teeny, tiny, toy, wee.

antonym giant.

minimal *adj* insignifcant, least (possible), little, minimum, minuscule, minute, nominal, slight, small, token.

minimize *v* abbreviate, attenuate, belittle, curtail, decrease, decry, dedramatize, de-emphasize, deprecate, depreciate, diminish, discount, disparage, downplay, lessen, make light of, make little of, play down, prune, reduce, shrink, underestimate, underrate.

antonym maximize.

minimum *n* bottom, least (amount), lowest point, nadir, slightest.

antonym maximum.

adj bottom, least (possible), littlest, lowest, minimal, slightest, smallest, teeniest, teensiest, tiniest, weest.

antonym maximum.

minion *n* backscratcher, bootlicker, creature, darling, favourite, flatterer, flunky, follower, groupie, hanger-on, heeler, henchman, hireling, lackey, lickspittle, myrmidon, parasite, pawn, pet, sycophant, toady, underling, yes man.

minister[1] *n* administrator, adviser, agent, aide, ambassador, assistant, cabinet member, delegate, diplomat, envoy, executive, instrument, ministrant, officeholder, official, plenipotentiary, servant, vizier.

v accommodate, administer, aid, attend, bring hope (to), care (for), cater (to), help, nurse, serve, succour, support, take care (of), tend.

minister[2] *n* chaplain, churchman, churchwoman, clergyman, clergywoman, cleric, divine, dominie, ecclesiastic, Levite, man (or woman) of the cloth, parson, pastor, preacher, priest, rector, vicar.

ministration *n* aid, assistance, care, favour, help, office(s), patronage, relief, service, succour, supervision, support.

ministry[1] *n* administration, bureau, cabinet, council, department, ministers, office.

ministry[2] *n* clergy, clerics, holy orders, ministers, the church, the cloth, the pastorate, the priesthood.

minor *adj* inconsequential, inconsiderable, inferior, insignificant, junior, lesser, light, lower, negligible, paltry, petty, piddling, secondary, second-class, slight, small, smaller, subordinate, trifling, trivial, unclassified, unimportant, younger.

antonym major.

minstrel *n* balladeer, bard, jongleur, musician, poet, rhymer, rimer, singer, street musician, troubadour.

mint *v* cast, coin, construct, create, devise, fabricate, fashion, forge, invent, make, make up, manufacture, monetize, originate, produce, punch, stamp, strike.

adj A-one, as good as new, brand-new, excellent, first-class, immaculate, in perfect shape, perfect, unblemished, undamaged, untarnished.

n an arm and a leg, bundle, fortune, heap, killing, king's ransom, million, packet, pile, stack, wad.

minuscule *adj* diminutive, fine, infinitesimal, itsy-bitsy, Lilliputian, little, microscopic, miniature, minute, small-scale, teensy, teeny, tiny.

antonyms gigantic, huge.

minute[1] *n* flash, instant, jiffy, mo, moment, sec, second, shake, trice, twinkling of an eye, two shakes.

minute[2] *adj* close, critical, detailed, diminutive, exact, exhaustive, fine, inconsiderable,

infinitesimal, intricate, itsy-bitsy, Lilliputian, little, meticulous, microscopic, miniature, minim, minuscule, negligible, painstaking, paltry, petty, picayune, piddling, precise, punctilious, puny, slender, slight, small, tiny, trifling, trivial, unimportant.

antonyms gigantic, huge, immense.

minutely *adv* carefully, closely, critically, exactly, exhaustively, in detail, fully, meticulously, painstakingly, precisely, scrupulously, systematically, with a fine-toothed comb.

minutes *n* details, memoranda, notes, proceedings, record(s), report(s), tapes, transactions, transcript.

minutiae *n* details, ins and outs, intricacies, niceties, particulars, subtleties, trifles, trivialities.

miracle *n* deus ex machina, marvel, miraculum, phenomenon, prodigy, thaumaturgy, wonder.

miraculous *adj* amazing, astonishing, astounding, extraordinary, incredible, inexplicable, magical, marvellous, otherworldly, phenomenal, preternatural, prodigious, stupendous, superhuman, supernatural, thaumaturgic, unaccountable, unbelievable, unheard of, wonderful, wondrous.

antonyms natural, normal.

mirage *n* Fata Morgana, figment, of the imagination, hallucination, (optical) illusion, phantasm.

mire *n* bog, difficulties, dirt, fen, marsh, morass, muck, mud, murky, muskey, ooze, quag, quagmire, slime, slush, swamp, trouble.

mirror *n* copy, double, glass, hand glass, image, likeness, looking glass, model, reflection, reflector, replica, representation, speculum, spit and image, spitting image, twin.

v copy, depict, echo, emulate, follow, imitate, mimic, portray, reflect, represent, resemble, show.

mirth *n* amusement, cheerfulness, festivity, frolic, fun, gaiety, gladness, glee, hilarity, jocosity, jocularity, jocundity, jollity, joviality, joyousness, laughter, levity, merriment, merrymaking, pleasure, rejoicing, revelry, sport.

antonyms gloom, glumness, melancholy.

mirthful *adj* amused, amusing, blithe, cheerful, cheery, festive, frolicsome, funny, gay, glad, gladsome, happy, hilarious, jocose, jocular, jocund, jolly, jovial, laughable, laughing, light-hearted, merry, playful, sportive, uproarious, vivacious.

antonyms gloomy, glum, melancholy, mirthless.

misadventure *n* accident, bad luck, calamity, cataclysm, catastrophe, contretemps, debacle, disaster, failure, grief, ill fortune, ill luck, mischance, misfortune, mishap, reverse, setback, tragedy.

misanthropic *adj* antisocial, cynical, distrustful, egoistic, hostile, inhumane, malevolent, surly, suspicious, Timonistic, unfriendly, unsociable, unsympathetic.

antonym philanthropic.

misapply v abuse, exploit, misappropriate, misemploy, mismanage, misuse, pervert.

misapprehend v err, get the wrong idea, miscomprehend, misconceive, misconstrue, mishear, misinterpret, misjudge, misread, mistake, misunderstand, take amiss.

misapprehension n delusion, error, fallacy, misbelief, misconception, misconstruction, misinterpretation, misjudgment, misreading, mistake, misunderstanding.

misappropriate v abuse, defalcate, divert, embezzle, feather one's nest with, misapply, mismanage, misspend, misuse, peculate, pervert, pocket, steal, swindle.

misappropriation n defalcation, embezzlement, misapplication, mismanagement, misuse, peculation, pocketing, stealing, theft.

misbegotten adj dishonest, disreputable, harebrained, ill-advised, ill-conceived, illegitimate, ill-gotten, illicit, indiscreet, monstrous, pitiable, poorly thought-out, purloined, shady, stolen, unlawful.

misbehave v act up, be naughty, carry on, cut up, disobey, get into mischief, horse around, kick over the traces, mess around, muck around, offend, sow one's wild oats, transgress, trespass.

antonym behave.

misbehaviour n disobedience, disorderliness, hooliganism, impropriety, incivility, indiscipline, insubordination, mayhem, mischief, misconduct, misdeeds, misdemeanour, monkey business, naughtiness, rudeness, shenanigans, unruliness.

antonym good behaviour.

misbelief n delusion, error, fallacy, heresy, heterodoxy, illusion, misapprehension, misconception, miscreance, unorthodoxy.

miscalculate v blunder, err, get wrong, misjudge, overestimate, overrate, overvalue, slip up, underestimate, underrate, undervalue.

miscarriage n abortion, botch, breakdown, error, failure, misadventure, mischance, misfire, mishap, mismanagement, miss, perversion, thwarting, undoing.

antonym success.

miscarry v abort, bite the dust, bomb, come to grief, come to nothing, fail, fall through, flounder, go wrong, miss fire, miss the mark, warp.

antonym succeed.

miscellaneous adj assorted, confused, diverse, diversified, farraginous, heterogeneous, indiscriminate, jumbled, manifold, many, mingled, mixed, motley, multifarious, multiform, omnifarious, promiscuous, sundry, varied, various.

miscellany n anthology, assortment, collection, conglomeration, diversity, farrago, gallimaufry, hash, hodgepodge, jumble, medley, mélange, mixed bag, mixture, odds and ends, pastiche, potpourri, salmagundi, variety.

mischance n accident, bad break, bad luck, blow, calamity, contretemps, disaster, ill fortune, ill luck, infelicity, misadventure, misfortune, mishap, tragedy.

mischief[1] n bane, damage, detriment, devilment, deviltry, diablerie, disruption, evil, harm, hurt, impishness, injury, misbehaviour, misfortune, monkey business, monkeyshines, naughtiness, pranks, roguery, roguishness, shenanigans, trouble, waywardness, wrong, wrongdoing.

mischief[2] n imp, (little) devil, mischief-maker, monkey, nuisance, pest, prankster, rascal, rogue, scallywag, scamp, scapegrace, villain.

antonym angel.

mischievous adj arch, bad, damaging, deleterious, destructive, detrimental, elfish, elfin, evil, exasperating, frolicsome, harmful, hurtful, impish, injurious, malicious, malignant, naughty, pernicious, playful, puckish, rascally, roguish, sinful, spiteful, sportive, teasing, tricksy, troublesome, vexatious, vicious, wayward, wicked.

antonyms good, well-behaved.

misconceive v misapprehend, misconstrue, misinterpret, misjudge, misread, mistake, misunderstand.

misconception n delusion, error, fallacy, false notion, misapprehension, misconstruction, misreading, misunderstanding, wrong idea.

misconduct n delinquency, dereliction, hanky-panky, immorality, impropriety, malfeasance, malpractice, malversation, misbehaviour, misdemeanour, misfeasance, mismanagement, naughtiness, rudeness, transgression, wrongdoing.

misconstrue v misapprehend, misconceive, misinterpret, misjudge, misread, misreckon, mistake, mistranslate, misunderstand, take the wrong way.

miscreant n bad egg, bad guy, blackguard, caitiff, criminal, dastard, degenerate, evildoer, knave, malefactor, mischief-maker, profligate, rascal, reprobate, rogue, scallywag, scamp, scapegrace, scoundrel, sinner, troublemaker, vagabond, varlet, villain, wretch, wrongdoer.

antonym worthy.

misdeed n crime, criminal act, delinquency, fault, felony, malefaction, malfeasance, misconduct, misdemeanour, misfeasance, offence, peccadillo, sin, transgression, trespass, villainy, wrong.

misdemeanour n fault, indiscretion, infringement, lapse, malfeasance, misbehaviour, misconduct, misdeed, offence, peccadillo, summary offence, transgression, trespass.

miser n cheapskate, curmudgeon, Mammonist, moneygrubber, niggard, penny-pincher, pinchpenny, save-all, Scrooge, Silas Marner, skinflint, tightwad.

antonym spendthrift.

miserable *adj* abject, adverse, anguished, bad, base, blue, broken-hearted, caitiff, cheerless, contemptible, crestfallen, crushed, dejected, deplorable, depressed, desolate, despicable, despondent, destitute, detestable, disconsolate, disgraceful, dismal, distressed, doleful, dolorous, down, downcast, dreary, forlorn, gloomy, glum, hapless, heartbroken, ignominious, impoverished, (in) the dumps, indigent, joyless, lachrymose, lamentable, lousy, low, low-spirited, luckless, lugubrious, meagre, mean, measly, melancholic, melancholy, mere, mournful, needy, niggardly, out of sorts, paltry, pathetic, penniless, piteous, pitiable, pitiful, pleasureless, poor, sad, scanty, scurvy, shabby, shameful, sordid, sorrowful, sorrowing, sorry, squalid, stricken, tearful, unhappy, vile, woebegone, woeful, worthless, wretched.

antonyms cheerful, comfortable, generous, honourable, noble.

miserly *adj* avaricious, beggarly, cheap, cheeseparing, close, close-fisted, covetous, curmudgeonly, grasping, grudging, illiberal, mean, mercenary, money-grubbing, niggardly, parsimonious, penny-pinching, penurious, Scroogelike, sparing, stingy, thrifty, tight, tight-fisted, ungenerous.

antonyms generous, lavish, prodigal, spendthrift.

misery[1] *n* abjectness, adversity, affliction, agony, anguish, bale, bane, bitter pill (to swallow), blues, burden, calamity, catastrophe, cross, curse, depression, desolation, despair, destitution, disaster, discomfort, discontent, distress, dolour, extremity, gloom, grief, hardship, heartache, heartbreak, humiliation, indigence, infelicity, living death, load, low spirits, melancholia, melancholy, misfortune, mortification, need, oppression, ordeal, penury, poverty, privation, prostration, sadness, sordidness, sorrow, squalor, suffering, torment, torture, trial, tribulation, trouble, unhappiness, want, woe, wretchedness.

antonyms comfort, happiness, joy.

misery[2] *n* bear, crosspatch, griper, grouch, Jeremiah, Job's comforter, killjoy, moaner, moper, party pooper, pessimist, prophet of doom, ray of sunshine, sourpuss, spoilsport, wet blanket, whiner.

antonym sport.

misfire *v* abort, bomb, come a cropper, come to grief, come to nothing, fail, fall flat, fall short, fall through, fizzle out, flop, founder, go phut, go wrong, miscarry.

antonym succeed.

misfit *n* drop-out, eccentric, fish out of water, individualist, lone wolf, loner, maverick, nonconformist, odd man out, oddball, rogue, square peg in a round hole, weirdo.

antonym conformist.

misfortune *n* accident, adversity, affliction, bad luck, blow, buffet, calamity, catastrophe, disaster, failure, grief, hardship, harm, ill luck, infelicity, loss, misadventure, mischance, misery, mishap, reversal, reverse, setback, tragedy, trial, tribulation, trouble, woe.

antonyms luck, success.

misgiving *n* anxiety, apprehension, backward glance, compunction, distrust, doubt, dubiety, fear, foreboding, hesitation, misdoubt, presentiment, qualm, reservation, scruple, second thoughts, suspicion, uncertainty, unease, worry.

antonym confidence.

misguided *adj* deluded, erring, erroneous, foolish, ill-advised, ill-considered, ill-judged, imprudent, incautious, injudicious, misconceived, misled, misplaced, mistaken, rash, unreasonable, unsuitable, unwarranted, unwise.

antonym sensible.

mishandle *v* ball up, botch, bungle, fumble, louse up, make a hash of, make a mess of, mess up, misconduct, misjudge, mismanage, mistreat, misuse, muff, screw up.

antonyms cope, manage.

mishap *n* accident, adversity, calamity, contretemps, disaster, ill fortune, ill luck, misadventure, mischance, misfortune, misventure, setback, wreck.

mishmash *n* conglomeration, farrago, gallimaufrey, hash, hodgepodge, jumble, medley, mélange, mess, mixed bag, muddle, pastiche, potpourri, rat's nest, salad, salmagundi.

misinform *v* bluff, deceive, give a bum steer, hoodwink, lead down the garden path, misdirect, misguide, mislead, mistell, snow, string someone a line, take for a ride.

misinformation *n* baloney, bluff, bum steer, deception, disinformation, eyewash, guff, hype, lies, misdirection, nonsense, snow job.

misinterpret *v* distort, garble, get wrong, misappreciate, misapprehend, misconceive, misconstrue, misjudge, misread, misrepresent, mistake, misunderstand, pervert, take (in) the wrong way, warp, wrest.

misjudge *v* miscalculate, miscount, misinterpret, mistake, overestimate, overrate, underestimate, underrate, undervalue.

mislead *v* beguile, bluff, deceive, delude, fool, give a bum steer, hoodwink, lead astray, lead down the garden path, misadvise, misdirect, misguide, misinform, pull the wool over someone's eyes, snow, take for a ride, take in, throw off-track.

misleading *adj* ambiguous, biassed, casuistic, confusing, deceitful, deceptive, delusive, delusory, disingenuous, distorted, equivocatory, evasive, fallacious, false, illusory, loaded, mendacious, sophistic, specious, spurious, tricky, unreliable.

antonyms authentic, authoritative, informative, plain, unequivocal.

mismanage *v* ball up, botch, bungle, fluff, foul up, louse up, make a hash of, make a mess of, maladminister, mangle, mar, mess up, misconduct, misdirect, misgovern, mishandle, misjudge, misrule, misspend, misuse, muff, screw up, squander, waste.

mismatched *adj* antipathetic, clashing, discordant, disparate, ill-assorted, incompatible, incongruous, irregular, misallied, misjoined, mismated, unmatching, unreconcilable, unsuited.

antonyms compatible, matching.

misogynist *n* antifeminist, male chauvinist, male supremacist, sexist, woman-hater.

misplaced *adj* inappropriate, lost, misapplied, misassigned, misdirected, misfiled, mislaid, missing.

misprint *n* corrigendum, erratum, error, mistake, transposition, typo, typographical error.

misprize *v* belittle, depreciate, disdain, disparage, hold cheap, hold in contempt, look down on, slight, underestimate, underrate, undervalue.

antonyms appreciate, cherish.

misquote *v* distort, falsify, garble, misinterpret, misreport, misrepresent, misstate, muddle, pervert, twist.

misrepresent *v* belie, bend, colour, disguise, distort, exaggerate, falsify, garble, load, minimize, miscolour, misconstrue, misinterpret, misquote, misstate, pervert, slant, twist.

misrule *n* anarchy, chaos, confusion, disorder, disorganization, indiscipline, lawlessness, maladministration, misgovernment, mismanagement, riot, tumult, turbulence, turmoil.

miss¹ *v* avoid, be short, be without, bypass, circumvent, err, escape, evade, fail, fail to notice, fall short (of), forego, go wide, lack, leave out, leave undone, let go, let slip, lose, miscarry, misfire, mistake, obviate, omit, overlook, pass over, pass up, sidestep, skip (over).

n blunder, error, failure, fiasco, flop, mistake, omission, oversight.

miss² *v* be homesick for, feel the want of, grieve for, lack, lament, long for, mourn, need, pine for, regret, sorrow for, want, whistle for, wish, yearn for.

miss³ *n* child, damsel, demoiselle, flapper, Fraülein, girl, Jungfrau, junior miss, kid, lass, lassie, mademoiselle, maid, maiden, missy, Ms., nymphet, schoolgirl, spinster, sweet young thing, teenager.

missal *n* Book of Common Prayer, breviary, formulary, Mass book, prayer book, service book.

misshapen *adj* abnormal, contorted, crippled, crooked, deformed, distorted, grotesque, ill-made, ill-proportioned, malformed, monstrous, twisted, ugly, ungainly, unshapely, unsightly, warped, wry.

antonyms regular, shapely.

missile *n* arrow, ball, bolt, bomb, dart, flying bomb, grenade, ICBM, projectile, rocket, scud, shaft, shell, shot, torpedo, weapon.

missing *adj* absent, disappeared, gone astray, lacking, lost, minus, mislaid, misplaced, short, strayed, unaccounted-for, unfound, wanting.

antonyms found, present.

mission *n* aim, assignment, business, calling, campaign, charge, commission, crusade, delegates, delegation, deputation, duty, embassy, errand, goal, job, legation, mandate, ministry, object, office, operation, purpose, pursuit, quest, raison d'être, task, task force, trust, undertaking, vocation, work.

missionary *n* ambassador, apostle, campaigner, champion, crusader, emissary, envoy, evangelist, exponent, preacher, promoter, propagandist, proponent, proselytizer, teacher.

missive *n* bulletin, communication, communiqué, dispatch, epistle, letter, line, memo, memorandum, message, note, report.

misspent *adj* dissipated, frittered away, idle, idled away, misapplied, mismanaged, misused, prodigal, profitless, squandered, thrown away, unprofitable, wasted.

antonym profitable.

misstate *v* distort, falsify, garble, misquote, misrelate, misreport, misrepresent, mistell, pervert, twist.

mist *n* brume, cloud, condensation, dew, dimness, drizzle, film, fog, fogginess, haze, mistiness, obscurity, smog, spray, steam, vapour, veil.

v becloud, bedim, befog, blur, cloud, dim, film, fog, glaze (over), obscure, steam (up), veil.

antonym clear.

mistake *n* aberration, bêtise, bloomer, blooper, blunder, boner, booboo, clanger, clinker, corrigendum, erratum, error, fallacy, false move, fault, faux pas, folly, foul-up, gaffe, gaucherie, goof, howler, human error, inaccuracy, indiscretion, inexactitude, lapse, lapsus, lapsus calami, lapsus linguae, lapsus memoriae, malapropism, misapprehension, miscalculation, miscarriage, misconception, misjudgment, misprint, mispronunciation, misreading, miss, misspelling, misunderstanding, mix, oversight, screw-up, slip, slip of the tongue, slip-up, solecism, typo.

v confound, confuse, get wrong, goof on, misapprehend, miscalculate, misconceive, misconstrue, misinterpret, misjudge, misobserve, misread, misreckon, misunderstand, screw up, slip up on, take, take wrongly.

mistaken *adj* deceived, deluded, erroneous, fallacious, false, faulty, ill-judged, inaccurate, inappropriate, incorrect, in error, inexact, misguided, misinformed, misinstructed, mislead, misplaced, off base, unfair, unfounded, unjust, unsound, untrue, wide of the mark, wrong.

antonyms correct, justified.

mistakenly *adv* by mistake, erroneously, fallaciously, falsely, inaccurately, inadvertently, inappropriately, incorrectly, in error, misguidedly, unfairly, unjustly, wrongly.

antonyms appropriately, correctly, fairly, justly.

mistimed *adj* ill-timed, inconvenient, infelicitous, inopportune, malapropos, tactless, unfortunate, unseasonable, unsynchronized, untimely.

antonym opportune.

mistreat *v* abuse, batter, brutalize, bully, harm, hurt, ill-treat, ill-use, injure, knock around, maltreat, manhandle, maul, mishandle, misuse, molest, push around, rough up, savage.

antonyms pamper, treat well.

mistreatment *n* abuse, battering, brutalization, bullying, cruelty, harm, ill-treatment, ill-usage, ill-use, injury, maltreatment, manhandling, mauling, mishandling, misuse, molestation, unkindness.

antonyms cosseting, pampering.

mistress *n* amante, chatelaine, concubine, courtesan, demimondaine, doxy, fancy woman, girlfriend, hetaera, inamorata, kept woman, lady, ladylove, lover, odalisque, owner, paramour, popsy, proprietress, sweetheart, teacher, woman.

mistrust *n* apprehension, caginess, caution, chariness, distrust, doubt, dubiety, fear, hesitancy, misdoubt, misgiving, reservations, scepticism, suspicion, uncertainty, wariness.

antonym trust.

v be wary (or leery) of, beware, disbelieve, distrust, doubt, fear, fight shy of, have one's doubts about, look askance at, misdoubt, question, suspect.

antonym trust.

mistrustful *adj* apprehensive, cagey, cautious, chary, cynical, distrustful, doubtful, dubious, fearful, hesitant, leery, sceptical, shy, suspicious, uncertain, wary.

antonym trustful.

misty *adj* bleary, blurred, blurry, cloudy, dim, faint, filmy, foggy, fuzzy, gauzy, hazy, indeterminate, indistinct, murky, muzzy, nebulous, obscure, opaque, out of focus, shadowy, smoky, translucent, unclear, vague, veiled.

antonyms bright, clear.

misunderstand *v* get the wrong idea, get wrong, misapprehend, miscomprehend, misconceive, misconstrue, mishear, misinterpret, misjudge, misread, miss the point, mistake, take wrong.

antonyms grasp, understand.

misunderstanding *n* argument, breach, clash, conflict, difference (of opinion), difficulty, disagreement, discord, disharmony, dispute, dissension, error, misapprehension, misconception, misconstruction, misinterpretation, misjudgment, misreading, mistake, mix-up, quarrel, rift, rupture, squabble, variance.

antonyms agreement, reconciliation.

misunderstood *adj* ill-judged, misapprehended, misconceived, misconstrued, misheard, misinterpreted, misjudged, misread, misrepresented, mistaken, unappreciated, unrecognized.

misuse *n* abuse, barbarism, catachresis, corruption, desecration, dissipation, distortion,

exploitation, harm, ill-treatment, ill-usage, injury, malapropism, maltreatment, manhandling, misapplication, misappropriation, misemployment, mismanagement, mistreatment, misusage, perversion, profanation, prostitution, solecism, squandering, wastage, waste.

v abuse, brutalize, corrupt, defile, desecrate, dissipate, distort, exploit, harm, ill-treat, ill-use, injure, maltreat, manhandle, maul, misapply, misappropriate, misemploy, mismanage, misquote, mistreat, molest, overload, overtax, pervert, pollute, profane, prostitute, squander, strain, waste, wrong.

mite *n* atom, grain, iota, jot, micron, modicum, morsel, ounce, scrap, smidgen, spark, trace, whit.

mitigate *v* abate, allay, alleviate, assuage, blunt, calm, check, decrease, diminish, dull, ease, extenuate, lessen, lighten, moderate, modify, pacify, palliate, quiet, reduce, relax, relieve, remit, slake, soften, soothe, still, subdue, temper, tone down, weaken.

antonyms aggravate, exacerbate, increase.

▲ *confusable word* militate.

mitigating *adj* alleviating, assuaging, exculpatory, extenuating, justificatory, justifying, lenitive, mitigative, modifying, palliative, qualifying, relieving, softening, vindicating.

mitigation *n* abatement, allaying, alleviation, assuagement, decrease, diminution, easement, extenuation, falling off, lessening, let up, moderation, palliation, qualification, reduction, relief, remission, softening, subduing, tempering.

antonyms aggravation, exacerbation, increase.

mix *v* admix, adulterate, alloy, amalgamate, associate, blend, coalesce, combine, commingle, commix, compound, consort, cross, dash, fold (in), fraternize, fuse, hobnob, homogenize, incorporate, infiltrate, infuse, inject, integrate, interlard, intermix, interpolate, interpose, intersperse, interweave, introduce, join, jumble, merge, mingle, rub shoulders with, shuffle, socialize, stir, synthesize, unite.

antonym separate.

n alloy, amalgam, assortment, blend, combination, composite, compound, conglomerate, fusion, medley, mishmash, mixture, pastiche, synthesis.

mix up befuddle, bewilder, blend, combine, complicate, confound, confuse, embroil, entangle, fluster, garble, implicate, involve, jumble, mix, muddle, perplex, puzzle, scramble, snarl up, throw together.

mixed *adj* alloyed, amalgamated, ambivalent, assorted, blended, co-ed, combined, composite, compound, cosmopolitan, crossbred, desegregated, diverse, diversified, ecumenical, equivocal, fused, heterogeneous, hybrid, incorporated, indecisive, integrated, interbred, interdenominational, international, merged, mingled, miscegenate, miscellaneous, mongrel, motley, multicultural, multinational,

multiracial, promiscuous, uncertain, unsegregated, varied.

mixed up befuddled, bewildered, chaotic, complicated, confused, disordered, disoriented, distracted, distraught, disturbed, helter-skelter, jumbled, maladjusted, muddled, perplexed, puzzled, scrambled, screwed up, topsy-turvy, unbalanced, upset.

mixer *n* everybody's friend, extrovert, joiner, life (and soul) of the party, party animal, socializer.

antonyms introvert, loner, recluse.

mixture *n* admixture, alloy, amalgam, amalgamation, association, assortment, blend, brew, coalescence, combination, combine, composite, compost, compound, concoction, conglomeration, cross, fusion, gallimaufry, half-caste, hodgepodge, hybrid, interfusion, intermixture, jumble, macédoine, medley, mélange, merger, miscegenation, miscellany, mix, mixed bag, mongrel, omnium-gatherum, pastiche, potpourri, preparation, salad, salmagundi, solution, synthesis, union, variety.

mix-up *n* ball-up, chaos, complication, confusion, disorder, foul-up, jumble, mess, mistake, misunderstanding, muddle, schmozzle, screw-up, snafu, snarl-up, tangle.

moan *n* beef, bellyache, bitch, complaint, gripe, groan, grouch, grouse, grumble, howl, keen, keening, lament, lamentation, murmur, sigh, snivel, sob, sough, ululation, wail, whimper, whine.

v beef, bellyache, bemoan, bewail, bitch, carp, complain, deplore, grieve, gripe, groan, grouch, grouse, grumble, howl, keen, kick up a fuss, lament, mourn, murmur, sigh, sing the blues, snivel, sob, sough, ululate, wail, weep, whimper, whine.

antonym rejoice.

mob *n* assemblage, bevy, body, bunch, canaille, collection, common herd, commonalty, company, crew, crowd, crush, dregs of society, drove, flock, gang, gathering, great unwashed, group, herd, hoi polloi, horde, host, lot, many-headed beast (or monster), mass, masses, multitude, pack, plebs, populace, press, rabble, riffraff, rout, scum (of the earth), set, swarm, throng, tribe, troop.

v besiege, charge, cram, crowd, crowd around, descend on, fill, jam, jostle, overrun, pack, pester, set upon, surround, swarm around.

antonym shun.

mobile *adj* active, agile, ambulatory, animated, changeable, changing, energetic, ever-changing, expressive, flexible, fluid, in motion, itinerant, lively, locomotive, mercurial, migrant, motile, movable, moving, nimble, on the go, on the move, peripatetic, portable, quick, roaming, roving, supple, travelling, wandering.

antonym immobile.

mobility *n* activeness, agility, animation, changeability, expressiveness, flexibility, fluidity, locomotion, locomotivity, mobilizability,

motility, motion, movability, movableness, portability, suppleness.

antonyms immobility, inflexibility, rigidity.

mobilize *v* activate, animate, assemble, call to arms, call up, enlist, galvanize, levy, marshal, motivate, muster, organize, prepare, put into action, rally, ready, set into motion, shift, stir, summon.

mob rule *n* anarchy, chaos, lawlessness, law of the jungle, lynch law, mobocracy, ochlocracy, Reign of Terror.

mock *v* ape, burlesque, caricature, chaff, cheat, debunk, deceive, defy, deride, disappoint, disparage, dupe, flout, frustrate, gibe (at), imitate, insult, jeer (at), joke (about), lampoon, laugh at, laugh in (someone's) face, laugh to scorn, make fun of, make light of, make sport of, mimic, parody, parrot, pasquinade, poke fun at, rag, razz, revile, ride, ridicule, roast, satirize, scoff at, scorn, send up, sneer, take off (on), taunt, tease, thwart, travesty, twit.

antonyms flatter, praise.

adj artificial, bogus, counterfeit, dummy, ersatz, fake, false, feigned, fraudulent, imitation, phony, pinchbeck, plastic, pretended, pseudo, sham, simulated, substitute, spurious, synthetic.

mocker *n* derider, detractor, flouter, iconoclast, jeerer, lampooner, lampoonist, pasquinader, reviler, ridiculer, satirist, scoffer, scorner, sneerer, tease, tormentor.

antonyms flatterer, supporter.

mockery *n* burlesque, caricature, contempt, contumely, deception, derision, disappointment, disdain, disrespect, farce, gibes, iconoclasm, imitation, insults, jeering, joke, lampoon, lampoonery, letdown, mimicry, misrepresentation, parody, pasquinade, poor excuse (for), pretence, ridicule, sarcasm, satire, scoffing, scorn, sendup, sham, spoof, takeoff, travesty, wisecracks.

antonyms flattery, praise.

mocking *adj* contemptuous, contumelious, cynical, derisive, derisory, disdainful, disrespectful, iconoclastic, impudent, insulting, irreverent, jeering, reviling, sarcastic, sardonic, satiric, satirical, scoffing, scornful, snide, taunting.

antonym laudatory.

mode[1] *n* approach, condition, convention, course, form, look, manner, method, plan, practice, procedure, process, quality, rule, state, system, technique, vein, way.

mode[2] *n* craze, custom, fad, fashion, latest thing, rage, style, trend, vogue.

model *n* analogy, archetype, (classic) example, conceptualization, configuration, copy, criterion, design, draft, dummy, embodiment, epitome, exemplar, facsimile, figure, form, hypothesis, ideal, image, imitation, lodestar, manikin, mannequin, maquette, miniature, mock-up, mode, mould, norm, original, paradigm, paragon, pattern, personification, plan, praxis, prototype, replica, representation, reproduction, sketch, standard, style, subject, template, touchstone, type, version, yardstick.

adj archetypal, classic, consummate, dummy, exemplary, ideal, illustrative, miniature, par excellence, paradigmatic, perfect, prototypical, quintessential, representative, standard, typical.

v base, carve, cast, create, design, display, fashion, form, make, mould, pattern, plan, sculpt, shape, show off, sport, wear, work.

moderate *adj* abstemious, average, calm, centrist, continent, controlled, deliberate, disciplined, equable, fair, frugal, gentle, judicious, just, limited, measured, medium, middle-of-the-road, middling, mild, modest, neutral, non-extreme, ordinary, passable, rational, reasonable, restrained, sensible, sober, sparing, steady, temperate, tepid, tolerable, unexceptional, well-regulated.

v abate, allay, alleviate, blunt, calm (down), check, control, curb, cushion, decrease, diminish, dwindle, ease, lessen, limit, mediate, mitigate, modify, modulate, palliate, play down, quiet, regulate, restrain, slake, slow (down), soften, soft-pedal, stabilize, subdue, subside, tame, temper, tone down.

moderately *adv* fairly, frugally, gently, in moderation, modestly, pretty, quite, rather, reasonably, relatively, slightly, soberly, somewhat, sparingly, temperately, to a certain degree, to a certain extent, to some extent, tolerably, unpretentiously, within limits, within measure, within reason.

antonym immoderately.

moderation *n* abatement, abstemiousness, alleviation, calmness, caution, centrism, composure, continence, control, decrease, diminution, discipline, discretion, easing, equanimity, extenuation, fairness, frugality, gentleness, golden mean, judiciousness, justice, justness, lenity, letup, limitation, middle course, mildness, mitigation, moderateness, modification, modulation, palliation, reason, reduction, restraint, self-control, sobriety, temperance, tempering, via media.

antonyms increase, intemperance.

modern *adj* advanced, avant-garde, contemporary, current, emancipated, fashionable, fresh, in, innovative, late, latest, modernistic, modish, neoteric, new, newfangled, novel, now, of today, present, present-day, progressive, recent, stylish, today's, trendy, up-to-date, up-to-the-minute, with it, young.

antonyms antiquated, old, old-fashioned.

modernity *n* contemporaneity, currency, fashionableness, freshness, innovation, innovativeness, modernism, newness, novelty, originality, recentness.

antonyms antiquatedness, antiquity.

modernize *v* bring up to date, do up, improve, modify, neoterize, redesign, reform, refresh, refurbish, rejuvenate, remake, remodel, renew, renovate, revamp, streamline, transform, update.

modest *adj* bashful, blushing, chaste, coy, demure, diffident, discreet, fair, humble, limited, maidenly, meek, middling, moderate, ordinary, proper, quiet, reserved, respectable, reticent, retiring, seemly, self-deprecating, self-effacing, shy, simple, small, subdued, unassertive, unassuming, unexceptional, unostentatious, unpresuming, unpresumptuous, unpretending, unpretentious.

antonyms conceited, immodest, pretentious, vain.

modesty *n* bashfulness, coyness, decency, demureness, diffidence, discreetness, humbleness, humility, meekness, moderateness, propriety, quietness, reserve, reticence, seemliness, self-effacement, shyness, simplicity, unobtrusiveness, unostentatiousness, unpretentiousness.

antonyms conceit, immodesty, vanity.

modicum *n* atom, bit, crumb, dab, dash, drop, fragment, grain, hint, inch, iota, jot, little, mite, ounce, particle, pinch, scrap, shred, smidgen, speck, suggestion, tinge, tittle, touch, trace, whit.

modification *n* accommodation, adaptation, adjustment, alteration, change, customization, limitation, moderation, modulation, mutation, qualification, refinement, reformation, restriction, revision, shift, tempering, variation.

modify *v* abate, adapt, adjust, allay, alter, change, convert, customize, improve, lessen, limit, lower, moderate, modulate, mutate, qualify, recast, redesign, redo, reduce, refashion, reform, remodel, reorganize, reshape, restrain, restrict, revise, rework, shift, soften, temper, tone down, transform, vary.

modish *adj* à la mode, all the rage, avant-garde, chic, contemporary, current, fashionable, hip, in, jazzy, latest, modern, modernistic, now, smart, stylish, trendy, ultramodern, up-to-the-minute, vogue, with it.

antonyms dowdy, old-fashioned.

modulate *v* adjust, alter, attune, balance, change, harmonize, inflect, lower, moderate, qualify, regulate, soften, shift, tone down, tune, vary.

antonyms increase, raise.

modulation *n* accent, adjustment, alteration, change, inflection, intonation, moderation, qualification, regulation, shade, shift, tone, tuning, variation.

modus operandi line of action, manner, method, plan, procedure, rule, rule of thumb, standard process, style, system, technique, usual practice, way.

mogul *n* baron, bashaw, big cheese, big gun, big noise, big shot, big wheel, bigwig, grandee, high muckamuck, magnate, magnifico, Mr. Big, nabob, notable, panjandrum, pasha, personage, potentate, top dog, tycoon, VIP.

antonym nobody.

moist *adj* clammy, damp, dampish, dank, dewy, dripping, drizzly, humid, marshy, muggy, rainy, soggy, swampy, tearful, vaporous, watery, wet, wettish.

antonyms arid, dry.

moisten *v* bathe, bedew, damp, dampen, embrocate, humidify, imbue, irrigate, lick, moisturize, slake, soak, splash, spray, sprinkle, spritz, squirt, water, wet.

antonym dry.

moisture *n* clamminess, condensation, damp, dampness, dankness, dew, humidity, liquid, moistness, mugginess, perspiration, sweat, tears, vapour, water, wateriness, wet, wetness.

antonym dryness.

mole¹ *n* barrier, breakwater, dike, embankment, groin, jetty, levee, pier, seawall.

mole² *n* birthmark, freckle, lentigo, mark, naevus, strawberry mark.

molest *v* abuse, accost, annoy, assail, attack, badger, beset, bother, bug, bully, disturb, harass, harm, harry, hassle, hector, hound, hurt, ill-treat, ill-use, injure, maltreat, manhandle, meddle with, mistreat, persecute, pester, plague, tease, torment, vex, victimize, violate, worry.

mollify *v* abate, allay, appease, assuage, blunt, calm, compose, conciliate, cushion, ease, lessen, lull, mellow, mitigate, moderate, modify, pacify, placate, propitiate, quell, quiet, relax, relieve, soften, soothe, sweeten, temper.

antonyms aggravate, anger.

mollycoddle *v* baby, cater to, coddle, cosset, indulge, mother, overprotect, pamper, pander to, pet, spoil, spoon-feed.

antonyms ill-treat, neglect.

moment¹ *n* flash, hour, instant, jiffy, juncture, less than no time, millisecond, minute, mo, point (in time), second, shake, split second, stage, time, trice, twinkling, two shakes.

moment² *n* concern, consequence, gravity, import, importance, influence, interest, note, seriousness, significance, substance, value, weight, weightiness, worth.

antonym insignificance.

momentarily *adv* at any moment, briefly, fleetingly, for a moment, for a second, for an instant, from moment to moment, temporarily.

momentary *adj* brief, elusive, ephemeral, evanescent, fleeting, flying, fugitive, hasty, passing, quick, short, short-lived, temporary, transient, transitory.

antonyms lasting, permanent.

momentous *adj* apocalyptic, consequential, critical, crucial, decisive, earth-shaking, earth-shattering, epoch-making, eventful, fateful, grave, historic, important, life-changing, major, monumental, pivotal, serious, significant, tremendous, vital, weighty.

antonym insignificant.

momentum *n* drive, energy, force, impetus, impulse, incentive, power, propulsion, push, speed, stimulus, strength, thrust, urge, velocity.

monarch *n* crowned head, despot, dynast, emperor, empress, king, potentate, prince, princess, queen, ruler, sovereign, throne, tyrant.

monarchy *n* absolutism, autarchy, autocracy, despotism, dynasty, empire, kingdom, kingship, majesty, monocracy, princedom, principality, principate, realm, royal family, rule, sovereignty, throne, tyranny.

monastery *n* abbey, ashram, cenobium, cloister, convent, friary, house, lamasery, nunnery, priory.

monastic *adj* anchoritic, ascetic, austere, celibate, cenobitic, cloistered, cloistral, contemplative, conventual, eremitic, hermitical, monasterial, monkish, monklike, reclusive, secluded, sequestered, withdrawn.

antonyms gregarious, materialistic, worldly.

monasticism *n* anchoritism, asceticism, austerity, cenobitism, eremitism, friarhood, monkery, monkhood, reclusion, seclusion.

monetary *adj* budgetary, capital, cash, economic, financial, fiscal, money, pecuniary.

money *n* baksheesh, banknotes, bankroll, boodle, brass, bread, capital, cash, chips, coin, currency, dibs, dough, (filthy) lucre, finances, funds, gold, gravy, greenstuff, hard cash, hard money, legal tender, loot, mazuma, means, mint, money of account, moola, notes, pelf, ready money, rhino, riches, roll, scrip, shekels, shinplasters, silver, specie, sugar, the ready, the wherewithal, wad, wealth.

in the money affluent, flush, loaded, opulent, prosperous, rich, rolling in it, wealthy, well-heeled, well-off, well-to-do.

moneyed *adj* affluent, comfortable, filthy rich, flush, loaded, opulent, prosperous, rich, rolling in the money, wealthy, well-fixed, well-heeled, well-off, well-to-do.

antonym impoverished.

moneygrubbing *adj* acquisitive, avaricious, grasping, greedy, mammonistic, mercenary, miserly, money-hungry, money-mad.

mongrel *n* cross, crossbreed, cur, hybrid, lurcher, mule, mutt.

adj bigeneric, crossbred, hybrid, mixed, mongrelly, nondescript.

antonyms pedigreed, purebred.

monitor *n* adviser, detector, guide, invigilator, overseer, prefect, proctor, recorder, scanner, screen, sensor, supervisor, VDT, VDU, watchdog.

v check, detect, follow, keep an eye on, keep track of, keep under surveillance, note, observe, oversee, proctor, record, scan, screen, supervise, survey, trace, track, watch.

monk *n* abbot, ascetic, brother, celibate, cenobite, contemplative, conventual, friar, hermit, mendicant, monastic, prior, religious.

monkey¹ *n* ape, primate, simian.

monkey² *n* imitator, imp, jackanapes, (little) devil, mischief, mischief-maker, prankster, rapscallion, rascal, rogue, scallywag, scamp.

v fiddle, fidget, fool, interfere, meddle, mess, play, putter around, tamper, tinker, trifle.

monkey business carryings-on, chicanery, clowning, dishonesty, foolery, hanky-panky, hocus-pocus, jiggery-pokery, jugglery, legerdemain, mischief, monkey tricks, pranks,

prestidigitation, shenanigans, skulduggery, sleight-of-hand, tomfoolery, trickery.
antonyms honesty, probity.

monochrome *adj* black-and-white, monochroic, monochromatic, monotone, monotonous, sepia, unicolour, unicoloured.
antonym kaleidoscopic.

monolith *n* column, megalith, menhir, obelisk, shaft, standing stone.

monolithic *adj* colossal, faceless, giant, gigantic, homogeneous, huge, immobile, immovable, impersonal, inflexible, intractable, massive, monumental, of a piece, rigid, solid, undifferentiated, uniform, unvarying, vast.

monologue *n* harangue, homily, lecture, oration, sermon, soliloquy, solo, speech, spiel.
antonyms conversation, dialogue, discussion.

monomania *n* bee in one's bonnet, complex, fanaticism, fetish, fixation, hobbyhorse, idée fixe, mania, neurosis, obsession, one track mind, preoccupation, ruling passion, single-mindedness, thing.

monopolize *v* appropriate, buy up, control, corner, dominate, engross, fill (up), hog, occupy, possess, preoccupy, take over, take up, tie up.
antonym share.

monopoly *n* ascendancy, control, corner, domination, exclusive right, monopolization, monopsony, sole right.

monotonous *adj* blah, boring, colourless, drab, dreary, droning, dull, flat, humdrum, monochrome, monotone, plodding, prosaic, relentless, repetitious, repetitive, routine, same old, singsong, soul-destroying, tedious, tiresome, toneless, unbroken, unchanging, uneventful, uniform, uninflected, unrelieved, unvaried, unvarying, wearisome.
antonyms colourful, lively, varied.

monotony *n* boredom, broken record, colourlessness, dullness, flatness, humdrumness, prosaicness, repetitiousness, repetitiveness, routine, sameness, staleness, tediousness, tedium, the same old thing, tiresomeness, uneventfulness, uniformity, wearisomeness.
antonyms colour, liveliness.

monster *n* barbarian, basilisk, beast, behemoth, bogeyman, brute, centaur, chimera, cockatrice, colossus, Cyclops, demon, devil, dragon, fiend, freak, gargoyle, giant, Gorgon, harpy, hellhound, hippogriff, Hydra, jabberwock, lamia, leviathan, mammoth, manticore, Medusa, Minotaur, monstrosity, mutant, Ogopogo, ogre, ogress, savage, Sphinx, teratism, titan, villain, vampire, wendigo, werewolf, wyvern.
adj Brobdingnagian, colossal, cyclopean, enormous, gargantuan, giant, gigantic, huge, immense, jumbo, mammoth, massive, monstrous, outsize, prodigious, stupendous, titanic, tremendous, vast.
antonym minute.

monstrosity *n* abnormality, atrocity, dreadfulness, enormity, evil, eyesore, freak, frightfulness, heinousness, hellishness, hideousness, horror, loathsomeness, monster, monstrousness, mutant, obscenity, ogre, teratism, ugliness.

monstrous *adj* abhorrent, abnormal, appalling, atrocious, base, colossal, criminal, cruel, cyclopean, depraved, devilish, diabolical, disgraceful, dreadful, egregious, elephantine, enormous, evil, fiendish, foul, freakish, frightful, gargantuan, giant, gigantic, great, grotesque, gruesome, heinous, hellish, hideous, horrendous, horrible, horrific, horrifying, huge, hulking, immense, infamous, inhuman, intolerable, loathsome, mammoth, massive, misshapen, monster, obscene, odious, outrageous, prodigious, repugnant, satanic, scandalous, shocking, stupendous, teratoid, terrible, titanic, towering, tremendous, ugly, unconscionable, unnatural, vast, vicious, villainous, wicked.

monument *n* antiquity, barrow, cairn, cenotaph, commemoration, cross, dolmen, evidence, gravestone, headstone, marker, martyry, mausoleum, memento, memorial, obelisk, pillar, record, relic, remembrance, reminder, shaft, shrine, statue, testament, token, tombstone, tumulus, witness.

monumental *adj* abiding, awe-inspiring, awesome, catastrophic, classic, colossal, commemorative, conspicuous, cyclopean, durable, egregious, enduring, enormous, epic, epoch-making, funerary, gigantic, great, heroic, historic, huge, immense, immortal, important, imposing, impressive, lasting, magnificent, majestic, massive, memorable, memorial, monolithic, notable, outstanding, overwhelming, prodigious, significant, staggering, statuary, stupendous, tremendous, vast, weighty, whopping.
antonyms insignificant, unimportant.

mooch *v* beg, borrow, cadge, freeload, sponge, steal.

mood(s) *n* ambience, atmosphere, blues, caprice, depression, disposition, doldrums, dumps, feeling, fit, frame of mind, grumps, humour, melancholy, pique, spirit, state of mind, sulk, temper, tenor, the sulks, tone, vein, whim.

in the mood disposed, in the right frame of mind, inclined, interested, keen, minded, of a mind, willing.

moody *adj* angry, atrabilious, bad-tempered, blue, broody, cantankerous, capricious, changeable, choleric, crabby, cranky, cross, crotchety, crusty, dejected, depressed, dismal, doleful, dour, downcast, down in the dumps, erratic, faddish, fickle, fitful, flighty, gloomy, glum, grumpy, huffy, ill-humoured, inconstant, in the doldrums, introspective, irascible, irritable, listless, long faced, lugubrious, melancholy, mercurial, miserable, mopish, mopy, morose, peevish, pensive, petulant, piqued, sad, saturnine, short-tempered, splenetic, sulky, sullen, temperamental, testy, touchy, unpredictable, unsettled, unsociable, unstable, unsteady, up and down, volatile, waspish, withdrawn.

antonyms cheerful, equable.

moon[1] *v* brood, daydream, dream, fantasize, idle, languish, loaf, mope, muse, pine.

moon[2] *n* crescent, Cynthia, Diana, full moon, half moon, lune, lunette, meniscus, moonlight, Phoebe, Selene.

moonlike *adj* crescent, crescentic, crescentlike, crescentshaped, lunar, lunate, meniscoid, moon-shaped, moony.

moonshine[1] *n* baloney, bilage, blather, blather, bosh, bull, bunk, bunkum, claptrap, crap, eyewash, gammon, gas, guff, hogwash, hokum, hooey, hot air, humbug, malarkey, nonsense, piffle, poppycock, rot, rubbish, stuff, taradiddle, tommyrot, tripe, twaddle, wind.

antonym sense.

moonshine[2] *n* bootleg, home brew, hootch, hootchinoo, moosemilk.

moor[1] *v* anchor, berth, bind, dock, drop anchor, fasten, fix, hitch, lash, secure, tie up.

antonym loose.

moor[2] *n* brae, downs, fell, heath, moorland, upland, wasteland, wold.

moot *v* advance, argue, bring forward (or up), broach, debate, discuss, introduce, pose, propose, propound, put forward, raise, submit, suggest, ventilate.

adj academic, arguable, conjectural, contestable, controversial, debatable, disputable, disputed, doubtful, iffy, in doubt, insoluble, knotty, open, open to debate, problematic, questionable, undecided, undetermined, unresolvable, unresolved, unsettled.

moot point bone of contention, controversial issue, crux, difficulty, (Gordian) knot, open question, poser, problem, question mark, vexed question.

mop *n* crop, head of hair, mane, mass, mat, shock, sponge, squeegee, swab, thatch.

v absorb, clean, soak (up), sponge, swab, wash, wipe.

mop up absorb, account for, clean up, clear out, eliminate, finish (off), neutralize, rid off, round up, soak up, sponge, swab, take care of, tidy up, wash, wipe.

mope *v* brood, despair, despond, droop, eat one's heart out, fret, grieve, languish, moon, pine, sulk.

n depressive, grouch, grump, introvert, killjoy, melancholiac, misery, moaner, moper, pessimist, sourpuss.

moral *adj* blameless, chaste, clean-living, decent, equitable, ethical, good, high-minded, honest, honourable, incorruptible, innocent, just, meritorious, moralistic, noble, principled, proper, pure, responsible, right, righteous, scrupulous, square, straight, temperate, upright, upstanding, virtuous.

antonym immoral.

n adage, aphorism, apothegm, dictum, epigram, gnome, import, lesson, maxim, meaning, message, motto, point, precept, proverb, saw, saying, significance, teaching.

▲ *confusable word* morale.

morale *n* attitude, confidence, courage, esprit de corps, heart, mettle, mood, resolve, self-esteem, spirit, spirits, state of mind, temper.

▲ *confusable word* moral.

morality *n* chastity, decency, deontology, equity, ethicality, ethics, goodness, honesty, ideals, integrity, justice, moral climate, moral code, morals, mores, philosophy, principle(s), probity, propriety, rationale, rectitude, righteousness, scruple(s), standards, uprightness, values, virtue.

antonym immorality.

moralize *v* admonish, discourse, jaw, lecture, pontificate, preach, sermonize, soapbox, wag one's finger.

morals *n* behaviour, conduct, conscience, deontics, deontology, ethics, ideals, integrity, morality, mores, principles, probity, propriety, rectitude, scruples, standards, values.

morass *n* bog, can of worms, chaos, clutter, confusion, fen, jam, jumble, marsh, marshland, mess, mire, mix-up, muddle, quagmire, quicksand, slough, swamp, tangle.

moratorium *n* ban, delay, embargo, freeze, halt, pause, postponement, standstill, stay, stop, suspension.

antonyms go-ahead, green light.

morbid *adj* brooding, corrupt, deadly, diseased, dreadful, frightful, ghastly, ghoulish, gloomy, grim, grisly, gruesome, hideous, horrible, horrid, lugubrious, macabre, malignant, melancholy, neurotic, pathological, perverted, pessimistic, sick, sombre, unhealthy, unsalubrious, unsound, unwholesome, vicious.

mordant *adj* acerbic, acid, acidic, acidulous, acrid, acrimonious, astringent, biting, bitter, caustic, corrosive, cutting, edged, harsh, incisive, mordacious, pungent, sarcastic, scathing, sharp, stinging, tart, trenchant, venomous, vicious, waspish, wounding.

antonyms gentle, sparing.

more *adj* added, additional, extra, fresh, further, greater, increased, new, renewed, repeated, spare, supplementary.

adv again, further, in addition, longer, more and more.

moreover *adv* additionally, also, as well, besides, further, furthermore, in addition, into the bargain, likewise, I might add, more to the point, to boot, too, what is more, withal.

moribund *adj* at a standstill, at death's door, collapsing, comatose, crumbling, dead and alive, declining, done for, doomed, dwindling, dying, ebbing, fading, failing, given up for dead, in extremis, languishing, near death, obsolescent, on one's last legs, on the way out, senile, sick unto death, stagnant, stagnating, waning, wasting away, weak, with one foot in the grave.

antonyms alive, flourishing, lively, nascent.

morning *n* a.m., break of day, cockcrow, dawn, daybreak, daylight, dayspring, first thing, forenoon, morn, sunrise, sunup.

adj antemeridian, auroral, dawn, forenoon, matutinal.

moron *n* ass, blockhead, bonehead, clod, cretin, dimwit, dolt, dope, dullard, dumbbell, dummy, dunce, dunderhead, fool, half-wit, idiot, imbecile, klutz, mental defective, mooncalf, muttonhead, natural, numbskull, schmo, schmuck, simpleton, vegetable, zombie.

moronic *adj* asinine, brainless, cretinous, daft, defective, dimwitted, doltish, dopey, dumb, foolish, gormless, half-witted, idiotic, imbecilic, lacking, mindless, retarded, simple, simple-minded, stupid, subnormal, thick, unintelligent.

morose *adj* blue, brooding, cheerless, churlish, crabby, cross, crusty, dejected, depressed, dour, down, gloomy, glum, grim, grouchy, gruff, huffy, humourless, ill-humoured, ill-natured, ill-tempered, long-faced, low, melancholy, misanthropic, moody, mopish, mournful, perverse, pessimistic, saturnine, sour, stern, sulky, sullen, surly, taciturn, testy, unsociable.

antonyms cheerful, communicative.

morsel *n* atom, bit, bite, crumb, dainty, delicacy, fraction, fragment, grain, modicum, mouthful, nibble, part, piece, scrap, segment, slice, smidgen, snack, soupçon, taste, tidbit.

mortal *adj* agonizing, awful, bodily, corporeal, deadly, death-dealing, deathful, dire, earthly, enormous, ephemeral, extreme, fatal, fleshly, grave, great, human, impermanent, intense, irreconcilable, killing, lethal, passing, perishable, relentless, remorseless, severe, sublunary, temporal, terrible, transient, unrelenting, worldly.

n being, body, creature, earthling, human, human being, individual, living soul, man, person, sublunary, woman.

antonyms god, immortal.

mortality *n* bloodshed, caducity, carnage, corruptibility, death, destruction, ephemerality, fatality, humanity, humanness, humans, impermanence, killing, mankind, mortals, perishability, temporality, transience, transitoriness.

antonym immortality.

mortgage *v* pawn, pledge, put in hock stake.
n bond, debenture, deed, lien, loan, pledge, security.

mortification *n* abasement, abashment, asceticism, chagrin, chastening, confounding, conquering, control, defeat, denial, discipline, discomfiture, dissatisfaction, embarrassment, humiliation, ignominy, loss of face, overthrow, punishment, self-control, shame, subduing, subjugation, vexation.

mortified *adj* abashed, ashamed, chagrined, chastened, confounded, crushed, deflated, discomfited, disconcerted, discountenanced, embarrassed, humbled, humiliated, overcome, put to shame, shamed, vexed.

antonym jubilant.

mortify *v* abase, abash, chagrin, chasten, confound, conquer, control, corrupt, crush, deflate, deny, disappoint, discipline, discomfit, disconcert, discountenance, embarrass, humble, humiliate, put to shame, shame, subdue, vex.

mostly *adv* almost entirely, as a rule, characteristically, chiefly, commonly, customarily, essentially, for the most part, generally, in most cases, largely, mainly, normally, on the whole, particularly, predominantly, primarily, principally, substantially, typically, usually.

mote *n* atom, grain, iota, jot, mite, particle, speck, spot, trace.

moth-eaten *adj* aged, ancient, antiquated, archaic, dated, decayed, decrepit, dilapidated, mangy, moribund, mouldy, musty, obsolete, old-fashioned, outdated, out-of-date, outworn, ragged, seedy, shabby, stale, tattered, threadbare, worn-out.

antonyms fresh, new.

mother *n* dam, mama, mater, materfamilias, mom, mommy, old lady, old woman.
v baby, bear, care for, cherish, cosset, foster, fuss over, indulge, nurse, nurture, overprotect, pamper, produce, protect, raise, rear, spoil, tend.

antonym neglect.

motherly *adj* affectionate, caring, comforting, fond, gentle, indulgent, kind, kindly, loving, maternal, protective, solicitous, tender, warm.

antonyms indifferent, neglectful, uncaring.

motif *n* concept, decoration, design, device, figure, form, idea, leitmotif, logo, notion, ornament, pattern, shape, strain, subject, theme, topic.

motion *n* action, activity, change, dynamics, flow, flux, gesticulation, gesture, kinesics, kinesis, kinetics, locomotion, mechanics, mobility, motility, move, movement, moving, nod, passage, passing, progress, proposal, proposition, recommendation, sign, signal, submission, suggestion, transit, travel, wave.
v beckon, direct, flag, gesticulate, gesture, give the nod, nod, sign, signal, usher, wave.

in motion afoot, functioning, going, in progress, moving, on the go, operational, running, sailing, travelling, under way.

motionless *adj* at a standstill, at rest, calm, fixed, frozen, halted, immobile, inactive, inanimate, inert, lifeless, paralysed, petrified, quiescent, resting, rigid, stagnant, standing, static, stationary, still, stock-still, stopped, transfixed, unmoving.

antonym active.

motivate *v* actuate, arouse, bring, cause, draw, drive, encourage, impel, incite, induce, inspire, inspirit, instigate, kindle, lead, move, nudge, persuade, prompt, propel, provoke, push, spark, spur, stimulate, stir, trigger, urge.

antonyms deter, prevent.

motivation *n* actuation, ambition, desire, drive, hunger, impulse, incentive, incitement, inducement, inspiration, instigation, interest, momentum, motive, persuasion, prompting, provocation, push, reason, spur, stimulus, urge, wish.

antonyms discouragement, prevention.

motive *n* cause, consideration, design, desire, grounds, impulse, incentive, incitement, inducement, influence, inspiration, intention, mainspring, motivation, object, occasion, purpose, rationale, reason, source, spur, stimulus, thinking, urge.

antonyms deterrent, discouragement, disincentive.

adj activating, actuating, agential, driving, impelling, initiating, motivating, motor, moving, operative, prompting, propellent.

antonyms deterrent, inhibitory, preventive.

motley *adj* assorted, checkered, colourful, disparate, dissimilar, diverse, diversified, haphazard, heterogeneous, ill-assorted, kaleidoscopic, miscellaneous, mixed, multicoloured, parti-coloured, patchwork, polychromatic, polychrome, prismatic, promiscuous, rainbow, unlike, varied, variegated.

antonyms homogeneous, monochrome, uniform.

mottled *adj* blotchy, brindled, calico, checkered, dappled, flecked, freckled, jaspe, marbled, patchy, pinto, piebald, pied, skewbald, speckled, splotchy, spotted, stippled, streaked, tabby, variegated, veined, watered.

antonyms monochrome, plain, uniform.

motto *n* adage, aphorism, apothegm, byword, catchword, cry, dictum, epigraph, formula, gnome, golden rule, inscription, maxim, precept, proverb, rule, saw, saying, slogan, war cry, watchword.

mould¹ *n* arrangement, build, calibre, cast, character, configuration, construction, cut, design, die, fashion, form, format, frame, framework, ilk, kidney, kind, line, make, makeup, matrix, model, moulage, nature, pattern, shape, sort, stamp, structure, style, temperament, template, type.

v affect, carve, cast, construct, contour, control, create, design, direct, fashion, fit, forge, form, hew, influence, make, model, sculpt, sculpture, shape, stamp, tailor, work.

mould² *n* black, black spot, blight, dry rot, fungus, mildew, mouldiness, must, mustiness, rot, rust.

mould³ *n* clods, dirt, earth, ground, humus, loam, rot, smut, soil.

moulder *v* break up, crumble, decay, decompose, disintegrate, fall to pieces, perish, rot, turn to dust, waste away.

mouldy *adj* bad, blighted, decaying, fusty, mildewed, mouldering, musty, old, old-fashioned, outdated, out-of-date, putrid, rotten, rotting, smutty, spoiled, stale.

antonyms fresh, wholesome.

mound *n* bank, barrow, bulwark, butte, drift, dune, earthwork, elevation, embankment, heap, hill, hillock, hummock, knob, knoll, mow,

pile, pingo, rampart, rick, ridge, rise, stack, swell, tuffet, tumulus.

mount¹ *v* accumulate, ascend, bestraddle, bestride, clamber up, climb, climb on, climb up on, copulate, cover, display, emplace, enchase, escalade, exhibit, fit, frame, get astride, get on, get up, get up on, go up, hop on, horse, install, jump on, launch, lift, place, position, prepare, produce, put in place, put in position, put on, ready, ride, scale, set, set in motion, set off, set up, stage, straddle.

n backing, base, fixture, foil, frame, horse, mountain, mounting, pedestal, podium, setting, stand, steed, support.

mount² *v* accumulate, build (up), climb, crescendo, escalate, grow, heighten, increase, intensify, multiply, pile up, rise, rocket, snowball, soar, swell.

mountain *n* abundance, alp, berg, elevation, eminence, fell, heap, height, hill, mass, massif, mound, mount, peak, pile, stack, ton.

mountainous *adj* alpine, daunting, enormous, formidable, gigantic, great, gross, high, highland, hilly, huge, hulking, immense, mammoth, mighty, monumental, ponderous, prodigious, rocky, rugged, soaring, steep, towering, unwieldy, upland.

antonyms easy, flat, small.

mountebank *n* charlatan, cheat, con man, confidence man, fake, fraud, huckster, impostor, phony, pretender, quack, rogue, spieler, swindler, trickster.

mourn *v* bemoan, bewail, deplore, grieve, keen, lament, miss, regret, rue, sigh, sorrow, wail, weep.

antonyms bless, rejoice.

mourner *n* griever, keener, lamenter, sorrower, the bereaved.

mournful *adj* broken-hearted, calamitous, cheerless, chapfallen, dejected, depressed, desolate, dirgelike, disconsolate, dismal, distressing, doleful, dolorous, downcast, elegiac, funereal, gloomy, grief-stricken, grieving, grievous, heartbroken, heavy, heavy-hearted, joyless, lachrymose, lamentable, long-faced, lugubrious, melancholy, miserable, painful, piteous, plaintive, plangent, rueful, sad, sombre, sorrowful, sorrowing, stricken, tragic, unhappy, woeful.

antonyms cheerful, joyful.

mourning *n* bereavement, black, desolation, grief, grieving, keening, lamentation, sackcloth and ashes, sadness, sorrow, wailing, weeds, weeping, widow's weeds, woe.

antonym rejoicing.

mouselike *adj* cowardly, cowering, diffident, diminutive, fearful, mousy, murine, shy, timid, timorous, unassertive.

mousey *adj* brownish, characterless, colourless, diffident, drab, dull, fearful, grey, indeterminate, ineffectual, introverted, mouselike, plain, quiet, self-effacing, shy, timid, timorous, unassertive, unforthcoming, uninteresting, withdrawn.

mouth[1]

antonyms assertive, bright, extroverted, irrepressible.

mouth[1] *n* aperture, cavity, chops, crevice, debouchment, door, embouchure, entrance, estuary, gab, gateway, gob, inlet, jaw, kisser, lips, mandibles, maw, moue, mug, muzzle, opening, oral cavity, orifice, outlet, portal, pout, threshold, trap, vent, yap.
v articulate, declaim, elegize, enunciate, form, pronounce, say, shape, speak, spout, utter, whisper.

mouth[2] *n* backchat, backtalk, boasting, braggadocio, bragging, cheek, effrontery, gas, hot air, impudence, insolence, lip, rudeness, sauce.

mouthful *n* bit, bite, drop, forkful, gob, gobbet, gulp, morsel, sample, sip, slug, spoonful, sup, swallow, taste, tidbit.

mouthpiece *n* agent, delegate, journal, organ, propagandist, representative, spokesman, spokesperson, spokeswoman, voice.

movable *adj* adjustable, alterable, changeable, conveyable, detachable, flexible, mobile, portable, removable, transferable, transportable.
antonyms fixed, immovable.

movables *n* belongings, chattels, effects, furniture, gear, goods, impedimenta, possessions, property, stuff, things.

move *v* act, activate, actuate, adjust, advance, advocate, affect, agitate, be on one's way, be on the move, budge, carry, cause, change, cover ground, decamp, depart, disturb, drift, drive, ease (into position), edge, excite, flit, get going, go, go away, gravitate, impel, impress, incite, induce, influence, inspire, jiggle, lead, leave, locomote, make progress, make strides, march, migrate, motivate, move away, move house, move in, move on, operate, persuade, proceed, progress, prompt, propel, propose, pull, push, put forward, put in motion, recommend, relocate, remove, rouse, run, sell, set out, shift, shove, start off, stimulate, stir, submit, suggest, surge, swing, switch, touch, transfer, transport, transpose, travel, turn, urge, walk.
n act, action, deed, démarche, dodge, draft, go, manoeuvre, measure, migration, motion, movement, ploy, relocation, ruse, shift, step, stratagem, stroke, tack, tactic, transfer, turn.

on the move active, advancing, astir, moving, on the go, progressing, stirring, succeeding.

movement *n* act, action, activity, advance, agitation, beat, cadence, campaign, cause, change, crusade, current, development, displacement, division, drift, drive, evolution, exercise, faction, flow, front, gesture, ground swell, group, grouping, innards, machinery, manoeuvre, measure, mechanism, metre, motion, move, moving, nod, operation, organization, pace, pacing, party, passage, progress, progression, rhythm, section, shift, steps, stir, stirring, swing, tempo, tendency, transfer, travel, trend, turn, workings, works.

movie *n* feature, film, flick, motion picture, picture, silent, talkie, video.

movies *n* acting, cinema, film(s), flicks, Hollywood, pictures, picture shows, silver screen.

moving *adj* affecting, ambulant, ambulatory, arousing, compelling, dynamic, eloquent, emotional, emotive, evocative, exciting, impelling, impressive, in gear, inspirational, inspiring, locomotive, mobile, motile, motivating, persuasive, pitiful, poignant, progressive, rousing, running, shifting, stimulating, stimulative, stirring, touching, travelling.
antonyms fixed, stationary, unemotional.

mow *v* clip, crop, cut, scythe, shear, swatch, trim.

mow down butcher, cut down, cut to pieces, decimate, destroy, fell, massacre, raze, shoot down, slaughter.

much *adv* considerably, copiously, decidedly, exceedingly, far, frequently, greatly, often, substantially, very.
adj a lot of, abundant, ample, considerable, copious, great, plenteous, plenty of, substantial, tons of.
n heaps, lashings, loads, lots, oodles, plenty, scads.
antonym little.

muck *n* dirt, droppings, dung, feces, fertilizer, filth, grime, grunge, gunk, manure, mire, mud, ooze, ordure, scum, sewage, slime, sludge.

muck up botch, bungle, make a mess of, mar, mess up, muff, ruin, screw up, spoil, waste, wreck.

mucky *adj* begrimed, bespattered, dirty, filthy, grimy, grungy, messy, miry, mud-caked, muddy, mud-spattered, oozy, soiled, sticky.
antonym clean.

mucous *adj* gelatinous, glutinous, gummy, mucilaginous, mucuslike, slimy, snotty, viscid, viscous.

mud *n* adobe, clay, dirt, gley, mire, muck, ooze, silt, slime, slop, sludge, slush.

muddle *v* addle, befog, befuddle, bewilder, bungle, complicate, confound, confuse, daze, disarrange, disorder, disorganize, disorient, fuddle, jumble, make a mess of, mess, mix up, perplex, scramble, spoil, stupefy, tangle.
n chaos, clutter, confusion, daze, disarray, disorder, disorganization, jumble, mess, mix-up, perplexity, plight, predicament, puzzlement, snarl-up, tangle.

muddle through cope, get along, get by, make it, manage, muddle along, scrape by.

muddled *adj* addled, at sea, befuddled, bewildered, chaotic, confused, dazed, disarrayed, disordered, disorganized, disoriented, flustered, higgledy-piggledy, in a fog, incoherent, jumbled, loose, messy, mixed-up, muddle-headed, perplexed, puzzled, rattled, scrambled, stupefied, tangled, unclear, vague, woolly.

muddy *adj* bespattered, blurred, boggy, cloudy, colourless, confused, dingy, dirty, dredgy, dull, foggy, foul, fuzzy, grimy, hazy, impure, indistinct, marshy, miry, mucky, mud-caked, muddled, mud-spattered, murky, obscure, opaque, quaggy, sloppy, soiled, swampy, turbid, unclear, vague, woolly.

antonyms clean, clear, lucid.

v bedaub, begrime, bespatter, cloud, confuse, dirty, fog, muddle, obscure, obfuscate, smear, smirch, soil.

antonym clean.

muff *v* botch, bungle, fluff, fumble, mess up, mishandle, mismanage, miss, spoil.

muffle *v* burke, cloak, conceal, cover, damp down, dampen, deaden, disguise, dull, envelop, gag, hood, hush (up), mask, mute, muzzle, quieten, shroud, silence, soften, stifle, suppress, swaddle, swathe, wrap up.

antonyms amplify, uncover.

mug[1] *n* beaker, cup, flagon, jug, pot, stein, stoup, tankard, toby.

mug[2] *n* countenance, face, features, gab, kisser, mouth, physiognomy, puss, trap.

mug[3] *v* ambush, assault, attack, bash, batter, beat up, fall upon, garrote, hold up, jump (on), rip off, rob, roll, set upon, steal from, stick up, swarm, waylay.

muggy *adj* clammy, close, damp, dank, heavy, humid, moist, oppressive, sticky, stifling, stuffy, sudorific, sultry, sweltering.

antonym dry.

mulish *adj* balking, bloody-minded, bullheaded, cross-grained, defiant, difficult, headstrong, inflexible, intractable, intransigent, obstinate, perverse, pig-headed, recalcitrant, refractory, rigid, self-willed, stiff-necked, stubborn, unreasonable, willful, wrong-headed.

mull over *v* chew on, consider, contemplate, deliberate, examine, meditate on, muse on, ponder, reflect on, review, ruminate, study, think about, think over, turn over in the mind, weigh.

multifarious *adj* different, diverse, diversified, legion, manifold, many, miscellaneous, multifold, multiform, multiphase, multiple, multiplex, multitudinous, numerous, sundry, varied, variegated.

multiple *adj* manifold, many, multifarious, multiplex, multitudinous, numerous, plural, several, sundry, various.

multiplicity *n* abundance, array, diversity, heaps, host, loads, lot, lots, manifoldness, mass, multitude, myriad, number, numerousness, oodles, piles, plurality, profusion, scores, stacks, tons, variety.

multiply *v* accumulate, augment, boost, breed, build up, expand, extend, increase, intensify, procreate, proliferate, propagate, reproduce, spread.

antonyms decrease, lessen.

multitude *n* army, assemblage, assembly, collection, commonalty, concourse, congregation, crowd, herd, hive, hoi polloi, horde, host, legion, lot, lots, mass, mob, myriad, people, populace, proletariat, public, rabble, sea, swarm, throng.

antonyms handful, scattering.

multitudinous *adj* abounding, abundant, considerable, copious, countless, great, infinite, innumerable, legion, manifold, many, myriad, numerous, profuse, swarming, teeming, umpteen.

mum *adj* close-lipped, close-mouthed, dumb, mute, quiet, reticent, secretive, silent, taciturn, tight-lipped, uncommunicative, unforthcoming.

mumbo jumbo *n* abracadabra, cant, chant, charm, claptrap, conjuration, double talk, gibberish, gobbledygook, hocus-pocus, humbug, incantation, jargon, magic, mummery, nonsense, rigmarole, rite, ritual, spell, superstition.

munch *v* chew, chomp, crunch, eat, masticate, nibble, nosh, snack.

mundane *adj* banal, commonplace, day-to-day, earthly, everyday, fleshly, human, humdrum, material, mortal, ordinary, prosaic, routine, secular, subastral, sublunary, temporal, terrestrial, unimaginative, workaday, worldly.

antonyms cosmic, extraordinary, supernatural.

municipal *adj* borough, burg, city, civic, community, public, town, urban.

municipality *n* borough, burgh, city, district, precinct, town, township.

munificence *n* beneficence, benevolence, big-heartedness, bounteousness, bounty, generosity, generousness, hospitality, largesse, liberality, magnanimousness, open-handedness, open-heartedness, philanthropy.

antonyms niggardliness, stinginess.

munificent *adj* beneficent, benevolent, big-hearted, bounteous, bountiful, freehanded, generous, hospitable, lavish, liberal, magnanimous, open-handed, open-hearted, philanthropical, princely, rich, unstinting.

antonyms niggardly, stingy, ungenerous.

murder *n* agony, assassination, bloodshed, butchery, carnage, difficult, foul play, fratricide, genocide, hell, homicide, infanticide, killing, liquidation, manslaughter, massacre, matricide, misery, next to impossible, ordeal, parricide, patricide, slaughter, slaying.

v assassinate, bump off, burke, butcher, cut down, destroy, dispatch, do in, eliminate, execute, exterminate, gun down, hit, kill, mangle, massacre, mow down, rub out, slaughter, slay, take the life of, terminate, waste.

murderer *n* assassin, butcher, cutthroat, fratricide, hired gun, hit man, homicide, killer, liquidation, matricide, parricide, patricide, slaughterer, slayer.

murderous *adj* arduous, barbarous, bloodthirsty, bloody, brutal, cruel, cutthroat, dangerous, deadly, death-dealing, destructive, devastating, difficult, exhausting, fatal, fell, ferocious, harrowing, hellish, homicidal, internecine, killing, lethal, sanguinary, sapping, savage, slaughterous, strenuous, unpleasant, withering.

murky *adj* cloudy, dark, dim, dingy, dismal, dreary, dull, dusky, enigmatic, foggy, gloomy, grey, hazy, impenetrable, misty, mysterious, obscure, overcast, thick, veiled.
antonyms bright, clear.

murmur *n* babble, burble, buzz, buzzing, complaint, croon, drone, grumble, hum, humming, moan, mumble, murmuring, muttering, purl, purling, purr, rippling, rumble, rustle, susurration, undertone, whisper, whispering.
v babble, burble, burr, buzz, drone, gurgle, hum, mumble, mutter, purl, purr, ripple, rumble, rustle.

muscle *n* bicep, brawn, clout, depressor, force, forcefulness, influence, levator, might, muscularity, potency, power, sinew, stamina, strength, sturdiness, teeth, tendon, thews, weight.

muscle in butt in, elbow one's way in, force one's way in, horn in, impose oneself, jostle, push in, shove, strong-arm, use force.

muscular *adj* athletic, beefy, brawny, hefty, husky, powerful, powerfully-built, sinewy, stalwart, strapping, strong, sturdy, well-built, well-knit, wiry.
antonyms delicate, feeble, flabby, puny, weak.

muse *v* brood, chew, cogitate, consider, contemplate, daydream, deliberate, dream, meditate, mull (over), ponder, reflect, review, ruminate, speculate, think, think (over), weigh.

mush *n* cornmeal, glop, goo, mash, mawkishness, mushiness, pap, paste, pulp, schmaltz, sentimentality, slop, slush, swill.

mushroom *v* balloon, boom, burgeon, expand, flourish, grow, increase, luxuriate, proliferate, shoot up, spread, spring up, sprout.

mushy *adj* cloying, doughy, maudlin, mawkish, pappy, pulpy, saccharine, sappy, schmaltzy, sentimental, sloppy, slushy, soft, squishy, squelchy, sugary, syrupy, weak.

musical *adj* dulcet, euphonious, harmonious, lilting, lyrical, melodic, melodious, sweet, sweet-sounding, tuneful.
antonym unmusical.

musician *n* accompanist, artist, bard, composer, conductor, entertainer, instrumentalist, minstrel, performer, player, singer, vocalist.

musing *n* absent-mindedness, abstraction, brown study, cerebration, cogitation, contemplation, daydreaming, dreaming, introspection, meditation, pondering, reflection, reverie, rumination, thinking, woolgathering.

must *n* basic, duty, essential, fundamental, imperative, necessity, obligation, prerequisite, provision, requirement, requisite, sine qua non, stipulation.

mustache *n* face fungus, facial hair, handlebar (mustache), mustachio, peach fuzz, soup-strainer, walrus, whiskers.

muster *v* assemble, call to arms, call together, call up, collect, come together, congregate, convene, convoke, enlist, enrol, gather, group, marshal, mass, meet, mobilize, rally, round up, summon, throng.
n assemblage, assembly, call to arms, collection, concourse, congregation, convention, convocation, gathering, mass, meeting, mobilization, muster roll, rally, roundup, throng.

musty *adj* airless, ancient, antediluvian, antiquated, banal, clichéd, dank, decayed, dull, frowzy, fusty, hackneyed, hoary, malodorous, mildewed, mildewy, moth-eaten, mouldy, obsolete, old, old-fashioned, old hat, out-dated, out-of-date, outworn, smelly, stale, stuffy, trite, worn-out.

mutability *n* alterability, changeability, inconstancy, interchangeability, permutability, transcience, variability, variation.

mutable *adj* adaptable, alterable, changeable, changing, fickle, flexible, inconsistent, inconstant, interchangeable, irresolute, permutable, transient, uncertain, undependable, unreliable, unsettled, unstable, unsteady, vacillating, variable, volatile, wavering.
antonyms constant, invariable, permanent.

mutation *n* alteration, anomaly, change, deviant, deviation, evolution, metamorphosis, modification, mutant, transfiguration, transformation, transmutation, variation, vicissitude.

mute *adj* aphonic, dumb, dumbfounded, dumbstruck, mum, noiseless, silent, speechless, unexpressed, unpronounced, unspeaking, unspoken, voiceless, wordless.
antonyms articulate, vocal, voluble.
v baffle, cushion, dampen, deaden, dull, lower, moderate, muffle, silence, soften, soft-pedal, subdue, tone down, understate.

muted *adj* dampened, dull, faint, low-key, muffled, quiet, restrained, soft, stifled, subdued, subtle, suppressed, understated.

mutilate *v* adulterate, amputate, bowdlerize, butcher, censor, cut, cut to pieces, cut up, damage, detruncate, disable, disfigure, dismember, distort, expurgate, hack, injure, lacerate, lame, maim, mangle, mar, savage, spoil, tear apart.

mutinous *adj* contumacious, defiant, disobedient, insubordinate, insurgent, rebel, rebellious, recusant, refractory, revolutionary, riotous, seditious, subversive, striking, turbulent, uncompliant, ungovernable, unmanageable, unruly, unsubmissive.
antonyms compliant, dutiful, obedient.

mutiny *n* coup d'état, defiance, disobedience, insubordination, insurgence, insurrection, putsch, rebellion, resistance, revolt, revolution, riot, rising, strike, uprising.
v disobey, kick over the traces, protest, rebel, resist, revolt, riot, rise up, strike.

mutt *n* canine, cur, dog, mongrel, pooch.

mutter *v* complain, drone, grouch, grouse, grumble, grump, mumble, murmur.

mutual *adj* common, communal, complementary, conjoint, exchanged, interchangeable, interchanged, joint, reciprocal, reciprocated, returned, shared.

muzzle n bit, curb, gag, guard, jaws, mouth, nose, restraint, silencer, snaffle, snout.
v censor, choke, curb, gag, mute, restrain, silence, stifle, suppress.

muzzy adj addled, befuddled, bemused, bewildered, blurred, confused, dazed, drunk, hazy, indistinct, muddled, tipsy, vague.

myopic adj half blind, near-sighted, poorly planned, poor-sighted, short-sighted, undiscerning, unwise.
antonym far-sighted.

myriad adj boundless, countless, immeasurable, incalculable, innumerable, legion, limitless, multitudinous, numberless, untold.
n army, flood, horde, host, millions, mountain, multitude, scores, sea, swarm, thousands, throng.

mysterious adj abstruse, arcane, baffling, concealed, covert, cryptic, curious, dark, enigmatic, esoteric, furtive, hidden, impenetrable, incomprehensible, inexplicable, inscrutable, insoluble, mystical, mystifying, obscure, perplexing, puzzling, recondite, secret, secretive, strange, unaccountable, uncanny, unfathomable, unknown, veiled, weird.
antonyms comprehensible, frank, straightforward.

mystery n arcanum, conundrum, enigma, inexplicability, problem, puzzle, question, riddle, secrecy, secret, the unknown.

mystical adj abstruse, arcane, cabalistic, cryptic, enigmatic, esoteric, hidden, inscrutable, metaphysical, mysterious, mystic, numinous, occult, otherworldly, paranormal, preternatural, supernatural, transcendental.

mystify v baffle, bamboozle, beat, bewilder, boggle (the mind), confound, confuse, floor, nonplus, perplex, puzzle, stump.

mystique n appeal, awe, charisma, charm, fascination, glamour, magic, spell.

myth n allegory, crock, delusion, fable, fairy tale, fallacy, fancy, fantasy, fiction, fictionalization, figment, illusion, invention, legend, old wives' tale, parable, saga, story, superstition, tradition, untruth.

mythical adj fabled, fabricated, fabulous, fairy-tale, fanciful, fantasy, fictional, fictionalized, fictitious, imaginary, invented, legendary, made-up, make-believe, mythological, non-existent, pretended, unhistoric, unreal.
antonyms actual, historical, real, true.

mythological adj fabulous, fictional, fictitious, folkloric, legendary, mythical, traditional.

mythology n fiction, folklore, folk tales, legend, lore, myth(s), mythos, tales, tradition(s).

N

nab *v* apprehend, arrest, capture, catch, collar, grab, nail, seize, snatch.

nabob *n* big wheel, bigwig, billionaire, celebrity, Croesus, financier, luminary, magnate, millionaire, mogul, multimillionaire, panjandrum, personage, tycoon, VIP.

nadir *n* all-time low, bottom, depths, lowest point, low point, low-water mark, minimum, perigee, rock bottom, zero.

antonyms acme, apex, peak, zenith.

nag¹ *v* annoy, badger, be on someone's case (or back), berate, carp, chivvy, criticize, find fault, goad, harass, harp, harry, henpeck, irritate, kvetch, pester, plague, remind, scold, torment, upbraid, vex.

n harpy, harridan, kvetcher, scold, shrew, tartar, termagant, virago.

nag² *n* hack, horse, jade, plug, rip, Rosinante.

nagging *adj* annoying, continuous, critical, distressing, faultfinding, haunting, irritating, on one's case (or back), painful, persistent, scolding, shrewish, tormenting, upsetting, worrying.

nail *v* apprehend, attach, capture, catch, clinch, collar, fasten, fix, hammer, join, nab, pin, secure, seize, tack.

n brad, hobnail, peg, pin, rivet, screw, skewer, spike, staple, tack.

nail down ascertain, determine, fix, narrow down, pin down, settle, track down.

naïve *adj* artless, callow, candid, childlike, confiding, credulous, dewy-eyed, doe-eyed, facile, frank, green, guileless, gullible, idealistic, ignorant, inexperienced, ingenuous, innocent, jejune, open, simple, simplistic, small-town, starry-eyed, trusting, uncritical, uninformed, unknowing, unrealistic, unsophisticated, unsuspecting, unsuspicious, unworldly, wide-eyed.

antonyms cynical, experienced, sophisticated.

naïvety *n* artlessness, callowness, candour, credulity, frankness, guilelessness, gullibility, idealism, inexperience, ingenuousness, innocence, openness, simplicity, unsophistication.

naked *adj* adamic, bald, bare, blatant, defenceless, denuded, disrobed, divested, evident, exposed, helpless, in one's birthday suit, in the altogether, insecure, in the buff, manifest, nude, open, overt, patent, plain, self-conscious, simple, skyclad, stark, starkers, stark naked, stripped, unadorned, unaided, unclothed, unconcealed, uncovered, undisguised, undraped, undressed, unexaggerated, unguarded, unmistakable, unprotected, unqualified, unvarnished, vulnerable.

antonyms clothed, concealed, covered.

nakedness *n* baldness, bareness, nudity, plainness, simplicity, starkness, undress, vulnerability.

namby-pamby *adj* anemic, colourless, emasculated, feeble, insipid, mawkish, prim, prissy, sentimental, sloppy, spineless, vapid, weak, wimpy, wishy-washy.

name *n* acronym, alias, appellation, character, cognomen, denomination, designation, epithet, fame, handle, label, moniker, nickname, pen name, pseudonym, reputation, repute, signature, sobriquet, stage name, term, title.

v appoint, baptize, call, choose, christen, cite, commission, denominate, designate, entitle, enumerate, identify, know as, label, mention, nominate, select, specify, style, tell (off), term, title.

call names abuse, defame, hurl epithets at, insult, slander, swear at, taunt.

in name only nominal(ly), ostensible, ostensibly, phony, professed, pseudo, purported(ly), so-called, soi-disant, spurious, supposed(ly), titular, token, would-be.

in the name of for, for the cause of, for the sake of, in the interest of, on behalf of, on the authority of, representing.

(make) a name for oneself distinction, (earn or achieve) celebrity, fame, glory, notoriety, renown.

nameless *adj* abominable, anonymous, dreadful, fearsome, horrendous, horrible, incognito, indescribable, indeterminate, ineffable, inexpressible, innominate, obscure, strange, terrible, undesignated, undistinguished, unfamiliar, unheard-of, unidentifiable, unknown, unmentionable, unnamed, unsayable, unspeakable, unsung, untitled, unutterable.

antonyms famous, identifiable, known.

namely *adv* i.e., specifically, that is, that is to say, to wit, videlicet, viz.

nap¹ *v* catch forty winks, catnap, cop z's, doze, drop off, drowse, go down (for a nap), kip, lie down, nod (off), rest, sleep, snooze.

n catnap, forty winks, kip, lie-down, rest, shuteye, siesta, sleep.

nap² *n* down, downiness, fibre, fuzz, grain, pile, shag, weave.

narcissistic *adj* conceited, egocentric, egomaniacal, egotistic, self-absorbed, self-centred, self-loving, vain.

narcotic *n* analgesic, anesthetic, anodyne, dope, drug, hop, kef, opiate, painkiller, sedative, tranquillizer.

adj analgesic, calming, dulling, hypnotic, Lethean, mood-altering, numbing, painkilling, sedative, somniferous, soothing, soporific, stupefacient, stupefying, tranquillizing.

narrate *v* chronicle, describe, detail, recite, recount, rehearse, relate, repeat, report, set forth, state, tell, unfold.

narration *n* description, explanation, reading, recital, recountal, rehearsal, relation, storytelling, telling, voice-over.

narrative *n* account, chronicle, history, parable, report, statement, story, tale.

narrator *n* annalist, author, bard, chronicler, commentator, raconteur, reciter, relator, reporter, storyteller, writer.

narrow *adj* attenuated, biassed, bigoted, blinkered, circumscribed, close, confined, constricted, contracted, cramped, dogmatic, exclusive, fine, illiberal, incapacious, intolerant, limited, literal, meagre, mean, mercenary, narrow-minded, parochial, pinched, prejudiced, provincial, reactionary, restricted, scanty, select, simplistic, slender, slim, small-minded, spare, straitened, tapering, thin, tight, ungenerous.

antonyms broad, liberal, tolerant, wide.

v circumscribe, constrict, contract, cramp, diminish, limit, reduce, restrict, simplify, straiten, taper, tighten.

antonyms broaden, increase, loosen, widen.

narrowly *adv* barely, by a hair's-breadth, by a whisker, carefully, closely, dogmatically, exclusively, finely, just, literally, only just, painstakingly, parochially, precisely, scarcely, strictly, tightly, ungenerously.

narrow-minded *adj* biassed, bigoted, blinkered, closed-minded, conservative, dogmatic, hidebound, illiberal, insular, intolerant, mean, opinionated, parochial, petty, prejudiced, provincial, reactionary, short-sighted, small-minded, strait-laced.

antonyms broad-minded, open-minded.

narrowness *n* bigotry, closed-mindedness, closeness, constriction, crowdedness, dogmatism, exclusiveness, insularity, intolerance, limitation, meagreness, meanness, narrow-mindedness, parochialism, restrictedness, slenderness, small-mindedness, thinness, tightness.

antonyms breadth, liberality, width.

nascent *adj* advancing, budding, developing, embryonic, evolving, growing, incipient, rising, young.

antonym dying.

nasty *adj* abusive, angry, annoying, bad, bad-tempered, beastly, despicable, dirty, disagreeable, disgusting, distasteful, filthy, foul, gross, horrible, hostile, loathsome, low-down, malicious, malodorous, mean, mephitic, nauseating, noisome, noxious, obnoxious, odious, offensive, painful, poisonous, putrid, repellent, repugnant, repulsive, revolting, severe, sickening, sordid, spiteful, unappetizing, unpleasant, unsavoury, venomous, vicious, vile, waspish.

antonyms agreeable, appealing, civil, kind, mild, sweet.

nation *n* citizenry, commonwealth, community, country, dominion, ethnic group, people, population, realm, society, state, tribe.

national *adj* civil, countrywide, domestic, federal, general, governmental, internal, nationwide, public, social, state, widespread.

n citizen, indigene, inhabitant, native, resident, subject.

nationalism *n* allegiance, chauvinism, ethnocentricity, fealty, flagwaving, jingoism, loyalty, national (or ethnic) pride, patriotism, xenophobia.

nationalistic *adj* chauvinistic, ethnocentric, flagwaving, jingoistic, loyal, patriotic, xenophobic.

native *adj* aboriginal, autochthonous, built-in, congenital, domestic, endemic, first, hereditary, home, homebred, homegrown, homemade, inborn, inbred, indigenous, ingrained, inherent, inherited, innate, instinctive, intrinsic, local, mother, natal, natural, original, vernacular.

n aborigine, autochthon, homebrew, indigene.

antonyms immigrant, newcomer, visitor.

natter *v* blather, chatter, gab, gabble, go on, gossip, jabber, jaw, prate, prattle, rap, rattle on, talk, yak.

natty *adj* chic, dapper, elegant, fashionable, neat, ritzy, sharp, smart, snazzy, spruce, stylish, swanky, trim, well-dressed.

natural *adj* artless, automatic, biological, birth, candid, characteristic, congenital, constitutional, ecological, essential, frank, genuine, human, inborn, indigenous, inherent, innate, instinctive, intrinsic, intuitive, legitimate, lifelike, logical, native, normal, open, ordinary, organic, plain, pure, real, realistic, reflexive, relaxed, raw, simple, spontaneous, to be expected, typical, unaffected, unbleached, unconstrained, understandable, unforced, unlaboured, unlearned, unmixed, unpolished, unpretentious, unprocessed, unrefined, unregenerate, unself-conscious, unsophisticated, unstudied, untaught, whole.

antonyms abnormal, affected, artificial, supernatural, unnatural.

naturalistic *adj* graphic, lifelike, natural, photographic, realistic, real-life, representational, true-to-life.

naturalize *v* acclimate, acclimatize, acculturate, accustom, adapt, adopt, domesticate, endenizen, enfranchise, establish, familiarize, habituate, settle.

naturally *adj* absolutely, artlessly, as a matter of course, as per expectation, biologically, by birth, by nature, candidly, frankly, genuinely, humanly, informally, inherently, innately, instinctively, intuitively, justifiably, logically, normally, obviously, of course, plainly, simply, spontaneously, typically, unaffectedly, understandably, unpretentiously.

naturalness *n* artlessness, candour, frankness, genuineness, humanness, informality, ingenuousness, innateness, instinctiveness, intuitiveness, logic, openness, plainness, simplicity, spontaneity, unaffectedness, unpretentiousness, unself-consciousness.

nature[1] *n* attributes, bent, category, character, complexion, constitution, description, disposition, essence, features, humour, inbeing, instincts, kind, make-up, outlook, quality, sort, species, style, temper, temperament, traits, type, variety, way.

nature[2] *n* cosmos, country, countryside, creation, earth, ecological balance, environment, instinct, landscape, natural history, natural order, (physical) universe, scenery.

naught *n* diddly-squat, nil, nothing, nothingness, nought, zero, zilch, zip.

naughty *adj* bad, bawdy, blue, daring, disobedient, exasperating, fractious, improper, indecent, lewd, misbehaved, mischievous, obscene, off-colour, refractory, ribald, risqué, roguish, sinful, wayward, wicked.

antonyms good, polite, well-behaved.

nausea *n* abhorrence, aversion, biliousness, disgust, loathing, motion sickness, queasiness, repugnance, retching, revulsion, sickness, squeamishness, vomiting.

nauseate *v* disgust, gross out, horrify, make one's gorge rise, offend, repel, repulse, revolt, sicken, turn one's stomach.

nauseating *adj* abhorrent, abominable, detestable, disgusting, distasteful, foul, fulsome, gross, loathsome, noisome, noxious, offensive, repugnant, repulsive, revolting, sickening.

nautical *adj* boating, marine, maritime, naval, navigational, oceanic, sailing, seafaring, seagoing, yachting.

naval *adj* marine, maritime, nautical, sea.

navel *n* belly button, centre, hub, middle, omphalos, umbilicus.

navigate *v* con, cross, cruise, direct, drive, find one's way, guide, handle, helm, journey, manage, manoeuvre, pilot, plan, plot the course of, sail, skipper, steer, voyage.

navigation *n* aviation, cruising, helmsmanship, pilotage, sailing, seamanship, steering, voyaging.

navigator *n* explorer, guide, helmsman, mariner, pilot, seaman.

navvy *n* digger, ganger, labourer, worker, workman.

navy *n* argosy, armada, fleet, flotilla, marine force, ships, warships.

near *adj* accessible, adjacent, adjoining, akin, allied, alongside, approaching, at close quarters, at hand, beside, bordering, close (by), connected, contiguous, dear, familiar, forthcoming, handy, hither, imminent, impending, in the offing, intimate, just around the corner, looming, near at hand, nearby, neighbouring, next, nigh, proximal, related, touching.

antonyms distant, far, remote.

a near thing a close shave, a narrow escape, a near miss, nip and tuck, touch and go.

nearby *adj, adv* accessible, adjacent, at close quarters, close at hand, close by, convenient, handy, in the vicinity, near, neighbouring, to hand, within reach.

antonyms faraway, remote.

nearly *adv* about, all but, almost, approaching, approximately, around, as good as, coming on (or up) to, going on (or for), just about, just short of (or under), more or less, nigh on to, not quite, practically, pretty much, pretty well, roughly, virtually, well-nigh.

nearness *n* accessibility, availability, closeness, contiguity, dearness, familiarity, handiness, immediacy, imminence, intimacy, juxtaposition, kinship, propinquity, proximity, vicinity.

neat *adj* adept, adroit, apt, careful, clean-cut, clever, crisp, deft, dexterous, efficient, effortless, elegant, expert, fastidious, graceful, handy, methodical, natty, nice, nimble, orderly, precise, properly aligned, pure, shipshape, skilful, smart, spick-and-span, spruce, square, straight, systematic, tidy, trim, uncluttered, undiluted, unmixed, well-groomed, well-judged.

antonyms disordered, disorderly, messy, untidy.

neaten *v* arrange, clean up, groom, put in order, set to rights, smarten, spruce up, square away, straighten, tidy (up), trim.

neatness *n* adeptness, adroitness, aptness, cleverness, deftness, dexterity, efficiency, elegance, expertness, fastidiousness, good grooming, good housekeeping, grace, gracefulness, handiness, methodicalness, niceness, nimbleness, order, orderliness, precision, skilfulness, smartness, spruceness, straightness, tidiness, trimness.

nebulous *adj* ambiguous, amorphous, cloudy, confused, dim, fuzzy, hazy, ill-defined, imprecise, indefinite, indeterminate, indistinct, misty, murky, obscure, shadowy, shapeless, uncertain, unclear, unformed, unspecific, vague.

antonym clear.

necessarily *adv* automatically, axiomatically, by definition, certainly, compulsorily, incontrovertibly, ineluctably, inescapably, inevitably, inexorably, naturally, of course, of necessity, perforce, willy-nilly.

necessary *adj* a must, compulsory, de rigueur, essential, fated, imperative, indispensable, ineluctable, inescapable, inevitable, inexorable, mandatory, needed, needful, obligatory, required, requisite, unavoidable, vital.

antonyms inessential, redundant, unimportant, unnecessary.

necessitate *v* call for, compel, constrain, demand, entail, force, impose, involve, require.

necessities *n* basics, essentials, exigencies, fundamentals, indispensables, necessaries, needs, requirements.

necessity *n* compulsion, demand, desideratum, destiny, destitution, essential, exigency, extremity, fate, fundamental, indigence, indispensability, inevitability, inexorability, necessary, need, needfulness, obligation, penury, poverty, prerequisite, privation, requirement, sine qua non, want.

necklace *n* carcanet, chain, choker, gorget, lavaliere, locket, pendant, torc, torque.

necromancy *n* conjuration, demonology, divination, enchantment, evil arts, hoodoo, magic, sorcery, voodoo, witchcraft, witchery, wizardry.

need *v* call for, crave, cry out for, demand, lack, miss, must, require, take, want.

n demand, deprivation, desideratum, destitution, distress, egence, egency, emergency, essential, exigency, extremity, impecuniousness, inadequacy, indigence, insufficiency, lack, longing, necessity, neediness, obligation, paucity, penury, poverty, privation, requirement, requisite, shortage, urgency, want, wish.

antonym sufficiency.

needed *adj* called for, compulsory, de rigueur, desired, essential, indispensable, lacking, mandatory, necessary, needful, obligatory, required, requisite, stipulated, wanted, wanting.

antonyms unnecessary, unneeded.

needle *v* aggravate, annoy, bait, bug, chivvy, goad, harass, incite, irk, irritate, nag, nettle, pester, prick, prod, provoke, rile, spur, sting, taunt, tease, torment.

needless *adj* causeless, dispensable, excessive, expendable, gratuitous, groundless, inessential, non-essential, pointless, purposeless, reasonless, redundant, superfluous, uncalled-for, unnecessary, unwanted, useless.

antonyms necessary, needful.

needy *adj* deprived, destitute, disadvantaged, impecunious, impoverished, indigent, in want, penniless, penurious, poor, poverty-stricken, underprivileged.

antonyms affluent, wealthy, well-off.

ne'er-do-well *n* black sheep, good-for-nothing, idler, layabout, loafer, rapscallion, scapegrace, wastrel.

nefarious *adj* abominable, atrocious, base, criminal, depraved, detestable, dreadful, evil, execrable, foul, heinous, horrible, infamous, infernal, iniquitous, monstrous, odious, opprobrious, satanic, shameful, sinful, unholy, vicious, vile, villainous, wicked.

antonym exemplary.

negate *v* abrogate, annul, cancel, contradict, countermand, deny, disallow, disprove, gainsay, invalidate, neutralize, nullify, oppose, quash, refute, repeal, rescind, retract, reverse, revoke, undo, veto, void, wipe out.

antonym affirm.

negation *n* abrogation, annulment, antithesis, cancellation, contradiction, contrary, converse, counterpart, denial, disaffirmation, disavowal, gainsaying, inverse, neutralization, nullification, opposite, rejection, repeal, reverse, veto.

antonym affirmation.

negative *adj* argumentative, below zero, contrary, counterproductive, critical, cynical, damaging, dampening, deleterious, destructive, detrimental, disagreeable, disapproving, dissenting, gloomy, harmful, hurtful, injurious, invalidating, jaundiced, neutralizing, nullifying, pessimistic, prejudicial, unco-operative, unenthusiastic, unhelpful, uninterested, unobliging, unwilling.

antonyms affirmative, optimistic, positive, uplifting.

n contradiction, denial, inverse, opposite, refusal.

neglect *v* disregard, fail (to), forget, ignore, leave alone, let fall by the wayside, let go, let slide, omit, overlook, pass by, pigeonhole, shirk, short-change, slight.

antonyms attend to, cherish, keep up with, treasure.

n carelessness, default, dereliction, disregard, failure, forgetfulness, heedlessness, inattention, indifference, laches, laxity, laxness, neglectfulness, negligence, oversight, slackness, slovenliness, unconcern.

neglected *adj* abandoned, derelict, disregarded, forgotten, ignored, overgrown, unappreciated, uncared-for, uncultivated, undervalued, unhusbanded, unmaintained, untended, untilled, unweeded.

antonyms cherished, well-maintained.

neglectful *adj* careless, forgetful, heedless, inattentive, inconsiderate, indifferent, lax, negligent, oblivious, remiss, thoughtless, uncaring, unmindful.

antonyms attentive, careful.

negligence *n* carelessness, default, dereliction, disregard, forgetfulness, heedlessness, inadvertence, inattention, inattentiveness, indifference, irresponsibility, laxity, laxness, neglect, neglectfulness, remissness, slackness, stupidity, thoughtlessness.

antonyms attentiveness, care, regard.

negligent *adj* careless, forgetful, heedless, inattentive, indifferent, irresponsible, lax, neglectful, nonchalant, offhand, remiss, slack, thoughtless, uncareful, uncaring, unmindful, unthinking.

antonyms attentive, careful, heedful, scrupulous.

negligible *adj* ignorable, imperceptible, inconsequential, insignificant, low, minor, minute, nugatory, petty, slight, small, trifling, trivial, unimportant, unnoticeable, virtually nonexistent.

antonym significant.

negotiate *v* adjudicate, agree on, arbitrate, arrange, bargain, broker, clear, close, come to the table, compromise, confer, consult, contract, cross, deal, debate, dialogue, discuss, get past, hammer out, handle, hash out, manage, mediate, parley, pass, reach, settle (on), surmount, transact, traverse, treat (for), work out.

negotiation *n* arbitration, bargaining, compromise, debate, dialogue, diplomacy, discussion, mediation, parley, summitry, transaction, wheeling and dealing.

negotiator *n* adjudicator, ambassador, arbitrator, broker, delegate, diplomat, facilitator, go-between, intermediary, mediator, moderator, third party.

neighbourhood *n* area, block, community, confines, district, environs, locale, locality, neck of the woods, precincts, purlieu(s), quarter, region, surroundings, vicinage, vicinity.

neighbouring *adj* abutting, adjacent, adjoining, bordering, connecting, contiguous, near, nearby, nearest, next, surrounding, vicinal.

antonyms distant, faraway, remote.

neighbourly *adj* amiable, chummy, civil, companionable, considerate, friendly, genial, helpful, hospitable, kind, obliging, sociable, social, solicitous.

nemesis *n* destiny, destruction, fate, punishment, retribution, vengeance.

nerve *n* audacity, boldness, brass, bravery, brazenness, cheek, chutzpah, cool, coolness, courage, daring, determination, effrontery, endurance, face, fearlessness, firmness, force, fortitude, gall, gameness, grit, guts, hardihood, impertinence, impudence, insolence, intrepidity, mettle, pluck, resolution, sauce, spirit, spunk, steadfastness, temerity, valour, will.

antonyms cowardice, timidity, weakness.

v bolster, brace, embolden, encourage, fortify, gird, hearten, invigorate, prepare, psych up, steel, strengthen.

antonym unnerve.

nerveless *adj* afraid, cowardly, debilitated, demoralized, enervated, feeble, flabby, gutless, inert, irresolute, nervous, slack, spineless, spiritless, timid, unnerved, weak, weak-kneed, weak-willed, wimpy, wishy-washy, yellow.

antonyms bold, strong.

nerves *n* anxiety, butterflies in one's stomach, fidgets, fretfulness, jitters, nervousness, panic attack, shakes, stage fright, strain, stress, tension, worry.

get on one's nerves aggravate, annoy, bother, bug, drive one crazy, drive one up the wall, exasperate, get one's goat, get to one, get under one's skin, irritate, make one's blood boil, nettle, send around the bend, set one's teeth on edge, tick off, torment, upset, vex.

nerve-wracking *adj* agonizing, annoying, anxious, difficult, disquieting, distracting, distressing, draining, exasperating, frightening, harassing, harrowing, maddening, stressful, suspenseful, tense, tormenting, torturous, trying, unnerving, worrisome, worrying.

nervous *adj* agitated, anxious, apprehensive, discomposed, disquieted, distracted, edgy, excitable, fearful, fidgety, flustered, hesitant, highly-strung, high-strung, hung up, hysterical, insecure, jittery, jumpy, nervy, neurotic, on edge, panicky, psyched out, restless, self-conscious, shaky, stammering, stressed out, tense, timid, timorous, tongue-tied, twitchy, uneasy, unquiet, uptight, worked up, worried.

antonyms bold, calm, confident, cool, relaxed.

nervousness *n* agitation, anxiety, apprehension, butterflies in one's stomach, discomposure, disquiet, edginess, excitability, fear, fluster, insecurity, jitters, jumpiness, nerves, panic attack, perturbation, self-consciousness, shakiness, stage fright, stress, tension, timidity, touchiness, tremulousness, uneasiness, uptightness, white knuckles, willies, worry.

antonyms calmness, coolness.

nest *n* breeding-ground, burrow, den, earth, form, formicary, haunt, hideaway, hotbed, nidus, refuge, resort, retreat.

nest egg *n* cache, deposit, funds, reserve(s), savings, store.

nestle *v* cradle, cuddle, curl up, ensconce oneself, hide, huddle, nuzzle, settle oneself, snuggle.

nestling *adj* baby, chick, fledgling, hatchling, suckling, weanling.

net¹ *n* drag, dragnet, drift, drift net, mesh, netting, network, openwork, reticulum, seine, tracery, trawl (net), web.

v apprehend, bag, capture, catch, enmesh, ensnare, entangle, nab, reel in, snag, snare, trap.

net² *adj* after deductions, after tax, clear, final, lowest, take-home.

v bring in, clear, earn, gain, make (a profit of), realize, take home.

nether *adj* basal, below, beneath, bottom, inferior, infernal, lower, Plutonian, Stygian, under, underground.

nettle *v* anger, annoy, chafe, discountenance, exasperate, fret, goad, harass, incense, irritate, needle, pique, provoke, ruffle, sting, tease, tick off, vex.

nettled *adj* aggrieved, angry, annoyed, chafed, cross, exasperated, galled, goaded, harassed, hot and bothered, huffy, incensed, irritated, miffed, peeved, peevish, piqued, provoked, riled, ruffled, stung, vexed.

network *n* arrangement, circuitry, complex, connections, grid, interconnections, labyrinth, maze, mesh, meshwork, net, nexus, organization, plexus, rete, reticulation, structure, syndicate, system, tracks, web.

neurosis *n* abnormality, chronic anxiety, deviation, disorder, disturbance, hang-up, instability, maladjustment, mental imbalance, morbidity, obsession, phobia.

neurotic *adj* abnormal, anxious, compulsive, deviant, disordered, distraught, disturbed, erratic, hung up, maladjusted, manic, mentally unbalanced, morbid, nervous, obsessive, overwrought, phobic, unhealthy, unstable, uptight, wearisome.

antonyms normal, stable.

neuter *v* caponize, castrate, emasculate, fix, spay, unsex.

neutral *adj* colourless, disinterested, dispassionate, drab, dull, even-handed, expressionless, impartial, indifferent, intermediate, lukewarm, non-aligned, non-belligerent, non-committal, nondescript, non-partisan, non-sectarian, objective, unbiassed, uncommitted, undecided, uninvolved, unprejudiced.

antonyms biassed, prejudiced.

neutrality *n* detachment, disinterest, disinterestedness, impartiality, impartialness, non-alignment, non-belligerence, non-intervention, non-involvement, non-partisanship, non-sectarianism, objectivity, unbiassedness.

neutralize *v* cancel (out), compensate for, counteract, counterbalance, counterpoise, frustrate, invalidate, negate, nullify, offset, undo.

never *adv* at no time, not at all, not once, not on your life, on no account, over my dead body, under no circumstances, when hell freezes over, when pigs fly.

antonym always.

never-ending *adj* boundless, ceaseless, constant, continual, continuous, endless, eternal, everlasting, incessant, inexhaustible, infinite, interminable, non-stop, permanent, perpetual, persistent, relentless, Sisyphean, unbroken, unceasing, unchanging, uninterrupted, unremitting.

antonyms fleeting, transitory.

nevertheless *adv* anyhow, anyway, but, despite that, even so, however, in any case, nonetheless, notwithstanding, regardless, still, yet.

new *adj* added, additional, advanced, altered, avant-garde, brand (spanking) new, changed, contemporary, current, different, fresh, improved, inexperienced, innovative, latest, modern, modernized, modernistic, modish, more, neo-, newborn, newfangled, novel, original, recent, redesigned, renewed, restored, revised, supplementary, trendy, ultra-modern, unfamiliar, unknown, untried, unused, unusual, updated, up-to-date, up-to-the-minute, virgin.

antonyms broken in, former, hackneyed, old, outdated.

newcomer *n* arrival, arriviste, beginner, cheechako, colonist, immigrant, Johnny-come-lately, neophyte, nouveau riche, novice, parvenu, probationer, settler, stranger, upstart.

newfangled *adj* contemporary, fashionable, futuristic, gimmicky, modern, modernistic, new, novel, recent, trendy.

antonyms old-fashioned, tried and true.

newly *adv* afresh, anew, differently, freshly, just, lately, latterly, recently.

newness *n* alteration, change, difference, freshness, innovation, novelty, originality, recency, rejuvenation, renewal, strangeness, unfamiliarity, uniqueness, unusualness, youth.

antonyms oldness, ordinariness, sameness, tiredness.

news *n* account, advice, bulletin, communiqué, development(s), disclosure, dispatch, exposé, gen, gossip, headlines, hearsay, information, intelligence, knowledge, latest, leak, lowdown, newscast, release, report, revelation, rumour, scandal, scoop, statement, story, tidings, update, word.

newspaper *n* daily, gazette, journal, newsprint, organ, paper, periodical, publication, rag, sheet, tabloid, weekly.

newsworthy *adj* arresting, important, interesting, intriguing, notable, noteworthy, remarkable, reportable, significant, stimulating, unusual.

next *adj* adjacent, adjoining, closest, coming, earliest, ensuing, following, nearest, neighbouring, sequent, subsequent, succeeding, upcoming.

antonyms preceding, previous.

adv afterwards, later, subsequently, then, thereafter, thereupon.

nibble *n* bit, bite, crumb, morsel, peck, piece, snack, taste, tidbit.

v bite, eat, gnaw, munch, nip, nosh, peck.

nice *adj* accurate, agreeable, amiable, attractive, careful, charming, considerate, courteous, cultured, dainty, decent, delicate, delightful, discriminating, elegant, exact, exacting, fastidious, fine, friendly, genteel, good, helpful, kind, likable, mannerly, meticulous, minute, neat, obscure, particular, personable, pleasant, pleasurable, polite, precise, prepossessing, proper, punctilious, purist, refined, respectable, rigorous, scrupulous, skilful, strict, subtle, thoughtful, tidy, trim, virtuous, well-bred, well-mannered.

antonyms careless, disagreeable, haphazard, nasty, unpleasant.

niceness *n* accuracy, agreeableness, amiability, attractiveness, care, carefulness, charm, courtesy, daintiness, decency, delicacy, delightfulness, discrimination, elegance, exactitude, exactness, fastidiousness, fineness, friendliness, gentility, goodness, helpfulness, kindness, likableness, mannerliness, meticulousness, minuteness, neatness, obscurity, personableness, pleasantness, pleasurableness, politeness, preciseness, precision, propriety, punctilio, punctiliousness, purism, refinement, respectability, rigorousness, rigour, scrupulosity, scrupulousness, strictness, subtleness, subtlety, thoughtfulness, tidiness, trimness, virtue.

antonyms carelessness, disagreeableness, haphazardness, nastiness, unpleasantness.

nicety *n* accuracy, daintiness, delicacy, detail, discrimination, distinction, exactness, fastidiousness, fine point, finesse, finicality, meticulousness, minuteness, nuance, precision, punctilio, refinement, subtlety, T.

niche *n* alcove, calling, corner, cubbyhole, hollow, home, métier, nook, opening, pigeonhole, place, position, recess, slot, spot, vocation.

nick *n* chip, cut, dent, mark, notch, scar, score, scratch, snick.

v chip, cut, damage, dent, mark, notch, scar, score, scratch, snick.

nickname *n* cognomen, diminutive, epithet, familiarity, label, moniker, pet name, sobriquet.

nifty *adj* adroit, agile, apt, chic, clever, cool, deft, excellent, handy, ingenious, neat, sharp, smart, spiffy, spruce, stylish.

niggardly *adj* avaricious, beggarly, cheeseparing, close, covetous, frugal, grudging, hard-fisted, inadequate, insufficient, meagre, mean, mercenary, miserable, miserly, near, paltry, parsimonious, penurious, poor, scanty, skimpy, small, sordid, sparing, stingy, tight-fisted, ungenerous, ungiving, wretched.

antonyms bountiful, generous.

night *n* bedtime, benightedness, dark, darkness, day's end, dead of night, evening, hours of darkness, nightfall, nighttime.

antonyms day, daybreak, daytime, enlightenment, light.

nightclub *n* cabaret, club, disco, discothèque, nightspot, singles' club, watering hole.

nightfall *n* crepuscule, dark, dusk, eve, evening, eventide, gloaming, moonrise, sundown, sunset, twilight, vespers.

antonyms dawn, daybreak, first light, sunrise.

nightmare *n* agony, bad dream, hallucination, hell, horror, incubus, ordeal, succubus, terror, torment, torture, trial, tribulation.

nightmarish *adj* agonizing, alarming, creepy, disturbing, dreadful, fell, frightening, harrowing, horrible, horrific, scary, terrifying, unreal.

nihilism *n* abnegation, agnosticism, anarchy, atheism, chaos, cynicism, denial, disbelief, disorder, emptiness, lawlessness, meaninglessness, negation, negativism, oblivion, pessimism, rejection, renunciation, repudiation, scepticism, solipsism, terrorism.

nihilist *n* absurdist, agnostic, anarchist, antinomian, atheist, cynic, denier, disbeliever, extremist, negationist, negativist, pessimist, revolutionary, sceptic, solipsist, terrorist.

nil *n* diddly-squat, goose egg, love, naught, nihil, none, nothing, zero, zilch, zip.

nimble *adj* active, adroit, agile, alert, brisk, deft, dexterous, fleet, graceful, light-footed, lissome, lively, proficient, quick, quick-witted, ready, sharp, skilful, skilled, smart, sprightly, spry, swift, volant.

antonyms awkward, clumsy.

nimbleness *n* adroitness, agility, alacrity, alertness, deftness, dexterity, ease, finesse, grace, lightness, liveliness, proficiency, quickness, readiness, skill, smartness, sprightliness, spryness, swiftness.

nimbly *adv* actively, agilely, alertly, briskly, deftly, dexterously, easily, fast, featly, fleetly, proficiently, quickly, quick-wittedly, readily, sharply, smartly, snappily, speedily, spryly, swiftly.

antonyms awkwardly, clumsily.

nincompoop *n* blockhead, dimwit, dolt, dope, dunce, dunderhead, fool, idiot, ignoramus, ninny, nitwit, numskull, sap, simpleton.

nip[1] *v* arrest, bite, catch, check, clip, cut off, grip, nibble, pinch, snag, snap, snip, squeeze, sting, tweak.

n bit, bite, edge, flavour, morsel, mouthful, nibble, pinch, sharpness, snip, squeeze, sting, tang, taste, tweak, zip.

nip[2] *n* dram, draft, drop, finger, mouthful, peg, portion, shot, sip, slug, snifter, soupçon, sup, swallow, taste.

nipple *n* breast, dug, pap, teat, udder.

nippy *adj* astringent, biting, chilly, cold, crisp, fresh, frosty, pungent, sharp, stinging, strong, tangy, zippy.

nirvana *n* bliss, ecstasy, enlightenment, exaltation, joy, oblivion, paradise, peace, perfection, serenity, tranquillity.

nit-picking *adj* captious, carping, cavilling, faultfinding, finicky, fussy, hair-splitting, hard-to-please, hypercritical, pedantic, pettifogging, petty, picky, quibbling.

nitwit *n* bubblebrain, dimwit, dope, dummy, dunce, fool, half-wit, idiot, imbecile, lamebrain, nincompoop, moron, ninny, numskull, simpleton.

nob *n* aristocrat, big shot, bigwig, celebrity, fat cat, nabob, personage, VIP.

nobility *n* aristocracy, blue blood, dignity, élite, eminence, excellence, first estate, generosity, gentlefolk, gentry, grandeur, greatness, high society, honour, illustriousness, incorruptibility, integrity, loftiness, lordliness, lords and ladies, magnanimity, magnificence, majesty, nobleness, nobles, patricians, peerage, stateliness, sublimity, superiority, titled class, upper class, uprightness, virtue, worthiness.

antonyms baseness, proletariat.

noble *n* aristocrat, baron(ess), blue blood, count(ess), dame, duchess, duke, gentilhomme, grande dame, grand seigneur, lady, lord, marchioness, marquis(e), nobleman, noblewoman, patrician, peer, viscount(ess).

antonyms pleb, prole.

adj aristocratic, august, blue-blooded, dignified, distinguished, elevated, eminent, excellent, generous, gentle, glorious, grand, great, high, highborn, honourable, honoured, idealistic, illustrious, imposing, impressive, lofty, lordly, magnanimous, magnificent, majestic, patrician, splendid, stately, titled, upper-class, upright, virtuous, worthy.

antonyms base, ignoble, lowborn.

nobody *n* also-ran, cipher, lightweight, loser, menial, minnow, nonentity, no-name, no one, nothing, straw man, unknown, zero.

antonyms big name, somebody.

nod *v* acknowledge, agree, assent, beckon, bob, bow, concur, dip, doze, droop, drop off, drowse, duck, gesture, indicate, nap, salute, sign, signal, sleep, slip up, slump, snooze, snore, yawn.

n acknowledgment, affirmative, approval, beck, bob, bow, cue, dip, gesture, green light, greeting, indication, salute, sign, signal, thumbs up.

node *n* bud, bump, burl, caruncle, growth, intersection, knob, knot, lump, nodule, point, process, protuberance, swelling.

no doubt assuredly, certainly, doubtless, indubitably, most likely, of course, presumably, probably, surely, undoubtedly, unquestionably, without a doubt.

noise *n* babble, babel, ballyhoo, blare, brouhaha, buzz, clamour, clang, clangour, clash, clatter, coil, commotion, cry, din, disturbance, fracas, hubbub, hue and cry, hullabaloo, hum, hype, interference, knocking, outcry, pandemonium, racket, rattle, roar, row, ruckus, rustle, sound, static, talk, tumult, uproar, whine.

antonyms quiet, silence.

v advertise, announce, bruit, circulate, gossip, publicize, repeat, report, rumour, spread, tell.

noiseless *adj* hushed, inaudible, mute, muted, quiet, silent, soundless, still.

antonyms loud, noisy.

noisome *adj* bad, baneful, deleterious, disgusting, fetid, foul, fulsome, harmful, hurtful, injurious, malodorous, mephitic, mischievous, noxious, offensive, pernicious, pestiferous, pestilential, poisonous, putrid, reeking, repulsive, revolting, smelly, stinking, unhealthy, unwholesome.

antonyms balmy, pleasant, wholesome.

▲ *confusable word* noisy.

noisy *adj* blaring, boisterous, cacophonous, chattering, clamorous, clangorous, deafening, ear-piercing, ear-splitting, loud, obstreperous, piercing, plangent, rackety, riotous, strident, tumultuous, turbulent, uproarious, vocal, vociferous.

antonyms peaceful, quiet, silent.

▲ *confusable word* noisome.

nomad *n* drifter, gypsy, hobo, itinerant, migrant, rambler, roamer, rover, traveller, vagabond, vagrant, wanderer.

nomadic *adj* drifting, gypsy, itinerant, migrant, migratory, peregrinating, peripatetic, roaming, roving, travelling, unsettled, vagrant, wandering.

nom de plume alias, allonym, assumed name, nom de guerre, pen name, pseudonym.

nomenclature *n* classification, codification, lexis, locution, naming, phraseology, taxonomy, terminology, vocabulary.

nominal *adj* formal, in name only, insignificant, minimal, ostensible, pretended, professed, puppet, purported, self-styled, small, so-called, soi-disant, supposed, symbolic, theoretical, titular, token, trifling, trivial.

antonyms actual, genuine, real, true.

nominate *v* appoint, assign, choose, cite, commission, designate, elect, mention, name, present, propose, put up, recommend, select, slate, submit, suggest.

nomination *n* appointment, assignment, choice, citation, designation, election, mention, proposal, recommendation, selection, submission, suggestion.

nominee *n* appointee, assignee, candidate, contestant, entrant, protégé, runner.

non-aligned *adj* impartial, independent, maverick, neutral, unallied, uncommitted, undecided.

nonchalance *n* aplomb, calm, casualness, composure, cool, detachment, equanimity, impassivity, imperturbability, indifference, insouciance, offhandedness, sang-froid, self-possession, unconcern.

antonyms excitement, overreaction, worriedness.

nonchalant *adj* airy, apathetic, blasé, calm, careless, casual, collected, cool, detached, dispassionate, impassive, indifferent, insouciant, offhand, unconcerned, unemotional, unperturbed.

antonyms anxious, concerned, excited, worried.

non-committal *adj* ambiguous, cautious, equivocal, evasive, guarded, hedging, indefinite, neutral, politic, reserved, tactful, temporizing, tentative, unrevealing, vague, wary.

non compos mentis crazy, deranged, insane, irresponsible, mentally ill, of unsound mind, unbalanced, unhinged.

antonyms sane, stable.

nonconformist *n* anti-establishmentarian, counterculturalist, deviant, dissenter, dissentient, eccentric, heretic, iconoclast, individualist, maverick, oddball, protester, radical, rebel.

antonym conformist.

nonconformity *n* counterculturalism, deviation, dissent, eccentricity, heresy, heterodoxy, individualism, protest, rebellion, unconventionality.

antonym conformity.

nondescript *adj* characterless, commonplace, drab, dull, featureless, forgettable, indeterminate, mousy, ordinary, plain, uncategorizable, unclassifiable, undistinctive, undistinguished, unexceptional, uninspiring, uninteresting, unmemorable, unremarkable, vague.

none *pron* nil, nobody, no one, not any, not (a single) one, zero, zilch, zip.

nonentity *n* cipher, lightweight, mediocrity, nobody, no-name, nothing, unknown, zero.

non-essential *adj* decorative, dispensable, expendable, extra, extraneous, extrinsic, frill, gratuitous, inessential, non-core, ornamental, peripheral, superfluous, supplementary, unimportant, unnecessary.
antonym essential.

nonetheless *adv* anyway, despite this, even so, howbeit, however, natheless, nevertheless, notwithstanding, still, yet.

non-existence *n* illusoriness, insubstantiality, nothingness, oblivion, unbeing, unreality.
antonyms existence, reality.

non-existent *adj* fancied, fictional, hallucinatory, hypothetical, illusory, imaginary, imagined, immaterial, incorporeal, insubstantial, legendary, missing, mythical, null, unreal.
antonyms actual, existing, real.

non-flammable *adj* fireproof, fire-resistant, flame-resistant, incombustible, unignitable, uninflammable.
antonyms flammable, inflammable.

non-partisan *adj* detached, dispassionate, even-handed, impartial, independent, neutral, objective, unbiassed, unprejudiced.
antonym partisan.

nonplus *v* astonish, astound, baffle, bewilder, confound, confuse, disconcert, discountenance, dumfound, embarrass, flabbergast, floor, flummox, make speechless, mystify, perplex, puzzle, stump, stun, take aback, throw for a loop, throw (off).

nonsense *n* absurdity, a crock, bafflegab, balderdash, baloney, bilge, blah, blather, bombast, bosh, bull, bunk, business, cardboard, claptrap, codswallop, crap, drivel, eyewash, fandango, fatuity, fiddle-de-dee, fiddle-faddle, fiddlesticks, flapdoodle, folly, foolishness, gibberish, gobbledygook, guff, hanky-panky, hogwash, hooey, humbug, inanity, ludicrousness, malarkey, moonshine, old wives' tales, piffle, pulp, ridiculousness, rot, rubbish, senselessness, silliness, stuff, stupidity, taradiddle, tomfoolery, tommyrot, trash, twaddle, unreason.
antonym sense.

nonsensical *adj* absurd, crazy, daft, fatuous, foolish, inane, incomprehensible, irrational, ludicrous, meaningless, ridiculous, senseless, silly.
antonyms logical, sensible.

non-stop *adj* ceaseless, constant, continuous, direct, endless, express, incessant, interminable, never-ending, ongoing, relentless, round-the-clock, steady, unbroken, unceasing, unending, unfaltering, uninterrupted, unrelenting, unremitting.
antonyms intermittent, occasional.
adv ceaselessly, constantly, continuously, directly, endlessly, express, incessantly, interminably, relentlessly, round-the-clock, steadily, unbrokenly, unceasingly, unendingly, unfalteringly, uninterruptedly, unrelentingly, unremittingly.
antonyms intermittently, occasionally.

non-violent *adj* amicable, anti-war, bloodless, dovish, irenic, pacifist, peaceable, peaceful, quiet.
antonyms bloody, violent.

nook *n* alcove, cavity, corner, cranny, crevice, cubbyhole, hide-out, inglenook, nest, niche, opening, recess, retreat, shelter.

norm *n* average, benchmark, canon, convention, criterion, mean, measure, model, par, pattern, reference, rule, standard, type, yardstick.

normal *adj* accustomed, acknowledged, average, characteristic, common, conventional, customary, habitual, healthy, mainstream, natural, ordinary, par for the course, rational, reasonable, regular, routine, run-of-the-mill, sane, standard, straightforward, typical, unexceptional, usual, well-adjusted.
antonyms abnormal, irregular, odd, peculiar.

normally *adv* as a rule, as per (the) usual, characteristically, commonly, conventionally, customarily, habitually, naturally, ordinarily, regularly, typically, usually.
antonym abnormally.

northern *adj* Arctic, boreal, hyperborean, north, northerly, northwardly, polar.
antonyms austral, southern.

nose *n* beak, bill, cap, cone, muzzle, proboscis, prow, schnozz, schnozzle, sniffer, snout, tip.
v detect, inquire, intrude, meddle, nudge, nuzzle, pry, push, search, shove, smell, sniff, snoop.

nose-dive *n* dive, drop, header, plummet, plunge.
v dive, drop, fall sharply, plummet, plunge.

nosegay *n* bouquet, boutonnière, corsage, posy, spray.

nosey *adj* curious, eavesdropping, inquisitive, interfering, intrusive, meddlesome, meddling, officious, prying, snooping.

nostalgia *n* bittersweet, homesickness, longing, pining, regret, remembrance, reminiscence, romanticism, sentimentality, wistfulness, yearning.

nostalgic *adj* bittersweet, emotional, homesick, longing, maudlin, regretful, romantic, sentimental, wistful, yearning.

nosy *see* **nosey**

notability *n* big name, big shot, celebrity, dignitary, distinction, eminence, esteem, fame, luminary, magnate, notable, notoriety, personage, renown, somebody, VIP, worthy.
antonym nonentity.

notable *adj* celebrated, conspicuous, distinguished, eminent, extraordinary, famous, impressive, marked, memorable, noteworthy, noticeable, notorious, outstanding, overt, pre-eminent, pronounced, rare, remarkable, renowned, signal, striking, uncommon, unusual, well-known.
antonyms commonplace, ordinary, usual.
n big name, big shot, celebrity, dignitary,

luminary, notability, personage, somebody, VIP, visiting fireman, worthy.

antonyms nobody, nonentity.

notably *adv* conspicuously, distinctly, eminently, especially, impressively, markedly, noticeably, outstandingly, particularly, remarkably, signally, strikingly, uncommonly.

notation *n* alphabet, characters, code, record, script, shorthand, signs, symbols, system, writing.

notch *n* cleft, crenation, cut, degree, grade, incision, indentation, kerf, level, mark, nick, rank, rung, score, serration, serrulation, snip, step.

v cut, indent, mark, nick, pink, scallop, score, scratch, serrate.

notched *adj* crenate, emarginate, indented, jagged (-edged), pinked, serrate, serrulate.

note *n* annotation, apostil, celebrity, certificate, clarification, comment, communication, consequence, distinction, eminence, endnote, epistle, epistolet, explanation, fame, fistnote, footnote, gloss, heed, importance, indication, jotting, letter, line, mark, memo, memorandum, message, notice, observation, postscript, prestige, record, remark, reminder, renown, reputation, signal, symbol, token.

v cite, denote, designate, detect, enter, flag, indicate, mark, mention, notice, observe, perceive, record, refer to, register, remark, see, witness, write down.

make a note of file for future reference, flag, keep in mind, notice, observe, pay attention to, record, remember, write down.

noted *adj* acclaimed, celebrated, distinguished, eminent, famous, great, illustrious, notable, notorious, outstanding, prominent, recognized, renowned, respected, well-known.

notes *n* commentary, cue cards, impressions, jottings, minutes, musings, outline, record, report, (rough) draft, sketch, synopsis, thoughts.

noteworthy *adj* exceptional, extraordinary, important, interesting, notable, on the map, outstanding, remarkable, signal, significant, special, unusual.

antonyms commonplace, ordinary, unexceptional, usual.

nothing *n* bagatelle, cipher, emptiness, naught, nix, nobody, nonentity, non-existence, nothingness, nought, nullity, trifle, void, zero, zilch, zip.

antonyms everything, something.

nothingness *n* black hole, emptiness, nihility, non-existence, nullity, oblivion, vacuum, void.

notice *v* be aware or conscious of, descry, detect, discern, distinguish, espy, heed, mark, mind, N.B., nota bene, note, observe, perceive, remark, see, spot.

antonyms ignore, overlook.

n advertisement, announcement, attention, awareness, bill, civility, cognizance, communication, consideration, declaration, heed, information, intelligence, intimation,

news, note, notification, observation, poster, regard, resignation, review, sign, warning.

noticeable *adj* appreciable, clear, conspicuous, decided, distinct, dramatic, evident, manifest, marked, measurable, observable, obtrusive, obvious, perceptible, plain, pronounced, significant, striking, unmistakable.

antonyms hidden, insignificant, obscure.

notification *n* announcement, declaration, information, intelligence, message, notice, statement, warning.

notify *v* acquaint, advise, alert, apprise, inform, tell, warn.

notion *n* abstraction, apprehension, belief, caprice, concept, conception, construct, desire, fancy, idea, image, impression, impulse, inclination, inkling, intention, knowledge, opinion, sentiment, understanding, view, whim, wish.

notional *adj* abstract, conceptual, fanciful, hypothetical, ideational, imaginary, speculative, thematic, theoretical, unfounded, unreal, visionary.

antonym real.

notoriety *n* celebrity, dishonour, disrepute, (ill) fame, infamy, obloquy, opprobrium, renown.

notorious *adj* dishonourable, disreputable, famous, infamous, opprobrious, renowned, well-known.

notwithstanding *adv, conj, prep* although, despite (this or the fact that), even so, howbeit, however, in any case, natheless, nevertheless, nonetheless, still, though, yet.

nourish *v* cherish, cultivate, feed, foster, harbour, maintain, nurse, nurture, strengthen, supply, support, sustain.

nourishing *adj* beneficial, good, healthful, health-giving, high-energy, nutritious, nutritive, substantial, sustaining, wholesome.

nourishment *n* aliment, alimentation, diet, food, goodness, maintenance, nutriment, nutrition, support, sustenance.

novel *adj* brand-new, creative, different, fresh, imaginative, innovative, neoteric, new, newfangled, original, singular, strange, surprising, uncommon, unconventional, unfamiliar, unique, unusual.

antonyms familiar, ordinary.

n bestseller, epic, fiction, narrative, paperback, romance, saga, story, tale, yarn.

novelty *n* bagatelle, bauble, curiosity, freshness, gadget, gewgaw, gimcrack, gimmick, innovation, knick-knack, memento, neoterism, newness, originality, souvenir, strangeness, surprise, trifle, trinket, unfamiliarity, uniqueness.

novice *n* amateur, apprentice, beginner, catechumen, cheechako, convert, cub, greenhorn, learner, neophyte, newcomer, novitiate, probationer, proselyte, pupil, rookie, tenderfoot, tyro.

antonyms doyen, expert, professional.

now *adv* at once, at present, at this time, currently, directly, immediately, instantly, next,

nowadays, presently, promptly, straightaway, these days, today.

now and then at times, desultorily, from time to time, infrequently, intermittently, now and again, occasionally, on and off, once in a while, on occasion, periodically, sometimes, spasmodically, sporadically.

nowadays *adv* any more, currently, in this day and age, now, these days, today.

noxious *adj* baneful, corrupting, deadly, deleterious, destructive, detrimental, foul, harmful, hurtful, injurious, insalubrious, mephitic, noisome, pernicious, pestilential, poisonous, unhealthy, unwholesome.

antonyms innocuous, wholesome.

nuance *n* connotation, degree, distinction, gradation, hint, nicety, overtone, refinement, shade, soupçon, subtlety, suggestion, suspicion, tinge, touch, trace.

nub *n* centre, core, crux, essence, gist, heart, kernel, nitty-gritty, nucleus, pith, point.

nubile *adj* attractive, desirable, marriageable, ripe, sexy, voluptuous.

nucleus *n* basis, centre, core, crux, focus, heart, hub, kernel, nub, pivot.

nude *adj* au naturel, bare, disrobed, exposed, in one's birthday suit, in the altogether, in the buff, naked, starkers, stark naked, stripped, unattired, unclad, unclothed, uncovered, undraped, undressed, without a stitch on.

antonyms clothed, covered, dressed.

nudge *v, n* bump, dig, jog, poke, prod, prompt, push, shove, tap, touch.

nudity *n* bareness, dishabille, exposure, nakedness, naturism, nudism, undress.

nugatory *adj* bootless, futile, inadequate, inconsequential, ineffective, ineffectual, inoperative, insignificant, invalid, null and void, trifling, trivial, unavailing, useless, vain, valueless, worthless.

antonyms important, significant.

nugget *n* choice bit, chunk, clump, gem, hunk, lump, mass, piece, tidbit.

nuisance *n* annoyance, bore, bother, botheration, drag, drawback, hassle, inconvenience, irritation, pain, pest, plague, problem, trouble, vexation.

null *adj* characterless, empty, immaterial, incorporeal, ineffectual, inoperative, invalid, meaningless, non-existent, powerless, useless, vain, valueless, void, worthless.

antonym valid.

nullify *v* abolish, abrogate, annul, bring to nothing, cancel, counteract, countervail, destroy, do away with, invalidate, negate, neutralize, quash, repeal, rescind, revoke, undermine, undo, veto, vitiate, void, wipe out.

antonym validate.

nullity *n* characterlessness, emptiness, immateriality, incorporeality, ineffectualness, invalidity, meaninglessness, non-existence, powerlessness, uselessness, voidness, worthlessness.

antonym validity.

numb *adj* benumbed, dead, deadened, frozen, immobilized, insensate, insensible, insensitive, inured, paralysed, stunned, stupefied, torpid, unfeeling.

antonym sensitive.

v anesthetize, benumb, deaden, desensitize, dull, freeze, harden, immobilize, inure, obtund, paralyse, stun, stupefy.

antonym sensitize.

number[1] *n* aggregate, amount, collection, company, count, crowd, figure, horde, index, integer, many, multitude, plurality, quantity, several, sum, throng, total.

v add up, calculate, compute, count, enumerate, include, inventory, reckon, tell, total.

number[2] *n* character, digit, figure, folio, integer, numeral.

number[3] *n* copy, edition, impression, imprint, issue, printing, volume.

numberless *adj* countless, endless, infinite, innumerable, multitudinous, myriad, uncounted, unnumbered, unsummed, untold, without number.

numbness *n* anesthesia, anesthetization, deadness, dullness, freezing, hardness, immobility, insensateness, insensibility, insensitivity, paralysis, stupefaction, torpor, unfeelingness.

antonym sensitivity.

numeral *n* character, cipher, digit, figure, folio, integer, number.

numerous *adj* abundant, copious, diverse, manifold, many, multifarious, multifold, multiple, multiplex, multitudinous, myriad, plentiful, profuse, several, sundry.

antonyms few, scanty.

numerousness *n* abundance, copiousness, manifoldness, multiplexity, multiplicity, multitudinousness, plentifulness, plurality, profusion.

antonyms scantiness, scarcity.

numskull *n* blockhead, bonehead, buffoon, dimwit, dolt, dope, dullard, dummy, dunce, dunderhead, fathead, fool, idiot, ninny, nitwit, sap, simpleton, twit.

nun *n* abbess, bride of Christ, mother superior, prioress, religious, sister, vestal.

nunnery *n* abbey, cloister, convent, priory.

nuptial *adj* bridal, conjugal, connubial, epithalamic, hymeneal, marital, matrimonial, wedded, wedding.

nuptials *n* bridal, espousal, marriage, matrimony, spousals, wedding.

nurse *v* breastfeed, care for, cherish, cultivate, encourage, feed, foster, harbour, keep, nourish, nurture, preserve, promote, succour, suckle, support, sustain, tend, treat, wet-nurse.

n amah, attendant, caregiver, health professional, home nurse, nanny, nursemaid, public health nurse, R.N., sister of mercy, V.O.N., wet nurse.

nurture *n* care, cultivation, development, diet, discipline, education, food, fostering, instruction, nourishment, rearing, socialization, training, upbringing.

v bring up, care for, cherish, cultivate, develop, discipline, educate, feed, foster, instruct, nourish, nurse, rear, school, socialize, support, sustain, tend, train.

nut[1] *n* kernel, nutmeat, pip, seed, stone.

nut[2] *n* brain, head, mind, noggin, noodle, reason, senses.

nut[3] *n* addict, crackpot, crank, eccentric, enthusiast, extremist, fan, fanatic, flake, fruitcake, loony, lunatic, madman, maniac, nutcase, psychopath, weirdo.

nutriment *n* aliment, diet, feed, food, foodstuff, nourishment, nutrition, pabulum, provender, subsistence, support, sustenance.

nutrition *n* eutrophy, feeding, food, nourishment, nutriment, sustenance.

nutritious *adj* alimental, beneficial, good, healthful, health-giving, high-energy, invigorating, nourishing, nutrient-rich, nutritive, solid, square, strengthening, substantial, sustaining, wholesome.

antonyms bad, unwholesome.

nuts *adj* bananas, batty, crazy, demented, deranged, eccentric, insane, irrational, loony, loopy, mad, moonstruck, nutty, off one's rocker, out of one's tree (or mind or senses), psychopathic, unbalanced, unglued, unhinged.

antonym sane.

nuts about   crazy about, ecstatic about, enthusiastic about, fond of, infatuated with, (madly or head over heels) in love with, smitten with, taken with, wild about.

nuts and bolts   basics, bits and pieces, brass tacks, components, details, essentials, fundamentals,   minutiae,   nitty-gritty, practicalities.

nuzzle *v* burrow, cuddle, fondle, nestle, nose, nudge, pet, snuggle.

nymph *n* damsel, dryad, girl, hamadryad, houri, lass, maid, maiden, naiad, oread, sprite, sylph, undine.

O

oaf *n* baboon, blockhead, bonehead, booby, boor, brute, clod, dolt, dullard, dummy, dunce, dunderhead, fool, goon, gorilla, half-wit, hick, hobbledehoy, hulk, lout, lummox, meathead, nincompoop, nitwit, numskull, sap, schlemiel, schlep, simpleton.

oafish *adj* awkward, blockish, boneheaded, boorish, bovine, brutish, bungling, clumsy, crass, dense, dim, dimwitted, doltish, dull, dumb, heavy, loutish, lubberly, lumbering, moronic, obtuse, schleppy, stupid, thick, thickheaded.

oasis *n* enclave, haven, island, refuge, resting-place, retreat, sanctuary, sanctum, watering hole.

oath *n* affirmation, assurance, avowal, bad language, blasphemy, bond, curse, cuss, expletive, guarantee, imprecation, malediction, obscenity, pledge, plight, profanity, promise, swearword, vow, word, word of honour.

obdurate *adj* adamant, callous, dogged, firm, fixed, flinty, hard, hard-hearted, harsh, immovable, implacable, inexorable, inflexible, intransigent, iron, mulish, obstinate, perverse, pig-headed, relentless, stiff-necked, stony, stubborn, unbending, unfeeling, unrelenting, unshakable, unyielding.

antonyms submissive, tender.

obedience *n* accordance, acquiescence, agreement, allegiance, amenableness, compliance, conformability, deference, docility, dutifulness, duty, observance, passivity, respect, reverence, submission, submissiveness, subservience, tractability.

antonym disobedience.

obedient *adj* acquiescent, amenable, biddable, compliant, co-operative, deferential, docile, duteous, dutiful, law-abiding, observant, passive, regardful, respectful, submissive, subservient, tractable, unquestioning, unresisting, well-disciplined, well-trained, yielding.

antonyms disobedient, rebellious, refractory, unruly, wilful.

obeisance *n* bow, congé, curtsy, deference, genuflection, homage, kowtow, prostration, respect, reverence, salaam, salutation, salute.

obese *adj* bulky, chubby, corpulent, Falstaffian, fat, fleshy, gross, heavy, outsize, overweight, paunchy, plump, ponderous, portly, potbellied, pudgy, pursy, roly-poly, rotund, stout, tubby.

antonyms skinny, slender, thin.

obesity *n* bulk, chubbiness, corpulence, embonpoint, fatness, fleshiness, grossness, middle-age spread, overweight, portliness, stoutness, tubbiness.

antonyms skinniness, slenderness, thinness.

obey *v* abide by, act upon, adhere to, be ruled by, bow to, carry out, comply, conform, defer to, discharge, embrace, execute, fall in line (with), follow, fulfil, give in (to), give way (to), heed, implement, keep, knuckle under (to), mind, observe, perform, respond, serve, submit, surrender, take orders from, toe the line, yield.

antonym disobey.

object[1] *n* article, body, entity, fact, item, phenomenon, reality, thing.

object[2] *n* aim, butt, design, end, focus, goal, idea, intent, intention, motive, objective, point, purpose, raison d'être, reason, recipient, target, victim.

object[3] *v* argue, complain, demur, dissent, expostulate, oppose, protest, rebut, refuse, repudiate, take exception.

antonyms accede, acquiesce, agree, assent.

objection *n* cavil, censure, challenge, complaint, counter-argument, demur, doubt, exception, niggle, opposition, protest, remonstrance, scruple.

antonyms agreement, assent.

objectionable *adj* abhorrent, antisocial, deplorable, despicable, detestable, disagreeable, dislikable, displeasing, distasteful, exceptionable, indecorous, insufferable, intolerable, loathsome, noxious, obnoxious, offensive, regrettable, repugnant, unacceptable, undesirable, unpleasant, unseemly.

antonyms acceptable, pleasant, welcome.

objective *adj* calm, detached, disinterested, dispassionate, equitable, even-handed, fair, impartial, impersonal, judicial, just, open-minded, sensible, sober, unbiassed, unemotional, unimpassioned, uninvolved, unprejudiced.

antonyms biassed, subjective.

n aim, ambition, aspiration, destination, end, goal, hope, idea, intention, mark, object, point, prize, purpose, target.

objectivity *n* detachment, disinterest, disinterestedness, dispassion, equitableness, even-handedness, impartiality, impersonality, open mind, open-mindedness.

antonyms bias, subjectivity.

obligation *n* accountability, accountableness, agreement, bond, burden, charge, commitment, compulsion, constraint, contract, debt, due(s), duty, engagement, indebtedness, liability, must, onus, promise, requirement, responsibility, stipulation, trust, understanding.

antonyms choice, discretion.

obligatory *adj* binding, coercive, compulsory, de rigueur, due, enforced, essential, imperative, mandatory, necessary, required, requisite, statutory, unavoidable.

antonym optional.

oblige *v* accommodate, assist, benefit, bind, coerce, compel, constrain, do a favour for, favour, force, gratify, help, impel, indulge, make, necessitate, obligate, please, require, serve.

obliged *adj* appreciative, beholden, bound, compelled, constrained, forced, grateful, gratified, in debt, indebted, obligated, required, thankful, under an obligation, under compulsion.

obliging *adj* accommodating, agreeable, amiable, civil, complaisant, considerate, co-operative, courteous, eager, friendly, good-natured, helpful, kind, polite, willing.

antonyms inconsiderate, unhelpful, unkind.

oblique *adj* angled, aslant, at an angle, backhanded, circuitous, circumlocutory, evasive, inclined, indirect, periphrastic, roundabout, sidelong, skew, slanted, slanting, sloped, sloping, tilted, transverse.

obliquely *adv* askance, askant, aslant, aslope, at an angle, circuitously, diagonally, evasively, in a roundabout way, indirectly, not in so many words, slantwise.

obliterate *v* annihilate, blot out, cancel, delete, destroy, devastate, efface, eliminate, eradicate, erase, expunge, exterminate, extirpate, level, raze, rub out, stamp out, vaporize, wipe out.

oblivion *n* abeyance, blankness, coma, darkness, disregard, eclipse, extinction, forgetfulness, insensibility, Lethe, limbo, neglect, Nirvana, nothing, nothingness, obliviousness, obscurity, stupor, unawareness, unconsciousness, void.

antonyms awareness, consciousness.

oblivious *adj* blind, careless, comatose, deaf, disregardful, forgetful, heedless, ignorant, inattentive, insensible, neglectful, negligent, nescient, regardless, unaware, unconcerned, unconscious, unmindful, unobservant.

antonyms aware, conscious.

obloquy *n* abuse, animadversion, aspersion, attack, bad press, blame, calumny, censure, contumely, criticism, defamation, detraction, discredit, disfavour, disgrace, dishonour, humiliation, ignominy, infamy, invective, odium, opprobrium, reproach, shame, slander, stigma, vilification.

obnoxious *adj* abhorrent, abominable, detestable, disagreeable, disgusting, dislikable, foul, fulsome, hateful, horrid, insufferable, loathsome, nasty, nauseating, nauseous, noisome, objectionable, odious, offensive, repellent, reprehensible, repugnant, repulsive, revolting, sickening, unpleasant.

antonyms agreeable, likable, pleasant.

obscene *adj* atrocious, bawdy, blue, coarse, dirty, disgusting, evil, filthy, foul, gross, heinous, immodest, immoral, improper, impure, indecent, lewd, licentious, loathsome, loose, offensive, outrageous, pornographic, prurient, Rabelaisian, ribald, salacious, scabrous, scurrilous, shameless, shocking, sickening, smutty, suggestive, unchaste, unwholesome, vile, vulgar, wicked.

antonyms clean, decent, decorous.

obscenity *n* abomination, affront, atrocity, bawdiness, blight, blueness, coarseness, dirtiness, evil, expletive, filthiness, foulness, four-letter word, grossness, immodesty, impropriety, impurity, indecency, indelicacy, lewdness, licentiousness, offence, outrage, pornography, profanity, prurience, salacity, scurrility, smut, smuttiness, suggestiveness, swear-word, vileness, vulgarism.

obscure *adj* abstruse, ambiguous, arcane, blurred, clear as mud, clouded, cloudy, complex, complicated, concealed, confusing, cryptic, dark, deep, Delphic, dim, doubtful, dusky, enigmatic, esoteric, faint, gloomy, hazy, hermetic, hidden, humble, incomprehensible, inconspicuous, indefinite, indistinct, inglorious, intricate, involved, little-known, lowly, minor, misty, murky, mysterious, nameless, obfuscated, occult, opaque, oracular, out-of-the-way, recondite, remote, riddling, shadowy, shady, sombre, tenebrous, tenebrose, twilight, unclear, undistinguished, unheard-of, unhonoured, unimportant, unknown, unlit, unnoted, unobvious, unrenowned, unseen, unsung, vague, veiled.

antonyms clear, definite, explicit, famous, lucid.

v bedim, befog, block out, blur, cloak, cloud, conceal, cover, darken, dim, disguise, dull, eclipse, hide, mask, muddy, obfuscate, overshadow, screen, shade, shadow, shroud, veil.

antonyms clarify, illuminate.

obscurity *n* abstruseness, ambiguity, complexity, darkness, dimness, dusk, duskiness, fogginess, gloom, haze, haziness, impenetrability, incomprehensibility, inconspicuousness, indistinctness, ingloriousness, insignificance, intricacy, lowliness, murk, murkiness, namelessness, reconditeness, shadowiness, shadows, unimportance, vagueness.

antonyms clarity, fame, lucidity.

obsequious *adj* abject, cringing, deferential, fawning, flattering, grovelling, ingratiating, menial, oily, servile, slavish, slimy, smarmy, submissive, subservient, sycophantic, toadying, unctuous.

antonym assertive.

observable *adj* apparent, appreciable, clear, detectable, discernible, evident, measurable, noticeable, obvious, open, patent, perceivable, perceptible, recognizable, significant, visible.

observance *n* adherence, attention, celebration, ceremonial, ceremony, compliance, custom, discharge, fashion, form, formality, fulfilment, heeding, honouring, notice, obedience, observation, orthodoxy, performance, practice, rite, ritual, service, tradition.

observant *adj* alert, attentive, eagle-eyed, eagle-sighted, heedful, mindful, perceptive, percipient, perspicacious, quick, sharp-eyed, vigilant, watchful, wide-awake.

antonyms inattentive, unobservant.

observation *n* annotation, attention, cognition, comment, consideration, discernment, examination, experience, finding, information, inspection, knowledge, monitoring, note, notice, obiter dictum, opinion, perception, pronouncement, reading, reflection, remark, review, scrutiny, study, surveillance, thought, utterance, watching.

observe *v* abide by, adhere to, animadvert, celebrate, commemorate, comment, comply, conform to, contemplate, declare, detect, discern, discover, espy, follow, fulfil, heed, honour, keep, keep an eye on, keep tabs on, mention, mind, monitor, note, notice, obey, opine, perceive, perform, regard, remark, remember, respect, say, scrutinize, see, solemnize, spot, state, study, survey, view, watch, witness.

antonyms break, miss, overlook, violate.

observer *n* beholder, bystander, commentator, discerner, eyewitness, looker-on, noter, onlooker, spectator, spotter, viewer, watcher, witness.

obsess *v* bedevil, consume, dominate, engross, grip, haunt, hold, monopolize, nag, plague, possess, preoccupy, prey on, rule, torment.

obsessed *adj* bedevilled, beset, dominated, gripped, hagridden, haunted, hounded, hung up (on), immersed (in), in the grip (of), infatuated, plagued, preoccupied.

antonyms detached, indifferent, unconcerned.

obsession *n* bee in one's bonnet, complex, enthusiasm, fetish, fixation, hang-up, idée fixe, infatuation, mania, monomania, neurosis, phobia, preoccupation, ruling passion, thing (about).

obsessive *adj* besetting, compulsive, consuming, fixed, gripping, haunting, maddening, nagging, tormenting, unforgettable.

obsolescent *adj* ageing, declining, disappearing, dying out, fading, moribund, on the decline, on the wane, on the way out, past its prime, waning.

obsolete *adj* anachronistic, ancient, antediluvian, antiquated, antique, archaic, bygone, dated, dead, démodé, discarded, disused, extinct, horse-and-buggy, musty, old, old-fashioned, old hat, out, out of date (or

fashion), outmoded, outworn, passé, superannuated.

antonyms contemporary, current, modern, new, up-to-date.

obstacle *n* bar, barrier, block, brick wall, catch, check, chicane, difficulty, drawback, hindrance, hitch, hurdle, impediment, interference, interruption, obstruction, pons asinorum, problem, snag, stop, stumbling-block.

antonyms advantage, help.

obstinacy *n* doggedness, firmness, frowardness, inflexibility, intransigence, mulishness, obduracy, perseverance, persistence, pertinacity, perversity, pig-headedness, resoluteness, stubbornness, tenacity, wilfulness, wrong-headedness.

antonyms flexibility, submissiveness.

obstinate *adj* adamant, bull-headed, bullish, camelish, contumacious, determined, dogged, firm, hard-core, headstrong, immovable, inflexible, intractable, intransigent, mulish, obdurate, opinionated, persistent, pertinacious, perverse, pervicacious, pig-headed, recalcitrant, refractory, self-willed, set in one's ways, steadfast, stiff-necked, strong-minded, stubborn, sturdy, tenacious, unpersuadable, unyielding, uppity, wilful, wrong-headed.

antonyms co-operative, flexible, pliant, submissive.

obstreperous *adj* boisterous, clamorous, disorderly, intractable, loud, noisy, out of hand, rackety, rambunctious, rampaging, raucous, refractory, restive, riotous, rip-roaring, roistering, roisterous, rough, rowdy, tempestuous, tumultuous, turbulent, uncontrolled, undisciplined, unmanageable, unruly, uproarious, vociferous, wild.

antonyms calm, disciplined, quiet.

obstruct *v* arrest, bar, barricade, block, check, choke, clog, cut off, encumber, frustrate, hamper, hinder, hold up, impede, inhibit, interfere with, interrupt, occlude, prevent, shut off, stall, stonewall, stop, thwart.

antonym help.

obstruction *n* bar, barricade, barrier, block, blockage, check, difficulty, filibuster, hindrance, holdup, impediment, obstacle, occlusion, stoppage, traverse.

antonym help.

obstructive *adj* awkward, difficult, unaccommodating, unco-operative, unhelpful.

antonym helpful.

obtain[1] *v* achieve, acquire, attain, come by, compass, earn, gain, get, procure, secure.

obtain[2] *v* be customary, be in force, be prevalent, be the case, exist, hold, prevail, reign, rule, stand.

obtainable *adj* accessible, achievable, at hand, attainable, available, in stock, on call, on tap, procurable, ready, realizable, to be had.

antonym unobtainable.

obtrusive *adj* blatant, forward, importunate, interfering, intrusive, manifest, meddling, nosey, noticeable, obvious, officious, prominent, protruding, protuberant, prying, pushy.

antonym unobtrusive.

obtuse *adj* blunt, boneheaded, crass, dense, dopey, dull, dull-witted, dumb, imperceptive, inattentive, insensitive, rounded, slow, stolid, stupid, thick, uncomprehending, unintelligent.

antonyms bright, sharp.

▲ *confusable word* abstruse.

obviate *v* anticipate, avert, counter, counteract, divert, forestall, preclude, prevent, remove.

obvious *adj* apparent, clear, conspicuous, discernible, distinct, evident, glaring, indisputable, manifest, noticeable, open, open-and-shut, overt, palpable, patent, perceptible, plain, prominent, pronounced, recognizable, self-evident, self-explanatory, straightforward, transparent, unconcealed, undeniable, undisguised, unmistakable, unsubtle, visible.

antonyms obscure, unclear.

obviously *adv* certainly, clearly, distinctly, evidently, manifestly, of course, palpably, patently, plainly, undeniably, unmistakably, unquestionably, visibly, without doubt.

occasion *n* affair, call, case, cause, celebration, chance, convenience, event, excuse, experience, ground(s), incident, inducement, influence, instance, justification, moment, motive, occurrence, opening, opportunity, prompting, provocation, reason, time.

v bring about, bring on, cause, create, effect, elicit, engender, evoke, generate, give rise to, induce, influence, inspire, lead to, make, originate, persuade, produce, prompt, provoke.

occasional *adj* casual, desultory, fitful, incidental, infrequent, intermittent, irregular, odd, periodic, rare, scattered, sporadic, uncommon.

antonym frequent.

occasionally *adv* at intervals, at times, every so often, from time to time, infrequently, irregularly, now and again, now and then, off and on, on and off, on occasion, once in a while, periodically, sometimes, sporadically.

antonym frequently.

occult *adj* abstruse, arcane, cabalistic, concealed, esoteric, faint, hidden, impenetrable, invisible, magical, mysterious, mystic, mystical, mystifying, obscure, preternatural, recondite, secret, supernatural, unknown, unrevealed, veiled.

occultism *n* diabolism, magic, mysticism, sorcery, spiritualism, supernaturalism, witchcraft.

occupancy *n* domiciliation, habitation, holding, inhabitancy, occupation, ownership, possession, residence, tenancy, tenure, term, use.

occupant *n* addressee, denizen, holder, householder, incumbent, indweller, inhabitant, inmate, lessee, occupier, resident, squatter, tenant, user.

occupation[1] *n* absorption, activity, business, calling, craft, employment, job, line, post, profession, pursuit, trade, vocation, walk of life, work.

occupation[2] *n* billet, conquest, control, habitation, holding, invasion, occupancy, possession, residence, seizure, subjugation, takeover, tenancy, tenure, use.

occupied *adj* absorbed, busy, employed, engaged, engrossed, full, hard at it, in use, inhabited, lived-in, peopled, settled, taken, tenanted, tied up, unavailable, working.

antonym unoccupied.

occupy[1] *v* absorb, amuse, beguile, busy, cover, divert, employ, engage, engross, entertain, immerse, interest, invade, involve, keep busy, monopolize, preoccupy, take up, tie up.

occupy[2] *v* capture, conquer, dwell in, engage, ensconce (or establish) oneself in, fill, garrison, hold, inhabit, invade, keep, live in, overrun, own, permeate, pervade, possess, reside in, seize, stay in, take over, take possession of, tenant, use.

occur *v* appear, arise, be found, be met with, be present, befall, betide, chance, come about, come off, come to pass, crop up, develop, eventuate, exist, happen, intervene, manifest itself, materialize, obtain, result, show itself, take place, transpire, turn up.

occur to come to mind, come to one, cross one's mind, dawn on, enter one's head, present itself, spring to mind, strike one, suggest itself.

occurrence *n* action, adventure, affair, appearance, case, circumstance, development, episode, event, existence, happening, incident, instance, manifestation, materialization, proceeding, transaction.

ocean *n* briny, chuck, main, sea, the deep, the drink, the water.

odd[1] *adj* abnormal, atypical, bizarre, curious, deviant, different, eccentric, erratic, exceptional, extraordinary, fantastic, flukey, freak, freakish, freaky, funky, funny, idiosyncratic, irregular, kinky, oddball, original, outlandish, peculiar, quaint, queer, rare, remarkable, singular, strange, uncanny, uncommon, unconventional, unexplained, unusual, weird, whimsical.

antonym normal.

odd[2] *adj* auxiliary, casual, fragmentary, ill-matched, incidental, irregular, left-over, lone, miscellaneous, occasional, only, periodic, random, remaining, seasonal, single, solitary, spare, sundry, surplus, uneven, unmatched, unpaired, varied, various.

oddity *n* abnormality, anomaly, bizarreness, card, character, crank, curiosity, eccentricity, extraordinariness, freak, freakishness, idiosyncrasy, incongruity, irregularity, kink, maverick, misfit, oddball, oddness, outlandishness, peculiarity, phenomenon, queerness, quirk, rara avis, rarity, screwball, singularity, strangeness, unconventionality, unnaturalness, weirdo.

oddment *n* bit, end, fragment, leftover, offcut, patch, remnant, scrap, shred, sliver, snippet.

odds *n* advantage, allowance, ascendancy, balance, chances, difference, discrepancy, disparity, dissimilarity, distinction, edge, lead, likelihood, probability, superiority.

at odds at daggers drawn, at enmity, at loggerheads, at one another's throats, at outs, at swords' points, at variance, feuding, in conflict, in dispute, on the outs, on opposite wavelengths, opposed (to), quarrelling.

odds and ends bits, bits and pieces, flotsam and jetsam, junk, leavings, litter, oddments, remnants, scraps, this and that.

odious *adj* abhorrent, abominable, annoying, detestable, disgusting, execrable, foul, hateful, heinous, horrible, horrid, insufferable, loathsome, obnoxious, offensive, repellent, repugnant, repulsive, revolting, unpleasant, vile.

antonym pleasant.

odium *n* abhorrence, animosity, antipathy, censure, condemnation, contempt, detestation, disapprobation, disapproval, discredit, disfavour, disgrace, dishonour, dislike, disrepute, execration, hatred, infamy, obloquy, opprobrium, reprobation, shame.

odorous *adj* aromatic, balmy, fragrant, high, odoriferous, perfumed, pungent, redolent, scented, smelly, sweet-smelling.

antonym odourless.

odour *n* air, aroma, atmosphere, aura, bouquet, breath, emanation, essence, exhalation, flavour, fragrance, perfume, quality, redolence, scent, smell, spirit, stench, stink.

odyssey *n* journey, travels, voyage, wandering.

of course certainly, definitely, doubtlessly, indubitably, naturally, no doubt, obviously, undoubtedly.

off *adj* abnormal, absent, bad, below par, cancelled, free, gone, green about the gills, high, inaccurate, inoperative, mouldy, postponed, rancid, rotten, sickish, sour, turned, under the weather, wrong.

adv apart, aside, at a distance, away, elsewhere, out.

off and on fitfully, from time to time, intermittently, now and again, now and then, occasionally, on and off, once in a while, periodically, sometimes, sporadically.

off-duty at leisure, at liberty, free, not at work, off, off work, on holiday.

off guard by surprise, napping, unawares, unprepared, unready, unwary, with one's defences down, with one's pants down.

off the cuff ad lib, extempore, impromptu, improvised, offhand, off the top of one's head, spontaneous, spontaneously, unofficially, unprepared, unrehearsed, unscripted.

off the hook acquitted, cleared, exonerated, in the clear, scot-free, vindicated.

off the record confidential, confidentially, private, privately, sub rosa, unofficial, unofficially.

antonym officially.

off-colour *adj* faded, ill, indecent, indisposed, off form, out of sorts, pasty-faced, peaked, poorly, queasy, sick, under the weather, unwell.

offence[1] *n* affront, crime, delinquency, fault, harm, infraction, indignity, infringement, injury, injustice, insult, lapse, misdeed, misdemeanour, outrage, peccadillo, put-down, sin, slight, snub, transgression, trespass, violation, wrong, wrongdoing.

offence[2] *n* anger, annoyance, displeasure, hard feelings, huff, hurt, indignation, injury, ire, pique, resentment, umbrage, wrath.

offend *v* affront, annoy, disgruntle, disgust, displease, fret, gall, hurt, insult, irritate, miff, nauseate, outrage, pain, pique, provoke, put off, repel, repulse, rile, sicken, slight, snub, transgress, turn off, upset, vex, violate, wound, wrong.

antonym please.

offended *adj* affronted, disgruntled, disgusted, displeased, huffy, in a huff, miffed, outraged, pained, piqued, put off, put out, resentful, smarting, stung, ticked off, upset, wounded.

antonym pleased.

offender *n* criminal, culprit, delinquent, guilty party, law-breaker, malefactor, miscreant, sinner, transgressor, wrongdoer.

offensive *adj* abominable, abusive, aggressive, annoying, attacking, detestable, disagreeable, discourteous, disgusting, displeasing, disrespectful, embarrassing, grisly, impertinent, insolent, insulting, intolerable, invading, irritating, loathsome, nasty, nauseating, noisome, objectionable, obnoxious, odious, rank, repellent, repugnant, revolting, rude, sickening, uncivil, unmannerly, unpalatable, unpleasant, unsavoury, vile.

antonyms defensive, pleasing.

n attack, charge, drive, onslaught, push, raid, sortie, thrust.

offer *v* advance, afford, bid, extend, furnish, give, hold out, make available, move, present, proffer, propose, propound, provide, put forth, put forward, show, submit, suggest, tender, volunteer.

n approach, attempt, bid, endeavour, essay, overture, presentation, proposal, proposition, submission, suggestion, tender.

offering *n* contribution, donation, gift, oblation, present, sacrifice, subscription.

offhand *adj* abrupt, aloof, brusque, careless, casual, cavalier, curt, glib, informal, offhanded, perfunctory, take-it-or-leave-it, unappreciative, uncaring, unceremonious, unconcerned, uninterested.

antonyms calculated, planned.

adv at once, extempore, immediately, off the cuff, off the top of one's head, on the spur of the moment, straightaway.

office *n* appointment, business, capacity, charge, commission, duty, employment, function, obligation, occupation, place, post, responsibility, role, room, service, situation, station, trust, work.

officer *n* administrator, agent, appointee, bureaucrat, dignitary, executive, functionary, officeholder, official, public servant, representative.

offices *n* advocacy, aegis, aid, auspices, backing, backup, favour, help, intercession, intermediation, intervention, mediation, patronage, recommendation, referral, support.

official *adj* accredited, approved, authentic, authenticated, authorized, authoritative, bona fide, certified, ex cathedra, formal, legitimate, licensed, on the record, proper, sanctioned.
antonym unofficial.
n agent, bureaucrat, executive, functionary, gauleiter, hakim, intendant, mandarin, officebearer, officer, representative.

officiate *v* adjudicate, chair, conduct, emcee, manage, oversee, preside, referee, serve, superintend, umpire.

officious *adj* bustling, dictatorial, forward, impertinent, inquisitive, interfering, intrusive, meddlesome, meddling, mischievous, nosey, obtrusive, opinionated, overzealous, pragmatical, pushy, self-important.

offish *adj* aloof, cool, haughty, stand-offish, stuck-up, unsociable.
antonyms friendly, sociable.

off-key *adj* discordant, dissonant, ill-timed, improper, inappropriate, indecent, inharmonious, jarring, out of keeping, out of tune, unsuitable.

offload *v* deposit, disburden, discharge, drop, dump, get rid of, jettison, shift, transfer, unburden, unload, unship.

off-putting *adj* daunting, demoralizing, deterring, discomfiting, disconcerting, discouraging, disheartening, dismaying, dispiriting, disturbing, formidable, frustrating, intimidating, unnerving, unsettling, upsetting.

offset *v* balance out, cancel out, compare, compensate for, counteract, counterbalance, counterpoise, countervail, juxtapose, make up for, neutralize.
n balance, compensation, counterbalance, counterweight, equipoise, equivalent, redress.

offshoot *n* adjunct, appendage, arm, branch, by-product, development, embranchment, limb, outgrowth, spin-off, sprout, spur.

offspring *n* brood, child, children, creation, descendant, descendants, family, fry, heir, heirs, issue, kids, litter, progeny, quiverful, result, scion, seed, spawn, successor, successors, young.
antonym parent(s).

often *adv* again and again, frequently, generally, habitually, many a time, much, oft, over and over, regularly, repeatedly, time after time, time and again.
antonym seldom.

ogle *v* check out, eye, eye up, leer, look, make eyes at, stare.

ogre *n* bogey, bogeyman, brute, bugaboo, bugbear, demon, devil, fiend, giant, monster, spectre, villain.

oil *v* anoint, dress, embrocate, grease, lubricate.
n balm, cream, grease, kerosene, liniment, lotion, lubricant, ointment, oleum, salve, unguent.

oily *adj* fatty, flattering, fulsome, glib, greasy, hypocritical, obsequious, oiled, oleaginous, plausible, sebaceous, servile, slick, slippery, smarmy, smeary, smooth, unctuous.

ointment *n* balm, balsam, cerate, cream, demulcent, embrocation, emollient, liniment, lotion, moisturizer, salve, sunscreen, unction, unguent.

okay *adj* acceptable, accurate, adequate, all right, approved, convenient, correct, fair, fine, good, in order, not bad, OK, passable, permitted, reasonable, right as rain, satisfactory, tolerable.
n agreement, approbation, approval, assent, authorization, consent, endorsement, go-ahead, green light, OK, permission, sanction, say-so, seal of approval, support.
v accredit, agree to, approve, authorize, consent to, countersign, endorse, give the go-ahead to, give the green light to, OK, pass, rubber-stamp, sanction, validate.
interj agreed, all right, fine, OK, right, very good, very well, yes.

old *adj* aboriginal, aged, age-old, ancient, antediluvian, antiquated, antique, archaic, bygone, cast-off, crumbling, dated, decayed, decrepit, done, earlier, early, elderly, erstwhile, ex-, experienced, familiar, former, fossilized, grey, grey-haired, grizzled, hackneyed, hardened, hoary, immemorial, long-established, long-standing, mature, obsolete, of old, of yore, olden, old-fashioned, one-time, original, out, out-of-date, outdated, outmoded, outworn, over the hill, passé, patriarchal, practised, prehistoric, previous, primeval, primitive, primordial, pristine, quondam, remote, senescent, senile, skilled, stale, superannuated, time-honoured, timeworn, traditional, unfashionable, unoriginal, venerable, versed, veteran, vintage, weathered, worn-out.
antonym young.

old age advancing years, age, agedness, dotage, elderliness, second childhood, senescence, senility, twilight of one's life.
antonym youth.

old-fashioned *adj* ancient, antiquated, archaic, behind the times, corny, dated, dead, démodé, fog(e)yish, fusty, horse-and-buggy, musty, neanderthal, obsolescent, obsolete, old-fogeyish, old hat, old-time, out, out-of-date, outdated, outmoded, out of style, passé, past, retro, rinky-dink, square, superannuated, unfashionable.
antonyms contemporary, modern, up-to-date.

old-world *adj* archaic, ceremonious, chivalrous, conservative, courtly, formal, gallant, old-fashioned, picturesque, quaint, traditional.

Olympian *adj* elevated, exalted, glorious, godlike, Jovian, lofty, majestic, rarefied, splendid, sublime.

omen *n* augury, auspice, bad feeling, boding, foreboding, foretoken, harbinger, indication, portent, premonition, presage, prognostic, prognostication, sign, straw in the wind, warning, writing on the wall.

ominous *adj* baleful, bodeful, dark, fateful, inauspicious, menacing, minatory, portentous, premonitory, presageful, sinister, threatening, unpromising, unpropitious.
antonym auspicious.

omission *n* avoidance, bowdlerization, default, ellipsis, exclusion, failure, forgetfulness, gap, lack, neglect, oversight.
antonyms addition, inclusion.

omit *v* disregard, drop, edit out, eliminate, exclude, fail, forget, give something a miss, leave out, leave undone, let slide, miss out, neglect, overlook, pass over, pretermit, skip.
antonyms add, include.

omnibus *adj* across-the-board, all-embracing, compendious, comprehensive, encyclopedic, inclusive, overall, sweeping, wide-ranging.
antonym selective.

omnipotence *n* divine right, invincibility, mastery, plenipotence, sovereignty, supremacy.
antonym impotence.

omnipotent *adj* all-powerful, almighty, plenipotent, supreme.
antonym impotent.

omnipresent *adj* pervasive, ubiquitary, ubiquitous, universal.

omniscient *adj* all-knowing, all-seeing, pansophic.

on
For phrases such as *on duty*, *on the ball*, *on thin ice*, see the first noun after *on*.

on and off discontinuously, fitfully, from time to time, intermittently, now and again, now and then, off and on, on occasion, periodically, sometimes, spasmodically, sporadically.

once *adv* at one time, formerly, heretofore, in the old days, in the past, in times gone by, in times past, long ago, once upon a time, previously.

at once as one, at one go, at the same time, directly, forthwith, immediately, in concert, in unison, instantly, now, promptly, right away, simultaneously, straight away, this minute, together, unhesitatingly, with one voice, without delay.

once (and) for all conclusively, decisively, definitively, finally, for good, for the last time, permanently, positively.

once in a blue moon hardly ever, infrequently, rarely, seldom.

oncoming *adj* advancing, approaching, forthcoming, gathering, imminent, impending, looming, onrushing, upcoming.

one *adj* alike, compatible, complete, entire, equal, harmonious, identical, like-minded, united, whole.

oneness *n* completeness, consistency, distinctness, identicalness, identity, individuality, sameness, singleness, unity, wholeness.

onerous *adj* backbreaking, burdensome, crushing, demanding, difficult, exacting, exhausting, exigent, formidable, grave, hard, heavy, herculean, laborious, oppressive, responsible, taxing, troublesome, weighty.
antonyms easy, light.

one-sided *adj* asymmetrical, biassed, discriminatory, inequitable, lopsided, partial, partisan, prejudiced, unequal, unfair, unilateral, unjust.
antonym impartial.

one-time *adj* erstwhile, ex-, former, late, previous, quondam, sometime, whilom.

ongoing *adj* advancing, continuing, continuous, current, developing, evolving, extant, growing, in progress, lasting, progressing, successful, unfinished, unfolding.

onlooker *n* beholder, bystander, eyewitness, gawker, looker-on, observer, passer-by, rubberneck, spectator, viewer, watcher, witness.

only *adv* at most, barely, exclusively, just, merely, purely, simply, solely.
adj exclusive, individual, lone, single, sole, solitary, unique.

onrush *n* career, cascade, charge, flood, flow, onset, onslaught, push, rush, stampede, stream, surge.

onset *n* assault, attack, beginning, charge, commencement, inception, kick-off, onrush, onslaught, outbreak, outset, start.
antonyms end, finish.

onslaught *n* assault, attack, barrage, blitz, bombardment, charge, offensive, onrush, onset.

onus *n* burden, duty, encumbrance, liability, load, obligation, responsibility, task.

onward *adv* ahead, beyond, forth, forward, frontward, in front, on.
antonym backward.

oodles *n* abundance, bags, heaps, lashings, loads, lots, masses, piles, tons.
antonym scarcity.

oomph *n* animation, bounce, energy, enthusiasm, exuberance, get-up-and-go, pep, pizzazz, sparkle, vigour, vitality, vivacity, zing.

ooze *v* bleed, discharge, drain, dribble, drip, drop, emit, escape, exude, filter, leach, leak, overflow with, percolate, seep, strain, sweat, transude, weep.
n alluvium, deposit, mire, muck, mud, sediment, silt, slime, sludge.

oozy *adj* dewy, dripping, miry, moist, mucky, muddy, slimy, sloppy, sludgy, sweaty, weeping.

opacity *n* cloudiness, density, dullness, filminess, impermeability, milkiness, murkiness, obfuscation, obscurity, opaqueness, unclearness.

antonym transparency.

opaque *adj* abstruse, baffling, clouded, cloudy, cryptic, difficult, dim, dull, enigmatic, filmy, hazy, impenetrable, incomprehensible, inexplicable, lustreless, muddied, muddy, murky, obfuscated, obscure, turbid, unclear, unfathomable, unintelligible.

antonym transparent.

open *adj* aboveboard, accessible, agape, airy, ajar, apparent, arguable, artless, available, avowed, bare, barefaced, blatant, bounteous, bountiful, candid, champaign, clear, conspicuous, debatable, disinterested, downright, evident, expanded, exposed, extended, extensive, fair, filigree, flagrant, frank, free, fretted, gaping, general, generous, guileless, holey, honest, honeycombed, impartial, ingenuous, innocent, lacy, liberal, lidless, loose, manifest, moot, munificent, natural, navigable, noticeable, objective, obvious, overt, passable, plain, porous, public, receptive, revealed, rolling, sincere, spacious, spongy, spread out, sweeping, transparent, unbarred, unbiassed, unclosed, uncluttered, uncommitted, unconcealed, unconditional, uncovered, uncrowded, undecided, undefended, undisguised, unenclosed, unengaged, unfastened, unfenced, unfolded, unfortified, unfurled, unlidded, unlocked, unobstructed, unoccupied, unprejudiced, unprotected, unqualified, unreserved, unresolved, unrestricted, unroofed, unsealed, unsettled, unsheltered, unwalled, upfront, vacant, visible, wide, wide-open, yawning.

antonyms closed, shut.

v begin, clear, come apart, commence, crack, disclose, divulge, exhibit, explain, expose, inaugurate, initiate, launch, lay bare, pour out, rupture, separate, set in motion, show, split, spread (out), start, throw wide, unbar, unbare, unblock, unclose, uncork, uncover, undo, unfasten, unfold, unfurl, unlatch, unlid, unlock, unroll, unseal, unshutter.

antonyms close, shut.

open to accessible, disposed, exposed, liable, susceptible, vulnerable.

open-and-shut *adj* obvious, simple, straightforward.

open-handed *adj* bountiful, eleemosynary, free, generous, large-hearted, lavish, liberal, munificent, unstinting.

antonym tight-fisted.

opening *n* adit, aperture, beginning, birth, breach, break, cavity, chance, chasm, chink, cleft, commencement, crack, cranny, dawn, doorway, fissure, fistula, foramen, gap, hole, inauguration, inception, initiation, interstice, kick-off, launch, launching, occasion, onset, opportunity, orifice, ostiole, outset, perforation, place, portal, rent, rupture, slot, space, split, start, vacancy, vent, vista.

antonyms closing, closure.

adj beginning, commencing, early, first, inaugural, inceptive, initial, initiatory, introductory, maiden, primary.

antonym closing.

openly *adv* blatantly, brazenly, candidly, face to face, flagrantly, forthrightly, frankly, glaringly, in full view, in public, overtly, plainly, publicly, shamelessly, unabashedly, unashamedly, unhesitatingly, unreservedly, wantonly.

antonyms secretly, slyly.

open-minded *adj* broad, broad-minded, catholic, dispassionate, enlightened, free, impartial, latitudinarian, liberal, objective, reasonable, receptive, tolerant, unbiassed, unprejudiced.

antonyms bigoted, intolerant, prejudiced.

open-mouthed *adj* agape, amazed, astounded, dumfounded, expectant, flabbergasted, gaping, slack-jawed, spellbound, thunderstruck.

operate *v* act, function, handle, manage, manoeuvre, perform, run, use, utilize, work.

operation *n* action, activity, affair, agency, assault, business, campaign, course, deal, effect, effort, employment, enterprise, exercise, force, influence, instrumentality, manipulation, manoeuvre, motion, movement, performance, procedure, proceeding, process, surgery, transaction, undertaking, use, utilization, working.

operational *adj* functional, going, in service, in working order, on duty, operative, prepared, ready, usable, viable, workable, working.

antonym out of order.

operative *adj* active, crucial, current, effective, efficient, engaged, functional, functioning, important, in action, in force, in operation, indicative, influential, key, operational, relevant, serviceable, significant, standing, workable.

antonym inoperative.

n artisan, employee, hand, labourer, machinist, mechanic, operator, worker.

operator *n* administrator, conductor, contractor, dealer, director, driver, handler, machinator, machinist, manager, manipulator, mechanic, mover, operant, operative, practitioner, shyster, speculator, technician, trader, wheeler-dealer, worker.

opiate *n* anodyne, bromide, depressant, downer, drug, narcotic, nepenthe, pacifier, sedative, soporific, stupefacient, tranquillizer.

opine *v* believe, conceive, conclude, conjecture, declare, guess, judge, presume, say, suggest, suppose, surmise, suspect, think, venture, volunteer.

opinion *n* assessment, belief, conception, conjecture, conventional wisdom, doxy, estimation, feeling, idea, impression, judgment, mind, notion, perception, persuasion, point of view, sentiment, stance, tenet, theory, view, voice, vox populi.

in my opinion as far as I'm concerned, for my money, in my view, the way I see it.

opinionated *adj* adamant, biassed, bigoted, bull-headed, cocksure, dictatorial, doctrinaire, dogmatic, inflexible, obdurate, obstinate, overbearing, partisan, pig-headed, prejudiced, self-assertive, single-minded, stubborn, uncompromising, wilful.

antonym open-minded.

opponent *n* adversary, antagonist, challenger, competitor, contender, contestant, disputant, dissentient, dissident, enemy, foe, objector, opposer, opposition, rival.

antonyms ally, proponent.

opportune *adj* advantageous, appropriate, apt, auspicious, convenient, favourable, felicitous, fit, fitting, fortunate, good, happy, lucky, pertinent, proper, propitious, seasonable, suitable, timely, well-timed.

antonym inopportune.

opportunism *n* adventurism, expediency, exploitation, Machiavellianism, making hay while the sun shines, pragmatism, realism, Realpolitik, taking advantage, trimming, unscrupulousness.

opportunity *n* break, chance, convenience, hour, moment, occasion, opening, scope, shot, time, turn.

oppose *v* bar, beard, breast, check, combat, compare, confront, contradict, contrary, contrast, contravene, controvert, counter, counterattack, counterbalance, defy, face, fight, fly in the face of, gainsay, hinder, obstruct, pit against, play off, prevent, resist, stand up to, take a stand against, take issue with, thwart, withstand.

antonyms favour, support.

opposed *adj* against, antagonistic, anti, antipathetic, antithetical, clashing, conflicting, contrary, contrasted, dissentient, hostile, in opposition, incompatible, inimical, opposing, opposite.

antonym in favour.

opposing *adj* antagonistic, antipathetic, clashing, combatant, conflicting, contentious, contrary, disputatious, enemy, hostile, incompatible, irreconcilable, opposed, opposite, oppugnant, rival, warring.

opposite *adj* adverse, antagonistic, antipodal, antipodean, antithetical, conflicting, contradictory, contrary, contrasted, corresponding, different, differing, diverse, facing, fronting, hostile, inconsistent, inimical, irreconcilable, opposed, reverse, unlike.

antonym same.

n antipode(s), antipole, antithesis, contradiction, contrary, converse, inverse, reverse.

antonym same.

opposition *n* antagonism, antagonist, clash, competition, contraposition, contrariety, counteraction, disapproval, foe, hostility, obstruction, obstructiveness, opponent, other side, polarity, prevention, resistance, rival, syzygy, unfriendliness.

antonyms co-operation, support.

oppress *v* abuse, afflict, burden, crush, depress, dispirit, grind down, harass, harry, lie hard on, lie heavy on, maltreat, overpower, overwhelm, persecute, sadden, subdue,

subjugate, suppress, torment, trample, tyrannize, vex, weigh heavy (on).

oppressed *adj* abused, browbeaten, burdened, disadvantaged, disenfranchised, downtrodden, enslaved, harassed, henpecked, maltreated, misused, persecuted, prostrate, slave, subject, subjugated, troubled, tyrannized, underprivileged.

antonym free.

oppression *n* abuse, brutality, calamity, cruelty, hardship, harshness, injury, injustice, jackboot(s), maltreatment, misery, persecution, severity, subjection, suffering, tyranny.

oppressive *adj* airless, brutal, burdensome, close, coercive, cruel, despotic, draining, enervating, grinding, harsh, heavy, inhuman, intolerable, muggy, onerous, overbearing, overpowering, overwhelming, repressive, severe, stifling, stuffy, suffocating, sultry, torrid, tyrannical, unendurable, unjust.

antonyms gentle, invigorating.

oppressor *n* autocrat, bully, despot, dictator, harrier, intimidator, persecutor, scourge, slave driver, taskmaster, tormentor, tyrant.

opprobrious *adj* abusive, calumniatory, calumnious, contemptuous, contumelious, damaging, defamatory, derogatory, insolent, insulting, invective, offensive, scandalous, scurrilous, vitriolic, vituperative.

opprobrium *n* calumny, censure, contumely, debasement, degradation, discredit, disfavour, disgrace, dishonour, disrepute, ignominy, infamy, obloquy, odium, reproach, scurrility, shame, slur, stigma.

opt *v* choose, decide (on), elect, go (for), plump (for), prefer, select.

optimistic *adj* assured, bright, bullish, buoyant, cheerful, confident, encouraged, expectant, heartened, hopeful, idealistic, Panglossian, Pollyannish, positive, rosy, sanguine, upbeat, Utopian.

antonym pessimistic.

optimum *adj* A-one, best, choicest, highest, ideal, most fitting, optimal, peak, perfect, superlative, top.

antonym worst.

n best, peak, zenith.

option *n* alternative, choice, election, possibility, preference, selection.

optional *adj* discretionary, elective, extra, open, possible, unforced, voluntary.

antonym compulsory.

opulence *n* abundance, affluence, copiousness, cornucopia, easy street, fortune, fullness, lavishness, luxuriance, luxury, plenty, profusion, prosperity, riches, richness, sumptuousness, superabundance, wealth.

antonyms penury, poverty.

opulent *adj* abundant, affluent, copious, lavish, luxuriant, luxurious, moneyed, plentiful, profuse, prolific, prosperous, rich, sumptuous, superabundant, wealthy, well-heeled, well-off, well-to-do.

antonyms penurious, poor.

opus *n* brainchild, composition, creation, lucubration, oeuvre, piece, production, work.

oracle *n* adviser, answer, augur, augury, authority, divination, guru, high priest, mastermind, mentor, prediction, prognostication, prophecy, prophet, pundit, python, revelation, sage, seer, sibyl, soothsayer, vision, wizard.

oracular *adj* ambiguous, arcane, auspicious, authoritative, cryptic, Delphic, dictatorial, dogmatic, equivocal, grave, haruspical, mantic, mysterious, obscure, ominous, portentous, positive, predictive, prescient, prognostic, prophetic, pythonic, sage, sibylline, significant, two-edged, vatic, vaticinal, venerable, wise.

oral *adj* buccal, spoken, unwritten, verbal, vocal.

antonym written.

orate *v* declaim, discourse, harangue, hold forth, pontificate, sermonize, speak, speechify, talk.

oration *n* address, declamation, discourse, eulogy, harangue, homily, lecture, sermon, speech, spiel.

orator *n* declaimer, demagogue, lecturer, phrasemaker, phrasemonger, public speaker, rhetorician, speaker, spellbinder, spieler.

oratorical *adj* bombastic, Ciceronian, declamatory, Demosthenic, elocutionary, eloquent, grandiloquent, high-flown, magniloquent, rhetorical, silver-tongued, smooth-tongued, sonorous.

oratory *n* declamation, diction, elocution, eloquence, grandiloquence, public speaking, rhetoric, speech, speechifying, speechmaking.

orb *n* ball, circle, globe, globule, mound, ring, round, sphere, spherule.

orbit *n* ambit, circle, circumgyration, circumvolution, compass, course, cycle, domain, ellipse, influence, path, range, reach, revolution, rotation, scope, sphere, sphere of influence, sweep, track, trajectory.

v circle, circumnavigate, encircle, revolve.

orchestrate *v* arrange, compose, concert, co-ordinate, fix, integrate, organize, prepare, present, score, stage-manage.

ordain *v* anoint, appoint, call, consecrate, decree, destine, dictate, elect, enact, enjoin, fate, fix, foredoom, foreordain, frock, instruct, intend, invest, lay down, legislate, nominate, order, predestine, predetermine, prescribe, pronounce, require, rule, set, will.

ordeal *n* affliction, agony, anguish, nightmare, pain, persecution, suffering, test, torture, trial, tribulation(s), trouble(s).

order¹ *n* arrangement, array, calm, categorization, classification, codification, control, cosmos, discipline, disposal, disposition, grouping, harmony, law and order, layout, line, line-up, method, neatness, ordering, orderliness, organization, pattern, peace, placement, plan, progression, propriety, quiet, regularity, sequence, structure, succession, symmetry, system, tidiness, tranquillity.

antonym disorder.

in order acceptable, all right, allowed, A-OK, appropriate, arranged, called for, correct, done, fine, fitting, hunky-dory, in (good) condition, in sequence, neat, OK, orderly, permitted, right, shipshape, suitable, tidy.

antonyms disallowed, out of order.

order² *n* application, behest, booking, chit, command, commission, decree, dictate, diktat, direction, directive, injunction, insistence, instruction, law, mandate, ordinance, precept, prescription, regulation, request, requisition, reservation, rule, stipulation.

order³ *n* association, breed, brotherhood, cast, caste, class, community, company, degree, family, fraternity, genre, genus, grade, guild, hierarchy, ilk, kind, league, lodge, organization, pecking order, phylum, position, rank, sect, sisterhood, society, sodality, sort, species, status, subclass, tribe, type, union.

order⁴ *v* adjure, adjust, align, arrange, authorize, bid, book, catalogue, charge, class, classify, command, conduct, control, decree, direct, dispose, enact, engage, enjoin, group, instruct, lay out, manage, marshal, neaten, ordain, organize, prescribe, put to rights, regulate, request, require, reserve, sort out, systematize, tabulate, tidy.

antonym disorder.

in order to in order that, in preparation for, intending to, so as to, so that, to, with a view to, with the intention of, for the purpose of.

orderly *adj* businesslike, controlled, cosmic, decorous, disciplined, in order, law-abiding, methodical, neat, non-violent, peaceable, quiet, regular, restrained, scientific, shipshape, systematic, systematized, tidy, trim, well-behaved, well-organized, well-regulated.

antonym disorderly.

ordinance *n* canon, ceremony, command, decree, dictum, directive, edict, enactment, fiat, injunction, institution, law, observance, order, practice, precept, prescript, regulation, rite, ritual, rule, ruling, sacrament, statute, usage.

ordinarily *adv* as a rule, commonly, conventionally, customarily, familiarly, generally, habitually, in general, normally, usually.

ordinary *adj* accustomed, average, common, common-or-garden, commonplace, conventional, customary, established, everyday, fair, familiar, habitual, homespun, household, humble, humdrum, inconsequential, indifferent, inferior, mean, mediocre, modest, normal, pedestrian, plain, prevailing, prosaic, quotidian, regular, routine, run-of-the-mill, settled, simple, standard, stock, typical, undistinguished, unexceptional, unmemorable, unpretentious, unremarkable, usual, wonted, workaday.

antonyms extraordinary, special, unusual.

ordnance *n* arms, artillery, big guns, cannon, guns, matériel, missiles, munitions, weapons.

ordure *n* dirt, dung, excrement, filth, waste products.

organ *n* agency, channel, device, element, forum, implement, instrument, journal, means, medium, member, mouthpiece, newspaper, paper, part, periodical, process, publication, structure, tool, unit, vehicle, voice.

organic *adj* anatomical, animate, biological, biotic, constitutional, formal, fundamental, inherent, innate, integral, integrated, live, living, methodical, natural, ordered, organized, structural, structured, systematic, systematized.

organism *n* animal, being, body, cell, creature, entity, living thing, structure.

organization *n* arrangement, assembling, assembly, association, body, business, chemistry, combine, company, composition, concern, confederation, configuration, conformation, consortium, constitution, construction, co-ordination, corporation, design, disposal, federation, firm, format, formation, formulation, framework, group, grouping, institution, league, make-up, management, method, methodology, organism, outfit, pattern, plan, planning, regulation, running, standardization, structure, structuring, syndicate, system, unity, whole.
antonym disorganization.

organize *v* arrange, catalogue, classify, codify, constitute, construct, co-ordinate, dispose, establish, form, frame, group, marshal, pigeonhole, regiment, run, see to, set up, shape, structure, systematize, tabulate.
antonym disorganize.

organized *adj* arranged, neat, orderly, planned, well-run.
antonym disorganized.

orgy *n* bacchanal, bacchanalia, binge, bout, carousal, debauch, excess, indulgence, love-in, overindulgence, revel, revelry, saturnalia, splurge, spree, surfeit.

orient *v* acclimatize, accommodate, adapt, adjust, align, familiarize, get one's bearings, habituate, orientate.

orientation *n* acclimatization, adaptation, adjustment, assimilation, attunement, bearings, collimation, co-ordination, direction, familiarization, introduction, location, position, sense of direction, settling in.

orifice *n* aperture, cleft, hole, inlet, mouth, opening, perforation, pore, rent, slit, vent.

origin *n* ancestry, base, basis, beginning, beginnings, birth, cause, commencement, creation, dawning, derivation, descent, emergence, etymology, etymon, extraction, family, font, foundation, fountain, fountainhead, genesis, heritage, inauguration, inception, incunabula, launch, lineage, occasion, origination, outset, parentage, paternity, pedigree, provenance, root, roots, source, spring, start, stock, wellspring.
antonyms end, termination.

original *adj* aboriginal, archetypal, authentic, autochthonous, commencing, creative, earliest, early, embryonic, fertile, first, first-hand, fresh, genuine, imaginative, infant, ingenious, initial, innovative, innovatory, introductory, inventive, master, new, novel, opening, primal, primary, primitive, primordial, pristine, prototypical, resourceful, rudimentary, seminal, starting, unborrowed, unconventional, unhackneyed, unprecedented, unusual.
antonym unoriginal.
n archetype, case, character, cure, eccentric, master, model, nonconformist, oddity, paradigm, pattern, prototype, queer fish, standard, type, weirdo.

originality *n* boldness, cleverness, creative spirit, creativeness, creativity, daring, eccentricity, freshness, imagination, imaginativeness, individuality, ingenuity, innovation, innovativeness, inventiveness, newness, novelty, resourcefulness, singularity, unconventionality, unorthodoxy.

originally *adv* at first, at the outset, at the start, by birth, by derivation, first, in origin, in the beginning, initially.

originate *v* arise, be born, begin, come, commence, conceive, create, derive, develop, discover, emanate, emerge, establish, evolve, flow, form, formulate, generate, give birth to, inaugurate, initiate, institute, introduce, invent, issue, launch, pioneer, proceed, produce, result, rise, set up, spring, start, stem.
antonyms end, terminate.

originator *n* architect, author, creator, designer, father, founder, generator, innovator, inventor, mother, pioneer, prime mover, the brains.

ornament *n* accessory, adornment, bauble, decoration, doodad, embellishment, fallal, flower, frill, furbelow, garnish, gaud, honour, jewel, leading light, pride, treasure, trimming, trinket.
v adorn, beautify, bedizen, bespangle, brighten, caparison, deck, decorate, dress up, embellish, festoon, garnish, gild, grace, prettify, prink, trim.

ornamental *adj* attractive, beautifying, decorative, embellishing, flashy, for show, grandiose, showy.

ornamentation *n* adornment, decoration, elaboration, embellishment, embroidery, foofaraw, frills, garniture, ornateness.

ornate *adj* arabesque, aureate, baroque, bedecked, busy, complicated, convoluted, elaborate, fancy, florid, flowery, fussy, intricate, ornamented, overdecorated, rococo, sumptuous.
antonyms austere, plain.

orotund *adj* dignified, imposing, magniloquent, pompous, pretentious.

orthodox *adj* accepted, approved, conformist, conventional, correct, customary, doctrinal, established, kosher, official, received, sound, traditional, true, usual, well-established.
antonym unorthodox.

orthodoxy *n* authenticity, authoritativeness, authority, conformism, conformity, conventionality, devotion, devoutness, faithfulness, inflexibility, properness, received wisdom, soundness, traditionalism, trueness.

oscillate *v* fluctuate, seesaw, sway, swing, vacillate, vary, vibrate, waver, yo-yo.

oscillation *n* fluctuation, instability, seesawing, shilly-shallying, swing, swinging, vacillation, variation, wavering.

ossified *adj* bony, fixed, fossilized, frozen, hardened, indurate(d), inflexible, petrified, rigid, solid, stiff.

ostensible *adj* alleged, apparent, avowed, exhibited, manifest, outward, plausible, presumed, pretended, professed, purported, put-on, seeming, so-called, specious, superficial, supposed.

ostensibly *adv* apparently, professedly, purportedly, reputedly, seemingly, supposedly.

ostentation *n* affectation, boasting, display, exhibitionism, flamboyance, flashiness, flaunting, flourish, foppery, pageantry, parade, pomp, pretension, pretentiousness, show, showiness, showing off, swank, tinsel, trappings, vaunting, window-dressing.

antonym unpretentiousness.

ostentatious *adj* aggressive, boastful, conspicuous, extravagant, flamboyant, flash, flashy, garish, gaudy, loud, obtrusive, pretentious, self-advertising, showy, splashy, swanking, swanky, vain, vulgar.

antonyms quiet, restrained.

ostracism *n* avoidance, banishment, boycott, cold-shouldering, exclusion, excommunication, exile, expulsion, isolation, proscription, rejection.

antonyms acceptance, reinstatement, welcome.

ostracize *v* avoid, banish, bar, blackball, blacklist, boycott, cast out, cold-shoulder, cut, debar, exclude, excommunicate, exile, expatriate, expel, reject, segregate, send to Coventry, shun, shut out, snub.

antonyms accept, receive, reinstate, welcome.

other *adj* added, additional, alternative, auxiliary, contrasting, different, differing, dissimilar, distinct, diverse, extra, fresh, further, more, new, remaining, separate, spare, supplementary, unlike, unrelated.

otherworldly *adj* absent-minded, bemused, dreamy, ethereal, fey, preoccupied, rapt.

antonyms mundane, solid, substantial, worldly.

ounce *n* atom, crumb, drop, grain, iota, jot, modicum, morsel, particle, scrap, shred, speck, spot, trace, whit.

oust *v* depose, disinherit, dislodge, displace, dispossess, drive out, eject, evict, expel, overthrow, replace, supplant, throw out, topple, turn out, unseat, upstage.

antonyms ensconce, install, reinstate, settle.

out[1] *adj* abroad, absent, away, disclosed, elsewhere, evident, exposed, gone, manifest, not at home, outside, public, revealed.

out of bounds banned, barred, disallowed, forbidden, off-limits, prohibited, taboo.

out of date antiquated, archaic, behind the times, dated, horse-and-buggy, moribund, obsolete, old, old hat, old-fashioned, out, outmoded, passé.

antonyms fashionable, modern, new.

out of focus blurred, blurry, fuzzy, hazy, ill-defined, indistinct, muzzy.

antonyms clear, sharp.

out of order broken, broken down, burst, conked out, haywire, in disrepair, inoperative, kaput, non-functional, not working, on the blink, on the fritz, out of commission.

antonym functioning.

out of place disarranged, in disorder, inappropriate, malapropos, tactless, topsy-turvy, unbecoming, unfitting, unseemly, unsuitable.

antonyms appropriate, apropos.

out of sorts below par, depressed, down in the dumps, down in the mouth, gloomy, ill, moody, off-colour, poorly, sick, under the weather.

antonyms cheerful, well.

out of the blue all of a sudden, suddenly, unexpectedly.

out of the wood(s) home and dry, in the clear, on dry land, out of danger, out of difficulty, safe, safe and sound, secure.

antonyms insecure, vulnerable.

out of this world excellent, fabulous, fantastic, great, incredible, indescribable, marvellous, phenomenal, remarkable, superb, unbelievable, wonderful.

antonyms mundane, ordinary.

out of work idle, jobless, laid off, redundant, unemployed, workless.

antonyms busy, employed, occupied.

out[2] *adj* antiquated, banned, dated, dead, démodé, disallowed, ended, excluded, exhausted, expired, extinguished, finished, forbidden, impossible, not on, old-fashioned, out-of-date, passé, square, taboo, unacceptable, unfashionable, used up.

antonyms acceptable, fashionable, in.

out-and-out *adj* absolute, arrant, complete, consummate, downright, dyed-in-the-wool, inveterate, outright, perfect, thoroughgoing, total, uncompromising, unmitigated, unqualified, utter, whole-hog.

outbreak *n* burst, ebullition, epidemic, eruption, excrescence, explosion, flare-up, flash, outburst, rash, spasm, upsurge.

outburst *n* access, attack, discharge, eruption, explosion, fit, fit of temper, flare-up, gale, gush, outbreak, outpouring, paroxysm, seizure, spasm, storm, surge, volley.

outcast *n* abject, castaway, derelict, exile, leper, outsider, pariah, persona non grata, refugee, reject, reprobate, unperson, untouchable, vagabond, wretch.

antonyms favourite, idol.

outclass *v* beat, eclipse, excel over, leave standing, outdistance, outdo, outrank, outrival, outshine, outstrip, overshadow, put in the shade, surpass, top, transcend.

outcome *n* after-effect, aftermath, conclusion, consequence, effect, end, end result, harvest, issue, payoff, result, sequel, upshot.

outcry *n* clamour, commotion, complaint, cry, exclamation, flap, howl, hue and cry, hullabaloo, noise, outburst, protest, row, scream, screech, uproar, vociferation, yell.

outdated *adj* antediluvian, antiquated, antique, archaic, behind the times, dated, démodé, obsolescent, obsolete, old-fashioned, out, out-of-date, out of style, outmoded, passé, square, unfashionable, unmodish.
antonyms fashionable, modern, modish.

outdistance *v* leave behind, leave standing, outpace, outrun, outstrip, overhaul, overtake, pass, pull ahead of, shake off, surpass.

outdo *v* beat, best, eclipse, excel over, get the better of, outclass, outdistance, outfox, outmanoeuvre, outshine, outsmart, outstrip, outwit, overcome, surpass, top, transcend.

outdoor(s) *adj, adv* alfresco, en plein air, in the open air, open-air, outside.
antonym indoor(s).

outer *adj* distal, distant, exterior, external, further, outlying, outside, outward, peripheral, remote, superficial, surface.
antonyms central, inner, mesial, proximal.

outface *v* beard, brave, brazen out, confront, defy, outstare, stare down.
antonyms capitulate, succumb.

outfit¹ *n* accoutrements, clothes, costume, duds, ensemble, equipage, equipment, garb, gear, get-up, kit, paraphernalia, rig, suit, threads, toggery, trappings, turnout.
v accoutre, apparel, appoint, attire, equip, fit out, fit up, furnish, kit out, provision, stock, supply, turn out.

outfit² *n* business, clan, clique, company, corps, coterie, crew, firm, galère, gang, group, organization, set, set-up, squad, team, unit.

outfitter *n* clothier, costumer, costumier, costumière, couturier, couturière, dressmaker, haberdasher, modiste, tailor.

outflow *n* debouchment, discharge, drainage, ebb, effluence, effluent, effluvium, efflux, effusion, emanation, emergence, gush, jet, outfall, outpouring, rush, spout.

outflowing *adj* debouching, discharging, effluent, emanant, gushing, leaking, rushing, spurting.

outgoing¹ *adj* departing, ex-former, last, past, retiring, withdrawing.

outgoing² *adj* affable, approachable, chatty, communicative, cordial, demonstrative, easy, expansive, extrovert, friendly, genial, gregarious, informal, open, sociable, sympathetic, unreserved, warm.
antonyms incoming, introvert, new, unsociable.

outgrowth *n* consequence, effect, emanation, excrescence, offshoot, product, protuberance, shoot, sprout, swelling.

outing *n* excursion, expedition, jaunt, picnic, pleasure trip, ramble, spin, trip.

outlandish *adj* alien, barbarous, bizarre, eccentric, exotic, extraordinary, fantastic, foreign, grotesque, odd, outré, preposterous, queer, strange, unheard-of, weird.
antonyms familiar, ordinary.

outlandishness *n* bizarreness, eccentricity, exoticness, grotesqueness, oddness, queerness, strangeness, weirdness.
antonyms commonplaceness, familiarity.

outlast *v* come through, outlive, outstay, ride, survive, weather.

outlaw *n* bandit, brigand, criminal, convict, dacoit, desperado, freebooter, fugitive, highwayman, marauder, outcast, outsider, pariah, proscript, robber.
v ban, banish, bar, condemn, debar, disallow, embargo, exclude, excommunicate, forbid, illegalise, illegitimate, interdict, prohibit, proscribe, waive.
antonyms allow, legalize.

outlawed *adj* banished, banned, condemned, disallowed, embargoed, excommunicated, proscribed.

outlay *n* costs, disbursal, disbursement, expenditure, expenses, investment, payment, price.

outlet *n* avenue, channel, debouchment, duct, egress, emissary, exit, market, opening, orifice, outfall, release, safety valve, vent, way out.
antonyms entry, inlet.

outline *n* bare bones, bare facts, configuration, contour, delineation, draft, drawing, figure, form, frame, framework, layout, lineament(s), plan, profile, recapitulation, résumé, rough, rundown, scenario, schema, shape, silhouette, skeleton, sketch, summary, synopsis, thumbnail sketch, tracing.
v adumbrate, block (out), delineate, draft, frame, plan, recapitulate, rough out, silhouette, sketch, summarize, trace.

outlive *v* come through, live through, outlast, survive, weather.
antonym predecease.

outlook *n* angle, aspect, attitude, expectations, forecast, frame of mind, future, lookout, panorama, perspective, point of view, prognosis, prospect, scene, slant, standpoint, vantage point, view, viewpoint, views, vista.

outlying *adj* distant, faraway, far-flung, far-off, fringe, further, outer, outlandish, peripheral, provincial, remote.
antonyms central, inner.

outmanoeuvre *v* beat, circumvent, fake out, get the better of, outdo, outflank, outfox, outgeneral, outsmart, outthink, outwit.

outmoded *adj* anachronistic, antediluvian, antiquated, antique, archaic, behind the times, bygone, dated, démodé, fossilized, horse-and-buggy, obsolescent, obsolete, olden, old-fashioned, old-fogeyish, outdated, out-of-date, outworn, passé, square, superannuated, superseded, unfashionable, unmodish, unusable.

antonyms fashionable, fresh, modern, modish, new.

out-of-the-way *adj* abnormal, abstruse, curious, distant, exceptional, extraordinary, faraway, far-flung, far-off, inaccessible, isolated, little-known, lonely, obscure, odd, outlandish, outlying, peculiar, remote, secluded, strange, uncommon, unfamiliar, unfrequented, unusual.

outpace *v* beat, outdistance, outdo, outrun, outstrip, overhaul, overtake, pass, surpass.

outpouring *n* cascade, debouchment, deluge, effluence, efflux, effusion, emanation, flood, flow, flux, gush, logorrhoea, outflow, spate, spurt, stream, torrent.

output *n* achievement, manufacture, outturn, printout, product, production, productivity, readout, yield.
antonym input.

outrage *n* hurt, abuse, affront, anger, atrocity, barbarism, crime, desecration, disgrace, enormity, evil, fury, grand guignol, horror, indignation, indignity, inhumanity, injury, insult, offence, profanation, rape, ravishing, resentment, scandal, shock, violation, violence, wrath.
v abuse, affront, astound, defile, desecrate, disgust, incense, infuriate, injure, insult, madden, make someone's blood boil, maltreat, offend, rape, ravage, ravish, repel, scandalize, shock, violate.

outrageous *adj* abominable, atrocious, barbaric, beastly, disgraceful, egregious, excessive, exorbitant, extortionate, extravagant, flagrant, godless, heinous, horrible, immoderate, infamous, inhuman, iniquitous, inordinate, monstrous, nefarious, offensive, preposterous, scandalous, shocking, steep, turbulent, unconscionable, ungodly, unholy, unreasonable, unspeakable, villainous, violent, wicked.
antonyms acceptable, irreproachable.

outrider *n* advance guard, attendant, bodyguard, escort, guard, harbinger, herald, precursor, scout, squire, vanguard.

outright *adj* absolute, arrant, categorical, complete, consummate, definite, direct, downright, flat, out-and-out, perfect, point-blank, pure, straightforward, thorough, thoroughgoing, total, uncompromising, unconditional, undeniable, unequivocal, unmitigated, unqualified, utter, wholesale.
antonyms ambiguous, indefinite, provisional.
adv absolutely, at once, attached, cleanly, completely, directly, explicitly, immediately, instantaneously, instantly, on the spot, openly, positively, straightaway, straightforwardly, straight out, there and then, thoroughly, unhesitatingly, with no strings attached, without restraint.

outrun *v* beat, exceed, excel, leave behind, lose, outdistance, outdo, outpace, outstrip, overhaul, overtake, pass, shake off, surpass.

outset *n* beginning, commencement, early days, inauguration, inception, kick-off, opening, start.

antonyms conclusion, end, finish.

outshine *v* beat, best, eclipse, excel, outclass, outdo, outrank, outstrip, overshadow, put in the shade, surpass, top, transcend, upstage.

outside¹ *adj* exterior, external, extramural, extraneous, extreme, outdoor, outer, outermost, outward, superficial, surface.
antonym inside.
n cover, exterior, façade, face, front, skin, superficies, surface, topside.
antonym inside.

outside² *adj* distant, faint, improbable, infinitesimal, marginal, minute, negligible, remote, slight, slim, small, unlikely.
antonyms likely, real, substantial.

outsider *n* alien, foreigner, immigrant, incomer, interloper, intruder, layman, misfit, newcomer, non-member, non-resident, observer, odd man out, outcast, outlander, outlier, settler, stranger.
antonyms inhabitant, insider, local, member, native, resident, specialist.

outskirts *n* borders, boundary, edge, environs, faubourgs, fringes, margin, periphery, purlieus, suburbia, suburbs, vicinity.
antonyms centre, downtown, inner city.

outsmart *v* beat, best, deceive, dupe, get the better of, outfox, outmanoeuvre, outperform, outthink, outwit, trick.

outspoken *adj* abrupt, blunt, candid, direct, explicit, forthright, frank, free, open, plain-spoken, pointed, Rabelaisian, rude, sharp, trenchant, unceremonious, unequivocal, unreserved.
antonyms diplomatic, tactful.

outspread *adj* expanded, extended, fanned out, flared, open, opened, outstretched, spread out, stretched, unfolded, unfurled, wide, wide-open.

outstanding¹ *adj* ace, arresting, celebrated, conspicuous, crack, distinguished, egregious, eminent, excellent, exceptional, extraordinary, eye-catching, great, important, impressive, marked, memorable, notable, noteworthy, pre-eminent, prominent, remarkable, salient, signal, singular, special, striking, superior, superlative, surpassing.
antonyms ordinary, unexceptional.

outstanding² *adj* due, left, ongoing, open, over, owing, payable, pending, remaining, uncollected, undone, unpaid, unresolved, unsettled.

outstrip *v* beat, best, better, eclipse, exceed, excel, gain on, leave behind, leave standing, outclass, outdistance, outdo, outpace, outperform, outrun, outshine, overhaul, overtake, pass, surpass, top, transcend.

outward *adj* alleged, apparent, avowed, evident, exterior, external, noticeable, observable, obvious, ostensible, outer, outside, professed, public, superficial, supposed, surface, visible.
antonyms inner, private.

outwardly *adv* apparently, at first sight, evidently, externally, in appearance, officially, on the surface, ostensibly, seemingly, superficially, supposedly, to all appearances, to the eye.

antonyms internally, inwardly, privately.

outweigh *v* cancel out, compensate for, eclipse, make up for, outbalance, overcome, override, overrule, predominate, preponderate, prevail over, take precedence over, tip the scales in favour of, transcend.

outwit *v* beat, best, better, cheat, circumvent, deceive, defraud, dupe, get the better of, gull, make a fool of, make a monkey of, outfox, outmanoeuvre, outsmart, outthink, swindle, trick.

outworn *adj* abandoned, antiquated, clichéd, defunct, discredited, disused, exhausted, fogeyish, hackneyed, horse-and-buggy, moth-eaten, obsolete, out-of-date, outdated, outmoded, overused, rejected, stale, superannuated, threadbare, tired, trite, worn-out.

antonyms fresh, new.

oval *adj* egg-shaped, ellipsoidal, elliptical, lens-shaped, lenticular, obovate, obovoid, ovate, oviform, ovoid, ovoidal.

ovation *n* acclaim, acclamation, applause, bravos, cheering, cheers, clapping, éclat, laudation, plaudits, praises, tribute.

antonyms abuse, boos, catcalls, mockery.

over[1] *adj* accomplished, bygone, closed, completed, concluded, done (with), ended, finished, forgotten, gone, in the past, past, settled, up.

over[2] *prep* above, exceeding, in charge of, in command of, in excess of, more than, on, on top of, superior to, upon.

adv above, aloft, beyond, extra, in addition, in excess, left, on high, overhead, remaining, superfluous, surplus, unclaimed, unused, unwanted.

over and above added to, along with, as well as, besides, in addition to, let alone, not to mention, on top of, plus, together with.

over and over (again) ad infinitum, ad nauseam, again and again, continually, endlessly, frequently, often, repeatedly, time and (time) again.

overabundance *n* embarrassment of riches, excess, glut, oversupply, plethora, profusion, superabundance, superfluity, surfeit, surplus, too much of a good thing.

antonyms dearth, lack.

overact *v* chew the scenery, emote, exaggerate, ham, ham up, overdo, overplay.

antonyms underact, underplay.

overall *adj* all-embracing, all-inclusive, allover, blanket, broad, complete, comprehensive, general, global, inclusive, panoramic, total, umbrella.

antonyms narrow, short-term.

adv by and large, generally speaking, in general, in the long term, on the whole.

overawe *v* abash, alarm, awe, browbeat, cow, daunt, disconcert, dismay, frighten, intimidate, petrify, scare, terrify, unnerve.

antonym reassure.

overbalance *v* capsize, fall over, keel over, lose (one's) balance, lose one's footing, overset, overturn, slip, tip over, topple over, trip, tumble, turn turtle, upset.

overbearing *adj* arrogant, autocratic, bossy, cavalier, despotic, dictatorial, dogmatic, domineering, haughty, high and mighty, high-handed, imperious, lordly, magisterial, officious, oppressive, overweening, peremptory, pompous, supercilious, superior, tyrannical.

antonyms modest, unassertive, unassuming.

overcast *adj* black, clouded, clouded over, cloudy, dark, darkened, dismal, dreary, dull, grey, hazy, leaden, lowering, murky, sombre, sunless, threatening.

antonyms bright, clear, sunny.

overcharge *v* burn, cheat, do, extort, fleece, gouge, gyp, mulct, rip off, rook, short-change, soak, sting, surcharge, take (for).

antonym undercharge.

overcome *v* beat, best, better, conquer, crush, defeat, euchre, expunge, lick, master, overpower, overthrow, overwhelm, prevail, rise above, subdue, subjugate, surmount, survive, triumph over, vanquish, weather, worst.

adj affected, beaten, bowled over, broken, defeated, exhausted, overpowered, overwhelmed, speechless, swept off one's feet.

overconfident *adj* arrogant, brash, cocksure, cocky, foolhardy, hubristic, incautious, overoptimistic, overweening, presumptuous, rash, sanguine, temerarious.

antonyms cautious, diffident.

overcritical *adj* captious, carping, cavilling, fastidious, faultfinding, hairsplitting, hard to please, hypercritical, nit-picking, overnice, overparticular, pedantic, pernickety, purist.

antonyms easygoing, tolerant, uncritical.

overcrowded *adj* chock-a-block, chock-full, choked, congested, crammed full, jam-packed, overloaded, overpopulated, packed, packed out, seething, swarming.

antonyms deserted, empty.

overdo *v* do to death, exaggerate, gild the lily, go to extremes, go too far, labour, lay it on thick, overact, overexert, overindulge, overplay, overreach, overstate, overtax, overuse, overwork.

antonyms neglect, underuse.

overdone *adj* burnt, burnt to a cinder, charred, dried up, effusive, exaggerated, excessive, fulsome, histrionic, immoderate, inordinate, over the top, overcooked, overelaborate, overplayed, overstated, preposterous, spoiled, supererogatory, undue, unnecessary.

antonyms raw, underdone, underplayed, understated.

overdue *adj* behind schedule, behindhand, belated, delayed, late, owing, slow, tardy, unpunctual.

antonyms early, on time.

overeat *v* binge, eat like a horse, gluttonize, gorge, gormandize, guzzle, make a pig of oneself, overindulge, pack away, stuff, stuff oneself.

antonyms abstain, starve.

overeating *n* bingeing, bulimia, gluttony, gourmandise, gourmandism, guzzling, overindulgence.

antonyms abstemiousness, abstention.

overemphasize *v* belabour, exaggerate, labour, overdramatize, overstress.

antonyms belittle, minimize, underplay, understate.

overexert oneself burn oneself out, burn the candle at both ends, drive oneself too hard, fatigue, knock oneself out, overdo it, overstrain oneself, overtax oneself, overtire oneself, overwork, push oneself too hard, strain oneself, wear oneself out, work oneself to death.

antonyms idle, laze.

overflow *v* brim over, bubble over, pour over, soak, spill, surge, swamp, well over.

n flood, inundation, overabundance, overspill, spill, superfluity, surplus.

overflowing *adj* abounding, bountiful, brimful, copious, inundant, plenteous, plentiful, profuse, rife, superabundant, swarming, teeming, thronged.

antonyms lacking, scarce.

overgrowth *n* escalation, hypertrophy, overabundance, overdevelopment, superabundance.

antonyms decline, failure, shrinkage, wasting.

overhang *v* beetle, bulge, extend, impend, jut (out), loom, menace, project, protrude, stick out, threaten.

overhanging *adj* beetling, impending, jutting, pensile, projecting, protruding.

overhaul[1] *v* check, do up, examine, fix, inspect, mend, recondition, re-examine, repair, restore, service, survey.

n check, check-up, examination, going-over, inspection, reconditioning, repair, restoration, service.

overhaul[2] *v* gain on, outpace, outstrip, overtake, pass, pull ahead of.

overhead *adv* above, aloft, on high, up above, upward.

antonyms below, underfoot.

adj aerial, elevated, overhanging, roof, upper.

antonyms floor, ground, underground.

overheads *n* burden, expenses, operating costs, running costs.

overheated *adj* agitated, excited, fiery, flaming, impassioned, inflamed, overexcited, overwrought, passionate, roused.

antonyms calm, cool, dispassionate, impassive.

overheating *n* heatstroke, hyperpyrexia, hyperthermia, sunstroke.

antonyms chill, hypothermia.

overindulge *v* binge (on), booze, gluttonize, gorge, gormandize, guzzle, overdo it, overeat.

antonym abstain.

overindulgence *n* binge, debauchery, excess, immoderation, intemperance, overeating, surfeit.

antonyms abstemiousness, abstention.

overjoyed *adj* delighted, delirious, ecstatic, elated, enraptured, euphoric, in raptures, joyful, jubilant, on cloud nine, over the moon, rapturous, thrilled, tickled pink, transported, walking on air.

antonyms disappointed, sad.

overlap *v* coincide, cover, flap over, imbricate, overlay, overlie, shingle.

overlapping *adj* coinciding, covering, imbricated, layered, overlying, shingled.

overload *v* burden, encumber, oppress, overburden, overcharge, overtax, saddle, strain, surcharge, tax, weigh down.

overlook[1] *v* condone, disregard, excuse, forget, forgive, ignore, let go, let pass, let ride, miss, neglect, omit, pardon, pass, pass over, skip, slight, turn a blind eye to, wink at.

antonyms animadvert, note, notice, penalize, record, remember.

overlook[2] *v* command a view of, face, front on to, give upon, look on to.

overlooked *adj* unconsidered, unheeded, unhonoured, unnoted, unprized, unregarded, unremarked, unvalued.

antonyms appreciated, prized, sought-after, valued.

overly *adv* exceedingly, excessively, immoderately, inordinately, over, too, unduly, unreasonably.

antonyms inadequately, insufficiently.

overnice *adj* finicky, nit-picking, overfastidious, overmeticulous, overparticular, overprecise, overscrupulous, oversensitive, oversubtle, pernickety.

antonyms casual, uncritical.

overpower *v* beat, best, conquer, crush, defeat, floor, immobilize, master, overcome, overthrow, overwhelm, quell, subdue, subjugate, vanquish.

overpowering *adj* compelling, convincing, extreme, forceful, insuppressible, invincible, irrefutable, irrepressible, irresistible, nauseating, oppressive, overwhelming, powerful, sickening, strong, suffocating, telling, unbearable, uncontrollable.

overrate *v* blow up, magnify, make too much of, overestimate, overpraise, overprize, oversell, overvalue.

antonym underrate.

override *v* abrogate, annul, cancel, countermand, disregard, ignore, nullify, outweigh, overrule, quash, rescind, reverse, ride roughshod over, set aside, supersede, trample, upset, vanquish.

overriding *adj* cardinal, compelling, determining, dominant, essential, final, first, major, number one, overruling, paramount, pivotal, predominant, prevailing, primary, prime, prior, ruling, supreme, ultimate.

antonyms insignificant, unimportant.

overrule *v* abrogate, annul, cancel, countermand, disallow, invalidate, outvote, override, overturn, recall, repeal, rescind, reverse, revoke, set aside, veto, vote down.

antonyms allow, approve.

overrun[1] *v* choke, infest, inundate, invade, occupy, overflow, overgrow, overspread, overwhelm, permeate, ravage, run riot, spread over, surge over, swamp, swarm over.

antonyms desert, evacuate.

overrun[2] *v* exceed, overdo, overshoot, overstep.

overseas *adj* exotic, extracontinental, foreign, international, ultramarine.

antonyms domestic, home.

adv abroad, in(to) foreign climes, in(to) foreign parts.

n abroad, foreign climes, foreign parts (or shores).

antonym home.

overseer *n* boss, chief, foreman, forewoman, gaffer, manager, master, super, superintendent, superior, supervisor, surveyor.

overshadow *v* adumbrate, becloud, bedim, blight, cloud, darken, dim, dominate, dwarf, eclipse, excel, mar, obfuscate, obscure, outshine, outweigh, protect, put in the shade, rise above, ruin, shelter, spoil, surpass, tower above, veil.

oversight[1] *n* administration, care, charge, control, custody, direction, guidance, handling, inspection, keeping, management, responsibility, superintendence, supervision, surveillance.

oversight[2] *n* blunder, booboo, carelessness, delinquency, error, fault, inattention, lapse, laxity, mistake, neglect, omission, slip, slip-up.

overt *adj* apparent, avowed, evident, manifest, observable, obvious, open, patent, plain, professed, public, unconcealed, undisguised, visible.

antonyms covert, secret.

overtake *v* befall, catch up with, come upon, draw level with, engulf, happen, hit, outdistance, outdo, outstrip, overhaul, pass, pull ahead of, strike.

overthrow *v* abolish, beat, bring down, conquer, crush, defeat, demolish, depose, destroy, dethrone, displace, knock down, level, master, oust, overcome, overpower, overturn, overwhelm, raze, ruin, subdue, subjugate, subvert, topple, unseat, upset, vanquish.

antonyms install, reinstate.

n confounding, coup d'état, defeat, deposition, destruction, dethronement, discomfiture, disestablishment, displacement, dispossession, downfall, end, fall, humiliation, ousting, prostration, rout, ruin, subjugation, subversion, suppression, undoing, unseating.

overtone *n* association, connotation, feeling, flavour, hint, implication, innuendo, intimation, nuance, sense, slant, something, suggestion, undercurrent.

overture *n* advance, approach, introduction, invitation, motion, move, offer, opening, (opening) gambit, opening move, prelude, proposal, proposition, signal, suggestion, tender.

overturn *v* abolish, abrogate, annul, capsize, countermand, depose, destroy, invalidate, keel over, knock down, knock over, overbalance, overset, overthrow, quash, repeal, rescind, reverse, set aside, spill, tip over, topple, tumble, unseat, upend, upset, upturn.

overused *adj* bromidic, clichéd, commonplace, hackneyed, platitudinous, played out, stale, stereotyped, threadbare, tired, trite, unoriginal, worn.

antonyms fresh, original.

overweening *adj* arrogant, cavalier, cocksure, cocky, conceited, egotistical, excessive, extravagant, haughty, high-handed, hubristic, immoderate, inflated, insolent, lordly, opinionated, overblown, pompous, presumptuous, proud, self-confident, supercilious, swollen, vain, vainglorious.

antonyms diffident, unassuming.

overweight *adj* ample, bulky, buxom, chubby, chunky, corpulent, fat, flabby, fleshy, gross, heavy, hefty, huge, massive, obese, outsize, plump, pudgy, portly, potbellied, stout, tubby, well-padded, well-upholstered.

antonyms emaciated, skinny, thin, underweight.

overwhelm *v* bowl over, bury, confuse, crush, cut to pieces, defeat, deluge, destroy, devastate, engulf, floor, inundate, throw for a loop, overcome, overpower, overrun, prostrate, rout, snow under, stagger, submerge, swamp.

overwhelming *adj* breathtaking, crushing, devastating, foudroyant, insuppressible, invincible, irrepressible, irresistible, overpowering, shattering, stunning, towering, uncontrollable, vast.

antonyms insignificant, negligible, resistible.

overwork *v* burden, burn the midnight oil, exhaust, exploit, fatigue, oppress, overburden, overload, overstrain, overtax, overuse, prostrate, strain, sweat, tax, wear out, weary, work one's fingers to the bone.

overwrought *adj* agitated, beside oneself, distracted, emotional, excited, frantic, keyed up, on edge, overcharged, overexcited, overheated, overworked, stirred, strung up, tense, uptight, worked up, wound up.

antonyms calm, cool, impassive.

owing *adj* due, in arrears, outstanding, overdue, owed, payable, unpaid, unsettled.

owing to as a result of, because of, imputable to, on account of, thanks to.

own[1] *adj* idiosyncratic, individual, inimitable, particular, personal, private.

on one's own alone, by oneself, independently, isolated, off one's own bat, single-handedly, singly, solo, unaccompanied, unaided, unassisted.

own[2] *v* acknowledge, admit, agree, allow, avow, concede, confess, disclose, enjoy, grant, have, hold, keep, possess, recognize, retain.

own up admit, come clean, confess, make

a clean breast of it, spill the beans, tell the truth.

owner *n* deedholder, franklin, freeholder, holder, landlady, landlord, lord, master, mistress, possessor, proprietor.

ownership *n* dominion, freehold, possession, proprietary rights, proprietorship, right of possession, title.

ox *n* bison, buffalo, bullock, carabao, clod, dolt, gaur, lout, oaf, steer.

P

pace *n* celerity, clip, gait, lick, measure, momentum, motion, movement, progress, quickness, rapidity, rate, speed, step, stride, tempo, time, tread, velocity, walk.
v count, determine, gauge, march, mark out, measure, pad, patrol, pound, step, stride, tramp, tread, walk.

pacific *adj* appeasing, calm, complaisant, conciliatory, diplomatic, dovelike, dovish, equable, friendly, gentle, halcyon, irenic, meek, mild, non-belligerent, non-violent, pacificatory, pacifist, peaceable, peaceful, peacekeeping, peace-loving, peacemaking, placatory, placid, propitiatory, quiet, restful, serene, smooth, still, tranquil, unruffled.
antonyms aggressive, belligerent, contentious, pugnacious, warring.

pacifism *n* non-combat, non-violence, passive resistance, satyagraha.
antonym warmongering.

pacifist *n* conchie, conscientious objector, dove, passive resister, peace lover, peacemaker, peacemonger, peacenik, satyagrahi.
antonyms hawk, warmonger.

pacify *v* allay, ameliorate, appease, assuage, calm, compose, conciliate, humour, lull, moderate, mollify, placate, propitiate, put down, quell, quiet (down), repress, silence, smooth down, soften, soothe, still, subdue, tame, tranquillize.
antonyms aggravate, anger.

pack[1] *n* assemblage, bale, band, bunch, bundle, burden, collection, company, crew, crowd, deck, drove, flock, gang, group, herd, kit, load, lot, mob, outfit, package, packet, parcel, set, troop, truss.
v batch, box, bundle, burden, carry, charge, compact, compress, cram, crowd, fill, jam, load, mob, overload, package, press, ram, steeve, store, stow, stuff, tamp, throng, thrust, wedge.

pack[2] *n* backpack, haversack, kitbag, knapsack, rucksack, sack.

package *n* agreement, amalgamation, arrangement, bale, box, carton, case, combination, container, deal, entity, kit, pack, packet, parcel, proposal, proposition, unit, whole.
v batch, box, combine, pack, pack up, parcel, parcel up, wrap, wrap up.

packed *adj* brimful, chock-a-block, chock-full, compact, congested, crammed, crawling, crowded, filled, full, jammed, jam-packed, overflowing, overloaded, swarming, teeming.
antonyms deserted, empty.

packet *n* bag, carton, case, container, pack, package, packing, parcel, poke, pouch, roll, sachet, sack, wrapper, wrapping.

pact *n* accord, agreement, alliance, arrangement, bargain, bond, cartel, compact, concord, concordat, contract, convention, covenant, deal, entente, league, protocol, treaty, understanding.
antonyms breach, disagreement, quarrel.

pad[1] *n* bedding, buffer, cushion, jotter, notepad, pillow, protection, stiffening, stuffing, tablet, wad, writing pad.
v amplify, augment, cushion, drag out, elaborate, expand, fill, fill out, flesh out, increase, inflate, lengthen, line, pack, protect, protract, shape, spin out, stretch, stuff, wrap.

pad[2] *n* foot, footprint, paw, print, sole.
v lope, move, run, step, tiptoe, tramp, tread, trudge, walk.

pad[3] *n* apartment, flat, hangout, home, penthouse, place, quarters, room, rooms.

padding *n* bombast, circumlocution, cushioning, filling, hot air, packing, prolixity, redundancy, stuffing, verbiage, verbosity, wadding, waffle, wordiness.

paddle[1] *n* oar, pole, scull, sweep.
v oar, ply, propel, pull, row, scull, spank, steer.

paddle[2] *v* dabble, dip, plash, play, splash, trail, wade.

paean *n* anthem, dithyramb, doxology, encomium, eulogy, hymn, ode, ovation, panegyric, psalm, song.
antonyms denunciation, satire.

pagan *n* atheist, heathen, idolater, infidel, polytheist, unbeliever.
adj atheistic, godless, heathen, heathenish, idolatrous, infidel, irreligious, polytheistic.
antonym religious.

page[1] *n* chapter, episode, epoch, era, event, folio, incident, leaf, period, phase, point, recto, sheet, side, stage, time, verso, written record.

page[2] *n* attendant, bellboy, bellhop, boy, errand boy, footman, messenger, pageboy, servant, squire.

v announce, beep, bid, call (for), call out, come, seek, send for, summon.

pageant *n* display, extravaganza, masque, parade, play, procession, representation, scene, show, spectacle, tableau, tableau vivant.

pageantry *n* ceremony, display, drama, extravagance, glamour, glitter, grandeur, magnificence, melodrama, ostentation, parade, pomp, show, showiness, spectacle, splash, splendour, stateliness, theatricality.

pail *n* bail, bucket, churn, container, tub.

pain *n* ache, affliction, aggravation, agony, anguish, annoyance, bitterness, bore, bother, burden, cramp, discomfort, distress, dole, dolour, drag, grief, hassle, headache, heartache, heartbreak, hurt, inconvenience, irritation, misery, nuisance, pang, pest, smart, soreness, spasm, suffering, tenderness, throb, throe, torment, torture, tribulation, trouble, twinge, vexation, woe, wretchedness.

v afflict, aggrieve, agonize, annoy, chagrin, cut to the quick, disappont, disquiet, distress, exasperate, gall, grieve, harass, hurt, irritate, nettle, rile, sadden, torment, torture, vex, worry, wound, wring.

antonyms gratify, please.

pained *adj* aggrieved, anguished, chagrined, cut to the quick, cut up, disappointed, distressed, grieved, hurt, injured, nettled, offended, reproachful, saddened, stung, upset, wounded.

antonyms gratified, pleased.

painful *adj* aching, achy, afflictive, agonizing, arduous, bitter, difficult, disagreeable, distasteful, distressing, dolorous, excruciating, grievous, hard, harrowing, hurtful, hurting, laborious, saddening, severe, sharp, smarting, sore, tender, troublesome, trying, unpleasant, vexatious.

antonyms easy, painless.

painfully *adv* agonizingly, alarmingly, deplorably, distressingly, dreadfully, excessively, excruciatingly, markedly, pitiably, pitifully, sadly, terribly, unfortunately, woefully, wretchedly.

painkiller *n* alleviative, analgesic, anesthetic, anodyne, drug, lenitive, palliative, remedy, sedative.

antonym irritant.

painless *adj* downhill, easy, effortless, fast, painfree, plain sailing, quick, simple, troublefree, undemanding.

antonyms difficult, painful.

pains *n* assiduity, assiduousness, attention to detail, birth pangs, bother, care, contractions, cramps, diligence, effort, industry, labour, sedulity, sedulousness, spasms, throes, trouble.

painstaking *adj* assiduous, careful, conscientious, dedicated, devoted, diligent, earnest, exacting, hardworking, industrious, meticulous, perfectionist, persevering, punctilious, rigorous, scrupulous, sedulous, strenuous, thorough, thoroughgoing.

antonyms careless, negligent.

paint *n* colour, colouring, cosmetics, distemper, dye, emulsion, enamel, glaze, greasepaint, lacquer, lake, make-up, maquillage, oils, pigment, primer, stain, tint, undercoat, warpaint, wash, water colour, whitewash.

v apply, coat, colour, cover, daub, decorate, delineate, depict, describe, distemper, evoke, glaze, lacquer, limn, picture, portray, recount, render, represent, whitewash.

painter *n* artist, colourist, dauber, delineator, depicter, limner, miniaturist, muralist, oil-painter, water-colourist.

painting *n* aquarelle, daubery, depiction, fresco, illustration, landscape, masterpiece, miniature, mural, oil, oil painting, picture, portrait, portraiture, portrayal, representation, scene, seascape, still life, tableau, water-colour.

pair *n* brace, combination, couple, deuce, doublet, duo, dyad, match, mates, partners, span, twins, two, two of a kind, twosome, yoke.

v bracket, combine, couple, double up, join, juxtapose, link, marry, match (up), mate, pair off (or up), put together, splice, team, twin, unite, wed, yoke.

antonyms dissever, sever.

paired *adj* associated, bracketed, combined, coupled, didymous, double, in twos, joined, linked, married, matched, mated, partnered, twinned, yoked.

antonym single.

pal *n* amigo, (boon) companion, bosom friend, buddy, chum, comrade, confidant(e), crony, friend, intimate, mate, partner, roomie, sidekick, soul mate.

antonym enemy.

palace *n* alcazar, basilica, castle, château, mansion, palazzo, schloss.

antonyms dump, hovel.

palatable *adj* acceptable, agreeable, appetizing, attractive, enjoyable, fair, pleasant, pleasing, sapid, satisfactory, savoury, tasty, toothsome.

antonyms unacceptable, unpleasant.

palate *n* appetite, appreciation, enjoyment, gusto, heart, liking, relish, stomach, taste, zest.

palatial *adj* deluxe, grand, grandiose, illustrious, imposing, luxurious, magnificent, majestic, opulent, plush, posh, regal, spacious, splendid, stately, sumptuous, swanky.

antonyms cramped, shabby.

palaver *n* activity, ado, babble, blather, bustle, carryings-on, chatter, colloquy, confab, conference, confusion, discussion, fuss, get-together, goings-on, hubbub, nonsense, parley, performance, powwow, prattle, rigmarole, session, song and dance, to-do, tongue-wagging, yak.

v blab, blather, chatter, confab, confer, discuss, gabble, go on (about), gossip, jabber, jaw, natter, parley, powwow, prattle, tattle, yak.

pale *adj* anemic, ashen, blanched, bleached, bloodless, chalky, colourless, deathly, dim, etiolated, faded, faint, feeble, ghostly, grey, inadequate, indistinct, light, livid, pallid, pasty, poor, sallow, thin, wan, washed-out, waxy, weak, whey-faced, white, white-faced, white-livered, whitish.
antonym ruddy.
v blanch, decrease, dim, diminish, dull, etiolate, fade, lessen, lose colour, shrink, whiten.
antonyms blush, colour.

palisade *n* barricade, bulwark, defence, enclosure, fence, fortification, paling, palisado, stockade.

pall[1] *n* cloud, cold water, damp, damper, gloom, mantle, melancholy, shadow, shroud, veil.

pall[2] *v* bore, cloy, glut, jade, lose flavour, sate, satiate, sicken, surfeit, tire, weary.

palliate *v* abate, allay, alleviate, assuage, cloak, conceal, cover, diminish, ease, excuse, extenuate, lessen, lighten, minimize, mitigate, moderate, mollify, relieve, soften, soothe, temper.

palliative *adj* alleviative, anodyne, assuasive, calming, demulcent, lenitive, mitigating, mitigative, mollifying, relieving, sedative, soothing.
antonym irritant.
n alleviative, analgesic, anodyne, calmative, demulcent, lenitive, painkiller, remedy, sedative, tranquillizer.

pallid *adj* anemic, ashen, bloodless, cadaverous, colourless, doughy, etiolated, insipid, lifeless, livid, pale, pasty, pasty-faced, sallow, spiritless, sterile, tame, tired, uninspired, uninteresting, vapid, wan, waxen, waxy, whey-faced, white-faced, whitish.
antonyms ruddy, vigorous.

palm *n* hand, mitt, paw.
palm off fob, fob off, foist, foist off, offload, pass off, unload.

palmy *adj* balmy, blooming, booming, carefree, flourishing, glorious, golden, halcyon, happy, joyous, luxurious, prosperous, salad, thriving, triumphant.

palpable *adj* apparent, blatant, clear, concrete, conspicuous, evident, manifest, material, obvious, open, overt, patent, plain, real, solid, substantial, tangible, touchable, unmistakable, visible.
antonyms elusive, impalpable, imperceptible, intangible.

palpitate *v* beat, flutter, go pitapat, pitapat, pitter-patter, pound, pulsate, pulse, quiver, shiver, throb, thump, tremble, vibrate.

palsied *adj* agued, arthritic, atonic, crippled, debilitated, disabled, helpless, paralysed, paralytic, rheumatic, sclerotic, shaking, shaky, shivering, trembling, tremulous.

paltry *adj* base, beggarly, contemptible, derisory, despicable, dime-a-dozen, inconsiderable, insignificant, laughable, low, meagre, mean, measly, minor, miserable, negligible, pathetic, pettifogging, petty, picayune, piddling, piffling, pitiful, poor, puny, slight, small, sorry, tinpot, trifling, trivial, two-bit, twopenny, unimportant, worthless, wretched.
antonyms significant, substantial.

pamper *v* baby, cater to, coddle, cosset, fondle, give in to, gratify, humour, indulge, mollycoddle, mother, overindulge, pet, spoil.
antonyms ill-treat, neglect.

pamphlet *n* booklet, broadside, brochure, chapbook, circular, flyer, folder, handout, leaflet, literature, tract, tractate, treatise.

pan[1] *n* casserole, container, fryer, marmite, pot, saucepan, skillet, spider, stewpot, vessel, wok.
pan out be realized, come about, come off (or out), come to fruition, come true, happen, materialize, turn out, work out.

pan[2] *v* censure, criticize, flay, hammer, knock, pick to pieces, pull to pieces, roast, slam, trash.
antonym praise.

pan[3] *v* circle, follow, move, scan, sweep, swing, track, traverse, turn.

panacea *n* catholicon, cure-all, elixir, nostrum, panpharmacon, theriac, universal remedy.

panache *n* brio, dash, élan, enthusiasm, flair, flamboyance, flashiness, flourish, grand manner, ostentation, pizzazz, spirit, style, swagger, theatricality, verve, vigour, zest.

pandemonium *n* babel, bedlam, brouhaha, chaos, clamour, commotion, confusion, din, disorder, Donnybrook, free-for-all, frenzy, hubbub, hue and cry, hullabaloo, racket, riot, ruckus, rumble, rumpus, to-do, tumult, turbulence, turmoil, uproar.
antonyms calm, order, peace.

pander *v* furnish, pimp, procure, provide, purvey.
n bawd, go-between, pimp, procurer, procuress, white slaver, whoremonger.
pander to cater to, gratify, indulge, pamper, please, satisfy, serve, truckle to, wait on hand and foot.

panegyric *n* accolade, citation, commendation, encomium, eulogium, eulogy, homage, paean, praise, tribute.
antonym censure.
adj approbative, commendatory, complimentary, eulogistic, favourable, flattering, glowing, laudatory, panegyric, praiseful, praising.
antonyms censorious, damning.

pang *n* ache, agony, anguish, crick, discomfort, distress, gripe, pain, prick, spasm, stab, sting, stitch, throe, twinge, twitch, wrench.

panic *n* agitation, alarm, consternation, dismay, fear, fright, horror, hysteria, scare, terror, tizzy.
antonyms assurance, confidence.
v alarm, frighten, go to pieces, lose one's cool, lose one's nerve, overreact, put the wind

up, scare, scare the life (or wits) out of, startle, terrify, throw up one's hands, unnerve.
antonyms reassure, relax.

panic-stricken *adj* aghast, agitated, alarmed, appalled, beside oneself (with fear), fearful, frenzied, frightened, horrified, horror-stricken, hysterical, in a cold sweat, panicky, perturbed, petrified, scared, scared stiff, startled, stunned, stupefied, terrified, terror-stricken, unnerved.
antonyms confident, laid-back, relaxed.

panoply *n* armour, array, attire, (ceremonial) dress, equipage, equipment, garb, gear, get-up, insignia, raiment, regalia, show, suit of armour, trappings, turnout.

panorama *n* bird's-eye view, full extent, landscape, overview, perspective, prospect, scene, scenery, spectacle, survey, sweep, view, vision, vista.

panoramic *adj* across-the-board, bird's-eye, broad, complete, comprehensive, extensive, far-reaching, general, inclusive, overall, scenic, sweeping, universal, whole, wide.
antonym limited.

pant *v* ache, be out of breath, blow, breath hard (or heavily), covet, crave, desire, gasp, hanker, heave, huff, huff and puff, hunger, long, palpitate, pine, puff, sigh, thirst, throb, want, wheeze, yearn, yen.
n gasp, huff, puff, throb, wheeze.

panting *adj* anxious, breathless, eager, gasping, huffing and puffing, impatient, longing, out of breath, puffing, short-winded, thirsty, winded.

pantomime *n* charade, dumb show, gestures, hand motions, mime, sign language.

paper *n* analysis, archive, article, assignment, composition, critique, daily, diary, dissertation, document, essay, examination, gazette, instrument, journal, letter, monograph, news, newspaper, note, notepaper, organ, rag, record, report, script, stationery, study, thesis, treatise.

papers *n* authorization, certificate, credentials, deed, documentation, documents, dossier, file.

papery *adj* delicate, flimsy, fragile, frail, insubstantial, light, lightweight, paper-thin, thin, translucent.

par *n* accordance, average, balance, correspondence, equal footing, equality, equilibrium, equivalence, level, mean, median, norm, parity, similarity, standard.
on a par with according to, commensurate with, comparable to, equal to, equivalent to, in the same league as, on the same level as.
not up to par below average, inadequate, not up to scratch (or snuff), not up to standard, substandard, unsatisfactory.

parable *n* allegory, apologue, exemplum, fable, homily, lesson, story.

parade *n* array, cavalcade, ceremony, column, display, exhibition, flaunting, march, marchpast, motorcade, ostentation, pageant, pageantry, pomp, procession, promenade, review, show, spectacle, train, vaunting.
v air, display, exhibit, file, flaunt, make a show of, march, peacock, process, promenade, show, show off, strut, swagger, vaunt.

paradigm *n* archetype, example, exemplar, framework, ideal, model, original, pattern, prototype, standard.

paradise *n* bliss, City of God, cloud nine, delight, Eden, Elysian fields, Elysium, eternal bliss, felicity, garden of delights, Garden of Eden, heaven, heavenly kingdom, land of milk and honey, lotus land, Olympus, Promised Land, seventh heaven, Shangri-La, utopia, Valhalla, Zion.
antonyms Hades, hell.

paradox *n* absurdity, ambiguity, anomaly, contradiction, contrariety, conundrum, dilemma, enigma, equivocation, incongruity, inconsistency, mystery, oddity, oxymoron, puzzle, riddle.

paradoxical *adj* absurd, ambiguous, baffling, conflicting, confounding, contradictory, enigmatic, equivocal, illogical, impossible, improbable, incongruous, inconsistent, puzzling, self-contradictory.

paragon *n* apotheosis, archetype, crème de la crème, criterion, cynosure, epitome, exemplar, ideal, jewel, masterpiece, model, nonesuch, nonpareil, paradigm, pattern, prototype, quintessence, shining example, standard.

paragraph *n* clause, item, notice, part, passage, piece, portion, section, subdivision, subsection.

parallel *adj* akin, aligned, alongside, analogous, co-extensive, collateral, comparable, connate, correspondent, corresponding, equidistant, homologous, like, matching, resembling, similar, uniform.
antonyms divergent, separate.
n analogue, analogy, comparison, corollary, correlation, correspondence, counterpart, duplicate, equal, equivalent, homologue, likeness, match, parallelism, resemblance, similarity, twin.
v agree with, be analogous to, compare with, conform to, correlate with, correspond to, duplicate, emulate, equal, match.
antonyms diverge, separate.

paralyse *v* anesthetize, arrest, benumb, clamp down on, cripple, debilitate, disable, freeze, halt, immobilize, incapacitate, lame, numb, obtund, petrify, stun, stupefy, transfix.

paralysis *n* arrest, breakdown, halt, hemiplegia, immobility, monoplegia, palsy, paraplegia, paresis, quadriplegia, shutdown, stagnation, standstill, stoppage, torpor.

parameter(s) *n* boundary, bounds, constant, criterion, framework, given, guideline, horizons, indication, limits, limitation, measure, restriction, specification, variable.

paramount *adj* best, capital, cardinal, chief, dominant, eminent, first, foremost, highest, leading, main, outstanding, predominant, pre-eminent, premier, primary, prime, principal, superior, supreme, topmost, top-ranked.
antonyms inferior, last, lowest.

paramour n beau, concubine, courtesan, doxy, gigolo, hetaera, inamorata, inamorato, kept man, kept woman, lover, mistress.

paranoia n complex, delusions, distrust, megalomania, monomania, obsession, persecution, psychosis, suspicion.

parapet n barbican, bartisan, bastion, battlement, bulwark, fortification, rampart.

paraphernalia n accessories, accoutrements, apparatus, appurtenances, baggage, belongings, bits and pieces, clutter, effects, equipage, equipment, gear, impedimenta, kit, material, odds and ends, rig, stuff, tackle, things, trappings.

paraphrase n (free or loose) translation, gloss, interpretation, recapitulation, rehash, rendering, rendition, rephrasing, restatement, rewording, version.
    antonym literal translation.
    v gloss, interpret, recapitulate, rehash, render, repeat verbatim, rephrase, restate, reword, translate literally, translate (loosely or freely).

parasite n bloodsucker, endophyte, entozoon, epiphyte, epizoon, freeloader, hanger-on, leech, moocher, scrounger, sponge, sponger, sucker, tick.

parcel n batch, bunch, bundle, carton, collection, company, crew, crowd, gang, group, lot, pack, package, packet, piece, plot, portion, property, quantity, set, tract.
    v bundle, collect, pack, package, tie up, wrap.
    parcel out allocate, allot, apportion, carve up, deal out, dispense, disperse, distribute, divide, divvy up, dole out, mete out, portion out, separate, share.

parch v blister, burn, dehydrate, desiccate, dry out, dry up, exsiccate, roast, scorch, sear, shrivel, wither.

parched adj arid, brittle, burned, dehydrated, dried up, droughty, dry, scorched, shrivelled, shrunken, thirsty, waterless, withered.

parchment n certificate, charter, diploma, document, palimpsest, scroll, vellum.

pardon v absolve, acquit, amnesty, condonation, condone, emancipate, exculpate, excuse, exonerate, forgive, free, let off, liberate, overlook, release, remit, reprieve, respite, vindicate.
    n absolution, acquittal, amnesty, condonation, discharge, exculpation, excusal, excuse, exoneration, forgiveness, grace, indulgence, mercy, release, remission, reprieval, reprieve.

pardonable adj allowable, condonable, excusable, forgivable, justifiable, minor, permissible, remissible, understandable, venial, warrantable.
    antonym inexcusable.

pare v clip, crop, cut, cut away (or back), decrease, diminish, dock, lessen, lop (off), peel, prune, reduce, retrench, shave (off), shear, skin, trim.

parent n ancestor, architect, author, begetter, cause, creator, father, forerunner, guardian, mother, origin, originator, procreator, progenitor, prototype, root, sire, source.

parentage n affiliation, ancestry, birth, bloodline, derivation, descent, extraction, family, filiation, line, lineage, origin, paternity, pedigree, race, source, stirps, stock.

parenthetic adj adventitious, bracketed, elucidative, explanatory, extraneous, extrinsic, incidental, in parentheses, inserted, interjectional, interposed, intervening, qualifying.
    antonyms basic, original.

pariah n black sheep, castaway, exile, leper, outcast, outlaw, undesirable, untouchable.

paring n clipping, cutting, flake, fragment, peel, peeling, rind, shaving, shred, skin, slice, sliver, snippet.

parish n brethren, church, churchgoers, community, congregation, district, flock, fold, parishioners, vicariate.

parity n affinity, agreement, analogy, conformity, congruence, congruity, consistency, consonance, correspondence, equality, equivalence, evenness, likeness, par, parallelism, resemblance, sameness, similarity, similitude, uniformity, unity.

park n estate, garden, grounds, parkland, pleasance, pleasure garden, preserve, recreation area, reserve, woodland.

parlance n argot, cant, diction, idiom, jargon, language, lingo, phraseology, speech, talk, tongue.

parley n colloquy, confab, conference, council, debate, deliberation, dialogue, discussion, exchange, get-together, huddle, meeting, negotiation, palaver, powwow, rap session, talk(s), tête-à-tête.
    v confabulate, confer, consult, debate, deliberate, discuss, get together, negotiate, palaver, powwow, speak, talk.

parliament n assembly, conclave, congress, convocation, council, diet, house, legislative body, legislature, senate.

parliamentary adj congressional, deliberative, governmental, lawmaking, legislative, senatorial.

parochial adj blinkered, confined, constricted, insular, inward-looking, limited, narrow, narrow-minded, petty, provincial, restricted, small-minded.

parody n burlesque, caricature, imitation, lampoon, mimicry, pasquinade, satire, sendup, skit, spoof, takeoff, travesty.
    v burlesque, caricature, irritate, lampoon, make fun of, mimic, mock, pasquinade, ridicule, satirize, send up, spoof, take off (on), travesty.

paroxysm n attack, convulsion, eruption, explosion, fit, flare-up, frenzy, outbreak, outburst, seizure, spasm, tantrum.

parrot n ape, copycat, imitator, mimic.
    v ape, copy, ditto, echo, imitate, mimic, reiterate, repeat (mindlessly).

parrot-fashion *adv* automatically, by rote, mechanically, mindlessly, unthinkingly.

parry *v* avert, avoid, block, circumvent, deflect, divert, dodge, duck, evade, fence, fend off, field, forestall, obviate, rebuff, repel, repulse, shun, sidestep, stave off, turn aside, ward off.

parsimonious *adj* cheeseparing, close, close-fisted, economical, frugal, grasping, miserly, moneygrubbing, niggardly, penny-pinching, penny-wise, penurious, saving, scrimping, sparing, stingy, stinting, tight-fisted.
antonyms generous, liberal, open-handed.

parsimony *n* economy, frugality, niggardliness, penny-pinching, saving, scrimping, stinginess, thrift, tight-fistedness.
antonyms generosity, liberality.

parson *n* chaplain, churchman, clergyman, cleric, curate, divine, ecclesiastic, incumbent, man of God, man of the cloth, minister, padre, pastor, preacher, priest, rector, reverend, vicar.

part *n* allotment, area, aspect, behalf, bit, bite, branch, capacity, character, charge, chunk, clause, complement, component, concern, constituent, detail, district, division, duty, element, faction, factor, feature, fraction, fragment, function, half, ingredient, interest, involvement, limb, lines, lot, member, module, neck of the woods, neighbourhood, organ, particle, party, percentage, piece, place, portion, proportion, quarter, region, responsibility, role, scrap, section, sector, segment, share, side, slice, some, stake, task, territory, tip of the iceberg, unit, vicinity.
v break, break up (or apart), cleave, come apart, detach, disband, disconnect, disjoin, dismantle, disperse, disunite, diverge, divide, divvy up, force apart, go separate ways, open, parcel, part company, pull apart, rend, scatter, separate, sever, split, split up, sunder, tear (apart).

for the most part chiefly, commonly, generally, in the main, largely, mainly, mostly, normally, on the whole, principally, usually.

in good part cheerfully, cordially, good-naturedly, laughingly, well.
antonyms angrily, touchily.

in part a little, in some measure, part-way, partially, partly, slightly, somewhat, to a certain extent, to some degree.
antonym wholly.

part from depart from, go away from, go from, leave, quit, take (one's) leave of, withdraw from.

part with abandon, cede, discard, forgo, give away, give up, jettison, leave behind, let go of, relinquish, renounce, sacrifice, spend, surrender, yield.

partake *v* be involved, engage, enter, form a part of, participate, share, take part.

partake of consume, drink, eat, evince, have, have a hint of, have a part (or share) of, manifest, receive, share (in), show, smack of, suggest, take.

partial¹ *adj* fragmentary, imperfect, incomplete, inexhaustive, limited, part, uncompleted, unfinished.
antonyms complete, exhaustive, total.

partial² *adj* affected, biassed, coloured, discriminatory, ex parte, influenced, interested, lopsided, one-sided, partisan, predisposed, prejudiced, tendentious, unfair, unjust.
antonyms disinterested, fair, unbiassed.

partial to crazy about, fond of, keen on, mad about, nuts about, taken with, wild about.

partiality *n* affinity, bias, discrimination, favouritism, fondness, inclination, liking, lopsidedness, love, one-sidedness, partisanship, penchant, predilection, predisposition, preference, prejudice, proclivity, propensity, soft spot, taste, weakness.
antonyms dislike, justice.

partially *adv* fractionally, imperfectly, in part, incompletely, not wholly, partly, somewhat, to a degree, to some extent, unfairly, with undue bias.

participant *n* associate, contributor, co-operator, helper, member, partaker, participator, party, shareholder, worker.

participate *v* be involved, chip in, co-operate, engage, enter, have a voice, join, muck in, partake, perform, share, take part.

participation *n* a piece of the action, assistance, complicity, contribution, co-operation, engagement, involvement, mucking in, partaking, partnership, sharing.

particle *n* atom, bit, crumb, drop, electron, grain, iota, jot, kaon, micron, mite, molecule, morsel, mote, neutrino, neutron, photon, piece, pion, proton, scrap, shred, sliver, smidgen, snippet, speck, tittle, whit.

parti-coloured *adj* motley, multicoloured, patchwork, piebald, polychromatic, polychromic, variegated, versicolour.
antonyms monochromatic, plain.

particular¹ *adj* blow-by-blow, circumstantial, detailed, distinct, especial, exact, exceptional, express, individual, itemized, marked, minute, notable, noteworthy, peculiar, precise, remarkable, several, singular, special, specific, uncommon, unique, unusual.
antonym general.
n circumstance, detail, fact, feature, instance, item, point, specific, specification.

in particular distinctly, especially, exactly, expressly, in detail, particularly, specifically.

particular² *adj* careful, choosy, critical, dainty, demanding, discriminating, exacting, fastidious, finicky, fussy, hard to please, meticulous, nice, overnice, painstaking, pernickety, picky, selective, thorough.
antonyms careless, casual.

particularity¹ *n* characteristic, circumstance, detail, distinctiveness, fact, feature, idiosyncrasy, individuality, instance, item, mannerism, peculiarity, point, property, quirk, singularity, trait, uniqueness.

particularity² *n* accuracy, carefulness, choosiness, fastidiousness, fussiness, meticulousness, precision, thoroughness.

particularize *v* detail, enumerate, individualize, individuate, itemize, specify, stipulate.

particularly *adv* decidedly, distinctly, especially, exceptionally, explicitly, expressly, extraordinarily, in particular, markedly, notably, noticeably, outstandingly, peculiarly, remarkably, singularly, specifically, surprisingly, uncommonly, unusually.

parting *n* adieu, breaking, departure, detachment, disbandment, disjunction, disunion, divergence, division, farewell, fork, going, goodbye, leave-taking, partition, rift, rupture, separation, severance, split, valediction.

antonyms convergence, meeting.

adj closing, concluding, deathbed, departing, dying, farewell, final, last, stirrup (cup), swan (song), valedictory.

antonyms arriving, first.

partisan *n* adherent, backer, champion, devotee, disciple, follower, guerrilla, irregular, liner, loyalist, party-liner, party member, stalwart, supporter, upholder, votary.

adj biassed, discriminatory, factional, factious, guerrilla, interested, irregular, one-sided, partial, predisposed, prejudiced, resistance, sectarian, tendentious, underground, unjust.

partition¹ *n* allocation, allotment, apportionment, distribution, dividing, division, part, portion, rationing, section, segregation, separation, severance, share, splitting.

v allocate, allot, apportion, assign, divide, parcel out, portion, ration, section, segment, separate, share, split up, subdivide.

partition² *n* barrier, diaphragm, divider, membrane, room divider, screen, separation, septum, traverse, wall.

v bar, compartmentalize, divide, fence off, screen, separate, wall off.

partly *adv* halfway, incompletely, in part, moderately, partially, relatively, slightly, somewhat, to a (certain) degree, to a certain extent, up to a point.

antonyms completely, in toto, totally.

partner *n* accomplice, ally, associate, bedfellow, buddy, cohabitator, cohort, collaborator, colleague, companion, comrade, confederate, consort, co-partner, helper, helpmate, helpmeet, husband, mate, participant, sidekick, spouse, teammate, wife.

partnership *n* affiliation, alliance, association, brotherhood, combination, combine, companionship, company, conglomerate, connection, co-operation, co-operative, co-partnership, corporation, fellowship, firm, fraternity, house, interest, participation, sharing, sisterhood, society, syndicate, union.

party¹ *n* assembly, at-home, ball, bash, blowout, ceilidh, celebration, do, entertainment, -fest, festa, festivity, fiesta, function, gathering, get-together, hootenanny, housewarming, jollification, potlach, rave, reception, rout, shindig, social, soirée, tea.

party² *n* alliance, association, band, body, bunch, cabal, caucus, clique, coalition, combination, company, confederacy, contingent, coterie, crew, detachment, faction, gang, gathering, group, grouping, junto, league, set, side, squad, team, unit.

party³ *n* contractor, defendant, individual, interest, litigant, participant, person, plaintiff.

parvenu *n* arriviste, new money, nouveau riche, pretender, social climber, upstart, vulgarian.

adj nouveau riche, upstart, vulgarian.

pass¹ *v* accept, ace, adopt, advance, approve, authorize, beat, befall, beguile, blow over, cease, come to an end, come up, come up to scratch, communicate, convey, declare, decree, deliver, depart, devote, die, die away, disappear, discharge, disregard, dissolve, do, dwindle, ebb, elapse, eliminate, enact, end, establish, evacuate, evaporate, exceed, excel, exchange, excrete, expel, expire, fade, flow, fulfil, get through, give, go, go away, go beyond, go by, go past, graduate, hand, happen, lapse, leave, legislate, make it, march on, melt away, move, move by, move on, occupy, occur, ordain, outdistance, outdo, outstrip, overtake, pass muster, proceed, pronounce, qualify, ratify, roll by, run, sanction, send, serve, spend, succeed, suffice, surmount, surpass, take place, terminate, throw, toss, transcend, transfer, transmit, utter, validate, vanish, void, waft, wane, while away.

pass² *n* admission slip, advances, approach, attempt, authorization, chit, condition, crisis, feint, free ticket, identification, jab, juncture, licence, lunge, overture, passage, passport, permission, permit, pinch, play, plight, predicament, proposition, safe-conduct, situation, stage, state, state of affairs, straits, success, swing, thrust, ticket, warrant.

pass away cease to exist, come to an end, croak, decease, die, expire, give up the ghost, kick the bucket, pass on, pass over.

pass by disregard, elapse, forget, ignore, leave out, miss, neglect, omit, overlook, pass, pass over, pretermit.

pass muster be adequate, be up to scratch (or snuff), fill the bill, make the grade, measure up, meet with approval, qualify, stand the test.

pass off palm off, represent, fob off, misrepresent.

pass oneself off as act the part of, disguise oneself as, impersonate, masquerade as, pose as, pretend to be, profess to be, purport to be, represent oneself to be.

pass out¹ black out, die, drop, faint, flake out, keel over, lose consciousness, swoon.

pass out² circulate, deal out, dispense, distribute, dole out, give out, hand out, share (out).

pass over die, ignore, miss, neglect, omit, overlook, pretermit, skip (over), slight.

pass[3] *n* canyon, col, defile, gap, ghat, gorge, ravine, valley.

passable *adj* acceptable, adequate, admissible, all right, allowable, average, clear, fair, mediocre, middling, moderate, navigable, OK, open, presentable, so-so, tolerable, traversable, unblocked, unexceptional, unobstructed.

passably *adv* after a fashion, fairly, moderately, rather, reasonably, relatively, somewhat, tolerably, to some extent.

passage *n* acceptance, access, adit, advance, alley, approach, arcade, authorization, avenue, breezeway, change, channel, citation, clause, communication, conduit, conversion, corridor, course, crossing, doorway, drifting, duct, enactment, entrance, entrance hall, excerpt, exit, extract, fistula, flow, gallery, hall, hallway, journey, lane, lapse, leave to pass, march, migration, motion, movement, opening, orifice, paragraph, part, passageway, passing, path, piece, portion, progress, progression, quotation, ratification, reading, right to pass, road, route, safe-conduct, section, sentence, spiracle, text, thoroughfare, throughway, ticket, transit, transition, trek, vent, verse, vestibule, visa, voyage, way.

passageway *n* aisle, alley, avenue, channel, corridor, entrance, exit, hall, hallway, lane, lobby, opening, passage.

passé *adj* antiquated, dated, démodé, obsolete, old-fashioned, old hat, out, outdated, outmoded, out-of-date, outworn, past one's best, past one's prime, unfashionable, yesterday's news.

antonyms fashionable, in.

passenger *n* commuter, fare, hitchhiker, pillion rider, rider, traveller.

passer-by *n* bystander, looker-on, onlooker, spectator, witness.

passing *adj* brief, casual, cursory, ephemeral, evanescent, fleeting, fly-by-night, fugitive, glancing, hasty, impermanent, incidental, momentary, quick, shallow, short, short-lived, slight, superficial, temporary, transient, transitory.

antonyms long-lasting, permanent.

n death, decease, demise, end, expiration, finish, loss, quietus, termination.

in passing accidentally, by the by, by the way, en passant, incidentally.

passion *n* adoration, affection, anger, animation, ardour, arousal, attachment, avidity, bug, chafe, concupiscence, craving, craze, dander, desire, devotion, eagerness, emotion, enthusiasm, excitement, fanaticism, fancy, fascination, feeling, fervency, fervour, fire, fit, flame, fondness, frenzy, furor, fury, heat, idol, indignation, infatuation, intensity, ire, itch, keenness, love, lust, mania, monomania, obsession, rage, rapture, spirit, storm, transport, vehemence, warmth, weakness, worship, wrath, yen, zeal.

antonyms calm, coolness, self-possession.

passionate *adj* amorous, animated, ardent, aroused, burning, choleric, desirous, eager,

emotional, enthusiastic, excitable, excited, explosive, fanatic, fascinated, fervent, fervid, fierce, fiery, flaming, frenzied, heartfelt, heated, hot, hot-headed, hot-tempered, impassioned, impetuous, impulsive, incensed, inflamed, inspirited, intense, irascible, irate, loving, lustful, mad, peppery, quick-tempered, stormy, strong, sultry, tempestuous, torrid, turned-on, vehement, violent, volcanic, warm, wild, zealous.

antonyms frigid, laid-back, passionless, phlegmatic.

passionless *adj* apathetic, callous, calm, cold, cold-blooded, cold-hearted, detached, dispassionate, emotionless, frigid, frosty, icy, impartial, impassive, indifferent, insensible, neutral, restrained, uncaring, unemotional, unfeeling, uninvolved, unloving, unresponsive, withdrawn.

antonyms caring, passionate, sensitive, sympathetic.

passive *adj* acquiescent, apathetic, compliant, docile, enduring, impassive, inactive, indifferent, indolent, inert, lifeless, long-suffering, non-participating, non-violent, patient, quiescent, resigned, submissive, supine, unaffected, unassertive, uninvolved, unresisting.

antonyms active, involved, lively.

passive resistance civil disobedience, non-violence, peaceful demonstration, satyagraha.

passport *n* authorization, entree, in, key, pass, permit, safe-conduct, ticket, visa.

password *n* countersign, open sesame, shibboleth, signal, watchword.

past *adj* accomplished, ancient, behind one, bygone, completed, dead and buried, defunct, done, early, elapsed, ended, erstwhile, expired, extinct, finished, foregone, forgotten, former, gone, gone by, late, long gone, no more, of long ago, of yore, olden, over, over and done with, preceding, previous, prior, quondam, recent, spent, vanished.

n antiquity, auld lang syne, background, days gone by, days of yore, experience, former times, good old days, history, life, olden days, old times, times past, track record, yesteryear.

past one's prime has-been, not what one was, over the hill, passé, past one's best.

paste *n* adhesive, cement, dough, glue, gum, mastic, mucilage, pastry, putty.

v beat, cement, fasten, fix, glue, gum, hammer, hit, pound, punch, stick, thrash, thump.

pastel *adj* delicate, faint, gentle, light, muted, pale, soft, soft-coloured, soft-hued, subdued.

n chalk, crayon, drawing, pastille, sketch, vignette.

pastiche *n* assortment, blend, conglomeration, farrago, gallimaufrey, hodgepodge, medley, mélange, miscellany, mixed bag, mixture, patchwork, potpourri.

pastille *n* confection, cough drop, incense, joss stick, jujube, lozenge, pastel, tablet, troche.

pastime *n* activity, amusement, avocation, distraction, diversion, divertisement, entertainment, game, hobby, play, recreation, relaxation, sideline, sport.
antonyms business, employment, occupation, vocation, work.

pastor *n* canon, churchman, churchwoman, clergyman, clergywoman, cleric, curate, divine, ecclesiastic, man (or woman) of the cloth, minister, parson, priest, rector, vicar.

pastoral *adj* agrarian, Arcadian, bucolic, clerical, countrified, country, ecclesiastical, georgic, idyllic, ministerial, priestly, rural, rustic, simple.
antonyms oppidan, urban.

pasture *n* grass, grassland, grazing, herbage, lea, mead, meadow, pasturage, pasture land, prairie, range.

pasty *adj* anemic, colourless, doughy, gluey, glutinous, mucilaginous, pale, pallid, pasty-faced, quaggy, sallow, sickly, starchy, sticky, unhealthy-looking, viscous, wan, waxy, whey-faced.
antonyms healthy-looking, rubicund.

pat[1] *v* caress, clap, dab, daub, fondle, pet, slap, stroke, tap, touch.
n cake, caress, chunk, clap, dab, lump, piece, portion, slap, square, stroke, tap, touch.

pat[2] *adv* down pat, exactly, faultlessly, flawlessly, fluently, glibly, just right, opportunely, perfectly, plumb, precisely, relevantly, right on, seasonably, without a hitch.
antonyms imprecisely, wrongly.
adj apposite, appropriate, apropos, apt, automatic, bang on, easy, facile, felicitous, fitting, glib, just right, pertinent, ready, relevant, right, right (on), simplistic, slick, smooth, suitable, superficial, to the point, trite, well-chosen.
antonyms irrelevant, unsuitable.

patch *n* area, bit, connection, ground, hookup, land, lot, pad, parcel, piece, plot, scrap, shred, splotch, spot, square, stretch, tract.
v cover, fix, mend, reinforce, repair, sew up, stitch, vamp.

patchwork *n* confusion, farrago, gallimaufrey, hash, hodgepodge, jumble, medley, mishmash, mixture, pastiche.

patchy *adj* discontinuous, erratic, fitful, incongruous, inconsistent, inharmonious, irregular, maculate, mixed, non-uniform, random, sketchy, spotted, spotty, uneven, variable, varying.
antonyms consistent, even, regular, uniform.

patent *adj* apparent, blatant, clear, clear-cut, conspicuous, downright, evident, explicit, flagrant, glaring, indisputable, manifest, obvious, open, ostensible, outright, overt, palpable, plain, transparent, unconcealed, unequivocal, unmistakable.
antonyms hidden, opaque.
n certificate, copyright, exclusive right, invention, licence, privilege, registered trademark.

paternal *adj* benevolent, concerned, fatherlike, fatherly, indulgent, loving, patrilineal, patrimonial, protective, solicitous, vigilant.

paternity *n* authorship, descent, extraction, family, fatherhood, fathership, lineage, male line, origination, parentage, seed, stock.

path *n* avenue, course, direction, footpath, footway, gate, lane, pad, passage, pathway, road, route, spoor, towpath, track, trail, walk, walkway, way.

pathetic *adj* beneath contempt, contemptible, crummy, deplorable, disgraceful, dismal-looking, distressing, feeble, heartbreaking, heart-rending, inadequate, lamentable, meagre, measly, mere, miserable, moving, paltry, petty, piteous, pitiable, pitiful, plaintive, poignant, poor, puny, sad, sorry, tender, touching, uninteresting, useless, woebegone, woeful, worthless, wretched.
antonyms admirable, cheerful.

pathos *n* misery, pitiableness, pitifulness, plaintiveness, poignancy, sadness.

patience *n* calmness, composure, constancy, cool, diligence, endurance, equanimity, forbearance, fortitude, indefatigability, long-suffering, perseverance, persistence, resignation, restraint, self-control, serenity, stoicism, staying power, submission, sufferance, tirelessness, tolerance, toleration.
antonyms impatience, intolerance.

patient[1] *adj* accepting, accommodating, calm, composed, diligent, enduring, even-tempered, forbearing, forgiving, indefatigable, indulgent, lenient, long-suffering, mild, persevering, persistent, philosophical, quiet, resigned, restrained, self-controlled, self-possessed, serene, steady, stoical, submissive, tolerant, uncomplaining, understanding, untiring.
antonyms impatient, intolerant.

patient[2] *n* case, client, in-patient, invalid, out-patient, shut-in, sickie, sufferer.

patois *n* argot, cant, dialect, jargon, lingo, lingua franca, patter, slang, vernacular.

patriarch *n* elder, father, founder, grand old man, grandfather, greybeard, paterfamilias, sire.

patrician *n* aristocrat, blue blood, gentleman, grandee, noble, nobleman, peer.
antonyms commoner, pleb.
adj aristocratic, blue-blooded, genteel, highborn, high-class, lordly, noble, thoroughbred, titled, wellborn.
antonyms common, humble.

patrimony *n* bequest, birthright, estate, heritage, inheritance, legacy, portion, revenue, share.

patriotic *adj* chauvinistic, flag-waving, jingoistic, loyal, nationalistic, public-spirited, ultranationalistic.

patrol *n* beat, defence, garrison, guard, lookout, policing, protection, sentinel, surveillance, walk, watch, watchman.
v cruise, guard, inspect, keep watch, make the rounds, perambulate, police, tour, walk.

patron *n* advocate, backer, benefactor, buyer, champion, client, customer, defender, frequenter, friend, guardian, guardian angel, habitué, helper, Maecenas, partisan, philanthropist, protector, regular, shopper, sponsor, subscriber, supporter, sympathizer.

patronage *n* aegis, aid, assistance, backing, benefaction, business, championship, clientele, commerce, custom, encouragement, help, participation, promotion, protectorship, sponsorship, subscription, support, sustenance, trade, trading, traffic.

patronize *v* assist, back, befriend, condescend to, deal with, do business with, encourage, foster, frequent, fund, habituate, help, humour, maintain, promote, shop at, sponsor, support, talk down to.

patronizing *adj* arrogant, condescending, contemptuous, disdainful, haughty, high-handed, imperious, lofty, overbearing, paternalistic, snobbish, stooping, supercilious, superior.
antonym humble.

patter[1] *v* beat, pat, pelt, pitapat, pitter-patter, rat-a-rat, scurry, scuttle, skip, spatter, tap, tiptoe, trip.
n pattering, pitapat, pitter-patter, rat-a-tat, scuttle, tapping.

patter[2] *n* argot, babbling, cant, chatter, gab, gabble, glib talk, jabber, jargon, line, lingo, monologue, patois, pitch, prattle, slang, spiel, vernacular, yak.

pattern *n* archetype, arrangement, cast, configuration, criterion, cycle, cynosure, delineation, design, device, diagram, examplar, example, figuration, figure, Gestalt, guide, instructions, kind, master, matrix, method, model, motif, norm, order, orderliness, original, paradigm, paragon, plan, predictability, prototype, regularity, rhythm, sample, sequence, shape, sort, specimen, standard, stencil, stereotype, structure, style, system, template, theme, type, variety.
v copy, design, form, model, mould, order, shape, stencil, style.

patterned *adj* decorated, figured, moiré, moulded, ornamented, printed, stamped, stereotyped, watered.

paucity *n* dearth, deficiency, exiguousness, fewness, insufficiency, lack, meagreness, paltriness, poverty, rarity, scantiness, scarcity, shortage, slenderness, slightness, smallness, sparseness, sparsity, want.
antonym abundance.

paunch *n* abdomen, beer-belly, beer-gut, belly, breadbasket, gut, pot, potbelly, spare tire, tummy.

paunchy *adj* adipose, bloated, corpulent, distended, fat, portly, potbellied, pudgy, roly-poly, rotund, tubby.

pauper *n* bankrupt, beggar, churchmouse, down-and-outer, have-not, indigent, insolvent, mendicant.

pause *v* break, catch one's breath, delay, hesitate, interrupt, let up, linger, recess, rest, stop for breath, take a break, take a breather, take five, take time out, wait, waver.
n abatement, break, breather, caesura, cessation, delay, discontinuance, discontinuity, gap, halt, hesitation, interlude, intermission, interruption, interval, letup, lull, recess, respite, rest, slackening, stay, stop, stoppage, suspension, time out, wait.

pave *v* asphalt, blacktop, concrete, cover, floor, macadamize, resurface, revet, slab, surface, tar, tile.

pavement *n* asphalt, bed, causeway, floor, footway, sidewalk, surface.

paw *v* feel up, finger, grab, manhandle, maul, mishandle, molest, palm.
n foot, forefoot, forepaw, hand, pad.

pawn[1] *n* cat's-paw, creature, dupe, instrument, plaything, puppet, stooge, tool, toy.

pawn[2] *v* deposit, gage, hazard, hock, mortgage, pledge, risk, stake, wager.
n bond, deposit, forfeit, gage, hostage, pledge, security.

pay *v* ante, benefit, be worthwhile, bestow, bring in, clear, compensate, cough up, disburse, discharge, dish out, extend, foot, fork over, get even with, give, grant, hand over, honour, indemnify, liquidate, make, meet, offer, pay out, present, produce, proffer, profit, punish, reciprocate, recompense, reimburse, remit, remunerate, render, repay, requite, return, reward, serve, settle, spend, square, square up, yield.
n allowance, compensation, consideration, earnings, emoluments, fee, hire, honorarium, income, payment, recompense, reimbursement, remuneration, reward, salary, stipend, takings, wage(s).

pay back avenge, chasten, get even with, get one's own back on, get (or take) revenge on (or for), make restitution, punish, reciprocate, recompense, refund, reimburse, repay, retaliate, return, settle up, settle with, square with.

pay (for) answer for, atone, compensate, face the music, get one's (just) deserts, make amends, suffer.

pay off bribe, clear, discharge, get even with, grease the palm of, liquidate, pay back, pay in full, recompense, retaliate, satisfy, settle, square, succeed, work.

pay out cough up, disburse, dish out, expend, fork out, hand over, lay out, render, shell out, spend.

payable *adj* due, in arrears, mature, obligatory, outstanding, owed, owing, receivable, unpaid.

payment *n* advance, alimony, ante, consideration, defrayal, deposit, discharge, expenditure, fee, hire, instalment, outlay, paying, portion, premium, punishment, remittance, remuneration, reward, settlement, wage.

payoff *n* bribe, climax, clincher, conclusion, consequence, crunch, culmination, day of reckoning, denouement, judgment, moment of truth, outcome, payment, punch line, reimbursement, result, retribution, reward, settlement, upshot.

peace *n* accord, agreement, amity, armistice, calm, calmness, cease-fire, conciliation, concord, contentment, harmony, hush, order, pacification, pax, peacefulness, placidity, quiet, quietude, reconciliation, relaxation, repose, rest, serenity, silence, stillness, tranquillity, treaty, truce.

antonyms disagreement, disturbance, war.

peaceable *adj* amiable, amicable, compatible, conciliatory, dovelike, dovish, easygoing, friendly, gentle, inoffensive, mild, non-belligerent, pacific, peaceful, peace-loving, placid, unwarlike.

antonyms belligerent, offensive, warlike.

peaceful *adj* amicable, at peace, becalmed, calm, conciliatory, friendly, gentle, halcyon, harmonious, irenic, non-violent, pacific, peaceable, peacekeeping, peace-loving, placatory, placid, quiet, restful, serene, still, tranquil, unagitated, undisturbed, unruffled, untroubled, unwarlike.

antonyms at war, disturbed, noisy, troubled.

peacemaker *n* appeaser, arbitrator, conciliator, intercessor, intervener, mediator, pacifier, peacekeeper, peacemonger.

peacemaking *adj* appeasing, conciliatory, irenic, mediating, mediative, mediatory, pacific, peacemongering.

peak *n* acme, aiguille, apex, apogee, arête, brow, climax, crag, crest, crown, culmination, cusp, high, high noon, high point, maximum, ne plus ultra, pinnacle, point, summit, tip, top, visor, zenith.

antonyms nadir, trough.

v climax, come to a head, crest, culminate, tower.

peaked *adj* drooping, droopy, emaciated, green about the gills, ill, off-colour, pale, pinched, poorly, sick, sickly, under the weather, unwell, wan, washed-out, wilting.

antonyms healthy, in the pink.

peal *n* blast, boom, carillon, chime, clamour, clang, clangour, clap, clash, crash, knell, resounding, reverberation, ring, ringing, roar, tintinnabulation.

v chime, clash, crack, crash, knell, resonate, resound, reverberate, ring (out), roll, sound, tintinnabulate, toll, vibrate.

peanuts *n* a (mere) pittance, a trifling amount, chicken feed, pennies, small potatoes, starvation wages.

peasant *n* boor, bumpkin, churl, countryman, hillbilly, kulak, lout, muzhik, oaf, provincial, rustic, swain, yokel.

antonym sophisticate.

peccadillo *n* booboo, delinquency, error, fault, indiscretion, infraction, lapse, misdeed, misdemeanour, slip, slip-up.

peck *n* buss, jab, kiss, strike.

v buss, criticize, eat, find fault, jab, kiss, nibble, pick.

peculiar¹ *adj* abnormal, bizarre, curious, eccentric, exceptional, extraordinary, far out, freakish, funky, funny, odd, offbeat, outlandish, out-of-the-way, quaint, queer, singular, strange, uncommon, unconventional, unusual, way out, weird.

antonyms normal, ordinary.

peculiar² *adj* appropriate, characteristic, differentiating, discriminative, distinct, distinctive, distinguishing, endemic, idiosyncratic, indicative, individual, local, particular, personal, private, quintessential, restricted, special, specific, unique.

antonyms general, uncharacteristic.

peculiarity¹ *n* abnormality, bizarreness, eccentricity, exception, foible, freakishness, kink, oddity, queerness, quirk, whimsicality.

peculiarity² *n* attribute, characteristic, distinctiveness, feature, idiosyncrasy, mannerism, mark, particularity, property, quality, singularity, trait.

pecuniary *adj* capital, commercial, financial, fiscal, monetary, nummary.

pedagogue *n* dogmatist, don, educationalist, educator, instructor, master, pedant, preceptor, schoolmaster, schoolmistress, schoolteacher, teacher.

pedagogy *n* education, instruction, pedagogics, schooling, teaching, training, tuition, tutelage, tutoring.

pedant *n* casuist, doctrinaire, dogmatist, grammarian, hairsplitter, literalist, mandarin, nit-picker, pedagogue, pettifogger, phrasemonger, precisian, precisionist, purist, quibbler, scholastic, stickler.

pedantic *adj* abstruse, academic, bookish, cavilling, didactic, donnish, erudite, formal, fussy, hairsplitting, learned, nit-picking, particular, pedagogical, perfectionist, pompous, precise, punctilious, scholastic, schoolmasterly, sententious, stilted, studious.

antonyms casual, imprecise, informal.

peddle *v* dispense, flog, hawk, huckster, market, push, retail, sell, tout, trade, vend.

pedestal *n* base, dado, foot, foundation, mounting, pier, platform, plinth, podium, socle, stand, support, understructure.

pedestrian *adj* banal, boring, commonplace, dull, flat, humdrum, indifferent, mediocre, mundane, ordinary, plodding, prosaic, run-of-the-mill, stodgy, tolerable, unimaginative, uninspired, uninteresting.

antonyms bright, brilliant, exciting, imaginative.

pedigree *n* ancestry, blood, breed, derivation, descent, dynasty, extraction, family, family tree, genealogy, heritage, line, lineage, parentage, race, stem, stirps, stock, strain, succession.

pedigreed *adj* aristocratic, full-blooded, purebred, registered, thoroughbred.

pedlar *n* cheapjack, colporteur, distributor, gutter merchant, hawker, huckster, pusher, seller, sidewalk salesman, (street) vendor.

peek *v* glance, look, peep, peer, pry, spy, take a peek.

n blink, (casual) glance, gander, glimpse, look, look-see, peep, (sideways) glance.

peel *v* debark, decorticate, denude, flake (off), pare, scale, shuck, skin, strip (off), undress.

n epicarp, exocarp, integument, peeling, rind, skin, zest.

peep *v* blink, emerge, glimpse, issue, peek, peep out, peer, pry, show.

n blink, gander, glimpse, look, look-see, peek.

peephole *n* aperture, chink, cleft, crack, crevice, fissure, hole, interstice, keyhole, lookout, opening, pinhole, slit, spyhole.

peer[1] *v* appear, blink, come out, emerge, gaze, look closely, peep, snoop, spy, squint.

peer at examine, go over with a fine-toothed comb, inspect, investigate, look closely at, scan, scrutinize.

peer[2] *n* compeer, counterpart, equal, equipollent, equivalent, fellow, like, match, mate.

peerage *n* aristocracy, lords and ladies, nobility, titled class, upper crust.

peerless *adj* beyond compare, excellent, incomparable, matchless, nonpareil, outstanding, paramount, second to none, superlative, supreme, unbeatable, unequalled, unexcelled, unique, unmatched, unparalleled, unrivalled, unsurpassed, without equal.

peeved *adj* annoyed, exasperated, galled, huffy, irked, irritated, miffed, nettled, piqued, provoked, put out, riled, sore, upset, vexed.

peevish *adj* acrimonious, cantankerous, captious, churlish, complaining, crabby, cranky, cross, crotchety, crusty, discontented, fractious, fretful, grumpy, huffish, ill-natured, ill-tempered, irritable, miffed, perverse, petulant, querulous, ratty, short-tempered, snappy, splenetic, sulky, sullen, surly, testy, touchy, waspish.

antonym good-tempered.

peg *v* attach, categorize, control, fasten, fix, freeze, hold, identify, join, label, limit, mark, pierce, pigeonhole, score, secure, set.

n dowel, hook, knob, marker, notch, pin, post, stake, thole, toggle.

peg away apply oneself, beaver away, drudge (away), hang in, keep at it, persevere, persist, plod along, plug away, slog away, stick at it, work away.

pejorative *adj* bad, belittling, condemnatory, damning, debasing, deprecatory, depreciatory, derogatory, detractive, disparaging, negative, slighting, uncomplimentary, unflattering, unpleasant.

antonyms complimentary, laudatory.

pellet *n* ball, bead, bee-bee, bullet, missile, pill, shot, wad.

pell-mell *adv* feverishly, full tilt, hastily, headlong, heedlessly, helter-skelter, hurriedly, hurry-scurry, impetuously, posthaste, precipitously, rashly, recklessly.

adj chaotic, confused, disordered, disorganized, haphazard, headlong, helter-skelter, hurry-scurry, indiscriminate, scrambled, tumultuous.

pelt[1] *v* assail, batter, beat, belabour, belt, bombard, bucket, career, cast, charge, dash, hit, hurl, hurry, hurtle, pepper, pound, pour, pummel, rain cats and dogs, rush, shoot, shower, sling, speed, strike, tear, teem, thrash, throw, wallop, whiz.

pelt[2] *n* coat, fell, fleece, fur, hide, skin.

pen[1] *v* author, compose, draft, jot down, scribble, write.

pen name alias, allonym, nom de plume, pseudonym.

pen[2] *n* cage, coop, corral, crib, enclosure, fold, hutch, kraal, stall, sty.

v cage, confine, coop (up), corral, crib, enclose, fence, hedge in, hem in, mew (up), shut in (or up).

penalize *v* amerce, correct, disadvantage, discipline, handicap, mulct, punish.

antonym reward.

penalty *n* amende, amercement, disadvantage, fine, forfeit, forfeiture, handicap, mulct, price, punishment, retribution.

antonym reward.

penance *n* atonement, mortification (of the flesh), penalty, placation, propitiation, punishment, reparation, sackcloth and ashes.

penchant *n* affinity, bent, bias, disposition, fondness, inclination, leaning, liking, partiality, predilection, predisposition, preference, proclivity, proneness, propensity, soft spot, taste, tendency, turn.

antonym dislike.

pendant *n* drop, lavaliere, locket, medallion, necklace.

pendent *adj* dangling, drooping, hanging, pendulous, pensile, suspended, swinging.

pending *adj* forthcoming, hanging, imminent, impending, in abeyance, in the balance, in the offing, on the back burner, undecided, undetermined, unfinished, unsettled.

antonyms finished, settled.

pendulous *adj* dangling, drooping, droopy, hanging, pendent, sagging, suspended, swaying, swinging.

penetrable *adj* accessible, clear, comprehensible, explicable, fathomable, intelligible, open, passable, permeable, pervious, porous, understandable, vulnerable.

antonym impenetrable.

penetrate *v* affect, bore into, come across, come home, comprehend, decipher, discern, enter, fathom, get through (to), get to the bottom of, grasp, impress, infiltrate, infuse, pass into, pass through, perforate, perfuse, permeate, pervade, pierce, prick, probe, register, see through, seep (through or into), sink, soak (through or into), spread through, stab, strike, touch, unravel.

penetrating *adj* acute, astute, biting, critical, discerning, discriminating, harsh, incisive, intelligent, intrusive, keen, observant, penetrative, perceptive, percipient, perspicacious, pervasive, piercing, profound, pungent, quick, sagacious, searching, sharp, sharp-witted, shrewd, shrill, stinging, strong, trenchant.

antonyms gentle, obtuse, soft.

penetration *n* acumen, acuteness, astuteness, discernment, entrance, entry, incision, infusion, inroad, insight, interpenetration, invasion, keenness, perception, perforation, permeation, perspicacity, piercing, puncturing, sagacity, sharpness, shrewdness, wit.

penitence *n* compunction, contrition, regret, regretfulness, remorse, repentance, rue, self-reproach, shame, sorrow.

penitent *adj* abject, apologetic, atoning, conscience-stricken, contrite, humble, in sackcloth and ashes, regretful, remorseful, repentant, rueful, sorrowful, sorry.

antonym unrepentant.

pennant *n* banderole, banner, burgee, ensign, flag, gonfalon, oriflamme, pennon, standard, streamer.

penniless *adj* bankrupt, broke, busted, cleaned out, destitute, down-and-out, flat broke, impecunious, impoverished, in desperate straits, indigent, moneyless, necessitous, needy, on one's uppers, on the rocks, penurious, poor, poverty-stricken, ruined, stone-broke, strapped, strapped for cash.

antonyms rich, wealthy.

penny-pincher *n* cheapskate, meanie, miser, niggard, pinchpenny, screw, Scrooge, skinflint, tightwad.

penny-pinching *adj* cheap, cheeseparing, close-fisted, frugal, mean, miserly, niggardly, parsimonious, penurious, scrimping, stingy, thrifty, tight-fisted, ungenerous.

antonyms generous, open-handed.

pension *n* allowance, annuity, benefit, maintenance, stipend, superannuation.

pensive *adj* absent-minded, absorbed, cogitative, contemplative, dreamy, grave, meditative, melancholy, musing, preoccupied, reflective, ruminative, serious, sober, solemn, thoughtful, wistful.

pent-up *adj* bottled-up, bridled, checked, constrained, contained, curbed, inhibited, repressed, restrained, smothered, stifled, suppressed.

penurious *adj* beggarly, busted, cheeseparing, close, close-fisted, deficient, destitute, flat broke, frugal, grudging, impecunious, impoverished, inadequate, indigent, in need, meagre, mean, miserable, miserly, near, needy, niggardly, paltry, parsimonious, penniless, poor, poverty-stricken, scanty, skimping, stingy, tight-fisted, ungenerous.

antonyms generous, wealthy.

penury *n* bare subsistence, beggary, dearth, deficiency, destitution, hand-to-mouth existence, indigence, lack, mendicancy, need, neediness, pauperism, poverty, privation, straitened circumstances, straits, want.

antonym prosperity.

people *n* citizens, clan, commonalty, community, crowd, family, folk, general public, gens, grass roots, hoi polloi, human beings, humanity, humankind, humans, inhabitants, kinsfolk, many-headed beast, many-headed monster, masses, mob, mortals, multitude, nation, persons, plebs, populace, population, public, rabble, race, rank and file, relatives, the herd, the million, tribe.

v colonize, inhabit, occupy, populate, settle, stock, tenant.

pep *n* animation, energy, enthusiasm, exuberance, get-up-and-go, gusto, high spirits, life, liveliness, pizzazz, spirit, verve, vigour, vim, vitality, vivacity, zip.

pep up animate, energize, enliven, excite, exhilarate, inspire, invigorate, jazz up, perk up, quicken, spice up, stimulate, vitalize, vivify.

peppery *adj* astringent, biting, caustic, choleric, fiery, hot, hot-tempered, incisive, irascible, irritable, nippy, piquant, pungent, quick-tempered, sarcastic, sharp, snappish, spicy, stinging, testy, touchy, trenchant, waspish.

perceive *v* appreciate, apprehend, be aware of, behold, catch, comprehend, conclude, deduce, descry, detect, discern, discover, distinguish, espy, feel, gather, get, grasp, intuit, know, learn, make out, note, notice, observe, realize, recognize, remark, see, sense, spot, take in, understand.

perceptible *adj* apparent, appreciable, clear, conspicuous, detectable, discernible, distinct, distinguishable, evident, manifest, measurable, noticeable, observable, obvious, palpable, perceivable, recognizable, salient, tangible, visible.

antonym imperceptible.

perception *n* apprehension, awareness, cognizance, conception, consciousness, discernment, feeling, grasp, idea, impression, insight, intellection, notion, observation, percept, perspicacity, recognition, sagacity, sensation, sense, taste, understanding, uptake, view.

perceptive *adj* acute, alert, astute, aware, discerning, insightful, observant, penetrating, percipient, perspicacious, quick, responsive, sagacious, sapient, sensitive, sharp.

antonym unobservant.

perch *v* alight, balance, drop, land, light, rest, roost, settle, sit.

percipient *adj* alert, alive, astute, aware, discerning, discriminating, insightful, intelligent, intuitive, judicious, observant, penetrating, perceptive, perspicacious, quick-witted, sagacious, sensitive, sharp, wide-awake.

antonyms obtuse, unaware.

percolate *v* drain, drip, exude, filter, filtrate, leach, leak, ooze, penetrate, permeate, pervade, seep, strain, transfuse.

perdition *n* condemnation, damnation, destruction, doom, downfall, everlasting torment, fire and brimstone, hell, hellfire, ruin, ruination.

peremptory *adj* abrupt, absolute, arbitrary, assertive, authoritative, autocratic, bossy, categorical, commanding, compelling, curt, decisive, dictatorial, dogmatic, domineering, final, high-handed, imperative, imperious, incontrovertible, irrefutable, obligatory, overbearing, pontifical, summary, undebatable, undeniable.

perennial *adj* abiding, ceaseless, chronic, constant, continual, continuing, continuous, deathless, enduring, eternal, evergreen, everlasting, immortal, imperishable, incessant, inveterate, lasting, lifelong, never-ending, never-failing, permanent, perpetual, persistent, recurrent, sempiternal, unceasing, unchanging, undying, unfailing, uninterrupted.

perfect *adj* absolute, accomplished, accurate, adept, blameless, complete, completed, consummate, correct, entire, exact, excellent, experienced, expert, faithful, faultless, finished, flawless, full, ideal, immaculate, impeccable, irreproachable, masterly, model, polished, practised, precise, pure, right, sheer, sinless, skilful, skilled, splendid, spotless, strict, sublime, superb, superlative, supreme, thorough, true, unadulterated, unalloyed, unblemished, unerring, unimpeachable, unmarred, unmitigated, untarnished, utter, whole, wonderful.

antonyms flawed, imperfect.

v accomplish, achieve, carry out, complete, consummate, develop, effect, elaborate, fine-tune, finish, fulfil, hone, perfectionate, polish, realize, refine.

perfection *n* completeness, completion, consummation, culmination, development, evolution, exactness, excellence, exquisiteness, faultlessness, fine-tuning, flawlessness, fulfilment, honing, ideal, impeccability, integrity, maturity, polish, precision, purity, realization, refinement, sinlessness, spotlessness, sublimity, superiority, wholeness.

antonyms flaw, imperfection.

perfectionist *n* formalist, idealist, nit-picker, precisian, precisionist, purist, stickler.

perfidious *adj* corrupt, deceitful, dishonest, disloyal, double-dealing, duplicitous, faithless, false, Machiavellian, Punic, recreant, traitorous, treacherous, treasonous, two-faced, unfaithful, untrustworthy.

antonyms faithful, honest, loyal.

perfidy *n* betrayal, deceit, disloyalty, double-dealing, duplicity, faithlessness, falsity, infidelity, perfidiousness, Punic faith, traitorousness, treachery, treason.

antonyms faithfulness, honesty, loyalty.

perforate *v* bore, drill, honeycomb, penetrate, pierce, prick, punch, puncture.

perforation *n* bore, cut, dotted line, fenestration, hole, prick, puncture, slit, space.

perforce *adv* ineluctably, inevitably, necessarily, of necessity, unavoidably, willy-nilly.

perform *v* accomplish, achieve, act, appear as, bring about, bring off, carry out, complete, depict, discharge, dispatch, do, effect, enact, execute, fulfil, function, keep, manage, observe, play, portray, practise, present, produce, pull off, put on, render, represent, satisfy, stage, transact, work.

performance *n* accomplishment, account, achievement, act, acting, action, behaviour, business, carrying out, ceremony, completion, conduct, consummation, discharge, efficiency, execution, exercise, exhibition, exploit, feat, fulfilment, functioning, fuss, gig, implementation, interpretation, melodrama, operation, play, portrayal, practice, presentation, production, productivity, rendition, representation, rigmarole, running, show, to-do, work, working.

performer *n* actor, actress, artiste, entertainer, mummer, play-actor, player, Thespian, trouper.

perfume *n* aroma, attar, balm, balminess, bouquet, cologne, essence, fragrance, incense, odour, redolence, scent, smell, sweetness, toilet water.

perfunctory *adj* automatic, brief, careless, cursory, heedless, hurried, inattentive, indifferent, mechanical, negligent, offhand, routine, sketchy, slipshod, slovenly, superficial, wooden.

antonym cordial.

perhaps *adv* conceivably, feasibly, for all one knows, maybe, mayhap, peradventure, perchance, possibly, you never know.

peril *n* danger, exposure, hazard, imperilment, insecurity, jeopardy, menace, pitfall, risk, threat, uncertainty, vulnerability.

antonyms safety, security.

perilous *adj* chancy, dangerous, desperate, dicey, difficult, dire, exposed, hairy, hazardous, menacing, parlous, precarious, risky, threatening, unreliable, unsafe, unsure, vulnerable.

antonyms safe, secure.

perimeter *n* ambit, border, borderline, boundary, bounds, circumference, confines, edge, fringe, frontier, limit(s), margin, periphery.

antonyms centre, heart, middle.

period¹ *n* age, course, cycle, date, days, duration, end, eon, epoch, era, generation, interval, season, space, span, spell, stage, stint, stop, stretch, term, time, turn, while, years.

period² *n* friend, menses, menstrual flow, menstruation, monthlies, the curse.

periodic *adj* cyclic, cyclical, desultory, etesian, infrequent, intermittent, occasional, recurrent, regular, repeated, seasonal, spasmodic, sporadic.

periodical *n* gazette, journal, magazine, monthly, organ, paper, publication, quarterly, review, serial, weekly.

peripatetic *adj* ambulant, ambulatory, itinerant, journeying, migrant, mobile, nomadic, roaming, roving, travelling, vagabond, vagrant, wandering.

antonym fixed.

peripheral *adj* borderline, exterior, external, incidental, inessential, irrelevant, marginal, minor, outer, outermost, outlying, outside, perimetric, secondary, superficial, surface, surrounding, tangential, unimportant, unnecessary.
antonyms central, crucial.

periphery *n* ambit, border, boundary, bounds, brim, brink, circuit, circumference, edge, exterior, fringe, hem, margin, outskirts, perimeter, rim, skirt, verge.
antonyms centre, nub.

perish *v* collapse, croak, crumble, decay, decline, decompose, decrease, die, die off, disappear, disintegrate, end, expire, fall, moulder, pass away, rot, spoil, vanish, waste, wither.

perishable *adj* biodegradable, corruptible, decomposable, destructible, ephemeral, fast-decaying, fast-deteriorating, mortal, short-lived, unstable.

perjury *n* false oath, false statement, false swearing, false witness, falsification, forswearing, mendacity.

perk *n* benefit, bonus, dividend, extra, freebie, fringe benefit, perquisite, plus.

perk up brighten, buck up, cheer up, improve, liven up, look up, pep up, rally, recover, recuperate, revive, take heart, upturn.

perky *adj* animated, bouncy, bright, bubbly, buoyant, cheerful, cheery, chipper, effervescent, gay, jaunty, lively, peppy, spirited, sprightly, sunny, vivacious.
antonyms cheerless, dull, gloomy.

permanence *n* changelessness, constancy, continuance, continuity, deathlessness, dependability, durability, duration, endurance, finality, fixedness, fixity, immortality, imperishability, indestructibility, lastingness, longevity, perdurability, perpetuity, stability, survival.
antonym impermanence.

permanent *adj* abiding, changeless, constant, durable, enduring, everlasting, fixed, immutable, imperishable, indelible, indestructible, ineffaceable, ineradicable, inerasable, invariable, lasting, long-lasting, perennial, perpetual, persevering, persistent, stable, standing, steadfast, unchanging, unfading.
antonyms ephemeral, fleeting, temporary.

permanently *adv* always, ceaselessly, constantly, continually, endlessly, eternally, ever more, everlastingly, forever, for keeps, indelibly, in perpetuity, once and for all, unendingly, unremittingly.
antonym temporarily.

permeable *adj* absorbent, absorptive, passable, penetrable, pervious, porous, spongy.
antonyms impermeable, watertight.

permeate *v* fill, filter through, imbue, impenetrate, impregnate, infiltrate, infuse, interfuse, interpenetrate, pass through,

penetrate, percolate, pervade, saturate, seep through, soak through, spread through.

permissible *adj* acceptable, admissible, allowable, allowed, all right, authorized, kosher, lawful, legit, legitimate, licit, OK, permitted, proper, sanctioned.
antonym prohibited.

permission *n* allowance, approval, assent, authorization, consent, dispensation, freedom, go-ahead, green light, imprimatur, leave, liberty, licence, permit, sanction, sufferance.
antonym prohibition.

permissive *adj* acquiescent, complaisant, easygoing, forbearing, free, indulgent, latitudinarian, lax, lenient, liberal, non-restrictive, open-minded, overindulgent, tolerant.
antonym strict.

permit *v* admit, agree to, allow, authorize, consent to, empower, enable, endorse, endure, give leave, grant, let, make possible, sanction, warrant.
antonym prohibit.
n authorization, carnet, liberty, licence, pass, passport, permission, sanction, visa, warrant.
antonym prohibition.

permutation *n* alteration, change, commutation, rearrangement, shift, transformation, transmutation, transposition, transubstantiation.

pernicious *adj* bad, baleful, baneful, damaging, dangerous, deadly, deleterious, destructive, detrimental, evil, fatal, harmful, hurtful, injurious, maleficent, malevolent, malicious, malign, malignant, noisome, noxious, offensive, pestilent, poisonous, ruinous, toxic, unhealthy, unwholesome, venomous, wicked.
antonym innocuous.

pernickety *adj* careful, carping, detailed, exacting, fastidious, fiddly, fine, finicky, fussy, hairsplitting, hard to please, nice, nit-picking, overprecise, painstaking, particular, punctilious, tricky.

peroration *n* closing remarks, conclusion, recap, recapitulation, recapping, reiteration, summary, summing up.

perpendicular *adj* orthogonal, plumb, precipitous, sheer, straight, upright, vertical.
antonym horizontal.

perpetrate *v* carry out, commit, do, effect, enact, execute, inflict, perform, practise, wreak.

perpetual *adj* abiding, ceaseless, constant, continual, continuous, deathless, endless, enduring, eternal, everlasting, immortal, incessant, infinite, interminable, lasting, never-ending, never-failing, perennial, permanent, persistent, recurrent, repeated, sempiternal, unceasing, unchanging, undying, unending, unfailing, unflagging, uninterrupted, unremitting, unvarying.
antonyms ephemeral, intermittent, transient.

perpetuate *v* commemorate, continue, eternalize, immortalize, keep alive, keep up, maintain, preserve, protract, sustain.

perplex *v* baffle, befuddle, bewilder, bother, complicate, confound, confuse, dumfound, embrangle, entangle, gravel, mix up, muddle, mystify, nonplus, pother, puzzle, stump, thicken, throw.

perplexed *adj* at a loss, baffled, bamboozled, befuddled, bewildered, confounded, confused, disconcerted, fuddled, muddled, mystified, nonplussed, puzzled, stumped, worried.

perplexing *adj* baffling, bewildering, complex, complicated, confusing, cryptic, difficult, distractive, enigmatic, hard, inexplicable, intricate, involved, knotty, labyrinthine, mysterious, mystifying, obscure, paradoxical, puzzling, strange, taxing, thorny, tough, unaccountable, vexatious, weird.
antonyms easy, simple.

perplexity *n* bafflement, bewilderment, brain teaser, brain twister, complexity, confusion, conundrum, difficulty, dilemma, enigma, incomprehension, intricacy, involvement, labyrinth, mystery, mystification, nonplus, obfuscation, obscuration, obscurity, paradox, poser, puzzle, puzzlement, puzzler, snarl, stupefaction, teaser.

perquisite *n* appanage, baksheesh, benefit, bonus, dividend, extra, fringe benefit, gratuity, perk, plus, tip.

persecute *v* afflict, annoy, badger, bait, bother, castigate, crucify, distress, dragoon, harass, haze, hound, hunt, ill-treat, injure, maltreat, martyr, molest, oppress, pester, pursue, tease, torment, torture, tyrannize, vex, victimize, worry.
antonyms accommodate, humour, indulge, pamper.

▲ *confusable word* prosecute.

persecution *n* abuse, baiting, bashing, castigation, discrimination, ill treatment, maltreatment, mistreatment, molestation, oppression, punishment, subjugation, suppression, torture, tyranny.

perseverance *n* assiduity, constancy, continuance, dedication, determination, diligence, doggedness, endurance, indefatigability, patience, persistence, pertinacity, purposefulness, resolution, sedulity, stamina, steadfastness, tenacity.

persevere *v* carry on, continue, endure, go on, hang in there, hang on, hold fast, hold on, keep at it, keep going, persist, plug away, pursue, remain, soldier on, stand firm, stick at it.
antonyms desist, discontinue, give up, stop.

persist *v* abide, carry on, continue, endure, insist, keep at it, last, linger, live on, persevere, remain, stand fast, stand firm.
antonyms desist, stop.

persistent *adj* assiduous, ceaseless, constant, continual, continuous, demanding, determined, dogged, endless, enduring, fixed, immovable, incessant, indefatigable, indomitable, insistent, interminable, lingering, never-ending,

obdurate, obstinate, perpetual, persevering, pertinacious, relentless, repeated, resolute, steadfast, steady, stubborn, tenacious, tireless, unceasing, unflagging, unrelenting, unremitting, zealous.

person *n* being, blighter, bod, body, cat, character, codger, cookie, customer, entity, fish, human, human being, individual, living soul, party, soul, specimen, type.
in person as large as life, in propria persona, personally.

persona *n* character, façade, face, front, image, mask, part, personality, public face, role.

personable *adj* affable, agreeable, amiable, attractive, charming, good-looking, handsome, likable, nice, outgoing, pleasant, pleasing, prepossessing, presentable, warm, winning.
antonyms disagreeable, unattractive.

personage *n* big shot, celebrity, dignitary, headliner, luminary, name, notable, personality, public figure, somebody, VIP, worthy.

personal[1] *adj* bodily, confidential, corporal, corporeal, exclusive, exterior, face-to-face, idiosyncratic, individual, inmost, innermost, intimate, material, own, particular, peculiar, physical, private, privy, special, tête-à-tête.
antonyms general, public, universal.

personal[2] *adj* ad hominem, cutting, derogatory, disparaging, insulting, nasty, nosey, offensive, pejorative, pointed, probing, slighting.

personality *n* attractiveness, celebrity, character, charisma, charm, disposition, dynamism, humour, identity, individuality, likableness, magnetism, make-up, nature, notable, personage, pleasantness, psyche, selfhood, selfness, star, temperament, traits.

personally *adv* alone, face to face, idiosyncratically, independently, individually, in person, oneself, privately, solely, specially, subjectively.

personification *n* delineation, embodiment, image, incarnation, likeness, living example, manifestation, personation, portrayal, recreation, representation, semblance.

personify *v* embody, epitomize, exemplify, express, image forth, incarnate, mirror, personate, portray, represent, symbolize, typify.

personnel *n* crew, employees, helpers, human resources, manpower, members, people, staff, workers, work force.

perspective *n* angle, aspect, attitude, context, mindset, objectivity, outlook, overview, panorama, proportion, prospect, relation, scene, slant, view, vista.

perspicacious *adj* acute, alert, astute, aware, clear-eyed, clear-sighted, clever, discerning, discriminating, far-sighted, keen, knowing, observant, penetrating, perceptive, percipient, sagacious, sharp, sharp-witted, shrewd.
antonyms obtuse, unobservant.

perspicacity *n* acuity, acumen, acuteness, brains, cleverness, discernment,

discrimination, insight, keenness, penetration, perceptiveness, percipience, perspicaciousness, perspicuity, sagaciousness, sagacity, sharpness, shrewdness, understanding, wisdom, wit.
antonym obstuseness.

perspicuity *n* clarity, clearness, comprehensibility, comprehensibleness, distinctness, explicitness, intelligibility, lucidity, penetrability, plainness, precision, straightforwardness, transparency.
antonyms incomprehensibility, unintelligibility.

perspicuous *adj* apparent, clear, comprehensible, crystal-clear, distinct, explicit, intelligible, lucid, manifest, obvious, plain, self-evident, straightforward, transparent, unambiguous, understandable.
antonyms muddled, opaque.

perspiration *n* diaphoresis, exudation, hidrosis, lather, moisture, sudor, sweat, water, wetness.

perspire *v* drip, exude, glow, secrete, sweat, swelter.

persuadable *adj* acquiescent, agreeable, amenable, compliant, flexible, gullible, impressionable, influenceable, malleable, persuasible, pliable, receptive, susceptible.
antonyms firm, inflexible, stubborn.

persuade *v* actuate, advise, allure, bring around, cajole, coax, convert, convince, counsel, entice, fast-talk, impel, incite, induce, influence, inveigle, lead on, lead to believe, lean on, prevail upon, prompt, satisfy, sell (on), sucker into, sway, sweet-talk, talk into, urge, wheedle, win over, work on.
antonyms discourage, dissuade.

persuasion *n* belief, blandishment, cajolery, camp, certitude, cogency, come-on, conversion, conviction, credo, creed, cult, denomination, eloquence, enticement, exhortation, faction, faith, fast talk, firm belief, force, inducement, influence, inveiglement, kind, opinion, party, persuasiveness, sales talk, school (of thought), sect, side, sort, stripe, suasion, sweet talk, view, wheedling.

persuasive *adj* assuring, cajoling, cogent, compelling, convincing, credible, effective, eloquent, forceful, honeyed, impelling, impressive, inducing, influential, logical, moving, persuasory, plausible, potent, powerful, sound, telling, touching, valid, weighty, winning.

pert *adj* audacious, bold, brash, brassy, brisk, cheeky, cocky, daring, flip, flippant, forward, fresh, gay, impertinent, impudent, insolent, jaunty, lively, nimble, perky, presumptuous, saucy, smart, spirited, sprightly, vivacious.
antonyms coy, shy.

pertain to *v* appertain to, apply to, be appropriate to, be part of, be relevant to, bear on, befit, belong to, come under, concern, refer to, regard, relate to.

pertinacious *adj* determined, dogged, headstrong, inflexible, intractable, mulish, obdurate, obstinate, persevering, persistent,

perverse, purposeful, relentless, resolute, self-willed, strong-willed, stubborn, tenacious, uncompromising, unyielding, willful.

pertinent *adj* ad rem, admissible, analogous, applicable, apposite, appropriate, apropos, apt, befitting, fit, fitting, germane, material, pat, proper, relevant, suitable, to the point, to the purpose.
antonyms inappropriate, irrelevant, unsuitable.

perturb *v* agitate, alarm, bother, confuse, disarrange, discompose, disconcert, discountenance, disorder, disquiet, disturb, excite, faze, fluster, muddle, ruffle, trouble, unsettle, upset, vex, worry.
antonyms compose, reassure.

perturbed *adj* agitated, alarmed, anxious, discomposed, disconcerted, disturbed, fearful, flappable, flurried, flustered, in a dither, in a tizzy, nervous, restless, shaken, troubled, uncomfortable, uneasy, unsettled, upset, worried.
antonym unperturbed.

perusal *n* browse, check, examination, inspection, look, read, run-through, scrutiny, study.

peruse *v* browse through, check, examine, inspect, look through, pore over, read, scan, scrutinize, study, vet.

pervade *v* affect, diffuse, extend throughout, fill, imbue, infuse, overspread, penetrate, percolate, permeate, saturate, spread throughout, suffuse.

pervasive *adj* common, diffuse, extensive, general, immanent, inescapable, omnipresent, permeating, pervading, prevalent, rife, ubiquitous, universal, widespread.

perverse *adj* aberrant, abnormal, balky, bloody-minded, cantankerous, contradictory, contrary, contumacious, cross-grained, cussed, delinquent, depraved, deviant, disobedient, dogged, fractious, froward, headstrong, ill-natured, ill-tempered, improper, incorrect, intractable, intransigent, irascible, miscreant, mulish, obdurate, obstinate, peevish, petulant, pig-headed, rebellious, recalcitrant, refractory, spiteful, stubborn, surly, troublesome, twisted, unhealthy, unmanageable, unreasonable, unwholesome, unyielding, warped, wayward, wicked, willful, wrong, wrong-headed, wry.
antonyms normal, reasonable.

perversion *n* aberration, abnormality, anomaly, corruption, debauchery, depravity, deviance, deviation, distortion, falsification, immorality, kink, kinkiness, misapplication, misconstruction, misinterpretation, misrepresentation, misuse, twisting, unnaturalness, vice, vitiation, wickedness.

perversity *n* contradictoriness, contrariety, contrariness, contumacy, cussedness, disobedience, frowardness, intransigence, irascibility, obduracy, obstinacy, refractoriness, waywardness, wrong-headedness.

pervert *v* abuse, bend, corrupt, debase, debauch, degrade, deprave, distort, divert, falsify, garble, lead astray, misapply, misconstrue, misinterpret, misrepresent, misuse, subvert, twist, vitiate, warp, wrest.

n debauchee, degenerate, deviant, psycho, weirdo.

perverted *adj* aberrant, abnormal, corrupt, debased, debauched, depraved, deviant, distorted, evil, freakish, immoral, kinky, misguided, sick, twisted, unhealthy, unnatural, vicious, vitiated, warped, wicked.

pessimism *n* cynicism, defeatism, dejection, depression, despair, despondency, distrust, gloom, gloominess, glumness, hopelessness, melancholy, negativism, Weltschmerz.

antonym optimism.

pessimist *n* Cassandra, cynic, defeatist, doom merchant, doomsayer, gloom and doom merchant, killjoy, melancholic, negativist, wet blanket, worrier, worrywart.

antonym optimist.

pessimistic *adj* bearish, bleak, cynical, dark, defeatist, dejected, depressed, despairing, despondent, dismal, distrustful, downbeat, downhearted, gloomy, glum, hopeless, melancholy, misanthropic, morose, negative, resigned, sad, worried.

antonym optimistic.

pest *n* annoyance, bane, blight, bore, bother, bug, canker, curse, irritation, nuisance, pain (in the neck), scourge, thorn in one's flesh, tormentor, trial, vexation.

pester *v* annoy, badger, bedevil, bother, bug, chivvy, disturb, dog, drive round the bend, drive up the wall, fret, get at, harass, harry, hassle, hector, hound, irk, nag, pick on, plague, ride, torment, worry.

pestilential *adj* annoying, bothersome, catching, communicable, contagious, contaminated, corrupting, dangerous, deadly, deleterious, destructive, detrimental, diseased, disease-ridden, evil, foul, galling, harmful, hazardous, infected, infectious, injurious, irksome, irritating, malignant, noxious, pernicious, pesky, pestiferous, plague-ridden, poisonous, ruinous, tainted, tiresome, troublesome, venomous, vexing, vicious.

pet *n* apple of one's eye, darling, doll, duck, ewe-lamb, favourite, idol, jewel, treasure.

adj beloved, cherished, dearest, favoured, favourite, particular, preferred, prized, special.

v baby, canoodle, caress, coddle, cosset, cuddle, dote on, fondle, indulge, kiss, mollycoddle, neck, pamper, pat, smooch, spoil, stroke, touch.

peter out cease, come to nothing, dissolve, drop off, dwindle, ebb, evaporate, fade, fail, stop, taper off, wane.

antonym come to fruition.

petite *adj* bijou, dainty, delicate, elfin, little, slight, small, tiny.

antonyms big, large.

petition *n* address, appeal, application, boon, entreaty, imploring, invocation, plea, prayer, request, round robin, solicitation, suit, supplication.

v appeal (to or for), apply to, ask, beg,

beseech, bid, call upon, entreat, implore, plead (with or for), pray, press, solicit, sue, supplicate, urge.

pet name *n* cognomen, diminutive, endearment, hypocorism, nickname, sobriquet.

petrified *adj* aghast, appalled, benumbed, calcified, dazed, dumfounded, fossilized, frozen, gorgonized, hardened, horrified, horror-stricken, immobilized, numb, ossified, paralysed, scared stiff, shocked, speechless, stone, stunned, stupefied, terrified, terror-stricken, transfixed.

petticoat *n* crinoline, farthingale, half slip, kirtle, slip, underskirt.

pettifogging *adj* argumentative, captious, casuistic, cavilling, circumlocutary, equivocating, faultfinding, hairsplitting, hypercritical, niggling, nit-picking, over-refined, quibbling, sophistic, subtle.

petty *adj* cheap, contemptible, grudging, illiberal, inessential, inferior, insignificant, junior, lesser, little, lower, mean, measly, minor, negligible, one-horse, paltry, picayune, piddling, quibbling, secondary, slight, small, small-minded, small-town, spiteful, stingy, subordinate, trifling, trivial, ungenerous, unimportant.

antonyms generous, important, large-hearted, significant, vital.

petulance *n* bad temper, crabbiness, discontent, ill humour, ill temper, irritability, peevishness, pettishness, pique, querulousness, spleen, sulkiness, sullenness, waspishness, whine, whining.

antonyms cheerfulness, good-humour.

petulant *adj* bad-tempered, captious, cavilling, crabby, cross, discontented, fretful, ill-humoured, impatient, irascible, irritable, moody, peevish, perverse, plaintive, querulous, snappish, sour, sulky, sullen, ungracious, waspish, whiny.

antonyms cheerful, good-humoured.

phantom *n* apparition, chimera, eidolon, figment (of the imagination), ghost, hallucination, illusion, manes, phantasm, revenant, shade, simulacrum, spectre, spirit, spook, vision, wraith.

adj ghostly, illusory, imagined, immaterial, spectral, wraithlike.

pharisaic *adj* canting, goody-goody, holier-than-thou, hypocritical, insincere, moralizing, pietistic, preachy, sanctimonious, self-righteous.

pharisee *n* deceiver, dissembler, dissimulator, fraud, humbug, hypocrite, phony, pietist, whited sepulchre.

phase *n* aspect, chapter, episode, facet, juncture, period, point, position, season, spell, stage, state, step, time.

phase out close, deactivate, discontinue, dispose of, ease out, eliminate, get rid of, remove, replace, run down, taper off, terminate, wind down, withdraw.

phenomenal *adj* amazing, eventful, exceptional, extraordinary, fantastic, marvellous, miraculous, outstanding, prodigious, remarkable, sensational, singular, stupendous, unbelievable, uncommon, unique, unparalleled, unusual, wonderful, wondrous.

phenomenon *n* appearance, circumstance, curiosity, episode, event, fact, happening, incident, marvel, miracle, nine day's wonder, occurrence, prodigy, rarity, sensation, sight, spectacle, wonder.

philanderer *n* Casanova, dallier, Don Juan, flirt, gallant, gay deceiver, ladies' man, lecher, libertine, Lothario, playboy, seducer, stud, trifler, wolf, woman chaser, womanizer.

philanthropic *adj* almsgiving, altruistic, beneficent, benevolent, benignant, bounteous, bountiful, charitable, eleemosynary, giving, gracious, humane, humanitarian, kind, kind-hearted, kindly, munificent, public-spirited.
antonym misanthropic.

philanthropist *n* almsgiver, altruist, angel, benefactor, contributor, donor, giver, good fairy, humanitarian, patron.
antonyms misanthrope, misanthropist.

philanthropy *n* agape, almsgiving, altruism, beneficence, benevolence, benignity, bounty, charitableness, charity, generosity, humanitarianism, kind-heartedness, liberality, munificence, open-handedness, patronage, public-spiritedness, unselfishness.

Philistine *n* barbarian, boor, bourgeois, Goth, ignoramus, lowbrow, Neanderthal, roughneck, vulgarian, yahoo.
antonym aesthete.
adj boorish, bourgeois, brutish, crass, ignorant, lowbrow, uncultivated, uncultured, uneducated, unlettered, unread, unrefined.

philosopher *n* dialectician, epistemologist, ethicist, intellectual, logician, metaphysician, sage, theorist, thinker, wise man.

philosophical *adj* abstract, analytical, calm, collected, composed, cool, dispassionate, epistemological, equanimous, erudite, impassive, imperturbable, learned, logical, metaphysical, patient, rational, resigned, sagacious, serene, stoical, theoretical, thoughtful, tranquil, unruffled, wise.

philosophy *n* aesthetics, attitude, beliefs, convictions, doctrine, epistemology, ideology, knowledge, logic, metaphysics, principle(s), rationale, rationalism, reason, reasoning, school, system, tenets, theory, thinking, thought, values, viewpoint, Weltanschauung, wisdom, worldview.

phlegmatic *adj* apathetic, bovine, calm, cool, dull, equanimous, even-keeled, heavy, impassive, imperturbable, indifferent, lethargic, listless, lukewarm, lymphatic, matter-of-fact, nonchalant, placid, sluggish, stoical, stolid, unconcerned, undemonstrative, unemotional, unflappable.
antonyms demonstrative, passionate.

phobia *n* abhorrence, anxiety, aversion, detestation, dislike, distaste, dread, fear, hang-up, hatred, horror, loathing, neurosis, obsession, repulsion, revulsion, terror, thing.
antonyms liking, love.

phony *adj* affected, assumed, bogus, counterfeit, fake, false, forged, imitation, pseudo, put-on, quack, sham, spurious, trick, ungenuine.
antonyms real, true.
n counterfeit, fake, faker, forgery, fraud, humbug, imposter, mountebank, pretender, quack, sham.

phosphorescent *adj* bright, fluorescent, glowing, luminescent, luminous, noctilucent, radiant, refulgent.

photograph *n* angiogram, daguerreotype, ferrotype, hologram, image, likeness, mug shot, photo, picture, print, shot, slide, snap, snapshot, still, transparency, ultrasound, x-ray.
v capture on film, film, record, shoot, snap, take, take a picture of, video.

photographic *adj* accurate, cinematic, detailed, exact, faithful, filmic, graphic, lifelike, minute, natural, naturalistic, pictorial, precise, realistic, representational, retentive, visual, vivid.

phrase *n* construction, expression, idiom, locution, maxim, motto, remark, saying, tag, utterance.
v couch, express, formulate, frame, present, pronounce, put (into words), say, style, term, utter, voice, word.

phraseology *n* argot, cant, diction, expression, idiom, jargon, language, parlance, patois, phrase, phrasing, speech, style, syntax, wording.

physical *adj* actual, bodily, carnal, concrete, corporal, corporeal, earthly, fleshly, incarnate, material, mortal, natural, palpable, real, sensible, solid, somatic, substantial, tangible, visible.
antonyms mental, spiritual.

physician *n* doc, doctor (of medicine), general practitioner, G.P., hakim, healer, intern, leech, M.D., medic, medical practitioner, medico, specialist.

physiognomy *n* countenance, face, features, kisser, looks, mug, visage.

physique *n* body, build, chassis, constitution, figure, form, frame, make-up, shape, structure.

picayune *adj* nit-picking, petty, small, small-minded, trifling, trivial.

pick *v* break (open), choose, crack, cull, cut, decide on, elect, fix upon, gather, handpick, harvest, opt for, pick at, pick out, pluck, prefer, provoke, pull, select, settle on, sift out, single out, start.
antonym reject.
n best, brightest and best, choice, choicest, cream, crème de la crème, decision, elite, flower, gem, jewel, option, pièce de résistance, preference, pride, prize, selection.
pick at nibble at, peck, play with, toy with.
pick off detach, gun down, hit, kill, plug, remove, shoot (at), snipe at.
pick on badger, bait, blame, bug, bully, carp at, cavil at, criticize, find fault with, get at, harp at, nag, needle, quibble with, single out, tease, torment.
pick out choose, cull, differentiate,

discriminate, distinguish, extract, handpick, notice, perceive, recognize, select, separate, single out, tell apart.

pick up acquire, apprehend, arrest, bust, buy, call for, capture, collar, collect, come across, earn, fetch, find, gain, gain ground, garner, gather, go (and) get, go for, grasp, happen on, haul in, hoist, improve, increase, learn, lift (up), master, mend, nab, obtain, perk up, pinch, pull in, purchase, raise, rally, recover, recuperate, refresh, run in, score, snap up, summon, take on board, take up, tidy up, uplift.

picket *n* demonstrator, dissenter, guard, lookout, outpost, paling, palisade, patrol, peg, picketer, post, protester, scout, sentinel, sentry, spotter, stake, stanchion, upright, vedette, watchman.
v blockade, boycott, corral, demonstrate, enclose, fence, hedge in, palisade, pen in, protest.

pickings *n* booty, earnings, gain, gravy, loot, plunder, proceeds, profits, returns, rewards, spoils, take, yield.

pickle *n* bind, crisis, difficulty, dilemma, exigency, fix, hot water, jam, pinch, predicament, quandary, scrape, spot, strait(s), tight spot.
v conserve, cure, marinade, preserve, steep.

pick-me-up *n* boost, cordial, fillip, refresher, refreshment, restorative, shot in the arm, stimulant, tonic.

pickpocket *n* cutpurse, dip, purse snatcher, thief.

picnic *n* breeze, cinch, duck soup, mere child's play, piece of cake, pushover, sinecure, snap.

pictorial *adj* diagrammatic, expressive, graphic, illustrated, photographic, representational, scenographic, schematic, striking, vivid.

picture *n* account, archetype, carbon copy, copy, dead ringer, delineation, depiction, description, double, drawing, duplicate, effigy, embodiment, engraving, epitome, essence, example, film, flick, graphic, icon, idea, ideogram, illustration, image, impression, likeness, look-alike, motion picture, movie, painting, personification, photograph, portrait, portrayal, print, re-creation, replica, representation, scene, similitude, sketch, spit, spitting image, tablature, twin, view, visualization.
v conceive of, delineate, depict, describe, draw, envisage, envision, illustrate, image, imagine, paint, photograph, portray, render, represent, see, show, sketch, visualize.

picturesque *adj* attractive, beautiful, charming, colourful, descriptive, graphic, pretty, quaint, scenic, striking, vivid.

piebald *adj* brindled, dappled, flecked, mottled, pied, pinto, skewbald, speckled, spotted.

piece *n* allotment, article, bit, chunk, coin, component, composition, constituent, creation, division, element, example, fraction, fragment, instance, item, length, morsel, mouthful, objet d'art, part, portion, production, quantity, sample, scrap, section, segment, share, shred, slice, snippet, specimen, stroke, study, work, work of art.

in pieces broken, burst, damaged, disintegrated, in bits, in smithereens, kaput, piecemeal, ruined, shattered, smashed, totalled.

piece together assemble, attach, compose, fit, fix, join, mend, patch, put together, repair, restore, unite.

pièce de résistance *n* chef-d'oeuvre, crowning achievement, jewel, magnum opus, masterpiece, masterwork, prize, showpiece.

piecemeal *adv* at intervals, bit by bit, by degrees, fitfully, in dribs and drabs, intermittently, little by little, one by one, piece by piece, separately, severally, slowly.
antonyms all at once, all together.
adj discrete, fragmentary, intermittent, interrupted, partial, patchy, scattered, unsystematic.
antonyms complete, entire, whole, wholesale.

pied *adj* brindled, dappled, flecked, irregular, motley, mottled, multicoloured, parti-coloured, piebald, skewball, spotted, streaked, varicoloured, variegated.

pie-in-the-sky *adj* fantastic, idealistic, impractical, lofty, romantic, unattainable, unrealistic, utopian, visionary.

pier *n* buttress, column, jetty, landing, landing place, pile, piling, pillar, post, promenade, quay, support, upright, wharf.

pierce *v* affect, barb, bite, bore (into), comprehend, cut, discern, drill, enter, fathom, gore, grasp, hurt, impale, injure, lancinate, move, pain, penetrate, perforate, pink, plumb, prick, probe, puncture, run through, see through, spike, stab, stick (into), sting, stir, strike, thrust, touch, transpierce, understand, wound.

piercing *adj* acute, agonizing, algid, arctic, biting, bitter, cold, deep-felt, discerning, earpiercing, earsplitting, excruciating, exquisite, fierce, freezing, frosty, gelid, high-pitched, icy, intense, keen, loud, nippy, numbing, painful, penetrating, powerful, probing, racking, raw, searching, severe, sharp, shattering, shooting, shrill, Siberian, stabbing, wintry.

piety *n* devotion, devoutness, dutifulness, duty, faith, godliness, grace, holiness, piousness, religion, religiosity, reverence, saintliness, sanctity, veneration.
antonym impiety.

piffle *n* balderdash, baloney, bunk, drivel, eyewash, foolishness, guff, hogwash, hooey, humbug, malarkey, nonsense, poppycock, rot, rubbish, taradiddle, tommyrot, trash, tripe, twaddle.

pig *n* animal, beast, boar, boor, brute, glutton, gormandizer, gourmand, greedy guts, grunter, guzzler, hog, piggy, piglet, porker, shoat, slob, sloven, sow, swine.

pigeonhole *n* box, category, class, classification, compartment, cubbyhole, cubicle, locker, niche, place, section, slot.

v alphabetize, catalogue, characterize, classify, codify, compartmentalize, defer, file, label, peg, postpone, put away, put off, shelve, slot, sort, typecast.

piggish *adj* beastly, boorish, brutish, coarse, filthy, gluttonous, gormandizing, greedy, slobby, slovenly, swinish, unmannerly.

pig-headed *adj* bull-headed, contrary, cross-grained, dense, froward, inflexible, intractable, intransigent, mulish, obstinate, perverse, self-willed, stiff-necked, stubborn, stupid, unyielding, willful, wrong-headed.

antonyms flexible, tractable.

pigment *n* colour, colorant, colouring, colouring matter, dye, dyestuff, hue, paint, stain, tempera, tincture, tint.

pile[1] *n* accumulation, assemblage, assortment, building, bundle, cock, collection, edifice, erection, fortune, heap, hoard, killing, mass, mint, mound, mountain, mow, packet, pot, stack, stockpile, store, structure, wad.

v charge, climb, crowd, crush, flock, flood, heap, jam, load (up), pack, rush, stack, store, stream.

pile up accumulate, amass, assemble, build up, collect, gather, hoard (up), stack (up), stockpile, store up.

pile[2] *n* bar, beam, column, foundation, pier, piling, post, rib, stake, stanchion, support, upright.

pile[3] *n* down, fur, fuzz, fuzziness, hair, nap, plush, shag.

piles *n* a great deal, a lot, heaps, loads, masses, millions, oceans, oodles, plenty, quantities, scads, stacks, tons.

pilfer *v* appropriate, embezzle, filch, finger, help oneself to, lift, make off with, mooch, palm, peculate, pinch, purloin, rifle, snaffle, steal, swipe, thieve.

pilgrim *n* crusader, haji, peregrine, traveller, wanderer, wayfarer.

pilgrimage *n* crusade, excursion, expedition, haj, journey, mission, odyssey, peregrination, quest, tour, trip.

pill *n* ball, bolus, capsule, contraceptive, globule, pellet, tablet.

pillage *v* despoil, freeboot, loot, maraud, plunder, raid, ransack, ravage, raze, rifle, rob, sack, seize, spoil, spoliate, strip, vandalize, wreck.

n booty, depredation, devastation, harrying, loot, looting, marauding, plunder, plundering, rapine, robbery, sack, seizure, spoils, spoliation.

pillar *n* baluster, bastion, column, leader, leading light, mainstay, mast, pier, pilaster, piling, post, prop, rock, shaft, stanchion, support, supporter, tower of strength, upholder, upright, worthy.

pillory *v* brand, cast a slur on, denounce, hold up to shame, lash, mock, pour scorn on, revile, ridicule, show up, stigmatize.

pilot *n* airman, airwoman, aviator, captain, conductor, coxswain, director, flier, guide, helmsman, leader, navigator, operator, steersman.

v boss, conduct, control, direct, drive, fly, guide, handle, lead, manage, navigate, operate, run, shepherd, steer.

adj experimental, model, test, trial.

pimp *n* bawd, fleshmonger, go-between, pander, procurer, white slaver, whoremaster, whoremonger.

pimple *n* blackhead, blemish, boil, mark, pustule, spot, swelling, whelk, whitehead, zit.

pin *v* affix, attach, fasten, fix, hold down, hold fast, immobilize, join, nail, pin down, pinion, press, restrain, secure, skewer, staple, tack.

n bolt, breastpin, brooch, clip, fastener, nail, peg, rivet, screw, spike, spindle, stickpin, tack, tiepin.

on pins and needles agitated, anxious, edgy, excited, impatient, in suspense, jittery, nervous, uneasy, unsettled.

pin down bind, confine, constrain, determine, fix, hold, hold down, home in on, identify, immobilize, locate, nail, nail down, name, pinpoint, put one's finger on, restrain, specify, tie down, transfix, zero in on.

pincers *n* chelae, forceps, nippers, pliers, tweezers, vice.

pinch *v* apprehend, arrest, bust, chafe, collar, compress, confine, cramp, crush, distress, economize, filch, grasp, hurt, lift, limit, nab, nip, oppress, pain, pick up, pilfer, press, purloin, run in, scrimp, skimp, snaffle, snatch, snitch, spare, squeeze, steal, stint, swipe, tweak.

n bit, crisis, dash, difficulty, distress, emergency, exigency, hardship, jam, jot, mite, necessity, nip, oppression, pain, pass, pickle, plight, predicament, pressure, soupçon, speck, squeeze, strait, stress, taste, tweak.

pinched *adj* careworn, clamped, constricted, drawn, gaunt, haggard, narrowed, nipped, peaked, starved, straitened, thin, worn.

pine *v* ache, crave, decline, deteriorate, droop, dwindle, fade (away), flag, grieve, hanker, hunger, languish, long, sicken, sigh, sink, thirst, waste away, weaken, wilt, wish, wither (away), yearn, yen.

pinion *v* bind, chain, confine, fasten, fetter, hobble, immobilize, manacle, pin (down), shackle, tie, truss.

pink[1] *n* acme, best, extreme, flower, height, peak, perfection, summit, top.

adj blushing, flushed, reddish, rose, roseate, rosy, salmon.

pink[2] *v* incise, notch, perforate, prick, punch, puncture, scallop, score, serrate.

pinnacle *n* acme, apex, apogee, cap, cone, crest, crown, culmination, eminence, height, needle, obelisk, peak, pyramid, spire, steeple, summit, top, tower, turret, vertex, zenith.

pinpoint *v* define, distinguish, home in on, identify, locate, place, put one's finger on, spot, zero in on.

pitiless

pint-sized *adj* diminutive, dwarf, little, midget, miniature, pocket, pocket-size, small, tiny, wee.

antonyms giant, huge.

pioneer *n* colonist, colonizer, developer, explorer, founder, founding father, frontiersman, innovator, leader, settler, trailblazer, vanguard.

v begin, blaze a trail, break new ground, create, develop, discover, establish, found, initiate, instigate, institute, invent, launch, lead, open up, originate, prepare, start.

pious *adj* dedicated, devoted, devout, God-fearing, godly, good, goody-goody, holier-than-thou, holy, hypocritical, moral, pietistic, religiose, religious, reverent, righteous, saintly, sanctimonious, self-righteous, spiritual, unctuous, virtuous.

antonym impious.

pipe *n* briar, clay, conduit, conveyor, corncob, duct, fife, fistula, flue, hookah, horn, hose, line, main, meerschaum, passage, pipeline, toot, tooter, tube, whistle.

v carry, channel, cheep, chirp, conduct, convey, funnel, peep, play, sing, siphon, sound, supply, toot, tootle, transmit, trill, tweet, twitter, warble, whistle.

pipe dream *n* castle in Spain, castle in the air, chimera, daydream, delusion, dream, fancy, fantasy, illusion, mirage, notion, reverie, romance, vagary.

pipeline *n* channel, conduit, conveyor, duct, line, passage, pipe, tube.

pipsqueak *n* hobbledehoy, midget, nobody, nonentity, nothing, shrimp, squirt, twerp, upstart, whippersnapper.

antonym somebody.

piquancy *n* bite, colour, edge, excitement, flavour, ginger, interest, juice, kick, pep, pepperiness, pizzazz, punch, pungency, raciness, relish, sharpness, spice, spiciness, spirit, tang, vigour, vitality, zest, zip.

piquant *adj* appetizing, biting, interesting, lively, peppery, poignant, provocative, pungent, racy, salty, savoury, scintillating, sharp, sparkling, spicy, spirited, stimulating, stinging, tangy, tart, titillating, zesty.

antonyms banal, bland.

pique *n* anger, annoyance, displeasure, huffiness, irritation, offence, resentment, umbrage, vexation, wounded pride.

v affront, annoy, arouse, displease, excite, gall, galvanize, get (to), goad, incense, irk, irritate, kindle, mortify, nettle, offend, peeve, provoke, put out, rile, rouse, spur, stimulate, sting, stir, vex, whet, wound.

piracy *n* bootlegging, brigandage, buccaneering, copyright, freebooting, hijacking, infringement, plagiarism, rapine, robbery, stealing, theft.

pirate *n* brigand, buccaneer, copyright infringer, corsair, filibuster, freebooter, marauder, picaroon, plagiarist, raider, rover, sea rat, sea robber, sea rover, sea wolf, water rat.

v appropriate, borrow, copy, crib, lift, pinch, plagiarize, poach, reproduce (illegally), steal.

pirouette *v* gyrate, pivot, spin, turn, twirl, whirl.

pistol *n* automatic, derringer, gat, gun, handgun, iron, piece, revolver, rod, sidearm, six-shooter, zip gun.

pit *n* abyss, alveolus, cavity, chasm, coal mine, crater, dent, depression, dimple, excavation, gulf, hole, hollow, indentation, mine, oubliette, pitfall, pockmark, pothole, trap, trench.

pit against fight (with), match, oppose, set against.

pitch *v* bung, cast, chuck, dive, drop, erect, fall headlong, fix, fling, flounder, heave, hurl, hustle, launch, lob, locate, loft, lurch, place, plant, plunge, push, raise, roll, sell, settle, set up, sling, slope, stagger, station, throw, topple, toss, tumble.

n advertisement, angle, cant, commercial, degree, dip, frequency, gradient, ground, harmonic, height, incline, level, line, lurch, modulation, park, patter, playing field, plug, plunge, point, position, sales talk, slope, spiel, sports field, steepness, throw, tilt, timbre, tone, toss.

pitch-dark *adj* black, dark, inky, jet-black, pitch-black, pitchy, Stygian, unilluminated, unlit.

pitcher *n* bottle, can, container, crock, ewer, jar, jug, urn, vessel.

piteous *adj* affecting, deplorable, distressing, doleful, dolorous, grievous, heart-rending, heart-rending, lamentable, miserable, mournful, moving, pathetic, pitiable, pitiful, plaintive, poignant, sad, sorrowful, touching, woeful, wretched.

pitfall *n* catch, danger, difficulty, downside, drawback, hazard, hidden danger, peril, snag, snare, stumbling-block, trap.

pith *n* consequence, core, crux, depth, essence, force, gist, gravamen, heart, import, importance, kernel, marrow, matter, meaning, meat, moment, nub, point, power, pulp, quintessence, salient point, significance, strength, substance, value, weight.

pithy *adj* aphoristic, apothegmatic, brief, cogent, compact, concise, epigrammatic, expressive, forceful, laconic, meaningful, pointed, short, succinct, telling, terse, trenchant.

antonyms prolix, verbose, wordy.

pitiable *adj* contemptible, distressed, distressful, distressing, doleful, grievous, lamentable, miserable, mournful, pathetic, piteous, poor, sad, sorry, woeful, wretched.

pitiful *adj* abject, base, beggarly, contemptible, deplorable, despicable, disgraceful, distressing, grievous, heartbreaking, heart-rending, hopeless, inadequate, insignificant, lamentable, low, mean, miserable, paltry, pathetic, piteous, pitiable, sad, scurvy, shabby, sorry, vile, woeful, worthless, wretched.

pitiless *adj* brutal, callous, cold-blooded, cold-hearted, cruel, flinty, hard-hearted, harsh, heartless, implacable, inexorable, inhuman, merciless, obdurate, relentless, ruthless, uncaring, unfeeling, unmerciful, unpitying, unsympathetic.

antonyms compassionate, gentle, kind, merciful.

pittance *n* chicken feed, crumb, drop (in the ocean), mite, modicum, peanuts, trifle.

pitted *adj* blemished, dented, dinted, gouged, holey, indented, lacunal, marked, nicked, notched, pockmarked, pocky, potholed, punctuated, riddled, rough, rutty, scarred, scratched.

pity *n* charity, clemency, commiseration, compassion, condolence, crime, crying shame, fellow feeling, forbearance, kindness, mercy, misfortune, regret, shame, sin, sympathy, tenderness, understanding.

antonyms cruelty, disdain, scorn.

v bleed for, commiserate with, condole with, feel for, grieve for, sympathize with, take pity on, weep for.

pivot *n* axis, axle, centre, focal point, fulcrum, heart, hinge, hub, kingpin, linchpin, spindle, swivel.

v depend, hang, hinge, lie, rely, revolve, rotate, spin, swing, swivel, turn, twirl.

pivotal *adj* axial, central, climactic, critical, crucial, decisive, determining, focal, important, key, vital.

pixie *n* brownie, elf, fairy, gnome, goblin, imp, leprechaun, puck, sprite.

placard *n* advertisement, bill, billboard, poster, public notice, sandwich board, sign, sign board, sticker.

placate *v* appease, assuage, calm, conciliate, humour, lull, mollify, pacify, propitiate, quiet, satisfy, soothe, win over.

antonyms anger, enrage, incense, infuriate.

place *n* abode, accommodation, affair, apartment, appointment, area, arena, berth, billet, building, business, city, concern, district, domicile, duty, dwelling, employment, flat, function, home, house, job, locale, locality, location, locus, manor, mansion, neighbourhood, office, pad, point, position, post, prerogative, property, quarter, rank, region, residence, responsibility, right, role, room, seat, site, situation, space, spot, station, status, stead, town, venue, vicinity, village, whereabouts.

v allocate, appoint, arrange, assign, associate, charge, class, classify, commission, deposit, dispose, dump, entrust, establish, fix, give, grade, group, identify, impose, install, invest, know, lay, locate, order, plant, position, put, put one's finger on, rank, recognize, remember, rest, set, settle, situate, sort, stand, station, stick.

in place of as an alternative to, as a replacement for, as a substitute for, in exchange for, in lieu of, instead of.

placement *n* appointment, arrangement, assignment, attribution, classification, deployment, disposition, distribution, emplacement, employment, engagement, grouping, installation, locating, location, ordering, positioning, ranking, stationing.

placid *adj* calm, collected, composed, cool, equable, even, even-tempered, gentle, halcyon, imperturbable, irenic, level-headed, mild, peaceful, quiet, reposeful, restful, self-possessed, serene, still, tranquil, undisturbed, unexcitable, unmoved, unruffled, untroubled.

antonyms agitated, jumpy.

plagiarism *n* appropriation, borrowing, copying, counterfeiting, cribbing, imitation, infringement, lifting, piracy, reproduction, theft.

plagiarize *v* appropriate, borrow, counterfeit, crib, infringe, lift, pirate, reproduce, steal, thieve.

plague *n* affliction, aggravation, annoyance, bane, blight, bother, calamity, cancer, contagion, curse, death, disease, epidemic, evil, infection, irritant, nuisance, pain, pandemic, pest, pestilence, problem, scourge, thorn in the flesh, torment, trial, vexation, visitation.

v afflict, annoy, badger, bedevil, bother, distress, disturb, fret, harass, harry, hassle, haunt, hound, molest, pain, persecute, pester, tease, torment, torture, trouble, vex.

plain *adj* apparent, artless, audible, austere, bare, basic, blunt, candid, clear, clinical, common, commonplace, comprehensible, direct, discreet, distinct, downright, dull, even, everyday, evident, flat, forthright, frank, frugal, guileless, homebred, homely, homespun, honest, humble, ill-favoured, ingenuous, legible, level, lowly, lucid, manifest, modest, muted, obvious, open, ordinary, patent, plain-spoken, plane, pure, restrained, self-coloured, self-evident, severe, simple, sincere, smooth, Spartan, stark, straightforward, transparent, ugly, unadorned, unaffected, unambiguous, unattractive, unbeautiful, understandable, undistinguished, unelaborate, unembellished, unfigured, unhandsome, unlovely, unmistakable, unobstructed, unornamented, unostentatious, unpatterned, unprepossessing, unpretentious, untrimmed, unvarnished, visible, workaday.

antonyms abstruse, attractive, elaborate, exaggerated, ostentatious, rich, striking, unclear.

n flat, flats, grassland, llano, lowland, open country, pampas, plateau, prairie, steppe, tableland, veld.

plain-spoken *adj* blunt, candid, direct, downright, explicit, forthright, frank, free-spoken, honest, open, outright, outspoken, plain, straightforward, truthful, unequivocal.

plaintive *adj* disconsolate, dismal, doleful, dolorous, grief-stricken, grievous, heart-rending, melancholy, mournful, pathetic, piteous, pitiful, rueful, sad, sorrowful, wistful, woebegone, woeful.

plan *n* aim, blueprint, chart, contrivance, delineation, design, device, diagram, drawing, goal, idea, illustration, intention, layout, map, method, plot, procedure, program, project, proposal, proposition, representation, scenario, schedule, scheme, sketch, strategy, suggestion, system.

v aim, arrange, concoct, conspire, contemplate, contrive, design, devise, draft, envisage, formulate, frame, intend, invent, mean, organize, outline, plot, premeditate, prepare, propose, purpose, scheme.

plane¹ *n* class, condition, degree, echelon, footing, level, position, rank, rung, stage, stratum.

adj even, flat, flush, horizontal, level, plain, planar, regular, smooth, uniform.

plane² *n* airplane, aircraft, airliner, bomber, fighter, glider, jet, jumbo, jumbo jet, seaplane, VTOL.

v fly, glide, sail, skate, skim, soar, volplane, wing.

plangent *adj* clangorous, deep, loud, mournful, plaintive, resonant, resounding, reverberating, ringing, sonorous, sorrowful, vibrant.

plant¹ *n* bush, flower, herb, shrub, vegetable, weed, wort.

v bury, embed, establish, fix, found, implant, inlay, insert, inset, institute, lodge, put in the ground, root, scatter, seed, set, set out, settle, sow, transplant.

plant² *n* apparatus, equipment, factory, foundry, gear, machinery, mill, shop, works, workshop, yard.

plaque *n* badge, cartouche, medal, medallion, panel, plate, shield, slab, tablet.

plaster *n* adhesive plaster, bandage, compress, dressing, gypsum, mortar, plaster of Paris, poultice, stucco.

v bedaub, besmear, coat, cover, daub, overlay, smear, smooth, spackle, spread.

plastic *adj* changeable, compliant, docile, ductile, fictile, flexible, impressionable, malleable, manageable, mouldable, pliable, pliant, receptive, responsive, soft, submissive, supple, teachable, tractable.

antonyms inflexible, rigid.

plate *n* charger, course, covering, dish, helping, illustration, lame, lamella, lath, layer, lithograph, palette, panel, plateful, platter, portion, print, scale, serving, sheet, slab, trencher.

v anodize, coat, cover, electroplate, face, galvanize, gild, laminate, nickel, overlay, silver, tin, veneer, zinc.

plateau *n* grade, highland, level, mesa, plain, stability, stage, table, tableland, upland.

platform *n* dais, gantry, manifesto, objective(s), party line, podium, policy, policies, principle(s), program, rostrum, stage, stand, tenet(s).

platitude *n* banality, bromide, chestnut, cliché, commonplace, inanity, pat answer, truism.

platitudinous *adj* banal, clichéd, commonplace, corny, dull, flat, hackneyed, overworked, pat, set, stale, stock, timeworn, tired, trite, truistic, vapid, well-worn.

platonic *adj* chaste, ideal, idealistic, incorporeal, intellectual, non-physical, spiritual, transcendent.

platoon *n* battery, company, group, outfit, patrol, squad, squadron, team, unit.

platter *n* charger, dish, plate, salver, tray, trencher.

plaudits *n* acclaim, acclamation, accolade(s), a hand, applause, approbation, approval, bouquet(s), clapping, commendation, congratulations, hurrahs, kudos, ovation, praise, standing ovation.

plausible *adj* believable, colourable, conceivable, convincing, credible, fair-spoken, glib, likely, logical, persuasive, possible, probable, reasonable, smooth, smooth-talking, smooth-tongued, specious, tenable.

antonyms implausible, improbable, unlikely.

play *v* act, bet, bet on, caper, challenge, chance, compete, contend, direct, execute, fiddle, fidget, flirt, fool around, frisk, frolic, gamble, gambol, have fun, hazard, impersonate, interfere, participate (in), perform, personate, portray, represent, revel, risk, rival, romp, speculate (on), sport, string along, take, take on, take part (in), take the part of, trifle, vie with, wager.

antonym work.

n action, activity, amusement, caper, comedy, diversion, drama, elbowroom, entertainment, exercise, farce, foolery, freedom, frolic, fun, gambling, gamboling, game, gaming, give, humour, jest, joking, lark, latitude, leeway, margin, masque, motion, move, movement, operation, pastime, performance, piece, range, recreation, romp, room, rope, scope, show, space, sport, sweep, swing, teasing, tragedy, transaction, working.

play around dally, flirt, fool around, mess around, philander, trifle.

play ball collaborate, co-operate, do business, go along, play along, reciprocate, respond, show willingness, team up, work together.

play by ear ad-lib, do offhand, extemporize, fake, improvise, wing it.

play down de-emphasize, gloss over, make light of, make little of, minimize, soft-pedal, underplay, underrate, undervalue.

play for time delay, drag one's feet, filibuster, hang fire, hesitate, procrastinate, stall, temporize.

play havoc with confuse, demolish, destroy, devastate, disorganize, disrupt, mess up, ruin, wreck.

play on abuse, affect, capitalize on, exploit, make use of, milk, misuse, profit by, take advantage of, trade on, turn to (good) account, utilize.

play the fool clown around, fool around, horse around, mess around, monkey around, skylark.

play the game acquiesce, conform, keep in step, play by the rules, play fair, toe the line, yield.

play up accentuate, dramatize, emphasize,

exaggerate, exploit, highlight, magnify, make an issue of, overemphasize, spotlight.

play up to blandish, bootlick, butter up, court, curry favour with, dance attendance on, fawn on, flatter, ingratiate oneself with, make up to, soft-soap, suck up to, toady to.

play with fire ask for trouble, burn one's fingers, court disaster, flirt with danger, go in harm's way, skate on thin ice, take risks, tempt, Providence, walk a thin line.

playboy *n* debauchee, ladies' man, libertine, man about town, philanderer, rake, roué, socialite, womanizer.

player *n* actor, actress, artist, artiste, athlete, bandsman, competitor, contender, contestant, entertainer, gambler, gamester, instrumentalist, jock, musician, participant, performer, sportsman, sportswoman, teammate, Thespian, trouper.

playful *adj* animated, arch, cheerful, coltish, coquettish, coy, flirtatious, frisky, frolicsome, full of fun, gamesome, gay, good-natured, humorous, impish, jesting, joking, joyous, kittenish, lively, merry, mischievous, prankish, puckish, roguish, rollicking, spirited, sportive, sprightly, tongue-in-cheek, vivacious, waggish.

antonyms serious, stern.

playmate *n* buddy, chum, companion, comrade, friend, mate, neighbour, pal, playfellow.

plaything *n* amusement, bauble, game, gewgaw, gimcrack, pastime, puppet, toy, trifle, trinket.

playwright *n* dramatist, dramatizer, dramaturge, screenwriter, scriptwriter.

plea *n* action, allegation, appeal, argument, asking, begging, cause, claim, defence, entreaty, excuse, explanation, extenuation, intercession, invocation, justification, petition, prayer, pretext, reason, request, suit, supplication, vindication.

plead *v* adduce evidence, allege, answer, appeal, argue, ask, assert, beg, beseech, crave, entreat, implore, importune, maintain, moot, offer as an excuse, petition, put forward, request, solicit, speak for, supplicate, urge.

pleasant *adj* acceptable, affable, agreeable, amiable, amusing, appealing charming, cheerful, cheery, congenial, cool, delectable, delightful, engaging, enjoyable, euphoneous, fair, fine, friendly, genial, good-humoured, gratifying, likable, lovely, nice, pleasing, pleasurable, refreshing, satisfying, sunshiny, toothsome, welcome, winsome.

antonyms distasteful, nasty, repugnant, unpleasant.

pleasantry *n* badinage, banter, bon mot, jest, joke, persiflage, quip, sally, teasing, witticism.

please *v* amuse, be to one's liking, captivate, cater to, charm, cheer, choose, content, delight, desire, enchant, entertain, gladden, go for, gratify, humour, indulge, like, make one happy, opt, pleasure, prefer, rejoice, satisfy, see fit, suit, think fit, tickle, tickle pink, want, will, wish.

antonyms anger, annoy, displease.

pleased *adj* contented, delighted, elated, euphoric, glad, gratified, happy, in high spirits, on cloud nine, over the moon, satisfied, thrilled, tickled (pink).

antonyms annoyed, displeased.

pleasing *adj* acceptable, agreeable, amiable, amusing, attractive, charming, congenial, delightful, engaging, enjoyable, entertaining, good, gratifying, likable, nice, pleasant, pleasurable, polite, satisfying, to one's liking, welcome, winning.

antonym unpleasant.

pleasurable *adj* agreeable, amusing, congenial, delightful, diverting, enjoyable, entertaining, fun, good, gratifying, lovely, nice, pleasant, pleasing.

antonyms bad, disagreeable.

pleasure *n* amusement, bliss, choice, comfort, command, complacency, contentment, delectation, delight, desire, diversion, ease, enjoyment, gladness, gratification, happiness, inclination, joy, mind, option, pleasantness, preference, purpose, recreation, satisfaction, solace, will, wish.

antonyms displeasure, pain, sorrow, trouble.

pleat *v* crease, crimp, flute, fold, gather, goffer, plait, pucker, shirr, tuck.

plebeian *adj* base, baseborn, blue-collar, coarse, common, homespun, ignoble, low, lowborn, lower-class, mean, peasant, proletarian, uncultivated, unrefined, vulgar, working-class.

antonyms aristocratic, noble, patrician.

n average citizen, common man, commoner, person in the street, peasant, pleb, proletarian, worker.

antonyms aristocrat, noble, patrician.

plebiscite *n* ballot, poll, referendum, straw vote, vote.

pledge *n* assurance, bail, bond, collateral, covenant, deposit, earnest, gage, guarantee, health, oath, pawn, promise, security, surety, toast, token, undertaking, vow, warranty, word, word of honour.

v bind, contract, drink to, engage, ensure, gage, guarantee, mortgage, plight, promise, secure, swear, toast, undertake, vouch, vow, warrant.

plenary *adj* absolute, complete, entire, full, general, integral, open, sweeping, thorough, unconditional, unlimited, unqualified, unrestricted, whole.

plenipotentiary *n* ambassador, dignitary, diplomat, emissary, envoy, legate, minister, nuncio.

plenitude *n* abundance, amplitude, bounty, completeness, copiousness, cornucopia, entirety, excess, fullness, muchness, overflow, plenteousness, plentifulness, plenty, plethora, prodigality, profusion, repletion, store, wealth.

antonym scarcity.

plentiful *adj* abounding, abundant, a dime a dozen, ample, aplenty, bounteous, bountiful, bumper, complete, copious, enough and to spare, fertile, fruitful, galore, generous, inexhaustible, infinite, lavish, liberal, luxuriant, overflowing, plenteous, productive, profuse, prolific, superabundant.

antonyms rare, scanty, scarce.

plenty *n* abundance, affluence, a fund, a plethora, a profusion, copiousness, enough, fertility, fruitfulness, heap(s), lots, luxury, mass, masses, milk and honey, mountain(s), oodles, opulence, overabundance, pile(s), plenitude, plenteousness, plentifulness, prosperity, quantities, stack(s), ton(s), volume(s), wealth.

antonyms lack, need, scarcity, want.

plethora *n* excess, glut, overabundance, overfullness, oversupply, profusion, superabundance, superfluity, surfeit, surplus.

pliable *adj* accommodating, adaptable, amenable, bendable, biddable, compliant, conformable, docile, ductile, easily led, flexible, impressionable, influenceable, limber, lithe, malleable, manageable, persuadable, plastic, pliant, receptive, responsive, suggestible, supple, susceptible, teachable, tractable, yielding.

antonyms inflexible, rigid.

plight¹ *n* adversity, bind, circumstance(s), condition, crunch, difficulty, dilemma, extremity, hardship, hole, jam, perplexity, pickle, predicament, quandary, scrape, situation, spot, state, straits, tight spot, trouble.

plight² *v* affiance, contract, covenant, engage, give one's word (of honour), guarantee, pledge, promise, propose, swear, vouch, vow.

plod *v* clump, drag, drudge, grind, grub, labour, lumber, moil, peg, persevere, plough, plug, slog, soldier, stomp, sweat, toil, tramp, tread, trudge.

plodder *n* drudge, dullard, foot-dragger, grub, hack, slogger, slowpoke, stick-in-the-mud, toiler, workhorse.

antonym highflier.

plot¹ *n* action, cabal, conspiracy, design, diagram, intrigue, machination(s), map, outline, plan, scenario, scheme, story, story line, stratagem, subject, theme, thread.

v brew, cabal, calculate, chart, collude, compass, compute, conceive, concoct, conspire, contrive, cook up, design, devise, draft, draw, frame, hatch, imagine, intrigue, lay, locate, machinate, manoeuvre, map, mark, outline, plan, position, premeditate, project, scheme.

plot² *n* allotment, area, field, green, ground, lot, parcel, patch, tract.

plotter *n* caballer, conspirator, contriver, intriguer, Machiavellian, machinator, planner, schemer, strategist.

plough *v* break, cultivate, cut, dig, furrow, plod, ridge, spade, till.

ploy *n* artifice, contrivance, device, dodge, gambit, game, manoeuvre, move, ruse, scheme, stratagem, subterfuge, tactic, trick, wile.

pluck¹ *n* backbone, boldness, bravery, courage, determination, fortitude, gameness,

grit, guts, hardihood, heart, intrepidity, mettle, nerve, resolution, spirit, spunk, tenacity.

antonyms cowardice, weakness.

pluck² *v* catch, clutch, collect, depilate, deplume, divest of, draw, extract, gather, harvest, jerk, pick, plunk, pull, pull off, pull out, rob, snatch, strum, swindle, thrum, tug, twang, tweak, yank.

plucky *adj* bold, brave, courageous, daring, doughty, game, gritty, gutsy, hardy, heroic, intrepid, mettlesome, resolute, spirited, spunky, tenacious, unflinching, valiant.

antonyms feeble, weak.

plug *n* ad, advert, advertisement, bung, cake, chew, cork, dottle, good word, hype, mention, piece, pigtail, publicity, push, quid, recommendation, spigot, spile, stopper, stopple, tampion, tampon, twist, wad.

v advertise, block, build up, bung up, choke, close (off), cork, cover, drudge, fill, grind, hype, labour, mention, pack, peg away, plod, promote, publicize, push, recommend, seal, slog, stop, stopper, stopple, stop up, stuff, talk up, tamp, toil.

plum *n* bonus, catch, find, pick, prize, sinecure, treasure, trophy.

plumb *n* lead, plumb bob, plummet, sinker, weight.

adv absolutely, bang, completely, dead, exactly, perpendicularly, precisely, slap, smack-dab, spot (on), square, squarely, up and down, vertically.

v delve (into), explore, fathom, gauge, investigate, mark, measure, penetrate, probe, search, sound, unravel.

plume *n* aigrette, crest, feather, pappus, pinion, quill, tuft.

plume oneself on be proud of, boast about, congratulate oneself on, exult in, glory in, pat oneself on the back for, pique oneself on, preen oneself on, pride oneself on.

plummet *v* crash, descend, dive, drop, fall, hurtle, nose-dive, plunge, stoop, swoop, tumble.

antonym soar.

plump¹ *adj* ample, beefy, burly, buxom, chubby, corpulent, dumpy, endomorphic, fat, fleshy, full, obese, portly, pudgy, roly-poly, rotund, round, stout, tubby, well-upholstered.

antonyms skinny, thin.

plump² *v* collapse, descend, drop, dump, fall, flop, sink, slump.

adv abruptly, directly, heavily, straight, suddenly.

plump for back, champion, choose, favour, opt for, select, side with, support, vote for.

plunder *v* despoil, devastate, loot, pillage, raid, ransack, ravage, rifle, rob, sack, spoil, spoliate, steal, strip.

n booty, despoilment, ill-gotten gains, loot, pickings, pillage, prey, prize, rapine, spoils, swag.

plunge *v* career, cast, charge, dash, decrease, descend, dip, dive, dive-bomb, douse, drop, fall, go down, hurtle, immerse, jump, lurch, nose-dive, pitch, plummet, rush, sink, submerge, swoop, tear, throw, tumble.

n chance, collapse, decrease, descent, dive, drop, fall, immersion, jump, lowering, submersion, swoop, tumble.

plurality *n* bulk, diversity, galaxy, majority, mass, most, multiplicity, multitude, numerousness, preponderance, profusion, variety.

plus *n* advantage, asset, benefit, bonus, credit, extra, gain, good point, perk, surplus.
antonym minus.

plush *adj* affluent, costly, deluxe, grandiose, lavish, luxurious, luxury, opulent, palatial, rich, ritzy, sumptuous.

plutocrat *n* billionaire, capitalist, Croesus, Dives, fat cat, magnate, millionaire, moneybags, multimillionaire, rich man (or woman), tycoon.

ply[1] *v* assail, be busy at (or doing), beseige, beset, bombard, carry on, cruise, employ, exercise, follow, handle, harass, importune, manipulate, navigate, practise, press, pursue, run, sail, set upon, swing, urge upon, use, utilize, wield, work at (or with).

ply[2] *n* fold, layer, leaf, sheet, strand, thickness, twist.

poach *v* appropriate, encroach, pilfer, plunder, rob, steal, trespass.

pocket *n* bag, compartment, envelope, hollow, pouch, receptacle, reticule, sack.
adj abridged, compact, concise, dwarf, little, mini, miniature, pint-sized, pocket-size, portable, small.
v appropriate, filch, help oneself to, lift, pilfer, pinch, purloin, snaffle, steal, take.

pockmark *n* blemish, pit, pock, pustule, scar, spot.

pod *n* case, hull, husk, legume, shell, shuck.

podium *n* dais, platform, rostrum, soapbox, stage, stand.

poem *n* acrostic, ballad, ballade, dithyramb, ditty, eclogue, elegy, epic, epicedium, epigram, epithalamion, epode, epopee, fabliau, idyll, jingle, lay, limerick, lyric, madrigal, monody, ode, palinode, rhyme, rondeau, rondel, song, sonnet, threnody, verse, versicle.

poet *n* bard, iambist, idyllist, librettist, lyricist, Meistersinger, metricist, minnesinger, minstrel, monodist, odist, Parnassian, poetaster, poet laureate, rhapsodist, rhymer, rhymester, skald, sonneteer, troubadour, versemonger, verser, verse-smith, versifier.

poetic *adj* artistic, elegiac, evocative, expressive, figurative, flowing, graceful, inspiring, lyric, lyrical, metrical, moving, rhythmic, romantic, speaking.
antonym prosaic.

poetry *n* free verse, iambics, lyrics, Parnassus, poems, poesy, rhyme, rhyming, verse, vers libre, versification, versing.

poignant *adj* acrid, acute, affecting, agonizing, biting, bitter, caustic, deep-felt, distressing, eloquent, heartbreaking, heart-rending,

intense, keen, moving, painful, pathetic, penetrating, piercing, piquant, pointed, pungent, sad, severe, sharp, stinging, tender, touching, upsetting.

point[1] *n* aim, aspect, attribute, burden, characteristic, circumstance, condition, core, crux, degree, design, detail, dot, drift, end, essence, extent, extremity, facet, feature, full stop, gist, goal, import, instance, instant, intent, intention, item, juncture, location, (main) idea, mark, marrow, matter, meaning, message, moment, nicety, nub, object, objective, particular, peculiarity, period, pith, place, position, proposition, purpose, quality, question, reason, score, speck, spot, stage, stop, subject, tally, text, theme, thrust, time, topic, trait, unit, use, usefulness, utility.
v aim, align, direct, face, hint, level, punctuate, sharpen, train.

point of view angle, approach, attitude, belief, judgment, opinion, orientation, outlook, perspective, position, slant, stance, standpoint, view, viewpoint.

point out allude to, bring up, call attention to, identify, indicate, mention, reveal, show, specify.

point to allude to, augur, be attributable to, call (or draw) attention to, denote, designate, evidence, identify, indicate, point at, point out, signal, suggest.

point up accentuate, emphasize, headline, spotlight, stress, underline, underscore.

to the point applicable, apposite, appropriate, apropos, apt, brief, fitting, germane, pertinent, pithy, pointed, relevant, short, suitable, terse.
antonym irrelevant.

point[2] *n* apex, bill, cape, crest, end, fastigium, foreland, head, headland, hook, needle, ness, nib, peninsula, pinnacle, promontory, prong, spike, spire, spit, spur, summit, tang, tine, tip, top.

point-blank *adj* abrupt, blunt, categorical, direct, downright, explicit, express, flat, forthright, outright, plain, plain-spoken, straight, straightforward, unreserved.
adv bluntly, brusquely, candidly, directly, explicitly, flatly, forthrightly, frankly, in plain words, openly, outright, plainly, square, squarely, straightforwardly, straight (out), unequivocally.

pointed *adj* accurate, aciculate, aciform, aculeate, acuminate, acute, barbed, biting, cuspidate, cutting, edged, emphatic, expressive, fastigiate, incisive, keen, lanceolate, lancet, penetrating, pertinent, sharp, telling, trenchant.

pointer *n* caution, finger post, guide, hand, hint, indication, indicator, information, needle, recommendation, sign, suggestion, tip, warning, word of advice.

pointless *adj* absurd, aimless, bootless, fruitless, futile, gratuitous, hopeless, inane, ineffectual, irrational, irrelevant, meaningless, nonsensical, profitless, purposeless, senseless, silly, stupid, unavailing, unbeneficial, unproductive, unprofitable, useless, vain, worthless.

antonyms meaningful, profitable.

poise *n* aplomb, assurance, calmness, carriage, collectedness, composure, cool, coolness, dignity, elegance, equanimity, equilibrium, grace, presence, presence of mind, sangfroid, savoir-faire, self-assurance, self-confidence, self-possession, serenity, steadiness, sureness.

poised *adj* balanced, calm, collected, composed, cool, dignified, expectant, floating, graceful, hanging, held, hovering, nonchalant, positioned, prepared, ready, self-confident, self-possessed, serene, suave, supported, sure of oneself, suspended, unruffled, urbane, waiting.

poison *n* aconite, bane, blight, cancer, canker, contagion, contamination, corruption, malignancy, miasma, toxin, venom, virus.

v adulterate, contaminate, corrupt, defile, deprave, embitter, empoison, envenom, harm, infect, kill, murder, pervert, pollute, subvert, taint, undermine, vitiate, warp, work (its) evil on.

poisonous *adj* aconitic, baleful, baneful, corruptive, deadly, evil, fatal, harmful, lethal, malicious, mephitic, mortal, noxious, pernicious, pestiferous, pestilential, toxic, venomous, vicious, virulent.

poke *v* butt, dig, elbow, hit, jab, nose, nudge, prod, punch, push, shove, stab, stick, thrust.

n butt, dig, jab, nudge, prod, punch, shove, thrust.

poke fun at chaff, guy, jeer, lampoon, laugh at, make a mockery of, make fun of, mock, parody, rag, razz, rib, ridicule, roast, send up, spoof, tease.

poke one's nose into butt into, interfere in, intrude in, meddle in, pry into, snoop in, tamper with.

pokey¹ *adj* crawling, dawdling, slow, unenergetic, unhurried.

pokey² *adj* confined, cramped, crowded, incommodious, narrow, small, tight, tiny.

antonym spacious.

polarity *n* ambivalence, antithesis, antonymy, contradiction, contraposition, contrariety, dichotomy, duality, extreme, oppositeness, opposition, paradox.

pole¹ *n* bar, beam, lug, mast, post, rod, shaft, spar, staff, stake, standard, stick.

pole² *n* antipode, extremity, limit, terminus, (ultima) Thule.

poles apart antithetical, at opposite extremes, complete opposites, incompatible, irreconcilable, like chalk and cheese, like night and day, worlds apart.

polemic *n* argument, controversy, debate, dispute.

adj argumentative, contentious, controversial, disputatious, eristic, polemical, quarrelsome.

polemicist *n* arguer, contender, controversialist, debater, disputant, disputer, logomachist.

polemics *n* argument, argumentation, contention, controversy, debate, disputation, dispute.

police *n* constabulary, fuzz, gendarmerie, law, law enforcement agency, myrmidons of the law, police force, RCMP.

v check, control, defend, guard, keep a check on, keep guard over, keep in order, keep the peace, monitor, observe, oversee, patrol, protect, regulate, stand guard over, supervise, watch.

police officer *n* arm of the law, bobby, catchpole, constable, cop, copper, flatfoot, fuzz, gendarme, gumshoe, law enforcement agent, mountie, officer, peace officer, policeman, policewoman.

policy *n* action, approach, code, course, custom, discretion, good sense, guideline, line, plan, position, practice, procedure, program, protocol, prudence, rule, sagacity, scheme, shrewdness, stance, stratagem, theory, wisdom.

polish *v* brighten (up), brush up, buff, burnish, clean, cultivate, emend, emery, enhance, file, finish, furbish, glaze, gloss, improve, lustre, perfect, planish, refine, rub, shine, sleek, slick (down), smooth, touch up, wax.

antonyms dull, tarnish.

n breeding, brightness, brilliance, burnish, class, cultivation, elegance, expertise, finesse, finish, glaze, gloss, grace, lustre, perfectionism, proficiency, refinement, rub, savoir-faire, sheen, shine, smoothness, sophistication, sparkle, style, suavity, urbanity, varnish, veneer, wax.

antonyms clumsiness, dullness, gaucherie.

polish off bolt (down), bump off, consume, devour, dispose of, down, eat, eliminate, finish, gobble (down or up), kill, liquidate, murder, put away, rub out, stuff, wolf (down).

polished *adj* accomplished, adept, bright, burnished, civilized, courtly, cultivated, educated, elegant, expert, faultless, fine, finished, flawless, furbished, genteel, glassy, gleaming, glossy, graceful, gracious, impeccable, improved, lustrous, masterly, outstanding, perfected, polite, professional, refined, sheeny, shining, shiny, skilful, sleek, slippery, smooth, sophisticated, suave, superlative, urbane, well-bred.

antonyms clumsy, dull, gauche, inexpert, tarnished.

polite *adj* affable, attentive, civil, civilized, complaisant, considerate, cordial, courteous, courtly, cultured, deferential, diplomatic, discreet, elegant, genteel, gentlemanly, gracious, ladylike, mannerly, obliging, polished, refined, respectful, solicitous, tactful, thoughtful, urbane, well-behaved, well-bred, well-mannered.

antonyms impolite, uncultivated.

politeness *n* attention, civility, complaisance, considerateness, cordiality, courtesy, courtliness, cultivation, culture, deference, diplomacy, discretion, elegance, gentility, gentlemanliness, good manners, grace, graciousness, mannerliness, manners, polish, refinement, respect, respectfulness, tact, thoughtfulness.

antonym impoliteness.

politic *adj* advantageous, advisable, artful, astute, canny, crafty, cunning, designing, diplomatic, discreet, expedient, ingenious, intriguing, judicious, Machiavellian, opportune, prudent, sagacious, sage, scheming, sensible, shrewd, sly, subtle, tactful, unscrupulous, wise.

antonym impolitic.

politician *n* agitator, legislator, Machiavellian, machinator, manipulator, Member of Parliament, MP, opportunist, politico, statesman, statist, stirrer, tactician, wheeler-dealer.

politics *n* affairs of state, civics, diplomacy, government, ideology, Machiavellianism, machination, manipulation, political affairs, political science, polity, power politics, Realpolitik, statecraft, statesmanship, Weltpolitik, wheeling and dealing.

poll *n* ballot, canvass, census, count, figures, head, plebiscite, polls, questionnaire, returns, sampling, straw poll, survey, tally, vote, voting.

v canvass, clip, cut back, cut off, cut short, dehorn, pollard, prune, shear, trim.

pollute *v* adulterate, befoul, besmirch, canker, contaminate, corrupt, debase, debauch, defile, deprave, desecrate, dirty, dishonour, foul, infect, mar, poison, profane, soil, spoil, stain, sully, taint, violate, vitiate.

pollution *n* adulteration, befoulment, contamination, corruption, defilement, desecration, dirt, dirtying, foulness, impurity, infection, profanation, stain, taint, uncleanness, violation, vitiation.

antonyms purification, purity.

polychromatic *adj* kaleidoscopic, many-coloured, many-hued, motley, mottled, multicoloured, parti-coloured, polychrome, rainbow, varicoloured, variegated.

antonyms monochromatic, monochrome.

polymath *n* all-rounder, fount of knowledge, mine of information, oracle, pansophist, Renaissance man (or woman), walking encyclopedia.

antonym ignoramus.

pomp *n* ceremonial, ceremoniousness, ceremony, display, éclat, flourish, formality, grandeur, grandiosity, magnificence, ostentation, pageant, pageantry, parade, pomp and circumstance, pomposity, ritual, show, solemnity, splendour, state, vainglory.

antonyms austerity, simplicity.

pomposity *n* affectation, airs, arrogance, bombast, euphuism, fustian, grandiloquence, grandiosity, loftiness, magniloquence, orotundity, pompousness, pontificating, pontification, portentousness, preachiness, presumption, pretension, pretentiousness, ranting, rhetoric, self-importance, stuffiness, turgidity, vainglory, vanity.

antonyms economy, simplicity.

pompous *adj* affected, arrogant, bloated, bombastic, chesty, elevated, euphuistic, flatulent, full of oneself, fulsome, fustian, grandiloquent, grandiose, highfalutin, high-flown, high-sounding, imperious, inflated, lofty, magisterial, magniloquent, orotund, ostentatious, overbearing, overblown, pontifical, portentous, pretentious, prosy, ranting, self-important, stilted, stuffy, supercilious, turgid, vainglorious, windy.

antonyms economical, modest, simple, unaffected, unassuming.

ponder *v* analyse, brood (over), cerebrate, chew over, chew the cud, cogitate, contemplate, consider, deliberate upon, digest, examine, excogitate, give thought to, incubate, meditate (on), mull over, muse (on or upon), puzzle over, ratiocinate, reason, reflect, ruminate over, sleep on (it), study, think, weigh.

ponderous *adj* awkward, bulky, clumsy, cumbersome, cumbrous, dreary, dull, elephantine, graceless, heavy, heavy-footed, heavy-handed, hefty, huge, humourless, laborious, laboured, lifeless, long-winded, lumbering, massive, pedantic, pedestrian, plodding, portentous, prolix, serious, slow-moving, stilted, stodgy, stolid, tedious, uninteresting, unwieldy, verbose, weighty.

antonyms delicate, light, simple.

poniard *n* bodkin, dagger, dirk, misericord, skean, stiletto, stylet.

pontifical *adj* apostolic, bloated, condescending, didactic, dogmatic, ecclesiastical, homiletic, imperious, magisterial, overbearing, papal, peremptory, pompous, portentous, preachy, prelatic, pretentious, self-important, sermonizing.

antonyms reticent, unassuming.

pontificate *v* declaim, dogmatize, expound, harangue, hold forth, lay down the law, lecture, moralize, perorate, preach, pronounce, sermonize, sound off.

pooh-pooh *v* belittle, brush aside, deride, disdain, dismiss, disparage, disregard, make light (or little) of, minimize, play down, reject, ridicule, scoff, scorn, slight, sneer at, sniff at, spurn, turn up one's nose at.

antonyms consider, exaggerate, magnify, regard.

pool[1] *n* lagoon, lake, mere, pond, puddle, reservoir, swimming pool, tarn, wading pool, water hole, watering hole.

pool[2] *n* accumulation, bank, cartel, collective, combine, consortium, co-operative, funds, group, jackpot, kitty, pot, purse, reserve, ring, stakes, syndicate, team, trust.

v amalgamate, chip in, combine, contribute, merge, put together, share.

poor[1] *adj* badly off, bankrupt, beggared, beggarly, broke, destitute, distressed, embarrassed, exiguous, feeling the pinch, hard up, impecunious, impoverished, inadequate, indigent, in reduced circumstances, insufficient, lacking, meagre, miserable, moneyless, necessitous, needy, niggardly, on one's beam-ends, on one's uppers, on the rocks, pauperized, penniless, penurious, pinched, pitiable, poverty-stricken, reduced, scanty, skimpy, slight, sparse, stone-broke, straitened, without means, without the wherewithal.

antonyms affluent, opulent, wealthy.

poor² *adj* bad, bare, barren, base, below par, deficient, depleted, exhausted, faulty, feeble, fruitless, grotty, humble, imperfect, impoverished, inferior, infertile, insignificant, jejune, low-grade, lowly, meagre, mean, mediocre, modest, paltry, pathetic, pitiful, plain, rotten, second-rate, seedy, shabby, shoddy, sorry, spiritless, sterile, substandard, thin, third-rate, trivial, unfruitful, unimpressive, unproductive, unsatisfactory, valueless, weak, worthless.

antonyms excellent, superior.

poor³ *adj* accursed, cursed, forlorn, hapless, ill-fated, luckless, miserable, pathetic, pitiable, star-crossed, unfortunate, unhappy, unlucky, wretched.

antonym lucky.

poorly *adv* badly, crudely, faultily, feebly, inadequately, incompetently, inexpertly, insufficiently, meagrely, meanly, pathetically, rottenly, shabbily, shoddily, unjustly, unsatisfactorily, unskilfully, unsuccessfully.

antonym well.

adj ailing, below par, frail, green about the gills, groggy, ill, indisposed, off-colour, out of sorts, rotten, shaky, sick, sickly, under the weather, unhealthy, unwell.

antonyms healthy, robust.

pop *v* bang, blast, bulge, burst (open), crack, down, explode, go bang, go off, push, report, shoot, snap, spring.

pop in breeze in, burst in, come in, drop in, enter, insert, look in, put in, shove in, slide in, stick in, visit.

pop up appear, arise, arrive, bob up, burst into view, come out of nowhere, crop up, emerge, put in an appearance, rise, show up, spring up, surface, turn up. *n* bang, burst, crack, explosion, noise, report, snap.

popinjay *n* beau, buck, coxcomb, dandy, dude, exquisite, fop, jackanapes, macaroni, pansy, peacock, spark, swell.

antonyms he-man, macho.

poppycock *n* babble, balderdash, baloney, bilge, bosh, bunk, drivel, eyewash, gibberish, gobbledygook, guff, hogwash, hooey, hot air, malarkey, nonsense, rot, rubbish, taradiddle, tommyrot, trash, twaddle.

antonym sense.

populace *n* canaille, common herd, commonalty, crowd, general public, hoi polloi, inhabitants, masses, mob, multitude, people, plebs, population, proletariat, public, rabble, rank and file, throng.

antonyms aristocracy, elite, nobility.

popular *adj* accepted, accessible, approved, beloved, celebrated, common, conventional, current, customary, democratic, demotic, famous, fashionable, favoured, favourite, feted,

general, hip, household, idolized, in, in demand, in favour, in vogue, liked, lionized, modish, overpopular, overused, prevailing, prevalent, public, sought-after, standard, stock, trite, ubiquitous, universal, usual, vernacular, voguish, vulgar, well-liked, widespread.

antonyms exclusive, unpopular, unusual.

popularity *n* acceptance, acclaim, adoration, adulation, applause, approbation, approval, celebrity, currency, esteem, fame, fashionableness, favour, glory, idolization, kudos, lionization, mass appeal, recognition, regard, renown, reputation, repute, vogue, worship.

antonym unpopularity.

popularize *v* debase, democratize, disseminate, familiarize, give currency to, propagate, simplify, spread, universalize, vulgarize.

antonym discredit.

popularly *adv* commonly, conventionally, customarily, generally, in the vernacular, ordinarily, regularly, traditionally, universally, usually, vernacularly, vulgarly, widely.

populate *v* colonize, establish oneself in, inhabit, live in, make one's home in, occupy, overrun, people, put down roots in, settle, tenant.

population *n* citizenry, citizens, community, denizens, folk, inhabitants, natives, occupants, people, populace, residents, society.

populous *adj* crawling, crowded, frequented, overpeopled, overpopulated, packed, populated, swarming, teeming, thickly populated, thronged.

antonyms deserted, unfrequented.

pore over *v* brood over, con, contemplate, devour, dwell on, examine, go over, peruse, ponder, read, scan, scrutinize, study.

pornographic *adj* bawdy, blue, coarse, dirty, filthy, gross, indecent, lewd, obscene, off-colour, offensive, porn, prurient, raunchy, ribald, risqué, salacious, smutty.

antonyms innocent, inoffensive.

pornography *n* bawdiness, dirt, erotica, filth, grossness, indecency, obscenity, porn, ribaldry, sexploitation, skin flick, smut.

porous *adj* absorbent, absorptive, cellular, foraminous, holey, honeycombed, penetrable, permeable, pervious, pitted, sievelike, spongelike, spongy.

antonyms impermeable, impervious.

port *n* anchorage, asylum, harbour, harbourage, haven, refuge, sanctuary, seaport.

portable *adj* carryable, compact, convenient, conveyable, handy, light, lightweight, manageable, movable, transportable.

antonyms fixed, immovable.

portend *v* adumbrate, announce, augur, bespeak, betoken, bode, forebode, forecast, foreshadow, foretell, foretoken, forewarn, harbinger, herald, indicate, omen, point to, predict, presage, prognosticate, promise, signify, threaten, warn of.

portent n augury, foreboding, forecast, forerunner, foreshadowing, forewarning, harbinger, indication, omen, precursor, prefiguration, premonition, presage, presentiment, prodrome, prognostic, prognostication, sign, signification, threat, warning.

portentous adj alarming, amazing, astounding, awe-inspiring, bloated, charged, consequential, crucial, earth-shaking, earth-shattering, epoch-making, extraordinary, fateful, heavy, important, menacing, minatory, miraculous, momentous, ominous, phenomenal, pompous, ponderous, pontifical, pregnant, prodigious, remarkable, self-important, significant, sinister, solemn, threatening.

antonyms insignificant, unimportant, unimpressive.

porter[1] n baggage attendant, baggage man, bearer, carrier, redcap.

porter[2] n caretaker, commissionaire, concierge, doorkeeper, doorman, gatekeeper, janitor.

portion n allocation, allotment, allowance, amount, assignment, bit, cup, destiny, division, dowry, fate, fortune, fraction, fragment, helping, kismet, lot, luck, measure, meed, moiety, morsel, parcel, part, piece, quantity, quota, rakeoff, ration, scrap, section, segment, serving, share, slice, something, whack.

v allocate, allot, apportion, assign, carve up, deal, distribute, divide, divvy up, dole (out), parcel (out), partition, segment, share (out), slice up.

portliness n ampleness, beefiness, chubbiness, corpulence, dumpiness, embonpoint, fleshiness, fullness, heaviness, obesity, paunchiness, plumpness, rotundity, roundness, stoutness, tubbiness.

portly adj ample, beefy, bulky, chubby, corpulent, dumpy, embonpoint, fat, fleshy, full, heavy, large, obese, overweight, paunchy, plump, rotund, round, stout, tubby.

antonyms slight, slim.

portrait n account, caricature, characterization, depiction, description, icon, image, likeness, miniature, mug shot, painting, photograph, picture, portraiture, portrayal, profile, representation, sketch, thumbnail (sketch), vignette.

portray v act, capture, characterize, delineate, depict, describe, draw, emblazon, encapsulate, evoke, figure, illustrate, impersonate, limn, paint, personate, personify, picture, play, present, render, represent, sketch, suggest.

portrayal n acting, characterization, delineation, depiction, description, evocation, impersonation, interpretation, performance, picture, portrait, presentation, rendering, representation, sketch.

pose n act, affectation, air, attitude, bearing, charade, con, façade, front, mark, masquerade, mien, position, posture, pretence, role, sham, stance.

v advance, arrange, assert, attitudinize, claim, model, place, posit, position, posture, present, propose, propound, put, put forward, put on an act, set, sham, sit, state, strike an attitude, submit.

pose as act the part of, disguise oneself as, impersonate, masquerade as, pass for, pass oneself off as, pretend to be, profess to be, represent oneself to be, take the guise of.

poser[1] n brain teaser, brain twister, Chinese puzzle, conundrum, enigma, mystery, problem, puzzle, puzzler, question, riddle, stumper, tough nut to crack, vexed question.

poser[2] n attitudinizer, model, phony, poseur, posturer, pretender, sitter.

poseur n attitudinizer, charlatan, exhibitionist, impostor, masquerader, mountebank, phony, poser, posturer, quack.

posh adj chic, classy, deluxe, elegant, exclusive, fancy, fashionable, grand, grandiose, high-class, lavish, luxurious, luxury, opulent, plummy, plush, ritzy, select, smart, stylish, sumptuous, swanky, swell, swish, upper-class, upscale.

antonyms cheap, inferior.

posit v advance, assert, assume, pose, postulate, predicate, presume, propound, put forward, state, submit.

position n angle, area, arrangement, attitude, bearings, belief, berth, capacity, circumstances, deployment, disposition, duty, employment, footing, function, importance, job, level, locale, locality, location, niche, occupation, office, opinion, orientation, outlook, pass, perspective, pinch, place, placement, placing, plight, point, point of view, policy, pose, positioning, post, posture, predicament, premise, prestige, rank, reputation, role, set, setting, site, situation, slant, slot, spot, stance, stand, standing, standpoint, station, stature, status, ubiety, view, viewpoint, whereabouts.

v arrange, array, deploy, dispose, fix, lay out, line up, locate, place, pose, put, range, set, settle, stand, stick.

positive adj absolute, actual, affirmative, ameliorative, arrant, assertive, assured, authoritative, beneficial, categorical, certain, clear, clear-cut, cocksure, complete, conclusive, concrete, confident, constructive, consummate, convinced, decided, decisive, definite, direct, dogmatic, downright, effective, efficacious, emphatic, explicit, express, firm, forceful, forward-looking, good, helpful, hopeful, incontestable, incontrovertible, indisputable, indubitable, irrefragable, irrefutable, open-and-shut, opinionated, optimistic, out-and-out, peremptory, perfect, plus, practical, productive, progressive, promising, rank, raving, real, realistic, resolute, secure, self-evident, sheer, stubborn, sure, thorough, thoroughgoing, uncompromising, undeniable, undoubted, unequivocal, unmistakable, unmitigated, unqualified, unquestioning, useful, utter.

antonyms indecisive, indefinite, negative, uncertain.

positively adv absolutely, assuredly, authoritatively, beyond a doubt, categorically, certainly, conclusively, constructively, decidedly, decisively, definitely, dogmatically, emphatically, expressly, finally, firmly, incontestably, incontrovertibly, indisputably, surely, uncompromisingly, undeniably, unequivocally, unmistakably, unquestionably.

possess v bedevil, be endowed with, bewitch, boast, command, consume, control, dominate, enjoy, get into one, haunt, have, hold, obsess, obtain, occupy, own, seize, take over.

possessed adj bedevilled, berserk, besotted, bewitched, consumed, crazed, cursed, demented, dominated, enchanted, frenzied, hagridden, haunted, infatuated, insane, maddened, mesmerized, obsessed, raving.

possession n colony, control, custody, dependency, dominion, enjoyment, fruition, hold, mandate, occupancy, occupation, ownership, proprietorship, protectorate, province, tenure, territory, title.

possessions n assets, baggage, belongings, chattels, effects, estate, gear, goods, goods and chattels, junk, movables, paraphernalia, pelf, property, riches, stuff, things, trappings, wealth, worldly wealth.

possessive adj acquisitive, clinging, covetous, dominating, domineering, grasping, jealous, overprotective, proprietorial, selfish.

antonyms generous, sharing, unassertive.

possibilities n capabilities, expectations, potential, potentiality, promise, prospects, talent.

antonyms disadvantages, liabilities.

possibility n achievability, chance, conceivability, feasibility, hazard, hope, latency, liability, likelihood, odds, off chance, plausibility, potentiality, practicability, probability, prospect, realizability, risk, workableness.

antonym impossibility.

possible adj accomplishable, achievable, alternative, attainable, available, conceivable, credible, doable, feasible, hopeful, hypothetical, imaginable, latent, likely, potential, practicable, probable, promising, realizable, tenable, viable, workable.

antonym impossible.

possibly adv at all, by (any) chance, by any means, Deo volente, D.V., feasibly, God willing, haply, hopefully, in any way, maybe, mayhap, on an off chance, peradventure, perchance, perhaps, very like(ly).

post¹ n baluster, banister, column, leg, newel, pale, palisade, picket, pier, pillar, pin, pole, shaft, stake, stanchion, standard, stock, strut, support, upright.

v advertise, affix, announce, denounce, display, give notice of, make known, placard, proclaim, promulgate, publicize, publish, put up, report, stick up.

post² n appointment, assignment, beat, berth, employment, incumbency, job, office, outpost, place, position, situation, station, vacancy.

v appoint, assign, establish, locate, move,

place, position, put, second, send, shift, situate, station, transfer.

post³ n collection, delivery, dispatch, mail, mailbox, postal service.

v acquaint, advise, apprise, brief, dispatch, fill in on, inform, keep posted, mail, notify, report to, send, transmit.

poster n advertisement, announcement, bill, handbill, notice, placard, sign, sticker.

posterior adj after, back, behind, dorsal, ensuing, following, hind, hinder, later, latter, rear, rearward, subsequent, succeeding.

antonyms anterior, front, previous.

n backside, behind, bottom, bum, butt, buttocks, croup, haunches, hindquarters, rear, rear end, rump, seat, tail.

posterity n children, descendants, family, future, future generations, heirs, issue, offspring, progeny, scions, seed, successors.

antonyms ancestors, antiquity, forebears, past.

posthaste adv at once, directly, double-quick, full tilt, hastily, immediately, on the double, promptly, pronto, quickly, speedily, straightaway, swiftly, with all speed.

antonyms eventually, gradually, slowly.

post-mortem n analysis, autopsy, dissection, examination, necropsy, review.

postpone v adjourn, defer, delay, freeze, hold off, hold over, pigeonhole, prorogue, put aside, put back, put off, put on ice, shelve, sleep on, suspend, table, waive.

antonyms advance, forward.

postponed adj adjourned, deferred, frozen, in abeyance, on ice, pigeonholed, shelved, suspended.

antonym advanced.

postponement n adjournment, deferment, deferral, delay, freeze, moratorium, prorogation, putting off, respite, stay, suspension.

postscript n addendum, addition, afterthought, afterword, appendix, codicil, epilogue, P.S., supplement.

antonyms introduction, prologue.

postulate v advance, assume, claim, hypothesize, lay down, posit, predicate, presuppose, propose, stipulate, suppose, take for granted, theorize.

n a priori principle, axiom, fundamental principle, necessary condition, premise, self-evident truth, truism, truth.

posture n attitude, bearing, carriage, disposition, mien, port, pose, position, set, stance.

v affect, attitudinize, pose, put on airs, show off, strike attitudes, strut.

posy n bouquet, boutonniere, buttonhole, corsage, nosegay, spray.

pot n basin, beaker, bowl, coffee pot, crock, crucible, cruse, cupel, flask, gallipot, jar, marmite, pan, pig, pipkin, planter, receptacle, samovar, teapot, urn, vase, vessel.

potbellied *adj* bloated, corpulent, distended, fat, obese, overweight, paunchy, portly, pudgy, roly-poly, rotund, tubby.

potbelly *n* beer belly, belly, gut, love handles, paunch, pot, spare tire.

potency *n* authority, capacity, cogency, control, effectiveness, efficaciousness, efficacy, energy, force, headiness, influence, kick, might, muscle, persuasiveness, potentiality, power, puissance, punch, strength, sway, vigour.
antonyms impotence, weakness.

potent *adj* authoritative, cogent, commanding, compelling, convincing, dominant, dynamic, effective, efficacious, eloquent, forceful, formidable, heady, impressive, influential, intoxicating, mighty, moving, persuasive, powerful, puissant, pungent, strong, telling, vigorous, weighty.
antonyms impotent, weak.

potentate *n* chief, chieftain, despot, dictator, dynast, emperor, empress, head of state, king, leader, mogul, monarch, overlord, prince, queen, ruler, sovereign, tyrant.

potential *adj* budding, concealed, conceivable, dormant, embryonic, future, hidden, imaginable, in embryo, inherent, latent, likely, possible, probable, promising, prospective, undeveloped, unrealized.
n ability, aptitude, capability, capacity, flair, possibility, potentiality, power, talent, the makings, the wherewithal, what it takes.

potentiality *n* ability, aptitude, capability, capacity, latency, likelihood, possibility, potential, promise, prospect.

potion *n* beverage, brew, concoction, cup, dose, draft, drink, electuary, elixir, medicine, mixture, philtre, potation, tonic.

potpourri *n* assortment, collection, combination, conglomeration, gallimaufry, hodgepodge, jumble, medley, mélange, miscellany, mixed bag, mixture, motley, pastiche, patchwork, salad, salmagundi.

pottery *n* ceramics, china, chinaware, crockery, delft, earthenware, porcelain, stoneware, terra cotta, ware.
adj ceramic, china, clay, earthenware, fictile, porcelain, stoneware.

potty *adj* balmy, bananas, barmy, bonkers, crackers, crazy, daft, demented, dippy, dotty, eccentric, flaky, foolish, kooky, loony, nuts, nutty, screwball, screwy, silly, soft, touched.

pouch *n* bag, container, marsupium, pocket, poke, purse, reticule, sac, sack, sporran, wallet.

pounce *n* assault, attack, bound, dive, grab, jump, leap, lunge, spring, swoop. *v* dive, jump, leap, lunge, spring, swoop.
pounce on ambush, attack, dash at, dive on, fall upon, grab, jump, leap at, lunge at, rush at, seize, snatch, spring, strike at, swoop down on.

pound[1] *v* ache, bang, bash, baste, batter, beat, belabour, bray, bruise, clobber, clump, comminute, crush, drub, drum, hammer, hit, knock, lick, palpitate, pelt, powder, pulsate, pulse, pulverize, pummel, rap, smash, stomp, strike, strum, thrash, throb, thrum, thud, thump, thunder, tramp, triturate, wallop.

pound[2] *n* compound, corral, enclosure, fold, pen, yard.

pour *v* cascade, come down in buckets (or sheets or torrents), course, crowd, decant, effuse, emit, exude, flow, gush, rain, rain cats and dogs, rain run, rush, spew, spill, spout, stream, swarm, teem, throng, tumble.
pour out debouch, decant, discharge, disgorge, emit, gush (forth), issue, share, spew forth, spit out, unbosom, unburden, vent.

pout *v* glower, grimace, lower, mope, pull a face, scowl, sulk.
antonyms grin, smile.
n glower, grimace, long face, moue, scowl.
antonyms grin, smile.

poverty *n* aridity, bareness, barrenness, beggary, dearth, deficiency, depletion, destitution, distress, exhaustion, hand-to-mouth existence, hardship, ill-being, impoverishment, inadequacy, indigence, infertility, insolvency, insufficiency, jejuneness, lack, meagreness, necessitousness, necessity, need, paucity, pauperism, pennilessness, penury, poorness, privation, reduced circumstances, scarcity, shortage, sterility, thinness, unfruitfulness, want.
antonyms affluence, fertility, fruitfulness, riches, richness.

poverty-stricken *adj* bankrupt, beggared, broke, destitute, distressed, down-and-out, down at heel, flat broke, impecunious, impoverished, indigent, necessitous, needy, on one's beam-ends, on one's uppers, penniless, penurious, poor, stone-broke, strapped.
antonyms affluent, rich.

powder *n* bran, dust, pounce, talc, triturate.
v bray, comminute, cover, crumble, crush, dredge, dust, granulate, grind, pestle, pound, pulverize, scatter, sprinkle, strew, triturate.

powdery *adj* chalky, crumbling, crumbly, crushed, dry, dusty, fine, friable, grainy, granular, loose, mealy, powdered, pulverized, sandy.

power *n* ability, ascendancy, autarchy, authorization, authority, brawn, brute force, capability, capacity, clout, clutches, command, competence, control, dominance, domination, dominion, dynamism, dynamo, efficacy, eloquence, energy, faculty, force, forcefulness, hegemony, horsepower, imperium, influence, intensity, juice, licence, mastery, might, muscle, muscularity, omnipotence, potency, potential, prepotency, prerogative, privilege, puissance, pull, right, rule, sovereignty, steam, strength, supremacy, sway, teeth, vehemence, vigour, virtue, vis, voltage, warrant, weight.

powerful *adj* ascendant, authoritative, cogent, commanding, compelling, controlling, convincing, dominant, dynamic, effective, effectual, eloquent, energetic, forceful, forcible, impressive, influential, leading, masterful, mighty, muscular, omnipotent, persuasive, plutocratic, potent, pre-eminent, prepotent, prevailing, puissant, robust, souped-up, sovereign, stalwart, strapping, strong, sturdy, supreme, telling, vehement, vigorous, weighty, winning.

antonyms impotent, ineffective, weak.

powerless *adj* debilitated, defenceless, dependent, disabled, effete, feeble, frail, helpless, impotent, incapable, incapacitated, ineffective, ineffectual, inefficacious, infirm, nerveless, paralysed, prostrate, subject, tied, unable, unarmed, unenforceable, vulnerable, weak, weak-kneed.

antonyms commanding, potent, powerful.

practicability *n* feasibility, operability, performability, possibility, practicality, realizability, usefulness, utility, value, viability, workability, workableness.

antonym impracticability.

practicable *adj* accomplishable, achievable, attainable, doable, expedient, feasible, negotiable, performable, possible, practical, realizable, viable, workable.

antonym impracticable.

practical *adj* active, applicative, applied, businesslike, common-sense, commonsensical, convenient, down-to-earth, efficient, empirical, everyday, expedient, experimental, factual, feasible, functional, hands-on, handy, hard-headed, hard-nosed, level-headed, material, matter-of-fact, mundane, nuts-and-bolts, ordinary, practicable, pragmatic, proficient, realistic, sensible, serviceable, sound, unsentimental, usable, useful, utilitarian, virtual, workable, workaday, working.

antonym impractical.

practicality *n* basics, common sense, experience, feasibility, nitty-gritty, nuts and bolts, possibility, practicability, practicalities, practicalness, practice, pragmatism, realism, sense, serviceability, soundness, usefulness, utility, workability.

practically¹ *adv* actually, all but, almost, as good as, essentially, for all practical purposes, fundamentally, in effect, in practice, in principle, just about, nearly, not quite, pretty nearly, pretty well, very nearly, virtually, well-nigh.

practically² *adv* clearly, from a commonsense angle, matter-of-factly, rationally, realistically, reasonably, sensibly, unsentimentally.

practice *n* action, application, business, career, clientele, convention, custom, discipline, drill, dry run, exercise, experience, habit, ism, method, mode, modus operandi, observance, operation, patronage, performance, policy, practicalities, practicum, praxis, preparation, procedure, process, profession, rehearsal, repetition, routine, rule, run-through, study, system, tradition, training, trial run, usage, use, vocation, way, wont, work, workout.

in practice actually, effectively, in effect, in fact, in reality, practically.

antonyms in theory, on paper, theoretically.

put into practice actualize, apply, carry out,

effect, implement, perform, put into effect, work out.

practise *v* apply, carry out, discipline, do, drill, enact, engage in, execute, exercise, follow, go over, implement, live up to, observe, perfect, perform, ply, prepare, pursue, put into practice, rehearse, repeat, run through, study, train, undertake, warm up.

practised *adj* able, accomplished, consummate, experienced, expert, finished, highly-developed, knowing, knowledgeable, masterly, perfected, proficient, qualified, refined, seasoned, skilful, skilled, trained, versed, veteran, well-trained.

antonyms inexpert, unpractised.

pragmatic *adj* businesslike, down-to-earth, efficient, expedient, factual, functional, hard-headed, opportunistic, practical, realistic, sensible, unidealistic, unsentimental, utilitarian.

antonyms idealistic, romantic, unrealistic.

pragmatism *n* ad hockery, functionalism, hard-headedness, opportunism, practicality, practicalness, realism, unidealism, utilitarianism.

antonyms idealism, romanticism.

praise *n* acclaim, acclamation, accolade(s), acknowledgment, adoration, adulation, applause, approbation, approval, bouquet(s), buildup, cheering, commendation, compliment, compliments, congratulation(s), encomium, eulogium, eulogy, exaltation, extolment, flattery, glorification, glory, homage, honour, kudos, laud, laudation, ovation, panegyric, pat on the back, plaudit(s), puff, rave, recognition, salvos, testimonial, thanks, thanksgiving, tribute, worship.

antonyms criticism, revilement.

v acclaim, acknowledge, admire, adore, applaud, approve, bless, build up, celebrate, cheer, compliment, congratulate, cry up, eulogize, exalt, extol, flatter, give thanks to, glorify, hail, honour, laud, magnify, make much of, panegyrize, pat on the back, pay tribute to, promote, puff, rave about, recognize, tout, wax lyrical about, worship.

antonyms bad-mouth, criticize, revile.

praiseworthy *adj* admirable, commendable, creditable, deserving, estimable, excellent, exemplary, fine, honourable, laudable, meritorious, reputable, sterling, worthy.

antonyms discreditable, dishonourable, ignoble.

prance *v* bound, caper, capriole, caracole, cavort, curvet, dance, frisk, frolic, gambol, jump, leap, parade, peacock, romp, skip, spring, stalk, strut, strut one's stuff, swagger, swank, vault.

prank(s) *n* antics, caper, dido, escapade, frolic, jape, joke, lark, monkeyshines, piece of mischief, practical joke, shenanigans, spree, stunt, trick, vagary.

prate *v* babble, blather, bleat, boast, brag, burble, chatter, drivel, gab, gas, jabber, jaw, maunder, palaver, prattle, ramble, rattle (on), run off at the mouth, shoot off one's mouth, yak.

prattle v babble, blather, chat, chatter, clack, drivel, gabble (on), gibber, go on, gossip, jabber, patter, rattle (on), run on, talk nonsense, tittle-tattle, twitter.

n blather, chat, chatter, clack, drivel, foolishness, gab, gas, gibberish, gossip, guff, hot air, jaw, maundering, nonsense, palaver, prating, talk, tattle, twaddle.

prattler n airhead, babbler, bigmouth, blabbermouth, blatherskite, chatterbox, chatterer, gabber, gabbler, gossip, loudmouth, magpie, prater, prattlebox, rattlebrain, talker, tattler, windbag.

antonym clam.

pray v adjure, ask, beg, beseech, call on, crave, entreat, implore, importune, invoke, petition, plead, press, request, solicit, sue, supplicate, urge.

prayer n appeal, collect, communion, devotion, entreaty, invocation, litany, orison, paternoster, petition, plea, request, solicitation, suffrage, suit, supplication.

prayer book n Book of Common Prayer, breviary, euchology, formulary, machzor, missal, ordinal, siddur.

preach v address, admonish, advocate, discourse, evangelize, exhort, expound, harangue, hold forth, lecture, moralize, orate, pontificate, preachify, prose, sermonize, urge.

preacher n cantor, chaplain, clergyman, evangelist, expounder, homilist, man (or woman) of the cloth, minister, missionary, moralizer, parson, pontificater, predicant, pulpiteer, ranter, reverend, revivalist, sermonizer, sky pilot.

preachiness n cant, didacticism, dogmatism, moralizing, pharisaism, pietism, pomposity, portentousness, preachment, pulpitry, religiosity, sanctimoniousness, sanctimony, self-righteousness, sermonizing, soapboxing.

preaching n discourse, doctrine, dogma, evangelism, exhortation, gospel, homiletics, homilies, instruction, lecture, message, pontification, preachification, precepts, sermonizing, sermon(s), teaching.

preachy adj canting, declamatory, didactic, dogmatic, edifying, exhortatory, holier-than-thou, homiletic, hortatory, moralizing, pharisaic, pietistic, pontifical, pontificating, preceptive, religiose, sanctimonious, self-righteous, sententious, sermonizing.

preamble n exordium, foreword, introduction, lead-in, overture, preface, preliminaries, prelude, preparation, proem, prolegomenon, prologue.

antonyms epilogue, postscript.

precarious adj chancy, critical, dangerous, delicate, dicey, doubtful, dubious, hairy, hazardous, iffy, insecure, parlous, perilous, problematic, risky, shaky, slippery, ticklish, touch-and-go, tricky, uncertain, unpredictable, unreliable, unsafe, unsettled, unstable, unsteady, unsure, vulnerable.

antonyms certain, safe, secure.

precaution n anticipation, backstop, buffer, care, caution, circumspection, foresight, forethought, insurance, preparation, preventive measure, prophylactic, prophylaxis, protection, providence, provision, prudence, safeguard, safety measure, security, surety, wariness.

precautionary adj anticipatory, cautious, foresighted, foresightful, judicious, preliminary, preparatory, preventive, prophylactic, protective, provident, provisional, prudent, safety, self-protective.

precede v antecede, antedate, anticipate, come first, forerun, front, go before, head, herald, introduce, lead, outrank, preface, prefix, prelude, take precedence.

antonym follow.

▲ *confusable word* proceed.

precedence n antecedence, first place, lead, pre-eminence, preference, pride of place, primacy, priority, rank, seniority, superiority, supremacy.

▲ *confusable word* precedents.

precedent n antecedent, authority, citation, criterion, example, exemplar, guideline, instance, judgment, model, paradigm, past instance, pattern, prototype, ruling, standard, yardstick.

▲ *confusable word* precedence.

preceding adj above, aforementioned, aforesaid, antecedent, anterior, earlier, foregoing, former, past, precedent, precursive, previous, prior, supra.

antonyms following, later.

precept n axiom, behest, belief, bidding, byword, canon, charge, command, commandment, convention, decree, dictum, direction, directive, guideline, injunction, instruction, law, mandate, maxim, motto, order, ordinance, principle, regulation, rubric, rule, saying, sentence, statute.

precinct n area, bound, boundary, confine, district, division, enclosure, limit, quarter, section, sector, zone.

precincts n area, borders, bounds, confines, district, environment, environs, limits, locality, milieu, neighbourhood, premises, region, surrounds, vicinity.

preciosity n affectation, artificiality, chi-chi, floweriness, overfastidiousness, overrefinement, preciousness, pretentiousness.

precious[1] adj adored, beloved, beyond price, cherished, chi-chi, choice, costly, darling, dear, dearest, expensive, exquisite, favourite, fine, idolized, inestimable, invaluable, irreplaceable, loved, overfastidious, priceless, prized, rare, treasured, valuable, valued.

precious[2] adj affected, artificial, chi-chi, exaggerated, fastidious, flowery, namby-pamby, overdone, overnice, over-refined, recherché.

precipice n bluff, brink, cliff, cliff face, crag, drop, escarpment, height, scarp, steep.

precipitate v accelerate, advance, bring on, cast, cause, chuck, discharge, drive, expedite, fling, forward, further, hasten, hurl, hurry up, induce, launch, occasion, pitch, quicken, speed (up), throw, trigger.

adj abrupt, breakneck, brief, frantic, hasty, headlong, heedless, hot-headed, hurried, impatient, impetuous, impulsive, incautious, indiscreet, madcap, pell-mell, plunging, precipitous, premature, quick, quixotic, rapid, rash, reckless, rushing, sudden, swift, unannounced, unexpected, violent.

antonym cautious.

▲ *confusable word* precipitous.

precipitous *adj* abrupt, dizzy, giddy, hasty, high, perpendicular, rash, reckless, sheer, steep, sudden, vertiginous.

antonyms gradual, sloping.

▲ *confusable word* precipitate.

précis *n* abbreviation, abridgment, abstract, aperçu, compendium, condensation, conspectus, contraction, digest, encapsulation, epitome, outline, overview, résumé, rundown, sketch, summary, survey, synopsis, table.

v abbreviate, abridge, abstract, compress, condense, contract, digest, encapsulate, epitomize, outline, shorten, sum up, summarize, synopsize.

antonyms amplify, expand.

precise *adj* absolute, accurate, actual, authentic, bang-on, blow-by-blow, careful, clear-cut, correct, dead-on, definite, delimitative, detailed, determinate, distinct, exact, explicit, express, factual, faithful, fastidious, finicky, fixed, formal, identical, literal, meticulous, minute, nice, particular, prim, punctilious, rigid, rigorous, scrupulous, specific, strict, succinct, unequivocal, verbatim, well-defined, word-for-word.

antonym imprecise.

precisely *adv* absolutely, accurately, bang, blow by blow, conscientiously, correctly, dead, distinctly, exactly, just, just so, literally, meticulously, minutely, on the dot, plumb, punctually, slap, smack, smack dab, square, squarely, strictly, verbatim, word for word.

precision *n* accuracy, care, correctness, definiteness, detail, exactitude, exactness, explicitness, expressness, faithfulness, fastidiousness, fidelity, meticulousness, minuteness, neatness, niceness, nicety, particularity, preciseness, punctilio, punctiliousness, rigour, scrupulosity, specificity.

antonym imprecision.

preclude *v* eliminate, exclude, forestall, hinder, inhibit, make impossible, obviate, prevent, prohibit, restrain, rule out, stop.

antonyms incur, involve.

precocious *adj* advanced, ahead, bright, clever, developed, fast, forward, gifted, mature, premature, quick, smart.

antonym backward.

preconceive *v* anticipate, assume, conceive, conceptualize, envisage, ideate, imagine, picture, prejudge, presume, presuppose, project, visualize.

preconception *n* anticipation, assumption, bias, conjecture, expectation, notion, predisposition, prejudgment, prejudice, presumption, presupposition.

precondition *n* essential, must, necessity, need, prerequisite, proviso, requirement, requisite, sine qua non, stipulation.

precursor *n* antecedent, forebear, forerunner, foreshadowing, forewarning, harbinger, herald, indication, indicator, messenger, originator, pathfinder, pioneer, predecessor, prodrome, sign, trailblazer, usher, vanguard, warning, warning sign, way-maker.

antonyms after-effect, aftermath.

predatory *adj* acquisitive, avaricious, carnivorous, covetous, despoiling, greedy, hunting, looting, lupine, marauding, pillaging, plundering, predacious, preying, rapacious, raptorial, ravaging, ravening, thieving, voracious, vulturine, wolfish.

predecessor *n* ancestor, antecedent, antecessor, forebear, forefather, forerunner, precursor, progenitor.

antonyms descendant, successor.

predestination *n* destiny, doom, election, fate, foreordainment, foreordination, karma, lot, necessity, portion, predestiny, predetermination, preordainment, preordination.

predestine *v* destine, doom, fate, foredoom, foreordain, intend, mean, predetermine, pre-elect, preordain.

predetermined *adj* agreed upon, certain, cut and dried, decided beforehand, deliberate, fixed, foregone, foreordained, prearranged, preordained, preplanned, set, set up, settled.

predicament *n* bind, can of worms, corner, crisis, dilemma, embarrassment, emergency, fix, hole, hot water, impasse, jam, kettle of fish, mess, pickle, pinch, plight, quandary, scrape, situation, spot, state, trouble.

predicate *v* affirm, assert, aver, avouch, avow, base, build, contend, declare, establish, found, ground, maintain, posit, postulate, premise, proclaim, rest, state.

predict *v* anticipate, augur, call for, divine, expect, forebode, forecast, foresee, foreshow, forespeak, foretell, portend, presage, prognosticate, project, prophesy, see coming, see up ahead, soothsay, vaticinate.

predictable *adj* anticipated, boring, calculable, certain, consistent, conventional, dependable, determinate, divinable, dull, expected, finite, foregone, foreseeable, foreseen, humdrum, imaginable, likely, presumable, probable, regular, reliable, risk-free, routine, safe, stodgy, sure, unexciting, wonted.

antonym unpredictable.

prediction *n* augury, divination, forecast, foretelling, fortune-telling, prognosis, prognostication, prophecy, second sight, soothsaying, vaticination.

predictive *adj* augural, diagnostic, divinatory, foretelling, premonitory, prognostic, prophetic.

predilection *n* affection, affinity, bent, bias, enthusiasm, fancy, fondness, inclination, leaning, liking, love, partiality, penchant, predisposition, preference, proclivity, proneness, propensity, soft spot, taste, tendency, weakness.

antonyms antipathy, disinclination.

predispose *v* bias, dispose, encourage, head, incline, induce, influence, lead, lean, make, make liable, make susceptible, prejudice, prepare, prime, prompt, sway.

predisposed *adj* agreeable, amenable, biassed, disposed, favourable, inclined, liable, minded, prejudiced, prepared, prone, ready, subject, susceptible, well-disposed, willing.

predisposition *n* bent, bias, disposition, inclination, leaning, liability, likelihood, mind, penchant, potentiality, predilection, preference, prejudice, proclivity, proneness, propensity, susceptibility, tendency, vulnerability, willingness.

predominance *n* ascendancy, control, dominance, dominion, edge, hegemony, hold, influence, leadership, mastery, numbers, power, predomination, pre-eminence, preponderance, prepotency, prevalence, superiority, supremacy, sway, upper hand, weight, whip hand.

antonyms ineffectiveness, weakness.

predominant *adj* ascendant, capital, chief, controlling, dominant, forceful, governing, important, influential, leading, main, paramount, potent, powerful, pre-eminent, preponderant, prepotent, prevailing, prevalent, primary, prime, principal, prominent, ruling, reigning, sovereign, strong, superior, supreme.

antonyms ineffective, lesser, minor, weak.

predominate *v* dominate, excel, have the upper (or whip) hand, obtain, outnumber, outweigh, override, overrule, overshadow, preponderate, prevail, reign, rule, tell, transcend.

pre-eminence *n* distinction, excellence, fame, incomparability, matchlessness, peerlessness, predominance, prestige, prominence, renown, repute, superiority, supremacy, transcendence.

pre-eminent *adj* authoritative, chief, consummate, distinguished, excellent, exceptional, first, foremost, incomparable, inimitable, leading, matchless, nonpareil, outstanding, paramount, peerless, predominant, prominent, renowned, superior, superlative, supreme, surpassing, top, transcendent, unequalled, unmatched, unparallelled, unrivalled, unsurpassed.

antonyms undistinguished, unknown.

pre-eminently *adv* conspicuously, eminently, emphatically, especially, exceptionally, exclusively, incomparably, inimitably, matchlessly, notably, par excellence, particularly, peerlessly, signally, singularly, strikingly, superlatively, supremely, surpassingly.

pre-empt *v* acquire, anticipate, appropriate, arrogate, assume, bag, forestall, secure, seize, usurp.

preen *v* adorn, array, beautify, clean, deck, doll up, do up, dress up, groom, plume, prank,

prettify, primp, prink, slick, smarten up, spiff up, spruce up, tart up, titivate, trick out, trim.

preen oneself on be proud of, congratulate oneself on, exult in, gloat about, pique oneself on, plume oneself on, pride oneself on.

antonym be ashamed of.

preface *n* exordium, foreword, intro, introduction, preamble, preliminaries, prelims, prelude, proem, prolegomena, prolegomenon, prologue.

antonyms afterthought, epilogue, postscript.

v begin, introduce, launch, lead up to, open, precede, prefix, prelude, premise, start.

antonyms append, complete, finish.

prefatory *adj* antecedent, exordial, explanatory, introductory, opening, preambulatory, precursory, preliminary, preludial, preparatory, proemial, prolegomenal.

antonyms closing, final.

prefer[1] *v* adopt, advocate, back, be partial to, choose, desire, elect, endorse, fancy, favour, go for, incline toward, lean toward, like better, opt for, pick, plump for, recommend, select, single out, support, vote for, want, wish, would rather, would sooner.

antonym reject.

prefer[2] *v* bring, file, lodge, place, present, press, propose, register, submit, tender.

antonym drop.

prefer[3] *v* advance, aggrandize, dignify, elevate, exalt, kick upstairs, promote, raise, up, upgrade.

antonym demote.

preferable *adj* advantageous, advisable, best, better, chosen, eligible, expedient, favoured, more desirable, nicer, of choice, preferred, stronger, superior, to be preferred, worthier.

antonyms ineligible, inferior, undesirable.

preferably *adv* by choice, by preference, first, rather, sooner.

preference[1] *n* bag, choice, cup of tea, desire, druthers, election, fancy, favourite, first choice, inclination, liking, option, partiality, pick, predilection, selection, wish.

preference[2] *n* advantage, favour, favouritism, precedence, preferential treatment, priority, special consideration, special treatment.

preferential *adj* advantageous, better, biassed, favourable, favoured, partial, partisan, prior, privileged, special, superior.

antonym equal.

preferment *n* advancement, aggrandizement, betterment, dignity, elevation, exaltation, furtherance, improvement, promotion, rise, step up, upgrading.

antonym demotion.

preferred *adj* approved, authorized, chosen, desired, favoured, of choice, recommended, sanctioned, selected.

antonyms rejected, undesirable.

pregnancy *n* childbearing, conception, fertilization, gestation, gravidity, impregnation.

pregnant[1] *adj* big, big-bellied, big with child, delicate, enceinte, expectant, expecting, gravid, impregnated, in a condition, in the family way, knocked up, parturient, PG, preggers, with child.

pregnant[2] *adj* charged, eloquent, expressive, full, heavy, laden, loaded, meaning, meaningful, ominous, pithy, pointed, significant, speaking, suggestive, telling, weighty.

antonyms blank, empty.

prehistoric *adj* ancient, antediluvian, antiquated, archaic, earliest, early, hoary, obsolete, old, outmoded, out-of-date, primeval, primitive, primordial.

antonym modern.

prejudge *v* anticipate, assume, forejudge, judge prematurely, jump to conclusions about, predetermine, prejudicate, presume, presuppose.

prejudice[1] *n* bias, bigotry, chauvinism, discrimination, favouritism, inclination, injustice, intolerance, leaning, narrow-mindedness, one-sidedness, partiality, partisanship, preconception, predilection, preference, prejudgment, racism, sexism, tendency, unfairness, warp.

antonyms fairness, tolerance.

v bend, bias, colour, condition, distort, incline, indoctrinate, influence, jaundice, load, poison, predispose, prepossess, slant, sway, twist, warp, weight.

prejudice[2] *n* damage, detriment, disadvantage, harm, hurt, impairment, injury, loss, mischief, ruin, vitiation, wreck.

antonyms advantage, benefit.

v damage, compromise, destroy, harm, hinder, hurt, impair, injure, jeopardize, mar, ruin, spoil, threaten, undermine, vitiate, wreck.

antonyms advance, benefit, help.

prejudiced *adj* biassed, bigoted, chauvinistic, conditioned, discriminatory, distorted, ex parte, illiberal, influenced, intolerant, jaundiced, loaded, narrow-minded, one-sided, opinionated, partial, partisan, playing favourites, prepossessed, racist, sexist, subjective, unenlightened, unfair, unobjective, warped, weighted.

antonyms fair, tolerant.

prejudicial *adj* counter-productive, damaging, deleterious, detrimental, disadvantageous, harmful, hostile, hurtful, inimical, injurious, mischievous, noxious, pernicious, ruinous, undermining, unfavourable.

antonyms advantageous, beneficial.

preliminaries *n* basics, beginning, first round, formalities, foundations, groundwork, initiation, introduction, opening, preamble, preface, prelims, prelude, preparation, proem, prolegomena, rudiments, start.

preliminary *adj* earliest, early, embryonic, exordial, experimental, exploratory, first, inaugural, initial, initiative, initiatory, introductory, opening, pilot, precursory, prefatory, preparatory, primary, prior, qualifying, test, trial.

antonyms closing, final.

prelude *n* beginning, commencement, curtain raiser, exordium, foreword, intro, introduction, opener, overture, praeludium, preamble, precursor, preface, preliminary, preparation, prodrome, proem, prolegomenon, prologue, start, taster.

antonyms aftermath, epilogue, postscript.

premature *adj* abortive, early, embryonic, forward, green, half-formed, hasty, ill-considered, ill-timed, immature, imperfect, impulsive, incomplete, inopportune, overhasty, precipitate, precocious, preterm, previous, rash, raw, soon, undeveloped, unfledged, unprepared, unready, unripe, unseasonable, untimely.

antonyms late, tardy.

premeditated *adj* aforethought, calculated, cold-blooded, conscious, considered, contrived, deliberate, intended, intentional, planned, plotted, prearranged, prepense, preplanned, studied, willful.

antonyms spontaneous, unpremeditated.

premeditation *n* deliberateness, deliberation, design, determination, forethought, intention, intentionality, malice aforethought, planning, plotting, prearrangement, predetermination, purpose, scheming.

antonyms impulse, spontaneity.

premier *n* chancellor, chief minister, first minister, head of government, prime minister, secretary of state.

adj arch, cardinal, chief, earliest, first, foremost, head, highest, initial, leading, main, most important, original, paramount, pre-eminent, primary, prime, principal, supreme, top.

premise *v* assert, assume, hypothesize, lay down, posit, postulate, predicate, presuppose, state, stipulate, take as true.

n a priori principle, argument, assertion, assumption, axiom, basis, ground, hypothesis, position, postulate, postulation, predication, presupposition, proposition, statement, stipulation, supposition, thesis.

premises *n* building, establishment, estate, grounds, office, place, precincts, property, site.

premonition *n* anxiety, apprehension, fear, feeling (in one's bones), foreboding, forewarning, hunch, idea, intuition, misgiving, omen, portent, presage, presentiment, sign, suspicion, unease, uneasiness, warning, worry.

preoccupation *n* absence of mind, absent-mindedness, absorption, abstraction, bemusement, brown study, concern, daydreaming, distraction, engrossment, enthusiasm, fixation, hang-up, hobbyhorse, idée fixe, immersion, inattention, inattentiveness, musing, oblivion, obliviousness, obsession, pensiveness, raptness, reverie, thoughtfulness, woolgathering.

preoccupied *adj* absent-minded, absorbed, abstracted, bemused, daydreaming, distracted, distrait, engrossed, faraway, fixated, heedless, immersed, intent, lost in thought, oblivious, obsessed, pensive, rapt, taken up, unaware, woolgathering, wrapped in thought, wrapped up.

preordain v decree, destine, doom, fate, foreordain, order, prearrange, predestine, predetermine.

preparation[1] n alertness, anticipation, arrangement, assignment, basics, development, expectation, foresight, foundation, grooming, groundwork, homework, imposition, lesson, measure, plan, precaution, preliminaries, prep, preparedness, provision, readiness, readying, revision, rudiments, safeguard, schoolwork, study, task, training.

preparation[2] n application, composition, compound, concoction, lotion, medicine, mixture, potion, tincture.

preparatory adj basic, elementary, exordial, fundamental, initial, introductory, opening, prefatory, preliminary, prerequisite, primary, proemial, rudimentary.

preparatory to before, in advance of, in anticipation of, in expectation of, previous to, prior to.

prepare v accoutre, adapt, adjust, anticipate, arm, arrange, assemble, brace, brief, coach, combine, compose, concoct, condition, confect, construct, contrive, develop, devise, dispose, do one's homework, draft, draw up, dress, equip, fashion, fit, fit out, fix (up), forearm, form, format, fortify, furnish, get ready, gird, groom, instruct, limber up, make, make ready, make up, mix up, order, outfit, plan, practise, predispose, prime, produce, provide, psych up, put together, ready, rehearse, steel, strengthen, supply, throw together, train, trim, warm up, whip up.

prepare oneself arm oneself, brace oneself, fortify oneself, get psyched up, get ready, gird oneself, grit one's teeth, limber up, psych oneself up, ready oneself, steel oneself.

prepared adj able, alert, all set, arranged, briefed, disposed, equipped, expectant, fit, forearmed, good and ready, inclined, minded, planned, predisposed, prepped, primed, psyched up, ready, set, waiting, well-rehearsed, willing.
antonyms unprepared, unready.

preparedness n alertness, anticipation, competence, expectancy, fitness, order, preparation, readiness.
antonym unreadiness.

preponderance n ascendancy, bulk, dominance, domination, dominion, extensiveness, force, lion's share, majority, mass, power, predominance, prevalence, superiority, supremacy, sway, weight.

preponderant adj ascendant, chief, controlling, dominant, extensive, foremost, greater, larger, most important, overriding, overruling, paramount, predominant, prevailing, prevalent, significant, superior.

prepossessing adj alluring, amiable, appealing, attractive, beautiful, bewitching, captivating, charming, delightful, disarming, enchanting, engaging, fair, fascinating,

fetching, good-looking, handsome, inviting, likable, lovable, magnetic, personable, pleasing, striking, taking, winning, winsome.
antonyms unattractive, unprepossessing.

prepossession n absorption, bias, engrossment, inclination, leaning, liking, partiality, predilection, predisposition, prejudgment, prejudice, preoccupation.

preposterous adj absurd, asinine, bizarre, crazy, derisory, excessive, exorbitant, extravagant, extreme, fatuous, foolish, imbecile, impossible, inane, incredible, insane, intolerable, irrational, laughable, ludicrous, monstrous, nonsensical, outrageous, ridiculous, risible, senseless, shocking, unbelievable, unconscionable, unreasonable, unthinkable.
antonym reasonable.

prerequisite adj basic, essential, fundamental, imperative, indispensable, mandatory, necessary, needed, needful, obligatory, required, requisite, vital.
antonym unnecessary.
n condition, essential, imperative, must, necessity, precondition, preparation, provision, proviso, qualification, requirement, requisite, sine qua non.
antonym extra.

prerogative n advantage, authority, birthright, carte blanche, choice, claim, droit, due, exemption, immunity, liberty, licence, perquisite, privilege, right, sanction, title.

presage v adumbrate, augur, betoken, bode, divine, feel, forebode, forecast, forefeel, foreknow, foresee, foreshadow, foretell, foretoken, forewarn, intuit, omen, point to, portend, predict, prognosticate, prophesy, sense, signify, soothsay, vaticinate, warn of.
n apprehension, augury, auspice, bad vibes, boding, feeling, foreboding, forecast, foreknowledge, forewarning, funny feeling, harbinger, intimation, intuition, misgiving, omen, portent, prediction, premonition, presentiment, prodrome, prognostic, prognostication, prophecy, sign, warning.

prescience n clairvoyance, far-sightedness, foreknowledge, foresight, precognition, predetermination, prevision, prophecy, second sight.

prescient adj clairvoyant, discerning, divinatory, divining, far-seeing, far-sighted, foreknowing, foreseeing, foresighted, mantic, perceptive, previsional, prophetic, psychic.
antonym imperceptive.

prescribe v advise, appoint, assign, command, decree, define, dictate, direct, enjoin, fix, impose (on), lay down, limit, ordain, order, proper, require, rule, set, set bounds to, specify, stipulate.
▲ *confusable word* proscribe.

prescribed adj assigned, decreed, established, formulaic, formulary, laid down, official, ordained, orthodox, prescription, proper, set, specified, stipulated, textbook.

prescription *n* direction, directive, drug, formula, instruction, medicine, mixture, preparation, recipe, remedy, treatment.

prescriptive *adj* authoritarian, commanding, customary, dictatorial, didactic, dogmatic, instructive, legislative, preceptive, prescribing, rigid, usual.

presence *n* air, apparition, appearance, aspect, attendance, aura, bearing, carriage, closeness, company, comportment, demeanour, ease, existence, ghost, immanence, immediacy, manifestation, mien, nearness, occurrence, personality, phantom, poise, propinquity, proximity, revenant, self-assurance, shade, spectre, spirit, statuesqueness, vicinity.
antonym absence.

presence of mind alertness, aplomb, calmness, composure, cool, coolness, gumption, imperturbability, level-headedness, quickness, sang-froid, self-assurance, self-command, self-possession, wits.
antonyms agitation, confusion.

present¹ *adj* at hand, attendant, attending, available, contemporary, current, existent, extant, here, here and now, immanent, immediate, instant, near, now, on hand, ready, there, to hand.
antonyms absent, out-of-date, past.

for the present for a while, for now, for the moment, for the nonce, for the time being, in the interim, in the meantime, pro tem, pro tempore, provisionally, temporarily.

present² *v* acquaint (with), address, adduce, advance, award, bestow, confer, declare, demonstrate, display, donate, entrust, exhibit, expound, extend, furnish, give, grant, hand over, hold out, introduce, manifest, mount, offer, pose, produce, proffer, provide, put on, raise, recount, relate, show, stage, state, submit, suggest, tender, unveil.
antonym take.
n benefaction, boon, bounty, donation, endowment, favour, gift, grant, gratuity, largesse, offering, presentation, surprise.

presentable *adj* acceptable, becoming, clean, decent, neat, passable, pleasing, proper, respectable, satisfactory, suitable, tidy, tolerable.
antonyms unpresentable, untidy.

presentation *n* appearance, arrangement, award, bestowal, conferral, consecration, delivery, demonstration, display, donation, exhibition, exposition, gift, giving, introduction, investiture, lecture, offering, pageant, performance, production, proposal, rendition, representation, seminar, show, showing, staging, submission, talk.

present-day *adj* contemporary, current, existing, fashionable, living, modern, present, up-to-date.
antonyms future, past.

presentiment *n* anticipation, apprehension, bad vibes, expectation, fear, feeling in one's bones, foreboding, foreknowledge, forewarning, (funny) feeling, hunch, intimation, intuition, misgiving, premonition, presage.

presently *adv* anon, at present, at the moment, before long, by and by, directly, immediately, in a minute, in due time, now, shortly, soon.

preservation *n* conservation, defence, keeping, maintenance, perpetuation, protection, retention, safeguarding, safekeeping, safety, salvation, security, storage, support, upholding, upkeep.
antonyms destruction, ruination.

preserve *v* care for, conserve, continue, cure, defend, embalm, guard, hold on to, keep, maintain, perpetuate, protect, reserve, retain, safeguard, save, secure, shelter, shield, store, sustain, uphold.
antonyms destroy, neglect, ruin.
n area, bird sanctuary, confection, confiture, conserve, domain, field, game preserve, jam, jelly, marmalade, national park, purview, realm, refuge, reservation, reserve, sanctuary, sole, specialism, specialty, sphere, wilderness preserve, wildlife preserve.

preside *v* administer, chair, conduct, control, direct, govern, head, lead, manage, officiate, run, supervise.

press¹ *v* afflict, assail, beg, beset, besiege, clasp, cluster, coax, compel, compress, condense, constrain, crowd, crush, demand, depress, disquiet, dun, embrace, encircle, enfold, enforce, enjoin, entreat, exhort, finish, flatten, flock, force, force down, gather, harass, hasten, herd, hug, hurry, implore, importune, insist on, iron, jam, mangle, mash, mill, petition, plague, plead, pressure, push, push against, push on, rush, seethe, smooth, squeeze, steam, stuff, sue, supplicate, surge, swarm, throng, thrust, torment, trouble, urge, vex, worry.
antonyms expand, hang back, lighten, relieve.
n bunch, bustle, crowd, crowding, crush, demand, flock, hassle, herd, horde, host, hurry, mob, multitude, pack, pressure, push, strain, stress, swarm, throng, thrust, urgency.

press² *n* columnists, correspondents, Fleet Street, fourth estate, hacks, journalism, journalists, news media, newspapers, newswriters, paparazzi, papers, photographers, reporters.

pressed *adj* browbeaten, bullied, coerced, constrained, forced, harassed, hurried, pressured, pushed, rushed, short (of), strapped, under pressure.
antonyms unhurried, well-off.

pressing *adj* acute, burning, compelling, constraining, crowding, crucial, crushing, essential, exigent, high-priority, imperative, important, importunate, serious, thronging, urgent, vital.
antonyms trivial, unimportant.

pressure *n* adversity, affliction, burden, coercion, compressing, compression, compulsion, constraint, crushing, demands, difficulty, distress, duress, exigency, force, hassle, heat, heaviness, hurry, influence, insistence, load, obligation, power, power play, press, squeeze, squeezing, strain, stress, sway, urgency, weight.

v browbeat, bulldoze, bully, coerce, compel, constrain, dragoon, drive, force, impel, importune, induce, lean on, manipulate, oblige, persuade, press, pressurize, put pressure on, put the screws to, railroad, squeeze, twist one's arm, urge, work on.

prestige *n* authority, cachet, celebrity, clout, credit, distinction, eminence, esteem, fame, honour, importance, influence, kudos, pull, regard, renown, reputation, respect, standing, stature, status, weight.

antonyms humbleness, unimportance.

prestigious *adj* blue-chip, celebrated, classy, eminent, esteemed, estimable, exalted, great, high-status, illustrious, important, imposing, impressive, influential, notable, posh, prominent, renowned, respected, upscale.

antonyms humble, modest.

presumably *adv* apparently, (as) like as not, doubtless, doubtlessly, in all likelihood, in all probability, most likely, no doubt, probably, seemingly, supposedly.

presume *v* assume, bank on, believe, conjecture, count on, dare, depend on, entail, expect, figure, go so far as, have the audacity, hypothesize, imagine, impose (upon), infer, make (so) bold, posit, postulate, presuppose, reckon, rely on, suppose, surmise, take advantage (of), take for granted, take it, take the liberty, take upon oneself, think, trust, undertake, venture.

presumption[1] *n* arrogance, audacity, boldness, brass, cheek, chutzpah, effrontery, forwardness, gall, imposition, impudence, insolence, nerve, presumptuousness, temerity.

antonyms humility, politeness.

presumption[2] *n* anticipation, assumption, basis, belief, chance, conjecture, entailment, expectation, grounds, guess, hypothesis, inference, likelihood, opinion, plausibility, premise, presupposition, probability, reason, supposition, surmise.

presumptive *adj* apparent, assumed, believable, believed, conceivable, credible, designate, expected, evidential, hypothetical, inferred, likely, plausible, possible, probable, prospective, reasonable, supposed, suppositional, understood.

antonyms known, unlikely.

presumptuous *adj* arrogant, audacious, big-headed, bold, conceited, familiar, foolhardy, forward, impertinent, impudent, insolent, obtrusive, overconfident, overfamiliar, overweening, presuming, pushy, rash.

antonym modest.

presuppose *v* accept, assume, consider, entail, imply, posit, postulate, premise, presume, suppose, take for granted.

presupposition *n* assumption, belief, hypothesis, preconception, prejudgment, premise, presumption, supposition, theory.

pretence *n* act, acting, affectation, appearance, artifice, charade, claim, cloak, cover, deceit, deception, display, excuse, fabrication, façade, fakery, faking, falsehood, feigning, garb, guise, humbug, invention, make-believe, mask, masquerade, play-acting, posing, posturing, pretentiousness, pretext, profession, ruse, semblance, sham, show, simulation, smoke and mirrors, subterfuge, trickery, veil, veneer, wile.

antonyms honesty, openness.

pretend *v* act, affect, allege, aspire, assume, claim, counterfeit, dissemble, dissimulate, fake, falsify, feign, go through the motions, imagine, impersonate, make believe, pass oneself off, play-act, profess, purport, put on, sham, simulate, suppose.

pretended *adj* alleged, assumed, avowed, bogus, counterfeit, fake, false, feigned, fictitious, imaginary, ostensible, phony, pretend, professed, pseudo, purported, sham, so-called, specious, spurious, supposed, supposititious, would-be.

antonym real.

pretender *n* aspirant, claimant, claimer, fake, fraud, impersonator impostor, phony, pseud, wolf in sheep's clothing.

pretension *n* affectation, airs, aspiration, assertion, assumption, claim, conceit, demand, display, fakery, grandiloquence, hypocrisy, ostentation, pomposity, pretence, pretentiousness, pretext, profession, self-importance, show, showiness, snobbery, snobbishness, vainglory, vanity.

antonyms humility, modesty, simplicity, straightforwardness.

pretentious *adj* affected, ambitious, assuming, bombastic, chi-chi, conceited, euphuistic, exaggerated, extravagant, flaunting, grandiloquent, grandiose, highfalutin, high-flown, high-sounding, hollow, inflated, magniloquent, mannered, orotund, ostentatious, overambitious, overassuming, pompous, pseud, pseudo, showy, snobbish, snooty, specious, uppity, vainglorious.

antonyms humble, modest, simple, straightforward.

pretext *n* appearance, cloak, cover, device, excuse, guise, mask, ploy, pretence, rationale, ruse, semblance, show, simulation, veil.

prettify *v* adorn, beautify, bedeck, deck, deck out, decorate, doll up, do up, dress up, embellish, fancy up, garnish, gild, ornament, pretty up, primp, smarten up, spiff up, tart up, titivate, trick out, trim.

antonyms mar, uglify.

pretty *adj* appealing, attractive, beautiful, bijou, bonny, charming, comely, cute, dainty, decorative, delicate, elegant, fair, fine, good-looking, graceful, lovely, neat, nice, personable, pleasing, pretty as a picture, sightly, tasteful, trim.

antonyms tasteless, ugly.

adv fairly, moderately, passably, quite, rather, reasonably, somewhat, to some degree, tolerably.

prevail v abound, be in general use, endure, excel, obtain, overcome, overrule, predominate, preponderate, reign, rule, succeed, triumph, win.
antonym lose.

prevail on bring around, convince, induce, influence, persuade, prompt, sway, talk around, talk into, twist one's arm, win over.

prevailing *adj* chief, common, controlling, current, customary, dominant, established, fashionable, general, influential, in style, in vogue, main, mainstream, operative, ordinary, overall, popular, predominating, preponderating, prepotent, prevalent, principal, ruling, set, usual, victorious, widespread.
antonyms minor, uncommon.

prevalence n acceptance, ascendancy, commonness, currency, extensiveness, frequency, hold, mastery, omnipresence, pervasiveness, popularity, predominance, preponderance, prepotency, primacy, profusion, regularity, rule, sway, ubiquity, universality.
antonym uncommonness.

prevalent *adj* accepted, ascendant, common, commonplace, compelling, current, customary, dominant, epidemic, established, everyday, extensive, fashionable, frequent, general, governing, habitual, popular, powerful, predominant, prevailing, rampant, regnant, rife, successful, superior, ubiquitous, universal, usual, victorious, widespread.
antonyms subordinate, uncommon.

prevaricate v be evasive, cavil, deceive, dodge, equivocate, fib, hedge, lie, palter, quibble, shift, shuffle, stretch the truth, temporize, tergiversate.

prevarication n cavil, cavilling, deceit, deception, equivocation, evasion, falsehood, falsification, fibbing, fib(s), half-truth, lie, misrepresentation, pretence, quibbling, tergiversation, untruth.

prevaricator n Ananias, casuist, caviller, deceiver, dissembler, dodger, equivocator, evader, falsifier, fibber, hypocrite, liar, pettifogger, quibbler, sophist.

prevent v anticipate, avert, avoid, bar, block, check, counteract, debar, defend against, deter, foil, forestall, frustrate, get in the way of, hamper, head off, hinder, impede, inhibit, intercept, keep (from), obstruct, obviate, preclude, prohibit, restrain, stave off, stop, stymie, thwart, ward off.
antonyms cause, foster, help.

prevention n anticipation, avoidance, bar, check, deterrence, elimination, forestalling, forethought, frustration, hindrance, impediment, interruption, obstacle, obstruction, obviation, precaution, preclusion, prohibition, prophylaxis, safeguard, stoppage, thwarting.
antonyms causing, fostering, help.

preventive *adj* counteractive, deterrent, hampering, hindering, impeding, inhibitory, obstructive, precautionary, preventative, prohibitive, prophylactic, protective, shielding.
antonyms causative, fostering.

n block, condom, deterrent, hindrance, impediment, neutralizer, obstacle, obstruction, prevention, prophylactic, protection, protective, remedy, safeguard, shield.
antonyms cause, encouragement, incitement.

previous *adj* antecedent, anterior, earlier, erstwhile, ex-, foregoing, former, one-time, past, preceding, precipitate, premature, prior, quondam, sometime, untimely, whilom.
antonyms later, timely.

previously *adv* before, beforehand, earlier, formerly, heretofore, historically, hitherto, in the past, once.
antonym later.

prey n booty, dupe, fall guy, game, kill, mark, mug, plunder, quarry, target, victim.

prey on blackmail, bleed, bully, burden, despoil, devour, distress, eat, eat away, exploit, feed on, gnaw at, haunt, hunt, intimidate, live off, oppress, ravage, seize, take advantage of, terrorize, trouble, victimize, waste, weigh down, weigh heavily, worry.

price n amount, assessment, bill, bounty, charge, consequences, consideration, cost, damage, estimate, expenditure, expense, fee, figure, levy, outlay, payment, penalty, rate, sacrifice, sum, toll, valuation, value, worth.
v assess, cost, estimate, evaluate, offer, put, rate, valorize, value.

priceless[1] *adj* beyond price, cherished, costly, dear, expensive, incalculable, incomparable, inestimable, invaluable, irreplaceable, precious, prized, rare, rich, treasured, without price.
antonyms cheap, run-of-the-mill.

priceless[2] *adj* absurd, a hoot, amusing, a scream, comic, droll, funny, hilarious, killing, rib-tickling, rich, ridiculous, riotous, risible, sidesplitting, too funny for words.

pricey *adj* costly, dear, excessive, exorbitant, expensive, extortionate, high-priced, steep, upscale.
antonym cheap.

prick v bite, bore, goad, hurt, itch, jab, jag, pain, perforate, pierce, pink, point, prickle, punch, puncture, raise, rise, smart, stab, sting, thorn, tingle, touch, trouble.
n goad, jag, pang, perforation, pinhole, prickle, puncture, smart, spasm, sting, twinge, wound.

prickle n aculeus, barb, needle, point, smart, spike, spine, spur, sting, thorn, tickle, tingle, tingling.
v itch, jab, nick, nip, prick, smart, sting, tingle.

prickly *adj* aculeate, barbed, brambly, bristly, cantankerous, complicated, crawling, delicate, difficult, echinate, edgy, fractious, grumpy, intricate, involved, irritable, itchy, jaggy, knotty, peevish, pettish, petulant, prickling, pricking, scratchy, sharp, short-tempered, smarting, spiny, stinging, tetchy, thorny, ticklish, tingling, touchy, tricky, troublesome, trying, waspish.
antonyms easygoing, simple, smooth.

pride *n* amour-propre, arrogance, best, big-headedness, conceit, cream, crème de la crème, delight, dignity, egotism, elite, flower, gem, glory, gratification, haughtiness, hauteur, high spirits, honour, hubris, jewel, joy, loftiness, magnificence, mettle, ostentation, pick, pleasure, presumption, pretension, pretentiousness, pride and joy, prize, satisfaction, self-esteem, self-importance, self-love, self-respect, smugness, snobbery, splendour, superciliousness, treasure, vainglory, vanity.

antonym humility.

pride oneself on be proud of, boast about, brag about, congratulate oneself on, crow about, exult in, flatter oneself on, glory in, pat oneself on the back for, pique oneself on, plume oneself on, preen oneself on, revel in, take pride in, vaunt.

antonyms belittle, humble.

priest, priestess *n* abbé, canon, churchman, clergyman, clergywoman, cleric, curate, curé, divine, ecclesiastic, father, father confessor, flamen, holy man (or woman), lama, Levite, Magus, man (or woman) of God, man (or woman) of the cloth, minister, padre, rector, religious, vestal, vicar.

priestly *adj* canonical, churchly, clerical, ecclesiastical, hieratic, ministerial, pastoral, priestlike, sacerdotal.

prig *n* bluenose, goody-goody, Mrs. Grundy, precisian, prude, puritan, snob.

priggish *adj* fastidious, goody-goody, holier-than-thou, narrow-minded, pedantic, prim, prudish, puritanical, self-righteous, self-satisfied, smug, snobbish, snooty, starchy, stiff, stuffy.

antonyms broad-minded, informal.

prim *adj* demure, fastidious, formal, fussy, governessy, old-maidish, particular, precise, priggish, prissy, proper, prudish, puritanical, rigid, schoolmarmish, sedate, starchy, stiff, strait-laced.

antonyms broad-minded, informal.

primacy *n* ascendancy, command, dominance, dominion, importance, leadership, paramountcy, pre-eminence, seniority, sovereignty, superiority, supremacy.

antonym inferiority.

primal *adj* basic, central, chief, earliest, essential, first, fundamental, greatest, highest, initial, main, major, original, paramount, primary, prime, primeval, primitive, primordial, principal, pristine, ur-.

antonyms later, minor.

primarily *adv* at bottom, at heart, basically, chiefly, especially, essentially, first (and foremost), fundamentally, generally, mainly, mostly, principally.

antonym secondarily.

primary *adj* aboriginal, basic, beginning, best, capital, cardinal, chief, dominant, earliest, elemental, elementary, essential, first, foremost, fundamental, greatest, highest, initial, introductory, leading, main, most important, original, paramount, primal, prime,

primeval, primitive, primordial, principal, pristine, radical, rudimentary, simple, top, ultimate, underlying.

antonym secondary.

prime[1] *adj* basic, beginning, best, capital, chief, choice, earliest, excellent, first-class, first-rate, foremost, fundamental, highest, leading, main, original, predominant, pre-eminent, primary, primitive, principal, quality, ruling, select, selected, senior, superior, top, underlying.

antonyms minor, secondary, second-rate.

n beginning, dawn, flower, flowering, height, heyday, maturity, morning, opening, peak, perfection, spring, springtide, springtime, start, youth, zenith.

prime[2] *v* brief, charge, clue in, coach, cram, equip, fill, fill in, groom, inform, notify, prepare, train.

primer *n* ABC, basics, introduction, manual, prodrome, reader, rudiments, textbook.

primeval *adj* ancient, earliest, early, first, old, original, prehistoric, primal, primitive, primordial, pristine, ur-.

antonyms developed, later, modern.

primitive *adj* backward, barbarian, barbaric, childlike, crude, earliest, early, elementary, first, naïve, neanderthal, original, primal, primary, primeval, primordial, pristine, rough, rude, rudimentary, savage, simple, uncivilized, uncouth, uncultivated, undeveloped, unrefined, unsophisticated, untrained, untutored, ur-.

antonyms advanced, civilized, developed.

primordial *adj* basic, beginning, earliest, elemental, first, first-formed, first-made, fundamental, original, prehistoric, primal, primeval, primitive, pristine, radical, ur-.

antonyms developed, later, modern.

prince, princess *n* lady, lord, mogul, monarch, nabob, nawab, nobleman, noblewoman, potentate, ruler, sovereign.

princely *adj* august, bounteous, bountiful, dignified, generous, gracious, grand, imperial, imposing, lavish, liberal, lofty, magnanimous, magnificent, majestic, munificent, noble, open-handed, regal, rich, royal, sovereign, stately, sumptuous.

antonyms humble, mean.

principal *adj* capital, cardinal, chief, controlling, dominant, essential, first, foremost, highest, key, leading, main, most important, paramount, predominant, pre-eminent, primary, prime, strongest.

antonyms least, lesser, minor.

n boss, chief, dean, director, educator, first violin, head, head honcho, head teacher, headmaster, headmistress, lead, leader, main party (or character), master, prima ballerina, prima donna, rector, star, superintendent, superior.

▲ *confusable word* principle.

principally *adv* above all, chiefly, especially, first and foremost, mainly, mostly, particularly, predominantly, primarily.

principle *n* assumption, axiom, basis, belief, canon, code, conscience, credo, criterion, dictum, doctrine, dogma, element, ethic, formula, fundamental, golden rule, grounds, honour, institute, integrity, law, maxim, moral, morality, morals, postulate, precept, principium, probity, proposition, rectitude, rule, scruples, standard, tenet, truth, uprightness, verity, virtue.

antonyms corruption, wickedness.

▲ *confusable word* prinicpal.

in principle en principe, ideally, in essence, in theory, theoretically.

principled *adj* clear, clear-cut, conscientious, correct, decent, ethical, full of integrity, high-minded, honourable, just, logical, moral, rational, reasoned, righteous, right-minded, scrupulous, sensible, upright, virtuous, well-founded, well thought-out.

antonym unprincipled.

print *v* engrave, impress, imprint, issue, mark, process, produce, publish, reproduce, run off, stamp, write.

n books, characters, copy, design, die, edition, engraving, face, fingerprint, font, fount, impression, imprint, ink, lettering, letters, magazines, mark, mould, newspapers, periodicals, photo, photograph, picture, publications, reproduction, snap, stamp, type, typeface, typescript.

prior *adj* aforementioned, antecedent, anterior, earlier, foregoing, former, preceding, pre-existent, previous.

antonym later.

prior to before, earlier than, preceding, preparatory to, previous to.

antonym after.

priority *n* importance, precedence, pre-eminence, preference, prerogative, privilege, rank, right of way, seniority, superiority, supremacy, the lead.

antonyms inferiority, subordinateness.

priory *n* abbey, cloister, convent, monastery, nunnery, religious house.

prison *n* bastille, big house, bridewell, brig, cage, calaboose, can, cell, clink, concentration camp, confinement, cooler, coop, correctional facility, dungeon, gulag, hoosegow, house of correction, house of detention, imprisonment, jail, jug, lockup, pen, penal institution, penitentiary, pokey, reformatory, slammer, solitary confinement, stalag, stir, tank, the hole.

prisoner *n* captive, con, convict, detainee, hostage, inmate, internee, jailbird, lifer, P.O.W., prisoner of war.

prissy *adj* effeminate, fastidious, finicky, fussy, old-maidish, overnice, precious, prim, prim and proper, prudish, schoolmarmish, squeamish, starchy, strait-laced.

antonyms broad-minded, informal.

pristine *adj* earliest, first, former, initial, innocent, natural, original, primal, primary, primeval, primitive, primordial, uncorrupted, undamaged, undefiled, unspoiled, unsullied, untouched, unused, virgin.

antonyms developed, later, polluted, spoiled.

privacy *n* confidentiality, isolation, quietness, quietude, personal space, retirement, retreat, seclusion, separateness, sequestration, solitude.

antonym publicness.

private *adj* aloof, clandestine, closet, concealed, confidential, exclusive, hush-hush, in camera, independent, individual, inner, inside, intimate, intraparietal, inward, isolated, off-the-record, own, particular, personal, privy, reserved, retired, secluded, secret, self-contained, separate, sequestered, solitary, special, unofficial, withdrawn.

antonyms open, public.

in private behind closed doors, in camera, in confidence, in private conference, in secret, privately, secretly, sub rosa, under the rose.

antonym openly.

private detective P.I., gumshoe, pinkerton, private eye, private investigator, shamus, sleuth, sleuthhound.

privateer *n* buccaneer, corsair, freebooter, marque, pirate, sea robber, sea wolf.

privation *n* absence, affliction, austerity, bereavement, deprivation, destitution, (dire) need, distress, hardship, indigence, lack, loss, misery, necessary, neediness, penury, poverty, suffering, want.

antonyms affluence, wealth.

privilege *n* advantage, benefit, birthright, claim, concession, droit, due, entitlement, exemption, franchise, freedom, immunity, liberty, licence, prerogative, right, sanction, title.

antonym disadvantage.

privileged *adj* advantaged, allowed, authorized, classified, confidential, elite, empowered, entitled, exempt, favoured, free, granted, honoured, indulged, inviolable, licensed, permitted, powerful, protected, ruling, sacrosanct, sanctioned, special, vested.

antonyms disadvantaged, underprivileged.

privy *n* can, cloaca, john, latrine, lavatory, loo, outhouse, toilet, watercloset, w.c.

adj confidential, hidden, hush-hush, intimate, off-the-record, personal, private, secret, top-secret.

antonym public.

privy to apprised of, aware of, cognizant of, in on, informed about, in the know about, party to, wise to.

antonym unaware of.

prize¹ *n* accolade, award, conquest, gain, goal, haul, honour, hope, jackpot, premium, purse, reward, stake(s), trophy, windfall, winnings.

adj award-winning, best, champion, excellent, first-rate, outstanding, top, top-notch, winning.

antonyms second-rate, worst.

v appreciate, cherish, esteem, hold dear, rate highly, revere, reverence, set store by, treasure, value.

antonyms despise, undervalue.

prize² *n* booty, capture, conquest, haul, loot, pickings, pillage, plunder, spoils, trophy.

probability *n* chances, expectation, (good) chance, liability, likelihood, likeliness, odds, prospect.
antonym improbability.

probable *adj* apparent, credible, expected, feasible, in (or on) the cards, likely, odds-on, plausible, possible, predicted, presumed, reasonable, seeming, verisimilar.
antonym improbable.

probably *adv* as likely as not, doubtless, in all likelihood, in all probability, like as not, like enough, likely, little doubt, maybe, most (or very) likely, perhaps, possibly, presumably.
antonym improbably.

probation *n* apprenticeship, novitiate, testing, test (period), trial (period).

probe *v* examine, explore, go into, investigate, look into, penetrate, pierce, poke, prod, query, scrutinize, search (into), sift, sound (out), test.
n bore, drill, examination, exploration, inquest, inquiry, investigation, research, scrutiny, study, test.

probity *n* equity, fairness, fidelity, goodness, honesty, honour, honourableness, integrity, justice, morality, principle, rectitude, righteousness, sincerity, trustworthiness, truthfulness, uprightness, virtue, worth.
antonym improbity.

problem *n* brain teaser, brain twister, bug, complication, conundrum, difficulty, dilemma, disagreement, dispute, doubt, enigma, kink, mystery, no laughing matter, obstacle, snag, poser, predicament, puzzle, quandary, question, riddle, trouble, vexed question.
adj delinquent, difficult, intractable, perverse, refractory, uncontrollable, unmanageable, unruly.
antonyms manageable, well-behaved.

problematic *adj* chancy, debatable, dicey, difficult, doubtful, dubious, enigmatic, iffy, moot, puzzling, questionable, thorny, tricky, uncertain, unestablished, unsettled, unsure.
antonym certain.

procedure *n* approach, business, ceremony, course (of action), custom, form, formula, method, modus operandi, move, operation, performance, plan of action, policy, practice, process, routine, scheme, step, strategy, system, transaction.

proceed *v* advance, arise, begin, carry on, come forth, continue, derive, emanate, ensue, flow, follow, go ahead, go on (or forward), issue, move on (or forward), originate, pass (on), press on, progress, result, set in motion, spring, start, stem, take action, take steps.
antonyms retreat, stop.
▲ *confusable word* precede.

proceedings *n* account, action, affair, affairs, annals, archives, business, course of action, dealings, deeds, doings, event(s), lawsuit, litigation, matters, measures, minutes, moves, procedure, process, record(s), report, steps, transactions, undertaking.

proceeds *n* earnings, emoluments, gain, income, monies raised, profit, receipts, returns, revenue, takings, yield.
antonyms losses, outlay.

process *n* action, advance, approach, case, course, course of action, development, evolution, formation, growth, manner, means, measure, method, mode, movement, operation, performance, practice, procedure, proceeding, proceedings, progress, stage, step(s), suit, summons, system, transaction, trial, unfolding.
v alter, convert, deal with, digitize, dispose of, fill, handle, make, prepare, refine, transform, treat.

processing *n* conversion, handling, manufacture, preparation, refinement, treatment.

procession *n* cavalcade, column, concatenation, cortege, course, cycle, file, march, marchpast, motorcade, parade, run, sequence, series, string, succession, train.

proclaim *v* advertise, affirm, announce, annunciate, bear witness (to), blaze, blazon, circulate, declare, enounce, enunciate, give out, herald, indicate, issue a statement, make known, profess, promulgate, pronounce, publicize, publish, show, testify, trumpet.

proclamation *n* affirmation, announcement, annunciation, ban, bulletin, declaration, decree, edict, interlocution, manifesto, notice, notification, press conference, promulgation, pronouncement, pronunciamento, publication, ukase.

proclivity *n* bent, bias, disposition, facility, inclination, leaning, liability, penchant, predilection, predisposition, preference, proneness, propensity, tendency, weakness.
antonym disinclination.

procrastinate *v* adjourn, dally, dawdle, defer, delay, dilly-dally, drag one's heels, gain time, Penelopize, play for time, postpone, prolong, protract, put off, retard, stall, temporize, waste time.
antonyms advance, proceed.

procrastination *n* dallying, deferral, delaying, dilly-dallying, foot-dragging, stalling, temporizing.

procreate *v* beget, breed, conceive, engender, father, generate, mother, produce, propagate, reproduce, sire, spawn.

procure *v* acquire, appropriate, bag, bring about, buy, come by, earn, effect, find, gain, get, induce, lay hands on, obtain, pander, pick up, pimp, purchase, secure, win.
antonym lose.

procurer *n* bawd, madam, pander, pimp, procuress, white slaver, whoremonger.

prod *v* dig, drive, egg on, elbow, encourage, goad, impel, incite, jab, motivate, move, nudge, poke, prick, prompt, propel, push, rouse, shove, spur, stimulate, stir up, urge (on).
n boost, cue, dig, elbow, jab, nudge, poke,

prompt, push, reminder, shove, signal, stimulus.

prodigal *adj* bounteous, bountiful, copious, excessive, extravagant, exuberant, generous, immoderate, improvident, intemperate, lavish, luxuriant, profligate, profuse, reckless, spendthrift, squandering, sumptuous, superabundant, teeming, unsparing, unthrifty, wanton, wasteful.
antonyms modest, parsimonious, thrifty.
n big spender, profligate, spendthrift, squanderer, waster, wastrel.

prodigality *n* abandon, abundance, amplitude, bounteousness, bounty, copiousness, dissipation, excess, extravagance, exuberance, immoderation, intemperance, lavishness, luxuriance, overabundance, plenteousness, plenty, profligacy, profusion, recklessness, richness, squandering, sumptuousness, superabundance, unthrift, unthriftiness, wantonness, waste, wastefulness.
antonyms modesty, parsimony, thrift.

prodigious *adj* amazing, astounding, colossal, enormous, exceptional, extraordinary, fabulous, fantastic, flabbergasting, giant, gigantic, huge, immeasurable, immense, impressive, inordinate, mammoth, marvellous, massive, miraculous, monstrous, monumental, phenomenal, remarkable, spectacular, staggering, startling, striking, stupendous, tremendous, unprecedented, unusual, vast, wonderful.
antonyms commonplace, small, unremarkable.

prodigy *n* child genius, curiosity, genius, gifted child (or person), marvel, master, mastermind, miracle, natural, phenomenon, rara avis, rarity, sensation, spectacle, superstar, talent, virtuoso, whiz, whiz kid, wizard, wonder, wonder child, wunderkind.

produce *v* adduce, bear, bear fruit, beget, breed, bring about, bring forth, cause, compose, construct, create, deliver, demonstrate, develop, direct, effect, engender, exhibit, fabricate, factuate, furnish, generate, give, give rise to, invent, make, manufacture, mount, occasion, offer, originate, present, provoke, put forward, put on, render, result in, secrete, show, stage, supply, yield.
antonyms consume, result from.
n crop, fruit, harvest, product, vegetables, yield.

producer *n* creator, director, farmer, grower, impresario, maker, manager, manufacturer, presenter, régisseur.

product *n* artefact, commodity, concoction, consequence, creation, effect, end result, facture, fruit, goods, invention, issue, legacy, merchandise, offshoot, offspring, outcome, output, produce, production, result, returns, spinoff, upshot, work, yield.
antonym cause.

production *n* assembly, construction, creation, direction, fabrication, facture, formation, fructification, making, management, manufacture, manufacturing, origination, preparation, presentation, producing, staging.
antonym consumption.

productive *adj* abundant, advantageous, beneficial, constructive, creative, dynamic, effective, energetic, fecund, fertile, fructiferous, fruitful, gainful, generative, gratifying, inventive, plentiful, prodigal, producing, profitable, prolific, rewarding, rich, teeming, useful, valuable, vigorous, voluminous, well-spent, worthwhile.
antonyms fruitless, unproductive.

productivity *n* abundance, fecundity, fertility, fruitfulness, output, production, productiveness, yield.
antonym unproductiveness.

profane *adj* abusive, blasphemous, coarse, crude, dirty, disrespectful, filthy, forbidden, foul, godless, heathen, idolatrous, impious, impure, irreligious, irreverent, lay, obscene, pagan, sacrilegious, secular, sinful, temporal, unclean, unconsecrated, ungodly, unhallowed, unholy, uninitiated, unsanctified, vulgar, wicked, worldly.
antonyms initiated, permitted, religious, sacred.
v abuse, blaspheme (against), contaminate, debase, defile, degrade, desecrate, misemploy, misuse, pervert, pollute, prostitute, violate, vitiate.
antonym revere.

profanity *n* abuse, blasphemy, curse, cursing, execration, expletive, foul (or obscene) language, four-letter word(s), impiety, imprecation, irreverence, malediction, obscenity, profaneness, sacrilege, swearing, swearword.
antonyms politeness, reverence.

profess *v* acknowledge, admit, affirm, allege, announce, assert, asseverate, avouch, avow, certify, claim, confess, confirm, declare, enunciate, fake, feign, lay claim to, maintain, make out, own, pretend, proclaim, propose, propound, purport, sham, state.

professed *adj* acknowledged, alleged, avowed, certified, confirmed, declared, ostensible, pretended, proclaimed, purported, self-acknowledged, self-confessed, self-styled, so-called, soi-disant, supposed, would-be.

profession *n* acknowledgment, affirmation, assertion, attestation, avowal, business, calling, career, claim, confession, declaration, employment, job, line (of work), manifesto, métier, occupation, office, position, sphere, statement, testimony, vocation, vow, walk of life.

professional *adj* accomplished, adept, competent, crack, efficient, experienced, expert, finished, masterly, polished, practised, proficient, qualified, skilful, skilled, slick, trained, virtuoso.
antonyms amateur, unprofessional.
n adept, authority, dab hand, expert, maestro, master, past master, pro, proficient, specialist, virtuoso, wizard.

proffer v advance, extend, hand, hold out, offer, present, propose, propound, submit, suggest, tender, volunteer.

proficiency n ability, accomplishment, aptitude, capability, competence, conversancy, dexterity, excellence, expertise, expertness, facility, finesse, knack, know-how, mastery, skilfulness, skill, talent, virtuosity.
antonyms clumsiness, incompetence.

proficient adj able, accomplished, adept, apt, capable, clever, competent, conversant, efficient, excellent, experienced, expert, first-rate, gifted, masterly, qualified, skilful, skilled, talented, trained, versed, virtuoso.
antonyms clumsy, incompetent.

profile n analysis, biography, biopic, characterization, chart, contour, description, diagram, drawing, examination, figure, form, graph, outline, portrait, review, shape, side view, silhouette, sketch, study, survey, table, thumbnail sketch, vignette.

profit n advancement, advantage, a fast buck, avail, benefit, boot, bottom line, earnings, emoluments, fruit, gain, good, graft, gravy, grist, interest, melon, percentage, pickings, proceeds, receipts, return, revenue, surplus, takings, use, value, velvet, winnings, yield.
antonym loss.
v advance, advantage, aid, avail, benefit, be of use, better, clean up, contribute to, do good, forward, gain, help, improve, learn, line one's pockets, make a bundle, promote, serve, stand (one) in good stead.
antonyms harm, hinder.
profit by (or from) capitalize on, cash in on, exploit, learn from, put to good use, reap the benefit of, take advantage of, turn to (good) account, turn to advantage, use, utilize.
antonym lose by.

profitable adj advantageous, beneficial, commercial, cost-effective, expedient, fruitful, gainful, helpful, lucrative, money-making, paying, plummy, productive, remunerative, rewarding, serviceable, useful, utile, valuable, worthwhile.
antonym unprofitable.

profiteer n exploiter, extortionist, racketeer, shakedown artist.
v exploit, extort, fleece, make a fast buck, make a (quick) killing, overcharge, racketeer.

profiteering n exploitation, extortion, highway robbery, racketeering, usury.

profitless adj bootless, fruitless, futile, gainless, idle, ineffective, ineffectual, pointless, thankless, unavailing, unproductive, unprofitable, unremunerative, unrewarding, useless, vain, worthless.
antonym profitable.

profligacy n abandon, baseness, corruption, debauchery, degeneracy, depravity, dissipation, dissoluteness, excess, extravagance, immorality, improvidence, lavishness, laxity, libertinism, licentiousness, prodigality, promiscuity, recklessness, squandering, unrestraint, unthriftiness, wantonness, waste, wastefulness.
antonyms morality, parsimony, thrift, uprightness.

profligate adj abandoned, base, corrupt, debauched, degenerate, depraved, dissipated, dissolute, extravagant, gone to the dogs, immoderate, immoral, improvident, iniquitous, libertine, licentious, loose, prodigal, promiscuous, reckless, reprobate, shameless, spendthrift, squandering, unchaste, unprincipled, vicious, vitiated, wanton, wasteful, whorish, wicked, wild.
antonyms moral, parsimonious, thrifty, upright.
n debauchee, degenerate, libertine, prodigal, racketeer, rake, reprobate, roué, spendthrift, squanderer, waster, wastrel.

profound adj abject, absolute, abstruse, abysmal, acute, awful, bottomless, complete, consummate, deep, deep-felt, deep-seated, discerning, erudite, exhaustive, extensive, extreme, far-reaching, fathomless, fervent, great, heartfelt, heart-rending, hearty, huge, intense, keen, learned, penetrating, philosophical, pronounced, radical, recondite, sagacious, sage, serious, sincere, skilled, subtle, thoroughgoing, thoughtful, total, utter, weighty, wise.
antonyms mild, shallow, slight.

profundity n abstruseness, acuity, acumen, depth, erudition, extremity, insight, intelligence, intensity, learning, penetration, perceptiveness, perspecuity, perspicacity, sagacity, seriousness, severity, strength, wisdom.
antonym shallowness.

profuse adj abundant, ample, bountiful, copious, effusive, exaggerated, excessive, extravagant, exuberant, fulsome, generous, immoderate, lavish, liberal, luxuriant, open-handed, overflowing, over the top, plentiful, prodigal, prolific, teeming, unstinting.
antonyms sparing, sparse.

profusion n abundance, bounty, copiousness, cornucopia, excess, extravagance, exuberance, glut, lavishness, luxuriance, multitude, plenitude, plenty, plethora, prodigality, profuseness, quantity, riot, superabundance, superfluity, surplus, wealth.
antonyms sparingness, sparsity.

progenitor n ancestor, antecedent, begetter, father, forebear, forefather, forerunner, founder, instigator, mother, originator, parent, precursor, predecessor, primogenitor, procreator, source.

progeny n breed, brood, children, descendants, family, fruit, heirs, inheritors, issue, lineage, offspring, posterity, race, scions, seed, stock, young.

prognosis n diagnosis, expectation, forecast, judgment, outlook, prediction, prognostication, projection, prospect, speculation, surmise.

prognosticate v augur, betoken, divine, forecast, foreshadow, foretell, harbinger, herald, indicate, portend, predict, presage, prophesy, soothsay.

prognostication n expectation, forecast, horoscope, prediction, prognosis, projection, prophecy, speculation, surmise.

program n agenda, broadcast, curriculum, design, line-up, list, listing, order of events, order of the day, performance, plan, plan of action, presentation, procedure, production, project, schedule, scheme (of things), show, syllabus, transmission.

v arrange, bill, book, brainwash, design, engage, formulate, indoctrinate, itemize, lay on, line up, list, map out, plan, prearrange, schedule, work out.

progress n advance, advancement, amelioration, betterment, breakthrough, continuation, course, development, gain, growth, headway, improvement, increase, journey, movement, passage, procession, progression, promotion, step forward, way.

antonyms decline, deterioration.

v advance, ameliorate, better, blossom, come on, continue, develop, evolve, forge ahead, gain, gain ground, gather momentum, grow, improve, increase, make headway, make strides, mature, move, move forward, proceed, prosper, travel.

antonyms decline, deteriorate.

in progress going on, happening, occurring, proceeding, under way.

progression n advance, advancement, chain, concatenation, continuation, course, cycle, furtherance, gain, headway, moving forward, order, progress, sequence, series, string, succession.

antonyms decline, deterioration.

progressive adj accelerating, advanced, advancing, avant-garde, continuing, continuous, developing, dynamic, enlightened, enterprising, escalating, forward-looking, gradual, growing, increasing, incremental, intensifying, liberal, modern, ongoing, radical, reactionary, reformist, regressive, revolutionary, up-and-coming.

prohibit v ban, bar, constrain, debar, disallow, embargo, exclude, forbid, hamper, hinder, impede, interdict, obstruct, outlaw, preclude, prevent, proscribe, restrain, restrict, rule out, stop, veto.

antonym permit.

prohibited adj banned, barred, disallowed, embargoed, excluded, forbidden, interdicted, off-limits, proscribed, taboo, verboten, vetoed.

antonym permitted.

prohibition n ban, bar, constraint, disallowance, embargo, exclusion, forbidding, injunction, interdict, interdiction, negation, obstruction, prevention, proscription, restraint, restriction, temperance, veto.

antonym permission.

prohibitive adj excessive, exclusive, exorbitant, extortionate, forbidding, impossible, preposterous, prohibiting, proscriptive, repressive, restraining, restrictive, sky-high, steep, suppressive, unaffordable.

antonyms encouraging, reasonable.

project n activity, assignment, conception, design, enterprise, idea, job, occupation, plan, program, proposal, purpose, scheme, task, undertaking, venture, work.

v beetle, bulge, calculate, cast (forth), come across, contemplate, contrive, design, devise, discharge, draft, estimate, exsert, extend, externalize, extrapolate, extrude, fling, forecast, gauge, hurl, intend, jut, launch, map out, outline, overhang, plan, predetermine, predict, present, propel, prophesy, propose, protrude, purpose, reckon, represent, scheme, shoot (forth), stand out, stick out, throw, transmit.

projectile n ball, bullet, grenade, ICBM, missile, rocket, shell, shot, torpedo.

projecting adj beetling, exsertile, extrusive, overhanging, protrudent, protruding, protrusive.

projection n blueprint, bulge, calculation, computation, diagram, estimate, estimation, extrapolation, forecast, jut, jutting, ledge, map, outline, overhang, plan, prediction, process, prominence, protrusion, protuberance, reckoning, representation, ridge, shelf, sill.

proletariat n canaille, commonalty, commoners, common people, great unwashed, herd, hoi polloi, lower classes, masses, mob, plebs, proles, rabble, rank and file, working class.

proliferate v breed, burgeon, escalate, expand, exuberate, increase, multiply, mushroom, procreate, run riot, snowball.

antonym dwindle.

proliferation n buildup, concentration, duplication, escalation, expansion, extension, increase, intensification, multiplication, mushrooming, procreation, productiveness, snowballing, spread.

antonym decrease.

prolific adj abounding, abundant, bountiful, copious, fecund, fertile, fruitful, generative, luxuriant, productive, profuse, rank, reproductive, rich, teeming, voluminous.

antonyms infertile, scarce.

prolix adj diffuse, digressive, discursive, lengthy, long, long-winded, maundering, overlong, prolonged, prosy, protracted, rambling, tedious, tiresome, verbose, windy, wordy.

antonym succinct.

prolixity n boringness, circuitousness, circuity, diffuseness, discursiveness, long-windedness, maundering, pleonasm, prosiness, rambling, tediousness, verbiage, verboseness, verbosity, wandering, windiness, wordiness.

antonym succinctness.

prologue n exordium, foreword, introduction, preamble, preface, preliminary, prelude, proem, prolegomena.

prolong v continue, delay, drag out, draw out, extend, lengthen, perpetuate, produce, protract, spin out, stretch, stretch out, string out, sustain.

antonym shorten.

promenade¹ *n* boardwalk, boulevard, esplanade, parade, terrace, walkway.

promenade² *n* airing, breather, constitutional, saunter, stroll, turn, walk, walkabout.
v amble, mosey, parade, perambulate, sally forth, saunter, stroll, strut, swagger, walk.

prominence¹ *n* bulge, bump, cliff, crag, crest, elevation, headland, height, hummock, hump, jutting, lump, mound, pinnacle, process, projection, promontory, protrusion, protuberance, rise, spur, swelling.

prominence² *n* celebrity, conspicuousness, distinction, eminence, fame, greatness, importance, markedness, name, notability, outstandingness, precedence, pre-eminence, prestige, rank, reputation, repute, salience, specialness, standing, top billing, visibility, weight.
antonyms inconspicuousness, unimportance.

prominent *adj* beetling, bulging, celebrated, chief, conspicuous, distinguished, eminent, eye-catching, famous, foremost, high-profile, important, jutting, leading, main, noted, noticeable, obtrusive, obvious, outstanding, popular, pre-eminent, projecting, pronounced, protruding, protrusive, protuberant, remarkable, renowned, respected, salient, standing out, striking, top, unmistakable, weighty, well-known.
antonyms inconspicuous, unimportant.

promiscuity *n* abandon, amorality, debauchery, depravity, disorder, dissipation, immorality, laxity, laxness, lechery, libertinism, licentiousness, looseness, permissiveness, profligacy, promiscuousness, unchastity, wantonness, whoring.
antonym chastity.

promiscuous *adj* abandoned, accidental, careless, casual, chaotic, confused, debauched, disordered, dissipated, dissolute, diverse, fast, haphazard, heterogeneous, ill-assorted, immoral, indiscriminate, intermingled, intermixed, jumbled, libertine, licentious, loose, mingled, miscellaneous, mixed, motley, of easy virtue, profligate, random, unbridled, unchaste, uncontrolled, undiscriminating, unselective, wanton, whorish, wild.
antonyms chaste, controlled, selective.

promise *v* assure, augur, bespeak, betoken, bid fair, contract, denote, engage, foretoken, give hope of, guarantee, hint at, indicate, look like, pledge, plight, predict, presage, prophesy, stipulate, suggest, swear, take an oath, undertake, vouch, vow, warrant.
n ability, aptitude, assurance, bond, capability, capacity, commitment, compact, covenant, engagement, guarantee, hope, indication, oath, omen, pledge, potential, talent, undertaking, vow, word, word of honour.

promised land heaven, Kingdom, land of milk and honey, land of opportunity, paradise, Shangri-La, utopia, Zion.

promising *adj* able, auspicious, bright, encouraging, favourable, gifted, good, hopeful, likely, propitious, reassuring, rising, rosy, talented, up-and-coming.
antonym unpromising.

promontory *n* cape, foreland, head, headland, hook, ness, peninsula, point, projection, ridge, spur.

promote *v* advance, advertise, advocate, aggrandize, aid, assist, back, blazon, boost, champion, commend, contribute to, develop, dignify, elevate, encourage, endorse, espouse, exalt, forward, foster, further, help, honour, hype, kick upstairs, nurture, plug, popularize, prefer, publicize, puff, push, raise, recommend, sell, sponsor, stimulate, support, tout, trumpet, upgrade, urge.
antonyms demote, disparage, obstruct.

promotion *n* advancement, advertising, advocacy, aggrandizement, backing, ballyhoo, boosting, campaign, cultivation, development, elevation, encouragement, ennoblement, espousal, exaltation, fanfare, furtherance, honour, hype, plugging, preferment, promo, propaganda, publicity, puffery, pushing, raise, selling, support, trumpeting, upgrading.
antonyms demotion, disparagement, obstruction.

prompt *adj* alert, brisk, eager, early, efficient, expeditious, immediate, instant, instantaneous, on time, punctual, quick, rapid, ready, responsive, smart, speedy, swift, timely, unhesitating, willing.
antonyms dilatory, slow.
v advise, assist, call forth, cause, cue, elicit, evoke, give rise to, impel, incite, induce, influence, inspire, instigate, jog (the memory), motivate, move, occasion, prod, produce, provoke, remind, result in, spur, stimulate, urge.
antonym dissuade.
n cue, help, hint, instigation, jog, jolt, prod, reminder, spur, stimulus.

prompting *n* admonition, advice, assistance, direction, encouragement, hint, incitement, influence, jogging, persuasion, pressing, pressure, prodding, pushing, reminder, reminding, stimulation, suggestion, urging.
antonym dissuasion.

promptly *adv* directly, eagerly, forthwith, immediately, instantly, on time, PDQ, posthaste, pronto, punctually, quickly, right away, speedily, straightaway, swiftly, unhesitatingly, without delay.

promptness *n* alacrity, alertness, briskness, celerity, dispatch, eagerness, expedition, haste, promptitude, punctuality, quickness, readiness, speed, swiftness, willingness.
antonym tardiness.

promulgate *v* advertise, announce, broadcast, circulate, communicate, declare, decree, disseminate, issue, notify, proclaim, promote, publicize, publish, spread.

prone¹ *adj* apt, bent, disposed, given, inclined, liable, likely, minded, predisposed, subject, susceptible, tending, vulnerable, wont.
antonym unlikely.

prone² *adj* face down, flat, full-length, horizontal, procumbent, prostrate, recumbent, stretched.

antonym upright.

proneness *n* aptness, bent, bias, disposition, inclination, leaning, liability, penchant, proclivity, propensity, susceptibility, tendency, weakness.

antonym dislike.

prong *n* fork, point, projection, spike, spur, tine, tip.

pronounce *v* accent, accentuate, affirm, announce, articulate, assert, declaim, declare, decree, deliver, enunciate, judge, pass, proclaim, say, sound, speak, stress, utter, vocalize, voice.

pronounceable *adj* articulable, enunciable, expressible, sayable, speakable, utterable.

antonym unpronounceable.

pronounced *adj* accentuated, broad, clear, conspicuous, decided, definite, distinct, evident, highlighted, marked, noticeable, obvious, positive, striking, strong, unmistakable.

antonyms unnoticeable, vague.

pronouncement *n* affirmation, announcement, assertion, declaration, decree, dictum, edict, ipse dixit, judgment, manifesto, notification, proclamation, promulgation, pronunciamento, statement.

pronunciation *n* accent, accentuation, articulation, diction, elocution, enunciation, inflection, intonation, modulation, speech, stress.

proof *n* attestation, authentication, certification, confirmation, corroboration, demonstration, documentation, evidence, manifestation, print, substantiation, support, sure sign, test, testimony, trial, verification, voucher.

adj impenetrable, impervious, protected, rainproof, repellent, resistant, safe, sealed, secure, strong, tight, treated, waterproof, weatherproof, windproof.

antonyms permeable, untreated.

prop *v* bolster, buttress, lean, maintain, prop up, rest, set, shore, stand, stay, strengthen, strut, support, sustain, truss, underpin, uphold.

n brace, buttress, mainstay, stanchion, stay, strut, support, truss.

propaganda *n* advertising, agitprop, ballyhoo, brainwashing, double talk, hype, indoctrination, promotion, publicity, puffery.

propagandist *n* advocate, canvasser, evangelist, indoctrinator, pamphleteer, plugger, promoter, proponent, proselytizer, publicist, spin doctor.

propagate *v* beget, breed, broadcast, circulate, diffuse, disperse, disseminate, engender, generate, increase, multiply, proclaim, procreate, produce, proliferate, promote, promulgate, publicize, publish, reproduce, spawn, spread, transmit.

propel *v* drive, force, impel, launch, motivate, move, push, send, shoot, shove, start, thrust, waft.

antonyms slow, stop.

propensity *n* aptness, bent, bias, disposition, foible, inclination, leaning, liability, penchant, predisposition, proclivity, proneness, readiness, susceptibility, tendency, weakness.

antonym disinclination.

proper *adj* accepted, accurate, appropriate, apt, becoming, befitting, characteristic, complete, conventional, correct, decent, decorous, due, established, exact, fit, fitting, formal, genteel, gentlemanly, just, kosher, ladylike, legitimate, mannerly, meet, orthodox, particular, peculiar, polite, precise, prim, prissy, punctilious, refined, respectable, respective, right, rightful, sedate, seemly, special, specific, strait-laced, strict, suitable, suited, thorough, thoroughgoing, well-chosen.

antonyms common, general, improper.

property¹ *n* acres, assets, belongings, building(s), capital, chattels, effects, estate, freehold, goods, holding(s), house(s), land, means, possessions, premises, real estate, realty, resources, riches, stuff, title, wealth.

property² *n* ability, attribute, characteristic, feature, hallmark, idiosyncrasy, mark, nature, peculiarity, quality, trait, virtue.

prophecy *n* augury, divination, forecast, foretelling, prediction, prognosis, prognostication, revelation, second sight, soothsaying, vaticination.

prophesy *v* augur, divine, forecast, foresee, foretell, forewarn, predict, presage, prognosticate, soothsay, vaticinate.

prophet *n* augur, Cassandra, clairvoyant, divinator, diviner, forecaster, foreteller, Nostradamus, oracle, prognosticator, prophesier, seer, sibyl, soothsayer, tipster, vaticinator, visionary.

prophetic *adj* augural, divinatory, fatidic, fey, foreshadowing, forewarning, mantic, oracular, predictive, presaging, prescient, prognostic, sibylline, vatic, vaticinal.

antonym unprophetic.

propinquity *n* adjacency, affiliation, affinity, blood, blood relationship, closeness, connection, consanguinity, contiguity, immediacy, kinship, nearness, neighbourhood, proximity, relation, relationship, tie, vicinity.

antonym remoteness.

propitiate *v* appease, calm, conciliate, make peace with, mollify, pacify, placate, reconcile, satisfy, smoothe (over), soothe.

antonyms anger, provoke.

propitiatory *adj* appeasing, assuaging, atoning, conciliatory, irenic, mollifying, pacificatory, pacifying, peacemaking, placatory, reconciliatory, soothing.

antonym provocative.

propitious *adj* advantageous, auspicious, beneficial, benevolent, benign, bright, encouraging, favourable, fortunate, friendly, gracious, happy, kindly, lucky, opportune, promising, prosperous, reassuring, rosy, timely, well-disposed.

antonym inauspicious.

proponent *n* advocate, apologist, backer, champion, defender, enthusiast, exponent, friend, partisan, patron, proposer, subscriber, supporter, upholder, vindicator.
antonym opponent.

proportion *n* amount, balance, comparison, congruity, correspondence, cut, degree, distribution, division, eurhythmy, fraction, harmony, measure, part, percentage, portion, ratio, relationship, segment, share, symmetry.
antonyms disproportion, imbalance.

proportional *adj* balanced, commensurate, comparable, comparative, compatible, consistent, correspondent, corresponding, equitable, even, fair, just, proportionate, pro rata, prorated.
antonyms disproportionate, unjust.

proportions *n* amplitude, breadth, bulk, capacity, dimensions, expanse, extent, magnitude, measurements, range, scope, size, volume.

proposal *n* bid, design, draft, intention, manifesto, motion, offer, outline, overture, plan, platform, presentation, proffer, program, project, proposition, recommendation, scheme, sketch, suggestion, suit, tender, terms.

propose *v* advance, advise, bring up, design, enunciate, have in mind, intend, introduce, invite, lay (before), mean, move, name, nominate, pay suit, plan, pop the question, postulate, present, proffer, propound, purpose, put forward, put up, recommend, scheme, submit, suggest, table, tender.
antonyms oppose, withdraw.

proposition *n* assertion, manifesto, motion, plan, program, project, proposal, recommendation, scheme, statement, suggestion, tender.
v accost, invite, make advances, make a pass (at), solicit.

propound *v* advance, advocate, contend, enunciate, lay down, move, postulate, present, propose, put forward, set forth, submit, suggest.
antonym oppose.

proprieties *n* civilities, conventions, decencies, decorum, etiquette, niceties, protocol, p's and q's, social graces, the done thing.
antonym boorishness.

proprietor *n* chatelaine, deed holder, freeholder, landlady, landlord, landowner, owner, patron, possessor, titleholder.

propriety *n* appropriateness, aptness, becomingness, breeding, correctness, courtesy, decency, decorum, delicacy, etiquette, fitness, gentlemanliness, manners, modesty, politeness, protocol, punctilio, rectitude, refinement, respectability, rightness, seemliness, suitableness.
antonym impropriety.

propulsion *n* drive, impetus, impulse, impulsion, momentum, power, pressure, push, thrust.

prosaic *adj* banal, boring, bromidic, businesslike, commonplace, dry, dull,

everyday, flat, hackneyed, humdrum, matter-of-fact, mundane, ordinary, pedestrian, plain, routine, simple, stale, tame, trite, unadorned, unimaginative, uninspired, uninspiring, unpoetic, vapid, workaday.
antonyms imaginative, interesting.

proscribe *v* ban, banish, bar, blackball, boycott, censure, condemn, damn, denounce, deport, disallow, doom, embargo, exclude, excommunicate, exile, expatriate, expel, forbid, interdict, ostracize, outlaw, prohibit, reject, taboo.
antonyms admit, allow.
▲ *confusable word* prescribe.

proscription *n* ban, banishment, bar, barring, boycott, censure, condemnation, damning, denunciation, deportation, ejection, embargo, eviction, exclusion, excommunication, exile, expatriation, expulsion, injunction, interdict, ostracism, outlawry, prohibition, rejection, taboo.
antonyms admission, allowing.

prosecute *v* arraign, bring suit against, bring to trial, carry on, carry out, conduct, continue, direct, discharge, engage in, execute, follow through, indict, litigate, manage, perform, persevere, persist, practise, prefer charges, pursue, put on trial, see through, sue, summon, take to court, try, work at.
antonym desist.
▲ *confusable word* persecute.

proselytize *v* bring into the fold, bring to God, convert, convince, evangelize, make converts, persuade, propagandize, spread the gospel, spread the (good) word, win over.

prospect *n* anticipation, chance, eventuality, expectation, future, hope, landscape, likelihood, odds, opening, outlook, panorama, perspective, plan, possibility, presumption, probability, promise, proposition, scene, sight, spectacle, thought, view, vision, vista.
antonym unlikelihood.
v explore, mine, nose, pan, quest, search, seek, survey.

prospective *adj* anticipated, approaching, awaited, coming, designate, designated, destined, eventual, expected, forthcoming, future, imminent, intended, likely, possible, potential, soon-to-be, to come, -to-be.
antonyms agreed, current.

prospectus *n* account, announcement, catalogue, conspectus, list, manifesto, outline, pamphlet, plan, platform, program, scheme, statement, syllabus, synopsis.

prosper *v* advance, bloom, boom, burgeon, fare well, flourish, flower, get ahead, grow rich, make good, progress, succeed, thrive, turn out well.
antonym fail.

prosperity *n* affluence, boom, ease, fortune, good fortune, good times, luxury, plenty, prosperousness, riches, success, the big time, the good life, weal, wealth, well-being.
antonym poverty.

protruding

prosperous *adj* affluent, blooming, booming, burgeoning, flourishing, fortunate, in the money, lucky, moneyed, on easy street, opulent, palmy, profitable, rich, successful, thriving, wealthy, well-heeled, well-off, well-to-do.

antonym poor.

prostitute *n* bawd, call girl, cocotte, courtesan, drab, floozie, harlot, hooker, hustler, moll, streetwalker, strumpet, tart, trollop, trull, whore, woman of the town, working girl.

v cheapen, compromise, debase, degrade, demean, devalue, misapply, misuse, pander, pimp, procure, pervert, profane, sell.

prostitution *n* harlotry, meretriciousness, pandering, pimping, streetwalking, the oldest profession, whoredom, whoring.

prostrate *adj* abject, brought to one's knees, crushed, defenceless, dejected, depressed, desolate, disarmed, done, drained, exhausted, fagged, fallen, flat, helpless, horizontal, impotent, inconsolable, kowtowing, overcome, overwhelmed, paralysed, pooped, powerless, procumbent, prone, recumbent, reduced, shattered, spent, worn out.

antonyms elated, erect, hale, happy, strong, triumphant.

v conquer, crush, depress, disarm, drain, exhaust, fatigue, knock down, lay low, overcome, overthrow, overturn, overwhelm, paralyse, poop, reduce, render powerless, ruin, sap, shatter, tire, wear out, weary.

antonyms elate, exalt, strengthen.

prostrate oneself abase oneself, bend the knee, bow down, cringe, grovel, kneel, kowtow, submit.

antonym exalt oneself.

prostration *n* abasement, bow, collapse, dejection, depression, desolation, despair, despondency, exhaustion, genuflection, grief, helplessness, kneeling, kowtow, obeisance, paralysis, slough of despond, submission, weakness, weariness.

antonyms elation, exaltation, happiness, triumph.

protagonist *n* advocate, champion, chief character, exponent, hero, heroine, lead, leader, mainstay, prime mover, principal, proponent, standardbearer, supporter.

protean *adj* amoebic, changeable, ever-changing, inconstant, many-sided, mercurial, multiform, mutable, polymorphic, polymorphous, variable, volatile.

antonyms stable, unchanging.

protect *v* care for, chaperone, convoy, cover, cover up for, defend, escort, guard, harbour, keep (safe), look after, preserve, safeguard, save, screen, secure, shelter, shield, stand guard over, support, watch over.

antonyms attack, threaten.

protection *n* aegis, aid, armour, backstop, barrier, buffer, bulwark, care, charge, cover, custody, defence, guard, guardianship, guarding, precaution, preservation, prophylactic, protecting, refuge, safeguard,

safekeeping, safety, screen, security, shelter, shield, tutelage, umbrella, wardship.

antonyms attack, neglect.

protective *adj* careful, conservationist, covering, custodial, defensive, fatherly, insulating, jealous, maternal, motherly, paternal, possessive, precautionary, preservative, prophylactic, safeguarding, sheltering, shielding, tutelary, vigilant, warm, watchful.

antonyms aggressive, neglectful.

protector *n* advocate, benefactor, bodyguard, champion, counsel, defender, father figure, guard, guardian, patron, safeguard.

antonyms abuser, attacker.

protégé *n* charge, dependant, discovery, favourite, pupil, student, ward.

antonym guardian.

protest *n* assertion, complaint, declaration, demur, demurral, dharna, disapproval, dissent, formal complaint, objection, outcry, protestation, remonstrance, resistance, sit-in.

antonym acceptance.

v affirm, argue, assert, asseverate, attest, avow, complain, contend, cry out, declare, demonstrate, demur, disagree, disapprove, expostulate, insist, maintain, object, oppose, profess, remonstrate, resist, squawk, take exception, testify, vow.

antonym accept.

protestation *n* affirmation, assertion, asseveration, assurance, avowal, complaint, declaration, disagreement, dissent, expostulation, oath, objection, outcry, pledge, profession, protest, remonstrance, remonstration, statement, vow.

protester *n* agitator, demonstrator, dissenter, dissident, rebel, remonstrant, remonstrator.

protocol *n* conventions, courtesies, customs, decorum, etiquette, formalities, good form, manners, procedure(s), proprieties, propriety, p's and q's.

antonym boorishness.

prototype *n* archetype, example, exemplar, mock-up, model, original, paradigm, pattern, precedent, standard, template, type.

protract *v* continue, drag on, draw out, extend, keep going, lengthen, prolong, spin out, stretch out, sustain.

antonym shorten.

protracted *adj* dragged out, drawn-out, endless, extended, interminable, lengthy, long, long-drawn, overlong, prolix, prolonged, wearisome, wordy.

antonym shortened.

protrude *v* bulge, come through, emerge, exsert, extend, extrude, jut out, obtrude, point, pop, project, protuberate, stand out, start, stick out.

protruding *adj* bulging, exsertile, extrusive, jutting, popping, projecting, prominent, protrudent, protrusive, protuberant, proud.

antonyms flat, flush.

protrusion *n* bulge, bump, extrusion, jut, lump, outgrowth, process, projection, protuberance, swelling.

protuberance *n* bulb, bulge, bump, excrescence, extrusion, knob, lump, outgrowth, process, projection, prominence, protrusion, swelling, tuber, tubercle, tumour, wart, welt.

protuberant *adj* beetling, bulbous, bulging, bunched, exsertile, extrusive, gibbous, jutting, popping, prominent, protrudent, protruding, protrusive, swelling, swollen.

antonym flat.

proud *adj* appreciative, arrogant, august, boastful, conceited, dignified, disdainful, distinguished, egotistic, eminent, exalted, glad, glorious, grand, gratified, gratifying, great, haughty, high and mighty, high-nosed, hoity-toity, honoured, illustrious, imperious, imposing, lofty, lordly, magnificent, majestic, memorable, noble, overbearing, overweening, pleased, pleasing, presumptuous, prideful, puffed up, raised, red-letter, rewarding, satisfied, satisfying, self-important, self-satisfied, smug, snobbish, snooty, splendid, stately, stuck-up, supercilious, uppity, vainglorious, vain.

antonym humble.

provable *adj* amenable to proof, attestable, confirmable, corroborable, demonstrable, establishable, evincible, substantiable, testable, verifiable.

antonym unprovable.

prove *v* analyse, ascertain, assay, attest, authenticate, bear out, check, confirm, corroborate, demonstrate, determine, document, establish, evidence, evince, examine, justify, show, substantiate, test, try, turn out, verify.

antonyms discredit, disprove, falsify.

proven *adj* accepted, attested, authentic, authenticated, certified, checked, confirmed, corroborated, definite, dependable, established, proved, reliable, tested, tried, tried and true, trustworthy, undoubted, valid, verified.

antonym unproven.

provenance *n* birthplace, derivation, genesis, origin, rise, root, source.

provender *n* comestibles, eats, edibles, fare, feed, fodder, food, foodstuffs, forage, groceries, grub, nosh, provisions, rations, supplies, sustenance, victuals.

proverb *n* adage, aphorism, apothegm, bromide, byword, dictum, gnome, maxim, precept, saw, saying.

proverbial *adj* accepted, acknowledged, aphoristic, apothegmatic, archetypal, axiomatic, bromidic, conventional, customary, famed, famous, legendary, notorious, self-evident, time-honoured, traditional, typical, unquestioned, well-known.

provide *v* accommodate, add, afford, anticipate, arrange for, bring, cater, contribute, determine, equip, forearm, furnish, give, impart, lay down, lend, outfit, plan for, prepare

for, present, produce, provision, render, require, serve, specify, state, stipulate, stock up, suit, supply, take measures, take precautions, yield.

antonyms remove, take.

provide for care for, dower (with), endow (with), fend for, keep, maintain, support, sustain.

antonyms ignore, neglect.

provided *conj* as long as, contingent upon, given (that), if on condition, on the assumption, on the understanding, providing, subject to, with the proviso, with the stipulation.

providence *n* care, caution, destiny, discretion, divine intervention, farsightedness, fate, foresight, forethought, fortune, God's will, karma, kismet, perspicacity, predestination, predetermination, presence of mind, prudence, the will of the gods.

antonym improvidence.

provident *adj* canny, careful, cautious, circumspect, discreet, economical, equipped, far-seeing, farsighted, frugal, imaginative, judicious, long-sighted, prudent, sagacious, shrewd, thrifty, vigilant, wary, well-prepared, wise.

antonym improvident.

providential *adj* convenient, fortuitous, fortunate, happy, heaven-sent, lucky, opportune, timely, welcome.

antonym untimely.

provider *n* angel, benefactor, breadwinner, donor, earner, funder, giver, mainstay, patron, purveyor, source, supplier, supporter.

province *n* area, bailiwick, business, capacity, charge, colony, concern, county, department, dependency, district, division, domain, duty, employment, field, function, line, orbit, part, post, region, responsibility, role, section, sphere, territory, tract, zone.

provincial *adj* insular, inward-looking, limited, local, narrow, narrow-minded, parochial, small-minded, small-town, uninformed, unsophisticated.

antonyms sophisticated, urban.

provincialism *n* insularity, localism, narrow-mindedness, parochialism, provinciality, regionalism.

antonym sophistication.

provision *n* accoutrement, agreement, arrangement, catering, clause, condition, demand, equipping, fitting out, furnishing, plan, prearrangement, precaution, preparation, prerequisite, providing, proviso, purveyance, purveying, requirement, specification, stipulation, supply, term, victualling.

antonyms neglect, removal.

provisional *adj* conditional, contingent, interim, limited, makeshift, pro tem, provisory, qualified, stopgap, temporary, tentative, transitional.

antonyms definite, fixed, permanent.

provisionally *adv* conditionally, for the time being, in the interim, in the meantime, meanwhile, pro tem, pro tempore, temporarily, tentatively.

provisions n comestibles, eatables, eats, edibles, fare, food, foodstuffs, groceries, grub, provender, rations, stores, supplies, sustenance, viands, viaticum, victuals.

proviso n clause, condition, limitation, provision, qualification, requirement, reservation, restriction, rider, small print, stipulation.

provisory adj conditional, interim, provisional, qualified, temporary, tentative.

antonyms definite, fixed, permanent.

provocation n affront, aggravation, annoyance, casus belli, challenge, dare, grievance, grounds, incitement, indignity, inducement, injury, instigation, insult, (just) cause, justification, motivation, motive, offence, reason, red flag, stimulus, taunt, vexation.

provocative adj abusive, aggravating, alluring, annoying, antagonizing, arousing, challenging, controversial, disturbing, erotic, exciting, galling, goading, incensing, infuriating, insulting, inviting, leading, offensive, outrageous, provoking, seductive, sexy, stimulating, suggestive, tantalizing, teasing, tempting, thought-provoking.

antonyms pacificatory, unprovocative.

provoke v affront, aggravate, anger, annoy, antagonize, bait, cause, chafe, elicit, enrage, evoke, exasperate, excite, fire, gall, generate, give rise to, goad, incense, incite, induce, inflame, infuriate, inspire, instigate, insult, irk, irritate, kindle, madden, motivate, move, occasion, offend, pique, precipitate, produce, promote, prompt, put out, rile, rouse, stimulate, stir, vex.

antonyms pacify, please.

provoking adj aggravating, annoying, antagonizing, exasperating, galling, infuriating, irking, irksome, irritating, maddening, obstructive, offensive, pesky, pestiferous, provocative, tiresome, vexatious, vexing.

antonyms pacificatory, pleasing.

prow n beak, bow, cutwater, fore, forepart, front, head, nose, stem.

antonym stern.

prowess n ability, accomplishment, adeptness, adroitness, aptitude, attainment, bravery, command, courage, daring, dauntlessness, dexterity, doughtiness, excellence, expertise, expertness, facility, genius, heroism, mastery, skill, talent, valour.

antonyms clumsiness, mediocrity.

prowl v creep, cruise, hunt, lurk, nose, patrol, range, roam, rove, scavenge, search, skulk, slink, sneak, stalk, steal, wander.

proximity n adjacency, closeness, contiguity, juxtaposition, nearness, neighbourhood, propinquity, vicinity.

antonym remoteness.

proxy n agent, attorney, delegate, deputy, factor, locum tenens, representative, stand-in, substitute, surrogate.

prude n goody-goody, Mrs. Grundy, old maid, prig, puritan, schoolmarm, Victorian.

prudence n canniness, care, caution, circumspection, common sense, discretion, economy, farsightedness, foresight, forethought, frugality, good judgment, good sense, heedfulness, husbandry, judiciousness, planning, policy, precaution, preparedness, providence, sagacity, saving, thrift, vigilance, virtue, wariness, wisdom.

antonym imprudence.

prudent adj canny, careful, cautious, circumspect, discerning, discreet, economical, farsighted, foresighted, frugal, judicious, moderate, politic, provident, sagacious, sage, sensible, shrewd, sparing, thrifty, vigilant, wary, well-advised, wise.

antonym imprudent.

prudish adj demure, fastidious, goody-goody, narrow-minded, old-maidish, overmodest, overnice, priggish, prim, prim and proper, prissy, proper, puritanical, schoolmarmish, squeamish, starchy, strait-laced, stuffy, ultra-virtuous, Victorian.

antonyms easygoing, lax.

prune v clip, cut (down or off), dehorn, dock, lop, pare, reduce, shape, shorten, snip, thin out, trim.

prurient adj concupiscent, desirous, dirty, erotic, indecent, itching, lascivious, lecherous, lewd, libidinous, lustful, obscene, pornographic, salacious, smutty, voyeuristic.

antonym decent.

pry v delve, dig, ferret, interfere, intrude, meddle, nose, peek, peep, peer, poke, poke (or stick) one's nose in, snoop, spy.

antonym mind one's own business.

prying adj curious, inquisitive, interfering, intrusive, meddlesome, meddling, nosey, peering, snooping, snoopy, spying.

antonym uninquisitive.

psalm n canticle, chant, doxology, hymn, paean, song.

pseudo adj artificial, bogus, counterfeit, ersatz, fake, false, imitation, mock, phony, pretended, quasi-, sham, spurious, unnequine.

antonym genuine.

pseudonym n alias, allonym, anonym, assumed name, false name, incognito, moniker, nom de guerre, nom de plume, pen name, professional name, stage (or screen) name.

psyche n anima, awareness, consciousness, individuality, intellect, intelligence, mind, personality, pneuma, self, soul, spirit, subconscious, understanding.

psychiatrist n analyst, headshrinker, psychoanalyst, psychologist, psychotherapist, shrink, therapist.

psychic adj clairvoyant, cognitive, extrasensory, intellectual, mental, mystic, mystical, occult, preternatural, psychogenic, psychological, spiritual, spiritualistic, supernatural, telekinetic, telepathic.

psychological *adj* affective, cerebral, cognitive, emotional, imaginary, intellectual, irrational, mental, psychiatric, psychosomatic, subconscious, subjective, unconscious, unreal.

psychopath *n* lunatic, madman, maniac, psycho, psychotic, sociopath.

psychotic *adj* certifiable, demented, deranged, insane, lunatic, mad, psychopathic, unbalanced.

antonym sane.

puberty *n* adolescence, awkward age, maturescence, nubility, pubescence, teens, youth.

antonyms childhood, immaturity.

public *adj* accessible, acknowledged, circulating, civic, civil, common, communal, community, exposed, general, high-profile, important, known, national, notorious, obvious, open, overt, patent, plain, popular, prominent, published, recognized, respected, social, state, universal, unrestricted, well-known, widespread.

antonym private.

n audience, buyers, citizens, clientele, commonalty, community, country, electorate, everyone, followers, following, masses, multitude, nation, patrons, people, populace, population, society, supporters, voters.

in public for all to see, in full view, in open view, in the open, openly, overtly, publicly.

antonyms in camera, in secret.

publication *n* advertisement, airing, announcement, appearance, book, booklet, broadcasting, brochure, declaration, disclosure, dissemination, divulgence, flyer, handbill, issue, leaflet, magazine, newspaper, notification, pamphlet, periodical, printing, proclamation, promulgation, publishing, reporting, vent.

publicity *n* advertising, attention, ballyhoo, boost, buildup, exposure, hype, plug, press, promotion, public notice, puffery, splash.

antonym secrecy.

publicize *v* advertise, blaze, blazon, broadcast, expose, hype, plug, promote, puff, push, spotlight, spread (around).

antonym keep secret.

public-spirited *adj* altruistic, charitable, community-minded, conscientious, generous, humanitarian, philanthropic, unselfish.

antonym selfish.

publish *v* advertise, announce, bring out, broadcast, circulate, communicate, declare, diffuse, disclose, distribute, divulge, expose, issue, leak, print, proclaim, produce, promulgate, publicize, reveal, spread, vent.

antonym keep secret.

pucker *v* compress, contract, crease, crinkle, crumple, furrow, gather, purse, ruck, ruckle, ruffle, screw up, shirr, shrivel, tighten, wrinkle.

n crease, crinkle, crumple, fold, ruck, ruckle, shirr, wrinkle.

puckered *adj* creased, gathered, pursed, rucked, ruckled, wrinkled.

antonym smooth.

puckish *adj* frolicsome, high-spirited, impish, mischievous, naughty, playful, prankish, roguish, sly, sportive, teasing, waggish, whimsical.

antonym solemn.

pudenda *n* genitalia, genitals, private parts, privates.

pudgy *adj* chubby, chunky, corpulent, dumpy, fat, fleshy, paunchy, plump, roly-poly, rotund, squat, stout, stubby, stumpy, tubby.

puerile *adj* babyish, childish, foolish, immature, inane, infantile, irresponsible, jejune, juvenile, naïve, petty, ridiculous, silly, simple-minded, trifling, trivial, weak.

antonym mature.

puff *n* advertisement, blast, breath, commendation, drag, draft, emanation, flurry, gust, mention, plug, publicity, pull, smoke, waft, whiff.

v bloat, blow, breathe, dilate, distend, do in, drag, draw, exaggerate, exhale, expand, gasp, gulp, hype, inflate, inhale, pant, plug, praise, promote, publicize, pull, push, smoke, swell, waft, wheeze, whiff, whiffle.

puffed-up *adj* arrogant, big-headed, conceited, exaggerated, full of oneself, high and mighty, prideful, proud, swollen-headed, too big for one's britches (or boots), vain.

antonym modest.

puffing *adj* all in, blowing, breathless, done in, exhausted, gasping, out of breath, panting, wheezing, winded.

antonym vigorous.

puffy *adj* bloated, distended, edematous, enlarged, inflamed, inflated, puffed-up, swollen.

antonym flat.

pugilism *n* boxing, fighting, fisticuffs, prizefighting, sparring, the noble art of self-defence, the prize-ring, the ring.

pugilist *n* boxer, bruiser, fighter, prizefighter, pug, scrapper.

pugnacious *adj* aggressive, antagonistic, argumentative, bareknuckle, bellicose, belligerent, chippy, choleric, combative, contentious, disputatious, hostile, hot-tempered, irascible, petulant, quarrelsome.

antonym easygoing.

puke *v* barf, be sick, bring up, chuck up, disgorge, egest, heave, regurgitate, retch, spew, throw up, upchuck, vomit.

pull *v* attract, cull, dislocate, drag, draw, draw out, entice, extract, gather, haul, heave, jerk, lengthen, lure, magnetize, pick, pluck, remove, rend, rip, schlep, sprain, strain, stretch, take out, tear, tow, track, trail, tug, tweak, uproot, weed out, wrench, yank.

antonyms deter, push, repel.

n advantage, allurement, attraction, clout, drag, draw, drawing power, effort, exertion, force, forcefulness, heave, influence, inhalation, jerk, leverage, lure, magnetism, muscle, power, puff, seduction, swig, tug, twitch, weight, yank.

antonyms deterring, push, repelling.

pull a face   frown, glower, grimace, knit one's brows, lower, pout, scowl, sulk.

pull a fast one on   cheat, con, deceive, defraud, grift, hoodwink, outwit, put one over on, sting, swindle, take for a ride, trick.

pull apart   attack, be critical of, carp at, criticize, dismember, find fault with, flay, knock, lay into, pan, part, pick holes in, pull to pieces, run down, separate, slam, slate, sunder.
antonym praise.

pull down[1]   bulldoze, demolish, destroy, dismantle, knock down, raze, remove.
antonym put up.

pull down[2]   bring in, clear, draw, earn, gross, make, pocket, receive, take home.

pull off   accomplish, achieve, bring about, bring off, carry out (or off), make happen, manage, succeed, swing.
antonym fail.

pull out (of)   abandon, depart (from), desert, evacuate, leave, quit, retreat (from), withdraw (from).
antonym join.

pull someone's leg   chaff, deceive, fool, make fun of, tease, trick.

pull the wool over someone's eyes bamboozle, con, deceive, delude, dupe, fool, hoodwink, lead down the garden path, pull a fast one on, put one over on, snow, take in, trick.

pull through   get over, get well, make it, rally, recover, recuperate, survive, weather (the storm).
antonym fail.

pull together   collaborate, co-operate, team up, work together.
antonym fight.

pull up   brake, draw in, draw up, halt, stop.

pull up short   admonish, bawl out, castigate, chastise, haul on the carpet, rake over the coals, rebuke, reprimand, reprove, scold, take to task, tell off.

pulp *n* flesh, marrow, mash, mush, pap, paste, pomace, soft part, triturate.
v crush, liquidize, mash, pulverize, squash, triturate.

pulpit *n* dais, lectern, platform, podium, rostrum, soapbox.

pulpy *adj* fleshy, mushy, pappy, sloppy, soft, squashy, succulent.
antonym hard.

pulsate *v* beat, drum, hammer, oscillate, palpitate, pound, pulse, quiver, throb, thud, thump, tick, vibrate.

pulsating *adj* oscillating, palpitating, periodic, pulsing, vibratile, vibrating, vibrational, vibratory.

pulse *n* beat, beating, drumming, ictus, oscillation, periodicity, pulsation, rhythm, stroke, throb, throbbing, thudding, vibration.
v beat, drum, pulsate, throb, thud, tick, vibrate.

pulverize *v* annihilate, bray, comminute, crush, defeat, demolish, destroy, flatten, granulate, grind, hammer, mill, pestle, pound, powder, shatter, smash, triturate, vanquish, wreck.

pummel *v* bang, batter, beat, drub, hammer, knead, knock, paste, pound, punch, strike, thump, wallop.

pump *v* catechize, cross-examine, debrief, drive, extract, force, grill, inject, interrogate, pour, probe, push, question, quiz, send, supply.

pump out   bail out, drain, draw off, empty, force out, siphon.

pump up   blow up, dilate, distend, increase, inflate, intensify, puff up, rouse, step up, turn up.

pun *n* double entendre, paronomasia, play on words, quip, witticism, wordplay.

punch[1] *v* bash, biff, bop, box, clout, hit, jab, land one, plug, pummel, slam, slug, smash, sock, strike, wallop, zap.
n bash, biff, bite, blow, bop, clout, drive, effectiveness, force, forcefulness, hit, impact, jab, knock, knuckle sandwich, panache, pizzazz, plug, point, pungency, sock, thump, verve, vigour, vim, wallop, zip.
antonym feebleness.

punch[2] *v* bore, cut, drill, perforate, pierce, pink, prick, puncture, stamp.

punch-drunk *adj* befuddled, confused, dazed, dizzy, groggy, knocked silly, punchy, reeling, slap-happy, staggering, stupefied, unsteady, woozy.

punch-up *n* argument, brawl, Donnybrook, dustup, fight, free-for-all, melee, row, ruckus, scrap, scuffle, set-to, shindy.

punchy *adj* aggressive, dynamic, effective, forceful, incisive, lively, powerful, spirited, vigorous, zappy, zippy.
antonym feeble.

punctilio *n* attention to detail, ceremony, convention, delicacy, distinction, exactitude, exactness, fine point, finickiness, formality, meticulousness, nicety, particular, particularity, preciseness, precision, punctiliousness, refinement, scrupulousness, strictness.
antonyms boorishness, informality.

punctilious *adj* careful, ceremonious, conscientious, exact, fastidious, finicky, fussy, meticulous, nice, overnice, particular, precise, proper, scrupulous, strict.
antonyms boorish, easy-going, informal.

punctual *adj* early, exact, in good time, on the dot, on time, precise, prompt, punctilious, ready, strict, timely.
antonym unpunctual.

punctuality *n* promptitude, promptness, readiness, regularity, strictness.
antonym unpunctuality.

punctually *adv* exactly, on the dot, on time, precisely, promptly, sharp.
antonym unpunctually.

punctuate *v* accentuate, break, dot, emphasize, interject, interrupt, intersperse, pepper, sprinkle.

puncture *n* break, cut, fissure, flat (tire), hole, leak, nick, opening, perforation, rupture, slit.

v bore, cut, deflate, discourage, disillusion, disprove, flatten, humble, nick, penetrate, perforate, pierce, poke holes in, prick, rupture, take down a peg or two.

pundit *n* authority, buff, expert, guru, maestro, master, specialist, teacher.

pungent *adj* acid, acrid, acrimonious, acute, aromatic, barbed, biting, bitter, caustic, cutting, hot, incisive, keen, mordant, painful, penetrating, peppery, piercing, piquant, poignant, pointed, sarcastic, scathing, seasoned, sharp, sour, spicy, stinging, stringent, strong, tangy, tart, telling, trenchant.

antonyms feeble, mild, tasteless.

punish *v* abuse, batter, beat, castigate, chasten, chastise, correct, crucify, discipline, flog, harm, hurt, injure, keelhaul, lash, maltreat, manhandle, misuse, oppress, pay back, penalize, rake over the coals, reprimand, retaliate (against), rough up, scourge, teach a lesson to, torture, trounce.

punishable *adj* actionable, blameworthy, chargeable, contrary to law, convictable, criminal, culpable, illegal, indictable, unlawful, wrongful.

punishing *adj* arduous, backbreaking, burdensome, chastising, demanding, exhausting, fatiguing, grinding, gruelling, hard, laborious, punitive, strenuous, taxing, tiring, wearing.

antonym easy.

punishment *n* abuse, beating, castigation, chastening, chastisement, comeuppance, consequences, correction, damnation, discipline, just (deserts), maltreatment, manhandling, medicine, pain, penalty, penance, reprisal, retribution, sanction, torture, victimization, what one has coming.

punitive *adj* castigatory, penal, punishing, retaliatory, retributive, revengeful, vindictive.

puny *adj* diminutive, dwarfish, feeble, frail, inconsequential, inferior, insignificant, little, meagre, minor, paltry, petty, piddling, runty, scrawny, sickly, slight, stunted, thin, tiny, trifling, trivial, underdeveloped, underfed, undersized, undeveloped, weak, worthless.

antonyms important, large, strong.

pupil *n* beginner, catechumen, disciple, learner, neophyte, novice, protégé, scholar, schoolboy, schoolgirl, student, tutee, tyro.

antonym teacher.

puppet *n* agent, cat's-paw, creature, doll, dupe, figurehead, gull, instrument, marionette, mouthpiece, nonentity, pawn, quisling, stooge, tool, yes man.

puppy *n* braggart, cub, dandy, jackanapes, popinjay, pup, shaver, whelp, whippersnapper.

purchase *v* achieve, acquire, attain, buy, earn, gain, invest in, obtain, pay for, procure, ransom, realize, secure, win.

antonym sell.

n acquisition, asset, buy, buying, edge, foothold, footing, gain, grasp, grip, hold, influence, investment, lever, leverage, possession, property, ransoming, support, toehold.

antonym sale.

purchaser *n* buyer, client, consumer, customer, patron, prospect, shopper, vendee.

pure *adj* absolute, abstract, academic, antiseptic, authentic, blameless, chaste, clean, clear, disinfected, extreme, flawless, genuine, germ-free, guileless, high-minded, honest, hygienic, immaculate, innocent, maidenly, mere, modest, natural, neat, pasteurized, perfect, philosophical, pious, real, refined, righteous, sanitary, Saturnian, sheer, simple, sincere, single-minded, snow-white, speculative, spiritous, spotless, stainless, sterile, sterilized, straight, theoretical, thorough, true, unadulterated, unalloyed, unblemished, uncontaminated, uncorrupted, undefiled, unmingled, unmitigated, unmixed, unpolluted, unqualified, unsoiled, unspoiled, unspotted, unstained, unsullied, untainted, untarnished, untouched, upright, utter, virgin, virginal, virtuous, wholesome, without blemish.

antonyms adulterated, applied, defiled, immoral, impure, polluted, tainted.

purebred *adj* blooded, full-blooded, highbred, pedigreed, pure-blooded, thoroughbred.

antonyms crossbred, hybrid, mixed, mongrel.

purely *adv* absolutely, completely, entirely, exclusively, just, merely, only, plainly, sheerly, simply, solely, thoroughly, totally, utterly, wholly.

purgation *n* atonement, catharsis, cleansing, clearing, evacuation, exculpation, exoneration, justification, penance, purge, purging, purification, release, riddance, ridding, vindication.

purgative *n* aperient, atonement, cathartic, cleansing agent, emetic, enema, evacuant, laxative, purge.

adj aperient, atoning, cathartic, cleansing, evacuant, laxative, purging, relieving.

purge *v* absolve, absterge, acquit, clean out, cleanse, clear, depose, dismiss, eject, eradicate, exonerate, expel, expiate, exterminate, extract, forgive, get rid of, kill, liquidate, oust, pardon, purify, release, remove, rid, root out, scour, wash, wipe out.

n aperient, catharsis, cathartic, cleansing, cleansing agent, ejection, elimination, emetic, enema, eradication, expulsion, extermination, laxative, liquidation, purgative, removal, witch hunt.

purification *n* ablution, absolution, catharsis, clarification, cleaning, cleansing, decontamination, deodorization, desalination, disinfection, expurgation, filtration, fumigation, furbishing, hallowing, lustration, lustre, lustrum, mundification, purgation, redemption, refinement, sanctification, sanitization.

antonyms contamination, defilement, pollution.

purify *v* absolve, chasten, clarify, clean, cleanse, decontaminate, deodorize, desalinate, disinfect, expurgate, filter, fumigate, furbish, hallow, lustrate, redeem, refine, sanctify, sanitize, shrive, sterilize, sublimize, wash.

antonyms contaminate, defile, pollute.

purifying *adj* atoning, cathartic, cleansing, expiatory, lustral, penitential, propitiatory, purgative, purging, purificatory, redeeming, refining.

antonyms contaminating, defiling, polluting.

purism *n* Atticism, austerity, classicism, fastidiousness, formalism, fussiness, orthodoxy, overprecision, pedantry, perfectionism, precisianism, precisionism, restraint, strictness.

antonyms liberality, open-mindedness, tolerance.

purist *n* Atticist, classicist, formalist, mandarin, nit-picker, pedant, perfectionist, precisian, precisionist, quibbler, stickler.

antonym liberal.

puristic *adj* austere, captious, fastidious, finicky, fussy, hypercritical, nit-picking, orthodox, overexact, overmeticulous, overparticular, overprecise, pedantic, punctilious, quibbling, strict, uncompromising.

antonyms liberal, open-minded, tolerant.

puritan *n* ascetic, bluenose, disciplinarian, moralist, pietist, prude, rigorist, zealot.

antonyms hedonist, libertarian.

adj ascetic, austere, disciplinarian, hard-line, hidebound, moralistic, narrow, narrow-minded, prim, prudish, puritanical, self-disciplined, severe, stern, strait-laced, strict, uncompromising.

antonyms broad-minded, hedonistic, indulgent, liberal.

puritanical *adj* abstemious, abstinent, ascetic, austere, disciplinarian, fastidious, narrow, narrow-minded, orthodox, prim, prim and proper, proper, prudish, puritan, rigid, severe, stern, stiff, strait-laced, strict, stuffy, uncompromising, zealous.

antonyms broad-minded, hedonistic, indulgent, liberal.

purity *n* blamelessness, chasteness, chastity, clarity, classicism, cleanliness, cleanness, clearness, decency, faultlessness, fineness, genuineness, honesty, immaculateness, incorruption, innocence, integrity, morality, perfection, piety, pureness, rectitude, refinement, righteousness, sanctity, simplicity, sincerity, single-mindedness, spotlessness, stainlessness, truth, unspottedness, untaintedness, uprightness, virginity, virtue, virtuousness, wholesomeness.

antonyms immorality, impurity.

purlieus *n* arena, borders, bounds, confines, environs, fringes, limits, neighbourhood, outskirts, perimeter, periphery, precincts, suburbs, vicinity.

purloin *v* abstract, appropriate, filch, finger, lift, make off with, palm, pilfer, pinch, pocket, remove, rob, scrounge, snaffle, snitch, steal, swipe, take, thieve.

purport *v* allege, argue, assert, betoken, claim, convey, declare, denote, express, give

out, imply, import, indicate, intend, maintain, mean, portend, pose as, pretend, proclaim, profess, seem, show, signify, suggest.

n bearing, direction, drift, effect, gist, idea, implication, import, meaning, point, sense, significance, spirit, substance, tendency, tenor, theme, thrust.

purpose *n* advantage, aim, ambition, aspiration, assiduity, avail, benefit, constancy, contemplation, decision, dedication, design, determination, devotion, drive, effect, end, firmness, function, gain, goal, good, hope, idea, ideal, intent, intention, meaning, motive, object, objective, outcome, persistence, pertinacity, plan, point, principle, profit, project, rationale, reason, resolution, resolve, result, return, scheme, service, single-mindedness, steadfastness, target, tenacity, use, usefulness, utility, view, vision, will, wish, zeal.

v aim, aspire, contemplate, decide, design, desire, determine, intend, mean, meditate, plan, propose, resolve.

on purpose deliberately, designedly, intentionally, knowingly, premeditatedly, purposely, wilfully, wittingly.

antonym accidentally.

purposeful *adj* assiduous, calculated, decided, deliberate, determined, firm, fixed, intentional, meaningful, motivated, persevering, persistent, pertinacious, positive, purposive, resolute, resolved, sedulous, settled, single-minded, steadfast, strong-willed, studied, teleological, tenacious, unfaltering, unswerving.

antonym purposeless.

purposeless *adj* aimless, empty, goalless, gratuitous, meaningless, motiveless, needless, nonsensical, objectless, pointless, senseless, thoughtless, unasked-for, uncalled-for, unnecessary, useless, vacuous, vain, wanton.

antonym purposeful.

purposely *adv* by design, calculatedly, consciously, deliberately, designedly, expressly, intentionally, knowingly, on purpose, pointedly, premeditatedly, purposefully, specifically, willfully, with malice aforethought, wittingly.

antonyms impulsively, spontaneously, unpremeditatedly.

purse *n* award, bag, burse, coffers, exchequer, finances, funds, handbag, means, money, money-bag, money belt, pocketbook, pouch, prize, resources, reward, sporran, treasury, wallet, wealth.

v close, compress, contract, draw together, pucker, pucker up, tighten, wrinkle.

pursuance *n* accomplishment, achievement, carrying out, completion, discharge, effecting, effectuation, execution, following, fulfilment, performance, prosecution, pursuing, pursuit.

pursue *v* adhere to, aim at, aim for, aspire to, attend, bedevil, beset, besiege, carry on, carry out, chase, check out, conduct, court, cultivate, desire, dog, engage in, follow, follow up, go after, go for, gun for, harass, harry, haunt, hold to, hound, hunt, inquire into, investigate, keep on with, maintain, perform, persecute, persevere in, persist in, plague, ply, practise, proceed along (in), prosecute, purpose, seek, set one's cap at, shadow, stalk, strive for, tackle, tail, track, trail, try for, wage, woo.

antonyms eschew, shun.

pursuit¹ *n* chase, chevy, following, hounding, hue and cry, hunt, hunting, inquiry, investigation, quest, search, seeking, stalking, tracking, trail, trailing.

pursuit² *n* activity, craft, hobby, interest, line, occupation, pastime, pleasure, sideline, specialty, vocation.

purvey *v* cater, communicate, deal in, disseminate, furnish, pass on, peddle, propagate, provide, provision, publicize, publish, put out, retail, sell, spread, stock, supply, trade in, transmit, victual.

purveyor *n* caterer, communicator, dealer, disseminator, donor, merchant, peddler, propagator, provider, provisioner, pusher, retailer, seller, stocker, supplier, trader, transmitter, victualler.

push *v* advance, advertise, agitate, boost, browbeat, bulldoze, bully, campaign, coerce, constrain, deal (in), depress, dragoon, drive, edge, egg on, elbow, encourage, expedite, extend, force, hurry, hustle, hype, incite, influence, inveigle, jockey, jog, jostle, lobby, manhandle, manoeuvre, move, oblige, peddle, persuade, plug, poke, press, prod, promote, propagandize, propel, publicize, puff, put pressure on, ram, shoulder, shove, spur, squeeze, thrust, urge, wedge.

n advance, ambition, assault, attack, bunt, butt, campaign, charge, determination, drive, dynamism, effort, energy, enterprise, force, go, impetus, impulse, initiative, jog, jolt, knock, notice, nudge, offensive, onset, onslaught, poke, power, pressure, prod, shove, thrust, vigour, vim, vitality, zip.

push off   be off, depart, go away, leave, make a move, make tracks, move, push along, shift, shove off, start out.

push-over *n* child's play, cinch, dupe, easy mark, fall guy, gull, mug, picnic, piece of cake, sinecure, sitting duck, sitting target, soft touch, stooge, sucker, walkover.

antonym challenge.

pushy *adj* aggressive, ambitious, arrogant, assuming, bold, bossy, brash, bumptious, forceful, forward, high-powered, insistent, insolent, intrusive, loud, obtrusive, offensive, officious, overassertive, overconfident, presumptuous, self-assertive.

antonyms quiet, restrained, unassertive, unassuming.

pusillanimity *n* cowardliness, cravenness, faint-heartedness, fearfulness, feebleness, gutlessness, poltroonery, recreancy, spinelessness, timidity, timorousness, weakness, yellow streak.

pusillanimous *adj* chicken, chicken-hearted, cowardly, craven, dastardly, faint-hearted, fearful, feeble, gutless, lily-livered, mean-spirited, poltroon, recreant, scared,

spineless, timid, timorous, unassertive, unenterprising, weak, weak-kneed, yellow.

antonyms ambitious, courageous, forceful, strong.

pussyfoot *v* beat around the bush, creep, equivocate, hedge, lurk, mess around, pad, prevaricate, prowl, sidestep, slink, steal, tergiversate, tiptoe, walk on eggs.

pustule *n* abscess, blemish, blister, boil, bulla, carbuncle, eruption, fester, furuncle, gathering, papilla, pimple, pock, swelling, ulcer, whelk, whitlow.

put *v* advance, apply, assign, attribute, bring, bring forward, cast, commit, condemn, consign, constrain, couch, deploy, deposit, dispose, drive, employ, enjoin, establish, express, fit, fix, fling, force, formulate, forward, frame, heave, hurl, impel, impose, induce, inflict, land, lay, levy, lob, make, oblige, offer, park, phrase, pitch, place, plunk, pose, position, post, present, propose, push, render, require, rest, send, set, set down, settle, situate, state, station, subject, submit, suggest, tender, throw, thrust, toss, utter, voice, word, write.

put across   bring home, communicate, convey, explain, express, get through, make clear, put over, spell out.

put an end to   abolish, annihilate, annul, cancel, check, destroy, discontinue, jugulate, kibosh, knock on the head, nullify, put a stop to, put paid to, put the kibosh on, put the lid on, stem, stop, terminate.

put aside¹   cache, deposit, hoard, keep, lay by, put by, reserve, retain, salt away, save (for a rainy day), set aside, slash, stockpile, store, stow.

put aside²   abandon, bury, discard, discount, dispense with, disregard, forget, ignore, put behind one, remove, set aside.

put away   certify, commit, consume, divorce, eat, imprison, institutionalize, kill, put aside, remove, renounce, replace, repudiate, return, save, secrete, shift, store, tidy, wolf (down).

put back   delay, move back, postpone, replace, repulse, reschedule, return.

put down¹   enter, inscribe, log, note, record, register, report, state, transcribe, write down.

put down²   abash, condemn, conquer, crush, defeat, deflate, degrade, depreciate, destroy, dismiss, disparage, humble, humiliate, kill, mortify, put away, put to sleep, quash, quell, reject, repress, ridicule, shame, show up, silence, slight, snub, squelch, suppress, take down a peg, topple.

put down³   ascribe, assign, attribute, chalk up, impute.

put forward   advance, introduce, move, nominate, offer, present, press, proffer, propose, recommend, submit, suggest, table, tender.

put in   arrive, enter, input, insert, install, key in, plant, spend.

put off   avoid, daunt, defer, delay, demoralize, deter, disconcert, discourage, dishearten, dismay, dispirit, dissuade, divert, faze, nonplus, postpone, rattle, repel, reschedule, throw off, unnerve.

antonym encourage.

put on add, affect, affix, apply, assume, attach, bet, deceive, do, don, dress, exert, fake, feign, fool, gain, host, impose, increase (by), kid, make believe, mislead, mount, place, present, pretend, produce, pull (someone's) leg, sham, show, simulate, stage.

put one's finger on discover, find out, hit the nail on the head, hit upon, identify, indicate, isolate, locate, name, pin down, pinpoint, place, recall, remember.

put out[1] affront, anger, annoy, bother, exasperate, hurt, irk, irritate, let go, nettle, offend, pay, perturb, provoke, spend, upset, vex.

put out[2] announce, broadcast, circulate, give out, issue, produce, publish, release.

put out[3] be a burden to, bother, discommode, disturb, impose on, incommode, inconvenience, trouble.

put out[4] blow out, douse, extinguish, quench, smother, snuff (out).

put the wind up agitate, alarm, daunt, discourage, frighten, make suspicious, panic, perturb, scare, sound the alarm for, startle, unnerve.

antonym reassure.

put through accomplish, achieve, bring about, bring off, bring to fruition, conclude, effect, execute, finalize, manage.

put to death execute, exterminate, kill, liquidate, martyr, put to the sword.

put to shame disgrace, eclipse, excel, humble, humiliate, outclass, outdo, outshine, outstrip, shame, show up, surpass.

put up[1] accommodate, billet, board, entertain, house, lodge, put forward, quarter, shelter.

put up[2] assemble, build, construct, erect, fabricate, pitch, raise, set up.

put up[3] advance, float, give, invest, pay, pledge, provide, supply.

put up[4] nominate, offer, present, propose, put forward, submit.

put up[5] can, lay up, pack, prepare, preserve.

put upon exploit, impose on, inconvenience, take advantage of, use, victimize.

put up to abet, encourage, goad, incite, instigate, prompt, urge.

antonyms discourage, dissuade.

put up with abide, allow, bear, brook, endure, lump, permit, stand, stand for, stomach, submit to, suffer, swallow, take, take lying down, tolerate.

antonyms object to, protest against, reject.

put wise alert, apprise, clue in, enlighten, fill in, inform, make wise, notify, put in the picture, tell, tip off, warn, wise up.

putative *adj* alleged, assumed, conjectural, hypothetical, imputed, presumed, presumptive, reported, reputed, supposed, suppositional, supposititious.

put-down *n* affront, dig, disparagement, gibe, humiliation, insult, jab, rebuff, sarcasm, slap in the face, slight, sneer, snub.

put-off *n* barrier, damper, deterrent, discouragement, disincentive, hindrance, obstacle, stumbling-block, turnoff.

antonyms encouragement, incentive.

put on *n* act, affectation, hoax, kidding, joke, pretension, tease, trick.

putrefy *v* addle, canker, corrupt, decay, decompose, deteriorate, fester, gangrene, go bad, mortify, mould, necrose, perish, rot, spoil, stink.

putrescent *adj* decaying, decomposing, festering, mephitic, perishing, putrefying, rotting, stinking.

putrid *adj* addled, bad, contaminated, corrupt, decayed, decomposed, fetid, foul, gangrenous, malodorous, mephitic, mouldy, necrosed, noisome, off, putrefied, rancid, rank, reeking, rotten, rotting, spoiled, stinking, tainted.

antonyms fresh, wholesome.

putter *v* dabble, doodle, fiddle, fidget, fritter, idle, keep busy, mess around, moon, piddle, tinker, waste time.

put-upon *adj* abused, beset, exploited, harassed, harried, henpecked, ill-used, imposed on, inconvenienced, overworked, persecuted.

puzzle[1] *v* baffle, bamboozle, beat, bewilder, confound, confuse, floor, flummox, gravel, mystify, nonplus, perplex, stump, trouble, worry.

n acrostic, anagram, brain teaser, brain twister, confusion, conundrum, crossword, difficulty, dilemma, enigma, jigsaw, knot, koan, maze, mind bender, mystery, paradox, perplexity, poser, problem, quandary, question, rebus, riddle, Sphinx, tickler.

puzzle[2] *v* brood, cogitate, consider, deliberate, figure, meditate, mull over, muse, ponder, rack one's brains, ratiocinate, reason, ruminate, study, think, wonder, worry.

puzzle out clear up, crack, decipher, decode, excogitate, figure out, reason out, resolve, see, solve, sort out, think out, unravel, unriddle, untangle, work out.

puzzled *adj* at a loss, at sea, baffled, bamboozled, beaten, bemused, bewildered, confounded, confused, doubtful, flummoxed, lost, mixed up, mystified, nonplussed, perplexed, stuck, stumped, stymied, uncertain.

antonyms certain, clear.

puzzlement *n* astonishment, bafflement, bamboozlement, bewilderment, confusion, disorientation, doubt, incertitude, mystification, perplexity, surprise, uncertainty, wonder.

antonyms certainty, clarity, lucidity.

puzzling *adj* abstruse, ambiguous, baffling, bewildering, bizarre, cabalistic, circuitous, confusing, cryptic, curious, enigmatic, equivocal, impenetrable, inexplicable, intricate, involved, knotty, labyrinthine, mind-bending, mind-boggling, misleading, mysterious, mystical, mystifying, peculiar, perplexing, queer, riddling, Sphynxlike, strange, tangled, tortuous, unaccountable, unclear, unfathomable.

pygmy n dwarf, fingerling, half pint, homunculus, Lilliputian, manikin, midget, runt, shrimp, Tom Thumb.

antonym giant.

adj baby, diminutive, dwarf, dwarfish, elfin, half-pint, Lilliputian, midget, miniature, minuscule, minute, pint-sized, pocket, small, stunted, tiny, toy, undersized, wee.

antonym gigantic.

Q

quack *n* charlatan, cowboy, fake, fraud, horse doctor, humbug, impostor, masquerader, medicaster, mountebank, phony, pretender, pseud, quacksalver, sham, spieler, swindler, trickster, witch doctor.

adj bogus, counterfeit, fake, false, fraudulent, phony, pretended, pseudo, sham, so-called, spurious, supposed, unqualified.

antonym genuine.

quackery *n* charlatanism, fraud, fraudulence, humbug, imposture, mountebankery, phoniness, sham.

quaff *v* chug, down, drain, drink, gulp, guzzle, imbibe, knock back, swallow, swig, swill, tipple, tope, toss off.

n cup, dram, draft, drink, jorum, nip, slug, snifter, snort, swig, tot.

quagmire *n* bog, everglade, fen, marsh, mire, morass, moss, mud flat, quag, quicksand, slough, swamp.

quail *v* back away, blanch, cower, droop, faint, falter, flinch, pull back, quake, recoil, shake, shrink, shudder, shy away, tremble, wince.

quaint *adj* absurd, antiquated, antique, charming, curious, droll, eccentric, fanciful, funky, ingenious, odd, old-fashioned, old-time, old-world, peculiar, picturesque, queer, rum, singular, strange, unconventional, unusual, weird, whimsical.

quake *v* convulse, heave, jolt, move, pulsate, quail, quiver, rock, shake, shiver, shudder, sway, throb, totter, tremble, vibrate, waver, wobble.

qualification[1] *n* ability, accomplishment, adequacy, aptitude, attribute, capability, capacity, certification, competence, credential, eligibility, fitness, preparedness, skill, suitability, suitableness, training.

qualification[2] *n* adaptation, adjustment, allowance, caveat, condition, criterion, exception, exemption, limitation, modification, objection, provision, proviso, reservation, restriction, stipulation.

qualified[1] *adj* able, accomplished, adept, adequate, apt, capable, certified, competent, efficient, eligible, equipped, experienced, expert, fit, knowledgeable, licensed, practised, prepared, proficient, skilful, suitable, talented, trained.

antonym unqualified.

qualified[2] *adj* bounded, cautious, circumscribed, conditional, confined, contingent, equivocal, guarded, limited, modified, provisional, reserved, restricted.

antonyms categorical, unequivocal.

qualify[1] *v* authorize, befit, capacitate, certificate, empower, enable, endow, entitle, equip, fit, graduate, permit, prepare, sanction, shape, train.

antonym unfit.

qualify[2] *v* be eligible, be fit, meet criteria, pass the test, satisfy requirements.

qualify[3] *v* abate, adapt, adjust, categorize, characterize, circumscribe, define, delimit, describe, designate, diminish, distinguish, ease, extenuate, lessen, limit, mitigate, moderate, modify, modulate, reduce, regulate, restrain, restrict, soften, temper, vary, weaken.

quality *n* aspect, attribute, calibre, capacity, character, characteristic, class, complexion, condition, constitution, distinction, essence, excellence, feature, fineness, first water, grade, kidney, kind, make, mark, merit, nature, peculiarity, position, pre-eminence, property, rank, refinement, role, sort, standing, status, superiority, talent, timbre, tone, trait, value, water, worth.

qualm *n* anxiety, apprehension, compunction, disquiet, doubt, fear, hesitation, misgiving, pang, presentiment, regret, reluctance, remorse, scruple, twinge, uncertainty, unease, uneasiness, worry.

quandary *n* bewilderment, confusion, corner, difficulty, dilemma, doubt, embarrassment, entanglement, fix, hole, imbroglio, impasse, jam, kettle of fish, mess, perplexity, plight, predicament, problem, puzzle, uncertainty.

quantity *n* abundance, aggregate, allotment, amount, breadth, bulk, capacity, content, dosage, expanse, extent, greatness, length, lot, magnitude, mass, measure, number, part, plenty, portion, proportion, quantum, quota, share, size, spread, strength, sum, total, volume, weight.

quarantine *n* confinement, detention, isolation, lazaretto, segregation.

quarrel *n* affray, altercation, argument, battle, beef, bicker, brawl, breach, breeze, broil, clash, commotion, conflict, contention, controversy, coolness, debate, difference, disagreement, discord, disputation, dispute, dissension, dissidence, disturbance, dustup, estrangement, falling-out, feud, fight, fracas, fray, misunderstanding, objection, quibble, row, rupture, schism, scrap, scuffle, shouting match, skirmish, slanging match, spat, split, squabble, strife, tiff, tumult, tussle, vendetta, war of words, wrangle.

antonyms agreement, harmony.

v altercate, argue, be at loggerheads, be at variance, bicker, brawl, carp, cavil, clash, contend, differ, disagree, dispute, dissent, fall out, fight, find fault, have a falling out, object, pick a fight, pick holes, question, row, spar, spat, squabble, take exception, tiff, wrangle.

antonym agree.

quarrelling *n* altercation, argumentation, bickering, contention, discord, disharmony, disputation, dissension, feuding, hostilities, rowing, scrapping, strife, variance, wrangling.

antonyms concord, harmony.

adj at loggerheads, at odds, at swords' points, at variance, bickering, clashing, contending, discordant, dissentient, feuding, fighting, hostile, rowing, scrapping, sparring, squabbling, warring, wrangling.

antonyms amicable, friendly.

quarrelsome *adj* antagonistic, argumentative, bellicose, belligerent, cantankerous, captious, chippy, choleric, combative, contentious, contrary, cross, disputatious, easily provoked, fractious, ill-tempered, irascible, irritable, litigious, peevish, perverse, petulant, pugnacious, querulous, shrewish, testy, touchy, truculent, wranglesome.

antonyms peaceable, placid.

quarry *n* game, goal, kill, mine, object, objective, pit, prey, prize, target, victim.

quarter[1] *n* area, direction, district, division, locality, location, neighbourhood, part, place, point, position, province, quartier, region, section, sector, side, spot, station, territory, vicinity, zone.

quarter[2] *n* clemency, compassion, favour, forgiveness, grace, indulgence, leniency, mercy, pardon, pity.

quarter[3] *v* accommodate, bed, billet, board, canton, house, install, lodge, place, post, put up, settle, shelter, station.

quarters *n* abode, accommodations, apartment, barracks, billet, cantonment, casern, chambers, digs, domicile, dwelling, habitation, housing, lodging, lodgings, post, residence, rooms, shelter.

quash *v* annul, cancel, crush, declare null and void, defeat, hush up, invalidate, nullify, overrule, overthrow, quell, put down, repress, rescind, reverse, revoke, set aside, squash, squelch, subdue, suppress, void.

antonyms confirm, justify, reinstate, vindicate.

quaver *v* break, crack, flicker, flutter, oscillate, pulsate, quake, quiver, shake, shudder, tremble, trill, twitter, vibrate, warble.

n break, quaveriness, quiver, shake, sob, throb, tremble, trembling, tremolo, tremor, trill, vibration, vibrato, warble.

quay *n* dock, harbour, jetty, levee, pier, wharf.

queasy *adj* bilious, dizzy, faint, giddy, green, green around the gills, groggy, ill, indisposed, light-headed, nauseated, nauseous, off-colour, qualmish, queer, seasick, sick (to one's stomach), squeamish, unwell.

queen *n* beauty, belle, consort, czarina, diva, doyenne, empress, goddess, grande dame, idol, maharani, mistress, monarch, nonpareil, prima donna, princess, rani, ruler, sovereign, star, sultana, Venus.

queenly *adj* dignified, gracious, grand, imperial, imperious, majestic, noble, regal, royal, sovereign, stately.

antonym undignified.

queer *adj* aberrant, abnormal, absurd, anomalous, atypical, bizarre, crazy, curious, daft, demented, deranged, deviant, disquieting, dizzy, doubtful, droll, dubious, eccentric, eerie, eldritch, erratic, exceptional, extraordinary, faint, fanciful, fantastic, fey, fishy, flaky, freakish, funny, giddy, grotesque, homosexual, idiosyncratic, ill, irrational, irregular, light-headed, mad, mysterious, odd, offbeat, out in left field, outlandish, out of the ordinary, outré, peculiar, preternatural, puzzling, quaint, queasy, questionable, reeling, remarkable, rum, screwy, shady, shifty, singular, skewed, strange, suspect, suspicious, touched, twisted, unaccountable, unbalanced, uncanny, uncommon, unconventional, uneasy, unhinged, unnatural, unorthodox, unusual, unwell, unwonted, weird.

antonyms common, ordinary, straightforward, unexceptional, usual.

v botch, endanger, foil, frustrate, harm, impair, imperil, injure, jeopardize, mar, ruin, spoil, stymie, thwart, upset, wreck.

queerness *n* aberrance, abnormality, absurdity, anomalousness, atypicalness, bizarreness, craziness, curiousness, deviance, drollness, dubiety, dubiousness, eccentricity, eeriness, fishiness, grotesqueness, idiosyncrasy, individuality, irrationality, irregularity, light-headedness, madness, mysteriousness, mystery, oddity, oddness, outlandishness, peculiarity, puzzle, quaintness, shadiness, shiftiness, singularity, skewness, strangeness, suspiciousness, uncanniness, uncommonness, unconventionality, unnaturalness, unorthodoxy, unusualness, unwontedness.

quell *v* allay, alleviate, appease, assuage, blunt, calm, compose, conquer, crush, deaden, defeat, dull, extinguish, hush (up), mitigate, moderate, mollify, overcome, overpower, pacify, put down, quash, quench, quiet, reduce, silence, soothe, squash, stifle, subdue, subjugate, suppress, vanquish.

quench *v* allay, appease, check, cool, crush, damp down, destroy, douse, end, extinguish, overcome, put out, quash, quell, sate, satisfy, silence, slake, smother, snuff out, stifle, suppress.

querulous *adj* cantankerous, captious, carping, cavilling, censorious, complaining, crabby, critical, cross, cross-grained, crusty, discontented, dissatisfied, exacting, faultfinding, fretful, fussy, grouchy, grumbling, hypercritical, ill-humoured, intolerant, irascible, irritable, peevish, perverse, petulant, plaintive, quarrelsome, sour, testy, waspish, whining, whiny.

antonyms contented, equable, placid, uncomplaining.

querulousness *n* cantankerousness, captiousness, censoriousness, crabbiness, criticalness, crossness, crustiness, discontent, discontentedness, dissatisfaction, faultfinding, fretfulness, fussiness, grouchiness, grumbling, ill-humour, intolerance, irascibility, irritability, peevishness, perversity, petulance, plaintiveness, quarrelsomeness, sourness, testiness, waspishness.

antonyms contentedness, equableness, placidity.

query *v* ask, be curious about, be sceptical (or doubtful) of, call into question, challenge, disbelieve, dispute, distrust, doubt, express doubt about, inquire (into), misdoubt, mistrust, quarrel with, question, suspect.

antonym accept.

n doubt, hesitation, inquiry, misdoubt, misgiving, objection, problem, question, question mark, quibble, reservation, scepticism, suspicion, uncertainty.

quest *n* adventure, crusade, enterprise, expedition, exploration, hunt, inquiry, investigation, journey, mission, pilgrimage, pursuit, search, undertaking, venture, voyage. *v* adventure, explore, hunt, search, seek, pursue.

question *v* ask, be sceptical of, catechize, challenge, controvert, cross-examine, debrief, defy, disbelieve, dispute, distrust, doubt, examine, grill, impugn, inquire into, interpellate, interrogate, interview, investigate, misdoubt, mistrust, oppose, probe, pump, quarrel with, query, quiz, suspect.

n argument, confusion, contention, controversy, debate, difficulty, dispute, doubt, dubiety, examination, if, inquiry, interpellation, interrogation, interrogative, investigation, issue, misdoubt, misgiving, motion, point, problem, proposal, proposition, query, quibble, subject, theme, topic, uncertainty.

questionable *adj* arguable, borderline, controversial, debatable, disputable, doubtful, dubious, dubitable, equivocal, fishy, iffy, impugnable, moot, open to question, problematic, queer, shady, suspect, suspicious, uncertain, unclear, undetermined, unproven, unreliable, unsettled, vexed.

antonyms certain, indisputable, straightforward.

questioner *n* agnostic, catechizer, catechist, disbeliever, doubter, examiner, inquirer, inquiring mind, inquisitor, interlocutor, interrogator, interviewer, investigator, sceptic.

questionnaire *n* catechism, form, quiz, survey, test.

queue *n* file, line, line-up, order, procession, sequence, series, string, succession, tail, train.

quibble *v* carp, cavil, chop logic, equivocate, find fault, niggle, nit-pick, pettifog, prevaricate, shift, split hairs.

n casuistry, cavil, complaint, criticism, equivocation, evasion, objection, pettifoggery, prevarication, query, quip, quirk, sophism, subterfuge.

quibbler *n* casuist, caviller, equivocator, faultfinder, hair splitter, logic-chopper, niggler, nit-picker, pettifogger, sophist.

quibbling *adj* ambiguous, argumentative, captious, carping, casuistic, cavilling, critical, equivocating, evasive, faultfinding, hairsplitting, logic-chopping, niggling, nit-picking, overnice, pettifogging, sophistic.

n carping, cavilling, nit-picking, pettifoggery, sophistry.

quick *adj* able, active, acute, adept, adroit, agile, alert, animated, apt, astute, awake, brief, bright, brisk, clever, cursory, deft, dexterous, discerning, eager, energetic, expeditious, express, fast, fleet, flying, hasty, headlong, hurried, immediate, instant, instantaneous, intelligent, keen, lively, nimble, penetrating, perceptive, perfunctory, precipitate, prompt, quick-witted, rapid, ready, receptive, responsive, sharp, short, shrewd, skilful, smart, snappy, speedy, spirited, sprightly, spry, sudden, summary, swift, teachable, transient, unhesitating, vivacious, wide-awake, willing, winged.

antonyms dull, slow.

quicken *v* accelerate, activate, advance, animate, arouse, come (or bring) to life, dispatch, energize, enliven, excite, expedite, facilitate, galvanize, hasten, hurry, impel, incite, inspire, invigorate, kindle, precipitate, reactivate, refresh, reinvigorate, resuscitate, revitalize, revive, revivify, rouse, sharpen, speed, stimulate, strengthen, vitalize, vivify.

antonyms dull, retard.

quickly *adv* abruptly, before you can say Jack Robinson, briskly, by leaps and bounds, cursorily, eagerly, expeditiously, express, fast, hastily, hell for leather, hotfoot, hurriedly, immediately, instantaneously, instantly, lickety-split, like a bat out of hell, on the double, perfunctorily, posthaste, promptly, pronto, quick as a wink, rapidly, readily, shortly, soon, speedily, swiftly, unhesitatingly, with alacrity.

antonyms slowly, tardily, thoroughly.

quickness *n* acuteness, agility, alertness, alacrity, aptness, astuteness, briskness, deftness, dexterity, eagerness, expedition, expeditiousness, hastiness, immediacy, instantaneousness, intelligence, keenness, liveliness, nimbleness, penetration, precipitation, promptitude, promptness, quick-wittedness, rapidity, readiness, receptiveness, sharpness, shrewdness, speed, speediness, suddenness, summariness, swiftness, teachability, transience, turn of speed.

antonyms dullness, slowness, tardiness.

quick-tempered *adj* choleric, excitable, explosive, fiery, hot-tempered, impatient, impulsive, irascible, irritable, petulant, quarrelsome, shrewish, snappy, splenetic, temperamental, testy, touchy, volcanic, waspish.

antonyms cool, dispassionate.

quick-witted *adj* acute, alert, astute, bright, clever, crafty, ingenious, intelligent, keen, nimble-witted, penetrating, perceptive, ready-witted, resourceful, sharp, shrewd, smart, wide awake, witty.

antonyms dull, slow, stupid.

quiescent *adj* asleep, calm, dormant, in abeyance, inactive, inert, latent, motionless, passive, peaceful, placid, quiet, reposeful, resting, serene, silent, sleeping, smooth, still, tranquil, undisturbed, untroubled.

antonym active.

quiet *adj* calm, composed, conservative, contemplative, contented, covert, docile, dumb, even-tempered, gentle, hushed, inaudible, isolated, lonely, low, low-pitched, meek, mild, modest, motionless, noiseless, out-of-the-way, pacific, passive, peaceable, peaceful, placid, plain, private, removed, reserved, restful, restrained, retiring, secluded, secret, sedate, self-effacing, sequestered, serene, shy, silent, simple, smooth, sober, soft, soundless, still, stilly, subdued, taciturn, tasteful, thoughtful, timid, tranquil, uncommunicative, undisturbed, uneventful, unexcitable, unexciting, unforthcoming, unfrequented, uninterrupted, unobtrusive, untroubled.

antonyms busy, noisy, obtrusive.

n calm, calmness, ease, hush, lull, order, peace, quiescence, quietness, quietude, repose, rest, serenity, silence, stillness, tranquillity.

antonyms bustle, disturbance, noise.

v abate, allay, alleviate, appease, assuage, blunt, calm, compose, deaden, diminish, dull, ebb, fall silent, hush, lull, mitigate, mollify, muffle, mute, pacify, palliate, quell, quieten, reduce, silence, smooth, sober, soothe, stifle, still, stop, subdue, tranquillize.

antonyms aggravate, discompose, disturb, exacerbate.

quietly *adv* calmly, composedly, confidentially, contentedly, demurely, diffidently, dispassionately, docilely, gently, humbly, inaudibly, meekly, mildly, modestly, mutely, noiselessly, obediently, on the q.t., patiently, peacefully, placidly, privately, secretly, serenely, silently, softly, soundlessly, surreptitiously, tastefully, tranquilly, undemonstratively, unobtrusively, unostentatiously, unpretentiously.

antonyms noisily, obtrusively.

quietness *n* calm, calmness, composure, dullness, hush, inactivity, inertia, lull, noiselessness, order, peace, peacefulness, placidity, quiescence, quiet, quietude, repose, serenity, silence, still, stillness, tranquillity, uneventfulness.

antonyms activity, bustle, commotion, disturbance, noise, racket.

quietus *n* acquittance, coup de grâce, defeat, death, deathblow, decease, demise, discharge, dispatch, end, extinction, finishing stroke, quittance, release, riddance, silencing.

quilt *n* bedcover, bedspread, blanket, comforter, counterpane, cover, coverlet, duvet, eiderdown.

quintessence *n* core, distillation, embodiment, essence, exemplar, extract, gist, heart, kernel, marrow, pattern, pith, soul, spirit, sum and substance, sum total.

quintessential *adj* archetypal, complete, consummate, definitive, entire, essential, ideal, model, par excellence, perfect, prototypical, ultimate.

quip *n* bon mot, crack, epigram, gag, gibe, jest, jeu d'esprit, joke, mot, one-liner, pleasantry, retort, riposte, sally, (snappy) comeback, wisecrack, witticism.

v crack a joke, gag, gibe, jest, joke, quibble, retort, riposte, wisecrack.

quirk *n* aberration, caprice, characteristic, curiosity, eccentricity, fancy, fetish, foible, freak, habit, idiosyncrasy, kink, mannerism, oddity, oddness, peculiarity, singularity, trait, turn, twist, vagary, warp, whim.

quisling *n* betrayer, collaborationist, double-crosser, fifth columnist, Judas, rat, renegade, snake in the grass, traitor, turncoat.

quit *v* abandon, abdicate, apostatize, back out, cease, conclude, decamp, depart, desert, disappear, discontinue, drop, drop out, end, exit, forsake, give up, go, halt, leave, relinquish, renege, renounce, repudiate, resign, retire, stop, surrender, suspend, vamoose, vanish, withdraw.

quit of clear of, discharged from, done with, finished with, free of, released from, rid of.

quite *adv* absolutely, comparatively, completely, entirely, exactly, fairly, fully, moderately, perfectly, positively, precisely, rather, relatively, somewhat, totally, utterly, very, wholly.

quits *adj* equal, even, even stephen, square, tied.

quitter *n* apostate, defector, delinquent, deserter, rat, recreant, renegade, shirker.

quiver *v* agitate, convulse, flicker, flutter, oscillate, palpitate, pulsate, quake, quaver, shake, shiver, shudder, tremble, vibrate, wobble.

n convulsion, flicker, flutter, oscillation, palpitation, pulsation, shake, shiver, shudder, spasm, throb, tic, tremble, tremor, vibration, wobble.

quixotic *adj* chivalrous, extravagant, fanciful, fantastic, idealistic, impetuous, impracticable, impulsive, romantic, starry-eyed, unrealistic, unworldly, Utopian, visionary, with one's head in the clouds.

antonyms hard-headed, practical, realistic.

quiz *n* catechism, examination, investigation, questioning, questionnaire, test.

v ask, catechize, cross-examine,

cross-question, debrief, examine, grill, interrogate, investigate, pump, question.

quizzical *adj* amused, arch, bantering, curious, humorous, inquiring, mocking, questioning, ridiculing, sardonic, satirical, sceptical, teasing, waggish, whimsical.

quota *n* allocation, allotment, allowance, assignment, cut, limit, maximum, part, percentage, portion, proportion, ratio, share, slice, whack.

quotation[1] *n* citation, excerpt, extract, locus classicus, passage, piece, quote, reference, repetition.

quotation[2] *n* charge, cost, estimate, figure, price, quote, rate, tender.

quote *v* adduce, attest, cite, detail, echo, instance, name, parrot, recall, recite, recollect, refer to, repeat, reproduce, retell.

quoted *adj* above-mentioned, aforementioned, cited, instanced, referred to, reported, reproduced, stated.

quotidian *adj* common, commonplace, customary, daily, day-to-day, diurnal, everyday, habitual, normal, ordinary, recurrent, regular, repeated, routine, workaday.

R

rabble n canaille, commonalty, commoners, crowd, dregs (of society), herd, hoi polloi, horde, masses, mob, peasantry, plebs, populace, proles, proletariat, raffle, raggle-taggle, ragtag (and bobtail), riffraff, scum, swarm, the great unwashed, throng, trash.

antonyms aristocracy, elite, nobility.

rabble-rouser n agitator, demagogue, firebrand, fomenter, incendiary, inciter, instigator, mischief-maker, mob-orator, troublemaker, tub thumper.

Rabelaisian adj barrack-room, bawdy, blue, broad, coarse, earthy, gross, indecent, lewd, lusty, obscene, racy, raunchy, ribald, risqué, salacious, satirical, scabrous, smutty, uninhibited, unrestrained, vulgar.

rabid adj berserk, crazed, extreme, fanatical, foaming (or frothing) at the mouth, frantic, frenzied, furious, hydrophobic, hysterical, infuriated, intemperate, irrational, mad, maniacal, narrow-minded, obsessive, overzealous, raging, raving, stark raving mad, unreasoning, violent, wild, wild-eyed, zealous.

race¹ n chase, competition, contention, contest, course, dash, derby, footrace, marathon, pursuit, quest, rat race, regatta, rivalry, scramble, sprint, steeplechase.

v career, compete (with), contest, dart, dash, fly, gallop, hare, hasten, hurry, make haste, run, rush, speed, sprint, tear, zoom.

race² n ancestry, blood, breed, clan, descent, family, folk, house, issue, kin, kind, kindred, line, lineage, nation, offspring, people, progeny, seed, stirps, stock, strain, tribe, type.

racetrack n circuit, course, hippodrome, raceway, route, speedway, track, turf.

racial adj ancestral, ethnic, ethnological, folk, genealogical, genetic, inherited, national, tribal.

rack¹ n frame, framework, gantry, gondola, hack, shelf, stand, structure.

rack² n affliction, agony, anguish, distress, misery, pain, pangs, persecution, strain, suffering, torment, torture.

v afflict, agonize, convulse, crucify, distress, excruciate, harass, harrow, lacerate, oppress, pain, punish, shake, strain, stress, stretch, tear, torment, torture, wrench, wrest, wring.

racket¹ n babel, ballyhoo, clamour, clangour, commotion, din, disturbance, fuss, hubbub,

hullabaloo, hurly-burly, kafuffle, noise, outcry, pandemonium, row, shouting, tumult, uproar.

racket² n business, con, deception, dodge, fiddle, fraud, game, scam, scheme, swindle, trick.

racy adj animated, bawdy, blue, boisterous, breezy, broad, buoyant, distinctive, doubtful, dubious, dynamic, ebullient, energetic, entertaining, enthusiastic, exciting, exhilarating, fresh, gamy, heady, immodest, indecent, indelicate, jaunty, lewd, lively, naughty, off-colour, piquant, pungent, Rabelaisian, ribald, rich, risqué, salacious, sharp, smutty, sparkling, spicy, spirited, stimulating, strong, suggestive, tangy, tasty, vigorous, zestful, zippy.

antonyms dull, ponderous.

radiance n beauty, brightness, brilliance, delight, effulgence, glare, gleam, glitter, glow, happiness, incandescence, joy, lambency, light, luminosity, lustre, refulgence, resplendence, shine, splendour, sunniness, warmth.

radiant adj aglow, alight, beaming, beamish, beatific, beautiful, blissful, bright, brilliant, delighted, ecstatic, effulgent, gleaming, glittering, glorious, glowing, gorgeous, happy, illuminated, incandescent, joyful, joyous, lambent, luminous, lustrous, rapturous, refulgent, resplendent, shining, sparkling, splendid, sunny.

antonym dull.

radiate v beam, branch out, diffuse, disseminate, diverge, emanate, emit, eradiate, give light, give out, gleam, issue, pour, scatter, send forth, shed, shine, spread (out).

radiation n dispersion, emanation, emission, insolation, radioactivity, rays.

radical adj basic, causal, complete, comprehensive, constitutional, deep, essential, excessive, extreme, extremist, fanatical, far-reaching, fundamental, inherent, innate, intrinsic, native, natural, organic, primary, profound, revolutionary, root, sweeping, thorough, thoroughgoing, total, violent.

antonym superficial.

n extremist, fanatic, Jacobin, left-winger, militant, reformer, reformist, revolutionary.

raffish adj bohemian, boorish, careless, casual, churlish, coarse, crude, dashing, devil-may-care, disreputable, dissipated, dissolute, flamboyant, flashy, garish, gaudy, gross, improper, jaunty, loud, meretricious, rakish, rowdy, showy, sporty, tasteless, tawdry, trashy, uncouth, vulgar.

antonyms decorous, proper, sedate, staid.

raffle *n* draw, lottery, lotto, sweep, sweepstake, tombola.

rag *v* badger, bait, bullyrag, chaff, jeer at, mock, razz, rib, ridicule, taunt, tease, torment, twit.

ragamuffin *n* beggar child, gamin(e), guttersnipe, street rat, tatterdemalion, urchin, waif.

ragbag *n* assemblage, confusion, hodgepodge, jumble, medley, miscellany, mixture, pastiche, potpourri, salad.

rage *n* agitation, anger, chafe, conniption (fit), craze, dernier cri, enthusiasm, fad, fashion, fit, frenzy, fury, ire, madness, mania, obsession, passion, style, tantrum, temper, the latest thing, vehemence, violence, vogue, wrath.

v bluster, chafe, explode, fulminate, fume, inveigh, ramp, rampage, rant, rave, seethe, storm, surge, thunder.

ragged *adj* broken, deckledged, desultory, disorganized, down-at-heel, erratic, fragmented, frayed, imperfect, irregular, jagged, moth-eaten, non-uniform, notched, patchy, poor, raggedy, rent, ripped, rough, rugged, scraggly, serrated, shabby, shaggy, tattered, tatty, threadbare, torn, uneven, unfinished, unkempt, worn-out.

raging *adj* enraged, frenzied, fulminating, fuming, furious, incensed, infuriated, irate, ireful, mad, rabid, rampageous, raving, seething, storming, stormy, violent, wrathful.

rags *n* attire, duds, gladrags, raggedness, remnants, shreds, tatters, threads.

raid *n* attack, break-in, bust, descent, foray, incursion, inroad, invasion, irruption, onset, onslaught, plundering, sack, sally, seizure, sortie, strike, swoop.

v attack, bust, descend on, forage, foray, invade, loot, maraud, pillage, plunder, ransack, rifle, rush, sack.

raider *n* attacker, brigand, despoiler, forager, freebooter, invader, looter, marauder, pirate, plunderer, ransacker, robber, rustler, sacker, thief.

rail at (or **against**) *v* abuse, arraign, attack, castigate, censure, criticize, decry, denounce, fulminate against, inveigh against, jeer at, mock, revile, ridicule, scoff at, upbraid, vituperate, vociferate against.

railing *n* balustrade, banister, barrier, fence, paling, parapet.

raillery *n* badinage, banter, chaff, irony, jeering, jesting, joke, joking, kidding, mockery, persiflage, pleasantry, ragging, razzing, repartee, ribbing, ridicule, satire, sport, teasing.

railway *n* el, elevated, LRT, metro, railroad, subway, the rails, the tube, the underground track, tramway.

rain *n* cloudburst, deluge, downpour, drizzle, flood, hail, moisture, monsoon, precipitation, raindrops, rainfall, shower(s), spate, stream, torrent, volley.

v bestow, deluge, deposit, drizzle, drop, expend, fall, heap, lavish, pour, precipitate, rain cats and dogs, shower, spit, sprinkle, teem.

rainbow *n* arc, iridescence, iris, prism, spectrum.

adj iridescent, kaleidoscopic, multicoloured, nacreous, opalescent, prismatic, rainbowlike, shot, spectral, variegated.

antonym monochrome.

rainy *adj* damp, dripping, drizzly, pluvious, showery, wet.

antonym dry.

raise *v* accumulate, advance, aggrade, aggrandize, aggravate, amass, amplify, arouse, assemble, augment, awaken, boost, breed, bring up, broach, build, cause, collect, conjure up, construct, create, cultivate, develop, drum up, elate, elevate, elicit, emboss, engender, enhance, enlarge, ennoble, erect, escalate, establish, evoke, exaggerate, exalt, excite, foment, form, foster, gather, gentrify, get, gladden, grow, heave, heighten, hoist, incite, increase, inflate, instigate, intensify, introduce, kindle, levy, lift (up), lighten, loft, magnify, mention, mobilize, moot, motivate, muster, nurture, obtain, occasion, originate, pose, prefer, produce, promote, propagate, provoke, rally, rear, recruit, reinforce, rouse, set up, sky, start, stir up, strengthen, sublime, suggest, up, upgrade, uplift, utter.

antonyms debase, decrease, degrade, dismiss, lower, reduce, suppress.

rake[1] *v* bombard, comb, drag, enfilade, examine, graze, harrow, hoe, hunt through, make, pepper, ransack, scan, scour, scrape, scratch, scrutinize, search, strafe, sweep.

rake in accumulate, amass, collect, gather, haul in.

rake over the coals bawl out, castigate, censure, chastise, haul on the carpet, give heck, pull (or bring) up short, ream out, reprimand, tell off.

rake[2] *n* blood, debauchee, degenerate, dissolute, hedonist, lecher, libertine, playboy, pleasure-seeker, prodigal, profligate, roué, sensualist, spendthrift, swinger, voluptuary.

antonyms ascetic, puritan.

rakish *adj* abandoned, breezy, dapper, dashing, debauched, debonair, degenerate, depraved, devil-may-care, dissipated, dissolute, flamboyant, flashy, immoral, jaunty, lecherous, libertine, licentious, loose, natty, prodigal, profligate, raffish, sharp, sinful, smart, snazzy, sporty, stylish, wanton.

rally[1] *v* assemble, call together, cluster, collect, come, come together, congregate, convene, embolden, encourage, gather, hearten, improve, join (together), marshal, mass, mobilize, muster, organize, pick up, pull together, rally round, reassemble, recover, recuperate, re-form, regroup, reorder, reorganize, revive, round up, summon, unite.

n assembly, comeback, concourse, conference, congregation, convention, convocation, gathering, improvement, jamboree, meeting, recovery, recuperation, regrouping, renewal, reorganization, resurgence, reunion, revival.

rally around be there for, cheer on, come to the aid of, encourage, help out, stand (or stick) by, support, sustain, take up the cause of.

rally² *v* chaff, make fun of, mock, rag, rib, ridicule, send up, taunt, tease, twit.

ram *v* butt, cram, crash, crowd, drive, drum, force, hammer, hit, impact, jam, pack, pound, push, railroad, ramrod, slam, smash, strike, stuff, tamp, thrust.

ramble *v* amble, babble, chatter, digress, divagate, drift, expatiate, maunder, meander, perambulate, peregrinate, range, rattle (on), roam, rove, saunter, snake, straggle, stray, stroll, traipse, tramp, walk, wander (around), wind, zigzag.

n amble, divagation, excursion, hike, perambulation, peregrination, roaming, roving, saunter, stroll, tour, traipse, trip, walk.

rambler *n* drifter, globetrotter, hiker, peregrinator, roamer, rolling stone, rover, stroller, walker, wanderer, wayfarer.

rambling *adj* circuitous, desultory, diffuse, digressive, disconnected, discursive, disjointed, excursive, incoherent, irregular, long-drawn-out, long-winded, loose, peripatetic, periphrastic, prolix, sprawling, spreading, straggling, trailing, unfocussed, wandering, wordy.

antonym direct.

rambunctious *adj* boisterous, clamorous, disorderly, exuberant, loud, noisy, obstreperous, refractory, robust, roisterous, roistering, rollicking, rough, rowdy, unmanageable, unruly, uproarious, wayward, wild, willful.

antonyms quiet, restrained, sensible.

ramification *n* branch, complication, consequence, development, dichotomy, divarication, division, excrescence, extension, fork, limb, offshoot, outgrowth, ramus, result, sequel, subdivision, upshot.

ramp *n* grade, gradient, incline, rise, slope.

rampage *v* rage, rant, rave, run amuck, run riot, run wild, rush, storm, tear.

n destruction, frenzy, furor, fury, rage, rush, spree, storm, tantrum, tempest, tumult, outburst, uproar, violence, warpath.

on the rampage amok, berserk, frenzied, in a frenzy, rampageous(ly), rampant(ly), riotous(ly), violent(ly), wild(ly).

rampant *adj* aggressive, dominant, epidemic, erect, excessive, exuberant, fierce, flagrant, luxuriant, outrageous, prevalent, prodigal, profuse, raging, rampaging, rank, rearing, rife, riotous, standing (up), unbridled, unchecked, uncontrollable, uncontrolled, ungovernable, unrestrained, upright, vehement, violent, wanton, widespread, wild.

rampart *n* barricade, barrier, bastion, bulwark, buttress, defence, earthwork, embankment, fence, fort, fortification, guard, security, stronghold, wall.

ramshackle *adj* broken-down, crumbling, decrepit, derelict, dilapidated, flimsy, haywire, jerry-built, rickety, shaky, shoddy, tottering, tumbledown, unsafe, unsteady.

antonyms solid, stable.

ranch *n* estancia, estate, farm, hacienda, plantation, station.

rancid *adj* bad, fetid, foul, fusty, malodorous, musty, off, putrid, rank, reasty, rotten, sour, spoiled, stale, tainted, unsavoury.

antonym sweet.

rancorous *adj* acrimonious, bitter, hostile, implacable, malevolent, malicious, malignant, resentful, spiteful, splenetic, vengeful, venomous, vindictive, virulent.

rancour *n* acrimony, animosity, animus, antipathy, bitterness, enmity, grudge, hate, hatred, hostility, ill feeling, ill will, malevolence, malice, malignity, resentfulness, resentment, spite, spleen, venom, vindictiveness.

random *adj* accidental, adventitious, aimless, arbitrary, casual, chance, desultory, fortuitous, haphazard, incidental, indiscriminate, purposeless, scattered, scattergun, scattershot, spot, stray, unfocussed, unordered, unplanned, unpremeditated.

antonyms deliberate, systematic.

at random accidentally, adventitiously, aimlessly, arbitrarily, by chance, capriciously, casually, desultorily, fortuitously, haphazardly, indiscriminately, irregularly, purposelessly, randomly, unsystematically, without rhyme or reason.

randy *adj* amorous, aroused, concupiscent, hot, lascivious, lecherous, lustful, raunchy, satyric, sexy, turned-on.

range *n* amplitude, area, assortment, band, bounds, chain, class, collection, compass, confines, diapason, distance, distribution, domain, earshot, extent, field, file, gamut, grassland, kind, latitude, limits, line, lot, mountain range, orbit, order, palette, parameters, pastureland, plain, province, purview, radius, rank, reach, row, scale, scope, selection, sequence, series, sort, span, spectrum, sphere, steppe, string, sweep, tessitura, tier, variety, view.

v aim, align, arrange, array, bracket, catalogue, categorize, class, classify, direct, dispose, explore, extend, fluctuate, go, grade, graze, group, level, order, pasture, pigeonhole, point, ramble, rank, reach, roam, rove, run, straggle, stray, stretch, stroll, sweep, train, traverse, vary, wander, wander over.

rangy *adj* gangling, lanky, leggy, long-legged, skinny, slender, weedy.

antonyms compact, dumpy.

rank¹ *n* authority, caste, class, classification, column, condition, degree, dignity, division, echelon, estate, état, file, formation, grade, group, level, line, nobility, order, place, position, prestige, quality, range, row, series, standing, station, status, stratum, tier.

v align, arrange, array, class, classify, dispose, evaluate, grade, judge, locate, marshal, order, organize, place, position, prioritize, range, sort.

rank² *adj* absolute, abundant, arrant, atrocious, bad, blatant, coarse, complete, crass, dense, disagreeable, disgusting, downright, egregious, excessive, extravagant, extreme, exuberant, fetid, filthy, flagrant, flourishing, foul, fusty, gamy, glaring, gross, indecent, lush, luxuriant, malodorous, mephitic, musty, noisome, noxious, obscene, off, offensive, out-and-out, outrageous, outright, profuse, pungent, putrid, rampant, rancid, repulsive, revolting, scurrilous, sheer, shocking, stale, stinking, tainted, thorough, thoroughgoing, total, undisguised, unmitigated, unsavoury, utter, vigorous, vulgar.

antonyms sparse, sweet.

rankle *v* anger, annoy, chafe, embitter, fester, gall, irk, irritate, nettle, peeve, rile.

ransack *v* comb, despoil, explore, gut, loot, maraud, pillage, plunder, raid, rake (through), ravage, rifle (through), rummage (through), sack, scour, search (through), strip.

ransom *n* deliverance, liberation, money, payment, payoff, price, redemption, release, rescue.

v buy out, deliver, extricate, liberate, redeem, release, rescue.

rant *v* bellow, bluster, cry, declaim, mouth off, rave, roar, shout, spout, tub thump, vociferate, yell.

n bluster, bombast, declamation, diatribe, fanfaronade, harangue, philippic, rhetoric, storm, tirade, tub-thumping, vociferation.

rap¹ *v* bark, castigate, censure, crack, criticize, hit, knock, pan, reprimand, scold, strike, tap.

n blame, blow, castigation, censure, chiding, clout, conviction, crack, discussion, knock, punishment, rebuke, reprimand, responsibility, sentence, tap.

rap² *v* chat, confabulate, converse, discourse, talk.

n chat, colloquy, confabulation, conversation, dialogue, discourse, talk.

rapacious *adj* avaricious, esurient, extortionate, grasping, greedy, insatiable, marauding, plundering, predatory, preying, ravening, ravenous, sharklike, usurious, voracious, vulturine, wolfish.

rapacity *n* avarice, avidity, cupidity, esurience, graspingness, greed, greediness, insatiability, insatiableness, predatoriness, rapaciousness, ravenousness, usury, voraciousness, voracity, wolfishness.

rape *n* abuse, defilement, deflowering, depredation, desecration, despoilment, despoliation, exploitation, maltreatment, pillage, plundering, rapine, ravaging, ravishment, sack, spoliation, violation.

v abuse, assault, deflower, desecrate, despoil, loot, pillage, plunder, ransack, ravage, ravish, sack, spoliate, violate.

rapid *adj* accelerated, brisk, expeditious, express, fast, fleet, flying, hasty, headlong, hurried, precipitate, prompt, quick, speedy, swift.

antonyms leisurely, slow, sluggish.

rapidity *n* alacrity, briskness, celerity, dispatch, expedition, expeditiousness, fleetness, haste, hurry, precipitateness, promptitude, promptness, quickness, rush, speed, speediness, swiftness, velocity.

antonym slowness.

rapidly *adv* at a good clip, briskly, by leaps and bounds, expeditiously, fast, hastily, headlong, hurriedly, lickety-split, like a house afire, posthaste, precipitately, promptly, quickly, speedily, swiftly.

antonym slowly.

rapine *n* depredation, despoilment, despoliation, looting, marauding, pillage, plunder, ransacking, rape, ravaging, robbery, sack, sacking, seizure, spoliation, theft.

rapport *n* affinity, bond, compatibility, empathy, harmony, link, relationship, sympathy, understanding.

rapprochement *n* accord, agreement, détente, harmonization, reconciliation, reunion, softening.

rapscallion *n* blackguard, cad, cur, good-for-nothing, knave, mischief-maker, ne'er-do-well, rascal, reprobate, rogue, scallywag, scamp, scapegrace, scoundrel, wastrel, wretch.

rapt *adj* absorbed, beatific, bewitched, captivated, charmed, delighted, ecstatic, enchanted, engrossed, enraptured, enthralled, entranced, fascinated, gripped, held, intent, preoccupied, rapturous, ravished, spellbound, transported.

rapture *n* bliss, delectation, delight, ecstasy, enthusiasm, entrancement, euphoria, exaltation, felicity, happiness, joy, ravishment, rhapsody, spell, transport.

rapturous *adj* blissful, delighted, ecstatic, enthusiastic, entranced, euphoric, exalted, happy, in (seventh) heaven, joyful, joyous, on cloud nine, overjoyed, rhapsodic, transported.

rare *adj* atypical, choice, curious, excellent, exceptional, exquisite, extraordinary, extreme, few, few and far between, fine, great, incomparable, infrequent, invaluable, matchless, one-of-a-kind, peerless, precious, priceless, recherché, remarkable, rich, scarce, singular, sparse, sporadic, strange, superb, superlative, surpassing, uncommon, unusual.

antonyms abundant, common, usual.

rarefied *adj* elevated, exalted, high, lofty, noble, purified, refined, sublime, subtle.

rarely *adv* atypically, exceptionally, extraordinarily, finely, hardly, hardly ever, infrequently, notably, remarkably, scarcely, seldom, singularly, uncommonly, unusually.

antonyms frequently, often.

raring *adj* agog, anxious, athirst, avid, chomping at the bit, desperate, eager, enthusiastic, impatient, itching, keen, longing, ready, willing, yearning.

rarity *n* choiceness, curio, curiosity, excellence, exquisiteness, find, fineness, incomparability, incomparableness, infrequency, marvel, one of a kind, paucity, peerlessness, preciousness, pricelessness, scarcity, shortage, singularity, sparseness, strangeness, treasure, uncommonness, unusualness.

antonyms commonness, commonplace.

rascal *n* blackguard, caitiff, devil, good-for-nothing, hellion, imp, knave, mischief-maker, miscreant, ne'er-do-well, rake, rapscallion, reprobate, rogue, scallywag, scamp, scapegrace, scoundrel, varmint, villain, wastrel, wretch.

rascally *adj* bad, base, blackguardly, crooked, dishonest, disreputable, evil, good-for-nothing, knavish, low, low-down, mean, nasty, recreant, reprobate, scoundrelly, unscrupulous, vicious, vile, villainous, wicked.

rash¹ *adj* adventurous, audacious, brash, careless, foolhardy, harebrained, harum-scarum, hasty, headlong, headstrong, heedless, helter-skelter, hot-headed, ill-advised, ill-considered, impetuous, imprudent, impulsive, incautious, indiscreet, injudicious, madcap, precipitate, premature, reckless, slap-bang, slapdash, temerarious, thoughtless, unguarded, unthinking, unwary, venturesome.

antonyms calculating, careful, considered, wary.

rash² *n* epidemic, eruption, exanthem, flood, hives, outbreak, plague, series, spate, succession, urticaria, wave.

rashness *n* adventurousness, audacity, brashness, carelessness, foolhardiness, hastiness, heedlessness, impulsiveness, incaution, incautiousness, indiscretion, precipitation, precipitousness, recklessness, temerity, thoughtlessness.

antonyms carefulness, cautiousness.

rasp *n* croak, grating, grinding, harshness, hoarseness, scrape, scratch.

v abrade, croak, file, grate, grind, irk, irritate, jar, rub, sand, scour, scrape.

rasping *adj* creaking, croaking, croaky, grating, gravelly, gruff, harsh, hoarse, husky, jarring, raspy, raucous, rough, scratchy, stridulating.

rat *n* cad, double-crosser, ratfink, renegade, snake in the grass, swine, traitor, turncoat.

rate¹ *n* amount, charge, class, cost, degree, duty, fee, figure, gait, grade, measure, pace, percentage, price, proportion, quantity, rank, rating, ratio, relation, scale, speed, standard, tariff, tax, tempo, time, toll, value, velocity, worth.

v adjudge, appraise, assess, class, classify, consider, count, deserve, esteem, estimate, evaluate, figure, grade, judge, measure, measure up, merit, place, price, rank, reckon, regard, value, weigh.

rate² *v* admonish, berate, blame, castigate, censure, chastise, chide, criticize, dress down, lecture, rake over the coals, rebuke,

reprimand, reprove, roast, scold, tell off, tongue-lash, upbraid.

rather *adv* a bit, fairly, instead, kind of, moderately, noticeably, on the contrary, preferably, pretty, quite, relatively, significantly, slightly, somewhat, sooner, sort of, to a degree, very.

ratify *v* affirm, approve, authenticate, authorize, certify, confirm, corroborate, endorse, establish, legalize, recognize, sanction, sign, uphold, validate.

antonyms reject, repudiate.

rating¹ *n* class, classification, degree, designation, estimate, evaluation, grade, grading, judgment, measurement, order, placing, position, rank, rate, sort, sorting, standing, status, valuation.

rating² *n* castigation, chastisement, chiding, dressing-down, lecture, rebuke, reprimand, reproof, roasting, scolding, telling-off, tongue-lashing, upbraiding.

ratio *n* balance, correlation, correspondence, equation, fraction, percentage, proportion, quotient, rate, relation, relationship.

ration *n* allocation, allotment, allowance, amount, dole, helping, measure, part, portion, provision, quota, share.

v allocate, allot, apportion, budget, conserve, control, deal, dispense, distribute, dole (out), issue, limit, mete (out), restrict, save, supply.

rational *adj* balanced, cerebral, cognitive, compos mentis, enlightened, intelligent, judicious, logical, lucid, mental, normal, ratiocinative, realistic, reasonable, reasoning, sagacious, sane, sensible, sound, thinking, well-founded, well-grounded, wise.

antonyms crazy, illogical, irrational.

rationale *n* excuse, explanation, exposition, grounds, logic, motivation, philosophy, pretext, principle, raison d'être, reason(s), theory, the whys and wherefores.

rationalize *v* defend, demystify, demythologize, excuse, explain (away), extenuate, justify, organize, reason (out), streamline, trim, vindicate.

rations *n* commons, food, provender, provisions, stores, supplies.

rattle *v* bang, bounce, bump, clang, clank, clatter, confuse, crepitate, discomfit, discompose, disconcert, discountenance, disturb, faze, fluster, frighten, jangle, jolt, jounce, perturb, scare, shake, upset, vibrate.

rattle off enumerate, itemize, list, recite, reel off, rehearse, repeat, rhyme off, run through, spiel off.

rattle on blather, cackle, chatter, gab, gabble, gibber, jabber, prate, prattle, yak.

ratty¹ *adj* dowdy, frayed, out at the elbows, patchy, raggedy, ripped, scruffy, shabby, tacky, tattered, torn.

ratty² *adj* angry, annoyed, crabbed, cross, impatient, irritable, peeved, short, short-tempered, snappish, testy, touchy.

antonyms calm, patient.

raucous *adj* dissonant, grating, harsh, hoarse, husky, loud, noisy, rasping, rough, rusty, strident.

ravage *v* demolish, desolate, despoil, destroy, devastate, gut, lay waste, loot, pillage, plunder, ransack, raze, ruin, sack, shatter, spoil, wreck.

n damage, defilement, demolition, depredation, desecration, desolation, destruction, devastation, havoc, pillage, plunder, rapine, ruin, ruination, spoliation, waste, wreckage.

ravaged *adj* battle-torn, desolate, destroyed, devastated, pillaged, ransacked, ruined, shattered, spoiled, war-torn, wasted, wrecked.
antonym unspoilt.

rave *v* babble, bluster, declaim, fulminate, fume, harangue, rage, ramble, rant, roar, splutter, storm, thunder.
adj ecstatic, enthusiastic, excellent, fantastic, favourable, laudatory, wonderful.

rave about be (or go) gaga over, enthuse about, fuss over, go on about, gush over, praise (or puff) to the skies, swoon over, wax eloquent about.

ravenous *adj* avaricious, covetous, devouring, esurient, famished, ferocious, gluttonous, grasping, greedy, hungry, insatiable, insatiate, predatory, rapacious, ravening, starved, starving, voracious, wolfish.

ravine *n* arroyo, canyon, clough, coulee, crevasse, defile, flume, gap, gorge, gulch, gully, pass.

raving *adj* berserk, blustering, bonkers, crazed, crazy, delirious, frantic, frenzied, furious, hysterical, incoherent, infuriated, insane, irrational, mad, manic, rabid, raging, violent, wild.

ravish *v* abuse, captivate, charm, deflower, delight, enchant, enrapture, entrance, fascinate, outrage, overjoy, rape, spellbind, transport, violate.

ravishing *adj* alluring, beautiful, bewitching, charming, dazzling, delightful, enchanting, entrancing, gorgeous, lovely, radiant, seductive, stunning.

raw *adj* abraded, bare, basic, biting, bitter, bleak, bloody, blunt, brutal, callow, chafed, chill, chilly, coarse, cold, crass, crude, damp, earthy, freezing, fresh, grazed, green, gross, harsh, ignorant, immature, inexperienced, naked, natural, new, open, organic, piercing, plain, rough, rude, scraped, scratched, sensitive, skinned, sore, tender, unadorned, uncooked, undeveloped, undisciplined, undisguised, undressed, unfinished, unpleasant, unpolished, unpractised, unprepared, unprocessed, unrefined, unripe, unseasoned, unskilled, untrained, untreated, untried, unvarnished, verdant, vulgar, wet, wet behind the ears.
antonyms cooked, experienced, refined.

ray *n* bar, beam, flash, flicker, gleam, glimmer, glint, hint, indication, scintilla, shaft, spark, stream, trace.

raze *v* bulldoze, demolish, destroy, dismantle, efface, erase, expunge, extinguish, extirpate, flatten, level, obliterate, remove, ruin, tear down.

re *prep* about, anent, apropos, concerning, pertaining to, regarding, respecting, touching, with reference to, with regard to, with respect to.

reach *v* amount to, arrive at, attain, contact, drop to, extend (to), fall to, get to, hand, land at, make, pass, rise, sink (to), stretch (to), strike.

n ambit, capacity, clutches, compass, distance, extension, extent, grasp, influence, jurisdiction, latitude, power, purview, range, scope, spread, stretch, sweep.

react (to) *v* acknowledge, act, answer, be affected, behave, counteract, emote, reply, respond, work.

reaction *n* acknowledgment, answer, backlash, backwash, compensation, conservatism, counteraction, counterbalance, counterpoise, counter-revolution, feedback, furor, obscurantism, recoil, reflex, reply, response, stir.

reactionary *adj* conservative, counter-revolutionary, die-hard, obscurantist, obstructive, old-line, reversional, rightist, right-wing.
antonyms progressive, radical, revolutionary.
n Colonel Blimp, conservative, counter-revolutionary, die-hard, obscurantist, obstructionist, old-liner, reactionist, rightist, right-winger.
antonyms progressive, radical, revolutionary.

read *v* announce, be worded, comprehend, con, construe, decipher, deliver, discover, give a lecture, indicate, interpret, introduce, measure, peruse, pore over, proofread, recite, register, render, scan, see, show, sound out, speak, study, understand.

readable *adj* accessible, clear, compelling, comprehensible, decipherable, enjoyable, entertaining, enthralling, gripping, intelligible, interesting, legible, plain, understandable, unputdownable.
antonyms illegible, unreadable.

readily *adv* cheerfully, eagerly, easily, effortlessly, fain, freely, gladly, lief, promptly, quickly, smoothly, speedily, unhesitatingly, voluntarily, willingly, with alacrity.

readiness *n* adroitness, alacrity, alertness, aptitude, aptness, dexterity, eagerness, ease, facility, fitness, foresight, gameness, handiness, inclination, keenness, maturity, preparation, preparedness, promptitude, promptness, quickness, rapidity, ripeness, skill, tendency, willingness.

reading *n* book learning, conception, construction, edification, education, emendation, erudition, examination, excerpt, extract, grasp, homily, impression, inspection, interpretation, knowledge, learning, lecture, lesson, measure, passage, performance, perusal, recital, rendering, rendition, review, scholarship, scrutiny, sermon, study, treatment, understanding, version.

ready *adj* around, accessible, acute, agreeable, alert, apt, arranged, astute, available, bright, clever, close (at hand), completed, convenient, deft, dexterous, disposed, eager, equipped, expert, facile, finished, fit, game, handy, inclined, intelligent, keen, liable, likely, minded, near, on call, on tap, organized, perceptive, predisposed, prepared, primed, prompt, prone, quick, quick-witted, rapid, resourceful, ripe, set, sharp, skilful, smart, willing.

antonyms unprepared, unready.

v alert, arrange, brace, equip, fit (out), gird, order, organize, prepare, prime, set, train.

real *adj* absolute, actual, authentic, bona fide, certain, certified, essential, existent, factual, genuine, heartfelt, honest, legitimate, positive, right, rightful, simon-pure, sincere, substantial, substantive, sure-enough, tangible, true, unaffected, undoubted, unfeigned, unquestionable, valid, veritable.

antonyms imaginary, unreal.

realism *n* authenticity, common sense, hard-headedness, lifelikeness, naturalism, objectivity, practicality, pragmatism, sensibleness, truthfulness, verisimilitude.

realistic *adj* authentic, businesslike, clear-eyed, clear-sighted, common-sense, detached, down-to-earth, faithful, genuine, graphic, hard-headed, level-headed, lifelike, matter-of-fact, natural, naturalistic, objective, practical, pragmatic, rational, real, real-life, representational, sensible, sober, true, true-to-life, truthful, unromantic, unsentimental.

antonyms fanciful, impractical, irrational, unrealistic.

reality *n* actuality, authenticity, certainty, corporeality, fact, factuality, genuineness, materiality, nitty-gritty, palpability, realism, tangibility, truth, validity, verisimilitude, verity.

realization *n* accomplishment, achievement, actualization, appreciation, apprehension, awareness, cognizance, completion, comprehension, conception, concretization, knowledge, consciousness, consummation, effectuation, fruition, fulfilment, grasp, perception, recognition, understanding.

realize *v* accomplish, achieve, actualize, appreciate, apprehend, attain, catch on, clear, complete, comprehend, concretize, consummate, do, earn, effect, effectuate, fulfil, gain, get, grasp, implement, know, make, net, obtain, perform, produce, reap, recognize, take in, twig to, understand.

really *adv* absolutely, actually, assuredly, categorically, certainly, essentially, genuinely, indeed, intrinsically, positively, surely, truly, undoubtedly, verily.

realm *n* area, bailiwick, branch, country, department, domain, dominion, empire, field, jurisdiction, kingdom, land, monarchy, orbit, principality, province, region, sphere, state, territory, world, zone.

reap *v* acquire, collect, crop, cut, derive, gain, garner, gather, get, harvest, mow, obtain, realize, secure, win.

rear[1] *n* back, backside, bottom, buttocks, croup, end, hindquarters, posterior, rear guard, rump, stern, tail.

antonym front.

adj aft, after, back, following, hind, hindmost, last.

antonym front.

rear[2] *v* breed, bring up, build, construct, cultivate, educate, elevate, erect, fabricate, foster, grow, hoist, lift (up), loom, nurse, nurture, parent, raise, rise, soar, tower, train.

rearrange *v* adjust, alter, reorder, reorganize, reposition, restructure, shift, vary.

reason *n* aim, apologia, apology, apprehension, argument, basis, bounds, brains, cause, common sense, comprehension, consideration, defence, design, end, excuse, explanation, exposition, goal, (good) sense, ground(s), impetus, incentive, inducement, intellect, intention, justification, limits, logic, mentality, mind, moderation, motive, nous, object, occasion, propriety, purpose, ratiocination, rationale, rationality, reasonableness, reasoning, sanity, sensibleness, soundness, target, thought, understanding, vindication, warrant, wisdom.

v argue, conclude, debate, deduce, infer, intellectualize, ratiocinate, resolve, solve, syllogize, think, work (out).

reason with argue, dissuade, expostulate with, get through to, move, persuade, remonstrate with, talk to (or with), urge.

reasonable *adj* acceptable, advisable, arguable, average, believable, credible, equitable, fair, fit, honest, inexpensive, intelligent, judicious, just, justifiable, logical, moderate, modest, OK, passable, plausible, possible, practical, proper, rational, reasoned, right, sane, satisfactory, sensible, sober, sound, tenable, tolerable, viable, well-advised, well-thought-out, wise.

antonyms crazy, extravagant, irrational, outrageous, unreasonable.

reasoned *adj* clear, judicious, logical, methodical, rational, sensible, sound, systematic, well-thought-out.

antonyms illogical, unsystematic.

reasoning *n* analysis, argument, case, cogitation, deduction, explication, exposition, hypothesis, interpretation, logic, proof, ratiocination, rationale, reason, supposition, thinking, thought.

reassure *v* bolster, brace, comfort, encourage, give hope, hearten, inspirit, nerve.

rebate *n* allowance, bonus, deduction, discount, reduction, refund, repayment.

rebel *v* defy, disobey, dissent, flinch, kick over the traces, mutiny, recoil, resist, revolt, rise up, run riot, shrink.

n apostate, dissenter, heretic, insurgent, insurrectionist, Jacobin, malcontent, mutineer, nonconformist, revolutionist, schismatic, secessionist, subversive.

adj insubordinate, insurgent, insurrectionary, malcontent, mutinous, rebellious, revolutionary, subversive.

rebellion *n* apostasy, defiance, disobedience, dissent, heresy, insubordination, insurgence, insurrection, jacquerie, mutiny, nonconformity, resistance, revolt, revolution, rising, schism, sedition, uprising.

rebellious *adj* contumacious, defiant, difficult, discontented, disloyal, disobedient, disorderly, incorrigible, insubordinate, insurgent, insurrectionary, intractable, malcontent(ed), mutinous, obstinate, rebel, recalcitrant, refractory, resistant, revolutionary, seditious, subversive, ungovernable, unmanageable, unruly.

antonyms obedient, submissive.

rebirth *n* reactivation, re-animation, regeneration, reincarnation, rejuvenation, renaissance, renascence, renewal, restoration, resurgence, resurrection, revitalization, revival.

rebound *v* backfire, boomerang, bounce (back), misfire, recoil, redound, resound, return, reverberate, ricochet, spring back.

n backwash, bounce, recoil, reflection, repercussion, return, reverberation, ricochet.

rebuff *v* brushoff, cold-shoulder, cut, discourage, give the brush off, put someone's nose out of joint, refuse, reject, repulse, resist, send packing, slight, snub, spurn, turn down.

n brushoff, check, cold shoulder, defeat, discouragement, flea in one's ear, opposition, refusal, rejection, repulse, set-down, slight, snub.

rebuild *v* reassemble, reconstruct, redo, re-establish, refashion, remake, remodel, renovate, restore.

antonyms demolish, destroy.

rebuke *v* admonish, bawl out, berate, blame, call on the carpet, call to account, castigate, censure, chew out, chide, dress down, lecture, rake over the coals, rate, rap on the knuckles, read the riot act to, reprehend, reprimand, reproach, reprove, scold, slap down, tell off, trim, upbraid.

antonyms compliment, praise.

n admonition, blame, castigation, censure, dressing-down, going-over, lecture, rap on the knuckles, reaming-out, reprimand, reproach, reproof, reproval, scolding, talking-to, telling-off, tongue-lashing, what for.

antonyms compliment, praise.

rebut *v* confute, contradict, defeat, discredit, disprove, explode, give the lie to, invalidate, negate, oppose, overturn, quash, refute.

rebuttal *n* confutation, defeat, disproof, invalidation, negation, overthrow, refutation.

recalcitrant *adj* contrary, contumacious, defiant, disobedient, insubordinate, intractable, non-compliant, obstinate, refractory, resistant, stubborn, uncontrollable, unco-operative, ungovernable, unmanageable, unruly, unsubmissive, unwilling, wayward, willful.

antonym amenable.

recall *v* annul, call back, call to mind, cancel, cast one's mind back, countermand, evoke, mind, nullify, place, recognize, recollect, remember, reminisce about, repeal, rescind, retract, revoke, think back (to), withdraw.

n abrogation, annulment, cancellation, memory, nullification, recollection, remembering, remembrance, repeal, rescission, retraction, revocation, withdrawal.

recant *v* abjure, abrogate, apostatize, deny, disavow, disclaim, disown, forswear, recall, reject, relinquish, renounce, repudiate, rescind, retract, revoke, unsay, withdraw.

recantation *n* abjuration, apostasy, denial, disavowal, disclaimer, disownment, rejection, renunciation, repudiation, retraction, revocation, withdrawal.

recapitulate *v* give a summary (of), recap, recount, reiterate, repeat, restate, review, summarize, sum up, synopsize.

recede *v* abate, decline, decrease, diminish, dwindle, ebb, fade, lessen, regress, retire, retreat, retrogress, return, shrink, sink, slacken, subside, wane, withdraw.

antonyms advance, proceed.

receipt *n* acceptance, acknowledgment, counterfoil, delivery, receiving, reception, slip, stub, ticket, voucher.

receipts *n* gains, gate, income, proceeds, profits, return, take, takings.

receive *v* accept, accommodate, acquire, admit, apprehend, bear, collect, derive, encounter, entertain, experience, gather, get, greet, hear, meet, obtain, perceive, pick up, react to, respond to, suffer, sustain, take (in), undergo, welcome.

antonyms donate, give.

recent *adj* contemporary, current, fresh, late, latter, latter-day, modern, neoteric, new, novel, present-day, up-to-date, young.

antonyms dated, old, out-of-date.

recently *adv* currently, freshly, in the recent past, lately, latterly, newly.

receptacle *n* container, holder, reliquary, repository, urn, vessel.

reception *n* acceptance, acknowledgment, admission, do, durbar, entertainment, function, greeting, levee, party, reaction, receipt, receiving, recognition, response, shindig, (social) gathering, soirée, tea, treatment, welcome.

receptive *adj* accessible, alert, amenable, approachable, bright, favourable, friendly, hospitable, influenceable, interested, open, open-minded, perceptive, responsive, sensitive, suggestible, susceptible, sympathetic, teachable, welcoming.

recess *n* alcove, apse, bay, break, cavity, cessation, closure, corner, depression, embrasure, holiday, hollow, indentation, intermission, interval, niche, nook, oriel, pause, respite, rest, vacation.

recesses *n* bowels, depths, heart, innards, interior, inward parts, reaches, retreats.

recession *n* decline, depression, downturn, hard times, regression, retreat, slump, stagflation.

antonyms boom, upturn.

recherché *adj* abstruse, affected, arcane, choice, esoteric, exotic, far-fetched, precious, rare, refined, select, unusual.

antonym commonplace.

recipe *n* directions, formula, ingredients, instructions, method, prescription, procedure, process, program, system, technique.

recipient *n* assignee, beneficiary, donee, endorsee, grantee, legatee, receiver.

antonyms donor, giver.

reciprocal *adj* alternating, complementary, correlative, corresponding, equivalent, give-and-take, interchangeable, interdependent, mutual, reciprocatory, shared.

reciprocate *v* alternate, co-operate, correspond, echo, equal, give in return, interchange, match, reply, requite, respond, return.

recital *n* account, concert, description, detailing, enumeration, interpretation, narration, narrative, performance, reading, recapitulation, recitation, rehearsal, relation, rendering, rendition, repetition, statement, story, tale, telling.

recitation *n* lecture, narration, (party) piece, passage, performance, reading, recital, rendering, rendition, speech, telling.

recite *v* articulate, deliver, describe, detail, enumerate, itemize, narrate, orate, perform, quote, recapitulate, recount, rehearse, relate, repeat, state, summarize, tell (of).

reckless *adj* careless, daredevil, devil-may-care, foolhardy, harebrained, hasty, headlong, heedless, ill-advised, impetuous, imprudent, inattentive, incautious, indiscreet, irresponsible, madcap, mindless, negligent, precipitate, rash, thoughtless, unconcerned, unwise, wild.

antonyms calculating, careful, cautious.

recklessness *n* carelessness, foolhardiness, heedlessness, imprudence, inattention, incaution, irresponsibility, madness, mindlessness, negligence, rashness, thoughtlessness, unconcern, wildness.

antonym carefulness.

reckon *v* account, add up, adjudge, appraise, assess, believe, calculate, compute, conjecture, consider, count, dare say, deem, enumerate, esteem, estimate, evaluate, expect, fancy, gauge, guess, hold, imagine, judge, number, opine, rate, regard, suppose, surmise, tally, think, total.

reckon on bank on, bargain on, believe in, calculate on, count on, depend on, expect, figure on, hope for, plan on, rely on, trust in.

reckon with anticipate, bargain for, bear in mind, consider, cope with, deal with, expect, face, factor in, foresee, not lose sight of, plan for, settle with, take into account, take into consideration.

to be reckoned with consequential, considerable, formidable, important, influential, powerful, significant, strong, weighty.

reckoning *n* account, adding (up), bill, calculation, charge, computation, count, counting, enumeration, estimate, fee, judgment, numeration, score, settlement, sum, summation, working.

reclaim *v* recapture, recover, redeem, reform, regain, regenerate, rehabilitate, reinstate, rescue, restore, retrieve, salvage, save.

recline *v* couch, lean, lie, loll, lounge, repose, rest, sprawl, stretch out.

recluse *n* anchorite, ascetic, eremite, hermit, monk, shut-in, solitary.

reclusive *adj* ascetic, cloistered, eremitic, hermitic, isolated, monastic, recluse, retiring, secluded, sequestered, shut-in, solitary, withdrawn.

recognition *n* acceptance, acknowledgment, admission, allowance, appreciation, approval, avowal, awareness, cognizance, commendation, detection, discovery, enlightenment, gratitude, greeting, honour, identification, notice, perception, realization, recall, recollection, remembrance, respect, salute, thanks, understanding.

recognize *v* accept, acknowledge, admit, allow, appreciate, approve, avow, commend, concede, confess, detect, grant, greet, honour, identify, know, notice, own, perceive, place, realize, recall, recollect, remember, respect, salute, see, spot, tell, understand.

recoil *v* backfire, boomerang, falter, flinch, kick, misfire, quail, react, rebound, redound, shrink (back).

n backlash, kick, reaction, rebound, repercussion.

recollect *v* bear in mind, call up, cast one's mind back, mind, place, recall, reflect on, remember, reminisce on, think back on.

recollection *n* image, impression, memory, recall, remembrance, reminiscence, retrospection, souvenir.

recommend *v* advance, advise, advocate, approve, commend, counsel, endorse, enjoin, exhort, plug, praise, propose, puff, push (for), suggest, urge, vouch for.

antonyms disapprove, veto.

recommendation *n* advice, advocacy, approbation, approval, blessing, commendation, counsel, endorsement, plug, praise, proposal, puff, reference, sanction, suggestion, testimonial, urging.

antonyms disapproval, veto.

recompense *v* atone (for), compensate, guerdon, indemnify, make amends for, make restitution, pay, pay back, redress, reimburse, remedy, remunerate, repay, requite, reward, satisfy.

n amends, atonement, compensation, damages, emolument, guerdon, indemnification, indemnity, payment, remediation, remuneration, reparation, repayment, requital, restitution, return, reward, satisfaction, wages.

reconcile v adjust, appease, build a bridge between, conciliate, harmonize, pacify, placate, propitiate, rectify, resolve, reunite, settle, square.
antonym estrange.

reconcile oneself to accept, accommodate, adjust to, resign oneself to, submit to, yield to.
antonyms fight against, reject.

reconciliation n accommodation, adjustment, agreement, appeasement, bridge-building, compromise, conciliation, détente, harmony, pacification, propitiation, rapprochement, rectification, reunion, settlement, understanding.
antonyms estrangement, separation.

recondite adj abstruse, arcane, cabalistic, complicated, concealed, dark, deep, difficult, esoteric, hidden, intricate, involved, little-known, mysterious, mystical, obscure, occult, profound, secret.
antonyms simple, straightforward.

recondition v fix, overhaul, refurbish, remodel, renew, renovate, repair, restore, revamp.

reconnaissance n examination, exploration, inspection, investigation, observation, patrol, probe, reconnoitring, scan, scouting, scrutiny, survey.

reconnoitre v case, examine, explore, inspect, investigate, observe, patrol, probe, scan, scout out, scrutinize, spy out, survey.

reconsider v modify, reassess, re-examine, rethink, review, revise, think better of, think over, think twice.

reconstruct v reassemble, rebuild, recreate, re-establish, refashion, reform, reformulate, regenerate, remake, remodel, renovate, reorganize, restore.

record n account, album, annals, archives, background, career, chronicle, copy, curriculum vitae, diary, disc, document, documentation, dossier, entry, evidence, file, form, gramophone record, history, journal, log, LP, memoir, memorandum, memorial, minute, (past) performance, platter, recording, register, registry, release, remembrance, report, single, testimony, trace, tracing, track record, witness.
v chalk up, chronicle, contain, cut (a record), document, enregister, enrol, enter, indicate, inscribe, keep (track of), log, minute, note, preserve, read, register, report, say, show, take down, tape, tape-record, transcribe, video, videotape, write (down).

recorder n annalist, archivist, chronicler, clerk, diarist, historian, minute-taker, registrar, scorekeeper, scribe, stenographer.

recording n cut, CD, compact disc, disc, gramophone record, record, release, sound recording, tape, video.

recount v communicate, delineate, depict, describe, detail, enumerate, narrate, portray, recite, rehearse, relate, repeat, report, summarize, tell.

recoup v compensate, indemnify, make good, recover, redeem, refund, regain, reimburse,

remunerate, repay, requite, retrieve, satisfy, win back.

recourse n access, alternative, appeal, choice, expedient, fallback, option, refuge, remedy, resort.

have recourse to appeal to, avail oneself to, fall back on, resort to, turn to.

recover v be on the mend, bounce back, convalesce, get better, heal, improve, mend, pick up, pull through, rally, recapture, reclaim, recoup, recuperate, redeem, regain, repair, replevy, repossess, rescue, restore, retake, retrieve, revive.
antonyms forfeit, lose, worsen.

recovery n amelioration, comeback, convalescence, healing, improvement, mending, rally, recapture, reclamation, recuperation, redemption, rehabilitation, repair, replevy, repossession, rescue, restoration, retrieval, revival, second wind, upturn.
antonyms forfeit, loss, worsening.

recreation n amusement, distraction, diversion, enjoyment, entertainment, exercise, fun, games, hobby, leisure activity, pastime, play, pleasure, refreshment, relaxation, relief, sport.

recrimination n come back, counter accusation, counterattack, counterblow, countercharge, retaliation, retort.

recruit v augment, conscript, draft, engage, enlist, enrol, gather, headhunt, impress, mobilize, muster, obtain, procure, proselytize, raise, refresh, reinforce, renew, replenish, restore, sign up, strengthen, supply, trawl (for).
n apprentice, beginner, conscript, convert, draftee, greenhorn, helper, initiate, learner, neophyte, novice, proselyte, rookie, trainee, tyro.

rectify v adjust, amend, correct, distil, emend, fix, improve, mend, purify, put to rights, redress, refine, reform, remedy, repair, right, separate, square, straighten.

rectitude n accuracy, correctness, decency, equity, exactness, goodness, honesty, honour, incorruptibility, integrity, irreproachability, justice, morality, precision, principle, probity, righteousness, rightness, scrupulousness, sinlessness, soundness, unimpeachability, uprightness, verity, virtue.

recumbent adj flat, horizontal, leaning, lounging, lying (down), prone, prostrate, reclining, resting, sprawling, supine.
antonyms erect, upright.

recuperate v be on the mend, convalesce, get better, improve, mend, pick up, rally, recoup, recover, regain, revive.
antonym worsen.

recur v persist, reappear, repeat, return.

recurrent adj continued, cyclical, frequent, habitual, haunting, intermittent, periodic, recurring, regular, repeated, repetitive.

recycle v reclaim, reconstitute, rehash, reprocess, reuse, salvage, save.

red adj auburn, bay, bloodshot, bloodstained, bloody, blooming, blushing, cardinal, carmine, carroty, cherry, chestnut, coral, crimson, damask, embarrassed, ensanguined, flame-coloured, flaming, florid, flushed, glowing, gory, gules, healthy, incarnadine, inflamed, maroon, pink, radical, reddish, rose, roseate, rosy, rubicund, rubied, ruby, ruby-red, ruddy, sanguine, scarlet, shamefaced, suffused, titian, vermilion, wine.

in the red bankrupt, in arrears, in debt, insolvent, on the rocks, overdrawn.

antonym in credit.

red-blooded *adj* hearty, lively, lusty, manly, robust, spirited, strong, vigorous, virile, vital.

redden *v* blush, colour, crimson, flush, suffuse.

reddish *adj* bloodshot, copper-coloured, coppery, ginger, pink, rosy, rubicund, ruddy, rufous, russet, rust-coloured.

redeem *v* absolve, acquit, atone for, buy back, cash (in), change, compensate for, convert, convert into cash, defray, deliver, discharge, emancipate, exchange, extricate, free, fulfil, keep, liberate, make good, make up for, meet, offset, outweigh, pardon, pay (off), perform, ransom, reclaim, recoup, recover, recuperate, redress, regain, rehabilitate, reinstate, repossess, repurchase, rescue, retrieve, salvage, satisfy, save, trade in.

redemption *n* amends, atonement, compensation, conversion, deliverance, discharge, emancipation, exchange, expiation, fulfilment, liberation, pardon, performance, ransom, reclamation, recovery, rehabilitation, reinstatement, release, reparation, repossession, repurchase, rescue, retrieval, salvation, trade-in.

redolent *adj* aromatic, evocative, fragrant, odoriferous, odorous, perfumed, remindful, reminiscent, scented, suggestive, sweet-smelling.

antonym malodorous.

redoubtable *adj* awesome, courageous, doughty, dreadful, fearful, fearsome, formidable, heroic, mighty, powerful, strong, terrible, valiant.

redound *v* accrue, conduce, contribute, lead, rebound, recoil, result, serve, tend.

redress *v* adjust, amend, balance, correct, ease, expiate, make amends for, mend, recompense, rectify, reform, regulate, relieve, remedy, repair, repay, square.

n amends, atonement, compensation, correction, expiation, indemnification, justice, payment, quittance, recompense, rectification, relief, remedy, reparation, repayment, requital, restitution, satisfaction.

reduce *v* abate, abridge, bankrupt, break, cheapen, compress, condense, conquer, contract, curtail, cut, cut back (on), debase, decimate, decrease, degrade, demote, deoxidize, depress, diet, dilute, diminish, discount, downgrade, drive, ease, force, humble, humiliate, impair, impoverish, lessen, limit, lower, mitigate, moderate, muffle, mute, narrow, overpower, pauperize, rebate, ruin, shorten, simplify, slacken, slake, slash, slenderize, slim, subdue, trim, truncate, vanquish, weaken.

antonyms boost, fatten, increase, upgrade.

reduction *n* abatement, abbreviation, abridgment, abstraction, alleviation, attenuation, compression, condensation, constriction, contraction, curtailment, cut, cutback, decline, decrease, deduction, degradation, demotion, deoxidization, deposal, depreciation, devaluation, diminution, discount, drop, easing, ellipsis, limitation, loss, miniature, mitigation, moderation, modification, muffling, muting, narrowing, rebate, refund, restriction, shortening, shrinkage, shrinking, slackening, softening, subtraction, summarization, summary, syncope, weakening.

antonyms enlargement, improvement, increase.

redundancy *n* excess, overabundance, pleonasm, prolixity, repetition, superfluity, surplus, tautology, uselessness, verbosity, wordiness.

redundant *adj* de trop, diffuse, excessive, extra, inessential, inordinate, padded, periphrastic, pleonastic, prolix, repetitious, supererogatory, superfluous, supernumerary, surplus, tautological, unemployed, unnecessary, unneeded, unused, unwanted, verbose, wordy.

antonyms concise, essential, necessary.

reef *n* atoll, cay, key, ridge, sand bank, sand bar, shoal.

reek (of) *v* exhale, exude, fume, give off, smell, smoke, spew, stink.

n effluvium, exhalation, fumes, mephitis, odour, smell, smoke, stench, stink, vapour.

reel *v* flounder, gyrate, lurch, pitch, revolve, rock, roll, spin, stagger, stumble, sway, swim, swirl, totter, twirl, waver, wheel, whirl, wobble.

refer *v* advert, allude, apply, ascribe, assign, attribute, commit, consign, direct, go, guide, hint, impute, pertain, point, recommend, relate, send, submit, transfer, turn over.

refer to adduce, avail oneself of, cite, consult, denote, invoke, look up, make mention of, mean, mention, speak of, touch on, turn to.

referee *n* adjudicator, arbiter, arbitrator, judge, ref, umpire.

v adjudicate, arbitrate, judge, ref, umpire.

reference *n* allusion, applicability, bearing, certification, character, citation, concern, connection, consideration, credentials, endorsement, illustration, instance, mention, note, quotation, recommendation, regard, relation, remark, respect, testimonial.

refine *v* civilize, clarify, cultivate, distil, elevate, exalt, filter, hone, improve, perfect, polish, process, purify, rarefy, sensitize, sharpen, spiritualize, sublimate, temper, tighten up, touch up.

refined *adj* Attic, Augustan, civil, civilized, clarified, clean, cleansed, courtly, cultivated, cultured, delicate, discerning, discriminating, distilled, elegant, exact, fastidious, filtered, fine, genteel, gentlemanly, gracious, improved, ladylike, nice, perfected, polished, polite, precise, processed, punctilious, pure, purified, sensitive, sophisticated, sublime, subtle, urbane, well-bred, well-mannered.

antonyms   brutish, coarse, earthy, rude, vulgar.

refinement *n* civilization, civility, clarification, cleansing, courtesy, courtliness, cultivation, culture, delicacy, discrimination, distillation, elegance, fastidiousness, filtering, fineness, finesse, finish, gentility, (good) breeding, grace, graciousness, improvement, manners, nicety, nuance, polish, politeness, precision, processing, purification, rarefaction, rectification, sophistication, style, subtlety, taste, urbanity.

antonyms   coarseness, earthiness, vulgarity.

reflect *v* bespeak, cogitate, communicate, consider, contemplate, deliberate, demonstrate, display, echo, evince, exhibit, express, imitate, indicate, manifest, meditate, mirror, mull (over), muse, ponder, reproduce, return, reveal, ruminate, show, think, wonder.

reflection *n* aspersion, censure, cerebration, cogitation, consideration, contemplation, counterpart, criticism, deliberation, derogation, echo, expression, idea, image, impression, imputation, indication, manifestation, meditation, memoir, mirroring, musing, observation, opinion, pondering, reflex, remembrance, reproach, retrospection, rumination, slur, study, thinking, thought, view.

reflective *adj* absorbed, cogitating, contemplative, deliberative, dreamy, meditative, pensive, pondering, reasoning, ruminative, thoughtful.

reform *v* ameliorate, amend, better, change for the better, correct, emend, improve, mend, purge, rebuild, reclaim, reconstitute, reconstruct, rectify, regenerate, rehabilitate, remodel, renew, renovate, reorganize, repair, restore, revamp, revolutionize, turn over a new leaf.

n amelioration, amendment, betterment, change, correction, improvement, purge, rectification, rehabilitation, renovation, shake-up.

reformer *n* activist, do-gooder, radical, revolutionary, whistle-blower.

refractory *adj* balky, cantankerous, contentious, contumacious, difficult, disobedient, disputatious, headstrong, intractable, mulish, non-compliant, obstinate, perverse, recalcitrant, resistant, restive, stubborn, uncontrollable, unco-operative, ungovernable, unmanageable, unruly, willful.

antonyms   co-operative, malleable, obedient.

refrain *n* burden, chorus, epistrophe, falderal, melody, slogan, song, theme, tune, undersong.

refrain from *v* abstain from, avoid, cease, desist, eschew, forbear, leave off, quit, renounce, stop, swear off.

refresh *v* brace, cheer, cool, energize, enliven, freshen, inspirit, invigorate, jog, prod, prompt, reanimate, rejuvenate, renew, renovate, repair, replenish, restore, revitalize, revive, revivify, stimulate.

antonyms   exhaust, tire.

refreshing *adj* bracing, cooling, different, energizing, fresh, inspiriting, invigorating, new, novel, original, restorative, revivifying, stimulating, thirst-quenching, tonic.

antonyms   exhausting, tiring.

refreshment *n* enlivenment, freshening, invigoration, reanimation, renewal, renovation, repair, restoration, revitalization, revival, stimulation, strengthening, tonic.

refreshments *n* aliment, drinks, food, goodies, provisions, snacks, sustenance, tidbits.

refrigerate *v* chill, congeal, cool, freeze.

antonyms   heat, warm.

refuge *n* asylum, bolt-hole, harbour, haven, hideaway, hideout, protection, resort, retreat, sanctuary, security, shelter.

refugee *n* boat person, displaced person, D.P., émigré, escapee, evacuee, exile, fugitive, runaway, stateless person.

refulgent *adj* beaming, bright, brilliant, gleaming, glistening, glittering, irradiant, lambent, lustrous, radiant, resplendent, shining.

refund *v* pay back, rebate, reimburse, repay, restore, return.

n rebate, reimbursement, repayment, return.

refurbish *v* mend, overhaul, recondition, re-equip, refit, remodel, renovate, repair, restore, revamp.

refusal *n* choice, denial, nay, negation, no, non-compliance, option, rebuff, rejection, repudiation, unwillingness.

antonym   acceptance.

refuse[1] *v* decline, deny, naysay, reject, repel, repudiate, repulse, spurn, turn away, withhold.

antonyms   accept, allow.

refuse[2] *n* chaff, dregs, dross, excrementa, garbage, hogwash, husks, junk, landfill, leavings, lees, leftovers, litter, mullock, offscourings, rejectamenta, rubbish, scraps, scum, sediment, slops, sweepings, tailings, trash, waste.

refutation *n* confutation, counter argument, counterclaim, denial, disproof, elenchus, negation, overthrow, rebuttal.

refute *v* confute, counter, discredit, disprove, give the lie to, negate, overthrow, rebut, silence.

regain *v* re-attain, recapture, reclaim, recoup, recover, redeem, re-establish, repossess, retake, retrieve, return to.

regal *adj* kingly, magnificent, majestic, monarchal, monarchic, noble, princely, proud, queenly, royal, sovereign, stately.

regale *v* amuse, captivate, delight, divert, entertain, fascinate, feast, feed, gratify, ply, refresh, serve.

regard v account, adjudge, attend, behold, believe, cherish, concern, consider, contemplate, deem, esteem, eye, heed, hold, judge, look at, mark, mind, note, notice, observe, pertain to, rate, relate to, remark, respect, scrutinize, see, suppose, think (of), value, view, watch.

antonyms despise, disregard.

n account, affection, aspect, attachment, attention, care, concern, connection, consideration, count, deference, detail, esteem, favour, feature, gaze, glance, heed, honour, look, love, matter, mind, note, notice, particular, point, reference, relation, relevance, reputation, repute, respect, score, scrutiny, stare, store, sympathy, thought.

antonyms contempt, disapproval, disregard.

regardful adj attentive, aware, careful, circumspect, considerate, dutiful, heedful, mindful, observant, respectful, thoughtful, watchful.

antonyms heedless, inattentive, regardless, unobservant.

regarding prep about, apropos, as for, as regards, as to, concerning, in re, in respect of, in the matter of, on the subject of, pertaining to, re, relating to, respecting, touching, with reference to, with regard to, with respect to.

regardless adj careless, disregardful, heedless, inattentive, inconsiderate, indifferent, neglectful, negligent, nonchalant, rash, reckless, remiss, uncaring, unconcerned, unmindful.

antonyms attentive, heedful, regardful.

adv anyhow, anyway, by hook or by crook, come what may, despite everything, even so, in any case, nevertheless, no matter what, nonetheless, notwithstanding, one way or another, willy-nilly.

regards n compliments, devoirs, good wishes, greetings, (one's) best, respects, salutations.

regenerate v change, inspirit, invigorate, reawaken, reconstitute, reconstruct, recreate, re-establish, refresh, re-invigorate, rejuvenate, remake, renew, renovate, reproduce, restore, revive, revivify, uplift.

regeneration n homomorphosis, rebirth, reconstitution, reconstruction, re-establishment, re-invigoration, rejuvenation, renewal, renovation, reproduction, restoration, revival.

regime n administration, command, control, establishment, government, leadership, management, reign, rule, system.

regiment n band, battery, body, brigade, cohort, company, crew, gang, group, platoon, squadron.

regimented adj controlled, co-ordinated, disciplined, institutional, methodical, ordered, organized, regulated, severe, standardized, stern, strict, structured, systematic.

antonyms disorganized, free, lax, loose.

region n area, biome, clime, country, district, division, domain, expanse, field, land, locality, neighbourhood, part, place, province, quarter, range, realm, scope, section, sector, sphere, terrain, territory, tract, vicinity, world, zone.

regional adj district, geographical, local, localized, parochial, provincial, sectional, territorial, zonal.

register n almanac, annals, archives, catalogue, chronicle, diary, file, ledger, list, log, memorandum, record, roll, roster, scale, schedule.

v assimilate, bespeak, betray, catalogue, chronicle, comprehend, compute, display, enlist, enrol, enter, exhibit, express, indicate, inscribe, list, log, manifest, mark, note, read, record, reflect, reveal, say, scale, score, show, sign up, sink in.

regress v backslide, degenerate, deteriorate, ebb, lapse, recede, relapse, retreat, retrocede, retrogress, return, revert, wane.

antonym progress.

regret v bemoan, be sorry about, bewail, deplore, grieve, lament, miss, mourn, repent, rue, sorrow over.

n bitterness, compunction, contrition, disappointment, grief, lamentation, nostalgia, penitence, remorse, repentance, ruefulness, self-reproach, shame, sorrow.

regretful adj apologetic, ashamed, conscience-stricken, contrite, disappointed, mournful, penitent, remorseful, repentant, rueful, sad, sorrowful, sorry.

antonyms impenitent, unashamed.

▲ *confusable word* regrettable.

regrettable adj deplorable, disappointing, distressing, ill-advised, lamentable, pitiable, sad, shameful, sorry, unfortunate, unhappy, unlucky, woeful.

antonyms fortunate, happy.

▲ *confusable word* regretful.

regular adj absolute, approved, balanced, bona fide, classic, common, commonplace, complete, consistent, constant, consuetudinary, conventional, correct, customary, daily, dependable, established, even, everyday, fixed, flat, formal, frequent, habitual, level, methodical, normal, official, ordered, orderly, ordinary, orthodox, out-and-out, outright, periodic, prevailing, proper, recurrent, rhythmic, routine, set, smooth, standard, standardized, steady, straight, symmetrical, systematic, thorough, time-honoured, total, traditional, typical, uniform, unvarying, usual, well-balanced, well-proportioned.

antonyms irregular, sporadic, unconventional.

regulate v adjust, administer, arrange, balance, bring into line, conduct, control, direct, fine-tune, fit, govern, guide, handle, limit, manage, moderate, modulate, monitor, order, organize, oversee, regiment, rule, run, settle, standardize, superintend, supervise, systematize.

regulation n adjustment, administration, arrangement, code, commandment, control, decree, dictate, direction, edict, fine-tuning, governance, government, guideline, law, management, modulation, order, ordinance, precept, prodecure, regimentation, requirement, rule, standard, standardization, statute, supervision.

adj accepted, customary, mandatory, normal, official, prescribed, required, standard, stock, usual.

regurgitate *v* back, disgorge, parrot, puke, repeat, spew, throw up, upchuck, vomit.

rehabilitate *v* adjust, clear, convert, mend, normalize, rebuild, recondition, reconstitute, reconstruct, redeem, redintegrate, re-establish, reform, reinstate, reintegrate, re-invigorate, renew, renovate, restore, save.

rehash *n* rearrangement, reshuffle, restatement, reworking, rewrite.

v alter, change, rearrange, recycle, refashion, reshuffle, restate, reword, rework, rewrite, warm over.

rehearsal *n* account, description, drill, dry run, enumeration, list, narration, practice, preparation, reading, recital, recounting, relation, report, run-through, telling.

rehearse *v* act, delineate, depict, describe, detail, drill, enumerate, list, narrate, practise, prepare, ready, recite, recount, relate, repeat, review, run through, spell out, study, tell, train, trot out.

reign *n* ascendancy, authority, command, control, dominion, empire, government, hegemony, influence, kingship, monarchy, power, rule, sovereignty, supremacy, sway, term, throne.

v administer, command, govern, hold sway, influence, predominate, prevail, rule.

reimburse *v* compensate, indemnify, recompense, refund, remunerate, repay, requite, restore, return, square up.

rein *n* brake, bridle, check, checkrein, control, curb, harness, hold, restraint, restriction, slow down.

rein in phrase arrest, bridle, check, control, curb, halt, hold, hold back, limit, pull up, restrain, restrict, slow down, stop.

reinforce *v* add to, augment, back up, bolster, buttress, confirm, emphasize, fortify, harden, increase, prop (up), recruit, shore (up), steel, stiffen, strengthen, stress, supplement, support, toughen, underline.

antonyms undermine, weaken.

reinforcements *n* addition, aid, amplification, augmentation, backup, brace, buttress, confirmation, emphasis, enlargement, fortification, hardening, increase, prop, shore, stay, strengthening, supplement, support.

reinforcement *n* auxiliaries, backup, fresh troops, relief, reserves, support.

reinstate *v* reappoint, recall, re-establish, rehabilitate, reinstall, replace, restore, return.

reiterate *v* go back over the same ground, iterate, recapitulate, repeat, resay, restate, retell.

reject *v* abandon, condemn, decline, deny, despise, disallow, disbelieve, discard, eliminate, exclude, jettison, jilt, rebuff, refuse, renounce, repel, reprobate, repudiate, repulse,

scrap, spurn, throw out, turn away, turn down, turn one's back on, veto.

antonyms accept, select.

n cast-off, discard, second.

rejection *n* brushoff, Dear John letter, denial, disapproval, dismissal, elimination, exclusion, rebuff, refusal, renunciation, repudiation, veto.

antonyms acceptance, selection.

rejoice *v* celebrate, delight, exult, glory, joy, jubilate, make merry, revel, triumph.

rejoicing *n* celebration, cheer, delight, elation, exultation, festivity, gaiety, gladness, happiness, joy, jubilation, merrymaking, revelry, triumph.

rejoin *v* answer, counter, quip, rebut, repartee, reply, respond, retort, riposte.

rejoinder *n* answer, comeback, counter, countercharge, counterclaim, quip, repartee, reply, response, retort, riposte.

rejuvenate *v* give a new lease on life (to), re-animate, recharge, refresh, regenerate, re-invigorate, rekindle, renew, restore, revitalize, revivify.

relapse *v* backslide, degenerate, deteriorate, fade, fail, lapse, regress, retrogress, return, revert, sicken, sink, weaken, worsen.

n backsliding, deterioration, hypostrophe, lapse, recidivism, recurrence, regression, retrogression, reversion, setback, weakening, worsening.

relate *v* ally, appertain, apply, associate, chronicle, communicate, compare, connect, convey, correlate, couple, describe, detail, empathize, feel (for), identify (with), impart, join, link, narrate, pertain, present, recite, recount, refer, rehearse, report, sympathize, tell, tie in, understand.

related *adj* accompanying, affiliated, affinal, affined, akin, allied, associated, cognate, concomitant, connected, consanguineous, correlated, germane, interconnected, joint, kin, kindred, linked, relevant.

antonyms different, unconnected, unrelated.

relation *n* account, affiliation, affine, affinity, application, bearing, bond, comparison, connection, consanguinity, correlation, description, interdependence, involvement, kin, kindred, kinship, kinsman, kinswoman, link, narration, narrative, pertinence, propinquity, recital, recountal, reference, regard, relationship, relative, report, sib, similarity, story, tale, tie-in.

relations *n* affairs, associations, clan, communications, connections, contact, dealings, doings, family, interaction, intercourse, kin, kindred, kinsfolk, liaison, meetings, people, rapport, relationship, relatives, terms, tribe, truck.

relationship *n* affair, association, bond, communications, conjunction, connection, contract, correlation, dealings, exchange, intercourse, kinship, liaison, link, parallel, proportion, rapport, ratio, similarity, tie-up.

relative *adj* allied, applicable, apposite, appropriate, appurtenant, apropos, associated, comparative, connected, contingent, correlative, corresponding, dependent, germane, interrelated, pertinent, proportionate, reciprocal, related, relevant, respective.

n cognate, connection, kinsman, kinswoman, relation, sib.

relatively *adv* comparatively, fairly, pretty, quite, rather, somewhat.

relax *v* abate, calm down, diminish, ease (up), ebb, lessen, let up, lighten up, loosen, loosen up, lower, mellow out, mitigate, moderate, reduce, relent, relieve, remit, rest, slacken, slow down, soften, tranquillize, unbend, unclench, unwind, weaken.

antonyms intensify, tighten.

relaxation *n* abatement, amusement, decrease, détente, diminution, distraction, easing, enjoyment, entertainment, fun, leisure, lessening, letup, loosening, moderation, pleasure, recreation, reduction, refreshment, relenting, rest, slackening, weakening.

antonyms intensification, tension.

relaxed *adj* calm, carefree, casual, collected, composed, cool, downbeat, easygoing, even-tempered, happy-go-lucky, informal, insouciant, laid-back, lax, mellow, mild, nonchalant, placid, serene, together, tranquil, unhurried.

antonyms edgy, nervous, stiff, tense, uptight.

relay *n* broadcast, communication, dispatch, message, program, shift, transmission, turn.

v broadcast, carry, communicate, convey, pass on, rebroadcast, send, spread, supply, transmit.

release *v* absolve, acquit, break, circulate, declassify, decontrol, deliver, discharge, disengage, disenthral, dismiss, dispense, disseminate, distribute, drop, emancipate, exempt, excuse, exonerate, extricate, free, furlough, issue, launch, let go, let off (or out), liberate, loose, manumit, present, publish, relinquish, set free, unbind, uncage, unchain, undo, unfasten, unfetter, unhand, unleash, unloose, unshackle, untie, unveil.

antonyms check, detain.

n absolution, acquittal, acquittance, announcement, catharsis, closure, deliverance, delivery, discharge, dismissal, dispensation, emancipation, exemption, exoneration, freedom, issue, let-off, liberation, liberty, manumission, offering, proclamation, publication, quittance, relief, relinquishment.

antonym detention.

relegate *v* assign, banish, consign, delegate, demote, deport, dispatch, downgrade, eject, entrust, exile, expatriate, expel, refer, transfer.

antonym promote.

relent *v* acquiesce, capitulate, drop, ease (up), fall, forbear, give in, have pity, let up, melt, relax, slacken, slow, soften, unbend, weaken, yield.

relentless *adj* cruel, fierce, grim, hard, harsh, implacable, incessant, inexorable, inflexible, merciless, non-stop, persevering, persistent, pitiless, punishing, remorseless, ruthless, stern, sustained, unabated, unbroken,

uncompromising, undeviating, unfaltering, unflagging, unforgiving, unrelenting, unrelieved, unremitting, unstoppable, unyielding.

antonyms submissive, yielding.

relevant *adj* ad rem, admissible, applicable, apposite, appropriate, appurtenant, apt, congruous, fitting, germane, material, pertinent, proper, related, relative, significant, suitable, suited.

antonym irrelevant.

reliable *adj* certain, constant, dependable, faithful, honest, predictable, regular, reputable, responsible, safe, solid, sound, stable, staunch, sure, true, trusted, trustworthy, trusty, unfailing, upright.

antonyms doubtful, suspect, unreliable, untrustworthy.

reliance *n* assurance, belief, confidence, credence, credit, dependence, faith, trust.

relic *n* fragment, keepsake, memento, potsherd, record, remembrance, remnant, scrap, souvenir, survival, token, trace, vestige.

relief *n* abatement, aid, alleviation, assistance, assuagement, balm, break, breather, comfort, cure, deliverance, diversion, ease, easement, help, letup, load off one's mind, mitigation, palliation, reinforcement(s), relaxation, release, remedy, remission, respite, rest, solace, succour, support, sustenance.

relieve *v* abate, aid, alleviate, appease, assuage, break, brighten, calm, comfort, console, cure, deliver, diminish, discharge, disembarrass, disencumber, dull, ease, exempt, free, help, interrupt, lighten, mitigate, mollify, palliate, relax, release, rid, salve, slacken, soften, solace, soothe, spell (off), stand in for, substitute for, succour, support, sustain, take over from, take the place of, unburden, vary.

antonyms aggravate, intensify.

religious *adj* assiduous, churchgoing, churchy, conscientious, devotional, devout, divine, doctrinal, exact, faithful, fastidious, God-fearing, godly, holy, inspirational, meticulous, pious, punctilious, pure, reverent, righteous, rigid, rigorous, sacred, scriptural, scrupulous, sectarian, spiritual, strict, theological, unerring, unswerving.

antonyms irreligious, lax, ungodly.

relinquish *n* abandon, abdicate, cede, desert, discard, drop, forgo, forsake, give up, hand over, leave, quit, release, renounce, repudiate, resign, surrender, vacate, waive, yield.

antonyms keep, retain.

relish *v* appreciate, enjoy, fancy, have a taste for, lap up, like, prefer, revel in, savour.

n appetite, appreciation, condiment, enjoyment, fancy, flavour, fondness, gout, gusto, liking, love, partiality, penchant, piquancy, predilection, sauce, savour, seasoning, spice, stomach, tang, taste, trace, zest.

reluctance *n* aversion, disinclination, dislike, distaste, hesitancy, indisposition, loathing, recalcitrance, repugnance, resistance, slowness, unwillingness.

antonyms eagerness, willingness.

reluctant *adj* averse, disinclined, grudging, hesitant, indisposed, loath, recalcitrant, resistant, slow, squeamish, unenthusiastic, unwilling.

antonyms eager, willing.

▲ *confusable word* reticent.

rely *v* bank, believe (in), bet, count, depend, lean, reckon, swear by, trust, trust (in).

remain *v* abide, bide, cling, continue, delay, dwell, endure, last, linger, persist, prevail, rest, sojourn, stand, stay, survive, tarry, wait.

antonyms depart, go, leave.

remainder *n* balance, dregs, excess, leavings, residual, residue, residuum, rest, surplus, trace, vestige(s).

remaining *adj* abiding, enduring, extant, lasting, left, leftover, lingering, outstanding, persisting, residual, surplus, surviving, unfinished, unspent, unused.

remains *n* ashes, balance, body, cadaver, carcass, corpse, crumbs, debris, detritus, dregs, fragments, leavings, leftovers, oddments, pieces, relics, remainder, remnants, residue, rest, scraps, traces, vestiges.

remark *v* animadvert, comment, declare, espy, heed, mark, mention, note, notice, observe, perceive, reflect, regard, say, see, state.

n acknowledgment, assertion, attention, comment, consideration, declaration, heed, mention, notice, observation, opinion, recognition, reflection, regard, say, statement, thought, utterance, word.

remarkable *adj* amazing, conspicuous, distinguished, exceptional, extraordinary, famous, impressive, miraculous, notable, noteworthy, odd, outstanding, phenomenal, pre-eminent, prominent, rare, signal, singular, strange, striking, surprising, uncommon, unusual, wonderful.

antonyms average, commonplace, ordinary.

remedy *n* aid, antidote, corrective, counteractive, countermeasure, cure, medicament, medicine, nostrum, panacea, physic, redress, relief, restorative, solution, specific, therapy, treatment.

v alleviate, ameliorate, assuage, control, correct, counteract, cure, ease, fix, heal, help, mitigate, palliate, put right, rectify, redress, reform, relieve, repair, restore, solve, soothe, treat.

remember *v* call to mind, commemorate, look back (on), place, recall, recognize, recollect, reminisce, retain, summon up, think back (to), think of, view in retrospect.

antonym forget.

remembrance *n* commemoration, keepsake, memento, memorial, memory, mind, monument, recall, recognition, recollection, regard(s), relic, remembrancer, reminder, reminiscence, retrospect, retrospection, souvenir, testimonial, thought, token, trophy.

remind *v* cue, give a hint to, jog one's memory, prompt, put (one) in mind, refresh one's memory, take one back.

reminder *n* aide-mémoire, cue, hint, memento, memo, memorandum, nudge, prompt, remembrance, souvenir, suggestion.

reminisce *v* hark back, look back, recall, recollect, remember, retrospect, review, think back.

reminiscence *n* anecdote, memoir, memory, personalia, recall, recollection, reflection, remembrance, retrospection, review.

reminiscent *adj* evocative, nostalgic, redolent, remindful, similar, suggestive.

remiss *adj* careless, culpable, delinquent, derelict, dilatory, fainéant, forgetful, heedless, inattentive, indifferent, lackadaisical, lax, neglectful, negligent, regardless, slack, slipshod, sloppy, slothful, slow, tardy, thoughtless, unmindful.

antonyms careful, scrupulous.

remission *n* abatement, abeyance, absolution, acquittal, alleviation, amelioration, amnesty, cessation, decrease, diminution, discharge, ebb, excuse, exemption, exoneration, forgiveness, indulgence, interruption, lessening, letup, lull, moderation, pardon, pause, reduction, relaxation, release, relinquishment, reprieve, respite, slackening, suspension.

remit *v* abate, acquit, alleviate, cancel, decrease, defer, delay, desist, desist from, diminish, dispatch, dwindle, forbear, forgive, forward, halt, mail, mitigate, moderate, pay, post, postpone, put back, put off, reduce, relax, repeal, rescind, send, send back, shelve, sink, slacken, soften, stop, suspend, transfer, transmit, wane, weaken.

remnant *n* balance, bit, end, fragment, hangover, leftover, piece, remainder, residue, residuum, rest, rump, scrap, shred, survival, trace, vestige.

remonstrance *n* complaint, expostulation, grievance, objection, petition, protest, protestation, reprimand, reproof.

remonstrate *v* argue, challenge, complain, dispute, dissent, expostulate, gripe, object, protest.

remorse *n* anguish, bad conscience, compassion, compunction, contrition, grief, guilt, penitence, pity, regret, repentance, ruefulness, self-reproach, shame, sorrow.

remorseful *adj* apologetic, ashamed, chastened, compunctious, conscience-stricken, contrite, guilt-ridden, guilty, penitent, regretful, repentant, rueful, sad, sorrowful, sorry.

antonyms impenitent, remorseless.

remorseless *adj* callous, cruel, hard, hard-hearted, harsh, implacable, inexorable, inhumane, merciless, pitiless, relentless, ruthless, savage, shameless, stern, undeviating, unforgiving, unmerciful, unrelenting, unremitting, unstoppable.

antonyms remorseful, sorry.

remote *adj* abstracted, alien, aloof, backwoods, cold, detached, distant, doubtful, dubious, extraneous, extrinsic, faint, far, faraway, far-off, foreign, godforsaken, implausible, inaccessible, inconsiderable, indifferent, introspective, introverted, isolated, lonely, meagre, negligible, outlying, out-of-the-way, outside, poor, removed, reserved, secluded, slender, slight, slim, small, standoffish, unconnected, uninterested, uninvolved, unlikely, unrelated, unsociable, withdrawn.

antonyms adjacent, close, nearby, significant.

removal *n* ablation, abstraction, departure, deposal, dislodgement, dismissal, displacement, dispossession, divestiture, ejection, elimination, eradication, erasure, evacuation, expulsion, expunction, extraction, metastasis, moving, purge, purging, relocation, riddance, stripping, subtraction, transfer, uprooting, withdrawal.

remove *v* ablate, abolish, abstract, amputate, assassinate, blot (out), delete, depart, depose, detach, dethrone, discharge, dislodge, dismiss, displace, divest, doff, efface, eject, eliminate, erase, execute, expunge, extract, kill, liquidate, move, murder, obviate, oust, purge, quit, relegate, relocate, shave, shear, shed, sideline, strike, take off (or away), transfer, transmigrate, transport, unseat, vacate, withdraw.

remunerate *v* compensate, guerdon, indemnify, pay, recompense, redress, reimburse, repay, requite, reward.

remuneration *n* compensation, earnings, emolument, fee, guerdon, income, indemnity, pay, payment, profit, recompense, reimbursement, remittance, reparation, repayment, retainer, return, reward, salary, stipend, wages.

remunerative *adj* fruitful, gainful, lucrative, moneymaking, paying, profitable, rewarding, rich, worthwhile.

renaissance *n* awakening, new birth, new dawn, re-appearance, re-awakening, rebirth, recrudescence, re-emergence, regeneration, rejuvenation, renascence, renewal, restoration, resurgence, resurrection, revival.

renascent *adj* born-again, re-animated, re-awakened, reborn, redivivus, re-emergent, renewed, resurgent, resurrected, revived, revivified.

rend *v* afflict, break, burst, cleave, crack, dissever, distress, disturb, disunite, divide, fracture, hurt, lacerate, pain, pierce, pull, rip, rive, rupture, separate, sever, shatter, smash, splinter, split, stab, sunder, tear, torment, wound, wrench, wring.

render *v* act, cede, clarify, construe, contribute, deliver, depict, display, do, evince, exchange, exhibit, explain, furnish, give, give back (or up), hand over, interpret, leave, make, make up, manifest, melt, pay, perform, play, portray, present, provide, put, relinquish, repay, represent, reproduce, restate, restore, return, show (forth), submit, supply, surrender, swap, tender, trade, transcribe, translate, yield.

rendezvous *n* appointment, assignation, date, engagement, haunt, meeting, meeting place, resort, tryst, trysting place, venue.

v assemble, collect, convene, converge, gather, meet, muster, rally.

rendition *n* arrangement, construction, delivery, depiction, execution, explanation, interpretation, performance, portrayal, presentation, reading, rendering, transcription, translation, version.

renegade *n* apostate, backslider, betrayer, defector, deserter, dissident, mutineer, outlaw, rebel, recreant, runaway, tergiversator, traitor, turncoat.

antonyms adherent, disciple, follower.

adj apostate, backsliding, disloyal, dissident, mutinous, outlaw, perfidious, rebel, rebellious, recreant, runaway, traitorous, unfaithful.

renege *v* abandon, apostatize, back out, break one's word, cop out, default, repudiate, welsh, withdraw.

renew *v* continue, extend, fix up, mend, modernize, overhaul, prolong, re-affirm, recommence, recreate, re-establish, refashion, refit, refresh, refurbish, regenerate, rejuvenate, remodel, renovate, reopen, repair, repeat, replace, replenish, restate, restock, restore, resume, revitalize, revive, revivify, transform.

renewal *n* instauration, kiss of life, new lease on life, recommencement, reconditioning, reconstitution, reconstruction, re-creation, refurbishment, re-invigoration, reiteration, rejuvenation, renovation, repair, replenishment, resumption, resurrection, resuscitation, revitalization, revival, revivification.

renounce *v* abandon, abdicate, abjure, abnegate, decline, deny, discard, disclaim, disown, eschew, forgo, forsake, forswear, give up, put away, quit, recant, reject, relinquish, repudiate, resign, spurn, surrender, swear off, throw off (or over).

renovate *v* do up, fix up, improve, modernize, overhaul, rebuild, recondition, re-create, redecorate, redo, refit, re-form, refurbish, rehabilitate, remodel, renew, repair, restore, revamp.

renovation *n* facelift, improvement, modernization, overhaul, reconditioning, redecoration, refit, refurbishment, renewal, repair, restoration.

renown *n* acclaim, celebrity, distinction, eminence, fame, glory, honour, illustriousness, kudos, lustre, mark, notability, note, reputation, repute, stardom.

antonyms anonymity, obscurity.

renowned *adj* acclaimed, celebrated, distinguished, eminent, esteemed, famed, famous, illustrious, notable, noted, pre-eminent, well-known.

antonyms anonymous, obscure, unknown.

rent[1] *n* fee, hire, lease, payment, rental, tariff.

v charter, hire, lease, let, sublet, take.

rent[2] *n* breach, break, chink, cleavage, crack, dissension, disunion, division, flaw, gash, hole, opening, perforation, rift, rip, rupture, schism, slash, slit, split, tear.

renunciation *n* abandonment, abdication, abjuration, abnegation, abstention, apostasy, denial, disavowal, disclaimer, eschewal, forgoing, forswearing, recantation, rejection, relinquishment, repudiation, resignation, spurning, surrender, waiver.

repair¹ *v* debug, fix (up), heal, mend, patch up, re-cover, rectify, redress, renew, renovate, restore, retrieve, square.
n adjustment, condition, darn, fettle, form, improvement, mend, overhaul, patch, restoration, shape, state.

repair² *v* go, wend one's way, move, remove, resort, retire, turn, withdraw.

reparable *adj* correctable, corrigible, curable, recoverable, rectifiable, remediable, repairable, restorable, retrievable, salvageable, savable.
antonym irreparable.

reparation *n* amends, atonement, compensation, damages, indemnity, propitiation, recompense, redress, renewal, repair, requital, restitution, satisfaction.

repartee *n* badinage, banter, comeback, jesting, persiflage, pleasantry, raillery, riposte, sally, waggery, wit, witticism, wittiness, wordplay.

repast *n* collation, feed, food, meal, nourishment, refection, snack, spread, victuals.

repay *v* avenge, compensate, get even with, make restitution, pay, pay back, rebate, reciprocate, recompense, refund, reimburse, remunerate, requite, restore, retaliate, return, revenge, reward, settle the score, square.

repayment *n* amends, avenging, compensation, rebate, reciprocation, recompense, redress, refund, reimbursement, remuneration, reparation, requital, restitution, retaliation, retribution, revenge, reward, vengeance.

repeal *v* abolish, abrogate, annul, cancel, countermand, do away with, invalidate, nullify, quash, recall, rescind, reverse, revoke, set aside, void, withdraw.
antonyms enact, establish.
n abolition, abrogation, annulment, cancellation, invalidation, nullification, quashing, rescission, reversal, revocation, withdrawal.
antonyms enactment, establishment.

repeat *v* copy, duplicate, echo, iterate, quote, rebroadcast, recapitulate, recite, redo, rehearse, reiterate, relate, renew, replay, reproduce, rerun, reshow, restate, retell.
n copy, duplicate, echo, encore, rebroadcast, recapitulation, reiteration, repetition, replay, reproduction, rerun, reshowing.

repeatedly *adv* again and again, frequently, often, oftentimes, ofttimes, over and over, recurrently, time after time, time and (time) again.

repel *v* check, disgust, drive away (or off), fend off, fight back, hold off, keep away, nauseate, offend, parry, rebuff, refuse, reject, repulse, resist, sicken, ward off.
antonym attract.

repellent *adj* abhorrent, abominable, disgusting, distasteful, hateful, horrid, loathsome, nauseating, noxious, obnoxious, odious, offensive, off-putting, rebarbative, repugnant, repulsive, resistant, revolting, sickening.
antonym attractive.

repent *n* be sorry (for), bewail, deplore, lament, regret, relent, rue, sorrow.

repentance *n* change of heart, compunction, contrition, grief, guilt, penitence, regret, remorse, self-reproach, sorriness, sorrow.

repentant *adj* apologetic, ashamed, chastened, compunctious, contrite, penitent, regretful, remorseful, rueful, sorry.
antonym unrepentant.

repercussion *n* aftermath, backlash, backwash, consequence, echo, reaction, rebound, recoil, result, reverberation, side effect.

repertory *n* collection, list, range, repertoire, repository, reserve, reservoir, stock, store, supply.

repetition *n* anaphora, assonance, duplication, echo, echolalia, imitation, iteration, reappearance, recapitulation, recital, recurrence, redundancy, rehearsal, reiteration, relation, renewal, repeat, repetitiousness, replication, restatement, return, tautology.

repetitious *adj* battological, long-winded, pleonastic, prolix, redundant, repetitive, tautological, tedious, verbose, windy, wordy.

repetitive *adj* boring, dull, habitual, interminable, mechanical, monotonous, recurrent, repetitious, tedious, unchanging, unvaried.

rephrase *v* paraphrase, recast, restate, reword, rewrite.

repine *v* beef, brood, complain, fret, grieve, grouse, grumble, lament, languish, moan, mope, murmur, sulk.

replace *v* follow, oust, put back, re-establish, reinstate, restore, substitute, succeed, supersede, supplant.

replacement *n* double, fill-in, proxy, spare, stand-in, substitute, successor, surrogate, understudy.

replenish *v* fill, furnish, provide, recharge, recruit, refill, reload, renew, replace, restock, restore, stock (up), supply, top up.

replete *adj* abounding, brimful, brimming, charged, chock-a-block, chock-full, crammed, filled, full, full up, glutted, gorged, jammed, jam-packed, sated, satiated, stuffed, teeming, well-provided, well-stocked.
▲ *confusable word* complete.

repletion *n* completeness, fullness, glut, overfullness, plenty, plethora, satiation, satiety, superabundance, superfluity.

replica *n* clone, copy, duplicate, facsimile, imitation, model, reconstruction, reproduction.

replicate *v* ape, clone, copy, duplicate, follow, mimic, re-create, reduplicate, repeat, reproduce.

reply *v* acknowledge, answer, counter, echo, react, reciprocate, rejoin, repartee, respond, retaliate, retort, return, riposte.

n acknowledgment, answer, comeback, counter, echo, reaction, reciprocation, rejoinder, repartee, response, retaliation, retort, return, riposte.

report *n* account, announcement, article, bang, blast, boom, bruit, character, commentary, communication, communiqué, crack, crash, debriefing, declaration, description, detail, detonation, discharge, dispatch, explosion, gossip, hearsay, information, message, narrative, news, noise, note, notification, paper, piece, procès-verbal, recital, record, regard, relation, reputation, repute, reverberation, rumour, sound, statement, story, summary, tale, talk, tidings, version, word, write-up.

v air, announce, answer, appear, broadcast, bruit, circulate, come, communicate, cover, declare, describe, detail, document, inform (on), mention, narrate, note, notify (of), present oneself, proclaim, publish, recite, record, recount, relate, relay, state, tattle on, tell (on), tell tales.

reporter *n* announcer, correspondent, hack, journalist, legman, newscaster, newshound, newspaperman, newspaperwoman, pressman, presswoman, stringer, writer.

repose¹ *n* aplomb, calm, calmness, composure, dignity, ease, equanimity, inactivity, peace, poise, quiet, quietness, quietude, relaxation, respite, rest, restfulness, self-possession, serenity, sleep, slumber, stillness, tranquillity.

antonyms activity, strain, stress.

v laze, lie, recline, relax, rest, sleep, slumber.

repose² *v* confide, deposit, entrust, invest, lodge, place, put, set, store.

repository *n* archive, depository, depot, emporium, magazine, promptuary, receptacle, repertory, store, storehouse, treasury, vault, warehouse.

reprehensible *adj* bad, blamable, blameworthy, censurable, condemnable, culpable, delinquent, discreditable, disgraceful, errant, erring, ignoble, objectionable, opprobrious, remiss, shameful, unworthy.

antonyms creditable, good, praiseworthy.

represent *v* act, act for, appear as, be, betoken, delineate, denote, depict, describe, designate, embody, enact, epitomize, equal, evoke, exemplify, exhibit, express, illustrate, mean, outline, perform, personify, picture, portray, produce, render, reproduce, show, sketch, speak for, stage, stand for, substitute for, symbolize, typify.

representation *n* account, bust, compliant, delineation, depiction, description, drawing, exhibition, explanation, exposition, expostulation, icon, idol, illustration, image, likeness, model, narration, narrative, performance, petition, picture, play, portrait, portrayal, production, protest, relation, remonstrance, representative, resemblance, show, sign, sketch, spectacle, statue, symbol.

representative *n* agent, archetype, commissioner, councillor, delegate, deputy, embodiment, epitome, exemplar, member, MP, personification, proxy, rep, salesman, saleswoman, spokesman, spokesperson, spokeswoman, type.

adj archetypal, characteristic, chosen, delegated, elected, elective, emblematic, evocative, exemplary, illustrative, normal, symbolic, typical, usual.

antonyms atypical, unrepresentative.

repress *v* bottle up, chasten, check, control, crush, curb, gag, hamper, hinder, impede, inhibit, keep down, lean on, master, muffle, overcome, overpower, put down, quash, quell, restrain, silence, smother, stifle, subdue, subjugate, suppress, swallow.

repression *n* authoritarianism, censorship, coercion, constraint, control, denial, despotism, domination, gagging, inhibition, restraint, subjugation, suffocation, suppression, tyranny.

repressive *adj* absolute, authoritarian, autocratic, coercive, despotic, dictatorial, harsh, iron-handed, oppressive, prohibitive, severe, tough, tyrannical.

reprieve *v* abate, allay, alleviate, mitigate, palliate, pardon, redeem, release, relieve, rescue.

n abatement, abeyance, alleviation, amnesty, deferment, delay, letup, mitigation, palliation, pardon, postponement, redemption, release, relief, remission, rescue, respite, suspension.

reprimand *n* admonition, castigation, censure, dressing-down, lecture, rebuke, reprehension, reproach, reproof, schooling, scolding, talking-to, telling-off, tongue-lashing, warning.

v admonish, bawl out, call on the carpet, castigate, censure, check, chew out, chide, dress down, give (someone) what for, lecture, rebuke, reprehend, reproach, reprove, scold, tell off, tongue-lash, upbraid.

reprisal *n* evening of the score, getting even, requital, retaliation, retribution, revenge, vengeance.

reproach *v* abuse, accuse, blame, censure, chide, condemn, criticize, defame, discredit, disparage, rebuke, reprehend, reprimand, reprove, scold, take to task, upbraid.

n abuse, accusation, blame, blemish, censure, condemnation, contempt, disapproval, discredit, disgrace, dishonour, disrepute, ignominy, indignity, obloquy, odium, opprobrium, reproof, scorn, shame, slight, slur, stain, stigma, upbraiding.

reproachful *adj* admonitory, aggrieved, castigatory, censorious, condemnatory, critical, denunciatory, disappointed, disapproving, faultfinding, opprobrious, reproving, scolding, upbraiding.

antonym complimentary.

reprobate *adj* abandoned, bad, base, condemnatory, corrupt, damned, degenerate, depraved, dissolute, hardened, immoral, incorrigible, profligate, shameless, sinful, unprincipled, vile, wicked.

antonym upright.

n blackguard, degenerate, evildoer, knave, miscreant, ne'er-do-well, outcast, pariah, profligate, rake, rascal, rogue, roué, scamp, scoundrel, sinner, villain, wastrel, wretch, wrongdoer.

reproduce *v* ape, breed, copy, duplicate, echo, emulate, facsimile, generate, imitate, increase, match, mirror, multiply, parallel, parrot, print, procreate, proliferate, propagate, recreate, regurgitate, repeat, replicate, represent, simulate, spawn, transcribe.

reproduction *n* amphimixis, breeding, copy, duplicate, ectype, facsimile, fructification, gamogenesis, generation, imitation, increase, multiplication, picture, print, procreation, proliferation, propagation, replica.

antonym original.

reproductive *adj* generative, genital, procreative, progenitive, propagative, sex, sexual.

reproof *n* admonition, blame, castigation, censure, chiding, condemnation, correction, criticism, dressing-down, lecture, rap on the knuckles, rebuke, reprehension, reprimand, reproach, reproval, reproving, scolding, sermon, slap on the wrist, talking-to, telling-off, tongue-lashing, upbraiding.

antonym praise.

reprove *v* admonish, berate, blame, censure, check, chide, condemn, lecture, rap (on the knuckles), rate, rebuke, reprehend, reprimand, scold, take to task, upbraid.

antonym praise.

repudiate *v* abandon, abjure, cast off, deny, desert, disaffirm, disavow, discard, disclaim, disown, divorce, forsake, recant, reject, renounce, rescind, retract, reverse, revoke.

antonyms admit, own.

repudiation *n* abjuration, denial, disaffirmation, disavowal, disclaimer, disowning, recantation, rejection, renouncement, renunciation, retraction.

antonym acceptance.

repugnance *n* abhorrence, abhorring, antipathy, aversion, disgust, dislike, disrelish, distaste, hatred, inconsistency, loathing, reluctance, repulsion, revulsion.

antonyms liking, pleasure.

repugnant *adj* abhorrent, abominable, adverse, antagonistic, antipathetic, averse, contradictory, contrary, disgusting, distasteful, foul, hateful, horrid, hostile, incompatible, inconsistent, inimical, loathsome, nauseating, objectionable, obnoxious, odious, offensive, opposed, repellent, revolting, sickening, unacceptable, unsavoury, vile.

antonyms acceptable, consistent, pleasant.

repulse *v* beat off, check, defeat, disdain, disregard, drive back, drive off, fend off, fight back (or off), rebuff, refuse, reject, repel, snub, spurn.

antonyms accept, welcome.

n check, defeat, disappointment, failure, rebuff, refusal, rejection, repudiation, reverse, snub, spurning.

antonyms acceptance, success.

repulsion *n* abhorrence, aversion, detestation, disgust, disrelish, distaste, hatred, loathing, repugnance, revulsion.

antonym liking.

repulsive *adj* abhorrent, abominable, cold, disagreeable, disgusting, distasteful, forbidding, foul, hateful, hideous, horrid, loathsome, nauseating, objectionable, obnoxious, odious, offensive, repellent, revolting, sickening, ugly, unpleasant, vile.

antonyms friendly, pleasant.

reputable *adj* creditable, dependable, estimable, excellent, good, honourable, honoured, irreproachable, legitimate, principled, reliable, respectable, trustworthy, unimpeachable, upright, worthy.

antonyms disreputable, fly-by-night, infamous.

reputation *n* bad name, character, distinction, esteem, estimation, fame, good name, honour, infamy, name, renown, repute, standing, stature.

repute *n* celebrity, distinction, esteem, estimation, fame, good name, name, notability, renown, reputation, standing, stature.

antonym infamy.

reputed *adj* accounted, alleged, apparent, believed, considered, deemed, estimated, held, ostensible, putative, reckoned, regarded, rumoured, said, seeming, supposed, thought.

antonym actual.

reputedly *adv* allegedly, apparently, ostensibly, putatively, reportedly, seemingly, supposedly.

antonym actually.

request *v* ask, ask for, beg (for), beseech, demand, desire, entreat, importune, petition, pray, requisition, seek, solicit, supplicate.

n appeal, application, asking, begging, call, demand, desire, entreaty, impetration, petition, prayer, representation, requisition, solicitation, suit, supplication.

require *v* ask (of), bid, command, compel, constrain, crave, demand, direct, enjoin, entail, exact, force, have need of, instruct, involve, lack, make, miss, necessitate, need, obligate, oblige, order, prescribe, take, want, wish.

required *adj* compulsory, demanded, essential, imperative, mandatory, necessary, needed, obligatory, prescribed, recommended, requisite, set, stipulated, unavoidable, vital.

antonyms inessential, optional.

requirement *n* demand, desideratum, essential, lack, must, necessity, need, precondition, prerequisite, provision, proviso, qualification, requisite, rule, sine qua non, specification, stipulation, term, want.

antonym inessential.

requisite *adj* essential, imperative, indispensable, mandatory, necessary, needed, needful, obligatory, prerequisite, required, vital.

antonyms inessential, optional.

n condition, desideratum, essential, must, necessity, need, precondition, prerequisite, requirement, sine qua non.

antonym inessential.

requisition *v* appropriate, commandeer, confiscate, demand, order, put in (a request) for, request, seize, take.

n application, appropriation, call, commandeering, demand, order, request, seizure, summons, takeover, use.

requital *n* amends, compensation, indemnification, indemnity, payment, payoff, quittance, recompense, redress, reparation, repayment, restitution, satisfaction.

requite *v* avenge, compensate, make amends, pay (to or for), reciprocate, recompense, redress, reimburse, remunerate, repay, respond (to), retaliate (against), return, reward, satisfy.

rescind *v* abrogate, annul, cancel, countermand, invalidate, negate, nullify, overturn, quash, recall, repeal, retract, reverse, revoke, void.

antonym enforce.

rescission *n* abrogation, annulment, cancellation, invalidation, negation, nullification, recall, repeal, retraction, reversal, revocation, voidance.

antonym enforcement.

rescue *v* deliver, extricate, free, liberate, ransom, recover, redeem, release, salvage, save.

antonym capture.

n aid, deliverance, delivery, extrication, liberation, recovery, redemption, release, relief, salvage, salvation, saving.

antonym capture.

research *n* analysis, delving, examination, experimentation, exploration, fact-finding, groundwork, inquiry, investigation, probe, quest, scrutiny, search, study.

v analyse, examine, experiment (with), explore, ferret (out), inquire into, investigate, probe (into), scrutinize, search, study.

researcher *n* analyst, boffin, field worker, inquirer, inspector, investigator, student.

resemblance *n* affinity, analogy, assonance, closeness, comparability, comparison, conformity, correspondence, counterpart, facsimile, image, kinship, likeness, parallel, parity, sameness, semblance, similarity, similitude.

antonym dissimilarity.

resemble *v* approach, be comparable to, be like, be reminiscent of, be similar to, duplicate, echo, favour, mirror, parallel, suggest, take after.

antonym differ from.

resent *v* begrudge, chafe at, dislike, grudge, grumble at, object to, take amiss, take exception to, take offence at, take umbrage at.

antonyms accept, like.

resentful *adj* aggrieved, angry, annoyed, bitter, discontented, embittered, exasperated, grudging, huffish, huffy, hurt, incensed, indignant, irate, ireful, jealous, miffed, offended, peeved, piqued, put out, rancorous, revengeful, unforgiving, wounded.

antonym contented.

resentment *n* anger, animosity, bitterness, disaffection, discontent, discontentment, displeasure, fury, grudge, huff, hurt, ill feeling, ill will, indignation, ire, irritation, malice, pique, rage, rancour, umbrage, vexation, vindictiveness, wrath.

antonym contentment.

reservation *n* apprehension, arrière pensée, condition, demur, doubt, hesitancy, hesitation, inhibition, proviso, qualification, restraint, scepticism, scruple, second thought, stipulation, uncertainty.

reserve¹ *v* allot, bespeak, book, conserve, defer, earmark, engage, hoard, hold (back), husband, keep (back), postpone, prearrange, preserve, put by, retain, save, secure, set apart (or aside), spare, stockpile, store, store up, withhold.

antonym use up.

n backlog, cache, capital, fund, hoard, park, preserve, reservoir, sanctuary, savings, stock, stockpile, store, substitute, supply, tract.

adj additional, alternate, auxiliary, extra, secondary, spare, substitute.

reserve² *n* aloofness, constraint, coolness, formality, limitation, modesty, reluctance, reservation, restraint, restriction, reticence, secretiveness, shyness, silence, taciturnity.

antonyms friendliness, informality.

reserved¹ *adj* booked, bound, designated, destined, earmarked, engaged, fated, held, intended, kept, meant, predestined, put aside, restricted, retained, saved, set aside, spoken for, taken.

antonym unreserved.

reserved² aloof, cautious, close-mouthed, cold, cool, demure, formal, modest, prim, restrained, reticent, retiring, secretive, shy, silent, stand-offish, taciturn, unapproachable, uncommunicative, uncompanionable, unconversable, undemonstrative, unforthcoming, unresponsive, unsociable.

antonyms friendly, informal.

reservoir *n* accumulation, basin, container, fund, holder, lake, pond, pool, receptacle, repository, reserves, source, stock, stockpile, storage place, store, supply, tank.

reshuffle *n* change, interchange, re-alignment, rearrangement, redistribution, regrouping, reorganization, restructuring, revision, shake-up, upheaval.

v change, interchange, realign, rearrange, reassign, redistribute, regroup, reorganize, restructure, revise, shake up, shift, shuffle.

reside *v* abide, consist, dwell, exist, inhabit, inhere, lie, live, lodge, remain, settle, sit, sojourn, stay.

residence *n* abode, countryhouse, countryseat, domicile, dwelling, habitation, hall, home, house, household, lodge, lodging, manor, mansion, occupancy, occupation, pad, palace, place, quarters, seat, sojourn, stay, tenancy, villa.

resident *n* citizen, denizen, dweller, inhabitant, local, lodger, occupant, tenant.

antonym non-resident.

adj dwelling, en poste, indwelling, inhabiting, intrinsic, live-in, living, local, neighbourhood, permanent, settled.

antonym non-resident.

residual *adj* leftover, net, reliquary, remaining, residuary, unconsumed, unused, vestigial.

antonym core.

residue *n* balance, difference, dregs, excess, extra, leftovers, overflow, overplus, remainder, remains, remnant, residuum, rest, surplus.

antonym core.

resign *v* abandon, abdicate, cede, deliver, forgo, forsake, give up, leave, quit, relinquish, renounce, sacrifice, stand down, surrender, vacate, waive, yield.

antonyms join, maintain.

resign oneself accede, accept, acquiesce, bow, comply, endure, give in, knuckle under, reconcile oneself, submit, yield.

antonym resist.

resignation *n* abandonment, abdication, acceptance, acquiescence, apathy, compliance, defeatism, departure, endurance, forbearance, fortitude, leaving, non-resistance, notice, passivity, patience, relinquishment, renunciation, retirement, submission, sufferance, surrender.

antonym resistance.

resigned *adj* accepting, acquiescent, apathetic, compliant, defeatist, forbearing, long-suffering, passive, patient, stoical, subdued, submissive, unprotesting, unresisting.

antonym resisting.

resilience *n* adaptability, bounce, buoyancy, elasticity, flexibility, give, hardiness, plasticity, pliability, rebound, recoil, spring, springiness, strength, suppleness, toughness.

antonyms inflexibility, rigidity.

resilient *adj* adaptable, bouncy, buoyant, elastic, flexible, hardy, irrepressible, plastic, pliable, springy, strong, supple, tough.

antonyms downcast, rigid.

resist *v* avoid, battle, check, combat, confront, counteract, countervail, curb, defy, dispute, fight back, forbear, forgo, hinder, keep from, oppose, refuse, repel, stand against, thwart, weather, withstand.

antonyms accept, submit.

resistance *n* battle, combat, contention, counteraction, counterstand, defiance, dissidence, fight, fighting, freedom fighters, friction, guerrillas, hindrance, immunity, impedance, impediment, intransigence, Maquis, non-compliance, non-co-operation, obstruction, opposition, partisans, refusal, resistant, resistors, stand, struggle, underground, unwillingness.

antonyms acceptance, submission.

resistant *adj* antagonistic, combative, defiant, dissident, hard, hostile, immune, impervious, insusceptible, intractible, intransigent, opposed, recalcitrant, resistive, stiff, strong, tough, ungovernable, unsusceptible, unwilling, unyielding.

antonyms compliant, yielding.

resolute *adj* bold, constant, determined, dogged, firm, fixed, indissuadable, indivertible, inflexible, obstinate, persevering, purposeful, relentless, set, staunch, steadfast, stout, strong-minded, strong-willed, stubborn, sturdy, tenacious, unbending, undaunted, unflinching, unshakable, unshaken, unwavering, zealous.

antonym irresolute.

resolution[1] *n* boldness, constancy, courage, dedication, determination, devotion, doggedness, earnestness, energy, firmness, fortitude, obstinacy, perseverance, pertinacity, purpose, relentlessness, resoluteness, resolve, sincerity, staunchness, steadfastness, stubbornness, tenacity, will power, zeal.

antonym indecision.

resolution[2] *n* aim, decision, declaration, finding, intent, intention, judgment, motion, verdict.

resolution[3] *n* answer, conclusion, denouement, end, outcome, settlement, solution, solving, unravelling.

resolve *v* agree, alter, analyse, anatomize, answer, banish, break up, change, clear (up), close, conclude, convert, crack, decide, design, determine, disentangle, disintegrate, dispel, dissect, dissipate, dissolve, elucidate, end, explain, fathom, fix, intend, liquefy, make up one's mind, melt, metamorphose, purpose, reduce, relax, remove, separate, settle, solve, transform, transmute, undertake, unravel.

antonyms blend, waver.

n boldness, conviction, courage, decision, design, determination, earnestness, firmness, intention, objective, purpose, resoluteness, resolution, sense of purpose, steadfastness, undertaking, will power.

antonym indecision.

resonant *adj* booming, echoing, full, plummy, resounding, reverberant, reverberating, rich, ringing, sonorous, vibrant.

antonym faint.

resort *n* alternative, chance, course, expedient, hangout, haunt, health resort, hope, possibility, recourse, reference, refuge, retreat, solution, spa, spot, watering-place.

resort to[1] avail oneself of, employ, exercise, go so far as to, lower oneself to, make use of, stoop to, turn to, use, utilize.

resort to[2] frequent, go to, haunt, hie to, repair to, withdraw to.

resound *v* boom, echo, peal, re-echo, resonate, reverberate, ring, sound, thunder.

resounding *adj* booming, conclusive, crushing, decisive, echoing, full, loud, plangent, powerful, resonant, reverberating, rich, ringing, sonorous, sounding, thorough, vibrant, vocal.

antonyms faint, slight.

resource *n* ability, aid, cache, capability, cleverness, contrivance, course, expedient, hoard, ingenuity, initiative, inventiveness, means, quick-wittedness, reserve, resort, resourcefulness, shift, skill, source, stockpile, storehouse, strength, supply, talent.

antonym unimaginativeness.

resourceful *adj* able, bright, capable, clever, creative, fertile, imaginative, ingenious, innovative, inventive, originative, quick-witted, sharp, skilled, talented, versatile.

antonym unimaginative.

resourceless *adj* feckless, feeble, helpless, hopeless, inadequate, shiftless, useless.

antonym resourceful.

resources *n* assets, capital, funds, holdings, materials, means, money, pelf, property, purse, reserves, riches, supplies, wealth, wherewithal.

respect *n* admiration, appreciation, approbation, approval, aspect, connection, consideration, courtesy, deference, detail, esteem, estimation, facet, feature, homage, honour, matter, particular, point, recognition, reference, regard, relation, reverence, sense, veneration, way.

antonym disrespect.

v admire, appreciate, approve of, attend (to), be considerate of, esteem, follow, heed, honour, obey, observe, pay attention to, pay homage to, recognize, regard, relate to, revere, reverence, value, venerate.

antonym scorn.

respectable *adj* acceptable, admirable, ample, appreciable, clean-living, considerable, decent, decorous, dignified, estimable, fair, good, goodly, honest, honourable, large, passable, presentable, proper, reasonable, reputable, respected, seemly, sizable, substantial, tidy, tolerable, upright, venerable, well-to-do, worthy.

antonyms disreputable, miserly, unseemly.

respectful *adj* civil, courteous, courtly, deferential, dutiful, filial, gracious, humble, mannerly, obedient, polite, regardful, reverent, reverential, self-effacing, solicitous, submissive, subservient, well-mannered.

antonym disrespectful.

respecting *prep* about, concerning, considering, in respect of, regarding, with regard to, with respect to.

respective *adj* corresponding, individual, own, particular, personal, relevant, separate, several, special, specific, various.

respects *n* compliments, devoirs, duty, greetings, regards, salutations.

respite *n* adjournment, break, breather, cessation, delay, gap, halt, hiatus, intermission, interruption, interval, letup, lull, moratorium, pause, postponement, recess, relaxation, relief, remission, reprieve, rest, stay, suspension.

resplendent *adj* beaming, bright, brilliant, dazzling, effulgent, fulgent, gleaming, glittering, glorious, irradiant, luminous, lustrous, radiant, refulgent, shining, splendid, splendiferous.

antonym dull.

respond *v* acknowledge, answer, answer back, come back, counter, react, reciprocate, rejoin, reply, retort, return.

response *n* acknowledgment, answer, comeback, counterattack, feedback, reaction, rejoinder, reply, retort, return, riposte.

antonym query.

responsibility *n* accountability, amenability, answerability, authority, blame, burden, business, care, charge, conscientiousness, culpability, dependability, duty, fault, guilt, job, level-headedness, liability, maturity, obligation, office, onus, power, reliability, sense, sensibleness, stability, trust, trustworthiness.

antonym irresponsibility.

responsible *adj* accountable, adult, amenable, answerable, at fault, authoritative, bound, chargeable, conscientious, culpable, decision-making, dependable, duty-bound, ethical, executive, guilty, high, important, level-headed, liable, mature, of age, public-spirited, rational, reliable, right, sensible, sober, sound, stable, steady, subject, trustworthy.

antonym irresponsible.

responsive *adj* alive, appreciative, answering, awake, aware, forthcoming, impressionable, influenceable, open, perceptive, pliant, reactive, receptive, respondent, sensitive, sharp, susceptible, sympathetic.

antonym unresponsive.

rest¹ *n* base, break, breather, breathing space, breathing spell, calm, cessation, cradle, death, doze, forty winks, halt, haven, holder, holiday, idleness, inactivity, interlude, intermission, interval, leisure, lie-down, lie-in, lull, motionlessness, nap, pause, peace, pit stop, prop, refreshment, refuge, relaxation, relief, repose, respite, retreat, shelf, shelter, shut-eye, siesta, sleep, slumber, snooze, somnolence, spell, stand, standstill, stillness, stop, support, the grave, tranquillity, vacation.

antonyms action, activity, restlessness.

v base, be based, be found, be supported, cease, depend, desist, discontinue, doze, halt, hang, hinge, idle, lay, laze, lean, lie, lie back, lie down, lie in, perch, prop, recline, relax, rely, remain, repose, reside, settle, sit, sleep, slumber, snooze, spell, stand, stay, stop, take a breather, take it easy, turn.

antonyms change, continue, work.

at rest asleep, at a standstill, at peace, calm, dead, idle, immobile, inactive, motionless, peaceful, resting, sleeping, still, stopped, tranquil, unmoving.

rest² *n* balance, excess, leftovers, others, remainder, remains, remnants, residue, residuum, surplus.

restaurant *n* automat, bistro, brasserie, buffet, café, cafeteria, coffee shop, diner, dining car, dining room, eatery, grill, lunchroom, pizzeria, snack bar, steakhouse, tearoom.

restful *adj* calm, calming, comfortable, easeful, languid, pacific, peaceful, placid, quiet, relaxed, relaxing, serene, sleepy, soothing, tranquil, tranquillizing, undisturbed, unhurried.

antonyms disturbed, disturbing.

restitution *n* amends, atonement, compensation, damages, indemnification, indemnity, payment, recompense, redress, refund, reimbursement, remuneration, reparation, repayment, requital, restoration, restoring, return, satisfaction.

restive *adj* agitated, edgy, fidgety, fractious, fretful, impatient, jittery, jumpy, nervous, obstinate, recalcitrant, refractory, restless, uneasy, unmanageable, unquiet, unruly.

antonyms calm, relaxed.

restless *adj* active, agitated, antsy, anxious, bustling, changeable, disturbed, edgy, fidgety, fitful, footloose, fretful, hurried, impatient, inconstant, irresolute, jumpy, moving, nervous, nomadic, restive, roving, shifting, sleepless, transient, troubled, turbulent, uneasy, unquiet, unresting, unruly, unsettled, unstable, unsteady, wakeful, wandering, worried.

antonyms calm, relaxed.

restlessness *n* activity, agitation, ants in one's pants, anxiety, bustle, disquiet, dissatisfaction, disturbance, edginess, fitfulness, fretfulness, heebie-jeebies, hunger, hurry, hurry-scurry, inconstancy, inquietude, insomnia, instability, itch, jitteriness, jitters, jumpiness, movement, nervousness, restiveness, sleeplessness, transience, turbulence, turmoil, uneasiness, unrest, unsettledness, wakefulness, wanderlust, worriedness.

antonyms calmness, relaxation.

restoration *n* instauration, kiss of life, reconstruction, recovery, re-establishment, refreshment, refurbishing, rehabilitation, re-installation, reinstatement, rejuvenation, renewal, renovation, repair, replacement, restitution, return, revitalization, revival.

antonyms damage, removal, weakening.

restore *v* fix, fix up, mend, re-animate, rebuild, recondition, reconstitute, reconstruct, re-cover, redintegrate, re-enforce, re-establish, refresh, refurbish, rehabilitate, re-impose, reinstate, re-institute, re-introduce, rejuvenate, renew, renovate, repair, replace, retouch, return, revitalize, revive, revivify, strengthen.

antonyms damage, remove, weaken.

restrain *v* arrest, bind, bit, bridle, chain, check, confine, constrain, control, curb, curtail, debar, detain, fetter, govern, hamper, handicap, harness, hinder, hold, hold back, hold down, imprison, inhibit, jail, keep, keep a lid on, keep in check, keep within limits, limit, manacle, moderate, muzzle, pinion, prevent, rein in, repress, restrict, stay, subdue, suppress, tie.

antonyms encourage, liberate.

restrained *adj* bound, calm, controlled, discreet, low-key, mild, moderate, muted, quiet, reasonable, reticent, self-controlled, shackled, soft, steady, subdued, tasteful, temperate, undemonstrative, understated, unemphatic, unobtrusive.

antonym unrestrained.

restraint *n* arrest, ban, bondage, bonds, bridle, captivity, chains, check, coercion, command, compulsion, confinement, confines, constraint, control, cramp, curb, curtailment, dam, detention, discipline, embargo, fetters, grip, hindrance, hold, imprisonment, inhibition, interdict, lid, limit, limitation, manacles, moderation, order, pinions, prevention, rein, reserve, restriction, reticence, self-control, self-discipline, self-possession, self-restraint, shackles, stint, straitjacket, suppression, taboo, temperance, tie.

antonym freedom.

restrict *v* bound, circumscribe, condition, confine, constrain, contain, cramp (one's style), demarcate, hamper, handicap, impede, inhibit, limit, narrow, regulate, restrain, stint on, tie, tie one's hands.

antonyms broaden, encourage, free.

restriction *n* check, condition, confinement, constraint, containment, control, curb, demarcation, handicap, inhibition, limitation, regulation, restraint, rule, squeeze, stint, stipulation.

antonyms broadening, encouragement, freedom.

restroom *n* bathroom, can, comfort station, john, ladies' room, lavatory, men's room, powder room, public convenience, washroom.

result *n* conclusion, consequence, development, effect, end, end product, event, fruit, issue, outcome, product, reaction, sequel, termination, upshot.

antonyms beginning, cause.

v arise, come (after or out of), culminate, derive, develop, emanate, end, ensue, eventuate, finish, flow, follow, issue, proceed, spring, stem, terminate.

antonyms begin, cause.

resume *v* continue, pick up, proceed, recommence, re-institute, reopen, restart, take up.

antonym cease.

résumé *n* abstract, digest, epitome, overview, précis, recap, recapitulation, review, run-down, summary, synopsis.

resumption *n* continuation, recommencement, re-establishment, renewal, reopening, restart, resurgence.

antonym cessation.

resurgence *n* rebirth, recrudescence, re-emergence, renaissance, renascence, resumption, resurrection, return, revival, revivification.

antonym decrease.

resurrect *v* bring back (to life), breathe new life into, come to life, dig up (or out), disinter, dust off, re-introduce, remake, renew, restore, revive.

antonyms bury, kill off, quash.

resurrection *n* comeback, reactivation, re-appearance, rebirth, renaissance, renascence, renewal, restoration, resurgence, resuscitation, return, revival, revivification.

antonyms burying, killing off, quashing.

550

resuscitate v bring back to life, quicken, re-animate, re-invigorate, renew, rescue, restore, resurrect, revitalize, revive, revivify, save.

resuscitated adj back from the dead, reborn, redintegrated, redivivus, restored, resurrected, revived.

retain v absorb, assimilate, commission, contain, employ, engage, grasp, hire, hold, hold back, hold on to, keep, keep in mind, maintain, memorize, pay, preserve, recall, recollect, remember, reserve, save, support, sustain.

antonyms release, spend.

retainer[1] n attendant, dependant, domestic, flunky, footman, hanger-on, lackey, menial, servant, supporter, valet, vassal.

retainer[2] n advance, deposit, fee, retaining fee.

retaliate v even the score, fight back, get back, get even, get one's own back, give as good as one gets, give tit for tat, have one's revenge, hit back, reciprocate, repay in kind, reply, respond, retort, return like for like, revenge oneself, strike back, take revenge.

antonyms accept, submit.

retaliation n a taste of one's own medicine, counterattack, counterstroke, reciprocation, repayment (in kind), reprisal, requital, retort, retribution, revenge, tit for tat, vengeance.

antonyms acceptance, submission.

retard v arrest, brake, check, clog, decelerate, defer, delay, detain, encumber, handicap, hinder, impede, inhibit, keep back, obstruct, slow, stall.

antonym advance.

retardation n delay, hindering, hindrance, impeding, incapability, incapacity, lag, mental deficiency, mental disability, obstruction, slowing, slowness.

antonym advancement.

retch v barf, be nauseated, disgorge, gag, heave, puke, regurgitate, spew, throw up, upchuck, vomit.

reticence n muteness, quietness, reserve, restraint, secretiveness, silence, taciturnity, uncommunicativeness, unforthcomingness.

antonyms communicativeness, effusiveness, forwardness, frankness.

reticent adj close-lipped, close-mouthed, mum, mute, quiet, reserved, restrained, retiring, secretive, silent, taciturn, tight-lipped, uncommunicative, undemonstrative, unforthcoming, unspeaking.

antonyms communicative, effusive, forward, frank.

▲ confusable word reluctant.

retinue n aides, attendants, cortege, entourage, escort, followers, following, personnel, retainers, servants, staff, suite, train.

retire v decamp, depart, depose, discard, draw back, ebb, exit, get rid of, go to bed, leave, pay off, recede, remove, resign, retreat, withdraw.

antonyms enter, join.

retired adj emeritus, ex-, former, past.

retirement n abdication, departure, disuse, exit, flight, life of leisure, loneliness, obscurity, privacy, resignation, retreat, seclusion, solitude, withdrawal.

antonyms advancement, company, limelight, starting out.

retiring adj bashful, coy, demure, diffident, humble, introverted, meek, modest, mousy, quiet, reclusive, reserved, reticent, self-effacing, shamefaced, shrinking, shy, timid, timorous, unassertive, unassuming, withdrawn.

antonyms advancing, assertive, forward.

retort v answer, come back, counter, make a comeback, rejoin, repartee, reply, respond, retaliate, return, riposte.

n answer, comeback, quip, rejoinder, repartee, reply, response, riposte, sally, witticism.

retract v abjure, cancel, deny, disavow, disclaim, disown, pull back, recall, recant, renounce, repeal, repudiate, rescind, reverse, revoke, take back, unsay, withdraw.

antonym maintain.

retreat v back down, beat a (hasty) retreat, depart, do an about-face, ebb, fall back, leave, pull back, quit, recede, recoil, retire, shrink, turn back, turn tail, withdraw.

antonym advance.

n asylum, den, departure, ebb, evacuation, flight, haunt, haven, hibernaculum, hideaway, hide-out, privacy, recession, refuge, resort, retirement, sanctuary, seclusion, shelter, withdrawal.

antonyms advance, company, limelight.

retrench v curtail, cut (back), decrease, diminish, economize, husband, lessen, limit, pare, prune, reduce, restrain, save, slim down, tighten one's belt, trim.

antonym increase.

retrenchment n contraction, cost cutting, curtailment, cut, cutback(s), economy, paring, pruning, reduction, restraint, shrinkage.

antonym increase.

retribution n compensation, justice, nemesis, payment, punishment, reckoning, recompense, redress, repayment, reprisal, requital, restitution, retaliation, revenge, reward, satisfaction, talion, vengeance.

retrieve v fetch, make good, recall, recapture, recoup, recover, redeem, regain, repair, repossess, rescue, restore, return, salvage, save.

antonym lose.

retrograde adj backward, declining, degenerative, denigrating, deteriorating, downward, inverse, negative, regressive, relapsing, retreating, retrogressive, reverse, reverting, waning, worsening.

antonym progressive.

retrogress v backslide, decline, degenerate, deteriorate, drop, ebb, fall, recede, regress, relapse, retire, retreat, retrograde, return, revert, sink, wane, withdraw, worsen.

antonym progress.

retrogression *n* decline, deterioration, drop, ebb, fall, recidivism, regression, relapse, return, reversion, worsening.

antonyms increase, progress.

retrospect *n* afterthought, contemplation, hindsight, recollection, re-examination, regard, remembrance, reminiscence, retrospection, review, survey.

antonym prospect.

return *v* announce, answer, choose, communicate, convey, deliver, earn, elect, give back, pay back, pick, produce, put back, re-appear, rebound, reciprocate, recoil, recompense, recur, redound, re-elect, re-establish, refund, reimburse, reinstate, relapse, rejoin, remit, render, repair, repay, replace, reply, report, requite, respond, restore, retort, retreat, revert, send back, volley, yield.

antonyms leave, take.

n account, advantage, answer, benefit, comeback, compensation, form, gain, homecoming, income, interest, proceeds, profit, quip, re-appearance, rebound, receipts, reciprocation, recoil, recompense, recovery, recrudescence, recurrence, redound, re-establishment, regression, reimbursement, reinstatement, rejoinder, relapse, reparation, repayment, replacement, reply, report, requital, response, restoration, retaliation, retort, retreat, revenue, reversion, reward, riposte, sally, statement, summary, takings, yield.

antonyms disappearance, expense, loss, payment.

revamp *v* overhaul, rebuild, recast, recondition, reconstruct, redo, refit, refurbish, rehabilitate, renovate, repair, restore, revise.

reveal *v* announce, bare (all), betray, blow the lid off, broadcast, communicate, disclose, display, divulge, exhibit, expose, impart, leak, let on, let out, let slip, manifest, open, proclaim, publish, show, spill the beans, tell (all), unbosom, uncover, unearth, unfold, unmask, unveil.

antonym hide.

revel *v* carouse, celebrate, go on a spree, live it up, make merry, paint the town red, raise the roof, roister, whoop it up.

n bacchanal, carousal, carouse, celebration, debauch, festivity, gala, jollification, merrymaking, party, saturnalia, spree.

revel in bask in, crow over, delight in, enjoy, gloat about, glory in, indulge, joy, lap up, luxuriate in, rejoice in, relish, savour, take pleasure in, thrive on, wallow in.

antonym dislike.

revelation *n* announcement, apocalypse, betrayal, broadcasting, communication, disclosure, discovery, display, exhibition, exposé, exposition, exposure, giveaway, leak, manifestation, news, proclamation, publication, surprise, telling, uncovering, unearthing, unveiling.

reveller *n* bacchanal, bacchant, carouser, celebrator, merrymaker, party animal, party-goer, pleasure-seeker, roisterer, wassailer.

revelry *n* carousal, carouse, celebration, conviviality, debauch, debauchery, festivities, festivity, fun, jollification, jollity, merrymaking, party, revel-rout, riot, roistering, saturnalia, spree, wassail, wassailing.

antonym sobriety.

revenge *n* a dose (or taste) of one's own medicine, an eye for an eye, reprisal, requital, retaliation, retribution, revengement, satisfaction, tit for tat, vengeance, vindictiveness.

v avenge, even (or settle) the score, get one's own back, get satisfaction, repay, requite, retaliate, vindicate.

revengeful *adj* bitter, implacable, malevolent, malicious, malignant, resentful, spiteful, unforgiving, vengeful, vindictive.

antonym forgiving.

revenue *n* gain, income, interest, proceeds, profits, receipts, returns, rewards, take, takings, yield.

antonym expenditure.

reverberate *v* echo (back), rebound, recoil, re-echo, reflect, resound, ring, vibrate.

reverberation *n* echo, rebound, recoil, re-echoing, reflection, resonance, resounding, ringing, vibration.

reverberations *n* consequences, effects, repercussions, results, ripples, shock wave(s).

revere *v* adore, cherish, defer to, exalt, hold in awe, honour, pay homage to, respect, reverence, venerate, worship.

antonyms despise, scorn.

reverence *n* admiration, adoration, awe, deference, devotion, esteem, genuflection, homage, honour, latria, obeisance, respect, veneration, worship.

antonym scorn.

v acknowledge, admire, adore, hold in awe, honour, respect, revere, venerate, worship.

antonyms despise, scorn.

reverent *adj* adoring, awed, decorous, deferential, devout, dutiful, humble, loving, meek, pious, respectful, reverential, solemn, worshipful.

antonym irreverent.

reverie *n* absent-mindedness, abstraction, brown study, daydream, daydreaming, inattention, musing, preoccupation, trance, woolgathering.

reversal *n* about-face, abrogation, annulment, cancellation, countermanding, defeat, delay, difficulty, disaster, mirror image, misfortune, mishap, nullification, problem, repeal, rescinding, rescission, reverse, revocation, setback, turnabout, turnaround, upset, U-turn, volte face.

antonyms advancement, progress.

reverse *v* about-face, advance to the rear, alter, annul, backtrack, back up, cancel, change, countermand, do a 180, invalidate, invert, negate, overrule, overset, overthrow, overturn, quash, repeal, rescind, retract, retreat, revert, revoke, transpose, turn inside out, turn upside down, undo, upend, upset.

antonym enforce.

n adversity, affliction, antithesis, back, blow, check, contradiction, contrary, converse, defeat, disappointment, failure, hardship, inverse, misadventure, misfortune, mishap, opposite, repulse, reversal, setback, tail, trial, tribulation, underside, verso, vicissitude.

adj backward, contrary, converse, inverse, inverted, opposite, verso.

revert *v* backslide, change back, lapse, regress, relapse, retrogress, return, reverse.

antonym progress.

review *v* assess, cram, critique, criticize, discuss, evaluate, examine, inspect, judge, look back on, look over, reassess, recall, recapitulate, recollect, reconsider, re-evaluate, re-examine, refresh one's memory, rehearse, remember, reread, rethink, scrutinize, study, survey, think over, weigh.

n analysis, assessment, commentary, criticism, critique, evaluation, examination, journal, judgment, magazine, notice, periodical, reassessment, recapitulation, recension, reconsideration, re-evaluation, re-examination, report, rereading, rethink, retrospect, revision, scrutiny, study, survey.

reviewer *n* arbiter, commentator, connoisseur, critic, essayist, judge, observer.

revile *v* abuse, berate, blackguard, calumniate, curse, defame, denigrate, insult, jeer at, libel, malign, miscall, reproach, scorn, slander, smear, traduce, vilify, vilipend, vituperate.

antonym praise.

revise *v* alter, amend, change, correct, edit, emend, modify, recast, reconsider, reconstruct, redo, remake, rework, revamp, rewrite, update.

revision *n* alteration, amendment, change, correction, editing, emendation, modification, new version, recast, recasting, recension, reconstruction, re-examination, rewrite, rewriting, updating.

revitalize *v* re-activate, re-animate, refresh, rejuvenate, renew, restore, resurrect, revive, revivify.

antonyms dampen, suppress.

revival *n* awakening, quickening, re-activation, re-animation, re-awakening, rebirth, recrudescence, reformation, renaissance, renascence, renewal, restoration, resurgence, resurrection, resuscitation, revitalization, revivification.

antonym suppression.

revive *v* animate, awaken, breathe (new) life into, cheer (up), come to life, dig up, dust off, invigorate, quicken, rally, re-activate, re-animate, recover, refresh, rekindle, renew, renovate, restore, resurrect, resuscitate, revitalize, revivify, rouse.

antonyms suppress, weary.

revivify *v* energy, inspirit, invigorate, re-activate, re-animate, refresh, renew, restore, resuscitate, revive.

antonyms dampen, depress.

reviving *adj* bracing, enheartening, exhilarating, invigorating, re-animating, refreshening, regenerating, re-invigorating, restorative, revivifying, stimulating, strengthening, tonic.

antonyms disheartening, exhausting.

revocation *n* abolition, annulment, cancellation, countermanding, nullification, quashing, repeal, repealing, repudiation, rescinding, rescission, retraction, reversal, revoking, withdrawal.

antonym enforcement.

revoke *v* abolish, abrogate, annul, cancel, countermand, disclaim, dissolve, invalidate, negate, nullify, quash, recall, recant, renounce, repeal, repudiate, rescind, retract, reverse, take back, withdraw.

antonym enforce.

revolt[1] *n* breakaway, counteraction, defection, insurgence, insurrection, jacquerie, mutiny, putsch, rebellion, resistance, revolution, rising, secession, sedition, strike, uprising.

v balk, defect, dig in one's heels, mutiny, rebel, resist, riot, rise (up), strike.

antonym submit.

revolt[2] *v* disgust, nauseate, offend, outrage, repel, repulse, scandalize, shock, sicken.

antonym please.

revolting *adj* abhorrent, abominable, appalling, disgusting, distasteful, fetid, foul, horrible, horrid, loathsome, nasty, nauseating, nauseous, noisome, obnoxious, obscene, offensive, repellent, repugnant, repulsive, shocking, sickening, ugly.

antonym pleasant.

revolution *n* cataclysm, change, circle, circuit, coup (d'état), cycle, gyration, innovation, insurgency, jacquerie, lap, metamorphosis, metanoia, mutiny, orbit, paradigm shift, putsch, radical change, rebellion, reformation, revolt, rising, rotation, round, shift, spin, transformation, turn, upheaval, uprising, volution, wheel, whirl.

revolutionary *n* anarchist, insurgent, insurrectionary, insurrectionist, Jacobin, mutineer, radical, rebel, reformer, revolutionist, subversive, Trotskyite.

adj anarchistic, anti-establishment, avant-garde, countercultural, different, drastic, experimental, extremist, fundamental, innovative, insurgent, insurrectionary, leading-edge, mutinous, new, novel, progressive, radical, rebel, rebellious, seditious, subversive, thoroughgoing.

antonyms commonplace, establishment.

revolve *v* circle, gyrate, orbit, rotate, spin, turn, wheel, whirl.

revulsion *n* abhorrence, abomination, aversion, detestation, disgust, dislike, distaste, hatred, loathing, recoil, repugnance, repulsion.

antonym pleasure.

reward *n* award, benefit, bonus, bounty, comeuppance, compensation, desert, gain, guerdon, honour, meed, merit, payment, payoff, premium, prize, profit, punishment, recompense, remuneration, repayment, requital, retribution, return, wages, what's coming to one.

antonym punishment.

v compensate, guerdon, honour, pay, recompense, remunerate, repay, requite.

antonym punish.

rewarding *adj* advantageous, beneficial, edifying, enriching, fruitful, fulfilling, gainful, gratifying, pleasing, productive, profitable, remunerative, rich, satisfying, valuable, worthwhile.

antonym unrewarding.

reword *v* paraphrase, recast, rehash, rephrase, restate, revise, translate.

rewrite *v* correct, edit, emend, recast, redraft, revise, reword, rework.

rhetoric *n* bombast, declamation, discourse, eloquence, fustian, grandiloquence, hyperbole, magniloquence, oratory, pomposity, propoganda, rant, verbosity, wordiness.

rhetorical *adj* artificial, bombastic, declamatory, decorative, false, flamboyant, flashy, florid, flowery, grandiloquent, high-flown, high-sounding, hyperbolic, inflated, insincere, magniloquent, oratorical, ornamental, pompous, pretentious, showy, silver-tongued, stylistic, verbal, verbose, windy.

antonym simple.

rhyme *n* chime, ditty, doggerel, jingle, limerick, ode, poem, poetry, song, verse.

rhyme off parrot, recite, spiel off, spout, trot out.

rhythm *n* accent, beat, cadence, cycle, eurhythmy, flow, lilt, measure, metre, movement, pattern, periodicity, pulsation, pulse, regularity, swing, tempo, time.

rhythmic *adj* cadenced, cyclical, flowing, harmonious, lilting, melodious, metrical, musical, periodic, pulsating, regular, throbbing.

antonym unrhythmical.

rib[1] *n* band, bar, bone, costa, moulding, purlin, ribbing, ridge, spine, support, vein, wale.

rib[2] *v* chaff, josh, make fun of, needle, rag, razz, ridicule, taunt, tease, twit.

ribald *adj* base, bawdy, blue, broad, coarse, derisive, earthy, filthy, foul-mouthed, gross, indecent, jeering, licentious, low, mean, mocking, naughty, obscene, off-colour, Rabelaisian, racy, risqué, rude, scurrilous, smutty, vulgar.

antonym polite.

ribaldry *n* baseness, bawdiness, billingsgate, coarseness, derision, earthiness, filth, grossness, indecency, jeering, licentiousness, lowness, mockery, naughtiness, obscenity, raciness, rudeness, scurrility, smut, smuttiness, vulgarity.

ribbon *n* award, band, cord, fillet, hairband, headband, sash, shred, strip, tatter.

rich *adj* abounding, abundant, affluent, ample, bright, copious, costly, creamy, deep, delicious, elaborate, elegant, expensive, exquisite, exuberant, fatty, fecund, fertile, fine, flavourful, flush, fruitful, fulfilling, full, full-bodied, full-flavoured, full-throated, funny, heavy, highly-flavoured, hilarious, humorous, in the money, intense, juicy, laughable, lavish, loaded, ludicrous, luscious, lush, luxurious, mellifluous, mellow, moneyed, opulent, ornate, oversweet, palatial, pecunious, plenteous, plentiful, plutocratic, precious, priceless, productive, prolific, propertied, prosperous, resonant, rewarding, ridiculous, risible, rolling (in dough), savoury, side-splitting, spicy, strong, succulent, sumptuous, superb, tasty, valuable, vibrant, vivid, warm, wealthy, well-heeled, well-off, well-provided, well-stocked, well-supplied, well-to-do.

antonyms harsh, infertile, miserly, plain, poor, simple, tasteless, thin.

riches *n* abundance, affluence, assets, a well-lined purse, fortune, gold, mint, money, money to burn, opulence, pelf, plenty, property, resources, richness, substance, treasure, wealth.

antonym poverty.

richly *adv* abundantly, amply, appropriately, condignly, elaborately, elegantly, expensively, exquisitely, fully, gorgeously, lavishly, luxuriously, opulently, palatially, properly, splendidly, suitably, sumptuously, thoroughly, well.

antonyms poorly, scantily.

rickety *adj* broken, broken-down, decrepit, derelict, dilapidated, feeble, flimsy, frail, imperfect, infirm, insecure, jerry-built, precarious, ramshackle, shaky, tottering, tottery, unsound, unstable, unsteady, weak, wobbly.

antonyms stable, strong.

rid *v* clear, deliver, disabuse, disburden, disembarrass, disencumber, free, purge, relieve, unburden.

antonym burden.

get rid of abolish, cast off, chase away, chuck, clear away, delete, dispose of, do away with, eliminate, eradicate, lose, scrap, shed, throw out.

riddance *n* clearance, deliverance, disposal, ejection, elimination, expulsion, extermination, freedom, purgation, release, relief, removal.

antonym burdening.

riddle[1] *n* brain teaser, brain twister, charade, conundrum, enigma, logogram, logograph, mystery, paradox, poser, problem, puzzle, rebus.

riddle[2] *v* corrupt, fill, filter, infest, invade, make holes in, mar, pepper, perforate, permeate, perplexity, pervade, pierce, puncture, puzzler, screen, shoot full of holes, sift, strain, winnow.

ride *v* be contingent, control, depend, dominate, drive, enslave, float, handle, haunt, hurl, journey, make fun of, manage, move, oppress, progress, ride roughshod over, rib,

554

ridge

ridicule, sit, survive, tease, travel, turn, tyrannize, weather.

n drive, gallop, jaunt, journey, joyride, lift, outing, spin, trip, whirl.

ridge *n* arête, band, costa, crinkle, drum, drumlin, escarpment, esker, hill, hogback, hummock, lump, reef, ripple, saddle, sastruga, summit, wale, weal, welt.

ridicule *n* banter, chaff, contempt, derision, gibe, irony, jeering, jeers, laughter, mockery, raillery, sarcasm, satire, scorn, sneers, taunting.

antonym praise.

v burlesque, caricature, cartoon, chaff, crucify, depreciate, deride, humiliate, jeer (at), josh, lampoon, make fun of, mock, parody, pillory, pooh-pooh, put down, rib, satirize, scoff (at), send up, sneer at, taunt.

antonym praise.

ridiculous *adj* absurd, amusing, comical, contemptible, derisory, farcical, foolish, funny, hilarious, incredible, laughable, ludicrous, nonsensical, outrageous, preposterous, rich, risible, silly, stupid, unbelievable.

antonym sensible.

rife *adj* abounding, abundant, common, commonplace, current, epidemic, frequent, general, plentiful, prevailing, prevalent, raging, rampant, teeming, ubiquitous, universal, widespread.

antonym scarce.

riffraff *n* canaille, hoi polloi, mob, rabble, raggle-taggle, ragtag (and bobtail), scum, the great unwashed, trash, undesirables.

rifle¹ *v* burgle, despoil, gut, loot, maraud, pillage, plunder, ransack, rob, rummage, sack, strip.

rifle² *n* air gun, carbine, firearm, firelock, flintlock, fusil, gun, musket, shotgun.

rift *n* alienation, breach, break, chink, cleavage, cleft, crack, cranny, crevice, difference, disaffection, disagreement, division, estrangement, falling-out, fault, flaw, fracture, gap, opening, quarrel, schism, separation, space, split.

antonym unity.

rig¹ *v* accoutre, equip, fit out, furnish, kit out, outfit, provision, supply.

n accoutrements, apparatus, costume, ensemble, equipage, equipment, fittings, fixtures, gear, get-up, installation, machinery, outfit, tackle.

rig out accoutre, array, attire, caparison, clothe, costume, dress, dress up, equip, fit, fit out, fit up, furnish, kit out, outfit.

rig up arrange, assemble, build, construct, erect, fix up, improvise.

antonym dismantle.

rig² *v* arrange, cook, doctor, engineer, fake, falsify, fiddle with, fix, gerrymander, juggle, manipulate, prearrange, set up, stack, tamper with, trump up.

right *adj* absolute, accurate, admissible, advantageous, appropriate, approved, apt, authentic, balanced, bang on, becoming, comme il faut, complete, compos mentis, conservative, conventional, correct, deserved, desirable, dexter, dextral, direct, done, due, equitable, ethical, exact, factual, fair, favourable, fine, fit, fitting, genuine, good, healthy, honest, honourable, ideal, in the right, just, lawful, left-hand, lucid, moral, normal, opportune, ordained, orthodox, out-and-out, perpendicular, precise, prescribed, proper, propitious, rational, reactionary, real, reasonable, right-angled, righteous, rightful, right hand, rightist, rightward, right-wing, sane, satisfactory, seemly, sound, spot on, straight, suitable, thorough, thoroughgoing, tory, true, unerring, unimpaired, upright, utter, valid, veracious, verifiable, veritable, virtuous, well.

antonyms left, left-wing, mad, unfit, wrong.

adv absolutely, accurately, advantageously, altogether, appropriately, aptly, aright, bang, befittingly, beneficially, completely, correctly, directly, entirely, ethically, exactly, extremely, factually, fairly, favourably, fittingly, fortunately, genuinely, honestly, honourably, immediately, instantly, just, justly, morally, perfectly, precisely, promptly, properly, quickly, quite, righteously, rightly, rightward, satisfactorily, slap, square, squarely, straight, straightaway, suitably, thoroughly, to rights, totally, truly, utterly, very, virtuously, well, wholly.

antonyms incorrectly, left, unfairly, wrongly.

n authority, business, call, claim, droit, due, equity, fair treatment, freedom, good, goodness, honour, integrity, interest, justice, lawfulness, legality, liberty, licence, morality, permission, power, prerogative, privilege, propriety, reason, rectitude, righteousness, rightfulness, rightness, title, truth, uprightness, virtue.

antonyms depravity, wrong.

v avenge, correct, fix, make right, put to rights, rectify, redress, remedy, repair, settle, stand up, straighten, vindicate.

in the right justified, right.

antonym in the wrong.

right away at once, chop-chop, directly, forthwith, immediately, instantly, now, promptly, pronto, right off, straight off, straightaway, this instant, tout de suite, without delay, without hesitation, yesterday.

antonym eventually.

righteous *adj* blameless, equitable, ethical, fair, God-fearing, good, guiltless, holy, honest, honourable, incorrupt, just, law-abiding, moral, pious, pure, saintly, sinless, upright, virtuous.

antonym unrighteous.

righteousness *n* blamelessness, dharma, equity, ethicalness, faithfulness, goodness, holiness, honesty, honour, integrity, justice, morality, piety, probity, purity, rectitude, uprightness, virtue.

antonym unrighteousness.

rightful *adj* authentic, authorized, bona fide, correct, de jure, due, just, lawful, legal, legitimate, licit, prescribed, proper, real, suitable, true, valid.

antonyms incorrect, unlawful.

rightfully *adv* by rights, correctly, de jure, justifiably, justly, lawfully, legally, legitimately, properly, rightly.

antonyms incorrectly, unjustifiably.

rigid *adj* adamant, austere, cast-iron, exact, fixed, formal, harsh, inflexible, intransigent, invariable, rigorous, set, severe, starch(y), stern, stiff, stony, strict, stringent, tense, unalterable, unbending, unchanging, uncompromising, undeviating, unrelenting, unyielding.

antonym flexible.

rigmarole *n* balderdash, bother, carryings-on, ceremony, fuss, gibberish, hassle, jargon, nonsense, palaver, performance, procedure, red tape, schmozzle, to-do, trash, twaddle.

rigorous *adj* accurate, austere, challenging, conscientious, demanding, exact, exacting, extreme, firm, hard, harsh, inclement, inflexible, inhospitable, meticulous, nice, painstaking, precise, punctilious, Rhadamanthine, rigid, scrupulous, severe, Spartan, stern, strict, stringent, thorough, tough, unsparing.

antonyms lenient, mild.

rigour *n* accuracy, asperity, austerity, conscientiousness, exactitude, exactness, firmness, hardness, hardship, harshness, inflexibility, meticulousness, ordeal, preciseness, precision, privation, punctiliousness, rigidity, rigourousness, severity, sternness, strictness, stringency, suffering, thoroughness, trial.

antonyms leniency, mildness.

rile *v* anger, annoy, bug, exasperate, gall, get (to), irk, irritate, miff, nettle, peeve, pique, provoke, put out, upset, vex.

antonym soothe.

rim *n* border, brim, brink, circumference, edge, lip, margin, skirt, verge.

antonym centre.

rind *n* crust, epicarp, husk, integument, peel, skin, zest.

ring[1] *n* annulation, annulet, annulus, arena, association, band, cabal, cartel, cell, circle, circuit, circus, clique, collar, combine, coterie, crew, enclosure, gang, group, gyre, halo, hoop, knot, loop, mob, organization, rink, round, syndicate.

v circumscribe, close in, encircle, enclose, encompass, gird, girdle, mark, surround.

ring[2] *v* buzz, call (up), chime, clang, clink, peal, phone, resonate, resound, reverberate, sound, tang, telephone, ting, tinkle, tintinnabulate, toll.

n buzz, call, chime, clang, clink, knell, peal, phone call, tang, ting, ting, tinkle, tintinnabulation.

ringleader *n* bellwether, brains, chief, instigator, leader, spokesperson.

rinse *v* bathe, clean, cleanse, dip, sluice, splash, swill, wash, wet.

n bath, dip, dye, splash, tint, wash, wetting.

riot *n* anarchy, ball, boisterousness, burst, carousal, commotion, confusion, debauchery, disorder, display, disturbance, Donnybrook, excess, extravaganza, festivity, flourish, fray, free-for-all, frolic, high jinks, hoot, insurrection, jollification, lawlessness, merrymaking, quarrel, revelry, revolt, riotousness, romp, rout, row, ruffle, shindig, splash, strife, tumult, turbulence, turmoil, uproar.

antonyms calm, order.

v carouse, frolic, go on the rampage, rampage, rebel, revel, revolt, rise up, roister, romp, run riot, run wild.

riotous *adj* anarchic, boisterous, disorderly, insubordinate, insurrectionary, lawless, loud, luxurious, mutinous, noisy, orgiastic, rambunctious, rampageous, rebellious, refractory, roisterous, rollicking, rowdy, saturnalian, side-splitting, tumultuous, ungovernable, unrestrained, unruly, uproarious, violent, wanton, wild.

antonyms orderly, restrained.

rip *v* burst, claw, cut, gash, hack, lacerate, rend, rupture, score, separate, slash, slit, split, tear.

n cleavage, cut, gash, hole, laceration, rupture, slash, slit, split, tear.

rip off cheat, con, defraud, diddle, do, dupe, exploit, filch, fleece, lift, mulct, overcharge, pilfer, pinch, rob, rogue, rook, steal, sting, swindle, swipe, thieve, trick.

ripe *adj* accomplished, auspicious, complete, developed, favourable, finished, grown, ideal, mature, mellow, opportune, perfect, prepared, promising, propitious, ready, right, ripened, seasoned, suitable, timely.

antonyms inopportune, untimely.

ripen *v* age, burgeon, develop, mature, mellow, prepare, season.

rip-off *n* cheat, con, daylight robbery, diddle, exploitation, fraud, robbery, scam, sting, swindle, theft, trick.

riposte *n* answer, comeback, quip, rejoinder, repartee, reply, response, retort, return, sally.

v answer, quip, reciprocate, rejoin, reply, respond, retort, return.

ripple *n* babble, burble, disturbance, eddy, gurgle, lapping, purl, undulation, wave, wimple, wrinkle.

rise *v* advance, appear, arise, ascend, buoy, climb, crop up, emanate, emerge, enlarge, eventuate, evolve, flow, get up, grow, happen, improve, increase, intensify, issue, levitate, lift, loom, mount, mutiny, occur, originate, progress, prosper, rebel, resist, revolt, slope upward, soar, spring, spring up, stand up, surface, swell, tower, wax.

antonyms descend, fall.

n acclivity, advance, advancement, aggrandizement, ascent, climb, development, elevation, emergence, evolution, hillock, improvement, incline, increase, increment, intensification, origin, progress, progression, promotion, reaction, rising, upsurge, upswing, upturn, upward slope, upward turn.

antonyms descent, fall.

risible *adj* absurd, amusing, comic, comical, droll, farcical, funny, hilarious, humorous, laughable, ludicrous, rib-tickling, ridiculous, sidesplitting.

antonyms serious, unfunny.

rising *n* insurrection, revolt, revolution, riot, uprising.

adj advancing, approaching, ascending, assurgent, emerging, growing, increasing, intensifying, mounting, soaring, swelling.

antonym decreasing.

risk *n* adventure, chance, danger, gamble, hazard, jeopardy, peril, possibility, probability, speculation, uncertainty, venture.

antonyms certainty, safety.

v adventure, chance, dare, endanger, gamble (with), hazard, imperil, jeopardize, speculate, take chances (with), venture.

risky *adj* chancy, dangerous, dicey, dodgy, fraught, hazardous, iffy, perilous, precarious, riskfilled, touch-and-go, tricky, uncertain, unsafe.

antonym safe.

risqué *adj* bawdy, blue, coarse, crude, daring, earthy, immodest, improper, indecent, indecorous, indelicate, naughty, off-colour, Rabelaisian, racy, ribald, suggestive.

antonym decent.

rite *n* act, ceremonial, ceremony, custom, form, formality, liturgy, mystery, observance, office, ordinance, practice, procedure, ritual, sacrament, service, solemnity, usage, worship.

ritual *n* ceremonial, ceremony, convention, custom, form, formality, habit, liturgy, mystery, observance, ordinance, practice, prescription, procedure, rite, ritualistic, routine, service, solemnity, tradition, wont.

adj ceremonial, ceremonious, conventional, customary, formal, formulary, habitual, prescribed, procedural, ritualistic, routine, stereotyped.

antonyms informal, unusual.

rival *n* adversary, antagonist, challenger, competitor, contender, contestant, emulator, equal, equivalent, fellow, match, opponent, peer.

antonyms associate, colleague, co-worker.

adj competing, competitive, conflicting, emulative, emulous, opposed, opposing.

antonyms associate, co-operating.

v compare (favourably) with, compete with (or against), contend with, emulate, equal, hold a candle to, match, oppose, vie with.

antonym co-operate.

rivalry *n* antagonism, competition, competitiveness, conflict, contention, contest, duel, emulation, opposition, struggle, vying.

antonym co-operation.

river *n* beck, burn, creek, flood, flow, gush, riverway, rush, spate, stream, surge, tributary, waterway.

riveting *adj* absorbing, arresting, captivating, engrossing, enthralling, fascinating, gripping, hypnotic, magnetic, spellbinding.

antonym boring.

road *n* autoroute, avenue, boulevard, carriageway, course, crescent, direction, drift, drive, driveway, expressway, freeway, highway, lane, motorway, path, pathway, roadway, route, street, thoroughfare, track, way.

roam *v* drift, meander, peregrinate, prowl, ramble, range, rove, squander, stray, stroll, travel, walk, wander.

antonym stay.

roar *v* bawl, bay, bell, bellow, blare, clamour, crash, cry, guffaw, hoot, howl, rumble, shout, thunder, vociferate, yell.

antonym whisper.

n bellow, belly laugh, blare, clamour, crash, cry, guffaw, hoot, howl, outcry, rumble, shout, thunder, yell.

antonym whisper.

rob *v* bereave, bunco, burglarize, cheat, con, defraud, deprive, despoil, dispossess, do, fleece, gyp, heist, hold up, loot, mug, pillage, plunder, raid, ramp, ransack, rifle, rip off, roll, sack, stick up, sting, strip, swindle, thieve.

antonyms give, provide.

robber *n* bandit, brigand, burglar, cat burglar, cheat, con man, dacoit, fraud, highwayman, hijacker, land pirate, looter, mugger, pickpocket, pirate, plunderer, raider, stealer, stick-up artist, swindler, thief, vulture.

robbery *n* burglary, depredation, embezzlement, filching, fraud, heist, holdup, job, larceny, mugging, pillage, plunder, purse snatching, raid, rapine, rip-off, spoliation, stealing, stick-up, swindle, theft, thievery.

robe *n* bathrobe, costume, dressing gown, gown, habit, housecoat, peignoir, vestment, wrap, wrapper.

v apparel, attire, clothe, drape, dress, garb, vest.

robot *n* android, automaton, cyborg, golem, machine, zombie.

robust *adj* able-bodied, athletic, boisterous, brawny, coarse, down-to-earth, earthy, fit, hale, hard-headed, hardy, healthy, hearty, husky, indecorous, lusty, muscular, powerful, practical, pragmatic, raw, realistic, roisterous, rollicking, rough, rude, rugged, sensible, sinewy, sound, staunch, sthenic, stout, straightforward, strapping, strong, sturdy, thick-set, tough, unsubtle, vigorous, well.

antonyms mealy-mouthed, unhealthy, unrealistic, weak.

rock¹ *n* anchor, boulder, bulwark, cornerstone, danger, foundation, hazard, mainstay, obstacle, pebble, problem, protection, stone, support.

rock² *v* astonish, astound, daze, dumfound, jar, lurch, pitch, reel, roll, shake, shock, stagger, stun, surprise, sway, swing, tilt, tip, toss, wobble.

rocky¹ *adj* craggy, flinty, hard, pebbly, rocklike, rough, rugged, stony.

antonyms smooth, soft.

rocky² *adj* dizzy, doubtful, drunk, ill, inebriated, intoxicated, rickety, shaky, sick, sickly, staggering, tipsy, tottering, uncertain,

undependable, unpleasant, unreliable, unsatisfactory, unstable, unsteady, unwell, weak, wobbly, wonky.
antonyms dependable, steady, well.

rod *n* bar, baton, birch, cane, dowel, ferule, mace, pole, sceptre, shaft, spoke, staff, stick, strut, switch, verge, wand.

rogue *n* blackguard, charlatan, cheat, con man, crook, deceiver, fraud, knave, mischief-maker, miscreant, mountebank, nasty piece (or bit) of work, ne'er-do-well, picaroon, rapscallion, rascal, reprobate, scamp, scapegrace, scoundrel, sharper, swindler, vagrant, villain, wag.
antonym saint.

roguish *adj* arch, bantering, cheeky, confounded, coquettish, criminal, crooked, deceitful, deceiving, dishonest, fraudulent, frolicsome, impish, knavish, mischievous, playful, puckish, raffish, rascally, roguing, shady, sportive, swindling, unprincipled, unscrupulous, villainous, waggish.
antonyms honest, serious.

roguishly *adv* archly, cheekily, coquettishly, en badinant, impishly, mischievously, playfully.
antonym seriously.

roguishness *n* archness, badinage, bantering, cheekiness, coquettishness, deceitfulness, dishonesty, fraud, impishness, mischief, mischievousness, playfulness, roguery, tricks, unscrupulousness, villainy, waggishness.
antonym seriousness.

roister *v* bluster, boast, brag, carouse, celebrate, frolic, make merry, paint the town red, revel, rollick, romp, strut, swagger, whoop it up.

roisterer *n* blusterer, boaster, braggart, carouser, ranter, reveller, roister, swaggerer.

roisterous *adj* boisterous, clamorous, disorderly, exuberant, loud, noisy, obstreperous, roistering, rowdy, uproarious, wild.
antonyms orderly, restrained.

role *n* capacity, character, duty, function, impersonation, job, part, portrayal, position, post, representation, task.

roll *v* billow, boom, coil, curl, drum, echo, even, flatten, flow, furl, grumble, gyrate, level, lumber, lurch, pass, pitch, pivot, press, reel, resound, reverberate, revolve, rise and fall, roar, rob, rock, rotate, rumble, run, smooth (out), spin, spread, stagger, swagger, swathe, sway, swing, swivel, thunder, toss, trill, trundle, tumble, turn, twirl, twist, undulate, waddle, wallow, welter, wheel, whirl, wind, wrap.
n annals, ball, bobbin, boom, bun, bundle, catalogue, census, chronicle, cycle, cylinder, directory, drumming, growl, grumble, gyration, index, inventory, list, record, reel, register, resonance, reverberation, revolution, rise and fall, roar, roller, roster, rotation, rumble, run, schedule, scroll, spin, spool, table, thunder, turn, twirl, undulation, wheel, whirl.

rollicking *adj* boisterous, carefree, cavorting, devil-may-care, exuberant, frisky, frolicsome,

hearty, jaunty, jovial, joyous, lively, merry, playful, riproaring, roistering, roisterous, romping, spirited, sportive, sprightly, swashbuckling.
antonyms restrained, serious.

rolling *adj* heaving, hilly, rippling, rising and falling, surging, undulant, undulating, waving.
antonym flat.

roly-poly *adj* buxom, chubby, fat, overweight, plump, pudgy, rotund, round, tubby.
antonym slim.

romance *n* adventure, affair, amour, attachment, colour, exaggeration, excitement, fabrication, fairy tale, falsehood, fantasy, fascination, fiction, geste, glamour, idealism, idealization, idyll, intrigue, invention, legend, liaison, lie, love affair, love story, melodrama, mystery, novel, passion, relationship, sentiment, soap opera, story, tale, tearjerker.
v court, daydream, exaggerate, fantasize, lie, overstate, woo.

romantic *adj* amorous, charming, colourful, dreamy, exaggerated, exciting, exotic, fabulous, fairy-tale, fanciful, fantastic, fascinating, fictitious, fond, glamorous, high-flown, idealistic, idealized, idyllic, imaginary, imaginative, impractical, improbable, legendary, lovey-dovey, loving, made-up, mushy, mysterious, passionate, picturesque, quixotic, romanticized, sentimental, sloppy, soppy, starry-eyed, tender, unrealistic, utopian, visionary, whimsical.
antonyms humdrum, practical, real, sober, unromantic.
n Don Quixote, dreamer, idealist, romancer, sentimentalist, utopian, visionary.
antonym realist.

Romeo *n* Casanova, Don Juan, ladies' man, Lothario, lover.

romp *v* caper, cavort, frisk, frolic, gambol, play, revel, roister, rollick, skip, sport.
n caper, frolic, lark, spree.

rook *v* bilk, cheat, clip, con, defraud, diddle, do, fleece, mulct, overcharge, rip off, soak, sting, swindle.

room *n* allowance, apartment, area, capacity, chamber, chance, compartment, compass, elbowroom, expanse, latitude, leeway, margin, occasion, office, opportunity, play, range, rope, salon, saloon, scope, space, territory, volume.

roomy *adj* ample, broad, capacious, commodious, extensive, generous, large, sizable, spacious, voluminous, wide.
antonym cramped.

root¹ *n* base, basis, beginning(s), bottom, cause, core, crux, derivation, essence, foundation, fountainhead, fundamental, germ, heart, mainspring, nub, nucleus, origin, radicle, radix, rhizome, root cause, seat, seed, source, starting point, stem, tuber.
v anchor, embed, entrench, establish, fasten, fix, ground, implant, moor, set, sink, stick.

root² *v* burrow, delve, dig, ferret, forage, grout, hunt, nose, poke, pry, rootle, rummage.

root out abolish, clear away, destroy, dig

out, discover, efface, eliminate, eradicate, erase, exterminate, extirpate, ferret out, get rid of, produce, remove, root up, turn up, uncover, unearth, uproot.

antonyms cover, establish.

roots *n* background, beginning(s), birthplace, cradle, family, heritage, home, origins.

rope *n* cable, cord, hawser, lariat, lasso, latitude, leeway, line, marline, noose, room, strand, warp.

v bind, catch, fasten, hitch, lash, lasso, moor, pinion, tether, tie.

rope in embroil, engage, enlist, inveigle, involve, lure, persuade.

antonym keep out.

roster *n* list, listing, register, roll, rota, schedule, table.

rostrum *n* dais, hustings, platform, podium, stage.

rosy *adj* auspicious, blooming, blushing, bright, cheerful, encouraging, favourable, fresh, glowing, healthy-looking, hopeful, optimistic, pink, promising, reassuring, red, reddish, rose, roseate, rose-coloured, rose-hued, roselike, rose-pink, rose-red, rose-scented, rosy-cheeked, rubicund, ruddy, sunny.

antonyms depressed, depressing, sad.

rot *v* corrode, corrupt, crumble, decay, decline, decompose, degenerate, deteriorate, disintegrate, fester, go bad, languish, moulder, perish, putrefy, ret, spoil, taint.

n balderdash, blight, bosh, bunk, bunkum, canker, claptrap, collapse, corrosion, corruption, decay, decomposition, deterioration, disintegration, drivel, flapdoodle, guff, hogwash, moonshine, mould, nonsense, poppycock, putrefaction, putrescence, rubbish, taradiddle, tommyrot, twaddle.

rotary *adj* gyrating, revolving, rotating, rotational, spinning, turning, whirling.

antonym fixed.

rotate *v* alternate, gyrate, interchange, pirouette, pivot, reel, revolve, spell, spin, switch, swivel, turn, twiddle, wheel.

rotation *n* alternation, cycle, gyration, interchanging, orbit, pirouette, reel, revolution, round, sequence, spin, spinning, succession, switching, turn, turning, volution, wheel.

rotten *adj* addled, bad, base, below par, bent, contemptible, corroded, corrupt, crooked, crumbling, crummy, dastardly, decayed, decaying, deceitful, decomposed, decomposing, degenerate, deplorable, despicable, dirty, disagreeable, disappointing, dishonest, dishonourable, disintegrating, disloyal, faithless, festering, fetid, filthy, foul, grotty, ill-considered, ill-thought-out, immoral, inadequate, inferior, lousy, low-grade, mangy, mean, mercenary, mouldering, mouldy, nasty, off-colour, perfidious, perished, poor, poorly, punk, putrescent, putrid, rank, regrettable, rough, scurrilous, sick, sorry, sour, stinking, substandard, tainted, treacherous, unacceptable, unfortunate, unlucky, unpleasant, unsatisfactory, unsound,

untrustworthy, unwell, venal, vicious, vile, wicked.

antonyms good, honest, practical, sensible, well.

rotter *n* bastard, blackguard, blighter, bounder, cad, cur, dastard, fink, louse, rat, scoundrel, stinker, swine.

antonym saint.

rotund *adj* bulbous, chubby, corpulent, fat, fleshy, full, globular, grandiloquent, heavy, magniloquent, obese, orbicular, orblike, orotund, pear-shaped, plump, portly, pudgy, resonant, rich, roly-poly, round, rounded, sonorous, spheral, spherical, spherular, stout, tubby.

antonyms flat, gaunt, slim.

roué *n* debauchee, lecher, libertine, profligate, rake, sensualist, wanton.

rough *adj* agitated, amorphous, approximate, arduous, austere, basic, bluff, blunt, boisterous, boorish, bristly, broken, brusque, bumpy, bushy, cacophonous, chippy, choppy, churlish, coarse, craggy, crude, cruel, cursory, curt, difficult, discordant, discourteous, dishevelled, disordered, draft, drastic, estimated, extreme, fuzzy, general, grating, gruff, hairy, hard, harsh, hasty, husky, ill, ill-bred, ill-mannered, imperfect, impolite, imprecise, inclement, incomplete, inconsiderate, indelicate, inexact, inharmonious, irregular, jagged, jarring, loutish, nasty, off colour, quick, rasping, raspy, raucous, raw, rocky, rough-and-ready, rowdy, rude, rudimentary, rugged, rusty, scabrous, severe, shaggy, sharp, sick, sketchy, spartan, squally, stony, stormy, tangled, tempestuous, tough, tousled, turbulent, unceremonious, uncivil, uncomfortable, uncouth, uncultured, uncut, uneven, unfeeling, unfinished, ungracious, unjust, unmannerly, unmusical, unpleasant, unpolished, unprocessed, unrefined, unshaven, unshorn, untutored, unwell, unwrought, vague, violent, vulgar, wild.

antonyms accurate, calm, harmonious, mild, polite, smooth, well.

n bruiser, bully, draft, hooligan, mock-up, model, outline, roughneck, rowdy, ruffian, sketch, thug, tough.

rough up bash, batter, beat up, do, knock around, maltreat, manhandle, maul, mistreat, mug, thrash.

rough-and-ready *adj* adequate, approximate, crude, improvised, makeshift, provisional, sketchy, stopgap, temporary, unpolished, unrefined.

antonyms exact, refined.

rough-and-tumble *n* affray, brawl, Donnybrook, dustup, fight, fracas, melee, punch-up, rout, ruffle, rumpus, scrap, scuffle, shindy, struggle.

roughen *v* abrade, coarsen, granulate, graze, harshen, rough, scuff.

antonym smooth.

roughneck *n* apache, bruiser, bully, hoodlum, hooligan, rough, rowdy, ruffian, thug, tough.

round *adj* ample, annular, approximate, ball-shaped, blunt, bowed, bulbous, candid, circular, complete, curved, curvilinear, cylindrical, direct, discoid, disc-shaped, entire, explicit, fleshy, forthright, frank, full, full-fleshed, globular, mellifluous, orbicular, orotund, outspoken, plain, plump, resonant, rich, ring-shaped, roly-poly, rotund, rounded, solid, sonorous, spheral, spherical, straightforward, unbroken, undivided, unmodified, whole.

antonyms evasive, niggardly, partial, thin.

n ball, band, beat, bout, bullet, cartridge, circle, circuit, compass, course, cycle, disc, discharge, division, globe, lap, level, orb, period, ring, rotation, routine, schedule, sequence, series, session, shell, shot, sphere, spheroid, spherule, stage, succession, tour, turn.

v bypass, circle, circumnavigate, encircle, flank, sail round, skirt, turn.

round off cap, close, complete, conclude, crown, end, finish, finish off, settle.

antonym begin.

round on abuse, assail, attack, bite (someone's) head off, retaliate, snap at, turn on.

round the bend barmy, batty, bonkers, crazy, cuckoo, daft, dotty, eccentric, insane, mad, nuts, nutty, off one's rocker, screwy.

antonym sane.

round up assemble, collect, drive, gather, gather up (or together), group, herd, marshal, muster, rally.

antonym disperse.

roundabout *adj* ambiguous, circuitous, circumlocutory, devious, discursive, evasive, indirect, meandering, oblique, periphrastic, tortuous, twisting, winding.

antonyms direct, straight, straightforward.

roundly *adv* bluntly, completely, fiercely, forcefully, forthrightly, frankly, in no uncertain terms, intensely, openly, outspokenly, rigorously, severely, sharply, thoroughly, vehemently, violently.

antonym mildly.

roundup *n* assembly, collation, collection, gathering, herding, marshalling, muster, rally.

antonym dispersal.

rouse *v* agitate, anger, animate, arouse, awaken, bestir, call, disturb, enkindle, excite, exhilarate, flush, galvanize, incite, inflame, instigate, move, provoke, start, startle, stimulate, stir, unbed, wake (up), whip up.

antonym calm.

rousing *adj* brisk, electrifying, energizing, excitant, exciting, exhilarating, inflammatory, inspiring, invigorating, lively, moving, spirited, stimulating, stirring, vigorous.

antonym calming.

rout *n* beating, brawl, clamour, crowd, debacle, defeat, disturbance, Donnybrook, drubbing, flight, fracas, fuss, hiding, licking, mob, overthrow, pack, rabble, riot, rookery, ruffle, ruin, shambles, stampede, thrashing.

antonyms calm, win.

v beat, best, chase, conquer, crush, defeat, destroy, discomfit, dispel, drive off, drub, hammer, lick, overthrow, scatter, thrash, worst.

route *n* avenue, beat, circuit, course, direction, flightpath, itinerary, journey, passage, path, road, round, run, way.

v convey, direct, dispatch, forward, send.

routine *n* act, bit, custom, formula, grind, groove, habit, jog trot, line, method, order, pattern, performance, piece, practice, procedure, program, rut, spiel, usage, way, wont.

adj banal, boring, clichéd, conventional, customary, day-to-day, dull, everyday, familiar, habitual, hackneyed, humdrum, mundane, normal, ordinary, predictable, regular, run-of-the-mill, standard, tedious, tiresome, typical, unimaginative, uninspired, unoriginal, usual, wonted, workaday.

antonyms exciting, unusual.

rove *v* cruise, drift, gallivant, meander, ramble, range, roam, stray, stroll, traipse, travel, wander.

antonym stay.

rover *n* drifter, gadabout, gypsy, itinerant, nomad, rambler, ranger, transient, traveller, vagrant, wanderer.

antonym stay-at-home.

row[1] *n* bank, colonnade, column, file, line, queue, range, rank, sequence, series, string, tier.

row[2] *n* altercation, brawl, castigation, commotion, controversy, dispute, disturbance, Donnybrook, dressing-down, falling-out, fight, fracas, fray, fuss, lecture, noise, quarrel, racket, reprimand, reproof, rout, ruckus, ruction, ruffle, rumpus, scrap, shemozzle, shindig, shindy, slanging match, spat, squabble, talking-to, telling-off, tiff, tongue-lashing, trouble, tumult, uproar.

antonym calm.

v argue, argufy, brawl, dispute, fight, quarrel, scrap, squabble, wrangle.

rowdy *adj* boisterous, disorderly, loud, loutish, noisy, obstreperous, rambunctious, roisterous, roisting, rough, unruly, uproarious, wild.

antonyms quiet, restrained.

n brawler, hoodlum, hooligan, rough, roughneck, ruffian, tough, yahoo.

royal *adj* august, grand, imperial, impressive, kinglike, kingly, magnificent, majestic, monarchical, princely, queenlike, queenly, regal, sovereign, splendid, stately, superb, superior.

rub *v* abrade, apply, caress, chafe, clean, embrocate, fray, grate, knead, massage, polish, put, scour, scrape, shine, smear, smooth, spread, stroke, wipe.

n caress, catch, difficulty, drawback, friction, hindrance, hitch, impediment, kneading, massage, obstacle, polish, problem, shine, snag, stroke, trouble, wipe.

rub out assassinate, cancel, delete, efface, erase, expunge, kill, murder, obliterate, remove.

rub the wrong way anger, annoy, bug, get,

get one's goat, get to, get under one's skin, irk, irritate, needle, niggle, peeve, vex.

antonym calm.

rubbish *n* balderdash, baloney, bosh, bunk, claptrap, crap, deadwood, debris, dreck, drivel, dross, eyewash, flotsam and jetsam, garbage, gibberish, gobbledegook, guff, hogwash, junk, kibosh, kitsch, landfill, leavings, litter, lumber, moonshine, nonsense, offal, offscourings, piffle, poppycock, raffle, refuse, riddlings, rot, scoria, scrap, stuff (and nonsense), sweepings, taradiddle, tommyrot, trash, truck, trumpery, twaddle, waste.

antonym sense.

ruddy *adj* blooming, blushing, crimson, florid, flushed, fresh, glowing, healthy, pink, red, reddish, roseate, rose-hued, rose-pink, rosy, rosy-cheeked, rubicund, ruby, sanguine, scarlet, sunburnt.

antonyms pale, unhealthy.

rude *adj* abrupt, abusive, artless, barbarous, blunt, boorish, brusque, brutish, cheeky, churlish, coarse, common, crude, curt, discourteous, disrespectful, graceless, gross, harsh, ignorant, illiterate, ill-mannered, impertinent, impolite, impudent, inartistic, inconsiderate, inelegant, insolent, insulting, loutish, low, makeshift, oafish, obscene, offhand, peremptory, primitive, raw, rough, rustic, savage, scurrilous, sharp, short, simple, startling, sudden, uncivil, uncivilized, uncouth, uncultured, uneducated, ungracious, unlearned, unmannerly, unpleasant, unpolished, unrefined, untutored, violent, vulgar.

antonyms graceful, polished, polite, smooth.

rudeness *n* abruptness, abuse, abusiveness, bad manners, barbarism, bluntness, boorishness, brusqueness, cheek, churlishness, curtness, discourtesy, disrespect, ill manners, impertinence, impoliteness, impudence, incivility, insolence, oafishness, sharpness, uncouthness, vulgarity.

antonym politeness.

rudimentary *adj* abecedarian, basic, beginning, early, elementary, embryonic, emerging, fundamental, germinal, immature, inchoate, initial, introductory, primary, primitive, primordial, undeveloped, vestigial.

antonyms advanced, developed.

rudiments *n* ABCs, basics, beginnings, elements, essentials, foundation, fundamentals, principia, principles, prolegomena.

rue *v* bemoan, bewail, deplore, grieve, lament, mourn, regret, repent.

antonym rejoice.

rueful *adj* conscience-stricken, contrite, dismal, doleful, grievous, long-visaged, lugubrious, melancholy, mournful, penitent, pitiable, pitiful, plaintive, regretful, remorseful, repentant, sad, self-reproachful, sorrowful, sorry, woebegone, woeful.

antonym glad.

ruffian *n* apache, bruiser, brute, bully, cutthroat, hood, hoodlum, hooligan, miscreant, rascal, rogue, rough, roughneck, rowdy, scoundrel, street fighter, thug, tough, villain.

ruffle *v* agitate, annoy, confuse, derange, disarrange, discompose, disconcert, dishevel, disorder, disquiet, disturb, fluster, harass, irritate, mess up, muss up, nettle, peeve, perturb, provoke, rattle, rumple, stir, torment, tousle, trouble, unsettle, upset, vex, worry, wrinkle.

antonym smooth.

rugged *adj* arduous, austere, barbarous, beefy, blunt, brawny, broken, bumpy, burly, churlish, craggy, crude, demanding, difficult, dour, exacting, graceless, gruff, hale, hard, hard-featured, hardy, harsh, husky, irregular, jagged, laborious, muscular, ragged, rigorous, robust, rocky, rough, rude, severe, stark, stern, strenuous, strong, sturdy, taxing, tough, trying, uncompromising, uncouth, uncultured, uneven, unpolished, unrefined, vigorous, weather-beaten, weathered, worn.

antonyms easy, refined, smooth.

ruin *n* bankruptcy, breakdown, collapse, crash, damage, decay, defeat, destitution, destruction, devastation, disintegration, disrepair, dissolution, downfall, failure, fall, havoc, heap, insolvency, nemesis, overthrow, ruination, subversion, undoing, Waterloo, wreck, wreckage.

antonyms development, reconstruction.

v bankrupt, be the death of, botch, break, crush, damage, defeat, demolish, destroy, devastate, disfigure, euchre, impoverish, injure, mangle, mar, mess up, overthrow, overturn, overwhelm, pauperize, raze, scupper, scuttle, shatter, smash, spoil, thwart, undo, unmake, wreck.

antonyms develop, restore.

ruinous *adj* baleful, baneful, broken-down, calamitous, cataclysmic, catastrophic, crippling, deadly, decrepit, deleterious, derelict, destructive, devastating, dilapidated, dire, disastrous, extravagant, fatal, immoderate, injurious, murderous, noxious, pernicious, ramshackle, ruined, shattering, wasteful, withering.

antonym beneficial.

ruins *n* ashes, chaos, debris, devastation, havoc, shambles, shattered remains, tatters.

rule *n* administration, ascendancy, authority, axiom, canon, command, condition, control, convention, course, criterion, custom, decree, direction, domination, dominion, empire, form, formula, governance, government, guide, guideline, influence, institute, jurisdiction, law, leadership, maxim, method, norm, order, ordinance, policy, power, practice, precept, prescript, principle, procedure, regime, regulation, reign, routine, ruling, sovereignty, standard, supremacy, sway, tenet, way, wont.

v adjudge, adjudicate, administer, command, control, decide, declare, decree, determine, direct, dominate, establish, find, govern, guide, judge, lead, manage, obtain, order, pass judgment, predominate, preponderate, prevail, pronounce, regulate, reign, resolve, settle.

as a rule characteristically, customarily,

run-down

generally, habitually, in most cases, mainly, most often, normally, ordinarily, regularly, typically, usually.

rule out ban, debar, disallow, dismiss, eliminate, exclude, forbid, obviate, preclude, prevent, prohibit, proscribe, reject.

ruler *n* commander, controller, dictator, emperor, empress, governor, gubernator, head of state, imperator, king, leader, lord, monarch, potentate, prince, princess, queen, sovereign, suzerain.

antonym subject.

ruling *n* adjudication, decision, declaration, decree, finding, judgment, pronouncement, resolution, ukase, verdict.

adj chief, commanding, controlling, dominant, governing, leading, main, number-one, predominant, pre-eminent, preponderant, prevailing, prevalent, principal, regnant, reigning, supreme, top, upper.

ruminate *v* brood, chew over, chew the cud, cogitate, consider, contemplate, deliberate, meditate, mull over, muse, ponder, reflect, revolve, think.

rummage *v* delve, dig, hunt, poke around, ransack, root, rout, search.

rumour *n* breeze, bruit, bush telegraph, buzz, canard, gossip, grapevine, hearsay, news, report, story, talk, tidings, whisper, word.

v advertise, bruit, circulate, gossip, noise abroad, publish, put around, report, say, tell, whisper.

rump *n* backside, bottom, bum, buttocks, croup, dock, haunch, hindquarters, nache, posterior, rear, seat.

rumple *v* crease, crinkle, crumple, crush, disarrange, dishevel, disorder, muss (up), pucker, ruffle, scrunch, tousle, wrinkle.

antonym smooth.

rumpus *n* ballyhoo, brouhaha, commotion, confusion, disruption, disturbance, Donnybrook, foofaraw, fracas, free-for-all, furor, fuss, hullabaloo, kafuffle, noise, rout, row, schmozzle, shindig, shindy, tumult, uproar.

antonym calm.

run *v* abscond, administer, bear, beat it, bleed, bolt, boss, career, carry, cascade, circulate, clear out, climb, conduct, continue, control, convey, co-ordinate, course, creep, dart, dash, decamp, depart, direct, discharge, display, dissolve, drive, escape, extend, feature, flee, flow, function, fuse, gallop, glide, go, gush, hare, hasten, head, hie, hightail it, hotfoot, hurry, incur, issue, jog, ladder, last, lead, leak, light out, liquefy, lope, manage, manoeuvre, mastermind, melt, move, operate, oversee, own, pass, perform, ply, pour, print, proceed, propel, publish, race, range, ravel, regulate, roll, rush, scamper, scarper, scramble, scud, scurry, skedaddle, skim, slide, smuggle, speed, spill, spout, spread, sprint, stream, stretch, superintend, supervise, take off, tear, tick, trail, transport, unravel, work.

antonyms stay, stop.

n chain, coop, course, current, cycle, dash, demand, direction, drift, drive, duration, enclosure, excursion, flow, gallop, jaunt, jog, journey, ladder, movement, outing, passage, path, pen, period, pressure, progress, race, ride, rip, round, rush, season, sequence, series, snag, spell, spin, sprint, spurt, streak, stream, stretch, string, tear, tide, trend, trip, variety, way.

run after chase, follow, hound, hunt down, pursue, stalk, tag along after, tail.

antonym flee.

run away (or off) abscond, beat it, bolt, clear out, decamp, elope, escape, flee, scarper, scoot, scram, skedaddle, take it on the lam.

antonym stay.

run down belittle, capture, criticize, debilitate, decrease, decry, defame, denigrate, deteriorate, disparage, drop, exhaust, flag, hit, knock, knock over, reduce, revile, run over, run to earth, strike, tire, vilify, weaken, wind down.

antonyms increase, miss, praise.

run for it bolt, escape, flee, fly, head for the hills, make a break for it, make off, retreat, scarper, scram, skedaddle.

antonym stay.

run in apprehend, arrest, bust, capture, collar, jail, nab, pick up.

run into bash, collide with, come across, crash into, encounter, hit, meet, ram, strike.

antonyms avoid, miss.

run off abscond, bolt, decamp, drain, drive off (or away), duplicate, elope, escape, flee, make off, print, produce, scarper, siphon, skedaddle, take to one's heels.

antonym stay.

run out cease, close, dry up, elapse, end, expire, fail, finish, terminate.

run over hit, knock down, overflow, practise, rehearse, repeat, reiterate, review, run down, spill, strike, survey.

run riot cut loose, go on the rampage, kick over the traces, rampage, run amuck, run rampant, sow one's wild oats, spread.

run through dissipate, examine, exhaust, fritter away, impale, pierce, practise, read, rehearse, review, spend, spit, squander, stab, stick, survey, transfix, waste.

run together amalgamate, blend, coalesce, combine, commingle, fuse, intermingle, intermix, join, merge, mingle, mix, unite.

antonym separate.

runaway *n* absconder, deserter, escapee, escaper, fugitive, refugee, truant.

adj escaped, fleeing, fugitive, loose, uncontrolled, wild.

rundown *n* briefing, outline, précis, recap, résumé, review, run-through, sketch, summary, synopsis.

run-down *adj* badly maintained, broken-down, debilitated, decrepit, dilapidated, dingy, drained, enervated, exhausted, fatigued, grotty, ill-kept, neglected, peaked, ramshackle, scabby, seedy, shabby, tumbledown, unhealthy, weak, weary, worn-out.

antonym well-kept.

run-in *n* altercation, argument, brush, confrontation, contretemps, difference of opinion, dispute, dustup, encounter, fight, quarrel, set-to, skirmish, tussle, wrangle.

runner[1] *n* athlete, competitor, courier, harrier, jogger, messenger, miler, participant, sprinter.

runner[2] *n* flagellum, offshoot, sarmentum, shoot, sprig, sprout, stem, stolon, tendril.

running *adj* consecutive, constant, continuous, current, cursive, flowing, incessant, moving, ongoing, perpetual, streaming, successive, unbroken, unceasing, uninterrupted.

antonyms broken, ceased, occasional.

n administration, charge, competition, conduct, contention, contest, control, co-ordination, direction, functioning, going, leadership, maintenance, management, operation, organization, pace, performance, race, regulation, superintendency, supervision, working.

runny *adj* dilute, diluted, flowing, fluid, liquefied, liquid, melted, molten, watery.

antonym solid.

run-of-the-mill *adj* average, common, commonplace, everyday, fair, mediocre, middling, modest, ordinary, passable, routine, tolerable, undistinguished, unexceptional, unexciting, unimaginative, unimpressive, unremarkable.

antonym exceptional.

rupture *n* altercation, breach, break, breaking off, burst, bust-up, cleavage, cleft, contention, crack, disagreement, disruption, dissolution, estrangement, falling-out, feud, fissure, fracture, hernia, hostility, quarrel, rent, rift, schism, split, splitting, tear.

v break, burst, cleave, crack, disrupt, dissever, divide, fracture, puncture, rend, separate, sever, split, sunder, tear.

rural *adj* agrarian, agricultural, Arcadian, bucolic, countrified, country, pastoral, rustic, sylvan.

antonym urban.

ruse *n* artifice, blind, deception, device, dodge, hoax, imposture, manoeuvre, ploy, sham, stall, stratagem, subterfuge, trick, wile.

rush *v* accelerate, attack, bolt, bustle, capture, career, charge, dart, dash, dispatch, expedite, fly, gush, hasten, hightail it, hotfoot, hurry, hustle, overcome, pour, press, push, quicken, race, run, scour, scramble, scurry, shoot, speed, speed up, sprint, stampede, storm, tear, wallop, whoosh.

n assault, attack, buzz, charge, dash, dispatch, expedition, flood, flow, haste, high, hurry, onslaught, push, race, scramble, spate, speed, stampede, storm, streak, surge, swiftness, tantivy, tear, urgency.

adj eleventh-hour, express, emergency, expeditious, fast, last-minute, priority, speedy, urgent.

rushed *adj* breathless, careless, cursory, hasty, hurried, last-minute, precipitate, pressed for time, running late, slapdash, taken (or done) on the fly.

rust *n* blight, corrosion, fungus, mildew, mould, must, oxidation, patina, rot, stain, verdigris.

v atrophy, corrode, corrupt, decay, decline, degenerate, deteriorate, oxidize, rot, stagnate, tarnish.

rust-coloured *adj* auburn, chestnut, copper, coppery, ginger, gingery, red, reddish, reddish-brown, russet, rusty, sandy, tawny, titian.

rustic *adj* agrarian, Arcadian, artless, awkward, boorish, bucolic, churlish, cloddish, clodhopping, clownish, clumsy, coarse, countrified, country, crude, graceless, hick, homey, homespun, loutish, lumpish, maladroit, oafish, pastoral, plain, provincial, rough, rude, rural, simple, sylvan, unaffected, uncouth, uncultured, unmannerly, unpolished, unrefined, unsophisticated, yokelish.

antonyms cultivated, polished, sophisticated, urban, urbane.

n boor, bumpkin, churl, clod, clodhopper, clown, country cousin, countryman, countrywoman, farmer, hayseed, hick, hillbilly, hind, kern, oaf, peasant, ploughboy, provincial, swain, yokel.

antonyms dandy, man-about-town, sophisticate.

rustle *v* crackle, crepitate, susurrate, swish, whish, whisper.

n crackle, crepitation, crinkling, rustling, susurration, swish, whish, whisper, whispering.

rusty *adj* aeruginous, ancient, antiquated, antique, corroded, creaking, creaky, croaking, croaky, dated, discoloured, dull, encrusted, hoarse, old-fashioned, outmoded, oxidized, passé, raucous, rough, rust-covered, rusted, sluggish, stagnated, stale, stiff, tarnished, timeworn, unpractised, weak.

rut *n* channel, ditch, furrow, gouge, groove, gutter, habit, indentation, pattern, pothole, routine, score, sulcus, system, track, trough, wheelmark.

v channel, cut, furrow, gouge, groove, hole, indent, mark, score.

ruthless *adj* adamant, adamantine, barbarous, brutal, callous, cruel, cutthroat, despotic, dog-eat-dog, ferocious, fierce, hard, hard-hearted, harsh, heartless, implacable, inexorable, inhuman, iron-fisted, merciless, pitiless, relentless, remorseless, savage, severe, stern, stony, unfeeling, unmerciful, unpitying, unrelenting.

antonyms compassionate, merciful.

S

sable *adj* black, coal-black, dark, dusky, ebon, ebony, inky, jet, jetty, midnight, pitch-black, pitch-dark, pitchy, raven.

sabotage *v* cripple, damage, destroy, disable, disrupt, incapacitate, mar, nullify, ruin, scupper, spoil, subvert, thwart, undermine, vandalize, vitiate, wreck.

n damage, destruction, disablement, disruption, impairment, marring, subversion, treachery, treason, undermining, vandalism, vitiation, wrecking.

sac *n* bag, bladder, bursa, capsule, cyst, follicle, pocket, pod, pouch, theca, vesica, vesicle.

saccharine *adj* cloying, honeyed, maudlin, mawkish, nauseating, oversweet, schmaltzy, sentimental, sickly, sickly-sweet, sloppy, soppy, sugary, syrupy, treacly.

antonyms bitter, tart.

sack¹ *v* axe, discharge, dismiss, fire, lay off, make redundant.

antonym hire.

sack² *v* demolish, desecrate, despoil, destroy, devastate, lay waste, level, loot, maraud, pillage, plunder, raid, rape, ravage, raze, rifle, rob, ruin, spoil, strip, waste.

antonym build (up).

n depredation, desecration, despoliation, destruction, devastation, levelling, looting, marauding, pillage, plunder, plundering, rape, rapine, ravage, razing, ruin, waste.

the sack discharge, dismissal, notice, one's marching orders, one's walking papers, pink slip, the axe, the boot, the bum's rush, the sack.

sacred *adj* blessed, consecrated, dedicated, devotional, divine, ecclesiastical, godly, hallowed, heavenly, holy, inspirational, inviolable, inviolate, priestly, protected, religious, revered, sacrosanct, saintly, sanctified, secure, solemn, spiritual, venerable, venerated.

antonyms mundane, profane, temporal.

sacrifice *v* abandon, destroy, forego, forfeit, give up, immolate, let go, lose, offer, relinquish, renounce, slaughter, surrender.

n cost, destruction, expense, hecatomb, holocaust, immolation, loss, oblation, offering, renunciation, surrender, victim, votive offering.

sacrificial *adj* atoning, expiatory, oblatory, propitiatory, reparative, votive.

sacrilege *n* blasphemy, defilement, desecration, disrespect, heresy, impiety, impiousness, irreverence, mockery, outrage, profanation, profaneness, profanity, violation.

antonyms piety, respect, reverence.

sacrilegious *adj* blasphemous, desecrating, disrespectful, heretical, impious, irreligious, irreverent, profanatory, profane, ungodly, unholy.

antonyms pious, respectful, reverent.

sacrosanct *adj* hallowed, holy, impregnable, inviolable, inviolate, revered, sacred, sanctified, untouchable.

sad *adj* bad, blue, calamitous, cheerless, chapfallen, crestfallen, crushed, dark, dejected, deplorable, depressed, depressing, desolated, despairing, despondent, disastrous, disconsolate, discouraged, disheartened, dismal, dispirited, distressed, distressing, doleful, dolorous, dour, down, downcast, downhearted, (down) in the dumps, drear, dreary, dull, funereal, gloomy, glum, grave, grief-stricken, grieved, grieving, grievous, heartbreaking, heartbroken, heart-rending, heavy, heavy-hearted, hopeless, in the doldrums, jaw-fallen, joyless, lachrymose, lamentable, long-faced, low, low-spirited, lugubrious, melancholy, miserable, mournful, moving, painful, pathetic, pensive, piteous, pitiable, pitiful, plainting, pleasureless, poignant, regrettable, saddened, sombre, sorrowful, sorry, tearful, touching, tragic, uncheerful, unfortunate, unhappy, upsetting, wistful, woebegone, woeful, wretched.

antonyms cheerful, fortunate, happy, lucky.

sadden *v* aggrieve, cast a pall over, dash, deject, depress, desolate, discourage, dishearten, dispirit, distress, grieve, hurt, oppress, upset.

antonyms cheer, delight, gratify, please.

saddle *v* burden, charge, encumber, impose, land, load, lumber, task, tax.

sadistic *adj* atrocious, barbarous, bestial, brutal, callous, cruel, heartless, inhuman, malevolent, perverted, ruthless, savage, unnatural, vicious.

sadness *n* bleakness, cheerlessness, darkness (of the soul), dejection, depression, desolation, despair, despondency, disconsolateness, dismalness, distress, dole, dolefulness, dolour, gloominess, glumness, gravity, grief, hopelessness, joylessness, low spirits, lugubriousness, melancholy, misery, misfortune, mournfulness, pain, pathos, poignancy, regret, sombreness, sorrow, sorrowfulness, tearfulness, tragedy, unhappiness, wanness, wistfulness, woe, wretchedness.

antonyms cheerfulness, delight, happiness.

safe *adj* alive and well, all in one piece, all right, careful, cautious, certain, circumspect, conservative, dependable, discreet, fail-safe, foolproof, guarded, hale (and hearty), harmless, immune, impregnable, innocuous, intact, in the clear, invulnerable, non-poisonous, non-toxic, OK, out of danger, out of harm's way, out of the woods, protected, proven, prudent, reliable, risk-free, scatheless, secure, sound, sure, tame, tested, tried (and true), trustworthy, unadventurous, uncontaminated, undamaged, unfailing, unharmed, unhurt, uninjured, unscathed, wholesome.

antonyms exposed, harmful, unsafe, vulnerable.

n coffer, deposit box, (money) chest, repository, strongbox, strongroom, vault.

safe-conduct *n* authorization, convoy, escort, laissez passer, licence, pass, passport, permit, safeguard, warrant.

safeguard *v* assure, defend, guard, insure, preserve, protect, screen, secure, shelter, shield.

antonyms endanger, jeopardize.

n armour, assurance, bulwark, convoy, cover, defence, escort, guarantee, guard, insurance, palladium, precaution, preventive (measure), protection, security, shield, surety.

safekeeping *n* aegis, care, charge, custody, guard, guardianship, keeping, lock and key, protection, preservation, supervision, surveillance, trust, tutelage, vigilance, ward, wardship, watch, watchful eye.

safety *n* assurance, cover, deliverance, dependability, harmlessness, immunity, impregnability, invulnerability, protection, refuge, reliability, safeguard, salvation, sanctuary, security, shelter, sureness.

antonyms danger, jeopardy.

adj precautionary, preventive, prophylactic, protective, security.

sag *v* bag, decline, dip, drag, droop, drop, dwindle, fail, fall (off), flag, give, give way, hang, settle, sink, slide, slip, slump, wane, weaken, wilt.

antonyms bulge, rise.

n decline, depression, dip, downturn, drop, dwindling, fall, low, low point, reduction, slide, slip, slump.

antonyms peak, rise.

saga *n* adventure, chronicle, epic, epopee, epos, history, narrative, romance, roman-fleuve, soap opera, story, tale, yarn.

sagacious *adj* able, acute, apt, astute, canny, cogent, discerning, far-sighted, foresightful, insightful, intelligent, judicious, knowing, long-headed, long-sighted, penetrating, perceptive, percipient, perspicacious, quick,

sage, sapient, sharp, shrewd, smart, wide-awake, wise.

antonyms foolish, obtuse, short-sighted.

sagacity *n* acumen, acuteness, astuteness, canniness, discernment, foresight, insight, judgment, judiciousness, knowingness, penetration, perception, percipience, perspicacity, prudence, sapience, sense, sharpness, shrewdness, understanding, wisdom.

antonyms folly, foolishness, obtuseness.

sage *adj* astute, canny, discerning, intelligent, judicious, knowing, knowledgeable, learned, perspicacious, politic, prudent, sagacious, sapient, sensible, wise.

antonym foolish.

n authority, elder, expert, guru, maharishi, mahatma, master, Nestor, oracle, philosopher, pundit, rishi, savant, Solomon, Solon, teacher, wise man.

antonym ignoramus.

sail *v* captain, cruise, drift, embark, float, fly, glide, navigate, pilot, plane, put to sea, scud, set sail, shoot, skim, skipper, soar, steer, sweep, take ship, voyage, waft, weigh anchor, wing.

sail into assault, attack, criticize, fly at, fly into, lambaste, lay into, let fly at, light into, pitch into, set upon, tear a strip off, tear into.

sailor *n* AB, able-bodied seaman, able seaman, hearty, Jack Tar, leatherneck, limey, marine, mariner, matelot, navigator, rating, salt, seafarer, seaman, tar.

saintliness *n* blessedness, chastity, devoutness, faith, godliness, goodness, holiness, morality, piety, purity, righteousness, sanctity, self-denial, selflessness, self-sacrifice, spirituality, spotlessness, unselfishness, uprightness, virtue.

antonyms godlessness, unholiness, wickedness.

saintly *adj* angelic, beatific, blameless, blessed, celestial, devout, God-fearing, godly, good, holy, immaculate, innocent, pious, pure, religious, righteous, sainted, saintlike, seraphic, sinless, spotless, stainless, upright, virtuous, worthy.

antonyms godless, unholy, unrighteous, wicked.

sake *n*

for the sake of for the benefit of, for the gain (or good) of, for the purpose of, for the welfare (or well-being) of, in (or for) the cause (or interest) of, on account (or behalf) of, on the principle of, out of consideration for, out of regard (or respect) for, out of the motive of, with the aim (or objective) of.

salacious *adj* bawdy, blue, carnal, coarse, concupiscent, dirty, erotic, improper, indecent, lascivious, lecherous, lewd, libidinous, lustful, obscene, pornographic, prurient, raunchy, ribald, ruttish, scurrilous, sexually explicit, sexy, smutty, steamy, sultry, wanton.

antonyms clean, decent, proper.

salaried *adj* paid, regular, remunerated, stipendiary, waged.

antonyms honorary, unpaid, voluntary.

salary *n* earnings, emolument, honorarium, income, pay, remuneration, stipend, wage, wages.

sale *n* auction, deal, disposal, marketing, sell, selling, trade, traffic, transaction, vending, vendition, vendue.

saleable *adj* desirable, marketable, merchantable, sought-after, vendible.

antonyms unmarketable, unsaleable.

salesperson *n* agent, clerk, sales agent, sales assistant, salesclerk, saleslady, salesman, saleswoman, seller, shop assistant, shopkeeper, vendeuse.

salient *adj* arresting, chief, conspicuous, important, jutting, main, marked, notable, noticeable, obvious, outstanding, principal, projecting, prominent, pronounced, protruding, remarkable, signal, significant, striking.

sallow *adj* anemic, bilious, colourless, pale, pallid, pasty, sickly, unhealthy, wan, yellowish.

antonyms rosy, sanguine.

sally[1] *v* breeze, charge, erupt, foray, issue, mosey, promenade, retire, rush, saunter, set, sortie, start, stroll, surge, venture.

antonym retreat.

n assault, dash, drive, escapade, excursion, foray, incursion, jaunt, journey, offensive, raid, rush, sortie, surge, thrust, trip, venture.

antonym retreat.

sally[2] *n* bon mot, comeback, crack, jest, joke, quip, retort, riposte, wisecrack, witticism.

salt *n* acuteness, Attic salt (or wit), bite, dryness, flavour, liveliness, piquancy, punch, pungency, relish, saltiness, sarcasm, savour, seasoning, sharpness, smack, taste, trenchancy, vigour, wit, wittiness, zest, zip.

adj Attic, brackish, briny, saline, salted, salty, witty.

antonyms bland, fresh.

salt away accumulate, amass, bank, cache, collect, hide, hoard, lay in (or by), put away for a rainy day, save, squirrel away, stash, stockpile, stock up, store up, stow away.

antonyms spend, squander.

salty *adj* brackish, briny, colourful, dry, humorous, keen, lively, piquant, pungent, racy, saline, salt, salted, spicy, tangy, tart, witty, wry, zestful.

salubrious *adj* beneficial, bracing, healthful, health-giving, healthy, hygienic, invigorating, refreshing, restorative, salutary, sanitary, tonic, wholesome.

antonyms insalubrious, unwholesome.

salutary *adj* advantageous, beneficial, good (for one), healthful, healthy, helpful, much-needed, practical, profitable, salubrious, seasonable, timely, useful, valuable, wholesome.

salutation *n* address, greeting, homage, obeisance, respects, reverence, salaam, salute, welcome.

salute *v* accost, acknowledge, address, applaud, bow to, greet, hail, honour, kiss, nod, pay homage to, recognize, salaam, wave, welcome.

n acknowledgment, address, bow, gesture, greeting, hail, handshake, hello, homage, kiss, nod, obeisance, recognition, reverence, salaam, salutation, salvo, tribute, wave.

salvage *v* conserve, glean, preserve, reclaim, recover, recuperate, redeem, repair, rescue, restore, retrieve, salve, save.

antonyms abandon, lose, waste.

salvation *n* deliverance, escape, liberation, lifeline, preservation, reclamation, redemption, rescue, restoration, retrieval, safety, saving, soteriology.

antonyms damnation, loss.

salve *n* application, balm, cream, dressing, embrocation, emollient, liniment, lotion, lubricant, medication, ointment, preparation, unguent.

same *adj* aforementioned, aforesaid, alike, analogous, changeless, comparable, consistent, corresponding, duplicate, equal, equivalent, homologous, identical, indistinguishable, interchangeable, invariable, matching, mutual, one, one and the same, reciprocal, selfsame, similar, substitutable, synonymous, twin, unaltered, unchanged, undiminished, unfailing, uniform, unvarying, very.

antonyms changeable, different, incompatible, inconsistent, variable.

sameness *n* changelessness, consistency, déja vu, duplication, identicalness, identity, indistinguishability, invariability, likeness, monotony, oneness, predictability, repetition, resemblance, similarity, standardization, tedium, uniformity.

antonyms difference, inconsistency, variety.

sample *n* cross section, demonstration, example, exemplification, foretaste, free sample, freebie, illustration, indication, instance, model, pattern, representative, sampling, sign, specimen, swatch, taste, template.

v experience, inspect, investigate, sip, taste, test, try out.

adj demonstration, illustrative, pilot, representative, specimen, test, trial, trial-size.

sanctify *v* anoint, bless, cleanse, consecrate, dedicate, exalt, hallow, make holy, purify, sanction.

antonyms defile, degrade, desecrate.

sanctimonious *adj* canting, false, goody-goody, holier-than-thou, hypocritical, moralizing, pharisaic, pietistic, pious, preaching, preachy, priggish, self-righteous, self-satisfied, smug, superior, unctuous, zealous.

antonym humble.

sanctimoniousness *n* cant, canting, complacency, hypocrisy, moralizing, pharisaism, pietism, preachiness, priggishness, religiosity, self-righteousness, self-satisfaction, smugness, unctuousness.

antonym humility.

sanction *n* accreditation, agreement, allowance, approbation, approval, authorization, authority, backing, cachet, consent, countenance, endorsement, fiat, go-ahead, green light, imprimatur, legalization, licence, OK, permission, ratification, seal, seal of approval, support.

antonyms disapproval, veto.

v accredit, allow, approve, authorize, back, consent to, countenance, countersign, endorse, legalize, license, permit, ratify, support, underwrite, warrant.

antonyms disallow, disapprove, veto.

sanctions *n* ban, boycott, embargo, interdict, penalty, prohibition, proscription, restrictions.

sanctity *n* devotion, godliness, goodness, grace, holiness, inviolability, piety, purity, religiousness, righteousness, sacredness, sacrosanctity, saintliness, saintship, sanctitude, spirituality, venerableness.

antonyms godlessness, impurity, secularity, unholiness, worldliness.

sanctuary *n* altar, ark, asylum, chancel, church, harbourage, haven, hiding place, holy of holies, inner sanctum, naos, presbytery, protection, refuge, retreat, sanctum, sanctum sanctorum, seclusion, shelter, shrine, tabernacle, temple.

sanctum *n* cubbyhole, den, growlery, hideaway, hide-out, hidey-hole, holy of holies, refuge, retreat, sanctuary, sanctum sanctorum, shrine, snuggery, study.

sand *n* beach, gravel, grit, sands, shore, strand.

sandbank *n* bar, barachois, cay, dune, key, reef, sand bar, sandspit.

sandy *adj* arenaceous, brownish-yellow, ginger, grainy, granular, gritty, light-brown, reddish-yellow, tawny, xanthous, yellow, yellowish, yellowy.

sane *adj* all there, balanced, compos mentis, dependable, in one's right mind, judicious, level-headed, lucid, moderate, normal, of sound mind, rational, reasonable, reliable, right-minded, sensible, sober, sound, stable.

sang-froid *n* aplomb, assurance, calmness, composure, cool, cool-headedness, coolness, dispassion, equanimity, imperturbability, indifference, nerve, nonchalance, phlegm, poise, self-control, self-possession, unexcitability, unflappability.

antonyms discomposure, excitability, hysteria, panic.

sanguinary *adj* bloodied, bloodstrained, bloodthirsty, bloody, brutal, cruel, fell, gory, grim, merciless, murderous, pitiless, ruthless, savage, warring, warlike.

sanguine[1] *adj* animated, ardent, assured, buoyant, cheerful, confident, expectant, hopeful, lively, optimistic, roseate, spirited, unabashed, unappalled, unbowed.

antonyms cynical, depressive, gloomy, melancholy, pessimistic.

sanguine[2] *adj* florid, flushed, fresh, fresh-complexioned, pink, red, roseate, rosy, rubicund, ruddy.

antonyms pale, sallow.

sanitary *adj* aseptic, clean, disinfected, germ-free, healthy, hygienic, pure, salubrious, uncontaminated, unpolluted, wholesome.

antonyms insanitary, unwholesome.

sanity *n* balance of mind, common sense, judiciousness, level-headedness, lucidity, mental health, moderation, normalcy, rationality, reason, reasonableness, right mind, saneness, sense, sound mind, soundness of mind, stability.

antonyms foolishness, insanity.

sap *v* bleed, deplete, devitalize, diminish, drain, enervate, exhaust, impair, reduce, rob, undermine, weaken.

antonyms build up, increase, strengthen.

sarcasm *n* acidity, bitterness, contempt, cynicism, derision, diatribe, invective, irony, mockery, mordancy, satire, scorn, sneering, venom, vitriol.

sarcastic *adj* acerbic, acid, acrimonious, biting, caustic, contemptuous, cutting, cynical, derisive, disparaging, incisive, mocking, mordant, sardonic, satirical, scathing, sharp, sharp-tongued, sneering, stinging, taunting, vitriolic, withering.

sardonic *adj* biting, bitter, cynical, derisive, dry, heartless, jeering, malevolent, malicious, malignant, mocking, mordant, quizzical, sarcastic, satirical, scornful, sneering, wry.

sash *n* baldric, belt, cincture, cummerbund, girdle, surcingle, vitta, waistband, zone.

Satan *n* Apollyon, archenemy, archfiend, Beelzebub, Belial, Lucifer, Mephistopheles, Old Harry, Old Nick, Old Scratch, Prince of Darkness, the Adversary, the Devil, the Enemy, the Evil One, the Tempter.

satanic *adj* accursed, demoniac, demoniacal, demonic, devilish, diabolical, evil, fell, fiendish, hellish, infernal, inhuman, iniquitous, malevolent, malignant, Mephistophelian, vicious, wicked,.

antonyms benevolent, benign, divine, godlike, godly, heavenly, holy.

sate *v* cloy, fill, glut, gorge, gratify, overfill, satiate, satisfy, saturate, sicken, slake, surfeit, weary.

antonyms deprive, dissatisfy, starve.

satellite *n* adherent, aide, attendant, dependant, disciple, follower, hanger-on, lackey, minion, moon, parasite, puppet, retainer, sidekick, sputnik, subordinate, sycophant, tributary, vassal, votary.

satiate *v* cloy, engorge, glut, gorge, jade, nauseate, overfeed, overfill, overload, sate, satisfy, slake, stuff, surfeit.

antonyms deprive, dissatisfy, underfeed.

satiety *n* fullness, gratification, overfullness, overindulgence, repleteness, repletion, satiation, satisfaction, saturation, surfeit.

satire *n* burlesque, caricature, diatribe, farce, invective, irony, lampoon, parody, pasquinade, raillery, ridicule, sarcasm, sendup, skit, spoof, squib, takeoff, travesty, wit.

satirical *adj* biting, bitter, burlesque, caustic, cutting, cynical, derisive, incisive, ironic, irreverent, mocking, mordant, pungent, Rabelaisian, sarcastic, sardonic, satiric, taunting.

satirize *v* abuse, burlesque, caricature, censure, criticize, deride, lampoon, make fun of, make sport of, mock, parody, pasquinade, pillory, ridicule, send up, squib, take off (on), travesty.

antonyms acclaim, celebrate, honour.

satisfaction *n* achievement, amends, appeasment, assuagment, atonement, comfort, compensation, complacency, content, contentedness, contentment, damages, ease, enjoyment, fulfilment, fullness, gratification, guerdon, happiness, indemnification, justice, pacification, payment, pleasure, pride, quittance, recompense, redress, reimbursement, remuneration, reparation, repayment, repleteness, repletion, requital, resolution, restitution, reward, satiety, self-satisfaction, sense of achievement, settlement, vindication, well-being.

antonyms discontent, displeasure, dissatisfaction, frustration.

satisfactory *adj* acceptable, adequate, all right, average, competent, convincing, fair, fit, good enough, OK, passable, proper, sufficient, suitable, tickety-boo, up to scratch (or snuff), up to the mark.

antonyms inadequate, unacceptable, unsatisfactory.

satisfied *adj* appeased, complacent, content, contented, convinced, full, happy, mollified, pacified, persuaded, pleased, positive, quenched, reassured, replete, sated, satiated, self-satisfied, slaked, smug, sure.

antonyms dissatisfied, hungry, unconvinced.

satisfy *v* answer, appease, assuage, assure, atone (for), compensate, content, convince, delight, discharge, do, feed, fill, fulfil, glut, gratify, guerdon, indemnify, indulge, meet, mollify, pacify, pay (in full), persuade, placate, please, qualify, quench, quiet, reassure, recompense, reimburse, remunerate, replete, requite, reward, sate, satiate, serve, settle, slake, square up, suffice, surfeit.

antonyms disappoint, dissatisfy, fail, frustrate, thwart.

satisfying *adj* cheering, convincing, cool, filling, fulfilling, gratifying, persuasive, pleasing, pleasurable, satisfactory.

antonyms dissatisfying, frustrating, thwarting, unsatisfactory.

saturate *v* douse, drench, imbue, impregnate, infuse, permeate, ret, soak, souse, steep, suffuse, waterlog.

saturated *adj* drenched, dripping, imbued, impregnated, permeated, soaked, soaking, sodden, soggy, sopping, soused, steeped, suffused, waterlogged, wet through, wringing.

saturnine *adj* austere, dismal, dour, dull, gloomy, glum, grave, grim, heavy, melancholy, mirthless, moody, morose, phlegmatic, severe, sombre, stern, taciturn, uncommunicative, withdrawn.

antonyms cheerful, jovial.

satyr *n* faun, goat, lecher, Pan, philanderer, womanizer.

saucy *adj* arch, audacious, brassy, brazen, cheeky, dashing, disdainful, disrespectful, flip, flippant, forward, fresh, gay, impertinent, impudent, insolent, irreverent, jaunty, lippy, malapert, mouthy, perky, pert, presumptuous, provocative, rakish, rude, sassy, smart, sporty.

antonyms polite, respectful.

saunter *v* amble, dally, dander, dawdle, linger, loiter, meander, mosey, perambulate, promenade, ramble, roam, rove, sally forth, stroll, wander.

n airing, amble, breather, constitutional, outing, perambulation, promenade, ramble, sally, stroll, turn, walk.

savage *adj* barbarous, beastly, bestial, blistering, bloodthirsty, bloody, brutal, brutish, cruel, devilish, diabolical, dog-eat-dog, enraged, fell, feral, ferocious, fierce, harsh, infuriated, inhuman, merciless, murderous, pitiless, primitive, ravening, rough, rude, rugged, ruthless, sadistic, sanguinary, uncivilized, uncouth, uncultivated, undomesticated, uneducated, unenlightened, unsparing, untamed, untaught, vicious, violent, warlike, warring, wild.

antonyms benign, civilized, humane.

n animal, barbarian, bear, beast, boor, brute, fiend, Goth, monster, oaf, philistine, primitive, roughneck, yahoo.

v abuse, attack, claw, hammer, lacerate, mangle, maul, mistreat, pan, scarify, shred, tear to pieces.

savagery *n* barbarity, bestiality, bloodthirstiness, brutality, brutishness, cruelty, ferity, ferocity, fierceness, inhumanity, mercilessness, murderousness, pitilessness, primitiveness, roughness, ruthlessness, sadism, viciousness, violence, wildness.

antonyms civilization, civility, humanity.

savant *n* authority, guru, intellectual, man of letters, master, mastermind, philosopher, pundit, rishi, sage, scholar.

antonyms amateur, duffer, ignoramus.

save *v* cache, collect, conserve, cut back, deliver, economize, free, gather, guard, hinder, hoard, hold, husband, keep, lay up, liberate, obviate, preserve, prevent, protect, put aside, put by, reclaim, recover, redeem, rescue, reserve, retain, retrench, safeguard, salt away, salvage, screen, shield, spare, squirrel away, stash, store up.

antonyms discard, spend, squander, waste.

saving *adj* careful, compensatory, economical, economizing, efficient, extenuating, frugal, mitigating, preservative, qualifying, redeeming, sparing, thrifty.

antonyms damning, wasteful.

n bargain, conservation, cut, discount, economy, preservation, reclamation, redemption, reduction, rescue, retrenchment, salvage, salvation.

antonyms expense, loss, waste.

savings *n* capital, fund, nest egg, reserve fund, reserves, resources, store(s).

saviour *n* champion, defender, emancipator, guardian, knight errant, liberator, messiah, preserver, protector, redeemer, rescuer, salvation.

antonyms destroyer, enemy.

savoir-faire *n* acumen, address, assurance, confidence, diplomacy, discretion, expertise, finesse, know-how, mannerliness, poise, savvy, social graces, social skills, tact, urbanity, worldly wisdom.

antonyms awkwardness, clumsiness, incompetence, inexperience.

savour *n* flavour, piquancy, relish, salt, smack, smell, spice, tang, taste, zest.

v appreciate, bask in, delight in, dwell on, enjoy, gloat over, like, luxuriate in, relish, revel in.

antonyms shrink from, wince at.

savoury *adj* agreeable, appetizing, aromatic, decent, delectable, delicious, edifying, full-flavoured, gamy, good, honest, luscious, mouthwatering, palatable, piquant, reputable, respectable, rich, salubrious, scrumptious, spicy, tangy, tasty, toothsome, wholesome.

antonyms insipid, tasteless, unappetizing.

n appetizer, canapé, delicacy, hors d'oeuvre.

saw *n* adage, aphorism, apothegm, axiom, byword, commonplace, dictum, epigram, gnome, maxim, mot, proverb, saying.

say *v* add, affirm, allege, announce, answer, assert, assume, bruit, claim, comment, communicate, conjecture, convey, declare, deliver, disclose, divulge, enunciate, estimate, express, go, guess, imagine, imply, intimate, judge, maintain, mention, observe, opine, orate, perform, presume, pronounce, put into words, read, recite, reckon, rehearse, rejoin, remark, render, repeat, reply, report, respond, retort, reveal, rumour, signify, speak, state, suggest, surmise, tell, utter, voice.

n authority, chance, choice, clout, influence, power, say-so, suppose, sway, turn, two cents' worth, voice, vote, weight, word.

saying *n* adage, aphorism, apothegm, axiom, byword, dictum, gnome, maxim, mot, motto, precept, proverb, saw, slogan.

sayings *n* Analects, bon mots, dicta, gems, mots, obiter dicta, quotations, quotes, remarks, words of wisdom.

say-so *n* affirmation, agreement, approval, assertion, asseveration, assurance, authorization, authority, backing, consent, dictum, guarantee, OK, permission, ratification, sanction, word.

scale¹ *n* calibration, compass, continuum, degree, degrees, extent, gamut, gradation, grading, graduation, hierarchy, ladder, measure, order, progression, proportion, range, ranking, ratio, reach, register, scope, sequence, series, spectrum, spread, steps.

v adjust, level, move, proportion, prorate, regulate, shift, size.

scale² *n* crust, encrustation, film, flake, furfur, lamella, lamina, layer, plate, scurf, scutellum, shield, squama.

v clean, exfoliate, flake, peel, scrape.

scale³ *v* ascend, clamber up (or over), climb (up), escalade, mount, scramble up, shin up, surmount, swarm up.

scaly *adj* flaky, furfuraceous, leprous, scabby, scabrous, scurfy, squamate, squamous, squamulose.

scamp *n* blighter, devil, imp, knave, mischief, mischief-maker, monkey, prankster, rascal, rogue, ruffian, scalawag, scapegrace, tyke, whippersnapper.

scamper *v* chevy, dart, dash, fly, frisk, frolic, gambol, hasten, hurry, pelt, romp, run, rush, scoot, scurry, scuttle, skedaddle, sprint.

scan *v* check, con, examine, glance through, investigate, look over, pan over, scrutinize, search (through), skim (over), survey, sweep (over).

n check, examination, investigation, probe, review, scanning, screening, scrutiny, search, survey.

scandal *n* abuse, aspersion, backbiting, calumniation, calumny, crime, defamation, detraction, dirt, discredit, disgrace, dishonour, embarrassment, enormity, evil, furor, gossip, gossiping, ignominy, infamy, iniquity, muckraking, obloquy, odium, offence, opprobrium, outcry, outrage, reproach, rumours, shame, sin, slander, stigma, talk, tattle, traducement, uproar, wrongdoing.

scandalize *v* affront, appal, astound, disgust, dismay, horrify, nauseate, offend, outrage, repel, revolt, shock, sicken.

scandalmonger *n* busybody, calumniator, defamer, gossip, gossipmonger, muckraker, quidnunc, talebearer, tattletale, tattler, telltale, traducer.

scandalous *adj* abominable, atrocious, bad, calumnious, defamatory, disgraceful, dishonourable, disreputable, evil, exorbitant, extortionate, gamy, gossiping, immoderate, improper, infamous, libellous, monstrous, odious, opprobrious, outrageous, scurrilous, shameful, shocking, slanderous, unconscionable, unseemly, unspeakable, untrue, wrong.

scant *adj* bare, barely enough, deficient, hardly any, inadequate, in short supply, insufficient, limited, little, little or no, minimal, sparse.

antonyms adequate, ample, sufficient.

scanty *adj* bare, beggarly, deficient, exiguous, inadequate, insubstantial, insufficient, light, meagre, narrow, parsimonious, poor, restricted, scant, scrimpy, short, shy, skimpy, slender, sparing, sparse, thin.

antonyms ample, plentiful, substantial.

scapegoat *n* fall guy, patsy, victim, whipping boy.

scapegrace *n* blighter, good-for-nothing, imp, mischief-maker, ne'er-do-well, rapscallion, rascal, reprobate, rogue, scalawag, scamp.

scar *n* blemish, cicatrix, injury, lesion, mark, proud flesh, scar tissue, scarring, stigma, trauma, wound.
v blemish, brand, cicatrize, damage, disfigure, mark, stigmatize, traumatize.

scarce *adj* deficient, few (and far between), hard to get, in demand, infrequent, in short supply, insufficient, lacking, rare, scanty, sparse, thin on the ground, uncommon, unusual, wanting.
antonyms common, copious, plentiful.

scarcely *adv* barely, hardly, just and no more, not readily, not willingly, only just, scarce.

scarcity *n* dearth, deficiency, fewness, infrequency, insufficiency, lack, niggardliness, paucity, poverty, rareness, rarity, scantiness, shortage, sparseness, uncommonness, want.
antonyms abundance, enough, glut, plenty, sufficiency.

scare *v* affright, alarm, appal, daunt, dismay, frighten, give one a turn, intimidate, panic, put the wind up, shock, spook, startle, terrify, terrorize, unnerve.
antonym reassure.
n agitation, alarm, consternation, dismay, fright, hysteria, panic, shock, start, terror, the jitters.
antonym reassurance.

scared *adj* affrighted, agitated, anxious, appalled, cowering, dismayed, fearful, frightened, in a cold sweat, jittery, nervous, panicky, panic-stricken, petrified, shaken, spooked, startled, terrified, unnerved, worried.
antonyms confident, reassured.

scaremonger *n* alarmist, Cassandra, doom and gloom merchant, pessimist, prophet of doom.

scarf *n* babushka, boa, cravat, fichu, headscarf, headsquare, kerchief, muffler, neckerchief, shawl, stole.

scarper *v* abscond, beat it, bolt, clear off, decamp, depart, disappear, escape, flee, flit, go, go on the lam, hightail it, make tracks, run away, run for it, scram, skedaddle, take off, vamoose, vanish.

scary *adj* alarming, anxious, bloodcurdling, chilling, creepy, disturbing, eldritch, fearsome, frightening, hair-raising, hairy, horrendous, horrible, horrifying, intimidating, shocking, spine-chilling, spooky, terrifying, unnerving, upsetting, weird, worrying.

scathing *adj* acid, acrimonious, biting, bitter, brutal, caustic, critical, cutting, excoriating, harsh, lacerating, mordant, sarcastic, savage, scornful, searing, trenchant, unsparing, virulent, vitriolic, withering, wounding.
antonym complimentary.

scatter *v* bestrew, break up, broadcast, diffuse, disarrange, disband, disintegrate, dispel, disperse, disseminate, dissipate, disunite, divide, drive off, fling, litter, propagate, separate, shower, sow, spatter, spread, sprinkle, squander, strew.
antonyms collect, concentrate.

scatterbrained *adj* absent-minded, birdbrained, careless, dizzy, empty-headed, featherbrained, flighty, forgetful, frivolous, giddy, inattentive, irresponsible, madcap, silly, slaphappy, thoughtless, undependable, unreliable.
antonyms careful, efficient, sensible, sober.

scattering *n* break-up, diaspora, diffusion, dispersal, dispersion, dissemination, dissipation, dissolution, few, fistful, handful, propagation, scatter, separation, smatter, smattering, sprinkling.
antonyms abundance, mass.
adj disintegrative, dispersive, disseminative, dissipative, divisive.
antonym unifying.

scavenger *n* cleaner, beachcomber, forager, garbage collector, raker, rummager, scrounger, street cleaner, (street) sweeper.

scenario *n* case, outline, plan, plot, projection, résumé, rundown, schema, scheme, sequence, situation, skeleton, sketch, story line, summary, synopsis.

scene *n* act, area, arena, backdrop, background, business, carrying-on, chapter, circumstances, commotion, confrontation, display, disturbance, division, drama, environment, episode, exhibition, focus, fuss, incident, landscape, locale, locality, location, melodrama, milieu, mise en scène, outburst, pageant, panorama, performance, picture, place, position, prospect, representation, row, set, setting, show, sight, site, situation, spectacle, spot, stage, tableau, tantrum, to-do, upset, view, vista, whereabouts, world.

scenery *n* backdrop, background, décor, flats, landscape, mise en scène, outlook, panorama, set, setting, sight, surroundings, terrain, view, vista.

scenic *adj* awe-inspiring, beautiful, breathtaking, grand, impressive, magnificent, panoramic, picturesque, pretty, spectacular, striking, stupendous.
antonyms dreary, dull, unspectacular.

scent *n* aroma, bouquet, fragrance, odour, perfume, redolence, smell, spoor, trace, track, trail, waft, whiff.
antonym stink.
v detect, discern, nose, nose out, perceive, recognize, sense, smell, sniff, sniff out.

scented *adj* aromatic, fragrant, odoriferous, perfumed, redolent, sweet-smelling.
antonyms malodorous, noisome, stinking.

sceptic *n* agnostic, atheist, cynic, disbeliever, doubter, doubting Thomas, questioner, rationalist, scoffer, unbeliever.
antonym believer.

sceptical *adj* agnostic, cynical, disbelieving, distrustful, doubtful, doubting, dubious, hesitating, incredulous, leery, mistrustful, pessimistic, questioning, quizzical, scoffing, suspicious, unbelieving, uncertain, unconvinced, unpersuaded, untrustful.

antonyms convinced, naïve, trusting.

scepticism *n* agnosticism, atheism, cynicism, disbelief, distrust, doubt, incredulity, leeriness, pessimism, rationalism, suspicion, unbelief.

antonyms belief, faith, naïvety.

schedule *n* agenda, calendar, catalogue, diary, form, inventory, itinerary, list, plan, program, scheme, scroll, table, timetable.

v appoint, arrange, book, list, organize, plan, program, slot, table, time.

schematic *adj* diagrammatic, graphic, illustrative, representational, simplified, simplistic, symbolic.

scheme *n* arrangement, blueprint, chart, codification, configuration, conformation, conspiracy, contrivance, design, device, diagram, disposition, dodge, draft, game, idea, intrigue, layout, machinations, manoeuvre, method, outline, pattern, plan, plot, ploy, procedure, program, project, proposal, proposition, racket, ruse, schedule, schema, set-up, shape, shift, stratagem, strategy, subterfuge, suggestion, system, tactics, theory, trick.

v collude, conspire, contrive, design, devise, frame, imagine, intrigue, machinate, manipulate, manoeuvre, mastermind, plan, plot, project, pull strings, pull strings (or wires), use influence, work out.

schemer *n* conniver, deceiver, éminence grise, fox, intriguer, Machiavellian, machinator, mastermind, plotter, politician, wangler, wheeler-dealer, wire puller.

scheming *adj* artful, calculating, conniving, crafty, cunning, deceitful, designing, devious, dishonest, duplicitous, foxy, insidious, Machiavellian, manipulative, slippery, sly, tricky, underhand, unscrupulous, wily.

antonyms artless, honest, open, transparent.

schism *n* breach, break, cleavage, discord, disunion, division, estrangement, faction, falling-out, quarrel, rift, rupture, sect, separation, severance, splinter group, splintering, split, sunderance.

scholar *n* academic, authority, bookworm, egghead, expert, great mind, intellectual, man (or woman) of letters, pupil, savant, scholastic, schoolboy, schoolchild, schoolgirl, student, thinker.

antonyms dullard, dunce, ignoramus, illiterate, philistine.

scholarly *adj* academic, analytical, bookish, critical, educational, erudite, intellectual, knowledgeable, learned, lettered, scholastic, scientific, studious, thorough, well-read, well-researched.

antonyms illiterate, unscholarly.

scholarship¹ *n* academe, academia, book learning, education, erudition, insight, knowledge, learnedness, learning, lore, scholarliness, studiousness, wisdom.

scholarship² *n* award, bursary, endowment, fellowship, grant.

scholastic *adj* academic, analytical, bookish, educational, formal, learned, lettered, literary, pedagogical, pedantic, precise, scholarly, school.

school *n* academy, adherents, alma mater, CEGEP, circle, class, classroom, clique, college, collegiate, creed, denomination, department, devotees, disciples, discipline, doctrine, dogma, faction, faculty, faith, followers, following, group, institute, institution, lycée, outlook, persuasion, pupils, sect, seminary, set, students, teaching, view, votaries.

v coach, discipline, drill, educate, habituate, harden, indoctrinate, instruct, inure, prepare, prime, train, tutor, verse.

schooling *n* book learning, booklore, coaching, drill, education, grounding, guidance, inculcation, indoctrination, instruction, preparation, schoolcraft, teaching, training, tuition, tutelage, tutoring.

schoolteacher *n* dominie, educator, instructor, master, mistress, pedagogue, schoolmarm, schoolmaster, schoolmistress, teacher.

science *n* art, discipline, knowledge, ology, proficiency, skill, specialization, study, systematic, technique, technology.

scientific *adj* accurate, analytical, controlled, empirical, exact, mathematical, methodical, precise, rational, scholarly, systematic, thorough.

scintillate *v* blaze, coruscate, flash, gleam, glint, glisten, glitter, shine, spark, sparkle, twinkle, wink.

scintillating *adj* animated, blazing, blinding, bright, brilliant, coruscant, coruscating, dazzling, ebullient, exciting, flashing, glittering, lively, shining, sparkling, stimulating, vivacious, winking, witty.

antonym dull.

scion *n* branch, child, descendant, graft, heir, imp, offshoot, offspring, shoot, slip, sprig, sprout, successor, twig.

scoff¹ (at) *v* belittle, deride, despise, flout, gibe, jeer at, knock, make fun of, make light of, mock, poke fun at, pooh-pooh, rail, revile, rib, ridicule, scorn, sneer at, taunt, twit.

antonyms compliment, flatter, praise.

scoff² *v* bolt, consume, cram, devour, fill one's face, gobble, gulp, guzzle, pig out on, put away, shift, wolf (down).

antonym abstain.

n chow, comestibles, commons, eatables, eats, edibles, fare, feed, fodder, food, grub, meal, nosh, provisions, rations, tuck, victuals.

scoff³ *v* filch, make off with, pilfer, snitch, steal.

scoffing *adj* cynical, derisive, derisory, disbelieving, jeering, Mephistophelian, mocking, ridiculing, sarcastic, sneering, tuck away, tuck into.

scold *v* admonish, bawl out, berate, blame, call on the carpet, castigate, censure, chew out, chide, dress down, find fault with, give (someone) what for, jaw, jawbone, lecture, nag at, rake over the coals, rate, read the riot act, rebuke, remonstrate with, reprimand, reproach, reprove, take to task, tell off, tongue-lash, upbraid, vituperate.

antonyms commend, praise.

scolding *n* a piece of one's mind, bawling-out, castigation, chewing-out, dressing-down, earful, going-over, jaw, jawing, lecture, rebuke, reprimand, reproof, talking-to, telling-off, the riot act, tongue-lashing, upbraiding, what for.

antonym commendation.

scoop[1] *n* backhoe, bail, bailer, bucket, dipper, lade, ladle, shovel, spoon.

v bail, dig, dip, empty, excavate, gather, gouge, hollow, lade, ladle, lift, pick up, remove, scrape, shovel, sweep.

scoop[2] *n* dirt, exclusive, exposé, facts, information, inside story, latest, lowdown, poop, revelation.

scoot *v* beat it, bolt, bowl, career, dart, dash, hurry, run, scamper, scarper, scud, scurry, scuttle, shoot, skedaddle, sprint, step on it, tear, vamoose, zip.

scope *n* ambit, application, area, breadth, capacity, compass, competence, confines, coverage, elbowroom, extent, freedom, latitude, liberty, opportunity, orbit, outlook, purview, range, reach, room, space, span, sphere, terms of reference, tessitura.

scorch *v* blacken, blister, burn, castigate, char, criticize, dry up, parch, roast, scald, sear, shrivel, singe, sizzle, torrefy, wither.

scorched *adj* arid, baked, blackened, blistered, burnt, charred, cracked, dried-up, dry, parched, sere, seared, shrivelled, torrid, withered.

scorching *adj* baking, biting, blistering, boiling, broiling, burning, caustic, fiery, flaming, hot, parching, red-hot, roasting, scalding, scathing, searing, sizzling, sweltering, torrid, tropical, withering.

score *n* a bone to pick, account, amount, basis, bill, cause, charge, cut, debt, due, gash, grade, gravamen, grievance, ground, grounds, grove, grudge, injury, injustice, line, mark, notation, notch, obligation, outcome, points, reason, reckoning, record, result, scratch, sum total, tab, tally, total, wrong.

v achieve, adapt, amass, arrange, attain, be one up, benefit, chalk up, compose, count, cut, deface, earn, engrave, furrow, gain, gouge, grave, graze, groove, hatch, have the advantage, have the edge, impress, incise, indent, make, make a hit, mark, nick, notch, notch up, orchestrate, profit, realize, record, register, scrape, scratch, set, slash, tally, total, win.

scores *n* crowds, droves, heaps, hosts, hundreds, legions, loads, lots, masses, millions, multitudes, myriads, scads, shoals, swarms, tons.

scorn *n* contempt, contemptuousness, contumely, defiance, derision, disdain, disgust, dismissiveness, disparagement, mockery, ridicule, sarcasm, scornfulness, slight, sneer.

antonyms admiration, respect.

v be above, contemn, deride, despise,

disdain, dismiss, flout, have no time for, hold in contempt, laugh at, laugh in the face of, look down on, misprise, pooh-pooh, refuse, reject, ridicule, scoff at, slight, sneer at, spurn, thumb one's nose at.

antonyms admire, respect.

scornful *adj* arrogant, contemptuous, contumelious, defiant, derisive, derisory, disdainful, dismissive, disparaging, haughty, insulting, jeering, mocking, rejecting, sarcastic, sardonic, scathing, scoffing, slighting, sneering, supercilious, withering.

antonyms admiring, complimentary, respectful.

scornfully *adv* arrogantly, contemptuously, derisively, disdainfully, dismissively, disparagingly, haughtily, scathingly, slightingly, sneeringly, superciliously, witheringly.

antonyms admiringly, respectfully.

scot-free *adj* clear, free, free and clear, safe, scatheless, undamaged, unharmed, unhurt, uninjured, unpunished, unrebuked, unreprimanded, unreproached, unscathed, with impunity, without a scratch, without penalty.

scoundrel *n* blackguard, blighter, caitiff, cheat, cur, dastard, good-for-nothing, heel, hound, knave, louse, miscreant, ne'er-do-well, picaroon, rascal, rat, reprobate, rogue, rotter, ruffian, scab, scalawag, scamp, scapegrace, stinker, swine, vagabond, villain.

scour[1] *v* abrade, buff, burnish, clean, clear (out), cleanse, dig (out), flush, furbish, polish, purge, rub, scrape, scrub, wash, whiten.

scour[2] *v* beat, comb, drag, forage, go over, hunt, rake, ransack, search, turn upside-down.

scourge *n* affliction, bane, cat, cat-o'-nine-tails, curse, evil, flagellum, infliction, knout, lash, menace, misfortune, penalty, pest, pestilence, plague, punishment, strap, switch, terror, thong, torment, visitation, whip.

antonyms benefit, blessing, boon, godsend.

v afflict, beat, belt, cane, castigate, chastise, curse, devastate, discipline, excoriate, flagellate, flail, flog, harass, horsewhip, lambaste, lash, lather, leather, oppress, plague, punish, tan, terrorize, thrash, torment, trounce, visit, wallop, whale, whip.

scout *v* case, check (out), explore, hunt (for), investigate, look, observe, probe, reconnoitre, search, seek, snoop, spy, spy out, survey, track, watch.

n emissary, escort, lookout, outrider, precursor, reconnoitrer, spy, vanguard.

scowl *v* frown, glare, glower, grimace, lower.

n frown, glare, glower, grimace, moue.

antonyms beam, grin, smile.

scrabble *v* clamber, claw, dig, grope, grub, paw, root, scramble, scrape, scratch, scrawl, scribble, struggle.

scraggy *adj* angular, bony, emaciated, gangling, gangly, gaunt, lank, lanky, lean, meagre, rawboned, scraggly, scrawny, skinny, spare, undernourished, wasted.

antonyms plump, rounded, sleek.

scram *v* beat it, bolt, clear off, clear out, depart, disappear, flee, get lost, go away, leave, quit, scarper, scoot, shove off, skedaddle, take to one's heels, vamoose.

scramble *v* clamber, climb, contend, crawl, hasten, hustle, jostle, jumble, mix up, push, run, rush, scale, scrabble, shuffle, sprawl, strive, struggle, swarm, vie.

n climb, commotion, competition, confusion, contention, free-for-all, hustle, jumble, melee, muddle, race, rat race, rivalry, rush, strife, struggle, tussle.

scrap[1] *n* atom, bit, bite, crumb, fraction, fragment, grain, iota, junk, leftover, mite, modicum, morsel, mouthful, part, particle, piece, portion, remnant, rubbish, shard, shred, sliver, smidgen, snatch, snippet, trace, vestige, waste, whit.

v abandon, axe, break up, cancel, chuck, demolish, discard, ditch, drop, jettison, junk, shed, throw out, toss (out), write off.

antonyms reinstate, restore, resume.

on the scrap-heap discarded, ditched, dumped, forgotten, jettisoned, outmoded, redundant, rejected, written off.

scrap[2] *n* argument, battle, brawl, disagreement, dispute, dustup, falling-out, fight, quarrel, row, ruckus, rumpus, scuffle, set-to, shindy, squabble, tiff, wrangle.

antonyms agreement, peace.

v argue, bicker, clash, fall out, fight, spat, squabble, wrangle.

antonym agree.

scrape *v* abrade, bark, claw, clean, erase, file, grate, graze, grind, pinch, rasp, remove, rub, save, scour, scrabble, scratch, scrimp, scuff, skimp, skin, squeak, stint.

n abrasion, difficulty, dilemma, distress, fix, graze, mess, pickle, plight, predicament, pretty kettle of fish, rub, scratch, scuff, shave, spot, trouble.

scrappy[1] *adj* chippy, disjointed, fragmentary, incomplete, perfunctory, piecemeal, sketchy, slapdash, slipshod, superficial.

antonyms complete, finished.

scrappy[2] *adj* agressive, belligerent, combative, contentious, disputatious, feisty, fighting, full of flight, quarrelsome, trigger-happy, truculent, warlike, warring.

antonyms pacific, peaceful.

scraps *n* bits (and pieces), crumbs, leavings, leftovers, odds and ends, remains, scrapings, shavings, snippings.

scratch *v* annul, cancel, carve, claw, cut, damage, delete, eliminate, engrave, erase, etch, grate, graze, incise, lacerate, mark, obliterate, retire, rub, scarify, score, scrabble, scrape, scribble, strike (out), withdraw.

n abrasion, blemish, claw mark, gash, graze, laceration, mark, scrape, scribble, streak.

adj haphazard, impromptu, improvised, rough, rough-and-ready, unrehearsed.

antonym polished.

scrawl *n* cacography, chicken scratching, scrabble, scratch, scribble, squiggle, writing.

scrawny *adj* angular, bony, emaciated, gaunt, lanky, lean, rawboned, scraggy, skeletal, skinny, thin, underfed, undernourished.

antonym plump.

scream[1] *v* bawl, cry, holler, roar, screech, shriek, shrill, squeal, wail, yell, yelp, yowl.

n howl, outcry, roar, screech, shriek, squeal, wail, yell, yelp, yowl.

antonym whisper.

scream[2] *n* card, caution, character, comedian, comic, good one, hoot, howler, joker, laugh, panic, riot, sensation, wit.

antonym bore.

screech *v* cry, screak, scream, shriek, squawk, squeal, ululate, yelp.

antonym whisper.

screen *v* cloak, conceal, cover, cull, defend, evaluate, examine, filter, gauge, grade, guard, hide, mask, process, protect, riddle, safeguard, scan, shade, shelter, shield, shroud, sieve, sift, sort, veil, vet.

antonyms broadcast, present, show, uncover.

n awning, bluff, canopy, cloak, concealment, cover, divider, guard, hedge, hoarding, mantle, mesh, net, partition, safeguard, shade, shelter, shield, shroud.

screw *v* adjust, bleed, cheat, coerce, compress, constrain, contort, contract, crumple, distort, extort, extract, fasten, force, oppress, overcharge, press, pucker, put (the) pressure on, put the screws to, squeeze, swindle, take (unfair) advantage of, tighten, turn, twist, wind, wrest, wring, wrinkle.

screw up ball up, botch, bungle, contort, crumple, disrupt, distort, knot, louse up, make a hash of, mess up, mishandle, mismanage, pucker (up), queer, spoil, wrinkle.

antonyms manage, unscrew.

screwy *adj* batty, cracked, crackers, crazy, daft, dotty, eccentric, flaky, mad, nutty, odd, queer, round the bend, weird.

antonym sane.

scribble *v* dash off, doodle, jot, pen, scratch, scrawl, write.

scribe *n* amanuensis, clerk, copyist, notary, penman, scrivener, secretary, writer.

scrimmage *n* affray, brawl, disturbance, dustup, fight, fray, free-for-all, melee, riot, row, scrap, scramble, scrum, scrummage, scuffle, set-to, shindy, skirmish, squabble, struggle.

antonym calmness.

scrimp *v* curtail, economize, limit, pinch, reduce, restrict, save, scrape, scrimp and save, skimp, stint.

antonym spend.

script *n* book, calligraphy, chirography, copy, hand, handwriting, letters, libretto, lines, longhand, manuscript, penmanship, text, words, writing.

scroll *n* inventory, list, parchment, record(s), roll, volume, volute.

Scrooge *n* cheapskate, meanie, miser, moneygrubber, niggard, penny-pincher, skinflint, tightwad.

antonym spendthrift.

scrounge *v* beg, bum, cadge, freeload, mooch, purloin, sponge, wheedle.

scrounger *n* beggar, bum, cadger, freeloader, moocher, parasite, sponger.

scrub *v* abandon, abolish, abrade, call off, can, cancel, clean, cleanse, delete, discontinue, ditch, drop, forget, get rid of, give up, rub, scour, stop, wash, wipe out.

scruffy *adj* dirty, disreputable, dog-eared, draggletailed, frowzy, grotty, ill-groomed, mangy, messy, ragged, ratty, run-down, scrubby, seedy, shabby, slatternly, slovenly, sluttish, squalid, tattered, ungroomed, unkempt, untidy.

antonyms tidy, well-dressed.

scrumptious *adj* appetizing, delectable, delicious, delightful, exquisite, luscious, magnificent, moreish, mouth-watering, succulent, yummy.

antonym unappetizing.

scrunch *v* crinkle, crumple, crunch, crush, grate, grind, hunch, mash, pulverize, squash, squeeze, squish.

scruple *v* balk (at), demur (at), falter, hesitate, object (to), recoil (from), shrink (from), stick (at), vacillate, waver.

n caution, compunction, difficulty, doubt, hesitation, misgiving, pang, perplexity, qualm, reluctance, squeamishness, uneasiness.

scrupulous *adj* careful, conscientious, conscionable, dutiful, exact, fastidious, honourable, meticulous, minute, moral, nice, observant, painstaking, precise, principled, punctilious, rigorous, squeaky-clean, strict, upright.

antonym careless.

scrutinize *v* analyse, dissect, examine, explore, give the once-over, inspect, investigate, peruse, probe, scan, search, sift, study.

scrutiny *n* analysis, examination, exploration, inquiry, inspection, investigation, once-over, perusal, search, sifting, study.

scud *v* blow, dart, fly, hasten, race, sail, shoot, skim, speed.

scuff *v* abrade, brush, drag, graze, rub, scratch, shuffle, skin, wear.

scuffle *v* clash, contend, fight, grapple, jostle, struggle, tussle.

n affray, brawl, commotion, disturbance, dogfight, fight, fray, ruck, ruckus, rumpus, scramble, scrap, set-to, skirmish, tussle.

sculpt *v* carve, chisel, cut, fashion, form, hew, model, mould, represent, sculp, sculpture, shape.

scum *n* algae, canaille, crust, dregs, dross, film, froth, impurities, offal, offscourings, pellicle, rabble, rag-tag and bobtail, riff-raff, rubbish, scruff, spume, trash.

scupper *v* defeat, demolish, destroy, disable, euchre, overthrow, throw (or put) a monkey wrench (or spanner) in the works, ruin, spoil, thwart, torpedo, wreck.

antonyms advance, promote.

scurf *n* dandruff, flakiness, furfur, scabrousness, scaliness.

scurfy *adj* flaky, furfuraceous, leprous, scabious, scaly.

scurrility *n* abuse, abusiveness, billingsgate, coarseness, grossness, indecency, invective, nastiness, obloquy, obscenity, offensiveness, rudeness, scurrilousness, vituperation, vulgarity.

antonym politeness.

scurrilous *adj* abusive, coarse, defamatory, dirty, foul, foul-mouthed, gross, indecent, insulting, low, nasty, obscene, offensive, Rabelaisian, ribald, rude, salacious, scabrous, scandalous, slanderous, vituperative, vulgar.

antonym polite.

scurry *v* dart, dash, fly, hurry, hustle, race, rush, scamper, scoot, scud, scuttle, skedaddle, skim, sprint, trot, whisk.

antonym stroll.

n flurry, hustle and bustle, scampering, whirl.

antonym calm.

scurvy *adj* abject, bad, base, caddish, contemptible, despicable, dirty, dishonourable, ignoble, low, low-down, mean, pitiful, rotten, scabby, shabby, sorry, vile, worthless.

antonyms good, honourable.

scuttle *v* bustle, hare, hasten, hurry, run, rush, scamper, scoot, scramble, scud, scurry, trot.

antonym stroll.

sea *n* abundance, (briny) deep, drink, expanse, main, mass, multitude, ocean, plethora, profusion, waves.

at sea adrift, astray, baffled, bewildered, confused, disoriented, insecure, lost, mystified, perplexed, puzzled, upset.

adj aquatic, marine, maritime, naval, ocean, ocean-going, oceanic, pelagic, salt, saltwater, seagoing.

antonyms air, land.

seafaring *adj* marine, maritime, nautical, naval, oceanic, sailing.

antonym land.

seal *v* assure, attest, authenticate, bung, clinch, close, conclude, confirm, consummate, cork, enclose, establish, fasten, finalize, plug, ratify, secure, settle, shake hands on, shut, stamp, stop, stopper, validate, waterproof.

antonym unseal.

n assurance, attestation, authentication, bull, bung, confirmation, imprimatur, insignia, ratification, signet, stamp.

seal off block (off), close (off), cut off, fence off, isolate, quarantine, segregate, shut off.

antonym open up.

sealed *adj* airtight, closed, corked, hermetic, plugged, shut, watertight.

antonym unsealed.

seam *n* closure, crack, furrow, joint, layer, line, lode, ridge, scar, stratum, suture, vein, wrinkle.

seaman *n* AB, able (-bodied), deck-hand, hand, Jack Tar, matelot, sailor, seafarer, steersman, tar.

seamy *adj* corrupt, dark, degraded, disagreeable, disreputable, low, nasty, rough, sleazy, sordid, squalid, unpleasant, unwholesome.

antonyms pleasant, respectable.

sear *v* blight, brand, brown, burn, cauterize, desiccate, dry up, harden, scorch, seal, shrivel (up), sizzle, wilt, wither.

search *v* check, comb, examine, explore, ferret, forage, frisk, hunt, inquire, inspect, investigate, look, probe, pry, quest, ransack, rifle, rummage, scour, scrutinize, sift, test.

n examination, exploration, going-over, hunt, inquiry, inspection, investigation, pursuit, quest, research, rummage, scrutiny.

searching *adj* close, in-depth, intent, keen, minute, penetrating, piercing, probing, quizzical, severe, sharp, thorough.

antonyms superficial, vague.

season[1] *n* division, interval, period, span, spell, term, time.

v acclimatize, accustom, anneal, condition, cure, discipline, habituate, harden, inure, mature, temper, toughen, train.

season[2] *v* colour, enliven, flavour, imbue, lace, leaven, mitigate, moderate, prepare, qualify, salt, spice.

seasonable *adj* appropriate, convenient, fit, opportune, providential, suitable, timely, well-timed.

antonym unseasonable.

seasoned *adj* acclimatized, accustomed, battle-scarred, experienced, hardened, long-serving, mature, old, practised, time-served, veteran, weathered, well-versed.

antonym novice.

seasoning *n* condiment, dressing, flavouring, herb, pepper, relish, salt, sauce, spice.

seat *n* abode, axis, base, bed, bench, bottom, bum, butt, buttocks, capital, cause, centre, chair, constituency, cradle, footing, foundation, ground, groundwork, headquarters, heart, house, hub, incumbency, location, mansion, membership, pew, place, residence, settle, shooting stick, site, situation, source, stall, station, stool, throne, tush.

v accommodate, assign, contain, deposit, establish, fit, fix, hold, install, locate, place, set, settle, sit, slot, take.

seating *n* accommodation, chairs, places, room, seats.

seaweed *n* gulf weed, kelp, laver, rockweed, sargasso, sea moss, sea wrack, wrack.

secede from *v* apostatize, desert, disaffiliate, leave, quit, resign, retire, separate, split off, withdraw.

antonyms join, unite with.

secession *n* apostasy, break, defection, desertion, disaffiliation, schism, seceding, split, withdrawal.

antonyms amalgamation, unification.

secluded *adj* cloistered, cloistral, concealed, cut off, hermitlike, isolated, lonely, out-of-the-way, private, reclusive, remote, retired, secret, sequestered, sheltered, solitary, unfrequented.

antonyms busy, public.

seclusion *n* concealment, hiding, isolation, privacy, purdah, reclusiveness, remoteness, retirement, retreat, shelter, solitude.

second[1] *adj* additional, alternate, alternative, double, duplicate, extra, following, further, inferior, lesser, lower, next, other, repeated, reproduction, secondary, subordinate, subsequent, succeeding, supplementary, supporting, twin.

n assistant, backer, helper, supporter.

v advance, agree with, aid, approve, assist, back, encourage, endorse, forward, further, help, promote, ratify, support.

second[2] *n* instant, jiffy, minute, moment, split second, trice, twinkling, two shakes.

secondary *adj* alternate, auxiliary, backup, consequential, contingent, derivative, derived, extra, indirect, inessential, inferior, lesser, lower, minor, relief, reserve, resultant, resulting, second, second-hand, second-rate, spare, subordinate, subsidiary, supporting, unimportant.

antonym primary.

second-class *adj* déclassé, indifferent, inferior, mediocre, second-best, second-rate, undistinguished, uninspired, uninspiring.

second-hand *adj* borrowed, derivative, hand-me-down, old, plagiarized, used, vicarious, worn.

antonym new.

second-rate *adj* cheap, cheap and nasty, grotty, inferior, jerry-built, low-grade, mediocre, poor, shoddy, substandard, tacky, tawdry, undistinguished, uninspired, uninspiring.

antonym first-rate.

secrecy *n* clandestineness, concealment, confidence, confidentiality, covertness, furtiveness, mystery, privacy, retirement, seclusion, secretiveness, silence, solitude, stealth, stealthiness, surreptitiousness.

antonym openness.

secret *adj* abstruse, arcane, backdoor, backroom, backstairs, cabalistic, camouflaged, clandestine, classified, cloak-and-dagger, close, closet, concealed, confidential, conspiratorial, covered, covert, cryptic, deep, discreet, disguised, esoteric, furtive, hidden, hole-and-corner, hush-hush, inly, invisible, mysterious, occult, out-of-the-way, private, privy, recondite, reticent, retired, secluded, secretive, sensitive, shrouded, sly, stealthy, tête-à-tête, undercover, underground, underhand, under-the-counter, undisclosed, unfrequented, unknown, unpublished, unrevealed, unseen.

antonyms open, public.

n arcanum, code, confidence, enigma, formula, key, mystery, recipe.

in secret in confidence, inly, inwardly, on the q.t., on the quiet, secretly, sub rosa, under the rose.

antonym openly.

secretary *n* assistant, clerk, executive assistant, minute-taker, office administrator, P.A., personal assistant, person Friday, recorder, registrar, stenographer.

secrete¹ *v* emanate, emit, exude, give off, produce, release.

secrete² *v* bury, cache, conceal, cover, hide (away), keep secret, put away, put out of sight, shroud, squirrel away, stash (away), stow, veil.

antonym reveal.

secretion *n* discharge, emission, excretion, extravasation, exudation, osmosis.

secretive *adj* cagey, close, close-lipped, close-mouthed, cryptic, deep, enigmatic, quiet, reserved, reticent, tight-lipped, uncommunicative, unforthcoming, withdrawn.

antonyms communicative, open.

secretly *adv* clandestinely, confidentially, covertly, furtively, in camera, in confidence, in private, in secret, on the q.t., on the quiet, on the sly, privately, privily, quietly, stealthily, surreptitiously, unobserved.

antonym openly.

sect *n* camp, denomination, division, faction, group, party, school, splinter group, subdivision, wing.

sectarian *adj* bigoted, clannish, cliquish, denominational, doctrinaire, dogmatic, exclusive, factional, fanatic, fanatical, insular, limited, narrow, narrow-minded, parochial, partisan, prejudiced, rigid, schismatic, ultra.

antonyms broad-minded, cosmopolitan, non-sectarian.

n adherent, bigot, denominationalist, disciple, dogmatist, extremist, fanatic, factionalist, partisan, zealot.

section *n* area, article, class, component, cross section, department, district, division, fraction, fragment, instalment, part, passage, piece, portion, region, sample, sector, segment, slice, subdivision, wing, zone.

antonym whole.

sectional *adj* class, divided, exclusive, factional, local, localized, partial, partisan, racial, regional, sectarian, separate, separatist.

antonyms general, universal.

sector *n* area, category, district, division, part, quarter, region, section, stratum, subdivision, zone.

antonym whole.

secular *adj* civil, laic, lay, materialistic, non-religious, profane, state, temporal, worldly.

antonym religious.

secure *adj* absolute, assured, certain, conclusive, confident, definite, dependable, easy, fast, fastened, firm, fixed, fortified, immovable, immune, impregnable, in the bag, nailed down, on velvet, protected, reassured, reliable, safe, sheltered, shielded, solid, stable, steadfast, steady, sure, tight, unassailable, undamaged, unharmed, well-founded.

antonyms insecure, uncertain.

v acquire, assure, attach, batten down, bolt, chain, clinch, ensure, fasten, fix, gain, get, get

hold of, guarantee, insure, land, lash, lock, lock up, moor, nail, obtain, padlock, procure, rivet, seize, tie (down or up).

antonyms lose, unfasten.

security *n* assurance, asylum, care, certainty, collateral, confidence, conviction, cover, custody, defence, faith, gage, guarantee, guards, hostage, immunity, insurance, pawn, pledge, positiveness, precautions, preservation, protection, refuge, reliance, retreat, safeguards, safekeeping, safety, sanctuary, sureness, surety, surveillance, warranty.

antonym insecurity.

sedate *adj* calm, collected, composed, cool, decorous, deliberate, demure, dignified, earnest, grave, imperturbable, proper, quiet, seemly, serene, serious, slow-moving, sober, solemn, staid, tranquil, unflappable, unhurried, unruffled.

antonyms flippant, hasty, undignified.

sedative *adj* allaying, anodyne, calming, depressant, lenitive, relaxing, palliative, sleep-inducing, soothing, soporific, tranquillizing.

antonym rousing.

n anodyne, calmative, dope, downer, narcotic, opiate, pacifier, sleeping pill, soporific depressant, tranquillizer.

sedentary *adj* desk, desk-bound, inactive, motionless, seated, sitting, stationary, still, torpid, unmoving.

antonym active.

sediment *n* deposit, dregs, feculence, grounds, lees, precipitate, residue, residuum, settlings, sludge.

sedition *n* agitation, disloyalty, factiousness, incitement, rabble-rousing, subversion, treason, tumult.

antonyms calm, loyalty.

seditious *adj* disloyal, dissident, factious, insubordinate, mutinous, rebellious, refractory, revolutionary, seditionary, subversive, traitorous.

antonyms calm, loyal.

seduce *v* allure, attract, beguile, bewitch, corrupt, debauch, deceive, decoy, deflower, deprave, dishonour, ensnare, entice, inveigle, lure, mislead, ruin, tempt, win over.

seducer *n* cad, Casanova, charmer, debaucher, deceiver, Don Juan, flirt, deceiver, libertine, Lothario, philanderer, tempter, wolf, womanizer.

seduction *n* allure, allurement, come-on, corruption, debauchment, defloration, ensnarement, enticement, lure, seducement, snare, temptation.

seductive *adj* alluring, attractive, beguiling, bewitching, captivating, come-hither, come-on, desirable, enchanting, enticing, flirtatious, honeyed, inviting, irresistible, provocative, ravishing, seducing, sexy, siren, specious, tempting.

antonym unattractive.

seductress n Circe, femme fatale, Lorelei, siren, temptress, vamp.

sedulous adj assiduous, busy, conscientious, constant, determined, diligent, hardworking, industrious, laborious, painstaking, persevering, persistent, resolved, tireless, unflagging, unremitting, untiring.

antonym half-hearted.

see v accept, accompany, anticipate, appreciate, ascertain, attend, behold, call on, come across, comprehend, consider, consult, court, date, decide, descry, detect, determine, discern, discover, distinguish, divine, encounter, ensure, entertain, envisage, escort, espy, experience, fathom, feel, find (out), follow, foresee, foretell, get, glimpse, go (out) with, grasp, guarantee, identify, imagine, interview, investigate, judge, know, learn, look at, make out, make sure, mark, meet, mind, note, notice, observe, perceive, picture, realize, receive, recognize, reflect, regard, run into, show, sight, spot, take, think of, understand, usher, view, visit, visualize, walk, witness.

see eye to eye accord, agree, be at one, be of the same mind, coincide, concur, get along, get on, harmonize, jibe, speak the same language, subscribe.

antonym disagree.

see red blow one's top, blow up, boil over, get hot under the collar, get mad, get one's back up, get steamed, lose it, lose one's temper, seethe.

see to arrange, attend to, deal with, do, fix, handle, look after, manage, organize, repair, sort out, take care of, take charge of, undertake.

seed n beginning, children, descendants, egg, embryo, germ, grain, heirs, issue, kernel, nucleus, offspring, ovule, ovum, pip, progeny, race, scions, semen, source, spawn, sperm, spore, start, successors, suspicion.

antonym ancestors.

seedy adj ailing, crummy, decaying, dilapidated, faded, grotty, grubby, grungy, ill, mangy, off-colour, poorly, run-down, scruffy, shabby, sick, sickly, sleazy, slovenly, squalid, tatty, unkempt, unwell, worn.

antonyms posh, well.

seek v aim, ask, aspire to, attempt, beg, desire, endeavour, entreat, essay, follow, hunt, inquire, invite, petition, pursue, request, solicit, strive, try, want.

seeker n disciple, inquirer, novice, petitioner, pursuer, searcher, student.

seem v appear, appear to be, give the impression (of or that), look, look like, pretend, sound like.

seeming adj apparent, appearing, illusory, ostensible, outward, pseudo, quasi-, specious, surface.

antonym real.

seemingly adv allegedly, apparently, as far as one can see, at first blush, on the face of it, on the surface, ostensibly, outwardly, superficially.

antonym really.

seemly adj appropriate, attractive, becoming, befitting, comely, comme il faut, decent, decorous, fit, fitting, handsome, maidenly, meet, nice, proper, suitable, suited.

antonym unseemly.

seep v exude, leak, ooze, percolate, permeate, soak, trickle, weep, well.

seepage n exudation, infiltration, leak, leakage, oozing, osmosis, percolation.

seer n augur, prophet, prognosticator, sibyl, soothsayer.

seesaw v alternate, fluctuate, oscillate, pitch, shilly-shally, swing, teeter, wigwag.

n alternation, oscillation, pendulum, teeter-totter, wigwagger.

seethe v boil, bubble, churn, ferment, fizz, foam, foam at the mouth, froth, fume, marinate, rage, rise, saturate, see red, simmer, smoulder, soak, souse, steep, storm, surge, swarm, swell, teem.

see-through adj clear, diaphanous, filmy, flimsy, gauzy, gossamer, sheer, translucent, transparent.

antonym opaque.

segment n bit, compartment, division, part, piece, portion, section, slice, wedge.

antonym whole.

v analyse, anatomize, apportion, cut up, divide, halve, separate, slice, split.

segregate v cut off, discriminate against, dissociate, exclude, isolate, quarantine, seclude, separate, set apart.

antonym unite.

segregation n apartheid, discrimination, isolation, quarantine, separation.

antonym unification.

seize v abduct, annex, apprehend, appropriate, arrest, capture, catch, claw, clutch, collar, commandeer, confiscate, crib, distrain, fasten, fix, grab, grasp, grip, hijack, impound, nab, snatch, take, take custody of, take possession of, usurp.

antonym let go.

seizure n abduction, annexation, apprehension, arrest, attachment, attack, capture, commandeering, confiscation, convulsion, distraint, fit, grabbing, paroxysm, spasm, taking.

antonym release.

seldom adv hardly, infrequently, occasionally, rarely, scarcely.

antonym often.

select v choose, cull, pick, prefer, single out, specify.

adj best, chosen, choice, élite, excellent, exclusive, first-class, first-rate, hand-picked, limited, particular, picked, posh, preferable, prime, privileged, rare, selected, special, superior, top, top-notch.

antonyms general, second-rate.

selection n anthology, assortment, choice, choosing, collection, line-up, medley, miscellany, option, palette, pick, potpourri, preference, range, variety.

selective adj careful, choosy, discerning, discriminating, discriminatory, eclectic, fastidious, particular.

antonym unselective.

self n ego, I, identity, person, personality, psyche, soul.

self-assertive adj aggressive, authoritarian, bossy, commanding, dictatorial, domineering, forceful, heavy-handed, high-handed, overbearing, overweening, peremptory, pushing, pushy.

antonym compliant.

self-assured adj assured, cocksure, cocky, collected, composed, confident, overconfident, self-possessed, sure, sure of oneself.

antonyms humble, unsure.

self-centred adj egocentric, egotistic, looking out for number one, narcissistic, self-absorbed, self-interested, selfish, self-seeking, self-serving.

antonym altruistic.

self-confident adj assured, collected, composed, confident, cool, fearless, poised, secure, self-assured, self-possessed, self-reliant.

antonyms humble, unsure.

self-conscious adj affected, awkward, bashful, coy, diffident, embarrassed, ill at ease, insecure, nervous, retiring, self-effacing, shamefaced, sheepish, shrinking, uncomfortable.

antonyms natural, unaffected.

self-control n calmness, composure, cool, coolness, discipline, restraint, self-command, self-discipline, self-government, self-mastery, self-restraint, temperance, willpower.

self-denial n abstemiousness, altruism, asceticism, moderation, renunciation, self-abandonment, self-abnegation, selflessness, self-renunciation, self-sacrifice, temperance, unselfishness.

antonym self-indulgence.

self-esteem n amour-propre, dignity, pride, self-assurance, self-confidence, self-pride, self-regard, self-respect.

antonym humility.

self-evident adj axiomatic, clear, incontrovertible, inescapable, manifest, obvious, self-explanatory, undeniable, unquestionable.

self-government n autarky, autonomy, democracy, home rule, independence, self-sovereignty.

antonym subjection.

self-important adj arrogant, big-headed, bumptious, cocky, conceited, consequential, overbearing, pompous, pushy, self-consequential, strutting, swaggering, vain.

antonym humble.

self-indulgence n dissipation, dissoluteness, excess, extravagance, high living, incontinence, indiscipline, intemperance, profligacy, self-gratification, sensualism.

antonyms self-denial, self-discipline, restraint.

self-indulgent adj dissipated, dissolute, extravagant, intemperate, profligate, sensualistic, undisciplined.

antonym abstemious.

self-interest n egocentrism, egotism, self, self-absorption, self-aggrandizement, self-centredness, selfishness, self-love, self-regard, self-serving.

antonym selflessness.

selfish adj egocentric, egoistic, egotistic, greedy, looking out for number one, mean, mercenary, narrow, self-absorbed, self-centred, self-interested, self-seeking, self-serving.

antonym unselfish.

selfishness n egocentrism, egoism, egotism, greed, meanness, self-centredness, self-interest, self-love, self-regard, self-seeking, self-serving.

antonym selflessness.

selfless adj altruistic, generous, giving, magnanimous, self-denying, self-sacrificing, ungrudging, unselfish.

antonym selfish.

self-possessed adj calm, collected, composed, confident, cool, poised, self-assured, self-collected, together, unruffled.

antonym worried.

self-possession n aplomb, calmness, composure, confidence, cool, coolness, equanimity, poise, sang-froid, self-command, self-confidence, unflappability.

antonym worry.

self-reliance n autarky, independence, self-sufficiency, self-support.

antonym dependence.

self-reliant adj autarkic, independent, self-sufficient, self-supporting, self-sustaining.

antonym dependent.

self-respect n amour-propre, dignity, pride, self-assurance, self-confidence, self-esteem, self-pride, self-regard.

antonym self-doubt.

self-restraint n abstemiousness, forbearance, moderation, patience, self-command, self-control, self-denial, self-discipline, self-government, temperance, willpower.

antonym licence.

self-righteous adj complacent, goody-goody, holier-than-thou, hypocritical, pharisaic, pietistic, pious, priggish, sanctimonious, self-satisfied, smug, superior.

antonym understanding.

self-sacrifice n altruism, generosity, self-abandonment, self-abnegation, self-denial, selflessness, self-renunciation.

antonym selfishness.

self-satisfaction n complacency, pride, self-appreciation, self-approbation, self-approval, self-content, smugness.

antonym humility.

self-satisfied *adj* complacent, puffed-up, self-approving, self-congratulatory, self-contented, self-righteous, smug.
antonym humble.

self-seeking *adj* acquisitive, calculating, careerist, fortune-hunting, gold-digging, mercenary, on the make, opportunistic, self-centred, self-interested, selfish, self-loving, self-serving.
antonym altruistic.

self-styled *adj* professed, pseudo, self-appointed, so-called, soi-disant, would-be.

self-supporting *adj* autarkic, independent, self-financing, self-reliant, self-sufficient, self-sustaining.
antonym dependent.

self-willed *adj* balky, bullheaded, headstrong, intractable, mulish, obstinate, opinionated, pig-headed, refractory, self-opinionated, stiff-necked, stubborn, ungovernable, willful.
antonym complaisant.

sell *v* barter, cheat, convince, deal in, exchange, handle, hawk, market, merchandise, peddle, persuade, promote, retail, sell out, stock, trade, trade in, traffic in, vend, wholesale.
antonym buy.

sell out betray, compromise, double-cross, fail, fink on, inform on, rat on, sell down the river, stab in the back, two-time.
antonym back.

seller *n* agent, dealer, merchant, peddler, rep, representative, retailer, salesperson, storekeeper, tradesman, vendor, wholesaler.
antonym buyer.

selling *n* commence, dealing, marketing, merchandising, merchanting, promotion, sales, salesmanship, trading, traffic, trafficking, transactions, vendition.
antonym buying.

semblance *n* air, appearance, aspect, bearing, façade, figure, form, front, guise, image, likeness, mask, mien, pretence, resemblance, show, similarity, veneer.

seminal *adj* creative, formative, groundbreaking, imaginative, important, influential, innovative, original, productive.
antonym derivative.

seminary *n* academy, college, institute, institution, (divinity) school.

send *v* broadcast, cast, charm, communicate, consign, convey, courier, delight, deliver, direct, discharge, dispatch, drive, electrify, emit, enrapture, enthral, excite, exude, fire, fling, forward, hurl, impel, inspire, intoxicate, mail, move, please, propel, radiate, ravish, refer, remit, shoot, stir, thrill, throw, titillate, transmit.

send for call for, fetch, summon.
antonym dismiss.

send up burlesque, imitate, lampoon, make fun of, mimic, mock, parody, roast, satirize, spoof, take off (on).

send-off *n* departure, farewell, going away, leave-taking, start, valediction.
antonym arrival.

sendup *n* imitation, mockery, parody, satire, skit, spoof, takeoff.

senile *adj* anile, decrepit, doddering, doting, failing, senescent.

senility *n* caducity, decrepitude, dotage, infirmity, second childhood, senescence, senile dementia.

senior *adj* doyenne, elder, first, higher, high-ranking, major, older, superior.
antonym junior.

seniority *n* precedence, priority, rank, standing, superiority.
antonym juniority.

sensation *n* agitation, awareness, commotion, consciousness, emotion, excitement, feeling, furor, hit, impression, perception, scandal, sense, stir, success, surprise, thrill, tingle, vibes, vibrations, wow.

sensational *adj* amazing, astounding, blood-and-thunder, breathtaking, dramatic, electrifying, excellent, exceptional, exciting, fabulous, great, impressive, incredible, lurid, marvellous, melodramatic, mind-blowing, revealing, scandalous, sensationalistic, shocking, smashing, spectacular, staggering, startling, superb, thrilling, yellow.
antonym run-of-the-mill.

sense *n* a head on one's shoulders, appreciation, atmosphere, aura, awareness, brains, clear-headedness, common sense, consciousness, definition, denotation, discernment, discrimination, drift, faculty, feel, feeling, flair, gist, gumption, horse sense, implication, import, impression, intelligence, interpretation, intuition, judgment, level-headedness, logic, marbles, meaning, message, mother wit, nuance, opinion, perception, point, premonition, presentiment, purport, purpose, rationality, reason, reasonableness, sagacity, savvy, sensation, sensibility, significance, signification, substance, understanding, use, value, way, wisdom, wit(s), worth.
antonym foolishness.
v appreciate, comprehend, detect, divine, feel, grasp, intuit, notice, observe, perceive, realize, see, suspect, understand.

senseless *adj* absurd, anesthetized, asinine, crazy, daft, deadened, dotty, fatuous, foolish, halfwitted, idiotic, ill-advised, illogical, imbecilic, inane, incongruous, inconsistent, insane, insensate, insensible, irrational, ludicrous, mad, meaningless, mindless, moronic, nonsensical, numb, numbed, out for the count, out of it, pointless, ridiculous, silly, simple, stunned, stupid, unconscious, unfeeling, unintelligent, unreasonable, unreasoning, unwise.
antonym sensible.

sensibility *n* appreciation, awareness, cognizance, consciousness, delicacy, discernment, discrimination, insight, intuition, perceptiveness, responsiveness,

sensitiveness, sensitivity, sentience, susceptibility, taste.
antonym insensibility.

sensible *adj* appreciable, canny, considerable, discernable, discreet, discriminating, down-to-earth, far-sighted, intelligent, judicious, level-headed, logical, matter-of-fact, noticeable, palpable, perceptible, practical, prudent, rational, realistic, reasonable, right-thinking, sagacious, sage, sane, shrewd, significant, sober, solid, sound, tangible, visible, well-advised, well-thought-out, wise.
antonyms imperceptible, senseless.

sensible of acquainted with, alive to, appreciative of, aware of, cognizant of, conscious of, convinced of, mindful of, observant of, sensitive to, understanding of.
antonym unaware of.

sensitive *adj* acute, alive, controversial, delicate, discriminating, excitable, fine, hyperesthetic, hyperconscious, hypersensitive, impressionable, irritable, keen, perceptive, precise, prickly, quick to take offence, reactive, receptive, responsive, secret, sensitized, sentient, susceptible, temperamental, tender, thin-skinned, touchy, tuned in, umbrageous.
antonym insensitive.

sensitivity *n* delicacy, discrimination, hyperesthesia, hyperconsciousness, irritability, prickliness, reactiveness, reactivity, receptiveness, responsiveness, sensitiveness, susceptibility, thin skin, touchiness.
antonym insensitivity.

sensual *adj* animal, bodily, carnal, epicurean, erotic, fleshly, lascivious, lecherous, lewd, libidinous, licentious, lustful, luxurious, physical, randy, raunchy, self-indulgent, sexual, sexy, voluptuous, worldly.
antonyms ascetic, puritan.

▲ *confusable word* sensuous.

sensualist *n* bon vivant, debauchee, epicure, epicurean, gourmand, gourmet, hedonist, libertine, profligate, roué, sybarite, voluptuary.
antonyms ascetic, Puritan.

sensuality *n* animalism, animal magnetism, carnality, debauchery, eroticism, gourmandise, lasciviousness, lecherousness, lewdness, libertinism, libidinousness, licentiousness, lustfulness, profligacy, prurience, salaciousness, sexiness, voluptuousness.
antonyms asceticism, Puritanism.

sensuous *adj* epicurean, gratifying, hedonistic, lush, luxurious, pleasurable, rich, sensory, sumptuous, sybaritic, voluptuous.
antonyms ascetic, plain, simple.

▲ *confusable word* sensual.

sentence *n* condemnation, decision, decree, doom, judgment, legal, opinion, order, pronouncement, ruling, verdict.
v condemn, consign, damn, doom, judge, pass judgment on, penalize, pronounce judgment on.

sententious *adj* aphoristic, axiomatic, brief, canting, compact, concise, epigrammatic, gnomic, laconic, moralistic, moralizing, pithy, pointed, pompous, ponderous, preachy, sanctimonious, short, succinct, terse.
antonyms humble, prolix.

sentient *adj* aware, conscious, feeling, live, living, reactive, responsive, sensible, sensitive.
antonym insentient.

sentiment *n* belief, emotion, emotionalism, feeling, idea, judgment, mawkishness, maxim, mental attitude, mush, mushiness, opinion, persuasion, romanticism, saying, sensibility, sentimentalism, sentimentality, slush, soft-heartedness, tenderness, thought, view, warm fuzzies.
antonyms hard-heartedness, straightforwardness.

sentimental *adj* corny, dewy-eyed, drippy, emotional, gushing, gushy, impressionable, lovey-dovey, maudlin, mawkish, mushy, nostalgic, pathetic, pulpy, romantic, sappy, schmaltzy, simpering, sloppy, slushy, soft, soft-hearted, soppy, tearful, tearjerking, tender, touching, treacly, weepy.
antonym unsentimental.

sentimentality *n* bathos, corniness, emotionalism, gush, mawkishness, mush, nostalgia, pulp, romanticism, schmaltz, sentimentalism, sloppiness, slush, soppiness, tenderness.

sentry *n* guard, lookout, picket, sentinel, vedette, watch, watchman.

separable *adj* detachable, distinguishable, divisible, scissile, severable.
antonym inseparable.

separate *v* abstract, bifurcate, come between, decompose, decouple, departmentalize, detach, disaffiliate, disally, disband, disconnect, disentangle, disjoin, dissever, dissolve, distance, disunite, diverge, divide, divorce, estrange, exfoliate, fall out, isolate, open, part, part company, partition, quarantine, remove, secede, seclude, segregate, sever, split, split up, sunder, uncouple, unlink, winnow.
antonyms join, unite.
adj alone, apart, autonomous, detached, disconnected, discrete, disjointed, disjunct, disparate, distinct, divided, divorced, independent, individual, isolated, particular, several, single, solitary, unattached, unconnected, unrelated.
antonyms attached, together.

separated *adj* alienated, apart, disjoined, disjointed, dissociated, disconnected, disunited, divided, divorced, isolated, parted, segregated, separate, split up, sundered.
antonyms attached, together.

separately *adv* alone, apart, discretely, discriminately, independently, individually, personally, severally, singly.
antonym together.

separating *adj* disjunctive, dividing, divisive, intervening, isolating, partitioning, segregating.
antonym unifying.

separation *n* break, break-up, detachment, dialysis, dieresis, dichotomy, disconnection, disengagement, disjunction, disseverance, dissociation, dissolution, distance, disunion, divergence, division, divorce, estrangement, falling-out, farewell, gap, leave-taking, parting, partition, quarantine, rift, segregation, severance, solution, split, split-up.

antonyms togetherness, unification.

septic *adj* contaminated, diseased, festering, infected, poisoned, purulent, putrefactive, putrefying, putrid, suppurating, tainted.

sepulchral *adj* cheerless, deep, dismal, funereal, gloomy, grave, hollow, lugubrious, melancholy, morbid, mournful, reverberating, sad, sepultural, sombre, sonorous, woeful.

antonym cheerful.

sepulchre *n* burial chamber, crypt, grave, mausoleum, tomb, vault.

sequel *n* aftermath, conclusion, consequence, continuation, development, end, end result, follow-up, issue, outcome, payoff, result, upshot.

sequence *n* arrangement, chain, course, cycle, order, procession, progression, run, series, set, succession, track, train.

sequestered *adj* cloistered, isolated, lonely, out-of-the-way, private, quiet, reclusive, remote, retired, secluded, unfrequented.

antonyms busy, frequented, public.

seraphic *adj* angelic, beatific, blissful, celestial, divine, heavenly, holy, innocent, pure, saintly, sublime, virtuous.

antonym demonic.

serene *adj* calm, composed, cool, halcyon, imperturbable, irenic, pacific, peaceful, placid, quiet, tranquil, unclouded, undisturbed, unflappable, unruffled, untroubled.

antonym troubled.

serf *n* bondmaid, bondservant, bondsman, bondwoman, helot, servant, slave, thrall, villein.

antonym master.

series *n* arrangement, catena, chain, concatenation, course, cycle, line, order, progression, run, scale, sequence, set, string, succession, train.

serious *adj* acute, alarming, critical, crucial, dangerous, deep, deliberate, determined, difficult, earnest, far-reaching, fateful, genuine, grave, great, grim, heavy, honest, humourless, important, long-faced, momentous, pensive, pressing, resolute, resolved, sedate, severe, significant, sincere, sober, solemn, staid, stern, straight-faced, thoughtful, unsmiling, urgent, weighty, worrying, zealous.

antonyms facetious, light, slight, smiling, trivial.

seriously *adv* acutely, all joking aside, badly, critically, dangerously, distressingly, earnestly, gravely, grievously, severely, sincerely, solemnly, sorely, thoughtfully, urgently, zealously.

antonyms casually, slightly.

seriousness *n* danger, earnestness, gravity, humourlessness, importance, moment, sedateness, significance, sobriety, solemnity, staidness, sternness, urgency, weight.

antonyms casualness, slightness, triviality.

sermon *n* address, dressing-down, exhortation, harangue, homily, lecture, preachment, reproof, talking-to.

serpentine *adj* circuitous, coiling, crooked, cunning, meandering, serpentiform, sinuous, snakelike, snaking, snaky, tortuous, treacherous, twisting, winding.

antonym straight.

serrated *adj* notched, sawlike, serrulate, toothed.

antonym smooth.

serried *adj* close, close-set, compact, crowded, dense, massed.

antonym scattered.

servant *n* amah, ancillary, assistant, attendant, ayah, bearer, boy, butler, daily, day-worker, domestic, drudge, flunkey, footman, garçon, gardener, gentleman's gentleman, gossoon, handmaid, handmaiden, help, helper, hireling, housekeeper, kitchenmaid, knave, lackey, lady's maid, liveryman, maid, maid of all work, maidservant, maître d'hôtel, major-domo, man, man of all work, manservant, menial, ministrant, nanny, retainer, seneschal, slave, steward, subordinate, underling, valet, vassal.

antonyms master, mistress.

serve *v* act, aid, answer, assist, attend, be of use, content, dance attendance on, deal, deliver, discharge, distribute, do, duty, fulfil, function, further, help, minister to, oblige, officiate, pass, perform, present, provide, satisfy, succour, suffice, suit, supply, tend, treat, undergo, wait on, work, work for.

service *n* advantage, agency, aid, allegiance, assistance, avail, benefit, ceremony, check, duty, employ, employment, expediting, favour, function, good turn, help, homage, labour, liturgy, maintenance, ministrations, obedience, observance, office, overhaul, performance (of duties), rite, servicing, supply, use, usefulness, utility, work, worship.

v check, maintain, overhaul, recondition, repair, tune (up).

serviceable *adj* advantageous, beneficial, convenient, dependable, durable, efficient, functional, handy, hard-wearing, helpful, operative, plain, practical, profitable, simple, strong, tough, unadorned, usable, useful, utilitarian, working.

antonym unserviceable.

servile *adj* abject, bootlicking, craven, cringing, deferential, fawning, grovelling, humble, low, mean, menial, obeisant, obsequious, slavish, subject, submissive, subservient, sycophantic, toadying, unctuous.

antonyms aggressive, bold.

servility *n* abjection, abjectness, bootlicking, deference, fawning, grovelling, meanness, obeisance, obsequiousness, self-abasement, slavishness, subjection, submissiveness, subservience, sycophancy, toadeating, toadyism, unctuousness.

antonyms aggressiveness, boldness.

servitude *n* bondage, bonds, chains, enslavement, obedience, serfdom, slavery, subjection, subjugation, thralldom, thrall, vassalage, villeinage.

antonym freedom.

session *n* assembly, conference, discussion, get-together, hearing, meeting, period, semester, sitting, term, year.

set¹ *v* adjust, agree on, aim, allocate, allot, appoint, arrange, assign, cake, cohere, condense, congeal, co-ordinate, crystallize, decree, deposit, designate, determine, dip, direct, embed, establish, fasten, fix, form, gel, gelatinize, go down, harden, impose, install, jell, lay, locate, lodge, mount, name, ordain, order, park, place, plant, plump, plunk, point, position, prepare, prescribe, put, regulate, resolve, rest, schedule, seat, settle on, shape, sink, situate, solidify, specify, stake, station, stick, stiffen, synchronize, thicken.

n bearing, carriage, course, direction, drift, fit, form, hang, inclination, mise en scène, orientation, position, posture, scene, scenery, setting, tendency, trend, turn.

adj agreed, appointed, arranged, conventional, customary, decided, definite, determined, entrenched, established, firm, fixed, formal, hackneyed, immovable, inflexible, planned, prearranged, predetermined, prepared, prescribed, regular, rehearsed, resolved, rigid, routine, scheduled, settled, standard, stereotyped, stock, strict, stubborn, traditional, trite, unspontaneous, usual.

antonyms free, movable, off-the-cuff, spontaneous, undecided.

set about begin, go about, set to work, start, tackle, wade into.

set against alienate from, antagonize against, balance with, compare with, contrast with, estrange from, juxtapose, weigh against.

set apart choose, consecrate, dedicate, devote, differentiate, put aside, segregate, separate, single out.

set aside abrogate, allot, annul, cancel, commit, devote, discard, dismiss, disregard, keep, keep back, lay aside, nullify, overrule, overturn, put aside, quash, reject, repeal, repudiate, reserve, reverse, save, select, separate, waive.

set back delay, hamper, hinder, hold up, impede, interrupt, retard, slow (down).

set eyes on behold, clap eyes on, come across, come upon, encounter, lay eyes on, meet, meet with, notice, observe, see.

set free decontrol, deliver, disembarrass, disentangle, emancipate, extricate, free, liberate, loose, manumit, ransom, release, rescue, rid, save, unpen.

antonyms confine, enslave.

set off depart, detonate, display, embark, enhance, explode, ignite, leave, light, make tracks, sally forth, show off, start out, touch off, trigger.

set on assail, assault, attack, beat up, fall upon, fly at, go for, incite, instigate, lay into,

mug, pitch into, sail into, set upon, turn on, urge.

set out arrange, array, begin, describe, detail, display, dispose, elaborate, elucidate, embark, exhibit, explain, intend, lay out, make a move, make tracks, plan, present, sally forth, set off, spread out, start, start out.

set up arrange, assemble, back, begin, boost, build, constitute, construct, contrive, create, elevate, erect, establish, finance, fit out, form, found, frame, fund, inaugurate, initiate, install, institute, introduce, organize, prearrange, prepare, promote, raise, sponsor, start, subsidize, support.

set² *n* apparatus, assemblage, assortment, band, batch, circle, class, clique, collection, company, compendium, coterie, covey, crew, crowd, faction, gang, group, kit, lot, outfit, pack, sequence, series.

setback *n* blow, check, defeat, delay, disappointment, hitch, holdup, misfortune, problem, rebuff, regression, relapse, reverse, snag, upset.

antonyms advance, advantage, boost, help.

setting *n* adjustment, arena, backdrop, background, context, environment, frame, locale, location, milieu, mise en scène, mounting, period, perspective, position, scene, scenery, set, site, surroundings.

settle *v* adjust, agree, alight, appoint, arrange, bed, calm, choose, clear, colonize, come to rest, come to terms (with), compact, complete, compose, conclude, confirm, deal with, decide, decree, descend, determine, discharge, dispose of, dower, drop, dwell, end, endow, ensconce, establish, fall, fix, found, hush, inhabit, land, lay, light, liquidate, live, lower, lull, occupy, ordain, order, pacify, pay, people, pioneer, plant, plump, populate, put (or lay) to rest, quell, quiet, quieten, quit, reassure, reconcile, relax, relieve, reside, resolve, sedate, sink, soothe, square, square up, subside, tranquillize.

settlement¹ *n* accommodation, adjustment, agreement, allowance, arrangement, coming to terms, completion, compromise, conclusion, confirmation, decision, defrayal, discharge, disposition, endowment, establishment, income, liquidation, payment, putting in order, resolution, satisfaction, termination.

settlement² *n* colonization, colony, community, encampment, frontier town, hamlet, immigration, kibbutz, occupation, outpost, peopling, population.

settlement³ *n* compacting, drop, fall, sinkage, sinking, subsidence.

settler *n* colonizer, colonist, frontier dweller, immigrant, incomer, newcomer, pioneer, squatter.

set-to *n* altercation, argument, brush, conflict, contest, disagreement, dispute, dustup, exchange, fight, fracas, quarrel, row, scrap, spat, squabble, wrangle.

setup *n* arrangement, frame-up, ménage, organization, plan, prearrangement, preparation, put-up job, régime, structure, system.

sever v alienate, bisect, break off, cleave, cut, cut off, detach, disconnect, disjoin, dissever, dissociate, dissolve, disunite, divide, estrange, part, rend, separate, split, sunder, terminate.

antonyms join, unite.

several adj a few, assorted, different, discrete, disparate, distinct, diverse, individual, particular, respective, separate, single, some, some few, specific, sundry, various.

severally adv discretely, individually, one by one, particularly, respectively, separately, seriatim, singly.

antonyms simultaneously, together.

severe adj acute, arduous, ascetic, astringent, austere, biting, bitter, caustic, cold, critical, cruel, cutting, dangerous, demanding, difficult, disapproving, dour, draconian, exacting, excruciating, extreme, fierce, flinty, forbidding, functional, grave, grim, grinding, hard, harsh, inclement, inexorable, intense, ironfisted, iron-handed, oppressive, painful, piercing, pitiless, plain, punishing, relentless, restrained, Rhadamanthine, rigid, rigorous, scathing, serious, sharp, shooting, simple, sober, Spartan, stabbing, stark, stern, strait-laced, strict, stringent, taxing, tight-lipped, tough, trying, tyrannical, unadorned, unbending, unembellished, ungentle, unkind, unrelenting, unsmiling, unsparing, unsympathetic, violent.

antonyms compassionate, kind, lenient, mild, sympathetic.

severely adv acutely, austerely, badly, bitterly, coldly, critically, dangerously, disapprovingly, dourly, excruciatingly, extremely, gravely, grimly, hard, harshly, rigorously, sharply, sorely, sternly, strictly, unsympathetically.

severity n acuteness, asceticism, austerity, coldness, gravity, hardness, harshness, plainness, rigour, seriousness, severeness, sharpness, simplicity, starkness, sternness, stringency, strictness, toughness, ungentleness, unkindness.

antonyms compassion, kindness, leniency, mildness.

sex n coitus, congress, copulation, fornication, gender, genitals, intercourse, intimacy, libido, lovemaking, reproduction, sexual intercourse, sexual relations, sexuality, union, venery, whoopee.

sex appeal allure, desirability, glamour, magnetism, nubility, seductiveness, sensuality, sexiness, sexual attraction, voluptuousness.

sexless adj asexual, neuter, parthenogenetic, undersexed, unfeminine, unmasculine, unsexed, unsexual.

sexton n caretaker, gravedigger, sacristan, verger.

sexual adj carnal, coital, erotic, gamic, genital, intimate, procreative, reproductive, sensual, sex, sex-related, venereal.

antonym asexual.

sexual intercourse carnal knowledge, coitus, commerce, congress, consummation, copulation, coupling, going all the way, lovemaking, making it, mating, penetration, scoring, sex, sleeping together, the marriage act, union, whoopee.

sexuality n carnality, desire, eroticism, lust, sensuality, sexiness, sexual drive, sexual instincts, sexual urges, virility, voluptuousness.

sexy adj arousing, come-hither, curvaceous, erotic, flirtatious, hot, inviting, kissable, lascivious, lustful, naughty, nubile, pornographic, provocative, provoking, racy, raunchy, seductive, sensual, sensuous, sexual, slinky, steamy, stimulating, suggestive, titillating, virile, voluptuous.

antonym sexless.

shabby adj bad, base, cheap, contemptible, dastardly, despicable, dilapidated, dingy, dirty, dishonourable, disreputable, dog-eared, faded, frayed, ignoble, inferior, low, low-down, lowlife, mangy, mean, moth-eaten, neglected, niggardly, out at the elbows, paltry, pokey, poor, ragged, ratty, rotten, run-down, scruffy, seedy, shameful, shoddy, squalid, tacky, tattered, tatty, threadbare, ungentlemanly, unworthy, worn, worn-out.

antonyms honourable, smart.

shack n cabin, dump, hellhole, hole, hovel, hut, hutch, lean-to, shanty, shed.

antonym mansion.

shackle n ball and chain, bond, bracelets, chain, fetter, gyve, hamper, handcuff, hobble, iron, leg-iron, manacle, restraint, rope, shackles, tether, trammel.

v bind, chain, constrain, curb, encumber, fetter, gyve, hamper, hamstring, handcuff, handicap, hobble, hogtie, impede, inhibit, limit, manacle, obstruct, pinion, restrain, restrict, secure, tether, thwart, tie, trammel.

shade n amount, apparition, awning, blind, canopy, cloud, colour, coolness, cover, covering, curtain, dash, degree, difference, dimness, drape, eidolon, ghost, gradation, grade, hint, hue, manes, nuance, obscurity, penumbra, phantasm, phantom, screen, semblance, semidarkness, shadiness, shadow, shadows, shelter, shield, shroud, shutter, spark, spectre, spirit, stain, suggestion, suspicion, tinge, tint, tone, touch, trace, umbra, umbrage, umbrella, variation, variety, veil, wraith.

v cloud, conceal, cover, darken, dim, hide, mute, obscure, overshadow, protect, screen, shadow, shield, shroud, veil.

shadow n affliction, blight, cloud, companion, cover, darkness, degree, detective, dimness, dusk, echo, follower, ghost, gloaming, gloom, gloominess, hanger-on, hint, image, inseparable, obscurity, pal, phantom, protection, reflection, remnant, representation, sadness, shade, shelter, sidekick, silhouette, sleuth, spectre, spirit, suggestion, suspicion, tail, tenebrity, trace, umbrage, vestige.

v darken, dog, follow, obscure, overhang, overshadow, screen, shade, shield, stalk, tail, track, trail, watch.

shadowy adj crepuscular, dark, dim, dreamlike, dusky, elusive, faint, ghostly, gloomy, half-remembered, hazy, illusory, imaginary, impalpable, indistinct, intangible, murky, nebulous, obscure, shaded, shady, spectral, tenebrous, tenuous, umbrageous, umbral, undefined, unreal, unsubstantial, vague, wraithlike.

antonyms clearly defined, sunlit.

shady¹ *adj* bosky, cool, dark, dim, shaded, shadowy, tenebrous, treed, umbrageous, umbral, umbriferous, wooded.

antonyms bright, sunlit, sunny.

shady² *adj* crooked, discreditable, dishonest, disreputable, dubious, fishy, fly-by-night, fraudulent, not kosher, questionable, shifty, slippery, suspect, suspicious, underhand, unethical, unscrupulous, untrustworthy.

antonyms honest, trustworthy.

shaft¹ *n* arbor, arrow, axle, barb, beam, column, cut, dart, gibe, gleam, haft, handle, hole, missile, passage, pit, pole, ray, rod, shank, spear, stalk, stem, stick, streak, thrust, upright, well, winze.

shaft² *v* burn, cheat, con, diddle, do out of, exploit, give the shaft (to), gyp, have, screw, sell a bill of goods (to), stick it to, swindle.

shaggy *adj* disorderly, hairy, hirsute, longhaired, napped, rough, tousled, unkempt, unshorn.

antonyms bald, shorn.

shake *n* agitation, convulsion, disturbance, flutter, instant, jar, jerk, jiffy, jolt, jounce, moment, no time (at all), pulsation, quaking, sec, second, shiver, shock, shudder, split second, trembling, tremor, trice, twitch, vibration.

v agitate, brandish, break (the habit), bump, churn, concuss, convulse, daunt, distress, disturb, flourish, fluctuate, frighten, heave, jar, joggle, jolt, jounce, oscillate, quake, quiver, rattle, rock, rouse, shake up, shimmy, shiver, shock, shudder, sway, totter, tremble, twitch, undermine, unnerve, unsettle, upset, vibrate, wag, waggle, wave, waver, weaken, wobble.

shake a leg get a move on, get cracking, get on the stick, hurry (up), look lively, step on it.

shake (off) dislodge, elude, get rid of, give the slip (to), shrug off, leave behind, lose, outdistance, outpace, outstrip.

shake (up) agitate, discompose, distress, disturb, frighten, intimidate, jar, jolt, psych out, rattle, rock, rouse, shock, startle, unnerve, unsettle, upset, weaken.

shake-up *n* disturbance, rearrangement, reorganization, reshuffle, upheaval.

shaky *adj* dubious, faltering, flimsy, inexpert, insecure, precarious, questionable, quivery, rickety, rocky, suspect, tottering, uncertain, undependable, unreliable, unsafe, unsound, unstable, unsteady, unsupported, untrustworthy, weak, wobbly.

antonyms firm, strong.

shallow *adj* empty, flimsy, foolish, frivolous, idle, ignorant, meaningless, puerile, simple, skin-deep, slight, superficial, surface, trivial, unanalytical, unintelligent, unscholarly.

antonyms analytical, deep.

sham *n* charlatan, counterfeit, fake, feint, forgery, fraud, gold brick, hoax, humbug, imitation, impostor, imposture, mountebank, phony, pretence, pretender, pretext.

adj artificial, bogus, cardboard, counterfeit, ersatz, fake, faked, false, feigned, imitation, mock, pasteboard, phony, pinchbeck, pretend, pseudo, put-on, simulated, spurious, synthetic.

antonym genuine.

v affect, counterfeit, fake, feign, pretend, put on, simulate.

shaman *n* angakoq, charmer, magician, medicine man (or woman), powwow, sorcerer, witch doctor.

shambles *n* anarchy, battlefield, bedlam, chaos, confusion, disarray, disorder, disorganization, havoc, madhouse, mess, muddle, pigsty, wreck.

shambling *adj* awkward, clumsy, disjointed, loose, lumbering, lurching, shuffling, unco-ordinated, ungainly, unsteady.

antonyms agile, neat, nimble, spry.

shame *n* bashfulness, blot, chagrin, compunction, contempt, degradation, derision, discredit, disgrace, dishonour, disrepute, embarrassment, guilt (feelings), humiliation, ignominy, infamy, mortification, obloquy, odium, opprobrium, remorse, reproach, scandal, shamefacedness, stain, stigma.

antonyms distinction, honour, pride.

v abash, confound, debase, defile, degrade, discomfit, disconcert, discredit, disgrace, dishonour, embarrass, humble, humiliate, mortify, put to shame, reproach, ridicule, show up, sully, taint.

shamefaced *adj* abashed, apologetic, ashamed, bashful, blushing, chagrined, conscience-stricken, contrite, diffident, discomfited, embarrassed, guilty, hat in hand, hesitant, humiliated, modest, mortified, red-faced, remorseful, sheepish, shrinking, shy, timid, uncomfortable.

antonyms proud, unashamed.

shameful *adj* abominable, appalling, atrocious, base, contemptible, dastardly, degrading, discreditable, disgraceful, dishonourable, embarrassing, humiliating, ignominious, indecent, inexcusable, infamous, low, mean, mortifying, outrageous, reprehensible, scandalous, shaming, unbecoming, unconscionable, unworthy, vile, wicked, wrong.

antonyms creditable, honourable.

shameless *adj* abandoned, audacious, barefaced, blatant, bold, brash, brazen, corrupt, defiant, depraved, dissolute, flagrant, hardened, immodest, improper, impudent, incorrigible, indecent, insolent, profligate, reprobate, unabashed, unashamed, unblushing, unprincipled, unrepentant, unscrupulous, wanton.

antonyms ashamed, contrite, shamefaced.

shanty *n* cabin, hovel, hut, hutch, lean-to, shack, shed.

antonym mansion.

shape *n* apparition, appearance, aspect, build, condition, configuration, conformation, contour, cut, dimensions, fettle, figure, form, format, frame, Gestalt, guise, health, image, kilter, likeness, lines, make, model, mould, outline, pattern, physique, profile, semblance, silhouette, spectre, state, structure, template, trim.

v accommodate, adapt, conform, construct, contour, create, define, develop, devise, embody, fashion, forge, form, frame, guide, make, model, modify, mould, plan, prepare, produce, redact, regulate, remodel.

shapeless *adj* amorphous, asymmetrical, characterless, dumpy, embryonic, formless, inchoate, indeterminate, irregular, nebulous, obscure, undeveloped, unformed, unshapely, unstructured, vague.

antonyms clear-cut, definitely, shapely, structured.

shapely *adj* comely, curvaceous, elegant, graceful, pretty, trim, voluptuous, well-formed, well-proportioned, well-set-up, well-shaped, well-turned.

antonym dumpy, shapeless.

share *v* allot, apportion, assign, chip in, distribute, divide (up), divvy (up), go Dutch, go fifty-fifty, go halves, partake in (or of), participate in, split, whack up.

antonyms monopolize.

n a piece of the action, allotment, allowance, contribution, cut, dividend, division, divvy, due, finger, lot, part, portion, proportion, quota, ration, stint, whack.

shark *n* adept, chiseller, crook, expert, extortionist, fleecer, no slouch, parasite, predator, pro, sharp, sharper, slicker, swindler, usurer, wheeler-dealer.

sharp *adj* abrupt, acerbic, aciculate, acid, acidulous, acrid, acrimonious, acute, alert, angular, apt, artful, astute, attractive, barbed, biting, bitter, bright, brisk, brusque, burning, canny, caustic, chic, chiselled, classy, clear, clear-cut, clever, cold, crafty, crisp, cunning, cutting, deep, deep-felt, discerning, dishonest, distinct, dressy, eager, edged, excruciating, extreme, fashionable, fierce, harsh, honed, hot, hurtful, incisive, intense, jagged, keen, knife-edged, knifelike, knowing, long-headed, marked, natty, nimble-witted, noticing, observant, painful, penetrating, perceptive, piercing, piquant, pointed, pungent, quick, quick-witted, rapid, razor-sharp, ready, sarcastic, sardonic, scathing, serrated, severe, sharpened, shooting, shrewd, shrill, sly, smart, snappy, snazzy, spiky, stabbing, stinging, strident, stylish, subtle, sudden, tart, trenchant, trendy, unblurred, undulled, unscrupulous, vinegary, violent, vitriolic, waspish, watchful, wily.

antonyms blunt, dull, mild, obtuse, slow, stupid.

adv abruptly, exactly, on the dot, precisely, promptly, punctually, suddenly, unexpectedly.

sharpen *v* acuminate, de-blur, edge, file, focus, grind, hone, improve, increase, stimulate, strop, taper, whet.

antonym blunt.

sharpness *n* acuity, acuteness, alertness, astuteness, causticity, discernment, eagerness, fierceness, incisiveness, intensity, keenness, penetration, perceptiveness, pungency, quickness, severity, shrewdness, stridence, whet.

antonyms dullness, sloth.

sharp-sighted *adj* cat-eyed, clear-eyed, eagle-eyed, gimlet-eyed, hawk-eyed, keen-sighted, lynx-eyed, noticing, observant, perceptive, sharp-witted.

antonyms short-sighted, unobservant.

shatter *v* blast, blight, break, burst, crack, crack open, crush, dash, demolish, destroy, devastate, disable, dumfound, explode, impair, implode, overturn, overwhelm, pulverize, reduce to smithereens, ruin, shiver, smash, splinter, split, stun, torpedo, undermine, upset, wreck.

shattered *adj* broken, crushed, damaged, demolished, destroyed, devastated, disabled, overturned, overwhelmed, pulverized, reduced to smithereens, ruined, smashed, undermined.

shave *v* barber, crop, cut close, cut (off), fleece, graze, pare, plane, scrape, shear, shorten, tonsure, trim.

sheaf *n* armful, batch, bunch, bundle, lot, packet, truss.

sheath *n* armour, case, casing, coat, coating, covering, envelope, plating, protective layer, shell, sleeve, tube, scabbard.

shed[1] *v* cast, cast aside, cast off, diffuse, discard, drop, effuse, emit, exfoliate, exuviate, get rid of, give, give forth, lose, moult, peel off, pour, radiate, repel, scatter, shower, slough, spill, throw off.

shed light on clarify, clear up, elucidate, explain, illuminate, simplify.

shed[2] *n* barn, hut, lean-to, outbuilding, outhouse, shack, shanty.

shedding *n* casting, diffusion, discarding, ecdysis, effusion, emission, exfoliation, exuviation, moulting, radiation, scattering, sloughing.

sheen *n* brightness, brilliance, burnish, gleam, gloss, lustre, patina, polish, shimmer, shine, shininess.

antonyms dullness, tarnish.

sheepish *adj* abashed, ashamed, chagrined, chastened, embarrassed, foolish, mortified, self-conscious, shamefaced, silly, uncomfortable.

antonym unabashed.

sheer[1] *adj* abrupt, absolute, arrant, complete, downright, mere, out-and-out, perpendicular, precipitous, pure, rank, stark, steep, thorough, thoroughgoing, total, unadulterated, unalloyed, unmingled, unmitigated, unqualified, utter, vertical.

sheer[2] *adj* diaphanous, fine, flimsy, gauzy, gossamer, pellucid, see-through, thin, translucent, transparent.

antonyms heavy, thick.

sheet *n* blanket, broadsheet, broadside, circular, coat, covering, expanse, film, flyer, folio, handbill, handout, lamina, layer, leaf, leaflet, membrane, newspaper, overlay, page, pane, panel, piece, plate, shroud, skin, slab, stratum, surface, veneer.

shelf *n* bank, bar, bench, bracket, ledge, mantel, mantelpiece, platform, projection, reef, sandbank, sand bar, shoal, step, terrace.

shell *n* carapace, cartridge, case, casing, chassis, covering, crust, exterior, frame, framework, hull, husk, nacelle, pod, projectile, rind, shuck, skeleton, structure.

v attack, barrage, batter, blitz, bomb, bombard, cannonade, fire upon, hull, husk, shuck, strafe, strike.

shell out ante (up), contribute, cough up, disburse, donate, expend, fork out, give, lay out, pay out, spend, subscribe.

shelter *v* accommodate, cover, defend, ensconce, guard, harbour, hide, house, protect, put up, safeguard, screen, shade, shadow, shield.

antonym expose.

n accommodations, aegis, asylum, bunker, cover, covert, coverture, defence, dugout, guard, harbour, harbourage, haven, lean-to, lee, lodgings, protection, refuge, retreat, roof (over one's head), safety, sanctuary, sconce, screen, security, shade, shadow, umbrage, umbrella.

antonym exposure.

sheltered *adj* cloistered, conventual, cosy, hermitic, isolated, lee, protected, quiet, reclusive, retired, screened, secluded, shaded, shielded, snug, unworldly, warm, withdrawn.

antonym exposed.

shelve *v* defer, dismiss, freeze, halt, mothball, pigeonhole, postpone, put aside, put in abeyance, put off, put on hold, put on ice, suspend, table.

antonyms expedite, implement.

shepherd *n* guardian, guide, herd, herder, pastor, protector, shepherd boy, shepherdess.

v conduct, convoy, escort, guide, herd, lead, marshal, steer, usher.

shield *n* aegis, buckler, bulwark, cover, defence, écu, escutcheon, guard, protection, rampart, safeguard, screen, scutum, shelter, targe.

v cover, defend, guard, protect, safeguard, screen, shade, shadow, shelter.

antonym expose.

shift *v* adjust, alter, budge, change, change course, convert, deviate, dislodge, displace, drift, fluctuate, manoeuvre, move, quit, rearrange, relocate, remove, reposition, swerve, switch, transfer, transpose, vacillate, vary, veer.

n alteration, artifice, change, contrivance, conversion, deviation, device, displacement, dodge, expedient, fluctuation, housedress, manoeuvre, modification, move, permutation, rearrangement, removal, ruse, scheme, shifting, sleight, stratagem, subterfuge, switch, tactic, transfer, trick, veering, wile.

shiftless *adj* aimless, directionless, feckless, goalless, good-for-nothing, idle, incompetent, indolent, ineffectual, inefficient, inept, irresponsible, lackadaisical, lazy, resourceless, slothful, unambitious, unenterprising.

antonyms ambitious, aspiring, eager, enterprising.

shifty *adj* contriving, crafty, crooked, deceitful, devious, dishonest, disingenuous, dubious, duplicitous, evasive, fly-by-night, furtive, scheming, shady, slippery, tricky, underhand, unprincipled, unreliable, untrustworthy, wily.

antonyms honest, open.

shilly-shally *v* back and fill, dilly-dally, dither, falter, fluctuate, hem and haw, hesitate, mess around, prevaricate, seesaw, teeter, vacillate, waver.

shimmer *v* coruscate, gleam, glisten, glitter, phosphoresce, scintillate, twinkle.

n coruscation, gleam, glimmer, glitter, glow, incandescence, iridescence, lustre, phosphorescence.

shimmering *adj* aventurine, gleaming, glimmering, glistening, glittering, glowing, incandescent, iridescent, luminous, lustrous, phosphorescent, sheeny, shining, shiny, sparkling.

antonyms dull, matt.

shin *v* ascend, clamber (up), climb, mount, scale, scramble (up), shinny, swarm.

shine *v* beam, be good (at), brush, buff, burnish, coruscate, excel, flash, glare, gleam, glimmer, glisten, glitter, glow, lustre, polish, radiate, scintillate, shimmer, sparkle, stand out, twinkle.

n brightness, burnish, effulgence, glare, glaze, gleam, gloss, glow, lambency, light, luminosity, lustre, patina, polish, radiance, sheen, shimmer, sparkle.

shining *adj* beaming, bright, brilliant, celebrated, conspicuous, distinguished, effulgent, eminent, fulgent, gleaming, glistening, glittering, glorious, glowing, illustrious, leading, lucent, luminous, outstanding, radiant, resplendent, rutilant, shimmering, shiny, sparkling, splendid, twinkling.

shiny *adj* agleam, aglow, bright, burnished, gleaming, glistening, glossy, luminous, lustrous, polished, satiny, sheeny, shimmery, shining, sleek.

antonyms dark, dull.

ship *n* airplane, airship, argosy, barque, boat, ferry, freighter, frigate, galleon, galley, liner, schooner, spacecraft, steamer, steamship, tanker, trawler, vessel, warship, yacht.

shipshape *adj* businesslike, neat, orderly, seamanlike, spick-and-span, spruce, tidy, trim, well-organized, well-planned, well-regulated.

antonyms disorderly, untidy.

shirk *v* avoid, dodge, duck, duck out of, evade, get out of, goldbrick, leave undone, malinger, neglect, shun, sidestep, slack.

shirker *n* absentee, clock watcher, dodger, goldbricker, idler, layabout, loafer, malingerer, quitter, shirk, slacker.

shiver *v* palpitate, quake, quiver, shake, shudder, tremble, vibrate.

n flutter, frisson, quiver, shaking, shudder, start, thrill, tremble, trembling, tremor, twitch, vibration.

shivery *adj* chilled, chilly, cold, fearful, fluttery, jittery, nervous, quaking, quivery, shaking, trembly.

shoal *n* assemblage, crowd, flock, horde, mass, mob, multitude, swarm, throng.

shock *v* agitate, appal, astound, confound, disgust, dismay, disquiet, electrify, horrify, jar, jolt, nauseate, numb, offend, outrage, paralyse, revolt, scandalize, shake, sicken, stagger, startle, stun, stupefy, traumatize, unnerve, unsettle.

antonyms delight, gratify, please, reassure.

n blow, bombshell, concussion, consternation, dismay, distress, disturbance, fright, impact, jar, jolt, perturbation, stupefaction, stupor, thunderbolt, trauma, turn, upset.

antonyms delight, pleasure.

shocking *adj* abhorrent, abominable, appalling, astounding, atrocious, deplorable, detestable, disgraceful, disgusting, disquieting, distressing, dreadful, execrable, foul, frightful, ghastly, hideous, horrible, horrific, horrifying, insufferable, intolerable, loathsome, monstrous, nauseating, odious, offensive, outrageous, repugnant, repulsive, revolting, scandalous, sickening, stupefying, unbearable, unspeakable.

antonyms acceptable, delightful, pleasant, satisfactory.

shoddy *adj* cheap, cheapjack, flimsy, gimcrack, inferior, jerry-built, junky, poor, schlocky, second-rate, schlocky, shabby, slipshod, sloppy, tacky, tatty, tawdry, trashy, trumpery, worthless.

antonyms fine, well-made.

shoot¹ *v* bag, blast, bolt, charge, dart, dash, discharge, dump, emit, enfilade, film, fire, flash, fling, gun down, hit, hurl, hurtle, immunize, inject, kill, launch, open fire, photograph, pick off, plug, precipitate, project, propel, race, radiate, rake, rocket, rush, scoot, send, speed, spring, sprint, streak, take a picture of, tear, whiz, wound, zap.

shoot² *n* branch, bud, offshoot, scion, slip, sprig, sprout, stem, tendril, twig, vimen.

v bolt, bud, burgeon, detonate, germinate, grow, shoot up, sprout, stretch, tower.

shop *n* boutique, business, chain, deli, emporium, garage, groceteria, market, mart, megastore, practice, repair shop, store, supermarket, workshop.

shore *n* beach, border, coast, foreshore, lakefront, lakeside, littoral, margin, offing, sands, seaboard, seacoast, seafront, seashore, seaside, strand, waterfront, water's edge, waterside.

v bolster (up), brace, buttress, hold up, prop up, reinforce, stay, strengthen, support, underpin.

shorn *adj* bald, beardless, bereft, crewcut, cropped, deprived, divested, naked, polled, shaved, shaven, sheared, stripped.

short *adj* abbreviated, abridged, abrupt, blunt, brief, brittle, brusque, compendious, compressed, concise, crisp, crumbly, crusty, curt, curtailed, deficient, diminutive, direct, discourteous, dumpy, ephemeral, evanescent, fleeting, friable, gruff, impolite, inadequate, insufficient, lacking, laconic, limited, little, low, meagre, momentary, offhand, passing, petite, pithy, poor, précise, sawed-off, scant, scanty, scarce, sententious, sharp, shortened, short-handed, short-lived, short-term, slender, slim, small, snappish, snappy, sparse, squat, straight, succinct, summarized, summary, tart, terse, tight, tiny, transitory, uncivil, understaffed, unplentiful, wanting, wee.

antonyms adequate, ample, expansive, large, lasting, long, long-lived, polite, tall.

short of apart from, away from, deficient in, except, lacking, less than, low on, missing, other than, pushed for, short on, strapped for, wanting (in).

shortage *n* absence, dearth, deficiency, deficit, failure, inadequacy, insufficiency, lack, leanness, meagreness, need, paucity, poverty, scantiness, scarcity, shortfall, sparseness, want.

antonyms abundance, sufficiency.

shortcoming *n* defect, drawback, failing, falling short, fault, flaw, foible, frailty, imperfection, inadequacy, weakness, weak point.

shorten *v* abbreviate, abridge, condense, contract, crop, curtail, cut (back), decrease, diminish, dock, foreshorten, lessen, lop (off), précis, prune, reduce, take up, telescope, trim, truncate.

antonyms amplify, enlarge, lengthen.

shortened *adj* abbreviated, abridged, abstracted, compendious, concise, condensed, summarized.

antonym amplified.

short-lived *adj* brief, ephemeral, evanescent, fleeting, here today and gone tomorrow, impermanent, momentary, passing, short, temporary, transient, transitory.

antonyms abiding, enduring, lasting, long-lived.

shortly¹ *adv* anon, any time, before long, by and by, directly, in a (little) while, momentarily, presently, soon.

shortly² *adv* abruptly, briefly, brusquely, curtly, huffily, laconically, sharply, tartly, tersely.

short-sighted *adj* careless, hasty, ill-advised, ill-considered, impolitic, impractical, improvident, imprudent, injudicious, myopic, near-sighted, unimaginative, unthinking.

antonyms far-sighted, hyperopic, long-sighted, sagacious.

short-tempered *adj* choleric, chippy, crusty, fiery, hot-headed, hot-tempered, impatient, irascible, irritable, peppery, quick-tempered, ratty, testy, touchy.

antonyms calm, patient, placid.

short-winded *adj* breathless, gasping, out of breath, panting, puffing, pursy.

shot¹ *n* attempt, ball, bash, blast, bullet, cannon ball, chance, crack, discharge, dram, drink, dose, effort, essay, guess, injection, lead, lob, marksman, opportunity, pellet, photograph, picture, projectile, range, reach, shooter, shy, slug, stab, stroke, throw, try, turn.

shot in the arm boost, encouragement, fillip, fresh talent, impetus, incentive, lift, nudge, spur, stimulus, uplift.

shot in the dark blind guess, conjecture, guess, guesswork, (pure) speculation, surmise, wild guess.

shot² *adj* iridescent, moiré, mottled, variegated, watered.

shoulder *v* accept, assume, bear, carry, elbow, jostle, press, push, shove, sustain, take on, thrust.

shout *n* bay, bellow, belt, call, cheer, cry, holler, roar, scream, shriek, yell.

v bawl, bay, bellow, belt (out), call, cheer, cry, holler, roar, scream, shriek, whoop, yell.

shove *v* barge, crowd, drive, elbow, force, impel, jostle, press, propel, push, shoulder, thrust.

shove off beat it, clear off, clear out, depart, get lost, leave, push off, put out, scarper, scram, skedaddle, vamoose.

shovel *n* backhoe, bail, bucket, scoop, spade.

v convey, dredge, heap, ladle, load, move, scoop, shift, spade, spoon, toss.

show *v* accompany, accord, attest, bestow, betray, conduct, confer, demonstrate, disclose, display, divulge, elucidate, escort, evidence, evince, exemplify, exhibit, explain, grant, guide, illustrate, indicate, lead, manifest, offer, play, point out, present, protrude, prove, register, reveal, teach, testify to, usher, witness (to).

antonym hide.

n affectation, air, appearance, demonstration, display, éclat, entertainment, exhibition, exhibitionism, expo, exposition, extravaganza, façade, fair, flamboyance, gig, indication, likeness, manifestation, movie, movie theatre, ostentation, pageant, pageantry, parade, performance, play, pose, presentation, pretence, pretext, production, profession, representation, semblance, sight, sign, spectacle, view.

show off advertise, boast (about), brag (about), brandish, demonstrate, display, enhance, exhibit, flaunt, grandstand, hot dog, parade, peacock, set off, strut, strut one's stuff, swagger, swank.

show up appear, arrive, come, disgrace, embarrass, expose, highlight, humiliate, lay bare, let down, mortify, outshine, overshadow, pinpoint, reveal, shame, show, stand out, turn up, unmask.

showdown *n* clash, climax, confrontation, crisis, culmination, dénouement, exposé, face-off.

shower *n* abundance, barrage, deluge, douche, downpour, drift, fusillade, hail, lots, plenty, plethora, precipitation, rain, spout, spray, stream, torrent, volley.

v deluge, douche, douse, heap, inundate, lavish, load, overwhelm, pour, pour down, rain, spray, sprinkle, wet.

showiness *n* flamboyance, flashiness, gaudiness, glitter, glitz, ostentation, pizzazz, razzle-dazzle, razzmatazz, splashiness, swank.

antonym restraint.

showing *n* account, appearance, display, evidence, exhibition, impression, indication, past performance, performance, presentation, record, representation, show, staging, statement, track record.

showing-off *n* boasting, braggadocio, bragging, egotism, exhibitionism, peacockery, self-advertisement, swagger, swank, vainglory.

antonym modesty.

showman *n* entertainer, impresario, performer, publicist, ringmaster, show-off.

show-off *n* boaster, braggadocio, braggart, egotist, exhibitionist, peacock, self-advertiser, swaggerer, swanker, vaunter.

showy *adj* euphuistic, exotic, flamboyant, flashy, florid, garish, gaudy, glitzy, loud, meretricious, ostentatious, pompous, pretentious, specious, splashy, swanking, swanky, tawdry, tinselly.

antonyms quiet, restrained.

shred *n* atom, bit, fragment, grain, iota, jot, mite, piece, rag, ribbon, scrap, sliver, snippet, strip, tatter, trace, whit, wisp.

shrew *n* dragon, Fury, harridan, henpecker, nag, scold, spitfire, termagant, virago, vixen, Xanthippe.

shrewd *adj* acute, arch, artful, astute, calculated, calculating, canny, clever, crafty, cunning, discerning, discriminating, far-seeing, far-sighted, guileful, intelligent, judicious, keen, knowing, long-headed, observant, penetrating, perceptive, perspicacious, sagacious, sharp, sly, smart, well-advised, wily, wise.

antonyms naïve, obtuse, unwise.

shrewdly *adv* artfully, astutely, cannily, cleverly, craftily, far-sightedly, judiciously, knowingly, perceptively, perspicaciously, sagaciously, wisely.

shrewdness *n* acumen, acuteness, astuteness, canniness, craftiness, cunning, discernment, grasp, intelligence, judgment, penetration, perceptiveness, perspicacity, sagacity, sharpness, smartness, wisdom.

antonyms foolishness, naïvety, obtuseness.

shrewish *adj* bad-tempered, captious, complaining, discontented, faultfinding, henpecking, ill-humoured, ill-natured, ill-tempered, nagging, peevish, petulant, quarrelsome, querulous, scolding, sharp-tongued, vixenish.

shriek

shriek

shriek *v* bellow, blare, caterwaul, cry, holler, howl, scream, screech, shout, squeal, wail, yell.
n bellow, caterwaul, cry, howl, scream, screech, shout, squeal, wail.

shrill *adj* acute, carrying, ear-piercing, ear-splitting, high, high-pitched, penetrating, piercing, piping, screaming, screeching, screechy, sharp, strident, treble.
antonyms gentle, low, soft.

shrine *n* chapel, fane, martyry, memorial, sanctuary, stupa, tabernacle, temple, tope.

shrink *v* back away, balk, contract, cower, cringe, decrease, deflate, diminish, draw back, dwindle, flinch, lessen, narrow, pull back, quail, recoil, retire, shorten, shrivel, shy away, wince, withdraw, wither.
antonyms embrace, expand, stretch, warm to.

shrivel *v* burn, dehydrate, desiccate, dwindle, frizzle, parch, pucker, scorch, sear, shrink, wilt, wither, wizen, wrinkle.

shrivelled *adj* desiccated, dried up, dry, emaciated, puckered, sere, shrunken, withered, wizened, wrinkled.

shroud *v* blanket, cloak, conceal, cover, enshroud, envelop, enwrap, hide, screen, sheet, swathe, veil, wrap.
antonyms expose, uncover.
n cerecloth, cerement, cloud, covering, grave clothes, mantle, pall, screen, veil, winding sheet.

shrouded *adj* blanketed, cloaked, clouded, concealed, covered, enshrouded, enveloped, hidden, swathed, veiled, wrapped.
antonyms exposed, uncovered.

shrunken *adj* cadaverous, contracted, emaciated, gaunt, reduced, shrivelled, shrunk, stunted.
antonyms full, generous, rounded, sleek.

shudder *v* convulse, heave, quake, quiver, shake, shiver, tremble.
n convulsion, frisson, quiver, spasm, trembling, tremor.

shuffle¹ *v* drag, hobble, limp, scrape, scuff, scuffle, shamble.

shuffle² *v* chop and change, confuse, disarrange, disorder, intermix, jumble, mix, rearrange, reorganize, shift, shift around, switch around.

shun *v* avoid, cold-shoulder, elude, eschew, evade, ignore, ostracize, shy away from, spurn, steer clear of.
antonyms accept, embrace.

shut *v* bar, bolt, cage, close, fasten, latch, lock, seal, secure, slam.
antonym open.

shut down cease, close (up), discontinue, go bankrupt, go belly-up, halt, inactivate, shut up, stop (work), suspend, switch off, terminate, turn off.

shut in box in, circumscribe, confine, enclose, hedge round, hem in, imprison, incarcerate.

shut off cut off, isolate, remove, seclude, segregate, separate, sequester, turn off.

shut out banish, bar, conceal, cover, debar, defeat, exclude, hide, lock out, mask, muffle, ostracize, overwhelm, screen, trounce, veil.

shut up cage, clam up, confine, coop up, gag, hold one's tongue, hush up, immure, imprison, incarcerate, intern, jail, muzzle, pipe down, silence.

shuttle *v* alternate, carry, commute, ferry, go to and fro, ply, seesaw, shunt, travel.

shy *adj* backward, bashful, cautious, chary, coy, diffident, distrustful, farouche, fearful, hesitant, inhibited, modest, mousy, nervous, reserved, reticent, retiring, self-conscious, self-effacing, shrinking, suspicious, timid, timorous, tongue-tied, unassertive, wary.
antonyms bold, confident.
v back away, balk, buck, flinch, quail, rear, recoil, shrink, start, swerve, wince.

sibyl *n* oracle, prophetess, Pythia, pythoness, seer, seeress, sorceress, wise woman.

sick *adj* ailing, below par, blasé, bored, diseased, disgusted, disgusting, displeased, fed up, feeble, ghoulish, glutted, green about the gills, icky, ill, indisposed, jaded, laid up, morbid, mortified, nauseated, off-colour, off one's feed, pining, poorly, puking, qualmish, queasy, sick and tired, sick at heart, sickly, tired, under the weather, unwell, vomiting, weak, weary.
antonyms healthy, well.

sicken *v* disgust, nauseate, offend, put off, repel, revolt, turn off.
antonyms attract, delight.

sickening *adj* cloying, disgusting, distasteful, foul, icky, loathsome, mephitic, nauseating, offensive, putrid, repulsive, revolting, vile.
antonyms attractive, delightful, pleasing.

sickly *adj* ailing, bilious, bloodless, cloying, colourless, delicate, faint, feeble, frail, indisposed, infirm, lacklustre, languid, mawkish, nauseating, pale, pallid, peaked, pining, revolting, saccharine, syrupy, treacly, unhealthy, wan, weak, weakly.
antonyms robust, sturdy.

sickness *n* affliction, ailment, bug, complaint, disease, disorder, ill health, illness, indisposition, infirmity, malady, nausea, pestilence, qualmishness, queasiness, vomiting.
antonym health.

side *n* angle, aspect, bank, border, boundary, brim, brink, camp, cause, department, direction, division, edge, elevation, face, facet, faction, flank, flitch, fringe, gang, hand, limit, margin, opinion, page, part, party, perimeter, periphery, position, quarter, region, rim, sect, sector, slant, stand, standpoint, surface, team, twist, verge, view, viewpoint.
adj flanking, incidental, indirect, irrelevant, lateral, lesser, marginal, minor, oblique,

roundabout, secondary, subordinate, subsidiary.

side with agree with, back, befriend, favour, join with, second, support, team up with, vote for.

sidelong *adj* covert, indirect, oblique, sideward, sideways.

antonyms direct, overt.

sidestep *v* avoid, bypass, circumvent, dodge, duck, elude, evade, find a way round, shirk, shy away (from), skip, skirt.

antonym tackle.

sidetrack *v* deflect, distract, divert, head off, shunt, switch, turn aside.

sideways *adv* askance, crabwise, crosswise, edgeways, laterally, obliquely, sidelong, sidewards.

adj oblique, side, sidelong, sideward, slanted.

sidle *v* creep, edge, inch, ingratiate, insinuate, slink, sneak, steal, wriggle.

siesta *n* catnap, doze, forty winks, nap, relaxation, repose, rest, sleep, snooze.

sieve *v* remove, riddle, screen, separate, sift, strain.

n colander, riddle, screen, sifter, strainer.

sift *v* analyse, consider the pros and cons of, discriminate (between or among), examine, explore, filter, investigate, pan, part, probe, review, riddle, screen, scrutinize, separate, sieve, sort, sprinkle, winnow.

sigh *n* moan, sough, suspiration.

v breathe, complain, grieve, lament, moan, sorrow, sough, suspire.

sigh for bemoan, grieve, lament, languish, long for, mourn, pine for, weep for, wish for, yearn for.

sight *n* aim, appearance, apprehension, display, estimation, exhibition, eye, eyes, eyeshot, eyesight, eyesore, field of vision, fright, glance, glimpse, good bit, judgment, ken, look, mess, monstrosity, observation, opinion, pageant, perception, range, reach, scene, seeing, show, sight for sore eyes, something to behold, spectacle, view, viewing, visibility, vision, vista.

v aim, behold, discern, distinguish, glimpse, observe, perceive, see, spot.

at first sight at first blush, on first acquaintance, on the surface, prima facie, superficially, to the outsider, to the uninitiated, to the untrained eye.

sightseer *n* excursionist, holidaymaker, rubberneck, tourist, tripper, visitor.

sign *n* advertisement, augury, auspice, badge, beck, betrayal, billboard, board, broad hint, character, cipher, clue, cue, device, emblem, ensign, evidence, figure, foreboding, forewarning, gesture, giveaway, hieroglyph, hint, indication, indicium, insignia, intimation, logo, logogram, logograph, manifestation, mark, marker, miracle, nod, notice, omen, placard, pointer, portent, poster, presage, proof, reminder, representation, rune, signal, signature, signification, signpost, spoor,

suggestion, symbol, symptom, token, trace, trademark, vestige, warning, wink.

v autograph, beckon, endorse, gesticulate, gesture, indicate, initial, inscribe, motion, signal, subscribe, wave.

sign over consign, deliver, entrust, make over, surrender, transfer, turn over.

sign up appoint, contract, employ, engage, enlist, enrol, hire, join, join up, recruit, register, sign on, take on, volunteer.

signal *n* alarm, alert, beacon, beck, cue, flare, flash, gesture, go-ahead, impulse, indication, indicator, light, mark, OK, password, rocket, sign, SOS, tip-off, token, transmitter, waft, warning, watchword.

adj conspicuous, distinguished, eminent, exceptional, extraordinary, famous, glorious, impressive, memorable, momentous, notable, noteworthy, outstanding, remarkable, significant, striking.

v beckon, communicate, gesticulate, gesture, indicate, motion, nod, sign, telegraph, waft, wave.

signature *n* autograph, endorsement, initials, inscription, John Henry, mark, sign.

significance *n* consequence, consideration, force, implication, implications, import, importance, impressiveness, interest, matter, meaning, meaningfulness, message, moment, point, purport, relevance, sense, signification, solemnity, weight.

antonym unimportance.

significant *adj* appreciable, considerable, critical, denoting, eloquent, expressing, expressive, important, indicative, knowing, material, meaning, meaningful, momentous, noteworthy, ominous, pregnant, serious, solemn, suggestive, symbolic, symptomatic, telling, vital, weighty.

antonyms meaningless, negligible, unimportant.

significantly *adj* appreciably, considerably, critically, crucially, eloquently, greatly, knowingly, materially, meaningfully, meaningly, noticeably, perceptibly, suggestively, vitally.

signify *v* announce, augur, betoken, carry weight, communicate, connote, convey, count, denote, evidence, exhibit, express, imply, indicate, intimate, matter, mean, omen, portend, presage, proclaim, represent, show, stand for, suggest, symbolize, transmit.

silence *n* calm, dumbness, hush, lull, muteness, noiselessness, peace, quiescence, quiet, quietness, reserve, reticence, secrecy, secretiveness, speechlessness, stillness, taciturnity, uncommunicativeness.

v deaden, dumfound, extinguish, gag, muffle, muzzle, quell, quiet, quieten, stifle, still, strike dumb, subdue, suppress.

silent *adj* aphonic, dumb, hushed, idle, implicit, inaudible, inoperative, mum, mute, muted, noiseless, quiet, reticent, soundless, speechless, still, tacit, taciturn, tongue-tied, uncommunicative, understood, unexpressed, unforthcoming, unpronounced, unsounded, unspeaking, unspoken, voiceless, wordless.

antonyms loud, noisy, talkative.

silently *adv* dumbly, inaudibly, mutely, noiselessly, quietly, soundlessly, speechlessly, tacitly, unheard, wordlessly.

silhouette *n* delineation, figure, form, outline, profile, shadow, shadowgraph, shape.

silky *adj* fine, satiny, silken, sleek, smooth, soft, velvety.

silly *adj* absurd, addled, asinine, benumbed, birdbrained, brainless, childish, cuckoo, daffy, daft, dazed, dimwitted, dizzy, dopey, drippy, fatuous, featherbrained, flighty, foolhardy, foolish, frivolous, gaga, giddy, goofy, groggy, idiotic, illogical, immature, imprudent, inane, inappropriate, inept, irrational, irresponsible, meaningless, mindless, moronic, pointless, preposterous, puerile, ridiculous, scatterbrained, senseless, simpering, spoony, stunned, stupefied, stupid, thoughtless, unwise, witless.

antonyms collected, mature, sane, sensible, wise.

n airhead, clod, dope, duffer, flibbertigibbet, goof, goose, half-wit, ignoramus, ninny, rattlepate, simpleton, twit.

silt *n* alluvium, deposit, mud, ooze, residue, sediment, sludge.

silt up block up, choke up, clog up, congest, dam up.

similar *adj* alike, analogous, close, comparable, compatible, congruous, corresponding, homologous, kin, like, parallel, related, resembling, uniform.

antonym different.

similarity *n* affinity, agreement, analogy, closeness, coincidence, comparability, compatibility, concordance, congruence, correspondence, equivalence, likeness, parallel, relation, relationship, resemblance, sameness, similitude, uniformity.

antonym difference.

similarly *adv* by analogy, by the same token, correspondingly, likewise, uniformly.

simmer *v* boil, bubble, burn, fizz, fume, rage, seethe, smart, smoulder.

simmer down calm down, chill out, collect oneself, contain oneself, control oneself, cool down, cool off, get a hold of oneself, keep one's shirt on, recollect oneself, settle down, take it easy.

simpering *adj* affected, arch, coy, giggling, mincing, schoolgirlish, self-conscious, silly.

simple *adj* artless, bald, bare, bare bones, basic, brainless, childlike, classic, classical, clean, clear, credulous, dense, direct, dumb, easy, elementary, everyday, feeble, feeble-minded, foolish, frank, genuine, green, guileless, gullible, half-witted, homely, honest, humble, idiot-proof, ignorant, ingenuous, innocent, intelligible, lowly, lucid, manageable, mere, modest, moronic, naïve, naked, natural, obtuse, one-celled, ordinary, plain, pure, rudimentary, rustic, Saturnian, shallow, sheer,

silly, sincere, single, slow, Spartan, stark, straightforward, stupid, thick, unadorned, unaffected, unalloyed, unblended, uncluttered, uncombined, uncomplicated, undeniable, understandable, undisguised, undivided, unelaborate, unembellished, unfussy, uninvolved, unlearned, unmixed, unornate, unpretentious, unschooled, unskilled, unsophisticated, unsuspecting, unvarnished, user-friendly.

antonyms artful, clever, complicated, difficult, fancy, intricate.

simple-minded *adj* addle-brained, artless, backward, brainless, cretinous, dimwitted, dopey, feeble-minded, foolish, goofy, idiot, idiotic, imbecilic, inexperienced, moronic, natural, retarded, simple, stupid, unsophisticated.

antonyms bright, clever.

simpleton *n* blockhead, booby, born fool, dolt, dope, dough-head, dullard, dunce, dupe, fool, gaby, gander, goof, goofball, goon, goose, green goose, greenhorn, idiot, imbecile, jackass, moron, nincompoop, ninny, numskull, stupid, twerp.

antonym brain.

simplicity *n* artlessness, baldness, bareness, candour, clarity, classicism, clearness, directness, ease, easiness, elementariness, guilelessness, ignorance, innocence, intelligibility, modesty, naïveté, naturalness, obviousness, openness, plainness, purity, restraint, rusticity, simpleness, sincerity, straightforwardness, uncomplicatedness, unsophistication.

antonyms difficulty, guile, intricacy, sophistication.

simplify *v* abridge, decipher, disentangle, facilitate, pare down, prune, reduce, streamline.

antonyms complicate, elaborate.

simplistic *adj* naïve, oversimplified, pat, schematic, shallow, simple, superficial, sweeping, unanalytical, undeveloped.

antonyms analytical, detailed.

simply *adv* absolutely, altogether, artlessly, baldly, clearly, completely, directly, easily, in plain words, intelligibly, just, merely, modestly, naturally, obviously, only, plainly, purely, quite, really, sincerely, solely, straightforwardly, totally, unaffectedly, undeniably, unpretentiously, unquestionably, unreservedly, utterly, wholly.

simulate *v* act like, affect, assume, counterfeit, duplicate, echo, fabricate, fake, feign, imitate, mimic, parrot, pretend, put on, reflect, reproduce, resemble, sham.

simulated *adj* artificial, assumed, bogus, fake, feigned, imitation, inauthentic, insincere, make-believe, manufactured, mock, phony, pinchbeck, pretend, pseudo, put-on, sham, spurious, substitute, synthetic, ungenuine.

antonyms genuine, real.

simultaneous *adj* accompanying, coincident, coinciding, concomitant, concurrent, contemporaneous, parallel, synchronic, synchronous.

antonyms asynchronous, separate.

sin *n* crime, debt, error, evil, fault, guilt, impiety, iniquity, lapse, misconduct, misdeed, misdemeanour, offence, sinfulness, transgression, trespass, ungodliness, unrighteousness, wickedness, wrong, wrongdoing.

v do wrong, err, fall, fall from grace, go astray, lapse, misbehave, offend, stray, transgress, trespass.

sincere *adj* artless, bona fide, candid, deep-felt, earnest, frank, genuine, guileless, heartfelt, heart-whole, honest, honest-to-goodness, natural, open, open-hearted, plain-spoken, pure, real, serious, simple, simple-hearted, single-hearted, soulful, straightforward, true, true-hearted, truthful, unadulterated, unaffected, unfeigned, unmixed, wholehearted.

antonym insincere.

sincerely *adv* earnestly, genuinely, honestly, in earnest, in good faith, really, seriously, simply, truly, truthfully, unaffectedly, wholeheartedly.

sinecure *n* cinch, cushy job, gravy train, money for jam, picnic, plum job, soft option.

sinewy *adj* athletic, brawny, lusty, muscular, powerful, robust, stringy, strong, sturdy, tendinous, tough, vigorous, wiry.

sinful *adj* bad, corrupt, criminal, decadent, depraved, erring, evil, fallen, guilty, immoral, impious, iniquitous, irreligious, peccable, peccant, ungodly, unholy, unrighteous, unvirtuous, wicked, wrong, wrongful.

antonyms righteous, sinless.

sinfulness *n* corruption, decadence, depravity, guilt, immorality, impiety, iniquity, peccability, sin, transgression, ungodliness, unrighteousness, wickedness.

antonym righteousness.

sing *v* belt out, betray, blow the whistle, cantillate, carol, caterwaul, chant, chirp, croon, entertain, finger, fink, hum, inform, intone, lilt, melodize, peach, pipe, proclaim, purr, quaver, rat, render, ring, screech, serenade, spill the beans, squeal, talk, tell all, trill, turn informer, vocalize, warble, whistle, yodel.

sing out bawl, bellow, call, cooee, cry, halloo, holler, shout, yell.

singe *v* blacken, burn, cauterize, char, scorch, sear.

singer *n* balladeer, bard, cantor, caroller, chanteuse, choirboy, choirgirl, choir member, chorister, crooner, diva, entertainer, jongleur, Meistersinger, minstrel, performer, precentor, prima donna, psalmodist, songster, troubadour, vocalist.

single *adj* celibate, distinct, exclusive, free, individual, lone, man-to-man, one, one-fold, one-on-one, one-to-one, only, particular, separate, simple, sincere, single-minded, singular, sole, solitary, unattached, unblended, unbroken, uncombined, uncompounded, undivided, unique, unmarried, unmixed, unshared, unwed, wholehearted.

single out choose, cull, distinguish, hand-pick, highlight, isolate, pick, pinpoint, select, separate, set apart.

single-handed *adv, adj* alone, independent(ly), on one's own, solo, unaccompanied, unaided, unassisted.

single-minded *adj* dedicated, determined, devoted, dogged, fixed, hellbent, intent, monomaniacal, resolute, steadfast, stubborn, tireless, undeviating, unswerving, unwavering.

singular *adj* atypical, bizarre, conspicuous, curious, eccentric, eminent, exceptional, extraordinary, individual, noteworthy, odd, out-of-the-ordinary, out-of-the-way, outstanding, peculiar, pre-eminent, private, prodigious, proper, puzzling, queer, rare, remarkable, separate, single, sole, strange, uncommon, unique, unparalleled, unusual, weird.

antonyms normal, usual.

singularity *n* abnormality, curiosity, curiousness, eccentricity, extraordinariness, idiosyncrasy, irregularity, oddity, oddness, oneness, particularity, peculiarity, queerness, quirk, strangeness, twist, uniqueness, unity.

antonym normality.

singularly *adv* bizarrely, conspicuously, curiously, eminently, especially, exceptionally, extraordinarily, notably, oddly, outstandingly, particularly, prodigiously, remarkably, signally, singly, surprisingly, uncommonly, uniquely, unusually.

sinister *adj* adverse, bad, creepy, dire, disastrous, disquieting, evil, inauspicious, injurious, malevolent, malign, malignant, menacing, ominous, shady, threatening, underhand, unlucky, wicked.

antonyms harmless, innocent.

sink *v* abandon, abate, bore, collapse, conceal, decay, decline, decrease, defeat, degenerate, degrade, descend, destroy, dig, diminish, dip, disappear, drill, drive, droop, drop, drown, dwindle, ebb, engulf, excavate, fade, fail, fall, fall in, finish, flag, founder, go down, invest, languish, lay, lessen, lower, overwhelm, penetrate, plummet, plunge, recede, relapse, retrogress, ruin, sag, scupper, settle, slip, slope, slump, stoop, submerge, subside, succumb, vanish, weaken, worsen.

antonyms float, rise, uplift.

sinless *adj* faultless, guiltless, immaculate, impeccable, innocent, pure, unblemished, uncorrupted, undefiled, unspotted, unsullied, virtuous.

antonym sinful.

sinner *n* backslider, evildoer, malefactor, miscreant, offender, reprobate, transgressor, trespasser, wrongdoer.

sinuous *adj* coiling, crooked, curved, curvy, lithe, mazy, meandering, serpentine, slinky, supple, tortuous, twisting, undulating, winding.

antonym straight.

sip *v* sample, savour, sup, taste.
n drop, mouthful, spoonful, swallow, taste, thimbleful.

siren *n* bewitcher, charmer, Circe, femme fatale, houri, Lorelei, seductress, temptress, vamp, witch.

sissy *n* baby, coward, crybaby, gutless wonder, jellyfish, milksop, mollycoddle, namby-pamby, softy, weakling.
adj cowardly, effeminate, feeble, namby-pamby, sissified, soft, sucky, unmanly, weak.

sister *n* associate, chum, colleague, companion, compeer, comrade, cousin, fellow, fellow worker, friend, kin, kinswoman, mate, nun, nurse, pal, partner, relation, relative, religious, sibling, soul mate.

sisterhood *n* alliance, association, circle, community, confederation, coterie, fellowship, guild, league, partnership, society, sorority, union.

sisterly *adj* affectionate, amicable, caring, concerned, cordial, friendly, kind, loving, neighbourly, sympathetic, understanding, warm.

sit *v* accommodate, assemble, befit, brood, contain, convene, deliberate, hold, meet, officiate, perch, pose, preside, reside, rest, seat, settle.

site *n* arena, ground, location, lot, place, plot, position, setting, spot, station, theatre.
v install, locate, place, position, set, situate, station.

sitting *n* assembly, consultation, get-together, hearing, meeting, period, seat, session, spell.

situation *n* ballgame, berth, case, circumstances, condition, employment, environment, job, kettle of fish, lie of the land, locale, locality, location, office, place, placement, plight, position, post, predicament, scenario, seat, setting, set-up, site, spot, state, state of affairs, station, status.

sizable *adj* biggish, considerable, decent, decent-sized, fair-sized, goodly, good-sized, large, largish, respectable, significant, substantial, tidy.
antonym small.

size *n* amount, amplitude, bigness, bulk, dimensions, extent, greatness, height, hugeness, immensity, largeness, magnitude, mass, measurements, proportions, range, vastness, volume.

size up appraise, assess, estimate, evaluate, gauge, measure.

sizzle *v* crackle, fry, hiss, scorch, sear, spit, sputter.

skedaddle *v* abscond, beat it, bolt, decamp, disappear, flee, hop it, run away, scarper, scoot, scram, split, take off, vamoose.

skeletal *adj* cadaverous, drawn, emaciated, fleshless, gaunt, haggard, hollow-cheeked, lean, shrunken, skin-and-bone, wasted.

skeleton *n* bag of bones, barebones, draft, endoskeleton, frame, framework, outline, sketch, skin and bones, structure.

sketch *v* block out, delineate, depict, describe, draft, draw, outline, paint, pencil, plot, portray, represent, rough out.
n delineation, depiction, description, design, draft, drawing, outline, plan, scenario, skeleton, vignette.

sketchily *adv* cursorily, hastily, imperfectly, inadequately, incompletely, patchily, perfunctorily, roughly, vaguely.
antonym fully.

sketchy *adj* crude, cursory, imperfect, inadequate, incomplete, insufficient, outline, perfunctory, rough, scrappy, skimpy, slight, superficial, unfinished, vague.
antonym full.

skilful *adj* able, accomplished, adept, adroit, apt, canny, clever, competent, deft, dexterous, experienced, expert, handy, masterly, nimble-fingered, practised, professional, proficient, quick, ready, skilled, trained.
antonyms awkward, clumsy, inept.

skill *n* ability, accomplishment, adroitness, aptitude, art, cleverness, competence, dexterity, experience, expertise, expertness, facility, finesse, handiness, ingenuity, intelligence, knack, proficiency, quickness, readiness, savoir-faire, savvy, skilfulness, talent, technique, touch.

skilled *adj* able, ace, accomplished, crack, experienced, expert, first-class, masterly, practised, professional, proficient, schooled, skilful, trained.
antonym unskilled.

skim *v* browse, brush, coast, cream, dart, float, fly, glide, plane, sail, scan, scratch the surface, separate, skip, soar.

skimp *v* conserve, cut corners, economize, pinch, scant, scrimp, stint, withhold.

skimpy *adj* beggarly, exiguous, inadequate, insufficient, meagre, measly, miserly, niggardly, scanty, short, sketchy, sparse, thin, tight.
antonym generous.

skin *n* casing, coating, crust, epidermis, exterior, fell, film, hide, hull, husk, integument, membrane, mouton, outer layer, outside, peel, pellicle, pelt, rind.
v abrade, bark, beat, best, cheat, excoriate, flay, fleece, graze, peel, scrape (off), strip (off), swindle.

skin-deep *adj* artificial, empty, external, meaningless, outward, shallow, superficial, surface.

skinflint *n* cheeseparer, meanie, miser, niggard, penny-pincher, Scrooge, tightwad.

skinny *adj* attenuated, bony, emaciated, gangling, lean, scraggy, skeletal, skin-and-bone, thin, twiggy, underfed, undernourished, weedy.
antonym fat.

skip *v* bob, bounce, bypass, caper, cavort, cut, dance, eschew, flee, flit, frisk, gambol, hooky (or truant), hop, jump, leap, leave, leave out, miss, omit, overleap, play, pass over, prance, trip.

skirmish *n* affair, affray, battle, brush, clash, combat, conflict, contest, dustup, encounter, engagement, fight, fracas, incident, scrap, scrimmage, set-to, spat, tussle.

v clash, collide, contend, do battle, scrap, tussle.

skirt *v* avoid, border, bypass, circle, circumambulate, circumnavigate, circumvent, detour, edge, evade, flank, go around, steer clear of.

skit *n* burlesque, caricature, parody, satire, shtick, sketch, spoof, takeoff, travesty.

skittish *adj* coltish, excitable, fickle, fidgety, frisky, frivolous, high-strung, jumpy, kittenish, lively, nervous, playful, restive.

skulduggery *n* chicanery, dishonesty, double-dealing, duplicity, foul play, fraudulence, jiggery-pokery, machinations, sharp practice, shenanigans, swindling, trickery, underhandedness, unscrupulousness.

skulk *v* creep, lie in wait, loiter, lurk, pad, prowl, pussyfoot, slink, sneak.

sky *n* atmosphere, azure, blue, empyrean, ether, firmament, heaven(s), outer space, vault of heaven, welkin.

slab *n* bar, block, briquette, chunk, hunk, lump, piece, portion, slice, wedge.

slack *adj* baggy, careless, dull, easy, easygoing, flaccid, flexible, idle, inactive, inattentive, lackadaisical, lax, lazy, limp, loose, neglectful, negligent, permissive, quiet, relaxed, remiss, slow, slow-moving, sluggish, tardy, weak, workshy.

antonyms busy, diligent, quick, rigid, stiff, taut.

n excess, give, inactivity, latitude, leeway, looseness, play, relaxation, room, rope.

slack off fail, flag, goldbrick, neglect one's duty, relax one's efforts, shirk, take it easy, tire.

antonyms increase, quicken, tighten.

slacken *v* abate, decrease, diminish, ease up (or off), lessen, let up, loosen, moderate, relax, release, slow (down).

slacker *n* clock-watcher, dawdler, dodger, do-nothing, fainéant, good-for-nothing, idler, layabout, loafer, malingerer, ne'er-do-well, passenger, shirker.

slake *v* abate, allay, assuage, deaden, extinguish, gratify, mitigate, moderate, moisten, quench, reduce, relieve, sate, satiate, satisfy, slacken, subside.

slam *v* attack, bang, castigate, clap, crash, criticize, damn, dash, denounce, excoriate, fling, hurl, lambaste, lash out against, pan, pillory, slate, smash, swat, throw, thump, trash, vilify.

slander *n* aspersion, backbiting, calumniation, calumny, defamation, detraction, libel, misrepresentation, muckraking, obloquy, scandal, smear, traducement.

v asperse, backbite, calumniate, decry, defame, disparage, libel, malign, muckrake, scandalize, slur, smear, traduce, vilify, vilipend.

antonyms glorify, praise.

slanderous *adj* abusive, aspersive, calumnious, damaging, defamatory, libellous, malicious.

slang *v* abuse, berate, castigate, excoriate, insult, lambaste, malign, rail at, revile, scold, vilify, vituperate.

antonym praise.

slanging match altercation, argument, dispute, quarrel, row, set-to, shouting match, spat.

slant *v* angle, bend, bevel, bias, cant, colour, distort, incline, lean, list, misrepresent, shelve, skew, slope, tilt, twist, warp, weight.

n angle, attitude, bias, camber, declination, deviation, diagonal, emphasis, gradient, inclination, incline, leaning, obliquity, perspective, pitch, prejudice, rake, ramp, skewness, slope, tilt, twist, viewpoint.

slanting *adj* angled, askew, aslant, asymmetrical, bent, canted, diagonal, inclined, kitty-cornered, oblique, sideways, skewed, slanted, slantwise, sloping, tilted, tilting.

antonym level.

slap *n* bang, blow, clap, clout, cuff, smack, spank, swat, wallop, whack.

v bang, clap, clout, cuff, daub, hit, plaster, plunk, smack, spank, strike, whack.

adv bang, dead, directly, exactly, plumb, precisely, right, slap-bang, smack.

slap down berate, keelhaul, put in one's place, rebuke, reprimand, restrain, scold, squash, upbraid.

slap in the face affront, blow, humiliation, indignity, insult, put-down, rebuff, rebuke, rejection, repulse, snub.

slapdash *adj* careless, clumsy, disorderly, haphazard, hasty, hit-or-miss, hurried, last-minute, messy, negligent, offhand, perfunctory, rash, reckless, slipshod, sloppy, slovenly, thoughtless, thrown-together, untidy.

antonyms careful, orderly.

slaphappy *adj* boisterous, carefree, dazed, giddy, giggly, happy-go-lucky, irresponsible, nonchalant, punch-drunk, reckless, reeling, woozy.

slapstick *n* buffoonery, comedy, farce, horseplay, knockabout, tomfoolery.

slap-up *adj* bang-up, elaborate, elegant, excellent, extravagant, first-class, first-rate, lavish, luxurious, magnificent, princely, splendid, sumptuous, superb, superlative.

slash *v* criticize, cut (or back) down, gash, hack, lacerate, lash, lower, reduce, rend, rip, slit.

n cut, gash, incision, laceration, lash, rent, rip, slit.

slashing *adj* aggressive, biting, brutal, ferocious, harsh, savage, searing, severe, unsparing, vicious, violent.

slate *v* abuse, berate, blame, castigate, censure, criticize, lambaste, pan, rebuke, reprimand, roast, scold, slam, slang.

antonym praise.

n agenda, list, record, schedule.

slatternly *adj* bedraggled, dirty, dowdy, draggle-tailed, frowzy, frumpy, slipshod, sloppy, slovenly, sluttish, unclean, unkempt, untidy.

slaughter *n* battue, blood bath, bloodshed, butchery, carnage, extermination, genocide, holocaust, killing, liquidation, massacre, murder, purge, slaying.
v butcher, crush, defeat, destroy, exterminate, hammer, kill, liquidate, massacre, murder, overwhelm, purge, slay, trounce, vanquish, wipe out.

slave *n* bondservant, bondsman, bondswoman, captive, drudge, helot, mameluke, scullion, serf, servant, thrall, vassal, villein.
v drudge, grind, labour, slog, struggle, sweat, toil.
antonyms goof off, shirk, sit on one's hands.

slaver *v* dribble, drivel, drool, salivate, slobber.

slavery *n* bondage, captivity, duress, enslavement, impressment, serfdom, servitude, subjugation, thralldom, thrall, vassalage, yoke.
antonym freedom.

slavish *adj* abject, base, conventional, cringing, fawning, grovelling, imitative, laborious, literal, low, mean, menial, obsequious, servile, strict, submissive, sycophantic, unimaginative, uninspired, unoriginal, unquestioning, unthinking.
antonyms independent, original.

slay *v* amuse, annihilate, assassinate, break one up, butcher, destroy, dispatch, eliminate, execute, exterminate, kill, massacre, murder, rub out, slaughter.

slaying *n* annihilation, assassination, butchery, destruction, dispatch, elimination, extermination, killing, massacre, murder, slaughter.

sleazy *adj* crummy, disreputable, low, run-down, seedy, sordid, squalid, tacky.

sleek *adj* elegant, glossy, insinuating, lustrous, plausible, shiny, slick, smooth, smug, trim, well-fed, well-groomed.

sleep *v* be dormant, catnap, cop z's, doss (down), doze, drop off, drowse, flop, get some shut-eye, hibernate, nap, nod off, repose, rest, slumber, snooze, snore, take forty winks.
n coma, dormancy, doss, doze, forty winks, hibernation, nap, repose, rest, shut-eye, siesta, slumber(s), snooze, unconsciousness.

sleepiness *n* doziness, drowsiness, heaviness, languor, lethargy, oscitancy, somnolence, torpor.
antonyms alertness, wakefulness.

sleeping *adj* asleep, becalmed, daydreaming, dead, dormant, dreaming, hibernating, idle, inactive, inattentive, inert, latent, off guard, passive, slumbering, unaware, unconscious.
antonyms alert, awake.

sleepless *adj* alert, disturbed, insomniac, insomnious, restless, unsleeping, vigilant, wakeful, watchful, wide-awake.

sleep-walking *n* noctambulation, noctambulism, somnambulation, somnambulism.

sleepy *adj* drowsy, dull, groggy, half asleep, heavy, hypnotic, inactive, languid, lethargic, nodding, quiet, slow, sluggish, slumberous, slumbersome, slumbery, somnolent, soporific, tired, torpid, yawning.
antonyms alert, awake, restless, wakeful.

sleight of hand adroitness, artifice, dexterity, juggling, legerdemain, magic, manipulation, prestidigitation, skill, trick, trickery.

slender *adj* aciculate, faint, feeble, flimsy, fragile, gracile, inadequate, inconsiderable, insufficient, lean, little, meagre, narrow, poor, remote, scanty, slight, slim, small, spare, svelte, sylphlike, tenuous, thin, thready, wasp-waisted, weak, willowy.
antonyms considerable, fat, thick.

sleuth *n* bloodhound, detective, dick, gumshoe, private eye, private investigator, shadow, tail, tracker.

slice *n* cross section, cut, frustum, helping, layer, piece, portion, rasher, sample, section, segment, share, slab, sliver, task, wafer, wedge, whack.
v carve, chop, cut, divide, segment, sever, sliver, whack, whittle.

slick *adj* adroit, deft, dexterous, glib, ingenious, meretricious, oily, plausible, polished, professional, sharp, shrewd, skilful, sleek, slippery, smooth, sophistic, specious, stylish, trim.
antonyms amateurish, clumsy, coarse.

slide *v* coast, decline, glide, glissade, lapse, skate, skim, slip, slither, toboggan, veer.

slight *adj* delicate, feeble, flimsy, fragile, frail, gracile, inconsiderable, insignificant, insubstantial, light, meagre, minor, modest, negligible, paltry, scanty, slender, slim, small, spare, superficial, tenuous, trifling, trivial, unimportant, weak.
antonyms considerable, large, major, significant.
v affront, cold-shoulder, cut, despise, disdain, disparage, disrespect, ignore, insult, neglect, overlook, scorn, snub.
antonyms compliment, flatter.
n affront, cold shoulder, contempt, discourtesy, disdain, disregard, disrespect, inattention, indifference, insult, neglect, rebuff, rudeness, slur, snub.
antonyms compliment, flattery.

slighting *adj* abusive, belittling, defamatory, derogatory, disdainful, disparaging, disrespectful, insulting, offensive, scornful, slanderous, supercilious, uncomplimentary.
antonym complimentary.

slightly *adv* a little, a tad, a touch, barely, by a hair, negligibly, only just, scantily, somewhat, to a slight degree.
antonyms a lot, hugely, to a large degree.

slim *adj* ectomorphic, faint, gracile, lean, narrow, poor, remote, slender, slight, svelte, sylphlike, thin, trim.

antonyms bulky, chubby, fat.

slim down count calories, diet, lose weight, reduce, shed kilos, slenderize, slim, take off weight, weight-watch.

slime n bitumen, filth, goo, gunk, mess, muck, mucus, mud, ooze.

slimy adj clammy, creepy, disgusting, glutinous, grovelling, miry, mucous, muddy, obsequious, oily, oozy, repulsive, servile, slippery, smarmy, soapy, sycophantic, toadying, unctuous, viscous.

sling v cast, catapult, chuck, dangle, fling, hang, heave, hurl, lob, pitch, shy, suspend, swing, throw, toss.
n band, bandage, catapult, loop, strap, support, throw.

slink v creep, prowl, pussyfoot, sidle, skulk, slip, sneak, steal.

slinky adj clinging, close-fitting, feline, figure-hugging, furtive, lean, sinuous, skin-tight, sleek, sneaking.

slip[1] v blunder, creep, decline, disappear, dislocate, elude, err, escape, fall, fall off, get away (from), glide, goof (up), lapse, let go, loose, miscalculate, misjudge, mistake, skate, skid, slide, slink, slip up, slither, sneak, steal, trip.
n blooper, blunder, boner, booboo, bungle, error, failure, fault, imprudence, indiscretion, lapsus, lapsus linguae, mistake, omission, oversight, slip-up.

slip[2] n cutting, piece, runner, scion, shoot, sliver, sprig, sprout, stem, strip.

slipper n flip-flop, loafer, moccasin, mule, pump, sandal, thong.

slippery adj crafty, cunning, deceitful, devious, dishonest, duplicitous, elusive, evasive, false, foxy, glassy, greasy, icy, oily, perilous, precarious, shifty, skiddy, slick, slimy, smooth, sneaky, treacherous, tricky, two-faced, uncertain, unpredictable, unreliable, unsafe, unstable, unsteady, untrustworthy.

slipshod adj careless, casual, jerry-built, loose, negligent, schlocky, slapdash, sloppy, slovenly, unsystematic, untidy.
antonyms careful, fastidious, neat, tidy.

slit v cut, gash, groove, knife, lance, pierce, rip, slash, slice, split.
n cleft, crack, cut, fissure, gash, groove, incision, opening, rent, split, tear, vent.
adj cleft, cut, grooved, rent, split, torn.

slither v glide, slide, slink, slip, snake, undulate.

sliver n chip, flake, fragment, paring, shaving, shiver, shred, slip, splinter.

slob n boor, brute, churl, frump, lout, oaf, philistine, sloven, yahoo.

slobber v dribble, drivel, drool, salivate, slaver, splutter, water at the mouth.

slog v bash, belt, grind, hit, labour, persevere, plod, plough (through), slave, slug, smite, sock, strike, thump, toil, tramp, trek, trudge, wallop, work.

n effort, exertion, grind, hike, labour, struggle, tramp, trek, trudge.

slogan n battle cry, catch phrase, catchword, chant, jingle, motto, rallying cry, war cry, watchword.

slop v overflow, slobber, slosh, spatter, spill, splash, splatter, wash.

slope v camber, cant, fall, incline, lean, pitch, rise, slant, tilt, verge.
n acclivity, brae, cant, declination, declivity, descent, downgrade, escarpment, glacis, gradient, inclination, incline, ramp, rise, slant, tilt, versant.

sloping adj acclivitous, bevelled, canting, declivitous, inclined, inclining, leaning, oblique, slanting.
antonym level.

sloppy adj amateurish, banal, careless, clumsy, gushing, hit-or-miss, ill-fitting, inattentive, loose, mawkish, messy, mushy, schmaltzy, sentimental, slapdash, slipshod, slovenly, sludgy, slushy, soppy, splashy, trite, unkempt, untidy, watery, weak, wet.
antonyms careful, exact, precise.

slosh v flounder, plash, pour, shower, slog, slop, sluice, splash, spray, swash, wade.

slot n aperture, channel, crack, gap, groove, hole, niche, opening, place, position, slit, space, time, vacancy.
v adjust, assign, fit, insert, pigeonhole, place, position, schedule.

sloth n fainéance, idleness, inactivity, indolence, inertia, laziness, listlessness, slackness, slothfulness, slowness, sluggishness, torpor.
antonyms diligence, industriousness, sedulity.

slothful adj do-nothing, fainéant, idle, inactive, indolent, inert, lackadaisical, lazy, listless, slack, slow, sluggardly, sluggish, torpid, workshy.
antonyms diligent, industrious, sedulous.

slouch v droop, hunch, idle, loll, shamble, shuffle, slump, stoop.

slouching adj careless, disorderly, drooping, heedless, loose, negligent, shambling, shuffling, slack, slapdash, slatternly, slipshod, sloppy, slovenly, unkempt, untidy.

slow adj adagio, backward, behind, behindhand, boring, bovine, conservative, crawling, creeping, dawdling, dead, dead-and-alive, delayed, deliberate, dense, dilatory, dim, disinclined, dull, dull-witted, dumb, easy, gradual, hesitant, inactive, lackadaisical, laggard, lagging, late, lazy, leaden, leisurely, lingering, loath, loitering, long-drawn, measured, obtuse, one-horse, plodding, ponderous, prolonged, protracted, quiet, reluctant, retarded, slack, sleepy, slow-moving, slow-witted, sluggardly, sluggish, stagnant, stupid, tame, tardy, tedious, thick, time-consuming, uneventful, unhasty, unhurried, uninteresting, unproductive, unprogressive, unpunctual, unresponsive, wearisome.

antonyms active, busy, fast, quick, rapid, swift.

v brake, check, curb, decelerate, delay, detain, draw rein, handicap, hold up, inhibit, lag, relax, restrict, retard.

slowly *adv* adagio, gradually, inchmeal, larghetto, largo, lazily, leisurely, lento, ploddingly, ponderously, sluggishly, steadily, unhurriedly.

antonym quickly.

sludge *n* dregs, gunk, mire, muck, mud, ooze, residue, sediment, silt, slag, slime, slop, slush, swill.

slug *v* bash, hit, punch, slap, sock, strike, swat, take a swipe at, thump, thwack, wallop.

sluggish *adj* apathetic, dilatory, dull, heavy, inactive, indolent, inert, lethargic, lifeless, listless, lymphatic, phlegmatic, slothful, slow, slow-moving, torpid, unresponsive.

antonyms brisk, dynamic, eager, quick, vigorous.

sluice *v* cleanse, drain, drench, flow, flush, irrigate, pour, rush, slosh, steam, swill, wash.

slumber *v* doze, drowse, nap, repose, rest, sleep, snooze, take forty winks.

slump *v* bend, collapse, crash, decline, deteriorate, droop, drop, fall, hunch, loll, plummet, plunge, sag, sink, slip, slouch, worsen.

n collapse, crash, decline, depreciation, depression, downturn, drop, failure, fall, falloff, hard times, low, recession, reverse, stagnation, trough, worsening.

antonym boom.

slur *n* affront, aspersion, blot, brand, calumny, discredit, disgrace, disparagement, innuendo, insinuation, insult, put-down, reproach, slander, slight, smear, snide remark, stain, stigma.

sly *adj* arch, artful, astute, canny, clever, conniving, covert, crafty, crazy like a fox, cunning, devious, foxy, furtive, guileful, impish, insidious, knowing, mischievous, roguish, scheming, secret, secretive, shifty, shrewd, stealthy, subtle, surreptitious, underhand, vulpine, wily.

antonyms frank, honest, open, straightforward.

on the sly clandestinely, covertly, furtively, on the quiet (or q.t.), privately, secretly, surreptitiously, underhandedly.

antonym openly.

smack *v* box, clap, cuff, hit, pat, slap, sock, spank, strike, tap, thwack, whack.

n blow, box, crack, cuff, hit, pat, slap, sock, spank, stroke, tap, thwack, whack.

adv bang, directly, exactly, plumb, point-blank, precisely, right, slap, slap-bang, squarely, straight.

small *adj* bantam, base, cramped, dainty, diminutive, dwarfish, humble, illiberal, inadequate, incapacious, inconsiderable, insignificant, insufficient, itsy-bitsy, limited, little, meagre, mean, measly, mignon, mignonne, mini, miniature, minor, minuscule, minute, modest, narrow, negligible, paltry, peewee, petite, petty, piddling, pint-sized, pocket, pocket-size, poor, puny, pygmy, scanty, selfish, slight, small-scale, thin, tight, tiny, trifling, trivial, undersized, unimportant, unpretentious, wee.

antonyms big, huge, large.

small-minded *adj* bigoted, envious, grudging, hidebound, insular, intolerant, mean, narrow-minded, parochial, petty, rigid, ungenerous.

antonyms broad-minded, liberal, tolerant.

small-time *adj* bush-league, inconsequential, insignificant, minor, no-account, petty, piddling, unimportant.

antonyms important, major.

smarmy *adj* bootlicking, crawling, fawning, fulsome, greasy, ingratiating, obsequious, oily, servile, smooth, soapy, suave, sycophantic, toadying, unctuous.

smart[1] *adj* acute, adept, agile, alert, apt, astute, bright, brisk, canny, chic, clever, dandy, effective, elegant, fashionable, fine, impertinent, impudent, ingenious, intelligent, jaunty, keen, lively, modish, natty, neat, nimble, nimble-witted, nobby, pert, pointed, quick, quick-witted, rattling, ready, ready-witted, saucy, sharp, shrewd, smart-alecky, snappy, spanking, spirited, spruce, stylish, swagger, swish, trim, vigorous, vivacious, well-appointed, witty.

antonyms dowdy, dumb, slow, stupid, unfashionable, untidy.

smart aleck know-it-all, smarty, smartypants, wiseacre, wise guy.

smart[2] *v* be sore, burn, hurt, pain, sting, throb, tingle, twinge.

adj hard, keen, painful, piercing, resounding, sharp, stinging.

n pain, pang, smarting, soreness, sting, twinge.

smarten *v* beautify, clean, groom, improve, neaten, polish, primp, prink, spiff up, spruce up, tidy.

smash *v* break, collide, crash, crush, dash, defeat, demolish, destroy, disintegrate, lay waste, overthrow, pulverize, ruin, shatter, shiver, total, wipe out, wreck.

n accident, collapse, collision, crash, defeat, destruction, disaster, downfall, failure, hit, impact, pile-up, ruin, shattering, smash-up, success, wipeout, wreck.

smashing *adj* excellent, exhilarating, fabulous, fantastic, first-class, first-rate, great, magnificent, marvellous, sensational, smash, stupendous, super, superb, superlative, terrific, tremendous, wonderful.

smattering *n* basics, bit, dash, elements, modicum, rudiments, smatter, soupçon, sprinkling.

smear *v* apply, asperse, bedaub, besmirch, blacken, blur, calumniate, coat, cover, dab, daub, dirty, drag (someone's) name through the mud, malign, plaster, rub on, slander,

smudge, soil, splotch, spread (over), stain, stigmatize, sully, tarnish, traduce, vilify.

n blemish, blot, blotch, calumny, daub, defamation, libel, mudslinging, slander, smudge, splotch, stain, stigma, streak, vilification, whispering campaign.

smell *n* aroma, bouquet, fragrance, mephitis, nose, odour, perfume, redolence, scent, sniff, stench, stink, trace, whiff.

v be malodorous, detect, inhale, nose, reek, scent, sense, sniff, snuff (up), stink, stink to high heaven, take a whiff (of), whiff.

smelly *adj* bad, evil-smelling, fetid, foul, foul-smelling, high, malodorous, mephitic, noisome, odorous, off, putrid, reeking, stinking, strong, strong-smelling.

smirk *n* grin, leer, simper, sneer, snigger.

smitten *adj* afflicted, beguiled, beset, bewitched, blown away, bowled over, captivated, charmed, enamoured, gaga, hard hit, impressed, infatuated, in love, plagued, struck, taken, troubled.

smoke *n* exhaust, film, fog, fume, gas, mist, reek, smog, vapour.

v cure, dry, fume, fumigate, reek, smoulder, vent.

smoky *adj* begrimed, black, grey, grimy, hazy, murky, reeky, sooty, thick.

smooth *adj* agreeable, bland, calm, cunning, easy, effortless, eloquent, equable, even, facile, fair-spoken, finished, flat, flowing, fluent, flush, frictionless, glasslike, glassy, glib, glossy, hairless, harmonious, horizontal, ingratiating, level, mellow, mild, mirrorlike, peaceful, persuasive, plain, plane, pleasant, polished, pressed, problem-free, regular, serene, shiny, silken, silky, sleek, slick, slippery, smarmy, smoothfaced, soft, soothing, steady, straight, suave, tranquil, unbroken, unctuous, undisturbed, uneventful, uniform, uninterrupted, unpuckered, unruffled, unrumpled, untroubled, unwrinkled, urbane, velvety, well-oiled, well-ordered.

antonyms coarse, hairy, harsh, irregular, rough, unsteady.

v allay, alleviate, appease, assuage, calm, ease, extenuate, facilitate, flatten, iron (out), level, mitigate, mollify, palliate, plane, polish, press, soften, straighten (out), unknit, unwrinkle.

antonym roughen.

smoothly *adv* calmly, easily, effortlessly, equably, evenly, fluently, ingratiatingly, legato, like clockwork, mildly, peacefully, pleasantly, problem-free, quietly, serenely, slickly, soothingly, steadily, suavely, tranquilly, without a hitch.

smoothness *n* calmness, ease, efficiency, effortlessness, evenness, facility, finish, flow, fluency, glassiness, glibness, levelness, lubricity, oiliness, placidity, polish, regularity, rhythm, serenity, silkiness, sleekness, slickness, smarminess, softness, stillness, suavity, unbrokenness, urbanity, velvetiness.

antonyms coarseness, harshness, roughness.

smooth-talking *adj* bland, facile, glib, persuasive, plausible, silver-tongued, slick, smooth, suave.

smother *v* choke, cocoon, conceal, cover, deaden, envelop, extinguish, hide, hush up, inundate, kill, muffle, oppress, overlie, overwhelm, put out, repress, shower, shroud, snuff (out), stifle, strangle, suffocate, suppress, surround.

smoulder *v* boil, burn, fester, fume, rage, seethe, simmer, smoke.

smudge *v* blacken, blur, daub, dirty, mark, smear, smirch, soil, spot, stain.

n blemish, blot, blur, smear, smut, spot, stain.

smug *adj* cocksure, complacent, conceited, holier-than-thou, priggish, self-opinionated, self-righteous, self-satisfied, superior, unctuous.

antonym modest.

smuggler *n* bootlegger, contrabandist, courier, gunrunner, moonshiner, mule, rumrunner, runner, wrecker.

smutty *adj* bawdy, blue, coarse, crude, dirty, filthy, gross, improper, indecent, indelicate, lewd, obscene, off-colour, pornographic, prurient, racy, raunchy, ribald, risqué, salacious, suggestive, vulgar.

antonyms clean, decent.

snack *n* bite, break, elevenses, light meal, munchies, nibble, nosh, refreshment(s), tidbit, tiffin.

snag *n* bug, catch, complication, difficulty, disadvantage, drawback, hitch, inconvenience, obstacle, pitfall, problem, stumbling block.

v acquire, catch, get hold of, hinder, hook, ladder, pick up, pull, rip, tear.

snap *v* bark, bite, break, catch, click, crack, crackle, crepitate, flash, grip, growl, nip, pop, retort, seize, separate, snarl, snatch, spark.

n bite, break, breeze, cinch, crack, crackle, energy, fillip, flick, get-up-and-go, go, grab, liveliness, nip, pizzazz, pop, snarl, snatch, vigour, zip.

adj abrupt, hasty, immediate, impulsive, instant, offhand, off-the-cuff, on-the-spot, sudden, unexpected, unpremeditated.

snap up grab, grasp, nab, pick up, pluck, pounce on, seize, snatch.

snappy *adj* brisk, brusque, chic, crabbed, crabby, cross, curt, dapper, edgy, energetic, fashionable, hasty, ill-natured, irritable, modish, natty, quick-tempered, smart, snappish, snazzy, stylish, tart, testy, touchy, trendy, up-to-the-minute, waspish.

snare *v* bag, catch, ensnare, entrap, net, seize, springe, trap, trepan, wire.

n catch, cobweb, gin, lure, net, noose, pitfall, springe, toils, trap, wire.

snarl[1] *v* complain, growl, grumble.

snarl[2] *v* complicate, confuse, embroil, enmesh, entangle, entwine, gnarl, hamper, jam, knot, muddle, ravel, tangle.

snarl-up *n* confusion, entanglement, jumble, mess, mix-up, muddle, tangle, traffic jam.

snatch v abduct, clutch, gain, grab, grasp, grip, jerk, kidnap, nab, pluck, pull, rescue, seize, spirit, steal, take, win, wrench, wrest.
n bit, clutch, fragment, grab, grasp, part, piece, section, segment, smattering, snippet, spell.

snazzy adj attractive, dashing, fashionable, flamboyant, flashy, jazzy, raffish, ritzy, showy, smart, snappy, sophisticated, sporty, stylish, swinging, with-it.
antonyms drab, unfashionable.

sneak v cower, creep, cringe, lurk, pad, sidle, skulk, slink, slip, smuggle, snoop, spirit, steal.
n coward, informer, snake in the grass, tattletale, telltale.
adj clandestine, covert, furtive, quick, secret, stealthy, surprise, surreptitious, underhand.

sneaking adj contemptible, cowardly, cowering, dim, furtive, half-formed, hidden, intuitive, mean, nagging, niggling, persistent, private, secret, sly, sneaky, stealthy, suppressed, surreptitious, two-faced, uncomfortable, underhand, unexpressed, unvoiced, worrying.

sneaky adj backdoor, backstairs, base, contemptible, cowardly, cowering, cunning, deceitful, devious, dishonest, disingenuous, double-dealing, furtive, guileful, low, low-down, malicious, mean, nasty, secretive, shady, shifty, slippery, sly, snide, surreptitious, underhand, unethical, unreliable, unscrupulous, untrustworthy.
antonyms honest, open.

sneer v deride, disdain, gibe, jeer, laugh, look down (on), mock, put down, ridicule, scoff, scorn, snicker, sniff (at), snigger, turn up one's nose (at).
n derision, disdain, gibe, jeer, mockery, put-down, ridicule, scorn, smirk, snicker, snide remark, snigger.

snicker v, n giggle, laugh, sneer, snigger, snort, titter.

snide adj base, cynical, derogatory, dishonest, disparaging, hurtful, ill-natured, insinuating, malicious, mean, nasty, sarcastic, scornful, sneering, spiteful, unkind.

sniff v breathe, inhale, nose, smell, snuff, snuffle, vent.

sniffy adj condescending, contemptuous, disdainful, haughty, scoffing, scornful, sneering, supercilious, superior.

snip v clip, crop, cut, nick, notch, prune, shave, slit, trim.
n bit, clipping, fragment, piece, runt, scrap, shred, slit, snippet.

snippet n fragment, part, particle, piece, portion, scrap, section, segment, shred, snatch.

snitch[1] v filch, lift, palm, pilfer, pinch, snatch, steal, swipe.

snitch[2] v blab, blow the whistle, inform (on), peach, rat (on), squeal, tattle, tell all, tell (on), turn informer.

snivelling adj blubbering, crying, mewling, moaning, sniffling, snuffling, weeping, whimpering, whining.

snobbery n airs, arrogance, condescension, haughtiness, loftiness, lordliness, pretension, pride, snobbishness, snootiness, uppitiness.

snobbish adj arrogant, condescending, haughty, high and mighty, high-hat, hoity-toity, lofty, lordly, patronizing, pretentious, snooty, stuck-up, supercilious, superior, uppity, upstage.

snoop v interfere, meddle, nose (around), pry, sneak, spy.
n busybody, meddler, Nosey Parker, pry, spy.

snooze v catnap, doze, drowse, get some shut-eye, nap, nod off, sleep, take forty winks.
n catnap, doze, forty winks, nap, shut-eye, siesta, sleep.

snout n muzzle, nose, proboscis, schnozzle, snoot, trunk.

snub v brush off, check, cold-shoulder, cut, humble, humiliate, mortify, rebuff, rebuke, shame, slight, squash, squelch, wither.
n affront, brushoff, check, humiliation, insult, put-down, rebuff, rebuke, slap in the face.

snug adj close, close-fitting, comfortable, comfy, compact, cosy, formfitting, homey, intimate, neat, safe, sheltered, trim, warm.

snuggle v cuddle, embrace, hug, nestle, nuzzle.

soak v bathe, damp, drench, imbue, immerse, infuse, interfuse, marinate, moisten, penetrate, permeate, saturate, souse, steep, wet.
soak up absorb, drink in, eat up, imbibe, immerse oneself in, inhale, lap up, sop up, suck up.

soaking adj drenched, dripping, saturated, soaked, sodden, soggy, sopping, streaming, waterlogged, wet, wet through, wringing.
antonym dry.

soar v ascend, climb, escalate, fly, mount, plane, rise, rocket, tower, wing.
antonym plummet.

sob v bawl, blubber, boohoo, cry, howl, mewl, moan, shed tears, snivel, weep.

sober adj abstemious, abstinent, calm, clear-headed, composed, cool, dark, dignified, dispassionate, drab, grave, level-headed, lucid, moderate, plain, practical, quiet, rational, realistic, reasonable, reflective, restrained, sedate, sensible, serene, serious, severe, solemn, sombre, sound, staid, steady, subdued, temperate, thoughtful, unexcited, unintoxicated, unruffled, weighty.
antonyms drunk, excited, frivolous, intemperate, irrational.

so-called adj alleged, nominal, ostensible, pretended, professed, pseudo, self-styled, soi-disant, supposed, would-be.

sociability n affability, amiability, chumminess, companionability, congeniality, conviviality, cordiality, friendliness, gregariousness, neighbourliness.

sociable *adj* accessible, affable, amiable, approachable, chummy, communicative, companionable, convivial, cordial, familiar, friendly, genial, gregarious, neighbourly, outgoing, social, talkative, warm.
antonyms unfriendly, unsociable, withdrawn.

social *adj* collective, common, communal, community, companionable, friendly, general, gregarious, group, neighbourly, public, sociable, societal.
n ceilidh, do, gathering, get-together, hootenanny, party.

socialism *n* collectivism, communism, leftism, Leninism, Marxism, Stalinism, Trotskyism, welfarism.

socialist *adj* collectivist, commie, communist, leftist, left-wing, pink, red, Trotskyite.
n collectivist, commie, communist, leftist, left-winger, red, Trotskyite, welfarist.

socialize *v* chat, consort, entertain, fellowship, fraternize, get together, go out, hang out, mingle, mix, party.

society *n* association, brotherhood, circle, civilization, club, community, companionship, company, corporation, culture, fellowship, fraternity, friendship, gesellschaft, group, guild, humanity, humankind, institute, league, organization, people, population, sisterhood, the public, the world, union, Verein.

sodden *adj* boggy, drenched, marshy, miry, saturated, soaked, soggy, sopping, waterlogged, wet, wet through.
antonym dry.

so far hitherto, thus far, till now, to date, up to now.

soft *adj* balmy, bendable, bland, caressing, comfortable, compassionate, cottony, creamy, crumby, cushioned, cushiony, cushy, daft, delicate, diffuse, dim, dimmed, doughy, downy, ductile, dulcet, easy, easygoing, effeminate, elastic, faint, feathery, feeble-minded, fine, flabby, flaccid, fleecy, flexible, flowing, fluid, foolish, furry, gelatinous, gentle, impressible, indulgent, kind, lax, lenient, liberal, light, limp, low, malleable, mellifluous, mellow, melodious, mild, mouldable, muffled, murmured, muted, namby-pamby, non-alcoholic, out of practice, out of shape, overindulgent, pale, pampered, pastel, permissive, pitying, plastic, pleasant, pleasing, pliable, pulpy, quaggy, quiet, restful, rusty, sensitive, sentimental, shaded, silky, silly, simple, smooth, soothing, soppy, spineless, spongy, squashy, subdued, supple, swampy, sweet, sympathetic, temperate, tender, tender-hearted, undemanding, understated, unprotected, velvety, weak, whispered, yielding.
antonyms firm, hard, harsh, heavy, loud, rigid, rough, severe, strict.

soft spot fondness, liking, partiality, penchant, vulnerability, weakness.

soften *v* abate, allay, alleviate, appease, assuage, calm, come around, cushion, decline, decrease, digest, diminish, ease, ease up, extenuate, lessen, lighten, lower, macerate, melt, mitigate, moderate, modify, mollify, muffle, palliate, quell, relax, relent, soothe, still, subdue, temper.
antonyms anneal, harden.

soften up conciliate, disarm, melt, persuade, soft-soap, weaken, win over.

soft-hearted *adj* benevolent, charitable, clement, compassionate, generous, indulgent, kind, merciful, pitying, sentimental, sympathetic, tender, tender-hearted, warm-hearted.
antonym hard-hearted.

soft-pedal *v* de-emphasize, go easy on, moderate, muffle, play down, subdue, tone down.
antonyms emphasize, play up.

soggy *adj* boggy, damp, dripping, moist, mushy, pulpy, saturated, soaked, sodden, sopping, soppy, spongy, waterlogged, wet.

soil[1] *n* clay, country, dirt, dust, earth, glebe, ground, humus, land, loam, region, terra firma.

soil[2] *v* bedraggle, befoul, begrime, besmirch, corrupt, defile, dirty, foul, maculate, muddy, pollute, smear, spatter, spot, stain, sully, tarnish.

soiled *adj* corrupted, dirty, grimy, maculate, polluted, spotted, stained, sullied, tarnished.
antonyms clean, immaculate.

sojourn *n* rest, stay, stop, stopover, visit.
v abide, dwell, lodge, reside, rest, stay, stop, tarry, visit.

solace *n* alleviation, assuagement, comfort, consolation, relief, succour, support.
v allay, alleviate, assuage, comfort, console, mitigate, soften, soothe, succour, support.

soldier *n* cavalryman, fighter, G.I., guardsman, hoplite, infantryman, Jäger, Janizary, kern, lancer, leatherneck, Mameluke, man-at-arms, marine, officer, poilu, private, redcoat, reservist, rifleman, sepoy, serviceman, Tommy, trooper, warrior.

sole *adj* alone, exclusive, individual, one, only, single, singular, solitary, unique.
antonyms multiple, shared.

solecism *n* absurdity, anacoluthon, blunder, booboo, breach, error, faux pas, gaffe, gaucherie, impropriety, incongruity, indecorum, lapse, malapropism, mistake, nonstandard usage, slip.

solely *adv* alone, completely, entirely, exclusively, merely, only, purely, simply, single-handedly, singly, uniquely.

solemn *adj* august, awed, awe-inspiring, ceremonial, ceremonious, devotional, dignified, earnest, formal, gloomy, glum, grand, grave, hallowed, holy, imposing, impressive, majestic, momentous, pompous, portentous, reflective, religious, reverent, ritual, sacred, sanctified, sedate, serious, sober, sombre, staid, stately, thoughtful, venerable, weighty.
antonyms frivolous, gay, light-hearted.

solemnities *n* celebration, ceremonial, ceremony, formalities, observance, pomp, proceedings, rite, ritual.

solemnity n dignity, earnestness, grandeur, gravity, impressiveness, momentousness, portentousness, sacredness, sanctity, seriousness, stateliness.

antonym frivolity.

solemnize v celebrate, commemorate, dignify, formalize, honour, keep, observe.

solicit v ask, beg, beseech, canvass, crave, entreat, implore, importune, petition, pray, request, seek, sue, supplicate.

solicitor n advocate, attorney, barrister, lawyer, notary (public), QC.

solicitous adj anxious, apprehensive, ardent, attentive, careful, caring, concerned, eager, earnest, fearful, troubled, uneasy, worried, zealous.

solicitude n anxiety, attentiveness, care, concern, considerateness, consideration, disquiet, regard, uneasiness, worry.

solid adj chunky, compact, complete, concrete, constant, continuous, cubical, decent, dense, dependable, estimable, excellent, firm, genuine, good, hard, law-abiding, level-headed, massed, pure, real, reliable, respectable, sensible, serious, sober, sound, square, stable, stalwart, sterling, stocky, stout, straight, strong, sturdy, substantial, thorough, trusty, unalloyed, unanimous, unbroken, undivided, uninterrupted, united, unmixed, unshakeable, unvaried, upright, upstanding, weighty, worthy.

antonyms broken, insubstantial, liquid.

solidarity n accord, camaraderie, cohesion, concord, concordance, consensus, co-operation, esprit de corps, harmony, like-mindedness, soundness, stability, team spirit, unanimity, unification, unity.

antonyms discord, division, schism.

solidify v cake, clot, coagulate, cohere, congeal, crystallize, gel, harden, jell, set, strengthen.

antonyms dissolve, liquefy, soften.

solitary adj alone, cloistered, companionless, desolate, friendless, hermitlike, hidden, isolated, lone, lonely, lonesome, only, out-of-the-way, reclusive, remote, retired, secluded, separate, sequestered, single, sole, unfrequented, unsociable, unsocial, untrodden, unvisited, withdrawn.

antonyms accompanied, gregarious.

solitude n aloneness, desert, emptiness, isolation, loneliness, privacy, reclusiveness, retirement, seclusion, waste, wasteland, wilderness.

antonym companionship.

solution n answer, blend, clarification, compound, decipherment, denouement, disconnection, dissolution, elucidation, emulsion, explanation, explication, key, liquefaction, melting, mix, mixture, resolution, result, solvent, solving, suspension, unfolding, unravelling.

solve v answer, clarify, clear up, crack, decipher, disentangle, dissolve, elucidate, explain, figure out, get to the bottom of, interpret, resolve, settle, unbind, unfold, unravel, work out.

sombre adj dark, depressing, dim, dingy, dismal, doleful, drab, dull, dusky, funereal, fuscous, gloomy, grave, grey, joyless, lacklustre, lugubrious, melancholy, mournful, obscure, sad, sepulchral, shadowy, sober, solemn, subfusc.

antonyms bright, cheerful, happy.

somebody n big name, big noise, big shot, big wheel, bigwig, celebrity, dignitary, heavyweight, household name, luminary, magnate, mogul, nabob, name, notable, panjandrum, personage, someone, star, superstar, VIP.

antonym nobody.

somehow adv by fair means or foul, by hook or by crook, come hell or high water, come what may, if it's the last thing one does, one way or another.

sometimes adv at times, every so often, from time to time, now and again, now and then, occasionally, off and on, once in a while.

antonyms always, never.

somnolent adj comatose, dopey, dozy, drowsy, half-asleep, half-awake, heavy-eyed, languid, oscitant, sleepy, soporific, torpid.

son n boy, descendant, disciple, inhabitant, lad, native, offspring.

song n air, anthem, ballad, barcarole, canon, canticle, cantilena, canto, canzonet, carol, chanson, chant, chorus, ditty, elegy, epicedium, epithalamion, folk song, hymn, lay, lied, lilt, lullaby, lyric, madrigal, melody, number, ode, paean, poem, psalm, round, shanty, strain, tune, volkslied.

song and dance ado, commotion, disturbance, flap, foofaraur, furor, fuss, hoo-ha, hullabaloo, kafuffle, performance, shindig, shindy, spiel, squall, stir, tizzy, to-do, tumult, turmoil, variety, vaudeville.

songster n balladeer, chansonnier, chansonnière, chanter, chanteuse, chorister, crooner, minstrel, singer, songbird, troubadour, vocalist, warbler.

sonorous adj full, full-mouthed, full-throated, full-voiced, grandiloquent, high-flown, high-sounding, loud, orotund, pear-shaped, plangent, plummy, resonant, resounding, rich, ringing, rounded, sounding.

soon adv anon, any time now, before long, betimes, early, in a minute, in a sec, in a short time, in the near future, momentarily, presently, shortly.

soothe v allay, alleviate, appease, assuage, calm, coax, comfort, compose, ease, hush, lull, mitigate, mollify, pacify, quiet, reassure, relieve, salve, settle, soften, still, tranquillize.

antonyms annoy, irritate, vex.

soothing adj assuaging, balmy, balsamic, calming, comforting, demulcent, easeful, emollient, lenitive, palliative, quieting, reassuring, relaxing, restful, sedative, tranquillizing.

antonyms annoying, irritating, vexing.

soothsayer *n* augur, Chaldee, diviner, foreteller, oracle, predictor, prophet, psychic, seer, sibyl.

sophisticated *adj* advanced, blasé, citified, civilized, complex, complicated, cosmopolitan, couth, cultivated, cultured, elaborate, experienced, highly-developed, intricate, jetset, multifaceted, refined, seasoned, subtle, urbane, worldly, worldly-wise, world-weary.

antonyms artless, naïve, simple, unsophisticated.

sophistication *n* culture, elegance, experience, finesse, poise, savoir-faire, savoir-vivre, urbanity, worldliness.

antonyms naïvety, simplicity.

sophistry *n* casuistry, elenchus, fallacy, quibble, sophism.

soporific *adj* hypnagogic, hypnotic, poppied, sedative, sleep-inducing, sleepy, somniferous, somnolent, tranquillizing.

antonyms invigorating, stimulating.

n anesthetic, hypnotic, narcotic, opiate, sedative, tranquillizer.

antonym stimulant.

soppy *adj* cloying, corny, drippy, gushy, lovey-dovey, mawkish, mushy, schmaltzy, sentimental, silly, slushy, soft, weepy.

sorcerer *n* enchanter, mage, magician, necromancer, sorceress, warlock, witch, wizard.

sorcery *n* charm, diablerie, divination, enchantment, hoodoo, incantation, magic, necromancy, spell, warlockry, witchcraft, witchery, witching, wizardry.

sordid *adj* avaricious, base, contemptible, corrupt, covetous, debauched, degenerate, degraded, despicable, dingy, dirty, disreputable, filthy, foul, grasping, greedy, low, mean, mercenary, miserly, money-grubbing, niggardly, rapacious, seamy, seedy, selfish, self-seeking, shabby, shameful, sleazy, slovenly, squalid, tawdry, unclean, ungenerous, venal, vicious, vile, wretched.

sore *adj* acute, afflicted, aggrieved, angry, annoyed, annoying, burning, chafed, critical, desperate, dire, distressing, extreme, grieved, grievous, harrowing, hostile, hurt, inflamed, irked, irritable, irritated, pained, painful, peeved, pressing, raw, reddened, resentful, sensitive, severe, sharp, smarting, stung, tender, touchy, troublesome, upset, urgent, vexed.

n abscess, boil, canker, carbuncle, chafe, gathering, inflammation, swelling, ulcer, wound.

sorrow *n* affliction, anguish, blow, distress, dolour, grief, hardship, heartache, heartbreak, lamentation, misery, misfortune, mourning, regret, sadness, trial, tribulation, trouble, unhappiness, woe, worry.

antonyms happiness, joy.

v agonize, bemoan, bewail, grieve, lament, moan, mourn, pine, weep.

antonym rejoice.

sorrowful *adj* afflicted, brokenhearted, dejected, depressed, disconsolate, distressing, doleful, grief-stricken, grieving, grievous, heartbroken, heart-rending, heavy-hearted, lamentable, lugubrious, melancholy, miserable, mournful, painful, piteous, plaintive, rueful, sad, sorry, tearful, unhappy, woebegone, woeful, wretched.

antonyms happy, joyful.

sorry *adj* abject, apologetic, base, commiserative, compassionate, conscience-stricken, contrite, deplorable, disconsolate, disgraceful, dismal, distressed, distressing, grieved, guilt-ridden, mean, melancholy, miserable, mournful, moved, paltry, pathetic, penitent, piteous, pitiable, pitiful, pitying, poor, regretful, remorseful, repentant, sad, self-reproachful, shabby, shamefaced, sorrowful, sympathetic, unhappy, unworthy, vile, wretched.

antonym glad.

sort *n* brand, breed, category, character, class, denomination, description, family, genre, genus, group, ilk, kidney, kind, make, nature, order, quality, race, species, stamp, style, type, variety.

v arrange, assort, catalogue, categorize, class, classify, distribute, divide, file, grade, group, neaten, order, rank, screen, select, sift, systematize, tidy.

sort out clarify, clear up, divide, figure out, get to the bottom of, organize, resolve, segregate, select, separate, sift, solve, tidy up, work out.

so-so *adj* adequate, average, fair, fair to middling, indifferent, mediocre, middling, moderate, neutral, not bad, OK, ordinary, passable, run-of-the-mill, tolerable, undistinguished, unexceptional.

soul *n* anima, animation, ardour, being, body, courage, creature, element, embodiment, emotion, energy, essence, expression, expressiveness, feeling, fervour, force, heart, incarnation, individual, inner nature, inspiration, inspirer, intellect, leader, life, life force, man, mind, mortal, nobility, person, personification, pneuma, psyche, quintessence, reason, spirit, type, vital force, vitality, vivacity, warmth, woman.

soulful *adj* eloquent, emotional, expressive, heartfelt, meaningful, mournful, moving, profound, sensitive.

soulless *adj* callous, cold, cruel, dead, heartless, ignoble, inanimate, inhuman, lifeless, mean, mean-spirited, mechanical, soul-destroying, spiritless, unfeeling, uninteresting, unkind, unsympathetic.

sound¹ *n* description, din, earshot, hearing, noise, range, report, resonance, reverberation, tenor, tone, utterance, voice.

v announce, appear, articulate, blare, chime, declare, echo, enunciate, express, knell, look, peal, proclaim, pronounce, resonate, resound, reverberate, ring, seem, signal, sing, toll, utter, voice.

sound² *adj* correct, deep, entire, established, fair, firm, fit, good, hale, healthy, hearty, in one piece, intact, just, level-headed, logical, orthodox, peaceful, perfect, proper, proven, prudent, rational, reasonable, recognized, reliable, reputable, responsible, right, right-thinking, robust, safe, secure, sensible, solid, solvent, stable, sturdy, substantial, thorough, tried-and-true, true, trustworthy, unbroken, undamaged, undisturbed, unhurt, unimpaired, uninjured, uninterrupted, unscathed, untroubled, valid, vigorous, well, well-founded, well-grounded, whole, wise.

antonyms shaky, unfit, unreliable, unsound.

sound³ *v* examine, fathom, inspect, investigate, measure, plumb, probe, test.

sound out ask, canvass, examine, feel out, probe, pump, question.

sound⁴ *n* channel, estuary, fiord, firth, inlet, passage, strait.

soup *n* bisque, broth, chowder, consommé, julienne, potage.

sour *adj* acerbic, acetic, acid, acidulous, acrid, acrimonious, bad, bad-tempered, biting, bitter, churlish, crabby, curdled, cynical, disagreeable, discontented, embittered, fermented, grouchy, grudging, ill-natured, ill-tempered, inharmonious, jaundiced, off, peevish, pungent, rancid, rank, sharp, spoiled, tart, turned, ungenerous, unpleasant, unsavoury, unsuccessful, unsweet, unwholesome, vinegary, waspish.

antonyms good-natured, sweet.

v acidify, alienate, curdle, disenchant, embitter, envenom, exacerbate, exasperate, go bad, spoil.

source *n* author, authority, begetter, beginning, bottom, cause, commencement, derivation, fountainhead, genesis, headwaters, informant, mine, origin, original, originator, primordium, rise, spring, wellspring.

sourpuss *n* crosspatch, grouch, grouse, grumbler, grump, killjoy, kvetch, misery, shrew, wet blanket, whiner.

souse *v* douse, drench, dunk, immerse, marinate, pickle, plunge, soak, steep.

souvenir *n* gift, keepsake, memento, memory, relic, remembrance, reminder, token.

sovereign *n* autarch, chief, czar, dynast, emperor, empress, kaiser, king, monarch, potentate, prince, queen, ruler, shah.

adj absolute, august, chief, dominant, excellent, greatest, imperial, independent, kingly, majestic, monarchal, monarchical, paramount, powerful, predominant, principal, queenly, regal, royal, ruling, self-governing, supreme, unlimited.

sovereignty *n* ascendancy, dominion, imperium, independence, kingship, primacy, raj, regality, self-government, supremacy, suzerainty, sway.

sow *v* broadcast, disperse, disseminate, drill, implant, inseminate, lodge, plant, scatter, seed, spread, strew.

space *n* accommodation, berth, blank, capacity, chasm, distance, duration, elbowroom, expanse, extension, extent, freedom, gap, interval, lacuna, leeway, margin, omission, opening, period, place, play, room, rope, scope, seat, spaciousness, span, time, volume.

spacious *adj* ample, big, broad, capacious, comfortable, commodious, expansive, extensive, huge, large, roomy, sizable, uncrowded, vast, voluminous, wide.

antonyms confined, cramped, narrow, small.

spadework *n* dirty work, donkey-work, drudgery, foundation, groundwork, labour, preparation.

span *n* amount, compass, distance, duration, extent, length, period, reach, scope, spell, spread, stretch, term.

v arch, bridge, cover, cross, encompass, extend, join, link, overarch, traverse, vault.

spank *v* belt, cane, cuff, lather, slap, slipper, smack, strap, tan, wallop, whack.

spanking *adj* brand-new, brisk, energetic, fast, fine, gleaming, invigorating, lively, quick, smart, snappy, speedy, swift, vigorous.

antonym slow.

spar *v* argue, bicker, box, contend, contest, dispute, fall out, fight, quarrel, scrap, skirmish, spat, squabble, tiff, wrangle, wrestle.

spare *adj* additional, economical, emergency, extra, free, frugal, gaunt, lank, lean, leftover, meagre, modest, odd, remaining, reserve, scanty, slender, slight, slim, sparing, superfluous, supernumerary, surplus, thin, unoccupied, unused, unwanted, wiry.

antonyms corpulent, necessary, profuse.

v afford, allow, bestow, do without, give quarter, grant, have mercy on, leave, let off, pardon, part with, refrain from, release, relinquish.

sparing *adj* careful, chary, cost-conscious, economical, frugal, parsimonious, prudent, saving, stingy, thrifty.

antonyms lavish, liberal, unsparing.

spark *n* atom, flake, flare, flash, flicker, gleam, glint, hint, jot, scintilla, scintillation, scrap, spit, trace, vestige.

v animate, cause, excite, inspire, kindle, motivate, occasion, precipitate, provoke, set off, start, stimulate, stir, trigger.

sparkle *v* beam, bubble, coruscate, dance, effervesce, fizz, fizzle, flash, gleam, glint, glisten, glister, glitter, glow, scintillate, shimmer, shine, spark, twinkle, wink.

n animation, brilliance, coruscation, dash, dazzle, effervescence, élan, flash, flicker, gaiety, gleam, glint, glitter, life, liveliness, panache, pizzazz, radiance, scintillation, spark, spirit, twinkle, vim, vitality, vivacity, zip.

sparkling *adj* animated, bubbly, carbonated, coruscating, effervescent, fizzy, flashing, gleaming, glistening, glittering, lively, scintillating, twinkling, witty.

antonyms dull, flat.

sparse *adj* dispersed, few and far between, infrequent, meagre, scanty, scarce, scattered, sporadic.
antonyms dense, lush, thick.

Spartan *adj* abstemious, abstinent, ascetic, austere, bleak, disciplined, extreme, frugal, hardy, harsh, joyless, plain, rigorous, self-denying, severe, stark, stern, strict, stringent, temperate, unflinching.

spasm *n* access, burst, contraction, convulsion, eruption, fit, frenzy, jerk, outburst, paroxysm, seizure, shaking, throe, twitch.

spasmodic *adj* convulsive, erratic, fitful, intermittent, irregular, jerky, occasional, paroxysmal, sporadic.
antonyms continuous, uninterrupted.

spat *n* argument, disagreement, fight, quarrel, row, squabble, tiff, wrangle.
v argue, bicker, fight, quarrel, row, squabble, wrangle.

spate *n* deluge, downpour, epidemic, eruption, flood, flow, inundation, outpouring, rush, torrent.

spatter *v* bedaub, bespatter, besprinkle, bestrew, daub, dirty, scatter, soil, speckle, splash, splotch, spot, spray, sprinkle.

speak *v* address, advert to, allude to, argue, articulate, breathe, comment on, communicate, converse, deal with, declaim, declare, discourse, discuss, enunciate, express, harangue, lecture, make a speech, mention, plead, pronounce, refer to, say, speechify, spiel, state, talk, utter, voice.

speak to accost, address, admonish, apostrophize, berate, bring to book, dress down, give a piece of one's mind, have a word with, lecture, rebuke, reprimand, scold, take aside, take to task, tell off, upbraid, warn.

speaker *n* lecturer, megaphone, mouthpiece, orator, speechifier, speechmaker, spieler, spokesman, spokesperson, spokeswoman, voice.

spearhead *v* be on the vanguard (of), front, head, initiate, launch, lead, pioneer.

special *adj* appropriate, certain, characteristic, chief, choice, detailed, distinctive, distinguished, especial, exceptional, exclusive, extraordinary, festive, gala, important, individual, intimate, main, major, memorable, momentous, particular, peculiar, precise, primary, red-letter, select, significant, specialized, specific, uncommon, unique, unusual.
antonyms common, normal, ordinary, usual.

specialist *n* adept, authority, connoisseur, consultant, expert, master, professional, proficient.

specialty *n* area of experience, bag, field, focus, forte, métier, particular, peculiarity, pièce de resistance, scene, special, strength, talent, thing.

species *n* breed, category, class, collection, denomination, description, genus, group, kind, sort, type, variety.

specific *adj* characteristic, clear-cut, definite, delimitative, distinguishing, especial, exact, explicit, express, limited, particular, peculiar, precise, special, unambiguous, unequivocal.
antonyms general, vague.

specification *n* condition, description, detail, enumeration, item, itemization, listing, particular, qualification, requirement, stipulation.

specify *v* cite, define, delineate, describe, designate, detail, enumerate, indicate, individualize, itemize, list, mention, name, particularize, spell out, stipulate.

specimen *n* copy, embodiment, example, exemplar, exemplification, exhibit, illustration, individual, instance, model, paradigm, pattern, person, proof, representative, sample, type.

specious *adj* casuistic, deceptive, fallacious, false, hollow, misleading, plausible, sophistic, unsound, untrue.
antonym valid.

speck *n* atom, bit, blemish, blot, defect, dot, drop, fault, flaw, fleck, grain, impurity, iota, jot, macula, mark, mite, modicum, mote, particle, shred, smidgen, speckle, spot, stain, tittle, trace, whit.

speckled *adj* brindled, dappled, dotted, flecked, freckled, lentiginous, mottled, pied, spotted, spotty, sprinkled, stippled.

spectacle *n* curiosity, display, event, exhibition, extravaganza, marvel, pageant, parade, performance, phenomenon, scene, show, sight, wonder.

spectacles *n* eyeglasses, glasses, goggles, lorgnette, opera glasses, pince-nez, specs.

spectacular *adj* amazing, astounding, breathtaking, daring, dazzling, dramatic, eye-catching, fabulous, fantastic, grand, impressive, magnificent, marked, remarkable, sensational, splendid, staggering, striking, stunning.
antonyms ordinary, unspectacular.
n display, event, extravaganza, pageant, show, spectacle.

spectator *n* beholder, bystander, eyewitness, looker-on, observer, onlooker, passer-by, viewer, watcher, witness.
antonyms contestant, participant, player.

spectral *adj* disembodied, eerie, ghostly, illusory, incorporeal, insubstantial, phantasmal, phantom, shadowy, spooky, supernatural, uncanny, unearthly, weird.

spectre *n* apparition, ghost, phantom, presence, revenant, shade, shadow, spirit, vision, wraith.

speculate *v* cogitate, conjecture, consider, contemplate, deliberate, gamble, guess, hazard, hypothesize, invest, meditate, muse, predict, reflect, risk, scheme, suppose, surmise, theorize, venture, wonder.

speculation *n* conjecture, consideration, contemplation, deliberation, flight of fancy, gamble, gambling, guess, guesswork, hazard, hypothesis, ideology, investment, opinion, prediction, risk, supposition, surmise, theory.

speculative adj abstract, academic, chancy, conjectural, dicey, hazardous, hypothetical, iffy, notional, projected, reflective, risky, suppositional, tentative, theoretical, thoughtful, uncertain, unpredictable.

speech n address, articulation, colloquy, communication, conversation, dialect, dialogue, diction, discourse, discussion, disquisition, enunciation, harangue, homily, idiom, intercourse, jargon, language, lecture, lingo, oration, parlance, parole, peroration, say, spiel, talk, tongue, utterance, voice, winged words, words.

speechless adj aghast, amazed, astounded, dazed, dumb, dumfounded, dumbstruck, inarticulate, mum, mute, shocked, silent, tacit, thunderstruck, tongue-tied, unspoken, wordless.

speed n acceleration, celerity, clip, dispatch, expedition, fleetness, haste, hurry, lick, momentum, pace, precipitation, quickness, rapidity, rush, swiftness, tempo, velocity.
  v advance, aid, assist, belt, bomb, boost, bowl along, career, dispatch, expedite, facilitate, flash, fleet, further, gallop, hasten, help, highball, hurry, impel, lick, press on, promote, quicken, race, rush, sprint, step on it, step on the gas, tear, urge on, vroom, whiz, zap, zip, zoom.
  antonyms delay, hamper, restrain, slow.

speedily adv fast, hastily, hurriedly, posthaste, promptly, quickly, rapidly, swiftly.
  antonym slowly.

speedy adj clipping, expeditious, express, fast, fleet, hasty, headlong, hurried, immediate, nimble, precipitate, prompt, quick, rapid, summary, swift, winged, zappy.
  antonyms dilatory, slow, tardy.

spell[1] v augur, herald, imply, indicate, mean, portend, presage, promise, signal, signify, suggest.

spell[2] n abracadabra, allure, bewitchment, charm, conjuration, enchantment, exorcism, fascination, glamour, hex, incantation, jinx, magic, open sesame, paternoster, philtre, rune, sorcery, trance, witchery.

spell[3] n bout, course, innings, interval, patch, period, season, shift, stint, stretch, term, time, turn.

spell out clarify, elucidate, emphasize, explain, make explicit, specify.

spellbound adj bemused, bewitched, captivated, charmed, enchanted, engrossed, enthralled, entranced, fascinated, gripped, hooked, hypnotized, mesmerized, possessed, rapt, transfixed, transported.

spend v apply, bestow, blow, concentrate, consume, cough up, deplete, devote, disburse, dispense, dissipate, drain, employ, empty, exhaust, expend, fill, fork out, fritter away, invest, lavish, lay out, occupy, pass, pay out, shell out, squander, use, use up, waste.
  antonyms hoard, save.

spendthrift n big spender, poor manager, prodigal, profligate, spender, squanderer, waster, wastrel.
  antonyms hoarder, miser, saver.
  adj extravagant, improvident, prodigal, profligate, thriftless, wasteful.
  antonyms saving, thrifty.

spent adj all in, burnt out, bushed, consumed, dead beat, dead on one's feet, debilitated, dog-tired, done in, drained, exhausted, expended, finished, gone, played out, prostrate, tired out, used up, wasted, weakened, wearied, weary, whacked, worn out, worn to a frazzle, zonked.

spew v belch, disgorge, gush, jet, puke, regurgitate, retch, spit (out), throw up, vomit.

sphere n arena, ball, capacity, circle, compass, department, domain, field, function, globe, globule, milieu, orb, province, range, rank, realm, scope, spheroid, spherule, station, stratum, territory.

spherical adj ball-shaped, globate, globed, globelike, globe-shaped, globoid, globose, globular, orbicular, rotund, round, spheroidal, spherular.

spice n colour, excitement, flavouring, gusto, kick, life, pep, piquancy, relish, salt, savour, seasoning, tang, zap, zest, zip.

spick-and-span clean, immaculate, neat, polished, scrubbed, shipshape, spotless, spruce, tidy, trim, well-kept.
  antonyms dirty, untidy.

spicy adj aromatic, flavoursome, fragrant, hot, improper, indecorous, indelicate, lively, off-colour, piquant, pungent, racy, ribald, risqué, savoury, scandalous, seasoned, sensational, showy, suggestive, tangy, titillating, unseemly.
  antonym bland.

spiel v declaim, harangue, hold forth, lecture, orate, recite, rhyme (off), sermonize, speechify, spout.
  n harangue, oration, patter, pitch, recital, routine, sales patter, sermon, speech.

spike n barb, nail, point, prong, spica, spicule, spine, spire, thorn, tine.
  v block, foil, fortify, frustrate, impale, lace, pierce, puncture, spear, spit, stab, stick, stop, thwart.

spill v discharge, disgorge, overflow, overturn, scatter, shed, slop, slosh, upset.
  n accident, cropper, fall, overturn, tumble, upset.

spill the beans blab, blow the gaff, give the game away, inform, let slip, let the cat out of the bag, rat, show, squeal, tattle.

spin v birl, concoct, develop, gyrate, invent, make up, narrate, pirouette, recount, reel, reel off, relate, revolve, rotate, swim, swirl, tell, turn, twirl, twist, unfold, wheel, whirl.
  n agitation, bias, commotion, drive, flap, gyration, panic, pirouette, revolution, ride, roll, rotation, run, state, tizzy, turn, twist, whirl.

spin out amplify, delay, draw out, extend,

lengthen, maintain, pad out, prolong, protract, sustain.

spindle *n*   arbor, axis, axle, pivot.

spindly *adj*   attenuated, gangling, gangly, lanky, leggy, skeletal, skinny, spidery, spindleshanked, thin, twiggy, weedy.

antonyms   stocky, thickset.

spine *n*   backbone, barb, courage, moral strength, needle, quill, rachis, ray, resolve, ridge, spicule, spiculum, spike, spur, support, thorn, vertebrae, vertebral column.

spine-chilling *adj*   bloodcurdling, eerie, frightening, hair-raising, horrifying, scary, spine-tingling, spooky, terrifying.

spineless *adj*   cowardly, faint-hearted, feeble, gutless, inadequate, ineffective, irresolute, lily-livered, soft, spiritless, squeamish, submissive, vacillating, weak, weak-kneed, weak-willed, wimpy, wishy-washy, yellow.

antonyms   brave, strong.

spiny *adj*   acanthine, briery, difficult, knotty, perplexing, pointed, prickly, spiculate, spiniferous, spinose, thistly, thorny.

spiral *adj*   circular, cochleate, coiled, corkscrew, gyratory, helical, scrolled, spiraliform, volute, whorled, winding.

n   coil, convolution, corkscrew, curlicue, gyre, helix, screw, volute, volution, whorl.

spire *n*   cone, flèche, peak, pinnacle, point, shoot, spike, sprout, stalk, steeple, summit, tip, top.

spirit *n*   air, anima, animation, apparition, ardour, atmosphere, attitude, backbone, bravura, breath, brio, character, complexion, courage, daemon, dash, dauntlessness, deva, disposition, earnestness, élan, energy, enterprise, enthusiasm, esprit, essence, familiar, faun, feeling(s), fervour, fire, force, gameness, genie, genius, genius loci, ghost, ghoul, gist, grit, guts, heart, inner nature, intent, intention, jinni, Ka, kobold, life, life force, liveliness, manitou, meaning, mettle, mood, morale, motivation, outlook, phantom, pluck, pneuma, psyche, purport, purpose, quality, resolution, resolve, revenant, sense, shade, shadow, soul, sparkle, spectre, spook, sprite, spunk, stout-heartedness, substance, sylph, temper, temperament, tenor, tone, totem, verve, vigour, vision, vitality, vivacity, warmth, water nymph, water sprite, will, will power, Zeitgeist, zest.

spirit away   abduct, abstract, carry off, convey, kidnap, purloin, remove, run off with, shanghai, snaffle, steal, whisk off.

spirited *adj*   active, animated, ardent, bold, courageous, eager, energetic, enthusiastic, feisty, game, hearty, high-spirited, lively, mettlesome, plucky, sparkling, sprightly, spunky, vigorous, vivacious.

antonyms   lazy, spiritless, timid.

spiritless *adj*   anemic, apathetic, dejected, depressed, despondent, dispirited, droopy, dull, lacklustre, languid, lifeless, listless, low, melancholy, mopish, torpid, unenthusiastic, unmoved, unmoving.

antonym   spirited.

spirits *n*   alcohol, firewater, hard stuff, hooch, liquor, moonshine, strong drink, strong liquor.

spiritual *adj*   airy, devotional, divine, ecclesiastical, ethereal, ghostly, holy, immaterial, incorporeal, otherwordly, pious, pure, religious, sacred, unfleshly, unworldly.

antonyms   carnal, material, physical.

spit *v*   discharge, drizzle, eject, expectorate, hawk, hiss, spew, splutter, sputter.

n   dribble, drool, expectoration, phlegm, saliva, slaver, spittle, sputum.

spite *n*   animosity, bitchiness, gall, grudge, hate, hatred, hostility, ill nature, malevolence, malice, malignity, pique, rancour, spitefulness, spleen, venom, viciousness.

antonyms   affection, good will.

v   annoy, discomfit, gall, harm, hurt, injure, irk, irritate, needle, nettle, offend, peeve, pique, provoke, put out, vex.

in spite of   despite, even with, irrespective of, notwithstanding, regardless of.

spiteful *adj*   barbed, bitchy, catty, cruel, ill-disposed, ill-natured, malevolent, malicious, malignant, nasty, rancorous, snide, splenetic, vengeful, venomous, vindictive, waspish.

antonyms   affectionate, charitable.

spitting image   clone, dead ringer, dead spit, double, (exact) replica, likeness, look-alike, picture, ringer, spit, twin.

splash *v*   bathe, bespatter, blazon, break, broadcast, dabble, dash, display, flaunt, headline, moisten, paddle, plash, plaster, plop, plunge, publicize, shower, slop, slosh, spatter, splatter, splotch, spray, spread, sprinkle, squirt, strew, surge, tout, trumpet, wade, wallow, wash, wet.

n   burst, dash, display, effect, excitement, impact, ostentation, patch, publicity, sensation, show, spattering, splatter, splotch, spot, sprinkle, stir, touch.

spleen *n*   acrimony, anger, animosity, animus, bad temper, bile, biliousness, bitterness, gall, hatred, hostility, ill humour, ill will, malevolence, malice, malignity, peevishness, petulance, pique, rancour, resentment, spite, spitefulness, venom, vindictiveness, wrath.

splendid *adj*   admirable, beaming, bright, brilliant, costly, dazzling, excellent, exceptional, fantastic, fine, first-class, glittering, glorious, glowing, gorgeous, grand, grandiose, great, heroic, illustrious, imposing, impressive, lavish, lustrous, luxurious, magnificent, marvellous, ornate, outstanding, phenomenal, radiant, rare, refulgent, remarkable, renowned, resplendent, rich, shining, splendiferous, splendorous, sterling, sublime, sumptuous, superb, supreme, tiptop, top-flight, top-notch, wonderful.

antonyms   drab, ordinary, run-of-the-mill.

splendour *n*   beauty, brightness, brilliance, ceremony, display, effulgence, glory, gorgeousness, grandeur, lustre, magnificence, majesty, pomp, radiance, refulgence, renown, resplendence, richness, show, solemnity, spectacle, stateliness, sumptuousness.

splenetic *adj* acid, atrabilious, bad-tempered, bilious, bitchy, choleric, churlish, crabby, cross, envenomed, fretful, ill-tempered, irascible, irritable, morose, peevish, petulant, rancorous, resentful, sour, spiteful, sullen, testy, touchy.

splice *v* bind, braid, entwine, graft, interlace, interlink, intertwine, intertwist, interweave, join, knit, marry, mesh, plait, tie, unite, wed, yoke.

splinter *n* chip, flake, flinder, fragment, needle, paring, shaving, sliver, spall, spicule.
v break up, disintegrate, fracture, fragment, shatter, shiver, smash, spall, split.

split *v* allocate, allot, apportion, bifurcate, branch, break, burst, cleave, crack, decamp, delaminate, depart, disband, distribute, disunite, diverge, divide, flee, fork, gape, halve, leave, open, parcel out, part, partition, rend, rip, rive, section, separate, sever, share out, slash, slice up, slit, sliver, snap, splinter, take off.
n breach, break, break-up, cleft, crack, dichotomy, difference, discord, disruption, dissension, disunion, divergence, division, estrangement, falling-out, fissure, gap, opening, partition, rent, rift, rip, rupture, schism, scission, separation, slash, slit, tear.
adj ambivalent, bisected, broken, cleft, cloven, cracked, divided, dual, fractured, riven, ruptured, severed, twofold.

split hairs cavil, find fault, nit-pick, overrefine, pettifog, quibble.

split up break up, disband, dissolve, divorce, fall out, go separate ways, part, part company, separate.

spoil *v* addle, baby, blemish, bungle, butcher, coddle, cosset, curdle, damage, debase, decay, decompose, deface, despoil, destroy, deteriorate, detract from, disfigure, feather-bed, go bad, go off, harm, impair, indulge, injure, louse up, mar, mildew, mollycoddle, pamper, plunder, putrefy, queer, rot, ruin, screw up, spoon-feed, thwart, turn, upset, wreck.

spoils *n* acquisitions, boodle, booty, gain, haul, loot, pickings, pillage, plunder, prey, prize(s), rapine, spoliation, swag, winnings.

spoilsport *n* damper, dog in the manger, killjoy, misery, party pooper, skeleton at the feast, wet blanket.

spoken *adj* declared, explicit, expressed, oral, phonetic, said, stated, told, unwritten, uttered, verbal, viva voce, voiced.
antonyms tacit, unspoken, written.

sponge *v* cadge, freeload, mooch, scrounge.

sponger *n* bloodsucker, cadger, deadbeat, freeloader, hanger-on, leech, moocher, parasite, scrounger.

spongy *adj* absorbent, bibulous, cushioned, cushiony, elastic, light, porous, springy.

sponsor *n* angel, backer, financer, godparent, guarantor, patron, promoter, supporter, surety, underwriter.
v back, finance, fund, guarantee, patronize, promote, subsidize, support, underwrite.

spontaneous *adj* extempore, free, impromptu, impulsive, instinctive, natural, unbidden, uncompelled, unconstrained, unforced, unhesitating, unlaboured, unpremeditated, unprompted, unstudied, untaught, voluntary, willing.
antonyms forced, planned, studied.

spontaneously *adv* extempore, freely, impromptu, impulsively, instinctively, off the cuff, of one's own accord, on impulse, on the spur of the moment, unprompted, voluntarily, willingly.

spoof *n* bluff, burlesque, caricature, con, deception, fake, game, hoax, joke, lampoon, mockery, parody, prank, satire, sendup, takeoff, travesty, trick.

spooky *adj* chilling, creepy, eerie, eldritch, frightening, ghostly, hair-raising, mysterious, scary, sinister, spine-chilling, supernatural, uncanny, unearthly, weird.

spoon-feed *v* baby, cosset, feather-bed, indulge, mollycoddle, pamper, spoil.

sporadic *adj* erratic, infrequent, intermittent, irregular, isolated, occasional, random, scattered, spasmodic, uneven.
antonyms frequent, regular.

sport *n* activity, amusement, athletics, badinage, banter, brick, contest, dalliance, derision, diversion, entertainment, exercise, frolic, fun, game, good egg, jest, joking, kidding, laughingstock, merriment, mirth, mockery, pastime, play, plaything, raillery, recreation, ridicule, sportsman, teasing.
v amuse oneself, caper, dally, display, disport, exhibit, flirt, frolic, gambol, philander, play, romp, show off, toy, trifle, wear.

sporting *adj* considerate, decent, fair, fair-minded, generous, sportsmanlike.
antonyms unfair, unsporting.

sportive *adj* coltish, frisky, frolicsome, gamesome, gay, jaunty, joyous, kittenish, lively, merry, playful, prankish, rollicking, skittish, sprightly.

sporty *adj* athletic, casual, dashing, energetic, flamboyant, flashy, gay, hearty, informal, jaunty, jazzy, loud, natty, outdoor, raffish, rakish, showy, snazzy, stylish, trendy.

spot *n* bit, blemish, blot, blotch, daub, difficulty, discoloration, flaw, little, locality, location, macula, mark, mess, morsel, pimple, place, plight, point, position, predicament, pustule, quandary, scene, site, situation, smudge, speck, splash, stain, stigma, taint, trouble.
v besmirch, blot, descry, detect, dirty, discern, dot, espy, fleck, identify, maculate, mark, mottle, observe, recognize, see, sight, soil, spatter, speckle, splotch, stain, sully, taint, tarnish, variegate.

spotless *adj* blameless, chaste, clean, faultless, flawless, gleaming, immaculate, innocent, irreproachable, perfect, pure, shining, snowy, spick-and-span, unblemished, unimpeachable, unstained, unsullied, untarnished, virgin, virginal.
antonyms dirty, impure, spotted.

spotlight *v* accentuate, emphasize, feature, focus on, highlight, illuminate, point up, throw into relief.

n attention, emphasis, fame, interest, limelight, notoriety, public eye, publicity.

spotted *adj* brindled, dappled, dotted, flecked, guttate, macled, maculate, mottled, piebald, pied, polka-dot, specked, speckled, variegated. *antonym* spotless.

spotty *adj* blotchy, pimpled, pimply, speckled, spotted.

spouse *n* better half, companion, consort, helpmate, helpmeet, husband, mate, other half, partner, wife.

spout *v* declaim, discharge, emit, erupt, expatiate, gush, jet, orate, pontificate, ramble (on), rant, rhyme off, sermonize, shoot, speechify, spiel, spray, spurt, squirt, stream, surge.

n chute, fistula, fountain, gargoyle, geyser, jet, nozzle, outlet, rose, spray.

sprawl *v* flop, loll, lounge, ramble, recline, repose, slouch, slump, spread, straggle, stretch out, trail, tumble.

spray[1] *v* atomize, diffuse, douse, drench, moisten, scatter, shower, sprinkle, wet.

n aerosol, atomizer, drizzle, droplets, foam, froth, mist, moisture, rain, shower, spindrift, sprinkler, volley.

spray[2] *n* bough, branch, corsage, garland, shoot, sprig, wreath.

spread *v* advertise, arrange, array, blazon, bloat, broadcast, broaden, bruit, cast, circulate, couch, cover, diffuse, dilate, disseminate, distribute, divulge, effuse, expand, extend, fan out, furnish, increase, lay (out), metastasize, multiply, mushroom, open (out), overlay, pass, prepare, proclaim, proliferate, promulgate, propagate, publicize, publish, radiate, scatter, shed, sprawl, stretch, strew, swell, transmit, unfold, unfurl, unroll, widen.

antonyms close, compress, contain, fold.

n advance, advancement, array, banquet, blowout, compass, contagion, cover, development, diffusion, dispersion, dissemination, divulgence, expanse, expansion, extension, extent, feast, increase, period, proliferation, radius, ranch, range, reach, repast, span, stretch, suffusion, sweep, term, transmission.

spree *n* bacchanalia, bender, binge, bust, carouse, debauch, drinking bout, drunk, fling, jag, jamboree, junket, orgy, revel, splurge.

sprightly *adj* active, agile, airy, alert, alive, animated, blithe, brisk, cheerful, energetic, frolicsome, gamesome, gay, hearty, jaunty, joyous, lively, nimble, perky, playful, spirited, sportive, spry, vivacious.

antonym inactive.

spring[1] *v* bounce, bound, dance, hop, jump, leap, rebound, recoil, vault.

n bounce, bounciness, bound, buck, buoyancy, elasticity, flexibility, give, hop, jump, leap, rebound, recoil, resilience, springiness, vault.

spring[2] *n* beginning, cause, eye, fountainhead, origin, root, source, well, wellspring.

spring up appear, arise, burgeon, come, derive, descend, develop, emanate, emerge, grow, issue, mushroom, originate, pop up, proceed, shoot up, sprout, start, stem.

springy *adj* bouncy, buoyant, elastic, flexible, resilient, rubbery, spongy, stretchy.

antonyms rigid, stiff.

sprinkle *v* asperse, diversify, dot, dredge, dust, moisten, pepper, powder, scatter, seed, shower, spatter, spray, strew.

sprinkling *n* admixture, dash, dusting, few, handful, moistening, pinch, scatter, scattering, smattering, sprinkle, touch, trace.

sprint *v* belt, dart, dash, gallop, hare, hotfoot, race, run, scamper, shoot, speed, tear, whiz.

sprite *n* apparition, brownie, dryad, elf, fairy, goblin, imp, kelpie, leprechaun, naiad, nymph, pixie, puck, spirit, sylph.

sprout *v* bud, develop, germinate, grow, pullulate, push, shoot, spring, vegetate.

spruce *adj* chic, dainty, dapper, elegant, natty, neat, sleek, slick, smart, trim, well-groomed, well-turned-out.

antonyms dishevelled, untidy.

spruce up dress up, groom, gussy up, neaten, preen, primp, smarten up, spiff up, tidy, titivate.

spry *adj* active, agile, alert, brisk, energetic, lively, nimble, nippy, peppy, quick, ready, sprightly, supple.

antonyms doddering, inactive, lethargic.

spunk *n* backbone, chutzpah, courage, gameness, grit, guts, heart, mettle, nerve, pluck, resolution, spark, spirit, toughness, what it takes.

antonyms spinelessness, wimpiness.

spur *v* animate, drive, goad, impel, incite, poke, press, prick, prod, prompt, propel, stimulate, urge.

antonym curb.

n fillip, goad, impetus, impulse, incentive, incitement, inducement, motive, prick, rowel, stimulus.

antonym curb.

on the spur of the moment capriciously, impetuously, impromptu, impulsively, on impulse, on the spot, thoughtlessly, unpremeditatedly, unthinkingly.

spurious *adj* adulterate, apocryphal, artificial, assumed, bastard, bogus, contrived, counterfeit, deceitful, fake, false, feigned, forged, illegitimate, imitation, mock, phony, pretend, pretended, pseudo, sham, simulated, specious, suppositious, unauthentic.

antonyms authentic, genuine, real.

spurn *v* cold-shoulder, contemn, cut, despise, disdain, disregard, eschew, rebuff, refuse, reject, repulse, resist, scorn, slight, snub, stoop to, turn away from, turn down.

antonym embrace.

spurt v burst, effuse, erupt, gush, jet, shoot, spew, squirt, surge.

n access, burst, effusion, fit, rush, spate, surge.

spy n double agent, fifth columnist, foreign agent, mole, scout, secret agent, snoop, spook, undercover agent.

v descry, detect, discover, espy, glimpse, notice, observe, see, spot.

squabble v argue, bicker, brawl, clash, dispute, fall out, fight, quarrel, row, scrap, spat, tiff, wrangle.

n argument, clash, disagreement, dispute, falling-out, fight, quarrel, rhubarb, row, scrap, set-to, spat, tiff, wrangle.

squad n band, brigade, company, crew, force, gang, group, outfit, team, troop, unit.

squalid adj broken-down, decayed, dingy, dirty, disgusting, fetid, filthy, foul, low, nasty, neglected, poverty-stricken, repulsive, run-down, seedy, sleazy, slovenly, sordid, uncared-for, unclean, unkempt, wretched.

antonyms clean, pleasant.

squall n blast, blow, gale, gust, hurricane, storm, tempest, williwaw, windstorm.

squally adj blowy, blustery, foul, gusty, rough, stormy, tempestuous, turbulent, wild, windy.

squalor n decay, dinginess, filth, foulness, meanness, seediness, sleaziness, squalidness, wretchedness.

squander v blow, consume, dissipate, expend, fritter away, lavish, misspend, misuse, scatter, spend, splurge, throw away, waste.

square v accommodate, accord, adapt, adjust, agree, align, appease, balance, bribe, conciliate, conform, correspond, corrupt, discharge, equalize, fit, fix, harmonize, level, match, pay in full, reconcile, regulate, rig, satisfy, settle (with), suborn, suit, tailor, tally, win over.

adj aboveboard, bourgeois, broad, complete, conformist, conservative, conventional, decent, equitable, ethical, even, exact, fair, fair and square, fitting, full, genuine, honest, just, level, old-fashioned, on the level, orthodox, quadrate, right-angled, satisfying, solid, straight, straightforward, strait-laced, stuffy, suitable, thickset, traditional, true, unequivocal, unhip, upright.

n antediluvian, conformer, conformist, conservative, conventionalist, die-hard, fuddy-duddy, (old) fogey, stick-in-the-mud, traditionalist.

squash v annihilate, compress, crowd, crush, distort, flatten, humiliate, mash, nip in the bud, pound, press, pulp, pulverize, put an end (or a stop) to, quash, quell, silence, smash, snub, squelch, stamp out, stifle, suppress, trample.

antonyms encourage, expand, nurture.

squashy adj mushy, pappy, pulpy, soft, spongy, squelchy, squishy, yielding.

antonym firm.

squat adj chunky, corpulent, dumpy, short, squabby, stocky, stubby, stumpy, thickset.

antonyms lanky, slender.

v bend, camp out, crouch, hunch, hunker, settle, stoop.

squawk v cackle, complain, cry, cry foul, grouse, hoot, protest, screech, shriek, squeal, yelp.

squeak v chirp, peep, pipe, shrill, squeal, whine, yelp.

squeal n scream, screech, shriek, ululation, wail, yell, yelp, yowl.

v betray, blab, complain, inform on, peach (on), protest, rat (on), scream, screech, shout, shriek, shrill, snitch, squawk, ululate, wail, yelp.

squeamish adj coy, delicate, fastidious, finicky, nauseous, particular, prissy, prudish, punctilious, qualmish, queasy, queer, reluctant, scrupulous, sick, sickish, stickling, strait-laced.

squeeze v bleed, clasp, clutch, compress, cram, crowd, crush, cuddle, embrace, enfold, extort, force, grip, hug, jam, jostle, lean on, milk, nip, oppress, pack, pinch, press, pressure, put the pressure on, ram, scrounge, squash, squish, strain, stuff, thrust, wedge, wrest, wring.

n clasp, congestion, crowd, crush, embrace, grasp, handclasp, hold, hug, jam, pinch, predicament, press, pressure, restriction, squash.

squire v accompany, attend, conduct, escort, usher.

squirm v agonize, fidget, flounder, move, shift, squiggle, twist, wiggle, wriggle, writhe.

squirt v discharge, ejaculate, eject, emit, expel, jet, shoot, spew, spout, spritz, spurt.

n jet, spray, spurt.

stab v bayonet, cut, dirk, gore, injure, jab, knife, pierce, pink, puncture, spear, stick, thrust, transfix, wound.

n ache, attempt, endeavour, essay, gash, incision, jab, pain, pang, pink, prick, puncture, rent, thrust, try, twinge, venture, wound.

stab in the back betray, deceive, double-cross, inform on, let down, sell out, slander.

stabbing adj acute, painful, piercing, sharp, shooting, stinging.

stability n constancy, continuity, durability, firmness, fixity, permanence, reliability, security, solidity, soundness, steadfastness, steadiness, strength, sturdiness.

antonyms insecurity, instability, unsteadiness, weakness.

stable adj abiding, constant, continuing, deep-rooted, durable, enduring, established, fast, firm, fixed, immutable, invariable, lasting, permanent, reliable, secure, self-balanced, sound, static, steadfast, steady, strong, sturdy, sure, unalterable, unchangeable, unwavering, well-balanced, well-founded, well-grounded.

antonyms shaky, unstable, weak, wobbly.

stack n accumulation, cock, heap, hoard, load, mass, mound, mountain, pile, rick, stockpile.

v accumulate, amass, assemble, gather, load, pile, save, stockpile, store.

staff[1] *n* crew, employees, officers, organization, personnel, team, workers, workforce.

staff[2] *n* caduceus, cane, crook, crosier, pole, prod, rod, stave, (walking) stick, wand.

stage[1] *n* division, juncture, lap, leg, length, level, period, phase, point, step, storey, subdivision, tier.

stage[2] *n* arena, background, floor, (live) theatre, platform, set, setting.
v arrange, do, engineer, give, mount, orchestrate, organize, perform, present, produce, put on, stage-manage.

stagger *v* alternate, amaze, astonish, astound, confound, dumfound, falter, flabbergast, flounder, fluctuate, hesitate, lurch, nonplus, overlap, overwhelm, reel, shake, shock, stun, stupefy, surprise, sway, teeter, totter, vacillate, waver, wobble, zigzag.

stagnant *adj* becalmed, brackish, inert, lethargic, motionless, sluggish, stale, standing, still, torpid.

stagnate *v* decay, decline, degenerate, deteriorate, fester, idle, languish, rot, rust, vegetate.

staid *adj* calm, composed, decorous, demure, grave, quiet, sedate, self-restrained, serious, sober, solemn, steady, Victorian.
antonyms debonair, frivolous, jaunty, sportive.

stain *v* besmirch, blemish, blot, colour, contaminate, corrupt, defile, deprave, dirty, discolour, disgrace, dye, imbue, mark, smudge, soil, splotch, spot, stigmatize, sully, taint, tarnish, tinge.
n blemish, blot, discoloration, disgrace, dishonour, dye, infamy, reproach, shame, slur, smirch, smudge, soil, splotch, spot, stigma, tint.

stake[1] *n* pale, paling, picket, pile, pole, post, spike, standard, stave, stick.
v brace, fasten, pierce, prop, secure, support, tether, tie, tie up.
stake out define, delimit, demarcate, keep an eye on, mark out, outline, reconnoitre, reserve, stake off, survey, watch.

stake[2] *n* ante, bet, chance, claim, concern, hazard, interest, investment, involvement, jackpot, peril, pledge, prize, risk, share, venture, wager.
v ante, bet, chance, gamble, hazard, imperil, jeopardize, pledge, risk, venture, wager.

stale *adj* antiquated, banal, clichéd, cliché-ridden, common, commonplace, decayed, drab, dry, effete, faded, fetid, flat, fusty, hackneyed, hard, insipid, musty, old, overused, platitudinous, repetitious, sour, stagnant, stereotyped, tainted, tasteless, trite, unoriginal, vapid, worn-out, yesterday's news.
antonym fresh.

stalemate *n* deadlock, draw, halt, impasse, standstill, stop, tie.
antonym progress.

stalk[1] *v* approach, follow, haunt, hunt, march, pace, pursue, shadow, stride, strut, tail, track.

stalk[2] *n* bole, branch, shaft, shoot, spire, stem, trunk.

stall[1] *n* bay, bench, berth, booth, box, compartment, concession, cowshed, cubicle, pew, seat, stable, table.

stall[2] *v* delay, drag one's feet, equivocate, hedge, hem and haw, obstruct, Penelopize, play for time, prevaricate, stonewall, temporize.
antonym advance.

stalwart *adj* athletic, beefy, brawny, courageous, daring, dependable, determined, hefty, husky, indomitable, intrepid, lusty, muscular, redoubtable, resolute, robust, rugged, sinewy, staunch, steadfast, stout, strapping, strong, sturdy, valiant, vigorous.
antonyms timid, weak.

stamina *n* endurance, energy, fibre, force, fortitude, grit, indefatigability, lustiness, perseverence, pluck, power, resilience, resistence, staying power, stick-to-itiveness, strength, toughness, vigour.
antonym weakness.

stammer *v* falter, gibber, hesitate, splutter, stumble, stutter.

stamp *v* brand, categorize, characterize, engrave, etch, fix, identify, impress, imprint, incuse, inscribe, label, mark, mint, mould, pound, print, pronounce, reveal, stomp, strike, trample.
n attestation, authorization, brand, breed, cast, character, cut, description, die, earmark, evidence, fashion, form, hallmark, impression, imprint, kind, mark, mould, postage, seal, sign, signature, sort, type.
stamp out annihilate, crush, destroy, eliminate, end, eradicate, extinguish, extirpate, kill, put an end to, quell, quench, suppress, wipe out.
antonym encourage.

stampede *n* charge, dash, debacle, flight, rout, rush, scattering, sprint.
v charge, dash, flee, fly, gallop, hightail it, hotfoot it, run, rush, scurry, shoot, sprint, tear.
antonyms walk, wander.

stance *n* angle, attitude, bearing, carriage, deportment, point of view, position, posture, stand, standpoint, station, viewpoint.

stand *v* abide, allow, bear, belong, brook, continue, countenance, endure, exist, experience, face, hack, halt, handle, hold, last out, mount, obtain, pause, place, position, prevail, put, rank, remain, rest, rise, set, stay, stick (it) out, stomach, stop, suffer, support, sustain, take, take a position, tolerate, undergo, wear, weather, withstand.
antonym advance.
n attitude, base, booth, bracket, cradle, dais, determination, erection, frame, grandstand, halt, holder, loss, opinion, place, platform, position, rack, rank, rest, stage, staging, stall, stance, standpoint, standstill, stay, stop, stopover, stoppage, support, table, view, witness box.
stand by adhere to, back, befriend,

champion, defend, hold to, reiterate, repeat, speak for, stick up for, support, uphold.

antonym   let down.

stand down   abandon, abdicate, cede, give away, give up, quit, resign, step down, withdraw.

antonyms   ascend, join.

stand for   allow, bear, betoken, brook, champion, countenance, denote, embody, endure, epitomize, exemplify, indicate, mean, permit, personify, represent, signify, suffer, symbolize, tolerate, typify.

stand in for   cover for, deputize for, hold the fort for, replace, spell (off), substitute for, understudy.

stand out   catch the eye, jut out, large, loom, obtrude, project, stare one in the face, stick out, stick out a mile, stick out like a sore thumb.

stand up   cohere, hold up, hold water, stand, wash.

stand up for   champion, defend, fight for, side with, speak (up) for, stand the test, stick up for, support, uphold.

antonym   attack.

stand up to   beard, brave, confront, defy, endure, face, face up to, front, meet head-on, oppose, resist, withstand.

antonym   give in to.

standard¹   *n*   average, benchmark, canon, criterion, example, exemplar, gauge, grade, guide, guideline, level, measure, model, norm, pattern, principle, requirement, rule, sample, specification, touchstone, type, yardstick.

adj   accepted, approved, authoritative, average, basic, classic, customary, definitive, established, mainstream, normal, official, orthodox, popular, prevailing, recognized, regular, set, staple, stock, typical, usual.

antonyms   abnormal, irregular, unusual.

standard²   *n*   banner, colours, ensign, flag, gonfalon, labarum, pennant, pennon, rallying-point, streamer, vexillum.

standardize   *v*   assimilate, equalize, institutionalize, normalize, regiment, stereotype.

antonym   differentiate.

standards   *n*   ethics, ideals, morals, norms, principles.

standing   *n*   condition, continuance, credit, duration, eminence, estimation, existence, experience, footing, position, prestige, rank, reputation, repute, seniority, station, state, status.

adj   erect, fixed, lasting, long-term, on one's feet, permanent, perpendicular, perpetual, rampant, regular, repeated, upended, upright, vertical.

antonyms   horizontal, lying.

stand-offish   *adj*   aloof, cold, distant, haughty, remote, reserved, unapproachable, uncommunicative, unsociable, untalkative.

antonym   friendly.

standpoint   *n*   angle, point of view, position, post, stance, station, vantage point, viewpoint, Weltanschauung.

standstill   *n*   arrest, blockage, cessation, deadlock, halt, impasse, logjam, lull, moratorium, pause, reprieve, respite, rest, stalemate, stay, stop, stoppage, termination.

antonym   progress.

staple   *adj*   basic, chief, essential, fundamental, key, leading, main, major, predominant, primary, principle.

antonym   minor.

star¹   *n*   asterisk, asteroid, comet, étoile, meteor, meteorite, nova, planet, pulsar, quasar, red dwarf, red giant, satellite, shooting star, starlet, sun, supernova, white dwarf.

star²   *n*   celebrity, draw, idol, lead, leading lady, leading man, luminary, main attraction, name, starlet.

adj   brilliant, celebrated, chief, illustrious, leading, major, number-one, paramount, pre-eminent, principal, prominent, talented, top, well-known.

antonym   minor.

starchy   *adj*   ceremonious, conventional, formal, prim, punctilious, rigid, stiff, strait-laced, stuffy.

antonym   informal.

stare   *v*   gape, gawk, gawp, gaze, glare, goggle, look, ogle.

n   evil eye, gaze, glare, glower, leer, look, ogle, scowl.

stark   *adj*   absolute, arrant, austere, bald, bare, barren, bleak, blunt, cold, complete, consummate, depressing, desolate, downright, drear, dreary, entire, flagrant, forsaken, grim, harsh, out-and-out, palpable, patent, plain, pure, severe, sheer, simple, solitary, stern, stiff, strong, total, unadorned, unalloyed, unmitigated, unyielding, utter.

antonyms   mild, slight.

adv   absolutely, altogether, clean, completely, entirely, quite, stoutly, totally, utterly, wholly.

antonyms   mildly, slightly.

stark naked   *adj*   in one's birthday suit, in the altogether, in the buff, in the nude, in the raw, naked, nude, stark, stripped, unclad, unclothed, undressed.

antonym   clothed.

start¹   *v*   activate, arise, begin, break away, commence, create, engender, establish, father, found, galvanize, ignite, inaugurate, initiate, instigate, institute, introduce, issue, kick off, launch, light, open, originate, pioneer, rouse, sally forth, set off, set out, set up, shoot, switch on.

antonyms   finish, stop.

n   advantage, backing, beginning, birth, break, chance, commencement, convulsion, dawn, edge, foundation, inauguration, inception, initiation, introduction, kickoff, lead, onset, opening, opportunity, outset, point of departure, sponsorship, spurt, starting gate, starting point, takeoff point.

antonyms   finish, stop.

start² *v* blench, dart, flinch, jerk, jump, recoil, shy, spring forward, twitch.

n fright, jar, jerk, jolt, jump, spasm, twitch.

startle *v* agitate, alarm, amaze, astonish, astound, electrify, flush, frighten, jump, scare, shock, spook, start, surprise.

antonym calm.

startling *adj* alarming, astonishing, astounding, dramatic, electric, electrifying, extraordinary, shocking, staggering, sudden, surprising, unexpected, unforeseen.

antonyms boring, calming, ordinary.

starvation *n* famine, famishment, hunger, inanition, malnutrition, underfeeding, undernourishment, want.

antonym plenty.

starve *v* deprive, die of starvation, diet, fast, hunger, perish.

antonyms gorge, provide for.

starving *adj* famished, hungering, hungry, in need, ravenous, starved, underfed, undernourished.

antonym fed.

stash *v* cache, closet, conceal, hide, hoard, lay up, salt away, save up, secrete, stockpile, store, stow.

antonyms bring out, uncover.

state¹ *v* affirm, articulate, assert, asseverate, aver, declare, enumerate, explain, expound, express, formalize, formulate, formulize, make explicit, present, profess, propound, put, report, say, specify, voice.

n attitude, bother, category, circumstances, condition, flap, humour, mode, mood, panic, pass, phase, plight, position, pother, predicament, rank, shape, situation, spirits, stage, status, style, tizzy.

antonym calmness.

in a state agitated, anxious, distressed, disturbed, excited, flustered, hassled, heated, in a stew, in a tizzy, panic-stricken, ruffled, steamed, troubled, upset, worked up, worried.

state of affairs case, circumstances, condition, crisis, juncture, kettle of fish, lie of the land, mess, plight, position, predicament, situation.

state² *n* body politic, ceremony, commonwealth, country, dignity, federation, glory, government, grandeur, kingdom, land, leviathan, majesty, nation, pomp, republic, splendour, style, territory.

adj ceremonial, ceremonious, formal, governmental, magnificence, magnificent, national, official, pompous, public, solemn.

stately *adj* august, ceremonious, deliberate, dignified, elegant, grand, grandiose, imperial, imposing, impressive, Junoesque, kingly, lofty, majestic, measured, noble, pompous, princely, queenly, regal, royal, solemn.

antonyms informal, unimpressive.

statement *n* account, affadavit, affirmation, announcement, articulation, assertion, asseveration, bill, bulletin, communication, communiqué, declaration, deposition, explanation, formulation, ipse dixit, manifesto,

proclamation, profession, recital, relation, remark, report, testimony, utterance.

static *adj* at rest, changeless, constant, fixed, immobile, inert, motionless, resting, stable, stagnant, stationary, still, unmoving, unvarying.

antonyms active, dynamic, moving.

station *n* appointment, base, business, calling, centre, depot, employment, grade, habitat, headquarters, location, occupation, office, place, position, post, rank, seat, situation, sphere, stance, standing, standing place, status, stopping place, terminal.

v appoint, assign, establish, fix, garrison, install, locate, mount, place, post, send, set.

stationary *adj* fixed, immobile, inert, moored, motionless, parked, permanent, resting, settled, standing, static, stock-still, unmoving.

antonym moving.

▲ *confusable word* stationery.

statue *n* acrolith, bronze, bust, carving, caryatid, effigy, figure, figurine, head, idol, inukshuk, statuette.

statuesque *adj* classic, dignified, imposing, majestic, regal, stately, tall.

antonyms dumpy, small.

stature *n* consequence, distinction, eminence, height, importance, prestige, prominence, rank, size, standing, weight.

antonym unimportance.

status *n* character, condition, consequence, degree, distinction, eminence, face, grade, importance, position, prestige, rank, standing, state, station, weight.

antonym lowliness.

statute *n* act, bill, decree, edict, enactment, fiat, law, legislation, ordinance, regulation, rescript, rule, ruling, ukase.

staunch¹ *adj* constant, dependable, faithful, firm, hearty, loyal, reliable, resolute, sound, stalwart, steadfast, stout, strong, sure, true, true-blue, trustworthy, trusty, watertight, yeomanly, zealous.

antonyms unreliable, wavering, weak.

staunch² *v* arrest, block, check, dam, halt, plug, stay, stem, stop.

antonyms increase, promote.

stave off avert, delay, evade, fend off, foil, hold off, keep at bay, keep back, parry, ward off.

antonyms cause, encourage.

stay¹ *v* abide, adjourn, allay, arrest, check, continue, curb, defer, delay, detain, discontinue, dwell, endure, halt, hinder, hold, hold out, hover, impede, last, linger, live, lodge, loiter, obstruct, pause, postpone, prevent, prorogue, remain, reside, restrain, settle, sojourn, stand, stem, stop, stop over, suspend, tarry, visit, wait.

antonyms advance, leave.

n continuance, deferment, delay, halt, holiday, pause, postponement, remission, reprieve, sojourn, stop, stopover, stopping, suspension, visit.

stay² *n* brace, buttress, mainstay, prop, reinforcement, shoring, stanchion, support.

v buttress, hold up, prop, prop up, shore up, support, sustain.

steadfast *adj* constant, dedicated, dependable, enduring, established, faithful, fast, firm, fixed, intent, loyal, persevering, reliable, resolute, single-minded, stable, stalwart, staunch, steady, unfaltering, unflinching, unswerving, unwavering.

antonyms unreliable, wavering, weak.

steady *adj* balanced, calm, ceaseless, confirmed, consistent, constant, continuous, dependable, equable, equanimous, even, even-keeled, faithful, firm, fixed, habitual, immovable, imperturbable, incessant, industrious, level-headed, non-stop, perpetual, persistent, regular, reliable, rhythmic, safe, sedate, sensible, serene, serious-minded, settled, sober, stable, staid, steadfast, substantial, unbroken, unchangeable, unexcitable, unfaltering, unfluctuating, unhurried, uniform, uninterrupted, unremitting, unswerving, unvarying, unwavering.

antonyms unsteady, wavering.

v balance, brace, firm, fix, secure, stabilize, support.

steal *v* appropriate, bag, boost, cop, creep, embezzle, filch, heist, lift, make off with, misappropriate, nab, palm, peculate, pilfer, pinch, pirate, plagiarize, poach, purloin, relieve someone of, rip off, rustle, scoff, shoplift, slink, slip, snaffle, snatch, sneak, snitch, swipe, take, thieve, tiptoe.

antonym return.

stealing *n* embezzlement, larceny, misappropriation, peculation, pilferage, pilfering, plagiarism, rip-off, robbery, shoplifting, theft, thievery, thieving.

stealth *n* covertness, cunning, furtiveness, secrecy, slyness, sneakiness, stealthiness, surreptitiousness, unobtrusiveness.

antonym openness.

stealthy *adj* catlike, clandestine, covert, cunning, furtive, quiet, secret, secretive, skulking, sly, sneaking, sneaky, surreptitious, underhand.

antonym open.

steam *n* condensation, dampness, haze, mist, moisture, vapour.

steamy *adj* close, damp, erotic, gaseous, hazy, hot, humid, misty, muggy, salacious, sexy, steaming, stewy, sticky, sultry, sweaty, sweltering, vaporous, vapourish.

steed *n* charger, hack, horse, jade, mount, nag, Rosinante.

steel *v* brace, fortify, harden, nerve, strengthen, toughen.

antonym weaken.

steep¹ *adj* abrupt, bluff, excessive, exorbitant, extortionate, extreme, headlong, high, overpriced, precipitous, sheer, stiff, uncalled-for, unreasonable.

antonyms gentle, moderate.

steep² *v* bathe, brew, drench, fill, imbrue, imbue, immerse, infuse, macerate, marinate, moisten, permeate, pervade, saturate, seethe, soak, souse, submerge, suffuse.

steer *v* con, conduct, control, direct, govern, guide, pilot.

steer clear of avoid, bypass, circumvent, dodge, escape, eschew, evade, give a wide berth, shun, skirt.

antonym seek.

stem¹ *n* ancestry, axis, branch, family, house, line, lineage, peduncle, race, shoot, stalk, stirps, stock, trunk.

stem from arise from, come from, derive from, develop from, emanate from, flow from, issue from, originate in, spring from.

antonym give rise to.

stem² *v* arrest, check, contain, curb, dam, oppose, resist, restrain, staunch, stay, stop, tamp.

antonyms encourage, increase.

stench *n* mephitis, odour, reek, stink, whiff.

step *n* act, action, advance, advancement, deed, degree, demarche, doorstep, expedient, footfall, footprint, footstep, gait, grade, level, little way, manoeuvre, means, measure, move, pace, phase, point, procedure, proceeding, process, progression, rank, remove, round, rung, stage, stair, stone's throw, stride, trace, track, tread, walk.

v move, pace, stamp, tread, walk.

step by step bit by bit, gradually, in stages, little by little, one step at a time, slowly.

step down abdicate, bow out, decrease, leave, lower, quit, reduce, resign, retire, stand down, withdraw.

antonyms ascend, increase, join.

step on someone's toes affront, annoy, bruise (feelings), discommode, disgruntle, hurt, inconvenience, infringe, injure, irk, offend, upset, vex.

antonym soothe.

step up accelerate, augment, boost, build up, escalate, increase, intensify, raise, speed up, up.

antonyms decrease, reduce.

stereotype *n* convention, formula, mould, pattern.

v categorize, conventionalize, pigeonhole, standardize, typecast.

antonym differentiate.

stereotyped *adj* banal, clichéd, cliché-ridden, conventional, corny, hackneyed, overused, platitudinous, stale, standard, standardized, stock, threadbare, tired, trite, unoriginal.

antonyms different, unconventional.

sterile *adj* abortive, acarpellous, antiseptic, aseptic, bare, barren, disinfected, dry, empty, fruitless, germ-free, ineffective, infecund, pointless, sanitary, sterilized, unfruitful, unimaginative, unproductive, unprofitable, unprolific.

antonyms fruitful, septic.

sterility *n* asepsis, barrenness, cleanness, fruitlessness, futility, impotence, ineffectiveness, inefficacy, infecundity, pointlessness, purity, unfruitfulness, uselessness. *antonyms* fertility, fruitfulness.

sterilize *v* clean, cleanse, disinfect, fumigate, purify, sanitize. *antonyms* contaminate, infect.

sterling *adj* authentic, excellent, first-class, genuine, great, pure, real, sound, standard, substantial, superlative, true, worthy. *antonyms* false, poor.

stern *adj* austere, authoritarian, bitter, cruel, flinty, forbidding, frowning, grim, hard, harsh, inflexible, relentless, rigid, rigorous, serious, severe, stark, steely, strict, unrelenting, unsmiling, unsparing, unyielding. *antonym* mild.

stew *v* agonize, boil, braise, cook, fret, fricassee, fuss, jug, perspire, seethe, simmer, sweat, swelter, worry. *n* agitation, bother, bouillabaisse, chowder, dither, fluster, fret, fuss, goulash, hash, lobscouse, mulligan, pot-au-feu, pother, predicament, ragout, scouse, tizzy, worry.

steward *n* chamberlain, factor, head servant, head waiter, husband, maître d'hôtel, major-domo, manager, marshal, trustee.

stick¹ *v* abide, adhere, affix, attach, bind, bond, catch, cement, cheat, cleave, cling, clog, cohere, con, defraud, dig, endure, fasten, fix, fleece, fuse, glue, gore, gouge, gyp, have, hold, insert, install, jab, jam, join, linger, lodge, paste, persist, pierce, pin, place, plant, plonk, poke, position, prod, puncture, put, put up with, remain, set, snag, spear, stab, stand, stay, sting, stomach, stuff, take, thrust, tolerate, transfix, weld. *antonym* unstick.

stick at balk at, demur at, draw the line at, hesitate at, recoil from, resist, scruple at, shrink from, stop at.

stick out¹ be noticeable, be obvious, bulge (out), extend, jut, obtrude, project, protrude, show, stand out, stare one in the face.

stick out² (or at) continue, endure, hang in, keep at, persevere in, persist, plug away at, stand, stay with. *antonym* give up.

stick to adhere to, cleave to, honour, keep to, persevere in, stand by. *antonyms* give up, quit.

stick up for back, be on the side of, champion, defend, speak (up) for, stand up for, support, take the part (or side) of, uphold. *antonym* attack.

stick² *n* bar, baton, birch, bludgeon, branch, cane, lug, piece, pole, quarterstaff, rod, sceptre, staff, stake, stave, switch, twig, wand, whip, withe.

stick-in-the-mud *adj* antediluvian, antiquated, conservative, die-hard, fogeyish, fossilized, old fogey, old-school, outmoded, reactionary, stodgy, unadventurous, Victorian. *antonyms* adventurous, modern. *n* conservative, die-hard, fogey, fossil,

fuddy-duddy, old fogey, reactionary, stuffed shirt, wet blanket, Victorian.

stickler *n* fanatic, fusspot, maniac, martinet, nut, pedant, perfectionist, precisianist, purist.

sticky *adj* adhesive, awkward, clammy, clinging, clingy, close, delicate, difficult, discomforting, embarrassing, gluey, glutinous, gooey, gummy, hairy, humid, muggy, nasty, oppressive, painful, stifling, suffocating, sultry, sweaty, sweltering, syrupy, tacky, tenacious, thorny, tricky, unpleasant, viscid, viscous. *antonyms* cool, dry, easy.

stiff *adj* arduous, arthritic, artificial, austere, awkward, brisk, brittle, buckram, ceremonious, chilly, clumsy, cold, constrained, creaky, cruel, difficult, drastic, exacting, excessive, exorbitant, expensive, extreme, fatiguing, firm, forced, formal, formidable, graceless, hard, hardened, harsh, heavy, high, inelastic, inelegant, inexorable, inflexible, jerky, laborious, laboured, mannered, oppressive, out of practice, pertinaceous, pitiless, pokerish, pompous, powerful, priggish, prim, punctilious, resistant, rheumaticky, rigid, rigorous, rusty, severe, solid, solidified, stand-offish, starchy, stark, stilted, strict, stringent, strong, stubborn, taut, tense, tight, toilsome, tough, trying, unbending, uneasy, ungainly, ungraceful, unnatural, unrelaxed, unsupple, unyielding, uphill, vigorous, wooden. *antonyms* easy, flexible, graceful, informal, limber, mild.

stiffen *v* ankylose, brace, coagulate, congeal, crystallize, freeze, harden, jell, reinforce, rigidify, set, solidify, starch, strengthen, tense, thicken, toughen.

stiff-necked *adj* arrogant, bull-headed, contumacious, haughty, obstinate, opinionated, pig-headed, proud, self-willed, stubborn, uncompromising, willful. *antonyms* flexible, humble.

stifle *v* asphyxiate, check, choke, control, curb, dampen, extinguish, hold back, hush, muffle, prevent, repress, restrain, silence, smother, stop, strangle, suffocate, suppress, swallow. *antonym* encourage.

stigma *n* blemish, blot, brand, disgrace, dishonour, imputation, mark, reproach, shame, slur, smirch, spot, stain. *antonym* credit.

stigmatize *v* brand, cast aspersions on, condemn, defame, defile, denounce, discredit, label, mark, pillory, vilify, vilipend. *antonym* praise.

still *adj* calm, hushed, inert, lifeless, motionless, noiseless, pacific, peaceful, placid, quiet, restful, serene, silent, smooth, soundless, stagnant, stationary, stilly, subdued, tranquil, undisturbed, unmoving, unruffled, unstirring. *antonyms* agitated, busy, disturbed, noisy. *v* allay, alleviate, appease, calm, hush, lull, pacify, put (or lay) to rest, quiet, quieten, restrain, settle, silence, smooth, soothe, subdue, tranquillize. *antonyms* agitate, stir up.

adv but, even so, even then, however, nevertheless, nonetheless, notwithstanding, yet.

stillness *n* hush, peace, peacefulness, quiet, quietness, silence, soundlessness, still, tranquillity.

antonyms agitation, disturbance, noise.

stilted *adj* affected, artificial, awkward, bombastic, constrained, forced, formal, grandiloquent, high-flown, high-sounding, inflated, laboured, mannered, pedantic, pompous, pretentious, stiff, unnatural, wooden.

antonyms flowing, fluent.

stimulant *n* analeptic, bracer, energizer, excitant, fillip, hype, incitant, pep pill, pick-me-up, restorative, reviver, shot in the arm, tonic, upper.

antonym depressant.

stimulate *v* animate, arouse, dynamize, encourage, energize, excite, fan, fire, foment, get psyched up, goad, hype (up), impel, incite, inflame, instigate, jog, motivate, prompt, provoke, psych (oneself) up, quicken, rouse, spur, titillate, urge, whet.

antonym discourage.

stimulating *adj* energizing, excitant, exciting, exhilarating, galvanic, inspiring, intriguing, provocative, provoking, rousing, stirring, thought-provoking.

antonyms boring, depressing, uninspiring.

stimulus *n* carrot, encouragement, fillip, ginger, goad, incentive, incitement, inducement, prick, provocation, shot in the arm, spur.

antonyms deterrent, discouragement.

sting *v* anger, burn, cheat, con, cut, defraud, do, fleece, gall, goad, hurt, incense, inflame, infuriate, nettle, overcharge, pain, pique, provoke, rile, rip off, smart, stiff, swindle, tingle, wound.

antonym soothe.

n agony, anguish, bite, bitterness, distress, goad, incentive, incitement, nip, prick, pungency, smarting, spur, stimulus, tingle, torment, torture, woe.

stinging *adj* aculeate, biting, burning, caustic, nippy, painful, prickly, smarting, tingling.

antonyms mild, soothing.

stingy *adj* avaricious, chary, cheeseparing, close-fisted, illiberal, inadequate, insufficient, meagre, mean, measly, miserly, near, niggardly, parsimonious, penny-pinching, penurious, save-all, scanty, scrimping, selfish, small, sparing, tight-fisted, ungenerous, ungiving.

antonym generous.

stink *v* reek, smell, smell bad, smell to high heaven.

n brouhaha, commotion, disturbance, fetidness, foulness, fuss, hubbub, malodour, mephitis, odour, row, rumpus, scandal, stench, stir, to-do, uproar, upset, whiff.

stinker *n* affliction, beast, bummer, cad, creep, cur, dastard, difficulty, fink, heel, poser, problem, rat, rotter, scab, scoundrel, shocker, skunk, swine.

stinking *adj* contemptible, disgusting, fetid, foul, foul-smelling, grotty, ill-smelling, low, low-down, malodorous, mean, mephitic, noisome, offensive, reeking, rotten, smelly, unpleasant, vile, wretched.

antonyms good, pleasant.

stint *n* assignment, bit, period, quota, share, shift, spell, stretch, term, time, tour, trick, turn.

v economize, pinch, save, scrimp, skimp on.

stipulate *v* agree, contract, covenant, engage, guarantee, insist upon, lay down, pledge, postulate, promise, provide, require, settle, specify.

antonym imply.

stipulation *n* agreement, clause, condition, contract, engagement, precondition, prerequisite, provision, proviso, qualification, requirement, restriction, settlement, sine qua non, small print, specification, term.

antonym implication.

stir *v* affect, agitate, beat, bestir, be up and about, budge, bustle, disturb, electrify, excite, fire, flutter, fold, hasten, hum, inspire, look lively, mix, move, quiver, roil, rustle, shake, shake a leg, thrill, touch, tremble.

antonyms bore, calm, stay.

n activity, ado, agitation, bustle, commotion, disorder, disturbance, excitement, ferment, flurry, furor, fuss, hue and cry, hustle and bustle, movement, outcry, sensation, to-do, tumult, uproar.

antonym calm.

stir up agitate, animate, arouse, awaken, egg on, excite, incite, inflame, instigate, jog, kindle, mix, prompt, provoke, quicken, raise, rouse, spur, stimulate, urge.

antonyms calm, discourage.

stirring *adj* animating, dramatic, eloquent, emotive, exciting, exhilarating, heady, impassioned, inspiring, intoxicating, lively, moving, rousing, spirited, stimulating, thrilling.

antonyms calming, uninspiring.

stock *n* ancestry, array, assets, assortment, background, block, breed, broth, cache, capital, cattle, choice, commodities, descent, equipment, estimation, extraction, family, flocks, forebears, fund, funds, goods, herds, hoard, horses, house, inventory, investment, kindred, line, lineage, livestock, log, merchandise, parentage, pedigree, post, property, race, range, repertoire, repute, reserve, reservoir, resources, root, selection, sheep, source, stem, stockpile, store, strain, stump, supply, trunk, type, variety, wares.

adj banal, basic, bromidic, clichéd, commonplace, conventional, customary, formal, hackneyed, ordinary, overused, pat, platitudinous, regular, routine, run-of-the-mill, set, standard, staple, stereotyped, traditional, trite, usual, worn-out.

antonym original.

v deal in, handle, keep, sell, supply, trade in.

stock up (on) accumulate, amass, equip,

fill, furnish, gather, hoard, lay in, pile up, provision, replenish, save, stockpile, store (up), supply.

stocky *adj* chunky, dumpy, mesomorphic, short, solid, stubby, stumpy, sturdy, thickset.

antonyms skinny, tall.

stodgy *adj* boring, dull, formal, fuddy-duddy, heavy, laboured, leaden, old-fashioned, out-of-date, solemn, spiritless, staid, starchy, stuffy, tedious, turgid, unenterprising, unexciting, unimaginative, uninspired.

antonyms exciting, informal, light.

stoical *adj* calm, cool, dispassionate, impassive, imperturbable, indifferent, long-suffering, patient, philosophical, phlegmatic, resigned, stolid, uncomplaining, unexcitable.

antonyms anxious, depressed, furious, irascible.

stoicism *n* acceptance, ataraxia, calmness, dispassion, fatalism, forbearance, fortitude, impassivity, imperturbability, indifference, long-suffering, patience, resignation, stolidity, unexcitability.

antonyms anxiety, depression, fury.

stolid *adj* apathetic, beefy, blockish, bovine, doltish, dull, heavy, impassive, lumpish, obtuse, slow, stoical, stupid, unemotional, unexcitable, unimaginative, wooden.

antonyms interested, lively.

stomach *n* abdomen, appetite, belly, breadbasket, craw, desire, gizzard, gut, inclination, inside(s), maw, mind, paunch, pot, potbelly, relish, spare tire, taste, tummy.

v abide, bear, deal with, endure, hack, put up with, stand, submit to, suffer, swallow, take, tolerate.

stone *n* boulder, cobble, concretion, endocarp, flag, flagstone, gem, gemstone, gravestone, headstone, jewel, kernel, lapis, monument, pebble, pip, pit, rock, seed, slab, tombstone.

stonewall *v* block, gain time, hem and haw, hold out, hold up, obstruct, play for time, resist, stall, thwart, use delay tactics.

stony *adj* adamant, blank, callous, chilly, expressionless, frigid, hard, heartless, hostile, icy, indifferent, inexorable, lapilliform, lithic, lithoid, merciless, obdurate, pebbly, pitiless, rocky, rough, steely, stonelike, unfeeling, unforgiving, unresponsive.

antonyms forgiving, friendly, soft, soft-hearted.

stooge *n* butt, cat's paw, dupe, fall guy, foil, henchman, lackey, patsy, pawn, puppet.

stoop¹ *v* bend, bow (down or over), crouch, descend, duck, hunch, incline, kneel, lean, squat.

n droop, inclination, round-shoulderedness, sag, slouch, slump.

stoop² *v* condescend, deign, descend, go so far as, go so low as, lower oneself, resort, sink, vouchsafe.

stop *v* arrest, bar, block, break, cease, check, close, close down, come to an end, conclude, daunt, delay, desist, discontinue, end, finish,

forestall, frustrate, halt, hinder, impede, intercept, intermit, interrupt, knock off, leave off, lodge, obstruct, pack (it) in, pack up, parry, pause, plug, prevent, put an end to, quit, refrain, repress, rest, restrain, shut down, seal, silence, sojourn, stall, staunch, stay, stem, stymie, swear off, suspend, tarry, terminate, ward off.

antonyms advance, continue, start.

n bar, block, break, bung, cessation, check, conclusion, control, cork, depot, destination, discontinuation, end, finish, halt, hindrance, impasse, impediment, plug, rest, sojourn, stage, standstill, station, stay, stopover, stoppage, stopper, termination, terminus, visit.

antonyms continuation, start.

interj avast, cease, cease and desist, cool it, cut it out, desist, easy, enough already, give it a rest, give over, halt, hang on, hold it, hold on, hold your horses, just a minute, lay off, stop it, wait, wait a minute, whoa.

stopgap *n* expedient, improvisation, makeshift, resort, shift, substitute.

adj emergency, expediential, impromptu, improvised, makeshift, provisional, rough-and-ready, temporary.

antonyms finished, permanent.

stoppage *n* abeyance, arrest, blockage, check, close, closure, curtailment, cutoff, delay, desistance, discontinuance, halt, hindrance, interruption, layoff, obstruction, occlusion, shutdown, standstill, stasis, stopping, strike, walkout.

antonyms continuation, start.

store *v* accumulate, cupboard, deposit, garner, gather, hive, hoard, husband, keep, lay aside, lay by, lay up, put away, reserve, salt away, save, stash, stock, stockpile, stow (away), treasure.

antonym use.

n abundance, accumulation, bank, cache, cupboard, depository, emporium, fund, hoard, market, mart, mine, outlet, plenty, plethora, provision, quantity, repository, reserve, reservoir, shop, stock, stockpile, storage place, storehouse, storeroom, supermarket, supply, warehouse, wealth.

antonym scarcity.

storehouse *n* armoury, arsenal, barn, cellar, depository, depot, elevator, entrepôt, fund, garner, granary, hold, larder, pantry, repertory, repository, silo, storage place, treasury, vault, warehouse.

storey *n* deck, étage, flight, floor, level, stage, stratum, tier.

storm *n* agitation, anger, assault, attack, blast, blitz, blitzkrieg, blizzard, clamour, commotion, cyclone, disturbance, dust devil, furor, gale, gust, hubbub, hurricane, offensive, onset, onslaught, outbreak, outburst, outcry, paroxysm, passion, roar, row, rumpus, rush, squall, stir, strife, tempest, tornado, tumult, turmoil, violence, whirlwind.

antonym calm.

v assail, assault, beset, blow, bluster, charge, complain, flounce, fly, fume, rage, raid, rampage, rant, rave, rush, scold, stalk, stamp, stomp, thunder.

stormy *adj* blustering, blustery, boisterous, choppy, dirty, foul, gusty, inclement, raging, rough, squally, tempestuous, turbulent, violent, wild, windy.

antonym calm.

story *n* account, anecdote, article, chronicle, episode, fable, fabrication, fairy tale, falsehood, feature, fib, fiction, history, legend, lie, myth, narration, narrative, news, novel, plot, recital, record, relation, report, romance, rumour, scoop, spiel, tale, untruth, version, yarn.

storyteller *n* anecdotist, author, bard, chronicler, fabulist, fibber, liar, narrator, novelist, raconteur, raconteuse, romancer, telltale.

stout *adj* able-bodied, athletic, beefy, big, bold, brave, brawny, bulky, burly, chunky, corpulent, courageous, dauntless, determined, doughty, enduring, fat, fearless, fleshy, firm, gallant, hardy, heavy, hulking, husky, intrepid, lion-hearted, lusty, muscular, obese, overweight, plucky, plump, portly, resolute, robust, rotund, solid, stalwart, steadfast, stocky, stout-hearted, strapping, strong, sturdy, substantial, thick, tough, tubby, valiant, valorous, vigorous.

antonyms slim, timid, weak.

stove *n* cookstove, furnace, grill, heater, kiln, oven, range.

stow *v* bundle, cram, deposit, dump, jam, load, pack, put (away), secrete, sling, stash, store, stuff, tuck.

antonym unload.

straggle *v* amble, dilly-dally, drift, lag, loiter, ramble, range, roam, rove, scatter, spread (out), stray, string out, trail, wander.

straggly *adj* aimless, disorganized, drifting, irregular, loose, rambling, random, spreading, spread out, straggling, straying, strung out, untidy.

antonyms grouped, organized, tidy.

straight *adj* accurate, aligned, arranged, balanced, blunt, bourgeois, candid, consecutive, conservative, continuous, conventional, correct, decent, direct, downright, equitable, erect, even, fair, flat, forthright, frank, heterosexual, honest, honourable, horizontal, just, law-abiding, level, neat, non-stop, normal, orderly, ordinary, organized, orthodox, outright, outspoken, perpendicular, plain, plane, plumb, point-blank, pure, reliable, respectable, right, running, shipshape, smooth, solid, square, straightforward, successive, sustained, through, tidy, traditional, true, trustworthy, unadulterated, undeviating, undiluted, uninterrupted, unmixed, unqualified, unrelieved, unswerving, upright, vertical, virtuous.

antonyms bent, circuitous, dilute, dishonest, evasive, indirect, roundabout.

adv candidly, directly, flatly, flat out, frankly,

honestly, outspokenly, point-blank, squarely, unflinchingly, unswervingly, upright.

straightaway *adv* at once, directly, immediately, instantly, now, promptly, right away, right off, there and then, this minute.

antonym eventually.

straighten (out) *v* arrange, clear up, correct, disentangle, neaten, order, rectify, reform, regularize, resolve, settle, sort out, unsnarl, untwist, work out.

antonym muddle.

straightforward *adj* candid, clear-cut, direct, easy, elementary, forthright, frank, genuine, guileless, honest, intelligible, open, open-and-shut, routine, simple, sincere, truthful, uncomplicated, undemanding.

antonyms complicated, devious, evasive.

strain¹ *v* compress, distend, drive, embrace, endeavour, exert, express, extend, fatigue, filter, hug, injure, labour, make an effort, overdo, overextend, overstretch, overtax, overwork, percolate, pull, purify, refine, restrain, riddle, screen, seep, separate, sieve, sift, sprain, squeeze, stretch, strive, struggle, tax oneself, tear, tighten, tire, try, tug, twist, weaken, wrench, wrest.

n anxiety, burden, effort, endeavour, force, injury, overdoing, overexertion, overextension, pressure, pull, sprain, stress, struggle, tautness, tension, wrench.

strain² *n* ancestry, blood, class, descent, extraction, family, humour, kind, lineage, manner, pedigree, race, spirit, stem, stock, streak, style, suggestion, suspicion, temper, tendency, tone, trace, trait, vein, way.

strained *adj* artificial, awkward, constrained, difficult, embarrassed, false, forced, laboured, self-conscious, stiff, tense, uncomfortable, uneasy, unnatural, unrelaxed.

antonym natural.

strains *n* air, lay, measure, melody, music, song, theme, tune.

strait *n* channel, gut, narrows, sound.

straitened *adj* difficult, distressed, embarrassed, impoverished, limited, poor, reduced, restricted.

antonyms easy, well-off.

strait-laced *adj* moralistic, narrow, narrow-minded, old-maidish, prim, proper, prudish, puritanical, strict, stuffy, upright, Victorian.

antonyms broad-minded, easy-going.

straits *n* crisis, difficulty, dilemma, distress, embarrassment, emergency, extremity, hardship, hole, mess, need, perplexity, plight, poverty, predicament.

strand *n* fibre, fibril, filament, length, lock, rope, string, thread, tress, twist.

stranded *adj* abandoned, aground, ashore, beached, grounded, helpless, high and dry, homeless, in difficulty, in the lurch, marooned, penniless, shipwrecked, snowbound, stuck, wrecked.

strange *adj* abnormal, alien, astonishing, awkward, bewildered, bizarre, curious, disoriented, eccentric, eerie, exceptional, exotic, extraordinary, fantastic, foreign, freak(y), funny, ill at ease, irregular, lost, marvellous, mystifying, new, novel, odd, out of place, out-of-the-way, peculiar, perplexing, queer, rare, remarkable, remote, singular, sinister, unaccountable, unaccustomed, unacquainted, uncanny, uncomfortable, uncommon, unexplained, unexplored, unfamiliar, unheard of, unknown, unrelated, untried, unusual, weird, wonderful.

antonyms comfortable, common, familiar, ordinary.

stranger *n* alien, foreigner, guest, incomer, newcomer, non-member, outlander, outsider, unknown, visitor.

antonyms local, native.

strangle *v* asphyxiate, choke, constrict, gag, garrote, inhibit, jugulate, repress, smother, stifle, strangulate, suffocate, suppress, throttle.

strap *n* band, belt, leash, strip, thong, tie.

v beat, belt, bind, buckle, fasten, flog, lash, scourge, secure, tie, truss, whip.

strapping *adj* beefy, big, brawny, burly, hefty, hulking, husky, powerful, robust, stalwart, strong, sturdy, well-built, whopping.

antonym puny.

stratagem *n* artifice, device, dodge, feint, intrigue, manoeuvre, plan, plot, ploy, ruse, scheme, subterfuge, trick, wile.

strategic *adj* calculated, cardinal, critical, crucial, decisive, deliberate, diplomatic, important, key, planned, politic, vital.

antonym unimportant.

strategy *n* approach, design, manoeuvre(s), means, plan, planning, policy, procedure, program, scheme, tactic(s), way.

stratum *n* bed, bracket, caste, category, class, grade, group, layer, level, lode, rank, region, seam, station, stratification, table, tier, vein.

stray *v* backslide, deviate, digress, diverge, drift, err, get lost, go off the beaten path, leave the straight and narrow, meander, ramble, range, roam, rove, straggle, wander (off).

adj abandoned, accidental, chance, erratic, freak, homeless, lost, odd, random, roaming, scattered, vagrant, wandering.

streak *n* band, dash, daub, element, layer, line, slash, smear, strain, strip, stripe, stroke, touch, trace, vein.

v band, dart, daub, flash, fleck, fly, gallop, hurtle, slash, smear, speed, sprint, striate, stripe, sweep, tear, variegate, whistle, whiz, zoom.

streaked *adj* banded, barred, brindled, flecked, lined, streaky, striated, striped, variegated, veiny.

stream *n* beck, brook, burn, course, creek, current, drift, flow, freshet, gush, outpouring, procession, rill, river, rivulet, run, runnel, rush, surge, tide, torrent, tributary.

v cascade, course, emerge, emit, float, flood, flow, glide, gush, issue, pour, rain, run, shed, spill, spout, surge, well out.

streamer *n* banner, ensign, flag, gonfalon, pennant, pennon, plume, ribbon, standard.

streamlined *adj* efficient, graceful, modernized, organized, simplified, sleek, slick, smooth, smooth-running, superior, tight, time-saving, up-to-the-minute, well-run.

antonyms clumsy, inefficient, old-fashioned.

strength *n* advantage, anchor, asset, backbone, brawn, cogency, concentration, courage, effectiveness, efficacy, endurance, energy, firmness, force, fortitude, health, intensity, lustiness, mainstay, might, muscle, potency, power, puissance, resolution, robustness, security, sinew, spirit, stamina, stoutness, sturdiness, toughness, vehemence, vigour.

antonyms timidity, weakness.

strengthen *v* add to, bolster, brace, buttress, confirm, consolidate, corroborate, edify, encourage, enhance, establish, firm up, fortify, harden, hearten, heighten, increase, intensify, invigorate, justify, nerve, nourish, reinforce, rejuvenate, restore, steel, stiffen, substantiate, support, tone, toughen.

antonym weaken.

strenuous *adj* active, arduous, bold, demanding, determined, eager, earnest, energetic, exacting, exhausting, hard, heated, herculean, laborious, persistent, resolute, spirited, strong, taxing, tireless, toilsome, tough, uphill, urgent, vehement, vigorous, zealous.

antonyms easy, effortless.

stress *n* accent, accentuation, anxiety, beat, burden, emphasis, force, hardship, hassle, importance, oppression, pressure, significance, strain, tautness, tension, trauma, urgency, weight, worry.

antonym relaxation.

v accent, accentuate, belabour, dwell on, emphasize, play up, punctuate, repeat, strain, underline, underscore.

antonym relax.

stretch *n* area, bit, challenge, distance, exaggeration, expanse, extensibility, extension, extent, period, reach, run, space, spell, spread, stint, strain, sweep, term, time, tract.

v bend, bloat, challenge, cover, distend, draw out, elongate, expand, extend, falsify, grow, inflate, lengthen, pull, rack, reach, spread, strain, swell, tighten, overstate, unfold, unroll.

antonyms relax, squeeze.

stretch one's legs exercise, go for a walk, move around, promenade, stroll, take a breather, take a walk, take the air.

stretch out draw out, hold out, lengthen, lie down, prolong, protract, put out, reach out, relax, stretch forth, string out.

antonyms draw back, shorten.

stretch the truth exaggerate, fib, hyperbolize, lay it on, lay it on (too) thick, overstate, talk big, tell fish stories, tell half-truths.

strew *v* bespread, besprinkle, bestrew, disperse, litter, scatter, spread, sprinkle, toss.

antonym gather (up).

stricken *adj* affected, afflicted, expunged, heartbroken, hit, injured, smitten, struck, wounded.

antonym unaffected.

strict *adj* absolute, accurate, austere, authoritarian, close, complete, conscientious, demanding, exact, exacting, faithful, fastidious, firm, harsh, meticulous, no-nonsense, orthodox, particular, perfect, precise, regimented, religious, restricted, rigid, rigorous, scrupulous, severe, stern, strait-laced, stringent, thoroughgoing, total, true, unsparing, utter, Victorian.

antonyms easy-going, flexible, mild.

stricture *n* animadversion, blame, censure, constriction, criticism, disapproval, flak, narrowing, rebuke, reproof, restriction.

antonyms applause, commendation, praise.

strident *adj* cacophonous, clamorous, clashing, discordant, dissonant, grating, harsh, jangling, jarring, loud, rasping, raucous, screeching, shrill, stridulant, unmusical, vociferous.

antonyms quiet, sweet.

strife *n* animosity, battle, bickering, combat, conflict, contention, contest, controversy, discord, dispute, dissension, disunity, enmity, feuding, friction, hostility, quarrel, rivalry, row, squabbling, struggle, warfare, wrangling.

antonym peace.

strike *n* attack, bop, buffet, discovery, hit, mutiny, protest, raid, refusal, stoppage, success, swipe, thump, walkout, wallop, work-to-rule.

v achieve, affect, afflict, arrange, assail, assault, assume, attack, attain, bang, beat, bop, box, buffet, chastise, clap, clobber, clout, collide with, come to, cuff, delete, devastate, discover, dismantle, douse, drive, effect, encounter, enter upon, find, go on strike, hammer, hit, impress, invade, knock, mutiny, occur to, overcome, penetrate, pierce, pound, print, punish, ratify, reach, register, remove, revolt, shoot, slap, smack, smite, sock, sound, stamp, stumble across, stumble upon, surrender, swat, swipe, take a swipe at, take down, thrust, thump, touch, turn up, uncover, unearth, walk out, wallop, whack, wham, work to rule, zap.

strike down afflict, assassinate, destroy, kill, murder, ruin, slay, smite.

strike out cancel, cross out, delete, efface, erase, excise, expunge, fail, fail to score, lash out, obliterate, remove, rub out, scratch (out), set out, start off, strike, strike through.

antonym add.

striking *adj* arresting, astonishing, conspicuous, dazzling, distingué, extraordinary, forcible, foudroyant, impressive, memorable, noticeable, outstanding, overwhelming, remarkable, salient, significant, stunning, vivid, wonderful.

antonym unimpressive.

string *n* bunch, chain, cord, fibre, file, line, number, procession, queue, row, sequence, series, strand, succession, train, twine.

v festoon, hang, link, loop, sling, stretch, suspend, thread, tie up.

string along bluff, deceive, dupe, flatter, fool, hoax, humbug, lead down the garden path, lead on, play fast and loose with, play (someone) false, put one over on, snow, string (someone) a line, take (someone) for a ride.

string along with accept, accompany, agree, assent, collaborate, co-operate, follow, go along.

antonym dissent.

string out disperse, draw out, extend, fan out, lengthen, prolong, protract, space out, spin out, spread out, straggle, stretch out, wander.

antonyms gather, shorten.

stringent *adj* binding, demanding, exacting, inflexible, rigid, rigorous, severe, strict, tight, tough.

antonyms flexible, lax, mild.

strings *n* catch, conditions, limitations, obligations, prerequisites, provisos, qualifications, requirements, restrictions, stipulations.

stringy *adj* chewy, fibrous, gristly, ropy, sinewy, tough, wiry.

antonym tender.

strip¹ *v* bare, bereave, clear, clear out, defoliate, denude, deprive, despoil, disfranchise, dismantle, disrobe, divest, doff, empty, excoriate, expose, gut, husk, lay bare, loot, milk, peel off, pillage, plunder, pull off, ransack, remove, rob, sack, skin, spoil, take away, tear off, unclothe, uncover, undress.

antonyms cover, provide.

strip² *n* band, belt, bit, fillet, lath, length, line, piece, ribbon, sash, screed, shred, slat, slip, spline, strake, strap, swath, swathe, tape, thong, tongue.

stripe *n* band, bar, belt, chevron, flash, fleck, streak, striation, vitta.

striped *adj* banded, barred, streaked, streaky, striated, stripy, vittate.

stripling *n* adolescent, boy, fledgling, hobbledehoy, juvenile, lad, sapling, shaver, teenager, youngling, youngster, youth.

strive *v* attempt, compete, contend, endeavour, fight, labour, push (oneself), strain, struggle, toil, try, work.

stroke *n* accomplishment, achievement, apoplexy, attack, beat, blow, clap, collapse, dot, feat, fit, flourish, hit, instant, knock, line, move, movement, pat, piece, rap, seizure, shock, squiggle, thump.

v caress, fondle, pat, pet, rub, touch.

stroll *v* amble, dawdle, meander, mosey, promenade, ramble, saunter, take the air, toddle, wander.

n airing, constitutional, dawdle, excursion, meander, promenade, ramble, saunter, toddle, turn, walk.

strong *adj* accented, acute, aggressive, athletic, beefy, biting, bold, brave, brawny, bright, brilliant, burly, capable, clear, clear-cut, cogent, compelling, competent, concentrated, convincing, courageous, dazzling, dedicated, deep, deep-rooted, determined, devout, distinct, drastic, durable, eager, effective, efficient, emphasized, enduring, energetic, excelling, extreme, fast-moving, fervent, fervid, fierce, firm, forceful, forcible, formidable, glaring, great, grievous, gross, hale, hard, hard-nosed, hard-wearing, hardy, heady, healthy, hearty, heated, heavy-duty, herculean, highly-flavoured, highly-seasoned, hot, intemperate, intense, intoxicating, iron, irresistible, keen, lasting, loud, lusty, marked, muscular, numerous, offensive, overpowering, persuasive, piquant, pithy, plucky, potent, powerful, pungent, pure, rank, redoubtable, reinforced, resilient, resistant, resolute, resourceful, robust, self-assertive, severe, sharp, sinewy, skilled, sound, spicy, stalwart, stark, staunch, steadfast, sthenic, stout, stout-hearted, strapping, stressed, sturdy, substantial, telling, tenacious, thewy, thriving, tough, trenchant, undiluted, unmistakable, unseemly, unwavering, unyielding, urgent, vehement, violent, virile, vivid, weighty, well-armed, well-built, well-established, well-founded, well-knit, well-protected, well-rooted, well-set, well-versed, zealous.

antonyms mild, weak.

strong point advantage, aptitude, asset, bag, bent, cup of tea, forte, gift, long suit, métier, specialty, strength, strong suit, talent, thing.

strong-arm *adj* aggressive, bullying, coercive, forceful, intimidating, oppressive, physical, terrorist, threatening, thuggish, violent.

antonym gentle.

stronghold *n* bastion, bulwark, castle, centre, citadel, fastness, fort, fortification, fortress, keep, redoubt, refuge.

structural *adj* configurational, constructional, design, formal, formational, organizational, systemic, tectonic.

structure *n* arrangement, boundaries, building, composition, configuration, conformation, construction, contexture, design, edifice, erection, fabric, form, formation, framework, make-up, organization, pile, regimentation, scaffolding, set-up, system.

v arrange, assemble, build, construct, design, form, order, organize, regiment, set up, shape.

struggle *v* agonize, battle, compete, contend, endeavour, exert oneself, fight, grapple, labour, scuffle, strain, strive, toil, work, wrestle.

antonyms give in, rest.

n agony, battle, brush, clash, combat, conflict, contention, contest, effort, encounter, exertion, fight, grind, hostilities, labour, pains, scramble, scuffle, skirmish, strife, toil, tussle, work.

antonyms ease, submission.

strut *v* parade, peacock, prance, stalk, swagger.

stub *n* butt, counterfoil, end, remnant, stump, tail, tail end.

stubborn *adj* bullheaded, contumacious, cross-grained, determined, difficult, dogged,

dour, fixed, hard to get rid of, headstrong, inflexible, intractable, intransigent, mulish, obdurate, obstinate, opinionated, persistent, pertinacious, pig-headed, recalcitrant, refractory, resolute, rigid, self-willed, stiff, stiff-necked, tenacious, tough, unbending, unmanageable, unshakable, unyielding, willful.

antonym compliant.

stubby *adj* blunt, bristly, chunky, dumpy, prickly, pudgy, pug, rough, short, squat, stocky, stumpy, thickset.

antonyms long, tall, thin.

stuck *adj* at an impasse, baffled, beaten, bogged down, cemented, fast, fastened, firm, fixed, flummoxed, glued, joined, marooned, mired, nonplussed, stranded, stumped, stymied.

antonym loose.

stuck on crazy about, dotty about, enthusiastic about, (far) gone on, gaga over, infatuated with, in love with, keen on, mad about, nuts about, obsessed with, smitten with, sweet on, taken with, wild about.

antonym indifferent to.

stuck-up *adj* arrogant, big-headed, conceited, condescending, exclusive, haughty, high and mighty, hoity-toity, overweening, patronizing, prideful, proud, snobbish, snooty, too big for one's britches, uppity.

antonym humble.

studded *adj* beaded, bejewelled, bespangled, dotted, flecked, ornamented, scattered, set, spangled, speckled, spotted, sprinkled.

student *n* apprentice, bookman, co-ed, contemplator, disciple, freshman, learner, observer, pupil, scholar, seminarian, undergraduate.

studied *adj* affected, calculated, conscious, deliberate, forced, intentional, overelaborate, planned, premeditated, purposeful, unnatural, willful.

antonyms natural, unplanned.

studio *n* atelier, school, workroom, workshop.

studious *adj* academic, assiduous, attentive, bookish, careful, diligent, eager, earnest, hardworking, heedful, intellectual, intent, meditative, reflective, scholarly, sedulous, serious, solicitous, studentlike, thoughtful.

antonym lazy.

study *v* analyse, bone up (on), cogitate, con, consider, contemplate, cram, deliberate, dig into, examine, inquire into, inspect, investigate, learn, lucubrate, meditate (on), peruse, ponder, pore over, read, read up (on), research, review, scan, scrutinize, survey.

n analysis, application, cogitation, consideration, contemplation, cramming, critique, examination, inclination, inquiry, inspection, interest, investigation, learning, lessons, lucubration, memoir, monograph, reading, report, research, review, scrutiny, survey, thesis, thought, treatise.

stuff *v* binge, compress, cram, crowd, fill, force, gluttonize, gobble, gorge, gormandize, guzzle, jam, load, overindulge, overload, pack, pad, push, ram, sate, satiate, shove, squeeze, steeve, stow, wedge.

antonyms nibble, unload.

n belongings, cloth, effects, equipment, essence, fabric, furniture, gear, goods, impedimenta, junk, kit, luggage, material, materials, matériel, matter, objects, paraphernalia, possessions, provisions, quintessence, substance, tackle, textile, things, trappings.

stuffing *n* dressing, filler, filling, forcemeat, kapok, packing, quilting, wadding.

stuffy *adj* airless, boring, close, conventional, deadly, dreary, dull, fetid, fogeyish, frowzy, fusty, heavy, humourless, muggy, musty, narrow-minded, old-fashioned, oppressive, pokey, pompous, priggish, prim, staid, stale, stifling, stilted, stodgy, stopped up, strait-laced, suffocating, sultry, uninteresting, unventilated, Victorian.

antonyms airy, informal, interesting, modern.

stultify *v* benumb, blunt, dull, frustrate, hebetate, numb, repress, smother, stifle, stupefy, suppress, thwart.

antonym sharpen.

stultifying *adj* dulling, hebetating, numbing, stupefying, unstimulating.

antonym electrifying.

stumble *v* blunder, bungle, fall, falter, flounder, fluff, hesitate, lurch, reel, slip, stagger, stammer, stutter, titubate, trip.

stumble on blunder upon, chance upon, come across, discover, encounter, find, happen upon, light upon.

stumbling-block *n* bar, barrier, difficulty, fly in the ointment, hindrance, hitch, hurdle, impediment, obstacle, obstruction, offence, pons asinorum, snag.

antonym boost.

stump *v* baffle, bamboozle, bewilder, clump, confound, confuse, defeat, dumfound, floor, flummox, foil, lumber, mystify, nonplus, outwit, perplex, plod, puzzle, stomp, stop, stymie, thwart, trudge.

antonym assist.

stumped *adj* at an impasse, baffled, bamboozled, floored, flummoxed, nonplussed, perplexed, stuck, stymied.

stumpy *adj* chunky, dumpy, dwarf, dwarfish, heavy, short, squat, stocky, stubby, thick, thickset.

antonyms long, tall, thin.

stun *v* amaze, astonish, astound, bewilder, confound, confuse, daze, deafen, devastate, dumfound, flabbergast, overcome, overpower, shock, stagger, startle, stupefy.

stung *adj* angered, bitten, cut (to the quick), exasperated, goaded, hurt, incensed, irked, needled, nettled, peeved, piqued, resentful, roused, wounded.

antonym soothed.

stunning *adj* amazing, astonishing, beautiful, brilliant, dazing, dazzling, deadening, devastating, gorgeous, great, heavenly, impressive, lovely, marvellous, ravishing,

remarkable, sensational, shocking, smashing, spectacular, striking, wonderful.

antonyms poor, ugly.

stunt[1] *n* act, antic, deed, enterprise, exploit, feat, feature, gest, performance, prank, tour de force, trick, turn.

stunt[2] *v* arrest, check, cramp, dwarf, hamper, hinder, impede, inhibit, restrict, slow, stop.

antonym promote.

stunted *adj* diminutive, dwarfed, dwarfish, little, runtish, runty, small, tiny, undersized.

antonyms large, sturdy.

stupefaction *n* amazement, astonishment, awe, bafflement, bewilderment, wonder, wonderment.

stupefy *v* amaze, astound, baffle, benumb, bewilder, boggle, confound, daze, dumfound, flabbergast, hocus, numb, overwhelm, shock, stagger, stun.

stupendous *adj* amazing, astounding, breathtaking, colossal, enormous, extraordinary, fabulous, fantastic, gigantic, huge, marvellous, mind-blowing, mind-boggling, overwhelming, phenomenal, prodigious, staggering, stunning, superb, tremendous, vast, wonderful.

antonym unimpressive.

stupid *adj* absurd, addle-pated, anserine, asinine, birdbrained, blockish, boring, bovine, brainless, chuckleheaded, clueless, crack-brained, crass, crazy, cretinous, cuckoo, daft, dazed, deficient, dense, dim, dizzy, doltish, dopey, dozy, drippy, dull, dumb, dunderheaded, fatheaded, fatuous, feeble-minded, foolhardy, foolheaded, foolish, gormless, groggy, gullible, half-baked, half-witted, idiotic, ill-advised, imbecilic, inane, indiscreet, inept, insane, insensate, insipient, irresponsible, laughable, ludicrous, lumpish, lunatic, meaningless, mindless, moronic, naïve, nonsensical, oafish, obtuse, opaque, pointless, puerile, punch-drunk, rash, semiconscious, senseless, short-sighted, silly, simple, simple-minded, slow, slow-witted, sluggish, stunned, stupefied, thick, thick-headed, thick-witted, thoughtless, unintelligent, unthinking, unwise, vacuous, vapid, witless, wooden-headed.

antonyms alert, clever.

stupor *n* apathy, coma, daze, inertia, insensibility, lethargy, numbness, oscitancy, sluggishness, stupefaction, torpor, trance, unconsciousness.

antonym alertness.

sturdy *adj* athletic, brawny, determined, durable, firm, flourishing, hardy, hearty, husky, lusty, muscular, obstinate, powerful, resolute, robust, secure, solid, stalwart, staunch, steadfast, stout, strong, substantial, vigorous, well-built, well-made.

antonyms decrepit, puny.

stutter *v* falter, hesitate, mumble, splutter, stammer, stumble.

style *n* approach, bon ton, category, chic, comfort, cosmopolitanism, custom, cut, dash, design, diction, dressiness, dress sense, élan, elegance, expression, fashion, fashionableness, flair, flamboyance, form, genre, grace, grandeur, kind, luxury, make, manner, method, mode, model, panache, pattern, phraseology, phrasing, pizzazz, polish, rage, refinement, savoir-faire, smartness, sophistication, sort, spirit, strain, stylishness, taste, technique, tenor, tone, treatment, trend, type, urbanity, variety, vein, vogue, way, wording.

antonym inelegance.

v adapt, address, arrange, call, christen, create, cut, denominate, design, designate, dress, entitle, fashion, label, name, set, shape, tailor, term, title.

stylish *adj* à la mode, chic, chi-chi, classy, cool, dapper, dressy, fashionable, groovy, hip, in, in style, in vogue, modish, natty, polished, smart, snappy, snazzy, trendy, urbane, voguish.

antonym unstylish.

stylus *n* gnomon, graver, index, needle, pen, pointer, probe, style.

stymie *v* baffle, balk, bamboozle, block, confound, defeat, euchre, flummox, foil, frustrate, hinder, mystify, nonplus, puzzle, snooker, stall, stump, thwart.

antonym assist.

suave *adj* affable, agreeable, bland, charming, civilized, courteous, diplomatic, gracious, obliging, oily, pleasing, polite, smooth, smooth-tongued, soft-spoken, sophisticated, unctuous, urbane, worldly.

antonym unsophisticated.

subconscious *adj* hidden, inner, innermost, intuitive, latent, repressed, subliminal, suppressed, unconscious.

antonym conscious.

n id, superego, unconscious.

subdue *v* allay, alleviate, break, bring to heel, check, conquer, control, cow, crush, damp, dampen, daunt, defeat, discipline, humble, master, mellow, moderate, muffle, overcome, overpower, overrun, quash, quell, quieten, reduce, repress, restrain, soften, soft-pedal, subject, subjugate, suppress, tame, tone down, trample, vanquish.

antonym arouse.

subdued *adj* abated, chastened, cowed, crestfallen, dejected, dim, docile, downcast, grave, hushed, low-key, mellow, muffled, muted, pastel, quiet, repentant, repressed, reserved, restrained, reticent, serious, shaded, sober, soft, solemn, subfusc, subtle, unobtrusive, vanquished.

antonyms aroused, lively.

subject *n* affair, business, case, citizen, curriculum area, discipline, focus, grounds, issue, matter, mind, object, participant, patient, point, question, score, specialty, subordinate, substance, theme, topic, vassal.

antonym master.

adj captive, dependent, enslaved, inferior, satellite, subjugated, subordinate, subservient.

antonyms free, superior.

v expose, lay open, subdue, submit, subordinate.

subject to answerable to, conditional on, contingent on, dependent on, disposed to, liable to, open to, prone to, susceptible to, vulnerable to.

subjection *n* bondage, captivity, chains, crushing, defeat, domination, enslavement, mastery, oppression, quelling, servitude, shackles, slavery, subduing, subjugation, thrall, thralldom, vassalage.

subjective biassed, emotional, idiosyncratic, individual, instinctive, introspective, intuitive, personal, prejudiced.

antonym objective.

subjugate *v* conquer, crush, defeat, enslave, enthrall, master, overcome, overpower, overthrow, put down, quash, quell, reduce, subdue, suppress, tame, thrall, vanquish.

antonym free.

sublimate *v* channel, divert, elevate, exalt, heighten, purify, redirect, refine, sublime, transfer, transmute.

antonym let out.

sublime *adj* elevated, eminent, empyreal, exalted, glorious, grand, great, high, imposing, lofty, magnificent, majestic, noble, transcendent.

antonym lowly.

submerge *v* bury, cover, deluge, dip, duck, dunk, engulf, flood, immerse, inundate, overflow, overwhelm, plunge, sink, submerse, swamp.

antonym surface.

submerged *adj* buried, concealed, covered, demersal, drowned, hidden, immersed, inundated, obscured, subaquatic, subaqueous, submarine, submersed, sunken, swamped, undersea, underwater, unseen.

submission *n* acquiescence, assent, capitulation, compliance, contention, deference, docility, entry, meekness, obedience, offer, passivity, presentation, proposal, report, resignation, submissiveness, suggestion, surrender, tender, tendering, tractability, yielding.

antonym intractability.

submissive *adj* abject, accommodating, acquiescent, amenable, assenting, biddable, bootlicking, complaisant, compliant, consenting, deferential, docile, dutiful, humble, ingratiating, malleable, meek, obedient, obeisant, obsequious, passive, patient, pliant, resigned, servile, subdued, subservient, supine, tractable, uncomplaining, unresisting, yielding.

antonym intractable.

submit *v* accede, acquiesce, advance, affirm, agree, argue, assert, bend, bow, capitulate, claim, commit, comply, contend, defer, endure, enter, file, hand in, knuckle under, move, present, proffer, propose, propound, put (forward), state, subject, succumb, suggest, surrender, table, tender, tolerate, yield.

antonym struggle.

subordinate *adj* ancillary, auxiliary, dependent, inferior, junior, lesser, lower, menial, minor, secondary, subject, subservient, subsidiary, supplementary.

antonym superior.

n adjunct, aide, assistant, attendant, dependant, inferior, junior, second, second banana (or fiddle), stooge, sub, subaltern, underdog, underling.

antonym superior.

subordination *n* inferiority, servitude, subjection, submission, subservience.

antonym superiority.

subscribe *v* contribute, cough up, donate, endorse, fork out, give, offer, pledge, promise, shell out, sign, underwrite.

subscribe to acquiesce in, advocate, agree with, approve of, consent to, countenance, favour, (give) assent to, go along with, ratify, support.

subscription *n* contribution, donation, dues, fee, gift, offering, payment.

subsequent *adj* after, consequent, consequential, ensuing, following, later, resulting, succeeding.

antonym previous.

subsequently *adv* after (that), afterwards, consequently, later (on).

antonym previously.

subservient *adj* abject, ancillary, auxiliary, bootlicking, conducive, cringing, deferential, helpful, inferior, instrumental, obsequious, serviceable, servile, slavish, subject, submissive, subordinate, subsidiary, sycophantic, truckling, useful.

antonyms domineering, rebellious, unhelpful.

subside *v* abate, collapse, decline, decrease, descend, diminish, drop, dwindle, ease, ebb, fall, lessen, lower, moderate, quieten, recede, settle, sink, slacken, wane.

antonym increase.

subsidence *n* abatement, decline, decrease, de-escalation, descent, detumescence, diminution, ebb, lessening, settlement, settling, sinking, slackening.

antonym increase.

subsidiary *adj* aiding, ancillary, assistant, auxiliary, branch, contributory, co-operative, helpful, helping, lesser, minor, secondary, serviceable, subordinate, subservient, supplemental, supplementary, supporting, useful.

antonym chief.

n affiliate, branch, division, offshoot, part, section, subsection.

subsidize *v* aid, assist, back, endow, finance, fund, promote, sponsor, support, underwrite.

subsidy *n* aid, allowance, assistance, backing, bursary, contribution, endowment, financing, grant, help, sponsorship, subvention, support.

subsist *v* continue, endure, exist, hold out, inhere, last, live, remain, survive.

subsistence *n* aliment, existence, food, keep, livelihood, living, maintenance, nourishment, provision, rations, support, survival, sustenance, upkeep, victuals.

substance *n* actuality, affluence, assets, body, burden, concreteness, content, depth, drift, element, entity, essence, estate, fabric, force, foundation, gist, gravamen, grounds, import, material, matter, meaning, means, nitty-gritty, pith, property, reality, resources, significance, solidity, stuff, subject, subject matter, texture, theme, topic, wealth.

substandard *adj* damaged, imperfect, inadequate, inferior, jerry-built, mediocre, poor, second-rate, shoddy, tawdry, unacceptable.

antonym first-rate.

substantial *adj* actual, ample, big, bulky, considerable, corporeal, durable, enduring, essential, existent, firm, full-bodied, generous, goodly, hefty, important, influential, large, massive, material, meaningful, positive, real, significant, sizable, solid, sound, stout, strong, sturdy, tidy, true, valid, weighty, well-built, worthwhile.

antonyms insignificant, small.

substantially *adv* essentially, in the main, largely, materially, on the whole, significantly, to all intents and purposes.

antonym slightly.

substantiate *v* affirm, authenticate, confirm, corroborate, establish, prove, support, validate, verify.

antonym disprove.

substitute *v* change, commute, exchange, interchange, make do with, replace, subrogate, swap, switch.

n agent, alternate, deputy, double, dummy, equivalent, ersatz, locum tenens, makeshift, pinchhitter, proxy, relief, replacement, replacer, representative, reserve, ringer, scapegoat, stand-in, stopgap, sub, surrogate, temp, understudy, vicar.

adj acting, additional, alternative, deputy, ersatz, proxy, relief, replacement, reserve, second, supply, surrogate, temporary, vicarious.

substitute for act for, cover for, deputize for, double for, fill in for, relieve, stand in for, sub for, take the rap for.

substitution *n* change, exchange, interchange, replacement, swap, swapping, switch, switching.

subterfuge *n* artifice, deception, deviousness, dodge, duplicity, evasion, excuse, expedient, feint, machination, manoeuvre, ploy, pretence, pretext, ruse, scheme, shift, stall, stratagem, trick.

antonyms honesty, openness.

subtle *adj* abstruse, artful, astute, clever, crafty, cunning, deep, delicate, designing, devious, discerning, discriminating, elusive, faint, fine, fine-drawn, fine-spun, impalpable, implied, indirect, ingenious, insidious, insinuated, keen, Machiavellian, nice, penetrating, profound, rarefied, refined, scheming, shrewd, slight, sly, sophisticated, tenuous, tricky, understated, wily.

antonyms open, unsubtle.

subtlety *n* acumen, acuteness, artfulness, astuteness, cleverness, complexity, craftiness, cunning, delicacy, deviousness, discernment, discrimination, finesse, guile, intricacy, nicety, penetration, refinement, sagacity, skill, slyness, sophistication, wiliness.

antonyms openness, unsubtlety.

subtract *v* debit, deduct, detract, diminish, remove, take away, withdraw.

antonyms add, add to.

suburbs *n* bedroom communities, commuter belt, environs, exurbia, faubourg, outskirts, precincts, purlieus, suburbia.

antonyms centre, downtown, heart.

subversive *adj* destructive, disruptive, incendiary, inflammatory, insurrectionary, overthrowing, rebel, revolutionary, seditious, treasonous, underground, undermining.

antonym loyal.

n deviationist, dissident, fifth columnist, freedom fighter, insurrectionist, quisling, rebel, revolutionary, saboteur, seditionary, seditionist, terrorist, traitor.

subvert *v* contaminate, corrupt, debase, demolish, demoralize, deprave, destroy, disrupt, overthrow, overturn, pervert, poison, raze, ruin, sabotage, undermine, vitiate, wreck.

antonyms boost, uphold.

succeed *v* arrive, be a hit, bring off, ensue, flourish, follow, make good, make it, prevail, prosper, pull off, replace, result, supersede, supervene, thrive, triumph, work.

antonyms fail, precede.

succeed to accede to, come into, enter upon, inherit, take over.

antonyms abdicate, precede.

succeeding *adj* coming, ensuing, following, later, next, subsequent, successive, to come.

antonym previous.

success *n* accomplishment, ascendancy, bestseller, celebrity, eminence, fame, (good) fortune, happiness, hit, luck, prosperity, sensation, somebody, star, triumph, VIP, winner.

antonym failure.

successful *adj* accomplished, acknowledged, bestselling, booming, efficacious, famous, favourable, flourishing, fortunate, fruitful, lucrative, moneymaking, paying, profitable, prosperous, rewarding, satisfactory, satisfying, thriving, top, unbeaten, victorious, wealthy, well-known, well-to-do.

antonym unsuccessful.

successfully *adv* beautifully, famously, fine, great, smoothly, swimmingly, victoriously, well.

antonym unsuccessfully.

succession *n* accession, assumption, chain, concatenation, continuation, course, cycle, descendants, descent, flow, inheritance, line, lineage, order, procession, progression, run, sequence, series, train.

successive *adj* back-to-back, consecutive, following, in succession, sequent, straight, succeeding.

succinct *adj* brief, compact, compendious, concise, condensed, gnomic, laconic, pithy, short, summary, terse.

antonym wordy.

succour *v* aid, assist, befriend, comfort, encourage, foster, help, help out, lend a helping hand, nurse, relieve, support.

antonym undermine.

n aid, assistance, comfort, help, helping hand, ministrations, relief, support.

succulent *adj* fleshy, juicy, luscious, lush, mellow, moist, mouthwatering, rich, sappy, tasty.

antonym dry.

succumb *v* capitulate, collapse, deteriorate, die, fall, give in, knuckle under, submit, surrender, yield.

antonym overcome.

suck *v* absorb, drain, draw, draw in, drink, extract, imbibe, take in.

suck up to bootlick, curry favour with, fawn on, flatter, ingratiate oneself with, toady to, truckle to.

sucker *n* cat's-paw, dupe, fool, gull, mark, patsy, pushover, sap, stooge, victim.

sudden *adj* abrupt, hasty, hurried, impulsive, precipitate, prompt, quick, rapid, rash, snap, startling, swift, unexpected, unforeseen, unusual.

antonym slow.

suddenness *n* abruptness, haste, hastiness, hurriedness, impulsiveness, unexpectedness.

antonym slowness.

sue *v* apply, beg, beseech, charge, entreat, indict, litigate, petition, plead, prosecute, solicit, summon, supplicate, take to court.

suffer *v* ache, agonize, allow, bear with, brook, deteriorate, endure, experience, feel, grieve, hurt, let, permit, sorrow, sustain, tolerate, undergo.

suffering *n* ache, affliction, agony, anguish, discomfort, distress, hardship, martyrdom, misery, ordeal, pain, pangs, torment, torture.

suffice *v* answer, content, do, measure up, satisfy, serve.

sufficiency *n* adequacy, adequateness, competence, enough, enough to get by on, plenty, satiety.

antonym insufficiency.

sufficient *adj* adequate, ample, decent, effective, enough, good enough, satisfactory, tolerable, up to scratch (or snuff), up to the mark.

antonyms insufficient, poor.

suffocate *v* asphyxiate, choke, smother, stifle, strangle, throttle.

suffuse *v* bathe, colour, cover, flood, imbue, infuse, mantle, permeate, pervade, spread over, transfuse.

suggest *v* advise, advocate, be reminiscent of, bring to mind, call up, conjure up, connote, evoke, hint (at), imply, indicate, insinuate, intimate, move, propose, raise, recommend, smack of.

antonyms demonstrate, order.

suggestion *n* breath, clue, hint, indication, innuendo, insinuation, intimation, motion, proposal, proposition, recommendation, suspicion, tinge, trace, whisper.

antonyms demonstration, order.

suggestive *adj* bawdy, blue, evocative, expressive, immodest, improper, indecent, indelicate, indicative, insinuating, meaning, off-colour, provocative, prurient, racy, redolent, reminiscent, ribald, risqué, smutty, spicy, titillating, unseemly.

antonyms clean, unevocative.

suicide *n* hara-kiri, kamikaze, self-destruction, self-immolation, self-murder, self-slaughter, suttee.

suit *v* accommodate, adapt, adjust, agree, answer, become, be convenient (for), befit, conform to, correspond, do, fashion, fit, gear, gratify, harmonize, match, modify, please, proportion, satisfy, tailor, tally.

antonyms clash, displease.

n action, addresses, appeal, case, cause, clothing, costume, courtship, dress, ensemble, entreaty, get-up, habit, invocation, lawsuit, outfit, petition, prayer, proceeding, prosecution, request, series, solicitation, trial, wooing.

suitable *adj* acceptable, accordant, adequate, applicable, apposite, appropriate, apt, becoming, befitting, conformable, congenial, congruent, consonant, convenient, correspondent, due, eligible, expedient, fit, fitting, opportune, pertinent, proper, relevant, right, satisfactory, seemly, square, suited.

antonym unsuitable.

suitably *adv* acceptably, accordingly, appropriately, expediently, fitly, fittingly, properly, quite.

antonym unsuitably.

suite *n* apartment, attendants, collection, entourage, escort, followers, furniture, group, retainers, retinue, rooms, series, servants, set, train.

suitor *n* admirer, beau, follower, swain, wooer, young man.

sulk *v* brood, grouch, grump, mope, pet, pout.

sulky *adj* aloof, churlish, cross, disgruntled, grouchy, ill-humoured, moody, morose, perverse, petulant, put out, resentful, sullen.

antonym cheerful.

sullen *adj* baleful, brooding, cheerless, cross, dark, dismal, dull, farouche, gloomy, glowering, glum, heavy, ill-humoured, moody, morose, obstinate, perverse, silent, sombre, sour, stubborn, sulky, surly, unsociable.

antonym cheerful.

sully *v* befoul, besmirch, blemish, contaminate, darken, defile, dirty, disgrace, dishonour, mar, pollute, soil, spoil, spot, stain, taint, tarnish.

antonyms cleanse, honour.

sultry *adj* close, come-hither, erotic, hot, humid, indecent, lurid, muggy, oppressive, passionate, provocative, seductive, sensual, sexy, sticky, stifling, stuffy, sweltering, torrid.

antonyms cold, cool.

sum *n* aggregate, amount, entirety, extent, gist, quantity, reckoning, result, score, substance, summary, sum total, tally, total, totality, whole.

sum up add up, calculate, perorate, précis, recapitulate, review, summarize, total.

summarily *adv* abruptly, arbitrarily, expeditiously, forthwith, hastily, immediately, peremptorily, promptly, speedily, swiftly, without delay.

summarize *v* abbreviate, abridge, condense, encapsulate, epitomize, outline, précis, review, shorten, sum up.

antonym expand (on).

summary *n* abridgment, abstract, compendium, condensation, digest, epitome, essence, extract, outline, précis, recapitulation, résumé, review, rundown, summation, summing up, synopsis.

adj arbitrary, brief, compact, compendious, concise, condensed, cursory, expeditious, hasty, laconic, peremptory, perfunctory, pithy, prompt, short, speedy, succinct, swift.

antonym lengthy.

summer house *n* arbour, belvedere, bower, gazebo, pavilion, pergola.

summit *n* acme, apex, apogee, crown, culmination, head, height, peak, pinnacle, point, tip, top, vertex, zenith.

antonyms bottom, nadir.

summon *v* arouse, assemble, beckon, bid, call (for), cite, conjure (up), convene, convoke, fetch, gather, invite, invoke, mobilize, muster, rally, rouse.

antonym dismiss.

sumptuous *adj* costly, dear, expensive, extravagant, gorgeous, grand, grandiose, lavish, luxurious, magnificent, opulent, plush, posh, princely, rich, ritzy, splendid, superb.

antonym mean.

sunbathe *v* bake, bask, bronze, brown, insolate, sun (oneself), take the sun, tan.

sunburned *adj* blistered, bronzed, brown, burned, peeling, red, ruddy, tanned, weather-beaten.

antonym pale.

sunder *v* chop, cleave, cut, dissever, divide, part, rive, separate, sever, split.

antonym join.

sundry *adj* a few, assorted, different, divers, miscellaneous, separate, several, some, varied, various.

sunk *adj* done for, doomed, finished, lost, ruined, toast, up the creek, up the spout.

sunken *adj* buried, concave, depressed, drawn, emaciated, gaunt, haggard, hollow, hollowed, lower, recessed, submerged.

sunless *adj* bleak, cheerless, cloudy, dark, depressing, dismal, dreary, gloomy, grey, hazy, overcast, sombre.

antonym sunny.

sunny *adj* beaming, blithe, bright, brilliant, buoyant, cheerful, cheery, clear, cloudless, fine, genial, happy, joyful, light-hearted, luminous, optimistic, pleasant, radiant, smiling, summery, sunlit, sunshiny.

antonym gloomy.

sunrise *n* aurora, cockcrow, crack of dawn, dawn, daybreak, daylight, dayspring, sunup.

sunset *n* crepuscule, dusk, evening, eventide, gloaming, nightfall, sundown, twilight.

super *adj* excellent, first-class, glorious, incomparable, magnificent, marvellous, matchless, outstanding, peerless, sensational, smashing, superb, super-duper, superior, superlative, terrific, top-notch, wonderful.

antonym poor.

superannuated *adj* aged, antiquated, decrepit, moribund, obsolete, old, past it, pensioned off, put out to grass (or pasture), retired, senile.

antonym young.

superb *adj* admirable, breathtaking, choice, excellent, exquisite, fine, first-rate, gorgeous, grand, magnificent, marvellous, splendid, superior, unrivalled.

antonym poor.

supercilious *adj* arrogant, condescending, contemptuous, disdainful, haughty, hoity-toity, imperious, insolent, lofty, lordly, overbearing, patronizing, proud, scornful, snobbish, snooty, snotty, stuck-up, uppity, upstage, vainglorious.

antonym humble.

superficial *adj* apparent, casual, cosmetic, cursory, desultory, empty, empty-headed, evident, exterior, external, frivolous, hasty, hurried, lightweight, nodding, ostensible, outward, passing, perfunctory, peripheral, seeming, shallow, silly, sketchy, skin-deep, slapdash, slight, surface, trivial, unanalytical, unreflective.

antonyms deep, detailed, thorough.

superficially *adv* apparently, externally, hastily, ostensibly, seemingly.

antonym in depth.

superfluity *n* excess, extravagance, exuberance, glut, pleonasm, plethora, profusion, redundancy, superabundance, surfeit, surplus.

antonym lack.

superfluous *adj* de trop, excess, excessive, extra, needless, otiose, pleonastic, redundant, remaining, residuary, spare, superabundant, supererogatory, supernumerary, surplus, uncalled-for, unessential, unnecessary, unneeded, unneedful, unwanted.

antonym necessary.

superhuman *adj* divine, great, herculean, heroic, immense, paranormal, phenomenal, preternatural, prodigious, stupendous, supernatural, valiant.

antonyms average, ordinary.

superintend *v* administer, control, direct, guide, inspect, manage, overlook, oversee, run, steer, supervise.

superintendent *n* administrator, chief, conductor, controller, curator, director,

governor, inspector, manager, overseer, super, supervisor.

superior *adj* admirable, arrogant, better, choice, condescending, deluxe, disdainful, distinguished, excellent, exceptional, exclusive, fine, first-class, first-rate, good, grander, greater, haughty, high-class, higher, hoity-toity, incomparable, lofty, lordly, of quality, par excellence, patronizing, predominant, preferred, pretentious, prevailing, remarkable, respectable, snobbish, snooty, snotty, stuck-up, supercilious, superordinate, surpassing, top-flight, top-notch, transcendent, unrivalled, upper, uppity, upstage, worthy.

antonyms humble, inferior.

n boss, chief, director, foreman, forewoman, gaffer, head, higher-up, manager, principal, senior, supervisor.

antonyms inferior, junior, subordinate.

superiority *n* advantage, ascendancy, edge, excellence, lead, precedence, predominance, pre-eminence, supremacy.

antonym inferiority.

superlative *adj* consummate, crack, excellent, greatest, highest, magnificent, matchless, nonpareil, outstanding, peerless, supreme, surpassing, transcendent, unbeatable, unbeaten, unparalleled, unrivalled, unsurpassed.

antonym poor.

supernatural *adj* abnormal, dark, divine, ghostly, hidden, hyperphysical, metaphysical, miraculous, mysterious, mystic, occult, paranormal, phantom, preternatural, psychic, spectral, spiritual, superhuman, superlunary, supersensible, supersensory, uncanny, unearthly, unnatural.

antonym natural.

supernumerary *adj* excess, excessive, extra, extraordinary, redundant, spare, superfluous, surplus.

antonym necessary.

supersede *v* annul, displace, oust, overrule, remove, replace, succeed, supplant, suspend, take the place of, usurp.

superstition *n* delusion, fable, myth, old wives' tale, voodooism.

superstitious *adj* delusive, fallacious, false, fetishistic, groundless, irrational, voodooistic.

supervise *v* administer, conduct, control, direct, govern, handle, inspect, keep tabs (or an eye) on, manage, oversee, preside over, run, superintend.

supervision *n* administration, auspices, care, charge, control, direction, government, guidance, instruction, leading strings, management, oversight, stewardship, superintendence, surveillance.

supervisor *n* administrator, boss, chief, foreman, forewoman, gaffer, inspector, manager, overseer, steward, superintendent.

supervisory *adj* administrative, directorial, executive, governing, managerial, overseeing, superintending.

supine _adj_ apathetic, bored, careless, flat, heedless, horizontal, idle, inactive, incurious, indifferent, indolent, inert, languid, lazy, lethargic, listless, negligent, passive, prostrate, recumbent, resigned, slothful, sluggish, spineless, spiritless, torpid, uninterested, unresisting.
antonyms alert, upright.

supplant _v_ displace, dispossess, oust, overthrow, remove, replace, succeed, supersede, topple, undermine, unseat, usurp the place of.

supple _adj_ adaptable, bending, double-jointed, elastic, flexible, limber, lithe, loose-limbed, plastic, pliable, pliant, willowy, yielding.
antonym rigid.

supplement _n_ addendum, addition, appendix, codicil, complement, extra, insert, postscript, pull-out, rider, sequel, supplementary.
_v_ add to, augment, complement, eke out, extend, fill up, reinforce, supply, top up.
antonym deplete.

supplementary _adj_ above and beyond, accompanying, additional, ancillary, auxiliary, complementary, extra, reinforcing, secondary, supplemental.
antonym core.

suppliant _adj_ begging, beseeching, craving, entreating, imploring, importunate, petitioning, supplicating.
_n_ applicant, petitioner, pleader, postulant, suitor, supplicant.

supplication _n_ appeal, entreaty, invocation, orison, petition, plea, pleading, prayer, request, rogation, solicitation, suit.

supplicatory _adj_ begging, beseeching, imploring, imprecatory, petitioning, praying, supplicating.

supplier _n_ dealer, furnisher, hawker, peddler, provider, purveyor, retailer, seller, shopkeeper, storekeeper, sutler, vendor, wholesaler.

supplies _n_ equipment, food, foodstuffs, groceries, materials, matériel, necessities, provender, provisions, rations, stores, victuals.

supply _v_ afford, contribute, donate, endow, equip, fill, furnish, give, grant, outfit, produce, provide, purvey, satisfy, stock, store, victual, yield.
antonym take.
_n_ cache, fund, hoard, materials, necessities, provender, provisions, quantity, rations, reserve, reservoir, resources, source, stock, stockpile, store, stores.
antonym lack.

support _v_ advocate, aid, assist, authenticate, back, bear, bear out, bolster, brace, buttress, carry, champion, cherish, confirm, corroborate, countenance, crutch, defend, document, donate to, endorse, endure, favour, finance, foster, fund, handle, help, hold (up), keep (up), maintain, nourish, promote, prop (up), propound, provide for, rally around, reinforce, second, service, shore (up), sponsor, stand behind, stand (for), stay, stomach, strengthen, strut, subsidize, substantiate, succour, suffer, sustain, take (someone's) part, tolerate, underpin, underwrite, uphold, verify.
antonyms contradict, oppose.
_n_ abutment, aid, alimony, approval, assent, assistance, backbone, backer, backing, backstay, backstop, blessing, brace, championship, comfort, comforter, corroboration, crutch, encouragement, evidence, financing, foundation, friendship, fulcrum, furtherance, girdle, help, helper, jockstrap, keep, loyalty, mainstay, maintenance, patronage, pillar, post, prop, protection, reinforcement, relief, second, service, sheet anchor, shore, stanchion, stay, stiffener, subsidy, substantiation, succour, supporter, tower of strength, underpinning, upkeep.
antonym opposition.

supporter _n_ adherent, advocate, ally, apologist, backer, champion, co-worker, defender, donor, fan, financer, follower, friend, heeler, helper, patron, proponent, seconder, sponsor, support, upholder, well-wisher.
antonym opponent.

supportive _adj_ affirmative, approving, attentive, caring, confirming, encouraging, favourable, helpful, positive, reassuring, sympathetic, understanding.
antonym discouraging.

suppose _v_ assume, believe, calculate, conceive (of), conclude, conjecture, consider, expect, fancy, guess, hypothesize, imagine, imply, infer, judge, opine, posit, postulate, presume, presuppose, pretend, surmise, suspect, think.
antonym know.

supposed _adj_ accepted, alleged, assumed, believed, conjectured, hypothetical, imagined, ostensible, presumed, presupposed, professed, putative, reported, reputed, rumoured, so-called, suspected.
antonym known.

supposed to designed to, expected to, intended to, meant to, obliged to, required to.

supposedly _adv_ allegedly, assumedly, avowedly, hypothetically, ostensibly, presumably, professedly, purportedly, putatively, reportedly, reputedly, theoretically.
antonym really.

supposition _n_ assumption, conjecture, guess, guesstimate, guesswork, hypothesis, idea, notion, opinion, postulate, presumption, speculation, surmise, theory.
antonym knowledge.

suppress _v_ censor, check, choke back, conceal, conquer, contain, crush, end, extinguish, hold back, muffle, muzzle, overpower, overthrow, put down, quash, quell, repress, restrain, silence, smother, snuff out, squelch, stamp out, stifle, stop, strangle, subdue, submerge, swallow, vote down, withhold.
antonyms encourage, incite.

suppression _n_ blackout, censorship, check, clampdown, containment, crackdown, crushing, elimination, extinction, inhibition, prohibition, quashing, quelling, restraint, repression, smothering, squelching, termination.

antonyms encouragement, incitement.

suppurate v discharge, fester, form pus, gather, matter, maturate, ooze, run, weep.

suppuration n festering, purulence, pus.

supremacy n ascendancy, dominance, domination, dominion, hegemony, lordship, mastery, predominance, pre-eminence, primacy, sovereignty, sway.

supreme adj best, cardinal, chief, consummate, crowning, culminating, extreme, final, first, foremost, greatest, head, highest, incomparable, leading, matchless, nonpareil, number one, paramount, peerless, predominant, pre-eminent, prevailing, prime, principal, second-to-none, sovereign, superlative, surpassing, top, transcendent, ultimate, unbeatable, unbeaten, unsurpassed, utmost.

antonyms lowly, poor, slight.

sure adj absolute, accurate, assured, beyond question, bound, certain, clear, confident, convinced, decided, definite, dependable, effective, fast, firm, fixed, foolproof, guaranteed, indisputable, indubitable, ineluctable, inescapable, inevitable, infallible, irrevocable, persuaded, positive, precise, reliable, safe, satisfied, secure, solid, stable, steadfast, steady, sure-fire, trustworthy, trusty, undeniable, undoubted, unerring, unfailing, unmistakable, unquestionable, unswerving, unwavering.

antonyms doubtful, unsure.

surely adv absolutely, assuredly, certainly, confidently, definitely, doubtless(ly), firmly, indubitably, ineluctably, inevitably, inexorably, positively, safely, undeniably, undoubtedly, unerringly, unfailingly, unmistakably, unquestionably, without a doubt.

surety n bail, bond, bondsman, certainty, deposit, guarantee, guarantor, hostage, indemnity, insurance, mortgagor, pledge, safety, security, sponsor, warranty.

surface n covering, exterior, façade, face, facet, outside, outward appearance, plane, side, skin, superficies, top, veneer.

antonym interior.

adj apparent, exterior, external, outer, outside, outward, shallow, superficial.

antonym interior.

v appear, come to light, emerge, materialize, pop up, rise, transpire, turn up.

antonyms disappear, sink.

surfeit n bellyful, excess, glut, overindulgence, plethora, satiety, superabundance, superfluity.

antonym lack.

v cloy, cram, fill to overflowing, glut, gorge, overfeed, overfill, overload, satiate, stuff.

surge v billow, eddy, gush, heave, rise, roll, rush, seethe, swell, swirl, undulate.

n access, billow, breaker, efflux, flood, flow, gurgitation, gush, increase, intensification, outpouring, roller, rush, swell, uprush, upsurge, wave.

surly adj bad-tempered, brusque, churlish, crabby, cross, crusty, curmudgeonly, grouchy, gruff, grumpy, ill-natured, ill-tempered, morose, perverse, rude, sulky, sullen, testy, uncivil, unfriendly, ungracious.

antonym pleasant.

surmise v assume, believe, conclude, conjecture, consider, deduce, fancy, guess, imagine, infer, opine, presume, speculate, suppose, suspect.

antonym know.

n assumption, conclusion, conjecture, deduction, guess, hypothesis, idea, inference, notion, opinion, possibility, presumption, speculation, supposition, suspicion, thought.

antonym certainty.

surmount v conquer, exceed, get over, master, overcome, surpass, triumph over, vanquish.

surpass v beat, best, eclipse, exceed, excel, outdistance, outdo, outshine, outstrip, override, overshadow, surmount, top, tower above, transcend.

surpassing adj exceptional, extraordinary, incomparable, inimitable, matchless, outstanding, phenomenal, rare, superior, supreme, transcendent, unrivalled, unsurpassed.

antonym poor.

surplus n balance, excess, overage, overplus, plethora, remainder, residue, superabundance, superfluity, surfeit, surplusage.

antonym lack.

adj excess, extra, redundant, remaining, spare, superfluous, unused.

antonym essential.

surprise v amaze, astonish, astound, bewilder, catch off guard, confuse, disconcert, dismay, dumfound, flabbergast, nonplus, shock, stagger, startle, stun, take unawares, throw, throw for a loop.

n amazement, astonishment, bewilderment, bolt out of the blue, bombshell, dismay, eye-opener, incredulity, jolt, revelation, shock, start, stupefaction, wonder.

antonym composure.

surprised adj amazed, astonished, astounded, disconcerted, flabbergasted, incredulous, nonplussed, open-mouthed, shocked, speechless, staggered, startled, stunned, thunderstruck, unprepared.

antonyms composed, unsurprised.

surprising adj amazing, astonishing, astounding, extraordinary, incredible, marvellous, out of the blue, remarkable, shocking, staggering, startling, stunning, sudden, unexpected, unforeseen, unlooked-for, unpredictable, unusual, unwonted, wonderful.

antonyms expected, unsurprising.

surrender v abandon, capitulate, cede, concede, forego, give in, give up, quit, relinquish, remise, renounce, resign, submit, succumb, waive, yield.

antonym fight on.

n abandonment, appeasement, capitulation, delivery, relinquishment, remise, renunciation, white flag, yielding.

surreptitious *adj* backdoor, behind closed doors, clandestine, covert, deceitful, furtive, secret, sly, sneaking, stealthy, unauthorized, underhand, veiled.

antonym open.

surrogate *n* deputy, fill-in, proxy, replacement, representative, stand-in, substitute.

surround *v* begird, besiege, compass, embosom, encase, encircle, enclose, encompass, envelop, environ, girdle, invest, ring.

surrounding *adj* adjacent, adjoining, ambient, bordering, circumambient, circumjacent, encircling, enclosing, encompassing, environing, environmental, nearby, neighbouring.

surroundings *n* ambience, background, environment, environs, locale, milieu, neighbourhood, setting, vicinity.

surveillance *n* care, charge, check, control, direction, guardianship, inspection, monitoring, observation, regulation, scrutiny, stewardship, superintendence, supervision, vigilance, watch.

survey *v* appraise, assess, consider, contemplate, estimate, examine, inspect, look over, measure, observe, peruse, plan, plot, prospect, reconnoitre, research, review, scan, scrutinize, study, supervise, triangulate, view.

n appraisal, assessment, conspectus, examination, inquiry, inspection, investigation, measurement, overview, perusal, review, sample, scrutiny, study, triangulation, viewing.

survive *v* endure, exist, hang on, last, last out, live, live out, live through, outlast, outlive, remain, ride out, stay, subsist, weather, withstand.

antonym succumb.

susceptibility *n* defencelessness, liability, openness, predisposition, proclivity, proneness, propensity, sensitivity, suggestibility, tendency, vulnerability, weakness.

antonyms impregnability, resistance.

susceptible *adj* defenceless, disposed, given, impressionable, inclined, influenceable, liable, open, predisposed, pregnable, prone, receptive, sensitive, subject, suggestible, teachable, unprotected, vulnerable.

antonyms impregnable, resistant.

suspect *v* believe, call in question, conjecture, distrust, doubt, fancy, feel, guess, infer, mistrust, opine, speculate, suppose, surmise.

adj debatable, doubtful, dubious, fishy, questionable, shady, suspicious, unauthoritative, uncertain, under suspicion, unreliable, untrustworthy.

antonyms acceptable, innocent, straightforward.

suspend *v* adjourn, append, arrest, attach, cease, dangle, debar, defer, delay, disbar, discontinue, dismiss, expel, freeze, hang, hold in abeyance, hold (off), interrupt, postpone,

put off, send home, shelve, sideline, stay, stop, swing, waive, withhold.

antonyms continue, expedite, reinstate, restore.

suspended *adj* dangling, hanging, in abeyance, pendent, pending, pensile, put on hold, put on ice, shelved, unenforced, waived.

suspense *n* anticipation, anxiety, apprehension, doubt, excitement, expectancy, expectation, incertitude, indecision, irresolution, pins and needles, tension, tenterhooks, uncertainty.

antonyms certainty, knowledge.

suspension *n* abeyance, adjournment, break, cessation, deferment, deferral, delay, diapause, disbarment, discontinuation, dismissal, ellipsis, dormancy, intermission, interruption, moratorium, postponement, remission, respite, standstill, stay.

antonyms continuation, reinstatement, restoration.

suspicion *n* apprehension, chariness, conjecture, distrust, doubt, (funny) feeling, glimmer, guess, hint, hunch, idea, impression, intuition, jealousy, leeriness, misgiving, mistrust, notion, presentiment, scepticism, shade, shadow, soupçon, suggestion, supposition, surmise, suspiciousness, tinge, touch, trace, wariness.

antonym trust.

suspicious *adj* apprehensive, chary, distrustful, doubtful, dubious, fishy, incredulous, irregular, jealous, leery, mistrustful, peculiar, queer, questionable, sceptical, shady, suspect, suspecting, unbelieving, uneasy, wary.

antonyms innocent, trustful, unexceptionable.

sustain *v* aid, approve, assist, bear, bear up, buoy up, carry, comfort, confirm, continue, endorse, endure, experience, feel, foster, help, hold up, incur, keep going, keep up, lend support to, maintain, nourish, nurture, prolong, protract, provide for, ratify, sanction, stay, suffer, support, undergo, uphold, validate, verify, withstand.

sustained *adj* constant, continuous, long-drawn, non-stop, perpetual, prolonged, protracted, steady, unremitting.

antonyms broken, intermittent, interrupted, occasional, spasmodic.

sustenance *n* aliment, board, comestibles, commons, eatables, edibles, fare, food, livelihood, maintenance, nourishment, nutriment, pabulum, provender, provisions, rations, refection, refreshments, subsistence, support, upkeep, viands, victuals.

svelte *adj* elegant, graceful, lissome, lithe, shapely, slender, slim, streamlined, sylphlike, willowy.

antonyms bulky, ungainly.

swagger *v* bluster, boast, brag, crow, gasconade, hector, parade, peacock, prance, roister, show off, strut, swank.

n arrogance, bluster, boastfulness, boasting, braggadocio, display, fanfaronade, gasconade, ostentation, rodomontade, show, showing off, swank, vainglory.

antonyms diffidence, modesty, restraint.

swaggerer *n* attitudinizer, blusterer, boaster, braggadocio, braggart, cock of the walk, gascon, hector, loudmouth, peacock, poser, poseur, posturer, roisterer, scaramouch, show-off, strutter, swank, swashbuckler.

swallow *v* absorb, accept, assimilate, believe, buy, choke down (or back), consume, devour, down, drink, eat, eat up, engorge, engulf, gobble, gulp down, guzzle, imbibe, ingest, ingurgitate, keep back, knock back, quaff, repress, stifle, suppress, swig, swill, wash down.

swallow up absorb, consume, deplete, destroy, drain, eat up, engulf, envelop, exhaust, gobble up, overwhelm, use up, waste.

swamp *n* bog, everglades, fen, marsh, mire, morass, muskeg, quagmire, quicksand, slough, wash, wetland.

v besiege, deluge, drench, engulf, flood, inundate, overload, overwhelm, saturate, submerge, waterlog.

swampy *adj* boggy, fenny, marshy, miry, mushy, quaggy, soggy, squelchy, waterlogged, wet.

antonyms arid, dehydrated, dry.

swank *v* attitudinize, boast, parade, peacock, posture, preen oneself, show off, strut, swagger.

n boastfulness, conceit, conceitedness, display, ostentation, pretentiousness, self-advertisement, show, showing-off, swagger, vainglory.

antonyms modesty, restraint.

swanky *adj* chic, deluxe, exclusive, expensive, fancy, fashionable, flashy, glamorous, grand, lavish, luxurious, magnificent, ostentatious, plush, posh, pretentious, rich, ritzy, showy, smart, stylish, sumptuous, swell, swish.

antonyms discreet, unobtrusive.

swap *v* bandy, barter, exchange, interchange, substitute, switch, trade, traffic, transpose.

swarm *n* army, bevy, concourse, crowd, drove, flock, herd, horde, host, mass, mob, multitude, myriad, shoal, throng.

v congregate, crowd, flock, flood, mass, overrun, stream, throng.

swarm with abound with, bristle with, crawl with, teem with.

swarthy *adj* black, brown, dark, dark-coloured, dark-complexioned, dark-skinned, dusky, tawny.

antonyms fair, pale.

swashbuckling *adj* adventurous, blustering, boasting, bold, bullying, daredevil, dashing, exciting, flamboyant, gallant, hectoring, mettlesome, rip-roaring, roisterous, spirited, swaggering.

antonyms tame, unadventurous, unexciting.

swathe *v* bandage, bind, cloak, drape, enfold, enshroud, envelop, enwrap, fold, lap, sheathe, shroud, swaddle, wind, wrap (up).

antonyms unwind, unwrap.

sway *v* affect, bend, control, divert, fluctuate, induce, influence, lean, lurch, move, oscillate, overrule, persuade, pitch, reel, rock, roll, swerve, swing, teeter, veer, wave.

n ascendency, authority, clout, command, control, dominion, government, hegemony, influence, jurisdiction, leadership, power, predominance, rule, sovereignty, supremacy, swerve, swing.

swear¹ *v* affirm, assert, asseverate, attest, avow, declare, depose, insist, promise, testify, vow, warrant.

swear² *v* blaspheme, curse, cuss, imprecate, maledict, take the Lord's name in vain, turn the air blue, use profanity.

swearing *n* bad language (or words), billingsgate, blasphemy, cursing, cussing, expletives, foul language, imprecations, invective, maledictions, profanity.

swearword *n* blasphemy, curse, dirty word, expletive, four-letter word, imprecation, oath, obscenity, profanity.

sweat *n* agitation, anxiety, chore, dew, diaphoresis, distress, drudgery, effort, exudation, fag, flap, hidrosis, labour, panic, perspiration, strain, sudor, toil, work, worry.

v agonize, chafe, exude, fret, glow, perspire, strain, swelter, toil, work, worry.

sweaty *adj* bathed in sweat, clammy, damp, glowing, moist, perspiring, sticky, sweating.

antonyms cool, dry.

sweep *v* brush, career, carry (along), clean, clear, dust, flounce, fly, glance, glide, hurtle, knock, pass (over), remove, sail, scud, skim, tear, whisk, zoom.

n arc, bend, clearance, compass, curve, expanse, extent, gesture, impetus, move, movement, onrush, panorama, range, scope, span, stretch, stroke, swing, vista.

sweeping *adj* across-the-board, all-embracing, all-encompassing, all-inclusive, blanket, broad, comprehensive, exaggerated, extensive, far-reaching, global, indiscriminate, overdrawn, overgeneralized, oversimplified, overstated, radical, simplistic, thoroughgoing, unanalytical, unqualified, wholesale, wide, wide-ranging.

sweet¹ *adj* adorable, affectionate, agreeable, amiable, appealing, aromatic, attractive, balmy, beautiful, beloved, benign, charming, cherished, clean, cloying, cute, darling, dear, dearest, delightful, dulcet, endearing, engaging, euphonic, euphonious, fair, fragrant, fresh, gentle, good-natured, gracious, gratifying, harmonious, honeyed, lovable, luscious, mellow, melodious, melting, mild, musical, new, perfumed, pet, pleasing, precious, pure, redolent, saccharine, sickly, silver-toned, silvery, soft, suave, sugary, sweetened, sweet-smelling, sweet-sounding, sweet-tempered, syrupy, taking, tender, toothsome, treasured, tuneful, unselfish, wholesome, winning, winsome.

antonyms acid, bitter, cacophonous, discordant, malodorous, salty, sour, unpleasant.

sweet² *n* bonbon, candy, confection, dessert, sweetmeat.

sweeten *v* alleviate, appease, candy, candy-coat, cushion, honey, mellow, mollify, pacify, soften, soothe, sugar, sugar-coat, take the sting out of, temper.

antonyms aggravate, embitter, jaundice.

sweetheart *n* admirer, beau, beloved, betrothed, boyfriend, darling, dear, Dulcinea, flame, follower, girlfriend, inamorata, inamorato, ladylove, love, lover, Romeo, steady, suitor, swain, sweetie, truelove, valentine.

sweetness *n* amiability, balminess, charm, euphony, fragrance, freshness, harmony, kindness, loveliness, lusciousness, mellowness, suavity, succulence, sugariness, sweet temper, syrup, tenderness, winsomeness.

antonyms acidity, bitterness, cacophony, nastiness, saltness, sourness.

sweet-smelling *adj* ambrosial, aromatic, balmy, fragrant, odoriferous, odorous, perfumed, redolent, sweet-scented.

antonyms fetid, malodorous.

swell¹ *v* aggravate, augment, balloon, belly, billow, bloat, bulge, dilate, distend, enhance, enlarge, expand, extend, fatten, grow, heave, heighten, increase, inflate, intensify, intumesce, mount, protrude, rise, surge, tumefy.

antonyms contract, dwindle, shrink.

n billow, bore, bulge, distension, eagre, enlargement, increase, rise, surge, swelling, undulation, wave.

swell² *adj* deluxe, exclusive, fashionable, flashy, grand, grandiose, posh, ritzy, smart, stylish, swanky, swish.

antonyms seedy, shabby.

swelling *n* blister, boll, bulb, bulge, bump, dilation, distension, edema, emphysema, enlargement, gathering, gout, inflammation, intumescence, lump, protuberance, puffiness, tuber, tubercle, tumefaction, tumescence, tumour.

sweltering *adj* airless, baking, broiling, burning, hot, humid, oppressive, perspiring, scorching, steamy, stifling, suffocating, sultry, sweating, torrid, tropical.

antonyms airy, breezy, chilly, cold, cool, fresh.

swerve *v* bend, deflect, deviate, diverge, sheer, shift, skew, stray, sway, swing, turn (aside), veer, wander.

swift *adj* abrupt, agile, expeditious, express, fast, fleet, fleet-footed, flying, hurried, immediate, limber, nimble, precipitate, prompt, quick, rapid, ready, speedy, sudden, summary, swift-footed, winged.

antonyms slow, sluggish, tardy.

swiftly *adj* at full tilt, double-quick, expeditiously, express, fast, hotfoot, hurriedly, immediately, instantly, on the double, posthaste, promptly, quickly, rapidly, speedily, summarily, without delay.

antonyms slowly, tardily.

swiftness *n* celerity, dispatch, expedition, fleetness, immediacy, immediateness, instantaneousness, promptness, quickness, rapidity, readiness, speed, speediness, suddenness, velocity.

antonyms delay, slowness, tardiness.

swill *v* booze, consume, drain, drink, gulp, guzzle, imbibe, knock back, quaff, swallow, swig, swizzle, toss off.

n hogwash, mash, mush, offal, pigswill, refuse, scourings, slops, waste.

swill out cleanse, drench, flush, rinse, sluice, wash down, wash out.

swindle *v* bamboozle, bilk, bunco, cheat, chicane, chisel, con, deceive, defraud, diddle, do, dupe, fiddle, finagle, fleece, flimflam, grift, gull, gyp, hornswoggle, overcharge, rip off, rook, scam, sell one a bill of goods, sell smoke, skin, trick.

n chicanery, con, deceit, deception, double-dealing, fakery, fiddle, fraud, grift, gyp, knavery, racket, rip-off, roguery, scam, sharp practice, shenanigans, skin game, trickery.

swindler *n* charlatan, cheat, chiseller, con artist, con man, crook, flimflammer, fraud, grifter, impostor, knave, mountebank, rascal, rogue, rook, shark, sharper, slicker, spieler, trickster.

swine *n* beast, boar, boor, brute, cad, heel, hog, pig, reptile, rotter, scoundrel, slob.

swing *v* accomplish, arrange, bat, brandish, bring off, carry off, dangle, fluctuate, fly, hang, hurl, influence, manage, oscillate, rock, strike (at), succeed, suspend, sway, swerve, swivel, vary, veer, vibrate, wave, whirl.

n fluctuation, impetus, oscillation, rhythm, scope, stroke, sway, sweep, vibration, waving.

swing round curve, gyrate, pivot, revolve, rotate, spin, swivel, turn, twirl, wheel (round).

swinging *adj* contemporary, dynamic, fashionable, fast, groovy, hip, jetsetting, lively, modern, stylish, tony, trendy, up-to-date, up-to-the-minute, with it.

antonyms old-fashioned, square.

swipe *v* appropriate, bat, clip, filch, hit, lift, make off with, nip, pilfer, pinch, purloin, slap, snaffle, snitch, sock, steal, strike, thwack, walk off with, wallop, whack.

n blow, clip, clout, cuff, slap, smack, thwack, wallop, whack.

swirl *v* agitate, boil, churn, eddy, purl, spin, twirl, twist, wheel, whirl.

swish *v* lash, rustle, stir, swirl, switch, swoosh, thrash, twitch, wave, whish, whisk, whistle, whiz(z), whoosh.

switch¹ *v* about-face, change course (or direction), change (over), chop and change, convert, deflect, deviate, divert, exchange, interchange, rearrange, replace, shift, shunt, substitute, swap, take turns, trade, turn, veer.

n about-face, about turn, alteration, change, change of direction, changeover, conversion, exchange, interchange, reversal, shift, shunt, substitution, swap, transition.

switch² v birch, flog, jerk, lash, swish, twitch, wave, whip, whisk.
n birch, cane, jerk, rod, twig, whip, whisk.

swivel v gyrate, pirouette, pivot, revolve, rotate, spin, swing round, turn, twirl, wheel.

swollen adj bloated, bulbous, bulging, distended, dropsical, edematous, emphysematous, enlarged, full, inflamed, intumescent, puffed up, puffy, tumescent, tumid, turgid, ventricular.
antonyms contracted, emaciated, shrunken.

swoop v descend, dive, drop, fall, lunge, plunge, pounce, rush, stoop, sweep.
n attack, descent, drop, lunge, onslaught, plunge, pounce, rush, stoop, sweep.

sword n bilbo, blade, broadsword, claymore, cutlass, épée, Excalibur, foil, rapier, sabre, scimitar, steel.

sworn adj attested, confirmed, devoted, eternal, implacable, inveterate, relentless.

sybarite n bon vivant, epicure, hedonist, one of the idle rich, playboy, pleasure seeker, sensualist, voluptuary.
antonyms ascetic, toiler.

sybaritic adj easy, epicurean, hedonistic, Lucullian, luxurious, luxury-loving, pleasure-loving, pleasure-seeking, self-indulgent, sensual, voluptuous.
antonym ascetic.

sycophant n apple-polisher, backscratcher, bootlicker, cringer, fawner, flatterer, flunky, groveller, hanger-on, lackey, lickspittle, slave, toadeater, toady, truckler, yes man.

sycophantic adj backscratching, bootlicking, cringing, fawning, flattering, grovelling, ingratiating, kowtowing, obsequious, servile, slavish, slimy, smarmy, timeserving, toadeating, toadying, truckling, unctuous.

syllabus n calendar, catalogue, course, curriculum, plan, program, schedule, timetable.

syllogism n argument, deduction, proposition.

sylphlike adj elegant, graceful, lithe, slender, slight, slim, streamlined, svelte, willowy.
antonyms bulky, plump.

sylvan adj arboreal, arboreous, bosky, forestal, forested, leafy, tree-covered, treed, wooded, woodland.
antonym treeless.

symbiotic adj commensal, co-operative, endophytic, epizoic, interactive, interdependent, synergetic.

symbol n badge, character, emblem, figure, ideogram, image, logo, logogram, mandala, mark, representation, rune, sign, token, type.

symbolic adj allegorical, allusive, emblematic, figurative, iconic, indicative, metaphorical, representative, ritual, significant, symbolic, token, typical.

symbolize v betoken, connote, denote, designate, emblematize, exemplify, mean, personate, personify, represent, signify, stand for, typify.

symmetrical adj balanced, corresponding, isometric, parallel, proportional, regular, well-balanced, well-proportioned, well-rounded.
antonyms asymmetrical, irregular.

symmetry n agreement, balance, correspondence, evenness, form, harmony, isometry, order, parallelism, proportion, regularity.
antonyms asymmetry, irregularity.

sympathetic adj affectionate, agreeable, appreciative, caring, comforting, commiserating, companionable, compassionate, compatible, concerned, condoling, congenial, consoling, empathetic, exorable, feeling, friendly, in accord, interested, kind, kindly, like-minded, pitying, responsive, sensitive, supportive, tender, understanding, warm, warm-hearted, well-intentioned, well-wishing.
antonyms antipathetic, callous, indifferent, unsympathetic.

sympathize v agree, commiserate, condole, empathize, feel (for), identify (with), pity, relate (to), respond (to), side (with), understand.
antonyms disapprove, dismiss, disregard, ignore, oppose.

sympathizer n adherent, admirer, backer, condoler, fan, fellow traveller, friend, partisan, supporter, well-wisher.
antonyms enemy, opponent.

sympathy n accord, affinity, agreement, comfort, commiseration, compassion, condolence, condolences, congeniality, correspondence, empathy, fellow feeling, harmony, pity, rapport, responsiveness, tenderness, thoughtfulness, understanding, warmth.
antonyms callousness, disharmony, incompatibility, indifference.

symptom n concomitant, diagnostic, evidence, expression, feature, hint, indication, manifestation, mark, note, sign, syndrome, token, warning (sign).

symptomatic adj associated (with), characteristic, evidential, indicative, suggestive, typical.

syndicate n alliance, association, bloc, cartel, combination, combine, group, ring.

synonymous adj co-extensive, comparable, corresponding, equal, equivalent, exchangeable, identical, interchangeable, parallel, similar, substitutable, tantamount, the same.
antonyms antonymous, dissimilar, opposite.

synopsis n abridgment, abstract, aperçu, compendium, condensation, conspectus, digest, epitome, outline, précis, recapitulation, résumé, review, run-down, sketch, summary, summation.

synthesis n alloy, amalgam, amalgamation, blend, coalescence, combination, composite, compound, fusion, integration, pastiche, syncretization, unification, union, welding.

synthesize v amalgamate, blend, coalesce, combine, compound, fuse, integrate, manufacture, merge, syncretize, unify, unite, weld.

antonyms   analyse, resolve, separate.

synthetic *adj*   artificial, bogus, ersatz, fake, imitation, manufactured, mock, plastic, pseudo, simulated.

antonyms   genuine, real.

system   *n*   arrangement, classification, co-ordination, logic, method, methodicalness, methodology, mode, modus operandi, orderliness, organization, plan, practice, procedure, process, regularity, routine, rule, scheme, setup, structure, systematization, tabulation, taxis, taxonomy, technique, theory, usage, way.

systematic *adj*   businesslike, efficient, habitual, intentional, logical, methodical, ordered, orderly, organized, planned, precise, regular, standardized, systematized, well-ordered, well-planned.

antonyms   disorderly, inefficient, unsystematic.

systematize   *v*   arrange, classify, dispose, make uniform, methodize, order, organize, plan, rationalize, regiment, regulate, schematize, standardize, tabulate.

T

tab *n* bill, check, cost, docket, flag, flap, label, marker, sticker, tag, ticket.

tabby *adj* banded, brindled, moiré, mottled, streaked, striped, stripy, variegated, watered, wavy.

table *n* agenda, altar, array, bench, board, booth, buffet, catalogue, chart, counter, diagram, diet, digest, display, fare, flat(s), flatland, food, graph, index, inventory, list, paradigm, plain, plan, plateau, record, register, roll, schedule, slab, spread, stall, stand, syllabus, synopsis, tableland, victuals.

v propose, put forward, submit, suggest.

tableau *n* diorama, picture, portrayal, representation, scene, spectacle, tableau vivant, vignette.

taboo *adj* accursed, anathema, banned, forbidden, inviolable, outlawed, prohibited, proscribed, sacrosanct, unacceptable, unmentionable, unsayable, unthinkable, verboten.

antonym acceptable.

n anathema, ban, curse, disapproval, interdict, interdiction, prohibition, proscription, restriction.

tabulate *v* arrange, catalogue, categorize, chart, classify, codify, index, list, order, range, sort, systematize, table, tabularize.

tacit *adj* implicit, implied, inferred, silent, ulterior, undeclared, understood, unexpressed, unprofessed, unspoken, unstated, unuttered, unvoiced, voiceless, wordless.

antonyms explicit, express, spoken, stated.

taciturn *adj* aloof, antisocial, cold, distant, dumb, mute, quiet, reserved, reticent, saturnine, silent, tight-lipped, uncommunicative, unconversable, unforthcoming, unsociable, withdrawn.

antonyms communicative, forthcoming, sociable, talkative.

tack *n* approach, attack, bearing, course, direction, harness, heading, line, loop, method, nail, path, pin, plan, procedure, pushpin, route, staple, stitch, tactic, thumbtack, way.

v add, affix, annex, append, attach, baste, change direction, fasten, fix, join, nail, pin, staple, stitch, zigzag.

tackle¹ *n* accoutrements, apparatus, equipment, gear, harness, implements, outfit, paraphernalia, rig, rigging, tackling, tools, trappings.

v attach, harness.

tackle² *n* attack, block, challenge, interception, intervention, stop.

v approach, attack, attempt, begin, block, challenge, clutch, confront, deal with, embark upon, encounter, engage in, essay, face head-on, face up to, go about, grab, grapple with, grasp, halt, intercept, lunge at, seize, set about, stop, take a crack (or stab) at, take on, throw, try, undertake, wade into.

antonyms avoid, sidestep.

tacky *adj* adhesive, cheap, crass, gimcrack, gluey, gummy, messy, nasty, schlocky, scruffy, seedy, shabby, shoddy, sleazy, sticky, tasteless, tatty, tawdry, vulgar, wet.

antonyms classy, elegant.

tact *n* address, adroitness, consideration, delicacy, diplomacy, discernment, discretion, finesse, grace, judgment, perception, prudence, savoir-faire, sensitivity, skill, thoughtfulness, understanding.

antonyms clumsiness, indiscretion, tactlessness.

tactful *adj* careful, considerate, delicate, diplomatic, discerning, discreet, graceful, judicious, perceptive, polished, polite, politic, prudent, sensitive, skilful, subtle, thoughtful, understanding.

antonym tactless.

tactic(s) *n* approach, campaign, course, device, gambit, game plan, line (of attack), manoeuvre(s), means, method, move(s), plan of attack, plan(s), ploy(s), policy, procedure, ruse, scheme, shift, stratagem(s), strategy, subterfuge, tack, trick, way.

tactical *adj* adroit, artful, calculated, clever, cunning, diplomatic, judicious, politic, prudent, shrewd, skilful, smart, strategic.

antonym impolitic.

tactician *n* brain, campaigner, co-ordinator, director, mastermind, orchestrator, planner, politician, (smooth) operator, strategist.

tactless *adj* blundering, boorish, careless, clumsy, crass, discourteous, gauche, hurtful, ill-timed, impolite, impolitic, imprudent, inappropriate, inconsiderate, indelicate, indiscreet, inept, insensitive, maladroit, oafish, rough, rude, thoughtless, uncivil, undiplomatic, unfeeling, unkind, unsubtle.

antonym tactful.

tag *n*   aglet, aiguillette, appellation, badge, designation, docket, epithet, identification, label, mark, marker, name, note, slip, sticker, stub, tab, tally, ticket.
v   add, adjoin, affix, annex, append, call, christen, designate, earmark, fasten, identify, label, mark, name, nickname, style, tack, term, ticket.

tag along   accompany, attend, dog, follow, hang round, shadow, tail, trail.

tail *n*   appendage, backside, behind, bottom, bum, butt, buttocks, conclusion, croup, detective, duff, empennage, end, extremity, follower, line, posterior, queue, rear, rear end, retinue, rump, scut, suite, tailpiece, train.
v   dog, follow, shadow, spy on, stalk, stay with, track, trail.

tail off   decrease, die, die out (or away), drop, dwindle, fade, fail, fall away, peter out, tail away, taper off, wane.

antonyms   grow, increase.

tailor *n*   clothier, costumer, costumier, costumière, couturier, couturière, dressmaker, garment maker, modiste, outfitter, seamstress.
v   accommodate, adapt, adjust, alter, convert, customize, cut, fashion, fit, modify, mould, shape, style, suit, trim.

tailor-made *adj*   custom-built, custom-made, fitted, ideal, made-to-measure, perfect, right, suitable, suited.

antonyms   ill-adapted, unsuitable.

taint *v*   adulterate, besmirch, blacken, blemish, blight, blot, brand, contaminate, corrupt, damage, defile, deprave, dirty, disgrace, dishonour, envenom, foul, infect, muddy, poison, pollute, ruin, shame, smear, smirch, soil, spoil, stain, stigmatize, sully, tarnish, vitiate.
n   blemish, blot, contagion, contamination, corruption, defect, disgrace, dishonour, fault, flaw, infamy, infection, obloquy, odium, opprobrium, pollution, shame, smear, smirch, spot, stain, stigma.

take *v*   abduct, abide, abstract, accept, accommodate, accompany, acquire, adopt, appropriate, arrest, ascertain, assume, attract, bear, believe, betake, bewitch, blight, book, brave, bring, brook, buy, call for, captivate, capture, carry, cart, catch, charm, clutch, conduct, consider, consume, contain, convey, convoy, deduct, deem, delight, demand, derive, detract, do, drink, eat, effect, eliminate, enchant, endure, engage, ensnare, entrap, escort, execute, fascinate, ferry, fetch, filch, gather, glean, grasp, grip, guide, haul, have, have room for, hire, hold, imbibe, ingest, inhale, lead, lease, make, measure, misappropriate, necessitate, need, observe, obtain, operate, perceive, perform, photograph, pick, pinch, please, pocket, portray, presume, purchase, purloin, receive, regard, remove, rent, require, reserve, secure, seize, select, stand, steal, stomach, strike, subtract, succeed, suffer, swallow, swipe, tolerate, tote, transport, undergo, understand, undertake, usher, weather, win, withstand, work.
n   bottom line, catch, gate, haul, income, proceeds, profits, receipts, return, revenue, takings, yield.

take aback   astonish, astound, bewilder, disconcert, dismay, flabbergast, floor, nonplus, stagger, startle, stun, surprise, throw for a loop, upset.

take apart   analyse, disassemble, dismantle, resolve, take down, take to pieces.

take back   eat (one's words), recant, reclaim, regain, repossess, retract, unsay, withdraw.

take down   abase, cut down to size, deflate, demolish, disassemble, dismantle, humble, humiliate, level, lower, minute, mortify, note, put down, put in one's place, raze, record, reduce, set down, strike, take apart, transcribe, unstep, write.

take effect   act, be effective, become operative, begin, come into force, kick in, work.

take heart   brighten up, buck up, cheer up, perk up, rally, revive.

antonym   despair.

take in   absorb, accommodate, admit, annex, appreciate, assimilate, bamboozle, bilk, bluff, catch, cheat, clip, comprehend, comprise, con, contain, cover, cozen, deceive, digest, do, dupe, embrace, enclose, encompass, fool, furl, grasp, gull, hoodwink, imagine, include, incorporate, kid, mislead, note, notice, observe, realize, receive, register, shelter, soak, subdue, swindle, tighten, trick, understand.

take issue with   call in question, challenge, disagree, dispute, object to, oppose, quarrel, question, take exception to.

take off   beat it, bloom, burgeon, caricature, decamp, deduct, depart, disappear, discard, divest, doff, drop, expand, flourish, go, imitate, lampoon, leave, mimic, mock, parody, remove, rise, rush away, satirize, scarper, send up, soar, spoof, start, strip, subtract, take wing, travesty, vamoose.

take offence   be miffed, be put out (or off), get huffy, sulk, take it amiss.

take on   accept, acquire, assume, complain, contend with, employ, engage, enlist, enrol, face, fight, grieve, lament, oppose, retain, tackle, undertake, vie with.

take part   associate oneself, be instrumental, be involved, join, partake, participate, play a part, share, take a hand.

take pity on   feel compassion for, forgive, give quarter, have mercy on, pardon, pity, reprieve, show mercy, spare.

take place   befall, betide, come about, come off, come to pass, fall, happen, occur, transpire.

take stock   appraise, assess, check out, estimate, size up, survey, weigh up.

take the plunge   commit oneself, cross the Rubicon, decide, pop the question.

take to task   blame, bring up short, censure, chew out, criticize, lecture, rebuke, reprimand, reproach, reprove, scold, tell off, upbraid.

antonyms   commend, praise.

take up absorb, accept, adopt, affect, assume, begin, carry on, consume, continue, cover, engage in, engross, fill, lift, monopolize, occupy, pick up, proceed with, raise, recommence, restart, resume, shorten, start, use up.

takeoff *n* burlesque, caricature, imitation, lampoon, mimicry, parody, pasquinade, spoof, travesty.

takeover *n* amalgamation, coalition, combination, coup, incorporation, merger.

taking *adj* alluring, appealing, attractive, beguiling, captivating, catching, charming, compelling, delightful, enchanting, engaging, fascinating, fetching, intriguing, pleasing, prepossessing, winning, winsome.

antonyms repellent, repulsive, unattractive.

takings *n* earnings, emoluments, gain, gate, haul, income, pickings, proceeds, profits, receipts, returns, revenue, take, yield.

tale *n* account, anecdote, fable, fabrication, falsehood, fib, fiction, legend, lie, myth, narration, narrative, relation, report, rigmarole, romance, rumour, saga, spiel, story, superstition, tall story, tradition, untruth, yarn.

talent *n* ability, aptitude, bent, capacity, endowment, faculty, feel, flair, forte, genius, gift, knack, long suit, power, strength.

antonyms inability, ineptitude, weakness.

talented *adj* able, accomplished, adept, adroit, apt, artistic, brilliant, capable, clever, deft, gifted, ingenious, inspired.

antonyms clumsy, inept, maladroit.

talisman *n* amulet, charm, fetish, juju, mascot, phylactery.

talk *v* articulate, blab, blather, breathe, buzz, chat, chatter, commune, communicate, confabulate, confer, converse, gab, gossip, inform, jaw, natter, negotiate, palaver, parley, prate, prattle, rap, rattle on, say, sing, speak, squeak, squeal, utter, verbalize, whisper, yak.
n address, argot, blather, bull session, buzz, causerie, chat, chatter, chinwag, chit-chat, colloquy, conclave, confab, confabulation, conference, consultation, conversation, dialect, dialogue, discourse, discussion, disquisition, dissertation, dope, gab, gossip, harangue, hearsay, hot air, jargon, jaw, jawing, language, lecture, lingo, meeting, natter, negotiation, oration, palaver, parley, patois, patter, pitch, rap, rumour, scuttlebutt, seminar, sermon, slang, speech, spiel, symposium, tête-à-tête, tittle-tattle, utterance, words.

talk big bluster, boast, brag, crow, exaggerate, mouth off, swank, talk it up, vaunt.

talk into argue into, bring around, coax, convince, encourage, influence, overrule, persuade, sway, win over.
antonym dissuade.

talk out of caution, deter, discourage, dissuade, expostulate with (about), head off, put off, remonstrate with (about).

talkative *adj* chatty, communicative, conversational, effusive, expansive, forthcoming, gabby, garrulous, gossipy, long-tongued, long-winded, loquacious, prating, prolix, unreserved, verbose, vocal, voluble, wordy.

antonyms reserved, taciturn.

talker *n* blabbermouth, blatherskite, chatterbox, conversationalist, gabber, gossip, natterer, prattler, spieler, windbag, yakker.

talking-to *n* criticism, dressing-down, earful, jaw, lecture, rebuke, reprimand, reproach, reproof, row, scolding, slating, telling-off,.

antonyms commendation, congratulation, praise.

tall[1] *adj* big, elevated, giant, great, high, lanky, leggy, lofty, soaring, steep, towering.

antonyms low, short, small.

tall[2] *adj* absurd, dubious, embellished, exaggerated, far-fetched, grandiloquent, implausible, improbable, incredible, overblown, preposterous, remarkable, unbelievable, unlikely.

antonym reasonable.

tally *v* accord, add, agree, chalk up, check (out), coincide, compute, concur, conform, correspond, figure, fit, harmonize, jibe, jive, mark, match, parallel, reckon, record, register, score, square, suit, tie in, total.

antonyms differ, disagree.

n account, check mark, count, counterfoil, counterpart, credit, duplicate, label, mark, match, mate, notch, reckoning, record, score, stub, tab, tag, total.

tame *adj* amenable, biddable, bland, bloodless, boring, broken, compliant, cultivated, disciplined, docile, domesticated, dull, feeble, flat, gentle, humdrum, insipid, lifeless, manageable, meek, obedient, prosaic, safe, spiritless, subdued, submissive, tedious, tractable, unadventurous, unenterprising, unexciting, uninspired, uninspiring, uninteresting, unresisting, vapid, wearisome.

antonyms exciting, rebellious, unmanageable, wild.

v break in, bridle, calm, conquer, curb, discipline, domesticate, enslave, gentle, house-train, humble, master, mellow, mitigate, mute, pacify, quell, repress, soften, subdue, subjugate, suppress, temper, train.

tamper (with) *v* alter, bribe, cook, corrupt, damage, fiddle, fix, influence, interfere, intrude, juggle, manipulate, meddle, mess, rig, tinker.

tang *n* aroma, bite, flavour, hint, kick, overtone, piquancy, pungency, savour, scent, sharpness, smack, smell, suggestion, tartness, taste, tinge, touch, trace, whiff.

tangible *adj* actual, concrete, corporeal, definite, discernible, evident, manifest, material, objective, observable, palpable, perceptible, physical, positive, real, real live, sensible, solid, substantial, tactile, touchable.

antonym intangible.

tangle *n* coil, complication, confusion, convolution, embroilment, entanglement, fix, hassle, hodgepodge, imbroglio, jam, jumble, jungle, knot, labyrinth, mass, mat, maze, mesh, mess, mix-up, muddle, raffle, ravel, snarl, snarl-up, twist, web.

v catch, coil, confuse, convolve, embroil, enmesh, ensnare, entangle, entrap, hamper, implicate, interlace, interlock, intertwine, intertwist, interweave, involve, jam, knot, mat, mesh, muddle, ravel, snarl, trap, twist.

antonym disentangle.

tangled *adj* complex, complicated, confused, convoluted, dishevelled, entangled, intricate, involved, jumbled, knotted, knotty, matted, messy, mixed-up, muddled, ravelled, scrambled, snarled, tortuous, tousled, twisted, unkempt.

antonyms clear, free.

tangy *adj* biting, bitter, fresh, gamy, piquant, pungent, savoury, sharp, spicy, strong, tart.

antonym insipid.

tank *n* aquarium, basin, boiler, cistern, container, reservoir, vat.

tantalize *v* baffle, bait, balk, entice, frustrate, lead on, play upon, provoke, taunt, tease, thwart, titillate, torment, torture.

antonym satisfy.

tantamount (to) *adj* as good as, commensurate (with), equal (to), equivalent (to), synonymous (with), the same (as), virtually.

tantrum *n* fit, flare-up, fury, hysterics, outburst, paroxysm, rage, scene, storm, temper.

tap[1] *v* beat, clip, dab, drum, knock, pat, rap, slap, strike, touch.

n beat, clip, dab, knock, pat, rap, rat-tat, slap, touch.

tap[2] *n* bung, faucet, plug, receiver, spigot, spile, spout, stopcock, stopper, valve.

v access, bleed, broach, drain, draw (on), exploit, give access to, milk, mine, open, pierce, quarry, siphon off, unplug, use, utilize, wiretap.

tape *n* band, binding, magnetic tape, ribbon, strip, tape measure.

v bind, measure, mend, record, seal, secure, stick, tape-record, video, wrap.

taper (off) *v* attenuate, decrease, die away, die out, dwindle, ebb, fade, lessen, narrow, peter out, reduce, slim, subside, tail off, thin, wane, weaken.

antonyms increase, swell, widen.

tardily *adv* at the eleventh hour, at the last minute, belatedly, late, late in the day, slowly, sluggishly, unpunctually.

antonyms promptly, punctually.

tardy *adj* backward, behindhand, belated, dawdling, delayed, dilatory, eleventh-hour, lag, last-minute, late, loitering, overdue, procrastinating, retarded, slack, slow, sluggish, unpunctual.

antonyms prompt, punctual.

target *n* aim, ambition, bull's-eye, butt, destination, end, goal, intention, mark, object, objective, prey, purpose, quarry, scapegoat, victim.

tariff *n* assessment, bill of fare, charges, customs, duty, excise, impost, levy, menu, price list, rate, schedule, tax, toll.

tarnish *v* befoul, blacken, blemish, blot, darken, dim, discolour, dull, mar, rust, soil, spoil, spot, stain, sully, taint.

antonyms brighten, enhance, polish up.

n blackening, blemish, blot, discoloration, film, patina, rust, spot, stain, taint.

antonyms brightness, polish.

tarry *v* abide, dally, dawdle, delay, dwell, lag, linger, loiter, pause, remain, rest, sojourn, stay, stop, wait.

tart[1] *n* pastry, pie, quiche, tartlet.

tart[2] *adj* acerb, acerbic, acid, acidulous, acrimonious, astringent, barbed, biting, bitter, caustic, cutting, incisive, piquant, punchy, pungent, sardonic, scathing, sharp, short, sour, tangy, trenchant, vinegary.

tart[3] *n* call girl, drab, harlot, hooker, prostitute, slut, streetwalker, strumpet, trollop, whore.

task *n* assignment, burden, business, charge, chore, duty, employment, enterprise, exercise, imposition, job, labour, mission, occupation, piece (or unit) of work, toil, undertaking, work.

v burden, charge, commit, encumber, entrust, exhaust, load, oppress, overload, push, saddle, strain, tax, test, weary.

taste *n* appetite, appreciation, bent, bit, bite, choice, correctness, cultivation, culture, dash, decorum, delicacy, desire, discernment, discretion, discrimination, drop, elegance, experience, fancy, finesse, flavour, fondness, goût, grace, gustation, inclination, judgment, leaning, liking, morsel, mouthful, nibble, nicety, nip, palate, partiality, penchant, perception, polish, politeness, predilection, preference, propriety, refinement, relish, restraint, sample, savour, sensitivity, sip, smack, soupçon, spoonful, style, swallow, tact, tactfulness, tang, tastefulness, tidbit, touch.

v assay, differentiate, discern, distinguish, encounter, experience, feel, know, meet, nibble, perceive, relish, sample, savour, sip, smack, test, try, undergo.

tasteful *adj* aesthetic, artistic, attractive, charming, comme il faut, correct, cultivated, cultured, delicate, discreet, discriminating, elegant, exquisite, graceful, harmonious, judicious, polished, refined, restrained, smart, stylish, well-judged.

antonym tasteless.

tasteless *adj* barbaric, bland, boring, cheap, coarse, crass, crude, dilute, dull, flashy, flat, flavourless, garish, gaudy, graceless, gross, improper, inartistic, indecorous, indelicate, indiscreet, inelegant, inharmonious, insipid, low, mild, rude, schlocky, stale, tacky, tactless, tame, tatty, tawdry, thin, uncouth, undiscriminating, uninspired, uninteresting, unseemly, vapid, vulgar, watered-down, watery, weak.

antonym tasteful.

tasty *adj* appetizing, delectable, delicious, flavourful, flavoursome, gusty, luscious, mouthwatering, palatable, piquant, sapid, savoury, scrumptious, succulent, toothsome, yummy.

antonyms disgusting, insipid, tasteless.

tattered *adj* frayed, in ribbons, in shreds, in tatters, lacerated, ragged, raggedy, rent, ripped, tatty, threadbare, torn.

antonyms neat, trim.

tattle *v* betray, blab, blather, divulge, gossip, inform, rat, reveal, squeal, talk, tell, tittle-tattle. *n* dirt, gossip, hearsay, rumour, tales, talk.

tattler *n* busybody, gossip, newsmonger, quidnunc, rumourmonger, scandalmonger, talebearer, taleteller, tattletale, telltale.

taunt *v* bait, boo, bug, call names, deride, gibe, insult, jeer (at), mock, provoke, razz, revile, rib, ridicule, roast, sneer (at), take a fling at, tease, torment, twit. *n* barb, boo, brickbat, catcall, censure, cut, derision, dig, gibe, insult, jab, jeer, provocation, ribbing, ridicule, sarcasm, sneer, teasing.

taut *adj* contracted, rigid, strained, stressed, stretched, tense, tensed, tight, tightened, unrelaxed.

antonyms loose, relaxed, slack.

tautology *n* duplication, iteration, otiosity, pleonasm, redundancy, repetition, repetitiousness, repetitiveness, superfluity.

antonyms economy, succinctness.

tavern *n* alehouse, bar, barroom, beer garden, beer hall, beer parlour, hostelry, inn, joint, pub, public house, roadhouse, watering hole.

tawdry *adj* cheap, cheapjack, flashy, garish, gaudy, gimcrack, glittering, loud, meretricious, pinchbeck, plastic, raffish, schlocky, showy, tacky, tasteless, tatty, tinsel, tinselly, vulgar, worthless.

antonyms excellent, fine, superior.

tawny *adj* fawn, fulvous, golden, sandy, tan, xanthous, yellow.

tax *n* assessment, burden, charge, contribution, customs, demand, drain, duty, excise, imposition, impost, levy, load, pressure, rate, strain, tariff, tithe, toll, tribute. *v* accuse, arraign, assess, blame, burden, censure, charge, demand, drain, enervate, exact, exhaust, extract, impeach, impose, impugn, incriminate, load, overburden, overtax, push, rate, reproach, sap, strain, stretch, task, tithe, try, weaken, weary.

taxing *adj* burdensome, demanding, draining, enervating, exacting, exhausting, heavy, onerous, punishing, stressful, tiring, tough, trying, wearing, wearisome.

antonyms easy, gentle, mild.

teach *v* accustom, advise, coach, counsel, demonstrate, direct, disciple, discipline, drill, edify, educate, enlighten, explain, ground, guide, impart, implant, inculcate, inform, instil, instruct, prepare (how), school, show, train, tutor, verse.

teacher *n* coach, counsellor, educationalist, educator, guide, guru, instructor, lecturer, luminary, maharishi, master, mentor, mistress, pedagogue, professor, pundit, rabbi,

schoolmarm, schoolmaster, schoolmistress, schoolteacher, trainer, tutor.

teaching *n* didactics, doctrine, dogma, education, gospel, grounding, indoctrination, instruction, pedagogy, precept, principle, schooling, tenet, training, tuition.

team *n* band, body, bunch, company, corps, crew, duo, gang, group, line-up, pair, partnership, set, shift, side, span, squad, stable, troupe, workgroup, yoke. *v* combine, couple, join, link, match, yoke.

team up band together, combine, co-operate, join, unite.

teamwork *n* collaboration, concerted effort, co-operation, co-ordination, esprit de corps, fellowship, harmony, interaction, joint effort, partnership, team spirit.

antonyms disharmony, disunity.

tear[1] *v* claw, divide, drag, gash, grab, lacerate, mangle, mutilate, pull, rend, rip, rive, rupture, scratch, seize, sever, shred, snag, snatch, split, sunder, wrench, wrest, yank. *n* hole, laceration, rent, rip, run, rupture, scratch, snag, split.

tear[2] *v* bolt, career, charge, dart, dash, fly, gallop, hurry, race, run, rush, shoot, speed, sprint, zoom.

tearful *adj* blubbering, crying, distressing, dolorous, emotional, inconsolable, lachrymose, lamentable, maudlin, mournful, pathetic, pitiable, pitiful, poignant, sad, snivelling, sobbing, sorrowful, upsetting, weeping, weepy, whimpering, woeful.

tears *n* blubbering, crying, distress, lamentation, mourning, pain, regret, sadness, snivelling, sobbing, sorrow, wailing, waterworks, weeping, whimpering, woe.

tease *v* aggravate, annoy, badger, bait, bedevil, bother, bug, chaff, get a rise out of, gibe, goad, hassle, irritate, josh, laugh at, mock, needle, pester, pick on, plague, provoke, rag, razz, rib, ride, ridicule, tantalize, taunt, torment, twit, vex, worry.

technique *n* address, adroitness, approach, art, artistry, course, craft, craftsmanship, delivery, execution, expertise, facility, fashion, knack, know-how, manner, means, method, mode, modus operandi, performance, procedure, proficiency, skill, style, system, touch, way.

tedious *adj* annoying, banal, boring, dead, deadly, drab, draggy, dreary, dry as dust, dull, fatiguing, ho-hum, humdrum, irksome, laborious, lifeless, long-drawn, monotonous, prolonged, prosaic, prosy, soporific, tiresome, tiring, unexciting, uninteresting, vapid, wearisome.

antonyms exciting, interesting.

tedium *n* banality, boredom, drabness, dreariness, dullness, ennui, lifelessness, monotony, prosiness, routine, sameness, tediousness, vapidity.

teem *v* abound, bear, brim, bristle, burst, come down in sheets (or buckets or torrents), increase, multiply, overflow, overspill, pour, produce, proliferate, pullulate, rain cats and dogs, swarm.

antonyms lack, want.

teeming *adj* abundant, alive, brimful, brimming, bristling, bursting, chock-a-block, chock-full, crawling, fruitful, full, lush, numerous, overflowing, packed, pregnant, proliferating, pullulating, replete, swarming, thick.

antonyms lacking, rare, sparse.

teenage *adj* adolescent, immature, juvenile, pre-adult, pubescent, teen, young, youthful.

teeny *adj* diminutive, itsy-bitsy, microscopic, miniature, minuscule, minute, teeny-weeny, tiny, wee.

teeter *v* balance, fluctuate, lurch, oscillate, pitch, pivot, rock, seesaw, stagger, sway, titubate, totter, tremble, vacillate, waver, wobble.

telegram *n* bulletin, cable, cablegram, dispatch, telegraph, telex, wire.

telegraph *n* cable, radiotelegraph, telegram, teleprinter, telex, wire.

v cable, flash, radio, send, signal, telex, transmit, wire.

telepathy *n* clairvoyance, E.S.P., mind reading, sixth sense, thought transference.

telephone *n* blower, handset, horn, line, phone.

v buzz, call, call up, contact, dial, get in touch, get on the horn (or blower), give someone a buzz (or ring), page, phone, ring (up).

telescope *v* abbreviate, abridge, compress, condense, contract, crush, curtail, cut, reduce, shorten, shrink, squash, trim, truncate.

television *n* idiot box, programming, receiver, set, small screen, the box, the tube, TV, TV set.

tell *v* acquaint, announce, apprise, authorize, betray, bid, blab, calculate, chronicle, command, communicate, comprehend, compute, confess, count, depict, describe, differentiate, direct, discern, disclose, discover, discriminate, distinguish, divulge, enjoin, enumerate, express, foresee, give notice, identify, impart, indicate to, inform, instruct, mention, militate, narrate, notify, number, order, portray, predict, proclaim, rat, reckon, recognize, recount, register, rehearse, relate, report, require, reveal, say, see, speak, squeal, state, summon, tally, tattle, understand, utter, weigh.

tell off bawl out, berate, castigate, censure, chew out, chide, dress down, give (someone) what for, lecture, objurgate, rebuke, reprimand, reproach, reprove, scold, take to task, tear off a strip, tick off, upbraid.

telling *adj* cogent, convincing, conclusive, definite, effective, efficacious, expressive, forceful, powerful, revealing, significant, striking, suggestive, telltale.

temerity *n* assurance, audacity, boldness, brass, brazenness, cheek, chutzpah, daring, effrontery, forwardness, gall, heedlessness, impudence, impulsiveness, intrepidity, nerve, pluck, rashness, recklessness.

antonym caution.

temper *n* anger, annoyance, attitude, bait, calm, calmness, character, composure, constitution, cool, coolness, disposition, equanimity, fury, heat, humour, ill humour, irascibility, irritability, irritation, mind, moderation, mood, nature, passion, peevishness, pet, petulance, rage, resentment, sang-froid, self-control, surliness, taking, tantrum, temperament, tenor, tranquillity, vein, wrath.

v abate, admix, allay, anneal, assuage, calm, harden, indurate, lessen, mitigate, moderate, modify, mollify, palliate, restrain, season, soften, soothe, strengthen, tone down, toughen.

temperament *n* anger, bent, character, complexion, constitution, disposition, excitability, explosiveness, hot-headedness, humour, impatience, make-up, mettle, moodiness, moods, nature, outlook, personality, petulance, quality, soul, spirit, stamp, temper, tendencies, tendency, volatility.

temperamental *adj* capricious, congenital, constitutional, emotional, erratic, excitable, explosive, fiery, highly-strung, hot-headed, hypersensitive, impatient, inborn, inconsistent, ingrained, inherent, innate, irritable, mercurial, moody, natural, neurotic, over-emotional, passionate, petulant, sensitive, touchy, undependable, unpredictable, unreliable, volatile, volcanic.

antonyms calm, serene, steady.

temperance *n* abstemiousness, abstinence, continence, discretion, forbearance, moderation, prohibition, restraint, self-abnegation, self-control, self-denial, self-discipline, self-restraint, sobriety, teetotalism.

antonyms excess, intemperance.

temperate *adj* abstemious, abstinent, agreeable, balanced, balmy, calm, clement, composed, continent, controlled, cool, dispassionate, equable, even-tempered, fair, gentle, mild, moderate, pleasant, reasonable, restrained, sensible, sober, soft, stable.

antonyms excessive, extreme, intemperate.

tempest *n* blizzard, commotion, cyclone, disturbance, duster, duststorm, ferment, furor, gale, hurricane, snowstorm, squall, storm, thunderstorm, tornado, tumult, turbulence, twister, typhoon, upheaval, uproar, whirlwind.

tempestuous *adj* agitated, blustery, boisterous, breezy, emotional, excited, feverish, furious, gusty, heated, hysterical, impassioned, intense, passionate, raging, squally, stormy, troubled, tumultuous, turbulent, uncontrolled, violent, wild, windy.

antonyms calm, quiet.

temple *n* church, fane, house, house of God (or worship), joss house, masjid, mosque, pagoda, sanctuary, shrine, stupa, synagogue, tabernacle.

tempo n beat, cadence, measure, metre, pace, pulse, rate, rhythm, speed, time, velocity.

temporal adj carnal, civil, earthly, evanescent, fleeting, fleshly, fugitive, impermanent, lay, material, momentary, mortal, mundane, passing, profane, secular, short-lived, sublunary, temporary, terrestrial, transient, transitory, unspiritual, worldly.

antonym spiritual.

temporarily adv briefly, fleetingly, for the meantime, for the moment, for the nonce, for now, for the short term, for the time being, in the interim, momentarily, pro tem, provisionally, transiently, transitorily.

antonym permanently.

temporary adj ad hoc, brief, ephemeral, evanescent, fleeting, fugitive, impermanent, interim, jury-rigged, makeshift, momentary, passing, perishable, pro tem, provisional, short-lived, stopgap, transient, transitory.

antonyms everlasting, permanent.

temporize v delay, drag one's feet, equivocate, filibuster, hang back, hem and haw, pause, play for time, procrastinate, stall, tergiversate.

tempt v allure, attract, bait, coax, dare, decoy, draw, enamour, entice, incite, inveigle, invite, lure, provoke, risk, seduce, tantalize, test, try, woo.

antonyms discourage, dissuade.

temptation n allurement, appeal, attraction, attractiveness, bait, blandishments, coaxing, come-on, decoy, draw, enticement, fascination, forbidden fruit, inducement, invitation, lure, persuasion, pull, seduction, snare.

tempting adj alluring, appetizing, attractive, enticing, inviting, mouthwatering, seductive, tantalizing.

antonyms unattractive, uninviting.

temptress n Circe, coquette, Delilah, enchantress, femme fatale, flirt, seductress, siren, sorceress, vamp.

tenable adj arguable, believable, credible, defendable, defensible, justifiable, maintainable, plausible, rational, reasonable, sound, supportable, viable.

antonyms indefensible, unjustifiable, untenable.

tenacious adj adamant, clinging, coherent, determined, dogged, fast, firm, forceful, inflexible, intransigent, obdurate, obstinate, persistent, pertinacious, resolute, retentive, single-minded, solid, staunch, steadfast, strong, strong-willed, stubborn, sure, tight, tough, unshakeable, unswerving, unwavering, unyielding.

antonyms loose, slack, weak.

tenacity n adhesiveness, application, clinginess, determination, diligence, doggedness, fastness, firmness, force, forcefulness, indomitability, inflexibility, intransigence, obduracy, obstinacy, perseverance, persistence, pertinacity, power, resoluteness, resolution, resolve, retention, retentiveness, single-mindedness, solidity, solidness, staunchness, steadfastness, stick-to-it-iveness, strength, stubbornness, toughness.

antonyms looseness, slackness, weakness.

tenancy n holding, incumbency, lease, leasehold, occupancy, occupation, possession, renting, residence, tenure.

tenant n inhabitant, landholder, leaseholder, lessee, occupant, occupier, renter, resident.

tend[1] v affect, aim, bear, bend, conduce, contribute, go, gravitate, head, incline, influence, lead, lean, move, point, trend, verge.

tend[2] v attend, care for, comfort, control, cultivate, feed, guard, handle, keep, look after, maintain, manage, minister to, nurse, nurture, protect, see to, serve, succour.

antonym neglect.

tendency n bearing, bent, bias, course, direction, disposition, drift, drive, heading, inclination, leaning, liability, movement, partiality, penchant, predilection, predisposition, proclivity, proneness, propensity, purport, readiness, susceptibility, tenor, thrust, trend, turning.

tender[1] adj aching, acute, affectionate, amoroso, amorous, benevolent, breakable, bruised, callow, caring, chary, compassionate, complicated, considerate, dangerous, delicate, difficult, emotional, fond, fragile, gentle, green, humane, immature, impressionable, inexperienced, inflamed, irritated, kind, loving, merciful, moving, new, painful, pitying, poignant, raw, romantic, scrupulous, sensitive, sentimental, smarting, soft, soft-hearted, sore, sweet, sympathetic, tender-hearted, ticklish, touching, touchy, tricky, vulnerable, warm, warm-hearted, young, youthful.

antonyms callous, chewy, hard, harsh, rough, severe, tough.

tender[2] v advance, extend, give, offer, present, proffer, propose, submit, suggest, volunteer.

n bid, currency, estimate, medium, money, offer, payment, proffer, proposal, proposition, specie, submission, suggestion.

tender-hearted adj affectionate, benevolent, benign, caring, compassionate, considerate, empathetic, feeling, fond, gentle, humane, kind, kind-hearted, kindly, loving, merciful, mild, pitying, responsive, sensitive, sentimental, soft-hearted, sympathetic, understanding, warm, warm-hearted.

antonyms callous, cruel, hard-hearted, unfeeling.

tenderness n ache, aching, affection, amorousness, attachment, benevolence, bruising, callowness, care, compassion, consideration, delicateness, devotion, discomfort, fondness, fragility, gentleness, greenness, humaneness, humanity, immaturity, impressionableness, inexperience, inflammation, irritation, kindness, liking, love, loving-kindness, mercy, newness, pain, painfulness, pity, rawness, sensitivity, sentimentality, soft-heartedness, softness, soreness, sweetness, sympathy, tender-heartedness, touchiness, vulnerability, warm-heartedness, warmth, youth, youthfulness.

antonyms cruelty, hardness, harshness.

tenet *n* article of faith, assumption, belief, canon, conviction, credo, creed, doctrine, dogma, maxim, opinion, precept, principle, rule, teaching, thesis, view.

tenor *n* burden, course, direction, drift, essence, evolution, gist, intent, meaning, path, point, purport, purpose, sense, spirit, substance, tendency, theme, tone, trend, way.

tense *adj* antsy, anxious, apprehensive, edgy, electric, exciting, fidgety, jittery, jumpy, moving, nerve-racking, nervous, overwrought, restless, rigid, stiff, strained, stressed out, stressful, stretched, strung up, suspenseful, taut, tight, uneasy, uptight, worrying.

antonyms calm, lax, loose, relaxed.

v brace, contract, strain, stretch, tighten.

antonyms loosen, relax.

tension *n* anxiety, apprehension, butterflies, edginess, hostility, nervousness, pressure, restlessness, rigidity, stiffness, strain, straining, stress, stretching, suspense, tautness, tightness, tone, unease, worry.

antonyms calm(ness), laxness, looseness, relaxation.

tent *n* big top, canvas, marquee, tabernacle, tepee, tilt, tupik, wigwam, yurt.

tentative *adj* cautious, conjectural, diffident, doubtful, experimental, exploratory, faltering, hesitant, iffy, indefinite, provisional, speculative, timid, uncertain, unconfirmed, undecided, unformulated, unsettled, unsure.

antonyms conclusive, decisive, definite, final.

tenuous *adj* attenuated, delicate, doubtful, dubious, fine, flimsy, gossamer, insignificant, insubstantial, nebulous, questionable, rarefied, shaky, sketchy, slender, slight, slim, thin, weak.

antonyms significant, strong, substantial.

tenure *n* habitation, holding, incumbency, occupancy, occupation, possession, proprietorship, residence, tenancy, term, time.

tepid *adj* apathetic, cool, half-hearted, indifferent, lukewarm, unenthusiastic, warmish.

antonyms animated, cold, hot, passionate.

tergiversation *n* apostasy, defection, desertion, equivocation, evasion, fencing, flip-flop, hedging, prevarication, seesaw, shift, shilly-shallying, shuffle, vacillation, wavering.

term[1] *n* appellation, denomination, designation, epithet, expression, locution, name, phrase, title, word.

v call, denominate, designate, entitle, label, name, style, tag, title.

term[2] *n* bound, boundary, close, conclusion, confine, course, culmination, duration, end, finish, fruition, interval, limit, period, season, session, space, span, spell, terminus, time, while.

terminal *adj* bounding, concluding, deadly, extreme, fatal, final, incurable, killing, last, lethal, limiting, mortal, ultimate, utmost.

antonym initial.

n boundary, depot, end, extremity, limit, station, termination, terminus.

terminate *v* abort, cease, close, complete, conclude, cut off, discontinue, drop, end, expire, finish, issue, lapse, result, stop, wind up.

antonyms begin, initiate, start.

termination *n* abortion, cessation, close, completion, conclusion, consequence, dénouement, discontinuation, effect, end, ending, expiry, finale, finis, finish, issue, result, wind-up.

antonyms beginning, initiation, start.

terminology *n* argot, cant, -ese, jargon, language, lingo, nomenclature, phraseology, terms, vocabulary, wording, words.

terminus *n* boundary, close, depot, destination, end, extremity, furthermost point, garage, goal, limit, station, target, termination.

terms *n* agreement, charges, compromise, conditions, fees, footing, language, particulars, payment, phraseology, position, premises, price, provisions, provisos, qualifications, rates, relations, relationship, settlement, specifications, standing, status, stipulations, terminology, understanding.

terrain *n* country, countryside, ground, land, landscape, territory, topography.

terrestrial *adj* earthbound, earthly, global, mundane, subastral, sublunary, tellurian, worldly.

antonyms cosmic, empyreal, heavenly.

terrible *adj* abhorrent, abominable, appalling, awful, bad, beastly, dangerous, desperate, dire, disgusting, distressing, dread, dreaded, dreadful, extreme, fearful, fell, formidable, foul, frightful, grim, grisly, gruesome, harrowing, hateful, hideous, horrendous, horrible, horrid, horrific, horrifying, loathsome, lousy, monstrous, obnoxious, odious, offensive, outrageous, poor, repulsive, revolting, rotten, serious, severe, shocking, unpleasant, vile, wretched.

antonyms great, pleasant, superb, wonderful.

terribly *adv* awfully, decidedly, desperately, exceedingly, extremely, frightfully, gravely, greatly, much, seriously, shockingly, thoroughly, very.

terrific *adj* ace, amazing, awesome, awful, breathtaking, brilliant, dreadful, enormous, excellent, excessive, extreme, fabulous, fantastic, far out, fearful, fierce, fine, gigantic, great, harsh, horrific, huge, intense, magnificent, marvellous, monstrous, outstanding, prodigious, sensational, severe, smashing, stupendous, super, superb, terrible, tremendous, wonderful.

terrified *adj* alarmed, appalled, awed, dismayed, frightened, horrified, horror-struck, intimidated, panic-stricken, petrified, scared (stiff or out of one's wits), spooked.

terrify v affright, alarm, appal, awe, consternate, dismay, frighten, horrify, intimidate, petrify, scare (the daylights out of), shock, terrorize.

territorial adj area, district, geographical, localized, regional, sectional, topographic, zonal.

territory n area, bailiwick, country, dependency, district, domain, home ground, jurisdiction, land, park, preserve, province, region, sector, state, stomping ground, terrain, tract, zone.

terror n affright, alarm, anxiety, awe, blue funk, bogeyman, bugbear, consternation, devil, dismay, dread, fear, fiend, fright, hellion, horror, intimidation, monster, panic, rascal, rogue, scourge, shock.

terrorize v alarm, appal, awe, browbeat, bully, coerce, dismay, frighten, horrify, intimidate, menace, oppress, petrify, scare, shock, strong-arm, terrify, threaten.

terse adj abrupt, aphoristic, brief, brusque, clipped, compact, concise, condensed, crisp, curt, economical, elliptical, epigrammatic, gnomic, incisive, laconic, neat, pithy, sententious, short, snappy, succinct.

antonyms long-winded, prolix, repetitious.

test v analyse, assay, assess, check, examine, experiment, investigate, prove, screen, try, verify.

n analysis, assessment, attempt, catechism, check, dry run, evaluation, examination, hurdle, investigation, moment of truth, ordeal, pons asinorum, probation, proof, shibboleth, trial, tryout.

testament n attestation, demonstration, devise, earnest, evidence, exemplification, proof, testimony, tribute, will, witness.

testify v affirm, assert, asseverate, attest, avow, certify, corroborate, declare, depone, depose, evince, give evidence, show, state, swear, vouch, witness.

testimonial n blurb, certificate, character, citation, commendation, credential, endorsement, gift, good word, memorial, plug, recommendation, reference, tribute.

testimony n affidavit, affirmation, asseveration, attestation, avowal, confirmation, corroboration, declaration, demonstration, deposition, evidence, indication, information, manifestation, profession, proof, statement, submission, support, verification, witness.

testy adj bad-tempered, cantankerous, captious, crabby, cranky, cross, crusty, edgy, fractious, fretful, grumpy, impatient, inflammable, irascible, irritable, peevish, peppery, petulant, quarrelsome, quick-tempered, short-tempered, snappish, splenetic, sullen, tetchy, touchy, waspish.

antonyms even-tempered, good-humoured.

tether n bond, chain, cord, fastening, fetter, halter, lead, leash, line, restraint, rope, shackle.

v bind, chain, fasten, fetter, lash, leash, manacle, picket, restrain, rope, secure, shackle, tie (up).

text n argument, body, contents, lection, libretto, matter, motif, paragraph, passage, reader, reading, script, sentence, source, subject, textbook, theme, topic, verse, wording, words.

texture n character, composition, consistency, constitution, fabric, feel, grain, quality, structure, surface, tissue, weave, weft, woof.

thankful adj appreciative, beholden, contented, grateful, indebted, obliged, pleased, relieved.

antonyms thankless, unappreciative, ungrateful.

thankless adj unappreciated, ungrateful, unrecognized, unrequited, unrewarded, unrewarding.

antonym rewarding.

thanks n acknowledgment, appreciation, credit, grace, gratefulness, gratitude, recognition, thanksgiving.

thanks to as a result of, because of, by reason of, due to, in consequence of, on account of, owing to, through.

thaw v defrost, dissolve, liquefy, melt, soften, unbend, uncongeal, unfreeze, unthaw, warm.

antonym freeze.

theatre n amphitheatre, auditorium, cinema, concert hall, filmhouse, hall, lyceum, movie house, music hall, odeon, opera house, playhouse, repertory, stage.

theatrical adj affected, artificial, ceremonious, dramatic, dramaturgic, exaggerated, extravagant, grandstand, histrionic, mannered, melodramatic, ostentatious, overdone, pompous, scenic, showy, stagy, stilted, theatric, Thespian, unreal.

theft n abstraction, embezzlement, filching, fraud, heist, kleptomania, larceny, lifting, misappropriation, pilfering, pinching, plunder, purloining, rip-off, robbery, stealing, taking, thievery, thieving.

the limit beyond endurance, beyond the pale, enough, insufferable, intolerable, more than one can take, the final blow, the last straw, the limit, the worst, too much, unbearable, unendurable.

the masses hoi polloi, the common people, the commonalty, the crowd, the general populace, the great unwashed, the majority, the many, the mob, the multitude, the people, the plebs, the proles, the proletariat, the rank and file.

thematic adj conceptual, notional, subject-oriented, taxonomic, theme-based, topical, classificatory.

theme n argument, burden, composition, dissertation, essay, exercise, idea, keynote, leitmotif, matter, motif, mythos, paper, subject, subject matter, text, thesis, topic.

theological adj divine, doctrinal, ecclesiastical, hierological, religious.

theorem *n* deduction, dictum, formula, hypothesis, postulate, principle, proposition, rule, statement, thesis.

theoretical *adj* abstract, academic, conjectural, doctrinaire, doctrinal, hypothetical, ideal, impractical, on paper, pure, speculative.

antonyms applied, concrete, practical.

theorize *v* conjecture, formulate, guess, hypothesize, postulate, project, propound, speculate, suppose.

theory *n* abstraction, assumption, conjecture, guess, guesswork, hypothesis, ism, philosophy, plan, postulation, presumption, proposal, scheme, speculation, supposition, surmise, system, thesis.

antonyms certainty, practice.

therapeutic *adj* ameliorative, analeptic, beneficial, corrective, curative, good, healing, recuperative, remedial, restorative, salubrious, salutary, sanative, tonic.

antonym harmful.

therapy *n* cure, healing, prophylaxis, tonic, treatment.

therefore *adv* accordingly, as a result, consequently, ergo, for that reason, hence, so, then, thence, thus.

thesaurus *n* dictionary, encyclopedia, lexicon, repository, storehouse, synonymy, treasury, vocabulary, wordbook.

thesis *n* argument, assumption, composition, contention, disquisition, dissertation, essay, hypothesis, idea, monograph, opinion, paper, postulate, premise, proposal, proposition, statement, subject, supposition, surmise, theme, theory, topic, tract, tractate, treatise, view.

thick *adj* abundant, brainless, brimming, bristling, broad, brushy, bulky, bursting, chock-a-block, chock-full, chummy, close, clotted, coagulated, compact, concentrated, condensed, confidential, covered, crass, crawling, crowded, deep, dense, devoted, dim-witted, distorted, dopey, dull, excessive, familiar, fat, foggy, frequent, friendly, full, gross, guttural, hard to take, heavy, hoarse, husky, impenetrable, inarticulate, indistinct, insensitive, inseparable, intimate, lush, luxuriant, marked, moronic, much, muffled, numerous, obtuse, opaque, packed, profuse, pronounced, replete, rich, slow, slow-witted, solid, soupy, squab, strong, stupid, substantial, swarming, teeming, thick-headed, throaty, turbid, unreasonable, wide.

antonyms acceptable, brainy, clever, slender, slight, slim, thin, unfriendly, watery.

n centre, focus, heart, hub, middle, midst.

thicken *v* cake, clot, coagulate, condense, congeal, deepen, gel, incrassate, inspissate, jell, set.

antonym thin.

thicket *n* bosk, brake, bush, clump, coppice, copse, covert, deadfall, grove, maquis, scrub, spinney, wood, woodland.

thick-headed *adj* asinine, blockheaded, brainless, dense, dim-witted, doltish, dopey,

dull-witted, idiotic, imbecilic, lamebrain, moronic, obtuse, slow, slow-witted, stupid, thick, witless.

antonyms brainy, clever, intelligent, sharp.

thickness *n* body, breadth, bulk, bulkiness, density, diameter, layer, ply, sheet, stratum, viscosity, width.

antonym thinness.

thickset *adj* beefy, brawny, bulky, burly, dense, heavy, muscular, solid, squat, stocky, stubby, sturdy, thick, well-built.

antonyms lanky, thin.

thick-skinned *adj* callous, case-hardened, hard-boiled, hardened, impervious, insensitive, inured, obdurate, pachydermatous, stolid, tough, unfeeling.

antonym thin-skinned.

thief *n* bandit, burglar, cheat, cracksman, crook, cutpurse, dip, embezzler, filcher, housebreaker, kleptomaniac, larcenist, mugger, pickpocket, pilferer, plunderer, purloiner, purse snatcher, rip-off artist, robber, shoplifter, stealer, swindler.

thieve *v* abstract, boost, cheat, embezzle, filch, heist, hook, knock off, lift, misappropriate, peculate, pilfer, pinch, plunder, poach, purloin, rip off, rob, steal, swindle, swipe, walk off with.

thieving *n* banditry, burglary, crookedness, embezzlement, kleptomania, larceny, mugging, peculation, pilferage, pilfering, piracy, plundering, robbery, shoplifting, stealing, theft, thievery.

thievish *adj* crooked, dishonest, fraudulent, larcenous, light-fingered, piratical, predatory, rapacious, sly, stealthy, sticky-fingered, thieving.

thin *adj* attenuate, attenuated, bony, deficient, delicate, diaphanous, dilute, diluted, emaciated, feeble, filmy, fine, fine-drawn, flimsy, gaunt, gossamer, inadequate, insubstantial, insufficient, lanky, lean, light, meagre, narrow, poor, rarefied, runny, scant, scanty, scarce, scattered, scraggy, scrawny, see-through, shallow, sheer, skeletal, skimpy, skinny, slender, slight, slim, spare, sparse, spindly, superficial, tenuous, translucent, transparent, unconvincing, undernourished, underweight, unsubstantial, washy, watery, weak, wishy-washy, wispy.

antonyms broad, dense, fat, solid, strong, thick.

v attenuate, dilute, diminish, emaciate, extenuate, prune, rarefy, reduce, refine, trim, water down, weaken, weed out.

thing *n* act, action, affair, apparatus, article, aspect, attitude, being, body, circumstance, concept, contrivance, creature, deed, detail, device, dislike, entity, event, eventuality, facet, fact, factor, feat, feature, fetish, fixation, gadget, hang-up, happening, idée fixe, implement, incident, instrument, item, liking, machine, mania, matter, means, mechanism, monomania, object, obsession, occurrence, part, particular, phenomenon, phobia, point, portion, possession, preoccupation, problem, proceeding, quirk, something, statement, substance, thought, tool.

things n baggage, belongings, bits and pieces, clothes, effects, equipment, gear, goods, impedimenta, junk, luggage, odds and ends, paraphernalia, possessions, stuff, traps, utensils.

think v anticipate, believe, be under the impression, brood, calculate, cerebrate, cogitate, conceive, conclude, consider, contemplate, deem, deliberate, design, determine, envisage, envision, esteem, estimate, expect, foresee, hold, ideate, imagine, intellectualize, intend, judge, meditate, mull over, muse, ponder, presume, purpose, ratiocinate, reason, recall, reckon, recollect, reflect, regard, remember, revolve, ruminate, see (as), suppose, surmise, understand, view (as).
n assessment, cogitation, consideration, contemplation, deliberation, meditation, reflection.

think much of admire, esteem, prize, rate, respect, set store by, think highly of, value.
antonym abominate.

think over chew over, consider, contemplate, meditate, mull over, ponder, reflect upon, ruminate, weigh up.

think up conceive, concoct, contrive, create, design, devise, dream up, imagine, improvise, invent, plan, visualize.

thinkable adj cogitable, conceivable, feasible, imaginable, likely, possible, reasonable, supposable.
antonym unthinkable.

thinker n brain, ideologist, intellect, mastermind, philosopher, sage, theorist.

thinking n assessment, cogitation, conclusions, conjecture, contemplation, deliberation, idea, introspection, judgment, meditation, opinion, outlook, philosophy, position, ratiocination, reasoning, theory, thoughts, view.
adj analytical, cerebral, contemplative, cultured, intelligent, introspective, meditative, philosophical, ratiocinative, rational, reasonable, reasoning, reflective, sophisticated, thoughtful.

thin-skinned adj hypersensitive, irascible, irritable, sensitive, snappish, soft, susceptible, tender, testy, touchy, vulnerable.
antonym thick-skinned.

third-rate adj bad, cheap and nasty, cheapjack, indifferent, inferior, low-grade, mediocre, poor, shoddy.

thirst n appetite, craving, desire, drought, drouth, dryness, eagerness, hankering, hunger, hydromania, keenness, longing, lust, passion, thirstiness, voracity, yearning, yen.

thirsty adj arid, athirst, avid, burning, craving, dehydrated, desirous, drouthy, dry, dying, eager, greedy, hankering, hungry, hydropic, itching, longing, lusting, parched, thirsting, voracious, yearning.

thorn n affliction, annoyance, bane, barb, bother, curse, irritant, irritation, nuisance, pest, plague, prickle, scourge, spike, spine, torment, torture, trouble.

thorny adj awkward, barbed, bristly, difficult, fraught, harassing, hard, irksome, pointed, prickly, problematic, sharp, spiky, spinelike, spiny, sticky, ticklish, tough, troublesome, trying, unpleasant, upsetting, vexatious, vexed, worrying.

thorough adj absolute, all-embracing, all-inclusive, all-out, arrant, assiduous, A to Z, careful, complete, comprehensive, conscientious, deep-seated, downright, efficient, entire, exhaustive, extensive, full, in-depth, intensive, methodical, meticulous, out-and-out, painstaking, perfect, pure, root-and-branch, scrupulous, sheer, sweeping, thoroughgoing, total, unmitigated, unqualified, utter, widespread.
antonyms careless, haphazard, partial.

thoroughfare n access, avenue, boulevard, causeway, concourse, expressway, freeway, highway, main drag, parkway, passage, passageway, road, roadway, street, strip, throughway, turnpike, way.

thoroughly adv absolutely, assiduously, carefully, completely, comprehensively, conscientiously, dead, downright, efficiently, entirely, every inch, exhaustively, fully, inside out, intensively, like crazy, meticulously, painstakingly, perfectly, quite, root and branch, scrupulously, sweepingly, totally, utterly, with a fine-toothed comb.
antonyms carelessly, haphazardly, partially.

though conj albeit, allowing, although, even if, granted, howbeit, notwithstanding, while.
adv all the same, even so, for all that, however, in spite of the fact that, nevertheless, nonetheless, notwithstanding, still, yet.

thought¹ n aim, anticipation, anxiety, aspiration, assessment, attention, attentiveness, belief, brainwork, care, cerebration, cogitation, compassion, concept, conception, concern, conclusion, conjecture, considerateness, consideration, contemplation, conviction, deliberation, design, dream, estimation, excogitation, expectation, heed, hope, idea, intention, introspection, judgment, kindness, meditation, musing, notion, object, opinion, plan, prospect, purpose, reflection, regard, resolution, rumination, scrutiny, solicitude, study, sympathy, thinking, thoughtfulness, view.

thought² n bit, dash, hair, hint, jot, little, suspicion, tad, tinge, touch, trace, trifle, whisker.

thoughtful adj absorbed, abstracted, astute, attentive, canny, careful, caring, cautious, circumspect, considerate, contemplative, deliberate, deliberative, discreet, heedful, helpful, introspective, kind, kindly, meditative, mindful, musing, pensive, prudent, rapt, reflective, ruminative, serious, solicitous, studious, thinking, unselfish, wary, wistful.
antonym thoughtless.

thoughtless *adj* absent-minded, careless, foolish, heedless, ill-considered, impolite, imprudent, inadvertent, inattentive, inconsiderate, indiscreet, injudicious, insensitive, mindless, neglectful, negligent, rash, reckless, regardless, remiss, rude, selfish, silly, stupid, tactless, uncaring, undiplomatic, unkind, unmindful, unobservant, unreflecting, unthinking.
antonym thoughtful.

thralldom *n* bondage, enslavement, serfdom, servitude, slavery, subjection, subjugation, vassalage, villeinage.
antonym freedom.

thrash *v* beat, belt, birch, cane, chastise, clobber, crush, defeat, drub, flagellate, flail, flog, hammer, heave, horsewhip, jerk, lambaste, larrup, lather, lay into, leather, maul, overwhelm, paste, plunge, punish, rout, scourge, slaughter, spank, squirm, swish, tan, thresh, toss, trounce, wallop, whale, whap, whip, whop, writhe.

thrash out debate, discuss, negotiate, resolve, settle, solve.

thrashing *n* beating, belting, caning, chastisement, defeat, drubbing, flogging, hammering, hiding, lashing, leathering, mauling, pasting, punishment, rout, tanning, trouncing, whaling, whipping.

thread *n* cotton, course, direction, drift, fibre, filament, filum, fimbria, line, motif, plot, storyline, strain, strand, string, tenor, theme, yarn.
v ease, inch, meander, pass, string, weave, wind.

threadbare *adj* clichéd, cliché-ridden, commonplace, conventional, corny, frayed, hackneyed, moth-eaten, old, outworn, overused, ragged, scruffy, shabby, stale, stereotyped, stock, tattered, tatty, tired, trite, used, well-worn, worn, worn-out.
antonyms fresh, luxurious, new, plush.

threadlike *adj* fibrillar, fibrillated, fibrillose, filamentary, filamentous, filiform, filose, fine, slender, stringy, thin, thready.

threat *n* commination, danger, foreboding, foreshadowing, hazard, menace, omen, peril, portent, presage, risk, sabre-rattling, warning.

threaten *v* browbeat, bully, comminate, cow, endanger, forebode, foreshadow, impend, imperil, intimidate, jeopardize, menace, portend, presage, pressure, terrorize, warn.

threatening *adj* baleful, bullying, cautionary, comminatory, Damoclean, grim, inauspicious, intimidatory, menacing, minacious, minatory, ominous, sinister, terrorizing, warning.

threesome *n* trey, triad, trilogy, trine, trinity, trio, triple, triplet, triplex, triptych, triumvirate, triune, troika.

threshold *n* beginning, brink, dawn, door, doorsill, doorstep, doorway, entrance, inception, level of tolerance, minimum, opening, outset, sill, start, starting point, verge.

thrift *n* carefulness, conservation, economy, frugality, husbandry, parsimony, prudence, saving, thriftiness.
antonyms profligacy, waste.

thriftless *adj* dissipative, extravagant, immoderate, improvident, imprudent, lavish, prodigal, profligate, spendthrift, squandering, unthrifty, wasteful.
antonym thrifty.

thrifty *adj* careful, conserving, economical, frugal, parsimonious, provident, prudent, saving, scrimping, sparing.
antonyms prodigal, profligate, thriftless, wasteful.

thrill *n* adventure, bang, buzz, charge, flutter, fluttering, frisson, glow, kick, pleasure, quiver, sensation, shiver, shudder, stimulation, throb, tingle, titillation, tremble, tremor, vibration.
v arouse, electrify, excite, flush, flutter, glow, move, quake, quiver, send, shake, shudder, stimulate, stir, throb, tingle, titillate, tremble, turn on, vibrate, wow.

thrilling *adj* electrifying, exciting, exhilarating, gripping, hair-raising, heart-stirring, quaking, riproaring, riveting, rousing, sensational, shaking, shivering, shuddering, soul-stirring, stimulating, stirring, trembling, vibrating.

thrive *v* advance, bloom, blossom, boom, burgeon, develop, flourish, gain, grow, increase, make good, mushroom, profit, prosper, succeed, wax.
antonyms die, fail, languish, stagnate.

thriving *adj* affluent, blooming, blossoming, booming, burgeoning, comfortable, developing, flourishing, growing, healthy, prosperous, successful, wealthy, well.
antonyms ailing, dying, failing, languishing, stagnating.

throat *n* craw, esophagus, fauces, gorge, gullet, throttle, weasand, windpipe.

throaty *adj* deep, gruff, guttural, hoarse, husky, low, rasping, raucous, thick.

throb *v* beat, palpitate, pound, pulsate, pulse, thump, vibrate.
n beat, palpitation, pounding, pulsating, pulsation, pulse, thump, thumping, vibration, vibrato.

throes *n* agony, anguish, death agony, distress, pain, pangs, struggle, suffering, torture, travail.

throng *n* assemblage, bevy, concourse, congregation, crowd, crush, flock, gathering, herd, horde, host, jam, mass, mob, mob scene, multitude, pack, press, swarm.
v bunch, cluster, congregate, converge, cram, crowd, fill, flock, gather, herd, jam, mill around, pack, press, swarm.

throttle *v* asphyxiate, choke, control, gag, garrote, inhibit, silence, smother, stifle, strangle, strangulate, suppress.

through *prep* as a result of, because of, between, by, by means of, by reason of, by virtue of, by way of, during, in, in and out of, in consequence of, in the middle of, past, thanks to, throughout, using, via.

adj completed, direct, done, ended, express, finished, non-stop, terminated.

through and through altogether, completely, entirely, from top to bottom, fully, thoroughly, totally, to the core, unreservedly, utterly, wholly.

throughout *adv* all over (or around), all through, everywhere, extensively, ubiquitously. *prep* all over (or around), all through, during the whole of, everywhere in, extensively in, for the (full) duration of, in all parts of, -wide, widely in.

throw *v* astonish, baffle, bemuse, bring down, cast, chuck, confound, confuse, defeat, discomfit, disconcert, dislodge, dumfound, execute, fell, fling, floor, heave, hurl, jaculate, launch, lob, overturn, perform, perplex, pitch, produce, project, propel, put, send, shy, sling, slug, toss, unhorse, unsaddle, unseat, upset. *n* attempt, cast, chance, essay, fling, gamble, hazard, heave, lob, pitch, projection, put, shy, sling, spill, toss, try, venture, wager.

throw away blow, cast off, discard, dispense with, dispose of, ditch, dump, fritter away, jettison, lose, reject, scrap, squander, toss out, waste.

antonyms keep, preserve, rescue, salvage.

throw dust in the eyes of con, confuse, cozen, deceive, delude, dupe, fool, have on, hoodwink, mislead, snow, take in.

throw off abandon, cast off, catch off guard, confuse, discard, disconcert, disturb, doff, drop, elude, faze, fluster, shake off, throw (for a loop), unsaddle, unseat, unsettle, upset.

throw out discard, dislocate, dismiss, ditch, dump, eject, emit, evict, expel, give off, jettison, offer, put a kink in, put out, radiate, reject, scrap, suggest, throw, throw a monkey wrench into, toss out, turf out, turn down, unhouse, warp.

throw over abandon, chuck, desert, discard, drop, finish with, forsake, jilt, leave, quit, reject.

throw up abandon, build, chuck, disgorge, give up, heave, leave, produce, puke, quit, raise, regurgitate, relinquish, renounce, resign, retch, reveal, slap together, spew, vomit.

throwaway *adj* careless, casual, cheap, disposable, offhand, passing, undramatic, unemphatic, wasteful.

thrust *v* bear, butt, drive, force, impel, intrude, jab, jam, lunge, pierce, plunge, poke, press, prod, propel, push, ram, shove, stab, stick, urge, wedge. *n* drive, impetus, lunge, momentum, poke, prod, push, shove, stab.

thud *n, v* bang, bash, clump, clunk, crash, knock, smack, thump, thwack, wallop, wham.

thug *n* animal, assassin, bandit, bruiser, bully boy, cutthroat, gangster, goon, gorilla, heavy, hood, hoodlum, hooligan, killer, mugger, murderer, robber, ruffian, tough.

thumb one's nose at defy, deride, flout, guy, jeer at, laugh at, mock, ridicule, scoff, scorn.

thumb (through) browse, flick, flip, glance (at), leaf, peruse, riffle, scan, skim.

thumbnail *adj* brief, capsule, compact, concise, condensed, miniature, pithy, quick, short, small, succinct.

thumbs down bad review, denial, disapproval, negation, no, pan, rebuff, refusal, rejection, turn-down, veto.

antonym thumbs up.

thumbs up acceptance, affirmation, approval, encouragement, go-ahead, good review, green light, OK, sanction, yes.

antonym thumbs down.

thump *n* bang, blow, box, clout, clunk, crash, cuff, knock, rap, smack, thud, thwack, wallop, whack. *v* bang, batter, beat, belabour, box, clout, crash, cuff, dent, hit, knock, lambaste, pound, rap, smack, strike, thrash, throb, thud, thwack, wallop, whack.

thumping *adj* big, colossal, enormous, excessive, exorbitant, gargantuan, gigantic, great, huge, immense, impressive, mammoth, massive, monumental, terrific, thundering, titanic, towering, tremendous, whopping.

antonyms insignificant, petty, piddling, trivial.

thunder *n* boom, booming, clap, cracking, crash, crashing, detonation, explosion, pealing, roll, rumble, rumbling. *v* bark, bellow, blast, boom, clap, crack, crash, curse, declaim, denounce, detonate, explode, fulminate, inveigh, peal, rail, resound, reverberate, roar, rumble, shout, threaten, yell.

thundering *adj* enormous, excessive, great, monumental, remarkable, thumping, tremendous, unmitigated.

thunderous *adj* booming, deafening, earsplitting, loud, noisy, resounding, reverberating, roaring, stentorian, tumultuous.

thunderstruck *adj* agape, aghast, amazed, astonished, astounded, dazed, dumfounded, flabbergasted, floored, flummoxed, nonplussed, open-mouthed, paralysed, petrified, shocked, staggered, stunned.

thus *adv* accordingly, as follows, consequently, ergo, hence, in this way, like so, like this, so, then, therefore, thusly.

thwack *v* bash, beat, buffet, clout, cuff, flog, hit, slap, smack, thump, wallop, whack. *n* bash, blow, buffet, clout, cuff, slap, smack, thump, wallop, whack.

thwart *v* baffle, balk, check, defeat, euchre, foil, frustrate, hinder, impede, obstruct, oppose, outwit, prevent, spite, stop, stymie, traverse.

antonyms abet, aid, assist.

tic *n* jerk, spasm, twitch.

tick *n* check, check mark, clack, click, clicking, mark, stroke, tap, tapping, tick-tick, tick-tock. *v* beat, choose, clack, click, indicate, mark (off), select, tally, tap.

tick off aggravate, anger, annoy, bug, cheese off, displease, exasperate, get on one's nerves, get to, irritate, tell off, upset.

antonym praise.

ticket *n* card, certificate, coupon, docket, label, marker, pass, slip, sticker, tab, tag, tessera, token, voucher.

tickle *v* amuse, cheer, delight, divert, enchant, entertain, excite, gratify, please, thrill, titillate.

ticklish *adj* awkward, critical, delicate, difficult, dodgy, hazardous, precarious, risky, sensitive, thorny, touchy, tricky, uncertain, unstable, unsteady.

antonyms easy, straightforward.

tidbit *n* appetizer, dainty, delicacy, goody, morsel, scrap, snack, tidbit, treat.

tide *n* course, current, direction, drift, ebb, flow, flux, movement, stream, tendency, tenor, trend.

tidings *n* advice, announcement, bulletin, communication, dope, gen, greetings, information, intelligence, message, news, notice, notification, report, word.

tidy *adj* ample, businesslike, clean, cleanly, considerable, fair, generous, good, goodly, handsome, healthy, large, largish, methodical, neat, ordered, orderly, organized, respectable, shipshape, sizable, spick-and-span, spruce, substantial, systematic, trim, uncluttered, well-groomed, well-kept.

antonyms disorganized, untidy.

v arrange, clean, groom, neaten, order, organize, spruce up, straighten (up or out).

tie *v* attach, bind, confine, connect, draw, equal, fasten, hamper, hinder, hold, interlace, join, knot, lash, ligature, limit, link, match, moor, oblige, restrain, restrict, rope, secure, strap, tether, truss, unite.

n affiliation, allegiance, band, bond, commitment, connection, contest, copula, cord, dead heat, deadlock, draw, duty, encumbrance, fastening, fetter, hindrance, joint, kinship, knot, liaison, ligature, limitation, link, match, obligation, relationship, restraint, restriction, rope, stalemate, string.

tie up attach, bind, conclude, delay, detain, end, engage, engross, finish off, hinder, lash, ligate, lock in, make certain, moor, occupy, pinion, restrain, rope, secure, settle, sew up, stop, terminate, tether, truss, wind up, wrap up.

tie-in *n* affiliation, association, connection, co-ordination, liaison, link, relation, relationship, tie-up.

tier *n* band, belt, echelon, floor, gradin(e), layer, level, line, rank, row, stage, storey, stratification, stratum, zone.

tiff *n* difference (of opinion), disagreement, dispute, dustup, falling-out, hassle, huff, ill humour, pet, quarrel, row, run-in, scrap, set-to, spat, squabble, sulk, tantrum, temper, words.

tight[1] *adj* close, close-fitting, compact, competent, concise, constricted, cramped, dangerous, dense, difficult, even, evenly-balanced, fast, firm, fixed, grasping, harsh, hazardous, hermetic, impervious, inflexible, mean, miserly, narrow, near, niggardly, parsimonious, penurious, perilous, precarious, precise, problematic, proof, rigid, rigorous, scarce, sealed, secure, severe, snug,

sound, sparing, stern, sticky, stiff, stingy, stretched, strict, stringent, taut, tense, terse, ticklish, tight-fisted, tough, tricky, troublesome, uncompromising, unyielding, watertight, well-matched, worrisome.

antonyms lax, loose, slack.

tight[2] *adj* blotto, drunk, in one's cups, inebriated, intoxicated, pickled, pie-eyed, plastered, smashed, sozzled, stewed, stoned, tanked, three sheets to the wind, tipsy, under the influence.

antonym sober.

tighten *v* close, constrict, cramp, crush, fasten, fix, narrow, screw, secure, squeeze, stiffen, stretch, tense.

antonyms loosen, relax.

tight-fisted *adj* cheap, cheeseparing, close, close-fisted, grasping, mean, miserly, niggardly, parsimonious, penny-pinching, penurious, Scroogelike, sparing, stingy, tight.

antonym generous.

tight-lipped *adj* close-lipped, close-mouthed, mum, mute, quiet, reserved, reticent, secretive, silent, taciturn, uncommunicative, unforthcoming.

antonyms garrulous, talkative.

till *v* cultivate, dig, dress, farm, plough, turn (over), work.

tilt[1] *v* cant, heel, incline, lean, list, pitch, slant, slope, tip.

n angle, cant, inclination, incline, list, lists, pitch, slant, slope.

tilt[2] *v* aim, attack, charge, clash, contend, duel, fight, have an encounter, joust, overthrow, spar, thrust.

n clash, combat, duel, encounter, fight, joust, set-to, thrust, tournament, tourney.

full tilt at top speed, flat out, full force, full speed, full throttle.

timber *n* beams, boarding, boards, forest, logs, lumber, planking, planks, trees, wood.

timbre *n* colour, resonance, ring, tonality, tone, (voice) quality.

time *n* age, beat, chronology, date, day, duration, epoch, era, generation, heyday, hour, instance, interval, juncture, life, lifespan, lifetime, measure, metre, occasion, peak, period, point, rhythm, season, space, span, spell, stage, stretch, tempo, term, tide, while.

v clock, control, count, judge, measure, meter, regulate, schedule, set.

at a time at once, at one time, concurrently, in one fell swoop, in one go (or try), in (or at) one sitting, simultaneously, synchronously, together, with one shot (or blow).

for the time being for now, for the moment, for the nonce, for the present, in the meantime, meantime, meanwhile, pro tem, pro tempore, temporarily.

from time to time at times, every now and then, every so often, intermittently, now and then, occasionally, once in a while, on occasion, sometimes, spasmodically, sporadically.

antonym constantly

in (good) time ahead of time, early, in advance, in plenty of time, on time, promptly, punctually, soon enough, with time to spare.

in no time before you could say (...), immediately, in a jiffy, in a split second, in a twinkling, in seconds (flat), instantaneously, instantly, in two ticks.

mark time count the hours (or minutes or days, etc.), do nothing, kill time, sit on one's hands, sit tight, twiddle one's thumbs, wait.

time and again frequently, many times, often, on many occasions, over and over again, recurrently, repeatedly, time after time.

time-honoured *adj* accustomed, age-old, ancient, conventional, customary, established, fixed, historic, long-established, old, traditional, usual, venerable.

timeless *adj* abiding, ageless, amaranthine, ceaseless, changeless, deathless, endless, enduring, eternal, everlasting, immortal, immutable, imperishable, indestructible, lasting, permanent, perpetual, persistent, undying.

timely *adj* appropriate, convenient, judicious, opportune, prompt, propitious, punctual, seasonable, suitable, well-timed.

antonyms ill-timed, inappropriate, unfavourable.

timetable *n* agenda, calendar, curriculum, diary, list, listing, program, roster, rota, schedule.

timeworn *adj* aged, ancient, broken-down, bromidic, clichéd, dated, decrepit, dog-eared, hackneyed, hoary, lined, out of date, outworn, passé, ragged, ruined, run-down, shabby, stale, stock, threadbare, tired, trite, weathered, well-worn, worn, wrinkled.

antonyms fresh, new.

timid *adj* afraid, apprehensive, bashful, chicken, cowardly, coy, diffident, faint-hearted, fearful, irresolute, modest, mousy, nervous, pusillanimous, retiring, scared, shrinking, shy, spineless, timorous.

antonyms audacious, bold, brave.

timorous *adj* afraid, apprehensive, aspen, bashful, cowardly, coy, diffident, faint-hearted, fearful, inadventurous, irresolute, modest, mousy, nervous, pusillanimous, retiring, shrinking, shy, tentative, timid, trembling.

antonyms assertive, assured, bold.

tincture *n* aroma, colour, dash, flavour, hint, hue, seasoning, shade, smack, stain, suggestion, tinct, tinge, tint, touch, trace.

v colour, dye, flavour, imbue, infuse, permeate, scent, season, stain, suffuse, tinge, tint.

tinge *n* bit, cast, colour, dash, drop, dye, flavour, pinch, shade, smack, smattering, sprinkling, stain, suggestion, tinct, tincture, tint, touch, trace, wash.

v colour, dye, imbue, shade, stain, suffuse, tint.

tingle *v* itch, prickle, ring, sting, thrill, throb, tickle, vibrate.

n frisson, goose flesh, goose pimples, itch, itching, pins and needles, prickling, quiver, shiver, stinging, thrill, tickle, tickling.

tinker *v* dabble, fiddle, meddle, monkey, play, putter, toy, trifle.

tinsel *adj* cheap, flashy, gaudy, gimcrack, meretricious, ostentatious, pinchbeck, plastic, sham, showy, specious, superficial, tawdry, tinselly, trashy.

n artificiality, display, flamboyance, frippery, garishness, gaudiness, glitter, insignificance, meaninglessness, ostentation, pinchbeck, pretension, sham, show, spangle, triviality, worthlessness.

tint *n* cast, colour, dye, hint, hue, rinse, shade, stain, streak, suggestion, tinct, tincture, tinge, tone, touch, trace, wash.

v affect, colour, dye, influence, rinse, stain, streak, taint, tincture, tinge.

tiny *adj* baby, bantam, diminutive, dwarfish, infinitesimal, insignificant, itsy-bitsy, Lilliputian, little, microscopic, midget, mini, miniature, minuscule, minute, negligible, peewee, petite, pint-sized, pocket, pocket-size, puny, pygmy, slight, small, teeny, teeny-weeny, trifling, wee.

antonyms big, immense.

tip[1] *n* acme, apex, cap, crown, end, extremity, ferrule, head, nib, peak, pinnacle, point, summit, top.

v cap, crown, finish, pinnacle, surmount, top.

tip[2] *v* cant, capsize, ditch, dump, empty, heel, incline, lean, list, overturn, pour out, slant, spill, tilt, topple over, unload, upend, upset.

tip[3] *n* baksheesh, clue, forecast, gen, gift, gratuity, hint, information, inside information, perquisite, pointer, pourboire, suggestion, tip-off, warning, word, word of advice.

v advise, caution, forewarn, inform, remunerate, reward, suggest, tell, warn.

tipple *v* drink, imbibe, indulge, quaff, swig, tope.

n alcohol, booze, drink, liquor.

tippler *n* boozer, dipsomaniac, drinker, drunk, drunkard, inebriate, lush, soak, sot, sponge, toper, winebibber.

tipsy *adj* drunk, elevated, fuddled, happy, high, mellow, merry, slaphappy, squiffed, squiffy, tight, unsteady, woozy.

antonym sober.

tirade *n* abuse, denunciation, diatribe, fulmination, harangue, invective, lecture, outburst, philippic, rant, vituperation.

tire *v* annoy, bore, burn out, drain, droop, enervate, exasperate, exhaust, fag, fail, fatigue, flag, harass, irk, irritate, jade, sink, wear out, weary.

antonyms energize, enliven, exhilarate, invigorate, refresh.

tired *adj* all in, aweary, beat, bone-weary, burned out, bushed, clichéd, conventional, corny, dead beat, dead (tired), dog-tired, done in, drained, drooping, drowsy, effete, enervated, exhausted, fagged out, familiar, fatigued, flagging, hackneyed, jaded, old, outworn, pooped, sleepy, spent, stale, stock, threadbare, trite, tuckered out, weary, well-worn, whacked, wiped out, worn out.

antonyms active, energetic, fresh, lively, rested.

tireless *adj* determined, diligent, energetic, indefatigable, industrious, relentless, resolute, sedulous, unflagging, untiring, unwearied, vigorous.

antonyms tired, unenthusiastic, weak.

tiresome *adj* annoying, boring, bothersome, dull, exasperating, fatiguing, flat, irksome, irritating, laborious, monotonous, pesky, tedious, troublesome, trying, uninteresting, vexatious, wearing, wearisome.

antonyms easy, interesting, stimulating.

tiring *adj* arduous, demanding, draining, enervating, exacting, exhausting, fatiguing, laborious, strenuous, tough, wearing, wearying.

tissue *n* accumulation, agglomeration, collection, combination, concatenation, conglomeration, fabric, fabrication, gauze, mass, mesh, network, pack, paper, series, structure, stuff, texture, tissue paper, web.

titan *n* Atlas, colossus, giant, Hercules, leviathan, superman.

titanic *adj* Brobdingnagian, colossal, cyclopean, enormous, giant, gigantic, great, herculean, huge, humungous, immense, jumbo, mammoth, massive, mighty, monstrous, monumental, mountainous, prodigious, stupendous, towering, vast.

antonyms insignificant, small.

tit for tat an eye for an eye, blow for blow, counterattack, counterblow, countercharge, like for like, measure for measure, quid pro quo, requital, retaliation, revenge, talion.

titillate *v* arouse, captivate, excite, interest, intrigue, provoke, stimulate, tantalize, tease, thrill, tickle, turn on.

titillating *adj* arousing, captivating, exciting, interesting, intriguing, lewd, lurid, provocative, sensational, stimulating, suggestive, teasing, thrilling.

titivate *v* doll up, make up, prank, preen, primp, prink, refurbish, smarten up, tart up, touch up.

title *n* appellation, caption, championship, claim, credit, crown, denomination, designation, entitlement, epithet, handle, heading, headline, inscription, label, laurels, legend, letterhead, moniker, name, nickname, nom de plume, ownership, prerogative, privilege, pseudonym, right, sobriquet, style, term.

v call, christen, designate, entitle, label, name, style, term.

titter *v* chortle, chuckle, giggle, laugh, mock, snicker, snigger, tee-hee.

tittle-tattle *n* babble, blather, cackle, chat, chatter, chitchat, dope, gossip, hearsay, jaw, natter, poop, prattle, rumour, scuttlebutt, tongue-wagging, twaddle, yak, yak-yak, yakety-yak, yap.

v babble, blab, blather, cackle, chat, chatter,

chit-chat, gossip, jaw, natter, prattle, tell tales, wag one's tongue, yak, yakety-yak, yap.

titular *adj* formal, honorary, nominal, puppet, putative, so-called, token.

to

For phrases such as *to a fault, to all intents and purposes, to the full,* see the first noun after *to.*

toady *n* apple-polisher, bootlicker, crawler, creep, fawner, flatterer, flunky, groveller, hanger-on, jackal, lackey, lickspittle, minion, parasite, suck-up, sycophant, timeserver, toadeater, truckler, yes man.

v bootlick, bow and scrape, butter up, crawl, creep, cringe, curry favour, fawn, flatter, grovel, kiss the feet (of), kowtow, play up, suck up, truckle.

toast¹ *v* broil, brown, grill, heat, roast, warm.

toast² *n* compliment, darling, drink, favourite, grace cup, health, hero, heroine, pledge, salutation, salute, tribute, wassail.

to-do *n* agitation, botheration, brouhaha, bustle, commotion, disturbance, excitement, flap, flurry, furor, fuss, hubbub, hue and cry, hullabaloo, outcry, palaver, performance, pother, quarrel, rumpus, scene, stew, stir, tumult, turmoil, unrest, uproar.

together *adv* all at once, as a unit, as one, as one body, at the same time, cheek by jowl, closely, collectively, concurrently, consecutively, contemporaneously, continuously, en masse, fixed, hand in glove, hand in hand, in a body, in a row, in concert, in co-operation, in succession, in unison, jointly, mutually, on end, shoulder to shoulder, side by side, simultaneously, successively, with one voice.

antonym separately.

adj calm, commonsensical, composed, cool, down-to-earth, level-headed, on top of things, sensible, stable, well-adjusted, well-balanced, well-integrated, well-ordered, well-organized.

toil *n* application, donkey-work, drudgery, effort, elbow grease, exertion, industry, labour, pains, slog, sweat, travail.

v drudge, grind, grub, labour, persevere, plug away, slave, slog, strive, struggle, sweat, work.

toiler *n* donkey, drudge, labourer, menial, navvy, slave, slogger, struggler, workaholic, worker, workhorse.

antonyms idler, loafer, shirker.

toilet *n* ablutions, backhouse, bathing, bathroom, can, closet, comfort station, convenience, dressing, grooming, john, ladies' room, latrine, lavatory, loo, men's room, outhouse, powder room, privy, rest room, toilette, urinal, washroom, water closet, W.C.

toilsome *adj* arduous, backbreaking, burdensome, difficult, fatiguing, hard, herculean, laborious, painful, severe, strenuous, taxing, tedious, tiresome, tough, uphill, wearisome.

token *n* badge, clue, demonstration, earnest, emblem, evidence, expression, index, indication, keepsake, manifestation, mark, memento, memorial, note, pledge, proof, remembrance, reminder, representation, sign, souvenir, symbol, tessera, testimony, voucher, warning.

adj emblematic, hollow, inconsiderable, minimal, nominal, perfunctory, superficial, symbolic.

tolerable *adj* acceptable, adequate, allowable, all right, average, bearable, endurable, fair, fair to middling, good enough, indifferent, liveable, mediocre, middling, not bad, OK, ordinary, passable, run-of-the-mill, so-so, sufferable, supportable, unexceptional.

antonym intolerable.

tolerance *n* allowance, broad-mindedness, charity, endurance, fluctuation, forbearance, fortitude, hardiness, hardness, indulgence, lenity, magnanimity, open-mindedness, patience, permissiveness, play, resilience, resistance, rope, stamina, sufferance, swing, sympathy, toughness, variation.

antonyms bigotry, intolerance, narrow-mindedness, prejudice.

tolerant *adj* broad-minded, catholic, charitable, complaisant, easy-going, fair, forbearing, indulgent, kind-hearted, latitudinarian, lax, lenient, liberal, long-suffering, magnanimous, open-minded, patient, permissive, soft, sympathetic, understanding, unprejudiced.

antonyms biassed, bigoted, intolerant, prejudiced, unsympathetic.

tolerate *v* abide, accept, admit, allow, bear, brook, buy, condone, connive at, countenance, endure, indulge, permit, put up with, receive, sanction, stand, stomach, suffer, swallow, take, turn a blind eye to, undergo, wink at.

toleration *n* acceptance, allowance, condoning, connivance, endurance, indulgence, permissiveness, sanction, sufferance.

toll[1] *v* announce, call, chime, clang, knell, peal, ring, send, signal, sound, strike, summon, warn.

toll[2] *n* assessment, charge, cost, customs, damage, demand, dues, duty, fee, impost, inroad, levy, loss, payment, penalty, rate, tariff, tax, tithe, tribute.

tomb *n* burial chamber, burial place, catacomb, cenotaph, crypt, dolmen, grave, mastaba, mausoleum, pyramid, resting place, sepulchre, sepulture, vault.

tombstone *n* gravestone, headstone, marker, memorial, monument, stone.

tome *n* book, opus, volume, work.

tomfoolery *n* antics, balderdash, baloney, bilge, bosh, buffoonery, bunk, childishness, claptrap, clowning, foolishness, hogwash, hooey, horseplay, idiocy, inanity, larking around, larks, messing around, monkey business, monkeyshines, nonsense, poppycock, rot, rubbish, shenanigans, silliness, skylarking, stupidity, tommyrot, trash, twaddle.

tone *n* accent, air, approach, aspect, attitude, cast, character, colour, drift, effect, emphasis, feel, force, frame, grain, harmony, hue, inflection, intonation, manner, modulation, mood, note, pitch, quality, shade, spirit, strength, stress, style, temper, tenor, timbre, tinge, tint, tonality, vein, volume.

v blend, harmonize, intone, match, sound, suit.

tone down alleviate, assuage, dampen, dim, mitigate, moderate, modulate, palliate, play down, reduce, restrain, soften, soft-pedal, subdue, temper.

tone up brighten, freshen, invigorate, limber up, shape up, sharpen up, touch up, trim, tune up.

tongue *n* argot, articulation, clapper, dialect, discourse, idiom, language, languet, lingo, parlance, patois, speech, talk, utterance, vernacular, voice.

tongue-tied *adj* dumb, dumbstruck, dumfounded, inarticulate, mute, silent, speechless, voiceless.

antonyms garrulous, talkative, voluble.

tonic *n* analeptic, boost, bracer, cordial, fillip, inspiration, livener, pick-me-up, refresher, restorative, shot in the arm, stimulant, upper.

too[1] *adv* additionally, also, as well (as), besides, further, furthermore, in addition, into the bargain, likewise, moreover, to boot, what's more.

too[2] *adv* excessively, exorbitantly, extremely, immoderately, inexcusably, inordinately, intolerably, over, overly, ridiculously, to excess, to extremes, unduly, unjustifiably, unreasonably, very.

tool *n* agency, agent, apparatus, appliance, cat's-paw, contraption, contrivance, creature, device, dupe, flunkey, front, gadget, hireling, implement, instrument, intermediary, jackal, lackey, machine, means, medium, minion, pawn, puppet, stooge, toady, utensil, vehicle, weapon.

v chase, cut, decorate, fashion, machine, ornament, shape, work.

tooth *n* cog, denticle, fang, incisor, jag, masticator, molar, prong, spur, tush, tusk.

toothless *adj* edentate, edentulous, fangless, ineffective, powerless, unenforceable.

toothsome *adj* agreeable, ambrosial, appetizing, attractive, curvaceous, dainty, delectable, delicious, enjoyable, flavoursome, luscious, mouth-watering, nice, palatable, sapid, savoury, scrumptious, shapely, sweet, tasty, tempting, voluptuous, yummy.

antonyms disagreeable, plain, unpleasant.

top *n* ace, acme, apex, apogee, beginning, cap, cork, cover, crest, crown, culmination, head, height, high point, lead, lid, maximum, meridian, peak, pinnacle, start, stopper, summit, tip, vertex, zenith.

antonyms base, bottom, nadir.

adj best, chief, crack, crowning, culminating, dominant, elite, finest, first, foremost, greatest, head, highest, lead, leading, pre-eminent, prime, principal, ruling, sovereign, superior, topmost, upmost, upper, uppermost.

v ascend, beat, best, better, cap, climb, command, cover, crest, crop, crown, decorate, eclipse, exceed, excel, finish, finish off, garnish, head, lead, lop, outdo, outshine, outstrip, poll, pollard, roof, rule, scale, surmount, surpass, tip, transcend.

on top of the world ecstatic, elated, exhilarated, exultant, flying, happy, on cloud nine, over the moon, overjoyed, thrilled, walking on air.

topic *n* issue, matter, motif, point, question, subject, subject matter, talking point, text, theme, thesis.

topical *adj* contemporary, current, familiar, immediate, local, newsworthy, popular, relevant, timely, up-to-date, up-to-the-minute.

topmost *adj* apical, dominant, foremost, highest, leading, loftiest, maximum, paramount, principal, supreme, tiptop, top, ultimate, upper, uppermost.

antonyms bottom, bottommost, lowest.

topple *v* capsize, collapse, oust, overbalance, overthrow, overturn, totter, tumble, unseat, upset.

topsy-turvy *adj* back-to-front, chaotic, confused, disarranged, disorderly, disorganized, higgledy-piggledy, inside out, jumbled, messy, mixed up, untidy, upside down.

antonyms ordered, tidy.

torch *n* brand, cresset, firebrand, flambeau, flame, link.

torment *v* afflict, agitate, agonize, annoy, bedevil, bother, chivvy, crucify, devil, distort, distress, excruciate, harass, harrow, harry, hound, irritate, nag, pain, persecute, pester, plague, provoke, rack, tease, torture, trouble, vex, worry, wrack.

n affliction, agony, angst, anguish, annoyance, bane, bother, distress, harassment, hassle, hell, irritation, misery, nag, nagging, nuisance, pain, persecution, pest, plague, provocation, scourge, suffering, torture, trouble, vexation, worry.

torn[1] *adj* cut, lacerated, ragged, rent, ripped, slit, split.

torn[2] *adj* dithering, divided, irresolute, uncertain, undecided, unsure, vacillating, wavering.

tornado *n* cyclone, gale, hurricane, monsoon, squall, storm, tempest, twister, typhoon, whirlwind, windstorm.

torpid *adj* apathetic, benumbed, dormant, drowsy, dull, fainéant, hebetudinous, inactive, indolent, inert, lackadaisical, languid, languorous, lazy, lethargic, listless, lymphatic, motionless, numb, passive, pokey, slothful, slow, slow-moving, sluggish, somnolent, stagnant, supine.

antonyms active, lively, vigorous.

torpor *n* accidie, apathy, dormancy, drowsiness, dullness, hebetude, inactivity, inanition, indolence, inertia, inertness, languor, laziness, lethargy, listlessness, numbness, passivity, sloth, sluggishness, somnolence, stagnancy, stupidity, stupor, the blahs, torpidity.

antonyms activity, animation, vigour.

torrent *n* barrage, cascade, deluge, downpour, effusion, flood, flow, gush, outburst, rush, spate, stream, tide, volley.

torrid *adj* ardent, arid, blistering, boiling, broiling, burning, dried, dry, emotional, erotic, fervent, fiery, hot, intense, parched, parching, passionate, scorched, scorching, sexy, sizzling, steamy, stifling, sultry, sweltering, tropical.

antonym arctic.

tortuous *adj* ambiguous, bent, Byzantine, circuitous, complicated, convoluted, crooked, cunning, curved, deceptive, devious, evasive, indirect, involved, labyrinthine, mazy, meandering, misleading, roundabout, serpentine, sinuous, tricky, twisted, twisting, winding, zigzag.

antonyms straight, straightforward.

torture *v* afflict, agonize, crucify, distress, excruciate, harrow, lacerate, martyr, pain, persecute, rack, torment, wrack.

n affliction, agony, anguish, distress, hell, laceration, martyrdom, misery, nightmare, pain, pang(s), persecution, rack, suffering, torment.

toss *v* agitate, cant, cast, chuck, disturb, fling, flip, heave, hurl, jiggle, joggle, jolt, labour, launch, lob, lurch, pitch, project, propel, rock, roll, shake, shy, sling, thrash, throw, tumble, wallow, welter, wriggle, writhe.

n cast, chuck, fling, lob, pitch, shy, sling, throw.

total *n* aggregate, all, amount, ensemble, entirety, lot, mass, sum, totality, whole.

adj absolute, all-consuming, all-encompassing, all-inclusive, all-out, complete, comprehensive, consummate, downright, entire, exhaustive, full, gross, integral, out-and-out, outright, perfect, rank, root-and-branch, sheer, sweeping, thorough, thoroughgoing, unconditional, undisputed, undivided, unmitigated, unqualified, unreserved, utter, whole, whole-hog.

antonyms limited, partial, restricted.

v add (up), amount to, be all together, come to, count (up), destroy, make, reach, reckon, ruin, smash, sum (up), wreck.

totalitarian *adj* absolute, authoritarian, despotic, dictatorial, monocratic, monolithic, omnipotent, one-party, oppressive, tyrannical, tyrannous, undemocratic.

antonym democratic.

totality *n* aggregate, all, completeness, comprehensiveness, cosmos, entireness, entirety, everything, fullness, inclusiveness, plenitude, singleness, sum, thoroughness, total, universe, whole, wholeness.

totally *adv* absolutely, completely, comprehensively, consummately, entirely, fully, perfectly, quite, thoroughly, unconditionally, undisputedly, undividedly, unmitigatedly, unreservedly, utterly, whole-heartedly, wholly.

antonym partially.

totter *v* dodder, falter, lurch, quiver, reel, rock, shake, stagger, stumble, sway, teeter, tremble, waver.

touch *n* ability, acquaintance, adroitness, approach, art, artistry, awareness, bit, blow, brush, caress, characteristic, command, communication, contact, correspondence, dash, deftness, detail, direction, drop, effect, facility, familiarity, feel, feeling, flair, fondling, hair, hand, handiwork, handling, hint, hit, influence, intimation, jot, knack, manner, mastery, method, mite, palpation, pat, pinch, push, skill, smack, smattering, soupçon, speck, spot, stroke, style, suggestion, suspicion, tactility, tad, tap, taste, technique, thought, tinge, trace, trademark, understanding, virtuosity, way, whiff.

v abut, adjoin, affect, attain, border, brush, caress, cheat, compare with, concern, consume, contact, converge, disturb, drink, eat, equal, feel, finger, fondle, graze, handle, hit, hold a candle to, impress, influence, inspire, interest, mark, match, meet, melt, move, palp, palpate, parallel, pat, pertain to, push, reach, regard, rival, soften, stir, strike, stroke, tap, tinge, upset, use, utilize.

touch off actuate, arouse, begin, cause, fire, foment, ignite, inflame, initiate, light, provoke, set off, spark off, trigger (off).

touch on allude to, broach, cover, deal with, mention, refer to, remark on, speak of.

touch up arouse, brush up, enhance, finish off, fondle, improve, patch up, perfect, polish up, renovate, retouch, revamp, round off, stimulate, titivate.

touch-and-go *adj* a near thing, close, critical, dangerous, delicate, dicey, hairy, hazardous, iffy, nerve-wracking, nip and tuck, offhand, perilous, precarious, risky, sticky, suspenseful, tricky, uncertain.

touched *adj* affected, barmy, batty, bonkers, crazy, cuckoo, daft, disturbed, dotty, eccentric, impressed, mad, melted, moved, nuts, nutty, softened, stirred, swayed, unbalanced, upset.

touchiness *n* bad temper, captiousness, crabbiness, grouchiness, grumpiness, irascibility, irritability, peevishness, pettishness, petulance, surliness, testiness, tetchiness.

touching[1] *adj* affecting, emotional, emotive, haptic, heartbreaking, melting, moving, pathetic, piteous, pitiable, pitiful, poignant, sad, stirring, tender.

touching[2] *adj* abutting, adjacent, cantiguous, in contact.

touching[3] *prep* about, concerning, regarding, relating to, relevant to, respecting, to do with.

touchstone *n* benchmark, criterion, gauge, measure, norm, proof, standard, yardstick.

touchy *adj* bad-tempered, captious, chippy, crabby, cross, feisty, grouchy, grumpy, huffy, irascible, irritable, peevish, petulant, querulous, quick-tempered, sensitive, snippety, snuffy, sore, splenetic, surly, testy, tetchy, thin-skinned.

antonyms calm, imperturbable, serene, unflappable.

tough *adj* adamant, arduous, bad, baffling, brawny, callous, chewy, cohesive, difficult, durable, exacting, exhausting, firm, fit, gristly, hard, hard-bitten, hard-boiled, hardened, hard-hearted, hard-nosed, hardy, herculean, inflexible, intractable, irksome, knotty, laborious, lamentable, leathery, merciless, obdurate, obstinate, perplexing, pugnacious, puzzling, refractory, regrettable, resilient, resistant, resolute, rigid, rough, ruffianly, rugged, ruthless, seasoned, severe, solid, stalwart, stern, stiff, stout, strapping, strenuous, strict, strong, stubborn, sturdy, tenacious, thewy, thorny, troublesome, unbending, unforgiving, unfortunate, unlucky, unyielding, uphill, vicious, vigorous, violent.

antonyms brittle, delicate, easy, fragile, liberal, soft, tender, vulnerable, weak.

n bravo, bruiser, brute, bully, bully boy, gorilla, hooligan, rough, roughneck, rowdy, ruffian, thug, yahoo.

toughness *n* arduousness, callousness, difficulty, durability, firmness, fitness, grit, hardiness, hardness, inflexibility, intractability, laboriousness, obduracy, obstinacy, pugnacity, resilience, resistance, rigidity, roughness, ruggedness, ruthlessness, severity, solidity, sternness, stiffness, strength, strenuousness, strictness, sturdiness, tenacity, viciousness.

antonyms fragility, liberality, softness, vulnerability, weakness.

tour *n* airing, circuit, course, drive, excursion, expedition, jaunt, journey, junket, outing, peregrination, progress, ride, round, run, stroll, trek, trip, voyage, walk.

v drive, explore, journey, ride, sightsee, stroll, travel, trek, visit, voyage.

tourist *n* excursionist, globetrotter, holiday-maker, jetsetter, journeyer, out-of-towner, rubberneck, sightseer, sojourner, traveller, tripper, visitor, voyager.

tournament *n* championship, competition, contest, event, joust, lists, match, meeting, series, tourney.

tousled *adj* disarranged, dishevelled, disordered, messed up, mussed (up), ruffled, rumpled, tangled, tumbled, unkempt.

tow *v* drag, draw, haul, lug, pull, tote, trail, transport, trawl, tug, yank.

toward *prep* a little short of, about, almost, approaching, around, close to, coming up to, concerning, for, getting on for, in the direction of, in the vicinity of, just before, nearing, nearly, on the way to, regarding, to, -ward, with regard to, with respect to.

tower *n* barbican, bastille, bastion, belfry, castle, citadel, column, donjon, fort, fortification, fortress, highrise, keep, Martello (tower), minaret, obelisk, peel, pillar, refuge, skyscraper, steeple, stronghold, turret.

v ascend, dominate, exceed, loom, mount, overlook, overtop, rear, rise, soar, surpass, top, transcend.

towering *adj* burning, colossal, elevated, excessive, extraordinary, extreme, fiery, gigantic, great, high, immoderate, imposing, impressive, inordinate, intemperate, intense, lofty, magnificent, mighty, monumental, outstanding, overpowering, paramount, passionate, prodigious, sky-high, soaring, sublime, superior, supreme, surpassing, tall, transcendent, vehement, violent.

antonyms minor, small, trivial.

town *n* borough, burg, burgh, city, metropolis, municipality, settlement, township.

antonym country.

toxic *adj* baneful, deadly, fatal, harmful, lethal, mortal, noxious, pernicious, pestilential, poisonous, septic, unhealthy, virulent.

antonym harmless.

toy *n* bagatelle, bauble, doll, game, gewgaw, kickshaw(s), knick-knack, plaything, trifle, trinket.

v dally, fiddle, flirt, play, putter, sport, tinker, trifle, wanton.

trace *n* bit, dash, drop, evidence, footmark, footprint, footstep, hint, indication, iota, jot, mark, path, record, relic, remains, remnant, scintilla, shadow, sign, smack, soupçon, spoor, spot, suggestion, survival, suspicion, tincture, tinge, token, touch, track, trail, trifle, vestige, whiff.

v ascertain, chart, copy, delineate, depict, detect, determine, discover, draw, find, follow, keep track of, map, mark, outline, pursue, record, seek, shadow, show, sketch, source, stalk, track (down), trail, traverse, unearth, write.

track *n* beat, channel, course, drift, footmark, footprint, footstep, line, mark, orbit, path, pathway, piste, rail, rails, road, scent, sequence, spoor, trace, trail, train, trajectory, wake, way.

v chase, dog, follow, hunt, pursue, shadow, spoor, stalk, tail, trace, trail, travel, traverse.

track down apprehend, capture, catch, dig up, discover, expose, ferret out, find, hunt down, locate, run to earth, sniff out, trace, unearth.

tract[1] *n* area, district, estate, expanse, extent, lot, plot, quarter, region, section, stretch, territory, zone.

tract[2] *n* article, booklet, brochure, discourse, disquisition, dissertation, essay, homily, leaflet, monograph, pamphlet, sermon, tractate, treatise.

tractable *adj* amenable, biddable, complaisant, compliant, controllable, docile, ductile, fictile, governable, malleable, manageable, obedient, persuadable, plastic, pliable, pliant, submissive, tame, tractile, willing, workable, yielding.

antonyms headstrong, intractable, obstinate, refractory, rigid, stubborn, unruly, wilful.

traction *n* adhesion, drag, draft, drawing, friction, grip, haulage, propulsion, pull, pulling, purchase, resistance.

trade *n* avocation, barter, business, calling, clientele, commerce, commodities, craft, custom, customers, deal, dealing, employment, exchange, interchange, job, line, market, métier, occupation, patrons, profession, pursuit, skill, swap, traffic, transactions, truck.

v bargain, barter, commerce, deal, do business, exchange, negotiate, peddle, swap, switch, traffic, transact, truck.

trademark *n* badge, brand name, crest, emblem, hallmark, identification, idiograph, insignia, label, logo, logotype, name, proprietary name, sign, symbol, trade.

trader *n* barterer, broker, buyer, dealer, marketer, merchandiser, merchant, seller, sutler.

tradesperson *n* artisan, crafter, dealer, journeyman, mechanic, merchant, retailer, seller, skilled worker, storekeeper, vendor.

tradition *n* convention, custom, customs, folklore, habit, institution, lore, practice, praxis, ritual, routine, usage, way, wont.

traditional *adj* accustomed, ancestral, apocryphal, conventional, customary, deep-rooted, established, fixed, folk, historic, legendary, long-established, old, oral, time-honoured, transmitted, unconventional, unwritten, usual.

traduce *v* abuse, asperse, calumniate, decry, defame, denigrate, deprecate, depreciate, detract, disparage, knock, malign, misrepresent, revile, run down, slander, smear, vilify.

traffic *n* barter, business, commerce, communication, dealing, dealings, doings, exchange, freight, intercourse, movement, passengers, peddling, relations, smuggling, trade, transport, transportation, truck, vehicles.

v bargain, barter, deal, do business, exchange, intrigue, market, merchandise, peddle, smuggle, trade, truck.

trafficker *n* broker, dealer, merchant, peddler, pusher, smuggler, trader.

tragedy *n* adversity, affliction, blow, calamity, catastrophe, disaster, misfortune, unhappiness.

antonyms prosperity, success, triumph.

tragic *adj* anguished, appalling, awful, calamitous, catastrophic, deadly, dire, disastrous, doleful, dreadful, fatal, grievous, heartbreaking, heart-rending, heart-wrenching, ill-fated, ill-starred, lamentable, miserable, mournful, pathetic, pitiable, ruinous, sad, shocking, sorrowful, thespian, unfortunate, unhappy, woeful, wretched.

antonyms comic, successful, triumphant.

trail *v* chase, dangle, dawdle, drag, draw, droop, extend, follow, hang, haul, hunt, lag, linger, loiter, pull, pursue, shadow, stalk, straggle, stream, sweep, tail, tow, trace, track, traipse.

n appendage, drag, footpath, footprints, footsteps, mark, marks, path, road, route, scent, spoor, stream, tail, trace, track, train, wake, way.

trail away (or **off**) decrease, die away, diminish, disappear, dwindle, fade (away), fall away, lessen, peter out, shrink, sink, subside, tail off, taper off, weaken.

train v aim, coach, condition, direct, discipline, drill, educate, exercise, focus, guide, improve, instruct, lesson, level, point, prepare, rear, rehearse, school, teach, tutor, work out.

n appendage, attendants, caravan, chain, column, concatenation, convoy, cortege, course, court, entourage, file, followers, following, household, order, process, procession, progression, retinue, sequence, series, set, staff, string, succession, suite, tail, trail.

trainer n coach, handler, instructor, teacher, tutor.

training n coaching, conditioning, discipline, dressage, education, exercise, grounding, guidance, instruction, manège, practice, preparation, schooling, teaching, tuition, tutelage, upbringing, workout.

traipse v drag, plod, schlep, slog, slouch, trail, tramp, trek, trudge, walk, wander.
n plod, slog, tramp, trek, trudge, walk, wander.

trait n attribute, characteristic, feature, idiosyncrasy, lineament, mannerism, peculiarity, quality, quirk.

traitor n apostate, back-stabber, betrayer, deceiver, defector, deserter, double agent, double-crosser, fifth columnist, fink, informer, Judas, miscreant, quisling, rat, rebel, renegade, stool pigeon, turncoat, two-timer.

traitorous adj apostate, dishonourable, disloyal, double-crossing, double-dealing, faithless, false, perfidious, renegade, seditious, treacherous, treasonable, two-timing, unfaithful, untrue.
antonyms faithful, loyal, patriotic.

trajectory n course, flight, line, path, route, track, trail.

trammel n bar, block, bond, chain, check, clog, curb, entanglement, fetter, hamper, handicap, hindrance, impediment, obstacle, rein, shackle, stumbling-block, toils.
v bar, block, capture, catch, check, clog, curb, enmesh, ensnare, entangle, entrap, fetter, hamper, handicap, hinder, hobble, hogtie, impede, inhibit, net, pinion, restrain, restrict, shackle, snag, tie.

tramp v crush, footslog, hike, march, plod, ramble, range, roam, rove, slog, stamp, stomp, stump, toil, traipse, trample, tread, trek, trudge, walk, wander.
n bindlestiff, derelict, down-and-outer, drifter, footfall, footstep, hike, hobo, march, ramble, slog, stamp, stiff, street dweller, street person, traipse, tread, trek, vagabond, vagrant, wanderer.

trample (on) v crush, flatten, hurt, infringe, oppress, ride roughshod over, squash, stamp, tread, violate.

trance n abstraction, another world, brown study, catalepsy, daydream, daze, dream, ecstasy, muse, rapture, reverie, spell, stupefaction, stupor, unconsciousness, woolgathering.

tranquil adj at peace, calm, composed, cool, dispassionate, pacific, peaceful, placid, quiet, reposeful, restful, sedate, serene, still, undisturbed, unexcited, unperturbed, unruffled, untroubled.
antonyms agitated, disturbed, noisy, troubled.

tranquillize v calm, compose, deaden, dull, hush, lull, pacify, quell, quiet, relax, sedate, settle, soothe, still.
antonyms agitate, disturb, upset.

tranquillizer n barbiturate, bromide, downer, narcotic, opiate, opium, sedative.

tranquillity n ataraxia, calm, calmness, composure, coolness, equanimity, hush, imperturbability, peace, peacefulness, placidity, quiet, quietness, quietude, repose, rest, restfulness, sedateness, serenity, silence, stillness.
antonyms agitation, disturbance, noise.

transact v accomplish, carry on, carry out, conclude, conduct, discharge, dispatch, do, enact, execute, handle, manage, negotiate, perform, prosecute, settle.

transaction n action, affair, arrangement, bargain, business, coup, deal, deed, enterprise, event, execution, matter, negotiation, occurrence, proceeding, undertaking.

transactions n affairs, annals, concerns, doings, goings-on, minutes, proceedings, record(s).

transcend v eclipse, exceed, excel, outdo, outrival, outshine, outstrip, overleap, overstep, overtop, surmount, surpass.

transcendence n ascendancy, excellence, greatness, incomparability, matchlessness, predominance, pre-eminence, sublimity, superiority, supremacy.

transcendent adj consummate, exceeding, extraordinary, foremost, incomparable, matchless, peerless, pre-eminent, sublime, superior, transcendental, unequalled, unique, unparalleled, unrivalled, unsurpassed.

transcribe v copy, engross, interpret, note, record, render, reproduce, rewrite, take down, tape, tape-record, transfer, translate, transliterate.

transcript n copy, duplicate, manuscript, note, notes, record, recording, reproduction, tenor, transcription, translation, transliteration, version.

transfer v carry, cede, change, consign, convey, decal, decant, demise, displace, grant, hand over, move, relocate, remove, second, shift, switch, translate, transmit, transplant, transport, transpose.
n change, changeover, crossover, decantation, displacement, move, relocation, removal, shift, switch, switchover, transference, translation, transmission, transposition.

transfigure v alter, apotheosize, change, convert, exalt, glorify, idealize, metamorphose, transform, translate, transmute.

transfix v engross, fascinate, fix, hold, hypnotize, impale, mesmerize, paralyse, petrify, pierce, puncture, skewer, spear, spellbind, spike, spit, stick, stun, transpierce.

antonyms bore, release.

transform v alter, change, convert, metamorphose, reconstruct, remodel, renew, revolutionize, transfigure, translate, transmogrify, transmute, transverse.

antonym preserve.

transformation n alteration, change, conversion, metamorphosis, metanoia, metastasis, renewal, revolution, sea change, transfiguration, translation, transmogrification, transmutation.

antonym preservation.

transfuse v imbue, instil, permeate, pervade, suffuse, transfer.

transgress v breach, break, contravene, defy, disobey, encroach, err, exceed, infringe, lapse, misbehave, offend, overstep, sin, trespass, violate.

antonym obey.

transgression n breach, contravention, crime, debt, encroachment, error, fault, infraction, infringement, iniquity, lapse, misbehaviour, misdeed, misdemeanour, offence, peccadillo, sin, trespass, violation, wrong, wrongdoing.

transgressor n criminal, culprit, debtor, delinquent, evildoer, felon, lawbreaker, malefactor, miscreant, offender, scofflaw, sinner, trespasser, villain, wrongdoer.

transient adj brief, deciduous, ephemeral, evanescent, fleeting, fly-by-night, flying, fugitive, impermanent, momentary, passing, short, short-lived, short-term, temporary, transitory.

antonym permanent.

transit n alteration, carriage, cartage, carting, change, changeover, conversion, conveyance, crossing, haulage, motion, movement, passage, portage, shift, shipment, transfer, transition, transport, transportation, travel, traverse.

transition n alteration, change, changeover, conversion, development, evolution, flux, metamorphosis, metastasis, passage, passing, progress, progression, shift, switch, transformation, transit, transmutation, upheaval.

antonyms beginning, end.

transitional adj changing, developmental, fluid, intermediate, passing, provisional, temporary, transitionary, unsettled.

antonyms final, initial.

transitory adj brief, deciduous, ephemeral, evanescent, fleeting, flying, fugitive, impermanent, momentary, passing, short, short-lived, short-term, temporary, transient, vanishing.

antonym lasting.

translate v alter, carry, change, construe, convert, convey, decipher, decode, elucidate, enrapture, explain, improve, interpret, metamorphose, move, paraphrase, remove, render, renovate, send, simplify, spell out, transcribe, transfer, transfigure, transform, transliterate, transmogrify, transmute, transplant, transport, transpose, turn.

translation n alteration, change, conversion, conveyance, crib, decoding, elucidation, explanation, gloss, interpretation, metamorphosis, move, paraphrase, removal, rendering, rendition, rephrasing, rewording, simplification, transcription, transference, transfiguration, transformation, transliteration, transmutation, transposition, version.

translator n dragoman, exegete, glosser, interpreter, linguist, paraphraser.

translucent adj clear, diaphanous, limpid, lucent, pellucid, translucid, transparent.

antonym opaque.

transmigration n metempsychosis, Pythagoreanism, rebirth, reincarnation, transformation.

transmission n broadcast, broadcasting, carriage, communication, conveyance, diffusion, dispatch, dissemination, passage, program, relaying, remission, sending, shipment, show, showing, signal, spread, trajection, transfer, transference, transit, transport, transportation.

antonym reception.

transmit v broadcast, communicate, convey, diffuse, dispatch, disseminate, forward, impart, network, radio, relay, remit, send, spread, traject, transfer, transport.

antonym receive.

transmute v alter, change, convert, metamorphose, remake, transfigure, transform, translate, transmogrify.

antonym retain.

transparency[1] n apparentness, candidness, clarity, clearness, diaphanousness, directness, distinctness, explicitness, filminess, forthrightness, frankness, gauziness, limpidity, limpidness, obviousness, openness, patentness, pellucidity, pellucidness, perspicuousness, plainness, sheerness, straightforwardness, translucence, translucency, transparence, unambiguousness.

antonyms ambiguity, opacity, unclearness.

transparency[2] n photograph, picture, plate, slide.

transparent adj aboveboard, apparent, artless, candid, clear, crystal-clear, crystalline, diaphanous, direct, distinct, easy, evident, explicit, filmy, forthright, frank, gauzy, hyaline, hyaloid, ingenuous, limpid, lucent, lucid, manifest, obvious, open, patent, pellucid, perspicuous, plain, plain-spoken, recognizable, see-through, sheer, straight, straightforward, translucent, unambiguous, understandable, undisguised, unequivocal, up front.

antonyms ambiguous, opaque, unclear.

transpire v appear, arise, become known, befall, betide, chance, come about, come out, come to light, develop, emerge, happen, leak out, occur, take place, turn out.

transplant v displace, graft, relocate, remove, repot, resettle, shift, transfer, uproot.

transport v banish, bear (away), bring, captivate, carry, carry away, convey, delight, deport, electrify, enchant, enrapture, entrance, exile, fetch, haul, move, ravish, remove, run, ship, spellbind, take, transfer, turn on, waft.
 n bliss, carriage, cartage, carting, conveyance, delight, ecstasy, enchantment, euphoria, happiness, haulage, heaven, rapture, ravishment, removal, rush, shipment, shipping, transference, transportation, vehicle.

transportation n carriage, cartage, carting, conveyance, haulage, postage, transfer, transit, transport.

transpose v alter, change, exchange, interchange, metathesize, move, rearrange, relocate, reorder, shift, substitute, swap, switch, transfer.
 antonym leave.

transverse adj cross, crossways, crosswise, diagonal, oblique, transversal.

trap n ambush, bunker, danger, deception, gin, hazard, net, noose, pitfall, ruse, snare, spring, springe, stratagem, subterfuge, toils, trapdoor, trick, trickery, wile.
 v ambush, beguile, catch, corner, deceive, dupe, enmesh, ensnare, entrap, inveigle, net, snare, take, tangle, trick.

trapped adj ambushed, beguiled, caught, cornered, deceived, duped, ensnared, entangled, inveigled, netted, snared, stuck, surrounded, tricked.
 antonym free.

trapper n backwoodsman, frontiersman, hunter, huntsman, voyageur.

trappings n accompaniments, accoutrements, adornments, apparatus, appurtenances, clothes, decorations, dress, equipment, finery, fittings, fixtures, fripperies, furnishings, gear, housings, livery, ornaments, panoply, paraphernalia, raiment, things, trimmings.

trash n balderdash, bull, dreck, dregs, drivel, dross, garbage, hogwash, junk, kitsch, litter, nonsense, offscourings, refuse, rot, rubbish, scoria, sweepings, tripe, trumpery, twaddle, waste.
 antonyms sense, treasure.

trashy adj catchpenny, cheap, cheapjack, flimsy, grotty, inferior, kitschy, meretricious, pinchbeck, shabby, shoddy, tawdry, third-rate, tinsel, valueless, worthless.
 antonyms first-rate, valuable.

trauma n agony, anguish, damage, disturbance, hurt, injury, jolt, lesion, ordeal, pain, scar, shock, strain, suffering, torture, upheaval, upset, wound.
 antonyms healing, relaxation.

traumatic adj agonizing, damaging, distressing, disturbing, frightening, hurtful, injurious, painful, scarring, shocking, unpleasant, upsetting, wounding.
 antonyms healing, relaxed, relaxing.

travail n birth pangs, childbirth, distress, drudgery, effort, exertion, grind, labour, labour pains, moil, pain, slavery, slog, strain, stress, struggle, suffering, sweat, tears, throes, toil, tribulation, trouble.
 antonym rest.

travel v commute, cross, drift, go, globetrot, junket, journey, locomote, move, peregrinate, proceed, progress, ramble, roam, rove, take a trip, tour, traverse, trek, voyage, walk, wander, wend.
 antonym stay.

traveller n agent, bird of passage, drummer, excursionist, explorer, globetrotter, gypsy, hiker, hitchhiker, holiday-maker, itinerant, journeyer, migrant, nomad, passenger, peregrinator, rep, representative, salesperson, tinker, tourist, vagrant, voyager, wanderer, wayfarer.

travelling adj itinerant, migrant, migratory, mobile, movable, moving, nomadic, on the move, peregrinating, peripatetic, roaming, roving, touring, vagrant, wandering, wayfaring.
 antonyms fixed, stay-at-home.

travels n excursion, expedition, globetrotting, journey, passage, peregrination, ramble, tour, travel, trip, voyage, walk, wanderings.

traverse v balk, bridge, check, consider, contradict, contravene, counter, counteract, cover, cross, deny, dispute, examine, eye, frustrate, hinder, impede, inspect, intersect, investigate, move, negotiate, obstruct, oppose, peregrinate, peruse, ply, range, review, roam, scan, scrutinize, span, study, swing, thwart, turn, wander.
 antonyms aid, confirm, remain.

travesty n apology, botch, burlesque, caricature, distortion, lampoon, mockery, parody, perversion, sendup, sham, takeoff.
 v burlesque, caricature, deride, distort, lampoon, mock, parody, pervert, pillory, ridicule, send up, sham, spoof, take off.

treacherous adj back-stabbing, dangerous, deceitful, deceptive, disloyal, double-crossing, double-dealing, duplicitous, faithless, false, hazardous, icy, perfidious, perilous, precarious, Punic, recreant, risky, slippery, traitorous, treasonable, tricky, unfaithful, unreliable, unsafe, unstable, untrue, untrustworthy.
 antonyms dependable, loyal.

treachery n betrayal, disloyalty, double cross, double-dealing, duplicity, faithlessness, falseness, infidelity, Judas kiss, lese-majesty, perfidiousness, perfidy, Punic faith, stab in the back, treason.
 antonyms dependability, loyalty.

tread v hike, march, pace, pad, plod, stamp, step, stride, tramp, trudge, walk, walk on.
 n footfall, footstep, gait, pace, step, stride, walk.

tread underfoot crush, have contempt for, oppress, put down, repress, squash, squelch, step on, stomp on, subdue, subjugate, trample, walk all over, walk on.

treason n disaffection, disloyalty, duplicity, lese-majesty, mutiny, perfidy, sedition, subversion, traitorousness, treachery.

antonym loyalty.

treasonable *adj* disloyal, false, insurrectionary, mutinous, perfidious, seditious, subversive, traitorous, treacherous.

antonym loyal.

treasure *n* apple of one's eye, cash, darling, flower, fortune, funds, gem, gold, jewel, jewels, money, nonpareil, paragon, pearl, precious, pride and joy, prize, riches, valuables, wealth.

v adore, cherish, esteem, idolize, love, preserve, prize, revere, value, venerate, worship.

antonym disparage.

treasurer *n* bursar, cashier, purser, quaestor.

treasury[1] *n* assets, bank, cache, capital, coffers, exchequer, finances, funds, hoard, money, repository, resources, revenues, store, storehouse, vault.

treasury[2] *n* chrestomathy, corpus, Parnassus, thesaurus.

treat *n* celebration, delight, enjoyment, entertainment, excursion, fun, gift, goody, gratification, joy, little something, outing, party, pleasure, satisfaction, surprise, sweet, thrill.

antonym punishment.

v attend to, bargain, care for, confer, consider, contain, deal with, discourse upon, discuss, doctor, entertain, give, handle, manage, medicament, medicate, medicine, negotiate, nurse, parley, provide, regale, regard, stand, use.

treatise *n* disquisition, dissertation, essay, exposition, monograph, pamphlet, pandect, paper, prolegomena, study, thesis, tract, tractate, work, writing.

treatment *n* care, conduct, cure, deal, dealing, discussion, handling, healing, management, manipulation, medication, medicine, prescript, reception, regimen, remedy, surgery, therapeutics, therapy, usage, use.

treaty *n* agreement, alliance, bargain, bond, compact, concordat, contract, convention, covenant, entente, negotiation, pact.

treble *adj* high, high-pitched, piping, sharp, shrill, soprano, threefold, triple.

antonyms deep, rumbling.

tree *n* bush, conifer, cross, evergreen, pollard, sapling, seedling, shrub.

trek *n* expedition, footslog, hike, journey, march, migration, odyssey, safari, slog, traipse, tramp, trip, walk.

v footslog, hike, journey, march, migrate, plod, range, roam, rove, schlep, slog, traipse, tramp, travel, trudge.

tremble *v* flutter, heave, oscillate, palpitate, quail, quake, quaver, quiver, rock, shake, shiver, shudder, teeter, totter, vibrate, wobble.

n flutter, oscillation, palpitation, quake, quaver, quiver, shake, shiver, shudder, tremor, vibration.

antonym steadiness.

trembling *n* oscillation, quaking, quavering, quivering, rocking, shakes, shaking, shivering, shuddering, trepidation, vibration.

antonym steadiness.

tremendous *adj* ace, amazing, appalling, awe-inspiring, awesome, awful, colossal, deafening, dreadful, enormous, excellent, exceptional, extraordinary, fabulous, fantastic, fearful, fearsome, formidable, frightful, gargantuan, gigantic, great, hell of a, herculean, huge, immense, incredible, mammoth, marvellous, monstrous, prodigious, sensational, spectacular, stupendous, super, terrible, terrific, titanic, towering, vast, whopping, wonderful.

antonyms boring, run-of-the-mill, tiny.

tremor *n* agitation, earthquake, paroxysm, quake, quaking, quaver, quavering, quiver, quivering, shake, shaking, shiver, shock, spasm, thrill, tremble, trembling, trepidation, trill, twitch, udder, vibration, wobble.

antonym steadiness.

tremulous *adj* afraid, agitated, agog, anxious, apprehensive, aspen, diffident, dithery, excited, faltering, fearful, frightened, jittery, jumpy, nervous, quavering, quivering, quivery, scared, shaking, shivering, shy, timid, trembling, trembly, vibrating, wavering, weak.

antonyms calm, firm.

trench *n* channel, conduit, cut, ditch, drain, duct, earthwork, entrenchment, excavation, fosse, furrow, gullet, gutter, pit, rill, sap, trough, waterway.

trenchant *adj* acerbic, acid, acidulous, acute, astringent, biting, caustic, clear, clear-cut, cogent, crisp, cutting, distinct, driving, effective, effectual, emphatic, energetic, explicit, forceful, forthright, hurtful, incisive, keen, mordant, penetrating, piquant, pointed, potent, powerful, pungent, sarcastic, scratching, severe, sharp, strong, tart, unequivocal, vigorous.

antonym woolly.

trend *n* bias, course, craze, current, dernier cri, direction, drift, fad, fashion, flow, inclination, leaning, look, mode, rage, style, tendency, thing, vogue.

trendy *adj* fashionable, funky, groovy, hip, in, latest, modish, stylish, up to the minute, voguish, with it.

antonym unfashionable.

trepidation *n* agitation, alarm, anxiety, apprehension, butterflies, cold sweat, consternation, dismay, disquiet, disturbance, dread, emotion, excitement, fear, fright, jitters, misgivings, nervousness, palpitation, perturbation, qualms, quivering, shaking, trembling, tremor, unease, uneasiness, willies, worry.

antonym calm.

trespass *v* encroach, err, infringe, injure, intrude, invade, obtrude, offend, poach, sin, transgress, violate, wrong.

antonyms keep to, obey.

n breach, contravention, crime, delinquency, encroachment, error, evildoing, fault, infraction, infringement, iniquity, injury, intrusion, invasion, misbehaviour, misconduct, misdeed, misdemeanour, offence, poaching, sin, transgression, wrongdoing.

trespasser *n* criminal, delinquent, evildoer, infringer, interloper, intruder, invader, malefactor, offender, poacher, sinner, transgressor, wrongdoer.

tress *n* braid, bunch, curl, lock, pigtail, plait, queue, ringlet, tail.

trial *n* adversity, affliction, assay, attempt, audition, bane, bother, burden, check, contest, crack, distress, dry run, effort, endeavour, examination, experience, experiment, grief, hardship, hassle, hearing, irritation, litigation, load, misery, nuisance, ordeal, pain, pest, plague, probation, proof, shot, sorrow, stab, suffering, taste, temptation, test, testing, tribulation, tribunal, trouble, try, trying, unhappiness, venture, vexation, woe, worry, wretchedness.

antonyms happiness, rest.

adj experimental, exploratory, pilot, probationary, provisional, testing.

triangular *adj* cuneiform, three-cornered, three-sided, trigonal, trilateral.

tribe *n* blood, branch, bunch, caste, clan, class, crowd, division, dynasty, family, gens, group, house, ilk, nation, people, phratry, race, seed, sept, stock.

tribulation *n* adversity, affliction, blow, burden, care, curse, distress, grief, heartache, misery, misfortune, ordeal, pain, reverse, sorrow, suffering, travail, trial, trouble, unhappiness, vexation, woe, worry, wretchedness.

antonyms happiness, rest.

tribunal *n* bar, bench, court, examination, forum, hearing, inquisition, trial.

tribute *n* acclaim, acclamation, accolade, acknowledgment, applause, charge, commendation, compliment, contribution, credit, customs, duty, encomium, esteem, eulogy, excise, gift, gratitude, homage, honour, impost, laudation, offering, panegyric, payment, praise, ransom, recognition, respect, subsidy, tax, testimonial, testimony, toll.

antonym blame.

trice *n* flash, instant, jiffy, minute, moment, sec, second, shake, twinkling.

trick *n* ability, antic, art, artifice, caper, characteristic, chicane, command, con, craft, deceit, deception, device, dodge, expedient, expertise, feat, feint, flimflam, foible, fraud, frolic, gag, gambol, gift, gimmick, habit, hang, hoax, idiosyncrasy, imposition, imposture, jape, joke, josh, knack, know-how, legerdemain, mannerism, manoeuvre, peculiarity, ploy, practical joke, practice, prank, put-on, quirk, ruse, secret, skill, sleight, spell, stratagem, stunt, subterfuge, swindle, technique, toy, trait, trap, turn, wile.

v bamboozle, beguile, cheat, con, cozen, deceive, defraud, delude, diddle, dupe, fool, gull, hoax, hoodwink, hornswoggle, lead on, mislead, outwit, pull a fast one on, put one over on, sell, snow, swindle, trap.

trick out adorn, array, attire, bedeck, bedizen, decorate, doll up, dress up, ornament, prink, spruce up, tart up, trick up.

trickery *n* cheating, chicanery, con, deceit, deception, dishonesty, double-dealing, flimflam, fraud, funny business, guile, hanky-panky, hoax, hocus-pocus, imposture, jiggery-pokery, jugglery, monkey business, pretence, shenanigans, skulduggery, sleight, sleight of hand, smoke and mirrors, swindling, tricksiness.

antonym honesty.

trickle *v* dribble, drip, drop, exude, filter, gutter, leak, ooze, percolate, run, seep.

antonyms gush, stream.

n dribble, driblet, dribs and drabs, drip, seepage.

antonyms gush, stream.

trickster *n* cheat, con man, cozener, deceiver, diddler, fraud, hoaxer, impostor, joker, pretender, swindler, tricker.

tricky *adj* artful, complicated, crafty, cunning, deceitful, deceptive, delicate, devious, difficult, foxy, Gordian, knotty, problematic, risky, scheming, slippery, sly, sticky, subtle, thorny, ticklish, touch-and-go, trickish, tricksy, wily.

antonyms easy, honest.

trifle *n* bagatelle, bauble, bit, dash, drop, falderal, finicality, foolishness, gewgaw, gimcrack, jot, knick-knack, little, nonsense, nothing, pinch, pittance, plaything, spot, touch, toy, trace, trinket, triviality.

v coquet, dabble, dally, dawdle, fiddle, fiddle-faddle, flirt, fool, fritter, frivol, idle, meddle, niggle, palter, play, play with, sport, toy, wanton, waste.

trifler *n* dallier, dilettante, good-for-nothing, idler, layabout, loafer, ne'er-do-well, piddler, waster.

trifles *n* inessentials, minor considerations, minutiae, trivia, trivialities.

antonym essentials.

trifling *adj* empty, frivolous, idle, inconsiderable, insignificant, minuscule, negligible, nugatory, paltry, petty, picayune, piddling, piffling, puny, shallow, silly, slight, small, tiny, trivial, two-bit, unimportant, valueless, worthless.

antonym important.

trigger *v* activate, actuate, cause, elicit, generate, initiate, produce, prompt, provoke, set off, spark off, start.

n catch, goad, lever, release, spur, stimulus, switch.

trill *v* cheep, chirp, chirrup, sing, tweet, twitter, warble, whistle.

trim *adj* clean-limbed, compact, dapper, natty, neat, orderly, shipshape, slender, slim, smart, soigné, soignée, spick-and-span, spruce, streamlined, svelte, well-dressed, well-groomed, willowy.

antonym scruffy.

v adjust, adorn, arrange, array, balance, barber, beautify, bedeck, clip, crop, curtail, cut, decorate, distribute, dock, dress, embellish, embroider, garnish, lop, order, ornament, pare, prepare, prune, settle, shave, shear, tidy.

n adornment, array, attire, border, clipping, condition, crop, cut, decoration, disposition, dress, edging, embellishment, equipment, fettle, fitness, fittings, form, frill, fringe, garnish, gear, health, humour, nick, order, ornament, ornamentation, piping, pruning, repair, shape, shave, shearing, situation, state, temper, trappings, trimming.

trimming *n* adornment, border, braid, decoration, edging, embellishment, fimbriation, frill, fringe, frou-frou, furbelow, garnish, gingerbread, ornamentation, piping, rickrack, trim, window dressing.

trimmings *n* accessories, accompaniments, additions, appurtenances, clippings, cuttings, ends, extras, frills, garnish, ornaments, paraphernalia, parings, remnants, shavings, trappings.

trinity *n* threefoldness, threesome, triad, trilogy, trio, triple, triplet, triumvirate, triune, triunity, troika.

trinket *n* bagatelle, bauble, bibelot, bijou, doodad, gewgaw, gimcrack, kickshaws, knick-knack, nothing, ornament, toy, trifle.

trio *n* threesome, triad, trilogy, trine, trinity, triple, triplet, triptych, triumvirate, triune.

trip *n* blunder, errand, error, excursion, expedition, fall, faux pas, foray, indiscretion, jaunt, journey, lapse, misstep, outing, ramble, run, skip, slip, step, stumble, tour, travel, voyage.

v activate, blunder, caper, confuse, dance, disconcert, engage, err, fall, flip, flit, frisk, gambol, go, hop, lapse, miscalculate, misstep, pull, ramble, release, set off, skip, slip, slip up, spring, stumble, switch on, throw, tilt up, tip up, tour, trap, travel, tumble, unsettle, voyage.

tripe *n* balderdash, blah, bosh, bull, bunk, claptrap, drivel, eyewash, garbage, guff, hogwash, inanity, nonsense, poppycock, rot, rubbish, trash, trumpery, twaddle.

antonyms sense, treasure.

triple *adj* ternate, three-branched, threefold, three-ply, three-way, treble, trinal, trinary, tripartite, triplex, triplicate, triploid.

n threefoldness, threesome, triad, trilogy, trine, trinity, trio, triplet, triplex, triplicity, triumvirate, triune, triunity.

v treble, triplicate.

triplet *n* tercet, threesome, triad, trilogy, trine, trinity, trio, triple, triplicity, tripling, triumvirate, triune, troika.

tripper *n* excursionist, holiday-maker, sightseer, tourist, voyager.

trite *adj* banal, bromidic, clichéd, common, commonplace, corny, dull, hack, hackneyed, ordinary, overworn, pedestrian, routine, run-of-the-mill, stale, stereotyped, stock, threadbare, tired, uninspired, unoriginal, well-trodden, well-worn, worn, worn out.

antonym original.

triumph (over) *v* best, celebrate, crow, defeat, dominate, exult, gloat, glory, have the last

laugh, humble, humiliate, jubilate, overcome, overwhelm, prevail, prosper, rejoice, revel, subdue, succeed, swagger, vanquish, win.

antonym fail.

n accomplishment, achievement, ascendancy, attainment, conquest, coup, elation, exultation, feat, happiness, hit, joy, jubilation, master stroke, mastery, pride, rejoicing, sensation, smash, smash hit, success, tour de force, victory, walkaway, walkover, win.

antonym disaster.

triumphant *adj* boastful, celebratory, conquering, dominant, elated, exultant, gloating, glorious, joyful, jubilant, proud, rejoicing, successful, swaggering, triumphal, undefeated, victorious, winning.

antonyms defeated, humble.

trivia *n* details, irrelevancies, minutiae, trifles, trivialities.

antonym essentials.

trivial *adj* commonplace, dinky, everyday, frivolous, incidental, inconsequential, inconsiderable, insignificant, little, meaningless, minor, negligible, nugatory, paltry, pettifogging, petty, piddling, piffling, puny, slight, small, snippety, trifling, trite, unimportant, valueless, worthless.

antonym significant.

triviality *n* detail, frivolity, futility, inconsequence, inconsequentiality, insignificance, littleness, meaninglessness, minor matter, negligibility, nothing, nugatoriness, paltriness, pettiness, slightness, smallness, technicality, trifle, triteness, unimportance, valuelessness, worthlessness.

antonyms essential, importance.

trivialize *v* belittle, depreciate, devalue, downplay, minimize, scoff at, underestimate, underplay, undervalue.

antonym exalt.

troop *n* assemblage, band, body, bunch, company, contingent, crew, crowd, division, drove, flock, gang, gathering, group, herd, horde, multitude, pack, squad, squadron, swarm, team, throng, trip, unit.

v crowd, flock, go, march, pack, parade, stream, swarm, throng, traipse, turn.

troops *n* army, military, servicemen, servicewomen, soldiers, soldiery.

trophy *n* award, booty, cup, laurels, memento, memorial, prize, souvenir, spoils.

tropical *adj* equatorial, hot, humid, lush, luxuriant, steamy, stifling, sultry, sweltering, torrid.

antonyms arctic, cold, cool, temperate.

trot *v* bustle, canter, jog, lope, pace, run, scamper, scurry, scuttle.

n canter, jog, jog trot, lope, run.

trot out adduce, bring forward, bring up, drag up, exhibit, recite, rehearse, reiterate, relate, repeat.

troubadour *n* balladeer, jongleur, minnesinger, minstrel, poet, singer.

trouble *n* affliction, agitation, ailment, annoyance, anxiety, attention, bother, care, commotion, complaint, concern, danger, defect, difficulty, dilemma, disability, discontent, discord, disease, disorder, disquiet, dissatisfaction, distress, disturbance, effort, exertion, failure, grief, heartache, illness, inconvenience, irritation, labour, malfunction, mess, misfortune, nuisance, pain, pains, pest, pickle, predicament, problem, row, scrape, solicitude, sorrow, spot, strife, struggle, suffering, thought, torment, travail, trial, tribulation, tumult, uneasiness, unrest, upheaval, upset, vexation, woe, work, worry.

antonyms calm, peace.

v afflict, agitate, annoy, bother, burden, discomfort, discommode, discompose, disconcert, disquiet, distress, disturb, fret, grieve, harass, incommode, inconvenience, molest, muddy, pain, perplex, perturb, pester, plague, sadden, torment, upset, vex, worry.

antonyms help, reassure.

troublemaker *n* agent provocateur, agitator, firebrand, heller, hellion, hellraiser, incendiary, instigator, meddler, mischief-maker, rabble-rouser, ringleader, stirrer, tub thumper.

antonym peacemaker.

troublesome *adj* annoying, arduous, bothersome, burdensome, demanding, difficult, disorderly, harassing, hard, importunate, inconvenient, insubordinate, irksome, irritating, laborious, oppressive, pestilential, plaguey, rebellious, recalcitrant, refractory, rowdy, spiny, taxing, thorny, tiresome, tricky, trying, turbulent, unco-operative, undisciplined, unruly, upsetting, vexatious, violent, wearisome, worrisome, worrying.

antonyms easy, helpful, polite.

trough *n* channel, conduit, crib, depression, ditch, duct, flume, furrow, gully, gutter, hollow, manger, trench, tub.

trounce *v* beat, best, blank, clobber, crush, drub, hammer, lick, overwhelm, paste, punish, rebuke, rout, slaughter, thrash, whale, whitewash.

troupe *n* band, cast, company, group, set, troop.

trouper *n* actor, artiste, entertainer, old hand, performer, player, theatrical, thespian, veteran.

trousers *n* bloomers, breeches, breeks, culottes, denims, ducks, dungarees, flannels, jeans, knickerbockers, lederhosen, Levis, pantaloons, pants, pedal pushers, plus fours, shorts, slacks.

truce *n* armistice, break, cease-fire, cessation, intermission, interval, letup, lull, moratorium, peace, respite, rest, stay, suspension, treaty.

antonym hostilities.

truck[1] *n* barrow, camion, cart, drag, float, handcart, lorry, trailer, trolley, van, wagon, wheelbarrow.

truck[2] *n* business, commerce, communication, connection, contact, dealings, exchange, intercourse, relations, trade, traffic.

truculent *adj* aggressive, antagonistic, bad-tempered, bellicose, belligerent, combative, contentious, cross, defiant, fierce, hostile, ill-tempered, obstreperous, pugnacious, quarrelsome, savage, scrappy, sullen, violent.

antonyms co-operative, good-natured.

trudge *v* clump, hike, labour, lumber, march, mush, plod, slog, stump, traipse, tramp, trek, walk.

n haul, hike, march, mush, slog, traipse, tramp, trek, walk.

true *adj* absolute, accurate, actual, apodictic, authentic, bona fide, confirmed, conformable, constant, correct, corrected, dedicated, devoted, dutiful, exact, factual, faithful, fast, firm, genuine, honest, honourable, legitimate, loyal, natural, perfect, precise, proper, pure, real, right, rightful, sincere, sooth, square, staunch, steady, true-blue, true-born, true-hearted, trustworthy, trusty, truthful, typical, unerring, unswerving, upright, valid, veracious, veridical, veritable.

antonyms faithless, false, inaccurate.

adv accurately, correctly, exactly, faithfully, honestly, perfectly, precisely, properly, rightly, truly, truthfully, unerringly, veraciously, veritably.

antonyms falsely, inaccurately.

true-blue *adj* card-carrying, committed, confirmed, constant, dedicated, devoted, dyed-in-the-wool, faithful, loyal, orthodox, staunch, true, trusty, uncompromising, unwavering.

antonyms superficial, wavering.

truism *n* axiom, bromide, cliché, commonplace, platitude, proverb, saw, saying, truth, verity.

truly *adv* accurately, authentically, constantly, correctly, devotedly, dutifully, exactly, exceptionally, extremely, factually, faithfully, firmly, genuinely, greatly, honestly, honourably, indeed, indubitably, in good sooth, in reality, in truth, legitimately, loyally, precisely, properly, really, rightly, sincerely, soothly, staunchly, steadfastly, steadily, truthfully, undeniably, veraciously, verily, veritably, very.

antonyms faithlessly, falsely, incorrectly, slightly.

trumped-up *adj* concocted, contrived, cooked-up, fabricated, fake, faked, false, falsified, invented, made-up, phony, spurious, untrue.

antonym genuine.

trumpery *adj* cheap, flashy, grotty, meretricious, nasty, pinchbeck, shabby, shoddy, tawdry, trashy, trifling, useless, valueless, worthless.

antonym first-rate.

trumpet *n* bellow, blare, blast, bray, bugle, call, clarion, cry, honk, horn, roar.

v advertise, announce, bellow, blare, blast, bray, broadcast, call, extol, honk, proclaim, publish, roar, shout, tout.

trump up *v* concoct, contrive, cook up, create, devise, fabricate, fake, invent, make up.

truncate *v* abbreviate, clip, crop, curtail, cut, cut short, lop, maim, pare, prune, shorten, trim.

antonym lengthen.

truncheon *n* baton, billy, club, cudgel, knobkerrie, nightstick, shillelagh, staff.

trunk¹ *n* body, bole, frame, shaft, stalk, stem, stock, torso, tube.

trunk² *n* bin, box, case, chest, coffer, crate, footlocker, locker, luggage, suitcase.

trunk³ *n* nose, proboscis, snout.

truss *v* bind, bundle, fasten, hogtie, pack, pinion, secure, strap, tether, tie.

antonym untie.

n bale, bandage, beam, binding, brace, bundle, buttress, joist, prop, shore, stanchion, stay, strut, support.

trust *n* affiance, assurance, belief, care, certainty, certitude, charge, confidence, conviction, credence, credit, custody, duty, expectation, faith, fidelity, guard, guardianship, hope, obligation, protection, reliance, responsibility, safekeeping, trusteeship.

antonym mistrust.

v assign, assume, bank on, believe, command, commit, confide, consign, count on, credit, delegate, depend on, entrust, expect, give, hope, imagine, presume, rely on, suppose, surmise, swear by.

antonym mistrust.

trustee *n* administrator, agent, custodian, depositary, executor, fiduciary, guardian, keeper, school trustee.

trusting *adj* confiding, credulous, gullible, innocent, naïve, optimistic, simple, trustful, unguarded, unquestioning, unsuspecting, unsuspicious, unwary.

antonyms cautious, distrustful.

trustworthy *adj* authentic, dependable, ethical, foursquare, honest, honourable, level-headed, mature, principled, reliable, responsible, righteous, sensible, steadfast, true, trusty, truthful, upright.

antonym unreliable.

trusty *adj* dependable, faithful, firm, honest, loyal, reliable, responsible, solid, staunch, steady, straightforward, strong, supportive, true, trustworthy, upright.

antonym unreliable.

truth *n* accuracy, actuality, axiom, candour, certainty, constancy, dedication, devotion, dutifulness, exactness, fact, facts, factuality, factualness, faith, faithfulness, fidelity, frankness, genuineness, historicity, honesty, integrity, law, legitimacy, loyalty, maxim, precision, realism, reality, sooth, truism, truthfulness, uprightness, validity, veracity, veridicality, verity.

antonym falsehood.

truthful *adj* accurate, candid, correct, exact, faithful, forthright, frank, honest, literal, naturalistic, plain-spoken, precise, realistic, reliable, sincere, sooth, soothfast, straight, straightforward, true, trustworthy, veracious, veridical, verist, veristic, veritable.

antonym untruthful.

truthfulness *n* candour, frankness, honesty, openness, righteousness, sincerity, straightness, uprightness, veracity, verism.

antonym untruthfulness.

try *v* adjudge, adjudicate, afflict, aim, annoy, appraise, attempt, catechize, endeavour, essay, evaluate, examine, experiment, hear, inconvenience, inspect, investigate, irk, irritate, pain, plague, prove, sample, seek, strain, stress, strive, struggle, taste, tax, test, tire, trouble, undertake, upset, venture, vex, wear out, weary.

n appraisal, attempt, bash, crack, effort, endeavour, essay, evaluation, experiment, fling, go, inspection, sample, shot, stab, taste, taster, test, trial, whack.

try out appraise, check out, evaluate, inspect, sample, taste, test, try on.

trying *adj* aggravating, annoying, arduous, bothersome, difficult, distressing, exasperating, fatiguing, hard, irksome, irritating, searching, severe, stressful, taxing, testing, tiresome, tough, troublesome, upsetting, vexing, wearisome.

antonym calming.

tub *n* barrel, basin, bath, bathtub, bucket, butt, cask, hogshead, keg, pail, puncheon, tun, vat.

tubby *adj* buxom, chubby, corpulent, fat, obese, overweight, paunchy, plump, portly, pudgy, roly-poly, stout.

antonym slim.

tube *n* channel, conduit, cylinder, duct, hose, inlet, main, outlet, pipe, shaft, spout, trunk, vas.

tubular *adj* pipelike, tubate, tubelike, tubulate, tubulous.

tuck¹ *v* cram, crease, fold, gather, insert, push, stuff.

n crease, fold, gather, pinch, pleat, pucker.

tuck² *n* comestibles, eats, food, grub, nosh, scoff, victuals.

tuck in devour, dine, eat, eat up, fall to, feast, gobble, gorge, scarf, scoff, sup.

tuft *n* beard, bunch, clump, cluster, collection, crest, dollop, floccus, flock, knot, shock, tassle, topknot, truss, tussock.

tug *v* drag, draw, haul, heave, jerk, jiggle, lug, pluck, pull, tow, wrench, yank.

n drag, haul, heave, jerk, pluck, pull, tow, traction, wrench, yank.

tuition *n* education, instruction, lessons, pedagogy, schooling, teaching, training, tutelage, tutoring.

tumble *v* disorder, drop, fall, flop, jumble, overthrow, pitch, plummet, roll, rumple, stumble, topple, toss, trip up.

n collapse, drop, fall, flop, plunge, roll, spill, stumble, toss, trip.

tumbledown *adj* broken-down, crumbling, crumbly, decrepit, dilapidated, disintegrating, ramshackle, rickety, ruined, ruinous, shaky, tottering.

antonym well-kept.

tumbler[1] *n* acrobat, contortionist, gymnast.

tumbler[2] *n* beaker, cup, drinking glass, glass, goblet, mug, schooner.

tumid *adj* affected, bloated, bombastic, bulbous, bulging, distended, enlarged, euphuistic, flowery, fulsome, fustian, grandiloquent, grandiose, high-flown, inflated, magniloquent, orotund, overblown, pompous, pretentious, protuberant, puffed up, puffy, sesquipedalian, stilted, swollen, tumescent, turgid.

antonyms flat, simple.

tumour *n* cancer, carcinoma, growth, lump, lymphoma, melanoma, myeloma, neoplasm, sarcoma, swelling, tubercle.

tumult *n* ado, affray, agitation, altercation, bedlam, brawl, brouhaha, bustle, clamour, coil, commotion, din, disorder, disturbance, Donnybrook, excitement, fracas, hubbub, hullabaloo, outbreak, pandemonium, quarrel, racket, riot, rout, row, ruffle, stir, strife, to-do, turmoil, unrest, upheaval, uproar.

antonym calm.

tumultuous *adj* agitated, boisterous, clamorous, confused, disorderly, disturbed, excited, fierce, hectic, noisy, obstreperous, passionate, raging, restless, riotous, rowdy, stormy, tempestuous, troubled, turbulent, unrestrained, unruly, uproarious, violent, vociferous, wild.

antonym calm.

tune *n* agreement, air, attitude, concert, concord, consonance, demeanour, disposition, euphony, frame of mind, harmony, melody, mood, motif, pitch, song, strain, sympathy, temper, theme, unison.

v adapt, adjust, attune, harmonize, pitch, regulate, set, synchronize, temper.

tuneful *adj* catchy, euphonious, harmonious, mellifluous, mellow, melodic, melodious, musical, pleasant, sonorous.

antonym tuneless.

tuneless *adj* atonal, cacophonous, clashing, discordant, dissonant, harsh, unmelodic, unmelodious, unmusical.

antonym tuneful.

tunnel *n* burrow, channel, chimney, drift, gallery, hole, passage, passageway, sap, shaft, subway, underpass.

v burrow, dig, excavate, mine, penetrate, sap, undermine.

turbid *adj* clouded, cloudy, confused, dense, dim, disordered, feculent, foggy, foul, fuzzy, hazy, impure, incoherent, muddled, muddy, murky, opaque, roily, thick, unclear, unsettled.

antonym clear.

▲ *confusable word* turgid.

turbulence *n* agitation, boiling, chaos, commotion, confusion, disorder, disruption, instability, pandemonium, roughness, storm, tumult, turmoil, unrest, upheaval.

antonym calm.

turbulent *adj* agitated, blustery, boiling, boisterous, chaotic, choppy, confused, disordered, disorderly, foaming, furious, insubordinate, obstreperous, raging, rebellious, riotous, rough, rowdy, stormy, tempestuous, tumultuous, unbridled, undisciplined, ungovernable, unruly, unsettled, unstable, uproarious, violent, wild.

antonym calm.

turf *n* clod, divot, glebe, grass, green, lawn, sod, sward.

turf out banish, bounce, chuck out, discharge, dismiss, dispossess, eject, evict, expel, fire, fling out, kick out, oust, sack, throw out, turn out.

turgid *adj* affected, bloated, bombastic, bulging, congested, dilated, distended, extravagant, flowery, fulsome, fustian, grandiloquent, grandiose, high-flown, inflated, magniloquent, orotund, ostentatious, overblown, pompous, pretentious, protuberant, puffy, sesquipedalian, stilted, swollen, tumescent, tumid, windy.

antonyms flat, simple.

▲ *confusable word* turbid.

turmoil *n* agitation, bedlam, brouhaha, bustle, chaos, combustion, commotion, confusion, disorder, disquiet, disturbance, Donnybrook, dust, ferment, flurry, noise, pandemonium, pother, rout, row, ruffle, stir, strife, trouble, tumult, turbulence, uproar, violence, welter.

antonym calm.

turn *v* adapt, alter, apostatize, appeal, apply, approach, become, caracole, change, circle, construct, convert, corner, crank, curdle, defect, deliver, depend, desert, divert, double, execute, fashion, fit, form, frame, go, gyrate, hang, hinge, infatuate, influence, issue, look, make, metamorphose, mould, move, mutate, nauseate, negotiate, pass, perform, persuade, pivot, prejudice, remodel, renege, resort, retract, return, reverse, revolve, roll, rotate, shape, shift, sicken, sour, spin, spoil, swerve, switch, swivel, taint, transfigure, transform, translate, transmute, twirl, twist, upset, veer, wheel, whirl, write.

n act, action, airing, aptitude, bend, bent, bias, bout, caracole, cast, chance, change, circle, circuit, constitutional, crack, crank, crisis, culmination, curve, cycle, deed, departure, deviation, direction, distortion, drift, drive, excursion, exigency, fashion, favour, fling, form, format, fright, gesture, guise, gyration, heading, innings, jaunt, make-up, manner, mode, mould, occasion, opportunity, outing, performance, performer, period, pivot, promenade, reversal, revolution, ride, rotation, round, saunter, scare, service, shape, shift, shock, shot, spell, spin, start, stint, stroll, style, succession, surprise, swing, tendency, time, trend, trick, try, turning, twist, U-ie, U-turn, vicissitude, walk, warp, way, whack, whirl.

to a turn correctly, exactly, perfectly, precisely, to perfection.

turn away avert, deflect, depart, deviate, discharge, dismiss, reject.

antonym accept.

turn back beat off, do a U-turn, drive back, drive off, force back, go back, rebuff, repel, repulse, resist, retrace one's steps, return, revert.

antonyms go on, stay.

turn down decline, diminish, fold, invert, lessen, lower, moderate, muffle, mute, quieten, rebuff, refuse, reject, repudiate, soften, spurn.

antonyms accept, turn up.

turn in deliver, enter, exchange, give back, give up, go to bed, hand in, hand over, hit the sack, register, retire, return, submit, surrender, tender, trade in.

antonyms get up, give out, keep.

turn of events change in fortune, development, outcome, result, twist of fate.

turn off alienate, bore, branch off, cut out, depart from, deviate, discourage, disenchant, disgust, displease, divert, irritate, leave, nauseate, offend, put off, put out, quit, repel, repulse, shut, shut down, sicken, stop, switch off, turn out, unplug.

antonym turn on.

turn on activate, arouse, assail, assault, attack, attract, balance, depend, energize, excite, expose, fall on, hang, hinge, ignite, inform, initiate, introduce, pivot, please, rest, round on, rouse, show, start, start up, stimulate, switch on, thrill, titillate, trip, turn against, work up.

antonym turn off.

turn out accoutre, apparel, appear, assemble, attend, attire, banish, become, cashier, clean out, clear, clothe, come, come about, come out right, crop up, deport, develop, discharge, dismiss, dispossess, dress, drive out, drum out, emerge, empty, end up, eventuate, evict, evolve, expel, fabricate, finish, fire, fit, fly, gather, go, happen, kick out, make, manufacture, muster, oust, outfit, process, produce, result, sack, show up, succeed, switch off, throw out, transpire, turf out, turn inside out, turn off, turn up, unplug, unseat, work out.

antonyms bomb, flop, take in, turn on, welcome.

turn over activate, assign, break up, capsize, commend, commit, consider, contemplate, deliberate, deliver, dig, examine, give over, give up, hand over, keel over, mull over, overturn, pass on, plough, ponder, reflect on, render up, reverse, revolve, ruminate, start up, surrender, switch on, think about, think over, transfer, upend, upset, yield.

antonym stand firm.

turn over a new leaf amend, begin anew, change, change one's ways, improve, mend one's ways, pull one's socks up, reform.

antonym persist.

turn tail escape, flee, high-tail it, make off, retreat, run away, run for it, run off, scarper, skedaddle, take off, take to one's heels, vamoose.

antonym stand firm.

turn up amplify, appear, arrive, attend, boost, come, crop up, dig up, disclose, discover, expose, find, increase, intensify, invert, pop up, raise, reveal, show, show up, surface, transpire, unearth.

antonyms stay away, turn down.

turncoat *n* apostate, defector, deserter, fink, rat, recreant, renegade, scab, seceder, tergiversator, traitor.

turning *n* bend, crossroads, curve, flexure, fork, junction, turn, turnoff.

turning point *n* change, climacteric, crisis, crossroads, crux, cusp, moment of truth, watershed.

turn out *n* array, assemblage, assembly, attendance, attire, audience, company, congregation, costume, crowd, dress, equipage, equipment, gate, gear, get-up, number, outfit, output, outturn, product, production, productivity, rig, throng, turnover, volume, yield.

turnover *n* business, change, flow, income, movement, output, outturn, production, productivity, profits, replacement, volume, yield.

turpitude *n* badness, baseness, corruption, corruptness, criminality, degeneracy, depravity, evil, flagitiousness, foulness, immorality, iniquity, nefariousness, rascality, sinfulness, viciousness, vileness, villainy, wickedness.

antonym honour.

tussle *v* battle, brawl, compete, contend, fight, grapple, scramble, scrap, scuffle, struggle, vie, wrestle.

n battle, bout, brawl, competition, conflict, contention, contest, dustup, fight, fracas, fray, melee, punch-up, race, scramble, scrap, scrimmage, scrum, scuffle, set-to, struggle.

tutelage *n* aegis, care, charge, custody, education, eye, guardianship, guidance, instruction, patronage, preparation, protection, schooling, teaching, tuition, vigilance, wardship.

tutor *n* coach, educator, guardian, guide, guru, instructor, lecturer, master, mentor, preceptor, supervisor, teacher.

v coach, control, direct, discipline, drill, edify, educate, guide, instruct, lecture, school, supervise, teach, train.

tutorial *n* class, lesson, seminar.

adj coaching, didactic, educative, guiding, instructional, teaching.

twaddle *n* balderdash, blather, bull, bunk, chatter, claptrap, drivel, eyewash, gabble, garbage, gobbledygook, gossip, guff, hogwash, hot air, inanity, nonsense, piffle, poppycock, rigmarole, rot, rubbish, stuff, trash.

antonym sense.

tweak *v, n* jerk, nip, pull, pinch, snatch, squeeze, tug, twist, twitch.

tweezers *n* forceps, pincers, tongs.

twiddle *v* adjust, fiddle, finger, jiggle, juggle, swivel, turn, twirl, twist, wiggle.

twig[1] *n* branch, offshoot, ramus, shoot, spray, stick, wattle, withe, withy.

twig[2] **(to)** *v* catch on, comprehend, cotton on, fathom, get, grasp, see, tumble to, understand.

twilight *n* crepuscule, decline, demi-jour, dimness, dusk, ebb, evening, eventide, gloaming, half-light, sundown, sunset, wane.

adj crepuscular, darkening, declining, dim, dying, ebbing, evening, final, last, shadowy.

twin *n* clone, counterpart, doppelgänger, double, duplicate, fellow, likeness, look-alike, match, mate, ringer.

adj balancing, corresponding, didymous, double, dual, duplicate, geminate, identical, matched, matching, paired, parallel, symmetrical, twofold.

v combine, couple, join, link, match, pair, yoke.

twine *n* cord, string, twist, yarn.

v bend, braid, coil, curl, encircle, entwine, interlace, interweave, knit, loop, meander, plait, snake, spiral, splice, surround, tie, twist, weave, wind, wrap, wreathe, wriggle, zigzag.

twinge *n* bite, gripe, pain, pang, pinch, prick, qualm, spasm, stab, stitch, throb, throe, tweak, twist, twitch.

twinkle *v* blink, coruscate, flash, flicker, gleam, glint, glisten, glitter, scintillate, shimmer, shine, sparkle, vibrate, wink.

n amusement, blink, coruscation, flash, flicker, gleam, glimmer, glistening, glitter, glittering, light, quiver, scintillation, shimmer, shine, spark, sparkle, wink.

twinkling *adj* blinking, bright, coruscating, flashing, flickering, gleaming, glimmering, glistening, glittering, polished, scintillating, shimmering, shining, sparkling, winking.

n flash, instant, jiffy, moment, no time, sec, second, shake, trice, twinkle, two shakes.

twirl *v* birl, coil, gyrate, pirouette, pivot, revolve, rotate, spin, swivel, turn, twiddle, twist, wheel, whirl, wind.

n coil, convolution, gyration, gyre, helix, pirouette, revolution, rotation, spin, spiral, turn, twiddle, twist, wheel, whirl, whorl.

twirling *adj* gyral, gyratory, pirouetting, pivoting, revolving, rotating, rotatory, spinning, swivelling, whirling.

twist *v* alter, change, coil, contort, corkscrew, crinkle, crisp, curl, distort, encircle, entangle, entwine, garble, intertwine, meander, misinterpret, misquote, misrepresent, pervert, pivot, revolve, rick, screw, spin, sprain, squirm, strain, swivel, turn, tweak, twine, warp, weave, wind, wrap, wreathe, wrench, wrest, wriggle, wring, writhe, zigzag.

n aberration, arc, bend, bent, braid, break, change, characteristic, coil, confusion, contortion, convolution, curl, curlicue, curve, defect, deformation, development, distortion, eccentricity, entanglement, fault, flaw, foible, hank, idiosyncrasy, imperfection, jerk, kink, knot, meander, mess, mix-up, nuance, oddity, peculiarity, plug, proclivity, pull, quid, quirk, revelation, roll, screw, slant, snarl, spin, sprain, squiggle, surprise, swivel, tangle, tortion, trait, turn, twine, undulation, variation, warp, wind, wrench, wrest, zigzag.

twist someone's arm bulldoze, bully, coerce, dragoon, force, intimidate, lean on, persuade, pressure.

twisted *adj* abnormal, bent, biassed, bitter, coiled, contorted, convoluted, curled, deformed, depraved, deviant, devious, distorted, garbled, intertwined, jaundiced, misshapen, morbid, perverse, perverted, quirky, sick, torqued, tortile, tortuous, unnatural, warped, wound, woven, wry.

antonyms straight, straightforward.

twit[1] *v* chaff, deride, hassle, jeer (at), mock, rib, scoff (at), scorn, taunt, tease.

twit[2] *n* ass, blockhead, buffoon, chump, clown, dolt, dope, fool, halfwit, idiot, nerd, nincompoop, ninny, nitwit, noodle, silly ass, simpleton, twerp, twirp.

twitch *v* blink, flutter, jerk, jump, pinch, pluck, pull, snatch, tug, tweak, yank.

n blink, convulsion, flutter, jerk, jump, nervous habit, pluck, pull, spasm, tic, tremor, tweak, twinge.

twitter *v* chatter, cheep, chirp, chirrup, giggle, prattle, simper, sing, snigger, titter, trill, tweet, warble, whistle.

n agitation, anxiety, call, chatter, cheeping, chirping, chirruping, cry, dither, excitement, flurry, fluster, flutter, song, tizzy, trill, tweeting, warble.

two-faced *adj* deceitful, deceiving, devious, dissembling, double-dealing, duplicitous, false, hypocritical, insincere, Janus-faced, lying, mendacious, perfidious, treacherous, untrustworthy.

antonyms candid, frank, honest.

tycoon *n* baron, big cheese, big noise, big shot, big-time operator, big wheel, bigwig, capitalist, captain of industry, Croesus, entrepreneur, fat cat, financier, industrialist, magnate, mogul, nabob, plutocrat, potentate.

type[1] *n* archetype, breed, category, class, classification, description, designation, emblem, embodiment, epitome, essence, example, exemplar, form, genre, group, ilk, insignia, kidney, kind, mark, model, order, original, paradigm, pattern, personification, prototype, quintessence, sort, species, specimen, stamp, standard, strain, subdivision, variety.

type[2] *n* case, characters, face, font, lettering, print, printing.

typhoon *n* cyclone, hurricane, squall, storm, tempest, tornado, twister, whirlwind, windstorm.

typical *adj* archetypal, average, characteristic, classic, conventional, distinctive, essential, illustrative, indicative, model, normal, orthodox, quintessential, representative, standard, stock, symptomatic, usual, vintage.

antonyms atypical, untypical.

typify *v* characterize, embody, encapsulate, epitomize, exemplify, illustrate, incarnate, personify, represent, symbolize.

tyrannical *adj* absolute, arbitrary, authoritarian, autocratic, coercive, despotic, dictatorial, domineering, high-handed, imperious, inexorable, iron-handed, magisterial, oppressive, overbearing, overpowering, overweening, peremptory, ruthless, severe, tyrannous, unjust, unreasonable.

antonyms liberal, tolerant.

tyrannize *v* browbeat, bully, coerce, crush, dictate, domineer, enslave, intimidate, oppress, subjugate, terrorize.

tyranny *n* absolutism, authoritarianism, autocracy, coercion, despotism, dictatorship, harshness, high-handedness, imperiousness, injustice, oppression, peremptoriness, relentlessness, ruthlessness.

antonyms democracy, liberality.

tyrant *n* absolutist, authoritarian, autocrat, bully, despot, dictator, martinet, monarch, oppressor, satrap, slave driver, sovereign, taskmaster.

tyro *n* apprentice, beginner, catechumen, cheechako, freshman, greenhorn, initiate, learner, neophyte, novice, novitiate, pupil, starter, student, tenderfoot, trainee.

antonyms old hand, veteran.

U

ubiquitous *adj* all over, common, (encountered) worldwide, everpresent, everywhere, frequent, global, omnipresent, pervasive, universal.

antonyms localized, rare.

ubiquity *n* commonness, frequency, omnipresence, pervasiveness, popularity, prevalence, universality.

antonym rarity.

ugliness *n* danger, deformity, disgrace, enormity, evil, frightfulness, heinousness, hideousness, homeliness, horridness, horror, menace, monstrosity, monstrousness, nastiness, offensiveness, plainness, repulsiveness, unattractiveness, unloveliness, unpleasantness, unsightliness, vileness.

antonyms beauty, charm, goodness, pleasantness.

ugly *adj* angry, bad-tempered, dangerous, dark, deformed, disagreeable, disgusting, distasteful, distorted, evil, forbidding, frightful, haggish, haglike, hard-featured, hideous, homely, horrid, ill-favoured, ill-looking, malevolent, menacing, misshapen, monstrous, nasty, objectionable, offensive, ominous, plain, repugnant, repulsive, revolting, shocking, sinister, spiteful, sullen, surly, terrible, threatening, truculent, unattractive, unlovely, unpleasant, unprepossessing, unsightly, vile.

antonyms beautiful, charming, good, pretty.

ulcer *n* abscess, boil, canker, fester, gumboil, lesion, sore, ulceration.

ulterior *adj* concealed, covert, hidden, personal, private, secondary, secret, selfish, undisclosed, unexpressed, unrevealed.

antonyms declared, overt.

ultimate *adj* basic, concluding, conclusive, consummate, decisive, elemental, end, endmost, eventual, extreme, farthest, final, fundamental, furthest, greatest, highest, last, maximum, paramount, perfect, primary, radical, remotest, superlative, supreme, terminal, topmost, utmost.

n consummation, culmination, epitome, extreme, granddaddy, greatest, height, peak, perfection, summit.

ultimately *adv* after all, at last, basically, eventually, finally, fundamentally, in origin, in the end, originally, primarily, sooner or later.

ultra *adj* avant-garde, exceptional, excessive, extravagant, extreme, fanatical, far-out, immoderate, rabid, radical, revolutionary, way-out.

ultra- *adv* especially, exceptionally, excessively, extra, extraordinarily, extremely, remarkably, unusually, very.

ululate *v* bawl, cry, holler, hoot, howl, keen, lament, moan, mourn, scream, screech, sob, wail, weep.

umbrage *n* anger, chagrin, disgruntlement, displeasure, grudge, (high) dudgeon, huff, indignation, offence, pique, resentment, sulks.

umbrella *n* aegis, agency, cover, parasol, patronage, protection, sunshade, umbel.

umpire *n* adjudicator, arbiter, arbitrator, judge, linesman, mediator, moderator, negotiator, ref., referee.

v adjudicate, arbitrate, call, control, judge, moderate, negotiate, referee, settle.

umpteen *adj* a good (or great) many, considerable, countless, innumerable, millions, numerous, plenty, uncounted.

antonym few.

unabashed *adj* blatant, bold, brazen, composed, confident, unawed, unblushing, unconcerned, undaunted, undismayed, unembarrassed.

antonyms abashed, sheepish.

unable *adj* impotent, inadequate, incapable, incompetent, ineffectual, not up (to), powerless, unequipped, unfit, unfitted, unqualified.

antonyms able, capable.

unabridged *adj* complete, entire, full, full-length, uncondensed, uncut, unexpurgated, unshortened, whole.

antonyms abridged, partial.

unacceptable *adj* beyond the pale, disagreeable, displeasing, distasteful, improper, inadmissible, insupportable, objectionable, offensive, ugly, undesirable, unpleasant, unsatisfactory, unwelcome.

antonyms acceptable, correct.

unaccommodating *adj* disobliging, inflexible, intransigent, obstinate, perverse, rigid, stubborn, unbending, uncomplaisant, uncompromising, unco-operative, unhelpful, unyielding.

antonyms flexible, obliging.

unaccompanied *adj* a cappella, alone, lone, single, solitary, solo, stag, unattended, unescorted.

antonym accompanied.

unaccountable[1] *adj* astonishing, baffling, extraordinary, impenetrable, incomprehensible, inexplicable, inscrutable, mysterious, odd, peculiar, puzzling, singular, strange, uncommon, unexplainable, unfathomable, unheard-of, unintelligible, unusual, unwonted.

antonyms accountable, explicable.

unaccountable[2] *adj* clear, exempt, free, immune, irresponsible, unanswerable, unliable, unresponsible, unsubject.

unaccustomed *adj* different, extraordinary, exceptional, green, inexperienced, new, rare, remarkable, special, strange, surprising, unacquainted, uncommon, unexpected, unfamiliar, unheard-of, unpractised, unprecedented, unused, unusual, unwonted.

antonyms accustomed, customary.

unacquainted (with) *adj* ignorant (of), strange (to), unaccustomed (to), unfamiliar (with).

unadorned *adj* austere, outright, plain, restrained, severe, simple, stark, straightforward, undecorated, unembellished, unornamented, unvarnished.

antonyms decorated, embellished, ornate.

unaffected[1] *adj* aloof, blasé, impassive, impervious, indifferent, proof, remote, stoic, stolid, unaltered, unchanged, unconcerned, unemotional, unfazed, unfeeling, unimpressed, uninfluenced, unmoved, unresponsive, untouched.

antonyms affected, moved.

unaffected[2] *adj* artless, candid, down-to-earth, frank, genuine, guileless, honest, ingenuous, naïve, natural, open, plain, simple, sincere, spontaneous, straightforward, unassuming, unpretentious, unsophisticated, unspoiled, unstudied.

antonyms affected, pretentious.

unafraid *adj* confident, daring, dauntless, fearless, imperturbable, intrepid, unshakeable.

antonyms afraid, timid.

unalterable *adj* final, fixed, immutable, inflexible, invariable, permanent, rigid, steadfast, unchangeable, unchanging, unyielding.

antonyms alterable, flexible.

unanimity *n* accord, agreement, chorus, communion, concert, concord, concurrence, consensus, consent, correspondence, harmony, like-mindedness, rapport, unison, unity.

antonyms disagreement, disunity.

unanimous *adj* agreed, common, concerted, concordant, harmonious, in accord, in agreement, joint, solid, united.

antonyms disunited, split.

unanimously *adv* by common consent, conjointly, in concert, nem. con., unopposed, without exception, without opposition.

unanswerable[1] *adj* moot, problematic, undecidable, undeterminable, unresolvable, unsolvable, vexed, wide-open.

unanswerable[2] *adj* absolute, conclusive, final, incontestable, incontrovertible, indisputable, irrefragable, irrefutable, unarguable, undeniable, unquestionable.

antonyms disputable, refutable.

unappetizing *adj* disagreeable, distasteful, insipid, off-putting, tasteless, unappealing, unattractive, unexciting, uninteresting, uninviting, unpalatable, unpleasant, unsavoury.

antonyms appetizing, inviting.

unapproachable *adj* aloof, distant, forbidding, formidable, frigid, godforsaken, inaccessible, intimidating, remote, reserved, stand-offish, unfriendly, unreachable, unsociable, withdrawn.

antonyms accessible, approachable.

unapt *adj* improbable, inapplicable, inapposite, inappropriate, inapt, malapropos, unfit, unfitted, unlikely, unqualified, unseasonable, unskilful, unsuitable, unsuited, untimely.

antonyms apt, fitting.

unarmed *adj* assailable, defenceless, exposed, helpless, open, pregnable, unarmoured, unequipped, unprotected, vulnerable, weak, weaponless.

antonyms armed, equipped.

unashamed *adj* impenitent, open, shameless, unabashed, unconcealed, undisguised, unrepentant.

unasked *adj* gratuitous, spontaneous, unbidden, undemanded, undesired, uninvited, unprompted, unrequested, unsolicited, unsought, unwanted, voluntary.

antonyms invited, solicited.

unassailable *adj* absolute, conclusive, impregnable, incontestable, incontrovertible, indisputable, invincible, inviolable, invulnerable, irrefutable, positive, proven, sacrosanct, secure, sound, undeniable, well-armed, well-fortified, well-protected.

antonyms assailable, defenceless.

unassertive *adj* backward, bashful, diffident, meek, mousy, quiet, retiring, self-effacing, shy, timid, timorous, unassuming.

antonyms assertive, brash.

unassuming *adj* diffident, humble, low-key, meek, mild, modest, natural, quiet, reserved, restrained, retiring, self-effacing, simple, unassertive, unobtrusive, unostentatious, unpresuming, unpretentious.

antonyms presumptuous, pretentious.

unattached *adj* adrift, autonomous, available, fancy-free, footloose, free, independent, loose, non-aligned, single, unaffiliated, uncommitted, unconnected, unengaged, unhooked, unmarried.

antonyms attached, committed, connected, engaged.

unattended *adj* abandoned, alone, disregarded, forgotten, ignored, unaccompanied, unescorted, unguarded, unsupervised, unwatched.

antonyms attended, escorted.

unattractive *adj* disagreeable, disgusting, distasteful, homely, ill-favoured, objectionable, offensive, off-putting, plain, repellent, ugly, unappealing, unappetizing, uncomely, undesirable, unexciting, uninviting, unlovely, unpalatable, unpleasant, unprepossessing, unsavoury, unsightly, unwelcome.
antonyms attractive, inviting.

unauthorized *adj* illegal, illicit, irregular, unlawful, unofficial, unsanctioned, unwarranted, wildcat.
antonyms authorized, legal, official.

unavailing *adj* abortive, barren, bootless, fruitless, futile, idle, ineffective, ineffectual, inefficacious, pointless, unproductive, unprofitable, unsuccessful, useless, vain.
antonyms productive, successful.

unavoidable *adj* certain, compulsory, fated, ineluctable, inescapable, inevitable, inexorable, mandatory, necessary, obligatory, ordained, predestined.
antonyms avoidable, optional.

unaware *adj* forgetful, heedless, ignorant, incognizant, insensible, oblivious, out of it, unconscious, unenlightened, uninformed, unknowing, unmindful, unsuspecting, unsuspicious.
antonyms alert, aware.

unawares *adv* aback, abruptly, accidentally, by surprise, inadvertently, mistakenly, off guard, suddenly, unconsciously, unexpectedly, unintentionally, unknowingly, unprepared, unthinkingly, unwittingly.

unbalanced *adj* asymmetrical, biassed, crazy, demented, deranged, disproportionate, disturbed, eccentric, erratic, inequitable, insane, irrational, irregular, lopsided, lunatic, mad, off-balance, off-centre, one-sided, partial, partisan, prejudiced, shaky, top-heavy, touched, unequal, uneven, unfair, unhinged, unjust, unsound, unstable, unsteady, wobbly.
antonyms balanced, steady.

unbearable *adj* insufferable, insupportable, intolerable, outrageous, too much, unacceptable, unendurable, unspeakable.
antonyms acceptable, bearable.

unbeatable *adj* indomitable, invincible, matchless, nonpareil, supreme, unconquerable, unstoppable, unsurpassable.
antonyms inferior, weak.

unbeaten *adj* supreme, triumphant, unbowed, unconquered, undefeated, unsubdued, unsurpassed, unvanquished, victorious, winning.
antonyms defeated, vanquished.

unbecoming *adj* discreditable, dishonourable, ill-suited, improper, inappropriate, incongruous, indecorous, indelicate, infelicitous, offensive, tasteless, unattractive, unbefitting, unfit, unflattering, unmeet, unseemly, unsightly, unsuitable, unsuited.
antonyms becoming, proper.

unbelief *n* agnosticism, atheism, disbelief, distrust, doubt, incredulity, scepticism.

antonyms belief, faith.

unbelievable *adj* astonishing, far-fetched, implausible, impossible, improbable, inconceivable, incredible, outlandish, preposterous, questionable, staggering, unconvincing, unimaginable, unlikely, unthinkable.
antonyms believable, credible.

unbeliever *n* agnostic, atheist, disbeliever, doubter, doubting Thomas, infidel, nihilist, sceptic.
antonyms believer, supporter.

unbelieving *adj* disbelieving, distrustful, doubtful, doubting, dubious, incredulous, sceptical, suspicious, unconvinced, unpersuaded.
antonyms credulous, trustful.

unbend *v* loosen up, relax, straighten, thaw, unbutton, uncoil, uncurl, unfreeze.
antonyms stiffen, withdraw.

unbending *adj* aloof, distant, firm, forbidding, formal, formidable, frozen, hard-line, inexorable, inflexible, intransigent, obdurate, obstinate, reserved, resolute, Rhadamanthine, rigid, set, severe, stiff, strict, stubborn, tough, uncompromising, unyielding, wooden.
antonyms approachable, friendly, relaxed.

unbiassed *adj* detached, disinterested, dispassionate, equitable, even-handed, fair, fair-minded, impartial, independent, just, neutral, objective, open-minded, square, uncoloured, uninfluenced, unprejudiced.
antonyms biassed, unfair.

unbidden *adj* free, spontaneous, unasked, unforced, uninvited, unprompted, unsolicited, unwanted, unwelcome, voluntary, willing.
antonyms invited, solicited.

unbind *v* free, liberate, loose, loosen, release, unchain, undo, unfasten, unfetter, unloose, unloosen, unshackle, untie, unyoke.
antonyms bind, restrain.

unblemished *adj* clear, flawless, immaculate, irreproachable, perfect, pure, spotless, unflawed, unimpeachable, unspotted, unstained, unsullied, untarnished.
antonyms blemished, flawed, imperfect.

unblinking *adj* assured, calm, composed, confident, cool, emotionless, fearless, impassive, imperturbable, nerveless, steady, sure, unafraid, unemotional, unfaltering, unflinching, unshrinking, unwavering.
antonyms cowed, faithful, fearful.

unblushing *adj* amoral, blatant, bold, brazen, immodest, shameless, unabashed, unashamed, unembarrassed.
antonyms abashed, ashamed.

unborn *adj* awaited, coming, embryonic, expected, fetal, future, hereafter, later, subsequent, succeeding.

unbosom *v* acknowledge, admit, bare, come clean, confess, confide, disburden, disclose, divulge, expose, lay bare, let out, pour out, reveal, spill, tell, unburden, uncover.
antonyms conceal, suppress.

unbounded *adj* absolute, boundless, endless, immeasurable, infinite, lavish, limitless, prodigal, unbridled, unchecked, unconstrained, uncontrolled, unlimited, unrestrained, vast.

antonym limited.

unbreakable *adj* armoured, durable, indestructible, indivisible, infrangible, inviolable, lasting, permanent, proof, resistant, rugged, shatterproof, solid, strong, tough, toughened.

antonyms breakable, fragile.

unbridled *adj* excessive, immoderate, intemperate, licentious, profligate, rampant, riotous, unchecked, unconstrained, uncontrolled, uncurbed, ungovernable, ungoverned, unrestrained, unruly, violent, wanton.

unbroken *adj* ceaseless, complete, constant, continuous, endless, entire, incessant, intact, integral, non-stop, perpetual, progressive, solid, total, unbowed, unceasing, undamaged, undisturbed, undivided, unimpaired, uninterrupted, unremitting, unsubdued, untamed, whole.

antonyms cowed, fitful, intermittent.

unburden *v* confess, confide, disburden, discharge, disclose, disencumber, empty, lay bare, lighten, offload, pour out, relieve, reveal, tell all, unbosom, unload.

antonyms conceal, hide, suppress.

uncalled-for *adj* gratuitous, impertinent, inappropriate, needless, rude, undeserved, unheeded, unjust, unjustified, unmerited, unnecessary, unprovoked, unwanted, unwarranted, unwelcome.

antonym timely.

uncanny *adj* astonishing, astounding, bizarre, creepy, eerie, eldritch, exceptional, extraordinary, fantastic, incredible, inspired, marvellous, miraculous, mysterious, preternatural, prodigious, queer, remarkable, scary, singular, spooky, strange, supernatural, unaccountable, unearthly, unerring, unheard-of, unnatural, unusual, weird, wonderful.

uncaring *adj* callous, inconsiderate, indifferent, negligent, unconcerned, unfeeling, uninterested, unmoved, unresponsive, unsympathetic.

antonyms concerned, solicitous.

unceasing *adj* ceaseless, constant, continual, continuing, continuous, endless, incessant, never-ending, non-stop, perpetual, persistent, relentless, unbroken, unending, unfailing, uninterrupted, unrelenting, unremitting.

antonyms intermittent, spasmodic.

uncertain *adj* ambiguous, ambivalent, chancy, changeable, conjectural, dicey, dithery, doubtful, dubious, erratic, fitful, hazardous, hazy, hesitant, iffy, incalculable, inconstant, indefinite, indeterminate, indistinct, insecure, in the lap of the gods, irregular, irresolute, precarious, problematic, questionable, risky, shaky, speculative, unclear, unconfirmed, undecided, undetermined, unfixed, unforeseeable, unpredictable, unreliable,

unresolved, unsettled, unsure, vacillating, vague, variable, wavering.

antonym certain.

uncertainty *n* ambiguity, bewilderment, confusion, diffidence, dilemma, doubt, doubtfulness, dubiety, hesitancy, hesitation, incalculability, inconclusiveness, indecision, insecurity, irresolution, misgiving, perplexity, puzzlement, qualm, quandary, risk, scepticism, unpredictability, vagueness.

antonym certainty.

unchallengeable *adj* absolute, conclusive, final, impregnable, incontestable, incontrovertible, indisputable, irrefragable, irrefutable.

antonyms contestable, inconclusive.

unchangeable *adj* final, fixed, habitual, immutable, intransmutable, invariable, inveterate, irreversible, permanent, unalterable.

antonyms alterable, changeable.

unchanging *adj* abiding, changeless, constant, continuing, deathless, enduring, eternal, fixed, immutable, imperishable, invariable, lasting, permanent, perpetual, phaseless, steadfast, steady, unchanged, unfading, unvarying.

antonyms changing, temporary.

uncharitable *adj* callous, captious, cruel, hard-hearted, hypercritical, inhumane, insensitive, mean, merciless, pitiless, stingy, unfeeling, unforgiving, unfriendly, ungenerous, unkind, unsympathetic.

antonyms charitable, sympathetic.

uncharted *adj* foreign, mysterious, new, novel, strange, undiscovered, unexplored, unfamiliar, unknown, unplumbed, virgin.

antonyms familiar, well-known.

unchaste *adj* degenerate, depraved, dishonest, dissolute, immodest, immoral, impure, lewd, libertine, licentious, loose, promiscuous, shameless, wanton.

antonyms chaste, innocent.

uncivil *adj* abrupt, bad-mannered, boorish, brusque, churlish, curt, discourteous, disrespectful, gruff, ill-bred, ill-mannered, impolite, rude, surly, uncouth, ungracious, unmannerly.

antonyms civil, polite.

uncivilized *adj* antisocial, barbarian, barbaric, barbarous, boorish, brutish, churlish, coarse, gross, heathenish, ill-bred, illiterate, philistine, primitive, savage, uncouth, uncultivated, uncultured, uneducated, unpolished, unsophisticated, untamed, vulgar, wild.

antonyms civilized, cultured.

unclassifiable *adj* atypic(al), doubtful, elusive, ill-defined, indefinable, indefinite, indescribable, indeterminate, indistinct, uncertain, unconformable, undefinable, unidentifiable, vague.

antonyms conformable, definable, identifiable.

unclean *adj* contaminated, corrupt, defiled, dirty, evil, filthy, foul, impure, insalubrious, nasty, polluted, soiled, spotted, stained, sullied, tainted, unhygienic, unwholesome.

antonyms clean, pure.

unclear *adj* ambiguous, as clear as mud, dim, doubtful, dubious, equivocal, hazy, indefinite, indiscernible, indistinguishable, obscure, uncertain, vague.

antonyms clear, understandable.

unclothed *adj* bare, disrobed, in one's birthday suit, in the altogether, in the buff, naked, nude, stark naked, stripped, unclad, undraped, undressed.

antonyms clothed, dressed.

uncomfortable *adj* awkward, bleak, confused, conscience-stricken, cramped, disagreeable, discomfited, discomfortable, discomposed, disquieted, distressed, disturbed, embarrassed, hard, ill-fitting, incommodious, irritating, painful, pokey, self-conscious, sheepish, troubled, troublesome, uneasy.

antonyms comfortable, easy.

uncommitted *adj* available, fancy-free, floating, free, neutral, non-aligned, non-partisan, single, unattached, undecided, uninvolved.

antonyms bound, committed.

uncommon *adj* abnormal, atypical, bizarre, curious, distinctive, exceptional, extraordinary, incomparable, infrequent, inimitable, notable, noteworthy, novel, odd, outstanding, peculiar, queer, rare, recherché, remarkable, scarce, singular, special, strange, superior, unfamiliar, unparalleled, unprecedented, unusual, unwonted.

antonyms common, customary, ordinary.

uncommonly *adv* abnormally, amazingly, exceptionally, extremely, infrequently, inordinately, occasionally, outstandingly, particularly, peculiarly, rarely, remarkably, seldom, singularly, strangely, unusually, very.

antonyms commonly, frequently, usually.

uncommunicative *adj* brief, close, curt, guarded, laconic, quiet, reserved, reticent, retiring, secretive, short, shy, silent, taciturn, tight-lipped, unforthcoming, unresponsive, unsociable, withdrawn.

antonyms chatty, communicative.

uncompromising *adj* decided, die-hard, firm, hard-core, hard-line, inexorable, inflexible, intransigent, obdurate, obstinate, rigid, set, steadfast, strict, stubborn, tough, unaccommodating, unbending, unyielding.

antonyms flexible, open-minded.

unconcealable *adj* clear, insistent, insuppressible, irrepressible, manifest, obvious, plain, uncontrollable, undisguisable.

unconcealed *adj* admitted, apparent, blatant, conspicuous, evident, frank, ill-concealed, manifest, naked, noticeable, obvious, open, overt, patent, self-confessed, unashamed, undisguised, visible.

antonyms hidden, secret.

unconcern *n* aloofness, apathy, callousness, detachment, indifference, insouciance, jauntiness, negligence, nonchalance, remoteness, uninterestedness.

antonyms care, concern.

unconcerned *adj* aloof, apathetic, blithe, callous, carefree, careless, complacent, composed, cool, detached, dispassionate, distant, easy, incurious, indifferent, insouciant, nonchalant, oblivious, relaxed, serene, uncaring, uninterested, uninvolved, unmoved, unperturbed, unruffled, unsympathetic, untroubled, unworried.

antonyms concerned, sympathetic.

unconditional *adj* absolute, categorical, complete, downright, entire, full, implicit, out-and-out, outright, plenary, positive, thoroughgoing, total, unequivocal, unlimited, unqualified, unreserved, unrestricted, utter, whole-hearted.

antonyms conditional, partial.

uncongenial *adj* antagonistic, antipathetic, disagreeable, discordant, displeasing, distasteful, incompatible, unappealing, unattractive, uninviting, unpleasant, unsavoury, unsuited, unsympathetic.

antonyms agreeable, congenial.

unconnected *adj* detached, disconnected, disjoined, disjointed, divided, illogical, incoherent, independent, irrational, irrelevant, off-line, separate, unattached, unrelated.

antonyms connected, relevant.

unconquerable *adj* enduring, indomitable, ingrained, insuperable, insurmountable, inveterate, invincible, irrepressible, irresistible, overpowering, unbeatable, undefeatable, unyielding.

antonyms weak, yielding.

unconscionable *adj* amoral, criminal, excessive, exorbitant, extravagant, extreme, immoderate, inordinate, outrageous, preposterous, unethical, unjustifiable, unpardonable, unprincipled, unreasonable, unscrupulous, unwarrantable.

unconscious *adj* accidental, automatic, comatose, concussed, heedless, ignorant, inadvertent, innate, insensible, instinctive, involuntary, knocked out, latent, oblivious, out, out cold, out for the count, reflex, senseless, stunned, subconscious, subliminal, unaware, unintended, unintentional, unknowing, unmindful, unsuspecting, unwitting.

antonyms aware, conscious.

unconstraint *n* abandon, freedom, laissez-faire, liberality, openness, relaxation, unreserve.

uncontrollable *adj* frantic, furious, intractable, irrepressible, irresistible, irrestrainable, mad, recalcitrant, refractory, strong, ungovernable, unmanageable, unruly, violent, wild.

antonyms controllable, manageable.

uncontrolled *adj* boisterous, furious, rampant, riotous, unbridled, unchecked, uncurbed, undisciplined, ungoverned, unhindered, unrestrained, unruly, untrammelled, violent, wild.

antonyms contained, controlled.

unconventional *adj* abnormal, alternative, atypical, bizarre, bohemian, different, eccentric, extraordinary, far-out, flaky, freaky, idiosyncratic, individual, individualistic, informal, irregular, nonconforming, odd, offbeat, original, unconformable, unorthodox, unusual, way-out, wayward.
antonyms conventional, ordinary.

unconvincing *adj* doubtful, dubious, feeble, fishy, flimsy, implausible, improbable, inconclusive, lame, questionable, specious, suspect, tall, thin, unlikely, unpersuasive, weak.
antonyms convincing, plausible.

unco-ordinated *adj* awkward, bumbling, clodhopping, clumsy, diffuse, disjointed, disorganized, graceless, inept, lumbering, maladroit, unconcerted, ungainly, ungraceful, unorganized.
antonyms concerted, graceful, systematic.

uncouth *adj* awkward, barbarian, barbaric, boorish, clownish, clumsy, coarse, crude, gauche, gawky, graceless, gross, hayseed, ill-mannered, loutish, lubberly, oafish, rough, rude, rustic, uncivilized, uncultivated, ungainly, unmannerly, unrefined, unseemly, vulgar.
antonyms polished, polite, refined, urbane.

uncover *v* bare, blow (or lift) the lid off, detect, disclose, discover, disrobe, divulge, exhume, expose, open, reveal, show, strip, unearth, unmask, unveil, unwrap.
antonyms conceal, cover, suppress.

uncritical *adj* accepting, casual, credulous, indiscriminate, naïve, non-judgmental, superficial, trusting, undiscerning, undiscriminating, unexacting, unfussy, unscholarly, unselective, unthinking.
antonyms critical, discriminating, sceptical.

unctuous *adj* fawning, glib, greasy, gushing, ingratiating, insincere, obsequious, oily, pietistic, plausible, sanctimonious, slick, smarmy, smooth, suave, sycophantic.

uncultivated *adj* fallow, natural, rough, uncultured, wild.
antonyms cultivated, groomed.

uncultured *adj* awkward, boorish, coarse, crude, hayseed, hick, raw, rustic, uncivilized, uncouth, uncultivated, unrefined, unsophisticated.
antonyms cultured, sophisticated.

undaunted *adj* bold, brave, courageous, dauntless, fearless, gallant, indomitable, intrepid, resolute, steadfast, unbowed, undashed, undeterred, undiscouraged, undismayed, unfaltering, unflinching, unperturbed, unshrinking.
antonyms cowed, timorous.

undecided *adj* ambivalent, debatable, dithering, doubtful, dubious, hesitant, indefinite, in two minds, irresolute, moot, open, pending, tentative, torn, uncertain, uncommitted, unconcluded, undetermined, unfinished, unfixed, unsettled, unsure, vague, vexed, wavering.
antonyms certain, decided, definite.

undecorated *adj* austere, classical, functional, plain, severe, simple, stark, unadorned, unembellished, unornamented.
antonyms decorated, ornate.

undefended *adj* defenceless, exposed, naked, open, pregnable, unarmed, unfortified, unguarded, unprotected, vulnerable, weak.
antonyms armed, defended, fortified.

undefiled *adj* chaste, clean, clear, flawless, immaculate, intact, inviolate, pure, sinless, spotless, unblemished, unsoiled, unspotted, unstained, unsullied, virginal.

undefined *adj* formless, hazy, ill-defined, imprecise, indefinite, indeterminate, indistinct, inexact, nebulous, shadowy, tenuous, unclear, unexplained, unspecified, vague, woolly.
antonyms definite, precise.

undemonstrative *adj* aloof, cold, contained, cool, distant, formal, impassive, phlegmatic, reserved, restrained, reticent, stiff, stolid, unbending, uncommunicative, unemotional, unresponsive, withdrawn.
antonyms demonstrative, gushing.

undeniable *adj* certain, clear, evident, incontestable, incontrovertible, indisputable, indubitable, irrefragable, irrefutable, manifest, obvious, patent, proven, sound, sure, unassailable, undoubted, unmistakable, unquestionable.

undependable *adj* capricious, changeable, erratic, fair-weather, fickle, inconsistent, inconstant, irresponsible, mercurial, treacherous, uncertain, unpredictable, unreliable, unstable, untrustworthy, variable.
antonyms dependable, reliable.

under *prep* belonging to, below, beneath, governed by, included in, inferior to, junior to, led by, less than, lower than, secondary to, subject to, subordinate to, subservient to, underneath.
adv below, beneath, down, downward, less, lower.

under an obligation beholden, bound, duty-bound, grateful, honour-bound, in debt, in honour bound, indebted, obligated, obliged, thankful.

under the weather ailing, below par, groggy, hung over, ill, indisposed, nauseous, off-colour, out of sorts, poorly, queer, seedy, sick, squeamish, the worse for wear.

under way afoot, begun, going, in motion, in operation, in progress, launched, moving, on the go, on the move, started.

undercover *adj* clandestine, closed-door, closet, concealed, confidential, covert, furtive, hidden, hush-hush, intelligence, private, secret, spy, stealthy, surreptitious, underground.
antonyms open, unconcealed.

undercurrent *n* atmosphere, aura, connotation, cross-current, drift, eddy, feeling, flavour, hint, movement, murmur, overtone, rip, riptide, sense, suggestion, tendency, tenor, tide, tinge, trend, undertone, undertow, vibes, vibrations.

undercut v excavate, gouge out, hollow out, mine, sacrifice, scoop out, underbid, undercharge, undermine, underprice, undersell.

underestimate v belittle, dismiss, fail to appreciate, minimize, miscalculate, misprize, sell short, talk down, underrate, undervalue.

antonyms exaggerate, overestimate.

undergo v bear, brook, endure, experience, live through, put up with, run the gauntlet, stand, stomach, submit to, suffer, sustain, swallow, weather, withstand.

underground adj alternative, avant-garde, buried, clandestine, concealed, covered, covert, experimental, hidden, hypogeal, hypogene, radical, revolutionary, secret, subterranean, subversive, sunken, surreptitious, undercover.

undergrowth n bracken, brambles, briers, brush, brushwood, ground cover, scrub, underbrush.

underhand adj clandestine, crafty, crooked, deceitful, deceptive, devious, dishonest, dishonourable, fraudulent, furtive, immoral, improper, shady, shifty, sly, sneaky, stealthy, surreptitious, treacherous, underhanded, unethical, unscrupulous.

antonym above board.

underline v accent, accentuate, emphasize, highlight, italicize, mark, point up, press, reiterate, stress, underscore, urge.

antonyms play down, soft pedal.

underling n flunkey, hireling, inferior, lackey, menial, minion, nobody, nonentity, retainer, servant, slave, subordinate.

antonyms boss, leader.

underlying adj basal, basic, concealed, elementary, essential, fundamental, hidden, implicit, intrinsic, latent, lurking, primary, prime, root, subjacent, substructural, veiled.

undermine v debilitate, disable, erode, excavate, impair, mar, mine, sabotage, sap, subvert, threaten, tunnel, undercut, vitiate, weaken, wear away.

antonyms fortify, strengthen.

underprivileged adj deprived, destitute, disadvantaged, impecunious, impoverished, indigent, needy, poor, poverty-stricken.

antonyms affluent, fortunate, privileged.

underrate v belittle, deprecate, depreciate, discount, dismiss, disparage, misprize, underestimate, undervalue.

antonyms exaggerate, overrate.

undersell v cut, depreciate, disparage, mark down, play down, reduce, slash, undercharge, undercut, understate.

undersized adj achondroplastic, atrophied, dwarfish, miniature, minute, puny, pygmy, runty, small, stunted, tiny, underdeveloped, underweight.

antonyms big, oversized, overweight.

understand v accept, appreciate, apprehend, assume, believe, commiserate, comprehend, conceive, conclude, cotton on, discern, fathom, follow, gather, get, get the idea (or message or picture), grasp, hear, know, learn, penetrate, perceive, presume, realize, recognize, see, see daylight, suppose, sympathize, think, tolerate, tumble to, twig.

antonym misunderstand.

understanding n accord, agreement, appreciation, arrangement, awareness, bargain, belief, comprehension, conclusion, discernment, estimation, grasp, idea, impression, insight, intellect, intelligence, interpretation, judgment, knowledge, notion, opinion, pact, penetration, perception, reading, sense, view, viewpoint, wisdom.

adj accepting, compassionate, considerate, discerning, forbearing, forgiving, kind, kindly, loving, patient, perceptive, responsive, sensitive, sympathetic, tender, tolerant.

antonyms impatient, insensitive, intolerant, unsympathetic.

understate v belittle, deprecate, dismiss, make light of, make little of, minimize, play down, soft pedal, underplay, undersell.

understood adj accepted, assumed, axiomatic, implicit, implied, inferred, presumed, tacit, unspoken, unstated, unwritten.

understudy n alternate, backup, deputy, double, fill-in, pinch hitter, replacement, reserve, standby, stand-in, substitute.

undertake v accept, agree, assume, attempt, begin, commence, contract, covenant, embark on, endeavour, engage, guarantee, pledge, promise, shoulder, stipulate, tackle, try.

undertaking n adventure, affair, assurance, attempt, business, commitment, effort, endeavour, enterprise, game, operation, pledge, project, promise, task, venture, vow, word.

undertone n atmosphere, aura, connotation, current, feeling, flavour, hint, murmur, sense, suggestion, tinge, touch, trace, undercurrent, whisper.

undervalue v deprecate, depreciate, discount, dismiss, disparage, disprize, minimize, misjudge, misprize, underestimate, underrate.

antonyms exaggerate, overrate.

underwater adj subaquatic, subaqueous, submarine, submerged, sunken, undersea.

underwear n lingerie, underclothes, underclothing, undergarments, underlinen.

underweight adj emaciated, half-starved, puny, skinny, thin, undernourished, undersized.

antonym overweight.

underwrite v approve, authorize, back, consent, countenance, countersign, endorse, finance, fund, guarantee, initial, insure, okay, sanction, sign, sponsor, subscribe, subsidize, validate.

undesirable adj disagreeable, disliked, disreputable, distasteful, dreaded, objectionable, obnoxious, offensive, repugnant, unacceptable, unattractive, unpleasant, unpopular, unsavoury, unsuitable, unwanted, unwelcome, unwished-for.

antonyms desirable, welcome.

undeveloped *adj* dwarfish, embryonic, immature, inchoate, latent, potential, primordial, stunted, unformed.
antonyms developed, mature.

undignified *adj* foolish, improper, inappropriate, indecorous, inelegant, infra dig, petty, unbecoming, ungentlemanly, unladylike, unrefined, unseemly, unsuitable.
antonyms dignified, stately.

undisciplined *adj* disobedient, disorganized, green, obstreperous, raw, uncontrolled, unpredictable, unreliable, unrestrained, unruly, unschooled, unsteady, unsystematic, untrained, wayward, wild, willful.
antonyms disciplined, organized.

undisguised *adj* apparent, blatant, confessed, evident, explicit, frank, genuine, ill-concealed, manifest, naked, obvious, open, out-and-out, outright, overt, patent, stark, thoroughgoing, transparent, unadorned, unashamed, unconcealed, unmistakable, utter, whole-hearted.
antonyms concealed, hidden, secret.

undisguisedly *adj* blatantly, frankly, obviously, openly, outright, overtly, patently, transparently, unreservedly.
antonym secretly.

undisputed *adj* accepted, acknowledged, certain, conclusive, definite, incontestable, incontrovertible, indisputable, irrefragable, irrefutable, recognized, sure, unchallenged, uncontested, undeniable, undoubted, unequivocal, unmistakable, unquestioned.
antonyms dubious, uncertain.

undistinguished *adj* banal, common, commonplace, everyday, indifferent, inferior, mediocre, no big deal, nothing special, ordinary, pedestrian, plain, prosaic, run-of-the-mill, so-so, unexceptional, unexciting, unimpressive, unremarkable.
antonyms distinguished, exceptional.

undisturbed *adj* calm, collected, composed, equable, even, motionless, placid, quiet, serene, tranquil, unaffected, unconcerned, uninterrupted, unperturbed, unruffled, untouched, untroubled.
antonyms disturbed, ruffled.

undivided *adj* combined, complete, concentrated, concerted, entire, exclusive, full, solid, thorough, tightknit, unanimous, unbroken, united, whole, whole-hearted.

undo *v* annul, cancel, defeat, destroy, disengage, euchre, invalidate, loose, loosen, mar, neutralize, nullify, offset, open, overturn, quash, reverse, ruin, separate, shatter, spoil, subvert, unbutton, unchain, undermine, unfasten, unlink, unlock, unloose, unloosen, unmake, untie, unwind, unwrap, upset, vitiate, wreck.
antonyms fasten, make.

undoing *n* bane, besetting sin, blight, collapse, curse, defeat, destruction, disgrace, downfall, humiliation, misfortune, overthrow, overturn, reversal, ruin, ruination, shame, tragic fault, trouble, weakness.

undomesticated *adj* feral, natural, savage, uncivilized, unpractical, untamed, wild.
antonyms domesticated, tame.

undone[1] *adj* betrayed, destroyed, lost, ruined.
antonyms rescued, saved.

undone[2] *adj* forgotten, incomplete, left, neglected, omitted, outstanding, unaccomplished, uncompleted, unfinished, unfulfilled, unperformed.
antonyms accomplished, complete, done.

undone[3] *adj* loose, open, unbraced, unbuttoned, unfastened, unlaced, unlocked, untied.
antonyms fastened, secured.

undoubted *adj* accepted, acknowledged, certain, definite, evident, incontrovertible, indisputable, indubitable, obvious, patent, recognized, sure, unchallenged, undisputed, unquestionable, unquestioned.

undoubtedly *adv* absolutely, assuredly, categorically, certainly, definitely, doubtless, indubitably, of course, positively, surely, undeniably, unmistakably, unquestionably.

undreamed-of *adj* astonishing, inconceivable, incredible, miraculous, unexpected, unforeseen, unheard-of, unhoped-for, unimagined, unsuspected.

undress *v* disrobe, divest, peel off, remove, shed, strip.
n deshabille, disarray, nakedness, nudity.

undressed *adj* disrobed, naked, nude, stark naked, stripped, unclad, unclothed.

undue *adj* disproportionate, excessive, extravagant, extreme, immoderate, improper, inordinate, intemperate, needless, overmuch, supererogatory, uncalled-for, undeserved, unnecessary, unreasonable, unseemly, unwarranted.
antonym reasonable.

undulate *v* billow, heave, ripple, rise and fall, roll, surge, swell, wave.

undulating *adj* billowing, rippling, rolling, sinuous, undulant, wavy.
antonym flat.

unduly *adv* disproportionately, excessively, extravagantly, immoderately, inordinately, over, overly, overmuch, too, unjustifiably, unnecessarily, unreasonably.
antonym reasonably.

undutiful *adj* careless, defaulting, delinquent, disloyal, neglectful, negligent, remiss, slack, unfilial.
antonym dutiful.

undutifulness *n* default, defection, delinquency, dereliction, desertion, disloyalty, neglect, negligence, remissness.
antonyms dutifulness, loyalty.

undying *adj* abiding, constant, continuing, deathless, eternal, everlasting, immortal, imperishable, indestructible, inextinguishable, infinite, lasting, perennial, permanent, perpetual, sempiternal, undiminished, unending, unfading.
antonyms impermanent, inconstant.

unearth *v* detect, dig up, discover, disinter, dredge up, excavate, exhume, expose, ferret out, find, grub up, reveal, uncover.

unearthly *adj* abnormal, eerie, eldritch, ethereal, extraordinary, ghostly, haunted, heavenly, nightmarish, otherworldly, phantom, preposterous, preternatural, spectral, strange, sublime, supernatural, uncanny, unnatural, unreasonable, weird.

uneasiness *n* agitation, alarm, anxiety, apprehension, apprehensiveness, disquiet, doubt, dysphoria, inquietude, misgiving, nervousness, perturbation, qualms, suspicion, unease, worry.

antonyms calm, composure.

uneasy *adj* agitated, anxious, apprehensive, awkward, constrained, discomposed, disquieting, disturbed, disturbing, edgy, fidgety, ill at ease, impatient, insecure, jittery, jumpy, nervous, niggling, on edge, perturbed, precarious, put out, queasy, restive, restless, shaky, strained, tense, troubled, troubling, uncomfortable, unquiet, unsettled, unstable, upset, upsetting, worried, worrying.

antonyms calm, composed.

uneducated *adj* benighted, ignorant, illiterate, lowbrow, philistine, uncultivated, uncultured, uninstructed, unlettered, unread, unschooled, untaught.

antonyms educated, highbrow.

unembellished *adj* austere, bald, bare, basic, functional, modest, plain, severe, simple, spare, stark, unadorned, undecorated, unelaborated, unornamented, unvarnished.

antonyms embellished, ornate.

unemotional *adj* apathetic, cold, cool, dispassionate, formal, impassive, indifferent, laid-back, low-key, objective, passionless, phlegmatic, reserved, stiff, undemonstrative, unexcitable, unfeeling, unimpassioned, unresponsive.

antonyms emotional, excitable.

unemphatic *adj* downbeat, played-down, soft-pedalled, underplayed, understated, unobtrusive, unostentatious.

unemployed *adj* idle, jobless, laid off, out of work, redundant, resting, unoccupied, workless.

antonyms employed, working.

unending *adj* ceaseless, constant, continual, endless, eternal, everlasting, incessant, interminable, never-ending, non-stop, perpetual, unceasing, undying, unrelenting, unremitting.

antonyms intermittent, transient.

unendurable *adj* insufferable, insupportable, intolerable, overwhelming, shattering, unbearable.

antonyms bearable, endurable.

unenthusiastic *adj* apathetic, blasé, bored, cool, half-hearted, indifferent, lukewarm, neutral, nonchalant, unimpressed, uninterested, unmoved, unresponsive.

antonyms enthusiastic, keen.

unenviable *adj* disagreeable, painful, thankless, uncomfortable, uncongenial, undesirable, unpalatable, unpleasant, unsavoury.

antonyms desirable, enviable.

unequal *adj* asymmetrical, different, differing, disparate, disproportionate, dissimilar, ill-equipped, ill-matched, inadequate, incapable, incompetent, insufficient, irregular, unbalanced, uneven, unlike, unmatched, variable, varying.

antonym equal.

unequalled *adj* exceptional, incomparable, inimitable, matchless, nonpareil, paramount, peerless, pre-eminent, supreme, surpassing, transcendent, unmatched, unparalleled, unrivalled, unsurpassed.

unequivocal *adj* absolute, certain, clear, clear-cut, crystal-clear, decisive, definite, direct, distinct, evident, explicit, express, incontrovertible, indubitable, manifest, plain, positive, straight, unambiguous, uncontestable, unmistakable, well-defined.

antonyms ambiguous, vague.

unerring *adj* accurate, certain, exact, faultless, impeccable, infallible, perfect, right on, sure, uncanny, unfailing.

antonym fallible.

unerringly *adv* accurately, infallibly, unfailingly.

unethical *adj* dirty, discreditable, dishonest, dishonourable, disreputable, illegal, illicit, immoral, improper, shady, underhand, unfair, unprincipled, unprofessional, unscrupulous, wrong.

antonyms ethical, right.

uneven *adj* asymmetrical, broken, bumpy, changeable, coarse, disparate, erratic, fitful, fluctuating, ill-matched, inconsistent, intermittent, irregular, jerky, lopsided, lumpy, odd, one-sided, patchy, rough, spasmodic, unbalanced, unequal, unfair, unsteady, variable.

antonyms even, smooth.

uneventful *adj* boring, commonplace, dull, humdrum, monotonous, ordinary, quiet, routine, run-of-the-mill, tame, tedious, unexceptional, unexciting, uninteresting, unmemorable, unremarkable, unvaried.

antonyms eventful, memorable.

unexampled *adj* incomparable, never before seen, novel, prototypical, unequalled, unheard-of, unique, unmatched, unparalleled, unprecedented.

unexceptional *adj* average, commonplace, conventional, indifferent, insignificant, mediocre, normal, ordinary, pedestrian, run-of-the-mill, typical, undistinguished, unimpressive, unmemorable, unremarkable, usual.

antonyms exceptional, impressive.

unexcitable *adj* calm, composed, contained, cool, dispassionate, easygoing, impassive, imperturbable, laid-back, passionless, phlegmatic, relaxed, self-possessed, serene, unimpassioned.

antonyms excitable, nervous.

unexpected adj abrupt, accidental, amazing, astonishing, chance, fortuitous, startling, sudden, surprising, unaccustomed, unanticipated, unforeseen, unlooked-for, unpredictable, unusual, unwonted.
antonyms expected, normal, predictable.

unexpectedly adv abruptly, by chance, fortuitously, out of the blue, suddenly, surprisingly, unpredictably, without warning.

unexpressive adj blank, deadpan, emotionless, expressionless, immobile, impassive, inexpressive, inscrutable, poker-faced, vacant.
antonyms expressive, mobile.

unfading adj abiding, durable, enduring, fadeless, fast, fixed, imperishable, lasting, permanent, undying, unfailing.
antonyms changeable, transitory.

unfailing adj certain, constant, dependable, faithful, infallible, loyal, reliable, staunch, steadfast, steady, sure, true, undying, unfading.
antonyms fickle, impermanent, transient.

unfair adj arbitrary, biassed, bigoted, crooked, discriminatory, dishonest, dishonourable, inequitable, one-sided, partial, partisan, prejudiced, uncalled-for, undeserved, unethical, unjust, unmerited, unprincipled, unscrupulous, unsporting, unwarranted, wrongful.
antonyms fair, just.

unfairness n bias, bigotry, discrimination, inequity, injustice, one-sidedness, partiality, partisanship, prejudice.
antonyms equity, fairness.

unfaithful adj adulterous, deceitful, dishonest, disloyal, faithless, false, false-hearted, fickle, godless, inconstant, perfidious, recreant, traitorous, treacherous, treasonable, two-timing, unbelieving, unreliable, untrue, untrustworthy.
antonyms faithful, loyal.

unfaltering adj constant, dogged, firm, fixed, indefatigable, pertinacious, resolute, steadfast, steady, tireless, unfailing, unflagging, unflinching, unswerving, untiring, unwavering.
antonyms faltering, uncertain, wavering.

unfamiliar adj alien, curious, different, foreign, new, novel, out-of-the-way, strange, unaccustomed, unacquainted, uncharted, uncommon, unconversant, unexplored, unknown, unpractised, unskilled, unusual, unversed.
antonyms customary, familiar.

unfashionable adj antiquated, dated, démodé, obsolete, old-fashioned, out, outmoded, out-of-date, passé, square, unpopular.
antonyms fashionable, trendy.

unfasten v detach, disconnect, loosen, open, separate, unbolt, unchain, uncouple, undo, unlace, unlock, unloose, unloosen, untie.
antonym fasten.

unfathomable adj abstruse, baffling, bottomless, deep, esoteric, fathomless, hidden, immeasurable, impenetrable, incomprehensible, indecipherable, inexplicable, mysterious, profound, unknowable, unplumbed, unsounded.
antonyms comprehensible, explicable, penetrable.

unfavourable adj adverse, bad, contrary, counter, critical, disadvantageous, discouraging, hostile, ill-suited, inauspicious, infelicitous, inimical, inopportune, low, negative, ominous, opposed, poor, threatening, uncomplimentary, unfortunate, unfriendly, unlucky, unpromising, unpropitious, unseasonable, unsuited, untimely, untoward.
antonyms favourable, good.

unfeeling adj apathetic, callous, cold, cruel, hard, hardened, hard-hearted, harsh, heartless, inhuman, inhumane, insensitive, pitiless, soulless, stony, uncaring, unsympathetic.
antonym concerned.

unfeigned adj candid, earnest, frank, genuine, heartfelt, natural, pure, real, sincere, spontaneous, straightforward, unaffected, unforced, whole-hearted.
antonyms feigned, insincere, pretended.

unfettered adj free, unbridled, unchecked, unconfined, unconstrained, unhampered, unhindered, uninhibited, unrestrained, unshackled, untrammelled.
antonyms constrained, fettered.

unfinished adj bare, crude, deficient, half-done, imperfect, incomplete, lacking, natural, partial, raw, rough, rude, sketchy, unaccomplished, uncompleted, undone, unfulfilled, unpolished, unrefined, wanting.
antonyms complete, finished, polished, refined.

unfit adj debilitated, decrepit, feeble, flabby, flaccid, ill-adapted, ill-equipped, inadequate, inappropriate, incapable, incompetent, ineffective, ineligible, unequal, unhealthy, unprepared, unqualified, unsuitable, unsuited, untrained, useless.
antonyms competent, fit, healthy, suitable.

unflagging adj constant, dogged, fixed, gritty, indefatigable, never-failing, persevering, persistent, resolute, single-minded, staunch, steadfast, steady, tenacious, tireless, unceasing, undeviating, unfailing, unfaltering, unremitting, unswerving, untiring.
antonyms faltering, inconstant.

unflappable adj calm, collected, composed, cool, equable, impassive, imperturbable, level-headed, phlegmatic, self-possessed, unexcitable, unruffled, unworried.
antonyms excitable, nervous, temperamental.

unflattering adj blunt, candid, critical, honest, outspoken, unbecoming, uncomplimentary, unfavourable, unprepossessing.
antonyms complimentary, flattering.

unflinching adj bold, constant, determined, firm, fixed, gritty, resolute, stalwart, staunch, steadfast, steady, sure, unblinking, unfaltering, unshaken, unshrinking, unswerving, unwavering.

antonyms cowed, scared.

unfold *v* clarify, describe, develop, disclose, disentangle, divulge, elaborate, evolve, expand, explain, flatten, grow, illustrate, mature, open, present, reveal, show, spread, straighten, stretch out, uncoil, uncover, undo, unfurl, unravel, unroll, unwrap.

antonyms fold, suppress, withhold, wrap.

unforeseen *adj* abrupt, accidental, fortuitous, startling, sudden, surprise, surprising, unanticipated, unavoidable, unexpected, unheralded, unlooked-for, unpredicted.

antonyms expected, predictable.

unforgettable *adj* exceptional, extraordinary, historic, impressive, memorable, momentous, notable, noteworthy.

antonyms unexceptional, unmemorable.

unforgivable *adj* deplorable, disgraceful, indefensible, inexcusable, reprehensible, shameful, unconscionable, unjustifiable, unpardonable, unwarrantable.

antonyms excusable, forgivable.

unfortunate *adj* adverse, calamitous, cursed, deplorable, disastrous, doomed, hapless, hopeless, ill-advised, ill-fated, ill-starred, ill-timed, inappropriate, infelicitous, inopportune, jinxed, lamentable, luckless, poor, regrettable, ruinous, star-crossed, tactless, unbecoming, unfavourable, unhappy, unlucky, unprosperous, unsuccessful, unsuitable, untimely, untoward, woebegone, wretched.

antonyms fortunate, lucky.

unfortunately *adv* regrettably, sadly, sad to relate, sad to say, unhappily, unluckily, worse luck.

antonyms fortunately, luckily.

unfounded *adj* apocryphal, baseless, fabricated, false, gratuitous, groundless, idle, spurious, trumped-up, unjustified, unmerited, unproven, unsubstantiated, unsupported, vain.

antonym justified.

unfrequented *adj* deserted, desolate, godforsaken, isolated, lone, lonely, remote, secluded, sequestered, solitary, uninhabited, unvisited.

antonyms busy, crowded, populous.

unfriendly *adj* alien, aloof, antagonistic, chilly, cold, critical, disagreeable, distant, hostile, ill-disposed, inauspicious, inhospitable, inimical, quarrelsome, sour, stand-offish, surly, unapproachable, unbending, uncongenial, unfavourable, unneighbourly, unsociable, unwelcoming.

antonyms agreeable, amiable, friendly.

unfrock *v* degrade, demote, depose, dismiss, suspend.

antonyms reinstate, restore.

unfruitful *adj* arid, barren, exhausted, fruitless, impoverished, infecund, infertile, sterile, unproductive, unprofitable, unprolific, unrewarding.

antonyms fruitful, productive.

ungainly *adj* awkward, clumsy, gangling, gauche, gawky, inelegant, klutzy, loutish, lubberly, lumbering, slouching, unco-ordinated, uncouth, unwieldy.

antonyms elegant, graceful.

ungodly *adj* blasphemous, corrupt, depraved, dreadful, extreme, godless, horrendous, immoral, impious, intolerable, irreligious, outrageous, profane, shocking, sinful, unearthly, unreasonable, unseasonable, unseemly, unsocial, vile, wicked.

ungovernable *adj* disorderly, out of control, out of hand, rebellious, refractory, uncontrollable, ungoverned, unmanageable, unrestrainable, unruly, wild.

ungracious *adj* bad-mannered, boorish, churlish, discourteous, disrespectful, graceless, ill-bred, impolite, offhand, rude, uncivil, unmannerly.

antonyms gracious, polite.

ungrateful *adj* disagreeable, heedless, ill-mannered, ingrate, selfish, thankless, unappreciative, ungracious, unmindful, unpleasant.

antonyms grateful, pleasant.

unguarded[1] *adj* careless, foolhardy, foolish, heedless, ill-considered, impolitic, imprudent, incautious, indiscreet, rash, thoughtless, uncircumspect, undiplomatic, unheeding, unthinking, unwary.

antonyms cautious, guarded.

unguarded[2] *adj* defenceless, exposed, pregnable, undefended, unpatrolled, unprotected, vulnerable.

antonyms guarded, protected.

unhandy *adj* awkward, bungling, clumsy, cumbersome, fumbling, heavy-handed, ill-contrived, incompetent, inconvenient, inept, inexpert, maladroit, unco-ordinated, unskilful, unwieldy.

antonyms adroit, deft, handy, manageable.

unhappy *adj* awkward, blue, clumsy, contentless, crestfallen, cursed, dejected, depressed, despondent, disconsolate, dismal, dispirited, down, downcast, gloomy, hapless, ill-advised, ill-chosen, ill-fated, ill-omened, ill-timed, inappropriate, inapt, inept, infelicitous, injudicious, long-faced, luckless, lugubrious, malapropos, melancholy, miserable, mournful, sad, sorrowful, sorry, tactless, uneasy, unfortunate, unlucky, unsuitable, wretched.

antonyms fortunate, happy.

unharmed *adj* intact, safe, scot-free, sound, undamaged, unhurt, unimpaired, uninjured, unscarred, unscathed, untouched, whole, without a scratch.

antonyms damaged, harmed, impaired.

unhealthy *adj* ailing, bad, baneful, corrupt, corrupting, degrading, deleterious, delicate, detrimental, feeble, frail, harmful, infirm, insalubrious, insanitary, invalid, morbid, noisome, noxious, polluted, poorly, sick, sickly, undesirable, unhygienic, unsound, unwell, unwholesome, weak.

antonyms healthy, hygienic, robust, salubrious.

unheard-of *adj* disgraceful, extreme, inconceivable, new, novel, obscure, offensive, out of the question, outrageous, preposterous, shocking, singular, unacceptable, unbelievable, undiscovered, undreamed-of, unexampled, unfamiliar, unimaginable, unique, unknown, unprecedented, unregarded, unremarked, unsung, unthinkable, unthought-of, unusual.

antonyms famous, normal, usual.

unheeded *adj* disobeyed, disregarded, forgotten, ignored, neglected, overlooked, unnoticed, unobserved, unremarked.

antonyms heeded, noted, observed.

unheralded *adj* surprise, unadvertised, unannounced, unexpected, unforeseen, unnoticed, unproclaimed, unpublicized, unrecognized, unsung.

antonyms advertised, publicized, trumpeted.

unhesitating *adj* automatic, immediate, implicit, instant, instantaneous, knee-jerk, prompt, ready, resolute, spontaneous, steadfast, unfaltering, unquestioning, unreserved, unswerving, unwavering, whole-hearted.

antonyms hesitant, tentative, uncertain.

unhinge *v* confuse, craze, derange, disorder, distract, drive mad, madden, unbalance, unnerve, unsettle, upset.

unholy *adj* appalling, base, corrupt, depraved, dishonest, dreadful, evil, godless, heinous, immoral, iniquitous, irreligious, outrageous, profane, shocking, sinful, taboo, unconscionable, unearthly, ungodly, unnatural, unreasonable, vile, wicked.

antonyms godly, holy, pious, reasonable.

unhoped-for *adj* incredible, surprising, unanticipated, unbelievable, undreamed-of, unexpected, unforeseen, unimaginable, unlooked-for.

unhurried *adj* calm, deliberate, easy, easygoing, laid-back, leisurely, relaxed, sedate, slow.

antonyms hasty, hurried.

unidentified *adj* anonymous, incognito, mysterious, nameless, unclaimed, unclassified, unfamiliar, unknown, unmarked, unnamed, unrecognized, unspecified.

antonyms identified, known, named.

unification *n* alliance, amalgamation, coalescence, coalition, combination, confederacy, confederation, consolidation, enosis, federation, fusion, incorporation, merger, synthesis, union, uniting.

antonyms separation, split.

uniform *n* costume, dress, garb, gear, habit, insignia, livery, outfit, regalia, rig, robes, suit.

adj alike, consistent, constant, equable, equal, even, homogeneous, homomorphic, homomorphous, identical, like, monochrome, montonous, of a piece, regular, same, selfsame, similar, smooth, unbroken, unchanging, undeviating, unvarying.

antonyms changing, colourful, varied.

uniformity *n* constancy, drabness, dullness, evenness, flatness, homogeneity, homomorphism, invariability, monotony, regularity, sameness, similarity, similitude, tedium.

antonyms difference, dissimilarity, variation.

unify *v* amalgamate, bind, combine, confederate, consolidate, federalize, federate, fuse, join, marry, merge, unite, weld.

antonyms separate, split.

unifying *adj* combinatory, consolidating, henotic, reconciling, uniting.

antonym divisive.

unimaginable *adj* absurd, fantastic, impossible, inconceivable, incredible, indescribable, ineffable, mind-blowing, mind-boggling, out of the question, unbelievable, undreamed-of, unheard-of, unhoped-for, unknowable, unthinkable.

unimaginative *adj* banal, barren, blinkered, commonplace, derivative, dry, dull, hackneyed, lifeless, matter-of-fact, myopic, ordinary, pedestrian, predictable, prosaic, routine, short-sighted, tame, uncreative, uninspired, unoriginal.

antonyms imaginative, original.

unimpeachable *adj* blameless, faultless, flawless, immaculate, impeccable, irreproachable, perfect, spotless, unassailable, unblemished, unchallengeable, unexceptionable, unobjectionable, unquestionable.

antonyms blameworthy, faulty.

unimpeded *adj* all-round, clear, free, open, unblocked, unchecked, unconstrained, unhampered, unhindered, uninhibited, unrestrained, untrammelled.

antonyms hampered, impeded.

unimportant *adj* bush-league, immaterial, inconsequential, insignificant, irrelevant, low-ranking, minor, minuscule, negligible, nondescript, nugatory, off the map, paltry, peanuts, petty, slight, small-time, trifling, trivial, worthless.

antonyms important, significant.

unimpressive *adj* average, commonplace, dull, indifferent, mediocre, ordinary, undistinguished, unexceptional, uninteresting, unremarkable, unspectacular.

antonyms impressive, memorable, notable.

uninhibited *adj* abandoned, candid, frank, free, informal, instinctive, liberated, natural, open, relaxed, spontaneous, unbridled, unchecked, unconstrained, uncontrolled, uncurbed, unrepressed, unreserved, unrestrained, unrestricted, unselfconscious.

antonyms constrained, inhibited, repressed.

uninspired *adj* boring, commonplace, dull, humdrum, indifferent, ordinary, pedestrian, prosaic, stale, stock, trite, undistinguished, unexciting, unimaginative, uninspiring, uninteresting, unoriginal.

antonyms inspired, original.

unintelligent *adj* brainless, dense, dull, dumb, empty-headed, fatuous, foolish, half-witted, obtuse, silly, slow, stupid, thick, unreasoning, unthinking.

antonyms intelligent, thoughtful.

unintelligible *adj* garbled, illegible, inapprehensible, inarticulate, incoherent, incomprehensible, indecipherable, indistinct, jumbled, meaningless, muddled, unfathomable.

antonyms clear, intelligible.

unintentional *adj* accidental, chance, fortuitous, inadvertent, involuntary, spontaneous, unconscious, undeliberate, unintended, unpremeditated, unthinking, unwitting.

antonyms deliberate, intentional.

uninterested *adj* apathetic, blasé, bored, distant, impassive, inattentive, incurious, indifferent, listless, unconcerned, unenthusiastic, uninvolved, unresponsive.

antonyms concerned, enthusiastic, interested, responsive.

▲ *confusable word* disinterested.

uninteresting *adj* boring, commonplace, drab, dreary, dry, dull, flat, humdrum, monotonous, tame, tedious, tiresome, uneventful, unexciting, unimpressive, uninspiring, wearisome.

antonyms exciting, interesting.

uninterrupted *adj* constant, continual, continuous, non-stop, peaceful, quiet, solid, steady, sustained, unbroken, undisturbed, unending.

antonyms broken, intermittent.

uninvited *adj* unasked, unbidden, unsolicited, unsought, unwanted, unwelcome.

antonyms invited, solicited.

uninviting *adj* disagreeable, distasteful, nasty, offensive, off-putting, repellent, repulsive, revolting, unappealing, unappetizing, unattractive, undesirable, unpleasant, unsavoury, unwelcoming.

antonyms inviting, welcome.

uninvolved *adj* disengaged, fancy-free, footloose, free, independent, unattached, uncommitted, unengaged, unhampered, unhindered, untrammelled.

antonyms attached, committed.

union *n* accord, agreement, alliance, amalgam, amalgamation, association, blend, coalition, coitus, combination, compact, concert, concord, concrescence, concurrence, confederacy, confederation, confluence, conjugation, conjunction, consensus, convergence, copulation, coupling, enosis, federation, fusion, harmony, intercourse, junction, juncture, league, marriage, matrimony, mixture, pool, syndicate, syndication, synthesis, unanimity, unison, uniting, unity, wedlock.

antonyms alienation, disunity, estrangement, separation.

unique *adj* incomparable, inimitable, lone, matchless, nonpareil, only, peerless, single, singular, sole, solitary, sui generis, unequalled,

unexampled, unmatched, unparalleled, unprecedented, unrivalled.

antonyms average, commonplace.

unison *n* accord, accordance, agreement, concert, concord, co-operation, harmony, homophony, monophony, unanimity, unity.

antonyms disharmony, polyphony.

unit *n* component, constituent, detachment, element, entity, group, item, measure, measurement, member, module, monad, one, part, piece, portion, quantity, section, segment, system, whole.

unite *v* accrete, ally, amalgamate, associate, band, blend, coalesce, cohere, combine, confederate, conjoin, conjugate, connect, consolidate, converge, co-operate, couple, federate, fuse, incorporate, join, join forces, league, link, marry, merge, mix, pool, splice, syndicate, unify, wed.

antonyms separate, sever.

united *adj* affiliated, agreed, allied, collective, combined, concerted, concordant, conjoined, conjoint, conjunct, conjunctive, corporate, federated, in accord, in agreement, leagued, like-minded, linked, one, pooled, syndicated, unanimous, unified.

antonyms differing, disunited, separated, unco-ordinated.

unity *n* accord, agreement, community, concord, concurrence, consensus, entity, harmony, integrity, oneness, peace, singleness, solidarity, unanimity, unification, union, wholeness.

antonyms disagreement, disunity.

universal *adj* across-the-board, all-embracing, all-inclusive, all-round, common, entire, general, global, omnipresent, total, ubiquitous, unlimited, whole, widespread, worldwide.

universality *n* all-inclusiveness, commonness, completeness, comprehensiveness, entirety, generalization, generality, predominance, prevalence, totality, ubiquity.

universally *adv* always, everywhere, invariably, ubiquitously, uniformly.

universe *n* cosmos, creation, firmament, macrocosm, nature, world.

unjust *adj* biassed, gratuitous, groundless, inequitable, one-sided, partial, partisan, prejudiced, undeserved, unethical, unfair, unjustified, unmerited, wrong, wrongful.

antonyms fair, just.

unjustifiable *adj* excessive, immoderate, indefensible, inexcusable, outrageous, steep, unacceptable, unforgivable, unjust, unpardonable, unreasonable, unwarrantable, wrong.

antonyms acceptable, justifiable.

unkempt *adj* bedraggled, blowsy, disarranged, dishevelled, disordered, frowzy, messy, mussed (up), ratty, rumpled, scruffy, shabby, shaggy, slatternly, sloppy, slovenly, sluttish, tousled, uncombed, ungroomed, untidy.

antonyms neat, tidy.

unkind *adj* callous, cruel, disobliging, hard, hard-hearted, harsh, inconsiderate, inhuman, inhumane, insensitive, malevolent, malicious, mean, merciless, nasty, severe, spiteful, thoughtless, unamiable, uncaring, uncharitable, unfeeling, unforgiving, unfriendly, unsympathetic.

antonyms considerate, gentle, kind.

unkindness *n* callousness, cruelty, disobligingness, hard-heartedness, harshness, ill-turn, inhumanity, insensitivity, maliciousness, meanness, spite, uncharitableness, unfriendliness.

antonyms charity, friendship, kindness.

unknowable *adj* incalculable, infinite, in the lap of the gods, unascertainable, unfathomable, unforeseeable, unimaginable, unpredictable, untold.

unknown *adj* alien, anonymous, concealed, dark, foreign, hidden, incognito, mysterious, nameless, new, obscure, secret, strange, uncharted, undisclosed, undiscovered, unexplored, unfamiliar, unheard-of, unidentified, unnamed, unrecognized, unsung, untold.

antonyms familiar, known.

unladylike *adj* boyish, coarse, hoydenish, ill-bred, impolite, indelicate, inelegant, rough, rude, tomboyish, uncivil, unfeminine, ungracious, unmannerly, unrefined, unseemly.

antonyms ladylike, seemly.

unlawful *adj* actionable, banned, contraband, criminal, felonious, forbidden, illegal, illegitimate, illicit, larcenous, outlawed, prohibited, proscribed, unauthorized, unconstitutional, unlicensed, unsanctioned.

antonyms authorized, lawful.

unleash *v* free, loose, release, unchain, unloose, untether, untie.

antonym restrain.

unlettered *adj* ignorant, illiterate, uneducated, unlearned, unschooled, untaught, untutored.

antonym educated.

unlike *adj* contrasted, different, disparate, dissimilar, distinct, divergent, diverse, ill-matched, incompatible, opposed, opposite, unequal, unrelated.

antonyms related, similar.

unlikely *adj* doubtful, dubious, faint, fishy, implausible, improbable, incredible, questionable, remote, slight, suspect, suspicious, unbelievable, unconvincing, unexpected, unimaginable, unpromising.

antonyms likely, plausible.

unlikeness *n* contrast, difference, disparity, dissemblance, dissimilarity, divergence, diversity, incompatibility.

antonym similarity.

unlimited *adj* absolute, all-encompassing, boundless, complete, countless, endless, extensive, full, great, illimitable, immeasurable, immense, incalculable, inexhaustible, infinite, interminable, limitless, never-ending, numberless, total, unbounded, uncircumscribed, unconditional, unconstrained, unfettered, unhampered, unqualified, unrestricted, vast.

antonyms circumscribed, limited.

unload *v* disburden, discharge, disencumber, dump, empty, offload, relieve, unburden, unpack.

unlock *v* bare, disengage, free, open, release, unbar, unbolt, unchain, undo, unfasten, unlatch.

antonyms fasten, lock.

unlooked-for *adj* chance, fortuitous, fortunate, lucky, surprise, surprising, unanticipated, undreamed-of, unexpected, unforeseen, unhoped-for, unpredicted, unthought-of.

antonyms expected, predictable.

unloved *adj* despised, detested, disliked, forsaken, hated, loveless, neglected, rejected, spurned, uncared-for, uncherished, unpopular, unwanted.

antonyms beloved, loved.

unlucky *adj* cursed, disastrous, doomed, hapless, ill-fated, ill-omened, ill-starred, inauspicious, jinxed, luckless, miserable, ominous, star-crossed, unfavourable, unfortunate, unhappy, unpropitious, unsuccessful, untimely, wretched.

antonyms favourable, lucky.

unmanageable *adj* awkward, bulky, cumbersome, difficult, disorderly, fractious, inconvenient, intractable, obstreperous, recalcitrant, refractory, uncontrollable, unco-operative, unhandy, unruly, unwieldy, wild.

antonyms docile, manageable.

unmannerly *adj* badly-behaved, bad-mannered, boorish, discourteous, disrespectful, graceless, ill-bred, ill-mannered, impolite, low-bred, rude, uncivil, uncouth, ungracious.

antonym polite.

unmarried *adj* available, bachelor, celibate, fancy-free, footloose, maiden, single, unattached, unwed, unwedded, virgin.

antonym married.

unmask *v* bare, come out (of the closet), detect, disclose, discover, expose, reveal, show, uncloak, uncover, unveil.

unmatched *adj* beyond compare, consummate, incomparable, matchless, nonpareil, paramount, peerless, supreme, unequalled, unexampled, unparalleled, unrivalled, unsurpassed.

unmentionable *adj* abominable, disgraceful, disreputable, immodest, indecent, scandalous, shameful, shocking, taboo, unnamable, unspeakable, unutterable.

unmerciful *adj* brutal, callous, cold-blooded, cruel, flinty, hard, heartless, implacable, merciless, pitiless, relentless, remorseless, ruthless, sadistic, uncaring, unfeeling, unrelenting, unsparing.

antonyms kind, merciful.

unmethodical *adj* confused, desultory, disorderly, haphazard, illogical, irregular, muddled, random, unco-ordinated, unorganized, unsystematic.

antonyms methodical, organized.

unmindful *adj* absent-minded, careless, forgetful, heedless, inattentive, indifferent, lax, neglectful, negligent, oblivious, regardless, remiss, slack, unaware, unconscious, unheeding.

antonyms aware, heedful, mindful.

unmistakable *adj* certain, clear, conspicuous, crystal-clear, decided, distinct, downright, evident, explicit, flaming, for-sure, glaring, indisputable, manifest, obvious, palpable, patent, plain, positive, pronounced, sure, unambiguous, undeniable, undisputed, unequivocal, unquestionable.

antonyms ambiguous, unclear.

unmitigated *adj* absolute, all-out, arrant, complete, consummate, downright, grim, harsh, intense, oppressive, out-and-out, outright, perfect, persistent, pure, rank, relentless, sheer, thorough, thoroughgoing, unabated, unalleviated, unbroken, undiminished, unmodified, unqualified, unredeemed, unrelenting, unrelieved, unremitting, utter.

unmoved *adj* adamant, cold, determined, dispassionate, dry-eyed, fast, firm, impassive, indifferent, inflexible, obdurate, phlegmatic, resolute, resolved, steadfast, steady, unaffected, unchanged, undeviating, unfeeling, unimpressed, unresponsive, unshaken, untouched, unwavering.

antonyms affected, moved, shaken.

unnatural *adj* aberrant, abnormal, affected, anomalous, artificial, assumed, bizarre, brutal, callous, cold-blooded, contrived, cruel, evil, extraordinary, factitious, false, feigned, fiendish, forced, freakish, heartless, inhuman, insincere, irregular, laboured, mannered, monstrous, odd, outlandish, perverse, perverted, phony, queer, ruthless, sadistic, savage, self-conscious, stagey, stiff, stilted, strained, strange, studied, supernatural, theatrical, unaccountable, uncanny, unfeeling, unspontaneous, unusual, wicked.

antonyms acceptable, natural, normal.

unnecessary *adj* dispensable, expendable, inessential, needless, non-essential, otiose, pleonastic, redundant, supererogatory, superfluous, supernumerary, tautological, uncalled-for, unjustified, unneeded, unwanted, useless.

antonyms indispensable, necessary.

unnerve *adj* confound, daunt, deflate, deject, demoralize, discomfit, disconcert, discourage, dishearten, dismay, dispirit, disquiet, faze, fluster, frighten, intimidate, perturb, rattle, scare, shake (up), throw, unhinge, unsettle, upset, worry.

antonyms brace, nerve, steel.

unnoticed *adj* disregarded, ignored, neglected, overlooked, passed over, unconsidered, undiscovered, unheeded, unobserved, unperceived, unrecognized, unrecorded, unremarked, unseen.

antonyms noted, remarked.

unobtrusive *adj* humble, inconspicuous, low-key, meek, modest, quiet, restrained, retiring, self-effacing, subdued, unassertive, unassuming, unemphatic, unnoticeable, unostentatious, unpretentious.

antonyms obtrusive, ostentatious.

unobtrusively *adv* inconspicuously, modestly, on the q.t., on the quiet, quietly, surreptitiously, unostentatiously.

antonyms obtrusively, ostentatiously.

unoccupied *adj* disengaged, empty, free, idle, inactive, uninhabited, untenanted, vacant.

antonyms busy, occupied.

unofficial *adj* backyard, casual, confidential, illegal, informal, personal, private, ulterior, unauthorized, unconfirmed, undeclared, unsanctioned, wildcat.

antonyms authorized, official.

unoriginal *adj* cliché-ridden, copied, cribbed, derivative, derived, second-hand, stale, stock, trite, unimaginative, uninspired.

antonyms imaginative, original.

unorthodox *adj* abnormal, alternative, fringe, heterodox, irregular, nonconformist, unconventional, unusual, unwonted.

antonyms conventional, orthodox.

unpaid *adj* due, free, honorary, outstanding, overdue, owing, payable, unremunerative, unsalaried, unsettled, voluntary.

antonyms paid, settled.

unpalatable *adj* bitter, disagreeable, displeasing, distasteful, inedible, insipid, offensive, repugnant, unappetizing, unattractive, uneatable, unenviable, unpleasant, unrelished, unsavoury.

antonyms palatable, pleasant.

unparalleled *adj* consummate, exceptional, incomparable, matchless, nonpareil, peerless, rare, singular, superlative, supreme, surpassing, unequalled, unexampled, unique, unmatched, unprecedented, unrivalled, unsurpassed.

unpardonable *adj* deplorable, disgraceful, indefensible, inexcusable, irremissible, outrageous, scandalous, shameful, shocking, unconscionable, unforgivable.

antonyms forgivable, understandable.

unperturbed *adj* calm, collected, composed, cool, impassive, placid, poised, self-possessed, serene, tranquil, undisturbed, unexcited, unflinching, unflustered, unruffled, untroubled, unworried.

antonyms anxious, perturbed.

unpleasant *adj* abhorrent, bad, disagreeable, displeasing, distasteful, godawful, ill-natured, irksome, mean, nasty, objectionable, obnoxious, pesky, repulsive, sticky, traumatic, troublesome, unattractive, unpalatable, yucky.

antonym pleasant.

unpleasantness *n* annoyance, bother, embarrassment, furor, fuss, ill feeling, nastiness, scandal, trouble, upset.

unpolished *adj* coarse, crude, rough, rough and ready, rude, sketchy, uncivilized, uncouth, uncultivated, uncultured, unfashioned, unfinished, unrefined, unsophisticated, unworked, vulgar.

antonyms finished, polished, refined.

unpopular *adj* avoided, detested, disliked, hated, neglected, out, rejected, shunned, undesirable, unfashionable, unloved, unsought-after, unwanted, unwelcome.

antonyms fashionable, popular.

unprecedented *adj* abnormal, anomalous, atypical, exceptional, extraordinary, freakish, new, novel, original, prototypical, remarkable, revolutionary, singular, unexampled, unheard-of, unknown, unparalleled, unrivalled, unusual.

unpredictable *adj* chance, changeable, doubtful, erratic, fickle, flukey, iffy, inconstant, in the lap of the gods, random, squirrelly, unforeseeable, unreliable, unstable, variable.

antonyms predictable, reliable.

unprejudiced *adj* balanced, detached, dispassionate, enlightened, even-handed, fair, fair-minded, impartial, just, non-partisan, objective, open-minded, unbiassed, uncoloured.

antonyms narrow-minded, prejudiced.

unpremeditated *adj* extempore, fortuitous, impromptu, impulsive, offhand, off-the-cuff, on-the-spot, spontaneous, spur-of-the-moment, unintentional, unplanned, unprepared, unrehearsed, unstudied.

antonyms planned, premeditated.

unprepared *adj* ad-lib, by surprise, casual, extemporaneous, half-baked, ill-considered, ill-equipped, ill-trained, improvised, incomplete, napping, off-the-cuff, spontaneous, surprised, taken aback, unawares, unfinished, ungirded, unplanned, unready, unrehearsed, unsuspecting.

antonyms prepared, ready.

unpretentious *adj* homey, honest, humble, modest, natural, plain, simple, straightforward, unadorned, unaffected, unassuming, unimposing, unobtrusive, unostentatious, unpretending, unsophisticated, unspoiled.

antonyms ostentatious, pretentious.

unprincipled *adj* amoral, corrupt, crooked, deceitful, devious, discreditable, dishonest, dishonourable, immoral, shady, sharp, underhand, unethical, unprofessional, unscrupulous.

antonyms ethical, scrupulous.

unproductive *adj* arid, barren, bootless, dry, fruitless, futile, idle, ineffective, inefficacious, infertile, otiose, sterile, unavailing, unfruitful, unprofitable, unprolific, unremunerative, unrewarding, useless, vain, valueless, worthless.

antonyms fertile, productive.

unprofessional *adj* amateur, amateurish, bush, improper, inadmissible, incompetent, inefficient, inexperienced, inexpert, lax, negligent, unacceptable, unbecoming, unbusinesslike, unethical, unfitting, unprincipled, unseemly, unskilled, untrained, unworthy.

antonyms professional, skilful.

unpromising *adj* adverse, depressing, discouraging, dispiriting, doubtful, gloomy, inauspicious, ominous, unfavourable, unpropitious.

antonyms hopeful, promising.

unprotected *adj* defenceless, exposed, helpless, insecure, liable, naked, open, pregnable, unarmed, unattended, undefended, unfortified, unguarded, unsheltered, unshielded, unvaccinated, vulnerable, weak.

antonyms immune, protected, safe.

unprovable *adj* indemonstrable, indeterminable, unascertainable, undemonstrable, unverifiable.

antonym verifiable.

unqualified *adj* absolute, categorical, complete, consummate, downright, ill-equipped, incapable, incompetent, ineligible, not cut out for, not equal to, out-and-out, outright, pure, sheer, thorough, thoroughgoing, total, uncertificated, unconditional, unfit, unmitigated, unmixed, unprepared, unreserved, unrestricted, untrained, utter, whole-hearted.

antonyms conditional, tentative.

unquestionable *adj* absolute, certain, clear, conclusive, definite, faultless, flawless, incontestable, incontrovertible, indisputable, indubitable, irrefutable, manifest, obvious, patent, self-evident, sure, unchallenged, undeniable, unequivocal, unmistakable.

antonyms dubious, questionable.

unquestioning *adj* implicit, unconditional, unhesitating, unqualified, whole-hearted.

antonym doubtful.

unravel *v* break, clear up, crack, disentangle, dope out, explain, extricate, figure out, free, interpret, penetrate, puzzle out, ravel out, resolve, separate, solve, sort out, straighten out, undo, unknot, unlock, unroll, untangle, unwind, work out.

antonyms complicate, tangle.

unreal *adj* academic, artificial, fabulous, factitious, fairy-tale, fake, false, fanciful, fantastic, fictitious, hypothetical, illusory, imaginary, immaterial, impalpable, insincere, insubstantial, intangible, made-up, make-believe, mock, moonshiny, mythical, nebulous, ostensible, phantasmagorical, pretended, seeming, sham, storybook, synthetic, vaporous, visionary.

antonyms genuine, real.

unrealistic *adj* fanciful, half-baked, idealistic, impracticable, impractical, improbable, infeasible, off-the-wall, quixotic, romantic, starry-eyed, theoretical, unworkable.

antonyms pragmatic, realistic.

unreasonable *adj* absurd, arbitrary, biassed, blinkered, capricious, crazy, cussed, erratic, excessive, exorbitant, extortionate, extravagant, far-fetched, foolish, froward, headstrong, illogical, immoderate, inconsistent, irrational, mad, nonsensical, off-the-wall, opinionated, perverse, preposterous, quirky, senseless, silly, steep, stupid, uncalled-for, undue, unfair, unjust, unjustifiable, unjustified, unwarranted, wacky.

antonyms moderate, rational, reasonable.

unrecognizable *adj* altered, changed, disguised, incognito, unidentifiable, unknowable.

unrefined *adj* boorish, coarse, crude, imperfect, inelegant, raw, rude, uncultivated, uncultured, unfinished, unperfected, unpolished, unpurified, unsophisticated, untreated, vulgar.

antonyms finished, refined.

unregenerate *adj* abandoned, hardened, impenitent, incorrigible, intractable, obdurate, obstinate, persistent, recalcitrant, refractory, shameless, sinful, stubborn, unconverted, unreformed, unrepentant, wicked.

antonyms reformed, repentant.

unrelated *adj* different, discrete, disparate, dissimilar, distinct, extraneous, inapplicable, inappropriate, irrelevant, separate, unassociated, unconnected, unlike.

antonyms related, similar.

unrelenting *adj* ceaseless, constant, continual, continuous, cruel, endless, implacable, incessant, inexorable, insistent, intransigent, merciless, perpetual, pitiless, relentless, remorseless, ruthless, steady, stern, tough, unabated, unalleviated, unbroken, unceasing, uncompromising, unmerciful, unremitting, unsparing.

antonyms intermittent, spasmodic.

unreliable *adj* deceptive, delusive, disreputable, erroneous, fair-weather, fallible, false, implausible, inaccurate, inauthentic, irresponsible, mistaken, specious, uncertain, unconvincing, undependable, unsound, unstable, untrustworthy.

antonyms reliable, sound.

unremitting *adj* assiduous, ceaseless, conscientious, constant, continual, continuous, diligent, incessant, indefatigable, perpetual, relentless, remorseless, sedulous, tireless, unabated, unbroken, unceasing, unrelenting.

antonym spasmodic.

unrepentant *adj* callous, hardened, impenitent, incorrigible, obdurate, shameless, unabashed, unashamed, unregenerate, unremorseful, unrepenting.

antonyms penitent, repentant.

unreserved *adj* absolute, candid, complete, demonstrative, direct, entire, extrovert, forthright, frank, free, full, open, open-hearted, outgoing, outspoken, total, unconditional, unhesitating, uninhibited, unlimited, unqualified, unrestrained, whole-hearted.

antonyms inhibited, tentative.

unreservedly *adv* completely, entirely, outright, totally, unhesitatingly, utterly, whole-heartedly.

unresisting *adj* docile, like a lamb to the slaughter, meek, obedient, passive, submissive.

antonyms protesting, resisting.

unresolved *adj* doubtful, iffy, inconclusive, indefinite, moot, pending, problematic, unanswered, undecided, undetermined, unsettled, unsolved, up in the air, vague, vexed, wide-open.

antonyms definite, determined.

unresponsive *adj* aloof, apathetic, cool, echoless, flat, indifferent, unaffected, uninterested, unmoved, unsympathetic.

antonyms responsive, sympathetic.

unrest *n* agitation, anxiety, apprehension, disaffection, discontent, discord, disquiet, dissatisfaction, dissension, dissent, distress, perturbation, protest, rebellion, restlessness, sedition, strife, tumult, turmoil, unease, uneasiness, unquiet, worry.

antonyms calm, peace.

unrestrained *adj* abandoned, boisterous, free, immoderate, inordinate, intemperate, irrepressible, natural, rampant, unbounded, unbridled, unchecked, unconstrained, uncontrolled, unhindered, uninhibited, unrepressed, unreserved, uproarious.

antonym inhibited.

unrestricted *adj* absolute, all-round, clear, free, free-for-all, freewheeling, open, public, unbounded, uncircumscribed, unconditional, unhindered, unimpeded, unlimited, unobstructed, unopposed, unregulated.

antonyms limited, restricted.

unripe *adj* green, immature, undeveloped, unready, unripened.

antonyms mature, ripe.

unrivalled *adj* incomparable, inimitable, matchless, nonpareil, peerless, superlative, supreme, surpassing, unequalled, unexcelled, unmatched, unparalleled, unsurpassed, without equal.

unruffled *adj* calm, collected, composed, cool, even, impassive, imperturbable, level, level-headed, peaceful, placid, poised, serene, smooth, tranquil, unbroken, undisturbed, unflustered, unmoved, unperturbed, untroubled.

antonyms anxious, troubled.

unruly *adj* disobedient, disorderly, fractious, headstrong, insubordinate, intractable, lawless, mutinous, obstreperous, out of control (or hand), rampageous, rebellious, refractory, riotous, rowdy, turbulent, unbridled, uncontrollable, undisciplined, ungovernable, unmanageable, wayward, wild, willful.

antonym manageable.

unsafe *adj* chancy, dangerous, exposed, hazardous, insecure, parlous, perilous, precarious, risky, threatening, treacherous, uncertain, unreliable, unsound, unstable, vulnerable.

antonyms safe, secure.

unsaid *adj* undeclared, unexpressed, unmentioned, unpronounced, unspoken, unstated, unuttered, unvoiced.

antonym spoken.

unsatisfactory *adj* deficient, disappointing, displeasing, dissatisfying, frustrating, inadequate, incomplete, inferior, insufficient, lacking, leaving a lot to be desired, mediocre, poor, unacceptable, unsatisfying, unsuitable, unworthy, weak.

antonyms complete, satisfactory.

unsavoury *adj* disagreeable, distasteful, nasty, nauseating, objectionable, obnoxious, offensive, repellent, repugnant, repulsive, revolting, sickening, sordid, squalid, tasteless, unappetizing, unattractive, undesirable, unpalatable, unpleasant.

antonyms palatable, pleasant.

unscathed *adj* intact, safe, scot-free, sound, unharmed, unhurt, unimpaired, uninjured, unmarked, unscarred, unscratched, untouched, whole.

antonyms harmed, injured.

unscrupulous *adj* corrupt, crooked, cynical, discreditable, dishonest, dishonourable, double-dealing, immoral, improper, ruthless, shameless, two-timing, unethical, unprincipled.

antonyms honest, scrupulous.

unseasonable *adj* ill-timed, inappropriate, inopportune, malapropos, mistimed, unsuitable, untimely.

antonyms seasonable, timely.

unseasoned *adj* green, unmatured, unprepared, unprimed, untempered, untreated.

unseat *v* depose, dethrone, discharge, dismiss, displace, oust, overthrow, remove, throw, topple, unhorse.

unseemly *adj* discreditable, disreputable, improper, inappropriate, indecorous, indelicate, shocking, unbecoming, unbefitting, undignified, undue, ungentlemanly, unladylike, unrefined, unsuitable.

antonyms decorous, seemly.

unseen *adj* concealed, hidden, invisible, lurking, obscure, overlooked, undetected, unnoticed, unobserved, unobtrusive, unperceived, veiled.

antonyms observed, visible.

unselfish *adj* altruistic, charitable, dedicated, devoted, disinterested, generous, humanitarian, kind, liberal, magnanimous, noble, open-handed, philanthropic, self-denying, selfless, self-sacrificing, ungrudging, unstinting.

antonyms mean, selfish.

unsentimental *adj* cynical, hard as nails, hard-headed, level-headed, practical, pragmatic, realistic, shrewd, tough.

antonyms sentimental, soft.

unsettle *v* agitate, bother, confuse, destabilize, discomfit, discompose, disconcert, disorder, disorient, disturb, fluster, flutter, perturb, psych (out), rattle, ruffle, shake, throw, trouble, unbalance, upset, weaken.

antonyms compose, settle.

unsettled *adj* agitated, anxious, changeable, changing, confused, debatable, disorderly, disoriented, disturbed, doubtful, due, edgy, flustered, iffy, inconstant, insecure, moot, open, outstanding, overdue, owing, payable, pending, perturbed, problematic, restive,

restless, shaken, shaky, tense, troubled, uncertain, undecided, undetermined, uneasy, unnerved, unpredictable, unresolved, unstable, unsteady, upset, variable.

antonyms certain, composed, settled.

unshakable *adj* absolute, adamant, constant, determined, firm, fixed, immovable, resolute, stable, staunch, steadfast, sure, unassailable, unswerving, unwavering, well-founded.

antonym insecure.

unsheathe *v* draw, expose, reveal, uncover.

antonyms retract, sheathe.

unsightly *adj* disagreeable, displeasing, hideous, horrid, off-putting, repellent, repugnant, repulsive, revolting, ugly, unattractive, unpleasant, unprepossessing.

antonym pleasing.

unskilful *adj* amateurish, awkward, bungling, clumsy, fumbling, gauche, incompetent, inept, inexperienced, inexpert, maladroit, unapt, uneducated, unhandy, unpractised, unprofessional, unqualified, unskilled, untalented, untaught, untrained.

antonyms skilled, skilful.

unsociable *adj* aloof, chilly, cold, distant, farouche, hostile, inhospitable, introverted, reclusive, remote, reserved, retiring, shy, stand-offish, taciturn, uncommunicative, uncongenial, unforthcoming, unfriendly, unneighbourly, unsocial, withdrawn.

antonyms friendly, sociable.

unsolicited *adj* gratuitous, spontaneous, unasked, uncalled-for, unforced, uninvited, unrequested, unsought, unwanted, unwelcome, voluntary.

antonyms invited, solicited.

unsophisticated *adj* artless, childlike, green, guileless, hick, homespun, inexperienced, ingenuous, innocent, naïve, natural, plain, raw, simple, small-town, straightforward, unaffected, uncomplicated, uncouth, uninvolved, unpretentious, unrefined, unspecialized, unspoilt, untutored, unworldly.

antonyms complex, pretentious, sophisticated.

unsound *adj* ailing, defective, delicate, deranged, dicey, diseased, erroneous, fallacious, fallible, false, faulty, flawed, frail, ill, ill-founded, illogical, insecure, invalid, shaky, specious, unbalanced, unhealthy, unhinged, unreliable, unsafe, unstable, unsteady, unwell, weak, wobbly.

antonyms safe, sound.

unsparing[1] *adj* abundant, bountiful, generous, lavish, liberal, munificent, open-handed, plenteous, prodigal, profuse, ungrudging, unstinting.

antonyms forgiving, mean, sparing.

unsparing[2] *adj* flint-hearted, hard, hard-hearted, harsh, implacable, inexorable, merciless, pitiless, relentless, rigorous, ruthless, scathing, severe, stern, stony-hearted, stringent, uncompromising, unforgiving, unmerciful.

unspeakable *adj* abhorrent, abominable, appalling, disgusting, dreadful, evil, execrable, fantastic, frightful, heinous, horrible, inconceivable, indescribable, ineffable, inexpressible, loathsome, monstrous, odious, overwhelming, repellent, shocking, unbelievable, unimaginable, unutterable, wonderful.

unspectacular *adj* boring, dull, methodical, ordinary, plodding, systematic, unexciting, unimpressive, unremarkable.

unspoiled *adj* artless, innocent, intact, natural, perfect, preserved, scatheless, unaffected, unaltered, unassuming, unblemished, unchanged, undamaged, unharmed, unimpaired, unscathed, unsophisticated, unstudied, untouched, wholesome.

antonyms affected, spoiled.

unspoken *adj* assumed, implicit, implied, inferred, mute, silent, speechless, tacit, undeclared, understood, unexpressed, unsaid, unstated, unuttered, voiceless, wordless.

antonym explicit.

unstable *adj* capricious, changeable, deranged, erratic, fitful, fluctuating, inconsistent, inconstant, insecure, irrational, labile, precarious, rickety, risky, shaky, shifting, swaying, teetering, ticklish, tippy, tottering, tottery, unbalanced, unhinged, unpredictable, unsettled, unsteady, untrustworthy, vacillating, variable, volatile, wobbly.

antonyms stable, steady.

unsteady *adj* changeable, dicey, erratic, flickering, flighty, fluctuating, frail, inconstant, infirm, insecure, irregular, precarious, reeling, rickety, shaky, skittish, tippy, tottering, tottery, treacherous, tremulous, unbalanced, unreliable, unsafe, unstable, unsteeled, vacillating, variable, volatile, wavering, wobbly.

antonyms firm, steady.

unstinting *adj* abounding, abundant, ample, bountiful, full, generous, large, lavish, liberal, munificent, plentiful, prodigal, profuse, ungrudging, unsparing.

antonyms grudging, mean.

unsubstantial *adj* airy, cheap, dreamlike, dubious, ephemeral, fanciful, feeble, flimsy, fragile, frail, idle, ill-founded, illusory, imaginary, immaterial, impalpable, inadequate, incorporeal, insubstantial, light, makeshift, poor, rickety, shaky, slight, superficial, tenuous, thin, unreal, unsound, unsupported, vaporous, visionary, weak.

antonyms real, solid, valid.

unsubstantiated *adj* debatable, dubious, questionable, unattested, unconfirmed, uncorroborated, undemonstrated, unestablished, unfounded, unproved, unproven, unsupported, unverified.

antonyms proved, supported.

unsuccessful *adj* abortive, balked, bootless, crossed, failed, foiled, fruitless, frustrated, futile, ill-fated, inadequate, ineffective, ineffectual, losing, luckless, manqué, otiose, sterile, thwarted, unavailing, unfortunate, unlucky, unproductive, unsatisfactory, useless, vain.

antonyms effective, successful.

unsuitable *adj* improper, inapposite, inappropriate, inapt, incompatible, incongruous, inconsistent, indecorous, ineligible, infelicitous, malapropos, out of keeping, out of place, unacceptable, unbecoming, unbefitting, unfitting, unlikely, unseasonable, unseemly, unsuited.

antonyms seemly, suitable.

unsullied *adj* clean, immaculate, intact, perfect, pristine, pure, spotless, stainless, unblemished, uncorrupted, undefiled, unsoiled, unspoiled, unspotted, unstained, untarnished, untouched.

antonyms dirty, stained.

unsung *adj* anonymous, disregarded, forgotten, nameless, neglected, obscure, overlooked, unacknowledged, uncelebrated, unhailed, unheard-of, unhonoured, unknown, unnamed, unrecognized, unrenowned.

antonyms famous, renowned.

unsure *adj* agnostic, distrustful, doubtful, dubious, hesitant, insecure, in (or of) two minds, irresolute, mistrustful, sceptical, suspicious, tentative, uncertain, unconvinced, undecided, unpersuaded.

antonyms resolute, sure.

unsurpassed *adj* consummate, exceptional, incomparable, matchless, nonpareil, paramount, peerless, sublime, superlative, supreme, surpassing, transcendent, unequalled, unexcelled, unparalleled, unrivalled.

unsuspecting *adj* childlike, confiding, credulous, green, gullible, inexperienced, ingenuous, innocent, naïve, off guard, trustful, trusting, unconscious, uncritical, unsuspicious, unwary, unwitting, wide-eyed.

antonyms conscious, knowing.

unswerving *adj* constant, dedicated, devoted, direct, firm, fixed, immovable, resolute, single-minded, staunch, steadfast, steady, sure, true, undeviating, unfaltering, unflagging, untiring, unwavering.

antonyms irresolute, tentative.

unsympathetic *adj* antagonistic, antipathetic, apathetic, callous, cold, compassionless, cruel, hard, hard as nails, hard-hearted, harsh, heartless, indifferent, inhuman, insensitive, soulless, stony, uncharitable, uncompassionate, unconcerned, unfeeling, unkind, unmoved, unpitying, unresponsive.

antonyms compassionate, sympathetic.

unsystematic *adj* chaotic, confused, desultory, disorderly, disorganized, haphazard, hodgepodge, illogical, indiscriminate, irregular, jumbled, mixed-up, muddled, random, scrambled, slapdash, sloppy, unco-ordinated, unmethodical, unorganized, unplanned, untidy.

antonyms logical, systematic.

untamed *adj* barbarous, feral, fierce, savage, unbroken, undomesticated, unmellowed, untameable, wild.

antonyms domesticated, tame.

untangle *v* clear up, disentangle, explain, extricate, resolve, solve, straighten out, undo, unravel, unsnarl.

antonyms complicate, tangle.

untarnished *adj* bright, burnished, clean, glowing, immaculate, impeccable, intact, polished, pristine, pure, shining, spotless, stainless, unblemished, unimpeachable, unsoiled, unspoiled, unspotted, unstained, unsullied.

antonyms blemished, tarnished.

untenable *adj* fallacious, flawed, illogical, indefensible, insupportable, shaky, unmaintainable, unreasonable, unsound, unsustainable.

antonyms sound, tenable.

unthinkable *adj* absurd, illogical, implausible, impossible, improbable, incomprehensible, inconceivable, incredible, insupportable, outrageous, preposterous, shocking, unbelievable, undreamed-of, unheard-of, unimaginable, unlikely, unreasonable.

unthinking *adj* automatic, careless, heedless, impulsive, inadvertent, incautious, inconsiderate, indiscreet, insensitive, instinctive, mechanical, negligent, oblivious, rash, rude, selfish, senseless, tactless, thoughtless, unconscious, undiplomatic, unguarded, vacant, witless.

antonyms conscious, deliberate, witting.

untidy *adj* bedraggled, chaotic, cluttered, dishevelled, disorderly, every which way, higgledy-piggledy, jumbled, littered, messy, muddled, rumpled, scruffy, slipshod, sloppy, slovenly, sluttish, topsy-turvy, unkempt, unsystematic.

antonyms systematic, tidy.

untie *v* free, loosen, release, unbind, unchain, undo, unfasten, unknot, unlace, unloose, unloosen, untether.

antonyms fasten, tie.

untimely *adj* awkward, early, ill-timed, inappropriate, inauspicious, inconvenient, inopportune, malapropos, mistimed, premature, unfortunate, unseasonable, unsuitable.

antonyms opportune, timely.

untiring *adj* constant, dedicated, determined, devoted, dogged, incessant, indefatigable, patient, persevering, persistent, staunch, steady, tenacious, tireless, unfailing, unfaltering, unflagging, unremitting, unwearied.

antonym inconstant.

untold *adj* boundless, countless, hidden, incalculable, indescribable, inexhaustible, inexpressible, infinite, innumerable, measureless, myriad, numberless, private, secret, umpteen, uncountable, uncounted, undisclosed, undreamed-of, unimaginable, unknown, unnumbered, unpublished, unreckoned, unrecounted, unrelated, unreported, unrevealed, unspoken, unthinkable, unutterable.

untouched *adj* indifferent, intact, safe, scatheless, unaffected, unaltered, unconcerned, undamaged, undiscussed, unhandled, unharmed, unhurt, unimpaired, unimpressed, uninjured, unmentioned, unmoved, unscathed, unstirred, untainted, untasted.

antonyms affected, dealt with, impaired, moved.

untoward *adj* adverse, annoying, awkward, bad, contrary, disastrous, ill-timed, improper, inappropriate, inauspicious, inconvenient, indecorous, inimical, inopportune, irritating, ominous, troublesome, unbecoming, unexpected, unfavourable, unfitting, unfortunate, unlucky, unpropitious, unseemly, unsuitable, untimely, vexatious, worrying.

antonyms auspicious, suitable.

untrained *adj* amateur, green, inexperienced, inexpert, raw, uneducated, unpractised, unprofessional, unqualified, unschooled, unskilled, untaught, untutored.

antonyms expert, trained.

untried *adj* experimental, exploratory, innovative, new, novel, unestablished, unproved, untested.

antonyms proven, tested.

untroubled *adj* calm, composed, cool, impassive, peaceful, placid, serene, steady, tranquil, unconcerned, undisturbed, unexcited, unflappable, unflustered, unperturbed, unruffled, unstirred, unworried.

antonyms anxious, disturbed.

untrue *adj* cockeyed, deceitful, deceptive, deviant, dishonest, disingenuous, disloyal, distorted, erroneous, faithless, fallacious, false, forsworn, fraudulent, imitation, inaccurate, inauthentic, inconstant, incorrect, lying, mendacious, misleading, mistaken, perfidious, sham, specious, spurious, traitorous, treacherous, two-faced, unfaithful, untrustworthy, untruthful, wrong.

antonyms honest, true.

untrustworthy *adj* capricious, deceitful, devious, dishonest, disloyal, disreputable, dubious, duplicitous, fair-weather, faithless, false, fickle, fly-by-night, shady, slippery, treacherous, tricky, two-faced, undependable, unfaithful, unreliable, unsafe, untrue, untrusty.

antonyms reliable, trustworthy.

untruth *n* deceit, deceitfulness, dishonesty, duplicity, fabrication, falsehood, falsification, falsity, fib, fiction, inexactitude, invention, inveracity, lie, lying, mendacity, perjury, prevarication, story, tale, trick, untruthfulness, whopper.

antonyms honesty, truth.

untruthful *adj* crooked, deceitful, deceptive, dishonest, dissembling, false, hypocritical, lying, mendacious, shifty, untrustworthy, unveracious.

antonyms honest, truthful.

untwine *v* disentangle, disentwine, uncoil, unravel, untwist, unwind.

antonyms twine, wind.

untwist v disentangle, uncoil, unravel, untwine, unwind.

antonyms twist, wind.

untutored *adj* artless, ignorant, illiterate, inexperienced, inexpert, simple, uneducated, unlearned, unlessoned, unpractised, unrefined, unschooled, unsophisticated, untrained, unversed.

antonyms educated, trained.

unused *adj* available, extra, fresh, idle, intact, left, leftover, new, original, pristine, remaining, unaccustomed, unconsumed, unemployed, unexercised, unexploited, unfamiliar, untouched, untried, unutilized.

unusual *adj* abnormal, anomalous, atypical, bizarre, curious, different, eccentric, exceptional, extraordinary, odd, phenomenal, queer, rare, remarkable, singular, strange, surprising, uncommon, unconventional, unexpected, unfamiliar, unwonted.

antonyms normal, usual.

unutterable *adj* egregious, extreme, indescribable, ineffable, overwhelming, unimaginable, unspeakable.

unvarnished *adj* bare, candid, frank, honest, naked, plain, pure, sheer, simple, sincere, stark, straight, straightforward, unadorned, undisguised, unembellished.

antonyms disguised, embellished.

unveil v bare, bring to light, disclose, discover, divulge, expose, open, reveal, uncover, unfold, unshroud, unwrap.

antonyms cover, hide.

unwanted *adj* de trop, extra, ostracized, otiose, outcast, rejected, superfluous, surplus, unasked, uncalled-for, undesired, uninvited, unnecessary, unneeded, unrequired, unsolicited, unsought, unwelcome, useless.

antonyms necessary, needed, wanted.

unwarranted *adj* baseless, gratuitous, groundless, indefensible, inexcusable, uncalled-for, unjust, unjustified, unprovoked, unreasonable, vain, wrong.

antonyms justifiable, warranted.

unwary *adj* careless, credulous, hasty, headlong, heedless, imprudent, incautious, indiscreet, rash, reckless, thoughtless, unchary, uncircumspect, unguarded, unthinking, unwatchful.

antonyms cautious, wary.

unwavering *adj* consistent, dedicated, determined, resolute, single-minded, staunch, steadfast, steady, sturdy, tenacious, undeviating, unfaltering, unflagging, unquestioning, unshakable, unshaken, unswerving, untiring.

antonyms fickle, wavering.

unwelcome *adj* disagreeable, displeasing, distasteful, excluded, rejected, thankless, unacceptable, undesirable, uninvited, unpalatable, unpleasant, unpopular, unwanted, upsetting, worrying.

antonyms desirable, welcome.

unwell *adj* ailing, ill, indisposed, off-colour, poorly, sick, sickly, unhealthy.

antonyms healthy, well.

unwholesome *adj* anemic, bad, corrupting, degrading, deleterious, demoralizing, depraving, evil, foul, harmful, immoral, injurious, innutritious, insalubrious, insalutary, insanitary, junk, noxious, pale, pallid, pasty, pernicious, perverting, poisonous, sickly, tainted, unclean, unhealthy, unhygienic, wan, wicked.

antonyms salubrious, wholesome.

unwieldy *adj* awkward, bulky, burdensome, clumsy, cumbersome, cumbrous, gangling, hefty, hulking, inconvenient, massive, ponderous, ungainly, unhandy, unmanageable, weighty.

antonyms manageable, neat.

unwilling *adj* averse, disinclined, forced, grudging, indisposed, involuntary, laggard, loath, opposed, reluctant, resistant, slow, unenthusiastic.

antonyms enthusiastic, willing.

unwillingness n backwardness, disinclination, hesitancy, indisposition, lack of enthusiasm, reluctance, slowness.

antonyms enthusiasm, willingness.

unwind v calm down, disentangle, quieten down, relax, slacken, uncoil, undo, unravel, unreel, unroll, unswathe, untwine, untwist, unwrap, wind down.

antonyms twist, wind.

unwise *adj* bone-headed, dumb, foolhardy, foolish, ill-advised, ill-considered, ill-judged, impolitic, improvident, imprudent, inadvisable, indiscreet, inexpedient, injudicious, irresponsible, rash, reckless, senseless, short-sighted, silly, stupid, thoughtless, unintelligent.

antonyms prudent, wise.

unwitting *adj* accidental, chance, ignorant, inadvertent, innocent, involuntary, unaware, unconscious, unintended, unintentional, unknowing, unmeant, unplanned, unsuspecting, unthinking.

antonyms conscious, deliberate.

unwonted *adj* atypical, exceptional, extraordinary, freakish, infrequent, peculiar, rare, singular, strange, unaccustomed, uncommon, uncustomary, unexpected, unfamiliar, unheard-of, unusual.

antonyms usual, wonted.

unworldly *adj* abstract, celestial, ethereal, extramundane, extra-terrestrial, green, idealistic, impractical, inexperienced, innocent, metaphysical, naïve, otherworldly, religious, spiritual, transcendental, unearthly, unsophisticated, visionary.

antonyms earthly, materialistic, practical.

unworried *adj* calm, collected, composed, cool, downbeat, unabashed, undismayed, unperturbed, unruffled, untroubled.

antonym anxious.

unworthy *adj* base, contemptible, degrading, discreditable, disgraceful, dishonourable, disreputable, ignoble, improper, inappropriate, ineligible, inferior, shameful, unbecoming,

unbefitting, undeserving, unfitting, unprofessional, unseemly, unsuitable, unsuited.

antonyms commendable, worthy.

unwritten *adj* accepted, conventional, customary, implicit, oral, recognized, tacit, traditional, understood, unformulated, unrecorded, verbal, vocal, word-of-mouth.

antonyms recorded, written.

unyielding *adj* adamant, determined, firm, hard-line, immovable, implacable, inexorable, inflexible, intractable, intransigent, obdurate, obstinate, relentless, resolute, rigid, solid, staunch, steadfast, stubborn, tough, unbending, uncompromising, unrelenting, unwavering.

antonyms flexible, yielding.

up *adj, adv* abreast (with), aloft, at bat, awake, due, heavenward, higher, informed, in line, in the market (or running), on high, skyward, stirring, well-read.

up to one's eyes busy, engaged, inundated, overwhelmed, preoccupied, tied up.

antonyms free, idle.

up to scratch acceptable, adequate, capable, comme il faut, competent, OK, satisfactory, sufficient.

antonym unsatisfactory.

up-and-coming ambitious, assertive, eager, enterprising, promising, pushing, rising.

upbeat *adj* bright, bullish, buoyant, cheerful, cheery, encouraging, favourable, forward-looking, heartening, hopeful, optimistic, positive, promising, rosy.

antonyms downbeat, gloomy.

upbraid *v* admonish, bawl out, berate, blame, castigate, censure, chew out, chide, condemn, criticize, dress down, jaw, lecture, rate, rebuke, reprimand, reproach, reprove, scold, take to task, tell off.

antonyms commend, praise.

upbringing *n* breeding, bringing-up, care, cultivation, education, instruction, nurture, parenting, raising, rearing, tending, training.

update *v* amend, correct, modernize, renew, renovate, revamp, revise.

upgrade *v* advance, ameliorate, better, elevate, enhance, gentrify, improve, promote, raise, rehabilitate, renovate, restore.

antonyms degrade, downgrade.

upgrading *n* advancement, amelioration, betterment, elevation, enhancement, gentrification, improvement, promotion, rehabilitation, renovation, restoration.

upheaval *n* blow up, cataclysm, chaos, confusion, disorder, disruption, disturbance, earthquake, eruption, overthrow, revolution, shake-up, turmoil, upset.

uphill *adj* arduous, ascending, climbing, difficult, exhausting, gruelling, hard, laborious, mounting, punishing, rising, strenuous, taxing, tough, upward, wearisome.

antonyms downhill, easy.

uphold *v* advocate, aid, approve, back, bear, bolster, buttress, champion, confirm, countenance, defend, encourage, endorse, fortify, hold to, justify, maintain, promote, stand by, strengthen, support, sustain, vindicate.

upkeep *n* care, conservation, costs, expenditure, expenses, keep, maintenance, operating costs, outlay, overhead, preservation, repair, running, running costs, subsistence, support, sustenance.

antonym neglect.

uplift *v* advance, ameliorate, better, boost, civilize, cultivate, edify, elate, elevate, enlighten, exalt, heave, hoist, improve, inspire, lift, raise, refine, upgrade.

n advancement, betterment, boost, cultivation, edification, enhancement, enlightenment, enrichment, improvement, lift, refinement.

upper *adj* elevated, eminent, exalted, greater, high, higher, important, loftier, senior, superior, top, topmost, uppermost.

antonyms inferior, junior, lower.

upper hand advantage, ascendancy, control, dominance, domination, dominion, edge, mastery, superiority, supremacy, sway.

upper-class *adj* aristocratic, blue-blooded, educated, élite, exclusive, gentle, highborn, high-class, noble, patrician, swanky, top-drawer, well-born, well-bred.

antonym lower-class.

uppermost *adj* chief, dominant, first, foremost, greatest, highest, leading, loftiest, main, paramount, predominant, pre-eminent, primary, principal, prominent, supreme, tiptop, top, topmost, upmost.

antonym lowest.

uppity *adj* affected, arrogant, assuming, big-headed, bumptious, cocky, conceited, hoity-toity, impertinent, overweening, presumptuous, self-important, snobbish, stuck-up, supercilious.

antonym humble.

upright *adj* conscientious, decent, erect, ethical, fair, faithful, good, high-minded, honest, honourable, incorruptible, just, law-abiding, noble, perpendicular, principled, righteous, square, straight, straightforward, true, trustworthy, unimpeachable, upstanding, vertical, virtuous.

antonyms dishonest, flat, horizontal, prone, supine.

uprising *n* coup d'état, insurgence, insurgency, insurrection, mutiny, rebellion, revolt, revolution, rising, sedition, upheaval.

uproar *n* brawl, brouhaha, clamour, commotion, confusion, din, disorder, furor, hubbub, hullabaloo, hurly-burly, noise, outcry, pandemonium, racket, riot, ruckus, rumpus, to-do, tumult, turbulence, turmoil.

uproarious *adj* boisterous, clamorous, confused, convulsive, deafening, disorderly, gleeful, hilarious, hysterical, killing, loud, noisy, rib-tickling, riotous, riproaring, roistering, rollicking, rowdy, sidesplitting, tempestuous, tumultuous, turbulent, unrestrained, wild.

antonym sedate.

uproot *v* deracinate, destroy, disorient, displace, eliminate, eradicate, exile, exterminate, extirpate, grub up, remove, rip up, root out, weed out, wipe out.

upset *v* agitate, bother, capsize, change, confuse, conquer, defeat, destabilize, discombobulate, discompose, disconcert, dismay, disorder, disorganize, disquiet, distress, disturb, faze, fluster, grieve, hurt, overcome, overthrow, overturn, perturb, rattle, rock the boat, ruffle, shake (up), spill, spoil, tip, topple, trouble, tumble, unnerve, unsteady.
n agitation, bother, bug, complaint, defeat, disorder, disruption, disturbance, illness, indisposition, reverse, shake (up), shock, sickness, surprise, trouble, upheaval, worry.
adj agitated, angry, bothered, capsized, chaotic, choked up, confused, disconcerted, dismayed, disordered, disquieted, distressed, disturbed, frantic, grieved, hurt, ill, messed-up, miffed, muddled, overturned, overwrought, pained, poorly, put out, queasy, rattled, ruffled, shattered, sick, spilled, ticked off, toppled, topsy-turvy, troubled, tumbled, worried.

upshot *n* conclusion, consequence, culmination, end, event, finale, finish, issue, outcome, payoff, result.

upside down at sixes and sevens, chaotic, confused, disordered, higgledy-piggledy, inverted, jumbled, muddled, overturned, topsy-turvy, upset, upturned, wrong side up.

antonym shipshape.

upstanding *adj* decent, erect, ethical, firm, good, honest, honourable, incorruptible, law-abiding, moral, principled, respectable, solid, square, stalwart, strong, true, trustworthy, upright.

antonym untrustworthy.

upstart *n* arriviste, nobody, nouveau riche, parvenu, social climber, status seeker.

uptight *adj* anxious, edgy, hung-up, irritated, nervy, prickly, tense, uneasy.

antonyms calm, cool, relaxed.

up-to-date *adj* à la mode, all the rage, contemporary, current, fashionable, in, latest, modern, modish, newest, now, popular, smart, stylish, swinging, trendy, up-to-the-minute, vogue, voguish, with it.

antonym old-fashioned.

upturn *n* advancement, amelioration, boost, improvement, increase, recovery, revival, rise, upsurge, upswing.

antonyms downturn, drop, setback.

urban *adj* built-up, burghal, city, civic, inner-city, metropolitan, municipal, oppidan, town, urbanized.

antonyms country, rural, rustic.

urbane *adj* bland, civil, civilized, cosmopolitan, courteous, cultivated, cultured, debonair, easy, elegant, mannerly, polished, refined, smooth, sophisticated, suave, well-bred, well-mannered.

antonyms gauche, uncouth.

urbanity *n* blandness, charm, civility, courtesy, cultivation, culture, ease, elegance, grace, mannerliness, polish, refinement, smoothness, sophistication, suavity, worldliness.

antonyms awkwardness, gaucheness.

urchin *n* brat, gamin, gamine, guttersnipe, imp, kid, ragamuffin, tatterdemalion, waif.

urge *v* advise, advocate, beg, beseech, champion, compel, constrain, counsel, drive, emphasize, encourage, entreat, exhort, force, goad, hasten, impel, implore, incite, induce, instigate, nag, plead, press, propel, push, recommend, solicit, spur, stimulate, support, underline, underscore.

antonyms deter, dissuade.

n compulsion, desire, drive, eagerness, fancy, impulse, inclination, itch, libido, longing, wish, yearning, yen.

antonym disinclination.

urgency *n* exigence, exigency, extremity, gravity, hurry, immediacy, imperativeness, importance, importunity, instancy, necessity, need, pressure, seriousness, stress.

urgent *adj* clamorous, compelling, critical, crucial, demanding, eager, earnest, exigent, immediate, imperative, important, importunate, insistent, instant, intense, persistent, persuasive, pressing, top-priority.

urinate *v* ease oneself, make water, micturate, pass water, pee, piddle, piss, relieve oneself, tinkle.

usable *adj* available, current, exploitable, functional, operating, operational, practical, serviceable, utilizable, valid, working.

antonyms unusable, useless.

usage *n* application, control, convention, custom, employment, etiquette, form, habit, handling, management, method, mode, operation, practice, procedure, protocol, regime, regulation, routine, rule, running, tradition, treatment, use, wont.

use *v* apply, bring, consume, employ, enjoy, exercise, exhaust, expend, exploit, handle, manipulate, misuse, operate, ply, practise, spend, treat, usufruct, utilize, waste, wield, work.
n advantage, application, avail, benefit, call, cause, custom, employment, end, enjoyment, exercise, habit, handling, help, meaning, necessity, need, object, occasion, operation, point, practice, profit, purpose, reason, service, treatment, usage, usefulness, usufruct, utility, value, way, wont, worth.

use up absorb, consume, deplete, devour, drain, eat into, exhaust, finish, fritter away, sap, squander, swallow, waste.

used *adj* accustomed, castoff, dog-eared, familiar, hand-me-down, nearly new, reach-me-down, second-hand, worn.

antonyms fresh, new, unused.

useful *adj* advantageous, all-purpose, beneficial, convenient, effective, expedient, fruitful, general-purpose, handy, helpful, practical, productive, profitable, salutary, serviceable, valuable, worthwhile.

antonym useless.

useless *adj* bootless, disadvantageous, feckless, fruitless, futile, hopeless, idle, impractical, incompetent, ineffective, ineffectual, inefficient, inept, no good, of no use, pointless, profitless, shiftless, stupid, unavailing, unproductive, unworkable, vain, valueless, weak, worthless.

antonym useful.

uselessness *n* futility, hopelessness, idleness, impracticality, incompetence, ineffectiveness, ineffectuality, ineptitude.

antonyms effectiveness, usefulness.

usher *n* attendant, doorkeeper, escort, guide, usherette.

v conduct, direct, escort, guide, lead, pilot, shepherd, steer.

usher in announce, herald, inaugurate, initiate, introduce, launch, precede, ring in.

usual *adj* accepted, accustomed, common, constant, conventional, customary, everyday, expected, familiar, fixed, general, habitual, normal, ordinary, recognized, regular, routine, standard, stock, typical, unexceptional, wonted.

antonyms unheard-of, unusual.

usually *adv* as a rule, by and large, chiefly, commonly, customarily, generally, generally speaking, habitually, in the main, mainly, mostly, normally, on the whole, ordinarily, regularly, routinely, traditionally, typically.

antonym exceptionally.

usurp *v* annex, appropriate, arrogate, assume, commandeer, seize, steal, take, take over, wrest.

utensil *n* apparatus, contrivance, device, gadget, gizmo, implement, instrument, tool.

utilitarian *adj* convenient, down-to-earth, effective, efficient, functional, lowly, practical, pragmatic, sensible, serviceable, unpretentious, useful.

antonyms decorative, impractical.

utility *n* advantage, advantageousness, avail, benefit, convenience, efficacy, expedience, fitness, point, practicality, profit, satisfactoriness, service, serviceableness, use, usefulness, value.

antonym pointlessness.

utilize *v* adapt, appropriate, employ, exploit, make use of, put to use, resort to, take advantage of, turn to account, use.

utmost *adj* extreme, farthest, final, first, furthest, greatest, highest, last, maximum, outermost, paramount, remotest, supreme, ultimate, uttermost.

n best, hardest, maximum, most, uttermost.

utopia *n* bliss, Eden, Elysium, heaven, heaven on earth, paradise, seventh heaven, Shangri-La, Utopia.

utopian *adj* airy, dream, Elysian, fanciful, fantastic, ideal, idealistic, illusory, imaginary, impractical, perfect, romantic, unworkable, visionary, wishful.

utter[1] *adj* absolute, arrant, complete, consummate, dead, downright, entire, out-and-out, perfect, sheer, stark, thorough, thoroughgoing, total, unalleviated, unmitigated, unqualified.

utter[2] *v* articulate, declare, deliver, divulge, enounce, enunciate, express, proclaim, promulgate, pronounce, publish, reveal, say, sound, speak, state, tell, tongue, verbalize, vocalize, voice.

utterance *n* announcement, articulation, comment, declaration, delivery, ejaculation, expression, opinion, pronouncement, remark, speech, statement, verbalization, vocalization, vociferation.

utterly *adv* absolutely, completely, dead, diametrically, entirely, extremely, fully, perfectly, thoroughly, totally, wholly.

U-turn *n* about-turn, backtrack, reversal, tergiversation, volte face.

V

vacancy *n* accommodation, emptiness, gap, job, opening, opportunity, place, position, post, room, situation, space, vacuity, vacuousness, vacuum, void.

vacant *adj* abstracted, available, bare, blank, brainless, deadpan, disengaged, dreaming, dreamy, empty, expressionless, free, idle, inane, inattentive, incurious, spare, thoughtless, to let, unemployed, unengaged, unfilled, unoccupied, untenanted, unthinking, vacuous, void.

antonyms engaged, occupied.

vacate *v* abandon, depart (from), desert, evacuate, leave, quit, resign (from), withdraw.

vacillate *v* fluctuate, hesitate, oscillate, shilly-shally, shuffle, sway, temporize, tergiversate, waver.

vacillating *adj* hesitant, indecisive, irresolute, oscillating, shilly-shallying, shuffling, temporizing, uncertain, unresolved, wavering.

antonyms resolute, unhesitating.

vacillation *n* fluctuation, hesitancy, hesitation, inconstancy, indecision, indecisiveness, irresolution, shilly-shallying, temporization, tergiversation, unsteadiness, wavering.

vacuity *n* apathy, blankness, emptiness, inanity, incomprehension, incuriosity, nothingness, space, vacuousness, vacuum, void.

vacuous *adj* apathetic, blank, empty, idle, inane, incognizant, incurious, stupid, uncomprehending, unfilled, unintelligent, vacant, void.

vacuum *n* chasm, emptiness, gap, nothingness, space, vacuity, void.

vagabond *n* hobo, itinerant, migrant, nomad, outcast, rascal, rover, runabout, tramp, vagrant, wanderer, wayfarer.

vagary *n* caprice, crotchet, fancy, humour, megrim, notion, prank, quirk, whim, whimsy.

vagrant *n* beggar, bum, down-and-out, hobo, itinerant, rolling stone, stroller, tramp, wanderer.

adj footloose, homeless, itinerant, nomadic, roaming, rootless, roving, shiftless, travelling, vagabond, wandering.

vague *adj* amorphous, blurred, dim, doubtful, evasive, fuzzy, generalized, hazy, ill-defined, imprecise, indefinite, indeterminate, indistinct, inexact, lax, loose, misty, nebulous, obscure, shadowy, uncertain, unclear, undefined, undetermined, unknown, unspecific, unspecified, woolly.

antonyms certain, clear, definite.

vaguely *adv* absent-mindedly, dimly, faintly, imprecisely, inexactly, obscurely, slightly, vacantly.

vagueness *n* ambiguity, amorphousness, dimness, faintness, fuzziness, haziness, imprecision, inexactitude, looseness, obscurity, uncertainty, woolliness.

antonyms clarity, precision.

vain *adj* abortive, affected, arrogant, baseless, big-headed, cocky, conceited, egotistical, empty, fruitless, futile, groundless, hollow, idle, inflated, mindless, narcissistic, nugatory, ostentatious, overweening, peacockish, pointless, pretentious, proud, purposeless, self-important, self-satisfied, senseless, stuck-up, swaggering, swanky, time-wasting, trifling, trivial, unavailing, unimportant, unproductive, unprofitable, unsubstantial, useless, vainglorious, vaporous, worthless.

antonyms modest, self-effacing.

in vain bootlessly, fruitlessly, ineffectually, to no avail, unsuccessfully, uselessly, vainly.

valediction *n* adieu, farewell, godspeed, goodbye, leave-taking, send-off, vale.

antonyms greeting, welcome.

valet *n* body servant, gentleman's gentleman, man, manservant.

valetudinarian *adj* delicate, feeble, frail, hypochondriac, infirm, invalid, neurotic, sickly, weakly.

antonym stoical.

valiant *adj* bold, brave, courageous, dauntless, doughty, fearless, gallant, gutsy, heroic, indomitable, intrepid, plucky, red-blooded, redoubtable, stalwart, staunch, stout, stout-hearted, valorous, worthy.

antonym cowardly.

valid *adj* approved, authentic, binding, bona fide, cogent, conclusive, convincing, efficacious, efficient, genuine, good, just, lawful, legal, legitimate, logical, official, potent, powerful, proper, rational, reliable, sound, substantial, telling, weighty, well-founded, well-grounded.

antonyms invalid, unsound.

validate *v* attest to, authenticate, authorize, certify, confirm, corroborate, endorse, legalize, ratify, stamp, substantiate, underwrite, warrant.

validity n authority, cogency, force, foundation, grounds, justifiability, lawfulness, legality, legitimacy, logic, point, power, soundness, strength, substance, weight.

antonyms invalidity, weakness.

valley n barranca, clough, combe, coulee, dale, defile, dell, depression, dingle, gap, glen, graben, gulch, gully, hollow, ravine, vale.

valorous adj bold, brave, courageous, dauntless, doughty, fearless, gallant, hardy, heroic, intrepid, lion-hearted, mettlesome, plucky, redoubtable, stalwart, valiant.

antonyms cowardly, weak.

valour n boldness, bravery, courage, derring-do, doughtiness, fearlessness, fortitude, gallantry, hardiness, heroism, intrepidity, lion-heartedness, mettle, spirit.

antonyms cowardice, weakness.

valuable adj advantageous, beneficial, blue-chip, cherished, costly, dear, esteemed, estimable, expensive, fruitful, handy, helpful, high-priced, important, invaluable, precious, prizable, prized, productive, profitable, serviceable, treasured, useful, valued, worthwhile, worthy.

antonyms useless, valueless.

valuation n acknowledgment, appraisal, assessment, computation, determination, estimate, evaluation, survey.

value n account, advantage, avail, benefit, consequence, consideration, cost, desirability, equivalent, gain, good, help, importance, merit, moment, price, profit, rate, significance, use, usefulness, utility, weight, worth.

v account, admire, appraise, appreciate, apprize, assess, cherish, compute, esteem, estimate, evaluate, hold dear, love, price, prize, rate, regard, respect, survey, treasure.

antonyms disregard, neglect, undervalue.

valued adj admired, beloved, cherished, dear, esteemed, highly regarded, loved, prized, respected, treasured.

values n customs, ethics, ideals, institutions, morals, principles, standards.

vamoose v clear off, decamp, disappear, make oneself scarce, quit, scram, skedaddle, vanish.

vanish v dematerialize, depart, die out, disappear, disperse, dissipate, dissolve, evanesce, evaporate, exit, fade, fizzle out, melt, vaporize.

antonyms appear, materialize.

vanity n affectation, airs, arrogance, big-headedness, complacency, conceit, conceitedness, egotism, emptiness, frivolity, fruitlessness, futility, hollowness, idleness, inanity, narcissism, ostentation, peacockery, pointlessness, pretension, pride, self-admiration, self-conceit, self-love, self-satisfaction, smugness, triviality, unreality, unsubstantiality, uselessness, vainglory, worthlessness.

antonyms modesty, worth.

vanquish v beat, best, confound, conquer, crush, defeat, humble, overcome, overpower, overwhelm, quell, reduce, repress, rout, subdue, subjugate, triumph over, trounce.

vapid adj banal, bland, bloodless, boring, colourless, dead, dull, flat, flavourless, insipid, jejune, lifeless, limp, stale, tame, tasteless, tedious, tiresome, trite, uninspiring, uninteresting, watery, weak, wishy-washy.

antonyms interesting, vigorous.

vaporous adj fanciful, flimsy, foggy, fuming, gaseous, insubstantial, misty, steamy, vain.

antonym substantial.

vapour n breath, brume, cloud, damp, dampness, exhalation, film, fog, fumes, gas, haze, miasma, mist, pollution, reek, smog, smoke, steam.

variable adj capricious, chameleonlike, changeable, diverse, diversified, fickle, fitful, flexible, fluctuating, inconstant, mercurial, moody, mutable, protean, shifting, temperamental, unpredictable, unstable, unsteady, vacillating, varied, varying, versicolour, wavering.

antonym invariable.

n factor, parameter.

variance n difference, disagreement, discord, discrepancy, disharmony, dissension, dissent, divergence, division, inconsistency, quarrelling, strife, variability, variation.

antonyms agreement, harmony.

variant adj alternative, derived, deviant, different, divergent, exceptional, modified.

antonyms normal, standard, usual.

n alternative, development, modification, rogue, sport, variation.

variation n alteration, change, departure, deviation, difference, discrepancy, diversification, diversity, elaboration, inflection, innovation, modification, modulation, novelty, variant, variety.

antonyms monotony, similitude, uniformity.

varied adj assorted, different, diverse, heterogeneous, manifold, miscellaneous, mixed, motley, multifarious, sundry, various.

antonyms similar, uniform.

variegated adj dappled, diversified, many-coloured, motley, mottled, multicoloured, parti-coloured, pied, polychrome, streaked, varicoloured, veined, versicolour.

antonyms monochrome, plain.

variety n array, assortment, brand, breed, category, change, class, collection, difference, discrepancy, diversification, diversity, genre, intermixture, kind, make, manifoldness, many-sidedness, medley, miscellany, mixed bag, mixture, multifariousness, multiplicity, order, potpourri, range, sort, species, strain, type, variation.

antonyms monotony, similitude, uniformity.

various adj assorted, different, differing, disparate, distinct, divers, diverse, diversified, heterogeneous, many, many-sided, miscellaneous, multifarious, omnifarious, several, sundry, varied, variegated, varying.

varnish n coating, glaze, gloss, japan, lac, lacquer, polish, resin, shellac.

vary v alter, alternate, change, depart, differ, disagree, diverge, diversify, fluctuate, inflect, intermix, modify, modulate, permutate, recombine, reorder, transform.

vase n amphora, container, cruse, ewer, jar, jug, pitcher, receptacle, urn, vessel.

vassal n bondservant, liege, liegeman, retainer, serf, slave, subject, thrall, villein.

vassalage n bondage, dependence, serfdom, servitude, slavery, subjection, subjugation, thralldom, villeinage.

vast adj astronomical, boundless, capacious, colossal, cyclopean, enormous, extensive, far-flung, fathomless, gigantic, great, huge, illimitable, immeasurable, immense, limitless, mammoth, massive, measureless, monstrous, monumental, never-ending, prodigious, stupendous, sweeping, tremendous, unbounded, unlimited, voluminous, wide.

vat n barrel, cask, cauldron, container, kier, tank, tub.

vault¹ n arch, cavern, cellar, concave, crypt, depository, mausoleum, repository, roof, span, strongroom, tomb, wine cellar.

vault² v bound, clear, hurdle, jump, leap, leapfrog, spring.

vaunt v blazon, boast about, brag about, celebrate, crow about, exult in, flaunt, parade, show off, trumpet.

antonyms belittle, minimize.

veer v change (direction), sheer, shift, swerve, tack, turn, wheel.

vegetables n greens, greenstuff, legumes, plants, produce, truck.

vegetarian adj grass-eating, herbivorous, Pythagorean, vegan.

vegetate v coast, degenerate, deteriorate, go to seed, grow, idle, languish, loaf, moulder, relax, rest, rust, rusticate, sprout, stagnate.

vehemence n animation, ardour, eagerness, earnestness, emphasis, energy, enthusiasm, fervency, fervour, fire, force, forcefulness, heat, impetuosity, intensity, keenness, passion, urgency, verve, vigour, violence, warmth, zeal.

antonym indifference.

vehement adj animated, ardent, eager, earnest, emphatic, energetic, enthusiastic, fervent, fervid, fierce, forceful, forcible, heated, hot, impassioned, impetuous, intense, keen, passionate, powerful, strong, urgent, violent, zealous.

antonyms apathetic, indifferent.

vehicle n agency, apparatus, channel, conveyance, instrument, means, mechanism, medium, organ, tool, transport, transportation.

veil v camouflage, cloak, conceal, cover, dim, disguise, dissemble, dissimulate, hide, mantle, mask, obscure, screen, shade, shadow, shield.

antonyms expose, uncover.

n blind, camouflage, cloak, cover, curtain, disguise, film, haze, mask, screen, shade, shadow, shroud, velum.

vein n blood vessel, channel, course, current, disposition, frame of mind, hint, humour, lode, mode, mood, note, seam, strain, stratum, streak, striation, stripe, style, temper, tenor, thread, tone, trait.

veined adj marbled, mottled, streaked, striated, variegated.

velocity n celerity, fleetness, pace, quickness, rapidity, rate, speed, swiftness.

venal adj bent, bribable, buyable, corrupt, corruptible, grafting, mercenary, purchasable, simoniacal.

antonym incorruptible.

▲ *confusable word* venial.

vendetta n bad blood, bitterness, blood feud, enmity, feud, quarrel, rivalry.

veneer n appearance, casing, coating, façade, facing, front, gloss, guise, layer, mask, overlay, pretence, semblance, show, surface.

venerable adj aged, ancient, august, dignified, esteemed, grave, honoured, respected, revered, reverenced, reverend, sage, sedate, venerated, wise, worshipful.

venerate v adore, esteem, hallow, honour, respect, revere, reverence, worship.

antonyms anathematize, disregard, execrate.

veneration n adoration, awe, deference, devotion, esteem, respect, reverence, worship.

vengeance n reprisal, requital, retaliation, retribution, revenge, tit for tat.

antonym forgiveness.

vengeful adj avenging, implacable, punitive, rancorous, relentless, retaliatory, retributive, revengeful, spiteful, unforgiving, vindictive.

antonym forgiving.

venial adj excusable, forgivable, insignificant, minor, negligible, pardonable, slight, tolerable, trifling, trivial.

antonyms unforgivable, unpardonable.

▲ *confusable word* venal.

venom n acrimony, bane, bitterness, gall, grudge, hate, hatred, ill will, malevolence, malice, maliciousness, malignity, poison, rancour, spite, spitefulness, spleen, toxin, venin, vindictiveness, virulence, virus, vitriol.

venomous adj baleful, baneful, envenomed, hostile, malicious, malign, malignant, mephitic, noxious, poison, poisonous, rancorous, savage, spiteful, toxic, vicious, vindictive, virulent, vitriolic.

vent n air hole, aperture, blowhole, duct, hole, opening, orifice, outlet, passage, slit, spiracle, split.

v air, discharge, emit, express, let fly, release, split, unloose, utter, voice.

ventilate v air, broadcast, debate, discuss, examine, expound, express.

antonym suppress.

venture v advance, adventure, chance, dare, endanger, hazard, imperil, jeopardize, make bold, presume, put forward, risk, speculate, stake, suggest, take the liberty, volunteer, wager.

n adventure, chance, endeavour, enterprise, fling, gamble, hazard, operation, project, risk, speculation, undertaking.

venturesome adj adventurous, audacious, bold, courageous, daredevil, daring, dauntless, doughty, enterprising, fearless, intrepid, plucky, spirited.
antonyms pusillanimous, unenterprising.

veracious adj accurate, credible, dependable, exact, factual, faithful, frank, genuine, honest, reliable, straightforward, true, trustworthy, truthful, veridical.
antonym untruthful.

veracity n accuracy, candour, credibility, exactitude, frankness, honesty, integrity, precision, probity, rectitude, trustworthiness, truth, truthfulness, verity.
antonym untruthfulness.

verbal adj lexical, oral, spoken, unwritten, verbatim, word-of-mouth.

verbatim adv exactly, literally, precisely, to the letter, word for word.

verbiage n circumlocution, periphrasis, pleonasm, prolixity, repetition, verbosity.
antonyms economy, succinctness.

verbose adj circumlocutory, diffuse, garrulous, long-winded, loquacious, periphrastic, pleonastic, prolix, windy, wordy.
antonyms economical, laconic, succinct.

verbosity n garrulity, logorrhea, long-windedness, loquaciousness, loquacity, prolixity, verbiage, verboseness, windiness, wordiness.
antonyms economy, succinctness.

verdant adj flourishing, fresh, grassy, green, leafy, lush, teeming, viridescent.

verdict n adjudication, assessment, call, conclusion, decision, finding, judgment, opinion, ruling, sentence.

verdure n foliage, freshness, grass, greenery, greenness, herbage, leafage, meadows, pasture, verdancy, vigour, viridescence.

verge n border, boundary, brim, brink, edge, edging, extreme, limit, lip, margin, roadside, threshold.

verge on approach, border on, come close to, incline toward, lean toward, near, tend toward.

verification n affirmation, attestation, authentication, checking, confirmation, corroboration, proof, substantiation, validation.

verify v affirm, attest, authenticate, back up, bear out, check, clinch, confirm, corroborate, establish, prove, substantiate, support, testify, validate.
antonyms discredit, invalidate.

verisimilitude n authenticity, colour, credibility, likeliness, plausibility, realism, resemblance, ring of truth, semblance.
antonym implausibility.

verity n actuality, authenticity, factuality, soundness, truth, truthfulness, validity, veracity.
antonym untruth.

vernacular adj colloquial, common, endemic, indigenous, informal, local, mother, native, popular, vulgar.

n argot, cant, dialect, idiom, jargon, language, lingo, parlance, patois, speech, tongue.

versatile adj adaptable, adjustable, all-round, flexible, functional, general-purpose, handy, many-sided, multifaceted, multipurpose, protean, resourceful, variable.
antonym inflexible.

verse n canto, doggerel, elegiac, fit, iambic, jingle, poesy, poetastery, poetry, rhyme, stanza, stave, strophe, versicle, versification.

versed adj accomplished, acquainted, au fait, competent, conversant, experienced, familiar, informed, knowledgeable, learned, practised, proficient, qualified, savvy, seasoned, skilled, up on.

versifier n poet, poetaster, poetess, rhymer, rhymester.

version n account, adaptation, design, form, interpretation, kind, model, paraphrase, portrayal, reading, rendering, rendition, style, translation, type, variant.

vertex n acme, apex, apogee, cap, crown, culmination, extremity, height, meridian, peak, pinnacle, summit, tip, top, zenith.
antonym nadir.

vertical adj erect, on end, perpendicular, plumb, upright, upstanding.
antonym horizontal.

vertigo n dizziness, giddiness, light-headedness, megrim.

verve n animation, brio, dash, élan, energy, enthusiasm, force, gusto, life, liveliness, pizzazz, punch, relish, sparkle, spirit, vigour, vim, vitality, vivacity, zeal, zing, zip.
antonym apathy.

very adv absolutely, acutely, awfully, decidedly, deeply, eminently, exceeding(ly), excessively, extremely, greatly, highly, noticeably, particularly, passing, rattling, really, remarkably, superlatively, surpassingly, terribly, truly, uncommonly, unusually, wonderfully.
antonyms hardly, scarcely, slightly.
adj actual, appropriate, bare, exact, express, identical, mere, perfect, plain, precise, pure, real, same, selfsame, sheer, simple, unqualified, utter.

vessel n boat, canister, container, craft, holder, jar, pot, receptacle, ship, utensil.

vestibule n anteroom, entrance, entrance hall, entranceway, foyer, hall, lobby, porch, portico.

vestige n evidence, glimmer, hint, indication, print, relic, remainder, remains, remnant, residue, scrap, sign, suspicion, token, trace, track, whiff.

vestigial adj functionless, imperfect, incomplete, reduced, rudimentary, surviving, undeveloped.

vet v appraise, audit, check, examine, inspect, investigate, review, scan, scrutinize, survey.

veteran n dean, doyen, doyenne, master, old hand, old soldier, old-timer, past master, pro, trouper, war horse.
antonyms novice, recruit.

adj ace, adept, battle-scarred, crack, experienced, expert, long-serving, masterly, mature, old, practised, professional, proficient, ripened, seasoned, skilled.

antonyms inexperienced, raw.

veto *v* ban, disallow, embargo, forbid, interdict, kill, negative, prohibit, quash, reject, rule out, stop, turn down.

antonyms approve, sanction.

n ban, embargo, interdict, prohibition, rejection, stop, thumbs down.

antonyms approval, assent.

vex *v* afflict, aggravate, agitate, annoy, bother, bug, chagrin, displease, distress, disturb, exasperate, fret, gall, get (to), goad, harass, hassle, irritate, miff, molest, needle, nettle, offend, peeve, perplex, pester, pique, plague, provoke, rile, spite, tease, torment, trouble, upset, worry.

antonym soothe.

vexation *n* aggravation, anger, annoyance, bore, bother, chagrin, difficulty, displeasure, dissatisfaction, exasperation, frustration, fury, hassle, headache, irritant, misfortune, nuisance, pain, pique, problem, trouble, upset, worry.

vexatious *adj* afflicting, aggravating, annoying, bothersome, burdensome, disagreeable, disappointing, distressing, doggone, exasperating, harassing, infuriating, irksome, irritating, nagging, pesky, pestiferous, pestilent, pestilential, plaguy, provoking, teasing, tormenting, troublesome, trying, unpleasant, upsetting, worrisome, worrying.

antonyms pleasant, soothing.

vexed *adj* afflicted, aggravated, agitated, annoyed, bedevilled, bored, bothered, chagrined, confused, contested, controversial, displeased, disputed, distressed, disturbed, exasperated, harassed, hassled, irritated, miffed, moot, nettled, peeved, perplexed, provoked, put out, riled, ruffled, tormented, troubled, upset, worried.

viable *adj* achievable, applicable, feasible, operable, possible, practicable, serviceable, usable, workable.

antonyms impossible, unworkable.

vibes *n* ambience, atmosphere, aura, emanation, emotions, feel, feelings, reaction, response, sensations, vibrations.

vibrant *adj* alive, animated, bright, colourful, dynamic, electric, electrifying, jazzy, oscillating, palpitating, peppy, pulsating, quivering, responsive, sensitive, sparkling, spirited, trembling, vivacious, vivid.

vibrate *v* fluctuate, judder, oscillate, pulsate, pulse, quiver, resonate, resound, reverberate, shake, shimmy, shiver, shudder, sway, swing, thrill, throb, tremble, undulate.

vibration *n* frisson, judder, juddering, oscillation, pulsation, pulse, quiver, resonance, reverberation, shaking, shudder, throb, throbbing, trembling, tremor.

vicarious *adj* acting, commissioned, delegated, deputed, empathetic, indirect, second-hand, substituted, surrogate.

vice *n* bad habit, besetting sin, blemish, corruption, defect, degeneracy, depravity, evil, evildoing, failing, fault, immorality, imperfection, iniquity, misdeed, profligacy, shortcoming, sin, transgression, venality, weakness, wickedness, wrong.

antonym virtue.

vicinity *n* area, district, environs, locality, neighbourhood, precincts, propinquity, proximity, purlieu, vicinage.

vicious *adj* abhorrent, atrocious, backbiting, bad, barbarous, bitchy, brutal, catty, corrupt, cruel, dangerous, debased, defamatory, degenerate, depraved, diabolical, fiendish, foul, heinous, immoral, infamous, malicious, mean, monstrous, nasty, perverted, profligate, rancorous, savage, sinful, slanderous, spiteful, unprincipled, venomous, vile, vindictive, violent, virulent, vitriolic, wicked, worthless, wrong.

antonyms gentle, good, virtuous.

viciousness *n* badness, bitchiness, brutality, corruption, cruelty, degeneracy, depravity, ferocity, immorality, malice, profligacy, rancour, savagery, sinfulness, spite, spitefulness, venom, virulence, wickedness.

antonyms gentleness, goodness, virtue.

vicissitude *n* alteration, alternation, change, deviation, divergence, fluctuation, mutability, mutation, revolution, rotation, shift, succession, turn, twist, variation.

victim *n* casualty, dupe, fall guy, fatality, gull, injured party, innocent, mark, martyr, patsy, pigeon, prey, quarry, sacrifice, scapegoat, sitting target, sucker, sufferer.

victimize *v* bully, cheat, con, deceive, defraud, discriminate against, dupe, exploit, fool, gull, hoodwink, oppress, persecute, pick on, prey on, shaft, snow, sucker in, swindle, take, use.

victor *n* champ, champion, conqueror, first, subjugator, top dog, vanquisher, winner.

antonyms loser, vanquished.

victorious *adj* champion, conquering, first, on top, prize-winning, successful, top, triumphant, unbeaten, winning.

antonyms losing, unsuccessful.

victory *n* conquest, laurels, mastery, palm, prize, subjugation, success, superiority, triumph, vanquishment, win.

antonyms defeat, loss.

victuals *n* aliment, bread, chow, comestibles, eatables, eats, edibles, food, grub, meat, nosh, nourishment, provisions, rations, stores, supplies, sustenance, viands.

vie *v* challenge, compete, contend, contest, fight, rival, strive, struggle.

view *n* aspect, attitude, belief, contemplation, conviction, display, estimation, examination, eyeshot, feeling, glimpse, impression, inspection, judgment, ken, landscape, look, notion, opinion, outlook, panorama, perception, perspective, picture, prospect, scan, scene, scrutiny, sentiment, sight, spectacle, survey, viewing, vision, vista.

v behold, consider, contemplate, deem, examine, explore, eye, inspect, judge, observe, perceive, read, regard, scan, speculate, survey, take in, watch, witness.

viewer *n* observer, onlooker, spectator, watcher.

viewpoint *n* angle, attitude, feeling, opinion, perspective, point of view, position, sentiment, slant, stance, standpoint.

vigil *n* lookout, sleeplessness, stake-out, wake, wakefulness, watch.

vigilance *n* alertness, attentiveness, carefulness, caution, circumspection, guardedness, observation, wakefulness, wariness, watchfulness.

vigilant *adj* alert, Argus-eyed, attentive, careful, cautious, circumspect, guarded, on one's guard, on one's toes, on the alert, on the lookout, on the qui vive, sleepless, unsleeping, wakeful, wary, watchful, wide-awake.

antonyms careless, forgetful, lax, negligent.

vigorous *adj* active, brisk, dynamic, effective, efficient, energetic, enterprising, flourishing, forceful, forcible, full-blooded, hale, hardy, healthy, hearty, intense, lively, lusty, mettlesome, powerful, red-blooded, robust, sound, spanking, spirited, stout, strenuous, strong, virile, vital, zippy.

antonyms feeble, lethargic, weak.

vigorously *adv* briskly, eagerly, energetically, forcefully, hard, heartily, lustily, powerfully, strenuously, strongly.

antonyms feebly, weakly.

vigour *n* activity, animation, dash, dynamism, energy, force, forcefulness, gusto, health, liveliness, might, oomph, pep, potency, power, punch, robustness, snap, soundness, spirit, stamina, strength, verve, vim, vitality, zing, zip.

antonyms impotence, sluggishness, weakness.

vile *adj* abandoned, abject, appalling, bad, base, coarse, contemptible, corrupt, debased, degenerate, degrading, depraved, despicable, disgraceful, disgusting, earthly, evil, foul, horrid, humiliating, ignoble, impure, loathsome, low, mean, miserable, nasty, nauseating, nefarious, noxious, offensive, perverted, repellent, repugnant, repulsive, revolting, scabbed, scabby, scandalous, scurvy, shocking, sickening, sinful, ugly, vicious, vulgar, wicked, worthless, wretched.

vileness *n* baseness, coarseness, corruption, degeneracy, depravity, dreadfulness, enormity, evil, foulness, meanness, noxiousness, offensiveness, outrage, profanity, ugliness, viciousness, wickedness.

vilification *n* abuse, aspersion, calumniation, calumny, contumely, criticism, defamation, denigration, disparagement, invective, mudslinging, revilement, scurrility, vituperation.

vilify *v* abuse, asperse, bad-mouth, berate, calumniate, contemn, criticize, debase, decry, defame, denigrate, denounce, disparage, dump on, malign, revile, run down, slander, smear, stigmatize, traduce, vituperate.

antonyms adore, compliment, eulogize, glorify.

village *n* barrio, community, hamlet, kampong, kraal, pueblo, settlement, township.

villain *n* antihero, antiheroine, baddie, bad guy, blackguard, bravo, cad, caitiff, criminal, devil, evildoer, heavy, knave, libertine, louse, malefactor, miscreant, profligate, rapscallion, rascal, rat, reprobate, rogue, scoundrel, wretch.

antonyms hero, heroine.

villainous *adj* atrocious, bad, base, blackguardly, criminal, cruel, debased, degenerate, depraved, detestable, diabolical, disgraceful, evil, fiendish, hateful, heinous, ignoble, infamous, inhuman, malevolent, mean, nefarious, opprobrious, outrageous, ruffianly, scoundrelly, sinful, terrible, thievish, vicious, vile, wicked.

antonyms good, heroic.

villainy *n* atrocity, badness, baseness, crime, criminality, delinquency, depravity, devilry, deviltry, iniquity, knavery, rascality, roguery, sin, turpitude, vice, viciousness, wickedness.

vindicate *v* absolve, acquit, clear, confirm, defend, establish, exculpate, excuse, exonerate, justify, maintain, restore, support, uphold, verify.

antonyms accuse, convict.

vindication *n* acquittal, apology, assertion, confirmation, defence, exculpation, excuse, exoneration, extenuation, justification, plea, restoration, substantiation, support, verification.

antonyms accusation, conviction.

vindictive *adj* implacable, malevolent, malicious, malignant, merciless, punitive, rancorous, relentless, resentful, retributive, revengeful, spiteful, unforgiving, unrelenting, vengeful, venomous.

antonyms charitable, forgiving, merciful.

vintage *adj* best, choice, classic, fine, mature, old, prime, quintessential, rare, ripe, select, superior, venerable, veteran.

violate *v* abuse, assault, befoul, break, contravene, debauch, defile, desecrate, dishonour, disobey, disregard, flout, infract, infringe, invade, outrage, pollute, profane, rape, ravish, transgress.

antonyms obey, observe, respect, uphold.

violation *n* abuse, breach, contravention, defilement, desecration, disruption, encroachment, infraction, infringement, offence, profanation, rapine, sacrilege, spoliation, transgression, trespass.

antonyms obedience, observance, respect.

violence *n* abandon, acuteness, bestiality, bloodshed, bloodthirstiness, boisterousness, brutality, conflict, cruelty, destructiveness, ferocity, fervour, fierceness, fighting, force, frenzy, fury, harshness, hostilities, intensity, murderousness, passion, power, roughness, savagery, severity, sharpness, storminess, strength, terrorism, thuggery, tumult, turbulence, vehemence, wildness.

antonyms passivity, peacefulness.

violent *adj* acute, agonizing, berserk, biting, bloodthirsty, blustery, boisterous, brutal, cruel, destructive, devastating, excruciating, extreme, fiery, forceful, forcible, furious, harsh, headstrong, homicidal, hot-headed, impetuous, intemperate, intense, maddened, maniacal, murderous, outrageous, painful, passionate, powerful, raging, riotous, rough, ruinous, savage, severe, sharp, strong, tempestuous, tumultuous, turbulent, uncontrollable, ungovernable, unrestrained, vehement, vicious, wild.

antonyms calm, gentle, moderate, passive, peaceful.

VIP *n* big cheese, big gun, big name, big noise, big shot, big wheel, bigwig, celebrity, dignitary, headliner, heavyweight, lion, luminary, notable, personage, somebody, star, visiting fireman.

antonyms nobody, nonentity.

virago *n* battle-axe, dragon, fury, gorgon, harridan, hellcat, scold, shrew, tartar, termagant, vixen, Xanthippe.

virgin *n* bachelor, celibate, damsel, girl, maid, maiden, spinster, vestal.

adj chaste, fresh, immaculate, intact, maidenly, modest, new, pristine, pure, snowy, spotless, stainless, uncorrupted, undefiled, unsullied, untouched, untrodden, unused, vestal, virginal.

virginity *n* chasteness, chastity, maidenhead, maidenhood, purity, virtue.

virile *adj* forceful, hairy-chested, husky, lusty, macho, male, manlike, manly, masculine, potent, red-blooded, robust, rugged, strong, vigorous.

antonyms effeminate, impotent, weak.

virility *n* huskiness, machismo, maleness, manhood, manliness, masculinity, potency, ruggedness, vigour.

antonyms effeminacy, impotence, weakness.

virtual *adj* effective, essential, implicit, implied, indirect, potential, practical, substantial, tacit.

antonym actual.

virtually *adv* almost, as good as, effectively, effectually, in effect, in essence, just about, nearly, practically, to all intents and purposes.

virtue *n* advantage, asset, attribute, chastity, credit, excellence, goodness, high-mindedness, honour, incorruptibility, innocence, integrity, justice, merit, morality, plus, probity, purity, quality, rectitude, redeeming feature, righteousness, strength, uprightness, virginity, worth, worthiness.

antonym vice.

virtuosity *n* bravura, brilliance, éclat, expertise, finesse, finish, flair, mastery, panache, polish, skill, wizardry.

virtuoso *n* ace, artist, crackerjack, dab, dab hand, genius, maestro, magician, master, prodigy, whiz, wizard.

adj ace, bravura, brilliant, crack, crackerjack, dazzling, expert, masterly, wizard.

virtuous *adj* blameless, celibate, chaste, clean-living, continent, ethical, excellent, exemplary, good, high-principled, honest, honourable, incorruptible, innocent, irreproachable, moral, praiseworthy, pure, righteous, spotless, squeaky-clean, unimpeachable, upright, virginal, worthy.

antonyms bad, dishonest, immoral, vicious, wicked.

virulent *adj* acrimonious, baneful, bitter, deadly, envenomed, hostile, infective, injurious, lethal, malevolent, malicious, malignant, noxious, pernicious, poisonous, rancorous, resentful, septic, spiteful, splenetic, toxic, venomous, vicious, vindictive, vitriolic.

viscera *n* bowels, chitterlings, entrails, guts, innards, insides, intestines, vitals.

viscous *adj* adhesive, clammy, gelatinous, gluey, glutinous, gummy, mucilaginous, mucous, sticky, syrupy, tacky, tenacious, thick, treacly, viscid.

antonyms runny, thin, watery.

visible *adj* apparent, clear, conspicuous, detectable, discernible, discoverable, distinct, distinguishable, evident, manifest, noticeable, observable, obvious, open, palpable, patent, perceivable, perceptible, plain, salient, unconcealed, undisguised, unmistakable.

antonym invisible.

vision *n* apparition, chimera, concept, conception, construct, daydream, delusion, discernment, dream, eyes, eyesight, fantasy, far-sightedness, foresight, ghost, hallucination, idea, ideal, illusion, image, imagination, insight, intuition, mirage, penetration, perception, phantasm, phantom, picture, prescience, revelation, seeing, sight, spectacle, spectre, view, wraith.

visionary *adj* delusory, dreaming, dreamy, fanciful, fantastic, ideal, idealistic, idealized, illusory, imaginary, impractical, prophetic, quixotic, romantic, speculative, starry-eyed, unreal, unrealistic, unworkable, utopian.

n daydreamer, Don Quixote, dreamer, enthusiast, fantasist, idealist, mystic, prophet, rainbow-chaser, romantic, seer, theorist, utopian, zealot.

antonym pragmatist.

visit *v* afflict, assail, attack, attend, befall, call (in), chat, chew the fat, converse, drop in (or by or over), haunt, inflict, inspect, look in, look up, pop in, punish, rap, see, send, shoot the breeze, smite, stay at, stay with, stop by, take in, trouble.

n call, chat, conversation, excursion, sojourn, stay, stop, talk.

visitation *n* appearance, bane, blight, calamity, cataclysm, catastrophe, disaster, examination, infliction, inspection, manifestation, nemesis, ordeal, punishment, retribution, scourge, trial, visit.

visitor *n* caller, company, guest, habitué, holidaymaker, patron, regular, tourist.

vista *n* outlook, panorama, perspective, prospect, scene, sight, view.

visual *adj* discernible, observable, ocular, optic, optical, perceptible, visible.

visualize *v* conceive, conjure up, envisage, envision, ideate, imagine, picture.

vital *adj* alive, animate, animated, animating, basic, cardinal, critical, crucial, decisive, dynamic, energetic, essential, forceful, fundamental, generative, imperative, important, indispensable, invigorating, key, life-giving, life-or-death, live, lively, living, necessary, quickening, requisite, significant, spirited, urgent, vibrant, vigorous, vivacious, zestful.

antonyms inessential, lethargic, peripheral.

vitality *n* animation, energy, exuberance, go, life, liveliness, lustiness, oomph, pep, robustness, sparkle, stamina, strength, vigour, vim, vivaciousness, vivacity, zip.

vitiate *v* blemish, blight, contaminate, corrupt, debase, defile, deprave, deteriorate, devalue, harm, impair, injure, invalidate, mar, nullify, pervert, pollute, ruin, spoil, sully, taint, undermine.

antonym purify.

vitriolic *adj* acerbic, acid, bitchy, biting, bitter, caustic, destructive, envenomed, malicious, sardonic, scathing, venomous, vicious, virulent, withering.

vituperate *v* abuse, berate, blame, castigate, censure, denounce, execrate, rate, reproach, revile, slam, slang, slate, upbraid, vilify.

antonyms applaud, eulogize, extol, praise.

vituperation *n* abuse, blame, castigation, censure, contumely, diatribe, execration, faultfinding, flak, invective, objurgation, obloquy, phillipic, rebuke, reprimand, reproach, revilement, scurrility, vilification.

antonyms acclaim, eulogy, praise.

vituperative *adj* abusive, belittling, calumniatory, censorious, defamatory, denunciatory, derogatory, fulminatory, harsh, insulting, malign, objurgatory, opprobrious, sardonic, scornful, scurrilous, sharp-tongued, withering.

antonym laudatory.

vivacious *adj* animated, bubbling, bubbly, cheerful, chipper, ebullient, effervescent, frisky, frolicsome, gay, high-spirited, jolly, light-hearted, lively, merry, scintillating, sparkling, spirited, sportive, sprightly, vital.

antonym languid.

vivacity *n* animation, brio, bubbliness, ebullience, effervescence, energy, friskiness, gaiety, high spirits, jollity, life, liveliness, pep, quickness, sparkle, spirit, sprightliness, zip.

antonym languor.

vivid *adj* active, animated, bright, brilliant, clear, colourful, distinct, dramatic, dynamic, eidetic, energetic, expressive, flamboyant, glowing, graphic, highly-coloured, intense, lifelike, lively, memorable, powerful, quick, realistic, rich, sharp, spirited, stirring, striking, strong, telling, vibrant, vigorous.

antonyms dull, lifeless.

vividness *n* brightness, brilliancy, clarity, distinctness, glow, immediacy, intensity, life, liveliness, lucidity, radiance, realism, refulgence, resplendence, sharpness, sprightliness, strength.

antonyms dullness, lifelessness.

vixen *n* beldam, bitch, fury, harpy, harridan, hellcat, scold, shrew, spitfire, termagant, virago, Xanthippe.

vocabulary *n* dictionary, glossary, idiom, language, lexicon, lexis, lingo, nomenclature, terminology, thesaurus, wordbook, word list, words.

vocal *adj* articulate, clamorous, eloquent, expressive, forthright, frank, free-spoken, noisy, oral, outspoken, plain-spoken, shrill, spoken, strident, uttered, vociferous.

antonyms inarticulate, quiet.

vocation *n* bag, business, calling, career, craft, employment, job, métier, mission, niche, office, post, profession, pursuit, role, thing, trade, work.

vociferous *adj* clamorous, deafening, loud, loud-mouthed, noisy, obstreperous, ranting, shouting, shrill, stentorian, strident, thundering, uproarious, vehement, vocal.

antonyms quiet, silent.

vogue *n* acceptance, craze, currency, custom, day, dernier cri, fashion, fashionableness, favour, last word, mode, popularity, prevalence, style, the latest, the rage, the thing, trend, usage, use.

adj current, fashionable, in, modish, now, popular, prevalent, stylish, trendy, up-to-the-minute, voguish, with it.

voice *n* agency, articulation, decision, expression, inflection, instrument, intonation, language, medium, mouthpiece, opinion, organ, part, say, sound, speech, spokesman, spokesperson, spokeswoman, tone, utterance, vehicle, view, vote, will, wish, words.

v air, articulate, assert, bruit, convey, declare, disclose, divulge, enunciate, express, say, speak of, utter, vent, ventilate.

void *adj* bare, blank, cancelled, clear, dead, drained, emptied, empty, free, hollow, inane, ineffective, ineffectual, inoperative, invalid, nugatory, null, tenantless, unenforceable, unfilled, unoccupied, useless, vacant, vacuous, vain, worthless.

antonyms full, valid.

n blank, blankness, cavity, chasm, emptiness, gap, hiatus, hollow, lack, opening, space, vacancy, vacuity, vacuum, want.

v abnegate, annul, cancel, countermand, defecate, discharge, drain, eject, elimate, emit, empty, evacuate, invalidate, nullify, pass, rescind, vitiate.

antonyms fill, validate.

volatile *adj* airy, changeable, erratic, explosive, fickle, flighty, gay, giddy, hot-headed, hot-tempered, inconstant, lively, mercurial, sprightly, temperamental, unsettled, unstable, unsteady, variable, volcanic.

antonyms constant, steady.

volition *n* choice, choosing, decision, determination, discretion, election, option, preference, purpose, resolution, taste, will.

volley *n* barrage, blast, bombardment, burst, cannonade, discharge, enfilade, explosion, fusillade, hail, salvo, shower.

voluble *adj* articulate, chatty, fluent, forthcoming, gabby, garrulous, glib, loquacious, talkative.

antonyms laconic, reserved, reticent.

volume *n* aggregate, amount, amplitude, bigness, body, book, bulk, capacity, compass, dimensions, fascicle, heft, mass, part, publication, quantity, tome, total, treatise.

voluminous *adj* abounding, ample, big, billowing, bulky, capacious, cavernous, commodious, copious, full, large, massive, prolific, roomy, vast.

antonyms scanty, slight.

voluntarily *adv* by choice, consciously, deliberately, freely, intentionally, of one's own accord, of one's own free will, on one's own initiative, purposely, spontaneously, willingly.

antonyms involuntarily, unwillingly.

voluntary *adj* conscious, deliberate, discretional, free, gratuitous, honorary, intended, intentional, optional, spontaneous, unconstrained, unforced, unpaid, volunteer, willing.

antonyms compulsory, forced, involuntary, unwilling.

volunteer *v* advance, communicate, extend, offer, present, proffer, propose, put forward, step forward, submit, suggest, tender.

voluptuary *n* bon vivant, debauchee, epicurean, hedonist, libertine, playboy, pleasure-seeker, profligate, sensualist, sybarite.

antonym ascetic.

voluptuous *adj* ample, buxom, curvaceous, enticing, epicurean, erotic, hedonistic, licentious, luscious, luxurious, pleasure-loving, provocative, seductive, self-indulgent, sensual, shapely, sybaritic.

antonym ascetic.

voluptuousness *n* buxomness, carnality, curvaceousness, licentiousness, lusciousness, opulence, seductiveness, sensuality, shapeliness.

antonym asceticism.

vomit *v* barf, bring up, cough up, disgorge, eject, emit, gag, heave, puke, ralph, regurgitate, retch, spew out, spew up, throw up, toss one's cookies, upchuck.

vomiting *n* ejection, emesis, emission, puking, regurgitation, retching, sickness, spewing.

voracious *adj* acquisitive, avid, devouring, edacious, gluttonous, greedy, hungry, insatiable, omnivorous, piggish, prodigious, rapacious, ravening, ravenous, uncontrolled, unquenchable.

voracity *n* acquisitiveness, avidity, eagerness, edacity, greed, hunger, piggishness, rapacity, ravenousness.

vortex *n* black hole, eddy, maelstrom, whirl, whirlpool, whirlwind.

votary *n* addict, adherent, aficionado, believer, devotee, disciple, follower, monk.

vote *n* ballot, election, franchise, plebiscite, poll, referendum, show of hands, suffrage.

v ballot, choose, declare, elect, judge, opt, plump for, pronounce, propose, recommend, return, suggest.

voucher *n* certificate, check, chit, coupon, receipt, ticket, token, warrant.

vouch for affirm, assert, asseverate, attest to, avouch, back, certify, confirm, endorse, guarantee, recommend, sponsor, support, swear to, uphold.

vouchsafe *v* accord, bestow, cede, confer, deign, grant, impart, yield.

vow *v* affirm, avouch, consecrate, dedicate, devote, maintain, pledge, profess, promise, swear.

n avouchment, oath, pledge, promise, troth, word.

voyage *n* crossing, cruise, expedition, journey, passage, peregrination, travels, trip.

vulgar *adj* blue, boorish, cheap and nasty, coarse, common, crude, dirty, flashy, gaudy, general, gross, ill-bred, impolite, improper, indecent, indecorous, indelicate, insensitive, lewd, low, lowlife, low-minded, nasty, naughty, obscene, ordinary, plebeian, ribald, risqué, rude, suggestive, tacky, tasteless, tawdry, uncouth, unmannerly, unrefined, vernacular.

antonyms correct, decent, elegant, noble, polite, refined.

vulgarian *n* arriviste, barbarian, boor, nouveau riche, parvenu, philistine, upstart.

vulgarity *n* coarseness, crudeness, crudity, dirtiness, gaudiness, grossness, indecency, indecorum, indelicacy, insensitivity, lewdness, ribaldry, rudeness, suggestiveness, tastelessness, tawdriness.

antonyms decency, politeness.

vulnerable *adj* accessible, assailable, defenceless, exposed, pregnable, sensitive, susceptible, tender, thin-skinned, unprotected, weak, wide open.

antonyms protected, strong.

W

wacky *adj* crazy, daffy, daft, eccentric, erratic, irrational, loony, nutty, odd, screwball, screwy, silly, unpredictable, wild, zany.
antonym sensible.

wad *n* ball, block, bundle, chunk, gob, hunk, mass, pile, plug, roll.

wadding *n* cotton batting, cotton wool, filler, lining, packing, padding, stuffing.

waddle *v* rock, shuffle, sway, toddle, totter, wiggle, wobble.

waffle *v* blather, duck, equivocate, fudge, jabber, prate, prattle, prevaricate, sidestep, spout.
n blather, claptrap, evasion, gobbledegook, guff, jabber, nonsense, padding, prating, prattle, prolixity, verbiage, verbosity, wordiness.

waft *v* bear, carry, convey, drift, float, glide, ride, transmit, transport, whiffle, winnow.
n breath, breeze, current, draft, puff, scent, whiff.

wag[1] *v* bob, bobble, flap, flutter, jiggle, nod, oscillate, quiver, rock, shake, stir, vibrate, waggle, wave, wiggle, wigwag.

wag[2] *n* banterer, card, clown, comedian, comic, droll, fool, humorist, jester, joker, wit.

wage *n* allowance, compensation, earnings, emolument, fee, guerdon, hire, pay, payment, recompense, remuneration, reward, salary, stipend, wages.
v carry on, conduct, engage in, practise, prosecute, pursue, undertake.

wager *n* bet, gage, gamble, hazard, pledge, speculation, stake, venture.
v bet, chance, gamble, hazard, lay, lay odds, pledge, risk, speculate, stake, venture.

waggish *adj* amusing, arch, bantering, comical, droll, facetious, frolicsome, funny, humorous, impish, jesting, jocose, jocular, merry, mischievous, playful, puckish, risible, roguish, sportive, witty.
antonyms grave, serious, staid.

waggle *v* flutter, jiggle, oscillate, shake, wag, wave, wiggle, wobble.

wagon *n* buggy, carriage, cart, dray, float, train, truck, tumbrel, van.

waif *n* foundling, orphan, stray.

wail *v* bemoan, bewail, complain, cry, deplore, grieve, howl, keen, lament, mewl, moan, ululate, weep, yammer, yowl.
n caterwaul, complaint, cry, grief, howl, keen, lament, lamentation, moan, ululation, weeping, yowl.

wait *v* abide, bide one's time, dally, delay, hang around, hang back, hang fire, hesitate, hold back, hover, linger, loiter, mark time, pause, remain, rest, sit tight, stand by, stand in line, stay, stick around, tarry.
antonyms depart, go, leave.
n delay, halt, hesitation, hiatus, holdup, interval, pause, rest, stay.

waive *v* abandon, cede, defer, delay, disclaim, forgo, pass up, postpone, relinquish, remit, renounce, resign, surrender, yield.
antonyms claim, maintain.

waiver *n* abandonment, abdication, deferral, disclaimer, postponement, relinquishment, remission, renunciation, resignation, surrender.

wake[1] *v* activate, animate, arise, arouse, awake, awaken, bestir, enliven, excite, fire, galvanize, get up, kindle, provoke, quicken, rise, rouse, stimulate, stir, unbed.
antonyms relax, sleep.
n deathwatch, funeral, vigil, watch.

wake[2] *n* aftermath, backwash, path, rear, track, trail, train, wash, wave.

wakeful *adj* alert, alive, attentive, heedful, insomniac, observant, restless, sleepless, unblinking, unsleeping, vigilant, wary, watchful.
antonyms inattentive, sleepy, unwary.

waken *v* activate, animate, arouse, awake, awaken, enliven, fire, galvanize, ignite, kindle, quicken, rouse, stimulate, stir, whet.

walk *v* accompany, advance, amble, ambulate, convoy, escort, hike, hoof it, march, move, pace, perambulate, plod, promenade, saunter, step, stride, stroll, traipse, tramp, tread, trek, trudge.
n airing, aisle, alley, ambulatory, avenue, carriage, cloister, constitutional, esplanade, footpath, gait, hike, lane, march, pace, path, pathway, perambulation, promenade, ramble, saunter, sidewalk, step, stride, stroll, trail, traipse, tramp, trek, trudge, turn.

walk of life activity, area, arena, calling, career, course, field, line, métier, occupation, profession, pursuit, social position, sphere, trade, vocation.

walker *n* ambulator, backpacker, footslogger, hiker, pedestrian, rambler, wayfarer.

walkout *n* industrial action, protest, rebellion, revolt, stoppage, strike.

walkover *n* child's play, cinch, picnic, piece of cake, pushover, snap, walk, walkaway.

walkway *n* ambulatory, cloister, esplanade, footpath, lane, path, pathway, promenade, sidewalk.

wall *n* bailey, barricade, barrier, block, breastwork, bulkhead, bulwark, dike, divider, embankment, enclosure, fence, fortification, hedge, impediment, membrane, obstacle, obstruction, palisade, panel, parapet, partition, rampart, screen, septum, stockade.

wallet *n* billfold, pocketbook, pouch, purse.

wallop *v* batter, beat, belt, best, buffet, clobber, crush, defeat, drub, hammer, hit, lambaste, lick, paste, pound, pummel, punch, rout, slug, smack, strike, swat, swipe, thrash, thump, thwack, trounce, vanquish, whack, worst.

n bash, belt, blow, haymaker, hit, kick, punch, slug, smack, swat, swipe, thump, thwack, whack.

wallow *v* bask, delight, enjoy, flounder, glory, indulge, lie, lurch, luxuriate, relish, revel, roll, splash, stagger, stumble, tumble, wade, welter.

wan *adj* anemic, ashen, bleak, bloodless, cadaverous, colourless, dim, discoloured, faint, feeble, ghastly, livid, mournful, pale, pallid, pasty, sickly, waxen, weak, weary, whey-faced, white.

wand *n* baton, mace, rod, sceptre, sprig, staff, stick, twig, verge, withe.

wander *v* babble, cruise, depart, deviate, digress, divagate, diverge, drift, err, lapse, meander, mill around, mooch, mosey, peregrinate, ramble, range, rave, roam, rove, saunter, straggle, stray, stroll, swerve, traipse, veer.

n cruise, excursion, meander, peregrination, ramble, saunter, stroll, traipse.

wanderer *n* backpacker, drifter, gadabout, gypsy, hiker, hobo, itinerant, migrant, nomad, rambler, ranger, rolling stone, rover, strag, straggler, stray, stroller, traveller, vagabond, vagrant, voyager, wayfarer.

wandering *n* aberration, deviation, digression, divagation, divergence, drift(ing), journey(ing), meander(ing), odyssey, peregrination, travels, walkabout.

adj aberrant, drifting, homeless, itinerant, migratory, nomadic, peregrinatory, peripatetic, rambling, rootless, roving, strolling, travelling, vagabond, vagrant, voyaging, wayfaring.

wane *v* abate, atrophy, contract, decline, decrease, dim, diminish, droop, drop, dwindle, ebb, fade, fail, lessen, shrink, sink, subside, taper off, weaken, wither.

antonyms increase, wax.

n abatement, atrophy, contraction, decay, decline, decrease, diminution, drop, dwindling, ebb, fading, failure, fall, lessening, sinking, subsidence, tapering off, weakening.

antonym increase.

on the wane declining, degenerating, deteriorating, dropping, dwindling, ebbing, fading, lessening, moribund, obsolescent, on its last legs, on the decline, on the way out, subsiding, tapering off, weakening, withering.

antonym on the increase.

wangle *v* arrange, bring off, contrive, engineer, fiddle, finagle, fix, machinate, manage, manipulate, manoeuvre, pull off, pull strings, scheme, swing, work.

want *v* call for, covet, crave, demand, desire, fancy, hanker after, hunger for, lack, long for, miss, need, pine for, require, thirst for, wish, yearn for, yen.

n absence, appetite, craving, dearth, default, deficiency, demand, desideratum, desire, destitution, famine, fancy, hankering, hunger, indigence, insufficiency, lack, longing, necessity, need, neediness, paucity, pauperism, penury, poverty, privation, requirement, scantiness, scarcity, shortage, thirst, wish, yearning, yen.

antonyms abundance, plenty, riches.

wanting *adj* absent, defective, deficient, disappointing, faulty, imperfect, inadequate, incomplete, inferior, insufficient, lacking, less, missing, patchy, poor, short, shy, sketchy, substandard, unsatisfactory, unsound.

antonyms adequate, sufficient.

wanton *adj* abandoned, arbitrary, careless, coltish, cruel, dissipated, dissolute, evil, extravagant, fast, gratuitous, groundless, heedless, immoderate, immoral, intemperate, lavish, lecherous, lewd, libertine, libidinous, licentious, loose, lustful, malevolent, malicious, motiveless, needless, outrageous, promiscuous, rakish, rash, reckless, senseless, shameless, spiteful, uncalled-for, unchaste, unjustifiable, unjustified, unprovoked, unrestrained, vicious, wicked, wild, wilful.

n Casanova, debauchee, Don Juan, harlot, lecher, libertine, mort, profligate, prostitute, rake, rip, roué, satyr, slut, strumpet, tart, trollop, voluptuary, whore.

war *n* battle, bloodshed, combat, conflict, contention, contest, crusade, enmity, fighting, hostilities, hostility, jihad, strife, struggle, warfare.

antonym peace.

v battle, clash, combat, contend, contest, crusade, fight, skirmish, strive, struggle, take up arms, wage war.

war cry battle cry, rallying cry, slogan, war whoop, watchword.

warble *v* chirp, chirrup, quaver, sing, trill, twitter, yodel.

n call, chirp, chirrup, cry, quaver, song, trill, twitter.

ward *n* area, care, charge, cubicle, custody, dependant, district, division, guardianship, keeping, minor, precinct, protection, protégé, pupil, quarter, room, safekeeping, vigil, watch, zone.

ward off avert, avoid, beat off, block, deflect, disperse, evade, fend off, forestall, parry, repel, repulse, stave off, thwart, turn aside, turn away.

warden n administrator, captain, caretaker, castellan, chatelaine, concierge, curator, custodian, guardian, janitor, keeper, ranger, steward, superintendent, warder, watchman.

warder n custodian, guard, jailer, keeper, prison officer, screw, turnkey, wardress.

wardrobe n apparel, attire, closet, clothes, costumes, cupboard, outfit.

warehouse n depository, depot, entrepôt, repository, stockroom, store, storehouse.

wares n commodities, goods, lines, merchandise, produce, products, stock, stuff, vendibles.

warfare n arms, battle, blows, combat, conflict, contention, contest, discord, fighting, hostilities, passage of arms, strife, struggle, war.

antonyms harmony, peace.

warily adv apprehensively, cagily, carefully, cautiously, charily, circumspectly, distrustfully, gingerly, guardedly, hesitantly, leerily, suspiciously, uneasily, vigilantly, watchfully.

antonyms heedlessly, recklessly, thoughtlessly, unwarily.

wariness n alertness, apprehension, attention, caginess, care, carefulness, caution, circumspection, discretion, distrust, foresight, heedfulness, hesitancy, mindfulness, prudence, suspicion, unease, vigilance, watchfulness.

antonyms heedlessness, recklessness, thoughtlessness.

warlike adj aggressive, antagonistic, armed, bellicose, belligerent, bloodthirsty, combative, hawkish, hostile, inimical, jingoistic, martial, militant, militaristic, military, pugnacious, sabre-rattling, scrappy, truculent, unfriendly.

antonym peaceable.

warlock n conjurer, demon, enchanter, magician, magus, necromancer, sorcerer, witch, wizard.

warm adj affable, affectionate, amiable, amorous, angry, animated, ardent, balmy, cheerful, cordial, cosy, dangerous, disagreeable, earnest, effusive, emotional, enthusiastic, excited, fervent, friendly, genial, glowing, happy, hazardous, hearty, heated, hospitable, impassioned, incalescent, intense, irascible, irritable, keen, kindly, lively, loving, lukewarm, passionate, perilous, pleasant, quick, recent, sensitive, short, spirited, stormy, sunny, tender, tepid, thermal, touchy, tricky, uncomfortable, unpleasant, vehement, vigorous, violent, zealous.

antonyms cool, indifferent, safe, unfriendly.

v animate, awaken, excite, heat, heat up, interest, melt, put some life into, reheat, rouse, stimulate, stir, thaw, turn on.

antonym cool.

warm-blooded adj ardent, earnest, emotional, enthusiastic, excitable, fervent, hot-blooded, impetuous, lively, passionate, rash, red-blooded, spirited, vivacious.

warm-hearted adj affectionate, ardent, compassionate, cordial, generous, genial, kind-hearted, kindly, loving, sympathetic, tender, tender-hearted.

antonyms cold, unsympathetic.

warmth n affability, affection, amorousness, animation, ardour, cheerfulness, cordiality, eagerness, earnestness, effusiveness, empressement, enthusiasm, excitement, fervency, fervour, fire, happiness, heartiness, heat, hospitableness, hotness, intensity, kindliness, love, passion, spirit, tenderness, vehemence, vigour, violence, warmness, zeal, zest.

antonyms coldness, coolness, unfriendliness.

warn v acquaint, admonish, advise, alert, apprise, caution, counsel, forewarn, give notice, inform, notify, put on one's guard, tell, tip off.

warning n admonishment, admonition, advance notice, advice, advisory, alarm, alert, augury, caution, caveat, foretoken, forewarning, harbinger, hint, lesson, notice, notification, omen, premonition, presage, prodrome, sign, signal, siren, threat, tip, tip-off, token, word, word to the wise.

adj admonitory, aposematic, cautionary, monitory, ominous, premonitory, prodromal, prodromic, threatening.

warp v bend, contort, deform, deviate, distort, kink, misshape, pervert, turn, twist.

antonym straighten.

n bend, bent, bias, contortion, deformation, deviation, distortion, irregularity, kink, perversion, quirk, turn, twist.

warrant n authorization, authority, commission, guarantee, licence, permission, permit, pledge, sanction, security, voucher, warranty.

v affirm, answer for, approve, assure, attest, authorize, avouch, be bound, call for, certify, commission, declare, demand, empower, entitle, excuse, guarantee, justify, license, necessitate, permit, pledge, require, sanction, secure, underwrite, uphold, vouch for, vouchsafe.

warrantable adj accountable, allowable, defensible, excusable, justifiable, lawful, legal, necessary, permissible, proper, reasonable, right.

antonyms indefensible, unjustifiable, unwarrantable.

warranty n assurance, authorization, bond, certificate, contract, covenant, guarantee, justification, pledge.

warring adj at daggers drawn, at war, belligerent, combatant, conflicting, contending, embattled, fighting, hostile, opposed, opposing.

warrior n brave, champion, combatant, fighter, man-at-arms, soldier, wardog, warhorse.

wart n excrescence, growth, lump, protuberance, verruca.

wary adj alert, apprehensive, attentive, cagey, careful, cautious, chary, circumspect, distrustful, guarded, hawk-eyed, heedful, leery, on one's guard, on the lookout, on the qui vive, prudent, suspicious, vigilant, watchful, wide-awake.

antonyms careless, foolhardy, heedless, reckless, unwary.

wash¹ *v* bath, bathe, clean, cleanse, flush, launder, moisten, rinse, scrub, shampoo, shower, sluice, sponge, swill, wet.

n ablution, bath, cleaning, cleansing, coat, coating, ebb and flow, film, flow, laundering, laundry, layer, overlay, rinse, screen, scrub, shampoo, shower, souse, stain, suffusion, surge, sweep, swell, washing, wave.

wash one's hands of abandon, abdicate responsibility, give up on, have nothing to do with, leave to someone's own devices.

wash² *v* bear examination, bear scrutiny, carry weight, hold up, hold water, pass muster, stand up, stick.

washed-out *adj* all in, beat, blanched, bleached, bushed, colourless, dead on one's feet, dog-tired, drained, drawn, etiolated, exhausted, faded, fatigued, flat, haggard, lacklustre, pale, pallid, pooped, spent, tired, tired out, wan, weary, worn out.

washout *n* disappointment, disaster, dud, failure, fiasco, flop, incompetent, lead balloon, lemon, loser, mess.

antonyms success, triumph, winner.

washroom *n* bathroom, head, john, ladies' room, lavatory, loo, men's room, powder room, privy, (public) convenience, rest room, toilet, urinal.

waspish *adj* bad-tempered, bitchy, cantankerous, captious, crabby, cross, crotchety, fretful, grouchy, grumpy, ill-tempered, irascible, irritable, peevish, peppery, petulant, prickly, snappish, splenetic, testy, touchy.

waste *v* atrophy, blow, burn up, consume, corrode, crumble, debilitate, decay, decline, deplete, despoil, destroy, devastate, disable, dissipate, drain, dwindle, eat away, ebb, emaciate, enfeeble, erode, exhaust, fade, fritter away, gnaw, kill (time), lavish, lay waste, misspend, misuse, perish, pillage, rape, ravage, raze, rig, ruin, run through, sack, shrink, sink, spend, spoil, squander, throw away, undermine, wane, wanton, wear out, wither.

n debris, desert, desolation, destruction, devastation, dissipation, dregs, effluent, erosion, expenditure, extravagance, garbage, havoc, leavings, leftovers, litter, loss, misapplication, misuse, offscourings, prodigality, ravage, refuse, rubbish, ruin, scrap(s), slops, solitude, spoilage, squandering, sweepings, trash, void, wastefulness, wasteland, wild, wilderness.

adj bare, barren, desolate, devastated, dismal, dreary, empty, extra, leftover, superfluous, supernumerary, uncultivated, uninhabited, unproductive, unprofitable, unused, unwanted, useless, wild, worthless.

wasted *adj* abandoned, atrophied, cadaverous, debauched, depleted, dissipated, dissolute, emaciated, exhausted, finished, gaunt,

profligate, shrivelled, shrunken, spent, tabescent, wanton, washed-out, withered.

antonyms healthy, robust.

wasteful *adj* dissipative, extravagant, improvident, lavish, prodigal, profligate, ruinous, spendthrift, thriftless, uneconomical, unthrifty.

antonyms economical, frugal, thrifty.

wasteland *n* barrenness, desert, solitude, void, waste, wilderness, wild(s).

waster *n* drone, goldbricker, good-for-nothing, idler, layabout, loafer, lounger, malingerer, ne'er-do-well, profligate, shirker, spendthrift, wastrel.

antonym worker.

wasting *n* atrophy, degeneration, dystrophy, emaciation, marasmus.

adj destroying, devastating, dystrophic, emaciating, enfeebling, marasmoid, tubescent.

antonym strengthening.

watch¹ *v* attend, contemplate, eye, gaze at, guard, keep, keep an eye open, look, look after, look at, look on, look out, mark, mind, note, observe, ogle, pay attention, peer at, protect, regard, see, spectate, stare at, superintend, take care of, take heed, tend, view, wait.

n alertness, attention, eye, heed, inspection, lookout, notice, observation, supervision, surveillance, vigil, vigilance, wake, watchfulness.

watch out be careful, be on guard, have a care, keep a weather eye open, keep one's eyes open, keep one's eyes peeled, watch oneself.

watch over baby-sit, defend, guard, keep an eye on, keep tabs on, look after, mind, preserve, protect, shelter, shield, stand guard over, supervise, tend.

watch² *n* chronometer, clock, ticker, timepiece, wristwatch.

watchdog *n* custodian, guard dog, guardian, inspector, monitor, ombudsman, protector, scrutineer, vigilante.

watcher *n* Argus, lookout, member of the audience, observer, onlooker, peeping Tom, spectator, spy, viewer, voyeur, witness.

watchful *adj* alert, attentive, cautious, circumspect, guarded, heedful, observant, on one's guard, on the lookout, on the qui vive, on the watch, suspicious, vigilant, wary, wide-awake.

antonym inattentive.

watchfulness *n* alertness, attention, attentiveness, caution, cautiousness, circumspection, heedfulness, suspicion, suspiciousness, vigilance, wariness.

antonym inattention.

watchman *n* caretaker, custodian, guard, security guard, sentry.

watchword *n* battle cry, buzz word, byword, catch phrase, catchword, countersign, magic word, maxim, motto, password, rallying cry, shibboleth, signal, slogan.

water *n* Adam's ale, aqua, fluid, lake, moisture, ocean, rain, river, saliva, sea, stream, sweat, tears, urine.
v adulterate, damp, dampen, dilute, douse, drench, drink, flood, hose, irrigate, moisten, soak, souse, spray, sprinkle, thin, water down, weaken, wet.
antonyms dry out, purify, strengthen.

water down adulterate, dilute, mitigate, mix, qualify, soften, thin, tone down, water, weaken.
antonyms purify, strengthen.

watercourse *n* arroyo, canal, channel, ditch, river, stream, water channel.

waterfall *n* cascade, cataract, chute, fall, torrent.

waterproof *adj* coated, impermeable, impervious, proofed, rubberized, water-repellent, water-resistant.
antonym leaky.

watertight *adj* airtight, firm, flawless, foolproof, hermetic, impregnable, incontrovertible, perfect, sealed, sound, unassailable, waterproof.
antonyms leaky, unsound.

watery *adj* adulterated, aqueous, damp, dilute, diluted, flavourless, fluid, humid, hydatoid, insipid, liquid, marshy, moist, poor, rheumy, runny, soggy, squelchy, tasteless, tear-filled, tearful, thin, washy, watered-down, weak, weepy, wet, wishy-washy.
antonyms solid, strong.

wave[1] *v* beckon, brandish, curl, curve, direct, flap, flourish, flutter, gesticulate, gesture, indicate, oscillate, quiver, ripple, shake, sign, signal, stir, sway, swing, undulate, waft, wag, waggle, waver, weave, wield, wigwag.

wave[2] *n* billow, breaker, comber, current, drift, flood, ground swell, movement, outbreak, rash, ripple, roller, rush, stream, surge, sweep, swell, tendency, tidal wave, trend, tsunami, undulation, unevenness, upsurge, wavelet, white horse.

waver *v* blow hot and cold, dither, falter, flicker, fluctuate, gutter, hem and haw, hesitate, quiver, reel, rock, seesaw, shake, shilly-shally, sway, teeter, totter, tremble, undulate, vacillate, vary, wave, weave, whiffle, wobble.
antonyms decide, stand.

wavering *adj* dithering, dithery, doubtful, doubting, hesitant, in two minds, shilly-shallying.
antonym determined.

wavy *adj* curly, curvy, flamboyant, ridged, ridgy, rippled, ripply, serpentine, sinuate(d), sinuous, snaky, undulating, winding, wrinkled, zigzag.
antonyms flat, smooth.

wax *v* become, blow up, develop, dilate, enlarge, expand, fill out, grow, increase, magnify, mount, mushroom, rise, swell.
antonym wane.

waxen *adj* anemic, ashen, bloodless, colourless, ghastly, livid, pale, pallid, wan, white, whitish.
antonym ruddy.

waxy *adj* ceraceous, impressible, impressionable, pallid, pasty, soft, waxen.

way *n* access, advance, aim, ambition, approach, area, aspect, avenue, channel, characteristic, choice, circumstance, condition, conduct, course, custom, demand, desire, detail, direction, distance, district, elbow room, fashion, feature, fettle, gate, goal, habit, headway, highway, idiosyncrasy, journey, lane, length, manner, march, means, method, mode, movement, nature, opening, particular, passage, path, pathway, personality, plan, pleasure, point, practice, procedure, process, progress, region, respect, road, room, route, scheme, sense, shape, situation, space, state, status, street, stretch, style, system, technique, thoroughfare, track, trail, trait, usage, will, wish, wont.

wayfarer *n* bird of passage, globetrotter, gypsy, itinerant, journeyer, migrant, nomad, rover, traveller, trekker, voyager, walker, wanderer.
antonyms resident, stay-at-home.

wayfaring *adj* drifting, itinerant, journeying, migrant, nomadic, peripatetic, rambling, roving, travelling, voyaging, walking, wandering.
antonyms resident, stay-at-home.

waylay *v* accost, ambush, attack, buttonhole, catch, hold up, intercept, lie in wait for, seize, set upon, surprise.

way out *adj* advanced, amazing, avant-garde, bizarre, crazy, eccentric, excellent, experimental, extraordinary, fantastic, far out, freaky, great, marvellous, offbeat, outlandish, progressive, satisfying, tremendous, unconventional, unorthodox, unusual, weird, wild, wonderful.
antonym ordinary.

ways and means capability, capacity, capital, cash, funds, methods, procedure, reserves, resources, tools, way, wherewithal.

wayward *adj* capricious, changeable, contrary, contumacious, cross-grained, disobedient, erratic, fickle, flighty, froward, headstrong, inconstant, incorrigible, insubordinate, intractable, mulish, obdurate, obstinate, perverse, rebellious, refractory, self-willed, stubborn, undependable, ungovernable, unmanageable, unpredictable, unruly, uppity, wilful.
antonyms complaisant, good-natured.

weak *adj* anemic, asthenic, cowardly, debilitated, decayed, decrepit, defenceless, deficient, delicate, dilapidated, diluted, dim, dull, effete, enervated, exhausted, exposed, faint, faint-hearted, faltering, faulty, feeble, fibreless, flimsy, fragile, frail, half-baked, helpless, hollow, imperceptible, impotent, inadequate, incapable, inconclusive, indecisive, ineffective, ineffectual, infirm, insipid, invalid, irresolute, lacking, lame, languid, limp, low, muffled, muted, namby-pamby, pathetic, poor, powerless, puny, quiet, rickety, runny, shaky, shallow, sickly, slight, small, soft, spent, spineless, substandard, tasteless, tender, thin, timorous, toothless, unconvincing, unguarded, unprotected, unresisting, unsafe, unsatisfactory, unsound, unsteady, unstressed, unsubstantial, untenable, vulnerable, wanting, wasted, watery, weak-kneed, weakly, weak-minded, wishy-washy.

antonym strong.

weaken *v* abate, adulterate, attenuate, cut, debase, debilitate, deplete, depress, dilute, diminish, drap, droop, dwindle, ease up, enervate, enfeeble, exhaust, fade, fail, fatigue, flag, give way, go downhill, handicap, impair, impoverish, invalidate, lessen, lower, mitigate, moderate, reduce, sap, soften up, temper, thin, tire, undermine, wane, water, water down.

antonym strengthen.

weakening *n* abatement, attenuation, depletion, dilution, diminishment, drop, dwindling, easing, fading, failing, fatigue, flagging, impoverishment, lessening, lowering, moderation, reduction, waning.

antonym strengthening.

weakling *n* coward, doormat, milksop, milquetoast, mouse, sissy, underdog, underling, wimp.

antonyms hero, stalwart.

weakness *n* Achilles' heel, asthenia, blemish, debility, decrepitude, defect, deficiency, enervation, enfeeblement, failing, faintness, fault, feebleness, flaw, foible, fondness, fragility, frailty, imperfection, impotence, inclination, infirmity, irresolution, lack, liking, loophole, partiality, passion, penchant, powerlessness, predilection, proclivity, proneness, shortcoming, soft spot, soft underbelly, underbelly, vulnerability, weak point, weediness.

antonyms dislike, strength.

weal *n* cicatrice, cicatrix, contusion, mark, ridge, scar, streak, stripe, wale, welt, wound.

wealth *n* abundance, affluence, assets, big bucks, bounty, capital, cash, copiousness, cornucopia, dough, estate, fortune, fullness, fund(s), gold mine, golden calf, goods, lucre, mammon, mazuma, means, millions, money, moolah, opulence, pelf, plenitude, plenty, possessions, profusion, property, prosperity, reserves, resources, riches, richness, store, storehouse, substance, treasure, wherewithal.

antonym poverty.

wealthy *adj* affluent, comfortable, easy, filthy rich, flush, (living) in clover, loaded, moneyed, on easy street, opulent, prosperous, rich, rolling in it, well-heeled, well-off, well-to-do.

antonym poor.

wear *v* abrade, annoy, bear, bear up, carry, consume, corrode, deteriorate, display, don, drain, dress in, endure, enervate, erode, exasperate, exhibit, fatigue, fly, fray, frazzle, gnaw, grind, harass, have on, hold up, irk, last, pester, put on, rub, scrap, show, sport, stand up, tax, undermine, use, vex, waste, weaken, weary.

n abrasion, apparel, attire, attrition, clothes, corrosion, costume, damage, depreciation, deterioration, dress, durability, employment, erosion, friction, garb, garments, gear, habit, outfit, service, things, use, usefulness, utility, wear and tear.

wear down abrade, chip away at, consume, corrode, diminish, erode, exhaust, fatigue, grind down, lessen, macerate, overcome, reduce, rub away, undermine, wear out, weary.

wear off abate, abrade, decrease, diminish, disappear, dwindle, ebb, efface, fade, lessen, rub away, subside, wane, weaken.

wear out consume, deteriorate, enervate, erode, exhaust, fatigue, fray, impair, prostrate, rub through, sap, tire (out), tucker (out), use up, wear down, wear through, weary.

weariness *n* drowsiness, enervation, ennui, exhaustion, fatigue, languor, lassitude, lethargy, listlessness, prostration, sleepiness, tiredness.

antonym freshness.

wearing *adj* corrosive, erosive, exhausting, fatiguing, irksome, oppressive, taxing, tiresome, tiring, trying, wearisome.

antonym refreshing.

wearisome *adj* annoying, boring, bothersome, burdensome, dreary, dull, exasperating, exhausting, fatiguing, humdrum, irksome, monotonous, oppressive, pestilential, prolix, prosaic, protracted, tedious, troublesome, trying, vexatious, weariful, wearing, wearying.

antonym refreshing.

weary *adj* all in, arduous, aweary, beat, bored, burned out, bushed, dead beat, dead on one's feet, discontented, dog-tired, done in, drained, drooping, drowsy, enervated, exhausted, fagged, fatigued, fed up, flagging, impatient, indifferent, irksome, jaded, laborious, pooped, shot, sick, sick and tired, sleepy, spent, taxing, tired, tiresome, tiring, tuckered out, wearied, wearing, wearisome, wearying, whacked, worn out.

antonyms excited, fresh, lively.

v annoy, bore, bug, burden, debilitate, drain, droop, enervate, exasperate, fade, fag, fail, fatigue, irk, irritate, plague, sap, sicken, tax, tire, tire out, wear out.

wearying *adj* exhausting, fatiguing, taxing, tiring, trying, wearing, wearisome.

antonym refreshing.

weather *n* climate, conditions, rainfall, temperature.

v brave, come through, endure, expose, harden, live through, overcome, pull through, resist, ride out, rise above, season, stand, stick (it) out, suffer, surmount, survive, toughen, weather out, withstand.

antonym succumb.

weave *v* blend, braid, build, construct, contrive, create, crisscross, entwine, fabricate, fuse, incorporate, intercross, interdigitate, interlace, intermingle, intertwine, introduce, knit, make, mat, merge, plait, put together, spin, twist, unite, wind, zigzag.

web *n* interlacing, lattice, mesh, net, netting, network, screen, snare, tangle, texture, toils, trap, weave, webbing, weft, woof.

wed *v* ally, blend, coalesce, combine, commingle, espouse, fuse, get hitched, interweave, join, link, marry, merge, splice, tie the knot, unify, unite, yoke.
antonym divorce.

wedding *n* bridal, espousals, marriage, matrimony, nuptials.
antonym divorce.
adj bridal, hymeneal, marriage, matrimonial, nuptial.

wedge *n* block, chock, chunk, cleat, lump.
v block, cram, crowd, force, jam, lodge, pack, push, ram, squeeze, stuff, thrust.
antonyms dislodge, space out, take out.

wedlock *n* holy matrimony, marriage, matrimony, union.

wee *adj* diminutive, insignificant, Lilliputian, little, microscopic, midget, miniature, minuscule, minute, negligible, small, teensy, teensy-weensy, teeny, teeny-weeny, tiny.
antonym large.

weed *v* hoe.
weed out cull, discard, eliminate, eradicate, extirpate, get rid of, purge, remove, root out.
antonyms entrench, preserve.

weep *v* bawl, bemoan, bewail, blubber, boohoo, complain, cry, drip, exude, keen, lament, leak, moan, mourn, ooze, pour out, rain, shed tears, snivel, sob, ululate, whimper.
antonym rejoice.
n cry, lament, moan, snivel, sob.

weepy *adj* blubbering, crying, labile, lachrymose, sobbing, snivelling, tearful, teary, weeping.
antonym dry-eyed.

weigh *v* bear down, burden, carry weight, consider, contemplate, count, deliberate, evaluate, examine, give thought to, impress, matter, meditate on, mull over, oppress, ponder, prey, reflect on, study, tell, think over.
antonyms cut no ice, hearten.
weigh down afflict, bear down, burden, depress, distress, encumber, get down, load, oppress, overburden, overload, press down, tax, trouble, weigh upon, weight, worry.
antonyms hearten, lighten, refresh.
weigh up assess, chew over, cogitate, consider, contemplate, deliberate, discuss, examine, mull over, ponder, ruminate on, think over.

weight *n* authority, avoirdupois, ballast, burden, clout, consequence, consideration, efficacy, emphasis, force, gravity, heaviness, heft, impact, import, importance, impressiveness, influence, load, mass, millstone, moment, onus, oppression, persuasiveness, ponderance, power, preponderance, pressure, significance, strain, substance, value.
antonym lightness.
v affect, ballast, bias, burden, charge, encumber, freight, handicap, hold down, impede, influence, keep down, load, oppress, overburden, slant, sway, unbalance, weigh down.

antonym lighten.

weightless *adj* airy, imponderous, insubstantial, light, unsubstantial.
antonym heavy.

weighty *adj* backbreaking, burdensome, consequential, considerable, convincing, critical, crucial, crushing, cumbersome, demanding, dense, difficult, exacting, forcible, grave, heavy, hefty, important, leading, massive, momentous, onerous, oppressive, ponderous, portentous, respected, revered, serious, significant, solemn, substantial, taxing, worrisome, worrying.
antonyms trivial, unimportant.

weird *adj* bizarre, creepy, eerie, eldritch, freakish, ghostly, grotesque, mysterious, odd, outlandish, preternatural, queer, spooky, strange, supernatural, uncanny, unearthly, unnatural, witching.
antonym normal.

weirdo *n* crackpot, crank, eccentric, freak, fruitcake, loony, nut, oddball, queer fish.

welcome *adj* acceptable, accepted, agreeable, allowed, appreciated, delightful, desirable, entitled, free, gratifying, permitted, pleasant, pleasing, refreshing.
antonym unwelcome.
n acceptance, greeting, hospitality, reception, red carpet, salaam, salutation, shalom.
v accept, approve of, embrace, greet, hail, meet, receive, roll out the red carpet for.
antonyms reject, snub.

weld *v* bind, bond, cement, connect, fuse, join, link, seal, solder, unite.
antonym separate.
n bond, joint, seal, seam.

welfare *n* advantage, benefit, comfort, good, happiness, health, interest, profit, prosperity, satisfaction, success, weal, well-being.
antonym harm.

well[1] *adv* ably, abundantly, accurately, adeptly, adequately, admirably, agreeably, amply, approvingly, attentively, capitally, carefully, clearly, closely, comfortably, completely, conscientiously, considerably, correctly, deeply, easily, effectively, efficiently, expertly, fairly, famously, favourably, fittingly, flourishingly, fully, glowingly, graciously, greatly, happily, heartily, highly, intimately, justly, kindly, nicely, personally, pleasantly, possibly, proficiently, profoundly, properly, prosperously, readily, rightly, satisfactorily, skilfully, smoothly, splendidly, substantially, successfully, sufficiently, suitably, thoroughly, warmly.
antonym badly.
adj able-bodied, advisable, agreeable, A-one, bright, fine, fit, fitting, flourishing, fortunate, good, great, hale, happy, healthy, hearty, in fine fettle, in good health, lucky, on top of the world, pleasing, profitable, proper, prudent, right, robust, satisfactory, sound, strong, thriving, up to par, useful.
antonyms bad, ill.

well² *n* bore, cavity, fount, fountain, hole, mine, pit, pool, repository, shaft, source, spring, waterhole, wellspring.

v brim over, flood, flow, gush, jet, ooze, pour, rise, run, seep, spout, spring, spurt, stream, surge, swell, trickle.

well-balanced *adj* graceful, harmonious, judicious, level-headed, nutritious, proportional, rational, reasonable, sane, sensible, sober, sound, symmetrical, together, well-adjusted, well-proportioned.

antonym unbalanced.

well-being *n* comfort, contentment, good, happiness, health, prosperity, weal, welfare.

antonyms discomfort, harm.

well-bred *adj* chivalrous, civil, courteous, courtly, cultivated, cultured, gallant, genteel, gentlemanly, highborn, ladylike, mannerly, polished, polite, refined, urbane, well-brought-up, well-mannered.

antonym ill-bred.

well-deserved *adj* appropriate, condign, deserved, due, fitting, just, justified, meet, merited, rightful.

antonym undeserved.

well-disposed *adj* agreeable, amicable, favourable, friendly, sympathetic.

antonym ill-disposed.

well-dressed *adj* chic, dapper, natty, neat, smart, spiffy, spruce, tidy, trim, well-groomed.

antonym scruffy.

well-known¹ *adj* celebrated, famed, familiar, famous, illustrious, notable, noted, popular, prominent, renowned.

antonym unknown.

well-known² *adj* common, customary, established, everyday, familiar, household, traditional, usual.

well-off *adj* affluent, comfortable, flourishing, flush, fortunate, in the money, loaded, lucky, moneyed, prosperous, rich, successful, thriving, warm, wealthy, well-heeled, well-to-do.

antonym poor.

well-thought-of *adj* admired, esteemed, highly regarded, honoured, reputable, respected, revered, venerated, weighty.

antonym despised.

well-to-do *adj* affluent, comfortable, flush, loaded, moneyed, prosperous, rich, warm, wealthy, well-heeled, well-off.

antonym poor.

well-wisher *n* fan, supporter, sympathizer.

well-worn *adj* bromidic, commonplace, hackneyed, overused, stale, stereotyped, stock, threadbare, timeworn, tired, trite.

antonym original.

welsh *v* cheat, defraud, do, evade, renege, swindle, welch.

welt *n* cicatrice, cicatrix, contusion, mark, ridge, scar, streak, stripe, wale, weal, wound.

welter *v* billow, flounder, heave, lie, pitch, roll, soak, souse, splash, stumble, toss, tumble, wade, wallow, writhe.

n commotion, confusion, hodgepodge, jumble, mess, mishmash, muddle, tangle, web.

wet *adj* aqueous, boggy, clammy, damp, dank, dewy, drenched, dripping, drizzling, humid, misty, moist, moistened, muggy, pouring, raining, rainy, saturated, showery, silly, sloppy, soaked, soaking, sodden, soggy, sopping, soppy, soused, spongy, steamy, sweaty, teeming, watered, waterlogged, watery.

antonyms dry, resolute, strong.

n clamminess, condensation, damp, dampness, dew, drizzle, humidity, liquid, moistness, moisture, rain, rains, sap, seepage, shower, water, wetness.

antonym dryness.

v bedew, damp, dampen, dip, douse, drench, humidify, imbue, irrigate, moisten, saturate, sluice, soak, splash, spray, sprinkle, steep, souse, water.

antonym dry.

wet behind the ears callow, green, immature, inexperienced, innocent, naïve, new, raw, untrained.

antonym experienced.

wetness *n* clamminess, condensation, damp, dampness, dankness, dew, humidity, liquid, moisture, soddenness, sogginess, steam, sweat, water, wet.

antonym dryness.

whack¹ *v* bang, bash, beat, belabour, belt, biff, box, buffet, clobber, clout, cuff, hit, lambaste, rap, slap, slug, smack, sock, strike, thrash, thump, thwack, wallop, whale.

n attempt, bang, bash, belt, biff, blow, box, buffet, clout, crack, cuff, hit, rap, shot, slap, slug, smack, sock, stab, stroke, thump, thwack, try, turn, wallop, wham.

whack² *n* allotment, bit, cut, part, portion, quota, share.

wham *n* bang, bash, biff, crack, slam, smack, splat, thump, thwack, wallop, whack.

wharf *n* dock, dockyard, jetty, landing stage, marina, pier, quay.

wheedle *v* cajole, charm, coax, court, draw, entice, flatter, importune, inveigle, persuade.

antonym force.

wheel *n* circle, gyration, pirouette, pivot, revolution, roll, rotation, spin, turn, twirl, whirl.

v birl, circle, gyrate, orbit, pirouette, revolve, roll, rotate, spin, swing, swivel, turn, twirl, whirl.

wheeze¹ *v, n* cough, gasp, hiss, rasp, whistle, whiz(z).

wheeze² *n* anecdote, catch phrase, chestnut, crack, gag, joke, one-liner, practical joke, prank, slogan, story.

whereabouts *n* location, place, position, site, situation, vicinity.

wherewithal *n* capital, cash, funds, means, money, reserves, resources, supplies.

whet v acuminate, arouse, awaken, file, grind, hone, incite, increase, kindle, pique, prick, provoke, quicken, rouse, sharpen, stimulate, stir, strop, titillate.
antonyms blunt, dampen.

whiff n aroma, blast, blow, breath, draft, gale, gust, hint, odour, puff, reek, scent, smell, sniff, stench, stink.

whim n caprice, chimera, conceit, crank, craze, crotchet, fad, fancy, freak, humour, impulse, notion, quirk, urge, vagary, whimsy.

whimper v blubber, cry, mewl, moan, snivel, sob, weep, whine.
n moan, snivel, sob, whine.

whimsical adj capricious, chimeric(al), crotchety, curious, droll, eccentric, fanciful, fantastic(al), freakish, funny, mischievous, odd, peculiar, playful, quaint, queer, singular, unusual, waggish, weird.
antonym sensible.

whine n beef, bellyache, complaint, cry, fuss, gripe, grouch, grouse, grumble, moan, sob, wail, whimper.
v beef, bellyache, carp, complain, crab, cry, fuss, gripe, grouch, grouse, grumble, kvetch, moan, sob, wail, whimper.

whip v agitate, beat, best, birch, cane, castigate, clobber, compel, conquer, dart, dash, defeat, dive, drive, drub, flagellate, flash, flit, flog, flounce, fly, goad, hammer, hound, incite, jambok, jerk, knout, lash, leather, lick, outdo, overcome, overpower, overwhelm, paddle, prick, prod, provoke, pull, punish, push, rout, rush, scourge, shoot, snatch, spank, spur, stir, strap, switch, tan, tear, thrash, trounce, urge, whale, whisk, whop, worst.
n birch, bullwhip, cane, cat, cat-o'-nine-tails, crop, flagellum, horsewhip, knout, lash, paddle, quirt, rawhide, riding crop, scourge, switch, thong.
whip up agitate, arouse, excite, foment, incite, inflame, instigate, kindle, provoke, psych up, stir up, work up.
antonyms dampen, deter.

whipping n beating, belting, birching, caning, castigation, flagellation, flogging, hiding, lashing, leathering, paddling, pasting, spanking, tanning, thrashing.

whirl v birl, circle, gyrate, pirouette, pivot, reel, revolve, roll, rotate, spin, swirl, swivel, turn, twirl, twist, wheel.
n agitation, bustle, circle, commotion, confusion, daze, dither, flurry, giddiness, gyration, gyre, hubbub, hullabaloo, hurly-burly, merry-go-round, pirouette, reel, revolution, roll, rotation, round, series, spin, stir, succession, swirl, tumult, turn, twirl, twist, uproar, vortex, wheel, whorl.
antonym calm.

whirling adj gyrating, gyratory, pirouetting, pivoting, reeling, revolving, rotating, spinning, turning, twirling, twisting, vertiginous, vortical, vorticose, vortiginous, wheeling.
antonym stationary.

whirlpool n maelstrom, vortex, whirl.

whirlwind n cyclone, dust devil, snow devil, tornado, vortex, waterspout.
adj hasty, headlong, impetuous, impulsive, lightning, precipitate, quick, rapid, rash, short, speedy, split-second, swift.
antonyms deliberate, slow.

whisk v beat, brush, dart, dash, flick, fly, grab, hasten, hurry, race, rush, scoot, shoot, speed, sweep, swipe, tear, twitch, whip, wipe.

whisker n bristle, hair, hair's-breadth, vibrissa.

whisky n Barley corn, bourbon, John Barleycorn, malt, rye, Scotch, whiskey.

whisper v breathe, buzz, divulge, gossip, hint, hiss, insinuate, intimate, murmur, rustle, sigh, sough, susurrate, tittle-tattle.
antonym shout.
n breath, buzz, gossip, hint, hiss, innuendo, insinuation, murmur, report, rumour, rustle, shadow, sigh, sighing, soughing, soupçon, suggestion, suspicion, susurration, susurrus, swish, tinge, tittle-tattle, trace, undertone, whiff, word.
antonym roar.

whistle n call, cheep, chirp, siren, song, warble.
v call, cheep, chirp, pipe, sing, warble, wheeze.

whit n atom, bit, crumb, dash, drop, fragment, grain, hoot, iota, jot, little, mite, modicum, particle, piece, pinch, scrap, shred, speck, tittle, trace.
antonym lot.

white adj alabaster, ashen, bleached, bloodless, bright, canescent, clean, colourless, ghastly, ghostly, grey, grizzled, hoar, hoary, immaculate, incandescent, pale, pallid, pasty, silver, snowy, spotless, stainless, unsullied, wan, waxen, whey-faced.
antonyms black, dark, ruddy, unclean, unreliable.

white-collar adj clerical, executive, non-manual, office, professional, salaried.
antonyms blue-collar, manual.

whiten v blanch, bleach, blench, decolour, etiolate, fade, pale, whitewash.
antonyms blacken, colour, darken.

whitewash[1] n camouflage, concealment, cover-up, deception, extenuation.
antonym exposure.
v camouflage, conceal, cover up, euphemize, extenuate, gloss over, make light of, suppress.
antonym expose.

whitewash[2] v beat, best, blank, clobber, crush, drub, hammer, lick, paste, thrash, trounce, whale.

whittle v carve, cut, hew, pare, scrape, shape, shave, trim.
whittle away consume, destroy, diminish, eat away, erode, pare down, reduce, undermine, wear away.

whole adj complete, cured, entire, faultless, fit, flawless, full, good, hale, healed, healthy, in one piece, intact, integral, integrate, inviolate, mint, perfect, recovered, robust, sound, strong, total, unabbreviated, unabridged, unbroken, uncut, undamaged, undivided, unedited, unexpurgated, unharmed, unhurt, unimpaired, uninjured, unmutilated, unscathed, untouched, well.

antonyms damaged, ill, partial.

n aggregate, all, ensemble, entirety, entity, everything, fullness, Gestalt, lot, piece, total, totality, unit, unity.

antonym part.

on the whole all in all, all things considered, as a rule, by and large, for the most part, generally, generally speaking, in general, in the main, mostly, predominantly.

whole-hearted *adj* committed, complete, dedicated, determined, devoted, earnest, emphatic, enthusiastic, genuine, heartfelt, hearty, passionate, real, sincere, true, unfeigned, unqualified, unreserved, unstinting, warm, zealous.

antonym half-hearted.

wholesale *adj* broad, comprehensive, extensive, far-reaching, indiscriminate, mass, massive, sweeping, total, wide-ranging.

antonym partial.

adv comprehensively, en bloc, extensively, indiscriminately, massively, totally.

antonym partially.

wholesome *adj* advantageous, beneficial, clean, clean-cut, decent, edifying, exemplary, good, healthful, healthy, helpful, honourable, hygienic, improving, innocent, invigorating, moral, nice, nourishing, nutritious, propitious, pure, respectable, righteous, salubrious, salutary, sanitary, squeaky-clean, uplifting, virtuous, worthy.

antonym unwholesome.

wholly *adv* absolutely, all, altogether, completely, comprehensively, entirely, exclusively, fully, in toto, only, perfectly, solely, thoroughly, through and through, totally, utterly.

antonym partly.

whoop *v, n* cheer, cry, holler, hoop, hoot, hurrah, roar, scream, shout, shriek, yell.

whopper *n* colossus, fable, fabrication, fairy story, falsehood, giant, lie, monster, tall story, untruth.

whopping *adj* big, enormous, extraordinary, giant, gigantic, great, huge, large, mammoth, massive, mighty, monstrous, monumental, prodigious, staggering, tremendous, whacking.

antonym tiny.

whore *n* broad, call girl, concubine, courtesan, demimondaine, drab, harlot, hooker, hustler, mistress, prostitute, streetwalker, strumpet, succubus, tart, tramp, trollop, wench, working girl.

whorehouse *n* bagnio, bawdy-house, bordello, brothel, cathouse, house of ill repute.

whorl *n* coil, convolution, corkscrew, helix, spiral, turn, twist, vortex.

wicked *adj* abandoned, abominable, ace, acute, agonizing, amoral, arch, atrocious, awful, bad, bothersome, corrupt, debased, depraved, destructive, devilish, difficult, dissolute, distressing, dreadful, egregious, evil, fearful, fiendish, fierce, flagitious, foul, galling, guilty, harmful, heinous, immoral, impious, impish, incorrigible, inexpiable, iniquitous, injurious, intense, irreligious, masterful, masterly, mighty, mischievous, nasty, naughty, nefarious, offensive, painful, rascally, roguish, scandalous, severe, shameful, sinful, skilful, spiteful, terrible, troublesome, trying, ungodly, unpleasant, unprincipled, unrighteous, vicious, vile, villainous, worthless.

antonyms good, harmless, modest, upright.

wickedness *n* abomination, amorality, atrocity, corruption, corruptness, depravity, devilishness, dissoluteness, enormity, evil, fiendishness, foulness, heinousness, immorality, impiety, iniquity, shamefulness, sin, sinfulness, unrighteousness, vileness, villainy.

antonym uprightness.

wide *adj* ample, away, baggy, broad, capacious, commodious, comprehensive, diffuse, dilated, distant, distended, encyclopedic, expanded, expansive, extensive, far-reaching, full, general, immense, inclusive, large, latitudinous, loose, off, off-course, off-target, outspread, outstretched, remote, roomy, spacious, sweeping, vast.

antonyms limited, narrow.

adv aside, astray, off course, off target, off the mark, out.

antonym on target.

wide-awake *adj* alert, astute, aware, conscious, fully awake, heedful, keen, observant, on one's toes, on the alert, on the ball, on the qui vive, quick-witted, roused, sharp, vigilant, wakened, wary, watchful.

antonym asleep.

widely *adv* extensively, generally, ubiquitously, universally.

widen *v* broaden, dilate, distend, enlarge, expand, extend, open out, splay, spread, stretch.

antonym narrow.

wide-open *adj* defenceless, expansive, exposed, gaping, indeterminate, lax, open, outspread, outstretched, splayed, spread, susceptible, uncertain, undecided, unfortified, unpredictable, unprotected, unsettled, vulnerable, wide.

antonyms closed, narrow.

widespread *adj* broad, common, epidemic, extensive, far-flung, far-reaching, general, pervasive, popular, prevailing, prevalent, rife, sweeping, universal, unlimited, wholesale.

antonyms limited, uncommon.

width *n* amplitude, beam, breadth, compass, diameter, extent, girth, measure, range, reach, scope, span, thickness, wideness.

wield *v* apply, brandish, command, control, employ, exercise, exert, flourish, handle, have, hold, maintain, manage, manipulate, ply, possess, swing, use, utilize.

wife n better half, bride, consort, helpmate, helpmeet, mate, missis, missus, partner, spouse, woman.

antonym husband.

wig n fall, hairpiece, periwig, peruke, rug, switch, toupee.

wiggle v, n grind, jerk, jiggle, shake, shimmy, squirm, twist, twitch, wag, waggle, wriggle, writhe.

wild adj barbaric, barbarous, berserk, blustery, boisterous, brutish, chaotic, chimeric(al), choppy, crazed, crazy, daft, delirious, demented, desert, deserted, desolate, dishevelled, disordered, disorderly, eager, empty, enthusiastic, excited, extravagant, fantastic, feral, ferocious, fierce, flighty, foolhardy, foolish, frantic, free, frenzied, furious, giddy, godforsaken, howling, hysterical, ill-considered, impetuous, impracticable, imprudent, inaccurate, indigenous, intense, irrational, lawless, mad, madcap, maniacal, native, natural, noisy, nutty, off-the-wall, outrageous, potty, preposterous, primitive, rabid, raging, rash, raving, reckless, riotous, rough, rowdy, rude, savage, self-willed, tempestuous, tousled, trackless, turbulent, unbridled, unbroken, uncheated, uncivilized, uncontrollable, uncontrolled, uncultivated, undisciplined, undomesticated, unfettered, ungovernable, uninhabited, unjustified, unkempt, unmanageable, unpopulated, unpruned, unrestrained, unruly, unsubstantiated, untamed, untidy, uproarious, violent, virgin, wayward, woolly.

antonyms civilized, peaceful, sane, sensible, tame, unenthusiastic.

wilderness n clutter, confusion, congeries, desert, jumble, jungle, mass, maze, muddle, tangle, waste, wasteland, welter, wild, wilds.

wilds n bush, desert, far reaches, hinterland, outback, the back of beyond, the boondocks, the middle of nowhere, the sticks, wasteland, wilderness.

wile n artfulness, artifice, cheating, chicanery, contrivance, craft, craftiness, cunning, deceit, device, dodge, expedient, fraud, guile, hanky-panky, imposition, lure, manoeuvre, ploy, ruse, slyness, stratagem, subterfuge, trick, trickery.

antonym guilelessness.

wilful adj adamant, bloody-minded, bullheaded, conscious, deliberate, determined, dogged, froward, headstrong, inflexible, intended, intentional, intractable, intransigent, mulish, obdurate, obstinate, persistent, perverse, pigheaded, purposeful, refractory, self-willed, stubborn, uncompromising, unyielding, volitional, voluntary.

antonyms complaisant, good-natured, unwitting.

will n aim, attitude, choice, command, decision, declaration, decree, desire, determination, discretion, disposition, fancy, feeling, inclination, intention, mind, option, pleasure, preference, prerogative, purpose, resolution, resolve, testament, volition, will power, wish, wishes.

v bequeath, bid, cause, choose, command, confer, decree, desire, determine, devise, direct, dispose of, elect, give, leave, opt, ordain, order, pass on, resolve, transfer, want, wish.

willing adj agreeable, amenable, biddable, compliant, consenting, content, desirous, disposed, eager, enthusiastic, favourable, game, happy, inclined, nothing loath, pleased, prepared, ready, volitional.

antonym unwilling.

willingly adv by choice, cheerfully, eagerly, freely, gladly, happily, nothing loath, readily, unhesitatingly, voluntarily.

antonym unwillingly.

willingness n agreeableness, agreement, complaisance, compliance, consent, desire, disposition, enthusiasm, favour, inclination, volition, will, wish.

antonym unwillingness.

willowy adj graceful, gracile, limber, lissome, lithe, lithesome, slender, slim, supple, svelte, sylphlike.

antonym buxom.

willpower n determination, drive, grit, resolution, resolve, self-command, self-control, self-discipline, self-mastery, single-mindedness.

willy-nilly adv compulsorily, necessarily, of necessity, perforce.

wilt v atrophy, diminish, droop, dwindle, ebb, fade, fail, flag, flop, languish, melt away, sag, shrivel, sink, wane, weaken, wither.

antonym perk up.

wily adj arch, artful, astute, cagey, crafty, crooked, cunning, deceitful, deceptive, designing, foxy, guileful, intriguing, long-headed, Machiavellian, scheming, sharp, shifty, shrewd, slick, slippery, sly, streetwise, tricky, underhand, wileful.

antonym guileless.

wimp n clot, clown, drip, fool, jellyfish, jerk, milksop, milquetoast, nerd, sap, softy, weakling.

win v accomplish, achieve, acquire, attain, bag, capture, catch, collect, come away with, conquer, earn, gain, get, net, obtain, overcome, pick up, prevail, procure, receive, secure, succeed, sweep the board, triumph.

antonym lose.

n conquest, mastery, success, triumph, victory.

antonym defeat.

win over allure, attract, carry, charm, convert, convince, disarm, dissuade, induce, influence, persuade, prevail upon, sway, talk round.

wince v blench, cower, cringe, draw back, flinch, jerk, quail, recoil, shrink, start.

n cringe, flinch, jerk, start.

wind[1] n air, babble, blast, blather, bluster, boasting, breath, breeze, bull, chinook, clue, concert, current, cyclone, draft, flatulence, flatus, gab, gale, gas, gust, harmattan, hint, hot air, humbug, hurricane, idle talk, inkling, intimation, khamsin, mistral, monsoon, notice, puff, report, respiration, rumour, sirocco, suggestion, talk, tidings, tornado, vanity, warning, whisper, williwaw, windiness, zephyr.

wind[2] *v* bend, coil, curl, curve, deviate, encircle, furl, loop, meander, ramble, reel, roll, snake, spiral, turn, twine, twist, wreathe, zigzag.

n bend, curve, dogleg, meander, oxbow, turn, twist, zigzag.

wind down decline, diminish, dwindle, lessen, quieten down, reduce, relax, slacken off, slow, slow down, subside, unwind.

antonyms increase, tense.

wind up close, close down, coil, conclude, crank up, end, end one's days, end up, excite, finalize, find oneself, finish, finish up, hoist, liquidate, raise, settle, terminate, tighten, work up, wrap up.

antonym begin.

windbag *n* bigmouth, blatherer, blatherskite, boaster, bore, braggart, gasbag, gossip.

winded *adj* breathless, out of breath, out of puff, panting, pooped, puffed, puffed out.

antonym fresh.

windfall *n* bonanza, find, godsend, jackpot, manna, stroke of luck, treasure-trove.

windiness *n* breeziness, flatulence, gustiness, storminess.

antonym calm.

winding *adj* bending, circuitous, coiling, convoluted, crooked, curved, curving, curvy, indirect, labyrinthine, mazelike, meandering, roundabout, serpentine, sinuate(d), sinuous, snaky, spiral, tortuous, turning, twining, twisting.

antonym straight.

window *n* dormer, dormer window, glass, light, opening, oriel, pane, rose window, skylight, vent.

windy *adj* blowy, blustering, blustery, boastful, boisterous, bombastic, breezy, changeable, conceited, diffuse, empty, flatulent, garrulous, gassy, gusty, long-winded, loquacious, pompous, prolix, rambling, squally, stormy, tempestuous, turgid, verbose, wild, windswept, wordy.

antonyms calm, modest.

wine *n* Champagne, claret, ice wine, plonk, Port, rosé, Sherry, vinho verde, vino, vin ordinaire, vintage.

wine glass *n* flute, glass, goblet, schooner.

wing *n* adjunct, annex, arm, branch, circle, clique, coterie, extension, faction, flank, group, grouping, pinion, section, segment, set, side.

v clip, fleet, flit, fly, glide, graze, hasten, hit, hurry, move, nick, pass, race, soar, speed, travel, wound, zoom.

wink *v* bat, blink, flash, flicker, flutter, gleam, glimmer, glint, nictitate, sparkle, twinkle.

n blink, flash, flutter, gleam, glimmering, glint, hint, instant, jiffy, moment, nictation, nictitation, second, sparkle, split second, twinkle, twinkling.

winner *n* champ, champion, conqueror, daisy, first, humdinger, master, vanquisher, victor, wow.

antonym loser.

winning *adj* alluring, amiable, attractive, bewitching, captivating, charming, conquering, delectable, delightful, disarming, enchanting, endearing, engaging, fascinating, fetching, lovely, on top, pleasing, prepossessing, successful, sweet, taking, triumphant, unbeaten, undefeated, victorious, winsome.

antonyms losing, unappealing.

winnings *n* booty, gains, prize money, prize(s), proceeds, profits, spoils, takings, velvet.

antonym losses.

winnow *v* comb, cull, divide, fan, pan, part, rack, riddle, screen, select, separate, sift, sort out, waft, weed out.

winsome *adj* agreeable, alluring, amiable, attractive, bewitching, captivating, charming, comely, delectable, disarming, enchanting, endearing, engaging, fair, fascinating, fetching, graceful, pleasant, pleasing, prepossessing, pretty, sweet, taking, winning.

antonym unattractive.

wintry *adj* algid, arctic, bitter, bleak, cheerless, chilly, cold, desolate, dismal, freezing, frigid, frosty, frozen, gelid, glacial, harsh, hibernal, hiemal, ice-cold, icy, rimy, snowy, wintery.

antonym summery.

wipe *v* absterge, brush, clean, clear, dry, dust, erase, mop, remove, rub, smooth, sponge, swab, swipe, take away, take off.

n brush, lick, rub, swab.

wipe out abolish, annihilate, blot out, demolish, destroy, do away with, efface, eradicate, erase, expunge, exterminate, extirpate, massacre, obliterate, put paid to, raze.

antonym establish.

wire-pulling *n* clout, conspiring, influence, intrigue, Machiavellianism, manipulation, plotting, pull, scheming.

wiry *adj* bristly, lean, sinewy, spare, stiff, strong, tough.

antonym puny.

wisdom *n* astuteness, circumspection, comprehension, discernment, enlightenment, erudition, foresight, gnosis, intelligence, judgment, judiciousness, knowledge, learning, penetration, prudence, reason, sagacity, sapience, smarts, understanding.

antonym folly.

wise *adj* astute, aware, clever, discerning, enlightened, erudite, informed, intelligent, judicious, knowing, long-headed, long-sighted, perceptive, politic, prudent, rational, reasonable, sagacious, sage, sapient, sensible, shrewd, smart, sound, understanding, well-advised, well-informed.

antonym foolish.

wiseacre *n* know-all, know-it-all, smart aleck, smartass, wise guy.

wisecrack *n* barb, funny, gag, jest, jibe, joke, one-liner, quip, witticism.

wish *v* ask, aspire, bid, command, covet, crave, desire, direct, hanker, hope, hunger, instruct, long, need, order, request, require, thirst, want, whim, yearn, yen.

antonyms dislike, fear, refuse.

n aspiration, bidding, command, desire, hankering, hope, hunger, inclination, intention, liking, order, request, thirst, urge, voice, want, whim, will, yearning, yen.

antonyms dislike, fear, refusal.

wishy-washy *adj* bland, feeble, flat, indecisive, ineffective, ineffectual, insipid, jejune, namby-pamby, tasteless, thin, vacillating, vapid, watered-down, watery, weak.

antonym strong.

wisp *n* lock, piece, shred, snippet, strand, thread, twist.

wispy *adj* attenuate, attenuated, delicate, diaphanous, ethereal, faint, fine, flimsy, flyaway, fragile, frail, gossamer, insubstantial, light, thin, unsubstantial.

antonym substantial.

wistful *adj* contemplative, disconsolate, dreaming, dreamy, forlorn, longing, meditative, melancholy, mournful, musing, pensive, reflective, sad, soulful, thoughtful, wishful, yearning.

wit *n* acumen, badinage, banter, brains, card, cleverness, comedian, common sense, comprehension, conceit, cut-up, discernment, drollery, epigrammatist, facetiousness, farceur, fun, humorist, humour, ingenuity, insight, intellect, intelligence, jocularity, joker, judgment, levity, mind, perception, pleasantry, punster, quipster, raillery, reason, repartee, sense, understanding, wag, wisdom, wordplay.

antonyms seriousness, stupidity.

witch *n* enchantress, hag, hex, lamia, magician, necromancer, occultist, pythoness, sorceress, sortileger.

witchcraft *n* black magic, conjuration, divination, enchantment, fascination, hoodoo, incantation, magic, myalism, necromancy, occultism, sorcery, sortilege, spell, the occult, voodoo, witchery, witching, wizardry.

witch doctor *n* angakoq, magician, medicine man, shaman.

witch hunt *n* hounding, hue and cry, McCarthyism.

withdraw *v* abjure, absent oneself, back out, depart, disavow, disclaim, disengage, draw back, draw out, drop out, extract, fall back, go, go away, leave, pull back, pull out, recall, recant, remove, repair, rescind, retire, retract, retreat, revoke, secede, subtract, take away, take back, take off, unsay, waive.

antonyms advance, deposit, persist.

withdrawal *n* abjuration, departure, disavowal, disclaimer, disengagement, disinvestment, exit, exodus, extraction, recall, recantation, removal, repudiation, rescission, retirement, retraction, retreat, revocation, secession, waiver.

antonyms advance, deposit, persistence.

withdrawn *adj* aloof, detached, distant, introversive, introverted, introvertive, isolated, quiet, remote, reserved, retiring, shrinking, shy, silent, solitary, taciturn, uncommunicative, unforthcoming, unresponsive, unsociable.

antonym outgoing.

wither *v* abash, blast, blight, decay, decline, desiccate, disintegrate, droop, dry, fade, humiliate, languish, miff, mortify, perish, put down, shame, shrink, shrivel, snub, wane, waste, wilt.

antonyms boost, thrive.

wither away decrease, die, die off, disappear, dwindle, fade away, shrink, shrivel, wilt.

withering *adj* contemptuous, deadly, death-dealing, destructive, devastating, humiliating, killing, mortifying, murderous, scathing, scornful, searing, slaughterous, snubbing, wounding.

antonym supportive.

withhold *v* check, conceal, deduct, detain, hide, keep back, refuse, repress, reserve, resist, restrain, retain, sit on, suppress, suspend.

antonyms accord, give.

with it fashionable, groovy, hip, in, modern, modish, progressive, trendy, up-to-date, up-to-the-minute, vogue.

antonym out-of-date.

without
For phrases such as *without delay*, *without doubt*, see the first noun after *without*.

withstand *v* bear, brave, combat, confront, cope with, defy, endure, face, grapple with, hold off, hold one's ground, hold out, last out, oppose, put up with, resist, stand, stand fast, stand one's ground, stand up to, survive, take, take on, thwart, tolerate, weather.

antonyms collapse, yield.

witless *adj* crazy, cretinous, daft, dull, empty-headed, foolish, half-witted, idiotic, imbecilic, inane, moronic, obtuse, senseless, silly, stupid.

antonym intelligent.

witness *n* attester, attestor, beholder, bystander, corroborator, deponent, eyewitness, looker-on, observer, onlooker, passer-by, spectator, testifier, viewer, voucher, watcher, witnesser.

v attend, attest, bear out, bear witness, confirm, corroborate, countersign, depone, depose, endorse, look on, mark, note, notice, observe, perceive, see, sign, testify, view, watch.

wits *n* acumen, astuteness, brains, cleverness, comprehension, faculties, gumption, ingenuity, intelligence, judgment, marbles, mother wit, reason, sense, understanding.

antonym stupidity.

at one's wits' end at a loss, at the end of one's rope (or tether), baffled, bewildered, desperate, finished, in despair, in dire straits, lost, resourceless, stuck, stumped, tearing one's hair out.

witticism *n* bon mot, epigram, good one, jest, joke, mot, one-liner, pleasantry, pun, quip, repartee, riposte, sally.

witty *adj* amusing, brilliant, clever, comic, droll, epigrammatic, facetious, fanciful, funny, humorous, ingenious, jocular, lively, original, piquant, salty, sparkling, waggish, whimsical.

antonyms dull, unamusing.

wizard¹ *n* conjurer, druid, enchanter, mage, magician, magus, merlin, seer, thaumaturge.

wizard² *n* ace, adept, crackerjack, expert, genius, hotshot, maestro, master, prodigy, pundit, star, virtuoso, whiz.

antonym duffer.

adj ace, brilliant, crackerjack, enjoyable, fantastic, good, great, marvellous, sensational, smashing, super, superb, terrific, tiptop, tremendous, wonderful.

antonym rotten.

wizardry¹ *n* black magic, conjuration, divination, enchantment, hoodoo, incantation, magic, myalism, necromancy, occultism, sorcery, sortilege, the occult, voodoo, witchcraft, witchery, witching.

wizardry² *n* artistry, brilliance, command, excellence, expertise, genius, mastery, proficiency, skill, talent, virtuosity.

wizened *adj* dessicated, dried-up, dry, gnarled, lined, sere, shrivelled, shrunken, thin, withered, worn, wrinkled.

antonyms plump, smooth.

wobble *v* dither, dodder, fluctuate, heave, hesitate, oscillate, quake, quiver, rock, seesaw, shake, shilly-shally, sway, teeter, totter, tremble, vacillate, vibrate, waggle, waver.

n oscillation, quaking, rock, shake, tremble, tremor, unsteadiness, vibration.

wobbly *adj* doddering, rickety, shaky, teetering, tottering, unbalanced, uneven, unsafe, unstable, unsteady, wonky.

antonym stable.

woe *n* adversity, affliction, agony, anguish, burden, curse, dejection, depression, disaster, distress, dole, dolour, gloom, grief, hardship, heartache, heartbreak, melancholy, misery, misfortune, pain, sadness, sorrow, suffering, tears, trial, tribulation, trouble, unhappiness, wretchedness.

antonym joy.

woebegone *adj* blue, crestfallen, dejected, disconsolate, dispirited, doleful, down in the dumps (or mouth), downcast, downhearted, forlorn, gloomy, grief-stricken, hangdog, long-faced, lugubrious, miserable, mournful, sad, sorrowful, tearful, tear-stained, troubled, wretched.

antonym joyful.

woeful *adj* agonizing, appalling, awful, bad, calamitous, catastrophic, cruel, deplorable, disappointing, disastrous, disconsolate, disgraceful, distressing, doleful, dreadful, feeble, gloomy, grieving, grievous,

heartbreaking, heart-rending, heartsick, hopeless, inadequate, lamentable, lousy, mean, miserable, mournful, paltry, pathetic, piteous, pitiable, pitiful, plaintive, poor, rotten, sad, shocking, sorrowful, sorry, terrible, tragic, unhappy, wretched.

antonym joyful.

wolf *n* Casanova, dallier, Don Juan, ladies' man, lecher, Lothario, philanderer, Romeo, seducer, stud, womanizer.

wolf down bolt, cram, devour, gobble, gorge, gormandize, gulp, pack away, put away, scarf, scoff, shift, stuff.

antonym nibble.

wolf-man *n* lycanthrope, lycanthropist, werewolf.

woman¹ *n* adult, body, bride, crone, dame, daughter, dowager, female, girl, girlfriend, human, human being, individual, lady, lass, lover, maid, maiden, mate, matron, miss, mistress, partner, person, she, spinster, spouse, sweetheart, wife.

antonym man.

woman² *n* attendant, chambermaid, domestic, employee, follower, handmaid(en), hireling, housekeeper, lady in waiting, maid, maidservant, retainer, servant, subject, subordinate, vassal, worker.

womanhood *n* woman, womankind, women, womenfolk.

womanizer *n* Casanova, dallier, Don Juan, ladies' man, lecher, Lothario, philanderer, Romeo, seducer, stud, wolf.

womanizing *n* dalliance, lechery, philandering, venery, wenching, whoring.

womanly *adj* female, feminine, ladylike, matronly, mature, motherly.

antonym manly.

women *n* woman, womanhood, womankind, womenfolk.

wonder *n* admiration, amaze, amazement, astonishment, awe, bewilderment, curiosity, fascination, marvel, miracle, nonpareil, phenomenon, portent, prodigy, rarity, sight, spectacle, stupefaction, surprise, wonderment, wunderkind.

antonyms disinterest, ordinariness.

v ask oneself, boggle, cogitate, conjecture, deliberate, doubt, gape, gawk, inquire, marvel, meditate, muse, ponder, puzzle, query, question, reflect, speculate, stare, think.

wonderful *adj* ace, admirable, amazing, astonishing, astounding, awe-inspiring, awesome, brilliant, excellent, extraordinary, fabulous, fantastic, great, incredible, magnificent, marvellous, miraculous, odd, outstanding, peculiar, phenomenal, remarkable, sensational, smashing, staggering, startling, strange, stupendous, super, superb, surprising, terrific, tiptop, topping, tremendous, unheard-of, wizard, wondrous.

antonyms ordinary, rotten.

wonders *n* curiosities, magic, marvels, miracles, phenomena, prodigies, sights.

wonky *adj* amiss, askew, asquint, awry, groggy, infirm, shaky, skew(ed), unsound, unsteady, weak, wobbly, wrong.
antonyms stable, straight.

wont *adj* accustomed, given, habituated, used.
n custom, habit, practice, routine, rule, use, way.

wonted *adj* accustomed, common, conventional, customary, daily, familiar, frequent, habitual, normal, ordinary, regular, routine, usual.
antonyms unwonted, unusual.

woo *v* chase, court, cultivate, importune, look for, pay court to, pursue, seek, seek the hand of.

wood[1] *n* beams, boards, firewood, kindling, lathing, logs, lumber, planks, posts, siding, timber.

wood[2] *n* bluff, boscage, bosk, bush lot, coppice, copse, forest, grove, plantation, thicket, trees, woodland, woodlot, woods.

wooded *adj* bosky, forested, sylvan, timbered, tree-covered, woodsy, woody.
antonym open.

wooden *adj* awkward, blank, clumsy, colourless, deadpan, dull, emotionless, empty, expressionless, gauche, gawky, glassy, graceless, hollow, inelegant, inflexible, lifeless, ligneous, maladroit, mechanical, muffled, oaken, rigid, robotic, spiritless, stiff, timber, unbending, unemotional, ungainly, unresponsive, unyielding, vacant, woody, xyloid.
antonyms bright, lively.

woody *adj* bosky, forested, ligneous, sylvan, tree-covered, treed, wooded, xyloid.
antonym open.

wool *n* down, fleece, floccus, fluff, hair, yarn.

woolly *adj* blurred, chaotic, clouded, confused, disorganized, downy, fleecy, flocculent, fluffy, foggy, frizzly, frizzy, furry, fuzzy, hairy, hazy, ill-defined, indefinite, indistinct, laniferous, muddled, nebulous, shaggy, unclear, vague, woollen, woolly-haired.
n cardigan, guernsey, jersey, pullover, sweater.

woozy *adj* befuddled, bemused, blurred, confused, dazed, dizzy, fuddled, nauseated, pixilated, rocky, tipsy, unsteady, vague, wobbly, woolly.
antonyms alert, sober.

word *n* account, advice, affirmation, assertion, assurance, bidding, bulletin, chat, colloquy, command, commandment, comment, communication, communiqué, confab, confabulation, consultation, conversation, countersign, declaration, decree, discussion, dispatch, edict, expression, go-ahead, green light, guarantee, hint, information, intelligence, intimation, locution, mandate, message, news, notice, oath, order, parole, password, pledge, promise, remark, report, rescript, rumour, sign, signal, slogan, speech, talk, term, tête-à-tête, tidings, ukase, undertaking, unit, utterance, vow, war cry, watchword, will.

v couch, explain, express, phrase, put, say, write.
in a word briefly, concisely, in a nutshell, in short, in sum, in summary, succinctly, to be brief, to put it briefly, to sum up.

wordiness *n* bafflegab, garrulity, logorrhea, long-windedness, prolixity, verbal diarrhea, verbiage, verbosity, wordage.

wording *n* choice of words, diction, language, phraseology, phrasing, style, terminology, verbiage, words.

wordplay *n* paronomasia, punning, puns, repartee, wit, witticisms.

words *n* altercation, argument, bickering, contention, disagreement, dispute, libretto, lyrics, quarrel, row, run-in, set-to, squabble, text.

wordy *adj* diffuse, discursive, garrulous, long-winded, loquacious, phrasy, pleonastic, prolix, rambling, verbose, windy.
antonyms concise, laconic.

work *n* achievement, art, assignment, book, business, calling, chore, commission, composition, craft, creation, deed, doings, drudgery, duty, effort, elbow grease, employ, employment, exertion, grind, handiwork, industry, job, labour, line, livelihood, métier, occupation, oeuvre, office, opus, performance, piece, play, poem, production, profession, pursuit, service, skill, slog, stint, sweat, task, toil, trade, travail, undertaking, workload, workmanship.
antonyms hobby, play, rest.
v accomplish, achieve, act, arrange, beaver, bring about, bring off, cause, contrive, control, create, cultivate, dig, direct, drive, drudge, effect, encompass, execute, exploit, farm, fashion, fiddle, fix, force, form, function, go, grind, handle, implement, knead, labour, make, manage, manipulate, manoeuvre, moil, mould, move, operate, peg away, perform, ply, process, progress, pull off, run, shape, slave, slog, sweat, swing, till, toil, twitch, use, wield.
antonyms play, rest.
at work busy, on the job, working.
work on butter up, cajole, coax, influence, inveigle, nag, persuade, pester, soft-soap, sweet-talk, talk round, wheedle.
work out accomplish, achieve, add up to, amount to, arrange, attain, calculate, clear up, come out, come to, construct, contrive, crack, decode, develop, devise, drill, effect, elaborate, evolve, excogitate, exercise, exhaust, expiate, figure out, flourish, form, formulate, go, happen, pan out, plan, practise, prosper, put together, puzzle out, reach, resolve, result, solve, succeed, train, turn out, warm up, win, worry out.
work up agitate, animate, arouse, develop, elaborate, enkindle, enlarge, evolve, excite, expand, foment, generate, incite, increase, inflame, instigate, move, rouse, spur, stir up.

workable *adj* doable, feasible, possible, practicable, practical, realistic, viable.
antonyms impossible, unworkable.

workaday *adj* common, commonplace, dull, everyday, familiar, humdrum, labouring, mundane, ordinary, practical, prosaic, routine, run-of-the-mill, toiling, working.
antonym exciting.

worker *n* agent, artificer, artisan, craftsman, employee, hand, journeyman, labourer, mechanic, operative, operator, proletarian, staffer, tradesman, workhorse, workingman, working stiff, workingwoman.
antonym idler.

work force *n* employees, hands, labour, labour force, personnel, staff, workers.

working *n* action, functioning, manner, method, operation, routine, running.
adj active, employed, functioning, going, labouring, operational, operative, running.
antonyms idle, inoperative, retired, unemployed.

workings *n* diggings, excavations, mine, pit, quarry, shaft.

workmanlike *adj* adept, careful, efficient, expert, masterly, painstaking, professional, proficient, satisfactory, skilful, skilled, thorough.
antonym amateurish.

workmanship *n* art, artistry, craft, craftsmanship, execution, expertise, facture, finish, handicraft, handiwork, manufacture, skill, technique, work.

works[1] *n* factory, foundry, mill, plant, shop, workshop.

works[2] *n* actions, acts, books, canon, deeds, doings, oeuvre, output, plays, poetry, productions, writings.

works[3] *n* action, gearing, guts, innards, insides, machinery, mechanism, movement, (moving) parts, workings.

workshop *n* atelier, class, discussion group, factory, mill, plant, school, seminar, shop, studio, symposium, workroom.

world *n* age, area, class, creation, days, division, domain, earth, environment, epoch, era, existence, experience, field, globe, humanity, humankind, human race, kingdom, life, nature, people, period, planet, province, public, realm, society, sphere, star, system, times, universe.

worldly *adj* ambitious, avaricious, blasé, carnal, cosmopolitan, covetous, earthly, experienced, fleshly, grasping, greedy, knowing, lay, materialistic, mundane, physical, politic, profane, secular, selfish, sophisticated, sublunary, temporal, terrestrial, unspiritual, urbane, worldly-minded, worldly-wise.
antonym unworldly.

worldview *n* outlook, perspective, philosophy, take on life, understanding, Weltanschauung, value (or belief) system.

worldwide *adj* catholic, general, global, international, pandemic, ubiquitous, universal.
antonym local.

worn *adj* bromidic, careworn, clichéd, drawn, exhausted, fatigued, frayed, hackneyed, haggard, jaded, lined, pinched, played out,

ragged, shabby, shiny, spent, stock, tattered, tatty, threadbare, tired, trite, wearied, weary, wizened, worn-out.
antonyms fresh, new.

worn-out *adj* all in, beat, burned out, dead on one's feet, decrepit, dog-tired, done, done in, exhausted, fatigued, finished, fit to drop, frayed, moth-eaten, on its last legs, pooped, prostrate, ragged, shabby, spent, tattered, tatty, threadbare, tired, tired out, used, useless, weary, worn, zonked.
antonym fresh.

worried *adj* afraid, agonized, anxious, apprehensive, bothered, concerned, distracted, distraught, distressed, disturbed, fearful, fretful, frightened, ill at ease, nervous, on edge, overwrought, perturbed, strained, tense, tormented, troubled, uneasy, unquiet, upset.
antonyms calm, unconcerned, unworried.

worrisome *adj* agonizing, anxious, apprehensive, bothersome, disquieting, distressing, disturbing, fretful, frightening, insecure, irksome, jittery, nail-biting, nervous, perturbing, troublesome, uneasy, upsetting, vexing, worrying.
antonyms calm, reassuring, unworried.

worry *v* agonize, annoy, attack, badger, bite, bother, brood, disquiet, distress, disturb, faze, fret, gnaw at, go for, harass, harry, hassle, hector, importune, irritate, kill, lacerate, nag, perturb, pester, plague, savage, tantalize, tear, tease, torment, trouble, unsettle, upset, vex.
antonyms comfort, reassure.
n agitation, annoyance, anxiety, apprehension, care, concern, disturbance, fear, irritation, misery, misgiving, perplexity, pest, plague, problem, stew, tizzy, torment, trial, trouble, unease, vexation, woe, worriment.
antonyms comfort, reassurance.

worrying *adj* anxious, disquieting, distressing, disturbing, harassing, nail-biting, perturbing, troublesome, trying, uneasy, unsettling, upsetting, worrisome.
antonym reassuring.

worsen *v* aggravate, damage, decay, decline, degenerate, deteriorate, erode, exacerbate, go downhill, retrogress, sink, slide, slip, take a turn for the worse.
antonym improve.

worsening *n* aggravation, decay, decline, degeneration, deterioration, erosion, exacerbation, pejoration, retrogression, slide, slip.
antonym improvement.

worship *v* adore, adulate, deify, exalt, glorify, honour, idolatrize, idolize, laud, love, praise, pray to, respect, revere, reverence, venerate.
antonym despise.
n adoration, adulation, deification, devotion(s), exaltation, glorification, glory, homage, honour, laudation, love, praise, prayer(s), regard, respect, reverence.
antonym vilification.

worth *n* avail, benefit, cost, credit, desert(s), excellence, goodness, help, importance, merit,

price, quality, rate, significance, use, usefulness, utility, value, virtue, worthiness.
antonym worthlessness.

worthless *adj* abandoned, abject, base, beggarly, contemptible, cultus, depraved, despicable, futile, good-for-nothing, grotty, ignoble, ineffectual, insignificant, meaningless, miserable, no-account, no-good, no use, nugatory, paltry, pointless, poor, scabbed, scabby, screwy, trashy, trifling, trivial, unavailing, unimportant, unusable, useless, vain, valueless, vile, wretched.
antonym valuable.

worthwhile *adj* beneficial, constructive, gainful, good, helpful, justifiable, productive, profitable, useful, valuable, worthy.
antonym useless.

worthy *adj* admirable, appropriate, commendable, creditable, decent, dependable, deserving, estimable, excellent, fit, good, honest, honourable, laudable, meritorious, praiseworthy, reliable, reputable, respectable, righteous, suitable, upright, valuable, virtuous, worthwhile.
antonyms disreputable, unworthy.
n big cheese, big noise, big shot, bigwig, dignitary, eminence, luminary, name, notable, personage, somebody, VIP.

wound *n* anguish, blow, bruise, cut, damage, distress, gash, grief, harm, heartbreak, hurt, injury, insult, laceration, lesion, mortification, offence, pain, pang, scar, shock, slash, slight, stab, torment, torture, trauma.
v annoy, cut, cut to the quick, damage, distress, gash, grieve, harm, hit, hurt, injure, irritate, lacerate, mortify, offend, pain, pierce, shock, slash, slight, stab, sting, traumatize, wing.

wraith *n* apparition, ghost, phantom, revenant, shade, spectre, spirit, spook.

wrangle *n* altercation, argument, bickering, brawl, clash, contest, controversy, dispute, quarrel, row, rumpus, run-in, set-to, slanging match, spat, squabble, tiff, tussle.
antonym agreement.
v altercate, argue, bicker, brawl, contend, disagree, dispute, fall out, fight, have words, quarrel, row, scrap, squabble.
antonym agree.

wrap *v* absorb, bind, bundle up, cloak, cocoon, cover, encase, enclose, enfold, envelop, fold, immerse, muffle, pack, package, roll up, sheathe, shroud, surround, swathe, wind.
antonym unwrap.
n cape, cloak, mantle, pelisse, robe, shawl, stole.

wrap up adjourn, bring to a close, complete, conclude, end, finish off, knock off, package, pack up, parcel, quit, round off, terminate, wind up.
antonym begin.

wrapper *n* case, casing, cover, dust jacket, envelope, jacket, packaging, paper, sheath, sleeve, wrapping.

wrath *n* anger, bitterness, choler, displeasure, exasperation, fury, indignation, ire, irritation, passion, rage, resentment, spleen, temper.
antonyms calm, pleasure.

wrathful *adj* angry, bitter, displeased, enraged, furious, gusty, incensed, indignant, infuriated, irate, ireful, raging, wrathy, wroth.
antonyms calm, pleased.

wreak *v* bestow, bring about, carry out, cause, create, effect, execute, exercise, express, inflict, perpetrate, unleash, vent, visit, work.

wreath *n* band, chaplet, coronet, crown, festoon, garland, lei, loop, ring.

wreathe *v* adorn, coil, crown, encircle, enfold, entwine, envelop, enwrap, festoon, intertwine, interweave, snake, spiral, surround, swathe, twine, twist, weave, wind, wrap, writhe.

wreck *v* break, demolish, destroy, devastate, mar, play havoc with, ravage, ruin, shatter, smash, spoil, torpedo, total, trash, write off.
antonyms repair, save.
n derelict, desolation, destruction, devastation, disruption, hulk, mess, overthrow, ruin, ruination, shipwreck, smash-up, undoing, write-off.

wreckage *n* debris, flotsam, fragments, pieces, remains, rubble, ruin, wrack.

wrench *v* distort, force, jerk, pull, rip, sprain, strain, tear, tug, twist, wrest, wring, yank.
n ache, blow, jerk, pain, pang, pull, sadness, shock, sorrow, sprain, tear, tug, twist, upheaval, uprooting.

wrest *v* extract, force, pervert, pull, seize, strain, take, twist, win, wrench, wring.

wrestle *v* battle, combat, contend, contest, fight, grapple, scuffle, strive, struggle, tussle, vie.

wretch *n* blackguard, cad, caitiff, cur, good-for-nothing, miscreant, outcast, pauper, profligate, rapscallion, rascal, rat, rogue, rotter, ruffian, sad case, scoundrel, swine, vagabond, victim, villain, worm.

wretched *adj* abject, base, broken-hearted, caitiff, calamitous, cheerless, comfortless, contemptible, crestfallen, dejected, deplorable, depressed, despicable, disconsolate, distressed, doggone, doleful, downcast, forlorn, gloomy, grotty, hapless, hopeless, inferior, low, low-down, mean, melancholy, miserable, paltry, pathetic, pesky, pitiable, pitiful, poor, ratty, scurvy, shabby, shameful, sorry, unfortunate, unhappy, vile, woebegone, woeful, worthless.
antonyms excellent, happy.

wriggle *v* crawl, dodge, edge, extricate, jerk, jiggle, manoeuvre, sidle, slink, snake, sneak, squiggle, squirm, talk one's way out, turn, twist, wag, waggle, wiggle, worm, writhe, zigzag.
n jerk, jiggle, squirm, turn, twist, twitch, wag, waggle, wiggle.

wring *v* agonize, bleed, coerce, distress, exact, extort, extract, force, harrow, hurt, lacerate, mangle, pain, pierce, rack, rend, screw, shake down, squeeze, stab, tear, torment, torture, twist, wound, wrench, wrest.

wrinkle *n* corrugation, crease, crimp, crinkle, crow's foot, crumple, fold, furrow, gather, line, pucker, rumple.

v corrugate, crease, crimp, crinkle, crumple, fold, furrow, gather, line, pucker, ruck, rumple, shrivel.

wrinkled *adj* creased, crimped, crinkled, crinkly, crumpled, furrowed, puckered, ridged, rugose, rumpled, wrinkly.

antonym smooth.

writ *n* court order, decree, subpoena, summons.

write *v* compose, copy, correspond, create, draft, draw up, indite, inscribe, jot down, pen, record, scribble, scribe, set down, take down, tell, transcribe.

write off amortize, annul, cancel, cross out, dismiss, disregard, give up on, rule out, scrub.

writer *n* amanuensis, author, clerk, columnist, copyist, crime writer, diarist, dramatist, dramaturge, elegist, encomiast, epigrammatist, epistler, epistoler, essayist, farceur, fictionist, hack, journalist, librettist, littérateur, man (or woman) of letters, memoirist, novelist, panegyrist, penman, penpusher, penwoman, playwright, poet, scribbler, scribe, secretary.

writhe *v* coil, contort, jerk, squirm, struggle, thrash, thresh, toss, twist, wiggle, wreathe, wriggle.

writing *n* autography, belles-lettres, book, calligraphy, chirography, composition, document, hand, handwriting, letter, letters, literature, opus, penmanship, print, publication, scrawl, scribble, script, work.

written *adj* documentary, drawn up, recorded, set down, transcribed.

antonyms unwritten, verbal.

wrong *adj* abusive, amiss, askew, awry, bad, blameworthy, criminal, crooked, defective, dishonest, dishonourable, erroneous, evil, fallacious, false, faulty, felonious, funny, illegal, illicit, immoral, improper, inaccurate, inappropriate, inapt, incongruous, incorrect, indecorous, in error, infelicitous, iniquitous, inner, inside, in the wrong, inverse, malapropos, misinformed, mistaken, off base, off beam, off target, opposite, out, out of

commission, out of order, reprehensible, reverse, sinful, unacceptable, unbecoming, unconventional, under, undesirable, unethical, unfair, unfitting, unhappy, unjust, unlawful, unseemly, unsound, unsuitable, untrue, wicked, wide of the mark, wrongful.

antonym right.

adv amiss, askew, astray, awry, badly, erroneously, faultily, improperly, inaccurately, incorrectly, mistakenly, wrongly.

antonyms right, rightly.

n abuse, crime, error, grievance, immorality, inequity, infraction, infringement, iniquity, injury, injustice, misdeed, offence, sin, sinfulness, transgression, trespass, unfairness, wickedness, wrongdoing.

antonym right.

v abuse, cheat, discredit, dishonour, harm, hurt, ill-treat, ill-use, impose on, injure, malign, maltreat, misrepresent, mistreat, oppress, traduce.

in the wrong at fault, blameworthy, guilty, in error, mistaken, to blame.

antonym in the right.

wrongdoer *n* criminal, culprit, delinquent, evildoer, felon, lawbreaker, malefactor, miscreant, offender, sinner, transgressor, trespasser.

wrongdoing *n* crime, delinquency, error, evil, fault, felony, immorality, iniquity, maleficence, mischief, misdeed, offence, sin, sinfulness, transgression, wickedness.

wrongful *adj* blameworthy, criminal, dishonest, dishonourable, evil, felonious, illegal, illegitimate, illicit, immoral, improper, reprehensible, unethical, unfair, unjust, unlawful, wicked, wrong.

antonym rightful.

wrongly *adv* badly, by mistake, erroneously, inaccurately, incorrectly, in error, mistakenly.

antonym rightly.

wrought *adj* beaten, decorative, fashioned, hammered, made, manufactured, ornamental, ornamented, ornate, shaped.

wry *adj* askew, aslant, awry, contorted, crooked, deformed, distorted, droll, dry, ironic, mocking, perverse, sarcastic, sardonic, twisted, uneven, warped.

antonym straight.

XYZ

xenophobic *adj* ethnocentric, parochial, racist.
   antonyms hospitable, welcoming.

yak *v* blather, chatter, gab, gossip, jabber, jaw, prattle, quack, rattle on, run on, tattle, twaddle, yap.
   n blah, blather, chat, chinwag, confab, gossip, hot air, huddle, jaw, prattle, twaddle, yakety-yak, yap.

yank *v, n* haul, heave, jerk, pull, snatch, tug, wrench.

yap *v* babble, bark, blather, chatter, go on, gossip, jabber, jaw, prattle, talk, tattle, twaddle, yak, yammer, yelp, yip.

yard *n* clearing, compound, court, courtyard, enclosure, garden, grounds, quad, quadrangle.

yardstick *n* benchmark, comparison, criterion, gauge, guideline, measure, standard, touchstone.

yarn[1] *n* fibre, fingering, lisle, thread, wool.

yarn[2] *n* anecdote, bull, cock-and-bull story, fable, fabrication, megillah, song and dance, story, tale, tall story.

yawn *v* gape, open, split.

yawning *adj* cavernous, gaping, huge, vast, wide, wide-open.
   antonym narrow.

yearly *adj* annual, per annum, per year.
   adv annually, every year, once a year.

yearn for ache for, burn for, covet, crave, desire, hanker for, have one's heart set on, hunger for, itch for, long for, lust for, pine for, want, wish for, yen for.
   antonym dislike.

yell *v, n* bawl, bellow, cheer, holler, hoot, howl, roar, scream, screech, shout, shriek, squall, squeal, whoop, yelp, yowl.
   antonym whisper.

yellow *adj* flaxen, fulvous, gold, golden, lemon, primrose, saffron, vitelline, xanthic, xanthous.

yelp *v* bark, bay, cry, yap, yell, yip, yowl.
   n bark, cry, yap, yell, yip, yowl.

yen *n* craving, desire, hankering, hunger, itch, longing, lust, passion, thing, yearning.
   antonym dislike.

yes *interj* absolutely, affirmative, agreed, aye, certainly, definitely, exactly, indeed, of course, quite, right, roger, sure, uh-huh, undoubtedly, yea, yeah, yep, you bet, you said it.
   antonym no.

yes man *n* bootlicker, crawler, creature, flunkey, lackey, lickspittle, minion, sycophant, toadeater, toady.

yield[1] *v* afford, bear, bring forth, bring in, earn, fructify, fruit, furnish, generate, give, net, pay, produce, provide, return, supply.
   n crop, earnings, gate, harvest, income, output, proceeds, produce, product, profit, return, revenue, takings.

yield[2] *v* abandon, abdicate, accede, acquiesce, admit defeat, agree, allow, bow, capitulate, cave in, cede, comply, concede, consent, give, give in, give up, give way, go along with, grant, hand (over), knuckle under, part with, permit, relinquish, resign, resign oneself, submit, succumb, surrender, throw in the towel.
   antonym withstand.

yielding *adj* accommodating, acquiescent, amenable, biddable, complaisant, compliant, docile, easy, elastic, flexible, malleable, manageable, obedient, obliging, pliable, pliant, quaggy, resilient, soft, spongy, springy, submissive, supple, tractable, unresisting.
   antonyms obstinate, solid.

yoke *n* bond, bondage, burden, chain, collar, coupling, dominion, enslavement, harness, ligament, link, oppression, rule, service, servitude, slavery, subjugation, thralldom, tie.
   v bracket, connect, couple, enslave, harness, hitch, join, link, tie, unite.
   antonym unhitch.

yokel *n* boor, bucolic, bumpkin, clodhopper, cornball, country cousin, hayseed, hick, hillbilly, peasant, rustic.
   antonym sophisticate.

yore *n* bygone days, elder days, long ago, old, olden times, past times, yesteryear.

young *adj* adolescent, baby, callow, childish, cub, early, fledgling, green, growing, immature, infant, junior, juvenile, little, minor, new, recent, underage, unfledged, youthful.
   antonym old.
   n babies, brood, chicks, cubs, family, fledglings, issue, litter, little ones, offspring, progeny.

youngster *n* boy, girl, juvenile, kid, lad, lass, nipper, shaver, teenybopper, urchin, youth.

youth[1] *n* adolescence, boyhood, childhood, girlhood, immaturity, juvenescence, minority, pubescence, salad days, teens, the young, younger generation, young people.

antonym old age.

youth² *n* adolescent, boy, colt, ephebe, hobbledehoy, juvenile, kid, lad, shaver, stripling, swain, teenager, young man, youngster.

antonym senior (citizen).

youthful *adj* active, adolescent, boyish, callow, childish, ephebic, fresh, girlish, immature, inexperienced, juvenescent, juvenile, lively, pubescent, puerile, sprightly, spry, vigorous, vivacious, well-preserved, young.

antonym elderly.

yowl *v* bay, caterwaul, cry, howl, screech, squall, ululate, wail, yell, yelp.

n cry, howl, screech, wail, yell, yelp.

yucky *adj* beastly, dirty, disgusting, distasteful, filthy, foul, grotty, horrible, messy, mucky, revolting, saccharine, sentimental, sickly, squall, unpleasant.

antonym nice.

zany *adj* absurd, amusing, clownish, comical, crazy, daft, droll, eccentric, foolish, funny, goofy, kooky, loony, madcap, nutty, off the wall, screwy, wacky.

antonym serious.

n buffoon, card, clown, comedian, droll, fool, goof, jester, joker, kook, laugh, merry-andrew, nut, screwball, wag.

zeal *n* ardour, dedication, devotion, eagerness, earnestness, enthusiasm, fanaticism, fervency, fervour, fire, gusto, intensity, keenness, militancy, passion, spirit, verve, warmth, zest.

antonym apathy.

zealot *n* bigot, devotee, enthusiast, extremist, fanatic, fiend, freak, maniac, militant.

zealous *adj* ardent, burning, devoted, eager, earnest, enthusiastic, fanatical, fervent, fervid, fired, gung-ho, impassioned, keen, militant, passionate, rabid, spirited.

antonym apathetic.

zenith *n* acme, apex, apogee, climax, culmination, height, high point, meridian, peak, pinnacle, summit, the most, tip, top, vertex.

antonym nadir.

zero *n* bottom, cipher, duck, goose egg, love, nadir, nil, nothing, naught, nought, zilch, zip.

zero in on aim for, concentrate on, converge on, direct at, fix on, focus on, head for, home in on, level at, pinpoint, train on.

zest *n* appetite, charm, delectation, élan, enjoyment, flavour, gusto, interest, joie de vivre, keenness, kick, piquancy, pungency, relish, savour, smack, spice, tang, taste, zeal, zing.

antonyms apathy, dullness.

zigzag *v* meander, snake, wind, yaw.

adj meandering, serpentine, sinuous, winding, zigzagging.

antonym straight.

zing *n* animation, brio, dash, élan, energy, go, joie de vivre, life, liveliness, oomph, pizazz, sparkle, spirit, vigour, vitality, zest, zip.

antonym listlessness.

zip *n* brio, drive, élan, energy, enthusiasm, get-up-and-go, go, gusto, life, liveliness, oomph, pep, pizzazz, punch, sparkle, spirit, verve, vigour, vim, vitality, zest, zing.

antonym listlessness.

v dash, flash, fly, gallop, hurry, race, rush, scoot, shoot, speed, tear, whiz, whoosh, zoom.

zone *n* area, belt, district, region, section, sector, sphere, stratum, territory, tract.

zoo *n* animal park, aquarium, aviary, menagerie, safari park, wildlife reserve.

Appendixes

Appendix I: classified word lists

air and space vehicles   721
alphabets, writing systems   721
anatomical   721
architecture and building   722
art   723
astronomy   724
baby animals   724
cat breeds   725
cattle breeds   725
cheeses   725
chemical elements   725
cloths, fabrics   726
collective nouns   727
collectors, enthusiasts   727
colours   727
confections, dishes, foods   728
dances   729
dog breeds   730
First Nations   730

furniture, furnishings   731
garments, vestments   731
herbs, spices   733
jewels, gems   734
languages, language families   734
literature and logic   735
minerals   735
musical instruments   736
poetry   737
public offices in Canada   738
ranks in armed forces   738
titles of rulers and nobles   738
tools and hardware   739
units of measurement   740
vehicles   741
vessels, ships   741
zodiac signs   742

Appendix II: words listed by suffix

-archy   743
-ast   743
-cide   743
-cracy   743
-crat   743
-cratic   743
-culture   743
-cyte   743
-dom   743
-ferous   744
-gamy   744
-genesis   744
-genic   744
-gon   744

-gram   744
-graph   745
-graphy   745
-hedron, -hedral   745
-hood   746
-iac   746
-iasis   746
-iatric   746
-ician   746
-ics   746
-iform   747
-ism   747
-itis   751
-latry   752

-logous   752
-logue   752
-logy   752
-lysis   753
-lytic   753
-mancy   753
-mania   753
-meter   753
-metry   754
-monger   754
-morphic   754
-onym   754
-osis   754
-pathy   755

-phagous   755
-phobia   755
-phone   755
-phonic   756
-phyte   756
-saurus   756
-scope   756
-sophy   756
-stat   756
-therapy   756
-tomy   756
-urgy   757
-vorous   757

Appendixes

Appendix I: classified word lists

Appendix II: words listed by suffix

Appendix I

Classified word lists

air and space vehicles

aerodrome
aerostat
air ambulance
airbus
aircraft
airliner
airplane
airship
air taxi
amphibian
autogyro
balloon
biplane
blimp
bomber
cable car
canard
chopper
Comsat
convertiplane
crate
deltawing
dirigible
dive bomber
fanjet
fighter
flying boat
flying saucer
flying wing
glider
gondola
gyroplane
helicopter
hot air balloon
Hovercraft
hydrofoil
hydroplane
interceptor
jet
jetliner
jet plane
LEM
lunar lander
microlight
module
monoplane
plane
rocket
rocketsonde
sailplane
satellite
seaplane
sonde

space probe
spaceship
space shuttle
space station
spacecraft
spitfire
sputnik
step rocket
STOL
swing-wing
tanker
tractor
triplane
troop carrier
turbojet
two-seater
UFO
warplane
zeppelin

alphabets, writing systems

Arabic
Bengali
Chalcidian alphabet
cuneiform
Cyrillic
Devanagari
finger alphabet
futhork
Glagol
Glossic
Greek
Gujarati
Gurmukhi
hieroglyphs
hiragana
ideograms
kana
katakana
Kufic
Linear A
Linear B
logograph
nagari
naskhi
ogham
Oriya
pictograph
Punjabi
Roman
runic
syllabary
Tamil
Telugu

anatomical

abductor
acromion
adductor
alveolar ridge
alvine
areola
astragalus
aural
auricular
axilla
biceps
blade
bone
brachial
bregma
buccal
calcaneus
cardiac
carpus
cartilage
celiac
cephalic
cerebral
cervical
cervix
cholecyst
clavicle
coccyx
collarbone
colon
concha
coracoid
cornea
crural
cuboid
cuneiform
deltoid muscle
dental
derma
dermal
dermis
diaphragm
diencephalon
digital
diverticulum
dorsum
duodenal
duodenum
dura mater
earlap
elbow
enarthrosis
encephalic
encephalon

endocardial
endocardium
endocrine
epencephalic
epencephalon
epidermal
epidermis
epididymis
epigastrium
epiglottal
epiglottis
epithelium
erythrocyte
esophagus
ethmoid
extensor
Fallopian tubes
false rib
femur
fenestra
fibula
flexor
floating rib
fontanel
foramen magnum
forearm
forebrain
forefinger
foreskin
fovea
frenum
frontal
fundus
funny bone
gastric
gastrocnemius
gastro-intestinal
genial
genitalia
genu
gingival
glabella
glabellar
gladiolus
glossa
glossal
glottal
glottis
gluteus
gnathic
gristle
groin
gular
gullet
guttural
hallux

anatomical *(cont.)*
ham
hamate bone
hamstring
helix
hemal
hematic
hepatic
hindbrain
hipbone
hip joint
humeral
humerus
hymen
hyoid
hypogastrium
hypothalamus
iliac
ilium
incus
inguinal
innominate bone
intercostal
ischium
jugular
labial
lachrymal
laryngopharynx
larynx
leucocyte
ligament
lumbar
malar
malleus
mammary
mammilla
mammillary
mandible
mandibular
manubrium
mastoid
maxilla
maxillary
membrane
metacarpal
metatarsal
mons pubis
mons veneris
muscle
nasal
nates
navicular
neural
occipital
occiput
occlusion
ocular
odontoid
optical
oral
orbit
origin
otic
palatal
parietal

parotid
patella
patellar
pectoral
pedal
pelvic girdle
pelvis
perineum
periosteum
peritoneum
peroneal
phalanges
pharynx
plantar
prefrontal
premaxilla
premaxillary
prepuce
pronator
pubis
pudenda
pulmonary
quadriceps
radius
rectum
renal
retina
rhomboideus
rib
sacroiliac
sacrum
scapula
sciatic nerve
sclera
shoulder blade
skull
sphenoid
sphincter
spine
stapes
sternum
stirrup bone
supinator
sural
talus
tarsal
temporal
tendon
thigh bone
tibia
trapezium
trapezius
trapezoid
triceps
triquetrous
turbinate
tympanic
ulna
umbilicus
uterus
uvula
vagus
vas deferens
velum
vermiform appendix

vermiform process
vertebra
vertebrae
vertex
vesica
voice box
vomer
vulva
windpipe
wisdom tooth
womb
wrist
xiphisternum
xiphoid
zygapophysis
zygoma
zygomatic

architecture and building

abacus
abutment
acrolith
alcove
annulet
anta
antefix
arcade
architrave
ashlar
astragal
atrium
baguette
banderole
bargeboard
barge couple
barge course
baroque
bastion
battlement
bema
brattice
canephoros
cantilever
cartouche
caryatid
Catherine wheel
cavetto
centring
cinquefoil
Composite
concha
corbel
Corinthian
cornerstone
cornice
corona
crenel
crocket
dado
decorated
den
dentil
diaper

dinette
distyle
ditriglyph
dodecastyle
dogleg
dogtooth
dome
domed
domical
donjon
Doric
dormer
double glazing
drawbridge
drawing room
dressing
drip
dripstone
-drome
dromic
drum
dry-stone
duplex
Early English
eaves
echinus
Edwardian
egg and anchor
egg and dart
egg and tongue
egg crate
el
elevation
Elizabethan
embattlement
embrasure
engrail
entresol
epistyle
exedra
extrados
façade
fanlight
fan tracery
fan vaulting
fascia
fastigium
fenestella
fenestra
fenestral
fenestration
festoon
fillet
finial
flamboyant
flèche
fleuron
floor plan
flying buttress
foliation
footer
fornicate
fortalice
French window
frieze

art (cont.)
vitrine
volute
vorticism
woodblock
woodcarving
woodcut
wood engraving
xoanon
zoomorphic

astronomy
aberration
accretion disk
airglow
albedo
alignment
Alpha
altitude
anomaly
aphelion
apoapsis
apocynthion
apogalacticon
apogee
apolune
apsis
armillary sphere
ascending node
asterism
asteroid
asteroid belt
astrolabe
astronomical latitude
astronomical unit
Auger shower
aurora
axis
azimuth
Baily's beads
Beta
big bang
binary star
black hole
bolide
celestial equator
celestial meridian
celestial pole
Cepheid variable
Chandler wobble
chondrite
chromosphere
circumpolar star
cislunar
coelostat
colure
comet
coma
conjunction
constellation
Copernican system
corona
cosmic censorship
cosmic dust

cosmic noise
cosmic rays
cosmic year
cusp
declination
descending node
earthshine
eclipse
ecliptic
elongation
ephemeris
epicycle
equinox
escape velocity
ether
event horizon
exobiology
faculae
finder
fireball
Fraunhofer lines
fundamental star
galactic equator
galactic pole
galaxy
gas giant
gegenschein
geocentric
geostationary
giant
gravitational lens
gravitational wave
great year
halo
heliacal rising or
  setting
heliocentric
hour angle
hour circle
Hubble effect
Hubble's constant
Hubble's law
Hubble telescope
intergalactic medium
interplanetary
  medium
interstellar medium
Kepler's laws
Lagrangian points
Leonids
libration
light pollution
light year
limb
lunar calendar
lunation
magnetic field
magnetic storm
magnetosphere
magnitude
mare
mascon
mean sun
mean solar time
metagalaxy

meteor
meteorite
meteoroid
meteor shower
micrometeorite
Milky Way
moonquake
multiple star
nadir
nebula
nebular hypothesis
neutron star
nova
nutation
obliquity
occultation
opposition
optical double
orbit
orrery
parallax
parking orbit
parsec
penumbra
periapsis
pericynthion
perigalacticon
perihelion
perilune
perturbation
phase angle
photosphere
plage
planet
planetesimal
planetoid
planet X
planisphere
Platonic year
Pleiades
polar distance
precession
primary
prominence
Ptolemaic system
pulsar
quadrant
quadrature
quasar
radiant
radio galaxy
radio source
radio telescope
red giant
red shift
reflecting telescope
refracting telescope
regression
retrograde motion
revolution
right ascension
rille
Roche limit
rotation
saros

satellite
scintillation
secular acceleration
selenography
selenology
semidiameter
Seyfert galaxy
sidereal period
sidereal time
solar constant
solar cycle
solar flare
solar system
solar unit
solar wind
solstice
spectral type
spectroheliogram
spicule
spinar
spiral galaxy
stardust
steady-state theory
stellar wind
subdwarf
subgiant
substellar
sunspot
supergiant
superlunary
supernova
synodical period
syzygy
telemetry
telespectroscope
telluric lines
terminator
transit
tropical year
umbra
uranography
uranometry
Van Allen belt
variable star
variation
vertical circle
white dwarf
ylem
zenith
Zodiac
Zodiacal light

baby animals
batling
calf
chick
colt
craneling
cub
cygnet
duckling
eaglet
eyas
fawn

baby animals *(cont.)*

foal
gosling
gum baby
infant
joey
kid
kit
kitten
lamb
owlet
peachick
piglet
porcupette
poult
pup
shearling
shoat
squab
whelp
whitecoat

cat breeds

Abyssinian
American shorthair
American wirehair
Balinese
Birman
Bombay
British Angora
British shorthair
Burmese
Chantilly
Chartreux
Colourpoint shorthair
Cornish Rex
Cymric
Devon Rex
Domestic shorthair
Egyptian mau
Exotic shorthair
Havana brown
Himalayan
Japanese bobtail
Javanese
Kashmir
Korat
Maine Coon
Manx
Norwegian Forest
Cat
Oriental shorthair
Oriental Spotted
Tabby
Persian
Ragdoll
Russian Blue
Scottish Fold
Selkirk Rex
Siamese
Somali
Tiffany
Tonkinese
Turkish Angora

cattle breeds

Afrikander
Alderney
Angus
Australian Ilawarra
Shorthorn
Ayrshire
Blonde d'Aquitaine
Brahman
Brown Swiss
cattalo
Charolais
Chianina
Devon
Dexter
Durham
Friesian
Galloway
Guernsey
Hereford
Highland
Holstein
Jersey
Kerry
Latvian
Limousin
longhorn
Luing
Red Poll
Santa Gertrudis
shorthorn
Simmenthal
Ukrainian

cheeses

Bel Paese
Bleu d'Auvergne
Brick
Brie
brynza
Caerphilly
Camembert
Cheddar
Cheshire
Chevrotin
Colby
cook cheese
cottage cheese
Danish blue
Derby
Edam
egg cheese
Eierkäse
Emmentaler
Esrom
Farmer
Feta
Fynbo
Gjetost
Gloucester
Gorgonzola
Gouda
Gruyère
Havarti

Herrgårdsost
Herve
Huntsman
Hushållsost
Jarlsberg
Killarney
Kochkäse
Lancashire
Leicester
Limburger
marble
mascarpone
Monterey Jack
mozzarella
Munster
Neufchâtel
Oka
Parmesan
Pont-l'Eveque
Port Salut
Provolone
Raclette
ricotta
Romano
Roquefort
sage Derby
Samsø
sapsago
Schmierkäse
Stilton
Tilsiter
Wensleydale

chemical elements

actinium
aluminum
americium
antimony
argon
arsenic
astatine
barium
berkelium
beryllium
bismuth
boron
bromine
cadmium
calcium
californium
carbon
cerium
cesium
chlorine
chromium
cobalt
copper
curium
dysprosium
einsteinium
erbium
europium
fermium
fluorine

francium
gadolinium
gallium
germanium
gold
hafnium
hahnium
helium
holmium
hydrogen
indium
iodine
iridium
iron
krypton
kurchatovium
lanthanum
lawrencium
lead
lithium
lutetium
magnesium
manganese
mendelevium
mercury
molybdenum
neodymium
neon
neptunium
nickel
niobium
nitrogen
nobelium
osmium
oxygen
palladium
phosphorus
platinum
plutonium
polonium
potassium
praseodymium
promethium
protoactinium
radium
radon
rhenium
rhodium
rubidium
ruthenium
rutherfordium
samarium
scandium
selenium
silicon
silver
sodium
strontium
sulphur
tantalum
technetium
tellurium
terbium
thallium
thorium

chemical elements
(cont.)
thulium
tin
titanium
tungsten
unnilemium
unnilhexium
unniloctium
unnilpentium
unnilquadium
unnilseptium
uranium
vanadium
xenon
ytterbium
yttrium
zinc
zirconium

cloths, fabrics

abaca
acid-washed
airplane cloth
alpaca
angora
armure
astrakhan
bagging
Balbriggan
baldachin
barathea
barege
batiste
batting
bayadère
bearskin
beaver
beige
bengaline
berber
blanket cloth
blonde lace
bobbinet
bobbin lace
bombazine
bottomweight
bouclé
broadcloth
brocade
brocatelle
broché
brushed
Brussels lace
buckram
buckskin
budge
buff
bunting
Burberry
burlap
byssus
caddis
calamanco

calico
cambric
camel hair
camlet
candlewick
canvas
carpeting
cashmere
cassimere
challis
chambray
chamois
chantilly (lace)
charmeuse
cheesecloth
chenille
chino
chintz
corduroy
cotton
crepe
crinkle
Dacron
damask
delaine
denim
dhoti
dhurrie
diamanté
diaper
dimity
doeskin
doily
dornick
drab
drapery
dreadnought
drill
drugget
duchesse lace
duck
duffel
dungaree
duvetyn
ecru
eyelet
faille
fearnought
felt
ferret
filet
flannel
flannelette
fleece
foulard
frieze
fustian
gabardine
galatea
galloon
gauze
gazar
georgette
gingham
Gobelin

grass cloth
greige
grenadine
grogram
grosgrain
guipure
gunny
haircloth
herringbone
Hessian
hodden
holland
homespun
hopsacking
horsehair
hound's tooth
huckaback
jaconet
jacquard
jean
jersey
karakul
kersey
kerseymere
khaddar
khaki
kid
kidskin
kilt
lamé
lampas
lawn
leather
leatherette
leghorn
leno
levantine
linen
linsey
linsey-woolsey
llama
loden
longcloth
Lurex
lustre
lutestring
Lycra
mackintosh
madras
marquisette
Mechlin
melton
merino
Mexican
mohair
moire
moleskin
monk's cloth
moreen
morocco
mousseline
mousseline de laine
mousseline de soie
mull
mulmul

mungo
muslin
nainsook
nankeen
ninon
noil
nylon
oilcloth
organdie
organza
organzine
Orlon
osnaburg
paduasoy
paisley
panne
parachute cloth
parramatta
peau de soie
percale
percaline
Petersham
pile
piña cloth
pinstripe
piqué
plaid
plush
pointelle
point-lace
polycotton
polyester
pongee
poplin
prunella
purple
quilting
ramie
ratiné
ratteen
rayon
rep
roan
russet
sackcloth
sacking
sailcloth
samite
sarcenet
sateen
satin
satinette
saxony
scarlet
scrim
seersucker
sendal
serge
shagreen
shalloon
shantung
sharkskin
sheepskin
sheer
sheeting

cloths, fabrics
(cont.)

Shetland wool
shoddy
silesia
silk
split
spun silk
stammel
stone-washed
suede
suiting
surah
swan's-down
swanskin
tabby
tableclothing
taffeta
tarlatan
tarpaulin
tartan
tattersall
tatting
terry
Terylene
ticking
tiffany
toile
torchon lace
towelling
tram
tricot
tulle
tussah
tweed
twill
union
Valenciennes
veiling
Velcro
velour
velure
velvet
velveteen
vicuña
viscose
viyella
voile
waistcoating
webbing
whipcord
wigan
winceyette
wire gauze
woolsey
worcester
worsted
zephyr

collective nouns

army of frogs
bale of turtles
bed of snakes
bevy of deer
brood of chickens
building of rooks
business of ferrets
cast of hawks
cete of badgers
charm of goldfinches
chattering of choughs
clamour of rooks
clowder of cats
colony of ants
company of widgeon
convocation of eagles
coterie of prairie dogs
covert of coots
covey of partridges
crash of rhinoceroses
descent of
    woodpeckers
down of hares
drag of squirrels
drift of swine
drove of cattle
dule of doves
exaltation of larks
fall of woodcock
fesnyng of ferrets
flight of swallows
gaggle of geese
gam of whales
gang of elks
grist of bees
host of sparrows
hover of trout
husk of hares
kennel of dogs
kindle of kittens
leap of leopards
murder of crows
murmuration of
    starlings
muster of peacocks
mute of hounds
nide of pheasants
pace of asses
parliament of owls
pod of seals
pride of lions
rafter of turkeys
rag of colts
richness of martens
run of poultry
school of porpoises
shoal of roaches
siege of herons
skein of geese
skulk of foxes
sloth of bears
smack of jellyfish
sounder of boars
spring of teals
stand of plovers
stud of mares
swarm of eels
team of ducks
tok of capercaillies

troop of kangaroos
troop of monkeys
unkindness of ravens
walk of snipe
watch of nightingales

collectors, enthusiasts

abolitionist
ailurophile
angelologist
antiquary
antivaccinationist
antivivisectionist
apiculturist
arachnologist
arctophile
audiophile
balletomane
bibliomane
bibliophage
bibliophile
birder
caffeinophile
campanologist
canophile
cartophile
chirographer
chocaholic
cinephile
coleopterist
conservationist
Dantophilist
deltiologist
discophile
dog fancier
ecclesiologist
egger
entomologist
environmentalist
ephemerist
epicure
ex-librist
feminist
gastronome
gemmologist
gourmet
herpetologist
hippophile
homeopathist
iconophile
incunabulist
jazzophile
lepidoptertist
medallist
monarchist
myrmecologist
numismatist
oenophile
ophiophile
orchidomaniac
ornithologist
orthoepist
orthographist

palindromophile
pangrammatist
paronomasiast
pedant
perfectionist
philanthropist
philatelist
phillumenist
philogynist
philologist
philologue
prohibitionist
pteridophilist
reincarnationist
scripophile
sericulturist
speleologist
stegophile
supernaturalist
timbrologist
timbromaniac
timbrophile
toxophilite
tulipomane
tulipomaniac
ufologist
ultramontanist
vexillologist
virtuoso
vulcanologist
workaholic
xenophile
zoophile

colours

alabaster
antique
aquamarine
argent
ash
aurora
avocado
azure
bay
Berlin blue
beryl
bilious
biscuit
black
blood red
blue
bone
bottle green
brick red
(British) racing green
bronze
brown
buff
burgundy
canary
caramel
cardinal
carmine
carnation

colours *(cont.)*

celadon
cerise
cerulean
cervine
cesious
champagne
charcoal
chestnut
chocolate
cinnamon
coal black
cobalt blue
coffee
copper
coral
cornflower blue
cream
crimson
cyan
dandelion yellow
dove
drab
dun
earth tones
ebony
ecru
eggplant
eggshell
emerald
fawn
ferruginous
fire-engine red
flame
flavescent
flaxen
flesh colour
forest green
fuchsia
fulvous
fuscous
garnet
ginger
glaucous
gold
golden
green
greige
grey
griseous
grizzled
gules
guly
hoar
honey-coloured
hot pink
hunter green
hyacinth
ice blue
icterine
incarnadine
indigo
ivory
jacinth
jade

Kelly green
khaki
lateritous
leaden
lemon
lilac
lily white
lovat
lurid
luteous
lutescent
magenta
mahogany
maize
mandarin
maroon
mauve
milk white
minium
morel
mottled
mouse-coloured
mousy
mulberry
murrey
nacreous
navy
neon
Nile green
nut brown
oatmeal
ochre
off-white
olive
opalescent
orange
oxblood
Oxford blue
palatinate
pansy
pastel
peach
peacock
pearl
perse
pewter
piceous
pink
pitchy
plum
plumbeous
pongee
porphyry
puce
purple
purpure
red
reseda
roan
robin's-egg blue
rose
royal
rubicund
rubiginous
rubious

ruby
ruddy
rufescent
rufous
russet
rust-coloured
rusty
sable
saffron
sage
salmon
sand
sapphire
scarlet
school-bus yellow
sea green
sepia
sienna
silver
sky
slate
smalt
snowy
spice
steel blue
straw
taffy
tan
tangerine
taupe
tawny
teal
terra cotta
titian
tomato
tortoise-shell
turquoise
Tyrian
ultramarine
vermeil
vermilion
vinous
violet
virescent
vitelline
vitreous
walnut
wheaten
white
wine
xanthic
xanthous
yellow

confections, dishes, foods

ambrosia
andouille
angel (food) cake
baked Alaska
bannock
Belgian waffle
biryani
blanquette

Bombay duck
borsch
bouillabaisse
brown betty
bubble and squeak
burgoo
burrito
calzone
cannelloni
carbonara
carpetbag steak
cassoulet
chapati
charlotte russe
cherries jubilee
chili con carne
chocolate hail
chop suey
chorizo
chowder
chow mein
cioppino
cipaille
cockaleekie
cod tongue
colcannon
consommé
crêpes suzette
croquette
cruller
curry
dacquoise
Danish custard
devil
devil's food cake
Devonshire cream
dim sum
doughnut
dragée
duff
dumpling
éclair
eggnog
egg roll
eggs Benedict
enchilada
escargot
fajitas
falafel
fettucine
feuilleté
fishball
fishcake
fish sticks
flan
flapjack
float
flummery
foie gras
fondant
fondue
foo yong
forcemeat
fortune cookie
frangipani

confections, dishes, foods (cont.)

frankfurter
French toast
fricandeau
fricassee
frittata
fritter
fruitcake
fruit cocktail
fruit salad
frumenty
fudge
galantine
gallimaufrey
garam masala
garbanzos
gazpacho
gefilte fish
gelati
ghee
gingerbread
ginger nut
ginger snap
gnocchi
goulash
graham bread
graham crackers
granola
grits
gruel
guacamole
gumdrop
gyros
haggis
halvah
hamburger
hard sauce
hardtack
hero sandwich
hoecake
hominy
hot cross bun
hot dog
hot pot
humbug
hummus
hyson
jemmy
jerky
kedgeree
kippers
knish
lasagne
latke
linguini
maple syrup
matelote
matzo
Melba toast
mille-feuille
mincemeat
minestrone
moussaka
mousse

mulligan
mulligatawny
naan
navarin
olla podrida
omelette
paella
pakora
panada
pan dowdy
panettone
papadum
pastrami
pavlova
pea soup
Peking duck
pemmican
penuche
perogy
pesto
pettitoes
pilau
pinole
piroshki
pita
pizza
ploughman's lunch
plum pudding
poi
polenta
popover
porterhouse
pot-au-feu
potpie
poutine
prairie oyster
profiterole
prosciutto
pumpernickel
quenelle
quiche
raclette
ragout
ramekin
ratatouille
ravioli
refried beans
remoulade
rijsttafel
rillettes
risotto
rissole
roly-poly pudding
roti
rusk
Sachertorte
salmagundi
salmi
salsa
saltimbocca
sambal
samosa
sashimi
sauce hollandaise
sauerkraut

scampi
schnitzel
Scotch woodcock
shashlik
shepherd's pie
shish kebab
shoofly pie
sloppy Joe
smorgasbord
soufflé
souvlaki
spaetzle
spaghetti (alla) bolognese
spring roll
steak tartare
stroganoff
succotash
sukiyaki
summer sausage
sundae
sushi
syllabub
tabbouleh
taco
tahini
tamale
tandoori
tapioca
taramasalata
tartuffo
tea biscuit
tempura
teriyaki
timbale
tiramisu
toad-in-the-hole
torte
tortellini
tortilla
tourtière
trifle
truffles
turtle soup
tutti-frutti
velouté sauce
vermicelli
vichyssoise
Vienna sausage
vindaloo
vol-au-vent
water biscuit
welsh rabbit
white sauce
Wiener schnitzel
won ton soup
Worcestershire sauce
wurst
yogurt
Yorkshire pudding
zabaglione
Zwieback

dances

allemande
beguine
belly dance
bergamasca
black bottom
bolero
bossa nova
bourrée
branle
breakdown
bunny hug
cachucha
cakewalk
canary
cancan
carioca
carmagnole
cha-cha-cha
chaconne
Charleston
clog dance
conga
corroboree
cotillion
country-dance
courante
czardas
dos-à-dos
écossaise
fado
fandango
farruca
flamenco
fling
fox-trot
galliard
galop
gavotte
gigue
gopak
habanera
halling
hay
Highland fling
hoedown
hornpipe
hora
hula
jig
jitterbug
jive
jota
juba
kazachok
kolo
krakowiak
lancers
ländler
line dance
macarena
malaguena
mambo
maxixe
mazurka

dances *(cont.)*
minuet
morris dance
musette
onestep
pasodoble
passacaglia
passepied
pavane
polka
polonaise
poussette
quadrille
quickstep
rain dance
redowa
reel
rigadoon
rondeau
roundel
roundelay
rumba
salsa
saltarello
samba
saraband
sardana
schottische
seguidilla
shimmy
siciliano
spring
square dance
step dancing
stomp
strathspey
sword dance
tambourin
tango
tap dance
tarantella
toe dance
turkey trot
twist
two-step
Tyrolienne
valse
waltz
war dance
zapateado
zapateo

dog breeds

affenpinscher
Afghan hound
Airedale
basenji
basset hound
beagle
Bedlington terrier
Belgian sheepdog
Blenheim spaniel
bloodhound
boarhound

Border terrier
borzoi
Boston terrier
bouvier des Flandres
boxer
briard
Brittany spaniel
Brussels griffon
bulldog
bull mastiff
bull terrier
cairn terrier
chihuahua
chow chow
clumber spaniel
coach dog
cocker spaniel
collie
coonhound
dachshund
Dalmatian
Dandie Dinmont
deerhound
dhole
dingo
Doberman pinscher
English toy spaniel
Eskimo dog
foxhound
fox terrier
German shepherd
golden retriever
Great Dane
Great Pyrenees
greyhound
griffon
harrier
Irish terrier
Irish water spaniel
Irish wolf hound
Keeshond
King Charles spaniel
Komondor
Kuvasz
Labrador retriever
Lhasa apso
malamute
Maltese
mastiff
Mexican hairless dog
miniature pinscher
Newfoundland
Norwegian elkhound
Old English
   sheepdog
otter hound
papillon
Pekingese
pointer
Pomeranian
poodle
pudelpointer
pug
puli
retriever

Rhodesian ridgeback
Rottweiler
Saint Bernard
saluki
Samoyed
schipperke
schnauzer
Scottish terrier
Sealyham
setter
sheltie
Shetland sheepdog
Shih Tzu
Siberian husky
Skye terrier
spaniel
spitz
Springer spaniel
Staffordshire terrier
staghound
Sussex spaniel
Tahltan (bear) dog
terrier
toy poodle
vizsla
Weimaraner
Welsh corgi
Welsh terrier
whippet
Yorkshire terrier

First Peoples

Abenaki
Ahousaht
Algonquin
Assiniboine
Attikanek
Baffin Island Inuit
Bearlake
Beaver
Bella Bella
Bella Coola
Beothuk
Blackfoot
Blood
Caribou Inuit
Carrier
Cayuga
Central Coast Salish
Chickliset
Chilcotin
Chipewyan
Clayoquot
Copper Inuit
Cree
Dakota
Dene Nation
Ditidaht
Dogrib
Dunneza
Ehattesaht
Gitksan
Haida
Han

Hare
Hesquiaht
Huron
Iglulik Inuit
Innu
Interior Salish
Iroquois
Kabloona
Kaska
Kitamaat
Kootenay
Kutchin
Kwakiutl
Labrador Inuit
Mackenzie Inuit
Maliseet
Métis
Mi'kmaq
Mohawk
Mowachaht
Muchalaht
Nahani
Netsilik Inuit
Nicola-Similkameen
Nishga
Nootka
North Georgia Strait
   Coast Salish
Nutchatlaht
Ohiaht
Ojibwa
Oneida
Onondaga
Opetchesaht
Ottawa
Pacheenaht
Peigan
Petun
Sadlermiut Inuit
Sarcee
Sekani
Seneca
Sheshaht
Sioux
Slave
Stoney
Tagish
Tahltan
Tlingit
Toquaht
Tsetsaut
Tsimshian
Tutchone
Uchucklesaht
Ucluelet
Ungava Inuit
Western Arctic Inuit
Yellowknife

**furniture,
furnishings**

andiron
area rug
armchair

**furniture,
furnishings** *(cont.)*

armoire
arrow-back chair
banquette
bar stool
bassinet
beanbag chair
bidet
bistro chair
blind
bolster
bookcase
boulle
buffet
bunk bed
bureau
cabinet
café curtains
camelback
camp bed
canopy bed
card table
CD tower
chaise longue
chandelier
change table
chesterfield
chest of drawers
cheval glass
chifferobe
chiffonier
CO tower
coaster
cocktail table
coffee table
commode
cot
couch
cradle
credenza
crib
cupboard
curio shelf
davenport
day bed
deacon's bench
desk
divan
drape
drawer
drawing-table
dresser
dressing table
drop-leaf table
dumb waiter
easy chair
end table
escritoire
étagère
faldstool
fauteuil
fender
filing cabinet
firedog

fire screen
floor lamp
folding chair
footstool
four-poster
futon
gasalier
girandole
glider
grandfather clock
hallstand
hassock
hearth rug
highboy
highchair
hope chest
hutch
jardiniere
knick-knack shelf
lazy Susan
lectern
lounge
lounger
love seat
lowboy
magazine rack
mantelpiece
mate's bed
mattress
microwave stand
mirror
mobile
night stand
ottoman
pantry
pedestal desk
pelmet
phone table
piecrust table
pier glass
pier table
platform bed
pouf
prie-dieu
pulpit
Québec desk
radiator
recliner
rocking chair
rollaway bed
roll-top
runner
scatter rug
sconce
secretaire
settee
settle
sideboard
side table
sofa
sofa bed
spice rack
squab
steno chair
studio couch

swag lamp
swivel chair
tallboy
tapestry
tatami
teapoy
tea service
tea tray
tea wagon
tête-à-tête
throw rug
toilet
torchiere
toss cushion
toy chest
trestle table
tub chair
TV stand
umbrella stand
utility cart
valance
vanity
veilleuse
vitrine
wall unit
wardrobe
washstand
water bed
Welsh dresser
whatnot
wicker work
window seat
Windsor chair
wing chair
writing desk

**garments,
vestments**

aba
achkan
actionwear
afghan
alb
amaut
amice
anorak
anti-g suit
apron
arnaut
ascot
atigi
babushka
baby dolls
balaclava
balbriggans
balmoral
bandana
banyan
basinet
basque
bathing suit
beanie
bearskin
beaver

bed jacket
beret
Bermuda shorts
bertha
bib
big shirt
bike shorts
bikini
biretta
blazer
bloomers
blouse
blouson
blucher
boa
boater
boat shoe
bobbysocks
bodice
body stocking
bodysuit
bolero
bolo tie
bomber jacket
bonnet
bootee
bottine
bow tie
box coat
boxer shorts
bra, brassiere
breeches
breeks
breton
briefs
broadbrim
brogue
buckskins
buff
buffalo robe
bumfreezer
Burberry
burnoose
busby
bush jacket
bush pants
buskin
bustier
bustle
caftan
calash
calotte
calpac
camise
camisole
camp shirt
cap
cape
capote
capri pants
capuche
capuchin
carcanet
car coat
cardigan

garments, vestments *(cont.)*

cardinal
Carmagnole
cashmere
casque
cassock
casuals
cerecloth
cerement
chador
chaparejos
chapeau
chaplet
chaps
chasuble
choli
chopine
cilice
civvies
clamdiggers
clerical collar
clogs
corselet
corset
court shoe
cowl
crop top
cross trainers
culottes
cummerbund
dalmatic
dashiki
décolletage
deerstalker
derby
dhoti
diadem
diaper
dickey
dinner jacket
dirndl
dishabille
divided skirt
djellaba
Dolly Varden
dolman
domino
doublet
drawers
dreadnought
dressing gown
dress pants
dress shirt
dress uniform
duffel coat
dungarees
earmuffs
epaulette
ephod
espadrille
Eton collar
Eton jacket
evening dress
fanny pack

fanon
farthingale
fascinator
fatigues
fedora
fez
fibula
fichu
filibeg
fillet
flip-flop
fob
fooler blouse
fraise
frock
frock coat
frog
frontlet
gaberdine
gaiter
galligaskins
galoshes
gambado
gambeson
garibaldi
gauchos
Geneva bands
geta
gilet
girandole
girdle
glengarry
glove
gorget
grego
gremial
G string
guernsey
gumboot
gumshoe
habergeon
haik
hair net
hairpiece
hair shirt
half boot
hat
hatpin
hauberk
havelock
headband
headcloth
hejab
helmet
henley
hikers
himation
hip-huggers
hipsters
hip waders
Homburg
hood
hot pants
housecoat
humeral veil

ihram
jabot
jackboot
jacket
jam shorts
jeans
jersey
jiz
jockey shorts
jockstrap
jodhpurs
jubbah
jumpsuit
jumper
kaffiyeh
kamees
kamik
kerchief
kilt
kimono
kirtle
knee breeches
knickers
kurta
lava-lava
lederhosen
leggings
leghorn
leg warmers
leotard
liberty cap
lingerie
loafer
loincloth
longjohns
lounger
lounge suit
lungi
mackinaw coat
mackintosh
madras
manta
mantelet
mantelletta
mantilla
mantle
maud
maxi
middy blouse
miniskirt
mink
mitre
mitt
mitten
mobcap
moccasin
mohair
moleskins
monkey jacket
montero
morning coat
morning dress
mortarboard
Mother Hubbard
mozzetta

muff
muffler
mufti
mukluk
mule
muscle shirt
muumuu
necktie
nehru collar
newmarket
nightgown
nightshirt
Norfolk jacket
obi
overalls
overcoat
oxford
paduasoy
palazzos
paletot
pallium
pantalettes
pantaloons
panties
pantofle
pants
pantsuit
pantyhose
pareu
parka
pea jacket
pectoral
pedal pushers
pelerine
pelisse
peplos
peplum
petasos
Petersham
petticoat
phylacteries
picture hat
pileus
pillbox
pinafore
pinner
pith helmet
plaid
plimsoll
plus fours
poke bonnet
polonaise
poloshirt
poncho
pontificals
pressure suit
princesse
pull-ons
pullover
pumps
puttee
pyjama
rabato
raglan
raincoat

**garments,
vestments** (cont.)
redingote
reefer
riding boots
riding habit
robe
robe-de-chambre
rochet
rollneck
rompers
roquelaure
ruff
rugby pants
rugby shirt
running shoe
sabot
sack
sack coat
safari jacket
safari suit
sagum
sailor hat
sailor suit
sanbenito
sandal
sari
sarong
sash
scapular
scarf
sealskin
separates
shako
shalwar
shawl
shell suit
Shetland
shift
shirt
shirtdress
shirtwaist
shoe
shortall
shorts
shovel hat
silk hat
singlet
ski jacket
ski pants
skirt
skivvies
skort
skullcap
slacks
sleeper
slicker
sling
slip
slip-on
slipper
slop
slouch hat
slouch socks
smallclothes

smalls
smock
smock frock
smoking jacket
sneaker
snood
snow boots
snowshoe
sock
solleret
sombrero
soubise
soutane
sou'-wester
spacesuit
spat
spatterdash
spencer
splash suit
sporran
sports jacket
sports shirt
stays
stephane
step-in
stirrup pants
stock
stocking cap
stocking(s)
stole
stomacher
stovepipe
straitjacket
strapless gown
straw hat
string tie
subfusc
sunbonnet
sundown
sundress
sun hat
sunsuit
surcingle
surcoat
surplice
surtout
suspenders
swaddling clothes
swaggerstick
swallowtail
sweatband
sweater
sweat pants
sweat shirt
sweat suit
swimsuit
swimwear
sword belt
tabard
tailcoat
tails
talaria
tallit
tam, tam-o'-shanter
tank top

tarboosh
tasse
teddy
ten-gallon hat
tennis shoe
terai
tiara
tie
tights
tile
tippet
toga
top boots
topcoat
top hat
topi
topper
toque
track shoe
track suit
trench coat
trews
tricorne
trilby
trunk hose
trunks
truss
T-shirt
T-strap
tube sock
tube top
tube skirt
tunic
tunicle
tuque
turban
turtleneck
tutu
tuxedo
twin set
ulster
underclothes
undergarments
underpants
undershirt
undershorts
underthings
underwear
undies
unmentionables
Vandyke
veil
veldschoen
vest
waistcoat
walking shorts
war bonnet
watch cap
watch chain
weeper
Wellington boot
wet suit
white tie
wig
wimple

windbreaker
wing collar
wrap
wraparound
yarmulke
yashmak
zoot suit
zucchetto

herbs, spices
anise
basil
caraway seeds
cardamom
cassia
cayenne
chervil
chili
chives
cinnamon
cloves
coriander
cumin
dill
dittany
endive
eyebright
fennel
fenugreek
finocchio
garlic
gentian
ginger
ginseng
groundsel
hellebore
henbane
horehound
horseradish
hyssop
juniper
lemon balm
licorice
lovage
lungwort
mace
marjoram
mint
motherwort
mustard
myrrh
nutmeg
oregano
orpine
paprika
parsley
peppermint
purslane
rampion
rape
rosemary
rue
saffron
sage

herbs, spices *(cont.)*
sassaparilla
savory
scallion
shallot
savory
stacte
tarragon
thyme
turmeric
vanilla
verbena
watercress
wintergreen
wormwood
woundwort
yerba buena

jewels, gems
agate
amber
amethyst
aquamarine
asteria
balas ruby
baroque pearl
beryl
bloodstone
brilliant
cairngorm
cameo
carbuncle
chalcedony
chrysoberyl
chrysolite
chrysoprase
coral
cornelian
crystal
diamond
emerald
fire opal
garnet
girasol
grossularite
heliodor
hyacinth
hyalite
hydrophane
intaglio
jacinth
jade
jargon
jasper
jet
lapis lazuli
ligure
marcasite
marquise
mocha stone
moonstone
morganite
mother-of-pearl
nacre

olivine
onyx
opal
papagon
pearl
peridot
pyrope
rhinestone
rhodolite
rhodonite
rose
ruby
sapphire
sard
sardonyx
smaragd
topaz
tourmaline
turquoise
water sapphire
zircon

**languages,
language families**
Aeolic
Afghan
Afrikaans
Afro-Asiatic
Akkadian
Albanian
Alemannic
Algonquian
Altaic
Ameslan
Amharic
Anatolian
Anglo-Saxon
Arabic
Aramaic
Arawak
Arawakan
Armenian
Armoric
Aryan
Assyrian
Attic
Austroasiatic
Austronesian
Avestan
Bahasa Indonesia
Balinese
Baltic
Baltoslavic
Baluchi
Bantu
Basque
Basuto
Belorussian
Bengali
Berber
Breton
Brythonic
Bulgarian
Burmese

Caddoan
Cajun
Cantonese
Carib
Catalan
Cebuano
Celtic
Chaldaic
Chari-Nile
Chinese
Circassian
Cornish
creole
Cushitic
Czech
Danish
Dard
Doric
Dravidian
Dutch
Efik
English
Erse
Esperanto
Estonian
Ethiopic
Etruscan
Faeroese
Fanti
Farsi
Finnish
Finno-Ugric
Flemish
Franglais
French
Frisian
Gaelic
Gaulish
Geëz
Georgian
German
Germanic
Goidelic
Greek
Guaraní
Gujarati
Gullah
Haitian Creole
Hausa
Hawaiian
Hebrew
Hellenic
High German
Hindi
Hindustani
Hittite
Hopi
Hottentot
Hungarian
Ibo
Icelandic
Ido
Indo-Aryan
Indo-European
Indo-Iranian

Interlingua
Inuktitut
Ionic
Iranian
Irish (Gaelic)
Italian
Italic
Japanese
Judezmo
Kalmuck
Kanarese
Kannada
Karen
Kennick
Khalkha
Khmer
Koine
Kurdish
Kwa
Ladin
Ladino
Lallans
langue d'oc
langue d'oil
Lapp
Latin
Latvian
Lettish
lingua franca
Lithuanian
Low German
Magyar
Malagasy
Malay
Malayalam
Maltese
Manchu
Mandarin
Mande
Mandean
Manx
Maori
Marathi
Median
Melanesian
Moeso-Gothic
Mon
Mongolian
Munda
Nahuatl
Navajo
Newspeak
Niger-Congo
Nilo-Saharan
Norwegian
Nynorsk
Old Norse
Oriya
Oscan
Ostyak
Pali
Papiamento
Pashto
Pawnee
Pehlevi

languages,
language families
(cont.)

Pennsylvania Dutch
Persian
Phoenician
Pictish
pig Latin
Pilipino
Plattdeutsch
Polish
Portuguese
Prakrit
Provençal
Punic
Punjabi
Québécois
Quechua
Rhaetic
Rhaeto-Romance
Romaic
Romance
Romanian
Romansch
Romany
Russian
Ruthenian
Samoyed
Sanskrit
Saxon
Scandinavian
Scythian
Semitic
Serbo-Croatian
Shan
Sinhalese
Sinitic
Sino-Tibetan
Siouan
Slavic
Slovak
Slovenian
Somali
Sorbian
Spanish
Sudanic
Sumerian
Suomi
Swahili
Swedish
Swiss German
Syriac
Tagalog
Tahitian
Tai
Taino
Tamil
Tatar
Telugu
Thai
Tibetan
Tibeto-Burman
Tocharian
Tswana
Tuareg

Tungus
Tupi
Turki
Turkish
Twi
Ugric
Ukrainian
Umbrian
Uralic
Urdu
Uzbek
Vietnamese
Volapuk
Volscian
Welsh
Wendish
West-Saxon
Wolof
Xhosa
Yakut
Yiddish
Yoruba
Zulu

literature and logic

alliteration
anachronism
anacoenosis
anacoluthia
anacoluthon
anadiplosis
analogism
analogy
anaphora
anastrophe
anochronism
antagonist
antetype
antiphrasis
antithesis
antonomasia
aphorism
aporia
apostrophe
apothegm
apposition
asyndeton
Bredermeier
catachresis
chiasmus
cleft sentence
climax
complication
conceit
contraposition
denouement
double entendre
dramatic irony
dysphemism
echoic
ecphonesis
ellipsis
enallage
enantiosis

enumeration
epagoge
epanadiplosis
epanalepsis
epanaphora
epanodos
epanorthosis
epexegesis
epigram
epilogue
epiphonema
epistrophe
episyllogism
euphemism
figure of speech
flashback
foreshadowing
hendiadys
holophrase
hypallage
hyperbaton
hyperbole
hypotyposis
hysteron proteron
imagery
imagism
increment
interior monologue
irony
litotes
major premise
malapropism
meiosis
metalepsis
metaphor
metaphrase
metonym
metonymy
middle term
minor premise
mixed metaphor
onomatopoeia
oxymoron
parable
parabole
paradox
parallelism
paralipsis
paraphrase
parenthesis
parody
paronomasia
pathetic fallacy
periodic structure
periphrasis
personification
posthumous
postscript
prolegomenon
prolepsis
protagonist
rhetorical question
satire
simile
Sturm und Drang

syllepsis
syllogism
symploce
synecdoche
synthesis
thesis
trope
type
vicious circle
zeugma

minerals

adularia
aegirine
almandine
alunite
amazonite
amianthus
amphibole
analcite
anatase
andesite
ankerite
aragonite
argil
arkose
asbestos
asphalt
augite
aventurine
azurite
balas
barilla
barite
basalt
bitumen
blackjack
black lead
blende
bloodstone
bluestone
blue vitriol
borane
borax
Borazon
boride
bornite
breccia
brownstone
buhrstone
cairngorm
calamine
calcite
caliche
Carborundum
carnotite
cassiterite
cat's-eye
celestite
cementite
cerussite
chalcedony
chalk
chert

minerals *(cont.)*

Chile saltpetre
china clay
chromite
chrysoberyl
chrysolite
chrysoprase
chrysotile
cinnabar
cinnamon stone
cipolin
coal
copper
cordierite
corundum
cryolite
cymophane
dendrite
diallage
diatomite
diopside
diorite
dolerite
dolomite
dunite
eclogite
emery
encrinite
enstatite
epidote
Epsom salt
erythrite
essonite
euclase
euxenite
fayalite
feldspar
felsite
flint
fluorite
franklinite
French chalk
fulgurite
fuller's earth
gabbro
gadolinite
gahnite
galena
gangue
ganister
garnet
glance
Glauber's salt
glauconite
gneiss
goethite
gossan
granite
granophyre
granulite
graphite
green earth
greenockite
greensand
greenstone

greisen
greywacke
grossularite
gummite
gypsum
halite
heavy spar
hematite
hemimorphite
heulandite
hiddenite
hornblende
hyacinth
hyalite
hypersthene
idocrase
ilmenite
ironstone
jacinth
jadeite
kainite
kaolinite
kieselguhr
kieserite
kimberlite
kunzite
lapis lazuli
lepidolite
leucite
lignite
limestone
limonite
lithomarge
malachite
manganite
marl
meerschaum
mica
molybdenite
morion
moss agate
muscovite
nepheline
nephelinite
nephrite
nitinol
obsidian
oligoclase
olivine
onyx
oolite
ophite
orpiment
orthoclase
ozokerite
peacock copper
pegmatite
pentlandite
peperino
pericline
peridotite
pipe clay
pipestone
pitchblende
plagioclase

porphyry
potstone
prase
pyrites
pyrope
pyrophyllite
pyroxene
pyrrhotite
quartz
quartzite
realgar
rhyolite
rutile
saltpetre
sandstone
sapphire
sapphirine
sard
sardonyx
scapolite
scheelite
schiller
schist
schorl
selenite
senarmontite
serpentine
shale
siderite
silica
sillimanite
siltstone
sinter
slate
soapstone
sodalite
spar
spelter
sperrylite
spessartite
sphalerite
sphene
spiegeleisen
spinel
spodumene
stinkstone
strontianite
syenite
sylvanite
sylvite
tachylyte
talc
terra alba
terra cotta
tharianite
thorite
thulia
tiger's-eye
till
tinstone
tourmaline
trachyte
trass
travertine
tremolite

tripoli
tufa
tuff
tungstite
turquoise
uintaite
umber
uralite
uraninite
uvarovite
vanadinite
variolite
veinstone
verd antique
vesuvianite
vitrain
wavellite
wernerite
whinstone
willemite
witherite
wolframite
wollastonite
wood coal
wulfenite
zaratite
zeolite
zinkenite
zircon
zoisite

musical instruments

accordion
aeolian harp
aerophone
alpenhorn
althorn
alto
Amati
American organ
archlute
autoharp
bagpipes
balalaika
bandore
banjo
baritone
barrel organ
baryton
bass clarinet
bass drum
basset horn
bass fiddle
bass horn
bassoon
bass tuba
bass viol
basset horn
bassoon
bazooka
bells
bombardon
bongo

musical instruments (cont.)

bouzouki
bucina
bugle
bull fiddle
calliope
carillon
castanets
celesta
cello
cembalo
chalumeau
chamber organ
chimes
chitarrone
chordophone
cimbalom
cithara
cittern
clarinet
clarion
clave
clavichord
concertina
conga
contrabassoon
cor anglais
cornet
crumhorn
crwth
cymbal
decachord
dichord
didgeridoo
double bass
drum
dulcimer
electric guitar
electric organ
electric piano
euphonium
fiddle
fife
fipple flute
flageolet
flügelhorn
flute
French horn
gamelan
gittern
glass harmonica
glockenspiel
gong
gourd
grand piano
guiro
guitar
gusle
hand organ
harmonica
harmonium
harp
harpsichord
hautboy

Hawaiian guitar
heckelphone
heptachord
horn
hornpipe
hunting horn
hurdy-gurdy
idiophone
Irish harp
jews'-harp
kantele
kazoo
kent-bugle
kettledrum
keyboard
koto
krummhorn
lituus
lute
lyra-viol
lyre
mandolin
mandora
maraca
marimba
marine trumpet
melodeon
melodica
membranophone
metallophone
mirliton
monochord
Moog synthesizer
mouth organ
mridangam
musette
musical glasses
musical saw
music box
naker
nose flute
oboe
oboe d'amore
oboe di caccia
ocarina
octachord
oliphant
ophicleide
orchestrion
organ
orpharion
pandora
panharmonicon
panpipe
pantaleon
piano
pianoforte
piccolo
pipe
pipe organ
player piano
polyphone
psaltery
rackett
rebec

recorder
reed organ
regal
rote
sackbut
salpinx
samisen
santir
sarod
sarrusophone
saxhorn
saxophone
serpent
shakuhachi
shawm
shofar
sistrum
sitar
snare drum
sousaphone
spinet
steel drum
steel guitar
Strad
Stradivarius
string bass
synthesizer
syrinx
tabla
tabor
taboret
tambour
tamboura
tambourin
tambourine
tamtam
tetrachord
theorbo
timbal
timbrel
timpani
tin whistle
triangle
trichord
trombone
trumpet
tuba
tubular bells (or chimes)
ukulele
vibraharp
vibraphone
vielle
vihuela
vina
viol
viola
viola da braccio
viola da gamba
viola d'amore
viola da spalla
violin
violoncello
violone
virginal

Welsh harp
whistle
woodwind
xylophone
zither

poetry

Alcaic
alexandrine
alliteration
amoebaean
amphibrach
amphimacer
Anacreontic
anacrusis
anadiplosis
anapaest
anastrophe
antibacchius
antistrophe
Archilochian
arsis
Asclepiadean
assonance
atonic
bacchius
bucolic
caesura
catalectic
choliamb
choriamb
cinquain
conceit
couplet
dactyl
decastich
decasyllable
dipody
dispondaic
dispondee
distich
disyllable
ditrochean
ditrochee
dizain
dodecasyllabic
dodecasyllable
eclogue
ecthlipsis
elide
elision
Elizabethan sonnet
enjambment
envoy
epic
epistrophe
epode
epopee
epos
extrametrical
eye rhyme
false quantity
feminine
fifteener

738

poetry *(cont.)*
free verse
gradus
haiku
head rhyme
hendecasyllable
heptameter
heptapody
heptastich
heptasyllable
heterostrophy
hexameter
hexapody
hexastich
Hudibrastic
huitain
hypercatalexis
hypermetric
iamb
ictus
idyll
Ionic
irrational
leonine
limerick
linked verse
logaoedic
long measure
macaronic(s)
masculine
Metaphysical
monometer
monorhyme
monostich
monostrophic
mora
ode
outride
oxytone
pantoum
pastoral
pentameter
pentastich
Petrarchan
Pindaric
poetic licence
poulter's measure
proceleusmatic
pyrrhic
quatorzain
quatrain
rhyme royal
rich rhyme
rime riche
rime suffisante
Romantic
rondeau
rondel
rove-over
Rubaiyat
run-on
Sapphics
scansion
senarius
septenarius

sestet
sestina
Shakespearean
sonnet
spondee
sprung rhythm
stich
stichometry
strophe
tetrabrach
tetrameter
tetrapody
tetrasemic
tetrastich
tetrasyllabic
thesis
tirade
tribrach
trimeter
triplet
tripody
tristich
trochee
true rhyme
villanelle
virelay
visual poetry

public offices in Canada

ambassador
Attorney General
Auditor General
cabinet minister
Chair of city council
Chief Electoral
  Officer
Chief Justice
Chief of the Defence
  Staff
Commissioner
Commissioner of
  Human Rights
Commissioner of
  Official Languages
councillor
customs officer
deputy minister
deputy premier
deputy prime minister
deputy speaker
government leader
Governor General
governor-in-council
Governor of the Bank
  of Canada
High Commissioner
Information
  Commissioner
Inspector General (of
  CSIS)
judge
Justice of the Peace

Leader of the
  Opposition
lieutenant-governor
magistrate
mayor
Member of
  Legislative
  Assembly
Member of
  Parliament
Member of Provincial
  Parliament
Ombudsman
parliamentary
  secretary
Police Commissioner
police constable
premier
President of the
  Treasury Board
Prime Minister
Privacy
  Commissioner
Privy Councillor
Receiver General
reeve
returning officer
senator
Solicitor General
Speaker of the House
Speaker of the
  Senate
Superintendent of
  Financial
  Institutions
Supreme Court
  Justice
Treasurer
trustee
vice premier (PQ)

ranks in armed forces

able seaman
acting sub lieutenant
admiral
brigadier-general
captain
chief petty officer
chief warrant officer
colonel
commandant
commander
commodore
corporal
fleet chief petty
  officer
general
leading seaman
lieutenant
lieutenant-colonel
lieutenant
  commander
lieutenant-general

major
major-general
master corporal
master seaman
master warrant officer
midshipman
officer
officer cadet
ordinary seaman
petty officer
private
quartermaster
rear-admiral
second lieutenant
sergeant
sergeant-major
sub lieutenant
superintendent clerk
vice admiral
warrant officer
wing commander

titles of rulers and nobles

Abuna
adelantado
aga
amir
ataman
atheling
autarch
ayatollah
ban
baron
baroness
baronet
begum
bey
boyar
burgomaster
burgrave
cacique
caesar
caliph
caudillo
chairman
chancellor
chief
consul
count
countess
czar
czarevitch
czarevna
czarina
Dan
dauphin
dauphine
dey
doge
Duce
duchess
duke
ealdorman

**titles of rulers and
nobles** *(cont.)*
earl
elector
emir
emperor
empress
ethnarch
exarch
Führer
governor
Graf
Gräfin
grave
Great Mogul
harmost
heptarch
hospodar
imperator
Inca
infanta
infante
jarl
kaiser
khan
khedive
king
kinglet
landgrave
langravine
magistrate
maharajah
maharani
mandarin
marchesa
marchese
marchioness
margrave
margravine
marquess
marquis
marquise
mikado
Mirza
monarch
Monseigneur
monsieur
Monsignor
nabob
nawab
Nizam
nomarch
oligarch
padishah
palatine
palsgrave
pasha
pendragon
pentarch
pharaoh
prince
prince imperial
prince regent
princess
princess regent

rajah
rajpramukh
Rajput
rana
rani
regent
sachem
sagamore
satrap
shah
sheik
sherif
shogun
sirdar
sovereign
stadholder
subadar
sultan
suzerain
theocrat
tribune
tuchun
vicegerent
vice-regent
viscount
viscountess
voivode
waldgrave
warlord

tools and hardware

aiguille
Allen key
alligator clip
ammeter
anvil
auger
auger bit
awl
axe
ball-peen hammer
band saw
block and tackle
bodkin
bolt borer
box wrench
brace
bradawl
broach
bucksaw
burin
burr
buzz saw
callipers
card
caulking gun
celt
centre bit
chain saw
chaser
chisel
chopper
chuck
circular saw

clamp
claw hammer
cleaver
cold chisel
compass
coping saw
cradle scythe
craft knife
crosscut saw
crowbar
cultivator
diamond drill
dibble
dolly
drawknife
drift
drill
drill press
drop hammer
drove (chisel)
earth rake
file
fillister
float
forceps
fretsaw
gad
gimlet
glue gun
gouge
grapnel
grapple
graver
grinder
hacksaw
hammer
handsaw
hatchet
hawk
hay fork
hex key
hod
hoe
jack
jackhammer
jack-knife
jackscrew
jigsaw
jointer
keyhole saw
lathe
leaf rake
level
levelling rod (or staff)
mallet
mattock
maul
mitre box
mitre saw
monkey
monkey wrench
mortar
mortarboard
muller
needlenose pliers

nippers
pachymeter
panga
paper knife
peavey
peel
penknife
pestle
Phillips
pick
pickaxe
picklock
pike-pole
pincers
pinch bar
pinking shears
pitchfork
plane
planer
plexor
pliers
plough
plumb (bob)
plumb line
plumb rule
plummet
plunger
pocketknife
poleaxe
probang
probe
prod
pruning hook
pruning knife
pruning shears
pry
punch
puncheon
punty
putty knife
quadrant
rabble
radial arm saw
rake
rasp
ratchet
retractor
riddle
riffle
ripper
ripple
ripsaw
Robertson
rototiller
router
rule
ruler
sander
saw
scalpel
scissors
scoop
scraper
screwdriver
scriber

tools and hardware (cont.)

scroll saw
scutcher
scythe
seam ripper
shave
shears
shovel
sickle
siphon
slate-axe
sledgehammer
snake
snips
socket
soldering iron
spade
spider
spokeshave
spray gun
spud
squeegee
stapler
steel
strickle
strigil
style
stylet
swage
Swedesaw
swingle
table saw
tedder
tenon saw
thresher
tinsnips
tire iron
tongs
torque wrench
trepan
trowel
T-square
turfing-iron
turnbuckle
tweezers
twist drill
ulu
utility knife
vacuum pump
vise
vise-grips
voltmeter
whipsaw
widener
wimble
winch
windlass
wire brush
wire cutters
wrench
xyster

units of measurement

acre
ampere
angstrom
anker
ardeb
are
arpent
arroba
as
bar
barleycorn
barn
barrel
bath
baud
becquerel
bel
bit
board-foot
Board of Trade Unit (BTU)
bolt
British Thermal Unit (BTU)
bushel
butt
byte
cab
cable's length
calorie
candela
candle
candle hour
carat
catty
cental
centimetre
centner
chain
chaldron
clove
cord
coulomb
cpi
cpm
cps
crore
cubit
curie
cusec
decibel
degree
demy
dessiatine
digit
dirham
dram
dyne
electronvolt
ell
em
en
ephah

erg
farad
faraday
fathom
fermi
firkin
foot
furlong
gal
gallon
gauss
gerah
gilbert
gill
grain
gram
gray
hand
hectare
henry
hertz
hin
hogshead
homer
hour
hundredweight
inch
joule
kelvin
kilderkin
kilogram
kilometre
kilopascal
kilowatt
kilowatt-hour
knot
lakh
league
li
light-year
link
litre
lumen
lux
maund
maxwell
megabyte
metre
mho
micrometre
micron
mile
mill
millilitre
millimetre
mina
minim
minute
mole
mph
mutchkin
nail
nanometre
nanosecond
nautical mile

newton
noggin
oersted
ohm
oke
omer
ounce
parasang
parsec
pascal
peck
perch
perm
phot
pica
picul
pint
pipe
poise
pole
pood
pound
poundal
quart
quarter
quartern
quintal
quire
rad
radian
ream
rem
revolution
rod
roentgen
rood
rpm
rps
rundlet
rutherford
sabin
scruple
second
seer
shekel
siemens
sievert
sone
span
stadium
standard atmosphere
steradian
stere
stilb
stokes
stone
tael
talent
tesla
tex
therm
tierce
tod
tola
ton

**units of
measurement**
(cont.)
tonne
torr
tun
vara
verst
virgate
volt
watt
weber
yard
yardland
year

vehicles
all-terrain vehicle
(ATV)
amtrac
armoured car
barouche
Bath chair
berlin
bicycle
Black Maria
bobsled
bogie
boneshaker
britzka
brougham
buckboard
buggy
bumper car
bus
cab
cable car
caboose
cabriolet
calash
calèche
camper
car
caravan
caravanette
cariole
caroche
carriage
carryall
Caterpillar
cat-train
chaise
charabanc
chariot
clarence
club car
coach
coaler
compact
convertible
conveyance
coupe
crate
cruiser

cutter
cycle
diesel
diligence
dirt bike
dogcart
dolly
double-decker
drag
dray
droshky
duck
dune buggy
fiacre
flatbed truck
forklift
four-in-hand
gharry
gig
go-kart
hack
hackney
handcar
hardcart
hatchback
hearse
herdic
hot rod
HUMV
jalopy
jaunting car
Jeep
jeepney
jinrikisha
jitney
juggernaut
kart
landau
landaulet
light rapid transit
(LRT)
limousine
litter
locomotive
minibus
monorail
moped
motorbike
motorbus
motor coach
motorcycle
motor scooter
mountain bike
multipurpose vehicle
off-road vehicle
omnibus
paddy wagon
palanquin
pantechnicon (van)
patrol wagon
pedicab
people mover
phaeton
pickup
post chaise

prairie schooner
Pullman car
quadriga
race
railway car
recreational vehicle
(RV)
rickshaw
roadster
rockaway
runabout
saloon car
scooter
sedan
sedan chair
semitrailer
sidecar
skateboard
sled
sledge
sleeper
sleeping car
sleigh
snowboard
snowmobile
snowplough
snowshoes
speedster
sport-utility wagon
squad car
stagecoach
stanhope
station wagon
steam engine
steam-roller
stock car
stoneboat
streetcar
stretch limo
subcompact
subway train
sulky
surrey
tallyho
tandem
tandem bike
tank
tank car
tank engine
tanker
tank truck
taxi
taxicab
T-bar
telpher
tender
tilbury
tin lizzie
tip cart
toboggan
tonga
tour bus
touring car
traction engine
tractor

tractor-trailer
trail bike
trailer
train
tram
tramcar
transport (truck)
trap
tricycle
trike
troika
trolley
trolley bus
trolley car
truck
tumbrel
Turbo
two-seater
two-wheeler
unicycle
velocipede
victoria
vis-à-vis
wagon
wagonette
wagon-lit
wain
wheelbarrow
wheelchair

vessels, ships
aircraft carrier
argosy
bark
barkentine
barque
bateau
battleship
bireme
boat
brig
brigantine
bumboat
cabin cruiser
caique
canal boat
canoe
caravel
carrack
casco
catamaran
catboat
clipper
coaler
coaster
coble
cockboat
cockleshell
collier
coracle
corsair
corvette
cruiser
cruise ship

vessels, ships
(cont.)

currach
cutter
dandy
destroyer
dhow
dinghy
diving bell
dogger
dreadnought
dredge
driving boat
dugout
faltboat
felucca
ferry
flagship
flatboat
fore-and-after
frigate
galiot
galleass
galleon
galley
gondola
grab
highliner
hooker
Hovercraft
hoy
hydrofoil
hydroplane
iceboat
icebreaker
Indiaman
ironclad
jolly boat
junk
kayak
ketch

laker
landing craft
lapstrake
launch
Liberty Ship
lifeboat
life raft
lightship
liner
longboat
lugger
mackinaw boat
merchantman
monitor
motorboat
motor ship
nacelle
nuggar
ocean liner
outrigger
packet (boat)
paddlewheeler
pair-oar
pedal boat
periagua
Peterborough
pink
pinnace
piragua
pirate (ship)
pirogue
pleasure craft
pocket battleship
pontoon
powerboat
pram
privateer
proa
punt
quinquereme
raft

razee
riverboat
rover
rowboat
sailboard
sailboat
sailing ship
sampan
schooner
scooter
scow
scull, sculler
shallop
ship
ship of the line
showboat
skiff
sloop
sloop of war
smack
speedboat
square-rigger
steamboat
steamer
steamship
stern-wheeler
submarine
supertanker
surface craft
surfboard
surfboat
tanker
tartan
tender
three-decker
torpedo boat
tour boat
trader
tramp
transport
trawler

trimaran
trireme
troop carrier
trooper
troopship
tub
tug, tugboat
U-boat
umiak
vaporetto
vedette
vessel
warship
water taxi
whaleboat
whaler
wherry
windjammer
xebec
yacht
yawl
York boat
zabra

zodiac signs

Aquarius
Aries
Cancer
Capricorn
Gemini
Leo
Libra
Pisces
Sagittarius
Scorpio
Taurus
Virgo

Appendix II

Words listed by suffix

-archy

anarchy
autarchy
diarchy
dyarchy
heptarchy
hierarchy
matriarchy
monarchy
oligarchy
patriarchy
tetrarchy

-ast

chiliast
dicast
dynast
ecclesiast
ecdysiast
encomiast
enthusiast
fantast
gymnasiast
gymnast
iconoclast
idoloclast
metaphrast
orgiast
pancratiast
paraphrast
pederast
peltast
scholiast

-cide

aborticide
algicide
bacillicide
bactericide
biocide
deicide
ecocide
ethnocide
feticide
filicide
fratricide
fungicide
genocide
germicide
herbicide
homicide
infanticide
insecticide

larvicide
liberticide
matricide
parasiticide
parricide
patricide
pesticide
regicide
rodenticide
sororicide
spermicide
suicide
taeniacide
tyrannicide
uxoricide
vaticide
vermicide
virucide

-cracy

aristocracy
autocracy
bureaucracy
democracy
Eurocracy
gerontocracy
gynecocracy
hagiocracy
hierocracy
isocracy
meritocracy
mobocracy
monocracy
nomocracy
ochlocracy
physiocracy
plutocracy
pornocracy
slavocracy
stratocracy
technocracy
thalassocracy
theocracy
timocracy

-crat

aristocrat
autocrat
bureaucrat
democrat
hierocrat
meritocrat
mobocrat
monocrat

ochlocrat
physiocrat
plutocrat
slavocrat
stratocrat
technocrat
theocrat

-cratic

aristocratic
autocratic
bureaucratic
democratic
Eurocratic
gerontocratic
gynecocratic
hierocratic
isocratic
meritocratic
mobocratic
monocratic
ochlocratic
pancratic
pantisocratic
physiocratic
plutocratic
stratocratic
technocratic
theocratic
timocratic
undemocratic

-culture

agriculture
apiculture
aquaculture
arboriculture
aviculture
criniculture
culture
floriculture
horticulture
mariculture
monoculture
ostreiculture
pisciculture
pomiculture
self-culture
sericulture
silviculture
subculture
sylviculture
viniculture
viticulture

zooculture

-cyte

erythrocyte
granulocyte
hemocyte
leucocyte
lymphocyte
macrocyte
microcyte
oocyte
phagocyte
spermatocyte
thrombocyte

-dom

Anglo-Saxondom
archdukedom
babudom
bachelordom
beadledom
beggardom
bishopdom
boredom
bumbledom
chiefdom
Christendom
clerkdom
cuckoldom
czardom
dukedom
earldom
fairydom
fandom
filmdom
flunkeydom
fogeydom
freedom
halidom
heathendom
heirdom
kaiserdom
kingdom
martyrdom
moviedom
officialdom
penny-wisdom
popedom
princedom
queendom
rascaldom
rebeldom
sachemdom
scoundreldom

-gram *(cont.)*
hexagram
histogram
hologram
ideogram
idiogram
isogram
kilogram
logogram
marconigram
meteorogram
microgram
monogram
myogram
nanogram
nephogram
nomogram
oscillogram
pangram
parallelogram
pentagram
phonogram
phraseogram
pictogram
pneumoencephalogram
program
pyelogram
radiogram
radiotelegram
roentgenogram
scintigram
seismogram
skiagram
sociogram
spectrogram
spectroheliogram
sphenogram
sphygmogram
stereogram
telegram
tetragram
thermogram
tomogram

-graph

allograph
anemograph
autograph
autoradiograph
ballistocardiograph
barograph
cardiograph
choreograph
chromatograph
chromolithograph
chronograph
cinematograph
coronograph
cryptograph
digraph
electrocardiograph
electroencephalograph
electrograph
electromyograph

encephalograph
epigraph
ergograph
flannelgraph
glyphograph
hectograph
heliograph
holograph
homograph
hyetograph
hygrograph
ideograph
kymograph
lithograph
logograph
meteorograph
micrograph
microphotograph
microseismograph
mimeograph
monograph
myograph
nephograph
nomograph
odograph
oleograph
orthograph
oscillograph
pantograph
paragraph
phonograph
photograph
photolithograph
photomicrograph
phototelegraph
pictograph
plethysmograph
polygraph
psychograph
radiograph
radiometeorograph
radiotelegraph
seismograph
serigraph
shadowgraph
skiagraph
spectrograph
spectroheliograph
sphygmograph
spirograph
stenograph
stereograph
stylograph
tachygraph
telegraph
telephotograph
thermograph
trigraph
xylograph
zincograph

-graphy

aerography
angiography

anthropography
autobiography
autography
autoradiography
ballistocardiography
bibliography
biogeography
biography
cacography
calligraphy
cardiography
cartography
chalcography
chirography
choreography
chorography
chromatography
chromolithography
chronography
cinematography
climatography
cosmography
cryptography
crystallography
dactylography
demography
discography
echocardiography
ectypography
electrocardiography
electroencephalography
electrography
electromyography
epigraphy
ethnography
filmography
geography
glossography
glyphography
glyptography
hagiography
heliography
historiography
holography
hydrography
hyetography
hypsography
ichnography
iconography
ideography
lexicography
lithography
logography
mammography
metallography
micrography
microphotography
myography
mythography
nomography
nosography
oceanography
oleography
organography
orography

orthography
paleogeography
paleography
paleontography
pantography
petrography
phonography
photography
photolithography
photomicrography
phototelegraphy
physiography
phytogeography
phytography
pictography
polarography
polygraphy
pornography
prosopography
pseudepigraphy
psychobiography
psychography
pyelography
pyrography
radiography
radiotelegraphy
reprography
roentgenography
scenography
scintigraphy
seismography
selenography
serigraphy
spectrography
sphygmography
stenography
stereography
stratigraphy
stylography
tachygraphy
technography
telegraphy
telephotography
thermography
tomography
topography
typography
ultrasonography
uranography
xerography
xeroradiography
xylography
zincography
zoogeography
zoography

-hedron, -hedral

chiliahedron
decahedron
dihedral
dodecahedron
enneahedron
hemihedral
hexahedron

-hedron, -hedral
(cont.)
holohedral
icosahedron
icositetrahedron
octahedron
pentahedron
polyhedron
rhombohedron
tetrahedron
trapezohedron
trihedral
trisoctahedron

-hood

adulthood
babyhood
bachelorhood
boyhood
brotherhood
childhood
falsehood
fatherhood
gentlemanhood
girlhood
godhood
hardihood
high-priesthood
knighthood
ladyhood
likelihood
livelihood
maidenhood
maidhood
manhood
matronhood
monkhood
motherhood
nationhood
neighbourhood
nunhood
orphanhood
parenthood
priesthood
provincehood
puppyhood
sainthood
selfhood
serfhood
sisterhood
spinsterhood
statehood
unlikelihood
widowerhood
widowhood
wifehood
womanhood

-iac

ammoniac
amnesiac
anaphrodisiac
Anglomaniac

aphasiac
aphrodisiac
bibliomaniac
cardiac
celiac
coprolaliac
demoniac
Dionysiac
dipsomaniac
egomaniac
elegiac
endocardiac
erotomaniac
hebephreniac
heliac
hemophiliac
hypochondriac
iliac
insomniac
kleptomaniac
maniac
megalomaniac
melancholiac
monomaniac
mythomaniac
necrophiliac
neurastheniac
nymphomaniac
orchidomaniac
paradisiac
paranoiac
pericardiac
pyromaniac
sacroiliac
simoniac
symposiac
Syriac
zodiac

-iasis

bilharziasis
elephantiasis
leishmaniasis
myiasis
psoriasis
schistosomiasis
trichomoniasis

-iatric

chemopsychiatric
geriatric
neuropsychiatric
orthopsychiatric
pediatric
podiatric
psychiatric

-ician

academician
acoustician
aeroelastician
aesthetician

arithmetician
beautician
clinician
cosmetician
diagnostician
dialectician
dietician
econometrician
ekistician
electrician
geometrician
geopolitician
geriatrician
logician
magician
mathematician
mechanician
metaphysician
mortician
musician
obstetrician
optician
patrician
Paulician
pediatrician
phonetician
physician
politician
practician
psychometrician
rhetorician
rubrician
statistician
tactician
technician
theoretician

-ics

acoustics
acrobatics
aerobatics
aerobics
aerodynamics
aeronautics
aerostatics
aesthetics
agonistics
apologetics
astrodynamics
astronautics
astrophysics
athletics
atmospherics
avionics
ballistics
bioastronautics
bioethics
biomathematics
biomechanics
biometrics
bionics
bionomics
biophysics
biosystematics

callisthenics
catoptrics
ceroplastics
chemotherapeutics
chromatics
civics
cliometrics
conics
cryogenics
cryonics
cryophysics
cybernetics
cytogenetics
dermatoglyphics
diagnostics
dialectics
dianetics
didactics
dietetics
dioptrics
dogmatics
dramatics
dynamics
dysgenics
econometrics
economics
ekistics
electrodynamics
electrokinetics
electromechanics
electronics
electrostatics
electrotherapeutics
electrothermics
energetics
epizootics
ergonomics
ethics
ethnolinguistics
eugenics
eurhythmics
euthenics
exegetics
floristics
fluidics
forensics
genetics
geodynamics
geophysics
geopolitics
geoponics
geotectonics
geriatrics
gerontotherapeutics
glyptics
gnotobiotics
graphemics
graphics
harmonics
hedonics
hermeneutics
hermetics
histrionics
homiletics
hydraulics

-ics *(cont.)*
hydrodynamics
hydrokinetics
hydromagnetics
hydromechanics
hydroponics
hydrostatics
hydrotherapeutics
hygienics
hysterics
irenics
isagogics
isometrics
kinesics
kinetics
linguistics
liturgics
logistics
macrobiotics
macroeconomics
magnetics
magnetohydrodynamics
magneto-optics
maieutics
mathematics
mechanics
melodics
metalinguistics
metamathematics
metaphysics
meteoritics
microeconomics
microelectronics
micrographics
microphonics
microphysics
mnemonics
morphemics
morphophonemics
nucleonics
numismatics
obstetrics
olympics
onomastics
optics
optoelectronics
orthodontics
orthogenics
orthopedics
orthoptics
orthotics
pataphysics
patristics
pedagogics
pediatrics
pedodontics
peptics
periodontics
pharmaceutics
pharmacodynamics
pharmacogenetics
pharmacokinetics
phonemics
phonetics
phonics

photics
physics
plastics
pneumatics
polemics
politics
prosthetics
prosthodontics
psychodynamics
psychogeriatrics
psycholinguistics
psychometrics
psychophysics
psychosomatics
psychotherapeutics
pyrotechnics
radionics
radiotherapeutics
rhythmics
robotics
semantics
semiotics
Semitics
sociolinguistics
sonics
sophistics
spherics
sphragistics
statics
strategics
stylistics
subatomics
subtropics
syllabics
systematics
tactics
technics
tectonics
theatrics
therapeutics
thermionics
thermodynamics
thermostatics
toreutics
ultrasonics
vitrics

-iform

aciform
acinaciform
aciniform
auriform
bacciform
bacilliform
biform
bursiform
calcariform
calceiform
calyciform
campaniform
cirriform
claviform
coliform
coralliform

cordiform
cribriform
cruciform
cubiform
cumuliform
cuneiform
cystiform
dendriform
dentiform
digitiform
dolabriform
ensiform
falciform
filiform
flabelliform
flagelliform
fungiform
fusiform
gasiform
infundibuliform
lamelliform
lanciform
limaciform
linguiform
lyriform
moniliform
multiform
napiform
oviform
panduriform
patelliform
penicilliform
piliform
pisiform
plexiform
pyriform
reniform
restiform
retiform
scalariform
scutiform
stalactiform
stelliform
stratiform
styliform
triform
tympaniform
unciform
unguiform
uniform
variform
vermiform
verruciform
villiform
vitriform
vulviform

-ism

abnormalism
abolitionism
absenteeism
absolutism
academicism
achromatism

actinism
activism
adiaphorism
adventurism
aeroembolism
aestheticism
Africanism
agism
agnosticism
agrarianism
Albigensianism
albinism
alcoholism
algorism
allotropism
alpinism
altruism
amateurism
Americanism
amoralism
amorphism
anabaptism
anabolism
anachronism
anarchism
aneurism
Anglicanism
anglicism
Anglo-Catholicism
animalism
animatism
animism
antagonism
anthropomorphism
anthropopathism
anticlericalism
antidisestablishmen-
   tarianism
antifederalism
anti-intellectualism
antinomianism
antiquarianism
anti-Semitism
antivaccinationism
antivivisectionism
apheliotropism
aphorism
apogeotropism
Arabism
Aramaism
archaism
Arianism
Aristotelianism
Arminianism
asceticism
asterism
astigmatism
asynchronism
atavism
atheism
athleticism
atomism
atonalism
Atticism
Augustinianism

-ism *(cont.)*

Shintoism
Sikhism
simplism
sinapism
sinecurism
singularism
Sinicism
Sivaism
Slavism
snobbism
socialism
Socinianism
solecism
solifidianism
solipsism
somnambulism
somniloquism
sophism
southernism
sovietism
specialism
speciesism
Spencerianism
Spinozism
spiritism
spiritualism
spoonerism
spread-eagleism
Stakhanovism
Stalinism
standpattism
statism
stereoisomerism
stereotropism
stigmatism
stoicism
strabism
structuralism
strychninism
subjectivism
sublapsarianism
substantialism
suffragism
Sufism
suggestionism
supernaturalism
supralapsarianism
supremacism
surrealism
Swedenborgianism
sybaritism
syllabism
syllogism
symbolism
synchronism
syncretism
syndactylism
syndicalism
synergism
synoecism
systematism
tachism
Tammanyism
tantrism

Taoism
tarantism
Tartuffism
tautologism
tautomerism
teetotalism
teratism
territorialism
terrorism
tetratheism
Teutonism
textualism
Thatcherism
theatricalism
theism
theomorphism
therianthropism
theriomorphism
thermotropism
thigmotropism
Thomism
thromboembolism
Titanism
Titoism
toadyism
tokenism
Toryism
totalitarianism
totemism
tourism
Tractarianism
traditionalism
traducianism
transcendentalism
transformationalism
transmigrationism
transsexualism
transvestism
traumatism
tribadism
tribalism
trichroism
trichromatism
tricrotism
trilingualism
triliteralism
trimorphism
Trinitarianism
tritheism
trivialism
troglodytism
troilism
tropism
Trotskyism
truism
ultraconservatism
ultraism
ultramontanism
unicameralism
uniformitarianism
unilateralism
unionism
Unitarianism
universalism
unrealism

urbanism
utilitarianism
utopianism
vagabondism
valetudinarianism
vampirism
vandalism
Vedantism
veganism
vegetarianism
ventriloquism
verbalism
verism
vernacularism
Victorianism
vigilantism
virilism
vitalism
vocalism
vocationalism
volcanism
Voltairism
voltaism
voluntarism
voodooism
voyeurism
vulcanism
vulgarism
vulpinism
vulturism
Wagnerism
Wahhabism
welfarism
werewolfism
Wesleyanism
westernism
Whiggism
wholism
Whorfianism
witticism
Wodenism
xanthochromatism
Yankeeism
zanyism
Zarathustrianism
Zionism
zombiism
zoomorphism
zoophilism
Zoroastrianism
Zwinglianism
zygodactylism
zygomorphism

-itis

adenitis
appendicitis
arteritis
arthritis
blepharitis
bronchitis
bursitis
carditis
cellulitis

cholecystitis
colitis
conjunctivitis
cystitis
dermatitis
diverticulitis
encephalitis
encephalomyelitis
endocarditis
enteritis
fibrositis
gastritis
gastroenteritis
gingivitis
glossitis
hepatitis
ileitis
iritis
keratitis
labyrinthitis
laminitis
laryngitis
lymphangitis
mastitis
mastoiditis
meningitis
mephitis
metritis
myelitis
myocarditis
nephritis
neuritis
oophoritis
ophthalmitis
osteitis
osteoarthritis
osteomyelitis
otitis
ovaritis
pancreatitis
parotitis
pericarditis
perinephritis
perineuritis
periostitis
peritonitis
pharyngitis
phlebitis
pneumonitis
poliomyelitis
polyneuritis
prostatitis
pyelitis
pyelonephritis
rachitis
retinitis
rhinitis
rhinopharyngitis
salpingitis
scleritis
sinusitis
spondylitis
staphylitis
stomatitis
synovitis

-itis *(cont.)*

tendinitis
thrombophlebitis
thyroiditis
tonsillitis
tracheitis
tympanitis
ureteritis
urethritis
uveitis
uvulitis
vaginitis
valvulitis
vulvitis

-latry

angelolatry
anthropolatry
astrolatry
autolatry
bibliolatry
cosmolatry
demonolatry
dendrolatry
doctrinolatry
ecclesiolatry
epeolatry
geolatry
hagiolatry
heliolatry
hierolatry
ichthyolatry
iconolatry
idolatry
litholatry
Mariolatry
necrolatry
ophiolatry
plutolatry
pyrolatry
symbololatry
thaumatolatry
theriolatry
zoolatry

-logous

analogous
antilogous
autologous
heterologous
homologous
isologous
tautologous

-logue

analogue
apologue
catalogue
collogue
Decalogue
dialogue
duologue

eclogue
epilogue
homologue
ideologue
isologue
monologue
prologue
Sinologue
travelogue
trialogue

-logy

acarology
aerobiology
aerology
agriology
agrobiology
agrology
agrostology
algology
amphibology
analogy
anemology
anesthesiology
angelology
anthology
anthropology
antilogy
apology
arachnology
archaeology
Assyriology
astrobiology
astrogeology
astrology
audiology
autecology
axiology
bacteriology
balneology
bioecology
biology
biotechnology
brachylogy
bryology
campanology
carcinology
cardiology
carpology
cetology
characterology
Christology
chronobiology
chronology
cine-biology
climatology
cometology
conchology
coprology
cosmetology
cosmology
craniology
criminology
cryobiology

cytology
dactylology
deltiology
demonology
dendrochronology
dendrology
deontology
dermatology
dialectology
doxology
ecclesiology
ecology
edaphology
Egyptology
electrobiology
electrophysiology
electrotechnology
embryology
emmenology
endocrinology
entomology
enzymology
epidemiology
epistemology
escapology
eschatology
ethnology
ethnomusicology
ethology
etiology
etymology
eulogy
exobiology
folk etymology
futurology
gastroenterology
gastrology
gemmology
genealogy
geochronology
geology
geomorphology
gerontology
glaciology
glottochronology
graphology
gynecology
hagiology
haplology
heliology
helminthology
hematology
heortology
hepaticology
hepatology
heresiology
herpetology
heterology
hierology
histology
histopathology
homology
horology
hydrobiology
hydrogeology

hydrology
hyetology
hygrology
hymnology
hypnology
ichnology
ichthyology
iconology
ideology
immunology
insectology
irenology
kinesiology
Kremlinology
laryngology
lepidopterology
lexicology
lichenology
limnology
lithology
liturgiology
malacology
mammalogy
Mariology
martyrology
menology
metapsychology
meteorology
methodology
metrology
microbiology
microclimatology
micrometeorology
microtechnology
mineralogy
misology
morphology
musicology
mycology
myology
myrmecology
mythology
necrology
nematology
neology
nephology
nephrology
neurobiology
neurology
neuropathology
neurophysiology
nomology
nosology
numerology
numismatology
oceanology
odontology
oenology
olfactology
oncology
oneirology
ontology
oology
ophiology
ophthalmology

-logy *(cont.)*
orchidology
ornithology
orology
osteology
otolaryngology
otology
otorhinolaryngology
paleoanthropology
paleoclimatology
paleoethnology
paleoichthyology
paleolimnology
paleontology
paleophytology
paleozoology
palynology
papyrology
paralogy
parapsychology
parasitology
pathology
pedology
penology
periodontology
petrology
pharmacology
pharyngology
phenology
phenomenology
philology
phonology
phraseology
phrenology
phycology
physiology
phytopathology
planetology
pneumatology
pomology
posology
primatology
proctology
protozoology
psephology
psychobiology
psychology
psychopathology
psychopharmacology
psychophysiology
pteridology
radiobiology
radiology
reflexology
rheology
rheumatology
rhinology
sarcology
scatology
Scientology
seismology
selenology
selenomorphology
semasiology
semiology

serology
sexology
sinology
sitology
sociobiology
sociology
somatology
soteriology
speleology
stomatology
symbology
symptomatology
synecology
syphilology
tautology
technology
teleology
teratology
terminology
tetralogy
thanatology
theology
thremmatology
tocology
topology
toxicology
tribology
trichology
trilogy
tropology
typology
ufology
uranology
urbanology
urology
venereology
vexillology
virology
volcanology
zoology
zoopathology
zoophytology
zoopsychology
zymology

-lysis
analysis
autocatalysis
autolysis
bacteriolysis
catalysis
cryptanalysis
cytolysis
dialysis
electroanalysis
electrolysis
hemodialysis
hemolysis
histolysis
hydrolysis
hypno-analysis
microanalysis
narcoanalysis
neurolysis

paralysis
photolysis
plasmolysis
pneumatolysis
proteolysis
psychoanalysis
pyrolysis
radiolysis
thermolysis
urinalysis
zymolysis

-lytic
analytic
anxiolytic
autocatalytic
autolytic
bacteriolytic
catalytic
cryptanalytic
cytolytic
dialytic
electro-analytic
electrolytic
hemodialytic
hemolytic
histolytic
hydrolytic
hypnoanalytic
neurolytic
paralytic
photolytic
plasmolytic
pneumatolytic
proteolytic
psychoanalytic
pyrolytic
radiolytic
sympatholytic
tachylytic
thermolytic
zymolytic

-mancy
bibliomancy
cartomancy
chiromancy
crystallomancy
dactylomancy
gastromancy
geomancy
gyromancy
hieromancy
hydromancy
lithomancy
necromancy
oenomancy
omphalomancy
oniromancy
ornithomancy
pyromancy
rhabdomancy
scapulimancy

spodomancy
tephromancy

-mania
acronymania
agromania
Anglomania
anthomania
arithmomania
balletomania
bibliomania
Celtomania
demonomania
dinomania
dipsomania
egomania
erotomania
glossomania
hydromania
hypomania
kleptomania
logomania
megalomania
melomania
methomania
monomania
morphinomania
mythomania
nostomania
nymphomania
oenomania
orchidomania
potichomania
pyromania
technomania
theatromania
toxicomania
tulipomania
ufomania
xenomania

-meter
absorptiometer
accelerometer
acidimeter
actinometer
aerometer
alcoholometer
alkalimeter
altimeter
ammeter
anemometer
atmometer
audiometer
barometer
bathometer
bolometer
calorimeter
centimeter
chlorimeter
chronometer
clinometer
colorimeter

-meter *(cont.)*
Comptometer
coulometer
craniometer
cryometer
cyanometer
cyclometer
declinometer
densimeter
densitometer
diameter
diaphanometer
diffractometer
dimeter
dosimeter
drosometer
drunkometer
dynamometer
electrodynamometer
electrometer
ergometer
evaporimeter
extensometer
Fathometer
flowmeter
fluorometer
galactometer
galvanometer
gasometer
geometer
geothermometer
goniometer
gradiometer
gravimeter
heliometer
heptameter
hexameter
hydrometer
hyetometer
hygrometer
hypsometer
inclinometer
interferometer
isoperimeter
lactometer
lysimeter
Machmeter
magnetometer
manometer
meter
micrometer
microseismometer
nephelometer
nitrometer
octameter
odometer
ohmmeter
ophthalmometer
optometer
osmometer
oximeter
pachymeter
parameter
pedometer
pelvimeter

pentameter
perimeter
phonometer
photometer
piezometer
planimeter
planometer
pleximeter
pluviometer
pneumatometer
polarimeter
potentiometer
potometer
psychrometer
pulsimeter
pulsometer
pycnometer
pyrheliometer
pyrometer
radiometer
refractometer
rheometer
roentgenometer
saccharimeter
saccharometer
salimeter
salinometer
scintillometer
sclerometer
seismometer
semi-diameter
semiperimeter
sensitometer
solarimeter
sonometer
spectrometer
spectrophotometer
speedometer
spherometer
sphygmomanometer
sphygmometer
spirometer
stalagmometer
tachometer
tachymeter
taximeter
telemeter
tellurometer
tensimeter
tensiometer
tetrameter
thermometer
tonometer
torquemeter
trimeter
udometer
urinometer
vaporimeter
variometer
vibrometer
viscometer
voltameter
voltmeter
volumeter
wattmeter

wavemeter
zymometer

-metry
anthropometry
asymmetry
biometry
dissymmetry
isometry
sociometry
stichometry
stoichiometry
symmetry
uranometry
zoometry

-monger
balladmonger
cheesemonger
costardmonger
costermonger
fearmonger
fellmonger
fishmonger
gossipmonger
hatemonger
ironmonger
jokemonger
lawmonger
mealmonger
miraclemonger
newsmonger
panicmonger
peacemonger
phrasemonger
piemonger
propagandamonger
rumourmonger
scandalmonger
scaremonger
starmonger
storymonger
versemonger
warmonger
whoremonger
witmonger

-morphic
actinomorphic
allelomorphic
anamorphic
anthropomorphic
dimorphic
ectomorphic
enantiomorphic
endomorphic
geomorphic
gynandromorphic
hemimorphic
heteromorphic
homeomorphic
homomorphic

hylomorphic
idiomorphic
isodimorphic
isomorphic
lagomorphic
mesomorphic
metamorphic
monomorphic
paramorphic
perimorphic
pleomorphic
polymorphic
pseudomorphic
theomorphic
theriomorphic
trimorphic
xenomorphic
zoomorphic
zygomorphic

-onym
acronym
anonym
antonym
autonym
cryptonym
eponym
heteronym
homonym
matronym
metonym
paronym
patronym
polyonym
pseudonym
synonym
tautonym
toponym

-osis
acidosis
actinomycosis
aeroneurosis
alkalosis
amaurosis
amitosis
anabiosis
anadiplosis
anamorphosis
anastomosis
ankylosis
anthracosis
anthropomorphosis
antibiosis
apodosis
aponeurosis
apotheosis
arteriosclerosis
asbestosis
aspergillosis
atherosclerosis
athetosis
autohypnosis